MOON HANDBOOKS®
SOUTH PACIFIC

© DAVID STANLEY

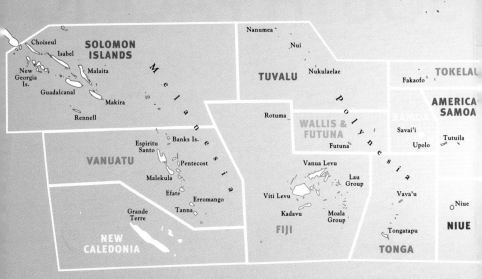

Marshall
Islands

NORTH

ohnpei

Kosrae

PACIFIC

Tarawa

Nauru   Gilbert
             Islands

Tabiteuea

Nanumea

Nui

Choiseul   SOLOMON
Isabel   ISLANDS   TUVALU   Nukulaelae   TOKELAI
New
Georgia   Malaita   Fakaofo
Is.
Guadalcanal   AMERICA
            Makira   Rotuma   SAMOA
Rennell   WALLIS &   SAMOA
                                                                 FUTUNA   Savai'i
                                                                                                Tutuila
                          Banks Is.   Futuna   Upolo
            Espiritu   Vanua Levu
VANUATU   Santo
                          Pentecost   Lau
            Malekula   Group   Vava'u
                  Efate   Viti Levu   Niue
                          Erromango   Moala
            Grande   Tanna   Kadavu   Group   NIUE
            Terre   FIJI   Tongatapu
            NEW
            CALEDONIA   TONGA

Norfolk   SOUTH   PACIFIC

AUSTRALIA

NEW
ZEALAND

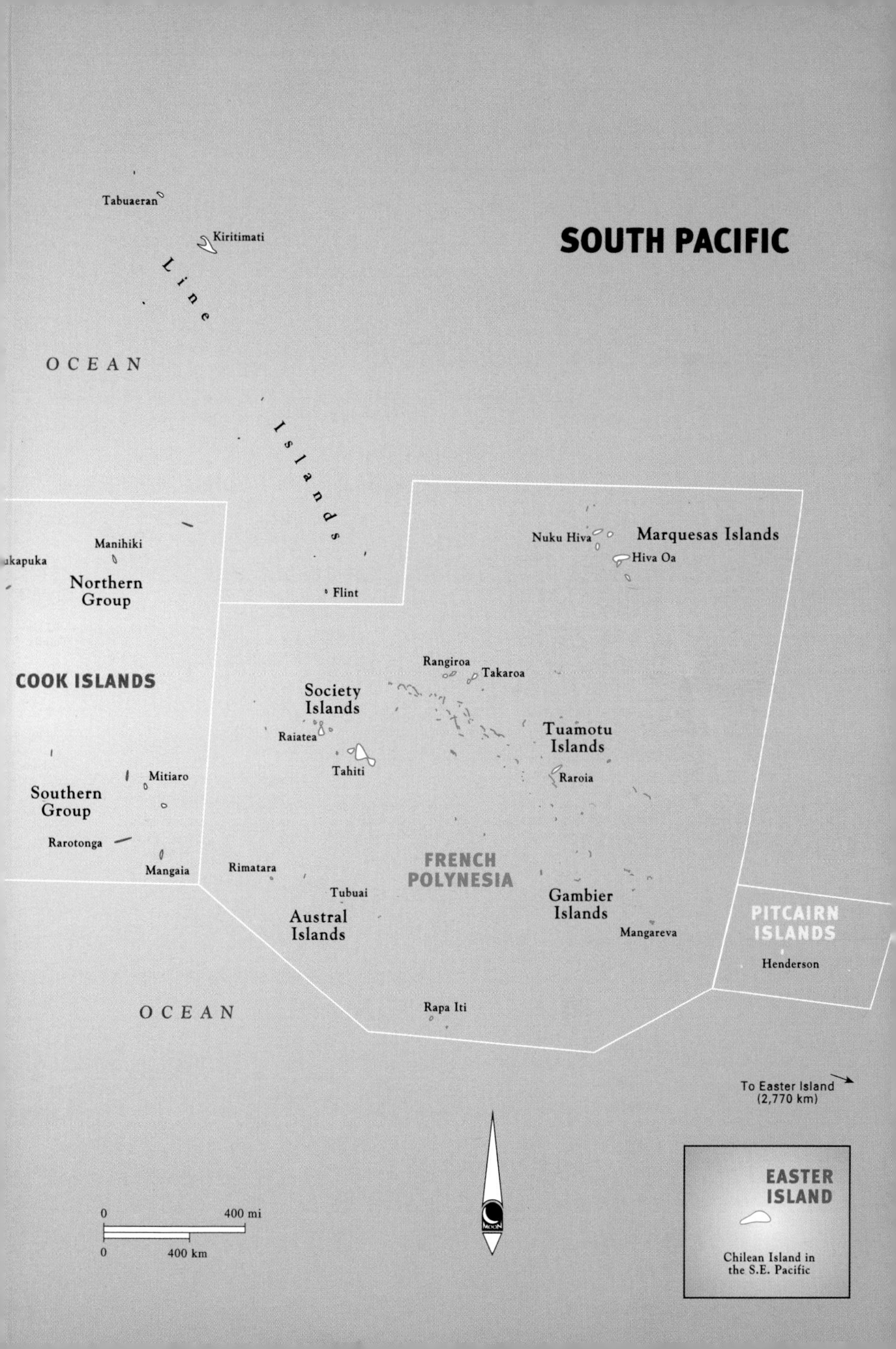

SOUTH PACIFIC

Tabuaeran

Kiritimati

Line Islands

OCEAN

ukapuka

Manihiki

Northern
Group

COOK ISLANDS

Southern
Group

Rarotonga

Mitiaro

Mangaia

Rimatara

Flint

Nuku Hiva

Marquesas Islands

Hiva Oa

Rangiroa

Takaroa

Society
Islands

Raiatea

Tahiti

Tuamotu
Islands

Raroia

FRENCH
POLYNESIA

Tubuai

Austral
Islands

Gambier
Islands

Mangareva

PITCAIRN
ISLANDS

Henderson

OCEAN

Rapa Iti

To Easter Island
(2,770 km)

EASTER
ISLAND

Chilean Island in
the S.E. Pacific

0   400 mi

0   400 km

MOON HANDBOOKS®
SOUTH PACIFIC

EIGHTH EDITION

DAVID STANLEY

AVALON
TRAVEL

Contents

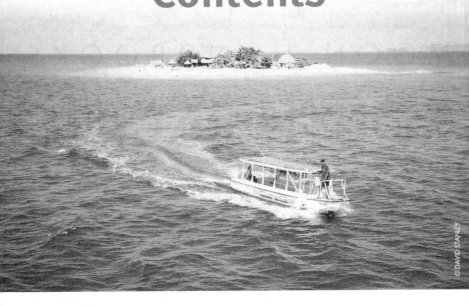

© DAVID STANLEY

French Polynesia 105

Made famous in the paintings of Paul Gauguin and the writings of James A. Michener, French Polynesia still embodies the South Pacific in the popular imagination, from Tahiti's verdant valleys to Bora Bora's perfect lagoon. But there are also lesser-known delights: traditional dancers recount legends through storytelling aparima, *and mysterious archeological ruins await on the little-visited Marquesas.*

Pitcairn Islands

Founded by English mutineers in 1790, this tiny British colony continues to tempt wayward travelers with its fortress of high cliffs, relics of the Bounty, *shell-strewn beaches, and reputation as the most remote destination in the Pacific.*

Easter Island

The mysteries of the largest collection of prehistoric monuments in the Pacific intrigue curious travelers and studious archaeologists alike. How were a thousand giant statues erected so far from their quarries? A question to ponder while hiking Rapa Nui's craters or diving its offshore caves.

Cook Islands

The best way to see the twisting valleys and steep ridges of Rarotonga, the Cooks' most populated and commercial island, is from the seat of a bicycle. If the main island becomes too familiar, escape to one of 14 outer islands, where your only companions will be coconut palms, the cool trade winds, and a handful of local fishermen.

Niue 382

*Butterflies dart between hibiscus and orchids,
crystal-clear waters harbor plentiful coral, and
limestone chasms support sheltered swimming.
With its green palms and golden sand Niue
promises a colorful escape.*

Kingdom of Tonga 395

*The regal culture of this last remaining
Polynesian monarchy is preserved in its
ancient stone monuments and traditional
arts and crafts. For those attracted by
natural wonders, the kingdom's dramatic
limestone cliffs and sacred flying foxes
won't disappoint.*

American Samoa 463

It's hot and humid on this string of islands, where wild coastlines meet gentle plains, cannery workers brush past day hikers at the bustling Fagotogo Public Market, and carefree yachties share warm waters with thousands of tropical fish.

Samoa 493

Samoans have fought hard to resist colonization, and today the fa'a Samoa, or Samoan way, is still prevalent. You'll find small villages of thatched oval fale ringing the two main islands, while countless waterfalls drop from the high interior.

Tokelau 552

This is outer-island Polynesia at its finest: a group of three atolls that greets you with plenty of coconuts, sunshine, and friendly smiles. With only one hotel available, it's likely you'll stay with a local family, who may invite you to go fishing or play a competitive game of cricket.

Wallis and Futuna 561

This trio of islands between Fiji and Samoa bears the imprint of French colonialism, from massive Catholic churches to properly attired gendarmes. But the physical landscape transcends these influences: corals and colorful fish inhabit Alofitai's shallow lagoon and spectacular red rock walls encircle Lake Lalolalo.

Tuvalu

A visit to one of the world's smallest and most isolated nations is expensive, but it's worth the effort for the 33 square kilometers of seabirds, turtles, coconut crabs, shellfish, and corals in the Funafuti Conservation Area and the idyllic, unspoiled atolls Nukufetau and Nukulaelae.

Fiji Islands

Fiji is an island escape and more, with a rich mixture of land- and seascapes, diverse cultures, and experiences found nowhere else. Dive beneath serene waters to explore vivid coral reefs. Laze on an isolated beach. Or drink kava at an open-air market. At this crossroads of the South Pacific, all visitors are welcomed with a hearty bula *(hello).*

New Caledonia 808

A complex melange of flashy Euro glamour and irrepressible indigenous customs, this French colony centers around cosmopolitan Nouméa, the Paris of the Pacific. Enjoy gourmet restaurants and designer boutiques before setting out for Grande Terre's dramatic east coast or the quiet white beaches of the outer islands.

Vanuatu

Espiritu Santo offers Champagne Beach, one of the South Pacific's finest, with talcum-white sands curving around a turquoise lagoon. Active volcanoes simmer underfoot on Ambrym. And, in a local custom that inspired bungee jumping, land divers plunge from dizzying heights on Pentecost. But it's the warmth of the people that makes it worth lingering on this island chain.

Solomon Islands

With welcoming people, plentiful diversions, and reasonable prices, the Solomons are perhaps the South Pacific's biggest surprise. Brilliant coral reefs and the ruins of the Japanese transport ship Toa Maru—*with sake bottles intact—draw diving enthusiasts, while crashing waterfalls and mist-enshrouded rainforests offer recreation on shore.*

Maps

MAP SYMBOLS

Symbol	Label	Symbol	Label	Symbol	Label
▬▬	Divided Highway	🛡 🛡	U.S. Interstate	⊙	State Capital
▬▬	Primary Road	⬭	U.S. Highway	○	City/Town
▬▬	Secondary Road	◯	State Highway	★	Point of Interest
....	Unpaved Road	✕	Airport	•	Accommodation
— - -	State Boundary	▲	State Park	▾	Restaurant/Bar
- - - - -	Trail	▲	Mountain	▪	Other Location
....	Ferry	⬏	Waterfall	ᴧ	Campground
		⬏	Swamp	✗	Ski Area

ABOUT THE AUTHOR
David Stanley

© M.E. DE VOS

David Stanley has spent much of the past three decades on the road. He has crossed six continents overland and visited 178 of the planet's 245 countries and territories. His travel guidebooks to the South Pacific, Micronesia, Alaska, Eastern Europe, and Cuba opened those areas to independent travelers for the first time.

For his first trip across the Pacific in 1978, Stanley bought the longest ticket ever issued in Canada by Pan American Airways. Since then he has returned many times, visiting and revisiting the islands. His career as a travel writer began with the letters he wrote to Bill Dalton and Tony Wheeler, the pioneers of budget travel to Asia in the 1970s. That feedback soon led to guides of his own. With over a million copies sold, he's still on the road researching guidebooks.

Though Stanley has traveled widely and become a specialist on many parts of the world, he always keeps returning to his favorite area, the South Pacific. One of the biggest treats for a guidebook writer is to meet people who are using their book. Stanley researches his books incognito, and the "Mystery Shopper" approach means he can't always admit who he is, but it's still fun hearing what unsuspecting readers think of his guidebook. Also the author of *Moon Handbooks Fiji* and *Moon Handbooks Tahiti,* Stanley enjoys receiving mail from those who have used his guides. His website www.southpacific.org provides contact details.

Introduction

The Pacific, greatest of oceans, has an area exceeding that of all dry land on the planet. Herman Melville called it "the tide-beating heart of earth." Covering more than a third of the planet's surface—as much as the Atlantic, Indian, and Arctic oceans combined—it's the largest geographical feature in the world. Its awesome 165,384,000 square km (up to 16,000 km wide and 11,000 km long) have an average depth of around 4,000 meters. Half the world's liquid water is stored here. You could drop the entire dry landmass of our planet into the Pacific and still have room for another continent the size of Asia. One theory claims the moon may have been flung from the Pacific while the world was still young.

The liquid continent of Oceania is divided between Melanesia, several chains of relatively large, mountainous land masses, and Polynesia, scattered groups of volcanic and coral islands. North of the equator are the coral and volcanic islands of Micronesia. It's believed that, in all, some 30,000 islands dot the Pacific basin—four times more than are found in all other oceans and seas combined. Of the 7,500 islands in the South Pacific, only 500 are inhabited. Something about those islands has always fascinated

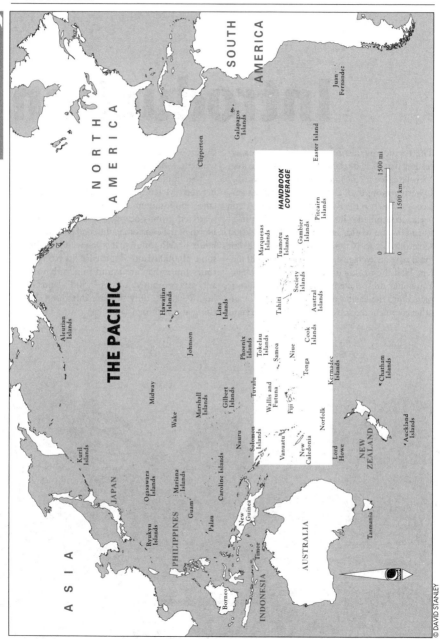

THE PACIFIC

ASIA

NORTH AMERICA

SOUTH AMERICA

JAPAN

PHILIPPINES

Ryukyu Islands

Ogasawara Islands

Mariana Islands

Guam

Palau

Caroline Islands

New Guinea

Borneo

Timor

INDONESIA

AUSTRALIA

Tasmania

Kuril Islands

Aleutian Islands

Midway

Wake

Marshall Islands

Gilbert Islands

Nauru

Solomon Islands

Vanuatu

New Caledonia

Norfolk

Lord Howe

NEW ZEALAND

Auckland Islands

Chatham Islands

Kermadec Islands

Tuvalu

Wallis and Futuna

Fiji

Tonga

Niue

Cook Islands

Samoa

Tokelau Islands

Phoenix Islands

Johnson

Hawaiian Islands

Line Islands

Austral Islands

Tahiti

Society Islands

Marquesas Islands

Tuamotu Islands

Gambier Islands

Pitcairn Islands

Easter Island

Galapagos Islands

Clipperton

Juan Fernandez

HANDBOOK COVERAGE

0   1500 mi
0   1500 km

© DAVID STANLEY

humans and made them want to learn what's there. Each one is a cosmos with a character of its own. This book is about some of those islands.

POLYNESIA

The Polynesian triangle between Hawaii, New Zealand, and Easter Island stretches 8,000 km across the central Pacific Ocean—a fifth of the earth's surface. Since the late 18th century, when Captain Cook first revealed Polynesia to European eyes, artists and writers have sung the praises of the graceful peoples of the "many islands." While there's homogeneity in Polynesia, there are also striking contrasts resulting from a history of American, French, and New Zealand colonial rule. (Hawaii and New Zealand are parts of Polynesia not covered herein as most visitors carry separate guidebooks to them.)

Polynesia consists of boundless ocean and little land. This vast region is divided into two cultural areas, Western Polynesia (Tonga and Samoa) and Eastern Polynesia (Hawaii, French Polynesia, the Cook Islands, and New Zealand). Of the three countries and eight territories included in this section, only French Polynesia and Samoa are larger than 1,000 square km, though both the Cook Islands and French Polynesia control sea areas well above a million square km.

Only French Polynesia, Tonga, and Samoa have populations of more than 100,000; American Samoa has nearly 60,000, while all the rest have less than 20,000 inhabitants. The mainly subsistence economies have inspired many Polynesians to emigrate to the Pacific rim: there are now more Samoans in the United States than in American Samoa itself, and more Cook Islanders in New Zealand than in their homeland. Only three Polynesian states are fully independent: Tonga, Samoa, and Tuvalu. All the rest still have legal ties to some outside power.

MELANESIA

Melanesia encompasses the hulking island chains of the Western Pacific from Fiji to New Guinea. A tremendous variety of cultures, peoples, languages, and attractions make up this relatively large region of mountainous islands. Prior to European colonization in the late 19th century, the 900 linguistic groups of Melanesia had little contact with one another, and unlike Polynesia, this was a largely classless society. Today parts of New Caledonia are as cosmopolitan as southern France, but on the outer islands of Vanuatu and the Solomon Islands people cling to their traditional ways. Custom and land ownership are intense issues everywhere.

Compared to Polynesia, the populations and islands are large. Densely populated Fiji is equal in inhabitants to New Caledonia, Vanuatu, and the Solomon Islands combined, yet in land area both New Caledonia and Solomon Islands are bigger than Fiji. In Vanuatu and the Solomon Islands, Melanesians still comprise the overwhelming majority of the population and few foreigners are seen outside the capitals, but in Fiji and New Caledonia, British and French colonialism introduced new ethnic groups leading to political instability. During WW II northern Melanesia became a pivotal battlefield. Today all of the countries of Melanesia except New Caledonia are independent. (We don't include Papua New Guinea herein because its extensive area merits a separate guidebook.)

The Land

Plate Tectonics

Much of the western Pacific is shaken by the clash of tectonic plates (a phenomenon once referred to as continental drift), when one section of earth's drifting surface dives beneath another. The northern and central Pacific rest on the Pacific Plate, while New Guinea, Australia, Fiji, New Caledonia, and part of New Zealand sit on the Indo-Australian Plate. The western edge of the Pacific Plate runs northeast from New Zealand up the eastern side of Tonga to Samoa, where it swings west and continues up the southwestern side of Vanuatu and the Solomons to New Britain. North of New Guinea the Pacific Plate faces the Eurasian Plate, with a series of ocean trenches defining the boundary. The greatest depths in any ocean are encountered in the western Pacific, reaching 10,924 meters in the Marianas Trench, the deepest point on earth.

The circum-Pacific "Ring of Fire" marks the boundary between the Pacific Plate and the plates to the west. West of this divide, much of New Caledonia remains from the submerged Australasian continent of Gondwana of 100 million years ago. To the east, only volcanic and coralline islands exist. Three-quarters of the world's active volcanoes occur around the edge of the Pacific Plate and 85 percent of the world's annual release of seismic energy occurs in this area. As the thinner Pacific Plate pushes under the thicker Indo-Australian Plate at the Tonga Trench it melts; under tremendous pressure, some of the molten material escapes upward through fissures, causing volcanoes to erupt and atolls to rise. Farther west the Indo-Australian Plate dives below the Pacific Plate, causing New Caledonia to slowly sink as parts of Vanuatu belch, quake, and heave. Fiji, between these two active areas, is relatively stable.

Darwin's Theory of Atoll Formation

The famous formulator of the theory of natural selection surmised that atolls form as high volcanic islands subside. The original island's fringing reef grows up into a barrier reef as the volcanic portion sinks. When the last volcanic material finally disappears below sea level, the coral rim of the reef/atoll remains to indicate how big the island once was.

Of course, all this takes place over millions of years, but deep down below every atoll is the old volcanic core. Darwin's theory is well-illustrated at Bora Bora, where a high volcanic island remains inside the rim of Bora Bora's barrier reef; this island's volcanic core is still sinking imperceptibly at the rate of one centimeter a century. Return to Bora Bora in 25 million years and all you'll find will be a coral atoll like Rangiroa or Manihiki.

Hot Spots

High or low, many of the islands have a volcanic origin best explained by the "Conveyor Belt Theory." A crack opens in the earth's crust and volcanic magma escapes upward. A submarine volcano builds up slowly until the lava finally breaks the surface, becoming a volcanic island. The Pacific Plate moves northwest approximately 11 centimeters a year; thus, over geologic eons the volcano disconnects from the hot spot or crack from which it emerged. As the old volcanoes dis-

PACIFIC AND INDO-AUSTRALIAN PLATES

AMERICAN PLATE

EURASIAN PLATE

PACIFIC PLATE

INDO-AUSTRALIAN PLATE

NEW ZEALAND

ANTARCTIC PLATE

© DAVID STANLEY

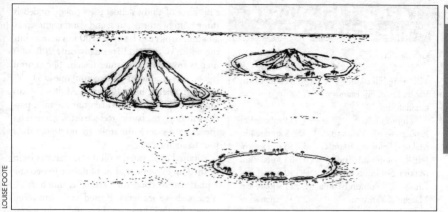

LOUISE FOOTE

Darwin's theory of atoll formation: As the volcanic portion of the island subsides, the fringing reef is converted into a barrier reef. After the volcanic core has disappeared completely into the lagoon, the remaining reef island is called an atoll.

connect from the crack, new ones develop over the hot spot to the southeast, and the older islands are carried away from the cleft in the earth's crust from which they were born.

The island then begins to sink as it's carried into deeper water, and erosion cuts into the now-extinct volcano. In the warm, clear waters a living coral reef begins to grow along the shore. As the island subsides, the reef continues to grow upward. In this way a lagoon forms between the reef and the shoreline of the slowly sinking island. This barrier reef marks the old margin of the original island.

As the sliding Pacific Plate moves northwest, the process is repeated, time and again, until whole chains of islands ride the blue Pacific. Weathering is most advanced on the composite islands and atolls at the northwest ends of the Society, Austral, Tuamotu, and Marquesas chains. Maupiti and Bora Bora, with their exposed volcanic cores, are the oldest of the larger Society Islands. The Tuamotus have eroded almost to sea level; the Gambier Islands originated out of the same hot spot and their volcanic peaks remain inside a giant atoll reef. In every case, the islands at the southeast end of the chains are the youngest.

By drilling into the Tuamotu atolls, scientists have proven their point conclusively: the coral formations are about 350 meters thick at the southeast end of the chain, 600 meters thick at Hao near the center, and 1,000 meters thick at Rangiroa near the northwest end of the Tuamotu Group. Clearly, Rangiroa, where the volcanic rock is now a kilometer below the surface, is many millions of years older than the Gambiers, where a volcanic peak still stands 482 meters above sea level.

Equally fascinating is the way ancient atolls have been uplifted by adjacent volcanoes. The outer crust of the earth is elastic, and when this envelope is stretched taut, the tremendous weight of a volcano is spread over a great area, deforming the seabed. In the Cook Islands, for example, Atiu, Mauke, Mitiaro, and Mangaia were uplifted by the weight of Rarotonga.

Island-building continues at an active undersea volcano called MacDonald, 50 meters below sea level at the southeast end of the Austral Islands. The crack spews forth about a cubic mile of lava every century and someday MacDonald too will poke its smoky head above the waves. The theories of plate tectonics, or the sliding crust of the earth, seem proven in the Pacific.

Life of an Atoll

A circular or horseshoe-shaped coral reef bearing

LARGEST ISLANDS IN THE SOUTH PACIFIC

Grande Terre, New Caledonia	16,648 square km
Viti Levu, Fiji Islands	10,531 square km
Vanua Levu, Fiji Islands	5,587 square km
Guadalcanal, Solomon Islands	5,353 square km
Espiritu Santo, Vanuatu	3,955 square km
Malaita, Solomon Islands	3,836 square km
Isabel, Solomon Islands	3,665 square km
Makira, Solomon Islands	3,190 square km
Choiseul, Solomon Islands	2,971 square km
Malekula, Vanuatu	2,041 square km
New Georgia, Solomon Islands	2,037 square km
Savaii, Samoa	1,718 square km
Lifou, New Caledonia	1,146 square km
Upolu, Samoa	1,125 square km
Tahiti, Society Islands	1,069 square km
Efate, Vanuatu	899 square km
Erromango, Vanuatu	888 square km
Kolombangara, Solomon Islands	688 square km
Ambrym, Vanuatu	667 square km
Rennell, Solomon Islands	660 square km
Mare, New Caledonia	657 square km
Vella Lavella, Solomon Islands	629 square km
Tanna, Vanuatu	555 square km
Vangunu, Solomon Islands	509 square km
Nendo, Solomon Islands	505 square km
Pentecost, Vanuatu	490 square km
Maramasike, Solomon Islands	480 square km
Kadavu, Fiji	450 square km
Epi, Vanuatu	445 square km
Taveuni, Fiji	442 square km
Rendova, Solomon Islands	411 square km
Ambae, Vanuatu	402 square km
Nggela, Solomon Islands	386 square km
Nuku Hiva, Marquesas Islands	345 square km
Vanua Lava, Vanuatu	335 square km
Gaua, Vanuatu	328 square km
Hiva Oa, Marquesas Islands	318 square km
Maewo, Vanuatu	303 square km
Niue	264 square km
Tongatapu, Tonga	259 square km

a necklace of sandy, slender islets *(motu)* of debris thrown up by storms, surf, and wind is known as an atoll. Atolls can be up to 100 km across, but the width of dry land is usually only 200–400 meters from inner to outer beach. The central lagoon can measure anywhere from one km to 50 km in diameter; huge Rangiroa Atoll is 77 km long. Entirely landlocked lagoons are rare; passages through the barrier reef are usually found on the leeward side. Most atolls are no higher than four to six meters.

A raised or elevated atoll is one that has been pushed up by some trauma of nature to become a platform of coral rock rising as much as 70 meters above sea level. Raised atolls are often known for their huge sea caves and steep oceanside cliffs. The largest coral platform of this kind in the South Pacific is 1,146-square-km Lifou in New Caledonia.

Where the volcanic island remains there's often a deep passage between the barrier reef and shore; the reef forms a natural breakwater, which shelters good anchorages. Soil derived from coral is extremely poor in nutrients, while volcanic soil is known for its fertility. Dark-colored beaches are formed from volcanic material; the white beaches of travel brochures are entirely calcareous. The black beaches are cooler and easier on the eyes, enabling plantlife to grow closer and providing patches of shade; the white beaches are generally safer for swimming, as visibility is better.

CORAL REEFS

To understand how a basalt volcano becomes a limestone atoll, it's necessary to know a little about the growth of coral. Coral reefs are the world's oldest ecological system covering some 200,000 square km worldwide, between 25 degrees north and 25 degrees south latitude. A reef is created by the accumulation of millions of calcareous skeletons left by myriad generations of tiny coral polyps, some no bigger than a pinhead. Though the skeleton is usually white, the living polyps are of many different colors. The individual polyps on the surface often live a long time, continuously secreting layers to the skeletal mass beneath the tiny layer of flesh.

CLIMATE CHANGE

The gravest danger facing the atolls and reefs of Oceania is the greenhouse effect, a gradual warming of the earth's environment due to fossil fuel combustion and the widespread clearing of forests. By the year 2030 the concentration of carbon dioxide in the atmosphere will have doubled from preindustrial levels. As infrared radiation from the sun is absorbed by the gas, the trapped heat melts mountain glaciers and the polar ice caps. In addition, seawater expands as it warms up, so water levels could rise almost a meter by the year 2100, destroying shorelines created 5,000 years ago.

A 1982 study demonstrated that sea levels had already risen 12 centimeters in the previous century; in 1995 2,500 scientists from 70 countries involved in the Intergovernmental Panel on Climate Change commissioned by the United Nations completed a two-year study with the warning that over the next century air temperatures may rise as much as 5°C and sea levels could go up 95 centimeters by 2100. Not only will this reduce the growing area for food crops, but rising sea levels will mean salt water intrusion into groundwater supplies—a troubling prospect if accompanied by the increasing frequency of droughts that have been predicted. Coastal erosion will force governments to spend vast sums on road repairs and coastline stabilization.

Increasing temperatures may already be contributing to the dramatic jump in the number of hurricanes in the South Pacific. For example, Fiji experienced only 12 tropical hurricanes 1941–1980, but 10 from 1981 to 1989. After a series of devastating hurricanes in Samoa, insurance companies announced in 1992 that they were withdrawing coverage from the country. In 1997 and 1998 the El Niño phenomenon brought with it another round of devastating hurricanes, many hitting Cook Islands and French Polynesia, which are usually missed by such storms. The usual hurricane season is November to April, but in June 1997 Hurricane Keli struck Tuvalu—the first hurricane ever recorded in the South Pacific in June. Hurricane Zoe, which swept across Tikopia and Anutu in the Solomon Islands in late December 2002, was the most powerful tropical storm ever recorded in the Pacific. Two weeks later, northern Fiji was battered by Hurricane Ami, the worst storm to hit Fiji in a decade.

Coral bleaching occurs when an organism's symbiotic algae are expelled in response to environmental stresses, such as when water temperatures rise as little as 1°C above the local maximum for a week or longer. Bleaching is also caused by increased radiation due to ozone degradation, and widespread instances of bleaching and reefs being killed by rising sea temperatures took place in French Polynesia, Cook Islands, and Fiji during the El Niño event of 1998. A "hot spot" over Fiji in early 2000 caused further damage. The earth's surface has warmed 1°C over the past century and by 2080 water temperatures may have increased 5°C, effectively bleaching and killing all of the region's reefs. By 2050 coral bleaching will become an annual event. Reef destruction will reduce coastal fish stocks and impact tourism.

As storm waves wash across the low-lying atolls, eating away the precious land, the entire populations of archipelagos such as Tokelau, Tuvalu, and the Tuamotus may be forced to evacuate long before they're actually flooded. The construction of seawalls to keep out the rising seas would be prohibitively expensive and may even do more harm than good by interfering with natural water flows and sand movement.

Unfortunately, those most responsible for the problem, especially the United States and Australia, have strongly resisted taking action to significantly cut greenhouse gas emissions, and new industrial polluters like India and China are sure to make matters much worse. And as if that weren't bad enough, the hydrofluorocarbons (HFCs) presently being developed by corporate giants like Du Pont to replace the ozone-destructive chlorofluorocarbons (CFCs) used in cooling systems are far more potent greenhouse gases than carbon dioxide. What to expect? A similar increase in temperature of just 6°C at the end of the Permian period 250 million years ago eventually wiped out 95 percent of species alive on earth at the time and it took 100 million years for species diversification to return to previous levels.

Coral polyps thrive in clear salty water where the temperature never drops below 18°C or goes over 30°C. They must also have a base not more than 50 meters below the water's surface on which to form. The coral colony grows slowly upward on the consolidated skeletons of its ancestors until it reaches the low-tide mark, after which development extends outward on the edges of the reef. Sunlight is critical for coral growth. Colonies grow quickly on the windward sides of reefs due to clearer water and a greater abundance of food. A strong, healthy reef can grow four to five centimeters a year. Fresh or cloudy water inhibits coral growth, which is why villages and ports all across the Pacific are located at the reef-free mouths of rivers. Hurricanes can kill coral by covering the reef with sand, preventing light and nutrients from getting through. Erosion caused by logging or urban development can have the same effect.

Polyps extract calcium carbonate from the water and deposit it in their skeletons. All limy reef-building corals also contain microscopic algae within their cells. The algae, like all green plants, obtain energy from the sun and contribute this energy to the growth of the reef's skeleton. As a result, corals behave (and look) more like plants than animals, competing for sunlight just as terrestrial plants do. Many polyps are also carnivorous; with minute stinging tentacles they supplement their energy by capturing tiny planktonic animals and organic particles at night. A small piece of coral is a colony composed of large numbers of polyps.

Coral Types

Corals belong to a broad group of stinging creatures, which includes polyps, soft corals, stony corals, sea anemones, sea fans, and jellyfish. Only those types with hard skeletons and a single hollow cavity within the body are considered true corals. Stony corals such as brain, table, staghorn, and mushroom corals have external skeletons and are important reef builders. Soft corals, black corals, and sea fans have internal skeletons. The fire corals are recognized by their smooth, velvety surface and yellowish brown color. The stinging toxins of this last group can easily penetrate

LONGEST REEFS IN THE WORLD

Great Barrier Reef, Australia	1,600 km
Southwest Barrier Reef, New Caledonia	600 km
Northeast Barrier Reef, New Caledonia	540 km
Sabana-Camaguey Reef, Cuba	400 km
Great Sea Reef, Fiji Islands	260 km
Belize Reef, Central America	250 km
South Louisiade Archipelago Reef, P.N.G.	200 km

human skin and cause swelling and painful burning that can last up to an hour. The many varieties of soft, colorful anemones gently waving in the current might seem inviting to touch, but beware: many are also poisonous.

The corals, like most other forms of life in the Pacific, colonized the ocean from the fertile seas of Southeast Asia. Thus the number of species declines as you move east. More than 800 species of reef-building coral make their home in the Pacific, compared to only 48 in the Caribbean. The diversity of coral colors and forms is endlessly amazing. This is our most unspoiled environment, a world of almost indescribable beauty.

Exploring a Reef

Until you've explored a good coral reef, you haven't experienced one of the greatest joys of nature. While one cannot walk through pristine forests due to a lack of paths, it's quite possible to swim over untouched reefs. Coral reefs are the most densely populated living space on earth—the rainforests of the sea! It's wise to bring along a high quality mask you've checked thoroughly beforehand as there's nothing more disheartening than a leaky, ill-fitting mask. Otherwise dive shops throughout the region sell or rent snorkeling gear, so do get into the clear, warm waters around you.

Conservation

Coral reefs are one of the most fragile and complex ecosystems on earth, providing food and

CORALS OF THE PACIFIC

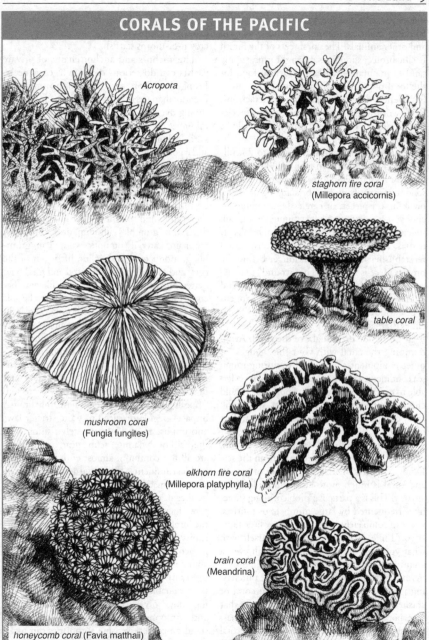

Acropora

staghorn fire coral
(Millepora accicornis)

table coral

mushroom coral
(Fungia fungites)

elkhorn fire coral
(Millepora platyphylla)

brain coral
(Meandrina)

honeycomb coral (Favia matthaii)

© DIANA LASICH HARPER

shelter for countless species of fish, crustaceans (shrimps, crabs, and lobsters), mollusks (shells), and other animals. The coral reefs of the South Pacific protect shorelines during storms, supply sand to maintain the islands, furnish food for the local population, form a living laboratory for science, and are major tourist attractions. Reefs worldwide host over two million species of life. Without coral, the South Pacific would be immeasurably poorer.

Hard corals grow only about 10 to 25 millimeters a year and it can take 7,000 to 10,000 years for a coral reef to form. Though corals look solid they're easily broken; by standing on them, breaking off pieces, or carelessly dropping anchor you can destroy in a few minutes what took so long to form. Once a piece of coral breaks off it dies, and it may be years before the coral reestablishes itself and even longer before the broken piece is replaced. The "wound" may become infected by algae, which can multiply and kill the entire coral colony. When this happens over a wide area, the diversity of marinelife declines dramatically.

Swim beside or well above the coral. Avoid bumping the coral with your fins, gauges, or other equipment and don't dive during rough sea conditions. Proper buoyancy control is preferable to excessive weight belts. Snorkelers should check into taking along a float-coat, which will allow equipment adjustments without standing on coral.

We recommend that you not remove seashells, coral, plantlife, or marine animals from the sea. Doing so upsets the delicate balance of nature, and coral is much more beautiful underwater anyway! This is a particular problem along shorelines frequented by large numbers of tourists, who can completely strip a reef in very little time. If you'd like a souvenir, content yourself with what you find on the beach (although even a seemingly empty shell may be inhabited by a hermit crab). Also think twice about purchasing jewelry or souvenirs made from coral or seashells. Genuine traditional handicrafts that incorporate shells are one thing, but by purchasing unmounted seashells or mass-produced coral curios you are contributing to the destruction of the marine environment. The triton shell, for example, keeps in check the reef-destroying crown-of-thorns starfish.

The anchors and anchor chains of private yachts can do serious damage to coral reefs. Pronged anchors are more environmentally friendly than larger, heavier anchors, and plastic tubing over the end of the anchor chain helps minimize the damage. If at all possible, anchor in sand. A longer anchor chain makes this easier, and a good windlass is essential for larger boats. A recording depth sounder will help locate sandy areas when none are available in shallow water. If you don't have a depth sounder and can't see the bottom, lower the anchor until it just touches the bottom and feel the anchor line as the boat drifts. If it "grumbles" lift it up, drift a little, and try again. Later, if you notice your chain grumbling, motor over the anchor, lift it out of the coral and move. Not only do sand and mud hold better, but your anchor will be less likely to become fouled. Try to arrive before 1500 to be able to see clearly where you're anchoring—Polaroid sunglasses make it easier to distinguish corals. If you scuba dive with an operator who anchors incorrectly, let your concerns be known.

There's an urgent need for stricter government regulation of the marine environment, and in some places coral reefs are already protected. Appeals such as the one above have only limited impact—legislators need to write stricter laws and impose fines. Unfortunately fishing with the help of dynamite, scuba gear, and poisons are all too common, almost entirely practiced by local residents. If you witness dumping or any other marine-related activity you think might be illegal, don't become directly involved but take a few notes and calmly report the incident to the local authorities or police at the first opportunity. You'll learn something about their approach to these matters and make them aware of your concerns.

Resort developers can minimize damage to their valuable reefs by providing public mooring buoys so yachts don't have to drop anchor and pontoons so snorkelers aren't tempted to stand on coral. Licensing authorities can make such amenities mandatory whenever appropriate, and in extreme cases, endangered coral gardens should be declared off limits to private boats. As consumerism spreads, once-remote areas become subject to the problems of pollution and overexploitation: the garbage is visibly piling up on many shores. As a visitor, don't hesitate to practice your conservationist attitudes, for as Marshall McLuhan said, "On Spaceship Earth, there are no passengers, we are all members of the crew."

CLIMATE

The Pacific Ocean has a greater impact on the world's climate than any other geographical feature on earth. By taking heat away from the equator and toward the poles, it stretches the bounds of the area in which life can exist. Broad circular ocean currents flow from east to west across the tropical Pacific, clockwise in the North Pacific, counterclockwise in the South Pacific. North and south of the "horse latitudes" just outside the tropics the currents cool and swing east. The prevailing winds move the same way: the southeast trade winds south of the equator, the northeast trade winds north of the equator, and the low-pressure "doldrums" in between. Westerlies blow east above the cool currents north and south of the tropics. This natural air-conditioning system brings warm water to Australia and Japan, cooler water to Peru and California.

The climate of the high islands is closely related to these winds. As air is heated near the equator it rises and flows at high altitudes toward the poles. By the time it reaches about 30 degrees south latitude it will have cooled enough to cause it to fall and flow back toward the equator near sea level. In the southern hemisphere the rotation of the earth deflects the winds to the left to become the southeast trades. When these cool moist trade winds hit a high island, they are warmed by the sun and forced up. Above 500 meters elevation they begin to cool again and their moisture condenses into clouds. At night the winds do not capture much warmth and are more likely to discharge their moisture as rain. The windward slopes of the high islands catch the trades head-on and are usually wet, while those on the leeward side may be dry.

Rain falls abundantly and frequently in the islands during the southern summer months (Nov.–April). This is also the hurricane season south of the equator, a dangerous time for cruising yachts. However, New Zealand and southern Australia, outside the tropics, get their finest weather at this time; many boats head south to sit it out. The southeast trade winds sweep the South Pacific from May to October, the cruising season. Cooler and drier, these are the ideal months for travel in insular Oceania, though the rainy season is only a slight inconvenience and the season shouldn't be a pivotal factor in deciding when to go.

Over the past few years climatic changes have turned weather patterns upside down, so don't be surprised if you get prolonged periods of rain and wind during the official "dry season" and drought when there should be rain. A recent analysis of data shows that in 1977 the belt of storms and winds abruptly shifted eastward, making Tonga and Melanesia drier and French Polynesia wetter. Hurricanes are also striking farther east and El Niño (the movement of warm water east toward South America) is expected to recur more frequently.

Temperatures range from warm to hot year-round; however, the ever-present sea moderates the humidity by bringing continual cooling breezes. The sun sets around 1800 year-round and there aren't periods when the days are shorter or longer. There's almost no twilight in the tropics, which makes Pacific sunsets brief. When the sun begins to go down, you have less than half an hour before darkness.

When to Go

Compared to parts of North America and Europe, the seasonal climatic variations in the South Pacific are not extreme. There is a hotter, more humid season from November to April and a cooler, drier time from May to October. These contrasts are more pronounced in countries closer to the equator such as Samoa and Solomon Islands and less noticeable in the Cook Islands, Tonga, Fiji, and New Caledonia. Hurricanes can also come during the "rainy" season but they only last a few days a year.

Seasonal differences in airfares are covered in the Getting There section in the Exploring the Islands chapter, and these should be more influential in deciding when to go. On Air New Zealand flights from North America to Fiji, Tonga, Samoa, and the Cook Islands, the low season is late April to August, the prime time in those countries. To Tahiti, on the other hand, June to September is the high tourist season for airfares, festivals, and tourism in general. French tourists are notorious for scheduling their trips in August,

and both Australians and New Zealanders crowd into the islands in July and August to escape winter weather in their home countries. Christmas is also busy with islanders returning home. In February and March many hotels stand half empty and special discounted rates are on offer.

In short, there isn't really any one season which is the "best" time to come. Go whenever you can, but book your airline seat well in advance as many flights from the United States run 90 percent full.

Flora and Fauna

FLORA

The flora and fauna of Oceania originated in the Malaysian region; in the two regions, ecological niches are filled by similar plants. One sees a steady decline in the variety of genera as one moves east: even in distant Hawaii very few native plants have an American origin. New Guinea has more than 5,000 vegetal species, New Caledonia 3,250, and French Polynesia only 1,000. Some species such as casuarinas and coconuts were spread by means of floating seeds or fruit, and wind and birds were also effective in colonization. The microscopic spores of ferns can be carried vast distances by the wind. Yet how creatures like Fiji's crested iguana or the flightless megapode bird of Niuafo'ou and Savo could have reached the Pacific islands remains a mystery. Later, humans became the vehicle: the Polynesians introduced taro, yams, breadfruit, plantains, coconuts, sugarcane, kava, paper mulberry, and much more to the islands.

The high islands of the South Pacific support a great variety of plantlife, while the low islands are restricted to a few hardy, drought-resistant species such as coconuts and pandanus. Rainforests fill the valleys and damp windward slopes of the high islands, while brush and thickets grow in more exposed locations. Hillsides in the drier areas are covered with coarse grasses. Yet even large islands such as Viti Levu have an extremely limited variety of plantlife when compared to Indonesia. The absence of leaf-eating

animals allowed the vegetation to develop largely without the protective spines and thorns found elsewhere.

Distance, drought, and poor soil have made atoll vegetation among the most unvaried on earth. Though a tropical atoll might seem "lush," no more than 15 native species may be present! On the atolls, taro, a root vegetable with broad heart-shaped leaves, must be cultivated in deep organic pits. The vegetation of a raised atoll is apt to be far denser, with many more species, yet it's likely that fewer than half are native.

Mangroves are often found along high island coastal lagoons. The cable roots of the saltwater-tolerant red mangrove anchor in the shallow upper layer of oxygenated mud, avoiding the layers of hydrogen sulfide below. The tree provides shade for tiny organisms dwelling in the tidal mudflats—a place for birds to nest and for fish or shellfish to feed and spawn. The mangroves also perform the same task as land-building coral colonies along the reefs. As sediments are trapped between the roots, the trees extend farther into the lagoon, creating a unique natural environment. The past two decades have seen widespread destruction of the mangroves.

Sugarcane probably originated in the South Pacific. On New Guinea the islanders have cultivated the plant for thousands of years, selecting vigorous varieties with the most colorful stems. The story goes that two Melanesian fishermen, To-Kabwana and To-Karavuvu, found a piece of sugarcane in their net one day. They threw it away, but after twice catching it again they decided to keep it and painted the stalk a bright color. Eventually the cane burst and a woman came forth. She cooked food for the men but hid herself at night. Finally she was captured and became the wife of one of the men. From their union sprang the whole human race.

Rainforests at Risk

In our day man has greatly altered the original vegetation by cutting the primary forests and introducing exotic species. For example, most of the plants now seen in the coastal areas of the main islands are introduced. The virgin rainforests of the world continue to disappear at the rate of 40 hectares a minute, causing erosion, silting, flooding, drought, climatic changes, and the extinction of countless life forms. The Solomon Islands and New Caledonia have been the hardest hit by commercial logging, but the forests of Vanuatu, Fiji, and Samoa are also suffering.

Locally operated portable sawmills have been promoted in Melanesia as an alternative to large-scale exploitation by foreign corporations. These low-tech sawmills can be operated by a couple of persons, and there's a ready market for the cut lumber. Logging roads and heavy equipment are not required, and nearly 100 percent of the income remains in the community. By providing villagers with a steady income from their forests, the *wokabout somils* make customary landowners far less ready to sign away their timber rights to large companies that devastate the environment. It is becoming recognized that what's needed is sustainable development rather than short-term exploitation, the creation of forest reserves, and better management across the board.

FAUNA

As with the flora, the variety of animal and bird species encountered in Oceania declines as you move away from the Asian mainland. The Wallace Line between Indonesia's Bali and Lombok was once believed to separate the terrestrial fauna of Southeast Asia from that of Australia. Although it's now apparent that there's no such clear-cut division, it still provides a frame of reference. Many of the marsupials and monotremes of Australia are also native to Papua New Guinea. Sea cows (dugongs) are found in New Guinea, the Solomons, and Vanuatu. The fauna to the east of New Guinea is much sparser, with flying foxes and insect-eating bats the only mammals that spread to all of Oceania (except Eastern Polynesia) without the aid of man.

Birds

Island birdlife is far more abundant than land-based fauna but still reflects the decline in variety from west to east. Bird-watching is a highly recommended pursuit for the serious Pacific traveler; you'll find it opens unexpected doors. Good field guides are few (ask at local bookstores, museums, and cultural centers), but a determined interest will bring you into contact with fascinating people and lead to great adventures. The best time to observe forest birds is in the very early morning—they move around a lot less in the heat of the day.

Introduced Fauna

Ancient Polynesian navigators introduced pigs, dogs, and chickens; they also brought along gray rats (a few species of mice are native to Australia and New Guinea). Captain Cook contributed cattle, horses, and goats; Captain Wallis left behind cats. The bird-eating mongoose was introduced to the region in the 1880s to combat the rats. Giant African snails *(Achatina fulica)* were brought to the islands by gourmets fond of fancy French food. Some of the snails escaped, multiplied, and now crawl wild, destroying the vegetation. They now exist in the Samoas, New Caledonia, French Polynesia, Vanuatu, and Wallis and Futuna.

Perhaps the most unfortunate newcomer of all is the hopping common mynah bird *(Acridotheres tristis),* introduced to many islands from Indonesia at the turn of the century to control insects, which were damaging the citrus and coconut plantations. The mynahs multiplied profusely and have become major pests, inflicting great harm on the very trees they were brought in to protect. Worse still, many indigenous birds are forced out of their habitat by these noisy, aggressive birds with yellow beaks and feet. This and rapid deforestation by man have made the South Pacific the region with the highest proportion of endangered endemic bird species on earth.

Sealife

The South Pacific's richest store of life is found in the silent underwater world of the pelagic and lagoon fishes. It's estimated that half the fish remaining on our globe are swimming in this great ocean. The Pacific reefs provide a habitat for over 4,000 fish species, five to 10 times the diversity of temperate oceans.

Coral pinnacles on the lagoon floor provide a safe haven for angelfish, butterfly fish, damselfish, groupers, soldierfish, surgeonfish, triggerfish, trumpet fish, and countless more. These fish seldom venture more than a few meters away from the protective coral, but larger fish such as barracuda, jackfish, parrot fish, pike, stingrays, and small sharks range across lagoon waters that are seldom deeper than 30 meters. The external side of the reef is also home to many of the above, but the open ocean is reserved for bonito, mahimahi, swordfish, tuna, wrasses, and the larger sharks. Passes between ocean and lagoon can be crowded with fish in transit, offering a favorite hunting ground for predators.

In the open sea the food chain begins with phytoplankton, which flourish wherever ocean upswellings bring nutrients such as nitrates and phosphates to the surface. In the western Pacific this occurs near the equator, where massive currents draw water away toward Japan and Australia. Large schools of fast-moving tuna ply these waters feeding on smaller fish, which consume tiny phytoplankton drifting near the sunlit surface. The phytoplankton also exist in tropical lagoons where mangrove leaves, sea grasses, and other plant material are consumed by far more varied populations of reef fish, mollusks, and crustaceans.

It's believed that most Pacific marine organisms evolved in the triangular area bounded by New Guinea, the Philippines, and the Malay Peninsula. This "Cradle of Indo-Pacific Marinelife" includes a wide variety of habitats and has remained stable through several geo-logical ages. From this cradle the rest of the Pacific was colonized.

Marine Mammals

While most people use the terms dolphin and porpoise interchangeably, a porpoise lacks the dolphin's beak (although many dolphins are also beakless). There are 62 species of dolphins, and only six species of porpoises. Dolphins leap from the water and many legends tell of their saving humans, especially children, from drowning (the most famous concerns Telemachus, son of Odysseus). Dolphins often try to race in front of ferries and large ships. The commercialization of dolphins in aquariums or enclosures for the amusement of humans is a questionable activity.

Whales generally visit the tropical South Pacific between July and October. Humpbacks arrive in Tonga about this time to give birth in the warm waters off Vava'u. Whales are also commonly seen in the Cook Islands. As the weather grows warmer they return to the summer feeding areas around Antarctica. (Sadly, Japanese whalers continue to hunt the animals in Antarctica for "scientific purposes," and endangered fin and humpback whales are hidden among the 400 minke whale kills reported each year. Whale meat is openly available at Tokyo restaurants.) Conservationists have demonstrated how a living whale can generate over a million dollars in tourism revenue during its lifetime, and by 2003 Australia, the Cook Islands, Fiji, French Polynesia, New Zealand, Niue, Papua New Guinea, Samoa, Tonga, and Vanuatu had all declared their exclusive economic zones marine mammal sanctuaries.

Sharks

Human activities threaten deepwater shark species with extinction. The National Marine Fisheries Service reports that 60,857 sharks were harvested in the central and western Pacific in 1998, a 25-fold increase in just seven years, with the vast majority taken only for their fins. These are used to make soup at Asian restaurants and the rest of the carcass is dumped back into the sea, a cruel, wasteful practice, which is gradually removing this top predator from the ecosystem. The consequences of these depredations are as yet unknown.

In contrast, the danger from sharks to swimmers has been greatly exaggerated. Of some 300 different species, only 28 are known to have attacked humans. Most dangerous are the white, tiger, and blue sharks. Fortunately, all of these inhabit deep water far from the coasts. An average of 70–100 shark attacks a year occur worldwide with 10 fatalities, so considering the number of people who swim in the sea, your chances of being involved are about one in a million. In the South Pacific, shark attacks on snorkelers or scuba divers are extremely rare and the tiny mosquito is a far more dangerous predator.

You're always safer if you keep your head underwater (with a mask and snorkel), and don't panic if you see a shark—you might attract it. Even if you do, they're usually only curious, so keep your eye on the shark and slowly back off. The swimming techniques of humans must seem very clumsy to fish, so it's not surprising if they want a closer look. Sharks are attracted by shiny objects (a knife or jewelry), bright colors (especially yellow and red), urine, blood, spearfishing, and splashing.

Sharks normally stay outside the reef, but get local advice. White beaches are safer than dark, and clear water safer than murky. Avoid swimming in places where sewage or edible wastes enter the water, or where fish have just been cleaned. You should also exercise care in places where local residents have been fishing with spears or even a hook and line that day.

Never swim alone if you suspect the presence of sharks. If you see one, even a supposedly harmless nurse shark lying on the bottom, get out of the water calmly and quickly, and go elsewhere. Studies indicate that sharks, like most other creatures, have a "personal space" around them that they will defend. Thus an attack could be a shark's way of warning someone to keep his distance, and it's a fact that more than half the victims of these incidents are not eaten but merely bitten. Sharks are much less of a problem in the South Pacific than in colder waters, where small marine mammals are commonly hunted by sharks. You won't be mistaken for a seal or otter here.

Let common sense be your guide, not irrational fear or carelessness. Many scuba divers actually come *looking* for sharks, and local divemasters seem able to swim among them with impunity. If you're in the market for some shark action, most dive shops can provide it. Just be aware that getting into the water with feeding sharks always entails some danger. Never snorkel on your own (without the services of an experienced guide) near a spot where shark feeding is practiced as you never know how the sharks will react to a surface swimmer without any food for them. Like all other wild animals, sharks deserve to be approached with respect.

Coconut Crabs

The coconut crab (*Birgus latro*) is a crustacean with a hard skeleton on the outside and no bones inside. The animal must periodically shed its skeleton as it grows: Young crabs change shells two or three times a year, while an old crab does so every other year. At these times, the crab is extremely vulnerable and it usually buries itself in the ground until a new shell grows, which can take a month.

The slow-growing crabs mature when they're five years old and can live as long as 40 years, at which time they might weigh four kilograms. The crabs rest in protected holes in the ground, under rocks, or in hollow trees in plantations and forests. Their diet includes fruits, rotting leaves, small animals, and occasionally other coconut crabs, but they're best known for their ability to open coconuts with their strong front claws.

Although coconut crabs live on land, their eggs hatch in the sea. The crabs mate during the rainy season and the female lays her eggs two or three weeks later. The mother carries the eggs around under her belly on land for over a month. When they are ready to hatch, she enters the sea during the evening at high tide and the eggs hatch immediately upon release. The larval crabs float in the water for a number of weeks, before settling in shallow water where the larvae change into tiny crabs. The babies hide in abandoned mollusk shells on the beach until they're large enough to move inland.

Coconut crabs have always been a favorite food of island inhabitants, but today with rising human populations and demand from tourists, they've become scarce in many areas. Often crabs with an upper body less than 2.5 centimeters long (not including the head and tail) are taken before they've had a chance to reproduce. The female crab has three flat, hairy legs under her body which she uses to hold her eggs. Conservation workers have tried to convince local residents not to harvest females at all, especially during the breeding season.

Sea Urchins

Sea urchins (living pincushions) are common in tropical waters. The black variety is the most dangerous: their long, sharp quills can go right through a snorkeler's fins. Even the small ones, which you can easily pick up in your hand, can pinch you if you're careless. They're found on rocky shores and reefs, never on clear, sandy beaches where the surf rolls in.

Most sea urchins are not poisonous, though quill punctures are painful and can become infected if not treated. The pain is caused by an injected protein, which you can eliminate by holding the injured area in a pail of very hot water for about 15 minutes. This will coagulate the protein, eliminating the pain for good. If you can't heat water, soak the area in vinegar or urine for a quarter hour. Remove the quills if possible, but being made of calcium, they'll decompose in a couple of weeks anyway—not much of a consolation as you limp along in the meantime. In some places sea urchins are considered a delicacy: The orange or yellow urchin gonads are delicious with lemon and salt.

Other Hazardous Creatures

Although jellyfish, stonefish, crown-of-thorns starfish, cone shells, eels, and poisonous sea snakes are dangerous, injuries resulting from any of these are rare. Gently apply methylated spirit, alcohol, or urine (but not water, kerosene, or gasoline) to areas stung by jellyfish. Inoffensive sea cucumbers (bêche-de-mer) punctuate the lagoon shallows. Stonefish also rest on the bottom and are hard to see due to camouflaging; if you happen to step on one, its dorsal fins inject a painful poison, which burns like fire in the blood. Fortunately, stonefish are not common.

It's worth knowing that the venom produced by most marine animals is destroyed by heat, so your first move should be to soak the injured part in very hot water for 30 minutes. (Also hold an opposite foot or hand in the same water to prevent scalding due to numbness.) Other authorities claim the best first aid is to squeeze blood from a sea cucumber scraped raw on coral directly onto the wound. If a hospital or clinic is nearby, go there immediately.

Never pick up a live cone shell; some varieties have a deadly stinger dart coming out from the pointed end. The tiny blue-ring octopus is only five centimeters long but packs a poison that can kill a human. Eels hide in reef crevices by day; most are harmful only if you inadvertently poke your hand or foot in at them. Of course, never tempt fate by approaching them (fun-loving divemasters sometimes feed the big ones by hand and stroke their backs).

Reptiles and Insects

Very few land snakes live in Oceania and the more common sea snakes are shy and inoffensive. This, and the relative absence of leeches, poisonous plants, thorns, and dangerous wild animals, makes the South Pacific a paradise for hikers. One creature to watch out for is the centipede, which often hides under stones or anything else lying around. It's a long, flat, fast-moving insect not to be confused with the round, slow, and harmless millipede. The centipede's bite, though painful, is not lethal to a normal adult.

Geckos and skinks are small lizards often seen on the islands. The skink hunts insects by day; its tail breaks off if you catch it, but a new one quickly grows. The gecko is nocturnal and has no eyelids. Adhesive toe pads enable it to pass along vertical surfaces, and it changes color to avoid detection. Unlike the skink, which avoids humans, geckos often live in people's homes, where they eat insects attracted by electric lights. Its loud clicking call may be a territorial warning to other geckos. Two species of geckos are asexual: In these, males do not exist and the unfertilized eggs hatch into females identical to the mother. Geckos are the highest members of the animal world where this phenomenon takes place. During the 1970s a sexual species of house gecko was introduced to Samoa and Vanuatu, and in 1988 it arrived on Tahiti. These larger, more aggressive geckos have drastically reduced the population of endemic asexual species.

Six of the seven species of sea turtles are present in the Pacific (the flatback, green, hawksbill, leatherback, loggerhead, and olive ridley turtles). These magnificent creatures are sometimes erroneously referred to as "tortoises," which are land turtles. All species of sea turtles now face extinction due to ruthless hunting, egg harvesting, beach destruction, and pollution. Sea turtles come ashore from November to February to lay their eggs on the beach from which they themselves originally hatched, but female turtles don't commence this activity until they are 30 years old. Thus a drop in numbers today has irreversible consequences a generation later, and it's estimated that breeding green, hawksbill, and leatherback females already number in the low hundreds. Turtles are often choked by floating plastic bags they mistake for food, or they drown in fishing nets.

History and Government

THE ERA OF DISCOVERY AND SETTLEMENT

Prehistory

Oceania is the site of many "lasts." It was the last area on earth to be settled by humans, the last to be discovered by Europeans, and the last to be both colonized and decolonized. It all began more than 50,000 years ago when Papuan-speaking Australoid migrants from Southeast Asia arrived in New Guinea and Australia, at a time when the two formed a single landmass. Buka Island in the North Solomons had already been settled by Papuans 30,000 years ago. During the Pleistocene (Ice Age), sea level was 150 meters lower and people could cross the narrow channels from Indonesia on primitive rafts more easily. Cut off by rising waters 10,000 years ago, the Australian Aboriginals maintained their Paleolithic (Old Stone Age) culture undisturbed until modern times.

Little is known about the prehistory of the Papuan peoples of New Guinea as their first coastal settlements are now covered by the sea, but they spoke non-Austronesian languages and were characterized by convex noses. Similar short, black peoples are found in various parts of Asia (the Philippine Negritos, for example). Some of the Dravidian peoples of southern India are also very short and dark, indicating the direction from which these migrations came. These pre-Austronesian societies were egalitarian, religious rites were performed communally, and a preference was shown for the curvilinear style in art.

The Austronesians

Next to arrive were the broad-nosed, lighter-skinned Austronesians who migrated from Taiwan to the Philippines around 3000 B.C., then from the Philippines and Indonesia to coastal Melanesia by 2000 B.C. They settled in enclaves along the coast of New Guinea and gradually populated the islands of Melanesia as far as Fiji. They mixed with the Papuans to become the Melanesians of today; in the Western Solomons the blue-black-skinned inhabitants still speak Papuan languages. The Papuans evolved their Neolithic (New Stone Age) culture long before the Austronesians passed this way: the earliest confirmed date for agriculture in the Western Highlands of Papua New Guinea is 4000 B.C., proving that the shift away from hunting and gathering was much earlier.

The Austronesians almost certainly introduced pottery and had more advanced outrigger canoes. Distinctive *lapita* pottery, decorated in horizontal geometric bands and dated from 1500 to 500 B.C., has been found at sites ranging from New Britain to New Caledonia, Tonga, and Samoa. *Lapita* pottery has allowed archaeologists not only to study Melanesian prehistory, but also to trace the migrations of an Austronesian-speaking race, the Polynesians, with some precision. These *Lapita* people were great traders: Obsidian from

INTRODUCTION

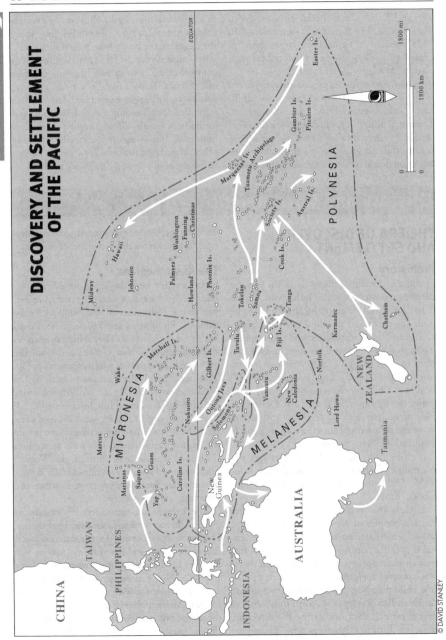

DISCOVERY AND SETTLEMENT OF THE PACIFIC

© DAVID STANLEY

New Britain Island in Papua New Guinea was exported to Santa Cruz in the Solomons—some 1,700 km away. By A.D. 300 at the latest the Polynesians had ceased to make pottery.

It's interesting to note that the third to second millenniums B.C. saw continuous movement of peoples from Southeast Asia and southern China into Indonesia. All insular Southeast Asian peoples are Austronesian-speaking, and the Polynesians were the advance guard of this migration. These population movements continue today with contemporary Javanese colonization of West Papua and Polynesian migration to New Zealand, Hawaii, and the American continent. Recent comparisons of DNA samples have confirmed that the Polynesians traveled from Taiwan to the Philippines, Indonesia, New Guinea, Fiji, and Samoa.

The colorful theory that Oceania was colonized from the Americas is no longer entertained. The Austronesian languages are spoken today from Madagascar through Indonesia all the way to Easter Island and Hawaii, half the circumference of the world! All of the introduced plants of old Polynesia, except the sweet potato, originated in Southeast Asia. The endemic diseases of Oceania, leprosy and the filaria parasite (elephantiasis), were unknown in the Americas. The amazing continuity of Polynesian culture is illustrated by motifs in contemporary tattooing and tapa, which are very similar to those on ancient *lapita* pottery.

The Colonization of Polynesia

Three thousand five hundred years ago the early Polynesians set out from Southeast Asia on a migratory trek that would lead them to make the "many islands" of Polynesia their home. Great voyagers, they sailed their huge double-hulled canoes far and wide, steering with huge paddles and pandanus sails. To navigate they read the sun, stars, currents, swells, winds, clouds, and birds. Sailing purposefully, against the prevailing winds and currents, the *Lapita* peoples reached the Bismarck Archipelago by 1500 B.C., Tonga (via Fiji) by 1300 B.C., and Samoa by 1000 B.C. Around the time of Christ they pushed out from this primeval area, remembered as Havaiki, into the eastern half of the Pacific.

Perhaps due to overpopulation in Samoa, some Polynesians pressed on to the Society Islands and the Marquesas by 300 B.C. About this time a backtracking movement settled the outliers of the Solomons, probably originating in Tuvalu or Futuna. Hawaii (A.D. 200), Easter Island (A.D. 300), and Mangareva (A.D. 900) were all reached by Polynesians from the Marquesas. Migrants to the Cook Islands (A.D. 800), the Tuamotus (A.D. 900), and New Zealand (A.D. 1100) were probably from the Society Islands. The stone food pounders, carved figures, and tanged adzes of Eastern Polynesia are not found in Samoa and Tonga (Western Polynesia), indicating that they were later, local developments of Polynesian culture.

These were not chance landfalls but planned voyages of colonization: The Polynesians could (and often did) return the way they came. That one could deliberately sail such distances against the trade winds and currents without the help of modern navigational equipment was proved in 1976 when the *Hokule'a*, a reconstructed oceangoing canoe, sailed 5,000 km south from Hawaii to Tahiti. The expedition's Micronesian navigator, Mau Piailug, succeeded in setting a course by the ocean swells and relative positions of the stars alone, which guided them very precisely along their way. Other signs used to locate an island were clouds (which hang over peaks and remain stationary), seabirds (boobies fly up to 50 km offshore, frigate birds up to 80 km), and mysterious *te lapa* (underwater streaks of light radiating 120–150 km from an island, disappearing closer in).

Since 1976 the *Hokule'a* has made several additional return trips to Tahiti; during 1985–1987 Hawaiian navigator Nainoa Thompson used traditional methods to guide the *Hokule'a* on a 27-month "Voyage of Rediscovery" that included a return west-east journey between Samoa and Tahiti. To date the vessel has logged well over 100,000 km using traditional methods, introducing Polynesian voyaging to countless thousands. In 1992 the canoe *Te Aurere* sailed from New Zealand to Rarotonga for the Festival of Pacific Arts—the first such voyage in 1,000 years—where it joined the *Hokule'a* and a fleet of other canoes in a dramatic demonstration of the current revival of traditional Polynesian navigation. In 1995 the *Hokule'a* led a three-canoe flotilla from Hawaii to Tahiti, returning in May with another three double-hulled canoes, which joined them in the Marquesas. In 1999 the vessel sailed to Easter Island. (For more information on the *Hokule'a,* click on http://leahi.kcc.hawaii .edu/org/pvs.)

The Polynesians were the real discoverers of the Pacific, completing all their major voyages long before Europeans even dreamed this ocean existed. In double canoes lashed together to form rafts, carrying their plants and animals with them, they penetrated as close to Antarctica as the South Island of New Zealand, as far north as Hawaii, and as far east as Easter Island—a full 13,000 km from where it's presumed they first entered the Pacific!

Neolithic Society

To some extent, the peoples of Polynesia, Micronesia, and Melanesia all kept gardens and a few domestic animals. Taro was cultivated on ingenious terraces or in organic pits; breadfruit was preserved by fermentation through burial (still a rare delicacy). Stone fishponds and fish traps were built in the lagoons. Pandanus and coconut fronds were woven into handicrafts. On the larger Polynesian islands these practices produced a surplus, which allowed the emergence of a powerful ruling class. The common people lived in fear of their gods and chiefs.

The Polynesians and Melanesians were cannibals, although the intensity of the practice varied from group to group: Cannibalism was rife in the Marquesas but relatively rare on Tahiti. Early European explorers were occasionally met by natives who would kneel beside them on the shore, squeezing their legs and pinching their posteriors to ascertain how tasty and substantial these white people would be to eat. It was believed that the mana or spiritual power of an enemy would be transferred to the consumer; to eat the body of one who was greatly despised was the ultimate revenge. Some Melanesians perceived the pale-skinned newcomers with "odd heads and removable skin" (hats and clothes) as evil spirits, perhaps ancestors intent on punishing the tribe for some violation of custom.

Jean-Jacques Rousseau and the 18th-century French rationalists created the romantic image of the "noble savage." Their vision of an ideal state of existence in harmony with nature disregarded the inequalities, cannibalism, and warfare that were a central part of island life, just as much of today's travel literature ignores the poverty and political/economic exploitation many Pacific peoples now face. Still, the legend of the South Pacific maintains its magic hold.

EUROPEAN CONTACT AND EXPLORATION
Hispanic Exploration

The first Europeans on the scene were Spaniards and Portuguese. The former were interested in gold and silver, new territories and colonies, and conversion of the heathen, while the latter were concerned with finding passages from Europe to the Moluccas, fabled Spice Islands of the East. Vasco Núñez de Balboa became the first to set eyes on this great ocean when he crossed the Isthmus of Panama in 1513 to discover the Mar del Sur, or South Seas (as opposed to the Mar del Norte, or North Seas, the Caribbean). On November 28, 1520, Ferdinand Magellan's three ships entered the Pacific around the bottom of South America. Pointing the vessels northwest, their next landfall was Guam, two months later. Though Magellan himself was killed in the Philippines, his surviving crew made it back to Spain in September 1522. The first circumnavigation in history had taken three years!

In 1568, Álvaro de Mendaña sailed from Peru to the Solomon Islands in search of gold. On his second trip to the Solomons in 1595 Mendaña discovered the southern Marquesas Islands. The voyage of Mendaña's pilot, Pedro Fernandez de Quirós, from Espiritu Santo in what is now Vanuatu to Mexico in 1606, against contrary winds in rotten ships with a starving, dying company, must rank as one of the greatest feats of Pacific journeying. The 16th-century Spaniards defined the bounds of the Pacific and added whole clusters of islands to geographic knowledge.

Terra Australis Incognita

The systematic European exploration of the Pacific was actually a search for *terra australis incognita,* a great southern continent believed to balance the continents of the north. There were many daring voyages during this period. The 17th century was the age of the Dutch explorations in search of new markets and trade routes. The first Dutch ships followed the routes pioneered by the Spanish and made few discoveries of significance. However, Anthony van Diemen, the Dutch governor-general of Batavia (present-day Jakarta) and a man of vision and great purpose, provided the backing for Abel Tasman's noteworthy voyage of 1642, which entered the Pacific from the west, rather than the east.

Tasman was instructed to find "the remaining unknown part of the terrestrial globe"—your basic Herculean task. Because of his meticulous and painstaking daily journals, Tasman is known as the historian of Pacific explorers. His observations proved invaluable to geographers, and

EUROPEAN CONTACT COUNTDOWN

DATE	EXPLORER AND NATIONALITY	LANDFALL
1513	Balboa, Spanish	Pacific Ocean
1521	Magellan, Spanish	Mariana Islands, Philippines
1526	Meneses, Portuguese	Irian Jaya
1527	Saavedra, Spanish	Marshall Islands
1543	Villalobos, Spanish	Caroline Islands
1545	Ortiz de Retes, Spanish	New Guinea
1568	Mendaña, Spanish	Tuvalu, Solomon Islands
1595	Mendaña, Spanish	Marquesas Islands
1606	Quirós, Spanish	Tuamotu Islands, Vanuatu
1606	Torres, Spanish	Australia
1616	Schouten/Le Maire, Dutch	Futuna
1642	Tasman, Dutch	Tasmania, New Zealand
1643	Tasman, Dutch	Tonga, Fiji
1722	Roggeveen, Dutch	Easter Island, Samoa
1765	Byron, English	Tokelau Islands
1767	Wallis, English	Tahiti, Wallis
1767	Carteret, English	Pitcairn
1769	Cook, English	Leeward Islands, Australs
1773	Cook, English	Cook Islands
1774	Cook, English	Niue, New Caledonia, Norfolk
1777	Cook, English	Christmas Island
1778	Cook, English	Hawaiian Islands
1781	Mourelle, Spanish	Vava'u
1791	Vancouver, English	Chatham Islands, Rapa
1798	Fearn, English	Nauru

he added Tasmania, New Zealand, Tonga, and parts of Fiji to Western knowledge. Tasman was the first to sail right around Australia. Jacob Roggeveen's voyage in 1722 also failed to discover the unknown continent, but he narrowed down the area of conjecture considerably.

The exploratory success of the 18th-century English was due to this 17th-century scientific labor. Although using 17th-century equipment, William Dampier explored with an 18th-century attitude. In 1745, the British Parliament passed an act promising £20,000 to the first British subject who could, in a British ship, discover and sail through a strait between Hudson's Bay and the South Seas. Thus many explorers were spurred to investigate the region. This route would have proven infinitely shorter than the one around Cape Horn, where the weather was often foul and the ships in perpetual danger; on Samuel Wallis's voyage of 1766–1767, his two ships took four months to round the chaotic Straits of Magellan. Captain John Byron (grandfather of the poet) ignored his orders to find a passage between the South Seas and Hudson's Bay and instead sought the Solomons, discovered initially by Mendaña. His circumnavigation took only two years. The great ocean was becoming an explorer's lake.

Captain Cook

The extraordinary achievements of James Cook (1728–1779) on his three voyages in the ships *Endeavor, Resolution, Adventure,* and *Discovery* left his successors with little to do but marvel over them. A product of the Age of Enlightenment, Cook was a mathematician, astronomer, practical physician, and master navigator. Son of a Yorkshire laborer, he learned seamanship on small coastal traders plying England's east coast. He joined the British Navy in 1755 and soon made a name for himself in Canada where he surveyed the St. Lawrence River, greatly contributing to the capture of Quebec City in 1759. Later he charted the coast of Newfoundland. Chosen to command the *Endeavor* in 1768 though only a warrant officer, Cook was the first captain to eliminate scurvy from his crew (with sauerkraut).

© WILLIAM HODGES

Omai, a Polynesian from Huahine, accompanied Captain Cook to England and returned.

The scientists of his time needed accurate observations of the transit of Venus, for if the passage of Venus across the face of the sun were measured from points on opposite sides of the earth, then the size of the solar system could be determined for the first time. In turn, this would make possible accurate predictions of the movements of the planets, vital for navigation at sea. Thus Cook was dispatched to Tahiti, and Father Hell (a Viennese astronomer of Hungarian origin) to Vardo, Norway.

So as not to alarm the French and Spanish, the British admiralty claimed Cook's first voyage (1768–1771) was primarily to take these measurements. His real purpose, however, was to further explore the region, in particular to find *terra australis incognita.* After three months on Tahiti, he sailed west and spent six months exploring and mapping New Zealand and the whole east coast of Australia, nearly tearing the bottom off his ship, the *Endeavor,* on the Great Barrier Reef in the process. Nine months after returning to England, Cook embarked on his second expedition (1772–1775), resolving to settle the matter of *terra australis incognita* conclusively. In the *Resolution* and *Adventure,* he sailed entirely around the bottom of the world, becoming the first to cross the Antarctic Circle and return to tell about it.

In 1773 John Harrison won the greater part of a £20,000 reward offered by Queen Anne in 1714 "for such Person or Persons as shall discover the Longitude at Sea." Harrison won it with the first marine chronometer (1759), which accompanied Cook on his second and third voyages. Also on these voyages was Omai, a native of Tahiti who sailed to England with Cook in 1774. Omai immediately became the talk of London, the epitome of the "noble savage," but to those who knew him he was simply a sophisticated man with a culture of his own.

In 1776 Cook set forth from England for a third voyage, supposedly to repatriate Omai but really to find a Northwest Passage from the Pacific to the Atlantic. He rounded the Cape of Good Hope and headed east to New Zealand, Tonga, and Tahiti. He then turned due north, discovering Kauai in what we now know as the Hawaiian Islands on January 18, 1778. After two weeks in Hawaii, Cook continued north via the west coast of North America but was forced back by ice in the Bering Strait. With winter coming, he returned to Hawaiian waters and located the two biggest islands of the group, Maui and Hawaii. On February 14, 1779, in a short, unexpected, petty skirmish with the Hawaiians, Cook was killed. Today he remains the giant of Pacific exploration. He'd dispelled the compelling, centuries-old hypothesis of an unknown continent, and his explorations ushered in the British era in the South Seas.

The Fatal Impact

Most early contacts with Europeans had a hugely disintegrating effect on native cultures. When introduced into the South Pacific, European sicknesses—mere discomforts to the white man—devastated whole populations. Measles, influenza, tuberculosis, dysentery, smallpox, typhus, typhoid, and whooping cough were deadly because the islanders had never developed resistance

to them. The white man's alcohol, weapons, and venereal disease further accelerated the process.

CONVERSION, COLONIALISM, AND WAR
Conversion

The systematic explorations of the 18th century were stimulated by the need for raw materials and markets as the Industrial Revolution took hold in Europe. After the American Revolution, much of Britain's colonizing energy was deflected toward Africa, India, and the Pacific. This gave them an early lead, but France and the U.S. weren't far behind.

As trade with China developed in the late 18th and early 19th centuries, Europeans combed the Pacific for products to sell to the Chinese. A very profitable triangular pattern of trade developed, in which European ships traded the islanders cheap whiskey, muskets, and glass beads for sandalwood, bêche-de-mer (sea cucumbers), pearls, and turtle shell, which were then sold to the Chinese for silk, tea, and porcelain. Ruffian whalers, sealers, and individual beachcombers flooded in. Most were unsavory characters who acted as mercenaries or advisers to local chiefs, but two, William Mariner and Herman Melville, left valuable accounts of early Polynesia.

After the easily exploited resources were depleted, white traders and planters arrived to establish posts and to create copra and cotton plantations on the finest land. Missionaries came to "civilize" the natives by teaching that all their customs—cannibalism, warring with their neighbors, having more than one wife, wearing leaves instead of clothes, dancing, drinking kava, chewing betel nut, etc.—were wrong. They taught hard work, shame, thrift, abstention, and obedience. Tribespeople now had to wear sweaty, rain-soaked, germ-carrying garments of European design. Men dressed in singlets and trousers, and the women in Mother Hubbards, one-piece smocks trailing along the ground. To clothe themselves and build churches required money, obtained only by working as laborers on European plantations or producing a surplus of goods to sell to European traders. In many instances

A PACIFIC CHRONOLOGY

50,000 B.C.	Papuan-speaking Australoid migrants arrive in New Guinea
8000 B.C.	Papuan hunters and gatherers colonize the Solomon Islands
1600 B.C.	Polynesians enter the Pacific from insular Southeast Asia
1300 B.C.	Polynesian *Lapita* people reach Tonga via Fiji
1000 B.C.	Polynesians reach Samoa (or Havaiki, the primeval homeland)
300 B.C.	Polynesians reach the Marquesas Islands and Tahiti from Samoa
A.D. 200	Polynesian canoes sail north to Hawaii from the Marquesas
A.D. 300	Polynesians from the Marquesas Islands reach Easter Island
A.D. 800	Polynesians reach the Cook Islands from Raiatea or the Marquesas
A.D. 900	Polynesians reach Mangareva in the Gambier Islands
A.D. 1100	Polynesians reach New Zealand for the Society or Cook islands
1520	Ferdinand Magellan becomes the first European to sail upon the Pacific Ocean
1768	Captain Cook's first Pacific voyage (to Tahiti, New Zealand, and Australia)
1779	Captain Cook killed during a brief, petty skirmish with the Hawaiians
1788	Australia becomes the British colony of New South Wales
1789	Fletcher Christian leads a mutiny against Capt. Bligh on the *Bounty*
1797	Protestant missionaries from the London Missionary Society reach Tahiti
1815	King Pomare II accepts Christianity on Moorea and reconquers Tahiti
1821	Protestant missionaries arrive at Aitutaki in the Cook Islands
1830	Rev. John Williams converts the Samoans to Protestantism
1836	the first French Catholic missionaries reach Tahiti and are expelled
1840	the Treaty of Waitangi with the Maori makes New Zealand a British colony
1842	Tahiti becomes a French protectorate over the objections of Queen Pomare IV
1845	George Tupou I becomes king of Tonga with the help of Wesleyan missionaries
1847	Tongans led by Enele Ma'afu invade eastern Fiji
1853	the French annex New Caledonia for use as a penal colony
1874	Ratu Seru Cakobau signs a Deed of Cession which makes Fiji a British colony
1875	King Tupou I signs the Victorian constitution still in use in Tonga today
1879	the first Indian indentured laborers arrive in Fiji on five-year contracts
1880	King Pomare V abdicates and French Polynesia becomes a full French colony
1888	the Cook Islands becomes a British protectorate to ward off French advances
1888	Chile annexes Easter Island for use as a naval coaling station
1893	Solomon Islands becomes a British protectorate to block German advances

1898	the U.S. annexes Hawaii after Queen Liliuokalani is deposed in an American coup
1899	Germany and the U.S. partition Samoa among themselves
1906	Britain and France assume joint control of the New Hebrides (Vanuatu)
1914	a New Zealand military force captures Samoa from Germany without a fight
1942	Japanese troops invade the Solomon Islands and occupy Guadalcanal
1947	South Pacific Commission (Secretariat of the Pacific Community) established
1959	Hawaii becomes the 50th state of the United States of Americaw
1962	Samoa achieves independence from New Zealand
1965	the Cook Islands becomes self-governing in free association with New Zealand
1966	France begins nuclear testing at Moruroa in the Tuamotu Islands
1968	the University of the South Pacific is founded at Suva, Fiji
1970	Fiji and Tonga achieve full independence from Great Britain
1971	South Pacific Forum is established by the Pacific's independent states
1974	Niue becomes internally self-governing in free association with New Zealand
1975	Papua New Guinea achieves independence from Australia
1978	Solomon Islands and Tuvalu are granted independence by Great Britain
1980	Vanuatu achieves independence from Great Britain and France
1985	French agents sink the *Rainbow Warrior* in Auckland harbor
1985	the South Pacific Nuclear-free Zone Treaty is signed at Rarotonga
1987	the South Pacific's first two military coups destabilize Fiji
1988	limited provincial autonomy is granted in New Caledonia by France
1990	universal suffrage is approved in Samoa
1992	France suspends its nuclear testing program in French Polynesia
1994	the Law of the Sea comes into force, greatly expanding island influence
1995	Jacques Chirac restarts French nuclear testing in French Polynesia
1996	Chirac halts French nuclear testing after worldwide protests
1997	constitutional democracy is restored in Fiji
1998	the Nouméa Accord signed in New Caledonia postpones independence
2000	governments in Fiji and the Solomon Islands are overthrown by civil coups
2001	democratic elections held in Fiji and the rule of law is reestablished
2003	Australia intervenes militarily in the Solomon Islands

this austere, harsh Christianity was grafted onto the numerous taboo systems of the Pacific.

Members of the London Missionary Society arrived at Tahiti in 1797, though it was not until 1815 that they succeeded in converting the Tahitians. One famous LMS missionary, Rev. John Williams, spread Protestantism to the Cook Islands (1823) and Samoa (1830). Methodists were active in Tonga (1822) and Fiji (1835). The children of some of the European missionaries who "came to do good, stayed to do well" as merchants. Later, many islanders themselves became missionaries: some 1,200 of them left their homes to carry the word of God to other islands. The first Catholic priests arrived in Polynesia in 1834. They competed with the Protestants for influence and divided islands on religious grounds.

Due to the inhospitable environment and absence of a chiefly class, the conversion and commercialization of Melanesia was not carried out until several decades later. After the 1840s, islanders were kidnapped by "blackbirders," who sold them as slaves to planters in Fiji and Queensland. Worst were the Peruvians, who took 3,634 islanders to Peru in 1862 and 1863, of whom only 148 were returned.

Colonialism

The first European colonies in Oceania were Australia (1788) and New Zealand (1840). Soon after, the French seized French Polynesia (1842) and New Caledonia (1853). A canal across Central America had already been proposed and Tahiti was seen as a potential port of call on the sea routes to Australia and New Zealand. New Caledonia was used first as a penal colony; nickel mining only began in the 1870s. The French annexed several other island groups near Tahiti in the 1880s.

Not wishing to be burdened with the expense of administering insignificant, far-flung colonies, Britain at first resisted pressure to officially annex other scattered South Pacific island groups, though Fiji was reluctantly taken in 1874 to establish law and order. In 1877 the Western Pacific High Commission was set up to protect British interests in the unclaimed islands.

Then the emergence of imperialist Germany and construction of the Panama Canal led to a

sudden rush of annexations by Britain, France, Germany, and the U.S. between 1884 and 1900. In 1899 Samoa was partitioned between Germany and the U.S., with Tonga and the Solomon Islands added to the British sphere of influence as compensation. The last island group to be taken over was New Hebrides (Vanuatu), declared a "condominium" by Britain and France in 1906 to forestall German advances.

Around the time of WW I Britain transferred responsibility for many island groups to Australia and New Zealand. The struggle for hegemony in imperialist Europe in 1914–1918 prompted Germany's colonies (New Guinea, Samoa, and Micronesia) to be taken by the British and Japanese empires. The South Pacific had become a British lake, economically dependent on Australia and New Zealand, a situation largely unchanged today.

By the late 19th century, the colonies' tropical produce (copra, sugar, vanilla, cacao, and fruits) had become more valuable and accessible; minerals—such as nickel and phosphates—and guano were also exploited. Total control of these resources passed to large European trading companies, which owned the plantations, ships, and retail stores. This colonial economy stimulated the immigration of Indian laborers to Fiji, the alienation of major tracts of native land in New Caledonia, and a drop in the indigenous populations in general by a third, not to mention the destruction of their cultures.

There were fundamental differences in approach between the British and French colonial administrations in the South Pacific. While the French system installed "direct rule" by French officials appointed by the French government, the British practiced "indirect rule" with the customary chiefs (Fiji) or royalty (Tonga) retaining most of their traditional powers. Not only was this form of government cheaper, but it fostered stability. British colonial officials had more decision-making authority than their French counterparts who had to adhere to instructions received from Paris. And while the French sought to undermine local traditions in the name of assimilation, the British defended the native land tenure on which traditional life was based.

War

World War II provided the United States with unparalleled opportunities to project power across the Pacific and grab territory. Although the United States had gained a toehold in the Pacific by annexing Hawaii and the Spanish colonies (Guam and the Philippines) in 1898, further expansion was frustrated by the British and Japanese. Japan had hoped to become the dominant force in Asia and the Pacific by establishing a "Greater East Asia Co-Prosperity Sphere." After the Japanese occupation of French Indochina in July 1941, an economic embargo on iron from the United States and oil from the Dutch East Indies presented the Japanese with a choice: strangulation, retreat, or war.

The history of the Pacific War can be found in many books. Half a million Japanese soldiers and civilians died far from their native shores. The only area covered in this handbook actually occupied by Japanese troops was the Solomon Islands; an account of the fighting there is included in that chapter's introduction. Large American staging and supply bases were created on Grande Terre, Espiritu Santo, Guadalcanal, and Bora Bora. The Americans built airfields on islands right across the South Pacific, while their ships controlled the southern supply routes to Australia and New Zealand.

DECOLONIZATION

In 1960 the United Nations issued a Declaration of Granting of Independence to Colonial Countries and Peoples, which encouraged the trend toward self-government, yet it was not until the independence of Samoa from New Zealand in 1962 that a worldwide wave of decolonization reached the region. During the 1960s and 1970s seven South Pacific countries (Fiji, Papua New Guinea, Solomon Islands, Tonga, Tuvalu, Vanuatu, and Samoa) became independent as Britain, Australia, and New Zealand dismantled their colonial systems.

The Cook Islands and Niue have achieved de facto independence in association with New Zealand. The French territories, French Polynesia, New Caledonia, and Wallis and Futuna, have varying degrees of internal autonomy, although great power continues to be wielded by appointed French officials who are not responsible to the local assemblies. Decolonization is a hot issue in these French colonies, where the South Pacific's only active independence movements are found (without forgetting the struggles for land and freedom in nearby Bougainville, West Papua, and Guam). American Samoa remains firmly tied to Washington by the subsidies it receives. Pitcairn is still a British colony, and New Zealand administers Tokelau, but this is at the request of the inhabitants. Easter Island is a colony of Chile.

French Colonialism

New Caledonia, French Polynesia, and Wallis and Futuna are part of a worldwide chain of French colonies also including Kerguelen, Guiana, Martinique, Guadeloupe, Mayotte, Reunion, and St. Pierre and Miquelon, under the DOM-TOM (Ministry of Overseas Departments and Territories). It costs France billions of Euros a year to maintain this system, a clear indicator that it's something totally different from colonial empires of the past, which were based on economic exploitation, not subsidies. For more than 40 years France has been willing to spend vast sums to perpetuate its status as a medium-sized world power.

These conditions contradict what has happened elsewhere in the South Pacific. During the 1960s and 1970s, as Britain, Australia, and New Zealand voluntarily withdrew from their Pacific colonies, French pretensions to global status grew stronger. This digging in created the anachronism of a few highly visible bastions of white colonialism in the midst of a sea of English-speaking self-governing nations. When French officials summarily rejected all protests against their nuclear testing and suppression of independence movements, most Pacific islanders were outraged.

The final round of nuclear testing in the Tuamotu Islands in 1995 was a watershed as French national prestige had seldom sunk as low, both in the Pacific and around the world. Since that debacle, France has tried to mend fences by supplying economic aid to the independent states and granting enhanced autonomy to its colonies. As France becomes fully integrated into the new Europe, it's quite likely that the ability and desire to maintain remote colonies will decline, and the decolonization process will finally be concluded.

Nuclear Testing

No other area on earth was more directly affected by the nuclear arms race than the Pacific. From August 6, 1945, until January 27, 1996, scarcely a year passed without one nuclear power or another testing their weapons of mass destruction here. The U.S., Britain, and France exploded more than 250 nuclear bombs at Bikini, Enewetak, Christmas Island, Moruroa, and Fangataufa, an average of more than six a year for more than 40 years, more than half of them by France. The U.S. and British testing was only halted by the 1963 Partial Nuclear Test Ban Treaty with the Soviets, while the French tests continued until unprecedented worldwide protests made it clear that the Cold War really was over (as usual, France was a slow learner).

The British and American test sites in Micronesia are now part of independent countries, but the Marshallese still suffer radiation sickness from U.S. testing in the 1940s and 1950s (some of it deliberately inflicted—the islanders were used as human guinea pigs), and the French are still covering up the consequences of their tests in French Polynesia. The end result of nuclear testing in Micronesia and Polynesia is ticking away in the genes of thousands of servicemen and residents present in those areas during the tests, and at the fragile underground Tuamotu test site used by the French.

The fact that the nuclear age began in their backyard at Hiroshima and Nagasaki has not been lost on the islanders. They have always seen few benefits coming from nuclear power, only deadly dangers. On August 6, 1985, eight member states of the South Pacific Forum signed the South Pacific Nuclear-Free Zone Treaty, also known as the Treaty of Rarotonga, which bans nuclear testing, land-based nuclear weapon storage, and nuclear waste dumping on their territories. Each country may decide for itself if nuclear-armed warships and aircraft are to be allowed entry. Of the five

nuclear powers, China and the USSR promptly signed the treaty, while the United States, France, and Britain only signed in March 1996 when it became obvious they could no longer use the region as a nuclear playground.

Regionalism

The postwar period also witnessed the growth of regionalism. In 1947 the South Pacific Commission (called the Secretariat of the Pacific Community since 1997) was established as a coordinating body by the colonial powers of the time. Today 22 island governments also belong to this technical assistance organization (www.spc.int). In 1971 the newly independent states formed the South Pacific Forum, renamed the Pacific Islands Forum (www.forumsec.org.fj) in 1999, a more vigorous regional body able to tackle political as well as social issues. The Forum Fisheries Agency (www.ffa.int), created in 1979, negotiates licensing agreements with 1,400 foreign fishing boats on behalf of the PIF members. The PIF also runs a regional shipping service, the Pacific Forum Line. The South Pacific Regional Environment Program (www.sprep.org.ws), set up in 1982 by the SPC, the PIF, and the United Nations, promotes sustainable development throughout the region. In 1988 Papua New Guinea, the Solomon Islands, and Vanuatu formed the Melanesian Spearhead regional grouping, which Fiji also joined in 1996.

Another major regional institution is the University of the South Pacific (www.usp.ac.fj), organized in 1967 to serve the English-speaking countries and territories. The initial campus was at Laucala, near Suva, and in 1977 the USP's School of Agriculture was established at Apia, Samoa. The major USP complex at Port Vila, Vanuatu, houses the Pacific Languages Unit and Law Department, and extension centers exist in all 12 member countries. The original aim of the USP was to facilitate the localization of posts held by expatriates until independence, but in recent years the emphasis has shifted from teacher training to business studies and technology. In 1987 the Université française du Pacifique was established with university centers at Tahiti (www.upf.pf) and Nouméa (www.univ-nc.nc).

OCEANIA AT A GLANCE

COUNTRY	POPULATION	LAND AREA	SEA AREA	HIGHEST POINT	CAPITAL	POLITICAL STATUS	CURRENCY
French Polynesia	245,405	3,543	5,030,000	2,241	Papeete	France 1842	CFP
Pitcairn Islands	50	47	800,000	347	Adamstown	Britain 1838	NZ$
Easter Island	3,800	171	355,000	507	Hanga Roa	Chile 1888	Peso
Cook Islands	18,027	240	1,830,000	653	Avarua	N.Z. 1901	NZ$
Niue	1,400	264	390,000	60	Alofi	N.Z. 1900	NZ$
Tonga	100,284	691	700,000	1,046	Nuku'alofa	Ind. 1970	Pa'anga
American Samoa	57,291	201	390,000	965	Utulei	U.S. 1900	US$
Samoa	174,140	2,842	120,000	1,858	Apia	Ind. 1962	Tala
Tokelau	1,507	12	290,000	5	Fakaofo	N.Z. 1925	NZ$
Wallis and Futuna	14,000	274	300,000	524	Mata-Utu	France 1887	CFP
Tuvalu	9,119	25	900,000	5	Funafuti	Ind. 1978	A$
Total Polynesia	**625,023**	**8,305**	**11,105,000**				
Fiji	806,268	18,272	1,290,000	1,323	Suva	Ind. 1970	F$
New Caledonia	215,904	18,735	1,740,000	1,639	Nouméa	France 1853	CFP
Vanuatu	186,678	12,189	680,000	1,879	Port Vila	Ind. 1980	Vatu
Solomon Islands	409,042	27,556	1,340,000	2,447	Honiara	Ind. 1978	SI$
Total Melanesia	**1,617,892**	**76,752**	**5,050,000**				

Land areas and sea areas (the ocean area included within the 200-nautical-mile Exclusive Economic Zone of each country, indicated on the map on p. 32) are expressed in square kilometers. The highest points are in meters. The category "political status" gives the year in which the country became independent, or the territory/province/state fell under colonial rule by the power named. The sea areas (and various other figures) were taken from Selected Pacific Economies: A Statistical Summary, published by the Secretariat of the Pacific Community, Nouméa.

One of the few regional grass roots coalitions is the Nuclear-Free and Independent Pacific (NFIP) movement, which organizes conferences periodically (Fiji 1975, Pohnpei 1978, Hawaii 1980, Vanuatu 1983, Manila 1987, New Zealand 1990, Fiji 1996, Tahiti 1999, Tonga 2003) to allow activists from groups from all around the Pacific to get together and map out strategy and solidarity in the struggle against militarism and colonialism. The directing body of the NFIP movement is the Pacific Concerns Resource Center (www.pcrc.org.fj).

THE PACIFIC TODAY

The modern world has transformed the Pacific. Outboards have replaced outriggers and Coca-Cola has been substituted for coconuts. Consumerism has caught on in the towns. As money becomes more important, the islanders learn the full meaning of urban unemployment, poverty, homelessness, inequality, and acculturation. Television is spreading, and attitudes are molded by the tens of thousands of VCRs that play pirated videotapes available at hundreds of corner stores. Villagers are trapped by material desires.

The diet is changing as imported processed foods take the place of fiber-rich fresh foods such as breadfruit, taro, and plantain. The ocean would seem a bountiful resource, but on many islands the reef waters are already overharvested, and the inhabitants often lack the ability to fish the open sea. Thus the bitter irony of Japanese canned mackerel.

Noncommunicable nutrition-related ailments such as heart disease, diabetes, and cancer now account for three-quarters of all deaths in urban Polynesia, but less than a quarter in predominantly rural Vanuatu and Solomon Islands, where infectious and parasitic diseases such as malaria, dengue fever, pneumonia, diarrhea, hepatitis, and tuberculosis prevail. Cigarette smoking is a major health problem; more than 50 percent of Pacific men are habitual smokers. Rural islanders tend to smoke more than those in the towns, and 88 percent of rural indigenous Fijian men are smokers.

Salaried employment leads inevitably to the replacement of the extended family by the nuclear family, and in Melanesia there's a growing gap between new middle classes with government jobs and the village-based populace. Western education has aroused expectations that the island economies are unable to fulfill, and the influx to the capitals has strained social services to the breaking point, creating serious housing and employment problems, especially among the young. Populations are growing faster than the local economies—leading to declining living standards—and oversized bureaucracies stifle development. Melanesian women are victimized by domestic violence, economic burdens, and cultural change.

Subsistence agriculture continues to play an important role in the South Pacific, and most land is still held communally by extended families or clans; however, pressure is mounting from outside agencies such as the World Bank and the International Monetary Fund (IMF) to convert communal land into individual ownership under the guise of "economic development." Western economic models give importance only to commodity crops useful to industrialized countries as raw materials, discounting the stabilizing effect of subsistence. When the tiller of the soil is no longer able to eat his own produce, he becomes a consumer of processed foods marketed by food-exporting countries such as Australia and New Zealand, and the country loses a measure of its independence.

Individually registered land can be taxed and sold on the open market, and throughout the third world the privatization of land has inevitably led to control of the best tracts passing into the hands of transnational corporations, banks, and the government. Pressure from agencies such as the IMF to force local governments to register land and allow it to be used as loan collateral is part of a stratagem to dispossess the islanders of their land. Once their communal land is gone, people are no longer able to fall back on their own produce when economies deteriorate, and they find themselves forced to take any job they can find. Acutely aware of the fate of the Hawaiians and the New Zealand Maoris, the islanders are highly sensitive about land rights, yet these instincts are coming under increasing pressure as local governments have "land mobilizations" forced upon them by foreign capital.

All across the South Pacific, regional stability is eroded by class differences, government corruption, uneven development, industrial exploitation, militarism, and the declining terms of trade. By making the economies dependent on external markets, much current "economic development" destabilizes societies once secure in "primitive affluence," and virtually every Pacific entity is now subservient to some degree of neocolonial control. Local interests are sacrificed for the benefit of transnational corporations and industrialized states far across the sea.

GOVERNMENT

Generally, the South Pacific is governed on the basis of constitutional law, an independent judiciary, and regular elections, with some regional idiosyncrasies. In Samoa only *matai* (Samoan chiefs) may stand as candidates for 47 of the 49 parliamentary seats, although since 1991 all adults can vote. Fiji has a constitution that segregates voting for 46 of the 71 members of parliament along racial lines, while in Tonga only

nine of the 30 members of parliament are elected directly by the people.

The two-party system is a relatively recent legacy of the last years of colonial rule. Traditionally, Melanesians governed themselves by consensus: those involved would sit down and discuss a problem until a compromise was reached, which everyone then accepted, and this bottom-up democracy still governs life throughout Melanesia. Governments in Melanesia today are typically weak coalitions of small parties dependent on skillful leaders to hold them together. There were no regional leaders or powerful chiefs in Melanesia before the arrival of Europeans. Polynesia, on the other hand, was governed by powerful hereditary chiefs and kings; the Fijian political system was strongly influenced by the Polynesians.

Although only six of the 15 political entities covered in this book are fully independent, most of the others are internally self-governing to some degree. Tokelau, a dependency of New Zealand, has resisted self-government out of fear that it might lead to a reduction in subsidies. The appointed French high commissioners in French Polynesia, Wallis and Futuna, and New Caledonia wield considerable power in those territories, although locally elected assemblies have growing control over economic and social matters.

Economy

External Aid

Countries like Tonga, Samoa, and the Cook Islands have classic "MIRAB" economies, based on migration, remittances, aid, and bureaucracy. An overwhelming proportion of aid money is given by metropolitan powers to their colonies, past or present. France spends US$750 million a year maintaining its three Pacific colonies, although much of the money returns to France to pay for French imports or services. In 2002–2003 Australia provided A$165 million in aid to the Pacific islands (excluding Papua New Guinea), of which A$36 million went to Solomon Islands, A$22 million to Vanuatu, A$19 million to Fiji, A$15 million to Samoa, and A$11 million to Tonga. New Zealand's

UN$75 million in aid is also evenly spread, while most of the US$161 million in U.S. aid is spent in American Samoa and the U.S.-related entities in Micronesia. The United States also pays US$21 million a year to the island states for fisheries access.

Other European countries such as Britain and Germany channel most of their aid through the European Union, which supplies soft loans, import quotas and subsidies, and technical assistance to the tune of around US$45 million. At US$150 million a year, Japan is one of the largest providers of bilateral aid to the independent countries, provided you don't count the large amounts of Australian money given to Papua New Guinea. The Asian Development Bank,

EXCLUSIVE ECONOMIC ZONES (EEZ)

© DAVID STANLEY

World Bank, and United Nations agencies are also significant players in the aid game.

Although the South Pacific absorbs the highest rate of per capita aid in the world, much of the money is wasted on doing things for people instead of helping them do things for themselves. Aid that empowers people by increasing their capacity to identify, understand, and resolve problems is the exception, while prestige projects like huge airports, sophisticated communications networks, and fancy government buildings, which foster dependence on outsiders, are the rule. The United States paid for the parliament building in Honiara and the Chinese government has bankrolled massive government complexes in Vanuatu and Samoa. In response, Taiwan has financed high profile buildings in Solomon Islands, Tuvalu, and Tonga. Direct budgetary aid to countries like Papua New Guinea is often siphoned off by corrupt politicians.

Japanese aid is intended primarily to ensure easy access for its fishing fleet and to support Japanese business activities in the islands. Virtually all Japanese aid is "tied," with most of the benefit going to Japanese companies. In contrast, Australia and New Zealand are to be commended for taking the trouble to develop low-profile microprojects to assist individual communities. The closest the United States comes to this is the Peace Corps, which is currently active in Samoa, Tonga, and Vanuatu.

Aid spent in the capitals prompts unproductive migrations to the towns. There's a growing imbalance between the cost of government in relation to locally generated revenues. Salaries for officials, consultants, and various other roving "experts" eat up much aid. The only Pacific country with a high per capita income that is not highly dependent on aid is Fiji.

Trade

Australia and New Zealand have huge trade surpluses with the Pacific islands. In 1999, for example, Australia sold them A$1,637 million in goods while purchasing only A$742 million worth. New Zealand sells 12 times more than it buys. Ten South Pacific countries participate in the Pacific Forum Line, a shipping company set up by the Pacific Islands Forum to facilitate trade with Australia and New Zealand, but in practice, the Line's large container ships run full northbound and empty southbound. The trade deficits make the industrialized, exporting nations the main beneficiaries of the island economies. Investment and tourism help to off-set the trade imbalances somewhat, but these also foster dependence.

The main products exported by the South Pacific countries are sugar (Fiji), seafood (American Samoa, Fiji, New Caledonia, and Solomon Islands), clothing and footwear (Fiji), minerals (Fiji, New Caledonia, and Solomon Islands), timber (Fiji, Solomon Islands, and Vanuatu), and black pearls (the Cook Islands and French Polynesia). The United Kingdom and Japan are the only major powers that purchase a lot more from the islands than they sell. The United Kingdom buys much of Fiji's sugar and fish while Japan purchases timber and fish from Solomon Islands and nickel ore from New Caledonia. In recent years Tonga has exported large quantities of squash (pumpkin) to Japan. In late 2001, the European Union imposed import restrictions on kava, reducing exports of the root crop from Fiji, Samoa, Tonga, and Vanuatu to a quarter previous levels. The stated reason for the ban was that natural kava-based medicines were suspected of causing liver damage but scientific proof for this claim has not appeared. In fact, the ban may have more to do with lobbying by powerful pharmaceutical firms anxious to prevent poor Pacific farmers from competing with their chemical anti-depressants.

Agricultural products such as bananas, cacao, coconut oil, coffee, copra, palm oil, pineapples, sugar, taro, tea, and vanilla are subject to price fluctuations over which local governments have no control, plus low demand and strong competition from other developing country producers. Most of these commodities are processed and marketed outside the islands by transnationals. Even worse, efforts to increase the output of commodities reduces subsistence food production, leading to imports of processed food. Bodies such as the World Bank push for cash cropping and expanded trade in food, usually at the expense of self-sufficiency. New Zealand meat exporters routinely ship low-quality "Pacific cuts" of fatty, frozen mutton flaps unsalable on world markets to countries like Tonga and Samoa. American companies dump junk foods such as "turkey tails" in the islands, and tinned mystery meats arrive from afar. Processed foods saturated with sugar and fat are popular in the islands due to their convenience and low cost; imported rice is less expensive than taro. Diet-related diseases such as diabetes are the hidden cost.

TRADING PARTNERS

(Figures are from 1999 and expressed in A$ million)

REGION	IMPORTS FROM	EXPORTS TO
Australia	1,637	742
New Zealand	534	45
South Pacific	199	58
France	612	150
United Kingdom	60	296
Other Europe	231	171
U.S.A.	838	229
Japan	481	301
Other Asia	455	170
Other countries	313	1,367
Total	**5,362**	**3,528**

Trade Agreements

Trade within the Pacific region is limited by a basic similarity of the island products and shipping tariffs which encourage bulk trade with Australia and New Zealand. In 1994 the Melanesian Spearhead countries signed the Melanesian Trade Agreement establishing free trade in beef from Vanuatu, canned tuna from Solomon Islands, and tea from Papua New Guinea. Fiji's decision to join the Spearhead in 1996 had a lot to do with a desire to gain access to this market, and in 1999 the list was expanded to over 200 products. The experience of Vanuatu and Solomon Islands was that arrangement favored large producers in Fiji and Papau New Guinea to the detriment of smaller companies in their countries, and in 2002 they dropped out. A Pacific Island Countries Trade Agreement (PICTA), launched at the 2002 meeting of the Pacific Islands Forum, was immediately signed by representatives of Fiji, Samoa, Tonga, and the Cook Islands but its viability is also in doubt.

The new order of colonialism in the Pacific is known as "globalization." The World Bank and other international banks aggressively market "project loans" designed to facilitate the production of goods for sale on world markets. The initial beneficiaries of these projects are the contractors, while the ability of transnational corporations to exploit the region's natural resources is enhanced. Subsistence food production is reduced and the recipient state is left with a debt burden it can only service through exports. Free trade forces Pacific countries to compete with low-wage producers in Asia and Latin America where human rights and the environment are of scant concern.

Should commodity exports fail, the International Monetary Fund steps in with emergency loans to make sure the foreign banks don't lose their money. Local governments are forced to accept "structural adjustment programs" dictated from Washington, and the well-paid Western bankers mandate that social spending be cut. Another favorite trick is to persuade governments to shift the tax burden from rich to poor by replacing income and company taxes with a value-added tax. Customs duties are removed and tottering administrations are forced to clearcut their rainforests or sell their soil to meet financial obligations. This kind of chicanery has caused untold misery in Africa, Asia, and Latin America, usually with the connivance of corrupt local officials.

A much fairer arrangement is the 20-year Cotonou Agreement (signed in 2000), previously known as the Lomé Convention, which provides for the preferential entry into the European Union at fixed prices of set quotas of agricultural commodities from 78 African, Caribbean, and Pacific countries. Many experts believe that trade subsidies of this kind are the most effective way of delivering aid to developing countries without the intervention of state bureaucracies. This type of arrangement is crucial to countries that rely on a single export for much of their foreign exchange. Eight Pacific countries are involved (half of Fiji's sugar crop enjoys free entry into the United Kingdom at three times the world market price thanks to Cotonou). The United States has lobbied vigorously against subsidized trading agreements of this kind in favor of "free trade" to allow American corporations based in Latin America to export tropical commodities produced cheaply through the use of semislave labor to Europe.

Since 1980 New Zealand and Australia have tried to help the island countries balance their trade deficits by allowing most of the products of the Pacific Islands Forum countries unrestricted duty-free entry on a nonreciprocal basis, provided they have 50 percent local content. The only exceptions are sugar, steel, motor vehicles, and clothing, which are subject to quotas in Australia. The South Pacific Regional Trade and Economic Cooperation Agreement (SPARTECA) has allowed Tonga, Samoa, and others to set up Small Industries Centers producing manufactured goods for export south. A large Japanese-owned factory in Samoa exports automotive electrical parts to Australia. Garments are now Fiji's largest export. Low wages, inadequate labor legislation, and weak unions combine with tax concessions, exemption from customs duties, and an open market in Australia and New Zealand to make Fiji attractive to foreign garment manufacturers. Women make up the vast majority of the workforce, earning less than a tenth as much as their counterparts in New Zealand, where working conditions are far better.

Critics of SPARTECA say the 50 percent local content rule discourages companies from operating efficiently by reducing local costs, and relegates them to the bottom end of the market since the raw materials required for quality products are not available in the islands. Now with universal trade barriers falling in the wake of the 1994 signing of the GATT, the value of selective trade agreements such as SPARTECA and Cotonou is decreasing, and in the future it will be much more difficult for Pacific island industries to compete with cheap-labor areas in Asia. The 1994 Bogor Declaration will reduce tariffs between the 19 members of the Asia Pacific Economic Cooperation (APEC) to zero by 2010, thereby eliminating the competitive advantage of SPARTECA by granting Asian producers similar access to Australia and New Zealand.

Business

Foreign investment in tourism, retailing, banking, construction, transportation, and mining is heavy. Foreign logging operations and local slash-and-burn agriculture threaten the rainforests of the high islands, and many governments lack the political will to enforce conservation. In Solomon Islands, Malaysian logging companies are cutting the forests at far beyond the sustainable rate while paying landowners a royalty of less than one percent of the value of the timber. An Australian study has shown how Vanuatu and Solomon Islands have lost hundreds of millions of dollars due to overcutting and underpaying by Asian loggers. Payoffs to local officials allow this practice to continue. Despite these depredations, three-quarters of the old growth forest in these two countries is still intact and capable of being saved.

The Asian economic crisis of 1997–1998 exacerbated a process already underway in the islands as national banks approached collapse, government indebtedness soared, and official corruption ran rampant. Like their counterparts in Jakarta, Kuala Lumpur, Bangkok, and Washington, many island political leaders have become hooked on the joys of borrowing, burdening their countries with unrepayable debts.

Minerals

The most important minerals are nickel in New Caledonia and gold in Fiji. Extensive mineral exploration has been conducted in the Solomon Islands, and there are potential oil basins around Tonga, Fiji, New Caledonia, Vanuatu, and the Solomons, though as yet no oil has been discovered.

More important are the undersea mineral nodules within the exclusive economic zones (EEZ) of French Polynesia, the Cook Islands, and Kiribati. Three known nodule deposits sit in more than 6,000 meters of water in the Pacific: one stretches from Mexico to a point southeast of Hawaii; another is between Hawaii and the Marshall Islands; a third is in French Polynesia and the Cook Islands. The potato-sized nodules contain manganese, cobalt, nickel, and copper; total deposits are valued at US$3 trillion, enough to supply the world for thousands of years. The South Pacific Applied Geoscience Commission or SOPAC (www.sopac.org.fj), a regional body set up by the United Nations in 1972, is in charge of assessing the development of mineral resources in the EEZs of the Pacific countries, though actual mining is still decades away. Over the past decade Japan has spent US$100 million on seabed surveys in preparation for eventual mining.

Fisheries

Tuna is the second-largest commercial fishing industry in the world (after shrimp and prawns), and about half the world's catch is taken in the central and western Pacific. Most of the two million metric tonnes of tuna (worth US$2 billion) fished from the region's seas each year is taken by about 1,200 foreign fishing boats, which pay a mere US$70 million in annual fees to work the EEZs of the island nations. The 200 large purse seiners from Taiwan, Korea, the United States, the Philippines, and Spain take about half the catch, with Chinese, Taiwanese, and Japanese longline and pole-and-line boats taking most of the rest. Only one percent is caught by trolling.

About 65 percent of the tuna pulled in are skipjack, with yellowfin, albacore, and bigeye accounting for the rest. Due to the introduction of purse seiners, catches have increased five fold since the early 1980s and the bigeye and yellowfin are already being harvested at close to maximum sustainable rates. Fears are growing that the entire resource could soon be ravaged as European high seas fleets are redeployed from oceans already stripped of fish. Fourteen of the huge Spanish factory ships that destroyed the North Atlantic fisheries began operating in Kiribati waters in 2000. The Spanish have a reputation for ignoring fishing rules and cheating, and their heavily subsidized purse seiners (twice the size of American purse seiners) pull in everything they can, including juvenile tuna and other species. These predators are now using the leverage of European Union aid money to gain access to the other South Pacific countries with potentially disastrous consequences. Overfishing by foreign boats has already led to dramatic falls in tuna catches by local boats in Samoa and Fiji.

The tuna fishery is of paramount importance because it's virtually the only area where the islands play a major role in the world economy, and tuna management and conservation in international waters have become key issues. Since 1987 Australia has donated several dozen 31-meter naval patrol boats to the island states to help police the island fisheries zones.

The Forum Fisheries Agency handles all fisheries agreements between the 14 FFA member states and foreign fishing interests. The Koreans and Taiwanese have a history of massively underreporting their catches to avoid paying proper access fees. World Bank figures report that the United States pays fees equivalent to 10 percent of the value of the catch, Spain 7 percent, Japan 5 percent, Taiwan 3.7 percent, and Korea only 2.2 percent. Although the Japanese report their catches more honestly than the other Asians, they've steadfastly refused to sign a multilateral fisheries agreement with the FFA. Instead the Japanese prefer to drive a hard bargain with each Pacific country individually, using aid money as bait. Smaller Pacific countries are often unable to stand up to this bullying, and the Asian fishing companies routinely pay bribes to island officials to avoid scrutiny or obtain licenses. In 2000 the Tuna Commission was created to regulate fishing

for migratory species in the entire central and western Pacific including international waters.

Some Pacific countries have established small pole-and-line fishing industries, but the capital-intensive, high-tech purse seiner operations carried out by foreign companies are beyond their means. A workable fishing fleet requires at least 10 boats plus large amounts of fresh water and electricity for processing. Also, U.S. customs regulations tax tuna heavily unless it's processed in an American territory, which is why the two canneries at Pago Pago, American Samoa, receive most of the purse seiner-caught fish. The other regional canneries at Levuka (Fiji) and Noro (Solomon Islands) benefit from a 24 percent duty advantage in the European Union thanks to the Cotonou Agreement. Without this they'd be unable to compete with low-wage canneries in Thailand and Indonesia. Longline vessels are used to supply the lucrative Japanese sashimi market with iced tuna, which is transshipped by air. Inshore fisheries net a mere 100,000 tonnes a year, a tenth the amount landed on the high seas. In all, about 10,000 Pacific islanders are directly employed on fishing boats or in canneries or packing plants.

Various Moneymaking Scams

In 1971 the New Hebrides (now Vanuatu) became the first Pacific entity to offer offshore banking facilities to foreign corporations attempting to avoid taxation in their home countries. In 1982 the Cook Islands also set up a tax haven, followed by Tonga in 1985 and Samoa in 1989. Almost 100 brass-plate banks and more than 1,000 dummy corporations now operate in Vanuatu with little or no staff, fixed assets, or capital. In 1990 Australia plugged the loopholes, which had been costing it millions of dollars a year in lost taxation, and most of the clients of the "financial centers" are now companies based in Asia.

Vanuatu also runs a "flag of convenience" shipping register that allows first-world shipping companies to evade Western safety, environmental, and labor regulations, while employing cheap third-world crews on their ships. Tonga has sold its sovereignty to affluent foreigners in the form of dummy Tongan passports intended to be used to slip into third countries. A sizable Chinese transient population is in Nuku'alofa awaiting the chance to move on to greener pastures. In past, Tuvalu and Niue have leased their international telephone circuits to the operators of sex-by-phone hot lines.

One of the largest sources of income for countries like Tonga, Samoa, and the Cook Islands is remittances sent home by emigrants living in New Zealand and Australia. The Diaspora also provides the bulk of visitors to countries like Tonga and Samoa.

TOURISM

Tourism is the world's largest and fastest-growing industry, accounting for 10 percent of world economic activity and one in 15 jobs worldwide. Some 750 million people a year currently travel abroad compared to only 25 million in 1950, and each year over 100 million first-world tourists visit developing countries, transferring US$110 billion from North to South. Tourism is the only industry that allows a net flow of wealth from richer to poorer countries, and in the islands it's one of the few avenues open for economic development, providing much-needed foreign exchange required to pay for imports. Unlike every other export, purchasers of tourism products pay their own transportation costs to the market.

Australia provides the largest percentage of the one million tourists who visit the South Pacific each year, followed by the United States, New Zealand, France, Japan, the United Kingdom, Canada, and Germany in that order. Australia is the main source of visitors to Fiji, Solomon Islands, and Vanuatu, while New Zealanders are the biggest group in the Cook Islands, Niue, Tonga, and Samoa. Americans and French are the largest single groups in French Polynesia, while the French and Japanese are tied in New Caledonia. On a per-capita basis, the Cook Islands gets the most tourists and Solomon Islands the fewest. It's the number-one industry in French Polynesia, Easter Island, the Cook Islands, Tonga, Samoa, Fiji, and Vanuatu, and some 45,000 islanders now rely on tourism as a way of making a living. Yet tourism is relatively

TOURIST ARRIVALS (2003)	
Fiji Islands	430,800
French Polynesia	212,767
New Caledonia	101,983
Samoa	92,313
Cook Islands	78,328
Papua New Guinea	52,623
Vanuatu	50,400
Tonga	40,110
Niue	2,758
Tuvalu	1,496

low key: overcrowded Hawaii gets 10 times as many annual visitors as the entire South Pacific combined. The "tyranny of distance" has thus far prevented the islands from being spoiled.

Arrival levels from Australia and New Zealand are expected to remain stable in coming years, and Japan, Europe, and North America are seen as the main growth markets for South Pacific tourism. The Japanese tend to go on short holidays, and only those countries with direct flights from Japan (Fiji, New Caledonia, and French Polynesia) receive sizable numbers of Japanese tourists. Increasing numbers of European and North American visitors can be expected if airfares remain low and the region's many advantages over competing Mediterranean and Caribbean destinations can be effectively marketed.

Only about 40 percent of the net earnings from tourism actually stays in the host country. The rest is "leaked" in repatriated profits, salaries for expatriates, commissions, imported goods, food, fuel, etc. Top management positions usually go to foreigners, with local residents offered low-paying service jobs. To encourage hotel construction, local governments must commit to crippling tax concessions and large infrastructure investments for the benefit of hotel companies. The cost of airports, roads, communications networks, power lines, sewers, and waste disposal can exceed the profits from tourism.

Tourism-related construction can cause unsightly beach erosion due to the clearing of vegetation and the extraction of sand. Resort sewage causes lagoon pollution, while the reefs are blasted to provide passes for tourist craft and stripped of corals or shells by visitors. Locally scarce water supplies are diverted to hotels, and foods such as fruit and fish can be priced beyond the reach of local residents. Access to the ocean can be blocked by wall-to-wall resorts.

Although tourism is often seen as a way of experiencing other cultures, it can undermine those same cultures. Traditional dances and ceremonies are shortened or changed to fit into tourist schedules, and mock celebrations are held out of season and context, and their significance is lost. Cheap mass-produced handicrafts are made to satisfy the expectations of visitors; thus, the New Guinea-style masks of Fiji, mock-Hawaiian tikis of Tonga, and Balinese carvings of Bora Bora. Authenticity is sacrificed for immediate profits. While travel cannot help but improve international understanding, the aura of glamour and prosperity surrounding tourist resorts can present a totally false image of a country's social and economic realities.

Foreign tour operators usually focus on luxury resorts and all-inclusive tours—the exotic rather than the authentic. Packaged holidays create the illusion of adventure while avoiding all risks and individualized variables, and on many tours the only islanders seen are maids and bartenders. This elitist tourism perpetuates the colonial master-servant relationship as condescending foreigners instill a feeling of inferiority in local residents and workers. Many island governments are publicly on record as favoring development based on local resources and island technology, yet inexplicably this concept is rarely applied to tourism. Without local participation, tourism can be the proverbial wolf in sheep's clothing.

The People

The Sea of Islands that is the Pacific is divided into three great cultural areas: Polynesia and Melanesia lie mostly below the equator while Micronesia is above it. The name Polynesia comes from the Greek words *poly* (many) and *nesos* (islands). The Polynesian Triangle has Hawaii at its north apex, New Zealand 8,000 km to the southwest, and Easter Island an equal distance to the southeast. Melanesia gets its name from the Greek word *melas* (black), probably for the dark appearance of its inhabitants as seen by the early European navigators. Micronesia comes from the Greek word *mikros* (small), thus, the "small islands."

The term Polynesia was coined by Charles de Brosses in 1756 and applied to all the Pacific islands. The present restricted use was proposed by Dumont d'Urville during a famous lecture at the Geographical Society in Paris in 1831. At the same time he also proposed the terms Melanesia and Micronesia for the regions that still bear those names. The terms are not particularly good, considering that all three regions have "many islands" and "small islands"; in Melanesia it is not the islands, but the people, that are black.

The notion that the Pacific islands and their peoples are all similar—if you've seen one you've seen 'em all—is a total fallacy. No other group of six million people anywhere on earth comes from such a variety of cultures. The population is divided between Melanesians (80 percent), Polynesians (7 percent), Asians (6 percent), Micronesians (5 percent), and Europeans (2 percent). Ninety percent of the people live on high islands, the rest on low islands and atolls. About a million reside in urban areas. The region's charming, gentle, graceful peoples are among its main attractions.

Population

The high birth rate (more than 3 percent a year in parts of Melanesia) and rapid urbanization severely tax the best efforts of governments with limited resources. The average population density across the region (excluding Papua New Guinea) is 27 persons per square km, though some atolls can have more than 1,000 people per square km.

The most densely populated Pacific countries are the Polynesian islands of American Samoa, Tokelau, Tonga, and Tuvalu, while the larger Melanesian countries have far fewer people per square km. Due to the absence of family planning, populations in Melanesia are doubling every 20 years and half the total population is under 18 years of age. Population growth rates vary from negative growth in the Cook Islands, Niue, and Tokelau, where people are emigrating, to just under three percent in Melanesia.

More developed countries like American Samoa, the Cook Islands, Fiji, New Caledonia, and French Polynesia are highly urbanized, with around half the population town dwellers. Samoa, Solomon Islands, and Vanuatu are the least urbanized, with about 85 percent still living in villages. The rapid growth of cities like Apia, Honiara, Nuku'alofa, Papeete, Port Vila, and Suva has led to high levels of unemployment and social problems such as alcoholism, petty crime, and domestic violence.

Emigration relieves the pressure a little and provides income in the form of remittances sent back. However, absenteeism also creates the problem of idled land and abandoned homes. Cook Islanders, Niueans, Tongans, and Samoans emigrate to New Zealand; American Samoans and Micronesians to the United States; Fiji Indians to Canada and Australia; people from the Australs, Tuamotus, and Marquesas to Tahiti; and Tahitians and Wallis Islanders to New Caledonia. In American Samoa, the Cook Islands, Niue, Tokelau, and Wallis and Futuna, more islanders now live off their home islands than on them. About 175,000 insular Polynesians live in New Zealand, another 65,000 in the United States. Some 25,000 former Indo-Fijians are in Canada.

Pacific Women

Traditionally, Pacific women were confined to the home, while the men would handle most matters outside the immediate family. In Melanesia the woman was responsible for working the land and doing most of the housework, thereby increasing the status of the man as head of the family; life was similar for Polynesian women, though they had greater influence.

Western education has caused many Pacific women to question their subordinate position and the changing lifestyle has made the old relationship between the sexes outmoded. As paid employment expands and—thanks to family planning—women are able to hold their jobs, they demand equal treatment from society. Polynesian women are more emancipated than their sisters in Melanesia, though men continue to dominate public life throughout the region. Tradition is often manipulated to deny women the right to express themselves publicly on community matters.

Cultural barriers hinder women's access to education and employment, and the proportion of girls in school falls rapidly as the grade level increases. Female students are nudged into low-paying fields such as nursing or secretarial services; in Fiji and elsewhere, export-oriented garment factories exploit women workers with low wages and poor conditions. Levels of domestic violence vary greatly. In Fiji, for example, it's far less accepted among indigenous Fijians than it is among Indo-Fijians, and in Fiji's Macuata Province women have a suicide rate seven times above the world average, with most of the victims being Indo-Fijians. Those little signs on buses reading "real men don't hit women" suggest the problem. Travelers should take an interest in women's issues.

Traditional Customs

Although the South Pacific is a region of great variety, there are a number of rituals and ceremonies that many islands have in common. The most important of these is the kava ceremony found in Fiji, Samoa, Tonga, and Vanuatu. Kava (called *yaqona* in Fiji) is a drink made from the crushed root of the pepper plant. The powder or pulp is strained or mixed with water in a large wooden bowl and drunk from a coconut-shell cup. Elaborate protocols accompany formal kava ceremonies although kava is also a social drink consumed by ordinary people when they get together to relax and chat. See the introductions to the Fiji Islands and Vanuatu chapters for more information.

Another widespread feature of Pacific culture is the making of bark cloth called tapa (*masi* in Fijian) used for clothing or decoration. This felt-like cloth with stenciled or printed designs is described under Arts and Crafts in this Introduction.

Other customs covered in this book include firewalking in Fiji, stone fishing in French Polynesia, the use of an earth oven called an *umu* in Polynesia or a *lovo* in Fiji, tattooing in Samoa and elsewhere in Polynesia, land diving on Pentecost in Vanuatu, shell money in the Solomon Islands, and the presentation of a whale's tooth called a *tabua* in Fiji. These unique traditions are a thread uniting the diverse peoples of the Pacific.

THE POLYNESIANS

The Polynesians, whom Robert Louis Stevenson called "God's best, at least God's sweetest work," have fine features, almost intimidating physiques, and a soft, flowing language. One theory holds that the Polynesians evolved their great bodily stature through a selective process on their long ocean voyages, as the larger individuals with more body fat were better able to resist the chill of evaporating sea spray on their bodies (polar animals are generally larger than equatorial animals of the same species for the same reason). Other authorities ascribe the Polynesian's huge body size to a high-carbohydrate vegetable diet.

The ancient Polynesians developed a rigid social system with hereditary chiefs; descent was usually through the father. In most of Polynesia there were only two classes, chiefs and commoners, but in Hawaii, Tahiti, and Tonga an intermediate class existed. Slaves were outside the class system entirely, but there were slaves only in New Zealand, the Cook Islands, and Mangareva. People lived in scattered dwellings rather than villages, although there were groupings around the major temples and chiefs' residences.

They lived from fishing and agriculture, using tools made from stone, bone, shell, and wood. The men were responsible for planting, harvesting, fishing, cooking, house and canoe building; the women tended the fields and animals, gathered food and fuel, prepared food, and made clothes and household items. Both males and females worked together in family or community groups, not as individuals.

The Polynesians lost the art of pottery making during their long stay in Havaiki (Western Polynesia) and had to cook their food in underground ovens *(umu)*. Breadfruit, taro, yams, sweet potatoes, bananas, and coconuts were cultivated (the Polynesians had no cereals). Pigs, chickens, and dogs were also kept for food, but the surrounding sea yielded the most important source of protein.

Numerous taboos regulated Polynesian life, such as prohibitions against taking certain plants or fish that were reserved for exploitation by the chiefs. Land was collectively owned by families and tribes, and there were nobles and commoners. Though the land was worked collectively by commoners, the chiefly families controlled and distributed its produce by well-defined customs. Large numbers of people could be mobilized for public works or war.

Two related forces governed Polynesian life: mana and *tapu*. Mana was a spiritual power of which the gods and high chiefs had the most and the commoners the least. In this rigid hierarchical system, marriage or even physical contact between persons of unequal mana was forbidden, and children resulting from sexual relations between the classes were killed. Our word "taboo" originated from the Polynesian *tapu*. Early missionaries would often publicly violate the taboos and smash the images of the gods to show that their mana had vanished.

Gods

The Polynesians worshipped a pantheon of gods, who had more mana than any human. The most important were Tangaroa (the creator and god of the oceans), and Oro, or Tu (the god of war), who demanded human sacrifices. The most fascinating figure in Polynesian mythology was Maui, a Krishna- or Prometheus-like figure who caught the sun with a cord to give its fire to the world. He lifted the firmament to prevent it from crushing mankind, fished the islands out of the ocean with a hook, and was killed trying to gain the prize of immortality for humanity. Also worth noting is Hina, the heroine who fled to the moon to avoid incest with her brother, and so the sound of her tapa beater wouldn't bother anyone. Tane (the god of light) and Rongo (the god of agriculture and peace) were other important gods.

MUSEUMS OF THE PACIFIC

The most important South Pacific history or anthropology museums are at Punaauia (Tahiti), Rarotonga, Nuku'alofa, Pago Pago, Suva, Nouméa, Port Vila, and Honiara, but most of the objects in their collections are of relatively recent origin. To see Pacific artifacts dating from the period of first European contact you must visit museums outside the region. The Museum of Man (or British Museum) in London, for example, has a huge collection covering the entire region, gathered by British officials and missionaries, but most of it is locked in storage for lack of display space and funding. The warehouses of many other European museums are also bulging with Pacific art objects inaccessible to the public for the same reason, yet very few are willing to return their treasures to the islands where they originated.

Some of the 2,000 objects brought back from the Pacific by Captain Cook can be seen in the Institut für Volkskunde, Göttingen, Germany; the Hunterian Museum, Glasgow, Scotland; and the Museo Borbonico, Naples, Italy. Many British universities, such as those of Cambridge, Oxford, and Aberdeen, have impressive Pacific collections. The ethnographical museums of Budapest, St. Petersburg, and Vienna have Oceanic artifacts from former imperial collections. The vast collections of the ethnographical museums of Germany were gathered by scientific expeditions during the German colonial period before 1914. The collection of Berlin's Dahlem Museum is perhaps the best displayed, but those of Bremen, Cologne, Dresden, and Hamburg are also outstanding.

Many objects in New England museums were brought back by whalers, including the rich array of objects from Fiji and Tonga in the Peabody Museum, Salem, Massachusetts. The collections of the American Museum of Natural History, New York, and the University Museum of Philadelphia were gathered by systematic collectors at the turn of the century. The Field Museum of Natural History, Chicago, has more than 50,000 Melanesian art objects, assembled by A.B. Lewis 1909–1913. The Bernice Bishop Museum, Honolulu, has been adding to its Polynesian collection for more than a century.

Mention must also be made of the Melanesian art at the Museum der Kulturen, Basel, plus the fine collections of the Royal Museum of Art and History, Brussels; the Museum of Man, Paris; the Musée Barbier-Muller, Geneva; the Asia and Pacific Museum, Warsaw; the Exeter City Museum; the Metropolitan Museum of Art, New York; the St. Louis Art Museum; and the de Young Memorial Museum, San Francisco. The museums of New Zealand, especially those of Auckland, Christchurch, Dunedin, and Wellington, hold a rich store of Pacific art, and a few have recently loaned objects for display at South Pacific museums such as the Museum of the Cook Islands on Rarotonga. The enormous wealth of Pacific art held by Australia's museums is mostly locked away in storerooms although the Australian Museum in Sydney occasionally mounts exhibitions. The Macleay Museum at the University of Sydney has a large Melanesian ethnographic collection dating from the 19th century.

This polytheism, which may have disseminated from Raiatea in the Society Islands, was most important in Eastern Polynesia. The *Arioi* confraternity, centered in Raiatea and thought to be possessed by the gods, traveled about putting on dramatic representations of the myths.

The Eastern Polynesians were enthusiastic temple builders, evidenced today by widespread ruins. Known by the Polynesian names *marae* or *me'ae*, these platform and courtyard structures of coral and basalt blocks often had low surrounding walls and internal arrangements of upright wooden slabs. Once temples for religious cults, they were used for seating the gods and for presenting fruits and other foods to them at ritual feasts. Sometimes, but rarely, human sacrifices took place on the *marae*. Religion in Western Polynesia was very low-key, with few priests or cult images. No temples have been found in Tonga and very few in Samoa. The gods of Eastern Polynesia were represented in human form. There was an undercurrent of ancestor worship, but this was nowhere as strong as in Melanesia. The ancestors were more important as a source of descent for social ranking, and genealogies were carefully preserved. Surviving elements of the old religion are the still-widespread belief in spirits *(aitu),* the continuing use of traditional medicine, and the influence of myth. More than 150 years after conversion by early missionaries, most Polynesians maintain their early Christian piety and fervid devotion.

Art

The Polynesians used no masks and few colors, usually leaving their works unpainted. Art forms were very traditional, and a defined class of artists produced works of remarkable delicacy and deftness. Three of the five great archaeological sites of Oceania are in Polynesia: Easter Island, Huahine, and Tongatapu (the other two are Pohnpei and Kosrae in Micronesia).

THE MELANESIANS

Most Melanesians live on high, volcanic islands and great differences exist between the bush people of the interiors and the saltwater people of the coasts. There's also great variety among the tribes of the interior; for centuries they waged wars with each other. Some clans were matrilineal, others patrilineal.

Art and Society

The Melanesians have developed a startling variety of customs, traditions, and cultures. The tremendous array of art objects and styles was due to the vast number of microsocieties; there was little variation within a single clan. Art among the Melanesians was a rigidly traditional medium of expression. If an object didn't correspond precisely to an accepted form, it couldn't capture the magic and the spirits, and thus would be meaningless and useless.

Melanesian society was based on consensus, gift giving, exchange, and obligation. Although there were a headman and a few sorcerers in each village, these were either elected at village councils or they "bought" their way up in society by giving feasts and pigs. Unlike Polynesian life, there were no hereditary classes of rulers or priests and no po-

litical unions outside the clan unit (the social structures in Fiji were influenced by Polynesia).

Secret societies existed and needed objects for initiation ceremonies and feasts to mark a man's passage to a higher grade. Some objects ensured fertility for man and the soil; others celebrated the harvest. Totemic figures (animals believed to be related to the clan by blood) were common. Everyday objects were artistically made, and almost everything was brightly painted. Many figures and masks were made specifically for a single ceremony, then discarded or destroyed.

More important than the social function of art was the religious function, especially in the cult of the dead. Ancestors were believed to remain in this world, and their advice and protection were often sought. The skull, considered the dwelling place of the soul, was often decorated and kept in the men's house. Sometimes carvings were made to provide a home for the spirits of the ancestors, or they were represented by posts or images. Masks were used to invoke the spirits in dance. The beauty of the objects was secondary; what the Melanesian artist sought was to create an embodied symbolism of the ancestors. In this rigid, ritual world the spirits of the dead possessed greater power than the living, and this power could be both harmful and beneficial.

RELIGION

Religion plays an important role in the lives of the Pacific islanders, holding communities together and defending moral values. No other non-European region of the world is as solidly Christian as the South Pacific, and unfortunately it sometimes seems to be one of the most uncritical, obedient, narrow-minded, and hypocritical strains of Christianity extant on the planet. The first missionaries to arrive were Protestants, and the Catholic fathers who landed almost 40 years later had to rely on French military backing to establish missions in Tahiti, the Marquesas, and New Caledonia. In Fiji 45 percent of the population is Hindu or Muslim due to the large Indo-Fijian population.

Since the 1960s, the old rivalry between Protestant and Catholic has been largely replaced by an avalanche of well-financed American fundamentalist missionary groups that divide families and spread confusion in an area already strongly Christian. While the indigenous churches have long been localized, the new evangelical sects are dominated by foreign personnel, ideas, and money. American televangelists proselytize from TV screens clear across the South Pacific Bible Belt from Rarotonga to Fiji. The ultraconservative outlook of the new religious imperialists continues the tradition of allying Christianity with colonialism or neocolonialism.

The established Protestant denominations are the Evangelicals of French Polynesia and New Caledonia, the Methodists of Tonga and Fiji, the Congregationalists of Samoa, the Presbyterians of Vanuatu, and the Anglicans of Solomon Islands. Catholics are present in every country. The ecumenical Pacific Conference of Churches began in 1961 as an association of the mainstream Protestant churches, but since 1976 many Catholic dioceses have been included as well. Both the Pacific Theological College (founded in 1966) and the Pacific Regional Seminary (opened in 1972) are in Suva, Fiji, and the South Pacific is one of the few areas of the world with a large surplus of ministers of religion.

Of course, the optimum way to experience religion in the South Pacific is to go to church on Sunday. Just be aware that the services can last 1.5 hours and will often be in the local language. If you decide to go, don't get up and walk out in the middle—see it through. You'll be rewarded by the joyous singing and fellowship, and you'll encounter the islanders on a different level. After church, people gather for a family meal or picnic and spend the rest of the day relaxing and socializing. If you're a guest in an island home you'll be invited to accompany them to church.

The Mormons

Mormon missionaries arrived on Tubuai in the Austral Islands as early as 1844, and today "Mormonia" covers much of the South Pacific. You don't have to travel far in the South Pacific to find the assembly-line Mormon chapels, schools, and sporting facilities, paid for by church members who are expected to tithe 10 percent of their incomes. The Mormon church spends more than US$500 million a year on foreign missions and sends out almost 50,000 missionaries, more than any other American church by far. According to Mormon doctrines, Polynesia was settled by American Indians, who were themselves descendants of the 10 lost tribes of Israel, and to hasten the second coming of Christ, these people must be reconverted! That explains why the present church is willing to spend so much time and money spreading the word.

The Mormons are especially successful in countries like Tonga and Samoa, which are too poor to provide public education for all. Mormon fascination with genealogy parallels the importance of descent in Polynesian society where it often determines land rights. There's a strong link to Hawaii's Brigham Young University, and many island students help pay for their schooling by representing their home country at the Mormon-owned Polynesian Cultural Center on Oahu. In Melanesia, Mormon missionary activity is a recent phenomenon, as prior to a "revelation" in 1978 blacks were barred from the Mormon priesthood. The pairs of clean-cut young Mormon "elders" seen on the outliers—each in shirt and tie, riding a bicycle or driving a minibus—are sent down from the States for two-year stays.

Other Religious Groups

More numerous even than the Mormons are adherents of the Seventh-Day Adventist Church, a politically ultra-conservative group that grew out of the 19th-century American Baptist movement. This is the largest nonhistorical religious group in the South Pacific, holding the allegiance of 10 percent of the population of Solomon Islands, and with large followings in French Polynesia, Tonga, Samoa, Fiji, and Vanuatu. The SDA Church teaches the imminent return of Christ, and Saturday (rather than Sunday) is observed as the Sabbath. SDAs regard the human body as the temple of the Holy Spirit, thus much attention is paid to health matters. Members are forbidden to partake of certain foods, alcohol, drugs, and tobacco, and the church expends considerable energy on the provision of medical and

THE PACIFIC IN LITERATURE

COURTESY OF HAWAII STATE ARCHIVES

Robert Louis Stevenson

Over the years a succession of European writers has traveled to the South Pacific in search of Bougainville's Nouvelle Cythère or Rousseau's noble savage. Brought to the stage and silver screen, their stories entered the popular imagination alongside Gauguin's rich images, creating the romantic myth of the South Seas paradise presently marketed by the travel industry. Only since independence have indigenous writers such as Epeli Hau'ofa, Julian Maka'a, Fata Sano Malifa, Raymond Pillai, John Saunana, Subramani, and Albert Wendt come to the fore.

Herman Melville, author of the whaling classic *Moby Dick* (1851), deserted his New Bedford whaler at Nuku Hiva in 1842 and *Typee* (1846) describes his experiences there. An Australian whaling ship carried Melville on to Tahiti, but he joined a mutiny on board, which landed him in the Papeete *calabooza* (prison). His second Polynesian book, *Omoo* (1847), was a result. In both, Melville decries the ruin of Polynesian culture by Western influence.

Pierre Loti's *The Marriage of Loti* (1880) is a sentimental tale of the love of a young French midshipman for a Polynesian girl named Rarahu. Loti's naiveté is rather absurd, but his friendship with Queen Pomare IV and his fine imagery make the book worth reading. Loti's writings influenced Paul Gauguin to come to Tahiti.

In 1888–1890 Robert Louis Stevenson, famous author of *Treasure Island* and *Kidnapped,* cruised the Pacific in his schooner, the *Casco.* His book *In the South Seas* describes his visits to the Marquesas and Tuamotus. In 1890 Stevenson and his family bought a large tract of land just outside Apia, Samoa, and built a large, framed house he called Vailima. In 1894 he was buried on Mt. Vaea, just above his home.

Jack London and his wife Charmian cruised the Pacific aboard their yacht, the *Snark,* in 1907–1909. A longtime admirer of Melville, London found only a wretched swamp at Taipivai in the Marquesas. His *South Sea Tales* (1911) was the first of the 10 books that he wrote on the Pacific. London's story "The House of Mapuhi," about a Jewish pearl buyer, earned him a costly lawsuit. London was a product of his time, and the modern reader is often shocked by his insensitive portrayal of the islanders.

In 1913–1914 the youthful poet Rupert Brooke visited Tahiti, where he fell in love with Mamua, a girl from Mataiea whom he immortalized in his poem "Tiare Tahiti." Later Brooke fought in WW I and wrote five famous war sonnets. He died of blood poisoning on a French hospital ship in the Mediterranean in 1915.

W. Somerset Maugham toured Polynesia in 1916–1917 to research his novel, *The Moon and Sixpence* (1919), a fictional life of Paul Gauguin. Of the six short stories in *The Trembling of a Leaf* (1921), "Rain" casts strumpet Sadie Thompson against the Rev. Mr. Davidson during an enforced stay at Pago Pago, "marooned in a dilapidated lodging house, upon whose corrugated roof the heavy tropical rain beat incessantly." Three film versions of the story have appeared. Maugham's *A Writer's Notebook*, published in 1984, 19 years after his death, describes his travels in the Pacific.

American writers Charles Nordhoff and James Norman Hall came to Tahiti after WW I, married Tahitian women, and collaborated on 11 books. Their most famous was the *Bounty Trilogy* (1934), which tells of Fletcher Christian's *Mutiny on the Bounty*, the escape to Dutch Timor of Captain Bligh and his crew in *Men Against the Sea*, and the mutineer's fate in *Pitcairn's Island*. Three generations of filmmakers have selected this saga as their way of presenting paradise.

Hall remained on Tahiti until his death in 1951 and he was buried on the hill behind his home at Arue. His last book, *The Forgotten One*, is a collection of true stories about expatriate intellectuals and writers lost in the South Seas. Hall's account of the 28-year correspondence with his American friend Robert Dean Frisbie, who settled on Pukapuka in the Cook Islands, is touching.

James A. Michener joined the U.S. Navy in 1942 and ended up visiting around 50 South Sea islands, among them Bora Bora. His *Tales of the South Pacific* (1947) tells of the impact of WW II on the South Pacific and the Pacific's impact on those who served. It was later made into the long-running Broadway musical, *South Pacific*. Michener's *Return to Paradise* (1951) is a readable collection of essays and short stories.

The literary traditions of the Pacific islanders themselves were largely oral until 1967 when the University of the South Pacific was established at Suva, Fiji. The student newspaper *Unispac* began carrying fiction by Pacific writers in 1968, but it was the formation of the South Pacific Creative Arts Society and its magazine *Mana* in 1973 that really stimulated the creation of a Pacific literature distinct from the expatriate writings that had prevailed up until that time. The first Festival of Pacific Arts held at Suva in 1972 greatly encouraged the development of a unique South Pacific culture.

Whereas the main characters in the expatriate writings are invariably Europeans with the islands and islanders treated only as exotic background, indigenous post-colonial writers deal with the real problems and concerns of the island people. The writings of outsiders such as Maugham and Michener often tell us more about the writers themselves than about the islands where their stories are set. In contrast to the Pacific paradise approach, island authors decry the impact of European colonialism and materialism on their traditional cultures and declare their own identity.

The Pacific's most famous contemporary writer is Samoan novelist Albert Wendt. His novels, such as *Sons for the Return Home* (1973), *Flying Fox in a Freedom Tree* (1974), *Pouliuli* (1977), and *Leaves of the Banyan Tree* (1979) portray the manipulative nature and complex social organization of Samoan society. Wendt studied in New Zealand for 12 years before returning to teach in Samoa in 1965, and he is now a professor of English literature at Auckland University.

Tongan poet and short-story writer Epeli Hau'ofa satirizes the foreign aid business and other aspects of island life in his humorous book *Tales of the Tikongs*. His 1977 essay "Our Crowded Islands" deals with overpopulation in Tonga and the Westernization of Tongan life. *Kisses in the Nederends* and *Corned Beef and Tapioca* are among his other books. Other Pacific writers of note include Samoa's Fata Sano Malifa *(Alms for Oblivion)* and Sia Figiel *(Where We Once Belonged)*, Fiji's Sudesh Mishra *(Tandava)* and Raymond Pillai *(The Celebration)*, and Solomon Island's John Saunana *(The Alternative)*. See Resources at the end of this book for more detailed reviews of some of these titles and a list of booksellers and publishers.

dental services. They're also active in education and local economic development. Like many of the fundamentalist sects, the SDAs tend to completely obliterate traditional cultures.

The Assemblies of God (AOG) is a Pentecostal sect founded in Arkansas in 1914 and presently headquartered in Springfield, Missouri. Although the AOG carries out some relief work, it opposes social reform in the belief that only God can solve humanity's problems. The sect is strongest in Fiji, where their numbers increased twelvefold between 1966 and 1992. A large AOG Bible College operates in Suva, and from Fiji the group has spread to other Pacific countries. Disgraced American tele-evangelists Jimmy Swaggart and Jim Bakker were former AOG ministers.

The Jehovah's Witnesses originated in 19th-century America and since 1909 their headquarters has been in Brooklyn, from whence their worldwide operations are financed. Jehovah's Witnesses' teachings against military service and blood transfusions have often brought them into conflict with governments, and they in turn regard other churches, especially the Catholic Church, as instruments of the Devil. Members must spread the word by canvassing their neighborhood door-to-door, or by standing on street-corners offering copies of *The Watchtower.* This group focuses mostly on Christ's return, and since "the end of time" is fast approaching, Witnesses have little interest in relief work. They're most numerous in French Polynesia, Fiji, New Caledonia, and Solomon Islands, but you'll find them in virtually every Pacific country.

LANGUAGE

Some 1,200 languages, a third of the world's total, are spoken in the Pacific islands, though most have very few speakers. The Austronesian language family includes more than 900 distinct languages spoken in an area stretching from Madagascar to Easter Island. Of all the Oceanic languages, only the Papuan languages spoken in New Guinea and the Solomons do not belong to this group. In all some 720 languages are spoken in Papua New Guinea, 113 in Vanuatu, and 87 in the Solomon Islands (the 250 languages spoken by the Australian Aborigines are unrelated to these). Many islanders are trilingual, equally fluent in the national lingua franca (pidgin), a local tribal tongue (or two), and an international language (either English or French). English is the predominant language of business and government in all but the French colonies.

Pidgin

Pidgin developed in Fiji and Queensland during the labor trade of the late 19th century. Because many separate local languages might be spoken on a single Melanesian island, often in villages only a few kilometers apart, the need for a common language arose when it became possible for people to travel beyond tribal boundaries. The three Pacific pidgins are Tok Pisin (P.N.G.), Pijin (Solomon Islands), and Bislama (Vanuatu). Solomons' Pidgin is the more Anglicized; the other two are surprisingly similar. Today pidgin is viewed as a pillar of a new Melanesian regional identity, although it's not spoken in Fiji or New Caledonia.

Pacific Pidgin, although less sophisticated than West African or China Coast Pidgin, is quite ingenious within its scope. Its vocabulary is limited, however, and pronouns, adverbs, and prepositions are lacking, but it has a bona fide Melanesian syntax. A very roundabout speech method is used to express things: "mine" and "yours" are *blong mifela* and *blong yufela,* and "we" becomes *yumi tufela.* Frenchman is *man wewi* (oui-oui), *meri* is woman, while *bulamakau* (bull and cow) means beef or cattle. Pidgin's internal logic is delightful.

Polynesian

The Polynesians speak about 21 closely related languages with local variations and consonantal changes. They're mutually unintelligible to those who haven't learned them, although they have many words in common. For instance, the word for land varies between *whenua, fenua, fanua, fonua, honua, vanua,* and *henua.* In the Polynesian languages the words are softened by the removal of certain consonants. Thus the Tagalog (Philippines) word for coconut, *niog,* became *niu, ni,* or *nu.* They're musical languages whose accent lies mostly on the vowels. Polynesian is rhetorical and poetical but not scientific, and to adapt to modern life many words have been borrowed from European languages; these too are infused with vowels to make them more melodious to the Polynesian ear. Thus in Tahitian governor becomes *tavana* and frying pan *faraipani*. Special vocabularies used to refer to or address royalty or the aristocracy also exist.

Conduct and Customs

Foreign travel is an exceptional experience enjoyed by a privileged few. Too often, tourists try to transfer their lifestyles to tropical islands, thereby missing out on what is unique to the region. Travel can be a learning experience if approached openly and with a positive attitude, so read up on the local culture before you arrive and become aware of the social and environmental problems of the area. A wise traveler soon graduates from hearing and seeing to listening and observing. It's not for nothing that we have two eyes and ears but only one mouth.

The path is primed with packaged pleasures, but pierce the bubble of tourism and you'll encounter something far from the schedules and organized efficiency: a time to learn how other people live. Walk gently, for human qualities are as fragile and subject to abuse as the brilliant reefs. The islanders are by nature soft-spoken and reserved. Often they won't show open disapproval if their social codes are broken, but don't underestimate them: They understand far more than you think. Consider that you're only one of thousands of visitors to their country, so don't expect to be treated better than anyone else. Respect is one of the most important things in island life and humility is also greatly appreciated.

Don't try for a bargain if it means someone will be exploited. What enriches you may violate others. Be sensitive to the feelings of those you wish to "shoot" with your camera and ask their permission first. Don't promise things you can't or won't deliver. Keep your time values to yourself; the islanders lead an unstressful lifestyle and assume that you are there to share it.

If you're alone you're lucky, for the single traveler is everyone's friend. Get away from other tourists and meet the people. There aren't many places on earth where you can still do this meaningfully, but the South Pacific is one. If you do meet people with similar interests, keep in touch by writing. This is no tourist's paradise, though, and local residents are not exhibits or paid performers. They have just as many problems as you, and if you see them as real people you're less likely to be viewed as a stereotypical tourist. You may have come to escape civilization, but keep in mind that you're just a guest.

Most important of all, try to see things their way. Take an interest in local customs, values, languages, challenges, and successes. If things work differently than they do back home, give thanks—that's why you've come. Reflect on what you've experienced and you'll return home with a better understanding of how much we all have in common, outwardly different as we may seem. Do that and your trip won't have been wasted.

The Pacific Way

A smile costs nothing but is priceless. Islanders smile at one another; tourists look the other way. In Western societies wealth is based on the accumulation of goods; in Pacific societies it's based on how much you can give away. Obligations define an individual's position in society, while sharing provides the security that holds a community together. If people are hospitable, look for some way of repaying their kindness and never exploit their goodwill. It's an island custom that a gift must be reciprocated, which is why tipping has never caught on.

Questions

The islanders are eager to please, so phrase your questions carefully. They'll answer yes or no according to what they think you want to hear—don't suggest the answer in your question. Test this by asking your informant to confirm something you know to be incorrect. Also don't ask negative questions, such as "you're not going to Suva, are you?" Invariably the answer will be "yes," meaning "yes, I'm not going to Suva." It also could work like this: "Don't you have anything cheaper?" "Yes." "What do you have that is cheaper?" "Nothing." Yes, he doesn't have anything cheaper. If you want to be sure of something, ask several people the same question in different ways.

Dress

It's important to know that the dress code in the islands is strict. Short shorts, halter tops, and bathing costumes in public are considered offensive; a *sulu* or pareu wrapped around you solves this one. Women should wear dresses that adequately cover their legs while seated. Nothing will mark you so quickly as a tourist nor make you more popular with street vendors than scanty dress. Of course, there *is* a place for it: on the beach in front of a resort hotel. In a society where even bathing suits are considered extremely risqué for local women, public nudity is unthinkable. Exceptions are Tahiti, Bora Bora, and Nouméa, where the French influence has led to topless beaches.

Women

In many traditional island cultures, a woman seen wandering aimlessly along a remote beach or country road was thought to be in search of male companionship, and "no" meant "yes." Single women hiking, camping, sunbathing, and simply traveling alone may be seen in the same light, an impression strongly reinforced by the type of videos available in the islands. In some cultures local women rarely travel without men, and some do-it-yourself day-hikes and interisland ship journeys mentioned in this book may be uncomfortable or even dangerous for women. Occasionally women on organized day tours ex-

perience low levels of sexual harrassment from guides or entertainers. Two women together will have less to worry about in most cases, especially if they're well covered and look purposeful.

Women traveling alone should avoid staying in isolated tourist bungalows by themselves—it's wise to team up with other travelers before heading to the outer islands. In many Polynesian cultures there's a custom known as "sleep crawling" in which a boy silently enters a girl's home at night and lies beside her to prove his bravery, and visiting women sometimes become objects of this type of unwanted attention, even in well-known resorts like Bora Bora.

A Swedish reader sent us this:

The South Pacific is an easy place for a single woman, as long as she's not stupid. I'm talking about shorts, minitops, bikinis, etc., which place an unnecessary barrier between you and the local women. In the handbook a lot of traditional ceremonies are described, and I think it's important to point out that some of them (such as a traditional kava party) are open to men only. On the other hand, as a woman I could sit down with the local women when they were weaving, cooking, etc. and get plenty of contact, something a man couldn't do. There's nothing like weaving a mat to make a Tongan woman more talkative! I've had "complicated" discussions I believe wouldn't have taken place if both of us hadn't been so occupied with those pandanus leaves! Don't attempt to be an "independent modern woman" trying to get a close look at every aspect of village life, but take advantage of those opportunities which come naturally from your being a woman.

Exploring the Islands

Few areas of the world are as rewarding to visit as the South Pacific. Life is relaxed, and the tremendous variety of cultures and choice of things to see and do make this the sort of place you just keep coming back to. When you tire of beachlife you can go to the mountains; city and town visits can alternate with stays in rural areas. There's no overcrowding, and you don't have to hassle with

vendors or be constantly on guard against thieves. It's relatively inexpensive, public transportation of all kinds is well developed, and you can easily sidestep the beaten tourist track and go native.

The South Pacific's distance from Europe and North America has saved it from becoming overrun, as Spain and the main Caribbean resorts are overrun. Only tiny New Zealand has the South Pacific in its backyard (Australians are more attracted to Bali and Thailand). Part of the higher amount you'll spend on airfare will come

back to you in the form of lower everyday prices. The islanders themselves are the region's greatest attraction: you'll seldom make friends as fast as you do here.

Each Pacific country is unique. Give yourself as much time in the islands as you can, and try to get to at least three different countries to be able to put things in perspective. No matter how hard you travel, you'll always have lots left over to see next time.

French Polynesia

Islands like Tahiti, Moorea, Huahine, and Bora Bora possess some of the most stirring scenery in the South Pacific, all of it easily accessible by sea or air. The electrifying Tahitian dancing is only the most visible aspect of a rich culture which combines well with the exquisite taste and style of the French. The world class shopping, restaurants, resorts, beaches, and attractions compensate for the higher cost of living.

Easter Island

The archaeological heart of Polynesia, mysterious Rapa Nui is also a rewarding destination for hikers, surfers, and scuba divers. It's the sort of place you have to visit at least once in your life.

Cook Islands

The Cook Islands has easygoing resort life on Rarotonga and Aitutaki, and unspoiled outer-island life everywhere else. Rarotonga resembles Moorea while Aitutaki has a lagoon like Bora Bora's. It's a great place to kick back and enjoy the good food, accommodations, entertainment, sporting activities, and local color at prices well below those of French Polynesia.

Tonga

Each of the three main island groups of Tonga has its own distinct character and Vava'u is an undiscovered pearl of the South Seas. Whalewatching, sailing, kayaking, fishing, scuba diving, and more await you at Vava'u. Tongatapu exhibits the symbols of the last ruling Polynesian dynasty, while Ha'apai is for the beach lover.

Samoa

Sultry Samoa is notable for its intact traditional life and vibrant Polynesian culture. Small villages of thatched oval *fale* ring the two main islands while countless waterfalls drop from the high verdant interiors. The capital, Apia, is a thriving South Seas metropolis with a bustling main market.

Fiji

Everyone likes Fiji, both for its excellent facilities and the fascinating variety of peoples and cultures. No other South Pacific destination can match the variety of things to see and do or places to go. There's exciting nightlife in the capital, Suva, old colonial towns such as Levuka and Savusavu, lush jungles and reefs on outer islands like Taveuni and Kadavu, and a long string of sunny resorts in the Mamanuca and Yasawa groups off western Viti Levu.

New Caledonia

New Caledonia is also a land of stirring contrasts. The capital, Nouméa, could have been lifted out of southern France, but on the east coast of the Grande Terre and on all the outer islands Melanesian culture predominates. The beaches of the Isle of Pines and Loyalty Islands are among the finest in the region.

Vanuatu

In Vanuatu you alternate between the polished capital and the unspoiled outer islands. Port Vila is the loveliest capital city in the South Pacific. Luganville on Espiritu Santo is a scuba diving destination, while Tanna offers an active volcano and intact traditional culture. This country is a melange unmatched anywhere in the world.

Solomon Islands

Solomon Islands is perhaps the South Pacific's biggest surprise: friendly welcoming people, reasonable prices, and lots of things to do. It's a land of adventure seldom visited by foreign tourists. The Western Solomons excels for its scenery, diving, and culture.

Sports and Recreation

Scuba Diving

Scuba diving is offered in resort areas throughout the South Pacific, with certification courses usually available. The waters are warm, varying less than one degree centigrade between the surface and 100 meters, so a wetsuit is not essential (although it will protect you from coral cuts). Lagoon diving is recommended for beginners; those with some experience will find the most beautiful coral along reef dropoffs and the most fish around passes into the lagoon.

Commercial scuba operators know their waters and will be able to show you the most amazing things in perfect safety. Dive centers at all the main resorts operate year-round, with marinelife most profuse July–November. Before strapping on a tank and fins you'll have to show your scuba certification card, and occasionally divers are also asked to show a medical report from their doctor indicating that they are in good physical condition. Serious divers will bring along their own mask, buoyancy compensator, and regulator.

Prices differ considerably across the region: a one-tank dive will cost about US$35 in the Cook Islands and Tonga, US$50 in Fiji, Samoa, Vanuatu, Easter Island, and the Solomons, US$60 in French Polynesia, and US$85 in New Caledonia. These prices include the US$10 or more most dive shops tack on for "equipment rental" (regulator, buoyancy compensator, and gauges) and frequent divers will save a lot by bringing their own. Precise information on scuba diving is provided throughout this handbook, immediately after the sightseeing sections.

Many of the scuba operators listed in this book offer introductory "resort courses" for those who only want a taste of scuba diving, and full CMAS, NAUI, or PADI open-water certification courses for those wishing to dive more than once or twice. Scuba training will enhance your understanding and enjoyment of the sea.

It should be noted here that the feeding of sharks, rays, eels, and other fish as widely practiced in French Polynesia and elsewhere is a highly controversial activity. Supplying food to wild creatures of any kind destroys their natural feeding habits and makes them vulnerable to human predators, and handling marinelife can have unpredictable consequences. More study is required to determine whether shark feeding by tourism operators tends to attract sharks to lagoons and beaches used for public recreation. Some scuba operators forego the easy profits to be made through shark or ray feeding and take their clients to places where things are still entirely natural. If this issue concerns you, avoid dive shops that promote fish feeding and direct your business to those whose first priority is protecting the natural environment.

Snorkeling

Even if you aren't willing to put the necessary money and effort into scuba diving, you should investigate the many snorkeling possibilities. Snorkeling is free—all you need is a mask and pipe. Be careful, however, and know the dangers. Practice snorkeling over a shallow sandy bottom and don't head into deep water or swim over coral until you're sure you've got the hang of it. Breathe easily; don't hyperventilate. When snorkeling on a fringing reef, beware of deadly currents and undertows in channels that drain tidal flows. Before going into the water, ask a local to point the channels out to you, and observe the direction the water is flowing before you swim into it. If you feel yourself being dragged out to sea through a reef passage, try swimming across the current rather than against it. If you can't resist the pull at all, it may be better to let yourself be carried out. Wait till the current diminishes, then swim along the outer reef face until you find somewhere to come back in. Or use your energy to attract the attention of someone onshore.

Snorkeling on the outer edge or drop-off of a reef is thrilling for the variety of fish and corals, but attempt it only on a very calm day. Even then it's wise to have someone stand onshore or paddle behind you in a canoe to watch for occasional big waves, which can take you by surprise and smash you into the rocks. Also, beware of unperceived currents outside the reef—you may not get a second chance. Many scuba operators will take snorkelers out on their regular trips for a third to a quarter the cost of diving. This is an easy way to reach some good snorkeling spots, just don't expect to be chaperoned for that price.

A far better idea is to limit your snorkeling to the protected inner reef and leave the open waters to the scuba diver. Yet while scuba diving quickly absorbs large amounts of money, snorkeling is free and you can do it as often as you like. You'll encounter the brightest colors in shallow waters anyway as beneath six meters the colors blue out as short wavelengths are lost. By diving with a tank you trade off the chance to observe shallow water species in order to gain access to the often larger deep water species. The best solution is to do a bit of both. In any case, avoid touching the reef or any of its creatures as the contact can be very harmful to both you and the reef. Take only pictures and leave only bubbles.

Surfing and Windsurfing

Polynesia's greatest gift to the world of sport is surfing. In 1771, Captain Cook saw Tahitians surfing in a canoe; board surfing was first observed off Hawaii in 1779. Surfing was revived at Waikiki, Hawaii, at the beginning of the 20th century and it's now the most popular sport among many young islanders.

Fiji's most renowned surfing camps are Club Masa (Kulukulu), Batiluva Beach Resort (Yanuca Island), Seashell Cove (Momi Bay), and Tavarua and Namotu Islands (Mamanuca Group). In French Polynesia, there's Pension Le Bon Jouir on Tahiti Iti, and in Tonga it's the Ha'atafu Beach Resort on Tongatapu. Other famous surfing spots include Tahiti's Papara Beach and Teahupoo, Huahine's Fare Reef, Easter Island, Laulii and Solosolo on Upolu, Salailua and Lano on Savai'i, Suva's Sandspit Lighthouse, and Grande Terre's Po'e Beach. The surfing in Samoa is not for beginners. The top season is generally July to September when the trade winds push the Antarctic swells north. During the hurricane season January to March tropical storms can generate some spectacular waves.

Prime locales for windsurfing include Rarotonga's Muri Lagoon and many others (but forget the Cook Islands for surfing). Pago Pago Harbor would be the windsurfing locale par excellence if the quality of the water weren't so poor.

Ocean Kayaking

This is a viable sport best practiced in sheltered lagoons, such as those of Raiatea/Taha'a, Bora Bora, Aitutaki, Vava'u, and New Georgia, or among Fiji's Yasawa Islands. You can rent kayaks in many places, but it's better to bring your own folding kayak if you're serious. See Getting Around, later in this chapter, for more information on kayaking.

Yachting

Cruising the South Pacific by yacht is also covered in Getting Around, and for those with less time there are several established yacht charter operations, the most important of which are based at Raiatea (French Polynesia), Vava'u (Tonga), Malololailai (Fiji), and Nouméa (New Caledonia). Turn to Yacht Tours and Charters in Getting There, which follows, and check the introductions to the chapters mentioned above.

Hiking

Hiking is an excellent, inexpensive way to see the islands. A few of the outstanding treks covered in this handbook are Mt. Aorai on Tahiti, Vaiare to Paopao on Moorea, the Cross-island Track on Rarotonga, Mt. Matafao on Tutuila, Lake Lanoto'o on Upolu, the Sigatoka River Trek on Viti Levu, White Sands to Port Resolution on Tanna, and the Mataniko River on Guadalcanal. There are many others.

Fishing

Sportfishing is a questionable activity—especially spearfishing, which is sort of like shooting a cow with a handgun. An islander who spearfishes to feed his family is one thing, but the tourist who does it for fun is perhaps worthy of the attention of sharks. Deep-sea game fishing from gas-guzzling powerboats isn't much better, and it's painful to see noble fish slaughtered and strung up just to inflate someone's ego. That said, one has to admit that taking fish from the sea one by one for sport is never going to endanger the stocks the way net fishing by huge trawlers does. On most big-game boats, the captain keeps the catch. Sportfishing is covered throughout this handbook.

Golf

The former British and New Zealand administrators left behind an abundance of golf courses in the islands, and virtually all are open to visitors. Major international competitions are held at Fiji's Pacific Harbor Golf Course and Tahiti's Olivier Breaud Golf Course. Greens fees vary considerably: Olivier Breaud Golf Course, US$55; Rarotonga Golf Club, US$9; Tonga Golf Club, US$5; Tutuila's 'Ili'ili Golf Course, US$7; Apia's Royal Samoa Country Club, US$7; Nadi Airport Golf Course, US$9; Nadi's Denarau Golf Club, US$57; Pacific Harbor Golf Course, US$17; Suva's Fiji Golf Club, US$12; Nouméa's Tina de Golf, US$65; Port Vila's White Sands Country Club, US$26; Port Vila Golf and Country Club, US$17; Honiara Golf Club, US$4. Club and cart rentals are usually available for a bit less than the greens fees and most of the courses have clubhouses with pleasant colonial-style bars.

Entertainment

Considering the strong Aussie presence and the temperature, it's not surprising that the South Seas has its fair share of colorful bars where cold beer is consumed in amazing quantities. These are good places to meet local characters at happy hour around 1700, and some bars become discos after 2200. Respectably attired visitors are welcome at the ex-colonial "clubs," where the beer prices are generally lower and the clientele more sedate. Barefoot (or flip-flop-shod) beachcombers in T-shirts and shorts may be refused entry, and you should take off your hat as you come in. Don't overlook the resort bars, where the swank surroundings cost only slightly more.

A small glass of draft beer at a normal bar will cost just over US$1 in Samoa, around

© M.E. DE VOS

Seated hand dancers performing a *meke* in a village on northern Taveuni.

EXPLORING THE ISLANDS

THE SOUTH SEAS ON THE SILVER SCREEN

Since the days of silent movies, Hollywood has shared the fascination with the South Pacific felt by poets and novelists. In fact, many of the best films about the region are based on books by Somerset Maugham, Charles Nordhoff, James Norman Hall, and James A. Michener. And like the printed works, most of the films are about Europeans temporarily in the islands rather than the islanders themselves. The clash between the simplicity of paradise and the complexity of civilization is a recurrent theme.

Somerset Maugham's famous short story *Rain* about a hooker and a repressed missionary thrown together beneath Samoa's monsoon rains has been filmed three times. In 1928 Gloria Swanson and Lionel Barrymore starred in the original silent movie version of *Sadie Thompson*. Four years later director Lewis Milestone cast Joan Crawford as Sadie Thompson in an outstanding remake titled *Rain*. Though set in Samoa, Milestone's production was actually shot on Catalina Island off Southern California. Rita Hayworth and José Ferrer starred in the 1953, 3-D version *Miss Sadie Thompson*.

Two classics of the silent movie era really were filmed in the region. In 1925 Robert Flaherty made *Moana of the South Seas* in Samoa. Six years later Flaherty teamed up with F. W. Murnau to create *Tabu*, the story of two lovers who flee to a tiny island on Bora Bora's barrier reef. In 1932 Douglas Fairbanks Sr. and Maria Alba traveled to the Society Islands by private yacht for the filming of *Mr. Robinson Crusoe*.

Three generations of filmmakers have used the Bounty saga popularized by American novelists Charles Nordhoff and James Norman Hall as their way of presenting paradise. In 1935 Frank Lloyd's *Mutiny on the Bounty* won the Oscar for Best Picture, with Charles Laughton starring as the cruel Captain Bligh and Clark Gable as gallant Fletcher Christian. Lloyd portrayed the affair as a simplistic struggle between good and evil, and the two subsequent remakes were more historically accurate.

The extravagant MGM production of *Mutiny on the Bounty* (1962) starring Trevor Howard as Captain Bligh and Marlon Brando as Fletcher Christian is well remembered in Tahiti due to Brando's ongoing ownership of Tetiaroa atoll. Unlike the 1935 Bounty movie filmed on Catalina Island, California, MGM captured the glorious color of Tahiti and Bora Bora in what may be the most spectacular movie ever made in the South Pacific.

The Bounty (1984), with Sir Anthony Hopkins as a purposeful Bligh and Mel Gibson portraying an ambiguous Christian, comes closer to reality than the other two Bounty films and the views of Moorea are stunning.

The theme of the despot is picked up by director John Ford who adapted Nordhoff and Hall's story of a young couple fleeing the haughty governor of tropical Manikoora in *The Hurricane* (1937). Surprisingly, this black and white movie remains an audiovisual feast, and the cli-

US$2 in the Cook Islands, Fiji, and Solomon Islands, less than US$2.50 in Tonga and Vanuatu, and US$3 or more in French Polynesia, New Caledonia, and American Samoa. Needless to say, Apia is a beer drinkers paradise. Don't worry about the quality as it's excellent everywhere, in fact, despite the price, Samoa's Vailima beer may be the region's best and Fiji Bitter is a close second.

Many big hotels run "island nights," or feasts where you get to taste the local food and see traditional dancing. If you don't wish to splurge on the meal it's sometimes possible to witness the spectacle from the bar for the price of a drink. These events are held weekly on certain days, so ask. On most islands Friday night is the time to let it all hang out; on Saturday many people are preparing for a family get-together or church on Sunday. Except in the French territories, everything grinds to a halt Saturday at midnight and

mactic storm is not soon to be forgotten. Dorothy Lamour stars in Ford's film. In 1978 Dino de Lautentiis remade *Hurricane* on Bora Bora with Mia Farrow and Trevor Howard in the starring roles.

The Moon and Sixpence, Albert Lewin's 1943 film version of Somerset Maugham's novel about the life of Paul Gauguin in Polynesia, appeals to the mind as much as to the senses. It's the dissonance between the main character's private mission and his social obligations gives this movie depth.

Although entirely filmed at Camp Pendleton, California, the wartime propaganda film *Guadalcanal Diary* (1943), starring William Bendix and Anthony Quinn, brings the battles in the Solomon Islands to life. *The Thin Red Line,* a 1999 reevaluation of the same battle, was far more sophisticated with a lyrical soundtrack and psychological musing.

Films based on James A. Michener's writings dominated the 1950s, beginning with *Return to Paradise* (1953) filmed on the Samoan island of Upolu. The beach where Gary Cooper played his role is now a popular tourist attraction.

James A. Michener's first book, *Tales of the South Pacific,* opened on Broadway as a Rodgers and Hammerstein musical in 1949. The 1958 screen version *South Pacific* was filmed on Kaua'i, Hawaii, starring Mitzi Gaynor as a wartime U.S. navy nurse in love with a middle-aged French planter on an enchanting South Seas isle.

Fiji wasn't discovered by Hollywood until the *The Blue Lagoon* (1980). In this romantic tale Fiji's Yasawa Islands are the setting for a pair of child castaways who fall in love on a deserted isle. This film is worth seeing for the lush beauty of the islands and not for Henry DeVere Stacpoole's rather insipid story. It stars Brooke Shields and Christopher Atkins. The 1991 sequel *Return to the Blue Lagoon* is about the two-year-old son from the first Blue Lagoon film. It was made on Taveuni with Milla Jovovich as the female lead.

Filmed on Monuriki Island in the Mamanucas, *Castaway* (2000) conveys well the savage beauty of Fiji's westernmost islands. Lead actor Tom Hanks had to lose 40 pounds and grow a ragged beard in the middle of production, forcing an eight month recess in the filming.

In all of the above films, the indigenous peoples of Oceania appear only as extras. The main characters are invariably Europeans who act out their roles against the exotic backdrop of the South Pacific. In Kevin Costner's 1994 production *Rapa Nui* about the ancient conflict between the "long ears" and the "short ears" on Easter Island, the islanders themselves become the main protagonists. Yet Costner's film was panned by the critics, and the filmmakers themselves were condemned by social activists for their negative impact on Easter Island.

Videos and DVDs of all of the films just mentioned can be ordered through www.south pacific.org/films.html.

Sunday is very quiet—a good day to go hiking or to the beach.

In the English-speaking countries it's cheap to go to the movies. Unfortunately it's usually romance, horror, or adventure, and as everywhere, good psychological films are the exception. In the French territories the films are just as bad, plus they're dubbed into French and admission is three times as high. Video fever is the latest island craze, and you often see throngs of locals crowded into some-

one's living room watching a violent and/or sexy tape rented from one of the ubiquitous video rental shops. Some guesthouses have video too, so make sure your room is well away from it.

Music and Dance

Traditional music and dance is alive and well in the South Pacific, be it the exciting *tamure* dancing of French Polynesia and the Cook Islands, the graceful *siva* of Samoa, the formalized *meke* of Fiji, or the *kastom* dances of Vanuatu. British ethnomusicologist David Fanshawe (see Resources) has suggested that the sitting dances common in Tonga, Fiji, and elsewhere may be related to the movements of the upper part of the body while paddling a canoe.

The slit-log gong (or *lali* in Fiji) beaten with a wooden stick is now a common instrument throughout Polynesia, even though the Eastern Polynesians originally had skin drums. The *to'ere* slit drum was only introduced to Tahiti from Western Polynesia after 1915, and it's marvelous the way the Tahitians have made it their own.

Melanesia has always excelled in the use of the flute, especially the panpipes of Solomon Islands. Flutes were known in Polynesia too, for example the nose flutes of Tonga and Tahiti. In the early 19th century, missionaries replaced the old chants of Polynesia with the harmonious gospel singing heard in the islands today, yet even the hymns were transformed into an original Oceanic medium. Contemporary Pacific music includes bamboo bands, brass bands, and localized Anglo-American pop. String bands have made European instruments such as the guitar and ukulele an integral part of Pacific music.

Holidays and Festivals

The special events of each island group are described in the respective chapters. Their dates often vary from year to year, so it's good to contact the local tourist information office soon after your arrival to learn just what will be happening during your stay.

The most important annual festivals are the Tapati Rapa Nui festival on Easter Island (late January or early February), American Samoa's Flag Day (April 17), the Independence Celebrations at Apia (first week of June), Nuku'alofa's Heilala Festival (first week in July), the Heiva i Tahiti at Papeete and Bora Bora (first two weeks of July), Solomon Islands Independence Day (July 7), Independence Day at Port Vila (July 30), the Constitution Celebrations on Rarotonga (early August), Suva's Hibiscus Festival (August), the Bourail Agricultural Show in New Caledonia in mid-August, and the Constitution Celebrations on Niue in mid-October. Catch as many as you can and try to participate in what's happening, rather than merely watching like a tourist.

Regional Events

The most important cultural event of the region is the Festival of Pacific Arts, held every four years (Suva, Fiji, 1972; Rotorua, N.Z., 1976; Port Moresby, P.N.G., 1980; Tahiti, 1985; Townsville, Australia, 1988; Rarotonga, 1992; Samoa, 1996; New Caledonia, 2000; Palau, 2004; American Samoa, 2008). The festival gathers in one place the cultures and folklores of all of Oceania. The coordination of each festival is in the hands of the Council of Pacific Arts, founded at Nouméa in 1977 under the auspices of the Secretariat of the Pacific Community. The Melanesian Arts and Cultural Festival of the five Melanesian Spearhead countries was held in Honiara in 1998 and in Port Vila in 2002 (the next will be in Fiji in 2006). Since 1987, a Marquesas Islands Festival has been held about every four years.

The South Pacific Games, the region's major sporting event, was created at the 1961 South Pacific Conference to promote friendship among the peoples of the Pacific and encourage the development of amateur sports. Since then the games have been held in Fiji (1963), New Caledonia (1966), P.N.G. (1969), French Polynesia (1971), Guam (1975), Fiji (1979), Samoa (1983), New Caledonia (1987), P.N.G. (1991), French Polynesia (1995), Guam (1999), Fiji (2003), and Samoa (2007) with the larger Pacific countries (New Caledonia, Fiji, P.N.G., and French Polynesia) dominating. Some 5,000 athletes from 22 countries gather for the games and, to give the smaller countries a better chance, Australia, Hawaii, and New Zealand don't participate. The five compulsory sports are athletics, basketball, soccer, swimming, and tennis, but almost any sport can be included if at least six teams approve it. The Mini South Pacific Games take place two years after the main games.

Arts and Crafts

The top countries in which to purchase handicrafts are Tonga, Samoa, Fiji, Vanuatu, and Solomon Islands. Not surprisingly, the traditional handicrafts that have survived best are the practical arts done by women (weaving, basketmaking, tapa). In cases where the items still perform their original function (such as the astoundingly intricate fine mats of Samoa—not for sale to tourists), they remain as vital as ever.

Whenever possible, buy handicrafts from local women's committee shops, church groups, local markets, or from the craftspeople themselves, but avoid objects made from turtle shell/leather, clam shell, or marine mammal ivory, which are prohibited entry into many countries under endangered species acts. Failure to declare such items to customs officers can lead to heavy fines. Also resist the temptation to purchase jewelry or other items made from seashells and coral, the collection of which damages the reefs. Souvenirs made from straw or seeds may be held for fumigation or confiscated upon arrival.

Weaving

Woven articles are the most widespread handicrafts, with examples in almost every South Seas country. Pandanus fiber is the most common, but coconut leaf and husk, vine tendril, banana stem, tree and shrub bark, the stems and leaves of water weeds, and the skin of the sago palm leaf are all used. On some islands the fibers are passed through a fire, boiled, then bleached in the sun. Vegetable dyes of very lovely mellow tones are sometimes used, but gaudier store dyes are much more prevalent. Shells are occasionally utilized to cut, curl, or make pliable the fibers. Polynesian woven arts are characterized by colorful, skillful patterns.

Tapa

To make tapa, the white inner bark of the tall, thin paper mulberry tree *(Broussonetia papyrifera)* is stripped and scraped with shells, rolled into a ball, and soaked in water. The sodden strips are then pounded with wooden mallets until they reach four or five times their original length and width. Next, several pieces are placed one on top of the other, pressed and pounded, and joined with a manioc juice paste. Sheets of tapa feel like felt when finished.

In Tonga, tapa *(ngatu)* is decorated by stitching coconut fiber designs onto a woven pandanus base that is placed under the tapa, and the stain is rubbed on in the same manner one makes temple rubbings from a stone inscription. The artisan then fills in the patterns freehand. In Fiji, stencils are used to decorate tapa *(masi)*. Sunlight deepens and sets the copper brown colors.

Each island group has its characteristic colors and patterns, ranging from plantlike paintings to geometric designs. On some islands tapa is still used for clothing, bedding, and room dividers, and as ceremonial red carpets. Tablecloths, bedcovers, place mats, and wall hangings of tapa make handsome souvenirs.

Woodcarving

Melanesia is especially well known for its woodcarvings, with designs passed down from generation to generation. Though shells are sometimes used for polishing the finest artifacts, steel tools are employed for the most part these days. Melanesian woodcarvings often suggest the mystic feelings of their former religious beliefs and the somber spirits of the rainforests. Polynesia also produces fine woodcarvings (especially kava bowls and war clubs), and those of the Marquesas Group are outstanding in detail.

Other Products

Other handicrafts include polished shell, inlays of shell in ebony, spears with barbs of splintered bone, thorn spines or caudal spines, "bride money," shell necklaces, and anklets. Among the European-derived items are the patchwork quilts *(tifaifai)* of Tahiti and the Cooks, and the hand-painted and silk-screened dress fabrics of Fiji, Samoa, the Cook Islands, and Tahiti.

Accommodations

Hotels

With the *Moon Handbooks South Pacific* in hand you're guaranteed a good, inexpensive place to stay on every island. To allow you the widest possible choice, all price categories are included herein and we've tried to indicate which properties offer value for money. If you think we're wrong or you were badly treated, be sure to send a written complaint to the author using the address on his website www.southpacific.org. Equally important, let us know when you agree with what's here or if you think a place deserves a better rave. Your letter will have an impact!

We don't solicit freebies from the hotel chains; our only income derives from the price you paid for this book. So we don't mind telling you that, as usual, most of the luxury hotels are just not worth the exorbitant prices they charge. Many simply recreate Hawaii at twice the price, offering far more luxury than you need. Even worse, they tend to isolate you in a French/American/Australian environment, away from the South Pacific you came to experience. Most are worth visiting as sightseeing attractions, watering holes, or sources of entertainment, but unless you're a millionaire, sleep elsewhere. There are always middle-level hotels that charge half what the top-end places ask, while providing adequate comfort. And if you really *can* afford US$500 a night and up, you might do better chartering a yacht!

Dormitory or backpacker accommodations are available on all of the main islands, with communal cooking facilities usually provided when meals aren't included. If you're traveling alone these are excellent, since they're just the place to meet other travelers. Couples can usually get a double room for a price only slightly above two dorm beds. For the most part, the dormitories are safe and congenial for those who don't mind sacrificing their privacy to save money.

Throughout the South Pacific, double rooms with shared bath at budget guesthouses average US$20–50, dorm beds US$6–20 pp. You can get a double room with shared bath for US$25 or less on Easter Island, Fiji, Niue, Samoa, Tonga, and Solomon Islands. Expect to pay around

© DAVID STANLEY

Choice accommodations in the South Pacific are thatched *bure* such as these.

ACCOMMODATIONS PRICE RANGES

Throughout this book, accommodations are generally grouped in the price categories which follow based on the lowest price of a double room. Of course, currency fluctuations and inflation can lead to slight variations.

Under US$25
US$25–50
US$50–100
US$100–150
US$150–250
US$250 and up

US$35 for the same in the Cook Islands, Tuvalu, and Vanuatu. The cheapest double rooms start at US$50 in American Samoa, French Polynesia, and New Caledonia. A dormitory bed for under US$10 can be obtained in Fiji, Tonga, and Solomon Islands. Moving into the medium-price category, you'll be able to get a quality air-conditioned room with all the facilities for US$75 double or less in American Samoa, Fiji, Samoa, Tonga, Tuvalu, and Solomon Islands. The same will cost around US$100 on Easter Island, Niue, and Wallis and Futuna. Expect to pay about US$120 in Vanuatu and the Cook Islands, or US$150 in French Polynesia and New Caledonia.

Needless to say, always ask the price of your accommodations before accepting them. This especially applies in remote areas of Melanesia where local guesthouses may be required to charge high prices by travel agencies, which would prefer that all bookings be channeled through them. In cases where there's a local and a tourist price, you'll always pay the higher tariff if you don't check beforehand. Asking first gives you the opportunity to bargain if someone quotes an absurdly high starting price, and by calling ahead you may be able to avoid a disastrous trip. Otherwise, hotel prices are usually fixed and bargaining isn't the normal way to go.

Be aware that some of the low-budget places included in this book are a lot more basic than what are sometimes referred to as "budget" accommodations in the States. The standards of

cleanliness in the common bathrooms may be lower than you expected, the furnishings "early attic," the beds uncomfortable, linens and towels skimpy, housekeeping nonexistent, and window screens lacking. Don't expect Sheraton service at motel prices.

When picking a hotel, keep in mind that although a thatched bungalow will be cooler and infinitely more attractive than a concrete box, it's also more likely to have insect problems. If in doubt, check the window screens and carry mosquito coils and/or repellent. Hopefully there'll be a resident lizard or two to feed on the bugs. Always turn on a light before getting out of bed to use the facilities at night, as even the finest hotels in the tropics have cockroaches.

A room with cooking facilities can save you a lot on restaurant meals, and some moderately priced establishments have weekly rates. If you have to choose a meal plan, take only breakfast and dinner (Modified American Plan or "half pension") and have fruit for lunch. As you check into your room, note the nearest fire exits. And don't automatically take the first room offered; if you're paying good money look at several, then choose.

Reserving Rooms

Booking accommodations in advance usually works to your disadvantage as full-service travel agents will begin by trying to sell you their most expensive properties (which pay them the highest commissions) and work down from there. The quite adequate middle and budget places included in this handbook often aren't on their screens or are sold at highly inflated prices. Few hotels charging under US$80 have the accounting wherewithal to process agency commissions. Herein we provide the rates for direct local bookings, and if you book through a travel agent abroad you could end up paying considerably more as multiple commissions are tacked on. Thus we suggest you avoid making any hotel reservations at all before arriving in the South Pacific (unless you're coming for a major event).

We don't know of any island where it's to your advantage to book ahead in the medium to lower price range, but you can sometimes obtain substantial discounts at the luxury hotels by including them as part of a package tour. Even then, you'll almost always find medium-priced accommodations for less than the package price and your freedom of choice won't be impaired. If, however, you intend to spend most of your time at a specific first-class hotel, you'll benefit from bulk rates by taking a package tour instead of paying the higher "rack rate" the hotels charge to individuals who just walk in off the street. Check the Getting There section of this chapter for agents specializing in package tours.

Homestays

In some countries such as French Polynesia there are bed and breakfast (logement chez l'habitant) programs, where you pay a set fee to stay with a local family in their own home. Meals may not be included in the price, but they're often available, tending toward your host family's fare of seafood and native vegetables. Ask about homestays at tourist information offices once you're in the islands.

A new development in Samoa is the appearance of basic beach resorts run by local families who supply meals, bedding, and *fale* (hut) accommodations at set rates. See the Samoa chapter for details. This is genuine ecotourism for you, and we hope people on some of the other islands catch on and start doing the same sort of thing.

Camping

There are organized campgrounds in French Polynesia, Easter Island, Samoa, Fiji, New Caledonia, and Vanuatu, and the only place where camping is totally forbidden is the Cook Islands. Many backpacker resorts allow camping. Otherwise, get permission of the landowner; you'll rarely be refused in places off the beaten track. Set a good precedent by not leaving a mess or violating custom. If you pitch your tent near a village or on private property without asking permission, you're asking for problems. Otherwise, camp out in the bush well away from gardens and trails.

Make sure your tent is water- and mosquito-proof, and try to find a spot swept by the trades. Never camp under a coconut tree, as falling coconuts hurt (actually, coconuts have two eyes so they only strike the wicked). If you hear a hurricane warning, pack up your tent and take immediate cover with the locals.

Food and Drink

The traditional diet of the Pacific islanders consists of root crops and fruit, plus lagoon fish and the occasional pig. The vegetables include taro, yams, cassava (manioc), breadfruit, and sweet potatoes. The sweet potato (kumara) is something of an anomaly—it's the only Pacific food plant with a South American origin. How it got to the islands is not known.

Taro is an elephant-eared plant cultivated in freshwater swamps. Although yams are considered a prestige food, they're not as nutritious as breadfruit and taro. Yams can grow up to three meters long and weigh hundreds of kilos. Papaya (pawpaw) is nourishing: a third of a cup contains as much vitamin C as 18 apples. To ripen a green papaya overnight, puncture it a few times with a knife. Don't overeat papaya—unless you *need* an effective laxative.

Raw fish (poisson cru) is an appetizing dish enjoyed in many Pacific countries. To prepare it, clean and skin the fish, then dice the fillet. Squeeze lemon or lime juice over it, and store in a cool place about 10 hours. When it's ready to serve, add chopped onions, garlic, green peppers, tomatoes, and coconut cream to taste. Local fishmongers know which species make the best raw fish, but know what you're doing before you join them—island stomachs are probably stronger than yours. Health experts recommend eating only well-cooked foods and peeling your own fruit, but the islanders swear by raw fish.

Lobsters have become almost an endangered species on some islands due to the high prices they fetch on restaurant tables. Coconut crabs are even more threatened and it's almost scandalous that local governments should allow them to be fed to tourists. Sea turtles and flying foxes are other delicacies to avoid, although these are seldom offered to tourists.

Never order "lamb" at a restaurant, because the lowest quality New Zealand mutton flaps (muscle fat and tissue from a sheep's belly) are dumped in the South Pacific and you could get some very fatty pieces. Also beware of "exotic" meats like goat to which your stomach may not be accustomed, and mystery meats like sausage. The turkey tails shipped in from the United States are solid chunks of fat. Chicken is safer provided it is freshly cooked. In general, the low-fat or diet foods popular in the States are unknown in the islands. Vegetarianism is only understood in Fiji where many Indo-Fijians spurn meat.

Islanders in the towns now eat mostly imported foods, just as we Westerners often opt for fast foods instead of meals made from basic ingredients. The Seventh-Day Adventists don't smoke, chew betel nut, dance, eat pork or rabbit, or drink tea, coffee, or alcohol. If you're going to the outer islands, take as many edibles with you as you can; they're always more expensive there. And keep in mind that virtually every food plant you see growing on the islands is cultivated by someone. Even sea shells washed up on a beach, or fish in the lagoon near someone's home, may be considered private property.

Restaurants

Eating out is an adventure, and first-rate restaurants are found in all the main towns, so whenever your travels start to get to you and it's time for a lift, splurge on a good meal and then see how the world looks. French Polynesia and New Caledonia have some of the finest restaurants in the region, with prices to match. Fiji is outstanding for the variety of cuisines you can sample, and prices are very reasonable. Nuku'alofa and Apia also offer an increasing number of good inexpensive places to eat. Unlike Australia and New Zealand, it's not customary to bring your own (BYO) alcohol into restaurants.

Cooking

The ancient Polynesians stopped making pottery over a millennium ago and instead developed an ingenious way of cooking in an underground earth oven known as an *umu, ahimaa,* or *lovo*. First a stack of dry coconut husks is burned in a pit. Once the fire is going well, coral stones are heaped on top, and when most of the husks have burnt away the food is wrapped in banana leaves and placed on the hot stones—fish and meat below, vegetables above. A whole pig may be cleaned, then stuffed with banana leaves and hot stones. This cooks the beast from inside out as well as outside in, and the leaves create steam. The food is then covered with more leaves and stones, and after about 2.5 hours everything is cooked.

Others

Betel chewing is a widespread practice among men, women, and children in the Western Pacific, as far southeast as Santa Cruz in the Solomons. First the unripe nut of the Areca palm is chewed, then the leaves of the fruit of the betel pepper. Lime from a gourd (made by burning coral or shells, or grinding limestone) is inserted into the mouth with a spatula, and the chewer's saliva turns bright red. It's said to relieve hunger and fatigue but also causes cancer of the mouth.

Kava drinking is easier to get into (see Customs in the Fiji chapter for a full description). While kava is extremely popular in Fiji and Tonga, extremely potent in Vanuatu, and extremely dignified in Samoa, it's unknown in Tahiti and Rarotonga.

Information and Services

INFORMATION

All the main countries have official tourist information offices. Their main branches in the capitals open during normal business hours but the information desks at the airports open only for the arrival of international flights, if then. Always visit the local tourist office to pick up brochures and ask questions. Their overseas offices, listed in this handbook's appendix, often mail out useful information on their country and all of them have Internet websites.

Be aware, however, that much of the information on the web is old, incomplete, and misleading. Most commercial websites are designed to promote specific companies, while individual sites usually don't examine all the travel options available. That's what we've tried to do herein, but things change and absolutes are rare in life, so we welcome feedback to help ensure that what appears in this handbook is as close to reality as possible. No comment will be disregarded. To contact us, visit www.southpacific.org.

VISAS AND OFFICIALDOM

If you're from an English-speaking country or Western Europe you won't need a visa to visit most of the South Pacific countries as a tourist. Unlike the United States, which is very sticky about visas, American Samoa does not require a visa of most tourists. Australia requires a visa of everyone except New Zealanders. This may be free if obtained "electronically" by your travel agent at the time you buy your plane ticket, but will cost around A$50 if obtained in person at a high commission, consulate, or airline office in the islands (airline offices used to issue electronic Australian visas free of charge but few do so any more).

Everyone must have a passport, sufficient funds, and a ticket to leave. Your passport should be valid six months beyond your departure date. Some officials object to tourists who intend to camp or stay with friends, so write the name of a likely hotel on your arrival card (don't leave that space blank). To avoid another problem, make sure the name on your passport is exactly the same as the name on your plane ticket (no nicknames or married names).

Immigration officials will often insist on seeing an air ticket back to your home country, no matter how much money you're able to show them. The easy way to get around this if you're on an open-ended holiday or traveling by yacht is to purchase a regular one-way ticket to Hawaii or Los Angeles from Air New Zealand. This will be accepted without question, and Air New Zealand offices throughout the Pacific will reissue the ticket, so you'll always have a ticket to leave from the next country on your itinerary. When you finally get home, you can turn in the unused coupons for a full refund. (See Getting There later in this chapter.)

The easiest way to obtain a residence permit in a South Pacific country is to invest money in a small business. Almost every country and territory has a special government department intended to facilitate investment and the local tourist office will be able to tell you who to contact. As little as US$50,000 capital may be required and lots of low-tech opportunities exist in the tourist industry. Drawbacks are that you may be obliged to accept a local partner, your residence permit will end as soon as you cease to be actively involved in the business, and you'll be subject to immediate deportation if you get on the wrong side of local politicians. Unconditional permanent residence and citizenship are rarely granted to persons of ethnic origins other than those prevailing in the countries.

Diplomatic Missions

The country with the widest representation in the South Pacific is New Zealand, which has high commissions in Apia, Honiara, Nuku'alofa, Port Vila, Rarotonga, and Suva, a consulate in Nouméa, and an honorary consul in Papeete. Australia has exactly the same level of diplomatic representation as New Zealand except that they lack offices in Papeete and on Rarotonga. Canada has a consulate at Nadi (Fiji), and in 1986 Canada and Australia signed a reciprocal agreement extending full consular service to Canadians at Australian missions throughout the region. Britain has high commissions in Honiara, Nuku'alofa, Port Vila, and Suva, and an honorary consul in Papeete. The United States is very poorly represented with heavily guarded embassies in Apia and Suva only.

France has embassies in Port Vila and Suva, high commissions in Nouméa and Papeete, and honorary consuls in Nuku'alofa and Rarotonga. China has embassies in Apia, Nuku'alofa, Port Vila, and Suva, while Taiwan has an embassy in Honiara. Japan has embassies in Honiara and Suva and a consulate in Nouméa. South Korea has an embassy in Suva, a consulate in Pago Pago, and honorary consuls in Apia, Nuku'alofa, and Papeete. Papua New Guinea has an embassy in Suva, a high commission in Honiara, and an honorary consul in Port Vila.

Numerous member countries of the European Union have consulates or honorary consuls in Nouméa and Papeete, and these are listed in the respective chapters. Other honorary consuls include those of Germany in Apia, Nuku'alofa, and Papeete; of Sweden in Apia, Nuku'alofa, Papeete, and Port Vila; of Switzerland in Nouméa and Papeete; of Spain in Nuku'alofa; of Chile in Papeete; and of Indonesia and Vanuatu in Nouméa.

Customs

Agricultural regulations in most Pacific countries prohibit the import of fresh fruit, vegetables, flowers, seeds, honey, eggs, milk products, meat (including sausage), live animals and plants, as well as any old artifacts that might harbor pests. If in doubt, ask about having your souvenirs fumigated by the local agricultural authorities and a certificate issued prior to departure. Processed food or beverages, biscuits, confectionery, sugar, rice, seafood, dried flowers, mounted insects, mats, baskets, and tapa cloth are usually okay. If you've been on a farm, wash your clothes and shoes before going to the airport, and if you've been camping, make sure your tent is clean.

MONEY

All prices quoted herein are in the local currency unless otherwise stated. If you have access to the Internet you'll find the rates for all Pacific currencies at www.xe.net/ucc/full.shtlm. There's strong opposition in the three French territories to the replacement of the Pacific franc (CFP) by the Euro, thereby bringing them under the jurisdiction of the European Central Bank in economic matters, and the Maastricht Treaty specifically exempts them from this fate.

Most South Pacific airports have banks changing money at normal rates (check the Airport listing at the end of each chapter Introduction) and the most convenient currencies to carry are Australian, N.Z., and U.S. dollars, although all major currencies are accepted. If you'll be visiting American Samoa, be sure to have enough U.S. dollar traveler's checks to see you through, as whopping commissions are charged on foreign currency. Banks in French Polynesia, Samoa, and New Caledonia also charge exorbitant commissions. Euros in cash are the best currency to carry to the French colonies as they're changed into CFP at a fixed rate without any commission (commission may be charged on Euro traveler's checks).

The bulk of your travel funds should be in traveler's checks, preferably American Express, although that company's representation in the region is dwindling. American Express has travel service offices in Papeete, Rarotonga, Suva, and Nouméa, but the American Express agencies in Pago Pago and Apia have closed and the company has no representation in Tonga, Vanuatu,

EXPLORING THE ISLANDS

EXCHANGE RATES

(approximate figures for orientation only)
US$1 = CFP 100 (French Pacific francs)
US$1 = NZ$1.60 (New Zealand dollars)
US$1 = A$1.40 (Australian dollars)
US$1 = T$2.00 (Tongan *pa'anga*)
US$1 = S$2.85 (Samoan *tala*)
US$1 = F$1.75 (Fiji dollars)
US$1 = Vt.115 (Vanuatu *vatu*)
US$1 = SI$7.50 (Solomon Islands dollars)

and Solomon Islands. Thomas Cook has large offices in Nadi and Suva, Fiji. To claim a refund for lost or stolen American Express traveler's checks call the local office (listed in the respective chapter) or their Sydney office collect (tel. 61-2/9271-8689). They'll also cancel lost credit cards, provided you know the numbers. Western Union has numerous agencies in the islands offering fast money transfers.

If you want to use a credit card, always ask beforehand, even if a business has a sign or brochure that says it's possible. Visa and MasterCard can be used to obtain cash advances at banks in most countries, but remember that cash advances are considered personal loans and accrue interest from the moment you receive the money. The use of bank cards such as Visa and MasterCard is expensive in Samoa and Solomon Islands because those currencies aren't recognized internationally. Thus the charge must first be converted into N.Z. or Australian dollars, then into your own currency, and you'll lose on the exchange several times. American Express is probably the best card to use, since they don't go through third currencies (this could vary—ask). Never use a credit card to pay an airport tax, even if it's allowed, as it will be treated as a cash advance and subject to service fees. Some cards have a daily limit that may be too low to cover large purchases and they're difficult to replace if lost.

When you rent a car the agency will probably ask you to sign a blank credit card charge slip as security on the vehicle. Room reservations are also commonly guaranteed by credit card. Whenever you provide your credit card number—especially if the company actually uses your card to make an imprint on a charge slip—you should let the charge go through and not switch to paying in cash at the last minute. All too often, such charges are processed "by accident" even though you paid in cash, and it's always a hassle trying to get things like this straightened out weeks or months later, even if you still have your signed cash receipt. On a long trip, you can avoid high interest charges by leaving an adequate deposit on your card.

Many banks now have automated teller machines (ATMs) outside their offices and these provide local currency at good rates against debit cards associated with the Cirrus, Maestro, and Plus networks. The charges can be deducted from your checking account automatically so you avoid interest charges. Be aware, however, that both your bank and the one providing the ATM may charge a surprisingly high fee for each transaction. Ask your bank how much they take and find out if you need a special personal identification number (PIN). Occasionally the machines don't work due to problems with the software and your password's numbers may not correspond to a foreign ATM's numerical keys. To avoid emergencies (such as if a machine were to "eat" your card), it's better not to be too dependent on ATMs.

Cost-wise, you'll find the Cook Islands, Fiji, Tonga, Samoa, and Solomon Islands to be the least expensive South Pacific countries, with French Polynesia and New Caledonia consistently dearer. The lack of budget accommodations makes the price of a visit to American Samoa stiff, while in Vanuatu it's the cost of interisland transportation that breaks your budget. Inflation is consistently low in New Caledonia and French Polynesia but high in Solomon Islands, Tonga, and Samoa, something to keep in mind when looking at the prices in this book.

Upon departure avoid getting stuck with leftover banknotes, as currencies such as the Fiji dollar, Pacific franc, Solomon Islands dollar, Vanuatu *vatu,* Samoan *tala,* and Tongan *pa'anga* are difficult to change and heavily discounted even in neighboring countries. Change whatever you have left over into the currency of the next country on your itinerary, but don't wait to do it at the airport. The Thomas Cook office in downtown Nadi, Fiji, buys and sells all Pacific currencies.

Bargaining is not common in the islands: The first price you're quoted is usually it. If you think it's too much, you could ask if they have a "second price" or if any "specials" are on. Tipping is *not* customary in the South Pacific and often generates more embarrassment than gratitude.

COMMUNICATIONS

Postal Services

Always use airmail when posting letters from the South Pacific. Airmail takes two weeks to reach North America and Europe, surface mail takes up to six months. Postage rates to the United States are very low from Solomon Islands and American Samoa, a wee bit more from Fiji, Tonga, and Samoa, medium-priced from the Cook Islands, and very expensive from French Polynesia, New Caledonia, and Vanuatu. Plan your postcard writing accordingly. Sending a picture postcard to an islander is a very nice way of saying thank you.

When collecting mail at poste restante (general delivery), be sure to check under the initials of your first and second names, plus any initial that is similar. Have your correspondents print and underline your last name. Parcels may be kept in a separate area.

PHILATELY

Postage stamps of the South Pacific are highly valued by collectors around the world, and many smaller Commonwealth countries such as the Cook Islands, Kiribati, Niue, Norfolk Island, Pitcairn, Samoa, Tokelau, Tonga, and Tuvalu earn a substantial portion of government revenue from the sale of stamps. In order to generate more revenue, the Cook Islands issues separate stamps for Penrhyn and Aitutaki, and Tonga has Niuafo'ou stamps. Some countries also try to boost income by increasing the number of annual issues, a practice that can cost them collectors. Bad actors in this regard are Cook Islands, Niue, and Tuvalu. Most of the stamps are printed in Britain, where the highest technical standards are employed.

Popular themes include birds, seashells, coral, maps, atoll scenes, fishing, dancing, musical instruments, and headdresses. As the bicentenaries of his voyages of discovery rolled around during the 1970s, Captain Cook was the subject of stamp issues by many of the islands he discovered. Easily obtained, inexpensive postage stamps and first-day covers make memorable souvenirs.

Telephone Services

The Cook Islands, Fiji, New Caledonia, Tonga, Solomon Islands, French Polynesia, and Vanuatu all have card telephones and these are very handy. If you'll be staying in a country more than a few days and intend to make your own arrangements, it's wise to purchase a local telephone card at a post office right away. In this handbook we provide all the phone numbers you'll need to make hotel reservations, check restaurant hours, find out about cultural shows, and compare car rental rates, saving you a lot of time and inconvenience.

By using a telephone card to call long distance you limit the amount the call can possibly cost and won't end up overspending should you forget to keep track of the time. On short calls you avoid three-minute minimum charges. International telephone calls placed from hotel rooms are always much more expensive than the same calls made from public phones using telephone cards. What you sacrifice is your privacy as anyone can stand around and listen to your call, as often happens. Card phones are usually found outside post offices or telephone centers. Check that the phone actually works before bothering to arrange your numbers and notes, as they're often out of service.

To place a call to a Pacific island from outside the region, first dial the international access code (check your phone book), then the country code, then the number. The country codes are:

- American Samoa 684
- Cook Islands 682
- Easter Island 56-32
- Fiji 679
- French Polynesia 689
- New Caledonia 687
- Niue 683
- Pitcairn Islands 872
- Samoa 685
- Solomon Islands 677
- Tokelau 690
- Tonga 676
- Tuvalu 688
- Vanuatu 678
- Wallis 681

EXPLORING THE ISLANDS

None of the Pacific countries have local area codes, but local telephone numbers have varying numbers of digits: four digits in Niue and Tokelau; five digits in the Cook Islands, Tonga, Samoa, Tuvalu, Vanuatu, and Solomon Islands; six digits in French Polynesia, Easter Island, Wallis and Futuna, and New Caledonia; and seven digits in American Samoa and Fiji.

You're better off calling from North America to the South Pacific in the evening as it will be mid-afternoon in the islands (plus you'll probably benefit from off-peak telephone rates). From Europe, call very late at night. In the other direction, if you're calling from the islands to North America or Europe, do so in the early morning as it will already be afternoon in North America and evening in Europe. The local time at almost any point worldwide is available at www.times.clari.net.au.

If a fax you are trying to send to the South Pacific doesn't go through smoothly on the first or second try, wait and try again at another time of day. If it still doesn't work, stop trying as the fax machine at the other end may not be able to read your signal and your telephone company will levy a minimum charge for each attempt. Call the international operator to ask what is going wrong.

Electronic Mail

An increasing number of tourism-related businesses in the South Pacific have email addresses, which makes communicating with them from abroad a lot cheaper and easier. We've tried to include the most useful email and website addresses herein, otherwise do a search on www.google.com. Email addresses tend to change faster than web addresses, and in the case of businesses which have both email and a website, we usually list the website herein. You should be able to find their current email address on their site, and maybe the answer to your question as well!

Websites and email addresses based in the islands are recognizable by their country codes: American Samoa (as), the Cook Islands (ck), Fiji (fj), French Polynesia (pf), New Caledonia (nc), Niue (nu), Pitcairn (pn), Samoa (ws), Solomon Islands (sb), Tokelau (tk), Tonga (to), Tuvalu (tv), Vanuatu (vu), and Wallis and Futuna (wf). Some countries have made a profitable business out of selling website domain names using these codes.

When sending email to the islands never include a large attached file (such as photos) with your message unless it has been specifically requested as the recipient may have to pay US$1 a minute in long distance telephone charges to download it. It's probably better not to email any attached files to the islands at all as the recipient may not have the latest virus scanning program and your message may be deleted unread.

Internet cafés on many islands now allow you to check your web-based email and we've included some of them in this book. In French Polynesia the computers usually have French keyboards, which vary slightly from English keyboards leading to annoying typing problems. Ask the operator if they have a machine with an English keyboard or to explain the quirks of the French keyboard.

Of course, in order to receive email online, you'll need a web-based electronic mailbox. Many servers now provide these to their clients, otherwise you should open a Yahoo or Hotmail account before leaving home. To do so, simply click "Email" at www.yahoo.com or "Sign Up" at www.hotmail.com. You must check your mail at least once a month, otherwise your free account will be canceled. Communicating has never been so easy!

MEDIA

Daily newspapers are published in French Polynesia (*La Dépêche de Tahiti* and *Les Nouvelles de Tahiti*), the Cook Islands (*Cook Islands News*), American Samoa (*The Samoa News*), Samoa (*The Samoa Observer*), Fiji (*The Fiji Times, The Fiji Sun,* and *The Daily Post*), New Caledonia (*Les Nouvelles Calédoniennes*), and Solomon Islands (*The Solomon Star*). Weekly or twice-weekly papers of note include the *Cook Islands Herald, Port Vila Presse, Tonga Chronicle, Trading Post,* and the *Tahiti Beach Press.*

The leading regional news magazines are *Islands Business* published in Fiji and *Pacific Magazine* from Honolulu. Copies of these are well worth picking up during your trip, and a subscription will help you keep in touch. Turn to Resources at the end of this book for more Pacific-oriented publications.

Radio

A great way to keep in touch with world and local affairs is to take along a small AM/FM shortwave portable radio. Your only expense will be the radio itself and batteries. Throughout this handbook we provide the names and frequencies of local stations, so set your tuning buttons to these as soon as you arrive. At least once a day the major local stations rebroadcast news reports from the BBC World Service, Radio Australia, and Radio New Zealand International, and we've tried to provide the times. In the Western Pacific, check Radio Vanuatu on shortwave at 3945 MHz and the Solomon Islands Broadcasting Corporation at 5020 MHz (a strong signal heard as far away as Australia and Fiji). None of the other countries have shortwave frequencies.

Health

For a tropical area, the South Pacific's a healthy place. The sea and air are clear and usually pollution-free. The humidity nourishes the skin and the local fruit is brimming with vitamins. If you take a few precautions, you'll never have a sick day. The information provided below is intended to make you knowledgeable, not fearful.

The government-run medical facilities mentioned in this book typically provide free medical treatment to local residents but have special rates for foreigners. It's usually no more expensive to visit a private doctor or clinic, and sometimes it's even cheaper. Private doctors can afford to provide faster service since everyone is paying, and we've tried to list local doctors and dentists throughout the handbook. In emergencies and outside clinic hours, you can always turn to the government-run facilities.

American-made medications may by unobtainable in the islands, so along bring a supply of whatever you think you'll need. If you need to replace anything, quote the generic name at the drug store rather than the brand name. Antibiotics should only be used to treat serious wounds, and only after medical advice. Check www.cdc.gov/travel/austspac.htm for up-to-the-minute information on Pacific health. Unfortunately, very few facilities are provided around the region for travelers with disabilities.

Travel Insurance

The sale of travel insurance is big business but the value of the policies themselves is often questionable. If your regular group health insurance covers you while you're on the road it's probably enough, as medical costs in the South Pacific are generally low. Most policies only pay the amount above and beyond what your national or group health insurance will pay and are invalid if you don't have any health insurance at all. You may also be covered by your credit card company if you paid for your plane ticket with the card. Buying extra travel insurance is about the same as buying a lottery ticket: there's always the chance it will pay off, but it's usually money down the drain.

If you do opt for the security of travel insurance, make sure emergency medical evacuations are covered. Some policies are invalid if you engage in "dangerous activities," such as scuba diving, parasailing, surfing, or even riding a motor scooter, so be sure to read the fine print. Scuba divers should be aware that the only recompression chambers in the South Pacific are at Papeete (Tahiti) and Suva (Fiji). Elsewhere you'll need an emergency medical evacuation to Australia or New Zealand and there isn't any point buying a policy that doesn't cover it. Medical insurance especially designed for scuba divers is available from **Divers Alert Network** (www.diversalertnetwork.org).

EXPLORING THE ISLANDS

A TRAVELER'S NOTES ON AIDS AND HIV

In 1981 scientists in the United States and France first recognized the Acquired Immune Deficiency Syndrome (AIDS), which was later discovered to be caused by a virus called the Human Immuno-deficiency Virus (HIV). HIV breaks down the body's immunity to infections leading to AIDS. The virus can lie hidden in the body for up to 10 years without producing any obvious symptoms or before developing into the AIDS disease and in the meantime the person can unknowingly infect others.

HIV lives in white blood cells and is present in the sexual fluids of humans. It is spread mostly through sexual intercourse, by needle or syringe sharing among intravenous drug users, in blood transfusions, and during pregnancy and birth (if the mother is infected). Using another person's razor blade or having your body pierced or tattooed are also risky, but the HIV virus cannot be transmitted by shaking hands, kissing, cuddling, fondling, sneezing, cooking food, or sharing eating or drinking utensils. One cannot be infected by saliva, sweat, tears, urine, or feces; toilet seats, telephones, swimming pools, or mosquito bites do not cause AIDS. Ostracizing a known AIDS victim is not only immoral but also absurd.

Most blood banks now screen their products for HIV, and you can protect yourself against dirty needles by only allowing an injection if you see the syringe taken out of a fresh unopened pack. The simplest safeguard during sex is the proper use of a latex condom. Unroll the condom onto the erect penis; while withdrawing after ejaculation, hold onto the condom as you come out. Never try to recycle a condom, and pack a supply with you as it's a nuisance trying to buy them locally.

HIV is spread more often through anal than vaginal sex because the lining of the rectum is much weaker than that of the vagina, and ordinary condoms sometimes tear when used in anal sex. If you have anal sex, only use extra-strong condoms and special water-based lubricants since oil, Vaseline, and cream weaken the rubber. During oral sex you must make sure you don't get any semen or menstrual blood in your mouth. A woman runs 10 times the risk of contracting AIDS from a man than the other way around, and the threat is always greater when another sexually transmitted disease (STD) is present.

Some companies will pay your bills directly while others require you to pay and collect receipts that may be reimbursed later. Ask if travel delays, lost baggage, and theft are included. In practice, your airline probably already covers the first two adequately and claiming something extra from your insurance company could be more trouble than it's worth. Theft insurance never covers items left on the beach while you're in swimming. All said, you should weigh the advantages and decide for yourself if you want a policy. Just don't be influenced by what your travel agent says as they'll only want to sell you coverage in order to earn another commission.

Acclimatizing

Don't go from winter weather into the steaming tropics without a rest before and after. Minimize jet lag by setting your watch to local time at your destination as soon as you board the flight. Westbound flights into the South Pacific from North America or Europe are less jolting since you follow the sun and your body gets a few hours extra sleep. On the way home you're moving against the sun and the hours of sleep your body loses cause jet lag. Airplane cabins have low humidity, so drink lots of juice or water instead of carbonated drinks, and don't overeat in-flight. It's also wise to forgo coffee, as it will only keep you awake, and alcohol, which will dehydrate you.

Scuba diving on departure day can give you a severe case of the bends. Before flying there should be a minimum of 12 hours surface interval after a nondecompression dive and a minimum of 24 hours after a decompression dive.

The very existence of AIDS calls for a basic change in human behavior. No vaccine or drug exists that can prevent or cure AIDS, and because the virus mutates frequently, no remedy may ever be totally effective. Other STDs such as syphilis, gonorrhea, chlamydia, hepatitis B, and herpes are far more common than AIDS and can lead to serious complications such as infertility, but most of them can usually be cured.

The euphoria of travel can make it easier to fall in love or have sex with a stranger, so travelers must be informed of these dangers. As a tourist you should always practice safe sex to prevent AIDS and other STDs. You never know who is infected or even if you yourself have become infected. It's important to bring the subject up *before* you start to make love. Make a joke out of it by pulling out a condom and asking your new partner, "Say, do you know what this is?" Or perhaps, "Your condom or mine?" Far from being unromantic or embarrassing, you'll both feel more relaxed with the subject off your minds and it's much better than worrying afterwards if you might have been infected. The golden rule is safe sex or no sex.

Currently an estimated 40 million people worldwide are HIV carriers, and millions have already died of AIDS. In the South Pacific, the number of cases is still extremely small compared to the hundreds of thousands of confirmed HIV infections in the United States. French Polynesia, New Caledonia, Papua New Guinea, and Guam are the most affected countries, yet it's worth noting that other STDs are rampant in the urban areas of Fiji, Vanuatu, and Solomon Islands, demonstrating that the type of behavior leading to the rapid spread of AIDS is present.

An HIV infection can be detected through a blood test because the antibodies created by the body to fight off the virus can be seen under a microscope. It takes at least three weeks for the antibodies to be produced and in some cases as long as six months before they can be picked up during a screening test. If you think you may have run a risk, you should discuss the appropriateness of a test with your doctor. It's always better to know if you are infected so as to be able to avoid infecting others, to obtain early treatment of symptoms, and to make realistic plans.

If you know someone with AIDS you should give them all the support you can (there's no danger in such contact unless blood is present).

Factors contributing to decompression sickness include a lack of sleep and/or the excessive consumption of alcohol before diving.

If you start feeling seasick onboard a ship, stare at the horizon, which is always steady, and stop thinking about it. Anti-motion-sickness pills are useful to have along; otherwise, ginger helps alleviate seasickness. Travel stores sell acubands that find a pressure point on the wrist and create a stable flow of blood to the head, thus miraculously preventing seasickness!

Frequently the feeling of thirst is false and only due to mucous membrane dryness. Gargling or taking two or three gulps of warm water should be enough. Keep moisture in your body by having a hot drink like tea or black coffee, or any kind of slightly salted or sour drink in small quantities. Salt in fresh lime juice is remarkably refreshing.

The tap water is safe to drink in the main towns, but ask first elsewhere. If in doubt, boil it or use purification pills. Tap water that is uncomfortably hot to touch is usually safe. Allow it to cool in a clean container. Don't forget that if the tap water is contaminated, the local ice will be too. Avoid brushing your teeth with water unfit to drink, and wash or peel fruit and vegetables if you can. Cooked food is less subject to contamination than raw.

Sunburn

Though you may think a tan will make you look healthier and more attractive, it's actually very damaging to the skin, which becomes dry, rigid, and prematurely old and wrinkled, especially on the face. Begin with short exposures to the sun, perhaps half an hour at a time, followed by an equal time in the shade. Drink plenty of liquids to keep your pores open and avoid the sun from 1000 to 1500, the most dangerous time. Clouds and beach umbrellas will not protect you fully. Wear a T-shirt while snorkeling to protect your back. Sunbathing is the main cause of cataracts to the eyes, so wear sunglasses and a wide-brimmed hat, and beware of reflected sunlight.

Use a sunscreen lotion containing PABA rather than oil, and don't forget to apply it to your nose, lips, forehead, neck, hands, and feet. Sunscreens protect you from ultraviolet rays (a leading cause of cancer), while oils magnify the sun's effect. A 15-factor sunscreen provides 93 percent protection (a more expensive 30-factor sunscreen is only slightly better at 97 percent protection). Apply the lotion *before* going to the beach to avoid being burned on the way, and reapply every couple of hours to replace sunscreen washed away by perspiration. Swimming also washes away your protection. After sunbathing take a tepid shower rather than a hot one, which would wash away your natural skin oils. Stay moist and use a vitamin E evening cream to preserve the youth of your skin. Calamine ointment soothes skin already burned, as does coconut oil. Pharmacists recommend Solarcaine to soothe burned skin. Rinsing off with a vinegar solution reduces peeling, and aspirin relieves some of the pain and irritation. Vitamin A and calcium counteract overdoses of vitamin D received from the sun. The fairer your skin, the more essential it is to take care.

As earth's ozone layer is depleted due to the commercial use of chlorofluorocarbons (CFCs) and other factors, the need to protect oneself from ultraviolet radiation is becoming more urgent as deaths from skin cancer are on the increase. Previously the cancers didn't develop until age 50 or 60, but now much younger people are affected.

Ailments

Cuts and scratches infect easily in the tropics and take a long time to heal. Prevent infection from coral cuts by immediately washing wounds with soap and fresh water, then rubbing in vinegar or alcohol (whiskey will do)—painful but effective. Use an antiseptic like hydrogen peroxide and an antibacterial ointment such as neosporin, if you have them. Islanders usually dab coral cuts with lime juice. All cuts turn septic quickly in the tropics, so try to keep them clean and covered.

For bites, burns, and cuts, an antiseptic such as Solarcaine speeds healing and helps prevent infection. Pure aloe vera is good for sunburn, scratches, and even coral cuts. Bites by *no-no* sandflies itch for days and can become infected if scratched. Not everyone is affected by insect bites in the same way. Some people are practically immune to insects, while traveling companions experiencing exactly the same conditions are soon covered with bites. You'll soon know which type you are.

Prickly heat, an intensely irritating rash, is caused by wearing heavy clothing that is inappropriate for the climate. When the glands are blocked and the sweat is unable to evaporate, the skin becomes soggy and small red blisters appear. Synthetic fabrics like nylon are especially bad in this regard. Take a cold shower, apply calamine lotion, dust with talcum powder, and take off those clothes! Until things improve, avoid alcohol, tea, coffee, and any physical activity that makes you sweat. If you're sweating profusely, increase your intake of salt slightly to avoid fatigue, but not without concurrently drinking more water.

Use antidiarrheal medications such as Lomotil or Imodium sparingly. Rather than take drugs to plug yourself up, drink plenty of unsweetened liquids like green coconut or fresh fruit juice to help flush yourself out. Egg yolk mixed with nutmeg helps diarrhea, or have a rice and tea day. Avoid dairy products, sweetened drinks, alcohol, and coffee. Most cases of diarrhea are self-limiting and require only simple replacement of the fluids and salts lost in diarrheal stools. If the diarrhea is persistent or you experience high fever, drowsiness, or blood in the stool, stop traveling, rest, and consider seeing a doctor. For constipation eat pineapple or any peeled fruit.

Malaria

Malaria is the most serious regional health hazard, but it's restricted to Vanuatu, Solomon Islands, and Papua New Guinea *only.* Guadalcanal ranks as one of the most malarial areas in the world, and Chloroquine-resistant *falciparum* malaria is widespread in all three countries. Read the relevant references in the Introductions to the Vanuatu and Solomon Islands chapters a couple of weeks before you embark for those islands. If you're only going to Fiji, New Caledonia, or any of the Polynesian countries, forget malaria entirely, as it's unknown there.

Malaria *can* be avoided, and even if you're unlucky, it won't kill you so long as you're taking prophylactics. So don't become alarmed or let fear of malaria prevent you from visiting northern Melanesia. Symptoms of malaria are chills, aches in the back, head, and joints, plus a high periodic fever. Doctors outside the area often misdiagnose these symptoms (which may not begin until months after you leave the area) as common flu. Yet once identified through a blood test, malaria can usually be cured.

The *Anopheles* carrier mosquitoes are most active from dusk to dawn, so try to avoid getting bitten at this time. Wear long shirts and pants, sleep in a screened room, burn a mosquito coil, and use an insect repellent containing a high concentration of N,N diethylmetatoluamide (deet). For some reason people taking vitamin B-1 aren't as attractive to mosquitoes. On the other hand perfumes, colognes, and scented soaps do attract them.

Begin taking an antimalarial drug a week before you arrive in Vanuatu or the Solomons and continue for four weeks after you leave. Malaria pills are a bit cheaper in the South Pacific than in North America or Australia, so you only need the minimum number required to get you started. In you're flying into Vanuatu, you could wait to buy the pills in Port Vila where malaria is not as serious a problem.

An often-recommended drug effective against *falciparum* malaria is Lariam, also known as Mefloquine, and the usual dose is one 250-mg tablet a week (Larium costs around US$5 a pill while Mefloquine is somewhat cheaper). Doxycycline (one 100-mg tablet each day) is also recommended by some authorities. Lariam/Mefloquine or Doxycycline are good choices if

you're going to Solomon Islands or northern Vanuatu but it would be overkill if you were only headed for Port Vila and southern Vanuatu where the risk is less. In southern Vanuatu, budget-priced Chloroquine (two 250-mg tablets once a week) may be sufficient but you should always take something.

There's vaccination against malaria and none of the various pills are 100 percent effective. It's something of a scandal in the medical profession that while hundreds of millions of dollars are spent annually on research into the lifestyle diseases of the affluent, such as cancer and heart disease, comparatively little is allocated to the tropical and parasitic diseases of the developing world. Vaccines only provide one percent of the profits of the big pharmaceutical companies, and just three percent of their research budgets are devoted to tropical diseases, largely because there's little money to be made.

Dengue Fever

Dengue fever is a mosquito-transmitted disease that first appeared in the South Pacific in the 1970s. Signs are headaches, sore throat, pain in the joints, fever, chills, nausea, and rash. This painful illness also known as "breakbone fever" can last anywhere from five to 15 days. Although you can relieve the symptoms somewhat, the only real cure is to stay in bed, drink lots of water, and wait it out. Avoid aspirin as this can lead to complications. No vaccine exists, so just try to avoid getting bitten (the *Aedes aegypti* mosquito bites only during the day). Dengue fever can kill infants so extra care must be taken to protect them if an outbreak is in progress.

In early 1998 a major outbreak in Fiji resulted in an estimated 25,000 cases and 14 deaths. During the 2001 dengue fever epidemic in French Polynesia—the worst in the territory's history—there were an estimated 30,000 cases with 10,000 requiring some form of hospital treatment. Of these, 4,000 cases were considered severe, and six deaths occurred among children aged six to 12. The Cook Islands and Easter Island also experienced dengue outbreaks about the same time. Fumigations and a clean-up campaign eventually overcame the disease.

EXPLORING THE ISLANDS

Toxic Fish

More than 400 species of tropical reef fish, including wrasses, snappers, groupers, jacks, moray eels, surgeonfish, shellfish, and especially barracudas are known to cause seafood poisoning (ciguatera). There's no way to tell if a fish will cause ciguatera: a species can be poisonous on one side of the island, but not on the other.

In 1976 French and Japanese scientists working in the Gambier Islands determined that a one-celled dinoflagellate algae or plankton called *Gambierdiscus toxicus* was the cause. Normally these microalgae are found only in the ocean depths, but when a reef ecosystem is disturbed by natural or human causes they can multiply dramatically in a lagoon. The dinoflagellates are consumed by tiny herbivorous fish and the toxin passes up through the food chain to larger fish where it becomes concentrated in the head and guts. The toxins have no effect on the fish that feed on them.

French Polynesia's 700–800 cases of ciguatera a year are more than in the rest of the South Pacific combined, leading to suspicions that the former French nuclear testing program is responsible. Ciguatera didn't exist on Hao atoll in the Tuamotus until military dredging for a 3,380-meter runway began in 1965. By mid-1968 43 percent of the population had been affected. Between 1971 and 1980 more than 30 percent of the population of Mangareva near the Moruroa nuclear test site suffered from seafood poisoning. Yet ciguatera has been around for a long time, having been reported in New Caledonia by Captain Cook.

The symptoms (numbness and tingling around the mouth and extremities, reversal of hot/cold sensations, prickling, itching, nausea, vomiting, erratic heartbeat, joint and muscle pains) usually subside in a few days. Induce vomiting, take castor oil as a laxative, and avoid alcohol if you're unlucky. Symptoms can recur for up to a year, and victims may become allergic to all seafoods.

Avoid biointoxication by cleaning fish as soon as they're caught, discarding the head and organs, and taking special care with oversized fish caught in shallow water. Small fish are generally safer. Whether the fish is consumed cooked or raw has no bearing on this problem. Local residents often know from experience which species may be eaten. Information on the new ciguatera test kit is available at www.cigua.com.

Other Diseases

Infectious hepatitis A (jaundice) is a liver ailment transmitted person to person or through unboiled water, uncooked vegetables, or other foods contaminated during handling. The risk of infection is highest among those who eat village food, so if you'll be spending much time in rural areas, consider getting an immune globulin shot, which provides six months protection. Better is a vaccine called Havrix, which provides up to 10 years protection (given in two doses two weeks apart, then a third dose six months later). If you've ever had hepatitis A in your life you are already immune. Otherwise, you'll know you've got the hep when your eyeballs and urine turn yellow. Time and rest are the only cure. Viral hepatitis B is spread through sexual or blood contact.

Cholera is rare in the South Pacific but there have been sporadic outbreaks in Micronesia. Cholera is acquired via contaminated food or water, so avoid uncooked foods, peel your own fruit, and drink bottled drinks if you happen to arrive in an infected area. Typhoid fever is also caused by contaminated food or water, while tetanus (lockjaw) occurs when cuts or bites become infected. Horrible disfiguring diseases such as leprosy and elephantiasis are hard to catch, so it's unlikely you'll be visited by one of those nightmares of the flesh.

Vaccinations

The overwhelming majority of visitors don't need to get any vaccinations at all before coming to the South Pacific. Tetanus, diphtheria, and typhoid fever shots are not required, but they're worth considering if you'll be going far off the beaten track for extended periods. Tetanus and diphtheria shots are given together, and a booster is required every 10 years. The oral typhoid fever vaccine is administered every seven years, if necessary. Polio is believed to have been eradicated from the region.

The cholera vaccine is only 50 percent effective and valid just six months, and bad reactions are common, which is why most doctors in developed countries won't administer it. Forget it unless you're sure you're headed for an infected area. If you'll be visiting Tuvalu or anywhere in Micronesia, ask your airline if a cholera vaccination is required. In that case you'll be able to obtain it locally without difficulty.

A yellow-fever vaccination is required if you've been in an infected area within the six days prior to arrival. Yellow fever is a mosquito-borne disease that only occurs in Central Africa and northern South America (excluding Chile), places you're not likely to have been just before arriving in the South Pacific. Since the vaccination is valid 10 years, get one if you're an inveterate globe-trotter.

Immune globulin (IG) and the Havrix vaccine aren't 100 percent effective against hepatitis A, but they do increase your general resistance to infections. IG prophylaxis must be repeated every five months. Hepatitis B vaccination involves three doses over a six-month period (duration of protection unknown) and is recommended mostly for people planning extended stays in the region.

What to Take

Packing

Assemble everything you simply must take and cannot live without—then cut the pile in half. If you're still left with more than will fit into a medium-size suitcase or backpack, continue eliminating. You have to be tough on yourself and just limit what you take. Now put it all into your bag. If the total (bag and contents) weighs more than 16 kilograms, you'll sacrifice much of your mobility. If you can keep it down to 10 kg, you're traveling *light*. Categorize, separate, and pack all your things into clear plastic bags or stuff sacks for convenience and protection from moisture. Items that might leak should be in resealable bags. In addition to your principal bag, you'll want a day pack or flight bag. When checking in for flights, carry anything that cannot be replaced in your hand luggage. *The biggest mistake of first-time travelers to the South Pacific is bringing too much baggage.*

Your Luggage

Veteran travelers often recommend a small suitcase with wheels and a retractable handle that you can sometimes take aboard flights as carry-on luggage. Officially, economy passengers are only allowed one item of cabin baggage with overall dimensions no greater than 115 centimeters. The bag must be able to fit under the seat in front of you, and must not weigh more than five kg. In first and business classes you may carry two bags aboard, which when added together do not exceed 115 cm or seven kg in weight. Larger bags must usually be checked in at the airline counter. All carry on luggage is subject to strict security controls.

Also ideal is a soft medium-size backpack with a lightweight internal frame or a small suitcase with wheels work best. The best packs have a zippered compartment in back where you can tuck in the hip belt and straps before turning your pack over to an airline or bus. This type of pack has the flexibility of allowing you to simply walk when motorized transport is unavailable or unacceptable; and with the straps zipped in it looks like a regular suitcase.

Make sure your pack allows you to carry the weight on your hips, has a cushion for spine support, and doesn't pull backwards. The pack should strap snugly to your body but also allow ventilation to your back. It should be made of a water-resistant material such as nylon and have a Fastex buckle.

Look for a pack with double, two-way zipper compartments and pockets you can lock with miniature padlocks. They might not *stop* a thief, but they will deter the casual pilferer. A 60-cm length of lightweight chain and another padlock will allow you to fasten your pack to something. Keep valuables locked in your bag, out of sight, as even upmarket hotel rooms aren't 100 percent safe.

Clothing and Camping Equipment

For clothes take loose-fitting cotton washables, light in color and weight. Synthetic fabrics are hot and sticky, and most of the things you wear at home are too heavy for the tropics—be prepared for the humidity. Dress is casual, with slacks and a sports shirt okay for men even at dinner parties. Local women often wear long colorful dresses in the evening, but respectable shorts are okay in daytime. If in doubt, bring the minimum with you and buy tropical garb upon arrival.

The *lavalava, sulu,* or pareu (par-RAY-o) is a bright two-meter piece of cloth both men and women wrap about themselves as an all-purpose garment. Any islander can show you how to wear it. Missionaries taught the South Sea island women to drape their attributes in long, flowing gowns, called muumuus in Hawaii. In the South Pacific, the dress is better known as a Mother Hubbard for the muumuu-attired nursery rhyme character who "went to the cupboard to fetch her poor dog a bone." In midwinter (July and August) it can be cool at night in the Cooks, Tonga, New Caledonia, and even Moorea, so a light sweater or windbreaker may come in handy.

Take comfortable shoes that have been broken in. Running shoes and rubber thongs (flip-flops) are handy for day use but will bar you from nightspots with strict dress codes. Scuba divers' wetsuit booties are lightweight and perfect for both crossing rivers and lagoon walking, though an old pair of sneakers may be just as good (never use the booties to walk on breakable coral). You'll need a disposable pair of shoes if you plan any serious interior trekking along river valleys as quality hiking boots would be ruined during the many river crossings.

A small nylon tent guarantees backpackers a place to sleep every night, but it *must* be mosquito- and waterproof. Get one with a tent fly, then waterproof both tent and fly with a can of waterproofing spray. You'll seldom need a sleeping bag in the tropics, so that's one item you can easily cut. A youth hostel sleeping sheet is ideal—all HI handbooks give instructions on how to make your own or buy one at your local hostel. You don't really need to carry a bulky foam pad, as the ground is seldom cold.

Below we've provided a few checklists to help you assemble your gear. The listed items combined weigh well over 16 kg, so eliminate what doesn't suit you:

- pack with internal frame
- day pack or airline bag
- sun hat or visor
- essential clothing only
- bathing suit
- sturdy walking shoes
- rubber thongs
- rubber booties
- nylon tent and fly
- tent-patching tape
- mosquito net
- sleeping sheet

Accessories

Bring some reading material, as good books can be hard to find in some countries. A mask and snorkel are essential equipment—you'll be missing half of the Pacific's beauty without them. Scuba divers will bring their own regulator, buoyancy compensator, and gauges to avoid rental fees and to eliminate the possibility of catching a transmissible disease from rental equipment. A lightweight three-mm Lycra wetsuit will provide protection against marine stings and coral.

Neutral gray eyeglasses protect your eyes from the sun and give the least color distortion. Take an extra pair (if you wear them).

A flashlight is essential if you'll be walking from your resort to nearby restaurants or bars after dark. There's no street lighting away from the main towns, and it can be slightly unnerving walking along a road in the pitch dark on a moonless night. Local bicycle and scooter riders often travel without lights and the sudden appearance of a barking dog can give you a fright.

Many pensions and hostels do not provide bath towels and even the deluxe resorts rarely supply face cloths. Beach towels may also be unavailable. A small travel towel will be required unless you're only staying at very upscale places.

- portable shortwave radio
- camera and 10 rolls of film

- compass
- pocket flashlight
- extra batteries
- candle
- pocket alarm calculator
- extra pair of eyeglasses
- sunglasses
- mask and snorkel
- padlock and lightweight chain
- collapsible umbrella
- string for a clothesline
- powdered laundry soap
- universal sink plug
- minitowel
- silicon glue
- sewing kit
- miniscissors
- nail clippers
- fishing line for sewing gear
- plastic cup and plate
- can and bottle opener
- corkscrew
- penknife
- spoon
- water bottle
- matches
- tea bags

Toiletries and Medical Kit

Since everyone has his/her own medical requirements and brand names vary from country to country, there's no point going into detail here. Note, however, that even the basics (such as aspirin) are unavailable on some outer islands, so be prepared. Bring medicated powder for prickly heat rash. Charcoal tablets are useful for diarrhea and poisoning (they absorb the irritants). Bring an adequate supply of any personal medications, plus your prescriptions (in generic terminology).

High humidity causes curly hair to swell and bush, straight hair to droop. If it's curly have it cut short or keep it long in a ponytail or bun. A good cut is essential with straight hair. Water-based makeup is preferable, as the heat and humidity cause oil glands to work overtime. High-quality locally made shampoo, body oils, and insect repellent are sold on all the islands,

and the bottles are conveniently smaller than those sold in Western countries. (See Health for more ideas.)

- wax earplugs
- soap in plastic container
- soft toothbrush
- toothpaste
- roll-on deodorant
- shampoo
- comb and brush
- skin creams
- makeup
- tampons or napkins
- toilet paper
- vitamin/mineral supplement
- insect repellent
- PABA sunscreen
- Chap Stick
- a motion-sickness remedy
- contraceptives
- iodine
- water-purification pills
- a diarrhea remedy
- Tiger Balm
- a cold remedy
- Alka-Seltzer
- aspirin
- antihistamine
- antifungal
- Calmitol ointment
- antibacterial ointment
- antiseptic cream
- disinfectant
- simple dressings
- adhesive bandages (such as Band-Aids)
- painkiller
- prescription medicines

Money and Documents

All post offices have passport applications. If you lose your passport you should report the matter to the local police at once, obtain a certificate or receipt, then proceed to your consulate (if any!) for a replacement. If you have your birth certificate with you it expedites things considerably. Don't bother getting an international driver's license, as your regular license is all you need to drive here (except in the Cook Islands and Tonga, where you'll be required to buy a local license).

Traveler's checks are recommended, and in the South Pacific, American Express is the most efficient company when it comes to providing refunds for lost checks. Bring along a small supply of US$1 and US$5 bills to use if you don't manage to change money immediately upon arrival or if you run out of local currency and can't get to a bank. In the French territories Euros are best currency to have by far as they're exchanged at a fixed rate.

Carry your valuables in a money belt worn around your waist or neck under your clothing; most camping stores have these. Make several photocopies of the information page of your passport, personal identification, driver's license, scuba certification card, credit cards, airline tickets, receipts for purchase of traveler's checks, etc.—you should be able to get them all on one page. On the other side, write the phone numbers you'd need to call to report lost documents. A brief medical history with your blood type, allergies, chronic or special health problems, eyeglass and medical prescriptions, etc., might also come in handy. Put these inside plastic bags to protect them from moisture, then carry the lists in different places, and leave one at home.

How much money you'll need depends on your lifestyle, but time is also a factor. The longer you stay, the cheaper it gets. Suppose you have to lay out US$1,000 on airfare and have (for example) US$50 a day left over for expenses. If you stay 15 days, you'll average US$117 a day (US$50 times 15 plus US$1,000, divided by 15). If you stay 30 days, you'll average US$83 a day. If you stay 90 days, the per-day cost drops to US$61. If you stay a year it'll cost only US$53 a day. Some countries are more expensive than others: while you'll certainly want to experience the spectacular scenery of Tahiti, spend those extra days lounging in the sun in budget-priced Fiji, Tonga, Samoa, or the Solomons.

- passport
- airline tickets
- scuba certification card
- driver's license
- traveler's checks
- some U.S. cash
- credit card
- photocopies of documents
- money belt
- address book
- notebook
- envelopes
- extra ballpoints

FILM AND PHOTOGRAPHY

Scan the ads in photographic magazines for deals on mail-order cameras and film, or buy at a discount shop in a large city. Run a roll of film through your camera to be sure it's in good working order; clean the lens with lens-cleaning tissue and check the batteries. Remove the batteries from your camera when storing it at home for long periods.

The type of camera you choose could depend on the way you travel. If you'll be staying mostly in one place, a heavy single-lens reflex (SLR) camera with spare lenses and other equipment won't trouble you. If you'll be moving around a lot for a considerable length of time, a 35-mm automatic compact camera will be better. The compacts are mostly useful for close-up shots; landscapes will seem spread out and far away. A wide-angle lens gives excellent depth of field, but hold the camera upright to avoid converging verticals. A polarizing filter prevents reflections from glass windows and water, and makes the sky bluer.

Take double the amount of film and mailers you think you'll need: only in American Samoa, Fiji, and Vanuatu is film cheap and readily available, and even then you never know if it's been spoiled by an airport X-ray on the way there. On a long trip mailers are essential as exposed film shouldn't be held for long periods. Choose 36-exposure film over 24-exposure to save on the number of rolls you have to carry. In French Polynesia and New Caledonia camera film costs more than double what you'd pay in the U.S., but you can import 10 rolls duty free. When purchasing film in the islands take care to check the expiration date. Specialty films like black-and-white or color slides are available only in main centers like Nadi or Suva; standard color print film will be about all you'll find in most places.

Films are rated by their speed and sensitivity to light, using ISO numbers from 25 to 1600. The higher the number, the greater the film's sensitivity to light. Slower films with lower ISOs (like 100-200) produce sharp images in bright sunlight. Faster films with higher ISOs (like 400) stop action and work well in low-light situations, such as in dark rainforests or at sunset. If you have a manual SLR, you can avoid overexposure at midday by reducing the exposure half a stop. From 1000 to 1600 the light is often too bright to take good photos, and panoramas usually come out best early or late in the day.

Keep your photos simple with one main subject and an uncomplicated background. Get as close to your subjects as you can and lower or raise the camera to their level. Include people in the foreground of scenic shots to add interest and perspective. Outdoors a flash can fill in unflattering facial shadows caused by high sun or backlit conditions. Most of all, be creative. Look for interesting details and compose the photo before you push the trigger. Instead of taking a head-on photo of a group of people, step to one side and ask them to face you. The angle improves the photo. Photograph subjects coming toward you rather than passing by. Ask permission before photographing people. If you're asked for money (rare) you can always walk away—give your subjects the same choice.

When packing, protect your camera against vibration. Checked baggage is scanned by powerful airport X-ray monitors, so carry both camera and film aboard the plane in a clear plastic bag and ask security for a visual inspection. Many airports will refuse to do this, however. A good alternative is to use a lead-laminated pouch. The old high-dose X-ray units are seldom seen these days but even low-dose inspection units can ruin fast film (400 ISO and above). Beware of the cumulative effect of X-ray machines. Digital camera images are not affected by X-rays.

Store your camera in a plastic bag during rain and while traveling in motorized canoes, etc. In the tropics the humidity can cause film to stick to itself; silica-gel crystals in the bag will protect film from humidity and mold growth. Protect camera and film from direct sunlight and load the film in the shade. When loading, check that the takeup spool revolves. Never leave camera or film in a hot place like a car floor, glove compartment, or trunk.

TIME

The international date line generally follows 180 degrees longitude and creates a difference of 24 hours in time between the two sides. It swings east at Tuvalu to avoid slicing Fiji in two. This can be confusing, as Tonga, which chooses to observe the same day as neighboring Fiji and New Zealand, has the same clock time as Samoa but is a day ahead! Everything in the Eastern Hemisphere west of the date line is a day later, everything in the Western Hemisphere east of the line is a day earlier (or behind). Air travelers lose a day when they fly west across the date line and gain it back when they return. Keep track of things by repeating to yourself, "If it's Sunday in Samoa, it's Monday in Manila."

In this book all clock times are rendered according to the 24-hour airline timetable system, i.e. 0100 is 1:00 A.M., 1300 is 1:00 P.M., 2330 is 11:30 P.M. The islanders operate on "coconut time"—the nut will fall when it is ripe. In the languid air of the South Seas punctuality takes on a new meaning. Appointments are approximate and the service relaxed. Even the seasons are fuzzy: sometimes wetter, sometimes drier, but almost always hot. Slow down to the island pace and get in step with where you are. You may not get as much done, but you'll enjoy life more. Daylight hours in the tropics run 0600–1800 with few seasonal variations.

WEIGHTS AND MEASURES

The metric system is used everywhere except in American Samoa. Study the conversion table in the back of this handbook if you're not used to thinking metric. Most distances herein are quoted in kilometers—they become easy to comprehend

PACIFIC TIME

	HOURS FROM GMT	STANDARD TIME AT 1200 GMT
Chile	-4	0800
Easter Island	-6	0600
California	-8	0400
Pitcairn	-8	0400
Marquesas Islands	-9.5	0230
Hawaii, Tahiti	-10	0200
Cook Islands	-10	0200
Niue, Samoa	-11	0100

	(International Date Line) yesterday	
	today	
Tonga	+13	0100
Fiji, Tuvalu	+12	2400
New Zealand	+12	2400
New Caledonia	+11	2300
Vanuatu, Solomons	+11	2300
NSW, Queensland	+10	2200
Japan	+9	2100

Note: *Chile, Easter Island, and New Zealand adopt daylight saving time October–February, while California does so April–October. The others do not. GMT is Greenwich Mean Time, the time at London, England.*

when you know that one km is the distance an average person walks in 10 minutes. A meter is slightly more than a yard and a liter is just over a quart. Unless otherwise indicated, north is at the top of all maps in this handbook.

Electric Currents

If you're taking along a plug-in razor, radio, computer, electric immersion coil, or other electrical appliance, be aware that two different voltages are used in the South Pacific. American Samoa uses 110 volts AC, while the rest of the region uses 220–240 volts AC. Take care, however, as some luxury hotel rooms provide 110-volt outlets as a

convenience to North American visitors. A 220-volt appliance will only run too slowly in a 110-volt outlet, but a 110-volt appliance will quickly burn out and be destroyed in a 220-volt outlet.

Most appliances require a converter to change from one voltage to another. You'll also need an adapter to cope with different socket types, which vary between flat two-pronged plugs in American Samoa, round two-pronged plugs in the French territories, and three-pronged plugs with the two on top at angles almost everywhere else. Pick up both items before you leave home, as they're hard to find in the islands. Some sockets have a switch that must be turned on. Remember voltages if you buy duty-free appliances: dual voltage (110/220 V) items are best.

Videos

Commercial travel videotapes make nice souvenirs, but always keep in mind that there are three incompatible video formats loose in the world: NTSC (used in North America, Japan, American Samoa, and Tonga), PAL (used in Britain, Germany, Australia, New Zealand, Fiji, the Cook Islands, and Samoa), and SECAM (used in France, French Polynesia, New Caledonia, and Russia). Don't buy prerecorded tapes abroad unless they're of the system used in your country.

Getting There

BOOKING TIPS

Preparations

First decide where and when you're going and how long you wish to stay. Some routes are more practical or available than others. Your plane ticket will be your biggest single expense, so spend some time considering the possibilities. Before going any further, read this entire section right through and check the Transportation sections in the various chapter introductions for more detailed information. If you're online, peruse the Internet sites of the airlines that interest you, then call them up directly over their toll-free 800 numbers to get current information on fares.

The major transit points for visitors are Auckland, Brisbane, Honolulu, Nadi, Nouméa, Tahiti, and Sydney; you'll notice how feeder flights radiate from these hubs. Most North Americans and Europeans will pass through Los Angeles International Airport (code-named LAX) on their way to Polynesia or Fiji, and Fiji's Nadi Airport (NAN) is something of a gateway to the Melanesian countries.

The following international airlines have flights to the South Pacific:

Aircalin: tel. 800/237-2747, www.aircalin.nc, flies from Nouméa to Auckland, Brisbane, Nadi, Osaka, Port Vila, Sydney, Tahiti, Tokyo, and Wallis

Air France: tel. 800/237-2747, www.airfrance .com/us, flies from Paris and Los Angeles to Tahiti

Air Nauru: tel. 310/670-7302 or 800/677-4277, flies from Nauru to Brisbane, Melbourne, Honiara, Nadi, and Tarawa

Air New Zealand: tel. 800/262-1234, www .airnewzealand.com, flies from Auckland and Los Angeles to Apia, Nadi, Nouméa, Rarotonga, Tahiti, and Tongatapu

Air Niugini: tel. 949/752-5440, www.airniugini .com.pg, flies from Port Moresby to Brisbane, Cairns, Honiara, Manila, Singapore, and Tokyo

Air Pacific: tel. 800/227-4446, www.airpacific .com, flies from Fiji to Apia, Auckland, Brisbane, Honiara, Honolulu, Los Angeles, Melbourne, Port Vila, Sydney, Tokyo, Tongatapu, and Vancouver

Air Tahiti Nui: tel. 877/824-4846, www.fly atn.com, flies from Tahiti to Auckland, Los Angeles, Melbourne, Paris, Osaka, Sydney, and Tokyo

Air Vanuatu: tel. 800/227-4500, www.airvan uatu.com, flies from Port Vila to Auckland, Brisbane, Honiara, Nadi, Nouméa, and Sydney

Aloha Airlines: tel. 800/367-5250, www.aloha airlines.com, flies from Honolulu to Pago Pago and Rarotonga

Hawaiian Airlines: tel. 800/367-5320, www .hawaiianair.com, flies from Honolulu to Pago Pago and Tahiti

Korean Air: tel. 800/438-5000, www.korean air.com.au, flies from Seoul to Nadi

LanChile Airlines: tel. 800/735-5526, www.lan chile.com, flies from Santiago to Easter Island and Tahiti

Polynesian Airlines: tel. 800/264-0823, www
.polynesianairlines.com, flies from Apia to Auckland, Honolulu, Melbourne, Nadi, Niue, Pago
Pago, Sydney, Tongatapu, and Wellington

Qantas Airways: tel. 800/227-4500, www
.qantas.com.au, flies from Australia to Nadi,
Nouméa, Port Vila, Tahiti, and Suva

Solomon Airlines: tel. 800/677-4277, www
.solomonairlines.com.au, flies from Honiara to
Brisbane, Nadi, and Port Vila

Virtually every airline flying to or around the
region is listed on www.southpacific.org/air.html.
Sometimes Canada and parts of the Unites States
have different toll-free numbers, so if the number
given above doesn't work, dial 800 information at
800/555-1212 (all 800, 866, 877, and 888 numbers are free). In Canada, Air New Zealand's toll-
free number is tel. 800/663-5494.

Call all of these carriers and say you want the
lowest possible fare. Cheapest are the excursion
fares but these often have limitations and restrictions, so be sure to ask. Some have an advance-
purchase deadline, which means it's wise to begin
shopping early. Also check the fare seasons.

If you're not happy with the answers you get,
call the number back later and try again. Many
different agents take calls on these lines, and
some are more knowledgeable than others. The
numbers are often busy during peak business
hours, so call first thing in the morning, after
dinner, or on the weekend. *Be persistent.*

Cheaper Fares

In recent years South Pacific airfares have been
deregulated and companies such as Air New
Zealand no longer publish specific fare price lists.
Their Internet websites are also evasive, usually
with tariff information undisclosed (they might
have prices for their all-inclusive package tours on
the web but not air prices alone). Finding your
way through this minefield can be the least enjoyable part of your before-trip planning, but
you'll definitely pay a premium if you take the
easy route and accept the first or second fare
you're offered.

With fares in flux, the airline employees you'll
get at the numbers listed above probably won't
quote you the lowest fare on the market, but at
least you'll have their official price to use as a
benchmark. After you're heard what they have
to say, turn to a "consolidator," specialist travel
agencies that deal in bulk and sell seats and rooms
at wholesale prices. Many airlines have more
seats than they can market through normal channels, so they sell their unused long-haul capacity
to "discounters" or "bucket shops" at discounts of
40–50 percent off the official tariffs. The discounters buy tickets on this gray market and pass
the savings along to you. Many such companies
run ads in the Sunday travel sections of newspapers like the *San Francisco Chronicle, New York
Times,* or *Toronto Star,* or in major entertainment weeklies.

Despite their occasionally shady appearance,
most discounters and consolidators are perfectly
legitimate, and your ticket will probably be issued
by the airline itself. Most discounted tickets look
and are exactly the same as regular full-fare tickets but they're usually nonrefundable. There may
also be penalties if you wish to change your routing or reservations, and other restrictions not associated with the more expensive tickets. Rates are
competitive, so allow yourself time to shop
around. A few hours spent on the phone, doing
time on hold and asking questions, could save
you hundreds of dollars.

Once you've done a deal with an agent and
have your ticket in hand, call the airline again
using their toll-free reservations number to check
that your flight bookings and seat reservations
are okay. If your agent said it was possible to
freely change your reservations, verify that this is
so. Considerable consumer protection is obtained
by paying by credit card.

Seasons

The date of outbound travel from your country
of origin determines which seasonal fare you'll
pay, and good advance planning could allow you
to reschedule your vacation slightly to take advantage of a lower fare.

On flights to Tahiti, the French carriers have
timed their high seasons to correspond to holiday

time in Europe: June–September and December. This also applies on Air New Zealand if you're only going as far as Tahiti.

The seasons are quite different on flights to the Cook Islands, Fiji, Samoa, and Tonga. If you're continuing from Tahiti to Rarotonga or Fiji, normal Air New Zealand fare seasons apply to the whole ticket. The following is Air New Zealand's fare season schedule for flights from North America to the South Pacific (excluding Tahiti):

- December 29–February 22—high season
- February 23–April 25—shoulder season
- April 26–June 17—low season
- June 18–July 18—shoulder season
- July 19–August 26—low season
- August 27–December 4—shoulder season
- December 5–December 11—high season
- December 12–December 28—peak season

Air New Zealand has made March–November—the top months in the South Pacific—their off-season because that's winter in Australia and New Zealand. If you're only going to the islands and can make it at that time, it certainly works to your advantage. Air Pacific's fare seasons are similar.

For travel to Fiji originating in New Zealand, the fare seasons are as follows:

- January 1–January 20—shoulder season
- January 21–March 9—low season
- March 10–May 31—shoulder season
- June 1–September 30—high season
- October 1–October 31—shoulder season
- November 1–November 30—low season
- December 1–December 17—shoulder season
- December 18–December 24—high season
- December 25–December 31—shoulder season

In Canada and Australia, the fare seasons are different again. Call the airlines to verify these dates as they vary slightly from year to year.

Internet Bookings

For an exact fare quote you can book instantly online, simply access an online travel agency. You type in your destination and travel dates, then watch as the site's system searches its database for the lowest fare. You may be offered complicated routings at odd hours, but you'll certainly get useful information.

Try a couple of sites for comparison, such as **Cheap Tickets** (www.cheaptickets.com), **Lowestfare.com** (www.lowestfare.com), **Microsoft Expedia** (www.expedia.com), **OneTravel.com** (http://air.onetravel.com), **Orbitz** (www.orbitz.com), and **Sabre Travelocity** (www.travelocity.com). **Priceline.com** (www.priceline.com) is unique in that it allows you to name your own price for your ticket! If your bid is accepted by an airline, your credit card will be charged immediately and the ticket cannot be changed, transferred, or canceled. Priceline promises an answer within 15 minutes. **TravelHUB, Inc.** (www.travelhub.com) offers last-minute specials on cruises and package tours as well as airfares.

All these companies are aimed at the U.S. market and a credit card with a billing address outside the United States may not be accepted. For the South Pacific, you'll need a paper ticket, and it's unlikely the agency will agree to send it to an address different from the one on your card. So despite the global reach of the Internet, you'll probably have to use a site based in your own country.

If you live in Europe, turn to **Flightbookers** (www.ebookers.com) in the United Kingdom and 11 other European countries. **Flights.com** (www.flights.com) is in Frankfurt, Germany, while **Travel Overland** (www.travel-overland.de) is in Munich. **Sabre Travelocity.ca** (www.travelocity.ca) is based in Canada and there are branches in Germany and the United Kingdom. **Expedia.ca** (www.expedia.ca) is in Canada and **Expedia.co.uk** (www.expedia.co.uk) is in the United Kingdom. Other sites for Canadians to try include **Destina.ca** (www.destina.ca) and **Cheap Flights Canada** (www.cheapflights.ca). In France there's **Anyway** (www.anyway.fr). In Australia it's **Travel.com.au** (www.travel.com.au) and **Flightcentre.com** (www.flightcentre.com.au). Flightcentre.com links to similar sites in Canada, New Zealand, South Africa, and the United Kingdom.

Many more online travel agencies are listed on www.etn.nl. When comparing prices, note whether taxes, processing fees, airline surcharges, and shipping are charged extra. Check beforehand if you're allowed to change your reservations or refund the ticket. After booking, print out your confirmation. If you're reluctant to place an order on an unfamiliar site, look for their contact telephone number and give them a call to hear how they sound (a listing here is not a recommendation). At all of these sites, you'll be asked to pay by credit card over their secure server. If that idea worries you, look for a local packager willing to order online on your behalf. Since you'll have already checked the price yourself, you'll know if you're getting a good deal. Let your agent surprise you by finding an even lower online fare. After all, they should know this business better than you.

Student Fares

Students and people under 26 years old can sometimes benefit from lower student fares by booking through **STA Travel** (www.sta-travel.com) with branches around the world. In the United States, call their toll-free number (tel. 800/781-4040) for information. **Student Universe** (100 Talcott Avenue East, Watertown, MA 02472, U.S.A.; tel. 617/321-3100 or 800/272-9676, www.studentuniverse.com) allows you to get quotes and purchase student tickets online. Canada's largest student travel organization is **Travel Cuts** (www.travelcuts.com).

Current Trends

High operating costs have caused the larger airlines to switch to wide-bodied aircraft and longhaul routes with less frequent service and fewer stops. In the South Pacific this works to your disadvantage, as even major destinations like Fiji get bypassed. Most airlines now charge extra for stopovers that once were free, or simply refuse to grant any stopovers at all on the cheapest fares.

Increasingly airlines are combining in global alliances to compete internationally. Thus Qantas is part of the "Oneworld" family (www.oneworldalliance.com) comprising Aer Lingus, American Airlines, British Airways, Cathay Pacific, Finnair, Iberia, and LanChile, while Air New Zealand is a member of the "Star Alliance" (www.star-alliance.com) of United Airlines, Air

INTERNATIONAL AIRPORT CODES

AKL—Auckland
APW—Apia/Faleolo
BNE—Brisbane
CHC—Christchurch
CNS—Cairns
DPS—Denpasar/Bali
FGI—Apia/Fagalii
FUN—Funafuti
GEA—Nouméa/Magenta
GUM—Guam
HIR—Honiara
HNL—Honolulu
ICN—Seoul
INU—Nauru
IPC—Easter Island
IUE—Niue
LAX—Los Angeles
MEL—Melbourne
MNL—Manila
NAN—Nadi
NLK—Norfolk Island
NOU—Nouméa/La Tontouta
OSA—Osaka
PNI—Pohnpei
POM—Port Moresby
PPG—Pago Pago
PPT—Papeete
RAR—Rarotonga
SCL—Santiago
SEA—Seattle
SFO—San Francisco
SIN—Singapore
SUV—Suva
SYD—Sydney
TBU—Tongatapu
TRW—Tarawa
TYO—Tokyo
VLI—Port Vila
WLG—Wellington
WLS—Wallis
YVR—Vancouver
YYZ—Toronto

Canada, Lufthansa, SAS, Singapore Airlines, Thai, All Nippon, and others. This is to your advantage as frequent flier programs are usually interchangeable within the blocks, booking becomes easier, flight schedules are coordinated, and through fares exist.

It's now possible to design some extremely wide-ranging trips by combining the networks of the two competing groups. For example, Oneworld's **Oneworld Explorer** fare allows as many as 20 stops selected from over 570 destinations in 134 countries. Even Easter Island is included!

Similar is the Star Alliance's **Round-the-World Ticket** valid on flights operated by the 15 members of the Star Alliance. You're allowed 29,000, 34,000, or 39,000 miles with a minimum of three and maximum of 15 stops. One transatlantic and one transpacific journey must be included, but the ticket is valid one year and backtracking is allowed. Fiji, Tahiti, and Rarotonga can be visited on this fare. Air New Zealand offices in North America sell these round-the-world tickets starting at US$3,530. In Britain you can buy the same thing for considerably less money.

Air New Zealand's **Circle-Pacific Fare** provides a trip around the Pacific (including Asia) on Air New Zealand and other Star Alliance carriers. With this one you get 22,000 or 26,000 miles starting at US$2,688 with all the stops you want (minimum of three). Travel must begin in either

Los Angeles or Vancouver (no add-ons). It's valid six months but you must travel in a continuous circle without any backtracking. No date changes are allowed for the outbound sector but subsequent changes are free. To reissue the ticket (for example, to add additional stops after departure) costs US$75, so plan your trip carefully.

In conjunction with Qantas, Northwest Airlines offers a Circle-Pacific Fare of US$3,277 from Los Angeles with add-on airfares available from other North American cities. This ticket allows four free stopovers in Asia and the South Pacific, additional stops US$75 each. Qantas and Air Pacific also have Circle-Pacific fares, so compare.

AIR SERVICES
From North America
Air New Zealand, Air Pacific, and Air Tahiti Nui are the major carriers serving the South Pacific out of Los Angeles. Fiji's **Air Pacific** flies nonstop from Los Angeles to Nadi four times a week (10.5 hours) and from Honolulu three times a week (six hours). From Los Angeles, a seven to 30-day round-trip ticket to Fiji on Air Pacific is US$1,088/1,328/1,608/1,688 low/shoulder/high/peak season. From Honolulu it's about US$200 cheaper. These are the midweek fares—weekend departures are US$70 more expensive—

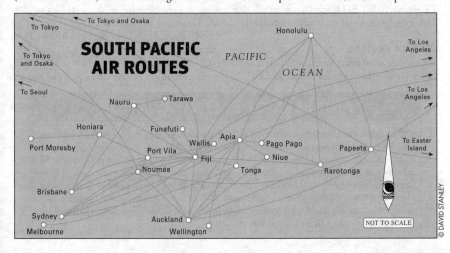

EXPLORING THE ISLANDS

© DAVID STANLEY

and some restrictions apply. When booking check the schedule carefully as some flights are overnight while others arrive just before midnight.

One of the few U.S. carriers serving the region is **Hawaiian Airlines,** which offers flights to Tahiti and Pago Pago via its base in Honolulu with connections to/from Las Vegas, Los Angeles, Portland, San Diego, San Francisco, and Seattle. From the West Coast to Tahiti a non-refundable, 14-day advance-purchase round-trip is US$735/835/935 low/shoulder/high season plus US$50 tax. From Honolulu, it's US$60 less. Fare seasons to Tahiti are complicated, so call well ahead. Date changes after ticketing are US$75. A free stop in Honolulu is available on this fare. To American Samoa, it's US$930/1,308 round-trip from Honolulu/Los Angeles with a US$250 discount if you book at least 30 days in advance.

In 2003 **Aloha Airlines** began flying twice weekly from Honolulu to Pago Pago and Rarotonga, with same-carrier connections from Burbank, Los Vegas, Oakland, Orange County, and Vancouver.

Other flights out of Honolulu include Polynesian Airlines to Apia. Passengers originating in Canada must pass U.S. security and immigration controls in Los Angeles or Honolulu. The only direct flight from Canada which doesn't require a change of planes in the U.S. is Air Pacific's twice weekly service from Vancouver, British Columbia, to Fiji via Hawaii (you must still clear U.S. immigration and security in Honolulu).

Air New Zealand

Air New Zealand offers more direct flights to the South Pacific than any other airline. In the 1950s the company pioneered its "Coral Route" using Solent flying boats, and today the carrier dominates long-haul air routes into the region by allowing stopovers in French Polynesia, the Cook Islands, Fiji, Samoa, and Tonga as part of through services between North America and New Zealand.

Air New Zealand's first priority is to fly people to Auckland, and it's sometimes cheaper to buy a return ticket to Auckland with a couple of free stops in the islands than a round-trip ticket from Los Angeles only as far as Tahiti-Rarotonga-Fiji. If you don't wish to visit New Zealand, you can transit Auckland airport the same day. Despite Air New Zealand's frequent services, travelers in North America and Europe often have difficulty booking stops in the islands on their way down under and it's advisable to reserve seats well ahead. Air New Zealand has the advantage of allowing you to include a number of countries in a single ticket if you do some advance planning.

Return tickets from Los Angeles to a single island are the cheapest. The lowest fare is the "APEX" at US$916/1,024 low/high round-trip between Los Angeles and Tahiti. You must purchase this ticket at least 14 days in advance, there's a 35 percent cancellation penalty, and the maximum stay is one month. From Los Angeles to either Rarotonga or Fiji, a return "No Stop Apex" ticket is US$1,088/1,328/1,608/1,688 low/shoulder/high/peak season if you leave Los Angeles at the beginning of the week. To set out on Thursday, Friday, Saturday or Sunday is US$80 more. From Los Angeles to Apia or Tongatapu, a "No Stop Apex" is US$1,217 mid-January–April and August–November or US$1,491 other months. The maximum stay is one month

PIONEERS OF PACIFIC AVIATION

The first flight from the United States to Australia took place in 1928. Charles Kingsford-Smith and Charles Ulm flew their trimotor Fokker VII-3M, the *Southern Cross,* from Oakland to Brisbane (11,906 km) in 83 hours and 38 minutes, with intermediate stops in Hawaii and Fiji. The original aircraft is now on display outside the domestic terminal of Brisbane's Eagle Farm Airport. In 1937 Pan American Airways began commercial flights between the United States and New Zealand, with stops at Hawaii and American Samoa. The flying boat service was tragically interrupted on the third flight when the *Samoa Clipper* exploded just after leaving Pago Pago on January 10, 1938.

and you must pay at least 21 days before departure (50 percent cancellation penalty). If you book on shorter notice the fare is almost 50 percent higher.

It's not that much more expensive to add a couple of other islands. Air New Zealand allows one stop plus your destination with additional stops available at US$150 each. Thus you can fly Los Angeles-Tahiti-Rarotonga-Fiji-Los Angeles for US$1,248/1,478/1,758/1,838 low/shoulder/high/peak season if you leave at the beginning of the week for a trip of three months maximum. Add US$150 if wish to extend your period of stay to six months, plus another US$70 if you'd like to set out on Thursday, Friday, Saturday, or Sunday. Drop either Tahiti, Rarotonga, or Fiji from your itinerary and you'll save US$160. Trips originating in Honolulu are US$200 cheaper in all cases. Remember that this fare must be purchased 14 days in advance and there's a US$125 penalty to change your flight dates. A 35 percent cancellation fee also applies after the 14-day ticket deadline.

For a more wide-ranging trip with fewer restrictions, ask for Air New Zealand's "12-month Excursion Pass," which costs US$2,098/2,388/2,668/2,748 low/shoulder/high/peak season. This worthwhile ticket allows you to fly Los Angeles-Tahiti-Rarotonga-Fiji-Auckland-Tongatapu-Los Angeles or vice versa. Extend the ticket to Australia for US$100 more. You can stay up to one year but rerouting costs US$125 (date changes are free). There's no advance purchase requirement and you can go any day.

In Canada, Air New Zealand offers similar fares called the "Explorer fare, 12 months multi stop," the "Stopover fare one month with no stops," and the "Bungy one and 12-month fare with one free stop." On most tickets special "add-on" fares to Los Angeles or Vancouver are available from cities right across the U.S. and Canada—be sure to ask about them. From Toronto, Air New Zealand's direct connections to/from Air Canada work better for Canadian passengers than the connections offered by Air Tahiti Nui, Air Pacific, and Qantas.

Air New Zealand's cabin service is professional, and you'll like the champagne breakfasts and outstanding food with complimentary beer and wine. Another plus are the relaxing seats with adjustable head rests and lots of leg room. The *Life in Pacifica* videos about their destinations are entertaining the first time you see them, but after a while you get bored. The only reading material provided is the *Panorama* inflight magazine, the *Skyshop* duty free catalog, and the *Primetime* entertainment magazine. These are unlikely to hold your attention for long, so bring along a book or magazine of your own (the daily newspaper is provided only to passengers in first class).

North American Ticket Agents

South Pacific Direct (8345 Kittyhawk Ave., Los Angeles, CA 90045-4226, U.S.A.; fax 310/568-8294, www.southpacificdirect.com) offers the same tour packages featured in glossy brochures and on fancy websites at a considerable savings to you. Its personalized service is available only by email, and the lower operating costs mean you get high quality hotel arrangements at the best possible price.

A wider selection of Fiji travel arrangements is available through **South Pacific Holidays** (10906 NE 39th St., Suite A-1, Vancouver, WA 98682-6789, U.S.A.; tel. 877/733-3454 or 360/944-1712, fax 360/253-3934, www.tropicalfiji.com).

Some of the cheapest round-trip tickets to Fiji are sold by **Fiji Travel** (8885 Venice Blvd., Suite 202, Los Angeles, CA 90034, U.S.A.; tel. 310/202-4220 or 800/500-3454, fax 310/202-8233, www.fijitravel.com). It makes its money through high volume, and to attract customers it keeps its profit margins as low as possible. Thus you should absorb the airline's time with questions about fare seasons, schedules, etc., and only call companies like Fiji Travel when you know exactly what you want and how much everyone else is charging.

Goway Travel (8651 Lincoln Blvd., Los Angeles, CA 90045, U.S.A.; tel. 800/387-8850, www.goway.com) with additional offices in Sydney, Toronto, and Vancouver offers competitive fares to Fiji. A leading Canadian specialist travel agency is **Pacesetter Travel** (3284 Yonge Street, Suite 301, Toronto, ON M4N 3M7, Canada; tel. 416/322-1031 or 800/387-8827, fax 416/322-7086, www.pacesettertravel.com), with offices in Calgary, Ottawa, Toronto, Vancouver, and Victoria.

For creative circle-Pacific or round-the-world fares try **Airtreks** (tel. 877/247-8735, www .airtreks.com) and **Air Brokers International** (tel. 415/397-1383 or 800/883-3273, www.air brokers.com), both based in San Francisco. In Canada there's **Long Haul Travel** (www.long haultravel.ca) in Toronto.

From Australia

You'll find nonstop flights from Sydney and Brisbane to all of the Melanesian countries, but to Polynesia most flights from Australia are via Auckland. Air Pacific offers nonstop flights to Fiji from Brisbane, Melbourne, and Sydney. There are also flights from Brisbane and Sydney to Nouméa on **Aircalin** and to Port Vila on **Air Vanuatu. Solomon Airlines** flies from Brisbane to Honiara.

Polynesian Airlines has direct flights to Apia and Tahiti from Melbourne and Sydney. **Air Tahiti Nui** flies to Tahiti from Melbourne and Sydney. Air New Zealand is competing fiercely in the Australian market, and they offer competitive fares to many South Pacific points via Auckland.

The low season ex-Australia is generally mid-January–June and October–November while high season is July–September and around Christmas. Apex (advance purchase excursion) tickets must be bought 14 days in advance and heavy cancellation penalties apply. Shop around as you can often find much better deals than the published Apex fares.

The airlines sometimes offer specials during the off months and you can usually get a better price by working through an agent specializing in bargain airfares rather than buying at the airline office itself. Check the travel sections in the weekend papers and call your local office of Flight Centres International (www.flightcentre.com.au). Also try **Trailfinders** (8 Spring St., Sydney, NSW 2000, Australia; tel. 02/9247-7666, www.trail finders.com.au), with additional offices in Brisbane, Cairns, Melbourne, and Perth. The South Pacific specialist is **Hideaway Holidays** (Val Gavriloff, P.O. Box 121, West Ryde, NSW 2114, Australia; tel. 02/9743-0253, fax 02/9743-3568,

www.hideawayholidays.com.au) and their website carries abundant information on air passes.

From New Zealand

Air New Zealand flies from their Auckland gateway to Apia, Nadi, Norfolk, Nouméa, Rarotonga, Tahiti, and Tongatapu. Other airlines with flights from Auckland include **Aircalin** to Nouméa, **Air Pacific** to Nadi and Suva, **Air Vanuatu** to Port Vila, and **Polynesian Airlines** to Tongatapu and Apia.

Air New Zealand offers reduced excursion fares from Auckland to all the main South Pacific islands with a maximum stay of 45 days to Tahiti or 90 days to Fiji, Tonga, and Samoa. Twenty-one-day advance purchase fares from Auckland to Rarotonga cost NZ$1,099/1,220/1,350 low/ shoulder/high season (see "Seasons" above for the applicable dates). The excursion fare from Auckland to Fiji is NZ$963/1,057/1,151. Seasonal "specials" are regularly available. It's sometimes cheaper to buy a package tour to the islands with airfare, accommodations, and transfers included, but these are usually limited to seven nights on one island and you're stuck in a boring touristic environment. Ask if you'll be allowed to extend your return date and still get the low inclusive tour price.

In early 2004 the New Zealand-based discount carrier Freedom Air (www.freedomair .co.nz) began weekly service from Hamilton and Palmerston North in New Zealand to Nadi. Their super-low discount fares are designed to cut into Air Pacific's market, and Air New Zealand has also begun offering cheaper "Express" fares to Fiji. To boot, Pacific Blue (www.flypacific blue.com), part of the Virgin airline empire of Sir Richard Branson, has announced its intention of launching budget-priced flights to Fiji and Vanuatu from Australia.

Agents to call include STA Travel and Flight Centres International (www.flightcentre.co.nz). The website of **Travel Online** (www.travel online.co.nz) provides specific quotes on flights to the South Pacific.

From South America

LanChile Airlines flies from Santiago to Tahiti

via Easter Island twice a week, with additional flights during the high southern summer season December–March. The regular one-way fare Santiago-Tahiti is US$961 economy class, plus US$50 for a stop on Easter Island. Santiago-Easter Island-Santiago is US$580 round-trip low season (March–November).

LanChile's round-trip fare between Tahiti and Easter Island costs US$435–727, depending on the season, how long you wish to stay, and who takes your booking. It's often cheaper to buy a tour package from one of the agencies mentioned in this book's Papeete section.

LanChile's Tahiti service is heavily booked between Easter Island and Santiago but seldom full between Easter Island and Tahiti. That makes it easier to travel westbound on a round-the-world trip.

From Europe

Since few European carriers reach the South Pacific, you'll probably have to use a gateway city such as Sydney, Honolulu, or Los Angeles. Air New Zealand offers daily nonstop flights London-Los Angeles with connections in Los Angeles to their Coral Route. Similarly, Lufthansa's daily Frankfurt-Los Angeles and Munich-Los Angeles flights code share with Air New Zealand's South Pacific flights. This means that European passengers can fly to the islands from London or Germany with only one change of aircraft (at Los Angeles). On Qantas you may transit Sydney instead of Los Angeles, a roundabout route that could be compensated for by a lower fare. From Paris, Air France and Air Tahiti Nui fly direct to Tahiti via Los Angeles. It may be cheaper to travel to Fiji via Seoul on Korean Air.

The British specialist in South Pacific itineraries is **Trailfinders** (1 Threadneedle St., London EC2R 8JX, United Kingdom; tel. 020/7628-7628, www.trailfinder.com), in business since 1970. Its 13 offices around the United Kingdom and Ireland offer a variety of discounted round-the-world tickets via the South Pacific which are often much cheaper than the published fares. It's easy to order a free copy of their magazine *Trailfinder* and brochures online.

Bridge the World (45-47 Chalk Farm Rd., Camden Town, London NW1 8AJ, United Kingdom; tel. 0870/443-2399, www.bridgetheworld.com) sells discounted round-the-world tickets which include Fiji, Rarotonga, Tahiti, and a variety of stops in Asia. **Western Air Travel** (Bickham, Totnes, Devon TQ9 7NJ, United Kingdom; tel. 0870/330-1100, fax 0870/330-1133, www.westernair.co.uk) explains round-the-world tickets on their website. Check the ads in the London entertainment magazines for other such companies.

Barron & De Keijzer Travel (Noordermarkt 16, 1015 MX Amsterdam, the Netherlands; tel. 020/625-8600, www.barron.nl), with additional offices in Antwerp, Den Bosch, and Rotterdam, specializes in the Pacific islands. Also try **Wereldcontact** (Hoofdstraat 166, Postbus 1200, 3970 BE Driebergen, The Netherlands; tel. 0343/530-530, www.wereldcontact.nl). In Sweden there's **Tour Pacific** (Sundstorget 3, SE-25110 Helsingborg, Sweden; tel. 042/179500, fax 042/143055, www.tourpacific.se).

In Switzerland try **Globetrotter Travel Service** (Rennweg 35, CH-8023 Zürich, Switzerland; tel. 01/213-8080, www.globetrotter.ch), with offices in Baden, Basel, Bern, Biel, Fribourg, Luzern, Olten, St. Gallen, Thun, Winterthur, Zug, and Zürich. You can order a free copy of their magazine, *Globetrotter*, through their website.

Bucket shops in Germany sell a "Pacific Airpass" on Air New Zealand from Frankfurt to the South Pacific that allows all the usual Coral Route stops and is valid six months. All flights must be booked prior to leaving Europe, and there's a charge to change the dates once the ticket has been issued. One of the most efficient agencies selling such tickets is **Jet-Travel e.K.** (Buchholzstr. 35, D-53127 Bonn, Germany; tel. 0228/284315, www.jet-travel.de). The websites of **Travel Overland** (Barerstr.73, D-80799 Munich, Germany; tel. 089/2727-6300, www.travel-overland.de) and **Adventure Holidays** (Wacholderbergstr. 29, D-90587 Veitsbronn, Germany; tel. 0911/979-9555, fax 0911/979-9588, www.adventure-holidays.com) quote exact fares on flights to the South Pacific.

Regional Airlines

Aside from the big international airlines described above, a number of island-based carriers fly around the South Pacific. For example, **Air Fiji** flies north to Funafuti and east to Tongatapu. Keep in mind that few regional flights operate daily and quite a few are only once or twice a week.

Within the South Pacific, many regional carriers have attempted to cut costs by pooling their services through "code sharing." This means that two or three different airlines will "own" seats on the same flight, which they sell under their own two-letter airline code. The weekly flight from Nadi to Honiara is designated both FJ (Air Pacific) and IE (Solomon Airlines) but is actually operated by Air Vanuatu. Few Qantas aircraft operate to the South Pacific and most of their services are now code shares with Air Pacific, Air Tahiti Nui, and Polynesian Airlines.

Regional Air Passes

The **Visit South Pacific Pass** allows travelers to include the services of nine regional carriers in a single ticket valid six months. You have to buy the initial two-leg air pass in conjunction with an international ticket into the region, but you can buy additional legs up to a maximum of eight after arrival. Only the first sector has to be booked ahead.

The flights are priced at three different levels. For US$200 per sector you can go Fiji-Apia/Tongatapu/Port Vila, Tongatapu-Apia/Niue, or Nouméa-Port Vila. For US$250 you have a choice of Honiara-Nadi/Port Vila/Port Moresby, Fiji-Nauru/Tarawa/Nouméa, or a variety of flights from Australia and New Zealand to the islands. For US$350 there's Tahiti-Nouméa or Sydney-Tongatapu/Apia. It's a great way of getting around the South Pacific.

Airlines which should know about this ticket include Air Pacific, Polynesian Airlines, Qantas, and Royal Tongan Airlines, so call them up on the toll-free 800 numbers provided earlier. Also try **Air Promotion Systems** (5757 West Century Blvd., Suite 660, Los Angeles, CA 90045-6407, U.S.A.; tel. 310/670-7302 or 800/677-4277, fax 310/338-0708, www.pacificislands.com).

Air New Zealand's **South Pacific Airpass** is valid on their flights between Tahiti, Rarotonga, and Fiji, or between Apia and Tongatapu, from NZ$400 a hop. It can also be used to travel to/from Australia and New Zealand. This Airpass can be purchased at Air New Zealand offices in the South Pacific within 30 days of arrival or in advance together with an international ticket. Passengers holding an Air New Zealand ticket into the region get a NZ$20 discount per sector. There are two fare options, standard and supersaver, based on availability. This pass is not available to residents of Australasia and at least two flights must be booked. It's an inexpensive way of extending your trip.

Aircalin has an **Oceania Pass** valid on flights between Nouméa and Port Vila (US$135), Nadi (US$135), Auckland (US$189), Brisbane (US$189), Sydney (US$189), and Papeete (US$334). This pass is not available to residents of Australasia and must be purchased prior to arrival. In practice, it's hard to find an agent able to sell this pass or book these flights.

From Australia, the **Circle South West Pacific Airfare** allows stops on two or more of Fiji, Samoa, Tonga, Solomon Islands, Vanuatu, and New Caledonia beginning at A$780. The maximum stay is 28 days and travel must begin and end at Sydney, Melbourne, or Brisbane. Accommodations must be prepaid for the entire period. Hideaway Holidays in Sydney (www.hideaway holidays.com.au) sells this fare.

Also consider regular one-way tickets with stopovers as a way of island hopping around the South Pacific, linking flights together with a free stop in the home country of the airline. For example, buy Auckland-Port Vila or Sydney-Fiji with a free stop in Nouméa from Aircalin, Brisbane-Fiji with a free stop in Honiara from Solomon Airlines, or Port Vila-Apia or Honiara-Nuku'alofa with a free stop in Fiji from Air Pacific, etc. You may have to buy these tickets directly from the airlines themselves as travel agents will want to add up all the sector fares, but full-fare tickets like these are valid one year and have virtually no restrictions. Compare prices and be creative.

Polynesian Airlines

Polynesian Airlines (www.polynesianairlines.com) offers a **Polypass** valid for 45 days unlimited travel between Fiji, Tonga, Samoa, and Pago Pago, plus one round-trip from Sydney, Melbourne, Auckland, or Wellington for US$1,099. From Honolulu the pass costs US$1,349; from any one of seven U.S. west coast airports it's US$1,699. Restrictions are that your itinerary must be worked out in advance and can only be changed once for free (subsequent changes US$50 each). Thus it's important to book all flights well ahead. A 20 percent penalty is charged to refund an unused ticket (no refund after one year) and the Polypass is not available in December and January. Unfortunately Polynesian Airlines services to Niue are not included in this pass, which is also known as the "Pacific Explorer Airpass." Still, if you've got a month and a half to see a slice of the South Pacific, this may be the ticket for you.

Air Pacific

Air Pacific has two different **Pacific Triangle Fares,** good ways to experience the region's variety of cultures: Fiji-Apia-Tonga-Fiji (US$484), Fiji-Nouméa-Port Vila-Fiji (F$850), Fiji-Honiara-Port Vila-Fiji (US$648). All three are valid for one year and can be purchased at any travel agency in Fiji or direct from the airline. Flight dates can be changed at no charge, but they're usually valid only for journeys commencing in Fiji. When booking these circular tickets, be aware that it's much better to go Fiji-Apia-Tonga-Fiji than vice versa, because the flights between Apia and Fiji are often fully booked while it's easy to get on between Tonga and Fiji. Also obtainable locally are Air Pacific's special 28-day round-trip excursion fares from Fiji to Apia (F$706), Tonga (F$714), Port Vila (F$649), and Honiara (F$1,176). Some of these fares have seasonal variations.

Air Nauru

Air Nauru, flag carrier of the tiny Republic of Nauru in Micronesia, has flights from Nadi to Tarawa twice a week. An Air Nauru 30-day round-trip excursion fare from Nadi to Tarawa costs F$1,445 from February–November, F$1,630 in December and January. If you just want to say you've been to Kiribati, a "weekend special" fare leaving Fiji on Friday and returning on Monday is F$890 round-trip. Kiribati visas can be obtained at the consulate in Suva.

Onward Tickets

All of the South Pacific countries require an onward ticket as a condition for entry. Although the immigration officials don't always check it, the airlines usually do. If you're planning a long trip including locally arranged sea travel between countries, this can be a nuisance. One way to satisfy the ticket-to-leave requirement is to purchase a full-fare ticket across the Pacific with stops in all the countries you'll visit, then use it *only* to satisfy check-in staff and immigration. When you finally complete your trip, return the ticket to the issuing office for a full refund. Remember that airline tickets are often refundable only in the place of purchase and that the sort of deals and discount airfares available elsewhere are not available in the South Pacific. Have your *real* means of departure planned.

Airport Taxes

When planning your route, keep airport departure taxes in mind, as they can add up fast on a trip with lots of stops. You'll pay about US$10 in American Samoa, Samoa, Solomon Islands, and Tonga, US$15 in the Cook Islands, Fiji, Niue, and Tuvalu, and US$25 in Easter Island and Vanuatu. You can often avoid paying the tax if you're in transit for less than 24 hours, and in many places, it's now included in the ticket price. You needn't worry in French Polynesia, where no such tax is collected.

Important Note

Airfares, rules, and regulations tend to fluctuate a lot, so some of the information above may have changed. This is only a guide; we've included a range of fares to give you a rough idea how much things might cost. Your travel agent will know what's available at the time you're ready to travel, but if you're not satisfied with his/her advice, keep shopping around. The

EXPLORING THE ISLANDS

biggest step is deciding to go—once you're over that, the rest is easy!

PROBLEMS

When planning your trip allow a minimum two-hour stopover between connecting flights at U.S. airports, although with airport delays on the increase even this may not be enough. In the islands allow at least a day between flights. Try to avoid flying on weekends and holidays when the congestion is at its worst. In some airports flights are not called over the public address system, so keep your eyes open. Whenever traveling, always have a paperback or two, some toiletries, and a change of underwear in your hand luggage.

If your flight is canceled due to a mechanical problem with the aircraft, the airline will cover your hotel bill and meals. If they reschedule the flight on short notice for reasons of their own or you're bumped off an overbooked flight, they should also pay. They may not feel obligated to pay, however, if the delay is due to weather conditions, a strike by another company, national emergencies, etc., although the best airlines still pick up the tab in these cases.

It's an established practice among airlines to provide light refreshments to passengers delayed two hours after the scheduled departure time and a meal after four hours. Don't expect to get this from a domestic carrier on an outer island, but politely request it if you're at a gateway airport. If you are unexpectedly forced to spend the night somewhere, an airline employee may hand you a form on which they offer to telephone a friend or relative to inform them of the delay. Don't trust them to do this, however. Call your party yourself if you want to be sure he or she gets the message.

Overbooking

To compensate for no-shows, most airlines overbook their flights. To avoid being bumped, ask for your seat assignment when booking, check in early, and go to the departure area well before flight time. Of course, if you *are* bumped by a reputable international airline at a major airport you'll be regaled with free meals and lodging, and sometimes even free flight vouchers (don't ex-

pect anything like this from a domestic carrier on a remote Pacific island).

Whenever you break your journey for more than 72 hours, reconfirm your onward reservations and check your seat assignment at the same time. Get the name of the person who takes your reconfirmation so they cannot later deny it. Failure to reconfirm could result in the cancellation of your complete remaining itinerary. This could also happen if you miss a flight for any reason. If you want special vegetarian food in-flight, request it when buying your ticket, booking, and reconfirming.

When you try to reconfirm your Air New Zealand flight the agent will tell you that this formality is no longer required. Theoretically this is true, but unless you request a seat assignment in advance, either at an Air New Zealand office or over the phone, you could be "bumped" from a full flight, reservation or no reservation. Air New Zealand's ticket cover bears this surprising message:

. . . no guarantee of a seat is indicated by the terms "reservation," "booking," "O.K." status, or the times associated therewith.

It does admit in the same notice that confirmed passengers denied seats may be eligible for compensation, so if you're not in a hurry, a night or two at an upmarket hotel with all meals courtesy of Air New Zealand may not be a hardship. Your best bet if you don't want to get "bumped" is to request seat assignments for your entire itinerary in advance. Any good travel agent selling tickets on Air New Zealand should know enough to automatically request your seat assignments as they make your bookings. Although you can't "reconfirm," Air New Zealand offices in the islands will still accept a local contact telephone number from you, a recommended way of confirming that you're still in their system and that the flight schedule hasn't changed.

Baggage

International airlines generally allow economy-class passengers 20 kilos of baggage. However, if any North American airport is included in your ticket, the allowance is two pieces not over 32 kilos each for all flights on that carrier. Under the piece system, neither bag must have a combined length, width, and height of over 158 centimeters (62 inches), and the two pieces together must not exceed 272 centimeters (107 inches). On most long-haul tickets to/from North America or Europe, the piece system should apply to all sectors, but check this with the airline and look on your ticket. The frequent flier programs of some airlines allow participants to carry up to 10 kilos of excess baggage free of charge. Small commuter carriers sometimes restrict you to as little as 10 kilos total, so it's better to pack according to the lowest common denominator. Polynesian Airlines allows only five kilograms on its domestic flights!

Bicycles, folding kayaks, and surfboards can usually be checked as baggage (sometimes for an additional US$60 "oversize" charge), but sailboards may have to be shipped airfreight. If you do travel with a sailboard, be sure to call it a surfboard at check-in.

Tag your bag with name, address, and phone number inside and out. Stow anything that could conceivably be considered a weapon (scissors, sewing needles, razor blades, corkscrews, sporting equipment, etc.) in your checked luggage. Metal objects such as flashlights and umbrellas which might require a security inspection should also be packed away. Electronic equipment in your hand luggage must be operational. Fireworks are prohibited aboard aircraft.

As you're checking in, look to see if the three-letter city codes on your baggage tag receipt and boarding pass are the same. Check your bag straight through to your final destination, otherwise the airline staff may disclaim responsibility if it's lost or delayed at an intermediate stop. If your baggage is damaged or doesn't arrive at your destination, inform the airline officials *immediately* and have them fill out a written report; otherwise future claims for compensation will be compromised. Keep receipts for any money you're forced to spend to replace missing items.

All checked luggage transferred through U.S. airports is now scanned for explosives, and the equipment used gives false positive readings 25 percent of the time. In such cases, the security staff will cut open locked baggage for a visual inspection. Of course, leaving your baggage unlocked makes it easy for handlers to pilfer items from inside, and if items are stolen in transit you must report the theft before leaving the customs hall in order to be eligible for compensation.

Claims for lost luggage can take weeks to process. Keep in touch with the airline to show your concern and hang on to your baggage tag until the matter is resolved. If you feel you did not receive the attention you deserved, write the airline an objective letter outlining the case. Get the names of the employees you're dealing with so you can mention them in the letter. Of course, don't expect any pocket money or compensation on a remote outer island. Report the loss, then wait till you get back to their main office.

ORGANIZED TOURS
Packaged Holidays

Any travel agent worth their commission would rather sell you a package tour instead of only a plane ticket, and it's a fact that some vacation packages actually cost less than regular round-trip airfare! While packaged travel certainly isn't for everyone, reduced group airfares and discounted hotel rates make some tours an excellent value. For two people with limited time and a desire to stay at first-class hotels, this is the cheapest way to go.

The "wholesalers" who put these packages together get their rooms at rates far lower than what individuals pay, and the airlines also give them deals. If they'll let you extend your return date to give you some time to yourself, this can be a great deal, especially with the hotel thrown in for "free." Special-interest tours are very popular among sportspeople who want to be sure they'll get to participate in the various activities they enjoy.

The main drawback to the tours is that you're on a fixed itinerary in a tourist-oriented environment, out of touch with local life. You may not like the hotel or meals you get, and singles pay a healthy supplement. You'll probably get prepaid vouchers to turn in as you go along and won't be escorted by a tour conductor. Some tour companies (including Brendan Tours, GoGo Worldwide Vacations, Happy Vacations, and Runaway Tours) do not accept consumer inquiries and require you to work through a travel agent. Do check all the restrictions.

The following companies based in the United States make individualized travel arrangements and offer package tours to five or six different South Pacific destinations:

Goway Travel, 8651 Lincoln Blvd., Los Angeles, CA 90045, U.S.A.; tel. 800/387-8850, www.goway.com

Newmans South Pacific Vacations, 6033 West Century Blvd., Suite 970, Los Angeles CA 90045, U.S.A.; tel. 800/421-3326, www.newmansvacations.com

Pacific Destination Center, 18685-A Main St, Suite 622, Huntington Beach, CA 92648 U.S.A.; tel. 714/960-4011 or 800/227-5317, www.pacific-destinations.com

South Pacific Direct, 8345 Kittyhawk Ave., Los Angeles, CA 90045-4226, U.S.A.; fax 310/568-8294, www.southpacificdirect.com

South Seas Adventures, 7171 North 63rd Street, Longmont, CO 80503, U.S.A.; tel. 303/440-8675 or 800/576-7327, fax 303/417-0557, www.south-seas-adventures.com

Sunspots International, 1918 N.E. 181st, Portland, OR 97230, U.S.A.; tel. 503/666-3893 or 800/334-5623, www.sunspotsintl.com

Companies specializing in French Polynesia, the Cook Islands, and Fiji include these:

Fiji Travel, 8885 Venice Blvd., Suite 202, Los Angeles, CA 90034, U.S.A.; tel. 310/202-4220 or 800/500-3454, www.fijitravel.com

Island Honeymoons, 1310 Cherry Ave., San Jose, CA 95125, U.S.A.; tel. 408/993-0572, www.islandhoneymoons.com

Islands in the Sun, 2381 Rosecrans Ave., Suite 325, El Segundo, CA 90245, U.S.A.; tel. 310/536-0051 or 800/828-6877, www.islandsinthesun.com

Pacific Escapes, 1605 N.W. Sammamish Rd., Suite 310, Issaquah, WA 98027, U.S.A.; tel. 425/657-1900 or 800/777-7992, www.pacificescapes.com

South Pacific Getaways, 4885 Mt. Elbrus Drive, San Diego, CA 92117, U.S.A.; tel. 858/560-6154 or 800/458-2499, www.southpacificgetaways.com

Tahiti Vacations, 9841 Airport Blvd., Suite 1124, Los Angeles, CA 90045, U.S.A.; tel. 310/337-1040 or 800/553-3477, www.tahitivacations.net

Wilcox Travel Cruise & Company, 615 Holly St., Junction City, OR 97448, U.S.A.; tel. 541/998-1605 or 800/234-1605, www.wilcoxtravel-cruise.com

Companies offering packages to French Polynesia and Fiji include:

Destination World, P.O. Box 1077, Santa Barbara, CA 93102, U.S.A.; tel. 800/707-3454, www.destinationworld.com

eTravelBound, 2312 Ryan Way, Bullhead City, AZ 86442, U.S.A.; tel. 888/540-8445 or 928/763-8255, www.etravelbound.com

Pleasant Holidays, 2404 Townsgate Road, Westlake Village, CA 91361, U.S.A.; tel. 800/742-9244, www.2tahiti.com

The following companies offer tours to French Polynesia only:

Griffin and Co. Travel, 406 West Main St., Flushing, MI 48433, U.S.A.; tel 888/292-4484 or 810/659-5584, www.griffin-travel.com

Manuia Tours, 59 New Montgomery St., San

Francisco, CA 94105, U.S.A.; tel. 866/682-4484 or 415/495-4500, www.tahitispecialist.com

Pacific for Less, 1993 South Kihei Road, Suite 21–130, Kihei, HI 96753, U.S.A.; tel. 808/249-6490 or 800/915-2776, www.pacificforless.com

Tahiti Honeymoons, 202 N. Curry St, Suite 100, Carson City, NV 89703, U.S.A.; tel. 888/226-2142 or 480/984-5245, www.come2 tahiti.com

Tahiti Legends, 19891 Beach Blvd, Suite 107, Huntington Beach, CA 92648, U.S.A.; tel. 714/374-5656 or 800/200-1213, www.tahiti-legends.com

Tahiti TravelNet, 6516 West 6th Street, Los Angeles, CA 90048, U.S.A.; tel. 323/655-2181 or 800/781-9356, www.tahititravel.com

Tahiti Travel Planners, New Millennium Travel, 461 Durand NE, Suite 100, Atlanta, GA 30307, U.S.A.; tel. 404/378-4983 or 800/772-9231, www.gotahiti.com

The following companies offer tours to Fiji only:

All Inclusive Fiji, 1505 S.W. Broadway, Portland, OR 97201, U.S.A.; tel. 866/444-8518 or 503/224-6659, fax 503/224-6216, www.all inclusivefiji.com

Fiji Fantasy Holidays, 207 East Highway 260, Payson, AZ 85541, U.S.A.; tel. 877/727-3454, fax 520/472-2580, www.fijifantasyholidays.com

South Pacific Holidays, 10906 NE 39th St., Suite A-1, Vancouver, WA 98682-6789, U.S.A.; tel. 877/733-3454 or 360/944-1712, fax 360/253-3934, www.tropicalfiji.com

Margi Arnold's **Creative Travel Adventures** (8500 East Jefferson Ave., Unit 5H, Denver, CO 80237, U.S.A.: tel. 303/694-8786 or 888/568-4432, www.honeymoonfiji.com) specializes in honeymoon travel to Fiji.

Far Horizons Trips (P.O. Box 91900, Albu-querque, NM 87199, U.S.A.; 505/343-9400 or 800/552-4575, www.farhorizon.com) and **Nature Expeditions International** (7860 Peters Road, Suite F-103, Plantation, FL 33324, U.S.A.; tel. 954/693-8852 or 800/869-0639, www.nature xp.com) organize tours to Easter Island.

From Australia

Since 1977 **Hideaway Holidays** (Val Gavriloff, P.O. Box 121, West Ryde, NSW 2114, Australia; tel. 02/9743-0253, fax 02/9743-3568, www.hide awayholidays.com.au) has been the Australian specialist on packages to Fiji and the South Pacific.

Other Australian tour operators specializing in the South Pacific include:

Adventure World, 3rd Floor, 73 Walker St, North Sydney, NSW 2060, Australia; tel. 02/8913-0755, fax 02/9956-7707, www.adven tureworld.com.au

ATS Pacific Pty Ltd, P.O. Box A2494, Sydney South, NSW 2000, Australia; tel. 02/9268-2111, fax 02/9267-9733, www.atspacific.com

Coral Seas Travel, Suite 502, 92 Pitt St., Sydney, NSW 2000, Australia; tel. 02/9231-2944, fax 02/9231-2029, www.coralseas.com.au

Essence Tours, 1666 Old Cleveland Road, Chandler, Queensland 4155, Australia; tel. 07/3245-7815, fax 07/3245-6372, www.essence tours.com.au

Executive Destinations, 38–40 Garden St., South Yarra, VIC 3141, Australia; tel. 03/9823-8300, fax 03/9823-8383, www.edfiji.com

Goway Travel, 350 Kent St., 8th floor, Sydney, NSW 2000, Australia; tel. 02/9262-4755, fax 02/9290-1905, www.goway.com

Orient Pacific Holidays, 14A Sandilands St., South Melbourne, Victoria 3205, Australia; tel. 03/9690-1500, fax 03/9690-1942, www.orient pacific.com.au

Pacific Specialist Holidays, Suite C15, Dalgety

Square, Ultimo Sydney, NSW 2007, Australia; tel 61-2/9080-1600, Fax 61-2/9080-1699, www.pacificholidays.com.au

Talpacific Holidays, Level 1, 91 York Street, Sydney, NSW 2000, Australia; tel. 02/9244-1850, fax 02/9262-6318, www.talpacific.com

Venture Holidays, 234 Sussex St., Sydney, NSW 2000, Australia; tel. 02/9236-5222, fax 02/9221-5394, www.ventureholidays.com

From New Zealand

Fathom South Pacific Travel (P.O. Box 2557, Shortland Street, Auckland, New Zealand; www.fathomtravel.com) is an adventure travel-oriented packager. It books rooms at all the top resorts, but also has numerous options for scuba diving and kayaking. Ninety-five percent of its bookings are via the Internet.

World Discovery Tours (P.O. Box 6145, Auckland, New Zealand; tel. 0800/367-868 or 64-9/366-0379, www.world-discovery.com) operates escorted small group tours to Fiji, Samoa, Tonga, the Cook Islands, and Tahiti. They also quote prices beginning from Los Angeles and Vancouver.

Ginz Travel (183 Victoria Street, Christchurch, New Zealand; tel. 64-3/366-4486, www.ginz.com) arranges flights, accommodations, rental cars, and package deals to French Polynesia and the Cook Islands.

Go Holidays (151 Victoria Street West, Level 4, Auckland, New Zealand; tel. 64-9/916-9910, www.goholidays.co.nz) has packaged tours and cruises to most of the areas covered in this book.

Talpacific Holidays (P.O. Box 297, Auckland, New Zealand; tel. 64-9/914-8728, www.talpacific.com) also offers package tours throughout the region.

From Europe

Austravel (17 Blomfield St., London EC2M 7AJ, United Kingdom; tel. 0870/166-2130, www.austravel.com), with nine locations in the United Kingdom, is a South Pacific-oriented tour company owned by the Thomson Travel Group. **Tailor Made Travel** (18 Port St., Evesham, Worchestershire, WR11 6AN, United Kingdom;

tel. 01386/712-005, www.tailor-made.co.uk) specializes in upscale South Pacific tours. **All Ways Pacific Travel** (7 Whielden Street, Old Amersham, Bucks HP7 0HT, United Kingdom; tel. 01494/432747, www.all-ways.co.uk) sells a variety of packages to the South Pacific.

The **Pacific Travel House** (Bayersstrasse 95, D-80335 München, Germany; tel. 49-89/530-9293, www.pacific-travel-house.com) and **Polynesia Tours** (Benekendorffstr. 87b, 13469 Berlin, Germany; tel. 49-30/4030-3085, www.polynesia-tours.de) offer a variety of package tours.

Similar are **Art of Travel** (Isartorplatz 1, D-80331 Munich, Germany; tel. 49-89/211-0760, www.artoftravel.de) and **Adventure Holidays** (Wacholderbergstr. 29, 90587 Veitsbronn, Germany; tel. 0911/ 979-9555, fax 0911/979-9588. www.adventure-holidays.com).

In Austria the South Pacific specialist is **Coco Weltweit Reisen** (Eduard-Bodem-Gasse 8, A-6020 Innsbruck; tel. 43-512/365-791, www.coco-tours.at).

Elsewhere in Europe, inclusive tours to French Polynesia are most easily booked through Nouvelles Frontières (www.nouvelles-frontieres.fr) offices. **Iles du Monde** (7 rue Cochin, Paris, France; tel. 01/4326-6868, fax 01/4329/1000, www.ilesdumonde.com) offers upscale tours to French Polynesia, the Cook Islands, Fiji, and New Caledonia.

Scuba Tours

The South Pacific is one of the world's prime scuba locales, and most of the islands have excellent facilities for divers. Although it's not that difficult to make your own arrangements as you go, you should consider joining an organized scuba tour if you want to cram in as much diving as possible. To stay in business, the dive travel specialists mentioned below are forced to charge prices similar to what you'd pay on the beach, and the convenience of having everything prearranged is often worth it. Before booking, find out exactly where you'll be staying and ask if daily transfers and meals are provided. Of course, diver certification is mandatory.

Before deciding, carefully consider booking a cabin on a "live-aboard" dive boat. They're a bit more expensive than hotel-based diving, but you're offered up to five dives a day and a total experience. Some repeat divers won't go any other way. Liveaboard dive boats operating in the South Pacific include the *Sere ni Wai, Beqa Princess,* and *Nai'a* in Fiji, the *Silent World* in Vanuatu, and the *Spirit of the Solomons* and *Bilikiki* in the Solomon Islands. **Live/Dive Pacific** (74-5588 Pawai Place, Building F, Kailua-Kona, HI 96740, U.S.A.; tel. 808/329-8182 or 800/344-5662, www.livedivepacific.com) specializes in liveaboards, especially the *Tahiti Aggressor* based at Rangiroa.

Companies specializing in dive tours to several South Pacific destinations include:

Dive Discovery, 77 Mark Dr., Suite 18, San Rafael, CA 94903, U.S.A.; tel. 415/444-5100 or 800/886-7321, fax 415/444-5560, www.divediscovery.com

Island Dreams, 1309 Antoine Dr., Houston, TX 77055, U.S.A.; tel. 713/973-9300 or 800/346-6116, fax 713/973-8585, www.islandream.com

Rainbowed Sea Tours, 74–5590 Luhia Street, Kailua-Kona, HI 96740, U.S.A.; tel. 808/326-7752 or 800/762-6827, fax 808/329-2608, www.rstours.com

South Pacific Island Travel, 537 North 137th Street, Seattle, WA 98133, U.S.A.; tel. 877/773-4846 or 206/367-0956, fax 509/695-8111, www.spislandtravel.com

Trip-N-Tour, 131 East Fig St., Ste 4, Fallbrook, CA 92028, U.S.A.; tel. 760/451-1001 or 800/348-0842, www.trip-n-tour.com

World of Diving, 301 Main St., El Segundo, CA 90245, U.S.A.; tel. 310/322-8100 or 800/900-7657, www.worldofdiving.com

Dive tours to Fiji only are available from:

Aqua-Trek, 601 Montgomery St., Suite 650, San Francisco, CA 94111, U.S.A.; tel. 800/541-4334, www.aquatrek.com

Poseidon Ventures Tours, 359 San Miguel Dr., Newport Beach, CA 92660, U.S.A.; tel. 800/854-9334, fax 949/644-5392, www.poseidontours.com

In Australia try **Dive Adventures** (Level 9, 32 York St., Sydney, NSW 2000; tel. 61-2/9299-4633, fax 61-2/9299-4644, www.diveadventures.com), a scuba wholesaler with packages to seven South Pacific destinations. They also have an office in Melbourne. **Allways Dive Expeditions** (168 High St., Ashburton, Melbourne, Victoria 3147, Australia: tel. 61-3/9885-8863, www.allwaysdive.com.au) organizes dive expeditions throughout the region. **Diversion Dive Travel** (P.O. Box 7026, Cairns 4870, Australia; tel. 61-7/4039-0200, fax 61-7/4039-0300, www.diversionoz.com) has dive tours to the Solomon Islands, while **Pro Dive International** (478 George St, Sydney, NSW 2000, Australia; tel. 800/820-820 or 61-2/9281-5066, fax 61-2/9281-0660, www.prodive.com.au) is a Vanuatu specialist.

Dive, Fish, 'n Snow Travel (15e Vega Pl., Mairangi Bay, Auckland 10, New Zealand; tel. 64-9/479-2210, fax 64-9/479-2214, www.divefishsnow.co.nz) arranges scuba and game fishing tours to Fiji, Solomon Islands, Tonga, and Vanuatu at competitive rates.

In Europe, **Scuba Safaris** (P.O. Box 8, Edenbridge, Kent, TN9 7ZS, United Kingdom; tel. 01342/851-196, fax 01342/851-197, www.scuba-safaris.com) offers dive tours to French Polynesia and Fiji. **Schöner Tauchen** (Hastedter Heerstr. 211, D-28207 Bremen; tel. 49-421/450-010, www.schoenertauchen.com) specializes in dive tours to Fiji, Tonga, Solomon Islands, and Vanuatu. A dive tour specialist in France is **Ultramarina** (37 rue Saint Léonard, 44032 Nantes Cedex 1, France; fax 02/4089-7489, www.ultramarina.com) with additional offices in Geneva, Lyon, Marseille, and Paris.

Alternatively, you can make your own arrangements directly with island dive shops. (Information about these operators is included under the heading Sports and Recreation in the respective destination chapters of this book.)

EXPLORING THE ISLANDS

Kayak Tours

From May–December the **Friendly Islands Kayak Company** (P.O. Box 142, Waitati, Otago 9060, New Zealand; tel./fax 64-3/482-1202, www.fikco.com) operates sea kayaking tours through Tonga's Vava'u and Ha'apai groups at US$578/1,465 for four/nine days (ground cost only). The packages include accommodations, meals, a Polynesian feast, and a farewell dinner. This eco-friendly company offers soft adventure tours emphasizing natural and cultural history interpretation.

Among the most exciting tours to the South Pacific are the nine-day kayaking expeditions offered from May–October by **Southern Sea Ventures** (Al Bakker, P.O. Box 781, Newport, NSW 2106, Australia; tel. 61-2/9999-0541, fax 61-2/9999-1357, www.southernseaventures.com). Their groups (limited to 12 people) paddle stable expedition sea kayaks through the sheltered tropical waters of the northern Yasawa chain. Accommodations are tents on the beach, and participants must be in reasonable physical shape, as three or four hours a day are spent on the water. The A$1,920 price doesn't include airfare. Southern Sea Ventures also operates kayak tours to Vanua Balavu in Fiji's Lau Group, to Ha'apai and Vava'u in Tonga, and to Epi and Ambrym in Vanuatu.

Tamarillo Tropical Expeditions (Anthony Norris, P.O. Box 9869, Wellington, New Zealand; tel. 04/239-9885, fax 04/239-9895, www.tamarillo.co.nz) organizes one-week kayaking trips to Ono and Kadavu year-round at NZ$2,150 all inclusive from Nadi. Two support boats carry the luggage and food. Nights are spent at small island resorts and in local villages, not in tents. Every third or fourth trip, Tamarillo offers a more rigorous "classic extreme" expedition (same price) for experienced kayakers who want to push the envelope a little further.

Kayak Solomons (P.O. Box 149, Mt Eliza, Victoria 3930, Australia; tel. 61-3/9787-7904, www.kayaksolomons.com) offers kayaking on Solomon Island's Marovo Lagoon. The packages begin at the Uepi Island Resort, costing US$135 pp a night including equipment, meals, and accommodations at rustic island lodges around the Marovo Lagoon.

Surfing Tours

The largest operator of surfing tours to the South Pacific is **The Surf Travel Company** (P.O. Box 446, Cronulla, NSW 2230, Australia; tel. 800/687-873 or 61-2/9527-4722, fax 61-2/9527-4522, www.surftravel.com.au) with packages to Fiji and Samoa.

Also in Australia, **Atoll Travel** (2 Bridge St., P.O. Box 205, Foster, Victoria 3960, Australia: tel 61-3/5682-1088, fax 61-3/5682-1202, www.atolltravel.com) books surfing tours to Samoa and Tonga. **World Surfaris Pty Ltd.** (P.O. Box 180, Suite 8/47 Brisbane Rd., Mooloolaba, Queensland 4557, Australia; tel. 61-7/5444-4011, fax 61-7/5444-4911, www.worldsurfaris.com) has tours to French Polynesia, Fiji, Tonga, Samoa, and New Caledonia.

For information on tours to Tavarua Island and the famous Cloudbreak contact **Tavarua Island Tours** (P.O. Box 60159, Santa Barbara, CA 93160, U.S.A.; tel. 805/686-4551, fax 805/683-6696, www.tavarua.com). A one-week package will run US$2,631 including airfare. Tavarua is often sold out six months in advance, but check with **Global Surf Trips** (2033 B San Elijo Ave., Suite 322, Cardiff By the Sea, CA 92007, U.S.A.; www.globalsurftravel.com) for "last minute opportunities."

One of the largest American companies offering surfing tours to Fiji, Samoa, Tahiti, and Tonga is **WaterWays Surf Adventures** (22611 Pacific Coast Highway, Malibu, CA 90265, U.S.A.; tel. 310/456-7744, fax 310/456-7755, www.waterwaystravel.com). Seven-night package tours to Fiji's Namotu Island Resort from Los Angeles with airfare, meals, and boat transfers included are US$2,598 pp.

Quiksilver Travel (15202 Graham St., Huntington Beach, CA 92649, U.S.A.; tel. 877/217-1091, fax 714/889-2250, www.quiksilvertravel.com), and **Wavehunters Surf Travel** (2424 Vista Way, Suite 203, Oceanside, CA 92054, U.S.A.; tel. 888/899-8823, fax 760/433-4476, www.wavehunters.com) has surfing tours to French Polynesia, Samoa, Fiji, and New Caledonia, and their website is a mine of information.

Tahitian Blue Water Dream (www.tahitianbluewaterdream.com) offers 10-day surfing and fishing cruises aboard the 19.5 live-aboard motor launch *Runaway*. The tour cost from Papeete without flights is US$2,500 and you can book online. **Vaimiti Tours** (www.vaimititours.com) also handles the *Runaway*.

Tours for Naturalists

Perhaps the most rewarding way to visit Fiji is with **Coral Cay Conservation** (The Tower, 13th Floor, 125 High Street, Colliers Wood, London SW19 2JG, United Kingdom; tel. 0870/750-0668, fax 0870/750-0667, www.coralcay.org). Its Fiji Reef Conservation Project helps protect vulnerable coral reefs and islands by gathering information urgently needed for new marine reserves and forest sanctuaries. Non-divers must first take a scuba certification course in Fiji, followed by a two-week training program. The length of time actually spent as a volunteer working in Fiji is optional. For dates and costs, check their website.

From June–October **Whale Discoveries** (P.O. Box 142, Waitati, Otago 9060, New Zealand; tel./fax 64-3/482-1202, www.whalediscoveries.com) offers a week of whalewatching at Vava'u, Tonga, for US$625 pp. The package includes five days of whalewatching, a day of sea kayaking, mountain biking or sailing, accommodations, and some meals (but not airfare). The knowledgeable staff provide an in-depth study of the playful humpback whales and their calves.

From August–October, Joel Simon's **Sea for Yourself** (729 College Ave., Menlo Park, CA 94025, U.S.A.; tel. 650/322-1494, www.seaforyourself.com) offers snorkeling tours to Fiji and Tonga. A 10-day tour with whale-watching in Tonga costs US$3,750 excluding airfare, while Joel's "remote reefs of Fiji" tour is US$3,250. Joel only takes a dozen people at a time, and he's usually sold out months in advance.

Reef and Rainforest Adventure Travel (298 Harbor Dr, Sausalito, CA 94965, U.S.A.; tel. 415/289-1760 or 800/794-9767, fax 415/289-1763, www.reefrainforest.com) books diving, kayaking, whale- or dolphin-watching, and other adventure tours to seven Pacific countries.

Outdoor Travel Adventures (2927-A Canon St., San Diego, CA 92106, U.S.A.; tel. 619/523-2137 or 877/682-5433, www.otadventures.com)

offers a 10-day adventure tour to Fiji which combines kayaking, hiking, cycling, rafting, and snorkeling. Offered from May–October, it's US$2,295 excluding airfare.

From Australia **Go Tours Travel** (7 Davenport St., Southport, Queensland 4217, Australia; tel. 07/5591-2199, fax 07/5532-1854, www.gotours.com.au) offers a variety of eco and adventure tours throughout the South Pacific including fishing, surfing, cruising, scuba diving, sea kayaking, and sailing.

An inbound tour operator dedicated to adventure/ecotourism in French Polynesia is **Tahiti Outfitters** (Frank Murphy, tel. 689/48-31-69, www.tahitioutfitters.com) in Papeete. Their main business is organizing expeditions for major U.S. adventure travel companies, but they can also put together custom trips for preformed groups, families, and even couples. These range from bird-watching groups to university field courses and active travelers who want to get out and do some hiking or sea kayaking. All of Tahiti Outfitter's trips have major natural and cultural history components, so the participants learn quite a lot about the place.

A Samoa-based company organizing nature tours is **Ecotour Samoa** (Steve Brown, www.ecotoursamoa.com), which uses their famous Green Turtle bus on one-week safaris around Upolu and Savai'i (US$188 a day and up).

Hiking Tours

Year-round **Adventure Fiji**, a division of Rosie The Travel Service (P.O. Box 9268, Nadi Airport; tel. 672-2755, fax 672-2607, www.rosiefiji.com) at Nadi Airport, runs adventuresome three/five-night hiking trips in the upper Wainibuka River area of central Viti Levu south of Rakiraki. Horses carry trekkers' backpacks, so the trips are feasible for almost anyone in good condition. Accommodation is in actual Fijian villages. The F$542/726 pp price includes transport to the trailhead, food and accommodations at a few of the 11 Fijian villages along the way, guides, and a bamboo raft ride on the Wainibuka River. Trekkers only hike about five hours a day, allowing lots of time to get to know the village people. You'll probably be required to ford rivers along the way, so have along a pair of cheap canvas shoes to avoid ruining your expensive hiking boots.

Tours for Veterans

Every August **Valor Tours Ltd.** (10 Liberty Ship Way, Sausalito, CA 94965, U.S.A.; tel. 415/332-7850 or 800/842-4504, fax 415/332-6971, www.valortours.com) organizes a tour of WW II battlefields in the Solomons at US$2,950 from Los Angeles (or US$4,100 including a seven-day cruise). Most tours are personally led by Valor's president, Robert F. Reynolds, who was the moving force behind construction of the U.S. war memorial in Honiara.

Tours for Seniors

Since 1989 the **Pacific Islands Institute** (354 Uluniu St., Suite 408, Kailua, HI 96734, U.S.A.; tel. 808/262-8942, www.pac-island.com) has operated educational tours to most of the South Pacific countries in cooperation with Hawaii Pacific University. Their **Elderhostel** people-to-people study programs designed for those aged 55 or over (younger spouses welcome) are offered between four and six times a year. A 19-day tour to French Polynesia and Rarotonga is US$4,985 from Los Angeles, otherwise it's US$8,451 for 27 days to Easter Island and the Marquesas.

Tours for Children

Rascals in Paradise (Theresa Detchemendy and Deborah Baratta, 1 Daniel Burnham Court, Suite 105-C, San Francisco, CA 94109, U.S.A.; tel. 415/921-7000 or 800/872-7225, www.rascals inparadise.com) has been organizing personalized tours to the South Pacific for families since 1987. Since then, they've have been instrumental in initiating numerous children's programs. The price is based on two adults with one or two children aged 2–11, and international airfares and transfers are additional. A single parent with child would have to pay two adult fares.

CRUISES AND CHARTERS

Tourist Cruises

Several times a year **Society Expeditions** (tel. 800/548-8669, www.societyexpeditions.com)

offers cruises to remote islands on the 85-stateroom expedition ship *World Discoverer.* Passengers land from Zodiacs and there are on-board lectures by leading authorities. The 17-night cruise "In the Wake of the *Bounty"* includes the Society, Tuamotu, and Marquesas islands, Pitcairn, and Easter Island, starting at US$6,215 pp double occupancy (cruise only). There's also an 14-day "Pearls of the South Pacific" cruise from Tahiti to Fiji starting at US$5,640 pp.

Several large cruise ships based at Papeete offer regular one-week cruises in the Society Islands. These include the *Paul Gauguin* of **Radisson Seven Seas Cruises,** the *Wind Star* of **Wind Star Cruises,** and the *Tahitian Princess* of **Princess Cruises.** Princess also sells cruises between Tahiti and Rarotonga. From Sydney, Australia, P&O Cruise's 1,620-passenger *Pacific Sky* operates cruises to Vanuatu and other western Pacific ports of call.

Companies like **Bora Bora Cruises** and **Archipels Croisieres** operate much smaller mini-cruise ships in French Polynesia. Also well worth considering are the adventure cruises to the Marquesas Islands aboard the passenger-carrying freighter *Aranui.* In Fiji, **Captain Cook Cruises** and **Blue Lagoon Cruises** run very popular deluxe cruises to the Yasawa Islands from Nadi or Lautoka. **Awesome Adventures** offers "Wanna Taki" cruises around Fiji's Yasawa Group for backpackers. **Tui Tai Adventure Cruises** also caters to younger travelers in Fiji. Turn to Transportation in the French Polynesia and Fiji introductions for detailed information on these cruises.

On all the cruises, check whether gratuities, port taxes, transfers, shore excursions, alcoholic drinks, and airfare are included when evaluating costs.

Yacht Tours and Charters

If you were planning on spending a substantial amount to stay at a luxury resort, consider chartering a yacht instead! Divided up among the members of your party the per-person charter price will be about the same, but you'll experience much more of the Pacific's beauty on a boat than you would staying in a hotel room. All charterers visit remote islands accessible only by small boat and thus receive special insights into island life unspoiled by normal tourist trappings. Of course, activities such as sailing, snorkeling, and general exploring by sea and land are included in the price.

Yacht charters are available either "bareboat" (for those with the skill to sail on their own) or "crewed" (in which case charterers pay a daily fee for a skipper plus his/her provisions). For specific information about French Polynesia yacht charters at Tahiti or Raiatea with Tahiti Yacht Charter, or at Raiatea with The Moorings and Stardust/Sunsail, turn to Transportation in the introduction to French Polynesia. The Moorings (www.moorings.com) also offers yacht charters at Vava'u, Tonga. In Fiji, Musket Cove Yacht Charters (www.musketcovefiji.com) offers fully crewed charters among the Mamanuca and Yasawa islands.

A few private brokers arranging bareboat or crewed yacht charters are listed below. Since they don't own their own boats, they'll be more inclined to fit you to the particular yacht that suits your individual needs.

Charter World Pty. Ltd., 23 Passchendaele St., Hampton, Melbourne 3188, Australia; tel. 61-3/9521-0033 or 800/335-039, www.charter world.com.au

Crestar Yacht Charters, 16/17 Pall Mall, London SW1Y 5LU, United Kingdom; tel. 020/7766-4329, www.crestaryachts.com

Paradise Adventures & Cruises, Heidi Gavriloff, P.O. Box 121, West Ryde, NSW 2114, Australia; tel. 61-2/9743-0253, www.paradiseadventures.com.au

Sail Connections Ltd., P.O. Box 90961, 8 Madden St., Auckland 1, New Zealand; tel. 64-9/358-0556, www.sailconnections.co.nz

The Windward Islands Cruising Company, 2672 NW 112th Ave., Miami, FL 33172, U.S.A.; tel. 305/593-8687, www.pacific-adventure.com

Yachting Partners International, 28–29 Richmond Pl., Brighton, East Sussex, BN2 9NA,

United Kingdom; tel. 800/626-0019 or 44-1273/571-722, www.ypi.co.uk

One of the most experienced brokers arranging such charters is **Ocean Voyages Inc.** (1709 Bridgeway, Sausalito, CA 94965, U.S.A.; tel. 415/332-4681 or 800/299-4444, fax 415/332-7460, www.oceanvoyages.com). For groups of four or six they can help select the right charter yacht for voyages from Tahiti or Mangareva to Pitcairn, charter programs out of Port Vila, Santo, Raiatea, Vava'u, Suva, Lautoka, and Taveuni, and extended tours of the entire South Pacific by classic square-rigger sailing boats. Ocean Voyages caters to a very select, professional clientele, and their crews are carefully chosen. More than 35 percent of the participants are repeaters—the best recommendation there is.

One of the classic "tall ships" cruising the South Pacific is the two-masted brigantine *Soren Larsen,* built in 1949. From May–November this 42 square meter rig vessel operates 10–17 day voyages to Tahiti, the Cook Islands, Tonga, Fiji, Vanuatu, and New Caledonia costing US$1,500–2,550. The 12-member professional crew is actively assisted by 22 voyage participants. For information contact **Square Sail Pacific** (P.O. Box 310, Kumeu, Auckland 1250, New Zealand; tel. 09/411-8755, fax 09/411-8484, www.sorenlarsen.co.nz). Their U.K. agent is **Explore Worldwide** (1 Frederick St., Aldershot, Hants GU11 1LQ, United Kingdom; tel. 01252/760-000, fax 01252/760-001, www.exploreworldwide.com). Ocean Voyages Inc. handles bookings in North America.

BY SHIP

Even as much Pacific shipping was being sunk during WW II, airstrips were springing up on all the main islands. This hastened the inevitable replacement of the old steamships with modern aircraft, and it's now extremely rare to arrive in the South Pacific by boat (private yachts excepted). Most islands export similar products and there's little interregional trade; large container ships headed for Australia, New Zealand, and the United States usually don't accept passengers.

EXPLORING THE ISLANDS

Those bitten by nostalgia for the slower pre-war ways may like to know that a couple of passenger-carrying freighters do still call at the islands, though their fares are much higher than those charged by the airlines. A specialized agency booking such passages is **TravLtips** (P.O. Box 580188, Flushing, NY 11358, U.S.A.; tel. 718/224-0435 or 800/872-8584, www.travltips.com). Also try **Freighter World Cruises** (180 South Lake Ave., Suite 335, Pasadena, CA 91101, U.S.A.; tel. 626/449-3106 or 800/531-7774, www.freighterworld.com).

These companies can place you aboard a British-registered **Bank Line** container ship on its way around the world from Europe via the Panama Canal, Tahiti, Nouméa, Suva, Lautoka, Port Vila, Santo, Honiara, and Papua New Guinea. A round-the-world ticket for the four-month journey is US$12,725, but segments are sold if space is available 30 days before sailing. Similarly, TravLtips books German-registered **Columbus Line** vessels, which make 45-day round-trips between Los Angeles and Australia via Suva. These ships can accommodate only about a dozen passengers, so inquire well in advance. Also ask about passenger accommodation on cargo vessels of the **Blue Star Line,** which call at Suva and Nouméa between Los Angeles and Auckland.

BY SAILING YACHT
Getting Aboard

It's possible to hitch rides into the Pacific on yachts from California, Panama, New Zealand, and Australia, or around the yachting triangle Papeete-Suva-Honolulu. If you've never crewed before, consider looking for a yacht already in the islands. In Tahiti, for example, after a month on the open sea, some of the original crew may have flown home or onward, opening a place for you. Pago Pago, Vava'u, Suva, Musket Cove, and Port Vila are other places to look for a boat. Cruising yachts are recognizable by their foreign flags, wind-vane steering gear, sturdy appearance, and laundry hung out to dry. Good captains evaluate crew on personality, attitude, and a willingness to learn more than experience, so don't lie. Be honest and open when inter-viewing with a skipper—a deception will soon become apparent.

It's also good to know what a captain's *really* like before you commit yourself to an isolated month with her/him. To determine what might happen should the electronic gadgetry break down, find out if there's a sextant aboard and whether he/she knows how to use it. A run-down-looking boat may often be mechanically unsound too. Also be concerned about a skipper who doesn't do a careful safety briefing early on, or who seems to have a hard time hanging onto crew. If the previous crew left the boat at an unlikely place such as the Marquesas, there must have been a reason. Once you're on a boat and part of the yachtie community, things are easy.

Time of Year

The weather and seasons play a deciding role in any South Pacific trip by sailboat and you'll have to pull out of many beautiful places, or be unable to stop there, because of bad weather. The prime season for rides in the South Pacific is May–October; sometimes you'll even have to turn one down. Be aware of the hurricane season: November–March in the South Pacific, July–December in the northwest Pacific (near Guam), and June–October in the area between Mexico and Hawaii. Few yachts will be cruising those areas at these times. A few yachts spend the winter at Pago Pago and Vava'u (the main "hurricane holes"), but most South Pacific cruisers will have left for hurricane-free New Zealand by October.

Also, know which way the winds are blowing; the prevailing trade winds in the tropics are from the northeast north of the equator, from the southeast south of the equator. North of the tropic of Cancer and south of the tropic of Capricorn the winds are out of the west. Due to the action of prevailing southeast trade winds, boat trips are smoother from east to west than west to east throughout the South Pacific, so that's the way to go.

Yachting Routes

The common yachting route or "Coconut Milk Run" across the South Pacific utilizes the northeast and southeast trades: from California to Tahiti via the Marquesas or Hawai'i, then Rarotonga, Niue, Vava'u, Suva, and New Zealand. Some yachts continue west from Fiji to Port Vila. In the other direction, you'll sail on the westerlies from New Zealand to a point south of the Australs, then north on the trades to Tahiti.

Some 300 yachts leave the U.S. west coast for Tahiti every year, almost always crewed by couples or men only. Cruising yachts average about 150 km a day, so it takes about a month to get from the U.S. west coast to Hawai'i, then another month from Hawai'i to Tahiti. Most stay in the South Seas about a year before returning to North America, while a few continue around the world. About 60–80 cross the Indian Ocean every year (look for rides from Sydney in May, Cairns or Darwin from June–August, Bali from August–October, Singapore from October–December); around 700 yachts sail from Europe to the Caribbean (from Gibraltar and Gran Canaria October–December).

To enjoy the finest weather conditions many yachts clear the Panama Canal or depart California in February to arrive in the Marquesas in March. From Hawai'i, yachts often leave for Tahiti in April or May. Many stay on for the *Heiva i Tahiti* festival, which ends on 14 July, at which time they sail west to Vava'u or Suva, where you'll find them in July and August. From New Zealand, the Auckland to Fiji yacht race in June brings many boats north. In mid-September the yachting season culminates with a race by about 40 boats from Musket Cove on Fiji's Malololailai Island to Port Vila (it's very easy to hitch a ride at this time). By late October the bulk of the yachting community is sailing south via New Caledonia to New Zealand or Australia to spend the southern summer there. In April or May on alternate years there's a yacht race from Auckland and Sydney to Suva, timed to coincide with the cruisers' return after the hurricane season. Jimmy Cornell's www.noonsite.com provides lots of valuable information for cruising yachties.

Blue Water Rallies (Peter Seymour, Windsor Cottage, Chedworth, Cheltenham, Gloucestershire GL54 4AA, United Kingdom; tel./fax 01285/720-904, www.yachtrallies.co.uk) organizes annual round-the-world yachting rallies, departing Europe each October. Inquiries from both owners and potential crew members are welcome for these 20-month circumnavigations that visit Galapagos, the Marquesas, Tahiti, Tonga, and Fiji. Blue Water's professional support services will help make that "voyage of a lifetime" a reality!

Life Aboard

To crew on a yacht you must be willing to wash and iron clothes, cook, steer, keep watch at night, and help with engine work. Other jobs might include changing and resetting sails, cleaning the boat, scraping the bottom, pulling up the anchor, and climbing the main mast to watch for reefs. Do more than is expected of you. A safety harness must be worn in rough weather. As a guest in someone else's home you'll want to wash your dishes promptly after use and put them, and all other gear, back where you found them. Tampons must not be thrown in the toilet bowl. Smoking is usually prohibited as a safety hazard.

Anybody who wants to get on well under sail must be flexible and tolerant, both physically and emotionally. Expense-sharing crew members pay US$50 a week or more per person. After 30 days you'll be happy to hit land for a freshwater shower. Give adequate notice when you're ready to leave the boat, but *do* disembark when your journey's up. Boat people have few enough opportunities for privacy as it is. If you've had a good trip, ask the captain to write you a letter of recommendation; it'll help you hitch another ride.

Food for Thought

When you consider the big investment, depreciation, cost of maintenance, operating expenses, and considerable risk (most cruising yachts are not insured), travel by sailing yacht is quite a luxury. The huge cost can be surmised from charter fees (US$600 a day and up for a 10-meter yacht). International law makes a clear distinction between passengers and crew. Crew members paying only for their own food, cooking gas, and part of the diesel are very different from charterers who do nothing and pay full costs. The crew is there to help operate the boat, adding safety, but like passengers, they're very much under the control of the captain. Crew has no say in where the yacht will go.

The skipper is personally responsible for crew coming into foreign ports: he's entitled to hold their passports and to see that they have onward tickets and sufficient funds for further traveling. Otherwise the skipper might have to pay their hotel bills and even return airfares to the crew's country of origin. Crew may be asked to pay a

share of third-party liability insurance. Possession of dope can result in seizure of the yacht. Because of such considerations, skippers often hesitate to accept crew. Crew members should remember that at no cost to themselves they can learn a bit of sailing and visit places nearly inaccessible by other means. Although not for everyone, it's *the* way to see the real South Pacific, and folks who arrive by yacht are treated differently than other tourists.

Getting Around

BY AIR

Domestic Air Services

Nearly every Pacific country has its local airline servicing the outer islands. These flights, described in the destination chapters of this guide, can be booked upon arrival. The most important local carriers are Air Calédonie (New Caledonia), Air Fiji (Fiji), Air Rarotonga (Cook Islands), Air Tahiti (French Polynesia), Inter Island Air (American Samoa), Polynesian Airlines (Samoa), fly Niu Airlines (Tonga), Solomon Airlines (Solomon Islands), Sun Air (Fiji), and Vanair (Vanuatu). Most fly small aircraft, so only 10 kilograms free baggage may be allowed. A typical interisland flight will cost just over US$50 in American Samoa and Solomon Islands, around US$70 in Tonga and Fiji, US$100 in New Caledonia and Wallis and Futuna, US$115 in the Cook Islands and Vanuatu, and US$150 in French Polynesia. Most runways are unlighted so few flights operate at night. These services are described in the respective chapters of this guide.

BY SEA

Ninety-nine percent of international travel around the South Pacific is by air. With few exceptions travel by boat is a thing of the past, and about the only regular international service left is Apia to Pago Pago. Local boats to the outer islands within a single country are available everywhere, however. Among the local trips you can

easily do by regularly scheduled ferry are Tahiti-Moorea, Tahiti-Bora Bora, Tongatapu-Vava'u, Tongatapu-'Eua, Upolu-Savai'i, Suva-Kadavu, Suva-Taveuni, Nabouwalu-Natovi, Natovi-Ovalau, Nouméa-Loyalty Islands, Port Vila-Espiritu Santo, Honiara-Malaita, and Honiara-Gizo. Details of these and other shipping possibilities are explored in the different destination chapters of this book.

OTHER TRAVEL OPTIONS

By Bus

Most of the main islands have highly developed bus systems serving the local people. In this handbook, we cover them all. Bus services are especially good in Fiji with all of the main centers connected by frequent services at very reasonable prices. Buses are also a good and inexpensive way to get around Tahiti, Rarotonga, Tongatapu, Tutuila, and Upolu. There's a good city bus service in Port Vila, but other than that, buses are few and far between in Vanuatu. A public bus ride to the international airport will cost less than US$0.50 in Fiji and Tonga, around US$0.75 in both Samoas and Vanuatu, US$1.50 in French Polynesia and the Cook Islands, and US$4 in New Caledonia.

By Car

A rental car with unlimited mileage will generally cost around US$35 a day in the Cook Islands, Niue, Samoa, Solomon Islands, and Tonga, US$50 on Easter Island, US$70 in American

© DAVID STANLEY

Ferries are the main way of island hopping in the South Pacific.

Samoa, Fiji, and Vanuatu, and over US$100 in French Polynesia and New Caledonia.

Because of the alternative means of travel available, the only places where you really need to consider renting a car are in New Caledonia (Grande Terre), French Polynesia, and Vanuatu (Efate), and perhaps also on Upolu in Samoa. Renting a car is an unnecessary luxury in American Samoa and Fiji due to the excellent public transportation in those countries. In the Cook Islands and Tonga one must purchase a local driver's license (international driver's license not recognized) and it's better to tour those countries by rented bicycle anyway. Bicycle is also the way to see Bora Bora.

The car rental business is very competitive and it's possible to shop around for a good deal upon arrival. Although the locally operated companies may offer cheaper rates than the international franchises, it's also true that the agents of Avis, Budget, Europcar, and Hertz are required to maintain recognized standards of service and they have regional offices where you can complain if anything goes seriously wrong. Always find out if insurance, mileage, and tax are included, and check for restrictions on where you'll be al-

lowed to take the car. If in doubt, ask to see a copy of their standard rental contract before making reservations.

Driving is on the right (as in continental Europe and North America) in American Samoa, New Caledonia, French Polynesia, Vanuatu, and Samoa, and on the left (as in Britain, New Zealand, and Japan) in the Cook Islands, Fiji, Solomon Islands, and Tonga. If you do rent a car, remember those sudden tropical downpours and don't leave the windows open. Also avoid parking under coconut trees (a falling nut might break the window), and never go off and leave the keys in the ignition. Lock the doors as you would at home.

By Bicycle

Bicycling in the South Pacific? Sure, why not? It's cheap, convenient, healthy, quick, environmentally sound, safe, and above all, *fun.* You'll be able to go where and when you please, stop easily and often to meet people and take photos, save money on taxi fares—really *see* the countries. Cycling every day can be fatiguing, however, so it's smart to have bicycle-touring experience beforehand. Most roads are flat along the coast, but be careful on coral roads, especially inclines: if you slip and fall you could hurt yourself badly. On the high islands interior roads tend to be very steep. Never ride your bike through mud.

You can rent bicycles on many islands. If you bring your own, a sturdy, single-speed mountain bike with wide wheels, safety chain, and good brakes might be ideal. Thick tires and a plastic liner between tube and tire will reduce punctures. Know how to fix your own bike. Take along a good repair kit (pump, puncture kit, freewheel tool, spare spokes, cables, chain links, assorted nuts and bolts, etc.) and a repair manual; bicycle shops are poor to nonexistent in the islands. Don't try riding with a backpack: sturdy, waterproof panniers (bike bags) are required; you'll also want a good lock. Refuse to lend your bike to *anyone*.

Most international airlines will carry a bicycle as checked luggage, usually free but sometimes at the standard overweight charge or for a flat US$50 fee. Verify the airline's policy when booking. Take off the pedals and panniers, turn the handlebars sideways and tie them down, deflate the tires, and clean off the dirt before checking in (or use a special bike-carrying bag) and arrive at the airport early. The commuter airlines usually won't accept bikes on their small planes. Interis-

land boats sometimes charge a token amount to carry a bike; other times it's free.

By Ocean Kayak and Canoe

Ocean kayaking is finally beginning to catch on in the South Pacific, and you can now rent kayaks in many resort areas. Almost every island has a sheltered lagoon ready-made for the excitement of kayak touring, but this effortless transportation mode hasn't yet arrived, so you can be a real independent 21st-century explorer! Many international airlines accept folding kayaks as checked baggage at no charge.

For a better introduction to ocean kayaking than is possible here, check at your local public library for sea kayaking manuals. Noted author Paul Theroux toured the entire South Pacific by kayak, and his experiences are recounted in *The Happy Isles of Oceania: Paddling the Pacific.* The kayaking tours mentioned previously are excellent value.

If you get off the beaten track, it's more than likely that a local friend will offer to take you out in his outrigger canoe. Never attempt to take a dugout canoe through even light surf: you'll be swamped. Don't try to pull or lift a canoe by its outrigger—it will break. Drag the canoe by holding the solid main body. A bailer is *essential* equipment.

French Polynesia

Introduction

Legendary Tahiti, isle of love, has long been the vision of "la Nouvelle Cythère," the earthly paradise. Explorers Wallis, Bougainville, and Cook all told of a land of spellbinding beauty and enchantment, where the climate was delightful, hazardous insects and diseases unknown, and the islanders, especially the women, among the handsomest ever seen. Rousseau's "noble savage" had been found! A few years later, Fletcher Christian and Captain Bligh acted out their drama of sin and retribution here.

The list of famous authors who came and wrote about these islands reads like a high-school literature course: Herman Melville, Robert Louis Stevenson, Pierre Loti, Rupert Brooke, Jack London, W. Somerset Maugham, Charles Nordhoff and James Norman Hall (the Americans who wrote *Mutiny on the Bounty*), among others. Exotic images of uninhibited dancers, fragrant flowers, and pagan gods fill the pages. Here, at least, life was meant to be enjoyed.

FRENCH POLYNESIA HIGHLIGHTS

lagoon tours, Bora Bora: snorkeling, marinelife, scenery (p. 238)

Maeva, Huahine: archaeology, nature, hiking (p. 210)

Marae and Le Belvédère, Moorea: archaeology, viewpoint (p. 189)

Papeete market, Tahiti: shopping, food, local color (p. 150)

Tiputa Pass, Rangiroa: drift diving, dolphins, sharks (p. 252)

The most unlikely PR man of them all was a once-obscure French painter named Paul Gauguin, who transformed the primitive color of Tahiti and the Marquesas into powerful visual images seen around the world. When WW II shook the Pacific from Pearl Harbor to Guadalcanal, rather than bloodcurdling banzais and saturation bombings, Polynesia got a U.S. serviceman named James A. Michener, who added Bora Bora to the legend. Marlon Brando arrived in 1961 on one of the first jets to land in Polynesia and, along with thousands of tourists and adventurers, has been coming back ever since.

The friendly, easygoing manner of the people of French Polynesia isn't only a cliché! Tahiti gets around 200,000 tourists a year (compared to the seven million that visit Hawaii) and many are French nationals visiting friends, so you won't be facing a tourist glut! Despite over a century and a half of French colonialism, the Tahitians retain many of their old ways, be it in personal dress, Polynesian dancing, or outrigger canoe racing. Relax, smile, and say *bonjour* to strangers—you'll almost always get a warm response. Welcome to paradise!

THE LAND

French Polynesia (or Te Ao Maohi as it is known to the Polynesians themselves) consists of five great archipelagos, the Society, Austral, Tuamotu, Gambier, and Marquesas islands, arrayed in chains running from southeast to northwest. The Society Islands are subdivided into the Windwards, or Îles du Vent (Tahiti, Moorea, Maiao, Tetiaroa, and Mehetia), and the Leewards, or Îles Sous-le-Vent (Huahine, Raiatea, Taha'a, Bora Bora, Maupiti, Tupai, Maupihaa/Mopelia, Manuae/Scilly, and Motu One/Bellinghausen).

Together the 35 islands and 83 atolls of French Polynesia total only 3,543 square km in land area, yet they're scattered over a vast area of the southeastern Pacific Ocean, between 7° and 28° south latitude and 131° and 156° west longitude. Papeete (149° west longitude) is actually eight degrees *east* of Honolulu (157° west longitude). Though French Polynesia is only half the size of Corsica in land area, if Papeete were Paris then the Gambiers would be in Romania and the Marquesas near Stockholm. At 5,030,000 square km the territory's 200-nautical-mile exclusive economic zone is by far the largest in the Pacific islands.

There's a wonderful geological diversity to these islands midway between Australia and South America—from the dramatic, jagged volcanic outlines of the Society and Marquesas islands, to the 400-meter-high hills of the Australs and Gambiers, to the low coral atolls of the Tuamotus. All of the Marquesas are volcanic islands, while the Tuamotus are all coral islands or atolls. The Societies and Gambiers include both volcanic and coral types.

Tahiti, around 4,000 km from both Auckland and Honolulu or 6,000 km from Los Angeles and Sydney, is not only the best known and most populous of the islands, but also the largest (1,069 square km) and highest (2,241 meters). Bora Bora and Maupiti are noted for their combination of high volcanic peaks framed by low coral rings. Rangiroa is one of the world's largest coral atolls while Makatea is an uplifted atoll. In the Marquesas, precipitous and sharply crenelated mountains rise hundreds of meters, with craggy peaks, razorback ridges, plummeting waterfalls, deep, fertile valleys, and dark broken coastlines pounded by surf. Compare them to the pencil-thin strips of yellow reefs, green vegetation, and white beaches enclosing the transparent Tuamotu lagoons. In all, French Polynesia offers some of the most varied and spectacular scenery in the entire South Pacific.

Climate

The hot and humid summer season runs November–April. The rest of the year the climate is somewhat cooler and drier. The refreshing southeast trade winds blow consistently May–August, varying to easterlies September–December. The northeast trades January–April coincide with the hurricane season. The trade winds cool the islands and offer clear sailing for mariners, making May–October the most favorable season to visit. (In fact, there can be long periods of fine, sunny weather anytime of year and these seasonal variations should not be a pivotal factor in deciding when to come.)

Hurricanes are relatively rare, although they do hit the Tuamotus and occasionally Tahiti (but almost never the Marquesas). From November 1980 to May 1983 an unusual wave of eight hurricanes and two tropical storms battered the islands due to the El Niño phenomenon. The next hurricane occurred in December 1991. In November 1997 two hurricanes struck Maupiti and neighboring isles, one passed over the Tuamotus in February 1998, and another hit Huahine in April 1998, again the fault of El Niño. A hurricane would merely inconvenience a visitor staying at a hotel, though campers and yachties might get blown into oblivion. The days immediately following a hurricane are clear and dry.

Rainfall is greatest in the mountains and along the windward shores of the high islands. The Societies are far damper than the Marquesas. In fact, the climate of the Marquesas is erratic: some years the group experiences serious drought, other years it could rain the whole time you're there. The low-lying Tuamotus get the least rainfall of all. French Polynesia encompasses such a vast area that latitude is an important factor: at 27° south latitude Rapa is far cooler than Nuku Hiva (9° south).

Winds from the southeast *(maraamu)* are generally drier than those from the northeast or north. The northeast winds often bring rain: Papenoo on the northeast side of Tahiti is twice as wet as rain-shadowed Punaauia. The annual rainfall is extremely variable, but the humidity is generally high, reaching 98 percent. In the evening the heat of the Tahiti afternoons is replaced by soft, fragrant mountain breezes called *hupe,* which drift down to the sea. French Poly-

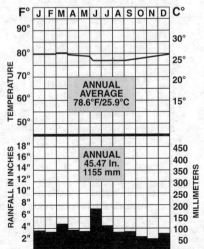

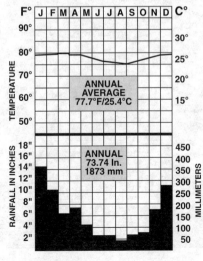

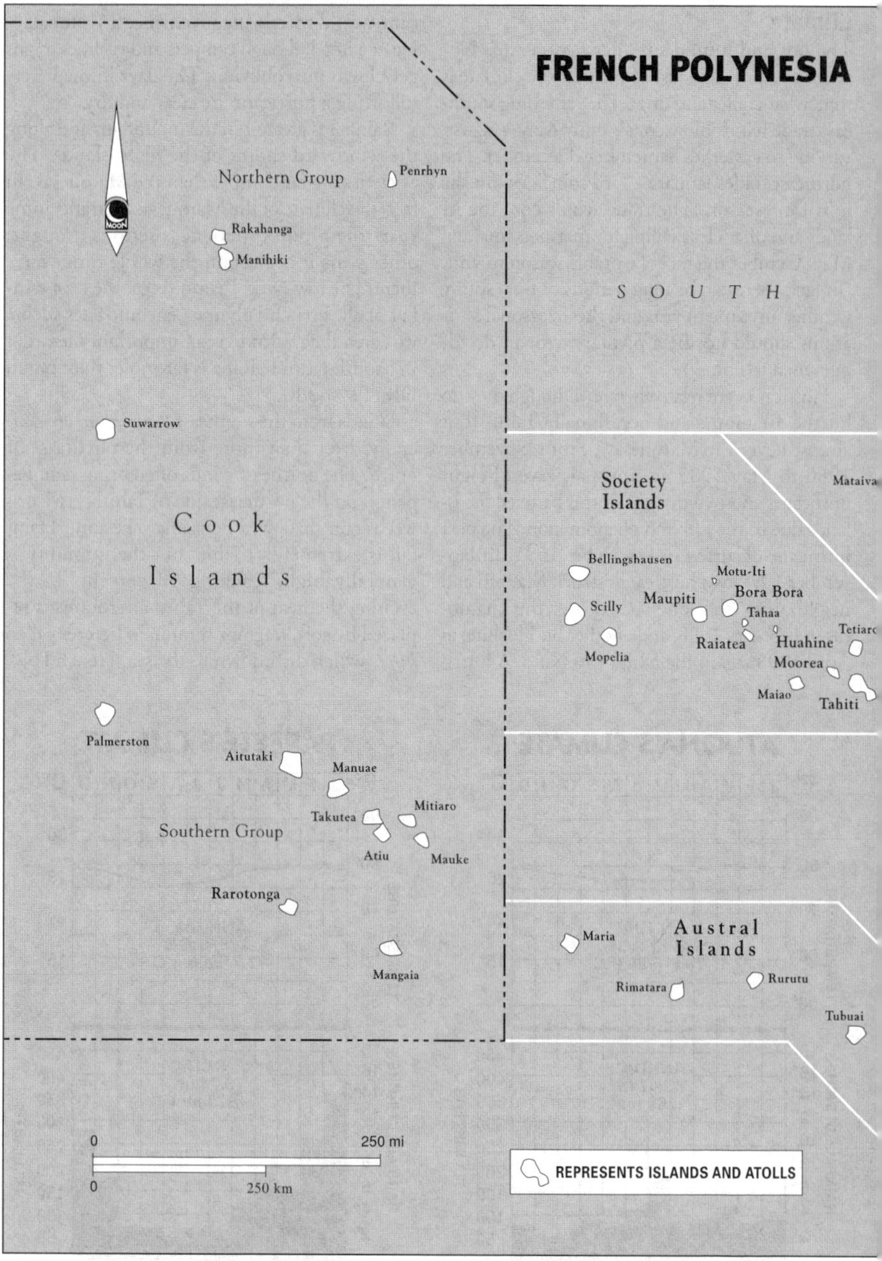

FRENCH POLYNESIA

Northern Group

Penrhyn

Rakahanga

Manihiki

S O U T H

Suwarrow

Society
Islands

Mataiva

C o o k

I s l a n d s

Bellingshausen

Motu-Iti

Scilly

Maupiti

Bora Bora

Tahaa

Mopelia

Raiatea

Huahine

Tetiarc

Moorea

Maiao

Tahiti

Palmerston

Aitutaki

Manuae

Takutea

Mitiaro

Southern Group

Atiu

Mauke

Rarotonga

Maria

Austral
Islands

Mangaia

Rimatara

Rururu

Tubuai

0   250 mi

0   250 km

REPRESENTS ISLANDS AND ATOLLS

FRENCH POLYNESIA

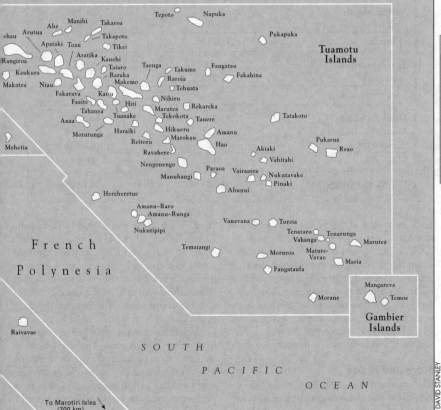

FRENCH POLYNESIA

FRENCH POLYNESIA AT A GLANCE

ISLAND	POPULATION (2002)	AREA (hectares)
Windward Islands	**184,224**	**118,580**
Tahiti	169,674	104,510
Moorea	14,226	12,520
Leeward Islands	**30,221**	**38,750**
Huahine	5,757	7,480
Raiatea	11,133	17,140
Taha'a	4,845	9,020
Bora Bora	7,295	2,930
Maupiti	1,191	1,140
Austral Islands	**6,386**	**14,784**
Rurutu	2,104	3,235
Tubuai	1,979	4,500
Tuamotu Islands	**14,765**	**72,646**
Rangiroa	2,334	7,900
Manihi	789	1,300
Gambier Islands	**1,097**	**4,597**
Marquesas Islands	**8,712**	**104,930**
Nuku Hiva	2,652	33,950
Hiva Oa	2,015	31,550
FRENCH POLYNESIA	**245,405**	**354,287**

nesia enjoys some of the cleanest air on earth—air that hasn't blown over a continent for weeks.

Tahiti and Moorea have a solar (rather than a lunar) tide which means that the low tides are at sunrise and sunset, high tides at noon and midnight. Because of this, snorkeling in or near a reef passage will be safest in the morning as the water flows in. Shallow waters are best traversed by yachts around noon when the water is high and slack, and visibility is at its peak.

Flora and Fauna

The national flower, the delicate, heavily scented *tiare Tahiti (Gardenia tahitiensis),* can have anywhere from six to nine white petals. It blooms year-round, but especially from September to April. In his *Plants and Flowers of Tahiti* Jean-Claude Belhay writes: "The tiare is to Polynesia what the lotus is to India: a veritable symbol." Follow local custom by wearing this blossom or a hibiscus behind your left ear if you're happily taken, behind your right ear if you're still available.

In the coastal areas of Tahiti most of the plants now seen have been introduced by humans. Avocado, banana, custard apple, guava, grapefruit, lime, lychee, mango, orange, papaya, pineapple, watermelon, and a hundred more are cultivated. Mountain bananas *(fei)* grow wild in the high country. *Mape* (Tahitian chestnut) grows along the streams, and other trees you'll encounter include almond, candlenut, casuarina (ironwood), flamboyant, barringtonia, *purau* (wild hibiscus), pistachio, and rosewood. A South American tree, *Miconia calvescens,* was planted at the botanical garden next to the Gauguin Museum in 1937, from which it spread across much of central Tahiti, supplanting the native vegetation.

Of the 104 species of birds in French Polynesia, half of the 30 species of native land birds are found only here. Among the 48 species of seabirds are the white-tailed tropic birds, brown and black noddies, white and crested terns, petrels, and boobies. The *itatae* (white tern), often seen flying about with its mate far from land, lays a single egg in the fork of a tree without any nest. The baby terns can fly soon after hatching. Its call is a sharp ke-ke-yek-yek. The *oio* (black noddy) nests in colonies, preferably in palm trees, building a flat nest of dead leaves, sticks, and stems. It calls a deep cra-cra-cra. Thirteen species of North American or Siberian land birds visit occasionally and another 13 species of introduced birds are always here. The most notorious among them is the hopping common mynah bird *(Acridotheres tristis)* with its yellow beak and feet which was introduced from Indonesia at the turn of the century to control insects. Today these noisy, aggressive birds are ubiquitous—feeding on fruit trees and forcing the native finches and blue-tinged doves out of their habitat.

HISTORY
Polynesian Culture

The eastern Polynesian islands, including those of French Polynesia, were colonized at uncertain dates around the start of the 1st millennium A.D. It's thought that about 300 B.C. the Polynesians reached the Marquesas from Samoa, and sometime before A.D. 300 they sailed on from the Marquesas to Hawaii and Easter Island. They were on the Society Islands by 600 and sailed from there to the Cooks and New Zealand before 1100, completing the occupation of the Polynesian triangle. On these planned voyages of colonization they carried all the plants and animals needed to continue their way of life.

The Polynesians lived from fishing and agriculture, using tools made from stone, bone, shell, and wood. The men were responsible for plant-

ing, harvesting, fishing, cooking, and house and canoe building; the women tended the fields and animals, gathered food and fuel, prepared food, and made tapa clothes and household items. Both men and women worked together in family or community groups, not as individuals.

The Polynesians lost the art of pottery making during their long stay in Havaiki (possibly Samoa) and had to cook their food in underground ovens *(umu)*. It was sometimes *tapu* (taboo) for men and women to eat together. Breadfruit, taro, yams, sweet potatoes, bananas, and coconuts were cultivated (the Polynesians had no cereals). Pigs, chickens, and dogs were also kept for food, but the surrounding sea yielded the most important source of protein.

Canoes were made of planks stitched together with sennit and caulked with gum from breadfruit trees. Clothing consisted of tapa (bark cloth). Both men and women wore belts of pandanus leaves or tapa when at work, and during leisure, a skirt that reached to their knees. Ornaments were of feathers, whale or dolphin teeth, and flowers. Both sexes were artfully tattooed using candlenut oil and soot.

For weapons there were clubs, spears, and slings. Archery was practiced only as a game to determine who could shoot farthest. Spear throwing, wrestling, boxing, kite flying, surfing, and canoe racing were popular sports. Polynesian music was made with nasal flutes and cylindrical sharkskin or hollow slit drums. Their dancing is still appreciated today.

The museums of the world possess many fine stone and wood tikis in human form from the Marquesas Islands, where the decorative sense was highly developed. Sculpture in the Australs was more naturalistic, and only here were female tikis common. The Tahitians showed less interest in the plastic arts but excelled in the social arts of poetry, oratory, theater, music, song, and dance. Life on the Tuamotus was a struggle for existence, and objects had utilitarian functions. Countless Polynesian cult objects were destroyed in the early 19th century by overzealous missionaries.

Prior to European contact three hereditary classes structured the Society Islands: high chiefs *(ari'i),* lesser chiefs *(raatira),* and commoners *(manahune).* A small slave class *(titi)* also existed. The various *ari'i* tribes controlled wedge-shaped valleys, and their authority was balanced. None managed to gain permanent supremacy over the rest. In this rigid hierarchical system, where high chiefs had more mana than commoners, marriage or even physical contact between persons of unequal mana was forbidden. Children resulting from sexual relations between the classes were killed.

Religion centered around an open-air temple, called a *marae,* with a stone altar. Here priests prayed to the ancestors or gods and conducted all the significant ceremonies of Polynesian life. An individual's social position was determined by his or her family connections, and the recitation of one's genealogy confirmed it. Human sacrifices took place on important occasions on a high chief's *marae.* Cannibalism was rife in the Marquesas and was also practiced in the Tuamotus.

Members of the Raiatea-based Arioi Society traveled through the islands performing ritual copulation and religious rites. The fertility god Oro had descended on a rainbow to Bora Bora's Mount Pahia, where he found a beautiful *vahine.* Their child was the first Arioi. In their pursuit of absolute *free* love, the Arioi shared spouses and killed their own children.

But the Arioi were not the only practitioners of infanticide in French Polynesia. The whole social structure could be threatened by a surplus of children among the chiefly class. Such children might demand arable land from commoners who supplied the chiefs with food. And a struggle between too many potential heirs could create strife. Thus the *ari'i* often did away with unwanted infants after birth (rather than before birth as happens today). The Arioi Society itself may have been a partial solution as unwanted *ari'i* children were assigned a benign role as Arioi with the assurance that they themselves would never produce any offspring.

European Exploration

While the Polynesian history of the islands goes back two millennia, the European period only began in the 16th century when the Magellan expedition sailed past the Tuamotus and Men-

daña visited the Marquesas. The Spaniard Quirós saw the Tuamotus in 1606, as did the Dutchmen Le Maire and Schouten in 1616, the Dutchman Roggeveen in 1722, and the Englishman Byron in 1765. But it was not until June 18, 1767 that Capt. Samuel Wallis on the HMS *Dolphin* happened upon Tahiti. He and most of his contemporary explorers were in search of *terra australis incognita,* a mythical southern landmass thought to balance the Northern Hemisphere.

At first the Tahitians attacked the ship, but after experiencing European gunfire they decided to be friendly. Eager to trade, they loaded the Englishmen down with pigs, fowl, and fruit. Iron was in the highest demand, and Tahitian women lured the sailors to exchange nails for love. Consequently, to prevent the ship's timbers from being torn asunder for the nails, no man was allowed onshore except in parties strictly for food and water. Wallis sent ashore a landing party, which named Tahiti "King George III Island," turned some sod, and hoisted the Union Jack. A year later the French explorer Louis-Antoine de Bougainville arrived on the east coast, unaware of Wallis's discovery, and claimed Tahiti for the king of France.

Wallis and Bougainville only visited briefly, leaving it to Capt. James Cook to really describe Polynesia to Europeans. Cook visited "Otaheite" four times, in 1769, 1773, 1774, and 1777. His first three-month visit was to observe the transit of the planet Venus across the face of the sun. The second and third were in search of the southern continent, while the fourth was to locate a northwest passage between the Pacific and Atlantic oceans. Some of the finest artists and scientists of the day accompanied Captain Cook. Their explorations added the Leeward Islands, two Austral islands, and a dozen Tuamotu islands to European knowledge. On Tahiti, Cook met a high priest from Raiatea named Tupaia, who had an astonishing knowledge of the Pacific and could name dozens of islands. He drew Cook a map that included the Cook Islands, the Marquesas, and perhaps also some Samoan islands!

In 1788 Tahiti was visited for five months by HMS *Bounty* commanded by Lt. William Bligh with orders to collect young breadfruit plants for transportation to the West Indies. However, the famous mutiny did not take place at Tahiti but in Tongan waters, and from there Bligh and loyal members of his crew managed to escape by navigating an open boat 6,500 km to Dutch Timor. In 1791, the HMS *Pandora* came to Tahiti in search of the *Bounty* mutineers, intending to take them to England for trial. They captured 14 survivors of the 16 who had elected to stay on Tahiti when Fletcher Christian and eight others left for Pitcairn. Although glamorized by Hollywood, the mutineers helped destroy traditional Tahitian society by acting as mercenaries for rival chiefs. In 1792 Bligh returned to Tahiti in another ship and completed his original mission.

By the early 19th century, ruffian British and American whalers were fanning out over the Pacific. Other ships traded with the islanders for sandalwood, bêche-de-mer, and mother-of-pearl, as well as the usual supplies. They brought with them smallpox, measles, influenza, tuberculosis, scarlet fever, and venereal diseases, which devastated the unprepared Polynesians. Slave raids, alcohol, and European firearms did the rest.

Kings and Missionaries

In March 1797 the ship *Duff* dropped off on Tahiti 18 Protestant missionaries and their wives after a 207-day journey from England. By this time Pomare, chief of the area adjoining Matavai Bay, had become powerful through the use of European tools, firearms, and mercenaries. He welcomed the missionaries but would not be converted; infanticide, sexual freedom, and human sacrifices continued. By 1800 all but five of the original 18 had left Tahiti disappointed.

In 1803 Pomare I died and his despotic son, Pomare II, attempted to conquer the entire island. After initial success he was forced to flee to Moorea in 1808. Missionary Henry Nott went with him, and in 1812 Pomare II turned to him for help in regaining his lost power. Though the missionaries refused to baptize Pomare II himself because of his heathen and drunken habits, his subjects on Moorea became nominal Christians. In 1815 this "Christian king" managed to regain Tahiti and overthrow paganism. Instead of being punished, the defeated clans were forgiven

and allowed to become Christians. The persistent missionaries then enforced the Ten Commandments and dressed the Tahitian women in "Mother Hubbard" costumes—dresses that covered their bodies from head to toe. Henceforth singing anything but hymns was banned, dancing proscribed, and all customs that offended puritanical sensibilities wiped away. Morality police terrorized the confused Tahitians in an eternal crusade against sin. Even the wearing of flowers in the hair was prohibited.

The Rape of Polynesia

Upon Pomare II's death from drink at age 40 in 1821, the crown passed to his infant son, Pomare III, but he passed away in 1827. At this juncture the most remarkable Tahitian of the 19th century, Aimata, half-sister of Pomare II, became Queen Pomare Vahine IV. She was to rule Tahiti, Moorea, and part of the Austral and Tuamotu groups for half a century until her death in 1877, a barefoot Tahitian Queen Victoria. She allied herself closely with the London Missionary Society (LMS), and when two fanatical French-Catholic priests, Honoré Laval and François Caret, arrived on Tahiti in 1836 from their stronghold at Mangareva (Gambier Islands), she expelled them promptly. (Turn to The Gambier Islands for more information on Père Laval.)

This affront brought a French frigate to Papeete in 1838, demanding $2,000 compensation and a salute to the French flag. Although the conditions were met, the queen and her chiefs wrote to England appealing for help, but none came. A Belgian named Moerenhout who had formerly served as the U.S. consul was appointed French consul to Queen Pomare in 1838, and in 1839 a second French gunboat arrived and threatened to bombard Tahiti unless 2,000 Spanish dollars were paid and Catholic missionaries given free entry. Back in Mangareva, Laval pushed forward a grandiose building program, which wiped out 80 percent of the population of the Gambiers from overwork.

In September 1842, while the queen and George Pritchard, the English consul, were away, Moerenhout tricked four local chiefs into signing a petition asking to be brought under French

FRENCH POLYNESIA

"protection." This demand was immediately accepted by French Admiral Abel Dupetit-Thouars, who was in league with Moerenhout, and on September 9, 1842 they forced Queen Pomare to accept a French protectorate. When the queen tried to maintain her power and keep her red-and-white royal flag, Dupetit-Thouars deposed the queen on November 8, 1843 and occupied her kingdom, an arbitrary act that was rejected by the French king, who reestablished the protectorate in 1844. Queen Pomare fled to Raiatea and Pritchard was deported to England in March 1844, bringing Britain and France to the brink of war. The Tahitians resisted for three years: old French forts and war memorials recall the struggle.

A French Protectorate

At the beginning of 1847, when Queen Pomare realized that no British assistance was forthcoming, she and her people reluctantly accepted the French protectorate. As a compromise, the British elicited a promise from the French not to annex the Leeward Islands, so Huahine, Raiatea, and Bora Bora remained independent until 1887. The French had taken possession of the Marquesas in 1842, even before imposing a protectorate on Tahiti. The Austral Islands were added in 1900 and only prior British action prevented the annexation of the Cook Islands. French missionaries attempted to convert the Tahitians to Catholicism, but only in the Marquesas were they fully successful.

Queen Pomare tried to defend the interests of her people as best she could, but much of her nation was dying: between the 18th century and 1926 the population of the Marquesas fell from 80,000 to only 2,000. In April 1774 Captain Cook had tried to estimate the population of Tahiti by counting the number of men he saw in a fleet of war canoes and ascribing three members to each one's family. Cook's figure was 204,000, but according to anthropologist Bengt Danielsson, the correct number at the time of discovery was about 150,000. By 1829 it had dropped to 8,568, and a low of 7,169 was reached in 1865. The name "Pomare" means "night cough," from *po,* night, plus *mare,* cough, because Pomare I's infant daughter died of tuberculosis in 1792.

Pomare V, the final, degenerate member of the line, was more interested in earthly pleasures than the traditions upheld by his mother. In 1880, with French interests at work on the Panama Canal, a smart colonial administrator convinced him to sign away his kingdom for a 5,000-franc-a-month pension. Thus, on June 29, 1880, the protectorate became the full French colony it is today, the Etablissements français de l'Océánie. In 1957 the name was changed to Polynésie française. Right up until the 1970s the colony was run by governors appointed in Paris who implemented the policies of the French government. There was no system of indirect rule through local chiefs as was the case in the British colonies: here French officials decided everything and their authority could not be questioned. Even the 18-member Conseil Générale created in 1885 to oversee certain financial matters had its powers reduced in 1899 and was replaced in 1903 by an impotent advisory council composed of French civil servants. The only elected official with any authority (and a budget) was the mayor of Papeete.

The most earthshaking event between 1880 and 1960 was a visit by two German cruisers, the *Scharnhorst* and *Gneisenau,* which shelled Papeete, destroying the marketplace on September 22, 1914. (Two months later both were sunk by the British at the Battle of the Falkland Islands.) A thousand Tahitian volunteers subsequently served in Europe, 300 of them becoming casualties. On September 2, 1940 the colony declared its support for the Free French, and soon after Pearl Harbor the Americans arrived to establish a base on Bora Bora. Polynesia remained cut off from occupied metropolitan France until the end of the war, although several hundred Tahitians served with the Pacific battalion in North Africa and Italy. In 1946 the colony was made an overseas territory or *territoire d'outre-mer* (TOM) endowed with an elected territorial assembly. Representation in the French parliament was also granted.

The economy of the early colonial period had been based on cotton growing (1865–1900), vanilla cultivation (1870–1960), pearl shell collecting (1870–1960), copra making, and phosphate mining (1908–1966). These were to be replaced by nuclear testing (1963–1996), tourism (1961–present), and cultured pearls (1968–present).

The Nuclear Era

The early 1960s were momentous times for Polynesia. Within a few years, an international airport opened on Tahiti, MGM filmed *Mutiny on the Bounty,* and the French began testing their atomic bombs. After Algeria became independent in July 1962 the French decided to move their Sahara nuclear testing facilities to Moruroa Atoll in the Tuamotu Islands, 1,200 km southeast of Tahiti. In 1963, when all local political parties protested the invasion of Polynesia by thousands of French troops and technicians sent to establish a nuclear testing center, President Charles de Gaulle simply outlawed political parties. The French set off their first atmospheric nuclear explosion at Moruroa on July 2, 1966, spreading contamination as far as Peru and New Zealand. In 1974 international protests forced the French to switch to the underground tests that continued until 1996. During those three decades of infamy 181 nuclear explosions, 41 of them in the atmosphere, rocked the Tuamotus.

In the 1960s–70s, as independence blossomed across the South Pacific, France tightened its strategic grip on French Polynesia. The spirit of the time is best summed up in the life of one man, Pouvanaa a Oopa, an outspoken WW I hero from Huahine. In 1949 he became the first Polynesian to occupy a seat in the French Chamber of Deputies. His party gained control of the territorial assembly in 1953 and in 1957 he was elected vice-president of the newly formed Government Council. In 1958 Pouvanaa campaigned for independence in a referendum vote, but when this failed due to a controversy over the imposition of an income tax, the French government reestablished central control and had Pouvanaa arrested on trumped-up charges of arson. He was eventually sentenced to an eight-year prison term, and exiled to France for 15 years. De Gaulle wanted Pouvanaa out of the way until French nuclear testing facilities could be established in Polynesia, and he was not freed until 1968. In 1971 he won the French Polynesian seat in the French Senate, a post he held until his death in early 1977. Tahitians refer to the man as *metua* (father), and his statue stands in front of Papeete's Territorial Assembly.

Pouvanaa's successors, John Teariki and Francis Sanford, were also defenders of Polynesian autonomy and opponents of nuclear testing. Their combined efforts convinced the French government to grant Polynesia a new statute with a slightly increased autonomy in 1977. A year later Faa'a mayor Oscar Temaru formed Tavini Huiraatira, the Polynesian Liberation Front, the leading antinuclear, pro-independence party in the territory. The 1982 territorial elections were won by the neo-Gaullist Tahoeraa Huiraatira (Popular Union), led by the pro-nuclear, anti-independence mayor of Pirae, Gaston Flosse, who still heads the local government today. To stem growing support for independence, Flosse negotiated enhanced autonomy for the territory in 1984 and 1996.

Flosse's reputation for fixing government contracts earned him the title "Mr. Ten Percent" from the Paris newspaper *Libération.* There have been numerous allegations of corruption in his administration, and in early 2000 Flosse was convicted of abuse of public funds and given an eight-month suspended sentence. Flosse and Tahoeraa Huiraatira remain in office thanks to the massive subsidies French Polynesia receives. The political reality here is that a majority of voters are unwilling to jeopardize their standard of living by electing to break French Polynesia's ties with France.

The independence cause was given impetus by France's last fling at nuclear testing. In April 1992, President Mitterrand halted the testing program at Moruroa, but in June 1995, newly elected President Jacques Chirac ordered a resumption of underground nuclear testing in the Tuamotus, and despite worldwide protests the first test was carried out on September 5, 1995. Early the next morning nonviolent demonstrators blocked the runway of Faa'a Airport after it was reported that Gaston Flosse was attempting to escape to France. When police charged the protesters to clear the runway, the demonstration turned into an ugly riot in which the airport and Papeete were ransacked.

Meanwhile at the Moruroa test site, two large Greenpeace protest vessels had been boarded by tear gas-firing French commandos and impounded (the ships were not released until six months later). Worldwide condemnation of the test series reached unprecedented levels, and in January 1996 the French announced that the testing had been completed. The facilities on Moruroa have since been decommissioned and it's highly unlikely the testing will ever resume, yet deadly radiation may already be leaking into the sea through cracks in the atoll's porous coral cap. A mantle of secrecy hangs over the France's former nuclear playground in the South Pacific and many of the 15,000 workers exposed to contamination during the 30 years of testing are now demanding an independent medical inquiry and compensation from France. (For more information, turn to The Nuclear Test Zone in the Tuamotu Islands section.)

Since 1996 Flosse and party have attempted to enhance the illusion of autonomy by developing the concept of Tahiti Nui or "Greater Tahiti." Tens of millions of Euros have been spent to build a new waterfront promenade and presidential palace (occupied by Flosse) in Papeete and an immense town hall and six-story general hospital at Pirae (Flosse's hometown). Raiatea has been given a new cruise ship terminal and five-star resorts have been erected on half a dozen islands. The government-sponsored airline, Air Tahiti Nui, has been granted landing rights in Paris, thereby forcing two French airlines (Air Lib and Corsair) to drop the route, and a territorial TV station, Tahiti Nui TV or "Télé Gaston," has been launched. In May 2004, a stunning upset occurred in elections for an expanded 57-seat Territorial Assembly. Flosse's party lost its majority for the first time in decades, and the pro-independence leader Oscar Temaru became president of French Polynesia. Temaru declared his willingness to negotiate with France and warned his followers that the road to true independence remained long. This dramatic change seems likely to speed up moves toward autonomy and the territory's integration into the South Pacific as a whole.

GOVERNMENT

In 1885 an organic decree created the colonial system of government, which remained in effect until the proclamation of a new statute in 1958. In 1977 the French granted the territory partial internal self-government, and Francis Sanford was elected premier of "autonomous" Polynesia. A new local-government statute, passed by the French parliament and promulgated on September 6, 1984, gave slightly more powers to the Polynesians, and in 1996 additional powers were transferred to the territory to slow the momentum toward full independence. Yet the constitution of the Republic of France remains the supreme law of the land and local laws can be overturned by a Constitutional Council comprised of French judges.

A Territorial Assembly elects the president of the government, who chooses 15 cabinet ministers (prior to 1984 the French high commissioner was the chief executive). The 57 assembly members are elected every five years from separate districts. In the May 2004 elections, the pro-independence Union for Democracy (UPD) won 27 seats, Flosse's Tahoeraa Huiraatira 26 seats, and two smaller parties one seat each. The territory is represented in Paris by two elected deputies, a senator (to be increased to two senators in 2007), and a social and economic counselor. The French government (www.outremer.gouv.fr), through its high commissioner (called governor until 1977), retains control over foreign relations, immigration, defense, justice, the police, the municipalities, higher education, radio and TV, property rights, and the currency.

French Polynesia is divided into 48 communes, each with an elected Municipal Council, which chooses a mayor from its ranks. Every main town on an island will have its *mairie* or *hôtel de ville* (town hall). These elected municipal bodies, however, are controlled by appointed French civil servants, who run the five administrative subdivisions. The administrators of the Windward, Tuamotu-Gambier, and Austral subdivisions are based at Papeete, while the headquarters of the Leeward Islands administration is at Uturoa (Raiatea), and that of the Marquesas Islands is at Taiohae (Nuku Hiva).

The territorial flag consists of horizontal red, white, and red bands with a double-hulled Polynesian sailing canoe superimposed on the white band. On the canoe are five figures representing the five archipelagos.

ECONOMY

The inflow of people and money since the early 1960s has stimulated consumerism, and except for tourism and cultured pearls, the economy of French Polynesia is now dominated by French government spending. The nuclear testing program provoked an influx of 30,000 French settlers, plus a massive infusion of capital, which distorted the formerly self-supporting economy into one totally dependent on France.

French Polynesia has the highest per capita gross domestic product (GDP) in the South Pacific, some CFP 1,910,000 pp in the year 2001 or nearly seven times as much as Fiji. Paris contributes little to the territorial budget, but it finances the many departments and services under the direct control of the high commissioner, spending an average of 1,000 million Euros a year in the territory or nearly a third of the GDP. Most of it goes to the military and to the 2,200 expatriate French civil servants who earn salaries 84 percent higher than those doing the same work in France. Of the total workforce of 58,000, about 40 percent work for some level of government while the other 60 percent are privately employed. Four out of every five jobs is in services. Unemployment is 13 percent.

In 1994 the territorial government introduced an income tax of 2 percent on earnings over CFP 150,000 a month, plus new taxes on gasoline, wine, telecommunications, and unearned income. Indirect taxes, such as licensing fees and customs duties long accounted for over half of territorial government revenue. In 1998 it was announced that customs duties would be reduced and the lost revenue replaced by a *taxe sur la valeur ajoutée* (TVA) or value-added tax (VAT) added to the price of most goods and services. In January 2002, the TVA was increased to 6 percent on groceries and hotel rooms, 10 percent on services, and 16 percent on goods. For decades the price of imported goods has been doubled by taxation and this new consumption tax has further increased the cost of living. Imports are now taxed at the rate of 15 percent (compared to 30 percent in 1999).

The conclusion of nuclear testing in 1996 meant that 1,000 local workers had to be laid off and tax revenues on military imports suddenly dropped. To compensate for this and to shore up the fortunes of their local political allies, the French government agreed to a "Pacte de Progrès," which provides the territory with an additional subsidy of CFP 18,000 million a year. Initially these payments were to have ended in 2006 but in mid-2002 they were extended infinitely.

Trade

Prior to the start of nuclear testing, trade was balanced. Only 35 years later, 2001 imports stood at CFP 140,948 million while exports amounted to just CFP 18,701 million, one of the highest disparities in the world. Much of the imbalance is consumed by the French administration itself. Foreign currency spent by tourists on imported goods and services also helps steady the situation.

Nearly 45 percent of the imports come from France, which has imposed a series of self-favoring restrictions. Imports include food, fuel, building material, consumer goods, and automobiles. The main agricultural export from the outer islands is copra; copra production has been heavily subsidized by the government since 1967 to discourage migration to Tahiti. The copra is crushed into coconut oil and animal feed at the Papeete mill. Cultured pearls from farms in the Tuamotus are the biggest export by far accounting for 75 percent of the total.

Agriculture and Fishing

Labor recruiting for the nuclear testing program caused local agriculture to collapse in the mid-'60s. Between 1962 and 1988 the percentage of the workforce employed in agriculture dropped from 46 percent to 10 percent, and today agriculture accounts for just under 5 percent of salaried employment. Vanilla and coconut oil combined now comprise only 3 percent of exports and the export of noni pulp to the U.S. for the making of juice is more important.

FRENCH POLYNESIA

About 80 percent of all food consumed locally is imported. Bread and rice are heavily subsidized by the government. Local vegetables supply half of local needs, while Tahitian coffee covers 20 percent of consumption. French Polynesia does manage, however, to cover three-quarters of its own fruit requirements, and the local pineapple and grapefruit crop goes to the fruit-juice factory on Moorea. Most industry is related to food processing (fruit-juice factory, brewery, soft drinks, etc.) or coconut products. It's rumored that marijuana *(pakalolo)* is now the leading cash crop, although you won't be aware of it. Large areas have been planted in Caribbean pine to provide for future timber needs. Considerable livestock is kept in the Marquesas.

Aquiculture is being developed, with tanks for freshwater shrimp, prawns, live bait, and green mussels. Until now most deep water fishing within the territory's huge exclusive economic zone has been done by foreign fleets, but their licenses are no longer being automatically renewed. Instead the territorial government has begun using some of the French structural adjustment money to build a tuna fishing fleet run by a territorial government-controlled company, Tahiti Rava'ai. The hope is to increase the tonnage of tuna landed locally tenfold by increasing the number of local boats from 30 to 150.

Cultured Pearls

According to myth, Oro, the Polynesian god of war, descended to earth on a rainbow to present a Bora Bora princess with a black pearl. Later pearls appeared on the mourning costumes of Tahitian priests at the funerals of important chiefs. The commercial quest for pearls began around 1870 as island divers wearing only tiny goggles plunged effortlessly to depths of 25–30 meters in the Tuamotu lagoons to collect oysters. Finding a pearl this way was one chance in 15,000, and the real objective was the shell which could be made into mother-of-pearl buttons. By 1960, overharvesting had depleted the slow-growing oyster beds and these days live oysters are collected only to supply cultured-pearl farms. The shell is now a mere by-product made into decorative items.

French Polynesia's cultured-pearl industry is now second only to tourism as a money earner, providing 75 percent of the territory's exports and around 10,000 jobs. It all began in 1963 when an experimental farm was established on Hikueru atoll in the Tuamotus. The first com-

BUYING A BLACK PEARL

The relative newness of this gemstone is reflected in varying prices. A radiant, perfectly round, smooth, and flawless pearl with a good depth of metallic green/blue can sell for many times more than a similar pearl with only one or two defects. The luster is more important than the color. Size can range 8–20 mm, with the larger pearls that much more expensive. Black pearls are now in fashion in Paris, so don't expect many bargains. A first-class necklace can cost as much as S$50,000 and individual pearls of the highest quality cost US$1,000 and up, but slightly flawed pearls are much cheaper (around US$100). The "baroque" pearls still make exquisite jewelry when mounted in gold and platinum. In recent years, prices have even come down as production begins to exceed demand.

Consider purchasing a loose pearl and having it mounted back home. If you think you might do this, check with your local jeweler before leaving for Tahiti or Rarotonga. Half the fun is in the shopping, so be in no hurry to decide and don't let yourself be influenced by a driver or guide who may only be after a commission. If no guide is involved the shop may even pay the commission to you in the form of a discount (ask). It's preferable to buy pearls at a specialized shop rather than somewhere that also sells pareus and souvenirs (and never buy a pearl from a person on the street). A reputable dealer will always give you an invoice or certificate verifying the authenticity of your pearl. If you've made an expensive choice ask the dealer to make a fresh X-ray right in front of you in order to be sure of the quality.

mercial farm opened on Manihi in 1968, but the real boom only commenced in the late 1980s, and today hundreds of cooperative and private pearl farms operate on 26 atolls, employing thousands of people. Although small companies and family operations are still able to participate in the industry, pearl production is becoming increasingly concentrated in a few hands due to the vertical integration of farming, wholesaling, and retailing. Robert Wan's Tahiti Perles now controls over half the industry and the next four companies account for another quarter of production.

The industry is drawing people back to ancestral islands they abandoned after devastating hurricanes in 1983. Pearl farming relieves pressure on natural stocks and creates an incentive to protect marine environments. Pollution from fertilizer runoff or sewage can make a lagoon unsuitable for pearl farming, which is why the farms are concentrated on lightly populated atolls where other forms of agriculture are scarcely practiced. On the down side, pearl farm workers often feed themselves with fish they catch in the lagoons, leading to a big decline in marine life. Another source of conflict are sea turtles, which crack open the oyster shells to get at one of their preferred foods. To prevent this, wire netting must be erected around the farms, although it's far easier for the farmers to simply to harvest the endangered turtles.

The strings of oysters must be constantly monitored and lowered or raised if there are variations in water temperature. The larger farms use high pressure hoses to clean the shells while smaller family operations often employ the traditional method of manually remove fouling organisms from the shells with a knife. Overcrowding can create disease hotspots that spread infections to other farms, and more research and government supervision will be required if this industry is to flourish in the long term.

Unlike the Japanese cultured white pearl, the Polynesian black pearl is formed only by the giant black-lipped oyster (Pinctada margaritifera), which thrives in the Tuamotu lagoons. It takes around three years for a pearl to form in a seeded oyster. A spherical pearl is formed when a Mississippi River mussel graft from Tennessee is introduced inside the coat; the oyster only creates a hemispherical half pearl if the graft goes between the coat and the shell. Half pearls are much cheaper than real pearls and make outstanding rings and pendants. Some of the grafts used are surprisingly large and the layer of nacre around such pearls may be relatively thin, but only an X-ray can tell. Thin coating on a pearl greatly reduces its value.

The cooperatives sell their production at Papeete auctions held twice a year. Local jewelers vie with Japanese buyers at these events, with some 60,000 black pearls in 180 lots changing hands for about CFP 750 million. Private producers sell their pearls through independent dealers or plush retail outlets in Papeete. Every year about a million black pearls worth CFP 15,000 million are exported to Japan, Hong Kong, the United States, France, and Switzerland, making the territory the world's second-largest source of loose pearls (after Australia which produces the smaller yellow pearls). To control quality and pricing, the export of loose reject pearls is prohibited, although finished jewelry is exempt. Pearl prices have fallen sharply in recent years due to overproduction and smuggling to avoid the export tax.

Tourism

French Polynesia is second only to Fiji as a South Pacific destination, with 189,003 visitors in 2002, a quarter of them from France and another quarter from the United States. Japan, New Zealand, Germany, Italy, Britain, Canada, and New Caledonia also account for significant numbers. Yet tourism is far less developed here than it is in Hawaii. A single Waikiki hotel could have more rooms than the entire island of Tahiti; Hawaii gets more visitors in 10 days than French Polynesia gets in a year.

Tourism by high-budget Japanese (especially honeymooners) is being vigorously promoted and the number of European visitors is growing. The CFP 47,000 million a year generated by tourism covers a third of French Polynesia's import bill and provides thousands of jobs, but 80 percent of the things tourists buy are also imported. Many of the luxury resorts are foreign owned and operated, and in some cases resort development has

© M.E. DE VOS

Papeete waterfront, Tahiti

been at the expense of the environment. Lagoons have been pillaged to provide sand for artificial beaches. We've received complaints from readers about improper waste disposal on Tahiti, Huahine, and Bora Bora. Tourism development contributed to the 20 percent increase in the populations of Moorea and Bora Bora between the 1996 and 2002 censuses.

THE PEOPLE

The 2002 population of 245,405 is around 63 percent Polynesian, 12 percent European, 17 percent Polynesian/European, 5 percent Chinese, and 3 percent Polynesian/Chinese. All are French citizens. About 69 percent of the total population lives on Tahiti (compared to only 25 percent before the nuclear-testing boom began in the 1960s), but a total of 65 far-flung islands are inhabited.

The indigenous people of French Polynesia are the Maohi or Eastern Polynesians (as opposed to the Western Polynesians in Samoa and Tonga), and some local nationalists refer to their country as Te Ao Maohi. The word *colon* formerly applied to Frenchmen who arrived long before the bomb and made a living as planters or

traders, and practically all of them married Polynesian women. Most of these *colons* have already passed away. Their descendants are termed *demis* or *afa* and they now dominate politics and the local bureaucracy. The present Europeans *(popa'a)* are mostly recently arrived metropolitan French *(faranis)*. Their numbers increased dramatically in the 1960s and 1970s, and most live in urban areas where they're involved in the administration, military, or professions. In contrast, very few Polynesians have migrated to France, although 7,000 reside in New Caledonia.

Local Chinese *(tinito)* dominate business throughout the territory. In Papeete and Uturoa entire streets are lined with Chinese stores, and individual Chinese merchants are found on almost every island. They're also prominent in pearl farming and tourism. During the American Civil War, when the supply of cotton to Europe was disrupted, Scotsman William Stewart decided to set up a cotton plantation on the south side of Tahiti. Unable to convince Tahitians to do the heavy work, Stewart brought in a contingent of 1,010 Chinese laborers from Canton in 1865–1866. When the war ended the enterprise went bankrupt, but many of the Chinese managed to stay on as market gardeners, hawkers, and opium dealers. Things began changing in 1964 when France recognized mainland China and granted French citizenship to the territory's Chinese (most other Tahitians had become French citizens right after WW II). The French government tried to assimilate the Chinese by requiring that they adopt French-sounding names and by closing all Chinese schools. Despite this, the Chinese community has remained distinct.

From 1976 to 1983 some 18,000 people migrated to the territory, 77 percent of them from France and another 13 percent from New Caledonia. Nearly 1,000 new settlers a year continue to arrive. Some 40,000 Europeans are now present in the territory, plus 8,000 soldiers, policemen, and transient officials. Most Tahitians would like to see this immigration restricted, as it is in virtually every other Pacific state. French citizens even have a tax incentive to come since they become legal residents after six months and one day in the territory and are thus exempt from French income tax (in French Polynesia the tax rate is only 2 percent). There's an undercurrent of anti-French sentiment; English speakers are better liked by the Tahitians.

Sex

Since the days of Wallis and Bougainville, Tahitian women have had a reputation for promiscuity. Well, for better or worse, this is largely a thing of the past, if it ever existed at all. As a short-term visitor your liaisons with Tahitians are likely to remain polite. Westerners' obsession with the sexuality of Polynesians usually reflects their own frustrations, and the view that Tahitian morality is loose is rather ironic considering that Polynesians have always shared whatever they have, cared for their old and young, and refrained from ostracizing unwed mothers or attaching shame to their offspring.

Polynesia's *mahus* or "third sex" bear little of the stigma attached to female impersonators in the West. A young boy may adopt the female role by his own choice or that of his parents, performing female tasks at home and eventually finding a job usually performed by women, such as serving in a restaurant or hotel. Generally only one *mahu*

exists in each village or community, proof that this type of individual serves a certain sociological function. George Mortimer of the British ship *Mercury* recorded an encounter with a *mahu* in 1789. Though Tahitians may poke fun at a *mahu,* they're fully accepted in society, seen teaching Sunday school, etc. Many, but not all, *mahus* are also homosexuals. Today, with money all-important, some transvestites have involved themselves in male prostitution and the term *raerae* has been coined for this category. Now there are even Miss Tane (Miss Male) beauty contests!

Religion

Though the old Polynesian religion died out in the early 19th century, the Tahitians are still a strongly religious people. Protestant missionaries arrived on Tahiti 39 years before the Catholics and 47 years before the Mormons, so 45 percent of the people now belong to the Evangelical Church, which is strongest in the Austral and Leeward Islands. Until the middle of the 20th century this church was one of the only democratic institutions in the colony and it continues to exert strong influence on social matters (for example, it resolutely opposed nuclear testing).

Of the 34 percent of the total population who are Catholic, half are Polynesians from the Tuamotus and Marquesas, and the other half are French. Another 5 percent are Seventh-Day Adventists and 10 percent are Mormons. A Mormon group called Sanitos, which rejects Brigham Young as a second prophet, has had a strong following in the Tuamotus since the 19th century. Several other Christian sects are also represented, and some Chinese are Buddhists. It's not unusual to see two or three different churches in a village of 100 people. All the main denominations operate their own schools. Local ministers and priests are powerful figures in the outer-island communities. One vestige of the pre-Christian religion is a widespread belief in ghosts *(tupapau).*

Protestant church services are conducted mostly in Tahitian, and Catholic services are in French. Sitting through a service (one to two hours) is often worthwhile just to hear the singing and to observe the women's hats. Never wear a pareu to church—you'll be asked to leave. Young missionaries from the Church of Latter-day Saints (Mormons) continue to flock to Polynesia from the United States for two-year stays. They wear short-sleeved white shirts with ties and travel in pairs—you may spot a couple.

Language

French is spoken throughout the territory, and visitors will sometimes have difficulty making themselves understood in English, although most of those involved in the tourist industry speak some English. Large Chinese stores often have someone who speaks English. Young Polynesians often become curious and friendly when they hear you speaking English. Still, unless you're on a package tour, everything will be a lot easier if you know at least a little French. Check out some French language recordings from your local public library to brush up your high school French before you arrive.

Contemporary Tahitian is the chiefly or royal dialect used in the translation of the Bible by early Protestant missionaries, and today, as communications improve, the outer-island dialects are becoming mingled with the predominant Tahitian. Tahitian or Maohi is one of a family of Austronesian languages spoken from Madagascar through Indonesia, all the way to Easter Island and Hawaii. The related languages of Eastern Polynesia (Hawaiian, Tahitian, Tuamotuan, Mangarevan, Marquesan, Rarotongan, Maori) are quite different from those of Western Polynesia (Samoan, Tongan). Among the Polynesian languages, the consonants did the changing rather than the vowels. The *k* and *l* in Hawaiian are generally rendered as a *t* and *r* in Tahitian.

Instead of attempting to speak French to the Tahitians—a foreign language for you both—turn to the Tahitian vocabulary at the end of this book and give it a try. Remember to pronounce each vowel separately, *a* as the *ah* in "far," *e* as the *ai* in "day," *i* as the *ee* in "see," *o* as the *oh* in "go," and *u* as the *oo* in "lulu"—the same as in Latin or Spanish. Written Tahitian has only eight consonants: *f, h, m, n, p, r, t, v*. Two consonants never follow one another, and all words end in a vowel. No silent letters exist in Tahitian, but there is a glottal stop, often marked with an apos-

trophe. A slight variation in pronunciation or vowel length can change the meaning of a word completely, so don't be surprised if your efforts produce some unexpected results!

Some of the many English words that have entered Tahitian through contact with early seamen include: *faraipani* (frying pan), *manua* (man of war), *matete* (market), *mati* (match), *moni* (money), *oniani* (onion), *painapo* (pineapple), *pani* (pan), *pata* (butter), *pipi* (peas), *poti* (boat), *taiete* (society), *tapitana* (captain), *tauera* (towel), and *tavana* (governor).

CONDUCT AND CUSTOMS

The dress code in French Polynesia is very casual—you can even go around barefoot. Cleanliness *is* important, however. Formal wear or jacket and tie are unnecessary (unless you're to be received by the high commissioner!). One exception is downtown Papeete, where scanty dress would be out of place. For clothing tips, see What to Take in the Exploring the Islands chapter.

People usually shake hands when meeting; visitors are expected to shake hands with everyone present. If a Polynesian man's hand is dirty he'll extend his wrist or elbow. Women kiss each other on the cheeks. When entering a private residence it's polite to remove your shoes.

All the beaches of French Polynesia are public to one meter above the high-tide mark, although some watchdogs don't recognize this. Topless sunbathing is completely legal in French Polynesia and commonly practiced at resorts by European tourists, though total nudity is only permissible on offshore *motu* and floating pontoons.

Despite the apparent laissez-faire attitude promoted in the travel brochures and this book, female travelers should take care: There have been sexual assaults by Polynesian men on foreign women. Peeping toms can be a nuisance in both budget accommodations and on beaches away from the main resorts, and women should avoid staying alone in isolated tourist bungalows or camping outside organized campgrounds.

Safety is commonly the one thing you hope not to have to think about when you arrive at your destination, and certainly in French Polynesia it is easy to become more lax about your surroundings. But with any situation—here or at home—use common sense. If you are making reservations for a tour, ask how many other people have reservations and find out the minimum number of people the company is willing to take. Speak up when you feel uncomfortable, ignore unwanted advances, and report problems to management.

Exploring the Islands

Highlights

French Polynesia abounds in things to see and do, including many in the "not to be missed" category. Papeete's colorful morning market and captivating waterfront welcome you to Polynesia. Travelers should not pass up the opportunity to take the ferry ride to **Moorea** and see the island's stunning Opunohu Valley, replete with splendid scenery, lush vegetation, and fascinating archaeological sites. Farther afield, an even greater concentration of old Polynesian *marae* (temples) awaits visitors to Maeva on the enchanting island of **Huahine.** The natural wonders of **Bora Bora** have been applauded many times, and neighboring **Maupiti** offers more of the same, though its pleasures are less well known. Polynesia's most spectacular atoll may be **Rangiroa,** where the Avatoru and Tiputa passes offer exciting snorkel rides on the tide flows. Mysterious **Nuku Hiva** and **Hiva Oa** in the Marquesas are seldom forgotten by those who get that far. The manta ray and shark viewing on Moorea, Raiatea, and Bora Bora, and dolphin or whale encounters at Moorea and Rurutu, are memorable experiences.

Sports and Recreation

As elsewhere in the South Pacific, **scuba diving** is the most popular sport among visitors, and well-established dive shops exist on Tahiti, Moorea, Huahine, Raiatea, Taha'a, Bora Bora, Rangiroa, Manihi, Tikehau, Fakarava, Ahe, and Nuku Hiva. Drift dives and swimming with sharks, rays, eels, dolphins, and even whales are all offered. In the warm waters of Polynesia wetsuits are not required. If you take a scuba certification course make sure it's PADI accredited as the French CMAS certification may not be recognized elsewhere. **Snorkeling** is possible at many of the same places and it has the big advantage of being free.

There's good **surfing** around Tahiti, Moorea, Huahine, and Raiatea, usually hurricane swells on the north shores October–March (summer) and Antarctic swells on the south shores from April–September (winter). The summer swells are the same ones that hit Hawaii three or four days earlier. The reef breaks off the north shore of Moorea work better than Tahiti's beach breaks. The most powerful, hollow waves are in winter. The reef breaks in the passes are a lot longer paddle than those off the beaches (where you can expect lots of company). To avoid bad vibes, make a serious effort to introduce yourself to the local surfers.

Excellent, easily accessible **hiking** areas exist on Tahiti, Moorea, and Nuku Hiva. **Horseback riding** is readily available on Moorea, Huahine, Raiatea, and in the Marquesas with the Huahine and Raiatea operations especially recommended. **Golfers** will certainly want to complete all 18 holes at the International Golf Course Olivier Breaud on Tahiti. The Leeward Islands are a sailor's paradise with numerous protected anchorages and excellent **sailing** weather, which is why most of French Polynesia's charter yacht operations are concentrated on Raiatea.

Entertainment

The big hotels on Tahiti, Moorea, Huahine, and Bora Bora offer exciting dance shows several nights a week. They're generally accompanied by a barbecue or traditional feast, but if the price asked for the meal is too steep, settle for a drink at the bar and enjoy the show (usually no cover charge). Many of the regular performances are listed in this book, but be sure to confirm the times and dates as these do change to accommodate tour groups.

On Friday and Saturday nights discos crank up in most towns and these are good places to meet the locals. The non-hotel bar scene is limited mostly to Papeete and Uturoa. The drinking age in French Polynesia is officially 18, but it's not strictly enforced. Consuming alcohol on the street is not allowed.

Music and Dance

Protestant missionaries banned dancing in the 1820s and the 19th-century French colonial administration forbade performances which disturbed Victorian decorum. Dancing began to reappear as early as 1853, but only after 1908 were the restrictions fully removed. Traditional Tahitian dancing experienced a revival in the 1950s with the formation of Madeleine Moua's Pupu Heiva dance troupe, followed in the 1960s by Coco Hotahota's Temaeva and Gilles Hollande's Ora Tahiti. Yves Roche founded the Takiti ma ensemble in 1962. These groups rediscovered the nearly forgotten myths of old Polynesia and popularized them with exciting music, dance, song, and costumes. During major festivals several dozen troupes consisting of 20–50 dancers and 6–10 musicians participate in thrilling competitions.

The Tahitian *tamure* or *'ori Tahiti* is a fast, provocative, erotic dance done by rapidly shifting the weight from one foot to the other. The rubber-legged men are almost acrobatic, though their movements tend to follow those of the women closely. The tossing, shell-decorated fiber skirts *(mores)*, the hand-held pandanus wands, and the tall headdresses add to the drama.

Dances such as the *aparima, 'ote'a,* and *hivinau* reenact Polynesian legends, and each movement tells part of a story. The *aparima* or "kiss of the hands" is a slow dance resembling the Hawaiian hula or Samoan siva executed mainly with the hands in a standing or sitting position. The hand movements repeat the story told in the accompanying song. The *'ote'a* is a theme dance executed to the accompaniment of drums with great precision and admirable timing by a group of men wearing tall headdresses and/or women with wide belts arrayed in two lines. The *ute* is a restrained dance based on ancient refrains.

Listen to the staccato beat of the *to'ere,* a slit rosewood drum, each slightly different in size and pitch, hit with a stick. A split-bamboo drum *(ofe)* hit against the ground often provides a contrasting sound. The *pahu* is a more conventional bass drum made from a hollowed coconut tree trunk with a sharkskin cover. Its sound resembles the human heartbeat. The smallest *pahu* is the *fa'atete,* which is hit with sticks. Another traditional Polynesian musical instrument is the bamboo nose flute *(vivo),* which sounds rather like the call of a bird, though today guitars and ukuleles are more often seen. The ukulele was originally the *braguinha,* brought to Hawaii by Portuguese immigrants a century ago. Homemade ukuleles with the half-shells of coconuts as sound boxes emit pleasant tones, while those sporting empty tins give a more metallic sound. The hollow, piercing note produced by the conch shell or *pu* once accompanied pagan ceremonies on the *marae.*

Traditional Tahitian vocal music was limited to polyphonic chants conveying oral history and customs, and the contrapuntal *himene* or "hymn" sung by large choirs today is based on those ancient chants. As the singers sway to the tempo, the spiritual quality of the *himene* can be electrifying, so for the musical experience of a lifetime attend church any Sunday.

Public Holidays and Festivals

Public holidays in French Polynesia include New Year's Day (January 1), Gospel Day (March 5), Good Friday and Easter Monday (March/April), Labor Day (May 1), Victory Day (May 8), Ascension Day (May), Pentecost or Whitmonday (May/June), Internal Autonomy Day (June 29), Bastille Day (July 14), Assumption Day (August 15), All Saints' Day (November 1), Armistice Day (November 11), and Christmas Day (December 25). Ironically, Internal Autonomy Day really commemorates June 29, 1880, when King Pomare V was deposed and French Polynesia became a full French colony, not September 6, 1984, when the territory achieved a degree of internal autonomy. *Everything* will be closed on these holidays (and maybe also the days before and after—ask).

The big event of the year is the two-week-long **Heiva i Tahiti** (www.tahiti-heiva.org), which runs from the end of June to Bastille Day (July 14). Formerly known as La Fête du Juillet or the Tiurai Festival (the Tahitian word *tiurai* comes from the English July), the Heiva originated way back in 1882. Long before that, a pagan festival was held around this time to mark the southern hemisphere solstice. Today it brings contestants and participants to Tahiti from all over the territory to take part in elaborate processions, competitive dancing and singing, feasting, and partying. There are bicycle, car, horse, and outrigger-canoe races, *pétanque*, archery, and javelin-throwing contests, fire walking, sidewalk bazaars, arts and crafts exhibitions, tattooing, games, and joyous carnivals. **Bastille Day** itself, which marks the fall of the Bastille in Paris on July 14, 1789, at the height of the French Revolution, features a military parade in the capital. Ask at the Visitors Bureau in Papeete about when to see the historical reenactments at Marae Arahurahu, the canoe race along Papeete waterfront, horse racing at the Pirae track, and the Taupiti nui dance competitions at the Tahua To'ata next to the Cultural Center. Tickets to most Heiva events are sold at the Cultural Center in Papeete or at the gate. As happens during carnival in Rio de Janeiro, you must pay to sit in the stands to watch the best performances (CFP 1,500–2,500), but you get four hours or more of unforgettable nonstop entertainment.

The July celebrations on Bora Bora are as good as those on Tahiti, and festivals are also held on Raiatea and Taha'a at that time. Note that all ships, planes, and hotels are fully booked around July 14, so be in the right place beforehand or get firm reservations, especially if you want to be on Bora Bora that day. At this time of year, races, games, and dance competitions take place on many different islands, and the older women often prove themselves graceful dancers and excellent singers. On Moorea, there's a canoe race around the island during the Heiva.

Chinese New Year in January or February is celebrated with dances and fireworks. **World Environment Day** (June 5) is marked by guided excursions to Tahiti's interior, and on the following weekend special activities are arranged at tourist sites around the island. The **Agricultural Fair** on Tahiti in mid-August involves the construction of a Tahitian village. Papeete's **Carnaval de Tahiti** at the end of October features dancing contests (waltz, foxtrot, rock), nightly parades along boulevard Pomare, and several gala evenings. On **All Saints' Day** (November 1) the locals illuminate the cemeteries at Papeete, Arue, Punaauia, and elsewhere with candles. On **New Year's Eve** the Papeete waterfront is beautifully illuminated and there's a seven-km foot race.

Major Sporting Events

The 42-km **Tahiti Nui Marathon** has been held on northern Moorea every February since 1988. In 1997 Patrick Muturi of Kenya set the record time for men of two hours, 21 minutes, and 31 seconds. The women's record is held by Gitte Karlshoj of Denmark who logged two hours, 50 minutes, and 23 seconds in 1999. In May there's the **Gotcha Tahiti Pro** surfing competition off Tahiti-iti. The **Tahiti Open** at the Atimaono golf course on Tahiti is in July.

The **Te Aito** individual outrigger canoe race is held on Tahiti around the end of July. The **Hawaiki Nui Va'a** outrigger canoe race in October is a stirring three-day event with almost 100 canoe teams crossing from Huahine to Raiatea (44.5 km) the first day, Raiatea to Taha'a (26 km) the second, and Taha'a to Bora Bora (58 km) the third. The **Va'a Hine,** a women-only canoe race from Raiatea to Taha'a and back (40 km), occurs a day or two before the men's race. Also in October is **L'Aitoman de Moorea** or "Iron Man" triathlon with swimming (3.8 km), bicycle riding (180 km), and running (41 km).

Shopping

Most local souvenir shops sell Marquesas-style wooden "tikis" carved from wood or stone. The original Tiki was a god of fertility, and really old tikis are still shrouded in superstition. Today they're viewed mainly as good luck charms and often come decorated with mother-of-pearl. Other items carved from wood include mallets (to beat tapa cloth), *umete* bowls, and slit *to'ere* drums. Carefully woven pandanus hats and mats come from the Australs. Other curios to buy include hand-carved mother-of-pearl shell, sharks'-tooth pendants, hematite (black stone) carvings, and bamboo fishhooks.

Black-pearl jewelry is widely available throughout French Polynesia. The color, shape, weight, and size of the pearl are important. The darkest pearls are the most valuable. Prices vary considerably, so shop around before purchasing pearls. Be aware that the export of large numbers of unset pearls is prohibited without a license and the folks operating the x-ray machines at the airport are on the lookout. Black pearl prices have fallen considerably since 2001 due to oversupply, smuggling, and poor quality control.

As this is a French colony, it's not surprising that many of the best buys are related to fashion. A tropical shirt, sundress, or T-shirt is a purchase of immediate usefulness. The pareu is a typically Tahitian leisure garment consisting of a brightly colored hand-blocked or painted local fabric about two meters long and a meter wide. There are dozens of ways both men and women can wear a pareu and it's the most common apparel for local women throughout the territory, including Papeete, so pick one up! Local cosmetics like Monoï Tiare Tahiti, a fragrant coconut-oil skin moisturizer, and coconut-oil soap will put you in form. Jasmine shampoo, cologne, and perfume are also made locally from the tiare Tahiti flower. Vanilla is used to flavor coffee.

Early missionaries introduced the Tahitians to quilting, and two-layer patchwork *tifaifai* have now taken the place of tapa (bark cloth). Used as bed covers and pillows by tourists, *tifaifai* is still used by Tahitians to cloak newlyweds and to cover coffins. To be wrapped in a *tifaifai* is the highest honor. Each woman has individual quilt patterns that are her trademarks and bold floral designs are popular, with contrasting colors drawn from nature. A complicated *tifaifai* can take up to six months to complete and cost US$1,000. The French artist Henri Matisse, who in 1930 spent several weeks at the former Hôtel Stuart on Papeete's boulevard Pomare, was so impressed by the Tahitian *tifaifai* that he applied the same technique and adopted many designs for his *"gouaches découpees."*

Those who have been thrilled by hypnotic Tahitian music and dance will want to take some Polynesian music home with them on cassette (CFP 2,000) or compact disc (CFP 3,200), available at hotels and souvenir shops throughout the islands. The largest local company producing these CDs is Editions Manuiti or Tamure Records. Among the well-known local singers and musicians appearing on Manuiti are Bimbo, Charley Manu, Guy Roche, Yves Roche, Emma Terangi, Andy Tupaia, and Henriette Winkler. Small Tahitian groups like the Moorea Lagon Kaina Boys, the Barefoot Boys, and Tamarii Punaruu, and large folkloric ensembles such as Maeva Tahiti, Tiare Tahiti, and Coco's Temaeva (often recorded at major festivals) are also well represented. The Tahitian recordings of the Hawaiian artist Bobby Holcomb are highly recommended. Visit www.southpacific.org/music.html for specific CD listings.

Hustling and bargaining are not practiced in French Polynesia: it's expensive for everyone. Haggling may even be considered insulting, so just pay the price asked or keep looking. Black pearl jewelry is an exception: Because the markups are so high, discounts are often available.

ACCOMMODATIONS AND FOOD

Accommodations

Hotel prices range from CFP 1,300 for a dormitory bed all the way up to CFP 260,000 double without meals plus tax for an overwater suite at the Bora Bora Sheraton! Price wars sometimes erupt between rival resorts, and at times you'll be charged less than the prices quoted herein! When things are really slow even the luxury hotels sometimes discount their rooms. If your hotel can't provide running water, electricity, air-conditioning, or something similar because of a hurricane or otherwise, ask for a price reduction. You might get 10 percent off.

The 11 percent hotel tax consists of a 5 percent room tax used to finance "tourism promotions" and the 6 percent value added tax (VAT). This 11 percent tax is on top of the rack room rates at the 44 "classified hotels" (seldom included in the quoted price). The 5 percent tourist development tax doesn't apply to pensions and small family-operated accommodations, but they must still collect the 6 percent VAT (often included in the basic rate). Many islands add a *taxe de séjour* (sojourn tax) to accommodation bills to cover municipal services. This varies from CFP 150 pp per day at the large hotels to CFP 50 at the pensions and it's almost always charged extra.

Be aware that the large hotels frequently tack a CFP 1,000 or 10 percent commission onto any rental cars, lagoon excursions, and scuba diving booked through their front desks. Many small hotels add a surcharge to your bill if you stay only one night and some charge a supplement during the high seasons (July, Aug., and mid-Dec.–mid-Jan.). Discounts may be offered during the low months of February, March, September, and October.

A wise government regulation prohibiting buildings higher than a coconut tree outside Papeete means that most of the hotels are low-rise affairs or consist of small Tahitian *fare*. The small hotels and bungalows often provide cooking facilities and this allows you to save a lot on food.

French Polynesia is one of the few South Pacific destinations where camping is a practical option and a tent can prove very convenient to fall back on. Regular campgrounds exist on Moorea, Huahine, Raiatea, and Bora Bora. On Rangiroa it's possible to camp at certain small hotels (listed herein). On the outer islands camping should be no problem, but ask permission of the landowner, or pitch your tent well out of sight of the road. Ensure this hospitality for the next traveler by not leaving a mess. Make sure your tent is water- and mosquito-proof, and never pitch a tent directly below coconuts hanging from a tree or a precariously leaning trunk.

There are no official youth hostels but all of the campgrounds and many of the guesthouses offer dormitory beds for only slightly more than you'd pay to pitch a tent. Communal cooking facilities are usually provided and it's a good way to meet other budget travelers. Separate dormitories for men and women are rare.

Hotel Chains

Of the large hotels, those belonging to the Sofitel/Accor/Coralia group are the oldest and most poorly maintained (Bora Bora's Sofitel Motu is an exception). Beachcomber Inter-Continental and Le Méridien are somewhere in the middle, and Sheraton has some of the newest but not necessarily best-value properties. Amanresorts and Orient Express each has one upscale property on Bora Bora, and Club Med is also at Bora Bora.

French Polynesia's homegrown hotel chain, Pearl Resorts (www.pearlresorts.com), offers an increasing number of tasteful hotels in both the middle and top-end price range. Most of the Pearl Resorts properties are owned by Air Tahiti, Banque Socredo, and other investors. Five hotels owned by the French travel company Nouvelles Frontières are currently being redeveloped by the Paladien hotel chain and will serve the middle market when ready. The Maitai chain currently has two medium-priced resorts which are managed by the owner of the Beachcomber chain.

Overwater Bungalows

The overwater bungalow was invented in French Polynesia in the 1960s and you'll now find them on Tahiti, Moorea, Huahine, Raiatea, Taha'a, Bora Bora, Rangiroa, and Manihi. They range in price from CFP 25,000 double plus tax at Club Bali Hai on Moorea to CFP 245,000 at the Bora Bora Sheraton.

There's no doubt that this type of accommodation is environmentally harmful. The coral formations are inevitably impacted during construction and unconcerned guests do further damage by touching the living corals while snorkeling around their rooms. Much of the coral near the existing bungalows is dead and fish are present only because they are fed. We've heard reports of improper waste disposal at overwater bungalows.

The lagoons of French Polynesia are in the public domain and the resort owners are clearly profiting by using them as building sites. To boot, some resorts have employed huge dredges to suck sand from the lagoon floors for the construction of artificial beaches, thereby destroying the spawning areas of fishes and further damaging the coral.

FRENCH POLYNESIA

Pensions

A unique accommodations option is the well-established network of homestays, in which you get a private room or bungalow provided by a local family. *Logement chez l'habitant* is available on all the outer islands, and even in Papeete itself; the Visitors Bureau does a good job of providing printed lists of these places. Most travel agents abroad won't book the pensions or lodgings with the inhabitants because no commissions are paid, but you can make reservations directly with the owners themselves either by email or phone. Calling ahead from Papeete works well.

One Papeete travel agency specializing in such bookings is **Tekura Tahiti Travel** (tel. 43-12-00, fax 42-84-60, www.tahiti-tekuratravel.com), in the Vaima Center near Hawaiian Airlines, although they tend to work with the more up-market places. Air Tahiti's "Séjours dans les îles" packages (www.islandsadventures.com) are built largely around pensions. Most pensions don't accept credit cards, and English may not be spoken. Many have a two-night minimum stay or charge extra if you leave after one night.

These private guesthouses can be hard to locate. There's usually no sign outside, and some don't cater to walk-in clients who show up unexpectedly. Also, the limited number of beds in each may all be taken (most pensions have under 10 rooms). Sometimes you'll get airport transfers at no additional charge if you book ahead. Don't expect hot water in the shower or a lot of privacy. Blankets and especially towels may not be provided and the room won't be cleaned every day. Often meals are included (typically seafood), which can make these places quite expensive. If you're on a budget, ask for a place with cooking facilities and prepare your own food. The family may loan you a bicycle and can be generally helpful in arranging tours, etc. It's a great way to meet the people while finding a place to stay.

Food and Drink

The restaurants are often exorbitant, but you can bring the price down by ordering only a single main dish. Fresh bread and cold water should come with the meal. Avoid appetizers, alcohol, and desserts. No service charges are tacked on, and tipping is unnecessary, so it's not as expensive as it looks! US$15 will usually see you through an excellent no-frills lunch of fried fish at a small French restaurant. The same thing in a deluxe hotel dining room will be about 50 percent more. Even the finest places are affordable if you order this way.

Most restaurants post their menu in the window. If not, have a look at it before sitting down. Check the main plates, as that's all you'll need to take. If the price is right, the ambience congenial, and the local French are at the tables, sit right down. Sure, food at a snack bar would be half as much, but your Coke will be extra, and in the end it's smart to pay a little more to enjoy excellent cuisine once in a while. A large plastic bottle of Eau Royale mineral water will add a couple of hundred francs to your bill, but you can always ask for free *eau ordinaire* (tap water). Also beware of set meals designed for tourists, as these usually cost double the average entree. If you can't order à la carte, walk back out the door.

Local restaurants offer French, Chinese, Vietnamese, Italian, and, of course, Tahitian dishes. The *nouvelle cuisine Tahitienne* is a combination of European and Asian recipes, with local seafood and vegetables, plus the classic *maa Tahiti* (Tahitian food). The French are famous for their sauces, so try something exotic. Lunch is the main meal of the day in French Polynesia, and many restaurants offer a *plat du jour* designed for regular customers. This is often displayed on a blackboard near the entrance and is usually good value. Most restaurants serve lunch from 1130–1400 and dinner from 1800–2100. Don't expect snappy service: what's the rush, anyway?

If it's all too expensive, groceries are a good alternative. There are lots of nice places to picnic, and at CFP 44 a loaf, that crisp French white bread is incredibly cheap and good. French baguettes are subsidized by the government, unlike that awful sliced white bread in a plastic package, which is CFP 250 a loaf! Cheap red wines like Selection Faragui are imported from France in bulk and bottled locally in plastic bottles. Add a nice piece of French cheese to the above and you're ready for a budget traveler's banquet. *Casse-croûtes* are big healthy sandwiches

THE MIRACULOUS NONI FRUIT

In 1996 an American company began promoting the therapeutic proprieties of the knobby green fruit of the endemic nono or noni tree *(Morinda citrifolia)*, an ingredient in traditional Polynesian medicine. Noni pulp has become French Polynesia's largest agricultural export and the tree is now widely cultivated. The ripe fruit has an unpleasant taste and smell which once made it fit only for pig feed, but mixed with other juices it's quite palatable.

Among the claims made for noni juice are that it increases mental clarity and energy levels, supports proper digestion, carries beneficial substances to the skin, enhances the immune system, relieves pain, fights bacteria, retards tumor growth, and promotes longevity.

Miracle cure or spurious elixir, the noni juice fad has created a mini-boom in producing areas like the Marquesas. The trees blossom yearround and a yellow dye is made from the roots. Apart from the juice, noni extract is used as an ingredient in many personal hygiene products such as soaps, creams, and shampoos. In the United States, the Morinda company has exclusive rights.

made with those long French baguettes at about CFP 250—a bargain.

There's also Martinique rum and Hinano beer (CFP 165 in grocery stores), brewed locally by the Brasserie de Tahiti. Founded in 1914, this company's first beer was called Aorai and today they produce Heineken as well as Hinano. Remember the deposit on Hinano beer bottles (CFP 60 on large bottles), which makes beer cheap to buy cold and carry out. Supermarkets aren't allowed to sell alcohol on Sundays or holidays (stock your fridge on Sat.).

The *maitai* is a cocktail made with rum, liqueur, and fruit juice. Moorea's famous Rotui fruit drinks are sold in tall liter containers in a variety of types. The tastiest is perhaps *pamplemousse* (grapefruit), produced from local Moorea fruit, but the pineapple juice is also outstanding. At about CFP 262 a carton, they're excellent value. At CFP 100 in supermarkets, bottled Eau Royale mineral water is also quite cheap.

If you're going to the outer islands, take as many edibles with you as possible; it's always more expensive there. Keep in mind that virtually every food plant you see growing on the islands is cultivated by someone. Even fishing floats or seashells washed up on a beach, or fish in the lagoon near someone's home, may be considered private property.

Tahitian Food

If you can spare the cash, attend a Tahitian *tamaaraa* (feast) at a big hotel and try some Polynesian specialties roasted in an *ahimaa* (underground oven). Basalt stones are preheated with a wood fire in a meter-deep pit, then covered with leaves. Each type of food is wrapped separately in banana leaves to retain its own flavor and lowered in. The oven is then covered with more banana leaves, wet sacking, and sand, and left one to three hours to bake: suckling pig, mahimahi, taro, *umara* (sweet potato), *uru* (breadfruit), and *fafa* (a spinachlike cooked vegetable made from taro tops).

Also sample the gamy flavor of *fei,* the red cooking banana that flourishes in Tahiti's uninhabited interior. The Tahitian chestnut tree *(mape)* grows near streams and the delicious cooked nuts can often be purchased at markets. *Miti hue* is a coconut-milk sauce fermented with the juice of river shrimp. Traditionally *ma'a Tahiti* is eaten with the fingers.

Poisson cru (ia ota), small pieces of raw bonito (skipjack) or yellowfin tuna marinated with lime juice and soaked in coconut milk, is enjoyable, as is *fafaru* ("smelly fish"), prepared by marinating pieces of fish in seawater in an airtight coconutshell container. As with the durian, although the smell is repugnant, the first bite can be addicting. Other typical Tahitian plates are chicken and pork casserole with *fafa,* pork and cabbage casserole *(pua'a chou),* and goat cooked in ginger.

Po'e is a sticky sweet pudding made of starchy banana, papaya, taro, or pumpkin flour, flavored with vanilla, and topped with coconut-milk sauce. Many varieties of this treat are made throughout Polynesia. *Faraoa ipo* is Tuamotu coconut bread. The local coffee is flavored with vanilla bean and served with sugar and coconut cream.

INFORMATION AND SERVICES

Information

French Polynesia has one of the best-equipped tourist offices in the South Pacific, Tahiti Tourisme (tel. 50-57-00, fax 43-66-19, www .tahiti-tourisme.pf). For a list of their overseas offices, turn to Resources at the back of this book. Within French Polynesia the same organization calls itself the Tahiti Manava Visitors Bureau and operates tourist information offices on Tahiti, Moorea, Huahine, Raiatea, and Bora Bora. These offices can provide free brochures and answer questions, but they're not travel agencies, so you must make your own hotel and transportation bookings (they won't make phone calls for you). Ask for their current information sheets on the islands you intend to visit.

Internet Resources

Tahiti Tourisme's site, **www.tahiti-tourisme.com,** has abundant links to other online resources, and there's an events calendar and address listings. Many of Tahiti Tourisme's overseas offices have sites of their own. Haere Mai, **www.haere-mai.pf,** the home page of the federation of guest houses and family accommodations, provides listings in all five archipelagoes. Tahiti Explorer, **www.tahiti-explorer.com,** clues you in on cruises, diving, flights, hotels, the weather, people and geography, and more. The photo albums and trip reports are a huge resource, and there's a travel forum. The Tahiti Traveler, **www.thetahititrav eler.com,** offers background information, island guides, hotel listings, a photo gallery, and screensavers. Tahiti Resorts, **www.tahiti.resortspa cific.com,** is an accommodation and resorts guide with maps and travel information. Tahiti Islands, **www.tahiti-islands.com,** also uses interactive maps to index hotel information and pictures.

The Tahiti Diving Guide, **www.diving-tahiti.com,** describes and maps 10 diving destinations. The underwater photography is unsurpassed. Tahiti Black Pearls, **www.perlesde tahiti.net,** is about the best primer you'll find on the subject—a must for anyone in the market for a black pearl. Tahiti1.Com, **www.tahiti1.com,** is the territory's news and information portal. You can sample Tahitian cooking and cocktails, view the flowers, visit surfing spots off Tahiti and Moorea, check boat timetables to the outer islands, read the legends of old Polynesia, learn about tattooing, and much more. Présidence du Gouvernement, **www.presidence.pf,** explains the system of government and takes you on a virtual tour of the new presidential palace in Papeete. The write-ups on the history, culture, geography, and economy of French Polynesia are precise, and it's an excellent source of information on the outer islands.

Visas and Officialdom

Everyone other than French citizens needs a passport valid six months beyond the departure date. French are admitted freely for an unlimited stay, and citizens of the European Union countries, Australia, Norway, and Switzerland, get three months without a visa. Citizens of the United States, Canada, New Zealand, Japan, and 13 other countries are granted a one-month stay free upon arrival at Papeete. If you need a visa for France, you'll also need one for French Polynesia. Call your airline beforehand to verify visa requirements, if in doubt.

If you do require a visa, make sure the words *valable pour la Polynésie Française* are endorsed on the visa, as visas for France are not accepted. Transit passengers only changing planes in Papeete also require a visa unless they fall into one of the categories above (this applies especially to South American passengers arriving from Chile in transit to New Zealand).

Extensions of stay are possible after you arrive, but they cost CFP 3,000 and you'll have to go to the post office to buy a stamp. You'll also need to show "sufficient funds" and your ticket to leave French Polynesia and provide one photo. The two immigration offices are listed in this book's Papeete section. Persons from countries outside the European Union are limited to three months total; if you know you'll be staying over a month, it's much better to get a three-month visa at a French consulate prior to arrival, making this formality unnecessary. To be married in French Polynesia involves a minimum of one month residence and considerable red tape (most of the marriage ceremonies performed at the resorts are not legally binding).

French Polynesia requires an onward or return ticket of everyone (including nonresident French citizens). If you arrive without one, you'll be refused entry or required to post a cash bond equivalent to the value of a full-fare ticket back to your home country.

Yacht Entry

The main port of entry for cruising yachts is Papeete. Upon application to the local gendarmerie, entry may also be allowed at Bora Bora, Hiva Oa, Huahine, Mangareva, Moorea, Nuku Hiva, Raiatea, Raivavae, Rangiroa, Rurutu, Tubuai, and Ua Pou. Have an accurate inventory list for your vessel ready. It's also best to have a French courtesy flag with you, as they're not always available in places like the Marquesas. Even after clearance, you must continue to report your arrival at each respective office every time you visit any of those islands (locations and phone numbers are provided throughout this book). The gendarmes are usually friendly and courteous, if you are. Boats arriving from Tonga, Fiji, and the Samoas must be fumigated (also those which have called at ports in Central or South America during the previous 21 days).

Anyone arriving by yacht without an onward ticket must post a bond or *caution* at a local bank equivalent to the airfare back to their country of origin. In Taiohae the bond is US$565 for New Zealanders, US$635 for Americans, and US$800 for Europeans. This is refundable upon departure at any Banque Socredo branch, less a 3 percent administrative fee. Make sure the receipt shows the currency in which the original deposit was made and get an assurance that it will be refunded in kind. To reclaim the bond you'll also need a letter from Immigration verifying that you've been officially checked out. If any individual on the yacht doesn't have the bond money, the captain is responsible. The bond can be charged to a credit card.

Once the bond is posted, a "temporary" three-month visa (CFP 3,000) is issued. Recently, the French authorities have been refusing extensions beyond the initial three months, so ask about this while checking in. Boats can be left at Raiatea Carenage if you have to leave temporarily, but yachts staying in French Polynesia longer than a total of one year in any two-year period are charged full customs duty on the vessel. Failure to comply can result in confiscation of the boat until any outstanding fees are paid. Actually, the rules are not hard-and-fast, and everyone has a different experience. Crew changes should be made at Papeete. Visiting yachts cannot be chartered to third parties without permission.

After clearing customs in Papeete, outbound yachts may spend the duration of their period of stay cruising the outer islands. Make sure every island where you *might* stop is listed on your clearance. Duty-free fuel may be purchased immediately after clearance. The officials want all transient boats out of the country by 31 October, the onset of the hurricane season.

Money

The French Pacific franc or CFP (for *cour de franc Pacifique)* is legal tender in French Polynesia, Wallis and Futuna, and New Caledonia (there is no difference between the banknotes circulating in those territories). There are beautifully colored big banknotes of CFP 500, 1,000, 5,000, and 10,000, and coins of CFP 1, 2, 5, 10, 20, 50, and 100. The 10,000 note is confusingly similar in color and design to the CFP 1,000, so when changing money, ask the clerk to give you CFP 5,000 notes instead.

The value of the CFP is pegged at exactly CFP 119.331 to the Euro buying or selling, so you can easily determine how many CFP you'll get for your dollar or pound by finding out how many Euros it's worth then multiplying by 119.331. At last report, US$1 = CFP 96, but a very rough way to convert CFP into U.S. dollars would be simply to divide by 100, so CFP 1,000 is US$10, etc. The Euro has not been adopted here over

THE FRENCH PACIFIC FRANC

The *cour de franc Pacifique* or CFP grew out of the dark days of WW II when France was under German occupation. During this period, the French franc (FF) lost two-thirds of its prewar value while prices remained stable in the Pacific. When the French colonies reestablished contact with metropolitan France after the war, a new currency was needed to avoid economic chaos. Thus the French Pacific franc was created in 1945 at the rate of 2.4 FF to one CFP. Over the next few years the French franc was devalued three times and each time the CFP was devalued against it, lowering the rate to 5.5 FF to one CFP by 1949. That year 100 old FF became one new FF, thus 5.5 new FF equaled 100 old CFP, a relationship which remained in place for over half a century. In 2002 France adopted the Euro but the CFP remained legal tender in France's three Pacific territories at the fixed rate of one Euro to CFP 119.331. Until 1967 the Banque de l'Indochine was responsible for issuing the Pacific franc, a function now carried out by the French government.

fears that the European Commission might gain the power to interfere in the local taxation system.

All banks levy a stiff commission on foreign currency transactions. The Banque de Polynésie (www.sg-bdp.pf) deducts CFP 411 commission, the Banque Socredo (www.websoc.pf) CFP 514, and the Banque de Tahiti (www.banque-tahiti.pf) CFP 566. Traveler's checks attract a rate of exchange about 1.5 percent higher than cash, but a passport is required for identification (photocopy sometimes accepted). The easiest way to avoid the high commissions and long bank lines is to change infrequently. When changing a large amount, it might be worth comparing the rates at all three banks as they do differ slightly.

The number-one currency to have with you is Euros as these are converted back and forth at a fixed rate. Traveler's checks in Euros are recommended, although U.S. dollar checks also work perfectly well. If you're from the States, you might also bring a few U.S. dollars in small bills to cover emergency expenses. Otherwise it's not a good idea to use cash U.S. dollars to cover expenses as these are usually converted at an unfavorable rate.

Credit cards are accepted in many places on the main islands, but Pacific francs in cash are easier to use at restaurants, shops, etc. If you wish to use a credit card at a restaurant, ask first. Visa and MasterCard are universally accepted in the Society Islands, but American Express and Diner's Club are not. The American Express representative on Tahiti is Tahiti Tours (tel. 54-02-50) at 15 rue Jeanne d'Arc near the Vaima Center in Papeete. Most banks will give cash advances on credit cards, but it's still wise to bring enough traveler's checks to cover all your out-of-pocket expenses, and then some.

An alternative are the ATM machines outside Banque Socredo offices throughout the territory (including at Faa'a airport). These give a rate slightly better than traveler's checks without commission, however checking account ATM cards may not work despite advertised links to international services like Cirrus and Maestro. Several readers have reported problems with ATMs that produced "amount too high" messages instead of banknotes. Other times, only French Cirrus was accepted. If the machine doesn't work the first time, don't try again as you could be charged for each attempt without receiving any cash! Go inside the bank and complain. This situation should improve as the banks upgrade their computer systems, meanwhile don't be too dependent on the ATMs. The weekly limit on ATM withdrawals is CFP 35,000 every seven days—if you'll need more, have several different cards.

On many outer islands credit cards, traveler's checks, and foreign banknotes won't be accepted, so it's essential to change enough money before leaving Papeete. Apart from Tahiti, there are banks on Bora Bora, Huahine, Hiva Oa, Moorea, Nuku Hiva, Raiatea, Rangiroa, Rurutu, Taha'a, Tubuai, and Ua Pou. All of these islands have Banque Socredo branches, and the Banque de Tahiti is represented on eight of them, the Banque de Polynésie on four. Bora Bora, Moorea, and Raiatea each have three different banks. If you're headed for any island other than these, take along enough CFP in cash to see you through.

Costs

Although Tahiti is easily the most expensive corner of the South Pacific, it also has the lowest inflation rate in the region. During the entire period from 1994 and 2001, there was only 8 percent inflation, or just over 1 percent a year, compared to 10 percent a year and up in many other South Pacific countries. The high price structure is directly related to the extremely high salaries paid to government employees. The minimum wage here is CFP 591 an hour.

Fortunately, facilities for budget travelers are now highly developed throughout the Society Islands, often with cooking facilities that allow you to save on meals. Bread (and indirectly the ubiquitous baguette sandwiches) are heavily subsidized and a real bargain. Beer, fruit juice, and mineral water from grocery stores are reasonable. Cheap transportation is available by interisland boat, and on Tahiti there's *le truck*. Bicycles can be hired in many places.

In 1998, a value-added tax (VAT) or *taxe sur la valeur ajoutée* (TVA) came into effect on many items. In 2002, the TVA was increased to 6 percent on groceries, rooms, and prepaid meals, 10 percent on services (including restaurants, bars, car rentals, and excursions), and 16 percent on

store purchases. Large "classified hotels" are taxed 11 percent, whereas small hotels and pensions charge 6 percent. Free of tax are *le truck* and public ferry fares. The TVA is usually hidden in the basic price but the hotel taxes are charged extra.

Time is what you need the most of to see French Polynesia inexpensively, and the wisdom to avoid trying to see and do too much. There are countless organized tours and activities designed to separate you and your money, but none are really essential and the beautiful scenery, spectacular beaches, challenging hikes, and exotic atmosphere are free. Bargaining is not common in French Polynesia, and no one will try to cheat you (with the exception of the odd taxi driver). There's *no tipping.*

Post

The 34 regular post offices (www.opt.pf) and 58 authorized agencies throughout French Polynesia are open weekdays 0700–1500. Main branches sell ready-made padded envelopes and boxes. Parcels with an aggregate length, width, and height of over 90 cm or weighing more than 20 kg cannot be mailed. Rolls (posters, calendars, etc.) longer than 90 cm are also not accepted. Letters cannot weigh over two kg, and when mailing parcels it's much cheaper to keep the weight under two kg. Registration *(recommandation)* is CFP 500 extra and insurance *(envois avec valeur déclarée)* is also possible. Always use airmail *(poste aérienne)* when posting a letter; surface mail takes months to arrive. Postcards can still take up to two weeks to reach the United States. Though twice as expensive as in Cook Islands or Fiji, the service is quite reliable.

To pick up poste restante (general delivery) mail, you must show your passport and pay CFP 55 per piece (or CFP 28 for newspapers or magazines). If you're going to an outer island and are worried about your letters being returned to sender after 15 days, pay CFP 2,000 per month for a *garde de courrier,* which obliges the post office to hold all letters for at least two months. If one of your letters has "please hold" marked on it, the local postmaster may decide to hold all your mail for two months, but you'll have to pay the CFP 2,000 to collect it. Packages may be returned after one month in any case. For a flat fee of CFP 2,000 you can have your mail forwarded for three months. Ask for an *"Ordre de Réexpédition Temporaire."*

There's no residential mail delivery in French Polynesia and what appear to be mail boxes along rural roads are actually bread delivery boxes! Since there are usually no street addresses, almost everyone has a post office box or B.P. *(Boîte Postale)*. French Polynesia issues its own colorful postage stamps—available at local post offices. They make excellent souvenirs.

Telecommunications

Public telephones are found almost everywhere in the territory but they accept local telephone cards only (no coins). Thus anyone planning on using the phone will have to pick up a telephone card *(télécarte),* sold at all post offices. They're valid for both local and international calls, and are available in denominations of 30 units (CFP 1,000), 60 units (CFP 2,000), and 150 units (CFP 5,000). Within French Polynesia, you're charged about one unit every four minutes within a single island, one unit every 2.5 minutes within an island group, and one unit every minute between island groups. From 2200–0600 it's half price.

Throughout this book we've tried to supply the local telephone numbers you'll need. Many tourist-oriented businesses will have someone handy who speaks English, so don't hesitate to call ahead. You'll get current information, be able to check prices and perhaps make a reservation, and often save yourself a lot of time and worry. If you need to consult the French Polynesia phone book, ask to see the *annuaire* at any post office. Online you can also search for numbers at www.annuaireopt.pf.

For long distance calls, using a card is cheaper than paying cash and you don't get hit with stiff three-minute minimum charges for operator-assisted calls (CFP 1,023 to the U.S.). With a card the cost of international calls per minute is CFP 100 to Australia, New Zealand, Japan, and North America, or CFP 166 to Britain and Germany. Calls to Germany and the UK are also CFP 100 a minute from midnight to 0600.

To dial overseas direct from Tahiti, listen for the dial tone, then push 00 (Tahiti's international access code). When you hear another dial tone, press the country code of your party (Canada and the United States are both 1), the city or area code, and the number. For information (in French), dial 3612 (a paid call); to get the operator, dial 19.

Operator-assisted long-distance calls are best placed at post offices, which also handle fax *(télécopier)* services. Calls made from hotel rooms are charged double or triple—you could be presented with a truly astronomical bill. Collect calls overseas are possible to Australia, Canada, France, New Zealand, Vanuatu, and the United States (but not to the U.K.): dial 19 and say you want a *conversation payable à l'arrivée.* North American AT&T telephone cards can be used in French Polynesia.

If calling from abroad, French Polynesia's telephone code is **689.** To call direct from the United States or Canada, one must dial 011-689 and the six-digit telephone number (there are no area codes). International access codes do vary, so always check in the front of your local telephone book.

Email and the internet were introduced to French Polynesia in 1995 and they've really caught on in recent years. We've included Tahiti-related websites and email addresses throughout this chapter. Internet cafes are found on all the main islands.

Media

Two morning papers appear daily except Sunday. *Les Nouvelles de Tahiti* (tel. 47-52-00, fax 47-52-09) was founded in 1961 and currently has a circulation of 6,700 copies. In 1964, *La Dépêche de Tahiti* (tel. 46-43-01, fax 41-25-68) merged with an existing paper and 14,000 copies a day are presently sold. Both are part of the Hersant publishing empire.

The free monthly *Tahiti Beach Press* (tel. 42-68-50, fax 42-33-56), edited by Jan Prince, includes tourist information and is well worth perusing to find out which local companies are interested in your business.

If you read French, the monthly magazine *Tahiti Pacifique* (www.tahiti-pacifique.com) is a lively observer of political and economic affairs (single copies CFP 600, airmail subscription US$85).

Television was introduced to Tahiti in 1965, and state-owned Réseau France Outre-Mer (RFO) broadcasts on two channels in French and (occasionally) Tahitian. A territorial station (Tahiti Nui TV), and two cable companies (Canal +, and Tahiti Nui Satellite) also operate.

There are 10 FM radio stations around Papeete. **Radio Polynésie** (RFO) is a government-run station which presents their main news of the day (in French) at 0630. **Radio 1** (www.radio1.pf) also gives a news report at 0630 and plays mostly French and Anglo-American music. Radio 1's sister station, **Tiare FM** (www.tiarefm.pf), plays more Tahitian music. Both these and **Star FM** (www.starfm.pf), the home of Anglo-American pop and reggae, are owned by the powerful Groupe Aline, which backs the political party of Gaston Flosse. Star FM's competitor, **NRJ,** owned by the newspaper *La Dépêche,* offers French and Anglo-American music. **Radio Maohi** based at Pirae is controlled by Gaston Flosse's political party. They play Tahitian music during the day but at night they compete with NRJ and Star FM for listeners. **Pacific FM,** based at Arue, features Tahitian, French, and international music. They rebroadcast the Radio France International news (in French) at 0530, 0630, 0730, 1200, 1300, 1700, and 1800. **Radio Bleue** (www.radiobleue.pf) based in Mahina presents a mix of Tahitian and Anglo-American music. **Radio Te Reo o Tefana** is a pro-independence Tahitian-language station based at Faa'a, which features Tahitian music. In Papeete, you'll find these stations at the following frequencies:

- 87.8 MHz—Pacific FM
- 88.2 MHz—Radio Maohi
- 88.6 MHz—NRJ
- 89.0 MHz—Radio Polynésie
- 91.4 MHz—Radio Despoire
- 91.8 MHz—Radio Polynésie
- 92.3 MHz—Radio Maohi
- 92.8 MHz—Radio Te Reo o Tefana
- 95.2 MHz—Radio Polynésie
- 96.0 MHz—Radio Bleue
- 96.4 MHz—Star FM
- 97.4 MHz—Radio Te Reo o Tefana
- 97.8 MHz—Star FM
- 98.7 MHz—Radio 1
- 100.0 MHz—Radio 1
- 101.1 MHz—Radio Bleue
- 103.0 MHz—NRJ
- 103.8 MHz—Radio 1
- 104.2 MHz—Tiare FM
- 105.5 MHz—Tiare FM
- 105.9 MHz—Star FM
- 106.4 MHz—Pacific FM

Outside Papeete the frequencies used by these stations varies. At Taravao, look for Radio Polynésie at 89.0 MHz, Radio 1 at 90.9 MHz, Radio Maohi at 94.8 MHz, Tiare FM at 98.3 MHz, and Star FM at 100.8 MHz. Radio Marquises uses 101.3 MHz at Nuku Hiva and 95 MHz at Hiva Oa. Radio Polynésie broadcasts throughout the territory over **738 kHz AM.** None of the local AM/FM stations broadcast in English.

Health

Public hospitals are found in Papeete (Tahiti), Taravao (Tahiti), Afareaitu (Moorea), Uturoa (Raiatea), Mataura (Tubuai), Taiohae (Nuku Hiva), and Atuona (Hiva Oa). Other islands have only infirmaries or dispensaries. Medical treatment is not free and in non-life-threatening situations it's better to see a private doctor or dentist. Their attention will cost you no more than you'd pay at a hospital but their services are generally more convenient. Private clinics are found throughout the Society Islands, but there are none in the eastern outer islands (over there, ask for the *infirmerie*). Papeete's Mamao Hospital (tel. 46-62-62) has one of only two recompression chambers in the South Pacific.

Business Hours and Time

The sun rises and sets early in French Polynesia. Businesses also open early, often closing for a two-hour siesta at midday. Normal office hours are weekdays 0730–1130/1330–1630. Many shops keep the same schedule but remain open until 1730 and Saturday 0730–1200. A few shops remain open at lunchtime and small convenience stores are often open

Saturday afternoon until 1800 and Sunday 0600–0800. Banking hours are variable, either 0800–1530 or 0800–1100/1400–1700 weekdays. A few banks in Papeete open Saturday morning (check the sign on the door). Most businesses are closed on Sunday.

French Polynesia operates on the same time as Hawaii, 10 hours behind Greenwich mean time or two hours behind California (except May–Oct., when it's three hours). The Marquesas are 30 minutes ahead of Tahiti and the Gambier Islands are an hour ahead of Tahiti. French Polynesia is east of the international date line, so the day is the same as that of the Cook Islands, Hawaii, and the United States, but a day behind Fiji, New Zealand, and Australia.

TRANSPORTATION

Getting There

Aircalin, Air France, Air New Zealand, Air Tahiti Nui, Hawaiian Airlines, LanChile Airlines, Polynesian Airlines, and Qantas Airways all have flights to Papeete. For more information on these, turn to the main Introduction. The local offices you may need to visit to reconfirm your flight are listed in the Papeete section.

Air Tahiti Nui (www.flyatn.com) only began service from Papeete in 1998, and they now fly to Los Angeles once or twice a day, to Paris five times a week, to Auckland four times a week, to Tokyo three times a week, and to Osaka weekly. The airline's political clout has allowed them to muscle in on routes previously served by other French carriers. In 2002 the French Polynesian government, which owns 66 percent of the airline's shares, paid 40 percent of the cost of Air Tahiti Nui's second A340 Airbus.

France's state-owned national airline, **Air France,** flies from Paris to Papeete via Los Angeles three times a week.

Air New Zealand has flights from Los Angeles to Papeete four times a week, with connections to/from many points in North America and Western Europe. These flights continue southwest to Auckland with one calling at Rarotonga

and Fiji. **Polynesian Airlines** has two flights a week direct from Auckland (not via Apia).

Qantas flies from Melbourne to Papeete via Auckland with connections from four other Australian cities. **Hawaiian Airlines** offers weekly service from Honolulu to Papeete with connections from Los Angeles, Las Vegas, San Francisco, Portland, San Diego, and Seattle.

Aircalin has flights from Nouméa to Papeete. **LanChile Airlines** operates a Boeing 767 service from Santiago to Papeete via Easter Island twice a week.

By Boat

The only scheduled international passenger-carrying freighter service to Tahiti is the monthly Bank Line ship from Le Havre (France) to Auckland via the Panama Canal. Europe to Tahiti takes just under a month. The local agent is **Agence Maritime de Fare Ute** (tel. 42-55-61, fax 42-86-08).

Getting Around by Air

The domestic carrier, **Air Tahiti** (www.air tahiti.pf), flies to 42 airstrips in every corner of French Polynesia, with important hubs at Papeete (Windward Islands), Bora Bora (Leeward Islands), Rangiroa (northern Tuamotus), Hao (eastern Tuamotus), and Nuku Hiva (Marquesas). Their fleet consists of five 66-seat ATR 72s, three 48-seat ATR 42s, and two 19-seat Dornier 228s. The Italian-made ATRs (Avions de Transport Regional) are economical in fuel consumption and maintenance requirements, and perform well under island conditions. The high-winged design makes them perfect for aerial sightseeing along the way.

Roundtrip tickets are about 15 percent cheaper than two one ways. Air Tahiti doesn't allow stopovers on their tickets, so if you're flying roundtrip from Tahiti to Bora Bora and want to stop at Raiatea on the way out and Huahine on the way back, you'll have to purchase four separate tickets (total CFP 36,300). Ask about their "Pass Bleu," which allows you to visit these islands plus Moorea for CFP 22,000 (certain restrictions apply).

No student discounts are available, but persons

under 25 and over 60 can get discounts of up to 50 percent on certain flights by paying CFP 1,000 for a discount card *(carte de réduction)*. Family reduction cards (CFP 2,000) provide a potential 50 percent reduction for the parents and 75 percent off for children under 12. Identification and one photo are required, and application must be made at least three working days before you wish to travel. The full discount is only given on off-peak flights and bookings can only be made from within French Polynesia.

Better than point-to-point fares are the Air Tahiti **Air Passes.** These are valid 28 days, but only one stopover can be made on each island included in the package. For example, you can go Papeete-Moorea-Huahine-Raiatea-Maupiti-Bora Bora-Papeete on a "Bora Bora Pass" for CFP 35,000. Otherwise pay CFP 48,000 for Papeete-Moorea-Huahine-Raiatea-Maupiti-Bora Bora-Rangiroa-Tikehau-Manihi-Fakarava-Papeete on a "Bora-Tuamotu Pass." This compares with an individual ticket price of CFP 51,000 to do the first circuit or CFP 90,000 for the second, which makes the air passes good value. A "Lagoon Pass" from Moorea or Papeete to Rangiroa, Manihi, Tikehau, and Fakarava costs CFP 37,000, while the "Discovery Pass" covers Moorea, Huahine, and Raiatea for CFP 23,000. These four air passes can be extended to include the Austral Islands for another CFP 20,000. To add Nuku Huva and Hiva Oa to a pass is CFP 45,000 extra. All flights must be booked in advance, and date changes and reroutings are not possible. Air Tahiti's agent in North America, Tahiti Vacations (tel. 800/553-3477, www.tahitivacations.net), will have current information. The passes are nonrefundable once travel has begun.

Air Tahiti also offers packages *(séjours)* to almost all their destinations including airfare, transfers, hotel rooms (double occupancy), and the occasional breakfast or excursion. Of course, they only use the more upmarket hotels, but if you were planning to stay in one of them anyway, Air Tahiti's packages are cheaper than what you'd pay directly. Cruise packages are also offered. All the possibilities are clearly outlined (in French) with exact prices quoted in Air Tahiti's well-designed timetable.

Air Tahiti tickets are refundable at the place of purchase, but you must cancel your reservations at least two hours before flight time to avoid a penalty. Do this in person and have your flight coupon amended as no-shows are charged 25 percent of the value of the ticket to make a new reservation (all existing reservations will be automatically canceled). Standby passengers are given any unclaimed seats 20 minutes before each flight.

If you're told a flight you want is full, keep checking back as local passengers often change their minds and seats may become available (except around major public holidays). It's not necessary to reconfirm reservations for flights between Tahiti, Moorea, Huahine, Raiatea, Bora Bora, Rangiroa, and Manihi, but elsewhere it's essential to reconfirm. (If your bookings were made from abroad, do reconfirm *everything* upon arrival in Papeete, as mix-ups in communications between foreign travel agencies and Air Tahiti are routine.) Beware of planes leaving 20 minutes early.

If you buy your ticket locally, the baggage allowance on domestic flights is 10 kg, but if your Air Tahiti flight tickets were purchased seven days prior to your arrival in French Polynesia, the allowance is 20 kg. All baggage above those limits is charged at the rate of the full fare for that sector divided by 80 per kilogram (surfboards over 1.8 meters long or items weighing over 32 kg are not accepted). Hand luggage is limited to three kg. Fresh fruit and vegetables cannot be carried from Tahiti to the Austral, Tuamotu, Gambier, or Marquesas islands.

On Bora Bora, Maupiti, and Mangareva passengers are transferred from the airport to town by boat. This ride is included in the airfare at Bora Bora but costs extra at Maupiti (CFP 500) and Mangareva (CFP 600). Smoking aboard the aircraft is prohibited and all flights are free seating.

The main Air Tahiti office (tel. 86-42-42, fax 86-40-69) in Papeete is at the corner of rue Maréchal Foch and rue Edouard Ahnne. They're closed on weekends. Check carefully to make sure all the flights listed in their published timetable are actually operating! Any travel agency in Papeete can book Air Tahiti flights for the

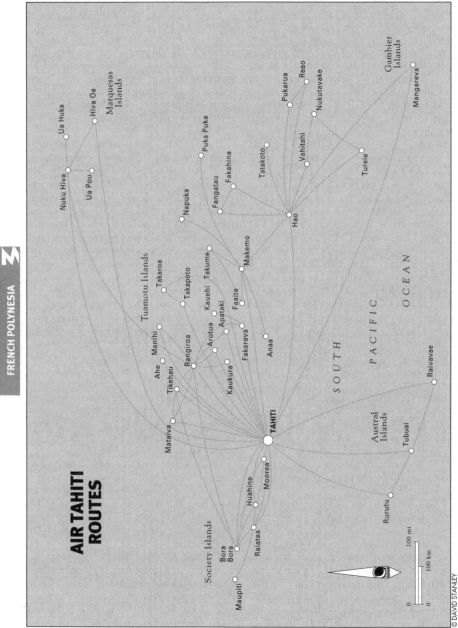

AIR TAHITI ROUTES

© DAVID STANLEY

same price as the Air Tahiti office, and the service tends to be better.

An Air Tahiti subsidiary, **Air Moorea** (tel. 86-41-41, fax 86-42-99), has flights between Tahiti and Moorea (CFP 4,000 one-way) leaving Papeete hourly 0600–1800. The Air Moorea terminal is in a separate building at the east end of Faa'a Airport. However, flying between Tahiti and Moorea is not recommended because going over by ferry is a big part of the experience and the transfer service to/from Moorea Airport is for persons on prebooked tours only. Persons traveling individually must take a taxi from Moorea airport to their hotel and they're very expensive. A cramped, stuffy plane ride at four times the cost of the relaxing 30-minute ferry is to be avoided.

Air Tahiti Services

Air Tahiti flies from Papeete to Huahine (CFP 10,000), Raiatea (CFP 11,400), and Bora Bora (CFP 15,000) four to eight times a day. Every day there's an expensive direct connection from Moorea to Huahine (CFP 19,700). The five weekly transversal flights from Bora Bora to Rangiroa and Tikehau (CFP 25,300) eliminate the need to backtrack to Papeete.

Flights between Papeete and Rangiroa (CFP 13,500) operate one to five times a day, continuing from Rangiroa to Tikehau (CFP 5,800) and Manihi (CFP 11,000) four times a week. Rangiroa-Fakarava (CFP 5,800) is only weekly. Air Tahiti also has flights to the East Tuamotu atolls and Mangareva. Many flights between outer islands of the Tuamotus operate in one direction only.

Flights bound for the Marquesas are the longest and most expensive of Air Tahiti's services. The ATR service from Papeete to Nuku Hiva (CFP 24,000) is daily. Once or twice a week these flights call at Hiva Oa on their way to or from Nuku Hiva, and one weekly ATR flight calls at Rangiroa. At Nuku Hiva the Papeete flights connect for Ua Pou (CFP 6,600), Hiva Oa (CFP 11,000), and Ua Huka (CFP 6,600). If you know you'll be going on to Hiva Oa, get a through ticket from Papeete; the fare is only CFP 2,800 more than a ticket as far as Nuku Hiva.

The Austral group is well connected to Papeete, with flights to Rurutu (CFP 20,300) and Tubuai (CFP 22,700) four or five times a week with alternating Papeete-Rurutu-Tubuai-Papeete or Papeete-Tubuai-Rurutu-Papeete routings. The twice weekly Tubuai-Rurutu leg costs CFP 10,400. When you add these fares up it becomes obvious that a visit to the Australs is only cost effective as an add-on to an air pass.

The fares quoted above are the low season fares in effect from January–March and November–mid-December. Other months you'll pay about 10 percent more. Air pass prices are more or less constant year-round—obviously, they're your best bet if you really want to get around.

During July and August, the peak holiday season, extra flights are scheduled. Air Tahiti is fairly reliable; still, you should avoid scheduling a flight back to Papeete on the same day that your international flight leaves Tahiti. It's always wise to allow some leeway in case there's a problem with the air service. Save your ride around Tahiti until the end.

Getting Around by Sea

To save money, many budget travelers tour French Polynesia by boat. There's a certain romance and adventure to taking an interisland freighter, and you can go anywhere by copra boat, including islands without airstrips and resorts. Ships leave Papeete regularly for the different island groups. You'll meet local people and fellow travelers and receive a gentle introduction to the island of your choice. Problems about overweight baggage, tight reservations, and airport transport are eliminated, and thanks to government subsidies, travel by ferry or passenger-carrying freighter is four times cheaper than the plane. Seasickness, cockroaches, diesel fumes, and the heavy scent of copra are all part of the experience.

Below you'll find specific information on the main interisland boats; the Visitors Bureau in Papeete also has lists. Prices and schedules have been fairly stable over the past few years, and new services are being added all the time. Lots of visitors travel this way to Moorea and Huahine, so don't feel intimidated if you've never done it before.

For the cheapest ride and the most local color, travel deck class. There's usually an awning in case of rain, and you'll be surrounded by Tahitians, but don't count on getting a lot of sleep if you go this way—probably no problem for one night, right? Lay your mat pointed to one side of the boat because if you lie parallel to the length of the boat you'll roll from side to side. Don't step over other peoples' mats, but if you must, first remove your shoes and excuse yourself. Otherwise take a cabin, which you'll share with three or four other passengers, still cheaper than an airplane seat. Food is only included on really long trips (ask), but snacks may be sold on board. On a long trip you're better off taking all your own food rather than buying a meal plan.

For any boat trip farther than Moorea check the schedule and pick up tickets the day before at the company office listed below. If you're headed for a remote island outside the Societies or want cabin class, visit the office as far in advance as possible. Take along your passport as they may insist on checking the expiration date of your visa before selling you a ticket to a point outside the Society Islands. Except on the tourist-class *Aranui*, it's not possible (nor recommended) to book your passage before arriving on Tahiti. If you really want to go, there'll be something leaving around the date you want. On an outer island, be wary when someone, even a member of the crew, tells you the departure time of a ship: they're as apt to leave early as late.

Boat trips are always smoother northwestbound than southeast-bound because you go with the prevailing winds. The ferry schedules are also more convenient northbound. Take this into consideration if you plan to fly one way, in which case it would be better to come back by air.

Ferries to Moorea

The Moorea ferries carry over a million passengers a year making Papeete the third-largest port under the French flag (after Calais and Cherbourg) as far as passenger movements go. Two types of ferries do this trip: fast catamarans carrying walk-on commuters only (30 minutes), and large car ferries with a capacity for 400 walk-on passengers and 80 vehicles (one hour). Departure times are posted at the ferry landing on the Papeete waterfront (punctual) and reservations are not required: you just buy your ticket before you board.

Most of the ferries mentioned below go to Vaiare Wharf on the east side of Moorea. Local buses meet the ferries at Vaiare and carry passengers to any part of Moorea for a flat CFP 300 fare (the bright yellow tourist buses charge CFP 500). Don't be too slow boarding as the buses do fill up at times.

The high-speed catamarans *Aremiti IV* (tel. 42-88-88) and *Moorea Jet* (tel. 42-37-42) make four to six trips a day between Tahiti and Vaiare at CFP 1,060 pp (bicycles CFP 210). On the Moorea catamarans you're allowed to sit or stand outside on the roof and get an all-round view, which makes them fun.

The large car ferries *Moorea Ferry* (tel. 45-00-30) and *Aremiti Ferry* shuttle four or five times a day between Papeete and Vaiare (CFP 850 one-way, students and children under 13 CFP 425, cars CFP 2,600, scooters CFP 725, bicycles CFP 210).

Unlike all the others, the high-speed monohull *Ono-Ono* (tel. 45-35-35, onoono@mail.pf) goes to a landing next to Paopao Fish Market at the head of Cook's Bay, Moorea. It runs 3-5 times a day and charge CFP 1,100. It's a wonderful introduction to Moorea to sail right into Cook's Bay, but unfortunately no buses meet the *Ono-Ono*.

Ferry to Huahine and Raiatea

The high-speed catamaran *Aremiti III* (tel. 74-39-40, fax 42-83-83) departs Papeete for Huahine (CFP 4,600) and Raiatea (CFP 5,200) every Monday and Friday morning at 0800. The return journey from Raiatea begins at 1400 those same days. The interisland fare between Huahine and Raiatea is CFP 1,700. You must be at the wharf an hour prior to departure. It's an excellent alternative to the slow, uncomfortable cargo ships and expensive flights. In windy weather, however, be prepared for a rough trip.

Cargo Ships to the Leeward Islands

All of the cargo ships depart Papeete's Motu Uta wharf, a 20-minute walk from town. Northbound the MV *Vaeanu* leaves Papeete Monday, Wednesday, and Friday at 1700; southbound it leaves Bora Bora Tuesday and Thursday at 1130, and Sunday at 0830. The MV *Hawaiki-Nui* (tel. 45-23-24, fax 45-24-44) departs Papeete for Huahine, Raiatea, and Bora Bora on Tuesday and Thursday at 1600. Beware of voyages marked "carburant" on the schedules because when fuel *(combustible)* is being carried, only cabin passengers are allowed aboard (this usually happens on the *Vaeanu's* Wednesday departures from Papeete). The cargo boat *Taporo VII* to Bora Bora no longer accepts passengers at all.

The timings are more civilized if you stay on the boat right through to Bora Bora northbound: you get to see the sunset over Moorea, go to bed, and when you awake you'll be treated to a scenic cruise past Taha'a and into the Bora Bora lagoon. Getting off at Huahine at 0130 is no fun (although there is a shelter on the wharf where you can spend the rest of the night for free). Southbound between Bora Bora, Raiatea, and Huahine you travel during daylight hours which makes it easy to island hop back. Southbound you board at Huahine at dusk and there will be no disturbances before Tahiti (where you'll be asked to disembark in the middle of the night).

Although the ships do make an effort to stick to their timetables, the times are approximate—ask at the company offices. They're more likely to be running late on the return trip from Bora Bora to Tahiti. Expect variations if there's a public holiday that week. In Papeete, board the ship at least an hour prior to departure to be sure of a reasonable place to sleep (mark your place with a beach mat). If you've got some time to kill before your ship leaves Papeete, have a look around the coconut-oil mill next to the wharf.

You can usually buy a deck ticket at the *Vaeanu* office (tel. 41-25-35, fax 41-24-34, torehiate tu@mail.pf) facing the wharf at Motu Uta a few hours prior to departure (except on holidays). Cabin space should be booked at least a day in advance. The *Hawaiki-Nui* accepts only 12 passengers, so the 120-passenger *Vaeanu* is a safer bet. Be sure to buy your ticket before boarding as there can be problems for anyone trying to pay once the ship is underway. In the Leeward Islands buy a ticket from the agent on the wharf as soon as the boat arrives. One-way fares from Papeete to any of the islands are CFP 1,786 deck (shared cabins begin at CFP 4,317 pp). The *Vaeanu* is the original *Aranui* which served the Marquesas Islands 1981–1990. It offers mats in the spacious hold down below or floor space on the enclosed upper rear deck (with the lights on all night). The passengers and crew are mostly Tahitian, and the *Vaeanu* is an excellent option for the adventurous traveler. Just don't expect a tourist cruise at those prices.

Barges to Maupiti

The government supply barges *Meherio* or *Maupiti to'u Aia* leave Papeete for Maupiti Wednesday afternoons (20 hours) calling at Raiatea on the way. Information is available from the **Groupement d'Intervention de la Polynésie** (tel. 50-66-88; weekdays 0730–1500) at Motu Uta. These ships don't carry foreign passengers very often, but they may make an exception in your case. If not, the fast ferry *Maupiti Express* (tel./fax 67-66-69) shuttles between Bora Bora and Maupiti three times a week.

Ships to the Austral Islands

The **Service de Navigation des Australes** (tel. 50-96-09, fax 42-06-09, snathp@mail.pf), in the building marked "Entrepot Tuhaa Pae" at the Tuamotu wharf, runs the *Tuhaa Pae III* to the Austral Islands. One-way deck/couchette/cabin fares from Papeete are CFP 3,969/5,556/7,641 to Rurutu, Rimatara, or Tubuai, CFP 5,722/8,010/11,017 to Raivavae, or CFP 7,823/10,953/15,060 to Rapa. Between Rurutu and Tubuai it's CFP 1,868/2,615/3,598. Otherwise it's CFP 30,120 cabin class for the entire 10-day roundtrip. Three meals a day cost CFP 3,000/5,000 pp a day extra at the cafeteria/officer's table (or take your own food).

The *Tuhaa Pae III* has nine four-bed, two two-bed, and two one-bed cabins. Some are below the waterline and are very hot with no portholes. The rear deck has a diesely romantic feel, for a day or two. For sanitary reasons the seats have been removed from the ship's toilets (you squat). The ship calls at Rimatara, Rurutu, Tubuai,

Raivavae three or four times a month. Rapa Iti is visited about once a month, Maria Atoll annually. The schedule changes at a moment's notice, so actually sailing on the *Tuhaa Pae III* requires persistence. Consider going out by boat and returning by plane.

Ships to the Tuamotus and Gambiers

The *Cobia II* runs to the Tuamotus, departing Monday at 1200 for Kaukura (Tues. 0800), Arutua (Tues. 1300), Apataki (Tues. 1630), Aratika (Wed. 0700), and Toau (Wed. 1330), returning to Papeete Friday at 1000 (CFP 3,120 one-way). No cabins are available and you must take all your own food. The office (tel. 43-36-43) is in the same building as the *Aranui* office at Motu Uta.

The *Vai-Aito* (tel. 43-99-96, fax 43-53-04) departs Motu Uta every 10 days for Tikehau (CFP 5,050 deck from Papeete), Rangiroa (CFP 5,050), Ahe (CFP 9,470), Manihi (CFP 10,100), Aratika (CFP 11,990), Kauehi (CFP 14,500), Raraka (CFP 15,150), and Fakarava (CFP 17,675). A complete roundtrip costs CFP 26,512, meals included.

Many smaller copra boats, such as the *Hotu Maru, Kura Ora III, Mareva Nui, Rairoa Nui,* and *Saint Xavier Maris Stella* also service the Tuamotus. The *Nuku Hau* and *Taporo V* go as far as the Gambier Islands. Ask about ships of this kind at the large warehouses west of Papeete's Motu Uta interisland wharf.

Cargo Ship to the Marquesas

Every other Thursday at 1700 the 75-meter cargo ship *Taporo VI* departs Papeete for Takapoto, Fatu Hiva, Tahuata, Hiva Oa, Ua Huka, Nuku Hiva, and Ua Pou. Passengers pay CFP 22,000/ 32,000 deck/cabin one-way from Papeete to any port in the Marquesas. Otherwise you can do the whole 12-day roundtrip for CFP 44,000/ 64,000 deck/cabin. To bring a bicycle is CFP 3,000. Only two to six hours are spent at each port, so you should plan on getting off somewhere and flying back. From Papeete, it takes three days on the open sea to reach the first Marquesan island.

The *Taporo VI* has two four-berth cabins and 12 seats on deck. Food is included but it's mar-ginal, so take extras and bring your own bowl. Meals are served at 0600, 1030, and 1730. No pillows or towels are supplied in the cabins and the shower is open only three hours a day. Moving cargo is their main business and they're sometimes selective about who they accept as a passenger. The agent is **Compagnie Française Maritime de Tahiti** (tel. 42-63-93, fax 42-06-17, taporo@mail.pf; weekdays 0730–1100/1330– 1700, Sat. 0730–1100) at Fare Ute. At island stops *Taporo VI* lowers a container onto the wharfs which it uses as an office. (The CFMT itself has a place in local history, having been founded in 1890 by Sir James Donald, who had the contract to supply limes to the British Pacific fleet. At the turn of the previous century Donald's schooner, the *Tiare Taporo,* was the fastest in Polynesia, and the CFMT is still the Lloyd's of London agent.)

The Aranui

The passenger-carrying freighter *Aranui* cruises 16 times a year between Papeete and the Marquesas. It calls at all of the inhabited Marquesas Islands, plus a couple of the Tuamotus. The routing might be Papeete-Takapoto-Ua Pou-Nuku Hiva-Hiva Oa-Fatu Hiva-Hiva Oa-Ua Huka-Nuku Hiva-Ua Pou-Rangiroa-Papeete. A vigorous daily program with fairly strenuous but optional hikes is included in the tour price. The only docks in the Marquesas are at Taiohae, Hakahau, and Atuona; elsewhere everyone goes ashore in whale boats, a potential problem for passengers with mobility limitations. Still, the *Aranui* is fine for the adventuresome visitor who wants to see a lot in a short time.

This 115-meter freighter had its inaugural sailing in 2003, replacing a smaller German-built boat that had served the Marquesas since 1990. It's clean and pleasant compared to the *Taporo VI,* but more expensive. The 208 passengers are accommodated in three classes of accommodations for the 16-day, eight-island cruise. The cheapest cabin with shared bath is US$3,023 pp roundtrip (double occupancy), all meals included. Cabins with private bath start at US$3,500 pp. Single occupancy costs 50 percent more. There's also an air-conditioned dormitory with upper and lower berths that costs US$1,980 pp and, of course, doesn't involve a single supplement. A US$285 port tax, cruise tax, and value added tax are extra. Deck passage is intended for local residents only, but it's sometimes possible for tourists to travel interisland within the Marquesas on deck (about CFP 3,000–8,000 a hop). The meals are good but with little choice. The roster of American/French/German passengers is congenial.

The *Aranui's* Papeete office (**Compagnie Polynésienne de Transport Maritime,** tel. 42-62-40, fax 43-48-89) is at the interisland wharf at Motu Uta. The CPTM's U.S. office is at 2028 El Camino Real South, Suite B, San Mateo, CA 94403, U.S.A. (tel. 650/574-2575 or 800/972-7268, www.aranui.com). In the United States bookings can be made through **TravLtips** (www.travltips.com). One Australian reader wrote: "The trip is fantastic and I hope to do it again soon."

Tourist Cruises

In addition to the *Aranui,* several conventional cruise ships ply the Society Islands from Tahiti to Bora Bora on one-week trips. The operators change regularly as such vessels enjoy a five-year tax holiday in French Polynesia and they tend to leave as soon as the incentives are used up. The main market is the United States' West Coast, which is almost as close to Tahiti as it is to the better-known cruising grounds in the Caribbean.

The best established vessel at the moment is the 320-passenger *Paul Gauguin,* built at St. Nazaire, France, in 1997 and presently operated by **Radisson Seven Seas Cruises** (tel. 800/525-5350, www.rssc.com). This ship does seven-night cruises from Papeete to Taha'a, Bora Bora, Raiatea, and Moorea year-round, beginning at US$2,835 pp a week double-occupancy for one of the 14 cabins on the bottom deck including airfare from Los Angeles (US$300 surcharge Apr.–Dec., plus US$195 pp port tax). Shore excursions and shipboard gambling cost extra. You can book through www.tahitivacations.net.

In 2002 **Wind Star Cruises** (www.windstar cruises.com) returned to Tahiti after an absence

of four years. Every Friday the 134-meter, four-mast- tall ship *Wind Star* takes 148 passengers from Papeete to Raiatea, Tahaa, Bora Bora and Moorea. Packages from Los Angeles begin around US$3,335 pp double occupancy, plus US$195 pp port tax.

P&O Princess Cruises (www.princess.com) operates the much larger 688-passenger *Pacific Princess* and *Tahitian Princess* on 10-day cruises out of Papeete. Three different itineraries are available on these huge love boats formerly operated by Renaissance Cruises, including Papeete to Bora Bora, Papeete to Rarotonga, and Papeete to the Marquesas. Shore excursions and alcoholic drinks are generally not included on this type of ship.

Smaller Vessels

The 67-meter, 37-cabin mini-cruise ships *Tu Moana* and *Tia Moana* do seven-day cruises around Huahine, Raiatea, Taha'a, and Bora Bora at CFP 336,000 pp. They're run by **Bora Bora Cruises** (tel. 43-43-03, fax 45-10-65, www.bora borapearlcruises.com), which also operates the 34-meter, 19-cabin catamaran *Haumana* on Tuamotu Islands cruises.

If scuba's your thing, the live-aboard *Tahiti Aggressor,* part of the **Aggressor Fleet** (tel. 800/348-2628, www.pac-aggressor.com), should be your choice. Based at Rangiroa, this 32-meter vessel does one-week cruises to remote Tuamotu atolls such as Kaukura, Fakarava, Toau, and Apataki. The 16 divers each pay about US$2,395 double occupancy, plus US$50 tax, for 5.5 days of extraordinary drift diving (airfare not included). Non-divers get a US$200 discount.

Archipels Croisieres (tel. 56-36-39, fax 56-35-87, www.archipels.com) operates all-inclusive cruises on their five 17-meter, eight-passenger catamarans. They offer a six-night tour of the Leeward Islands at US$1,975 pp or two/three nights cruising the Rangiroa lagoon at US$830/1,080 pp (both double occupancy). Shore excursions and almost everything other than interisland airfare and alcohol is included. For couples it's much cheaper than chartering a yacht and your crew does all the work. Just don't expect a luxury trip with gourmet cuisine, even though their brochure

FRENCH POLYNESIA

may suggest it. Hopefully your fellow passengers will be amenable.

Also consider yacht cruises in the same areas on lesser-known vessels, such as the *Eden Martin* (www.sailing-huahine.com) based at Huahine. **The Moorings** (www.moorings.com) offers six-night cruises of the Leeward Islands on a shared five-cabin yacht at US$3,276/4,368 single/double per cabin including meals and taxes (but not a suggested 15 percent gratuity). These happen four times a year between June and November.

Yacht Charters

Tahiti Yacht Charter (tel. 45-04-00, fax 42-76-00, www.vpm.fr), part of the Groupe Nouvelles Frontières, has 14 charter yachts available at Tahiti and Raiatea. Their Tahiti office is in the same Papeete complex as the Tahiti Manava Visitors Bureau. On Raiatea, they're based at the Marina Apooiti (tel. 66-28-86, fax 66-28-85), one km west of Raiatea Airport. Prices begin at CFP 272,720 a week for a three-cabin yacht and increase to CFP 629,090 for a large catamaran. There's a supplement in July and August and a discount from November to March. A skipper will be CFP 15,450 a day, a cook CFP 14,000. This may seem like a lot, but split among a nautical-minded group it's comparable to a deluxe hotel room.

The South Pacific's largest bareboat yacht charter operation is **The Moorings Ltd.** (tel. 66-27-13, fax 66-20-94, moorings@mail.pf), a Florida company with 25 yachts based at Raiatea's Marina Apooiti. Bareboat prices begin at US$3,990 a week for a yacht accommodating six and go up to US$6,090 for an eight-person catamaran. Prices are steeper during the April–September high season. Provisioning is US$32 pp a day (plus US$152 a day for a cook, if required). If you're new to sailing, a skipper must be hired at US$172 a day. Local tax is 6–16 percent, security insurance US$29 a day, and the starter kit US$87 and up. Charterers are given a complete briefing on channels and anchorages, and provided with a detailed set of charts. All boats are radio-equipped, and a voice from The Moorings is available to talk nervous skippers in and out. Travel by night is forbidden, but by day it's easy

sailing. All charters are from noon to noon. Book through The Moorings Ltd., 19345 US 19 North, Suite 402, Clearwater, FL 33764-3147, U.S.A. (tel. 888/952-8420, www.moorings.com). Ask about "specials" when calling.

A third yacht charter operation, **Stardust/Sunsail Yacht Charters** (tel. 60-04-85, fax 66-23-19, www.stardustyc.com), is based at Raiatea's Faaroa Bay. In the United States, they're known as Sunsail (www.sunsail.com). A four-person bareboat yacht will cost US$345/440/490 a day in the low/intermediate/high season with substantial reductions for periods over eight or 15 days. Their top-of-the-line eight-passenger deluxe catamaran is US$1,390/1,600/1,820 a day, including two crew, full board, and watersports such as windsurfing and waterskiing. There are eight other categories in between. The high season is July and August, intermediate April–June and September–November. If you can schedule a 15-day trip between January and March, you can have a bareboat yacht for as little as US$242 a day! Those without the required sailing skills will have to hire a skipper at US$140 a day.

Le Truck

Polynesia's folkloric *le truck* provides an entertaining unscheduled passenger service on Tahiti, Huahine, and Raiatea. Passengers sit on long wooden benches in back and there's no problem with luggage. Fares are fairly low and usually posted on the side of the vehicle. You pay through the window on the right side of the cab. The drivers are generally friendly and will stop to pick you up anywhere if you wave—they're all self-employed, so there's no way they'd miss a fare! Unfortunately, moves are underway to replace these colorful vehicles with air-conditioned Korean buses which only stop at official stops and require printed tickets.

On Tahiti the larger *trucks* and buses leave Papeete for the outlying districts periodically throughout the day until 1700; they continue running to Faa'a Airport and the Sofitel Maeva Beach until late. On Huahine and Raiatea service is usually limited to a trip into the main town in the morning and a return to the villages in the afternoon. On Moorea and Bora Bora buses or *trucks* meet the boats from Papeete. No public transportation is available on the roads of the Austral, Tuamotu, Gambier, or Marquesas islands.

Car Rentals

Car rentals are available at most of the airports served by Air Tahiti. On Tahiti there's sometimes a mileage charge, whereas on Moorea, Huahine, Raiatea, and Bora Bora all rentals come with unlimited mileage. Public liability insurance is included by law, but collision damage waiver (CDW) insurance is extra. The insurance policies don't cover a flat tire, stolen radios or accessories, broken keys, or towing charges if the renter is found to be responsible. If you can get a small group together, consider renting a minibus for a do-it-yourself island tour.

Unless you have a major credit card, you'll have to put a large cash deposit down on the car. Your home driver's license will be accepted, although you must have had your driver's license for at least a year. Some companies rent to persons aged 18–24, but those under 25 must show a major credit card and the deductible amount not covered by the CDW insurance will be much higher.

Except on Tahiti, rental scooters are usually available and a strictly enforced local regulation requires you to wear a helmet *(casque)* at all times (CFP 5,000 fine for failure to comply). On some outer islands you can rent an open two-seater "fun car" slightly bigger than a golf cart, and no helmet or driver's license is required for these. These and bicycles carry no insurance.

One major hassle with renting cars on the outer islands is that they usually give you a car with the fuel tank only a quarter full, so immediately after renting you must go to a gas station and tank up. Try to avoid putting in more gas than you can use by calculating how many kilometers you might drive, then dividing that by 10 for the number of liters of gasoline you might use. Don't put in over CFP 2,500 (about 20 liters) in any case or you'll be giving a nice gift to the rental agency (which, of course, is their hope in giving you a car that's not full). Gas stations are usually only in the main towns and open only on weekdays during business hours, plus perhaps a couple of hours on weekend mornings. Expect to pay around CFP 130 a liter for gas, which works out to just under US$4 per American gallon—the South Pacific's highest priced gasoline to drive the most region's expensive rental cars.

As in continental Europe and North America, driving is on the right-hand side of the road. Two traffic signs to know: a white line across a red background indicates a one-way street, while a slanting blue line on a white background means no parking. At unmarked intersections in Papeete, the driver on the right has priority. At traffic circles, the car already in the circle has priority over those entering. The seldom-observed speed limit is 40 kph in Papeete, 60 kph around the island, and 90 kph on the RDO expressway.

French Polynesia contains 70,000 registered vehicles and around 8,000 new cars are sold each year. Forget trying to park on the street in downtown Papeete on a weekday. Drive with extreme care in congested areas—traffic accidents are frequent (43 percent of fatal accidents involve alcohol and another 26 percent speeding). Persons aged 18–25 account for 57 percent of the dead and injured in accidents here.

A good alternative to renting a car are the 4WD jeep safaris offered on Tahiti, Moorea, Huahine, Raiatea, Tahaa, and Bora Bora. These take you along rough interior roads inaccessible to most rental vehicles and the guides know all the superlative spots. Prices vary CFP 3,500–8,000 pp depending on how far you go.

Others

French Polynesia has some of the most expensive taxis in the world and they're best avoided. If you must take one, always verify the fare before getting in. The hitching is still fairly good in Polynesia, although local residents along the north side of Moorea are fed up with it and may not stop. Hitching around Tahiti is only a matter of time.

Bicycling on the island of Tahiti is risky due to wild devil-may-care motorists, but most of the outer islands (Moorea included) have excellent, uncrowded roads. It's wiser to use *le truck* on Tahiti, though a bike would come in handy on the other islands where *le truck* is rare. The distances are just made for cycling!

International Airport

Faa'a Airport (PPT) is conveniently located 5.5 km southwest of Papeete. The runway was created in 1959–61, using material dredged from the lagoon or trucked in from the Punaruu Valley. A taxi into town is CFP 1,500, or CFP 2,500 after 2000, plus CFP 100 per piece of luggage. (The driver will *always* want CFP 2,500 if you don't verify the price beforehand. Some drivers even try to get CFP 2,500 per person!) *Le truck* up on the main highway will take you to the same place for only CFP 120 (CFP 200 after 1800) and starts running around 0530. Some *le truck* drivers ask CFP 100 for luggage, others don't. The tour buses at the airport are strictly for persons on prepaid packages. Lobbying by the taxi drivers prevents the hotels from providing airport shuttles.

Many flights to Tahiti arrive in the middle of the night, but you can stretch out on the plastic benches inside the terminal (open 24 hours a day). Be aware that the persons who seem to be staffing the tourist information counter at the airport during the night may in fact be taxi drivers who will say anything to get a fare. We've received complaints from readers who were driven all over town from one closed hostel to another, only to be presented with a tremendous bill (you have been warned!). Unless you're willing to spend a lot of money for the possibility of a few hours sleep, it's better to wait in the terminal until dawn.

The **Banque de Polynésie** (tel. 86-60-56), to the left as you come out of customs, opens Monday–Thursday 0800–1200/1300–1600, Friday 0800–1200/1300–1500, and one hour before and after the arrival and departure of all international flights (ATM accessible 24 hours). They charge a commission of CFP 411 on all traveler's checks. Euros are changed at a standard rate, but for other currencies the rate is 1 percent better for traveler's checks than it is for cash. There's also a **Banque Socredo** branch (tel. 83-86-95) next to the Air Tahiti ticket of-fice facing the parking lot at the far right (west) end of the airport. This office is not easily visible from inside the terminal, so search. It's open weekdays 0800–1145/1400–1700 (no exchanges after 1630) and an adjacent ATM is accessible 24 hours.

The airport luggage-storage office *(consigne a bagages)* is open weekdays 0600–1900, weekends 1200–1400, and two hours before international departures. They charge CFP 395 per day for a handbag, CFP 620 for a suitcase, backpack, or golf bags, CFP 730 for a bicycle, and CFP 1,040–2,500 for surfboards. This left-luggage office is poorly marked; it's behind the Fare Hei flower market in the middle of the parking lot.

Air Tahiti has a ticket office in the terminal open daily 0530–1730. These car rental companies have counters at the airport: Avis, Daniel, Europcar, Hertz, and Pierrot et Jacqueline. The airport post office is open weekdays 0600–1030/1200–1600, weekends 0600–0930. The post office sells cards for the public phones at airport. The snack bar is open 24 hours and is surprisingly reasonable (draft beer CFP 315, baguette sandwich CFP 385). Public toilets are located near the snack bar. The airport information number is tel. 86-60-61.

There's no bank in the departure lounge but you can spend your leftover Pacific francs at the duty-free shops in the departure lounge. Don't expect any bargains. The Fare Hei, just outside the terminal, sells inexpensive shell and flower leis which the locals give to arriving or departing friends.

All passengers arriving from Samoa or Fiji must have their baggage fumigated upon arrival, a process that takes about two hours (don't laugh if you're told this is to prevent the introduction of the "rhinoceros" into Polynesia—they mean the rhinoceros *beetle*). Fresh fruits, vegetables, and flowers are prohibited entry. There's no airport tax.

Tahiti

Tahiti, largest of the Societies, is an island of legend and song lying in the eye of Polynesia. Though only one of 118, this lush island of around 170,000 inhabitants is paradise itself to most people. Here you'll find an exciting city, big hotels, restaurants, nightclubs, things to see and do, valleys, mountains, reefs, trails, and history, plus transportation to everywhere. Since the days of Wallis, Bougainville, Cook, and Bligh, Tahiti has been the eastern gateway to the South Pacific.

Legends created by the early explorers, amplified in Jean-Jacques Rousseau's "noble savage" and taken up by the travel industry, make it difficult to write objectively about Tahiti. Though the Lafayette Nightclub is gone from Arue and Quinn's Tahitian Hut no longer graces Papeete's waterfront, Tahiti remains a delightful, enchanting place. In the late afternoon, as Tahitian crews practice canoe racing in the lagoon and Moorea gains a pink hue, the romance resurfaces. If you steer clear of the traffic jams and congestion in commercial Papeete and avoid the tourist ghettos west of the city, you'll get a taste of the magic Gauguin encountered in 1891. Whether you love or hate the capital, keep in mind that it's only on the outer islands, away from the motorists and military complexes, that the full flavor of old Polynesia endures.

The Land

The island of Tahiti (1,069 square km) accounts for almost a third of the land area of French Polynesia. Like Hawaii's Maui, Tahiti was formed over a million years ago by two or three shield volcanoes joined at the isthmus of Taravao. These peaks once stood 3,000 meters above the sea, or 12,700 meters high counting from the seabed. Today the rounded, verdant summits of Orohena (2,241 meters) and Aorai (2,066 meters) rise in the center of Tahiti-nui and deep valleys radiate in all directions from these central peaks. Steep slopes drop abruptly from the high plateaus to coastal plains. The northeast coast is rugged and rocky, without a barrier reef, and thus exposed to intense, pounding surf; villages lie on a narrow strip

between mountains and ocean. The south coast is broad and gentle with large gardens and coconut groves; a barrier reef shields it from the sea's fury.

Tahiti-iti (also called the Taiarapu Peninsula) is a peninsula with no road around it. It's a few hundred thousand years younger than Tahiti-nui, and Mount Rooniu (1,323 meters) forms its heart. The populations of big *(nui)* and small *(iti)* Tahiti are concentrated along the coast; the interior of both Tahitis is almost uninhabited. Contrary to the popular stereotype, mostly brown/black beaches of volcanic sand fringe this turtle-shaped island. To find the white/golden sands of the travel brochures, you must cross over to Moorea.

Orientation

Almost everyone arrives at Faa'a International Airport five km west of Papeete, the capital and main tourist center of French Polynesia. East of Papeete are Pirae, Arue, and Mahina, with a smattering of hotels and things to see, while south of Faa'a lie the commuter communities Punaauia, Paea, and Papara. On the narrow neck of Tahiti is Taravao, a refueling stop on your 117-km way around Tahiti-nui. Tahiti-iti is a backwater, with dead-end roads on both sides. Boulevard Pomare curves around Papeete's harbor to the Visitors Bureau near the market—that's where to begin. Moorea is clearly visible to the northwest.

PAPEETE

Papeete (pa-pay-EH-tay) means "Water Basket." The most likely explanation for this name is that islanders originally used calabashes enclosed in baskets to fetch water at a spring behind the present Territorial Assembly. Founded as a mission station by the Rev. William Crook in 1818, whalers began frequenting Papeete's port in the 1820s as it offered better shelter than Matavai Bay. It became the seat of government when young Queen Pomare IV settled here in 1827. The French governors who "protected" the island from 1842 also used Papeete as their headquarters.

TAHITI

SOUTH PACIFIC OCEAN

Point Venu
Matavai Bay
Papeete
Faaa
Pirae
Arue
Mahina
Araboho Blowhole
Tiarei
Papenoo
Mahaena
Hitiaa

Bain Loti
Fautaua Valley
Fautaua Falls
Punaruu Valley
Mt. Aorai (2,066 m)
Le Diademe (1,321 m)
Plateau of Oranges
Orofero Valley

OROFARA LEPER COLONY
FARE RAU APE
FARE HAMUTA
FARE MATO
FARE ATA

Tefa'aurumai Falls
Mt. Aramaoro (1,530 m)

Papenoo Valley
Pito Hiti (2,110 m)
Mt. Orohena (2,241 m)
RELAIS DE LA MAROTO

Vaiharuru Falls
Faaone
Faone

Lake Vaihiria
Mt. Tetufera (1,799 m)

Tahiti-nui

Mt. Ivirairai (1,696 m)

MARINA TAINA
IAORANA VILLA LAGOONARIUM
MUSEUM OF TAHITI
Punaauia
PENSION DE LA PLAGE
CHEZ ARMELLE
MAHANA PARK
TAAROA LODGE
PENSION TE MITI
MARAE OF ARAHURAHU

BEACHCOMBER INTER-CONTINENTAL
SOFITEL MAEVA BEACH HOTEL
HÔTEL MÉRIDIEN TAHITI

Paea
HITI MOANA VILLA
MARAA FERN GROTTO
PAPARA VILLAGE
Papara
MARAE OF MAHAIATEA
Atimaono
Mataiea
MARINA TEHORO
GAUGUIN MUSEUM
Papeari
RESTAURANT BAIE PHAETON
Port Phaeton
Taravao
PUUNUI MARINA
Vairao
PENSION MEHERIO ITI
Toahotu

FARE NANA'O
Afaahiti
PUNATEA VILLAGE
CHEZ JEANNINE
Pueu
VAIUFAUFA VIEWPOINT
Pari Coast
CHEZ MADO
Tautira
Vaitepiha Valley

Tahiti-iti (Taiarapu Peninsula)
Mt. Rooniu (1,323 m)
Vairao
Teahupoo
PENSION CHAYAN
PENSION VAIANI
TE PARI VILLAGE
PENSION LE BON JOUR
Vaipoiri Grotto
Pari Cliffs
Vaiarava Valley
Vaitepiha Valley

5 mi
5 km
0

© DAVID STANLEY

VICINITY OF PAPEETE

© DAVID STANLEY

FRENCH POLYNESIA

Today Papeete is the political, cultural, economic, and communications hub of French Polynesia. Over 100,000 people live in this cosmopolitan city, crowded between the mountains and the sea, and its satellite towns, Faa'a, Pirae, and Arue—over half the people on the island. "Greater Papeete" extends for 32 km from Paea to Mahina. The French Naval facilities in the harbor area were constructed in the 1960s to support nuclear testing in the Tuamotus.

Since the opening of Faa'a International Airport in 1961, Papeete has blossomed with large hotels, expensive restaurants, bars with wild dancing, radio towers, skyscrapers, and electric rock bands pulsing their jet-age beat. Where a nail or red feather may once have satisfied a Tahitian, VCRs and Renaults are now in demand. Over 35,000 registered vehicles jam Tahiti's 200 km of roads. Noisy automobiles, motorcycles, and mopeds clog Papeete's downtown and roar along boulevards Pomare and Prince Hinoï buffeting pedestrians with pollution and noise.

Yet along the waterfront the yachts of many countries rock luxuriously in their Mediterranean moorings (anchor out and stern lines ashore). Many of the boats are permanent homes for expatriate French working in the city. "Bonitiers" moored here fish for *auhopu* (bonito) for the local market. You should not really "tour" Papeete, just wander about without any set goal. Visit the highly specialized French boutiques, the Chinese stores trying to sell everything, and the Tahitians clustered in the market. Avoid the capital on weekends when life washes out into the countryside; on Sunday afternoons it's a ghost town. Explore Papeete, but make it your starting point—not a final destination.

SIGHTS

Papeete

Begin your visit at teeming **Papeete market** (rebuilt 1987) where you'll see Tahitians selling fish, fruit, root crops, and breadfruit; Chinese gardeners with their tomatoes, lettuce, and other vegetables; and French or Chinese offering meat and bakery products. The colorful throng is especially picturesque 1600–1700 when the fishmongers spring to life. Fish and vegetables are sold downstairs on the main floor, handicrafts, pareus, and snacks upstairs on the balcony. The flower displays outside make great photos and the vendors are quite friendly. The biggest market of the week begins around 0500 Sunday morning and is over by 0800.

The streets to the north of the market are lined with two-story Chinese stores built after the great fire of 1884. The US$14.5-million **Hôtel de Ville** (city hall) on rue Paul Gauguin was inaugurated in 1990 on the site of a smaller colonial building demolished to make way. The architect designed the three-story building to resemble the palace of Queen Pomare that once stood on Place Tarahoi near the present post office. A contemporary Marquesan stone tiki stands beside a pond in front of the building.

Notre Dame Catholic Cathedral (1875) is on rue du Général de Gaulle, a block and a half southeast of the market. Inside notice the Polynesian faces and the melange of Tahitian and Roman dress on the striking series of Gauguin-influenced paintings of the crucifixion.

Diagonally across the street from the cathedral is the **Vaima Center,** Papeete's finest window shopping venue, erected in 1977. The **Musée de la Perle** (tel. 45-21-22; Mon.–Sat. 0830–1830, Sun. 1100–1900; admission CFP 600, children under 15 CFP 300), on rue Jeanne d'Arc on the east side of the center, introduces Polynesia's famous black pearls. A 20-minute video presentation shown on request explains how cultured pearls are "farmed" in the Gambier Islands. The center is owned by a pioneer of the black pearl industry, Robert Wan, who operates nine farms in the Gambier and Tuamotu groups.

A few blocks west along rue du Général de Gaulle is Place Tarahoi. The **Territorial Assembly** on the left occupies the site of the former royal palace, demolished in 1966. The adjacent residence of the French high commissioner is private, but the assembly building and its lovely gardens are worth a brief visit. In front of the entrance gate is a monument erected in 1982 to **Pouvanaa a Oopa** (1895–1977), a Tahitian WW I hero who struggled all his life for the independence of his country. The plaque on the

PAPEETE

To Point Venus

To Bain Loti

Tahiti Island

Point Rahere

Lagoon

COURS DE L'UNION SACREE

AVE. DU COMMANDANT CHESSE

CHEMIN VICINAL DE TAUNOA

HINOI

AVE. DU PRINCE

TAUNOA

PATUTOA

AVE. DU CHEF PROMARE

VAIRAATOA

FARIIPITI

MAMAO

AVE. GEORGES CLEMENCEAU

KANTI CHINESE TEMPLE ★

MORMON TEMPLE ★

MAMAO PALACE CINEMA ■

MAMAO HOSPITAL ■

ARCHBISHOP'S PALACE ★

Papeava Stream

PENSION PUEA ■

MISSION

HOSTAL TEAMO ■

R. DE L'EVECHE

MGR. TEPANO JAUSSEN

CATHOLIC CATHEDRAL ★

OROVINI

500 yds
500 m

0
0

Rond Point des Remparts

R. DES REMPARTS

INDUSTRIAL AREA

FARE UTE

BUREAU TAPORO ■

NAVAL HQ

TOWN HALL ★

MARKET ■

GEORGES LAGARDE

R. DU GEN. DE GAULLE

TARAHOI

TERRITORIAL ASSEMBLY ★

PRESIDENTIAL PALACE

GENDARMERIE ●

R. DE SAINTE-AMELIE

Channel

NAUTI-SPORT ■

OIL TANKS

NAVAL ARSENAL

HOTEL KON TIKI PACIFIC ■

HOTEL ROYAL PAPEETE ■

HOTEL PRINCE HINOI ■

VISITORS BUREAU ■

HOTEL TIARE TAHITI ■

AVE. BRUAT

COURTHOUSE

HOTEL MAHINA TEA ●

SEE "CENTRAL PAPEETE" MAP

Taunoa Channel

BUREAU VAEANU ■

INTERISLAND WHARF

Motu Uta

TUAMOTU WHARF

OVERSEAS WHARF

Papeete Harbor

HOTEL VICTORIA ●

BOULEVARD POMARE

PROTESTANT CHURCH ★

CHAMPION SUPERMARKET ■

R. DES POILUS TAHITIENS

BUREAU ARANUI ■

ENTREPOT TUHAA PAE ■

GROUPEMENT D'INTERVENTION DE LA POLYNESIE

TAHUA TO'ATA

CULTURAL CENTER

PAOFAI

R. DU COMMANDANT DESTREMEAU

LYCÉE GAUGUIN

HOTEL MATAVAI ●

CHEZ MYRNA ●

SURFING SPOT

HANDICRAFT CENTER ■

MUNICIPAL SWIMMING POOL ■

URANIE CEMETERY ★

Passe de Papeete

Passe de Papeete

HOTEL SHERATON TAHITI ●

To Airport →

© DAVID STANLEY

FRENCH POLYNESIA

monument says nothing about Pouvanaa's fight for independence and against the bomb! In July 1995 nearly a third of the adult population of Tahiti gathered here to protest French nuclear testing in the Tuamotus.

Across the busy avenue from Place Tarahoi, beside the post office on the waterfront, is **Parc Bougainville.** A monument to Bougainville himself, who sailed around the world in 1766–69, is flanked by two old naval guns. One, stamped "Fried Krupp 1899," is from Count Felix von Luckner's famous raider *Seeadler,* which ended up on the Maupihaa reef in 1917; the other is off the French gunboat *Zélée,* sunk in Papeete harbor by German cruisers in 1914.

Much of the bureaucracy works along avenue Bruat just west, a gracious tree-lined French provincial avenue. The protectorate's first governor, Admiral Armand Bruat, set up a military camp here in 1843. You may observe French justice in action at the **Palais de Justice** (weekdays 0830–1200). The public gallery is up the stairway and straight ahead. Opposite the police station farther up avenue Bruat is the War Memorial.

In 1999 the Caserne Brioche, a military barracks dating back to 1886, was demolished to make way for the **Palais Présidentiel de Papeete,** official residence of the president of French Polynesia. This elegant neo-colonial structure near the gendarmerie at the top of avenue Bruat was built for Gaston Flosse, who has ruled the territory almost continuously since 1982. It's intentionally more impressive than the nearby French high commissioner's residence—a proud symbol of Tahiti Nui. You're allowed to enter the first courtyard and stroll around the fountain.

Facing the waterfront a few blocks west of avenue Bruat is the headquarters of the **Evangelical Church** in French Polynesia, with a church dating from 1875 but rebuilt in 1981. It was here that the London Missionary Society established Paofai Mission in 1818. From 1837 to 1958 the British consulate occupied the site of the six-story Paofai girl's hostel opposite the church, and George Pritchard, an early British consul, had his office here.

Continue west along the bay past the outrigger racing canoes to the **Tahua To'ata**

(www.toata.pf), a striking open-air venue created in 2000 for the annual Heiva i Tahiti festival held in July. Adjacent is the neo-Polynesian **Cultural Center** (1973) or Te Fare Tauhiti Nui, which houses a public library, notice boards, and auditoriums set among pleasant grounds. This complex is run by the Office Territorial d'Action Culturelle (OTAC), which organizes the annual Heiva Festival and many other events. The **municipal swimming pool** is on the coast beyond (go upstairs to the restaurant for a view). Return to the center of town along the waterfront.

Another walk takes you east from downtown to the Catholic **Archbishop's Palace** (1869), a lonely remnant of the Papeete that Gauguin saw. To get there, take rue Jaussen behind the Catholic cathedral, keep straight, and ask for the *archevêché catholique.* Without doubt, this is the finest extant piece of colonial architecture in a territory of fast-disappearing historic buildings. The park grounds planted in citrus and the modern open-air church nearby (to the right) also merit a look. The huge mango trees here were planted in 1855 by Tahiti's first bishop, Monseigneur Tepano Jaussen.

Fautaua Valley

If you'd like to make a short trip out of the city, go to the Hôtel de Ville and take a Mamao-Titioro *truck* to the **Bain Loti,** three kilometers up the Fautaua Valley from the Mormon Temple. A bust of writer Pierre Loti marks the spot where he had a love affair he later described in *The Marriage of Loti.* Today the local kids swim in a pool in the river here.

A dirt road continues three kilometers farther up the Fautaua Valley but because it's part of a water catchment, private cars are prohibited, so you must walk. From the end of the road, a trail straight ahead leads directly to **Fautaua Falls** (30 minutes) with several river crossings. Back a bit on the left, just before the end of the road, is a wooden footbridge across the river. Here begins a steep one-hour trail up to a 19th-century French fort at the top of the falls. The fort controlled the main trail into Tahiti's interior, and it's still an excellent hiking area. It's only open on weekdays and you should be back before 1530 when the gate is often closed.

Back on avenue Georges Clemenceau near the Mormon Temple is the impressive **Kanti Chinese Temple,** built in 1987, which is usually open mornings until noon.

Arue

Another easy sidetrip is east to Arue (a-roo-AY). Begin by taking an Arue or Mahina *truck* from near the Visitors Bureau to the colonial-style **Mairie de Arue** (1892) at PK 5.6. There has always been a degree of rivalry between Arue (www.arue.pf), heartland of the old Tahitian royal family, and neighboring Pirae, power base of pro-French politician Gaston Flosse.

From Arue town hall walk back a few minutes in the direction of Papeete to the **James Norman Hall Museum** (tel. 50-01-60; Tues.–Sat. 0900–1600, admission CFP 600) on the inland side of the road. Hall achieved fame during the 1930s as co-author of the **Bounty Trilogy** with Charles Nordhoff. He moved to Tahiti in 1920 and had this building erected in 1925. After his death in 1951, the house deteriorated to the point where it had to be completely rebuilt in 1991. The museum opened in 2002 and all captions on the exhibits are in English, French, and Tahitian. Some 3,000 books from Hall's personal library are on display and there's a comfortable lounge where you can sit and read excerpts from Hall's works.

Cross the highway from the museum and walk another 200 meters west toward Papeete to the École Maternelle Ahutoru at PK 5.4, Arue. Adjacent to this school is the little-known **Cimetière Royal Pomare** with the tombs of Pomare I, II, III, and IV. A map next to the cemetery clearly identifies the many Pomare graves, including that of Pomare V's successor Prince Hinoï. The most elevated tomb here belongs to Princess Elvina Pomare Buillard, who died in 1999. The Rev. Henry Nott (1774–1884), who translated the Bible into Tahitian, is buried directly behind the school (go around behind the building to see the ornate tomb). Nott arrived on the ship *Duff* in 1796 and served with the London Missionary Society for 18 years.

At PK 4.7 Arue, less than 10 minutes west of the Pomare cemetery on foot, is the **tomb of King Pomare V,** down a sideroad to a point of land on the lagoon. The mausoleum surmounted by a Grecian urn was built in 1879 for Queen Pomare IV, but her remains were subsequently removed to make room for her son, Pomare V, who died of drink in 1891 at the age of 52 (Paul Gauguin witnessed the funeral). A century earlier, on February 13, 1791, his grandfather, Pomare II, then nine, was made first king of Tahiti on the great *marae* that once stood on this spot. Pomare II became the first Christian convert and built a 215-meter-long version of King Solomon's Temple here, but nothing remains of either temple.

There's an excellent view of **Matavai Bay** from the Evangelical Church compound surrounding Pomare V's tomb. In 1767 Captain Samuel Wallis anchored in this bay after having "discovered" Tahiti, and most of the early English explorers (including Fletcher Christian and Captain Bligh) also came ashore here. The 8th Nuclear Free and Independent Pacific Conference was held in the church compound in 1999. To return to Papeete, simply walk back to the main highway and flag down the first westbound *truck.*

SPORTS AND RECREATION

Information on the **International Golf Course Olivier Breaud** on the south coast at Atimaono, can be found later in this chapter.

The Tahiti-based scuba operators cater mostly to local residents, so a knowledge of French will be helpful. Pascal Le Cointre and Arnauld Demier of **Scuba Tek Tahiti** (tel./fax 42-23-55, www.chez.com/scubatek) at the yacht club at PK 4, Arue, organize outings to offshore *faille* (faults) at 0900 and 1400 daily except Sunday afternoon and Monday. It's CFP 5,750 for one dive or CFP 26,950 for five dives. A certification course costs about the same as five dives, plus CFP 3,500 for PADI registration—good value.

On the other side of Papeete, **Tahiti Plongée** (tel. 41-00-62, fax 42-26-06, plongee.tahiti@mail.pf), also known as "Club Corail-Sub," offers scuba diving several times daily from its base at the former Hôtel Te Puna Bel Air opposite the

Tahiti Country Club, PK 7.5 Punaauia. The charge is CFP 5,000 per dive all-inclusive, or CFP 23,500/45,000 for a five/10-dive card. You can ocean dive Tuesday–Sunday at 0800 and on Wednesday and Saturday at 1400; lagoon diving is daily at 1000 and weekdays at 1400 (no diving on Monday). Divemaster Henri Pouliquen was one of the first to teach scuba diving to children. The youngest person Henri has dived with was aged two years, six months—the oldest was a woman of 72 on her first dive. Since 1979 Tahiti Plongée has arranged over 10,000 dives with children, certainly a unique achievement. Another specialty is diving with disabled persons. A fish-filled site called The Aquarium near their base is safe for all divers.

Eleuthera Plongée (Nicolas Castel and Joshua Rouger, tel. 42-49-29, fax 43-66-22, www.dive-tahiti.com), at the Marina Taina beside McDonald's at PK 9, Punaauia, charges CFP 5,700/10,500/25,000 for one/two/five dives. Exploration dives are at 0900 and 1400 daily. Their introductory dive is at 1100 daily (CFP 5,500). Eleuthera also offers dive tours to Marlon Brando's atoll Tetiaroa for CFP 15,500.

Iti Diving International (Gilles Jugel, tel./fax 57-77-93, www.itidiving.pf), at the Marina Puunui on the southeast side of the island, does scuba diving at CFP 5,700 a dive. Among the nearby dive sites are the Tetopa Pass grottoes and the Marado wall.

If you want to set out on your own, **Nauti-Sport** (tel. 50-59-59, fax 42-17-75; weekdays 0800–1145/1345–1700, Sat. 0730–1130) in Fare Ute sells every type of scuba gear and also rents tanks (CFP 2,550).

The **Ski Nautique Club de Tahiti** (tel. 77-22-62; Tues.–Fri. 1200–1800, weekends 0900–1800), on the waterfront at the former Hôtel Te Puna Bel Air opposite the Tahiti Country Club, Punaauia, offers water-skiing at CFP 260/15,000 a minute/hour. Training sessions are arranged.

Surfers often stay at Pension Te Miti or Taaroa Lodge in Paea on Tahiti-nui's west coast, with Moana David in Punaauia, or at Pension Vaiani or Pension Le Bon Jouir at Teahupoo on Tahiti-iti. A few of the surfing spots around Tahiti are mentioned in our circle-island tour.

The **École de Surf Tura'i Mataare** (Olivier Napias, tel./fax 41-91-37, surfschool@mail.pf), at Kelly Surf Boutique in the Fare Tony Commercial Center behind Big Burger in Papeete, teaches surfing and body surfing to persons aged eight and up. Courses with five three-hour lessons (CFP 19,500) or 10 lessons (CFP 26,500) are offered. Boards and transportation are supplied and a certificate is issued.

Papeete's **municipal swimming pool** (tel. 42-89-24) is open to the public Tuesday–Friday 1145–1600, weekends 0730–1700 (CFP 385). Most evenings after 1800 **soccer** is practiced in the sports field opposite the municipal swimming pool.

MOUNTAIN CLIMBING

Aorai

Tahiti's finest climb is to the summit of Aorai (2,066 meters), second-ranking peak on the island. (Some writers claim 2,110-meter Piti Hiti is the second-highest peak on Tahiti but it's actually a shoulder of Orohena.) A beaten 10-km track all the way to the top of Aorai makes a guide unnecessary, but food, water, flashlight, and long pants *are* required, plus a sleeping bag and warm sweater if you plan to spend the night up there. At last report the refuges at Fare Mato (1,400 meters) and Fare Ata (1,800 meters) were in good shape with drinking water available and splendid sunset views. Each refuge sleeps about 10 persons on the floor at no charge.

The road toward the summit begins beside the **Hôtel de Ville de Pirae,** an outlandish mock-colonial building surrounded by 66 massive Doric columns constructed in 2002 at a cost of CFP 1,120 million. It could be called "Gaston's folly" for ex-mayor Gaston Flosse who pushed the project through. Just inland from this building, take the first turn on the right and head up the hill to the access road on the left (if in doubt, ask). The trailhead is at Fare Rau Ape (600 meters) near **Le Belvédère** (tel. 42-73-44), a fancy French restaurant seven km up the narrow paved road from Pirae. Taxis want CFP 6,000 for the trip from Papeete and few people live up there, so hitching would be a case of finding tourists headed

© DAVID STANLEY

The track to the top of Aorai runs along this razor-back ridge.

for the restaurant, and weekends are best for this. You could rent a small car at the kilometer rate but parking near the restaurant is limited.

The restaurant does provide their clients with free *truck* transportation from most Papeete hotels and this the easiest way to get there. You can reserve the Belvédère *truck* at the Hôtel Tiare Tahiti reception in Papeete. Of course, in order to use it you'll be required to purchase a complete meal for CFP 4,950 including salad, dessert, coffee, and wine. The specialty is fondue bourguignon, a meat fondue, but you can substitute mahi mahi, steak, or shish kebab. The *truck* departs most Papeete hotels at 1130 and 1630, leaving the restaurant for the return trip to Papeete at 1430 and 2000.

To make a day of it, catch the 1130 *truck* up to the restaurant on the understanding that you'll be eating dinner and returning to town on the 2000 *truck* (make sure all of this is clearly understood before you pay—Tina Brichet at Le Belvédère speaks good English). This would give you all afternoon to cover part of the trail, although it's unlikely you'd have time to reach the top (even if you only get as far as Fare Mato, it's still well worth the effort). Take along a sandwich for

lunch. You should be able to leave some clean clothes at the restaurant to change into for dinner, and be sure to bring your bathing suit and a towel so you'll be able to take a dip in their swimming pool after the hike. If you can do all of this, the CFP 4,950 pp price becomes reasonable. Also consider the guided hikes mentioned below.

A large signboard outside the restaurant maps out the hike. Just above the restaurant is the French Army's Centre d'Instruction de Montagne, where you can sign a register. From Fare Rau Ape to the summit takes seven hours: an hour and a half to Hamuta, another two to Fare Mato (good view of Le Diadème, not visible from Papeete), then two and a half hours to Fare Ata, where most hikers spend the first night in order to cover the last 40 minutes to the summit the following morning. Just above Fare Mato cables have been fixed along the section of trail with the steepest drops on both sides. The hut at Fare Ata is in a low depression 100 meters beyond an open shelter.

The view from Aorai is magnificent, with Papeete and many of the empty interior valleys in full view. To the north is Tetiaroa atoll, while Moorea's jagged outline fills the west. Even on a cloudy day the massive green hulk of neighboring Orohena (2,241 meters) often towers above the clouds like Mt. Olympus. A bonus is the chance to see some of the original native vegetation of Tahiti, which survives better at high altitudes and in isolated gullies. In good weather Aorai is exhausting but superb; in the rain it's a disaster. Very few people do the climb, and if you go in the middle of the week you can expect to have the mountain to yourself.

Thousand Springs Trail

A much easier hike with better parking at the trailhead leads along the side of Aorai's neighbor Orohena. Turn off the coastal highway at the office of the Sheriff de Mahina, behind the Poissonnerie de Mahina (PK 11), and follow the paved road five km straight up through Mahinarama subdivision. At the top of the ridge at about 600 meters elevation the road ends. Park here—the trail is straight ahead. Anyone at Mahinarama will be able to direct you to the "Route des Mille Sources."

A jeep track built into the slope in 1975 follows the contour six km up the Tuauru River valley to the Thousand Springs at 900 meters elevation. The trail to the 2,241-meter summit of Orohena itself begins at the Thousand Springs and climbs steeply to Pito Iti where hikers spend the night before ascending Orohena the following morning. The Orohena climb involves considerable risks and a guide is required, but almost anyone can do the Thousand Springs hike on their own, enjoying the good views of the rounded peaks of Orohena to the left and Aorai's long ridge to the right. Since your car does most of the climbing, this is certainly the easiest way to see the island's unspoiled interior. There's nothing special to see at the Thousand Springs, so turn back whenever you like.

Mt. Marau

The road inland from directly opposite Faa'a Airport goes under the RDO bypass road and up the side of the island to an excellent viewpoint over northwestern Tahiti. It's a rough 10-km drive which should only be attempted by 4WD in dry weather. You must drive through a horrendous municipal dump on the way. From the TV tower at the end of the track it's only 30 minutes on foot to the summit of Mt. Marau (1,493 meters). From here you'll get another incredible view down into the Plateau of Oranges to the south, up the Fautaua Valley to the north, and along the ridge to Le Diadème and Aorai to the east. Several tour companies offer 4WD trips up here.

Guided Hikes

Numerous hikes around Tahiti are organized by Vincent Dubousquet of **Polynesian Adventure** (tel./fax 43-25-95, polynesianadv@mail.pf). He takes visitors on an easy walk up the Fautaua Valley near Papeete at CFP 6,200 pp. A bit more challenging are his climbs of Aorai and Mt. Marau (CFP 8,100 pp). The two-day trek along the Pari Coast is CFP 15,500 pp. These are only Vincent's most popular hikes and he knows many more. Call to find out which ones are scheduled during your stay.

Tahiti Evasion (tel./fax 56-48-77, www.tahitievasion.com) does day trips to Fautaua Falls or the Orofero Valley at CFP 8,900/6,900/5,200 pp for two/three/four persons. A three-day trek along the Pari Coast is CFP 23,500/18,000/15,500 on foot or CFP 32,500/24,000/20,000 by outrigger canoe. To climb Aorai in a day, they charge CFP 8,900/6,900/5,200 including the shuttle and a picnic lunch. Tahiti Evasion also offers several excellent hikes on Moorea.

Another professional guide, **Angélien Zéna** (tel. 57-22-67), specializes in three-day hikes around the Pari Coast at the east end of Tahiti-iti, "le Circuit Vert." Time is set aside for swimming and fishing. A boat from Vairao to Vaipoiri Grotto is used on the two-day hikes, and day trips can also be arranged. You can arrange to meet Angélien at Fare Nana'o, a pension near Taravao and easily accessible from Papeete by bus.

ACCOMMODATIONS

Most of the places to stay are in the congested Punaauia-to-Mahina strip engulfing Faa'a International Airport and Papeete, and they tend to offer poorer value for your money than comparable accommodations on Moorea. The hotel

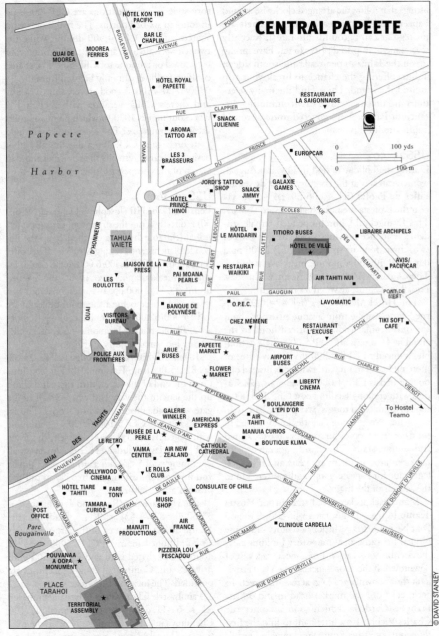

CENTRAL PAPEETE

HÔTEL KON TIKI PACIFIC
BAR LE CHAPLIN
QUAI DE MOOREA
MOOREA FERRIES
HÔTEL ROYAL PAPEETE
Papeete
Harbor
RESTAURANT LA SAIGONNAISE
SNACK JULIENNE
AROMA TATTOO ART
EUROPCAR
LES 3 BRASSERIES
JORDI'S TATTOO SHOP
SNACK JIMMY
GALAXIE GAMES
HÔTEL PRINCE HINOI
HÔTEL LE MANDARIN
TITIORO BUSES
LIBRAIRE ARCHIPELS
TAHUA VAIETE
HÔTEL DE VILLE
MAISON DE LA PRESS
RESTAURAT WAIKIKI
AVIS/ PACIFICAR
LES ROULOTTES
PAI MOANA PEARLS
AIR TAHITI NUI
PONT DE L'EST
BANQUE DE POLYNÉSIE
O.P.E.C.
LAVOMATIC
VISITORS BUREAU
CHEZ MÉMÈNE
RESTAURANT L'EXCUSE
TIKI SOFT CAFE
POLICE AUX FRONTIÈRES
ARUE BUSES
PAPEETE MARKET
AIRPORT BUSES
FLOWER MARKET
LIBERTY CINEMA
GALERIE WINKLER
BOULANGERIE L'EPI D'OR
AMERICAN EXPRESS
AIR TAHITI
MUSÉE DE LA PERLE
MANUIA CURIOS
To Hostel Teamo
LE RETRO
VAIMA CENTER
AIR NEW ZEALAND
BOUTIQUE KLIMA
CATHOLIC CATHEDRAL
HOLLYWOOD CINEMA
LE ROLLS CLUB
HÔTEL TIARE TAHITI
FARE TONY
CONSULATE OF CHILE
TAMARA CURIOS
MUSIC SHOP
POST OFFICE
Parc Bougainville
MANUITI PRODUCTIONS
AIR FRANCE
CLINIQUE CARDELLA
POUVANAA A OOPA MONUMENT
PIZZERIA LOU PESCADOU
PLACE TARAHOI
TERRITORIAL ASSEMBLY

0   100 yds
0   100 m

FRENCH POLYNESIA

© DAVID STANLEY

listings that follow are arranged clockwise around Papeete and Faa'a in each category. There are no regular campgrounds on Tahiti. Recently several medium-priced places to stay have sprung up on the Tahiti-iti peninsula and south side of Tahiti, offering the chance to break your trip around the island. These (and the many selections in Punaauia within easy commuting distance of Papeete) are covered under Around Tahiti later in this chapter.

US$25–50

During the holiday period in July and August, women can stay at the six-story **Foyer de Jeunes Filles de Paofai** (tel. 46-06-80, fax 46-06-81) near the Protestant church on boulevard Pomare. This Evangelical Church-operated female student's residence provides 116 beds in rooms of two, three, four, or six beds at CFP 2,000 pp a day, CFP 30,000 a month, breakfast included. There's a daily 2200 curfew, except Wednesday, Friday, and Saturday when it's midnight.

The **Hôtel Mahina Tea** (tel. 42-00-97), up rue Sainte-Amélie from avenue Bruat, is about the only regular economy-priced hotel in the city. The 16 rooms are CFP 5,000 single or double, reduced to CFP 4,200 if you stay three or more nights. A room with twin beds instead of a double bed is CFP 1,000 more. Six small studios with cooking facilities cost CFP 100,000 a month double. All rooms have private bath with hot water. No cooking facilities are provided in the daily rental rooms but you may use the shared fridge downstairs. This family-operated place has been around for many years and it's excellent value for Papeete. Dogs and roosters add to the sounds of the night.

Many backpackers head straight for **Hostel Teamo** (tel. 42-47-26, fax 43-56-95), 8 rue du Pont Neuf, Quartier Mission, a century-old house hidden behind a new four-story building near the Archbishop's Palace, just a short walk east of downtown. If the door is locked when you arrive, look for the owner at No. 3 across the street. To get there from the market head inland on rue François Cardella, which soon becomes rue Charles Vienot. It's a little hard to find the first time, but convenient once you know it. Dormi-

tory-style accommodations are CFP 2,000 pp in four- to six-bed dorms. The five rooms with shared bath are CFP 4,500 double, while the two with private bath are CFP 6,000. Bring your own towel or rent one for CFP 500. The shared cooking facilities can only be used from 0600–0900/1800–2100. A good grocery store is nearby and there's a nice veranda with French TV. Checkout time is 1000, at which point you must vacate the premises. The receptionist will hold your luggage at CFP 200 a day. It's all rather basic but Teamo remains the choice of those in search of the cheapest possible option.

US$50–100

Pension Dahl Fifi (Joséphine Dahl, tel. 82-63-30) is directly across the street from the airport terminal (the fourth house on the left up the hill beside Blanchisserie Pressing Mea Ma). They offer three rooms at CFP 3,500/6,000 single/double including breakfast, plus several four- and five-bed dorms at CFP 2,000 pp. Two additional rooms in a separate house behind the main building are CFP 4,000/6,000. Communal cooking facilities are available, but the location is noisy due to the nearby industrial laundry and airport.

To reach **Tahiti Airport Lodge** (tel. 82-23-68, fax 82-25-00) from Pension Dahl Fifi, continue up to the end of the street, turn right and climb up the lane to the very end where you'll find a gate with wide green and white stripes. The six rooms here are CFP 5,100/6,600 single/double with shared bath, CFP 8,800 double with private bath, breakfast included. There's a lovely small swimming pool overlooking airport. They'll pick you up from the airport for free if you call (no pickups after 2200).

The **Heitiare Inn** (Raymond Tarahu, tel. 83-33-52, fax 82-77-53) at PK 4.3, Faa'a, near the Mairie de Faa'a a km east of the airport, has six air-conditioned rooms at CFP 5,000 single or double with shared bath and CFP 6,500 with private bath. Communal cooking facilities are provided. The location isn't great.

Family-style **Chez Myrna** (Myrna Dammeyer, tel. 42-64-11, dammeyer.family@mail.pf), 106 Chemin vicinal de Tipaerui, is .5 km up the road from the Hôtel Matavai, almost opposite Limonaderie Singapour. They offer two shared-bath rooms at CFP 4,240/5,830 single/double with breakfast (minimum stay two nights). Dinner is CFP 1,500 (if desired). Myrna's husband, Walter, is a German expat who has been on Tahiti for decades. There's no sign outside, so call ahead.

The **Hôtel Victoria** (Bruno Gatto, tel. 43-13-93, fax 43-27-28), 10 rue du Commandant Destremeau, Papeete, has seven air-conditioned rooms with bath facing the noisy road at CFP 7,000 single or double. A dorm bed here is CFP 2,500. It's overpriced but uncrowded.

The timeworn **Hôtel Royal Papeete** (tel. 42-01-29, fax 43-79-09), 291 boulevard Pomare opposite the Quai de Moorea, has 78 large air-conditioned rooms beginning at CFP 9,000 single or double, CFP 10,500 triple, including tax. This hotel looks seedy from the outside but many tourists do stay there and it's very convenient if you happen to miss the last ferry. At last report both nightclubs in the Royal Papeete were closed and the hotel itself looks like it might not survive much longer.

An excellent new place to stay is **Pension Puea** (tel. 85-43-43, fax 42-09-35, pension.puea@mail.pf) at 87 rue Octave off avenue du Prince Hinoï 500 meters east of the Moorea ferry landing. The six rooms with shared bath in this two-story building are CFP 6,500 double or CFP 8,500 for a larger family room, breakfast included. Communal cooking facilities are available.

US$100–150

Opened in 1997, the six-story **Hôtel Tiare Tahiti** (tel. 43-68-48, fax 43-68-47, hotltiaretahiti@mail.pf), at 417 boulevard Pomare on the waterfront next to the post office, has 38 air-conditioned rooms with satellite TV beginning at CFP 13,600/16,000 standard/oceanview double, plus 11 percent tax. The standard rooms on the side of the hotel facing the post office are the quieter. The Tiare Tahiti should be your choice if you want quality accommodations without having to stay at the Sheraton.

The six-story **Hôtel Prince Hinoï** (tel. 42-32-77, fax 42-33-66, hotelprincehinoi@mail.pf), avenue du Prince Hinoï at boulevard Pomare, has 72 small air-conditioned rooms at CFP 12,800/13,600/14,500 single/double/triple, plus 11 percent tax. The rooms are okay but it's in a seedy area with prostitutes working the adjacent streets and heavy drinking going on in the bar downstairs.

The **Hôtel Kon Tiki Pacific** (tel. 54-16-16, fax 42-11-66, kontiki@mail.pf), 271 boulevard Pomare opposite the Quai de Moorea, has 36 spacious air-conditioned rooms beginning at CFP 11,250/14,730 single/double including tax (CFP 1,110 extra for two beds, additional persons CFP 2,150). Don't accept one of the noisy rooms near the elevator, which are always offered first, and avoid rooms on the lower floors, which are subjected to disco noise. Instead, get one with a balcony on the upper front side of the building. You'll have an excellent view straight into the adjacent French naval base.

US$150–250

The French-owned **Sofitel Maeva Beach** (tel. 86-66-00, fax 43-84-70) at PK 7.5, Punaauia, was built by UTA French Airlines in the late 1960s. The 224 air-conditioned rooms in this pyramidal high-rise cost CFP 23,000 single or double garden view, CFP 27,700 lagoon view, CFP 30,400 panoramic view, plus 11 percent tax (children under 12 free). The seven-story Maeva Beach faces a man-made white beach, but with pollution on the increase in the adjacent Punaauia Lagoon, most swimmers stick to the hotel pool. Tennis courts are available. The entire complex could use a facelift.

The 138-room **Hôtel Matavai** (tel. 42-67-67, fax 42-36-90, www.hotelmatavai.pf) is CFP 14,500/19,000/23,500 single/double/triple plus 11 percent tax with bath, TV, and two double beds. You can almost tell this four-floor edifice was once a Holiday Inn, but it has gone downhill since then. Tennis and squash courts, mini-golf, a swimming pool, and other sporting facilities are on the premises. This is the only hotel which Papeete's politically-connected taxi drivers allow to provide free airport transfers. We've received some negative feedback about the Matavai.

Hôtel Le Mandarin (tel. 50-33-50, fax 42-16-32, www.hotelmandarin.com), 51 rue Colette, is a modern six-story hotel whose 37 air-conditioned rooms are overpriced at CFP 14,000/16,500 single/double, plus 11 percent tax (children under 12 free). The levels of service and cleanliness at the Mandarin vary and the location in the heart of the market area isn't the best.

The **Hôtel Le Royal Tahitien** (tel. 50-40-40, fax 50-40-41, www.hotelroyaltahitien.com), off avenue du Prince Hinoï at PK 3.5, Pirae, is a peaceful two-story building facing beautifully kept grounds on a litter-strewn black-sand beach. You're unlikely to see anyone swimming here as the water is murky with no coral, but the windsurfing is good. The 40 air-conditioned rooms are CFP 17,000 single or double, CFP 20,000 triple, plus 11 percent tax. Breakfast and dinner are served on the attractive terrace overlooking the lagoon (in general, the food prices here are exorbitant). It's a long, boring walk into town (and no public transport back after 1700)—you'll get better value on Moorea for this kind of money.

US$250 and up

The **Tahiti Beachcomber Inter-Continental** (tel. 86-51-10, fax 86-51-30, www.tahiti.interconti.com), west of the airport at PK 7, Faa'a, is a former Travelodge built in 1974. It's a smart international hotel with a Polynesian flair—the largest resort in French Polynesia. The 232 air-conditioned rooms in the main buildings begin at CFP 30,900 single or double plus 11 percent tax; for one of the 32 overwater bungalows it's about double. Children under 15 sharing the room with their parents stay for free. A breakfast and dinner meal plan is CFP 7,600 pp extra. Tahitian dancing and crafts demonstrations are regular features. The beach is artificial but the swim-up bar is fun. The hotel pools are reserved for guests. Paid activities include water-skiing, snorkeling trips, and scuba diving is with the **Aquatica Dive Center** (tel. 53-34-96, fax 53-34-74, www.aquatica-dive.com). The Automatic Currency Exchange machine in the lobby of this hotel changes the banknotes of nine countries for a CFP 500 commission.

The **Hôtel Sheraton Tahiti** (tel. 86-48-48, fax 86-48-40, www.sheratontahiti.com), at PK 2.6 between Papeete and the airport, reopened in 1999 after being completely redeveloped by Louis Wane, brother of pearl baron Robert Wan. This site was once the residence of Princess Pomare, daughter of the last king of Tahiti, and from 1961 to 1996 a historic colonial-style hotel stood there. Outrigger Hotels of Hawaii managed the property initially but they withdrew after disagreements with Wane. The 200 air-conditioned rooms are in a series of four-story American-style buildings. Rates begin at CFP 33,000 plus 11 percent tax and increase to CFP 86,500 for the best suite. There's a large beachside freshwater swimming pool with a Jacuzzi on the knoll just above the waterfall, a spa, a 500-seat banquet hall, and an overwater restaurant with splendid sunset views of Moorea. Berhard Begliomini's TOPdive center offers scuba diving from the resort. The frequent Outumaoro *trucks* pass the Sheraton, Inter-Continental, and Maeva Beach until late at night. Europcar has desks at all three resorts.

In late 2004 the **Radisson Plaza Resort Tahiti** (tel. 48-88-88, fax 48-88-89, www.radissonasiapacific.com) opened on the black sands of Lafayette Beach facing Matavai Bay, seven km east of central Papeete. This new resort is just east of Arue, at the foot of the hill bearing the former Hôtel Tahara'a. The 86 ocean view rooms, 53 suites, and 26 duplex suites in seven blocks start at CFP 32,000 single or double. The core of the resort is a huge lagoon swimming pool with a sloping beach entry and waterfall edge. All the facilities of a five-star hotel are provided.

FOOD

Food Trailers

In the evening take a stroll along the Papeete waterfront past the dozens of gaily lit vans known as *les roulottes,* which form a colorful night market at **Tahua Vaiete** by the Quai d'honneur. Here you'll find everything from couscous, pizza, waffles, crêpes, and *brouchettes* (shish kebab) to steak with real *pommes frites.* There's no better place to sample *poisson cru.* As the city lights wink gently across the harbor, sailors promenade with their *vahine,* adding a touch of romance and glamour. The food and atmosphere are excellent, and even if you're not dining, it's a scene not to miss. On Friday and Saturday nights a live band will be playing in the bandshell. The most crowded *roulottes* generally have the best food, but you may have to wait as lots of people bring large bowls to be filled and taken home. The biggest drawback is that beer is not available. It all happens nightly from 1800–0100.

At **Tahua To'ata,** a 15-minute walk west along the waterfront, a similar atmosphere prevails. Here a row of outdoor terrace restaurants, including the Soledane Grill, Chez Jimmy, Snack Moeata, Snack Mado, and La Terrase, are always crowded with local residents. Pick the one that is most crowded. They're open daily.

Self-Service

Poly-Self Restaurant (tel. 43-75-32; weekdays 0530–1430), 8 rue Gauguin behind the Banque de Polynésie, dispenses unpretentious, filling Chinese-style plate lunches at about CFP 890. Additional seating is available upstairs.

Cafétéria La Palmerie (tel. 45-00-36; weekdays 1100–1400), upstairs off passage Cardella near the Vaima Center, offers a different main plate every day at CFP 950, or CFP 1,250 including an appetizer and dessert.

The **Foyer de Jeunes Filles de Paofai** (tel. 46-06-80), opposite the Protestant church on boulevard Pomare, has a good modern self-service cafeteria open weekdays for lunch 1130–1300. Alcohol is not available here.

Inexpensive grilled meat and fish dishes are the specialty at **Snack Paofai** (tel. 42-95-76; weekdays 0500–1430, Sat. 0500–1330) near Clinique Paofai. A complete meal chosen from among the specials listed on the blackboard and consumed on their airy terrace will run CFP 850, but arrive before 1300 or you'll find little left. On Thursday they prepare a special couscous dish—CFP 950 including a Coke.

Restaurant Oriane (tel. 42-03-06; weekdays 0630–1500), 75 avenue Georges Clemenceau halfway between Rond Point and Hospital Mamao, serves hearty meals to Tahitian workers. You can get a meat and rice lunch for only CFP 500 a plate.

Snack Bars

To sample the cuisine of the people, check out the Chinese/Tahitian eateries on rue Cardella right beside the market. Try *ma'a tinito,* a mélange of red beans, pork, macaroni, and vegetables on rice (CFP 850). A large Hinano beer at these places is around CFP 500.

Upstairs in the market under a thatched awning, **La Cafeteria de Marché** (Mon.–Sat. 0400–1500) serves a typical Tahitian breakfast of a large coffee with bread and butter for CFP 225. Have your lunch elsewhere.

Snack Julienne (tel. 42-86-49; daily 0500–1700), rues Clappier and Leboucher, is an unpretentious local place with some of the best prices in town. Their morning café au lait with bread and butter is CFP 280, while the cooked lunch plates go for CFP 650–1,050. The large baguette sandwiches *(casse-croûtes)* can't be beat at CFP 130–180.

Some of the freshest baguette sandwiches in town are sold over the counter at **Boulangerie L'Epi d'Or** (tel. 43-07-13), 26 rue du Maréchal Foch near the market.

For fruit juices, sandwiches, crepes, waffles, and ice cream cones, search no further than **Le Motu Tahiti** (tel. 41-33-59; closed Sun.), corner of rue du Général de Gaulle and rue Georges Lagarde behind the Vaima Center. The stand-up tables on the corner are very Parisian. **Vitamine Glacier Saladerie** (tel. 43-37-70; closed Sun.), just upstairs from Le Motu, has a happy combination of salads, draft beer, and tasty ice cream.

Asian

All of the best Chinese restaurants are along rue Colette east from the market. **Restaurant Snack Chez Méméne** (tel. 43-09-26; Mon.–Sat. 0530–1530), 25 rue Colette, is a nice open air locale with poisson cru (CFP 900), sashimi (CFP 1,200), shrimp (CFP 1,600), chicken (CFP 900), beef (CFP 1,260), and chow mein (CFP 900). Wash it down with draft beer.

Restaurant Hong Kong Pearls (weekdays 0800–1500/1700–2200, Sat. 0800–1500, Sun. 1700–2200), 45 rue Colette, serves ordinary Chinese market food. The menu posted in the window outside lists chow mein (CFP 750), seafood (CFP 1,000–1,600), chicken (CFP 850), and *steak frites* or duck (CFP 900).

Le Dragon d'Or (tel. 42-96-12; Tues.–Sun. 1130–1330/1830–2130), 49 rue Colette next to Hôtel Le Mandarin, serves more upscale Chinese food at CFP 1,500–2,000 a plate. The classic Tahitian-Chinese menu includes dishes like as pork with taro or steamed fish and you'll like the large portions and friendly, reliable service.

Snack Jimmy (tel. 43-63-32; Mon.–Sat. 1130–1400/1830–2100, Sun. 1830–2100), rue Colette at rue des Écoles near Hôtel Le Mandarin, features a clean, simple dining room with specialties like Thai curries (CFP 1,200–2,200), Vietnamese rice (CFP 950–1,100), Chinese plates (CFP 900–1,350), Chinese seafood (CFP 1,800), and filet mignon (CFP 1,800). Lobster is available at the market price.

Restaurant Waikiki (tel. 42-95-27; daily 1100–1300/1800–2100, closed Sun. lunch and Mon. dinner), rue Leboucher 20, is old and tired, but cheaper than the rest: chop suey and chow mein CFP 750, fried fish CFP 1,100. The staff doesn't speak English but the menu is in three languages. You'll probably have to ask for a spoon.

Restaurant La Saigonnaise (tel. 42-05-35; closed Sun.), 67 avenue du Prince Hinoï, has moderately expensive but fresh Vietnamese food served in a quiet setting. The Saigonese soup (CFP 1,150) makes a good lunch.

Finally, Papeete has it's own **Sushi Bar** (tel. 45-35-25; Mon.–Wed. 1115–1400, Thurs.–Sat. 1115–1400 and 1815–2200) near the Qantas office in the Vaima Center. You choose from the typical Japanese specialties floating in wooden bowls in a trough along the bar, and you're charged per dish depending on the color of the bowl (CFP 260–650 each). What better place to have sashimi?

Italian

For a taste of the Mediterranean, **Pizzeria Lou Pescadou** (tel. 43-74-26; Mon.–Sat. 1100–1430/1830–2300), on rue Anne-Marie Javouhey a long block back from the Vaima Center, is friendly, unpretentious, breezy, inexpensive, and fun. Their pizza pescatore (CFP 750) makes a good lunch, and a big pitcher of ice water is in-

cluded in the price. Owner Mario Vitulli may be from Marseilles, but you won't complain about his spaghetti—a huge meal for about CFP 800. And where else will you get unpitted olives on a pizza? Nonalcoholic drinks are on the house while you stand and wait for a table. The service is lively, and Lou Pescadou is very popular among local French, a high recommendation.

L'api'zzeria (tel. 42-98-30; Mon.–Sat. 1130–2200), 44 rue de Commandant Destremeau near the Protestant church, also prepares real pizza in a brick oven. This garden restaurant is a bit more expensive than Lou Pescadou (spaghetti CFP 780–1,300, pizzas CFP 770–1,400, fish CFP 1,390–2,380) but still good value. Draft beer is available.

French

For the aspiring gourmet, Papeete has much to offer. For example, **Café des Négociants** (tel. 48-08-48; Tues.–Sat. 1200–1430/1900–2200), 10 rue Gilbert next to Pai Moana Pearls, is a Parisian bistro offering a huge selection of beers and French and Tahitian dishes. Lunch mains cost CFP 800–2,000, dinner CFP 1,000–3,700.

Le Grillardin (tel. 43-09-90; Mon. 1130–1430, Tues.–Fri. 1130–1430/1900–2200, Sat. 1900–2200), rue Paul Gauguin opposite the Air Tahiti Nui office, offers fine French cuisine in a traditional country inn. Fish dishes are CFP 1,800–2,500, meat CFP 1,550–2,300.

La Petite Auberge (tel. 42-86-13; weekdays 1200–1330/1900–2130, Sat. 1900–2130), Pont de l'Est, is a fancy French country inn with linen tablecloths. Their menu lists appetizers (CFP 1,150–1,350), seafoods (CFP 1,950–2,550), grilled meats (CFP 1,500–1,750), and house specialties (CFP 2,150–3,350). Snails *(escargot)* as an appetizer is CFP 850 for a half a bowl.

Restaurant L'excuse (tel. 53-13-25; Tues.–Fri. 1200–1400/1900–2130, Sat. 1900–2130), 47 rue du Maréechal Foch, is a quality air-conditioned restaurant with meat dishes at CFP 1,950–2,800, fish at CFP 1,700–2,200.

Le Rubis Wine Bar (tel. 43-25-55; Mon. 1130–1500, Tues.–Sat. 1130–1500/1800–2100, Sun. 1800–2100), rue Jeanne d'Arc below the Vaima Center, is a good upscale French restaurant with seafood, salads, and meats (CFP 1,500–2,900). The chef Acajou has been running celebrated Papeete restaurants for a quarter century. Le Rubis claims to offer 130 different wines by the glass.

Restaurant L'O à la bouche (tel. 45-29-76; weekdays 1130–1300 and 1915–2200, Sat. 1915–2230), up passage Cardella opposite Air New Zealand, is an elegant French restaurant with funky blue decor. Their nouvelle cuisine includes mouth-watering mains at CFP 1,450–2,900, seafood at CFP 2,550–2,850, and meat at CFP 2,450–2,900. It's popular with trendy young French locals.

More fine French cuisine is available at **Restaurant Moana Iti** (tel. 42-65-24; closed Sun.), 483 boulevard Pomare next to Club 106 just west of avenue Bruat. The menu lists grilled meat (CFP 1,500–2,000), shellfish (CFP 1,660–1,950), and house specialties (CFP 1,950–3,520).

Pub Food

Recommended is **Les 3 Brasseurs** (tel. 50-60-25; daily 0800–0100), boulevard Pomare near avenue Prince Hinoï, with a fashionable sidewalk terrace overlooking the Moorea ferries. This northeastern French style microbrewery specializes in *flammekueche* (like a pizza made with unleavened bread and no tomato sauce). The "classique" with onions and ham is CFP 850 (or CFP 1,000 with a small beer). Otherwise a half chicken with beer is CFP 1,500, with *poisson cru* CFP 1,500. Sandwiches are also available. It's all spelled out in a menu resembling a French newspaper.

Brasserie des Remparts (tel. 42-80-00; weekdays 0630–2200, Sat. 1000–1500), rue des Remparts between La Petit Auberge and Tiki Soft Cafe, is a Belgian-style pub with draft beer at CFP 500/950 a half/full liter. The meals are CFP 1,450–1,900.

Big Burger Snack Bar (tel. 43-01-98; Mon.–Sat. 0600–2300), rue du Général de Gaulle and rue Georges Lagarde, is a world better than the McDonald's across the street. The *plat du jour* here is CFP 1,700, and if it's sold out you can get hamburgers (CFP 600–850), spaghetti (CFP 1,100), grilled meats (CFP 1,100–2,200). It's a

good place for an afternoon beer and there's often a live Tahitian group playing.

Café de la Gare (tel. 42-75-95; weekdays 0700–midnight, Sat. 1000–midnight), on rue du Général de Gaulle opposite McDonald's, is a typical French pub with draft beer. The only meal served here is lunch (CFP 1,200–1,750).

Other Restaurants

Carnivores may want to know about **Restaurant Le Gallieni** (tel. 42-05-23), on boulevard Pomare below the Hôtel Royal Papeete. Thursday–Saturday 1145–1400/1900–2130 they serve the house specialty, prime rib, at CFP 2,090–3,770. Add CFP 240 for the sauce and CFP 240 per vegetable side dish.

Jack Lobster (tel. 42-50-58; weekdays 1130–1400/1900–2130, Sat. 1900–2230), just upstairs from the newsstand in the corner of the Vaima Center closest to the port, is an upscale steakhouse with hearty grilled meats (CFP 1,700–2,500), surf and turf combos (CFP 2,500–5,000), seafood (CFP 1,700–2,500), lobster (CFP 4,100), and Tex-Mex (CFP 1,300–2,150).

Market Coffee (tel. 45-60-70; Mon.–Thurs. 0530–1600, Fri. and Sat. 0530–0100, Sun. 0700–1100), rue Edouard Ahnne behind Air Tahiti, is a lively unpretentious place with dancing on Saturday night. A full breakfast here will cost CFP 1,000. Meat and fish mains are CFP 1,200–2,400, grilled swordfish *(meka)* CFP 1,300. Also check the salads.

The Papeete equivalent of a Hard Rock Cafe is **Morrison's Café** (tel. 42-78-61; weekdays 1100–1430/1800–0100, Saturday 1800–0100), upstairs in the Vaima Center. Use the elevator on the side of the building just outside Air New Zealand. Morrison's offers a full menu (salads CFP 1,450–2,100, grilled dishes CFP 1,550–2,350) or a *plat du jour* (CFP 1,450) on a breezy rooftop terrace with a view of Tahiti. Some readers have reported that the lunch is of variable quality. There's an extensive wine list and live music is sometimes performed Tuesday–Saturday from 2230.

Cafés

Le Retro (tel. 42-86-83) on the boulevard Pomare side of the Vaima Center is *the* place to sit and sip a drink while watching the passing parade. The fruit-flavored ice cream is intense and for yachters, a banana split after a long sailing trip can be heavenly. The atmosphere here is thoroughly Côte d'Azur. A sign encourages tipping.

Cheaper meals and drinks are available at **Snack Hollywood** (tel. 54-59-51; daily 0700–2030), around the corner from Le Retro on pedestrians-only rue Georges Lagarde. The menu includes large salads (CFP 800), poisson cru (CFP 1,000), omelettes (CFP 250), grilled cheese (CFP 350), chicken and chips (CFP 750), and *steak frites* (CFP 1,000). Coffee, tea, and chocolate are CFP 200. It's a good bet on Sunday when many other places are closed.

Aux Delices Chez Louisette (tel. 45-46-46; weekdays 0600–1700, Sat. 0600–1130), on passage Cardella, the narrow street running inland almost opposite Air New Zealand, is good for ice cream, pastries, quiche, and coffee. It's clean and chic with most items displayed in window and nothing over CFP 1,000.

When the heat gets to you, **Pâtisserie La Marquisienne** (tel. 42-83-52; closed Mon.), 29 rue Colette, offers coffee and pastries in air-conditioned comfort. It's popular among French expats.

Tiki Soft Cafe (tel. 88-93-98; weekdays 0700–0100, Sat. 1400–0100), rue des Remparts at rue du Maréchal Foch, is venue for local French gays.

Restaurant Le Manava (tel. 42-02-91; weekdays 0500–2000, Sat. 0500–1100), avenue Bruat at Commandant Destremeau, has a nice open air sidewalk terrace, perfect for a coffee or beer.

Groceries

Downtown there's **Champion** (tel. 54-29-29; Mon.–Sat. 0700–1930, Sun. 0630–1200), a large supermarket on rue du Commandant Destremeau. Get whole barbecued chickens and chow mein in the deli section.

At PK 8.3 Punaauia, just south of the junction of the auto route to Papeete, is **Carrefour,** Tahiti's first enclosed shopping mall, which opened in 1986. Some of the cheapest groceries on the island are available at the large adjoining Continent supermarket (tel. 46-08-08; Mon.–Sat. 0800–2000, Sun. 0800–1200). The deli section has a

good selection of takeaway items including barbecued chickens, and there's also a fancy snack bar on the mall. The supermarket doesn't only sell groceries but also clothing and mass-produced souvenirs at the best prices on the island. Carrefour is easily accessible from Papeete on the frequent Outumaoro *truck* which finishes its route across the highway.

Other big supermarkets around the island include **Supermarche Venustar** (tel. 48-10-13; Mon.–Sat. 0630–1930, Sun. 0600–1130) at the turnoff to Point Venus on the circle island highway (PK 10), and **Champion** (tel. 57-16-76; Mon.–Sat. 0600–1900, Sun. 0600–1200) in Taravao. All of these are good places to pick up picnic supplies.

ENTERTAINMENT AND EVENTS

Five Papeete cinemas show B-grade films dubbed into French (admission CFP 850). The Concorde is in the Vaima Center; Hollywood I and II are on rue Georges Lagarde beside the Vaima Center; Liberty Cinema is on rue du Maréchal Foch near the market; and the Mamao Palace is near Mamao Hospital.

Nightlife

After dark local carousers and French sailors take over the little bars crowding the streets around rue des Écoles and east on boulevard Pomare. Yet for the glitzy capital of a leading French resort, the nightlife is surprisingly downmarket.

The places with live music or a show generally impose a CFP 1,000–1,500 cover charge on men, which includes one drink. Nothing much gets going before 2200, and by 0100 everything is very informal (many bars stay open until 0400). Male visitors should ensure they've got their steps right before inviting any local ladies onto the floor—or face immediate rejection.

French soldiers and sailors out of uniform patronize the bars along boulevard Pomare opposite the Quai de Moorea, including **Bar Le Chaplin** (tel. 42-73-05), next door to Paradise Night Club, and **Bar Le Taina Kaina** (tel. 42-64-40), 301 boulevard Pomare at rue Clappier.

Paradise Night Club (tel. 42-73-05; nightly 1900–0100, weekends until 0200), next to Hôtel

The **Piano Bar** (tel. 42-88-24), beside Hôtel Prince Hinoï on rue des Écoles, is the most notorious of Papeete's *mahu* (transvestite) discos. It's open daily 1500–0300 with a special show at 0130. Many of the persons dressed in sexy miniskirts along rue des Écoles are not exactly what they appear to be! Notice the folks beckoning from upstairs windows.

Café de l'amour (tel. 42-51-33), across rue des Écoles from the Piano Bar, has beer on tap and usually no cover. A lively crowd patronizes this colorful establishment, where a seasoned Tahitian band plays on weekends. Just don't believe the low drink prices advertised outside.

Bar Royal Kikiriri (tel. 43-58-64; Wed.–Sun. 2200–0300), rue Colette at rue des Écoles, is another Tahitian disco. Entry costs CFP 1,000 Friday and Saturday including one drink.

Le Rolls Club (tel. 43-41-42; Wed.–Sun. 2100–0400, Fri. 1400–0400, admission CFP 1,000), in the Vaima Center upstairs opposite Big Burger, was once a flashy youth disco but now they play mostly Tahitian dance music for a local crowd.

El Latino (tel. 42-40-01; weekdays 0900–0100, Sat. 1700–0300), rue Georges Lagarde behind El Retro, is an upscale pub with Mexican decor. There's disco dancing here after 2300 (no cover charge).

Club 106 (tel. 42-72-92; Thurs.–Sat. 2200–0400), 483 boulevard Pomare just west of avenue Bruat, caters to a slightly older crowd than the other places. They have a different DJ every night and admission for men is CFP 2,000, which includes a drink.

Cultural Shows for Visitors

A Tahitian dance show takes place in the Bougainville Restaurant, downstairs at the **Sofitel Maeva Beach** (tel. 86-66-00), Friday and Saturday at 2000. If you're not interested in having dinner, a drink at the Bar Moorea by the pool will put you in position to see the action (no cover charge). Sunday this hotel presents a full Tahitian feast at 1200, complete with earth oven *(ahimaa)* and dancing at 1300.

The **Tahiti Beachcomber Inter-Continental** (tel. 86-51-10) stages one of the top Tahitian

COURTESY OF TAHITI TOURISME

fire dancers at a Papeete resort

Kon Tiki and opposite the Moorea ferries, has West African and reggae music. Wednesday–Saturday after 2200 admission is CFP 2,000 pp including one drink. A dress code applies. Sunday–Tuesday nights it's karaoke. Their restaurant serves meals in the CFP 1,400–2,400 range Friday and Saturday 1900–midnight.

Le Manhattan Discotheque (tel. 42-63-65; Wed.–Sat. 2200–0400, CFP 1,500 cover charge), 271 boulevard Pomare below Hôtel Kon Tiki, is similar.

Le Grenier de Montmarte (tel. 45-47-77; Tues.–Sat. 2200–0300), 7 avenue Prince Hinoï, is a small Parisian-style nightclub with live music and no cover charge.

Mana Rock Café (tel. 48-36-36), boulevard Pomare at rue des Écoles in front of Hôtel Prince Hinoï, is a popular meeting place. There's karaoke from 2200 in the disco upstairs, dancing from 2300–0400 nightly (CFP 1,500–2,000 admission for males Fri. and Sat. nights). A small beer costs CFP 1,000.

FRENCH POLYNESIA

dance shows on the island; attend for the price of a drink at the bar near the pool (no cover charge). The Grand Ballet de Tahiti (Lorenzo) often performs here. The dancers' starting time is officially Wednesday, Friday, and Sunday at 2000, so arrive early and be prepared to wait. The seafood dinner show on Friday is CFP 6,950.

The **Hôtel Sheraton Tahiti** (tel. 86-48-48) has a Tahitian show in the restaurant Friday at 2030 and Sunday at 1300. **Hôtel Méridien Tahiti** (tel. 47-07-07) in Punaauia presents Tahitian dancing on Friday nights.

There's often Tahitian dancing in the **Captain Bligh Restaurant** (tel. 43-62-90) at the Punaauia Lagoonarium (PK 11.4) on Friday and Saturday nights at 2100. The buffet here is CFP 4,850 but you can also simply order a few drinks.

Be sure to check these times and days before going out of your way as things change. If you want dinner, do reserve.

SHOPPING

Normal shopping hours in Papeete are weekdays 0730–1130/1330–1730, Saturday 0730–1200. Papeete's largest shopping complex is the **Vaima Center,** where numerous shops sell black pearls, designer clothes, souvenirs, and books. It's certainly worth a look; then branch out into the surrounding streets. **Galerie Winkler** (tel. 42-81-77), 17 rue Jeanne d'Arc beside American Express, sells contemporary paintings of Polynesia.

Don't overlook the local fashions. Several shops along rue Paul Gauguin sell very chic island clothing.

If you're a surfer, check **Kelly Surf** (tel. 45-29-30), rue du 22 Septembre near the market, for boards, plus all attendant gear. **Magasin 360°** (tel. 42-98-86), 41 rue Colette, also sells trendy surfing gear.

Nauti-Sport (tel. 50-59-59) in Fare Ute carries a good selection of quality snorkeling/dive masks at reasonable prices.

The **Centre Philatelique** (tel. 41-43-35, www.tahitiphilatelie.pf) at the main post office sells the stamps and first-day covers of all the French Pacific territories. Some are quite beautiful and inexpensive.

Photo Lux (tel. 42-84-31), 30 rue du Maréchal Foch near the market, has some of the cheapest color print film you'll find, and they repair Minolta cameras.

Souvenirs

The best handicraft shopping is upstairs in Papeete Market. The pareus are outstanding. Surprisingly, handicrafts are often cheaper in Papeete than on their island of origin.

For Marquesan woodcarvings have a look in **Manuia Curios** (tel. 42-04-94), 7 run Jaussen on the east side of the cathedral. **Tamara Curios** (tel. 42-54-42), rue du Général de Gaulle opposite McDonald's, is another large craft shop with mass-produced objects.

Serious collectors should visit **Galerie Ganesha** (tel. 43-04-18), just down from Hawaiian Airlines in the Vaima Center. The top quality handicrafts here include Fatu Hiva tapa, tikis, bowls, Marquesas nose flutes, and carved mother of pearl. There are also objects from other areas, such as Fiji. Prices are high but fair.

Music

The **Music Shop** (tel. 42-85-63), 13 rue du Général de Gaulle behind the Vaima Center, has a large selection of compact discs of Tahitian music. You can use headphones to listen to the music.

If you're serious about building a Polynesian music collection, visit **Manuiti Productions** (tel. 42-82-39; weekdays 0900–1100/1200–1600), above Pharmacie Fare Rau on rue du Général de Gaulle (entry from the alley beside McDonald's, rear stairwell and up to the 2nd floor). They have the best selection of Tahitian music CDs and cassettes anywhere, including over 50 CDs and 100 cassettes from their own studio, founded by Yves Roche in 1962. They also sell sheet music and have manuals that teach Tahitian singing.

Pearls

Pai Moana Pearls (tel. 43-31-10), 8 rue Gilbert (down the alley between the Banque Socredo and La Maison de la Press from Tahua Vaiete), can give you a free copy of Rick Steger's excellent brochure *Pricing Pearls: The Consumer's Guide to Tahitian Black Pearls.*

O.P.E.C. (tel. 45-36-26), 20 rue Gauguin (upstairs), and **Tahiti Pearl Dream** (tel. 50-22-00), rue Leboucher 10 (upstairs), are black pearl sales rooms a block from the market. They'll show you a free video about the pearls if they think you're a potential buyer.

Several dozen other jewelers around Papeete, including **Vaima Perles** (tel. 42-55-57), **Tahiti Perles** (tel. 46-15-15), and **Sibani Perles** (tel. 54-24-24) in the Vaima Center, also sell pearls, and it's wise to visit several before making such an important purchase. Tahiti Perles specializes in classic settings using large pearls while Sibani uses slightly simpler settings. **Frédéric Misser Joaillier** (tel. 43-37-98), on boulevard Pomare just west of the Vaima Center, displays many original creations. At all the black pearl outlets, remember to ask for a discount on the sticker price.

Tattoo Shops

Many visitors leave Tahiti with a fresh Polynesian tattoo, and you can too. The shops mentioned below all have albums illustrating their designs and the proprietors usually speak English. Inquire about sanitary precautions, including clean razors and disposable needles—a listing here is no guarantee. Buy the antiseptic cream they tell you to buy, and don't expose your tattoo to salt water or the sun until it has healed.

Aroma Tattoo Art (tel. 78-06-73 or 41-29-00, demonaroma@yahoo.com; Mon.–Sat. 1000–1800), 303 boulevard Pomare at rue Clappier above Bar Le Taina Kaina, uses 80 colors in a freehand style with single tattoos priced CFP 5,000–40,000 (or CFP 800,000 for a complete body tattoo). The owner, Aroma Salmon, does beautiful work.

Jordi's Tattoo Shop (tel. 42-45-00, fax 83-04-91, www.jorditattoo.pf; Tues.–Sat. 1000–1200/1300–1900), 43 rue Leboucher directly behind Hôtel Prince Hinoï, is more expensive with tattoos starting at CFP 10,000. Established in 1980, Jordi's was the first professional tattoo shop in French Polynesia and tourists are their main clientele.

Mano Tattoos (tel. 74-69-14; Mon.–Sat. 0900–1700), upstairs in the Papeete market, applies Marquesan-style designs from CFP 5,000 and up.

INFORMATION

The **Tahiti Manava Visitors Bureau** (tel. 50-57-12, www.tahiti-manava.pf; weekdays 0730–1700, Sat. 0800–1200) is at Fare Manihini, a neo-Polynesian building between boulevard Pomare and the Quai d'honneur where the cruise ships tie up. They can answer questions and supply a free map of Papeete but they don't make phone calls or reservations on behalf of visitors. Pick up their lists of "small hotel" accommodations on virtually all of the islands, and inquire about special events or boats to the outer islands.

The **Institut Territorial de la Statistique** (tel. 54-32-32, fax 42-72-52, www.ispf.pf; Mon.–Thurs. 0730–1500, Fri. 0730–1200), 1st floor, Immeuble Uupa, rue Edouard Ahnne (next to Honolulu), puts out a useful annual abstract *La Polynésie en Bref.*

Bookstores

You'll find Papeete's biggest selection of books in English at **Libraire Archipels** (tel. 42-47-30, fax 45-10-27), 68 rue des Remparts.

The **Libraire du Vaima** (tel. 45-57-44, fax 45-53-45, vaimalib@mail.pf) in the Vaima Center is Papeete's largest French bookstore. They carry antiquarian books about the South Pacific, topographical maps, and posters.

There's a news kiosk (tel. 41-02-89) with magazines in English in front of the Vaima Center by the taxi stand on boulevard Pomare.

Maps

Topographical maps (CFP 1,500 a sheet) of many islands are available from the Section Topographie of the **Service de l'Urbanisme** (tel. 46-82-18, fax 43-49-83), 4th floor, Administrative Building, 11 rue du Commandant Destremeau.

La Boutique Klima (tel. 42-00-63, fax 43-28-24), 13 rue Jaussen behind the cathedral, sells nautical charts (CFP 3,000) and many interesting French books on Polynesia.

Nauti-Sport (tel. 50-59-59) in Fare Ute also retails French nautical charts of Polynesia at CFP 3,100 a sheet, and **Marine Corail** (tel. 42-82-22), next to the Canon Center nearby, has more of the same (compare).

FRENCH POLYNESIA

Library

A public library (tel. 54-45-44, fax 42-85-69; Mon.–Thurs. 0800–1700, Fri. 0800–1600) is located in the Cultural Center, 646 boulevard Pomare. Visitors cannot take books out but you're welcome to sit and read. The padded chairs in their air-conditioned reading room are great for relaxing.

Airline Offices

Reconfirm your international flight at your airline's Papeete office. Many of the airline offices are in the Vaima Center: Air New Zealand (tel. 54-07-47), Hawaiian Airlines (tel. 42-15-00), LanChile (tel. 42-64-55), and Qantas (tel. 43-88-38). Qantas represents Polynesian Airlines. Air Tahiti Nui (tel. 45-55-55) is at 61 rue Gauguin near the Hôtel de Ville. Air France (tel. 47-47-47), which also represents Aircalin, is on rue Georges Lagarde, inland from the Vaima Center. If the clerk tells you it's not necessary to reconfirm, check your seat assignment and leave a local contact phone number to ensure that your booking is still in their system.

SERVICES

Money

The **MG Change Office** (tel. 43-22-77; weekdays 0830–1200/1300–1600, Sat. 0800–1530, Sun. 0900–1200), adjacent to the Tahiti Manava Visitors Bureau on boulevard Pomare, changes cash or traveler's checks for a standard rate without commission. It's a good deal if you're changing US$150 or less, otherwise the banks give a fractionally better rate, which you must line up to receive.

The **Banque de Polynésie** (tel. 46-66-66; Mon.–Thurs. 0745–1530, Fri. 0745–1430), boulevard Pomare 355, directly across from the Visitors Bureau, takes CFP 411 commission. The **Banque de Tahiti** (tel. 50-42-42; weekdays 0800–1145/1330–1630, Sat. 0800–1130), on boulevard Pomare west of the Vaima Center, charges CFP 551 commission.

Several banks around town have automatic tellers where you can get cash if the machine's software recognizes your card. **Banque Socredo** (tel. 45-31-83), boulevard Pomare 411, on the waterfront just east of the post office, has an ATM accessible 24 hours a day. Adjacent is a nifty Automatic Currency Exchange machine, which changes the banknotes of nine countries for CFP 500 commission (an identical machine is at the Tahiti Beachcomber Inter-Continental). Complaints have been received about Tahiti ATMs which didn't work, so using one of these machines at a time when the bank itself is closed is not recommended.

Post and Telecommunications

The main post office (weekdays 0700–1800, Sat. 0800–1100) is on boulevard Pomare across from the yacht anchorage. Pick up poste restante (general delivery) mail downstairs (CFP 55 per piece). The public fax number at Papeete's main post office is fax 689/43-68-68 (you'll pay CFP 250 a page to pick up faxes sent to this number). The post office is also a place to make a long-distance telephone call, but there's a stiff three-minute minimum for operator-assisted calls and it's cheaper to use a telephone card for such calls.

Around Tahiti, small branch post offices with public telephones are found in Arue, Faa'a Airport, Mahina, Mataiea, Paea, Papara, Papeari, Pirae, Punaauia, and Taravao.

If you have an American Express card you can have your mail sent c/o Tahiti Tours, B.P. 627, 98713 Papeete, French Polynesia. Their office (tel. 54-02-50, fax 42-50-50, www.tahiti-tours.com) is at 15 rue Jeanne d'Arc next to the Vaima Center.

Courier Services

TTI-Tahiti (tel. 83-00-24, fax 83-76-27; Mon.–Thurs. 0730–1200/1300–1700, Fri. 0730–1200/1300–1530) is the DHL Worldwide Express agent. Their office is on the main highway in the first building toward Papeete from Faa'a Airport. Parcels to North America begin at CFP 5,650 for .5 kg (documents and shipments to California are slightly less). Specials include a 25-kg "Jumbo Box" costing CFP 26,600 and a 10-kg "Jumbo Junior" for CFP 17,000 (size limits apply). Optional insurance is 1.5 percent of value.

Cowan et Fils (tel. 82-44-25), upstairs above the Air Tahiti freight office in the airport itself, is the United Parcel Service agent. They're considerably more expensive than TTI-Tahiti.

Federal Express (tel. 45-36-45) has an office on avenue Bruat near boulevard Pomare.

Internet Access

La Maison de la Press (tel. 50-93-93; Mon.–Thurs. 0700–1900, Fri. and Sat. 0700–2200), 343 boulevard Pomare opposite Tahua Vaiete, has a very popular internet cafe upstairs (CFP 250 per 15 minutes). The service is friendly but all eight computers are often occupied.

Tiki Soft Cafe (tel. 88-93-98, contact@tikisoft.pf; weekdays 0700–0100, Sat. 1400–0100), rue des Remparts at rue du Maréchal Foch, also charges CFP 250 for 15 minutes internet access.

Galaxie Games (tel. 42-63-63; weekdays 0800–1700, Sat. 0800–1600), 91 rue des Remparts, provides internet access at CFP 100 per seven minutes.

Immigration Office

If you arrived by air, visa extensions are handled by the **Police Aux Frontières** (tel. 80-06-00; weekdays 0800–1200/1400–1700) at the airport (up the stairs beside the snack bar). Drop by at least a week before your current visa will expire. Yachters are handled by the Police Aux Frontières (tel. 42-40-74; weekdays 0730–1100/1400–1500) on the waterfront behind the Visitors Bureau in the center of town. If you wish to extend a three-month visa, ask the Visitors Bureau where you need to go to apply. Be patient and courteous with the officials if you want good service.

For those uninitiated into the French administrative system, the police station (in emergencies tel. 17) opposite the War Memorial on avenue Bruat deals with Papeete matters, while the gendarmerie (tel. 46-73-73) at the head of avenue Bruat is concerned with the rest of the island. The locally recruited Papeete police wear blue uniforms, while the paramilitary French-import gendarmes are dressed in khaki. The ubiquitous security personnel in red shirts along the Papeete waterfront belong to the Groupement d'Inter-

vention de la Polynésie (GIP), a body used to provide employment for Flosse supporters.

Consulates

The honorary consul of New Zealand (tel. 54-07-40) is upstairs in the Air New Zealand office in the Vaima Center. The Consulate of Chile (tel. 43-89-19; Wed.–Fri. 0900–1200) is at 3 passage Cardella near the Vaima Center. Other countries with honorary consuls in Papeete are Austria (tel. 43-91-14), Belgium (tel. 80-08-08), Denmark (tel. 54-04-54), Finland (tel. 43-60-67), Germany (tel. 42-99-94), Israel (tel. 42-41-00), Italy (tel. 43-45-01), Japan (tel. 45-45-45), Netherlands (tel. 42-49-37), Norway (tel. 43-79-72), South Korea (tel. 43-64-75), Sweden (tel. 42-73-93), and the United Kingdom (tel. 41-98-41).

Australia, Canada, China, and the United States are not represented in French Polynesia. All U.S. visa applications or requests for the replacement of lost American passports must go via the U.S. Embassy (tel. 679/331-4466; www.amembassy-fiji.gov) in Suva, Fiji. TTI-Tahiti (tel. 83-00-24) near Faa'a International Airport will send passports or documents to Fiji at CFP 7,200 with the return prepaid.

Launderettes

Lavomatic du Pont de l'Est (tel. 43-71-59; Mon.–Sat. 0630–1200/1330–1730), 64 rue Gauguin, charges CFP 750 to wash six kg, another CFP 750 to dry, and CFP 100 for soap.

Laverie Automatique "Lavex ça m'plein" (tel. 41-26-65; weekdays 0700–1730, Sat. 0630–1130), 303 boulevard Pomare opposite the Quai de Moorea, asks CFP 1,650 to wash and dry up to seven kilograms.

Public Toilets

Public toilets are found on Tahua Vaiete near the Visitors Bureau, beside the Flower Market, and at the Tahua To'ata west along the waterfront. Bring your own toilet paper.

Yachting Facilities

Yachts must report their arrival to the port authorities over VHF channel 12 before entering the pass. Customs and immigration are in the building behind the Visitors Bureau. A one-time entry fee and optional daily electricity and water hookup are charged. Yachts pay a daily fee based on the length of the vessel to moor Mediterranean-style (stern-to, bow anchor out) along the quay on boulevard Pomare.

It's cheaper to anchor at the **Marina Taina** (tel. 41-02-25, marina@mail.pf) at PK 9, Punaauia, accessible via the Faa'a Channel without exiting the lagoon. Otherwise visiting boats can use one of the anchor buoys at the **Yacht Club of Tahiti** (tel. 42-78-03) at PK 4, Arue, for a monthly fee. Another popular anchorage is Port Phaeton at Taravao. Tahiti's sunny west and south coasts are excellent cruising grounds, while there are few good anchorages on the windward, rainy, and often dangerous east and north coasts.

Health

Mamao Territorial Hospital (tel. 46-62-62) is always crowded with locals awaiting free treatment, so unless you've been taken to the recompression chamber there or it's an emergency, you're better off attending a private clinic. At the **Clinique Paofai** (tel. 46-18-18) on boulevard Pomare you can see a doctor anytime in the emergencies *(urgences)* department on the 1st floor (brief consultations CFP 3,300 from 0700–1900, CFP 7,300 from 1900–0700). The facilities and attention are excellent.

In case of emergencies around Papeete call S.O.S. Médecins at tel. 42-34-56. To call an ambulance dial 15.

Two dentists, Dr. Michel Ligerot and Dr. Valérie Galano-Serra (tel. 43-32-24), are on the 2nd floor of the building next to the Hôtel Tiare Tahiti at boulevard Pomare 415.

The Pharmacie de la Cathedrale (tel. 42-02-24), across the street from the Catholic cathedral, opens weekdays 0700–1800, Saturday 0730–1230. There are many other pharmacies around Papeete.

TRANSPORTATION

For information on air and sea services from Papeete to the other islands, see Transportation in the introduction to French Polynesia.

Le Truck

You can go almost anywhere on Tahiti by *le truck,* converted cargo vehicles with long benches in back. *Trucks* marked Outumaoro run from Papeete to Faa'a International Airport and the Sofitel Maeva Beach every few minutes throughout the day, with sporadic service after dark until midnight, then again in the morning from 0500 on. Weekdays the last trip from Papeete to Mahina, Paea, and points beyond is around 1700.

Trucks to Arue, Mahina, Papenoo, Taravao, and Tautira leave from both sides of boulevard Pomare near the Visitors Bureau. Those to the airport, Outumaoro, Punaauia, Paea, and Papara are found in front of the Banque de Tahiti on rue du Maréchal Foch. Local services to Motu Uta (infrequent), Mission, Mamao, Titioro, and Tipaeriu depart from rue Colette near the Hôtel de Ville.

Destinations and fares are posted on the side of the vehicle: CFP 120 to the airport (CFP 200 after 1800), CFP 140 to Punaauia, CFP 160 to Mahina, CFP 170 to Paea, CFP 180 to Papenoo, CFP 190 to Papara, CFP 220 to Mataiea, CFP 240 to Papeari, CFP 300 to Taravao, and CFP 350 to Teahupoo or Tautira. After dark all *truck* fares increase. Outside Papeete you don't have to be at a stop: *trucks* stop anywhere if you wave. Some drivers ask CFP 100 for luggage, others carry it free.

Sadly, a plan is being implemented to replace *le truck* with air-conditioned Korean buses, a change which will probably raise prices and reduce frequencies. Fixed bus stops, routes, schedules, and printed tickets may also be introduced. Local politics is involved as the territorial government has granted special concessions to Maeva Transport (a company controlled by supporters of President Gaston Flosse's party), while limiting the rival Tefana Rumana Transport group (which generally backs the pro-independence party) to less profitable rural areas. Check with the Visitors Bureau for current information on the public transportation system.

Taxis

Taxis in Papeete are extremely expensive, and it's important not to get in unless there's a meter that works or you've agreed to a flat fare beforehand. The basic fare is CFP 800 during the day (0600–2000) or CFP 1,200 at night (2000–0600). Add to that the per kilometer fee of CFP 120 by day or CFP 240 at night. The flat rate per hour is CFP 4,000 during the day or CFP 6,000 at night. Waiting time is CFP 2,000 an hour by day, CFP 3,000 at night. Baggage is CFP 50–100 per piece.

During the day expect to spend at least CFP 1,000 for a short trip within Papeete (including to the Sheraton), CFP 1,500 to the airport, or CFP 1,700 to the Beachcomber Inter-Continental or Maeva Beach. Taxi stands are found at the Vaima Center (tel. 42-33-60), Mana Rock Café (tel. 45-23-03), and airport (tel. 83-30-07). If you feel cheated by a taxi driver, take down the license number and complain to the Visitors Bureau, although what you consider a rip off may be the correct amount. We've received numerous complaints about Papeete taxi drivers; they're best avoided if at all possible.

Car Rentals

If you want to whiz across the island and pack in as many side trips as you can in a day, an un-limited-mileage car rental is for you, and with a few people sharing it's not a bad deal. Don't rent on a per-kilometer basis unless you plan to keep the car for at least three days and intend to use it only for short hops. Most agencies impose a 50-km daily minimum on their per-kilometer rentals to prevent you from traveling *too* slowly; most rentals are for a minimum of 24 hours. Almost all the car rental companies have kiosks inside Faa'a Airport, and most offer clients a free pickup and drop-off service to the hotels and airport.

Check the car as carefully as they check you; be sure to comment on dents, scratches, flat tires, etc. All the car rental agencies include third-party public liability insurance in the basic price, but collision damage waiver (CDW) varies from CFP 900 to CFP 3,500 extra per day with CFP 20,000 and up deductible (called the *franchise* in French). Most agencies charge the client for stolen accessories and damage to the tires, insurance or no insurance, and Tahiti insurance isn't valid if you take the car to Moorea. You'll also pay for towing if you are judged responsible. On Tahiti the car comes full of gas, and you'll see Mobil and Total gas stations all around the island.

Avis/Pacificar (tel. 54-10-10, fax 42-19-11, www.avis-tahiti.com), 56 rue des Remparts at pont de l'Est, at the east end of rue Paul Gauguin, is open weekdays 0600–1900, Saturday 0700–1830, Sunday 0800–1830. They also have a kiosk facing the Quai de Moorea, opposite the Hôtel Royal Papeete, and a desk at the airport. Avis/Pacificar has unlimited kilometer cars from CFP 9,600/18,000/26,000 for one/two/three days, including insurance.

Europcar (tel. 45-24-24, fax 41-93-41, fm europcar@mail.pf; Mon.–Sat. 0600–1930, Sun. 0700–1930) is at the corner of avenue du Prince Hinoï and rue des Remparts, two blocks back from the Quai de Moorea. Europcar desks are also found at several hotels and the airport. Their Fiat Pandas are CFP 1,875, plus CFP 41 a kilometer. With unlimited kilometers and insurance it's CFP 8,100/15,000/21,060 for one/two/three days. Their minimum age is 21 but the insurance coverage is limited for those under 25.

Hertz (tel. 42-04-71, fax 43-49-03, hertz@mail.pf) has a main office at the Peugeot dealer on rue du Commandant Destremeau at the west entrance to Papeete and a desk at the airport (tel. 82-55-86). Their cars begin at CFP 2,080 a day, plus CFP 41 a kilometer, plus CFP 1,400 insurance. Otherwise it's CFP 8,820/22,050/45,860 for one/three/seven days with unlimited mileage and insurance.

Robert Rent-a-Car (tel. 42-97-20, fax 42-63-00) on rue du Commandant Destremeau has cars from CFP 1,926 daily, plus CFP 43 a kilometer, plus CFP 954 insurance. Robert's unlimited kilometer rentals begin at CFP 6,800, plus CFP 954 insurance.

Location de Voitures Daniel (tel. 82-30-04, fax 85-62-64, tahiti.safari@mail.pf) at the airport terminal begins at CFP 2,033 a day, plus CFP 37 a kilometer, plus CFP 1,070 insurance. With unlimited mileage it's CFP 7,800/12,840/18,840 for two/three/seven days, insurance included.

The least expensive car available from **Location de Voitures Pierrot et Jacqueline** (tel. 81-94-00, fax 81-07-77), also known as Tahiti Rent a Car, is CFP 1,800 a day, plus CFP 38 a kilometer and CFP 1,200 insurance. With unlimited kilometers it's CFP 7,800/14,000/17,700 for two/three/seven days, insurance included. They'll allow you to take their car to Moorea if you ask before, but the insurance won't be valid over there. In any case, drivers are responsible for the first CFP 50,000 in damages to the car. The minimum age to rent is 21. This friendly, efficient company has an office at the airport.

Parking

It's still free to park on the street anywhere in Papeete, which explains the heavy traffic. Double parking and parking on the sidewalk are commonplace, and European-style parking fee machines are long overdue! You're well advised to take public transportation into town.

If you must park, there's underground parking at the Hôtel de Ville (weekdays 0600–1800, Sat. 0600–1200), accessible from rue Colette opposite Hôtel Le Mandarin, costing CFP 120 the first hour, CFP 60 subsequent hours. Otherwise, Parking du Centre Vaima (tel. 42-44-14; Mon.–Thurs. 0700–1900, Fri. 0700–2200, Sat. 0700–1700), entrance from rue Georges Lagarde off rue du Général de Gaulle in front of Hollywood Cinema, asks CFP 170 an hour.

Bicycle Rentals

Unfortunately, the fast and furious traffic on Tahiti's main highways makes cycling dangerous and unpleasant, and motor scooter rentals have been discontinued after fatal accidents.

Garage Bambou (tel. 42-80-09), on avenue Georges Clemenceau near the Chinese temple, sells new Peugot bicycles from CFP 40,000 and does repairs. **Pacific Bike Shop** (tel. 42-49-00), 33 avenue Georges Clemenceau, also does bicycle repairs.

Local Tours

Patrice Bordes of **Tahiti Safari Expédition** (tel. 42-14-15, fax 42-10-07, www.tahiti-safari.com) offers 4WD jeep tours to Mt. Marau, the Papenoo Valley, and Lake Vaihiria. The highly recommended day trip across Tahiti via the Relais de la Maroto (CFP 8,000 with lunch) not only provides a rare glimpse of the interior but a good introduction to the flora and fauna of the island. Most hotel receptions (including the Hôtel Tiare Tahiti) will book this tour. You can arrange the same thing at CFP 6,000 without lunch by calling Patrice direct (four-person minimum participation).

Natura Exploration (Arnaud Luccioni, tel. 43-03-83, fax 43-03-99, www.natura-exploration.com) does the same trip across the island at CFP 7,500/6,500 with/without a picnic lunch. Natura does a half-day Mt. Marau 4WD trip at CFP 5,000 pp. **Patrick Adventure** (Patrick Cordier, tel. 83-29-29) also does cross-island tours.

Marama Tours (tel. 83-96-50, fax 82-16-75, www.maramatours.com), at the Sheraton and Maeva Beach hotels, does six-hour circle-island tours at CFP 4,415 (admission fees extra). They also sell the 4WD tours just mentioned at CFP 8,475 including a picnic lunch. **Tahiti Nui Travel** (tel. 54-02-00, www.tahitinuitravel.com) at the Vaima Center and various hotels also offers circle-island tours.

William Leeteg of **Adventure Eagle Tours** (tel. 77-20-03) takes visitors on a full-day tour around the island at CFP 4,500 (admissions and lunch not included). William speaks good English and offers special guided tours for groups of up to seven.

Day Cruises

Many of the yachts and catamarans tied up along boulevard Pomare opposite the Vaima Center offer excursions to Tetiaroa, deep-sea fishing, scuba diving, yacht charters, etc. Departures are often announced on notice boards and a stroll along the waterfront will yield current information.

Croisieres L'Escapade (tel. 72-85-31) does Tetiaroa day trips on a 14-meter yacht at CFP 10,000 pp including breakfast, lunch, and drinks. Weekend cruises (Fri. afternoon–Sun. night) are CFP 30,000 pp. **Biotherm Charters** (tel./fax 41-04-09) also does Tetiaroa day trips at CFP 10,000 pp. **Jet France** (tel. 56-15-62), on the waterfront opposite the Hôtel Tiare Tahiti, does this trip for CFP 11,000 on Wednesday, Saturday, and Sunday from 0700–2000.

Tours to Easter Island

From Tahiti it's cheaper to make a side trip to Easter Island than to go to the Marquesas! Most Papeete travel agencies sell three- and seven-night packages designed for Tahiti residents that include airfare, accommodations, transfers, and often sightseeing tours. There's usually no single supplement. Check several agencies as prices vary considerably, and inquire about the price of a return air ticket alone at the LanChile office in the Vaima Center (low off-season fares available Mar.–Nov.). You'll probably only need a passport to visit Easter Island.

Vahine Tahiti Travel (tel. 50-44-20, fax 43-60-06, www.vahine-tahiti.com), off boulevard Pomare below the Vaima Center, has three/seven-night packages to Easter Island costing CFP 75,500/92,100 all inclusive. They sell Papeete-Easter Island air tickets alone at US$435 roundtrip with a maximum stay of one week or US$515 roundtrip for over one week. **Tahiti Nui Travel** (tel. 54-02-00, fax 42-74-35, www.tahitinuitravel.com), adjacent to Vahini Tahiti Travel, lists tour prices on their website.

Also check **Manureva Tours** (tel. 43-69-63 or 50-91-00, fax 42-48-43, www.axciom.fr/manureva), on boulevard Pomare next to the Banque de Tahiti just west of the Vaima Center, **Tekura Tahiti Travel** (tel. 43-12-00, fax 42-84-60, www.tahiti-tekuratravel.com), in the Vaima Center near Hawaiian Airlines, **e-Tahiti Travel** (tel. 83-51-60, fax 83-61-94, www.etahiti-travel.com), also in the Vaima Center, **Pacifica Tahiti Travel** (tel. 42-93-85, fax 42-90-29), rue Georges Lagarde almost opposite Air France, and **Nouvelles Frontières** (tel. 53-41-64) on boulevard Pomare opposite the Quai de Moorea. Visit them all as prices do vary and check the vouchers carefully after you've booked.

Getting Away

The **Air Tahiti** booking office (tel. 47-44-00; weekdays 0800–1700, Sat. 0800–1100) is at the corner of rue du Maréchal Foch and rue Edouard Ahnne just inland from the market. **Air Moorea** (tel. 86-41-41) is at Faa'a International Airport. Interisland services by air and sea are covered in the introduction to French Polynesia.

The ferries to Moorea depart from the landing just behind the Visitors Bureau downtown. All other interisland ships, including the cargo vessels *Vaeanu* and *Hawaiki-Nui,* leave from the Tuamotu wharf or Quai des Caboteurs in Motu Uta, across the harbor from downtown Papeete. You can catch *le truck* directly to Motu Uta from the Hôtel de Ville, if you're lucky (it's very infrequent). The ticket offices of some of the vessels are in Fare Ute just north of downtown, while others are at Motu Uta (addresses given in the introduction to French Polynesia).

AROUND TAHITI

A 117-km Route de Ceinture (Belt Road) runs right around Tahiti-nui, the larger part of this hourglass-shaped island. Construction began in the 1820s as a form of punishment. For orientation you'll see red-and-white kilometer stones, called PK *(pointe kilométrique),* along the inland side of the road. These are numbered in each direction from the Catholic cathedral in Papeete, meeting at Taravao.

Go clockwise to get over the most difficult stretch first; also, you'll be riding on the inside lane of traffic and less likely to go over a cliff in case of an accident (an average of 55 people a year are killed and 700 injured in accidents on this island). Southern Tahiti is much quieter than the northwest, whereas from Paea to Mahina it's even hard to slow down as tailgating motorists roar behind you.

If you're adventurous, it's possible to do a circle-island tour on *le truck,* provided you get an early start and go clockwise with no stop until Taravao. *Trucks* don't run right around the island, although some go as far as Tautira and Teahupoo on Tahiti-iti. *Trucks* and buses to Taravao leave from boulevard Pomare near the Visitors Bureau regularly throughout the day. *Trucks* to Tautira go via the south coast, so if you want to do a full circle trip, ask for one going to Taravao via Papenoo. Avoid trying this on the weekend when service is reduced.

A large bus to Taravao via Papenoo leaves Papeete from the same side of boulevard Pomare as the Visitors Bureau weekdays at 0830, 0900, 1000, 1130, and 1600 (1.5-hours, CFP 300).

THE FIRST WOMAN TO CIRCUMNAVIGATE THE GLOBE

In late 1766, Louis-Antoine Bougainville set sail from France aboard the frigate *Boudeuse* on a voyage of discovery which would last 28 months. The expedition's second vessel, the *Etoile,* carried the king's botanist Philibert Commerson. The ships spent over a year off the east coast of South America on various missions. In Brazil Commerson collected a violet flowering climber, which he named *bougainvillea* for his captain.

After rounding Cape Horn, Bougainville and crew reached Tahiti in April, 1768. Commerson's passion for native plants was shared by his hardworking assistant, Bonnefoy. There had been speculation aboard the *Etoile* that the fresh-faced boy dressed in baggy clothes might be a female, and all doubt was removed when "Bonnefoy" stepped ashore at Hitiaa. Tahitians immediately surrounded the youth crying *vahine, vahine* (woman, woman) and offering to do her *les honneurs de l'isle* (the honors of the island). Jeanne Baret had to beat a hasty retreat to the ship. Years later Bougainville described the situation in his *Journal:*

With tears in her eyes Baret acknowledged that she was a girl, that she had misled her master (Commerson) by dressing in men's clothes, that she was an orphan from Burgundy, that a lawsuit had reduced her to poverty, and that news of a voyage around the world had piqued her interest. I considered her case unique and admired her courage and wisdom. I took measures to ensure that nothing unpleasant happened to her. The royal court, I believe, will forgive this infringement of the rules. She was neither plain nor pretty and hardly 25 years old.

When the expedition reached the French colony of Mauritius in the Indian Ocean, Commerson and Baret disembarked. There Commerson named the *baretia,* a plant species of dubious sex, for this "valiant young woman who, adopting the dress and temperament of a man, had the curiosity and audacity to traverse the whole world, by land and by sea, accompanying us without ourselves knowing anything."

Over the centuries Commerson has been largely forgotten due to his decision not to return directly to Europe with Bougainville. Though his work at Mauritius, Madagascar, and Reunion was important, many of his specimens and reports have been lost. After Commerson's death at Reunion in 1773, it became apparent that the only way Jeanne could return to France was by marrying a soldier, which she did. In 1785 Jeanne Baret, now Madame Dubernat, a widow living in Burgundy, was granted a naval pension at Bougainville's request. She died quietly in 1807.

The departure from Taravao to return to Papeete is at 0530, 0630, 0730, 0830, 1030, 1130, and 1400. Once at Taravao, look for a *truck* coming from Tautira or Teahupoo to take you back to Papeete along the south coast. The last *truck* from Taravao via Paea is around 1300, but it's not 100 percent reliable. Be aware that many of the *trucks* you see around Taravao are carrying students and they won't stop.

After Papara the *truck* frequency increases, so feel free to get out at Mara Fern Grotto or else-where. The Papara *trucks* stop running around 1500, but if you get stuck, it's comforting to know that hitchhiking *(l'autostop)* is fairly easy and relatively safe on Tahiti. There's abundant traffic along the south coast highway all day and it's almost certain you'll get a ride. However you travel around Tahiti, it's customary to smile and wave to the Tahitians you see (outside Papeete).

Toward Point Venus

East of Arue (covered in the Papeete section),

the highway climbs sharply to the **Point de View du Tahara'a** on One Tree Hill (PK 8), where there's a splendid view across Matavai Bay to Papeete and Moorea. Adjacent to the viewpoint is the entrance to the former Hôtel Tahara'a erected by Pan American Airways in 1968. From 1988 to 1997 this was a Hyatt Regency, then it became the Hôtel Royal Matavai Bay, run by Réginald Flosse, son of Gaston Flosse, before closing in 1998. The Tahara'a is presently empty and moves to convert the structure into a residential apartment complex have not been going well. If the main gate is open it's worth going in to get a closer look at this 190-room structure built on a spectacular series of terraces down the hillside to conform to a local regulation that no building should be more than two-thirds the height of a coconut tree. There's another glorious view from the Governor's Bench on the knoll beyond the swimming pool above the hotel door.

Continue to Mahina (PK 10) and turn left beside Supermarche Venustar to **Point Venus.** Captain Cook camped on this point between the river and the lagoon during his visit to observe the transit of the planet Venus across the sun on June 3, 1769. Captain Bligh also occupied Point Venus for two months in 1788, while collecting breadfruit shoots for transportation to the West Indies. On March 5, 1797, the first members of the London Missionary Society landed here, as a monument recalls. From Tahiti, Protestantism spread throughout Polynesia and as far as Vanuatu.

Today there's a park on the point, with a 25-meter-high lighthouse (1867) among the palms and ironwood trees. The view of Tahiti across Matavai Bay is superb, and twin-humped Orohena, highest peak on the island, is in view (you can't see it from Papeete itself). Weekdays, Point Venus is a peaceful place, the perfect choice if you'd like to get away from the rat race in Papeete and spend some time at the beach, but on weekends it gets crowded. Any Mahina *truck* will bring you here.

The Northeast Coast

The coast is very rugged all along the northeast side of Tahiti with no barrier reef at many points between Point Venus and Mahaena. The **leper colony** at Orofara (PK 13.2) was founded in 1914. Previously the colony was on Reao atoll in the Tuamotus, but this proved too remote to service. Although leprosy is now a thing of the past, about 50 of the former patients' children who grew up there have nowhere else to go and so remain at Orofara, along with a couple of elderly leprosy victims.

From November to March surfers ride the waves at Chinaman's Bay, Papenoo (PK 16), one of the best river-mouth beach breaks on the north side of the island. The bridge over the broad **Papenoo River** (PK 17.9) allows a view up the largest valley on Tahiti. A paved road leads a few km up the valley before becoming a rough track across the island. See The Interior in this chapter for a description of this route.

At the **Arahoho Blowhole** (PK 22), jets of water shoot up through holes in the lava rock beside the highway at high tide. It's dangerous to get too close to the blowhole as a sudden surge could toss you out to sea! A nice picnic area is provided here. Just a little beyond the blowhole, a road to the right leads 1.3 km up to the three **Tefa'aurumai Waterfalls** (admission free), also known as the Faarumai Falls. Vaimahuta Falls is accessible on foot in five minutes along the easy path to the right across the bridge. The 30-minute trail to the left leads to two more waterfalls, Haamaremare Iti and Haamaremare Rahi. The farthest falls has a pool deep enough for swimming. Bring insect repellent and carefully lock your rental car before heading off to see the falls (the same applies at the blowhole).

At **Mahaena** (PK 32.5) is the battleground where 441 well-armed French troops defeated a dug-in Tahitian force twice their size on April 17, 1844 in the last fixed confrontation of the French-Tahitian War. The Tahitians carried on a guerrilla campaign another two years until the French captured their main mountain stronghold. No monument commemorates the 100 Tahitians who died combating the foreign invaders here.

The French ships *La Boudeuse* and *L'Étoile,* carrying explorer Louis-Antoine de Bougainville, anchored by the southernmost of two islets off **Hitiaa** (PK 37.6) on April 6, 1768. Unaware that an Englishman had visited Tahiti a year before, Bougainville christened the island "New Cythera," after the Greek isle where love goddess Aphrodite rose from the sea. A plaque near the bridge recalls the event. A clever Tahitian recognized a member of Bougainville's crew as a woman disguised as a man, and an embarrassed Jeanne Baret entered history as the first woman to sail around the world. (Bougainville lost six large anchors during his nine days at this dangerous windward anchorage.)

From the bridge over the Faatautia River at PK 41.8 **Vaiharuru Falls** are visible in the distance. The American filmmaker John Huston intended to make a movie of Herman Melville's *Typee* here in 1957, but when Huston's other Melville film, *Moby Dick,* became a box-office flop, the idea was dropped.

Taravao

At Taravao (PK 53), on the strategic isthmus joining the two Tahitis where the PKs meet, is an **old fort** built by the French in 1844 to cut off the Tahitians who had retreated to Tahiti-iti after the battle mentioned above. Germans were interned here during WW II, and the fort is still occupied today by the 1st Company of the Régiment d'Infanterie de Marine du Pacifique.

The assortment of supermarkets, banks, post office, gasoline stations, and restaurants at Taravao (www.chez.com/otahiti) make it a good place to break your trip around the island. For lunch, consider **Restaurant L'Escale** (tel. 57-07-16; Tues.–Sat. 1000–1400/1800–2000, Sun. 1000–1400), an atmospheric old French country inn on the highway near Total gas station in Taravao. The *plat du jour* is indicated on a blackboard outside (CFP 1,500–1,700), otherwise order a seafood dish (CFP 1,450–2,500) from the menu. Another good choice is **Restaurant Baie Phaeton** (tel. 57-08-96; Wed.–Sat. 1000–1400/1800–2100, Sun. 1000–1400), between Taravao and the Gauguin Museum. The Chinese and French entrees are reasonably priced at CFP 900–1,100, and there's a lovely terrace overlooking the bay.

Tahiti-iti

If you have your own transportation, three roads are explorable on rugged Tahiti-iti. An excellent 18-km highway runs east from Taravao to quaint little **Tautira.** Two Spanish priests from Peru attempted to establish a Catholic mission here in 1774, but it lasted for only one year. Scottish author Robert Louis Stevenson stayed at Tautira for two months in 1888 and called it "the most beautiful spot, and its people the most amiable, I have ever found." The road peters out a few kilometers beyond Tautira, but you can continue walking 12 km southeast to the Vaiote River where there are petroglyphs, sacred rocks, and *marae*. These are difficult to find without a guide, and a few kilometers beyond are the high cliffs that make it almost impractical to try hiking around the Pari Coast to Teahupoo. Intrepid sea kayakers have been known to paddle the 30 km around, although there's a wild four-km stretch not protected by reefs. Most visitors go by speedboat.

Another paved nine-km road climbs straight up the Taravao Plateau from just before the hospital in Taravao, 600 meters down the Tautira road from Champion supermarket. Turn right, then left on the second road (no sign). If you have a car and only time to take in one of Tahiti-iti's three roads, this should be your choice. At the 600-meter level on top is the **Vaiufaufa Viewpoint,** with a breathtaking view of both Tahitis. You'll witness spectacular sunsets from here and the herds of cows grazing peacefully among the grassy meadows give this upland an almost Swiss air. A rough side road near the viewpoint cuts down to rejoin the Tautira road near the PK 3 marker.

The third road on Tahiti-iti runs 18 km along the south coast to Teahupoo. Seven km east of Taravao is a **marina** with an artificial beach (PK 7). American pulp Western writer Zane Grey had his fishing camp near here in the 1930s. Just east of the marina is **Toouo Beach,** a long stretch of natural white sand beside the road where you'll see fishermen spearing by torchlight on the opposite reef in the evening. In the afternoon it's a great picnic spot. The two huge moorings near the shore were used by ocean liners before Papeete harbor was developed in the 1960s, as this is the finest natural deep-water harbor on Tahiti. Some of Tahiti's best reef break surfing is possible out there in the Tapuaeraha Pass, but you'll need a boat. Yachts can tie up to a pier near the *mairie* in **Vairoa.** An oceanographic research station studying shrimp breeding is nearby.

The **Teahupoo** road ends abruptly at a river crossed by a narrow footbridge. There's an excellent mountain view from this bridge, and a walk east along the beach offers a glimpse of Polynesian village life. After a couple of kilome-

Vahine no te Tiare

Paul Gauguin's *Girl with Flower,* pictured here, is now in the Carlsberg Glyptotek, Copenhagen. Gauguin was one of the first patrons of the French impressionists. Before he turned professional painter, Gauguin was a successful broker who worked at the Paris exchange. He went further than most of his contemporaries to search out the exotic, to paint in strong flat color, and to employ broad, bold decorative patterns made popular in France by the widespread distribution of Japanese wood block prints. Whereas later painters borrowed from African masks and carvings, Gauguin traveled directly to the source of his inspiration, arriving in Tahiti on June 9, 1891.

COURTESY OF CARLSBERG GLYPTOTEK, COPPENHAGEN

ters, the going becomes difficult due to yelping dogs, seawalls built into the lagoon, fences, fallen trees, and *tapu* signs. Beyond is the one-time domain of the "nature men" who tried to escape civilization by living alone with nature almost a century ago.

Three hours on foot from the end of the road is **Vaipoiri Grotto,** a large water-filled cave best reached by boat. Try hiring a motorized canoe or hitch a ride with someone at the end of the road. Beyond this the 300-meter-high cliffs of the Pari Coast terminate all foot traffic along the shore; the only way to pass is by boat. All the land east of Teahupoo is well fenced off, so finding a campsite would involve getting someone's permission. Two pensions, Le Bon Jouir and Te Pari Village, on the Pari Coast east of Teahupoo, are listed in Accommodations Around Tahiti.

Gauguin Museum

Port Phaeton on the southwest side of the Taravao Isthmus is a natural "hurricane hole" with excellent holding for yachts in the muddy bottom and easy access to Taravao from the head of the bay. (The entire south coast of Tahiti is a paradise for yachties with many fine protected anchorages.) Timeless oral traditions relate that the first Polynesians to reach Tahiti settled at **Papeari** (PK 56—measured now from the west). In precontact times the chiefly family of this district was among the most prestigious on the island.

The Gauguin Museum (tel. 57-10-58; daily 0900–1700, CFP 600 admission) is at PK 51.7 in Papeari District, 12 km southwest of Taravao. The museum opened in 1965 thanks to a grant from the Singer Foundation (of sewing machine fame), and a couple of minor Gauguin prints, small woodcarvings, and other objects associated with the painter are in the collection. These are displayed in the air-conditioned "Salle Henri Bing" to the left of the entrance, but unfortunately the captions are only in French and it's hard to distinguish the originals from the copies (most of the copies are marked "Fac-simílé" in small letters). The other three exhibition rooms provide haphazard English translations. The display on the tormented life of Gauguin is well presented with numerous illustrations and explanations in English. Strangely, Gauguin's Tahitian mistresses receive little attention and his clashes with the colonial authorities are swept under the carpet. A hall at the back of the museum contains a model of Gauguin's "Maison de Jouîr" in Atuona, Hiva Oa, plus bronze replicas of his woodcarvings. The final room deals with Gauguin's influences and influences on Gauguin. Two huge stone tikis are in the garden outside. The one closest to the beach stands 272 cm tall, the largest ancient stone statue in Polynesia outside of Easter Island. It's said to be imbued with a sacred *tapu* spell, and Tahitians believe this tiki, carved on the island of Raivavae hundreds of years ago, still lives. The three Tahitians who moved it here from Papeete in 1965 all died mysterious deaths within a few weeks. A curse is still said to befall all who touch the tiki. A

campaign is now underway to have these statues returned to Raivavae.

A **botanical garden** rich in exotic species is part of the Gauguin Museum complex (CFP 500 additional admission). This 137-hectare garden was created in 1919–21 by the American botanist Harrison Smith (1872–1947), who introduced over 200 new species to the island, among them the sweet grapefruit (pomelo), mangosteen, rambutan, and durian. Two large Galapagos tortoises traipse through the east side of the gardens, the last of several such animals given to the children of writer Charles Nordhoff back in the 1930s. Yachts can enter the lagoon through Temarauri Pass and anchor just west of the point here.

The South Coast

At PK 49 is the **Jardin Public Vaipahi** with a lovely waterfall minutes from the road (admission free). It's a good substitute if you missed the botanical garden. A few hundred meters west of Vaipahi is the **Bain du Vaima,** a strong freshwater spring with several deep swimming pools. This is one of the favorite free picnic spots on the island and on weekends it's crowded with locals. Yachts can anchor offshore.

In 1891–93 Gauguin lived near the Oriental-style church at **Mataiea** (PK 46.5).

The **International Golf Course Olivier Breaud** (tel. 57-43-41; daily 0800–1700) at PK 41, Atimaono, stretches up to the mountainside on the site of Terre Eugenie, a cotton and sugar plantation established by Scotsman William Stewart at the time of the U.S. Civil War (1863). Many of today's Tahitian Chinese are descended from Chinese laborers imported to do the work, and a novel by A. T'Serstevens, *The Great Plantation,* was set here. The present 5,405-meter, 18-hole course was laid out by Californian Bob Baldock in 1970 with a par 72 for men, par 73 for women. If you'd like to play a round, the greens fees are CFP 5,315, plus CFP 2,500 for clubs and CFP 4,200 for a cart. Since 1981, the Tahiti Open in July has attracted golf professionals from around the Pacific. The course restaurant is said to be good.

The **Marae of Mahaiatea** (PK 39) at Papara was once the most hallowed temple on Tahiti,

THE PAINTER PAUL GAUGUIN

One-time Paris stockbroker Paul Gauguin arrived at Papeete in June 1891 at age 43 in search of the roots of "primitive" art. He lived at Mataiea with his 14-year-old mistress Teha'amana for a year and a half, joyfully painting. In August 1893 he returned to France with 66 paintings and about a dozen woodcarvings, which were to establish his reputation. Unfortunately, his exhibition flopped and in August 1895 Gauguin returned to Tahiti a second time, infected with VD and poor, settling at Punaauia. After an unsuccessful suicide attempt he recovered somewhat, and in 1901 a Paris art dealer named Vollard signed a contract with Gauguin, assuring him a monthly payment of 350 francs and a purchase price of 250 francs per picture. His financial problems alleviated, the painter left for Hiva Oa, Marquesas Islands, to find an environment uncontaminated by Western influences. During the last two years of his life at Atuona, Gauguin's eccentricities put him on the wrong side of the ecclesiastical and official hierarchies. He died in May 1903 at age 53, a near outcast among his countrymen in the islands, yet today a Papeete street and school are named after him!

dedicated to the sea god Ruahatu. After a visit in 1769, Captain Cook's botanist Joseph Banks wrote, "It is almost beyond belief that Indians could raise so large a structure without the assistance of iron tools." Less than a century later planter William Stewart raided the *marae* for building materials, and storms did the rest. All that's left of the 11-story pyramid today is a rough heap of stones. Still, it's worth visiting for its aura and setting, and you can swim off the beach next to the *marae* if you pay attention to the currents. The unmarked turnoff to the *marae* is a hundred meters west of Magasin Maruia Junior (large Coca Cola sign), then straight down to the beach. From April to October surfers often take the waves at black-colored **Taharuu Beach** on nearby Popoti Bay (PK 38.5), one of the top beach break sites on southern Tahiti.

Beside Temple Zion at **Papara** (PK 36) is the grave of Dorence Atwater (1845–1910), U.S. consul to Tahiti from 1871–88. During the American Civil War, Atwater recorded the names of 13,000 dead Union prisoners at Andersonville Prison, Georgia, from lists the Confederates had been withholding. Himself a Union prisoner, Atwater escaped with his list in March 1865. His tombstone provides details.

Maraa Fern Grotto (PK 28.5) is by the road just across the Paea border. An optical illusion, the grotto at first appears small but is quite deep and some Tahitians believe *varua ino* (evil spirits) lurk in the shadowy depths. Others say that if you follow an underground river back from the grotto you'll emerge at a wonderful valley in the spirit world. Paul Gauguin wrote of a swim he took across the small lake in the cave. You're welcome to jump in the blue-gray water. Also, fill your water bottle with fresh mineral water from eight spouts next to the parking lot. Maraa Pass is almost opposite the grotto and yachts can anchor in the bay.

The West Coast

Paea and Punaauia are Tahiti's sheltered "Gold Coast," with old colonial homes hidden behind trees along the lagoon side and *nouveau riche* villas dotting the hillside above. In recent years, Punaauia has been a fast-growing commune in the territory as French civil servants retire here from France to enjoy pensions specially indexed to the higher cost of living, as well as tax write-offs on real estate investments, usually apartments in newly-built high-rise buildings. From 1896 to 1901 Gauguin had his studio at Punaauia, but nothing remains of it; his *Two Tahitian Women* was painted there. The view of Moorea is excellent from all along here.

The **Marae Arahurahu** at PK 22.5, Paea, is easily the island's most beautiful archaeological site (open daily, admission free). It's up the road inland from Magasin Laut—take care, the sign faces Papeete, so it's not visible if you're traveling clockwise. This temple, lying in a tranquil, verdant spot under high cliffs, is perhaps Tahiti's only remaining pagan mystery. The ancient open altars built from thousands of cut stones were carefully restored in 1954, the first such restoration in French Polynesia. Historical pageants (CFP 1,500–3,000 admission) recreating pagan rites are performed here in July.

Mahana Park (admission free) at PK 18.3, Papehue, is a territorial beach park with a restaurant (tel. 48-19-99) and cafe. It's not as effected by pollution as the beaches closer to Papeete and is the perfect place to stop for an afternoon swim or even a sunset over Moorea.

At Pointe des Pêcheurs, Punaauia, is the **Museum of Tahiti and the Islands** (tel. 58-34-76, musee@mail.pf; Tues.–Sun. 0930–1730; admission CFP 600, groups CFP 500, students and children free), which opened in 1977. Located in a large air-conditioned complex on Punaauia Bay, about 600 meters down a narrow road from PK 14.7, this worthwhile museum has four halls devoted to the natural environment and settlement, Polynesian material culture, the social and religious life, and the history of Polynesia. Outside is an anchor Captain Cook lost at Tautira in 1773. Most of the captions are in French, Tahitian, and English (non-flash, non-commercial photography allowed).

If it's too late for any more sightseeing, don't worry—the museum makes an excellent half-day excursion from Papeete by *le truck*. Any of the Paea or Papara *trucks* on rue du Maréchal Foch near Papeete market will bring you to the turnoff

FRENCH POLYNESIA

in 30 minutes. The road to the museum begins beside a Total gas station, 100 meters south of the large bridge over the Punaruu River just beyond a major traffic circle (ask). Go in the morning as the last *truck* back to town is at 1600.

When the waves are right, you can sit on the seawall behind the museum and watch the Tahitian surfers bob and ride, with the outline of Moorea beyond. It's a nice picnic spot. On your way back to the main highway from the museum, look up to the top of the hill at an **old fort** used by the French to subjugate the Tahitians in the 1840s. The crown-shaped pinnacles of **Le Diadème** (1,321 meters) are also visible from this road.

At the traffic circle just north of the bridge, you have a choice of taking a fast bypass highway straight back to Papeete or continuing on the older coastal road to the Lagoonarium (the coastal road is the second, smaller exit from the circle). The **Lagoonarium** (tel. 43-62-90; closed Mon.), below the lagoon behind Captain Bligh Restaurant at PK 11.4, Punaauia, provides a vision of the underwater marinelife of Polynesia safely behind glass. The big tank full of black-tip sharks is a feature and the shark feeding takes place around noon. Entry is CFP 500 pp, open daily, free for restaurant customers, and CFP 300 for children under 12. Straight out from the Lagoonarium is the Passe de Taapuna, southern entrance to the Punaauia Lagoon and another popular surfing venue.

To continue north, you must rejoin the bypass briefly. At PK 8, Outumaoro, just past the huge Carrefour shopping center, is the turnoff for the RDO autoroute to Papeete, Tahiti's superhighway. Follow the Université signs from here up to the ultramodern campus of the **Université de la Polynésie française** (tel. 80-38-03, www.upf.pf) with its fantastic hilltop view of Moorea. The academic year for the 2,500 students runs from mid-September to mid-May.

On the old airport road just north are two of Tahiti's biggest hotels, the **Sofitel Maeva Beach** (PK 7.5) and **Beachcomber Inter-Continental** (PK 7), each worth a stop—though their beaches are polluted. From the point where the Beachcomber Inter-Continental is today, the souls of

deceased Tahitians once leapt on their journey to the spirit world. A sunset from either of these hotels, behind Moorea's jagged peaks across the Sea of the Moon, would be a spectacular finale to a circle-island tour. The **Mairie de Faa'a** (PK 5), just east of the airport, was erected in the traditional Maohi style in 1989 (Faa'a mayor Oscar Temaru is the territory's leading independence advocate).

The Interior

A dirt track across the center of Tahiti begins next to the bridge over the Papenoo River (PK 17.9) on the north coast. In the dry season, you could drive a rental car 15 km up the track to the suspension bridge across the Vaitamanu River and perhaps another kilometer to the Vaituoru Dam. Beyond that, only a 4WD vehicle could proceed, as a large sign proclaims. If you wish to go further, you'll have to park at the bridge or dam and continue on foot. In the rainy season use your own judgment as to how far you wish to drive.

From coast to coast it's a four-hour, 37-km trip by 4WD jeep, or two days on foot. The easiest (and probably best) way to do this trip is with one of the adventure tour operators that leave their brochures at the Visitors Bureau. Expect to pay CFP 8,000 pp including a good lunch. See "Local Tours" above for listings.

The Papenoo Valley is the caldera of Tahitinui's great extinct volcano, considered by the ancient Tahitians the realm of the gods. On the slopes of Mt. Orohena (2,241 meters), 10 km south of Papenoo, is the entrance to the **Parc naturel Te Faaiti,** Tahiti's first (and as yet undeveloped) territorial park. On the east side of the Papenoo Valley stands Mt. Aramaoro (1,530 meters). Since 1980, the rivers here have been harnessed for hydroelectricity and they now supply over a third of Tahiti's electric requirements.

Up a steep incline two kilometers south of the Vaituoru Dam, a side road to the right leads to **Marae Farehape** (admission CFP 200), a well restored archaeological site with an archery platform, a *marae* with stone backrests, and the outlines of other buildings. A large dam, the Barrage Tahinu, is a couple of kilometers west of Marae Farehape. A primitive campsite exists next to

Marae Farehape, and if anyone is around, it's CFP 300 pp to pitch a tent or CFP 600 pp to sleep in an on-site hut.

The tour groups stop for lunch at the **Relais de la Maroto** (tel. 57-90-29, fax 57-90-30, maroto@ mail.pf), at 217 meters elevation above the junction of the Vaituoru and Vainavenave rivers. It's only a kilometer from Marae Farehape, 18 km from Papenoo. This cluster of solid concrete buildings was built to house workers during construction of the hydroelectric installations here. The 10 rooms in a long block beside the parking lot rent for CFP 7,500 single or double, while the three bungalows on the ridge are CFP 9,500. Add CFP 1,100/2,500/5,100 pp for breakfast/lunch/dinner. If you wish to stay, call ahead to make sure the Relais is open and has a room for you (at last report it was for sale). Tahiti Safari Expedition may agree to bring you here on one of their tours at CFP 6,000 pp each way.

South of the Relais de la Maroto, the track climbs five km to 780 meters elevation where the 110-meter Urufau Tunnel (opened in 1989) cuts through to the south coast watershed. The track then winds down to **Lake Vaihiria,** Tahiti's only lake, at 473 meters elevation, 25 km south of Papenoo. Sheer cliffs and spectacular waterfalls squeeze in around this spring-fed lake. Native floppy-eared eels known as *puhi taria,* up to 1.8 meters long, live in these cold waters, as do prawns and trout. With its luxuriant vegetation, this rain-drenched spot is one of the most stunning on the island.

Just south of the lake, a concrete track with a 37-degree incline drops to a dam and upper power station. Four km beyond this is a smaller dam and lower power station, then it's seven km on a rough dirt track to PK 47.6 on the south coast highway near Mataiea.

ACCOMMODATIONS AROUND TAHITI

Taravao and Tahiti-iti

Fare Nana'o (Monique Meriaux, tel. 57-18-14, fax 57-76-10, www.farenanao.com) is an unusual place to stay. It's beside the lagoon in a colorful compound overflowing with vegetation and fragments of sculpture, very near the PK 52 marker, a km north of the old French fort at Taravao. The three thatched *fare* with shared bath are CFP 7,500 single or double. Another four with private bath and cooking facilities cost CFP 11,000. An additional person is CFP 1,000 extra in any of these. Although unique and wonderful, this Robinson Crusoe-style place is not for everyone: The walls are constructed of tree trunks and branches, and in the night you may be aware of the presence of crabs, lizards, and a marauding cat. You might have to wade through the lagoon or climb into a tree to get to your room. The Fare Nana'o website provides many photos.

A good sightseeing base is **Chez Jeannine** (Jeannine Letivier, tel./fax 57-07-49), also known as "L'Eurasienne," on the Route de Plateau five km above Taravao. You'll need a rental car to stay here because it's way up on the road to the Vaiufaufa Viewpoint and *le truck* doesn't pass anywhere nearby. The four two-story bungalows with cooking facilities and wicker furniture are CFP 8,000/45,000/100,000 double a day/week/ month, while the three rooms above the restaurant are CFP 5,000 double. The cool breezes and good views are complemented by a swimming pool. Jeannine's restaurant features Vietnamese dishes and seafood.

Punatea Village (tel./fax 57-71-00, www .punatea-village.pf) is at PK 4.6, between Taravao and Pueu on the road to Tautira. The four bungalows with private bath facing a black pebble beach are CFP 11,000 double plus tax, while the five rooms with shared bath in a long thatched building cost CFP 7,000. Meals are CFP 600/2,000/2,500 for breakfast/lunch/dinner (cooking facilities not provided). There's a swimming pool.

Right adjacent to the Punatea Village is **Pension Fare Maïthé** (Maïthé Romero, tel. 57-18-24, fax 57-18-24, www.chez-maithe.com) with two rooms with shared kitchen facilities and TV at CFP 6,500/7,000 single/double. It's in a quiet area near the sea with lush tropical vegetation.

The backpacker's best bet is **Chez Mado** (no phone), the snack bar on the east beach in Tautira. The friendly folks running the restaurant rent three rooms with shared bath in their own home, 500 meters down the beach beyond the end of the road. The CFP 3,500 pp charge includes all meals at the snack bar. Mado does her grocery shopping on Monday mornings, so if she's not there when you arrive, just wait around. It's a great place for lunch even if you're not staying, with dishes like *steak frites,* chow mein, and *poisson cru* for CFP 850–950.

On the opposite side of the Tahiti-iti peninsula is **Pension Meherio Iti** (Marie Maitere, tel./fax 52-17-50), at PK 11.9 in Vairao district on the road to Teahupoo. There are two bungalows with cooking facilities down near the lagoon, 400 meters off the road. These cost CFP 6,000/8,000 single/double (extra person CFP 1,000). They also rent a small flat in a house up near the main road for the same price, but it's not at all as nice. This place is usually fully booked by local French families on weekends but it's a possibility during the week.

Pension Chayan (tel./fax 57-46-00, www .pensionchayantahiti.pf) at PK 14, Vairao, has four bungalows at CFP 14,150 double. Breakfast/dinner are CFP 500/2,000. Kayaks are available for rent at CFP 200/500/1,000 an hour/half day/full day, and a Vaipori Cave excursion is offered at CFP 3,500 pp. From April to October you'll probably find surfers staying here.

Pension Vaiani (tel./fax 57-96-16) at PK 16.5, Teahupoo, operates mainly as a surfing camp with 14 beds in a large attractive house, plus two beach bungalows with another three beds each. It's CFP 6,500 pp including all meals and the surf boat to the reef. Boat trips to the grotto are CFP 1,000 pp, to Pari Coast CFP 1,500 pp (minimum of four persons). This place is always packed with surfers in April and May.

On the Pari Coast beyond the end of the road at Teahupoo is **Pension Le Bon Jouir** (Annick Paofai, tel. 57-02-15, fax 43-69-70, www.bon jouir.com). The six bungalows start at CFP 9,500 double, otherwise the six rooms with shared bath are CFP 7,000 (two nights minimum). Camping is CFP 1,200 pp. You can cook for yourself or order breakfast and dinner at CFP 4,000 pp a day. Return boat transfers (at 1200 and 1700) are CFP 1,600 pp and it costs CFP 500 a day for parking at the wharf in Teahupoo. Le Bon

Jouir is in a verdant location backed by hills and it makes a great base for exploring this area. It's right opposite the famous Teahupoo surfing break.

On the same coast but a bit closer to Teahupoo than Le Bon Jouir is **Te Pari Village** (www .tahiti1.com/tepari). They don't have a direct phone at the guesthouse, but you can call tel. 42-59-12 in Papeete for information. The three bungalows are CFP 20,900 double including all meals and boat transfers. The wharf where both these establishments pick up their guests is at PK 17.1, a km back from the end of the road.

Southwestern Tahiti

Papara Village (Thomas Chave, tel. 57-75-58, fax 57-79-00) is up on a hill a km off the south coast highway at PK 38.5, Papara. The two solid bungalows with private bath, fridge, and TV (but no cooking) are CFP 7,500/10,500 single/double. There's also a large family bungalow with kitchen at CFP 18,500 for up to four persons. A swimming pool is on the premises.

Hiti Moana Villa (Steve Brotherson, tel. 57-93-93, fax 57-94-44, www.papeete.com/ moanavilla), at PK 32, is right on the lagoon between Papara and Paea. The four bungalows with a kitchen, living room, TV, terrace, and private bath are CFP 9,500 single or double, or CFP 13,000 for four persons. Four additional units without kitchens are CFP 9,000 (tax included but CFP 2,000 surcharge for one night). There's a swimming pool and pontoon, and the manager has a boat and motor for rent at CFP 7,000. Airport transfers are CFP 1,500 pp each way. This place is often full—especially on weekends—and advance bookings are recommended.

One of the best low-budget places on Tahiti is **Pension Te Miti** (Frédéric and Crystal Cella, tel./fax 58-48-61, www.pensiontemiti.com) at PK 18.5, Paea, in Papehue village, 450 meters up off the main road. The six rooms in two adjacent houses cost CFP 6,000–7,000 double depending on the size of the room. Backpackers and surfers often choose one of the four beds available in each of the two dorms at CFP 2,500 pp. Breakfast is included. Amenities include a communal fridge, cooking facilities, TV corner, luggage storage, bicycles, and Internet access. Use of the washing machine is CFP 500. Airport transfers are CFP 1,000 pp but it's fairly easy to get there on *le truck*. Mahana Park and various shops and restaurants are nearby.

Taaroa Lodge (Ralph Sanford, tel. 58-39-21, www.taaroalodge.com), a large house right on a rocky beach behind Restaurant Snack PK 18 at PK 18.1, Paea, offers a 10-mattress dorm at CFP 2,300 pp, one room at CFP 5,000 single, and two bungalows at CFP 10,000 for up to three persons (two-night minimum stay). There's a common kitchen. Surfers are the main clientele, and several surf breaks including Sapinus Reef are nearby. The atmosphere is good.

Directly across the highway from the Taaroa Lodge access road at PK 18, Paea, is **Relais Fenua** (Laurent Lyon, tel./fax 45-01-98, www.relais-fenua.pf) with three rooms on each side of a new V-shaped building at CFP 8,750/9,350 single/double. Breakfast/dinner are CFP 900/2,500. Parking space is provided.

Iaorana Villa (tel./fax 54-49-11, iaorana villa@mail.pf), PK 10.8, Punaauia, was a vacation center for military personnel involved in the French nuclear testing program until 2001. It's right on the coast with 24 thatched air-conditioned garden bungalows at CFP 12,000/72,000/240,000 for one/seven/30 nights (higher in July, August, and around Christmas). The 20 non-air-conditioned standard rooms are CFP 8,000/45,000/150,000. Some of the rooms are in bad repair, so you might ask to see yours before accepting it. Avoid the units across the busy highway, away from the rest of the hotel and the beach. There's a high diving platform over the lagoon.

Chez Armelle (Raimana Rivière, tel. 58-42-43, fax 58-42-81, www.pension-armelle.com), at PK 15.5 in Punaauia (almost opposite a large Mobil service station), has eight rooms at CFP 5,900/7,550/8,650 single/double/triple. A bungalow is CFP 8,650 double. Breakfast and tax are included in all rates and dinner is available at CFP 1,500 pp. The minimum stay is two nights. There's a pleasant snack bar facing the beach but the rooms are ensconced in the complex. No parking space is provided and rental cars must be left overnight at a public beach park nearby. Snorkeling gear, canoes, kayaks, and bicycles are available. Airport transfers are CFP 500/1,000 pp day/night each way. This pension caters more to French migrants who pay by the month, but it's still worth a look.

Pension de la Plage (tel. 45-56-12, fax 82-85-48, www.pensiondelaplage.com), PK 15.4, Punaauia, across the highway from Chez Armelle, has two long motel-style blocks of six rooms each at CFP 7,700/9,900 single/double (CFP 8,000/10,400 with kitchenette). The rooms face a small pool and beach access is nearby.

In 1998 the **Hôtel Méridien Tahiti** (tel. 47-07-07, fax 47-07-08, www.lemeridien-tahiti.com) opened at PK 15, Punaauia, about nine km southwest of the airport. The 138 air-conditioned rooms in the four-story main building begin at CFP 39,000 single or double, while the 12 overwater bungalows are CFP 53,000 single or double, plus 11 percent tax. There's a huge sand-bottomed swimming pool linked to the beach and a 500-seat conference center. The waters off their sandy beach are pollution-free, the Museum of Tahiti and the Islands is just a 15-minute walk away, the atmosphere is pleasingly European, and the sunsets over Moorea are superb. Considerable controversy surrounded the building of this hotel because Tahitian protesters occupied the site for nearly four years to protect an ancient Moahi burial ground. In January 1996 French gendarmes were called in to evict the demonstrators and construction went ahead under tight security.

On the mountain side of the highway at PK 8.3, Punaauia, up the hill and above Carrefour shopping center, is a five-bed dormitory and one double room provided by **Moana Surf Tours** (Moana David, tel./fax 43-70-70, moana surftours@mail.pf). There's no sign, so ask. A bed here will set you back CFP 12,000 pp a day including breakfast, dinner, and unlimited transfers to the surf breaks off Tahiti. The busy season is April–November, and most surfers stay a week. Other months you can stay in the dorm at CFP 4,000 pp including breakfast. This place is of interest only to surfers and is overpriced for other guests.

OTHER WINDWARD ISLANDS

Maiao

Maiao, or Tapuaemanu, 70 km southwest of Moorea, is a low coral island with an elongated, 180-meter-high hill at the center. On each side of this hill is a large greenish-blue lake. Around Maiao is a barrier reef with a pass on the south side accessible only to small boats. Some 250 people live in a small village on the southeast side of 8.3-square-km Maiao, all of them Polynesians. Problems with an Englishman, Eric Trower, who attempted to gain control of Maiao for phosphate mining in the 1930s, have resulted in a ban on Europeans and Chinese residing on the island. Most of the thatch used in touristic constructions on Moorea and Tahiti originates on Maiao.

There are no tourist accommodations on Maiao and an invitation from a resident is required to stay. Proposals to develop the island for tourism have been rejected by the inhabitants and there's no airstrip. For information on the monthly supply ship *Taporo V* from Papeete, contact the **Compagnie Française Maritime de Tahiti** (tel. 42-63-93) at Fare Ute. A roundtrip voyage on this ship would at least give you a glimpse of Maiao for CFP 2,654 deck. Two nights will be spent aboard ship and it's possible to get off at Moorea on the return trip.

Mehetia

Mehetia is an uninhabited volcanic island about 100 km east of Tahiti. Although Mehetia is less than two km across, Mount Fareura reaches 435 meters. There's no lagoon and anchorage is untenable. Landing is possible on a black beach on the northwest side of the island, but it's difficult. Anglers from the south coast of Tahiti visit occasionally.

Tetiaroa

Tetiaroa, 55 km north of Tahiti, is a low coral atoll with a turquoise lagoon and 13 deep-green coconut-covered islets totaling 490 hectares. Only small boats can enter the lagoon. Tahuna Iti has been designated a seabird refuge (fenced off) and the lagoon is a marine reserve. The three-km-long Rimatuu islet served as a retreat for Tahitian royalty, and the remains of Polynesian *marae* and giant *tuu* trees may be seen.

In 1904 the Pomare family gave Tetiaroa, once a Tahitian royal retreat, to a Canadian dentist named Walter J. Williams to pay their bills. Dr. Williams, who served as British consul from 1916 until his death in 1937, had a daughter who sold Tetiaroa to actor Marlon Brando in 1966. Brando came to Tahiti in 1960 to play Fletcher Christian in the MGM film *Mutiny on the Bounty* and he ended up marrying his leading lady, Tarita Teriipaia (who played Mameetee, the chief's daughter). Until 2004, she and her family ran a small tourist resort on Motu Onetahi called the Hôtel Tetiaroa Village, but this has now closed. Tarita and Marlon had two children, son Teihotu, born in 1965, and daughter Cheyenne, born in 1970.

The gunshot death of Dag Drollet, Cheyenne's ex-boyfriend and father of her son Tuki, at the Brando residence in Los Angeles in 1990, resulted in a 10-year prison sentence for Cheyenne's half-brother, Christian Brando, on an involuntary manslaughter plea bargain. On Easter Sunday 1995, Cheyenne committed suicide and she was buried next to Dag in the Drollet family crypt at Papeete's Uranie Cemetery. Due to these tragedies, Brando seldom visited Tetiaroa during the years leading up to his death in 2004.

Getting to Tetiaroa

Yachts and catamarans tied up opposite the Vaima Center offer day trips to Tetiaroa and their departure times and rates are posted. Prices vary according to whether lunch is included and the quality of the boat. See Transportation in the Papeete section for listings of day cruises to Tetiaroa. On all of the boat trips from Papeete, be aware that up to three hours will be spent traveling each way, and on a day trip you'll only have about four hours on the atoll. The boat trip tends to be rough and many people throw up their fancy lunch on the way back to Papeete. (In 1995 Marlon Brando won a lawsuit to prohibit "floating hotels" in the Tetiaroa lagoon, so overnight trips are no longer possible.)

Cruising yachts with careless captains sometimes make an unscheduled stop at low-lying Tetiaroa since it's directly on the approach to Papeete from Hawaii. Several good boats have ended their days here.

Moorea

Moorea, Tahiti's heart-shaped sister island, is clearly visible across the Sea of the Moon, just 21 km northwest of Papeete. This enticing island offers the white-sand beaches rare on Tahiti, plus long, deep bays, lush volcanic peaks, and a broad blue-green lagoon. Much more than Tahiti, Moorea is the laid-back South Sea isle of the travel brochures. And while Bora Bora has a reputation as Polynesia's most beautiful island, easily accessible Moorea seems more worthy of the distinction (and it's a lot less expensive too). When Papeete starts to get to you, Moorea is only a hop away.

With a population of just 14,000, Moorea lives a quiet, relaxed lifestyle; coconut, pineapple, and vanilla plantations alternate with pleasant resorts and the vegetation-draped dwellings of the inhabitants. Tourism is concentrated along the north coast around Paopao and Tiahura; many of the locals live in the more spacious south. Yet like Bora Bora, Moorea is in danger of becoming overdeveloped and traffic already roars along the north coastal road all day. The choicest sections of shoreline have been barricaded by luxury resorts. On the plus side, most of the hotels are clusters of thatched bungalows, and you won't find many of the monstrous steel, glass, and cement edifices that scream at you in Hawaii. Still, the accommodations are plentiful and good, and weekly and monthly rentals make even extended stays possible. Don't try to see Moorea as a day trip from Tahiti: this is a place to relax!

The Land

This triangular, 125-square-km island is actually

FRENCH POLYNESIA

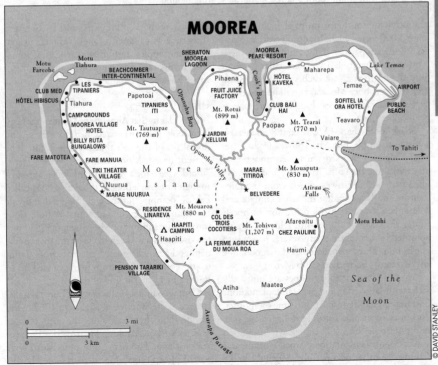

© DAVID STANLEY

© M.E. DE VOS

tour buses with shark-tooth-shaped Mouaroa soaring behind

the surviving southern rim of a shield volcano once 3,000 meters high. Moorea is twice as old as its Windward partner, Tahiti, and weathering is noticeably advanced. Two spectacular bays cut into the north coast on each side of Mt. Rotui (899 meters), once Moorea's core. The crescent of jagged peaks facing these long northern bays is scenically superb.

Shark-tooth-shaped Mouaroa (880 meters) is a visual triumph, but Mt. Tohivea (1,207 meters) is higher. Polynesian chiefs were once buried in caves along the cliffs. Moorea's peaks protect the north and northwest coasts from the rain-bearing southeast trades; the drier climate and scenic beauty explain the profusion of hotels along this side of the island. Moorea is surrounded by a coral ring with several passes into the lagoon. Three *motu* enhance the lagoon, one off Afareaitu and two off Club Med.

Moorea's interior valley slopes are unusually rich, with large fruit and vegetable plantations and human habitation. At one time or another, coconuts, sugarcane, cotton, vanilla, coffee, rice, and pineapples have all been grown in the rich soil of Moorea's plantations. Stock farming and fishing are other occupations. Vegetables like taro, cucumbers, pumpkins, and lettuce, and fruit such as bananas, oranges, grapefruit, papaya, star apples, rambutans, avocados, tomatoes, mangoes, limes, tangerines, and breadfruit make Moorea a veritable Garden of Eden.

History

Legend claims that Aimeho (or "Eimeo," as Captain Cook spelled it) was formed from the second dorsal fin of the fish that became Tahiti. The present name, Moorea, means "yellow" *(rea)* "lizard" *(moo)* for a yellow lizard which appeared to high priest in a dream. It has also been called Fe'e or "octopus" for the eight ridges that divide the island into eight segments. A hole right through the summit of Mt. Mouaputa (830 meters) is said to have been made by the spear of the demigod Pai, who tossed it across from Tahiti to prevent Mt. Rotui from being carried off to Raiatea by Hiro, the god of thieves.

Captain Samuel Wallis was the European discoverer of the Windward Islands in 1767. After leaving Tahiti, he passed along the north coast of Moorea without landing. He named it Duke of York's Island. The first European visitors were botanist Joseph Banks, Lieutenant Gore, the surgeon William Monkhouse, and Herman Sporie. Captain Cook anchored in Opunohu Bay for one week in 1777, but he never visited the bay that today bears his name! His visit was uncharacteristically brutal, as he smashed the islanders' canoes and burned their homes when they refused to return a stolen goat.

In 1792 Pomare I conquered Moorea using arms obtained from the *Bounty* mutineers. Moorea had long been a traditional place of refuge for defeated Tahitian warriors, thus in 1808 Pomare II fled into exile here after his bid to bring all Tahiti under his control failed. A party of English missionaries established themselves at Papetoai in 1811, and Moorea soon earned a special place in the history of Christianity: Here in 1812 the missionaries finally managed to convert Pomare II after 15 years of trying. On February 14, 1815, Patii, high priest of Oro, publicly accepted Protestantism and burned the old heathen idols at Papetoai, where the octagonal church is today. Shortly afterward the whole population followed Patii's example. The *marae* of Moorea were then abandoned and the Opunohu Valley depopulated. The first Tahitian translation of part of the Bible was printed on Moorea in 1817. From this island Protestantism spread throughout the South Pacific.

After Pomare II finally managed to reconquer Tahiti in 1815 with missionary help (the main reason for his "conversion"), Moorea again became a backwater. American novelist Herman Melville visited Moorea in 1842 and worked with other beachcombers on a sweet-potato farm in Maatea. His book *Omoo* contains a marvelous description of his tour of the island. Cotton and coconut plantations were created on Moorea in the 19th century, followed by vanilla and coffee in the 20th, but only with the advent of the travel industry has Moorea become more than a beautiful backdrop for Tahiti.

Orientation

If you arrive by ferry you'll probably get off at Vaiare, four km south of Temae Airport. Your hotel may be at Maharepa (Moorea Pearl Resort), Paopao (Club Bali Hai, Motel Albert), Pihaena (Sheraton Moorea Lagoon), or Tiahura (Club

Med, the campgrounds, Hôtel Moorea Village), all on the north coast. The Paopao hotels enjoy better scenery, but the beach is far superior at Tiahura. Add a CFP 150 pp per day municipal services tax to the accommodations prices quoted below.

The PKs (kilometer stones) on Moorea are measured in both directions from PK 0 at the access road to Temae Airport. They're numbered up to PK 35 along the north coast via Club Med and up to PK 24 along the south coast via Afareaitu, meeting at Haapiti halfway around the island.

Our circle-island tour and the accommodations and restaurant listings below begin at Vaiare Wharf and go counterclockwise around the island in each category.

SIGHTS

Northeast Moorea

You'll probably arrive on Moorea at **Vaiare Wharf,** which is officially PK 4 on the 59-km road around the island. To the north is the **Sofitel Ia Ora** (PK 1.3), built in the mid-1970s. If you have your own transport, stop for a look around the resort and a swim. It's also enjoyable to walk north along the beach from this hotel or even to go snorkeling. At PK 1 on the main road, high above the Ia Ora, is the fine **Toatea Lookout** over the deep passage, romantically named the Sea of the Moon, between Tahiti and Moorea.

One of the only public beach parks on Moorea is at **Temae,** about a km down a gravel road to the right a bit before you reach the airport access road. Watch out for black spiny sea urchins here. The Temae area is a former *motu* now linked to the main island and surfers will find an excellent long right wave around the point next to the airstrip. There's good snorkeling here. In 2002 the territorial government approved tax exemptions for a US$75 million 18-hole golf course and 150-room five-star hotel in this area, so watch out for construction. But don't take this for granted as Moorea residents have fought long and hard against golf courses and other tourism developments which strain the island's limited resources. In 1991 Moorea voters rejected a proposal to build an Arnold Palmer golf course and Sheraton hotel in the unspoiled Opunohu Valley. Moves to sweep sand from the lagoon to create artificial beaches at resorts have also been strongly opposed.

Around Cook's Bay

At PK 5.4 just west of the Moorea Pearl Resort on the mountain side of the road is the "White House," the stately mansion of a former vanilla plantation, now used as a pareu salesroom.

At the entrance to Cook's Bay (PK 7) is the **Galerie Aad Van der Heyde** (tel. 56-14-22), as much a museum as a gallery. Aad's paintings hang outside in the flower-filled courtyard; inside are his black-pearl jewelry, a large collection of Marquesan sculpture, and more paintings. The mock-colonial **Cook's Bay Resort Hôtel** at PK 7.2 is presently closed but it belongs to the same crowd that owns French Polynesia's three Sheratons and may be redeveloped eventually.

Paopao is the capital of Moorea with the gendarmerie, mairie, and several supermarkets serving the local community. The **Fish Market** is worth a stop to admire the large wall painting of a market scene by François Ravello. The fish market itself only opens Sunday 0500–0800. The catamaran *Ono-Ono* discharges passengers from Papeete here.

A rough four-km dirt road up to the paved Belvédère viewpoint road begins just west of the bridge at Paopao (PK 9), and it's nice to hike up past the pineapple plantations. This is a good shortcut to the Opunohu Valley easily covered by rental car or worth a walk.

On the west side of Cook's Bay, a km farther along the north-coast highway, is a new **Catholic church** (PK 10). In the older St. Joseph's Church next door is an interesting altar painting with Polynesian angels done by the Swedish artist Peter Heyman in 1948. Unfortunately this building is usually closed.

It's possible to visit the Distillerie de Moorea **fruit-juice factory** (tel. 56-11-33, fax 56-21-52), 300 meters up off the main road at PK 12. Aside from the excellent papaya, grapefruit, and pineapple juices made from local fruits, the factory produces apple, orange, and passion fruit juices from imported concentrate, with no preservatives added. They also make 40-proof brandies

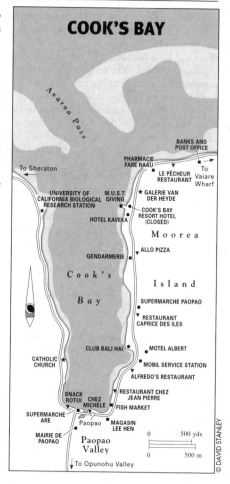

(carambola or "star fruit," ginger, grapefruit, mango, orange, and pineapple flavors) and 25-proof liqueurs (coconut, ginger, and pineapple varieties). These are for sale, and if they think you might buy a bottle, they'll invite you to sample the brews (no free samples for obvious backpackers). The sales room is open weekdays 0830–1630, but the factory 0800–1400 only.

Opunohu Bay to Le Belvédère

The Hôtel Sheraton Moorea Lagoon at PK 14 is the only large hotel between Paopao and Tiahura.

At PK 17.5 is the **Jardin Kellum Stop** (tel. 56-18-52), a tropical garden along Opunohu Bay with a colonial-style house built in 1925. Marie Kellum is an amateur archaeologist whose personal collection is full of interest and she can tell you anything you need to know about Tahitian medicinal plants. Until 1962 the Kellum family owned most of the Opunohu Valley. The garden is open Wednesday–Saturday mornings until noon. Ring the cow bell on the gate—it's CFP 500 pp admission. A famous yacht anchorage called Robinson's Cove is just offshore. Moorea residents have had to fight a running battle with developers to keep Opunohu Bay the way it is, and from the unspoiled surroundings it's easy to understand why the 1984 remake of *The Bounty* was filmed here.

Freshwater shrimp are bred in large basins at the head of Opunohu Bay (PK 18). From here a paved five-km side road runs up the largely uninhabited **Opunohu Valley** to the Belvédère viewpoint. After two km you reach the junction with the dirt connecting road from Cook's Bay previously mentioned, then another km up and on the right is the **Lycée Professionnel Agricole,** Moorea's agricultural high school. This worthy institution, with students from all the islands of French Polynesia, has hundreds of hectares planted in pineapples, vanilla, coffee, fruit trees, decorative flowers, and native vegetables on land seized from a German company in 1914.

Another km above this is **Marae Titiroa,** largest of a group of Polynesian temples restored in 1969 by Prof. Y.H. Sinoto of Honolulu. The small platform or *ahu* at the end of this *marae* was a sacred area reserved for the gods, and stone backrests for chiefs and priests are also seen. Here the people offered gifts of tubers, fish, dogs, and pigs, and prayed to their gods, many of whom were deified ancestors. Near the water tanks just 50 meters northwest of Marae Titiroa is a long council platform, and 50 meters farther are two smaller *marae* surrounded by towering Tahitian chestnut trees *(mape)*. The most evocative of the group is four-tiered **Marae Ahu o Mahine,** about 250 meters down the trail.

Some 500 ancient structures have been identified in this area, and if you're very keen, you should be able to find a few in the forest across the stream, evidence of a large population with a highly developed social system. Following the acceptance of Christianity in the early 19th century, the Opunohu Valley's importance declined sharply. Today lots of side trails lead nowhere in particular but you'll discover many crumbling marae walls. Naturalists will enjoy the natural vegetation.

Continue up the main road from Marae Titiroa about 200 meters and watch for some stone **archery platforms** on the left. Here kneeling nobles once competed to see who could shoot an arrow the farthest. The bows and arrows employed in these contests were never used in warfare. Just up on the left is access to another archery platform and **Marae Afareaito.** The stone slabs you see sticking up in the middle of the *marae* were backrests for participants of honor.

From the archaeological area the winding road climbs steeply another km to the **Belvédère,** or Roto Nui, a viewpoint high up near the geographical center of the island. Much of northern Moorea is visible from here and it's easy to visualize the great volcano that once existed. Mt. Rotui (899 meters) in front of you was once the central core of an island more than three times as high as the present. The north part is now missing, but the semicircular arch of the southern half is plain to see. (An ice cream from the *roulotte* in the parking lot may be a welcome treat.)

Although most easily toured by rental car, this intriguing area can also be explored on foot. If you're staying anywhere around Cook's Bay, begin by hiking up the four-km dirt road from the bridge in Paopao. If staying at Tiahura, take the boat bus to Cook's Bay to get started. After "doing" the *marae* and Belvédère, walk down the Opunohu Valley road if you're returning to Tiahura. For experienced hikers, a trail through the bush to Paopao begins at the rear left corner of the Belvédère parking lot. (Don't take a left turn near three pine trees as this branch only returns to the *marae.)* Carry lots of water and a picnic lunch and make a day of it.

Papetoai to Club Med

Back down on the coastal highway, continue west along Opunohu Bay. **Papetoai** (PK 22) is the oldest village on Moorea, where all the early explorers and missionaries initially came. The octagonal Protestant church behind the post office was built on the site of the temple of the god Oro in 1822. Despite having been rebuilt several times, the church is known as "the oldest European building still in use in the South Pacific."

At **Tiahura** the road begins to curve around the northwest corner of Moorea, passing a number of large resorts, including the Beachcomber Inter-Continental (PK 24.5), Club Med (PK 26.5), and the Hôtel Moorea Village (PK 27.9). Unfortunately, there are no public beaches anywhere along here, so walk through the grounds of one of the hotels. The beach at Tiahura looks nice but the water is rather shallow unless you go far out. The scuba operators or recreation people at the resorts will ferry you over to much better snorkeling areas off small islands like Tarahu and Tiahuru for a fee. For example, Scubapiti at Hôtel Les Tipaniers charges CFP 700 pp roundtrip for *motu* transfers. There's excellent reef break surfing in Taotai Pass off the Inter-Continental.

Patrice Bredel's **Galerie Api** (tel. 56-13-57, fax 56-28-27; Mon.–Sat. 1000–1200/1430–1730), in a stunning location overlooking the lagoon northeast of Club Med, displays the works of the late François Ravello who painted in a Gauguin-like style. Bredel's personal collection of old Pacific artifacts is fascinating.

In **Le Petit Village** shopping mall, across the street from Club Med, are a tourist information kiosk, bank, grocery store, snack bar, gas station, and many tourist shops. Drop into **Pai Moana Pearls** (tel. 56-25-25) between Club Med and Le Petit Village and ask for a free copy of owner Rick Steger's excellent brochure on pricing pearls. **Roonui Tattoo** (Roonui Mercer, tel. 56-37-53), opposite Club Med, does some beautiful work if you'd like a lifelong souvenir.

Southern Moorea

The south coast of Moorea is much quieter than the north. You'll drive for kilometers through the open coconut plantations past unspoiled villages and scenic vistas. At PK 31 is **Tiki Theater Village,** described below under **Entertainment,** the only one of its kind in the territory. Just past the

Fire Department at PK 31.5 Haapiti is **Marae Nuurua,** on the beach across the soccer field. This three-tiered *marae* restored in 1991 bears a petroglyph of a turtle, and beyond is the much higher rubble heap of an unrestored *marae.*

At PK 33 you can have your photo taken in front of a huge cement Tahitian warrior! You might also stop for an upmarket lunch or a drink at **Résidence Linareva** (PK 34). The Linareva's upscale floating seafood restaurant, the *Tamarii Moorea I,* is an old ferryboat that once plied between Moorea and Tahiti. Colorful reef fish swim around the dock, which also affords an excellent mountain view.

At PK 35/24, Haapiti, the kilometer numbering begins its descent to Temae Airport. The twin-towered **Église de la Sainte Famille** (1891) at Haapiti was once the head church of the Catholic mission on the island. There's good anchorage here for yachts entering Matauvau Pass and a tall left hander for the surfers out there.

Tiny Motu Hahi lies just off **Afareaitu** (PK 9), the administrative center of southern Moorea. After Papetoai, this was the second center of missionary activity on Moorea, and on June 30, 1817, at the printing works at Afareaitu, King Pomare II ceremonially printed the first page of the first book ever published on a South Pacific island, a Tahitian translation of the Gospel of St. Luke. Before the press was moved to Huahine a year later, over 9,000 books totaling more than half a million pages had been printed at Afareaitu! After 1821 the London Missionary Society established its Academy of the South Seas here to instruct the children of the missionaries and the Tahitian chiefs.

From opposite the old Protestant church (1912) in Afareaitu, the road between Magasin Ah Sing and a school leads up the **Afareaitu Valley** to a high waterfall, which cascades down a sheer cliff into a pool, a one-hour walk. You can drive a car two-thirds of the way up the valley. Park at the point where a normal car would have problems and hike on up the road to the right. When this road begins to climb steeply, look for a well-beaten footpath on the right, which will take you directly to the falls. You'll need a bit of intuition to find the unmarked way on your own.

You get a good view of **Mt. Mouaputa,** the peak pierced by Pai's spear, from the hospital just north of Afareaitu. The first road inland north of the hospital leads to a different waterfall, **Atiraa Falls.** The access road is very rough, so park just before a small concrete bridge and continue the 30-minute hike on foot.

Across the Island

An excellent day hike involves taking a morning bus to Vaiare Wharf, then hiking over the mountains to Paopao. From there you can catch another bus back to your accommodations, or try hitching. The shaded three-hour trail, partly marked by red, white, and green paint dabbed on tree and rock, does demand attention and perseverance, however. There are a few steep ascents and descents, and after rains it can be muddy and slippery.

Take the road inland beside Magasin Chez Meno, about 50 meters south of the first bridge south of the Vaiare ferry wharf. As you follow the dirt road up the valley, you'll take two forks to the right. Don't cross the stream after the second fork but go left and walk past some houses, just beyond which is an old Polynesian *marae* on the left. Further along you cross the stream and continue past a number of local gardens. The trail to Paopao leads off to the left near the last garden, and once you're on it it's fairly easy to follow if you keep your eyes open. When you see an old stone stairway on the left five minutes after leaving the gardens you'll know you're on the correct trail. All of the locals know about this trail and if you say "Paopao?" to them in a questioning way, they'll point you in the right direction.

When you reach the divide, go a short distance south along the ridge to a super viewpoint. On a clear day the rounded double peak of Orohena, Tahiti's highest, will be visible, plus the whole interior of Moorea. On the way down the other side avoid taking the wrong turn at a bamboo grove. You'll come out among the pineapple plantations of central Moorea behind Paopao. It's not possible to do this hike eastbound from Paopao to Vaiare without a guide, but westbound an experienced hiker should have no difficulty, and it's worth going simply to see a good cross section of the vegetation. Take water and wear sturdy shoes.

Transportation-wise, the easiest way to do this hike is as a day trip from Tahiti! If you take an early ferry from Papeete to Vaiare, you'll have ample time to do the hike before catching the afternoon *Ono-Ono* sailing back to Tahiti from Cook's Bay. The last departure from Paopao to Papeete is just after 1600 daily (check the exact time before leaving Papeete).

Sports and Recreation

TOPdive (Philippe Molle, tel. 56-17-32, fax 56-15-83, www.mooreaisland.com/mustdive), also known as M.U.S.T. Plongée, is centrally located near the Hôtel Kaveka on Cook's Bay. They offer diving daily at 0800, 1000, and 1400 for CFP 6,500/58,500 for one/10 dives. Guests at some hotels (such as the Kaveka and Hibiscus) are given a 15 percent discount.

Juan Pedro Duran's **Bathy's Club** (tel. 56-31-44, fax 56-38-10, bathys@mail.pf), at the Beachcomber Inter-Continental, offers scuba diving for CFP 5,500, plus CFP 1,500 for gear. This is the only PADI five-star facility in the territory, a classy and genuinely helpful outfit. Bathy's and TOPdive do underwater fish, eel, ray, and shark feeding. At sites like The Tiki the swarm of fish sometimes becomes so thick the guide is lost from sight, yet as the resident shark scatters the mass of fish to steal the bait, the divemaster is seen again patting *le requin* as it passes.

Scubapiti (Daniel Cailleux, tel./fax 56-20-38, www.scubapiti.com), at Hôtel Les Tipaniers at Tiahura, offers scuba diving daily at 0800 and 1400 (CFP 5,500 including gear). Instead of putting on a show, Daniel keeps things natural on his cave, canyon, and drift dives. Shark feeding and other gimmicks are not offered. He also offers PADI or CMAS scuba certification courses (CFP 34,000) and free hotel transfers from anywhere in northwestern Moorea.

Moorea's only female divemaster, Pascale Souquieres, runs **Moorea Fun Dive** (tel. 56-40-38, tel./fax 56-40-74, www.fundive.pf) at the Hôtel Moorea Village and the Sofitel Ia Ora. It's CFP 5,700 a dive or CFP 4,800 a dive for six dives or more including all gear (except a wetsuit). Ocean dives are at 0830 and 1400, lagoon diving at 1030, and hotel pickups are available from almost anywhere on northern Moorea. This is a professional yet laid-back operation we can recommend.

The "Activities Nautiques" kiosk on the wharf at the **Beachcomber Inter-Continental** (tel. 55-19-19) rents jet-skis or "wave runners" at CFP 7,750 for half an hour, CFP 12,180 for one hour, or try your hand at parasailing (CFP 6,460).

Surfing is possible in most of the passes around the island or off the beach next to the airstrip, but it's not quite as good as on Tahiti or Huahine. A boat or a long paddle is required to reach the reef breaks. Surfers often stay at Pension Tarariki Village on the south side of the island.

Deep-sea fishing is offered by **Tea Nui Charters** (Chris Lilley, tel./fax 56-15-08, teanui services@mail.pf), based at the Beachcomber Inter-Continental, at CFP 15,000 pp for a half/full day (four-person minimum).

Tiahura Ranch (tel. 56-28-55), across the highway from the Hôtel Moorea Village, offers horseback riding at 0845 and 1545 daily except Monday (CFP 5,000 for two hours). You must reserve at least an hour in advance.

Rupe-Rupe Ranch (tel. 56-26-52), at PK 2 between Vaiare Wharf and the Sofitel Ia Ora, also offers horseback riding. It's best to call ahead as they're not often there.

ACCOMMODATIONS

Camping

One of the South Pacific's nicest campgrounds is **Camping Chez Nelson** (Nelson and Josiane Flohr, tel. 56-15-18, www.camping-nelson.pf), near the Hôtel Hibiscus, just south of Club Med (PK 27, Tiahura). It's beautifully set in a coconut grove right on the beach. The camping charge is CFP 1,100 pp, with recently upgraded toilets, showers, refrigerator, and communal cooking facilities provided. No tents are for rent, but the 10 two-bed "dormitory" rooms go for CFP 1,300 pp (CFP 1,600 for one night). The five cabins are CFP 3,800 single or double (CFP 4,300 for one night); four larger rooms in a long building near the office are CFP 4,000 single or double (CFP 4,500 for

one night). The sunset cabin near the beach is CFP 5,300 (CFP 5,800 for one night). Kayaks and bicycles are for rent. The campground office is open only Monday–Saturday 0800–1800, Sunday 0800–1130. Josiane can be rather reserved at first, but she has a heart of gold. This place is clean, quiet, breezy, spacious, and well equipped, but don't leave valuables unattended or within reach of an open window at night.

A second campground is just a little south of Chez Nelson, near the Hôtel Moorea Village. Friendly **Moorea Camping** (tel. 56-14-47, fax 56-30-22), also known as "Chez Viri et Claude," faces the same white-sand beach and has nine four-bed dorms at CFP 1,300 pp (CFP 1,800 for one night), plus another 10 double rooms in a long building at CFP 2,400 single or double (CFP 3,400 for one night). The five beachfront bungalows are CFP 4,500 single or double (CFP 5,500 for one night). Camping is CFP 1,100 pp (CFP 1,200 for one night). All rooms at both campgrounds have only shared bath and French residents of Papeete often book all of the better units on weekends. The reception is open 0800–1200/1330–1700 only (closed Sun. afternoon). Communal kitchen and washing facilities are provided but sheets are not supplied in the dormitory. For CFP 1,500 pp they'll take you to a *motu* and their shark-feeding tours are very good. One-person kayaks are for rent at CFP 500/1,000 an hour/four hours. Bicycles are CFP 1,300 for eight hours. But as at Chez Nelson, we've heard of things going missing from the dorms, so take precautions. Both campgrounds are great for young low-budget travelers and other adventurers—you'll meet some wonderful people. Two grocery stores (with cold beer) are between the two camping grounds.

In 2003 **Haapiti Camping** (tel./fax 56-43-02, www.haapiti.com) opened near the Catholic church at PK 23.5 Haapiti on the south side of the island. It's CFP 1,000 pp to camp with your own tent, plus another CFP 1,500 pp to rent a tent with mattress, blanket, and pillow, if required. Several self-catering bungalows are available at CFP 5,000 double or CFP 2,000 pp for groups of three or four. A 10-bed dorm with shared kitchen, living room, and bath is CFP

2,000 pp. The owner, Mark Walker, lives in a treehouse on the property. During the Haapiti surfing season from May to October, this place is buzzing with surfers as some of the best waves on the island are nearby.

US$25–50

One of the least expensive places to stay is **Te Fare Oa Oa** (tel. 56-25-17, www.fareoaoa.com) at Pihaena, directly behind the PK 13 marker. It's down the road inland from Jean-Marc Fouchegu Avocat. Ask for Hervé. The four rooms with shared bath in a pleasant A-frame house are CFP 2,200/3,200 single/double or CFP 1,500 pp in the dorm, plus tax. Shared cooking and laundry facilities are provided. Bicycles are CFP 500 a half day.

Billy Ruta Bungalows (tel. 56-12-54) at PK 28.3, Tiahura, has 12 thatched A-frame bungalows lined up along the beach, beginning at CFP 5,700 double without kitchenette, CFP 6,800 double with kitchen. They're rented to French workers who pay by the month (CFP 65,000) and are often full. Another eight rooms in a long block with shared bath are CFP 3,000 single or double, but they're noisy due to permanent Tahitian residents who get up very early. On Saturday night, be prepared for disco dancing in an adjacent club until very late. Billy run the local bus service and is a very friendly guy. You'll find him in the house on the opposite side of the disco from the bungalows.

La Ferme Agricole du Moua Roa (Marie-Thérèse Buisson, tel./fax 56-58-62), off the south coast road at PK 21 between Haapiti and Maatea, is used mainly to accommodate school groups. This large colonial mansion has nine four-bed dorms at CFP 2,500 pp, plus CFP 3,000 pp for an organic breakfast and dinner. This hiking base camp is a 45-minute walk up a rough jeep track which begins next to a Mormon church. Guests are not allowed to drive in and must arrive on foot. You can climb most of Moorea's mountains from here.

US$50–100

Motel Albert (Iris Haring, tel. 56-12-76, fax 56-58-58, http://motelalbert.free.fr), on the slope opposite Club Bali Hai at Paopao (PK 8.5), catches splendid views across Cook's Bay. The four older apartments with one double bed, kitchen, and private bath are CFP 5,000 single or double, while four larger apartments with two double beds, kitchen, and private bath are CFP 6,000 double or triple (two-night minimum stay). The 10 two-bedroom bungalows with kitchen and private bath are CFP 8,500 for up to four persons. The larger apartments are often taken by monthly rentals. Each unit has cooking facilities, fridge, and hot water in a garden setting on spacious grounds. Several stores are nearby and the Mobil service station next door sells bread and groceries. It's good value and often full (try to make reservations).

Chez Dina (Dina Dhieux, tel./fax 56-10-39) is behind Magasin Pihaena at PK 13, Pihaena, a km east of the Sheraton. The three thatched bungalows are CFP 6,000 triple, CFP 7,000 for up to four (reductions on a weekly basis). Cooking facilities are provided, and the bathroom is communal.

Several small places rent bungalows near the Hôtel Sheraton Moorea Lagoon, PK 14, Pihaena. **Chez Nani** (Maeva Bougues, tel./fax 56-19-99) on the west side of the resort has three thatched bungalows with kitchenettes at CFP 8,000 single or double. The signposted **Faimano Village** (Faimano and Denis Feildel, tel. 56-10-20, fax 56-36-47, www.faimanovillage.com), next to Chez Nani, has seven lovely thatched *fare* with cooking facilities at CFP 12,500 for up to six persons or CFP 9,500/10,500 double/triple plus six percent tax (three-night minimum stay). Faimano Village has a nice garden setting facing the beach and easygoing atmosphere, but single women should avoid it as there have been reports of prowlers. The doors and windows cannot be properly locked. **Chez Francine** (Francine Lumen, tel./fax 56-13-24), 400 meters farther west, doesn't have a sign but look for three buildings with red tile roofs between the highway and the shore. A two-room house is CFP 8,500 double with kitchenette or CFP 6,500 double without kitchenette. The beach and view are excellent.

Repeat visitors to Moorea often stay at **Hôtel Tipaniers Iti** (tel. 56-12-67) at PK 21, Papetoai, on the west side of Opunohu Bay. It's a low-key place with five tin-roofed, self-catering bungalows in a garden setting from CFP 7,950, plus 11 percent tax, for up to four persons. Weekly rates are available. There's no beach but the long wooden deck offers great view of the bay. The reception is open from 0900–1300 only.

Hôtel Les Tipaniers (Geneviève Lemaire, tel. 56-12-67, fax 56-29-25, www.lestipaniers.com) at PK 25.9, Tiahura, is cramped around the reception, but spacious and attractive as you approach the beach. The 22 bungalows start at CFP 13,850 double, plus 11 percent tax (the 12 units with kitchen start at CFP 15,750). Four garden rooms are CFP 6,800 with fan. Les Tipaniers' well known restaurant offers Italian and seafood dishes. They'll shuttle you over to a nearby *motu* for snorkeling or loan you a bicycle or outrigger canoe at no charge. This hotel has a good reputation and a resident divemaster.

Moorea Fare Auti'ura (Viri Pere, tel. 56-14-47, fax 56-30-22), on the inland side of the road opposite Moorea Camping at PK 27.5, Tiahura, has six thatched bungalows on elevated concrete platforms at CFP 7,000 single or double (minimum stay two nights). Cooking facilities are provided. It's run by Moorea Camping, so check there if nobody seems to be around.

Fare Matotea (Iris Cabral, tel. 56-14-36, fax 56-32-54, mtt@mail.pf), on a spacious beach just south of Billy Ruta (PK 29, Tiahura), is CFP 9,000 for four, CFP 11,000 for six (minimum stay two nights). All nine large thatched *fare* on the spacious grounds have full cooking facilities and private bath. It's a good choice for families and small groups. Very little English is spoken.

Pension Tarariki Village (tel./fax 56-35-83), also known as "Fare Tatta'u" at PK 21.5, Haapiti, has four bungalows with private bath at CFP 7,520 single or double, one bungalow with shared bath at CFP 5,500, and a tiny individual cabin and common dorm at CFP 2,300 pp. There's a nice secluded beach below the pension's large treehouse and it's only a couple of kilometers to the pass for surfing. From May–October the owner provides boat transfers to Haapiti Pass for surfers at CFP 2,000 for one or two, plus CFP 1,000 each additional person. A grocery store is nearby.

Chez Pauline (Jean-Pierre Bouvier, tel./fax 83-71-21) at PK 9, Afareaitu, is between the two stores near the church. It's a lovely old colonial house with five rooms with double beds and shared bath at CFP 4,700/6,000/7,500 single/double/triple including breakfast. One larger room sleeping five is CFP 12,500. A picturesque restaurant with tikis on display rounds out this establishment, which has great atmosphere. Dinner here is around CFP 3,800 (fish and Tahitian vegetables) and it must be ordered in advance.

US$100–150

The **Hôtel Kaveka** (tel. 56-50-50, fax 56-52-63, www.hotelkaveka.com), PK 7.4 at the east entrance to Cook's Bay, has 24 wooden bungalows with fridge from CFP 9,800–23,800 double including tax. You'll need to burn a mosquito coil at night. The breakfast and dinner plan in their thatched restaurant is CFP 3,900 pp extra. The snorkeling is fine off their small artificial beach and there's a great view of Cook's Bay.

In early 2002 the 350-bungalow **Club Méditerranée** at PK 26.5, Tiahura, closed for major renovations and it's possible it may never open again. Labor costs have cut into Club Med's profitability and a huge investment will be required to bring this property up to the standards of the smaller, smarter Club Med on Bora Bora. It's rumored they've also had problems renewing their lease. At last report Club Med was still saying the Moorea property would reopen in early 2005, so check with their office in Papeete's Vaima Center (tel. 42-96-99, fax 42-16-83) to find out if anything's happening.

The **Hôtel Hibiscus** (tel. 56-12-20, fax 56-20-69, www.hotel-hibiscus.pf), on beach right next to Club Med (PK 27, Tiahura), offers 29 thatched bungalows beneath the coconut palms at CFP 13,200 triple in the garden or CFP 15,400 on the beach, plus 11 percent tax. A fourth person is CFP 1,650 extra. There's a 10 percent discount on a weekly basis but air-conditioned units cost more. The breakfast and dinner plan is CFP 5,250 pp, but all units have kitchenettes and fridge so this is a good choice for families. The location adjacent to Club Med has the advantage of fewer bugs due to frequent fumigations at the resort but the disadvantage of occasional noise from the disco. However, as long as Club Med remains closed, these factors don't apply.

Fare Vai Moana (tel./fax 56-17-14, farevaimoana@mail.pf) is next to a large restaurant overlooking the beach adjacent to Camping Chez Nelson at PK 27.1, Tiahura. The 12 attractive thatched bungalows are CFP 14,300 double in the garden or CFP 19,030 facing the beach, plus 11 percent tax. Half board at their seafood restaurant is CFP 6,720 pp extra.

The **Hôtel Moorea Village** (tel. 56-10-02, fax 56-22-11, www.mooreavillage.com) at PK 27.9, Tiahura, is also known as "Fare Gendron." It offers 70 fan-cooled thatched bungalows beginning at CFP 9,500/10,500 single/double plus 11 percent tax, or CFP 13,000 for up to four people. To be on the beach is another CFP 2,500. The 10 new units with kitchen are double price; all units have fridges. The breakfast and dinner plan costs CFP 4,600 pp but the quality of the food is uneven. Saturday at 1900 there's fire dancing; the Tahitian feast with Polynesian dancing is Sunday at noon. The eel and shark feeding tour is CFP 2,500. This place is somewhat of a hangout for local Tahitians and it's probably your best bet if you like to party.

Near the south end of the west coast strip (PK 30) is **Fare Manuia** (Jeanne Salmon, tel. 56-26-17, fax 56-10-30) with six *fare* with cooking facilities at CFP 10,200 for up to four people, CFP 13,000 for up to six people, or CFP 16,000 on the beach, plus tax. The minimum stay is two nights. Both this place and Fare Matotea are a little isolated from the restaurants and other facilities of Tiahura.

Résidence Linareva (tel./fax 56-15-35, www.linareva.com) sits amid splendid mountain scenery at PK 34 on the wild side of the island. Prices begin at CFP 11,500 double and increase to CFP 25,500 for four persons, with 10 percent weekly discounts (minimum stay two nights). Each of the eight units is unique, with TV, fan, and full cooking facilities. Bicycles and an outrigger canoe are loaned free. It's good value.

US$250 and up

The **Sofitel Ia Ora** (tel. 55-03-55, fax 56-12-

91), at PK 1.3 between Vaiare and the airport, sits on one of the finest beaches on the island with a splendid view of Tahiti. The 110 tastefully furnished thatched bungalows begin at CFP 38,350 single or double, plus 11 percent tax. Upgrade to air-conditioned if possible as many of the older units are inadequately screened. Breakfast and dinner are CFP 6,400 pp extra together. Scuba diving is CFP 6,000/25,000 for one/five dives. There's a Europcar desk in the lobby. Unfortunately, the service at the Ia Ora deteriorates when large groups are present.

In 2002 the **Moorea Pearl Resort** (tel. 55-17-50, fax 55-17-51, www.pearlresorts.com) at PK 5.3, Maharepa, was erected on the site of the former Hôtel Bali Hai dating back to 1961. The new resort features 30 rooms and suites in a long two-story concrete block with a thatched roof starting at CFP 25,000 double, 37 garden and beach bungalows from CFP 33,000, and 28 overwater bungalows on reinforced concrete piles beginning at CFP 51,000 (children under 13 sleep free). Add 11 percent tax to these rates. Breakfast and dinner are CFP 7,800 pp extra. The Polynesian and seafood buffets are CFP 6,200 pp (or CFP 1,500 if you've purchased a meal plan). Many banks, shops, and restaurants are only a short walk away.

Club Bali Hai (tel. 56-13-68, fax 56-13-27, www.balihaihotels.com) at PK 8.5, Paopao, has 20 rooms in the main two-story building starting at CFP 16,000 single or double, plus 19 beachfront or overwater bungalows CFP 24,000–32,000. Third persons pay CFP 5,000 and the 11 percent tax is extra (their website quotes lower prices in U.S. dollars—worth going after). Most rooms have a spectacular view of Cook's Bay. This is the last survivor of the famous Bali Hai hotel chain which once stretched clear across the Society Islands. To stay afloat, many units have been sold to Americans on a time-share basis, with each owner getting two weeks a year at the Club. There's a swimming pool by the bay. Avis has a desk here.

The **Hôtel Sheraton Moorea Lagoon** (tel. 55-11-11, fax 55-11-55, www.sheratonmoorea.com) at PK 14, Pihaena, has 52 garden and beach bungalows from CFP 42,000 double, plus

54 overwater bungalows beginning at CFP 77,500, plus 11 percent tax. There's excellent snorkeling offshore, a swimming pool, and a spa. The air-conditioned rooms are well equipped but the entire resort is crowded for the site. The service is surly and the location poor, with no local restaurants nearby. The activities desk tacks a 10 percent surcharge onto anything booked through them. The Sheraton was originally to have been managed by Outrigger Hotels of Hawaii, but they withdrew after falling out with property owner Louis Wane. As the resort was being built in 2000, local protesters in canoes surrounded a dredge attempting to pump lagoon sand onto the resort's artificial beach. Legal action eventually forced the construction company to withdraw the environmentally unfriendly dredge. In late 2002 Sheraton unveiled plans to build another 31 overwater bungalows to make the resort more profitable and local residents mounted a fresh campaign to confront this new threat to Moorea's ecosystem.

Unlike the Sheraton, the 147-room **Moorea Beachcomber Inter-Continental** (tel. 55-19-19, fax 55-19-55, www.moorea.interconti.com) at PK 24.5, has a friendly, welcoming atmosphere. The 48 standard air-conditioned rooms in the main building erected in 1987 start at CFP 34,400 single or double plus 11 percent tax, but it's better value to pay CFP 39,650 for a garden bungalow. Beach bungalows are CFP 48,600. For one of the 50 overwater bungalows, have your CFP 68,250 ready. Third persons pay CFP 6,660 for an uncomfortable extra bed, but children under 15 are free (this resort has a comprehensive children's activities program at additional cost). The breakfast and dinner plan is CFP 7,740 pp (alternative eateries are quite a walk away). This spacious resort has a large swimming pool and abundant paid sporting activities are available (only tennis and snorkeling gear are free for guests). The hotel's captive Hawaiian dolphins are a controversial attraction (admission is charged to the dolphin enclosure) and the snorkeling off the resort's artificial beach isn't very good. Europcar has a desk here.

A good alternative to the large resorts is family-style **Pension Anahoa** (tel. 56-35-32, www.pension-anahoa.com), down the street beside Chez Serge at Tiahura. The large two-room bungalows here are CFP 26,500 plus six percent tax for up to four persons including breakfast. Dinner can be ordered at CFP 3,250 pp plus 10 percent tax. Laurence and Coco are helpful in making restaurant or tour reservations, and they provide outrigger canoes, kayaks, and snorkeling gear free to guests. Ask them where to paddle out to see the manta rays.

FOOD

Maharepa

Restaurant Le Mahogany (tel. 56-39-73; Thurs.–Tues. 1100–1500/1800–2200), at PK 4, Maharepa, offers French and Chinese dishes in the CFP 1,550–2,000 range. A bit west is the popular **Restaurant Le Cocotier** (tel. 56-12-10; Wed.–Mon. 1130–1430/1830–2130) with meat dishes priced CFP 1,950–2,650 and fish at CFP 1,950–2,250. There's a menu at the entrance.

Snack Le Sylésie (tel. 56-15-88), next to the post office at PK 5.5, Maharepa, has a nice terrace and fast service—perfect for breakfast or lunch. It's also good for pastries, sandwiches, and crepes, and try the coconut ice cream. Of course, the coffee here is *magnifique!*

Le Pêcheur Restaurant (tel. 56-36-12; closed Sun.), also at Maharepa (PK 6), near the pharmacy at the east entrance to Cook's Bay, has an excellent reputation for its seafood dishes, which begin around CFP 2,200. The service is also good. If you lack transportation, they'll come and pick you up.

The overwater **Fishermen's Wharf Restaurant** (tel. 56-50-50) at the Hôtel Kaveka (PK 7.4) serves seafood in the CFP 1,800–2,100 range. Happy hour is 1800–1900 with live music provided. The view from their terrace is superb and there's even a beach.

Allo Pizza (tel. 56-18-22; Tues. 1700–2100, Wed.–Sat. 1100–1400/1700–2100), opposite the gendarmerie at PK 7.8, bakes 38 kinds of thin-crust takeaway pizzas costing CFP 900–1,900. You must consume these picnic-style elsewhere (the nearby TOPdive wharf is a good choice).

Paopao

Restaurant Caprice des Îles (tel. 56-44-24; closed Tues.), occupies a thatched pavilion next to Supermarché Paopao on the mountain side of the road, 150 meters north of Club Bali Hai. They offer Chinese dishes (CFP 1,300–1,500), fish (CFP 1,950–2,850), and meat (CFP 1,650–2,950)—more expensive than other places along this way. We've heard rave reviews of their seafood.

Restaurant Chez Jean Pierre (tel. 56-18-51; Sun. 1815–2115, Mon. 1115–1415, Tues. and Thurs.-Sat. 1115–1415 and 1815–2115), close to Paopao market, is one of the less expensive places. The specialty is roast suckling pig in coconut milk (CFP 2,200) served on Saturday night, but there's also chicken (CFP 1,150–1,250), duck (CFP 1,250), and seafood (CFP 1,150–1,950), plus Chinese dishes. Cheaper still is the outdoor snack bar at Paopao Market, which is only open in the evening.

Alfredo's Restaurante/Chez Jules et Claudine (tel. 56-17-71; closed Mon.), on the inland side of the road a few hundred meters south of Club Bali Hai, has pizza (CFP 1,450) and pasta (CFP 1,550–1,950), plus fish (CFP 1,900–2,450) and meat (CFP 1,950–2,750) dishes. Call for a free hotel pickup.

Also check **Chez Michèle** (tel. 56-34-80), by the river at the head of Cooks Bay, which lists their menu (CFP 1,200–1,500) on a blackboard facing their terrace.

Snack Rotui (tel. 56-18-16; Tues.-Sat. 0700–1700), just west of the bridge at Paopao, could be the cheapest place on the island with sandwiches (CFP 150–180), chicken wings, French fries, cake, egg rolls, and ice cream. Their terrace overlooks Cook's Bay, it's friendly, and English is spoken.

Tiahura

Aside from the selections that follow, remember the excellent Italian restaurant at **Hôtel Les Tipaniers** (tel. 56-12-67). The mahimahi with vanilla sauce and *tartare de thon* are excellent, and don't miss the homemade desserts, especially the crème brulée and coconut pie.

Restaurant L'Aventure (tel. 56-53-59; Tues. 1800–2130, Wed.-Sun. 1100–1400/1800–2130),

next to Hôtel Hibiscus, has pastas (CFP 1,020–1,980), meat and fish dishes (CFP 1,250–1,980), and vegetarian dishes (CFP 850–1,650). Specials are advertised on a blackboard menu.

Good pizza/pasta (CFP 1,100/1,200) and ocean views are available at beachfront **Le Sunset Pizzeria** (tel. 56-26-00; daily 1130–1430/1800–2130) at the Hôtel Hibiscus (but avoid the salads). **Pâtisserie Le Sylésie** (tel. 56-20-45) is nearby.

Snack Coco d'Isle (tel. 56-59-07), between the two campgrounds, has excellent lunch specials, such as swordfish or mahimahi in vanilla sauce for CFP 1,000. Their *poisson cru* is superb, and you can eat on a terrace beside the road. The fine French cuisine at **Restaurant Le Pitcairn** (tel. 56-55-46) nearby has been recommended by readers.

Rôtisserie Royal Chicken (tel. 78-53-53; Tues.-Sat. 1100–1330/1800–1930), a takeaway beside the road near Moorea Camping, sells huge, thick-crust half chickens for CFP 600. The proprietor, Alain, puts on quite a show, especially if someone gets him riled while he's trying to do six things at once. He's a great guy, so just stand back and enjoy. This is one of the best deals in French Polynesia—arrive soon after it opens as the chicken sell out fast.

Groceries

If you've got access to cooking facilities, shop at one of the many grocery stores spread around Moorea. The largest and cheapest is **Toa Moorea** (tel. 56-18-89; Mon.-Thurs. 0800–1900, Fri. 0800–1900, Sat. 0800–2000, Sun. 0600–1100), a km south of the Vaiare ferry wharf.

Libre Service Maharepa (tel. 56-35-90), at PK 5.5, is almost opposite the Banque de Tahiti in Maharepa. **Supermarché Pao Pao** (tel. 56-17-34), 150 meters north of Club Bali Hai, opens Monday–Saturday 0530–1200/1430–1800, Sunday 0500–0900.

At the head of Cook's Bay you have a choice of **Magasin Lee Hen** (tel. 56-15-02; Mon.-Sat. 0530–1200/1400–1830, Sunday 0500–1200) or **Supermarché Are** (tel. 56-10-28) just west of the bridge nearby. Lee Hen and some of the others sell lots of local takeaway snacks.

The nearest grocery store to the Sheraton is **Magasin Pihaena** at PK 13. The supermarket in **Le Petit Village** opposite Club Med opens Monday–Saturday 0700–1930 and Sunday 0700–1300/1600–1930.

All that you're likely to find in the **municipal market** at Paopao is a limited selection of fish. Fresh produce is much harder to obtain on Moorea than it is on Tahiti, so buy things when you see them and plan your grocery shopping carefully. Ask the stores what time the bread arrives, then be there promptly. The hybrid lime-grapefruit grown on Moorea has a thick green skin and a really unique taste.

ENTERTAINMENT

The **Iguana Rock Café** (tel. 56-17-16) at Le Petit Village in Tiahura has live music Saturday after 2000. It's expensive and not a lot happens there.

The disco at **Billy Ruta Bungalows** (tel. 56-18-12), at PK 28.3, Tiahura, is a nice, very Polynesian scene with a good music mix of Tahitian, French, American, reggae, etc. It's a fun place that gets very busy with some very talented dancers (Sat. from 2230, CFP 1,500 cover charge).

Cultural Shows for Visitors

See Tahitian dancing in the Sofitel Ia Ora's **La Pérouse Restaurant** (tel. 56-12-90) on Tuesday, Thursday, and Saturday at 2000 (buffet CFP 4,000–6,000). At **Club Bali Hai** (tel. 56-22-77) there's Polynesian dancing Wednesday at 1800. The Tahitian show at the **Moorea Beachcomber Inter-Continental** (tel. 55-19-19) is on Monday, Wednesday, and Saturday nights after 2000. The **Hôtel Moorea Village** (tel. 56-10-02) presents Polynesian dancing Friday and Saturday at 1900 and Sunday at lunchtime. These times often change, so check. The Tahitian feasts that come with the shows cost CFP 4,500 and up, but you can often observe the action from the bar for the price of a drink. It's well worth going.

Since 1986 Moorea has had its own instant culture village, the **Tiki Theater Village** (Olivier Briac, tel. 55-02-50, fax 56-10-86, www.tiki village.pf) at PK 31, Haapiti. The doors are open Tuesday–Saturday 1130–1500, with a charge of CFP 2,200 to visit the village and see the small dance show at 1300. The guided tour of the recreated Tahitian village is informative and the 32 dancers and other staff members who live in the village year-round are enthusiastic, but sometimes they're a little disorganized so you might obtain some details about the show time before parting with your francs. Lunch is available in the à la carte restaurant. On Tuesday, Wednesday, Friday, and Saturday at 1800 there's a big sunset show with a *tamaaraa* buffet and open bar (CFP 7,200, reservations required). Transportation is CFP 1,000 pp roundtrip, if required. If you've got CFP 135,000 to spare, a "royal" Tahitian wedding can be arranged at the village (bring your own partner, same sex couples welcome). The ceremony lasts two hours, from 1600 to sunset. The bridegroom arrives by canoe and the newlyweds are carried around in procession by four "warriors." Otherwise there's the less extravagant "princely" wedding for CFP 110,000, photos included. Yes, it's kinda tacky, but that's show biz! (Such weddings are not legally binding.)

INFORMATION AND SERVICES

Information

The Moorea Visitors Bureau (tel. 56-29-09; closed Sun.) has a poorly marked but helpful kiosk next to the gas station in front of Le Petit Village. Activities and tours can be booked here. An unstaffed tourist information counter at Temae Airport dispenses self-service brochures.

Kina Maharepa (tel. 56-22-44), next to the post office at PK 5.5, Maharepa, sells books and magazines in French. There's also a newsstand in Le Petit Village opposite Club Med. Newspapers in English are not available at either.

Services

The Banque Socredo, Banque de Polynésie, and Banque de Tahiti are all near the Moorea Pearl Resort at Maharepa. Banque Socredo has a second office opposite Vaiare Wharf. Another Banque de Polynésie branch is in Le Petit Village shopping mall opposite Club Med. None of these banks are open on Saturday but most have ATMs accessible 24 hours.

The main post office (tel. 56-10-12; Mon.–Thurs. 0730–1200/1330–1600, Fri. 0730–1200/1330–1500, Sat. 0730–0930) is near the banks at Maharepa. A branch post office (tel. 56-13-15) is found at Papetoai.

The gendarmerie (tel. 56-13-44) is at PK 7.8, Paopao, just south of the Hôtel Kaveka.

The Iguana Rock Café (tel. 56-17-16) at Le Petit Village in Tiahura provides internet access at CFP 25 a minute.

Health

The island's **hospital** (tel. 56-23-23) is at Afareaitu, on the opposite side of the island from most of the resorts. In case of need, it's much easier to see a private doctor or dentist. Moorea doctors charge around CFP 3,300 for office visits, or CFP 5,000 plus CFP 100 a km for hotel visits. Ask your hotel for the closest.

Pharmacie Tran Thai Thanh (tel. 56-10-51; weekdays 0730–1200/1400–1800, Sat. 0800–1200/1530–1800, Sun. 0800–1100) is at PK 6.5 between Maharepa and Paopao. There's also Pharmacie de Haapito (tel. 56-38-37; weekdays 0900–1200/1600–1830, Sun. 0900–1100) at PK 30.5, Haapiti, near Tiki Theater Village.

TRANSPORTATION AND TOURS

Air Moorea and **Air Tahiti** (both tel. 56-10-34) are based at Moorea Temae Airport. For information on the planes and ferries linking Tahiti, Moorea, and Huahine, turn to Transportation in the introduction to French Polynesia.

Buses await the ferries from Tahiti at Vaiare Wharf. Although they don't go right around the island, the northern and southern bus routes meet at Le Petit Village opposite Club Med, so you could theoretically effect a circumnavigation by changing buses there, provided you caught the last service back to Vaiare from Le Petit Village at 1530. You should have no problem catching a bus when you arrive on Moorea from Tahiti by ferry, but be quick to jump aboard.

Be aware that the bright yellow "Moorea Explorer" buses at the wharf charge CFP 500, while the older buses most of the locals use ask only

CFP 300. The fare is the same to anywhere on the island.

Buses leave Le Petit Village for the ferry weekdays at 0430, 0530, 0630, 0930, 1130, 1330, 1430, and 1530, Saturday at 0430, 0530, 0630, 0830, 0930, 1130, 1330, 1430, and 1530, and Sunday at 0430, 0630, 1230, 1330, 1430, and 1630. If you have to catch a bus somewhere along its route, add the appropriate traveling time and ask advice of anyone you can. Some of the buses run 30 minutes early.

A taxi on Moorea is actually a minibus with a white letter *T* inside a red circle. Taxis fares are exorbitant and you should consider bargaining. Hitching is wearing thin with Moorea motorists, although it's still possible. If you really need the ride, you'll probably get it; just be prepared to do some walking.

Car Rentals

Europcar (tel. 56-34-00, fax 56-35-05) has a main office opposite Club Med and branches at Vaiare Wharf, the Sofitel, Sheraton, and several other locations. Their unlimited-mileage cars begin at CFP 8,100/15,000/21,060 for one/two/three days. Scooters are CFP 4,500/5,000/5,500 four/eight/24 hours, bicycles CFP 1,000/1,500/2,000. Despite these prices many of Europcar's vehicles are in bad shape. If you don't have a credit card they'll want a cash deposit of CFP 100,000. Clients are responsible for the first CFP 100,000 in damages to the vehicle; to reduce this liability to CFP 25,000 a fee of CFP 1,400 a day must be paid.

Avis (tel. 56-32-68, www.avis-tahiti.com) at Vaiare wharf, the airport, Club Bali Hai, and opposite Club Med has cars from CFP 8,721/16,371 for one/two days including kilometers and insurance. These cheaper cars are often unavailable and you'll find yourself being quoted CFP 10,400/19,500. Though more expensive, their vehicles and service are superior to those of Europcar.

Rental cars and bicycles are also obtained at **Albert Activities Center** (tel./fax 56-10-42, alberttransport@mail.pf), with locations at the airport and opposite Club Bali Hai (tel. 56-19-28) and Club Med (tel. 56-33-75). Unlimited-mileage cars begin at CFP 7,000/8,000/14,500 for eight/24/48 hours, including insurance. Some of their vehicles are of the "rent a wreck" variety, so look the car over before signing the credit card voucher and insist on a replacement or a discount if it's a high-mileage bomb. Their scooters are CFP 4,500/5,000/9,000. Bicycles cost about CFP 1,000/1,300 for a half/full day.

If your time is limited, it's best to reserve an Avis or Europcar vehicle a day or two ahead at one of their offices in Papeete as all cars on Moorea are sometimes taken. There are five gasoline stations around Moorea: Mobil a km south of Vaiare Wharf, Shell opposite Vaiare Wharf, Total at the airport access road, another Mobil near Motel Albert at Paopao, and another Total opposite Club Med. The maximum speed limit is 60 kph.

Local Tours

Moorea Explorer (tel. 56-12-86, moorea.explorer@mail.pf) at the airport offers upscale bus and boat tours for people on package tours. Their bright yellow buses are newer than those of the other companies, but their tours tend to be rushed with fewer stops and little flexibility.

The tours offered by **Albert Activities** (tel. 56-13-53, fax 56-40-58, alberttransport@mail.pf), at the airport and opposite Club Bali Hai and Club Med, are much more personal than those of Moorea Explorer, and the guides are generally more receptive to individual requests. If you get one of the Haring brothers as your guide, you'll definitely enjoy it. Daily at 0900 Albert does a three-hour circle-island bus tour, including a visit to the Belvédère, at CFP 2,500 (lunch not included). Albert's five-hour 4WD jeep safari is CFP 3,500 pp (do it in the morning).

Several other companies, including **Ben Tours** (Benjamin Teraiharoa, tel. 56-26-50) at the airport, offer much the same. Whichever circle-island tour you choose, be prepared for a stop at whichever black pearl showroom is currently paying the guides the highest commission.
Tropic Escape (Rémy Costa, tel. 56-42-49) specializes in hiking and mountain climbing with half/full day trips at CFP 3,000/5,000.
Inner Island Safari Tours (Alexandre Haa-

matearii, tel. 56-20-09, fax 56-34-43), based at Maharepa, offers an exhilarating 4WD tour to various viewpoints and around Moorea for CFP 4,800 pp.

Archaeologist Mark Eddowes (tel. 56-34-20) leads a "Path of the Ancients" tour which visits numerous *marae* on a two-km hike through the Opunohu Valley. He does this half-day trip (CFP 5,750 pp) mostly for cruise ship passengers or when a group of at least 10 persons has booked. Call him up to find out what's scheduled.

Day Cruises

Archipels Croisières (tel. 56-58-41), based at PK 17 on Opunoho Bay near the Jardin Kellum, offers a day cruise around Moorea on the *Fetia Ura*, a 34-meter classic schooner, with various snorkeling and sightseeing stops. They visit "Le Monde de Mu," an underwater sculpture garden in the lagoon off Papetoai with 10 large tikis created in 1998 by the renowned Tahitian stone carver Tihoti. These trips operate Wednesday–Sunday 0830–1630 (CFP 11,500 including a buffet lunch). There's also a 1530–1830 sunset cruise daily except Thursday and Sunday (CFP 6,000).

At 0930 and 1400 daily the **Moorea Beachcomber Inter-Continental** (tel. 55-19-19) offers a three-hour cruise on the catamaran *Manu* at CFP 6,300 pp. The 1.5-hour sunset cruise is CFP 3,200 including drinks. You can take a one-hour ride in a glass-bottom motorboat called the *Aquascope* at CFP 3,200 pp and they'll go anytime between 0900 and 1200 (both have four-person minimums).

Snorkeling Trips

Albert Activities (tel./fax 56-10-42) runs a five-hour motorized aluminum canoe ride right around Moorea with a stop for snorkeling (gear provided), departing Tuesday, Wednesday, Friday, and Sunday at 0900 (CFP 5,000 pp, minimum of four). For a free pickup, inquire at one of the three Albert Activities centers around Moorea. You could see dolphins, whales, sharks, stingrays, and human surfers on this trip.

Other companies run a variety of trips, such a *motu* excursion by outrigger or a *motu* picnic party. On many of these, the canoes are without radios, life jackets, or flotation devices, and they can be frightening if you're not a good swimmer. The snorkeling itself is great. **Moorea Explorer** (tel. 56-12-86, fax 56-25-52) at the airport combines shark feeding with their island tours (CFP 6,500/7,500 pp by bus/4WD).

Moorea Camping (tel. 56-14-47) at Tiahura runs an excellent shark feeding tour to a *motu* at 1000 and 1400 daily. This trip costs CFP 1,500/2,000 for campground residents/non-residents, and if you're not staying at the campground, be sure to call ahead for information. Bring your own mask as theirs don't fit very well. The **Hôtel Moorea Village** (tel. 56-10-02) offers a similar tour for CFP 2,500.

Unfortunately, the shark feeding event has become just a bit too popular, especially when four boats each carrying 10 tourists arrive at the same time. The guides throw a few pieces of tuna to three or four well-fed little sharks, which sniff disinterestedly at the bait. Some of the tourists who get in the water become overexcited and begin thrashing around behind the rope that separates them from the beasts, trying to be in front. It's still unknown if this activity will eventually attract larger sharks into the Moorea lagoon but to date no incidents have been reported. The unexpected highlight of these trips is the chance to swim alongside groups of manta rays.

Dolphin-Watching

Dolphin Quest at the Moorea Beachcomber Inter-Continental (tel. 56-19-48, fax 56-16-67, dqfp@mail.pf) gives tourists the opportunity to pay CFP 16,500 each to spend 30 minutes wading around a shallow lagoon enclosure with four captive dolphins (touching and even kissing the penned mammals is allowed). These activities begin at 0930, 1330, and 1530. At 1030 and 1530 it's possible to don a mask and snorkel and actually swim with the dolphins in a deeper part of the enclosure at CFP 18,700 (the Inter-Continental tacks on a CFP 1,000 surcharge in either case if you're not a hotel guest). You're only in the water with the animals a short time and photos are charged extra. This whole business has environmental and moral implications. Dolphin

Quest's brochure claims that part of the proceeds "helps fund education, research, and conservation programs around the world" without being specific. The dolphins presently held here were flown in from Hawaii after the native dolphins proved impossible to tame and kept trying to escape. It's also clear that somebody is making a lot of money by exploiting these captive animals as a tourist attraction.

A quite different type of dolphin encounter is offered by Dr. Michael Poole of **Dolphin & Whale Watching Expeditions** (tel. 56-23-22 or 56-14-70, fax 56-14-70, criobe@mail.pf). Dr. Poole has been on Moorea researching dolphins and whales since 1987 and he's currently in charge of the Marine Mammal Research Program at CRIOBE, a French biological research station on Moorea. In May 2002 French Polynesia's government declared its entire exclusive economic zone a whale and dolphin sanctuary, protecting, forever, these animals in over five million square km of ocean. Dr. Poole was the author of this proposition, worked ten years to bring it to fruition, and wrote the original guidelines that were used as a basis for the legislation.

On his trips, small groups are taken out in boats to see acrobatic spinner dolphins—the only dolphins to spin vertically in the air like tops or ballerinas—in the wild. You may also observe dolphins surfing (!), and from July to October humpback whales are often seen. These 3.5-hour trips go out early on Thursday and Sunday mornings, costing CFP 6,700 pp with half price reductions for children 12 and under. Included in the price are boat pickups at all hotels between the Pearl Resort and the Moorea Village (bus transfers arranged from the Sofitel). Space is quite limited, so reserve well ahead through one of the Moorea activities offices, a hotel tour desk, or by calling the numbers above. Be sure to state clearly that you want "Dr. Poole's boat" as several unscientific imitators are trying to do the same thing with varying success. The activities desks at resorts like the Sheraton push the captive dolphin show at the Inter-Continental for the commissions they earn and may claim not to know of Dr. Poole.

Moorea Airport

Moorea Temae Airport (MOZ) is in the northeast corner of the island. The airport transfer service is only for people on prebooked tours, so unless you rent a car, you'll be stuck with a rip-off taxi fare in addition to the airfare: CFP 1,500 to Vaiare Wharf or the Moorea Pearl Resort, CFP 3,000 to the Sheraton, CFP 3,500 to the Inter-Continental, and CFP 4,000 to Club Med.

Thanks to intimidation from the taxi drivers, none of the hotels are allowed to offer airport pickups. The bright yellow Moorea Explorer transfer buses at the airport are only allowed to carry passengers with vouchers. Try to buy one as you're checking in for your flight to Moorea in Papeete. If you ask at the Moorea Explorer counter (tel. 56-12-86) inside the terminal you'll almost certainly be told to take a taxi. Your hotel reception should be able to book your return

trip to the airport on these buses for CFP 550. (Travel writers who enjoyed "hospitality" from Air Tahiti won't tell you about any of this.)

Albert, Avis, and Europcar have counters at the airport, but it's essential to reserve beforehand. Otherwise they may not have a car for you and you'll be subjected to the scam just mentioned.

Considering this, you should seriously consider using the ferry to/from Moorea. At a quarter the price of the plane (CFP 1,000 compared to CFP 4,000), the scenic 30-minute catamaran ride to/from Tahiti may end up being one of the highlights of your visit. It's mostly tourists on prepaid packages who arrive by air—those traveling individually usually take the ferry. If you do fly, try to sit on the left side of the aircraft on the way to Moorea and on the right on the way to Papeete.

Huahine

Huahine, the first Leeward island encountered on the ferry ride from Tahiti, is a friendly, inviting island, 175 km northwest of Papeete. In many ways, lush, mountainous Huahine (74 square km) has more to offer than overcrowded Bora Bora. The variety of scenery, splendid beaches, deep bays, exuberant vegetation, archaeological remains, and charming main town all invite you to visit. Huahine is a well-known surfing locale, with consistently excellent lefts and rights in the two passes off Fare (try to befriend the local surfers before entering their space). Schools of dolphins often greet ships arriving through Avapeihi Pass. Huahine's mosquito population is also surprisingly large.

It's claimed the island got its name because, when viewed from the sea, Huahine has the shape of a reclining woman—very appropriate for such a fertile, enchanting place. *Hua* means "phallus" (from a rock on Huahine-iti) while *hine* comes from *vahine* (woman). A narrow channel crossed by a concrete bridge slices Huahine into Huahine-nui and Huahine-iti (Great and Little Huahine, respectively). The story goes that the demigod Hiro's canoe cut this strait.

The almost entirely Polynesian population numbers 5,500, yet some of the greatest leaders in the struggle for the independence of Polynesia, Pouvanaa a Oopa among them, have come from this idyllic spot. The artist Bobby Holcomb and poet Henri Hiro are also well remembered.

In recent years Huahine has been discovered by international tourism, and deluxe hotels and bungalow-style developments are now found in different parts of the island. Luckily Huahine has been able to absorb this influx fairly painlessly, as it's a much larger island than Bora Bora, and the resorts are well scattered and constructed in the traditional Tahitian style. It's an oasis of peace after Papeete. The island has also become a major port of call for the yachts that anchor off Fare. Backpackers pioneered Huahine in the mid-1980s, and good facilities still exist for them too.

Archaeology

Archaeologists have found that human habitation goes back at least 1,300 years on Huahine; Maeva village was occupied as early as A.D. 850. In 1925 Dr. Kenneth P. Emory of Hawaii's Bishop Museum recorded 54 *marae* on Huahine, most of

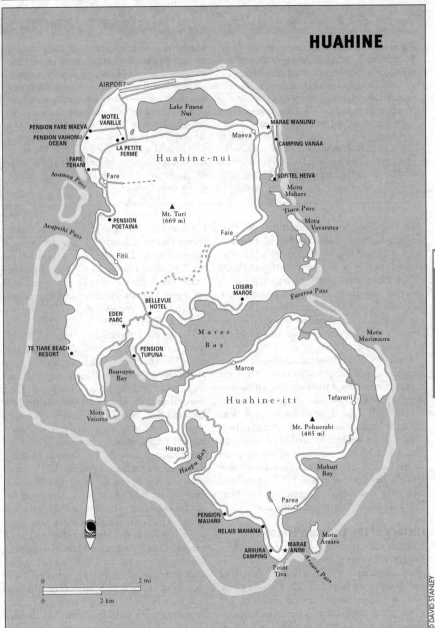

HUAHINE

AIRPORT

MOTEL VANILLE

Lake Fauna Nui

PENSION FARE MAEVA

PENSION VAIHONU OCEAN

MARAE MANUNU ★

Maeva

CAMPING VANAA

FARE TEHANI

LA PETITE FERME

Huahine-nui

Fare

SOFITEL HEIVA

Avamoa Pass

Motu Mahare

Tiare Pass

Avapehi Pass

Mt. Turi (669 m) ▲

PENSION POETAINA

Motu Vavaratea

Faie

Fitii

Farerea Pass

LOISIRS MAROE

BELLEVUE HOTEL

EDEN PARC ★

Maroe Bay

Motu Murimaora

TE TIARE BEACH RESORT

PENSION TUPUNA

Bourayne Bay

Maroe

Motu Vaiorea

Huahine-iti

Tefarerii

Mt. Pohuerahi (485 m) ▲

Haapu

Haapu Bay

Mahuti Bay

PENSION MAUARII

Parea

RELAIS MAHANA

MARAE ANINI ★

Motu Araara

ARIIURA CAMPING

Point Tiva

Araara Pass

0   2 mi

0   2 km

FRENCH POLYNESIA

POUVANAA A OOPA

Pouvanaa a Oopa was born at Maeva on Huahine in 1895 and during WW I he served in France. In 1942 he denounced war profiteers and was placed under arrest on Huahine. A year later he managed to escape with another man by canoe to Bora Bora in the hope of obtaining American help, but was arrested and returned to Huahine three days later. After the war Pouvanaa continued to oppose the colonial administration and to advocate a freer political alliance with France. He was elected a deputy to the French parliament in 1949, 1952, and 1956 on an autonomy program. In 1957 he became vice-president of the local administration and campaigned for independence in the 1958 referendum, but the No side got only 35 percent of the vote throughout the territory. Later that year he was falsely accused of trying to set Papeete aflame and was sentenced to 15 years imprisonment. Finally pardoned in 1968, Pouvanaa was elected a senator in the French parliament two years later, a post he held until his death in 1977. Known to the Tahitians as *metua* (spiritual father), Pouvanaa a Oopa remains a symbol of the Polynesian struggle for independence.

them built after the 16th century. In 1968 Prof. Yosihiko H. Sinoto found another 40. Huahine-nui was divided into 10 districts, with Huahine-iti as a dependency. As a centralized government complex for a whole island, Maeva, on the south shore of Lake Fauna Nui, is unique in French Polynesia. Here all the district chiefs on Huahine-nui lived side by side and worshiped their ancestors at their respective *marae*, twenty-eight of which are recorded here.

Since 1967 about 16 *marae* have been restored, and they can be easily visited today. The great communal *marae* at Maeva and Parea have two-stepped platforms *(ahu)* that served as raised seats for the gods. Like those of Raiatea and Bora Bora, the Huahine *marae* are constructed of large coral slabs, whereas comparable structures on Tahiti and Moorea are made of round basalt stones. During construction of the defunct Hôtel Bali Hai just north of Fare in 1972, a *patu* hand club was uncovered, suggesting that New Zealand's Maoris originated in this area.

History of the Leeward Islands

Huahine was settled by Polynesians around 850. Roggeveen, coming from Makatea in the Tuamotus, sighted (but did not land on) Bora Bora and Maupiti on June 6, 1722. Captain Cook "discovered" the other Leeward Islands in July 1769, which was quite easy since the Tahitians knew them well. In fact, Cook had the Raiatean priest Tupaia on board the *Endeavour* as a pilot.

Cook wrote: "To these six islands, as they lie contiguous to each other, I gave the names of Society Islands." Later the name was extended to the Windward Islands. In 1773 a man named Omai from Raiatea sailed to England with Cook's colleague, Captain Furneaux, aboard the *Adventure;* he returned Cook in 1777 and was dropped off on Huahine.

During the 19th century, American whalers spent their winters away from the Antarctic in places like Huahine, refurbishing their supplies with local products such as sugar, vegetables, oranges, salted pork, and *aito,* or ironwood. These visits enriched the island economy, and the New England sailors presented the islanders with foreign plants as tokens of appreciation for the hospitality received. English missionaries arrived in 1808 and later Pomare II extended his power to Huahine, abolishing the traditional religion. In 1822 missionary law was imposed. Among the missionaries was William Ellis whose book, *Polynesian Researches,* published in London in 1829, has left us a detailed picture of the island at that time.

Though Tahiti and Moorea fell under French control in 1842, the Leeward Islands remained a British protectorate until 1887 when these islands were traded for fishing rights off Newfoundland and a British interest in what was then New Hebrides (today Vanuatu). Marines from the French warship *Uranie* had attacked Huahine in 1846, but they were defeated at Maeva. A year later France promised Britain that it would not annex the Leeward Islands, yet in 1887 it proceeded to do so. The local chiefs refused to sign the annexation treaty until 1895, and resistance to France, especially on Raiatea, was only overcome by force in 1897. The French then expelled the English missionary group that had been there 88 years; nonetheless, today 80 percent of the population of the Leewards remains Protestant.

In 1918 a Spanish influenza epidemic wiped out a fifth of the population including the last queen, Tehaapapa III. Only in 1945 was missionary law finally abolished and French citizenship extended to the inhabitants. In the 1958 referendum, 7six percent of the population of Huahine voted in favor of independence.

Tourism began in 1973 with the building of the airstrip and the Hôtel Bali Hai. In 1999, a land dispute and strike led to the closing of this hotel, which is sad as it was one on finest of its kind in French Polynesia, tastefully placed between a lake and the beach. Several new upscale resorts have since appeared but they're much more expensive and isolated from town.

FARE

The unpretentious little town of Fare, with its tree-lined boulevard along the quay, is joyfully peaceful after the roar of Papeete. A beach runs right along the west side of the main street and local life unfolds without being overwhelmed by tourism. Local men play *pétanque* on the Fare waterfront around sunset. From here Bora Bora is visible in the distance to the left while the small twin peaks of Taha'a are to the right. The seven other villages on Huahine are linked to Fare by winding, picturesque roads. The snorkeling offshore north of town is great, but despite the easygoing atmosphere, it's unwise to leave valuables unattended on the beach (and beware of unperceived currents).

SIGHTS

After you've explored the Fare waterfront, visit the beautiful *mape* (chestnut) forest up the Faahia valley. Walk inland 15 minutes along the road that begins two houses south of the house marked "Oliveti" near the Total service station. This road becomes a jungle trail that you can easily follow another 15 minutes up a small stream into a tropical forest laced with vanilla vines and the sweet smell of fermenting fruit. By the stream is a long bedlike rock known as Ofaitere, or "Traveling Rock," but you'd need to have someone point it out to you. A guide will certainly be required to continue right to the summit of Huahine's highest peak, Mt. Turi (669 meters), in about three hours, as it's rough going.

A side road from Hôtel Bellevue, six km south of Fare, leads one km west to **Eden Parc** (tel. 68-86-58, www.edenparc.org; Mon.–Sat. 0900–1600, admission CFP 300), a commercial tropical garden where an organically-grown lunch (from CFP 1,000) and fruit drinks (CFP 400) are served to visitors.

Sports and Recreation

Pacific Blue Adventure (Didier Forget, tel. 68-87-21, fax 68-80-71, www.divehuahine.com) at Fare offers scuba diving at CFP 5,500/20,000 for one/four dives. Trips to sites like Avapeihi Pass, Fa'a Miti, Coral City, and Yellow Valley leave at 0900 and 1400, depending on demand. They'll take snorkelers only if things are really slow. They pick up at hotels around Fare.

La Petite Ferme (Pascale Liaudois, tel./fax 68-82-98, www.la-petiteferme.com), between Fare and the airport, offers riding with Pascale, Yvon, and their 16 small, robust Marquesan horses. A two-hour ride along the beach is CFP 4,500 pp, and they also offer a full day of riding into the mountains or along the beach for CFP 9,800. Call the day before to let them know you're coming. This is the number-one horseback-riding operation in French Polynesia—recommended.

ACCOMMODATIONS

US$25–50

Pension Chez Guynette (Marty and Moe Temahahe, tel./fax 68-83-75, chezguynette@mail.pf), also known as "Club Bed," is on the waterfront to the left as you get off the ship. The seven rooms, each with the name of a different Society island, are CFP 4,400/5,300/6,400 single/double/triple plus six percent tax with fan and private bath. The eight-bed dorm at the back of the building is CFP 1,750 pp. You can cook your own food in the communal kitchen here. It's a pleasant, clean place; no shoes are allowed in the house. Upon arrival peruse the list of rules and rates—rigorously applied (for example, it's lights out in the kitchen at 2200). On departure day the rooms must be vacated by 1000, but you can leave your bags at the reception until 1800 if catching a late ferry. Most readers say they liked the efficiency. Thankfully, the management doesn't allow overcrowding and will turn people away rather than pack them in for short-term gain.

Nearby on the waterfront is three-story **Hôtel Huahine** (tel. 68-82-69), at CFP 3,500/4,500/5,500 single/double/triple, or CFP 1,500 in a dorm. A supplement of CFP 500 is charged if you stay only one night. The 10 bare rooms are large, each with its own unreliable toilet and shower. No cooking facilities are provided. Fish dishes in the restaurant start at CFP 1,000, but you may also sit and watch TV for the price of a beer. Stalwart surfers who don't care for the house rules at Pension Guynette often stay here. Love it or leave it.

Under a km north of town is **Pension Vaihonu Ocean** (Etienne Faaeva, tel. 68-87-33, fax 68-77-57, vaihonu@mail.pf) with three *fare* at CFP 4,350 double and a six-bed dorm at CFP 1,650. Two self-catering duplexes with private bath are CFP 7,200 double plus six percent tax. Camping is CFP 1,620 pp. There's an open communal kitchen in the small compound jammed with potted flowers. Unfortunately access to the nearby beach is blocked by residential construction and you'll have to go back toward Fare to find a place to surf or swim.

La Petite Ferme (Pascale Liaudois, tel./fax 68-82-98, www.la-petiteferme.com), between Fare and the airport, has one room with shared bath at CFP 3,250/4,400 single/double and a six-bed dorm at CFP 1,850 pp, including breakfast (CFP 500 extra for one night). In addition, there's a self-catering bungalow at CFP 5,250/7,900/9,450 single/double/triple (two-night minimum stay). All prices include tax and airport

transfers. It's a great place to stay if you're at all interested in horseback riding.

US$50–100

Pension Enite (Enite Temaiana, tel./fax 68-82-37) is an eight-room boardinghouse at the west end of the waterfront beyond the snack bar. Rooms with shared bath are CFP 15,000 double with half board (two-night minimum stay, no room rentals without meals, no singles). The meals are served in a thatched cookhouse on the beach and the food is good. Middle-of-the-night arrivals mustn't knock on the door before 0700. This longstanding pension first opened in 1978 and French expats often stay here.

Just behind of Fare is **Pension Meri** (Milton Brotherson, tel. 68-82-44, fax 68-85-96), down the road behind Banque Socredo. The three bungalows with private bath and cooking facilities are CFP 8,500 single or double, or CFP 10,500 for up to four (minimum stay five nights).

Several good places to stay are between Fare and the airport, about 800 meters north of the wharf. Aside from Pension Vaihonu Ocean previously mentioned, **Pension Lovina** (Lovina Richmond, tel./fax 68-88-06) has five small *fare* with TV and shared bath at CFP 4,500/6,500 single/double. For families and groups, there are three oversized thatched bungalows with cooking and bathing facilities at CFP 6,600/8,000/12,000 single/double/triple, CFP 17,000 for up to five persons, CFP 24,500 for seven people. Dormitory accommodations are CFP 1,800 pp, and camping is CFP 1,250 pp. All guests have access to communal cooking facilities (and mosquitoes). The minimum stay is two nights, and discounts may be negotiable. Airport pickups cost CFP 1,200 pp return; from the harbor it's CFP 600 pp.

Chez Ella (Ella Mervin, tel./fax 68-73-07, ella@iaorana-huahine.com), next to Motel Vanille at the airport turnoff, has three bungalows with kitchen, fridge, and TV at CFP 7,500 single or double, CFP 10,000 triple or quad. You can ask to use the washing machine.

Motel Vanille (tel./fax 68-71-77, www.motel vanille.com) is on the corner of the airport access road and the Fare-Maeva highway. Their six thatched bungalows positioned around the swimming pool are CFP 9,500 single or double with bicycles and airport transfers included (two-night minimum stay). Breakfast and dinner are CFP 2,900 pp. It's all rather informal, but a kilometer from the beach.

Pension Fare Maeva (tel. 68-75-53, fax 68-70-68, faremaeva@mail.pf) is on a rocky shore, 900 meters down an access road west from the airport road. It's a bit less than two km from the airport or three km from Fare. The 10 self-catering bungalows are CFP 9,010 single or double, while the 10 motel-style rooms go for CFP 6,600, breakfast included. When booking, ask about packages including a car. There's a restaurant, swimming pool, and garden. They'll even do your laundry for a small fee. Airport transfers are free.

In a valley a km south of Fare (inland from the second bridge) is **Pension Poetaina** (Jean-Pierre Amo, tel./fax 68-89-49, pensionpoetaina@mail.pf), a large two-story building with spacious balconies and lounge. The four rooms with shared bath are CFP 7,500 single or double including breakfast, while two larger rooms with private bath are CFP 9,500 (two-night minimum stay). Communal cooking facilities are provided and there's a pool. Boat trips around Huahine are arranged at CFP 7,500 pp plus tax including lunch and snorkeling.

Chez Henriette (tel./fax 68-83-71) is a pleasant 15-minute walk south of Fare, beside the lagoon a few hundred meters beyond Pension Poetaina. The six thatched *fare* each have basic cooking facilities. The three smaller units with double bed, mosquito net, fridge, hot plate, and shared bath are CFP 6,675 double, while the three larger *fare* with two double beds and private bath are CFP 8,675 for up to four persons—okay for a family with two children. It's sort of like staying in a local village while retaining a measure of privacy.

The **Hôtel Bellevue** (tel. 68-82-76, fax 68-85-35), six km south of Fare, offers 10 bungalows without cooking facilities at CFP 8,900 double, plus 11 percent tax. The poor lighting makes it hard to read in the evening. There's a figure-eight shaped swimming pool. The restaurant has a lovely view of Maroe Bay but the meals are pricey. Roundtrip airport transfers are CFP 1,760 pp.

Considering the expense, isolation, and absence of a beach, the Bellevue has little going for it.

Idyllic **Pension Tupuna** (Loretta and Franck Souillard, tel./fax 68-70-36, www.huahine.com/tupuna) is in a rather isolated location on Bourayne Bay down the old road to the Huahine-iti bridge from Hôtel Bellevue. The three *fare* with shared bath are CFP 6,000 single or double, mosquito nets and breakfast included. Singles get a reduction to CFP 4,500 if they stay over two nights. Camping in the lovely garden is CFP 1,500 pp. You can cook your own food or order dinner for CFP 2,000. They'll pick you up at the airport for free if you call ahead.

US$100–150

Fare Tehani (Frédéric Girard, tel./fax 68-71-00) is on the beach down the road from the back entrance to Pension Lovina, between Fare and the airport. The three *fare* with kitchen and fridge are CFP 12,000/14,000 double/quad or CFP 70,000 a week. Nearby an American named **Rande Vetterli** (tel. 68-86-27, randesshack@mail.pf) has two self-catering houses right on the beach at CFP 7,200/12,000 for one/two bedrooms (three-night minimum stay). Bicycles and a row boat are loaned free.

US$250 and up

In 1999 the **Te Tiare Beach Resort** (tel. 60-60-50, www.tetiarebeachresort.com), part of the Pearl Resorts chain, opened on the west side of Huahine-nui. The 25 garden and beach bungalows start at CFP 32,000 double, while the 16 overwater bungalows with whirlpool bath are from CFP 70,000, plus 11 percent tax. Half board is CFP 7,500 pp. There's a freshwater swimming pool and overwater restaurant. To enhance the sense of isolation, this resort is accessible only by boat. Airport transfers are CFP 5,000 pp roundtrip.

Other campgrounds and hotels around Huahine are listed separately under Maeva and Huahine-iti below.

FOOD AND ENTERTAINMENT
Food Trailers

Between eight and 10 food trailers or *roulottes*

park at Fare Wharf at different times of day selling spring rolls, pastries, and long French sandwiches. Coffee and bread is CFP 200. At night you can get *steak frites*, chicken and chips, or *poisson cru* for CFP 800 and up. Look for the trailer that parks next to a row of telephone booths as it has excellent fish brochettes for CFP 150.

Restaurants

Opposite the car rental offices on the waterfront is **Restaurant Te Vaipuna** (tel. 68-70-45; Mon.–Sat. 1100–1430/1800–2130) with Chinese and French dishes. A cheaper snack bar is next door.

Pension Guynette (tel. 68-83-75) serves an inexpensive breakfast and lunch on its popular waterfront terrace bar, and this is also a good choice for only coffee and a snack. There's nowhere better to sit and watch the sunset while meeting old and new friends.

Restaurant Te Marara (tel. 68-81-70; closed weekends) at the west end of the waterfront has a nice terrace built over the lagoon, fine for a sunset beer. It's quite elegant, with fish dishes costing CFP 950–1,400, meat dishes CFP 1,100–1,400.

Restaurant Tiare Tipanier (tel. 68-80-52; Mon. 1800–2045, Tues.–Sat. 1130–1345/1800–2045), next to the *mairie* (town hall) at the north entrance to Fare, is a typical French rural restaurant without the tourist touches of some of the others. They serve meat and fish dishes in the CFP 1,300–1,800 range, while the set menu is CFP 2,200 including wine. A large Hinano is CFP 500.

Groceries

Super Fare-Nui (tel. 68-84-68; daily 0530–1900), on the Fare waterfront, sells groceries and cold beer. An alternative place to shop is **Libre Service Taahitini** (tel. 68-89-42; weekdays 0600–1200/1330–1900, Sat. 0600–1200/1600–1900, Sun. 0600–1100/1700–1900), just beyond the gendarmerie south of town. **Magasin Matehau** at Fitii also has groceries.

If you see a cruise ship tied up at Fare one morning, pop into the supermarket quickly to buy your daily bread before the ship's cook comes ashore to snap up the day's entire supply, a classic example of how tourism exploits small island communities. (Bread is heavily subsidized as an essential staple.)

The tap water on Huahine can be clouded after heavy rains.

Entertainment

There's traditional dancing at the **Sofitel Heiva Huahine** (tel. 60-61-60) at Maeva on Monday, Thursday, and Saturday nights, but you'll need motorized transportation to get there.

Les Dauphins (tel. 68-78-54), beside the post office north of town, offers disco dancing to local Tahitian groups on Friday and Saturday nights from 2100 (admission CFP 1,000 including a drink). They're also open for lunch daily except Sunday and Monday.

INFORMATION AND SERVICES

Information

The Comité du Tourisme information office (tel. 68-78-81, www.iaorana-huahine.com; weekdays 0730–1130) is below the internet place next to Photo Jojo on the main street.

Services

ATM machines are outside the Banque de Tahiti (tel. 68-82-46; weekdays 0745–1145/1330–1630), facing the Fare waterfront, and the Banque Socredo (tel. 68-82-71; weekdays 0730–1130/1330–1600), on the first street back from the waterfront.

The post office (Mon.–Thurs. 0700–1500, Fri. 0700–1400), on the road between the airport and Fare, has a convenient Coca-Cola vending machine. The gendarmerie (tel. 68-82-61) is opposite the hospital over the bridge at the south end of town.

An internet café is next to Pension Chez Guynette and upstairs.

Huahine Matic (tel. 23-61-70; Mon.–Fri. 0800–1630, Sat. 0800–1430), next to the Mobile gas station in Fare, is a laundromat charging CFP 700 a kilo to wash and dry. The price goes down as the number of kilos increases.

Public toilets and washbasins are in one of the yellow buildings on the waterfront (if open).

Health

A Gabinet Medical-Dentaire (tel. 68-82-20) is

next to the Mobil service station on the next street back from the wharf. Dr. Hervé Carbonnier and Dr. Pascal Matyka, general practitioners, see patients 0730–1200/1400–1600.

La Pharmacie de Huahine (tel. 68-80-90; weekdays 0730–1130/1400–1700, Sat. 0730–1130), is across the street from the Mormon church north of town on the way to the post office.

TRANSPORTATION
Getting There
Air Tahiti (tel. 68-82-65) has an office at the airport. For information on flights and ships to Huahine from Papeete, Moorea, Raiatea, and Bora Bora see Transportation in this chapter's Exploring the Islands section. Air Tahiti's direct flight between Huahine and Moorea would be great if it didn't cost CFP 13,700 when the flight to/from Papeete is only CFP 10,000.

The fast catamaran *Aremiti III* (tel. 73-52-73) departs Huahine for Raiatea (45 minutes, CFP 1,700) Monday and Friday at 1230. To Papeete (3.5 hours, CFP 4,600) it leaves Huahine the same days at 1500.

The Papeete cargo ships tie up to the wharf in the middle of town. If you arrive in the middle of the night you can sleep in the large open pavilion until dawn. Northbound, the *Vaeanu* calls at Huahine on Tuesday, Thursday, and Saturday at 0130; southbound on Tuesday and Thursday at 1830, and Sunday at 1500. Deck fares from Huahine are CFP 749 to Raiatea or CFP 1,786 to Papeete. The Thursday trip northbound may be carrying fuel, in which case only cabin passengers will be allowed. The *Hawaiki-Nui* also passes twice a week.

Tickets for *Vaeanu* go on sale at their office (tel. 68-73-73) adjoining the yellow warehouse on the wharf four hours before sailing or you can buy one as the ship is loading.

Getting Around
Getting around Huahine is not easy. A few *trucks* operate from outlying villages to Fare and back on weekday mornings—ask the drivers of any you see parked along the waterfront. Otherwise, the locals are fairly good about giving lifts. The only sure way of getting around is to rent something, although the 4WD excursions are a good alternative.

Europcar (tel. 68-82-59, fax 68-80-59, kake@mail.pf) is opposite the post office with branch offices at the airport, Sofitel Heiva, Relais Mahana, and Te Tiare Beach Resort. Their smallest car is CFP 3,600 a day plus CFP 58 a kilometer, or CFP 8,400/15,100 for one/two days with unlimited kilometers. Bicycles/scooters are CFP 2,000/5,900 a day. All prices include tax.

Avis (tel. 68-73-34, fax 68-73-35, www.avis-tahiti.com) is next to Super Fare-Nui on the waterfront, at the Mobil service station a block back, and at the airport. Their cars start at CFP 8,025/14,900 for one/two days including mileage (collision insurance CFP 1,500 a day extra). They also have bicycles/scooters at CFP 1,800/5,900 a day.

Huahine has only two gas stations, both in Fare: Mobil (tel. 68-81-41) is open weekdays 0630–1745, Saturday 0700–1100, Sunday 0630–0930, while Total (tel. 68-71-25) is open weekdays 0630–1700, Saturday 0630–1100, Sunday 0630–0930.

Huahine Lagoon (tel. 68-70-00), next to Restaurant Te Marara at the north end of the Fare waterfront, rents small aluminum boats with outboard motor for CFP 3,000/5,000/8,000 for two/four/eight hours (gas not included). Masks, snorkels, life jackets, anchor, oars, and an ice chest come with the boat. Bicycles are for rent here at CFP 1,500 a day, kayaks CFP 2,000/3,000 a half/full day.

Photos Jojo (tel. 68-89-16), next to Pension Guynette, also has bicycles and represents Europcar.

Local Tours
Island Eco Tours (tel./fax 68-79-67, islandecotours@mail.pf), based at Maeva village, offers four-hour 4WD tours of Huahine twice daily at CFP 5,000. What sets these trips apart from the usual photo-op affairs is the emphasis on archaeology and natural history. They also schedule hiking tours of the Maeva ruins upon request. Owner Paul Atallah is a former student of Prof. Yoshiko H. Sinoto who restored many of the

territory's ancient *marae* and he's the only guide on Huahine who has conducted scientific research on the sites he now shows his clients.

Félix Tours (tel. 68-81-69) does a three-hour morning archaeological tour at CFP 3,500 daily except Sunday.

Huahine Land (tel. 68-89-21, fax 68-86-84) offers 3.5-hour 4WD safaris at CFP 4,000 pp, which is a good alternative to renting a car.

Huahine Explorer (tel. 68-87-33, fax 68-77-57, h-explorer@mail.pf), based at Pension Vaihonu Ocean, offers a four-hour 4WD tour (CFP 4,240 pp) twice a day and a daily combined boat and 4WD tour (CFP 10,450, 7.5 hours). Experienced guides introduce the land and flora.

Sailing Huahine (Claude and Martine Bordier, tel./fax 68-72-49, www.sailing-huahine.com) offers snorkeling cruises on the 15-meter yacht *Eden Martin*. A half/full day costs CFP 6,500/12,500 pp including lunch or refreshments (minimum of four persons). It's also possible to charter the yacht for one-week cruises within the Society islands at CFP 69,000 a day including the skipper and fuel (meals and a CFP 11,000 "boat cleaning" fee are extra). The same in the Tuamotu islands is CFP 86,250 a day.

Huahine Nautique (tel. 68-83-15, www.huahine-nautique.com) offers a circle-island boat tour (CFP 7,500 pp) with a picnic lunch served on a *motu* and shark feeding.

Photos Jojo (tel. 68-89-16) runs a seven-hour boat trip Monday–Saturday at 1000 for CFP 7,500 pp including lunch.

Airport

The airport (HUH) is three km north of Fare. Make arrangements for the regular airport minibus (CFP 600 pp) at Pension Enite. Avis and Europcar have counters at the airport.

MAEVA

At Maeva, six km east of Fare, you encounter that rare combination of an easily accessible archaeological site in a spectacular setting. Here each of the 10 district chiefs of Huahine-nui had his own *marae*, and huge stone walls were erected to defend Maeva against invaders from Bora Bora (and later

France). The plentiful small fish in Lake Fauna Nui supported large chiefly and priestly classes (ancient stone fish traps can still be seen near the bridge at the east end of the village). In the 1970s Prof. Y.H. Sinoto of Hawaii restored many of the structures strewn along the lakeshore and older structures in the nearby hills. The two small stores in the village sell get cold drinks.

There's an **archaeological museum** (no phone, Mon.–Sat. 0900–1600, admission CFP 300) in round-ended Fare Pote'e, a replica of an old communal meeting house on the shores of the lake. **Marae Rauhuru** next to Fare Pote'e bears petroglyphs of turtles. From here, walk back along the road toward Fare about 100 meters, to a **fortification wall** on the left, built in 1846 with stones from the *marae* to defend the area against the French. Follow this inland to an ancient well at the foot of the hill, then turn right and continue around the base of the hill until you find the trail up onto Matairea Hill (opposite a stone platform). Twenty meters beyond a second, older fortification wall along the hillside is the access to **Marae Te Ana** on the right. The terraces of this residential area for chiefly families, excavated in 1986, mount the hillside.

Return to the main trail and continue up to the ruins of **Marae Tefano,** which are engulfed by an immense banyan tree. **Marae Matairea Rahi,** to the left, was the most sacred place on Huahine, dedicated to Tane, the principal god of Huahine associated with warfare and canoe building. The backrests of Huahine's principal chiefs are in the southernmost compound of the *marae,* where the most important religious ceremonies took place. Backtrack a bit and keep straight, then head up the fern-covered hill to the right to **Marae Paepae Ofata,** which gives a magnificent view over the whole northeast coast of Huahine.

Continue southeast on the main trail past several more *marae* and you'll eventually cross another fortification wall and meet a dirt road down to the main highway near **Marae Te Ava.** Throughout this easy two-hour hike, watch for stakes planted with vanilla by the present villagers (please don't touch).

When you get back down to the main road, walk south a bit to see photogenic **Marae Fare**

Miro, then backtrack to the bridge, across which is a **monument** guarded by seven cannon. Beneath it are buried French troops killed in the Battle of Maeva (1846), when the islanders successfully defended their independence against marauding French marines sent to annex the island. The ancient fish traps in the lagoon, recently repaired, are still being used. Fish enter the stone traps with the incoming and outgoing tides.

Seven hundred meters farther along toward the ocean and to the left is two-tiered **Marae Manunu,** the community *marae* of Huahine-nui, dedicated to the gods Oro and Tane. According to a local legend, Princess Hutuhiva arrived at this spot from Raiatea hidden in a drum. In the base of the *marae* is the grave of Raiti, the last great priest of Huahine. When he died in 1915 a huge stone fell from the *marae.* The road passing Marae Manunu runs another six km along the elevated barrier reef north of Lake Fauna Nui directly to Huahine Airport, an alternative route back to Fare. White beaches line this cantaloupe- and watermelon-rich north shore.

Faie

Below the bridge in the center of **Faie,** five km south of Maeva, is a river populated by sacred blue-eyed eels. Legend holds that it was the eels who brought fresh water to the village. You can buy fish to feed them at the red kiosk.

Also at Faie is the **Huahine Pearl Farm** (tel. 78-30-20, www.huahinepearlfarm.com; daily 1000–1600), which offers a free boat tour of their operation in the hope that you'll buy a pearl.

From Faie the very steep Route Traversiere crosses the mountains to Maroe Bay (2.5 km), making a complete circuit of Huahine-nui possible. Two hundred meters up this road from the bridge is **Faie Glace** (tel. 68-87-95; closed weekends), which manufactures ice cream from natural ingredients. If continuing south by bicycle don't begin coasting too fast on the other side as you may not be able to stop.

Accommodations

On the road to the Sofitel Heiva Huahine, a km from the bridge at Maeva, is **Camping Vanaa** (Vanaa Delord, tel. 68-89-51) with 13 small thatched *fare* on the beach at CFP 2,500/5,000 single/double including breakfast. Camping is CFP 1,000 pp. Meals in the restaurant are in the CFP 1,000–1,200 range. Your generous hosts try to make you feel at home, and it's a shady spot, conveniently located for exploring the *marae.* The huts are a bit better than those at Ariiura Camping (see below), but the beach isn't as good as the one at Parea. Bring insect repellent.

In 1989 the **Sofitel Heiva Huahine** (tel. 60-61-60, fax 68-85-25, www.sofitel-heiva.com) opened in a coconut grove on a *motu* two km southeast of Maeva. The 24 rooms in long blocks are CFP 24,500 single or double, the 12 thatched garden bungalows CFP 34,200, and the 18 beach bungalows CFP 51,500, plus 11 percent tax. Six overwater suites are CFP 62,700 single or double (children under 12 free). Don't drink the tap water. The breakfast and dinner plan is CFP 6,400 pp and it's prudent to be punctual at mealtimes as the staff will refuse to serve latecomers. Happy hour at the Manuia Bar is 1700–1800 (drinks two for one). One of the best Polynesian cultural shows you'll ever see usually takes place here on Monday, Thursday, and Saturday nights at 2000, complete with fire dancing, acrobatics, and coconut tree climbing.

Evocative neo-Polynesian paintings by the late artist/singer Bobby Holcomb highlight the decor in the public areas at the Heiva, and ancient *marae* are preserved in the gardens. Though picturesque, the rooms themselves are poorly constructed and rather dark. Unspoiled white beaches stretch all along this section of the lagoon and there's passable snorkeling off the oceanside beach. A swimming pool is available. The hotel tacks a hefty surcharge on any tours or activities arranged through their reception, but the Maeva archaeological area is only a 30-minute walk away. Europcar has a desk at this hotel. Airport transfers are CFP 2,100/3,400 pp roundtrip by bus/limousine.

Pension Te Nahe To'eto'e (tel./fax 68-71-43, www.pension-armelle.com), next to the pearl farm at Faie, has three rooms with shared bath at CFP 3,000/4,200 single/double. Breakfast/dinner can be ordered at CFP 500/1,500, or you can cook your own food. Bicycles and outrigger canoes are loaned free. There's a colorful common sitting room. This place is very popular with young French travelers, so call ahead. Airport transfers are free.

HUAHINE-ITI

Though the concrete "July Bridge" joins the two islands, Huahine-iti is far less accessible than Huahine-nui. It's 24 km from Fare to Parea via Haapu and another 16 km from Parea back to the bridge via Maroe.

Haapu village was originally built entirely over the water, for lack of sufficient shoreline to house it. The only grocery store on Huahine-iti is at Haapu, otherwise three grocery trucks circle the island several times daily; the locals will know when to expect them. There's a wide white beach along **Avea Bay** with good swimming right beside the road as you approach the southern end of the island. Yachts can follow a protected channel inside the barrier reef down the west coast of Huahine to the wonderful (if occasionally rough) anchorage at Avea Bay but shallows at Point Tiva force sailboats to return to Fare.

On another white beach on the east side of Point Tiva, one km south of Parea, is **Marae Anini**, the community *marae* of Huahine-iti. It was built by an ancestor of Hiro sometime between 1325 and 1400 as an offshoot of Marae Taputapuatea on Raiatea. Look for petroglyphs on this two-tiered structure, dedicated to the god of war Oro, where human sacrifices once took place. The *marae* is unmarked and hard to find. Go down the track without a bread delivery box, 900 meters north of Ariiura Camping or 500 meters south of Parea. After 200 meters this track reaches the beach, which you follow 100 meters to the right (south) to the huge stones of the *marae*. Surfing is possible in Araara Pass, beside the *motu* just off Marae Anini. If snorkeling here, beware of an outbound current in the pass.

Accommodations

Pension Hine Iti (Pablo and Repeta Serrano, tel./fax 68-74-58) at Haapu, 15 km south of Fare, has four rooms at CFP 3,000 pp (minimum stay two nights). A common kitchen is available downstairs.

Pension Mauarii (Vetea Breysse, tel./fax 68-86-49, www.mauarii.com), 20 km south of Fare, sits on Avea Bay's lovely shaded white beach. Some of the finest snorkeling in French Polynesia is available along here. Unscreened rooms in the main building are CFP 7,500 single or double, or CFP 9,000 in the mezzanine. The two newer beach rooms are also CFP 9,900 cfp. The two garden bungalows are CFP 11,000 double or CFP 15,000 for four persons. A beach bungalow is also CFP 16,650, all prices plus six percent tax. To reach the "private bathrooms" in most of the units you must go outside to a separate area! No cooking facilities are provided but a breakfast/dinner plan is available at CFP 3,000 pp. Their restaurant is open 1200–1400/1800–2000. If enough guests are present, there's a Friday buffet dinner from 1900–2300 with local music. Polynesian seafood is their specialty. The sports center here offers hobie sailing, windsurfing, boat rentals, and a snorkeling trip.

Relais Mahana (tel. 68-81-54, fax 68-85-08, www.relaismahana.com) is on the same long white beach as Pension Mauarii, a little over two km west of Parea. The 22 units with fridge are CFP 23,373 single or double, CFP 25,643 for a beach bungalow, plus 11 percent tax. For continental breakfast add another CFP 1,120 pp. Bicycles, kayaks, and snorkeling gear are loaned free. Recreational activities and the pool/beach are strictly for hotel guests only but the restaurant/bar is open to all, with excellent meals in the CFP 2,000–3,000 range. The Tahitian dance show here on Saturday night is CFP 4,000 (no additional charge for guests on meal plans). Annie's scuba diving center at the resort is also open to all, with dives from a zodiac at 0830 and 1330. Roundtrip airport transfers are CFP 2,544 pp.

Ariiura Camping (Hubert Bremond, tel./fax 68-85-20), 22 km south of Fare and 1,400 meters from Parea, shares the same lovely white beach with Relais Mahana, 800 meters northwest. There are 12 small open *fare*, each with a double bed and no lock on the door, at CFP 2,900/3,900 single/double. Camping is CFP 1,300 pp a day, and a communal kitchen and pleasant eating area overlook the turquoise lagoon. Bring food as no grocery stores are nearby, although grocery trucks pass daily, once in the morning and twice in the afternoon Monday–Saturday and twice in the morning on Sunday. Also bring insect repellent and coils. An outrigger canoe is available, and you may be able to rent bicycles at Relais Mahana. The snorkeling and surfing here are superb. The owner will pick you up at the airport or wharf at CFP 2,000 pp roundtrip; watch for his pickup truck on the wharf if you arrive by ferry from Papeete.

The **Huahine Beach Resort** (www.polyne sian-resort-hotels.com) at Parea has been redeveloped by the Paladien hotel chain. It's scheduled to reopen in mid-2004 at rates a bit above those of Relais Mahana.

Raiatea

At 171 square km, Raiatea is the second-largest island of French Polynesia. Its main town and port, Uturoa, is the business, educational, and administrative center of the Leeward Islands or Îles Sous-le-Vent (islands under the wind). The balance of Raiatea's population of about 12,000 lives in eight flower-filled villages around the island: Avera, Opoa, Puohine, Fetuna, Vaiaau, Tehurui, Tevaitoa, and Tuu Fenua. The west coast of Raiatea south of Tevaitoa is old Polynesia through and through.

Raiatea is traditionally the ancient Havai'i, the "sacred isle" from which all of eastern Polynesia was colonized. It may at one time have been reached by migrants from the west as the ancient name for Taha'a, Uporu, corresponds to Upolu, just as Havai'i relates to Savai'i, the largest islands of the Samoan chain. A legend tells how Raiatea's first king, Hiro, built a great canoe he used to sail to Rarotonga. Today Raiatea and Taha'a are mostly worth visiting if you want to get off the beaten tourist track. Though public transportation is scarce, the island offers good possibilities for scuba diving, charter yachting, and hiking, and the varied scenery is worth a stop.

The Land
Raiatea, 229 km northwest of Tahiti, shares a protected lagoon with Taha'a three km away. Legends tell how the two islands were cut apart by a mythical eel. About 30 km of steel-blue sea separates Raiatea from both Huahine and Bora Bora. The highest mountain is Toomaru (1,017 meters), and some of the coastlines are rugged and narrow. All of the people live on a coastal plain planted in coconuts, where cattle also graze.

According to Polynesian mythology the god Oro was born from the molten rage of Mt. Temehani (772 meters), the cloud-covered plateau that dominates the northern end of the island. *Tiare apetahi*, a sacred white flower that exists nowhere else on earth and resists transplantation, grows above the 400-meter level on the slopes around the summit. The fragile one-sided blossom represents the five fingers of a beautiful Polynesian girl who fell in love with the handsome son of a high chief, but was unable to marry him due to her lowly birth. The petals pop open forcefully enough at dawn to make a sound and local residents sometimes spend the night on the mountain to be there to hear it. These flowers are protected and there's a minimum CFP 50,000 fine for picking one. Small pink orchids also grow here.

No beaches are found on big, hulking Raiatea itself. Instead, picnickers are taken to picture-postcard *motu* in the lagoon. Surfing is possible at the 10 passes that open onto the Raiatea/Taha'a lagoon, and windsurfers are active. The Leeward Islands are the most popular sailing area in French Polynesia, and most of the charter boats are based at Raiatea. Many pearl farms dot the lagoon around Raiatea and Taha'a.

History
Originally called Havai'i, legend holds that the island was rechristened by Queen Rainuiatea in honor of her parents, Rai, a warrior from Tahiti, and Atea, queen of Opoa. Before European

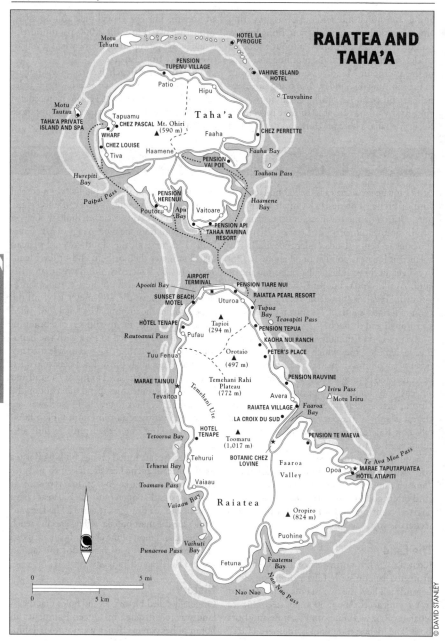

RAIATEA AND TAHA'A

Motu Tehutu

HOTEL LA PYROGUE

PENSION TUPENU VILLAGE

VAHINE ISLAND HOTEL

Patio   Hipu

Tuuvahine

Motu Tautau

TAHA'A PRIVATE ISLAND AND SPA

Tapuamu   **CHEZ PASCAL** Mt. Ohiri
▲ (590 m)

WHARF

CHEZ LOUISE

Tiva   Haamene

Taha'a

Faaha

CHEZ PERRETTE

Faaha Bay

PENSION VAI POE

Toahotu Pass

Hurepiti Bay

PENSION HERENUI

Poutoru   *Apu Bay*   Vaitoare

Paipai Pass

Haamene Bay

PENSION API

TAHAA MARINA RESORT

AIRPORT TERMINAL

Apooiti Bay

PENSION TIARE NUI

SUNSET BEACH MOTEL

Uturoa

RAIATEA PEARL RESORT

Tupua Bay

HÔTEL TENAPE

Tapioi
(294 m)

Teavapiti Pass

PENSION TEPUA

Rautoanui Pass

Pufau

KAOHA NUI RANCH

Tuu Fenua

Orotaio
▲ (497 m)

PETER'S PLACE

Temehani Rahi Plateau
(772 m)

PENSION RAUVINE

MARAE TAINUU

Tevaitoa

Temehani Ute

Avera

Iriru Pass

Motu Iriru

RAIATEA VILLAGE   *Faaroa Bay*

LA CROIX DU SUD

Tetooroa Bay

HOTEL TENAPE

▲ Toomaru
(1,017 m)

PENSION TE MAEVA

Tehurui

BOTANIC CHEZ LOVINE

Tehurui Bay

Vaiaau

Toamaro Pass

Faaroa Valley

Opoa

Te Ava Moa Pass

★ **MARAE TAPUTAPUATEA**

HÔTEL ATIAPITI

Vaiaau Bay

R a i a t e a

Oropiro
▲ (824 m)

Puohine

Vaihuti Bay

Punaeroa Pass

Fetuna

Faatemu Bay

Nao Nao Pass

Nao Nao

0   5 mi

0   5 km

© DAVID STANLEY

encroachment, Raiatea was the religious, cultural, and political center of what is now French Polynesia. Tradition maintains that the great Polynesian voyages to Hawaii and New Zealand departed from these shores.

These islands accepted Christianity soon after the Tahitians were converted. The noted Protestant missionary John Williams arrived in 1818, as recalled by a monument in the form of a black basalt pillar standing in front of the Protestant church just north of Uturoa. From Raiatea, Williams carried the gospel to Rarotonga in 1823 and Samoa in 1830. Later Queen Pomare IV spent the years 1844–1847 in exile on Raiatea. When France annexed the island in 1887, Chief Teraupoo launched a resistance campaign that lasted until 1897, when French troops and warships conquered the island. Teraupoo was captured after six weeks of fighting and deported to New Caledonia where he remained until 1905. The Queen of Raiatea and 136 of her followers were exiled to remote Eiao Island in the Marquesas.

UTUROA

Uturoa (pop. 4,000) is the territory's second city and the first stop on any exploration of the island. It's an easy place to find your way around with a row of Chinese stores along a main drag opening onto the new Gare Maritime. In 2001 the Uturoa waterfront was entirely redeveloped with a new cruise ship terminal, information offices, restaurants, and shops, plus a traditional style handicraft market. All of the ferries plying between Tahiti and Bora Bora call here and there's a frequent shuttle to Taha'a. The island's airport is three km west of town with the main yacht charter base, Marina Apooiti, a km beyond that.

Large cruise ships call here several times a week, flooding the little town with visitors. If you'd like to be able to sit at a waterfront cafe in peace or have the undivided attention of shop clerks, try to find out when love boats such as the *Paul Gauguin, Wind Surf,* and *Tahitian Princess* will be in port and avoid Uturoa those days. Rental cars will be in high demand, so reserve well ahead. If you're a cruise ship passenger yourself, be aware that the various excursions sold on board are highly inflated due to multiple commissions. You'll probably save money by dealing directly with the tour operators inside the Gare Maritime right on the wharf, although you could also miss out. The large groups on rushed tours don't have the same experience as those who take the time to spend a few days on these islands.

Hiking

For a view of four islands, climb **Tapioi Hill** (294 meters), the peak topped by a TV antenna behind Uturoa—one of the easiest and most satisfying climbs in French Polynesia. Take the road beside the gendarmerie. This is private property, and although the owners allow visitors to climb the hill on foot, they've posted a sign just before the cattle grid at the bottom of the hill asking that private cars not be used, and this request should be respected. The fastest time on record for climbing Tapioi is 17 minutes, but it's best to allow two or three hours to hike up and down.

Sports and Recreation

The coral at Raiatea is rather poor, but there's ample marinelife, including gray sharks, moray eels, barracudas, manta rays, and countless tropical fish in places like Tevavapiti Pass. Just off the Raiatea Pearl Resort is the century-old wreck of a 50-meter Dutch coal boat, the *Nordby,* the top of which is 18 meters down.

Hémisphère Sub (Hubert Clot, tel. 66-12-49, fax 66-28-63, VHF channel 68, www.diver aiatea.com), at the Marina Apooiti and Raiatea Hawaiki Nui Hotel, offers scuba diving at CFP 5,900 per dive (10 dives CFP 50,000). They go out daily at 0830 and 1430 and offer free pickups.

Diving is also offered by **Te Mara Nui Plongée** (tel. 72-60-19, tel./fax 66-11-88, www.temara nui.pf) at the marina just north of Uturoa. It's CFP 5,500/13,000 for one/two dives.

Nauti-Sports (tel. 66-35-83), next to the Kuomintang building at the south end of Uturoa, sells quality snorkeling gear.

There's good swimming in a large pool open to the sea at the **Centre Nautique** (*"la piscine"*) on the coast just north of Uturoa, beyond the new yacht harbor. The local Polynesians keep their long racing canoes here.

John's Tours (John and Ann Walker, tel./fax 66-33-44) offers fishing from an open speedboat at CFP 10,000 pp a half day (minimum of two).

The **Kaoha Nui Ranch** (Patrick Marinthe, tel./fax 66-25-46, www.tahitidecouvrir.com) at PK 6, Avera, a few hundred meters north of Pension Manava, charges CFP 4,000 for horseback riding (two hours). A half-day hiking tour to the waterfalls is CFP 2,500. You must reserve 24 hours in advance, and there's a two-person minimum.

Turn to Transportation in the French Polynesia introduction for information on yacht charters.

PRACTICALITIES

Most of the places to stay are on the northeast side of Raiatea and we've arranged them here from north to south in each price category. Accommodations in southern and western Raiatea are covered later under Around Raiatea. The proprietors often pick up guests who call ahead for reservations at the airport or harbor. The transfers are often free, but ask.

US$25–50

You can camp free on **Motu Iriru,** a tiny island on the south side of Iriru Pass off Avera. It's owned by the territory and serves as a public park with picnic tables, barbecue pits, outdoor showers, and flush toilets. A caretaker keeps the island clean. Permission to picnic or camp here is not required but take food and drinking water. To get there contact West Coast Charters (tel. 79-28-78 or 66-45-39) in the Gare Maritime d'Uturoa. Boat transfers to the *motu* are CFP 5,000 for one person, CFP 3,000 pp for two or three, CFP 2,500 pp for four or five, or CFP 2,000 pp for six or more. The owners of most of the pensions listed below will arrange transfers to Iriru at cheaper rates.

The backpacker's number-one choice on Raiatea is **Peter's Place** (Peter Brotherson, tel. 66-20-01) at Hamoa, six km south of Uturoa and just beyond Pension Manava. The eight neat double rooms in a long block are CFP 1,400 pp, or you can pitch a tent in the large grassy area facing the rooms at CFP 900 pp. A large open pavilion is used for communal cooking but there are no grocery stores nearby, so bring food. The pavilion doubles as a traveler's library with good lighting and it's very pleasant to sit there on a rainy night as torrents of water beat on the tin roof. Bicycles are for rent. Peter is the progeny of a Danish sea captain named Brotherson who left hundreds of descendants on Raiatea. He or his son Frame sometimes take guests on a hike up the valley to a picturesque waterfall with swimming in the river, fish feeding, and a tour of a vanilla plantation for a negotiable group price. Ask about guided hikes to the Temehani Plateau, taking about three hours up and two hours down, and boat trips. Peter might even loan you a dugout canoe free to paddle yourself around the lagoon. Transfers are CFP 600 pp roundtrip.

Pension Tepua (tel. 66-33-00, fax 66-32-00, www.raiatea.com/tepua) is by the lagoon just beyond Magasin Andre Chinese store, 2.5 km south of Uturoa. Three bungalows with kitchen and TV are CFP 9,000 in the garden or CFP 13,000 facing the lagoon. There's also a dormitory with 12 beds (CFP 2,000) and three rooms with shared bath at CFP 4,500–7,000 double. A supplement of up to CFP 1,000 is charged if you stay only one night. Common cooking facilities and a swimming pool are provided. Bicycles and a washing machine are for rent, and there's sometimes hot water. Boat trips are offered. The lagoon off Pension Tepua is good for windsurfing and there's surfing off Taoru Island in nearby Teavapiti Pass. Airport transfers are CFP 1,000 pp roundtrip.

Three of the best value places to stay on Raiatea are close together six km south of Uturoa, a CFP 1,500 taxi ride from Uturoa. Aside from Peter's Place previously mentioned, **Pension Kaoha Nui Ranch** (Patrick Marinthe, tel./fax 66-25-46, www.tahitidecouvrir.com) has four rooms with shared bath at CFP 3,600 single or double (or CFP 4,400 for one night). The two bungalows with private bath are CFP 6,500/7,500 double/triple. Communal cooking facilities are provided. It's the obvious selection if you have an interest in riding. Airport transfers are free.

Pension Manava (tel. 66-28-26, fax 66-16-66, www.manavapension.com), right next door to Kaoha Nui Ranch at PK 6, Avera, is run by Andrew and Roselyne Brotherson. This warm, sympathetic couple has four Polynesian-style bungalows with cooking facilities, private bath, and fan at CFP 6,000 or CFP 7,100 single or double, depending on the unit (plus CFP 1,000 per additional person or for one-night stays). Two rooms in a separate building are CFP 4,700 single or double with shared kitchen and bath. A half-day boat trip to southern Raiatea is CFP 4,000 pp, and they also do a full-day boat trip right around Taha'a at CFP 6,000 including lunch (six-person minimum)—these trips are also open to nonguests. *Motu* transfers are CFP 1,500 pp (four-person minimum). Bicycles are for rent. Ask Roselyne to show you how she paints Tahitian pareos. Call for a free airport and harbor pick-up.

US$50–100

The friendly **Sunset Beach Motel Apooiti** (Moana Boubée, tel. 66-33-47, fax 66-33-08, www.raiatea.com/sunsetbeach) is in a coconut grove five km west of Uturoa. It's on the point across the bay from Marina Apooiti, about 2.5 km west of the airport. The 21 comfortable, well-spaced bungalows with cooking facilities and private bath (hot water) are CFP 8,000/ 9,000/10,000/11,000 single/double/triple/ quad—good value for families (children under 13 are CFP 550 each, under three free). Camping is CFP 1,200 pp here, and there's a large communal kitchen. Discounts of 10 percent a fortnight and 20 percent a month are available, but there's a CFP 1,000 surcharge if you stay only one night. Bicycles are for rent and hitching into Uturoa is easy. It's one of the nicest places to stay in the islands and the managers speak English. Call for free airport transfers.

Pension Tiare Nui (Patrick Bardou, tel. 66-34-06, fax 66-16-06, europcar-loc@mail.pf) has four small bungalows with private bath for rent behind the Europcar office between the airport and Uturoa. It's CFP 5,300/5,830/6,360 single/double/triple, or pay CFP 10,930 double for a bungalow and an unlimited mileage car. It's a deal worth checking if you were planning to rent a car anyway, but cooking facilities are not provided. In Uturoa, Techni Isles Sarl (tel. 66-37-81;

weekdays 0730–1200/1330–1700, Sat. 0730–1200), between Champion Supermarket and Snack Moemoea, books rooms here with cars. At the airport, ask Europcar.

Bed and Breakfast Bellevue (Max Boucher, tel./fax 66-15-15, raiateabellevue@mail.pf) has five attractive rooms facing the swimming pool at CFP 7,000/7,900 single/double including breakfast. Each includes private bath, fridge, and TV, but no cooking facilities. It's on the north side of Uturoa, 700 meters up the hill from the Lycée des Îles Sous-le-Vent. Airport transfers are CFP 1,400 pp.

The **Hôtel Hinano** (Augustin Moulon, tel. 66-13-13, fax 66-14-14), conveniently located on the main street in the center of Uturoa, has 10 basic rooms at CFP 6,350/6,850 single/double (CFP 1,000 extra for one of the four air-conditioned rooms). Cooking facilities are not available.

Pension Rauvine (Josiah Bordes, tel./fax 66-25-50, pensionrauvine@mail.pf), at PK 8, Avera, has eight bungalows with cooking facilities at CFP 5,000 single or double, plus CFP 1,000 per extra person. Ask for Francis, who speaks good English and runs 4WD excursions at CFP 4,000. He'll take you over to Motu Iriru for picnicking free upon request. Airport transfers are free upon request.

Pension Yolande (Yolande Roopinia, tel./fax 66-35-28) is in an attractive location facing the lagoon at PK 10, Avera. The four rooms are CFP 5,000/6,000 single/double (private bath). Cooking facilities are provided, but you may be asked to take half pension (CFP 3,500 pp). You'll like the family atmosphere. Airport transfers are CFP 1,500 pp roundtrip.

The 12-unit **Raiatea Village** (Philippe Roopinia, tel. 66-31-62, fax 66-10-65, raiatea.village @mail.pf) is at the mouth of Faaroa Bay (PK 10). A garden bungalow with kitchenette and terrace is CFP 7,215/8,325/9,435/10,545 single/double/triple/quad. Airport transfers are CFP 1,100 pp extra.

On the hillside a little beyond is **Pension La Croix du Sud** (Annette and Eric Germa, tel./fax 66-27-55). The three rooms with bath are CFP 7,300/8,000 single/double including breakfast.

Cooking facilities are not provided but meals can be ordered. Facilities include a swimming pool and bicycles. Airport transfers are CFP 1,500 pp.

US$150–250

The 28-unit **Raiatea Hawaiki Nui Hotel** (tel. 66-20-23, fax 66-20-20, www.pearlresorts.com), 1.5 km south of Uturoa, is Raiatea's only luxury hotel. This is the former Raiatea Bali Hai, destroyed by a kitchen fire in 1992 and completely rebuilt in 1994 as the Hôtel Hawaiki Nui. In 1998 it was purchased by Pearl Resorts and it's currently at the bottom end of the chain in both services and price. The layout is attractive with a swimming pool overlooking the lagoon. There's no beach but you can snorkel off the end of their pier. The rates are CFP 19,000 double for one of the eight garden rooms, CFP 22,000 for the eight thatched garden bungalows, or CFP 42,000 for the 12 overwater bungalows, plus 11 percent tax. There's a Polynesian dance show Friday and Saturday nights at 2000. A Europcar desk is here. Airport transfers are CFP 1,500 pp each way.

Food

Unpretentious **Restaurant Michele** (tel. 66-14-66; weekdays 0500–1530/1800–2100, Sat. 0500–1430), below Hôtel Hinano (rear side of the building), is a good place for breakfast with coffee, bread, and butter at CFP 310. Chinese meals start around CFP 1,000, otherwise take one of the French dishes costing CFP 1,300–1,800 listed on the menu. Their *poisson cru* is CFP 800, a small glass of beer CFP 400.

Brasserie Maraamu (tel. 66-46-64; weekdays 0600–2100, Sat. 1000–1400), is in the corner of the new Gare Maritime facing town. The lunch menu tilts toward Chinese food with main plates CFP 950-1,550. There's also excellent *poisson cru* (CFP 600/950 small/large). A large Hinano is CFP 550.

Brasserie Le Quai des Pécheurs (tel. 66-43-19; daily 0930–2100), in the side of the Gare Maritime facing the small boat harbor, offers a nice view from its terrace and excellent food. The menu includes *poisson cru* (CFP 950), sashimi (CFP 1,150), fish (CFP 1,500–2,400),

meat dishes (CFP 1,600–2,200), bowls of ice cream (CFP 600–800), and draft beer (CFP 400). Ice cream cones are sold from a window facing the harbor. Le Quai des Pécheurs presents Polynesian dancing Saturday at 2030.

The **Sea Horse Restaurant** (tel. 66-16-34; Mon.–Sat. 1000–1330/1800–2130), on the side of the Gare Maritime facing the cruise ship wharf, serves Chinese dishes CFP 900–1,800 and seafood at CFP 1,500–1,800.

A more upscale choice would be the **Restaurant Jade Garden** (tel. 66-34-40; Wed.–Sat. 1100–1300/1830–2100) on the main street, offering some of the tastiest Chinese dishes this side of Papeete.

Snack Moemoea (tel. 66-39-84; weekdays 0600–1700, Sat. 0600–1400), on the small harbor, serves hamburgers (CFP 500) plus a range of French and Chinese dishes on their terrace. Despite the name it's rather upscale with meat dishes at CFP 1,300–1,700, fish at CFP 1,600, and Chinese food at CFP 1,200–1,500.

The largest supermarket is **Champion** (tel. 66-45-45; Mon.–Sat. 0730–1830), facing the small boat harbor. Whole barbecued chickens are CFP 790. A bit north is the **Marché Municipal de Uturoa** (Mon. 0630–1600, Tues.–Fri. 0530–1600, Sat. 0600–1130, Sun. 0430–0730).

Most of the stores in Uturoa close for lunch 1200–1330 and it's a ghost town after 1030 on Sunday.

Entertainment

Discothèque Le Zénith (tel. 66-27-49), above Super Marché Leogite opposite Banque Socredo, opens Friday and Saturday at 2200. Entry is free for men until 2230 (for women until 2300), then they begin collecting a CFP 1,000 cover charge.

Information and Services

In the Gare Maritime opposite the cruise ship wharf is a tourist office (tel. 60-07-77, fax 60-07-76; daily 0800–1600).

None of Uturoa's banks open on Saturday but ATMs accessible 24 hours are outside the Banque Socredo and Banque de Tahiti.

The large modern post office (tel. 66-35-50; Mon.–Thurs. 0730–1500, Fri. 0700–1400, Sat.

0800–1000) is opposite the new hospital just north of town, with the gendarmerie (tel. 66-31-07) about 50 meters beyond on the left.

For internet access, there's Phenix (tel. 66-24-79) out toward the airport.

There are free public toilets *(sanitaires publics)* in the Gare Maritime facing the main wharf, not far from the tourist office. It's hard to find, so ask.

A km west of the Sunset Beach Motel is Raiatea Carenage Services (tel. 66-22-96, raiatea carenage@mail.pf), a repair facility often used by cruising yachts. The only easily accessible slip facilities in French Polynesia are here (maximum 22 tons).

Health

Uturoa's public hospital (tel. 60-08-00) is on the north side of town.

Dr. Patrick Lazarini (tel. 66-23-01), general practitioner, has an office above La Palme d'Or in the center of Uturoa. It's open weekdays 0700–1200/1330–1730, Saturday 0800–1200.

Several private doctors have offices above the pharmacy opposite the Catholic church in central Uturoa. Among them are Dr. Alain Repiton-Préneuf and Dr. Bruno Bataillon, general practitioners.

The Pharmacy (tel. 66-34-44), opposite the Catholic church, is open weekdays 0730–1200/1330–1730, Saturday 0730–1200, Sunday 0930–1030.

TRANSPORTATION

Getting There and Away

The **Air Tahiti** office (tel. 60-04-44) is at the airport. Flights from Raiatea to Maupiti (CFP 6,600) operate three times a week. For information on flights and ships from Papeete, Huahine, and Bora Bora see Transportation in this chapter's Exploring the Islands section.

You can catch the *Vaeanu* and *Hawaiki-Nui* to Bora Bora, Huahine, and Papeete twice weekly. Consult the schedule in the introduction to French Polynesia. Tickets for the *Vaeanu* (tel. 66-22-22) are sold when the ship arrives. The *Hawaiki-Nui* office (tel. 66-42-10; weekdays 0800–1100) is at the south end of the main wharf.

The fast catamaran *Aremiti III* (tel. 77-90-99) uses the same office as the *Hawaiki-Nui* but tickets are only sold when the vessel arrives. It leaves for Huahine (CFP 1,700) and Papeete (CFP 5,200) Monday and Friday at 1400.

A government supply barge, the *Meherio III,* shuttles twice a month between Raiatea and Maupiti, usually departing Raiatea on Thursday. The exact time varies, so check with the Capitainerie Port d'Uturoa (tel. 66-31-52) on the interisland wharf.

The yellow and blue *Maupiti Express* (tel. 66-37-81, tel./fax 67-66-69), a fast ferry with 62 airline type seats, charges CFP 2,500/3,500 one-way/roundtrip between Raiatea and Bora Bora, departing Uturoa for Bora Bora Monday, Wednesday, and Friday afternoons. It's not possible to go directly from Raiatea to Maupiti on this vessel—you must overnight on Bora Bora—although you can buy a through ticket for CFP 3,500.

The fast ferries *(navettes)* of **S.A.R.L. Enota** (tel./fax 65-61-33) shuttle between Raiatea and Taha'a at CFP 850 pp each way (bicycles CFP 500). The fleet consists of two 57-seat ferries painted yellow and blue. The *Uporu* serves Taha'a's west coast (Taha'a Marina, Poutoru, Patii, Tiva, Tapuamu) while the *Iripau* serves the east coast (Haamene, Faaha Quai Amaru). Both leave Uturoa at 1045 and 1645 on weekdays, but one of the *Uporu's* trips terminates at the Taha'a Marina. On Monday, Wednesday, and Friday one of the *Iripau* trips has a bus connection between Faaha Quai Amaru and Patio. On Saturday only the west coast service operates—once in the morning. There's no schedule at all on Sunday and holidays.

The 66-passenger ferry *Tamarii Taha'a* (tel. 65-65-29) also operates between Raiatea and Taha'a twice on weekdays and once on Saturday morning. Verify the schedules a day before.

Getting Around

Getting around Raiatea by *le truck* isn't easy. You should be able to use them to get into town in the morning and the people where you're staying will know at what time you have to be waiting. In Uturoa the *trucks* usually park in front of Restaurant Michele and the drivers themselves are the only reliable source of departure information. In theory they leave Uturoa for Opoa at 1015 and 1515 and for Fetuna at 0930 and 1530 on weekdays only.

Raiatea Location Europcar (tel. 66-34-06 or 78-33-53, fax 66-16-06, europcar-loc@mail.pf), between the airport and Uturoa, is the main car rental operator on Raiatea. Their cars begin around CFP 9,000 a day, including mileage and insurance (minimum age 18). Ask about the package that gives you a bungalow behind their main office and a small car at CFP 10,930. Bicycles are CFP 1,700/2,200/3,300 for four/eight/24 hours (expensive). Apart from cars and bikes, Raiatea Location rents a four-meter boat with a six-horsepower motor at CFP 6,600/8,800 a four/eight hours. Scooter rentals are generally unavailable.

Avis (tel. 66-20-80, www.avis-tahiti.com) is at the airport only. Their cars start at CFP 9,000/16,371/23,754 for one/two/three days all inclusive.

Garage Motu Tapu (tel. 66-33-09), in a poorly marked building a few hundred meters east of the airport, also rents cars.

Local Tours

Many of the hotels and pensions run circle-island bus tours (www.raiateatourisme.com) and boat trips to a *motu* or Taha'a. **Raiatea Discovery** (Gérard and Maria, tel./fax 66-24-16, raidiscovery@mail.pf) offers 4WD excursions into the interior at CFP 4,400 (four-person minimum). The same as part of a full-day package including a boat trip, snorkeling, and picnic on a *motu* is CFP 9,000 (six-person minimum).

West Coast Charters (Anne-Marie and Tony Tucker, tel./fax 66-45-39), in the Gare Maritime, offers a full day boat tour around Taha'a or Raiatea (CFP 6,500 pp including lunch, minimum of six) and a half-day Faaroa River tour (CFP 4,500 pp, minimum of four).

Almost Paradise Tours (tel. 66-23-64), run by Faaroa Bay resident Bill Kolans, offers a very good three-hour minibus tour in American English at US$50 pp (minimum of four).

Airport

The airport (RFP) is three km northwest of Uturoa. A taxi from the Uturoa market taxi stand (tel. 66-20-60) to the airport is CFP 1,000 (double tariff late at night). Most of the hotels pick up clients at the airport free of charge upon request. Avis and Europcar both have car rental desks inside the terminal.

The Air Tahiti reservations office is in a separate building adjacent to the main terminal. The Tourist Board information kiosk at the airport is open at flight times only. The airport restaurant offers a good *plat du jour* at lunchtime.

AROUND RAIATEA

It will take the better part of a day to ride a bicycle the 150 km around Raiatea; by car you can take anywhere from a couple of hours to a leisurely day.

The road down the east coast circles fjordlike **Faaroa Bay,** associated with the legends of Polynesian migration. Stardust Marine has a yacht charter base on the north side of the bay, and from the anchorage there's a fine view of Toomaru, highest peak in the Leeward Islands. Boat trips are offered up the Apoomau River which drains the Faaroa Valley. It's navigable for about a kilometer, and if you're on a yacht you could explore it with your dingy. Yellow hibiscus flourishes along the river's banks.

At the head of Faaroa Bay is **Botanic Chez Lovine** (tel. 66-14-45; admission CFP 200), PK 14.5, which displays a wide variety of local plant species in a lush garden.

Instead of crossing the island, keep left and follow the coast around to a point of land just beyond Opoa, 32 km from Uturoa. Here stands **Marae Taputapuatea,** one of the largest and best preserved temples in Polynesia, its mighty *ahu* measuring 43 meters long, 7.3 meters wide, and between two and three meters high. Before it is a rectangular courtyard paved with black volcanic rocks. A small platform in the middle of the *ahu* once bore the image of Oro, god of fertility and war (now represented by a reproduction); backrests still mark the seats of high chiefs on the courtyard. Marae Taputapuatea is directly opposite Te Ava Moa Pass, and fires on the *marae* may once have been beacons to ancient navigators.

© M.E. DE VOS

Marae Taputapuatea on Raiatea is among the most sacred sites in Polynesia.

Several of the temple platforms have been restored. **Hauvivi** was the welcoming *marae* where guests would have been received as they disembarked from their canoes. They would then proceed to Marae Taputapuatea, the main temple, where rituals were performed. Meals were served on **Hiti Tai,** a temple platform on the north side of the complex. **Papa Ofeoro** was the place of sacrifice (some 5,000 skulls were discovered during excavations at the site). **Opu Teina** near the beach was the temple platform where visitors would say their farewells. Departing chiefs would often take a stone from this *marae* to be planted in new *marae* elsewhere, which would also receive the name Marae Taputapuatea.

In 1995 a fleet of traditional Polynesian voyaging canoes, including three from Hawaii and two each from Cook Islands and Tahiti, plus an Easter Island raft, gathered at Taputapuatea to lift a 650-year-old curse and rededicate the *marae.* The seven canoes then left for the Marquesas, navigating by the stars and swells. Some carried on to Hawaii and the west coast of the U.S. in an amazing demonstration of the current revival of this aspect of traditional culture. In April 2000, a Tattoo Festival took place at Marae Taputapuatea. During important events, fire-walking is practiced at a site across the road from the main temples.

The only places to buy food in the southern part of Raiatea are the two Chinese grocery stores at **Fetuna** and another at **Vaiaau,** on the west side of Raiatea. Vaiaau Bay marks the end of the protected inner channel from Uturoa around Raiatea clockwise and yachts must exit the lagoon through Toamaro Pass in order to continue northward. At Rautoanui Pass sailboats can come back in behind the barrier reef to continue the circumnavigation, with the possibility of a sidetrip south to Tevaitoa.

Behind Tevaitoa church is **Marae Tainuu,** dedicated to the ancient god Taaroa. Petroglyphs on a broken stone by the road at the entrance to the church show a turtle and some other indistinguishable figure. At Tevaitoa Chief Teraupo and his people fought their last battles against the French invaders in early 1897.

The territory's largest yacht charter base is the **Marina Apooiti,** which opened in 1982 one km west of the airport. Aside from The Moorings and Tahiti Yacht Charter, there's a large restaurant/bar here and a dive shop. For information on chartering, see Yacht Charters in this chapter's Exploring the Islands section.

Accommodations Around Raiatea

Pension Te Maeva (tel. 66-37-28, www.temaeva .com), at PK 23.5 Est toward Opoa, has two bungalows on the hillside at CFP 6,800/7,500 single/double. Camping is CFP 2,000/2,500. Both rates include breakfast and dinner can be ordered at CFP 3,000 pp. There's a swimming pool and free bicycles. Airport transfers are free if you stay two nights.

The **Hôtel Atiapiti** (Marie-Claude Rajaud, tel./fax 66-16-65, atiapiti@mail.pf), on the beach just south of Marae Taputapuatea at PK 31 Est, Opoa, has six self-catering beach bungalows and one garden bungalow from CFP 10,600 double or CFP 12,500 for up to five (children under 12

free). Half board is CFP 4,400 pp, or if you'd rather order a la carte, the restaurant has meat dishes (CFP 1,000–1,500) and fish (CFP 1,600–2,200). The managers organize excursions to a *motu* and around the island, and there's great snorkeling off their wharf. The view of Huahine from here is excellent. Bicycles are CFP 1,000 a day. The hotel's biggest drawback (or advantage!) is its isolation, but they'll pick you up at the port or airport if you call ahead (CFP 3,000 pp roundtrip). It's good for a couple of days of relaxation.

In 1999 the **Hôtel Tenape** (Marie-Hélène Viot, tel. 60-01-00, fax 60-01-01, hoteltenape@ yahoo.fr) opened at PK 10, Pufau, on the west coast. The 17 air-conditioned rooms in this long two-story building start at CFP 20,700 single or double (transfers CFP 1,500 pp). The rectangular swimming pool substitutes for a beach.

Taha'a

Raiatea's 90-square-km lagoonmate Taha'a is shaped like a hibiscus flower with four long bays cutting into its rugged south side. Mount Ohiri (590 meters), highest point on the island, got its name from Hiro, god of thieves, who was born here. Taha'a is known as the "vanilla island" for its plantations that produce 70 percent of the territory's "black gold." The Taha'a Festival in late October includes stone fishing, with a line of people in canoes herding the fish into a cove by beating stones on the surface of the lagoon. In November the Hawaiki Nui Outrigger Canoe Race passes Taha'a on its way from Huahine to Bora Bora.

It's a quiet island, with little traffic and few tourists. Most families use speedboats to commute to their gardens on the reef islets or to fishing spots, or to zip over to Raiatea on shopping trips, so they don't really need cars. Beaches are scarce on the main island but the string of *motu* off the northeast side of Taha'a has fine white-sand beaches. The pension owners and tour operators arrange picnics on a few of these, and pearl farms have been established on some. This is the only Society island you can sail a yacht or cruise ship right around inside the barrier reef,

and the many anchorages and central location between Raiatea, Huahine, and Bora Bora make Taha'a a favorite of both cruisers and charterers.

There aren't many specific attractions on Taha'a, and a dearth of inexpensive places to stay and lack of public transportation has kept this island off the beaten track. The easy way to visit Taha'a is still an all-day outrigger canoe tour from Raiatea. This could change, but meanwhile the isolation has made the 4,500 Taha'a islanders rather wary of outsiders.

Orientation

The administrative center is at Patio (or Iripau) on the north coast, where the post office, *mairie,* and gendarmerie (tel. 65-64-07) share one compound. A second post office is at Haamene where four roads meet. The ship from Papeete ties up to a wharf at Tapuamu, and there's a large covered area at the terminal where you could spread a sleeping bag in a pinch. The Banque Socredo branch is also at Tapuamu, while the Banque de Tahiti (tel. 65-63-14) is at Haamene.

The 67-km coral road around the main part of the island passes six of the eight villages; the other two are south of Haamene. A scenic road goes over the 141-meter Col Taira between Haamene and Tiva. There are ferries from Raiatea to Tapuamu and Haamene but no regular public transportation.

Sights

The mountain pass between Haamene and Tiva offers excellent views of Hurepiti and Haamene Bays, two of the four deep fjords cutting into the southern side of the island. You could also follow the rough track from Haamene up to the Col Vaitoetoe for an even better view. This track continues north, coming out near the hospital in Patio.

Rarahu, the girl immortalized in Pierre Loti's 1880 novel *The Marriage of Loti*, is buried near Vaitoare village at the south end of Taha'a, east of the Taha'a Marina Resort.

Activities

Shark Dive (Bertil Venzo, tel. 65-65-55, fax 65-65-60, www.dive.pf) at Hurepiti Bay visits over 20 diving spots around Raiatea and Taha'a islands for CFP 6,000 including gear.

ACCOMMODATIONS

US$25–50

The most convenient and least expensive place is **Chez Pascal** (Pascal Tamaehu, tel./fax 65-60-42). From the Tapuamu ferry wharf you'll see a small bridge at the head of the bay. Turn left as you leave the dock and head for this. Chez Pascal is the first house north of the bridge on the inland side. The rate for the four bungalows and two rooms is CFP 4,500 pp for bed, breakfast, and dinner, or CFP 3,000 pp with breakfast only. Boat trips to a *motu* and the loan of the family bicycle are possible.

Chez Louise (tel. 65-66-88) at Tiva has dormitory space for 12 persons at CFP 5,000 pp including all meals. Bicycles are for rent. Yachties often stop to have a meal here.

Pension Tupenu Village (Henri and Karine Manea, tel. 65-62-01) in Patio offers three rooms downstairs and two upstairs at CFP 5,000 single or double (two-night minimum stay). The bathrooms and kitchen are shared.

US$50–100

Pension Herenui (tel./fax 65-64-17) at Poutoru has three *fare* at CFP 8,100 single or double (children under 12 free), plus CFP 3,500 pp for half board. There's a circular swimming pool. It's easily accessible weekdays by ferry to Poutoru.

Pension Api (tel./fax 65-69-88, www.pensionapi.com) just east of the Marina Iti has two thatched bungalows in a garden setting at CFP 8,000 single or double, plus CFP 5,000 pp for all meals.

Hôtel L'Hibiscus (tel. 65-61-06, fax 65-65-65, www.tahaa-tahiti.com) is on the northeast side of Haamene Bay. The seven bungalows are CFP 9,434 single or double, plus tax and CFP 4,134/6,254 pp for half/full board. Cooking facilities and common drinking water are not supplied (bring bottled water). Verify all prices carefully upon arrival as misunderstandings have occurred in past.

Nearby on Haamene Bay and better value is **Pension Vai Poe** (Patricia and Daniel Amaru, tel./fax 65-60-83, http://vaipoe.webnui.com) with five self-catering bungalows at CFP 8,000 single or double. Call for boat transfers from Uturoa (CFP 3,000 pp roundtrip). Otherwise the ferry from Uturoa will drop you at Faaha Quai Amaru near here.

US$100–150

Chez Perrette (Perrette Tehuitua, tel. 65-65-78) is on a reasonable beach at Faaopore, 10 km east of Haamene. It's CFP 17,000 double with all meals in the one self-catering bungalow.

US$150–250

Pension Au Phil de Temps (tel./fax 65-64-19, moutte.junior@mail.pf) at Tapuamu has two *fare* at CFP 12,000 pp plus tax (three-night minimum stay). All meals, boat trips, and 4WD land tours are included.

The **Taha'a Marina Resort** (tel. 65-61-01, fax 65-63-87, VHF channel 68), also known as the Hôtel Marina Iti, sits at the isolated south tip of Taha'a on Taha'a's only sandy beach. From here there are marvelous views of the mountains of Taha'a and across to Raiatea. The five beach bungalows are CFP 22,000 single or double, or pay CFP 15,000 for the one garden bungalow. Third persons pay CFP 2,000. Cooking facilities are not provided and meals are CFP 5,200 pp extra for breakfast and dinner. Use of bicycles, canoe, and snorkeling gear is included, and scuba diving is available. As you'll have guessed, the Taha'a Marina caters to an upmarket crowd on yacht charters from Raiatea, and numerous cruising yachts anchor in the calm waters offshore. The ferry *Uporu* from Raiatea stops here.

In 2004 **Hôtel La Pirogue** (hotellapirogue@ yahoo.fr) opened on Motu Porou off Hipu village in northwestern Taha'a. The eight bungalows are priced CFP 22,000 double in the garden or CFP 28,000 on the beach (meals and tax extra). Airport transfers are CFP 6,000 pp.

US$250 and up

In 2002 the luxurious **Tahaa Private Island and Spa** (tel. 50-84-53, www.letahaa.com), formerly known as the Taha'a Pearl Beach Resort, opened on Motu Tautau opposite the shipping wharf at Tapuamu. The 12 spacious beach bungalows with private swimming pools start at CFP 80,000 double, while the 48 overwater bungalows are from CFP 85,000, plus 11 percent tax. Full board is another CFP 10,500 pp (breakfast delivered to your deck by canoe upon request). The horizon view swimming pool has a swim up bar. Verify the price of boat transfers from Raiatea beforehand is it can range from CFP 4,000–10,000 pp.

Hôtel Vahine Island (tel. 65-67-38, fax 65-67-70, VHF channel 68, www.vahine-island.com), on Motu Tuuvahine off the northeast side of the island, has six seafront bungalows at CFP 35,000 single or double, plus three overwater units at CFP 52,000, plus 11 percent tax. For half/full board add CFP 7,500/10,500 pp, for airport transfers CFP 6,000 pp. Outrigger canoes, windsurfing, snorkeling, and fishing gear are free, and moorings are provided for yachts.

OTHER PRACTICALITIES

Food

Village stores are at Tapuamu, Tiva, Haamene, and Patio. Grocery trucks circle the island daily except Sunday and any resident will know when to watch for them.

Health

There's a medical center (tel. 65-63-31) at Patio. Dr. Laurent Jereczek (tel. 65-60-60) is at Haamene.

Getting There

There's no airport on Taha'a. Large ships and ferries call at Tapuamu Wharf on the west side of Taha'a just behind the Total service station. There's a telephone booth on the wharf that you could use to call your hotel to have them pick you up.

The *Vaeanu* departs Taha'a for Raiatea, Huahine, and Papeete Tuesday and Thursday at 1500, and Sunday at 1130; it goes to Bora Bora Sunday at 0900. The *Hawaiki-Nui* visits Taha'a southbound only. The *Maupiti Express* leaves Taha'a for Bora Bora Monday, Wednesday, and Friday at 1615 (CFP 2,500).

The **Le Navette des Îles** leaves Taha'a for Raiatea at 0515 and 1210 on weekdays and only in the morning on Saturday (CFP 850 pp each way, bicycles CFP 500). Make sure to verify the routes and times, as they vary. For more information see Raiatea, above.

Getting Around

Trucks on Taha'a are for transporting schoolchildren only, so you may have to hitch to get around. It's not that hard to hitch a ride down the west coast from Patio to Haamene, but there's almost no traffic along the east coast.

Rental cars are available from **Europcar** (tel. 65-67-00, fax 65-68-08) at the Total station next to Tapuamu Wharf, **Taha'a Transport Services** (tel. 65-67-10) at the Taha'a Marina Resort, and **Avis** (tel. 65-66-77, www.avis-tahiti.com) at Haamene Wharf. The Taha'a Marina also rents bicycles. Avis charges CFP 7,900 a day with 100 km (extra kms CFP 40 each); Europcar is CFP 8,200 a day with unlimited kilometers and insurance. It's smart to book ahead if you want to be sure of a car.

Local Tours

Several companies offer full-day outrigger canoe trips right around Taha'a at CFP 10,500 pp, such as **Taha'a Pearl Tour** (Bruno Fabre, tel. 66-10-90, www.tahaa.net). Lunch, snorkeling, a visit to a pearl farm and vanilla plantation, and transfers on Raiatea are included. Bruno takes his guests to the best snorkeling spots around Taha'a, not just the convenient but less spectacular "coral gardens" off eastern Taha'a which the quickie tours from Raiatea prefer to visit. He doesn't cater to large groups off cruise ships.

Land tours by 4WD are popular on Taha'a. **Vai Poe Tours** (tel./fax 65-60-83), based at Pension Vai Poe on Haamene Bay, does a half-day trip including a drive across the island at CFP 5,000, or CFP 7,000 for a full day including a canoe ride and picnic lunch. **Edwin Mama** (tel. 65-62-18) at Haamene offers about the same. **Vanilla Tours** (Alain and Cristina Plantier, tel. 65-62-46, vanilla.tours@mail.pf), near Sophie Boutique at Hurepiti Bay, is a half-day, ethno-botanical tour by 4WD which operates whenever four persons have booked (CFP 5,000 pp without lunch). Alain is very knowledgeable about the island's botany and speaks English.

Bora Bora

Bora Bora, 260 km northwest of Papeete, is everyone's idea of a South Pacific island. Dramatic basalt peaks soar 700 meters above a gorgeous, multicolored lagoon. Slopes and valleys blossom with hibiscus. Some of the most perfect beaches you'll ever see are here, replete with topless sunbathers. Not only are the beaches good but there's plenty to see and do. The local population of 7,000 resides in three villages, Anau, Faanui, and Vaitape. Many are skilled dancers. To see them practicing in the evening, follow the beat of village drums back to their source.

The Land

Seven-million-year-old Bora Bora (29 square km) is made up of a 10-km-long main island, a few smaller high islands in the lagoon, and a long ring of *motu* on the barrier reef. Pofai Bay marks the center of the island's collapsed crater with Toopua and Toopuaiti as its eroded west wall. Mount Pahia's gray basalt mass rises 649 meters behind Vaitape, and above it soar the sheer cliffs of Otemanu's mighty volcanic plug (727 meters). The wide-angle scenery of the main island is complemented by the surrounding coral reef and numerous *motu,* one of which bears the airport. Motu Tapu of the travel brochures was featured in F.W. Murnau's classic 1931 silent movie *Tabu* about two young lovers who escape to this tiny island. Te Ava Nui Pass is the only entry through the barrier reef.

History

The letter *b* doesn't exist in Tahitian, so Bora Bora is actually Pora Pora, meaning "first born" since this was the first island created after Raiatea. The island's traditional name, Vava'u, suggests Tongan voyagers may have reached here centuries ago. It's believed Bora Bora has been inhabited since the year 900 and 42 *marae* ruins can still be found around the island. The Bora Borans of yesteryear were indomitable warriors who often raided Maupiti, Taha'a, and Raiatea.

"Discovered" by Roggeveen in 1722, Bora Bora was visited by Capt. James Cook in 1769 and 1777. The first European to live on the island was James O'Connor, a survivor of the British whaler *Matilda* wrecked at Moruroa atoll in 1793. O'Connor made his way to Tahiti where he married into the Pomare family, and eventually ended up living in a little grass shack on "Matilda Point," later corrupted to Matira Point. In 1895 the island was annexed by France.

In February 1942 the Americans hastily set up a refueling and regrouping base, code-named "Bobcat," on the island to serve shipping between the U.S. west coast or Panama Canal and Australia/New Zealand. You can still see remains from this time, including eight huge naval guns placed here to defend the island against a surprise Japanese attack that never materialized. The big lagoon with only one pass offered secure anchorage for as many as 100 U.S. Navy transports at a time. The Americans built Farepiti Wharf and a cable was

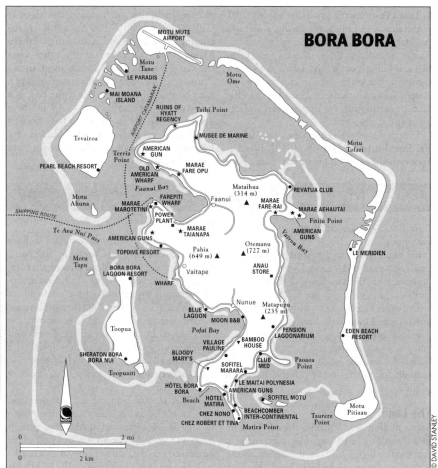

BORA BORA

MOTU MUTE AIRPORT

Motu Tane
LE PARADIS

Motu Ome

MAI MOANA ISLAND

RUINS OF HYATT REGENCY

Taihi Point

MUSEE DE MARINE

Tevairoa

AMERICAN GUN

Tereia Point

PEARL BEACH RESORT

OLD AMERICAN WHARF

MARAE FARE OPU

Faanui Bay

Motu Tofari

Motu Ahuna

MARAE MAROTETINI

FAREPITI WHARF

Faanui

Mataihua (314 m) ▲

MARAE FARE-RAI

REVATUA CLUB

MARAE AEHAUTAI

SHIPPING ROUTE

POWER PLANT

Fitiiu Point

Te Ava Nui Pass

AMERICAN GUNS

MARAE TAIANAPA

AMERICAN GUNS

Vaitou Bay

TOPDIVE RESORT

Pahia (649 m) ▲

Otemanu (727 m) ▲

LE MERIDIEN

Motu Tapu

BORA BORA LAGOON RESORT

Vaitape

ANAU STORE

WHARF

Nunue

Matapupu (235 m) ▲

Toopua

BLUE LAGOON

MOON B&B

PENSION LAGOONARIUM

Pofai Bay

VILLAGE PAULINE

BAMBOO HOUSE

EDEN BEACH RESORT

SHERATON BORA BORA NUI

BLOODY MARY'S

SOFITEL MARARA

CLUB MED

Paoaoa Point

Toopuaiti

HÔTEL BORA BORA

LE MAITAI POLYNESIA

AMERICAN GUNS

SOFITEL MOTU

Beach

HÔTEL MATIRA

CHEZ NONO

BEACHCOMBER INTER-CONTINENTAL

Taurere Point

Motu Pitiaau

CHEZ ROBERT ET TINA

Matira Point

© DAVID STANLEY

0   2 mi

0   2 km

stretched across Faanui Bay. Ships would hock onto the cable instead of dropping anchor. A road was built around the island and by April 1943 the present airfield on Motu Mute had been constructed. The 4,400 American army troops also left behind 130 half-caste babies, 40 percent of whom died of starvation when the base closed in June 1946 and the abandoned infants were forced to switch from their accustomed American baby formulas to island food. The survivors are now approaching ripe middle age. Novelist James A. Michener, a young naval officer at the time, left perhaps the most enduring legacy by modeling his Bali Hai on this "enchanted island," Bora Bora.

Orientation

You can arrive at Motu Mute airport and be carried to Vaitape Wharf by catamaran, or disembark from a ship at Farepiti Wharf, three km north of Vaitape. Most of the stores, banks, and offices are near Vaitape Wharf (and free public toilets are provided in the souvenir shop on the wharf itself). The finest beaches are at Matira Point at the island's southern tip.

SIGHTS

Vaitape

Behind the Banque de Tahiti at Vaitape Wharf is the **monument to Alain Gerbault,** who sailed his yacht, the *Firecrest,* solo around the world from 1923 to 1929—the first Frenchman to do so. Gerbault's first visit to Bora Bora was in 1926. He returned to Polynesia in 1933 and stayed until 1940. A supporter of the Pétian regime in France, he left Bora Bora when the colony declared its support for General de Gaulle and died at Timor a year later while trying to return to Vichy France.

To get an idea of how the Bora Borans live, take a stroll through Vaitape village: go up the road that begins just south of the Protestant church.

Around the Island

The largely paved and level 32-km road around the island makes it easy to see Bora Bora by rented bicycle. At the head of **Pofai Bay** notice the odd assortment of looted war wreckage across the road from Alain Linda Galerie d'Art. Surrounded by a barbed wire fence are a seven-inch American gun dragged here from Tereia Point in 1982 and two huge anchors. The locations of seven other MK II naval guns that have thus far escaped desecration are given below.

Stop at **Bloody Mary's Restaurant** to scan the goofy displays outside their gate, but more importantly to get the classic view of the island's soaring peaks across Pofai Bay as it appears in countless brochures. For an even better view go inland on the unmarked road that begins at a double electricity pole 100 meters north of Bloody Mary's. This leads to a jeep route with two concrete tracks up the 139-meter-high hill to a **radio tower,** a 10-minute hike. From the tower you get a superb view of the south end of the island.

The finest beach on the island stretches east from Hôtel Bora Bora to Matira Point. Some of the best **snorkeling,** with a varied multitude of colorful tropical fish, is off the small point at Hôtel Bora Bora. Enter from east of the hotel grounds (such as via the Bora Diving Center or the beach beyond) and let the current pull you toward the hotel jetty, as the hotel staff don't appreciate strangers who stroll through their lobby to get to the beach. From the way they approach you, the small fish are quite obviously accustomed to being fed here. Stay on the east side of the point, away from the overwater bungalows. For a more natural scene you could also snorkel due south to the northern edge of the barrier reef. Just beware of getting run over by a boat.

Two **naval guns** sit on the ridge above Hôtel Matira, but unfortunately residential construction has blocked the access route and it's no longer possible to visit.

Bora Bora's most popular public beach is **Matira Beach Park** in front of the huge open thatched pavilion directly across the street from the Beachcomber Inter-Continental on Matira Point. Don't leave valuables unattended here. At low tide you can wade from the end of **Matira Point** right out to the reef. These same shallows prevent yachts from sailing around the island inside the barrier reef. Northwest of the point is **Motu Piti uu Uta** with the Sofitel Motu Resort and more great snorkeling (if you swim over, don't enter the Sofitel Motu grounds as you won't be welcome).

Proceed north to the **Sofitel Marara,** a good

STONE FISHING

This traditional method of fishing is now practiced only on very special occasions in the Leeward Islands. Coconut fronds are tied end to end until a line a half km long is ready. Several dozen outrigger canoes form a semicircle. Advancing slowly together, men in the canoes beat the water with stones tied to ropes. The frightened fish are thus driven toward a beach. When the water is shallow enough, the men leap from their canoes, push the leaf line before them, yell, and beat the water with their hands. In this way the fish are literally forced ashore into an open bamboo fence, where they are caught. A famous scene in the Marlon Brando version of *Mutiny on the Bounty* depicts stone fishing at Bora Bora.

© M.E. DE VOS

cruise ship with Mount Pahia in background

place for a leisurely beer. Visitors are unwelcome at Club Med, which the road climbs over a hill to avoid. The two general stores at **Anau** can supply a cold drink or a snack.

On the north side of Vairou Bay the road begins to ascend a ridge. Halfway up the slope, look down to the right and by the shore you'll see the *ahu* of **Marae Aehautai,** the most intact of the three *marae* in this area. From the *marae* there's a stupendous view of Otemanu and you should be able to pick out Te Ana Opea cave far up on the side of the mountain. To visit the two American **seven-inch guns** on Fitiiu Point, follow the rough jeep track to the right at the top of the ridge a few hundred meters east (on foot) to a huge black rock from which you can see the guns. The steep unpaved road on the other side of this ridge can be dangerous on a bicycle, so slow down or get off and walk. There's a municipal dump in this area and you might catch a stench of burning garbage.

Just before Taihi Point at the north end of the main island is a **Musée de la Marine** (tel. 67-75-24; donations accepted) on the right, which is usually closed. Just beyond Taihi Point you'll notice a concrete trestle running right up the side of

the hill from the ruins of a group of platforms meant to be the overwater bungalows. This is all that remains an undercapitalized **Hyatt Regency hotel** project that went broke in the early 1980s. Actors Jack Nicholson and Marlon Brando are reputed to be among the owners of the overwater condominiums nearby.

One American **naval gun** remains on the hillside above the rectangular concrete water tank with a transformer pole alongside at Tereia Point. The housing of a second gun, vandalized in 1982, is nearby. The remains of several American concrete wharves can be seen along the north shore of **Faanui Bay.** Most of the American wartime occupation force was billeted around here and a few Quonset huts linger in the bush. Just beyond the small boat harbor (a former American submarine base) is **Marae Fare Opu,** notable for the petroglyphs of turtles carved into the stones of the *ahu.* Turtles, a favorite food of the gods, were often offered to them on the *marae.* (Mindless guides sometimes highlight the turtles in chalk for the benefit of tourist cameras.)

Between Faanui and Farepiti Wharf, just east of the Brasserie de Tahiti depot and the electricity-generating plant, is **Marae Taianapa;** its long *ahu,* restored in 1963, is visible on the hillside from the road. The most important *marae* on Bora Bora was **Marae Marotetini,** on the point near Farepiti Wharf—west of the wharf and accessible along the shore at low tide. The great stone *ahu,* 25 meters long and up to 1.5 meters high, was restored by Professor Sinoto in 1968 and can be seen from approaching ships.

The last two **American guns** are a 10-minute scramble up the ridge from the main road between Farepiti Wharf and Vaitape. Go straight up the concrete road a bit before you reach Otemanu Tours (where you see several *trucks* parked). At the end of the ridge there's a good view of Te Ava Nui Pass, which the guns were meant to defend, and Maupiti is farther out on the horizon. This is private property so ask permission to proceed of anyone you meet.

SPORTS AND RECREATION
Scuba Diving
The **Bora Diving Center** (Anne and Michel Condesse, tel. 67-71-84, fax 67-74-83, VHF channel 8, www.boradive.com), just east of Hôtel Bora Bora, offers scuba diving daily at 0845, 1345, and 1845. Prices are CFP 6,100/11,800 for one/two tanks, CFP 29,000 for a five-dive package, or CFP 7,100 for night dives. Snorkelers are welcome to tag along for CFP 1,800 when things are slow. Both PADI and CMAS open-water certification courses are offered at CFP 41,000 (three days). Gear is included. Ten different sites are visited (those around Toopua Island are recommended for snorkelers). They also have an activity called "Aqua Safari" (CFP 6,600) during which you walk along the lagoon floor wearing a diving helmet connected to their boat. Bookings can be made through their dive shop on Matira Beach (if you book through your hotel reception a 10 percent surcharge may be added). Hotel pickups are available to divers who have booked ahead.

Scuba diving can also be arranged through **Nemo World Diving** (tel./fax 67-77-85, www.nemodivebora.com) by the road between the Sofitel Marara and Bora Bora Beach Resort and at the Hôtel Méridien Bora Bora. They charge CFP 13,000 for two dives, gear included. Introductory dives (CFP 7,000) are offered in the afternoon and hotel pick-ups are available. Nemo's specialty is diving with huge manta rays off Fitiiu Point (worth doing to see the mantas, sharks, and turtles, though you won't see much else in that area as the coral is mostly dead and the waters fished out). Since it's a long way around to the single pass, most scuba diving at Bora Bora is within the lagoon and visibility is limited from January to April.

Bora Bora's newest scuba operator is **TOPdive** (tel. 60-50-50, fax 60-50-51, www.topdive.com), just north of Vaitape. They charge CFP 6,500/ 13,000/58,500 for one/two/10 tanks with free pickups. Their equipment is in good shape. They're the best positioned operation for dives outside the reef where the visibility is better and the schools of fish (especially sharks) are larger.

Mountain Climbing
If you're experienced and determined, it's possible to climb **Mount Pahia** in about four hours of rough going. Take the road inland just south of the Protestant church in Vaitape and go up the depression past a series of mango trees, veering slightly left. Circle the cliffs near the top on the left side, and come up the back of Snoopy's head and along his toes. (These directions will take on meaning when you study Pahia from the end of Vaitape's Wharf.) The trail is unmaintained and a local guide would be a big help. Avoid rainy weather, when the way will be muddy and slippery. Otemanu Tours (tel. 67-65-97) offers an all-day Mount Pahia hiking tour in the dry season (CFP 15,000 for one or two people, bring your own lunch).

Despite what some tourist publications claim, slab-sided **Otemanu,** the high rectangular peak next to pointed Pahia, has *never* been climbed. It's possible to climb up to the shoulders of the mountain, but the sheer cliffs of the main peak are inaccessible because clamps pull right out of the vertical, crumbly cliff face. Helicopters can land on the summit, but that doesn't count. Otemanu's name means "It's a bird."

Other Activities

Sportfishing from a luxury catamaran is a Bora Bora eccentricity invented by ex-Californian Richard Postma of **Taravana Charters** (tel./fax 67-77-79, www.taravana.com). His 15-meter *Taravana* based at Hôtel Bora Bora is fitted with a flybridge and two fighting chairs, and the sails and multihull stability make for a smooth, quiet ride. Any doubts you may have about fishing from a sailboat can be laid aside as this prototype vessel ranks among the best. A half-day fishing charter is CFP 95,400 for up to four people, while up to eight can go on a full day charter (CFP 127,200).

Parasailing at Hôtel Bora Bora begins at CFP 17,490 pp.

Horseback riding is available at **Ranch Reva Reva** (Olivier Ringeard, tel. 67-63-63) on Motu Pitiaau, the long coral island east of Matira Point. Organized riding is CFP 6,000 for 1.5 hours. Book through **Miki Miki Jet Ski** (tel. 67-76-44) at Matira, which arranges free transfers to the *motu*.

ACCOMMODATIONS

Be prepared for some of the highest room rates in the South Pacific: In all categories you'll pay about 50 percent more than you would for the same thing on Moorea. However, most guests at the top hotels arrive on prepaid packages and pay considerably less than the prices quoted herein. Tour operators engaged in packaging Bora Bora are listed in this book's main introduction. The places charging under US$100 seldom discount their rooms.

That said, there's a good choice of places to stay and only at holiday times—especially during the July festivities—does everything fill up. When things are slow, the budget hotel owners meet the airport ferry and interisland ships in search of guests. If someone from the hotel of your choice isn't on the dock when you arrive, get on the blue *truck* marked Vaitape-Anau and ask to be taken wherever you want to go. This should cost CFP 500 pp from Farepiti Wharf or CFP 350 pp from Vaitape Wharf, plus CFP 100 for luggage. However, if you're staying at a luxury resort you could be charged as much as CFP 4,200 pp return for airport transfers (ask).

Despite a desalination plant which opened in 2001, Bora Bora still suffers from water shortages, so use it sparingly, and protect yourself against theft by carefully locking your room when you go out. A daily CFP 50–150 pp municipal services tax is collected at all accommodations.

US$25–50

At the entrance to Pofai Bay three km south of Vaitape is **Blue Lagoon** (tel./fax 67-65-64) with five clean rooms with shared bath at CFP 2,200 pp (singles may be required to share). For another CFP 2,200 pp you get breakfast and dinner. Communal cooking facilities are not provided and there's considerable traffic noise and no beach. Their restaurant is open daily 1000–0200 with pizza on offer. Internet access is CFP 400 per 15 minutes and users are expected to order a drink. Transfers from the harbor are free (ask if you'll be required to buy a meal plan before agreeing to go and disregard suggestions that you might be able to camp here—you won't).

US$50–100

Moon B&B (Muna Teriitehau, tel./fax 67-74-36, moonbungalow@netcourrier.com), next to Galerie d'Art Alain Linda on Pofai Bay, has two well-constructed bungalows with fan and fridge at CFP 7,500/8,500 single/double plus six percent VAT (minimum stay two nights). Camping beside the lagoon is CFP 2,000 pp and you can use the kitchen in the house. This friendly place opened in 2001.

Pension Chez Rosina (tel./fax 67-70-91, ade saintpierre@mail.pf), next to Perlissima Boutique a few hundred meters north of Village Pauline on Pofai Bay, has seven rooms at CFP 5,500/7,000 single/double with private bath and shared cooking facilities. Two larger bungalows are CFP 13,000 for up to four persons. Add six percent VAT and CFP 50 pp local tax per day. Transfers are included. Rosina is friendly and her place is less crowded and less touristy than Pauline's, but there's no beach.

In 1997 **Village Pauline** (Pauline Youssef, tel. 67-72-16, fax 67-78-14, vpauline@mail.pf) moved from the white beach where the Hôtel Le Maitai Polynesia now stands to a new inland location on Pofai Bay. Despite the downgrade, prices went up and you'll now pay CFP 2,500 pp to camp (own tent), CFP 3,070 pp in the eight-bed dormitory, or CFP 7,000 single or double for one of the seven small bungalows with shared bath. The four larger thatched bungalows are CFP 12,000–15,000 triple. Add six percent VAT and a CFP 50 pp tax per day (children under 10 are free). Communal cooking facilities are provided for campers. Sacha's Snack (Mon.–Sat. 1000–1300/1700–2000) at Village Pauline serves meals in the CFP 1,200–1,400 range. Bicycles and kayaks (www.boraborakayak.com) are for rent. Heavy traffic on the adjacent road makes it a rather noisy place to camp.

On the Matira Point peninsula are two excellent alternatives to the upmarket hotels. **Pension Chez Nono** (Noël Leverd, tel. 67-71-38, fax 67-74-27) faces a great beach across from the Beachcomber Inter-Continental. They have two large bungalows (CFP 12,290), two smaller bungalows with private bath (CFP 9,110), and a six-room thatched guesthouse with shared kitchen at CFP 5,880/6,990 single/double per room, plus six percent tax. The CFP 1,000 breakfast isn't worth it. Ventilation spaces between the ceilings and walls mean you hear *everything* in the other rooms, but the atmosphere is amiable and all guests soon become good friends (though a few of the staff seem rather jaded). Tahitians from other islands and local French often stay here. Their garden is a pleasant place to sit, but the bungalows occasionally experience noise from beach parties. The solar hot water heating only works when the sun is shining. Bring mosquito coils and toilet paper. Their boat tour around the island 0930–1600 includes shark feeding (CFP 8,000 with lunch). Kayaks rent for CFP 2,500/3,500 a half/full day.

Also good is **Chez Robert et Tina** (tel. 67-63-55, fax 67-72-92), down the road from Chez Nono at the tip of Matira Point, with 15 rooms in three European-style houses at CFP 5,400/6,600 single/double. Shared cooking facilities are provided. Robert offers lagoon trips at CFP 7,000 pp. You'll enjoy it more if you know a little French. The location between two perfect snorkeling locales can't be beat.

In Anau village to the north of Club Med is **Pension Chez Teipo** (tel. 67-78-17, fax 67-73-24, teipobora@mail.pf), also known as Pension Anau, with six neat little thatched bungalows by the lagoon at CFP 7,000/9,500/11,000 single/double/triple (children under 12 free). Cooking facilities are provided. Transfers and bicycles are free.

The **Pension Lagoonarium** (tel. 67-71-34, fax 67-60-29, lagonarium@mail.pf), at Anau a km north of Club Med, has four rooms with shared bath at CFP 6,400 double, three bungalows with bath at CFP 8,600, and dorm beds at CFP 2,500 pp. Camping is CFP 1,600 pp. Communal cooking facilities are provided. It's right on the lagoon but there's no beach here.

US$100–150

Bungalows Temanuata (tel. 67-75-61, fax 67-62-48), just north of the Beachcomber Inter-Continental at Matira, has two thatched beachfront bungalows at CFP 16,000 double, seven garden bungalows at CFP 12,820, and two garden bungalows with kitchen at CFP 16,000. In 2004 four luxury beach bungalows opened at CFP 19,000. Extra persons are CFP 2,170, and tax is included.

The **Bora Bora Beach Lodge** (tel. 67-78-21, fax 67-77-57, www.boraborabeachlodge.pf), formerly known at the Bora Bora Motel, between Hôtel Le Maitai Polynesia and the Sofitel Marara at Matira, shares a white beach with the Sofitel. Their four studios with bedroom, living room, dining room, kitchen, and fridge are CFP 14,040 double, while the three slightly larger apartments are CFP 18,375 double, extra persons CFP 3,820 each. The one beachfront unit is CFP 20,440 (children under 13 years CFP 1,600, under age six free). You'll probably have an ocean view from your deck in this long thatched complex built in 1991. The cooking facilities make the lodge ideal for families and there's a supermarket across the street. Unfortunately mosquitoes can be a nuisance. Transfers from Vaitape are CFP 1,700 pp roundtrip.

US$150–250

Hôtel Matira (tel. 67-70-51, fax 67-77-02, www.hotelmatira.com), toward Matira Point, has four thatched bungalows with fridge near the restaurant at CFP 38,435 single or double. The 16 deluxe bungalows in the annex, 500 meters down the road toward the Beachcomber Inter-Continental, are CFP 21,285 to CFP 35,850, plus 11 percent tax. Prices have more than doubled here in recent years. The Matira's beachfront restaurant (0700–1000/1100–1400/1800–2100 daily) is reasonable with fish dishes around CFP 1,550, chicken at CFP 1,350, and Chinese dishes at CFP 1,050–1,550. Breakfast is rather expensive at CFP 1,335/1,890 continental/American, so visit one of the nearby cafes. The beach is excellent. Airport transfers are CFP 1,300 pp return.

The **Bora Bora Beach Resort** (tel. 60-59-50, fax 60-59-51, www.polynesian-resort-hotels.com), between the Bora Bora Beach Lodge and the Sofitel Marara, reopened in 2003 after being completely redeveloped by the Paladien hotel chain. This three-star hotel has 80 air-conditioned rooms in 10 thatched buildings at CFP 23,000 single or double, plus tax and CFP 4,500 pp for breakfast and dinner (if required). Scuba diving is with Nemo World.

US$250 and up

The **TOPdive Resort** (tel. 60-50-60, www.topdive.com), between Vaitape and Farepiti Wharf, has six tightly-packed thatched garden bungalows at CFP 31,910 double and three overwater bungalows (which aren't really overwater) at CFP 49,200, plus 11 percent tax. They cater mostly to scuba divers but it's an excellent alternative to the luxury resorts. There's a small swimming pool and an outstanding restaurant.

Hôtel Bora Bora (tel. 60-44-60, fax 60-44-66, www.amanresorts.com), which opened on a spectacular point in 1961, was the island's first large hotel and it's one of the most exclusive millionaire's playgrounds in the South Pacific. Actors Pierce Brosnan and Eddie Murphy are regulars. Garden rooms in this 55-unit resort begin at CFP 67,500 single or double, plus 11 percent tax. Rather than pay CFP 90,000 for a rather poorly situated overwater bungalow, take one of the eight pool *fare,* each with its own private swimming pool, for CFP 85,000. Beware of noisy rooms near the road. Breakfast and dinner are CFP 10,000 pp extra. The hotel restaurant's cuisine is exceptional though the table service is sullen. The beach is superb. Amanresorts manages the property.

The **Hôtel Beachcomber Inter-Continental** (tel. 60-49-00, fax 60-49-99, www.borabora.interconti.com), on a superb white-sand beach at Matira Point, opened in 1987. One of the 14 beachfront bungalows here will set you back CFP 71,150 single or double plus 11 percent tax; the 50 overwater bungalows are CFP 89,350 (children under 15 free). It's CFP 8,586 pp extra for breakfast and dinner (you can ask to have breakfast delivered to your room by outrigger canoe!). There's a swimming pool. The plumbing in their overwater bungalows could use an upgrade for such an expensive place. Inter-Continental has plans to build a 100-bungalow resort on one of the *motu.*

Hôtel Le Maitai Polynesia (tel. 60-30-00, fax 67-66-03, www.lemaitai.com) at Matira is the only major resort owned by a local Bora Boran, Pauline Youssef. Until 1997 there was a campground here, but this real estate was far too valuable for backpackers and in 1998 a deluxe, two-story hotel was built. The 28 air-conditioned rooms in the main building start at CFP 25,500 single or double, CFP 31,300 triple, plus 11 percent tax. The six beach bungalows go for CFP 41,000, while the 11 overwater bungalows are CFP 53,000. Ask for a room with a good view. A hundred meters north and behind Tiare Supermarket is **Vairupe Villas,** which is under the same management. The 10 spacious thatched villas with kitchen and TV are CFP 38,040. Although the cooking facilities are useful, the villas are not on the beach and seem rather exorbitant.

The **Hôtel Sofitel Marara** (tel. 60-55-00, fax 67-74-03), near the north end of the Matira hotel strip, was built in 1978 to house the crew filming Dino de Laurentiis's *Hurricane* with Mia Farrow and Trevor Howard. The film flopped but the hotel has been going strong ever since. The name Marara means "Flying Fish." The 32 garden bungalows are CFP 38,500 single or double, the 11 beach bungalows CFP 51,000, and the 21 larger overwater units are CFP 58,900, plus 11 percent tax. The "overwater" units are much closer to shore than those at the other resorts and you even get traffic noise. There's a swimming pool and watersports center. Guests staying at the Sofitel Marara are *not allowed* to take the free shuttle across to Sofitel Motu, but the water is shallow and you could just snorkel across. This entire property is becoming a little worn for the price but renovations are said to be in the pipeline. The food in the restaurant isn't highly rated and the service can be slow. Luckily there are lots of other restaurants nearby.

The 150-bungalow **Club Méditerranée** (tel. 60-46-04, fax 60-46-10) on the southeast side of Bora Bora is the largest resort on the island. Built in 1993 to replace an earlier Club Med north of Vaitape, the circuminsular road had to be rerouted around this US$30-million enclave just north of the Sofitel Marara. The guys at the gate are security freaks and it's not possible stroll in and rent a room at Club Med as only prepackaged guests are allowed inside. Book ahead at the Club Med office in Papeete's Vaima Center (tel. 42-96-99) or at any travel agency (two-night minimum stay). Lavish buffet meals and a wide range of nonmotorized nautical activities are included in the basic price. The gaudy orange and yellow bungalows go for CFP 15,820–26,155 pp plus 11 percent tax in the garden or CFP 18,985–31,385 pp on the beach, double occupancy (singles can be matched with other same-sex singles). The prices vary according to season with Christmas to New Years the most expensive period by far. Some of the "oceanview" units are far from the water. Club Med is good value for Bora Bora when you consider that all meals are included. The beach isn't that great for swimming but there are two or three boats a day to shuttle you out to a *motu* with fabulous snorkeling. Plenty of regimented "animation" is laid on by the staff, and the eclectic clientele can be fun, if you're sociable. The Club's disco is the top wildest nightspot on the island. Club Med's G.O.s *(gentils organisateurs)* tend to resist the unusual or nonroutine (such as requesting a specific room or not sitting where you're told in the restaurant), so try to "go with the flow" (i.e., conform). Unfortunately, bicycles are not available.

Offshore Resorts

Pension Le Paradis (Tipea et Tehapai Pahuiri, tel./fax 67-75-53, www.xroy.com/islv/paradis .htm), on Motu Paahi near the airport, offers seven thatched bungalows at CFP 15,000 double, plus CFP 1,000/2,500 pp for breakfast/dinner. Several of the units have only shared bath with cold water and these are half price. Airport transfers are CFP 1,000 pp roundtrip and trips to the main island can be arranged. It's your chance to experience life on a *motu* without blowing away your budget.

Mai Moana Island (Stan Wisnieswski, tel. 67-62-45, fax 67-62-39, www.mai-moana-island.com), on a tiny *motu* between the Pearl Beach Resort and the airport, has three thatched bungalows, at CFP 34,000/38,800 double with half/full board, plus six percent tax. It's possible to rent the entire island for two people at CFP 52,400 with half board—less than you'd pay for a single room at most of the other island resorts! The owner is a retired Polish filmmaker, and show business personalities often choose his place for a secluded getaway. Roundtrip transfers from the airport/Vaitape are CFP 2,400/4,800 for one or two persons. Island tours and scuba diving can be arranged.

The new **Bora Bora Pearl Beach Resort** (tel. 60-52-00, fax 60-52-22, www.pearlresorts.com), on Teveiroa Island between the airport and Vaitape, has 20 garden suites with private pool at CFP 48,000 double, 10 beach bungalows with whirlpool bath at CFP 62,000, and 50 overwater bungalows starting at CFP 65,000, plus 11 percent tax. Half/full pension is an extra CFP 7,800/10,800 pp, and the meals have received good reviews. There's a swimming pool, a Blue Nui Dive Center (Gilles Petre, tel./fax 67-79-07, www.bluenui.com), and a full range of activities, including a complimentary shuttle to Farepiti wharf (airport transfers CFP 5,000 pp).

The **Bora Bora Lagoon Resort** (tel. 60-40-00, fax 60-40-01, bblr@mail.pf), part of the Orient Express chain, is perched on Toopua Island opposite Vaitape. Opened in 1993, this place offers wonderful views of Mount Pahia, and the large swimming pool compensates for the average beach and shallow lagoon. The seven garden bungalows are CFP 59,375 double, the 21 beach bungalows CFP 70,625, the 41 overwater bungalows CFP 95,625, and the nine pontoon bungalows CFP 106,875, plus 11 percent tax. Rates include a buffet breakfast. Other meals are extra and it's forbidden to bring your own food and drink into the resort. Free activities include tennis, sailing, windsurfing, canoeing, the fitness center, and the launch to Vaitape or the airport. Check-in time is 1500.

In 2002, the 120-unit **Sheraton Bora Bora Nui Resort & Spa** (tel. 60-33-00, fax 60-33-01, www.boraboranui.com) opened on the west side of Motu Toopua. This is the most expensive place to stay in French Polynesia with 16 lagoon view suites beginning at CFP 72,000 double and increasing to a whopping CFP 260,000 for the two "overwater royal horizon suite bungalows." Add CFP 8,500/12,000 pp for half/full board. Of course, few pay these outlandish prices as the vast majority of guests at all of the luxury resorts arrive on all-inclusive packages.

Under separate management from the Sofitel Marara and much more luxurious is the **Sofitel Motu** (tel. 60-56-00, fax 60-56-66), which opened on Motu Piti uu Uta off the east side of the Matira peninsula in 1999. The 30 island/overwater bungalows are CFP 84,750/108,200 double, plus 11 percent tax. There's an artificial waterfall off the lobby and the service is excellent. The views of Bora Bora are unforgettable. Romantic couples are the target market here, and unlike almost every other resort in French Polynesia, there are no special deals for families with small children.

In 2001 the **Bora Bora Eden Beach Resort** (tel. 60-57-60, fax 67-69-76) was built by the lagoon on 10-km-long Motu Piti Aau south of the Hôtel Méridien Bora Bora. The eight garden bungalows are CFP 27,900 double and the seven beach bungalows CFP 37,900, plus 11 percent tax. This is much cheaper than Bora Bora's other offshore properties. Add CFP 6,100/8,000 pp for half/full board and CFP 4,200 pp for boat transfers. The Eden Beach prides itself in being the only "green" hotel in French Polynesia with solar energy, water conservation, and recycling.

In 1998 **Hôtel Le Méridien Bora Bora** (tel. 60-51-51, fax 60-51-52, www.lemeridien-bora bora.com) was built on Motu Piti Aau opposite Fitiiu Point with white sand everywhere you look. The 82 thatched overwater bungalows with plate glass floors start at CFP 76,500 single or double, while the 18 beach bungalows are CFP 65,400, plus 11 percent tax (children under 12 free). Add CFP 7,800/11,500 pp for two/three meals. All the usual sporting activities are offered, including scuba diving. Sea turtles are held in a lagoon enclosure for your snorkeling pleasure. A day tour to Tupai Atoll is CFP 15,000 pp. The resort launch goes to Anau rather than Vaitape, a disadvantage if you want to go shopping.

FOOD

Vaitape

Snack Bora Bora Burger (no phone; Mon.–Sat. 0800–1700), on the main road just south of the Banque de Polynésie near the wharf, serves hamburgers (CFP 660), French fries (CFP 300), baguette sandwiches (CFP 220), small/large coffees (CFP 200/300), and small beers (CFP 370).

Snack Chez Richard (tel. 67-69-09; Tues.–Sat. 1100–1300/1800–2030), near Farepiti Rent a Car opposite the Centre Artisanal, sells Chinese takeaway meals in the CFP 1,000–1,500 range. At night only they have waffles at CFP 250-500.

L'Appetisserie (tel. 67-78-88; Mon.–Sat. 0600–1800), at back of the Centre Commercial La Pahia opposite the Protestant church just north of the wharf, offers things like crepes (CFP 420–680), hot sandwiches (CFP 420–850), ice cream (CFP 150–700), cakes (CFP 300–450), coffee, and beer. At lunchtime the *plat du jour* will be around CFP 1,400. Internet access is available weekdays 0900–1300/1600–1800, Saturday 0900–1300, at CFP 40 a minute.

Snack Michel (tel. 67-71-43; weekdays 0600–1200), opposite the college just north of Magasin Chin Lee, serves filling meals for CFP 750 (but no alcohol). Try the *ma'a tinito*. You eat at picnic tables behind a thatched roof. This good local place is a little hard to find as the sign is not visible from the street.

Restaurant Bar Au Cocotier (tel. 67-74-18; Mon., Wed., and Fri. 0800–2030, Tues., Thurs., and Sat. 0800–1730), between Snack Michel and Pharmacie Fare Ra'au, serves Chinese dishes (CFP 1,200–2,000), meat dishes (CFP 1,300–2,000), and fish (CFP 1,200–2,100).

Ker Yann Pizza (tel. 67-68-00), next to Pharmacie Fare Ra'au, has takeaway pizza.

Surprisingly, one of the best restaurants on the island is at the **TOPdive Resort** (tel. 60-50-60; 0700–1000/1200–1400/1900–2200), between Vaitape and Farepiti Wharf. Dinner mains average CFP 2,900–3,400, and there's a nice harbor view from most tables. If you call, they'll provide free transportation.

Cold Hinano beer is available for a reasonable price at the **Jeu Association Amical Tahitien Club** next to Farepiti Wharf. You must consume your beer at one of their picnic tables as they don't want to lose any bottles. It's a good stop on your way around the island and the perfect place to sit and wait for your boat.

Pofai Bay

The **Bamboo House Restaurant** (Peter Eberhardt, tel./fax 67-76-24; daily 1130–1430/1830–2130), next to Le Jardin Gauguin on Pofai Bay, serves everything from pasta dishes (from CFP 1,500) to grilled lobster (CFP 5,500). Other specialties include mahimahi (CFP 2,800), scampi (CFP 3,000), crab (CFP 3,500), and sirloin steak (CFP 3,000). Free transportation is provided in the evening.

Bloody Mary's (tel. 67-72-86; Mon.–Sat. 1130–1500/1800–2100), on Pofai Bay a km south of Le Jardin Gauguin, is the longest established nonhotel restaurant on the island with a tradition dating back to 1979. A board outside lists "famous guests," including Jane Fonda and Baron George Von Dangel. The lunch menu includes teriyaki, fish kabob, and *poisson cru* (all CFP 1,250), though when things are slow they don't bother dishing out lunch at all. At dinner you choose from the upscale seafood (CFP 2,500–6,000) laid out in front of you. For ambience, menu, service, and staff it's hard to beat,

although the food itself is only so-so. Don't miss the zany toilets! Free hotel pickups for diners are available at 1830 if you call ahead.

Matira

Ben's Snack (tel. 67-74-54), between Hôtel Bora Bora and Hôtel Matira, turns out pizza (CFP 850–1,540), lasagna, pasta, steaks, and omelettes, but it's only open irregularly. Clients are not allowed to share meals in the evening. One reader said that her hamburger was reminiscent of a "where's the beef?" commercial. Frankly, the beachside Chinese restaurant at Hôtel Matira nearby may be better value.

Snack Matira (tel. 67-77-32; Tues.–Sun. 1000–1700), across the street and a bit east of Ben's, is the best place around for a budget lunch. The menu includes hamburgers (CFP 450), mahimahi with frites (CFP 1,000), *steak frites* (CFP 1,100), pizza (CFP 1,200–1,500), *poisson cru* (CFP 1,000), and big **casse-croûte** sandwiches (CFP 150–600). The food is good, but no beer is available on their nice beachfront terrace.

Snack Restaurant Moi Here (tel. 67-68-41; daily 0630–2200), right on Matira Beach between Hôtel Matira and the Beachcomber Inter-Continental, is good for the large *casse-croûte* sandwiches (CFP 200–600) and mahimahi with fries (CFP 1,300). Other meals are in the CFP 1,000–1,550 range. Their agreeable terrace overlooks the beach.

Restaurant Fare Manuia (tel. 67-68-08; Mon. 1800–2200, Tues.–Sat. 1130–1400/1800–2200), at Bungalows Temanuata near the turnoff to the Beachcomber Inter-Continental, offers excellent if rather expensive Chinese dishes and French specialties. Local seafood dishes are in the CFP 2,400–2,700 range, meat CFP 2,100–3,900. Try the prawns breaded with coconut, steak with mushrooms, or *poisson cru*. It fills up quickly in the evening.

Snack Mandarin (tel. 72-43-62), opposite Matira Pearls between the Beachcomber Inter-Continental and Hôtel Le Maitai Polynesia, has chow mein, *steak frites*, chicken, *poisson cru*, and mahi-mahi, all for around CFP 1,000.

Restaurant-Snack La Bounty (tel. 67-70-43; Tues.–Sun. 1130–1400/1830–2100), near

Taire Market close to the Bora Bora Beach Lodge, has an open air terrace under a thatched roof. Their lunch plates are CFP 1,400–1,600, dinner CFP 1,400–1,700, pizzas CFP 1,250–1,550. The largely French clientele doesn't seem to mind the slow service—reader reviews are favorable.

Snack Patoti (tel. 67-61-99; Mon.–Sat. 0800–1400/1900–2100), 300 meters north of the Sofitel Marara, serves hamburgers with fries (CFP 800), *poisson cru* (CFP 1,300), chow mein (CFP 1,300), *steak frites* (CFP 1,300), and beer (CFP 400).

Groceries

Bora Bora's best established supermarket is **Magasin Chin Lee** (tel. 67-63-07; Mon.–Sat. 0500–1900, Sun. 0500–1100), opposite the island's Mobil gas station north of Vaitape Wharf. Takeaway meals at the checkout counters are CFP 700. **Super To'a Amok** and the Total service station are farther north.

Tiare Market (tel. 67-61-38; Mon.–Sat. 0630–1900, Sun. 0630–1300/1500–1830), opposite the Bora Bora Beach Lodge at Matira, is very well stocked with a good wine section and even some fresh vegetables. It's always crowded with tourists from the upmarket hotels.

Other places to buy groceries are the two general stores at Anau (closed Sun.), halfway around the island, and a small grocery store at the head of Pofai Bay. A grocery truck passes Matira around noon and 1600 daily except Sunday.

ENTERTAINMENT AND EVENTS

Disco

Le Récife Bar (tel. 67-73-87), between Vaitape and Farepiti Wharf, is Bora Bora's after-hours club, open Friday and Saturday from 2230. Disco dancing continues almost until dawn, but expect loud, heavy-on-the-beat music with few patrons. Steer clear of the local drunks hanging around outside.

Otherwise, the evening activity on Bora Bora is geared toward honeymooners or couples rescuing their marriages, staring into each others eyes and trying to make this the romantic peak of their lives. Singles looking for some fun or an authentic island scene could leave a little disappointed.

Cultural Shows for Visitors

To see Polynesian dancing on the beach at **Hôtel Bora Bora** (tel. 60-44-60) grab a barside seat before it starts at 2030 on Friday night (buffet CFP 7,000).

Additional Tahitian dancing occurs after dinner Thursday night at 2030 at the **Beachcomber Inter-Continental** (tel. 60-49-00). You can watch it for the price of a drink.

Hôtel Le Maitai Polynesia (tel. 60-30-00) has Tahitian dancing in the restaurant Wednesday at 2000 (buffet CFP 6,000). Here too it's possible to watch the show from the bar for the price of a drink.

Another Tahitian dance show takes place at the **Sofitel Marara** (tel. 60-55-00) every Tuesday, Thursday, and Saturday night at 2000. Saturday at 1800 they open the earth oven and the feast begins. Unless you're taking the buffet (CFP 4,800, reservations required) you'll have to pay a CFP 2,000 cover charge (which includes one drink) to see the show at the Sofitel Marara.

Events

The **Fêtes de Juillet** are celebrated at Bora Bora with special fervor. The canoe and bicycle races, javelin throwing, flower cars, singing, and dancing competitions run until 0300 nightly. A public ball goes till dawn on the Saturday closest to 14 July. Try to participate in the 10-km foot race to prove that all tourists aren't lazy, but don't take the prizes away from the locals. If you win, be sure to give the money back to them for partying. You'll make good friends that way and have more fun dancing in the evening. The stands are beautiful because the top decorations win prizes, too.

SHOPPING AND SERVICES

Shopping

Plenty of small boutiques around Vaitape sell black coral jewelry, pearls, pareus, T-shirts, designer beachwear, etc. The **Centre Artisanal** near Vaitape Wharf is a good place to buy a shell necklace or a pareu directly from the locals.

A cluster of shops on Pofai Bay offers some of Bora Bora's best tourist shopping. **Boutique Gauguin** (tel. 67-76-67) has tropical clothing, T-shirts, souvenirs, and jewelry. Next door is an upmarket black pearl showroom called **O.P.E.C.** (tel. 67-61-62) where numbered black pearls complete with X-ray and certificate go for US$300–1,400. The pearls can be set in gold as earrings or necklaces in one day. A full pearl necklace will cost US$9,000–15,000—the gift of a lifetime.

Alongside O.P.E.C. is **Art du Pacifique** (tel. 67-63-85) with a display of woodcarvings from the Marquesas Islands. Just behind is the gallery of neo-impressionist Basque painter and sculptor **Garrick Yrondi** (tel. 67-79-66, www.yrondi.pf), who has spent most of his life in French Polynesia. These shops surround a small garden called *Le Jardin Gauguin* with a series of tacky plaster sculptures depicting scenes from Gauguin's paintings.

At photographer Erwin Christian's **Moana Art Boutique** (tel. 67-70-33, www.tahiti books.com), just north of Hôtel Bora Bora, you can buy striking postcards, photo books, and other souvenirs.

Information and Services

A Visitors Bureau (tel./fax 67-76-36; weekdays 0800–1500) is in the Centre Artisanal next to Vaitape Wharf.

The three main banks all have offices near Vaitape Wharf, but they're only open weekdays 0745–1130/1330–1600. Many yachties "check out" of French Polynesia at Bora Bora and reclaim their bond or *caution* at these banks. It's wise to check with the Banque Socredo (tel. 60-50-10) a few days ahead to make sure they'll have your cash or traveler's checks ready. At last report, such refunds were only available on Tuesday and Thursday.

The post office (tel. 67-70-74; Mon. 0800–1500, Tues.–Fri. 0730–1500, Sat. 0800–1000), gendarmerie (tel. 67-70-58), and health clinic (*Santé Publique*) are within a stone's throw of Vaitape Wharf.

In past, the Yacht Club de Bora Bora (tel. 67-70-69), near Farepiti Wharf and opposite Te Ava Nui Pass, has provided moorings, fresh water,

and showers for cruising yachties. These services were free to cruisers who splashed out in their upscale seafood restaurant, otherwise they cost CFP 2,500 per day per group, plus CFP 300 per shower (drinks at the bar were not good enough for free mooring). The Yacht Club was being rebuilt at press time and future conditions were still unknown. Beware of theft off yachts anywhere around this island.

Health

The private Cabinet Médical (tel. 67-70-62) behind Snack Bora Bora Burger is open weekdays 0700–1200/1500–1800, Saturday 0700–1200.

Dr. François Macouin's Cabinet Dentaire (tel. 67-70-55; weekdays 0730–1800, Sat. 0730–1200) is in the Centre Commercial Le Pahia opposite Magasin Chin Lee and the large Protestant church.

Dr. F. Duval (tel. 67-67-07; weekdays 0730–1130/1530–1800, Sat. 0730–1130, Sun. and holidays 0730–0830) is just north of Pharmacie Fare Ra'au. Consultations are CFP 3,000 (double price at night). Dr. Dominique Bourda (tel. 67-69-42; weekdays 0730–1200/1430–1730, Sat. 0730–1200), a dentist, is adjacent.

Pharmacie Fare Ra'au (tel. 67-70-30; weekdays 0800–1200/1530–1800, Sat. 0800–1200/1700–1800, Sun. 0900–0930) is north of the wharf.

TRANSPORTATION

Getting There

Air Tahiti (tel. 67-70-35; weekdays 0730–1130/1330–1630) is beside the Banque de Tahiti on Vaitape Wharf. Since Papeete–Bora Bora is primarily a tourist route, Air Tahiti has made it very expensive: CFP 15,000 one way. They do have a useful transversal flight direct from Bora Bora to Rangiroa and Tikehau (both CFP 25,300) five times a week. For information on flights and ships to Bora Bora from Papeete, Huahine, and Raiatea, see Transportation in this chapter's Exploring the Islands section.

Ships from Raiatea and Papeete tie up at Farepiti Wharf, three km north of Vaitape. The shipping companies have no representatives on Bora Bora, so for departure times just keep asking. Drivers of the *trucks* are the most likely to know. You buy your ticket when the ship arrives. Officially the *Vaeanu* (tel. 67-68-68) departs Bora Bora for Raiatea, Huahine, and Papeete Tuesday and Thursday at 1130, and Sunday at 0830 (CFP 749/1,786 deck to Raiatea/Papeete). The *Hawaiki-Nui* calls here twice a week. Beware of early departures.

A fast yellow-and-blue passenger ferry, the *Maupiti Express* (tel./fax 67-66-69), departs Vaitape Wharf for Maupiti, Taha'a, and Raiatea. It leaves for Maupiti on Tuesday, Thursday, and Saturday at 0830 (CFP 2,500), for Taha'a and Raiatea on Monday, Wednesday, and Friday at 0700 (CFP 2,500). Tickets are sold on board.

Getting Around

Getting around is a bit of a headache, as *le truck* service is irregular and at lunchtime everything stops. Public *trucks* usually meet the boats, but many of the *trucks* you see around town are for guests of the luxury hotels. If you do find one willing to take you, fares between Vaitape and Matira vary from CFP 350–500, plus CFP 100 for luggage. Taxi fares are high, so check before getting in. If you rent a bicycle, keep an eye on it when you stop to visit the sights.

Farepiti Rentacar (tel. 67-65-28, fax 67-65-29l, farepiticarhire@mail.pf; closed Sun.), opposite the Centre Artisanal in Vaitape, at the Hôtel Le Maitai Polynesia, and opposite the Sofitel Marara, has cars from CFP 4,800/5,800/6,600/7,300 for two/four/eight/24 hours with unlimited kms. The smaller cars are usually all taken, and it's likely you'll be charged CFP 6,000/7,000/8,000/9,000 for an air-conditioned car. Insurance is included. Scooters are CFP 3,800/4,350/5,400/6,500 (motorcycle license required). Bicycles cost CFP 850/1,000/1,250/1,850. You must leave a deposit of CFP 100,000/50,000/30,000 on the cars/scooters/bicycles.

Europcar (tel. 67-70-15, fax 67-79-95, europcarborabox@mail.pf; daily 0730–1800), next to the gendarmerie opposite Vaitape Wharf and with desks at the Inter-Continental, Sofitel Marara, Club Med, and Le Méridien, has Fiats from CFP 7,350/8,500 for an eight/24-hour day. The price includes insurance and unlim-

ited km. A two-seater Mini Cabriolet is CFP 6,800/8,400 for four/eight hours. They also have bicycles for CFP 1,400/1,800/1,900 for four/eight/24 hours.

If you rent a car and drive at night, watch out for scooters and bicycles without lights. However, to better enjoy the scenery and avoid disturbing the environment, we suggest you dispense with motorized transport here. Little Bora Bora is perfect for cycling as there's an excellent paved road right around the island (with only one unpaved stretch on the incline at Fitiiu Point), almost no hills, and lots of scenic bays to shelter you from the wind. Do exercise caution with fast-moving vehicles between Vaitape and Matira Point, however.

Land Tours

Otemanu Tours (tel. 67-70-49), just north of Vaitape, offers a two-and-a-half-hour truck tour around Bora Bora daily except Sunday at 1400 (CFP 2,750).

Tupuna Safaris (tel. 67-75-06, tupuna.bora@mail.pf), at Moana Art Boutique near Hôtel Bora Bora, does Land Rover tours up a steep ridge opposite Otemanu at CFP 6,500.

Héli-inter polynésia (tel. 67-62-59, helicotahiti@mail.pf), next to the Air Tahiti office at Vaitape wharf, charges CFP 14,000 for a 15-minute scenic flight (three-person minimum).

Day Cruises

Like Aitutaki in the Cook Islands, Bora Bora is famous for its **lagoon tours.** Prices vary depending on whether lunch is included, the length of the trip, the luxury of boat, etc., so check around. A seafood picnic lunch on a *motu,* reef walking, and snorkeling gear are usually included, and you get a chance to see giant clams, manta rays, and shark feeding. For the latter you don a mask and snorkel, jump into the shark-infested waters, and grasp a line as your guide shoves chunks of fish at a school of generally innocuous reef sharks in feeding frenzy. It's an encounter with the wild you'll never forget. See the Chez Nono and Chez Robert accommodations listings for two possibilities. Motorized canoe trips right around Bora Bora are also offered. An excursion of this kind is an essential part of the Bora Bora experience, so splurge on this one.

Moana Adventure Tours (tel. 67-61-41, fax 67-61-26, www.moanatours.com), on Pofai Bay near Village Pauline, does shark and ray feeding (CFP 6,600 pp) several times a week, departing around 1300. A half-day deep-sea fishing charter is CFP 38,500 for two persons.

Ioane (John) of **Matira Tour** (tel. 67-70-97), on Matira Point near Chez Robert et Tina, does lagoon tours from 0930–1500 at CFP 6,000 including lunch (minimum of six).

Three-hour tours to the **Bora Lagoonarium** (tel. 67-71-34, fax 67-60-29) on a *motu* off the main island occur daily except Saturday at 0915 and 1300 (CFP 6,990). The price is reduced to CFP 5,500 if you book directly at the Lagoonarium office at Anau, a km north of Club Med. A slightly different tour occurs at 1400 and 1630 (CFP 6,330/4,500 hotel/direct bookings). You'll see more colorful fish than you ever thought existed. Call for a free hotel pickup.

René et Maguy Boat Rental (tel. 67-60-61, fax 67-61-01), next to Tiare Supermarket at Matira, rents small boats with motor at CFP 6,050/7,150/8,250/11,550 two hours/three hours/half day/full day (gasoline extra). *Motu* transfers are CFP 1,815 pp return.

The **Aquascope** (tel. 67-61-92, www.boraboraisland.com/aquascope) is a step above a glass-bottom boat in that you view the marinelife through large windows. It departs Vaitape Wharf five times a day, charging CFP 5,000 pp for a one-hour trip inside the lagoon or CFP 10,000 for three hours beyond the pass.

On the submarine **Spirit of Pacific** (tel. 67-55-55, fax 67-65-67, www.spiritofpacific.com) you aren't tied to the surface. These vessel can descend to depths of 35 meters outside the lagoon to observe sharks and other marinelife. The six passengers each pay CFP 18,500 for their 30-minute dive including hotel transfers.

Airport

Bora Bora's vast airfield (BOB) on Motu Mute north of the main island was built by the Americans during WW II. The first commercial flight from Paris to French Polynesia landed here in October 1958, and until March 1961 all international flights used this airstrip; passengers were then transferred to Papeete by Catalina amphibious or Bermuda flying boat seaplanes. Today, a 25-minute catamaran ride brings arriving air passengers to Vaitape Wharf (included in the plane ticket). Make sure your luggage is loaded on/off the boat at the airport.

When the catamaran from the airport arrives at Vaitape Wharf, all of the luxury hotels will have guest transportation waiting, but the budget places don't always meet the flights (the deluxe places don't bother meeting the interisland boats). As you arrive at the wharf, shout out the name of your hotel and you'll be directed to the right *truck* (they don't have destination signs). At the airport the resorts use color-coded flower leis to sort out their guests.

If you're flying from Papeete to Bora Bora go early in the morning and sit on the left side of the aircraft for spectacular views—it's only from the air that Bora Bora is the most beautiful island in the world!

FRENCH POLYNESIA

Maupiti

Majestic Maupiti (Maurua), 52 km west of Bora Bora, is the least known of the accessible Society Islands. Maupiti's mighty volcanic plug soars above a sapphire lagoon, and the vegetation-draped cliffs complement the magnificent *motu* beaches. Almost every bit of level land on the main island is taken up by fruit trees, while watermelons thrive on the surrounding *motu*. Maupiti abounds in native seabirds, including frigate birds, terns, and others. The absence of Indian mynahs allows you to see native land birds that are almost extinct elsewhere.

The 1,125 people live in the adjacent villages of Vai'ea, Farauru, and Pauma. Tourism is not promoted because there aren't any regular hotels, which is a big advantage! It's sort of like Bora Bora was 30 years ago, before being "discovered" by the world of package tourism.

Sights

It takes only three hours to walk right around this 11-square-km island. The nine-km crushed-coral road, lined with breadfruit, mango, banana, and hibiscus, passes crumbling *marae,* freshwater springs, and a beach.

Marae Vaiahu, by the shore a few hundred meters beyond Hotuparaoa Massif, is the largest *marae.* Once a royal landing place opposite the pass into the lagoon, the *marae* still bears the king's throne and ancient burials. Nearby is the sorcerers' rock: light a fire beside this rock and you will die. Above the road are a few smaller *marae.*

Terei'a Beach, at the west tip of Maupiti, is the only good beach on the main island (excellent snorkeling). At low tide you can wade across from Terei'a's white sands to Motu Auira in waist-deep water.

Marae Vaiorie is a double *marae* with freshwater springs in between. As many as two dozen large *marae* are hidden in Maupiti's mountainous interior, and the island is known for its ghosts. Maupiti is well known among archaeologists for its black basalt stone pounders and fishhooks made from the seven local varieties of mother-of-pearl shell.

It's possible to climb to the 380-meter summit of Maupiti from the 42-meter-high saddle where the road cuts across Terei'a Point. You follow the ridge all the way to the top and the whole trip shouldn't take over three hours return.

Accommodations

Several of the inhabitants take paying guests, and they usually meet the flights and boats in search of clients. The absence of a regular hotel on Maupiti throws together an odd mix of vacationing French couples, backpackers, and "adventuresome" tourists in the guesthouses (none of which have signs). Agree on the price beforehand and check your bill when you leave. You could camp on the airport *motu,* but obtaining drinking water would be a problem and there are *no-nos* (insects). Maupiti experiences serious water shortages during the dry season.

Chez Mareta (Manuela Mohi, tel. 67-80-25), in the center of Vai'ea village, is the house with the sloping blue roof a few minutes' walk from the *mairie.* They offer three rooms at CFP 2,600 pp including breakfast. You can cook your own food or pay CFP 1,500 for dinner. An agreeable sitting room faces the lagoon downstairs. Upon request, they'll drop you on a *motu* for the day (beware of sunburn). Chez Mareta is okay for a couple of days, but not an extended stay. The church choir in the next building practices their singing quite loudly each night.

Chez Floriette Tuheiava (tel./fax 67-80-85) on the north side of Chez Mareta has two pleasant bungalows at CFP 6,100 pp including breakfast, dinner, activities, and airport transfers. Floriette speaks reasonable English. South of Chez Mareta is **Pension Eri** (Emmanuel Mohi, tel. 67-81-29) with four rooms in a separate house at CFP 5,500 pp with breakfast and dinner.

Pension Tamati (Ferdinand and Etu Tapuhiro, tel. 67-80-10), a two-story building at the south end of Vai'ea, rents nine bleak rooms at CFP 2,500 pp with breakfast or CFP 4,500 pp with half board. Unfortunately, tourists are usually given the inside rooms without proper ventilation, but communal cooking facilities are available.

Maupiti Loisirs (tel. 67-80-95), near Tereia Beach, provides camping facilities here or on Motu Auira at CFP 5,000 pp including breakfast and dinner. Bicycle rentals are CFP 1,000 a day.

Fare Pae'ao (Janine Tavaearii, tel. 67-81-01 or 67-80-08, fax 67-81-92) on Motu Pae'ao is quiet and offers a superb white beach with some of the finest snorkeling on Maupiti. The three thatched bungalows with bath are CFP 10,000 single or double, CFP 11,000 triple. Meals cost CFP 3,500/6,000 pp for two/three meals. Reservations are required to ensure an airport pickup (CFP 1,000 pp roundtrip). (In 1962 Kenneth Emory and Yosihiko Sinoto excavated a prehistoric cemetery on Pae'ao and found 15 adzes of six different types, providing valuable evidence for the study of Polynesian migrations.)

Pension Auira (Edna Terai, tel. 67-80-26) on Motu Auira, the *motu* opposite Terei'a Beach, has five unscreened thatched bungalows. The garden variety are CFP 8,500 pp a day including breakfast and dinner; the better quality beach bungalows are CFP 9,500 pp. Camping is CFP 2,000 pp. The food is great but the bathroom facilities are basic. Bring mosquito coils. You'll enjoy the good views and snorkeling. Transfers from the airport in an open boat cost CFP 2,000 pp return but they'll ferry you over to the mainland for free during your stay.

In addition, there are three small resorts on Motu Tiapaa, one of the islands framing Onoiau Pass. **Pension Papahani** (Vilna Tuheiava, tel./fax 67-81-58) has five thatched bungalows with private bath beginning at CFP 7,500 pp, breakfast and dinner included. Return airport transfers are CFP 1,000 pp. More upscale are the five *fare* with bath at the **Kuriri Village** (tel./fax 67-82-23, www.maupiti-kuriri.com) at CFP 22,800/27,600 double with half/full board. Also on Tiapaa is **Fare Rose des Îles** (Areti and Juliette Tauaroa, fax

67-82-00) with one bungalow at CFP 7,000 pp half board.

Services

Banque Socredo (tel. 67-81-95) has a branch on Maupiti, but it's not always operating, so change beforehand and don't count on using your credit cards. The post office and *mairie* are nearby. The bakery is in the power plant on the edge of town. It's important to check when the baguettes come out of the oven and to be punctual, as they sell out fast. The island youths come here an hour before and hang around waiting. Not all stores sell beer and the island's supply does run out at times.

Getting There

Maupiti's airport (MAU) is on a *motu* and you must take a launch to the main island (CFP 500 pp). **Air Tahiti** has flights to Maupiti from Raiatea (CFP 6,600 one-way) and Papeete (CFP 14,300) three times a week. At last report, the flights between Bora Bora and Maupiti weren't operating. Reconfirm with the Air Tahiti agent (tel. 67-80-20) near the *mairie*. The Air Tahiti boat to the main island is CFP 400 pp each way.

The 62-seat fast ferry *Maupiti Express* arrives from Bora Bora (CFP 2,500 each way) on Tuesday, Thursday, and Saturday mornings, returning to Bora Bora the same afternoon.

The government supply barges *Meherio III* or *Maupiti Tou Ai'a* depart Papeete for Raiatea and Maupiti Wednesday at 1900, departing Maupiti for the return Friday at 0800. See the French Polynesia introduction for more information.

Ships must enter the channel during daylight, thus the compulsory morning arrival, and the boats usually depart from Maupiti on the afternoon of the same day. Onoiau Pass into Maupiti is narrow, and when there's a strong southerly wind it can be dangerous—boats have had to turn back. At low tide a strong current flows out through this pass and the optimum time for a yacht to enter is around noon.

Other Leeward Islands

Tupai

Tupai or Motu Iti (Small Island), 24 km north of Bora Bora, is a tiny coral atoll measuring 1,100 hectares. The opposing horseshoe-shaped *motu* enclose a lagoon that small boats can enter through a pass on the east side. A small airstrip is in the northwest corner of the atoll. In 1860 the king of Bora Bora gave the atoll to a planter named Stackett and for decades a few dozen people were employed to make copra from coconuts off the 155,000 trees on Tupai. In 1997 the territorial government bought Tupai from its last owner, a Mr. Lejeune, for US$8 million with an eye to resort development. Although there are no permanent inhabitants at the moment, the 1,000 traditional landowners are contesting the title. Recently members of the Groupement d'Intervention de Polynésie (GIP), a militia created by Gaston Flosse, have undergone training on Tupai by former Foreign Legionnaires and army parachutists. The scuba operators on Bora Bora often arrange trips here.

Maupihaa

Tiny 360-hectare Maupihaa (Mopelia), 185 km southeast of Maupiti, is the only Society Islands atoll that can be entered by yachts but to attempt to do so in stormy weather is dangerous.

Narrow, unmarked Taihaaru Vahine Pass on Maupihaa's northwest side can only be found by searching for the strong outflow of lagoon water at low tide. Despite this, cruising yachts traveling between Bora Bora and Cook Islands or Samoa often anchor in the atoll's lagoon.

In July 1917 the notorious German raider *Seeadler* was wrecked at Maupihaa after capturing 15 Allied ships. The three-masted schooner was too large to enter lagoon, and while being careened outside the pass, a freak wave picked the vessel up and threw it onto the reef. Eventually the ship's chivalrous captain, Count Felix von Luckner, was able to carry on to Fiji in a small boat, where he was captured at Wakaya Island. Count von Luckner's journal, *The Sea Devil*, became a bestseller after the war.

About 50 people from Maupiti live on Maupihaa, where they run a nursery to supply oysters to black pearl farms in the Tuamotus. Sea turtles come to Maupihaa to lay their eggs only to be butchered for their flesh by poachers. Large numbers of terns, boobies, and frigate birds nest on the small *motu* and the seabird fledglings are slaughtered for their meager meat while the unhatched eggs are collected according to need. All of this is supposed to be pro-

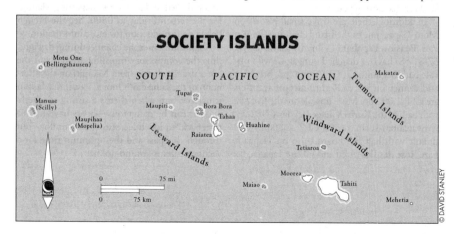

SOCIETY ISLANDS

hibited but it's hard to control what goes on in such an isolated place.

Manuae

Manuae (Scilly), 75 km northwest of Maupihaa, is the westernmost of the Society Islands. This atoll is 15 km in diameter but totals only 400 hectares. Pearl divers once visited Manuae. In 1855 the three-masted schooner *Julia Ann* sank on the Manuae reef. It took the survivors two months to build a small boat, which carried them to safety at Raiatea.

Motu One

Motu One (Bellingshausen), 65 km north of Manuae, got its second name from the Russian explorer Thadeus von Bellingshausen who visited Tahiti in 1820. Tiny 280-hectare Motu One is circled by a guano-bearing reef, with no pass into the lagoon. Of the 10 persons present on Motu One when Hurricane Martin swept through in November 1997, the sole survivor was a woman named Alice Haano who tied herself to a coconut tree.

Austral Islands

The inhabited volcanic islands of Rimatara, Rurutu, Tubuai, Raivavae, and Rapa, plus uninhabited Maria (or Hull) atoll, make up the Austral group. This southernmost island chain in the South Pacific is a 1,280-km extension of the same submerged mountain range as the southern Cook Islands, 900 km northwest. The islands of the Australs seldom exceed 300 meters, except Rapa, which soars to 650 meters. The southerly location makes these islands notably cooler and drier than Tahiti. Collectively the Australs are known as Tuhaa Pae, the "Fifth Part" or fifth administrative subdivision of French Polynesia. It's still a world apart from tourism.

History

Excavations carried out on the northwest coast of Rurutu uncovered 60 round-ended houses arranged in parallel rows, with 14 *marae* scattered among them, demonstrating the presence of humans here as early as A.D. 900. Ruins of *marae* can also be seen on Rimatara, Tubuai, and Raivavae. Huge stone tikis once graced Raivavae, but most have since been destroyed or removed. The terraced mountain fortifications, or *pa,* on Rapa are unique.

The Australs were one of the great art areas of the Pacific, represented today in many museums. The best-known artifacts are sculpted sharkskin drums, wooden bowls, fly whisks, and tapa cloth. Offerings that could not be touched by human hands were placed on the sacred altars with intricately incised ceremonial ladles. European contact effaced most of these traditions and the carving done today is crude by comparison.

Rurutu was spotted by Capt. James Cook in 1769; he found Tubuai in 1777. In 1789 Fletcher Christian and the *Bounty* mutineers attempted to establish a settlement at the northeast corner of Tubuai. They left after only three months, following battles with the islanders in which 66 Polynesians died. The European discoverer of Rapa was Capt. George Vancouver in 1791. Rimatara wasn't contacted until 1813, by the Australian captain Michael Fodger.

English missionaries converted most of the people to Protestantism in the early 19th century. Whalers and sandalwood ships introduced diseases and firearms, which decimated the Austral islanders. The French didn't complete their annexation of the group until 1901. Since then the Australs have gone their sleepy way.

The People

The 6,500 mostly Polynesian inhabitants are fishermen and farmers who live in attractive villages with homes and churches built of coral limestone. The rich soil and moderate climate stimulate agriculture with staple crops such as taro, manioc, Irish potatoes, sweet potatoes, leeks, cabbage, carrots, corn, and coffee. The coconut palm also thrives, except on Rapa. In recent years the population has declined slightly as many Austral people move to Papeete.

FRENCH POLYNESIA

Getting There

Air Tahiti has four or five flights a week to Rurutu and Tubuai. Two operate Papeete-Tubuai-Rurutu-Papeete, the other two Papeete-Rurutu-Tubuai-Papeete. One-way fares from Tahiti are CFP 20,300 to Rurutu and CFP 22,700 to Tubuai. Rurutu-Tubuai is CFP 10,400. In 2002 an airport was opened on Raivavae and another is under construction on Rimatara.

The Austral Islands are also accessible by boat. For information on the sailings of the *Tuhaa Pae III* from Papeete, see Transportation in this chapter's Exploring the Islands section.

RURUTU

This island, 565 km south of Papeete, is shaped like a miniature replica of the African continent. Rurutu is estimated to be 11 million years old, and it would normally have eroded to sea level, except that four million years ago it was uplifted by the movement of tectonic plates. This history accounts for the juxtaposition of coastal coral cliffs with volcanic interior hills. For the hiker, 32-square-km Rurutu is a more varied island to visit than Tubuai. Grassy, fern-covered Taatioe (389 meters) and Manureva (384 meters) are the highest peaks, and coastal cliffs on the southeast side of the island drop 30 meters to the sea. A narrow fringing reef surrounds Rurutu, but there's no lagoon.

The climate of this northernmost Austral island is temperate and dry. The recent history of Rurutu revolves around four important dates: 1821, when the gospel arrived on the island; 1889, when France declared a protectorate over the island; 1970, when Hurricane Emma devastated the three villages; and 1975, when the airport opened.

In January and July Rurutuans practice the ancient art of stone lifting or *amoraa ofai.* Men get three tries to hoist a 150-kg boulder coated with *monoï* (coconut oil) up onto their shoulders, while women attempt a 60-kg stone. Dancing and feasting follow the event. The women of Rurutu weave fine pandanus hats, bags, baskets, fans, lamp shades, and mats. A handicraft display is laid out for departing passengers. Rurutu's famous Manureva (Soaring Bird) Dance Group has performed around the world. The

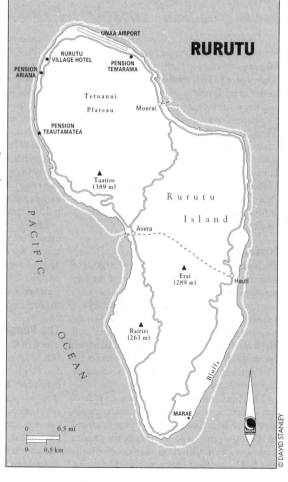

main evening entertainment is watching dancers practice in the villages.

Orientation

The pleasant main village, Moerai, boasts a post office, medical center, four small stores, two bakeries, and a bank. An Italian runs a goat cheese factory in Moerai. Two other villages, Avera and Hauti, bring the total island population to about 2,000. Neat fences and flower gardens surround the coral limestone houses. This is the Polynesia of 50 years ago: Though snack bars have appeared and electricity functions 24 hours a day, there's almost none of the flashy tourism development you see in the Society Islands nor the pearl farms common in the Tuamotus.

Public transportation is also lacking on the 36-km road around Rurutu, and even by bicycle it can be quite an effort to circle the island as the route climbs away from the coast on four occasions to avoid high cliffs. South of Avera the road reaches 190 meters, dropping back down to sea level at the southern tip, then rising again to 124 meters on the way up to Hauti. The direct road from Moerai to Avera also climbs to 168 meters. For hikers a three-km foot trail across the center of the island between Avera and Hauti makes a variety of itineraries possible. Beaches, waterfalls, valleys, bluffs, and limestone caves beckon the undaunted explorer.

One of the nicest spots is near **Toataratara Point** where a side road cuts back up the east coast to a *marae* and a few small beaches. It's quite easy to hike to the TV tower on the summit of **Manureva** from either the 200-meter-high Tetuanui Plateau toward the airport or the saddle of the Moerai-Avera road. Rurutu's highest peak, Taatioe, is nearby.

From July to October, the Raie Manta Club offers **humpback whale-watching** at Rurutu, costing CFP 10,000 a half day. You can even snorkel with the beasts. Scuba diving is available at different sites (see their website).

Accommodations

The **Hôtel Rurutu Village** (tel. 94-03-92, fax 94-05-01), on a beach a km southwest of the airport, is the only regular hotel in the Austral Is-

lands. The eight tin-roofed bungalows with bath go for CFP 4,500/5,500 single/double, or CFP 8,800/14,100 with breakfast and dinner. Facilities include a restaurant, bar, and swimming pool.

Pension Ariana (tel. 94-06-69, fax 94-07-14), near the Hôtel Rurutu Village, has two rooms at CFP 7,200/11,400 single/double and three bungalows at CFP 7,700/11,900, both rates including half board. The nice beach is just beyond pension's picturesque garden.

On the beach a few km south of the Rurutu Village and six km from Moerai is **Pension Teautamatea** (tel./fax 94-02-42, pension.teautamatea@free.fr) with three rooms at CFP 3,800/5,600 single/double. Half board is CFP 2,500 pp extra. They rent bicycles at CFP 1,000 a day.

Pension Temarama (tel./fax 94-02-17, pension.temarama@free.fr), between the airport and Moerai, has six rooms in a two-story house at CFP 3,800/4,800. Meals are extra (no cooking facilities). It's not right on the beach but provides a good base for visiting the village.

Pension Catherine (tel. 94-02-43), in a concrete building behind Moerai's Protestant church, has 10 rooms at CFP 4,500/5,500 single/double, or CFP 7,400/11,400 including half board.

Chez Paulette (tel. 94-05-82), near the wharf in Moerai, rents three rooms but their main business is their snack bar which serves good local meals.

Services and Transportation

Banque Socredo (tel. 94-04-75) and the post office are at Moerai. The gendarmerie (tel. 94-03-61) is at the east end of Moerai.

Unaa Airport (RUR) is at the north tip of Rurutu, four km from Moerai. All of the hotels offer free transfers to guests who have booked. **Air Tahiti** can be reached at tel. 94-03-57. The supply ship from Papeete ties up at Moerai.

TUBUAI

Ten-km-long by five-km-wide Tubuai, largest of the Australs, is 643 km south of Tahiti. Hills on the east and west sides of this oval 45-square-km island are joined by lowland in the middle; when seen from the sea Tubuai looks like two islands. Mount Taitaa (422 meters) is its highest point. Tubuai is surrounded by a barrier reef; a pass on the north side gives access to a wide turquoise lagoon bordered by brilliant white-sand beaches. Picnics are often arranged on the small reef *motu,* amid superb snorkeling grounds, and surfers are just discovering Tubuai's possibilities.

Tubuai has a mean annual temperature 3°C lower than Tahiti and it's at its driest and sunniest September–November. The brisk climate permits the cultivation of potatoes, carrots, cabbage, lettuce, oranges, and coffee, but other vegetation is sparse. Several *marae* are on Tubuai, but they're in extremely bad condition, with potatoes growing on the sites. The *Bounty* mutineers unsuccessfully attempted to settle on Tubuai in 1789 (though nothing remains of their Fort George, southeast of Taahuaia). Mormon missionaries arrived as early as 1844, and today there are active branches of the Church of Latter-day Saints in all the villages. The islanders weave fine pandanus hats, and some woodcarving is done at Mahu.

Most of the 2,050 inhabitants live in Mataura and Taahuaia villages on the north coast, though houses and hamlets are found all along the level 24-km road around the island. An eight-km paved road cuts right across the middle of Tubuai to Mahu village on the south coast, but even this presents no challenges for bicyclists (it's an easy hike to the summit of Mount Taitaa from this road). Mataura is the administrative center of the Austral Islands, and the post office, hospital, dental clinic, gendarmerie (tel. 95-03-33), and the branches of two banks are here. The two stores at Mataura bake bread.

Accommodations

Pension Yolande (Yolande and Sam Tahuhuterani, tel./fax 95-05-52), lagoonside in Mataura, has five rooms at CFP 5,300/6,880 single/double. For CFP 2,500 Yolande will serve you a huge dinner of up to seven courses (duck with tamarind sauce, chicken in lemon sauce, *poisson cru,* spring rolls, baked fish, etc.). Sam is a guitarist who also plays keyboard. An excellent beach is just 50 meters away.

Pension Vaitea Nui (Mélinda Bodin, tel. 93-22-40, fax 93-22-42, http://chez.mana.pf/~bodinm), inland a bit from Mataura, has five rooms with bath in a long block at CFP 3,300/5,300 single/double, plus CFP 3,400 pp for half board (no cooking facilities). There's a restaurant.

Near the college at the west end of Taahueia village, just under three km east of Mataura, is **Chez Karine and Talé** (Karine and Talé Tahuhuterani, tel./fax 95-04-52, charles@mail.pf) with one pleasant self-catering bungalow at CFP 5,000/8,000 single/double including breakfast.

Food

From **Restaurant Te Motu** (tel. 95-05-27) near Taahueia, you get a good view of the *motu.* The plat du jour is CFP 1,250 and smoked fish *(tazard), poisson cru,* mahimahi, and roast lamb are on the menu. You can order drinks.

Snack Vahinerii (tel. 95-03-97; closed Sun.), near the main wharf, has grilled fish, grilled chicken, chou mein, *poisson cru,* and grilled beef starting around CFP 750. No alcohol is served (but you can bring your own).

Getting There

Tubuai Airport (TUB), in the northwest corner of the island, opened in 1972. The best beach on the main island is beside the five-km road from the airport to Mataura. All the accommodations offer free transfers to guests. **Air Tahiti** (tel. 95-04-76) arrives from Rurutu and Papeete several times a week.

Ships enter the lagoon through a passage in the barrier reef on the north side and proceed to the wharf a km east of Mataura. Otherwise, the lagoon is too shallow for navigation.

Getting Around

There's no public transportation on Tubuai. You can rent a bicycle or car from **Tubuai Photo** (tel. 95-04-05) near Mataura. It's run by Donald Travers, an American from Los Angeles who has been on the island since 1974. Donald does day trips to *motu.* **Garage Le Guilloux** (tel. 95-06-01), near Tamatoa, also rents cars. The only gas station is run by a Canadian named Larry Miller near the wharf at Mataura.

OTHER AUSTRAL ISLANDS

Rimatara

Only a narrow fringing reef hugs Rimatara's lagoonless shore; arriving passengers are landed at Amaru or Mutua Ura by whaleboat and it's customary for newcomers to pass through a cloud of purifying smoke from beachside fires. The women of Rimatara make fine pandanus hats, mats, and bags, and shell necklaces. *Monoï* (skin oil) is prepared from gardenias and coconut oil. As yet without a harbor, wharf, hotels, restaurants, bars, and taxis, Rimatara is still a place to escape the world. This will change when the new airport begins receiving flights. The wreck of the interisland ship *Vaeanu II* sits on the reef at Rimatara, where it was lost in April, 2002.

This smallest (nine square km) and lowest (84 meters) of the Australs is home to fewer than 1,000 people. Dirt roads lead from Amaru, the main village, to Anapoto and Mutua Ura. **Pension Umarere** (Tama Aténi Tereopa, tel. 83-25-84), at Mutua Ura, five km southwest of Amaru, has two rooms with shared bath at CFP 2,500/4,000 single/double or CFP 60,000 a month. Cooking is possible but bring food and drink to Rimatara. Water is short in the dry season.

Uninhabited Maria (or Hull) is a four-islet atoll 192 km northwest of Rimatara, visited once or twice a year by men from Rimatara or Rurutu for fishing and copra making. They stay on the atoll two or three months, among seabirds and giant lobsters.

Raivavae

This appealing, nine-km-long and two-km-wide island is just south of the tropic of Capricorn, and thus outside the tropics. It's the third most southerly island in the South Pacific (only Rapa and Easter Island are farther south). For archaeology and natural beauty, this is one of the finest islands in Polynesia. Fern-covered Mt. Hiro (437 meters) is the highest point on 18-square-km Raivavae. A barrier reef encloses an emerald lagoon, but the 20 small coral *motu* are all located on the southern and eastern portions of the reef. The tropical vegetation is rich: rose and sandalwood are used to make perfumes for local use.

A few years after the arrival of Protestant missionaries in 1822, a malignant fever epidemic reduced the people of Raivavae from 3,000 to a mere 80 in 1834. The present population of around 1,050 lives in four coastal villages, Rairua, Mahanatoa, Anatonu, and Vaiuru, linked by a dirt road. A shortcut route direct from Rairua to Vaiuru crosses a 119-meter saddle, with splendid views of the island. The post office is in Rairua.

Different teams led by Frank Stimson (1917), Thor Heyerdahl (1956), and Donald Marshall (1957) have explored the ancient temples and defensive terraces of Raivavae. Many two- to three-meter-high red stone statues once stood on the island, but most have since been smashed, and two were removed to Tahiti where they can be seen on the grounds of the Gauguin Museum. One big tiki is still standing by the road between Rairua and Mahanatoa villages. Christian converts destroyed most of Raivavae's 92 *marae*. At **Pomoavao Marae** on the south side of the island huge stone blocks tilt upwards among the undergrowth.

Pension Moana (Haamoeura Teehu, tel./fax 95-42-66) at Mahanatoa has three rooms at CFP 2,500 pp, plus CFP 2,000 pp for half board. **Pension Ataha** (Odile Tamaititahio, tel./fax 95-43-69) and **Pension Rau'uru** (Edmond Flores, tel. 95-42-88) at Rairua are similar.

In 2002 an airport was constructed on land reclaimed from the lagoon south of Rairua, 6 km from Mahanatoa, and Air Tahiti operates flights from Papeete three times a week, usually via Tubuai. Ships enter the lagoon through a pass on the north side and tie up at the pier at Rairua. A boat calls at the island about every 10–14 days.

Rapa

At 27°38' south latitude, Rapa is the southernmost island in the South Pacific, and one of the most isolated and spectacular. Its nearest neighbor is Raivavae, 600 km away, and Tahiti is 1,244 km north. It's sometimes called Rapa Iti (Little Rapa) to distinguish it from Rapa Nui (Easter Island). Soaring peaks reaching 650 meters form a horseshoe around magnificent Haurei Bay, Rapa's crater harbor, the western portion of a drowned volcano. This is only one of 12 deeply indented bays around the island; the absence of reefs allows the sea to cut into the 40-square-km island's outer basalt coasts. Offshore are several sugarloaf-shaped islets. The east slopes of the mountains are bare, while large fern forests are found on the west. Coconut trees cannot grow in the foggy, temperate climate. Instead coffee and taro are the main crops.

A timeworn **Polynesian fortress** with terraces is situated on the crest of a ridge at Morongo Uta, commanding a wide outlook over the steep, rugged hills. Morongo Uta was cleared of vegetation by a party of archaeologists led by William Mulloy in 1956 and is still easily visitable. About a dozen of these *pa* (fortresses) are found above the bay, built to defend the territories of the different tribes of overpopulated ancient Rapa. Today the young men of Rapa organize eight-day bivouacs to hunt wild goats, which range across the island.

During the two decades following the arrival of missionaries in 1826, Rapa's population dropped from 2,000 to 300 due to the introduction of European diseases. By 1851 it was down to just 70, and after smallpox and dysentery arrived on a Peruvian ship in 1863 it was a miracle that anyone survived at all. The present population of about 550 lives at Area and Haurei villages on the north and south sides of Rapa's great open bay, connected only by boat.

If you're planning to stay on Rapa, it might be useful to write Le Maire, Rapa, Îles Australes, French Polynesia, well in advance, stating your name, nationality, age, and profession. Information may also be available from the Subdivision Administrative des Îles Australes (tel. 46-86-76, fax 46-86-79), rue des Poilus Tahitiens, Papeete.

Mrs. Titaua Jean (tel. 95-72-59, fax 95-72-60) rents a house with cooking facilities in Ahurei at CFP 5,000/60,000 a day/month. A number of local residents also rent rooms in their homes. The *Tuhaa Pae III* calls at Rapa monthly, so that's how long you'll be there.

Marotiri, or the "Bass Rocks," are nine uninhabited islets totaling just four hectares, 74 km southeast of Rapa. Amazingly enough, some of these pinnacles are crowned with man-made stone platforms and round "towers." One 105-meter-high pinnacle is visible from Rapa in very clear weather. Landing is difficult.

Tuamotu Islands

Arrayed in two parallel northwest-southeast chains scattered across an area of ocean 600 km wide and 1,500 km long, the Tuamotus are the largest group of coral atolls in the world. Of the 78 atolls in the group, 21 have one entrance (pass), 10 have two passes, and 47 have no pass at all. Some have an unbroken ring of reef around the lagoon, while others appear as a necklace of islets separated by channels. Although the land area of the Tuamotus is only 726 square km, the lagoons of the atolls total some 6,000 square km of sheltered water.

Variable currents, sudden storms, and poor charts make cruising this group by yacht extremely hazardous—in fact, the Tuamotus are popularly known as the Dangerous Archipelago, or the Labyrinth. Wrecks litter the reefs of many atolls. The breakers only become visible when one is within eight km of the reef, and once in, a yacht must carry on through the group. The usual route is to sail either between Rangiroa and Arutua after a stop at Ahe, or through the Passe de Fakarava between Toau and Fakarava. Winds are generally from the east, varying to northeast November–May and southeast June–October.

The resourceful Tuamotu people have always lived from seafood, pandanus nuts, and coconuts. They once dove to depths of 30 meters and more, wearing only tiny goggles, to collect mother-of-pearl shells. This activity has largely ceased as overharvesting has made the oysters rare. Today, cultured-pearl farms operate on Ahe, Aratika, Arutua, Fakarava, Hao, Hikueru, Katiu, Kaukura, Kauehi, Makemo, Manihi, Marutea South, Nengonengo, Raroia, Takapoto, Takaroa, Takume, Taenga, and others. Cultured black pearls *(Pinctada margaritifera)* from the Tuamotus and Gambiers are world famous. The pearl industry has reversed the depopulation of the atolls and spread prosperity through this remote region.

The scarcity of land and fresh water has always been a major problem. A total of around 14,500 people live on the 48 inhabited islands. Many of these dry, coconut-covered atolls have only a few hundred inhabitants. Although airstrips exist on 26 islands, the isolation has led many Tuamotuans to migrate to Papeete. Deluxe resorts exist on Rangiroa, Tikehau, Manihi, and Fakarava, and homestay accommodations are available on most of the other atolls. Beware of eating poisonous fish all across this archipelago.

Getting There

Air Tahiti has flights to Ahe, Apataki, Arutua, Fakarava, Kauehi, Kaukura, Manihi, Mataiva, Rangiroa, Takapoto, Takaroa, and Tikehau in the northern Tuamotus, and Anaa, Faaite, Fakahina, Fangatau, Hao, Makemo, Mangareva, Napuka, Nukutavake, Pukapuka, Pukarua, Reao, Takume, Tatakoto, Tureia, and Vahitahi in the south.

Interisland boats call at most of the Tuamotu atolls about once a week, bringing imported foods and other goods and returning to Papeete with fish. Information on the cargo boats from

Papeete is given in the introduction to French Polynesia. However you come, be aware that it's very difficult to change foreign currency on the atolls, so bring enough cash.

All the Tuamotu atolls offer splendid snorkeling possibilities (take snorkeling gear), though scuba diving is only developed on Fakarava, Manihi, Rangiroa, and Tikehau. The advantage of atolls other than Manihi, Rangiroa, and Tikehau is that the people will be far less impacted by packaged tourism. There it should be easy to hitch rides with the locals across to *le secteur* (uninhabited *motu*) as they go to cut copra or tend the pearl farms. Just don't expect many facilities on these tiny specks of sand scattered in a solitary sea.

RANGIROA

Rangiroa, 300 km northeast of Papeete, is the Tuamotus' most populous atoll. Its 1,020-square-km aquamarine lagoon is 78 km long, 24 km wide (too far to see), and 225 km around—the island of Tahiti would fit inside its reef. The name Rangiroa means "extended sky." Some 240 *motu* sit on this reef. Although Rangiroa is the largest atoll in eastern Polynesia, it's not the biggest in the South Pacific as all of the

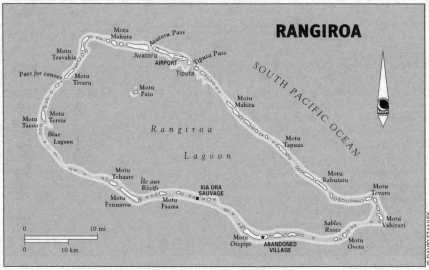

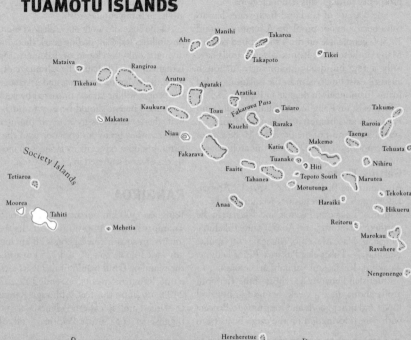

TUAMOTU ISLANDS

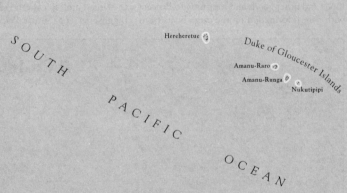

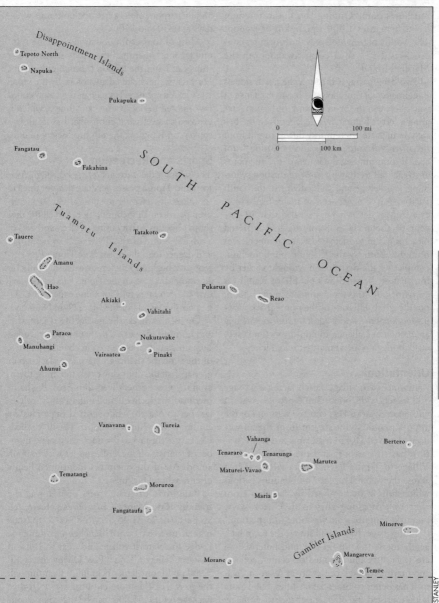

Disappointment Islands

Tepoto North

Napuka

Pukapuka

SOUTH PACIFIC OCEAN

0   100 mi
0   100 km

Fangatau

Fakahina

Tuamotu Islands

Tauere

Amanu

Hao

Tatakoto

Akiaki

Vahitahi

Pukarua

Reao

Paraoa

Manuhangi

Vairaatea

Nukutavake

Pinaki

Ahunui

Vanavana

Tureia

Vahanga

Tenararo   Tenarunga

Maturei-Vavao

Moruroa

Fangataufa

Maria

Bertero

Marutea

Tematangi

Morane

Gambier Islands

Mangareva

Temoe

Minerve

FRENCH POLYNESIA

brochures claim. Ontong Java in the Solomon Islands encloses 1,400 square km of lagoon. The world's biggest atoll—as the brochures concede—is 2,174-square-km Kwajalein in the Marshall Islands.

Two deep passages through the north side of Rangiroa's coral ring allow a constant exchange of water between the open sea and the lagoon, creating a fertile habitat. While lagoons in the Society Islands are often murky due to runoff from the main volcanic islands and pollution from coastal communities, the waters of the Tuamotus are clean and fresh, with some of the best swimming, snorkeling, and scuba diving in the South Pacific. You've never seen so many fish! However in May 1998 it was revealed that 80 percent of the reefs at Rangiroa had suffered bleaching due to increased water temperatures brought about by the El Niño phenomenon, completing the destruction wrought earlier by hurricanes. What draws people to Rangi (as everyone calls it) is the marinelife in the lagoon, not the coral. This one of the prime shark-viewing locales of the world. Most tourists to Rangiroa are French or Italian, and non-divers (and especially honeymooners) may get bored here.

Orientation

Rangiroa's twin villages, each facing a passage 500 meters wide, house 2,400 people. Avatoru village on Avatoru Pass is at the west end of the airport island, about six km from the airport itself. A paved 10-km road runs east from Avatoru past the airport and the Hôtel Kia Ora Village to Tiputa Pass. Tiputa village is just across the water. The accommodations listings which follow are arranged by category from west to east along this road. Check www.sejour-a-rangiroa.com for more information.

Both villages have small stores; the town hall, gendarmerie (tel. 96-03-61), and hotel school are at Tiputa, and the medical center, college, and marine research center are at Avatoru. Avatoru has better commercial facilities, but Tiputa is less touristed and offers the chance to escape by simply walking and wading southeast. **Gauguin's Pearl** (tel./fax 96-05-39, phcab@mail.pf; Mon.–Sat. 0830–1400), a pearl farm between Avatoru

and the airport, offers a free one-hour tour weekdays at 0830 and 1400.

Most of the accommodations face the tranquil lagoon rather than the windy sea, and large ships can enter the lagoon through either pass. For yachts, the sheltered anchorage by the Hôtel Kia Ora Village near Tiputa Pass is recommended (as opposed to the Avatoru anchorage, which is exposed to swells and chop). Far less English is spoken on Rangiroa than in the Society Islands.

Sports and Recreation

The strong tidal currents *(opape)* through **Avatoru** and **Tiputa passes** generate flows of three to six knots. It's exciting to shoot these 30-meter-deep passes on an incoming tide, and all the dive shops offer this activity using small motorboats or Zodiacs. Some of the dives tend to be longer and deeper than the norm. The Tiputa Pass current dive begins 45 meters down and is only for advanced divers; even the Tiputa Pass Shark Cave dive to 35 meters calls for some experience. Beginners should ask for the Motu Nuhi Nuhi dive.

On all the dives, the marinelife is fantastic, and humphead wrasses, manta rays, barracudas, dolphins, and sharks are seen in abundance. Most of the time the sharks are harmless black-tip or grey reef sharks (but don't risk touching them, even if you see other divers doing so). Big hammerhead sharks frequent Tiputa Pass from December to March, while spotted eagle rays are common from July to October. The dive schedules vary according to the tides, winds, and number of tourists on the atoll, and it's wise to book ahead. All of the operators mentioned below offer free hotel pickups.

Rangiroa's original scuba operator is the friendly **Raie Manta Club** (Yves Lefèvre, tel. 96-84-80 or 72-31-45, fax 96-85-60, http://raie mantaclub.free.fr), with branches near Rangiroa Lodge in Avatoru village and next to Pension Marie et Teina on Tiputa Pass. Diving costs CFP 5,900 pp for one tank, including a float through the pass. For the more enthusiastic, a 10-dive package is CFP 55,000 (can be shared by a couple and also used at Tikehau). Every dive is different (falling, pass, cave, undulating bottom, hollow, and night). Snorkelers can go along when practical, otherwise an introductory dive is CFP 6,500. Divers come from all parts of the world to dive with Yves and his highly professional seven-instructor team.

Rangiroa Paradive (Bernard Blanc, tel. 96-05-55, fax 96-05-50, www.chez.com/paradive) is next to Chez Glorine at Tiputa Pass. It's CFP 6,300 per dive; the package prices are CFP 30,000/58,000 for five/10 dives. Night dives are CFP 1,000 extra (minimum of five). You can ask for a small price reduction if you haven't booked ahead. Bernard isn't as aggressive about shark feeding as Yves but he does explore the shark caves and you'll see legions of sharks on his drift dives. He's obliging, hospitable, and one of the most highly qualified instructors in Polynesia. There's no provision for snorkelers here and divers must show their cards. Without a card you could still do an introductory dive for CFP 6,500.

The Six Passengers (Ugo Mazzavillani, tel. 96-03-05, fax 96-02-60, www.the6passengers .com) is in a hut between Chez Glorine and the Kia Ora. Ugo charges about the same as Yves and Bernard. Diving from a Zodiac is CFP 6,200/12,400/56,000 for one/two/10 tanks, night dives CFP 7,700, gear and pickups included. The name refers to the number of people he can take out each time. Snorkelers are not accepted, but a four-day CMAS certification course is offered at CFP 43,680.

TOPdive (tel. 96-05-60), on the beach just west of the Kia Ora, offers scuba diving at 0800, 1000, and 1400 (one/10 dives CFP 6,500/58,500). You can also use their 10-dive package at TOPdive centers on Moorea and Bora Bora.

The **Blue Dolphins Diving Center** (Junko Kida and Pascal Jagut, tel./fax 96-03-01, www .bluedolphinsdiving.com), based at the Hôtel Kia Ora Village, has Japanese-speaking monitors. Exploration/introductory dives are CFP 6,600/7,150.

Popular lagoon excursions include picnics to the **Blue Lagoon,** a fish-filled pool at Motu Taeoo, to the **Île aux Récifs,** a number of uplifted coral formations on the south side of the lagoon, to the **Sables Roses,** a stretch of pink sand at the southeast end of the lagoon, and to tiny **Motu Paio,** a mid-lagoon bird sanctuary. The waters of the lagoon can become rough when the wind is up, making these trips wet and even scary affairs.

Several companies offer a snorkel through the pass at CFP 4,200. A glass-bottom boat visit to **The Aquarium** at Motu Nuhi Nuhi near the Tiputa Pass with Tepa Matahi (tel. 96-84-48) is CFP 2,200. **Sharky Club Excursions** (tel. 96-84-73), at Chez Punua et Moana in Avatoru, organizes some good value trips starting at CFP 3,500. **Oviri Excursions** (Celine and Hugo, tel. 96-05-87) does excellent full day trips to Sables Roses at CFP 10,000 pp and to Île aux Récifs at CFP 7,500 pp (four-person minimum).

Accommodations

US$25–50: Rangiroa Lodge (Jacques and Rofina Ly, tel. 96-82-13, http://rangiroa.lodge .free.fr) in Avatoru has four rooms at CFP 4,240 double with shared bath or CFP 5,300 with private bath (plus CFP 200 for a fan, if desired). A place in one of the two three-bed dorms is CFP 1,800 pp. This is one of the few places with communal cooking facilities, though the proprietors also prepare meals upon request. The snorkeling just off the lodge is outstanding and they'll loan you gear if you need it. Divers from the adjacent Raie Manta Club often stay here.

Chez Nanua (Nanua and Marie Tamaehu, tel./fax 96-83-88), between the airport and Avatoru village, allows budget travelers to pitch their tents in a rather poor location at CFP 3,050 pp with two meals. The four simple thatched bungalows with shared/private bath are CFP 4,400/5,100 pp including two meals. You eat with the owners—a little fish and rice every meal. There's no hot water. Ask about bicycle and scooter rentals at Carole Pareo nearby.

US$50–100: Pension Henriette (Henriette Tamaehu, tel./fax 96-84-68), by the lagoon in Avatoru village, is a two-bungalow place charging CFP 5,400 pp with half pension. It can be a little noisy here but the food is excellent (especially the banana crêpes) and it's possible stop by for lunch even if you're staying elsewhere.

The son and daughter-in-law of the folks at Chez Nanua operate **Chez Punua et Moana** (Punua and Moana Tamaehu, tel. 96-84-73) in

Avatoru village. The three thatched bungalows are CFP 5,900 pp with half board. Camping is CFP 3,500 pp with half board. It's right by the road and can be noisy due to the activities of the surrounding village. Watch your gear here. For those who really want to get away, Punua can arrange overnight stays on Motu Teavahia. Otherwise all are welcome on the daily lagoon tours and "Sharky Club" excursions costing CFP 3,500 pp and up.

Pension Hinanui (René and Mareta Bizien, tel. 96-84-61), on a quiet beach near Avatoru, four km from the airport, has three bungalows at CFP 4,500/8,000/9,500 single/double/triple, plus CFP 2,500/3,500 pp for half/full board.

Pension Loyna (Loyna Fareea, tel. 96-82-09, www.membres.lycos.fr/pensionloyna), oceanside near Avatoru, has a large house with a dormitory and two rooms with shared bath on the mezzanine at CFP 5,565 pp, two rooms with shared bath downstairs at CFP 6,095 pp, and five rooms with private bath in two other buildings at CFP 6,625 pp. All prices include half board and Loyna speaks good English.

Next to Gauguin's Pearl on the lagoon between the airport and Avatoru is **Pension Cécile** (Alban and Cécile Sun, tel./fax 96-05-06) where the eight bungalows are CFP 4,500 pp, plus CFP 2,000 pp for half board (no cooking). Lobster is often on the menu. (Reader Rowland Burley writes that "this was the friendliest accommodation I found in French Polynesia. Cécile speaks excellent English, the units are spotlessly clean, and dinner is superb.") Alban does lagoon tours in his boat upon request. The beach in this vicinity is poor.

Pension Tuanake (Roger and Iris Terorotua, tel. 96-04-45, fax 96-03-29, www.tuanake.fr.st), by the lagoon next to Gauguin's Pearl two km west of the airport, has six thatched bungalows with bath (but no cooking facilities) at CFP 6,500/9,500 single/double (or CFP 10,500/15,500 with half board). Airport transfers are free.

The **Turiroa Village** (Olga Niva, tel./fax 96-04-27, pension.turiroa@mail.pf), less than a km west of the airport terminal, has four bungalows at CFP 6,000/8,000 for two/four persons. If required, half board is CFP 2,750 pp. No English is spoken.

Pension Martine (Martine and Corinne Tetua, tel. 96-02-51), by the lagoon near the airport terminal, has five fan-cooled bungalows with private bath and terrace (but no cooking) at CFP 6,500 pp with half board (lots of fresh fish). There's no single supplement if you're alone, and it's friendly, clean, and relaxed. Ask Corinne to show you around the family pearl farm.

Pension Marie et Teina (Tahuhu Maraeura, tel. 96-03-94, fax 96-84-44, rangiroa@mail.pf), behind Pension Glorine at Tiputa Pass, four km east of the airport, has six duplex garden rooms at CFP 6,500 pp and five thatched beach bungalows at CFP 7,500 pp, all including breakfast and dinner. The three three-bed dorms upstairs in a concrete house are CFP 3,500 including breakfast only. When things get crowded, a lounge is converted into another six-bed dorm. Communal cooking facilities are not provided. Transfers are free. This place gets mixed reviews.

Pension Lucien (Lucien and Esther Pe'a, tel. 96-73-55, http://pensionlucien.free.fr), near the pass in Tiputa village, offers three beach bungalows with private bath at CFP 6,600 pp with half board. Airport transfers are CFP 1,000 pp.

The **Pension Relais Mihiroa** (Maurice and Monique Guitteny, tel. 96-72-14, fax 96-75-13), in a coconut grove on Tiputa Island four km from the village, has four cubical bungalows with bath and terrace at CFP 7,200 for up to three people, plus CFP 2,400/3,900 pp for half/full board. Boat transfers from the airport are CFP 1,500 pp.

US$100–150: Pension Herenui (Victorine Sanford, tel./fax 96-84-71), next to the Raie Manta Club right in Avatoru village, four km from the airport, offers three thatched bungalows with private bath and terrace (but no cooking) at CFP 7,540 pp with breakfast and dinner.

The **Miki Miki Village** (tel. 96-83-83, fax 96-82-90), also known as the Rangiroa Village, is a rundown seven-bungalow resort on an unswimmable beach near Avatoru: CFP 11,000/19,000 single/double, including breakfast and dinner. It's not worth the price.

A five-minute walk west of the airport terminal is the **Ariitini Village** (Félix and Judith Tetua, tel. 96-04-41), previously known as Pension Félix, with nine beach bungalows at CFP 7,500 pp including breakfast and dinner.

A sister of the Henriette mentioned previously runs the popular **Pension Glorine** (Glorine To'i, tel. 96-04-05, fax 96-03-58, pensionglorine@ mail.pf), next to the wharf at Tiputa Pass, four km from the airport. The seven spacious thatched bungalows with private bath are CFP 7,500 pp including two meals (specialty fresh lagoon fish). Children under 13 are half price and bicycle rentals are available. Airport transfers are CFP 800. Nonguests can order meals here (reserve ahead).

US$150–250: Le Mérou Bleu (Friedrich Pierre and Sonya, tel. 79-16-82, http://le-meroubleu.ifrance.com), facing Avatoru Pass, has three thatched bungalows beginning at CFP 11,000/ 20,000 single/double with half board. For hot water add CFP 2,000 pp. Airport transfers are included. Some of Rangiroa's best surfing is just off their beach.

The **Raira Lagon** (Maxime and Pascale Boetsch, tel. 96-04-23, fax 96-05-86, www.rairalagon.pf), a bit over a km west of the airport terminal, offers 10 small thatched bungalows with private bath and fridge (but no cooking facilities) at CFP 21,600 double with half board and airport transfers. A few well-used bicycles are loaned free and it's right on the beach. Their beachfront restaurant is open to the public.

The **Rangiroa Beach Resort** (www.polynesian-resort-hotels.com), next to the Raira Lagon, reopened in late 2004 after being redeveloped by the Paladien hotel chain. Exact prices for the 38 bungalows were still unknown at press time.

Les Relais de Joséphine (Denise Thirouard, tel./fax 96-02-00, http://relaisjosephine.free.fr), facing directly onto Tiputa Pass, has three upscale bungalows with four-post beds and terrace at CFP 14,000/28,000 single/double, including tax, a light breakfast, dinner, and airport transfers. A third person pays CFP 10,500. Drinks are extra. Giant trees keep the mosquito-rich compound shady all day and the tall *fare* with their dysfunctional teak furnishings are consumately romantic. Dolphins frolic just offshore and the sound of the waves at night is wonderful (though

swimming would be dangerous due to the strong current). Several dive shops are nearby.

US$250 and up: Rangiroa's top resort is the **Hôtel Kia Ora Village** (tel. 96-03-84, fax 96-02-20, www.hotelkiaora.com), established in 1973 near Tiputa Pass, a bit over two km east of the airport by road. It's right on the best beach of this part of the island. The 30 beach bungalows are CFP 44,000 double, while the five larger garden bungalows are CFP 30,000, plus 11 percent tax. The 10 overwater units go for CFP 62,000. Add another CFP 7,400 pp for breakfast and dinner. Yachties anchored offshore are certainly not welcome to dingy in and use the facilities, but the pricey seafood restaurant is open to all (slow service, variable food, beautiful view). A wide range of lagoon excursions and activities are offered at higher than usual prices.

In 1991 the Kia Ora Village began offering accommodation in five thatched bungalows at **Kia Ora Sauvage** on Motu Avaerahi on the far south side of the lagoon. It's CFP 36,000 single or double, plus 11 percent tax, plus a compulsory three-meal plan at CFP 7,600 pp, plus CFP 8,000 pp for return boat transfers (two-night minimum stay). The boat leaves at 0900 daily, so you'll probably have to wait one night to go. Kia Ora Sauvage is a Robinson Crusoe experience most people rave about!

Food

Restaurant Le Kai Kai (tel. 96-03-39; no lunch Sun.), opposite Ana Gandy's pearl atelier west of the airport terminal, has a varied meat and seafood menu (main plates CFP 1,500–2,400). *Poisson cru* (CFP 1,100) is a good choice for lunch, and they have great desserts, like chocolate mousse, crème brûlée, and ice cream for around CFP 500. Their expressos come with chunks of dark chocolate. You eat on an outdoor terrace and the staff will switch on a fan to keep you cool.

Pizzeria Vaimario (tel. 96-05-96; closed Sun. and Mon.), on the ocean side of the road just west of the airport, has 10 tables on a tiled outdoor terrace and a couple more inside. There are hamburgers and sandwiches for lunch, and a more extensive menu at dinner. Try one of the exotic pizzas (CFP 1,600).

A great place for lunch is the **Relais** (no phone; Mon.–Sat. 0800–1500, Sun. 0530–0930), next to the wharf at Tiputa Pass on the Avatoru side. There's a nice terrace overlooking the lagoon, good atmosphere, and pleasant music. The menu includes a plat du jour (CFP 800), fried fish (CFP 1,000), *croques monsieur* grilled cheese (CFP 250), hamburgers (CFP 400), and other choices costing CFP 800–1,300. A large beer is CFP 350.

Services

The Banque de Tahiti (tel. 96-85-52) has a branch at Avatoru, while Banque Socredo (tel. 96-85-63) has branches at the *mairies* in both Avatoru and Tiputa. All branches are open limited hours according to a variable timetable (in Tiputa only on Mon., Tues., and Thurs.).

Post offices are found in Avatoru, Tiputa, and the airport. Taaroa Web (tel./fax 96-03-04, www.taaroa-web.com; daily 0830–1900), on the east side of the Hôtel Kia Ora Village, offers internet access at CFP 250 a quarter hour. They also sell black pearls.

There's a medical center (tel. 96-03-75) two km east of Avatoru, and an infirmary (tel. 96-73-96) at Tiputa. Dr. Guy Thirouard (tel. 96-04-44) has a private Cabinet Médical at Avatoru. It's prudent to drink bottled water on Rangiroa.

Getting There

Air Tahiti (tel. 96-03-41) flies Tahiti-Rangiroa several times daily (CFP 13,500 one-way). Five times a week a flight arrives direct from Bora Bora (CFP 21,500), but from Rangiroa to Bora Bora there's only a twice weekly flight. There's service four times a week from Rangiroa to Tikehau (CFP 4,600) and Manihi (CFP 9,200), weekly to Fakarava (CFP 4,600). A weekly flight operates from Rangiroa to Nuku Hiva and Hiva Oa in the Marquesas (CFP 25,500). Seats on flights to the Marquesas should be booked well in advance.

The motor vessel *Dory II* leaves Papeete every Monday at 1600 for Rangiroa (CFP 3,640), arriving Tuesday at 1800. It takes only 26 hours to go from Papeete to Rangiroa but 56 hours to return. Every 10 days the *Vai-Aito* departs Papeete for Rangiroa (CFP 5,050 including meals). To return to Papeete, ask about these vessels and the copra

boats *Rairoa Nui* and *Saint Xavier Maris Stella*. The *Aranui* stops at Rangiroa on the way back to Papeete from the Marquesas and you could disembark here. For more information on boats and flights to the Tuamotus, see Transportation in this chapter's Exploring the Islands section.

Archipels Croisieres (tel. 56-36-39, fax 56-35-87) offers two/three-night cruises around the Rangiroa lagoon on a 17.5-meter, eight-passenger catamaran at US$830/1,080 pp double occupancy (excluding airfare). It's a great way to explore the atoll and they'll go even if only two people reserve. When you consider that all meals and activities are included, it's no more expensive than staying at the Kia Ora.

Getting Around

There's no public transportation on Rangiroa although the scuba operators offer shuttles to their clients. To reach Tiputa village across Tiputa Pass from the airport island wait for a lift on the dock next to Chez Glorine (watch for dolphins in the pass). A boat ferrying school children across the Tiputa Pass leaves the airport side weekdays at 0600, returning from Tiputa at 1130 and 1600. The usual fee to be taken across is CFP 500 pp each way.

Europcar (tel./fax 96-03-28), with an office near Avatoru and a desk at the Kia Ora Village, has cars beginning at CFP 6,500/8,000 for four/eight hours, scooters at CFP 4,000/5,500, bicycles CFP 850/1,400. Two-person "fun cars" are slightly cheaper than the regular cars.

Avis (tel. 96-04-53, www.avis-tahiti.com) at the airport has cars at CFP 7,900/14,200 for one/two days including kms (collision insurance CFP 1,500 a day extra).

Arenahio Location (Carole Plovier, tel./fax 96-82-45, carpom@mail.pf), at Carole Pareo between the airport and Avatoru village, rents bicycles at CFP 700/1,300 a half/full day and scooters at CFP 3,800/5,200. Cars are available at CFP 6,000/8,000 and Carole speaks good English. Many of the pensions also rent bicycles.

Airport

The airstrip (RGI) is about six km from Avatoru village by road, accessible to Tiputa village by boat.

Most of the Avatoru pensions offer free airport transfers to those who have booked ahead (ask).

TIKEHAU

Rangiroa's smaller neighbor, Tikehau (400 inhabitants), is an almost circular atoll 26 km across with the shallow Passe de Tuheiava on its west side. Tuaherahera village and the airstrip share an island in the southwest corner of the atoll. Five pearl farms operate on Tikehau and tourism is growing fast. There's a far better choice of places to stay than you'll find on Manihi, and it's less developed than Rangiroa. Tikehau's beaches are unsurpassed.

All of the pensions organize boat trips to bird islands such as Puarua, picnics on a *motu*, snorkeling in the pass, visits to Eden Point, etc, costing CFP 3,500–8,000 pp.

Scuba diving (CFP 6,500) is available with the **Raie Manta Club** (Bertrand Varichon, tel./fax 96-22-53) based at the Tikehau Village. Prices are the same as those at the Raie Manta Club on Rangiroa and the 10-dive packages can be used at both centers. They'll show you huge manta rays, sea turtles, shark-infested caves, great schools of barracuda, and fabulous red reefs.

Accommodations

Pension Panau Lagon (Arai and Lorina Natua, tel./fax 96-22-99) sits on a white beach a few minutes walk from the airport. The four simple bungalows with bath are CFP 6,000 pp with breakfast and dinner. Camping may be possible.

Also in the direction away from the village and a few minutes beyond Pension Panau Lagon is **Chez Justine** (Justine and Laroche Tetua, tel. 96-22-87, fax 96-22-26) with two *fare* at CFP 6,500 pp with half board. Camping is CFP 2,500 pp with breakfast.

Pension Tematié (Nora Hoioré, tel./fax 96-22-65), near the airport, has three beach bungalows at CFP 7,500 pp plus six percent tax with half board.

The **Tikehau Village** (Caroline and Pa'ea Tefaiao, tel./fax 96-22-86), on the beach between the airstrip and the village, has nine *fare* starting at CFP 6,500 pp including two meals. Nonguests can order meals here.

Several residents of Tuherahera village provide rooms with shared bath in a family home at CFP 4,500–6,000 pp including breakfast and dinner. Among the people offering this are Isidore and Nini Hoiore (tel. 96-22-89) and Hélène Teakura (tel. 96-22-52).

The **Aito Motel Colette** (Colette Huri, tel. 96-22-47) in Tuherahera has five rooms with a shared kitchen at CFP 3,500 pp. The three *fare* are CFP 10,200/15,960 single/double with half board.

Pension Kahaia Beach (Merline Natua, tel. 96-22-77, 96-22-81), on the pink sands of Motu Kahaia between the village and the Pearl Beach Resort, has five *fare* at CFP 5,000 pp with half board and transfers. The owner doesn't speak English but hand gestures will do! The snorkeling is good and several other deserted *motu* are nearby.

In June 2001 the upscale **Tikehau Pearl Beach Resort** (tel. 96-23-00, fax 96-23-01, www.pearlresorts.com) opened on tiny Motu Tiano, a bit east of Motu Kahaia. There are 14 beach bungalows at CFP 38,000 single or double, plus 16 over water bungalows starting at CFP 52,000, plus 11 percent tax. Add CFP 6,900/9,800 pp for half/full board. Boat transfers are CFP 4,000 pp roundtrip. As if the excellent narrow beach wasn't enough, there's a small swimming pool. Diving is provided by the Blue Nui Dive Center (Carol Tilleffer, tel./fax 96-22-40, www.bluenui.com) on the wharf at the resort.

Getting There

Air Tahiti flies to Tikehau from Papeete (CFP 13,500) once or twice a day and from Rangiroa (CFP 4,600) four times a week. The airstrip is conveniently located a bit over a km east of Tuherahera village.

Every Monday at 1600 the motor vessel *Dory II* leaves Papeete for Tikehau, arriving the next morning at 1100. The return trip follows a roundabout route, so this service is only really practical eastbound. You can easily use it to go to Rangiroa, the next stop. You can also get to Tikehau (CFP 5,050 deck from Papeete, meals included) on the *Vai-Aito* (tel. 43-99-96, fax 43-53-04) every 10 days. These and other ships tie up to a lagoonside wharf.

FRENCH POLYNESIA

FAKARAVA

Fakarava is the second-largest Tuamotu atoll, about 250 km southeast of Rangiroa and 435 km northeast of Tahiti. A pass gives access to each end of this rectangular 60-by-25-km lagoon, which is dotted and flanked by 80 coconut-covered *motu*. There's spectacular snorkeling and drift diving in the passes or along the vertical dropoffs. Garuae Pass in the north is almost a km wide, nine meters deep, and the haunt of countless sharks, dolphins, barracuda, and rays. Tumakohua Pass in the south is smaller and accessible to snorkelers.

The French colonial administration for the Tuamotus moved here from Anaa in 1878 and Fakarava's Catholic church is one of the oldest in the group. Robert Louis Stevenson visited Fakarava aboard the yacht *Casco* in 1888 and spent two weeks living in a house near the church in the center of the village, Rotoava. French painter Henri Matisse visited briefly in 1930 and the beauty of the atoll influenced his art for years to come. The present airstrip, four km from village, only opened in 1995. About 500 people live on the atoll and a number of pearl farms have been established around the lagoon. Fakarava is still in the early stages of being developed for tourism.

Scuba Diving

Jean-Christophe Lapeyre operates the **Diving Center Te Ava Nui** (tel. 98-42-50, http://tuamotu.plongee.free.fr) at Rotoava. The spectacular Garuae Pass drift dive is for experienced divers only and shark feeding is unnecessary since the pass is already thick with sharks. Jean-Christophe's website provides details and many photos of Fakarava.

The **Fakarava Diving Center** (www.fakarava-diving-center.com) is run by Serge and Carine at Hôtel Le Maitai Dream who charge CFP 6,000/55,000 for one/10 dives.

Accommodations

Pension Havaiki Pearl (Joachim and Clotilde Petit-Dariel, tel./fax 98-42-16, http://chez.mana.pf/~havaiki), two km from the airport on a pot-holed road, has five nice bungalows at CFP 13,000/19,000/25,000 single/double/triple including full board and cold water showers (minimum stay three nights). Clotilde's meals are huge and tasty. The beach is good and a long pier points out into the lagoon toward Joachim's pearl farming shack. Kayaks and bicycles are loaned free.

The **Vahitu Dream** (Jacqueline Moeroa, tel. 98-42-63), on the beach next door, offers five basic rooms with shared bath at CFP 12,600 double including half board and taxes. Loud music is on in the snack bar all day and the folks here stay up late. It's used mostly by French scuba divers.

The least expensive place to stay is the **Relais Marama** (Marama Teanuanua, tel. 98-42-51), oceanside in Rotoava village, four km from the airstrip. The three rooms with shared bath in the main house are CFP 3,600/4,600/5,600 single/double/triple, otherwise it's CFP 4,400/5,400/6,400 for the garden bungalow. Cooking facilities are available and you can also camp here.

The three-star **Hôtel Le Maitai Dream Fakarava** (tel. 98-43-00, fax 98-43-01, www.lemaitai.com), seven km south of Rotoava, opened in 2003. The 30 units arranged in clusters of three range in price from CFP 43,500 double for a garden bungalow to CFP 53,950 for a premium beach bungalow, plus 11 percent tax. All meals are included and the restaurant/bar has a deck for sunset viewing.

At the other end of the atoll is the **Tetamanu Village** (Annabelle and Sané Richmond, tel. 43-92-40, fax 42-77-70, www.tetamanuvillage.pf). The six waterfront *fare* here are CFP 48,000 pp for three nights including all meals, activities, taxes, and airport transfers (1.5 hours each way by boat). A private bathing pontoon in the adjacent Tumakohua Pass facilitates snorkeling at slack tide. "Tetamanu Sauvage" on a small *motu* has another five beachfront fare at the same rates. Ask Sané to show you around his pearl farm.

Also near Tumakohua Pass, **Motu Aito Paradise** (Manihi and Tila Salmon, tel./fax 41-29-00, www.fakarava.org) offers rooms in a rustic thatched complex on a tiny coral *motu* at CFP 13,000 pp including all meals, transfers, and excursions (three-night minimum stay). Divers from Te Ava Nui often have lunch here after diving the pass. The sense of remoteness is perfect here. In Papeete, information is available from Salmon Aroma at Tattoo Tour Styles above Bar Le Taina, 303 boulevard Pomare.

Getting There

Air Tahiti flies from Papeete to Fakarava (CFP 14,500) six times a week with one flight going on to Rangiroa (CFP 5,800).

The supply boat *Vai-Aito* (tel. 43-99-96) leaves Papeete, Tikehau, Rangiroa, and Manihi for Fakarava about every 10 days. The voyage from Papeete costs CFP 17,675 deck, meals included. The ship returns directly to Papeete so you could use it to go back to Tahiti, but the eastbound trip is long and roundabout.

MANIHI

Manihi, 175 km northeast of Rangiroa, is also on the package tour circuit, with visions of white-sand beaches and cultured black pearls radiating from its glossy brochures. Unless you have a keen interest in pearl farming, scuba diving is the only reason to come. The accommodations are isolated and remarkably overpriced.

You can see right around Manihi's 6-by-30-km lagoon, and the 50,000 resident oysters on the 60 commercial pearl farms outnumber the 1,000 human inhabitants 50 to one. Due to the pearl industry, the people of Manihi have become more affluent than those on some of the other Tuamotu islands.

Turipaoa (or Paeua) village and its 50 houses face Tairapa Pass at the west end of a sandy strip just over a kilometer long. The airport island and main resort are just across the pass from Turipaoa, and many of the other *motu* are also inhabited.

Scuba Diving

Manihi Blue Nui (Stéphane Hamon, tel./fax 96-42-17, www.bluenui.com) at the Manihi Pearl Beach Resort offers year-round scuba diving on the outer reef walls. A one-tank dive is CFP 6,500 (or CFP 7,000 for night diving). Five/10-dive packages are CFP 30,000/60,000. Rental of a wetsuit or waterproof light is CFP 500. They'll

also take snorkelers on the boat at CFP 2,000 pp including mask and snorkel. Both PADI and CMAS certification courses are offered, otherwise a one-dive resort course is CFP 7,000.

It's exciting to shoot Tairapa Pass on the incoming tide, and since it's shallower than the passes at Rangiroa, you see more. Reef sharks are less common here but manta and eagle rays are often seen, as are countless Moorish idols. Just inside the lagoon at the mouth of the pass is a site called "The Circus" frequented by huge, science fiction–like rays with enormous socket eyes, and it's a fantastic experience to swim near them (also possible at Rangiroa).

The ocean drop-off abounds in gray sharks, Napoleon fish, giant jack fish, and huge schools of snappers, barracudas, and tuna. Each year, around late June or early July, thousands of marbled groupers gather here to breed in one of the most fascinating underwater events in the world. Among other favorite spots are "West Point" with fire, antler, and flower-petal coral in 65-meter visibility, and "The Break," where black-tip, white-tip, gray, and occasionally hammerhead sharks are seen.

Accommodations

The **Manihi Pearl Beach Resort** (tel. 96-42-73, fax 96-42-72, www.pearlresorts.com), by the lagoon one km from the airport, was known as the Kaina Village until a hurricane blew it away in 1993. Now rebuilt, the five standard beach bungalows are CFP 28,000 single or double, the 17 superior beach bungalows CFP 38,000, the 14 deluxe overwater bungalows CFP 52,000, and the five premium overwater bungalows CFP 60,000, all plus 11 percent tax. Add CFP 9,800 pp plus 10 percent tax for full board. Roundtrip airport transfers are CFP 2,200 pp (or walk it in 10 minutes). Almost all guests arrive on prepaid packages. There's a swimming pool facing the rather poor beach.

Nine km northeast of the airport is **Chez Jeanne** (Jeanne Huerta, tel. 96-42-90, fax 96-42-91), formerly known as Le Keshi, at Motu Taugaraufara. The two self-catering beach bungalows here are CFP 10,000 for up to three people, while the overwater unit is CFP 14,000 double (minimum stay two nights). Food, drinking water, and excursions are extra.

The **Vainui Perles Lodge** (Edmond and Vaiana Buniet, tel. 96-42-89, fax 96-43-30) is across the lagoon on Motu Marakorako. The six small duplex rooms with shared bath and one leaky-roofed beach bungalow go for CFP 17,600 double including meals. Bring a flashlight to be able to find the outhouse after they switch off the electricity at 2130. A free tour of the owner's pearl farm is offered. Airport transfers are CFP 1,000 pp.

Getting There

Manihi airport (XMH) is 2.5 km north of Turipaoa village by boat. Most Air Tahiti (tel. 96-43-34) flights to Manihi from Papeete (CFP 16,300) or Bora Bora (CFP 28,600) are via Rangiroa. Flights between Manihi and Rangiroa are CFP 11,000.

The motor vessels *Dory II* and *Vai-Aito* both travel from Papeete to Manihi (CFP 10,100 deck) regularly, a 46-hour trip. They enter the lagoon and tie up to a wharf at Turipaoa.

OTHER ISLANDS AND ATOLLS

Ahe

Ahe, 13 km west of Manihi, is often visited by cruising yachts, which are able to enter the 16-km-long lagoon through Tiarero Pass on the northwest side of the atoll. Tenukupara village is south across the lagoon. Facilities include two tiny stores, a post office, and a community center where everyone meets at night. Despite the steady stream of sailing boats, the 400 people are very friendly. All of the houses have solar generating panels supplied after a hurricane in the early 1980s. Only a handful of small children are seen in the village; most are away at school on Rangiroa or Tahiti. Many families follow their children to the main islands while they're at school, so you may even be able to rent a whole house. As well as producing pearls, Ahe supplies oysters to the pearl farms on Manihi.

The **Pension Coco Perle** (tel. 96-44-08, www.cocoperle.com), on Motu Maruaruki, 10 minutes by boat from the airport, has six bungalows at CFP 12,100 pp with half board and

shared bath or 13,800 pp with private bath. Airport transfers are included. Valérie et René at Ahe Plongée offer scuba diving on Ahe (see http://ahe.plongee.free.fr for details).

In 1998 the Foreign Legion constructed an airport on Ahe and Air Tahiti now has seven flights a week from Tahiti (CFP 17,200).

Anaa

Anaa is 424 km due east of Tahiti and it receives a weekly Air Tahiti flight from Papeete (CFP 15,600) continuing to Hao (CFP 15,200). Unlike most of the other atolls covered here, Anaa is part of the southern Tuamotu group that was out-of-bounds to non-French during the nuclear testing era. Devastating hurricanes hit Anaa in 1906 and 1983.

The 450 inhabitants live in five small settlements scattered around Anaa's broken coral ring and there's no pass into the shallow elongated lagoon. Anaa's tattooed warriors were once widely feared, yet this was the first Tuamotuan atoll to accept Christianity after a local missionary returned from training on Moorea in 1817. In 1845 an American named Benjamin Grouard converted the inhabitants to Mormonism. Catholic missionaries followed in 1851, leading to a mini-religious war and the banning of Mormon missionaries from the colony by the French authorities (they were not allowed to return until 1892). From 1853 to 1878 the French colonial administration of the Tuamotus was based here.

Joël Teaku operates **Toku Kaiga** (tel. 98-32-69 or 82-61-62) in Tokerau village, 400 meters from the airport on the northeast side of Anaa. The two bungalows here go for CFP 7,500/9,000 pp with half/full board.

Arutua

Numerous black pearl farms grace the 29-km-wide lagoon of this circular atoll between Rangiroa and Apataki. Rautini village near the only pass was rebuilt after devastating hurricanes in 1983, and among the 500 inhabitants are some locally renowned musicians and storytellers. **Pension Te Hinano** (Neri and Hinano Fau'ura, tel. 96-52-55) at Rautini has two rooms at CFP

6,000 pp including all meals. Arutua receives Air Tahiti flights from Papeete (CFP 14,600) three times a week. The airstrip is 30 minutes by boat north from the village (transfers CFP 2,000 pp roundtrip).

Hao

Hao Atoll (population 1,400) was visited by the Spaniard Quirós in 1606. Kaki Pass gives access to the 50-km-long lagoon from the north. The pass has been dredged to a depth of seven meters and medium-sized ships can enter and proceed eight km to the anchorage off Otepa village on the northeast side of the atoll.

Hao is strategically situated in the heart of French Polynesia, equidistant from Tahiti, Mangareva, and the Marquesas. From 1966 to 1996 a giant French air base on Hao served as the main support base for nuclear testing on Moruroa, 500 km southeast, allowing the French military to fly materials directly into the area without passing through Papeete's Faa'a Airport. Hao's 3,380-meter airport runway is the longest in the South Pacific, long enough to be considered a potential emergency landing site for the NASA space shuttles.

Prior to 1996 non-French visitors were forbidden to transit the atoll, but with the windup of nuclear testing on Moruroa in 1996, the French military base here has closed. Now moves are underway to convert Hao into a tax haven for foreign corporations! Some current Air Tahiti flights to Mangareva and the southern Tuamotus are via Hao.

Kaukura

A narrow pass gives limited access to Kaukura's shallow, 40-km-long lagoon, midway between Rangiroa and Fakarava. Air Tahiti has flights twice a week from Papeete to Kaukura (CFP 14,600). Accommodations are available at **Pension Rekareka** (Mrs. Titaua Parker, tel. 96-62-40, fax 96-22-39) in Raitahiti village, a km from the airstrip at the west end of the atoll. It's CFP 5,000 pp including meals in a six-room house in the village and they also have six self-catering *fare* on a *motu* at CFP 6,000 pp including meals. Fewer than 400 people live on Kaukura.

Makatea

Unlike the low coral atolls of the Tuamotus, Makatea, 230 km northeast of Tahiti, is an uplifted limestone block eight km long and 110 meters high. Gray cliffs plunge 50 meters to the sea. Phosphate was dug up here by workers with shovels from 1908 to 1966 and exported to Japan and New Zealand by the Compagnie française des Phosphates de l'Océanie. Between the world wars, 115,000 tons of raw ore was produced each year, increasing to 300,000 tons in the 1960s. During the first half of the 20th century this operation was the main element of the French Polynesian economy.

At one time 2,000 workers were present but today just over 50 people live here, hunting coconut crabs, fishing for lobster, and making copra. Five huge concrete pylons remaining from the mining era dominate the L-shaped landing on the west side of the island, and from here, a steep concrete ramp climbs to the central plateau. Half a dozen abandoned locomotives from the phosphate railway rust along the roadsides and near the contemporary villages, Temao, Moumu, and Vaitepau. Across the island at Moumu, a couple of km beyond Viatepau, is a long white beach. On the way there you'll pass a grotto with steps leading down to a pool. There are no flights to Makatea.

Mataiva

Tiny Mataiva, westernmost of the Tuamotus and 40 km from Tikehau, receives two Air Tahiti flights a week from Papeete (CFP 14,200). The airstrip is 400 meters from Pahua village on the west side of the atoll. The village is divided into two parts by a shallow pass crossed by a wooden bridge.

Only 10 km long and five km wide, Mataiva (population 225) is worth considering as an offbeat destination. A coral road covers most of the 35 km around the atoll with narrow concrete bridges over the nine shallow channels or "eyes" which gave the island its name (*mata* means eye, *iva* is nine). Exploratory mining of a 12-million-tonne phosphate deposit under the lagoon ended in 1982 and further mining has been strongly opposed by residents aware of the environmental devastation that would be inflicted.

Mr. Aroma Huri of Pahua runs a small resort called **Super Mataiva Cool** (tel./fax 96-32-53) on a white beach south of the pass. To stay in one of the four *fare* is CFP 5,500/10,000 single/double including two meals.

Ava Hei Pension (Benjamin Mahetau Lacour, tel. 96-32-39, fax 96-32-00), by the lagoon at Tevaihi 3.5 km south of the airport, offers three *fare* at CFP 7,000 pp plus six percent tax with half board. Lagoon excursions and airport transfers are included. Camping is CFP 1,500 pp.

Another place to stay is the **Mataiva Village** (Edgar Tetua, tel. 96-32-95), on a beach north of the pass, with five bungalows with bath at CFP 5,500 pp with half board. Camping is CFP 1,500 pp including breakfast. The guesthouses rent bicycles and arrange excursions.

Niau

The shark-free lagoon at Niau, 50 km southeast of Kaukura, is enclosed by an unbroken circle of land. Low-grade phosphate deposits on the island were judged too poor to mine. This lonely island of 450 souls does not receive any Air Tahiti flights.

Reao

No pass gives access to the lagoon of this easternmost inhabited Tuamotu atoll. In 1865 Catholic missionaries from Mangareva arrived on Reao and in 1901 they established a leper colony here that accepted patients from all over the Tuamotus and Marquesas until it was moved to Tahiti in 1914. Some 300 people live on the atoll today. Reao receives three Air Tahiti flights a month from Papeete (CFP 28,600).

Taiaro

In 1972 the private owner of Taiaro, Mr. W.A. Robinson, declared the atoll a nature reserve and in 1977 it was accepted by the United Nations as a biosphere reserve. Scientific missions studying atoll ecology sometimes visit tiny Taiaro, the only permanent inhabitants of which are a caretaker family. There are no flights to this isolated island northeast of Kauehi and Raraka.

Takapoto

Takapoto and Takaroa atolls are separated by only eight km of open sea, and on both the airstrip is within walking distance of the village. Air Tahiti flies three or four times a week from Papeete to Takapoto (CFP 17,200) and Takaroa (CFP 18,800). The freighter *Taporo VI* carries passengers from Papeete to Takapoto (36 hours, CFP 11,000/15,000 deck/cabin including meals) every two weeks, continuing on to the Marquesas. The more upscale *Aranui* also calls at Takapoto.

There's no pass into the lagoon but landing by whaleboat at Fakatopatere at the southwest end of the atoll is easy. Jacob Roggeveen lost one of his three ships on Takapoto's reef in 1722. Today the 16-km-long lagoon is a nursery for black pearl oysters and over 600 people live here.

The **Takapoto Village** (Pimati and Marie Toti, tel. 98-65-44, fax 98-64-81), right on the beach facing the lagoon a short walk from Fakatopatere, has two neat little bungalows with bath and fridge at CFP 6,700/12,400 single/double plus six percent tax including breakfast and dinner. A room with shared bath in the family home is CFP 1,000 pp cheaper.

Pension Tepuna Lagoon (tel./fax 98-64-75), on a pearl farm a 30-minute walk from the village, has one bungalow at CFP 6,500 pp plus six percent tax including breakfast and dinner. It's run by Miri and Tainui Ehu, who speak perfect English. Tainui makes jewelry from their pearls, while Miri creates pareus for sale to *Aranui* passengers. Airport transfers are free.

The **Faana Restaurant** (tel. 98-64-01) in Fakatopatere is a good place to have a cold beer.

Takaroa

This northeasterly atoll is 24 km long and up to eight km wide. The 30-meter-wide pass is barely three meters deep and the snorkeling here is second to none. On the outer reef near Takaroa's airstrip are two wrecks, one of a four-masted sailing ship here since 1906. Pearl farming flourishes in the Takaroa lagoon, which offers good anchorage everywhere. Since the appearance of this industry, visits by cruising yachts have been discouraged due to the danger of boats hitting poorly marked oyster platforms in the lagoon. Most of the 450 inhabitants of Teavaroa village belong to the Mormon church and their village is often called "little America." Tea, coffee, alcohol, and cigarettes are all frowned on but dog is considered a delicacy. *Marae* remains lurk in the bush.

Accommodations are available at **Chez Vahinerii** (Mrs. Vahinerii Temanaha, tel. 98-23-59), between the airport and the village, where a rooms with shared bath in the house is CFP 3,000 double. The one bungalow with cooking facilities is CFP 5,000/6,500 double/triple.

It's also possible to stay at a pearl farm on Motu Vaimaroro at the **Poerangi Village** (Eléonore Parker, tel. 98-23-82, fax 98-23-09). The three self-catering beach bungalows here are CFP 5,000/6,000 single/double. The food is good and the owners convivial.

Toau

Yachts can enter the lagoon at Toau, between Kaukura and Fakarava, though the pass is on the windward side. No flights land on Toau.

THE NUCLEAR TEST ZONE

The former French nuclear test site operated by the Centre d'Expérimentations du Pacifique until 1996 is at the southeastern end of the Tuamotu group, 1,200 km from Tahiti. The main site was 30-km-long Moruroa atoll, but Fangataufa atoll 37 km south of Moruroa was also used. In 1962 the French nuclear testing facilities in the Algerian Sahara had to be abandoned after that country won its independence, so in 1963 French president Charles de Gaulle officially announced that France was shifting the program to Moruroa and Fangataufa. Between 1966 and 1996 a confirmed 181 nuclear bombs, reaching up to 200 kilotons, were set off in the Tuamotus at the rate of six a year. By 1974 the French had conducted 41 *atmospheric* tests, 36 over or near Moruroa and five over Fangataufa. Five of these were megaton hydrogen bombs.

Way back in 1963, the U.S., Britain, and the USSR agreed in the Partial Test Ban Treaty to halt nuclear tests in the atmosphere. France chose not to sign. On June 23, 1973, the World Court urged France to discontinue the nuclear tests, which might drop radioactive material on surrounding territories. When the French government refused to recognize the court's jurisdiction in this matter, New Zealand Prime Minister Norman Kirk ordered the New Zealand frigate *Otago* to enter the danger zone off Moruroa, and on July 23 Peru broke diplomatic relations with France. On August 15 French commandos boarded the protest vessels *Fri* and *Greenpeace III*, attacking and arresting the crews.

In 1974, with opposition mounting in the Territorial Assembly and growing world indignation, French President Giscard D'Estaing ordered a switch to *underground* tests. Eighteen years and 134 tests later, as the Greenpeace *Rainbow Warrior II* confronted French commandos off Moruroa, French prime minister Pierre Bérégovoy suddenly announced on April 8, 1992, that nuclear testing was being suspended. President Boris Yeltsin had already halted Russian nuclear testing in October 1991, and in October 1992 U.S. president George Bush would follow suit by halting underground testing in Nevada. Despite the French moratorium, the testing facilities in the Tuamotus were maintained at great expense, and in June 1995 newly elected President Jacques Chirac ordered the testing to resume without bothering to consult the Polynesians.

On August 31, 1995, with the first test imminent, the Greenpeace ship *Rainbow Warrior II* reached Moruroa just over 10 years after its predecessor had been sunk by French terrorists at Auckland, New Zealand. As the ship crossed the 12-mile limit and launched six Zodiacs toward the French drilling rigs in the lagoon, the *Rainbow Warrior II* was boarded by French commandos who fired tear gas at the unresisting crew and smashed computers, generators, and the ship's engine. The MV *Greenpeace* was nearby in international waters at the time, and the French seized it too on the pretext that it had launched a helicopter that crossed the territorial limit. With the main protest vessels impounded and their crews deported, the French hoped they could carry on with the tests without further interference.

So on September 5, 1995, despite opposition from 63 percent of the French public and a large majority of Polynesians, the French military exploded the first of a planned series of eight bombs under Moruroa. This led to the worst rioting ever seen in French Polynesia as thousands of enraged Tahitians ran amok, ransacking Faa'a Airport and much of Papeete. The independence leader Oscar Temaru managed to calm the crowd, and the French brought in additional riot police to guard the capital. After a second blast on October 2 the South Pacific Forum carried out its threat to suspend France as a "dialogue partner."

In an attempt to deflect mounting worldwide condemnation, Chirac announced that the number of tests would be reduced from eight to six. Additionally, France, the U.S., and Britain said they would finally sign the protocols of the 1985 South Pacific Nuclear-Free Zone Treaty. The sixth and last test was carried out below Fangataufa atoll on January 27, 1996. Since then the facilities on Moruroa have been demolished and it's unlikely there will ever be another nuclear test in this area.

Moruroa

Obviously, an atoll, with its porous coral cap sitting on a narrow basalt base, is the most dangerous place in the world to stage underground nuclear explosions. This was not the initial intention. Moruroa was chosen for its isolated location, far from major population centers that might be affected by fallout. However by 1974, when atmospheric testing had to cease, the French military had a huge investment in the area. So rather than move to a more secure location in France or elsewhere, they decided to take a chance. Underground testing was to be carried out in Moruroa's basalt core, 500–1,200 meters below the surface of the atoll. Eventually 130 bombs were exploded below Moruroa and 10 below Fangataufa, making France the only nuclear state that has conducted tests *under* a Pacific island.

On September 10, 1966 President Charles de Gaulle was present at Moruroa to witness the atmospheric test of a bomb suspended from a balloon. Weather conditions caused the test to be postponed, and the following day conditions were still unsuitable, as the wind was blowing in the direction of inhabited islands to the west instead of toward uninhabited Antarctica to the south. De Gaulle complained that he was a busy man and could afford to wait no longer, so the test went ahead, spreading radioactive fallout across the Cook Islands, Niue, Tonga, Samoa, Fiji, and Tuvalu. Tahiti itself was the most directly affected island, but the French authorities have never acknowledged this fact.

Archive documentation published by the French weekly *Nouvel Observateur* in 1998 has confirmed that French defense officials knew very well that nearby islands such as Mangareva, Pukarua, Reao, and Tureia were receiving high doses of radiation during the 1966 tests, even as spokespersons publicly described the tests as "innocuous." France's radiological security service recommended at the time that the four islands be evacuated, but the newly discovered documents only note that "the hypothesis of an evacuation was excluded for political and psychological reasons."

A serious accident occurred on July 25, 1979, when a nuclear device became stuck halfway down an 800-meter shaft. Since army engineers were unable to move the device, they exploded it where it was, causing a massive chunk of the outer slope of the atoll to break loose. This generated a huge tsunami, which hit Moruroa, overturning cars and injuring seven people. After the blast, a crack 40 cm wide and two km long appeared on the surface of the island. As a precaution against further tsunamis and hurricanes, refuge platforms were built at intervals around the atoll. For an hour before and after each test all personnel had to climb up on these platforms.

By 1981 Moruroa was as punctured as a Swiss cheese and sinking two centimeters after every test, or a meter and a half between 1976 and 1981. In 1981, with the atoll's 60-km coral rim dangerously fractured by drilling shafts, the French switched to underwater testing in the Moruroa lagoon, in order to be closer to the center of the island's core. In 1987 the famous French underwater explorer Jacques Cousteau filmed spectacular cracks and fissures in the atoll as well as submarine slides and subsidence, and described the impact of testing on the atoll as creating "premature and accelerated aging." By 1988 even French officials were acknowledging that the 108 underground blasts had severely weakened the geological formations beneath Moruroa, and it was announced that, despite the additional cost involved, the largest underground tests would take place henceforth on nearby Fangataufa atoll. The military base remained on Moruroa, and small groups of workers and technicians were sent over to Fangataufa every time a test was made there.

The French government always claimed that it owned Moruroa and Fangataufa because in 1964 a standing committee of the Territorial Assembly voted three to two to cede the atolls to France for an indefinite period. This was never ratified by the full assembly, and French troops had occupied the islands before the vote was taken anyway. The traditional owners of Moruroa, the people of Tureia atoll, 115 km north, were not consulted and have never been compensated.

Impact

On June 21, 1987 Jacques Cousteau was present for a test at Moruroa and the next day he took water samples in the lagoon, the first time such independent tests had been allowed. Two samples collected by Cousteau nine km apart contained traces of cesium-134, an isotope with a half-life of two years. Though French officials claimed the cesium-134 remained from atmospheric testing before 1975, a 1990 study by American radiologist Norm Buske proved that this was not scientifically feasible, and that leakage from underground testing was the only possible explanation. Buske also found traces of cesium-134 in plankton collected in the open ocean, outside the 12-mile exclusion zone, indicating that the release of contamination into the Pacific from the numerous cracks and fissures had started.

A 1990 computer model of Moruroa developed by New Zealand scientists indicated that radioactive groundwater with a half-life of several thousand years may be seeping through fractures in the atoll at the rate of 100 meters a year and, according to Prof. Manfred Hochstein, head of

Auckland University's Geothermal Institute, "in about 30 years the disaster will hit us."

In July 1998 the International Atomic Energy Agency reported that about eight kilograms of plutonium and other dangerous elements still rest in sediments in the Moruroa and Fangataufa lagoons as a result of atmospheric testing and plutonium safety trials. With sea level rises, these sediments may eventually be swept into the ocean, but more worrisome are the tritium levels in the Moruroa lagoon, which are 10 times higher than those of the surrounding sea, a result of leakage from cavities created by the underground tests. In 1999, after years of secrecy and denials, France's Atomic Energy Commission (CEA) finally admitted that fractures exist in the coral cones of Moruroa and Fangataufa.

No one is allowed to visit Moruroa or Fangataufa without official approval and inspections by independent international observers are banned. Initially a detachment of foreign legionnaires kept watch over the abandoned wharf, airstrip, and concrete bunkers at the dismantled Moruroa test site while Fangataufa was abandoned. In January 2000 Admiral Jean Moulin, commander of the French forces in the territory, announced that the troops were being withdrawn over fears that a tsunami could be generated if the atoll's external coral cliffs were suddenly to collapse. Such an event would likely release a torrent of radioactivity into the Pacific Ocean and the CEA has installed satellite-controlled seismic sensors at the deserted site to give early warning of a collapse.

Unlike the U.S., which has paid millions of dollars in compensation money to the Marshallese victims of its nuclear testing program, France still refuses to acknowledge the obvious effects of its 41 atmospheric nuclear tests. From 1963 to 1983, no public health statistics were published in the territory, and now the rates of thyroid cancer, leukemia, brain tumors, and stillbirths are on the upswing in French Polynesia. The problem of seafood poisoning (ciguatera) in the nearby Gambier Islands is clearly related.

After the end of the testing, the Tahitian nongovernmental organization Hiti Tau surveyed 737 of the 12,000 Polynesians who worked at

Moruroa between 1966 and 1996, and found that many had experienced adverse health effects. Before being employed at the base, all workers at Moruroa had to sign contracts binding them to eternal silence and waiving access to their own medical records or to any right to compensation for future health problems. Yet in July 2001 the Association Moruroa e Tatou was founded, bringing together 1,160 former test site workers, and both they and a parallel group of over 900 French veterans are now demanding that their records be released and appropriate action taken. No official studies of this impact have been carried out as yet and no compensation has been paid. The archives are still closed. The story is far from over.

French radioactivity will remain in the Tuamotus for thousands of years and the future consequences of the tests are as uncertain as ever. The atolls remain wrapped in the same sinister mystery that has dogged them since 1966. (For more information on these matters, visit the website of the Centre de Documentation et de Recherche sur la Paix et les Conflits at www.obsarm.org.)

Gambier Islands

The Gambier (or Mangareva) Islands are just north of the tropic of Capricorn, 1,650 km southeast of Tahiti. The southerly location means a cooler climate. The archipelago, contrasting sharply with the atolls of the Tuamotus, consists of 10 rocky islands enclosed on three sides by a semicircular barrier reef 65 km long. In all, there are 46 square km of dry land. The Polynesian inhabitants named the main and largest island Mangareva, or "Floating Mountain," for 482-meter-high Mount Duff. Unlike the Marquesas, where the mountains are entirely jungle-clad, the Gambiers have hilltops covered with tall *aeho* grass. Black pearls are cultured on numerous platforms on both sides of the Mangareva lagoon. A local seabird, the *karako,* crows at dawn like a rooster.

History

Mangareva, which was originally settled from the Marquesas Islands before A.D. 1100, was the jumping-off place for small groups that discovered and occupied Pitcairn and perhaps Easter Island. In 1797 Capt. James Wilson of the London Missionary Society's ship *Duff* named the group for English Admiral James Gambier (1756-1833), a hero of the Napoleonic wars who had helped organize the expedition. France made the Gambiers a protectorate in 1871 and annexed the group in 1881.

Mangareva was the area of operations for a fanatical French priest, Father Honoré Laval of the Congregation for the Sacred Hearts. Upon hearing whalers' tales of rampant cannibalism and marvelous pearls, Laval left his monastery in Chile and with another priest reached the Gambiers in 1834. An old Mangarevan prophecy had foretold the coming of two magicians whose god was all-powerful, and Laval himself toppled the dreaded stone effigy of the god Tu on the island's sacred *marae.* He then single-handedly imposed a ruthless and inflexible moral code on the islanders, recruiting them as virtual slaves to build a 1,200-seat cathedral, convents, and triumphal arches—116 stone buildings in all—with the result that he utterly destroyed this once vigorous island culture and practically wiped out its people. During Laval's 37-year reign the population dropped from 9,000 to 500. You can still see his architectural masterpiece—the Cathedral of St. Michael with its twin towers of white coral rock from Kamaka and altar shining with polished mother-of-pearl—a monument to horror and yet another lost culture. The cathedral was built between 1839 and 1848 on the *ahu* of the island's principal *marae,* and Laval's colleague, Father François Caret, who died in 1844, lies buried in a crypt before the altar. In 1871 Laval was removed from Mangareva by a French warship, tried for murder on Tahiti, and declared insane.

Orientation

Most of the current 1,100 inhabitants of the

Gambiers live on 8-by-1.5-km Mangareva, of which Rikitea is the main village. A post office, seven small shops, a gendarmerie (tel. 97-82-68), an infirmary, schools, and a cathedral three times as big as the one in Papeete make up the infrastructure of this administrative backwater.

Sights

The tomb of Grégoire Maputeoa, the 35th and last king of Mangareva (died 1868), is in a small chapel behind the cathedral. Follow the path behind the church to the top of the hill and go through the gate on the left (close it after you as dogs dig up the graves). Among the walled ruins of Rouru convent in Rikitea one can pick out the chapel, refectory, infirmary, and a dormitory for 60 local nuns. On the opposite side of Rikitea is a huge nuclear-fallout shelter called the "Maison Nucléaire" built during the French atmospheric testing at Moruroa.

A 28-km road runs around Mangareva offering ever-changing views. At the north end of the island it passes St. Joseph's Chapel (1836) at Taku, place of worship of the Mangarevan royal family. The south coast of Mangareva is one of the most beautiful in Polynesia, with a tremendous variety of landscapes, plants, trees, smells, and colors.

The white sands of **Aukena** make a good daytrip destination by boat. The Church of St. Raphael here is the oldest in the Gambier Islands and to the south are the ruins of the Rehe Seminary (1840). The Church of Notre-Dame-de-la-Paix (1844) on abandoned **Akamaru** has twin towers added in 1862. Solitary **Makaroa** is a barren, rugged 136-meter-high island.

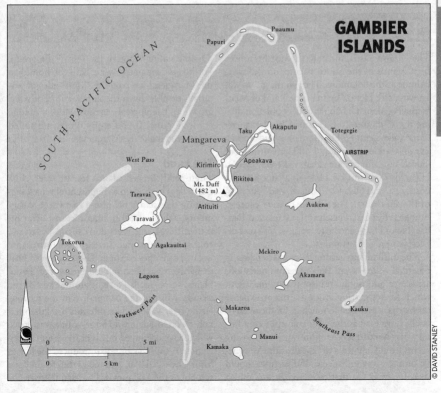

FRENCH POLYNESIA

© DAVID STANLEY

St. Gabriel Church (1868) on **Taravai** has a neo-Gothic facade decorated with seashells. In a cliffside cave on the uninhabited island of **Agakauitai** the mummies of 35 generations of cannibal kings are interred.

Accommodations

Chez Pierre et Mariette (tel. 97-82-87) near the wharf has three rooms at CFP 4,400 pp with half board.

Pension Bianca et Benoit (tel./fax 97-83-76, biancabenoit@mail.pf) is a modern two-story house with three rooms at CFP 6,180 pp including two meals. It's just above Rikitea and the view across to Aukena is lovely.

Five km north of the village is **Chez Jojo** (Jocelyne and Joseph Mamatui, tel./fax 97-82-61) with two rooms CFP 6,000 pp including two meals. Camping is possible here.

Tara Etu Kura (tel. 97-83-25) by the lagoon charges CFP 8,500 pp including all meals, plus CFP 1,000 pp for airport transfers.

Transportation

The airstrip (GMR) is on Totegegie, a long coral island eight km northeast of Rikitea. Arriving passengers pay CFP 600 pp each way for the boat ride to the village. The weekly Air Tahiti flights from Papeete (CFP 28,600 one way) are either nonstop or via Hao. Coming/going, remember the one-hour time difference between Tahiti and Mangareva.

The supply ships *Nuku Hau* and *Taporo V* from Papeete are only monthly. Large vessels can enter the lagoon through passes on the west, southwest, and southeast. Mr. Ioane Anania (tel. 97-82-92), nicknamed "Siki," offers speedboat charters and fishing trips.

The Marquesas Islands

The Marquesas Islands are the northernmost high islands of the South Pacific, on the same latitude as the Solomons. Though the group was known as Te Henua Enana (The Land of Men) by the Polynesian inhabitants, depopulation during the 19th and 20th centuries has left many of the valleys empty. The 10 main islands form a line 300 km long, roughly 1,400 km northeast of Tahiti, but only six are inhabited today: Nuku Hiva, Ua Pou, and Ua Huka in a cluster to the northwest, and Hiva Oa, Tahuata, and Fatu Hiva to the southeast. The administrative centers, Atuona (Hiva Oa), Hakahau (Ua Pou), and Taiohae (Nuku Hiva), are the only places with post offices, banks, gendarmes, etc.

The difficulty in getting there has kept many potential visitors away. Budget accommodations are scarce and public transport is nonexistent, which makes getting around a major expense unless you're prepared to rough it. Of the main islands, Hiva Oa has the most colorful recent history but Nuku Hiva is more varied. Cruising yachts from California often call at the Marquesas on their way to Papeete, and yachties should steer for Hiva Oa first to enjoy the smoothest possible sailing through the rest of the group. For hikers prepared to cope with the humidity, the Marquesas are paradise. Multitudes of waterfalls tumble down the slopes, and eerie overgrown archaeological remains tell of a golden era long gone. If you enjoy quiet, unspoiled places, you'll like the Marquesas.

The Land

These wild, rugged islands feature steep cliffs and valleys leading up to high central ridges, sectioning the islands off into a cartwheel of segments, which creates major transportation difficulties. Large reefs don't form due to the cold south equatorial current though there are isolated stretches of coral. The absence of protective reefs has prevented the creation of coastal plains, so no roads go right around any of the islands. Most of the people live in the narrow, fertile river valleys. The interiors are inhabited only by hundreds of wild horses, cattle, and goats, which have destroyed much of the original vegetation. A Catholic bishop introduced the horses from Chile in 1856, and today they're almost a symbol of the Marquesas. The islands are abundant with lemons, tangerines, oranges, grapefruit, bananas, mangoes, and papayas. Taro and especially breadfruit are the main staples. Birdlife is rich, and the waters around the Marquesas teem with lobster, fish, and sharks.

The subtropical climate is hotter and drier than that of Tahiti. July and August are the coolest months. The deep bays on the west sides of the islands are better sheltered for shipping, and the humidity is lower there than on the east sides, which catch the trade winds. The precipitation is uneven, with drought some years, heavy rainfall the others. The southern islands of the Marquesas (Hiva Oa, Tahuata, Fatu Hiva) are green and humid; the northern islands (Nuku Hiva, Ua Huka, Ua Pou) are brown and dry.

Pre-European Society

Marquesan houses were built on high platforms *(paepae)* scattered through the valleys (and still fairly easy to find). Every tribe had a rectangular ceremonial plaza *(tohua)* where important festivals took place. Archaeologists have been able to trace stone temples *(me'ae,* called *marae* elsewhere in French Polynesia), agricultural terraces, and earthen fortifications *('aka'ua)* half hidden in the jungle, evocative reminders of a vanished civilization. Then as now, the valleys were isolated from one another by high ridges and turbulent seas, yet warfare was vicious and cannibalism an important incentive. An able warrior could attain great power. Local hereditary chiefs exercised authority over commoners.

The Marquesans' artistic style was one of the most powerful and refined in the Pacific. The ironwood war club was their most distinctive symbol, but there were also finely carved wooden bowls, fan handles, and tikis of stone and wood, both miniature and massive. The carvings are noted for the faces: the mouth with lips parted and the bespectacled eyes. Both men and women wore carved ivory earplugs. Men's entire bodies were covered with bold and striking tattoos, a practice banned by the Catholic missionaries. Stilts were used by men in ceremonies and by boys for racing and mock fighting. This was about the only part of Polynesia where polyandry was common. There was a strong cult of the dead: the bodies or skulls of ancestors were carefully preserved. The northern Marquesas islands may have been inhabited as early as 300 B.C., and both Hawaii (around A.D. 200) and Easter Island (around A.D. 300) were colonized from here.

European Contact

The existence of these islands was long concealed from the world by the Spanish, to prevent the English from taking possession of them. The southern group was found by Álvaro de Mendaña in July 1595 during his second voyage of exploration from Peru. He named them Las Marquesas de Mendoza after his benefactor, the Spanish viceroy. The first island sighted (Fatu Hiva) seemed uninhabited, but as Mendaña's *San Jerónimo* sailed nearer, scores of outriggers appeared, paddled by about 400 robust, light-skinned islanders. Their hair was long and loose, and they were naked and tattooed in blue patterns. The natives boarded the ship, but when they became overly curious and bold, Mendaña ordered a gun fired, and they jumped over the side.

Then began one of the most murderous and shameful of all the white explorers' entries into the South Pacific region. As a matter of caution,

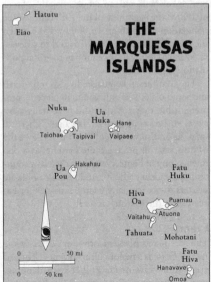

THE MARQUESAS ISLANDS

© DAVID STANLEY

Mendaña's men began shooting natives on sight, in one instance hanging three bodies in the shore camp on Santa Cristina (Tahuata) as a warning. They left behind three large crosses, the date cut in a tree, syphilis, and over 200 dead Polynesians. When Captain Cook arrived at Tahuata in 1774 it soon became obvious that knowledge of the earlier Spanish visit had remained alive in oral traditions, and Cook and his crew were shunned.

The northern Marquesas Islands were "discovered" by Joseph Ingraham of the American trading vessel *Hope* on April 19, 1791. After that, blackbirders, firearms, disease, and alcohol reduced the population. American whalers called frequently from 1800 onwards. Although France took possession of the group in 1842, Peruvian slavers kidnaped some Marquesans to South America in 1863 to work the plantations and mines. Those few able to return thanks to diplomatic lobbying by their French protectors brought a catastrophic smallpox epidemic. The Marquesans clung to their warlike, cannibalistic ways until 95 percent of their number had died—the remainder adopted Catholicism. (The Marquesas today is the only island group of French Polynesia with a Catholic majority.) From 80,000 at the beginning of the 19th century, the population fell to about 15,000 by 1842, when the French "protectors" arrived, and to a devastated 2,000 by 1926. Even today the total population is just 8,000.

The Marquesan language, divided into north and south dialects, is only about 50 percent comprehensible to a Tahitian and is actually a bit closer to Rarotongan and Hawaiian. There's a small separatist movement here that believes the Marquesas will receive more benefits as a distinct colony of France, or failing that, as a country independent of Tahiti. And just to complicate matters, twice as many Marquesans live in Papeete as in the Marquesas itself.

Events

The Marquesas Islands Festival or *Matava'a o te Henua Enata* is a major cultural event celebrated every four years in December with dancing, singing, drumming, and sports, plus handicraft displays and feasts. Aside from strengthening and reviving traditional knowledge and skills, numerous archaeological sites have been restored or rebuilt in preparation for these events. Previous festivals have been at Ua Pou (1987), Nuku Hiva (1989), Hiva Oa (1991), Ua Pou (1995), Nuku Hiva (1999), and Hiva Oa (2003). Future festivals will be on Ua Pou (2007) and Nuku Hiva (2011).

Getting There

Direct international flights to Nuku Hiva have been discussed for years, but nothing much has been done and an expensive roundtrip from Tahiti is still required. An **Air Tahiti** ATR flies from Papeete to Nuku Hiva daily (3.5 hours, CFP 24,000) with one of the flights via Rangiroa. Ask about Air Tahiti's "Extension Marquises" pass, which allows return flights from Papeete to Nuku Hiva and Hiva Oa for CFP 45,000 when purchased in combination with another Air Tahiti pass.

Dornier flights between Nuku Hiva and Ua Huka (CFP 6,600) operate weekly, connecting with one of the ATR flights from Papeete. From Nuku Hiva to Ua Pou (CFP 6,600) the flights are three times a week. To Hiva Oa (CFP 11,000) it's five times a week. No flight goes straight from Ua Pou to Ua Huka—you must backtrack to Nuku Hiva. Tahuata and Fatu Hiva are without air service. All flights are heavily booked. Coming or going, remember the 30-minute time difference between Tahiti and the Marquesas.

Two ships, the *Aranui* and *Taporo VI,* sail regularly from Papeete, calling at all six inhabited Marquesas Islands. The more convenient and comfortable of the two by far is the freighter *Aranui,* which does roundtrip voyages custom designed for tourists flown in from the U.S. and Europe. These trips cost cruise-ship prices and the other main interisland ship, *Taporo VI,* is much cheaper at CFP 22,000/32,000 deck/cabin including food one-way from Papeete to any Marquesan island. However, it's basic and only a few hours are spent in each port. The ships tie up to the wharves at Taiohae, Atuona, Vaipae'e, and Hakahau; at Tahauta and Fatu Hiva, passengers must go ashore by whaleboat. In stormy weather, the landings can be dangerous. For more information on boats and flights, turn to Transportation in this chapter's Exploring the Island section.

Getting Around

To island hop within the Marquesas, you can fly with Air Tahiti or try using the ships mentioned above, if they happen to be going where you want to go. Ask at local town halls about the supply boat *Ka'oha Nui,* a large luxury yacht owned by the territory that often sails among the islands picking up school children on holidays, etc. Private boats run from Taiohae to Ua Pou fairly frequently, and there are municipal boats from Atuona to Tahuata and Fatu Hiva at least once a week. Chartering boats interisland is extremely expensive, and to join a regular trip you just have to be lucky, persistent, and prepared to wait. You can also island-hop by helicopter if you've got the money.

Getting around the individual islands can be a challenge as there's no organized public transportation other than expensive airport transfers, and due to the condition of the roads, rental cars are limited to a few pricey vehicles at Taiohae and Atuona. It's fairly easy to hire a chauffeur-driven vehicle on Hiva Oa, Nuku Hiva, Ua Huka, and Ua Pou, but expect to pay CFP 15,000–20,000 a day. Since this amount can be shared among as many people as can fit inside, you'll want to join or form a group. While making your inquiries, keep your ears open for any mention of boat tours as these are often no more expensive than land tours.

Hitchhiking is complicated because many of the private vehicles you see out on the roads double as taxis, and drivers who depend on tourists for a large part of their incomes are unlikely to be eager to give rides for free. An option for hardy backpackers is just to count on having to walk the whole way and accept any lifts that happen to be offered. It's too far to walk in one day from Nuku Hiva airport to Taiohae or from Atuona to Pua-ma'u, but many other stretches can be covered on foot. If you're fit you can walk from Taiohae to Taipivai and from Taipivai to Hatiheu on Nuku Hiva, and from Atuona to Ta'aoa or the airport on Hiva Oa. Almost everywhere on Fatu Hiva, Tahuata, Ua Huka, and Ua Pou is accessible on foot, provided you've got the time and strength. If you pack a tent, food, and sufficient water, you'll be self sufficient and able to see the islands on a shoestring budget.

NUKU HIVA

Nuku Hiva is the largest (345 square km) and most populous (2,375 inhabitants) of the Marquesas. Taiohae (population 1,700) on the south coast is the administrative and economic center of the Marquesas. It's a modern little town with a post office, a hospital, a town hall, a bank, grocery stores, street lighting, and several hotels. Winding mountain roads lead northeast from Taiohae to Taipivai and Hatiheu villages or northwest toward the airport. In the center of the island Mt. Tekao (1,224 meters) rises above the vast, empty Toovii Plateau.

Taiohae Bay is a flooded volcanic crater guarded by two tiny islands called The Sentinels. Ua Pou is clearly visible across the waters. Though open to the south, Taiohae's deep harbor offers excellent anchorage. Cruising yachts toss in the hock on the east side of the bay, while the *Aranui* and *Taporo* tie up to a wharf at the southeast end of town. Take care with the drinking water at Taiohae. Unfortunately, many beaches around Nuku Hiva are infested with sandflies called *no-nos* that give nasty bites (the bugs disappear after dark). Luckily, Hiva Oa is free of these pests.

Sights of Taiohae

Taiohae's new post office is on a slight plateau in the heart of the official quarter, with the **Residence** of the subdivisional administrator just below toward the beach and the old **Administrative Center** across the street. On a grassy knoll topped by a navigational light above these buildings is the site of **Fort Collet,** which offers a sweeping view of Taiohae Bay. Nothing remains of Porter's original fort overlooking what he called Massachusetts Bay. Just north of this hill above the old marina is the colonial jail.

The **Monument to the Dead obelisk** (1928), marked by an anchor and cannon, is west along the waterfront past the bank.

Two towers retained from an earlier church give access to the open courtyard of **Notre-Dame**

Cathedral (1974) on the west side of central Taiohae. The cathedral's interior is notable for its fine woodcarvings, including a massive wooden pulpit bearing the symbols of the four evangelists. The floor behind the pulpit is paved with flower stones from Ua Pou. Among the outstanding wooden Stations of the Cross carved by Damien Haturau, note especially Station No 1 which depicts Jesus in the Garden of Breadfruit (instead of the Garden of Olives).

Across a small bridge just west of the cathedral is the **Temehea Tohua,** also known as the Tohua Piki Vehine, created for the Marquesas Islands Festival in 1989. Among the modern tikis on this platform are the figures of Temoana and Vaekehu, who were designated king and queen of the island by the French in 1842.

Next to a small cemetery 600 meters further west along the waterfront is the wooden **Typee Memorial** (1842–1992) by Séverin Kahe'e Taupotini (who also carved the cathedral's pulpit).

At the southwest end of the bay, just around corner from the Nuku Hiva Village Hôtel, is the **Boutique and Musée Hôtel Keikahanui** (tel. 92-03-82, rose.corser@mail.pf; donations) run by American art collector Rose Corser. Rose and her late husband Frank opened the original Keikahanui Inn in 1979, which in 1999 became the Keikahanui Pearl Lodge with Rose remaining an investor. A good part of her museum collection is on loan from Taiohae's bishop and other local residents. Her boutique displays a tasteful selection of Marquesan handicrafts, including Fatu Hiva tapa. Prices are comparable to those at other outlets around town. Many stone- and woodcarvers work on Nuku Hiva, and their wooden tikis, bowls, ukuleles, ceremonial war clubs, and paddles are keenly sought after.

The road now leaves the bay and climbs two km over the ridge to secluded **Haaotupa Bay,** also called Colette Bay, a nice picnic spot.

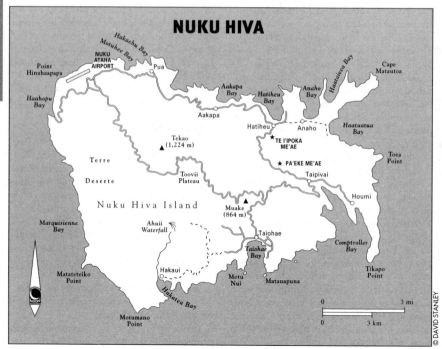

West of Taiohae

At Hakaui, 15 km west of Taiohae, a river runs down a narrow steep-sided valley. Fantastic 350-meter **Ahuii Waterfall,** highest in the territory, drops from the plateau at the far end of the valley, four km from the coast. It's a two-hour walk from Hakaui to the waterfall with a few thigh-high river crossings after rains (guide not required). The trail passes many crumbling platforms, indicating that the valley was once well populated. If you swim in the pool at the falls beware of falling pebbles. A boat from Taiohae to Hakaui would cost CFP 15,000 and up return, but an overgrown 12-km switchback trail also crosses the 535-meter ridge from above Haaotupa Bay to uninhabited Hakaui). You'll need to be adventurous and good at finding your own way to follow it (allow four hours each way between Taiohae to Hakaui).

Above Taiohae

For a sweeping view of Taiohae Bay, hike up to Muake (864 meters) on the ridge due north of town. A steep concrete road zigzags seven km to the point where the airport and Taipivai roads divide. Turn left toward the airport, then left again into the forest. There was once a Marquesan fort near where the radio tower presently stands. This is a favorite takeoff point for paragliders and groups from the *Aranui* have a picnic lunch here. Further west toward the airport is a market gardening area and agricultural station on the 900-meter-high **Toovii Plateau.** Herds of cattle range across the pine-covered plateau.

Sports and Recreation

Xavier Curvat's **Centre Plongée Marquises** (tel./fax 92-00-88; office hours Wed.–Fri. 1430–1700, Sat. 0900–1200), at the old marina in Taiohae, offers scuba diving daily at 0800 for CFP 5,500/10,000/45,000 for one/two/10 dives including gear. A maximum of eight peo-

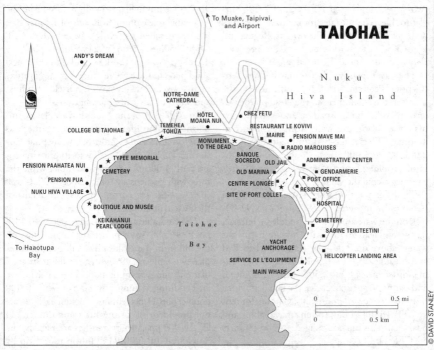

TAIOHAE

Nuku Hiva Island

To Muake, Taipivai, and Airport

ANDY'S DREAM

NOTRE-DAME CATHEDRAL

HÔTEL MOANA NUI

CHEZ FETU

RESTAURANT LE KOVIVI

COLLEGE DE TAIOHAE

TEMEHEA TOHŪA

MAIRIE

PENSION MAVE MAI

MONUMENT TO THE DEAD

RADIO MARQUISES

TYPEE MEMORIAL

BANQUE SOCREDO

OLD JAIL

ADMINISTRATIVE CENTER

PENSION PAAHATEA NUI

CEMETERY

OLD MARINA

GENDARMERIE

PENSION PUA

CENTRE PLONGÉE

POST OFFICE

NUKU HIVA VILLAGE

SITE OF FORT COLLET

RESIDENCE

BOUTIQUE AND MUSÉE

HOSPITAL

KEIKAHANUI PEARL LODGE

Taiohae

CEMETERY

SABINE TEIKITEETINI

Bay

YACHT ANCHORAGE

To Haaotupa Bay

HELICOPTER LANDING AREA

SERVICE DE L'EQUIPEMENT

MAIN WHARF

0   0.5 mi

0   0.5 km

© DAVID STANLEY

FRENCH POLYNESIA

ple are taken out every day, so book the day before. They also fill tanks for yachties at CFP 1,000 each. Xavier arrived in 1979 and he has thoroughly explored the archipelago during his years here. There's not much coral to be seen around Nuku Hiva but the underwater caves and spectacular schools of hammerhead sharks and pygmy orcas compensate. Snorkelers are welcome when space is available and the orcas are easily seen this way. The dive shop sells carvings and crafts.

Horseback riding is offered by Jean Paul and Sabine Teikiteetini (tel. 92-05-68), who live near the helicopter landing area above the main wharf in Taiohae. In the local area it's CFP 5,000 a half day, and rides from Taiohae to Taipivai are possible.

Accommodations

Pension Mave Mai (tel. 73-76-01, tel./fax 92-08-10, pension-mavemai@mail.pf), up the steep road between the old jail and Radio Marquises from near the old marina, has six rooms in a two-story building at CFP 6,200/7,200 single/double. The upstairs rooms have balconies with great views of bay. The owners, Regina and Jean-Claude, can provide meals and organize a variety of excursions at the usual rates.

The least expensive place to stay is **Chez Fetu** (Cyprien Peterano, tel. 92-03-66), just up the hill from the Monument to the Dead on the waterfront, off Taipivai Road behind Magasin Kamake, a 10-minute walk from the wharf in Taiohae. The three-bed bungalow is CFP 2,000/4,000/6,000 single/double/triple. Communal cooking facilities are available and there's a terrace facing the valley.

The friendly, two-story **Hôtel Moana Nui** (Charles Mombaerts, tel. 92-03-30, fax 92-00-02), on the waterfront in the middle of Taiohae, has seven clean rooms with private bath (hot water) above their popular restaurant/bar. Bed and breakfast is CFP 6,500/7,000 single/double, other meals CFP 2,500 each. Mosquitoes and bar noise are drawbacks, the excellent views from the terrace a definite plus. Cars are for rent at CFP 10,000 a day (often unavailable) and boat excursions can be arranged. Airport transfers are CFP 4,000.

Andy's Dream (André Teikiteetini, tel. 92-00-80) is at Hoata, about a km up from the Temehea Tohua. The small bungalow with bath is CFP 3,500 pp including breakfast or CFP 7,500 pp with all meals. The price of the bungalow is okay if you're able to cook your own food but you'll hear a lot of rooster noise at night. Andy's taxi tours are not the cheapest.

Pension Paahatea Nui (Justin and Julienne Mahiatapu, tel./fax 92-00-97), next to the Nuku Hiva Village Hôtel, has only a sign which reads "Sculpture La Maison Verte." It's up the road running inland from near the small cemetery beside the Typee Memorial. The two larger rooms with private bath are CFP 3,400 pp, while the four rooms with shared bath go for CFP 3,000 pp. The two bungalows are CFP 4,400 pp. Breakfast is included but use of the common kitchen is CFP 500 pp. Camping in the grassy yard is CFP 1,500 pp.

The rather rundown **Nuku Hiva Village Hôtel** (Bruno and Gloria Gendron, tel. 92-01-94, fax 92-05-97, nukuvillage@mail.pf), opposite the yacht anchorage on the west side of Taiohae Bay, has six thatched *fare* with private bath at CFP 6,500/7,500/8,500 single/double/triple, plus CFP 3,800 pp a day for breakfast and dinner. A local band plays in the large restaurant some Saturday nights. Excursions by 4WD, horseback riding, and scuba diving can be arranged.

In 2002 part of the Nuku Hiva Village compound came under separate management as **Pension Pua** (tel. 92-06-87, www.puaexcursions.pf). Their six bungalows without kitchens are CFP 4,000/5,500 single/double, while the three with kitchens are CFP 5,500/7,500. Check their website for current prices and details of their excursions.

The **Keikahanui Pearl Lodge** (tel. 92-07-10, fax 92-07-11, www.pearlresorts.com), just up the hill from the Nuku Hiva Village, was completely rebuilt in 1999 with a small but spectacular cliffside swimming pool. The 20 attractive air-conditioned bungalows start at CFP 29,000 double, plus 11 percent tax. Cooking facilities are not provided, so for breakfast and dinner add CFP 6,900 pp. Airport transfers arranged by the hotel are CFP 9,000/15,000 pp roundtrip by road/helicopter. The Keikahanui is named after a tattooed chief.

Food

The **Hôtel Moana Nui** (tel. 92-03-30) on the waterfront is famous for its pizza (CFP 1,000–1,500). It's a popular place to eat and drink.

Restaurant Le Kovivi (tel. 92-00-14; closed Sun.), near Banque Socredo, has a nice porch overlooking the bay. The plat du jour is around CFP 1,500, a large beer CFP 650.

If you're lucky, you might be able to buy fresh vegetables at the Saturday morning market at the old marina in Taiohae. Be there by 0500 as not much will be left at 0600. The only fresh produce available at the various supermarkets is potatoes and garlic (fresh veggies are easier to find on Hiva Oa).

Information

Tourist information is available from Comité Tourisme Nuku Hiva (Déborah Kimitete, tel. 92-08-24, tourisme@marquises.pf), at the Subdivision du Service de l'Urbanisme in the old jail (back door) between the *mairie* and the post office. They sell good topographical maps of the Marquesas at CFP 1,500.

Radio Marquises broadcasts from Taiohae over 101.3 MHz with the Réseau France Outre-Mer (RFO) news in French at 0700 and 1230.

Services

Central Taiohae boasts a Banque Socredo branch (tel. 92-03-63; weekdays 0730–1130/1330–1600). The post office on the east side of town sells telephone cards you can use at the public phone outside and at several other locations around the island. The post office also has public computer terminals for internet access at reasonable rates and sells the Tahiti newspapers.

Don't have your mail sent c/o poste restante at the post office as it will be returned via surface after 15 days. Instead have it addressed c/o Rose Corser, B.P. 21, 98742 Taiohae, Nuku Hiva, French Polynesia (tel. 92-03-82, fax 92-00-74). In a pinch, Rose will provide internet access at her Boutique and Musée below the Keikahanui Pearl Lodge at CFP 500 per 15 minutes.

The gendarmerie (tel. 92-03-61) is just up the road to the left of the post office, while the public hospital (tel. 92-03-75) is to the right. The Taiohae gendarmes invariably insist on yachties posting their arrival bonds, if they haven't already done so. A private dentist, Dr. Pierre Puech (tel. 92-00-83; weekdays 0730–1200), is next to Héli-Inter near the *mairie.*

Transportation

Air Tahiti (tel. 92-03-41) is in a poorly marked office behind Heli-Inter near the *mairie.*

Information on the *Ka'oha Nui, Meherio,* and other government boats can be obtained from the Service de l'Equipment next to the main wharf at Taiohae.

The only public transportation on Nuku Hiva is the expensive airport transfer. It's possible to walk from Taiohae to Taipivai and Hatiheu in two days if you're fit, camping or staying at local pensions along the way. A road now links Hatiheu to the airport via Aakapa and Pua.

Island tours by Land Rover are the usual way of getting around, but get ready for some astronomical charges, such as CFP 20,000 for a visit to Hatiheu. Car rentals often come with a driver and thus cost taxi prices. An example of this is **Teiki Transports** (Mr. Lucien Puhetini, tel. 92-00-90) which offers chauffeur-driven cars. To rent a car without a driver for something approaching normal rates, ask at the Hôtel Moana Nui (tel. 92-03-30), though their vehicles are often all taken.

Héli-Inter Marquises (tel. 92-02-17, heliconuku@mail.pf), next to the Mairie de Taiohae, does helicopter transfers from Taiohae to the airport or Hatiheu at CFP 7,500 pp. The helicopter will take pre-booked passengers from Hatiheu to the airport for the usual CFP 7,000, so it's not necessary to return to Taiohae. There are occasional trips from Taiohae to Ua Pou at CFP 12,500 pp, but only charters go to the other islands. In Taiohae, the helicopters use a heliport near the main wharf. The baggage allowance is 15 kg (or 20 kg with an international ticket).

Airport

Nuku Ataha Airport (NHV) is in the arid Terre Déserte at the northwest corner of Nuku Hiva,

32 km from Taiohae along a twisting dirt road over the Toovii Plateau. Upon arrival from Papeete or Rangiroa turn your watch ahead 30 minutes. A restaurant and hotel are near the terminal. The main drawback to flying into Nuku Hiva is the cost of airport transfers, which run CFP 4,000 pp each way by 4WD Toyota Landcruiser for the 2.5-hour drive or CFP 7,500 pp each way by helicopter. When shopping for woodcarvings during your stay on Nuku Hiva keep in mind the problem of getting the stuff back to Papeete. While waiting for your flight it's worth examining the excellent Marquesan low-relief woodcarvings made to decorate the airport's bar and shop when the airport was built in 1979.

Taipivai

Several hundred people live at Taipivai, a five-hour, 16-km walk from Taiohae over the Col Teavanui (576 meters). Vanilla grows wild throughout this valley. At Hooumi, on a fine protected bay near Taipivai, is a truly magical little church. The huge *tohua* of Vahangeku'a at Taipivai is a whopping 170 by 25 meters. Eleven great stone tikis watch over the **Pa'eke Me'ae,** a couple of km up the Taipi Valley toward Hatiheu then up the slope to the right. Robert Suggs excavated this site in 1957. About two km farther up the road to Hatiheu is a monument to the left of the road marking the spot where Herman Melville spent a month with his tattooed sweetheart Fayaway in 1842. In his novel, *Typee* (his spelling for Taipi), he gives a delightful account of the life of the great-grandparents of the present inhabitants.

By the river in Taipivai village, **Chez Martine Haiti** (tel. 92-01-19, fax 92-05-34) has two bungalows at CFP 2,000/3,500 single/double. You can cook for yourself or order dinner at CFP 2,000 pp. Call ahead as this pension was reported to have temporarily closed.

Tata Thomas at **Snack Heiau** (tel. 92-06-13), near the landing on the river in the center of Taipivai village, has one basic room for rent behind the snack bar (price negotiable).

Hatiheu and Anaho

From Taipivai it's another 12 km via the Col Teavaitapuhiva (443 meters) to Hatiheu on the north coast. Some spectacular falls are seen in the distance to the left of the road near the mountain pass. A statue of the Virgin Mary stands on a rocky peak high above Hatiheu Bay and its black sand beach. (Yachts are better off anchoring in protected Anaho Bay than here.) Hatiheu was destroyed by a tsunami in 1946 but 350 people live there today.

The restored **Hikoku'a Tohua** is a bit over a kilometer from Hatiheu back toward Taipivai. Several of the tikis on the structure were added during the 1989 Marquesas Islands Festival while others are old (notice the phallic fertility statue at the entrance on the left). In the jungle a kilometer farther up the road is the **Te I'ipoka Me'ae** where many human sacrifices were made to the goddess Te Vana'uau'a. The victims were kept in a pit beneath a huge sacred banyan tree until their turn arrived to be consumed at cannibal feasts. Up the steep wooded slope from here is the overgrown **Kamuihei Tohua** with petroglyphs. These sites are among the largest and most intriguing in the Marquesas.

Anaho is two km east of Hatiheu on horseback or foot over a 217-meter pass (no road). It's one of the most beautiful of Nuku Hiva's bays, with a powdery white beach and some of the finest snorkeling in the Marquesas (lovely coral and the possibility of seeing turtles or reef sharks).

From Anaho it's an easy 45-minute walk east along the south side of the bay and over the low isthmus to uninhabited **Haatuatua Bay** where you could camp wild. Ancient Marquesan stone platforms are hidden in the bush here (go inland on one of the grassy strips near the south end of the beach till you find a southbound trail). No one lives there, though wild horses are seen.

In Hatiheu village, **Chez Yvonne Katupa** (tel. 92-02-97, fax 92-01-28, hinakonui@mail.pf), also known as Pension Hinako Nui, offers five pleasant bungalows without cooking facilities or hot water at CFP 4,500/7,000 single/double, breakfast included. The bungalows are set in their own garden across a small bridge from Yvonne's restaurant, facing the beach on Hatiheu Bay. Passengers off the *Aranui* enjoy a superb fish and lobster lunch at Yvonne's. Ask to see her collection of artifacts at the *mairie*. It's possible to

rent sit-on-top kayaks here at CFP 500/1,500/
2,500 an hour/half day/full day or to hire horses
at CFP 5,000 a day. Yvonne arrange transfers
from Hatiheu to the airport (75 km) by 4WD at
CFP 5,000 pp.

You can also stay at **Te Pua Hinako** (Juliette
Vaianui, tel. 92-04-14), also known as Chez Juliette, at the northwest end of the beach at Anaho.
The two rooms with shared bath are CFP 2,500
pp with breakfast, or CFP 5,500 pp with all meals.

Juliette's son Raymond operates **Kaoha Tiare**
(Raymond Vaianui, tel. 92-00-08), next to Te
Pua Hinako. The five bungalows with bath are
CFP 2,500/5,000 single/double, plus CFP
3,000 pp for all meals. Juliette and Raymond
hosted TV crews from *Survivor* for several
months in late 2001.

UA POU

At 105 square km, Ua Pou is the third-largest
Marquesan island. This spectacular, diamond-
shaped island lies about 40 km south of Nuku
Hiva and it's very arid. Ua Pou is the only island
in the Marquesas with the sort of towering volcanic plugs seen on Moorea and Bora Bora. One
of these sugarloaf-shaped volcanic plugs inspired
Jacques Brel's song "La Cathédrale" and the name
Ua Pou itself means "the pillars." Mount Oave
(1,203 meters), highest point on Ua Pou, is often
cloud-covered.

The island's population of over 2,000 is larger
than that of Hiva Oa. The main village is Hakahau on the northeast coast, with solid concrete
streets, government services, and the only port. In
1988, 500 French foreign legionnaires rebuilt
the breakwater at Hakahau, and ships can now tie
up to the concrete pier.

Sights

The first stone church in the Marquesas was
erected at Hakahau in 1859, and the present
Church of Saint-Etienne (1981) has a pulpit
shaped like a boat carved from a single stump
by a group of sculptors. The wooden cross in
the church is by Damien Haturau.

The **Tenai Paepae** in the center of the village
was restored for the 1995 Marquesas Islands Fes-

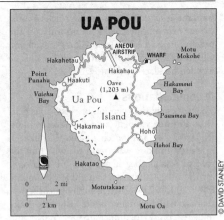

tival, the same occasion that saw the inauguration
of the small **Musée de Ua Pou** at the south end
of Hakahau.

Lovely **Anahoa Beach** is a scenic 30-minute
walk east of the marina, but unfortunately the
beach is infested with *no-nos*. There's a superlative
bird's-eye view from the cross overlooking Hakahau on the ridge halfway there.

South of Hakahau

A road leads south from Hakahau to a beach beyond Hohoi. On 88-meter-high **Motu Oa** off
the south coast, millions of seabirds nest.

The road from Hohoi to **Hakatao** on the
southwest coast crosses a high pass and the steep
descent to Hakatao is only possible in the dry
season. The track between Hakatao and **Hakamaii** can only be covered by canoe, hoof, or on
foot (a four-hour walk). You can drive the rest of
the way around the island.

West of Hakahau

West of Hakahau the road runs to the airport
(10 km), Hakahetau (16 km), and Haakuti (22
km). Sea turtles lay their eggs on the white sands
of uninhabited **Hakanahi Beach** between the
airport and Hakahetau, and large sharks wait
offshore to feed on the hatchlings (swimming
not advisable). You can often see the sharks from
the road above the beach.

Around 200 people live in the charming small
village of **Hakahetau.** Local handicrafts are made

from the *kea pua* (flower stone), a black volcanic stone with yellow streaks found only on the beaches here. Ask for Jean Marc Nguyen van Chinh (tel. 92-53-93), who produces unique wooden necklaces and bracelets.

Accommodations

The best established pension in Hakahao is **Pension Pukuéé** (Hélène and Doudou Kautai, tel./fax 92-50-83, http://chez.mana.pf/~pukuee), just a few minutes walk from the wharf on the road to Anahoa Beach. Set on a hill overlooking the village, the seven shared-bath rooms are CFP 3,000/5,500 single/double, plus six percent tax. Children under 12 are half price, under four free. Breakfast/dinner are CFP 500/2,500. Yachties often order seafood meals here. Airport transfers are CFP 2,000 per car (up to five passengers). Readers have liked it here.

Pension/Snack Vehine (Claire Teikiehuupoko, tel. 92-50-63), two blocks east of the Tenai Paepae, has two rooms for rent at CFP 3,000 pp. The restaurant (closed Sun.) serves good meals at the CFP 700–1,100 range with *poisson cru* at CFP 750. Claire also runs the island's traditional dance group (notice the photos along the bar). It's the best place to eat and drink on the island.

Pension Vaitiare (tel. 92-50-95), next to a general store at the western entrance to Hakahau from the airport, offers three rooms with bath at CFP 5,000 double including breakfast. Other meals are CFP 800–900. Make this your last choice.

Pension Chez Dora (Madame Dora Teikiehuupoko, tel./fax 92-53-69), in a quiet location south of town at the top of the hill beyond the museum, has three rooms at CFP 3,710 pp and two bungalows at CFP 4,240 pp, breakfast included. Dinner is CFP 2,000 pp. The room downstairs has a private bath, while those upstairs share a bath. Airport transfers are CFP 1,500 pp return.

In Hakahetau, ask for Étienne Hokaupoko (no phone) lives up on the hillside, a 10-minute walk from the port. His son lives next to the Protestant church in the village and should be able to provide information. In the past, Étienne has accommodated visitors at the usual rates and

you'll probably be welcome to stay with him and his wife. Étienne is currently working on an Marquesan-English dictionary and he knows many stories he's only too happy to share. Yachties often drop in to sign his guest book.

Food

CETAD (tel. 92-53-83) operates a culinary school at the Collège de Ua Pou opposite the beach not far from the wharf in Hakahau. Fridays at noon the students prepare an excellent lunch (CFP 1,500–2,000), which you can enjoy if you reserve a few days ahead.

Shopping

An Artisanat shop near the wharf at Hakahau sells local carvings and shell jewelry. Several woodcarvers work in Hakahau village—just ask for *les sculpteurs*. If you're buying, shop around at the beginning of your stay, as many items are unfinished and you should allow the time to have something completed.

Information and Services

Motu Haka (Georges "Toti" Teikiehuupoko, tel. 92-53-21) is a cultural organization that promotes Marquesan language instruction, archaeological projects, and traditional arts while rejecting cultural domination by Tahiti. The Marquesas Islands Festival is one of Motu Haka's projects. You can contact Toti through Pension Chez Dora.

The Banque Socredo (tel. 92-53-63), *mairie*, and a post office are all adjacent opposite the defunct market and not far from the beach. The gendarmerie (tel. 92-53-61) is a bit south. Infirmaries are in Hakahau, Hakatao, and Hakamaii. Six or seven stores are to be found in Hakahau.

Getting There

Ua Pou's Aneou airstrip (UAP) is on the north coast, 10 km west of Hakahau via a rough road over a ridge. It's in a valley just back from a long black beach between Hakahau and Hakahetau. The pensions in Hakahau offer airport transfers for CFP 1,500–2,000 pp return. You can reach Air Tahiti in Hakahau at tel. 92-53-41.

A launch from Nuku Hiva to Hakahau (1.5 hours each way, CFP 4,000 one-way or CFP 6,000 for a roundtrip the same day) operates irregularly. It's better to check on this a few days before.

UA HUKA

Ua Huka lies 35 km east of Nuku Hiva and 56 km northeast of Ua Pou. Crescent-shaped Ua Huka is the surviving northern half of an ancient volcano and its 575 inhabitants reside in the truncated crater in the south. Mount Hitikau (884 meters) rises northeast of Hane village. Vaipae'e is the main village of the island, although the hospital is at Hane.

Goats and wild horses range across this arid, 83-square-km island, while the tiny islands of Teuaua and Hemeni, off the southwest tip of Ua Huka, are a breeding ground for millions of *kaveka* (sooty terns). Sadly, local residents use these flat islands surrounded by sheer cliffs as a source of eggs.

Archaeological excavations by Prof. Y.H. Sinoto in 1965 dated a coastal site on Ua Huka to A.D. 300, which makes it the oldest in French Polynesia; two pottery fragments found here suggest that the island was probably a major dispersal point for the ancient Polynesians. Sinoto believes the migratory paths of Ua Huka's terns may have led the ancient Polynesians on their way to new discoveries.

Sights

Between the airport and Vaipae'e is a plantation that has been converted into a **Botanical Garden** (weekdays 0700–1430, free) complete with an aviary. Unfortunately the plants are not labeled.

Near the post office in Vaipae'e is a small but admirable **Musée Communal** (weekdays 0700–1400, free) of local artifacts and seashells, and replicas made by local artist Joseph Tehau Va'atete. Many other woodcarvers are active here. The craft shop adjacent to the museum only opens when tour groups are present.

In Hane is a **Centre Artisanal/Musée de la Mer,** by the beach just below the hospital. Three small tikis cut from red rock are in a mango for-

est up the valley behind Hane, a 25-minute walk from the Auberge Hitikau.

Accommodations

Chez Alexis (Alexis Scallamera, tel. 92-60-19, fax 92-60-12) in Vaipae'e village, a bit toward the wharf from the post office, is a two-room house with shared bath at CFP 4,700 pp including half board. You're also welcome to cook your own food. Alexis can arrange horseback riding (CFP 5,000) and boat excursions.

The **Mana Tupuna Village** (Teiki Taiaapu, tel. 92-60-08, fax 92-61-01) offers three bungalows on the hillside above the road on the north side of Vaipae'e at CFP 6,000/11,000 single/double including breakfast and dinner. Teiki or *le petit chef* is an affable guy.

Also in Vaipae'e is **Chez Christelle** (Christelle Fournier, tel./fax 92-60-85), a four-room house with shared bath at CFP 2,000 pp, plus CFP 1,000/2,000 for breakfast/dinner. It's run by the Air Tahiti agent and is down by the river on the north side of town.

In Hane village, the **Auberge Hitikau** (Céline and Jean Fournier, tel./fax 92-61-74) offers three rooms with shared bath next to their restaurant at CFP 2,500/4,000 single/double with breakfast. Lobster is served in their large restaurant at CFP 2,500—*Aranui* passengers often enjoy a meal here.

Also worth checking is **Chez Maurice et Delphine** (Maurice and Delphine Rootuehine, tel./fax 92-60-55) at Hokatu village, 13 km from the airport. The three rooms with shared bath in the family residence above their store in the village are CFP 2,200 pp with breakfast or CFP 5,200 pp with all meals. They also have three bungalows with private bath on a hill some distance away at CFP 2,700 pp with breakfast, or CFP 5,700 pp with all meals. Maurice can arrange a rental car.

Getting There

The airstrip (UAH) is on a hilltop between Hane and Vaipae'e, six km from the latter. The pensions generally provide free airport transfers. The Air Tahiti number is tel. 92-60-85. The *Aranui* enters the narrow fjord at Vaipae'e and anchors. It's quite a show watching the ship trying to turn around.

HIVA OA

Measuring 40 by 19 km, 318-square-km Hiva Oa (population 1,900) is the second largest of the Marquesas and main center of the southern cluster of islands. Mount Temetiu (1,276 meters), highest peak in the Marquesas, towers above Atuona to the west. Steep ridges falling to the coast separate lush valleys on this long crescent-shaped island. Ta'aoa, or "Traitors'," Bay is a flooded crater presently missing its eastern wall, while Puama'u sits in a younger secondary crater. The administrative headquarters for the Marquesas group has switched back and forth several times: Taiohae was the center until 1904, then it was Atuona until 1944, then Taiohae took over once again.

Atuona

The **Musée Gauguin** (admission CFP 400) in central Atuona displays 24 colorful reproductions of Gauguin's paintings created in 1997 and 1998 by Alin Marthouret (born 1945). In 1991 a replica of Gauguin's thatched "Maison du Jouîr" (House of Pleasure) was built next to the museum and a few reproductions of his prints are inside. Jacques Brel's aircraft *Jojo* is also on the grounds. Handicrafts are sold at the Fare Artisanal here. The *paepae* platforms near the museum were built for the Marquesas Islands Festival in December 1991. If the museum is closed when you arrive, ask for Jo Reus who lives nearby and has the key.

In 2003 Hiva Oa hosted its second Marquesas Islands Festival and a new **Cultural Center and Museum** was erected in the center of town to mark the centenary of Gauguin's death. The original well used by Gauguin during his stay here is on the site.

Back on the main street is **Magasin Gauguin** where Gauguin left an unpaid wine bill when he died. Go up the hill from beside the nearby gendarmerie and take the first fork in the road to the left to reach **Calvary Cemetery,** which hosts the graves of Jacques Brel (1929–1978) and Paul Gauguin (1848–1903). Gauguin's leading detractor, Monseigneur R.J. Martin (1849–1912), is buried under a large white tomb surrounded by a metal fence, higher up in the cemetery than Gauguin. The views of Atuona from here are excellent.

Other sights worth seeking out if you have the time include the **Catholic church** with its fine carved doors and interior visible through the open walls, and the Salle des Marriages at the **Mairie de Atuona** which contains another large Gauguin reproduction by Marthouret.

Chanson singer Jacques Brel lived at Atuona from 1975–1978. He intended to build his home on a ridge overlooking the entire valley, but died before the work could be done. The **Brel**

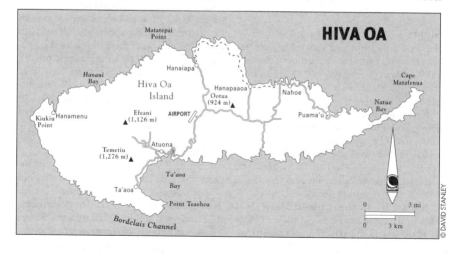

HIVA OA

Matatepai Point · Hanaui Bay · Hanaiapa · Hiva Oa Island · Hanapaaoa Ootua (924 m) · Nahoe · Cape Matafenua · Natue Bay · Efeani (1,126 m) · AIRPORT · Puama'u · Kiukiu Point · Hanamenu · Temetiu (1,276 m) · Atuona · Ta'aoa Bay · Ta'aoa · Point Teaehoa · Bordelais Channel · 0 3 mi · 0 3 km

© DAVID STANLEY

FAMOUS RESIDENTS OF ATUONA

Atuona was made forever famous when Paul Gauguin came to live here in 1901. Despite the attentions of his 14-year-old mistress, Vaeoho, he died of syphilis a year later at age 55 and is buried in the cemetery above the town. When Tioka, Gauguin's neighbor, found him stretched out with one leg hanging over the side of his bed, he bit him on the head as the Marquesans do to see if he really was dead. No, there was no doubt. *"Ua mate Koke!"* he cried, and disappeared. Gauguin was constantly in conflict with the colonial authorities, who disapproved of his heavy drinking sessions with the locals. Just a week before his death, Gauguin was summarily convicted of "libel of a gendarme in the course of his official duties," fined, and sentenced to three months in prison.

The famous Belgian *chanson* singer Jacques Brel and his companion Maddly Bamy came to the Marquesas aboard his 18-meter yacht, the *Askoy II*, in 1975. Jacques decided to settle at Atuona and sold his boat to an American couple. Maddly, who had been a dancer on her native Guadeloupe, gave dancing lessons to the local girls, while Jacques ran an open-air cinema. His plane, nicknamed *Jojo,* was kept at Hiva Oa airport for trips to Papeete, 1,500 km southwest. The album *Brel 1977* on the Barclay label includes one of his last songs, "Les Marquises." In 1978, chainsmoker Brel died of lung cancer and was buried in Atuona cemetery near Gauguin.

Belvédère is now accessible off the airport road, about six km out of Atuona. A plaque bears the inscription *Veux-tu que je te dise, Gémir n'est pas de mise, Aux Marquises.* The view from here is superb.

The beach at Atuona is poor and for better swimming, take the road six km southwest along the bay to the black beach at **Ta'aoa.** A big restored *tohua* with several *me'ae* platforms and a basalt tiki is found a bit over a kilometer up the river from there. This intriguing site was also restored for the festival in 2003.

Accommodations

The **Mairie de Atuona** (tel. 92-73-32, fax 92-74-95, communehivaoa@mail.pf) rents five well-equipped bungalows behind the town hall and post office at CFP 2,800/3,300 single/double. These have cooking facilities and private bath but they can only be booked directly at the *mairie* during business hours (weekdays 0730–1130/1300–1600). Ask for Claire.

Pension Gauguin (André Teissier, tel./fax 92-73-51, pens.gauguin@mail.pf), a bit east of Snack Make Make and up around the corner, charges CFP 6,900 pp with half board. It may be possible to get a room without meals at CFP 3,700 pp. There are two rooms downstairs and another four upstairs (the upstairs rooms are best). The upstairs terrace is most agreeable. Deep-sea fishing trips and excursions to the Brel Belvédère (CFP 4,000) and Puama'u (CFP 20,000) can be arranged.

Pension John Ozanne (Ozanne Rohi, tel./fax 92-73-43), up the hill from Pension Gauguin, offers a two-story bungalow in the yard at CFP 5,000. Cooking facilities are provided. Ozanne has a 12-meter boat called the *Denise II* which he uses for excursions and trips to Tahuata (CFP 20,000) or Fatu Hiva (CFP 50,000). Ask to see Ozanne's log books, which date back to the 1970s and contain dozens of entries by cruisers who have passed this way over the years.

For a longer stay, **Jean Saucourt** (tel. 92-73-33) rents rooms by the week in a house above the cemetery. Ask Aline Saucourt at the handicraft shop in the Cultural Center about this.

Pension Moehau (tel./fax 92-72-69, moehaupension@mail.pf) is at the east entrance to Atuona, just up the hill from Snack Make Make on the way to the harbor. It offers eight rooms in a new two-story building on the hillside at CFP 9,760/17,890/23,960 single/double/triple with half board.

Overlooking Tahauku Bay is the **Pension Temetiu Village** (Gabriel Heitaa, tel. 92-73-02, heitaagabyfeli@mail.pf), also known as Chez

Gabi, just up the hill from SMA des Marquises a km east of Atuona on the way to the harbor. The five bungalows with bath are CFP 8,300/12,600 single/double with half pension (no cooking facilities). Nonguests are welcome at their terrace restaurant. Gabriel rents out his eight-passenger boat, the *Pua Ote Tai*.

Atuona's upmarket place, the **Hanakéé Pearl Lodge** (tel. 92-75-87, fax 92-75-95, www.pearl resorts.com), is on the airport road about five km east of Atuona on the hillside overlooking Takauku Bay. There's a swimming pool with a panoramic deck. The 14 stylish bungalows and six suites start at CFP 26,000/31,000 double/triple, plus 11 percent tax. Breakfast and dinner are CFP 6,900 pp extra, airport transfers CFP 4,800 pp return. The manager sometimes allows yachties to check their email here at CFP 250 per eight minutes.

Food

Snack Make Make (tel. 92-74-26), also called Snack Atuona, 100 meters east of the post office and across the street, has juicy hamburgers (CFP 450), large *poisson cru* (CFP 950), grilled fish (CFP 1,050), and cold beer (CFP 400 a can). They're open for drinks weekdays 0730–1600 but meals served 1100–1330 only. The atmosphere is excellent.

Snack Kaupe (tel. 92-70-62; Tues.–Sun. 0900–1700, plus Fri. and Sat. nights), next to Magasin Gauguin, features specialties from Reunion Island in the Indian Ocean, including *curcuma* (chicken, CFP 1,300) and *Massalé de Thon* (spicy tuna, CFP 1,450). There's also good pizza (CFP 1,100–1,400), Chinese dishes (CFP 1,100–1,300), and fish (CFP 1,100–1,650). A large beer is CFP 500 and this is the only place with real ice cream (CFP 100 a scoop). The manager speaks some English—ask about their free transportation from the wharf. They do laundry for yachties.

Restaurant Hoa Nui (tel. 92-73-63), next to a school on the road up the Vaioa Valley just west of town, serves Chinese and Marquesan dishes nightly at 1900 by reservation only (CFP 2,300). *Aranui* passengers are often served a meal here.

Information and Services

Ernest Teapuaoteani at the Mairie de Atuona (tel. 92-73-32) is a great source of information and he speaks good English.

Banque Socredo (tel. 92-73-54) is next to the Air Tahiti office. The post office, town hall, dental center, and hospital (tel. 92-73-75) are two blocks east with the gendarmerie (tel. 92-73-61) diagonally opposite.

Transportation

A lighthouse on the point between Tahauku Bay and Atuona looks south across Traitors Bay. Yachts anchor behind the breakwater in Tahauku harbor, two km east of the center of town. The *Taporo* and *Aranui* also tie up here. The gas station at the wharf has a well stocked grocery store (if you want bread, order it the day before).

In theory, the cabin cruiser *Te Pua O Mioi* leaves Atuona for Tahuata Tuesday at noon, but this boat is often laid up with mechanical problems.

The catamaran *Auona II* should leave Atuona for Fatu Hiva Thursday at noon (CFP 4,000 pp) but it's often out of service.

Location David (Augustine Kaimuko, tel. 92-72-87), next to Magasin Chanson up from the museum, rents cars at around CFP 15,000 a day all inclusive. To hire a four-passenger Land Rover with driver from Atuona to Puama'u will run you CFP 20,000 for the vehicle.

Atuona Rent Car (tel. 92-76-07) has cars for a mere CFP 13,000 a day. You must call for a delivery.

Before renting a car, ask if the gas station at Tahauku wharf has any fuel available as they often run out.

Airport

The airstrip (AUQ) is on a 441-meter-high plateau, eight km northeast of Atuona. In 1991 the runway was upgraded to allow it to receive direct ATR 42 flights from Papeete (via Nuku Hiva). Air Tahiti is at tel. 92-73-41.

It's a two-hour downhill walk from the airport to Atuona. The normal taxi fare from the airport to Atuona is CFP 1,800 pp each way, but the amount collected by the various hotels seems to vary, so check when booking.

Companies like Taxi Marie-Thérèse (tel. 92-71-59) and Taxi Clark (tel. 92-71-33) should ask CFP 1,000 to Tahauku wharf, CFP 1,800 to the airport, CFP 8,000 to Taaoa, CFP 12,000 to Hanaiapa, CFP 20,000 to Puamau. In the case of the longer trips, this should be the price for the whole car round-trip.

The North Coast

A second village, **Puama'u**, is on the northeast coast of Hiva Oa, 30 km from Atuona over a winding mountain road. It's a good eight-hour walk from Atuona to Puama'u, up and down all the way. A few remote descendants of Gauguin are among the 300 people who live there today.

Aside from the village's golden beach, the main reason for coming are the five huge stone tikis to be seen on the **Me'ae Iiopona** among the breadfruit trees in the valley behind Puama'u, a 15-minute walk from the village soccer field. One named Takii stands 243 cm high—the largest old stone statue in the Marquesas. Notice the statue of the priestess who died in childbirth and the sculpted heads of victims of human sacrifice. The site was restored in 1991. You're supposed to pay the CFP 200 fee to visit the *me'ae* at Snack Aimee (tel. 92-71-53) on the waterfront.

You can stay in Puama'u at **Chez Heitaa** (Bernard and Marie-Antoinette Heitaa, tel. 92-72-27) in the upper part of the village, not far from the Me'ae Iipona. The two rooms with shared bath are CFP 5,720 pp including half board. Airport transfers are CFP 15,000 for up to four people. Horses are for hire at CFP 5,000. The tombs of the last queen of the area and her family are behind the pension.

At **Hanaiapa** on the north coast, ask for William who keeps a yachties' log. He's happy to have his infrequent visitors sign, and is generous with fresh fruit and vegetables. Barren **Hanamenu Bay** in the northwest corner of Hiva Oa is now uninhabited, but dozens of old stone platforms can still be seen. If you'd like to spend some time as a hermit in the desert, ask for Ozanne in Atuona, who has a house at Hanamenu he might be willing to rent. To the right of Ozanne's house is a small, crystal-clear pool. The trails into this area have become overgrown and it's now accessible only by boat.

TAHUATA

Tahuata (population about 650) is just six km south of Hiva Oa across Bordelais Channel. Fifteen km long by nine km wide, 69-square-km Tahuata is the smallest of the six inhabited islands of the Marquesas. A 17-km track crosses the island from Motopu to Vaitahu, the main village on the west coast. The anchorage at Hana Moe Noa north of Vaitahu is protected from the ocean swells. There's a lovely white beach and the water here is clear, as no rivers run into this bay.

Archaeological sites exist in the Vaitahu Valley and there's a small collection of artifacts in the school opposite the post office in Vaitahu. Tahuata was the point of first contact between Polynesians and Europeans anywhere in the South Pacific. Mendaña anchored in Vaitahu Bay in 1595, followed by Captain Cook in 1774. Here too, Admiral Abel Dupetit-Thouars took possession of the Marquesas in 1842 and established a fort, despite strong resistance led by Chief Iotete.

Sights

The **Catholic church** at Vaitahu was completed in 1988 to mark the 150th anniversary of the arrival here of missionaries. It has the largest stained glass window in the territory. Local sculptor Damien Haturau carved the huge wooden statue of the Virgin above the church entrance from a 400-year-old *temanu* tree.

Hapatoni village, farther south, is picturesque, with a century-old *tamanu*-bordered road and petroglyphs in the Hanatahau Valley behind. Coral gardens are found offshore and white-sand beaches skirt the north side of the island.

Accommodations

Pension Fara (Marguerite Kokauani, tel. 92-92-84), also known as Pension Amatea, in Vaitahu, has five rooms with shared bath at CFP 3,500 pp, plus CFP 500/2,000 for breakfast/dinner.

Ask about **Chez Leonie Teraiharoa** (tel. 92-93-07 or 20-74-99) on a brownish beach a 15-minute walk west of Vaitahu. Rates for the five bungalows were unknown at press time.

Getting There

There's no airport on Tahuata. To charter a six-passenger boat to/from Atuona is CFP 20,000–25,000 (one hour). Small boats leave Hiva Oa for Tahuata almost daily, so ask around at the harbor on Takauku Bay near Atuona.

When operating, the cabin cruiser *Te Pua O Mioi,* belonging to the Commune of Tahautu (tel. 92-92-19), shuttles between Atuona and Vaitahu on Tuesday and Thursday (one hour, CFP 1,000 pp each way). It leaves Tahuata around dawn, departing Hiva Oa for the return at noon. Southbound, take groceries with you.

FATU HIVA

Fatu Hiva (84 square km) is the southernmost and youngest of the Marquesas Islands, 56 km southeast of Tahuata. It's far wetter than the northern islands, and the vegetation is lush. Mount Tauaouoho (960 meters) is the highest point. Fatu Hiva was the first of the Marquesas to be seen by Europeans (Mendaña passed by in 1595). None landed until 1825 and Catholic missionaries couldn't convert the inhabitants until 1877. In 1937-38 Thor Heyerdahl spent one year on this island with his young bride Liv and wrote a book called *Fatu Hiva,* describing their far from successful attempt "to return to a simple, natural life."

This is the most remote of the Marquesas, and only a few French officials are present. With 650 inhabitants, Fatu Hiva has only two villages, Omoa and Hanavave, in the former crater on the western side of the island. Surfing off the rocky beach at Omoa can be pretty exciting! Hanavave on the Bay of Virgins offers one of the most fantastic scenic spectacles in all of Polynesia, with tiki-shaped cliffs dotted with goats. Yachts usually anchor here. Horses and canoes are for hire in both villages.

Fatu Hiva is one of the last places in French Polynesia where tapa cloth is still widely made. Until the 1960s, Fatu Hiva tapa bore no designs, instead the human body was decorated with tattoos. Today a revival of the old crafts is taking place and it's again possible to buy not only wooden sculptures but painted tapa cloth. Hats and mats are woven from pandanus. *Monoï* oils are made from coconut oil, gardenia, jasmine, and sandalwood.

Fatu Hiva doesn't have any *no-nos,* but ample mosquitoes. If you plan on staying over four months, get some free anti-elephantiasis pills such as Notézine at any clinic.

Activities

It takes about five hours to hike the 17-km dirt road linking Omoa and Hanavave, up and down over the mountains amid breathtaking scenery. It's a long gentle incline from Omoa to a 600-meter pass, followed by a very steep descent into Hanavave. **Vaiéé-Nui Falls** is a pleasant one-hour walk back into the valley from Hanavave. Unfortunately Hanavave is overrun by skinny half-starved dogs the locals use to hunt pigs.

Omoa is the main center for tapa production in all of French Polynesia. William Grelet has a small private museum with some exquisite woodcarvings behind the *mairie* and handicraft center at Omoa. A bakery and two small stores are also in Omoa.

Accommodations and Food

Several families in Omoa village take paying guests. **Chez Heimata** (Albertine Tetuanui; tel. 92-80-58) has two rooms at CFP 2,500 pp with breakfast, plus CFP 1,500 each for other meals. **Norma Ropati** (tel./fax 92-80-13) and **Cécile Gilmore** (tel. 92-80-54) rent rooms at similar rates.

Pension Chez Lionel (Lionel and Bernadette Cantois, tel./fax 92-80-80) at Omoa has one bungalow with cooking facilities at CFP 5,000 double.

Pension Manauea (Fernand Tholance, tel./fax 92-80-02), at the back of Omoa village toward the valley, has rooms at CFP 8,000/14,000 single/double including half board.

In Hanavave, **Pension Chez Noela** (Justine Pavaouau, tel./fax 92-80-60) has three rooms at CFP 3,000/4,000 single/double (meals available). Noela is a well known Fatu Hiva woodcarver.

Getting There

There's no airstrip on Fatu Hiva but the Mairie de Fatu Hiva (tel. 92-80-23) operates the 30-passenger catamaran *Auona II,* once a week between Atuona and Omoa. In past it has left Fatu Hiva on Tuesday and Thursday at 0600. From Atuona, it usually leaves Tuesday and Thursday at noon (ask), and on the return trip they may agree to drop you on Tahuata. The trip takes just over three hours and costs CFP 4,000 pp each way.

To hire a speedboat, such as the red and yellow *Rautea Nui* owned by Joel Coulon, from Omoa to Tahuata will cost around CFP 40,000 for the boat.

OTHER ISLANDS

Motane (Mohotani) is an eight-km-long island rising to 520 meters, about 18 km southeast of Hiva Oa. The depredations of wild sheep on Motane turned the island into a treeless desert. When the Spaniards "discovered" it in 1595, Motane was well-wooded and populated, but today it's uninhabited.

Uninhabited Eiao and Hatutu islands, 85 km northwest of Nuku Hiva, are the remotest (and oldest) of the Marquesas. **Eiao** is a 40-square-km island, 10 km long and 576 meters high, with rather difficult landings on the northwest and west sides. The French once used Eiao as a site of deportation for criminals or "rebellious" natives. The Queen of Raiatea and 136 Raiateans who had fought against the French were interned here from 1897 to 1900. In 1972 the French Army drilled holes 1,000 meters down into Eiao to check the island's suitability for underground nuclear testing, but deemed the basalt rock too fragile for such use. Wild cattle, sheep, pigs, and donkeys forage across Eiao, ravaging the vegetation and suffering from droughts. In contrast, the profusion of fishlife off Eiao is incredible.

Hatutu, the northernmost of the Marquesas, measures 7.5 square km. Thousands of birds nest here.

BASIC TAHITIAN

ahiahi: evening
ahimaa: earth oven
aita: no
aita e peapea: no problem
aita maitai: no good
aito: ironwood
amu: eat
ananahi: tomorrow
arearea: fun, to have fun
atea: far away
atua: god
avae: moon, month
avatea: midday (1000–1500)
e: yes, also *oia*
eaha te huru?: how are you?
e haere oe ihea?: where are you going?
e hia?: how much?
faraoa: bread
fare: house
fare iti: toilet
fare moni: bank
fare niau: thatched house
fare punu: tin-roofed house
fare pure: church
fare rata: post office
fare toa: shop
fenua: land
fetii: parent, family
fiu: fed up, bored
haari: coconut
haere: goodbye (to a person leaving)
haere mai io nei: come here
haere maru: go easy, take it easy
hauti: play, make love
hei: flower garland, lei

here hoe: number-one sweetheart
himene: song, from the English "hymn"
hoa: friend
ia orana: good day, may you live, prosper
i nanahi: yesterday
ino: bad
inu: drink
ioa: name
ite: know
ma'a: food
maeva: welcome
mahana: sun, light, day
mahanahana: warm
maitai: good, I'm fine; also a cocktail
maitai roa: very good
manava: welcome
manu: bird
manuia: to your health!
manureva: airplane
mao: shark
mauruuru: thank you
mauruuru roa: thank you very much
meka: swordfish
miti: salt water
moana: deep ocean
moemoea: dream
moni: money
nana: goodbye
naonao: mosquito
nehenehe: beautiful
niau: coconut-palm frond
oa oa: happy
ohipa: work
ora: life, health
ori: dance

oromatua: the spirits of the dead
otaa: bundle, luggage
oti: finished
pahi: boat, ship
painapo: pineapple
pape: water, juice
parahi: goodbye (to a person staying)
pareu: sarong
pia: beer
pohe: death
poipoi: morning
popaa: foreigner, European
poti'i: teenage girl, young woman
raerae: effeminate
roto: lake
taapapu: understand
taata: human being, man
tabu: forbidden
tahatai: beach
tama'a: lunch
tama'a maitai: bon appetit
tamaaraa: Tahitian feast
tamarii: child
tane: man, husband
taofe: coffee
taote: doctor
taravana: crazy
tiare: flower
to'e to'e: cold
tupapau: ghost
ua: rain
uaina: wine
uteute: red
vahine: woman, wife
vai: fresh water
veavea: hot

NUMBERS

hoe: 1
piti: 2
toru: 3
maha: 4
pae: 5
ono: 6
hitu: 7
vau: 8
iva: 9
ahuru: 10
ahuru ma hoe: 11
ahuru ma piti: 12
ahuru ma toru: 13
ahuru ma maha: 14
ahuru ma pae: 15
ahuru ma ono: 16
ahuru ma hitu: 17
ahuru ma vau: 18
ahuru ma iva: 19
piti ahuru: 20
piti ahuru ma hoe: 21
piti ahuru ma piti: 22
piti ahuru ma toru: 23
toru ahuru: 30
maha ahuru: 40
pae ahuru: 50
ono ahuru: 60
hitu ahuru: 70
vau ahuru: 80
iva ahuru: 90
hanere: 100
tauatini: 1,000
ahuru tauatini: 10,000
mirioni: 1,000,000

Pitcairn Islands

Introduction

Legendary Pitcairn, last refuge of HMS *Bounty's* mutinous crew, is the remotest populated place in the South Pacific. This tiny colony, founded in 1790 by nine fugitive Englishmen and 19 Polynesians, is presently more than 200 years old. It's one of the ironies of history that Pitcairn, born out of treason to the British crown, was the first Pacific island to become a British colony (in 1838) and remains today the last remnant of that empire in the Pacific.

The Land

Pitcairn Island, more than 2,200 km southeast of Tahiti, sits alone between Peru and New Zealand at 25° south latitude and 130° west longitude. Its nearest inhabited neighbor is Mangareva, a small island in French Polynesia 490 km to the northwest. Easter Island lies 1,900 km to the east. A high volcanic island, Pitcairn reaches 347 meters at the Pawala Ridge and is bounded by rocks and high cliffs on all sides. There's no coral reef, and breakers roll right in to the shore. The island is only 4.5 square km, almost half of which is fertile ground and well suited for human habi-

© PAUL J. LAREAU

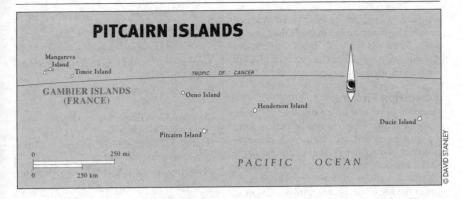

© DAVID STANLEY

tation. The uninhabited islands of Henderson, Ducie, and Oeno, belonging to Pitcairn, are described individually below. The tiny colony controls an exclusive economic zone of 800,000 square km, an important reason why Britain is in no hurry to leave.

Climate

Pitcairn enjoys an equitable climate, with mean monthly temperatures varying from 19°C in August to 24°C in February. Daily temperatures can vary from 13°C to 33°C. The 2,000 mm of annual rainfall is unevenly distributed, and prolonged rainy periods alternate with droughts. Moderate easterly winds predominate with short east-to-southeast gales occurring between April and September.

HISTORY

The Lost Civilization

Although Pitcairn was uninhabited when the nine *Bounty* mutineers arrived in 1790, the remains of a vanished civilization were clearly evident. The sailors found four platforms with roughly hewn stone statues, possibly smaller, simpler versions of those on Easter Island. Being good Christians, the Pitcairners destroyed these platforms and threw the images into the sea. Unfortunately, almost nothing remains of them today. The only surviving piece of sculpture resides in Dunedin's Otago Museum in New Zealand. Sporadic visits by European archaeologists have uncovered traces of ancient burials and stone axes,

and 22 petroglyphs are to be seen below "Down Rope." This evidence indicates that Pitcairn was occupied for a considerable period in the past, but where these ancient people came from and where they went remains a question.

European Discovery

Pitcairn was discovered in 1767 by Captain Carteret, on the HMS *Swallow.* The island was named for the son of Major Pitcairn of the marines, the first to sight it.

In 1788 the HMS *Bounty* sailed from England for the Pacific to collect breadfruit plants to supplement the diet of slaves in the West Indies. Because the *Bounty* arrived in Tahiti at the wrong time of year, it was necessary to spend a long five months there collecting samples, and during this time, part of the crew became overly attached to that isle of pleasure. On April 28, 1789, in Tongan waters, they mutinied against Lt. William Bligh under 24-year-old Master's Mate Fletcher Christian. Bligh was set adrift in an open boat with the 18 men who chose to go with him. He then performed the amazing feat of sailing 3,618 nautical miles in 41 days, reaching Dutch Timor to give the story to the world.

After the mutiny, the *Bounty* sailed back to Tahiti. An attempt to colonize Tubuai in the Austral Islands failed, and Fletcher Christian set out with eight mutineers, 18 Polynesians—men, women, and one small girl—to find a new home where they would be safe from capture. In 1791, the crew members who elected to remain on Tahiti were picked up by the HMS *Pandora* and

PITCAIRN ISLANDS

returned to England for trial. Three were executed. The *Bounty* sailed through the Cook Islands, Tonga, and Fiji, until Christian remembered Carteret's discovery. They changed course for Pitcairn and arrived on January 15, 1790.

Colonizing Pitcairn

After removing everything of value, the mutineers burned the *Bounty* to avoid detection. Right up until the present, each January 23 on the anniversary of the *Bounty*'s demise, a model of the ship is launched and burned at **Bounty Bay.** For 18 years after the mutiny, the world knew nothing of the fate of the *Bounty*, until the American sealer *Topaz* called at Pitcairn for water in 1808 and solved the mystery.

The first years on Pitcairn were an orgy of jealousy, treachery, and murder, resulting from a lack of women after the accidental death of one. By 1794, only four mutineers remained alive, and all of the Polynesian men had been killed. Three more men had died from a variety of causes by 1800, leaving only John Adams, nine women, and 19 children. Adams brought the children up according to strict Puritanical morality, and later the British Admiralty chose—all things considered—not to take action against him. Adams lived on Pitcairn until his death in 1829 at the age of 65; of the mutineers, he is the only one with a known burial site.

PITCAIRN TODAY

The British Dependent Territory of Pitcairn, Henderson, Ducie, and Oeno Islands is administered by the Pitcairn Island Administration in Auckland, New Zealand, on behalf of the South Pacific Department of the Foreign and Commonwealth Office in London. The highest resident official is the island magistrate, elected for three years. There's also a 10-member Island Council, four members of which are elected each year. In 1998, with Hong Kong off its hands, the British government conferred full citizenship on residents of all its remaining colonies, including Pitcairn.

The economy is self-sufficient, depending largely on subsistence agriculture, investment re-

PITCAIRN ISLANDS HIGHLIGHTS

Adamstown, Pitcairn: only settlement, historic relics (p. 294)

Bounty Bay, Pitcairn: where the *Bounty* was burned (p. 290)

Christian's Cave, Pitcairn: where Fletcher Christian ended his life (p. 294)

Henderson: UNESCO World Heritage Site (p. 295)

Oeno Atoll: remote coral island with a lagoon (p. 295)

turns, and postage stamp sales. Collectors value Pitcairn stamps due to the history depicted on the limited issues (under 600 Pitcairn stamps have been printed since 1940). British government aid is available for major capital expenditures from time to time. All the men work for the administration, mostly part-time. The fertile soil supports a variety of fruits and vegetables for local consumption, with three crops of sweet potatoes grown a year. The only domestic animals are goats, chickens, cats, and dogs. The islanders make baskets, small wooden carved sharks, and tiny models of the *Bounty*.

There are 6.5 km of dirt roads on Pitcairn (muddy after rains), and the islanders ride around on three- and four-wheeled all-terrain vehicles. There are also tractors, microwaves, freezers, and VCRs; diesel-generated electricity is on for around two hours in the morning and four hours in the evening. The quaint Pitcairn wheelbarrows are a thing of the past. The modern conveniences have brightened the lives of the islanders, reduced the number of people required to sustain the community, and convinced more of the young to stay.

Even so, a fifth of the present population is older than 59, double the regional norm, and the median age of 35 is 10 years above the next oldest Pacific country. It takes at least four men to operate one of the 13-meter longboats used to ferry passengers and goods from ship to shore and only eight working men remain on the island. Some Pitcairners feel that construction of an

A LETTER FROM JOHN ADAMS

John Adams was the only mutineer to survive the bloodshed of the first years on Pitcairn. In 1819, 10 years prior to his death, he wrote these words to his brother in England:

I have now lived on this island 30 years, and have a wife and four children, and considering the occasion which brought me here it is not likely I shall ever leave this place. I enjoy good health and except the wound which I received from one of the Otaheiteans when they quarreled with us, I have not had a day's sickness. . . . I can only say that I have done everything in my power in instructing them in the path of Heaven, and thank God we are comfortable and happy, and not a single quarrel has taken place these 18 years.

M.G.L. DOMENY DE RIENZI

airstrip is the only way to avoid an eventual evacuation but Britain has refused to finance such a project. An air service could only be made viable through the development of tourism via Mangareva and the cost would be considerable. In a March 2001 referendum, 22 Pitcairn residents voted in favor of tourism development while only six were against.

The People

Most of the fewer than 50 permanent inhabitants of Pitcairn are direct descendants of the mutineers and their Tahitian wives. In 1831, there was an attempt to resettle them on Tahiti, out of fear of drought, but the Pitcairners returned to their island the same year. In 1856, all 193 islanders were forcibly taken by the British to Norfolk Island, between New Zealand and New Caledonia, where many of their descendants live today (194 Pitcairners actually arrived

on Norfolk as a baby was born en route). Two families returned to Pitcairn in 1858, followed by four more in 1864. The present population is descended from those six families. Nearly half the people bear the surname Christian; all of the others are Warrens, Browns, and Youngs. The population peaked at 233 in 1937.

In 1967, David Silverman wrote in his book *Pitcairn Island* that there were around 1,500 true Pitcairners: 45 on Pitcairn, 150 in French Polynesia, 160 in New Zealand, 400 in Australia, and most of the rest on Norfolk Island.

The Pitcairners speak a local patois of English and Tahitian. For example, rough seas is *illi illi* from "hilly" plus Tahitian repetitive emphasis. There's a primary school with a N.Z. teacher who also assists the post-primary students with their N.Z. correspondence-school lessons. Scholarships are made available by the Island Council for older postprimary students wishing to further their education in New Zealand (and many never return).

In early 2000, a rape investigation led to accusations of the systematic sexual abuse of girls as young as seven dating back 40 years. In 2002 nine men were formally charged at a pre-trial hearing on Pitcairn. The saga is ongoing, and the island community is reeling from the case.

Exploring the Islands

Accommodations and Food

No hotels or guest houses exist on Pitcairn, and the two government hostels are usually reserved for official use. The island magistrate can organize paying guest accommodation with local families (around NZ$175 pp a week), but such arrangements must be made prior to arrival.

Visiting yachties are welcomed into the Pitcairners' homes. If you're headed for Pitcairn, take along a good supply of canned foods and butter, plus worthwhile books for the library, to repay the hospitality you'll receive. An American Seventh-Day Adventist missionary converted the Pitcairners in 1876, so pork, cigarettes, drugs, and alcohol are banned. Tea and coffee are frowned upon. To protect the island's beekeeping industry from disease, honey and bee products are prohibited imports.

The Cooperative Store opens for a few hours three times a week. Canned foods are usually obtainable, but flour, eggs, meat, and butter must be ordered from New Zealand several months in advance. Since no freight is charged to Pitcairn for foodstuffs, prices are about the same as in New Zealand, with a markup of 20 percent to cover losses.

Media and Information

The *Pitcairn Miscellany* is a delightful monthly newsletter sponsored by the Pitcairn Island School. One may become a subscriber by sending US$10 cash or an undated check to: *Pitcairn Miscellany,* Pitcairn Island, via New Zealand. Allow several months for your letter to reach Pitcairn.

The **Pitcairn Islands Study Group** publishes *The Pitcairn Log* quarterly (US$15 a year). It contains much interesting material on the people of Pitcairn, as well as the collecting of Pitcairn postage stamps. For more information, visit their website at www.pisg.org.

Internet Resources

The Official Pitcairn Island Government Website, **www.pitcairn.pn,** controlled by the Office of the Governor of Pitcairn in New Zealand, gives a history of Pitcairn, lists the rules and regulations involved in a visit, has a section devoted to the Pitcairn Island Philatelic Bureau, and even tells you how to register a .pn Pitcairn Island domain name. Paul J. Lareau's Pitcairn Island Web Site, **www.lareau.org/pitc.html,** is the mother of all Pitcairn websites with links to recent news articles about Pitcairn, precise information about each of the Pitcairners, an extensive photo album, bibliographies, genealogies, links, and much more. The Pitcairn Islands Study Center, **http://library.puc.edu/pitcairn,** based at Pacific Union College in Angwin, California, is a world-class study center about the mutiny on the Bounty. The Henderson Island Website, **www.winthrop.dk/hender.html,** offers photos, maps, and much useful information on uninhabited Henderson Island. Norfolk Island's Home on the Web, **www.pitcairners.org,** introduces the current home of the largest group of Pitcairn descendants.

Visas

No visa is required of passengers and crew who visit while their vessel is at Pitcairn. Anyone wishing to stay on Pitcairn after the ship has left requires a residence permit issued by the Commissioner for Pitcairn Islands, Pitcairn Island Administration, Private Box 105696, Auckland, New Zealand (tel. 64-9/366-0186, fax 64-9/366-0187). If you're in Auckland you can visit them at Level 10, 67 Customs St. Applications must be approved by the Island Council and the governor, and a processing fee of NZ$10 is payable in advance (plus another NZ$30 if communicating by fax). If granted, a "license to land and reside" on

Pitcairn for up to six months costs NZ$150. You'll be asked to provide a specific reason for wanting to go (journalists are not welcome).

Money

New Zealand currency is used, with local Pitcairn coins. No bank exists on Pitcairn, but the island secretary will change foreign cash and traveler's checks.

Communications

In 1992, an Inmarsat A Satellite Communications System was installed on Pitcairn and it's now possible to contact the island directly at tel. 872/762337766 (public telephone) or 872/762337765 (control room telephone). The fax number is fax 872/762337767. Incoming calls are answered by an operator at 0900, 1300, 1700, and 2100 local Pitcairn time. The island is eight hours behind GMT, so these times convert to 1700, 2100, 0100, and 0500 GMT. However, before dialing Pitcairn, check the cost with your long-distance operator as Inmarsat calls are extremely expensive (as much as US$10 a minute). Telephone cards are available for outgoing calls. Some Pitcairn locals are not very happy with this high-tech replacement of the much cheaper radio telephone link with New Zealand that went before.

A dozen Pitcairners are licensed ham radio operators, the highest proportion of amateur radio operators per capita in the world, and these days some residents also have email addresses. Pitcairn's top-level domain .pn internet registry is administered by the office of the governor in New Zealand.

Getting There

Talk of building an airstrip on Pitcairn has floated around for decades, and in 2001 it was announced that the residents had finally agreed to surrender a good part of their farmland for this purpose. Whether construction will actually go ahead remains to be seen but such a facility would change the island forever.

There's no harbor on Pitcairn. All shipping anchors in the lee, moving around when the wind shifts. This is why most passing ships don't drop anchor but only pause an hour or so to pick up and deliver mail. The islanders come out to meet boats anchored in Bounty Bay and ferry visitors ashore in their longboats (the use of zodiacs and dinghies isn't allowed).

There are two open anchorages: Bounty Bay when winds are blowing from the southwest, west, and northwest; Western Harbor when there's an east wind. Both have landings, but Bounty Bay is tricky to negotiate through the surf, and Western Harbor is far from the village. The unprotected jetty constructed at Bounty Bay by the Royal Engineers in 1976 is now in poor repair. The anchorage at Down Rope could be used in the event of north or northeast winds, but there's no way up the cliff except the proverbial rope. Gudgeon Harbor is another possibility, but be aware of the dangerous rocks lying off the south coast. The wind is irregular, so yachts must leave someone aboard in case it shifts.

The Pitcairn Island Administration in Auckland, New Zealand, will have information on container vessels that call at Pitcairn between New Zealand and the Panama Canal three or four times a year. Other ships occasionally stop at the discretion of the captain. Passage on these ships costs US$800–1,000 one-way. Return passage is usually a matter of chance, and it may be necessary to wait several months for the next ship.

Tours

Unless you own a yacht, the only practical way of visiting Pitcairn are the 15-day yacht tours arranged by **Ocean Voyages Inc.** (1709 Bridgeway, Sausalito, CA 94965, U.S.A.; tel. 415/332-4681 or 800/299-4444, fax 415/332-7460, www.oceanvoyages.com). These occur once or twice a year, usually involving a flight from Tahiti to Mangareva in the Gambier group, then a three-day sail to Pitcairn aboard a chartered yacht. One week is spent ashore as guests of the Pitcairners, and rather than lie idle, the yacht often does a wood run to Henderson and a fishing trip to Oeno during this period. In recent years the trip has taken place between April and June. The US$6,000 pp price includes the boat trip, lodging, and all meals on Pitcairn. Add US$550 for the return flight from Papeete to Mangareva, the cost of small gifts for the Pitcairners, and tips for the yacht's crew. Ocean Voyages has operated trips like this since 1980, but they only happen when enough people are willing to go.

If you can organize a small group, Ocean Voyages or any of the yacht charter brokers listed in the introduction to this book can book crewed Tahiti-based yachts for trips to Pitcairn via Mangareva anytime. The cost will be around US$8,000 a week for six persons, and three weeks must be allowed for the roundtrip sea journey, with the possibility of stops at the Tuamotus.

Luxury cruise ships also visit Pitcairn occasionally between Easter Island and Tahiti, but they spend only a few hours ashore and in bad weather they're unable to land at all. Check the listings for Society Expeditions and other companies in the introductory Getting There section.

Pitcairn Island

Scattered along a plateau 120 meters above the landing at Bounty Bay is **Adamstown,** the only settlement. At the top of the hill over the bay is The Edge, a restful spot with benches, shady trees, an old anchor, and a great view of everything. The original Bible from the *Bounty* is showcased in the church at Adamstown. The Bible, sold in 1839, was eventually acquired by the Connecticut Historical Society, which returned it to Pitcairn in 1949. The four-meter anchor of the *Bounty,* salvaged in 1957, is now mounted in the square outside the courthouse.

Nearby is a *Bounty* cannon recovered in 1999. Pitcairn postage stamps may be purchased at the post office between the courthouse and church. The library and dispensary are adjacent. A bell on the square is used to announce church services and the arrival of ships. The graves of John Adams, his wife Teio, and daughter Hannah are a short walk inland.

On the ridge west of Adamstown is **Christian's Cave** in which Fletcher Christian stayed during the period of strife on the island. He was finally killed by two Tahitians.

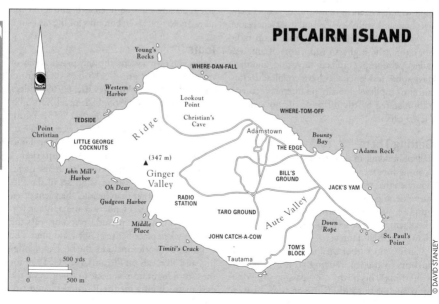

Oeno and Ducie

Grouped together with Pitcairn under the same administration are the uninhabited islands of Oeno, Henderson, and Ducie, annexed by Britain in 1902. The four islands together total 47.4 square km. Unlike Pitcairn and Henderson, both Ducie and Oeno have central lagoons inaccessible to shipping. Passing Japanese freighters often dump garbage in these waters and tankers illegally flush their holds, as the trash and tar littering the beaches of these remote atolls clearly proves.

Oeno, a tiny 5.1-square-km atoll 128 km northwest of Pitcairn, is visited by the Pitcairners from time to time to collect shells, coral, and pandanus leaves to use in their handicrafts. Small boats can enter the shallow lagoon through a passage on the north side. In 1969–70 Oeno was used by the U.S. Air Force as a satellite observation post. In 2001 a New Zealand company submitted a proposal to build a 1,200-meter runway and deluxe tourist lodge on Oeno, but nothing has yet been done.

Ducie atoll (6.4 square km) is 472 km east of Pitcairn. The poor soil and lack of fresh water

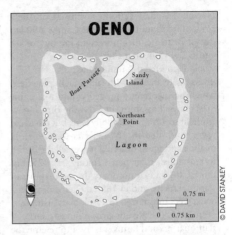

account for the sparse vegetation. Large whirlpools in the Ducie lagoon are caused by tunnels that drain the lagoon to the sea. Due to its inaccessibility, Ducie is rarely approached, and tens of thousands of petrels and other seabirds nest there.

Henderson

Henderson, a 31-square-km elevated atoll 169 km east-northeast of Pitcairn, is the largest of the Pitcairn Islands. The island measures 5 km by 10 km and is flanked by 15-meter-high coral cliffs on the west, south, and east sides. Geologists believe that Henderson was uplifted after a volcanic eruption on Pitcairn over a million years ago which tilted the earth's crust slightly with its weight.

Henderson is surrounded by a fringing reef with only two narrow passages: one on the north, the other on the northwest coast. The passages lead to a sandy beach on the island's north shore. Henderson's shoreline is littered with plastic refuse thrown overboard by passing ships. The interior of the island is a flat coral plateau about 33 meters high, but the dense undergrowth, prickly vines, and sharp coral rock make it almost impenetrable. There's said to be a freshwater spring visible only at low tide at the north end of the is-

land, but this is doubtful, and no other source of water on the island is known.

There are two unique species of land birds on the island: a black flightless rail (Henderson chicken) and a green fruit pigeon. Great numbers of seabirds nest here. Fish and lobster are also numerous, as are Polynesian rats. The Pitcairners visit Henderson to collect *miro* wood, which is excellent for carving.

Sometime between 1200 and 1500 AD Henderson was inhabited by Polynesians who died out or sailed away prior to the arrival of Europeans. Discovered by Europeans in 1818, it was first visited by the Pitcairners in 1851. There was talk of constructing an emergency runway on Henderson to support air services between South America and the South Pacific but this was rejected, and in 1988 the island was declared a World Heritage Site, the first South Pacific locale to be added to UNESCO's prestigious list.

PITCAIRN ISLANDS

Norfolk Island

Norfolk Island, 1,120 km northwest of Auckland, 800 km south of Nouméa, and 1,400 km east of Brisbane, measures eight km by five km and is 3,455 hectares in area. When Captain Cook discovered this uninhabited island in 1774 it was tightly packed with tall, straight pine trees, which he incorrectly judged would make fine masts for sailing ships. In 1788 the British government set up a penal colony here, but the island was abandoned in 1814. Fears that Norfolk might be occupied by a rival power led the British to reestablish their penal colony in 1825, but this facility gained notoriety through reports of wanton cruelty, and in 1855 the remaining prisoners were transferred to Tasmania, Australia.

In 1856, the existing prison infrastructure of staff quarters and farms was used to resettle the Pitcairn Islanders, and today more than a third of the 2,000 island residents have Pitcairn names. The Melanesian Mission established its headquarters on Norfolk in 1866, and until 1921 it had a college there used to train Solomon Islanders and others as pastors. The mission church and burial ground remain. Whaling was practiced by the islanders from the 1850s until 1962, but the event that changed Norfolk forever was the building of a wartime airport in 1944.

Today the island is a favorite vacation spot for middle-aged or retired Australians and New Zealanders who come for a quiet holiday. A small national park with hiking trails, the convict settlement, and lovely coastal scenery are the main attractions. The Pitcairn connection is heavily exploited by the local tourist industry, and there are Pitcairn museums, shows, film evenings, tours, and souvenirs.

Norfolk Island is a self-governing territory under Australian authority. Those making a return visit from Auckland do not require a visa for a stay of 30 days, but an Australian tourist visa is required of those continuing on to Australia (obtain beforehand). There are scheduled flights to Norfolk Island from Auckland, Brisbane, Melbourne, and Sydney. An A$25 airport tax is collected upon departure.

Tourism is tightly controlled by **Norfolk Island Tourism** (tel. 672-3/22147, fax 672-3/23109, www.norfolkisland.com.au) and only persons with prepaid accommodations are allowed entry. Camping, youth hostels, and most other forms of independent budget travel are strictly prohibited. There are about 45 official places to stay on the island and prices are reasonable for a couple of nights. Just be sure to get something with cooking facilities and perhaps a rental car included.

If your air ticket allows a stopover on Norfolk Island between New Zealand and Australia, contact **The Travel Center** (tel. 672-3/22502, fax 672-3/23205, www.travelcentre.nf), which can make direct accommodation bookings. Four or five days on the island should be enough. From Australia and New Zealand, package tours are offered by **Talpacific Holidays** (www.talpacific.com) with offices in Auckland, Brisbane, and Sydney.

Easter Island

Introduction

The mystery of Easter Island (Isla de Pascua) and its indigenous inhabitants, the Rapanui, has intrigued travelers and archaeologists for many years. Where did these ancient people come from? How did they transport almost 1,000 giant statues from the quarry to their platforms? What series of events caused them to overthrow all they had erected with so much effort? And most importantly, what does it all mean? With the opening of Mataveri airport in 1967, Easter Island became more easily accessible, and many visitors now take the opportunity to pause and ponder the largest and most awesome collection of prehistoric monuments in the Pacific. This is one of the most evocative places you will ever visit. (Herein we follow the convention of spelling the island name Rapa Nui and its people and their language Rapanui.)

The Land

Barren and detached, Easter Island lies midway between Tahiti and Chile, 4,050 km from the former and 3,700 km from the latter. Pitcairn Island, 1,900 km west, is the nearest inhabited land. At 109°26' west longitude and 27°09' south latitude, it's the easternmost and almost the southernmost island of the South Pacific (Rapa Iti

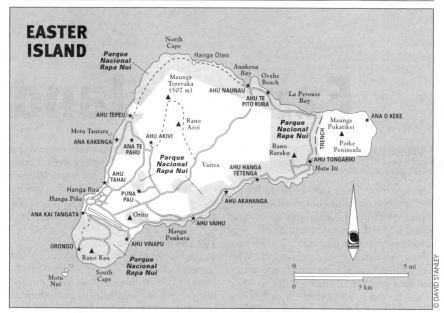

EASTER ISLAND

in French Polynesia is a bit farther south). Easter Island is triangular, with an extinct volcano at each corner. It measures 23 by 11 km, totaling 171 square km.

The interior consists of high plateaus and craters surrounded by coastal bluffs. Ancient lava flows from Maunga Terevaka (507 meters), the highest peak, covered the island, creating a rough, broken surface. Maunga Pukatikei and Rano Kau (to the east and south respectively) are nearly 400 meters high. Many parasitic craters exist on the southern and southeast flanks of Maunga Terevaka. Three of these, Rano Aroi, Rano Raraku, and Rano Kau, contain crater lakes, with the largest (in Rano Kau) over a kilometer across. Since 1935 about 40 percent of the island, including the area around Rano Kau and much of the island's shoreline, has been set aside as **Parque Nacional Rapa Nui** administered by the Corporación Nacional Forestal (CONAF). In 1995 the park was added to UNESCO's World Heritage List, the first place in Chile to be so honored.

Small coral formations occur along the shoreline, but the lack of any continuous reef has allowed the sea to cut cliffs around much of the island. These bluffs are high where the waves encountered ashy material, low where they beat upon lava flows. Lava tubes and volcanic caves are other peculiarities of the island. The only sandy beaches are at Ovahe and Anakena, on the north coast.

Climate

The sub-tropical climate is moderated by the cool Humboldt current and the annual average temperature is 20.3°C. The hottest month is February; the coolest are July and August. Winds can make it feel cooler. The climate is moist, and some rain falls 140 days a year. The rainiest months are March–June; the coolest months are generally July–October. The months August–December are the driest, although heavy rains are possible year-round (much of it falling at night). Drizzles and mist are common, and a heavy dew forms overnight. Snow and frost are unknown, however. The porous volcanic rock dries out quickly, so the dampness need not deter the well-prepared hiker.

Flora and Fauna

The forests of Easter Island were wiped out by the

EASTER I. CLIMATE

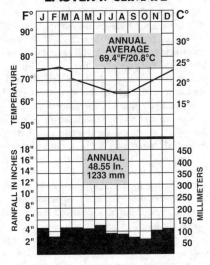

pretend to pick up a stone. Some 4,000 horses and cattle range across the island, damaging the archaeological sites.

HISTORY

Polynesian Genesis

It's believed that Easter Island was colonized around A.D. 300 by Polynesians from the Marquesas Islands or Mangareva, as part of an eastward migratory trend that originated in Southeast Asia around 2000 B.C. Here developed one of the most remarkable cultures in all of Polynesia.

Long platforms, or *ahu*, bearing slender statues known as *moai* were built near the coasts, with long retaining walls facing the sea. Each *ahu* generally carried four to six *moai* towering four to eight meters high. These statues, or *aringa ora* (living faces), were portraits of known ancestors, and they looked inland towards the villages to project the mana (protective power) of the *aku-aku* (ancestral spirits) they represented. Some 887 *moai* have been counted on Easter Island, of which 288 were actually erected on the *ahu*.

The vast majority of *moai* were all cut from the same quarry at Rano Raraku, the yellowish volcanic tuff shaped by stone tools. Some writers have theorized that the statues were "walked" to their platforms by a couple of dozen men using ropes to lean the upright figures from side to side while moving forward; others claim they were pulled along on a sledge or log rollers. Some statues bore a large cylindrical topknot (*pukao*) carved from the reddish stone of Puna Pau. Eyes of cut coral were fitted into the faces of *moai* standing on the *ahu*. South of Puna Pau, Maunga Orito contains black obsidian, which the islanders used for weapons and tools.

Other unique features of Easter Island are the strange canoe-shaped house foundations (*hare paenga*) with holes for wall supports, the so-called chicken houses (*hare moa*) thought to be tombs, and the incised wooden tablets (*rongorongo*), the only ancient form of writing known in Oceania. Only 25 examples survive, and Dr. Steven Roger Fischer, Director of the Institute of Polynesian Languages and Literatures in Auckland, has shown how the neat rows of symbols on the boards

indigenous inhabitants long ago, and during the 19th century sheep finished off most of the remaining native vegetation. The last indigenous *toromiro* tree died in the 1960s, and attempts to reintroduce the species from overseas botanical gardens have largely failed. Grasslands now envelop the green, windswept landscape; few endemic plants survive. Large tracts of eucalyptus were planted in the 1940s and 1950s. The crater lakes feature thick, floating bogs of peat; *nga'ata (totora)* reeds related to South American species surround and completely cover their surfaces. Pollen studies have determined that these reeds have existed here for at least 30,000 years.

Many of the native birds were wiped out by humans long ago. The sooty terns *(manutara)*, which once nested on Motu Nui in their thousands, are still seen here but in far fewer numbers. The frigate bird, often featured on the petroglyphs at Orongo, has been driven away. The brown hawks *(manu toketoke)*, small gray finches *(manu puhi)*, and tinamous *(vivi)* have all been introduced from the continent in recent years. The numerous dogs encountered in Hanga Roa are also new arrivals. Most are inoffensive and the others will soon retreat if you

EASTER ISLAND HIGHLIGHTS

Ahu Tongariki: statues, scenery (p. 307)

Anakena Beach: swimming, archaeology, hiking (p. 307)

Museo Antropológico, Hanga Roa: exhibition, shopping, information (p. 304)

Orongo: archaeology, scenery, hiking, volcano (p. 306)

Rano Raraku quarry: archaeology, statues, hiking, scenery (p. 307)

record procreation chants. Some scholars believe that the development of *rongorongo* was prompted by early exposure to European writing.

The oldest *ahu* (Ahu Tahai) is dated 690 A.D. and the most recent (Ahu Akivi) dated to 1460, after which the focus of the culture shifted from statue carving to the "birdman" cult at Orongo. Overpopulation, depletion of resources, and famine may explain the change. In 1774, Captain Cook reported internecine fighting among the islanders, with statues toppled and their platforms damaged, and by 1840 all of the *moai* had been thrown off their *ahu,* either by earthquakes or rival tribes.

Fantasy and Fact

The first comprehensive explorations of Easter Island were carried out by Katherine Routledge in 1914–1915, Alfred Métraux in 1934, and Thor Heyerdahl in 1955–1956. Earlier, in 1947, Heyerdahl had achieved notoriety by sailing some 6,500 km from South America to the Tuamotu Islands in a balsa raft, the *Kon Tiki.* His 1955 Norwegian Archaeological Expedition was intended to uncover proof that Polynesia was populated from South America, and Heyerdahl developed a romantic legend that still excites the popular imagination today.

Heyerdahl postulated that Easter Island's first inhabitants (the "long ears") arrived from South America around A.D. 380. They dug a three-km-long defensive trench isolating the Poike Peninsula and built elevated platforms of perfectly fitted basalt blocks. Heyerdahl noted a second

wave of immigrants, also from South America, who destroyed the structures of the first group and replaced them with the *moai*-bearing *ahu* mentioned above. Heyerdahl saw the toppling of the *moai* as a result of the arrival of Polynesian invaders (the "short ears") who arrived from the Marquesas and conquered the original inhabitants in 1680. According to Heyerdahl, the bird-man cult, centered on the sacred village of Orongo, was initiated by the victors.

Modern archaeologists discount the South American theory and see the statues as having developed from the typical backrests of Polynesian *marae.* The civil war would have resulted from over-exploitation of the island's environment, leading to starvation, cannibalism, and the collapse of the old order. Previous destruction of the forests would have deprived the inhabitants of the means of building canoes to sail off in search of other islands. The Poike trench was only a series of discontinuous ditches dug to grow crops, probably taro. Despite decades of study by some of the world's top archaeologists, no South American artifacts have ever been excavated on the island.

Heyerdahl argued that the perfectly fitted, polished stonework of the stone wall of Ahu Vinapu (Ahu Tahira) was analogous to pre-Incan stone structures in Cuzco and Machu Picchu, but fine stonework can be found elsewhere in Polynesia (for example, the *langi,* or stone-lined royal burial mounds, of Mu'a on Tongatapu). Easter Island's walls are a facade holding in rubble fill, while Peruvian stonework is solid block construction. In 1993, DNA evidence was used to prove that the Rapanui originated in Southeast Asia. In academic circles, Heyerdahl (who passed away in 2002) was always considered a maverick who started out with a conclusion to prove instead of doing his homework first. And his whole hypothesis is rather insulting to the island's present Polynesian population, as it denied them any credit for the archaeological wonders we admire today.

A sequel to this story occurred in 1999, when members of the Polynesian Voyaging Society sailed the catamaran *Hokule'a* from Hawaii to Easter Island and back using the traditional navigational techniques the ancients would have used. By crossing from Mangareva to Rapa Nui in just 17.5 days, the *Hokule'a* demonstrated vividly the mastery of the seas for which the Polynesians are renowned.

European Penetration

European impact on Easter Island was among the most dreadful in the history of the Pacific. When Jacob Roggeveen arrived on Easter Sunday, 1722, there were about 4,000 Rapanui (though the population had once been as high as 20,000). Roggeveen's landing party opened fire and killed a dozen islanders; then the great white explorer sailed off. González (1770), Cook (1774), and La Pérouse (1786) were the next to call, but contacts with whalers, sealers, and slavers were sporadic until 1862 when a fleet of eight Peruvian blackbirders kidnapped some 1,400 Rapanui to work in the coastal sugar plantations of Peru. Among those taken were the king and the entire learned class. Missionaries and diplomats in Lima protested to the Peruvian government, and eventually 15 surviving islanders made it back to their homes, where they sparked a deadly smallpox epidemic.

French Catholic missionaries took up permanent residence on Easter Island in 1866 and succeeded in converting the survivors; businessmen from Tahiti arrived soon after and acquired property for a sheep ranch. Both groups continued the practice of removing Rapanui from the island: The former sent followers to their mission on Mangareva, the latter sent laborers to their plantations on Tahiti. Returnees from Tahiti introduced leprosy. By 1877, the total population had been reduced to 110. One of the business partners, Jean Dutrou-Bornier, had the missionaries evicted in 1871 and ran the island as he wished until his murder by a Rapanui in 1876. The estate then went into litigation, which lasted until 1893.

The Colonial Period

In 1883, Chile defeated Peru and Bolivia in the War of the Pacific. With their new imperial power, the Chileans annexed Easter Island in 1888, erroneously believing that the island would become a port of call after the opening of the Panama Canal. Their lack of knowledge is illustrated by plans to open a naval base when no potential for harbor construction existed on the island. As this became apparent, they leased most of it to a British wool operation, which ran the island as a company estate until the lease was revoked in 1953. The tens of thousands of sheep devastated the vegetation, causing soil erosion, and stones were torn from the archaeological sites to build walls and piers. During this long period, the Rapanui were forbidden to go beyond the Hanga Roa boundary wall without company permission, to deter them from stealing the sheep.

In 1953, the Chilean Navy took over and continued the same style of paternal rule. The islanders remained confined to the area around Hanga Roa until 1966. After local protests, the moderate Christian Democratic government of Chile permitted the election of a local mayor and council in 1965. Elections were terminated by Pinochet's 1973 military coup, and Easter Island, along with the rest of Chile, suffered autocratic rule until the restoration of democracy in 1990. In 1984, archaeologist Sergio Rapu became the first Rapanui governor of Easter Island, and all subsequent governors have also been Rapanui. The 1993 filming of Kevin Costner's US$20 million epic *Rapa Nui* brought the world to Easter Island in the way the 1962 filming of *Mutiny on the Bounty* transformed Tahiti.

GOVERNMENT

Easter Island is part of the Fifth Region of Chile, with Valparaíso (Chile) as the capital. The president of Chile nominates the governor; the mayor and council are elected locally. Policy decisions affecting the island's development are made by officials in faraway Chile. Most Rapanui leaders want Easter Island made a separate region of Chile, a change that would greatly enhance local autonomy. This could happen when ex-dictator Pinochet finally dies and his 1980 constitution is replaced or fundamentally changed. The people of Easter Island pay no taxes and all government services on the island are underwritten by Chile. If the island were to become self-governing as a separate region, this might change.

The story is told that during the annexation ceremony in 1888, King Atamu Tekena leaned forward and pulled out a handful of grass which he gave to Captain Policarpo Toro with the words "this is for you." Then he picked up a handful of soil and put it in his pocket, saying, "this is for us." The Rapanui of today are becoming more assertive in reclaiming their rights and land.

Politics

After the return to democracy in Chile an indigenous rights group, the Consejo de Ancianos (Council of Elders), was created to represent the island's 36 original families. In 1994, the Consejo split into two factions over the question of land rights: the original Consejo No. 1 headed by former mayor Alberto Hotus, and a radical Consejo No. 2 led by Mario Tuki.

Most of Easter Island's land is still held by the Chilean State but any local will be able to tell you which part of the island once belonged to his/her original clan. In 1994, supporters of Consejo No. 2 set up a tent city outside the church in Hanga Roa with banners demanding the return of indigenous lands. To the embarrassment of Chile, this protest lasted five years.

In 1999, Chilean officials finally persuaded the demonstrators to take down their banners in exchange for the promise of a land redistribution. A Comisión de Desarrollo (development committee) comprised of six elected Rapanui, six members of various government agencies, the governor, and the mayor was established under Chile's Indigenous Law. In November 2001, clear title to over 1,400 hectares of land on the slopes of Maunga Terevaka was granted to 472 Rapanui individuals or families, but the redistribution was done by lottery with no attempt to match current residents with ancestral lands. In 2003, another 2,000 hectares of land south of Vaitea was due to be handed out in the same way.

These events have not pleased everyone. Many people were given rocky, eucalyptus-covered plots unsuitable for agriculture or cattle grazing. Only about 20 percent of the island is being distributed, and members of Consejo No. 2 have demanded that the government turn over most of the island, despite the very negative effect this would have on the environment and ancient sites. The rich farmlands around Vaitea, which have very little in the way of archaeological remain, are not on the table.

Hanga Roa is still the only sizable permanent settlement on Rapa Nui, but unserviced shacks are springing up all over the island. Fields are being plowed or bulldozed without any environmental impact studies being carried out and houses have been constructed on or near archaeological sites. As you travel around the island, watch for the Rapa Nui flags depicting a red *reimiro* or crescent-shaped pectoral on a white background that fly above the squatter camps.

The most provocative occupations have been inside Parque Nacional Rapa Nui itself, but the park authorities hesitate to expel anyone out of fear of provoking major unrest or losing their jobs. In 1999, the park's head, José Miguel Ramírez, was sacked for objecting to park land being redistributed. Among the Rapanui themselves, opinions on how to handle the land issue differ sharply, with many people concerned that redistributions could have a negative impact on tourism by damaging the visual esthetics of the island.

At times, officials in far-off Chile have come up with reckless development plans of their own, such as a proposed "monumental" lighthouse on a hill overlooking the airport flight path to proclaim Chilean sovereignty. The Sociedad Agrícola y Servicios Ltda. (SASIPA), which provides water and electricity to the island and operates a large cattle ranch, wants to exploit their valuable lands at Vaitea for a golf course, luxury resort, and botanical garden. "Progress" is catching up with this remote island and no coherent management plan exists for Easter Island as a whole. It's just one special interest group clawing against another—the world on a small scale.

THE PEOPLE

The original name of Easter Island was Te Pito o Te Henua, "navel of the world." The Rapanui believe they are descended from Hotu Matu'a, who arrived by canoe at Anakena Beach from Te Hiva, the ancestral homeland. The statues were raised by magic. The original inhabitants wore tapa clothing and were tattooed like Marquesans; in fact, there's little doubt that their forebears arrived from Eastern Polynesia. The language of the Rapanui is Austronesian, closely related to all the other languages of Polynesia, with no South American elements.

The Rapanui have interbred liberally with visitors for over a century, but the Polynesian element is still strong. Three-quarters of the 3,800 people on Easter Island are Rapanui or Rapanui-related. The island receives around 20,000 tourists a year from Chile, Europe, the United States, and Japan, and many Rapanui earn a living as innkeepers, guides, drivers, and craftspeople. Others are employed by the Chilean government. About a thousand *continentales* (mainlanders) also live here, most of them government employees and small shopkeepers. Many mainlanders live in Mataveri south of the airstrip.

Since 1966, the Rapanui have been Chilean citizens, and quite a few have emigrated to the mainland. Some 1,200 Rapanui live abroad, most of them in Chile and about 150 on Tahiti. People generally speak Rapanui in private, Spanish in public, French if they've been to Tahiti, and English if foreign tourists are important to them. Spanish is gradually supplanting Rapanui among the young, and it's feared the language will go out of everyday use within a generation or two. Television is diluting the local culture.

Conduct

The archaeological sites on Easter Island are fragile and easily damaged by thoughtless actions, such as climbing on the fallen statues or walking on petroglyphs. The volcanic tuff is soft and easily broken off or scuffed. Incredibly, some people have scraped ancient rock carvings with stones to make them easier to photograph! Cruise ships can unload hundreds of people a day, and the large groups often spin out of control, swarming over the quarry at Rano Raraku or standing on the stone house tops at Orongo (several of which have collapsed in recent years). The national park has had to erect stone walls around many sites to keep out rental vehicles and local residents have organized voluntary projects to pick up trash discarded by tourists.

Though it may seem that these places are remote from the world of high-impact consumer tourism, they are in fact endangered by the selfishness of some visitors and those locals who would profit from them. It's strictly prohibited to remove any ancient artifacts (such as spear heads, fishhooks, or basalt chisels) from the island. The warning signs erected in the park are there for a reason, and the bones occasionally encountered on the *ahu* and in the caves deserve to be left in peace (even if they're actually animal bones placed there by guides to give tourists something to photograph). In 2003, a Japanese and a British tourist who were caught scratching their initials on *moai* were each fined US$3,000.

Public Holidays and Festivals

Public holidays in Chile include New Year's Day (January 1), Easter Friday (March or April), Labor Day (May 1), Battle of Iquique Day (May 21), Corpus Christi (June), Saints Peter and Paul Day (June 29), Ascension Day (August 15), National Reconciliation Day (first Monday in September), Independence Day (September 18), Army Day (September 19), Columbus Day (October 12), All Saints' Day (November 1), Conception Day (December 8), and Christmas Day (December 25).

In late January or February is the carnival-like Tapati Rapa Nui festival, with traditional dancing, sporting events, canoe races, a horse race, fishing tournament, handicraft and agricultural exhibitions, statue-carving contest, shell-necklace-stringing competition, body-painting contest, *kai-kai* (string figure) performances, mock battles, feasts, and the election of Queen Tapati Rapa Nui (who is dramatically crowned on a spotlit Ahu Tahai). A unique triathlon at Rano Raraku involves male contestants in body paint who paddle tiny reed craft across the lake, pick up bunches of bananas on poles and run around the crater and up the hill, where they grab big bundles of *nga'ata* reeds to carry down and around the lake before a final swim across. There's also *haka pei*, which involves young men sliding down a grassy mountainside on banana-trunk sleds at great speed. Colored lights are strung up along the main street. Needless to say, all flights immediately before and after the festival are fully booked far in advance.

The Tokerau Singing Festival is in July. Chilean Independence Day (18 September) is celebrated with parades and a *fonda* (carnival). Everyone takes three days off for this big fiesta. On the day of their patron saint, the main families stage a traditional feast *(curanto)*, complete with an earth oven *(umu ta'o)*.

Exploring the Island

SIGHTS

Hanga Roa

The **Catholic church** (1964) in the center of town is notable for its woodcarvings. Buried next to the church entrance is Father Sebastián Englert, author of *Hotu Matu'a's Land* (1948), who served as parish priest from 1935 until his death in 1969 at the age of 80. Adjacent is the grave of Eugène Eyraud (1820–1868), who introduced Christianity and tuberculosis to the island.

The small boat harbor at **Caleta Hanga Roa** is appealing for its three restored statues, the row of local fishing boats, and the numerous surfers bobbing on the waves just offshore. North along the coast is **Hanga Vare Vare,** a public park featuring contemporary statues, petroglyphs, and sheltered places to swim.

Just north of town at **Ahu Tahai** are three *ahu,* one bearing five restored *moai,* and a large statue complete with a red 10-ton topknot reerected by the late Dr. William Mulloy in 1968. The statue's "eyes" are crude copies recently cemented in place for tourists. The Rapanui once launched their canoes down the ramp leading to the water between the *ahu.* This is a great place to be at sunset.

The **Museo Antropólogico Sebastián Englert** (tel. 551-020, www.museorapanui.cl; Tues.–Fri. 0930–1230/1400–1730, Sat.–Sun. 0930–1230; admission US$2, students US$1), near Ahu Tahai, first opened in 1973 but was modernized and rearranged in 1999. The museum has an excellent collection of old carvings and artifacts, plus a scale model of the island. Ask to borrow the English translation of the Spanish explanations, and don't miss the white coral and red scoria eye of the *moai* found at Anakena in 1978. The William Mulloy Research Library (weekdays 0930–1230/1400–1730) is adjacent to the museum.

North of Hanga Roa

Four km up the dirt road leading north from the museum is Motu Tautara, the first of two long lava islands pointing straight out from the coast. As you head down to the viewpoint over the islands, watch carefully on the left for the tiny entrance to **Ana Kakenga,** the Cave of the Two Windows. It's not far from the coastal road, near a curve in the track, and is easily missed. This remarkable lava tube gets much larger inside, with two openings in the cliffs directly above the sea.

A km north again, near where the rough coastal road turns sharply inland, is unrestored **Ahu Tepeu** and its fallen *moai.* The site is between the stone marker and the coastal cliffs, beyond the foundations of some canoe-shaped and round houses. Go around to the back of the ruined *ahu* to appreciate the megalithic stonework. In ancient times this area belonged to the powerful Miru clan.

Ana Te Pahu, a km southeast of Ahu Tepeu on the road inland, is one of the most spectacular lava tubes on the island. There's a stone marker but you'll know the cave from the banana trees and taro growing up through openings in the rock. You could drive a large truck a long distance through this cave (have a flashlight with you).

Inland again via the dirt track is **Ahu Akivi** (Siete Moai), with seven statues restored in 1960 by Dr. Mulloy. The seven much-photographed *moai* once overlooked a village but they now stare silently out to sea. Unfortunately, agricultural development in this area has obliterated many archaeological remains. If you're walking, the dirt track that begins opposite the nearby

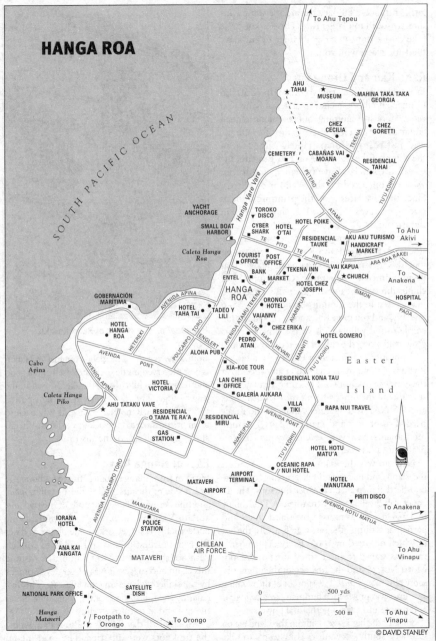

HANGA ROA

SOUTH PACIFIC OCEAN

To Ahu Tepeu

AHU TAHAI ★

MUSEUM ■

MAHINA TAKA TAKA GEORGIA ■

CHEZ CECILIA ■

CHEZ GORETTI ■

CEMETERY ■

CABAÑAS VAI MOANA ■

RESIDENCIAL TAHAI ■

YACHT ANCHORAGE

SMALL BOAT HARBOR

Caleta Hanga Roa

TOROKO DISCO ▼

CYBER SHARK ■

HOTEL O'TAI ■

HOTEL POIKE ■

RESIDENCIAL TAUKE ■

AKU AKU TURISMO ■

HANDICRAFT MARKET ★

To Ahu Akivi

TOURIST OFFICE ■

POST OFFICE ■

VAI KAPUA ■

To Anakena

ENTEL ■

BANK ■

MARKET ■

TEKENA INN ■

CHURCH ★

HANGA ROA

HOTEL CHEZ JOSEPH ■

GOBERNACIÓN MARITIMA ■

HOTEL TAHA TAI ■

TADEO Y LILI ■

ORONGO HOTEL ■

VAIANNY ■

HOSPITAL ■

HOTEL HANGA ROA ■

CHEZ ERIKA ■

HOTEL GOMERO ■

PEDRO ATAN ■

Easter

Cabo Apina

ALOHA PUB ■

Island

Caleta Hanga Piko

KIA-KOE TOUR ■

HOTEL VICTORIA ■

LAN CHILE OFFICE ■

RESIDENCIAL KONA TAU ■

AHU TATAKU VAVE ★

GALERÍA AUKARA ■

RESIDENCIAL O TAMA TE RA'A ■

RESIDENCIAL MIRU ■

VILLA TIKI ■

RAPA NUI TRAVEL ■

GAS STATION ■

HOTEL HOTU MATU'A ■

MATAVERI

OCEANIC RAPA NUI HOTEL ■

AIRPORT TERMINAL ■

HOTEL MANUTARA ■

IORANA HOTEL ■

MATAVERI AIRPORT

PIRITI DISCO ■

To Anakena

POLICE STATION ■

Avenida Hotu Matua

ANA KAI TANGATA ★

CHILEAN AIR FORCE

To Ahu Vinapu

MATAVERI

SATELLITE DISH ■

NATIONAL PARK OFFICE ■

0   500 yds

0   500 m

To Ahu Vinapu

Hanga Mataveri

Footpath to Orongo

To Orongo

© DAVID STANLEY

EASTER ISLAND

farm entrance, a bit back toward the coast, runs directly south to Hanga Roa. This 13-km circle hike can be done in a day if you're fit and have food and water with you.

Rano Kau and Orongo

From Hanga Roa, the six-km trip south to Orongo and the vast, circular crater of Rano Kau can be done in a morning, but take along a lunch and make a day of it if you have the time. On the way, just past the Iorana Hotel, at the foot of the cliff near the water, is **Ana Kai Tangata,** the so-called Cannibal Cave (whether cannibalism was ever practiced on the island is disputed). Since the cave faces west, the paintings of birds gracing the cave's ceiling are best photographed in the afternoon.

The road to Orongo swings left and up the side of 316-meter Rano Kau, but if you're on foot look for the shady footpath on the right that begins immediately after the CONAF office and climbs through the forest. Otherwise, a taxi from Hanga Roa to the summit should cost US$5–6 one-way, and you can easily walk back. Guavas (an edible round yellow fruit with a pink interior) grow wild along the side of the road to Orongo.

A one-time admission of US$10 (or a bit less if you pay in pesos) is charged at an office up at the entrance to Orongo. The entry fee may seem stiff, but all the other sites on the island are free, and CONAF is desperately short of the funds needed to protect and maintain Easter Island's monuments. Save your receipt if you plan a repeat visit up this way.

Orongo was the main ceremonial center on the island, and many high-relief carvings of frigate bird-headed men are on the rock outcrops. The 47 basalt slab dwellings here (restored by Dr. Mulloy in 1974–1976) were used by island chiefs and participants during the birdman festivals, the last of which occurred in 1866. Every September, a race was staged to the farthest offshore island, **Motu Nui,** to find the first egg of the migratory sooty tern *(manutara).* The sponsor of the winning swimmer was proclaimed birdman *(tangata manu)* and thought to have supernatural powers.

Some of the highest sea cliffs on the island are on Orongo's south side and it's risky to try to hike

two *moai* on the slopes of Rano Raraku

around the volcano. The island's original vegetation is best preserved inside the crater itself and a good alternative is to hike the 250 meters down to the water's edge. The trail begins at the sign-posted viewpoint over Rano Kao. On your way back to town, it's possible to cut back toward Ahu Vinapu along the south side of the airstrip.

East of Hanga Roa

Five km from Hanga Roa via the road along the north side of the airstrip are the 11 fallen *moai* and fine Peruvian-like stone walls of the two *ahu* at **Ahu Vinapu.** According to Heyerdahl, the perfectly fitted stonework of one platform dates from the earliest period and is due to contact with South America. Most authorities dispute this claim and suggest it was a later development by the skilled Polynesian stonemasons. This fascinating site is just south of the white oil tanks at the east end of the airport runway.

An easy half-day walk is to **Puna Pau,** where the topknots were quarried. The road inland from the north side of the church is the shortest way to go, but you must turn right on the back road to Anakena (ask). About 20 red topknots are in the quarry at Puna Pau, the largest weighing 11 tons. After seeing the topknots, climb to the three crosses atop neighboring Maunga Tangaroa (270 meters) for a great view of the center of the island. A pilgrimage is held here on Good Friday.

South Coast

Although many of the enigmatic statues *(moai)* are concentrated at moss-covered Rano Raraku (the statue quarry), they are found all around the island. Ninety-two important archaeological sites have been identified along the south coast alone. The stone walls seen at various places date from the English sheep ranch. The tour buses generally stop to visit the eight *moai* lying facedown at **Ahu Vaihu**, eight km east of Hanga Roa. The first king of the island, Hotu Matu'a, is buried at **Ahu Akahanga**, 3.5 km beyond Ahu Vaihu, where over a dozen toppled statues are seen.

The top sight on the island is certainly **Rano Raraku**, an extinct volcano 18 km east of Hanga Roa. The huge sculpture park here contains the island's most finely chiseled *moai,* including 70 standing on the inner or outer slopes of the crater and another 30 laying facedown on the ground. A kneeling statue called Tukuturi on the east side of Rano Raraku is unusual. In all, some 397 *moai* are still at the quarry in various stages of completion, allowing one to study the process. A few of the unfinished *moai* still attached to the cliffs resemble the reclining Buddhas of Thailand; one unhewn giant measures 21.6 meters long. Work on the statues seems to have ended rather abruptly, and many were abandoned en route to their *ahu*. From the summit of Rano Raraku, you can see clearly several dozen scattered along the ancient Ara O Te Moai, the Way of the Moai to the coast at Ahu Hanga Tetenga. Be aware that the quarry is usually crowded with tour groups around midday—if you arrive early or late you'll have this magical area all to yourself.

After climbing Rano Raraku, continue to nearby **Ahu Tongariki** at Hotu Iti, 20 km from Hanga Roa. This site was ravaged by a huge tsunami in 1960 that tossed the 15 massive statues around like cordwood. In 1994, Chilean archaeologists reconstructed the 200-meter-long *ahu* and reerected the *moai* using an enormous crane donated by the Japanese crane manufacturer Tadano. Some extraordinary petroglyphs of turtles and fish may be seen on the bedrock close to the *ahu* and at a nearby turn in the main road. The cliffs of the Poike Peninsula loom behind Ahu Tongariki.

North Coast

The tallest *moai* ever to stand on Easter Island is at **Ahu Te Pito Kura** on the north coast by La Pérouse Bay. The toppled 10-meter-long statue nicknamed "Paro" lies facedown beside the *ahu*, awaiting restoration. An egg-shaped stone next to the *ahu* is called Te Pito o Te Henua, meaning the Navel of the World. It's alleged that Hotu Matu'a brought the stone with him from Te Hiva, the legendary homeland of the Rapanui. The stone is believed to have magical powers.

The inviting white sands of palm-fringed **Anakena Beach** are 20 km northeast of Hanga Roa via the paved central highway, or 30 km via Rano Raraku. The national park has set up picnic tables, barbecue pits, toilets, and a campground here, and many locals come to swim or fish on Sunday. Anakena is the traditional disembarkation point of Hotu Matu'a. The one *moai* on **Ahu Ature Huki** here was reerected by Thor Heyerdahl in 1956, as is indicated on a bronze plaque—the first statue to be restored on the island. **Ahu Nau Nau** at Anakena bears seven *moai,* four with topknots. During the restoration of this *ahu* in 1978, archaeologist Sergio Rapu discovered the famous white coral eyes of the statues.

SPORTS AND RECREATION

Easter Island offers many outstanding **hiking** opportunities, but take PABA sunscreen, a wide-brimmed hat, and sturdy boots, because the terrain is rough and there's almost no shade. A folding umbrella could also come in handy when it's not too windy. Ample food and water are essential, as none are available outside Hanga Roa.

One of the most intriguing and practical hikes is along the rocky northwest coast from **Anakena to Hanga Roa.** If you know a bit of Spanish, you should be able to hire a taxi to Anakena for the peso equivalent of US$6–8 one way, then it will take a good six hours to walk back to town along the horse track around the outer edge of Maunga Terevaka. You'll pass several lava tube caves and ruined *ahu* with fallen *moai,* but the real attraction here is the dramatic scenery, which is at its best around Hanga Oteo.

You can also hike up a jeep track to the summit of **Maunga Terevaka** itself. The route begins near Ahu Akivi (not the road closest to the *ahu* but the other one 20 meters south). From the grassy 507-meter summit there's a rare 360° horizon view and a sweeping panorama of the entire island. Beyond the large eucalyptus forest just southeast of the summit, seven km from Ahu Akivi, is Rapa Nui's shallowest crater lake, Rano Aroi. From the lake one can follow the bed of a usually dry stream down through the fragrant forests another four km to the former English sheep farm at Vaitea.

The **scuba diving** off Easter Island is not for beginners, since one must dive in the open sea and the water is cool (Nov.–April is warmest). On the plus side are the unique caves, walls, corals, and fish.

The **Orca Diving Center** (tel. 550-877 or 550-375, fax 550-448, www.seemorca.co.cl), opposite the small boat harbor at Caleta Hanga Roa, is run by Michel García, a noted underwater photographer who arrived here in 1979. Michel and his brother Henri charge US$50/80 for one/two tanks (US$35 without gear). Certification is mandatory; otherwise take an introductory lesson for US$60. Their two-hour snorkeling trip to Motu Nui is US$30 pp (minimum of two). A three-hour boat trip to the north coast costs US$45. Orca also rents ocean kayaks at US$15/25 a half day for a single/double kayak, surfboards at US$20 a half day, and bodyboards at US$15 a half day.

Mike Rapu Diving (tel. 551-055), right next to Orca Diving on Caleta Hanga Roa, also does scuba diving at US$50 a tank (US$40 a tank after three tanks). It's US$65 for night dives.

The boat trip to the *motu* costs US$30 pp and is offered every Thursday at 0930.

Surfers will find a couple of consistent waves adjacent to town, such as the rights at Caleta Hanga Roa and Ahu Tahai and the left at Hanga Mataveri Otai. On the south side of the island, a powerful right plows into the lava at Hanga Poukura. Some of the highest walls are a couple of kilometers east at Cabo Koe Koe near Ahu Vaihu. Summer is the best season on the north coast, winter on the south (especially Mar.–Sept.).

Horseback riding is fun, and at about US$25/35 a half/full day, it's reasonable. Anakena is too far to go by horse and return in a day anyway, so look upon riding more as a change of pace than as a way of getting around. The area north of Hanga Roa is ideal to explore by horse.

ACCOMMODATIONS

The median price for guesthouse accommodation in the high season (Nov.–March) is US$35/50/75 single/double/triple. In the low season, subtract US$10 from these rates. The rooms are clean and simple, often facing a garden, and most have private bath. Many of the places called "hotels" are only larger guesthouses and virtually all are single story affairs. The fancy five-star resorts so common in French Polynesia haven't arrived here yet.

All prices include a continental breakfast, but for a full English breakfast you'll have to add US$5–10 pp. Beware if something extra is "offered," as you could end up paying an additional US$40 for one small frozen lobster. If you're asked to choose a meal plan, take only breakfast and dinner, as it's a nuisance to have to come back for lunch. Picnic fare can be purchased at local stores; otherwise some hotels will prepare a box lunch. Unfortunately, few places offer cooking facilities.

If you haven't booked a package, accommodations are easily arranged upon arrival, since most of the *residenciales* (guesthouses) have booking counters in the baggage collection hall at the airport. Once something is arranged you'll be given a free lift to the place. Don't promise to stay more than one night until you've seen the room and are happy. Many rooms are priced per person, which is a good deal if you're alone.

Room prices fluctuate according to supply and demand, and when things are slow, bargaining is possible. During the low season (Apr.–Oct.) the large hotels stand almost empty and rates are discounted by as much as 50 percent. The peak season with the highest visitor levels is November–February; June is the slackest month. More rooms are available than there are airline seats to fill them, so unless you're very fussy or specific about where you want to stay, reservations are not required, even during the Tapati Rapa Nui festival. You'll just have to pay more when it's busy.

If you want the security of a reservation, the best established travel agency on Easter Island itself is **Mahinatur** (Julio Lagos, tel./fax 551-513, www.mahinatur.cl) based Residencial O Tama Te Ra'a on Atamu Tekena. Also highly recommended is **Rapa Nui Travel** (Conny Martin, tel. 100-548, fax 100-165, www.rapanuitravel.com). Both can book hotel accommodations, excursions, and rental vehicles in advance, and their services are used by most overseas tour operators. Chile Hotels (www.chile-hotels.com/easteris.htm) also handles such bookings. All of the properties listed below (or anyone on the island) can be faxed at fax 56-32/100-105, the Entel telephone office, which will call the hotel and ask them to come and get their fax. Whenever possible, websites or email addresses are included in the listings.

Virtually everyone staying at the large hotels will have been put there by their travel agent or tour operator. Independent travelers invariably choose the smaller hotels and *residenciales,* which are a much better value. The rack rates at places like Hotel Iorana, Hotel Manutara, Hotel Hotu Matu'a, Hotel Hanga Roa, and Hotel Taha Tai are higher than what their rooms are worth. Especially avoid Hotel Hanga Roa, which has a dilapidated old wing, and Hotel Manutara, which is buffeted by rock music from a nearby disco on Friday and Saturday nights. Hotel Iorana is inconveniently far from everything but has some of the best rooms on the island.

If you're on a very low budget, ask about camping at a *residencial.* Residencial Chez Cecilia listed below provides some of the best camping facilities in Hanga Roa. Camping is also allowed behind the national park attendant's office at Rano Raraku and in the picnic park at Anakena. The park rangers may agree to replenish your water supply, but on very dry years no water is available for campers, so check beforehand. If you camp freelance elsewhere around the island, stay out of sight of motorized transport.

The listings which follow are not exhaustive because almost every family on the island is involved in tourism in some way (and unlike many other South Pacific destinations, tourism here is run almost exclusively by the local people). A few places, including Residencial Ana Rapu and Hostal Martín and Anita, have been deliberately left out. All of the 10 hotels and 40 *residenciales* are in Hanga Roa, arranged here beginning with those closest to the airport. None of the streets have numbers and most *residenciales* don't have signs, so never hesitate to ask directions. Some places are better known by the owner's name.

US$25–50

A friendly young school teacher named Diego Jaime runs **Residencial Kona Tau** (tel./fax 100-321, konatau@entelchile.net), on a hillside on Avareipua. The eight rooms are US$25, US$35, or US$45 pp high season, US$10, US$15, US$20, or US$25 pp low season, depending on the room. Breakfast is US$5 extra. It operates as a youth hostel and singles are expected to share their room with one or two other persons if need be. However, despite the large Hosteling International sign at the entrance, there's no HI discount. Camping is not allowed. A common kitchen and lounge are provided, and it's a good place to meet people.

Cabañas Vaianny (tel. 100-650, www5.gratisweb.com/vaiannyy), on Tuki Haka Hevari, has five rooms in a duplex and triplex at US$20/30 single/double including a good breakfast. It's friendly and central—ask for Teresa Araki at the airport.

Residencial Pedro Atan (tel. 551-027, ataraki@hotmail.com), also known at Hotel Atariki, on Tuki Haka Hevari just off Atamu Tekena, has 14 rooms in a long block at US$30/50 single/double with breakfast (or US$20 pp in the low season). It's run by Juan Atan Paoa, who worked with Thor Heyerdahl on the restoration of Ahu Ature Huki at Anakena in 1956.

A jovial lady named Janet Hei operates **Residencial Miru** (tel. 100-365), behind Gringos Pizza on Atamu Tekena. The three rooms with shared bath are US$10 pp, while the four with private bath go for US$20/30 single/double, breakfast included.

Across Atamu Tekena from Gringos Pizza is **Residencial O Tama Te Ra'a** (tel. 100-635, jlagos@mahinatur.cl) with three rooms at US$25 pp yearround. Dinner is US$10. This quiet guesthouse features a large garden and a greenhouse.

Residencial Tekena Inn (Gonzalo Nahoe, tel./fax 100-289), on Atamu Tekena beside Restaurant El Cuerito Regalón in the center of town, has 12 rooms, four inside the house and another eight in a corridor outside. It's US$15 pp without meals (US$17 pp in the high season), and you can use the common kitchen. All-day horseback riding tours are US$45 pp including a light lunch, and car rentals are also offered.

Residencial Tauke (Florentino Leiva Neira, tel. 100-253), on Calle Te Pito o Te Henua opposite the Liceo (high school), has four rooms at US$20/15 pp high/low season plus US$5 pp for breakfast.

Up a side street off Te Pito o Te Henu between Restaurant Kopakavana and the church, **Residencial Vai Kapua** (tel. 100-377) offers nine rooms, four in the main house and five facing the lovely garden outside. It's quiet and friendly, and at US$20/15 pp with breakfast high/low season, it's a good value.

On Pasaje Reimiro off Atamu Tekena in the northern part of town, **Residencial Tahai** (María Hey Paoa, tel. 100-395, mariahey@latinmail.com) resembles a rundown Spanish hacienda with a large garden out front. The seven rooms are US$25/40 single/double.

US$50–100

The **Oceanic Rapa Nui Hotel** (tel. 100-356, fax 100-985), on Tu'u Koihu a few minutes walk from the airport, has six attractive, spacious rooms in a quadrangle facing the large dining/sitting area. It's a tad expensive at US$50/100/130 single/double/triple high season, but good value at US$25 pp during the low season.

Residencial Villa Tiki (María Georgina Paoa Hucki, tel./fax 100-327, tiki@entelchile.net), on Ave. Pont, offers six rooms at US$45/70. There's a great view over Hanga Roa toward Terevaka from the rear garden of this quality establishment. Tiki Tours is based here.

Rapa Nui Travel (Conny Martin, tel. 100-548, fax 100-165), on Tu'u Koihu, has a two-bedroom house for rent next to their office, which is ideal for families of up to five. Cooking facilities are provided and the price varies from US$80 if the children are young to US$100 for a family with teens.

One of the nicer medium-priced places is **Hotel Gomero** (María Icka Araki, tel./fax 100-313, www.hotelgomero.com), on Tu'u Koihu, with 13 rooms in long blocks at US$49/76/95 single/double/triple. This tasteful, quiet hotel has a swimming pool, and Mani Iti Tours is based here.

Residencial Chez Erika (tel. 100-474), off Tuki Haka Hevari directly behind Cabañas Vaianny, offers 12 rooms at US$35/60 single/double high season, US$25 pp low season, breakfast included. It's quiet and friendly.

The **Hotel Orongo** (Juan Chávez, tel. 100-572, fax 100-294), on Atamu Tekena in the center of town, has 14 rooms at US$35/60/80 single/double/triple, breakfast included. A reduction of US$5 pp is possible in the low season. This hotel has a very good restaurant and a gift shop.

The seven-room **Hotel Victoria** (Jorge Edmunds, tel./fax 100-272, jedmunds@entelchile.net), off Avenue Pont, is US$50/70 single/double (or US$40/60 low season). A common kitchen is provided for guests. This comfortable hotel has a breezy hilltop location.

French speakers are catered to at **Residencial Tadeo y Lili** (Liliane Frechet, tel./fax 100-422, tadeolili@entelchile.net) at Avenue Apina and Policarpo Toro. Each of the seven rooms accommodates two to five persons at US$45/60/81 single/double/triple including breakfast. One three-bedroom house is US$25 pp. Lunch or dinner are US$15 each. The location facing Caleta Hanga Roa is excellent, although some of the rooms are not constructed in a way that takes full advantage of the site. Island tours and horseback riding are arranged.

Hotel Chez Joseph (José Arimereka Pacomio, tel. 100-373, fax 100-281, chezjoseph@entel chile.net), on Avareipua just up the street behind Restaurant Kopakavana, charges US$45/ 85/105 single/double/triple including breakfast for the 15 rooms (US$5 pp less low season). The quiet hilltop location and family atmosphere are its advantages.

The peaceful **Hotel Poike** (Carmen Cardinali, tel. 100-283, fax 100-366, ngaeheehe@ entelchile.net), on Petero Atamu a bit north of the church, has 13 rooms at US$40/30 pp high/low season including breakfast.

Cabañas Vai Moana (Edgard Hereveri, tel./fax 100-626, www.vai-moana.cl), on Atamu Tekena in the northern part of town, has five large duplex units containing a total of 10 rooms and three newer units in a triplex suite. It's US$40/60/90 single/double/triple (or US$5 less low season), plus US$12 for dinner. Many guests book through their website. Vai Moana rents bicycles, scooters, and jeeps.

Residencial Chez Cecilia (Cecilia Cardinali, tel. 100-499, www.chezcecilia.co.cl), off Atamu Tekena just behind Cabañas Vai Moana and near Ahu Tahai, has 10 rooms at US$40/70/95 single/double/triple high season, US$25/40/60 low season, breakfast included. Camping in a separate area behind the guesthouse is US$10 pp and there's a separate common kitchen and dining area for campers. Dinner is US$15.

Residencial Chez María Goretti (tel./fax 100-459, www.chezmariagoretti.cl), on Atamu Tekena north of Cabañas Vai Moana, has 15 large rooms at US$50/70/90 single/double/triple, plus US$10 pp for dinner. In the low season you can stay here for US$25 pp with breakfast. It's friendly, and there's a lovely garden and lounge. French is spoken.

Lucía Riroroko de Haoa runs **Mahina Taka Taka Georgia** (tel./fax 100-452, riroroco@ entelchile.net), at the north end of town near the museum. The four quiet rooms are US$30 pp (plus US$15 for dinner). You're really made to feel like part of the family.

US$100–150

The **Hotel Iorana** (tel./fax 100-312, www .ioranahotel.cl), on Policarpo Toro south of town, has 52 rooms with mini-fridge and cable TV. These begin at US$100/134 single/double for the 24 fan-cooled standard rooms on the north side of the complex. The 10 "turista" rooms (US$136/169) in the center are roasted by the afternoon sun and have very weak air-conditioning, so take one of the 18 superior rooms (US$179/200) on the south side of the Iorana if you want real air-conditioning. The bar next to the triangular swimming pool is worth a visit if you're returning from Orongo on foot, and the coastal views are fine.

The **Hotel Hotu Matu'a** (Orlando Paoa, tel. 100-242, fax 100-445, tokitour@entelchile.net) is at the east end of Avenue Pont not far from the airport. The 60 rooms are US$120/140/160 single/double/triple high season, US$60/100/ 120 low season including breakfast. Some rooms are rather old with worn carpets, so ask to see yours before accepting. There's a 10 percent surcharge if you pay by traveler's check or credit card. Lunch or dinner is US$20. This motel-style complex angles around a half-moon fresh-water swimming pool, and there's a bar. The owner's mini-museum off the lobby contains several intriguing artifacts. The LanChile flight crews always stay here.

Hotel Manutara (tel. 100-297, fax 100-768, manutarahotel@entelchile.net), on Hotu Matu'a east of the airport, has 28 rooms in an L-shaped building facing the pool at US$85/ 130/146 single/double/triple. The main problem here is the heavy disco beat from nearby PiRiti Disco, which continues all night on Fridays and Saturdays (don't allow your agent to book you here those nights). It's owned by Aku Aku Tourismo.

Hotel O'tai (Nico Haoa, tel. 100-250, fax 100-482, otairapanui@entelchile.net) is on Te Pito o Te Henua across from the post office. The 35 rooms are US$72/104 single/double, and there's a nice garden and swimming pool. Unfortunately the O'tai is just around the corner from island's other disco, the Toroko, so avoid staying here on a weekend.

US$150–250

The **Hotel Hanga Roa** (tel. 100-299, fax 100-426, reshangaroa@panamericanahoteles.cl), overlooking the bay at the west end of Avenue Pont, was used by Hollywood moviemakers for six months in 1993 and they really tore the place apart. A year later, the Hanga Roa was taken over by the Panamericana hotel chain, which added 10 bungalows, each containing three small air-conditioned rooms at US$270 double. The 60 worn rooms in the prefabricated main building are a poor value at US$130/150/175. In the low season the old rooms are reduced to US$72 single or double, the bungalows to US$100. Lunch or dinner is US$30.

Also not recommended is the **Hotel Taha Tai** (tel. 551-192, www.hotel-tahatai.co.cl), off Policarpo Toronto and Avenue Apina. Opened in 2001 and owned by Kia-Koe Tour, the Taha Tai has 30 rooms with no view in a main building, plus 10 cabañas in rows behind. It's way overpriced at US$140/165/180 single/double/triple—even the small pool is often dry.

FOOD AND ENTERTAINMENT

Food

A growing number of restaurants and snack bars exist along Atamu Tekena and Te Pito o Te Henua. The seafood is good, although the local lobsters (*langostas*) have become scarce (and expensive) due to overharvesting. Avoid *nanue* (rudderfish), an oily fish with a pungent taste much appreciated by the Rapanui but distasteful to the western pallet. Tuna (*kahi*) is a safer fish to order, and be sure to try *ceviche de pescado*, raw tuna marinated with lemon juice (US$6–8). Also watch for tasty local pastries called *empanadas*. A *completo* is a hot dog. Be wary of restaurants with prices quoted only in dollars!

The **Tunu-Ahi Barbecue** (Mon.–Sat. 0800–1500), on Atamu Tekena directly opposite the market (no sign), is a great place for a breakfast of *sopai pillos* (pancakes) at US$0.50 each with coffee for under a dollar. For lunch have a skewer of barbecued meat (US$3) or a large *ensalada poroto verde* salad (US$3). You can eat on their terrace.

Restaurant El Cuerito Regalón (tel. 551-232; daily 0900–midnight), just north on Atamu Tekena, features Chilean dishes, including *ceviche*, chicken, or tuna for US$7, red meat at US$9, and lobster for US$32. It's always crowded with tourists in the evening. The peso menu is less expensive than the one priced in dollars.

One of the cheapest places to eat is **Restaurante Tavake** (tel. 100-300), near the park on Atamu Tekena at the north end of the downtown strip. Sandwiches are US$3–4 and pizza US$4–5, but better value are the *platos económicos* for US$4. Vegetarian dishes cost the same.

A few blocks south on Atamu Tekena at the corner of Sebastián Englert is the **Aloha Pub** (tel. 551-383; Tues.–Sun. 1900–0300) with a coconut tree growing through the porch. It's more of a late night drinking place (large beer US$2.50) than a restaurant, but the light meals are fair value at US$5–8 (lobster US$39). The *ceviche* here is especially good.

Across Atamu Tekena and just down the hill from the Aloha Pub is **Ariki o te Pana** (Berta Hey, tel. 100-171; Mon.–Sat. 1000–midnight, Sun. 1000–1300) or The Queen of Empanadas. As usual there's no sign, but the *empanadas* made from cheese (US$1.50) or tuna (US$2) are really huge.

Easter Island's most expensive eatery by far is **Restaurant La Taverne Du Pêcheur** (tel. 100-619; Mon.–Sat. 1200–1400/1800–2200), near small boat harbor at Caleta Hanga Roa. The menu is priced exclusively in dollars: spaghetti US$11–15, fish or steaks US$13–15, lobster US$35–50. The portions are small and there's no view.

Restaurant Playa Pea (tel. 100-382; Tues.–Sun. 1200–1600), a bit south along the waterfront opposite Sernatur, is less expensive than La Taverne Du Pêcheur and the view is good. The menu includes a choice of seven fish dishes at US$8–10. The coffee and beer are reasonable, and you can sometimes get *empanadas* (US$1.50).

Restaurant Avarei Pua (tel. 100-431; Thurs.–Tues. 1200–2300), across the street from La Taverne Du Pêcheur, is much cheaper than it's neighbor (most dishes US$8).

Restaurant Caleta O'tai (tel. 100-607; Thurs.–Tues. 1100–2200), on Te Pito o Te Henua opposite Caleta Hanga Roa, is a good place for an afternoon drink with a nice sea view from the terrace. Main plates here are US$8, seafood soup US$6, and sandwiches US$4–6. It's run by the same people as Hotel Chez Joseph.

Despite the unpretentious appearance, **Restaurant La Tinita** (tel. 100-833; Mon.–Sat. 1200–1600/1800–2200), on Te Pito o Te Henua between hotels Manavai and O'tai, is one of the best restaurants in Hanga Roa. At US$8, the fish dishes, especially the tuna steak, are excellent. There's also fish soup for US$6 and sandwiches at US$3–5. The menu is in English and the portions large.

Finally, **Restaurant Kopakavana** (tel. 100-447; daily 1100–1500/1900–midnight) near the church offers a nice terrace with a view down Te Pito o Te Henua. The local fish dishes are US$8, lobster US$30.

The local tap water piped down from Rano Kao has a high magnesium content and may be a little brown, but it's quite safe to drink. Otherwise beer is available everywhere. Try the Chilean pisco (brandy) cocktails made from grapes. Liquor is sold cheaply in the local supermarkets.

Kai Nene Supermarket (tel./fax 100-492; weekdays 0930–1330/1700–2130, Sat. 0930–1400/1700–2130), on Atamu Tekena in the center of town, is the largest grocery store. The **Municipal Market** (Mon.–Sat. 0800–1200) or *feria municipal* on Atamu Tekena sells more handicrafts than food, and the best vegetables are sold out of the back of pick-up trucks across the street. The snack bar in the market has coffee and sandwiches for under a dollar.

Entertainment

The discos, **Toroko** on Policarpo Toro and **PiRiTi** on Avenue Hotu Matu'a, crank up on Friday and Saturday nights (admission US$3). During the peak summer season (Dec.–Feb.), they may operate other nights as well. The doors open around 2230, but nothing much happens before midnight; then the action continues until dawn.

The **Kari Kari Ballet Cultural** performs at Hotel Hanga Roa Tuesday or Wednesday and Saturday nights at 2200 (the days vary according to flight schedules). Admission is US$15. It's sometimes possible to purchase a package including dinner and the show for US$22, but

you must specifically request it at the hotel reception. December–February, Kari Kari also performs at Hotel Iorana on Fridays. This skillful traditional troupe, formed in 1996, is well worth seeing. September–February, a second group, the **Ballet Folklórico Polinesia,** performs at Restaurant Kopakavana (tel. 100-447) twice a week. Other cultural groups staging performances both here and abroad include Topatangi, Nga Poki, and Matato'a.

Sunday at 0900 there's singing in Rapanui in the Catholic church. April–October you can watch the local soccer teams compete in the field opposite Caleta Hanga Roa. Matches start at 2000 on Tuesday and Thursday, at 1400 on Sunday. Expect everything except church to start late.

Tito at **Rapa Nui Tattoo** (tel. 100-727), on Atamu Tekena a bit south of the LanChile office, does traditional tattooing beginning at US$20.

OTHER PRACTICALITIES
Shopping

Aside from shell necklaces and feather ornaments, the main things to buy here are woodcarvings, dance paddles, miniature stone *moai,* small pieces of tapa, and imitation *rongorongo* tablets. The onyx *moai* sold locally are imported from mainland Chile. Don't buy anything at all made from coral, as you'll only be encouraging unscrupulous individuals to damage the island's small reefs. Prices vary considerably from shop to shop.

The **Handicraft Market** (Mon.–Sat. 0930–1300/1600–1900, Sun. 1000–1300), opposite the church, sells overpriced woodcarvings, and is one of the only places in Polynesia where bargaining is expected. The vendors at this market are usually willing to trade woodcarvings for jeans, windbreakers, T-shirts, sneakers, toiletries, cosmetics, and rock music cassettes.

Handicrafts are also sold at the **Municipal Market** on Atamu Tekena, and inside a new pavilion in front of the airport terminal. The gift shop inside the **Museo Antropólogico Sebastián Englert** sells books, maps, videos, CDs, postage stamps, jewelry and T-shirts at rather high prices. Consider the surcharge a donation to the museum.

A commercial art gallery, the **Galería de Arte Aukara** (tel. 100–539), on Avenue Pont off Atamu Tekena not far from the LanChile office, displays museum-quality woodcarvings by internationally known sculptor Bene Tuki. These are priced US$100–700 and each is a unique work of art. Bene Tuki's wife, Ana María Arredondo, prepares numbered prints on tapa at US$15–50 apiece. This gallery doesn't keep regular hours so call ahead for an appointment to be sure someone will be there.

Information

There's a Sernatur tourist office (tel. 100-255; weekdays 0730–1300/1400–1800, Sat. 0830–1300) on Tu'u Maheke a few doors west of the bank. In Santiago de Chile, the Servicio Nacional de Turismo (tel. 56-2/731-8300, fax 56-2/251-8469), Ave. Providencia 1550, can supply a brochure and list of hotels on Easter Island.

Overpriced island maps of variable quality are sold locally at the museum and souvenir shops, such as Hotu Matu'a's Favorite Shoppe on Atamu Tekena.

Internet Resources

The site of the Easter Island Foundation, **www.islandheritage.org,** provides an online guide, history, legends, photos, and publications, plus a discussion of tourism's impact. The Easter Island Home Page, **www.netaxs.com/~trance/rapanui.html,** has useful historical and cultural introductions, and there's a sample of Rapa Nui music. The Rongorongo of Easter Island, **www.rongorongo.org,** presents the ancient culture of Easter Island, especially the mysterious rongorongo hieroglyphic script. There's even a Rapanui-English dictionary. Isla de Pascua, **www.rapanui.cl,** offers links to cultural resources, a directory of public services and institutions, news briefs, and listings of accommodations, restaurants and tour operators. The official tourism promotion website of the Cámara de Turismo Isla de Pascua, **www.turismo.rapanui.cl,** provides general information, history, legends, sightseeing, and activities. Portal Rapa Nui, **www.rapanuitours.com,** is a tourism site with general information, accommodations, car rentals, maps, tours, photos, and a local telephone directory. Iorana.net, **www.iorana.net,** is a Spanish portal with another Easter Island telephone directory, a Rapanui dictionary, news, music, and numerous links.

Money

The local currency is the Chilean peso (approximately US$1 = 650 pesos), which comes in notes of 500, 1,000, 2,000, 5,000, 10,000, and 20,000 pesos. Chilean currency is almost worthless outside Chile itself, so only change what you're sure you'll need, and get rid of the remainder before you leave. Duty-free purchases aboard LanChile flights can be paid for in pesos.

The Banco del Estado (tel. 100-221; weekdays 0800–1300), beside the tourist office in Hanga Roa, charges a flat US$10 commission to change any number of traveler's checks. U.S. dollars are changed without commission at the same rate. An ATM at the bank gives cash advances on MasterCard; cash advances on Visa cards are available at the counter (US$400 daily maximum). All cash advances are paid out in pesos, not dollars.

All tourist-oriented establishments accept dollars as payment, though not always at good rates. If you're coming from Santiago, bring a supply of pesos. Outside banking hours, the Shell gas station on Avenue Hotu Matu'a west of the airport changes U.S. cash at a rate 5 percent lower than the bank (posted in the office). Currencies other than U.S. dollars (including Polynesian CFP) can be difficult to exchange.

Credit cards are rarely usable on Easter Island, because those accepting them have to wait a long time to be paid. Some hotels levy a 10 percent service charge for the use of credit cards.

If you want to pay something approaching local prices, ask how much the item or service costs in pesos. Only tourists pay in U.S. dollars and dollar prices are invariably higher. When prices *are* quoted in dollars, you can usually save a small amount by asking to pay in pesos. Virtually all accommodations are priced (and can be paid) in dollars, but beware of restaurants, taxis, or shops quoting dollar prices. The prices in this book are given only in dollars to compensate for inflation and the depreciating Chilean peso, but almost everything can (and should) be paid for directly in pesos.

Post and Telecommunications

All mail is routed through Chile and Chilean postage stamps are used. The post office (tel. 100-332; weekdays 0900–1300/1430–1800, Sat. 0900–1230), on Te Pito o Te Henua opposite Hotel O'tai, sometimes has special Rapa Nui postage stamps only valid on the island. Occasionally they run out of stamps altogether. If you bring along your passport, the postmaster may be willing to stamp it too!

The Entel Telephone Center (fax 56-32/100-105; weekdays 0800–1800, Sat. 0800–1930), opposite the bank, sells telephone cards valued at US$1.50, US$4.50, US$8, and US$16, which can be used from all public telephones (the US$16 card will get you about 15 minutes to North America). You can receive faxes here for less that a dollar. The "AT&T Direct" access number from Easter Island is tel. 800/800-311. When calling Easter Island from abroad, dial your international access code plus 56 for Chile, 32 for Easter Island, and the six-digit local number (which always begins with 100, 550, or 551).

Interestingly, a phone call from Valparaíso, Chile, to Easter Island is a local call. However, from the island to Valparaíso is long distance.

Internet Access

Cyber Shark (tel./fax 100-600; Mon.–Sat. 1300–2000), next to Restaurant Caleta O'tai near Caleta Hanga Roa, offers internet access at US$1.50 per 15 minutes. Several shops and travel agencies along Atamu Tekena offer the same at similar rates.

Visas and Officialdom

Most visitors require only a passport valid six months ahead to stay 90 days in Chile. Visas are not necessary for North Americans, Australians, New Zealanders, and most Europeans. Check this at any LanChile Airlines office. An entry tax or *cobro por reciprocidad* is collected upon arrival in Chile, with the amount varying according to nationality (U.S. passports US$100, Canada US$55, Australia US$30, Mexico US$15, etc.). This tax is valid for the life of the passport and doesn't have to be paid again each visit. Try to have the exact change in cash, as the Chilean officials may not wish to give change. No vaccinations are required.

Yachting Facilities

Arriving yachts make contact over VHF channel 16. The Gobernación Marítima Hanga Roa (tel. 100-222) on Avenue Apina, the building on the coast with the Chilean flag, handles clearance.

Some 30 cruising yachts a year visit Easter Island between Galapagos/South America and Pitcairn/Tahiti. Due to Rapa Nui's remoteness, the boats will have been at sea two to four weeks before landfall. As Easter is well outside the South Pacific hurricane zone, they usually call January–March, so as to time their arrival in French Polynesia for the beginning of the prime sailing season there. The southeast trade winds extend south to Easter Island most reliably December–May, allowing for the easiest entry/exit. The rest of the year, winds are westerly and variable.

Anchorages include Hanga Roa, Vinapu, Hotu Iti, and Anakena/Ovahe, and a watch must be maintained over yachts at anchor at all times, as the winds can shift quickly in stormy weather. The anchorages are deep with many rocks to foul the anchor and little sand. Landing can be difficult through the surf. The frequent moves necessitated by changing winds can be quite exhausting, and crews often have only one or two days a week ashore. Luckily, the things to see are quite close to these anchorages.

A pilot is required to enter the small boat harbor at Hanga Piko and US$100 is charged. Entry through the breakers and rocks is only possible in calm weather. Mooring to the concrete wharf here is stern to as at Tahiti (no charge), but there's little space and this is only supposed to be done by boats in need of repairs. The harbor has 2.8 meters of water at low tide. Barges used to unload cargo from ocean-going ships are kept here.

Media

No newspapers or magazines are published on Easter Island, so the easiest way to keep in touch is to subscribe to Georgia Lee's *Rapa Nui Journal* (Easter Island Foundation, www.islandheritage.org). The *Journal* comes out twice a year, and contains an interesting mix of scientific studies, announcements, and local gossip—well worth the US$40 annual subscription price (US$50 airmail outside Canada and the U.S.).

EASTER ISLAND

Radio Manukena broadcasts in Rapanui over 88.9 MHz FM weekdays 0800–1100/1400–1700 (in Spanish at other times). The local TV station, channel 13 Mata Ote Rapa Nui, is on the air Friday–Sunday 1900–0100. Both are owned by the municipality. Chilean television programs are on at other times.

Health

The island hospital (tel. 100-215), on Simon Paoa, charges US$16 for medical consultations.

It's open 24 hours for emergencies. For non-emergencies, you must make an appointment a few days in advance. There's a pharmacy here (another is on Atamu Tekena in the center of town). To see the hospital's dentist, come in person around noon to get on the waiting list for that day (US$10 for a basic examination).

The private Consulta Médica (tel. 551-500; weekdays 1000–1400/1800–2200, Sat. 1100–1300), on Atamu Tekena next to Hotel Orongo, charges US$40 for consultations.

Transportation

Getting There

LanChile Airlines (www.lanchile.com) flies a Boeing 767 from Tahiti and Santiago to Easter Island twice a week. In the high season December–March, extra Santiago-Easter Island flights are added. From North America and Europe, LanChile has direct flights to Santiago from Los Angeles, Miami, New York, Madrid, and Frankfurt. See the Exploring the Islands chapter for sample fares. In North America, call LanChile toll-free at tel. 800/735-5526 for information. People in Europe and Australia can have Easter Island included in a cheap round-the-world ticket, something that usually isn't possible in North America.

Book and reconfirm your onward flight well ahead, as the plane is often overbooked between Easter Island and Santiago—a week is enough time to see everything. Between Easter Island and Tahiti, the plane is seldom full. We've heard from several readers who were forced to upgrade to business class when they tried to fly "standby" to Santiago. The local LanChile office (tel. 100-279; weekdays 0900–1300/1500–1730), on Atamu Tekena at Avenue Pont, will tell you there's no need to reconfirm your flight, but you should still visit their office and leave a local contact phone number to make sure your reservation is in their system. Don't be fooled by the nonchalant attitude of the LanChile employees—things go wrong on this route all the time.

The Gobernación Marítima Hanga Roa (tel. 100-222), on Avenue Apina near Hotel Hanga Roa, handles passenger bookings for the naval sup-

ply ship *Aquiles* to/from Valparaíso. It calls twice a year, usually in March and September, but you need to know someone with pull in the Chilean navy or administration to get aboard. If you do get on, passage costs around US$250 one way. On the continent, inquire at the Office of Naval Transport, Primera Zona Naval (weekdays 0800–1200), Plaza Sotomayor 594, Valparaíso, Chile.

Package Tours

Turn to Tours to Easter Island in the Papeete listings for information on package tours from Tahiti to Easter Island. Also see Organized Tours in the Exploring the Islands chapter introduction.

Getting Around

There's no public transportation, but the locals are pretty good about giving lifts. Sunday is an easy time to hitch a ride, since many people go fishing or to their gardens. Out on the island, drivers will often stop to offer you a ride even if you aren't hitchhiking.

Over 100 clearly-marked taxis patrol the streets of Hanga Roa, charging the locals US$1–2 for a ride around town or US$6–8 one-way to Anakena. Tourists are expected to pay much more and bargaining may be required. You'll get a better price dealing directly with a driver rather than by having your hotel receptionist call a taxi, in which case you'll pay the top tourist price.

For hikers, the taxis are handy to get somewhere in the morning with the intention of walking back to town. Sernatur has a list of official roundtrip taxi fares to many points with waiting time built in. To be expected to pay half that amount to be dropped somewhere without any waiting is unreasonable, yet some drivers still try and you may have to ask several of them. Flag a taxi down on the street and tell the driver straight away how many pesos you're willing to pay to be dropped somewhere. One-way, drop-off taxi fares from Hanga Roa start at US$5–6 to Orongo, US$6–8 to Anakena, and US$7–9 to Rano Raraku, paid in pesos. A knowledge of Spanish goes a long way here. The translation of "I only want to be dropped there" is *Solo quiero que me deje allá.*

The hotels and several offices along Atamu Tekena rent vehicles at US$40–60 a day. Most are 4WD jeeps due to the rugged terrain. Ask around, as prices vary (bargaining possible in the off season), and check to make sure the car has a spare tire *(neumático),* jack *(gata),* and gas tank cap. Insurance is not available, but gasoline is relatively cheap at US$2.25 a U.S. gallon and the distances are small. Scooters can be hired at US$30–45 a day, but a motorcycle license is mandatory. The roads to Anakena and Rano Raraku are now fully paved, making bicycling a lot more practical, and you should be able to rent a bike for US$10 a day.

Oceanic Rent a Car (tel. 100-985), on Atamu Tekena opposite Hotel Orongo, rents bicycles/motorcycles/jeeps at US$10/30/40.

Haunani Rent a Car (tel. 100-353, haunani@aclaris.cl), on Atamu Tekena next to Kai Nene Supermarket, rents bicycles/cars at US$8/40 a day. You can also arrange tours here with noted archaeologist Sergio Rapu of Easter Island Ecotours.

Several companies offer half/full day minibus tours of the island at US$25/35 pp. Boat tours to the *motu* off the southwestern tip of the island cost about US$30 pp a half day. The full day tour to Rano Raraku and Anakena is an excellent introduction to Easter Island, but unfortunately, all of the companies seem to do the same thing at the same time, so you're part of a moving crowd.

Aku Aku Turismo (tel. 100-770, www.akuaku turismo.cl), Tu'u Koihu just north of the church, has a half-day tour to Orongo and Tahai, and a full-day tour to Rano Raraku and Anakena. Their half-day "adventure tour" to Ana Kakenga and the summit of Maunga Terevaka by 4WD is US$30. Another adventure tour is to Ana o Keke, a cliffside cave on the Poike Peninsula. Horseback riding is also US$30. Lunch on the full-day tour costs US$15 extra, so take your own. Aku Aku is the largest tour company and the most likely to have the tour you want when you it. The narration will be in English and Spanish.

Kia-Koe Tour (tel. 100-852, fax 100-282, www.kiakoetour.co.cl), Atamu Tekena at Sebastián Englert, does much the same.

Rapa Nui Travel (tel. 100-548, fax 100-165), on Tu'u Koihu, caters to smaller groups and provides more personalized service for the same prices as Aku Aku and Kia-Koe. German-speaking guides can be provided. Rapa Nui's departures aren't as frequent as those of the others, so check early on in your stay. For a French-speaking tour, ask at **Residencial Tadeo y Lili** (tel./fax 100-422), Avenue Apina and Policarpo Toro.

Airport

At 3,353 meters long, Mataveri Airport (IPC) has the second longest runway in the South Pacific, only a little shorter than the one at the former French military base at Hao in the Tuamotu Islands. A rough airstrip was begun here in the early 1950s, and in the 1960s the U.S. Air Force improved it as an "ionospheric observation center." In fact, the Americans used the base to spy on the French nuclear testing. The Americans left after the election of Salvador Allende in 1970, but in 1986 they were back with Pinochet's blessing to extend both ends of the airstrip for use as an emergency landing strip by NASA space shuttles. Recently a plan to erect a new control tower in the form of a giant *moai* was scrapped after local objections.

The hotels and *residenciales* provide free airport transfers, or you can walk to any of them within a half hour. There's no bank, left-luggage office, or duty free shop, but there are many souvenir stands. The departure tax is US$26 to Tahiti or US$7 to Santiago, but it's usually included in the ticket price (ask). To control pests, it's prohibited to export fresh fruit or vegetables. *Iorana* means hello and goodbye in Rapanui.

Cook Islands

Introduction

The Cook Islands lie in the center of the Polynesian triangle about 4,500 km south of Hawaii. They range from towering Rarotonga, the country's largest island, to the low oval islands of the south and the solitary atolls of the north. Visitors are rewarded with natural beauty and colorful attractions at every turn. There is motion and excitement on Rarotonga and Aitutaki, peaceful village life on the rest. Since few tourists get beyond the two main islands, a trip to Atiu, Mangaia, or Mauke can be a fascinating experience. After Tahiti, the Cook Islands are inex-

pensive, and the local tourist industry is efficient and competitive. It's a safe, quiet place to relax, and you feel right at home. The local greeting is *kia orana* (may you live on). Other words to know are *meitaki* (thank you), *aere ra* (goodbye), and *kia manuia!* (cheers!).

The Land

These 15 islands and atolls, with a land area of only 240 square km, are scattered over 1.83 million square km of the South Pacific, leaving a lot of empty ocean in between. It's 1,433 km from Penrhyn to Mangaia. The nine islands in the southern group are a continuation of the Austral Islands of French Polynesia, formed as

© DAVID STANLEY

volcanic material escaped from a southeast/northwest fracture in the earth's crust. Five of the northern islands stand on the 3,000-meter-deep Manihiki Plateau, while Penrhyn rises directly out of seas 5,000 meters deep.

Practically every different type of oceanic island can be found in the Cooks. Rarotonga is the only high volcanic island of the Tahiti type. Aitutaki, like Bora Bora, consists of a middle-aged volcanic island surrounded by an atoll-like barrier reef, with many tiny islets defining its lagoon. Atiu, Mangaia, Mauke, and Mitiaro are raised atolls with a high cave-studded outer coral ring (*makatea*) enclosing volcanic soil at the center. It's believed these islands were uplifted during the past two million years due to the weight of Rarotonga on the earth's crust. There are low rolling hills in the interiors of both Atiu and Mangaia, while Mauke and Mitiaro are flat. The swimming and snorkeling possibilities at Atiu, Mangaia, Mauke, and Mitiaro are limited, as there's only a fringing reef with small tidal pools. Aitutaki and Rarotonga have protected lagoons where snorkeling is relatively safe. The rich, fertile southern islands account for 89 percent of the Cooks' land area and population.

Manihiki, Manuae, Palmerston, Penrhyn, Pukapuka, Rakahanga, and Suwarrow are typical lagoon atolls, while tiny Takutea and Nassau are sand cays without lagoons. All of the northern atolls are so low that waves roll right across them during hurricanes, and you have to be within 20 km to see them. This great variety makes the Cook Islands a geologist's paradise.

Climate

The main Cook Islands are about the same distance from the equator as Hawaii and have a similarly pleasant tropical climate. Rain clouds hang over Rarotonga's interior much of the year, but the coast is often sunny, and the rain often comes in brief, heavy downpours. The other islands are drier and can even experience severe water shortages. Winter evenings June–August can be cool. On both Rarotonga and Aitutaki, the best combination of prolonged hours of sunshine, fresh temperatures, and minimal rainfall runs July–September.

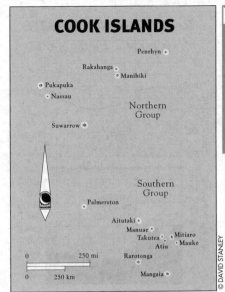

COOK ISLANDS

Penrhyn

Rakahanga
Manihiki

Pukapuka
Nassau

Northern Group

Suwarrow

Southern Group

Palmerston

Aitutaki
Manuae
Takutea · Mitiaro
Atiu · Mauke

0   250 mi   Rarotonga

0   250 km   Mangaia

© DAVID STANLEY

May–October, the trade winds blow steadily from the southeast in the southern Cooks and from the east in the more humid northern Cooks; the rest of the year winds are sometimes from the southwest or west (often a sign of bad weather). November–April is the summer hurricane season, with an average of one every other year, coming from the direction of Samoa. In December 2001, Hurricane Trina roared across Mangaia, flooding the taro fields and turning the sea red with eroded soil.

For weather information call the Meteorological Office (tel. 20-603) near Rarotonga Airport.

Flora and Fauna

The lush vegetation of the high islands includes creepers, ferns, and tall trees in the interior, while coconuts, bananas, and grapefruit grow on the coast. Avocados and papayas are so abundant that the locals feed them to their pigs. On the elevated atolls the vegetation in the fertile volcanic center contrasts brusquely with that of the infertile limestone *makatea*. Taro and yams are subsistence crops. The *au* is a native yellow-flowered hibiscus. The flower of this all-purpose plant is used for medicine, the leaves to cover the *umu*

RAROTONGA'S CLIMATE

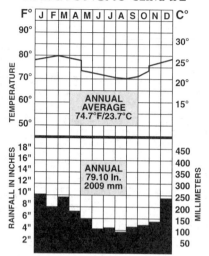

to 31 in the first two years. Humpback whales can sometimes be seen cruising along the shorelines July–September, having migrated 5,000 km north from Antarctica to bear their young. Pilot whales (up to six meters) are in the Cooks year-round. In 2001, the Cook Islands declared its large exclusive economic zone a whale sanctuary. Sharks are not a problem in the Cook lagoons.

HISTORY AND GOVERNMENT
Discovery

Though peppered across a vast expanse of empty ocean, the Polynesians knew all these islands by heart long before the first Europeans happened on the scene. One of several legends holds that Rarotonga was settled about A.D. 1200 by two great warriors, Karika from Samoa and Tangiia-nui from Tahiti. The story goes that Karika and Tangiia-nui met on the high seas but decided not to fight because there would be no one to proclaim the victor. Instead they carried on to Rarotonga together and divided the island among themselves by sailing their canoes around it in opposite directions, with a line between their starting and meeting points becoming the boundary. Even today, tribes in the Cooks refer to themselves as *vaka* (canoes), and many can trace their ancestry back to these chiefs.

Archaeologists believe Rarotonga was reached much earlier, probably before A.D. 800 from Raiatea or the Marquesas. The mythical chief Toi,

(earth oven), the fiber for skirts, reef sandals, and rope, and the branches for walling native cottages on outer islands. November–March, the flamboyant trees bloom red.

The only native mammals are bats and rats. The mynah is the bird most often seen, an aggressive introduced species that drives native birds up into the mountains and damages fruit trees. By 1989, only about 29 examples of the Rarotonga flycatcher, or *kakerori,* remained due to attacks on the birds' nests by ship rats. Fortunately, a local landowners group, the Takitumu Conservation Area, took an interest in the survival of *kakerori* and began laying rat poison in the nesting areas during the breeding season. By 2001, there were 241 *kakerori.*

Unfortunately, the activities of local sharpshooters have made the Cook Islands less attractive as a bird-watching venue, and spearfishing using scuba gear has done much damage to the marinelife. To control this, five lagoon areas around Rarotonga have been closed to fishing and shell collecting since 1998 under a traditional system known as *ra'ui.* In one of the *ra'ui* areas, the number of fish species increased from 14

COOK ISLANDS HIGHLIGHTS

island night, Aitutaki: dancing, culture, food, fun (p. 364)

makatea of Mangaia: geology, hiking, nature (p. 374)

Tapuaetai, Aitutaki: swimming at One Foot Island, lagoon trips (p. 366)

The Needle, Rarotonga: hiking, geology, nature (p. 340)

Titikaveka snorkeling, Rarotonga: marinelife (p. 339)

COOK ISLANDS AT A GLANCE

ISLAND	AREA (in hectares)	POPULATION (2001)
Rarotonga	6,718	12,206
Mangaia	5,180	745
Atiu	2,693	622
Mitiaro	2,228	230
Mauke	1,842	468
Aitutaki	1,805	1,937
Penrhyn	984	357
Manuae	617	0
Manihiki	544	516
Pukapuka	506	664
Rakahanga	405	161
Palmerston	202	48
Takutea	122	0
Nassau	121	69
Suwarrow	40	4
Cook Islands	**24,007**	**18,027**

who built the Ara Metua on Rarotonga, is associated with this earlier migration. Recent excavations of a *marae* on a *motu* in the Muri Lagoon point to an even earlier date, perhaps A.D. 500. Even earlier sites have been found on Mangaia. Atiu was a chiefly island that dominated Mauke, Mitiaro, Takutea, and sometimes Manuae.

The Spanish explorer Mendaña sighted Pukapuka in 1595, and his pilot, Quirós, visited Rakahanga in 1606. Some 500 inhabitants gathered on the beach to gaze at the strange ships. Quirós wrote, "They were the most beautiful white and elegant people that were met during the voyage— especially the women, who, if properly dressed, would have advantages over our Spanish women."

Then the islands were lost again to Europeans until the 1770s when Captain Cook contacted Atiu, Mangaia, Manuae, Palmerston, and Takutea—"detached parts of the earth." *He* named Manuae the Hervey Islands, a name others applied to the whole group; it was not until 1824 that the Russian cartographer, Johann von Krusenstern, labeled the southern group the Cook Islands. Cook never saw Rarotonga, and the Pitcairn-bound *Bounty* is thought to be its first European visitor (in 1789). The mutineers gave the inhabitants the seeds for their first orange trees. Aitutaki was discovered by Captain Bligh just before the famous mutiny. Mauke and Mitiaro were reached in 1823 by John Williams of the London Missionary Society.

European Penetration

Williams stopped at Aitutaki in 1821 and dropped off two Tahitian teachers. Returning two years later, he found that one, Papeiha, had done particularly well. Williams took him to Rarotonga and left him there for four years. When he returned in 1827, Williams was welcomed by Papeiha's many converts. The missionaries taught an austere, puritanical morality and believed the white man's diseases such as dysentery, measles, smallpox, and influenza, which killed two-thirds of the population, were the punishment of God descending on the sinful islanders. The missionaries became a law unto themselves; today, the ubiquitous churches full to overflowing on Sunday are their legacy. (The missionaries arrived from Australia, and since they weren't aware of the idea of an international date line, they held Sunday service on the wrong day for the first 60 years of their presence!) About 63 percent of the population now belongs to the Cook Islands Christian Church (CICC), founded by the London Missionary Society. Takamoa College, the Bible school they established at Avarua in 1837, still exists.

Reports that the French were about to annex the Cooks led the British to declare a protectorate over the southern group in 1888. The French warship approaching Manihiki to claim the islands turned back when it saw a hastily sewn Union Jack flying, and in 1889 the northern atolls were added to the protectorate at the behest of the missionaries. The local chiefs petitioned the British to have their islands annexed to the British Crown. Thus on June 11, 1901, both the northern and southern groups were included in the boundaries of New Zealand. During WW II, the United States built air bases on Aitutaki and Penrhyn.

A legislative council was established in 1946, followed by an assembly with greater powers in 1957. After decolonizing pressure from the United Nations, a new constitution was granted in 1964, and on August 4, 1965, the Cook Islands was made a self-governing state in free association with New Zealand. Today the Cook Islands manages its own internal and external affairs. The islanders are New Zealand and Cook Islands dual citizens and have the right of free entry to New Zealand and Australia. In fact, over three times more of them live in New Zealand and Australia than on their home islands. New Zealanders and Australians, on the other hand, do not have the reciprocal right to reside permanently in the Cook Islands. The Cook Islands belongs to many United Nations agencies but has never applied for full U.N. membership, as this might lead to New Zealand withdrawing

citizenship privileges. In recent years, the Cook Islands has sought closer economic and cultural ties with French Polynesia to balance their relationship with New Zealand.

Government

The Cook Islands' 25-member Parliament operates on the Westminster system, with a prime minister as the head of government (www.cookislands.gov.ck). The cabinet consists of up to eight ministers. While almost all members of parliament are men, most of the chiefly titles are held by women, who are also the main landowners. In theory, the 21-member House of Ariki (chiefs) should be consulted on custom and land issues, but in practice this seldom happens.

On all the outer islands there's an appointed chief administrative officer (CAO), formerly known as the resident agent. Although each island also has an elected Island Council, the CAO runs the local administration on behalf of the local and central governments.

Politics

Party politics, often based on personalities, can be vicious. The most dramatic event of the early years of self-government was the removal of Premier Albert Henry and the Cook Islands Party from office in 1978 by the chief justice of the High Court when it was proven that Henry had misused government funds to fly in his voters from New Zealand during the preceding election. Then, Queen Elizabeth II stripped Sir Albert of his knighthood. This was the first time in Commonwealth history that a court ruling had changed a government; the shock waves are still being felt on Rarotonga. Albert Henry died in 1981, it's said of a broken heart.

Albert Henry's successor, Sir Tom Davis of the Democratic Party, served as prime minister from 1978 until 1987. The Cook Islands Party, led by Sir Geoffrey Henry, a cousin of Albert, won the 1989 and 1994 elections. Henry's tenure was marked by financial disasters and a population collapse. In the 1999 elections, the vote was split between the Cook Islands Party, the Democratic Alliance Party, and the New Alliance Party, and the post of prime minister has been rotating as politicians switch sides for personal advantage. Office space, vehicles, expense accounts, jobs for relatives, and overseas travel are among the perks parliamentarians enjoy in addition to their generous salaries and pensions. After lengthy public consultations in 1998, a Commission of Inquiry into Political Reform called for a reduction in the number of members of parliament. In 2003, the controversial overseas seat in parliament was finally abolished, but calls to ban "party hopping" by self-serving politicians have been ignored.

ECONOMY

The Cook Islands has a severe trade imbalance, with imports outweighing exports by 11 times. Food imports alone cost three times the value of all exports. New Zealand benefits greatly from this situation by supplying 70 percent of the Cook Islands' imports. Around NZ$10 million comes back in the form of New Zealand aid to health, education, and special projects. Money remitted by Cook Islanders residing in New Zealand does its part to cover the country's import bill, and quite often durable goods included in the import figures are actually free gifts sent home by family members abroad. Tourism plays a vital role in correcting the balance of payments, and licensing fees from foreign fishing companies exploiting the exclusive economic zone bring in additional income. In 2003, a freezer plant was set up on Rarotonga by a company owned in part by the Japanese fishing company Sealord.

The largest exports are cultured pearls, fruits and vegetables, clothing, and fish and seafood in that order. Cultured pearls alone account for 90 percent of the country's exports and the percentage continues to grow. Fresh fruit production is hindered by the small volume, uneven quality, inadequate shipping, poor marketing, and the unreliability of island producers. Most food is imported and the local produce markets are usually empty.

The economy's small size is illustrated by the importance of the post office's Philatelic Bureau. A number of small clothing factories in Avarua supply tropical beachware to the local and tourist markets. Subsistence fishing and agriculture are important on the outer islands.

Future wealth may come from the mining of undersea deposits of cobalt, copper, and nickel inside the exclusive economic zone. In 1997, the Cook Islands signed a deal theoretically worth US$600 million with the American mining giant Bechtel Corporation. After a careful study in 2001, mining experts from Norway found that current world cobalt prices of around US$15 a pound made exploiting these reserves unviable. They did note that if prices were to increase to US$25, a 30 percent profit on investment was possible.

Finance

Since 1984, the Cook Islands has operated as an "international finance center," providing offshore banking facilities to foreign corporations and individuals attempting to avoid taxation and regulation in their home countries. In contrast to local businesses, which are heavily taxed and regulated, over 3,000 companies, trusts, banks, and insurance companies that don't operate in the Cooks are now registered in the Rarotonga "tax haven," bringing in about NZ$4 million a year in banking and licensing fees. Offshore "banks" can be owned by a single person, and it's believed that millions of illicit dollars have been laundered through Rarotonga. The number of Asian companies involved is significant.

Such arrangements allow individuals in other jurisdictions to transfer revenue to "asset protection trusts" in the Cook Islands that are safe from creditors in the event of a subsequent bankruptcy. Thus unscrupulous individuals can plunder their own companies elsewhere in order to build up tax-free nest eggs on Rarotonga. Profits can be routed through the Cook Islands to avoid taxation. Scams like these helped generate the Asian financial crisis of 1997, and teams of highly paid lawyers and accountants based on Rarotonga and abroad facilitate the process.

In June 2001, the 26-nation Financial Action Task Force of the Organization for Economic Cooperation and Development put the Cook Islands and 10 other countries on a blacklist of "uncooperative jurisdictions" with regulatory systems which make them attractive money laundering locations. Australia and New Zealand have revised their tax laws to restrict the use of tax havens by their citizens (penalties of up to 125 percent of the tax due and five years in prison). In 2003, the Cook Islands revised its banking laws under OECD pressure and 16 offshore banks withdrew from the country.

The country has a NZ$119 million national debt, most of it incurred during the administration of Sir Geoffrey Henry in the 1990s, for tourism-related developments such as the Sheraton Hotel project, the National Cultural Center, power generation, and telecommunications. Much of the money is owed to the governments of Italy and Nauru, which foolishly guaranteed huge unsecured loans to this tiny country, but NZ$27 million of it came from the Asian Development Bank, which has had to intervene several times to save the Cook Islands from bankruptcy.

In mid-1994, local branches of the ANZ and Westpac banks began to severely restrict private credit after the government proved unable to service its heavy debt load. A few months later, the banks stopped clearing checks drawn in the Cook Islands dollars through the New Zealand banking system and announced that these would have to be collected locally. Local businesses began moving money offshore, and in late 1994, the Reserve Bank of New Zealand confirmed that it no longer guaranteed the convertibility of the Cook Islands dollar. The threat of imminent financial collapse forced the government to withdraw the currency from circulation in 1995. New Zealand banknotes are presently used.

Until 1996, the Cook Islands had a bloated public service of 3,600 persons or 60 percent of the workforce. Then, after the Westpac Bank bounced official salary checks due to a US$5 million dollar overdraft in the government's current account, civil servants were forced to accept a 15 percent across the board pay cut. As interest on unpaid government loans continued to mount, it became clear that harsher measures were required. Thus it was announced that government employee numbers would be reduced to 1,200 and the pay cut increased to 65 percent. From 1996–1999, 3,969 Cook Islanders, a quarter of the population, voted with their feet and left for greener pastures in Australia and New Zealand. State assets (including four hotels and the telephone company) were hurriedly sold off and the number of government departments cut in half. The country is still recovering from this disaster.

The Cook Islands runs a discount "flag of convenience" ship registry that allows foreign shipping companies to avoid the more stringent safety and labor regulations of industrialized countries. Due to unexplained sinkings and other costly mishaps, most insurance companies won't touch ships registered in the Cooks. (Despite all the infighting and chicanery described herein, the Cook Islands is completely safe and stable for tourism. The Australian guidebooks conveniently leave out most of this information and are generally uncritical in order to curry favor on Rarotonga.)

Tourism

Since the opening of the international airport in 1973, tourism has been important, and directly or indirectly, it now employs more than a quarter of the workforce and accounts for NZ$103 million of the NZ$202 million gross national product. The Cook Islands has the highest tourist density in the South Pacific with four tourists a year for every local resident, compared to two Fijians, three Samoans, and four Tongans for every tourist visiting those countries. At times Rarotonga (with six tourists a year per Cook Islander) really has the feel of a little Hawaii.

After the civil coup in Fiji in May 2000, many tourists switched their holidays to the Cook Islands and arrivals jumped 50 percent. About a third of the 75,000-odd arriving tourists are New Zealanders who spend all their time at resorts on Rarotonga and Aitutaki on prepaid packaged holidays. The rest are fairly evenly divided between Americans, Australians, Canadians, and Europeans. Fears have been expressed that Rarotonga and Aitutaki's waste disposal, electricity generation, and water supply systems won't be able to keep pace with the rapid expansion of tourism, and tourist demand has led to double-digit inflation in the local housing market. Hundreds of low-wage Fijian workers have been imported to staff the resorts and hotels, and some have complained about long working hours and poor living conditions.

In 1984, "experts" from the United Nations Development Program advised that the way to make tourism more "profitable" was to allow more large hotels and to stop construction of the smaller, family-operated motels. Finding itself unable to attract the required foreign investment, the government itself decided to bankroll construction of a four-star luxury hotel, and in 1987, NZ$52 million was borrowed from an Italian bank. A year later, the Democratic Party government collapsed, and in 1989 Sir Geoffrey Henry's Cook Islands Party was voted in after promising to stop the project. Once in office, however, Sir Geoffrey did an about-face and announced that he now backed the hotel. A management contract was signed with the Sheraton chain and in May 1990, despite many objections from local residents, construction began on the south side of Rarotonga using Italian building materials and contractors.

The 204-room Cook Islands Sheraton Resort was conceived as a cluster of two-story buildings, similar to the Fiji Sheraton, with the inevitable 18-hole golf course. The project suffered repeated delays, and then it was announced that the Italian construction company had gone broke after spending NZ$30 million of the government's loan money without getting much done. A second Italian construction company (Stephany SpA) was brought in, and the government borrowed another NZ$20 million so work could resume. In mid-1993, the Italian government began its "clean hands" crackdown on Mafia activities, and several people involved in the Sheraton project were arrested in Italy, causing the Italian insurers to freeze coverage on the loans, and work on the Sheraton stopped again.

In late 1998, the government attempted to restart the project by letting their lease on the property lapse and turning the project over to Hawaiian/Japanese investors who paid the landowner a NZ$300,000 advance on the annual rent. A few months later, the Japanese partner was arrested for tax fraud and the deal collapsed. In late 2000, another company announced that they were willing to finish the hotel, which would become a Hilton, provided they got a casino license. This outraged the pious Rarotongans, who held meetings and circulated petitions vehemently opposed to gambling, and the casino idea had to be dropped. The uncertainty continues and demolition of the shell of what is now euphemistically called the "Vaimaanga Hotel" may be the only solution.

What has gone on behind the scenes in all of this is largely unknown and the Cook Islands Government claims it doesn't have the resources/ability to mount a proper investigation. Most of the records are said to be missing, and between 10 and 20 million New Zealand dollars have simply "disappeared." In 1998, the government's NZ$120 million Italian debt was rescheduled to NZ$55 million to be paid over 27 years. (Sheraton had nothing to do with the construction scandal and would only have become involved had the project been completed.)

Pearls

In 1982, research began into the possibility of creating a cultured-pearl industry in the Cook Islands similar to that of French Polynesia. The first commercial farms were set up on Manihiki in 1989, and today over a hundred farms on Manihiki produce cultured pearls from the two million oysters below the surface of the lagoon. By 1994, the Manihiki lagoon was thought to be approaching its maximum sustainable holding capacity and farms began being established on Penrhyn. Hundreds of thousands of oysters are presently hanging on racks in the Penrhyn lagoon, and a hatchery is adding to their numbers every day. Oyster farming has also begun on Rakahanga. A proposal to establish a pearl farm on uninhabited Suwarrow atoll was rejected in 2001 over fears that the atoll's large seabird colonies would be disturbed.

To build a farm, an investment of NZ$5,000 is required, and no return will be forthcoming for five years. There are currently over 300 farms in the Cook Islands with just 20 percent of them accounting for 80 percent of the oysters. The oysters are seeded once or twice a year by Japanese, Chinese, and Cook Islands experts screened by the Ministry of Marine Resources.

The pearl industry has reversed the depopulation of the northern atolls and brought a degree of prosperity to this remote region. Thanks to pearls, Air Rarotonga can afford to operate regular flights to Manihiki and Penrhyn, making life a little easier for the 1,750 inhabitants of the Northern Group.

Fluctuations in water temperature and overstocking can affect the amount of plankton available to the oysters and reduce the quality of the pearls. In 2001, a bacterial pearl shell disease outbreak at Manihiki, caused by a combination of overfarming and high water temperatures, wiped out almost half the juvenile oyster population, proving what some had been saying all along: that the rapid growth in pearl farming over the past decade has pushed some sections of the Manihiki lagoon well beyond their maximum carrying capacity of oysters. The algal bloom killed 15 percent of seeded oysters, resulting in an estimated loss of NZ$34 million over five years.

Despite this setback, annual production is around 200 kilograms and black pearls account for 90 percent of the Cook Islands' exports, bringing in NZ$15 million a year and employing 700 people. Japanese and Chinese dealers are the main buyers of the official production, and it's believed the industry is actually worth much more, since large quantities of pearls are smuggled out of the country each year to avoid customs duties. Pearl prices are currently falling as production increases, and some producers are worried that the pearl boom may already have peaked.

THE PEOPLE

About 84 percent of the people are Polynesian Cook Island Maoris, most of whom also have some other ancestry. They're related to the Maoris of New Zealand and the Tahitians, although the Pukapukans are unique in that they are closer to the Samoans. Almost everyone on Rarotonga and most people on the outer islands speak flawless English, while their mother tongue will be one of the 11 dialects of Cook Islands Maori. Rarotongan is now spoken throughout the southern group. Penrhyn is closely related to Rarotongan, Rakahanga-Manihiki is more distantly related, and Pukapukan is related to Samoan.

Over half the population resides on Rarotonga; only 13 percent live in the northern group. Cook Islanders reside near the seashore, except on Atiu and Mauke, where they are interior dwellers. The old-style thatched *kikau* houses have almost disappeared from the Cook Islands, even though they're cooler, more esthetic, and much cheaper to build than modern housing. A thatched pandanus roof can last 15 years.

While 18,027 (2001) Cook Islanders live in their home islands, some 60,000 reside in New Zealand and another 10,000 in Australia. Emigration to New Zealand increased greatly after the airport opened in 1973. During the 1980s, the migratory patterns reversed and many ex-islanders returned from New Zealand to set up tourism-related businesses, but due to the economic crisis, the steady flow of people to New Zealand and Australia resumed in 1996 and the total population has actually decreased. The loss of many teachers and students forced schools and classes to be amalgamated and led to an increase in the dropout rate among teenagers. Education is compulsory until the age of 15.

There are almost no Chinese in the Cooks due to a deliberate policy of discrimination initiated in 1901 by New Zealand Prime Minister Richard Seddon, although many islanders have some Chinese blood resulting from the presence of Chinese traders in the 19th century. A quarter of the population was born outside the South Pacific, and the proportion of Americans, New Zealanders, Australians, and others is increasing rapidly as "lifestyle investors" arrive to run businesses in the Cook Islands while the islanders themselves move in the opposite direction.

Under the British and New Zealand regimes, the right of the Maori people to their land was protected, and no land was sold to outsiders. These policies continue today, although foreigners can lease land for up to 60 years. The fragmentation of inherited landholdings into scattered mini-holdings hampers agriculture and many fine late 19th century stone buildings have fallen into ruins due to ownership disputes.

The powerful *ariki*, or chiefly class, that ruled in pre-European times, is still influential today. The *ariki* were the first to adopt Christianity, instructing their subjects to follow suit and filling leadership posts in the church. British and New Zealand colonial rule was established with the approval of the *ariki*. Today, materialism, party politics, and emigration to New Zealand are eroding the authority of the *ariki. Ariki* titles are tied to land and cannot be carried overseas (the title passes to another family member if a holder decides to migrate to New Zealand). Until self-government, Cook Islanders were only allowed to consume alcohol if they had a permit; now it's a serious social problem.

Dangers and Annoyances

When stepping out at night or choosing a place to stay, women should keep in mind that sexual assault is not unknown here. There's safety in numbers. Scanty dress outside the resorts will cause offense and maybe trouble. To go to church, women should wear a dress with long sleeves and a hat, while men need long trousers and a proper shirt. Be aware of petty theft, particularly if you're staying somewhere with young children running loose. Don't leave things unattended on a clothesline or the beach and keep your shoes in your room at night. Try to avoid being bitten by mosquitoes, as dengue fever epidemics have occurred on Rarotonga in recent years (see Health in the Exploring the Islands chapter of this book).

Exploring the Islands

Highlights

Everyone will arrive on **Rarotonga** and the short-list of "musts" includes an island night dance show, a bicycle ride around the island, a swim in the Muri Lagoon, and a hike up to the Needle on the Cross-Island Track. The main town Avarua has two museums and various monuments associated with 19th century missionaries. The finest snorkeling is at Titikaveka on the southeast side of the island.

The snorkeling at **Aitutaki** is even better and it's another nice place to hang loose. The lagoon trips by boat to One Foot Island are very popular and traditional dance shows are staged at the resorts almost every night.

However, to get a real feel for the Cook Islands, you must travel beyond this rather touristy pair to an outer island. Most of the people on **Atiu** live in the center of the island. Deep caves penetrate the island's uplifted limestone ring, and Atiu has the added attraction of *tumunus* where bush beer is served. **Mauke** is similar and even less visited. **Mangaia** has some of the most spectacular elevated coral formations in the world. All three islands have regular flights from Rarotonga and a few small lodgings, although other visitor facilities are scanty—they're that unspoiled.

Due to infrequent and expensive transportation, the Northern Group is seldom visited by tourists. In recent years, these far-flung atolls have been rediscovered thanks to the cultured pearl industry.

Sports and Recreation

Several professional scuba diving companies are based on Rarotonga and Aitutaki, and there are many snorkeling possibilities. Both islands offer lagoon tours by boat, with those at Aitutaki by far the better.

Operators based on Rarotonga's Muri Beach rent water-sports equipment, including windsurfers, sailboats, and kayaks, with training in their use available. The surfing possibilities are very limited in the Cook Islands—windsurfing's the thing to do. Horseback riding and deep-sea fishing are other popular activities.

Most of the hiking possibilities are on mountainous Rarotonga, but uplifted islands such as Atiu, Mauke, and Mangaia are also fascinating to wander around. The nine-hole golf courses on Aitutaki and Rarotonga aren't too challenging, but greens fees are low and the atmospheres amicable. Tournaments are held at both in September.

The spectator sports are cricket December–February, with matches every Saturday afternoon from 1300, and rugby May–July. Rugby is the main male team sport played in the Cooks; soccer is a more recent introduction (played year-round). On Rarotonga, ask about rugby matches at Tereora National Stadium, on the inland side of the airport, and in the sports ground opposite the National Cultural Center in Avarua. Netball is the most popular women's sport, especially in March and April.

Music and Dance

Among the main genres of Cook Islands music and dance are drum dancing (*'ura pa'u*), choreographed group dancing (*kaparima*) to string band music, dance dramas (*peu tupuna*) based on island legends, religious pageants (*nuku*), formal chants (*pe'e*), celebratory song/chants (*'ute*), and polyphonic choral music (*'imene tapu*) or hymns.

Among the drums used are the small *pate* or *to'ere* slit drum used to guide the dancers, the *pa'u*, a double-headed bass drum that provides the beat, and the upright *pa'u mango* that accompanies the *pa'u*. The larger *ka'ara* slit drum and the conch shell accompany chanting. Tahitian drummers have often copied Cook Island rhythms. String band music is based on the ukulele, although guitars are also used.

The top traditional dancing is seen during annual events on Rarotonga when the outer islanders arrive to compete. The drum dancing at hotel shows features the sensuous side-to-side hip movements of the women (differing somewhat from the circular movements seen on Tahiti) and the robust knee snapping of the men. In the Cook Islands the dancers keep their feet apart, while in Tahiti the feet are together. In the *hura* (equivalent of the Hawaiian *hula*) the female dancers must keep their feet flat on the ground and shoulders steady as they sway in a stunning display.

Public Holidays and Festivals

Public holidays include New Year's Day (January 1), ANZAC Day (April 25), Good Friday, Easter Monday (March/April), Queen Elizabeth's Birthday (first Monday in June), Constitution Day (August 4), National Gospel Day (October 26),

Christmas Day (December 25), and Boxing Day (December 26). On Rarotonga, Gospel Day is celebrated on July 26; elsewhere it's October 26.

The Dancer of the Year Competition is in late April. The 10-day Te Maeva Celebrations is the big event of the year, culminating on Constitution Day (August 4). There are parades, drumming and singing contests, sporting events, and an agricultural fair. The Round Raro Road Race is a 31-km marathon held on the first Saturday of October (the record time is 98 minutes set by Kevin Ryan in 1979). From mid-October–mid-November there's the annual *tivaevae* show at the National Museum on Rarotonga. National Gospel Day (October 26) recalls October 26, 1821, when the Rev. John Williams landed on Aitutaki. Ask about Biblical pageants (*nuku*) on that day. On All Souls Day (November 1) Catholics visit the cemeteries to place candles and flowers on the graves of family members. The third or fourth week in November is the Tiare Festival, with flower shows, a parade, and beauty contests.

Accommodations

There's an abundance of accommodations in all price categories on Rarotonga and Aitutaki, and most outer islands also have one or two places to stay. Accommodations accredited by the Cook Islands Tourism Corporation must meet certain standards and those that do can include a distinctive tick mark in their advertising. The accreditation system recognizes three categories: budget, self-catering, and hotels. Essentially, you have a "hotel" if you have a restaurant (and a few other minor things). In fact, many of the "self-catering" places are nicer than most of the hotels, so don't go by price alone. The non-accredited establishments aren't mentioned in the official tourist brochures, though the vast majority of them are also quite okay.

You'll save money and get closer to the people by staying at the smaller, locally owned "self-catering" motels and guesthouses. A "motel" in the Cooks is styled on the New Zealand type of motel, which means a fully equipped kitchen is built into each unit. Some of them are quite attractive, nothing like the dreary roadside motels of North America. The motels generally offer rooms with private bath and hot water, but some guesthouses and hostels do not, although communal cooking facilities are usually available.

The policy set by the Cook Islands Immigration Department is to have at least one night's accommodation booked before you arrive. Although many visitors wait to book their rooms upon arrival, they are taking the risk of being refused entry to the country if they happen to come on a day when everything is full. In practice this rarely happens, but to avoid the possibility, simply write the name of one of the places to stay listed herein on your arrivals card. As you come out of the airport terminal, ask for the representative of that place. If they're not there or the place happens to be full, ask for something similar.

The backpacker hostels always have empty dorm beds, but accommodation is sometimes tight in the medium-price range. If you're sure you want to stay at a particular place, you can easily make an advance booking by emailing the hostel or hotel directly (addresses provided in the back of this book). Most of the backpacker places have a two-night minimum stay and you shouldn't promise to stay longer than that. Then if you end up with something you don't like, you can easily move elsewhere (this advice may not apply at the more upscale places). Hotel rates tend to fluctuate in the Cook Islands, and when things are slow, some places cut their prices to attract guests, so in some cases you could end up paying less than the amounts quoted herein.

Camping is not allowed in the Cook Islands. There's a shortage of flights into the Cooks and airline seats are often at a premium. The government would rather see those seats being used by regular resort tourists who'll be spending more money and thereby paying more taxes. The main aim of campers is to save money, the exact opposite of what the government wants. And since the government makes the rules, camping has always been banned. The officials would also like to reduce the number of backpacker dormitories on Rarotonga, but the dorms are owned by local people and closing them now would have political repercussions.

Travel with Children

Unlike French Polynesia where children are welcome at virtually all of the resorts and charged reduced rates at most, many accommodations in the Cook Islands have a "no children" policy designed to enhance their appeal to "romantic couples" and honeymooners. The age limit varies and is noted in the listings whenever possible. Among the Rarotonga properties excluding young children are Maiana Guesthouse, Manuia Beach Hotel, Oasis Village, Paradise Inn, Rarotongan Sunset Motel, Reflections on Rarotonga, Shangri-La Beach Cottages, Sokala Villas, Sunhaven Beach Bungalows, Takitumu Romantic Villas, and The Little Polynesian. On Aitutaki, the Are Tamanu Beach Hotel doesn't admit children.

In contrast, the largest properties, including the Aitutaki Lagoon Resort, the Edgewater Resort, the Pacific Resort, and the Rarotongan Beach Resort, give discounts to families and have special programs for kids. Other Rarotonga accommodations with special deals for families include Lagoon Lodges, Palm Grove Lodges, and Moana Sands. If you suspect that the sight and sound of children might blemish your holiday, chose an adults-only property.

Booking Agencies

Island Hopper Vacations (tel. 22-576, fax 23-027, www.islandhoppervacations.com), west of the airport terminal, offers accommodation deals and outer island flights. They have an online booking facility at www.reservecooks.com. **Jetsave Travel** (tel. 27-707, fax 28-807, www.jetsave.co.ck), just west of the Westpac Bank, and **Tipani Tours** (www.tipanitours.com) are similar. These companies also offer transfers, wedding arrangements, and dive packages.

Be aware that these agents charge commissions as high as 35 percent to the owners, and you can often get a better rate by checking the hotel's website and emailing directly. On the plus side, the companies just mentioned do book the smaller, budget properties that travel agents outside the Cooks won't touch because the commissions are so small.

Food and Drink

The Rarotonga restaurant scene has improved in recent years and you now have a good choice. A few restaurants are found on Aitutaki, but none exist on the outer islands. When ordering, keep in mind that an "entree" is actually an appetizer and not a main dish. Garlic bread seems to appear on every menu regardless of cuisine!

By law all bars are required to close at midnight, except on Fridays when they can stay open until 0200 Saturday morning. On Sunday, no alcohol may be sold at grocery stores, and that day even restaurants are only allowed to serve alcohol with a meal, although this rule is not always followed. Wine is expensive at restaurants, due to high import duties, and drinking alcoholic beverages on the street is prohibited. You'll save a lot on meals if you stay at one of the many motels and guesthouses offering cooking facilities.

Rukau is Cook Islands *palusami,* made from spinachlike young taro leaves cooked in coconut cream. *Ika mata* is marinated raw fish with coconut sauce. Locals insist that slippery foods such as bananas lead to forgetfulness, while gluey foods like taro help one to remember. Dogs are sometimes eaten by young men on drinking sprees. Turn to the Atiu section for information on "bush beer" (called "home-brewed" on Rarotonga and Aitutaki).

INFORMATION AND SERVICES

Information

For advance information about the country, write to one of the overseas branches of the government-operated **Cook Islands Tourism Corporation** listed in the back of this book, or to their head office at P.O. Box 14, Rarotonga (www .cook-islands.com). Ask for their free magazine, *Jasons What's On in the Cook Islands,* and the color map *Jasons Passport Cook Islands.* Be aware that the Tourism Corporation's publications and website only list "accredited" businesses, and the Jasons publications are slanted toward their advertisers.

Elliot Smith's *Cook Islands Companion* is recommended for those who want more detailed information on the country than can be included here. It's possible to purchase a personally autographed copy directly from the author at Shangri-La Beach Cottages on Muri Beach.

Internet Resources

The official Cook Islands Tourism Corporation site, **www.cook-islands.com,** provides a business directory of their accredited partners. Details of accommodations and activities can be downloaded in PDF format, and there's a page about each island. A site titled simply Cook Islands, **www.ck,** contains a remarkable potpourri of useful information about the Cook Islands with maps, history, travel, recipes, and more.

Cook Islands Beaches, **www.cook.islands-beaches.com,** uses clickable maps to access information and photos of Cook Islands beaches and islands. Cook Islands Hotels, **www.the-cook-islands.com,** is a hotel guide to Rarotonga and Aitutaki, with more clickable photos and maps. Cook Islands Business and Tourism, **http://cook pages.com,** has a Cook Islands tourism directory covering lodging, dive shops, fishing, and vacation planning.

Cook Islands Aitutaki, **www.aitutaki.com,** is an online guide to Aitutaki. For Atiu, turn to **www.atiu.info.** Paka's Pearls, **www.maui pearls.com,** offers a buyer's guide with general information on Cook Islands black pearls. The prices quoted in U.S. dollars give you an idea of how much you'll need to budget.

Visas and Officialdom

No visa is required for a stay of up to 31 days, but you must show a ticket to leave (the airline can be fined as much as NZ$10,000 if they're caught carrying a passenger without an onward ticket). For NZ$70 you can get extensions up to six months in the Cooks. Apply at the Immigration office (tel. 29-347, fax 21-247, tutai@immigration.gov.ck) on the top floor of the Government Office Building behind the post office. Actually, one week is plenty of time to see Rarotonga and 31 days is sufficient to visit all of the southern Cook Islands.

If you're thinking of taking a boat trip to the northern group, be sure to get a visa extension before you leave Rarotonga. Otherwise you could have problems with Immigration if your entry permit has expired by the time you get back.

Persons with business skills or money to invest can obtain work and residence permits through the **Cook Islands Development Investment Board** (tel. 24-296, fax 24-298, www.cook islands-invest.com), a one-stop shop for "lifestyle investors." For details, consult their website listed in the back of this book.

Foreigners can obtain permanent residency in the Cook Islands after five years, but such status is only granted in exceptional circumstances, such as to those who have made significant financial investments in the country. Cook Islands citizenship has never been extended to Europeans.

Rarotonga, Aitutaki, and Penrhyn are ports of entry for cruising yachts; the only harbors for yachts are at Aitutaki, Penrhyn, Suwarrow, and Rarotonga.

Money

The currency is the New Zealand dollar, which was valued at US$1 = NZ$1.60 at press time. In 2003, the declining U.S. dollar made everything in the Cook Islands 20 percent more expensive for American visitors than was the case just a year before. After the financial crisis of 1995, the Cook Islands dollar, which had circulated at par with the New Zealand dollar since 1987, was withdrawn. Cook Islands coins are still in use, however, although these are worthless outside the Cook Islands. The Cook Islands dollar coin bearing an image of the god Tangaroa makes an offbeat souvenir.

Traveler's checks are worth about three percent more than cash at the banks. Changing money on an outer island is difficult or impossible—do it before you leave Rarotonga. The upmarket hotels and restaurants accept the main credit cards, and the banks will give cash ad-

vances. Many places won't allow credit cards to be used for petty charges.

A 12.5 percent value-added tax (VAT) is added to all sales, services, activities, and rentals. Most places include it in the price, but some add it on, so ask. Bargaining has never been a part of the local culture and some locals find it offensive when tourists try to beat prices down. The way to do it is to ask for "specials." Thankfully, tipping is still not widespread in the Cooks.

Communications

Telecom Cook Islands (tel. 29-680, fax 26-174, www.telecom.co.ck) charges a flat rate for international telephone calls with no off-hour discounts. Three-minute operator-assisted calls cost NZ$11.50 to the U.S., NZ$12.40 to New Zealand, and NZ$13 to Australia. Person-to-person calls attract an additional two-minute charge.

It's cheaper to use a local telephone card for international calls, as there's no three-minute minimum with a card (dial the international access code 00, the country code, the area code, and the number). More importantly, with a card you can't lose track of the time and end up being presented with a tremendous bill. The cards come in denominations of NZ$5, NZ$10, NZ$20, and NZ$50 and are good for all domestic and international calls. Calls to outer islands within the Cook Islands cost NZ$1 a minute with a card. You'll need a card to make local calls, since there aren't any coin telephones here.

Collect calls can be placed to Australia, Canada, Fiji, French Polynesia, Malaysia, Netherlands, New Zealand, Niue, Tonga, United Kingdom, and the United States only. To call collect, dial the international/outer island operator at tel. 015. Directory assistance numbers within the Cook Islands are tel. 010, international tel. 017 (NZ$0.20 fee). To look up numbers online, go to www.whitepages.co.ck or www.yellowpages.co.ck. The country code of the Cook Islands is 682.

For calls to the United States, the "AT&T Direct" service is more expensive than using a local telephone card, but perhaps useful in emergencies. To be connected to this service, dial 09-111 from any phone in the Cook Islands. The

Telecom New Zealand Direct number is tel. 0964-09682.

Many local businesses now have email and a directory of email addresses appears in the back of this book. Visitors can check their email at any of the numerous Internet outlets around Rarotonga at between NZ$0.20 and NZ$0.35 a minute. You may also find such a place on Aitutaki, and on the other islands your guesthouse may provide access for the usual fee.

Media

Be sure to pick up a copy of the *Cook Islands News* (tel. 22-999, fax 25-303, www.cinews.co.ck), published daily except Sunday (NZ$1 weekdays, NZ$1.35 Sat.). Its stories on island affairs really give you a feel for where you are, and local happenings are listed.

The *Cook Islands Herald* (tel. 29-460, www.ciherald.co.ck) is a weekly paper published on Rarotonga. Although published in Auckland, the weekly *Cook Islands Star* can be purchased on Rarotonga and it's worth purchasing for Jason Brown's investigative reporting. The *Cook Islands Sun* is a free tourist newspaper also published in New Zealand.

On Rarotonga, **Radio KC FM** (tel. 23-203) broadcasts over 103.3 MHz from 0530–2400 with overseas news at 0600 and 0700. The FM station can be difficult to pick up on the south side of Rarotonga, but **Radio Cook Islands** (tel. 29-560, www.radio.co.ck) at 630 kHz AM can be heard anywhere on the island (and even on nearby islands like Mauke in the evening). This station, the *Herald,* and Television Cook Islands are owned by the influential Pitt family.

Measurements and Time

The electric voltage is 240 volts DC, 50 cycles, the same as in New Zealand and Australia. American appliances will require a converter. The type of plug varies, but bring a three-pin adaptor. On outer islands other than Aitutaki electricity is only provided a few hours a day.

The time is the same as in Hawaii and Tahiti, two hours behind California and 22 hours behind Fiji and New Zealand. "Cook Islands time" also runs a bit behind "Western tourist's time," so

relax and let things happen. Most banks and government offices are closed on Saturday, although the shops and restaurants in Avarua are usually open until noon. In recent years, regulations have been relaxed and many small shops and car rental outlets on Rarotonga are now open on Sunday.

TRANSPORTATION

Getting There

Air New Zealand (tel. 26-300), with an office at Rarotonga Airport, has direct services to Rarotonga from Auckland (daily), Nadi (weekly), Papeete (weekly), and Los Angeles (three a week). In 2003, **Aloha Airlines** (www.alohaairlines.com) began flying to Rarotonga from Honolulu, with connections from the North American west coast.

Air services into Rarotonga are heavily booked, so reserve your inward and outward flights as far ahead as possible. If you try to change your outbound flight after arrival you could be put on standby.

Check in for your outgoing international flight at least one hour before the scheduled departure time, as the airlines are short of staff. If everyone is needed to attend to a flight arrival, they may simply close the check-in counter and you'll be out of luck.

Getting Around by Air

Air Rarotonga (tel. 22-888, fax 23-288, www.airraro.com) carries the distinction of being one of the only South Pacific airlines that is entirely privately owned and profitable to boot. It provides regular air service from Rarotonga to all of the main islands of the southern Cooks and a few of the northern group, although no flights operate on Sunday. They use a 34-seat SAAB 340 SF3 aircraft to Aitutaki; all other flights are in an 18-seat Embraer Bandeirante.

The flights to Aitutaki (NZ$158 one way, plus NZ$20 airport tax) are three times daily except Sunday. A reduced NZ$128 one-way fare to Aitutaki is available northbound on the afternoon flight and southbound on the morning flight. Air Rarotonga runs day tours from Rarotonga to Aitutaki at NZ$399 including roundtrip airfare, transfers, a lagoon tour, lunch, and drinks. On your northbound flight, sit on the left side of the aircraft for the best views.

Air Rarotonga flies from Rarotonga to Atiu (NZ$142) daily except Sunday, to Mauke (NZ$158) every weekday, to Mangaia (NZ$142) four times a week, and to Mitiaro (NZ$158) three times a week.

The interisland connection Atiu-Mitiaro-Mauke only works once a week, and interisland flights Atiu-Mitiaro and Mitiaro-Mauke are NZ$90 each. There's no flight Atiu-Mauke and you must stop over on Mitiaro at least one night en route to make the connection. Once a week you can fly between Atiu-Aitutaki-Atiu (NZ$142 one-way).

Air Rarotonga's "Island Discovery" ticket costs NZ$355 for a trip Rarotonga, Aitutaki, Atiu, Rarotonga. With Mitiaro included it's NZ$429. Add Mauke and it's NZ$505. To include Mangaia in any of the above is another NZ$107. This non-refundable pass is valid for 45 days maximum and date changes (but not route changes) are allowed. Advance reservations are required, as space is limited.

Manihiki (NZ$1,085 roundtrip) and Penrhyn (NZ$1,203 roundtrip) receive Air Rarotonga flights weekly. There's no flight Manihiki-Penrhyn and only charter flights operate to Pukapuka. The plane can't land at all on Rakahanga. Sitting in a Bandierante for four hours from Rarotonga to Manihiki or Penrhyn can be quite an experience!

Children under 12 pay half price. In late 2001, a NZ$4 per flight insurance surcharge was imposed and this will be added to all ticket prices above. Try to reconfirm your return flight, and beware of planes leaving early! Avoid scheduling your flight back to Rarotonga for the same day you're supposed to catch an international flight.

The baggage allowance is 16 kilos, though you can sometimes get by with more. On flights to Manihiki and Penrhyn the limit is 10 kilos. Overweight is not expensive, but if the plane is full and too heavy for the short outer-island runways they'll refuse excess baggage from all passengers. Thus it pays to stay below the limit.

Getting Around by Ship

Taio Shipping Ltd. (Teremoana Taio, tel. 24-905, fax 24-906), opposite the Ports Authority Building on Rarotonga's Avatiu Harbor, operates the interisland vessels *Manu Nui* and the smaller *Maungaroa*. Taio tries to run a ship around the southern and northern groups monthly. The schedule varies according to the amount of cargo waiting to move and the only way to find out is to ask at the office. Also ask about special trips to Apia in Samoa.

To do a four- to five-day roundtrip to the southern group costs NZ$130–150. To sail around the northern group for 12–13 days costs NZ$750. On a one-way basis it's NZ$65 from Rarotonga to any of the islands of the southern group, or NZ$25 deck between Atiu, Mauke, and Mitiaro only. One-way fares to the northern group are around NZ$300. Passengers must bring their own food.

Be forewarned that accommodations on this sort of ship are often next to noisy, hot engine rooms and tend to be cluttered with crates. Passengers may have to sleep under a canvas awning, and although it may be a little crowded, the islanders are friendly and easy to get along with. The *Manu Nui* has two three-bunk cabins, but the *Maungaroa* has only an open dorm. You usually go ashore by barge, as only Rarotonga and Penrhyn have wharves where ships can tie up. On the outer islands, check with the radio operator in the post office to find out when a ship from Rarotonga might be due in. Delays of a few days are routine. In practice, not many visitors travel this way.

Airport

Rarotonga International Airport (RAR) is 2.4 km west of Avarua. Immigration will stamp a 31-day entry permit onto your passport. Be sure to write the name of a hotel in the relevant space on your arrivals card—to leave blank that space will prompt the immigration clerk to ask where you plan to stay.

As you come out of customs you'll find representatives from most of the backpacker's hostels waiting to the left, at a counter marked "budget accommodations." State the name of the establishment you think best suits your needs and their representative will inform you whether they have any vacant rooms. Have a second name ready in case your first choice is fully occupied. Being prepared will make it easier for you to deal with the drivers eagerly jostling for your business. Most offer a free transfer to their lodging on the understanding that you'll stay at least two nights with them (the upscale places charge as much as NZ$20 each way for the transfer). A taxi to Avarua will cost around NZ$5.

All the main travel agencies and rental car companies have offices outside arrivals at the airport. There's a card telephone at the airport, otherwise you can use the public phone at the RSA Club across the street. If you're stuck here waiting for a flight, the RSA Club is a much better place to relax than the dreary airport terminal.

The Westpac Bank at the airport charges NZ$2.50 commission per transaction. The ANZ Bank has an ATM at the airport, just to the left as you leave the terminal. There are about a dozen left-luggage lockers around the side of the arrivals building near the airport fire department (NZ$5 a day). Raro Tours (tel. 25-325) at the airport holds luggage at NZ$6 a day per bag. Several duty-free shops open for international arrivals and departures, and arriving passengers are also allowed to duck into the duty-free liquor shop (tel. 29-297) to the right before clearing customs.

A NZ$25 departure tax is charged for international flights (children aged 2–11 pay NZ$10, and transit passengers staying fewer than 24 hours are exempt).

Rarotonga

The name Rarotonga means "in the direction of the prevailing wind, south," the place where the chief of Atiu promised early explorers they would find an island. It's fairly small, just 31 km around. Twisting valleys lead up to steep ridges covered with luxuriant green vegetation and towering mountains crowned in clouds. Yet, Te Manga (653 meters) is only a fraction of the height Rarotonga reached before the last volcanic eruption took place, over two million years ago.

Though Rarotonga is younger than the other Cook islands, continuous erosion has cut into the island, washing away the softer material and leaving the hard volcanic cones naked. The mountains are arrayed in a U-shaped arch, starting at the airport and then swinging south around to Club Raro, with Maungatea plopped down in the middle. Together they form the surviving southern half of the great broken volcanic caldera that became Rarotonga.

The reef circling the island defines a lagoon that is broad and sandy to the south, and narrow and rocky on the north and east. The finest beaches are on the southeast side near the south end of the Muri Lagoon, with crystal-clear water and a sandy bottom, but the best snorkeling is at Titikaveka. Elsewhere the water can be cloudy or shallow, with a lot of coral and shells that make wading difficult. You can't swim or snorkel at all anywhere from the top of the Muri Lagoon right around to the airport via the east and north coasts, as the reef is very close in. The south and west coasts are generally okay for snorkeling. Take care everywhere, as several snorkelers have drowned after being sucked out through the passes where a lot of water moves due to surf and tidal swings. Scuba diving on Rarotonga features coral drop-offs, canyons, caves, walls, sharks, wrecks, and swim-throughs. All beaches on the island are public.

In recent years, Rarotonga has become New Zealand's answer to Honolulu, with 75,000 visitors to an island of 12,000 inhabitants, the same six-to-one visitor/resident ratio experienced in Hawaii. Lodges and resorts completely encircle Rarotonga, and to find that "last heaven on earth" promised in the brochures, you must escape to an outer island. Yet Raro remains one of the most beautiful islands in Polynesia, somewhat reminiscent of Moorea (though only half as large). If you enjoy the excitement of big tourist resorts with plenty of opportunities for shopping and eating out, you'll like Rarotonga.

SIGHTS

Avarua

This attractive town of around 5,000 inhabitants is strung along the north coast beneath the green, misty slopes of Maungatea. The name means "two harbors." Somehow Avarua retains the air of a 19th-century South Seas trading post, and offshore in Avarua Harbor lies the boiler of the Union Steam Ship SS *Maitai*, wrecked in 1916. Near the bridge over Takuvaine Stream is the **Seven-in-One Coconut Tree** planted in 1906.

Inland and south of the post office is the stone on which in 1823 Papeiha preached the first Christian sermon on Rarotonga. It's set on a pedestal in the middle of the crossing with the Ara Metua, Rarotonga's old interior road. Turn left and follow the Ara Metua 150 meters east to a small bridge and a gate leading into the original missionary compound, now **Takamoa Theological College.** You pass a row of student residences, and at the next crossroad you'll find a monument to the missionaries of the London Missionary Society who have served in the Cook Islands. Across the street is an impressive monument to Polynesian missionaries from the college who carried the Gospel to other Pacific islands. In 1837, the third LMS missionary, Rev. Aaron Buzacott, erected the two-story **Takamoa Mission House** facing the monuments. The adjacent lecture hall dates from 1890.

Follow the road north between the monuments and you'll reach the **Cook Islands Library and Museum** (tel. 26-468; Mon.–Sat. 0900–1300, Tues. also 1600–2000, NZ$2 admission) with assorted artifacts, many of them on loan from museums in New Zealand. Across the street from the museum is the **Cook Islands Center** (tel. 29-415) of the University of the South Pacific, which is worth entering for the interesting books in the showcase on the right.

The massive white walls and roof of the **Cook Islands Christian Church** (1853) are visible from here. Check out the massive wooden balcony inside. It's worth being here Sunday morning at 1000, if only to see the women arrive in their Sunday best and to stand outside and listen to the wonderful singing (only go inside and sit down if you're prepared to stay for the entire service). Near the front of the church is the tomb of Albert Henry (1907–1981), topped by a lifelike statue of the man. American writer Robert Dean Frisbie (1895–1948), author of *The Book of Pukapuka* and *The Island of Desire,* is buried in the southwest corner of the cemetery.

Across the road, beyond some old graves, is the **Para O Tane Palace** of the Makea Takau Ariki, high chief of the landowning clan of most of the Avarua town area. **Marae Taputaputea** and a basalt investiture pillar are on the palace grounds.

Backtrack to the Cook Islands Center and turn left along a wide road to the massive green and white **Are-Karioi-Nui National Auditorium** with 2,000 seats. The four huge buildings to the left of this road are hostels used to house outer islanders when they visit Rarotonga. The auditorium itself forms part of the **National Cultural Center,** erected for the sixth Festival of Pacific Arts in 1992. The two yellow buildings beyond the auditorium contain the **National Library** (tel. 20-725; weekdays 0900–1600) in the building to the right, and the **National Museum** (tel. 20-725, www.culture.gov.ck/museum.htm; weekdays 0800–1600) in the one on the left. The museum has a collection of model canoes, old photos, carvings, paddles, drums, woven items, and costumes. This huge complex was one of the grandiose projects of the Honorable Sir Geoffrey Henry, who put his country millions of dollars into debt to finance construction of the island's second museum and library.

The Ara Metua

Two roads circle Rarotonga: the new coastal road (the Ara Tapu) and an old inner road (the Ara Metua). The main sights are arranged below for a counterclockwise tour of the island on the Ara Tapu with the distances from Avarua shown in parentheses. On a scooter you should be able to do it in four hours with stops; by bicycle give yourself a leisurely day.

On your second time around try using the scenic Ara Metua, which goes two-thirds of the way around the island. You'll encounter lush gardens, orchards, and good viewpoints. This inner

COOK ISLANDS

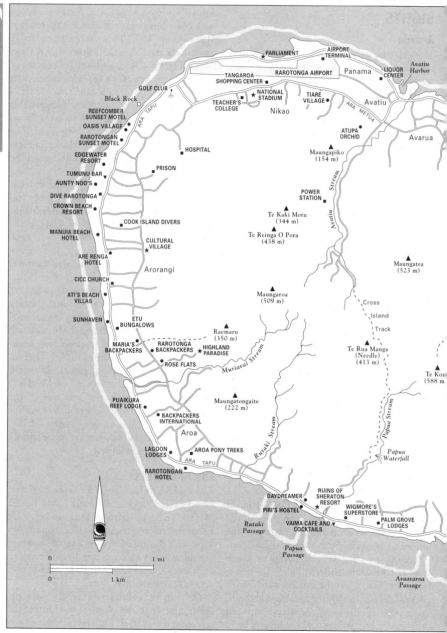

PARLIAMENT

AIRPORT
TERMINAL

Avatiu
Harbor

TANGAROA
SHOPPING CENTER

RAROTONGA AIROPORT

Panama

LIQUOR
CENTER

GOLF CLUB

NATIONAL
STADIUM

Avatiu

Black Rock

TEACHER'S
COLLEGE

TIARE
VILLAGE

Nikao

REEFCOMBER
SUNSET MOTEL

OASIS VILLAGE

ATUPA
ORCHID

Avarua

RAROTONGAN
SUNSET MOTEL

HOSPITAL

Maungapiko
(154 m)

EDGEWATER
RESORT

TUMUNU BAR

PRISON

AUNTY NOO'S

DIVE RAROTONGA

POWER
STATION

CROWN BEACH
RESORT

COOK ISLAND DIVERS

Te Kaki Motu
(344 m)

MANUIA BEACH
HOTEL

CULTURAL
VILLAGE

Te Reinga O Pora
(438 m)

ARE RENGA
HOTEL

Arorangi

Maungatea
(523 m)

CICC CHURCH

ATI'S BEACH
VILLAS

Maungaroa
(509 m)

Cross

SUNHAVEN

ETU
BUNGALOWS

Island

Raemaru
(350 m)

Track

MARIA'S
BACKPACKERS

RAROTONGA
BACKPACKERS

HIGHLAND
PARADISE

Te Rua Manga
(Needle)
(413 m)

Te Kou
(588 m

ROSE FLATS

PUAIKURA
REEF LODGE

Maungatongaite
(222 m)

BACKPACKERS
INTERNATIONAL

Aroa

Papua
Waterfall

LAGOON
LODGES

AROA PONY TREKS

RAROTONGAN
HOTEL

RUINS OF
SHERATON
RESORT

DAYDREAMER

WIGMORE'S
SUPERSTORE

PALM GROVE
LODGES

PIRI'S HOSTEL

Rutaki
Passage

VAIMA CAFE AND
COCKTAILS

Papua
Passage

Avaavaroa
Passage

0   1 mi

0   1 km

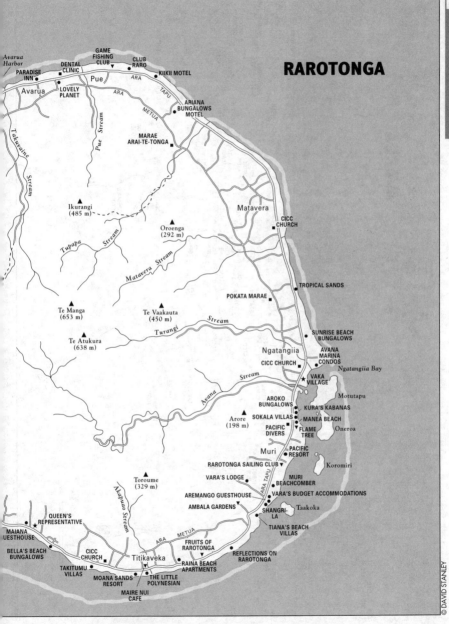

RAROTONGA

Avarua Harbor

PARADISE INN
DENTAL CLINIC
GAME FISHING CLUB
CLUB RARO
KIIKII MOTEL
LOVELY PLANET
Pue
ARA
ARA
TAPU
METUA
ARIANA BUNGALOWS MOTEL
Avarua

Takuvaine Stream

Pue Stream

MARAE ARAI-TE-TONGA

Ikurangi (485 m)

Matavera

CICC CHURCH

Oroenga (292 m)

Tupapa Stream

Matavera Stream

Te Manga (653 m)

Te Vaakauta (450 m)

POKATA MARAE

TROPICAL SANDS

Turangi Stream

Te Atukura (638 m)

SUNRISE BEACH BUNGALOWS

Ngatangiia

AVANA MARINA CONDOS

CICC CHURCH

Ngatangiia Bay

Avana Stream

VAKA VILLAGE

Motutapu

Arore (198 m)

AROKO BUNGALOWS

KURA'S KABANAS

SOKALA VILLAS

MANEA BEACH

PACIFIC DIVERS

FLAME TREE

Oneroa

Muri

PACIFIC RESORT

Koromiri

RAROTONGA SAILING CLUB

Toroume (329 m)

VARA'S LODGE

MURI BEACHCOMBER

Akapuao Stream

AREMANGO GUESTHOUSE

VARA'S BUDGET ACCOMMODATIONS

AMBALA GARDENS

SHANGRI-LA

Taakoka

QUEEN'S REPRESENTATIVE

TIANA'S BEACH VILLAS

MAIANA UESTHOUSE

ARA
METUA

FRUITS OF RAROTONGA

BELLA'S BEACH BUNGALOWS

CICC CHURCH

Titikaveka

REFLECTIONS ON RAROTONGA

TAKITUMU VILLAS

RAINA BEACH APARTMENTS

MOANA SANDS RESORT

THE LITTLE POLYNESIAN

MAIRE NUI CAFE

ARA TAPU

COOK ISLANDS

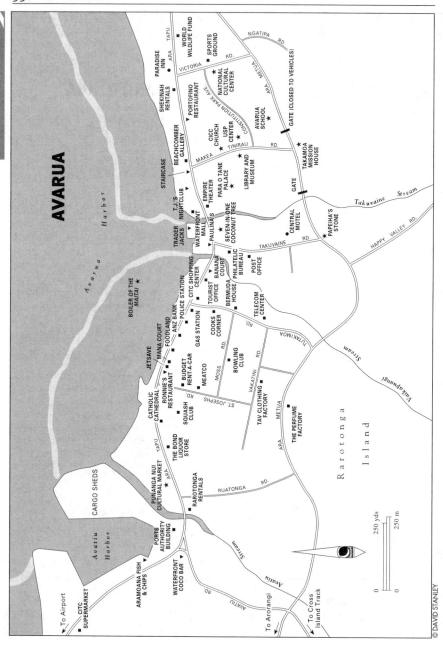

AVARUA

Avarua Harbor

Avatiu Harbor

Avatiu Harbor

Rarotonga Island

To Airport

CITC SUPERMARKET

CARGO SHEDS

PORTS AUTHORITY BUILDING

ARAMOANA FISH & CHIPS

WATERFRONT COCO BAR

To Arorangi

To Cross Island Track

Avatiu Stream

AVATIU RD.

RUATONGA RD.

RAROTONGA RENTALS

PUNANGA NUI CULTURAL MARKET

ARA TAPU

THE BOND LIQUOR STORE

SQUASH CLUB

ST JOSEPHS RD.

CATHOLIC CATHEDRAL

JETSAVE

RONNIE'S RESTAURANT

MANA COURT

FOODLAND

ANZ BANK

POLICE STATION

BUDGET RENT-A-CAR

MEATCO

MOSS RD.

BOWLING CLUB

VAKATINI RD.

TAV CLOTHING FACTORY

METUA ARA

THE PERFUME FACTORY

GAS STATION

COOKS CORNER

BERMUDA HOUSE

PHILATELIC BUREAU

TELECOM CENTER

TOURIST OFFICE

BANANA COURT

POST OFFICE

TUTAKIMOA RD.

Avatiu Stream

BOILER OF THE MAITAI ★

CITC SHOPPING CENTER

TRADER JACKS

WATERFRONT MALL

PAULINA'S

TJ'S NIGHTCLUB

SEVEN-IN-ONE COCONUT TREE

EMPIRE THEATER

PARA O TANE PALACE

LIBRARY AND MUSEUM

TAKUVAINE RD.

CENTRAL MOTEL

PAPEIHA'S STONE

GATE

Takuvaine Stream

HAPPY VALLEY RD.

Vakapuangi Stream

STAIRCASE

BEACHCOMBER GALLERY

MAKEA TINIRAU RD.

CICC CHURCH

USP CENTER

AVARUA SCHOOL

TAKAMOA MISSION HOUSE

CONSTITUTION PARK AVE.

PORTOFINO RESTAURANT

NATIONAL CULTURAL CENTER

GATE (CLOSED TO VEHICLES)

SHEKINAH RENTALS

PARADISE INN

ARA TAPU

WORLD WILDLIFE FUND

SPORTS GROUND

VICTORIA RD.

NGATIPA RD.

ARA METUA RD.

250 yds

250 m

© DAVID STANLEY

road is said to be the oldest in Polynesia, the coral-block foundation laid some 1,000 years ago by chief Toi. Up until the mid-19th century, when the missionaries concentrated the population in seven coastal villages, most of the people lived on the inland side of this road. During WW II, the road was resurfaced and much of it is now paved. There's very little traffic, which makes it perfect for cycling.

Around the Island

Just under a km west of Rarotonga airport is the **Parliament of the Cook Islands** in a building originally used to house workers during construction of the airport in 1973. Parliament meets briefly anytime February–March and July–September, and if you're properly dressed (no shorts or jeans), you can observe the proceedings from the public gallery (Mon., Tues., and Thurs. 1300–1700, Wed. and Fri. 0900–1300). Call 26-500 for information. Notice how all the important positions here are occupied by men.

For a cheap thrill, find out when an international flight will be arriving, then position yourself on the seawall below the end of the runway between Parliament and the Golf Club a bit beforehand. You'll get a rush when the huge aircraft passes just a few meters above your head!

Across the street from the Golf Club (see the Sports and Recreation section) west of the airport is a beach park with toilets and outdoor showers. From here it's not far to **Black Rock** (6 km), standing alone in a coral lagoon (good snorkeling at high tide). This rock marks the spot where the spirits of deceased Rarotongan Polynesians pass on their way back to the legendary homeland, Avaiki. The Tahitian missionary Papeiha is said to have swum ashore here holding a Bible above his head (in fact, he landed in a small boat).

Arorangi (8.5 km) was established by the Rev. Aaron Buzacott (who served in the Cooks 1828–1857) as a model village, and Papeiha is buried in the historic white cemetery at the old CICC church (1849). It was the LMS missionaries who resettled the people near the coast and built the **Tinomana Palace** beside the church for the last native ruler of this district.

Mount Raemaru (350 meters tall) rising up behind Arorangi has a flattened top—a local legend tells how Aitutaki warriors carried off the missing upper part. (To climb Raemaru, take the steep track off the Ara Metua when you see the sign for Maria's Backpackers Accommodation, then via a trail to the right up the fern-covered ridge to Raemaru's western cliffs. When you get close to the forest at the base of the cliffs, take the right fork of the trail up to the cliff itself. The final climb to the mountain's flat summit can be dangerous if the rocks on the cliff are wet and slippery, but once on top, you can see the whole western side of Rarotonga. There's an easier track down the back of Raemaru that you can use to return, but you'd probably get lost if you tried to climb it. Along this route you circle down a taro-filled valley back to the Ara Metua.)

Takitumu

The southeast side of Rarotonga is known as Takitumu. The skeletal **Sheraton Resort** with its ironic monument to the Honorable Sir Geoffrey A. Henry is the most visible physical reminder of the financial calamities that gripped these islands in the 1990s. The building with the flagpole a couple of kilometers east is the residence of the representative of Queen Elizabeth II (his salary comes out of local taxes). East again and on the corner before Kent Hall in **Titikaveka** is Te Pou Toru Marae. Beyond this, another fine coral-block CICC church (1841) stands beside the road, 19 km from Avarua counterclockwise or 14 km clockwise.

Some of the finest **snorkeling** on Rarotonga is off the beach opposite Raina Beach Apartments, behind the cemetery with the radio mast. Fruits of Rarotonga Café, a few hundred meters east, is another great base for snorkeling (the folks in the café will hold bags). There's not a lot of coral but plenty of small fish. Some of the scuba operators bring their clients here for diving.

Turn in at the Rarotonga Sailing Club, four km northeast, to see the lovely **Muri Lagoon,** with the nicest swimming, kayaking, and windsurfing area on the island. The southeast trades blow the mosquitoes away. At low tide you can wade across to uninhabited Koromiri Island, where hermit crabs forage as bathers enjoy the oceanside beach. Full nautical gear is for rent at the club (open daily) and Sails Restaurant serves a good lunch.

The road up the **Avana Valley** begins near the bridge over Avana Stream and runs along the south bank. You can cycle halfway up, then continue on foot.

On the right just beyond the Avana Stream bridge is **Vaka Village** with a monument marking the historic gathering of ocean voyaging and war canoes here during the 1992 Festival of Pacific Arts. Local fishing boats anchor on the spot today. A little beyond is another old white **CICC church** on the left, once the seat of the Rev. Charles Pitman who translated many works into Maori during his stay here 1827–1854. Across the street from the church is a small park with a good view of the tiny islands or *motu* in the Muri Lagoon and **Ngatangiia Harbor.** Legend claims that seven canoes departed from here in A.D. 1350 on a daring voyage to New Zealand, and the names of the canoes are inscribed on a monument. Cruising yachts sometimes anchor here, though it's rather exposed to the southeast trades.

Back near the bridge is a road in to the **Ara Metua.** On the right a short distance along this road is an old burial ground with a Polynesian *marae* among the trees on a hillock behind. Many other similar *marae* are in the vicinity.

Continue along the Ara Metua and turn left up the road alongside Turangi Stream, on the far side of a small bridge. The **Turangi Valley** is larger and more impressive than Avana, and swamp taro is grown in irrigated paddies. Once again, you cycle halfway up and continue on foot.

Toward Ikurangi

At **Matavera** there's yet another lovely CICC church (1865) beside the road. Farther along, just a few km before Avarua, watch for a signboard on Maotangi Road pointing the way in to **Marae Arai-te-tonga,** on the Ara Metua. Marae Arai-te-tonga, the most sacred on the island, was a *koutu,* or place where the *ta'unga* (priest) invested and anointed the high chiefs *(ariki)* of the island. The route of the ancient Ara Metua is quite evident here, and there are other stone constructions 100 meters along it to the east.

Take the road inland between these ruins as far as Tupapa Stream, where two rather difficult climbs begin. Just a km up the trail is a fork in the path: the right fork leads to the top of **Ikurangi** (485 meters), while the one up the stream continues to **Te Manga** (653 meters). Neither climb is easy, so a local guide would be a good idea. From the top of Ikurangi (Tail of the Sky) you can see the whole wave-washed reef, tomato patches, and plantations of grapefruit, orange, tangerine, and lemon trees. This climb is best done in the cool hours of the early morning.

The Cross-Island Track

From Avarua walk three km up the Avatiu Valley. Just beyond the power station you get your first view of Te Rua Manga, **the Needle** (413 meters). In another 10 minutes the road ends at a concrete water intake; you continue up a footpath for 15 minutes until you reach a huge boulder. Pass it and head up the steep forested incline. This climb is the hardest part of the trip, but when you reach the top, the Needle towers majestically above you (the hike from the end of the road to the top takes less than an hour).

There's a fork at the top of the ridge: the Needle on your right, the trail down to the south coast on the left. After scrambling around the Needle, start down the trail to the south coast, past the giant ferns along the side of Papua Stream. On this part of the trek you really get to see Rarotonga's interior rainforest. The road out begins at **Papua Waterfall,** also known as Wigmore's Waterfall, at the bottom of the hill. The stream above Papua is a drinking water source, and you're also not supposed to swim in the pool below the falls (which will be dry anyway unless there have been rains recently). The hapless Sheraton Resort is to your right just before you reach the main road.

Though sometimes slippery, the cross-island track can be covered in all weather, and even if it has been raining, you can still do the trip the next day. Parts of the track are badly eroded, so it might not be a good idea to go alone. Allow 45 minutes to walk up Avatiu Road, then an hour and a quarter to climb to the Needle. The descent down the Papua Valley takes two hours, and it's easier to do a roundtrip to the Needle from the end of the road on the Avatiu side, allowing a return to a parked vehicle. If you'll be hiking right across it's best to go Monday–Saturday, as onward bus service on the other side will be very limited on Sunday.

Several companies offer guided cross-island treks Monday–Saturday at 0930 if the weather is okay, but lots of visitors do this hike on their own and you don't really need a guide. Unfortunately, some hikers have inflicted environmental damage here. Don't attempt shortcuts by following the plastic water lines along the way; these lines can be damaged if you use them as handholds and they lead to very dangerous slopes. The trail will only remain open if visitors behave responsibly.

Commercial Visitor Attractions

Weekdays at 1000 the **Cultural Village** (tel. 21-314, fax 25-557, viltours@oyster.net.ck; admission NZ$54/27 adult/child), on the back road in Arorangi, enthusiastically demonstrates Cook Islands history, medicine, cooking, arts, crafts, dances, and traditions during an informative three-hour program, which includes a good lunch of local foods. Advance reservations through a hotel, travel agency, or directly by phone are required. Several readers have written in strongly endorsing the Cultural Village.

Another attraction accessible weekdays at 1000 is **Highland Paradise** (tel. 20-611; admission NZ$30 including lunch), a private botanical garden where old *marae* and other historic sites are scattered among the vegetation. The steep access road begins next to Rose Flats, a km south of the Cultural Village. The Arorangi people lived up here before being moved down to the coast by the missionaries.

Sports and Recreation

Dive Rarotonga (Ed Redman, tel. 21-873, fax 21-878, www.diverarotonga.com) offers scuba trips at 0800 and 1300 daily (including Sunday!). It's NZ$60/100/450 for one/two/10 tanks including gear (discount available if you have your own gear). Night dives are NZ$75. Snorkelers can go along for NZ$20 pp including snorkeling gear. Dive Rarotonga's PADI open water course is only NZ$350—what better place to learn?

Scuba diving is also offered by Greg Wilson's **Cook Island Divers** (tel. 22-483, fax 22-484, http://cookpages.com/CookIslandDivers), just up the road. Greg does two trips a day, at 0800 and 1300 (NZ$70 per dive), and he runs a highly professional show. His four-day NAUI or PADI scuba certification course is NZ$499. Call for their free hotel pickup. A reader's comment: "It was a really enjoyable day."

Pacific Divers (Graham and Christina McDonald, tel./fax 22-450, www.pacificdivers.co.ck), opposite the Flame Tree Restaurant at Muri Beach, offers dives on the nearby Titikaveka Reef at 0800 and 1300 daily (at 1230 only on Sunday). It's NZ$75/130 for one/two tanks and two people together get a NZ$10 discount. A PADI open water certification course (four days) will run NZ$485. The feedback we've received about Pacific Divers is mixed. All three scuba operators offer discounts for multiple dives.

Monday–Saturday at 1100 **Captain Tama's Aquasportz Center** (Tamaiva Tuavera, tel. 23-350, wedding@cookislands.co.ck), next to the Rarotonga Sailing Club on Muri Beach, offers lagoon cruises in a glass-bottom boat with a thatched sunroof for around NZ$60 pp including a barbecue lunch. Before signing up, check with the folks in the Beach Hut at the nearby Pacific Resort whose glass-bottom snorkeling cruise is only NZ20 (or NZ$37 with sandwiches for lunch). Captain Tama's rents double kayaks (NZ$12 an hour), windsurfers (NZ$15 an hour), and snorkeling gear (NZ$5 a half day). Lessons in windsurfing (NZ$35) are given. Equipment rental is possible every day.

The **Reef-Sub** (tel. 25-837) at Avatiu Harbor is a sort of glass-bottom boat with tiny jewelry case windows in an underwater viewing deck (it's not a real submarine). The 90-minute trips Monday–Saturday at 1000 and 1400 cost NZ$45.

Pacific Marine Charters (Wayne Barclay, tel. 21-237, fax 25-237, pacmarine@cookislands .co.ck) at Avatiu Harbor offers deep-sea fishing from its two cabin cruisers. Also at Avatiu is the larger 10-meter *Seafari* of **Seafari Charters** (Elgin Tetachuk, tel. 20-328, www.seafari.co.ck). Over four hours of fishing costs about NZ$100 pp (NZ$50 pp for nonfishing passengers), a light lunch included. Both boats depart weekdays around 0800 (weather permitting) and the fishing takes place right off Rarotonga, so you get very good views of the island and don't waste time commuting. Brent Fisher's **Fisher's Fishing Tours** (tel. 23-356, fax 23-354, www.ck/fisher) is based at Ngatangiia Harbor, and his boat, the *Corey-Anne,* goes out at 0800 or 1330 (NZ$70 pp). Another catamaran, the *Tangaroa III* based next to Trader Jack's at Avarua Harbor, is similar. Most of these operators will allow you to keep a few smaller fish for personal use, though larger fish belong to the boat. Ask about this before booking, if it matters. From August to October you might see whales from your boat!

For horseback riding it's **Aroa Pony Trek** (Georgina and Tiki Daniel, tel. 21-415, tiki gina@oyster.net.ck), up the road from Kaena Restaurant near the Rarotongan Beach Resort. Weekdays at 1000 and 1500 they offer two-hour rides to Papua Waterfall, returning along the beach (NZ$50/30 adult/child). Book ahead as participants are limited.

Try your swing at the nine-hole **Rarotonga Golf Club** (tel. 20-621; closed Sun.), under the radio towers near the end of the airstrip. Greens fees and club rentals are NZ$15 each. If you hit a mast, wire, or stay during your round, there's a compulsory replay; balls have been known to bounce back at players. Getting a tee time during the week is easy but on Saturday it's usually busy. There's an annual tournament here in late September and the club has a very pleasant colonial-style bar perfect for a cold beer (visitors are always welcome).

The bar at the **Rarotonga Bowling Club** (tel. 26-277) on Moss Road, Avarua, opens at 1600 weekdays, at 1000 on Saturday. If you've never tried lawn bowling before, do so—it's only NZ$1 greens fees plus NZ$1 bowls hire (a white outfit is required on Saturday).

The **Rarotonga Squash Club** (tel. 21-056; daily 0900–2230), directly behind the Catholic cathedral in Avarua, charges NZ$5 a session.

Both the Edgewater Resort and Rarotongan Beach Resort have **tennis court** open to the public, and the Edgewater also has squash courts.

Monday at 1730 you can jog with the **Hash House Harriers.** For the venue, call David Lobb at tel. 27-002 or scrutinize the back page of the Monday edition of the *Cook Islands News.* It's good fun and a nice way of meeting people.

ACCOMMODATIONS

There's such a glut of accommodations on Rarotonga that you'd have to be very unlucky to arrive on a day when everything was full. Bargaining for rooms isn't done but it's okay to ask if they have any "specials" on. The arrival of email has made booking ahead from overseas much easier and you sometimes get specially reduced rates through the hotel's own website. Most of the required email addresses are listed in this chapter.

If saving money is a concern, get a place with cooking facilities, as restaurant meals can add up. All of the budget and medium-priced hotels are self-catering, but many of the upmarket resorts are not. When choosing, keep in mind that the west coast is drier and gets beautiful sunsets, while the finest snorkeling is at windy Titikaveka in the south, and the top beach faces the gorgeous Muri Lagoon in the east. The places near Avarua are best for those more into shopping, sightseeing, and entertainment than beachlife.

Most places include the 12.5 percent VAT in the quoted rate but some charge it extra. Check out time at the motels is 1000. Most of the budget hotels provide free transfers from the airport to their properties (from international flights only) but charge NZ$10 for the ride back to the airport. The more upscale places charge NZ$15–20 each way. The listings below are arranged counterclockwise around the island in each price category.

Under US$25

Aunty Noo's Beach Lodge (tel. 21-253), halfway down to the beach behind Snowbird Laundry in Arorangi, offers the cheapest accommodations on Rarotonga and is thus the choice of backpackers on the barest of budgets. Beds in the crowded dorm are NZ$10 pp, the two four-bed "double" rooms are NZ$13 pp each, or you can camp in the back yard for NZ$8 pp. Rudimentary cooking facilities are provided and many guests sit and play cards at the picnic tables in the lounge all day. A party ensues whenever a duty-free bottle appears. Aunty Noo is rather eccentric (and she has quite a reputation on Rarotonga!) but it's unlikely you'll see much of her. This place isn't "accredited" so you won't find it in the official tourism brochures.

Maria's Backpackers Accommodations (Exham and Maria Wichman, tel. 21-180) is just off the Ara Metua in Arorangi, up near the trailhead of the Raemaru trek. From the main road in Arorangi, turn inland opposite Bunny's Diner. There are two self-catering rooms at NZ$20/36 single/double. Extra beds in the main house are NZ$15 pp. This is a place for people who like peace and quiet; those interested in meeting other travelers should head elsewhere.

Backpackers International Hostel (Mal and Tua Bates-Tuisila, tel./fax 21-847, www.backpackersinternational.com) is in the southwest corner of the island, only 100 meters from a grocery store, the Island Bus, an Internet outlet, and six km of white sandy beach. They offer six rooms with double beds and another 12 rooms with twin beds at NZ$28/35 single/double. In addition, there are six singles at NZ$28 and 21 dorm beds in rooms of three to eight at NZ$16 pp. A common TV lounge and cooking area are provided. It's convivial, and on Monday night the family prepares a special buffet dinner at NZ$20 pp (NZ$30 for nonguests).

Piri's Coconut Beach Hostel (tel. 20-309), on the beach just west of the Sheraton site, offers 16 mattresses in an open dorm at NZ$15 or a basic room at NZ$25. There are communal cooking facilities, but it's all really scruffy and to be avoided. Be aware, we've received many complaints about this place. The manager, Piri Puruto III, puts on tacky coconut tree climbing shows for tourists here and at other locations around the island.

Ariana Bungalows (Bob Healey, tel./fax 20-521, bobh@ariana.co.ck), a couple of km east of Avarua, offers quite a range of accommodations. The seven self-catering bungalows with bath are NZ$60 for up to three persons, whereas the six shared doubles are NZ$20/30 single/double. Three newer duplex studio rooms are NZ$65 for up to three. The nine-bed dorm is NZ$18 pp. On a weekly basis it's 25 percent off. Ariana is 400 meters off the main road and quite a distance from town or the beach. It's slightly run-down but almost never full—a good choice if you want to escape the crowds at Muri Beach. Airport pickups are free but departure transfers are NZ6 pp.

Lovely Planet Budget Accommodation (tel./fax 25-100) is opposite the Medical Clinic at Tupapa, a km east of central Avarua. The five four-bunk rooms start at NZ$20 pp. A shared kitchen, refrigerator, and laundry room are provided, and bicycles are for rent. Despite the name, this colonial-style home hostel with a spacious porch is run by Papa Ross Grant and has no connection with a certain mass-market Australian guidebook company.

A few travelers have managed to rent rooms in the large outer island hostels on Constitution Park Avenue opposite the Are-Karioi-Nui National Auditorium in Avarua. For example, the **Manihiki Hostel** charges about NZ$16 per person with communal cooking facilities. It's quite noisy due to the thin walls, but clean and convenient.

US$25–50

The first budget place to the west of town is **Atupa Orchid Units** (tel. 28-543, fax 28-546, www.atupaorchids.co.ck), run by a German woman named Ingrid Caffery who has been in the Cooks since 1970. There are nine rooms in four screened houses in a garden setting, each house with its own cooking facilities and hot water. Prices vary from NZ$30/44 single/double in a budget room to NZ$65/75 for a one/two-bedroom bungalow. It's an excellent value and discounts are available when things are slow. Quiet and comfortable, central Avarua is just a 10-minute walk away.

A 20-minute walk west of town are the A-frame chalets and guesthouse of the **Tiare Village Hostel** (Adrienne and Lucky Matapuku, tel. 23-466, fax 21-874, www.tiarevillage.co.ck). This

23-bed establishment has three fan-cooled, self-contained chalets, each with two singles and one double, at NZ$25/44 single/double, and three triples in the main house at NZ$20 pp to share. In addition, there are six self-catering duplex units facing a circular swimming pool at NZ$70 double. Guests staying in the dorms share the communal cooking facilities, lounge, and hot water showers, and the tropical garden is bursting with fruit there for the picking. Don't expect to get a lot of sleep, as this is a bit of a party hostel. Free luggage storage facilities and airport transfers are available.

The **Are Renga Motel** (tel. 20-050, fax 29-223, www.arerenga.com) at Arorangi has 20 simple, thin-walled units with well-equipped kitchens at NZ$60 single or double. The quality varies, so ask to see another room if the first one you're shown isn't to your liking. Beware of rooms with open ventilation spaces near the ceiling, as these let in every sound from adjacent rooms. The Are Renga offers a reduced "backpacker's rate" of NZ$25 per bed in six shared double rooms. The location is good with a store and other facilities nearby, and a lending library is available in the office. Use of their washing machine costs NZ$7, but there's no drier. In season you may harvest fruit from the large orchard behind the property. Airport transfers are free when you arrive, NZ$5 when you leave.

In late 2002, **Rarotonga Backpackers** (Paul and Rebecca, tel./fax 21-590, www.rarotonga backpackers.com) opened on a hillside off the Ara Metua in Arorangi, inland from Sunhaven Beach Bungalows. It's near the start of the invigorating hiking trail to the summit of Raemaru. There are two six-bed dorms at NZ$20 pp and four poolside rooms with shared bath at NZ$30/48 single/double in this multi-level complex. Common cooking and laundry facilities are available, and the large common area on the upper deck offers splendid sunset views. Unfortunately, the rooms are directly under this deck, which can be a nuisance if a group is partying late at night above. Rentals of bicycles/motorbikes (NZ$6/15) and surfboards (NZ$10) are possible. The Friday night barbecue and pub crawl (NZ$20) is a very popular event! Free airport

pickups are provided for those who have booked ahead through their website (NZ$6 pp for the departure transfer).

Etu Bungalows (tel./fax 25-588, www.etubun galows.com) in Arorangi has four self-catering bungalows at NZ$70 single or double.

A new place to stay is **Maiana Guesthouse** (Ina and Mano Pokia, tel./fax 20-438, www.maianaguesthouse.co.ck), just west of the residence of the Queen's Representative on the south coast. It has five rooms at NZ$35/50 single/double, three triple rooms at NZ$60, and one seven-bed dorm at NZ$20 pp (no children under 12 please). A common kitchen and fridge are provided. Maiana is cleaner and quieter than some of the Muri Beach places such as Vara's. Turoa Bakery and the Saltwater Café are next door and a white sandy beach is across the road.

One of the best established backpacker places is the **Aremango Guesthouse** (tel. 24-362, fax 24-363, www.ck/aremango), just 50 meters from Muri Beach, south of Vara's Budget Accommodation. The 10 spacious fan-cooled rooms with shared bath are NZ$22 pp. Singles must be prepared to share or pay for both beds. Reductions are offered if you stay three or more nights. Communal cooking facilities are available, and lockable cupboards for groceries are provided. Cleanliness could be an issue here, and peace and quiet will be up to your fellow guests. The feedback has been mixed, but it's still a good place if you click with the managers.

Vara's Budget Accommodation (Vara Hunter, tel. 23-156, fax 22-619, www.varas.co.ck), on the south side of the Muri Beachcomber, consists of two distinct sections. The beach complex includes several wooden buildings and a newer two-story block containing a mix of double rooms, upscale studios, and squashy dorms. Four hundred meters up the hillside are a "villa," "cottage," "apartment," and "lodge" with lots more rooms and dorms. At NZ$25 pp in a multi-bed dorm, NZ$55 double with shared bath, NZ$80 double with private bath, or NZ$120/130 single/double in a studio, both sections cost the same with a discount after three nights. The hillside accommodations are quieter, but Vara's is definitely for the backpacker who doesn't mind living in close quarters with lots of other backpackers. The fabulous beach draws people here, and all guests have access to laundry facilities (NZ$4), communal cooking facilities (a grocery store is adjacent), and cold showers. Bring your own toilet paper. Vara's office is up in the hillside section. If you want a double room, you should definitely reserve (no credit card number is required and they overbook to compensate for no-shows, so a reservation doesn't always guarantee a room).

US$50–100

The **Oasis Village** (Don and Pat Hawke, tel. 28-213, fax 28-214, www.ck/oasisvillage), near the beach in Arorangi, has four air-conditioned units starting at NZ$135/150/185 single/double/triple. Children under 12 are not accepted. Cooking facilities are not provided but there's a convenience store adjacent to the property.

Puaikura Reef Lodge (tel. 23-537, fax 21-537, www.puaikura.co.ck), on the southwest side of the island, offers 12 self-catering rooms in three single-story motel wings arranged around a cloudy swimming pool from NZ$135 single or double. A grocery store is adjacent, and the beach is just across the road with no houses blocking access to the sea. A paperback library is available for guests. The motel office is only open weekdays 0900–1600, Saturday 0900–1200, and the no-nonsense manager would prefer that you book ahead rather than just showing up unannounced on his doorstep.

Daydreamer Moemoea Apartments (Bruce and Nga Young, tel. 25-965, fax 25-964, byoung@daydreamer.co.ck), offers five attractive self-catering units in one long block just west of the Sheraton site and across the street from Piri's Hostel. It's NZ$120 single or double. The beach along here is great, but when snorkeling, beware of dangerous currents in passes draining the lagoon.

Bella's Beach Bungalows (Eugene Bella, tel. 26-004), east of the Queen's representative in Titikaveka, offers four quiet self-catering units on a white sandy beach at NZ$150. Kayaks and canoes are loaned free. Book through Shekinah Homes.

Raina Beach Apartments (tel. 23-601, fax 23-602, www.raina.com) in Titikaveka has four self-catering units in a three-story main building at NZ$150 single or double. Its main advantages are proximity to a good snorkeling area and the view from the roof. The same company also has six self-catering "villas" on the south side of the Manuia Beach Hotel in Arorangi, which go for NZ$390 double. These unscreened units are poorly maintained and not recommended.

Tiana's Beach Villas (tel. 24-452, www.tianas .com), at the south end of Muri Beach opposite Taakoka Island, is down the lane next to the Baha'i Center just south of Shangri-La Beach Cottages. The four bungalows with full cooking and laundry facilities begin at NZ$125 double. There's no on-site manager, so carefully lock up before you go out.

Daniel Roro's **Aroko Bungalows** (tel. 21-625 or 23-625, fax 24-625, aroko@bungalows.co.ck), at Ngatangiia, is one of the few medium-priced places facing Muri Beach. The 11 small bungalows with basic cooking facilities are NZ$110 single or double roadside or NZ$120 beachside. They're very tightly packed together, making the beachside units preferable.

The **Tropical Sands Bungalows** (tel. 23-564, www.tropicalsands.co.ck), at Ngatangiia a km north of Avana Marina Condominiums, has five self-catering units priced NZ$98–140 double.

The **Sunrise Beach Bungalows** (Caryn Kenny, tel. 20-417, fax 24-417, www.sunrise .co.ck) at Ngatangiia has four oceanfront and two garden bungalows at NZ$105/150 single/double, while the two duplex garden units are NZ$95/105. The rates are reduced when things are slow. All have cooking facilities, color TV, and laundry access—good value. The beach here is poor but there's a large swimming pool. It's peaceful and a store is close by. Some lovely nature hikes are available in the nearby valleys and it's an easy walk to Muri Beach.

Royal Palms (tel. 22-838, fax 22-836, www.royalpalms.co.ck), located inland at Matavera, has three thatched cottages at NZ$140 single or double (four-night minimum stay). There's a swimming pool.

Surfers often stay at **Seaview Lodge** (tel. 26-

240, fax 26-241, www.cookislandsurf.co.ck), a two-bedroom house on the hillside overlooking northern Rarotonga. It's NZ$100/130 double/triple and there's a fully equipped kitchen.

The clean, pleasant **KiiKii Motel** (Pauline and Harry Napa, tel. 21-937, fax 22-937, www.kii kiimotel.co.ck), a 30-minute walk west of Avarua, has an attractive swimming pool overlooking a rocky beach. The four older "budget rooms" in this solid two-story motel are NZ$70/90 single/double. The eight standard rooms in the west wing go for NZ$95/120/155 single/double/triple, while the 12 deluxe rooms are NZ$120/150 single/double (NZ$130/160 overlooking the sea). All 24 rooms have good cooking facilities, and the efficient staff is helpful in assisting with any special arrangements. KiiKii is probably the closest you'll come to a U.S.-style motel, although much nicer. Airport transfers are NZ$9 each way.

Club Raro (tel. 22-415, fax 24-415, www .clubraro.co.ck), two km east of Avarua, has 17 garden rooms at NZ$115 single or double, 20 poolside rooms at NZ$165, and 15 "beachfront" rooms at NZ$340 (a misnomer since there's no beach here). A swimming pool is provided but cooking facilities are not. It's walking distance from town.

A good bet very near Avarua's shopping, entertainment, and sightseeing possibilities is the **Paradise Inn** (Dianne Haworth, tel. 20-544, fax 22-544, www.paradiseinnrarotonga.com), just east of Portofino Restaurant. In a former existence "the Paradise" was the Maruaiai Dancehall, but it has been completely refurbished into a cozy little 16-room motel. The fan-cooled, split-level rooms are NZ$84/96/113 single/double/triple, and there are two smaller budget singles that are NZ$58. Cooking facilities are provided, and there's a large lounge and a nice terrace overlooking the ocean where you can sit and have a drink. Children under 12 are not accommodated.

The only hotel right in Avarua itself is the **Central Motel** (tel. 25-735, fax 25-740, www .cookpages.com/CentralMotel), up the road from the post office. The 16 units in this two-story concrete block edifice are NZ$95 single or double. No real cooking facilities are provided although a fridge, toaster, kettle, cups, and plates

have been placed in the units as an afterthought. It's clean and convenient and might be okay if you're there on business.

US$100–150

The **Reefcomber Sunset Motel** (tel. 25-673, fax 26-432, www.soltel.co.ck), opposite the road to the hospital a bit south of Black Rock, has 12 units from NZ$175. Cooking facilities are not provided.

The **Rarotongan Sunset Motel** (tel. 28-028, fax 28-026, www.rarotongansunset.co.ck), next door to the Oasis Village, has 19 self-catering units in long blocks of four or five units at NZ$175 double in the garden or from NZ$250 beachfront. These prices may be discounted 10 percent if you prepay direct. There's a swimming pool. It's a good value and often full. Children under 12 are not accepted.

Seashells Deluxe Serviced Apartments (tel.24-317, fax 24-318, www.seashells.co.ck), adjacent to the Manuia Beach Hotel in Arorangi, offers four two-bedroom duplex apartments at NZ$185 double, plus NZ$35 per additional person up to four maximum (children under 12 free). Full cooking facilities are provided.

Ati's Castaway Beach Villas (Dorothy and Cameron Robertson, tel. 21-546, fax 25-546, www.atiscastaway.co.ck), on the beach a little south of the church in Arorangi, offers 12 units with cooking facilities and hot water showers. It's NZ$160/200 double/triple for a pool unit, NZ$245/285 for a two-bedroom garden bungalow, or NZ$200/240 for a duplex beach bungalow. There's a communal TV lounge and a restaurant/bar beside the pool. A pole outside bears the flags of all the countries currently represented there, and the new owners from Scotland do their utmost to make guests feel at home. Airport transfers are NZ$15 pp return.

Sunhaven Beach Bungalows (Dennis and Patti Hogan, tel. 28-465, fax 28-464, www.ck/ sunhaven), south of Ati's Castaway and just north of Etu Bungalows, offers six new self-catering units at NZ$180–240 double (extra persons NZ$95). Five are right on the beach and the other is in the garden. There's an attractive swimming pool. Children under 12 are not accepted.

Lagoon Lodges Motel (tel. 22-020, www.la goonlodges.com), on spacious grounds near the Rarotongan Beach Resort, has 19 attractive self-catering units of varying descriptions beginning at NZ$180 double including breakfast. There's a swimming pool, terrace café, and NZ$25 Sunday night barbecue for in-house guests only. It's a good choice for families with small children, though it's not right on the beach. Lagoon Lodges is run by Des Eggelton, who arrived on Raro to help build the airport in 1973 and just couldn't bring himself to leave.

Palm Grove Lodges (Tom and Shirley Wills, tel. 20-002, fax 21-998, www.palmgrove.net), on the south side of the island, has 16 self-catering units beginning at NZ$205 single or double garden, NZ$315 beachfront, breakfast included. In the new beachfront units, you don't need to cross the road to swim.

At Titikaveka is the **Moana Sands Beachfront Hotel** (tel. 26-189, fax 22-189, www .moanasandshotel.co.ck) with 17 units packed together in a two-story building at NZ$235 for up to three persons including breakfast and the use of snorkeling gear and kayaks. A reduced rate may be available if you book ahead by email. The 12 standard units have limited cooking facilities but the five suites with better cooking facilities are NZ$2,800 a week for up to six persons. The beach is good and some water sports are offered.

Kura's Kabanas (Kura Bullen, tel./fax 27-010, www.kkabanas.co.ck), beside Sokala Villas on the Muri Lagoon, has four comfortable, self-catering units with large terraces facing the lagoon at NZ$200 double. Laundry facilities are available. Airport transfers are NZ$10 pp each way.

US$150–250

If your flight is delayed, Air New Zealand may accommodate you at the **Edgewater Resort Hotel** (tel. 25-435, fax 25-475, www.edgewater.co.ck), a tight cluster of two/three-story blocks and service buildings facing a mediocre beach. This is Raro's largest hotel, with 208 smallish air-conditioned rooms beginning at NZ$240 single or double for those in the most unfavorable locations and rising to NZ$550 for the VIP suite.

Third persons are NZ$80 extra. No cooking facilities are provided but many restaurants are nearby (avoid the hotel restaurant which has received mixed reviews). Traditional dancing is presented at the Edgewater twice a week. Frankly, this hotel is overpriced unless you're on a "cheap" package tour.

The **Manuia Beach Hotel** (tel. 22-461, fax 22-464, www.manuia.co.ck) at Arorangi has 20 Polynesian bungalows starting at NZ$295 double (children under 12 not admitted). Cooking facilities are not provided but there's a restaurant that has an island night on Saturdays. You can swim off their beach or use the swimming pool.

The **Rarotongan Beach Resort** (tel. 25-800, fax 25-799, www.rarotongan.co.ck), in the southwest corner of Rarotonga, has been the island's premier hotel since its opening in 1977. In 1997 the complex was fully renovated and made wheelchair accessible, one of the few South Pacific resorts where this is so. The 156 air-conditioned rooms in nine one- and two-story blocks begin at NZ$360 single or double (no cooking facilities). Children under 13 eat and sleep free, and other deals are available for families. Some water sports are also included. The beach and swimming pool are fine, there's an on-site spa, and island nights with traditional dancing are held twice a week. Airport transfers are NZ$35 pp roundtrip.

Takitumu Romantic Villas (tel. 24-682, fax 24-683, www.takitumuvillas.co.ck), near Kent Hall on the south side of the island, has 10 deluxe one-bedroom thatched villas between a swimming pool and the white sand beach (good snorkeling). It's self-catering and rates start at NZ$375. Children under 12 are not admitted.

The Little Polynesian (Dorice Reid & Jeannine Peyroux, tel. 24-280, fax 21-585, little poly@beach.co.ck), also at Titikaveka, has eight well-spaced self-catering duplex units at NZ$250 single or double, plus a lagoonside cottage at NZ$290. Children under 12 are not accepted. This quiet property faces one of the finest snorkeling beaches on the island (a swimming pool is also provided). Kayaks are available. Inquiries are only possible during office hours (weekdays 0800–1600, Sat. 0900–1200).

Travel writer Elliot Smith operates the deluxe

Shangri-La Beach Cottages (tel. 22-779, fax 22-775, www.shangri-la.co.ck) on the beach south of the Muri Beachcomber Motel. The 12 air-conditioned cottages start at NZ$250 single or double with whirlpool bath, microwave, fridge, TV/VCR, and lounge (no children under 18 years). A popular "early bird/self-servicing special" rate of only NZ$165 may be available through their website. There's a large pool, and kayaks and snorkeling gear are loaned free. The area between Ta'akoka islet and the barrier reef—maybe 100 meters from Shangri-La—is one of the best snorkeling spots on the island. After serving as a California judge for many years, Elliot dropped out of the legal profession and became a South Sea islander, sort of. His *Cook Islands Companion* is a best-seller on Rarotonga and he'll be able to tell you anything you want to know about the Cook Islands.

Near the south end of Muri Beach is the **Muri Beachcomber** (Phil and Juliet Wells, tel. 21-022, fax 21-323, www.beachcomber.co.ck) with 16 self-catering "seaview" units in eight older duplex blocks at NZ$240/260/340 single/double/triple. Children under 12 are only accepted in two larger air-conditioned garden units facing the pool, which cost NZ$270 for two adults and two children. Three "watergarden" units back near the road cost NZ$310/330/410.

The popular **Pacific Resort** (tel. 20-427, fax 21-427, www.pacificresort.com) at Muri offers 64 self-catering rooms beginning at NZ$300 single or double, NZ$350 triple (children under 12 free). Breakfast and airport transfers are included. Only 15 rooms face right onto the beach. A swimming pool, water-sports facility, Barefoot Bar, and evening entertainment are part of this well-rounded resort that fits nicely into its surroundings. The resort's restaurants are mediocre, however. The sandy beach is good for swimming but not for snorkeling.

Manea Beach (tel. 23-487, fax 25-320, www.manea.co.ck), between the Flame Tree Restaurant and Sokala Villas on Muri Beach, has five air-conditioned units with cooking, fridge, and terrace at NZ$250 single or double. A large three-bedroom beachfront villa is NZ$400. Opened in 2001, this place has a beachside swimming pool and complimentary kayaks.

Avana Marina Condominiums (tel. 20-836, fax 22-991, www.avanacondos.co.ck), on a rocky shore facing the north side of Ngatangiia Bay, has five two- and three-bedroom townhouses starting at NZ$325 double. These two-story self-catering units accommodate up to five persons. Also available are four studios with microwaves at NZ$280. The minimum stay is three nights. There's a swimming pool, and complimentary rowboats are provided to reach nearby secluded beaches.

US$250 and up

The most luxurious accommodations in the Cook Islands may be **Reflections on Rarotonga** (tel. 23-703, fax 23-702, www.reflections-rarotonga.com), southwest of Muri Beach and a few hundred meters east of Fruits of Rarotonga. Opened in 2002, this pair of two-story duplex units faces a white beach with excellent snorkeling. Each sleeps up to five persons at NZ$800 double in the master bedroom, then NZ$150 pp for the extra beds upstairs (no children please). Full kitchens and private swimming pools are provided. Behind these units is a self-catering "waterfall villa" at NZ$400 double. Airport transfers are included. Unfortunately, the whole complex is squeezed together on a tiny lot with little space even to park.

Crown Beach Resort (tel. 23-953, fax 23-951, www.crownbeach.com), south of the Edgewater Resort in Arorangi, opened in 1998. The 22 air-conditioned units start at NZ$525 single or double, continental breakfast included. All have small kitchenettes, and a swimming pool and watersports are available. The water off their beach is rather shallow for swimming. The Windjammer Restaurant (closed Tues.) is on the premises. The whole operation is overpriced.

Tucked away amid luxuriant vegetation next to the Flame Tree Restaurant is **Sokala Villas** (tel. 29-200, fax 21-222, www.sokala.com) with seven self-catering bungalows. The one garden villa without its own swimming pool is NZ$480 for up to three persons; the other six villas with pools or on the beach go as high as NZ$690. Children under 12 are not admitted. Office hours are weekdays 0900–1600, Saturday 0900–1300 only.

House Rentals

Renting an entire house by the week or month can be excellent value, and due to the outflow of Cook Islanders to New Zealand in the late 1990s, there are lots of places are available. Advertisements for furnished houses are often published in the classified section of the *Cook Islands News*, otherwise watch for signs around the island or ask at Cook Islands Tourism Corporation. Be aware of security when choosing a place, as break-ins (usually by teenagers) are not unknown here.

The houses available are far too numerous and subject to change to include in this book, but **Rarotonga Realty** (tel. 26-664, fax 26-665, www.rarorealty.co.ck) has a website that lists a large number of furnished homes for rent.

You could also try **Shekinah Homes** (tel. 26-004, fax 26-005, www.shekinahhomes.com), between the Paradise Inn and the Portofino Restaurant, which handles rentals at 30 properties (NZ$450–1,000 a week).

KiiKii Motel (tel. 21-937, fax 22-937, www.kiikiimotel.co.ck) rents four fully equipped two-bedroom cottages near the Rarotongan Beach Resort in Arorangi. These cost NZ$435 a week plus NZ$35 for electricity for up to four persons.

Jetsave Travel (tel. 27-707, www.jetsave.co.ck) books the studio at Muri Beach Cottages (www.ck/muribeachcottages) for NZ$175 per week.

FOOD

Some upmarket restaurants don't include the value-added tax in their menu prices. If in doubt, ask beforehand rather than get a 12.5 percent surprise on the bill. Most of the budget eateries popular among local residents are in Avarua, but you'll find fancy tourist restaurants all around the island, with a cluster near the Edgewater Hotel. Unless you don't mind waiting an hour or more, it's best to reserve if you'll be arriving for dinner after 1900.

Budget Eateries

Mama's Café (tel. 23-379; weekdays 0730–1530, Sat. 0730–1200), beside Foodland in Avarua, offers an interesting combination of healthy sandwiches and fattening desserts. The ice-cream cones are great!

Mae-Jo's Café (tel. 26-621; closed Sun.), beside the Island Bus stop at Cook's Corner, offers substantial Chinese meals, also available as takeaways.

Paulina's Polynesia Restaurant (tel. 28-889; Mon.–Sat. 0800 until late), near the traffic circle at Avarua Harbor, serves local foods, such as raw fish (NZ$8.50), sausage, eggs, and chips (NZ$8.50), and steaks (NZ$14.50). Breakfast is NZ$6.50–10. Seated at a picnic table between the Banana Court and Trader Jacks, you can wash it all down with beer.

At Avatiu Harbor there's **Aramoana Fish N' Chips** (tel. 21-250; weekdays 1000–2200, Sat. 1200–2200, Sun. 1200–2000) with a large fish and chips at NZ$7, parrot fish or flounder for NZ$5.50 a piece, plus oysters, mussels, calamari, and scallops. It's surprisingly pleasant with a nice terrace overlooking the harbor.

In Arorangi, **Flamboyant Place Takeaway** (tel. 23-958; daily 0800–0100), opposite Dive Rarotonga, serves inexpensive meals at their picnic tables. The ice-cream cones here are good.

Avarua

Much celebrated **Trader Jacks** (tel. 26-464; Mon.–Sat. 0900–2400, Sun. 1700–2200), on the waterfront at Avarua Harbor, serves pretty mediocre meals (NZ$16.50–24.40) and most people only consume *kati kati* bar snacks (NZ$9.50–12.50) and drink. The seafood chowder is said to be good. It's one of the few places away from the resorts where you can get a beer on Sunday night, and weekdays at happy hour you may meet some very senior, very drunk members of the local administration. It's lots of fun when the crew off one of the longliners working out of Avatiu Harbor rolls in. A 10-drink card, which can be used on different days by different people, is NZ$36. A live band plays here Friday nights from 2100.

The **Staircase Restaurant and Bar** (tel. 21-254; nightly from 1830), upstairs in the building beside the Beachcomber Gallery, has good value dinner specials advertised on blackboards outside (large portions). There's live music some nights, including Polynesian dancing Thursdays at 2030 (NZ$5 cover charge). After the show you too can dance the night away.

The **Portofino Restaurant** (tel. 26-480; Mon.–Sat. 1830–2100), on the east side of town, specializes in Italian dishes such as pizza (NZ$12–20), pasta (NZ$16–20), steaks (NZ$28–33), and seafood (NZ$27–35). It gets good reviews from readers ("good food, lots of it, and well prepared") and can be crowded, so try to reserve. Their takeaway pizzas are NZ$12/18 regular/large.

In mid-2004 veteran restaurateurs Sue Carruthers and Robbie Brown opened the **Tamarind House Restaurant** (tel. 26-487 or 26-488), near the Cook Islands Game Fishing Club just east of Avarua. They serve breakfast and lunch Tuesday–Sunday, dinners Tuesday–Saturday, closed Mondays. We still haven't had a chance to sample the cuisine, but if the food is typical Sue Carruthers', it will be the best food on the island.

Arorangi

Alberto's Steakhouse (tel. 23-597; Mon.–Sat. 1800–2100), near the Rarotongan Sunset Motel, offers steaks from NZ$23.50 to NZ$34.50 or pastas in the NZ$15–19 range. The cook is Swiss.

Hopsing's Chinese Restaurant (tel. 20-367), near the Edgewater Resort, serves some pretty decent Asian food. Expect main plates the size of side dishes in North America. The Mongolian beef arrives steaming at your table. Friday nights there's a buffet.

The much-advertised **Spaghetti House** (tel. 25-441; daily from 1700), at the entrance to the Edgewater Resort, offers pizzas, pastas, and meats.

Seafood, steaks, and chicken are available nightly 1800–2130 at the **Tumunu Tropical Garden Bar and Restaurant** (tel. 20-501), also near the Edgewater. The portions could be larger for the price. This spacious bar opened in 1979 and the bartender, Eric, offers sightseers a popular guided tour of his picturesque establishment for a NZ$1 tip. Ask the waitress if you can see Eric's scrapbooks of life on Raro in the early 1970s.

Titikaveka to Muri

The **Vaima Restaurant and Bar** (tel. 26-123; Thurs.–Tues. 1830–2200), on the south coast just east of the Sheraton site, has a reputation for good food (mains NZ$17.50–18.50). Try the mahimahi with coconut and papaya sauce. Friday–Monday nights there's live music. Call to ask about their NZ$4 hotel transfers.

Sails Restaurant (tel. 27-349, www.sailsrestaurant.co.ck; daily 1100–2300), at the Rarotonga Sailing Club, serves a classic baguette sandwich (NZ$9.50) at lunch. Dinner mains are NZ$17–24. The full à la carte menu is supplemented with a good selection of fresh seafood, fruits, and vegetables.

The **Flame Tree Restaurant** (tel. 25-123; nightly from 1830), on Muri Beach, has been the island's top restaurant since it opened in 1988. Every day they offer a different set three-course menu for NZ$28.50. À la carte starters are in the NZ$9–14 range and main plates running NZ$19–34. It opens at 1830 daily and reservations are recommended.

That's Pasta Italian Pasta Shop (tel. 22-232, www.thatspasta.com; Wed.–Sun. 1730–2100), next to The Internet Cafe at Muri, serves homemade pasta priced NZ$13.50–18.50, freshly prepared by Roberta and Stefano.

Cafés

The **Blue Note Café** (tel. 23-236; weekdays 0800–1730, weekends 0800–1400), on the Banana Court verandah, has the best coffee in town (NZ$3.50). It's a good choice for breakfast and there's a stack of New Zealand newspapers on the counter for free reading. Check out the adjacent art gallery.

The Café (tel. 21-283; weekdays 0730–1500, Sat. 0630–1300), between Avarua Harbor and T.J.'s Nightclub, is a spacious locale serving lunches at NZ$11–17 (Saturday brunch NZ$11–13), plus coffee and cakes all day.

Mairenui Botanical Garden and Café (tel. 22-796; weekdays 0900–1600, Sat. 1200–1600), opposite The Little Polynesian at Titikaveka, is a tropical garden you may visit for NZ$3 admission. The excellent café serves breakfast for under NZ$10, lunch for NZ$12.50. Tea or coffee is NZ$4, spaghetti on toast NZ$6.

Fruits of Rarotonga (tel. 21-509; weekdays 0800–1700, Sat. 0900–1700), by the road in the southeast corner of the island, sells a variety of jams, chutneys, pickles, sauces, and dried fruits made on the premises. It's a fine place to stop for coffee and muffins on your way around the island, and you can snorkel right off their beach.

Sunday Barbecues

Several of the hotels prepare a special Sunday barbecue dinner, or "roast," open to everyone. The favorite of those in the know takes place at 1900 at Ati's Castaway Beach Villas (tel. 21-546), a bit south of the church in Arorangi (NZ$20 pp, reservations required). Return minibus transfers from anywhere on the island can be arranged at NZ$10 pp.

At the main hotels, there a barbecue at the Rarotongan Sunset Motel (tel. 28-028) at 1730 (NZ$25 pp) and an Indian buffet at the Edgewater Resort (tel. 25-435) at 1830 (NZ$30). The Sunday barbecue (NZ$35) at The Rarotongan Beach Resort (tel. 25-800) comes with several hours of string band entertainment—a great way to watch the sun go down. Call ahead to check times, prices, transportation arrangements, and bookings. Other possibilities may be advertised in the local paper.

Groceries

Every budget hostel or motel provides kitchen facilities, so Rarotonga is perfect for those who enjoy preparing their own food. At the supermarkets, newcomers to the South Pacific will be surprised to find the milk and juice in boxes on the shelves and long loaves of unwrapped bread in barrels near the check-out. Unfortunately, it's almost impossible to buy fresh fish because the lagoons have been fished out and anything that does get caught goes straight to the hotel kitchens.

CITC Supermarket (tel. 22-777; Mon.–Wed. 0800–1700, Thurs. and Fri. 0800–1800, Sat. 0800–1600), west of Avatiu Harbor, is generally cheaper than Foodland Supermarket in town. Meatco (tel. 27-652), just down from Budget Rent-a-Car in Avarua, usually has the least expensive vegetables and the best meat (except pork).

For beer or liquor, go to the CITC Liquor Center (tel. 28-380; Mon.–Thurs. 0900–1700,

Fri. and Sat. 0900–1900) next to CITC Supermarket on the way to the airport.

Fresh milk and fruit juices are sold at Frangi Dairy (tel. 22-152), beside Parliament. You can also buy imported frozen meat and vegetables here, large containers of water, and super ice-cream cones.

On the south side of the island you can usually get everything you need at Wigmore's Super Store (tel. 20-206; Mon.–Sat. 0600–2100, Sun. 0600–0900 and 1400–2100) between the Sheraton site and Palm Grove Lodges. The food bar next to Wigmore's opens Tuesday–Saturday 1130–2030, Sunday 1130–1800.

The water on Rarotonga is safe to drink.

ENTERTAINMENT AND EVENTS

The Empire Theater (tel. 23-189) in Avarua projects feature films in two separate halls nightly except Sunday at 1930 and 2130 (NZ$5). On Tuesday you get two movies for NZ$5 and on Saturday there's a matinee at 1000. It's almost worth going just to experience the enthusiasm of the local audience!

The most famous watering hole on the island is the historic Banana Court (tel. 23-397) in central Avarua, in what was once a hostel for expatriate workers. This place just isn't what it used to be, but it still opens Monday–Saturday after 1700.

T.J.'s Nightclub (tel. 24-722), next to BECO Hardware Store just east of The Waterfront Mall, opens Wednesday–Saturday around 2000. There's karaoke singing and a disco. It's popular with the local teenagers, and dress regulations are in force to maintain standards.

The Arorangi Clubhouse, at the Raemaru Park Sports Ground near the CICC church in Arorangi, has a good bar open on Friday and Saturday nights only. There's often live music. A predominately local crowd comes here and it can get rough, but it's a good place to mix.

For a cheap thrill, find out when one of Air New Zealand's Boeing 767s will be arriving and position yourself on the sea wall at the west end of the runway a bit before. It's quite an experience to have a big jet pass only 15 meters above your head!

Bars

The only bars likely to be open on Sunday are those at Trader Jacks, the Edgewater Hotel, the Rarotongan Beach Resort, Sails Restaurant, and Club Raro.

Waterfront Coco Bar (tel. 20-340; Mon.–Sat. 1100–midnight, Fri. until 0200), across the street from Avarua Harbor, is a breezy hangout with mugs of cold beer and occasional live music. It's the sort of place where you might expect to meet a former prime minister and other colorful local characters. Special events are posted on the blackboard outside (NZ$5 cover charge Wed.–Sat. after 2000 if there's live music).

Another good drinking place is the **Cook Islands Game Fishing Club** (tel. 21-419; Mon.–Sat. 1200–midnight) near Club Raro east of town. There's a terrace out back with picnic tables overlooking the beach, and a large paperback library inside. This is a private club, but a little tact and charm will see you through. Other agreeable bars include those at the **Rarotonga Bowling Club** (tel. 26-277; opens at 1600 weekdays) in Avarua and at the **Rarotonga Golf Club** (tel. 20-621) west of the airport. Both are closed on Sunday.

The **Returned Services Association Club** or "RSA" (tel. 20-590; weekdays 1200–2400, Sat. 1100–2400, public holidays 1300–2400, closed Sun.), directly across the street from the airport terminal, is a good place for a beer while you're waiting for a flight. They also have two pool tables, but food service is erratic. Tom Neale, who wrote a well-known book about his experiences living alone on Suwarrow atoll in the northern Cooks, is buried in the cemetery next to the club.

Cultural Shows for Visitors

Cook Islands dancers are renowned and "island night" performances are staged regularly at the hotels and restaurants. A buffet of traditional Cook Island food *(umukai)* is laid out, and those ordering the meal can watch the show for free, otherwise there's usually a cover charge (NZ$5–20). Things change, so call the hotels to check. Best of all, try to attend a show related to some special local event when the islanders themselves participate (look in the newspaper for listings).

The **Edgewater Resort** (tel. 25-435) has island nights Tuesday and Saturday at 2030, costing NZ$49 for the buffet or NZ$15 cover if

musicians at island night

© DAVID STANLEY

you don't take dinner. The Taakoka Troupe often performs at the Edgewater on Tuesday with Orama on Saturday (ask). The **Rarotongan Beach Resort** (tel. 25-800) usually has shows Wednesday and Saturday at 2030 (NZ$45 buffet or NZ$20 cover). On Thursday there's an island night at the **Staircase Restaurant** (tel. 21-254) in Avarua (NZ$25 for dinner or NZ$5 show only). The **Pacific Resort** (tel. 20-427) at Muri has an island night with children dancing Friday at 1900 (dinner NZ$45). The **Manuia Beach Hotel** (tel. 22-461) in Arorangi has an island night on Saturday and to attend you must purchase the buffet (NZ$42).

SHOPPING

Shopping hours in Avarua are weekdays 0800–1600, Saturday 0800–1200 only. Supermarkets in Avarua stay open about an hour longer, and small general stores around the island are open as late as 2000 weekdays and also on weekends. The **Dive Shop** (tel. 26-675, www.palm.co.ck), in Mana Court in Avarua, sells quality snorkeling gear.

Raro Records (tel. 25-927), next to Empire Theater, sells Tahitian compact discs and cassettes a third cheaper than what you'd pay in Tahiti! **CITC Shopping Center** (tel. 22-000) nearby has more recordings of Cook Islands music.

The **Philatelic Bureau** (tel. 29-336, fax 22-428) next to the post office has colorful stamps, first-day covers, and mint sets of local coins, which make good souvenirs. In addition to the Cook Islands issues, they also sell stamps of Aitutaki and Penrhyn (only valid for postage on those islands). A crisp, new Cook Islands $3 bill costs NZ$7 here.

Crafts

Check out the **Punanga Nui Cultural Market** near Avatiu Harbor where you'll find grass skirts, baskets, dancing shakers, pandanus *rito* hats, and hat bands. *Tivaevae* quilts are available on request (NZ$250 and up for a medium-size one). Woods used by the carvers include beach hibiscus *(aue)* for tropical fish, ironwood *(toa)* for tangaroa figures, and mahogany *(tamano)* for slit

drums. Friday nights from 1600–2000 a large flea market occurs here with lots of local food (NZ$5 a plate) and live music. Saturday mornings are also lively. The large open area at Punanga Nui is used for cultural festivals.

More expensive but well worth a look is **Island Craft** (tel. 22-009, www.islandcraft.com), beside the Westpac Bank, selling teak or mahogany carvings of Tangaroa, the fisherman's god (a fertility symbol), white woven hats from Penrhyn, mother-of-pearl jewelry, and good, strong bags. Other popular items include handbags, fans, tapa cloth, replicas of staff gods, wooden bowls, food pounders, pearl jewelry, seats *(no'oanga)*, headrests, slit gongs *(tokere)*, and fishhooks. They've also got a branch at the airport that opens for international departures, but the selection in town is much better.

A branch of **Bergman and Sons** (tel. 21-901), between the Cook Islands Visitor Center and the Banana Court, also has a reasonable selection of woodcarvings. Also check **Tarani Crafts and Pearls** (tel. 21-124), next to Empire Theater, which has pandanus hats and black pearls.

Pearls and Souvenirs

The black pearls of Manihiki and Penrhyn may be inspected at the main **Bergman and Sons** store (tel. 21-902, fax 21-903, www.pearlcookislands.com) at Cooks Corner. Unfortunately, prices are not marked.

The **Beachcomber Gallery** (tel. 21-939, www.craftcookislands.com; weekdays 0930–1600, Sat. 0930–1200), at the corner of the Ara Tapu and Makea Tinirau Road, is housed in a former London Missionary Society school building (1843). It's worth entering this museumlike gallery to peruse the lovely black pearl jewelry and other artworks on sale.

The **Perfume Factory** (tel. 22-690, www.perfumes.co.ck), on the Ara Metua behind town, sells a variety of coconut oil-based lotions and soaps produced on the premises. They also have the distinctive Tangaroa coconut coffee liqueur sold in souvenir ceramic Tangaroa bottles at NZ$60 for a 350-ml bottle or NZ$25 for a 150-ml bottle. A regular 750-ml glass bottle of the same is NZ$35.

Clothing

Visit **Tav's Clothing Factory** (Ellena Tavioni, tel. 23-202), on Vakatini Road, for the attractive lightweight tropical clothing and swimsuits screen-printed and sewn on the premises. Special-size items can be made to measure. Tav's designer garments are presently in fashion in Australia.

Get into style with some bright tropical apparel from **Joyce Peyroux Garments** (tel. 20-201), opposite the Are Renga Motel in Arorangi. Joyce Peyroux and other retailers carry beautiful selections of hand-printed dresses, pareus, tie-dyed T-shirts, bikinis, etc.—all locally made.

INFORMATION AND SERVICES

Information

The government-run Cook Islands Tourism Corporation Visitor Center (tel. 29-435, fax 21-435; weekdays 0800–1600), has official brochures and information sheets giving current times and prices. Ask for a free copy of *Jasons What's On in the Cook Islands,* which contains a wealth of useful information about their advertisers. Jasons free island map is also excellent. This office does not make hotel or tour bookings.

The Statistics Office (tel. 29-511, fax 21-511), on the 2nd floor of the Government Office Building behind the post office, sells the informative *Annual Statistic Bulletin* (NZ$10).

The World Wide Fund for Nature (tel. 25-091, fax 25-093) is a bit beyond the Paradise Inn east of town.

The Bounty Bookshop (tel. 27-770, fax 24-555), next to post office in Avarua, carries books on the Cook Islands, the latest regional news magazines, and the *Cook Islands News.*

The University of the South Pacific Center (tel. 29-415), opposite the Cook Islands Library and Museum, has for sale an excellent selection of text books on the region.

The harbormaster (tel. 28-814; weekdays 0800–1200/1300–1600), at Avatiu Harbor, sells nautical charts of the Cook Islands, Tonga, and New Zealand at NZ$30 apiece.

Visitors can become temporary members of the Cook Islands Library and Museum (tel. 26-468; Mon.–Sat. 0900–1300, Tues. also 1600–2000) for an annual fee of NZ$25, of which NZ$10 is refunded upon departure. The library also sells good cultural books.

Island Hopper Vacations (tel. 22-576, fax 23-027, www.islandhoppervacations.com), west of the airport terminal, Jetsave Travel (tel. 27-707, fax 28-807, www.jetsave.co.ck), just west of the Westpac Bank, Matina Travel (tel. 21-780, fax 24-780, trvlsave@matinatravel.co.ck), and Tipani Tours (tel. 25-266, www.tipanitours.com) arrange package tours to the outer islands with flights and accommodations included.

Money

Two banks serve Rarotonga, the Westpac Bank (tel. 22-014, bank@westpac.co.ck; weekdays 0900–1500, Sat. 0900–1200), next to Island Craft on the main street, and the ANZ Bank (tel. 21-750; Mon.–Thurs. 0900–1500, Fri. 0900–1600), next to the Visitor Information Center. Both change traveler's checks and give cash advances on Visa and MasterCard. The Westpac branch at the airport charges NZ$2.50 commission on traveler's checks, while the branch of the same bank in Avarua charges no commission. The ANZ Bank charges NZ$2 commission on traveler's checks but gives a slightly better rate. If you're changing hundreds of dollars, check both banks and compare. The ANZ Bank has ATMs outside their downtown branch and at the airport. The Westpac Bank represents American Express.

Post and Telecommunications

The post office (tel. 29-940) in Avarua holds general delivery mail 28 days and there's no charge to pick up letters.

Telecom Cook Islands (tel. 29-680, fax 26-174) at the Earth Station Complex on Tutakimoa Road, Avarua, is open 24 hours a day for overseas telephone calls and telegrams. If you want to receive a fax here, the public fax number for Rarotonga is fax 682/26-174 and it costs NZ$2.20 to receive the first page, plus 55 cents each additional page.

TelePost (tel. 29-940; weekdays 0800–1600, Sat. 0830–1200), in CITC Shopping Center next to the ANZ Bank, will receive faxes sent to fax

682/29-873 at the same rate. To send a fax is NZ$5.50 a page, plus long distance charges (NZ$1.45 per minute to New Zealand, NZ$1.60 to Australia, NZ$3 to the U.S., and NZ$4 to Canada or the U.K.). TelePost has telephone cards that can be used in the public phones outside and around town. Postage stamps are sold.

Internet Access

Both Telecom Cook Islands and TelePost at the locations just mentioned offer Internet access from their "cyberbooths" at NZ$1.75 per five minutes. If you have a computer and are staying a while, you can get connected to the Internet at Telecom Cook Islands for NZ$25 registration plus NZ$7 an hour. Of course, you'll need access to a phone line.

Slightly cheaper internet access is available at Pacific Gifts and Souvenirs (tel. 23-458, www.gifts.co.ck; weekdays 0900–1600, Sat. 0900–1200), behind Cooks Corner, at NZ$0.30 a minute.

The Internet Shop (tel. 20-727; weekdays 0900–1700, Sat. 0900–1330), run by Pacific Computers in The Waterfront Mall opposite Empire Theater, charges NZ$0.20 a minute.

The Internet Cafe (tel. 27-242; Mon.–Sat. 1000–1800, Sun. 1200–1800), between the Pacific Resort and Flame Tree Restaurant at Muri Beach, provides access at US$0.25 a minute. They also rent bicycles at NZ$7/35 day/week. Blue Rock (weekdays 0930–1700, weekends 1030–1700) nearby at the entrance to Sokala Villas is slightly cheaper at US$0.20 a minute or NZ$10/18 per one/two hours.

Visas and Officialdom

For an extension of stay go, to the Immigration office (tel. 29-347) on the top floor of the Government Office Building behind the post office. Visa extensions cost NZ$70 to extend your initial 31 days to three months. Otherwise, you can pay NZ$120 and get a five-month extension on the spot. The maximum stay is six months. You must show a plane ticket valid for your scheduled departure date and proof of funds. If you lose your passport, report to the Ministry of Foreign Affairs in the same building.

The Honorary Consul of Germany is Dr. Wolfgang Losacker (tel. 23-306) near the tourist office in Avarua. The New Zealand High Commission (tel. 22-201; weekdays 1030–1430) is next to the Philatelic Bureau.

Other Services

Snowbird Laundry (tel. 20-952), next to the Tumunu Restaurant in Arorangi, will do your wash for NZ$9.50 a load including washing and drying.

There are public toilets at Cooks Corner and at the Punanga Nui Cultural Market.

Yachting Facilities

Yachts pay a fee to anchor Mediterranean-style at Avatiu Harbor and are subject to the NZ$25 pp departure tax. The harbor is overcrowded and it's wise to do exactly what the harbormaster (tel. 28-814; office hours weekdays 0800–1200/1300–1600) asks, as he's been around for a while. If you're trying to hitch a ride on a yacht to Aitutaki, Suwarrow, or points west, the harbormaster would be a good person to ask. There's a freshwater tap on the wharf, plus cold showers on the ground floor of the Ports Authority building. During occasional northerly winds November–March, this harbor becomes dangerous, and it would be a death trap for a small boat during a hurricane.

Health

Rarotonga's main hospital (tel. 22-664), on a hill between the airport and Arorangi, attends to emergencies 24 hours a day. To call an ambulance, dial 998.

The Tupapa Community Clinic (tel. 20-066) at Tupapa, a km east of town, is open weekdays 0800–1800, Saturday 0800–1100. Consultations are NZ$35. In the same building is Dental Services (tel. 29-312; weekdays 0900–1200/1300–1600). The registration fee here is NZ$12 and a full examination costs NZ$112.

It's usually more convenient to see a private practitioner, such as Dr. Tereapii Uka (tel. 23-680; weekdays 0800–1200/1330–1500, Sat. 0900–1200), upstairs in Ingram House opposite Avatiu Harbor. A private dentist, Dr. K. Henry (tel. 29-605; weekdays 0900–1500, Sat. 0900–1100), has an office adjacent to Dr. Uka.

You could also turn to Dr. Teariki Noovao (tel. 20-835), between the Teachers College and the Golf Club opposite Avatea School on the Ara Metua. His medical clinic is open weekdays 1630–2030, Saturday 0900–1200. A private Dental Surgery (tel. 20-169; weekdays 0800–1600) is a few hundred meters east along the same road back toward town.

Dr. Wolfgang Losacker (tel. 23-306; weekdays 1000–1300), operates a medical clinic and photo gallery between the Banana Court and the tourist office in Avarua. He's a specialist in internal and tropical medicine, cardiology, and parasitology, and at his office he sells his own Cook Islands photo books and postcards.

The CITC Pharmacy (tel. 29-292; weekdays 0800–1630, Sat. 0800–1200) is in central Avarua at CITC Shopping Center.

TRANSPORTATION

For information on air and sea services from Rarotonga to other Cook islands turn to this chapter's Exploring the Islands section.

By Road

The **Cook's Island Bus Passenger Transport Ltd.** (tel. 25-512, fax 25-513) operates a daily around-the-island bus service. These yellow, 32-seat buses alternate in traveling clockwise and counterclockwise. The clockwise buses leave Cooks Corner in Avarua on the hour Monday–Saturday 0700–1400, Sunday 0800–1200/1400–1600. The counterclockwise buses leave 25 minutes after the hour weekdays 0825–1630, Saturday 0825–1230.

The clockwise night bus leaves town Monday–Saturday at 1800, 2100, and 2200, plus midnight and 0130 on Friday. The counterclockwise night bus leaves Monday–Saturday at 1900 with some additional services (ask).

Current timetables are usually available at the Visitor Center and are reproduced in *What's On in the Cook Islands*. Fares are NZ$2.50 one-way, NZ$4 roundtrip. A 10-ride ticket, which can be shared, is NZ$17, a day pass NZ$9/16 adult/family. Tourists are the main users of this excellent, privately run service and the drivers make a point of being helpful.

Taxi rates are negotiable, but the service is slightly erratic. Ask the fare before getting in and clarify whether it's per person or for the whole car. Some drivers will drive you the long way around the island to your destination. Beware of pre-booking taxis to the airport over the phone, as they often don't turn up, especially at odd hours. Service is generally 0600–2200 only. Hitchhiking is not really accepted here.

Rentals

A Cook Islands Driver's License (NZ$10) is required to operate a motorized rental vehicle. This can be obtained in a few minutes at the police station (tel. 22-499) in the center of Avarua weekdays 0930–1430, Saturday 0830–1030, upon presentation of your home driver's license (minimum age 16 years). This whole exercise is purely a moneymaking operation and the International Driver's License is not accepted.

If you wish to operate a scooter they'll require you to show something that states explicitly that you're licensed to drive a motorcycle, otherwise you'll have to pass a test (NZ$5 extra fee) that involves riding one up and down the street without falling off. Bring your own scooter, and don't worry, nobody fails the test. (The person giving the driving tests knocks off for lunch 1200–1300, so don't come then if you need a test.) Without a license the insurance on the vehicle won't be valid and you'll be liable for a stiff fine if caught. No license is required to ride a bicycle.

You're supposed to wear a helmet while operating a motorbike. Although it's unlikely you'll ever see anybody with one on, an anti-tourist cop could always bring it up. Take care when getting on or off the motorbike, as many people receive burns on their lower right leg from the hot exhaust pipe.

Drive slowly, because local children tend to run onto the road unexpectedly, and beware of free-roaming dogs, which often cause accidents by suddenly giving chase at night. Take special care on Friday and Saturday nights, when there are often more drunks on the road than sober drivers. The radar-enforced speed limit is 40 km per hour in Avarua, 50 km per hour on the open road, and driving is on the left. Motorcycle accidents involving tourists are common.

The prices listed below are for the cheapest car. Rates include unlimited km, and the seventh consecutive day is usually free. Some places quote prices including the 12.5 percent government tax, others without the tax. Check all the agencies for special deals—most are also open on Sunday. Most cars and scooters rent for 24 hours, so you can use them for a sober evening on the town.

Budget/Polynesian (tel. 20-895, fax 20-838, www.budget.co.ck), in Avarua and at the Edgewater Resort and Rarotongan Beach Resort, has the best quality cars and bicycles. Their cars are NZ$79 a day, scooters NZ$27 a day, bicycles NZ$8 a day, tax included. You can also get a 12-passenger van, great if you want to organize your own group tour. Discounts are offered on rentals of three days or more. Insurance is included but you're still responsible for the first NZ$300 "insurance excess" on the scooters and NZ$1,000 on the cars.

Avis (tel. 22-833, fax 21-702, www.avis.co.ck), next to the Cook Islands Trading Company in Avarua, charges NZ$63 for cars. Avis also has scooters at NZ$23/108 a day/week. At Avis the 12.5 percent tax is charged extra and you're responsible for the first NZ$2,000 in "excess" damages.

Rarotonga Rentals (tel. 22-326, www.rarotongarentals.co.ck; weekdays 0800–1600, Sat. 0800–1200), next to Odds 'n Ends opposite the Punanga Nui Cultural Market, has cars from NZ$50 a day if you rent for three days and scooters at NZ$25 a day (or NZ$91 a week). Jeeps are also available.

Raymond Pirangi at **T.P.A. Rental Cars** (tel. 20-611), opposite the Rarotongan Sunset Motel in Arorangi, offers some of the cheapest car rentals on the island, so don't expect to receive a new car from him. Also try **Tipani Rentals** (tel. 22-328, fax 25-611), opposite the Edgewater Resort in Arorangi.

Many smaller companies rent motor scooters and bicycles—ask your hotel for the nearest. **Island Car & Bike Hire** (tel. 22-632, www.islandcarhire.co.ck), also known as Hogan Rentals, 250 meters north of the Are Renga Motel in Arorangi, rents cars/bicycles from NZ$40/12 a day. Island's 12-speed mountain bikes have baskets on the front and are fairly sturdy, but there are no lamps for night riding. **BT Bike Hire** (tel. 23-586), right next to the Are Renga Motel, also has bicycles and scooters.

There aren't enough women's bicycles to go around, but men's cycles are easy to rent. The main advantage to renting a bicycle for the week is that you have it when you want it. Rarotonga is small enough to be easily seen by bicycle, which makes renting a car or scooter an unnecessary expense—you also avoid the compulsory local driver's license rip-off. Bicycles are also quiet, easy on the environment, healthy, safe, and great fun. One of the nicest things to do on a sleepy Rarotonga Sunday is to slowly circle the island by bicycle.

Tours

The **Takitumu Conservation Area project** (tel. 29-906, kakerori@tca.co.ck) operates four-hour guided nature hikes into the bush on the south side of the island. You'll be shown the colorful flora and hopefully catch a glimpse of the endangered *kakerori* or Rarotonga flycatcher that the group is working to save. It's a gentle walk through lush forest suitable for all ages. Hikes start at 0930 Tuesday, Thursday, and Friday, costing NZ$45/20 pp adult/child including light refreshments and transfers.

Pa's Nature Walk (tel. 21-079, www.pasbungalows.co.ck) is another good way to get acquainted with the natural history of Rarotonga. The four-hour hike through the bush behind Matavera includes a light lunch; both it and Pa's more strenuous guided cross-island hike are NZ$60 pp with hotel transfers included. Pa's hikes are recommended for birdwatchers. With his blond Rastafarian good looks, Pa is quite a character and it's worth signing up just to hear his spiel. He also has two bungalows for rent at NZ$100 double.

Air Rarotonga (tel. 22-888, www.airraro.com) offers 20-minute scenic flights (NZ$65 pp) around Rarotonga out of their hangar, 500 meters west of the main terminal. The traditional time is

1400, but you can usually arrange this on the spur of the moment if there are two of you and a pilot and plane are available.

Hugh Henry (tel. 25-320, fax 25-420, tours@hughhenry.co.ck) and **Raro Tours** (tel. 25-324, coaches@rarotours.co.ck) offer 3.5-hour, NZ$25 circle-island tours weekday mornings. Call ahead and they'll pick you up at your hotel. Ask how much time will be spent on "shopping sprees" as some tours waste half the allotted time in souvenir shops. Sunday mornings at 0930 a church service is included in this tour (NZ$30).

Monday, Wednesday, and Friday at 1000 the **Cultural Village** (tel. 21-314) offers a full-day combined circle-island tour and cultural show for NZ$85 including lunch.

More adventurous tours in 4WD vehicles are offered by **Raro Mountain Safari Tours** (tel. 23-629, www.rarosafaritours.co.ck), opposite the Rarotongan Beach Resort. The 3.5-hour tours (NZ$60/30 adult/child) begin weekdays at 0900 and 1330, Sunday at noon. It's the best way to see the island's interior without walking.

The **Bond Liquor Store** (tel. 21-007), opposite the Punanga Nui Cultural Market, offers a free guided tour of their on-site brewery Monday–Thursday at 1400.

Aitutaki

Aitutaki, 259 km north of Rarotonga, is the second-most-visited Cook Island and the scenery of this "dream island" is actually quite lovely. The low, rolling hills are flanked by banana plantations, taro fields, and coconut groves. Atiu-type coffee is grown here. A triangular barrier reef 45 km around catches Aitutaki's turquoise lagoon like a fishhook. The maximum depth of this lagoon is 10.5 meters but most of it is less than five meters deep. The 15 picture-postcard *motu* (islets) and numerous sandbars on the eastern barrier reef all feature the soft white sands and aquamarine waters of your usual South Seas paradise.

The main island is volcanic: Its highest hill, Maungapu (124 meters), is said to be the top of Rarotonga's Raemaru, chopped off and brought back by victorious Aitutaki warriors. All of the *motu* are coralline except for Rapota and Moturakau, which contain some volcanic rock. Legend holds that just as the warriors were arriving back with their stolen mountain, they clashed with pursuing Rarotongans and pieces of Maungapu fell off creating Moturakau and Rapota. Moturakau served as a leper colony from the 1930s to 1967. Motikitiu at the south end of the lagoon is the nesting area of many of the Aitutaki's native birds, since mynahs have taken over the main island. Be on the lookout for the blue lorikeet *(kuramo'o)* with its white bib and orange beak and legs.

The 2,000 people live in eight villages strung along the roads on both sides of the main island. The roads are red-brown in the center of the island, coral white around the edge, and the locals generally get around on motor scooters. The administration and most local businesses are clustered near the wharf at Arutanga. All of the villages have huge community halls built mostly with money sent from New Zealand. There's tremendous rivalry among the villages to have the biggest and best one, although they're unused most of the time. The *motu* are uninhabited, and there aren't any dogs at all on Aitutaki.

Aitutaki is the only Cook island other than Rarotonga where there's a good choice of places to stay, entertainment, and organized activities. One way to go is to catch a Thursday or Friday flight up from Rarotonga so as to be on hand for "island night" that evening. Book a lagoon trip for Saturday and you'll still have Sunday to scooter around the island or laze on the beach. Fly back on Monday or Tuesday, having sidestepped Rarotonga's dull Sunday. This is probably too short a stay, however, and a week on the island would be better.

Aitutaki is north of Rarotonga and therefore warmer. During the hot season December–March, sand flies and mosquitoes are at their worst. They're more of a nuisance on the north side of the main island, far less so on the *motu*.

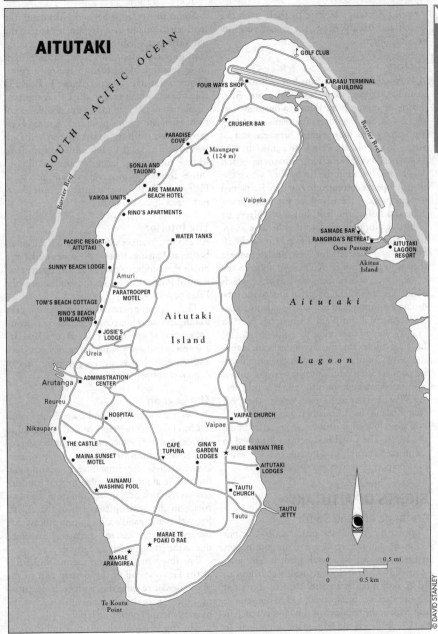

AITUTAKI

SOUTH PACIFIC OCEAN

Barrier Reef

Barrier Reef

GOLF CLUB

FOUR WAYS SHOP

KARAAU TERMINAL BUILDING

CRUSHER BAR

PARADISE COVE

Maungapu (124 m)

SONJA AND TAUONO

ARE TAMANU BEACH HOTEL

VAIKOA UNITS

Vaipeka

RINO'S APARTMENTS

WATER TANKS

SAMADE BAR
RANGIROA'S RETREAT

PACIFIC RESORT AITUTAKI

AITUTAKI LAGOON RESORT

Ootu Passage

SUNNY BEACH LODGE

Akitua Island

Amuri

PARATROOPER MOTEL

A i t u t a k i

TOM'S BEACH COTTAGE

RINO'S BEACH BUNGALOWS

Aitutaki

JOSIE'S LODGE

Island

L a g o o n

Ureia

ADMINISTRATION CENTER

Arutanga

Reureu

HOSPITAL

VAIPAE CHURCH

Nikaupara

Vaipae

THE CASTLE

CAFÉ TUPUNA

GINA'S GARDEN LODGES

HUGE BANYAN TREE

MAINA SUNSET MOTEL

AITUTAKI LODGES

VAINAMU WASHING POOL

TAUTU CHURCH

TAUTU JETTY

Tautu

MARAE TE POAKI O RAE

MARAE ARANGIREA

0   0.5 mi

0   0.5 km

Te Koutu Point

© DAVID STANLEY

Around Arutanga beware of theft from the beach and back yards of the guesthouses by small children.

History

A Polynesian myth explains how Aitutaki is a giant fish tethered to the seabed by a vine. After a perilous journey from Tubuai in the canoe *Little Flowers,* the legendary hero Ru landed here with four wives, four younger brothers, and 20 virgins to colonize the island. Ru named the atoll Utataki-enua-o-Ru-ki-te-moana, meaning "a land sought and found in the sea by Ru," which the first Europeans corrupted to Aitutaki. Ru named various parts of the island for the head, stomach, and tail of the fish, but more places he named for himself. His brothers became angry when most of the land was divided among the 20 virgins, and they left for New Zealand where they won great honor. Ru himself suffered the consequences of his arrogance when higher chiefs eventually arrived and relegated him to the subordinate position held by his descendants today.

Captain William Bligh "discovered" Aitutaki in 1789, only 17 days before the notorious mutiny. In 1821, this became the first of the Cook Islands to receive Christian missionaries when the Tahitian pastors Papeiha and Vahapata were put ashore. The Americans built the island's huge airfield during WW II. Tasman Empire Airways (now Air New Zealand) used Akaiami Island as a refueling stop for its four-engined Solent flying boats during the 1950s. The Coral Route, from Auckland to Tahiti via Suva and Apia, became obsolete when Faa'a Airport opened near Papeete in 1961.

SIGHTS OF AITUTAKI

Arutanga and the South

Opposite the Administration Center at Arutanga is the colonial-style residence of the government representative set amid lovely gardens. The limestone **CICC church** just south was begun in 1828, only a few years after Papeiha converted the islanders. It's usually solidly locked but you can still peek in the windows of this oldest church in the Cook Islands and admire the monument to missionaries John Williams and Papeiha out front.

South of Arutanga beyond Nikaupara, the road turns inland at a dry stream where the old **Vainamu Washing Pool** has been rebuilt. Continue east along this road, turning right at the junction of the road to Te Koutu Point. About 700 meters south is **Marae Te Poaki O Rae,** down a short trail to the left. A signpost visible east of the road marks this double row of stones beneath a huge puka tree. A more overgrown road running west toward the beach from the Te Poaki O Rae junction leads to **Marae Arangirea.** Look for another line of stones about 150 meters down on the left, in high grass just before you enter the eerie chestnut forest along the coast.

The Interior

An easy afternoon or sunset hike from the guesthouses at Arutanga is up to the **water tanks** on a hill in the middle of the island. Go up the road marked Pirake/Vaipeka on the south side of the Paratrooper Motel.

The trail to the radio towers on the summit of **Maungapu** starts from opposite Paradise Cove on the main road up the west side of the island. It's a leisurely half-hour jaunt up an obvious track and from the top you get a sweeping view of Aitutaki's entire barrier reef.

The Lagoon

At low tide you can walk and wade along a sandbar from the Pacific Resort Aitutaki right out to the reef, but wear something on your feet to protect yourself from the coral, sea urchins, eels, stonefish, algae, etc. Stonefish are not common, but they're almost impossible to spot until it's too late. At high tide, snorkel out from the black rocks on the beach just north of the resort. Snorkelers and paddlers must keep at least 200 meters inside the main reef entrance at Arutanga, due to the strong outgoing current.

The finest snorkeling off the main island is at the far west end of the airstrip and to the south. Beware of dangerous currents in the passes near the edge of the reef here. Elsewhere on the main island the snorkeling is poor.

The top beach on the main island is at the southeast end of the airstrip near the bridge to the

Aitutaki Lagoon Resort. It's fine to swim here, but snorkelers won't see many fish or corals.

Sports and Recreation

Neil Mitchell's **Aitutaki Scuba** (tel. 31-103, fax 31-310, scuba@aitutaki.net.ck) offers diving at the drop-off once or twice a day (except Sunday). If you have your own equipment, diving is NZ$75 per dive (NZ$10 extra if you need gear). Snorkelers are welcome to go along at NZ$35 pp when space is available. No reservations are required, but bring your own mask; wetsuits are handy June–December. The diving here is better March–November. Aitutaki is good place to learn to dive and Neil does four-day PADI certification courses for NZ$550 (minimum of two persons). You'll find Neil about a hundred meters down the side road that branches off the main road at Sunny Beach Lodge. Aitutaki is not an easy dive destination. The lagoon may be great for snorkeling, but it's too shallow for serious diving and the drop-off outside the reef is very steep (not for beginners).

Aitutaki Sea Charters (tel. 31-281) offers deep-sea fishing off the 10-meter cruiser *Foxy Lady*. Captain Jason and his father Don Watts live near the Crusher Bar toward the airport. Skipjack tuna, giant trevally, mahimahi, and barracuda are caught year-round off Aitutaki. The billfish (marlin) season is November–March, while in August and September wahoo are frequently caught.

The **Aitutaki Golf Club** (no phone) beside the airport welcomes visitors. Greens fees and club rentals are NZ$10 each. If your ball falls on the airstrip, it's considered out of bounds. The Aitutaki Open Golf Tournament is in mid-October.

ACCOMMODATIONS

There are lots of places to stay on Aitutaki in every price category and the rooms are almost never fully booked. Air Rarotonga or any travel agent on Rarotonga can reserve the places mentioned below, or you can call ahead and book your own room over the phone. If a travel agency tells you everything is full, it only means the rooms set aside for them are full and other rooms

may be available for direct bookings. Discounts are possible if you stay a week or more. Most of the cheaper places offer rooms with shared bath only.

Under US$25

Josie's Lodge (Josie Sadaraka, tel. 31-341, fax 31-518), an older island home in Arutanga, has five rooms with shared bath (cold showers) at NZ$20/40/51 single/double/triple. The rooms are screened to keep out insects, and communal cooking facilities are provided.

Junior Maoate's **Paradise Cove Lodge** (tel. 31-218, fax 31-456, mtl@aitutaki.net.ck) is at Anaunga, between the airstrip and the Pacific Resort Aitutaki. Spacious grounds lead down to a white sand beach with excellent snorkeling just offshore. The four rooms in the main house are NZ$25/35 single/double, while the six thatched Polynesian beach huts with shared bath are NZ$35/50. Six newer beach bungalows with balconies and private bath (hot water!) are NZ$150 single or double. The cheaper accommodations here are gradually being replaced by upscale units, so check prices beforehand if you're on a budget. In the meantime, Junior provides good communal cooking facilities and special reduced rates are sometimes offered.

US$25–50

The Castle (Teetu and Tschan Tatira, tel. 31-012), a 10-minute walk south of the post office in Arutanga, has one- and two-bedroom self-catering apartments in a two-story concrete building starting at NZ$60.

Tom's Beach Cottage (Taraota Tom, tel. 31-051, fax 31-409) is a large island-style house on the beach a bit north of Josie's. The seven rooms with old-fashioned brass beds and mosquito nets are NZ$32/48/58 single/double/triple, but the two facing the street get considerable traffic noise. A "honeymoon" bungalow a bit closer to the beach is NZ$86/94 single/double. When things are slow these rates are reduced. A communal kitchen is available (beware of mice), plus a lounge with a pool table and a sitting room with photos of the family. Local calls on the house phone are 50 cents each. Tom rents scooters (NZ$15) and bicycles (NZ$5) to guests.

The **Paratrooper Motel** (tel. 31-563 or 31-523) in Amuri consists of four wooden buildings in a crowded compound a block back from the beach. It's run by an ex-New Zealand paratrooper named Geoffrey Roi and his wife Maine. Geoffrey's rates are NZ$75/250 single or double a night/week for their two one-bedroom apartments with full cooking facilities. The three two-bedroom family units are NZ$120/350. The minimum stay is three nights.

Vaikoa Units (tel. 31-145), a km north of the Pacific Resort Aitutaki, offers seven self-catering units in parallel wooden blocks at NZ$40/80 single/double (no hot water). The nearest grocery store is a 15-minute walk away. It's right on one of the best snorkeling beaches on the main island. The managers are friendly but guests tend to keep to themselves.

Matriki Beach Huts (tel. 31-564, www.matriki.com), on a great beach next door to the fancy Are Tamanu Beach Hotel north of town, has three simple beach cabins at NZ$50/60 single/double. Each has cooking facilities and a private outdoor shower, but the shared toilet is beside the main house. Owners Matias and Riki rent scooters to guests at NZ$100 a week.

Josie's Beach Lodge (tel. 31-659), at Ootu Beach to the right as you approach the bridge over to the Aitutaki Lagoon Resort, has six double rooms with shared bath and cooking facilities in an older building at NZ$25 pp. They'll prepare an excellent breakfast for you at NZ$10. It's a good value. Information is available from Greta at Four Square Store (tel. 31-188) near the Administrative Center in Arutanga.

US$50–100

On the beach almost opposite Josie's Lodge in Arutanga is **Rino's Beach Bungalows** (Rino and Ngatere George, tel. 31-197, fax 31-559, rinos@aitutaki.net.ck) with four hotplate-equipped units in a two-story roadside block at NZ$70/111/137 single/double/triple. Four new beachfront duplex apartments are NZ$169–221 single or double complete with fridge, stove, and terrace. Rino's also has an older three-bedroom house across the street that is rented out at NZ$450 a week (up to six persons). Three large

apartments in a building on the hillside near Vaikoa Units are NZ$130.

Sunny Beach Lodge (tel./fax 31-446, sunnybeach@aitutaki.net.ck), on the beach toward the north end of the tourist strip, has a row of five self-catering units in a single-story block at NZ$75/85/100/115 single/double/triple/quad. The rooms face the wrong way and the beach is out of sight. If it's closed when you arrive, the owners live behind the Seventh-Day Adventist church across the street.

Ranginui's Retreat (Steve Schofield, tel. 31-657, fax 31-658, www.ranginuis.com), on Ootu Beach near the Samade Bar, has four self-catering duplex rooms at NZ$120/145 double/triple (no hot water). Children under 12 stay for free. They rent mini-cars at NZ$80 a day, scooters at NZ$15/20 a half/full day, and an outboard dingy at NZ$80. Return airport transfers are NZ$16. The location right next to the Aitutaki Lagoon Resort is great and several other budget resorts are planned or under construction in this vicinity.

In late 2002, **Popoara Ocean Breeze Villas** (Allen and Maria Mills, tel./fax 31-739, www.popoara.com) opened between Ranginui's Retreat and the Aitutaki Lagoon Resort. The 10 self-catering units are NZ$159 double. There's a restaurant and bar.

Gina's Garden Lodges (tel./fax 31-058, www.ginasaitutaki.com), between Arutanga and Tautu (just before Kingdom Hall), has four self-catering bungalows with lofts in a quiet garden setting at NZ$75/120/150 single/double/triple. An extra child is NZ$20. Two radio antennas are available for amateur ham operators. The inland location near Tautu is inconvenient to both Arutanga and the beach. Gina's is run by Queen Manarangi Tutai, one of the ariki of the island. She owns a beach house on lovely Akaiami Island which rents for NZ$180/300/375.

In 1995, the **Maina Sunset Motel** (tel. 31-511, fax 31-611, www.soltel.co.ck) opened in Nikaupara district, a 20-minute walk south of Arutanga. The 12 units are arranged in a U-shape around a freshwater swimming pool that faces an ugly boat passage dug out of the shallow lagoon (no beach). The eight rooms without cooking are NZ$160 double, while the four with cooking are NZ$195. It's peaceful, since you don't get a lot of traffic noise down here. Scooter hire is NZ$25 a day and airport transfers are NZ$16 pp roundtrip.

US$100–150

Aitutaki Lodges (tel. 31-334, fax 31-333, www .ck/aitutakilodges), near Tautu Jetty on the opposite side of the main island from Arutanga, offers six self-catering bungalows on stilts facing the lagoon at NZ$230 single or double, with reductions for three or more nights. You'll need to hire a scooter if you want to stay here, because it's far from everything. Although the lagoon view from your porch will be lovely, the beach below the units is too muddy for swimming and the water too murky for snorkeling. We've received several bitter complaints about the service here.

One Foot Hideaway (McBirney Enterprises, tel. 31-418, fax 31-486), on One Foot Island in the southeast corner of the lagoon, gives you the opportunity to spend a night on an otherwise uninhabited motu. It's NZ$180 double to sleep in this two-story bungalow a bit east of the One Foot Post Office (take insect repellent). The lighting is by kerosene lamp. Book through Kit Cat Lagoon Cruises at Mango Trading next to Mae Jo's Café in Amuri or Jetsave Travel. Transfers to the island are NZ$50 pp roundtrip.

US$250 and up

The **Are Tamanu Beach Hotel** (tel. 31-810, fax 31-816, www.aretamanu.com), on a white sandy beach between Arutanga and the airport, offers 12 thatched bungalows with full cooking facilities and fridge at NZ$425/510 double/triple (no children under 12). Only one unit actually faces the lagoon, the others face each other. There's no restaurant, but a complimentary tropical breakfast is served at the bar next to the swimming pool and sandwiches can be purchased all day. There's a barbecue Sunday at 1930 (NZ$25) and it's okay to bring your own booze to the bar or beach. This compact resort is run by local politician Mike Henry and all of the employees are his relatives. The Are Tamanu is off limits to outsiders, so don't bother trying to drop in for a

drink. Bicycles and canoes are loaned free to guests. It's often fully booked.

In October 2002, the **Pacific Resort Aitutaki** (tel. 31-720, fax 31-719, www.pacificresort.com) opened on the site of the former Rapae Motel just north of Arutanga. A branch of the Pacific Resort on Rarotonga, this property includes 19 bungalows at NZ$710/785 double/triple, six suites at NZ$930/1,005, and three villas at NZ$1,150/1,225, including breakfast, tax, and transfers. A pool and restaurant are provided. Ongoing construction is intended to increase the number of rooms to 75. The snorkeling here is good.

The **Aitutaki Lagoon Resort** (tel. 31-203, fax 31-202, www.aitutakilagoonresort.com), on Akitua Island near Ootu Beach at the east end of the airstrip, is connected to the main island by a small wooden bridge. Formerly known as the Aitutaki Pearl Beach Resort, in 2003 the property was acquired by Tata Crocombe, owner of the Rarotonga Beach Resort. The 16 air-conditioned garden bungalows with private bath and fridge are NZ$475 single or double, the nine lagoon bungalows NZ$620, the five beachfront bungalows NZ$765, and the seven so-called overwater bungalows NZ$1,095, tax included. Three garden rooms close to the main complex are NZ$320. Only the front deck of the "overwater" bungalows is partially overwater—the rear entrance is firmly anchored to the shore. Cooking facilities are not provided and full board is NZ$115 pp extra. The resort's Wednesday night seafood buffet and the Saturday barbecue both cost NZ$80 and come with traditional dancing. There's a swimming pool and the beach is lovely, but the water offshore is murky and there's nothing much to see through your mask. A NZ$5 surcharge is added to any tours or cruises booked through this resort.

FOOD AND ENTERTAINMENT

Food

The **Blue Nun Cafe** (tel. 31-604; Mon.–Thurs. 0800–2200, Wed., Fri., and Sat. 0800–midnight), in the Orongo Center, serves substantial portions of inexpensive food to be consumed at tables overlooking the lagoon. The name refers to the small *kuramoo* bird depicted on their sign, not religious nuns. The menu on the wall lists fish and chips (NZ$7), mussels and chips (NZ$9.50), curried chicken rice (NZ$8.50), and hamburgers (NZ$4–5). Wednesday and Saturday nights there's island dancing at 2030 (NZ$25 for the buffet dinner or you can watch for the price of a beer).

Mae Jo's Café (tel. 31-820), across the street from the Pacific Resort Aitutaki, formerly known as Fletcher's Bar & Grill, serves Chinese food.

Tauono's Garden Café (tel. 31-562), between Paradise Cove and Vaikoa Units, is easily the best place on the island for a home-cooked lunch (NZ$13.50) served in their garden. It's available daily from 1200–1400, but on Sundays you must book ahead.

The **Crusher Bar & Restaurant** (tel. 31-283), near Paradise Cove on the way to the airport, is a funky open-air bar with picnic tables under a tin roof. The Monday dinner and cultural show by Tamanu is only NZ$20 (or NZ$5 admission without dinner). Thursday night is **island night** with a Polynesian buffet (NZ$25.50 pp) followed by an excellent show by the dance group Tiare Aitutaki. The Friday special grilled fish or steak dinner with live entertainment is NZ$15.50. Saturday night is "backpackers nite," with main course and dessert at NZ$12.50, plus reduced drink prices and disco music after 2000. Sunday nights it's a roast or fish of the day. The à la carte menu (NZ$12.50–26.50) is available nightly from 1800. Animation is provided by the infamous lady-killer Riki de Von (also an excellent cook). Call ahead for reservations and NZ$5 hotel pickups.

The **Samade Bar** (tel. 31-526; closed Sat.), run by Sam and Adrienne at Ootu Beach, is a great escape for those staying at the nearby Aitutaki Lagoon Resort. For others it makes an excellent base for a day at the beach. You can order drinks on their white sand terrace all day, and weekdays they serve lunch (1100–1500) and dinner (from 1900). Choices include fish burgers (NZ$6.50) and steak burgers (NZ$8.50). There's an **island night** with traditional dancing Tuesday at 1930 (NZ$25 including dinner). The Friday night beach party and barbecue (NZ$25) and the generous Sunday *umukai* (earth oven) with

string band music at 1330 (NZ$18) are also recommended. It's best to reserve the evening meals, and Poo Bishop (tel. 31-109) does transfers at NZ$5 pp roundtrip.

Café Tupuna (tel. 31-678; daily 1730–2130), near Gina's Garden Lodges between Arutanga and Tautu, is good for a nicely presented, semi-upscale dinner (mains NZ$22–25). Tupuna Slattery is an ingenious cook, specializing in curries, steaks, and fish. Try the sashimi (NZ$12). A selection of wines is offered and the floor is pleasingly sandy. Book ahead, as seating is limited (transfers available at NZ$5 roundtrip).

Maina Traders Ltd. (tel. 31-055; Mon.–Sat. 0700–2000), near the wharf, offers a good selection of groceries, fresh vegetables, and drinks.

Rirei Store (Mon.–Sat. 0700–2000), the place with the Heineken sign a few hundred meters north of Rino's Beach Bungalows, scoops out ice-cream cones as well as selling fresh vegetables.

Ask the people where you're staying if the water is safe to drink. Rainwater is okay but the well water is sometimes slightly brackish and boiling won't help much in that case.

Entertainment

Polynesian dance shows take place almost nightly: Monday at the Crusher Bar (tel. 31-283), Tuesday at the Samade Bar (tel. 31-526), Wednesday at the Blue Nun (tel. 31-604) and the Aitutaki Lagoon Resort (tel. 31-200), Thursday at the Crusher Bar (tel. 31-283), and Saturday at the Blue Nun (tel. 31-604) and Aitutaki Lagoon Resort (tel. 31-203). Call ahead to confirm this schedule. Most of these venues provide roundtrip transfers at NZ$5 pp.

The **Aitutaki Game Fishing Club** (no phone, VHF channel 16; open Wed.–Sat. from 1600), in a container behind the Ports Authority on the way to the harbor, has cheap beer and is a good place to meet people at happy hour.

PRACTICALITIES
Shopping

Several handicraft stalls with bright pareus and beachware are in the **Orongo Center** (closed

Sunday), in the former banana packing house near Arutanga wharf.

Services

Traveler's checks can be cashed at the Westpac Bank agency (tel. 31-714; Mon. and Thurs. from 0930–1500), in the Administration Center opposite Arutanga wharf, where you'll also find an ATM, and the ANZ Bank agency (tel. 31-486; weekdays 0900–1500), next to Mae Jo's Café. It's smarter to change your money on Rarotonga beforehand, as the rates here are poor.

The post office (tel. 31-680; weekdays 0800–1600), in the Administration Center, sells local telephone cards (NZ$10, NZ$20, and NZ$50), which can be used for international calls at the public telephone outside (dial 00 for international access). If you need to receive a fax, the number is fax 682/31-683. The Aitutaki postage stamps sold here can only be used to post letter on Aitutaki itself (not accepted on Rarotonga).

M&S Video (tel. 31-712, marste@aitutaki .net.ck), just north of Tom's Beach Cottage, offers internet access.

Public toilets are behind the Blue Nun Cafe at the Orongo Center.

Outpatients are accepted at the hospital (tel. 31-002) Monday–Friday 0830–1200/1300–1600, Saturday 0830–1200, emergencies anytime.

TRANSPORTATION

Because Aitutaki's small population doesn't justify a regular ferry service from Rarotonga, getting here is more expensive than visiting similar outer islands in French Polynesia, Tonga, and Fiji, almost always involving a stiff plane ticket. A NZ$20 departure tax on flights from Rarotonga to Aitutaki was imposed in September, 2003. For flight and boat information see this chapter's Exploring the Islands section. **Air Rarotonga** (tel. 31-888, fax 31-414; weekdays 0800–1600, Sat. 0800–1200) has an office at Ureia.

The shipping companies have no local agent, but the people at the Ports Authority (tel. 31-050) near the wharf will know when a ship is due in. Dangerous coral heads and currents make passage through Aitutaki's barrier reef hazardous, so passengers and cargo on the interisland ships must be transferred to the wharf by lighters. The Americans built Arutanga Wharf during WW II. They had planned to dredge the anchorage and widen the pass, but the war ended before they got around to it. Blasting by the New Zealand military in 1986 improved Arutanga Passage somewhat, but it's still narrow, with a six-knot current draining water blown into the lagoon from the south. The depth in the pass is limited to two meters at high tide, but reader C. Webb reports that "the bottom of the pass is sand, so it's a good place to be somewhat aggressive." Once inside, the anchorage off Arutanga is safe and commodious for yachts. This is an official port of entry to the Cooks and the local customs officials readily approve visa extensions for yacht crews. "Having fun" is sufficient reason.

No taxis or buses operate on Aitutaki but there's considerable scooter and pickup traffic along the west coast. Paradise Tours does airport transfers at NZ$8 pp.

Aitutaki Walkabout Tours (tel./fax 31-757, www.aitutaki-walkabout.com.au) at Tautu offers a Maungapu trek (NZ$25), Aitutaki walkabout tour (NZ$30), and marae and feast tour (NZ$40 including lunch) daily except Sunday.

Rentals

Temporary Cook Islands driver's licenses can be obtained at the Police Department Center (tel. 31-015) in the Orongo Center for 2.50. No photo is required and they're also valid on Rarotonga.

The T & M Ltd. gasoline station (tel. 31-900), next to the Ports Authority at the wharf, opens weekdays 0700–2000, Saturday 0700–1230/1600–2030.

Rino's Rentals (tel. 31-197, fax 31-559), near Tom's Beach Cottage, has Suzuki jeeps (NZ$70 for 24 hours), cars (from NZ$85 daily), motor scooters (from NZ$25 the first day, NZ$20 subsequent days), and pushbikes (from NZ$5 daily). Rino's has a NZ$120 weekly rate for Honda 100s.

Some of the guesthouses and hotels also rent bicycles—all you really need.

The **Samade Bar** (tel. 31-526) at Ootu Beach rents kayaks at NZ$10/15/20 hour/half/day.

Call ahead if you want one. From Ootu you can paddle a kayak to Angarei in 15 minutes, Papua in an hour, and Akaiami in 2.5 hours. Hobie cat sailing with a captain is NZ$35 for the first hour, NZ$20 additional hours (four-hour maximum). Two can go for this price.

Lagoon Tours

Several companies offer boat trips to uninhabited *motu* around the Aitutaki Lagoon, such as Akaiami or **Tapuaetai** (One Foot Island). The swimming in the clear deep-green water at these islands is great, but the snorkeling is mediocre. Thus the boats take passengers to much better snorkeling spots on the reef. Unfortunately, the very popularity of these trips has become their undoing, as "desert islands" like Tapuaetai can get rather overcrowded when all of the tourist boats arrive!

Some trips also go to Maina, or "Bird Island," at the southwest corner of the lagoon. Only a few tropicbirds still nest on a sandbar called "Honeymoon Island" next to Maina; most have been scared off by marauding tourists and their guides. There's good snorkeling at Honeymoon Island, since the fish are fed here. But when the wind whips up the sea it gets hard to snorkel and you miss out on half the fun.

Different tour operators concentrate on varying aspects and the smaller independent operators tend to serve you a bigger and better lunch for a lower price. If snorkeling is your main interest, you should find out if their plan to spend all afternoon eating and drinking at Tapuaetai (also great fun). Bishop's Cruises is the most reliable company and they try to run on a schedule. This may be what you want if you have only one chance to get it right, but they're inevitably touristy and the amateur operators you learn about by word of mouth or from notices taped on the walls of the backpackers hostels are more personal (and less dependable and safe). It's also possible to arrange to be dropped off for the day on Akaiami or Maina.

Bishop's Lagoon Cruises (Teina Bishop, tel. 31-009, fax 31-493, bishopcruz@aitutaki.net.ck), inland from Arutanga Wharf, and **Kit Cat Lagoon Cruises** (tel. 31-418, mango@aitutaki

.net.ck), at Mango Trading next to Mae Jo's Café, offer lagoon trips daily except Sunday. One trip goes to Maina, another to Akaiami, and both continue to Moturakau and Tapuaetai. The Maina trip is the better and to get it you must specifically request a visit to Maina when booking, otherwise they'll only take you to Akaiami and Tapuaetai. Either way, the price is NZ$55 including lunch. **Paradise Islands Cruises** (Tai Herman, tel. 31-248, fax 31-398, lagoon@aitutaki.net.ck) operates the Aitutaki day tour cruises (NZ$65 cruise only) for Air Rarotonga using a large catamaran. You'll probably be whisked back to the main island earlier than you would have liked so that the day-trippers from Rarotonga can catch their flight.

Teariki George of **Teking Water Taxi Service** (tel. 31-582) at Tautu shuttles snorkelers over to Maina Island at NZ$35 pp including gear but no lunch.

If you're on a low budget, you can get comparable snorkeling off the west end of the airstrip for free. Whatever you decide, bring sunscreen and insect repellent.

Reef Tours

Sonja and Tauono Raela (tel. 31-562), who live between Paradise Cove and Vaikoa Units, offer unique reef tours in a traditional outrigger sailing canoe. The NZ$35 pp fee (NZ$45 if you go out alone) includes a light lunch, and they'll prepare any of the fish you catch for an additional fee of NZ$10–15, depending on what you want. You may also take your fish back to your guesthouse and cook it yourself. If you'd like to do any reef walking or fishing with a bamboo rod, you must go at low tide; the swimming and snorkeling are better at high tide. Tauono is a sensitive guide, more than willing to explain Aitutaki's delicate reef ecology during the four hours the trips usually last. Call the night before to arrange a time. Tauono and Sonja keep the only organic garden on Aitutaki and it's always worth stopping by to buy some vegetables, herbs, cakes, or fresh fish. Sonja will happily spend time with you providing cooking suggestions and general information on their produce and the cuisine of the islands.

Atiu

The original name of Atiu, third largest of the Cook Islands, was Enuamanu, meaning "land of birds." These days, native birds are found mostly around the coast, as the interior has been taken over by an influx of mynahs. In 2001, the 10 endangered Rarotonga flycatchers (*kakerori*) were introduced on Atiu in an effort to save the birds from extinction. Unlike neighboring Mauke and Mitiaro, which are flat, Atiu has a high central plateau (71 meters) surrounded by low swamps and an old raised coral reef known as a *makatea*. This is 20 meters high and covered with dense tropical jungle.

The red soil on Atiu's central plateau is formed from volcanic basalt rock and it's rather poor. The slopes up to the central plateau have been reforested to check erosion. Taro is the main crop and taro patches occupy the swamps along the inner edge of the *makatea*. Arabica coffee is grown, processed, roasted, packaged, and marketed as "Kaope Atiu."

Atiu is one of the only islands in Polynesia where the people prefer the center to the shore, and cooling ocean breezes blow across Atiu's plain. Once fierce warriors who made cannibal raids on Mauke and Mitiaro, the islanders became Christians after missionary John Williams converted high chief Rongomatane in 1823. Today the 650 Atiuans live peacefully in five villages on the high central plain. The villages radiate out from an administrative center where the main churches, hospital, PWD workshops, stores, and government offices are all found. Only 11 people on Atiu have full-time jobs, and from 1996–2001, a third of the island's people left for New Zealand. Pigs outnumber people four to one.

Atiu contrasts nicely with busier islands like Rarotonga and Aitutaki. The good beaches, varied scenery, and geological curiosities combine with satisfactory accommodations and enjoyable activities to make a visit well worthwhile. Atiu beckons the active traveler keen to experience a real slice of outer island life. It will appeal to hikers who want to explore the island's lonely roads, to adventurers who enjoy looking for caves and archaeological remains hidden in the bush, or to anyone in search of a restful holiday and a chance to spend some time on an unspoiled island without sacrificing creature comforts. Atiu has little to offer those interested in scuba diving, fancy resorts, or lagoon trips.

SIGHTS OF ATIU

The massive white walls of the **CICC church** dominate Teenui village in the exact center of the island. Just south, a road leads east toward Tengatangi village from almost opposite the Atiu Administration Building. On the right just beyond the house behind the tennis court is a stalagmite with twin inscribed stones in front. This marks the spot where John Williams preached in 1823. Next to the monument is a row of huge stalagmites or stalactites indicating the rectangular site of **Teapiripiri Marae.** Further south on the main road south into Areora village is the picturesque **Catholic mission.**

Andrea Eimke's **Atiu Fiber Arts Studio** (tel. 33-031; weekdays 0900–1500, Sat. 0900–1300), at the north end of Teenui village, makes wall hangings and bed spreads in the *tivaevae* quilt style, plus women's jackets, dresses, and vests.

The East Coast

The 20-km road around Atiu is best covered in stages. From Atiu Villas it's a 15-minute walk down to **Matai Landing** and its white-sand beach. You can swim here only if the sea is fairly calm, but it's a nice picnic spot anytime. About 800 meters east of Matai Landing you'll come into a partly cleared area where pigs have been kept. Here search for a small trail out to the coast, where two **sinkholes** drain the reef. The lagoon along the south coast is a meter above sea level, and when no waves are crashing over the reef sending water into the lagoon, the whole lagoon drains through these sinkholes. With nowhere else to go, all of the lagoon fish congregate in the

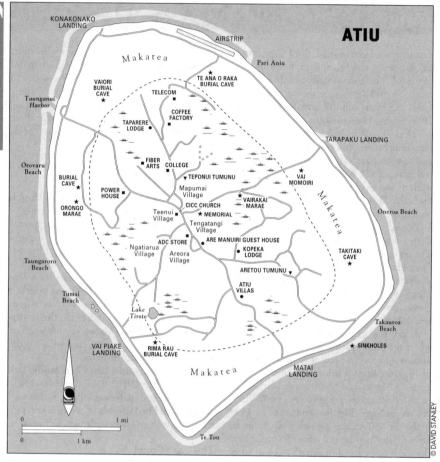

ATIU

© DAVID STANLEY

sinkholes, which become natural aquariums accessible to snorkelers. Due to the currents, it's safe to swim here only when the sea is very calm, and even then it's wise to remain on guard for changing or unexpected conditions. About 200 meters further east along the coast is a road down from the interior and a cut through the cliffs to **Takauroa Beach.** In calm weather at low tide you can also walk to the sinkholes along the reef from this beach.

A stretch of reefless shoreline on the northeast coast lets breakers roll right in to the cliffs. Look for the high white sands of **Oneroa Beach** and

continue to **Tarapaku Landing** where the islanders keep their dugout canoes. There's a ladder down to the water here. From the landing, take the Tengatangi road inland through the *makatea,* watching for **Vai Momoiri,** a large water-filled cave that tunnels under the track then opens up on both sides. The route crosses a taro swamp passing **Vairakaia Marae,** a wall of upright stones right beside the road, and **Vai Inano,** a pool where the legendary chief Rongomatane's 12 wives used to bathe. (Rongomatane later adopted Christianity and forsook all of his wives except the youngest.)

The West Coast

The coastal road up the west shore of the island runs through a beautiful shady forest. A few really huge *puka* trees sport low bird's-nest ferns to create a dense green cover. These leaves are used to wrap fish for cooking in the *umu*. **Taungaroro** is the nicest beach on Atiu, and one of the finest in the Cooks, with white sands descending far into the quiet blue-green lagoon, protected from ocean breakers by the surrounding reef. The cliffs of the *makatea* frame this scenic masterpiece.

Orovaru Beach, where Captain Cook arrived on April 3, 1777, is easily identified by a large coral rock that sits 15 meters out in the lagoon. On the island side of the road opposite Orovaru is a stone trail once used by Cook's crew to reach the main settlement of that time around **Orongo Marae,** the most important *marae* on Atiu. Once you're on the trail, it's fairly easy to follow, bending right toward the end and terminating at a pig farm on an interior road. This interesting hike offers a chance to view the vegetation on the *makatea* up close. Beyond the pigs, turn right and go about 100 meters south on the road to a track on the right toward a huge Barringtonia or *utu* tree. Orongo Marae is just behind the tree—one of the best-preserved archaeological sites in the Cook Islands. Cut coral slabs and giant stalagmites form the walls of several rectangular structures here.

Farther north is **Taunganui Harbor** with a striking zigzag configuration, constructed in 1975. Barges can dock here in all weather, but large ships must stand offshore. The swimming and snorkeling in the deep, clear harbor water is good, and if you're here at 1500 you may be able to purchase fresh fish from returning fishermen. Below the cliffs just south of the harbor is the wreckage of the SV *Edna,* a two-masted Dutch sailing vessel built in 1916. One stormy night in 1990, this magnificent metal vessel was wrecked here while carrying cargo to the island from Rarotonga. Fortunately, no lives were lost.

Lake Tiroto and Rima Rau Cave

According to legend, the eel Rauou dug Lake Tiroto and, when he was finished, traveled to Mitiaro to dig the lakes there. Eels still inhabit all these lakes! A tunnel runs under the *makatea* from Lake Tiroto right through to the seashore.

The Rima Rau burial cave near Lake Tiroto is said to contain the bones of those who died in a battle involving 1,000 Atiu warriors. Ask someone to tell you the legend of this cave's dead. Kiikii Tatuava (tel. 33-063) of Areora village can guide you to the cave, with side trips to the lake, taro fields, Katara Marae, and Vaitapoto Sinkhole.

Takitaki Cave

This cave is one of the few in the Cooks inhabited by birds: little *kopekas,* a type of swiftlet, nest in the roof. Their huge, saucerlike eyes help them catch insects on the wing. They never land nor make a sound while outside the cave; inside, they make a cackling, clicking sound, the echoes of which help them find their way through the dank dark. Fewer than 200 pairs of this bird remain and their nesting success is poor. Visitors to the cave should keep at least two meters away from bird nests and discourage their guide from catching the tiny creatures.

Takitaki is in the middle of the *makatea,* east of Atiu Villas, a taxing 40-minute hike in from the road. A guide (NZ$15) is required. The main part of the cave is large and dry, and you can walk in for quite a distance. Many stalactites, broken off by previous visitors, lie scattered about the floor. The story goes that Ake, wife of the hero Rangi, lived many years alone in this cave before being found by her husband, who was led to the spot by a *ngotare* (kingfisher) bird.

Keep an eye out for *unga* (coconut crabs) while exploring the *makatea,* and wear boots or sturdy shoes, as the coral is razor-sharp. Go slowly and take care, because a fall could lead to a very nasty wound.

PRACTICALITIES

Accommodations

Atiu Villas (Roger and Kura Malcolm, tel. 33-777, fax 33-775, www.atiuvillas.co.ck), eight km south of the airstrip, offers four comfortable self-catering chalets, each capable of accommodating four persons, at NZ$110/120/130 single/double/

triple. There's also a six-bed family unit at NZ$130 single, plus NZ$10 per additional guest. These unscreened A-frame units are constructed of native materials with beams of coconut-palm trunks and cupboard fronts of hibiscus. In your room's pantry and fridge you'll find almost everything you might wish to consume—except vegetables and bread. You mark what you've used on a stock list and settle up when you leave (normal prices). Otherwise, Kura will prepare a huge dinner for NZ$25 pp, sometimes including her famous pavlova (order by 1500). An entertainment evening is staged some Saturday nights in the bar overlooking the grass tennis court. Roger will give you a great introduction to Atiu during your drive up from the airport (NZ$8 pp each way).

A less expensive place to stay is the **Are Manuiri Guest House** (tel. 33-031, fax 33-032, www.adc.co.ck) opposite the bakery in Areora village, 200 meters south of ADC/ANZ Store and on the left. This three-room family house with communal cooking and bathing facilities is NZ$30 pp in a shared room, NZ$60 single or double in a private room, or NZ$75 for a larger family room. There's a lounge and verandah. It's run by Juergen Manske-Eimke, who arrived on Atiu in 1986 and runs the local coffee factory (rather good tours NZ$10 pp). Juergen often provides free coffee for his guests. Airport transfers are NZ$14 pp.

Kopeka Lodge (Tou Unuia, tel. 33-283, stay@kopekalodge-atiu.co.ck), west of Areora village, has two spacious two-bedroom wooden units with large porches at NZ$85/95 single/double, then NZ$20 for each additional person. Backpackers pay NZ$30 pp if they're willing to share. You can cook here.

In 2003, **Kia Orana Bungalows** (Moetaua Boaza, tel./fax 33-013) opened in Areora between Kopeka Lodge and Are Manuiri with six self-catering bungalows priced a bit above Kopeka Lodge.

Taparere Lodge (tel./fax 33-034), in a new concrete building on the north side of Teenui village, has two self-catering units at NZ$60/75/80 single/double/triple. It's run by local historian Paiere Mokoroa, who has many stories to tell about Atiu.

Food

There are three main shops on Atiu, and two bakers make bread weekdays and Sunday. **ADC/ANZ Store** (tel. 33-028; weekdays 0700–1900, Sat. 0700–0900/1700–1900), in Areora village, may have a few fresh vegetables and fruit (cabbage, lettuce, tomatoes, potatoes, papaya).

Kura Malcolm runs the **Center Store** (tel. 33-773; Mon.–Thur. 0700–1830, Fri. 0700–1930, Sat. 0700–1200/1700–1930), just beyond the CICC church, which dispenses liquor and cold drinks, as well as basic foodstuffs.

Purutu's Bakery is between ADC/ANZ shop and the tennis court in Areora village. **Akai Bakery** is a bit beyond Atiu College. Both sell bread around 1500 daily except Saturday.

Marshall Humphreys (tel./fax 33-041) sells fresh fruit and vegetables.

Entertainment

Tennis and volleyball are popular on Atiu, and village rivalry has produced no fewer than nine tennis courts (for under 650 people). Each village constructed its tennis court a little bigger than the last: The first village had a single netball court; the fourth built two tennis courts, two netball courts, and erected floodlights. The fifth village said it was "all too hard" and gave up.

Atiu won the Constitution Day dancing competitions on Rarotonga in 1982, 1983, 1984, 1985, 1988, 1992, 1993, and 1998, so ask where you can see them practicing. Special performances are held on Gospel Day and Christmas Day.

Bush Beer

Venerable institutions of note are the bush beer schools, of which there are seven on Atiu. Bush beer is a local moonshine made from imported yeast, malt, hops, and sugar. The concoction is fermented in a *tumunu,* a hollowed-out coconut tree stump about a meter high. Orange-flavored "jungle juice" is also made. The mixing usually begins on Wednesday, and the resulting brew ferments for two days and is ready to drink on the weekend. A single batch will last three or four nights; the longer it's kept, the stronger it gets.

Gatherings at a school resemble the kava ceremonies of Fiji, and the practice clearly dates back to the days before early missionaries banned kava drinking. Only the barman is permitted to ladle bush beer out of the *tumunu* in a half-coconut-shell cup, and the potent contents of the cup must be swallowed in one hearty gulp. Those who've developed a taste for the stuff usually refer to regular beer as "lemonade." The village men come together at dusk, and after a few rounds, the barman calls them to order by tapping a cup on the side of the *tumunu*. A prayer is said. Announcements are made by various members, and work details assigned to earn money to buy the ingredients for the next brew. After the announcements, guitars and ukuleles appear, and the group resumes drinking, dancing, and singing for as long as they can. The barman, responsible for maintaining order, controls how much brew each participant gets.

Nonmembers visiting a school are expected to bring along a kilo of sugar, or to put NZ$5 pp on the table, as their contribution (enough for the whole week). The two most reputable bush beer establishments are the **Aretou Tumunu** ("Sam and the boys"), down in the bush east of Areora, and the more commercial **Teponui Tumunu** in Mapumai.

Post and Telecommunications

You can make telephone calls using phone cards and buy postage stamps at Telecom Cook Islands (tel. 33-680; weekdays 0730–1600), north of Mapumai village. The Internet finally reached Atiu in September 2003, with access at NZ$10 an hour.

Transportation

The Air Rarotonga office (tel. 33-888) is a block back from the CICC church in the center of the island. There are six flights a week from Rarotonga (NZ$142), plus weekly services from Aitutaki (NZ$142) and Mitiaro (NZ$90). Most of the guesthouse owners provide airport transfers at NZ$8 pp each way.

Atiu Villas and some of the other places to stay rent bicycles/scooters/jeeps at NZ$10/25/60 a day.

The Humphreys family of **Atiu Tours** (tel./fax 33-041, atiutours.ck@ihug.co.nz) leads kopeka bird cave tours at NZ$15 pp and half-day island tours at NZ$35 pp. Young James Humphreys also offers a Rima Rau cave tour. "Birdman George" Mateariki (tel. 33-047) does a bird watch and bush walk for NZ$25 pp. These tours are worthwhile, because nothing is signposted on Atiu and finding your own way is hard.

Mauke

Mauke, the easternmost of the Cooks, is a flat, raised atoll. It and neighboring Mitiaro and Atiu are collectively known as Ngaputoru, "The Three Roots." As on its neighbors, the crops grow in the center of Mauke; the *makatea* ringing the island is infertile and rocky. Both the *makatea* and the central area are low, and you barely notice the transition as you walk along the road inland from the coast to the taro swamps and manioc plantations. Mauke exports bags of *maire* leaves to Hawaii, to be used in floral decorations, and taro is sent to Rarotonga. Pigs and chickens run wild across the island, and many goats can be seen. Thankfully, dogs are banned from Mauke.

The men fish for tuna just offshore in small outrigger canoes and the women weave fine pandanus mats with brilliant borders of blue, red, yellow, and orange. There are also wide-rimmed pandanus hats and *kete* baskets of sturdy pandanus with colorful geometric designs. The men carve the attractive white-and-black *tou* or red-and-brown *miro* wood into large bowls shaped like breadfruit leaves. They also carve large spoons and forks, miniature models of chiefs' seats, and small replicas of the canoe of Uke, legendary founder of Mauke, who gave the island its name.

Mauke has the best beaches of the three neighboring islands, but it's too shallow for snorkeling. Coral overhangs provide shade at many of the beaches, and in August and September whales are often seen off Mauke. It's a very friendly island to poke around for a few days and a good choice for a prolonged stay.

Sights of Mauke

The harbor, market, Catholic mission, government residency, and administration building are all at **Taunganui Landing.** The area behind the administration building is known as **Te Marae O Rongo,** with a stone circle and a large boulder once used as a seat by the chief. Inland at Makatea village, opposite a store with massive masonry walls, is the two-story concrete palace of the last queen of Mauke, who died in 1982. Unfortunately, the building is falling into ruins due to squabbles among her descendants. At one end of the taro swamp in the valley behind the palace is **Koenga Well,** a source of fresh drinking water in years gone by.

The **CICC church** (1882) at the hub of the island has an almost Islamic flavor, with its long rectangular courtyard, tall gateways, perpendicular alignment, and interior decoration of crescents and interlocking arches. Due to an old dispute between Areora and Ngatiarua villages, the church was divided across the center and each side was decorated differently. The dividing partition has been removed, but dual gateways lead to dual doors, one for each village. The soft pastels (green, pink, yellow, and blue) harmonize the contrasting designs, and the pulpit in the middle unifies the two. Inset into the railing in front of the pulpit are nine old Chilean pesos. Look carefully at the different aspects of this building; it's one of the most fascinating in the Cook Islands.

Vai Tango Cave is fairly easy to find. From the Telecom office, go 500 meters northeast through Ngatiarua village and turn left after the last house. The cave is 500 meters northwest of the main road, at the end of a trail along a row of hibiscus trees. A large circular depression with Barringtonia trees growing inside, Vai Tango has a clear, freshwater pool under the

overhanging stalactites. The locals swim and bathe here. There are large rooms further back in the cave but you'd need scuba gear and lamps to reach them.

A *marae* called **Paepae A,** 50 meters beyond the Vai Tango turnoff, was reconstructed from scratch in 1997. The stalagmites standing on the *marae* platform are two pieces of a single pillar once carried by the legendary chief Kai Moko (Eater of Lizards). On the ground behind Paepae A are four huge stones remaining from Marae Terongo. The origin of these volcanic rocks, unique on this coral island, is lost in time.

Back in Areora village, visit the woodcarvers who work in the house next to the Catholic church. One of their fine breadfruit leaf-shaped bowls would make a unique souvenir.

If you're still keen, you might wish to try to

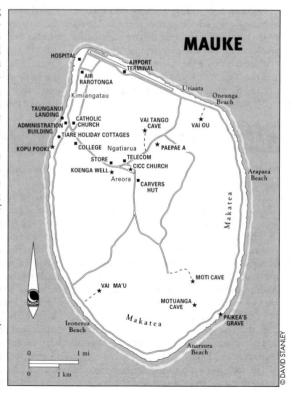

find **Moti Cave,** a large, open cave in the *makatea.* From the irrigation dam in the center of the island, follow the road south and take the left turn at a point where three roads separate. The cave is beyond the end of this road, and you'll probably spend some time searching unless you have a guide. A guide is definitely required to find the freshwater pools of **Motuanga Cave,** the "Cave of 100 Rooms," which is deeper into the *makatea* from here. Limestone growth has made all but the first three rooms inaccessible.

Around the Island

It's only 18 km around Mauke, and no one lives on the south or east sides of the island, so the secluded beaches there are ideal for those who want to be completely alone. There's good reef walking at low tide on the west side of Mauke, but ocean swimming is difficult everywhere. A coral trail just south of Tiare Cottages gives access to a small beach, and south around the point from this beach is a sea cave known as **Kopu Pooki** (Stomach Rock). It's about two meters deep and small fish congregate there.

About 450 meters southeast of Tukune junction, just past the second rock quarry, a trail leads 150 meters inland between the Barringtonia or *utu* trees to **Vai Ma'u,** a deep water-filled crack in the *makatea* with a tall coconut tree growing out. The water is very clear but the opening narrow and steep.

The finest beaches on Mauke are on the south side of the island and the white sands of **Ieoneroa** are just 500 meters southeast of Vai Ma'u. Also most inviting is the beach at **Anaraura,** where a long stretch of clean, white sand borders a green lagoon. This piece of paradise is flanked by rugged limestone cliffs and backed by palm, pine, and pandanus. A short track leads down to the beach.

Two upright stone slabs to the right of the road about a km beyond Anaraura mark the site of **Paikea's grave.** A secluded white beach is just behind. Yet another good beach is found at **Arapaea,** three km north of Paikea's Grave.

At Oneunga, just under two km northwest of Arapaea, two huge stones thrown up between the shore and the road have trees growing out of them. Directly opposite these two rocks is a trail leading across the *makatea* to **Vai Ou,** a series of three caves. You can swim in the first cave's pool, about 800 meters in from the coastal road. A five-minute scramble beyond Vai Ou is **Vai Moraro,** and beyond that **Vai Tunamea.** The coastal road meets the road to the interior villages and the airstrip less than a km west of Oneunga.

Accommodations and Food

Tiare Holiday Cottages (Tautara and Kura Purea, tel. 35-083), a few hundred meters south of Taunganui Landing, offers a duplex unit with two single rooms, two larger cottages with double beds, and one deluxe cottage with double beds. All units have their own fridge, but only the deluxe unit has a private bathroom and shower. There's no hot water. The accommodations with shared facilities are NZ$30/45/60 single/double/triple while the deluxe unit is NZ$100 single or double. A NZ$5 discount is offered if you stay more than three nights. A separate communal kitchen and dining area sits in the center of the compound. If you don't wish to cook (NZ$10 charge for gas), filling meals are served at reasonable prices, and tea, coffee, and tropical fruit are supplied free.

Bread is made on the island, and fresh tuna can be purchased directly from the fishermen at the landing. The brown insides of sea urchins, collected along the reef, are eaten raw (the egg cases are the most delicious part—the texture of raw liver and a strong taste of the sea).

M

Mangaia

Mangaia is pronounced Mahng-AH-ee-ah, not "man-gaia," as there's no "g" sound in the Polynesian languages. It's 204 km southeast of Rarotonga and just north of the tropic of Capricorn, a position that makes it the southernmost and coolest of the Cook Islands. South of here you don't strike land again until Antarctica. At 52 square km it's also the country's second-largest island, just slightly smaller than Rarotonga. Without soaring peaks or an azure lagoon, Mangaia doesn't fit the tropical island stereotype, and it remains an undiscovered tourist destination.

One of the major geological curiosities of the South Pacific, Mangaia is similar to Atiu and Mauke but much more dramatic. A *makatea,* or raised coral reef, forms a 60-meter-high ring around the island with sheer cliffs towering as high as 80 meters on the inland side. Lifted from the sea in stages over the past 18 million years, this outer limestone rim has eroded into quite remarkable rock formations with numerous caves hundreds of meters in length, some of them below sea level.

The volcanic earth inside the *makatea* is the only fertile soil on the island; this rises in rolling hills to slopes once planted with pineapples. At 169 meters elevation, Rangimotia is the island's highest point. Forested ridges radiate from this hill with the valleys between them used for farming. Near the inner edge of the *makatea,* where water is caught between the coral cliffs and the hills, low taro swamps are flanked by banana fields and miscellaneous crops. Nothing but bush and pandanus grow on the *makatea* itself, and pigs are kept there in makeshift pens. However, some areas of *makatea* are covered by lush green indigenous forest excellent for hiking.

Legend tells how Rongo rose from the deep with his three sons to colonize the island. Captain Cook "discovered" Mangaia in 1777 and Polynesian missionaries followed in 1826. Mangaia was the last Cook Island to accept Christianity, and traditionally the 750 Mangaians have a reputation for being a cautious lot, but you'll probably find them quite friendly when you get to know them. They live in three scattered coastal villages, Oneroa, Tamarua, and Ivirua. The population is continuing to drop as people depart for New Zealand and Australia with 33 percent of the inhabitants leaving between 1996–2001. The Mangaians speak a language similar to that of Rarotonga, part of the great Austronesian family.

Crafts

Mangaia is represented in museum collections around the world by large ceremonial adzes, which were used to decapitate prisoners taken in battles. The head, right arm, and right leg were regarded as prized possessions because of the mana they possessed. Later the missionaries had the adzes changed to incorporate "steeple stands," reproducing church steeples. This was used to symbolize church authority over the *ariki.* A local carver named Uria currently makes ceremonial adzes, which sell at NZ$150. Glen Tuara carves pendants and other items from stone.

The yellow *pupu* shell necklaces *(ei)* of Mangaia are also unique. The tiny gray *pupu* shells are found on the *makatea* only after rainfall. The yellow color comes from boiling them in caustic soda, though they can also be bleached white or dyed other colors. The shells are pierced one by one with a needle and threaded to make the *ei.*

© DAVID STANLEY

Sights of Mangaia

A 25-km road along the coastal strip rings most of the island. It's seven km from the airstrip to **Oneroa,** the main village, where a monument in front of the church recalls Mangaian church ministers and missionaries (such as the Rev. William Wyatt Gill, who served in the Cooks 1852–1883). If the church is open, enter to see the sennit rope bindings in the roof. On a large stone near Avarua landing are the footprints of the legendary giant, Mokea, and his son; both jumped across the island in a race to this spot. The huge stones on the reef to the north were thrown there by Mokea, to prevent a hostile canoe from landing. The queen of Mangaia still has a large flag given to her grandfather by Queen Victoria.

Tuara George (tel. 34-314) will guide you through **Teruarere Cave** for NZ$25 pp. Used as a burial ground in the past, the cave has old skeletons that add a skin-crawling touch of reality. The opening is small and you have to crawl in, but the cave goes on for a great distance. A lamp is necessary. Below Teruarere on the cliff is **Touri Cave.** There are two streams in this cave: one freshwater, the other salty.

An impressive cut leads up through the *makatea* from Oneroa. Follow a jeep track up to the flat summit of Rangimotia for varied views. From the plateau you can follow a footpath back down to Ivirua and return to Oneroa via **Tamarua,** a rather longish day hike. The church at Tamarua has a sennit-bound roof.

A water-filled cave at **Lake Tiriara** was the hiding place of the warlord Panako in the 1600s. Water from the lake runs through the cave under the *makatea* to the sea, and rises and falls slightly with the tide.

Beaches

There are several beautiful sandy beaches around the island. A spectacular one is **Araoa,** about 700 meters southwest of the airport terminal. As always around Mangaia, the lagoon is shallow, but at low tide you can wade out towards the north to a deep natural pool on the reef isolated from the ocean. Another beach is near Ara Moana Bungalows, although the water there is quite shallow. Four hundred meters southeast of this beach is an opening where freshwater from the interior comes out, resulting in a large natural pool on the reef called **Vai-Nga-Tara** where you can snorkel at low tide. You can also explore the watery tunnel in to about 50 meters, but you need a light.

Accommodations

Ara Moana Bungalows (tel. 34-278, fax 34-279, www.aramoana.com), on the coast just southeast of Ivirua village, about three km from the airport, is run by a Swede named Jan Kristensson and his wife Tu. There are four small thatched bungalows at NZ$60/80 single/double and two larger units at NZ$115/135/145 single/double/triple, all with private shower/toilet. Two tiny backpacker cabins without facilities are sometimes available at NZ$35/55 single/double. Airport transfers are included, but add NZ$35 pp a day for breakfast and a memorable dinner. Island nights with Polynesian dancing and singing are organized according to the number of guests present. Kawasaki 100 cc motorbikes are rented at NZ$30 a day. From Ara Moana, Teremanuia Tauakume (tel. 34-223) leads fascinating three-hour *makatea* hikes along the old village trail visiting four caves at NZ$35 pp. Island tours by 4WD vehicle or fishing trips which circumnavigate the island are NZ$50 each.

Babe's Guest House (tel. 34-092, fax 34-078), just south of Oneroa, has six rooms with bath at NZ$75/120/150 single/double/triple including all meals. There's a large common room with TV and a communal fridge (cooking facilities not provided). Four of the rooms are in a long block, the other two in a family house. The nearby bar gets lively during the Friday night dances. Clark's Tours does island tours from Babe's at NZ$50 pp. Clark occasionally takes guests on an inflatable boat ride across Lake Tiriara and to Tuatini Cave (NZ$30) near the lake. Bicycles and scooters can be arranged.

Mangaia Lodge (Torotoro Piiti, tel. 34-324, fax 34-239), near the hospital above Oneroa, charges NZ$25 pp including breakfast. A filling dinner is NZ$10 extra. It's basic, but has the advantage of providing cooking facilities for guests staying in the three rooms with shared bath in this large, colonial-style house. Airport transfers are NZ$5 each way.

Other Southern Islands

Mitiaro

Mitiaro, formerly known as Nukuroa, is a low island with two lakes and vast areas of swampland. Of the lakes, Rotonui is much longer and broader than Rotoiti. This surprisingly large lake is surrounded by an unlikely combination of pine trees and coconut palms. Before the arrival of Europeans, the people occupied the center of the island near their gardens. Today they all live in one long village on the west coast. The village is neat and clean, with white sandy roads between the Norfolk pines and houses. Four different sections of the village maintain the names of the four original villages, and each has a garden area inland bearing the same name.

It's 20 km around Mitiaro, but the road across the center of the island offers more variety than the coastal road (no shade on either road, so be prepared). A number of caves, *marae*, rock pools, and small golden beaches await visitors. Small, edible black tilapia are abundant in the lakes, providing food for the common black eels *('itiki)*. About 600 meters north of the Lake Rotonui road is the access road to **Vai Nauri,** a cool, crystal-clear freshwater cave pool. A stairway leads down to the water's edge, and on a hot afternoon a swim here is almost divine.

Mitiaro receives fewer than 50 tourists a year and there are no motels or tourist cottages. **Seabreeze Lodge** (Joe and Mikara Herman, tel. 36-153, fax 36-165), at the north end of the village, has one room with shared bath at NZ$65 pp including meals. **Nane Pokoati** (tel. 36-107), next to the *ariki's* house south of the church, accepts guests at NZ$50 pp including three good meals. She's also the Air Rarotonga agent. Due to flight connections, anyone flying from Atiu to Mauke will have to spend one night (not enough) or five nights (far too long) on Mitiaro.

Manuae

This small island consists of two islets, Manuae and Te Au O Tu, inside a barrier reef. The unspoiled wealth of marinelife in this lagoon has prompted the government to offer the atoll as an international marine park. It's said you can still catch large parrot fish in the lagoon by hand. There's no permanent habitation. Copra-cutting parties from Aitutaki once used an abandoned airstrip to come and go, though they haven't done so for years. In 1990, the 1,600 traditional Aitutaki-origin owners of Manuae rejected a government proposal to lease the island to an Australian company for tourism development. Captain Cook gave Manuae its other, fortunately rarely used, name, Hervey Island.

Takutea

Clearly visible 16 km off the northwest side of Atiu, to whose people it belongs, Takutea is in no place over six meters high. The island's other name, Enuaiti, means "Small Island." Until 1959, the people of Atiu called here to collect copra, but

the grave of William Marsters on Palmerston

Takutea gets few visitors now. There are a few abandoned shelters and a freshwater collection tank. The waters along the reef abound with fish; many red-tailed tropic birds and red-footed boobies nest on the land. Permission of the Atiu Island Council is required for visits.

Palmerston

Palmerston, 367 km northwest of Aitutaki, is an atoll 11 km across at its widest point. Some 35 tiny islands dot its pear-shaped barrier reef, which encloses the coral head-studded lagoon completely at low tide. Although Polynesians had once lived on what they called Ava Rau ("two hundred channels"), Palmerston was uninhabited when Captain Cook arrived in 1774.

William Marsters, legendary prolific settler, arrived here in 1863 to manage a coconut plantation. He brought with him from Penrhyn his Polynesian wife and her cousin, who were soon joined by another cousin. Marsters married all three, and by the time he died in 1899 at the ripe age of 78, he had begotten 21 children. Thousands of his descendants are now scattered around the Cook Islands, throughout New Zealand, and beyond, but the three Marsters branches on Palmerston are down to about 50. The grave of William Marsters the Patriarch may be seen beside the church. The current island patriarch, Rev. Bill Marsters (born 1923), has a mere 12 children.

The three Marsters families, the Tepou, Akakaingaro, and Mataiva, live on tiny Home or Palmerston Island on the west side of the atoll, where they grow taro and sugarcane in pits. All 35 islands are divided into sections between these three families, members of which cannot intermarry within their own group. Many of the older residents suffer from asthma. Like lonely Pitcairn Island, where the inhabitants are also of mixed British descent, on Palmerston the first language is English, the only island in the Cooks where this is so. And as in any small, isolated community, there's some tension between the families. In 1995, officials from Rarotonga arrived on Palmerston and by playing one group off against another, succeeded in undermining the authority of the island council and imposing centralized rule on independence-minded Palmerston.

The central government wants to build an airport on Toms Island, two islands away from Home Island, by 2005. Meanwhile, the launch *Marsters Dream* runs monthly from Rarotonga to Palmerston, bringing ordered supplies and taking away parrot fish. The vessel carries 13 passengers who must batten down inside for the 24-hour journey from Rarotonga (NZ$150/300 one way/roundtrip). Contact **Marsters Marine** (tel. 24-005) on Rarotonga. They'll also be able to arrange accommodations with families on the island at NZ$30 pp including meals.

About a dozen yachts call at Palmerston each year, and since boats drawing over 1.5 meters cannot enter the lagoon, they must anchor outside the reef. Yachties can hail "Palmerston Island" over VHF channel 16 when they're within 15 km of the atoll. The Republic of Palmsterston Yacht Club near the church in the center of the village provides cooking facilities, a washing machine, toilets, and hot showers (rain water) to yachties who pay NZ$20 for five years membership. Cold beer is sold daily except Sunday.

The Northern Group

The northern Cooks are far more traditional than the southern Cooks. Their location closer to the equator makes them much hotter than Rarotonga or Aitutaki. All of the northern atolls except Penrhyn sit on the 3,000-meter-deep Manihiki Plateau; the sea around Penrhyn is 5,000 meters deep. These low-lying coral rings are the very image of the romantic South Seas, but life for the inhabitants can be hard and large numbers have left for New Zealand in recent years. Reef fish and coconuts are abundant, but fresh water and everything else is limited. Now a commercial cultured pearl industry is bringing prosperity to several of the atolls.

All of the scattered atolls of the northern Cooks except Nassau have central lagoons. Only the Penrhyn lagoon is easily accessible to shipping, although yachts can anchor in the pass at Suwarrow. Until recently, these isolated islands were served only by infrequent ships from Rarotonga, and tourist visits were limited to the ship's brief stop, since to disembark would have meant a stay of several weeks or even months. Air Rarotonga has flights to Manihiki and Penrhyn, taking four and a half hours each way.

Anyone desiring a fuller picture of life of the northern atolls should read Robert Dean Frisbie's *The Book of Pukapuka*, serialized in the *Atlantic Monthly* in 1928. Though interesting, Frisbie's book may seem distorted to some contemporary eyes, catering to European stereotypes.

Suwarrow

In 1814, the Russian explorer Mikhail Lazarev discovered an uninhabited atoll, which he named for his ship, the *Suvarov*. A mysterious box containing US$15,000 was dug up in 1855, probably left by the crew of a wrecked Spanish galleon in 1742. Later, an additional US$2,400 was found. Early in the 20th century, Lever Brothers unsuccessfully attempted to introduce to the lagoon gold-lipped pearl oysters from Australia's Torres Straits. In the 1920s and 1930s, A.B. Donald Ltd. ran Suwarrow as a copra estate until the island became infested with termites and the

export of copra was prohibited. During WW II, New Zealand coast-watchers were stationed here—the few decrepit buildings on Anchorage Island date from that time.

At various times from 1952 onward, New Zealander Tom Neale lived alone on Suwarrow and wrote a book about his experiences titled, not surprisingly, *An Island to Oneself.* Tom never found the buried treasure he was searching for on Suwarrow, and in 1977 he died of cancer on Rarotonga. Today, coconut-watchers serve on Suwarrow to ensure that none of the termite-infested nuts are removed. The numerous rats are not afraid of humans. Officially, Suwarrow is a Marine Park, and the caretakers live in Tom Neale's house. A government meteorologist may also be present, and pearl divers from Manihiki and Penrhyn visit occasionally.

Yachts often call on their way from Rarotonga or Bora Bora to Samoa. The wide, easy lagoon entrance is just east of Anchorage Island on the northeast side of the atoll and a 40-meter-long coral rock jetty points to the deep anchorage. There's good holding, but in stormy weather the lagoon waters can become very rough. Though Suwarrow is not an official port of entry, yachts often stop without clearing in at Rarotonga or Aitutaki. Passports must be taken to the caretakers in Tom's house, who also accept outgoing mail (yachties often volunteer to carry mail to/from Rarotonga). The table and chairs outside the caretaker family's home provide welcome neutral ground for whiling away the time.

Of the 25 *motu*, only five are sizable. The snorkeling in the lagoon is fantastic, with lots of shark action—they won't usually bother you unless you're spearfishing. Scuba diving is not allowed. In the past, hurricanes have washed four-meter waves across the atoll, and during one storm in 1942, those present survived by tying themselves to a large tamanu tree (see *The Island of Desire,* by Robert Dean Frisbie). Thousands of seabirds, turtles, and coconut crabs nest on this historically strange and still mysterious island.

Nassau

Egg-shaped Nassau is the only northern island without an inner lagoon; instead, taro grows in gardens at the center of the island. The American whaler *Nassau* called in 1835. Europeans ran a coconut plantation here until 1945, when the government bought the island for £2,000 in order to get it back for the Pukapukans. In 1951, the chiefs of Pukapuka, 89 km to the northwest, purchased it from the government for the same amount and they've owned it ever since. Korean fishermen from Pago Pago stop illegally at Nassau to trade canned foods, fishing gear, and cheap jewelry for love. The children of these encounters add an exotic element to the local population. There's no safe anchorage and many ships have been lost here.

Pukapuka

An island sits at each corner of this unusual triangular atoll. Because of its treacherous reef, where no anchorage is possible, Pukapuka was formerly known as "Danger Island." The only landing place for small boats or canoes is on the west side of Wale. Discovered by Mendaña in 1595 and rediscovered by Byron in 1765, Pukapuka was outrageously victimized during a Peruvian slave raid in 1863. Captain Gibson of HMS *Curacao* annexed the island in 1892.

Pukapuka is closer to Samoa than to Rarotonga, so the people differ in language and custom from other Cook Islanders. Three villages on Wale (pronounced WAH-lay) island have coexisted since precontact times, each with its own island council. They compete enthusiastically with each other in singing, dancing, contests, and cricket. The people make copra collectively, each receiving an equal share in the proceeds. Bananas and papaya also grow here in limited quantities; their harvesting is controlled by the councils. Each village owns one of the three main islands. The nicest swimming and snorkeling are off Kotawa Island, also known as Frigate Bird Island for the thousands of seabirds that nest there. Pukapuka's Catholic church is beautifully decorated with cowry shells.

An airstrip was constructed over the lagoon on Pukapuka in 1994, but Air Rarotonga only

calls if there's sufficient demand. The Rarotonga office should know about this and any accommodation options.

Manihiki

One of the Pacific's most beautiful atolls, Manihiki's reef bears 39 coral islets enclosing a closed lagoon four km wide that's thick with sharks. The dark green, coconut-covered *motu* are clearly visible across the blue waters. Until 1852, Manihiki was owned by the people of Rakahanga, who commuted the 44 km between the two islands in outrigger canoes, with great loss of life. In that year the missionaries convinced the islanders to divide themselves between the two islands and give up the hazardous voyages. In 1889, some disenchanted Manihiki islanders invited the French to annex their island. When a French warship arrived to consummate the act, anxious missionaries speedily hoisted the Union Jack, so the French sailed off. The same August, Britain officially declared a protectorate over the island.

Today Manihiki is best known for its pearl farms. In November 1997, Hurricane Martin passed near Manihiki, leaving 20 people dead, Tauhunu village in a shambles, and pearl industry installations above water blown away. Fortunately, most of the oysters survived.

Manihiki is famous for its handsome people. The administrative center is Tauhunu on the

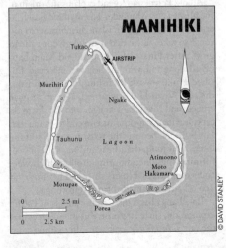

MANIHIKI

Tukao

✕ AIRSTRIP

Murihiti

Ngake

LAGOON

Tauhunu

Lagoon

Atimoono
Moto
Hakamaru

Motupae

Porea

0   2.5 mi

0   2.5 km

© DAVID STANLEY

west side of the atoll, and there's a second village at Tukao next to the airstrip. Permission of the chief of Tauhunu is required to dive in the lagoon. The anchorage off Tauhunu is not entirely safe. With the pearl boom in full swing, Air Rarotonga now flies here weekly from Rarotonga (1,204 km) and the airline can arrange accommodations in a local home at around NZ$75 pp including meals.

Rakahanga

Two opposing horseshoe-shaped islands almost completely encircle the lagoon of this rectangular atoll. The pearl industry is still in its infancy here, and this is a much quieter island than Manihiki. There are several small *motu* that can be reached on foot at low tide. Breadfruit and *puraka* (a tarolike vegetable) are the staples here, and copra is made for export. So that not too many coconuts are taken at one time, the island councils regulate visits to the *motu*. These usually take place only two or three times a year, so as to give nature a chance to regenerate. Coconut crabs, a delicacy on Rakahanga, are mostly caught on the small, uninhabited *motu*. Nivano village is at the southwest corner of the atoll. Although unable to enter the lagoon, ships can anchor offshore. An airstrip in the middle of the west side of the atoll was destroyed by Hurricane Wasa in December 1991 and has not been repaired.

An old Polynesian legend explains the origin of Rakahanga and Manihiki. The mythological fisherman Huku caught an island he considered too small to take, so he tied it up to give it time to grow. After Huku left, the demigod Maui happened along and, with the help of a mermaid, finished Huku's work by fishing the island from the sea. When Huku returned, a great struggle ensued, and Maui leapt straight into the sky to escape, leaving his footprints embedded in the reef. His fishhook became the stars, and such was the force of his jump that the island was split in two, forming these neighboring atolls, which were later colonized by Huku's sister and her husband Toa, a warrior banished from Rarotonga.

Rakahanga has a place in the annals of Pacific exploration, since it was on this island's reef that the raft *Tahiti Nui* met its end after sailing from

Tahiti to Chile and back between 1956 and 1958. The expedition's leader, Éric de Bisschop, died in the mishap after having proved that the ancient Polynesians could have sailed to South America and returned.

Penrhyn

Penrhyn's turquoise, 280-square-km lagoon is so wide that you can just see the roof of the church at Tautua from Omoka, the administrative center. The *motu* at the far end of the lagoon are too far away to be seen. The lagoon is thick with sharks, mostly innocuous black-tips; only the black shark is dangerous. The islanders ignore them as they dive for oysters. Now pearl farming is developing with 150,000 cultured oysters already hanging on racks in the lagoon and an oyster hatchery near Omoka.

Penrhyn was named for the British ship *Lady Penrhyn*, which arrived in 1788, although one of the Polynesian names is Tongareva. The legendary hero Vatea fished Penrhyn up from the sea using a hook baited with a piece of flesh from his own thigh. In 1863, four native missionaries on Penrhyn were tricked into recruiting as many as 472 members of their congregation for Peruvian slavers at $5 a head and sailed with them to Callao as overseers for $100 a month in the hope of obtaining enough money to build a new church! The blackbirders dubbed Penrhyn the "Island of the Four Evangelists" in gratitude. This tragedy wiped out the chiefly line and Penrhyn is today the only Cook Island without an *ariki*. Remnants of old graves and villages abandoned after the raid can still be seen on the *motu*, and the ruins of an unfinished church crumble away at Akasusu.

The island has a good natural harbor, one of the few in the Cook Islands, and vessels can enter the lagoon through Taruia Passage, just above Omoka, to tie up at Omoka wharf. In 1995, a fuel depot opened here for ships patrolling the fisheries zones of the Cook Islands and Kiribati (Penrhyn is closer to Christmas Island than it is to Rarotonga). Development plans by the Rarotonga government have been resisted as various local factions vie for influence. Fine pandanus *rito* hats and mother-of-pearl shell jewelry are made on Penrhyn and visiting yachties can trade kitchen- and tableware, dry cell batteries, rope, and small anchors for crafts and pearls.

American forces occupied Penrhyn during 1942–1946 and built a giant airfield at the south end of Omoka about five km from the present village. Aluminum from the wreck of a four-engined WW II Liberator bomber named *Go-Gettin' Gal* was used by the islanders to make combs, and not much is left other than three engines near Warwick Latham's house and a fourth engine in the village. Concrete building foundations from the war and from a base camp that supported British and American atmospheric nuclear tests on Christmas Island in the early 1960s can be seen. The waters around the atoll are a rich fishing ground, and Penrhyn is used as a base for patrol boats and planes monitoring the activities of foreign fishing fleets.

Air Rarotonga (penrhyn@airraro.co.ck) flies once a week from Rarotonga (1,365 km) to this most northerly Cook island. The airfare (NZ$1,203 return from Rarotonga) is high, due in part to an exorbitant landing fee levied by the island council. **Tarakore Guest House** (Doreen and Purua Heria, fax 42-683) and **Soa's Guest House** in the center of Omoka village accommodate visitors. In addition, the local Air Rarotonga agent Warwick Latham (tel. 42-888, fax 42-023) can arrange a house rental with schoolteacher Rara Taia (tel. 42-132).

Niue

A single, 264-square-km island, Niue is one of the world's smallest self-governing states (in free association with New Zealand). It stands alone 560 km southeast of Samoa, 386 km east of Vava'u, and 2,400 km northeast of New Zealand. The name comes from *niu* (coconut tree) and *e* (behold) and is pronounced NEW-way. This little-known island boasts some of the finest coastal limestone crevices and chasms in the South Pacific, all open to visitors and freely accessible. Each is unique—you'll need at least a week to do them justice.

Niue is for the explorer who likes to get out and make discoveries on his or her own, for the skin diver in search of clean clear water brimming with coral, fish, and sea snakes, and for those who want to relax in a peaceful, uncommercialized environment among charming, friendly people, without sacrificing creature comforts. Niue is perhaps the most unspoiled main island in the Pacific—it's an island of adventure.

The Land

Niue is an elevated atoll shaped like a two-tiered wedding cake with two terraces rising from the sea. It's one of the largest uplifted coral islands in the world (though 1,196-square-km Lifou in New Caledonia is much bigger). The lower terrace rises sharply, creating the 20-meter coastal

NIUE HIGHLIGHTS

Arches of Talava: seaside stone arches, caves (p. 389)

Huvalu Conservation Area: birdlife, fruit bats, hiking through rainforest (p. 389)

Matavai Resort: spectacular cliffside location (p. 392)

Togo Chasm: coral pinnacles, oasis, pools, crashing waves (p. 390)

Vaikona Chasm: deep chasm, cave, pools (p. 390)

cliffs that virtually surround the island. Inland, a second terrace rises abruptly from this coastal belt to a central plateau some 60 meters above the ocean. According to Professor Patrick Nunn of the University of the South Pacific, the uplifting continues and half a million years from now Niue will be 50–70 meters higher than it is today.

A fringing reef borders much of the coast, but in places the ocean breakers smash directly into precipitous cliffs. Faulting during the island's uplifting has created the chasms and crevices that are Niue's greatest attractions. Water dripping from their ceilings has added a touch of the surreal in the form of stalactites and stalagmites.

Cruise ships and yachts sailing between the Cook Islands and Tonga sometimes stop for snorkeling at Beveridge Reef, 200 km southeast of Niue and a possession of the country. Beveridge's horseshoe-shaped lagoon is easily entered through a pass on the west side. Like an oasis in the desert, this flourishing ecosystem is surrounded by vast expanses of open sea.

Climate

December to March are the hurricane months, with average temperatures of 27° C. The southeast trade winds blow from April to November and temperatures average 24° C. The 2,047 mm of annual rainfall is fairly well distributed throughout the year, with a slight peak during the hot southern summer. There's good anchorage at Alofi, except during strong westerly winds. In January 2004, the worst hurricane in living memory flattened buildings and vegetation on the southwest

side of Niue. Recorded tidal information and a local weather report can be heard at tel. 101.

Flora and Fauna

The waters off Niue are clear as can be, with countless species of colorful fish. There are also many varieties of sea snakes. Though they're poisonous, their mouths are too tiny to bite, and divers handle them with impunity. On most dives, underwater sightseers also spot white-tip reef sharks, but they're also not dangerous and add to the thrill.

Butterflies are everywhere, as are orchids, hibiscus, frangipani, and bougainvillea. One-fifth of the island's surface is covered by undisturbed primary forest, much of the rest by secondary growth. A profusion of huge "crow's nest" *(nidum)* and other ferns, rhododendron, and poinsettia grow wild, and there are ancient ebony trees. The birdlife is rich; white long-tailed terns, weka, swamp hens, pigeons, and parakeets abound. The Polynesian starling and Polynesian triller evolved into subspecies not found elsewhere.

History

Niue was colonized by the Samoans in the 9th or 10th century A.D., then Tongans invaded in the 16th century. The present Niuean language is related to both. Captain Cook made three landings in 1774, but he got a hostile reception from warriors with red-painted teeth! Cook called it Savage Island (as opposed to the Friendly Islands, Tonga), a name still heard from time to time. In 1830, the redoubtable missionary John Williams was also thrown back by force. A Samoa-trained Niuean named Peniamina managed to convert some of the islanders to Christianity in 1846, but it was a series of Samoan pastors, beginning in 1849, who really implanted the faith on the island. This paved the way for the first resident English missionary, George Lawes, who arrived in 1861.

Much of the early hostility to foreigners was motivated by a very real fear of European diseases. The islanders' reputation for ferocity had always kept the whalers away, but then in the 1860s came the Peruvians and Bully Hayes, who was able to entice Niuean men to leave their island voluntarily to mine phosphate for years at a time

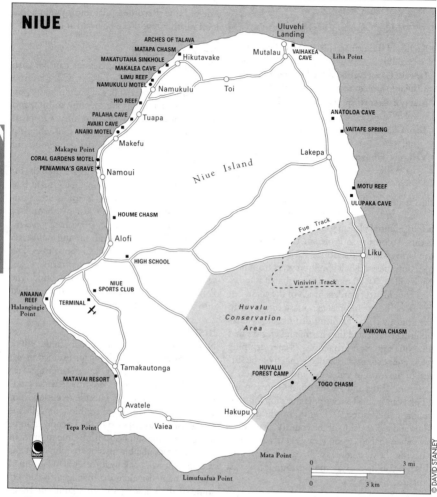

NIUE

Uluvehi Landing
ARCHES OF TALAVA
MATAPA CHASM
MAKATUTAHA SINKHOLE
Hikutavake
Mutalau
VAIHAKEA CAVE
Liha Point
MAKALEA CAVE
LIMU REEF
NAMUKULU MOTEL
Namukulu
Toi
HIO REEF
ANATOLOA CAVE
PALAHA CAVE
Tuapa
VAITAFE SPRING
AVAIKI CAVE
ANAIKI MOTEL
Makefu
Lakepa
Makapu Point
CORAL GARDENS MOTEL
PENIAMINA'S GRAVE
Namoui
Niue Island
MOTU REEF
HOUME CHASM
ULUPAKA CAVE
Alofi
Fue Track
HIGH SCHOOL
Liku
NIUE SPORTS CLUB
Vinivini Track
ANAANA REEF
TERMINAL
Huvalu Conservation Area
Halangingie Point
VAIKONA CHASM
Tamakautonga
HUVALU FOREST CAMP
MATAVAI RESORT
TOGO CHASM
Avatele
Hakupu
Tepa Point
Vaiea
Mata Point
Limufuafua Point
0   3 mi
0   3 km
© DAVID STANLEY

on distant Malden Island. Mataio Tuitonga was made king in 1876 and his successor, Fataaiki, appealed to Britain for protection. Finally, in 1900, Niue was taken over by the U.K. and a year later transferred to New Zealand.

Government

In 1959, the appointed Island Council was replaced by an elected Legislative Assembly (Fono Ekepule). Niue became internally self-governing in free association with New Zealand on Oc-

tober 19, 1974. The Assembly has 20 elected members who meet in the impressive Fale Fono (tel. 4200) in Alofi. The premier is elected by the Assembly from its own ranks by a show of hands. The premier in turn chooses three cabinet ministers from among the Assembly members. Local government is provided by the 14 village councils elected every three years.

Economy

Niue is totally dependent on official aid from

New Zealand, which supplies three-quarters of the local budget. Overseas aid totals about NZ$8 million a year, or NZ$5,750 per capita, one of the highest levels in the South Pacific. Most of the money is used to support the infrastructure, which maintains an artificial, consumer-oriented standard of living. Many government services are provided free and 450 island residents work for the government.

Imports are 13 times higher than exports, an imbalance only exceeded in the French colonies. Transportation difficulties have always hampered exports. Tourism, the sale of postage stamps to philatelists, and limited royalties from overseas fishing companies help balance the island's cash flow. Top level domain names bearing Niue's internet ending .nu are marketed worldwide through www.nunames.nu at US$60 for two years.

In 1993, Niue set up a "financial center" similar to those of Vanuatu and the Cook Islands to support overseas firms trying to avoid taxation in their real places of business. Since then, a Panama City law firm has registered over 6,000 "international business companies" in Niue, and the fees they pay account for 10 percent of government revenue. In 2001, rumors began circulating that the South American cocaine cartels were laundering money through Niue and several large American banks started blocking transfers to the island. After the Financial Action Task Force representing the world's largest economies threatened the country with sanctions in 2002, Niue announced that it was shutting down its offshore banking facilities but not the company register. Since then, the Task Force has taken Niue off its blacklist of "non-cooperative jurisdictions."

In 1996, the New Zealand government spent NZ$10 million extending the airport runway and building the Matavai Resort in the hope of promoting tourism to Niue. Even so, Niue's hotels stand empty most of the time. Of the 3,165 "tourists" who arrived in 2002, two-thirds were overseas Niueans visiting relatives and three-quarters of the remainder arrived on cheap packaged holidays from New Zealand. Sixty percent of visitors are New Zealanders and the average stay is two weeks.

Although attempts have been made to stimulate agriculture, the economy is continually undermined by the emigration of working-age Niueans to New Zealand (to which Niueans have unhindered entry). In the past, small quantities of passion fruit, lime juice, canned coconut cream, and honey have been exported. The coconut cream factory closed in 1989 after a hurricane wiped out the island's coconut plantations; in 1990, Hurricane Ofa destroyed the lime and passion fruit crops. Periodic droughts have also taken a heavy toll. Taro, yams, cassava, sweet potatoes, papaya, and bananas are actively cultivated in bush gardens for personal consumption by the growers. Local farmers also grow vanilla, and a few pigs, poultry, and beef cattle are kept. Saturday is bush day, when people go inland to clear, plant, and weed their gardens. Now farmers are turning to organic produce to serve the lucrative natural foods market in New Zealand. Efforts are being made to make Niue the first pesticide-free, entirely organic country in the world by 2010.

The People

Niueans are related to the Tongans and Samoans rather than to the Tahitians. The population is about 1,400 and falling (down from 4,000 at self-government in 1974). Another 20,000 Niueans reside in New Zealand (all Niueans are N.Z. citizens), and every year more people leave "the Rock" (Niue) to seek employment and opportunity abroad. Many of the landowners have left—you'll never see as many empty houses and near-ghost towns as you'll see here. The villages on the east coast give an idea of how Europe must have looked after a plague in the Middle Ages, as direct flights to Auckland have drained the population. Remittances from Niueans in New Zealand are an important source of income.

The remaining inhabitants live in small villages scattered along the coast, with a slight concentration near the administrative center, Alofi. After disastrous hurricanes in 1959 and 1960, the New Zealand government replaced the traditional lime-plastered, thatched-roofed houses of the people with tin-roofed "hurricane-resistant" concrete-block dwellings. Niue has the lowest population density of any Pacific country, and at 15 per thousand, Niue's birth rate is the lowest in the Pacific. Only about a quarter of the Niueans living in New Zealand can still speak their ancestral language proficiently.

All land is held by families. Three-quarters belong to the Ekalesia Niue, founded by the London Missionary Society. Other churches such as the Catholics and Mormons have only a few hundred members. There are no longer any chiefs, and lineage means little. Since the 1950s, education has been free and compulsory until the age of 14, and literacy is almost 100 percent. Two Polynesian dialects are spoken: Motu in the north and Tafiti in the south. Everyone on the island knows everyone else.

A major event for a teenage boy is his haircutting ceremony, when the long tail of hair he has kept since childhood is removed. Guests invited to the concurrent feast contribute hundreds of dollars to a fund that goes to the boy after the celebration expenses have been paid. For girls there's a similar ear-piercing ceremony. These gatherings are usually held on a Saturday in private homes; you may be invited to attend if you know someone.

Public Holidays and Festivals

Public holidays include New Year's Day, Commission Day (January 2), Waitangi Day (February 6), Good Friday, Easter Monday (March/April), ANZAC Day (April 25), White Sunday (second Sunday in May), Queen Elizabeth's Birthday (a Monday in early June), Constitution Days (October 19 and 20), Peniamina Day (fourth Monday in October), and Christmas Days (December 25 and 26).

Prayer Week and Takai Week are both held during the first week of January. The main event of the year is the Constitution Celebrations, which last three days around October 19. There are traditional dancing and singing, parades, sports, and a display of produce and handicrafts at the high school grounds two km inland from Alofi. A highlight is the exciting outrigger canoe race off Alofi wharf. Peniamina Day falls on the Monday during the Constitution Celebrations.

Accommodations and Food

Two large hotels and a number of smaller guesthouses and resorts are at your disposal. For a longer stay, ask around about renting a house by the week or month. There are usually plenty available. Unexpected complications can arise, however, as the house may have hundreds of owners, and visiting relatives might throw you out! Camping would be possible on the east coast, but get permission or keep out of sight. For indoor camping, unfurnished houses without hot water in Hakupu village start at NZ$50 a week.

Visas and Officialdom

Though you'll need a passport and onward ticket, no visa is required for a stay of up to 30 days. Extensions of stay up to three months total cost NZ$30. Resident expatriates who run afoul of government ministers are expelled from Niue with little ado. In a small community like Niue's, one has to take care not to step on the wrong toes.

Money

New Zealand currency is used. The Westpac Bank will change traveler's checks, though not always at a good rate. If you're arriving from New Zealand, bring sufficient N.Z. dollars rather than waiting to change money here. You can obtain a cash advance on a credit card for a NZ$10 fee, but no ATMs are available. Many hotels and restaurants accept credit cards, but ask first.

Media

The *Niue Star* (tel. 4293) is an independent weekly newspaper published in English and Niuean.

The Broadcasting Corporation of Niue (tel. 4026) provides television service 1800–2300 daily, and Radio Sunshine broadcasts over 91 and 102 MHz FM 0600–2130. Most TV programs are supplied by Television New Zealand.

Getting There

Polynesian Airlines operates a Boeing 737-800 on twice-weekly flights to Niue from Apia and Auckland. Flying from New Zealand you arrive a day earlier because Niue is across the international dateline (Niue and Samoa share the same day). Avoid coming around Christmas when the flights will be full of islanders returning home.

Reconfirm your flight reservations well ahead at **Peleni's Travel Agency** (Ida or Sonya Talagi, tel. 4317, fax 4322) in Alofi, the Polynesian Airlines agent. They can also help with general tourist information and can arrange car rentals and tours.

The freighter *Southern Express* sails monthly to Tonga and other Pacific countries. The agent is Des Hipa at Ali's Giftware (tel. 4054) in the Commercial Center, although passengers aren't usually accepted. Large ships must anchor offshore and their cargo is transferred to the wharf by lighters.

By Sailing Yacht

Yachts anchor in about 15 meters (good holding) in an open roadstead off Alofi and are well protected from all winds except those from the west. In summer especially, going ashore can be scary when there's a swell. The **Niue Island Yacht Club** (Box 129, Alofi, Niue, VHF channel 10, yachtclub@niue.nu) provides 16 secure moorings in Alofi Bay that can be used for NZ$5 a day. Water, toilets, and showers are available at the wharf, but it's necessary to have a bridle arrangement on the dingy to allow it to be lifted out of the water using an electronic winch.

Yachts must call "Niue Radio" on VHF channel 16 for clearance before coming ashore. Customs and immigration (tel. 4122, fax 4150) share an office just up the hill from the main wharf, but they're normally closed on weekends (exceptions are often made). The NZ$25 pp departure tax also applies to yachties. An annual yacht rally is held around the end of August if enough boats are in the bay. In good weather, Niue makes an excellent stop for yachts sailing between Rarotonga/Aitutaki and Vava'u.

Getting Around

There's no bus service on Niue, but taxi services are available from Cedric Tutaki (tel. 4245) and Mitaki's Café (tel. 4084). Hitching is easy along the west coast, but you could get stranded on the east. Don't underestimate the size of this island: it's a long, long way to walk. The road around the island is 64 km and the pavement doesn't extend beyond the west coast.

Niue Rentals (tel. 4216, fax 4065, www.niue rentals.nu; weekdays 0800–1600, Sat. 0830–1100), between the Hotel Niue and the hospital, has cars (NZ$45–50), trucks (NZ$50), vans (NZ$75), scooters (NZ$20), and bicycles (NZ$5). **Alofi Rentals** (Mary Saunders, tel. 4017, alofirentals@sin.net.nu) is between the airport road and Alofi. Rates are NZ$65/80 for a six/12-seater van, NZ$100 for a 15-seater minibus, NZ$45–55 for a car, NZ$25 for a motorbike, and NZ$10 for mountain bikes. On a weekly basis you usually get one day free. Car rentals include kilometers and insurance, but you're still responsible for the first NZ$3,000 in "excess" damages in case of an accident.

Before heading around the island on a scooter, make sure the tank is full and ask the renter if you can make it on one tank. All rental vehicles are in short supply, so don't wait until the last minute. A Niue driver's license must be obtained at the police station (no test required if you have another license). A temporary one-month license costs NZ$2 (NZ$5 for over 30 days). Driving is on the left and speed limits are 40 kph in the villages or 60 kph on the open road. The penalty for being caught inebriated at a roadside breath analyzer test is NZ$1,500.

Airport

Hanan International Airport (IUE) is three km southeast of Alofi. Some accommodations offer free airport transfers, while others charge up to NZ$10 each way. Otherwise it's fairly easy to hitch a ride into town. There's no bank or duty-free shop. The airport departure tax is NZ$25.

NIUE

Exploring the Island

SIGHTS

Virtually all of Niue's scenic attractions are within earshot of the sea, but while sites on the west coast are accessible from the road in a few minutes, those on the east coast are only reached over slippery rough trails requiring hikes of up to 40 minutes. Some of these trails, such as those through the fantastic petrified coral forests at Vaikona and Togo, are not well marked. Sturdy shoes are required to go almost anywhere off the road on Niue.

If you're a good walker, you could visit the sites south of Alofi on foot in under a day. Those to the north can be covered by a combination of walking, hitching, and good luck, but to get to the places on the northeast and southeast coasts and return to Alofi the same day, you'll need your own transportation. Take food and drink with you, as little is available in the villages.

Photographers should note that conditions on the east coast are best in the morning, on the west coast in the afternoon. Vaikona and Togo are definitely not afternoon trips, as the declining light in the forest makes the trails hard to discern. Also, limestone makes for slow walking.

Near Alofi

The **Huanaki Museum and Cultural Center** (tel. 4011, weekdays 0800–1500, admission free), next to the hospital near the junction of the airport and coastal roads, was severely damaged during the 2004 hurricane, but hopefully it will be rebuilt. According to a popular tradition, Captain Cook landed at **Opaahi Reef** opposite the Mormon church in Alofi. It's a scenic spot, well worth the short detour.

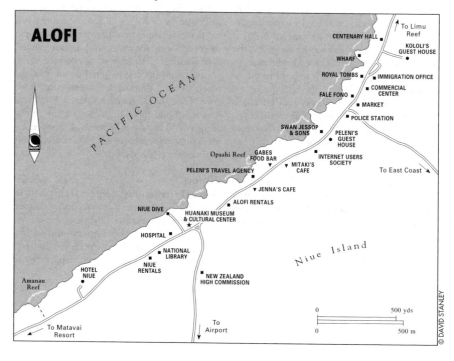

Two kings of Niue, Mataio Tuitonga (reigned 1876–1887) and Fataaiki (reigned 1888–1896), are buried at the **royal tombs** in front of the LMS Church opposite Alofi's post office. Nearby, adjoining the war memorial, are two stone backrests used by these kings. The last king of Niue, Togia (died 1917), ceded his kingdom to Britain on April 21, 1900, just four days after the Americans annexed Eastern Samoa. He's buried in front of the church at Tuapa.

If you're patient, you should be able to spot sea snakes in the clear water off Alofi's main wharf. It's fascinating to walk on the reef southwest of the wharf at low tide. Crevices, cliffs, and coral abound, and there are natural pools on the reef where you can safely swim. Beware of waves heralding the incoming tide, however. The Togalahi Sea Track across the street from the Niue Tourism Office leads down to the coast.

North of Alofi

Houme Chasm at Alofi North, about three km from town, is behind the house across the street and slightly north of the Catholic Mission. A flashlight is required to reach the pool.

Avaiki Sea Cave is another six km north and an easy five minutes from the road. The pool in the main cave just north of the landing contains a variety of marinelife and is a great place to swim, but this is often prohibited. The limestone formations are outstanding. Just 200 meters north of the Avaiki sign is the trail down to **Palaha Cave,** with stalagmites and stalactites. **Hio Reef,** a little over a km farther north, just before the point where the road divides, is a nice secluded sandy beach best for swimming at high tide. At low tide you can snorkel in the rock pool just north of here.

Farther north again, just beyond Namukulu, is the trail to **Limu Reef,** a perfect snorkeling locale with colorful coral and fish. A natural stone bridge over the lagoon is just a little north of here across the rocks. The trail to **Makalea Cave** is 200 meters north of the Limu signboard. Near the road just opposite the southernmost house in Hikutavake is **Makatutaha,** a large pothole containing a pool connected to the sea.

Two of Niue's highlights are **Matapa Chasm** and the **Arches of Talava,** reached along an extension of the coastal road just north of Hikutavake. Follow the road straight down to Matapa, a wide, sunken chasm that was once the bathing place of Niuean royalty—very good swimming and snorkeling. The Arches of Talava are harder to find. The trail branches off the Matapa track to the right just before the beginning of the descent. Keep straight on the trail about 15 minutes, then watch for yellow marks on the trees, which indicate the branch trail on the left to Talava. The site itself is entered through a cave. A great series of stone arches above the sea complement side caves with red and green stalactites and stalagmites in fantastic flowing formations. Behind the outermost arch is a large cave best entered at low tide with a flashlight. The constant roar of the surf adds to the overwhelming impression of the place.

Limu Reef and Matapa Chasm are good places to visit on Sunday, as swimming is allowed there that day when it's frowned upon elsewhere.

South of Alofi

From beyond the airport, the interior road drops to **Tamakautonga,** where you'll find a couple of small beaches behind the church. This is one of the best places on Niue for reef walking with the chance of observing shorebirds. Farther south at **Avatele** (pronounced Avasele), there's another poor excuse for a beach at the canoe landing. Return to Alofi along the coastal road with a stop at **Anaana** near Halangingie Point, where you can sit atop a cliff by the road and watch as tons of water are thrown at your feet.

Huvalu Conservation Area

A sizable chunk of southeastern Niue between Hakupu, Liku, and Alofi has been set aside as the Huvalu Conservation Area, a community project supported by the South Pacific Regional Environment Program. Eight-five percent of the reserve's 5,400 hectares is natural rainforest containing numerous species of banyan, Tahitian chestnut, and *kafika* trees. It's home to coconut crabs *(uga),* fruit bats *(peka),* and most of Niue's 29 species of birds.

The conservation area offers several excellent

hiking trails. The five-km **Fue Track** starts near an old quarry 1.5 km north of Liku and goes through mature forest. The seven-km **Vinivini Track** begins 3.5 km west of Liku just 300 meters west of the point where the Fue Track meets the Alofi-Liku Road. The first two km of the Vinivini Track passes bush gardens, but then it winds through the rainforest, finishing two km south of Liku. Although these tracks can be done on a motorbike, bird-watchers will wish to go quietly on foot.

The conservation area also includes a stretch of Niue's wild east coast with some of the most fantastic limestone features in the South Pacific. About four km northeast of Hakupu, the second-largest village on the island, is the trail to **Togo Chasm.** After a 20-minute walk, you reach a barren area of coral pinnacles much like the interior of Nauru Island. The path leads down to a wide chasm with coconut trees growing on the

A narrow ladder gives access to Togo Chasm.

© M.E. DE VOS

sandy bottom. Climb down the ladder to the sand, and swim in the pools at each end of the chasm. The green of the coconut trees combined with the golden sand contrasts sharply with the rocky wasteland, creating an almost North African effect—until you hear the ocean crashing into the cliffs just meters away; it's one of the scenic wonders of the Pacific.

From the Togo trailhead, travel northeast another four km to the trail to **Vaikona Chasm.** As you approach the coast through the pandanus brush covering the jagged limestone, you pass a sudden opening straight down into the chasm. Wind your way around the back of the opening and drop into a deep cave, grasping the stout orange rope provided for the purpose. You enter the chasm from the cave itself over huge rocks. There are two crystal clear pools to swim in, one at each end of Vaikona; tiny freshwater crayfish and black carp live here.

It would take a major expedition to explore all Vaikona Chasm has to offer. Resembling a ruined Gothic cathedral, the walls soar 30 meters to a canopy of vegetation, and huge blocks of the collapsed roof litter the floor. The stalagmites and stalactites of the entrance cave are like images on a broken medieval portal; by plunging into the cool, clear water of the pools, one has communion with the bowels of the earth. The crashing of breakers into the coast nearby is like the expurgation of sin—a spectacular visual experience. This awe-inspiring chasm is outstanding even for Niue.

The Northeast Coast

The trail to **Motu Reef** is about a kilometer south of Lakepa. There's a wide wooden stairway down to the reef from the cave where canoes are stored. A couple of km north of Lakepa, it's a 25-minute walk along an easy-to-follow trail from the trailhead to **Vaitafe Spring.** Fresh water from a crevice at the foot of a sheer cliff bubbles into a pool where you can swim or snorkel, but the area is accessible only at low tide. You can reef walk here.

At the north end of the island, opposite the church in **Mutalau** village, is a monument commemorating the arrival of the first Christian missionaries; the first Niuean convert, Peniamina (1846); and Paulo (1849), the first Samoan teacher. A jeep track across from the monument leads down to Uluvehi Landing, an easy five-minute walk. This was the main landing on the island in the early days; the islanders' sleek outrigger canoes are still stored in caves in the cliffs. To reach **Vaihakea Cave,** look for an overgrown trail just 100 meters inland from the streetlight at Uluvehi on the east side of the track. Once you get on the trail, it's only a five-minute walk to this fantastic submerged cave full of fish and coral, but you must climb down a sharp limestone cliff near the trail end. There's excellent swimming and snorkeling at low tide.

The sites mentioned above are only the *highlights* of Niue; there are many other caves for the avid spelunker to explore with the help of local guides.

Sports and Recreation

Niue Dive (Ian Gray and Annie Franklin, tel. 4311, fax 4028, VHF channel 14, www.dive.nu), behind the hospital, offers scuba diving from inflatable boats at NZ$120 for two tanks. Gear rental (if required) is NZ$40 a day. A certification card is necessary, otherwise a PADI open-water course will be NZ$495 pp. Featured are dives through caves to drop-offs and Niue's small, timid sea snakes. If you're very lucky, you may be able to dive with spinner dolphins (year-round) or migrating whales (June–Nov.). Due to the absence of rivers, the water is unbelievably clear—worth every penny. Niue Dive also arranges snorkeling or coastal sightseeing trips at NZ$30 pp. A three-hour whale-watching trip (July–Oct.) is NZ$50.

Game fishing is offered by **Akau Fishing Charters** (Jeff Wood, tel./fax 4025, jeffwood@niue.nu) at NZ$250 for four hours (maximum of four people). Fish caught belong to the boat. The main season for wahoo is July to November; marlin, sailfish, tuna, and mahi mahi are taken from November to April. Fishing on Sunday is prohibited by law.

Visitors are welcome at the nine-hole **golf course** (tel. 4292) near the airport. An annual tournament is in November.

Sporting events such as soccer (March–June),

rugby (June–Aug.), and netball (June–Aug.) take place on the high school grounds. Cricket (Dec.–Feb.) and softball matches are usually held in the villages on alternating Saturdays. The locals will know what's happening.

ACCOMMODATIONS

Under US$25

Peleni's Guest House (Fita and Sonya Talagi; tel. 4317 or 4153, fax 4322, pelenisguesthouse@niue.nu) is near Swan Jessops, just south of central Alofi. The three rooms with shared bath and cooking facilities are NZ$30/40 single/double. A three-bed family room costs NZ$54. Everything is clean, well maintained, and quiet. It's handy to swimming spots at Utuko and the wharf. They rent cars/vans to guests at NZ$35/40 a day. Airport transfers are free.

Kololi's Guest House (tel. 4171, rupina@niue.nu), 150 meters inland from the Commercial Center in central Alofi, charges NZ$38 single or double for the three standard rooms, NZ$45 for a larger room, and NZ$60 for the family room upstairs. A two-bedroom, self-catering unit is available next door at NZ$95. Your hosts Neil and Rupina Morrisey provide convenient communal cooking and laundry facilities in this stylishly designed guesthouse. Neal is a qualified chef who serves breakfast/lunch/dinner at NZ6.50/NZ$10/NZ$15–20.

The only place to stay on the east coast is the **Huvalu Forest Camp,** about 200 meters south of the trail to Togo Chasm (or three km northeast of Hakupu and eight km southwest of Liku). There's a bunkhouse where you'll pay NZ$15 pp for a dorm bed, and ample camping space at NZ$10 per tent. Communal toilets, showers, and cooking facilities are available in separate buildings. The Forest Camp is owned by Afele and Patiliva Paea (tel. 4244), who live at Namoui between Alofi and Makefu, but they're often off island so ask Niue Tourism for current information. The Forest Camp makes a great base for exploring the most beautiful part of the island, so long as you're prepared to rough it a bit. It's beautiful in the moonlight: wonderfully silent except for the sounds of the forest (and the occasional mosquito).

US$25-50

The **Coral Gardens Motel** (tel. 4235, fax 4237, www.coralgardens.nu), at Makapu Point six km north of Alofi, has five wooden clifftop bungalows with cooking facilities and excellent views at NZ$80 single or double. A monthly rate of NZ$1,000 is also offered. Sails Bar is on the premises, and there's an excellent swimming hole at the foot of the cliff for the agile and adventurous. Managers Stafford and Salome Guest are very helpful and can make any arrangements you may require.

Right above the Avaiki Caves a bit north of Makefu is the **Anaiki Motel** (Moka Misihepi; tel. 4321, anaiki@niue.nu) with five units in a long block at NZ$60/70 single/double. A hot plate is provided for heating up simple meals. It's a nice place from which to observe the sunset and watch the local fishermen launching their canoes on the evening tide. Your kind hosts will be happy to show you around the village or arrange any tours.

US$50-100

The two-story **Hotel Niue** (Colin Posimani, tel. 4091, fax 4372, niuehotel@niue.nu), on the coast between the airport and Alofi, was built by the government in 1975. In January 2004, the Hotel Niue and nearby hospital were destroyed by Hurricane Heta, and at press time it was still uncertain whether the 32-room hotel would be rebuilt.

The **Namukulu Motel** (Robyn and Joe Wright, tel. 4052, fax 3001, namukulu_motel@niue.nu), at Namukulu nine km north of Alofi, was also badly damaged by Hurricane Heta, so check the current status before heading that way. Prior to the hurricane they had three self-catering bungalows with fridge and TV at NZ$90/$125/$145/$165 single/double/triple/quad. Three of Niue's finest reef-swimming spots are nearby.

The stylish **Matavai Resort** (tel. 4360, fax 4361, matavai@niue.nu), perched on a precipice at the south end of Tamakautonga village, 10 km south of Alofi, was built in 1996 with New Zealand aid money. A collection of tapa and local crafts is displayed on the walls. Luckily, Heta did no damage here. The 24 rooms with fridge, movie channel TV, and seaview balcony in two-story

blocks begin at NZ$150/190 double/triple. The six rooms with air conditioning are the only air-conditioned accommodations on the island. Breakfast is NZ$12.50/18 continental/American (no cooking facilities). Specials may be available when business is slow. The dramatic location has made the managers reluctant to accept children under 12, who might be endangered, and parents or guardians are asked to sign a liability release. The resort features a restaurant, bars, two cliffside swimming pools, and a huge terrace from which you may spot dolphins, turtles, or humpback whales. Several nights a week local cultural groups provide entertainment here, especially after the Saturday night barbecue (NZ$18). Bicycles, golf clubs, and tennis rackets are loaned free. A taxi to or from Alofi might also be NZ$10. Airport transfers are NZ$10 roundtrip.

OTHER PRACTICALITIES

Food

Light snacks are served at **Tavana Cafeteria** (tel. 4334) in the Commercial Center in Alofi and at **Mitaki's Café and Bakery** (tel. 4084) south of town. **Jenna's Cafe** (tel. 4316) near the Mormon Church offers cappuccino, pizza, lasagna, spaghetti, and gelato.

Gabes Food Bar (tel. 4372; weekdays 0800–1400), just south of Alofi, serves burgers, chop suey, hot dogs, fish and chips, and beer. Wednesday nights there's an "island night buffet" featuring Polynesian vegetables and seafoods at NZ$20 pp. Included is a cultural show and live music—ask about this, as dates vary. The coastal views from Gabes are great.

The tap water is safe to drink on Niue.

Entertainment

Kifaga Theater, across the street from the Niue Tourism Office, shows DVDs Fridays at 1930 and Saturdays at 1600 (NZ$5 admission).

The **Niue Sports Club** (tel. 4292), better known as the Top Club, at the golf course near the airport, is nominally private, but visitors are welcome and bar prices low. Village dances take place on Friday and Saturday nights.

Every Wednesday night, provided at least 10

people are interested, the Niue Tourism Office (tel. 4224) organizes a *fia fia* at Hakupu village costing NZ$35 pp including transportation, a village tour, island food, and entertainment. It's well worth going.

Shopping

The **Commercial Center,** a small shopping mall in Alofi, houses the bank, telephone center, butcher shop, gift shop, stationery store, art gallery, and several handicraft shops. Culling's Butcher Shop (tel. 4346) in the Commercial Center sells Niue honey (NZ$3.50 a 500 gram jar) and vanilla.

Liquor is sold at the Bond Store (tel. 4122; Mon.–Thurs. 0900–1230 and 1300–1430, Fri. 0900–1230 and 1300–1530, Sat. 1000–1200) next to the immigration office beside the Commercial Center. Consuming alcohol on the street is prohibited. Alcoholism is a problem here and drunks can suddenly turn aggressive, so be careful what you say in such situations.

There's a market twice a week, held Tuesday 0900–1200 and Friday 0500–1200. The largest supermarkets are Swan-Son Ltd. (tel. 4306) and Jessop's and Daughters (tel. 4074), both in Alofi. Most shops open weekdays 0900–1600, Saturday 1600–1900.

The **Niue Philatelic and Numismatic Bureau** (tel. 4371, fax 4386), next to the post office in the Commercial Center, sells beautiful stamps.

Hinapoto Handcrafts (tel. 4340, tmhekau@ niue.nu) at the Commercial Center sells very fine, firmly woven baskets of pandanus, wound over a coconut-fiber core—among the sturdiest in Polynesia. Excellent pandanus hats are available. Avoid coral and rare shells that cannot be exported from Niue.

Information

The Niue Tourism Office (tel. 4224, fax 4225, www.niueisland.com; weekdays 0900–1600, Sat. 0900–1200) in Alofi's Commercial Center has a good selection of brochures and can answer most questions about the island. They also book activities. Ask for the free Jasons map of Niue.

The post office (tel. 4174) in the Commercial Center sells a 1:50,000 topographical map of Niue for NZ$6.

South Seas Traders (tel. 4295) in the Commercial Center sells a few books about Niue and local newspapers. They're also the local DHL Express agent.

The national library (tel. 4634; weekdays 0800–1600) near the hospital has a good Pacific section. The USP Extension Center (tel. 4049, fax 4315) at Niue High School sells a few books on Niue.

Internet Resources

The site of the Niue Tourism Office, **www.niue island.com,** covers just about everything related to a visit to the island, including fishing, diving, caving, yachting, nature tours, things to see and do, accommodations, eating out, events, medical, getting there, and island transportation. A more locally-oriented site titled simply Niue Island, **www.niueisland.nu,** has photos of communities and local beauty queens, a section on handicrafts, and some general information. The Okakoa Niue Homepage, **www.okakoa.nu,** is a Niue web portal with local news, music archives, a photo gallery, chat room, and a lively discussion forum. Niue News, **www.niuenews.nu,** provides a weather report and news updates. Niue Business News, **www.webpost.net/nb/nbn,** offers some business news but the flashing banner ads and pop-ups are a nuisance. Finally, the site of the Government of Niue, **www.gov.nu,** posts press releases and official news.

Services

The Commercial Center in Alofi contains the post office and the Westpac Bank (tel. 4221; weekdays 0900–1500).

Telecom Niue (tel. 4000; open 24 hours), next to the Niue Tourism Office in the Commercial Center, handles overseas calls and wires. Rates are NZ$1.60 a minute to New Zealand (reduced to NZ$1 2100–0800 weekdays and anytime weekends). To the United States and Europe it's NZ$4.20 a minute, to Australia NZ$2.30. Local calls can be placed for free at this office. You can send a fax to anyone on the island at fax 4010 and they'll be called and asked to pick it up. Niue's telephone code is 683.

The Internet Users Society (Richard Saint

Clair, tel. 1157, www.niue.nu; weekdays 0900–1200), just south of the center, provides free Internet access supported by the .nu domain name.

Public toilets are in front of the immigration office facing the parking lot on the north side of the Commercial Center.

Doctors and dentists are available at Lord Liverpool Hospital (tel. 4100; weekdays 0730–1500).

Land Tours

Island Hopper Vacations (tel. 4307, island.hopper.niue@niue.nu) in the Commercial Center is an inbound tour operator which arranges circle island tours and *fia fia* feasts for groups of at least eight persons.

Talitama Magatogia of **Tali's Tours** (tel. 3405) takes visitors to Ulupaka and Anatoloa caves at NZ$40 pp, including transportation, sandwiches, and lamps. Ulupaka (near Lakepa) is over a kilometer long and coated with black fungus, so be prepared to get a little dirty. Tali's circle-island tour on Monday morning is NZ$30. Pickups are at the Commercial Center in Alofi, otherwise an additional transfer charge applies (NZ$15 to the Matavai Resort).

Misa Kulatea of **Misa's Nature Tours** (tel. 4104) offers guided three-hour hikes in the Huvalu Conservation Area at NZ$35 pp. Unfortunately, some of Misa's trips involve the capture of endangered coconut crabs. Both Tali and Misa usually require at least five clients to run a tour.

Kingdom of Tonga

Introduction

The ancient Kingdom of Tonga, oldest and last remaining Polynesian monarchy, is the only Pacific nation never brought under foreign rule. Though sprinkled over 700,000 square km of ocean from Niuafo'ou between Fiji and Samoa, to the Minerva Reef 290 km southwest of Ata, the total land area of the kingdom is only 691 square km.

Tonga is divided into four main parts: the Tongatapu Group in the south, with the capital, Nuku'alofa; the Ha'apai Group, a far-flung archipelago of low coral islands and soaring volcanoes in the center; the Vava'u Group, with its immense landlocked harbor; and in the north, the isolated, volcanic Niuas. The four groups are pleasingly diverse, each with interesting aspects to enjoy: no other Pacific country is made up of components as scenically varied as these.

More than 100 km of open sea separate Tongatapu and Ha'apai, then it's another 100 km

between Ha'apai and Vava'u, then *another* 300 km north to remote Niuafo'ou and Niuatoputapu. In all, Tonga comprises 170 islands, 42 of them inhabited. Even though they're some of the most densely populated in the Pacific, the Tongan islands are set quite apart from the 21st century. Due to the position just west of the international date line, the Tonga Visitors Bureau uses the marketing slogan "where time begins," but they could just as well use "where time stands still."

The Land

Tonga sits on the eastern edge of the Indo-Australian Plate, which is forced up as the Pacific Plate pushes under it at the Tonga Trench. This long oceanic valley running 2,000 km from Tonga to New Zealand is one of the lowest segments of the ocean floor, in places over 10 km deep. Tonga is on the circum-Pacific Ring of Fire, which extends from New Zealand to Samoa, then jogs over to Vanuatu and the Solomons. Where Tongatapu (a raised atoll), Lifuka (a low coral island), and Vava'u (another uplifted atoll) are today, towering volcanoes once belched fire and brimstone. When they sank, coral polyps gradually built up the islands.

Study the map of Tonga and you'll distinguish four great atolls in a line 350 km long. The two central atolls (Ha'apai) are now largely submerged, with Lifuka and Nomuka the largest remaining islands of each. As Ha'apai sank under the weight of new volcanoes such as Kao and Tofua, the outermost groups, Vava'u and Tongatapu, tilted toward the center, creating cliffs on their outer edges and half-submerged islands facing in. Tonga is moving east-southeast at the rate of 20 millimeters a year and the crack in the earth's crust that originally built Tonga has shifted northwest. Thus, the active volcanoes of today are in a line 50 km west of Ha'apai-Vava'u: Fonuafo'ou, Tofua, Lateiki, Late, Fonualei, and Niuafo'ou have all erupted during the last 200 years.

Climate

The name Tonga means south; it's refreshingly cooler and less humid here than on islands closer to the equator (such as sultry Samoa). Decem-

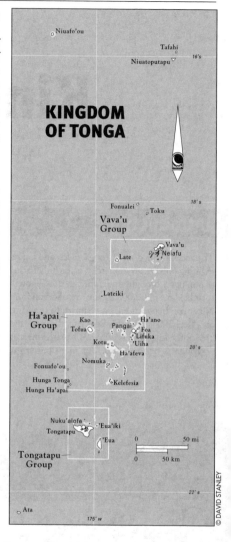

© DAVID STANLEY

ber–April is the hot, rainy season, with especially high humidity January–March. June–August can be cool enough to make a sweater occasionally necessary.

Tonga gets an average of two tropical hurricanes a year, usually between November and April, although they can occur as late as May. Rainfall, temperatures, and the probability of

TONGA HIGHLIGHTS

Lapaha Archaeological Area, Tongatapu: unexcavated pyramids over royal tombs (p. 432)

Li'angahuo 'a Maui, 'Eua: natural stone bridge, sea cliffs (p. 435)

Royal Palace, Nuku'alofa: Victoria structure symbolic of Tonga (p. 417)

Uoleva Island, Ha'apai: long deserted beach, semi-uninhabited island (p. 444)

whale-watching, Vava'u: humpbacks here May–October (p. 455)

hurricanes increase the farther north you go. The southeast trade winds prevail May–November, and easterlies the rest of the year; in Tonga, west and northwest winds herald bad weather. In February and March, north winds bring heat waves and heavy rains.

For local weather information, dial 23-401 in Nuku'alofa during business hours.

HISTORY AND GOVERNMENT

Prehistory

According to myth, the demigod Maui threw a fishhook from Samoa and yanked Tonga out of the sea. He then stomped on the islands to make them flat and suitable for gardening. The historic Polynesians reached Tonga from Fiji or Santa Cruz almost 3,000 years ago. These early arrivals made incised *lapita* pottery, though the art was lost around A.D. 200. Tangaloa, the creator god, descended from the sky and had a son, Aho'eitu, by a beautiful Tongan maiden named Va'epoua. This child became the first hereditary king, or Tu'i Tonga, perhaps around A.D. 950, initiating the "classical era" in Tongan history, which continued until about 1600. Many of the great monuments of Tongatapu were built during this period, which gradually ended after European contact. The Tu'i Tonga were absolute monarchs and the only Tongan males who were not tattooed or circumcised; there was an elaborate etiquette to be observed in all contacts with their subjects.

Fierce Tongan warriors traveled throughout Western Polynesia in large double-hulled canoes *(kalia)*, each capable of carrying up to 200 people. In the 13th century, the domain of the Tu'i Tonga extended all the way from Rotuma in the west through part of the Lau Group, Wallis and Futuna, Samoa, and Tokelau, to Niue in the east. The eventual collapse of this empire led to unrest and a series of Tu'i Tonga assassinations, so in 1470 the 24th Tu'i Tonga delegated much of his political power to a brother, the *hau* or temporal ruler, while retaining the spiritual authority. Later, the power of the *hau* was divided between the Tu'i Ha'atakalaua and Tu'i Kanokupolu, resulting in three distinct lines.

European Contact

Although the Dutchmen Schouten and Le Maire sighted the Niuas in 1616, another Dutchman, Abel Tasman, was the first European to visit Tongatapu and Ha'apai. Arriving on January 19, 1643, as Tongans approached his ship in narrow canoes, Tasman fired a gun—terrifying the chief. A trumpet, violin, and flute were then played in succession to this chief's further astonishment. Tasman received sorely needed food and water to carry on with his journey. At one point he escaped disaster by charging full-tilt over the Nanuku Reef, which was luckily covered with sufficient water to be traversed.

When Captain Cook visited Tonga in 1773, 1774, and 1777, he and his men were received with lavish friendliness—pyramids of food were offered them, and dances and boxing matches in which little girls and women took part were staged in their honor. (The skillful Tongan pugilists made short work of Cook's crew in a competition.) Some say the islanders intended to roast and eat Cook and his men as part of the feast, but Cook's profuse thanks at his reception prompted them to change their minds. Cook presented the Tu'i Tonga with a male Galapagos tortoise, which was left to wander blind in the royal garden right up until 1966, when it died at the ripe old age of over 200. Ever since Cook's visit, Tonga has been known as "The Friendly Islands." Cook never visited Vava'u, which was only "discovered" in 1781 by the Spaniard Antonio Mourelle.

KINGDOM OF TONGA

TONGA AT A GLANCE

ISLAND	POPULATION (2000 est.)	AREA (square km)
'Eua	5,060	87
Tongatapu	68,691	259
Ha'apai Group	8,346	109
Vava'u Group	16,117	119
Niuas*	2,070	72
Tonga	**100,284**	**646****

* Niuafo'ou, Niuatoputapu, Tafahi
** inhabited islands only

The Formation of a Nation

European contact led to a decline in population, as warring chiefs turned newly acquired muskets and cannons on each other. The new armaments also allowed Tongan warriors to conquer the Lau Group of Fiji about this time. Members of the London Missionary Society arrived in 1797, in the middle of these civil wars, but were unable to attract a following, and by 1804 all had left.

A British Wesleyan (Methodist) missionary, Rev. William Lawry, arrived in 1822. He and his associates built the first school in Tonga in 1829, and in 1831 printed the first book, the Bible of course. Their most noteworthy convert (in 1831) was Taufa'ahau, chief of Ha'apai, who defeated two rival dynasties with the missionaries' help and in 1845 became King George Tupou I, ruler of a united Tonga. In 1862, he freed the Tongan people from forced labor on the estates of the chiefs while making hereditary nobles of the chiefs. Tupou I decreed that each of his subjects be allotted a *tax'api* consisting of a town lot and 3.34 hectares of farmland for only T$3.20 annual rental. At the same time, the king established constitutional government, with a Privy Council of his choice and representation for both nobles and commoners in a Legislative Assembly.

This system, institutionalized in the Tongan Constitution of November 4, 1875, remains in force today. A year later, Germany concluded a Treaty of Friendship, which recognized Tongan independence and the sovereignty of the king. Similar treaties were signed with England (1879) and the United States (1888). The king's closest adviser in all of this was a Wesleyan missionary, Rev. Shirley Baker, who served as premier during the 1880s. Tupou I died in 1893 at 97 years of age, the creator of a unified Christian Tonga and one of the most remarkable men of the 19th century. The pervasive influence of the missionaries, who dominated Tonga from the early 19th century onward, can still be experienced any Sunday.

The 20th Century

Tonga (along with Japan, Thailand, Nepal, and a few Middle Eastern states) is one of the few countries in the world never to experience colonization by a European power. Germany had strong influence in Tonga during the late 19th century and wanted to include it in its colonial empire, but bowed out to the British in exchange for a free hand in Samoa. In 1900, Tupou I's grandson, King George Tupou II (ruled 1893-1918), signed a new Treaty of Friendship with Britain, which gave the latter control of Tonga's foreign affairs as a means of forestalling encroachments by other colonial powers. The British protection remained in effect until 1970, but the rule of the royal family continued unbroken.

Magnificent, much-loved Queen Salote Tupou III ruled Tonga from 1918 until her death in

VAVA'U'S CLIMATE

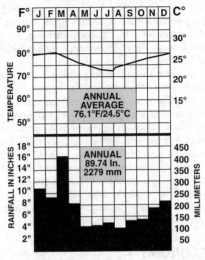

1965. Her achievements included the reunification of part of the Wesleyan church and the development of public health and education services. In 1953, she won the hearts of millions by riding through London in an open coach, despite torrential rain, at Queen Elizabeth's coronation. In fact, she was only observing the Tongan custom of showing respect for royalty by appearing before them unprotected in bad weather. (Actor Noel Coward quipped that the diminutive Asian sultan riding next to Salote in the carriage was "her lunch.")

Although just short of his mother's two-meter height, H.R.H. King Taufa'ahau Tupou IV, the present monarch, looks every bit the Polynesian king he is. As crown prince during WW II, he studied at the University of Sydney, becoming the first Tongan to earn a university degree. He served as prime minister from 1949 until his coronation in 1967. Tupou IV initiated a cautious modernization program, opening Tonga to the world by having the airport upgraded for jet aircraft and approving the construction of the first large hotels. On June 4, 1970, he reestablished Tonga's full sovereignty, which allowed Tonga to receive aid money from other countries.

For almost three decades, Tupou IV has steered Tonga on a conservative course. Yet way back in 1976, Tonga became the first South Pacific country to establish diplomatic relations with the Soviet Union, leading to an absurd panic over alleged Soviet expansionism in the Pacific. This worked to Tonga's advantage, as overdue aid money from Australia, New Zealand, and the United States came pouring in. Unlike Samoa, which has had diplomatic relations with the Peoples Republic of China for decades, Tonga recognized the Taiwan-based Republic of China until 1998. Then it abruptly switched recognition to Beijing, which facilitated Tonga's admission to the United Nations in 1999.

Government

Tonga's system of government (www.pmo.gov.to) is classified as a constitutional monarchy, though it would be more appropriate to call it a monarchy with a constitution, as the king rules absolutely here. He appoints the 12 members of the Cabinet, including the governors of Ha'apai and Vava'u, who retain their posts for life. They sit in the 30-seat Legislative Assembly or Parliament, along with nine members who represent the 33 Nobles of the Realm, and another nine members elected every three years to represent Tonga's 100,000 commoners. The king appoints one of the nobles as speaker of parliament (the king also decides who will hold the 33 noble titles). The king can dissolve parliament, dismiss ministers, veto legislation, suspend habeas corpus, and proclaim martial law at will.

Until 1998, the king's eldest son and heir, Crown Prince Tupouto'a, was minister of foreign affairs and defense. He resigned on his 50th birthday to devote himself to business activities, and the king's youngest son, Prince 'Ulukalala Lavaka Ata, replaced him. In 2000, Prince Lavaka also became prime minister. While Lavaka is an austere conservative in the mold of his father, Tupouto'a is a temperamental mover and shaker with no time for inefficiency. In a 1999 interview with a Tongan magazine, Tupouto'a lambasted the "incompetence and stupidity" of top Tongan bureaucrats and said Tongans preferred attending funerals to work. A long overdue shake up can be expected when he assumes the throne.

Although appointed by the king, the judiciary is independent, with the highest court of appeal consisting of three judges from other Commonwealth countries. Despite the absence of any external threat, Tonga maintains a 300-person defense force, with facilities behind the royal palace, at the airport, and near Queen Salote Wharf. These troops exercise with American Special Forces and are available to suppress pro-democracy unrest at any time. The bulk of the local media is government-owned, and formal criticism of the royal family is prohibited. There are no municipal councils; Nuku'alofa is administered directly by the central government.

Yet as educational levels increase and Tongan commoners become economically independent, the power of the privileged few is being called into question. There have been numerous allegations of corruption, and church leaders have backed increased democracy. In 1992, four of the nine people's representatives banded together to form a pro-democracy grouping, which in 1998 became the Human Rights and Democracy Movement in Tonga. Though not a political party, the HRDMT presently counts seven of the nine elected members of parliament as members. Tongatapu representative 'Akilisi Pohiva is a pioneer of the movement, and HRDMT leader Lopeti Senituli is well known around the region as a former director of the Pacific Concerns Resource Center in Fiji.

The old guard has a long history of using libel suits to intimidate the elected members, and journalists have been imprisoned for reporting on corruption or abuses of power. In 2003, an independent Tongan-language newspaper published in New Zealand was banned in Tonga, and requests by the HRDMT to be allowed to operate a radio station have been refused. New "anti-terrorism" legislation introduced in October 2002 includes provisions designed to terrorize the democratic opposition. As yet, no one questions the continued existence of the monarchy, but constitutional reform is very much a topic of discussion in Tonga these days. In recent years, pro-democracy candidates have won

a majority of the popular vote in every election, and the royalists only hold onto power thanks to Tonga's undemocratic laws. In October 2003, an unprecedented 8,000 Tongans marched through Nuku'alofa in a demonstration against a constitutional amendment suppressing freedom of the press.

In a way, Tonga's current political impasse is a direct result of the absence of colonization, because a European system of representative government was not instituted in Tonga as part of a normal decolonization process, as happened in virtually every other island state. The world has changed beyond recognition since 1875, yet Tonga's Victorian constitution remains the law of the land. This cannot last forever, and the future of the monarchy may well depend on its ability to adapt to the times and accept a parliament with an elected majority.

ECONOMY
Agriculture and Land

In Tonga's feudal system, all land is property of the crown but administered by nobles who allot it to the common people. The king and nobles retain 27 percent of the land for their own use, while the government owns another 18 percent. Although Tongan commoners still have a right to the 3.34-hectare *tax'api* granted them by King George Tupou I, there's no longer enough land to go around, and 10,000 Tongans are landless. This system has not been altered substantially since 1862, and a 1976 parliamentary law intended to redistribute unused land was vetoed by the king. Frustrations with the system are relieved by migration to New Zealand, Australia, and the United States. If those avenues were to close, Tonga would face serious unrest. Foreigners cannot purchase land, and even leasing requires cabinet approval.

Only half the population is involved in the cash economy; the rest live from subsistence agriculture, fishing, and collecting. The production of food, housing, and handicrafts used by the producer is higher than the value of all goods sold for cash, a situation rarely reflected in official statistics. The staples are yams, taro, manioc, and sweet potato. Crops are rotated, and up to two-thirds of a garden is left fallow at any time. Deforestation is a problem on islands like 'Eua, where land is still being cleared for agriculture (73 percent of Tonga's land is already used for pastures and crops, the highest level in the Pacific islands).

The biggest cash crop is pumpkins (squash), and since its introduction in 1987, this vegetable has become Tonga's biggest export by far, shipped mostly to Japan by air and worth T$15 million a year. Over 13,000 tonnes of Tongan pumpkins supply about half Japan's requirements for November and December, a "niche market" producers in other parts of the world can't cover for climatic reasons. Some 700 small farmers grow pumpkins July–December, and overproduction has led to soil degradation, groundwater pollution, deforestation, and an increase in pests. Tonga's overdependence on this monoculture carries with it the risk of economic collapse, should the Japanese market evaporate due to competition from other producers or a fall in yields caused by depleted soils, plant disease, or drought. Vanilla is seen as an alternative, and the production, though still small, fetches top prices on world markets. Coffee is another niche crop of growing importance.

Trade and Development

Tonga's main exports are pumpkins, vanilla, tuna, copra, handicrafts, kava, and taro. Although it had a favorable trade balance prior to 1960, Tonga now imports seven times as much as it exports, with food imports alone exceeding all exports. Australia and New Zealand profit most from the trade imbalance, selling food, machinery, manufactured goods, and fuels to Tonga. Japan, Australia, the European Union, New Zealand, the United Nations Development Program, and the Utah-based Church of Latter-day Saints are Tonga's largest aid donors, and total aid compensates for a third of the trade deficit. Fifty-five percent of the budget is currently spent on salaries for the cumbersome civil service.

In 1980, the government created a Small Industries Center (SIC) in the eastern section of Nuku'alofa for companies producing consumer goods for export to Australia and New Zealand under the regional free-trade agreement, SPARTECA, which was designed to correct the imbalance. In recent years, the value of SPARTECA had declined due to "globalization," and Tongan exports of knitwear, leather jackets, and footballs have been pushed off Australasian markets by competitors in Asia. Today, companies in the SIC produce mostly for the tariff-sheltered local market.

Traditional agricultural exports to New Zealand such as bananas have been wiped out by transnational producers and strict quarantine requirements. The replanting of Tonga's aging coconut plantations has been inadequate and copra exports have dwindled to almost nothing in recent years. Commercial fishing is on the increase, with longline vessels supplying tuna to the Pago Pago canneries. High quality fish such as red snapper is chilled and air freighted to restaurants in Honolulu and Tokyo. Fish now account for a quarter of Tonga's exports.

Tonga is very much a part of the third world. The T$70 million a year remitted by Tongans living abroad, the country's largest single source of income, is crucial to maintaining the balance of payments, covering over half of Tonga's import bill. In coming years, these amounts could decline as emigrants lose touch with relatives and friends back home. Meanwhile, rural areas are neglected as government facilities and light industry are concentrated in Nuku'alofa. A quarter of all Tongans now live in the capital, and hundreds more commute daily from outlying villages. Shanty-towns have sprung up in the suburbs of Nuku'alofa, and there's a growing gap between the haves and have-nots. Taxation has shifted from rich to poor as income tax and company taxes are replaced by a sales tax currently at five percent. Labor unions are banned.

As in places like Indonesia and the Philippines, the ruling family has used its political clout to assemble extensive business interests. Crown Prince Tupouto'a is a major shareholder in banking, brewing, fishing, electricity, telecommunications, insurance, and real estate companies (The Shoreline Group, www.tonfon.to), while Princess Pilolevu Tuita is involved in satellite communications and the duty-free trade (80 percent of cigarette sales in Tonga are "duty-free"). According to New Zealand journalist Michael Field, the crown prince and princess have been vying for influence, and Tonga's abrupt diplomatic switch from Taiwan to China in 1998 was a result of lobbying by Princess P. Though it appears that the princess currently has the king's ear, Prince Lavaka is known to support his elder brother.

Satellite Communications

In 1990, Tonga scored a coup by claiming half a dozen unoccupied orbital positions for geostationary satellites, which it registered with the International Telecommunications Union over the objections of most large satellite communications companies. A company called Tongasat was formed with Princess Pilolevu as 80 percent shareholder. The other 20 percent went to an American telecommunications expert named Matt Nilson, who came up with the original idea.

One condition for the registration was that the orbital slots actually had to be used within 10 years, so Tongasat has been actively engaged in leasing Tonga's valuable slots. Several satellites have been launched into orbit from Kazakhstan, and other slots have been sub-let to Asian companies (Beijing is the target market). Tongasat and the government have split income from this arrangement: *Forbes Magazine* reports that Princess P herself has pocketed a cool US$25 million. The Tongan government currently receives over US$1 million a year in royalties.

A similar scheme involves the marketing of Tonga's internet code .to for use in registering desirable domain names already occupied under the .com ending. Tonic (www.tonic.to), a joint venture between Crown Prince Tupouto'a and California computer experts, has sold thousands of domain names at US$50 a year each. (Despite all the high tech dabbling, Tonga's regular domestic telephone network is unchanged since the early 1950s, despite the expensive wireless cell phone service introduced in 2002.)

Sale of Passports and Flags

In recent years Tonga has peddled its nationality by selling Tongan passports to Hong Kong Chinese and others in need of an alternative nation-

ality. In 1983, Tonga began selling "Tongan Protected Persons" passports to all comers at US$10,000 a shot. Since the bearers still required a visa to enter Tonga, many countries refused to recognize them. Thus in 1984, legislation was passed allowing ordinary Tongan passports and naturalization certificates to be issued to anyone willing to pay US$20,000—among the takers were Imelda Marcos and her children. This was questioned by commoner members of the Tongan parliament, who pointed out that the five-year residency requirement was being ignored, so in 1988 the previous legislation was repealed, but the sales strangely continued.

In 1989, Mr. 'Akilisi Pohiva, the leading people's representative in parliament, filed suit against the government, claiming that the sale of passports to foreigners was unlawful. It took Pohiva a year to formulate his case, then another year to get a court date, and in 1991, just as the Supreme Court was about to act, the king called an emergency session of parliament to alter the constitution to legalize things. The government used its large majority of appointed members to ram through the amendment, and on March 7, 1991, 2,500 people marched through Nuku'alofa to the Royal Palace to present petitions protesting the constitutional changes, the largest popular demonstration of its kind in Tongan history.

Many countries, including Australia, New Zealand, and Fiji, do not recognize these mail-order passports, and genuine Tongans traveling on bona fide Tongan passports often face unexpected immigration hassles abroad as a result of the scam. Many of the buyers ended up in Nuku'alofa running small businesses in competition with existing Tongan businesses, and ethnic tensions have been aroused. By 1998, when the practice finally stopped, some 7,000 Tongan passports had been sold.

In 2001, most of the estimated US$26 million earned through the passport scheme was lost on dubious investments in a Nevada asset management company made on the advice of the king's official court jester, a former Bank of America employee named Jesse Bogdonoff. Two Tongan cabinet ministers were designated as scapegoats and sacked by Princess P, although the king himself was ultimately responsible. Some 600 Chinese business people and their families were given one year to leave the kingdom. Meanwhile the king pushed ahead with a new pet project, the ironic production of security nets against sharks!

A similar ill-fated scam involved a Tongan "flag of convenience" shipping registry. In 2001, a Greek businessman was granted the right to allow foreign vessels to fly the Tongan flag in order to avoid taxation and government regulation. This came to an ignominious end in early 2002 when a Tonga-registered ship owned by an Iraqi based in Yemen was seized in the Mediterranean by Israeli commandos, who found it to be loaded with 50 tons of weapons destined for Palestinian militants. Another Tongan-registered vessel was caught carrying 15 Pakistani men with al-Qaeda connections, and a third seized in Croatia allegedly had aboard missile parts destined for Iraq. After banner headlines in American newspapers about Tongan links to "terrorism," the king suspended the shipping registry, but not before the Greek registrar absconded with US$300,000 in fees owing to Tonga.

Biotechnology

From marketing the national identity, the government has passed to selling the physical identity of its people. In August 2000, the Ministry of Health agreed in principle to sell to an Australian biotechnology company exclusive rights to the DNA of the Tongan people. Tonga has an

THE WHALES OF TONGA

In June or July several hundred humpback whales arrive in Tonga from their summer feeding areas in Antarctica. They spend the austral winter in Tonga, mating and bearing their young, before heading south again in October or November. This annual migration is necessary because there's little food for whales in Tongan waters but the calves require warm seas to survive because they're poorly insulated at birth. During the first few months of their lives the baby whales grow at a rate of 45 kilograms a day. They're solely dependent on their mother's milk for sustenance, and by the end of the season a nursing female may have lost 25 percent of her body weight. As soon as the offspring are ready in spring, the animals return to their summer home thousands of kilometers south to fatten up on a tiny plankton called krill. Pregnancy lasts 12 months, just long enough for the mother to put on adequate weight in Antarctica to have a child in Tonga.

While in Tonga the humpbacks engage in elaborate courtship displays and mating rituals that can last for hours. The males sing complex songs that have been studied and found to contain syllables and rhyming phrases. During the displays the humpbacks often breach, and to see a 14.5-meter male rise from the sea, five-meter flippers flapping at his side, only to crash back on his side, is truly spectacular. A female chaperoning her calf is another favorite sight. Southern hemisphere humpbacks have a characteristic white belly, quite different from the black bellies of northern hemisphere humpbacks, and individuals are recognizable by their patterns.

Humpbacks prefer shallow waters close to shore, and are often curious about humans, characteristics that have worked to their disadvantage. From a population of around 100,000 in the 19th century, southern hemisphere humpback whales presently number only about 3,000, a drop of 97 percent. Subsistence shore whaling was only prohibited in Tonga in 1979 and the 10 whales previously taken each season did have an impact. However, it was the collapse of the Soviet Union in 1991 that contributed more to the whales' survival, since it put an end to illegal whaling from Soviet ships.

At a meeting of the International Whaling Commission in 2002, the South Pacific countries tried to establish a regional whale sanctuary. Sadly, strong opposition from Japan defeated the proposition (Japan is the only country that continues to hunt whales in the Pacific Ocean). In 2003, most countries around the region declared their 200-nautical-mile exclusive economic zones as whale sanctuaries, although the Japanese continue to do their dirty business in Antarctica.

extremely high 14 percent diabetes rate, and the researchers had hoped to identify genes related to diabetes with the intention of developing new drugs. Obesity, cancer, and heart disease were also to be studied. The Tongan's ethnic isolation and obsession with genealogy make them ideal subjects for such studies.

But as usual, the Tongans themselves weren't consulted about the sale of their own blood for use in mapping their genes, and after considerable controversy, the deal was stopped in August 2001. There were several attempts by American companies to patent the human T-cell lines of isolated groups of Pacific islanders during the 1990s, and bio-piracy has emerged as one of the last frontiers of colonization in the Pacific.

(The Australian guidebooks sweep most of the information just provided conveniently under the carpet and are generally uncritical in order to boost book sales in Nuku'alofa.)

Tourism

Earnings from tourism are higher than all exports combined, and a high proportion of the tourist dollar remains in Tonga because of the predominance of small, locally owned guesthouses and motels. Tonga is off the beaten track and is seldom overrun by tourists (Fiji gets 11 times as many visitors). About 35,000 tourists a year visit Tonga, coming from New Zealand, the United States, Australia, Germany, and Fiji, in that order. Nearly half are overseas Tongans visiting friends and relatives. The millions of government dollars spent subsidizing bankrupt Royal Tongan Airlines must be subtracted from tourism earnings.

There has been much talk of developing Vava'u as Tonga's main international tourism center, and the European Union has provided funds to upgrade Vava'u's airport to allow direct flights from Fiji. Yet almost all visitors are still channeled through less interesting Tongatapu. Vava'u has been a base for one of the South Pacific's most important yacht charter operations for many years, and since 1995, whale-watching has been developed. Scuba diving, kayaking, fishing, and cultural tourism are all readily available at Vava'u. The inefficient official infrastructure has

prevented Tonga from taking off as a major tourist destination.

THE PEOPLE

For visitors, Tonga is its culture and people. The Tongans are exceptionally relaxed, impassive toward delays, etc., and with the world's lowest death rate, it seems Tongans even pass away slowly. The happy lifestyle is summed up in expressions like *mo'ui fiemalie* (a contented life), *mo'ui nonga* (a peaceful life), *nofo fiefia* (living happily), and *nofo fakalata* (making others feel at home). It's also said that if a Tongan loses his identity, he will slowly become cold and die.

Tonga is typical of developing countries, with its large families and young population. Most Tongans reside in small villages near their bush gardens, and except in the Europeanized areas, isolated houses along the roads are rare. Most Tongans live in tin-roofed wooden or cement block houses with electricity and running water, and very few still live in traditional thatched *fale*. With 150 people per square km, Tonga is one of the most densely populated countries in the Pacific (twice as dense as the Cooks, three times as dense as Fiji). Yet despite a high birth rate, emigration has kept population figures stable at around 100,000 since the 1970s. Around 2,000 Tongans a year leave the country, many for good, and some 60,000 now live in the United States, 41,000 in New Zealand, and 35,000 in Australia.

In Tonga, women have traditionally enjoyed a higher social status than in some other parts of Polynesia, due to the *fahu* system, which gives Tongan women certain authority over male family members. The eldest sister is the family matriarch, exercising considerable control over younger brothers, nephews, and nieces. Public life in Tonga, however, is almost completely dominated by men, due to sexist succession and land ownership laws, as well as cultural norms.

The missionaries increased the importance of the family unit. Each family member has a role, with the older persons commanding the most respect. Children may reside with an aunt or uncle just as easily as with their parents and are taught obedience from an early age, which is why they are so much better behaved than Samoan children. The most important occasions in Tongan life are first and twenty-first birthdays, marriages, and funerals. Tonga has one of the highest levels of school enrollment in the South Pacific, and 99.6 percent of Tongans are literate.

Acculturation is proceeding fast in Nuku'alofa, where most families now have a VCR, and the dozens of video rental outlets do roaring business. There are few controls on videos, and Tongans can see everything from horror to soft pornography on their screens. The videos have effectively done away with *faka'apa'apa,* or respect between brother and sister, an old taboo that would never have allowed them to sit in the same room and watch a sex scene.

Tongans have a long traditional history, and many can name up to 39 generations by heart. There is little social mobility: A commoner can never become a noble, though a noble or a member of the royal family can be stripped of his title. Commoners have been appointed Cabinet ministers through education and ability, however, and may be elevated to the rank of *matapule* (talking chief), a spokesperson for the king or a noble. The nobles are fairly easy to spot. They're the overweight men in traditional costume who seem to command authority but do nothing. Ordinary Tongans must use a special dialect quite different from everyday Tongan when speaking to a noble or member of the royal family. An equivalent English example for "eating heartily" might go as follows: commoners *gorge,* the nobles *feed,* and the king *dines.*

To a Tongan, great physical size is the measure of beauty—Tongan women begin increasing prodigiously in beauty from age 15 onward.

Traditional Dress

The *ta'ovala* is the distinctive Tongan traditional skirt. The custom may have originated when Tongan mariners used canoe sails to cloak their nakedness. Made of a finely woven pandanus-leaf mat, the *ta'ovala* is worn around the waist. The men secure it with a coconut-fiber cord, while the women wear a *kiekie* waistband. The sight of a group of Tongan women on the road, each with a huge pandanus mat tied around herself, is truly striking. Worn especially on formal occasions, these mats are often prized heirlooms. The king and queen wear European dress to a European function, but dress in their plaited *ta'ovala,* tied around the waist over the *vala* (skirt or kilt), and wear sandals or go barefoot to a Tongan ceremony or entertainment. Tongans dress in black and wear huge *ta'ovalas* when mourning. If an important member of the royal family dies, the national period of mourning can last as long as six months, with Tongans required to dress in black and all places of sports or entertainment closed for the duration.

Religion

The bold red cross in the upper left corner of the royal red Tongan flag symbolizes the facts of life in this country. The Tongan Constitution (drafted by Methodist missionary Shirley Baker) declares the Sabbath day forever sacred: It's unlawful to work, hold sporting events, or trade on Sunday. Contracts signed that day are void. Most tours are also canceled, though picnic trips do run to the small islands off Nuku'alofa. All shops and most restaurants are closed on Sunday. The Sabbath is so strong that even the Seventh-Day Adventists here observe Sunday as the Lord's Day (not Saturday). They claim this is permissible because of the "bend" in the international date line, but it would be intolerable to have two Sundays in Tonga!

Tongans are great churchgoers—a third of all Tongans and most of the noble class are members of the mainstream Free Wesleyan Church. Three other branches of Methodism also have large followings in Tonga: the Free Church of Tonga, the Church of Tonga, and the Tokaikolo Christian Fellowship. In addition, there are 15,000 Mormons, 13,500 Roman Catholics, and 5,000 Seventh-Day Adventists. Smaller groups include the Anglicans, Assemblies of God, and Baha'is. In all, 16 official churches are active in the country, and missionaries from new groups are arriving all the time. Between 1966 and 1992, affiliation in the new religious groups increased from 9.7 percent to 29.5 percent of Tongans, as membership in all four Methodist churches declined.

Attend the service at Centenary Church (Free

CEMETERIES

Tongan cemeteries are unique. Usually set in a grove of frangipani trees, the graves are strange, sandy mounds marked with flags and banners, surrounded by inverted beer bottles, artificial flowers, seashells, and black volcanic rocks. Recent innovations are the miniature houses and concrete tombs, painted in the national colors red and white or decorated with art. Prior to emancipation in 1862 the graves of commoners were unmarked, and when popular cemeteries began to materialize, the Tongans adopted a scaled-down *langi* form that had been used for centuries by nobility. To honor the dead, valuable gifts such as tapa cloth, fine mats, quilts, and family heirlooms are placed on the graves, and these are *tapu*. Family members, great mats tied about their waists, spend several weeks after the funeral sitting next to the burial, leaving the area at night for fear of ghosts. They continue to visit with declining frequency for about a year, but after that the grave is abandoned as it's believed that the spirit of the deceased remains and can cause sickness among the living and even another death. On public holidays such as All Saint's Day and Christmas people return to the cemeteries to clean up the family plots.

Wesleyan) in Nuku'alofa Sunday at 1000 to hear the magnificent church choir and perhaps catch a glimpse of the royal family. Gentlemen are expected to wear coats and ties (although tourists are usually admitted without). After church, the rest of the day is spent relaxing, strolling, and visiting friends—what Tongans like to do anyway, so it wasn't hard for the missionaries to convince them to set aside a whole day for it.

The Mormons

Mormons account for around 15 percent of the population of Tonga, the highest such ratio in the world. The Church of Latter-day Saints has become the largest private employer in the kingdom, spending more on construction than even the government, and the American church sends far more financial aid to its Tongan flock than the U.S. government provides to Tonga as a whole. Mormon missionary efforts in Tonga are aimed at making this the first country on earth with a Mormon majority.

Assembly line Mormon churches (with their inevitable basketball courts) are popping up in villages all over Tonga, as the children of Israel convert in droves to be eligible for the free buildings, schools, sporting facilities, and children's lunches. Many Tongans become "school Mormons," joining as their children approach high school age and dropping out as they complete college in Hawaii. Unlike Cook Islanders and American Samoans, Tongans don't have the free right of entry to a larger country, so church help in gaining a toehold in Honolulu or Salt Lake City is highly valued.

Mormonism has a slightly lower profile in Nuku'alofa, however, because the king, a Wesleyan, is reputed to be uncomfortable with the new fast-faith religion. A building behind the International Date Line Hotel was a Mormon church until it was judged too close to the palace for comfort and was converted into a Chinese restaurant. The present Nuku'alofa Tonga Temple, the largest building in Tonga, is beside Mormon-operated Liahona High School near Houma on the opposite side of the island. Recently the king has been refusing to renew any Mormon land leases. Yet the Church of Jesus Christ of Latter-day Saints is a bastion of conservatism and a strong supporter of the political status quo (which is rather ironic in view of U.S. posturing on democracy and human rights in other selected parts of the world).

CONDUCT AND CUSTOMS

The key to getting things done in Tonga is knowing how to find the right person. Tongans hate to say no, and if you ask someone to do something that isn't really their responsibility, they may give the impression of agreeing to do it, but in fact nothing will happen. If a Tongan breaks a promise, the best approach is to pretend to be grateful, even if they've inconvenienced you. Causing a Tongan to lose face is the worst thing you can do.

Tongans in official positions may seem sluggish and could keep you waiting while they chat with friends over the phone or read the paper. Just keep smiling and be patient: they'll notice that and will usually go out of their way to be helpful once they get around to you. Impatiently demanding service will have the opposite effect. (It's illegal to anger or threaten a civil servant or member of the nobility in Tonga.)

Both men and women appearing in public topless are punished with a T$20 fine. Of course, this doesn't apply to men at the beach. As in Victorian England, the Tongans usually go swimming fully dressed—most of them don't even have bathing suits. For a Tongan woman to appear in a halter top and miniskirt is almost unthinkable, and female travelers, too, will feel more accepted in skirts or long pants than in shorts. A woman in a bathing suit on a beach anywhere other than in front of a resort will attract unwelcome attention, and it would be prudent to keep a T-shirt on at all times and to cover your legs with a *lavalava* while out of the water. It's also considered bad form to kiss or even hold hands in public. (Despite all the strident public morality, in private, Tongans are often sexually permissive, and it's commonplace for married men to have affairs.)

Be careful with your gear in Tonga, as thefts occur all too often—don't tempt people by leaving valuables unattended. Even hotel rooms are unsafe. Thus, *everything* left unattended will be pilfered, especially if it's out where anyone could

have taken it. This also applies to food left in the communal fridge at a guesthouse, or the drinks on your table if you get up to dance at a disco. Items left on the beach while you're swimming will have vanished by the time you come out of the water. Armed robbery, on the other hand, is almost unheard of.

Beware of Tongans bearing gifts—don't accept anything unless you're willing to pay for it. Often Tongan women and children will give unsuspecting tourists flowers, necklaces, or handicrafts with the sole intention of shaming them into paying money. When making purchases at shops or contracting services, pay attention to the price or you could easily be overcharged. The concept of "tourist price" is alive and well in Tonga.

Royal ownership of the land has led to several important differences with Samoa, where most land is village owned. Tonga's public beaches and roads tend to be much dirtier than those in Samoa, largely because the responsibility for keeping such places clean is not felt by the local Tongan villagers. On the plus side (for visitors), there are usually no customary admission fees to swim off Tongan beaches or visit caves, waterfalls, etc, since the king isn't likely to be around to collect the money. In Samoan villages, such fees are routinely charged by locals who have an incentive to keep their property clean.

Dogs can be a nuisance in Tonga, chasing cyclists and barking through the night. They can be especially aggressive as you approach a private residence, but pretending to pick up a stone will usually be enough to scare them away. (Looking at it another way, you'll see some of the most wretched, abused dogs in the world in Tonga, and it's not surprising that they bite.)

KINGDOM OF TONGA

Exploring the Islands

HIGHLIGHTS

Tonga stands out for its regal culture, which can be traced from the Ha'amonga trilithon on northeastern Tongatapu through the ancient *langi* or royal tombs of Mu'a to the gingerbread Royal Palace in downtown Nuku'alofa. Traditional arts and crafts are nurtured and preserved at the Tonga National Center just south of town. The country's most charming town, however, is Neiafu, which faces Vava'u's magnificent Port of Refuge Harbor. In fact, along with Levuka in Fiji and Gizo in the Solomons, Neiafu is one of the three most picturesque towns in the South Pacific.

Tonga's foremost natural feature is probably its coastal cliffs, especially the striking limestone formations at Keleti Beach Resort on Tongatapu, the east coast of 'Eua Island, and the north coast of Vava'u. Lovers of wildlife will not wish to miss the flying foxes of Kolovai on Tongatapu. Humpback whales come to Ha'apai and Vava'u to mate and calve July–October, and there are whale-watching cruises from Neiafu at this time.

SPORTS AND RECREATION

Although Tonga's preeminent hiking areas are on 'Eua and its only golf course is on Tongatapu, it is Vava'u that has the most to offer water sports enthusiasts. Vava'u is a famous sailing locale with one of the South Pacific's largest yacht charter operations. It's also perfect for ocean kayaking with lots of lovely protected waterways; a kayak touring company operates in this area. Deep-sea anglers too will find Tonga's top charter fishing boats based here. There's also undeveloped potential for windsurfing at Vava'u, but the mecca for regular reef-break surfers is Ha'atafu Beach on Tongatapu. In Samoa the surfing waves tend to be far offshore (boat required), while in Tonga you can often swim out from shore. It's no place for beginners, however. Southern swells arrive May–September, northern swells from December–February.

Scuba divers are well catered to by professional dive shops in Nuku'alofa, Lifuka, and Neiafu, with many outstanding diving possibilities. Snorkelers have even more options, beginning with the island resorts off Nuku'alofa, all of which operate day trips by boat. The finest snorkeling off Tongatapu itself is reputed to be at Ha'atafu Beach. At Ha'apai there's excellent snorkeling at the Captain Cook Beach Resort on Uoleva Island. At Vava'u, visitors can get in some excellent snorkeling by taking a day excursion from Neiafu by boat.

MUSIC AND DANCE

Music

Tongan church music is renowned and the singing of choir and congregation is often backed by a Salvation Army-style brass band. Traditionally a *lali* (slit drum) is beaten just before the service to call the faithful to prayer. The Tongans transformed the hymns taught by early missionaries, singing in minor instead of major. They also created hymns of their own, called *hiva usu*, which are closer to traditional chants than the imported hymns. The *hiva usu* are now most commonly sung at services of the Free Church of Tonga and the Church of Tonga, the more conservative of Tonga's four branches of Methodism.

Harmonious Polynesian singing can also be heard at kava-drinking sessions *(faikava)*, when groups of men sing popular Tongan songs to entertain themselves. Tonga's traditional string bands (guitar, violin, banjo, bass, and ukulele) have been upstaged by modern electric pop bands, though the former may still be heard at hotels, private parties, or even *faikava*. Public festivities and parades are animated by college brass bands. The traditional *fangufangu* (bamboo nose flute) would probably have died out had not the 'Atenisi Institute in Nuku'alofa begun to teach its use. The *'utete* (jew's harp) is a child's toy formed from a coconut leaf held horizontally across the mouth by a palm leaf midrib, which is twanged. Other Tongan instruments include the *nafa* (skin drum), *kele'a* (conch shell), and the *tutua* (tapa-beating mallet). The *mimiha* (panpipes) seen by Captain Cook are no longer used.

Dance

Traditional Tongan dances are stories sung by the singers and acted out by the dancers. As in Samoa, the words are represented by movements of the hands and feet, not the hips. The graceful movements of the female dancers contrast with those of the males, who dance with great vigor. A *punake* is a combination poet, composer, and choreographer who writes the songs then trains and leads the dancers.

The *lakalaka* is a standing dance that begins slowly but builds to a rhythmic finish. The male and female dancers stand on opposite sides of the stage, backed by a choir, and everyone sings a song especially composed for the occasion. A major *lakalaka* can involve hundreds of people and last half an hour. The *ma'ulu'ulu* is a sitting dance usually performed by groups of women accompanied by *nafa* on formal occasions. Standing girls perform the *ula*. Unlike these, the *kailao*, or war dance, has no accompanying song. The stamping feet, shouts of the leader, and insistent rhythm of the drums combine to make this dance popular among visitors. Very different is the dignified *tau'olunga*, in which a girl dances alone, knees held closely together, at weddings or village functions.

Your best chance to see real Tongan dancing is a fund-raising event (watch how the Tongans contribute, then give your share), on national holidays or during visits by VIPs. The Tonga National Center in Nuku'alofa presents two Tongan dance shows a week, as do some of the hotels and resorts. For a listing of compact discs of traditional Tongan music, visit www.south pacific.org/music.html.

PUBLIC HOLIDAYS AND FESTIVALS

Public holidays include New Year's Day, Good Friday, Easter Monday (March/April), ANZAC Day (April 25), Crown Prince's Birthday (May 4), Emancipation Day (June 4), King's Birthday (July 4), Constitution Day (Nov. 4), King Tupou I Day (Dec. 4), and Christmas Days (Dec. 26 and 26).

The **Vava'u Festival** during the first week of May features all sorts of sporting, cultural, and social events to mark Crown Prince Tupouto'a's birthday on May 4. The **Ha'apai Festival** coincides with Emancipation Day in early June. Nuku'alofa's **Heilala Festival,** with brass band and dancing contests, parades, and sporting competitions, occupies the week coinciding with the king's birthday, the first week in July. The Miss Galaxy beauty contest for *fakaleitis* (men dressed as women) is great fun and always sold-out. On the night of July 4 and again on New Year's Eve, Tongans standing along the beach light palm-leaf torches, illuminating the entire coast in rite called *tupakapakanava.*

Agricultural shows are held throughout Tonga during September and October, with the king in attendance at each. The ferry *Olovaha* makes special trips at these times, so ask and book early. Red Cross Week in May is marked by several fund-raising activities, including a grand ball. During the National Music Association Festival in late June and early July you can hear string bands, brass bands, electric bands, and singers. A military parade in Nuku'alofa marks the closing of parliament in late October. The Tonga Visitors Bureau should know what's happening.

ARTS AND CRAFTS

Most of the traditional handicrafts are made by women: woven baskets, mats, and tapa cloth. The weaving is mostly of tan, brown, black, and white pandanus leaves. The large sturdy baskets have pandanus wrapped around coconut-leaf midribs. A big one-meter-high laundry basket makes an excellent container to fill with other smaller purchases for shipment home. (Remember, however, that the post office will not accept articles more than a meter long or weighing over 10 kilograms by airmail or 20 kilograms by surface mail, though this does vary according to destination.) The soft, fine white mats from the Niuas, often decorated with colored wool, are outstanding but seldom sold.

Tonga's tapa cloth originates mostly on Tongatapu, where the paper mulberry tree *(Broussonetia papyrifera)* grows best. When the tree is about four meters high the bark is stripped and beaten into pieces up to 20 meters long, then hand-painted with natural brown and tan dyes. The cloth itself is called tapa but the painted product is known as *ngatu*. Big pieces of *ngatu* make excellent wall hangings or ceiling covers. In the villages, listen for the rhythmic pounding of tapa cloth mallets. The women are always happy to let you watch the process, and you may be able to buy something directly from them. Smaller pieces made for sale to tourists are often sloppily painted in a hurried fashion, and serving trays, fans, and purses made from tapa are often in poor taste.

Unfortunately too, Tongan woodcarving is now oriented toward producing imitation Hawaiian or Maori "tikis" for sale to tourists. Some shops will tell you the figures represent traditional Tongan gods, which is nonsense. Buy them if you wish, but know that they're not traditionally Tongan. The beautiful war clubs one sees in museums are rarely made today, perhaps out of fear they might be used! Tongan kava bowls are also vastly inferior to those made in Samoa and Fiji.

Many handicraft shops in Tonga sell items made from turtle shell, whale bone, ivory, black coral, seeds, and other materials that are prohibited entry into the United States, New Zealand, and many other countries, so be careful. Triton shells, conch shells, giant helmet shells, giant clamshells, winged oyster pearl shells, trochus shells, green snail shells, and other sea shells may also be banned. It's one of the negative aspects of tourism that such a catalog of endangered species should be so widely sold. Tonga's sea turtles have been hunted almost to the point of extinction.

ACCOMMODATIONS AND FOOD

All of the middle and upmarket hotels add 5 percent sales tax to their rates, plus a further 2.5 percent room tax that covers the salaries of the staff at the Tonga Visitors Bureau. These taxes usually won't be included in the amount you're quoted when you ask the price of a room and will be added when the time arrives to pay. The prices listed in this book don't usually include them, either.

Inexpensive accommodations are readily available, but upmarket places are less common, and even in the select few, the service is often lacking. Many of the larger upscale hotels are over a quarter of a century old and it shows. Be aware that some of the shoestring and budget lodgings listed herein are extremely basic. This has its advantages and its disadvantages, but for the adventurous traveler it's mostly advantageous. And although sometimes a bit more expensive than Samoa, Tonga has some beautifully situated places to stay.

Unless you're prepared to share a dorm with other backpackers, advance room reservations are a good idea from June to October, especially at Vava'u. Accommodation bookings made by the airlines or local travel agencies often don't go through and direct contact by email or telephone works better.

Some of the budget beach resorts will allow you to pitch your own tent on their grounds. In theory, camping is banned in Ha'apai, so if you're keen on unrolling the tent, don't stop there. Unlike in Fiji and Samoa (but as in the Cook Islands), you'll rarely be invited to spend the night in a local home. It's not forbidden to stay with the locals, it's just that the Tongans prefer to keep a certain distance between themselves and *palangi* tourists. If you do stay with a family, you should be aware of theft. On the plus side, you won't be expected to conform to a lot of complex social mores like you will in Samoa, and people tend to leave you alone.

Self-catering accommodations are harder to find than in Cook Islands or Fiji, and only a few of the guesthouses in Nuku'alofa have cooking facilities. At Ha'apai, most accommodations do allow cooking, but grudgingly, and they levy a T$2 pp charge for gas and electricity. Several places at Vava'u allow you to cook. Neiafu and Nuku'alofa have good public markets. Some stores sell fatty New Zealand mutton flaps called *sipi*, which unfortunately constitute the diet of many Tongans. Cheap canned corned beef and salty luncheon meat are also popular. Avoid cheap mystery meats like sausages and hot dogs, as you never know what goes into them. Tonga is an ice cream lover's paradise, with huge, inexpensive cones easy to find in Nuku'alofa. *Ota* is raw fish marinated in lime juice and coconut cream.

Of Tonga's gargantuan feasts, the most spectacular are those marking such important events as King Tupou IV's coronation or Queen Elizabeth's visit, which feature a whole roasted suckling pig for *each* of the thousands of guests. Literally tons of food are piled on long platters *(polas)* for these occasions, including taro, yams, cassava, breadfruit, sweet potato, fish, lobster, octopus, chicken, pork, corned beef, cooked taro leaves, and fruit. Cooking is done in an underground oven *(umu),* and coconut cream is added to everything. Less earthshaking feasts are put on for visitors to Tongatapu and Vava'u. Try to attend at least one.

In the main towns, the tap water is chlorinated and it won't bother you if you have a strong stomach; otherwise boil it or drink bottled water. Several readers have reported that the tap water made them sick. Well water should be considered highly suspect, whereas rainwater collected from roofs is usually okay. Unfortunately, beer is expensive in Tonga because it only comes in little 330-ml bottles, not the big 750-ml bottles used in most other Pacific countries. Crown Prince Tupouto'a owns the Royal Beer Co. (www.royal beer.to), Tonga's only brewery.

INFORMATION AND SERVICES
Information
The Tonga Visitors Bureau (tel. 25-334, fax 23-507) has information offices in Nuku'alofa, Lifuka, and Neiafu. Drop in for a supply of free brochures. These offices are good places to ask about events, and much useful data is posted on their information boards.

Internet Resources
The Tonga Visitors Bureau site, **www.vaca tions.tvb.gov.to,** provides useful background information on the country, plus a photo of H.R.H. Crown Prince Tupouto'a. Tonga Holiday,

(**www.tongaholiday.com**), has everything you need to know about holidaying in Tonga. Tonga's top attraction is whale-watching at Vava'u and Whale Discoveries, **www.whalediscoveries.com,** does it best. The Tonga Beach and Travel Guide, **www.tonga.islands-beaches.com,** has clickable maps that allow you to access photos and information about resorts throughout Tonga. Tonga Islands Hotels, **www.tonga-island.com,** also indicates the location of hotels on interactive maps.

Tonga on the Net, **www.tongatapu.net.to,** features Tongan stories and folklore. Planet Tonga, **www.planet-tonga.com,** is an online community website with news, people, events, links, and topics of interest to Tongans. The Government of Tonga site, **www.pmo.gov.to,** provides a good deal of useful information about Tonga and its government. The Tonga Star, **www.tongastar .com,** offers breaking news from Tonga, plus photos of the events of the week. Journalist Michael Field, **www.michaelfield.org,** is an authority on political developments in Tonga.

Visas and Officialdom
Visitors in possession of a passport and onward ticket do not require a visa for a stay of one month. Extensions of up to six months are possible at T$51 each (although the actual length of the extension is entirely up to the officers). Allow ample time for this. Visa over-stayers are harshly dealt with here regardless of their nationality. Drug smuggling carries a maximum penalty of 30 years hard labor.

Government authorization is required to do any sort of scientific research in Tonga, including archaeological excavations and sociological studies. The application fee of T$1,000 is refundable if your project is approved. Recently, one researcher on alcoholism had his application rejected. No drinking problems in Tonga, was the reply!

Ports of entry for cruising yachts are Niuafo'ou, Niuatoputapu, Vava'u, Lifuka, and Nuku'alofa. Yachts arriving from the east should call at Vava'u before Nuku'alofa (and Samoa before Tonga), as the prevailing winds make it much easier to sail from Vava'u to Nuku'alofa than vice versa and there are fewer hazardous reefs between Nuku'alofa and Fiji than between

Vava'u and Fiji. Customs and immigration are closed on weekends, and even on weekdays one can expect long waits before the officials come aboard to clear you in.

Money

The Tongan *pa'anga* (divided into 100 *seniti*) is worth a bit less than the Australian dollar (around US$1 = T$2.10), although the actual value fluctuates slightly. There are notes of one, two, five, 10, 20, and 50 *pa'anga,* and coins of one, five, 10, 20, and 50 *seniti.* Try to keep a supply of small coins in your pocket if you don't want petty expenditures to be rounded up to your disadvantage. Tongan banknotes are difficult to exchange outside Tonga, so get rid of them before you leave.

The banks are very crowded on Friday (pay day) but a few branches in Nuku'alofa and Neiafu are open Saturday mornings. The Westpac/Bank of Tonga branches in Nuku'alofa, 'Ononua ('Eua), Pangai (Lifuka), and Neiafu (Vava'u) charge T$8.10 commission per traveler's check. The MBf Bank charges T$2 commission, while the ANZ Bank charges only 10 cents per check (inquire about the commission before signing your checks as these things do change). Foreign banknotes are changed at a rate about 4 percent lower than traveler's checks. The ANZ Bank gives cash advances on credit cards for a T$8 commission. Cash advances through hotels cost about 10 percent commission and many businesses add 5 percent to all charges paid by credit card. Thus it's probably better to carry the bulk of your travel funds in traveler's checks. There's no American Express representative in Tonga.

Tipping and bargaining are not customary here, although monetary gifts *(fakapale)* are often given to performers at cultural events (Tongans stick small bills onto the well-oiled arms and shoulders of the dancers during the performance). A 5 percent sales tax is added to all goods and services. It's often hard to tell if this tax is included in sticker price. Many stores include it, but some add it on at the cash register. At hotels and restaurants, you really never know and the only way to be sure is to ask first.

Communications

The government-owned Tonga Telecommunications Corporation (tel. 24-255, fax 24-800, www.tcc.to) has a monopoly over telecommunications in Tonga. As in Samoa, the local telephone system is hasn't changed much since it was installed in the 1950s, and public telephones are few and far between. To place a local call, you must use your hotel phone or go to a central telephone office and have the clerk dial the number for you. When your party answers, the clerk will direct you to a booth and you'll pay for the time you're connected. This procedure must be repeated for each individual call you wish to make. Everyone in the office will hear everything you say, since you'll have to shout to be heard at the other end. The upside is that it's cheap: long-distance interisland calls within Tonga are only T$1.05/1.40 direct dial/operator assisted for three minutes. Urgent telegrams within Tonga cost 10 cents a word.

In 1995, telephone cards were introduced on Tongatapu, available in denominations of T$5, T$10, T$20, and T$50. Not only do they make calling easier and more private, but they're also cheaper, since three-minute minimums don't apply with the cards. The cards can be used for international calls, interisland calls, and local calls within Tongatapu. As with all direct-dial telephones in Tonga, the international access code is 00.

Three-minute direct-dial calls cost T$4.50 to Australia or New Zealand, or T$9 to Canada, the United States, or Europe. A T$1 international connection fee is added to the cost of each call. Person-to-person calls are T$2.50 extra. Collect calls are possible to Australia, New Zealand, the United States, and the United Kingdom (but not to Canada or Ger-

many). Internationally, faxing is a good alternative to telephoning.

The telephone exchanges where you can make phone calls are listed in the travel sections of this chapter. Calls placed from hotel rooms are much more expensive. Directory assistance is 910, the international operator 913, the interisland operator 915.

Tonga Telecom operates Tonga's kalianet.to email service, named for the double-hulled Tongan war canoe called the *kalia*. Nuku'alofa's cyber cafés are listed in the Nuku'alofa section.

Media

The government-owned *Tonga Chronicle* (tel. 23-302, fax 23-336, chroni@kalianet.to) comes out every Thursday and you can usually pick up a copy at the Friendly Islands Bookshop in Nuku'alofa. The English edition is less extensive than the one in Tongan. The Prime Minister's Office actually runs this newspaper, so don't expect any investigative journalism here. Instead, there's abundant coverage of the royal family.

Taimi 'o Tonga or Times of Tonga, a privately operated Tongan-language paper published twice weekly in New Zealand, has a larger circulation than the *Chronicle*. In 2003 it was banned in Tonga itself after publishing an exposé about cabinet ministers who were giving government contracts to certain private companies without public tenders. A constitutional amendment passed in October 2003 gives the government the right to shut down local newspapers and ban foreign papers at will. The penalty for anyone found in possession of over 12 copies of a banned publication is 10 years in prison.

Matangi Tonga (tel. 25-779, fax 24-749, www.matangitonga.to) is Tonga's bimonthly national news magazine. The same company publishes a free bimonthly tourist newspaper called *'Eva*.

In 2000, the Tonga Broadcasting Corporation launched Television Tonga, which provides a high level of local content. The BBC world service news comes on daily at 2000. For American religious programming, switch to TV7 (Oceania Broadcasting Network).

Radio

The government-run Tonga Broadcasting Commission (tel./fax 23-555) transmits in Tongan and English over 1017 kHz AM Monday–Saturday 0600–2400 and Sunday 1600–2300. Radio Tonga broadcasts in English Monday–Saturday 0630–2300 and Sunday 1600–2300 over FM 90.0 MHz. On both stations you can hear the BBC news at 0700 and Radio Australia news at 0800, followed by a weather report. The FM station presents the news in brief at 1100 and 1700, and major news bulletins at 0900, 1300, and 1900, while the AM station has the Radio Australia news at 2000. International news broadcasts are sometimes abruptly switched off if news about Tonga is coming up. An hour of classical music is broadcast over the AM station Sunday at 1630. The TBC transmitter at Vava'u was destroyed during a hurricane and you can only receive the AM station there very weakly. The AM is much stronger at Ha'apai and you should be able to receive both stations clearly on Tongatapu and 'Eua.

A private commercial station called Tonga Radio A3V (tel. 25-891, www.tongaradio.com) at FM 89.1 MHz broadcasts no news but plays the best selection of pop music you'll hear anywhere in the South Pacific. It's part of the empire of the Vea brothers, who also own Loni's Cinema and an adjacent video rental shop in Nuku'alofa.

Vava'u's local station, FM1 (tel. 70-777), is a private commercial operator broadcasting over 89.3 MHz 24 hours a day.

Business Hours and Time

Normal business hours are weekdays 0800–1300 and 1400–1700, Saturday 0800–1200. Government working hours are weekdays 0830–1230 and 1330–1630. Banking hours are weekdays 0900–1530. Post offices are open weekdays 0830–1600. Almost everything is closed on Sunday.

Due to its position just west of the international date line, Tonga is the first country in the world to usher in each new day. In fact, the date line seems to have so confused the local roosters that they crow constantly just to be safe. Tonga shares its day with Fiji, New Zealand, and Australia, but is one day ahead of Samoa, Niue,

Tahiti, and Hawaii. The time is the same as in Samoa, but one hour behind Hawaii and one ahead of Fiji and New Zealand.

Tonga's sacred Sunday adds to the fun of the date line confusion. Commercial flights (and most other transport) are banned in the kingdom that day. Don't get worried if you suddenly realize that it's Sunday on a flight to Tonga from Apia—you'll land on Monday. Just keep repeating: "If it's Sunday for the Samoans, it's Monday for the monarch."

Entertainment-wise, Friday is a much bigger party night than Saturday because most Tongans get paid on Friday, so there's money to spend and the fun doesn't have to stop at midnight. Only holy rolling is allowed on Sunday, but some bars, discos, and cinemas reopen a few minutes after midnight on Monday morning and try to make up for the time lost on the Sabbath. Expect a lot to happen late in Tonga.

Electricity

The electric voltage is 240 volts, 50 cycles, with a three-pronged plug used, as in Australia and New Zealand.

TRANSPORTATION
Getting There

Until recently, Tonga's government-owned flag carrier, **Royal Tongan Airlines,** used a leased Royal Brunei Airways Boeing 757 to fly to Auckland and Sydney. Royal Tongan's business plan also called for flights to Honolulu, but the approval process became stalled after the American authorities raised concerns over a Muslim-operated plane landing in Hawaii. By May, 2004, Royal Tongan had run up millions of dollars in leasing and servicing debts, and their oversized aircraft was seized by creditors at Auckland Airport. This fiasco bankrupted Royal Tongan Airlines and put the country deeply in debt. All international services to Tongan and domestic flights are now operated by other carriers.

Samoa's **Polynesian Airlines** (tel. 24-566) arrives from Apia (from T$336 roundtrip), Auckland, Melbourne, Sydney, and Wellington several times a week. The Fijian airline, **Air Pacific** (tel.

23-423), has service from Nadi to Tongatapu twice a week. **Air Fiji** (tel. 24-506) flies from Suva to Tongatapu twice a week. Around Christmas and the Heilala Festival July 4, all flights are fully booked by Tongans returning home.

Air New Zealand (tel. 23-828) has direct weekly flights from Apia and Los Angeles with connections from London. Their flights between Tonga and Auckland operate five times a week. This Coral Route connection is discussed under Getting There in the Exploring the Islands chapter.

Getting Around by Air

In 2004 **fly NiU Airlines** (tel. 28-280 or 28-281, fax 28-282, www.flyniu.com) began service using a 37-seat Dash 8 aircraft after the bankruptcy of Royal Tongan Airlines. They now have several flights daily from Tongatapu to 'Eua (T$36), Ha'apai (T$93), Vava'u (T$145), Niuatoputapu (T$274), and Niuafo'ou (T$324).

In addition, **Air Waves of Vava'u** (tel. 23-344, extension 162, fax 23-833), also known as Peau Vava'u Airlines and owned by Crown Prince Tupouto'a, uses a classic 28-seat DC3 aircraft on the Tongatapu-Ha'apai-Vava'u route. The flying time is twice as long as that on fly NiU, but it's a unique experience.

Neither airline operates on Sunday, and it's suggested that you book a northbound Friday or Saturday flight from Nuku'alofa to escape a depressing Sunday in the capital.

The baggage allowance on domestic flights in Tonga is only 10 kilos. Between Nuku'alofa and Vava'u, excess baggage is T$1.41 a kilogram. If the plane is judged overweight, the 10-kilo limit may be rigidly applied to everyone and anything heavier may have to come on a later flight. In that case, you should keep calling the airline office until it is delivered to your hotel. If you don't follow up, your luggage will remain at the airport.

In "emergencies" these airlines bump passengers with confirmed reservations if VIPs need their seats. This doesn't happen often, but be forewarned and check in early (never less than 30 minutes prior to the flight). Be sure to reconfirm your onward flight the day before as flight delays and cancellations happen all the time. Bookings are tight and you'll probably get bumped if you neglect to reconfirm. It's best not to schedule any tight connections with international flights, but if you do, let the airline know about it when you reconfirm and hopefully they'll bump someone else.

Getting Around by Ship

The government-owned **Shipping Corporation of Polynesia** (tel. 23-853, fax 22-617), at Queen Salote Wharf, Nuku'alofa, offers reliable boat service among the Tonga Islands. Their large car ferry, the 400-tonne MV *Olovaha*, departs Nuku'alofa every Tuesday at 1700, arriving at Pangai (T$34 deck) very early Wednesday morning and Vava'u (T$48 deck) on Wednesday afternoon. It leaves Vava'u again Thursday afternoon, calling at Pangai in the middle of the night and arriving back in Nuku'alofa Friday afternoon. In Ha'apai the ship calls at both Ha'afeva and Pangai. It's usually punctual.

Deck travel is sometimes very crowded, but when the ship isn't too full you can stretch out on the plastic benches or the floor in a clean, protected room. No meals are included. Cabins cost four times the deck fare, because you must book an entire twin room (T$128 double to Ha'apai, T$178 double to Vava'u). There are only four such cabins, and they can be just as noisy as deck, though more comfortable. The Shipping Corporation runs a boat from Vava'u to Niuatoputapu (T$51) and Niuafo'ou (T$60) every month or so. (During Hurricane Ami in January 2003, the *Olovaha* dragged its anchor at Nuku'alofa, slammed into another ship, and was thrown onto the reef. Salvagers managed to refloat the vessel and it was towed to New Zealand for repair. Check locally to find out if it's back in service.)

The private **Uata Shipping Lines** ('Uliti Uata, tel. 23-855, fax 23-860), also known as the Walter Shipping Lines, has three red-and-white ships, the MV *Tautahi*, the MV *'Ikale*, and the MV *Pulupaki*. The *Pulupaki* or *Tautahi* leaves Nuku'alofa Monday at 1700, reaching Pangai (T$31) in the middle of the night and Vava'u (T$46) Tuesday morning. It departs Vava'u for Ha'apai and Nuku'alofa Wednesday at 1300, stopping at Pangai late that night and reaching Nuku'alofa early Thursday morning.

No cabins are available, but long padded benches are provided. Take food, water, and anti-seasickness pills. The loud music broadcast over the ship's public address system all night is a disadvantage.

Other small ships serving Ha'apai irregularly include the wooden *Langi Fo'ou*, which leaves Nuku'alofa's Faua Jetty for Nomuka Wednesday mornings, an eight-hour trip.

Several boats shuttle back and forth between Nuku'alofa and 'Eua (1.5–2.5 hours, T$12). The blue-and-white *Alai Moana* departs Faua Jetty daily except Sunday at 1230, leaving 'Eua for the return around 0530 in the morning. You pay onboard. It's a safe metal ferry with rows of plastic seats. The 220-passenger *'Ikale* of the Uata Shipping Lines ferries also travels between Nuku'alofa and 'Eua. It's supposed to leave Faua Jetty Monday–Saturday at 1230, departing 'Eua for the return at 1730 weekdays with an extra trip at 0530 Monday, but it's canceled in choppy weather. However you go, be prepared for an extremely rough eastbound trip and a smoother, faster westbound voyage.

Note that all of the above information is only an indication of what might or should happen in ideal weather—the reality is often quite different. Make careful inquiries upon arrival and be prepared for a few delays. (For information on yacht charters and extended cruises, turn to the Vava'u section.)

Airport

Fua'amotu International Airport (TBU), 21 km southeast of Nuku'alofa, is closed on Sunday. The special airport bus (T$10 pp) meets most flights. If there are two or more of you, the T$15 taxi fare to town is better. Be sure to check the fare before getting into the taxi, and don't let the driver steer you to some hotel you never intended to stay at just so he can collect a commission. Often they will tell you the hotel you requested is closed with the aim of tricking you into going where *they* want. Know exactly where *you* want to go and how before you step out of the terminal. Hope that your flight doesn't arrive in Tonga late at night, as the taxis demand T$30 or more then. Some accommodations provide free transfers from the airport if they know you're coming (ask) but charge a fee to drive you back there. Avis and E.M. Jones Travel have car rental offices at the airport.

Airport-bound, the Teta Tours bus from the main hotels directly to the terminal costs T$10 pp. If you're on the lowest of budgets you could also take the infrequent Fua'amotu bus right to the airport access road, or any Mu'a bus to the crossroads at Malapo, then hitch the last six km.

The Tonga Visitors Bureau counter and the MBf Bank exchange office are to the right as you come out of arrivals. The MBf Bank at the airport changes traveler's checks at a rate similar to the banks in town, less a T$3 commission. The snack bar at the airport is reasonable and offers a good selection, and across the parking lot is a small farmers market with coconuts, pineapples, bananas, peanuts, etc. The duty-free shop in the departure lounge is also reasonably priced. Check in early as international flights are often over-booked and this airport is mildly chaotic. The departure tax on international flights is T$25 (only children under two years are exempt).

Tongatapu

Tongatapu's 259 square km are just over a third of the kingdom's surface area, yet two-thirds of Tonga's population lives here. Of coral origin, Tongatapu is flat with a slight tilt—from 18.2-meter cliffs south of the airport to partly submerged islands and reefs to the north. Some 20,000 years ago Tongatapu was blanketed with volcanic ash from an explosion on Tofua Island, creating the rich soil that today supports intensive agriculture.

Tongatapu, or "Sacred Tonga," is the heartland of Tongan culture, history, and political power. Here Captain James Cook conferred with the Tu'i Tonga, and the island is still the seat of Tongan royalty. The Tonga National Center outside the capital, Nuku'alofa, showcases Tongan culture, and compelling megalith monuments and royal tombs testify to Tongatapu's historical weight. Vying for visitors' attention are noisy colonies of sacred flying foxes, an admirable bird park, breathtaking beaches, remarkable coastlines, tapping tapa mallets, and evocative archaeological remains. And unlike Samoa, no "custom fees" are collected from visitors out to see the island's sights. Cook was enthralled by Tongatapu, and you will be too.

NUKU'ALOFA

Nuku'alofa (population 23,000) is just north of the azure Fanga'uta Lagoon, now sterile after sewage from adjacent Vaiola Hospital eliminated the fish and other marinelife. It's a dusty, ramshackle little town with trash strewn along the roadsides. Tourism, industry, commerce, and government are all concentrated here, and the slow-paced South Seas atmosphere hangs on. You'll find a good selection of places to stay, eat, and drink, reasonable entertainment (except on Sunday), a well-developed transportation network, and many reminders of Tonga's Victorian heritage. The name means "Abode of Love." A few days poking around are well spent, but the other islands have more to offer.

SIGHTS

Begin your visit at **Vuna Wharf,** the main port of entry to Tonga from 1906 until construction of Queen Salote Wharf in 1967. The **Treasury Building** (1928), opposite the wharf, was once Nuku'alofa's main post office. Nearby Railway Road is named for a former line that once carried copra to the wharf and it's still Nuku'alofa's only one-way street. The **House of Parliament** on Railway Road is a small wooden building prefabricated in New Zealand and reassembled here in 1894. The 30 members of parliament deliberate May–October. Walk through the park across the street from parliament, passing the **Tongan War Memorial,** and turn left on Taufa'ahau Road to the century-old **prime minister's office,** with its central tower.

Continue west across the soccer field beside the

Bank of Tonga to the Victorian **Royal Palace,** closed to the public but easily viewed from outside the grounds. This gingerbread palace was also prefabricated in New Zealand for reassembly here in 1867. The second-story veranda was added in 1882. The gables and scalloped eaves of this white frame building are crowned by a red roof and surrounded by Norfolk pines. The bronze statue of King Taufa'ahau Tupou IV in front of the palace was presented by the Chinese Embassy in 1999. The best vantage point for taking photos is around on the west side of the palace compound. (The king and queen no longer live here but rather in the Fua'amotu Palace south of the airport. The villa of the crown prince is at Pea, on the airport road, and across the street from it is the residence of Princess Pilolevu; a pair of white Bengali tigers guards the gate.)

Many old colonial-style residences line Vuna Road west of the palace, including the **British High Commissioner's residence,** with a flag-pole surrounded by cannon from the privateer *Port-au-Prince,* sacked at Ha'apai in 1806. South of the residence is **Mt. Zion,** site of an 18th-century Tongan fortress and, in 1830, the first missionary chapel. This hill is now crowned by several communications towers.

Centenary Church (1952), south of Mt. Zion, is the principle house of worship of the Free Wesleyan Church, the largest of Tonga's three Methodist denominations. Some 2,000 persons can be seated here, and most Sunday mornings the king and queen are among them for the 1000 service. The church's president lives in the impressive mansion (1871) on the west side of the church, a former residence of 19th-century missionary and Tongan premier Rev. Shirley Baker.

East on the south side of Laifone Road are the **Royal Tombs,** where Tongan royalty has been buried since 1893. Across Laifone Road from the Royal Tombs is another important Free

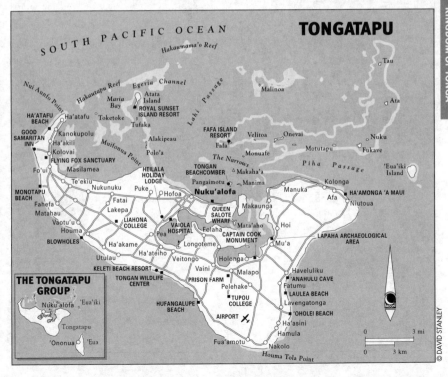

KINGDOM OF TONGA

NUKU'ALOFA

SOUTH PACIFIC OCEAN

500 yds
500 m
0
0

Tongatapu Island

Fanga'uta Lagoon

TOULIKI NAVAL BASE

To Friendly Islander Motel

To Blue Pacific Nightclub

QUEEN SALOTE WHARF

UATA SHIPPING

VAVA'U FERRY

SHIPPING CORP.

FISH MARKET

HARBOR VIEW MOTEL

LILY'S MOTEL

FAUA JETTY

EUA FERRY

TOM'S GUEST HOUSE

SMALL INDUSTRIES CENTER

BYPASS

ROAD

ROAD

VILLA MCKENZIE

TONGA TELECOM

KINIKINILAU SHOPPING CENTER

INTERNATIONAL DATELINE HOTEL

KIMIKO'S RESTAURANT

ALAMEA

TONGA BROADCASTING CORP.

TUNGI

TONGOLOA

SALOTE RD

TONGA CLUB

VISITORS BUREAU

YELLOW PIER

VUNA WHARF

LOCAL BUS STATION

LONG DISTANCE BUS STATION

VUNA

MARKET

AIRLINE OFFICE

ANGELA GUEST HOUSE

KAUSELA

LAVINIA

TELEPHONE EXCHANGE

DIVERS LODGE

BYPASS

SEAVIEW LODGE AND RESTAURANT

BRITISH HIGH COMMISSIONER'S RESIDENCE

ROYAL PALACE

VILAI BARRACKS

MT. ZION

POST OFFICE

PARLIAMENT

FRIEND'S CAFE

PACIFIC ROYALE HOTEL

HOTEL NUKU'ALOFA

LAFONE

MISA'S GUEST HOUSE

PHOENIX DISCO

NERIMA LODGE

SAVOY CLEANERS

MATEIALONA

ROAD

LONGOTEME

SELA'S GUESTHOUSE

FATAFEHI

TUPOULAHI

CENTENARY CHURCH

WELLINGTON RD

ROAD

SIPU

RD

CATHOLIC BASILICA

FRIENDLY ISLANDS BOOKSTORE

ROYAL TOMBS

QUEEN SALOTE HALL

RAILWAY ROAD

PIZZERIA LITTLE ITALY

ROAD

ATA

CAPTAIN COOK APARTMENTS

MOANA BEACH HOUSE

VUNA

'ATENISI INSTITUTE

ALIPATE

THE BACKPACKERS PLACE

TEUFAIVA STADIUM

VAHA'AKOLO

TAUFA'AHAU

TONGA NATIONAL CENTER

To Airport

To Kolovai

BYPASS

VAHA'AKOLO ROAD

WINNIE'S GUESTHOUSE

VAIOLA HOSPITAL

To Heilala Holiday Lodge

© DAVID STANLEY

© DAVID STANLEY

the Royal Palace at Nuku'alofa

Wesleyan church, which was only completed in 1985. The striking **Basilica of St. Anthony of Padua** (1980), back on Taufa'ahau Road, is worth visiting for its soaring interior.

Cultural Center

The **Tonga National Center** (tel. 23-022, fax 23-520), a complex of Polynesian-style buildings beside the Fanga'uta Lagoon opposite Vaiola Hospital, was built in 1988 using Japanese aid money. Here you'll see handicraft demonstrations (tapa and canoe making, woodcarving, basket making, mat weaving), contemporary art, and historical displays. The Center's impressive Exhibition Hall contains historic photos of Tonga and Samoa, a collection of war clubs and other carvings, and model canoes. The hall is open weekdays 0900–1600, admission T$2.

Weekdays at 1230 the Center prepares a barbecue lunch and traditional fashion show (T$15), and at 1400 the excellent two-hour guided cultural tour begins, featuring a kava ceremony, the telling of ancient legends and myths, and traditional Tongan dancing in the 450-seat amphitheater (T$8). The handicraft workshops will be operating at this time, and craft items may be purchased directly

from the artisans. Some of these activities are curtailed or canceled when not enough visitors are on hand, so you might check beforehand. Tuesday and Thursday are the usually the best days to come; otherwise just visit the museum and craft shop and come back for the evening performance another day. Advance reservations are required if you want to take lunch or dinner.

Not to be missed is the dinner show put on Tuesday and Thursday nights (T$20). The dancing is scheduled to begin at 1900 but it usually starts at 2000. The package includes a visit to the exhibition hall, string band entertainment, kava drinking, an all-you-can-eat buffet dinner of authentic Tongan cuisine, and some very good traditional dancing (take small banknotes to give to the dancers). An additional charge is collected for minibus hotel transfers. Reserve the evening shows before 1630 at either the Tonga Visitors Bureau or directly by phone. Admission for children under 12 is half price to all of the above events.

Sports and Recreation

The **Deep Blue Dive Center** (Herbert Keller, tel./fax 23-576, www.deep-blue-diving.to), on Vuna Road opposite Faua Jetty, is the only dive shop in Nuku'alofa. A full-day package, including two dives and lunch, is T$115/130 without/with equipment. Reductions are available for five or 10 dives, and snorkelers can go along for T$40. Their open-water certification course is T$530. Their 15-meter dive boat *Deep Blue* is always accompanied by a speedboat for fast pickups and deliveries. Exploring the underwater caves around 'Eua is a specialty.

One of the favorite local dive sites is **Hakau-mama'o Reef,** 14 km north of Nuku'alofa, a deep wall populated by large numbers of brilliant parrot fish. **Malinoa Island** to the southeast features a great variety of marinelife on the surrounding reef, plus a lighthouse and some old graves on the island itself. Both of the above are marine reserves, and taking fish, clams, or coral is prohibited (T$200 fine). Black coral can be seen at **Kings Reef** just off Nuku'alofa. Visibility ranges from 15 meters within the Tongatapu Lagoon to 50 meters on the barrier reefs. A wetsuit is recommended during the cooler months, April–August.

Neil Dalgety of **Flying Scotsman Charters** (tel. 23-348, fax 24-538) takes up to three anglers out game fishing at T$285/395 a half/full day.

The nine-hole **Tonga Golf Club** (no phone; closed Sun.) is opposite the indoor stadium at Alele near Veitongo on the road to the airport. Greens fees are T$10 and it may be possible to hire clubs. Saturday 1130–2100, the club bar is worth a stop. The Heilala Classic Golf Tournament is at the beginning of July. The club is easily accessible on the Folaha, Malapo, Vaini, or Veitongo buses.

Friday or Saturday at 1500 (April–June) catch a game of rugby at the Teufaiva Stadium. During the soccer season (May–July) you can watch the teams compete at the Pangai Soccer Field on the waterfront next to the Bank of Tonga Saturday at 1500. Joggers meet in front of the Bank of Tonga every Monday at 1700 for a recreational run. It's a good way to meet local expats.

ACCOMMODATIONS

The accommodations listings below are arranged beginning with those closest to Queen Salote

Wharf and Faua Jetty, then southwest through town. For accommodations around Tongatapu or on nearby islands, turn to those sections. Not all places in Nuku'alofa provide satisfactory communal cooking facilities, so ask check beforehand if this matters to you. The information board at the Tonga Visitors Bureau lists furnished apartments and houses for rent by the month. Unless otherwise stated, add 7.5 percent tax to all accommodation rates quoted below.

Under US$25

Lily's Motel (tel. 24-226, fax 24-389), opposite Faua Jetty, has six rooms with bath behind their large Chinese restaurant at T$30/35 single/double. Friday nights a live band plays until 0400.

Two-story **Angela Guest House** (tel. 23-930, fax 22-149), on Wellington Road in the center of town, has eight small rooms at T$20/30/45 single/double/triple. The Taiwanese managers provide guests with a tiny kitchen and fridge.

Moana Guest House (tel. 27-406), a km west of the palace on Vuna Road, is a pleasant wooden building with rooms at T$15/35 single/double with shared bath or T$60 with private bath.

Misa's Guest House (tel. 27-635, www.misas guesthouse.com), on Mateialona Road near Queen Salote Memorial Hall, was known as Toni's Guest House until the property owner took back the building in 2002. The 13 rooms with shared bath are T$20 pp (bring mosquito coils) and cooking facilities are provided. The Mu'a and Hihifo buses stop right across the street from the guesthouse if you'd like to organize your own island tour.

Though a bit out of the way, **Sela's Guest House** (Maria and 'Etoni Tonga, tel. 25-040, fax 23-775, mettonga@kalianet.to), south of town, has been a favorite of overseas volunteers working in Tonga since the mid-1970s. There are nine clean rooms with shared facilities at T$20/30 single/double, plus a T$10 six-bed dormitory. The six rooms with private bath and hot shower are T$40/50 double/triple. Discounts are available for long stays. Cooking facilities for guests are provided, or you can order a full breakfast for T$6 and a large dinner for T$15. Sela serves the best home-cooked meals you'll receive at any guesthouse in Nuku'alofa (which accounts for the many repeat visitors). If noise bothers you, however, ask for a room away from the VCR and dining room. On the positive side, you can sit and watch videos or CNN to your heart's content. It's a good family-style place to relax and local meet people, and it's seldom full. The Halaleva bus from opposite the Tonga Visitors Bureau will bring you to within a block and a half of the guesthouse (ask).

The Backpackers Place (tel. 26-230, fax 26-231), on Vaha'akolo Road beyond Teufaiva Stadium, has eight rooms with shared bath in two houses at $20/35 single/double. Dorm beds are T$15. Common cooking facilities are provided and all reports have been good.

Two-story **Helens Apartments** (tel. 24-873) is in an industrial area behind Winnie's Guesthouse at Havelulotu, two km south of town. The six units, starting at T$50 double, including cooking facilities, gas, electricity, and telephone (local calls free). A swimming pool is on the premises.

A variety of accommodations are available at **Heilala Holiday Lodge** (tel. 29-910, fax 29-410, www.heilala-holiday-lodge.com), in a pleasant rural setting at Tofoa, three km south of town (off the road to the airport). The four fan-cooled rooms upstairs in the main two-story house are T$35/48 single/double. Bathrooms are shared (hot water and *very* clean) and communal cooking facilities are provided. Out back in the garden are three thatched *fale* with bath costing T$55/68. The four superior bungalows with fridge are T$80/95. Rates include tax and breakfast (minimum stay two nights). A swimming pool and restaurant are on the premises. This place runs efficiently under the firm hand of a German woman named Waltraud Quick (or Maria as the Tongans call her) and her more laid-back son Sven. They arrange six-hour island tours with German-speaking guides at T$35 pp (minimum of four); one day they cover the west side of the island, another day the east side. Free luggage storage for a reasonable length of time is offered against a T$20 deposit that will be applied to future accommodation charges. Airport transfers are usually free—ask for Sven at the airport. Heilala is easily accessible to town by bus or taxi, and bicycles are available at T$8 a day.

Toni's Guest House (Toni, Kesi, and Vili, tel. 21-049 or 27-068, fax 21-049, www.geocities .com/tmatthias2000) is also at Tofoa, four km south of town, a bit beyond Heilala and to the right. There's a four-bed dorm, several bright green houses containing rooms with shared bath, and two *fale* with private bath. All cost T$11 pp and you get whatever happens to be available when you arrive. Communal cooking facilities, a library, and lounge are provided. A fish pond is the focal point of the extensive garden. Toni's is a good place to meet other travelers as guests swap stories around the kava bowl every evening. Kesi's full day minibus tour is the best of its kind at T$25 pp. Some travelers find Toni's English reserve and Kesi's forthright enthusiasm a bit odd, but you'll enjoy being with them if you accept them as they are. Toni charges T$6 pp for airport transfers. Don't believe airport taxi drivers who tell you this place is closed or full: They only want to take you elsewhere in order to collect a commission—insist on being driven straight to Toni's.

US$25–50

The two-story **Friendly Islander Hotel** (tel. 23-810, fax 24-199, http://kalianet.to/papiloa), on Vuna Road 500 meters beyond the Shell oil storage tanks three km east of town, has 26 rooms with fridge at T$50/60 single/double or T$60/75 for a *fale*. A few backpacker rooms with shared bath and kitchen are T$18 pp. A restaurant and swimming pool are on the premises. The Friendly Islander is run by Papiloa Foliaki, a former elected member of parliament and current head of the local transvestite association—an interesting person to meet! The hotel is easily accessible on the Va'epoua bus from opposite the Tonga Visitors Bureau.

The **Harbor View Motel** (tel. 25-488, fax 25-490, harbvmtl@kalianet.to), next to the Fakafanua Center opposite Queen Salote Wharf, has 12 clean rooms in a modern three-story building. Prices range from budget rooms downstairs with shared bath at T$40/60 single/double, to standard air-conditioned rooms on the middle floor with private bath at T$65/85, and deluxe rooms at T$105/115. No cooking facilities are available but breakfast is included. It's a good

KINGDOM OF TONGA

medium-priced choice near the interisland ferries and some colorful eating and drinking places.

Tom's Guest House (tel. 22-885, tomsgh@ kalianet.to), a block back from Davina's Restaurant at Faua Jetty, has five rooms in a nice European-style house at T$40/60 single/double with shared bath or T$80 with private bath including breakfast. Kitchen facilities are available.

The **Pacific Royale Hotel** (tel. 23-344, fax 23-833, royale@kalianet.to) on Taufa'ahau Road has seen better days. The 15 standard rooms are T$95 single or double, the 45 superior rooms T$142. All 60 rooms have private bath, fridge, and noisy air conditioners, but they're dimly lit and rather overpriced. Back from the reception area, just past the mediocre restaurant, is a miniature swimming pool. On Friday and Saturday nights the noisy One Night Stand disco here cranks up. Internet access is available here.

The German-owned **Hotel Nuku'alofa** (Uthana Sanft Taumoepeau, tel. 24-244, fax 23-154, hotelnuk@kalianet.to), above the MBf Bank on Taufa'ahua Road, has 14 spacious air-conditioned rooms with private bath and fridge at T$75/90/105 single/double/triple. There's a restaurant and bar.

Divers Lodge (tel. 23-379, fax 23-576), in Fasi off Tupoulahi Road, has five rooms in a new two-story building at T$37/70 single/double including breakfast. The common kitchen and lounge are fine. They cater mostly to people diving with Deep Blue Diving.

Nerima Lodge (Naoko Afeaki, tel. 25-533, fax 25-577, www.maca.to/english), off Fatafehi Road, has seven clean rooms in a two-story building at T$43/68 single/double with shared bath (the one room with private bath is T$55/80). Breakfast and tax are included. The home-cooked Japanese/Tongan meals are recommended at T$10–30, or you can cook for yourself.

Captain Cook Apartments (Phillip Vea, tel./fax 25-600, phil@captaincook.to), on Vuna Road facing the lagoon a kilometer west of the Royal Palace, offers six two-bedroom apartments accommodating up to four persons at T$80/ 90/99 single/double/triple plus tax. Each apartment has a kitchen, living room, and private

bath. It's an excellent choice for two couples traveling together, but book ahead.

Winnies Guesthouse (tel./fax 25-215, wg-house@tonfon.to), on Vaka'akolo Road near Vaiola hospital, two km south of the center, tries to recapture the atmosphere of an old South Seas guesthouse. The six rooms with shared bath are T$30 pp including a fruit and toast breakfast, and good communal cooking facilities are available. It's comfortable, with a plush sitting room where videos are shown nightly, and Winnie Santos and her son Marc are very helpful. Foreign medical interns working at the hospital often stay here. The Vaiola bus stops at their door.

US$50–100

John & Moira Forde's **Villa McKenzie** (tel./fax 24-998, villamac@kalianet.to) on Vuna Road offers four comfortable rooms with miniature bathrooms in a colonial-style house at T$115/135/150 single/double/triple including a full breakfast and tax. Dinner can be ordered Wednesday to Friday nights for around T$10. Though not cheap, this high-quality B&B is a good alternative to the International Dateline.

The three-story **International Dateline Hotel** (tel. 23-411, fax 23-410, www.dateline hotel.com) on Vuna Road was originally built in 1967 to accommodate guests at the coronation of King Taufa'ahau Tupou IV. Recently the Dateline was showing its age, but a complete refurbishment by Chinese investors has been announced. The 76 rooms with private bath, fridge, TV, and noisy air conditioning begin at T$105/120/135 single/double/triple in the old wing along Vuna Road. The rooms in the adjacent new wing on Tupoulahi Road are much better at T$142/165/180. The Dateline has a pleasant resort atmosphere and the location is excellent. Their reasonably priced restaurant is one of the few open to the public on Sunday (dinner only), and Polynesian dance shows are staged here Wednesday and Saturday nights at 2030. If you pay T$20 for the buffet (Wednesday) or the set three-course menu (Saturday), there's no cover charge. Otherwise T$5 is collected at the door. Despite the flip-flop-shod waiters, persons dressed in shorts, T-shirts, or sandals are not admitted to the dining room. A cold beer by the Dateline's pool is the perfect way to top off an afternoon and nonguests are allowed to swim upon payment of a T$5 fee (remember this if you're stuck in town on Sunday). Excursions to the islands just off Nuku'alofa can be booked at the hotel's helpful tours and information desk.

Seaview Lodge (tel. 23-709, fax 26-906, sea view@kalianet.to), on Vuna Road west of the palace, offers 11 air-conditioned rooms with bath and TV upstairs in a colonial-style house or in an adjacent building. The seven standard rooms in the annex are T$120 double. The upstairs rooms above the Seaview Restaurant are T$155 facing the rear garden or T$170 with a balcony overlooking the lagoon. Though the guesthouse section is new, the Seaview's restaurant downstairs has long been a local institution.

FOOD
Budget
'Pot Luck (tel. 25-091), down the street beside St. Mary's Catholic Cathedral opposite Queen Salote Wharf, serves a "pot luck" lunch at T$3–6 on Tuesday, Wednesday, and Friday 1200–1400. It's only open during the school year, March–November.

John's Place Takeaway (tel. 21-246), on Taufa'ahau Road in the center of town and opposite Vaiola Hospital (close to the Tonga National Center), dishes out greasy hamburgers, grilled chicken and chips, and cassava and curry. It's okay for a quick snack, but with a little effort you'll do better elsewhere for the same money. They're open until midnight, but closed Sunday.

Friends Café (tel. 26-323; weekdays 0800–2200, Sat. 0830–1930), on Taufa'ahau Road near the corner of Salote Road, is a nice clean place for breakfast or lunch ("large portions, good price"). The coffee and cakes are unsurpassed. Several readers have recommended it.

Akiko's Restaurant (tel. 25-339; Mon.–Fri. 1130–1400), in the basement of the Catholic basilica on Taufa'ahau Road, has long been a budget standby. The lunch special is good (alcohol is not served).

Chinese
One of the best value Chinese places is **Kimiko Restaurant** (tel. 22-170) on Vuna Road facing the waterfront: try the wonton soup. Kimiko's is one of the few places open on Sunday.

Emerald Chinese Restaurant (tel. 24-619, Mon.–Sat. 1130–1430 and 1800–2300, Sun. 1800–2300), next to the Tonga Visitors Bureau, has rice and noodle dishes (T$4–7), vegetables (T$5), chicken (T$6–7), and lobster (T$12–14).

The attractive **Fakalato Chinese Restaurant** (tel. 22-101, Mon.–Sat. 1800–2200), above a supermarket on Wellington Road, serves medium-priced Cantonese dishes of the type familiar to North Americans, so there will be no difficulty ordering. (While you're there, check out the Italian ice cream place nearby on the corner of Taufa'ahau Road.)

Upscale Restaurants
Several seafood restaurants are opposite the fish market at Faua Jetty, including **Davina's Restaurant** (tel. 23-385; closed Sun.), the **Waterfront Café** (tel. 21-004; weekdays from 1100, Sat. and Sun. from 1700), and **Lily's Chinese Restaurant** (tel. 24-226; daily 1100–1400 and 1800–2200). Davina's has an elegant indoor dining room with a piano (great steaks). The **Billfish Bar and Restaurant** (tel. 24-084, weekdays 1200–1400 and 1800–2200, Sat. 1800–2200), opposite Queen Salote Wharf, is known for its seafood.

Nuku'alofa's finest place to eat is the **Seaview Restaurant** (tel. 23-709; weekdays only) at Seaview Lodge, on Vuna Road west of the palace. The German chefs, Lothar and Martina, ensure that the food and atmosphere are excellent. Red snapper is T$27–29, lobster T$33–36, and steaks T$26–49 depending on the size. Tropical fruit appears in some dishes. They're open for dinner 1800–2200 (reservations recommended), and if you've got anything to celebrate or just want to treat yourself right, this should be your choice.

Pizzeria Little Italy (Angelo Crapanzano, tel. 25-053; Mon.–Sat. 1200–1400 and 1830–2300), west on the waterfront beyond the Seaview Restaurant, serves some of the tastiest pizza and pasta in Tonga.

Groceries

Talamahu Market (closed Sun.) has all the fruit and vegetables you'd expect, and most prices are posted (beware of overcharging if they're not). Unexpectedly, you're not allowed to eat in the market and the police may talk to you if you do.

Groceries are sold at **Molisi Tonga Supermarket** (tel. 23-355; Mon.–Thurs. 0800–1730, Fri. and Sat. 0800–2000), on Salote Road opposite the market.

Nuku'alofa's largest supermarket is the **Kinikinilau Shopping Center** (tel. 24-044; Mon.–Thurs. 0730–1730, Fri. 0730–2100, Sat. 0700–1400) on Salote Road toward Faua Jetty.

The **Tonga Cooperative Federation Store** (tel. 23-777), on Taufa'ahau Road opposite Tungi Arcade, is often cheaper than the others.

If you'll be spending a Sunday in Nuku'alofa, buy a few snacks on Saturday to tide you over, as the whole town will be dead.

ENTERTAINMENT

Nuku'alofa's only movie house is **Loni's Cinema** (tel. 23-621), also known as Finau Theater Twin. Films begin Monday–Saturday at 2000, with additional showings at 1300, 1500, 2200, and midnight on certain days. The Sunday midnight showing gets around Tonga's infamous blue laws, but all films are heavily censored. Expect the movie to start 20 minutes late if they think they can sell a few more tickets (admission T$3).

Friday is the big night at Nuku'alofa's discos because on Saturday they must be firmly shut by midnight. Amusingly, many of them reopen a few seconds after midnight on Sunday, and there's dancing until sunrise Monday morning. Such is the way of the Lord! At most of the places mentioned below, men must wear long pants and a shirt with a collar if they want to be admitted. These rules are for the convenience of doormen trying to keep out troublemakers, but there may be no exceptions. A $100 silk Gucci T-shirt won't do if it doesn't have a collar.

The Italian-operated **Ambassador Night Club** (tel. 23-906), just beyond the Tonga National Center south of town, has a nice location next to

Fanga'uta Lagoon and you can even get a table right beside the water. It's open Wednesday to Saturday from 2100—take a taxi to get there.

Also very popular is the **Blue Pacific International Night Club** (tel. 25-994), at Maufanga on the Bypass Road four km southeast of town (take a taxi). They're open Tuesday to Friday 2100–0400, Saturday 2100–midnight, playing rock music and reggae. When you tire of dancing inside, you can sit out on the terrace and chat. It's safe, and large crowds turn out for the various beauty pageants, including one for cross-dressers.

The downmarket **Phoenix Disco** (tel. 23-270) on Fatafehi Road has live music from 2000 Monday–Saturday. Occasional fistfights break out here among the local Tongans. It's an experience for single males but not recommended for women or couples.

Bars

Friday nights Wanda's Bar at the **Pacific Royale Hotel** has a happy hour from 1700–1800. **Davina's** (tel. 23-385) and the **Waterfront Café** (tel. 21-004) opposite Faua Jetty are other places where you kick off the evening on Fridays. Opposite Queen Salote Wharf farther east, **Billfish Bar** (tel. 24-084) is considered by many to be Nuku'alofa's best.

The **'Oua Inu Vai Bar** (tel. 25-430; closed Sun.), right next to the Tonga Visitors Bureau, has a good atmosphere. The name means "Don't Drink the Water." There's live music 2000–midnight (they open at 1600). Ask about the huts for rent in the rear garden.

Drink with the local elite at the **Tonga Club** (tel. 22-710). You're supposed to be a member, but you'll be welcome if you look all right. They're open daily until 2300 (on Sunday enter through the side door).

The quaint, old **Nuku'alofa Club** (tel. 25-160), on Salote Road near the Royal Palace, has been a hangout for local male expats and assorted nobles since 1914, and they're a bit selective about who they let in: Poorly dressed men and females of all descriptions are most unwelcome. Before you'll be served, the bartender will have to find someone to sign you in, and you'll probably be asked where you're staying (don't say the Pacific Royale unless it's true, as the manager is a regular here). Watch the reaction if you mention a backpacker hostel.

Cultural Shows for Visitors

Traditional Tongan dancing can be witnessed at the Tonga National Center on Tuesday and Thursday nights, at Fafa Island Resort on Wednesday nights, at the International Dateline Hotel on Wednesday and Saturday nights, at the Waterfront Café on Thursday nights, and at the Good Samaritan Inn on Friday nights. Package tours with dinner and transfers are available to all of the above.

Intellectual Activities

The privately run **'Atenisi Institute** (tel. 25-034 or 24-819, fax 24-819, http://kalianet.to/atenisi), in the western part of the city, began as an evening high school in 1963 but it now offers university-level courses right up to Ph.Ds. It has an international reputation for its classical school of thought—a bastion of critical mindedness and creative thinking in a conformist country. If you're an "expert" on anything, Professor Futa Helu may invite you to lecture the students. Write in advance or make an appointment soon after you arrive. There's no pay, but someone might end up buying you lunch. During the school year (February–October) there's a free public lecture at the Institute every Monday at 2000. It's a good opportunity to meet a few of the students over coffee, but you might call ahead or visit beforehand to check the subject and to make sure there really will be a lecture that week. The traditional graduation ceremonies in November are not to be missed if you happen to be there at the time. (The Institute receives no government or church funding, and is in urgent need of overseas assistance. Unfortunately, the Tongan Government has attempted to cripple this unique institution it doesn't control by insisting that all foreign funding proposals must go through official channels, then deliberately holding up the paperwork until the application deadlines have passed.)

SHOPPING

Handicraft prices in Tonga have increased sharply in recent years but you can still find bargains if you shop around. Baskets, mats, and occasionally tapa are reasonable buys, and there's no hard sell anywhere, so you can browse at leisure. A good place to begin is **Langafonua,** the Tongan Women's Association Handicraft Center (tel. 21-014) on Taufa'ahau Road in the center of town. Also try the **Friendly Islands Marketing Cooperative Handicraft Shop** (tel. 23-155), otherwise known as "FIMCO" or "Kalia Handicrafts," opposite the Tungi Arcade. A fishing goods store behind FIMCO sells snorkeling gear.

Also check upstairs at **Talamahu Market,** where you can buy directly from the craftspeople, but avoid buying anything at the market on a cruise-ship day when prices are jacked up. A "lane" or *langana* of tapa at the market should cost T$12 to T$15 (those with crown or Tongan seal designs are more expensive). Tapa is best purchased directly from the producers—just listen for the sound of the beating while you're touring the island.

The handicraft shop at the **Tonga National Center** is more expensive, and their woodcarvings are mostly nontraditional masks and tikis. The whalebone carvings sold here are prohibited entry into most countries under endangered species legislation, as is the black coral jewelry. It's a shame the center sells this type of tacky tourist art.

Ginette at **Tapa Craft** (tel. 26-760; weekdays 1200–1600), next to the Baha'i Temple on Lavina Road, makes small tapa souvenirs and dolls that are excellent souvenirs. She also trades paperbacks one for one. (If you love cats, drop in to visit Ginette's large family.)

Several shops along Taufa'ahau Road sell fancy Tonga shirts, including **Look Sharp Tonga** (tel. 26-056) and **Blue Banana Studios** (tel. 24-846).

The **Philatelic Bureau** (tel. 22-238), above the post office, sells attractive stamps and first-day covers from Tonga and Niuafo'ou.

Bring with you all the film you'll need, as it's rather expensive in Tonga.

INFORMATION AND SERVICES

Information

The Tonga Visitors Bureau (tel. 25-334, tourism@ kalianet.to; Mon.–Fri. 0800–1630, Sat. 0800– 1400) on Vuna Road is usually helpful and has lots of free brochures. Peruse their notice boards for all the latest tourist news. They'll also help you make your accommodation or tour bookings.

Maps

A few maps are still available at the dusty Lands and Survey Department (tel. 23-611) in the back yard of the Ministry Block.

Navigational charts (T$14 each) of Tonga, Samoa, and New Zealand are available at the Hydrographic Office (tel. 24-696; weekdays 0800–1600) at Touliki Naval Base, just east of Queen Salote Wharf. The hassle here is that you must first go the base to select your charts and get an invoice, then you must visit military head-quarters near Centenary Church in town to pay, then return to the base with the stamped invoice to pick up the charts.

Bookstores and Libraries

The Friendly Islands Bookshop (tel. 23-787, fax 23-631, fibs@kalianet.to), below Tungi Arcade, is one of the best in the South Pacific. Ask for books by local authors 'Epeli Hau'ofa, Pesi Fonua, Konai Helu Thaman, and Tupou Posesi Fanua. They also carry Tongan music cassettes and com-pact discs, and topographical maps of Tonga.

Family Christian Bookshop (tel. 25-723), op-posite the Tonga Development Bank on Fatafehi Road, has place mats and posters bearing mar-velous photos of Tongan lifestyle and culture.

The 'Utue'a Public Library (weekdays 1600–2000), below the Catholic basilica on Taufa'a-hau Road, charges T$5 annual membership. There's also a good library in the University of the South Pacific, Tonga Campus (tel. 29-055, fax 29-249) near the Golf Club at Ha'ateiho, out on the road to the airport. Ask to see their col-lection of antique Tongan war clubs.

Travel Offices

The Air New Zealand office (tel. 23-828) is in the Tungi Arcade. The Air Pacific agent is E.M. Jones Ltd. (tel. 23-423) on Taufa'ahau Road. Teta Tours at Railway and Wellington roads represents Air Fiji (tel. 26-125). The fly NiU Airlines office (tel. 28-280) is in the Royco Building on Fatafehi Road. Polynesian Airlines (tel. 24-560) is at the corner of Fatafehi and Salote roads.

If you need a travel agent, try Vital Travel (tel. 23-617) next to Loni's Cinema on Welling-ton Road.

Money

The main branch of the Westpac/Bank of Tonga (tel. 23-933; Mon.–Fri. 0900–1530, Sat. 0830–1130) is on Taufa'ahau Road. A smaller Bank of Tonga branch (weekdays 0900–1530) is opposite the entrance to Queen Salote Wharf. The Bank of Tonga has an ATM and gives cash advances on MasterCard and Visa for T$6 commission. They charge T$8.10 commission on traveler's checks.

The ANZ Bank (tel. 24-944, anztonga@ anz.com; Mon.–Fri. 0900–1600, Sat. 0900–1130), diagonally opposite the police station, has an ATM and changes traveler's checks without commission. They charge T$8 for cash advances.

The Malaysian-owned MBf Bank (tel. 24-600, mbfbank@kalianet.to), below Hotel Nuku'alofa, charges T$2 commission and doesn't give cash advances on credit cards.

Outside banking hours the Dateline Hotel will change money for about two percent less than the banks. Everywhere, you must show your passport to change money.

Post and Telecommunications

Postage in Tonga is inexpensive compared to other countries, but if you plan on making any heavy purchases, it's a good idea to visit the post office (tel. 21-700) beforehand to clarify the rules and rates. It should be possible to mail parcels up to 20 kilograms by surface mail, although this does vary according to the destination country. Poste restante mail is held until they get tired of seeing the letter, at which time it's sent back. If you're ex-pecting a parcel, ask them to check that too (and expect to pay customs duty if you get one). The DHL Worldwide Express agent (tel. 23-617) is next to Loni's Cinema on Wellington Road.

To make a domestic long-distance telephone call to 'Eua, Ha'apai, Vava'u, or anywhere else in Tonga you must go to the Telecom Telephone Exchange on Unga Road (open 24 hours daily).

The Tonga Telecom office (tel. 24-255; Mon.–Sat. 0700–2400, Sun. 1200–2400) on Salote Road accepts international telephone calls, faxes, and telegrams. You can receive faxes sent to fax 676/23-915 at 50 cents a page here.

You'll find card telephones outside the main post office, at the Telecom office on Salote Road, at the airport, and at a few other locations around Nuku'alofa. The post office sells the cards.

Internet Access

The Tonga Telecom office (tel. 24-255) on Salote Road provides internet access at T$2 per 15 minutes, but the computers are usually occupied.

Ants ICT Services (tel. 27-946, www.cafe .afe.to; weekdays 0900–1900, Sat. 0900–1400) operates an internet cafe on the ground floor of the Tungi Arcade behind Air New Zealand. They charge T$5 an hour with a T$1 minimum.

Internet access is also available at Friends Tourist Center (tel. 26-323; weekdays 0900–1700, Sat. 0900–1400), next to Friends Café on Taufa'ahau Road, at T$4 for 15 minutes.

Visas and Officialdom

You can get an extension of stay for T$51 from the Immigration Office (tel. 23-222; Mon., Tues., and Thurs. 0900–1200 and 1400–1600, Wed. and Fri. 0900–1200) at the central police station on Salote Road.

The countries with diplomatic representatives in Nuku'alofa are Germany (tel. 23-477), on Taufa'ahau Road between the Pacific Royale Hotel and Air Pacific, Korea (tel. 23-874), on Salote Road, New Zealand (tel. 23-122), on Salote Road opposite the post office, Sweden (tel. 22-855), on Salote Road opposite the Reserve Bank of Tonga, China (tel. 24-554), on Vuna Road, and the United Kingdom (tel. 24-285), on Vuna Road west of the Royal Palace. The Australian High Commission (tel. 23-244; weekdays 0900–1100), on Salote Road behind the International Dateline Hotel, also represents Canadians. The United States is not represented

in Tonga, and U.S. citizens in need of assistance must contact the embassy in Suva, Fiji (tel. 679/331-4466, fax 679/330-0081).

Laundry

Savoy Dry Cleaners (tel. 23-314; Mon.–Fri. 0800–1800, Sat. 0800–1400), on Fatafehi Road south of the center, washes and dries laundry at T$2 a kilo. Unfortunately, there have been reports of items going missing here and yachties with huge loads have been refused service for some odd reason.

Yachting Facilities

Cruising yachts can tie up to the seawall in the small boat harbor beside Queen Salote Wharf three km east of Nuku'alofa, though the channel is only 2.5 meters deep in the center. Customs is on the wharf, but immigration is at the police station in town. Keep valuables carefully stowed, as there have been many thefts from boats here.

Health

Medical and dental consultations are available at Vaiola Hospital (tel. 23-200), just outside town on the way to the airport.

Unless you have unlimited time and are on the barest of budgets, it's better to attend the German Clinic (Dr. Heinz Betz, tel. 22-736, after hours tel. 24-625), on Vaka'akolo Road opposite Vilai Barracks. Clinic hours are weekdays 0930–1230 and Saturday 1500–1700, but make an appointment.

A recommended dentist is Dr. Sione Ui Kilisimasi (tel. 24-780), beside Fasi Pharmacy on Salote Road near the Australian High Commission.

TRANSPORTATION

For information on air and sea services from Tongatapu to the other Tongan islands, see the Transportation section in the chapter introduction.

Ferries to 'Eua leave from Faua Jetty, but all ships to Ha'apai and Vava'u depart the adjoining Queen Salote Wharf. The offices of **Uata Shipping** (tel. 23-855) and the **Shipping Corporation of Polynesia** office (tel. 24-413) are at the entrance to Queen Salote Wharf.

KINGDOM OF TONGA

By Bus

A local bus station opposite the Tonga Visitors Bureau has city buses to Halaleva, Ma'ufanga, Va'epopua, and Vaiola. The Halalevu bus goes south to Fanga'uta Lagoon, then east to Queen Salote Wharf. The Va'epopua bus travels east to Queen Salote Wharf and the Friendly Islander Hotel. The Vaiola bus goes south to the hospital.

Opposite the Ministry Block farther west on the waterfront is another station with long-distance buses marked Fahefa or Ha'akame to the Houma blowholes, marked Hihifo or Masilamea to the Kolovai flying foxes and Ha'atafu Beach, marked Veitongo, Folaha, or Vaini to the golf course or Tongan Wildlife Center, marked Malapo, Lapaha, or Mu'a to the Lapaha archaeological area, and marked Niutoua to the Ha'amonga trilithon. Most fares are T$1.20 or less and visitors often use these buses.

The local bus to the airport from opposite the Ministry Block might be labeled Halaliku or Fua'amotu. Some (but not all) of the larger Liahona buses also pass the airport, as does the large green-and-yellow Malolelei Transport bus. It's unusual for a tourist to take one of these buses to the airport, as the entire tourism establishment assumes you'll want to use a special airport bus or a taxi.

The bus stations are rather chaotic but people are generally helpful. The bus service starts very early around 0600 but the last bus back to Nuku'alofa from Kolovai and Ha'amonga is at 1500. The buses stop running just before 1700 and don't run at all on Sunday. You pay as you get off. They're inexpensive and a great way to observe Tongan life.

Taxis

Throughout Tonga, registered taxis have a "T" on their license plate. Meterless taxis at the market are T$1.50 for a trip in town, T$3–4 for a longer trip in the vicinity, T$15 to the airport. Always ask the price beforehand and have small change. Taxis must purchase a special police permit to work on Sunday, so you won't see many on the road that day, and if you want one then, arrange it with a driver on Saturday and expect to pay a higher fare. Also, only telephone for a taxi at the exact moment you need it. If you call and ask them to come in 30 minutes, they'll probably forget and not come at all. City Taxi (tel. 24-666) has a stand near Teta Tours.

Some taxi drivers double as tour guides, and an island tour with them will run T$60–80 for up to four people (check the price beforehand). There have been reports of thefts from taxis, involving drivers who removed objects from handbags left in the car while visitors got out to take photos, etc., so be forewarned.

Tongan drivers often tailgate and speed. If it's a taxi or tour bus you're in and this starts happening, ask them to slow down right away, because accidents are commonplace and tourists have been seriously injured. (You can't really ask a local public bus to slow down, so sit a bit back if you're concerned.)

Car and Scooter Rentals

Foreign and international driver's licenses are not accepted in Tonga, so before renting a car or scooter you must first visit the Traffic Department at the Central Police Station (tel. 23-222; weekdays 0830–1230 and 1330–1630) on Salote Road to purchase a Tongan driver's license (T$15). You must queue up several times—once to get the form, another time to pay, then again to get a stamp—so allow at least an hour. This is strictly a revenue-generating operation and no practical test is required.

The speed limit is 40 kph in town and 65 kph on the open road. Speed limits are strictly enforced on Tongatapu by police with hand-held radar, and on-the-spot T$50 fines are routine. Avoid hitting a pig, as heavy compensation will have to be paid. Also beware of being hit from behind when you stop. Never drive a car in Tonga unless you're sure the insurance is valid, otherwise you'll have big problems in case of an accident. Driving is on the left.

Avis (tel. 21-179, fax 21-203, avis@kalianet.to), upstairs in the Tungi Arcade on Taufa'ahau Road, rents cars with unlimited mileage beginning at T$80 a day, including insurance on damage over T$1,000. To reduce your liability to T$250, a daily T$8 insurance surcharge must be paid. Five percent tax is extra. Weekend rates are available.

E.M. Jones Travel (tel. 23-423, http://kalia net.to/emjones), Taufa'ahau and Wellington roads, rents cars at T$80 a day including insurance.

Budget Rent a Car (tel. 23-510) is next to Asco Motors on Taufa'ahau Road south of town.

Alisei Ltd. (tel. 24-977) on Vuna Road rents scooters at T$20 a day.

By Bicycle

Rather than going to all the trouble and expense of renting a car, see Tongatapu by bicycle. From Nuku'alofa you can easily reach all the main sights in two days, visiting the east and west sides of the island on alternate days. The main roads are excellent without too much traffic, and steep hills don't exist. The open landscape invites you to look around at leisure and there are lots of small villages. Abundant road signs make it very easy to find your own way, but don't trust the posted distances. Cycling can be tiring and dusty, but the friendly islanders are quick to smile and wave at a pedaling visitor. And if you happen to see a black van with a police escort coming your way, pull over and let them pass: You're about to see the king and queen!

Quality 15-speed mountain bikes are for rent at **Niko Bicycle Rental** (theoretically Mon.–Sat. 0900–1700) on the waterfront opposite the Dateline Hotel. They charge T$2/10 an hour/day. Many guesthouses also rent bicycles. A bicycle tour is a good way to liven up a dull Tongan Sunday, provided you've reserved your bike by Saturday morning.

Local Tours

Kingdom Tours (tel. 25-200, fax 23-447, king domt@kalianet.to), in the Tungi Arcade next to Air New Zealand, offers a city sights tour (T$17), a cultural tour (T$20), a history tour to eastern Tongatapu (T$25), and a royal tour to western Tongatapu (T$53 including lunch). The all-day island cruise is T$45 with lunch. If you're interested, check well ahead, since they need a certain number of people to run a tour and don't go every day.

Friends Tourist Center (Paul Johansson, tel. 26-323, fax 25-730, friends@kalianet.to; weekdays 0900–1700, Sat. 0900–1400), next to

Friends Café on Taufa'ahau Road, and **Teta Tours** (tel. 24-506, fax 23-238, tetatour@kalianet.to), at Railway and Wellington roads, also offer sightseeing tours. The Tonga Visitors Bureau and most hotels can also help arrange sightseeing tours. Few of the road tours operate on Sunday and it's more common to do a boat trip to one of the islands off Nuku'alofa that day (see Getting There in the Offshore Islands section that follows).

Sione (John) Tohi's "Something to Do on Sunday" tour at 0930 includes a church service, visits to Christian sites, and a family *umu* feast. It's T$45 pp and you must book by Saturday at Friends Tourist Centre.

Also ask about the snorkeling tours operated by Soane Pasi of **Marine Adventures** (tel. 24-039) which cost T$40 for the day including an *umu* lunch.

WESTERN TONGATAPU

Take the Hihifo bus or ride a bicycle to Kolovai to see the **Flying Fox Sanctuary,** where countless thousands of the animals *(Pteropus tonganus)* hang in casuarina trees for about a kilometer along the road. Flying foxes are actually bats (the only mammals that can fly) with foxlike heads and wingspans of up to a meter across. Nocturnal creatures, they cruise after dark in search of food and hang upside down during the day. Legend says the bats were a gift from a Samoan maiden to an ancient Tongan navigator. Considered sacred, they may only be hunted by members of the royal family.

Just beyond Kolovai is the turnoff for the Good Samaritan Inn, 1.5 km off the main road. Farther west, behind the primary school at **Kanokupolu,** is the *langi*, or stone-lined burial mound of the Tu'i Kanokupolu, an ancestor of the present royal family. The stones to build this tomb were quarried at nearby **Ha'atafu Beach,** and a few partially cut slabs are still anchored to the bedrock at the water's edge, just where the access road meets the beach. The marinelife at Ha'atafu is good because it's a designated "reef reserve" and there's a T$200 fine for fishing. Ha'atafu is a *palangi* beach, which means there's no hassle about swimming on Sunday, but if you come for

FLYING FOXES

Flying foxes are found from Madagascar to the Cook Islands, with 55 species of the genus *Pteropus* living on different islands. In Western Polynesia, *Pteropus samoensis* is a daytime feeder that roosts alone or in small groups in the rainforest canopy, while the nocturnal *Pteropus tonganus* lives in colonies of several hundred, either in the forest or in trees along roads. Its feeding flights begin just before dusk and many species of rainforest trees and plants depend on the bats for pollination and seed dispersal. Flying foxes produce only one offspring per year and it's cared for by the mother for six to eight months. During the 1980s tens of thousands of flying foxes were slaughtered in Samoa for export to Guam, where they're considered a delicacy. Luckily this trade largely came to an end in 1989, when most island bats were listed as endangered species. Today habitat destruction is the gravest threat facing the animals in both Tonga and Samoa. On Tongatapu only one small tract of old growth rainforest still remains, although the surviving bats enjoy royal protection. In Samoa they are still hunted by villagers.

a picnic, don't leave any rubbish or you'll also be liable for a fine. The Kanokupolu Restaurant and Bar (open weekends only) between the Ha'atafu Beach Resort and 'Otuhaka Beach Resort serves lunch and dinner but the food isn't exceptional. There's excellent snorkeling, especially at high tide—you'll see dozens of species of fish. Just watch out for an east-to-west current. Some of the best reef-break surfing in Tonga is here, also at high tide, but even then it's challenging due to the shallow water, and a protective wetsuit is almost essential equipment. On the plus side, the waves are only 100 meters offshore.

Hihifo buses from Ha'atafu head straight back to town, but there's no bus from Fo'ui to Fahefa. If you want to go on to the blowholes discussed below, you'll find it a pleasant five-km walk (or hitch) with the possibility of a side trip to Monotapu Beach.

Accommodations

Since 1979, Tonga's premier surfing resort has been the **Ha'atafu Beach Resort** (tel. 41-088, www.surfingtonga.com). The Ha'atafu Beach is run by Australian surfer Steve Burling, who first came to Tongatapu in 1977, and whose son Michael is now Tonga's national surfing champion. No sign advertises this resort, as Steve doesn't cater to day-trippers who only drop in for lunch or drinks. The eight thatched *fale* with shared facilities are T$150 double including breakfast, buffet dinner, and nonmotorized sporting equipment. Shared rooms are T$82 pp. These are the walk-in, space-available rates. Through an agent it's T$163/189 single/double or T$113 pp for a shared double. Add a 20 percent high season surcharge December–February and June–September (the 7.5 percent tax is also extra). There's a 10 percent discount if you stay a month (many do). Ha'atafu only takes 15 guests at a time and is often full, so call ahead if you don't have a booking. Airport transfers are T$50 each way for up to four persons. The dining room, lounge, and public toilets have electricity, but kerosene lamp lighting is used in the *fale*. The meals are ample and excellent, and videos are shown every evening. When enough people are interested, Steve organizes boat trips for snorkeling, fishing, or surfing on outlying reefs (T$19 pp). The peak surfing season here is June, July, and August with five great left-handers within a 10-minute walk of the motel, as southern swells generated around New Zealand crash into the Ha'atafu coast. From January to March you have a choice of four right-handers and one left nearby, but at this time it's usually better to take a boat around to the reefs on the northwest side of Tongatapu, which catch waves rolling down from Hawaii. Steve knows all the better waves and his motel is *the* place for serious surfers (you must bring your own board).

The **'Otuhaka Beach Resort** (Phil Fie'eiki, tel. 21-266 or 41-599, fax 24-782, otuhaka@kalia net.to), at the south end of lovely Ha'atafu Beach west of Kanokupolu, has 16 simple bungalows starting at T$35/45 single/double with shared bath. Bungalows with private bath are T$65 or T$95, and there's a two-bedroom self-catering apartment at T$170. 'Otuhaka's restaurant/bar serves breakfast/lunch/dinner at T$4.50/10.50/13.50. Sporting equipment is available and tours can be arranged. Nonguests may be asked to pay T$2 to use the beach.

The **Good Samaritan Inn** (tel. 41-022, fax 41-095, gsi@kalianet.to) on Kolovai Beach, 18 km west of Nuku'alofa, is not such a great choice. The nine older bungalows with shared bath are T$30/50 single/double, while three newer bungalows with private bath are T$50/80/95 single/double/triple. One deluxe two-bedroom bungalow with private bath and cooking facilities is T$70/90/115. The bungalow prices include breakfast, and weekly rates are available. You can pitch your tent on the grounds for T$10 pp and the four-bed dorm is T$12 pp without breakfast. Cooking facilities are provided, or you can use the Inn's expensive and variable restaurant/bar, which sits on a large concrete terrace overlooking the rocky shore. Friday night there's a buffet dinner accompanied by Polynesian dancing (T$30 pp, plus T$5 pp for return bus transfers from Nuku'alofa, if required). On Sundays they prepare a popular barbecue lunch. On cruise-ship days the Inn overflows with day-tripping passengers (fortunately, they're not that frequent). Beware of currents if you snorkel here. Take the Hihifo bus to Kolovai, then walk 1.5 km to the Inn. A taxi from Nuku'alofa will cost T$15, from the airport T$25.

The **Princess Resort** (tel. 41-400, fax 24-530), in a nice location on gorgeous Monotapu Beach, has 10 bungalows ranging in price from T$40 single or double with shared bath to T$205 for a self-contained family room. A restaurant and bar are on the premises.

SOUTHERN TONGATAPU

Surf forced through naturally formed air vents creates spectacular **blowholes** on the rocky, terraced southwest coast near Houma, 15 km from Nuku'alofa. From the end of the road, walk along the path to the right. Waves batter the coral cliffs and spout water up to 30 meters in the air through eroded tunnels. These impressive blowholes number in the hundreds—come at high tide on a windy day! Bus service from Nuku'alofa to Houma is fairly frequent and continues west to Fahefa.

Just east of Utulau a dirt road branches off the paved highway (and bus route) between Houma and Nuku'alofa via Pea and runs along the south coast. Three km along this dirt road is Keleti Beach Resort (presently closed), with more blowholes and several small but strikingly beautiful beaches and pools protected from the open sea by unusual coral terraces. You can snorkel among the brightly colored tropical fish in the large tidal pools at the foot of the resort, just be aware of the currents. Keleti is down a road to the right, distinguishable from other similar roads by the electricity lines. As previously mentioned, there's no bus service east of the Utulau-Pea road, so you're better off coming by bicycle.

The **Tongan Wildlife Center** (tel./fax 29-449, birdpark@kalianet.to; daily 0900–1700), also known as the Veitongo Bird Park, is near the coast, a short distance east of Keleti on the south coast road 10 km from Nuku'alofa. To get there from Nuku'alofa, take the Folaha, Malapo, Vaini, or Veitongo buses to the turnoff, then it's a 2.5 km walk south from the main highway at Veitongo (a taxi from this corner will cost T$2 compared to T$8 from town). The Center is unique in Tonga for its small bird park and botanical garden. Examples of most native Tongan land birds are kept in aviaries brimming with vegetation—take the time to wait for them to appear. The small botanical garden displays all of the common Polynesian food plants, and at the entrance is an informative photo display on Tongan birds and reptiles. It's run by a nonprofit organization working to save endangered species of Tongan birds, so your T$3 admission fee goes to a good cause.

Also on the south coast is **Hufangalupe** ("Pigeon's Doorway"), a huge natural coral bridge with a sandy cove flanked by towering cliffs, six km east of the bird park and four km from Vaini, the closest bus stop. Make your way down the inside of the fault from the back to see the bridge and sea before you. As you return to the main south coast road, watch for a path on the left at the bottom of a slight dip, which leads down to a lovely white beach (beware of theft while you're in swimming).

EASTERN TONGATAPU

Tupou College (tel. 32-240) at Toloa is three km off the airport road. No bus service reaches the college, but you can take a Malapo, Lapaha, or Mu'a bus to Malapo, then walk south on the road beside the Mormon church. Tupou College is the oldest secondary school in the South Pacific, established by the Free Wesleyan Church in 1866, and it's believed that the first royal capital of Tonga was near here. The college has a small museum of dusty local relics, crafts, and artifacts. There are no fixed hours, but someone will let you in if you ask at the school office.

The main reason to come is the **Toloa Rainforest Reserve,** the last six hectares of natural forest remaining on Tongatapu. Most of the forest was cut down during the building of Fua'amotu Airport in 1940, and this remaining fragment is just 900 meters southeast of the college administration building. Take the road south beside a deep pit behind the library, and turn left onto a dirt road after 300 meters, then right to an old information shelter. Although the reserve is not as well cared for as might be desired, many of the trees are still labeled, and colorful butterflies flutter across the trails. More importantly, Toloa shelters a large colony of flying foxes, and it's much more intriguing to observe them here in their natural habitat than along the main road at Kolovai.

NORTHEASTERN TONGATAPU

Across the lagoon from Nuku'alofa, just southwest of Mu'a is a monument marking the spot where in 1777 Captain Cook landed from his ship the *Endeavor* and rested under a banyan tree (which has since disappeared). He then continued into Lapaha, the capital of Tonga at the time, to visit Pau, the Tu'i Tonga. Retrace Cook's footsteps into this richest archaeological area in western Polynesia.

For over 600 years beginning around A.D. 1200, **Lapaha** (Mu'a) was the seat of the Tu'i Tonga dynasty. Nothing remains of the royal residence today, but some 28 *langi* (burial mounds of ancient royalty) have been located in or near Mu'a. Due to local objections, none have yet been excavated. Several of these great rectangular platforms with recessed tiers of coralline limestone are clearly visible from the main road, including the *langi* of the last Tu'i Tonga (1865), a Catholic, which has a cross on top.

The finest of the terraced tombs, rather hidden down a side road, is the **Paepae 'o Tele'a,** built during the early 17th century for the 29th Tu'i Tonga. Notice in particular the gigantic L-shaped monoliths at the corners, the slanting upper surfaces, and the feet that extend underground. In its context, this mighty monument has all the power and emotional impact of a classical Greek temple. Adjacent to the Paepae 'o Tele'a is the **Namoala,** a three-tiered pyramid with the stone burial vault still intact on top. The **Hehea mound** opposite Namoala bears another two vaults.

The *langi* of Lapaha are the most imposing ancient tombs in the South Pacific and rank with the *moai* of Easter Island and Huahine's Maeva ruins as major archaeological sites. The beating of tapa mallets from houses all around the *langi* adds an otherworldliness to this magical place. Bus service from Nuku'alofa to Mu'a (20 km) is frequent throughout the day, making it easy to visit.

HA'AMONGA 'A MAUI

Catch the Niutoua bus to this famous trilithon, Tonga's most engaging relic, 32 km east of Nuku'alofa. The structure consists of an arch made from three huge rectangular blocks of nonstratified limestone. Two upright pillars of coral, each about five meters high, support a central lintel that is 5.8 meters long and weighs 816 kilos. The name means "The Burden of the God Maui" because, according to myth, the hero Maui brought the trilithon here on his shoulders all the way from Wallis Island using the connecting stone as his carrying pole.

Various other theories have been advanced to explain the origin of this massive 12-metric-ton stone archway. Some believe it was the gateway to Heketa, the old royal compound of Tonga. Others have called it Tonga's Stonehenge and assert that grooves incised on the upper side of the lintel could have been used in determining the seasons. To emphasize this concept, three tracks have been cut from the trilithon to the coast, the better to observe sunrise on the equinox, as well as the summer and winter solstices. This would have been useful to determine the planting and harvesting periods for yams or the sailing seasons. Most scholars believe, however, that the grooves were cut long after the trilithon was built and discount their utility as an astronomical calendar.

Since few archaeological excavations of ancient monuments have been conducted in Tonga, it's not known for sure when or why the Ha'a-monga 'a Maui was built. Local tradition attributes it to the 11th Tu'i Tonga, Tu'itatui, who reigned around A.D. 1200. Evidently this king feared that his two sons would quarrel after his death, so he had the trilithon erected to symbolize the bond of brotherhood uniting them. As long as the monument stood, its magic would uphold social harmony.

Nearby is a 2.7-meter-tall slab called the **'Esi Makafaakinanga** against which, it's said, this king would lean while addressing his people, a precaution to prevent anyone from spearing him in the back. His name means "the king who hits the knees" because Tu'itatui would administer a sharp slap with his staff to anyone who came too close to his regal person. The area between this slab and the Ha'amonga was the meeting place, or *mala'e,* where the king would receive tribute from Samoa, Futuna, Wallis, Rotuma, and Niue, all of which were subservient to Tonga at that time.

Beyond the slab is three-tiered **Langi Heketa,** believed to be the oldest of Tongatapu's *langi* and the prototype of those at Mu'a. It's believed that either Tu'itatui or a female member of his family is buried here. It was Tu'itatui's son Tal'atama who moved the capital to Mu'a, which offered far better anchorage for their large seagoing canoes. In the bush behind Langi Heketa are a number of large platforms, or *paepae,* on which the royal residences would have stood.

Bus service to the trilithon is about hourly until 1700, and the trilithon is just beside the road. If you have time, follow one of the tracks down to the rocky coast. Actually, you'll need more than an hour to visit this interesting area and read all the posted explanations. When you've seen enough, just start walking back along the road and flag down the first bus that passes.

THE EAST COAST

It's a three-km walk southeast from the bus stop at Mu'a Police Station to Haveluliku village (no bus service). Ask someone here to point out the *makatolo,* huge stones that the demigod Maui reputedly threw across from 'Eua Island at an errant chicken. **'Anahulu Cave** is on the coast near the village. You'll need a flashlight to explore the stalactite cave. The large freshwater pool inside is swimmable and the intrepid could swim back into another hidden cavern, but don't leave your possessions in too obvious a spot, as there have been thefts here. You may be charged an admission fee.

At low tide only, you can walk south from the cave to **Laulea Beach.** The beach continues unbroken for several km to **'Oholei Beach** where Tongan feasts were once staged in the Hina Cave. There's a fine view across to 'Eua Island. Sporadic bus service runs from Lavengatonga village near 'Oholei back to town.

OFFSHORE ISLANDS

Some of the many small islands off Tongatapu's north coast bear small tourist resorts that are favorite day-trip destinations for tourists staying in Nuku'alofa, especially on Sunday. Pangaimotu Island tends to cater to budget or independent travelers, while Fafa Island is more upmarket, and Atata Island is set up for packaged tourists from New Zealand. Scuba diving is possible upon prior arrangement, but these are mostly picnic places where you go to get some sun and have a day at the beach.

Accommodations

The **Tongan Beachcomber Island Village** (tel. 11-236, fax 23-759) on Pangaimotu Island is the closest island resort to Nuku'alofa and also the cheapest. It's owned by the royal family and the island name means "royal island." The four simple *fale* are T$30/50 single/double, while the six-bed dorm is T$15 pp and camping space is T$10 pp. No cooking facilities are provided, and meals at their restaurant are reasonable. The tap water is saline. The reef around the island is good, and there's even a half-sunken ship, the *Marner*, sticking up out of the water for snorkelers to explore. If you're a yachtie you'll want to know that Pangaimotu Island has excellent anchorage (all the other offshore islands are surrounded by treacherous reefs). Boat transfers are T$12 pp return. It's a day-trip island and somewhat of a local hangout. On Sunday many local expats come over to booze, and while it's not officially banned to bring over your own lunch, you'll be more comfortable having your picnic well away from the resort and other tourists.

Fafa Island Resort (Rainer Urtel, tel. 22-800, fax 23-592, www.fafa.to), quite a distance farther out than Pangaimotu Island, is one of the most tasteful resorts in Tonga. The eight standard *fales* with private bath (T$120/135 single/double) are rustic but adequate, while the eight superior beachside *fales* (T$240 single or double) are larger and more luxurious with open shower, sun deck, and garden. The marvelous meals in their pleasant thatched restaurant/bar are T$65/79 pp for two/three (no cooking facilities for guests). A full range of nonmotorized sporting activities is offered in the sapphire blue lagoon surrounding this delightful palm-covered, seven-hectare island. Snorkeling gear is loaned free but Hobie Cat riding is T$30 an hour. The initial 30-minute boat ride is T$28 pp roundtrip, but once you're staying they'll ferry you into town and back as often as you like at no extra cost. Their shuttle boat leaves the island at 0900 and 1630, leaves Faua Jetty at 1100 and 1730, so you can easily spend the day in town. Fafa can be a little quiet at times, and would not be a good choice if you were out for aggressive motorized watersports, sightseeing, or socializing.

The **Royal Sunset Island Resort** (David and Terry Hunt; tel./fax 21-254, www.invited.to/royalsunset), on Atata Island 11 km northwest of town, is the most remote of the small island hotels

off Tongatapu. The entire island is owned by the king's younger son, Prince Lavaka, and most of Royal Sunset's local employees are from the friendly, 233-person Tongan village on the island. The 26 bungalows with private bath, fridge, kitchenette, and overhead fan are T$120/150 single/double. If you book through a travel agent abroad you could pay considerably more (direct email bookings work best). Their three-meal plan is T$50 pp, and the food is not bad with large portions. Drinks at the bar are on the expensive side, so take along a couple of bottles of duty-free booze. There's a swimming pool, and free activities for guests include tennis, Hobie Cat sailing, paddleboarding, windsurfing, rowboating, and snorkeling. Scuba diving is T$60/80 for one/two tanks, plus T$24 for full gear. The resort is right on a broad white-sand beach but the off-shore snorkeling is poor. Deep-sea fishing is T$240/480 a half/full day and up to six people can go for that price. The resort has a three-cabin yacht, the 15-meter *Impetuous* (www.sailingtonga.com), available for overnight charters at T$1,126 a day double including food. Island transfers from Nuku'alofa on their large catamaran *Manutahi II* are T$26 pp roundtrip.

Getting There

The various day trips to offshore islands are cheap, and a leisurely boat trip to one of the island resorts described above is recommended. The Pangaimotu Island boat leaves daily at 1000 and 1100, with extra trips at 1200 and 1300 on Sunday (T$12 for transfers only). Children under 12 pay half price. Fafa Island also does excellent day trips daily at 1100 (T$35 including a good lunch). On Wednesday, Fafa Island Resort offers a romantic dinner cruise with a Polynesian floor show departing Nuku'alofa at 1730 (T$45). Royal Sunset's day trip departs Sunday at 1000 (T$35 including a barbecue lunch). All these leave from Faua Jetty near Nuku'alofa's fish market, and bookings can be made at Teta Tours or at the International Dateline Hotel tour desk (no booking required for the Pangaimotu Island shuttles). Provided the weather cooperates, they're an excellent way to pass Nuku'alofa's pious Sunday, and you'll have a better chance of meeting interesting people if you go that day.

'Eua Island

A rough 40-km boat ride from Nuku'alofa, 'Eua is a good place to go for the weekend. Since tourist facilities are undeveloped you won't feel as oppressed as you might on a Nuku'alofa Sunday, and you'll have to entertain yourself here anyway. Bony bareback horses can be hired, but all spots on the island are within walking distance.

'Eua's hills are a contrast to flat Tongatapu. The thickly forested spine down the east side of 'Eua drops to perpendicular cliffs, while the west half is largely taken up by plantations and villages. At 87 square km, it's Tonga's third-largest island.

Facilities on 'Eua are extremely basic; this is a chance to get off the beaten tourist track and see real Tongan life. It's a rather grubby, depressing place, indicative of why so many Tongans live in Auckland. Three full days are enough to get the feel of the island.

SIGHTS

Matalanga 'a Maui

Legend tells how the demigod Maui thrust his digging stick into 'Eua and pulled it back and forth in anger at his mother, threatening thereby to upset the island. To visit the great pothole that remains from this event, head south of the sawmill and Ha'atua Mormon Church, take the second bush road on the left, and walk inland about 10 minutes. You'll need intuition or a guide to locate the pit hidden in the middle of a plantation on the right, although the lower level of the trees growing in it is an indicator. Holding onto vines, you can get right down into Matalanga 'a Maui itself for an eerie view of jungle-clad walls towering around you.

Southern 'Eua

Most of the families in Pangai and farther south were relocated from Niuafo'ou Island after a devastating volcanic eruption there in 1946. The road south from the wharf terminates after 10 km at **Ha'aluma Beach.** The deserted beach is a weathered reef with sandy pools to swim in,

but it's only safe as long as you hug the shore. There are some small blowholes and a view of Kalau Island.

Just before the descent to the beach, take the road to the left and keep straight one hour almost to the south tip of the island. Here a track veers left through high grass and starts going north up the east coast past a gate. The first cliff you come to across the field from the track is **Lakufa'anga,** where Tongans once called turtles from the sea. So many have been slaughtered that none appear anymore. Look down on the grassy ledges below the cliffs and you'll spot the nesting places of seabirds.

Continue north on the track a short distance, watching on the left for a huge depression partly visible through the trees. This is **Li'angahuo 'a Maui,** a tremendous natural stone bridge by the sea, which you can pass right over without

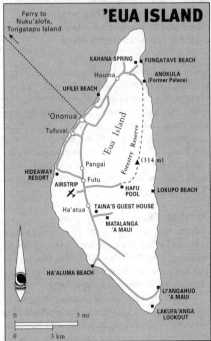

'EUA ISLAND

Ferry to Nuku'alofa, Tongatapu Island

KAHANA SPRING — FUNGATAVE BEACH
Houma — ANOKULA (Former Palace)
UFILEI BEACH
'Ononua
Tufuvai
Eua Island
Forestry Reserve
▲ (314 m)
Pangai
HIDEAWAY RESORT — Futu
AIRSTRIP — HAFU POOL
Ha'atua — LOKUPO BEACH
TAINA'S GUEST HOUSE
MATALANGA 'A MAUI
HA'ALUMA BEACH
LI'ANGAHUO 'A MAUI
LAKUFA'ANGA LOOKOUT

0   3 mi
0   3 km

© DAVID STANLEY

KINGDOM OF TONGA

© DAVID STANLEY

Legend tells how Li'angahuo 'a Maui on 'Eua Island was formed when the demigod Maui hurled his spear across the island.

realizing if you're not paying attention. Work your way around the side of the pothole for a clear view of the bridge. The story goes that after creating Matalanga, Maui threw his digging stick across 'Eua. It pierced the cliffs at this point and dove into the sea to carve out the Tonga Deep. After this impressive sight, continue up the coast a short distance to see more cliffs, which explain why the east side of 'Eua is uninhabited.

Northern 'Eua

Tufuvai village, two km south of 'Ononua wharf, is attractive but the undertow is deadly on an outgoing tide. Both this and **Ufilei Beach,** just two km north of the wharf across Tonga's only river bridge, are fine for a sunset stroll.

Tonga's most spectacular scenic viewpoint is just northeast of Houma village at **Anokula,** where in 1983 the king built himself a palace of which only the concrete foundations now re-

main. The soaring cliffs drop 120 meters straight into the coastal strip, creating an unsurpassed panorama of power and beauty.

After this visual blast look for a trail north up the coast to another access road that leads down to **Kahana Spring,** which supplies 'Eua with Tonga's purest water. Just beyond the spring is a second magnificent viewpoint over the east coast, directly above **Fungatave Beach.**

The Interior

Tonga's finest tropical forest is on the slopes just above Futu. Take the road inland from Sapa'ata toward the Forestry Experimental Farm. Continue east along the main road about 30 minutes till you reach the nursery. **Hafu Pool** is near the office, down a trail that continues straight ahead from the road on the right, but it's hardly worth the effort.

The forest, on the other hand, is well worth exploring for the many exotic species planted by the Ministry of Agriculture and Forestry (pine, red cedar, tree ferns) and the abundant birdlife, especially Pacific pigeons, crimson-crowned fruit doves, white-collared kingfishers, blue-crowned lorikeets, and red-breasted musk parrots. Now both forests and birds of 'Eua are threatened by villagers who burn the trees to clear land on which to plant their sweet potatoes and yams. After a few years the soil is depleted and the farmers move on, while the loss of trees lowers 'Eua's water table, threatening the island with drought.

The road on the left at the nursery leads through the forest reserve to Topuva'e 'a Maui (312 m), the highest point on the island, where there's the simple grave of a New Zealand soldier who died here during WW II. A track leads down to Lokupo Beach from just north of the grave.

PRACTICALITIES
Accommodations

The top place to stay on 'Eua is **Hideaway Resort** (tel. 50-255, fax 50-254, kw@kalianet.to), on the coast below Futu, a half hour walk south of 'Ononua Wharf. The six rooms with bath in a long wooden motel-style building start at

T$40/50 single/double including breakfast. Camping is T$10 pp. Their restaurant serves meals, and on Friday and Saturday nights a disco pumps up nearby. You can observe the sunset from their terrace, and even whales in season. Scuba diving with Deep Blue Diving, whale-watching, and hiking tours can be arranged.

Near the airport in the center of the island is **Highlight Guesthouse** (tel. 50-186) with four rooms with shared bath at T$30/45 single/double including breakfast. Eua's newest and largest place to stay is **Susan's Guest House** (tel. 50-088 or 50-070) with eight rooms in the same price range. You can cook your own food at Susan's.

South of the airport is **Taina's Guest House** (tel. 50-186), also known as the Scandic Motel, with four rooms with shared bath at T$20/25 single/double. Camping is T$12 per tent. To use the common kitchen in the main house is T$3 a day, or you can order meals. Bicycle and horse rentals or tours can be arranged. It's a pleasant place to stay.

Some of those who camped on the beach on the inhabited west side of the island have become victims of theft, and if you're interested in camping wild, a much better plan would be to trek around to the southeast side beyond Li'angahuo 'a Maui. Carry all the food and water you'll need.

Entertainment

The optimum time to come to 'Eua is late August or early September during the 'Eua Agricultural Show. The show grounds are right by the hospital at Futu.

The downmarket **Haukinima Bar** (tel. 50-088; closed Sun. and Mon.) near Futu in the center of the island is the local drinking place. A live band plays at **Maxi Disco Hall** across the street Friday and Saturday from 2000 and possibly a couple of other nights too. The hall is run by Taina of Taina's Guest House, who named it after her cat, Maxi. On dance nights the place is packed (foreign women have reported harassment here).

Services

What facilities 'Eua offers are near 'Ononua wharf, including the Bank of Tonga (tel. 50-145), post office (tel. 50-066), Telecom center (tel. 50-115), Friendly Islands Bookshop (tel. 50-167), and TCFS Supermarket (tel. 50-131). The bookshop sells an excellent map of 'Eua for T$3.

Kaufana Airport and several of the guesthouses are in the center of the island, three km south. Here too are the Forestry Division (tel. 50-116), with a good map on the wall, and Niu'eiki Hospital (tel. 50-111), a bit back toward 'Ononua.

Getting There

Fly NiU Airlines has flights between Nuku'alofa and 'Eua (T$36 one-way, T$66 roundtrip) four days a week.

The two boats shuttling between Nuku'alofa and 'Eua are described under Getting Around by Ship in the chapter introduction. In general, the boats leave 'Eua Monday–Saturday at 0530, departing Nuku'alofa's Faua Jetty for the return at 1300 the same days. Both charge T$12 each way. Due to the action of the southeast trades, the four-hour boat trip is far less rough westbound than eastbound, so if you're a terrible sailor you might want to fly over from Nuku'alofa and catch the boat back. In fact, so many people have figured that one out that the airline folks have made their roundtrip tickets slightly cheaper!

The harbor at 'Eua is less secure than the one at Nuku'alofa, so if strong winds are blowing or a hurricane warning has been issued for anywhere within a thousand km, that day's ferry trip will be canceled and the boat will remain tied up at Faua Jetty in Nuku'alofa. Of course, this happens more frequently during the southern summer (Dec.–April), but one should always be prepared to spend a day or two longer on 'Eua than planned or be willing to fly back. The Saturday trip from Nuku'alofa is the most likely to be canceled in bad weather, so it's safer to go over on Friday and not count on being able to come back on Monday. When the boat is canceled, the airline schedules additional flights.

ATA AND MINERVA

Ata Island, 136 km southwest of 'Eua, has been without permanent inhabitants since the 1860s, when King George Tupou I ordered the 200 villagers to move to 'Eua, where he could better protect them against the depredations of Peruvian slavers. The lack of a harbor and remote location have made resettlement unlikely, although in 2002 it was reported that juvenile delinquents were being sent to Ata for a survival course as part of their rehabilitation. Ata is an extinct volcano, and one of its twin peaks reaches 382 meters. It's the main breeding place in Tonga of the wedge-tailed shearwater, red-footed booby, Kermadec petrel, masked booby, blue-grey noddy, and red-tailed tropicbird.

Tonga ends at the two Minerva reefs, far to the south of Fiji's Lau Group and 290 km southwest of Ata. Minerva's only visitors are yachties who call occasionally between Vava'u and New Zealand, or New Zealand and Fiji. A deep pass on the northwest side of North Minerva's circular reef gives access to a protected lagoon five km wide with good anchorage on the north and east sides. At low tide you can walk across the reef's flat surface, but at high tide the only things visible between you and the breakers are old shipwrecks, a few coral boulders thrown up by storms, and a flagpole without a flag to the south. This recalls an attempt by right-wing American millionaires to seize Minerva Reef in the early 1970s for the creation of a taxless utopian state. In 1972, the king arrived in person to declare Tongan sovereignty. It's an eerie place, the outer edge of paradise.

The Ha'apai Group

This great group of 51 low coral islands and two volcanoes between Nuku'alofa and Vava'u is a beachcomber's paradise. Perfect white powdery beaches run right around the mostly uninhabited islands, but treacherous shoals keep cruising yachts away. There are two clusters: Nomuka is the largest of the seldom-visited southern islands, while Lifuka is at the center of a string of islands to the north. Over 8,000 people live on 16 of the islands. Ha'apai is mostly for beach people; if you're not a beach lover you'll soon get bored. Snorkelers and scuba divers have 150 km of untouched barrier reef, vast banks of soft and hard coral, and 1,600 species of tropical fish to keep them busy. Humpback whales (July–Oct.), spinner dolphins, and sea turtles add to the fun.

The first European to visit Ha'apai was Abel Tasman, who called at Nomuka in 1643. Captain Cook made prolonged stops on the same island in 1774 and 1777; on a visit to Lifuka in 1777 he coined the term "Friendly Islands," unaware of a plot by the Tongans on Lifuka to murder him. Later, off Tofua on April 28, 1789, Fletcher Christian and his mutineers lowered Captain William Bligh and 18 loyal members of his crew into a whaleboat, beginning one of the longest voyages in an open boat in maritime history, from Tongan waters to Timor in the Dutch East Indies (6,500 km)—a fantastic accomplishment of endurance and seamanship. Bligh's group suffered its only casualty of the trip, John Norton, quartermaster of the *Bounty*, when they landed on the southwest side of Tofua just after the mutiny and clashed with Tongans.

Tofua

Tofua (56 square km) is a flat-topped volcanic island about 505 meters high with a steep and rocky shoreline all the way around. The 10 abandoned houses and three churches at Hokula near the north coast, and Manaka, a tiny settlement on the east coast, are used by villagers from Kotu Island, who come to harvest Tofua's potent kava. It takes about an hour to climb up to Tofua's rim from Hokula. The large, steep-sided, four-km-wide caldera in the interior is occupied by a freshwater crater lake 30 meters above sea level and 250 meters deep. Tofua is still active: Steam and gases issue from a volcanic cone on the north side of the lake, and a hot pool is on the east side. Passing ships can see flames at night.

Until 1999, a seaplane based in Nuku'alofa ran charter flights to Tofua. The plane would make a photo pass over Kao and land on Tofua's crater lake. Passengers would then hike across the caldera for an hour to a smoking crater, and later there would be time for a swim in the lake. Unfortunately, there weren't enough customers and the operation has closed. The only way to get to Tofua now is to charter a small boat from Lifuka.

In Nuku'alofa, contact Branko Sugar of **Seataxi Charters** (tel. 22-795, fax 24-678, http://kalianet.to/seataxi). Branko's 10-meter cabin cruiser travels averages speeds of 25 knots but it still takes around four hours each way to cover the 145 km between Nuku'alofa and Tonga. The price is T$1,800 roundtrip for the boat (up to five persons), plus T$300 per night for waiting time (no waiting charge during the day). Ask if it will cost extra to cruise around Kao on the way back. You'll also pass the dormant volcanic islands of Hunga Tonga and Hunga Ha'apai on the way. Branko's clients generally sleep ashore under a large tarpaulin, which he ties between four trees. You must swim 10 meters to Tofua from the boat.

Kao

This extinct 1,046-meter-high volcano, four km north of Tofua, is the tallest in Tonga; on a clear day the classic triangular cone is visible from Lifuka, 56 km east. There's no anchorage, but it's possible to land on the south side of the uninhabited island in good weather. The lower slopes are well wooded, becoming barren higher up. Kao can be climbed in a long day.

Fonuafo'ou

One of the world's outstanding natural phenomena, this geographical freak 72 km northwest of Tongatapu was first observed in 1865 by the crew of HMS *Falcon*. Jack-in-the-box Fonuafo'ou (New Land) alternates between shoal and island. Sometimes this temperamental volcanic mound stands 100 meters high and three km long; other times the sea washes the exposed part away and it's completely under water. If you walk on it

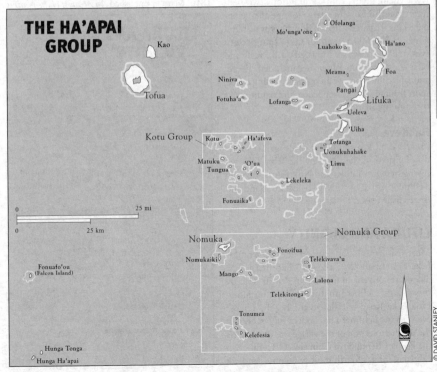

THE HA'APAI GROUP

Kao
Tofua

Ofolanga
Mo'unga'one
Luahoko
Ha'ano
Meama
Foa
Niniva
Pangai
Fotuha'a
Lofanga
Lifuka
Uoleva
'Uiha
Kotu Group
Kotu
Ha'afeva
Tofanga
Uonukuhahake
Matuku
'O'ua
Limu
Tungua
Lekeleka
Fonuaika

Nomuka Group
Nomuka
Nomukaiki
Fonoifua
Telekivava'u
Mango
Lalona
Telekitonga
Tonumea
Kelefesia
Fonuafo'ou
(Falcon Island)

Hunga Tonga
Hunga Ha'apai

0   25 mi
0   25 km

© DAVID STANLEY

KINGDOM OF TONGA

you're ankle deep in hot, black scoria (shaggy lava), an extremely desolate, blackened surface. At last report Fonuafo'ou was submerged again for the fifth time in the past 120 years.

Nomuka

Although the main island of the southern Ha'apai group, Nomuka has only 551 inhabitants and the number has fallen steadily in recent years. In the 18th century Nomuka was far from being the backwater it is today, and Tasman, Cook, and Bligh all called here to take on water from one of Nomuka's springs. A large brackish lake called Ano'ava sits in the middle of this triangular, seven-square-km coral island, each of the three sides of which is four km long.

Telekivava'u

This small island 69 km south of Pangai is notable for **Villa Mamana,** (Kendall Struxness, www.villamamana.com), a luxurious two-bedroom guesthouse with a large lounge and verandah. This "paparazzi-free" hideaway is available at a mere T$10,600 a week for up to four persons (yes, ten *thousand* six hundred). All meals and boat transfers from Pangai are included. Recreational facilities include an outrigger sailing canoe, sport fishing, surfing excursions, and nature walks through the island.

Ha'afeva

Ha'afeva, 42 km southwest of Pangai, is sometimes visited in the night by the ferry *Olovaka* plying between Lifuka and Nuku'alofa. Around 310 people live on this 181-hectare island but there's little reason for anyone else to get off here.

LIFUKA AND VICINITY

Most visitors to Ha'apai spend their time on Lifuka (11 square km) and its adjacent islands. There are convenient facilities in Pangai, a sleepy big village (3,000 inhabitants) strung along Holopeka Road parallel to the beach. There's even electric lighting! The modern high school in the northern section of the village was donated by the People's Republic of China in 2001. Although Lifuka is Tonga's fourth most populous island, it's

only a 10-minute walk out of this "metropolis;" then you're all alone among the coconut palms or strolling along an endless deserted beach. The most convenient and enjoyable way to explore Lifuka and Foa is by rented bicycle.

It was near the north end of Lifuka that Captain Cook was so well received in 1777 that he called these the Friendly Islands. On the same spot in 1806, the crew of the British privateer *Port-au-Prince* received a different welcome when Tongan warriors stormed aboard and murdered most of the crew. The captain's clerk, William Mariner, age 15, was spared and Chief Finau 'Ulukalala II took him under his protection. Mariner remained in Tonga four years, participating in 'Ulukalala's conquest of Tongatapu using a cannon taken from the ship. Eventually a passing ship carried him back to England, where he spent the rest of his life as a stockbroker, accidentally drowning in the Thames in 1853. In 1816, Mariner published *An Account of the Natives*

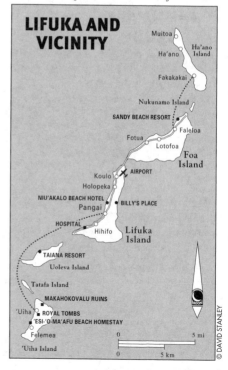

of the Tongan Islands in the South Pacific Ocean, the classic narration of pre-Christian Tonga.

Sights

On Holopeka Road at the south end of town is the **King's Palace,** with many fine old trees bordering the compound. The king visits Lifuka every September for the agricultural fair, which is held in the field across the street. The **Women's Island Development Handicraft Center** (weekdays 0900–1500), beyond the fairgrounds, displays local craft items.

Just north of the palace and inland a block on Faifekau Road is the Free Wesleyan Church, where a **miraculous cross** appeared in 1975. The spot is now outlined in cement on the grass outside the church. Palasi Road, the next street north runs right across the island to the long, lonely **beach** of high golden sands extending down the east side of Lifuka, only a 10-minute walk from town. Unfortunately, the locals have adversely affected the beauty of this beach by mining it for sand.

Virginia Watkins, a New Jersey woman who has been in Tonga since 1982, operates the **Afa Eli Historical Museum** (tel. 60-073; donations welcome) on Tuakolo Road. You'll see an odd assortment of handicrafts, tapa, lapita pottery, archaeological relics, fishing lures, children's toys, old books, seashells, fossilized turtle shells, corals, and lava rocks from Tofua. Virginia loves to chat and she'll show you around her garden.

Just north of Pangai is the grave and monument of Wesleyan missionary **Reverend Shirley Baker** (1836–1903), an adviser to King George Tupou I, who helped frame the Emancipation Edict of 1862 and the 1875 constitution. In 1880, Baker resigned his ministry and governed Tonga in the name of the elderly king. To increase his power he persuaded King George to break with Wesleyan headquarters in Australia and establish the independent Free Wesleyan Church. Baker's persecution of Tongan Wesleyans still loyal to the Australian church and his dictatorial rule prompted the British High Commissioner in Fiji to send a warship to collect him in 1890. Baker was later allowed to retire to Ha'apai and his children erected this monument after his death.

Sports and Recreation

Watersports Ha'apai (tel./fax 60-097, www.schwaranet.de/tonga.htm), based at the Niu'akalo Beach Hotel, can show you some pretty incredible things with the help of a snorkel or tank. It's run by a German named Roland Schwara who charges T$55/85 for one/two tanks, plus T$15 for gear. His scuba resort course is T$80 (no certificate), and he'll happily take you snorkeling at T$20 including a mask and snorkel. A guided day trip in a sea kayak is T$45 including lunch. If a group of six can be found, Roland will run a speedboat trip to the volcano on Tofua, costing T$75 pp for the boat, plus T$50 pp a day for guides and meals. Overnight trips almost anywhere in Ha'apai are possible.

Happy Ha'apai Divers (Herbert Mohr, tel. 60-600 between 0830–0930, www.tonga-dive.com) at the Sandy Beach Resort does introductory dives at T$125. An open-water certification course is T$510. The dive shop is closed in December and January.

ACCOMMODATIONS

Pangai

All of the guesthouses in Pangai village allow guests to cook their own food, but a small additional charge for cooking gas is levied to use the communal kitchen. Of course, they'd rather do the cooking for you at T$5–10 for breakfast and T$8–15 for dinner, but you must order in advance. Their food is good and the portions are gargantuan (as you'd expect in Tonga), but at those prices it gets expensive. If you really do want to cook for yourself, check out the kitchen as soon as you arrive and ask about extra charges for gas and electricity if you use it. Expect to have to share the facilities with the managers, who will be cooking for other guests. In addition to the places listed below, the **Government Rest House** (Ministry of Works, tel. 60-100), beside the Tonga Visitors Bureau, sometimes accepts tourists in the two rooms at T$10 pp.

Fifita's Guest House (Fifita Vi, tel. 60-213), near the center of the village, offers eight comfortable rooms in a two-story building at T$20/35 single/double including breakfast. You

KINGDOM OF TONGA

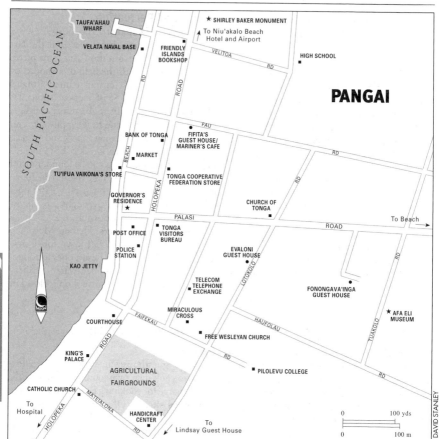

PANGAI

© DAVID STANLEY

can cook your own food. Bicycle rentals are T$8 and boat trips to Uoleva Island can be arranged at T$15 pp.

Evaloni Guest House (Mrs. Sitali Hu'akau, tel. 60-029), back behind the Visitors Bureau in Pangai, has three downstairs rooms with shared bath at T$20 pp, one downstairs room with private bath at T$45 double, and two upstairs rooms with bath, fan, fridge, and coffee making facilities at T$65 pp. Meals are available at T$7/12/20 for breakfast/lunch/dinner. Otherwise, it costs T$2 pp a day to use the cooking facilities and a small grocery store is attached. They're seldom full.

The friendly, nine-room **Fonongava'inga Guest House** (Mrs. Langilangi Vi, tel. 60-038,

vimahi@kalianet.to) nearby has five small rooms in the main building at T$15/30 single/double and four larger rooms in the annex at T$30/40. The bathroom facilities are communal in all cases, but only the new rooms have access to hot water. You can cook your own food in the owners' house next door at T$2 pp a day, or order excellent meals at T$8 for breakfast or T$20 for dinner. The atmosphere here is pleasant, with a large living room and front porch available to travelers. Langilangi is very kind and helpful. Airport transfers are T$6 pp each way.

In the southern section of Pangai is **Lindsay Guest House** (tel./fax 60-107) with shared-bath rooms at T$20/30 single/double, private-bath rooms at T$45 double, and family rooms at T$35/55 without/with bath. Meals are served or you can cook, and a small grocery store and bakery are on the premises. Bicycles are T$8 a day.

North of Town

The quiet **Niu'akalo Beach Hotel** (tel. 60-028), north of town between Pangai and Holopeka, offers 12 rooms on landscaped grounds facing a long, sandy beach only good for swimming at high tide. A small room with shared bath in a four-room standard unit is T$20/30 single/double, while larger rooms with private bath in the duplex deluxe units are T$30/37 single/double, or T$70 for a complete unit (up to six persons). Each cluster has a common living room shared by all guests, but there's only cold water. The Niu'akalo could use a facelift. The meals in the restaurant/bar aren't cheap and no cooking facilities are available for guests. Friday at 1900 there's a beach barbecue or a full Tongan feast, depending on how many guests are present. Rental snorkels, boats, and bicycles (T$10) are available. Your charming hosts, Mrs. Seletute Falevai, her husband, son, and two daughters, are very helpful.

Billy's Place (tel. 60-336), also known as Evaloni Beach Fales, is run by Viliami Hu'akau and his American wife Sandy with a bit of help from Milika. Unlike the places in Pangai, which are serenaded all night by barking dogs and rocked by legions of church bells at the crack of dawn, Billy's is in a coconut plantation on a long, unswimmable beach, 1.5 km north of town. It's on the breezy ocean side of the island, across narrow Lifuka from the Niu'akalo Beach Hotel. Watch for flying foxes headed north in the morning, south in the evening. Billy's five *fales* with lockable doors start at T$55 single or double, breakfast, bicycle, and snorkeling gear included (minimum stay two nights). Children under 12 are not accepted. Guests and nonguests alike can order surprisingly good burritos, fish, pizza, and pasta to be consumed on their pleasant patio (lunch is no problem, but order dinner in advance). Airport transfers are free.

The **Mele Tonga Guest House** (tel. 60-042) is on a reasonable beach at Holopeka about 500 meters south of the airstrip. At T$20/30 single/double with breakfast, there are two double rooms and a single in the main house, plus another double in an adjacent *fale*, and a communal kitchen in a separate building. It's run by a retired schoolteacher named Letty, and if she's not around when you arrive, ask at the small store beyond the church next to the guesthouse.

OTHER PRACTICALITIES

Food and Entertainment

The **Mariners Café** (tel. 60-374; Mon.–Sat. 0900–2100, Sun. 1800–2100), below Fifita Guest House, serves light meals such as fish and chips (T$6) and hamburgers (T$7). Antique bicycles can be rented at T$8 a day.

Pangai has several adequate stores opposite the Bank of Tonga and a small market selling little more than bananas and watermelon.

Ask around for dances in church halls on Friday and Saturday nights. You can drink kava all evening at several saloons around Pangai for a flat fee.

Information and Services

The Tonga Visitors Bureau (Mele Likiliki, tel. 60-733, fax 60-361, tvbhp@kalianet.to) on Holopeka Road in the center of Pangai can provide brochures and good local advice.

The Bank of Tonga (tel. 60-933; weekdays 0930–1230 and 1330–1530) changes traveler's checks.

The post office (tel. 60-666; weekdays 0830–1230 and 1330–1530) is next to fly NiU Airlines. Yachties should report their arrival at the post office even if they've already checked in at Vava'u.

The TCC telephone exchange (tel. 60-255; open 24 hours) is near the Miraculous Cross on the small street behind the Visitors Bureau. They sell telephone cards valued at T$5, T$10, T$20, and T$50 which you can to place long-distance calls at the public phones outside. If you want to fax anyone on Lifuka, or receive a fax yourself, direct those messages to fax 60-200 (the clerk will call whoever is named on the fax and ask them to come and pick it up).

Niu'ui Hospital (tel. 60-201) is two km south of the wharf.

Getting There

Fly NiU Airlines (tel. 13-066), next to the post office, flies to Ha'apai from Tongatapu (T$93) daily except Sunday, and from Ha'apai to Vava'u (T$77) three times a week. Pilolevu Airport (HPA) is at Koulo, five km north of Pangai. Some of the places to stay offer free transfers, otherwise a taxi will be T$3–5 for the car. (The main road to the north end of Lifuka crosses the airstrip and a gate must be closed during flight arrivals.)

Ferries between Nuku'alofa and Vava'u call regularly at Pangai, northbound very early Tuesday and Wednesday mornings, southbound in the middle of the night on Wednesday and Thursday. The *Tautahi* runs a day before the *Olovaha* in both directions. The *Olovaha* office (tel. 60-699) is inside the white container on Taufa'ahau Wharf. The office of the *Tautahi* (tel. 60-855) is in a nearby cream-colored shack (open only on ship days). Deck fares from Pangai are T$34 to Nuku'alofa and T$27 to Vava'u. Ships tie up to Taufa'ahau Wharf near the center of Pangai; turn right as you disembark. There's a large passenger shelter on the wharf where you can wait until dawn if you happen to arrive in the middle of the night (as is usually the case). When there are strong westerly winds, the ships may not risk landing at Pangai.

ISLANDS AROUND LIFUKA

Foa

A causeway links Lifuka and Foa (population 1,500). Weekdays from early morning until around 1600, and also on Saturday morning, buses leave Pangai intermittently for **Faleloa,** Foa's northernmost village. Continue 20 minutes on foot to Foa's northern tip to look across to **Nukunamo Island,** owned by the king. The beach is beautiful here and the snorkeling is fine at slack tide.

Outboard motorboats bring villagers from **Ha'ano Island** to the wharf at Faleloa, and you can go back with them most afternoons for about T$2 one-way.

The **Sandy Beach Resort** (tel./fax 60-600, sandybch@kalianet.to) opened in 1995 near the north end of Foa Island, 1.5 km from Faleloa. The 12 well-constructed beachfront bungalows with ceiling fan, fridge, 24-hour electricity, porch, and private bath cost T$240 single or double including tax and airport transfers. Cooking facilities are not provided for guests, and children under 16 are not accepted. Like the accommodations, the fancy food in the restaurant is geared to a more upscale clientele than the backpacker places on Lifuka (T$80 for breakfast and dinner). Non-guests are welcome to drop in for lunch (T$20) but not for dinner. The swimming and snorkeling are fine, even at low tide, and snorkeling gear, bicycles, kayaks, and canoes are loaned free. Dolphins swim offshore. Paid activities include bareback horse riding and boat trips. Happy Ha'apai Divers handles scuba diving. These facilities are for resort guests only. The Sandy Beach is run by a German couple named Jürgen and Sigi Stavenow, former managers of the Seaview Restaurant in Nuku'alofa, and before you leave you'll know all there is to know about them. The weekly Tongan cultural show is good too.

Uoleva

From the south end of Lifuka, 3.5 km from town, you can wade across the reef at low tide to sparsely populated Uoleva Island, which has super snorkeling off its southwest end. Check tide times at the Visitors Bureau in Pangai and don't set out if the tide is about to come in, since it takes at least 30 minutes to cross. Rubber booties or reef shoes will be required to protect your feet. Crossing this way involves a slight risk, because the currents can be unexpectedly strong. Sunday is a good day to go, as you won't meet any copra cutters.

Taiana Resort (tel. 60-292), on the northwest side of Uoleva, offers a real South Seas experience. The four *fale* with mosquito nets and mattresses on the floor are T$18/25 single/double. Breakfast/dinner are T$6/12, and transfers from Lifuka cost T$10 pp each way. It's a good value. You should also bring some food with you, because nothing can be purchased on the island, although water is supplied. The long white beach is fabulous and you'll share this sizable, coconut-covered island with only your fellow guests, the occasional local who comes to work his/her garden, and free-ranging cows, goats, and pigs. It's restful, just don't expect luxuries like electricity and running water. Enjoy the sunsets off their beach, the stars in the sky, and the utter tranquility. They usually light a bonfire on the beach later on.

The **Captain Cook Hideaway** (Soni Kaifoto, tel. 60-014), 200 meters south of Taiana Resort on Uoleva, has four rooms in two basic duplex units at T$15/20 single/double, plus T$12 pp for breakfast and dinner. The consensus is that Taiana Resort is nicer and serves better food, at a slightly higher price. To come/go by boat from Pangai costs about T$15 pp each way. Try contacting the owner, Soni Kaifoto, at his home on Haufolau Road in Pangai, or if you're staying at Fifita Guest House, ask Fifita, as Soni is her uncle. Otherwise the people at Tu'ifua Vaikona's store (tel. 60-605) on the Pangai waterfront can help you organize transfers to either place for the same price.

'Uiha

'Uiha Island (population 750), south of Lifuka, is more slow moving than Pangai, but there are things to see, accommodations, and fairly regular access by boat. The burial ground of the Tongan royal family was on 'Uiha until the move to Nuku'alofa. Also to be seen in front of the church in the middle of 'Uiha village is a cannon from the Peruvian slave ship *Margarita,* which was sacked off 'Uiha in 1863. A second cannon inside the church serves as a baptismal font. Also visit the Makahokovalu, an ancient monument composed of eight connecting stones at the north end of 'Uiha Island. Uninhabited Tatafa Island, between 'Uiha and Uoleva, can be reached from near here on foot at low tide.

The only place to stay is **'Esi-'O-Ma'afu Beach Homestay** (tel. 60-438), run by Hesse and Kaloni 'Aholelei. It's on the beach at Felemea village, a 15-minute walk south of the boat landing at 'Uiha village. The four Tongan *fale* with shared bath are T$20/25 single/double. Unfortunately, the *fale* are dark and rundown. Breakfast is T$6, dinner T$12 (or T$18 if lobster), or you can cook for yourself. An outrigger canoe can be borrowed.

'Uiha is fairly easy to get to on small open boats departing the beach at Pangai, but at best the service is only once a day, so you'll have to spend the night. The regular trip is about T$15 pp each way (T$25 if you're alone). The people at Tu'ifua Vaikona's store (tel. 60-605) on the Pangai waterfront can take you over to 'Uiha Island for a few hours of sightseeing and bring you back at around T$80 for the boat—worth considering if you can get a small group together.

The Vava'u Group

Vava'u is Tonga's most scenic region. It's an uplifted limestone cluster that tilts to cliffs in the north and submerges in a myriad of small islands to the south. A labyrinth of waterways winds between plateaus thrust up by subterranean muscle-flexing. In Vava'u one superb scenic vista succeeds another, all so varied you're continually consulting your map to discover just what you're seeing. Only Port Vila (Vanuatu) is comparable.

The Vava'u Group measures about 21 km east to west and 25 km north to south, and of the 34 elevated, thickly forested islands, 21 are inhabited. At 90 square km, the main island of Vava'u is Tonga's second largest. Ships approach Vava'u up fjordlike Ava Pulepulekai channel, which leads 11 km to picturesque, landlocked Port of Refuge Harbor, one of the finest in the South Pacific. The appealing main town of Neiafu, 275 km north of Nuku'alofa, looks out onto Puerto del Refugio, christened by Captain Francisco Antonio Mourelle, whose Spanish vessel chanced upon Vava'u in 1781 while en route from Manila to Mexico, making Vava'u one of the last South Pacific islands to be contacted by Europeans.

The many protected anchorages make Vava'u a favorite of cruising yachties, and it's also a prime

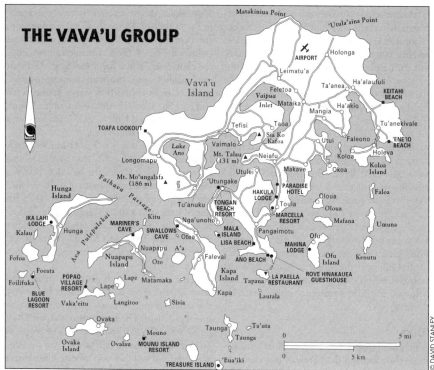

THE VAVA'U GROUP

Matakiniua Point

'Utula'aina Point

AIRPORT

Holonga

Leimatu'a

Vava'u
Island

Feletoa

Ha'alaufuli

Ta'anea

KEITAHI
BEACH

Vaipua
Inlet

Mataika

Ha'akio

Mangia

TOAFA LOOKOUT

Tefisi

Taoa

Tu'anekivale

Sia Ko
Kafoa

Utui

Faleono

'ENE'IO
BEACH

Lake
Ano

Vaimalo

Koloa

Holeva

Longomapu

Mt. Talau
(131 m)

Neiafu

Koloa
Island

Makave

Okoa

Faloa

Hunga
Island

Mt. Mo'ungalafa
(186 m)

Utulei

Utungake

PARADISE
HOTEL

Oloua

Faihava
Passage

Tu'anuku

HAKULA
LODGE

Oloua

IKA LAHI
LODGE

Kitu

Nga'unoho

TONGAN
BEACH
RESORT

Toula

Mafana

Umuna

Kalau

Hunga

MARINER'S
CAVE

SWALLOWS
CAVE

Otea

MARCELLA
RESORT

Pangaimotu

Ofu

Fofoa

Nuapapu
Island

Oto

A'a

MALA
ISLAND

Ofu
Island

Kenutu

Foeata

Lape

Falevai

LISA BEACH

MAHINA
LODGE

Foilifuka

POPAO
VILLAGE
RESORT

Lape

Matamaka

ANO BEACH

Kapa
Island

ROVE HINAKAUEA
GUESTHOUSE

BLUE
LAGOON
RESORT

Vaka'eitu

Langitoo

Sisia

Tapana

LA PAELLA
RESTAURANT

Kapa

Lautala

Ovaka

Mouno

Taunga

Ta'uta

Ovaka
Island

Ovalau

MOUNU ISLAND
RESORT

Taunga

TREASURE ISLAND

'Eua'iki

0   5 mi

0   5 km

© DAVID STANLEY

place to launch an ocean kayak. Waters on the west side of the archipelago are generally deeper and better protected than those on the east. Beaches can be hard to find on the main island but there are many on the islets to the south. There's a giant-clam breeding project at Falevai on Kapa Island and pearl-clam farming near Utulei in Port of Refuge Harbor and at three other locations. Vanilla plantations cover over 500 hectares, and Vava'u vanilla is among the best in the world. In 2002, a new high school was built at Neiafu with French aid money. Princess Pilolevu spends a fair bit of time in Vava'u; she's married to the governor, the Noble Tuita.

One of the South Pacific's two most important yacht charter operations is based here (the other is on Raiatea in French Polynesia). Places to stay abound, both in town and on the outer islands, the entertainment is varied, and watersports such as kayaking, sailing, scuba diving, and fishing

are well developed. July–October, this is the South Pacific's main whale-watching venue, and May–October is the prime time for yachting. Some hotels and activity operators raise their prices slightly during these months, but on the plus side, all of the restaurants will be open, Tongan feasts will be happening, and trips will be easily arranged. Hotel reservations may be worth obtaining at this time of year. In the off-season, November–April, many tourist facilities close down and everything happens more slowly. Anytime, Vava'u is one Pacific island group you can't afford to miss.

NEIAFU

Neiafu is Tonga's second "city," but it's still a sleepy little town of 6,000 inhabitants. It's a great place to explore on foot, visiting the markets or local attractions, shopping for handicrafts or groceries, dropping into a cafe or bar to hear yachties chatter, visiting travel offices to organize excursions, or hiking out into the unspoiled countryside all around. Neiafu is a much more colorful, attractive, appealing, and restful town than Nuku'alofa. The longer you stay, the more you'll like it, and the better you'll become attuned to the relaxed pace of life. You get the impression that this is a place where everyone knows one another, and where things can be arranged on short notice. The only drawback is that no swimmable beaches exist near town.

Be aware that virtually all shops, restaurants, and bars in Neiafu are closed on Sunday (except those at the Paradise Hotel). The only people you're likely to meet on the street on Sunday are those coming from or going to church. Sunday nights a church service consisting mostly of hymns accompanied by rock music is broadcast across Neiafu on loudspeakers. This really is an unusual place.

Sights

One of the overgrown burials in the **cemetery** between the Bank of Tonga and Mormon church is of the ancient *langi* type, and it's believed that a daughter of the 35th Tu'i Tonga is buried here. Also resting in this cemetery is the Rev. Francis Wilson, who established the first seminary in Tonga and died here in 1846. The nameless tombstone right next to Wilson's is that of early Methodist missionary David Cargill, who rendered the Tongan and Fijian languages into writing.

The old fig tree in front of Neiafu's red-and-white colonial-style **post office** is a local meeting place. Notice the Spanish monument across the street. The **Vava'u Club** up the hill is the former German Club, founded by trader Hermann Karl Guttenbeil in 1875. The old German cemetery is just a bit farther up the hill, past the club and on the left.

For a splendid view of Port of Refuge and much of the archipelago, climb **Mt. Talau** (131 meters), the flat-top hill that dominates Neiafu to the west. Take the road between the police station and the Flea Market and follow it west for 25 minutes high above the shoreline. Where the

road begins to descend and you reach an isolated house on the left, look for a trail up the hill on the right just beyond. Turn right at the top of the hill. This is an easy trip from town.

East of town is Neiafu's old harbor, which was used in the days of sail when it was more convenient to land on the beach. With the advent of steamships, interest shifted to the deeper Port of Refuge Harbor. There's another excellent walk at low tide along the shore from the old harbor to **Makave;** you pass a freshwater spring.

At **Toula** village, a half-hour walk south of Neiafu beyond the hotel, is a large cave called Ve'emumuni near the shore with a freshwater pool where the locals swim. To get there, turn left just beyond the Mormon church and go through the village, continuing up the hill past a cemetery to the cave. At low tide you can walk back to the old harbor along the beach in about an hour.

Sports and Recreation

Beluga Diving (Sybil and Huib Kuilboer, tel./fax 70-327, tel. 71-115, www.belugadivingvavau .com; Mon.–Sat. 0800–1700) beside Sunsail Yacht Charters offers two-tank boat dives at T$90/110 without/with equipment in the high season from May to November (T$10 less other months). Their open-water certification course is T$450 (or T$400 pp for two or more). They also fill tanks for T$8. A laminated chart of Vava'u is available at T$20. A travel agency in their office can book international flights. Reader reviews of Beluga have been positive.

Dolphin Pacific Diving (tel./fax 70-292, VHF channel 71, www.academydivers.co.nz), opposite The Moorings, does two-tank diving at T$80/90 without/with gear. Their five-day PADI open-water scuba certification course is T$400. Dolphin's boat leaves the Paradise Hotel wharf at 0815.

Scuba divers frequent the wreck of the 129-meter-long *Clan McWilliam,* a copra steamer that burned and sank in Port of Refuge Harbor in 1927. Huge fish and clams hang around the wreck 20 meters down, marked by a buoy just out past the yacht anchorage. Many other good dive sites are only 30 minutes by speedboat from

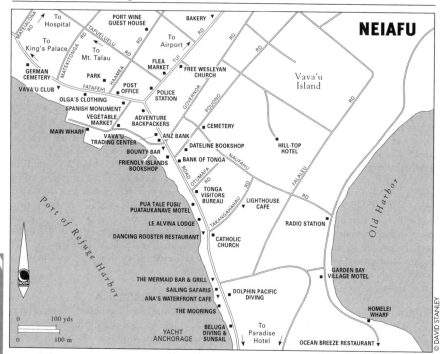

Neiafu. Most diving is drift diving and there aren't many spots where dive boats can anchor, so it's important to note the current.

The **Friendly Islands Kayak Company** (tel./fax 70-173, VHF channel 71, www.fikco .com), based at the Adventure Center at Toula and at the Tongan Beach Resort, runs guided kayaking trips of four to nine days at T$140 pp a day including meals, tents, kayaks, and snorkeling gear. The Canadian operators, Doug and Sharon Spence, also offer day-trips at T$70 pp including lunch. Mountain bike tours around Vava'u are T$25/40 a half/full day. These prices only apply to local bookings on a space-available basis from May to December. Kayaks are for rent for exploring the Port of Refuge at T$25/T$35 pp a half/full day.

Henk and Sandra Gros at Adventure Backpackers offer game fishing from the eight-meter powerboat *Target One* (tel./fax 70-647, www .invited.to/target1) at T$200 pp a day (minimum of three). **Ikapuna Store** (Paul Mead, tel.

70-698, fax 70-174), next to Vava'u Trading Center, offers sport fishing at T$200 pp a day (minimum of two).

Pat and Keith McKee's 10-meter *Kiwi Magic* (tel./fax 70-441, VHF channel 71, www.fish vavau.com) trolls for marlin, mahimahi, spearfish, and tuna along the drop-offs below 200-meter cliffs on the northwest side of the island. The McKee's, who are based at the Vava'u Guest House, charge T$750 a day (up to four anglers). On a per person basis they charge T$220 (minimum of two) but they reserve the right to sell up to four places on the boat.

See rugby Saturday afternoons (April–June) on the Fangatongo Rugby Ground, just off the road to Mt. Talau.

ACCOMMODATIONS
Under US$25
Adventure Backpackers (Henk and Sandra Gros, tel./fax 70-955, www.invited.to/back

packers), in a new concrete building just up from the main wharf, has three four-bed dorms at T$24 pp, one small room with shared bath at T$36/38 single/double, four better rooms with a balcony or harbor view but shared bath at T$48/58/78 single/double/triple, and one "suite" with private bath at T$68 single or double. Reduced rates are offered for long stays during the off-season November–May. The common cooking facilities are excellent. It's clean, convenient, inexpensive, and always crowded with backpackers. Adventure Backpackers books most activities around Vava'u and their notice board provides a wealth of information. Bicycle rentals here are T$13/20 a half/full day. Airport transfers are T$10 pp.

The **Port-Wine Guest House** (Louisa Pota, tel. 70-479), a block west of the Flea Market, has four rooms with shared bath at T$15/25 single/double. Two additional rooms are in the next building, in case of need. This comfortable wooden house with a large lounge and communal cooking facilities and fridge is very central, and well worth checking out if you're looking for the least expensive accommodations.

The **Puataukanave Motel** (tel. 70-644, fax 70-080), below S.F. Paea & Sons opposite the Tonga Visitors Bureau, has six fan-cooled rooms with private bath and balconies overlooking the bay at T$35/45 single/double. There are no cooking facilities for guests, and it's directly above a noisy disco open Friday and Saturday nights (free entry for motel guests), so only stay there if you'll be spending a lot of time drinking, dancing, or watching satellite TV in the lounge.

Mikio Filitonga's **Vava'u Guest House** (tel. 70-300, fax 70-441) is right across the street from the Paradise Hotel. The five basic rooms with shared bath in an old stone building are T$10/15 single/double, while the four bungalows with private bath, fan, and a table and chairs are T$30/50 single/double. A fee of T$2 is collected for use of the common cooking facilities. Be prepared for insect problems and nocturnal rooster/canine noise.

On the old harbor is the 13-room **Garden Bay Village Motel** (tel. 70-137, fax 70-025). The four duplex units (eight rooms) in the front row are T$25/35 single/double with private bath. Camping is T$10 pp. If you ask, they'll allow you to use the restaurant kitchen to cook your own food when things aren't too busy. Manager Marlene Moa arranges island tours. Loud music blares from the Garden Bay's nightclub on Wednesday, Friday, and Saturday nights (free admission for hotel guests).

US$25–50

The recently upgraded **Hill-Top Hotel** (tel./fax 70-209, sunset@kalianet.to) offers spectacular views of Neiafu and the harbor. The eight double rooms with bath are T$70/100 garden/seaview. The air-conditioned seaview rooms have verandahs with a view. Cooking facilities are not provided but the Sunset Restaurant and Pizzeria (tel. 70-838) is based here.

Le Alvina's Lodge (tel. 70-209, fax 70-873), just down from the Tonga Visitors Bureau, has eight rooms at T$35/55 single/double standard, T$45/65 superior. Breakfast on their terrace overlooking the harbor is included and you can cook your own dinner.

The **Paradise Hotel** (tel. 70-211, fax 70-184, tongaparadise@aol.com) stands on a hill overlooking Port of Refuge Harbor near Neiafu. Unfortunately, a recent change of ownership has made this hotel a little less inviting than it was. The 48 rooms with private bath start at T$83 double for an economy room, T$125 standard, T$168 garden view, and T$210 harbor view, all plus 7.5 percent tax. The fan-cooled economy rooms have older furnishings and cold showers only while the air-conditioned deluxe rooms are among Tonga's best (though tiny ants in the coffee-maker can be a nuisance). We've heard complaints about confirmed reservations not being honored here at peak periods and of billing mix-ups. The bar is still good and open all day Sunday (!) but skip the overpriced, poorly served meals in the restaurant (sandwiches at lunchtime T$10–12, dinner mains T$20–32). The hotel has a large pool (which non-guests can use for a T$2 fee) and there's good ocean swimming off their wharf. One-person fiberglass kayaks are for rent at T$10/20 a half/full day. Airport transfers are free for guests, T$4 for non-guests.

Twin View Motel (tel. 70-597, fax 70-622), on a breezy hilltop above the Vava'u Guest House, is run by Mikio's brother, Kapeliele Cocker. There are four spacious rooms at T$70/100 single/double and two larger rooms at T$85/120. All have cooking facilities and discounts are available for stays over a week. Scooters are for rent to guests only at T$12/20 half/full day. It's a good value.

Marcella Resort (tel. 70-687, fax 70-846, marcella@kalianet.to), on a hill directly behind the Three Stars Petroleum storage tanks at Toula, a 45-minute walk south of Neiafu, opened in 1996. The nine spacious duplex units with bath (but no cooking facilities) are T$65/85/105 single/double/triple plus tax. There's a reasonable view of Port of Refuge from the restaurant terrace. No beach is available but you can swim off their jetty. Whale-watching trips (T$95) are offered.

US$50–100

Hakula Lodge (Janine and Jeff Le Strange, tel. 70-872, fax 70-875, VHF channel 71, www.fish tonga.com), a km south of the Paradise Hotel, has two self-catering waterfront units with air conditioning at T$160/200/225 single/double/triple. Airport transfers are included. A full-day fishing charter is T$850 and whale-watching trips (www.whales-in-the-wild.com) are available July–October.

FOOD

The **Bounty Bar** (tel. 70-576, fax 70-493; closed weekends), across from the banks in the center of town, serves five kinds of burgers, fried rice, and sandwiches, but it's more of a place to come for drinks. It's a real yachtie hangout and you get a great view of everything (including sunsets) from the back porch, though it's often hard to find a table. Live entertainment is often offered on Friday nights during the high May–October season. Expensive Internet access is available.

The **Ifo Ifo Bar and Café** (tel. 70-285), behind Island Gas Station just below the Bounty Bar, has a terrace with a great view.

The **Pua Tale Fusi Restaurant & Garden Café** (tel. 70-704; Mon.–Sat. 1030–1430 and 1730–2200, Sun. 1730–2100) is right down on the water below S.F. Paea & Sons opposite the Tonga Visitors Bureau. Called the "Pua" for short, it's run by Ron Cherry, former owner of the Mermaid Bar and an expert cook. Lunch here will run T$9.50–12.50, dinner T$16–30 (tuna, lobster, chicken, steak). From July to September they put on a special "Tongan culinary night" every Saturday from 1730, with an eight-course menu made exclusively from local ingredients at T$35. Live string band music accompanies dinner from 1900 year-round (except Sun.) and there's a Tongan show with children dancing on Tuesday and Friday nights. You'll like the family atmosphere here. Yachties are welcome to leave their dinghies tied up to the Pua's dock while running errands around town.

The Dancing Rooster (tel. 70-886; Tues.–Sat. 1600–2200), down by the water opposite the prominent Catholic church in Neiafu, serves meals on their harborfront terrace. The menu includes fish and chicken dishes (T$14–19), sirloin steak (T$25–29), and lobster (T$27–32). Yachties can tie their dinghies to the dock.

The **Lighthouse Café** (closed Sunday), up from the Catholic church, serves breakfast from 0730. They're famous for their bread and pastries.

The Mermaid Bar & Grill (tel. 70-730; closed Sun.), next to The Moorings, is run by the same folks as Sailing Safaris nearby. You can feast on local specialties such as raw fish (T$8.50) delivered straight to the dock in their lively harborside bar.

Ana's Waterfront Cafe (tel. 70-664; closed Sun.), directly below The Moorings, serves breakfast and lunch, and is a good place to come at happy hour (weekdays 1700–1800). The waterside location facing a dingy dock makes it another yachtie hangout. It's in a sort of cave, or 'ana in Tongan—there's no person named Ana here (The Moorings owns the place).

The **Ocean Breeze Restaurant** (tel. 70-582, VHF channel 74) is on the old harbor southeast of Neiafu. Yachties anchored off Makave in the old harbor often use the Ocean Breeze's stone jetty to come for dinner. They specialize in upscale seafood such as lobster and fish curry, but also have steak, lamb, and chicken (prices range from T$20–32).

It's open daily 1200–1400 and 1800–2200 with reservations required. (Whenever at least three people want to go, English restaurateur John Dale runs day tours to outlying islands in his fiberglass speedboat. Ask to be shown the flying foxes.)

Groceries

'Utukalongalu Market near the main wharf is crowded with people selling bananas, cabbage, carrots, Chinese lettuce, coconuts, green beans, lettuce, manioc, onions, papaya, tomatoes, taro, yams, zucchini, and oranges. Everything is about T$1 a bunch, and you're only assured a fair selection of fresh vegetables if you arrive early. You can also have lunch here for about T$3. The largest market is on Saturday.

Neiafu's two largest supermarkets, the **Tonga Cooperative Federation** (tel. 70-224) and the **Vava'u Trading Center** (tel. 70-090), are across the street from one another. They close weekdays at 1630, Saturday 1230, so shop early. Buy fish directly from locals at the harbor (no fish poisoning problems here).

ENTERTAINMENT

The **Vava'u Club** (tel. 70-498), up the hill from the post office, has a great view but is more of a men's drinking place. They have two enormous pool tables where snooker and other such games are played; the bartender keeps sets of balls for eight-ball (hi-lo) and 15-ball pool. Beware of "mosquitoes," who will want you to buy them drinks.

From 2000 on Friday and Saturday nights a live dance band plays at the **Puataukanave Disco** (tel. 70-644), below S.F. Paea & Sons opposite the Tonga Visitors Bureau (cover charge T$2/3 for women/men). A slightly older crowd frequents the **Funga i Vava'u Nightclub** at the Garden Bay Village (tel. 70-137) which cranks up on Wednesday, Friday, and Saturday nights.

Cultural Shows for Visitors

Several "feasts" are organized weekly for both land-based and water-bound visitors. For a set fee of T$20–25 (half price for children under 10) you get a buffet-style meal of island foods such as roast suckling pig, octopus, fish, clams, lobster, crayfish, and taro, all baked in an *umu* (earth oven). Cooked papaya with coconut cream in the middle is served in half-coconut shells, and lots of watermelon is eaten while sitting on mats on the ground. Have a swim as soon as you arrive, then enjoy a drink (extra charge) to the strains of guitar music. Traditional dancing is performed later, and handicrafts are available for sale.

All of the feasts take place on outlying beaches. For example, John and Neti Tongia (tel. 70-898, VHF channel 16) prepare a "gigantic roast" with a kava ceremony and dancing by children at **Rove Hinakauea Beach** adjacent to Ano Beach on Thursdays. Ask other visitors for their recommendations, as conditions do vary.

You can book these feasts at the Paradise Hotel, the Bounty Bar, The Moorings, or the Tonga Visitors Bureau. Free minibus transfers are provided for visitors staying in Neiafu, though yacht charter clients and other yachties are the biggest customers. Often the feasts are canceled if not enough people sign up.

Events

The best time to be in Vava'u is the first week of May for the **Vava'u Festival,** marking the crown prince's birthday on May 4. There will be a display of handicrafts, sporting events, a game fishing tournament, a yacht regatta, boat parades, the Vava'u Marathon, island nights, concerts, dances, feasts, art exhibitions, church choir meetings, traditional Tongan games, a baby show, and a grand ball with the crowning of Miss Vava'u. The king usually attends the **Agricultural Show** in September. Hotel rooms should be booked ahead at these times.

The Sunday morning singing at the Free Wesleyan Church on Tui Road opposite the Flea Market is almost worth the plane fare to Vava'u.

Shopping

Aside from the items available at 'Utukalongalu Market, handicrafts can be purchased at the **Langafonua Shop** (tel. 70-356), next to the Tonga Visitors Bureau, **The Kalia Room,** opposite the Bank of Tonga, **Angela Handicraft,** opposite the Friend Islands Bookshop, and the **Vava'u Handicraft Shop,** in front of the post office.

a string band at Neiafu, Vava'u

© M.E. DE VOS

Fa Sea Souvenirs (tel. 70-853) in the Quo Vadis Center opposite the Paradise Hotel has tapa, woodcarvings, cultured pearls, and jewelry, some of it made from endangered species.

Uwe Schreiber runs **Vava'u Electronics and Booking Office** (tel./fax 70-247, VHF channel 13) in the Quo Vadis Center opposite the Paradise Hotel. Uwe does repairs and sells all manner of electronic parts for yachts. There's a paperback book exchange and a Vava'u chart for T$15. He can also book feasts and island tours during the yachting season.

With enough lead time, **Olga's Clothing** (tel. 70-064), between the post office and the Vava'u Club, makes clothes to order.

INFORMATION AND SERVICES
Information
The Tonga Visitors Bureau (tel. 70-115, fax 70-666, tvbvv@kalianet.to; closed Sat. afternoon and Sun.) in Neiafu has the usual brochures and can answer questions. Take the time to peruse their information boards to find out what's on around Vava'u. Teta Tours and the Paradise Hotel also have notice boards worth checking. The Bounty Bar has a VHF radio that can be used to contact yachts at Vava'u.

Books and Maps
The Friendly Islands Bookshop (tel. 70-505), diagonally opposite the Bank of Tonga, has postcards and a few good books about the islands.

The Dateline Bookshop (tel. 70-213), a bit up the side street from the Bank of Tonga, also sells books on Tonga.

The Moorings (tel. 70-016) produces a 32-page *Cruising Guide,* which comes with a chart indicating their 42 designated anchorages around Vava'u. Copies may be ordered through www.southpacific.org/books.html. The Friendly Islands Bookshop sells a reproduction of their chart.

Library
The Vava'u Public Library (Tues.–Fri. 1200–1700, Sat. 0830–1300) is in front of the post office.

Money
The Bank of Tonga (tel. 70-068), near the Tonga Visitors Bureau, and the ANZ Bank (tel. 70-944), next to the Vava'u Trading Center, change traveler's checks without commission. When the

banks are closed the Paradise Hotel changes money for a commission, provided they have sufficient funds on hand. The ATM machines at Neiafu's banks are often out of order.

Post and Telecommunications

Vava'u poste restante holds mail for one month. You can place local and long-distance telephone calls at the Telecom Telephone Exchange (tel. 70-255; open 24 hours) behind the post office. If you wish to receive a fax at Vava'u, you can have it sent here via fax 70-200 (T$1 a page to receive). Yachts, restaurants, and the police generally use VHF channel 16 to communicate.

Cafe Tropicana (tel. 70-037; Mon.–Sat. 0800–1800), next to Adventure Backpackers, has three computers providing Internet access at T$10 an hour. Coffee and cakes are also available.

Beluga Diving (tel. 71-115; Mon.–Sat. 0800–1700) beside Sunsail Yacht Charters has a computer in their office that you can use to send/receive email. Messages written offline and sent through their mailbox are T$1 each. Online access to an electronic mailbox like Hotmail costs T$0.50 a minute.

Visas

Officially, extensions of stay up to six months are available for T$51 at the immigration office at the Flea Market. In practice, however, it's entirely up to the officers how long you'll get, and your attitude could have a lot to do with it.

Laundry

Yachties are the clientel at Vava'u Laundry (tel. 70-519, VHF channel 9; Mon.–Wed. 0830–1630) opposite The Moorings.

Health

There's a great view of Neiafu from Ngu Hospital (tel. 70-201) on the northwest side of town, but you'll get better medical attention for T$35 at Dr. Alfredo Carafa's Italian Clinic (tel. 70-607; weekdays 0900–1300, Sat. 0900–1030), behind the Bank of Tonga.

TRANSPORTATION

By Air

Fly NiU Airlines (tel. 12-165), next to Adventure Backpackers, flies to Vava'u three times a week from Ha'apai (T$79), and weekly from Niuafo'ou (T$167) and Niuatoputapu (T$134). Service from Nuku'alofa (T$145) is two to four times a day except Sunday. The flights are often heavily booked, and cancellations occur without warning, so reconfirm early and don't plan tight connections.

Lupepau'u Airport (VAV) is nine km north of Neiafu. A double row of huge *ovava* trees leads up to the terminal. The Paradise Hotel bus is T$4 pp (free for hotel guests) and a taxi is T$8 for the car (T$15 to the Tongan Beach Resort). Local buses (50 cents) run to/from Leimatu'a village, two km south of the airport, sporadically on weekdays and Saturday mornings; otherwise, it's easy to hitch from the airport into town (offer the driver a couple of *pa'anga*). There's no bank at the airport.

By Ship

Ships tie up to the wharf. The **Uata Shipping Lines** ferry *Tautahi* leaves Neiafu for Ha'apai (T$27) and Nuku'alofa (T$48) Wednesday at 1400, whereas the **Shipping Corporation of Polynesia** ferry *Olovaha* leaves Thursday at 1600. Departures to the Niuas (T$92) are about once a month and usually very crowded. The office of the Shipping Corporation (tel. 70-128) is in the red container on the main wharf. The Uata Shipping office (tel. 70-490) is in the nearby white kiosk. See Transportation in this chapter's Exploring the Islands section for more information.

By Yacht

To crew on a cruising yacht, put up notices at the Bounty Bar and Ana's Waterfront Cafe, and ask around the bar at The Mermaid Bar and at the hotel. The yachting season is March–October. Until September try for a watery ride to Fiji; later most boats will be thinking of a run south to New Zealand.

Getting Around

Getting around Vava'u by public transport isn't

really practical, although passenger trucks and minibuses departing Neiafu do cover most of the roads on an unscheduled basis. Leimatu'a is fairly well serviced, as is Tu'anekivale. If you want to go to Holonga, you must take a bus as far as Mataika or Ha'alaufuli, then walk. Hitching is easy, but offer to pay if it looks like a passenger truck. They'll seldom ask more than T$1. Taxis charge about T$1.90 for the first kilometer, 80 cents each additional km. Waiting time is T$3.75 an hour. Verify the price beforehand.

Liviela Taxi (tel. 70-240), with a kiosk opposite the Bounty Bar, rents cars at T$70 a day. **JV Taxi** (tel. 70-136), opposite the Vava'u Trading Center, also charges T$70 a day. Before taking a car, you'll have to obtain a Tongan driver's license (T$15) at the police station around the corner (bring your home driver's license). Insurance is not available and serious problems can arise in the event of an accident, so take care (ask how much extra they'll charge to supply a driver with the car). The speed limit is 40 kph in town or 60 kph on the open road.

Though Vava'u is a lot hillier than Tongatapu, a bicycle is still a good way to get around.

Yacht Charters

Vava'u is one of the Pacific's top cruising grounds, with more than 50 "world class" anchorages. Florida-based **The Moorings** (tel. 70-016, fax 70-428, VHF channel 72, moorings.tonga@ kalianet.to) has a variety of charter vessels based here, beginning at US$400 a day for a two-cabin yacht in the low season and increasing to US$960 daily for a four-cabin catamaran in the high season (July and August). Add US$32 pp daily for provisioning, US$29 daily per yacht for security insurance, US$87–117 for a starter kit, and 7.5 percent tax. If you're new to sailing (they check you out) it's another US$132 a day for a skipper. Additional crew might include a cook (US$112 daily) and a guide (US$92 daily). To have a kayak aboard is yet another US$25 a day. These charges soon add up—a party of four can expect to spend US$5,000 a week to rent a small, uncrewed bareboat yacht, meals included. Tipping is extra. A 20 percent discount is possible if you book in person through the Vava'u office instead

of reserving ahead, although, of course, there'd be no guarantee they'd have a yacht available for you if you followed that route. It's not cheap, but The Moorings' boats are newer and better kept than those of their competitors.

Sunsail (tel. 70-646, fax 70-647, www.tonga sailing.com), down by the water on the east side of The Moorings, has five charter yachts based here in the off season (Jan.–March), a dozen in the full season (April–Dec.). It's a lot cheaper than The Moorings because their prices are based on New Zealand dollars (from NZ$335/425 daily off/full season, plus insurance, fuel, and tax). For more information contact Sunsail (tel. 64-9/378-7900, fax 64-9/378-8363).

Sailing Safaris (tel./fax 70-650, VHF channel 68, www.sailingsafaris.com), between Ana's Waterfront Cafe and the Mermaid Bar and Grill, is an independent boat charter company and marine center. Some of their yachts are smaller than those offered by The Moorings and Sunsail, allowing couples to experience bareboat chartering without the high costs associated with the larger charter yachts. They have a seven-meter yacht available at T$250 a day, plus T$200 for a skipper, if required. The minimum bareboat charter is three days. A five-passenger speedboat charter is T$250 a day including the skipper. Aside from chartering, they also do whale-watching at T$95 pp and snorkeling trips at T$65. The Sunday barbecue trip with snorkeling is T$65 (or T$110 if whale-watching is included). Their marine services facility offers fuel, water, slipway, engineering and fiberglass repairs and laundry to visiting yachties.

Day Cruises

A more economical way to experience sailing is to go out on the 12-meter trimaran *Orion*. It offers a cruise to Swallows Cave and other sites daily 1000–1630 at T$65 pp. Someone from the *Orion* is to be found near the swimming pool at the Paradise Hotel most afternoons at 1700. This cruise is very popular and many visitors take it twice during their stay.

Similar is the stylish, 15-meter ketch *Melinda* owned by **Melinda Sea Adventures**) (Christy Butterfield, tel. 70-975 or 70-861, www.sail

DANCING WITH WHALES

Some Tongan whale-watching companies advertise the possibility of swimming and snorkeling with humpback whales during the cetaceans' annual migration from July to October. This activity sounds appealing, yet there are a number of things to consider. To drop clients off within snorkeling distance of a whale, the swim boats must come closer than the 30 meters laid down in Tongan government guidelines in 1997. Engine noise from a maneuvering boat can startle a whale, and repeated disturbances can lead to the animals changing their behavior and even abandoning their traditional habitat. The nursing and resting routines of the pods can be disrupted, potentially threatening the health of the whales.

This high-risk activity is not covered by most travel insurance policies. The humpback whales of Tonga are wild animals with powerful fins, and swimming near one always involves some risk. The movements of these huge creatures can be fatal to a human swimmer, either accidentally or if the beast feels threatened, and a nursing mother with calf can be especially unpredictable. Swimming into the path of a whale greatly increases the danger. In Tonga, sharks are known to frequent areas where there are whales, especially calves, and at least one shark attack on a Tongan guide swimming with whales has been recorded. A tragic accident involving tourists seems to be only a matter of time.

Most whale encounters occur in deep waters where unperceived currents and wave action can soon tire a snorkeler and possibly lead to panic. For these reasons, responsible whale-watching companies do not offer snorkeling with whales. Of course, the demand is there, and pressure has come to bear on the Tongan Government to revise its guidelines to allow boats to come within 10 meters of a whale. Two new whale-watching licenses were issued in 2003, raising the number of commercial operators in this small area to 11, and at Vava'u, vessels often have to queue to drop off swimmers. Cases were observed of boats approaching to within five meters of whale pods, and of mother humpbacks and calves being pursued out to sea. The constant disturbances and harassment may have contributed to the animals' departure from Tonga's Vava'u Group several weeks early that year.

Visitors should be aware that by purchasing such an excursion, they could be adversely affecting the noble creatures they came to see. It's a good idea to discuss these matters with the operator before booking your trip and to avoid those who seem most interested in maximizing their own profits at the expense of the whales. Even if you decide to book such a tour, be aware that only 10 percent of swim-with attempts are successful, and there are no refunds. These concerns only apply to attempts to actually swim with whales, and whale-watching from a boat at a safe distance is no problem.

tonga.com), who charge T$65 pp for day sails or T$95 for whale-watching (minimum revenue T$200 to schedule a trip). Small groups can charter the *Melinda* for overnight trips at T$350/260 pp for two/four persons including a skipper, cook, and all meals. The minimum charter is two nights but five nights is more common.

If the *Orion* and *Melinda* have sailed away by the time you get there, ask around for something similar. Local operators like these know their waters and will take you on the South Seas adventure of your dreams.

Whale-Watching

Each winter July–October, over a hundred humpback whales come to Vava'u to bear their young before returning to the colder Antarctic waters for the southern summer. They generally stay on the western side of the group, in the lee of the prevailing trade winds. Lots of tour and fishing boats around Vava'u do whale-watching trips, and you'll easily see eight whales on a good day. Ask if there will be a roof on your boat, as the sun can be merciless. To maximize profits, the Tongan government requires all whale-watching operators to charge a minimum fare of T$95 pp. Standard practices regarding human/whale encounters in other parts of the world (not motoring directly toward whales or getting too close, for example) aren't always observed in Tonga.

Whale Discoveries (tel./fax 70-173, www.whalediscoveries.com), based at the Adventure Center in Toula, offers whale-watching from the 8.5-meter *Tropic Bird* at T$65/95 a half/full day. This eco-friendly company has decided to abstain from swimming with whales, as they believe this entails significant risks for the swimmer and has the potential to alter the behavior of the whales.

Whale Watch Vava'u (tel. 70-576, fax 70-493, www.whalewatch.to) uses a specially designed boat with a hydrophone that allows the mating songs of the males to be broadcast over speakers on board. Whale Watch offers full-day trips during the season, departing the Bounty Bar wharf at 0930 (T$95 pp, minimum of six). Lunch is T$15 extra. These trips can be booked at the Bounty Bar.

Whale-watching on the 10-meter fishing boat *Kiwi Magic* is T$95 pp with a minimum of four persons, maximum of six. Ask for Pat or Keith McKee (tel./fax 70-441) at the Vava'u Guest House.

SOUTH OF NEIAFU

The road south from Neiafu crosses two causeways before reaching **Nga'unoho** village (10 km), which has a lovely, clean beach. You can also swim at the Tongan Beach Resort at 'Utungake, and at Lisa and Ano Beaches south of Pangaimotu, although the snorkeling at all four is only fair. By bicycle, you'll find this is the hilliest part of Vava'u.

Accommodations

The **Tongan Beach Resort** (tel./fax 70-380, VHF channel 71, www.thetongan.com) is near 'Utungake village on 'Utungake Island, about nine km from Neiafu via a paved road. The beach here is fairly good and the 12 duplex bungalows (T$159 double including tax) are comfortable. The rooms cannot be locked, but a safety deposit box is available at the office. There's a three-night minimum stay, and children 12 and under are accommodated free if sharing with their parents. Scuba diving, game fishing, whale-watching, snorkeling tours, and yacht charters are offered. Snorkeling gear and kayaks are provided free and bicycles and a sailboat are for rent. One drawback is the cost of eating in their fancy thatched restaurant—it'll take some effort not to run up a daily food bill equal to the cost of your room (T$80 pp meal package available). Drinks at the bar are also expensive, so bring something along to put in your fridge (day-trippers from Neiafu are welcome to use the resort beach if they buy a few drinks). There's a Tongan show on Wednesday nights. Return airport transfers will be T$29 pp if arranged by the hotel, but you can get a taxi from Neiafu at T$10 for the car. If you book from abroad and pay in U.S. dollars, your costs will be about 25 percent higher than the prices quoted above. A water taxi leaves the resort for Neiafu most mornings at 0930, charging T$12 for three or more people.

The Tongia family operates **Rove Hinakauea Guesthouse** (tel. 70-898, VHF channel 16), on a lovely stretch of sand adjacent to Ano Beach at the south end of Pangaimotu Island, eight km from Neiafu. The four shabby concrete bungalows with bath are T$25/40 single/double. The meals served here are also poor and overpriced, but you may be able to do your own cooking (bring food). On the other hand, the T$20 feasts on Thursday evenings are reasonable value. Ask about this place at the Tonga Visitors Bureau in Neiafu. A taxi from Neiafu will be around T$7.

WEST OF NEIAFU

From the Seventh-Day Adventist church on Tui Road in Neiafu a highway leads west across the Vaipua Inlet causeway to western Vava'u. Beyond the causeway is a long steep incline at the top of which is a hill on the left called **Sia Ko Kafoa.** The track up the hill is on the left near the point where the road begins to descend again. Sia Ko Kafoa is an ancient burial mound built by the legendary chiefs Kafoa and Talau. It's an eerie, evocative spot with a good view of much of the island.

Keep straight (or left) at Tefisi and follow the rough track along the north side of **Lake Ano,** the still, fresh waters of which are easily accessible at one point. At Longomapu turn right and climb a long hill to **Toafa** at the west end of the island, where there's a splendid view of the cliffs of Hunga and many small islands trailing southward. If you have binoculars, you may see whales off Hunga July–October.

NORTHEAST OF NEIAFU

Two centuries ago, **Feletoa** was the center of power on Vava'u, and a Polynesian fortress was built here in 1808, but little remains today. Ask to see the burial place of Finau 'Ulukalala II behind the house opposite the primary school in Feletoa. The large, rectangular *langi* is surrounded by big stone slabs. It was Finau's father, Finau 'Ulukalala I, who had ordered the sacking of the British privateer *Port-au-Prince* at Ha'apai and who later adopted Will Mariner into his family. With the help of cannon from the ship and military advice from the survivors, 'Ulukalala II conquered Vava'u in 1808, and in 1810 he allowed Mariner to return to England. The dynasty came to an end when 'Ulukalala III's young son was deposed by King George Tupou I. 'Ulukalala II's tomb is unmarked, untended, and overgrown because he's still out of favor with the current Tongan dynasty.

For a splendid view of the north coast, travel due north from Neiafu to Holonga. About two km beyond the village, turn left when the trail begins to descend to the beach, then right some 500 meters farther along. With a little luck you'll come out on **'Utula'aina Point,** a sheer cliff a couple of hundred meters above the sea. The quiet beach here is fine for relaxing, but the water is too shallow for swimming. You could spend a whole day exploring this area.

OFFSHORE ISLANDS

The classic day tour at Vava'u encompasses Mariner's Cave, Swallows Cave, and Nuku Island. **Mariner's Cave** is a hollow in Nuapapu Island, southwest of Neiafu. You can approach it through an underwater tunnel in the island's stone face. The story goes that a young noble, fearing a despotic king might kill his sweetheart, hid her in this secret cave, coming back each night with food and water. Finally the young man and his friends built an oceangoing canoe and spirited the girl away to safety in Fiji. The cave gets its name from William Mariner, who told the story to the world.

To find it, go west along the cliff about 600 meters from the northeast tip of Nuapapu, watching for a patch of dark, deep water. White calcium deposits speckle the rocks to the right of the underwater opening; a single coconut tree standing high above also marks the place. Snorkeling gear is recommended for entry, though a strong swimmer could go in without. The opening is about one meter below sea level at low tide, and you have to swim about four meters underwater to get through (it's comparable to diving under a yacht). The water is illuminated by sunlight, but come up slowly to avoid banging your head on a ledge. Wave action causes the air inside to change constantly from foggy to clear. Swimming into Mariner's Cave is a bit like doing a bungee jump: it's certainly not for everyone, and claustrophobic souls should give it a miss. On upscale tours, a Tongan guide usually swims behind each guest to make sure they don't stop halfway.

Swallows Cave on Kapa Island is far more obvious, and a small boat can motor right inside. Inside Swallows Cave is a rock that rings like a bell when struck, and in front of the entrance to another cave next to Swallows is a huge round coral that looks like an underwater elephant. There are also sea snakes here and an exciting vertical dropoff. All these caves face west, so the best conditions for photography are in the afternoon. Day trips to these spots usually include a picnic on **Nuku Island,** where the snorkeling is good. One of the customary owners of Nuku may show up to collect a T$1 pp fee, one of the few places in Tonga where this happens.

Trips to the caves on village boats cost T$25–40 pp, depending on where you book, how many people are going, and whether lunch is included. The guesthouse owners should know which boats are going and they generally depart from the Bounty Wharf daily except Sunday at 1000, so long as at least four people have signed up. Some of the companies listed under Sports and Recreation, Yacht Charters, and Day Tours above also offer these trips at a somewhat higher price. Snorkeling on the Mala Island reef and along the dropoff at A'a Island are usually included in the Mariner's Cave trip.

If you enjoyed the Mariner's Cave tour and are staying longer, ask about the eastern islands boat tour from Neiafu's Old Harbor to Umuna Island (interesting cave), Kenutu Island (sea cliffs with huge breakers), and Ofu Island (nice beach). Neiafu tourist cafes like the Bounty Bar and Ana's are good sources of information about all tours and activities around Vava'u, and can quickly put you in touch.

Accommodations

A number of small resorts and restaurants exist on small islands south of Neiafu, and the easiest way to obtain current information on these is to check the information boards at the Bounty Bar, Tonga Visitors Bureau, Teta Tours, and Paradise Hotel.

Mahina Lodge (tel. 70-209, VHF channel 16), at anchorage 28 on Ofu Island, has five rooms starting at T$40/50 single/double, breakfast included. Transfers from Neiafu's Old Harbor are T$25 pp. This place has had its ups and downs in recent years, and you should check the current status before trying to go there.

La Paella Spanish Restaurant on Tapana Island off Ano Beach serves excellent set meals at T$35. Seven beaches are found on Tapana.

Mala Island Resort (tel./fax 70-852, www .malaisland.com), between Pangaimotu and Kapa islands, charges T$150 pp for one of the 16 *fale* and activities, plus T$50 for all meals if you book locally. Booked from overseas, it's about double that price. Swimmers should beware of strong currents around here.

Marcella Resort (tel. 70-687, marcella@ kalianet.to) in Neiafu has a branch called **Treasure Island** on Eua'iki Island on the south side of the Vava'u Group. The three-bedroom beachhouse here rents for T$100 double per room or T$250 for the whole house (minimum stay three nights). Transportation to the island is additional. An island-style restaurant and three *fale* will be

added in 2004. Combined stays with Marcella Resort are possible.

Whale Watch Vava'u operates upscale **Mounu Island Resort** (Allan and Lyn Bowe, tel. 70-747, fax 70-493, VHF channel 77, www.mounu.com), on a tiny beach-clad island a bit west of Eua'iki. The three *fale* are T$200 single or double (minimum stay three nights, children under 12 not accommodated). During off-season December–June it's reduced to T$175. The three-meal plan in their waters-edge restaurant is T$65 pp, return airport transfers T$50 pp. Whale-watching trips cost T$95 per head. Kayaks and snorkeling gear are loaned free. Information is available at the Bounty Bar.

Popao Village Resort (tel. 70-308, www .popao.net), on otherwise uninhabited Vaka'eitu Island near the southwest end of the Vava'u Group, tries to recapture the lifestyle of an old Tongan village of thatched *fales* decorated with tapa wall hangings. The complex is set in natural surroundings on a low hill with grand views with four deluxe *fale* with hard double beds, private bath, and wooden floors at T$140 single or double. Camping is free if you pay for transfers and meals. There's no electricity, generator, or traffic noise. Bucket showers are provided in a central bathhouse—you really experience everyday Tongan life as it was several decades ago. Bring insect repellent and a towel. Only fresh local foods are served here and a breakfast, afternoon tea, and dinner package costs T$50 pp. Guests are welcome to help with the cooking, which is done in the traditional way over an open fire or in a lavastone *umu*. Over a dozen types of bread and rolls are baked in a firewood stone oven. Yachties anchored offshore can also eat at Popao's Lighthouse Café if they announce their arrival over VHF channel 16 (and bring a flashlight). The snorkeling off the north end of Vaka'eitu is fantastic and small outrigger canoes are provided free. Fishing trips are organized using traditional methods such as the long spear and round throwing net *(kupenga)*. You can also try octopus fishing. You can rent a boat (without driver) at T$100 a day to tour the southernmost Vava'u islands not visited by the tour boats from Neiafu. Boat transfers from Neiafu to Popao cost T$62 pp each way. It's okay provided you don't mind roughing it a bit.

Blue Lagoon Resort (Friedyl and Ma'ata Pott, tel. 70-975, fax 70-976, www.kalianet.to/blue lagoon), on Foeata Island across the channel from Popao, has six thatched *fale* with bath at T$180/220 double/triple. Meals are T$55/75 for half/full board, airport transfers T$110 pp roundtrip. Free moorings are provided to yachties interested in patronizing their excellent seafood restaurant (four-course dinner T$33–50). Blue Lagoon is closed in February and March.

Ika Lahi Lodge (Steve Campbell and Caroline Hudson, tel./fax 70-611, VHF channel 71, www.tongafishing.com), on the western island of Hunga, has four rooms in two bungalows at T$185/225 double/triple. The three-meal plan is T$75 pp, and airport transfers cost another T$100 pp roundtrip. Safe swimming and snorkeling is available off their beach. Ika Lahi serves mostly as a base for fishing trips with Reel Obsession Charters (T$715–1,100 for up to four anglers including lunch and tackle). The protected anchorage here is good and seven moorings are available for restaurant/bar patrons.

OTHER ISLANDS OF VAVA'U

Late Island (17 square km), 52 km west of the main Vava'u Group, is visible from the west side of Vava'u on a clear day. This 519-meter-high dormant volcano last erupted in 1854. In the late 1860s, King George Tupou I evacuated the Late people to Hunga Island over worries of the residents being kidnapped for use as slave labor in the mines of Peru. Recently this densely forested, uninhabited island has itself become a resettlement area for the endangered Tongan megapode bird, or *malau,* which is threatened due to human activities on its native Niuafo'ou.

Fonualei (four square km) lies 70 km northwest of Vava'u, 19 km beyond smaller Toku Island. This dormant volcano 195 meters high last erupted in 1846, spewing ash across Vava'u. It's presently uninhabited. The Spaniard Mourelle called it Amargura, or "bitterness," in 1781 out of disappointment from not finding food and water there.

The Niuas

The isolated volcanic islands of Niuatoputapu, Tafahi, and Niuafo'ou sit midway between Vava'u and Samoa, and often share the devastating hurricanes common to the latter. Two owe their names to their ubiquitous coconut trees *(niu).* Surprisingly, these were the first Tongan Islands to be seen by Europeans (by Schouten and Le Maire in 1616). The number of visitors to the Niuas today is negligible, but the islands have a lot to offer and are well worth including in your trip, if you can afford the extra airfare (and if the air service is operating).

NIUATOPUTAPU

Niuatoputapu Island, 300 km north of Vava'u, is a triangular island of 18 square km with a long central ridge 150 meters high. You can climb this ridge from Vaipoa village in the north and explore the many bush trails, which lead to small garden patches on top. A plain surrounds the

ridge like the rim of a hat, and lovely white sandy beaches fringe the island, with a sheltered lagoon on the north side and pounding surf on the south. Much of the island is taken up by gardens producing copra and exquisite limes, but

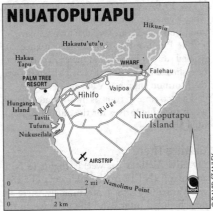

some fast-disappearing native forest remains in the south.

Niuatoputapu is a traditional island, where horse-drawn carts are still used and fine pandanus mats are made. All 1,300 inhabitants live in the three villages along the north coast. Hihifo, the administrative center, is about three km north of the airstrip. The wharf at Falehau offers good anchorage for yachties, good swimming for everyone.

The finest beaches are on **Hunganga Island,** accessible by wading at low tide. The channel between Hihifo and Hunganga is strikingly beautiful, with clean white sands set against curving palms, and the majestic cone of Tafahi Island looming in the distance. The waterways south of the village are not only scenic but also idyllic swimming areas. Within Hihifo itself is **Niutoua Spring,** a long freshwater pool in a crevice—perfect for an afternoon swim. Countless pigs forage on the beach at Hihifo, and from July–October, whales are numerous offshore.

Practicalities

Kalolaine's Guest House (tel. 85-021) in Hihifo has five rooms at T$18/22 single/double (shared facilities). Meals can be ordered here.

The **Palm Tree Island Resort** (tel. 85-090, fax 85-123, palmtreeislandtonga@yahoo.it), on Hunganga Island, has four screened beach bungalows with private bath at T$120/160 single/double. Meals at their restaurant cost T$8 for breakfast, T$12–15 for lunch, and T$18–30 for dinner. There's good swimming and snorkeling in the lagoon, and bicycles are available for guests' use.

The Produce Board maintains an adequate general store at Hihifo, and traveler's checks can be cashed at the post office. There's a bakery near the Mormon church at Vaipoa.

The top time to come is mid- to late August, when the king arrives for the annual Agricultural Show.

Getting There

Fly NiU Airlines has weekly flights to Niuatoputapu (NTT) from Nuku'alofa (T$274) and Vava'u (T$129). Unfortunately, there are no scheduled interisland flights between the Niuas and you must return to Vava'u to reach the other.

The supply ship from Nuku'alofa and Vava'u arrives about every month (T$92/368 deck/cabin from Vava'u). Niuatoputapu is a port of entry and clearance for cruising yachts, most of which call on their way from Samoa to Vava'u between June and September.

TAFAHI ISLAND

Fertile, cone-shaped Tafahi Island, 3.4 square km in size and nine km north of the Niuatoputapu wharf, produces some of the highest quality kava and vanilla in the South Pacific. Some 500 people live on the island and the only access is by small boat at high tide from Niuatoputapu. There are 154 concrete steps from the landing to clusters of houses on Tafahi's north slope.

The climb to the summit (555 meters) of extinct Tafahi volcano takes only three hours—get fresh water from bamboo stalks on top. On a clear day Samoa is visible from up there! You can also walk around the island in half a day, using the beach as your trail.

NIUAFO'OU

Niuafo'ou is Tonga's northernmost island, 574 km from Nuku'alofa and equidistant from Savai'i (Samoa), Taveuni (Fiji), and Vava'u. Despite the airstrip that opened in 1983, Niuafo'ou remains one of the most remote islands in the world. The supply ship calls about once a month, but there's no wharf on the island. Landings take place at Futu on the west side of the island.

For many years Niuafo'ou received its mail in kerosene tins wrapped in oilcloth thrown overboard from a passing freighter to waiting swimmers or canoeists, giving Tin Can Island its other name. In bad weather, rockets were used to shoot the mail from ship to shore. Early trader Walter George Quensell doubled as postmaster and brought fame to Niuafo'ou by stamping the mail with colorful postmarks. Special Niuafo'ou postage stamps, first issued in 1983, are prized by collectors.

The Land

Niuafo'ou (50 square km) is a collapsed volcanic cone once 1,300 meters high. Today the north rim of the caldera reaches 210 meters. The center of the island is occupied by a crater lake, **Vai Lahi,** nearly five km wide and 84 meters deep, lying 21 meters above sea level. From this lake rise small islands with crater lakes of their own—lakes within islands within a lake within an island. Grayish *lapila* fish live in these sulfurous waters.

Presently Niuafo'ou is dormant, but the southern and western sides of the island are covered by bare black **lava fields** from the many eruptions earlier this century. Lava flows emanating from fissures on the outer slopes of the caldera destroyed the villages of 'Ahau in 1853 and Futu in 1929. After Angaha disappeared under lava in 1946, the government evacuated the 1,300 inhabitants to 'Eua Island, where many live today. In 1958, some 200 refugees returned to Niuafo'ou, and by 1976 there were 678 people on the island once more (in 1996 735 people were present). Signs of the 1946 eruption are apparent in the vicinity of the airstrip.

Apart from the lava fields, the island is well forested. Incubator or megapode birds (*malau* in Tongan) lay eggs one-fifth the size of a grown bird in burrows two meters deep in the warm sands of the hot springs by the lake. Natural heating from magma close to the surface incubates the eggs, and after 50 days the megapode chicks emerge fully feathered and ready to fend for themselves. Unfortunately, those *malau* eggs that aren't collected by the islanders for food are dug up by free-ranging pigs, and the birds are facing extinction. Many tracks lead to the lake from all directions.

Facilities

Most government offices on Niuafo'ou are at

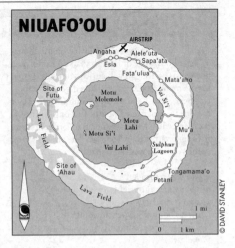

Esia, but the Telecom office and Civil Aviation offices are at Sapa'ata. There are no official accommodations on Niuafo'ou, though some of the locals will accept paying guests. The Catholic Mission also takes guests. The fly NiU Airlines agent on Niuafo'ou should be able to arrange accommodation, and the airline office in Vava'u will radio ahead to let them know you're coming. Camping on the crater is possible.

Getting There

Niuafo'ou (NFO) is theoretically accessible weekly on the **fly NiU Airlines** flights from Nuku'alofa (T$324) and Vava'u (T$179). In practice the plane has a 50-50 chance of landing, as Niuafo'ou's airstrip is placed in such a way that dangerously strong winds whip across it. When that happens, the plane has to fly all the way back to Vava'u, and the people on the island see their long-awaited cargo go back where it came from for another week.

BASIC TONGAN

Although Tongans generally have a much better knowledge of English than do Samoans, a few words of Tongan will enrich your stay. Listen for the many glottal stops (marked below by apostrophes), which sound something like co'n (for cotton) in American English. In Tongan, "ng" is pronounced as in longing, not as in longer, making it Tong-a, rather than Tong-ga. The vowels sound as they do in Spanish or Italian.

afe to'ohema: turn left
afe to'omata'u: turn right
alu: go (singular)
'alu a e: goodbye (to person going)
'alu hangatonu: go straight
bimi: later
fakaleiti: transvestite
fakamolemole: please (polite form)
fale: house
fe'unga: that's enough
fefe hake?: how are you?
fefine: woman
ha'u: come (singular)
hena: there (by you)
heni: here (beside me)
'i fe?: where?
ika: fish
'ikai: no
'ikai ha taha: none, nothing
'io: yes
kataki: please (common form)
kaukau: bath
kaume'a: friend
koau: I
ko e ha?: what?
ko e me'a 'e fiha?: how many?
Ko fe 'a e fale malolo?: Where is the toilet?
kohai ia?: who is it?
ko koe: you
ko moutolu: you (plural)
kovi: bad
lahi: big, much
ma'ama'a: cheap
mahalo: maybe
makona: full (of food)
malo: thank you

malo 'aupito: thank you very much
malo e lelei: hello
malohi: strong
malo pe: no thank you (at meals)
mamafa: expensive
mohe: sleep
mou nofo a e: goodbye (to several staying)
mou o a e: goodbye (to several going)
niu mata: drinking nut
niu motu'u: mature coconut
nofo a e: goodbye (to person staying)
o: go (plural)
'ofa: love
'oku fiha?: how much?
'oku mau: we
'oku nau: they
'Oku ou fieinua.: I'm thirsty.
'Oku ou fiekaia.: I'm hungry.
omai: come (plural)
palangi: foreigner
sai: good
sai pe: just fine
si'i: small
ta'ahine: girl
talitali fiefia: welcome
tamasi'i: boy
tangata: man
tulou: excuse me
tu'u: stop

NUMBERS
taha: 1
ua: 2
tolu: 3
fa: 4
nima: 5
ono: 6
fitu: 7
valu: 8
hiva: 9
hongofulu: 10
tahataha: 11
uanoa: 20
uanima: 25
teau: 100
tahaafe: 1,000
tahamano: 10,000

American Samoa

Introduction

American, or Eastern, Samoa, 4,000 km southwest of Hawaii, is the only U.S. territory south of the equator. Elbow-shaped Pago Pago Harbor (pronounced "Pahngo Pahngo"), made famous in Somerset Maugham's short story *Rain,* is one of the finest in the South Pacific, a natural hurricane shelter for shipping. It was this feature that attracted American attention in the late 19th century, as Germany built a vast commercial empire based around coconut cultivation on neighboring Upolu.

Until 1951 American Samoa was run as a naval base, but with advances in U.S. military technology it became obsolete, and control was turned over to the civilian colonial administrators who created the welfare state of today. To replace lost income from the base closure, U.S. companies were encouraged to build tuna canneries in the territory. Today traffic constantly winds along Tutuila's narrow south coast highway, and gun-totting, American-style cops prowl in big black-and-

white cruisers. Shopping centers and department stores have spread from the head of Pago Pago Harbor out into suburbia beyond the airport.

American Samoa is a fascinating demonstration of the impact of American materialism on a communal island society. Although the Samoans have eagerly accepted the conveniences of modern life, the *fa'a Samoa,* or Samoan way, remains an important part of their lives. Thus far the Samoans have obtained many benefits from the U.S. connection, without the loss of lands and influx of aliens that have overwhelmed the Hawaiians. While this part of Samoa will always be American, the Samoans are determined to prevent it from going the way of Hawaii.

The Land

American Samoa is composed of seven main islands. Tutuila, Aunu'u, and the Manu'a Group (Ofu, Olosega, Ta'u) are high volcanic islands; Rose and Swains are small coral atolls. Tutuila is about midway between the far larger island of Upolu and the smaller Manu'a Group.

Tutuila is by far the largest island, with a steep north coast cut by long ridges and open bays. The entire eastern half of Tutuila is crowded with rugged jungle-clad mountains, continuing west as a high broken plateau pitted with the verdant craters of extinct volcanoes. The only substantial flat area is in the wide southern plain between

THE SAMOAN ISLANDS

© DAVID STANLEY

> ## AMERICAN SAMOA HIGHLIGHTS
>
> **Blunt's Point, Tutuila:** huge naval guns emplaced in 1941 (p. 475)
>
> **Leone Falls, Tutuila:** freshwater swimming, lush jungle (p. 480)
>
> **National Park of American Samoa:** rainforests, mountains, coral reefs (p. 470)
>
> **Ofu and Olosega:** outer island jewels joined by a bridge (p. 490)
>
> **Rainmaker Mountain, Tutuila:** overlooking majestic Pago Pago Harbor (p. 475)

Leone and the airport. Fjordlike Pago Pago Harbor, which almost bisects Tutuila, is a submerged crater, the south wall of which collapsed millions of years ago. Despite the natural beauty, recent studies have shown that the harbor is dying biologically as a result of pollutants dumped by the two tuna canneries and local villagers, and the culminating effect of oil and ammunition spills by the U.S. Navy decades ago. The marinelife of inner Pago Pago harbor is poisonously contaminated by heavy metals and unfit for human consumption. Swimming in the harbor is not a wise idea.

Climate

Although the climate is hot and humid year-round, it's hotter and rainier from November to April (the hurricane season). The frequency of hurricanes has increased dramatically in recent years. The old rule of thumb was one every 7–10 years, but during the five-year period up to 1991, three major storms hit Tutuila. Many believe this is related to rising ocean temperatures caused by climate change—and things could get worse in the future. Most hurricanes move into the area from the north but they can also come from the east or west.

Temperatures are usually steady, but the stronger winds from May to October ventilate the islands. The prevailing tradewinds are from the east or southeast, with west or northwest winds and long periods of calm during the wetter season.

PAGO PAGO'S CLIMATE

As warm easterlies are forced up and over Tutuila's Rainmaker Mountain, clouds form that drop their moisture on the harbor just to the west. Apia receives only half the annual rainfall of Pago Pago. From December to March the rain can continue for days, while the rest of the year it often comes in heavy downpours. The exact amount of rain in any given month varies greatly from year to year, and much of it falls at night. Actually, the weather can change from bright sunshine to heavy rain within 5 or 10 minutes at any time of year.

You can hear a recorded weather report with tide times by calling 699-9333. Dial 633-4949 and you'll be told the date, time, and temperature.

Fauna

Some 64 species of birds are found in American Samoa, including forest birds such as the *lupe* (Pacific pigeon), *manutagi* (purple-capped fruit dove), *ve'a* (banded rail), and *'iao* (wattled honeyeater), and seabirds like the *fua'o* (red-footed booby) and *tava'e* (white-tailed tropicbird). The rarest of the territory's birds is the *manuma* (many-colored fruit dove), with only about 50 birds left in the wild. The only food the *manuma*

has ever been observed to eat is the fruit of the *aoa* (banyan) tree, and the bird is now facing extinction largely due to the disappearance of the *aoa,* many of which have been cut down by humans or blown over by hurricanes.

Hurricanes have also been blamed for an 85 percent drop in populations of the two species of *pe'a* (flying fox fruit bat) between 1987 and 1992. The white-throated flying fox is often seen soaring above the ridge tops around sunset as the bats leave their roosts to feed at night. The Samoan flying fox is more active during the morning and late afternoon. These native bats eat fruit and pollen, and are an essential link in the pollination of plants of the rainforest. Introduced bulbuls and mynahs are now common on Tutuila, but in the Manu'a Group there are only native birds. In an attempt to protect Samoa's endangered wildlife, a ban on hunting birds and bats was enacted in 1992.

Over 1,000 species of tropical fish dwell along American Samoa's coasts (twice the number found around Hawaii). Only 120 female hawksbill and green turtles still nest here, and there's a US$10,000 fine for killing a sea turtle. Humpback whales visit American Samoa from August to October to bear their young in these warm waters before returning to Antarctica, where they pass the southern summer. Sperm whales also call occasionally.

Two land snakes exist, neither poisonous. The blind potted soil snake, which looks rather like a plump earthworm, was introduced to Tutuila accidentally. The two-meter-long Pacific boa of Ta'u is found on islands from Indonesia to Samoa. Both are extremely rare and it's highly unlikely you'll ever see one.

History

The Polynesians emerged in Samoa some 3,000 years ago. By 600 B.C. they'd established a settlement on Tutuila at Tula. This nucleus (or a similar one in the Manu'a Group) may have been the jumping-off point for colonizing Eastern Polynesia (Tahiti and the Marquesas) about A.D. 300. The Samoans maintained regular contact by canoe with the other island groups of Western Polynesia, Tonga, and Fiji. Both Samoas belong

AMERICAN SAMOA

THE SAMOAS AT A GLANCE

ISLAND	POPULATION	AREA (square km)	HIGHEST POINT (m)
Savai'i	41,826 (2001)	1,718	1,858
Apolima	80 (2001)	1	168
Manono	955 (2001)	3	107
Upolu	131,279 (2001)	1,125	1,100
Samoa	**174,140 (2001)**	**2,842***	
Tutuila	55,400 (2000)	137	652
Aunuu	476 (2000)	2	88
Ofu	289 (2000)	7	494
Olosega	216 (2000)	5	639
Ta'u	873 (2000)	46	965
Rose	nil	1	5
Swains	37 (2000)	3	5
American Samoa	**57,291 (2000)**	**201**	

*The uninhabited islands of Nu'usafe'e, Nu'utele, Nu'ulua, Namu'a, and Fanuatapu are included in this total.

to a single cultural area: The chiefs of Tutuila were subordinate to those of Upolu.

The first European in Samoa was the Dutchman Jacob Roggeveen, who visited the Manu'a Group in 1722. In 1786 Antoine de Bougainville, who was French, christened Samoa the "Navigator Islands" for the islanders in canoes he observed chasing schools of tuna far offshore. Another Frenchman, La Pérouse, called in 1787 and had a bloody encounter with the islanders. The Samoans nicknamed these early visitors *papalagi*, or "sky bursters," shortened today to *palagi* and applied to all whites.

Protestant missionary John Williams arrived in 1830 with eight Tahitians and influenza. His son, John Williams, Jr., became one of the first European traders. Nearly 40 years later, American businessmen chose Pago Pago Harbor as an ideal coaling station for their new steamship service from San Francisco to Australia. In 1872, the U.S. Navy sent a ship to negotiate a treaty with local chiefs. Though never ratified by the U.S.

Senate, this agreement kept the other powers out of Tutuila. By the treaty of November 7, 1899, Germany and the United States partitioned Samoa between themselves, with British interests recognized in Tonga. In 1900, the United States annexed Tutuila and Aunu'u, adding the Manu'a Group in 1904. This act was not formally ratified by the U.S. Congress until 1929.

From 1900 to 1951 American Samoa was under the Navy Department; since then it has been the responsibility of the Department of the Interior. Thousands of U.S. Marines were trained on Tutuila during WW II, and concrete pillboxes built at that time still punctuate much of the island's coastline. The only action experienced, however, was a few shells lobbed from a Japanese sub on January 11, 1942, which ironically damaged the store of one of Tutuila's few Japanese residents, Frank Shimasaki.

The Americanization of Samoa

Outside the war years, little happened to alter

the centuries-old lifestyle of the Samoans until the early 1960s, when a United Nations mission visiting the U.S.-administered Trust Territory of the Pacific Islands in Micronesia, north of the equator, leveled criticism at Washington for its "benign neglect." In 1961, with neighboring Western Samoa on the verge of independence and U.S. "colonialism" in Samoa becoming an issue, President Kennedy appointed Governor H. Rex Lee, a Mormon, to dispense a giant infusion of federal funds. A massive public works program financed construction of roads, schools, housing, port facilities, electrification, a new hospital, a tuna cannery, a modern hotel, and an international airport. Lee's most publicized innovation was educational television, introduced in 1964; by the mid-1970s, however, the emphasis of the broadcasts had shifted to the usual commercial programming.

This excessive government spending has created an artificial American standard of living. The Samoans became so dependent that three times they voted down proposals to increase home rule for fear it would mean fewer subsidies from Uncle Sam. Only in 1976, after a short tenure by unpopular Gov. Earl B. Ruth, did they finally agree in a referendum to elect their own governor. Even today, American Samoans receive millions of dollars a year in food stamps, and lobbying for more money from Washington is the favorite pastime of local politicians. Meanwhile the territorial government is said to be riddled with corruption and fraud.

Government

While Samoa received independence from New Zealand in 1962, American Samoa (www.government.as) remains an "unincorporated" territory of the United States, meaning the U.S. Constitution and certain other laws don't apply. The Samoans have no desire to be brought under the jurisdiction of the U.S. Constitution, as this would mean an end to their system of chiefs and family-held lands, and would open the territory to uncontrolled migration and business competition from the U.S. mainland. Neither are they interested in independence so long as Washington is holding the purse strings and a majority of

their people reside in the United States itself. The territory does have observer status at the United Nations.

The territory is also defined as "unorganized," because it doesn't have a constitution sanctioned by the U.S. Congress. In 1966, federal officials authorized a Samoan constitution that included a bill of rights and gave legislative authority to the Fono (www.maotafono.info), a body composed of 20 representatives (two-year term) elected by the public at large and 18 senators (four-year term) chosen by the customary Samoan *matai* (chiefs). American Samoa's own colony, Swains Island, has a nonvoting representative. None of this has yet been made U.S. law by Congress.

The powers of the Fono increased during the 1970s; it now exercises considerable control over budget appropriations and executive appointments, though the Secretary of the Interior in Washington retains the right to cancel any law passed by the Fono, remove elected officials, and even cancel self-government itself without reference to the Samoans. The Secretary of the Interior appoints the Chief Justice of the High Court.

Every four years since 1977, American Samoans have elected their own governor and lieutenant governor. The governor can veto legislation passed by the Fono. Local political parties don't exist, although candidates often identify themselves with the U.S. Democratic or Republican parties. Since 1981 the territory has been represented in Washington by a nonvoting congressman elected every two years, and representative Eni F.H. Faleomavaega, a Democrat, has won every election since 1988.

Local government is conducted by three district governors, 15 county chiefs, and 55 *pulenu'u* (village mayors), all under the Secretary of Samoan Affairs, a leading *matai* himself.

Economy

The territorial government and the tuna canneries each employ about a third of the workforce. The Government of American Samoa receives an annual US$110 million in subsidies and grants from Washington. In fact, the territory gets more money in U.S. aid than the entire budget of independent Samoa, although American

Samoa has one-third the population. American Samoans receive a total of US$18 million a year in federal social security payments. This, and diverging living standards, ensure that the two Samoas will never be reunited. Residents of the territory pay exactly the same level of income tax as stateside taxpayers, and all such revenue is retained by the Government of American Samoa. Three-quarters of the local budget of US$225 million is spent on paying the salaries of the 5,000 government employees.

American Samoa's primary industry is tuna processing by the Samoa Packing Co., user of the "Chicken of the Sea" label, and StarKist Samoa, a subsidiary of Del Monte Foods. The first cannery opened in 1954, and American Samoa today is one of the world's tuna processors and the most important commercial fishing port under the U.S. flag (Dutch Harbor, Alaska, is a distant second). Canned fish, canned pet food (from the blood meat), and fish meal (from the skin, guts, and bones) now account for the bulk of the territory's industrial output.

Canneries thrive in this tiny U.S. territory because they allow Asian fishing companies to avoid U.S. import tariffs of up to 35 percent on processed fish. Goods have duty- and quota-free entry to the United States if 30 percent of their value is added in the territory. Federal law prohibits foreign commercial fishing vessels from offloading tuna at U.S. ports; however, American Samoa is exempted. Thus the greater part of the South Pacific tuna catch is landed here, supplying the United States with the bulk of its canned tuna, worth US$500 million a year. Even with this trade, imports into American Samoa are almost double exports (the biggest imports are manufactured goods, food, and fuel). On a per capita basis, American Samoa's foreign trade is far greater than that of any other South Pacific entity.

Both canneries pay virtually nothing in taxes to the local government and employ 5,000 cheap nonunion workers from independent Samoa, who put in two shifts. American Samoans themselves aren't at all interested in cleaning fish for US$3.26 an hour and instead work in business or government. Though they make millions on their tuna operations, the canneries have threatened to relocate if the minimum wage is raised or if the workers became unionized (the intimidated cannery workers have voted several times against becoming members of the International Brotherhood of Teamsters). American Samoa and the Northern Mariana Islands are the only U.S. jurisdictions where federal minimum wage legislation doesn't apply. Another looming threat is competition from low-wage canneries in Ecuador, which could soon gain access to the U.S. market under the North American Free Trade Agreement. StarKist has announced that it would terminate its Samoan operations in such a case.

The trend now is away from rust-eaten Korean and Taiwanese longline tuna boats, toward large California purse seiners worth a couple of million dollars apiece. Between 30 and 40 American purse seiners are based here. The more than one hundred Korean and Taiwanese longliners working out of Pago Pago provide only about 30 percent of the fish packed. Most of the fish are taken in Papua New Guinea and Federated States of Micronesia waters (the Samoa canneries don't can fish caught by setting nets around dolphins). In aggregate, the canneries contribute about US$25 million a year to the local economy in wages, and spend another US$40 million on support services, fuel, and provisioning.

The local government has recently established an industrial park at Tafuna near the airport where companies can lease land on which to build factories. The advantage here is the territory's low minimum wages and duty- and quota-free tariff relationship with the United States. In 1999, a Korean company, Daewoosa Samoa, began producing cheap men's jackets to be sold by major U.S. retailers. Daewoosa faced legal action and fines over the exploitation of its 300 female Vietnamese "guest workers," and in 2001, the sweatshop closed its doors. The factory owner Kil-Soo Lee and several managers were arrested by FBI agents and taken to Honolulu to face involuntary servitude and forced labor charges.

Tourism development has been hampered by unstable air connections to Honolulu, a reputation for unsuitable accommodations, environmental degradation, and poor marketing. Of the 88,650 international arrivals in 2001, only about

10 percent were actual tourists. The rest came on business, to visit relatives, for employment, or in transit. Most were from the other Samoa, with U.S. citizens a distant second. Air service is restricted by a federal "cabotage" law, which prohibits foreign airlines from carrying passengers between two American airports. Thus only U.S. carriers such as Hawaiian Airlines are allowed to operate between Pago Pago and Honolulu, leading to high fares and limited service. The government-owned Rainmaker Hotel has only made a profit during two years of its three decades of operations and repeated attempts to sell the hotel have failed. It's now hoped that the creation of National Park of American Samoa will stimulate tourism.

The People

Between 1980 and 2000, the population of American Samoa almost doubled, from 32,297 to 57,291. This is the fastest growth rate in the South Pacific, and at 285 persons per square km, American Samoa is the second most densely populated South Pacific entity (after Tuvalu). All of this growth was on Tutuila; the population of the Manu'a Group declined slightly. The population of the harbor area is growing almost 10 percent a year. This growth and needs of the canneries have put heavy pressure on the local water supply, and large investments have had to be made in catchments and fresh water pipelines.

American Samoans are U.S. "nationals," not citizens, the main difference being that nationals can't vote in U.S. presidential elections nor be drafted. American Samoans have free entry to the United States, and some 65,000 of them now live in California and Washington State, and another 20,000 are in Hawaii, most in the lower income bracket. Nearly 70 percent of high school graduates leave within a year of graduation, many of them to voluntarily join the Armed Forces. About 2,275 students attend the American Samoa Community College (www.amsamoacc.as) at Mapusaga, a two-year institution established in 1970.

The people of the two Samoan island groups are homogeneous in blood, speech, and traditions, and as fast as American Samoans leave for the States, people from the other Samoa migrate from west to east. Much intermarriage has occurred, and about 18,000 western Samoans now live in American Samoa. Some "American" Samoans look down on their western cousins, calling them *sulu'ie* for the traditional kilts they often wear instead of trousers, and immigration officials in Pago Pago often confiscate the passports of "real" Samoans upon arrival to ensure that they'll return home. Of course, without "western" Samoans to do the dirty work, much of American Samoa's economy would soon grind to a halt. Some 1,200 Tongans and 3,500 U.S.-born persons are also present, and only 56 percent of residents were actually born in the territory.

Although the young have largely forgotten their own culture in their haste to embrace that of the United States, the *fa'a Samoa* is tenaciously defended by those who choose to remain in their home villages. For a complete description of the *fa'a Samoa,* see the Introduction section in the Samoa chapter. Under treaties signed with the Samoan chiefs in 1900 and 1904, the U.S. government undertook to retain the *matai* system and protect Samoan land rights. To its credit, it has done just that. In addition, the innate strength and flexibility of "the Samoan way" has permitted its survival in the face of German, New Zealand, and American colonialism. It's remarkable how these people have adopted those American ways they considered useful, while remaining first and foremost Samoans.

On Tutuila, the people live in 60 villages along the coast. After a hurricane in 1966, the U.S. government provided funds to rebuild the thatched Samoan *fales* in plywood and tin, resulting in the hot, stuffy dwellings one sees today. The most farsighted act of the former naval administration was to forbid the sale of Samoan land to outsiders. Except for a small area owned by the government and the 2 percent freehold land alienated before 1900, 90 percent of all land in the territory is communally owned by Samoan extended families *(aiga),* who even bury relatives in front of their homes to reinforce their titles. The family *matai* assigns use of communal land to different members of the *aiga.* Non-Samoans can lease Samoan land for up to 55 years, however.

American Samoa's largest churches are the Congregational Christian Church (21,000 adherents), the Catholic Church (8,500 adherents), the Church of Jesus Christ of Latter-day Saints (5,000 adherents), the Methodist Church (4,000 adherents), the Assemblies of God (3,000 adherents), and the Seventh-Day Adventists (2,000 adherents).

Away from Pago Pago Harbor, if there's a village behind a beach, you're expected to ask permission before swimming. Never swim anywhere near a church on Sunday, and be aware that most Samoans don't wear bathing suits—they swim in shorts and T-shirts. Foreigners in swimsuits on a village beach could give offense, hence the necessity of asking permission first.

During *sa* every afternoon around 1830 villagers pause in whatever they're doing for a brief prayer. If you hear a village bell around this time, stop walking, running, or riding to avoid raising the Samoans' ire. Some remote villages also have a 2200 curfew.

Exploring the Islands

Highlights

American Samoa's throbbing heart is Fagatogo Market, where buses unload passengers from both ends of Tutuila. Mt. Alava, the canneries, Rainmaker Mountain, and Pago Pago Harbor are all visible from the market. Mt. Alava itself may be the island's second best sight, accessible on foot from the Fagasa road. A colorful island tour is easily arranged by boarding a bus to Tula or Leone. Those with more time can catch a flight to the twin islands of Ofu and Olosega with their spectacular beaches and cliffs. A week is ample time to see Tutuila, and with two weeks you could do all of the above.

National Park

In 1988, the U.S. Congress authorized the creation of the National Park of American Samoa, comprising 32 square km of tropical rainforest, coastal cliffs, and coral reef on Tutuila, Ofu, and Ta'u, and in 1993, nine villages signed 50-year leases involving annual fees of US$370,000 in total (this is the only U.S. national park in which the federal government leases the land).

On Tutuila the park stretches from Fagasa Bay to Afono Bay, encompassing everything north of the knifelike ridge. Countless seabirds nest on Pola Island. The largest unit is on Ta'u with Mt. Lata and the entire southeast corner of the island, including coastal, lowland, montane, and cloud forest communities. Ta'u's soaring cliffs and Laufuti Falls are spectacular. On Ofu, the lovely southeastern beach and coral reef are included. Two endangered species of *pe'a* (flying fox), pollinators of the rainforest, are protected in the park.

This splendid national park, which ranks with Yellowstone and the Grand Canyon in majesty, seems destined to become American Samoa's biggest tourist attraction if an appropriate infrastructure for visitors can be put in place. Current information is available from the park visitor center (tel. 633-7082, fax 633-7085) in Suite 114 of the Pago Plaza at Pago Pago. Park admission itself is free.

Public Holidays and Festivals

All standard U.S. public holidays are observed in American Samoa: New Year's Day (January 1), Martin Luther King Day (third Monday in January), Presidents' Day (third Monday in February), Flag Day (April 17), Good Friday and Easter Monday (March/April), Memorial Day (last Monday in May), Independence Day (July 4), Labor Day (first Monday in September), Columbus Day (second Monday in October), Veteran's Day (November 11), Thanksgiving (fourth Thursday in November), Christmas Day (December 25), and Family Day (December 26).

American Samoa's **Flag Day,** April 17, commemorates the first flying of the Stars and Stripes in 1900. This enthusiastic two-day celebration features *fautasi* (longboat) racing plus song and dance competitions in Fagatogo. National Tourism Week in early May sees barbecues, canoe races, cultural demonstrations, fireworks, music, a parade, and the crowning of Miss American Samoa at Utulei Beach. Manu'a Cession Day is July 16.

Although European explorers didn't find Samoa until 230 years after Christopher got to America, Columbus or "Discoverer's" Day (second Monday in October) is also a public holiday. In fact, it's one of the biggest holidays of the year because it happens to coincide with the **Moso'oi Tourism Festival** in mid-October. This is the occasion for sporting events, *fautasi* races, cultural performances, food and flower shows, a beauty pageant, and musical competitions. Most events are held at the Lee Auditorium.

Another important event is the rising of the palolo (coral worms) in late October or early November. When the moon and tide are just right and the palolo emerge to propagate, Samoans are waiting with nets and lanterns to scoop up this cherished delicacy, the caviar of the Pacific.

Information

The American Samoa Office of Tourism (P.O. Box 1147, Pago Pago, AS 96799, U.S.A.; tel. 633-1092, fax 633-2092, www.amerikasamoa.info), run by the Department of Commerce, mails out brochures upon request.

In the United States you can put your questions to American Samoa's congressman in Washington, the Hon. Eni F.H. Faleomavaega (tel. 202/225-8577, fax 202/225-8757, www.house.gov/faleomavaega).

Internet Resources

The Office of Tourism site, **www.amerika samoa.info,** has accommodation, restaurant, shopping, and transportation listings, plus a calendar of events and photos. The site of the National Park of American Samoa, **www.nps.gov/npsa,** lets you download detailed island maps, plus there's a Natural History Guide To American Samoa. The Fagatele Bay National Marine Sanctuary site, **www.fagatelebay.noaa.gov,** has excellent photo galleries and there's a good deal of information on corals.

Visit the site of the American Samoa Historic Preservation Office, **www.ashpo.org,** for John Enright's walking tour of Fagatogo and Utulei

featuring a clickable map and historic photos. Internet Manu'a, **www.geocities.com/imanua,** has a "Sights of Manu'a" section with the Skaggs collection of photos.

Amerika Samoa Net, **www.amsamoa.net,** is American Samoa's community website with links to the personal sites of Samoans in the islands and around the world. PagoPago.com, **www.pagopago.com,** allows you to look up American Samoan numbers in an online classified telephone directory. The official site of American Samoa's nonvoting congressman in Washington, D.C., Hon. Eni F.H. Faleomavaega, **www.house.gov/faleomavaega,** is useful for political news relating to the territory.

Visas and Officialdom

No visa is necessary for a stay of 30 days. Everyone requires a passport and onward ticket for entry. In the past, Americans could enter by showing a certified birth certificate, but since 9/11 Americans have also needed to present a passport. Non-U.S. passport holders should verify visa requirements (and entry fees!) with their airline in advance as they're subject to sudden change. "Alien" women more than six months pregnant are refused entry to American Samoa. In some cases, the local immigration authorities insist on holding passports to ensure that foreigners don't overstay their visas or become a security risk. Entry conditions are set by the Government of American Samoa—the U.S. Immigration and Naturalization Service does not exercise jurisdiction here.

Anyone with a Muslim sounding name or Middle Eastern appearance can expect heavy scrutiny upon arrival in American Samoa, and could be refused entry. Citizens of 25 predominately Muslim countries are banned from the territory unless they have the personal approval of the Attorney General of American Samoa. Initially this also applied to citizens of Fiji, although only 10 percent of the inhabitants of that country are Muslims and none had ever been accused of involvement in "terrorism." In early 2003, after a strong protest from Suva and adverse media coverage throughout the region, Fiji was removed from the list.

Visa extensions are very difficult to obtain and work permits almost impossible unless you have a special skill someone needs, in which case your sponsor will have to post a bond. The office of the Chief Immigration Officer is in the Executive Office Building in Utulei. If you're proceeding to Hawaii from Pago Pago and need a U.S. visa, be sure to pick it up at the U.S. Embassy in Apia or elsewhere, because there's no visa-issuing office here.

Before departing Hawaii for American Samoa, cruising yachts must obtain a U.S. Customs clearance. Pago Pago is the only port of entry for cruising yachts and few try to fight their way back to Ofu and Ta'u against the wind. At Pago Pago, US$25 clearance fees are charged, plus an additional US$25 departure fee. On both occasions you must take your boat to the customs dock, where the waves bang it against the rough concrete. Tutuila is infested with the giant African snail. Customs officials in neighboring countries know this and carefully inspect baggage and shipping originating in Pago Pago.

Money

U.S. dollars are used, and to avoid big problems and exorbitant commissions when changing money, non-U.S. residents should bring traveler's checks expressed in American currency. Samoan currency is difficult to change in American Samoa, and then at a poor rate. If you lose your traveler's checks or credit cards, you can report American Express cards and checks at the ANZ Amerika Samoa Bank and Visa at the Bank of Hawaii.

North American tourism has introduced tipping to the upmarket restaurants of the territory. The local saying goes, "it's not only accepted, it's expected." There's no bargaining in markets or shops.

Communications

Because U.S. postal rates apply, American Samoa is a cheap place for airmailing parcels to the United States (sea mail takes about 30 days to reach Oakland, California, by container). The mail service is reported to be erratic, so mark all mail to or from Pago Pago "priority post." The

U.S. postal code is 96799, and regular U.S. postage stamps are used.

Long-distance telephone calls to the United States are unexpectedly more expensive than from Apia. A three-minute call costs US$5.70 to New Zealand or Australia, US$6 to the United States, US$8 to Britain or Canada. Evenings and weekends you'll be eligible for a discount amounting to a few pennies on overtime charges to the United States but not elsewhere. Collect calls can be made to the United States only.

Blue Sky Communications (tel. 699-2759, www.blueskynet.as) at Pago Plaza sells prepaid telephone cards priced US$10, US$20, and US$50. These cards can be used from any Touch-Tone phone and are available at many locations around Tutuila. Blue Sky's long distance rates are much lower than those quoted above—ask.

Local telephone calls from public telephones anywhere in American Samoa cost only US$.10 each and the phones do work—get back into the habit of using them. Yes, it's only US$.10 to call the Manu'a Group from Tutuila. Local calls from private residences are free.

Local directory assistance is tel. 411. In emergencies, dial 911. American Samoa's telephone code is 684.

Media

The privately owned *Samoa News* (tel. 633-5599, fax 633-4864, www.samoanews.com), published daily except Sunday, has been around since the 1960s. Special deals on accommodations and airfares are sometimes advertised in the *News,* and you get local insights.

Channel 2 at government-operated KVZK-TV broadcasts PBS, CNN, and a couple of hours of local programming 0600–2400 daily (local programs are on in the evening). Catch CNN Headline News weekdays at 0800 and 1000, and KVZK local news weekdays at 1730. Commercial channel 4 has ABC/CBS/NBC programs 1500–2400 weekdays, 1200–2400 weekends. You can see the ABC world news weekdays at 1700, and the NBC nightly news weekdays at 1800. The tapes are broadcast with Hawaiian advertising. In 1995, satellite-generated cable television was introduced to the territory by two private companies, and although these cost about US$360 a year, dozens of channels are accessible 24 hours a day.

Radio KSBS-FM (tel. 633-7000, fax 633-5727, www.ksbsfm.com) at 92.1 MHz, broadcasts daily 0600–midnight, and you can pick it up everywhere on Tutuila. Throughout the day they play mostly island music and oldies, while in the evening there is also some top 40s for youthful listeners.

93KHJ-FM (tel. 633-7793, fax 633-4493, www.khjradio.com) broadcasts hit music over 93.1 MHz 24 hours a day.

TRANSPORTATION
Getting There
Hawaiian Airlines (tel. 699-1875) links Pago Pago to Honolulu twice a week, with connections in Honolulu to/from Los Angeles, Las Vegas, Portland, San Francisco, San Diego, and Seattle. Pago Pago-Honolulu costs US$930 roundtrip; Pago Pago-Los Angeles is US$1,308 roundtrip. Thirty-day advance purchase return fares are US$250 lower, but you must be physically there to buy such a ticket. One-way fares from Pago Pago are US$527 to Honolulu or US$650 to Los Angeles. Don't forget to reconfirm your onward flight if you want to avoid getting bumped.

In late 2003, Hawaii-based **Aloha Airlines** (www.alohaairlines.com) began twice weekly flights from Honolulu to Pago Pago, continuing to Rarotonga.

Polynesian Airlines (tel. 699-9126) also has frequent daily flights to Pago Pago from Apia, one or two leaving from Faleolo International Airport and the others from Fagali'i Airstrip. Always verify which airport they'll be using and reconfirm. Polynesian charges US$92/115 one-way/roundtrip from Pago Pago to Apia, and due to currency differences, tickets for the same route are a third cheaper when purchased in Apia rather than in American Samoa or elsewhere. Add US$9.50 tax to these fares. Most of the Apia flights are on 19-seater Twin Otter aircraft. Beware of baggage handling irregularities as damaged, delayed, or lost luggage is rou-

tine here—carry anything irreplaceable in your hand luggage.

Polynesian Airlines has connections in Apia to/from Australia, New Zealand, and Honolulu on their own aircraft, to/from Los Angeles on Air New Zealand, and to/from Fiji on Air Pacific. Polynesian's 45-day Polypass (US$1,099) is valid for travel between the Samoas, Tonga, Australia, and New Zealand. For US$250 extra you can begin in Honolulu and for US$600 extra it's good from Los Angeles and five other west coast airports.

For those interested in a quick prearranged side trip from independent Samoa, **Oceania Tours** (tel. 685/24-443, fax 685/22-255), in the Kitano Tusitala Hotel in Apia, offers overnight fly/drive packages to Pago Pago. Beginning at US$235/330 single/double plus tax, these include return airfare, one night's accommodations, and a car for 24 hours. They can also organize guided day trips from Apia at US$149 pp.

By Ship
The Samoa Shipping Corporation's ferry *Lady Naomi* leaves Pago Pago for Apia Thursday at 1600 (eight hours, US$40/50 one-way for a seat/bunk). On major public holidays the ship makes two weekly trips, departing Pago Pago at 1600 on Wednesday and Friday. Safety regulations limit the number of passengers aboard to 220, and when that number of tickets has been sold, the ship is "full." Thus it's wise to book before noon a day ahead (take your passport). If you have to buy your ticket at the wharf, you'll be the last person to board and you won't find a proper place to sleep. The booking agent is **Polynesia Shipping** (tel. 633-1211, fax 633-1265), across from Sadie's Restaurant. Make sure your name is added to the passenger list or you won't be allowed on board. As your departure date approaches, keep in close touch with the agent, since the schedule is subject to frequent change.

Boat fares are lower in the other Samoa, thus it's cheaper to buy only a one-way ticket to Apia and purchase your return portion there, although the Samoan ticket-to-leave requirement makes it difficult to take advantage of this savings. Coming from Apia, get a roundtrip ticket if you intend to return. Go aboard early to get a proper berth. The action of the southeast trade winds makes this a smoother trip westbound toward Apia than vice versa (but it can be rough anytime). Even veteran backpackers consider this a rough trip.

Immigration formalities at both ends are chaotic because everyone pushes to be the first person off. Non-Samoans arriving on Tutuila by boat can expect to be closely scrutinized by American Samoan immigration, so if there's anything at all "irregular" about your status, be sure to come by plane. Persons holding passports from places other than Western Europe, Canada, the United States, Japan, Australia, and New Zealand are singled out and could well be refused entry.

We don't know of any scheduled passenger boats from Pago Pago to Tonga, the Cook Islands, or Fiji. The main season for hitching rides to Tonga or Fiji on private yachts is mid-April to October. Somebody at the Utulei Yacht Club may be able to advise.

Getting Around

Inter-Island Air (tel. 699-7100, www.inter islandair.com) operates a Fairchild Dornier 228-212 high wing aircraft to Manu'a twice a day. Pago Pago to Ofu or Ta'u costs US$54/102 one-way/roundtrip, while flights *between* Ta'u and Ofu are US$31 one-way. Seats on the Manu'a flights are often fully booked a week ahead, so inquire early and try making a telephoned reservation well in advance, if you're sure you want to go. Carefully reconfirm every step of the way. The baggage limit on flights to Manu'a is 20 kilograms.

Inter-Island Shipping (tel. 258-7333 and ask for Seso) runs a landing craft-type supply vessel, the *Manu'a Tele III*, to the Manu'a Group, an eight-hour trip. The boat leaves every Wednesday at 2100, returning to Pago Pago on Thursday. The 30 passengers pay US$25 each way to Ofu and Ta'u on a first-come, first-served basis. It's unusual for a visitor to travel this way, so inquire well ahead.

Airport

Pago Pago International Airport (PPG) is built over the lagoon at Tafuna, 11 km southwest of Fagatogo. Transport to town is US$.75 by public bus or US$15 by taxi (agree on the price before and be sure you have exact change—the drivers *never* do). Public buses stop fairly frequently in front of the terminal (except on Sunday or after dark). Most of the car rental booths in the terminal open only for flights from Hawaii, although Avis stays open all day.

There's no tourist information desk or bank at the airport (bring some U.S. dollars in cash). The shops in front of the airline offices at the airport sell handicrafts, cheap ice-cream cones, and snacks. The duty-free shop in the departure lounge is generally more expensive than these and is often closed. The **Island Hut Café** (tel. 699-2329) at the airport serves filling American-style meals at reasonable prices. Watch your tickets and baggage tags carefully when you check in here, as the agents will happily book you through to wherever or strand you. The US$4.50 airport facility charge and US$5 "entry declaration fee" are usually included in the ticket price.

Tutuila

The main island of American Samoa, Tutuila, is shaped like a Chinese dragon, 32 km long and ranges 1–10 km wide. Alone it accounts for 68 percent of American Samoa's surface area and over 95 percent of its population. Surprisingly, this is one of the most varied and beautiful islands in the South Pacific. Its long mountainous spine twists from east to west with wild coastlines and cliffs on the north side, gentler landscapes and plains on the south. There are lots of good beaches scattered around, but for a variety of reasons, finding a good place to swim takes some doing. When it's calm, the snorkeling is fine off the empty golden beaches all along the north coast, and the reef-break surfing along the south coast is especially good from December to March.

Fagatogo, the largest town, looks out onto elbowlike Pago Pago Harbor, while government is centered at Utulei, just east of Fagatogo. Despite the oil slicks and continual flood of pollution from canneries, shipping, yachts, and residents, this harbor is dramatically scenic with many fine hikes in the surrounding hills. Among the seemingly incompatible elements thrown together here are slow-moving Samoan villagers, immigrant cannery workers, taciturn Asian fishermen, carefree yachties, and colorful American expatriates—only tourists are missing. It's an unusual, unpretentious place to poke around for a few days.

SIGHTS

Utulei

At **Blunt's Point,** overlooking the mouth of Pago Pago Harbor, are two huge six-inch naval guns emplaced in 1941. To reach them from Utulei, start walking southeast on the main road past the oil tanks, and keep watching on the right for a small pump house with two large metal pipes coming out of the wall. This pump is across the highway from a small beach, almost opposite two houses on the bay side of the road. The track up the hill begins behind the pump house. If arriving by bus from the west, get out as soon as

you see the oil tanks and walk back. The lower gun is directly above a large green water tank, while the second is about 200 meters farther up the ridge. Concrete stairways lead to both guns. To create a cross fire, two identical guns were positioned across the harbor mouth on the hillside near Breakers Point, where they remain to this day.

After visiting the guns, walk back toward town as far as the Yacht Club, where you'll see a few long *fautasi* longboats, then turn left to the US$10-million **Executive Office Building** erected in 1991 at Utulei. It's well worth going in to catch a glimpse of the territory's formidable bureaucracy. Behind this building is the **Feleti Barstow Library** (1998), and beyond it a paved road winds up to the former **cable-car terminal** on Solo Hill. Here a monument recalls a 1980 air disaster in which a U.S. Navy plane hit the cables and crashed into the Rainmaker Hotel, killing the six servicemen aboard and two tourists at the hotel. The hotel manager refused to allow the memorial to be erected on the hotel grounds.

The cableway, one of the longest single-span aerial tramways in the world, was built in 1965 to transport TV technicians to the transmitters atop Mt. Alava (491 meters). The car would sway for a kilometer and a half over Pago Pago Harbor, with mountains such as rugged Rainmaker (524 meters) in full view, making this the most spectacular aerial ride in the Pacific. In 1992, Hurricane Val put the cableway out of service and it has never been repaired. It's still worth visiting the Utulei terminal for the excellent view of **Rainmaker Mountain** from the viewpoint.

Also in Utulei is the **Lee Auditorium** (1962) and American Samoa's **television studios,** which may be visited weekdays around 1030. In 1964, American Samoa became the first Pacific country to acquire television, and although the original educational use has disappeared, KVZK-TV continues to broadcast commercially over two channels. Channel 2 is semi-educational, while Channel 4 is strictly commercial television. Channel 5 was blown off the air by Hurricane Val in

TUTUILA AND AUNU'U

AMERICAN SAMOA

S O U T H   P A C I F I C   O C E A N

Cape Matatula

Tula
Alao
Auasi
Olomoana Mtn.
Aoa
Onenoa
Masausi
Amouli
Alofau
Red Lake
Aunu'u Island
Aunu'u

Nafanua Bank

Masefau Bay
Fagatua
Masefau

Fagaitua Bay

Afono
Rainmaker Mtn.
Aua
Laulili
Pyramid Rock
Breakers Point
Pago Pago Harbor
Utulei
Faga'alu
Fau Rock
Taema Bank

TISA'S BAREFOOT BAR

Pola Island
Amalau Bay
Craggy Point
Afono Bay
Vaitu Bay
Vatia
Tafeu Cove

National Park
of American Samoa

Mt. Alava

Pago Pago
Fagatogo
HOSPITAL
Matafao Peak
(653 m)

Nu'uuli
Coconut Point
Pala Lagoon
PAGO PAGO INTERNATIONAL AIRPORT
TERMINAL
Freddie's Beach

Fagasa Bay
Fagasa
Nu'uuli
Tafuna

COMMUNITY COLLEGE
TRADEWINDS HOTEL
Ottoville
GOLF COURSE
Vaitogi

SHARK AND TURTLE LODGE
Larsen Bay
Steps Point

Massacre Bay

Aasu

Aoloaufou
Olotele Mtn.
(493 m)
Leone Falls
Pavaiai
Malaeloa
Futiga
Taputimu

Square Head

Aoloautai
Lealataalava Mtn.
(354 m)
Nua
Fagamutu
Asili
Leone
Leone Bay

ATAULOMA GIRLS SCHOOL
Vailoatai
Slides Rock
Fagatele Bay

Fagamalo
Maloata
Fagalii
Maloata Bay
Poloa
Amanave
Cape Taputapu

0   5 mi
0   5 km

AUNU'U ISLAND

0   500 yds
0   500 m

Aunu'u
AUASI SPEEDBOAT
Alofisau Point
Pala
Agaoleatu Point
Pola Hill
Ma'ama'a Cove
Red Lake
Fogatia Hill
Taufusitele Marsh
Aunu'u
Steacaria Point

© DAVID STANLEY

1992 and its equipment was cannibalized to keep the other two channels going.

Fagatogo

The **Governor's Mansion,** on a hilltop just west of the Rainmaker Hotel, was built in 1903 during the naval administration as the Commandant's Residence, becoming Government House in 1951. A large sign requests the public not to enter the grounds. The **Jean P. Haydon Museum** (tel. 633-4347; weekdays 1000–1500, admission free), farther west, was erected in 1917 as a naval commissary and served as the island's post office 1950–1971. The museum features exhibits on natural history, tapa making, and tattooing, plus a collection of war clubs, kava bowls, model canoes, and old photos.

Facing the Malae-O-Le-Talu field, where local chiefs ceded the island to the United States in 1900, is the **Fono Building** (1973), in which the territory's legislature convenes for 45-day sessions twice a year. The **police station,** across the field from the Fono, was originally the barracks of the Fitafita Guard, the former Samoan militia. Next to the police station is the **old jail** (1911), now the archives office.

Farther west just before the market is the old **courthouse** (1904), built in the U.S. Deep-South style. The **Fagatogo Public Market** is busiest early Saturday morning, when screaming red-faced evangelists backed up by ear-splitting gospel music harangue vendors selling tropical fruits and vegetables. Just inside the **Department of Marine and Wildlife Resources** office facing the bus station next to the market is a very good display of fish and birdlife of Samoa. Ask at the Education Office here for a copy of the booklet *American Samoa: Natural History and Conservation Topics.*

West of here is the former guesthouse where Somerset Maugham stayed in 1916, now **Sadie's Restaurant.** Today Maugham's tale of hooker Sadie Thompson and the repressed missionary, set here, is discussed over upscale seafood.

Pago Pago

Continue west to a sign reading National Park Visitor Center 1/4 Mile, where a road runs up the hill into Happy Valley. On this side road, you'll pass six WW II ammunition bunkers on the left before reaching a dirt road, also on the left, which leads to a large **concrete bunker** used during

Pago Pago Harbor as it looked in 1939 before roadbuilders broke out of the Bay Area

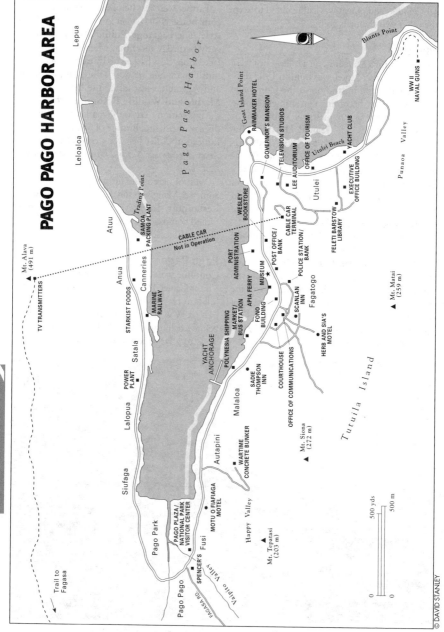

PAGO PAGO HARBOR AREA

Lepua

Leloaloa

Pago Pago Harbor

Blunts Point

WW II NAVAL GUNS ▪

Goat Island Point

RAINMAKER HOTEL

GOVERNOR'S MANSION

TELEVISION STUDIOS

OFFICE OF TOURISM

LEE AUDITORIUM

Utulei Beach

YACHT CLUB

Utulei

EXECUTIVE OFFICE BUILDING

Punaoa Valley

Atuu

Trading Point

SAMOA PACKING PLANT

Anua

CABLE CAR Not in Operation

WESLEY BOOKSTORE

FELETI BARSTOW LIBRARY

CABLE CAR TERMINAL

Mt. Alava ▲ (491 m)

TV TRANSMITTERS ▪

Canneries

STARKIST FOODS

MARINE RAILWAY

PORT ADMINISTRATION

POST OFFICE/ BANK

POLICE STATION/ BANK

Satala

Lalopua

POWER PLANT

Siufaga

Trail to Fagasa

Pago Park

SPENCER'S

Fusi

MOTU O FIAFIAGA MOTEL

PAGO PLAZA/ NATIONAL PARK VISITOR CENTER

Pago Pago

PACKARD RD

Vaipito Valley

Happy Valley

Autapini

Malaloa

WARTIME CONCRETE BUNKER

Mt. Tepatasi ▲ (203 m)

SADIE THOMPSON INN

COURTHOUSE

OFFICE OF COMMUNICATIONS

Mt. Siona ▲ (272 m)

YACHT ANCHORAGE

POLYNESIA SHIPPING

MARKET/ BUS STATION

APIA FERRY

FONO BUILDING

SCANLAN INN

Fagatogo

HERB AND SIA'S MOTEL

MUSEUM ★

Mt. Matai ▲ (259 m)

Tutuila Island

0 ⊢——— 500 yds
0 ⊢——— 500 m

© DAVID STANLEY

AMERICAN SAMOA

N

WW II as a naval communications headquarters. Many of these military structures are now inhabited, and you'll need to ask permission before approaching the bunker, which is in a backyard.

The **National Park Visitor Center** (tel. 633-7082, www.nps.gov/npsa; weekdays 0800–1630, Sat. 0800–1200, admission free), in Room 114 at Pago Plaza, contains a small collection of Samoan artifacts, seashells, coral, maps of American Samoa, and photos of the park. You can ask to see a brief video, and the friendly staff will answer questions. Their free brochure is excellent.

At the west end of the harbor is Pago Pago village, this area's namesake, and around on the north side of the harbor is the **Marine Railway,** which provides maintenance and repair facilities to the fishing fleet. The tuna canneries are nearby. To visit the Thai-owned **Samoa Packing Plant,** call the personnel office beforehand at tel. 644-5272 and make an appointment. You could also try asking at the gate. They'll want to know who you are, where you work, why you wish to visit, etc., and only persons wearing shoes and long pants are allowed inside the plant. **StarKist** (Del Monte Foods), the world's largest tuna processing plant, is less amenable to visitors. These plants process a thousand tons of tuna a day, filling a thousand shipping containers with canned tuna each month, all of it bound for the United States.

The North Coast

The easiest way to escape the congested Pago Pago harbor area is to jump on a bus to **Vatia** on Tutuila's north coast. Several buses (US$1.75) shuttle back and forth via Aua and Afono all day, so getting there is easy. Vatia is a picturesque village with a nice beach, and the scenery around here is superb with jungle-covered peaks surrounding the village on all sides. Look across to unforgettable Pola Island (also known as the "Cockscomb") with its sheer 100-meter cliffs and wheeling seabirds. Vatia is in the center of the Tutuila section of National Park of American Samoa, and if you're interested in some organized hiking or boating while at Vatia, call local resident Roy West (tel. 258-3527 or 644-1317) who offers boat trips at US$25–35 pp if there's

sufficient demand and who can arrange hiking guides at the same rate.

The East End

Eastern Tutuila is easily accessible on the frequent Tula buses that wind along the southeast coast through the day. At **Alao** and **Tula** are wide sandy beaches, but beware of the undertow. On Cape Matatula just past Tula is the **Samoa Observatory** (tel./fax 622-7455), established in 1974 by the National Oceanic and Atmospheric Administration (NOAA), one of five such climate monitoring laboratories around the world. The observatory stands on a ridge overlooking the bluest water you'll ever see. Walk left past the main building and cross the lawn to the top of a steep staircase down to high volcanic cliffs. You can see the Manu'a Group from here on a clear day. From Tula (the end of the bus route), the road continues around to the north side of Tutuila as far as Onenoa.

Aunu'u Island

There's a single village on Aunu'u Island off the southeast end of Tutuila, but no cars. Motorboats shuttle across to Aunu'u constantly from the small boat harbor at Auasi, taking passengers at US$2 pp each way or US$10 one-way for a charter trip. Go over first thing in the morning and you shouldn't have any trouble getting back. Don't come on a Sunday, though, as the locals don't appreciate *palagi* picnickers that day.

Aunu'u's eel-infested **Red Lake** in the sprawling crater is difficult to approach. Cliffs along the south coast and thick bushes make hiking around the island heavy going. Aunu'u's notorious stretch of red **quicksand** at Pala Lake is fairly close to the village, but you may have to wade through a swamp to get to it. The **taro swamps** just behind the village are easier to see, and a walk around to the new elementary school reveals an appealing slice of island life. At **Ma'ama'a Cove** on the east side of the island, waves rush into "the teacup" with much splashing. It's picturesque, but don't swim here.

Ottoville

At Ottoville on the Tafuna plain is **Holy Family**

AMERICAN SAMOA

Catholic Cathedral (1994), containing a wonderful picture of the Holy Family on a Samoan beach painted by Duffy Sheridan in 1991. Samoan carver Sven Ortquist did the 14 deep-relief Stations of the Cross and other woodcarvings in the cathedral and designed the stained glass windows.

Near the cathedral and adjacent to the Fatuoaiga Catholic Church Center is a small **historical park** with restored *tia seu lupe* (pigeon-catching mound) that in many ways resembles the later *marae* of Eastern Polynesia. Similar (if usually smaller) *tia* dot ridgelines and jungles in many parts of Tutuila. The park is well laid out and sits next to the only swatch of lowland rainforest still extant on Tutuila. It's accessible on the Tafuna bus and well worth a visit, especially around twilight if you're a birder.

Around Leone

The Leone bus will drop you at **Leala Sliding Rock,** between Vailoatai and Taputimu, where the local kids take a running slide down the large, flat rocks covered by slimy algae. It's dangerous to imitate unless you know exactly how. From here you can hike east along the lovely coast toward Fagatele Point, but only in dry weather at low tide, because the rocks become extremely slippery and dangerous when it rains. There are several clear tidal pools here where you can swim at low tide, and even a blowhole. Fagatele Bay, a drowned volcanic crater now a designated National Marine Sanctuary (www.fagatelebay.noaa.gov), cannot be reached from this side due to high cliffs.

From Sliding Rock, it's a pleasant two km walk (or another bus) northwest to Leone village. Just before you reach the intersection with the main south coast road, ask someone to direct you to the former **Fagalele Boys School,** on the coast behind a row of large banyan trees. Built in the mid-19th century, this is the oldest European-style building on the island, unfortunately destroyed by Hurricane Val in 1992.

Leone was the ancient capital of Tutuila, and when Samoa's first missionary, John Williams, visited Tutuila on October 18, 1832, it was here that he landed. A monument to Williams is in front of **Zion Church** (1900) at Leone, and the

LEGENDS OF SAMOA

Storytellers relate how once, at a time when food was scarce, a blind old woman took her granddaughter to a bluff at Vaitogi, and, holding hands, they leapt to the sea below. The young girl was transformed into a shark, while the old woman became a turtle. Villagers are still able to call the shark and the turtle to the shore with a certain chant (and for a small fee they'll happily perform the rite).

church itself is worth entering for its finely carved wooden ceiling. Until steamships were invented, Leone was the preferred anchorage of sailing ships unwilling to risk entering Pago Pago Harbor, and much of the early contact between Samoans and Europeans took place here. Two km up the road beginning beside the nearby Catholic church is **Leone Falls** (closed Sunday), where there's freshwater swimming.

Both Fagalele and Zion were built by the London Missionary Society, and a couple of kilometers west of Leone is the former **Atauloma Girls School** (1900), a third relic of LMS activity. Today the school building is owned by the territory and used as government housing for *palagi*—Samoans refuse to live there out of fear that it's haunted. When the sea is calm you can snorkel on the reef in front of Atauloma Girls School, and since there isn't a church in this village, it's usually okay to swim there even on Sunday. There's also surfing off the beaches at Atauloma and nearby Fagamutu.

Cape Taputapu

There's beautiful scenery along the road west of Leone. Get off the bus just beyond Amanave where the road swings north to Poloa. At low tide you can hike along the south coast from Amanave to **Cape Taputapu** in about 30 minutes, passing several lovely isolated beaches and rocky offshore islets. At high tide, look for the slippery, muddy trail that cuts behind several of the more difficult stretches. There's a lovely white-sand beach at uninhabited Loa Cove halfway to the cape. The cape itself is magnificent, and it's

the monument at Aasu to La Pérouse's
massacred crew members

exciting to stand on the rocky westernmost headland and watch the ocean rise and fall before you
as it crashes into the shore.

The Northwest Coast

Buses run fairly frequently between Pavaiai and
Aoloaufou, high in the center of the island. It's a
short walk up a paved road from Aoloaufou to
the radio towers on **Mt. Olotele** (493 meters)
for the view.

From beyond Aoloaufou, a muddy, slippery
trail leads down to Aasu village on **Massacre
Bay,** about an hour each way. Only one family
still lives here, and in front of one of the houses is
a monument erected in 1883 and surmounted by
a cross. This memorializes 11 French sailors from
the ships *Astrolabe* and *Boussole* of the ill-fated La
Pérouse expedition, who were killed here in an
encounter with the Samoans on December 11,
1787. The French had come ashore to fill their
casks with water, but as they were returning to
their ships the two longboats became stranded on

the reef due to a miscalculation of the tide, and
the Samoans attacked. A Chinese member of
the expedition and the 39 Samoans who also
died are not mentioned on the monument. A
year later, La Pérouse and all of his ships were
lost when a storm drove them onto a reef in the
Solomon Islands. Ask someone at Aasu to indicate the way to the waterfalls (and remember
that this whole area is private property).

Another trail from Aoloaufou goes down to
Aoloautuai; the trailhead is behind a house on
the left near the northwest end of the road.
Aoloautuai is a deserted village site on a lovely bay
where you could camp for a few days if you took
enough food. It may also be possible to hike
from Aoloaufou west to **Fagamalo,** putting yourself back on Tutuila's road network. The first half
of the way follows the ridge, and one should set
out early and not hesitate to turn back if the
final descent to Fagamalo looks impassable. This
route is seldom used and you'd be on your own if
anything went wrong.

SPORTS AND RECREATION
Hiking

One of Tutuila's easiest and most rewarding hikes
is through **National Park of American Samoa** to
the TV towers on **Mt. Alava** (491 meters). The
hourly Fagasa bus (US$.75) from Fagatogo Mar-
ket runs up to the trailhead at the pass, but ask
someone at the bus station where you should be
waiting, as the vehicle bears no destination sign.
Don't worry if you have to sit there a while, as it's
fun to observe the colorful locals coming and
going, and on the way back to town it's easy to
walk down through the village.

The TV towers on the summit are a two-hour
walk northeast along a five-km jeep track from the
Fagasa road (no chance of getting lost). A spectacular view of Pago Pago Harbor and Rainmaker
Mountain is obtained from Mt. Alava, and if
you're patient you may see an occasional flying fox
glide silently by, even at midday. An overgrown
trail down to Vatia on the north coast begins at the
circular observation pavilion on the very top of the
hill. Follow the ridge about 30 minutes east until
you see power lines, which you follow down to

AMERICAN SAMOA

Vatia. This overgrown trail is steep and should only be attempted in dry weather. Good boots and some hiking experience are essential. Hopefully, the park authorities will upgrade this trail to make it accessible to everyone.

Mt. Matafao (653 meters), Tutuila's highest peak, can be climbed in half a day via a trail that begins directly opposite the beginning of the Mt. Alava track on the pass just mentioned. Climb the white metal ladder up onto the ridge south of the road; the trail is fairly obvious on top. It'll take about three hours up through a beautiful rainforest—stay on the ridge all the way. No special gear is required for this climb and you could even go alone, but avoid rainy weather, when it gets slippery. In clear weather the view is one of the finest in the South Pacific.

Scuba Diving

Scuba diving is organized by the **Tutuila Dive Shop** (tel./fax 699-2842, tutuiladiveshop@samoatelco.com), under the big banyan tree in the center of Vaitogi village. It's run by John and Pisita Harrison: John has been diving Tutuila since 1986, Pisita runs the store and also dives. They charge US$85 for a two-tank dive including gear and a refreshment. John also arranges fishing trips, and can provide surfing shuttles.

At last report, **Pacific Underwater Construction** (tel. 258-4965, fax 633-4573, www.pucllc.com) had a diving decompression chamber on Tutuila (this could change).

Unfortunately, large areas of flat coral around Tutuila have been pulverized by fishermen standing on them or breaking off pieces to extract marinelife. On the upside, the currents aren't bad if the sea is flat, and spearfishing with the help of scuba gear (which decimates fish populations) has been banned.

Snorkeling

Snorkeling in the polluted waters off Utulei and Faga'alu is not recommended. The closest points outside the harbor are the open reefs opposite Aveina Bros. Market at Matu'u, or at Lauli'i. These can be treacherous when the southeast trade winds are blowing and there's a rather heavy break. If the water is quiet, get into one of the *avas*—the

channels going out—and enjoy undersea caves and canyons. Just beware of sneak bumper waves and strong currents in the channels: You might have to come back in over the reef, and the break varies considerably. Neither spot is outstanding, however, and you might see more trash than fish.

Better snorkeling locales are found at the east and west ends of Tutuila, but beware of strong currents and undertow. The north coast is best of all, as it's well protected from most pollution and the prevailing winds. However, better snorkeling by far is available at Ofu in the Manu'a Group. Shark attacks are extremely rare around American Samoa—coral cuts and undertow or currents are much more of a hazard.

Golf and Tennis

Visitors are welcome at the 18-hole **'Ili'ili Golf Course** (tel. 699-1762, biggydees@hotmail.com; open daily), maintained by the Department of Parks and Recreation at 'Ili'ili. You'll enjoy good views of the mountains and sea from the fairways, and inexpensive food and drink are available at the adjacent Country Club (tel. 699-2800). Greens fees for the 18 holes are US$5/7 weekdays/weekends. Cart hire is US$14, plus US$10 for clubs (bring your own balls and tees). It's not necessary to book starting times, but clubs and carts should be reserved, as they're in limited supply. The public tennis courts at Pago Pago and Tafuna are free.

ACCOMMODATIONS

Whether you love or hate Tutuila may well depend on the type of accommodations you get. Several good medium-priced places to stay do exist, but you should still expect to spend more than you would for similar accommodations elsewhere in the South Pacific. Knowing this in advance, it won't come as quite as much of a shock, and many other things such as food, drinks, groceries, toiletries, clothes, transportation, admissions, and telephone calls are relatively cheap, so it sort of averages out.

Under US$25

Camping is not allowed in public parks, and

about the closest you'll come to backpackers' accommodations on Tutuila is offered by **Roy West** (tel. 258-3527 or 644-1317), who lives in Vatia village on the north coast. He has a room for rent in the village at US$25 pp, and also has a secluded cabin at Amalau Bay, off the road to Vatia, which he rents at US$10 pp. (The Amalau valley is a prime bird- and bat-watching area.) In addition, Roy has a plantation shack and accommodation in tent sites at Tafeu Bay, west of Vatia, accessible by trail in three hours (US$25 pp for a guide) or by boat in 10 minutes (US$35 pp roundtrip), plus 20 minutes on foot. Roy knows of other options and is probably your best bet for low-budget accommodations on Tutuila, so call him up as soon as you arrive.

US$25–50

The **National Park** (tel. 633-7082), in Pago Plaza, has a homestay program of accommodations with village families at around US$45/60 single/double including food. These rates are not set by the National Park, which only acts as a liaison between visitors and host families. It's a great way to meet people and get a firsthand experience with the *fa'a Samoa*. Be prepared for huge meals with lots of meat and breadfruit, friendly people, little privacy, free rides around town, outdoor showers called "watertaps," and remote locations. The Samoans are warm, hospitable people, and if they like you, you'll immediately become part of the family. Highly recommended.

Tisa's Barefoot Bar (tel. 622-7447, tisasbarefootbar@hotmail.com), at Alega Beach on the southeast coast between Lauli'i and Avaio villages, has a *fale* sleeping four right on the beach at US$50.00 pp including breakfast and dinner, with pillows, mosquito nets, and mats provided. Running water is available, and Tisa's is in a secluded location away from the village. Bus service is fairly cheap and frequent, but call ahead to check availability.

Herb and Sia's Motel (tel. 633-5413), in the heart of Fagatogo, has gone downhill in recent years, although the prices haven't followed. The rooms, six with shared bath and three with private bath, all cost US$40/45 single/double. There's no hot water or cooking facilities, the air condi-

tioning and fridges may be out of order, and to be frank, the whole place is a dump. Avoid rooms five and six, which are without outside windows, and lock your door securely when you go out to the toilet. Be prepared for the sound of midnight "action" in adjacent rooms—women traveling alone shouldn't stay here.

Similar is the **Scanlan Inn** (tel. 633-4451) near Herb and Sia's in Fagatogo village with eight rooms at US$40 single or double with bath (plus US$10 for air-conditioning). Ask if they have any cheaper rooms with shared bath.

The top accommodation value in this category is without doubt **Barry's Bed and Breakfast** (tel. 688-2488, fax 633-9111), in a quiet residential area near the waterfalls at Leone. The four rooms in Barry's comfortable and solidly built two-story house go for US$40/50 single/double including a large breakfast. There are full cooking facilities, hot water showers, a washing machine, TV, and a large tropical garden at your disposal. You can even borrow Barry's set of golf clubs. Local telephone calls are free. Barry Willis, a fifth generation part-Samoan, will make you feel right at home. Although it may at first appear out of the way, it's actually a bit closer to the airport than Fagatogo. Barry's makes a great base for seeing western Tutuila and is easily accessible on public transport, with buses every 10 minutes throughout the day. Just be sure to catch the last bus back from town at 1700 and plan on spending Sunday around Leone. The bus rides back and forth from Fagatogo will be a memorable part of your visit.

US$50–100

Duke and Evalani's garishly decorated **Motu O Fiafiaga Motel** (tel. 633-7777, evalani_1@yahoo.com) is a big step up from Herb and Sia's for only a few dollars more. The 12 air-conditioned rooms with TV and shared bath are US$60 single or double if you stay only one night, US$50 for two or more nights, breakfast included. This well-maintained two-story building overlooks a noisy highway, so ask for one of the five rooms on the back side if traffic bothers you, and while you're at it, try to get one in the end of the building away from the cabaret.

Houseguests have access to an exercise room and sauna. The adjacent restaurant/bar under the same friendly management serves excellent and inexpensive American and Mexican food.

Tutuila's biggest hotel is the 181-room **Rainmaker Hotel** (tel. 633-4241, fax 633-5959), erected in 1959 by Pan American Airways but now government-owned. The oval neo-Samoan architecture echoes Rainmaker Mountain across the bay. Rates start at US$60 single or double standard, US$85 beachfront, US$90 deluxe (with TV). More expensive *fale* and suites are also available. Third persons pay US$15, but children under 12 are free. Unfortunately, it's rather rundown, so if the first room they give you is in bad condition, go back and ask for another. The upstairs rooms facing the beach are the nicest. Unpaid hydro bills have resulted in electricity blackouts at this hotel. The Rainmaker features the usual bars, restaurants, gift shops, swimming pool, car rental offices, and landscaped grounds. The location is convenient.

Le Fale Pule Lodge (Isabel Steffany-Hudson, tel. 633-5264 or 633-5648, fax 258-1422, lefale pule@samoatelco.com), high up on the hillside above Matafao Elementary School in Faga'alu, has five air-conditioned rooms with bath starting at US$85/100 single/double including breakfast. Lunch/dinner can be ordered at US$7.50/20 pp. Four of the rooms are in the main house, and there's also a separate cottage at US$135/150. The outdoor Jacuzzi accommodates six.

Pago Airport Inn (tel. 699-6333, fax 699-6336, pagoairportinn@samoatelco.com) is a large two-story concrete building in the middle of Tafuna village, two km from the airport (US$5 by taxi). The 20 air-conditioned rooms with bath, fridge, and TV are US$79/99/105 single/double/triple. Food can be a problem, because there are no cooking facilities in the rooms and no restaurant is nearby. It's not a convenient place to stay unless you're in transit for one night and don't wish to go into town.

Ethan's Place (Gwen and Victor Langkilde, tel. 699-6638, fax 699-2838, www.pagopago vacations.com), opposite Go See Cal Rental Cars and near Cost-U-Less in Tafuna, opened in 2004. The three air-conditioned apartments with

kitchens and cable/DVD TV are US$75 single or double for the smaller studio, US$90 triple for the larger studio, or US$115 for up to four persons in the one-bedroom unit. Continental breakfast and airport transfers are included.

Chande Lutu-Drabble operates **Ta'alolo Lodge** (tel. 699-7201, fax 699-7200, taalolo@samoa telco.com), an upscale bed and breakfast a few minutes walk from the 'Ili'ili Golf Course. This renovated two-story house has five air-conditioned rooms with bath, fridge, and TV varying in price from US$85 or US$105 single or double to US$125 for a junior suite, or US$135 for the master suite. Continental breakfast is included in the rates and dinner can be ordered. Guests are welcome to use the kitchen to cook their own meals at any time. A swimming pool, summerhouse, and outdoor bar are at your disposal, and office equipment business guests can be supplied. Chande is quite knowledgeable about Samoan culture and can help with your arrangements.

Tessarea's Vaitogi Inn (tel. 699-7793, fax 699-7790, tessa@samoatelco.com) at Vaitogi has eight air-conditioned hotel rooms with TV downstairs at US$90 single or double and five apartments upstairs at US$150. The Inn's two-story building faces a swimming pool.

The rather isolated **Turtle and Shark Lodge** (Roy and Juanita Hall, tel. 699-1212, fax 688-1821, www.turtleandshark.com) overlooks Larsen Bay beyond Vaitogi. The 10 air-conditioned rooms with TV and fridge in two buildings range from US$75 single or double with shared bath to US$125 with private bath, breakfast included. Other meals are not served and no restaurants are nearby, but you can use the common kitchen to cook your own food. A swimming pool, tennis court, gym, and laundry facilities are among the facilities. The beach is a half-hour hike away and you'll need to rent a car if you stay here (car and room packages available). Free airport transfers are provided.

US$100–150

In 2002, the **Sadie Thompson Inn** (Tom and Ta'aloga Drabble, tel. 633-5981, fax 633-5982, www.sadiethompsoninn.com) opened in Fagatogo above the famous restaurant of the same name. There are six standard rooms facing inland at US$135 single or double, six deluxe rooms overlooking the harbor at US$185, and two self-catering luxury rooms with spa tub at US$250 (children under 12 free).

The **Quality Inn Tradewinds Hotel** (tel. 699-1000, fax 699-1010, www.tradewinds.as), at Ottoville not far from the airport, opened in 2003. There are 104 large rooms starting at US$135 single or double (or US$165 and up for a suite). An extra person pays US$15. This three-story plantation style hotel caters mostly to business travelers, and there's a swimming pool and restaurant/bar. Airport transfers are free.

FOOD

Fast Food

An impressive selection of inexpensive eateries awaits you, although fried, high-sodium, and high-cholesterol foods are the norm at these. Most places provide the standard "bottomless" cup of coffee dear to American hearts. The American fast-food chains have also extended their tentacles to Tutuila, but boycott them in the name of culinary diversity.

Teo's Kitchen (tel. 633-2250; weekdays 0500–1700, Sat. 0500–1500), beside Fagatogo Market, offers filling US$2 lunch specials, and it's always full of locals watching TV.

Da Maks Island Style Restaurant (tel. 633-5838; weekdays 0700–1630), harborside behind the market, is more expensive with breakfast and "ono" lunch specials from US$5 a plate. You'll like Mel and Gretchen's mix of Samoan, Chinese, and Hawaiian foods, and the terrace just above the water is also nice.

Billy's Restaurant (tel. 633-1199), nearby on the water side of Fagatogo Square, is fast food heaven, with pizza, nachos, fried chicken, fish and chips, hamburgers, ice cream, and coffee.

Mom's Place (tel. 633-1414; closed Sun.), east of the post office at Fagatogo, is good for breakfast, or a soup and sandwich lunch.

Pinoy's Fast Foods (tel. 633-2125), near the Samoa Sports Building between the Rainmaker and town, serves tasty Filipino dishes beginning at 0800 weekdays and continuing until the food

runs out. The portions are huge and prices excellent. Longshoremen and sailors are the clientele.

Harbor Area Restaurants

The dining room at the **Rainmaker Hotel** (tel. 633-4241) offers a Samoan buffet lunch Friday 1130–1330 (US$15). Also try breakfast (0630–1100) or fish and chips in the surprisingly good hotel coffee shop (open daily until 1800). Saturday morning breakfast here is a local institution.

Sook's Sushi (tel. 633-5224; Mon.–Sat. 1000–2300), west of the market at Fagatogo, specializes in Japanese and Korean dishes.

Tutuila's top place to eat is recently renovated **Sadie's Restaurant** (tel. 633-5981; closed Sun.), just west of the market. Despite the Maugham theme, Sadie's is as unpretentious as everything else on Tutuila, and the American expats you see enjoying themselves at the tables are putting on no act. Dinner will set you back a lot farther than lunch, but the tuna dishes are said to be worth it.

Evie's Cantina (tel. 633-7777; lunch 1100–1400, dinner 1800–2200), at the Motu O Fiafiaga Motel in Pago Pago, dishes out some of the tastiest Mexican food in the South Pacific, plus karaoke nightly and a feature film with Sunday dinner. Avoid Evie's if you're a non-smoker.

Don't Drink The Water (tel. 633-5485; weekdays 0700–1700, Sat. 0700–1200), at Pago Plaza, is a trendy new internet café serving yuppie-style lunches for under US$10. Aside from the coffees, check out the sinfully rich deserts.

Nu'uuli

Sunny's Chinese Restaurant (tel. 699-5238; Mon.–Sat. 0900–2200, Sun. 1100–1400 and 1700–2200) is east of Transpac in Nu'uuli.

Hong Kong House (tel. 699-8983; Mon.–Sat. 1000–2200, Sun. 1630–2200), near the movie theater at Nu'uuli, is a bit more expensive than Sunny's, but it's nicely decorated and the menu is impressive. It's very popular.

The Deluxe Café (Sherry Butler, tel. 699-4000, deluxecafe@yahoo.com; Mon.–Sat. 0700–1400, Sun. 0900–1400), near the movie house on the main highway not far from the turnoff to the airport, is a typical American-style diner serving a good breakfast for US$8. Their generous lunches are medium priced. The locals call it the "Samoan Denny's."

Rubbles Tavern (tel. 699-4400; daily 1100–2300), in the Nu'uuli Shopping Center next to Transpac, is an air-conditioned Samoan-American sports bar. Steaks, fish, wings, nachos, and pasta dishes are on the medium-priced menu. Weekdays from 1630–1830 is happy hour and Sundays from 1100–1400 there's a Samoan buffet.

Mrs. Paul's Island Delites (tel. 699-6288, mrspaul@samoatelco.com; weekdays 0700-1400, Sat. 0700–1200), is a small family restaurant in Nu'uuli almost opposite Tropik-Traders. For breakfast there's steak and eggs, omelettes, and hotcakes, while lunch is fried or curry chicken, chop suey, and other local favorites.

Vegetarians will have no trouble ordering at **A & A Pizza Drive-Thru** (tel. 699-9428), at Malaeimi, a bit east of the Community College on the main road. It's the favorite pizza place outside the bay area.

Jeffrey's Bar and Grill (tel. 699-6560, jeffreys@pagopago.com; daily 1000–2300), in Ottoville near Cost-U-Less and only a five-minute walk from the new Quality Inn Tradewinds Hotel, claims to serve the best steaks and margaritas in town. Their all day breakfast runs US$5–7 without coffee, while the extensive lunch menu includes sandwiches, burgers, chicken, fish, or salads at around US$8. For dinner, it's mostly steaks and fish dishes (US$15–23).

ENTERTAINMENT

The **Wallace Theaters** (tel. 699-9334), a.k.a. Nu'uuli Place Cinemas, in Nu'uuli, screens recent Hollywood films in two halls. The usual admission is US$6.50, but the two shows before 1800 weekdays are reduced.

Bingo is played nightly except Sunday from 2000 in the former bowling alley across from Spencer's in Pago Pago. Huge traffic jams ensue when the bingo is finished as everyone tries to leave at the same time.

Evie's Nightclub (tel. 633-7777), at the Motu O Fiafiaga Motel in Pago Pago, has a spacious dance floor (dancing 2200 to closing), karaoke

from 1600–2200, and a nice crowd of chain-smoking locals. Co-owner Duke Wellington plays Tutuila's only grand piano during happy hours (1600–1900). The purse seiner guys tend to stand at the bar and cause trouble among themselves under the watchful eye of the mountainous bouncer.

Sadie's Restaurant (tel. 633-5981) has happy hours weekdays 1630–1830 with reduced beer prices (beer goes great with sashimi).

The Sadie Thompson Lounge off the main dining room at the **Rainmaker Hotel** has a consistently good happy hour band weekdays 1630–1830 (a favorite hangout of local politicians). Come early or you won't find a table. Shorts and bare feet are not permitted in the lounge after 1600; in fact, all of the places mentioned above except the bingo hall have strict dress codes in the evening. The drinking age in American Samoa is 21.

The **Maliu Mai Beach Resort** (Mapu Jamias, tel. 699-2830; open daily) is on Freddie's Beach at Fogagogo, a km off the road between the airport and 'Ili'ili. There's often live music here from Thursday to Saturday nights, with a special show on Fridays. Meals are available.

A good drinking place out beyond the airport is the **Country Club** (tel. 699-2800), next to 'Ili'ili Golf Course.

On Alega Beach between Lauli'i and Avaio villages is **Tisa's Barefoot Bar** (tel. 622-7447, tisasbarefootbar@hotmail.com; daily 1100–1900), subject of a number of magazine articles about a certain fertility tattoo on the proprietress. Tisa's is open on Sunday and you can swim and snorkel here—a good place to go that day. Call to find out if they'll be serving the traditional Sunday *umu* lunch. "Tisa's jungle hop," a guided three-hour hike through the rainforest to a waterfall behind the bar, is US$25 pp including lunch. Soak up the atmosphere while enjoying a Vailima beer.

SHOPPING

American Samoa is a poor place to shop for handicrafts, and many of the items sold at the airport shops and elsewhere are imported from Tonga.

About the easiest places to pick up souvenirs are the shops facing the airline offices at the airport (not the duty free shop in the departure lounge). Tropical clothing and *lavalava* can be a good buy here, and those long *puletasi* dresses make unique souvenirs. **Forsgren's** near the Office of Communications in Fagatogo has nice Samoan T-shirts and cut-rate clothes at some of the best prices in town. It's always crowded with nonresident Samoans who make the long pilgrimage from Apia just to shop here. **Tedi of Samoa** (tel. 633-4200) sells Samoan fashions and Reebok shoes in their Hawaiian-style store across from the courthouse in Fagatogo. While other local stores sell Chinese products, Tedi has mostly American-made clothing and sportswear but fewer bargains. **Spencer's** (tel. 633-4631) in Pago Pago also carries inexpensive clothing and shoes. Downtown closing time is inconveniently early at 1630 weekdays and 1200 on Saturday.

The **Transpac Corporation** (tel. 699-2589), in the Nu'uuli Shopping Center and below Sadie's Restaurant, has a good selection of imported goods. **Tropik-Traders** (tel. 699-5077), near Transpac in Nu'uuli, is the place to pick up magazines, compact discs, and gifts. You can buy tents at the hardware store across the street from Laufou Shopping Center in Nu'uuli.

In general, American Samoa is a cheap place to shop for consumer items because importers pay only 3 percent duty and there's no sales tax. Neighboring Samoa has a 12.5 percent sales tax and double-digit duties. When comparing prices, remember the three to one exchange rate between Samoan tala and dollars. Often it only *looks* cheaper.

INFORMATION AND SERVICES

Information

The Office of Tourism (tel. 633-1092; weekdays 0730–1600), in the back of an old wooden building by the shore between the Rainmaker Hotel and the Yacht Club, can supply the usual brochures and answer questions.

The Wesley Bookshop at Fagatogo carries books by Samoan novelist Albert Wendt, which are hard to find in Apia.

Hawaiian Airlines (tel. 699-1875), Polynesian Airlines (tel. 699-9126), and Inter-Island Air (tel. 699-7100, www.interislandair.com) all have their offices at the airport. If possible, reconfirm your flight out as soon as you arrive. The travel agencies directly above the post office in Fagatogo sell air tickets for the same price as the airlines, and they are usually less crowded and more helpful. For example, try Oceania Travel (tel. 633-1172, fax 633-1173, oceania@samoatelco.com) above the post office.

Money

The Bank of Hawaii (tel. 633-4226; weekdays 0900–1500), beside the post office in Fagatogo and at Pava'ia'i out toward Leone, will cash U.S.-dollar traveler's checks, but not those denominated in foreign currencies such as the Australian dollar unless you have an account. ATMs stand outside the Bank of Hawaii branches at Fagatogo and Tafuna, as well as at Laufou Shopping Center in Nu'uuli.

The ANZ Amerika Samoa Bank (tel. 633-5053), owned by the Australia New Zealand Banking Group, has branches next to the police station in Fagatogo and at Tafuna, both open weekdays 0900–1630, Saturday 0900–1200. They're a better bet for changing traveler's checks expressed in currencies other than U.S. dollars, but be prepared for high commission charges. ATMs are available at both of their branches, and at Cost-U-Less in Ottoville, at Pago Plaza, and at the Executive Office Building in Utulei.

Post and Telecommunications

The main post office (Mon. and Fri. 0730–1630, Tues.–Thurs. 0730–1500, Sat. 0730–1300) is in Fagatogo with a contract station at Leone. There is no residential mail delivery, but around 5,000 post office boxes are in use at the main post office. Mail addressed to General Delivery, Pago Pago, American Samoa, U.S.A. 96799, can be picked up at the main office weekdays 0930–1100 and 1300–1500, Saturday 1030–1130 (mail is held 30 days). If you're a yachtie, ask the clerk to also check under the name of your boat.

Place long-distance telephone calls at the

Office of Communications (www.samoatelco .com, open 24 hours), diagonally across from the Fono Building in Fagatogo. Go at odd hours, because this office is jammed around mid-afternoon. You can receive faxes addressed to fax 633-9111 here at a cost of US$2 for the first page, US$1 additional pages. Local telephone cards (available at many shops) are a cheaper, easier way of making long distance calls.

Internet access is available at Don't Drink The Water (tel. 633-5485; weekdays 0700–1700, Sat. 0700–1200), at Pago Plaza. They charge US$5 for half an hour.

The Feleti Barstow Library (tel. 633-5816, feletibarstow@yahoo.com; Mon., Wed., and Fri. 0900–1700, Tues. and Thurs. 0900–1900, and Sat. 1000–1400), a two-story tan building near the Executive Office Building in Utulei, provides free Internet access on 14 public terminals if you have a library card (available for a refundable US$25 deposit, identification required).

Launderettes and Toilets

Numerous launderettes around the island charge a dollar or less to wash or dry (ask the locals where they are).

Public toilets are next to the Jean P. Haydon Museum, near Da Maks Restaurant at the market, and at Pago Plaza.

Yachting Facilities

Harbormaster permitting, anchor your vessel as far away from the noise and smell of the canneries and power plant as you can. When all is calm, the stench can be almost unbearable and you feel this really is the armpit of the Pacific. There's bad holding in the harbor because the soft oozy bottom is covered with plastic bags. Lock your dinghy when you go ashore.

The Pago Pago Yacht Club (tel. 633-2465; Sun.–Thurs. 1130–1700, Fri. and Sat. 1130–2000) at Utulei is a friendly place worth frequenting in the late afternoon if you're looking to hitch a ride to Apia, Fiji, Wallis, Vava'u, or wherever. They can call any yachts in the vicinity over VHF channel 16. Check their notice board, or borrow a book from their exchange. Friday

1700–1800 the whole yachting community converges here for happy hour-priced drinks and free *pupu* (snacks). That's also the time when local club members break out their longboats (*fautasi*) for a row around the harbor. The weekday luncheon menu is also good and visitors are always most welcome (ignore the Members Only sign on the door).

Pago Pago is a good place for cruising yachts to provision—ask about case discounts. For example, there's Cost-U-Less (tel. 699-5975; Mon.–Fri. 0800–2000, Sat. 0800–1900, Sun. 1000–1800), a warehouse-style bulk store in Tafuna on the road from 'Ili'ili to the airport. It's also easy to order yacht supplies from the U.S. mainland.

Health

The 140-bed LBJ Tropical Medical Center in Faga'alu has doctors on call 24 hours a day in the Outpatients Department. There's also a dental section here. Several private medical clinics are at Nu'uuli.

The Drug Store (tel. 633-4630) has branches in Nu'uuli and on the road to the hospital.

GETTING AROUND

For an American territory, bus services on Tutuila are extremely good. Family-owned *aiga* buses offer unscheduled service from Fagatogo to all of the outlying villages. You can flag them down anywhere along their routes, and you bang on the roof when you want to get off. Not all the buses are marked with a destination, however; also, there's no service after 1600 on Saturday, and very little on Sunday or after dark any day. Bus service begins at 0400 to get workers to the first shift at the canneries—useful if you have to catch an early flight. No standing is allowed, so the rides are usually a lot of fun. Most buses play blaring music.

Bus fares are very reasonable. You pay as you leave and it's smart to carry small change: Ask someone how much the fare should be before you get on and just pay the exact amount. A trip anywhere in the congested zone from the canneries to the hospital is US$.25. Westbound to Tafuna and the airport is US$.75, US$1 to

Leone, US$1.25 to Amanave; US$1.50 to Faga-malo; eastbound it's US$.75 to Avaio or Fagasa, US$1 to Aoloaufou, US$1.25 to Tula. Service from Fagatogo to Leone is fairly frequent, and you can change buses at Leone for points west. Change at Pavaiai for Aoloaufou. The bus across the island to Vatia leaves from in front of Da Mak Restaurant at Fagatogo market about once an hour (US$1.75).

Taxis are expensive and it's important to agree on the price before getting into a meterless taxi anywhere on Tutuila. Expect to pay at least US$1 a mile. You'll find taxi stands at the market and airport (tel. 699-1179).

Car Rentals

Bus service to the north coast villages of Faga-malo, Fagasa, Masefau, Aoa, and Onenoa is in-frequent, so to reach them easily you'll need to rent a car. The main car rental companies have counters at the airport. If no one is present, use the nearby public telephones to call around, checking current prices and requesting a car de-livery to the airport.

The most professional car rental company on Tutuila is **Avis** (tel. 699-4408 at the main office at Pavaiai, tel. 699-2746 at the airport, fax 699-4305, res@avissamoa.com). Their Toy-otas are US$55–65 a day, plus US$10 colli-sion insurance.

Pavitts U-Drive (tel. 699-1456) usually has a representative at the airport during the day and also for all Hawaiian Airlines flights.

Go See Cal Rental Cars (tel. 699-6280, fax 699-6284, www.goseecal-samoa.com), 635 Airport Road, Tafuna, has cars starting at US$65/435 a day/week.

Oceania Rental Cars (tel. 633-1172, fax 633-1173, oceania@samoatelco.com), with an office above the post office in Fagatogo, charges US$67 including insurance.

Tropical Car Rental (tel. 633-2265, fax 633-2953, sandysatele@samoatelco.com) has cars starting at US$55, plus US$8 for insurance. Also try **Friendly Car Rental** (tel. 699-7186, fax 699-7187, cslater@friendlyhiking.com) at Tafuna.

All rates include unlimited mileage and all ve-hicles must have public liability insurance. Most of the agencies only rent to persons over the age of 25 and your home driver's license is honored here for 30 days. Lock your car and don't leave valuables in sight. One of the biggest problems with driving on Tutuila is the lack of places to pull over and get out. Most villages have open *fales* fac-ing the beach, so you'll often feel like an intruder.

Driving is on the right and the speed limit is 48 kph (30 mph) unless otherwise posted. You must stop if you see a yellow school bus load-ing or unloading, unless the driver signals you to proceed. Transporting open alcoholic bev-erage containers is illegal. Motorcyclists must wear helmets.

Local Tours

Roy West of **North Shore Tours** (tel. 258-3527 or 644-1317) offers a wide range of hiking, mountain climbing, bird-watching, snorkeling, and boat trips at very reasonable prices. Roy's ecotours cost US$25–35 pp for a full day, plus US$5 for lunch (if required). If you want to hike along Tutuila's rugged north coast, climb Rain-maker Mountain, or get dropped off at an in-accessible bay for a few days of real Robinson Crusoe living, Roy is the guy to call. He also has a good knowledge of Samoan plants. His base is at Vatia, so many of the trips leave from there.

Oceania Travel (tel. 633-1172), above the post office in Fagatogo, offers three-hour sight-seeing tours of either the east or west sides of Tutuila at US$40 pp (four-person minimum). For US$85 pp, you get a full day of sightseeing with lunch included.

The Manu'a Group

The three small islands of the Manu'a Group, 100 km east of Tutuila, offer spellbinding scenery in a quiet village environment. Ta'u is the territory's most traditional island, but the beaches are far better and more numerous on Ofu and Olosega. All three islands feature stimulating hiking possibilities and an opportunity for the adventurer to escape the rat race on Tutuila. The biggest hassle is canine: A real or pretended stone will keep the dogs at bay.

Although a couple of small guesthouses are available, few tourists make it to Manu'a. Regular air service from Tutuila has now made these islands more accessible, but book early, as local commuters fill the flights. Remember that telephone calls from Tutuila to the Manu'a Group cost only US$.10 each, so don't hesitate to call ahead to check on accommodations.

OFU AND OLOSEGA

Ofu and Olosega appear to be the remaining northern portions of a massive volcano whose southern side disintegrated into the sea. Some of the best snorkeling is around the concrete bridge that links these soaring volcanic islands; just be aware of currents. The strong current between Ofu and Nuutele islands makes snorkeling off Alaufau or Ofu villages risky, though the small-boat harbor just north of Alaufau is better protected than the one on Ta'u. The airstrip is by a long white beach on the south side of Ofu, about an hour's walk from Olosega village, and it's still possible to have to yourself this quintessential Polynesian paradise of swaying palms, magnificent reef, and rugged mountains rising out of the sea. The beach and reef between Papaloloa Point and the bridge are now part of National Park of American Samoa. Bring your own snorkeling gear, as none is available locally.

To climb to the television tower atop Ofu's **Tumutumu Mountain** (494 meters), take the five-km jeep track up the hill from near the wharf at Alaufau village and continue up to the ridge top, then over the well wooded mountain to Leolo Ridge (458 meters). Much of the way is through open secondary forest with little shade.

For Olosega's **Piumafua Mountain,** follow the shoreline south almost to Maga Point, then cut back up along the ridge to the 639-meter summit. The cloud forest atop the steep hill *after* you think you've hit the peak is like the Old Forest in *The Lord of the Rings*. No goblins—only mosquitoes—but be very careful not to get turned around, as the trees cut off the view, though the forests on Ofu and Olosega are open and easy to cross after the trails give out. This is one of Manu'a's best bird-watching trips, with nesting boobies on the point and ground-doves in the lower forest. It's well shaded and a good choice on a hot day. There's no trail along Olosega's forbidding east coast.

Accommodations and Food

Most visitors stay at **Vaoto Lodge** (tel. 655-1120 or 699-9628, www.vaotolodge.com), near the beach beside the airstrip on Ofu. The 10 fan-cooled rooms with private bath in five duplex

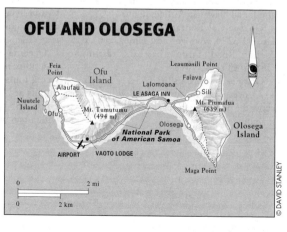

OFU AND OLOSEGA

Feia Point
Ofu Island
Alaufau
Nuutele Island
Ofu
Mt. Tumutumu (494 m)
Leaumasili Point
Faiava
Lalomoana
LE ASAGA INN
Sili
Mt. Piumafua (639 m)
Olosega
Olosega Island
National Park of American Samoa
AIRPORT   VAOTO LODGE
Maga Point

0   2 mi
0   2 km

© DAVID STANLEY

units are US$35/40/60 single/double/triple. Cooking facilities are not available but hosts Tito, Marty, and Marge Malae prepare good local meals at US$15 for all three. They'll make you feel like one of the family; ask Tito to tell you a ghost story.

Le Asaga Inn (Aliilelei Laolagi, tel. 655-1164, fax 655-1109, www.asagainn.com), on Ofu by the Ofu and Olosega Bridge, has six air-conditioned rooms US$50/60/85 single/double/triple. Weekly and monthly rates are available. Family style meals are available or you can cook your own in the communal kitchen. A grocery store is nearby. Airport transfers are free.

Call ahead for reservations, because all nine rooms on these islands are sometimes full. An alternative is the homestay program organized by the National Park Visitor Center (tel. 633-7082) in Pago Plaza on Tutuila, and this must be arranged in advance.

Rather than camp along Ofu's beautiful south coast beach, which is now part of the national park, keep east toward the bridge, then just before you reach the bridge cut down to the deserted beach on the north side of the island. You'll be less likely to have visitors here than you would by the road, but bring all the food and water you'll need.

TA'U

Ta'u is a rectangular island 10 km long and five km wide. It's only 11 km southeast of Olosega, with a submarine volcano between the two. Eons ago the south side of Ta'u collapsed, leaving dramatic 500-meter-high cliffs that rise directly from the southern sea. Five smaller craters dot the steep northern slopes of Lata Mountain (995 meters), the highest peak in American Samoa.

The entire southeast corner of Ta'u is included in National Park of American Samoa, the largest of the park's three units. Craters punctuate the island's wild, thickly forested interior, known for its steep slopes and gullies. Terrain and bush can change suddenly from easy hiking to difficult, and most of the upland area is inaccessible.

From Ta'u the Tui Manu'a ruled the entire group. In 1925, as a young woman of 24, Margaret Mead researched her book, *Coming of Age in*

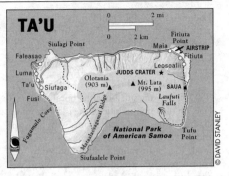

© DAVID STANLEY

Samoa, at Luma village on Ta'u. The present inhabitants of Ta'u live in villages at the northeast and northwest corners of the island. Small-boat harbors are at Luma and Faleasao, with the most sheltered anchorage for yachts at Faleasao. The reef pass is very narrow, and Luma harbor is used mostly by local fishing boats (not recommended for yachts). The airstrip is at Fitiuta in the northeast corner of the island.

Sights

At Luma village, see the tomb of the Tui Manu'a and other chiefly burials near the **Sacred Water,** or "royal pool" (dry). Also of interest is the **cave of Ma'ava,** the legendary giant. There's a nice beach at **Fagamalo Cove,** halfway down the west coast south of Fusi.

From Fitiuta, it's possible to hike south along the coast into American Samoa's extraordinary national park. Legend tells how the god Tangaloa created humans at Saua, a couple of km south of Fitiuata, and from here they colonized Polynesia. Everything south of here is included in the national park. The track continues south to Tufu Point, around which are views of waves crashing into Ta'u's rocky, volcanic southern coast, where sheer volcanic cliffs soar in two or three steps to cloud-covered Mt. Lata. It's possible to follow the shoreline a couple of km west to 450-meter-high **Laufuti Falls,** although fallen trees and huge rocks block the way in places. Beyond Laufuti, one must bushwhack.

Accommodations and Food

The most convenient place to stay is **Fitiuta**

AMERICAN SAMOA

Lodge (tel. 677-3501), in Fitiuta village a short walk from the airstrip. The eight rooms with shared bath are US$45 double and cooking facilities are provided. Try to reserve to ensure they'll be open.

The **Ta'u Motel** (Niumata Mailo, tel. 677-3504) is near the small-boat harbor in Luma village, on the opposite side of the island from the airstrip. It has nine clean rooms with bath and fridge at US$25 pp, and you can cook your own food. The entire motel is often booked by local contractors for extended periods, so call well ahead (it can be difficult to get a call through). They can pick you up at the airport at between US$10–20 for the trip (not pp), depending on whether they have to go anyway.

No restaurants are to be found on Ta'u, only small village stores. If your baggage isn't overweight, bring some food with you on the plane from Tutuila. There's no bakery on Ta'u, so it's a good idea to bring bread from Pago Pago.

CORAL ATOLLS
Rose Atoll
Discovered by French navigator Louis de Freycinet in 1819, Rose Atoll was visited by the U.S. Exploring Expedition under Commodore Charles Wilkes in 1839. In 1921, the United States claimed this uninhabited atoll, 125 km east of Ta'u. A reef of pink coral surrounds the square, three-by-three-km atoll with a pass into the lagoon. Of the atoll's two small islands, Rose is covered with coconut and other trees, while Sand is devoid of vegetation.

Large numbers of red-footed boobies and frigate birds nest near the top of Rose's large *buka* trees, while black noddies and white terns use the middle and lower branches. Green and hawksbill turtles lay eggs on the beach. To protect the turtles and seabirds, in 1973 Rose Atoll was included in the **Pacific Islands National Wildlife Refuges,** administered by the U.S. Fish and Wildlife Service (www.fws.gov). Special permission is required to land.

Swains Island
Swains Island, 340 km northwest of Tutuila, is a circular coral atoll about two km across and 13 km around the fringing reef. There's a large lagoon in the center not connected to the sea. Swains is far closer to Tokelau than to the rest of Samoa. In fact, its customary owners were the Tokelauans of Fakaofo, who knew it as Olohega. In 1856, a New England whaling captain, Eli Jennings, arrived to set up a coconut plantation with the help of Polynesian labor; his descendants still run it as a private estate today. At present, about two dozen people live on Swains.

Olohega was included in the Union Group (Tokelau), which Britain incorporated into the Gilbert and Ellice Islands Colony in 1916. In 1925, when Britain transferred Tokelau to N.Z. administration, the United States took advantage of the opportunity to annex Swains to American Samoa. Finally, in 1980, the U.S. government forced the Tokelauans to sign a treaty recognizing American sovereignty over Swains as a condition for the withdrawal of U.S. "claims" to the entire Tokelau Group and recognition of Tokelau's 200-nautical-mile fisheries zone.

Samoa

Introduction

The sultry, verdant isles of Samoa, two-thirds of the way from Hawaii to New Zealand, lie in the very heart of the South Pacific. Independent since 1962 and called Western Samoa until 1997, this is the larger portion of an archipelago split apart by colonialism in 1899. Although both Samoa and American Samoa sprang from the same roots, differing patterns of development are reflected in contrasting lifestyles—this highlights the impact of westernization on a Pacific people. Yet on both sides of the 100-km strait separating Upolu from Tutuila, Samoans have retained their ancient customs as nowhere else in Polynesia, and the *fa'a Samoa,* or Samoan way, continues to flourish.

In fact, travelers inbound from a dreary industrial world may be forgiven if they imagine they've arrived in the Garden of Eden, but there's more to it. In a series of provocative novels, Samoan author Albert Wendt has portrayed the conflicting pressures of *palagi* (foreign) life on his people. The protagonist in *Sons for the Return Home* finds he can no longer accept the *fa'a*-sanctioned authority of his mother, while *Leaves of the Banyan Tree* explores the universal themes of

SAMOA HIGHLIGHTS

Cape Mulinu'u, Savai'i: beach, westernmost point in the world (p. 544)

Piula Cave Pools, Upolu: natural swimming cave below a church (p. 518)

Pulemelei stone pyramid, Savai'i: largest ancient Polynesian structure, waterfall (p. 543)

Robert Louis Stevenson Museum, Apia: colonial mansion, garden, hiking, tomb (p. 517)

Saleapaga and Lalomanu, Upolu: beach *fale,* Samoan lifestyle (p. 537)

a changing Samoan society. In *Pouliuli,* the complex social relationships of village life unravel in a drama of compelling force. Wendt's books bring us closer to the complexity of a third-world Samoa shaken by economic crises, incompetence, and corruption, and searching desperately for a formula to reconcile timeworn traditions and contemporary consumer needs. "Gauguin is dead! There is no paradise!" shouts a character in Sia Figiel's novel *Where We Once Belonged.*

Paradoxically, although your status as a foreign tourist will never be in doubt, you'll find the Samoans to be among the South Pacific's most approachable peoples. You'll sight some really striking physical types and meet a few unforgettable characters. Some visitors find it too intense, but almost everyone will leave with a story to tell about Samoa. Alongside the human element, an outstanding variety of landscapes and attractions are packed into a small area made all the more accessible because this is one of the least expensive countries in the region. Everything is vividly colorful and well-groomed, and it's still undiscovered by mass tourism. Add it all up and you'll recognize Samoa as one of the world's top travel destinations and an essential stop on any South Pacific trip.

The Land

Samoa consists of four inhabited and five uninhabited islands totaling 2,842 square km, a bit bigger than the American state of Rhode Island. Unlike most Pacific countries, which are scattered across vast areas, all of these islands are in

one main cluster, which makes getting around fairly easy. Upolu is the more developed and populous, containing the capital, Apia; Savai'i is a much broader island. Together these two account for 96 percent of Samoa's land area and 99 percent of the population. Between them sit populated Apolima and Manono, while the five islets off southeast Upolu shelter only seabirds. The fringing reefs around the two big islands protect soft, radiantly calm coastlines.

Samoa's lush volcanic islands increase in age from west to east. Savai'i, though dormant, spewed lava only a century ago; the now-extinct cones of western Upolu erupted much more recently than those farther east. Well-weathered Tutuila and Manu'a in American Samoa are older yet, while 10-million-year-old Rose Island is a classic atoll.

Savai'i is a massive shield-type island formed by fast-flowing lava building up in layers over a long period. The low coast gradually slopes upward to a broad, 1,858-meter center of several parallel chains. Upolu's elongated 1,100-meter dorsal spine of extinct shield volcanoes slopes more steeply on the south than on the north. The eastern part of the island is rough and broken, while broad plains are found in the west.

Climate

Your first impression may be how slowly the Samoans move, and the climate has a lot to do with it. Samoa is closer to the equator than Fiji, Tonga, or Rarotonga, thus it's noticeably hotter and more humid year-round. May to October (winter) the days are cooled by the southeast trades; winds vary from west to north in the rainy season from November to April (summer). Practically speaking, the seasonal variations are not great, and long periods of sun are common even during the "rainy" months. Southern Upolu gets more rain than northern, but much of it falls at night. Upolu is generally wetter than Savai'i. The rainfall feeds Samoa's many spectacular waterfalls and supports the luxuriant vegetation.

December to March is hurricane time; ships at Apia should put out to sea at the first warning as the harbor is unsafe when a storm blows out of the north. In recent years, Samoa has suf-

APIA'S CLIMATE

ANNUAL AVERAGE
79.1°F/26.2°C

ANNUAL
115.20 In.
2926 mm

fered an increasing number of devastating hurricanes as the surrounding seas warm up due to climate change.

Flora and Fauna

Rainforests thrive in the mountain areas, where heavy rainfall nurtures huge tree ferns and slow-growing, moss-laden hardwoods. The vegetation is sparse in the intermediate zones, where more recent lava flows fail to hold moisture or soil. The richer coastal strip is well planted in vegetable gardens and coconut plantations. The national flower is the *teuila*, or red ginger *(Alpinia purpurata)*, an elongated stalk with many waxy red petals.

Although Upolu is smaller than Savai'i, its rich volcanic soil supports 72 percent of the population of Samoa; much of Savai'i is barren due to recent lava flows and the porousness of the soil, which allows rapid runoff of moisture. The rainforests of Samoa are threatened by exploitive logging operations for shortsighted economic gain, and already 80 percent of the lowland tropical rainforests have been replaced by plantations or logged. On a relative square kilometer basis, deforestation is occurring much faster than in the Amazon. Replanting is usually done in teak and mahogany, which native birds cannot use.

About 16 of 35 land bird species are unique to Samoa. One such species, the toothbilled pigeon, or *manumea (Didunculus strigirostris)*, is thought to be a living link with toothbilled birds of fossil times. Due to overhunting and habitat destruction, all native species of pigeons and doves are approaching extinction. Parliament has banned all hunting of fruit bats (flying foxes) and Pacific pigeons, but this is not enforced and the populations have not recovered from the carnage of the 1980s. From 1981 to 1986 over 30,000 flying foxes were exported from Samoa to Guam for gastronomical purposes, a trade that ended only in 1989 when the bats were added to the endangered species list. No snakes live on Upolu, although two harmless species are found on Savai'i. Attack dogs are a nuisance throughout Samoa, but unless you've actually entered someone's yard, they'll soon retreat when they see you reaching down to pick up a stone.

HISTORY AND GOVERNMENT
Prehistory

Samoa was named for the sacred *(sa)* chickens *(moa)* of Lu, son of Tagaloa, the god of creation. Samoan tradition asserts that Savai'i was Hawaiki, the legendary Polynesian homeland where the Samoans originated. Archaeologists confirm that the Polynesians had settled Samoa by 1000 B.C. and there they evolved their distinctive culture. It was a beautiful, comfortable, productive place to live. Their vegetables thrived in the rich volcanic soil, and the lagoon provided ample fish. They had found their true home; not for another millennium did small groups push farther east from this "cradle of Polynesia" to colonize Tahiti and the Marquesas.

The ancient Samoans maintained regular contact with Fiji and Tonga; Tongan invaders ruled Samoa from A.D. 950 to 1250 and the oral traditions of Samoa date back to the expulsion of the Tongans. This feat was accomplished by the first holder of what is still the highest chiefly title, Malietoa, meaning brave *(malie)* warrior *(toa)*. The legendary 15th-century queen, Salamasina,

SAMOA

became the only Samoan ruler ever to unite the four chiefly titles into one, and for 60 years Samoa enjoyed peace. The *matai,* or chiefly system, was well developed for almost 1,000 years before Europeans arrived in the late 18th century. Religion was less developed, and the chiefs were elected from high-ranking lineages: Everywhere else in Polynesia they were hereditary.

Christianity and Commercialization

Although several Dutch and French explorers sighted Samoa during the 18th century, none had any impact until Rev. John Williams of the London Missionary Society called at Savai'i aboard the *Messenger of Peace* in 1830. The ruling chief, Malietoa Vainu'upo, welcomed Williams, and by 1840 most Samoans had been converted to Protestantism. The missionaries taught the need for clothing, and white traders were soon arriving to sell the required cotton cloth. The first copra trader in Samoa was John Williams Jr., son of the missionary, who exported six tons in 1842. In 1844, Malua College was established on Upolu by the church. In true Samoan fashion, Malietoa's rival Mata'afa Iosefo converted to Catholicism in 1845.

In 1856, the German trading firm Johann Godeffroy and Son opened a store at Apia, and within a few years over a hundred Europeans resided in the new town, which soon became one of the main trading centers of the South Pacific. The first central government was formed by a group of district chiefs at Mulinu'u in 1868. During the 1870s, German businessmen purchased large tracts of family land from individual chiefs for the establishment of coconut plantations using Chinese and Melanesian labor. Germany, Britain, and the United States soon appointed consuls.

In 1873, an American, Col. A.B. Steinberger, assisted the Samoan chiefs in creating a constitution; two years later he had himself appointed premier. His role was not supported by the United States, however, although he was an official State Department agent. After five months in the premiership, Steinberger was arrested and taken to Fiji by the captain of a British warship who suspected him of German sympathies. He never returned.

COURTESY OF THE NAVAL HISTORICAL CENTER, WASHINGTON D.C.

wreckage from the March 1889 hurricane at Apia

Instability and Intrigue

The new Samoan government fumbled on and signed treaties of friendship with the United States and Germany. An intermittent civil war between the chiefly orator groups Pule and Tumua over the four highest ceremonial titles dragged on through most of the late 19th century. Rival Europeans sided with the different factions, but no one was able to establish a single, stable government. In 1879, the European residents of Apia took advantage of the situation to enact a municipal convention, which put control of the town in their hands.

In 1887, the German company Deutsche Handels-und Plantagen-Gesellshaft (successor to Godeffroy), tiring of the vicissitudes of native government in an area where they controlled 80 percent of the business, staged an unofficial coup. The nominal king, Malietoa Laupepa, was forced to flee, and the Germans installed a puppet in his place. The German regime, supported by German naval units but not sanctioned by Berlin, soon alienated the Samoans, British, and Americans.

In March 1889, an armed Samoan rebellion brought the warships of Germany, Britain, and the United States to Apia's port in a major international confrontation. This came to a ludicrous pass when the seven men-of-war refused to abandon Apia Harbor in the face of a hurricane, for fear of leaving the field to the opposing Great Powers. This colonial stupidity and arrogance caused the wreck of four ships; two others were beached and damaged; 92 German and 54 American lives were lost. The German ship *Adler* was thrown up onto the reef, and only the British *Calliope* escaped to the open sea. The Samoans saw it as an act of God. Robert Louis Stevenson compared the struggle between Britain and Germany for influence in Samoa to "two bald men fighting over a comb."

After this disaster, the military posturing abated, and in June 1889 a Tripartite Treaty was signed in Berlin under which the three powers agreed to the formation of a neutral government led by Malietoa Laupepa with the three consuls controlling Apia. Yet instability and open factional warfare alternated with ineffectual government until 1899, when new treaties were drawn up partitioning Samoa between Germany and the United States (see the American Samoa chapter). Britain, distracted at the time by the Boer War in South Africa, withdrew completely in exchange for German concessions in Tonga and the Solomons.

The Colonial Period

On March 1, 1900, the German flag was raised over Samoa. Under Governors Wilhelm Solf (1900–1912) and Erich Schultz (1912–1914), the Germans created the first public school system, built and staffed a hospital, and constructed the only roads that existed right up until 1942. Though both Solf and Schultz tried to work according to the principle that the Samoans could be guided but not forced, they deported Samoan resisters to the Mariana Islands in 1909. The Germans carefully studied traditional Samoan culture in order to play the rival factions off against each other. In Berlin, Samoa was seen as the brightest jewel of Germany's colonial empire.

On August 29, 1914, at the beginning of WW I, the last German governor surrendered without a fight to a New Zealand Expeditionary Force. The vast German plantations seized at the time are still held by the government-owned Samoa Land Corporation. Most of the 2,000 Chinese the Germans had brought from southern China to work the plantations were repatriated.

The new N.Z. administrators were real bunglers compared to the Germans. In November 1918, they allowed the SS *Talune* to introduce influenza to the territory, and 8,000 Samoans— 22 percent of the population—died; a stricter quarantine kept the epidemic out of American Samoa and Fiji. This awkward administration revived a strong opposition movement, the Mau, which had existed during German times. The Mau not only rejected colonial authority, but turned away from Western development and culture. Boycotts of imported goods were organized. In 1929, New Zealand crushed the Mau by military force, although the movement continued to enjoy the support of most of the villages, chiefs, and part-Samoan businessmen.

Only in 1947 was there a concrete step toward independence when a legislative assembly was created with some members elected from among the *matai* (chiefs). In 1960, a constitution was adopted; a year later both constitution and independence were approved in a plebiscite by universal ballot. And finally in 1962, with a Labor government in power in New Zealand, Samoa became the first Polynesian nation to reestablish its independence in the 20th century. In 1976, Samoa joined the United Nations.

Government

Samoa's government (www.govt.ws) is a parliamentary democracy with a prime minister elected by Parliament from its ranks. The prime minister chooses a 12-member Cabinet, also from among Parliament. Since independence, His Highness Malietoa Tanumafili II, Paramount Chief of Samoa, has been the ceremonial head of state, a position he may hold for life. The next head of state will be chosen by Parliament for a five-year term from among the four *tama aiga*, or paramount chiefs (Malietoa, Mata'afa, Tuimalealiifano, and Tupua Tamasese).

SAMOA

Initially 47 of the 49 members of parliament were elected every five years by the 20,000 registered chiefs, or *matai,* (most of them men) on a constituency basis, and only two by non-Samoan residents on the Individual Voters Roll. In 1990, all citizens aged 21 and over were allowed to vote in a referendum that approved universal suffrage and an extension of the term of office from three to five years. The old system of only allowing *matai* to run for the 47 Samoan seats was retained, however. An untitled person *(tautau)* can only be elected to parliament after he/she first becomes a *matai,* a situation which helps preserve traditional Samoan culture.

There are two main political parties: the Human Rights Protection Party and the Samoa National Development Party. As elsewhere in Anglophone Oceania, political parties revolve more around personalities than policies. In the past, campaign funds were used to "buy" votes and official corruption was rampant, but since the 2001 election, the Samoa Supreme Court has become more aggressive in removing parliamentarians who used bribery to win their seats. In 1999, Samoa saw its first political assassination since independence, when a cabinet minister was slain by a gunman linked to two former cabinet ministers involved in corruption scandals. At their trial, it was revealed that the ex-ministers' hit list also included the prime minister and a newspaper editor. The three murderers are currently serving life sentences.

The 11 administrative districts (A'ana, Aiga-i-le-Tai, Atua, Fa'asaleleaga, Gaga'emauga, Gagaifo-mauga, Palauli, Satupa'itea, Tuamasaga, Va'a-o-Fonoti, and Vaisigano) are used only for the organization of government services, and district officers don't exist. Samoa has no army and very few police: those responsibilities are assumed by the *matai.* The only police station on Upolu is the one in Apia; elsewhere the authority of village law prevails.

ECONOMY

Until the mid-1990s, Samoa's economy was battered by hurricanes, agricultural decline, and government mismanagement, but in recent years the economy has grown at an annual rate of around 4 percent. Despite the revenue collected from the 12.5 percent value-added tax (VAGST) initially imposed in 1994, the foreign debt has remained high at around S$500 million, owed mostly to international agencies such as the Asian Development Bank and the World Bank for infrastructure and agricultural loans. Vast sums have been squandered on flashy office buildings in Apia. In 1994, Samoa's chief auditor submitted a report alleging high-level corruption and nepotism, but this was successfully swept under the carpet and the chief auditor himself was given the boot. Many government departments keep no accurate financial records and no serious audits are carried out.

Samoa's per-capita gross domestic product is US$1,400 compared to US$8,000 in nearby American Samoa. Thus many Samoans migrate to Pago Pago to seek employment in the tuna canneries, where the starting rate is US$3.26 an hour (in independent Samoa the private-sector statutory minimum wage is S$1.60 or about US$0.50 an hour). Tens of thousands of Samoans now live in American Samoa, the United States, New Zealand, and Australia, and the S$100 million a year in private remittances they send home accounts for over a quarter of the country's gross domestic product.

Two-thirds of the workforce is engaged in subsistence agriculture—fisheries and agriculture make up more than a third of the gross domestic product, the highest such proportion in the Pacific. Since the opening of a freezer plant in Apia in 1997, longline fishing for tuna from 10-meter *alia* catamaran boats has experienced a boom with over 4,000 tonnes landed each year. However, 30 local fishermen have lost their lives on these small aluminum vessels and the government is encouraging a shift to larger boats. Only 27 percent of Samoans have non-agricultural employment, the lowest such percentage of any Polynesian country, and of these, 9,000 work for the government. Samoans have to hustle to obtain cash money, one reason why they look leaner and meaner than American Samoans (only those who have been to Tutuila will understand this comment).

In 1988, Samoa launched an off-shore banking center (www.samoaofc.ws) similar to those of Vanuatu and the Cook Islands. Foreign firms can pay a one-time registration fee that allows them to avoid taxation in their home country for 20 years (local companies are barred from participating and face strict bureaucratic regulation). Companies in Hong Kong, South Korea, Indonesia, and Eastern Europe especially, download their profits here. In 2000, the Samoan government was forced to bring in anti-money laundering legislation to avoid being blacklisted by international regulators. In 1997, a new scam was uncovered when it was revealed that regular Samoan passports were being sold under the counter to Chinese businessmen at US$26,000 apiece. A good part of Samoa's immigration department was implicated in the scandal.

Industry

To stimulate industry, the government has established a "small industries center" at Vaitele, on the airport highway five km west of Apia, where investing companies can obtain long-term leases at low rentals. Cheap labor and 15-year tax holidays are the main incentives to investing here. Most Samoan products have duty- and quota-free access to Australia and New Zealand under SPARTECA, to Europe under the Cotonou Agreement, and to the United States, Canada, and Japan under the Generalized System of Preferences (GSP) scheme as a "least developed country." Unfortunately, these competitive advantages are eroding as "globalization" expands worldwide.

The copra-crushing mill at Vaitele has experienced a turnaround since being privatized in 1993, and it now processes all local copra into coconut oil. To fully utilize the installed capacity, additional copra is imported from the Cook Islands and Tonga. The nearby government-owned Samoa Breweries has been highly successful with its excellent Vailima beer, and the Rothmans factory at Vaitele produces 50,000 cartons of cigarettes a month from raw materials imported from New Zealand. A Chinese-run garment factory began operating here in 1999.

In 1991, the Japanese corporation Yazaki transferred its automobile electrical wiring systems assembly plant from Melbourne to Vaitele, and Yazaki now exports A$75 million in automotive products to Australia each year. Since Yazaki pays low wages to its 2,000 mostly female Samoan employees, gets the factory rent-free from the government, and pays no company taxes, it's real value to the Samoan economy is far less than one would expect. All of the materials used at Yazaki's Vaitele plant are imported.

Trade and Aid

Imports run 10 times higher than exports; food imports alone exceed all exports. Bony junk food not sold in its place of origin is dumped in Samoa: chicken backs and turkey tails from the United States, mutton flaps and fatty canned corned beef from New Zealand. In 1996, even McDonald's got into the act. The main export items are fish, automotive electrical systems, garments, beer, coconut cream, nonu fruit, taro, and cocoa. Fresh fish grew from almost nothing to the top export item in 2002, but catches have begun to fall. American Samoa and the United States are the largest trading partners.

During the 1950s, Samoa exported 1.2 million cases of bananas a year to New Zealand, but shipping problems, hurricanes, disease, and inefficiency cost them this market, which is now supplied by Ecuador. Recently, however, the smaller, tastier Samoan bananas have reappeared in Auckland supermarkets, where they command high prices. Organic fruits and vegetables are a niche market in which small producers can compete with the pesticide-rich output of American conglomerates, and such exports are growing fast. Taro shipments to the Polynesian community in New Zealand were halted in 1994 due to an outbreak of taro leaf blight, but in 2002 they resumed after a blight-resistant variety was introduced. Infestations by rhinoceros beetles and giant African snails have hurt Samoan agriculture, and some 7,000 hectares of prime real estate is held by inept government agencies.

Japan, the United States, and New Zealand profit most from the trade imbalance—a classic case of economic neocolonialism. New Zealand exports 10 times more to Samoa than it buys, the United States 20 times more, Japan 2,000 times more! An exception is Australia, which buys more than it sells due to the Yazaki operation previously mentioned. Foreign aid covers about 10 percent of the trade imbalance with the main donors being China, the Asian Development Bank, Japan, Australia, New Zealand, the European Union, and the United Nations Development Program. Taiwan has funded the opposition in Samoa in an attempt to break this country's close relationship with mainland China. American aid is negligible.

Tourism

Tourism is Samoa's largest industry, earning S$130 million a year. The country gets around 88,000 foreign tourists annually, 40 percent of them from American Samoa and other Pacific countries, 26 percent from New Zealand, and about 10 percent each from Australia, the United States, and Europe. Well over half of these arrivals are expatriate Samoans visiting relatives and friends, and less than a third declare their purpose as tourism. About the only occasions on which Apia sees large numbers of tourists is during brief cruise-ship dockings, and this doesn't happen often.

Tourism development has been stifled by customary landowners, who have demanded exorbitant land-use fees for areas slated for resorts. When an attempt was made to locate the resorts on government lands, the chiefs laid claim to those lands too. Major chains like Inter-Continental and Marriott have withdrawn after seeing their costs spiral before they'd even turned a sod, and few new properties have opened in recent years. In desperation, the government formed a partnership with local investors in 2003 to begin construction of the 140-room Aggie Grey's Beach Resort on government land near Faleolo Airport. "Ecotourism" has been embraced by Samoan tourism planners, and at times it seems that almost everything is eco this or that: There are even aerial ecotours by helicopter! Business interests often exploit the term to justify eco-prices, but real ecotourism is alive and well out in the villages—the way to go in Samoa.

THE PEOPLE

Samoans are the second-largest group of full-blooded Polynesians in the world, behind the Maoris. About 89 percent of the population is Samoan and another 10 percent is part-Samoan (*afakasi*, or "half caste") with some European or Chinese blood. Although half of Samoa's people live in the northwest corner of Upolu, from Apia to the airport, only 21 percent live in the capital itself. Due to large-scale emigration to New Zealand and the United States, the population growth rate is very low, averaging only 0.5 percent a year. In all, 115,000 Samoans live in New Zealand and 60,000 in the United States (compared to around 175,000 in Samoa itself).

While almost everyone in Apia speaks good English, the same is not always true in the villages. The Samoan language has similarities to Tongan, but the k sound in Tongan is replaced in Samoan by a glottal stop (rather like the English sound oh-oh). It's among the most sweetly flowing of Polynesian languages, and an entire special vocabulary exists for formal or polite discourse among the various levels of society.

The Samoan approach to life is almost the opposite of the European: Property, wealth, and success are all thought of in communal or family rather than individual terms. Eighty percent of the country's land is owned communally by family groups (*aiga*) and cannot be sold or mortgaged. The *matai* work to increase the prosperity and prestige of their *aiga*.

Samoans are very conservative and resist outside interference in village affairs. The Samoans have an almost feudal concern for protocol, rank, and etiquette. They lead a highly complex, stylized, and polished way of life. Today, however, they are being forced to reconcile the *fa'a Samoa* with the competitive demands of Western society, where private property and the individual come first. The greatest burden of adjustment is on the young, and Samoa has one of the highest suicide rates in the world.

Social Structure

Since ancient times, Samoan society has been based on the *aiga,* a large extended family group with a *matai* as its head, who is elected by consensus of the clan. The *matai* is responsible for the *aiga*'s lands, assets, and distribution. He ensures that no relative is ever in need, settles disputes, sees to the clan's social obligations, and is the *aiga*'s representative on the district or village council *(fono)*. A *pulenu'u* (village mayor) appointed by the government presides over the *fono*. Around 85 percent of the total population lives under the direct authority *(pule)* of a *matai* (only residents of Apia are largely exempt from this). The 80 percent of Samoa's surface area that is customary land is under *matai* control (another 10 percent of the land is freehold and the government owns the balance).

The weight of traditional village law is enshrined in the Samoan constitution, and judges in the regular courts can take into account village fines or whether the offender has performed the traditional apology *(ifoga)* when passing sentence. A villager who chooses to ignore the rulings of his village *fono* faces ostracism, banishment, and worse. In exceptional cases, stoning, arson, and even murder have resulted.

Blood relationships count to a large extent in the elections of the *matai*, but even untitled persons can be elected on merit. (Foreigners can also be granted honorary *matai* titles, but these carry no social or legal weight.) In this formalized, ritualized society, the only way a person can achieve place is to become a *matai*. This semi democracy gives Samoan society its enduring strength.

A number of *aiga* comprise a village *(nu'u)* under an orator or talking chief *(tulafale)* and a titular or high chief *(ali'i)*. The high chiefs are considered too grand to speak for themselves at ceremonies, thus the need for orators. The *tulafale* conduct eloquent debates, give ceremonial speeches, and are the real sources of authority in the community. Direct conflicts are avoided through consensus decision-making. The villages are largely autonomous, and family welfare comes before individual rights—pure preindustrial socialism.

Villages

Samoans live in 362 villages near the seashore. Families share their work and food, and everyone has a place to live and a sense of belonging. It's difficult for individuals to get ahead in this communal society because as soon as anyone obtains a bit of money they're expected to spread it around among relatives and neighbors. Each immediate family has its own residence, called a *fale* (pronounced fah-LAY), which may be round or oval. Without walls, it's the least private dwelling on earth. The only furniture may be a large trunk or dresser. A *fale* is built on a stone platform, with mats covering the pebble floor. Mats or blinds are let down to shelter and shield the *fale* from storms—a very cool, clean, fresh place to live.

Most food is grown in village gardens, and cooking is done in an earth oven *(umu)*. Families are large, eight children being "about right." The men wear a vivid wraparound skirt known as a *lavalava*. The women of the village are often seen working together in the women's committee *fale*, making traditional handicrafts. The *fono* meets in the *fale taimalo*. Also a part of each village is the cricket pitch—looking like an isolated stretch of sidewalk. Notice too the *tia*, stone burial mounds with several stepped layers under which old chiefs are buried.

Kava and Tattoos

Unlike Fiji and Tonga, the Samoan kava *(ava)* ceremony is an exceptional occurrence held at important gatherings of *matai*, seldom witnessed by visitors. A *taupou* prepares the drink in a traditional wooden bowl; in the old days she was the fiercely guarded virgin daughter of a village high chief, a ceremonial princess. Chanting and dancing usually accompany this serving ceremony.

Tattooing is one of the few Polynesian cultural attributes adopted by Western civilization, and although missionaries a hundred years ago predicted its demise, it's still widespread among Samoan men. The navel-to-knees tattoos are a visual badge of courage, as 16 or more highly painful sessions are required to apply a full *pe'a* using purple candlenut dyes. Once the tattooing begins, it cannot end until completed, or the subject will be permanently marked with dishonor. Until recently, a full body tattoo could only be applied to a talking chief as a mark of his rank, but today anyone who can stand the pain is eligible. The designs originally represented a large fruit bat, although this is only recognizable today in the lines of the upper wings above the waist. The female equivalent, the *malu*, is more delicate. This art dates back to ancient times, and contemporary Samoan tattoo designs are strikingly similar to incised decorations on *lapita* pottery thousands of years old.

Religion

Ever since Rev. John Williams landed in 1830, the Samoans have taken Christianity very seriously and Samoan missionaries have gone on to convert the residents of many other island groups (Tuvalu, the Solomons, and New Guinea). Every Samoan banknote bears a radiant cross and the slogan *Fa'avae i le Atua Samoa* (Samoa is founded on God). Yet while the Samoans have embraced the rituals of Christianity, concepts such as individual sin are less accepted.

Some 61,500 Samoans belong to the Congregational Christian Church, 26,5000 are Methodist, 24,750 Catholic, and 22,500 Mormon. The numbers of Mormons, Seventh-Day Adventists, and Assemblies of God are growing fast as the Congregational Christian Church declines. During the 19th century, the main rivalry was between the British-connected Congregationals from the London Missionary Society active in Tahiti and the Cook Islands and the Australian-based Methodists or Wesleyans who dominated the Tongan and Fijian missionary fields. Although the Methodists landed in Samoa first, they later withdrew until 1857 at the behest of the church authorities in England.

Today each village has one or more churches, and the pastor's house is often the largest residence. Minister of religion is usually the best-paying job in the village and many pastors enjoy an affluent lifestyle at the expense of their congregations (often the pastor will be the only one in the village who owns a car). There's continuous pressure on villagers to contribute money to the church, and much of it goes into outlandishly huge and luxurious churches, which is rather scandalous in such a poor country. Donations are collected by parish treasurers at the church doors and the amount is read out with the person's name during the service. Those who haven't contributed can be asked to stand and explain why. Some villages have regulations that *require* villagers to attend church as many as three times on Sunday and choir practice weekly. Public education is neither free nor compulsory and many of the schools are church-operated.

There's a daily vespers called *sa* around 1800 for family prayers. All movement is supposed to cease at this time; some villages are rather paranoid about it and levy fines on offenders. It only lasts about 10 minutes, so sit quietly under a tree or on the beach until you hear a gong, bell, or somebody beating a pan to signal "all's clear." Even if you're in a car on the main road at vespers, some remote villages may not allow you to continue driving through the village, although most will. If you do get stopped by white-shirted morality police, just wait patiently in the car until you get an all clear signal after about 10 minutes (don't get out). Many villages also have a 2200 curfew.

CONDUCT AND CUSTOMS

Custom Fees

In many parts of Samoa it's an established village law that outsiders pay a set fee to swim at the local beach or waterhole, or to visit a cave, lava tube, waterfall, etc. Unlike Tonga, where the king owns all land and no entry fees need be paid, in Samoa such places are very much village property. Sometimes the required amount is posted on a sign and collected at a regular booth, but other times it's not. It's usually S$2 to S$5 either per person or per vehicle. In a few places, such as Falealupo on Savai'i, separate fees are charged for each individual thing you wish to see or do in the village. The upside of the fees is that such places are usually kept clean, and Samoa is generally a much tidier country than Tonga due to its communal ownership in which everyone has a stake.

However, you should be aware that a few rip-offs have become associated with this—sometimes an unauthorized person will demand payment, and you can't really tell if it's for real.

We recommend that you only pay customary fees of this kind if there's a sign clearly stating the amount or someone asks for the money *beforehand,* thus giving you the choice of going in or not. Resist paying anything if someone tries to collect as you're leaving (unless there's a sign), and *never* give the money to children. If there's a dispute or you're in doubt about the authenticity of a customary fee, politely say you want to give the money directly to the *pulenu'u.* He will straighten things out quickly. Keep your cool in all of this—the Samoans respect courtesy far more than anger or threats. To give you the opportunity to decide beforehand whether you feel a visit is still worthwhile, all customary fees we know about are listed in this book. Please let us know if we missed any.

Culture Shock

This can work two ways in Samoa, both you being intimidated by the unfamiliar surroundings and the Samoans being put off by your seeming affluence and intrusiveness. Because Samoan culture is a group culture, people can be overfriendly and unwilling to leave you alone. Of course, this doesn't apply in Apia, but in remote villages you may be viewed with suspicion, especially if you arrive in a taxi or rental car, the daily hire of which costs more than an average Samoan villager might earn in a month. You can easily smooth the situation over by smiling, waving, and saying *talofa* to those you meet. Be the first to say hello and everyone will feel a lot more comfortable. Another unique Samoan characteristic is *musu,* to be sullen. A previously communicative individual will suddenly become silent and moody. This often bears no relation to what's happening at the time, and when a Samoan becomes *musu,* the best approach is just to sit back and wait until they get a grip.

Requests

Samoan culture is extremely manipulative, and there's a saying that you can buy anything with a *fa'amolemole* (please). Samoans are constantly asking each other for things; it's not just a game they play with foreigners. If you're staying in a village for long, somebody from another household may eventually come and ask you for money or something you're carrying. It's important that you be firm with them. Explain that you're sharing what you have with your hosts, and you simply don't have money to give out. If you "loan" money, consider it a gift, for if you insist on being repaid you will only make an enemy without collecting anything. Samoans will often invite you home for a meal, or ask you to accompany them on an excursion, and they're usually sincere and only wish to share some time with you. Occasionally, however, it will be someone who only wants to get something out of you, such as to have you pay their expenses at a restaurant, bar, nightclub, or whatever. You have to form appropriate defenses in Samoa.

Theft and Violence

Nobody means any harm, and violent crime is almost unknown, but be careful: The concept of individual ownership is not entirely accepted by the Samoans. Don't leave valuables unattended. Someone might even steal your laundry off the line, so it's better to hang it up in your room. Theft from beach *fale* and hotel rooms is also not unusual. Your hosts will be able to suggest ways of avoiding this.

The wisest policy when visiting Samoa is to remain low-key. Don't put yourself in high-risk situations, and if you ever have to defend yourself, it's always better to try to run away. If confronted by a belligerent drunk (quite possible in the evening), humble yourself, apologize even if you did nothing wrong, and ease yourself out of the confrontation. If it ends in violence, you'll always lose, because the culture pressures relatives and friends to join in the attack even if their side is clearly in the wrong. Loyalty is priority number one, and proving that is a lifelong obligation.

Getting Stoned

Some Samoans in remote areas resent sightseers who drive through their village in rented automobiles, especially if they're going a little fast. Cases of local children shouting insults, baring their bottoms, and even stoning motorists are not unknown. Sometimes *palagi* on buses, cycling, or even walking get this reaction if they're

SAMOA

thought to be intruding. (Though the kids know how to throw stones with deadly accuracy, they seldom actually hit tourists.) Try to smile and keep your cool.

Children

At times village children can be a bit of a nuisance, calling to you and crowding around in an almost mocking way. You can forestall much of this by smiling and saying *talofa* (hello) as soon as you see them. Just keep smiling, keep going, and you'll soon leave them behind. It's important not to show any anger or irritation at their behavior, as this will only delight them and make them all the more unmannered with the next visitor who happens by.

If you're resting somewhere and don't really want to move on, the only way to get rid of annoying children is to complain very politely to their parents or to a local *matai*. Beware of ordering them away yourself, as tourists who thought they could do whatever they liked have been stoned by local children many times. As always, a kind smile is your best defense. Occasionally you'll be accosted by groups of children who have been given money by tourists and if they think you might do the same they'll stick to you like glue.

Fa'a Samoa

It's considered impolite to eat while walking through a village, or to talk or eat while standing in a *fale*. Sit down cross-legged on a mat, *then* talk and eat. Don't stretch out your legs when sitting: it's bad form to point your feet at anyone or prop them up, and also a discourtesy to turn your back on a *matai*. Swaying from side to side indicates anger or contempt, and gesturing with the hands is considered bad taste.

If you arrive at a house during the family prayer session, wait outside until they're finished. A sign that you are invited to enter is the laying out of mats for you to sit on. Walk around the mats, rather than over them. Shoes should be removed and left outside. Your host will give a short speech of welcome, to which you should reply by giving your impressions of the village and explaining your reason for coming, beginning with the words *susu mai* (listen). If you are offered food, try to eat a small amount even if you're not hungry.

Some villages object to the use of their beach on Sunday, and some object anytime. If someone's around, ask, or find a beach that's secluded. Public nudism is prohibited; cover up as you walk through a village. Women receive more respect when dressed in a *puletasi* (long dress) or *lavalava*, and not slacks or shorts. It's inappropriate to wear flowers or bright clothing to church.

This said, don't be intimidated by Samoan customs. Do your best to respect tradition, but rest assured that the Samoans are indulgent with foreigners who make an honest blunder. Samoans are fiercely proud of the *fa'a Samoa* and will be honored to explain it to you. It's all part of the Samoan experience, not an inconvenience at all.

In fact, the *fa'a Samoa* is open to interpretation, and even "world authorities" such as Margaret Mead and Derek Freeman can create diametrically opposed theories as to just what Samoan customs were or are. Mead's version of happy, uninhibited sexuality presented in *Coming of Age in Samoa* has been challenged by Freeman's description of a violent, competitive society that prizes virginity and forbids premarital sex (see Resources). Albert Wendt's 1979 novel, *Pouliuli*, is a superb analysis of that "laboratory of contradictions" that is Samoa.

Exploring the Islands

Highlights

Your most long-lasting impression of Samoa may be of people living in harmony with nature, and there's no better way to experience it than by sleeping in a Samoan *fale* at any of the growing number of beach *fale* resorts around the country. The bus rides from Apia to Aleipata and Lepa are also superb introductions to this exotic environment.

Samoa's most unforgettable sights draw their beauty from their natural surroundings, from the tomb of Robert Louis Stevenson on Mt. Vaea, to the Piula Cave Pool, the waterfall and pyramid at Savai'i's Letolo Plantation, and the nearby Taga blowholes. O Le Pupu-Pu'e National Park on Upolu's south side is Samoa's largest. You also won't want to miss a *fia fia* in Apia.

The east and west tips of the two main islands are the scenic highlights of this compact country. Samoa's most photographed beach is at Lalomanu, near Cape Tapaga in eastern Upolu, with Nu'utele Island lying offshore. Falealupo and Cape Mulinu'u at the west end of Savai'i are renowned for their beaches, rainforests, and local legends. Manase in northern Savai'i is the gateway to Mt. Matavanu, source of the island's huge lava fields, while Lefaga in southwestern Upolu is a quintessential South Seas paradise.

Sports and Recreation

The main **scuba diving** companies are based in Apia, but diving can be arranged at the Sinalei Reef Resort on Upolu and at Manase on Savai'i. A reasonable **snorkeling** locale, the Palolo Deep, is right in Apia, but Savai'i's Faga Beach is better. Other good snorkeling areas are Aleipata in eastern Upolu and around Manono Island. There are fewer options elsewhere, due in part to narrow fringing reefs, deadly currents, hurricane-impacted corals, and fishing with dynamite.

Samoa is a **surfing** paradise and the top waves are off the north-facing coasts in summer, off the south-facing coasts in winter. Thus optimum conditions are encountered at Lauli'i, Faleapuna, and Lano from December to March, and at Aufaga, Salani, Tafatafa, and Salailua from May to August. These powerful reef-break waves are mostly for experienced surfers only, and novices should learn to surf elsewhere. Check the websites of the Salani and Sa'Moana surf resorts included in the Upolu accommodation listings for details. Most villages on Savai'i collect a S$10 pp per day surfing fee from surfers.

Sea kayaking is becoming increasingly popular with several outfitters now operating from Apia. The tours often go to Aleipata and Manono, and many resorts rent kayaks.

Samoa Marine in Apia and the Sa'Moana Resort in southern Upolu offer deep-sea **fishing.** The Samoa International Game Fishing Association (www.fishing.ws) organizes an annual fishing tournament in May.

There are numerous opportunities for **hiking,** though the trails quickly become overgrown, which often makes local guides a good idea. Experienced hikers should be able to do the Lake Lanoto'o trip outside Apia on their own. O Le Pupu-Pu'e National Park in southern Upolu offers a number of hiking possibilities. Many good hikes are available on Savai'i.

If you bring your own **bicycle** on the flight, many wonderful opportunities to use it will present themselves here. Both main islands have excellent paved roads and there isn't much traffic except on northern Upolu. The only real hazard is sudden chases by dogs, but one must also be prepared for the heat. Allow a week or more to cycle around each island, staying at village *fale* resorts along the way. The 176-km road around Savai'i is flat, except for the stretch between Asau and Sasina, which at 229 meters elevation is still lower than the passes on Upolu. You'll need to find a place to spend the night before the evening prayers and carry your own food. (If you stop to talk to an adult on the road, be sure to get right off your bicycle, otherwise you might be seen as speaking down to a *matai*.)

Golfers will enjoy the 18-hole course at Apia.

Public Holidays and Festivals

Public holidays include New Year's Days (January

1, 2), Head of State's Birthday (first Monday in January), Good Friday, Easter Monday (March/April), ANZAC Day (April 25), Mothers of Samoa Day (a Monday in mid-May), Independence Days (June 1, 2), Labor Day (a Monday in early August), White Monday (the Monday after the second Sunday in October), Arbor Day (the first Friday in November), and Christmas Days (December 25, 26).

Don't expect to get any official business done during the three-week period beginning a week before Christmas and ending a week after New Year's, as most government employees knock off for extended holidays around then and many offices will be closed. Even basic public facilities such as the post office shut down for a week at a time! Also beware of Independence Days, since the two public holidays in a row mean that all banks, offices, and most stores will be closed for four consecutive days, at least. Easter is also a bad time to come if you have anything specific to do.

Many Western countries celebrate Mother's Day and Father's Day, but only Samoa has made Children's Day (White Monday, the day after White Sunday) a public holiday. On White Sunday, children dressed in white parade to church; after the service, they take the places of honor and eat first at family feasts.

The big event of the year is the **Independence Days** celebrations during the first week of June with dancing, feasting, speeches by *tulafale* (talking chiefs), horse races, and other sporting events. A highlight is the *fautasi* race on the Saturday closest to Independence Days, with teams of dozens of men rowing great longboat canoes. Though Samoa actually attained independence on January 1, 1962, the celebrations are held in June to avoid total paralysis around Christmas (which usually occurs anyway, however).

The **Teuila Tourism Festival** in early September is also a good time to be there. Among the many cultural activities are church choir competitions, dance and beauty contests, squash and cricket finals, *fautasi* (long-boat) races, traditional games, talent shows, etc.

Once a year, the palolo reef worm *(Eunice viridis)* rises from the coral before dawn according to a lunar cycle (October on Upolu, No-

vember on Savai'i). The Samoans wait with lanterns and nets to catch this prized delicacy, the "caviar of the Pacific." This remarkable event takes place in Samoa, Fiji, and some other islands, but never in Hawaii.

Dance

The *sasa* is a synchronized group dance in which the rhythm is maintained by clapping or by beating on a rolled mat or drum. The *siva* is a graceful, flowing dance in which the individual is allowed to express him/herself as he/she sees fit. The *fa'ataupati*, or slap dance, employs body percussion. Knife-fire dances are done solo or in small groups, and they can be dangerous to the performers. Tradition holds that only men who are afraid will be burned during the fire dance. The waving of flaming weapons was originally done in times of war, to warn a tribe of approaching enemies.

Arts and Crafts

The Samoan love of elaborate ceremony is illustrated in the fine mat *(ie toga)*. Exquisitely and tightly plaited from finely split pandanus leaves, a good example might take a woman a year of her spare time to complete. Fine mats are prized family heirlooms used as dowries, etc., and they increase in value as they're passed from person to person at ceremonial exchanges *(lafo)*. Mats of this kind cannot be purchased.

Samoan tapa cloth *(siapo)* is decorated by rubbing the tapa over an inked board bearing the desired pattern in relief. In Samoa the designs are usually geometric, but with a symbolism based on natural objects.

Traditional woodcarving includes kava bowls, drums, orator's staffs, and war clubs. In Tonga and Fiji, kava bowls have only four circular legs, while Samoan bowls are usually circular with a dozen or more round legs. A large kava bowl is an impressive object to carry home if you have six or seven kilograms to spare in your baggage allowance. Paradoxically, although carved from endangered trees such as the *ifilele,* the local production of kava bowls actually helps protect the rainforests, because it greatly increases the value of the trees in the eyes of local villagers who become far less willing to sign away their timber rights for a pittance. A tree used to make handicrafts could be worth S$2,000 while a logging company would only pay about S$30 to cut it down.

It's also interesting to note that the tikis you see here are mock Maori or Hawaiian, not Samoan—don't buy the grotesque, grimacing little devils. Also beware of imitation tapa crafts in the Tongan style imported from Pago Pago, New Guinea-style masks, and turtle-shell jewelry, which is prohibited entry into many countries. If what you see in the craft shops of Samoa seems less impressive than what you might encounter in some other Pacific countries, remember that oratory and tattooing were the maximum expressions of Samoan culture, followed by the kava ceremony itself.

ACCOMMODATIONS AND FOOD

Accommodations

The higher-priced hotels usually quote their rates in U.S. dollars to make them seem lower, but in this book we've converted all prices into *tala* to make them easier to compare. Whenever a hotel mentions dollars, be sure to clarify how they wish to be paid. If the amount has to be converted into *tala*, whether you're paying in *tala* cash or by credit card, your bill could be inflated about 15 percent due to the exchange rates used. You can sometimes avoid this by paying in U.S. dollars, cash or traveler's checks, otherwise ask them to quote a price in *tala*, as that could work out cheaper. In all cases, a 12.5 percent value-added tax is charged and you should ask if it's included. Failure to pay attention to these details could well result in a bill 25 percent higher than you'd expected!

During the off season (Jan.–April) some of the upscale hotels in outlying areas slash their rates to attract business. The hotels on Savai'i often do this, but those at Apia and Siumu don't. About the only way to find out about these specials is to call and ask. Other travelers may know about some of the deals. In Apia, plenty of rooms are available and there's no need to reserve. The only exceptions might be around Christmas and

during the Independence Celebrations at the beginning of June, but even then you'll invariably find something, as most of the people arriving for these events will be overseas Samoans who generally stay with family and friends. Accommodations and transfers booked from abroad are always much more expensive than what you'd pay locally.

Most of the regular hotels and guesthouses are in Apia, but an increasing number of places to stay are found on Savai'i and around Upolu. In the past few years numerous locally operated low-impact ecotourism resorts have opened on outlying beaches. These offer mattresses, pillows, sheets, blankets, and mats in Samoan *fale* right on the beach, with local meals provided at reasonable cost. Mosquito nets are also provided, but the shared bathrooms can be primitive. Virtually all are run by the villagers themselves, and they're an excellent way to combine hiking, snorkeling, swimming, surfing, and just plain relaxing with a sampling of Samoan life. They're covered in the Around Upolu and Savai'I sections of this chapter, and are highly recommended.

Staying in Villages

Staying in villages is a wonderful way to experience true Samoan culture and hospitality. The growing number of *fale* resorts makes it a simple matter to sleep on a beach adjacent to a village, such as at Saleapaga, Saluafata, Satapuala, and Sa'anapu on Upolu, and at Falealupo, Manase, and Satuiatua on Savai'i, to name only a few. It's also possible to stay right in the homes of local families themselves. Formal arrangements for this exist in villages that have organized conservation programs, such as Uafato on Upolu, and Letui, Sasina, Satoalepai, and Tafua-tai on Savai'i, but it's possible almost anywhere.

The Samoans are among the most hospitable people in the world, proud that a stranger can go to any house and request food or shelter and rarely be turned away. This admirable characteristic should not be abused, however. It's part of their culture that a gift will be reciprocated—if not now, then sometime in the future. Tourists who accept gifts (such as food and lodging) without reciprocating undermine the culture.

SAMOA

VAILIMA LAGER

Samoa's Vailima beer may be the South Pacific's top beer with more life, sparkle, and bite than any other lager you'll taste around this ocean. Since 1978 it's been brewed at Vaitele between Apia and Faleolo Airport by Samoa Breweries Ltd., presently owned by Fiji's Carlton Brewery, part of the Fosters group. The current brewmaster learned his craft in Bavaria. The version of Vailima sold in Samoa is 4.9 percent alcohol, but if you cross to American Samoa you should reduce your intake slightly because Vailima Export is 6.7 percent. Back in Apia, the same brewery's Eku Bavaria beer is 5.3 percent and excellent (brewed under license from Erste Kulmbacher Aktien-brauerei). In 1990, 1992, 1995, and 1998, Vailima was awarded the Grand Gold Medal at the Le Monde Selection in Brussels, Belgium, and as you sit in front of a cold one at the RSA Club, Otto's Reef, or any one of a dozen atmospheric Apia bars, you'll swear Samoa is paradise, and in this regard you will be right.

For this reason, it's strongly recommended that, in situations where there's no fixed price, you look for a way of repaying any courtesies received. Thanks is not enough, and a casual offer of payment might be offensive in situations where you were accommodated informally. The Samoans are a very proud people, among the proudest in the Pacific, and you must phrase things carefully to avoid misunderstandings. If your attitude is wrong, they will sense it.

Upon departure, sit down with your hosts for a formal thank you. Say something like, "Hospitality is not something that can be paid for, and I don't know how to show my appreciation fully, but I would like to leave a *mea alofa* (gift)." Then tender about the same amount you would have paid at a *fale* resort, or around S$50 pp per night. Give more if they've been especially helpful by taking you out fishing, guiding you through the mountains, etc. If you ask them to buy something for the children with the money, they'll smile and accept.

There's a Samoan proverb about guests who abuse hospitality, *ua afu le laufala* (the floor mats are sweating). Talk these matters over with your traveling companions before you set out, and don't go on a trip with one of the insensitive few. Foreigners who seem to be trying to take advantage of Samoans often become victims of theft.

Other Tips

It's a good idea to make known the approximate length of your stay as soon as a family invites you. If one of your hosts' neighbors invites you to come stay with them, politely refuse. This would bring shame on the first family. It's a Samoan custom that travelers may spend the night at the pastor's house. If you do, make an appropriate contribution to the church. The pastor's views on religion, values, and development in general will fascinate you.

Samoans are still unfamiliar with **camping** and might be offended if they feel you're refusing their hospitality. A tactful explanation of your desire to be close to nature might be accepted, though Samoans are naturally suspicious of those who try to remain apart from the group. Always ask permission of a responsible adult, or camp well out of sight of all roads, trails, and villages. To do otherwise is to place yourself beyond the protection of village law.

Food

Try *palusami*—thick coconut cream, onions, canned corned beef *(pisupo)*, and young taro leaves wrapped in a breadfruit leaf, then baked on hot stones and served on slices of baked taro—a very tasty dish when well prepared. Other traditional Samoan specialties include *taofolo* (kneaded breadfruit and sweet coconut cream wrapped in taro leaves and baked), *fa'ausi* (grated taro and coconut cream pudding), *lua'u* (taro leaves cooked in coconut cream), *suafa'i* (ripe bananas with coconut cream), *faia'ife'e* (octopus in coconut cream), *faiaipusi* (sea eel in coconut cream), and *oka* (marinated raw fish).

If you spend a night in a village or *fale* resort, notice how almost everything you eat is locally grown. Taro and breadfruit are the staples, but there's also pork, fish, chicken, *ta'amu* (a large root vegetable like taro), and bananas. If you're a strict vegetarian, mention it at the outset, although this concept is often not understood in Samoa. In the villages, food is normally eaten with the hands (no cutlery). After a meal with a family, linger a while; it's considered rude for a guest to get up and abruptly leave. Don't continue to occupy the table if others are awaiting their turn to eat, however. Samoans are *big* people. Most of us eat till we're full, but the Samoans eat till they're tired.

INFORMATION AND SERVICES

Information
The Samoa Tourism Authority (P.O. Box 2272, Apia, Samoa; tel. 685/63-500, fax 685/20-886, www.visitsamoa.ws) provides information through their website, by direct mail, or at the Apia office.

Internet Resources
The official website of the Samoa Tourism Authority, **www.visitsamoa.ws,** introduces the "Treasured Islands of the South Pacific." The Samoa Hotel Association's site, **www.samoa hotels.ws,** provides detailed listings of accommodations throughout the country. Samoa Islands Hotels, **www.samoa-islands.com,** uses interactive maps to show the location of hotels, plus pictures of beaches and scenery. Samoa Resorts Pacific, **www.samoa.resortspacific.com,** also uses clickable maps to access photos and information about resorts. Samoa Beaches, **www .samoa.islands-beaches.com,** has yet more clickable maps leading to information and photos of Samoan beaches.

Samoan Sensation, **www.samoan-sensation .com,** has extensive sections on visiting Samoa and Samoan culture. Samoan Tattoo, **samoan tattoo.tattooing-piercings.com,** provides the whole history of Samoan tattooing, with abundant photos of this ancient Polynesian art form. Samoa Live, **www.samoalive.com,** is Samoa's community website with loads of links and a family of message

boards wildly popular among Samoans around the world. The site of the Samoa Meteorology Division, **www.meteorology.gov.ws,** is the ideal place to get a feel for the weather conditions you'll encounter on your trip.

Visas and Officialdom
No visa is required for a stay of up to 30 days, although you must have a ticket to leave. This ticket may not be examined by the officials upon arrival at Apia airport, but it certainly will be requested by the airline staff as you're checking in for your flight to Samoa. Samoan immigration will stamp your passport to the date of your flight out, but you can get the 30 days without a struggle (if your onward flight is over 30 days ahead, the airline may want to see a Samoan visa before allowing you to board the plane). Extensions of stay are possible but not automatic (a brief side trip to American Samoa is an easy way to get an extension).

Apia is the only port of entry for cruising yachts and arriving boats can call customs over VHF channel 16. Clearance is done at the main wharf, then yachts anchor in the harbor off Aggie Grey's Hotel. Yachts may stop at Savai'i after checking out at Apia, provided they get prior permission from the Ministry of Foreign Affairs.

Money
The Samoan *tala* is divided into 100 *sene*. There are coins of 1, 2, 5, 10, 20, and 50 *sene* and one *tala,* and banknotes of 2, 5, 10, 20, 50, and 100 *tala.* The plastic S$2 banknotes make nice souvenirs. Samoans often speak of dollars when they mean *tala,* and many tourism-related businesses add to the confusion by quoting prices in U.S. dollars. Always note the currency carefully, as the difference is around three to one!

SAMOA

For consistency, we've quoted most prices in Samoan currency (S$).

Both banks charge exorbitant commissions on traveler's checks, the Westpac Bank S$7.50 and the ANZ Bank S$17.50. Several private currency exchange offices around Apia give similar rates without commission and you don't need to queue up! Traveler's checks attract an exchange rate about 4 percent higher than cash, but it's always good to have some U.S. currency in small bills in case you happen to run out of *tala,* as everyone will gladly accept it (though at a low rate). If you plan to go upmarket, also have an adequate supply of U.S. dollar traveler's checks in small denominations (see below).

Upmarket facilities that quote prices in dollars are often cheaper if you pay them the exact amount in U.S. dollars, cash or traveler's checks. If you pay by credit card, you risk having the charge inflated 15 percent because the dollar amount must be converted into *tala,* then the bank converts the *tala* into New Zealand dollars because all credit card charges are cleared through New Zealand, then the NZ$ are converted into your own home currency, all at rates unfavorable to you. This situation definitely applies to bank cards such as Visa and MasterCard; however, it may be possible to be charged the exact amount in U.S. dollars if you use a private card such as American Express (ask the merchant/hotel).

Tala are heavily discounted outside Samoa, so change only what you think you'll need. If you overestimate, excess *tala* can be changed back into U.S. dollars at the airport bank without question. As you're doing so, try to pick up some Tongan or Fijian banknotes, if that's where you're headed.

Camera film is expensive here and the selection is poor, so bring a good supply. When buying drinks at a grocery store, be aware that there's a S$.30 deposit on large beer or soft drink bottles, S$.10 on small bottles, although many stores refuse to refund the deposit. Tipping is discouraged, and one should avoid giving money to children, as this only creates a nuisance. There's a 12.5 percent sales tax, which is usually charged extra (not included in the sticker price).

Communications

Post offices sell telephone cards in denominations of S$5, S$10, S$20, and S$50 for use in public payphones. If you decide to make a call from your hotel, ask how much you'll be charged beforehand. Turn to the Apia section for the price of calls made from the main telephone company office.

To make an operator-assisted domestic call, dial 920. For the international operator, dial 900. If you have access to a direct-dial phone, the international access code is 0. For domestic directory assistance, dial 933; for international numbers, dial 910.

The country code for American Samoa is 684; for Samoa it's 685.

Samoa has three Internet service providers: Computer Services Ltd. (www.samoa.ws), Internet Pasifika Samoa (www.ipasifika.net), and Lesamoa.net (www.lesamoa.net). Four or five places around Apia offer Internet access at S$12 an hour. The two best established are in the Lotemanu Center near Air New Zealand.

Media

The main English-language newspaper is the *Samoa Observer* (tel. 21-099, fax 23-965, www.samoaobserver.ws), published daily except Mondays. Founded in 1978 by acclaimed poet and novelist Sano Malifa, the *Observer* has faced constant government harassment due its exposures of official corruption. Government advertising has been canceled, and to plug leaks, a law has been passed forcing journalists to reveal their information sources. The compulsory registration of publications and their employees has been imposed, and lawsuits against those accused of libeling government ministers are paid out of the public purse (all this, ironically, by the "Human Rights Protection Party" administration). In 1994, the paper's premises were gutted by arson, and in 1999, Malifa narrowly escaped being murdered. Of course, this situation only makes the *Observer* all the more worth reading.

Several other papers also appear, including *Newsline* (tel. 24-216), published on Wednesday, Friday, and Sunday, and *Le Samoa* (tel./fax

23-827), a weekly. *Savali* (tel. 26-397) is a government-run newspaper published on Friday.

Radio

The government-operated Broadcasting Department transmits over two AM radio frequencies. Radio 2AP at 540 kHz airs bilingual programs (English and Samoan) Monday to Saturday 0600–2300. Their local news in Samoan is at 0700 and 1200, the international news at 0800, 0900, 1000, and 1800 (rebroadcast from Australia or New Zealand). On Sundays Radio 2AP broadcasts nonstop Samoan hymns, so that day switch to 747 kHz AM for varied music introduced in English.

A private company, Radio Polynesia Ltd. (tel. 25-149, www.fmradio.ws), operates three FM stations which are on the air 24 hours a day. Magik FM broadcasts over 98.1 MHz to points west of Apia and over 99.9 MHz east of Apia. The same company runs Talofa FM at 96.1 MHz and K-Lite FM at 101.1 MHz. Magik 98 rebroadcasts the Radio New Zealand International news at 0700 and 0800. Local news comes before the 0700 international news weekdays, then again at noon, 1700, 1900, and 2200. On Saturday there's local news at 0700 and 1200. K-Lite plays the Radio New Zealand news weekdays at 0600, 0700, 0800, 1000, 1600, 1800, 1900, and 2000.

Health

Although no vaccinations are required (except yellow fever or cholera in the unlikely case that you're arriving directly from an infected area), it may be worthwhile to have been immunized against hepatitis A, typhoid fever, and tetanus (in case a dog bites you). Details of these are provided in the Exploring the Islands chapter. Body lice and intestinal parasites are widespread among Samoan villagers; any pharmacy will have a remedy for the former. Check the expiration date before buying any medicines in Samoa. And take care with the tap water in Apia—boiled water and beer are safer.

In case of need, you'll receive faster attention from any of the private doctors and dentists listed in this book's Apia section than you would at a government hospital or clinic.

Business Hours and Time

Business hours are weekdays 0800–1200 and 1330–1630, Saturday 0800–1200, with government offices closed on Saturday. Banks open weekdays 0900–1500, the post office 0900–1630 weekdays. Expect most businesses to be closed on Sunday, although Samoa's Sunday closing laws are much more lenient than those of Tonga. Grocery stores aren't supposed to sell beer on Sunday (but some will if nobody's watching).

Both Samoas share the same hour, and since the international date line is just west of here, this is where the world's day really ends. Tonga and Samoa are on the same hour, but Samoa is 24 hours behind Tonga. The Samoas are three hours behind California time, 21 hours behind eastern Australian time.

Weights and Measures

In American Samoa Imperial measurements (yards, miles) are used, while in Samoa it's all metric (meters, kilometers). Unlike American Samoa, where the electric voltage is 110 volts, in Samoa it's 240 volts AC, 50 cycles. However, if you plan to plug in an appliance (such as a hair drier or electric razor) at a deluxe hotel in Samoa, check the voltage carefully as some supply 110 volts instead of the usual 240 volts.

GETTING THERE

By Air

Polynesian Airlines (tel. 22-737, www.polynesian airlines.com), Samoa's government-owned flag carrier, connects Apia to Auckland, Honolulu, Melbourne, Nadi, Niue, Pago Pago, Sydney, Tongatapu, and Wellington. Their Polypass allows 45 days unlimited travel over most of Polynesian's South Pacific network (a roundtrip to/from Australia and New Zealand included) for a flat US$1,099. From Honolulu/Los Angeles, the Polypass costs US$1,349/1,699. Details of this and their triangle fares are provided under Getting Around in the Exploring the Islands chapter of this book. Polynesian's Los Angeles office can be reached at tel. 310/322-9727 or 800/264-0823.

Air Pacific (tel. 22-738) has a heavily booked weekly flight to Apia from Nadi. **Air New**

SAMOA

Zealand (tel. 20-825) arrives daily from Auckland and weekly from Los Angeles and Tongatapu. See Getting Around the Exploring the Islands chapter for information on circular tickets between Fiji, Apia, and Tonga.

Polynesian Airlines operates shuttles between Pago Pago and Apia four to seven times a day. For the Pago Pago flights, check carefully which airport you'll be using as Polynesian Airlines alternates between Faleolo and Fagali'i though the ticket may only say "Apia" (most of the Pago Pago flights are to/from Fagali'i). Fares from Apia to Pago Pago are S$165/260 one-way/roundtrip, and it's a third cheaper to buy your ticket in Samoa than elsewhere due to currency differences. Polynesia also has daily flights between Pago Pago and Maota airstrip on Savai'i (S$204/317 one-way/roundtrip). These should be booked before leaving Apia. American Samoan airport and customs taxes of US$9.50 are included in these prices but a S$11 Samoan insurance surcharge may be extra.

When the flight to/from Pago Pago is full all baggage may be bumped due to the limited carrying capacity of the aircraft. All passengers must be weighed and the average weight of Samoans is substantial (this may be one of the few places in the world where the flight attendant stands at the entrance to the plane with a bundle of extended seatbelts). When the baggage does arrive on a later flight, you'll have to go back to the airport and clear it personally through customs. Don't expect compensation for any of this, and be aware that the check-in staff probably won't inform you about what's going on until they're just about to close the aircraft door. If the flight is full and you see people in line with mountains of excess luggage, expect this to happen. In any case, carry everything you can't afford to lose or might need during the first few days in your hand luggage. (In 2003, a Pago Pago-based carrier, Samoa Air, went bankrupt, disrupting air service between the Samoas, so check these connections carefully.)

By Ship

The **Samoa Shipping Corporation** (tel. 20-935, fax 22-352, ssc@samoa.ws) runs the 220-passenger car ferry *Lady Naomi* from Apia to Pago Pago Wednesday at 2200 (156 km, seven hours, indoor seating S$60 one-way, 116 berths at S$80 one-way). Buy your ticket before 1200 on Tuesday at their office near the main wharf and be prepared to show your passport. If you wait to buy your ticket at the wharf, you won't be allowed aboard until the last minute and all of the good places to sleep on deck will have been taken (it's an overnight trip). After 220 tickets have been sold, standby passengers are turned away (due to stricter insurance conditions, they don't overload the ship anymore). Take seasickness precautions before boarding. During holiday periods the ship makes two trips, leaving Apia at 2200 on Tuesday and Thursday, and at these times it's often fully booked. If you'll be returning to Apia by boat, be sure to get a roundtrip ticket, as the fare charged in Pago Pago is much higher. But if you won't be returning, change excess *tala* back into dollars the day before, because there are no facilities on the wharf. Going by sea you save the S$30 airport departure tax paid by air travelers (although the US$5 American Samoan "entry declaration fee" must still be paid).

For information on the supply ship to the Tokelau Islands, contact the transport manager at the **Tokelau Apia Liaison Office** (P.O. Box 865, Apia; tel. 20-822, fax 21-761). There's service twice a month, and a cabin would run NZ$528 roundtrip. Turn to the Tokelau chapter for more information.

GETTING AROUND
By Air

For those who turn deep green at the thought of a 1.5 hour ferry ride between Upolu and Savai'i, **Polynesian Airlines** (tel. 22-737, www .polynesianairlines.com) operates flights to Savai'i from Fagali'i Airport (FGI), five km east of Apia. There are daily 10-minute flights to Maota airstrip, a few km west of Salelologa, costing S$49/95 one-way/roundtrip. A S$11 insurance surcharge is added to the cost flight coupon. Only 10 kilograms of checked baggage are allowed on this eight-passenger Islander aircraft, and overweight luggage is S$3.60 cents per kilo (make sure the overweight bag goes with you). If you fly, you'll have to pay a taxi fare upon arrival at Maota, costing S$10 to Salelologa, S$15 to Lalomalava, S$25 to Faga, or S$60 to Manase. At last report, the flights to Asau were cancelled. The Polynesian Airlines agent in Salelologa is Savai'i Tours and Travel (tel. 51-206) opposite the Westpac Bank.

By Boat

The **Samoa Shipping Corporation** (tel. 20-935) operates the 480-passenger car ferry MV *Lady Samoa II* between the wharfs at Mulifanua (Upolu) and Salelologa (Savai'i), departing each wharf two or three times daily. The ferry leaves Mulifanua Monday to Saturday at 0800, 1200, and 1600, and Sunday at 1200 and 1600. Departure times from Salelologa are Monday to Saturday at 0600, 1000, and 1400, Sunday at 1000 and 1400. Passenger fares are S$7 pp each way (children under 12 S$4); bicycles and motorcycles are S$5, cars S$55. Reservations are recommended for vehicles (and sometimes even foot passengers have to fight to obtain a ticket). To ensure that you'll get on the boat, buy a ticket as soon as your bus arrives at the dock and queue up when you see the others doing so—this may be the only time you'll ever see Samoans in a hurry. Sometimes a smaller ferry is used and you'll have to be fast to get a seat. The 24-km trip takes about one hour. On the way across, you get a good view of Apolima Island's single village cradled in the island's classic volcanic crater, and flying fish and dolphins are often spotted.

A faster passengers-only ferry also connects Mulifanua and Salelologa. The *Tausala Cedar o Samoa* operated by **Inter-Islander Express Services** (tel. 51-075, tuigasa@hotmail.com) takes only 30 minutes to cross at S$12 pp, departing each end shortly before the *Lady Samoa II*. There's outdoor seating on the roof and airline-style seating below. Tickets are sold at booths on the wharfs.

By Road

For information on buses, rental vehicles, and organized tours on Upolu and Savai'i, turn to the respective sections of this handbook.

AIRPORTS

Faleolo International Airport

Faleolo Airport (APW), Samoa's main international airport, is 35 km west of Apia. All flights to points outside the Samoas, as well as some services to Pago Pago, depart from here. Schuster's Shuttle Bus (tel. 23-014; S$12) will take you right to your Apia hotel, or you can wait on the highway for a public bus, which is only S$2, but very scarce after 1600 and on Sunday. Airport-bound, the airport bus departs Apia two hours before international flights. It picks up passengers in front on the Hotel Insel Fehmarn, then at Aggie Grey's Hotel, and finally at the Kitano Tusitala.

The airport taxi drivers often try to overcharge foreign tourists, so take the bus if you can. A taxi from the airport to Apia is around S$40 (40 *tala*) for the car but they will often insist on being paid US$40 in American currency, so be careful. It's much safer taking a taxi back to the airport, since they'll know you're already familiar with Samoan currency and probably won't try this trick. A taxi direct to Coconuts Beach Club or the Sinalei Reef Resort should cost S$65 for the car.

The Westpac Bank (S$7.50 commission) and the ANZ Bank (S$17.50 commission) in the arrivals area open for international flights (excluding those from Pago Pago) and change traveler's checks at similar rates. An ANZ Bank ATM is also available. For changing excess *tala* back, the banks in the departures hall are open for all international flights *except* those to Pago Pago. There's no left luggage room, but there is a tourist information desk. In a pinch, you can sleep on the floor upstairs in the terminal.

The airport post office (weekdays 0900–1530) sells philatelic stamps, a good way to unload excess *tala*. The duty-free shop in the departure lounge sells only expensive luxury goods and imported alcohol, so don't wait to do your shopping there. In general, alcohol and beer are relatively cheap in Samoa anyway.

The international departure tax is S$30 (children under 12 free). You don't have to pay the tax if you stay less than 24 hours (transit).

SAMOA

Fagali'i Airport

Fagali'i Airport (FGI) is near the golf course on the east side of Apia, just five km from the center of town. Polynesian Airlines flights to Savai'i leave from here. Some flights to Pago Pago use Fagali'i, others Faleolo, so check carefully to avoid disastrous mistakes. The local Fagali'i-uta bus should pass Fagali'i Airport Monday to Saturday, but service is irregular and not all of the Fagali'i buses come up here.

However, just 200 meters west of the airport is a junction where the more frequent Vaivase or Moata'a buses pass. Taxi drivers charge US$5 from Fagali'i to Apia but only S$8 from Apia to Fagali'i. If you're unwilling to pay this arbitrary premium, try bargaining or just walk off and look for a bus. The Westpac Bank has a branch at Fagali'i Airport and there's a duty-free shop. The usual international departure tax applies.

Upolu

Although much smaller than Savai'i, Upolu is Samoa's chief island with its capital, international airport, industry, business, attractions, visitor facilities, and three quarters of the total population. Physically, it's rather like Tahiti on a smaller scale with high verdant mountains in the background of Apia and a seaside boulevard encircling the harbor. The villages along the north coast also remind one of Tahitian villages, as do the valleys and black beaches. But Upolu is much wilder and more traditional than Tahiti, and less impacted by international tourism.

Although Savai'i commands a faraway mystique, Upolu is a more beautiful and varied island, especially the eastern half. Roads wind around the coast and across the center of the island. Some of the South Pacific's finest beaches are at Lepa and Aleipata with suitable facilities for budget travelers. Waterfalls cascade from the luxuriant green hillsides and there are countless places to swim. Hikers will feel rather like Tarzans and Janes cutting paths through the exuberant vegetation, and travelers will be enchanted by the easygoing Polynesian lifestyle. Upolu is an uncut insular jewel.

APIA AND ENVIRONS

Central Apia has been transformed in recent years, with enormous government buildings overshadowing the older churches and trading companies that still line the waterfront in the traditional South Seas movie-set manner. Yet away from the center, this city of 39,000 is only a cluster of villages. In Apia Harbor, where the Vaisigano River

has cut an opening in Upolu's protective reef, rock a motley assortment of container ships, fishing boats, interisland ferries, and cruising yachts. As at Papeete, you'll see teams of men paddling outrigger racing canoes around the harbor at sunset, about the only two towns in the South Pacific where this is so. Yet the languid inertia of Apia is pervasive. You can snorkel at the Palolo Deep, but the best beaches are on the south side of the island, about an hours drive away.

Apia makes a good base from which to explore northern Upolu, and there's lots of accommodation in all price brackets. The food and entertainment possibilities are also very good, so give yourself a break and see the city one step at a time. Get into the culture and prepare yourself for that big trip around Savai'i. Samoa is Polynesia's heart and Apia is the bright light around which the country revolves.

SIGHTS

By the harbor side where Falealili Street meets Beach Road is the **John Williams Memorial,** dedicated to the missionary who implanted Protestantism in Samoa in 1830. Nine years later Williams was killed and eaten by cannibals on Erromango Island in the New Hebrides (presently Vanuatu). Later his remains were returned to Samoa and buried beneath the porch of the old **Congregational Christian Church** (1898) across the street.

A block west on Beach Road is the historic wooden **Courthouse** dating from German

APIA AND ENVIRONS

SOUTH PACIFIC OCEAN

To Airport
Vaitele

APIA OBSERVATORY
APIA YACHT CLUB
PARLIAMENT Mulinu'u Peninsula
PENINSULA CLUB
GERMAN MONUMENT
MILLENIA HOTEL

PALOLO DEEP MARINE RESERVE

Pilot Point

SEE "CENTRAL APIA" MAP

Vaigaga
VAILIMA BREWERY
Vaiusu
Vaiusu Bay
Elisefou
Vailoa
Mangrove Swamp
Vaitoloa
Savalalo
POST OFFICE
Apia Harbor
Vaiala
Matautu
Vaipuna
Fagali'i Bay

TOMB OF TAMASESE
Lepea
River
Pesega
Fugalei
Leone
Apia Park
TENNIS COURTS
To Falefa

Tula'ele
MORMON TEMPLE
Lotopa
GERMAN CONSULATE
Lalovaea
Malifa
ANIVA'S PLACE
Faatoia
Fagali'i
COUNTRY CLUB

Sinamoga
Lalovaea Stream
SAMOAN OUTRIGGER HOTEL
NATIONAL HOSPITAL
PAVITTS U-DRIVE
HOTEL INSEL FEHMARN
Vaivase-Tai
NATIONAL UNIVERSITY OF SAMOA
FAGALI'I AIRPORT

Leufisa
Vaivase-Uta

To Aleisa and Paradise Beach
Alafua
SOUTH SEA STAR HOTEL
POSTAL RADIO FACILITY
Mulivai Stream
NAFANUA AGRICULTURAL COLLEGE
Nafanua
Papauta
MANGOES GRILL
Papaloloa Waterfall

UNIVERSITY OF THE SOUTH PACIFIC
SAMOA HOLIDAY HOTEL
Upolu Island
R. L. STEVENSON'S TOMB
Vailima
Vaivase Stream

Moamoa
Mt. Vaea (475 m)
STEVENSON MUSEUM
PAPASE'EA SLIDING ROCKS
CHANEL COLLEGE
Avele
To Siumu
MEDCEN PRIVATE HOSPITAL

0   1 mi
0   1 km

© DAVID STANLEY

times, which served as government headquarters until 1994. On Black Saturday, December 29, 1929, Tupua Tamasese Lealofi III, leader of the Mau Movement, was shot in the back in front of this building by the New Zealand Constabulary while trying to calm his people during a demonstration against the colonial regime. Eight other Samoans were also killed and five years of severe repression followed, only ending with a change of government in New Zealand. Today the **Falemataaga Museum of Samoa** (tel. 63-444, weekdays 1200-1600, admission free), upstairs in the courthouse, presents photos and exhibits on the culture and history of Samoa.

West again is imposing **Mulivai Catholic Cathedral** (1885–1905), formerly a landmark for ships entering the harbor, and **Matafele Methodist Church,** a fine building where marvelous singing may be heard during Sunday services.

Across the street is the gigantic eight-story **Government Building,** erected in 1994 with a S$35-million interest-free loan from the People's Republic of China. It and the neighboring seven-story **Central Bank of Samoa** wouldn't be out of place in Abu Dhabi, Dubai, or Kuwait, and stand

SAMOA

© DAVID STANLEY

Apia's Catholic cathedral on Beach Road

as stunning examples of third-world megalomania. At 0750 on weekday mornings, the police band marches from their barracks near the Courthouse and plays the national anthem here at the raising of the flag.

Nearby is the **Chief Post Office** with the modern headquarters of the **ANZ Bank** opposite. A block west in the center of the traffic circle where Vaea Street meets Beach Road is a **Clock Tower** built as a WW I memorial. On opposite corners of Vaea Street and Beach Road are the former Burns Philp store, now Chan Mow Supermarket, the **National Provident Fund** building housing the agency that administers the country's pension fund, and the **Nelson Memorial Public Library,** named for Olaf Nelson (1883–1944), a leader of the Mau Movement.

Farther west facing a small harbor is the **Savalalo Fish Market.** The numerous locally owned longline fishing boats here have made fish a leading export during the past few years, but safety standards are minimal and several boats and crews are lost each year. The **Flea Mar-**

ket nearby was Apia's main vegetable market until 1995, when it was moved three blocks inland. These days you can shop for handicrafts and clothing here, and cheap food stalls are along the side closest to the harbor. One of Apia's two bus stations is also here, and just beyond is a flashy **Women's Center,** built with another Chinese loan. The large wooden building almost across the street is the headquarters of the **Samoa Trust Estates Corporation.** These were once the premises of the German trading companies, whose assets were seized when New Zealand invaded in 1914.

Mulinu'u Peninsula

Just northwest of the old market is the **Kitano Tusitala Hotel,** which is well worth entering to appreciate the great hand-tied roofs of the main *fale*-like neo-Samoan buildings erected in 1974.

Continue northwest on Mulinu'u Street, past two monuments on the left commemorating the disastrous 1889 naval debacle when the German cruiser *Adler* and several other ships sank during a hurricane. There's also a monument on the right that recalls the raising of the German flag on March 1, 1900 *(die deutsche Flagge gehisst).*

The large beehive-style building farther along on the left is the neo-Samoan **Parliament of Samoa** (1972). The smaller old Fono House nearby now houses the office of the Ombudsman. Across the field is the **Independence Memorial** (1962), which declares, "The Holy Ghost, Council of all Mankind, led Samoa to Destiny," and behind it is the **Lands and Titles Court,** which reviews village council decisions, disagreements over customary lands, and *matai* title disputes.

At the end of the Mulinu'u Peninsula is the **Apia Observatory,** founded by the Germans in 1902. After the unexpected hurricane of 1889, the Germans weren't taking any more chances. Note the many impressive **royal tombs** of former paramount chiefs both here and down the road to the left. Mulinu'u is the heartland of modern Samoan history.

Vailima

In 1889, Robert Louis Stevenson, Scottish author of the adventure classic *Treasure Island,* purchased

REVEREND JOHN WILLIAMS

Credit for converting the Samoans to Christianity and establishing the Congregational Church in both Samoas goes to Rev. John Williams (1796-1839) of the London Missionary Society. In 1817 the young missionary and his wife Mary arrived at Tahiti, but the next year they shifted to Raiatea in the Leeward Islands, and this served as Williams' base for many years. With the help of native teachers, Williams spread his faith to Aitutaki (1821) and Rarotonga (1823) in the Cook Islands. At Rarotonga his converts constructed a ship, the *Messenger of Peace*, which Williams sailed to Samoa in 1830, landing at Sapapali'i on Savai'i. He happened to arrive at an auspicious moment, as a female prophet named Nafanua had predicted the coming of strangers bringing a new faith. The chief of Savai'i, Malietoa Vainu'upo, was receptive, and in 1832 Williams returned from Raiatea with Polynesian missionaries who stayed to teach the meaning of the new doctrine. This westward penetration of Williams' Tahiti-based London Missionary Society, or *Lotu Ta'iti*, was resented by the Tongans, who looked upon Samoa as their sphere of interest, and thus best evangelized by Wesleyanism or the *Lotu Toga*. A "gentlemen's agreement" between the parent churches in England led to several Wesleyan (or Methodist) missionaries—who had first visited Samoa two years before Williams—being recalled, much to the displeasure of the King of Tonga. Williams, meanwhile, had himself returned to England where he wrote a book, raised funds for his mission, and had a new ship constructed, the *Camden*. In 1838 he was back, setting up a fresh base at Malie on northern Upolu. In 1839 he sailed west again on what was to be his last voyage, for in 1839 he was killed and eaten by cannibals as he attempted to land on Erromango Island in the New Hebrides, today Vanuatu. Local tradition holds that his bones were later collected and reburied below the porch of the Congregational Church in Apia.

approximately 162 hectares of bushland at the foot of Mt. Vaea, three and a half km inland from Apia and high above the sea, for US$4,000. Stevenson named the place Vailima, meaning "five waters," for the small streams that ran across the property, and here he built his home and spent the last five years of his life.

During a power struggle between rival Samoan factions, some chiefs were imprisoned at Mulinu'u. Stevenson visited them in confinement, and to show their gratitude, these chiefs built him a road up to Vailima when they were released. The Samoans called Stevenson Tusitala, or "Teller of Tales." On December 3, 1894, at the age of 44, Stevenson suffered a fatal brain hemorrhage while helping his wife Fanny prepare dinner. He's buried just below the summit of Mt. Vaea, overlooking Vailima, as he'd requested.

The stately mansion with its beautiful tropical gardens was first sold to a retired German businessman, then bought by the German government as the official residence of their governor. Of the present complex, Stevenson had the central building erected in 1890, and in 1891-1892, the east wing was added to provide proper quarters for his mother. The Germans built the westernmost wing in 1897. The N.Z. regime took it over when they assumed power in 1914, and until the 1990s Villa Vailima was Government House, official residence of Samoa's head of state.

In early 1992, after Hurricane Val did serious damage to Vailima, Mormon businessmen from Utah and Arizona obtained a 60-year lease on the property with the intention of creating a museum. The complex was largely rebuilt, and in 1994 the **Robert Louis Stevenson Museum** (tel. 20-798) opened on the centenary of the writer's death. You'll be led through a series of bedrooms dedicated to various members of the Stevenson family, but all of the furniture and heirlooms on display are replicas except for three chairs and a few books. Temporary exhibits are housed in a gallery upstairs in the west wing and you may visit these on your own after the tour. There's a marvelous view from the breezy upper verandah.

A bit east of the Stevenson mansion is a smaller red-roofed house once occupied by a son of the head of state. Outside this building is an old-fashioned mahogany steering wheel inscribed "Fear God and Honor the King, Samoa 1889."

SAMOA

This is from the British ship *Calliope,* the only one to survive the naval debacle of that year. Britain donated the wheel to Samoa when the ship was broken up after WW II.

Entry to the museum grounds is free with admission to the house, S$15 for adults and S$5 for children under 11. It's open weekdays 0900–1600, Saturday 0900–1200, with the last tour commencing 30 minutes before closing.

In 1978, a **Botanical Garden Reserve** with a loop trail was established at the bottom of the hill adjoining Vailima. Adjacent is a pool for swimming and a small waterfall (dry except during the rainy months). The hiking trail up to Stevenson's grave on Mt. Vaea begins here, and both it and the gardens are open 24 hours, admission free. The hourly Avele or Vaoala buses (S$1.20) will bring you directly here from the markets, otherwise a taxi should cost around S$12.

Mount Vaea

An almost obligatory pilgrimage for all visitors to Samoa is the 45-minute climb along a winding trail to the tomb of Robert Louis Stevenson, just below the 475-meter summit of Mt. Vaea. After the small bridge turn left. Five hundred meters up, the trail divides with a shorter, steeper way to the right and a much longer less-used trail to the left. A good plan is to go up by the short trail and come back down the longer way. After rains, the trail can get muddy.

The path to the top was cut by 200 sorrowful Samoans as they carried the famous writer's body up to its final resting place in 1894. From the tomb there's a sweeping panorama of the verdant valley to the east with the misty mountains of Upolu beyond, and in the distance the white line of surf breaking endlessly on the reef. The red roof of Vailima directly below is clearly visible. This is the best bird-watching venue around Apia. It's utterly still—a peaceful, poignant, lonely place. Stevenson's requiem reads:

Under the wide and starry sky,
Dig the grave and let me lie.
Glad did I live and gladly die,
And I laid me down with a will.

This be the verse you grave for me:
Here he lies where he longed to be;
Home is the sailor, home from the sea,
And the hunter home from the hill.

Stevenson's wife Fanny died in California in 1914, and a year later her ashes were brought back to Samoa and buried at the foot of her husband's grave. The bronze plaque bears her Samoan name, Aolele, and the words of Stevenson:

Teacher, tender comrade, wife,
A fellow-farer true through life
Heart-whole and soul free,
The August Father gave to me.

Side Trip East

Buses marked Falefa, Falevao, and Lufilufi depart the Apia markets every hour or so for Falefa, 29 km east (you can also pick up these buses on Matautu Street). You'll get many fine views of Upolu's north coast as you pass along one of Upolu's finest summer surfing beaches, Lauli'i, a long right point break (beware of undertow). No barrier reef breaks the waves that crash onto these black sandy shores. Change rooms and showers (S$1 pp) are provided at **Saoluafata Beach,** but no visitors are allowed on Sunday.

A km east of Saoluafata Beach is Piula Theological College with the superb **Piula Cave Pool,** a natural freshwater pool fed by a spring directly below a large Methodist church. The water is unusually clear, despite all the carefree locals soaping up and washing clothes in it. Swim into the cave below the church. This is connected to a second cave by a small underwater opening on the left near the back. The second cave is long, dark, and deep, but can be explored with a mask and snorkel. The pool is open Monday to Saturday 0800–1630, admission S$2, and there are changing rooms. If you leave Apia in the morning you'll have time for a swim in the pool before catching a midday bus to the beach *fale* at Lalomanu or Lepa (ask).

Falefa Falls, two km east of Piula through Falefa village, is impressive during the rainy season and it's freely visible beside the road. The Falefa bus (S$2) turns around here.

Side Trip Southwest

Catch an hourly Seesee, Siusega, or Tafaigata bus (S$1.30) at the markets and ask the driver to drop you at the closest point to **Papase'ea Sliding Rocks.** You can also come on the Alafua bus to the University of the South Pacific (see below), but this will add about 15 minutes to your walking time. Even from the closest bus stop you'll still have to hike uphill two km and pay S$2 admission (don't give the money to children—only to the adult at the entrance). You slide down three rocks into freshwater pools—don't forget your bathing suit. It's open daily (Sunday included!).

At Alafua, below and to the east of this area, is the 30-hectare Samoan campus of the **University of the South Pacific** (the main campus is in Fiji). In 1977, the university's School of Agriculture was established here, with assistance from New Zealand. To the left of the main gate is an agricultural training center funded by the European Union. The university's two semesters run from February to the end of June and late July to mid-November. The university library (tel. 21-671) is open weekdays 0800–1200 and 1300–1600. In 1997, the campus of the National University of Samoa (www.nus.edu.ws) was established with Japanese assistance on the opposite side of Apia. The NUS has no connection to the USP, and its courses are oriented more toward Samoan studies, teacher training, and nursing.

On the way back to Apia notice the site of the **Apia Samoa Temple** (1983) on the airport highway. The Church of Jesus Christ of Latter-day Saints established its Samoan headquarters here in 1902, but in 2003 the temple burned to the ground as a result of undisclosed causes. A golden idol of the angel Moroni was saved, as it had been removed prior to the fire. Just a few minutes' walk west along the highway from the temple site is the impressive four-tier **tomb of Tupua Tamasese Lealofi III,** the slain Mau Movement leader.

Beer lovers might like to visit the **Vailima Brewery** at Vaitele on the road to the airport. You'll only be allowed in at 1000 on Thursday, and it's a good idea to call the Personnel Manager (tel. 20-200) beforehand to make sure he'll be available for a tour. Plenty of buses run out this way (including those marked Afega, Faleula, Puipa'a, Toamua, Vaigaga, Vaiusu, or Vaitele).

Central Upolu

For a bit of heavy hiking, catch a Mulivai, Salani, Sapunaoa, Siumu, or Vaovai bus up the Cross Island Highway to a turnoff on the right for **Lake Lanoto'o,** otherwise known as "Goldfish Lake," high in the center of Upolu at 590 meters above sea level. Walk straight west on the dirt access road for just under an hour until the road turns left (south). From here a sign and then red marks on trees should point the way west to the lake, another one-hour walk. When you arrive at a destroyed microwave reflector on top of a hill, the lake is just below you on the left.

The poorly marked way takes a bit of intuition to find and some of the locals living on the main road to the trail ask exorbitant fees such as S$40 to act as guides. There's no admission fee to the lake, and if you take your time and are good at finding your own way, you'll be okay. The route to the lake is very muddy following heavy rains, so only go after a couple of days of sunny weather. Expect fallen trees across the route and some confusion toward the end. This is a *very* strenuous hike, so be prepared. In 2003, Lake Lanoto'o was declared Samoa's second national park, so the trails and signposting should improve.

The opaque green waters of this seldom-visited crater lake are surrounded by mossy green bush dripping from the mist. Swimming in the lake is an eerie experience. To add to the otherworldliness of the place, Lake Lanoto'o is full of goldfish, but you'll have to wait patiently if you want to see any from shore (bring along bread to feed to them). This hike is ideal for seeing Upolu's high-altitude vegetation without going too far from town, but sturdy shoes and long pants are essential.

On your way back to Apia stop to visit the **Baha'i House of Worship** (1984), Mother Temple to all Baha'is in the region. The temple is at Tiapapata, eight km from Apia and a 30-minute walk down the highway from the Lanoto'o turnoff. The monumental dome soars 30 meters above the surrounding area and has nine sides, symbolizing the unity of the nine major religions of the world. Inside, the latticework of ribs forms a nine-pointed star at the apex of the dome. The seating is arranged facing the Holy Land (Israel) because this is the final resting place of Baha 'Ullah (1817–1892), Prophet-Founder of the Baha'i Faith. This majestic building, funded by Baha'is around the world, is open to all for prayer and meditation daily 0900–1700. Also visit the information center (tel. 24-192), to the left as you approach the temple. The Vaoala bus comes to within a 30-minute walk of the temple.

SPORTS AND RECREATION
Palolo Deep
One of Apia's nicest attractions is the **Palolo Deep Marine Reserve** (daily 0800–1800, admission S$2), a natural reef aquarium operated by the Division of Environment and Conservation. The signposted entrance to the reserve is near the main wharf at Matautu; in fact, the Deep's main draw is its convenience to Apia. You can easily wade out to the Deep at low tide if you have something to protect your feet. Although the reef has been heavily damaged by hurricanes, much of the coral has regenerated and there are plenty of colorful fish. Even if you don't intend to swim, the reserve garden is a very nice place to sit and read with lots of benches and relaxing lagoon views. This place is so peaceful it's hard to believe you're just a five-minute walk from the center of a capital city. The helpful staff do their best to serve visitors, but they also let you relax in privacy. Facilities include toilets, showers, and changing rooms. You can rent snorkeling gear (S$10) and buy cold soft drinks (no beer). The Deep is a perfect escape on Sunday—make an afternoon of it.

Scuba Diving
Moana Divers (Foua and Logo Toloa, tel./fax 24-858, www.divesamoa.ws), upstairs at Pasefika Inn, charges S$140/210 for one/two tank dives including gear. Their open-water certification course is S$990. Overnight dive packages to Aleipata are S$500 including two tanks, an ecotour, *fale* accommodations, and meals. One-week safaris to Tokelau can be arranged.

Pacific Quest Divers (Roger Christman, tel./fax 24-728, www.dive.ws), beside the Seaside Inn, offers sport fishing and kayak tours, as well as scuba diving (S$138/175 for one/two tanks). A no-experience introductory dive is S$225, and you can do a PADI or IDEA certification course for S$930.

Many of the reefs off Upolu's north coast have been damaged by hurricanes and local poachers who use dynamite or a type of poison to bring up fish, so the south coast is now favored for its calmer seas and variety of attractions. The reef channels teem with fish, best seen on an incoming tide. **Nu'usafe'e Island** just off Poutasi is a favorite for its coral heads, wavy coral, and variety of fishlife (including harmless sand sharks). You can hand-feed the tame fish. Five lava chutes penetrate 10–25 meters and open into clear water. If that sounds good, try going down the main lava chute at Lefaga through a strong current as the surf roars overhead, then over the edge of the reef. This is for experienced divers only.

Other good spots are the drop-offs at Nu'utele and Nu'ulua Islands in Aleipata, the western reef areas off Manono, and the edge of the barrier reef, three km offshore from Lalomalava, Savai'i.

Other Activities
Samoa Marine (tel. 23-898, fax 25-962, www.fishing.ws), near the Seaside Inn, offers deep sea fishing for marlin, mahimahi, wahoo, yellowfin, skipjack, and dog tooth tuna at S$925/1,550 a half/full day for up to three persons. This firm isn't there only for tourists: If nobody charters their powerboat, the *Ole Pe'a*, they'll often go out anyway in the hope of catching enough fish for sale on the local market to make it worth their while. Their guarantee is "no fish, no pay!"

Sea kayaking tours to the tiny islands off both ends of Upolu are offered by **Island Explorer** (Mats Arvidsson, tel. 22-401, fax 26-941, www.islandexplorer.ws). It's S$165 for a day tour, S$360 for an overnight tour, or S$190 per day for a multiday tour all inclusive.

The 18-hole golf course of the **Royal Samoa Country Club** (tel. 20-120) is just beyond Fagali'i Airport east of Apia (Fagali'i-uta bus). The clubhouse bar has a pleasant balcony overlooking the course and the sea—recommended for an

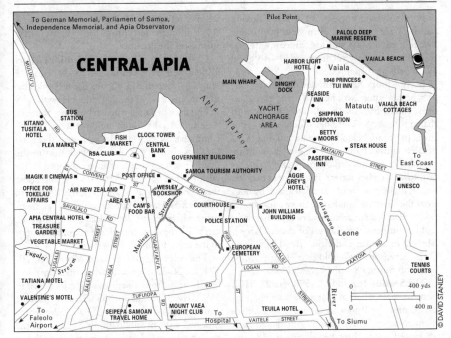

To German Memorial, Parliament of Samoa, Independence Memorial, and Apia Observatory

Pilot Point

CENTRAL APIA

PALOLO DEEP MARINE RESERVE

HARBOR LIGHT HOTEL · Vaiala

VAIALA BEACH

MAIN WHARF · DINGHY DOCK

1848 PRINCESS TUI INN

Apia Harbor

SEASIDE INN

Matautu

VAIALA BEACH COTTAGES

YACHT ANCHORAGE AREA

SHIPPING CORPORATION

BUS STATION

KITANO TUSITALA HOTEL

FLEA MARKET

FISH MARKET

CLOCK TOWER

CENTRAL BANK

RSA CLUB

GOVERNMENT BUILDING

SAMOA TOURISM AUTHORITY

BETTY MOORS

MATAUTU

STEAK HOUSE

To East Coast

PASEFIKA INN

STREET

MAGIK II CINEMAS

OFFICE FOR TOKELAU AFFAIRS

CONVENT

POST OFFICE

WESLEY BOOKSHOP

AIR NEW ZEALAND

AREA 51

CAM'S FOOD BAR

BEACH RD

COURTHOUSE

POLICE STATION

JOHN WILLIAMS BUILDING

AGGIE GREY'S HOTEL

UNESCO

Vaisigano

Leone

APIA CENTRAL HOTEL

TREASURE GARDEN

VEGETABLE MARKET

SAVALALO

STREET

SALEUFI

STREET

VAEA

Mulivai

Togafuafua

Stream

PIPE RD

EUROPEAN CEMETERY

LOGAN RD

TALELEU

STREET

FAATOIA RD

TENNIS COURTS

Fugalei

Fugalei Stream

TATIANA MOTEL

VALENTINE'S MOTEL

To Faleolo Airport

TUFUIOPA

SEIPEPA SAMOAN TRAVEL HOME

MOUNT VAEA NIGHT CLUB

To Hospital

TEUILA HOTEL

VAITELE STREET

To Siumu

River

0   400 yds

0   400 m

© DAVID STANLEY

---

afternoon drink. The course is open to non-members daily except Saturday (open to all on Sunday). Tuesday is Ladies Day with tee-off at 1330 and 1430. Greens fees are S$20. The big tournaments of the year are the Head of State Tournament in early January and the Samoa Open in late June or early July.

Saturday afternoons see exciting rugby or soccer from the grandstand at **Apia Park.** The main rugby season is February for "sevens" and July to November for league rugby. You shouldn't miss a chance to see a game by the famous national team, Manu Samoa. The gymnasium at Apia Park (a gift of the People's Republic of China for the 1983 South Pacific Games) hosts basketball (Tuesday and Thursday at 1700), badminton (Wednesday and Friday at 1900), and volleyball (Saturday from May to July) in the gym.

The **tennis courts** behind Apia Park are open to the public daily (nightly until 2200; S$5 pp an hour, plus S$10 an hour for night lights). The **Apia Squash Center** (tel. 20-554) is next to the Seaside Inn.

Kirikiti (cricket) is played mostly in rural villages at 1400 on Saturday throughout the year with the competition season July to September. Other traditional sports include *igavea* (hide and seek), *lape* (handball), *sioga afi* (fire making), and *oagapopo* (coconut husking).

ACCOMMODATIONS

Under US$25

The **Seipepa Samoan Travel Home** (tel./fax 25-447, www.samoa-experience.com), off Vaitele St. near the Mount Vaea Club, is an oasis of peace just a 10-minute walk from the city center. It's sort of like living in the middle of a village while still enjoying some privacy. There are four fan-cooled rooms with shared bath in a European-style house and six Samoan *fale* in the garden, three of them with an upper and lower floor! The overnight charge is whatever you wish to pay (offer at least S$35 pp) and includes a large tropical breakfast served Samoan style. Singles must be prepared to share or pay S$60 for a single room or *fale*. Cooking facilities are provided. Run by a hospitable Swede named Mats and his Samoan wife Sia, this place is highly recommended—so good all 20 beds are often full.

Betty Moors Accommodation (tel./fax 21-085, bettys@samoa.ws), just before the gas station on Matautu St., has 13 cell-like cubicles with shared bath at S$30/50 single/double. Ask about the better room behind the main building. Out of safety considerations, no cooking facilities are provided in this wooden building (also no breakfast, towels, or hot water). If you come back on foot at night, beware of a sudden attack by dogs from the adjacent launderette (have a few stones ready). Betty's an interesting person to chat with, and her husband was the son of trader Harry J. Moors, an adviser and close friend of Robert Louis Stevenson. She'll hold excess luggage while you're off touring Savai'i or south Upolu.

The **Seaside Inn** (tel. 22-578, fax 22-918), near the main wharf at Matautu, has a good location near the Palolo Deep and is also convenient to town. Three rooms with shared bath are rented out as three-bed dorms at S$32 pp. The 11 rooms with private bath are S$60/70/85 single/double/triple, and there's also a larger unit with fridge in the rear garden that costs a few *tala* more. The rooms aren't entirely soundproof and they're sometimes rented out to couples with "night exercise" on their minds. The rates include a uniform breakfast (served 0700–0900 only), and communal cooking facilities are available (shortage of utensils). A small bar is attached and there's a nice veranda overlooking the harbor. This place is usually full of travelers and it's a good place to meet people, although the toilets could use a cleaning. Occasional water problems are another drawback, and don't leave things lying around as there have been several reports of petty theft from the rooms. Lock your door at night. Car rentals are arranged and bicycles are available at S$20/22 a day to guests/nonguests.

Almost opposite the entrance to the main wharf at Matautu is the two-story **Harbour Light Hotel** (tel. 21-103). Its 18 motel-style rooms with private bath are S$66 single or double with fan or S$77 air-conditioned. There's

24-hour service and it's well worth a try if you arrive late on the ferry from Pago Pago. A small store is on the premises.

On the other side of town, **Valentine's Motel** (Valentine Parker, tel./fax 22-158, valentine@ samoa.ws), opposite JT's Sports Bar at Fugalei, has nine rooms at S$30/60 single/double on the airy second floor of an old wooden building. Showers, toilets, and a TV room are downstairs, but no communal cooking facilities are provided (a good breakfast is S$7 pp). A new block next to the main street has a couple of air-conditioned rooms with private bath at S$100 double and some three-bed dorms at S$25 pp (rarely crowded). There's a nice lawn out back where you can sunbathe whenever the sky is clear and maybe even camp. It's the most convenient accommodations to the vegetable market bus station.

The colonial-style **Tatiana Motel** (tel. 20-171, fax 26-829, www.tatiana-motel.com), just up the street from Valentine's Motel, opened in 1999. The 37 rooms are S$53/78 single/double with fan and shared bath, S$107/132 air-conditioned with private bath, or S$25 pp in the three garden *fale,* breakfast and tax included. A common kitchen is provided. A more upmarket annex at Tanugamanono up near the Robert Louis Stevenson Museum has 13 air-conditioned rooms starting at S$110/135 single/double.

US$25–50

The **Pasefika Inn** (tel. 20-971, fax 23-303, www .pasefikainn.ws), on Matautu St., has 26 rooms in a three-story building. Most rooms are air-conditioned with a fridge and access to common cooking facilities, and begin at S$135 single or double, plus S$34 extra if you want a balcony. Seven budget rooms without air conditioning are S$93 double. Breakfast is included in all rates, but to be frank, this place is overpriced.

Facing breezy Vaiala Beach is the 12-room **1848 Princess Tui Inn** (Alesi and George Hadley, tel. 23-432, fax 22-451, www.princesstui.ws), a six-minute walk from the main wharf. It occupies a stately old mansion built for Jonas Coe, the first American consul and father of the legendary "Queen Emma" (a plantation owner in New Guinea and the subject of several books). Room rates are S$70/85 single/double with fan and shared bath to S$95/105 with air conditioning or private bath, breakfast and tax included. Ocean-view rooms are S$105 double. A bed in one of the two dorms is S$32. Facilities include a communal kitchen and fridge, lounge, bar, mosquito nets, luggage storage, and a washing machine (S$8 a load). The sea views from the front lounge are very nice, and you'll enjoy sitting on the steps in the evening chatting with other guests. At night people staying here are often bitten on their way back from town by dogs from nearby houses, so consider taking a taxi.

Aniva's Place (Aniva and Bob Slater, tel./fax 23-431, anivas@lesamoa.net), not far from the National Hospital at Moto'otua, offers 12 fan-cooled rooms at S$95/115/135 single/double/triple including breakfast (plus S$20 for air-conditioning). Although this two-story building is clean and new, these prices are a bit high for accommodations with shared bath. There's a common kitchen, lounge, and swimming pool.

The **Samoan Outrigger Hotel** (Claus Hermansen, tel./fax 20-042, www.outrigger.net firms.com), on Moto'otua Road up near the National Hospital, is one of the best backpackers' hostels in the South Pacific. Rooms in this renovated colonial building are S$70/80 single/double with shared bath, S$80/100 with private bath, S$100/120 air-conditioned, or S$35 pp in the dorm, breakfast and tax included. Only couples are allowed to share the double rooms, and there are other rules and regulations. Facilities include a communal kitchen and fridge, lounge, bar, swimming pool, garden, and laundry facilities. A variety of excellent sightseeing tours are offered in the hotel minibus and car rentals can be arranged. Ask for their minibus at the airport.

Visiting academics might choose the **South Sea Star Hotel** (tel. 76-996, letagaloa@yahoo.com), at Alafua near the entrance to the University of the South Pacific. The 24 fan-cooled rooms with shared bath are S$100/120 single/double, almost double that with private bath and fridge, plus 12.5 percent tax. The minimum stay is two nights and there are weekly and monthly discounts. This two-story building (no sign) in a garden setting is accessible on the reg-ular Alafua bus. A free breakfast is included, but only if you request it. It's forbidden to consume alcohol in the rooms.

US$50–100

Apia Central Hotel (tel./fax 20-782, ahkams@lesamoa.net), formerly known as Ah Kam's Full-moon Inn, on Savalalo Rd. in downtown Apia, has three fan-cooled rooms at S$104/145/182 single/double/triple and 22 air-conditioned rooms at S$140/160/180. All rooms in this two-story motel have a mini-fridge and TV, and there's a nice little bar in the courtyard.

The Japanese-owned **Kitano Tusitala Hotel** (tel. 21-122, fax 23-652, www.kitano.ws), at the beginning of the Mulinu'u Peninsula, is a complex of two-story blocks containing 92 tatty but clean air-conditioned rooms with private bath in four categories, beginning at S$235/262 double/triple, including breakfast and tax. The open *fale* architecture of the main buildings is appealing, and perhaps because it's a little disorganized, the atmosphere is surprisingly relaxed. Mosquitoes permitting, the poolside bar is a pleasant place to visit in the afternoon or early evening, and the snack bar serves good food at reasonable prices (though the breakfast is very ordinary). Expect the waiters to try to shortchange you or to ask for a "loan" or a free trip to America. There's more local flavor than at Aggie's, just don't expect everything to work perfectly. For example, don't count on receiving your telephone messages or having your faxes go out. Occasionally, overseas Samoans throw all-night parties in the rooms and the night manager may be unwilling to try to control these regular guests just to please a one-time tourist like you.

A bit farther up the breezy Mulinu'u Peninsula is the three-story **Millenia Hotel** (Antonia Ah Him, tel. 28-284, fax 28-285, www.hotelmilleniasamoa.com) with 19 air-conditioned rooms from S$180 double including tropical breakfast. The Millenia has a large lounge and a good restaurant/bar (try Delilah's Bloody Mary). From Wednesday to Saturday there could be noise from an adjacent nightclub.

The two-story **Samoa Holiday Hotel** (tel. 28-017, fax 28-018, samoaholiday@lesamoa.net), on Moamoa Road two km south of the center, has 16 air-conditioned units with cooking facilities and TV at S$160/176 single/double.

The **Vaiala Beach Cottages** (tel. 22-202, fax 22-008, vaialabeach@samoa.ws), facing the lagoon at Vaiala, offers seven pleasant, fan-cooled bungalows with cooking facilities and fridge at S$200/230/260 single/double/triple, plus 12.5 percent tax. Children 12 and under are free. Discounts are possible for long stays if you book directly, but bookings made through a travel agent or airline are 10 percent higher. The aggressive guard dogs of this neighborhood make it unwise to walk back here from town late at night, so take a taxi.

The two-story **Teuila Hotel** (tel. 23-959, fax 23-935, teuila@lesamoa.net), on Vaitele St. opposite the Teachers College, has 15 air-conditioned rooms with fridge and private bath at S$135/195/255 single/double/triple, breakfast included.

US$100–150

Apia's premier tourist hotel, **Aggie Grey's** (tel. 22-880, fax 23-626, www.aggiegreys.com), on the east side of the harbor, originated in March 1942 as a hamburger stand catering to U.S. servicemen stationed in the area. Aggie's son Alan has continued the tradition of catering to American tastes, although the hotel lost some of its original South Seas atmosphere when the main waterfront building was reconstructed in mock-colonial style in 1989. The 156 rooms begin at S$292/308/325 single/double/triple in the old section around the pool. The 26 tightly packed bungalows are about S$62 more, rooms in the main lobby wing 50 percent more, the two suites 100 percent more. The cheaper rooms are rather shabby and stuffy, but the expensive ones facing the harbor are quite luxurious. Children under 16 are not allowed in the new wing or suites, but a fourth person in the old wing is S$15 regardless of age. Add 12.5 percent tax to these prices, and if you pay by credit card expect to have your bill inflated slightly due to the unfavorable exchange rates previously discussed. The restaurant lays out a very good buffet breakfast (S$25), and even if you aren't staying here, it's worth visiting for an afternoon coffee and pastry. Weekly events include the barbecue on Sunday night and the Samoan feast on Wednesday. Aggie's is often full of dull business guests and rather bored conference participants, but the bar is nice and there's even an island in the large swimming pool!

The three-story **Hotel Insel Fehmarn** (tel. 23-301, fax 22-204, insel@samoa.ws), up Falealili St. in Moto'otua, has 54 rooms at S$256/290/324 single/double/triple. Each air-conditioned unit has a fridge, full cooking facilities, video/TV, balcony, and private bath. The Insel Fehmarn caters to business travelers: typing, photocopying, email, and fax services are available. A swimming pool, tennis courts, guest launderette, restaurant, and bar are on the premises. Apia's top pizzeria is right across the street and there are several car rental agencies nearby offering good rates. This well-managed hotel is a good alternative to Aggie's and the Tusitala for those who want value for money. Ask for a room on the top floor for panoramic views.

Beach Fale East of Apia

The closest village-run beach resort to Apia is **Saoluafata Beach Fales** (tel. 40-317) on a nice beach near the Piula Cave Pool, 26 km east of Apia. To sleep in one of the three *fale* here costs S$25 pp, plus S$10 per meal. Picnickers pay S$1 pp. It's a good choice for a taste of this lifestyle without the long trip to Aleipata. Surfers come in summer (Dec.–Mar.) for the reef break right-hander, 90 meters off nearby Faleapuna. The Falefa, Falevao, and Lufilufi buses from the markets pass here.

FOOD
Budget

The food stalls at Apia's vegetable and flea markets are the cheapest places to eat (S$3–5), and it's hard to beat a breakfast of hot chocolate *(koko)* with buttered bread, or a large bowl of cocoa and rice. Surprisingly, there's quite a bit here for vegetarians, including *palusami* and roasted breadfruit. Less healthy barbecue takeaway meals (S$5) are available at several roadside locations around town. If available, *oka* (raw fish) is a better choice than the mutton flaps.

Skippy's (tel. 25-050; closed Sun.), in the arcade beside the Westpac Bank on Beach Rd., has fish and chips, hamburgers, and other rather fatty local meals.

Many of Apia's cheapest eateries are near the corner of Vaea and Convent Streets, most of them open only until 1600 weekdays and 1300 Saturday. Here you'll find **Betty's Restaurant,** which dishes out huge lunches to huge Samoans, but you'll need a strong stomach to join them. **Pinati's** (tel. 24-248), next to Betty's, has no sign outside and no menu inside, but the large crowd of locals tells you it's something good. There are only a few choices, including curry, chop suey, fish, and chicken, all around S$3 a big plate.

A step up is the **Gourmet Seafood and Grill** (tel. 24-625; Mon.–Sat. 0700–2200), on Convent St. a block back from the Chief Post Office, with lunch specials, sashimi, fried fish, and steaks. While the food certainly isn't "gourmet," the nautical decor is rather pleasant and their burgers are said to be the best in town (certainly more appealing than the predictable products doled out at the nearby McDonald's). You must pay the cashier first and get a number.

More Samoan-style fast food is scooped out at **Cam's Food Bar** (tel. 22-629; weekdays 0800–2100, Sat. 0800–1700), a block and a half behind the Chief Post Office (check the map). Cam's is great for lunch, passable at breakfast, but overpriced at dinner. The *oka* (raw fish) is a great bargain at S$2.70.

An Apia institution is **Maua's Restaurant and Takeaway** (tel. 23-942), near the Seaside Inn on Beach Road. A plate of grilled meat or fish and chips will around S$5. It's even open on Sunday.

Chinese

Apia insiders reckon that the finest Chinese food in town is served at the **Hua Mei Restaurant** (tel. 25-598; Mon.–Sat. 0800–2200, Sun. 0800–midnight), upstairs in the Lotemau Center behind Air New Zealand. The lunch specials are inexpensive and there's a good medium-priced dinner menu.

Substantial Chinese meals are served at the

Treasure Garden Restaurant (tel. 22-586; weekdays 1100–1400 and 1700–2200, Sat. 1700–2200) on Fugalei St. near the vegetable market. Although the food is good, the noisy TV set in the dining room is jarring and the air conditioning may give you a chill. On Sunday (0930–1200) all you can get is takeaways from the counter outside (always a good option if you've rented a car and want to carry a cheap dinner back to your hotel).

International Cuisine

Some of Apia's finest dining is available at **Sails Restaurant and Bar** (tel. 20-628, www.sails.ws; Mon.–Sat. 0900–2300, Sun. 1800–2300), above Fale Tifaga Tauese Mini Cinemas on Beach Road. Their airy terrace provides pleasing harbor views to complement the fancy seafood, steaks, pastas, and sashimi, just count on paying at least S$25/40 pp for lunch/dinner here. Proprietors Ian and Livia Black managed top hotels in Tahiti and Fiji before settling in Apia. Thanks to Samoa's location next to the international date line, Sails can claim to be the last restaurant in the world to close every day. The wooden restaurant building itself was built by trader Harry Moors, and Robert Louis Stevenson himself stayed here before Vailima was built.

The **Rainforest Restaurant** (tel. 25-736; weekdays 0900–1630 and 1800–2200), nearby on Beach Rd., really lives up to its name, with the wood shavings on the floor and potted plants. It's run by a Swiss/German couple named Barbara and Christian. They usually open weekdays only, serving breakfast and lunch 0900–1630, dinner from 1800 until late. You can also get handicrafts, postcards, and local guidebooks here.

Readers have recommended the **Look Out Restaurant** (tel. 24-065, weekdays 0700–2200, Sat. 0700–midnight, Sun. 1800–2100), on Beach Road next to Molesi Samoa Shop and not far from Aggie Grey's Hotel. The lobsters are *large* but the coffee is terrible. Main courses average S$15–22.

The **Steak House** (tel. 22-962; closed Sun.), on Matautu St. just east of the Mormon church, grills quality cuts at fair prices.

The **Apaula Heights Restaurant** (tel. 20-836; Tues.–Fri. 1600–midnight, Sat. noon–midnight),

SAMOA

on the lower slopes of Mt. Vaea up a winding road from the Mount Vaea Nightclub, serves upscale meals, including steaks and lobster, and the deserts and cocktails are excellent. It's best to come just before sunset to enjoy the wonderful view. There are about 30 steep steps up to the restaurant, which would be inconvenient for elderly or disabled people.

Giordano's Pizzeria (tel. 25-985; Tues.–Sat. 1500–2200, Sun. 1700–2100), near the Hotel Insel Fehmarn on the road connecting the National Hospital to the Cross Island Rd., has the best pizza in town and the candlelit courtyard dining area is agreeable.

Mangoes Bar & Grill (tel. 73-456; daily 1100–2300), on the Cross Island Rd. between the Hotel Insel Fehmarn and the Robert Louis Stevenson Museum, offers grilled meats on an outside terrace with a great view. The salad bar is excellent and the deserts are just fine.

Lighter Fare

The **Cappuccino Vineyard** (tel. 22-049; Mon.–Sat. 0700–2200), on Beach Rd. in the mall behind the National Bank of Samoa, is a trendy Internet café with specialty coffee, pastries, and upscale appetizers like sashimi, oysters, wings, satay, and American-style hamburgers. There's occasionally jazz in the evening. You can check email on the computers here.

Le Moana Café (tel. 24-828; weekdays 0730–2130, Sat. 0730–1400 and 1830–2130), in the Lotemau Center off Convent St. behind Air New Zealand, prepares good medium-priced meals and is also nice for a coffee.

Gensil's Ice Cream Parlor (tel. 74-342; weekdays 0600–1630, Sat. 0600–1200), on the back side of the Lotemau Center off Vaea St., has real two-scoop cones for S$2.50, plus milk shakes, sundaes, and banana splits. It's also good for breakfast.

Sunday

Sundays from 1200–1400, the Stevenson Restaurant at the **Hotel Kitano Tusitala** lays out an international buffet with lots of Samoan delicacies (S$36).

Another option is the *to'onai* served around noon on Sunday at the **Pasefika Inn.** For S$40 you can eat as much *umu*-baked Samoan specialties as you wish.

For Sunday night dinner consider the poolside barbecue at **Aggie Grey's Hotel,** which offers a good selection of Samoan dishes for S$45. There's no traditional dancing, but a corny hotel band is on the stage.

ENTERTAINMENT

Apia's top movie theater is **Magik II Cinemas** (tel. 28-126, www.magikcinemas.ws) on Convent St. which opened in 2001. Screenings in its two cinema halls begin at 1000 Monday to Saturday and from 1700 on Sunday (admission S$6). Several smaller cinemas around show downmarket adventure and romance videos.

Weekday mornings at 0750 the police band marches up Beach Road to the Government Building for the flag-raising ceremony at 0800, and all traffic is stopped. Church choirs are worth a listen on Sunday mornings (dress neatly and avoid bright clothing or shorts).

Nightclubs

The most popular club these days is **Area 51** opposite the Lotemau Center on Vaea Street. It gets extremely hot inside and there's often no place to sit. Upstairs is **Eye Spy** (tel. 20-805), a more expensive club popular among expats. After closing, beware of bottles being thrown into the street from up there.

The roughest place is the **Mount Vaea Nightclub** (tel. 21-627) on Vaitele St., open Monday to Saturday 1900–midnight, Apia's meet market since 1968. It's fast and loud with the best band in town, and there are lots of boys/girls. Things don't get going until late, and drunks often spin into squabbles, so stay out of the middle and be really polite to everyone. The trouble is usually between local Samoans, rarely tourists, and the huge bouncers intervene quickly.

As elsewhere in the South Pacific, places like this can be challenging for women. Many problematical situations revolve around the Samoan "nightclub custom" of asking any female to dance who is not currently dancing, whether she came with a date or not. It can be taken as an insult to say no in this situation, so a female who only wants to dance with her date must dance every dance with him or be bombarded with requests she cannot lightly refuse. Otherwise she can say that her foot hurts and forgo dancing with anyone, including her date.

The *fa'afefine* (transvestites) usually come in groups, so either they're somewhere or they're not. Drunken palagis often mistake them for women. The *crowd* also seems to shift from week to week.

At midnight the police begin making the rounds of the clubs and bars closing everything down, and by 0100 the city is dead. Everything except the hotel bars is tightly shut on Sunday and that day you're supposed to be a hotel guest to be drinking there.

Bars

Apia's favorite watering hole is the **RSA Club** (tel. 20-171; Mon.–Sat. 0900–midnight) on Beach Rd. in the center of Apia. The inexpensive food bar here is open the same hours (though closed on Monday and Tuesday). Whenever there's live music it's *loud*. (The RSA Band is rather uptight about piracy of their music, so talk to the manager before using your tape recorder, if you know what's good for you.) Foreign visitors are welcome here, there's ample seating, and active pool tables.

Otto's Reef (tel. 22-691) on Beach Rd. is a safe, casual place to drink or play pool (go elsewhere if you want to dance). Check out their Samoan *oka* (spicy raw fish) served after 1600.

Right next to Otto's is **The Coast Bar & Grill** (tel. 26-669; closed Sun.) with hamburgers and tuna steaks, and there's sometimes live music. **On the Rocks** (tel. 20-736), a few doors west and upstairs, is an air-conditioned cocktail lounge.

JT's Sports Bar (tel. 22-221; Mon.–Sat. 1100–midnight), on Fugalei St. south of the market, is popular for its pub food. It's run by former Manu Samoa player Junior Tonuu.

At the **Apia Yacht Club** (tel. 21-313), also out on the Mulinu'u Peninsula, you can get a great cheeseburger and a drink on Friday night, a barbecue on Sunday 1100–1600. All visitors are welcome *with* a member; polite, nicely dressed visitors *without* a member are usually invited in too.

Cultural Shows for Visitors

An essential part of any visit to Samoa is attendance at a *fia fia*, where the Polynesian dancing on stage comes with a buffet dinner of local foods (look over the whole spread before getting in line). There's usually a *fia fia* at **Aggie Grey's Hotel** (S$55) on Wednesday and at the **Kitano Tusitala** (S$50) on Friday. The show at the Kitano Tusitala includes dances from several Pacific countries, while the "We Are Samoa" program put on by the hotel staff at Aggie Grey's is strictly Samoan and usually includes a *siva* by your hostess Marina Grey, carrying on a tradition established by the late Aggie Grey herself. Another tacky touch at Aggie's is the Robert Louis Stevenson requiem set to music and sung in English and Samoan.

At Aggie's the show is before dinner at 1830, while at the Tusitala it's at 1900 (check these times). If you don't order the buffet, there's often a S$15 cover charge for the show alone. Patrons wearing T-shirts or shorts are not allowed in. These events aren't just for tourists—half the audience will be Samoan.

SHOPPING

Apia's colorful **vegetable market**, or *maketi fou*, three blocks inland on Fugalei or Saleufi Streets, throbs with activity 24 hours a day—families spend the night here rather than abandon their places. You'll see a marvelous array of local produce, all with prices clearly marked, plus an eating area and a great assortment of classic Polynesian types.

Go native in Samoa by changing into some colorful, eye-catching clothing. Female travelers especially will enhance their appearance and acceptance by wearing a long muumuu gown, a two-piece *puletasi*, or a simple wraparound *lavalava* available at the **Flea Market** on the waterfront. This is also a good place to shop for handicrafts.

Kava & Kavings Handicrafts (tel. 24-145), on Fugalei St., has war clubs, kava bowls, baskets,

SAMOA

fly whisks, tapa cloth, model canoes, slit drums, shell necklaces, and coconut shell jewelry. They carry mostly authentic traditional handicrafts at good prices. Handicrafts are also available at **Aggie's Gift Shop** (tel. 22-880), next to Aggie Grey's Hotel. Most shops are closed Saturday afternoon and Sunday.

The **Samoa Philatelic Bureau** (tel. 20-720) is in the Chief Post Office and at the airport—beautiful stamps at face value.

INFORMATION
Information
The government-run Samoa Tourism Authority (tel. 63-500, fax 20-886, www.visitsamoa.ws; weekdays 0800–1630, Sat. 0800–1200) is in a *fale* on Beach Rd. between the Government Building and the Catholic cathedral. Ask for your free copies of Jasons *Passport Map* and *What's On.*

Statistics and Maps
The Department of Statistics (tel. 63-600, fax 24-675), 1st floor, Government Buildings, sells an *Annual Statistical Abstract* (S$5).

Get large topographical maps of Apia and Samoa at the Lands, Surveys, and Environment Department (tel. 22-481) in the building marked "Matagaluega o Eleele, Faugafanua & Siosiomaga" next to the New Zealand High Commission on Beach Road. The *Samoa* map published by Hema Maps (S$15) is excellent, and it's available both here and at the Tourism Authority. The University of Hawaii's *Islands of Samoa* is better thanks to the detailed index and Aggie's Gift Shop sometimes has copies.

Bookstores and Library
The Wesley Bookshop (tel. 24-231) on Beach Rd. has a reasonable Samoa and Pacific section but the proprietors have long refused to sell the works of Samoa's leading novelist, Albert Wendt, which are too critical for their taste.

The place to buy Australian and New Zealand newspapers and magazines is Le Moana Café (tel. 24-828), in the Lotemau Center off Convent St. behind Air New Zealand.

The Information Resource Center at the South Pacific Regional Environmental Program (tel. 21-929, fax 20-231, www.sprep.org.ws), off the Cross Island Road a two-minute walk from the MedCen Private Hospital, sells many specialized publications on the South Pacific.

The Nelson Memorial Public Library (tel. 20-118; Mon.–Thurs. 0900–1630, Fri. 0800–1600, Sat. 0830–1200) is opposite the Clock Tower on Beach Road. Special permission of the librarian is required to enter the Pacific Room.

Travel Agencies and Airlines
Island Hopper Vacations (tel. 25-540, fax 26-941, samoa.sales@islandhopper.com.ws), in the Lotemau Center behind Air New Zealand, is an inbound tour operator that handles bookings from overseas.

Apia's airline offices are Air New Zealand (tel. 20-825), corner of Convent and Vaea Streets, Inter-Island Air, next to Molesi Supermarket on Beach Rd., and Polynesian Airlines (tel. 22-737), opposite the clock tower. Polynesian represents Air Pacific.

SERVICES
Money
The ANZ Bank and Westpac Bank give cash advances on Visa and MasterCard. Two ATMs are available outside the main branch of the ANZ Bank, but there are long lines. Another ANZ Bank ATM is inside Molesi Supermarket, a bit west on Beach Road.

The main branch of the ANZ Bank (tel. 22-422, www.anz.com/samoa) opposite the Chief Post Office changes traveler's checks weekdays Monday to Wednesday 0900–1500, Thursday and Friday 0900–1600. Several small agencies of the ANZ Bank around Apia will also change traveler's checks at the same rate. The ANZ Bank charges a rip off S$17.50 commission on traveler's checks, whereas the Westpac Bank (tel. 20-000) deducts S$7.50. The banks are often crowded with locals waiting to collect remittances from relatives overseas and (despite the high fees) the service is slow.

The locally owned National Bank of Samoa

(tel. 26-019, weekdays 0900–1500) on Beach Road opposite the RSA Club market charges 0.25 percent commission. Their vegetable market branch also changes traveler's checks Saturday 0830–1230.

Money Exchange Limited (tel. 23-276, money ex@ipasifika.net, weekdays 0800–1630, Sat. 0800–1200), on Vaea St. between Chan Mow and McDonald's, changes cash and traveler's checks without commission at rates similar to those offered by the banks. Samoa Money Transfer (tel. 22-316; weekdays 0800–1630, Sat. 0800–1200), on Fugalei St. near the Flea Market, also changes traveler's checks without commission.

The rate of exchange for traveler's checks is better than that for cash. Changing foreign currency outside Apia can be a nuisance, so do it here. On Saturday afternoon and Sunday, Aggie Grey's Hotel will change traveler's checks for a rate a bit lower than the bank. Allow extra time in any case as anything associated with bureaucracy moves very slowly in Samoa.

There's no American Express representative in Apia.

Post and Telecommunications

The Chief Post Office in central Apia is open weekdays 0830–1630. Poste restante mail is held three weeks at a counter in the room with the post office boxes. Branch post offices exist at Matautu, Pesega, and Faleolo Airport.

Make long-distance telephone calls from the International Telephone Bureau (www.samoa tel.ws, daily 0700–2200), behind the Lotemau Center. (This location is likely to change soon when SamoaTel's new office building is completed.) Three-minute station-to-station calls are S$7.50 to American Samoa, S$9 to Australia or New Zealand, S$13.50 to North America, and S$18 to Europe. Person to person service is only S$3 extra. These prices are among the lowest in the South Pacific. If you wish to receive a fax at this office, have it sent to fax 685/25-617. If you arrive to find a huge crowd of people waiting to place telephone calls at this office, be aware that they're probably waiting to place overseas calls *collect*. If you're willing to actually pay for your call, you'll get priority and can go straight to the counter without waiting.

Public card telephones have been installed at the Lotemanu Center, Fugalei Market, the Kitano Tusitala Hotel, both airports, the universities, and a few other locations.

Internet Access

Computer Services Ltd. (tel. 20-926, www.csl.ws, weekdays 0745–1630), across the street from Air New Zealand, charges S$12/30 an hour/three hours for Internet access. The Lesamoa Cyber Booth (tel. 21-016, www.lesamoa.net; weekdays 0800–1730, Sat. 0800–1200), in the Lotemau Center, charges the same rates. Several other Internet places are found around town.

Immigration Office

For a visa extension, go to Immigration (tel. 20-291), behind Molesi Supermarket opposite the Flea Market, with S$50, two photos, your onward ticket with a firm flight booking, sufficient funds, proof that you're staying at a hotel, and a good reason. You may also be asked to obtain a local sponsor who'll accept responsibility for you. Be super courteous to the officials here, even if they aren't.

Consulates

The Australian High Commission (tel. 23-411; Mon.–Thurs. 0830–1600, Fri. 0830–1200), next to The Rainforest Cafe on Beach Rd., also represents Canada in Samoa.

The Netherlands Consulate (tel. 24-337) is on the 4th floor of the John Williams Building on Beach Road. The New Zealand High Commission (tel. 21-711) is nearby on Beach Rd. opposite the John Williams Memorial.

In 2002, the United States Embassy (tel. 21-631; weekdays 0930–1230) moved to a new location on the Cross Island Road just south of the MedCen Private Hospital for security reasons.

The British consul is Bob Barlow (tel. 21-758), a solicitor with an office on the 2nd floor of the NPF Building above Polynesian Airlines. France is represented by Island Hopper Vacations (tel. 25-540).

SAMOA

The Swedish Consulate (tel. 20-346) is at the Samoa Ports Authority at the entrance to the main wharf. The German consul (tel. 22-634) is at the Rosenberg Clinic on the road up to the National Hospital. The Chinese Embassy (tel. 22-474) is at Vailima, a bit below the Robert Louis Stevenson Museum, down the road opposite the Carmelite Monastery.

Launderettes and Public Toilets

Cleanmaid Launderette (tel. 21-934; Mon.–Sat. 0700–1900), on Matautu St. between Betty Moors and the harbor, charges S$3 to wash, S$5 to dry. Bring your own laundry soap. At night, beware of vicious dogs here that often attack pedestrians headed for the restaurants and guesthouses down the road.

Near the vegetable market, Homestyle Laundromat, hidden behind A & S Hunt Service Center on Fugalei Street, and Launderette Sil, across the street, are both closed on Saturday.

Public toilets are behind the clock tower in the center of town.

HEALTH

You can see a doctor for S$20 anytime at the National Hospital (tel. 21-212), in Moto'otua south of the center, but bring along a thick book to read while you're waiting. To call an ambulance, dial tel. 999. The Moto'otua bus passes the hospital.

The MedCen Private Hospital (tel. 26-519), on the Cross Island Road up beyond the Robert Louis Stevenson Museum, charges S$55 per consultation, but the service is much better.

Another alternative to the hospitals is visiting a private doctor, most of which charge S$30 for a nonresident consultation. Dr. Toga T. Potai of L.T.P. Surgery (tel. 21-652), behind the post office and opposite Gourmet Seafood, specializes in aviation and travel medicine, plus ear, nose, and throat.

One of Apia's preeminent private doctors is Dr. John Atherton of **Soifua Manuia Clinic** (tel. 26-113), next to UNESCO above the post office at Matautu-uta. Call ahead for an appointment, if possible.

Dr. Peniamina Leavai (tel. 20-172) operates a dental surgery at the south end of Vaea Street.

Samoa Pharmacy (tel. 22-595) is next to the Westpac Bank on Beach Road. Both of the chemists (pharmacies) on Beach Rd. are only open weekdays 0800–1630, Saturday 0800–1230. Check the expiration dates of any medicines purchased here.

TRANSPORTATION

By Bus

Local buses for Apia and vicinity, and long-distance buses for points all around Upolu, leave from the bus stations adjacent to the two Apia markets: the Savalalo Flea Market on the waterfront and the Fugalei Food Market three blocks inland. The bus station at the Flea Market has separate areas marked Falelatai, Falealili, Taulaga, and Aleipata, but in practice these divisions are not followed.

The police do not allow buses to stand for long periods waiting for passengers at the vegetable market, so the buses make a loop between the two markets every 10 minutes or so until they're full. Long-distance buses have been known to drive around town for an hour looking for passengers. There are no set schedules, but you can find a bus to virtually anywhere if you're there by 1000 Monday to Saturday.

There are buses to the Robert Louis Stevenson Museum (marked Avele or Vaoala), the Papase'ea Sliding Rocks (Seesee, Siusega, or Tafaigata), the University of the South Pacific (Alafua), the main wharf (Matautu-tai), Fagali'i Airport (Fagali'i-uta or Vaivase), the National Hospital (Moto'otua), Piula Cave Pool (Falefa, Falevao, or Lufilufi), O Le Pupu-Pu'e National Park (Salani, Sapunaoa, or Vaovai), Faleolo Airport and the Savai'i ferry wharf (Falelatai, Manono, Mulifanua, Samatau, or Pasi Ole Va'a), and Manono Island (Falelatai, Manono, or Samatau).

Long-distance buses run to Lalomanu, Lepa, Safata, Sataoa, Siumu, and Lefaga. Buses to the Savai'i ferry wharf at Mulifanua begin their trips at the Food Market, whereas all of the other buses begin from the Flea Market and only visit the Food Market to pick up additional passengers. Buses to Mulifanua leave the Food Market two hours before the scheduled departure times of the ferries to Savai'i (if you board this particular bus at the Flea Market, you won't get a good seat).

On Friday afternoon, all buses departing Apia tend to be crowded with workers headed home. Saturday morning is a good time for buses, but on Saturday afternoon, Sunday, and evenings, service is very limited. It's not possible to make a day trip to Aleipata or Lepa from Apia by bus—you must spend the night there.

In outlying villages, only bus drivers are reliable sources of information about bus departure times. Others may give misleading information, so ask three or four people. On weekdays buses to Apia often leave villages in south and east Upolu at 0500, and then again at 1130. They often set out from Apia to return to their villages at 1100 and 1600.

Most of these colorful homemade wooden buses are village-owned, and trying to use them to go right around Upolu is very difficult, as they serve remote villages by different routes that don't link up. The Lalomanu bus goes via Falevao and Amaile, while the Lepa bus goes via Lotofaga to Saleapaga.

The Salani, Sapunaoa, and Vaovai buses follow the Cross Island Highway to Siumu, then run along the south coast via Poutasi toward Salani. Four buses serve this route, but they all seem to run about the same time, making three or four trips a day. The last bus back to Apia from Salani is at 1400 (important to know if you're making a day trip to O Le Pupu-Pu'e National Park).

There are good paved roads from Mafa Pass to Amaile and Lepa. The road along the south coast is paved from Siumu to Salani, but at Salani a river blocks eastbound vehicular traffic and cars must make a loop up and around via Sopo'anga Falls (no bus service). There's very little traffic along the south coast of Upolu if you intended to hitch.

Bus service is also very limited west of Siumu on the south coast. The Lefaga and Safata buses follow the north coast west to Leulumoega, then drive south through Tanumalamala to Matautu (Paradise Beach) or Tafitoala. There's no road between Lefaga and Falelatai. The only convenient way to go right around Upolu is to rent a car.

The buses are without cushions and you should avoid sitting at the back, since there's no suspension and the roads are bumpy. On the plus side, they do have destination signs and their fares are the lowest in the South Pacific. Buses around Apia cost 90 *sene;* S$2 to the Savai'i ferry wharf or Falefa; S$2.10 to Lefaga; SS$3.30 to Siumu; $3.40 to Lalomanu; S$4 to Saleapaga. The bus fare from Apia to Lalomanu is supposed to be S$3.40, but some drivers ask S$5. On local buses around Apia, you pay as you get off. On long-distance buses, tell the driver where you're going as you board. You'll make a better impression on everyone if you have small change to pay your fare. Standing isn't allowed, so once a bus is full, extra passengers must sit on the knees of existing passengers! (Half of all traffic convictions in Samoa are for overloading vehicles.) The stereo music is a bus plus.

Taxis

Taxis have license plates bearing the prefix "T." Taxis parked outside the two airports and at the upmarket hotels tend to be a rip-off, while those waiting at taxi stands used mostly by local people are usually okay. Average taxi prices from the taxi stand adjacent to the Flea Market bus station are S$3 to the main wharf, S$8 to Fagali'i Airport, S$12 to the Robert Louis Stevenson Museum, S$40 to Faleolo Airport or Coconuts Beach Club. The beginning fare for a short trip is S$2.

Since the taxis don't have meters, always agree on the price before you get in and make sure you're both talking Samoan *tala,* otherwise the driver could insist on the same amount in U.S. dollars (a favorite trick). If you intend to get out and have the driver wait awhile, ask the price of that too. Failure to do so will lead to unpleasant demands for extra money at the end of the trip and ugly threats if you resist. To hire a taxi should cost S$25 an hour. There's no additional charge for luggage, and tipping is unnecessary.

Beware of the taxis parked in front of Aggie Grey's Hotel, as these drivers are some of the most seasoned hustlers you'll ever meet. If you're staying at Aggie's and want a taxi, turn right as you come out the door, cross the bridge, and about a hundred meters in front you'll see a regular taxi stand. In general, taxis are abundant in Apia.

Car Rentals

The international driver's license isn't recognized in Samoa and you're supposed to get a local driver's license at the licensing office (open weekdays 0930–1200 and 1300–1500) opposite the main police station in Apia. A temporary 30-day driving permit costs S$10 with no photos required. The car rental company will probably also want to see your home driver's license.

Many side roads are too rough for a car and most agencies will tell you the insurance isn't valid if you drive on them. Make reservations well ahead if you want a jeep. A few of the car rental agencies are evasive about what is and isn't covered by the optional collision insurance, and some rental cars don't carry any collision insurance at all. Even with collision insurance you're still responsible for the "excess" or minimum deductible amount. Check the car *very carefully* before you drive off, and don't under any circumstances leave your passport as security on a car rental. Be suspicious; we get more than the usual number of complaints about car rentals at Apia (if you get the feeling that a company is unreliable, trust that impression and look elsewhere). On the positive side, car rental rates in Samoa are the lowest in the South Pacific. Despite occasional shortages, gasoline prices in Samoa and American Samoa are also among the best in the region.

As in American Samoa, driving is on the right. Speed limits are 40 kph in Apia or 56 kph on the open road (25 kph around schools). Drive very slowly and avoid hitting any people or animals—it can be as bad as in Mexico. Many drivers resist using their headlights after dark, and outside Apia pedestrians dominate the roadways. You'll often see people walking along a paved highway oblivious to approaching traffic, especially in the late afternoon. If you're forced to swerve dangerously to miss them or have to stop to avoid hitting another car, they'll just laugh. If you do hit something valuable like a large pig, drive back to Apia and turn yourself in to the police (tel. 22-222). If you stop you could be stoned, and heaven help you if you hit a Samoan! One Apia car rental company has this line in their brochure: "Stopping to verify the extend (sic) of possible injuries sustained to a third party could prove fatal to yourself." If you do become involved in a roadside dispute, don't react to excited bystanders—ask to speak to the *pulenu'u* right away. Occasionally, Samoan children throw stones at cars they think are driving through their village too quickly, and the rental agency will hold you responsible for the broken windshield. If you park a rental car in a village without permission, you risk having it vandalized.

Except for two gas stations near Fasito'outa out toward Faleolo Airport, fuel isn't usually available outside Apia, so plan ahead. Ask the car rental company which gas station they recommend, as some stations have tanks that let rainwater leak in. If you want to take the car to Savai'i make sure it's allowed before signing the rental contract (many agencies won't allow you to do this). You can reserve a car space on the ferry at the office of the Samoa Shipping Corporation (tel. 20-935) near the main wharf in Apia. However, taking a rental car from Upolu to Savai'i is always risky because if there's any problem with the car you'll be responsible for getting it repaired or towed back to Upolu.

Budget Rent-a-Car (tel. 20-561, fax 22-284), between Polynesian Airlines and the Westpac Bank in the center of town, has cars/jeeps at S$125/132 all included. Rent for six days and the seventh is free. The deductible insurance "excess" for which you are responsible is S$1,000 and you cannot take the vehicle to Savai'i.

Blue Pacific Car Hire (tel./fax 22-668, blue pacificsales@lesamoa.net), at Vaigaga village west of Apia, has Suzuki Samurais starting at S$110 a day including tax and insurance (S$2,000 deductible). They'll deliver free to Fagali'i Airport and Apia if you call.

P. K. Filo Car Rental (tel. 26-797, fax 25-574), at the Harbour Light Hotel opposite the wharf, has cars at S$110 a day for one or two days, including tax, mileage, and insurance (S$1,000 deductible). If you rent for six days the seventh is free. You must leave S$1,000 deposit but you may take the car to Savai'i.

Readers have recommended **Funway Rentals** (tel. 22-045, fax 25-008, funwayrentals@samoa.ws), near the main wharf, which charges similar rates to P.K. Filo (S$2,500 deductible insurance). They also allow their cars to be taken to Savai'i.

Also check **Pavitt's-U-Drive** (tel. 21-766, fax 24-667), between the National Hospital and Insel Fehmarn Hotel, and **Seven Seas Car Hire** (tel./fax 26-915) at the Samoan Outrigger Hotel.

Scooter and Bicycle Rentals

The agencies renting motorbikes change all the time, so ask at the Samoa Tourism Authority for current locations. With scooters the insurance is usually included, but the gas is extra. A cash deposit will be required.

Autopro Rentals (tel. 29-555, fax 29-556, www.autoprosamoa.ws), two blocks east of Aniva's Place, rents mountain bikes/scooters at S$30/70 a day.

Local Tours

Several companies offer organized day tours of Upolu from Apia. Prices vary according to the number of participants, whether you travel by private car or minibus, if lunch is included, etc. Don't expect much "narration" from the guide—it's mainly a way of getting around. The tours don't operate unless at least eight people sign up, so ask about that, and if it looks doubtful, check elsewhere. Even if organized sightseeing isn't your usual thing, the convenience and price makes it worth considering here. If nothing if happening, consider hiring a taxi for the day. A day trip to the beaches at Matareva or Lefaga should cost around S$150 for the car including waiting time.

Samoa Scenic Tours (tel. 22-880, fax 26-982, www.samoascenictours.com), next to Aggie Grey's Hotel, charges S$45 pp for an afternoon tour around town or a morning trip to the Piula Cave Pool. Full-day trips including lunch cost S$110 pp to Lefaga's Paradise Beach (Tuesday and Friday) or Aleipata (Wednesday and Saturday). Their full-day Manono Island excursion on Monday and Thursday is S$120 pp, lunch included.

Jane's Tours (tel. 20-954, fax 22-680, janes tours@samoa.ws) on Vaea St. offers full-day trips to Aleipata on Wednesday and Saturday, and

Paradise Beach on Thursday, both S$80 pp including lunch. The Manono trip on Tuesday is S$85 (half price for children under 12).

Oceania Tours (tel. 24-443, fax 22-255, www.oceania-travel.ws), at the Kitano Tusitala Hotel, has a variety of overnight tours to Savai'i and American Samoa. These trips are reasonable value for those with limited time, but compare prices and book ahead.

Ecotour Samoa Ltd. (Steve Brown, tel. 22-144 or 29-629, www.ecotoursamoa.com) does seven-day Samoan safaris, plus sea kayaking trips. They cater mostly to people who book from abroad (prices for individuals and couples vary between US$188 and US$300 pp a day). The same people run **Green Turtle Tours** (tel. 22-144 or 29-229, www.greenturtle.ws) which offers a local holiday package at S$110 a day including *fale* accommodations, bookings, and three meals. Unlimited ground transportation including buses and ferries is S$170 per island (S$340 for both Upolu and Savai'i). A ride right around Upolu in one day is S$90 with lunch, departing Apia at 0800 daily (including Sundays and holidays). They also have a daily bus trip around Savai'i for S$90, departing the ferry terminal at Salelologa at 0800. A Savai'i day tour by plane is S$199.

AROUND UPOLU

Like most other South Pacific "Bible Belt" towns, Apia is pretty dead on Saturday afternoon and Sunday. Luckily, a number of *fale* resorts have opened on beaches around Upolu and Savai'i in recent years, giving visitors the option of evacuating Apia on Saturday morning. There are basically two resort areas on Upolu, Aleipata/Lepa in the southeast corner of the island and Lefaga/Safata in the southwest. These also get quite a few Samoan day-trippers on the weekends, so be prepared.

There's no public bus service right around Upolu, and if you want to do a circle trip without renting a car or returning to Apia, you'll need several days and a willingness to walk for long stretches. If you must choose only one destination, Saleapaga is a good bet.

Northeastern Upolu

The bridge above Falefa Falls mentioned previously gives access to a little-traveled seven-km road east along Upolu's north coast to **Sauago** and **Saletele** villages, an unspoiled corner of old Samoa worth exploring if you have your own transport. After the twin village, the onward track to **Fagaloa Bay** becomes much worse and only passable in a vehicle with high clearance. Fagaloa Bay's flooded volcanic crater is more easily reached via a steep side road off the paved road to Aleipata, a bit north of Mafa Pass. A difficult road continues along Fagaloa Bay's south side to remote **Uafato** village, 14 km east of the turnoff. At Uafato one finds waterfalls, rainforests, flying foxes, and legendary sites associated with the demigod Moso, plus village *fale* accommodations (ask for Loi or his mother Sulia) and a daily bus to/from Apia. It's possible to hike east along the coast to Ti'avea.

Eastern Upolu

Some eight km south of Falefa Falls, the road works its way over **Mafa Pass** (276 meters), beyond which is a junction, with Aleipata to the left and Lepa to the right. If you take the left-hand highway or "Richardson Road" toward Amaile (Lalomanu bus) you'll pass alongside the **Afulilo Reservoir** where Afulilo Falls above Fagaloa Bay was harnessed in 1993 in a US$33-million, four-megawatt hydroelectric development. Over half of Upolu's electricity comes from this and other hydroelectric projects.

Aleipata and **Lepa** districts feature many excellent and unspoiled white-sand beaches with good swimming and snorkeling (lots of fish but unspectacular coral). The authentic ecotourism resorts of this area are covered below, and a stay at one of them would allow the time to explore this attractive area. A trail to the two volcanic craters behind Lalomanu begins behind the hospital in Lalomanu. A large colony of flying foxes lives in the intact lowland forest of the first crater and a guide would be useful. Visit the beautiful offshore islands at high tide with fishermen from Lalomanu. **Nu'utele Island,** a leper colony from 1916 to 1918, is now uninhabited, and two beautiful beaches flank the steep forested slopes that shelter most of Samoa's land bird species. Large colonies of seabirds also nest here, and with luck, sea turtles, coconut crabs, and even whales can be seen on or around Nu'utele. You can hire a boat out to Nu'utele at Ulutogia village just north of Lalomanu.

From Lalomanu it's seven km along the south coast to Saleapaga. The Lepa bus runs from Apia to Saleapaga via Mafa Pass and Lotofaga. Five km south of the pass, deep in the interior, are **Fuipisia Falls** (S$4 pp admission), signposted on the west side of the road. Just a 300-meter walk inland from the road, the falls plunge 56 meters down into a fern-filled valley of which you can get a good view from on top.

Three km south of Fuipisia, the same river plummets over 53-meter-high **Sopo'aga Falls** (admission S$6 per car or S$2 pp). The signposted viewpoint is just a few hundred meters south of the junction with the westbound road to O Le Pupu-Pu'e National Park. A trail heads down to the falls from the viewpoint.

If you don't have your own transportation, you'll probably have to walk the four km from Sopo'aga Falls to the Salani turnoff (this unpaved stretch can be messy after rains). Alternatively, you can wade across the river mouth from Sapoe to Salani at low tide. Buses run along the south coast from Salani to the National Park and Apia, but they're infrequent, and there's next to no traffic, so you're not likely to hitch a ride. The south coast of Upolu is more traditional than the north, and the people take pride in keeping their villages clean and attractively decorated with flowers.

O Le Pupu-Pu'e National Park

This 2,850-hectare national park (tel. 28-680), created in 1978, stretches along the insular divide from the summits of Mt. Le Pu'e (840 meters), the double-cratered peak east of Afiamalu, and Mt. Fito (1,100 meters), highest point on Upolu, right down to the lava fields of O Le Pupu and the south coast. The park is intended to provide a habitat for the endangered Tongan fruit bat, or flying fox (*Pteropus tonganus*). In the past, these giant bats with one-and-a-half-meter wingspans would soar above the treetops

SAMOA

at dusk, but illegal hunting has sharply reduced their numbers.

At Togitogiga, 28 km south of Apia via the Cross Island Highway, five km east of Siumu junction and just a short walk from the main road, are beautiful **Togitogiga Falls,** good for swimming, wading, and diving (middle pool). There are toilets, change rooms, and shelters at the falls. After heavy rains Togitogiga Falls becomes a raging torrent. It's crowded with Samoan picnickers on weekends (admission is free). With the permission of the park staff, you may camp free near the falls for two nights maximum.

An overgrown trail from the falls leads up to **Peapea Cave,** three hours roundtrip on foot. It's hard to find the way on your own, so consider hiring a guide at the house on the right just beyond a gate a few hundred meters up the track (S$10/20 a half/full day). Beyond the cave, a trail continues north up the stream another four km to a waterfall where you could camp.

A rough four-km road begins two km west of the falls and leads across the lava fields to the black coastal cliffs in the southern section of the park. It probably isn't worthwhile to hike all the way down on foot and the road is too rough for a normal car, but you could do it in a jeep for fun. The **O Le Pupu Trail** follows the coast east from the end of the road, but the spent shotgun shells seen along the way are disheartening.

It's possible to do O Le Pupu-Pu'e National Park as a day trip by catching a Salani, Sapunaoa, or Vaovai bus from the markets in Apia, but you'll probably only have an hour or two at Togitogiga Falls. Ask the driver what time he'll be returning to Apia, or better, get together with other travelers from your hotel and rent a vehicle for the day.

Southwest Upolu

The Cross Island Highway runs 23 km south from Apia to Siumu. To the right near the road, three km south of the Lake Lanoto'o turnoff (and 13.5 km from Apia), are **Papapapai-tai Falls,** also known as Tiavi Falls. The unmarked viewpoint (free) is near a store beside the road but it's only worth stopping if you have your own transportation.

From Siumu the South Coast Road continues west, reaching Sinalei Reef Resort and Coconuts Beach Club after one or two km, Salamumu Beach after 11 km, and Return to Paradise Beach after 13 km. Catching a bus along this way would be pure chance. One interesting south coast attraction is the **Sa'anapu-Sataoa Mangrove Forest,** accessible from either Sa'anapu or Sataoa villages. Each village has an information *fale* where you can pay S$2 pp to visit the mangroves on foot (only at low tide), or S$20 pp for an outrigger canoe tour (best at high tide). You'll see two types of mangroves here, the red mangrove with stilt roots and the oriental mangrove with buttress roots of knee-like extensions. Birds include the grey duck and reef heron. The locals practice aquaculture and crab harvesting. Both villages have guest *fale* where you can spend the night.

The paved Lefaga/Safata road follows an inland course a few km from the coast and you must pay fees to visit the beaches. **Return to Paradise Beach,** named for a 1953 Gary Cooper film based on a James Michener novel of the same name, is accessible via a rocky two-km side road (S$5 pp admission fee). It's a popular picnic spot on Saturdays but visits are discouraged on Sundays.

ACCOMMODATIONS

Beach Fale at Aleipata and Lepa

Over the past few years, several dozen basic ecotourism resorts have sprung up at Lalomanu (Aleipata), on the golden sands facing Nu'utele Island, and on a less-frequented beach at Saleapaga (Lepa). These clusters of small two-person beach *fale* are simple, and amenities like electricity, toilets, and running water are provided at some but not at others. As well as being great shoestring places to stay, they're a wonderful introduction to Samoan culture.

For around S$50 pp you'll get *fale* accommodation with a mat, mattress, pillow, sheets, and mosquito net, plus breakfast and dinner. Of course, these are open thatched *fale* with no walls or doors, so keep valuables well stowed at night, and if you go off during the day, it's wise to pack your bags and leave them with your hosts. Hurricanes tend to wipe these places out, but they're quickly rebuilt. There's always lots of space for visitors who show up unannounced (most of the owners don't have phones anyway).

At Saleapaga and Lalomanu the bus drops you right at the gates of the resorts, while at Lefaga in southwest Upolu you'll have a long hike down to the beach (which does enhance privacy). Picnickers pay S$2 pp or S$10 per car to use the facilities for the day (if you're just walking along the road and stop to sit down in an empty beach *fale* for a rest, someone will soon appear with a mat and the expectation of receiving the standard fee). Most day-trippers arrive on weekends, so during the week you could have the entire beach to yourself. It's lovely—the perfect antidote to Apia.

Namu'a Island

On Namu'a Island off Upolu's east end, **Namu'a Beach Fale** (tel. 20-566, kronfeldangie@hotmail.com) offers seven thatched *fale* right on the beach at S$80 pp including meals. Turtles are often seen here, and the snorkeling is excellent. The walk around the island at low tide is lovely (but bring insect repellant). The boat transfer from Mutiatele on the main island is included in the price.

Lalomanu

As you come down from Lalomanu village and go west along the coast you'll pass Litia Sini's, Taufua's, Sieni's, Romeo's, and Malo, in that order. **Litia Sini's Beach Fales** (tel. 41-050, talofalava65@yahoo.com) is the most developed with 16 mattress-equipped *fale* in a long row closed to the road but open to the sea (S$60 pp including meals).

Taufua's Beach Fales (tel. 25-389) has a small store you may visit but on weekends their beach is crowded with Samoan day-trippers. It's S$55 pp including reasonable meals. **Sieni's Beach Fales,** right next to Tuafua's, is also noisy and has poor security. **Romeo's** is part of the same strip. These three are used mostly by day-trippers and not recommended for an overnight stay.

Half a km west of Romeo's is **Malo Beach Fales** with 15 thatched *fale* which are better protected from the road and picnickers. Several unnamed collections of beach *fale* between Romeo's and Malo are cheaper and more basic.

Saleapaga

Whereas Lalomanu wins in the scenery category with its spectacular views of Nu'utele, Saleapaga offers a better choice of places to stay, fewer day-trippers, and good hiking possibilities in the hills overlooking the village. You may also find it quieter, friendlier, and safer—the whole South Seas dream.

Facing the white sands of Saleapaga Beach, seven km west of Lalomanu, are Lalopapa, Boomerang Creek, Tauiai, Gogosiva, Vaotea, Le Ta'alo, Faofao, Tagiilima, Tama o Le Aufuaina, Malaefono, Niusilani, Manusina, and Saleapaga Ocean View, cited here from east to west. Most of the *fale* resorts charge S$20 pp to sleep, plus S$10 per meal.

Lalopapa Beach Fales is nicely isolated a few hundred meters east of Boomerang Creek.

Boomerang Creek Beach Resort (Steve and Ana Harrison, tel. 40-358, boomerangcreek@yahoo.com) is different from all the other places in that it's run by an Australian/Samoan couple and the fan-cooled *fale* are lockable. The seven up on the hillside are S$35/65 single/double (S$5 extra with a verandah), while the four newer beachfront *fale* with toilet and shower go for S$50/80, breakfast included. The communal bathing facilities are clean, there's an excellent restaurant/bar and a guest library, and the security is good. Saturday is "island night" with a traditional *fia fia* featuring Samoan dancing and a buffet meal (S$30). Bicycles and kayaks are for rent, and various tours and hikes are organized. Needless to say, Boomerang Creek is very popular and often full.

Gogosiva Beach Fales (tel. 41-024) offers five thatched *fale* right on the beach. Electricity and running water are available, and the family that runs the place is very helpful. Though open to the road, Gogosiva has one of the finest views of the crashing surf, the sound of which will lull you to sleep.

Vaotea Beach Fales (tel. 41-153) is sheltered from the road by trees and flowers, and it offers a bit more space.

Tapu and Koroseta Legalo's **Faofao Beach Fales** (tel. 41-067, www.faofao.com) is the largest *fale* resort on the southeast coast with 18 beach *fale* at S$70 pp per night including all meals. It's protected from the road by bushes and a fence. Faofao's bar presents live music and firedancing at the Saturday night barbecue and *fia fia*. Day-trippers are welcome at the special Sunday *to'onai* (lunch) with local cuisine for S$30 pp (no additional charge for overnight guests). You can even rent a car here. **Le Ta'alo Beach Fales** (tel. 41-137) next door is run by a related family and charges about the same.

Buses leave Apia for Saleapaga almost hourly between 1000 and 1600. There's no need to rent a car to come to Saleapaga or Lalomanu—just catch a bus.

Aufaga

At Aufaga, a few km west of Saleapaga, are three adjacent *fale*-style resorts, but these are different in that they're at the bottom of a high cliff. Two face a wide sandy beach while the third is only separated from the others by a rocky headland. One *fale* is on a tiny island accessible only by canoe and another is on an isolated hill. The surfing is good at high tide. Recently these resorts have been leased by an American organization as a rehabilitation center for delinquent teenagers. At last report, this program had ended, and the Samoa Tourism Authority will know what's currently happening.

The more upscale **Vava'u Beach Fales** (tel. 26-940), a 10-minute walk west of Aufaga, has six attractive bungalows with kitchenettes at S$185 single or double (bring food). It's managed by the Sinalei Reef Resort and bookings are through Island Hopper Vacations in Apia. The coast here is fantastic with rock pools and a beach for swimming, but beware of the currents (ask for advice). Also ask about the nearby crater lake connected to the sea by a lava tube (S$5 custom fee collected).

Beach Fale in Southcentral Upolu

The **Salani Surf Resort** (tel./fax 41-069, www.surfsamoa.com), at the end of the paved road in Salani village, is right beside the Muli-vaifagatoloa River and near the beach. The eight fan-cooled bungalows have electric lighting with the toilets and showers in a separate building. The S$350 pp per day price is inclusive of room and board, surf guiding, kayaking, local tours, hammocks, and evening entertainment. No surfing is allowed on Sunday, so they usually take guests to the beach for a picnic. It's used almost exclusively by surfers who book through Waterways Travel (www.waterwaystravel.com) in California or Atoll Travel (www.atolltravel.com) in Australia, although non-surfers are always welcome. There's a great barreling right-hander as well as a hollow left-hander, both with plenty of power, out in the channel cut by the river. They receive surf year-round, though the best conditions here are from February to April and October to November. When the surf is down on this side of the island they'll drive you up to the north. Other activities include outrigger paddling or kayaking in the crystal clear lagoon or up the jade-green river to a waterfall, fishing, using the nearby village bathing pool, and exploring the south coast.

Parataiso Beach Fales, in Utulaelae village on the opposite (east) side of the river from the Salani Surf Resort, is much less expensive with six open *fale* at S$60 pp including all meals. Saturday is *fia fia* night (S$25), while on Sunday there's a traditional feast (S$20).

The **Maninoa Surf Camp** (Posala and Falanika Laumanuvae, tel. 29-162), also known as the Line Up Surf Resort, between the upscale Sinalei and Coconut Beach resorts at Siumu, has six beach *fale* at S$50/70 pp for non-surfers/surfers. Meals and shuttles to seven different surfing waves are included. It's a good inexpensive alternative to the Salani Surf and Sa'Moana Surf resorts.

Upscale Beach Resorts at Siumu

Samoa's best known resort is the American-operated **Coconuts Beach Club** (Jennifer and Barry Rose, tel. 24-849, fax 20-071, www.coconuts beachclub.com), which opened in 1992 at Maninoa on the south side of Upolu, a km west of Siumu. The 20 rooms are broken down into six categories, starting at S$450 single or double for a garden suite or tree house room and increasing to S$750 for a deluxe beach villa with kitchen (plus 12.5 percent tax). The spacious tree house rooms are cleverly designed with good ventilation and large covered balconies, and Tahitian-style overwater bungalows were added in 1997. The newest additions are the three two-room garden suites—the entire complex has been built using local materials and finishes. Returning guests will be impressed by the new reception and library/lounge *fale*. There's a gecko-shaped swimming pool with a swim-up bar. The three meal deal with unlimited house wine and local beer at lunch and dinner is S$135 pp when booked in advance. The minimum stay is three nights. Snorkeling gear is loaned free. On Saturday night, Coconuts has a *fia fia* on the beach under the stars (free admission to nonguests who order something at the restaurant or bar). Day visitors who patronize the beachside bar and seafood restaurant are welcome to use the facilities (except the pool), otherwise they'll be asked to leave. Day-trippers certainly aren't allowed to bring their own food or drink into the resort. How rude! For picnics, the adjacent village beach is available at S$5 per car. Coconuts has a more idiosyncratic, quirky character than the slick Sinalei Reef Resort next door, and a more interesting mix of guests, but it's also a bit less exclusive. Airport transfers are S$60 pp.

The **Sinalei Reef Resort** (tel. 25-191, fax 20-285, www.sinalei.com), next to Coconuts at Siumu, opened in 1996. This attractive international resort owned by Apia businessman Joe Annandale and family has a wonderfully cloistered feel and the gardens have matured beautifully. The 16 air-conditioned bungalows begin at S$550 single or double, S$650 triple (S$215 extra for ocean view), and there are four oceanside suites at S$900 single or double (plus 12.5 percent tax). The neat rectangular bungalows have open bathrooms for showering under the stars, and the reception, restaurant, and bar are in the traditional Samoan style. The food and service are good. Wednesday at 1900 there's a *fia fia* (S$60). Saturday nights at 1900 a fire-knife act is performed, followed by an island night dinner (S$60). Sunday lunch (S$50) is an *umu* affair.

The swimming pool is spectacular since the water is constantly replaced by a natural spring and it's strictly for house guests only. A 70-seat meeting room, nine-hole golf course, and two tennis courts are on the premises. Scuba diving is arranged with Pacific Quest Divers. Rental cars must be ordered from Apia. Airport transfers are included in the price.

Sa'anapu

There are a couple of places to stay at Sa'anaputai between Siumu and Lefaga. The **Manuia Wetlands Retreat** (Ray Hepehi, tel./fax 26-225) has three self-catering bungalows at S$80/120/150/170 single/double/triple/quad. To sleep in one of the seven open Samoan *fale* on their white beach is S$20 pp including bedding and a mosquito net. There's a bar and lots of free parking for overnight guests. Day visitors pay S$10 per car, plus another S$10 if the group wants a *fale* for the day, S$5 to use a barbecue, and S$20 to rent an outrigger canoe. It's a good bet if you want quality without the pricing of Coconuts and Sinalei resorts.

Sa'anapu Lagoon Lodges (tel. 20-196, fax 20-942), right on the same lovely white beach, has five budget cottages with private bath, fridge, and gas stove at S$66/110 single/double. One larger five-person unit is also S$150, and if you stay three nights the price drops to S$66 double. The resort has a bar and meals are available upon request.

Virgin Cove Resort (tel. 75-000, www.virgin-cove.ws) sits on a lovely white beach west of Sa'anapu village, about five km off the south coast road. The five open beach *fale* are S$60 pp for shared accommodations or S$85 single (S$10 pp extra for a larger "honeymoon" *fale* or one of the three traditional Fale Afa, single use S$105). The two garden bungalows with private facilities are S$180/210 single/double. If you stay six nights, the seventh is free. All rates include breakfast, dinner, and tax. The dinner menu rotates every 14 days, so there's variety in the meals. This resort uses only solar electricity and dining is by candlelight. A Samoan *fia fia* is staged on Saturday nights. Small lockers are provided for your valuables. Bookings can be made directly or through Seipepa Samoan Travel Home in Apia, which arranges free transfers every afternoon.

Beach Fale in Southwestern Upolu

The **Sa'Moana Surf Resort** (tel./fax 71-460, www.samoanaresort.com) is on Salamumu Beach, five km off the main road via an unpaved track. One double, one quad, and two six-bed *fale* with private bathroom stand along a lovely white beach flanked by black lava rock. At the waters edge, a saltwater swimming pool has been sculpted from the rock. Top Australian guides take guests surfing and game fishing (www .samoafishing.com), and activities such as scuba diving, golf, and ocean kayaking can be arranged at additional *cost*. A *fia fia* with traditional dancing is organized weekly, and there's a barbecue on Sunday nights. Most guests arrive on all-inclusive package deals booked through Wave Hunters (www.wavehunters.com) in the United States or World Surfaris (www.worldsurfaris.com) in Australia. Local bookings are only accepted on a space available basis at S$252 pp including accommodation and meals (plus S$50 for surf transfers, if required).

Matareva Beach Fales at Lefaga charges S$20 pp to stay overnight in one of their beach *fale*. Day use of the beach is S$5 per car or S$2 pp for pedestrians. Although there's a small store it's better to bring your own food from Apia. The money is collected up at main road, then it's a three km hike down to the beach. The swimming here is safer than at Paradise Beach, as there are no rocks and the location is nicely secluded. It's possible to hike along the beach from Matareva to Salamumu (30 minutes).

Another assortment of beach *fale* is found in Lefaga district, but these are quite a hike down from the main highway if you arrive on the Lefaga or Safata buses. It's possible to camp or sleep in a *fale* at famous **Return to Paradise Beach,** two km off the main road, but obtaining drinking water is sometimes a problem. More *fale* are at nearby Matautu.

West of Faleolo Airport

Airport Lodge (tel. 45-584, fax 45-582, airport lodge@lesamoa.net), two km southwest of the

Mulifanua ferry wharf or six km from the airport, opened 1997. The eight pleasant oval bungalows with fridge, fan, and private bath are S$110/125/140 single/double/triple including tax (or S$140/168/190 with air conditioning). A tropical breakfast in their restaurant is S$15, while the set dinner menu is S$30. A grocery store is only a short walk away. You get a nice view of Manono, Apolima, and Savai'i from their two beach *fale,* and there's safe swimming for children in the shallow water just off their beach (although no fish or corals to see). A traditional outrigger canoe is loaned free to guests. It's an agreeable budget place to relax after visiting Savai'i, if you don't wish to head straight back to Apia, and convenient to the ferries to Savai'i and Manono.

The American-operated **Samoan Village Resorts** (Bob Roberts, tel. 46-028, fax 46-098, www.samoanvillageresorts.com), on Cape Fatuosofia opposite Manono Island, 10 km southwest of the airport, has nine air-conditioned *fale* at S$310 single or double (plus S$30 per extra person to four maximum). The one honeymoon *fale* with its own whirlpool tub is S$460, plus 12.5 percent tax. Children under 15 stay free. These are the largest accommodation units on the island and each has its own bathroom, cooking facilities, veranda, and living room. From some you can even fish right off your porch. The resort features a swimming pool and restaurant/bar, and canoes and snorkeling gear are loaned free. The snorkeling here is poor, but the resort organizes a full-day tour to Manono at S$120 pp including lunch. You can watch the magnificent sunset over Manono while sipping a cocktail in the traditional Samoan *fale* on the point of the bay. Somehow the Samoan Village doesn't have the trendy atmosphere of Upolu's other two top resorts, but it's still a good value for the money. Airport transfers are free.

MANONO ISLAND

Three-km-square Manono Island, four km off the west end of Upolu, is sheltered within the larger island's protective reef. Four villages are on Manono (Faleu, Lepuia'i, Apai, and Salua)

but cars, dogs, and hotels aren't present, which makes it a delightful place (horses and bicycles are also banned). Electricity was installed on Manono in 1995, but as yet there are only a few small village stores, which are closed most of the time.

The trail around the island can be covered on foot in a little over an hour. Near the landing at Faleu is a monument commemorating the arrival of the first European Methodist missionary to Samoa, Rev. Peter Turner, who landed here on June 18, 1835. A five-minute walk west of the missionary monument is the **Grave of 99 Stones** (Pa Le Soo) at Lepuia'i, with one stone for each of the wives of the chief buried here. On a hill in the center of the island is an ancient **star mound** (Mauga Fetu), but a guide will be necessary to find it. Manono has a few nice beaches, and the tour groups use one on the less-populated northern side of the island facing Apolima.

You can spend the night at **Vaotu'ua Beach Fales** (tel. 46-077), run by Uili and Tauvela Vaotu'ua, who live in the large white house in Faleu village. They charge S$60 pp to sleep in one of their three basic *fale* including variable meals. Water problems are common here. We've received conflicting reports about this place. Also check the **Aiga I Le Tai Resort** (tel. 46-075, ask for Pale) which has six Samoan *fale*.

Getting There

Village boats to Manono depart from a landing just south of the Samoa Village Resorts at the west tip of Upolu. The Falelatai, Manono, and Samatau buses from Apia will bring you to the landing, and the boat leaves soon after the bus arrives. The boat operators always try to charge tourists S$20 per boat, while the Samoan passengers pay only S$2 per person. They'll tell you the next "regular" boat won't be for four or five hours, but if you say that's fine and sit down to wait, they'll begin loading the Samoan passengers after about 10 minutes and you'll also be able to go for S$2. There are two landings on Manono, at Faleu on the south side of the island and at Salua on the northeast side.

Some travel agencies in Apia offer full-day tours to Manono at S$120 pp, lunch included. Rather than taking the tour, get a small group together and charter a boat to Manono from the landing at S$20 each way for the whole boat. Pack a picnic lunch, because little is available on the island. You could also visit nearby Apolima Island, in the strait between Upolu and Savai'i, this way by paying S$180 return to charter a boat. It takes about two hours to hike right around Apolima, but you're supposed to be invited before you go.

Savai'i

Savai'i is just 20 km northwest of Upolu across the Apolima Strait. Although 50 percent larger and higher than its neighbor, Savai'i has less than a quarter as many people. If you thought Upolu was laidback, Savai'i is *slow*. This unspoiled big island offers ancient Polynesian ruins, waterfalls, clear freshwater pools, white beaches, vast black lava fields, massive volcanoes, innumerable churches, and traditional Samoan life. Most of the villages are by the seashore, strung along the fully paved circuminsular highway, and they're a pleasure to stroll through when the kids decide to leave you alone. Yet for an island, a visit to Savai'i is not sea-oriented since many of the attractions are away from the coast.

Savai'i is the largest island in Polynesia (out-side of Hawaii and New Zealand). Though about the same length as Upolu, it's 50 percent wider with broad lava plateaus in the interior. Most of the northeast side of this high volcanic island was transformed in the great eruptions of Mt. Matavanu between 1905 and 1911, which buried much fertile land and sent refugees streaming across to Upolu. Vast tracts of virgin rainforest survive despite agricultural clearings and heavy logging, but in 1998, large areas in the west were destroyed by forest fires facilitated by the drought associated with El Niño. Coral reefs are present along the east coast from Salelologa to Pu'apu'a, on the north coast from Saleaula to Sasina, then from Asau to Vaisala, and on the south coast

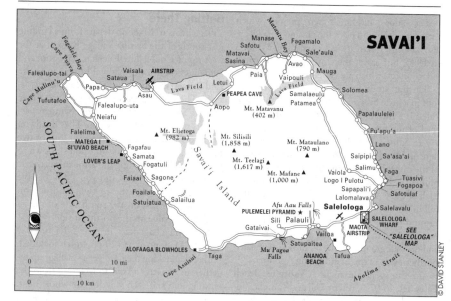

SAVAI'I

at Palauli. Expect to pay a custom fee of anywhere from S$2 pp to S$10 per car to a responsible adult (not a child or teenager) to use a village beach.

Orientation

Other than Salelologa, there's nothing that could be called a town on Savai'i; it's just one village after another around the coast, with large gaps on all sides. In recent years Salelologa has developed into a busy little town with a market, stores, launderette, several small restaurants and takeaways, and a couple of places to stay. The market and bus station are less than a km north of where the Upolu ferry lands.

Frankly, however, Salelologa is a dismal, uninteresting place best avoided by jumping directly on a bus to Lalomalava, Manase, Satuiatua, or Falealupo-tai.

Police stations are found at Asau and Fagamalo, but the main police station (tel. 53-515) is in the small government complex at Tuasivi, about 10 km north of Salelologa. There are post offices at Salelologa, Tuasivi, Fagamalo, Asau, and Salailua, and a district hospital at Tuasivi (tel. 53-511).

AROUND SAVAI'I

Tafua

The paved six-km side road to Tafua village begins directly opposite the access road to Maota Airport. To the left (east) of the road, two km before the village, is a grassy track around the north side of Tafua Crater (560 meters). The footpath up into the crater is 500 meters down this road: It's the second and larger trail to the right. It's worth the hike for a chance to see the crater's tooth-billed pigeons and diurnal flying foxes. In 1990, a Swedish environmental group and the Tafua villagers signed a covenant in which the villagers agreed to protect their forests from logging and other misuse for 50 years in exchange for Swedish financial aid to local health and education. Tafua village itself is just above the beach, and one can walk east along the coast to black cliffs where lava flows from the volcano entered the sea. A S$2 pp or S$5 per car entry fee to the Tafua Rainforest Reserve is collected at Maota at the start of the Tafua road.

Letolo Plantation

Catch a bus from the Salelologa ferry wharf to

Letolo Plantation, eight km west in Palauli District. The largest remaining prehistoric monument in Polynesia is here, as well as an idyllic waterfall and pool. The huge **Pulemelei stone pyramid** *(tia)*, on a slope about two km from the main circuminsular highway, was concealed by thick undergrowth until the 1960s. This immense three-tiered stone platform on a hillside in the middle of the coconut plantation is 65 meters long, 60 meters wide, and 12 meters high, and stones used in religious ceremonies are scattered around it. The structure is similar to some of the stone temple mounds of Tahiti and is possibly their predecessor, though its origins have been completely erased from the memories of present-day Samoans.

The route to the pyramid can be hard to follow. About 100 meters after a bridge just west of Vailoa village, turn right onto an unmarked farm road into Letolo Plantation. You can only drive a car 200 meters down the access road to the first river crossing. Continue on foot past a two-story concrete house on the right, where a S\$2 pp admission fee is charged. About 200 meters beyond the house you'll notice an entrance through a stone wall on the right. Here a faint track heads east through a coconut grove where cows are grazing to **Afu Aau Falls** (also known as Olemoe Falls). Rather than visit the falls immediately, however, continue north on the main track toward the pyramid and keep left.

About 20 minutes from the main road, start watching for a small stream with a sizable concrete drainage pipe across the road (the only such pipe you'll see). The trail to the pyramid is on the left at the top of a small slope about 100 meters beyond the pipe. The pyramid was cleared of ferns and bush during archaeological excavations in late 2002, and a trail runs right up and around the top. Radiocarbon dating demonstrated human activity in the area from A.D. 620 to A.D. 1690.

After exploring the pyramid, return to the falls for a well-deserved swim. The edge of the ravine is 400 meters straight east through the coconut plantation, and the steep path down to the pool is fairly obvious. The crystal-clear waters of Faleata Stream running down the east side of the plantation plunge over a cliff into a large,

deep pool into which you can dive from the sides. Brown prawns live in the pool: Drop in bread crumbs and wait for them to appear.

The Southwest Coast
Eight km west of Letolo Plantation at the east entrance to Gautavai village is the **Mu Pagoa Waterfall** where the Vaiola River—Samoa's largest—tumbles over black cliffs into the sea just below the highway bridge. The best view is from the west side (S\$2 custom fee).

The **Alofaaga Blowholes** are along the coast near Cape Asuisui, 16.5 km west of the Mu Pagoa bridge and 40 km from Salelologa wharf. Just a short walk from Taga village, this series of rather spectacular blowholes *(pupu)* are at their best at high tide. Throw in a coconut and watch the roaring jet propel it skyward. (If you allow a boy to perform this trick for you, he'll want a substantial tip.) Don't get between the blowholes and the ocean, as cases of people being dragged by the surge across the sharp rocks to their deaths are not uncommon. A S\$2 pp admission fee is collected at the turnoff.

There's good **surfing** in winter (June–Sept.) at high tide just off the point at Salailua, 13 km northwest of Taga. At Fagafau, 11.5 km northwest of Satuiatua Beach Resort, the sheer cliffs of **Lovers' Leap** drop precipitously to the sea (S\$2 pp fee if you stop by the road to peer down the cliffs). The story goes that due to family problems, an elderly blind woman and her only child jumped from the cliff. The woman turned into a turtle while the child became a shark. It's said that a certain magic chant can still bring the turtle and shark back to these shores. (The same story is told at Vaitogi on Tutuila, American Samoa.)

Matega i Si'uvao Beach (S\$2 pp admission, plus S\$5 for video cameras) is four km northwest of Lovers' Leap. Waves crash into the black rocky coast right next to the road, 600 meters beyond the Si'uvao Beach turnoff, and you can stop and look for free.

Falealupo
From Falealupo-uta on the circuminsular highway it's nine km down a paved road to

Falealupo-tai, which stretches 1.5 km along a white sandy beach. A unique attraction of this area is the highly publicized **Rain Forest Canopy Walkway,** two km up the Falealupo-tai access road. Stairways ascend a Garuga floribunda tree to a suspension bridge spanning a 30-meter gap to a large banyan tree. Then the stairways climb another five stories to a large platform high above the rainforest. Built in 1997 by the Seacology Foundation of Utah (www.seacology.org), it's part of a conservation project intended to provide local villagers with a financial incentive to preserve their lowland forests. At S$20 pp, admission to the walkway may seem expensive, but the money goes to supporting conservation efforts throughout this area. It's also possible to sleep on the uppermost platform at S$50 pp plus S$20 for two meals, although there would be no shelter in case of rain.

Four km beyond the Canopy Walkway is **Moso's Footprint,** on the right beside the road. Three meters long, it's said to have been left when the war god Moso leaped from Samoa to Fiji. You'll pay S$5 per group to stop and admire the print.

Another designated tourist attraction is the **House of Rocks,** in the bush 300 meters behind the ruined Methodist church at Falealupo-tai, three km beyond Moso's Footprint. Here your guide will point out a row of stone seats, the largest belonging to Maleatoa, in a lava tube with a hole in its roof. You'll pay either S$5 per person or per group (make sure the price is understood).

Falealupo-tai village was devastated by Hurricane Val in 1991, and the picturesque thatched *fale* of yesteryear have now been replaced by modern housing. To use the beach at Falealupo-tai is S$2 pp or S$5 per car. If you're staying at one of the *fale* resorts of this area, a good day hike is east along the coast to sandy Fagalele Bay and the lava cliffs of Cape Puava.

Three km southwest of Falealupo-tai is palm-covered **Cape Mulinu'u,** shaped like an arrow aimed against Asia and the spirit land of Pulotu. This lovely white beach is Samoa's westernmost tip and the place where the world's day comes to an end. Dubbed Sunset Beach for tourists, it's

controlled by Tufutafoe village and entry is S$10 per car. The rough track continues past Tufutafoe, 1.5 km southeast of the cape, to Neiafu on the main highway, a couple of hours walk.

As you may have gathered by now, the Falealupo/Tufutafoe locals are quite adept at collecting multiple customary fees from foreigners, and it's one of their few sources of income. If you're driving you can usually get everyone in your vehicle in for the basic amount (or just drive on), but individuals roughing it on public transport may have to pay the same fees per person (or bargain). Unless you have your own transport, getting to Falealupo is difficult—there's only one bus a day, which leaves the village for Salelologa wharf at 0500 every morning. This bus may only go as far as Falealupo-tai, although it's usually possible to hitch a ride in a pickup the last nine km to Falealupo. There's no store in Falealupo-tai village.

The North Coast

The road around the island continues past **Asau,** the main supply center on the north side of Savai'i. There's good holding for yachts in the well-protected small boat harbor in Asau Bay, but the channel is subject to silting, so seek local advice before attempting to enter. Asau wharf is seldom used but there's a large sawmill belonging to Samoa Forest Products.

From Asau, the newly paved road turns inland and climbs around a lava flow dating from an eruption in 1760. Very serious hikers can ascend **Mt. Silisili** (1,858 meters), Samoa's highest peak, from Aopo, 24 km east of Asau. The trail begins on the east side of the village and passes through some of the best bird-watching territory in Samoa. The charge for the three-day trip will be S$50 pp a day including a guide. A tent and warm clothing will be required. Accommodations in the village are easily arranged. **Peapea Cave,** a lava tube that runs under the highway five km northeast of Aopo, is S$3 pp admission. Numerous white swiftlets live in the cave.

Soon after you rejoin the coast, you reach Matavai, 9.5 km northeast of Peapea Cave. The **Matavai Pool** here is fed by a strong freshwater spring *(mata ole alelo)* and you can swim for S$5 pp. A *fale* is provided for resting. Ask a local to tell you the legend of "Sina and the spirit eel" associated with the pool. Robert Flaherty's classic, *Moana of the South Seas* (1926), was filmed in nearby **Safune.**

You'll find more freshwater pools *(vaisafe'e)* at **Safotu** village, three km east of Matavai. Three huge churches stand in a row in Safotu: Catholic, Congregational, and Methodist. A picturesque beach lined with small dugout fishing canoes is opposite the Catholic church.

Three km south of Safotu is **Paia** village with a lava tube *(nu'uletau)*, the "short people's cave," three km farther inland. You'll need guides and kerosene lamp to visit it (S$20 fee per group, plus S$5 for a lamp). People of small stature are said to live inside.

A grassy road beginning beside the Mormon church in Paia leads eight km south to the crater of **Mt. Matavanu** (402 meters), which the locals call *mata ole afi* (eye of the fire). This was the source of the 1905–1911 volcanic outbreak that covered much of northeast Savai'i with black lava. You don't really need a guide to find the crater—just look for a trail to the left where the road dips, about two and a half hours out of Paia. Beware of deep crevices and crumbling edges as you near the crater; they have claimed at least one life. There's no charge to come up here. If you're a really intrepid explorer you could hike northeast down the lava field from Mt. Matavanu and turn north on any road you meet, which should bring you through Vaipouli to the coast. You'll be on your own if anything goes wrong, and a guide would be advisable unless you're a very experienced hiker.

The main north coast tourist resorts, Stevenson's, Tanu Beach, and Jane's, are only four km east of the turnoff to Paia at Safotu. From May to October a safe, though exposed, yacht anchorage is found at Matautu Bay, two km farther east.

The Lava Field

The road south of Saleaula runs across a wide, barren lava flow. A large stone Methodist church, nearly engulfed by the lava at the beginning of the century, is on the northeast side of the road under a large tree about 100 meters off the road near the flow's northern edge. The so-called **Virgin's Grave** is about 150 meters east of the church near a mango tree. Look for a rectangular depression about two meters deep in the lava; the grave is clearly visible at the bottom. Someone will collect S$2 pp admission at this managed tourist site signposted "Saleaula village lava ruins (1905–1911)."

As the fast-flowing *pahoehoe* lava approached the coast here in the early years of this century, it built up behind the reef and spread out in both directions. The highway now runs across it for eight km. It's intriguing to stop anywhere and go for a walk on the lava to get a feel for this awesome geological event. Maunga village, 3.5 km southeast of the Virgin's Grave, is built around a circular crater.

The East Coast

Picturesque villages and intermittent white beaches run all along the route south from Pu'apu'a to the wharf. **Lano** is a favorite surfing beach in summer (Dec.–March), and there's good snorkeling at **Faga.** In front of the large Congregational Christian Church at **Sapapali'i,** eight km north of Salelologa wharf, is a stone monument to John Williams. This marks the site where the missionary arrived in 1830 and converted the local chiefs to Christianity in a couple of days. Several hotels are found around here.

Sports and Recreation

Dive and Fly Samoa (Patrick, Dirk, and Sandra, tel. 54-066, www.diveandflysamoa.com), based at Jane's Beach Fales in Manase, offers scuba diving at S$120/200 with one/two tanks, plus 10 percent for gear, if required. A PADI open-water certification course is S$990 (or pay S$180 for a no-experience introductory dive). Their favorite dive is on the mission ship *Juno,* which sank off Savai'i in 1840. Cave and canyon dives off the lava fields are also popular (all dives are boat dives). Guided snorkeling trips by boat are S$60, plus S$20 for gear.

Savai'i Surfaries (Keith Martin, tel. 58-248, fax 58-245, www.atolltravel.com) organizes surfing and fishing tours for people staying in the beach *fale* at Ananoa Beach just west of Salelologa.

PRACTICALITIES

Salelologa

A few minutes walk from the ferry wharf is the **Savai'i Ocean View Motel** (Tui and Maselina Retzlaff, tel. 51-409), with four self-contained rooms with fridge at S$77/99 single/double. There's a restaurant/bar (Mon.–Sat. 0700–2300).

Farther up before the market is **Taffy's Paradise Inn** (tel. 51-544, fax 51-354) with five rooms with shared bath in an airy European-style house overlooking the lagoon at S$35/60 single/double. This place would be noisy if full, but it seldom is.

The more upscale **Jet Over Motel** (tel. 51-565, fax 51-366, bbl@lesamoa.net), upstairs in the Bluebird Mall opposite the market, has 10 "budget" rooms with fridge and fan at S$80, plus "deluxe" rooms with kitchenette and air conditioning at S$150.

Food and Entertainment

The store opposite the Ocean View Motel at Salelologa serves a good plate lunch weekdays for about S$6.50. You can also get lunch at the food stalls in the market, but it and most shops close down by 1600. The **Kossara Restaurant and Takeaway** (tel. 51-216; weekdays 0830–1800) near the market serves chicken, steak and chips, Chinese dishes, and ice cream in a thatched, open-air setting.

The **Edgewater Bar & Grill** (tel. 51-497; daily 1100–1400 and 1700–2300) occupies an over-water locale overlooking the mangroves south of the wharf in Salelologa. The usual Samoan/Chinese food is served and you can get beer. A live band plays Wednesday to Saturday nights.

Other Practicalities

The ANZ Bank (tel. 51-213) is next to the market, and the Westpac Bank (tel. 51-208) is farther up the same way, near the T-junction with the circuminsular road. The ANZ Bank has an ATM. The National Bank of Samoa at Salelologa is open on Saturday mornings.

The **Savai'i Travel Centre** (tel. 51-206), next to the gas station near the intersection with the main island highway, provides Internet access at

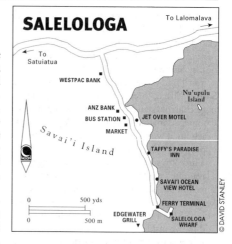

SALELOLOGA

To Lalomalava
To Satuiatua
WESTPAC BANK
Nu'upulu Island
ANZ BANK
BUS STATION
JET OVER MOTEL
MARKET
Savai'i Island
TAFFY'S PARADISE INN
SAVAI'I OCEAN VIEW HOTEL
FERRY TERMINAL
EDGEWATER GRILL
SALELOLOGA WHARF
0   500 yds
0   500 m
© DAVID STANLEY

S$8 per 15 minutes. Look for the Western Union sign; they're in the same office.

Internet access is also available at the **Savai'i Computer Training Center** (tel. 51-038) in the Blue Bird Mall opposite the market.

RESORTS AROUND THE ISLAND

Eastern Savai'i

The **Safua Hotel** (tel. 51-271, fax 51-272, safua hotel@lesamoa.net), in a garden setting at Lalomalava, six km north of the wharf, was the first hotel on Savai'i. The 12 Samoan *fale* with private facilities and fan are S$125/140/167 single/double/triple (discounts for groups, students, and long stayers). Rooms here are twice as expensive if booked through a travel agent overseas and one shouldn't expect luxury. Meals cost S$15/15/30 for breakfast/lunch/dinner if paid directly. The owner/hostess Moelagi Jackson and her family join guests at the nightly buffet dinner, and Sunday lunch is a special treat. Moelagi, one of the very few female *failauga* in Samoa, is an expert on tapa making, and she usually keeps a few high-quality pieces on hand to sell. She's very involved in ecotourism and has done more to promote appropriate development on Savai'i than anyone else on the island. Island tours by minibus are arranged, or just ask to be shown around the family plantation. The Safua is not on the beach but an informal bar faces a shady garden, and there's a large library. You'll enjoy sitting in the lounge chatting with the other guests and local personages.

The **Savaiian Hotel** (Roger and Ama Gidlow, tel. 51296 or 51206, fax 51439, savaiian@lesamoa.net), behind the gas station just south of the Safua at Lalomalava, has less Samoan atmosphere but more creature comforts. Built in 1992, it's on a rocky shore but is spacious and clean. The six air-conditioned duplex units with cooking facilities, fridge, and private bath (hot water) are S$125/150/175 single/double/triple, tax included. Four thatched *fale* at the back of the yard are S$44/66 single/double. These have a toilet, fan, and four beds but no cooking facilities. Rentals cars are available.

If you want to be at the beach, pick the **Siufaga Beach Resort** (tel. 53-518, fax 53-535, www.siufaga.com), also known as the Caffarelli Hotel, just a km north of the new hospital at Tuasivi and about six km north of Lalomalava. Created by an Italian doctor and his Samoan family, the resort has a large green lawn that faces lovely Faga Beach with some of the nicest swimming in Samoa. It's in something of a rain shadow so it's drier than Salelologa. The six *fale* with private bath and kitchenette start at S$110/120/135 single/double/triple (or S$210 for a much better "superior" unit). Campers are also welcome to pitch their tents in the shade of a big banyan tree for S$15 pp. There's a good grocery store opposite the post office, a 10-minute walk south of the resort, but no cooking facilities for campers. Excellent Italian/Samoan food is served on the upper balcony of Parenzo's Restaurant here. All-day mini-bus tours are S$60 pp. The Puapua bus (S$1) will bring you here from Salelologa wharf, otherwise a taxi from the wharf will run S$20 (or S$25 from Maota Airport).

Northeastern Savai'i

Way overpriced is **Le Lagoto Beach Resort** (Kuki and Sara Retzlaff, tel. 58-189, fax 58-249, www.lelagoto.ws), near Fagamalo Post Office at Savai'i's northernmost tip. The four individual *fale* facing the beach are S$320 single or dou-

ble. Each fan-cooled unit has a tiny kitchenette, fridge, TV, and private bath (hot water). The two-story, three-bedroom beach house is S$620. Meals are S$70 pp for all three, otherwise there's a large store opposite where you can buy groceries and drinks. In Samoan, "lagoto" means sunset and you'll enjoy some good ones sitting outside your unit. Unlike the local places that follow, at Le Lagoto people tend to keep to themselves and the atmosphere isn't very Samoan.

Tanu Beach Fales (Taito Muese Tanu, tel./fax 54-050, www.samoa-experience.com) sits on a nice beach at Manase village, a couple of km west of Fagamalo and 45 km northwest of Salelologa. There are 26 open Samoan *fale* at S$50 pp including breakfast and dinner. Drinking water, bananas, and nippy showers are free, and their store sells beer and cold drinks. The ample meals are served at a long common table and on Saturday nights they present a *fia fia* with Samoan dancing. The friendly managers arrange half-day tours covering most sites between here and the Taga blowholes. It makes a good base for visiting Mt. Matavanu and is a safe, convenient place to stop and unwind on your way around the island. Many backpackers stay here (and most readers said they liked it a lot).

Jane's Beach Fales (tel. 54-066) is a bit east of Tanu Beach Fales in Manase village. The 12 *fale* here also cost S$50 pp including breakfast and dinner, and they're a bit larger and more comfortable than those at Tanu. Each has a small balcony with chairs, a mosquito net over the bed, and lockable doors (the toilets and showers are shared). There's a *fia fia* on Saturday nights. A dive shop offering bicycle rentals is on the premises. **Vacations Beach Fales** (tel. 54-024) and **Regina's Beach Fales** nearby are similar. Vacations even has a bar.

Stevenson's at Manase (tel. 58-219, stevenson manase@lesamoa.net), right next to Tanu Beach Fales, is more upmarket with 12 small air-conditioned rooms in a long prefabricated block at S$100 single or double, plus five air-conditioned villas with fridge and TV at S$250, plus tax. These prices are sharply reduced when things are slow. Get a room away from the noisy generator. Meals in the hotel restaurant/bar are

BASIC SAMOAN

Although you can get by with English in both Samoas, knowing a few words of the Samoan language will make things more enjoyable. Written Samoan has only 14 letters. Always pronounce *g* as "ng," and *t* may be pronounced "k." Every letter is pronounced, with the vowels sounding as they do in Spanish. An apostrophe indicates a glottal stop between syllables.

afakasi: half-caste
afio mai: a Samoan greeting
afu: waterfall
'ai: eat
aiga: extended family
aitu: ghost, spirit
alia: catamaran fishing boat
ali'i: high chief
alofa: love
alu: go
Alu i fea?: Where are you going?
'ata: laugh
fa'afafine: transvestite
fa'afetai: thank you
fa'afetai tele: thank you very much
fa'amafu: home-brewed beer
fa'amolemole: please
Fa'apefea mai oe?: How are you?
fa'a Samoa: the Samoan way
fa'a se'e: surfing
fafine: woman

fa'i: banana
faia: sacred
faife'au: an ordained church minister
failauga: orator
fale: house
faleoloa: store
fautasi: a Samoan longboat
fia fia: happy; a Samoan feast
fono: council
fou: new
i: to, toward
i'a: fish
ietoga: fine mat
inu: drink
ioe: yes
lafo: a ceremonial exchange of gifts
lali: a large wooden drum
lavalava: traditional men's skirt
le: the
leai: no
leaga: bad
lelei: good
lelei tele: very good
le tau: the cost, price
lotu: religion
maamusa: girlfriend
malae: meeting ground
malaga: journey
malo: hi
malo lava: response to *malo*

expensive but good. The beach is also nice, but on nighttime strolls watch out for soft sinking sand around a small spring. Island tours are arranged at S$50/90 a half/full day. Transfers from Maota Airport are S$60 pp return, from Salelologa Wharf S$50.

Southwestern Savai'i

Savai'i's original backpackers camp is **Satuiatua Beach Resort** (tel./fax 56-026) at Satuiatua, 55 km west of Salelologa wharf. For S$55 pp you get a mattress in one of the 10 open Samoan beach *fale* with electric lighting, plus breakfast and dinner. The meals are huge with the emphasis on Samoan cuisine. Their small store across the road sells cold beer at normal prices (when available). The white beach is protected by a long lava ledge, making it safe for children, and you can snorkel. One of Samoa's best left-handers is nearby, and during the surfing season (June–Sept.) Satuiatua can get crowded. Tiny biting sand flies can be a problem. The whole complex is nestled in a row of huge *pulu* (banyan) trees. If you've got a couple of hours to spare, ask the staff to guide you to a lava tube up in the bush behind the resort. Otherwise hike west along the coast. A pickup truck is available for tours to Falealupo. Guests must present themselves at church on Sunday morning. The Fagafau bus, which meets all ferries from Upolu, will bring you directly here for S$3.

manogi: smell
manuia!: cheers!
manuia le po: good night
matafaga: beach
matai: head of an _aiga_
mau: opposition
mea alofa: gift
moe: sleep
motu: small island
musu: to be sullen
niu: coconut
nofo: sit
_nu'u:_ village
oi fea: where is
Ou te alofa ia te oe.: I love you.
Ou te toe sau.: I shall return.
paepae: the stone foundation of a _fale_
palagi: a non-Samoan; also _papalagi_
paopao: canoe
pe fia?: how much?
pisupo: canned corned beef
Poo fea a alu iai?: Where are you going?
pule: authority, power
pulenu'u: village mayor
puletasi: traditional women's dress
pupu: blowhole
_sa:_ taboo, sacred
sau: come
savali: walk
sene: a cent

siapo: tapa cloth
sili: best
siva: dance
soifua: good luck
sua: an important ceremonial presentation
taamu: giant taro
taavale: car
tai: sea, toward the coast
tala: dollar
talofa: hello
talofa lava: hello to you
tama: a boy
tamaloa: a man
tamo'e: run
tanoa: kava bowl
taulealea: untitled man
taupou: ceremonial virgin
tautau: untitled people, commoners
tele: much
tofa: goodbye
tofa soifua: fare thee well
tuai: old
tulafale: talking chief, orator
uku: head lice
ula: lei (flower necklace)
uma: finished
umu: earth oven
uta: inland
_va'a:_ boat

At Faiaai village, six km northwest of Satuiatua, you'll find a few _fale_ by the highway where you can stay for S$15 pp, plus another S$15 for meals. There's a lovely beach at the bottom of the cliff below the village and you might be able to camp there for a similar price. For information about this place, call 56-023.

Western Savai'i

Right in the center of Falealupo-tai village, **Utusou Beach Fales** offers three _fale_ with stone floors at S$40 pp a night including meals. The beach is lovely.

Tanumatiu Beach Fales, 800 meters southwest of Falealupo-tai, is on an even more spectacular beach with more privacy. The six _fale_ with mats on the floors are also S$40 pp with meals, or S$5 per car if you're just picnicking. It's run by the Gisa Seumanutafa family; they can supply buckets of water from their home a few hundred meters away. Take good care of your gear if you stay at either of these as thefts have occurred.

The only regular hotel on northwestern Savai'i is the **Vaisala Hotel** (tel. 58-016, fax 58-017, vaisala@ipasifika.net), four km west of Asau on the north coast. The 40 rooms in a cluster of European-style buildings overlooking a nice beach go for S$90/102 single/double (sometimes they offer specials). Ask for a room with a balcony overlooking the beach. The accommodations are good, with private bath, coffee-making facilities, and fridge (but no cooking). Breakfast and dinner in the restaurant will total around S$50 for both. The Vaisala makes a convenient base for exploring the northwest coast by rental car.

GETTING AROUND

For ferry and air services between Upolu and Savai'i, turn to Getting Around in the Exploring the Islands chapter. Travel around Savai'i is easy thanks to the broad paved highway that encircles the island, and bus service from the wharf is good. Yet all public transportation on Savai'i is a bit irregular, so don't plan tight itineraries or count on being able to get back to Upolu to catch an international flight the same day. If a storm came up and the ferries were canceled, you'd be as stranded as anyone else.

By Bus

Bus service on Savai'i focuses on the wharf at Salelologa, with departures to almost any point on the island immediately after a ferry comes in. Over a dozen buses will be revving up as the ferry arrives from Upolu, and they fill up fast, so quickly jump on the bus of your choice. They'll be marked Pu'apu'a or Tuasivi for the east coast, Letui, Paia, Sasina, or Safotu for the north coast, Gataivai or Sili for the south coast, or Asau or Fagafau for the west coast. Fares from Salelologa average S$1 to Lalomalava, Palauli, or Faga, S$2 to Taga, S$3 to Sasina or Satuiatua, S$5 to Falealupo, and around S$6 to Asau.

The buses pull out as soon as they're full, and you'll see as many as five buses racing along the same way, one right after another, then none until another ferry comes in. Buses that leave the wharf fully loaded won't stop to pick up additional passengers along the way, which can make it hard to carry on from places halfway around the island. If a ferry service is canceled, the buses will be too. Going back toward the ferry is much more inconvenient as early morning departures from villages in the northwest corner of Savai'i are a way of life. The last bus leaving Asau for the wharf via the west coast departs at 0600 and most buses leave Asau between 0300 and 0500!

Some of the Asau buses follow the north coast while others go via the south coast. The Tufutafoe bus generally uses the south road, while the Neiafu bus runs along the north coast (ask to be sure). Therefore, to go right around the island by bus, you could take the Tufutafoe bus from Salelologa to Falealupo, then after a couple of days at the beach *fale* there, try to get the Neiafu bus along the north coast as far as Manase where you could also stop. Getting back to the wharf from Manase is no problem. If you don't manage to catch the north coast bus in the very early morning, you could try hitching from Asau to Manase or go on the Forestry truck around 1300 weekdays (see below). Keep in mind that the Asau buses may not stop to pick up passengers in the middle of their runs (Manase or Satuiatua), so the only way to be sure of reaching Falealupo-tai without a tremendous struggle is to go directly there from the wharf and visit the midway points on the way back to Salelologa. The Tuasivi bus runs up and down the east coast fairly frequently throughout the day.

Hitchhiking

Hitchhiking is an option on Savai'I, as most vehicles will stop, and the completion of paving right around the island has seen an increase in traffic. It's always good to offer the equivalent of the bus fare, although most drivers will refuse payment from *palagi*. Traffic diminishes greatly after 1400.

One useful thing to know about is the flat-back truck jammed with plantation laborers, which leaves the Forestry Office near Asau Post Office for Safotu weekdays at 1300. The driver is usually willing to give travelers a lift, in which case a few *tala* would be welcome.

Car, Motorbike, and Bicycle Rentals

Rental vehicles are scarce on Savai'i, and some of the car rental agencies in Apia won't allow you to bring their vehicles over on the ferry (be sure to ask, otherwise the insurance won't be valid). It would be risky to do so anyway as you'd be fully responsible for getting the vehicle back to Apia in case of trouble.

Big Island Rentals (Hermann Retzlaff, tel.

51-499, fax 51-448) at Salelologa has Sidekick vehicles starting at S$149 a day including tax and insurance with discounts after three days (S$250 deposit). They don't pick up at the wharf but their office is only a 10-minute walk away.

Savai'i Car Rentals (tel. 51-392 or 23-431, fax 51-291, cars@lesamoa.net), based at the Savaiian Hotel, is reputable and charges S$140 and up for a vehicle. Tax and insurance (S$1,000 deductible) are included but a refundable deposit of S$350 must be made. You should call ahead from Apia to reserve.

While driving through villages on Savai'i go very slowly as the local kids often use passing cars as moving targets and the rental agency will hold you responsible if a stone goes through the windshield. By going slowly your chances of seeing trouble ahead increase and you can defuse the situation by reducing your speed to dead slow. Always lock the vehicle and stow your gear in the trunk, as break-ins are not unknown.

Beware of traffic cops around Tuasivi and Salelologa who will pull you over in the hope of receiving a bribe if you don't use your turn signal, fail to stop at a crosswalk, or commit any of the other minor infractions that most Samoan motorists commit all the time with impunity. Gas stations are found at Salelologa, Vaisala, Asau, Manase, and Lalomalava.

Dive and Fly Samoa (tel. 54-066), based at Jane's Beach Fales in Manase, rents motorbikes/bicycles at S$70/20 a day.

Taxis and Tours

Taxis are expensive on Savai'i, so be sure to settle the price before setting out. A full-day trip right around Savai'i by taxi will cost around S$300 for the whole car.

The easiest and safest way to get around is on an organized sightseeing tour conducted by retired geologist Warren Jopling from the Safua Hotel. Warren has achieved a measure of notoriety from descriptions in the mass-market Australian guidebooks, which, depending on his mood, he finds complimentary or an annoyance. He does very informative trips north across the lava fields to Mt. Matavanu and "short people's cave," and southwest to the Pulemelei stone pyramid and Taga blowholes, but only if four or five people sign up. The cost is S$60/100 pp for a half/full day tour (including lunch and custom fees). If only two people sign up, it could cost more.

Dive and Fly Samoa (tel. 54-066), at Jane's Beach Fales in Manase, does full-day circle island tours for S$80, plus admission fees. They can also take you flying in a micro light plane at S$120 for half an hour.

Tokelau

Tokelau, a dependent territory of New Zealand, consists of three atolls 500 km north of Samoa (Tokelau means "north"). In British colonial times it was known as the Union Group. The central atoll, Nukunonu, is 92 km from Atafu and 64 km from Fakaofo. Swains Island (Olohega), 200 km south of Fakaofo, traditionally belongs to Tokelau but it is now part of American Samoa.

Each atoll consists of a ribbon of coral *motus* (islets), 90 meters to six km long and up to 200 meters wide, enclosing a broad lagoon. At no point does the land rise more than five meters above the sea, which makes the territory vulnerable to rising sea levels caused by climate change. Together Atafu (3.5 square km), Fakaofo (four square km), and Nukunonu (4.7 square km) total only 12.2 square km of dry land, the smallest separate entity in the South Pacific. In water area, the three atolls include 165 square km of enclosed lagoons and 290,000 square km of territorial sea.

Life is relaxed in Tokelau. There are no large stores, hotels, restaurants, or bars, just plenty of coconuts, sand, and sun, and a happy, friendly people. This is outer-island Polynesia at its finest.

© MIKAELE MAIAVA

Climate

There's little variation from the 28°C annual average temperature. Rainfall is irregular but heavy (2,900 mm annually at Atafu); downpours of up to 80 mm in a single day are possible anytime. Tokelau is at the north edge of the main hurricane belt, but tropical storms sometimes sweep through between November and March. Since 1846, Tokelau had only experienced three recorded hurricanes; then in February 1990, waves from Hurricane Ofa broke across the atolls, washing topsoil away and contaminating the freshwater lens. Residual salt prevented new plant growth for months. Hurricane Val in 1992 did additional damage. The recent increase in such storms seems related to global warming.

History

Legend tells how the Maui brothers pulled three islands out of the ocean while fishing far from shore. Later the Polynesians arrived with taro, which supplemented the abundance of fish and coconuts. In the 18th century, the warriors of Fakaofo brought the other atolls under the rule of the Tui Tokelau.

The first European on the scene was Captain John Byron of HMS *Dolphin,* who saw Atafu in 1765. Ethnologist Horatio Hale of the U.S. Exploring Expedition of 1841 spent several days at Fakaofo and wrote an account of the inhabitants. Catholic and Protestant missionaries arrived between 1845 and 1863. In 1863, Peruvian slavers kidnapped several hundred Tokelauans, including nearly all of the able-bodied men, for forced labor in South America. Those who resisted were killed. A terrible dysentery epidemic from Samoa hit Tokelau the same year, reducing the total population to only 200.

The British belatedly extended official protection in 1877, but not until 1889, when it was decided that Tokelau might be of use in laying a transpacific cable, did Commander Oldham of the *Egeria* arrive to declare a formal protectorate. The British annexed their protectorate in 1916 and included it within the boundaries of the Gilbert and Ellice Islands Colony. This distant arrangement ended in 1925, when New Zealand, which ruled Samoa at that time,

TOKELAU HIGHLIGHTS

Atafu Atoll: wade/walk around the atoll in a day (p. 560)

Nukunono Atoll: broad lagoon, Catholic church, village with a bridge (p. 559)

Fale, Fakaofo: tiny island, densely populated village (p. 559)

MV *Tokelau,* the interisland ship: Tokelau is only accessible by boat (p. 557)

swimming pigs, Fakaofo: hundreds of pig pens along the reef (p. 559)

became the administering power. With the Tokelau Islands Act of 1948, New Zealand assumed full sovereignty, and the islanders became N.Z. citizens. A N.Z. proposal for Tokelau to unite with either Samoa or Cook Islands was rejected by the Tokelauans in 1964. In 1974, responsibility for Tokelau was transferred from New Zealand's Department of Maori and Island Affairs to the Ministry of Foreign Affairs. In a 1980, treaty signed with New Zealand, the United States government formally renounced claims to the group dating back to 1856. However, Tokelau's fourth atoll, Olohega (Swains Island), was retained by the United States. In 1999, Tokelau's elected leader restated his country's claim to Olohega at the United Nations.

Government

Tokelau is a dependency of New Zealand. The administrator of Tokelau is appointed by the N.Z. Ministry of Foreign Affairs and Trade (Private Bag 18-901, Wellington, New Zealand; tel. 64-4/473-2108, fax 64-4/494-8514) and resides in Wellington. He works through the Tokelau Apia Liaison Office (TALO) or "Tokalani" in Apia, Samoa. The administrator is represented on each island by a *faipule* (headman), who is elected locally every three years.

All three atolls have a *pulenuku* (mayor), also elected for a three-year term, who directs *nuku* (village) activities. Each island has a *taupulega* (island council) comprised of village elders or heads of families. Each *taupulega* chooses six delegates to the 18-member General Fono, which

THE RIDDLE OF THE JOYITA

One of the strangest episodes in recent Pacific history is indirectly related to Tokelau. On November 10, 1955, the crew of the trading ship *Tuvalu* sighted the drifting, half-sunken shape of the 21-meter MV *Joyita*, which had left Apia on October 3 bound for Fakaofo, carrying seven Europeans and 18 Polynesians. The *Joyita* had been chartered by Tokelau's district officer to take badly needed supplies to the atolls and pick up their copra, which was rotting on the beach. When the vessel was reported overdue, a fruitless aerial search began, which only ended with the chance discovery by the *Tuvalu* some 150 km north of Fiji. There was no sign of the 25 persons aboard, and sacks of flour, rice, and sugar had been removed from the ship. Also missing were 40 drums of kerosene, seven cases of aluminum strips, and the three life rafts.

The ghost ship was towed to Fiji and beached. Investigators found that the rudder had been jammed, the radio equipment wrecked, and the engines flooded due to a broken pipe in the saltwater cooling system. The navigation lights and galley stove were switched on. The *Joyita* hadn't sunk because the holds were lined with eight centimeters of cork. Though several books and countless newspaper and magazine articles have been written about the *Joyita* mystery, it has never been learned what really happened, nor have any of the missing persons ever been seen again.

meets twice a year (April and October) on alternate islands and has almost complete control over local matters.

In 1993, Tokelau received an added degree of self-government when a three-member Council of Faipule was created to act on behalf of the General Fono between sessions. The new position of *Ulu o Tokelau* (titular leader) is rotated annually among the three elected *faipule,* all of whom act as government ministers. In 1994, the powers of the Administrator were delegated to the General Fono and the Council of Faipule, giving Tokelau de facto internal self-government and the right to impose taxes. In 1996, the Parliament of New Zealand amended the Tokelau Islands Act of 1948 to make this system legal. In 2001, control of the public service was turned over to the Council of Faipule.

Rumors about the Tokelau Apia Liaison Office moving from Apia to one of the atolls have circulated for years, with the sticking point being disagreement over which atoll should become the host. Although Fakaofo seems the likely choice, there is great rivalry between the three and little "national" feeling. New Zealand would be happy to grant Tokelau full independence at any time, but there's considerable resistance to this in Tokelau itself where N.Z. aid is the main source of income. The right of free entry to New Zealand is also highly valued. The "Modern House of Tokelau" is a New Zealand-supported project aimed at developing Tokelau's governance, capacity and sustainable development on the path towards self-determination.

Economy

Tokelau receives more than NZ$8 million a year in N.Z. budgetary support and project assistance, over NZ$5,000 per capita. This subsidy is four times greater than all locally raised revenue, and exports of handicrafts are negligible (copra exports have ceased).

Tokelau earns several hundred thousand dollars a year from the sale of postage stamps and coins, but a more important source of revenue is licensing fees from American purse seiners, which pull tuna from Tokelau's 200-nautical-mile exclusive economic zone (EEZ). In recent years these fees have brought in twice as much revenue as local duties, registrations, and taxes. Inshore waters within 40 km of the reef are reserved for local fishing. New Zealand has declared that all income from the EEZ will go to Tokelau.

The 200 government jobs funded by New

Zealand are about the only regular source of monetary income in Tokelau today. Nearly all of these jobs are held by Tokelauans—there are few resident expatriates—and to avoid the formation of a privileged class, nearly half are temporary or casual positions that are rotated among the community. The Community Services Levy of 6–12 percent collected from wage earners is used to subsidize copra and handicraft production, further distributing the wealth. The *faka-Tokelau* (Tokelauan way of life) requires families to provide for their old and disabled.

Yet, limited resources have prompted many islanders to emigrate to New Zealand. Tokelauans are not eligible for N.Z. welfare payments unless they live in New Zealand and pay taxes there. However, since 1999 they have been allowed to receive their N.Z. pensions in Tokelau and this has stimulated some return migration.

The Changing Village
To be in the lee of the southeast trades, the villages sit on the west side of each atoll. The sandy soil and meager vegetation (only 61 species) force the Tokelauans to depend on the sea for protein. Coconut palms grow abundantly on the *motus:* What isn't consumed is dried and exported as copra. The islands are gradually being replanted with a high-yield coconut species from Rotuma. *Pulaka* (swamp taro) is cultivated in man-made pits up to two meters deep. Breadfruit is harvested November–March, and some bananas and papayas are also grown. Pandanus is used for making mats and other handicrafts or for thatching roofs; pandanus fruit is also edible. Pigs, chickens, and ducks are kept, and crabs are captured for food (but there are no dogs). Most land is held by family groups *(kaiga)* and cannot be sold to outsiders.

Today, as Tokelau enters a cash economy, imported canned and frozen foods are gaining importance. Aluminum motorboats have largely replaced dugout sailing canoes, and when gasoline is scarce the islanders cannot travel to the *motus* to collect their subsistence foodstuffs. European-style concrete housing is now the norm, and 98 percent of households depend on water channeled into storage tanks from the tin roofs. Some 39 percent

of houses have flush toilets. Most cooking is done on kerosene stoves, and appliances such as washing machines, electric irons, freezers, and VCRs are widespread. Trousers are gaining preference over the traditional *kie* (loincloth).

The changing values have also meant a decline in the traditional sharing system *(inati).* Outboard motors and electricity cost money: The rising standard of living has paralleled an increasing dependency on aid and remittances from relatives in New Zealand. Three-quarters of the adult population smoke. Imported foods and the changing lifestyle are largely to blame for the rapid increase in noncommunicable diseases such as hypertension, diabetes, heart disease, and gout. An average of one kilogram of sugar per person is consumed weekly, an 800 percent increase over the past 30 years. Dengue fever, influenza, and hepatitis are endemic in the population.

The People
The Tokelauans are closely related to the people of Tuvalu. Around 500 people live on each atoll, or 1,500 in Tokelau as a whole. Another 6,200 Tokelauans live "beyond the reef" in New Zealand (mainly around Wellington), the result of a migration that began in 1963, following overpopulation in Tokelau itself. A good many of the present islanders have been to New Zealand and the island population is actually declining as many working age adults join this migration.

Due to the work of early missionaries, Atafu is Congregationalist (LMS), Nukunonu Catholic, and Fakaofo a combination of the two. Since the Samoan Bible is used, all adults understand Samoan. Young people learn English at school, but everyone speaks Tokelauan at home. In Tokelau, authority is based on age, rather than lineage. Arguably, nowhere else in the world are senior citizens as respected. Traditionally, the women controlled family resources, but in recent years monetarism has led to this role being appropriated by men.

Conduct and Customs
In Tokelau, as elsewhere, proper conduct is mostly common sense. Take care not to expect better conditions than anyone else and avoid

causing a disturbance. Keep in mind that you're a guest in someone's home. Step aside for the elders and *never* tell them what to do. When passing in front of another person, bow slightly and say *tulou*.

If people invite you into a house for a cup of coffee or a meal, politely refuse, saying that you have just finished eating. Such invitations are usually only a form of greeting, and they may not even have what is offered. If they insist a second or third time, or it's someone you know quite well, then they probably mean it. Sit on the mat with your legs crossed or folded, not stretched out.

Village men work together a day or two a week on communal projects. If you can manage to join in with the group, known as the *aumaga*, you'll fit into the community better. You should also accompany your hosts to church on Sunday. Overt flirtations with members of the opposite sex are frowned upon. If you feel an attraction, simply mention it to one of his/her friends, and the word will be passed on. The women are crazy about bingo and stay up half the night playing it. You'll have to learn how to count (*tahi, lua, tolu, fa, lima, ono, fitu, valu, iva, helu*) if you want to join them (two *sene* a game). The men may offer to take you line fishing, rod fishing, spearfishing, net fishing, trolling (for bonito), etc.

Exploring the Islands

Arts and Crafts

Some of the finest traditional handicrafts in the Pacific are made in the Tokelau Islands, especially high-quality coconut-fiber hats and handbags, fans, and exquisite model canoes. Some of the handbags have a solid coconut-shell liner—handy for female self-defense. The coconut-shell water bottles are authentic and unique. The most distinctive article on display is the *tuluma*, a watertight wooden box used to carry valuables on canoe journeys; its buoyancy also makes it an ideal lifesaver. Unfortunately, little is produced these days.

Accommodations

Nukunonu has a small hotel, but on Fakaofo and Atafu you'll have to stay with a local family. This should be arranged in advance through the **Tokelau Apia Liaison Office** (P.O. Box 865, Apia, Samoa; tel. 685/20-822, fax 685/21-761). They'll forward your request to the respective island council and you'll pay about NZ$20 pp a day for food and accommodations. You could also write in advance to the *faipule* or *pulenuku* of the island of your choice to let them know your intentions—having a contact or local friend

TROPICAL CRICKET

Kilikiti (cricket) is the most popular team sport in Tokelau, involving teams of 55 players or more. On Fakaofo the men and women play together, while on Atafu they play separately. Batters stand at each end of a concrete pitch holding heavy Samoan hardwood bats that appear to be a cross between an American baseball bat and a Fijian war club. The bowler attempts to hit a wicket made from a wooden plank with overarm bowling mandatory on Atafu (on Fakaofo an underarm technique is used to bowl to ladies). The batters (one at each end) must hit the ball as far and fast as possible, and injuries often occur because the rubber ball is softer than an English cricket ball and travels much faster. The Fakaofo teams have special "runners" ready to run back and forth as soon as the ball is hit, while on Atafu the batters must run themselves. There are two innings per team per game, and the games can last anywhere from a few hours to three days. On Fakaofo the teams often take time off to go fishing in the middle of a game and the number of fish caught are added to each team's score.

makes everything easier. Once your stay has been approved, the Tokelau Apia Liaison Office will give you a visa application to complete and collect a NZ$20 processing fee.

When you go, take along a bottle of spirits for whomever made the arrangements, as well as gifts for the family. Suggested items are rubber thongs, housewares, tools, fishing gear (stainless steel fishhooks, fishing line, swivels, sinkers, lures, mask and snorkel, and spear-gun rubbers), and perhaps a rugby ball or volleyball. The women will appreciate perfumes, deodorants, cosmetics, printed cloth, and dyes. Kitchen knives and enamel mugs are always welcome.

You'll probably have to sleep on the floor and use communal toilets over the lagoon—there'll be little or no privacy. Still, the facilities are of a much higher standard than in comparable Samoan villages. Most families own land on one of the *motus,* so you could spend a few days camping on your own if you have a tent and a large enough water container. Before you leave an atoll where you've stayed between ships, you could receive a "summons" from the council of elders at which you'll be asked to explain the purpose of your visit. If you give the right answers you could be honored with a traditional gift.

Food

There's only one cooperative store on each atoll, selling rice, flour, sugar, canned fish and meat, spaghetti, gasoline, etc. Take as much food as you can—bags of taro, a sack of bananas, fruit such as pineapples and mangoes, garlic, instant coffee, and tea. Ask at the Tokelau Apia Liaison Office about agricultural import restrictions. Camera film is not available.

All three co-ops sell imported liquor, although the supply is often exhausted soon after the ship has left. Previously the locals made sour toddy, obtained by cutting the flower stem of a coconut tree and collecting the sap in a half-coconut container. The whitish fluid *(kaleve)* had many uses. It could be drunk fresh, or boiled and stored in a fridge. If kept in a container at room temperature for two days, it ferments into sour toddy beer. Boil fresh *kaleve* to a brown molasses for use in cooking or as a sauce. A tablespoon of boiled

kaleve in a cup of hot water makes an island tea. You can even make bread out of it by adding saltwater, flour, and fat, as all Tokelauan women know. Unfortunately, *kaleve* is now banned on all three atolls, because it was used mostly to make alcohol, leading to drinking problems. *Vaisalo* is a tasty hot drink made from boiled coconut milk and meat with sago added for taste.

Internet Resources

The Tokelau Web Site, **www.tokelau.org.nz** maintained by the Modern House of Tokelau Project, is the only serious site dedicated exclusively to the territory. Information is provided on the geography, history, people, culture, and economy, plus details of transportation and contacts for visitors. Websites dedicated to the individual atolls include **www.nukunonu.tk** and **www.fakaofo.tk.**

Services

The New Zealand dollar is the currency used on the islands. You can change money at the Finance Department in the Administration Center on each island.

In 1997, Tokelau became the last country in the world to be connected to the rest of the planet by satellite telephone. Tokelau's telephone code is 690.

If you wish to send a fax to anyone in Tokelau, the public fax numbers are: Atafu fax 690/2108, Fakaofo fax 690/3103, and Nukunonu fax 690/4108. Just put the person's name at the top and the clerk will deliver it for a small fee.

When writing to Tokelau, include the words "via Samoa" in the address. Collectors can order Tokelau postage stamps from the Tokelau Philatelic Bureau, P.O. Box 68, Wellington, New Zealand.

There's a hospital on all three atolls, and treatment is free. Bring a remedy for diarrhea.

Getting There

The seaplane service to Tokelau was suspended in 1983, but there's been talk of building an airstrip on Fenuafala (Fakaofo). Meanwhile, the only way to get there is on the 19-meter, 65-passenger monohull MV *Tokelau,* which leaves Apia, Samoa, for the three atolls about twice a month. It takes just under two days to reach the first island and seven to nine days to complete the roundtrip. The ship often runs out of food on the way back to Apia, so carry a reserve supply.

This is not a trip for the squeamish or fainthearted. On the MV *Tokelau* most passengers travel deck, and every available space on deck will be packed with the Tokelauans and their belongings. Cabin space is limited. Pray that you travel with the wind because against the wind it's extremely rough and the smell of diesel pervades the air. There's merry feasting when the boat arrives, and usually time for snorkeling and picnicking on the *motus*. The passengers are an interesting mix.

Tokelauans and officials get first priority on these trips, and tourists are only taken if there happens to be space left over. Advance reservations are not accepted, and cabins will be confirmed only a week prior to sailing. Check with the Tokelau Apia Liaison Office when you reach Apia—you may be lucky. Tokelauans pay only NZ$100 roundtrip on deck, but this price is heavily subsidized and NZ$286 (which you'll pay) is considered to be the real cost without any profit element built in. The cabin fare is NZ$528 pp roundtrip. Reduced rates are available for children 12 and under. You pass Samoan Immigration on the wharf in Apia, a unique way of renewing your Samoan tourist visa.

Getting Around

Passes for small boats have been blasted through the reefs, but the ships must stand offshore. Passengers and cargo are transferred to the landings in aluminum whaleboats, which roar through the narrow passes on the crest of a wave. In offshore winds there's poor anchorage at Fakaofo and Nukunonu, and none at all off Atafu. For safety's sake, interatoll voyages by outrigger canoe are prohibited, and everyone must use the fortnightly MV *Tokelau*. There are no cars or trucks in Tokelau, but most canoes are now fitted with outboards.

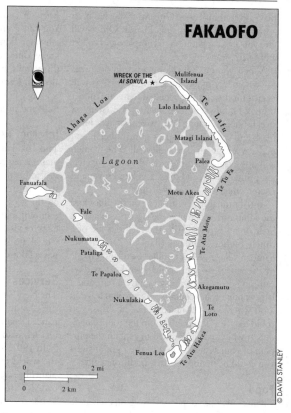

FAKAOFO

WRECK OF THE
AI SOKULA ★

Mulifenua Island

Ahaga Loa

Lalo Island

Te Lafu

Matagi Island

Lagoon

Palea

Fanuafala

Motu Akea

Te Tu Fa

Fale

Te Atu Motu

Nukumatau

Pataliga

Te Papaloa

Akegamutu

Nukulakia

Te Loto

Fenua Loa

Te Atu Hakea

0   2 mi

0   2 km

© DAVID STANLEY

The Tokelau Islands

Fakaofo

Fakaofo is the atoll closest to Samoa. Some 400 people live on tiny 4.5-hectare **Fale Island,** which is well shaded by breadfruit trees. The two-story administration building on Fale housing the transportation office, police station, post office, and village store was completed in 1989. To relieve the overcrowding, a second village was established in 1960 on the larger island of Fanuafala, about three km northwest. At low tide you can walk across the reef between the two. The school, hospital, and the TeleTOK (telephone company) headquarters are now on Fanuafala, which has a pleasant beach and good swimming on the lagoon side.

An ancient coral slab erected to the Tui Tokelau stands in the Fakafotu Falefono (meeting-house) at Fale. This stone may once have exercised supernatural power. On the lagoon-side beach opposite is the *hakava* (family meeting place) where visitors are sometimes accommodated in an upstairs room.

The freighter *Ai Sokula* can be seen on the reef at Ahaga Loa, where it was wrecked in 1987. Guano, a fertilizer formed from bird droppings, is collected on Palea, a tiny *motu* on the east side of the atoll, for use in nearby taro pits. Over a thousand **pigs** swim and forage for shellfish in reef pools near the settlements on Fakaofo (the only swimming pigs in the Pacific). Their pens and enclosures must be on the reef itself, since every bit of land on Fale is used for human housing.

small boat harbor at Fakaofo, Tokelau

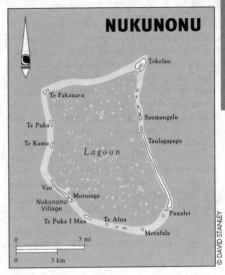

NUKUNONU

Tokelau
Te Fakanava
Saumangalu
Te Puka
Taulagapapa
Te Kamu
Lagoon
Vao
Motusaga
Nukunonu Village
Punalei
Te Puka I Mua
Te Afua
Motufala

0   3 mi
0   3 km

© DAVID STANLEY

Nukunonu

This largest atoll in both land and lagoon area sits in the center of the group. A New Zealand reader reported that he hiked right around the atoll in 2.5 days. One reef crossing lasted four hours but was possible. Since Nukunonu is Catholic (see the large whitewashed stone church), life is less restricted than on the Congregationalist islands. The village is divided into two parts by a reef pass spanned by a bridge. No dugout canoes are left on Nukunonu; everyone has switched to aluminum outboards. The rhinoceros beetle, a pest that attacks coconut trees, has established itself here.

Since 1995, Mr. Luhiano Perez, headmaster of the local school, and his wife Juliana have operated the **Luana Liki Hotel** (tel. 4140, fax 4108, matiti@wise.net.nz) near the school and a four-minute walk from the store. This solid, lilac-colored two-story building contains nine double rooms. They charge NZ$50 pp a night including all meals. Camping (own tent) on Sydney, Luhiano's private island, can be arranged.

Also available on Nukunonu is the **Falefa**

Resort (tel. 4137 or 4139, fax 4108), which charges NZ$25 pp a night including all meals.

Atafu

The smallest of the atolls, Atafu's lagoon totals only 17 square km (compared to 50 square km on Fakaofo and 98 square km at Nukunonu). It's claimed you can walk around the atoll in a day. This is the most traditional of the islands, the only one where dugout canoes are still made. Some houses with thatched roofs survive in the one village at the northwest corner of the atoll (few of these remain on the other atolls). There's a ceramic history of Tokelau on the side wall of Matauala Public School. The Office of the Council of Faipule (tel. 2133) and the University of the South Pacific Center are on Atafu. Be prepared for a NZ$50 fine if you get caught partaking of the local homebrew of yeast and sugar.

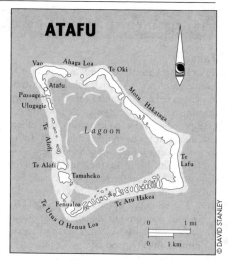

ATAFU

Vao Ahaga Loa Te Oki
Atafu Motu Hakataga
Passage
Ulugagie
Te Alofi
Lagoon
Te Alofi
Te Lafu
Tamaheko
Fenualoa Te Atu Hakea
Te Utua O Henua Loa

0   1 mi
0   1 km

© DAVID STANLEY

Wallis and Futuna

Introduction

This little-known corner of Polynesia lies between Fiji and Samoa, with Futuna almost as close to Vanua Levu as it is to Wallis. Smallest of France's three South Pacific territories, Wallis and Futuna (Uvéa mo Futuna) are isolated from its neighbors geographically, culturally, and politically. All the marks of French colonialism are here, from overpaid European officials controlling functionless staff to little French gendarmes in round caps and shorts.

Although Aircalin flights make the islands accessible from Nouméa and Fiji, high airfares and the lack of any moderately priced accommodations limit visitors to French officials, the eccentric, the adventuresome, and yachts' crews. Wallis and Futuna are well off the beaten track.

The Land

The islands of Wallis and Futuna, 250 km apart, are quite dissimilar. Wallis (159 square km including adjacent islands) is fairly flat, with verdant volcanic hillsides rising gently to Mt. Lulu Fakahega (145 meters). There are freshwater

© M.E. DE VOS

crater lakes (Lalolalo, Lanutavake, and others). The main island, Uvéa, and 10 other volcanic islands in the eastern half of the lagoon are surrounded by a barrier reef bearing 12 smaller coral islands, many with fine beaches. Five passes breach this reef, but large ships bound for Mata-Utu wharf enter the lagoon through Honikulu Pass, the southernmost.

Futuna and Alofi, together totaling 115 square km, are mountainous, with Mt. Puke on Futuna reaching 524 meters. Futuna is near a fracture where the Pacific Plate pushes under the Indo-Australian Plate and major earthquakes do occur. Though there are many freshwater springs on Futuna, Alofi two km to the southeast is uninhabited due to a lack of water. A reef fringes the sandy north coast of Alofi; the south coast features high cliffs. Futuna has no lagoon.

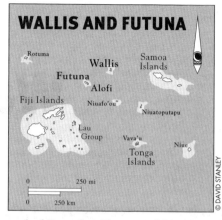

© DAVID STANLEY

Climate

As in neighboring Samoa, the climate is hot and humid year-round, with an annual average temperature of 27°C. Rainfall is heavy at more than 3,000 mm a year, usually falling in the late afternoon or night. The hurricane season in the islands is November–April, and many storms form in the area between Wallis and Samoa. During the drier season, May–October, the islands are cooled somewhat by the refreshing southeast trade winds.

History

Legend tells how the Polynesian god of creation Tangaloa caught an especially large fish in his net one night. He rushed home to get a knife, but upon seeing how huge the fish really was, decided to wait until daybreak to pull it in. As dawn rose in the east, Tangaloa saw that the large fish had changed into the island we call Uvéa, and some smaller fish also in the net were now little islets held together by the net itself, which had become a coral reef.

Although these islands were discovered by the Polynesians more than 3,000 years ago, not until April 26, 1616, did the Dutch navigators Schouten and Le Maire arrive at Futuna and Alofi. They named Futuna Hoorn, after their home port of Hoorn on the IJsselmeer, 42 km

north of Amsterdam. The name of Cape Horn, in South America, is derived from the same old port. Captain Samuel Wallis in HMS *Dolphin* was the first European to contact Wallis (on August 16, 1767). American whalers began to visit from 1820 onward.

Marist missionaries arrived on both Futuna and Wallis in 1837, and from Wallis Bishop Pierre Bataillon directed Catholic missionary efforts in Fiji, Samoa, and Tonga. Futuna is well known to Catholics around the Pacific as the site of the 1841 martyrdom of Pierre Chanel, patron saint of Oceania.

Wallis and Futuna was declared a French protectorate in 1887, and in 1924 the protectorate officially became a colony. This was the only French colony in the Pacific to remain loyal to the collaborating government in Vichy France until after Pearl Harbor. From 1942 to 1944, Wallis was an important American military base, with as many as 6,000 U.S. troops on the island. Hihifo airport dates from the war, as does an abandoned airstrip just south of Lake Kikila. In a 1959 referendum, the populace voted to upgrade Wallis and Futuna's status to that of an overseas territory, and this status was granted by the French Parliament in 1961.

Government

The French High Commissioner in Nouméa selects a senior administrator to control the local bureaucracy (www.adsupwf.org) from Mata-Utu on Wallis. An elected Territorial Assembly with 20 members (13 from Wallis and seven from Futuna) has limited legislative powers over local matters. The policy-making Territorial Council is composed of the Lavelua (king) of Wallis, two kings of Futuna (the Tuisigave of Sigave and the Tuiagaifo of Alo), and three members appointed by the French administrator, who presides. The three kings retain considerable influence, and every French administrator who has tried to challenge them has had to leave. The territory elects a deputy and a senator to the French Parliament in Paris. The traditional Polynesian monarchy and the Catholic Church continue to be powerful forces in the islands.

Economy

The territory of Wallis and Futuna buys a hundred times more than it sells: Trochus shells and a few bags of taro are the only exports. Most of the people employed on the island work for the French government, and what they produce is perhaps the most invisible export of all—the illusion of colonial glory. The strategic position of Wallis and Futuna at the heart of the South Pacific accounts for its continuing importance in France's global empire.

The US$30 million annual territorial budget and US$70 million in state expenditures come mostly out of the pockets of French taxpayers, although some local revenue is collected in customs duties. Nearly half this money is absorbed by administration costs. French civil servants on Wallis make a lot more than their counterparts in France, plus a respectable lump sum upon completion of their three-year contracts. All prices are set accordingly. The locals get free medical and dental care, and free education (in French) up to university level: With such French largess, independence is unthinkable. Considerable money also arrives in the form of remittances from Wallisian emigrants in New Caledonia.

The locals cultivate much of their own food in the rich volcanic soils. Taro, yam, manioc, breadfruit, and banana gardens are everywhere. The coconut plantations of Wallis were destroyed in the 1930s by the rhinoceros beetle, but this pest has been brought under control. All of the coconuts are now used to feed the prolific swine, an important source of food. The plantations of Futuna were saved, but today they only produce a couple of hundred tons of copra a year (also fed to the hogs). Archaeologists have found pig bones associated with *lapita* pottery dating from 1400 B.C., proving that these animals were introduced by the first humans. Introduced African snails continue to damage the vegetation.

The People

The 9,000 people on Wallis and 5,000 on Futuna are Polynesian: The Wallisians, or Uvéans, descended from Tongans, the Futunans from Samoans. The Wallis Islanders are physically huge, bigger than Tongans. There's little mixing between the two groups and only about 100 Uvéans and Futunans live on the other island. Some 800 French expats reside on Wallis, but only 100 on Futuna. They have a small subdivision on Wallis named Afala on a hill just north of Mata-Utu.

Another 17,600 people from both islands live and work 2,500 km away in Nouméa, New Caledonia, and 2,800 more are in France. Young Uvéans and Futunans often stay in New Caledonia after completing their compulsory military service, and many obtain employment in the nickel mining or construction industries. The many partially constructed or uninhabited dwellings on Wallis are a result of the migrations. Many residents still live in round-ended thatched *fales*. One compromise with the 21st century is the electric line entering through the peak of the roof. Property passes down through the female line.

Very little English is spoken on Wallis, and even less on Futuna, so a knowledge of French, Tongan, or Samoan makes life a lot easier. Wallisian and Futunan are distinct: Welcome is *malo te kataki/malo le ma'uli* in Wallisian/Futunan. Similarly, farewell said to someone leaving is *alu la/ano la.* Farewell said to someone staying is *nofo la* in both languages.

EXPLORING THE ISLANDS
Public Holidays and Festivals

Public holidays include New Year's Day, Easter Monday (March/April), Labor Day (May 1), Ascension Day, Pentecost, Assumption Day (August 15), All Saints' Day (November 1), Armistice Day (November 11), and Christmas Day. The biggest celebrations of the year center around St. Pierre Chanel Day (April 28) and Bastille Day (July 14). Territory Day (July 29) is also marked by traditional dancing and canoe races. Each of the three Wallis parishes has its own holiday: May 14 at Mu'a, June 29 at Hihifo (Vaitupu), and August 15 at Hahake (Mata-Utu). The Uvéans are expert sword dancers.

Accommodations

The handful of small pension-style hotels on these islands are mostly in our US$50–100 price range. Reserve in advance if you need an airport transfer. About the only alternative is to camp in the interior; the Uvéans are hospitable, and a request for permission to camp sometimes leads to an invitation to stay in their homes. Alofitai Beach on Alofi would be a nice place to camp.

Internet Resources

The Wallis and Futuna Website, **www.wallis-islands.com/index.gb.htm,** carries some general and travel information in English. Wallis and Futuna Hotels, **www.wallis-and-futuna .com,** provides detailed hotel listings in both English and French.

Visas and Officialdom

Entry requirements are the same as those of New Caledonia and French Polynesia. If you arrive by yacht, visit the gendarmerie in Mata-Utu. If you're going on to Futuna, return there for a *sortie* stamp, otherwise you could have trouble when you apply for an *entrée* stamp on Futuna.

Money

Three of the five hotels accept credit cards, but elsewhere they're seldom used. The bank in Mata-Utu gives cash advances but they deduct a high commission when changing traveler's checks. If you'll be visiting Tahiti or New Caledonia before going to Wallis and Futuna, buy your Pacific francs there, as exactly the same currency is used in all three French territories. Euros in cash are fairly easy to change. Though expensive, Wallis and Futuna has the lowest inflation rate in the South Pacific.

Media

The weekly newspaper, *Te Fenua Fo'ou* (tel./fax 72-17-46), is mostly in French with a couple of pages in Wallisian and Futunan. In mid-2002, this paper was forced to cease publication for seven months after a dispute with the local king, and only a change in ownership allowed publication to resume. The New Caledonian newspapers are also distributed on Wallis.

The government-operated radio station, Réseau France Outre-Mer or RFO (www.rfo.fr), broadcasts over FM 100 MHz and AM 1188 kHz from Uvéa, FM 91 MHz from Alo, and 89 and 90.5 MHz from Sigave.

Business Hours and Time

This being a French colony, many offices open only on weekdays 0730–1130 and 1400–1630. If you are planning on doing any shopping during the midday siesta, verify the opening hours beforehand.

The time in Wallis and Futuna is GMT plus 12 hours. Though the territory is actually east of the 180th meridian, in 1926 the international date line was moved east, so Wallis and Futuna could share New Caledonia's day. Thus it's the same day here as in Nouméa or Nadi, but one day later than in Papeete.

TRANSPORTATION

Getting There

The New Caledonian carrier **Aircalin** (tel. 72-28-80, fax 72-27-11) flies to Hihifo Airport on Wallis three times a week from Nouméa and twice a week from Nadi. The flights are heavily booked by Wallisian residents of New Caledonia, so reserve well ahead.

Private yachts sailing between Pago Pago and Fiji sometimes anchor in Wallis' sheltered lagoon. Un-fortunately, the container ship between Nouméa and Wallis no longer accepts passengers.

Getting Around

Aircalin also flies between Wallis and Futuna (CFP 8,900 one way) twice a day, four times a week. Only 10 kilos of baggage are allowed on the 19-passenger Twin Otter turboprop that does the Wallis-Futuna run, and it's often full.

There has been talk of establishing a high-speed catamaran service between Wallis and Futuna.

Wallis

Situated almost exactly midway between Tahiti and Nouméa, Wallis sits on the threshold of Polynesia and Melanesia. Around the year 1400, warriors sent by the Tu'i Tonga conquered the island and installed the first member of Uvéa's current ruling dynasty. The 15th century forts at Talietumu and Malama Tagata, built to enforce Tongan domination of Wallis, have recently been excavated. English explorer Samuel Wallis anchored off the island for two days in 1767, but he didn't disembark. Whalers began calling in 1825, and in 1832 they established a base on Nukuatea. Catholic missionaries arrived in 1837 and within five years the entire population had been converted. The missionaries protected the islanders from the excesses of other Europeans and controlled all aspects of society in congruence with the king. Massive stone churches were erected at Mata-Utu, Mu'a, and Vaitupu; the interior decoration of the one at Vaitupu is the best. Even today the bishop and king together carry more weight than the French prefect.

© DAVID STANLEY

The massive hulk of Mata Utu Cathedral is a very visible bulwark of Gaulish Catholicism.

WALLIS AND FUTUNA

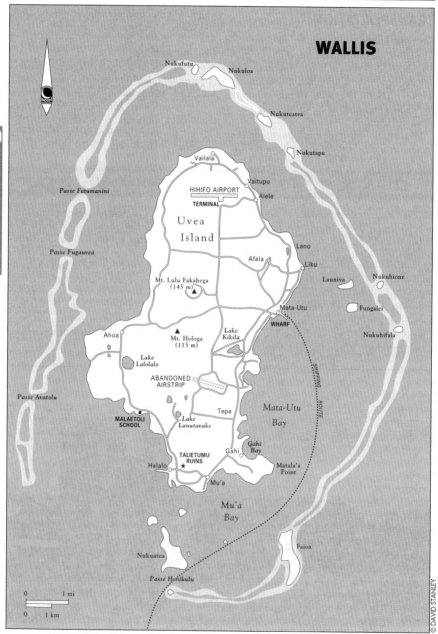

WALLIS

Nukufutu

Nukuloa

Nukuteatea

Nukutapu

Vailala

Vaitupu

HIHIFO AIRPORT

Alele

TERMINAL

Uvea
Island

Lano

Afala

Liku

Launiva

Nukuhione

Mt. Lulu Fakahega
(145 m)

Mata-Utu

Fungalei

WHARF

Ahoa

Mt. Hologa
(115 m)

Lake
Kikila

Nukuhifala

Lake
Lalolalo

ABANDONED
AIRSTRIP

Mata-Utu
Bay

MALAETOLI
SCHOOL

Tepa

Lake
Lanutavake

TALIETUMU
RUINS

Gahi

Gahi
Bay

Halalo

Matala'a
Point

Mu'a

Mu'a
Bay

Passe Fatumanini

Passe Fugauvea

Passe Avatolu

SHIPPING ROUTE

Nukuatea

Faioa

Passe Honikulu

0   1 mi

0   1 km

© DAVID STANLEY

SIGHTS

Near Town

Mata-Utu resembles a village, except for a massive **cathedral** of hand-cut blue volcanic stone with two blocklike towers overlooking the wharf. The Maltese cross between the towers also appears on the royal flag of Wallis. The **king's palace,** large but not ostentatious, is beside Mata-Utu Cathedral. On the waterfront opposite it is the **Fale Fono**, the main meeting place of the island's chiefs.

A rough road up to the tiny ruined chapel atop **Mt. Lulu Fakahega** (145 meters) brings you to the highest point on the island. Take the road west from Mata-Utu to the main north-south road in the center of the island: The track is on the left about 500 meters north of the cross-roads. From the summit the jungle-clad crater is fairly obvious, and you can descend to the taro plantation below along an easy trail. The view from Mt. Lulu Fakahega of Uvéa's rich red soil cloaked in greenery is quite good.

Farther Afield

Lake Lalolalo on the far west side of Wallis is spectacular: It's circular, with vertical red walls 30 meters high, which make the pea-green water almost inaccessible. At dusk flying foxes *(peka)* swoop over Lake Lalolalo from their perches on overhanging trees, and there are blind eels in the lake. Another of the crater lakes, **Lake Lanutavake,** is less impressive, but you can swim (approach it from the west side). The Americans dumped their war equipment into the lakes just before they left.

The ruins of the 15th century fortified Tongan settlement at **Talietumu** between Mu'a and Halalo have recently been excavated and restored.

There are no good beaches on the main island of Uvéa, but coralline **Faioa Island** on the reef southeast of Mu'a has the white sands bordering a turquoise lagoon of which South Seas dreams are made. When the easterlies are blowing hard, this is a protected place to anchor; nearby Gahi Bay is another good protected anchorage for yachts. Yachts also anchor off the wharves at Halalo and Mata-Utu, though it can be choppy if a wind is blowing.

PRACTICALITIES

Accommodations

Snack Oceania (tel. 72-19-64), at the end of Mata-Utu wharf, offers rooms with shared bath above their grocery store at CFP 5,000, breakfast included. Additional rooms are sometimes available at the waterside restaurant/bar next door.

Wallis' best-known hotel is the two-story **Hôtel Lomipeau** (Paola et Christian Ruotolo; tel. 72-20-21, fax 72-26-95, hotel.lomipeau@wallis.co.nc), beside the hospital 800 meters north of Mata-Utu. They have 12 a/c rooms with private bath and balcony at CFP 10,500/11,500 single/double, breakfast included. There's a lagoon view from the swimming pool. The Lomipeau arranges lagoon excursions and car rentals. Airport transfers are CFP 1,500.

The 28-room **Hôtel Moana Hou** (Palatomiano Kulikovi; tel./fax 72-21-35) is at Liku, on the waterfront about one km north of Mata-Utu. It's CFP 8,500/9,500 single/double, breakfast included. Airport transfers are CFP 1,500, and cars are for rent.

A retired French pilot named Jacques Bilco and his Wallisian wife operate **Hôtel Albatros** (tel./fax 72-18-27) at Alele, 200 meters from the airport terminal. The four a/c rooms with fridge in the main building are CFP 12,750 single or double, while the three neat little bungalows around the pool are CFP 16,000. Breakfast is included.

Food and Shopping

Snack Oceania (tel. 72-19-64) and **Restaurant du Quai** (Petelo Fuahea, tel. 72-24-55), both near the end of Mata-Utu Wharf, serve plates like steak frites and chicken at CFP 1,000 and up. **Restaurant Le Teone** (André Vaitootai, tel. 72-29-19), on the waterfront a bit north of the wharf, features Asian dishes, plus grilled meats and seafood. Late Friday and Saturday nights it becomes a disco.

Also in Mata-Utu is **Pizzeria Lelei** (tel. 72-25-54; daily 0600–2300). **Restaurant Paogo Togi** (Yannick Dinh, tel. 72-26-48; closed Sun.) on the main road south serves Vietnamese dishes costing CFP 1,350–1,500.

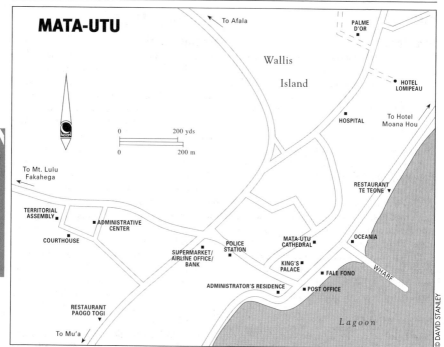

MATA-UTU

To Afala

PALME D'OR

Wallis

Island

HOTEL LOMIPEAU

To Hotel Moana Hou

HOSPITAL

0   200 yds

0   200 m

To Mt. Lulu Fakahega

RESTAURANT TE TEONE

TERRITORIAL ASSEMBLY

ADMINISTRATIVE CENTER

OCEANIA

COURTHOUSE

MATA-UTU CATHEDRAL

POLICE STATION

SUPERMARKET/ AIRLINE OFFICE/ BANK

KING'S PALACE

WHARF

FALE FONO

ADMINISTRATOR'S RESIDENCE

POST OFFICE

RESTAURANT PAOGO TOGI

Lagoon

To Mu'a

© DAVID STANLEY

At Liku just beyond the Hôtel Moana Hou north of town is a popular thatched locale called **La Terrasse de Liku** (Noella Taofifenua, tel. 72-27-37). Seafood is their specialty. At Mu'a try **Snack You You** (tel. 72-25-42).

The supermarkets of Mata-Utu offer a reasonable selection of goods but there's no fresh produce market. Meat is flown in from Nouméa weekly. The water is safe to drink on Wallis (but not on Futuna).

Palme d'Or, opposite the Hôtel Lomipeau, sells postcards and the excellent IGN topographical maps of Wallis and Futuna.

Services

The Banque de Wallis et Futuna (tel. 72-21-24; weekdays 0800–1200 and 1300–1600) in Mata-Utu is affiliated with the Banque Nationale de Paris. They charge CFP 1,000 commission on exchanges.

Card telephones are available at the post office near Mata-Utu wharf, the postal agencies at Mu'a and Vaitupu, the airport, and the Lycée. Wallis and Futuna's telephone code is 681.

Mata-Utu hospital (tel. 72-25-15) offers free consultations weekdays 0800–1000 and 1500–1600.

Getting Around

Most of the villages are on Wallis' east coast from Halalo to Vailala, which has a paved road along its length. No bus service is available on Wallis, but the hitching is very easy.

Some of the hotels rent cars, otherwise there's **Pacific Dinh Motoka** (François Dinh; tel./fax 72-26-57) in Mata-Utu and **Pacific Auto Location** (tel. 72-28-32, fax 72-29-33) near the airport.

Futuna and Alofi

Futuna (not to be confused with an island of the same name in Vanuatu) is a volcanic island five km wide by 20 km long (64 square km). The narrow southwestern coastal strip is 200 meters wide at most. Gardens are planted on the mountainside, which rises abruptly from the sea, and the terraced taro fields are quite ingenious. High cliffs on the north side of Futuna delayed completion of the road around the island until 1992, and the steep, narrow road from Ono to the airstrip and beyond is quite a feat of engineering.

Kava drinking has died out on Wallis (people would rather watch videos) but on Futuna the men imbibe large quantities nightly at the *tau'asu* (kava meetinghouses) found in each village. The Sunday meal is usually prepared in an *umu* (earth oven). The Futunans have also preserved their traditional Samoan-related handicrafts, such as tapa painted with a black dye made from cashew nut or a brown stain from the seed of a red fruit. Pandanus mats, kava bowls *(tanoa)*, war clubs, and outrigger canoes are also made.

Around 2,000 people live in Sigave Kingdom, which has the only anchorage for ships at Leava. Ono, between Leava and the airport, is the main village of Alo Kingdom with about 3,000 inhabitants. Two small hotels exist and the regular air service from Wallis makes a visit practical. Provided you know a little French and are willing to pay the price, it's a fascinating opportunity to see a part of the Pacific few English speakers know.

WALLIS AND FUTUNA

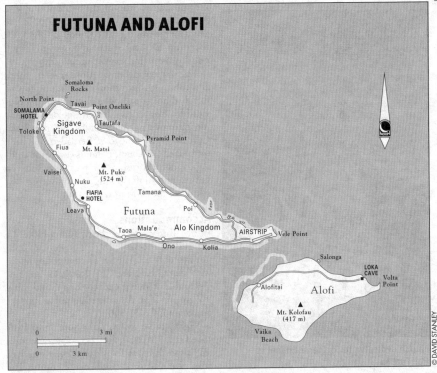

FUTUNA AND ALOFI

© DAVID STANLEY

Sights

A 35-km road circles Futuna with concrete paving from Poi to Ono, Leava, and Toloke via the south coast (the rest is a rough coral road). Both Ono and Nuku have old Catholic churches. The *fale fono* at Vaisei has a traditional fiber-bound ceiling.

At **Point Oneliki** a small chapel stands above the spot where a black lava flow once reached the sea. The blue hole just below the chapel is a great place to swim. A small black sand beach is just east of Point Oneliki at Tuatafa.

Futuna's most famous sight is the **Church of Pierre Chanel** at Poi on the northeast coast, a peculiar church with a stepped tower erected to honor Polynesia's first and only Catholic saint (canonized 1954). Chanel's relics were returned from France in 1976 and they're now kept in a smaller octagonal chapel next to the main church. His bones are held in a glass showcase near the entrance, and an adjacent silver casket contains

church dedicated to St. Pierre Chanel at Poi, Futuna

the saint's skull. A stone set in the chapel's floor marks the precise spot where Chanel was killed, and two of the war clubs used to kill him are on display. King Niuliki, who feared the missionary was usurping his position, had Chanel martyred on 28 April, 1841, four years after his arrival on the island. A small museum room behind the showcase contains other mementos.

The nicest place on Futuna to swim is off the white beach next to Vele Airport, but beware of the currents, because there's no lagoon.

With the help of a guide, it's possible to climb **Mt. Puke** (524 meters) from Taoa in about five hours return.

Alofi

Uninhabited Alofi (51 square km) is under the control of the King of Alo. People from Futuna spend the week tending their gardens on Alofi, returning to Futuna for church on Sunday. They keep their small boats on the beach next to Vele Airstrip, leaving for Alofitai around 0600. To hire a boat for the crossing will cost around CFP 3,000 roundtrip, although it should be easy to hitch a ride if you can find someone going anyway.

The shallow lagoon at **Alofitai** offers corals and colorful fish to snorkelers. A long row of thatched huts—each with electric lighting provided by solar panels—lines the golden beach at Alofitai, providing shelter for the gardeners. **Loka Cave,** where a shrine to St. Bernadette has been established, is a couple of hours east of the landing on foot. Large ships can pass easily between Futuna and Alofi, so long as they keep to the middle of the two-km-wide passage.

Accommodations

Patrick Tortey operates the two-story **Hôtel Le Fia Fia** (tel. 72-32-45, fax 72-35-56) at Nuku just west of Leava. The five air-conditioned rooms with shared bath are CFP 7,000/11,500 single/double. A lounge with cooking facilities and TV are provided. A substantial meal at Patrick's restaurant is CFP 1,500.

Slightly more upscale is the **Somalama Park Hôtel** (tel. 72-31-20, fax 72-31-75, www.wallis .co.nc/somalama) at Toloke, on a lovely stretch of coast near the northwestern tip of Futuna. The manager, Charles Gaveau, is one of the few English speakers on Futuna. Opened in 2001, this new concrete building has six air-conditioned rooms with private bath and satellite TV upstairs at CFP 10,500/11,500/13,000single/double/triple, breakfast included. Dinner is CFP 1,600. Car rentals are CFP 3,500 a day, plus CFP 50 per km. Airport transfers are CFP 1,500 pp for the 15 km. The Aoia 2000 Nightclub (open Fri. and Sat. nights) is nearby.

Practicalities

Five stores are in Sigave and three in Alo. A few shops are opposite Leava wharf. The small banking agency (tel. 72-36-40) at Leava is only open two days a month. The Aircalin office (tel. 72-32-04) is also at Leava. Card telephones are found at Leava and Ono post offices. The gendarmerie is just outside Leava on the road to Ono. The hospital is at Taoa. Gas stations are found at Leava and Mala'e.

Tuvalu

Introduction

Tuvalu is one of the world's smallest and most isolated independent nations. During British colonial times the group was known as the Ellice Islands, and while the current name Tuvalu means "cluster of eight," there are actually nine islands in all. The explanation lies with the smallest island, Niulakita, which was only resettled by people from Niutao in 1949. Internationally, Tuvalu is best known for its Internet address (.tv) and the threat posed by global warming.

Due to high airfares, this remote group of low coral atolls gets only a few dozen tourists a year and most never go beyond the crowded little government center on Funafuti. This makes the almost inaccessible outer islands one of the most idyllic and unspoiled corners of the Pacific, particularly Nukufetau and Nukulaelae. On these, time seems to stand still, yet rising sea levels due to greenhouse gas emissions far away may soon bring the world to them.

The Land

Legend tells how an eel *(te Pusi)* and a flatfish *(te Ali)* were carrying home a heavy rock and began to quarrel. The eel killed the flatfish and

© DAVID STANLEY

fed on his body, just as the tall coconut trees feed on the round, flat islands today. Then *te Pusi* broke the rock into eight pieces and disappeared into the sea.

The three islands and six atolls that make up Tuvalu together total only 25 square km in land area, curving northwest-southeast in a chain 676 km long on the outer western edge of Polynesia. Tuvalu's 900,000-square-km exclusive economic zone is 34,615 times bigger than the total land area, the highest ratio of its kind in the South Pacific by far. The country's reef area is 10 times greater than all dry land.

Funafuti, the administrative center, is more than 1,000 km north of Suva, Fiji. Funafuti, Nanumea, Nui, Nukufetau, and Nukulaelae are true atolls, with multiple islets less than four meters high and central lagoons, while Nanumaga, Niulakita, and Niutao are single table-reef islands, with small landlocked interior lakes. Vaitupu is also close to the table-reef type, though its interior lake or lagoon is connected to the sea. In all, the nine islands are composed of 129 islets, of which Funafuti accounts for 34 and Nukufetau 37. Ships can enter the lagoons at Nukufetau and Funafuti; elsewhere they must stand offshore.

It's feared that within a century, rising ocean levels will inundate these low-lying atolls and Tuvalu will cease to exist. Coastal erosion is already eating into the shorelines and seawater has seeped into the groundwater, killing coconut trees and flooding the taro pits. Sand mining from the beaches for construction purposes and causeway building is contributing to the problem. Recent spring tides on Funafuti have been the highest in recorded history, and if ocean levels continue to rise, the entire population of Tuvalu may have to evacuate, third-world victims of first-world affluence.

Climate

The climate is generally warm and pleasant, though hotter than Fiji due to the northerly location. The waters lapping these shores are among the warmest in the world, and those of the interior lagoons are several degrees warmer again. The mean annual temperature is 29°C and the

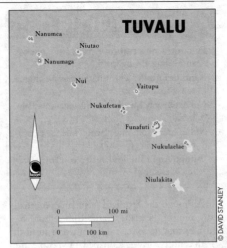

average annual rainfall 3,000 mm (the southernmost atolls are somewhat wetter). Rain falls on more than half the days of the year, usually heavy downpours followed by sunny skies. The trade winds blow from the east much of the year.

Strong west winds and somewhat more rain come between November and April, the hurricane season. Tuvalu is near the zone of hurricane formation, and these storms can appear with little warning and cause considerable damage. Tuvalu's climate is warming faster than anywhere else in the South Pacific, and this has led to an increase in the frequency and severity of hurricanes. Hurricane Bebe in 1972 was the first since 1894. Hurricanes Gavin and Hina spawned by the El Niño phenomena in 1997 eroded an estimated seven percent of Tuvalu's landmass! In June 1997 Hurricane Keli struck Niulakita with 180 kph winds, the first hurricane ever recorded in the South Pacific in June.

History

The Polynesians colonized Tuvalu some 2,000 years ago; Samoans occupied the southern atolls, while Tongans were more active in the north. Groups of warriors also arrived from Kiribati and their language is still spoken on Nui. Polynesian migrants reached the outliers of the Solomons and the Carolines from bases in Tuvalu.

TUVALU HIGHLIGHTS

Funafuti Conservation Area: nature reserve, snorkeling, diving (p. 583)

Nanumea Atoll: view from the massive church tower (p. 586)

Nui Atoll: only Micronesian inhabitants of Polynesian Tuvalu (p. 587)

Nukufetau Atoll: huge lagoon safe for navigation, war relics (p. 587)

Vaitupu Atoll: Tuvalu's largest secondary boarding school (p. 588)

Although the Spaniard Mendaña reportedly saw some of the islands in the 16th century, regular European contact did not occur until the 19th century. Slavers kidnaped 443 people from Funafuti, Nanumea, and Nukulaelae in 1863 to work as laborers in Peru—none returned. In 1861, a Cook Islands castaway named Elekana was washed up on Nukulaelae. He taught Christianity to the islanders, and after reporting back to Protestant missionaries in Samoa, returned in 1865 with Rev. A.W. Murray and an organized LMS missionary party. Soon, most Tuvaluans were converted, and they remained under the spiritual guidance of Samoan pastors right up to 1969. The LMS-descended Ekalesia Kelisiano Tuvalu retains the loyalty of 92 percent of the population today.

To keep out American traders, Britain declared a protectorate over Tuvalu in 1892, upgrading it to colonial status in 1916. The ensuing period was fairly uneventful, except for the American military bases established at Funafuti, Nukufetau, and Nanumea during WW II. Funafuti was home to the B-24 Liberator bombers of the U.S. Seventh Air Force, which launched raids against Japanese bases in the Gilberts and Marshalls. Warplanes en route from Wallis Island to the Gilberts were refueled here. Japanese planes did manage to drop a few bombs in return, but Tuvalu was spared the trauma of a Japanese invasion.

The United States built its airfield across the most fertile land on Funafuti, reducing the area planted in coconuts and *pulaka* (swamp taro) by a third. The enduring impact of this loss is reflected in the fact that *pulaka* is no longer a staple food of the Tuvaluans on Funafuti. The Americans left behind a few wrecked cranes and huge "borrow" pits where they extracted (borrowed) coral. Today garbage is dumped into the stagnant lakes in the American pits, forming perfect breeding grounds for mosquitoes and rats. A plan to fill the pits and reclaim the land has been under discussion for decades.

Until 1975, Tuvalu was part of the Gilbert and Ellice Islands Colony. In the early 1970s the Polynesian Ellice Islanders expressed their desire to separate from the Micronesian Gilbertese and proceed toward true independence. In a 1974 referendum, the Tuvaluans voted overwhelmingly to become a separate unit. Britain acceded to the wish in 1975, and on October 1, 1978, after only five months of full internal self-government, Tuvalu became a fully independent nation.

Political independence has greatly benefited Tuvalu, since it would have received far less attention and economic aid as an outer-island group of Kiribati. In 1995, politicians removed the Union Jack from the country's flag in a bid to establish a republic and out of dissatisfaction with the amount of financial assistance their country was receiving from Britain. Two years later there was a change of government and the old flag was brought back. With the country threatened by flooding, in 2002 Tuvalu began working on a lawsuit against the United States and Australian governments over their failure to limit greenhouse gas emissions. The case could take the form of a class-action suit in U.S. courts or be brought before the International Court of Justice in The Hague. Tuvalu is a member of the Commonwealth and United Nations.

Government

Tuvalu has an elected 15-member parliament headed by a prime minister chosen from its ranks. The six cabinet ministers and the house speaker are elected members of parliament. There are no political parties; instead, prominent families control politics and virtually all of the leading officials are men. A Tuvaluan governor-general represents the British Crown.

Since 1966, elected island councils (*kaupule*)

TUVALU AT A GLANCE

ISLAND	POPULATION (2002)	AREA (hectares)
Nanumea	669	361
Nanumaga	590	310
Niutao	664	226
Nui	555	337
Vaitupu	1,160	509
Nukufetau	558	307
Funafuti	4,493	254
Nukulaelae	395	166
Niulakita	35	41
Tuvalu	**9,119**	**2,511**

have provided local government on each outer island; in 1977 a town council replaced the island council on Funafuti. Previously the heads of families had met in *maneapa* or *falekaupule* (community halls) to discuss island affairs. Major attempts are underway to strengthen outer island local government by providing each island government with funds generated by the Falekaupule Trust Fund, a new source of budgetary revenue that each island government can spend according to certain guides.

Economy

Tuvalu's gross domestic product (A$21 million in 1998) is the smallest of any independent state. In 2000, imports cost A$23 million while exports were limited to small quantities of fish and copra. Despite this, Tuvalu has no foreign debts and is financially sound due to fiscal prudence, aid, remittances, and a series of unique monetary arrangements.

The Tuvalu Trust Fund was created in 1987 with grants of A$27.1 million from the governments of Australia, New Zealand, the United Kingdom, and Tuvalu itself. In March 2003 the fund had a market value of over A$71 million and was providing Tuvalu with a regular income of A$3 million a year on average. Tuvalu also receives about A$2 million a year in development aid from Taiwan and the European Union, plus another A$2 million from Australia for education and overseas scholarships, but not much of this money reaches the outer islands. Taiwan sharply increased its aid to Tuvalu in late 1998, after Tonga switched recognition to Beijing. Consequently, Taiwan established the first ever permanent diplomatic mission on Funafuti.

In 2003, American, Japanese, Korean, and Taiwanese tuna-fishing boats paid A$6.6 million in licensing fees to exploit Tuvalu's exclusive economic zone. The sale of postage stamps to collectors provides further government revenue, and remittances from Tuvaluans overseas, such as the 900 young men working as crew on foreign ships, bring in another A$7 million a year.

Tourism has long been hampered by stiff airfares, which effectively eliminate all but the most determined travelers. Of the 1,238 overseas visitors to Tuvalu in 2002, only about 10 percent declared their purpose as tourism, and not more than a handful of those got beyond Funafuti. Half the arrivals are on people on business and most of the rest are visiting friends and relatives.

In 1996, an earth satellite station was installed on Funafuti courtesy of Australian aid, creating excess international telephone service capacity that could be leased to a Hong Kong company which resold the connections to the operators of sex chat lines. In 1996, "live one to one" telephone sex advertisements bearing Tuvalu's international telephone access code 688 began appearing in pornographic magazines in Japan, the United States, and Britain. Although the calls were rerouted to "horny" operators in New Zealand, the arrangement caused embarrassment in a country where the national motto is "Tuvalu for God," and in 2000 the contract (worth A$2 million a year) was canceled.

Until 2000, the Tuvalu Trade Mission in Hong Kong was actively marketing Tuvaluan passports at US$11,000 for individuals or US$22,000 for a family of four. Although citizenship wasn't included, holders were allowed to reside in Tuvalu. Disappointing returns and bad publicity convinced the government to end the practice. Tuvalu has also bartered ambassadorships for favors, and in 1996 an Italian restaurateur snapped up the post of Ambassador to the Vatican, even though Tuvalu has less than 100 Catholics and no diplomatic relations with the Holy See (Vatican-accredited diplomats enjoy a special tax status that allows them to make huge profits on business dealings in Italy).

In early 2000 Tuvalu's internet address, .tv, began to be marketed by The .tv Corporation (www.tv), a California company which paid Tu-

valu royalties of US$22 million. In early 2002, the operation was purchased by VeriSign Inc. for US$45 million. Tuvalu received a US$9 million buyout and it's now paid US$500,000 a quarter on a 15-year contract. It costs US$50 a year to register an ordinary .tv domain name or US$1,000 and up for a "premium" name. Television companies are the target market.

The People

All nine atolls are inhabited, with one or two villages on each. The villages are often divided into two "sides" to foster competition. More than 70 percent of the people on the outer islands still live in traditional-style housing. The life of the people is hard—only coconuts and pandanus grow naturally, though bananas, papayas, and breadfruit are cultivated. A variety of taro (*pulaka*) has to be grown in pits excavated from coral rock. Reef fish and tuna are the main protein components in the diet. Chicken, both local and imported, is eaten quite regularly on Funafuti; pork is served on special occasions.

Tuvalu's population density (more than 400 persons per square km) is the highest in the South Pacific and one of the highest in the world. Since

© DAVID STANLEY

children playing in front of their home on Funafuti

1990, the number of persons per square km has doubled on Funafuti and nearly half the country's population now lives on this one atoll. Room to breathe is rapidly disappearing as additional people arrive continuously in search of government jobs. About 75 percent of the food consumed on Funafuti is now imported, and diet-related diseases such as diabetes, hypertension, and vitamin deficiency are on the increase. The waste disposal problems are immense.

While some 10,000 people live in Tuvalu, another 2,000 Tuvaluans reside in New Zealand and 500 more are in Fiji. After the separation from the Gilbert Islands in 1975, many Tuvaluans who had previously held government jobs on Tarawa or worked at the phosphate mine on Banaba returned home. A second influx occurred in 2003 when phosphate mining came to an end on Nauru, in Micronesia, and the 750 Tuvaluans employed there were repatriated. Some were resettled on overcrowded Funafuti but more continued on to New Zealand.

Mostly Polynesian, related to the Samoans and Tongans, the Tuvaluans' ancestry is evident in their language, architecture, customs, and *tuu mo aganu Tuvalu* (Tuvaluan way of life). Nui Island is an exception, with some Micronesian influence. Before independence, many Tuvaluans working on Tarawa took an I-Kiribati husband or wife, and there's now a large Gilbertese community on Funafuti. The Tuvaluan language is almost identical to that spoken in neighboring Tokelau, Wallis and Futuna, and on Tikopia in the Solomons.

Conduct and Customs

If you're planning to stop at an outer island, take along things like matches, chewing gum, volleyballs, fishhooks, T-shirts, cloth, and cosmetics to give as gifts. Don't hand them out at random like Santa Claus—give them to people you know as a form of reciprocation. It's the custom.

Scanty dress is considered offensive everywhere, so carry a *sulu* to wrap around you. Women should cover their legs while sitting down and their thighs at all times. Never stand upright before seated people, and try to enter a house or *maneapa* shoeless, and from the lagoon side rather than the ocean side.

Exploring the Islands

Entertainment

Tuvaluans love dancing, be it their traditional *fatele,* more energetic than Gilbertese dancing, or the predictable twist. Traditional dancing is performed on special occasions, such as when opening a building, greeting special visitors, or celebrating holidays. Get in on the singing, dancing, and general frivolity taking place at the *maneapa* almost every night. On Funafuti, migrants from each outer island have their own *maneapa,* so ask around to find out if anything is on. Or just listen for the rhythmic sounds and head that way. Sometimes the local I-Kiribati do Gilbertese dances. On festive occasions many people wear flower garlands called *fou* (rhymes with Joe) in their hair. Each island has its own style.

Ask where you can watch *te ano* (the ball), the national game. Two teams line up facing one another and competition begins with one member throwing the heavy ball toward the other team, who must hit it back with their hands. Points are scored if the opposite team lets the ball fall and the first team to reach 10 wins. Obviously, weak players are targeted and the matches can be fierce (but usually friendly). The game ends with the losers performing a funny song and dance routine intended to bring the winners back to earth.

Public Holidays and Festivals

Public holidays include New Year's Day, Commonwealth Day (second Monday in March), Good Friday, Easter Monday (March/April), Gospel Day (second Monday in May), the Queen's Birthday (June), National Children's Day (Aug.), Tuvalu National Days (early Oct.), Christmas (Dec. 25), and Boxing Day (Dec. 28). The period 25–28 December is the Christmas–Boxing Day Break.

Local Funafuti holidays include Bomb Day, which commemorates April 23, 1943, when a Japanese bomb fell through Funafuti's church roof and destroyed the interior. An American corporal had shooed 680 villagers out of the building only 10 minutes before, thus averting a major tragedy. Children's Day features kids' sports and crafts; dancing and a parade on Funafuti airstrip mark Independence Day (Oct. 1). On October 21, Hurricane Day, Tuvaluans recall 1972's terrible Hurricane Bebe. All of the outer atolls have a special holiday of their own, and that day everyone from that island gets the day off, even if they work on Funafuti.

Accommodations

One medium-priced hotel and a handful of small private guesthouses exist on Funafuti, but camping is not allowed. A 10 percent government room tax is added to all accommodations charges (not included in the prices quoted herein).

All of the outer islands except Niulakita have guesthouses run by the island councils where you can stay for A$15–30 pp. It's essential to announce your arrival by calling the particular island council from the Telecom Center opposite the post office in Vaiaku. Otherwise seek advice at the Ministry of Rural Development (tel. 20177), downstairs in the Tuvalu National Provident Fund building just south of the main government building next to the lagoon. It's also possible to arrange accommodations with local outer-island families, but be prepared to renounce all privacy. Vaitupu has a small privately run guesthouse, the first outside Funafuti. The guesthouse attendants will do laundry for an additional charge.

Some of the island council guesthouses ask surprisingly high amounts for food. In such cases, each guest may be given a tray laden with corned beef, fish, chicken, pork, rice, taro, breadfruit, bread, biscuits, and cake, plus an enormous pot of tea—far too much to finish. As soon as the guests stop eating, the trays are carried out to the veranda where a small crowd of women and children will finish everything off. It's hard to get around this unusual situation, and not all guesthouses provide cooking facilities. Inquire about

meal prices beforehand, as they vary from A$28–75 for three meals. If the quoted price is absurdly high, consider bringing groceries with you on the ship. The guesthouses themselves may not be as clean and tidy as you would wish.

Food and Drink

Pulaka (swamp taro) is eaten boiled or roasted or is made into pudding. Breadfruit, a staple, is baked, boiled with coconut cream, or fried in oil as chips. Plantain (cooking bananas) may also be boiled or chipped. Sweet potatoes, though becoming popular, are still only served on special occasions. Fish is eaten every day, both white-fish and tuna; pork, chicken, and eggs add a little variety. Reddish-colored fish caught in the lagoons may be poisonous. If you're interested in fishing, make it known and someone will take you out in their canoe. Imported foods such as rice, corned beef, sugar, and a variety of canned items are used in vast amounts.

When eating on the outer islands, ask for some of the local dishes such as *laulu* or *lolo* (a taro leaf in coconut cream, not unlike spinach and delicious), *palusami* (*laulu*, onions, and fish, usually wrapped in banana leaves), *uu* (coconut crab, only readily available on Nukulaelae and Nukufetau), and *ula* (crayfish).

The water should be considered suspect and boiled. There are no rivers or streams and the groundwater is not potable, so all water is collected in catchments or processed at a desalination plant. During droughts there's a serious water shortage.

Quench your thirst with *pi* (drinking coconut), *kaleve* (sweet coconut toddy, generally extracted morning and night), or supersweet coffee and tea. *Kao* is sour toddy produced by fermenting *kaleve* two or three days. Take care, as *kao* can quickly render you senseless and produces a vicious hangover. Drinking alcohol in public is prohibited.

Internet Resources

Tuvalu Online, **www.tuvaluislands.com,** contains a wealth of information on the country, including a detailed history, description, legends, island maps, island news, a Tuvaluan grammar, a photo album, flags, philately, a Tuvalu telephone directory, shopping, and numerous links.

Visas and Officialdom

Funafuti is the only port of entry. There are no visa requirements for any nationality, but make sure you have a passport valid for another six months and an onward ticket. Those arriving/departing by boat also require an air ticket to leave. Upon arrival by boat, immigration will inform you that it's prohibited to stay with the locals or to leave Funafuti. Diplomacy can usually overcome both obstacles.

The maximum stay is three months, but usually visitors are given only the time until their onward flight or 30 days. Sometimes you only get a week on arrival, with an extension to one month available for A$50 at the Immigration office (tel. 20706, fax 20241; weekdays 0800–1230 and 1330–1600) in the police station opposite the Vaiaku Lagi Hotel. Two additional months cost A$50 each (return ticket essential). Further extensions require government approval.

Money

Australian currency is used, with Tuvaluan coins (about US$1 = A$1.35). The Tuvaluan one-dollar coin is of the same size and edging as the Australian 50-cent piece. It pays to be alert when handling these coins, or face a 50 percent devaluation. Kiribati coins are not accepted even though both countries use Australian banknotes.

An office upstairs at the National Bank of Tuvalu (tel. 20803, fax 20802; Mon.–Thurs. 1000–1400, Friday 0900–1300) next to the airport at Funafuti will change traveler's checks for A$1 commission. Credit cards are not accepted by businesses in Tuvalu but the bank gives cash advances on Visa and MasterCard to a limit of A$200 a day (A$10 fee). For amounts over A$200, they must call for authorization and charge an additional A$25 fee.

Tuvaluans do not expect to be tipped.

Media

The free monthly national newspaper, *Tuvalu Echoes*, is available at the Broadcasting and Information Office (tel. 20731, fax 20732), opposite the Vaiaku Lagi Hotel.

Radio Tuvalu (tel. 20138, fax 20732) broadcasts from Funafuti in English and Tuvaluan from 0630–0800 and 1125–1300 and 1755–2200 (except Sunday morning). The news in English is at 0710 and 1910. When the local programming isn't on the air, the BBC World Service is broadcast over the same frequencies (621 kHz AM and 100.1 MHz FM).

Health

In 2003, the Japanese rebuilt Princess Margaret Hospital (tel. 20435, fax 20481; outpatients weekdays 0800–1100) on Funafuti to replace a building dating from 1978. The hospital has a pharmacist and dentist, but on the outer islands there are only "dressers." Hepatitis, cholera, dengue fever, and tuberculosis are occasional problems (the last major cholera outbreak was in 1990). Cuts can turn septic quickly, so one should pack and use an antiseptic such as hydrogen peroxide.

Recommended (but not compulsory) vaccinations for those who will be spending much time here include typhoid fever and immune globulin or the hepatitis A vaccine.

What to Take

Bring plenty of film, because what is sold locally has often expired. Only color print film is available (no black-and-white or color slides). Snorkelers should arrive with their own gear. Bring coffee too—it's priced out of reach here. Tampons can also be a problem. Don't count on being able to buy *any* imported goods on the outer islands; even staples such as rice, flour, and sugar can be sold out.

TRANSPORTATION

Getting There

Air Fiji (www.airfiji.net) flies a 30-seat Embraer Brasilia between Suva, Fiji, and Funafuti on Monday and Thursday, with an extra service on Sunday if there's a heavy backlog of bookings. At A$510 or F$650 each way between Fiji and Tuvalu, this is an expensive trip with no discounts

TUVALU

available. Even so, the flights are often heavily booked by local seamen and people on some sort of official business. Reconfirm your flight reservations upon arrival at Funafuti or not less than 72 hours in advance at the computerized Travel Office (tel. 20737, fax 20057, travel@ tuvalu.tv) in the airport terminal building beside the post office in Vaiaku. There can be long waiting lists, and you'll be bumped if you fail to reconfirm.

Funafuti's airport terminal is the center of town and the paved airstrip itself is used by the locals for sporting events, to dry clothes, for stargazing, etc. A siren sounds to clear the runway just before the flights arrive.

Tuvalu collects an A$20 departure tax, which yachties and ship passengers must also pay.

Getting There By Boat

About once a month the government-owned vessels *Nivaga II* and *Manu Folau* travel Suva-Funafuti (1,020 km). The one-way fare between Suva and Funafuti is A$58 deck, A$166 second class, A$234 first class, plus A$15/58 deck/cabin for meals (you'll need to pay for a roundtrip unless you have an onward air ticket). For information in Fiji, inquire at **Williams & Gosling Ltd. Ships Agency** (tel. 331-2633, fax 330-0105, www.wgfiji.com.fj), 80 Harris Rd., Suva, although they won't know anything until a week before the sailing. In Funafuti, ask at the Department of Marine and Port Services (tel. 20054) near the main wharf. The same ships also make occasional trips to Nauru (1,400 km), Tarawa, Tokelau, and Apia (1,000 km), carrying both passengers and cargo.

Another service from Fiji offered by Williams & Gosling Ltd. is the Kiribati Shipping Services vessel *Nei Matangare,* which leaves Suva for Funafuti and Tarawa about four times a year. The three-day trip to Funafuti costs A$99/198 deck/cabin one-way, meals included. On Funafuti, the folks at Su's Place (tel. 20612) act as *Nei Matangare* agents. In practice, for a tourist to use any of the above is highly unusual.

Getting Around

There are no internal flights but roughly every fortnight one of the two government-owned ships visits each of outer islands, stopping for about an hour depending on the tides. The southern trip to Nukulaelae and Niulakita takes three days; the northern trip visits two or three of the six islands up that way in four days. If you decide to stop off at one of the islands, you'll probably be there at least two weeks or maybe much more before a ship returns.

The 58-meter *Nivaga II* was donated by the British government in 1988 to mark Tuvalu's 10 years of independence. It has three twin first-class cabins with private bath and eight second-class cabins with shared facilities. The 120 deck passengers must bring their own mats, eating utensils, and food (unless meals have been ordered beforehand).

In 2002, Tuvalu got a second interisland ship, the 50-meter MV *Manu Folau,* as a gift of Japan. This ship has two four-bed and three two-bed first class cabins with private bath. The two four-bunk and seven two-bunk second class cabins all have shared bath. Third class is either a large air-conditioned room with a capacity for 40 persons or space outside on deck. A proper cafeteria is available for meals.

Distances from Funafuti with the corresponding one-way deck fares are 112 km to Nukulaelae (A$8), 221 km to Niulakita (A$15), 102 km to Nukufetau (A$8), 118 km to Vaitupu (A$9), 242 km to Nui (A$17), 301 km to Niutao (A$21), 352 km to Nanumaga (A$22), and 400 km to Nanumea (A$25). The first class fare on either vessel is three times the deck fare, plus A$25 pp a day. Second class is double the deck fare, plus A$20 a day. Meals are another A$22.50 pp a day. A roundtrip to two islands might cost around A$65/228/296 in deck/second/first class including meals (one way would be half those amounts). Tuvaluans pay cheaper fares, so always make sure you're being quoted the right amount.

No alcohol is sold aboard, though it's okay to bring your own (no refrigerators available). Don't offer booze to the crew, however, as disciplinary action would be taken against them if they imbibed. If you must drink, do it in your cabin.

Since the schedule varies a lot, the only practical way to arrange passage is to wait until you get to Funafuti, then visit the Department of Marine and Port Services office (tel. 20054; weekdays 0900–1200 and 1330–1500) near the main wharf to see what's available. If you happened to connect with a trip, you could then change your return flight reservations.

In busy periods women have a slightly better chance of getting cabin space than men, but even if you've booked and paid for a cabin you're not safe until the ship has actually sailed. VIPs such as the prime minister or a member of parliament have the right to requisition your cabin on short notice, and all the kicking and screaming in the world won't help a bit. As you'll be told, these vessels are heavily subsidized and not designed for tourism. Be prepared for a lot of seasick fellow passengers.

Funafuti

Captain Arent De Peyster "discovered" Funafuti in 1819 and named it Ellice, for Edward Ellice, the British member of parliament who owned the cargo that his ship, the *Rebecca,* was carrying. In 1841, Charles Wilkes, commander of the United States Exploring Expedition, applied the name to the entire Tuvalu group. Almost half the population of Tuvalu lives on 12-km-long Fongafale Islet on the east side of Funafuti Atoll, where the population density is over 1,600 per square km.

The government offices are at Vaiaku, 50 meters west of the airstrip, the Funafuti Fusi cooperative supermarket is a kilometer northeast, and the deepwater wharf is a little more than a kilometer beyond that. A Japanese fishing boat wrecked during Hurricane Bebe in 1972 is in the lagoon just north of the wharf. Most of the homes on Funafuti are prefabs put up after this same storm, which also left a beach of coral boulders along the island's east side.

The area between Vaiaku and the wharf has developed into a busy little township with a new hospital built by Japan in 2003. In 2004, the Taiwanese built an A$11 million administration building just behind the airport terminal (be aware that some gov-

ernment offices mentioned in this chapter may have relocated recently as a result).

Heavy motorcycle traffic circulates along the one main street, and the litter is piling up along the lagoon as imported cans and bottles dampen

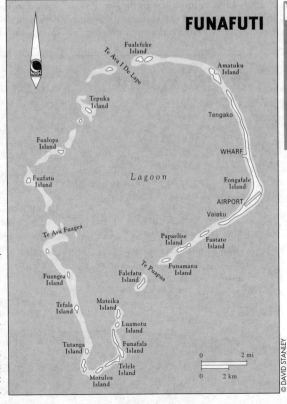

FUNAFUTI

TUVALU

Fualefeke Island

Te Ava I De Lape

Amatuku Island

Tepuka Island

Tengako

Fualopa Island

WHARF

Fuafatu Island

Lagoon

Fongafale Island

AIRPORT

Vaiaku

Te Ava Fuagea

Papaelise Island

Faatato Island

Te Puapua

Funamanu Island

Fuangea Island

Falefatu Island

Mateika Island

Tefala Island

Luamotu Island

Tutanga Island

Funafala Island

Telele Island

Motuloa Island

0   2 mi

0   2 km

© DAVID STANLEY

the South Seas dream. It's a crowded, dirty little place where women and children are often seen smoking. Author James A. Michener, who visited Funafuti during WW II, called it "a truly dismal island."

SIGHTS

Sights around Vaiaku include the open-sided government *maneapa* next to the airport building where parliament meets, and an old stone lighthouse next to the governor-general's residence to the south.

Not far from the hospital in the northeastern part of the village is the borehole known as **David's Drill.** Look for a round cement stone marked "NSEW" opposite a church labeled "Mainaga-Tou" near the Nanumaga *maneapa*. In 1896–1898, scientists sent by the Royal Society of London conducted experimental drilling at Funafuti to test Darwin's theory of atoll forma-

tion. The deepest bore (340 meters) failed to reach Funafuti's volcanic base. A second attempt in 1911 was also unsuccessful.

At the north end of the paved road up Fongafale Islet is a horrendous garbage dump. If it's a weekend, you may witness two seemingly incompatible activities here: groups of locals with flowers in their hair, playing volleyball or having a picnic, and vehicles dumping smelly refuse a few meters away. Skirt the debris and cut over to the lagoon side, where a lovely white sand beach extends to the north end of Fongafale, a 20-minute walk beyond the end of the road. Here a wartime bunker lies half buried in the sand.

Farther north is the **Tuvalu Maritime Training School** (tel. 20849) on Amatuku Island, which prepares young Tuvaluans for employment on oceangoing ships. Since the school opened in 1979, hundreds of young Tuvaluans have completed 12-month courses here. The classrooms include mock-ups of ship's cabins

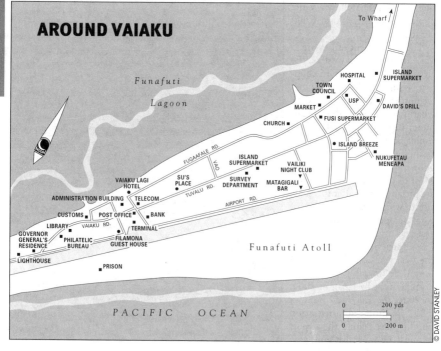

AROUND VAIAKU

and dining rooms, where steward trainees are taught how to make berths and set tables. At low tide you can walk across the reef to Amatuku (although you're expected to request advance permission before going).

One should use extreme caution when swimming on the ocean side of the atoll due to the big surf, currents, and coral heads. The lagoon beaches in the populated areas are often used as toilets or garbage dumps by the locals, which makes swimming (or simply walking along the shore) hazardous. In Vaiaku, a small beach where you can swim is beside the concrete wharf near the customs office, a block south of the hotel (there's no beach at the hotel itself).

Across the Lagoon

Of the outlying *motus* on the atoll's coral ring, Amatuku, Fualefeke, and Funafala are inhabited. A wartime bunker can be seen on Tepuka, which tourism planners dream of converting into a beach resort some day.

With funding from the South Pacific Regional Environmental Program, 33 square km of land and water along the western side of the atoll have been declared the **Funafuti Conservation Area.** The seabirds, turtles, coconut crabs, shellfish, and corals on or around the six uninhabited coral islets within the reserve are now fully protected, and the snorkeling and diving here are good. Visits are arranged through the Conservation Area Office (tel. 20489, fax 20664, fca@tuvalu.tv; Mon.–Thurs. 0900–1600, Fri. 0900–1330), upstairs in the Funafuti Town Council (or Kaupule). The A\$100 cost to charter their boat can be shared among up to six passengers (A\$120 on weekends). You must bring your own lunch. Scuba diving can be arranged at A\$30/50 for one/two tanks. These trips usually depart around 0800, returning at 1500. When inquiring, ask if anyone else is planning a trip that you could join, because you won't automatically be told.

Associated with this is the two-bed **Funafala Guesthouse** operated by the Funafuti Town Council (tel. 20422) on the beach at Funafala Island. To stay costs A\$25/35 pp for expatriates/tourists and you can cook on their kerosene stove (take your own food). Transfers from Fongafale can be arranged through the Conservation Area Office at A\$100 each way, though it's cheaper to arrange private transportation. This little tropical paradise is only an hour away from town.

ACCOMMODATIONS

Under US\$25

The **Island Breeze Motel** (Mr. Fanonga Isala, tel. 20606, fax 20675), in the center of the village, 100 meters east of the Funafuti Fusi, is a bit of a misnomer, as a hurricane would have to be raging for any breeze to reach there. Perhaps they're referring to the fans in the rooms! The smallest room with only enough space for one bed is A\$30 single or double. Two larger rooms with shared bath are A\$35, and the one room with a shower is A\$45. There's no hot water, but breakfast is included.

US\$25–50

Filamona Guest House (Penieli Metia, tel. 20833 or 20983), just beyond the *maneapa* next to the airport terminal, has one room with bath and fan at A\$35/45 single/double and four air-conditioned rooms with bath at A\$45/55. A communal kitchen is provided and there's a restaurant.

Su's Place (Semu and Susana Tafaaki, tel./fax 20612, susplace@hotmail.com), next to the Bahai Center, 250 meters northeast of Vaiaku post office up the main road, has four fan-cooled rooms with shared bath at A\$33/48 single/double. One self-catering air-conditioned flat in a different location one km north goes for A\$66 double. A restaurant/bar is on the premises.

German expat Rolf Köpke and his Tuvaluan wife Emily operate **Hideaway Guesthouse** (tel. 20365, fax 20835), a two-story European-style house in spacious surroundings about five km north of Vaiaku. Take a bus to the deepwater wharf, then walk along the lagoon 30 minutes (some buses continue this far). Rolf offers a self-catering apartment with private bath at A\$35/45/60 single/double/triple, plus two slightly cheaper rooms with private bath in the

TUVALU

annex. Cooking facilities are available. A 20 percent discount is given if you stay two weeks. Rolf's place is your best choice if you want a quiet holiday.

Saumalei Holiday Flats (Isa and Ben Paeniu, tel. 20373), a hundred meters beyond Hideaway, charges A$39/50 single/double for the three self-catering flats in a single-story building just across the road from the lagoon. It's usually booked by locals who pay A$100 a fortnight (foreigner rates negotiable).

US$50–100

The two-story, government-owned **Vaiaku Lagi Hotel** (tel. 20500 or 20502, fax 20503, tvlh@tuvalu.tv) faces the lagoon a few minutes walk from the airport terminal. The 16 air-conditioned rooms with private bath and fridge are A$80/90/100 single/double/triple, plus 10 percent tax (children under 12 free). Credit cards are not accepted. Traditional dancing is performed if sufficient guests are present or a government function is scheduled (ask). The Friday and Saturday night "twists" (discos) at the hotel can continue until 0200 accompanied by deafeningly loud music. Rowdy locals (often seamen on leave) demolish can after can of Victoria Bitter in the hotel's old wing bar (the bar in the new wing is more expensive). Insects in the rooms can also be a nuisance. The hotel staff are nice, friendly people who don't put themselves out for their guests in any way. You must make all your own transportation or tour arrangements.

OTHER PRACTICALITIES

Food

The **Kai Restaurant** (tel. 20833; daily 0900–1400 and 1600–2100), at Filamona Guest House near the airport, uses a blackboard to list their Chinese dishes (most are under A$5). Lunch at the Vaiaku Lagi Hotel is A$4.50 but it's nothing special. The snack bar at the airport has a cordial made from *kaleve* and water.

Su's Restaurant (tel. 20612) at Su's Place serves some of the best meals you'll find around here, when she's cooking, that is. Reservations are required (Su might not bother opening otherwise).

The **Vailiki Restaurant** (Mon.–Sat. 1000–1500 and 1800–2200, Sun. 1700–2100), above Vailiki Night Club a bit north of Su's, serves large portions of items like chopsuey, chowmein, black beans, curries, oysters, soups, eggs, and fried rice, all priced A$4.50–8. There's a nice terrace upstairs where you can eat.

Groceries

The cooperative **Funafuti Fusi** (tel. 20867), halfway between Vaiaku and the deepwater wharf, is the biggest self-service supermarket on Funafuti. The private **Island Supermarket** (tel. 20658), 500 meters north of the Fusi, is better stocked.

Bread and little else is sold at the small **municipal market** (closed Sun.) across the street from the Fusi. **Sangale Tutasi Bakery** (tel. 20644), next to Su's Place, also sells bread.

Most food on Funafuti is imported. The only animals kept here are the pigs held in pens along the east side of the airport runway. They're considered status symbols and the owners aren't usually eager to sell them, especially if any local feasts are planned.

Entertainment

The **Matagigali Bar** (tel. 20856), near the old seaplane hangar on the northwest side of the airstrip, has two pool tables. The weekend "twists" here often resemble saloon scenes out of Wild West movies. It's okay for males, but unescorted women will have problems with the local men (the name Matagigali means "Lovely Wind"). There's live music Thursday to Saturday from 2000 (A$2 admission).

The **Vailiki Night Club** in a former movie theater nearby is larger but dances only happen here for special events.

Sundays at 0900 catch the singing in the church not far from the Funafuti Fusi. Cricket *(kilikiti)* and soccer are played on Funafuti airstrip evenings and weekends, as is *te ano*. If you wish to use the tennis courts behind the Nukufetau *maneapa,* bring your own rackets and balls (the lights will be turned on at night for a small fee). This tennis court doubles as a basketball and volleyball court.

Shopping

The **Women's Handicraft Center** (tel. 20852, fax 20643; open office hours and at flight times), beside the airport terminal, has baskets, bags, mats, hats, fans, and necklaces from Funafuti and the outer islands. A booklet on Tuvaluan handicrafts is available at A$5. Women also sell crafts from private stalls at the airport on flight days.

Information

A good National Library (tel. 20711; weekdays 0800–1230 and 1330–1600) is near the government offices south of the airport at Vaiaku.

The Ministry of Tourism, Trade, and Commerce (Private Mail Bag, Funafuti; tel. 20184, fax 20829, mttc@tuvalu.tv), next to the National Library, has a few brochures.

The USP Extension Center (tel. 20811, fax 20704), near the hospital north of the center, sells books on Tuvalu and the region. The library here is open Monday to Thursday 0800–1230 and 1830–2030, Friday 0800–1230 and 1330–1600.

Nui Store (tel. 20623), opposite the USP Extension Center, sells the regional news magazines.

Basic maps of each of the atolls are available from the Lands & Survey Department (tel. 20170), beside one of two Island Supermarket outlets, between the airport terminal and the USP Extension Center.

Post and Telecommunications

The post office (tel. 20738; weekdays 0800–1200 and 1330–1500) near the airport terminal sells attractive Tuvalu stamps, though Tuvalu's mail service is chaotic. Local acquaintances may ask you to carry letters to Fiji to mail for them.

The Philatelic Bureau (tel. 20224, fax 20712), a few doors southwest of the National Library, offers a vast selection of Tuvalu stamps produced since independence. This is about the only place to buy postcards.

Manu Travel (tel. 20649), in a two-story building near the airport terminal, is the DHL Express agent.

Normal telephone, fax, and telex facilities are provided by satellite from the Telecom Center (tel. 20846; daily 0800–midnight) opposite the post office. Local calls are A$.10 each. Long-distance calls are A$.80 a minute to other atolls of Tuvalu, A$1.70 a minute to Australia, A$2.20 a minute to Fiji, or A$4.20 a minute to North America or Europe (three-minute minimum). Calls made using telephone cards (available in denominations of A$2, A$5, A$10, and A$20) are not subject to minimum charges and work out 10 percent cheaper. These cards cannot be used on islands other than Funafuti and they're often sold out anyway. Collect calls are not possible. Faxes can be sent for A$1/4 Tuvalu/overseas, plus the regular telephone charge. Faxes that arrive on the public fax 20800 are delivered free.

If you have access to a direct-dial telephone or are using a telephone card, you'll need to know that the international access code is 00. For direct-dial calls to the other atolls, the access code is 05 (except for Nuilakita, which uses the Funafuti line and requires no access code). For the local operator dial 010, for the international operator 012. Tuvalu's telephone code is 688. Try again if you don't get through the first time, as the operators go off duty at midnight.

Yachting Facilities

Te Ava Fuagea is the deepest (13 meters) of the three passes into the Funafuti lagoon; the others are only about eight meters deep. Large container ships can enter the lagoon and tie up to the main wharf. Yachties beware: Funafuti is probably the most poorly beaconed port of entry in the Pacific. At last report all the navigation buoys had disappeared from Te Ava Fuagea, making it an eyeball entrance. Navigation within the lagoon is also dangerous as it's studded with unmarked shoals, so yachts should proceed carefully along the marked channel to the anchorage off the main wharf. From October to April, westerly winds can make this anchorage risky.

Immigration is in the building across the street from the Vaiaku Lagi Hotel, while the customs office is opposite the Tuvalu National Provident Fund building south of the airport terminal. Funafuti is the only place where yachties can clear in and out of Tuvalu. If you get permission to also visit Nukufetau (the only other Tuvalu atoll with a navigable lagoon), you must still return to Funafuti to check out of the country.

You can buy diesel oil at the BP depot just north of the main wharf at prices 35 percent less than those charged at the Funafuti Fusi supermarket. Sammy's Service Station next to the Fusi and Mama's Petrol at the south end of the airstrip also sell gasoline and diesel.

To refill scuba tanks, try the workshop that supervises maintenance on Tuvalu's patrol boat at the main wharf. First, however, get authorization at their main office in the same building as immigration, opposite the hotel. If that fails, the Conservation Area Office at Funafuti Town Hall can refill scuba tanks.

Getting Around

Privately owned 26-seater buses run hourly between the Government Center at Vaiaku and the deepwater wharf 0700–2100 daily (A\$.60). Some buses continue to the north end of the island, usually in the morning and late afternoon. There are no bus stops—you just wave the buses down.

Asivai Motorcycle Hire (Sio Patiale, tel. 20053, fax 20790), on the main road near the hospital, rents scooters at A\$10 a day. Several places rent pick-up trucks. At night bicycles and motorcycles must carry a light, though a flashlight in hand will do. This regulation *is* enforced. Driving is on the left.

The **Fisheries Department** (tel. 20742, fax 20346) near the main wharf sometimes has fishing boats available for outer-island charters at A\$1,000–1,200 per day including meals. Be aware that they're usually broken down and unavailable. In 2002, only one of seven fishing boats donated by Japan in 1997 was still afloat, and it was anchored at Funafuti in need of repairs.

Other Islands of Tuvalu

Nanumaga

Nanumaga is a single island with only a narrow fringing reef. The main village is divided into the Tokelau (north) and Tonga (south) quarters, representing the island's two social groups. The Nanumaga people are conservative, but those few visitors who happen to call are warmly welcomed. If you visit, pay a courtesy call to the island chief, who belongs to the Mouhala clan. Fishing is prohibited on Tuesday and Wednesday.

Nanumaga's Island Council Guesthouse (tel. 33005) asks A\$40/60 single/double, plus A\$12/15/15 for breakfast/lunch/dinner.

Nanumea

Nanumea is the northwesternmost of the Tuvalu group, and its lagoon is considered by many to be the most beautiful. The two islands here are about five km apart. On Lakena Island is a small freshwater lake surrounded by palm and pandanus. American Passage, just west of Lolua village on Nanumea Island, was cut through the reef for 500 meters by the U.S. Army to allow small boats to enter the lagoon. It's said that yachts can reach an anchorage through this pass. A U.S. landing craft still sits on the reef as a reminder of the wartime U.S. base here and aircraft wreckage (mainly B-24s) is strewn around the atoll. If you have a head for heights, climb the pointed spire of the church—the view is worth it—but get permission from the pastor first. This German-style tower is one of the highest in the South Pacific, not at all what you'd expect to find on such a remote island.

The Nanumea Island Council Guesthouse (tel. 26005) costs A\$20 pp without meals. Guests may cook for themselves, which is a good idea as meals prepared by the attendant cost A\$25 each.

Niulakita

The southernmost, smallest, and least inhabited of the Tuvalu group, Niulakita is only a tiny coral dot just over a kilometer long. Niulakita sits up slightly higher than the other atolls, and the vegetation is lush. During the 19th century, the island was exploited by miners digging guano left by countless generations of seabirds. In 1926, the trading company Burns Philp set up a copra plantation here, which was sold to the British government in 1944. In 1946, the government ceded Niulakita to the people of Niutao, who have kept rotating groups here since 1949 (there never was any permanent population). They now live here making copra in shifts of a couple of years each. There's no guesthouse, but you can stay with local families.

Niutao

Legend has it that Pai and Vau, the two women who created Nanumea, also made Niutao, a tiny rectangular island about two km long with a small brackish lake. The people were converted by Protestant missionaries who arrived in 1870, and in 1991 a sturdy new church was completed, yet many traditional beliefs survive. Niutao is known for its decorative and durable pandanus floor mats.

Accommodation at the Island Council Guesthouse (tel. 28005) costs A$30 pp. Meals are overpriced at A$15/20/20 for breakfast/lunch/dinner.

Nui

A string of 11 coconut-covered islands surrounds the closed Nui lagoon on the northern, eastern, and southern sides. This six-km-long oval body of water is flanked by lovely white beaches. Terikiai islet is especially beautiful. Nui was the first of the Tuvalu islands to be spotted by Europeans (Mendaña in 1568). Though the Nui people speak Gilbertese, their culture is thoroughly Tuvaluan. The main, or "old," village (Tekawa Nikawai in Gilbertese) has recently been joined by Fakaifou, which means "new village" in Tuvaluan. The village houses sit in orderly rows.

The Island Council Guesthouse (tel. 23005) charges A$15 pp, plus A$10 for bedding. Meals are A$8/10/12 for breakfast/lunch/dinner. There's also a less expensive guesthouse without toilet facilities on Terikiai islet, which is usually only for locals.

Nukufetau

Nukufetau is the closest outer atoll to Funafuti (102 km) and the second largest after Funafuti in lagoon area. Unlike Funafuti's, the lagoon at Nukufetau is relatively safe for navigation and offers some protection from the westerlies. During WW II, the Americans constructed a wharf and an X-shaped airfield on Motolalo Island, eight km east of the present village across the la-

goon. Quite a bit of debris remains. Seabird colonies occupy some of the easternmost islands.

The Island Council Guesthouse (tel. 36005) is A$10 pp, plus A$5 for bedding and A$5 for the attendant. Meals are A$8/10/10 for breakfast/lunch/dinner. If outer island tourism is ever to be developed in Tuvalu, Nukufetau would be the logical choice for a resort.

Nukulaelae

Nukulaelae is the easternmost of Tuvalu's nine islands, only a half degree west of the 180th meridian and the international date line, its 10-km-long lagoon partly surrounded by long, sandy islands. There is no passage for ships. The Nukulaelae people are renowned dancers. Today, climate change threatens this isolated atoll and flooding has become a problem. Though the European Union has funded a seawall to slow the increasing erosion, salt water has already seeped into the large taro pits in the center of the main island. Pigpens stand on the mounds created when the pits were dug.

It was here in 1861 that a Cook Islander named Elekana made an unscheduled landfall after drifting west in his canoe from the Cook Islands. Elekana introduced Tuvalu to Christianity, as a monument on Nukulaelae now records, and it was here too that the first organized missionary party from Samoa landed in 1865.

In 1863, visitors of a different kind called, as three Peruvian ships appeared off the atoll. An old man came ashore to tell the islanders they were mission ships and everyone was invited aboard for religious services. The trusting Polynesians accepted, and after all the men were aboard and locked in the hold, the same rascal returned to the beach to say that the men had asked that the women and children join them. The ships then sailed off with 250 of Nukulaelae's 300 inhabitants to be used as slave labor in the mines of Peru. Only two men, who managed to jump overboard and swim 10 km back, ever returned.

The Island Council Guesthouse (tel. 35005) is A$20 pp to stay, plus another A$10 for bedding. Meals cost A$6/12/14 for breakfast/lunch/dinner. Unless you're really big on food, ask if they can cut some of those meals from your bill. This island is dry, so don't carry any alcohol with you if you go ashore here.

Vaitupu

Vaitupu is the largest of the nine Tuvalu islands in land area and, after Funafuti, the most Europeanized. The house of Herr Nitz, representative on Vaitupu of the German trading company J.C. Godeffroy for a quarter century in the late 19th century, still stands. In 1946, the *matai* (chiefs) of Vaitupu purchased Kioa Island in Fiji, where some 300 Vaitupu people now live.

The London Missionary Society opened a primary school at Motufoua on Vaitupu in 1905 to prepare young men for entry into the seminary in Samoa. Over the years this has developed into the large church/government Motufoua Secondary School, the only one in Tuvalu. A number of expatriate teachers are employed at the 600-student high school, which operates under a regime of strict authoritarian discipline. In early 2000, 18 girls aged 14–17 and an adult matron burned to death during a fire in a school dormitory. The girls were unable to escape because they had been locked in. The school has serious garbage disposal problems.

The Island Council Guesthouse (tel. 30005) in a wooden ex-missionary building charges A$15 pp, plus A$15 for bedding. Meals are A$10/13.50/15.50 for breakfast/lunch/dinner. There's a kitchen in the guesthouse, but no cooking utensils.

A local schoolteacher named Faleefa occasionally accepts paying guests in her own home. The two-story **Aliki Guest House** on Vaitupu has six rooms at A$25 pp. Meals are provided by the staff (extra charge). For more information, ask at the Island Breeze Motel on Funafuti.

BASIC TUVALUAN

ao: yes
Ea koe?: How are you?
e fia?: how much? how many?
fafine: women
fakafetai: thank you
fakafetai lasi: thank you very much
fakamolemole: please, sorry
fakatali: wait
fale: house
falefoliki: toilet
fesoasoani: help
fiafia: happy
foliki: small
gali: nice, good
igoa: name
ika: fish
ikai: no
inu: drink
kai: to eat
Koe e fano ki fea?: Where are you going?
Koi tou igoa?: What is your name?
kou kou: to wash, bathe
lasi: big, large
lei: fine, well
makalili: cold
makona: full
Malosi fakafetai.: I am well, thank you.
masaki: sick

masei: bad
mataku: afraid
meakai: food
meakaigali: good food
mea pusi: cigarettes
moa: chicken
moe: sleep
niu: coconut
palagi: non-Tuvaluan
pi: drinking coconut
poo: night
seai: none, none left
Seiloa ne au: I don't know.
sene: cent
taala: dollar
tagata: man
tai: salt water, the sea
taimi: time
talofa: hello, good morning
tamaliki: child
tapu: forbidden
ti: tea
tofaa: goodbye
Toku igoa ko . . . .: My name is . . .
vai: fresh water
vaka: boat, canoe
vakalele: airplane
vela: hot

TUVALU

Fiji Islands

Introduction

Once notorious as the "Cannibal Isles," Fiji is now the colorful crossroads of the South Pacific. Of the 322 islands that make up the Fiji Group, over 100 are inhabited by a rich mixture of exuberant Melanesians, Indo-Fijians, Polynesians, Micronesians, Chinese, and Europeans, each with a cuisine and culture of their own. Here Melanesia mixes with Polynesia, ancient India with the Pacific, and tradition with the modern world in a unique blend.

Fiji preserves an amazing variety of traditional customs and crafts such as kava, or *yaqona,* drinking, the presentation of the whale's tooth, firewalking, fish driving, turtle calling, *tapa* beating, and pottery making. Alongside this fascinating human history is a dramatic diversity of landforms and seascapes, all concentrated in a relatively small area. Fiji's sun-drenched beaches, blue lagoons, panoramic open hillsides, lush rainforests, and dazzling reefs are truly magnificent.

Fiji offers posh resorts, good food and accommodations, nightlife, historic sites, outer-island living, hiking, kayaking, camping, surfing, snorkeling, and scuba diving. Traveling is easy by small plane, interisland catamaran, car ferry,

local cargo boat, outboard canoe, open-sided bus, and air-conditioned coach. With even a month at your disposal you'll barely scratch the surface of all there is to see and do.

Best of all, Fiji is a visitor-friendly country with uncrowded, inexpensive facilities available almost everywhere. You'll love the vibrant, outgoing people whose knowledge of English makes communicating a breeze. In a word, Fiji is a traveler's country *par excellence,* and whatever your budget, Fiji gives you a good value for your money and plenty of ways to spend it. *Bula,* welcome to Fiji, everyone's favorite South Pacific country.

Important Note

When early British missionaries created a system of written Fijian in the middle of the 19th century, they established a unique set of orthographic rules followed to this day. In an attempt to represent the sounds of spoken Fijian more precisely, they rendered "mb" as *b,* "nd" as *d,* "ng" as *g,* "ngg" as *q,* and "th" as *c.* Thus Beqa is pronounced *Mbengga,* Nadi is *Nandi,* Sigatoka is *Singatoka,* Cicia is *Thithia,* etc. In order to be able pronounce Fijian names and words correctly, visitors must take a few minutes to learn these pronunciation rules. Turn to Language, which follows, for more information.

The Land

Fiji lies 5,100 km southwest of Hawaii and 3,150 km northeast of Sydney, astride the main air route between North America and Australia. Nadi is the hub of Pacific air routes, while Suva is a regional shipping center. The 180th meridian cuts through Fiji, but the international date line swings east so the entire group can share the same day.

The name Fiji is a Tongan corruption of the indigenous name "Viti." The Fiji Islands are arrayed in a horseshoe configuration with Viti Levu (great Fiji) and adjacent islands on the west, Vanua Levu (great land) and Taveuni to the north, and the Lau Group on the east. This upside-down, U-shaped archipelago encloses the Koro Sea, which is relatively shallow and sprinkled with the Lomaiviti, or central Fiji, group of islands. Together the Fiji Islands are

---

FIJI HIGHLIGHTS

Beach Street, Levuka, Ovalau: most picturesque street in Fiji (p. 763)

Bouma National Heritage Park, Taveuni: three waterfalls, hiking (p. 794)

Fiji Museum, Suva: lovely garden, outstanding exhibits (p. 704)

Sigatoka Sand Dunes, Viti Levu: visitor center, trails, accessible scenery (p. 684)

The Blue Lagoon, Yasawa Islands: swimming, snorkeling, natural beauty (p. 754)

---

scattered over 1,290,000 square km of the South Pacific Ocean.

If every single island were counted, the isles of the Fiji archipelago would number in the thousands. However, a mere 322 are judged large enough for human habitation, and of those only 106 are inhabited. That leaves 216 uninhabited islands, most of them prohibitively isolated or lacking fresh water.

Most of the Fiji Islands are volcanic oceanic islands. All of Fiji's volcanoes are presently dormant or extinct, although Vuna on Taveuni and Nabukelevu on Kadavu are classified as dormant, since they've both erupted within the past 2,000 years. There are as many as 50 groups of hot springs. The two largest islands, Viti Levu and Vanua Levu, together account for 87 percent of Fiji's 18,272 square km of land. Viti Levu has 57 percent of the land area and 75 percent of the people, while Vanua Levu, with 30 percent of the land, has 18 percent of the population. Viti Levu alone is bigger than all five archipelagos of French Polynesia. In fact, Fiji has more land and people than all of Polynesia combined.

Viti Levu

The 1,000-meter-high Nadrau Plateau in central Viti Levu is cradled between Tomaniivi (1,323 meters) on the north and Monavatu (1,131 meters) on the south. On different sides of this elevated divide are the Colo-East Plateau drained by the Rewa River, the Navosa Plateau drained by the Ba, the Colo-West Plateau drained by the Sigatoka, and the Navua Plateau drained by the

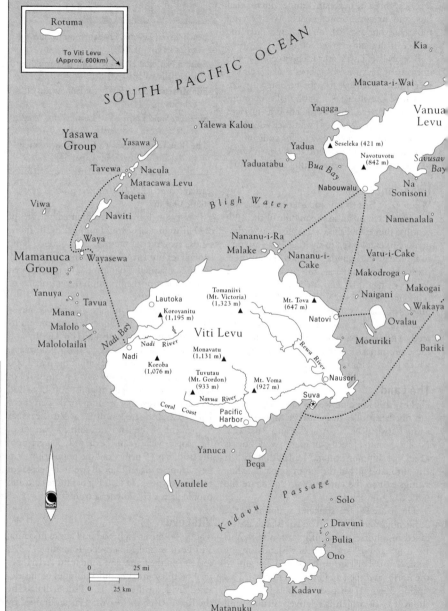

Rotuma

To Viti Levu
(Approx. 600km)

SOUTH PACIFIC OCEAN

Kia

Macuata-i-Wai

Vanua
Levu

Yaqaga

Yalewa Kalou

Yasawa
Group

Yasawa

Yadua

Seseleka (421 m)

Navotuvotu
(842 m)

Savusav
Bay

Tavewa
Nacula

Matacawa Levu

Yaduatabu

Bua Bay

Na
Sonisoni

Yaqeta

Nabouwalu

Viwa

Naviti

Bligh Water

Namenalala

Waya

Nananu-i-Ra

Mamanuca
Group

Wayasewa

Malake

Nananu-i-
Cake

Vatu-i-Cake

Makodroga

Yanuya

Tavua

Lautoka

Tomaniivi
(Mt. Victoria)
(1,323 m)

Mt. Tova
(647 m)

Naigani

Makogai

Wakaya

Mana

Koroyanitu
(1,195 m)

Natovi

Ovalau

Malolo

Viti Levu

Moturiki

Batiki

Malololailai

Nadi Bay

Nadi River

Monavatu
(1,131 m)

Rewa River

Nadi

Koroba
(1,076 m)

Tuvutau
(Mt. Gordon)
(933 m)

Mt. Voma
(927 m)

Nausori

Coral Coast

Navua River

Suva

Pacific
Harbor

Yanuca

Beqa

Kadavu Passage

Solo

Vatulele

Dravuni

Bulia

Ono

0   25 mi

0   25 km

Kadavu

Matanuku

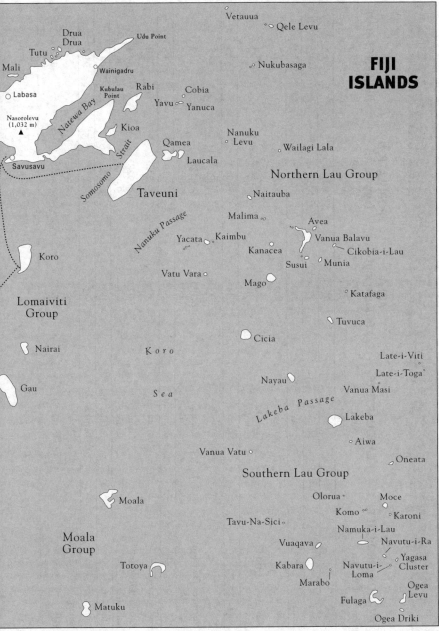

Vetauua
Qele Levu

Drua
Drua   Udu Point

Tutu   Nukubasaga

Mali

Labasa   Wainigadru   **FIJI ISLANDS**

Kubulau Point   Rabi   Cobia
Nasorolevu   Yavu   Yanuca
(1,032 m)   Kioa

Natewa Bay   Qamea   Nanuku Levu   Wailagi Lala

Savusavu   Laucala

Somosomo Strait   Northern Lau Group

Taveuni   Naitauba

Nanuku Passage   Malima   Avea
Yacata   Kaimbu   Vanua Balavu
Koro   Kanacea   Cikobia-i-Lau
Vatu Vara   Susui   Munia
Mago

Lomaiviti Group   Katafaga

Tuvuca

Nairai   Cicia

Koro   Late-i-Viti
Late-i-Toga
Gau   Nayau   Vanua Masi
Sea
Lakeba Passage   Lakeba

Aiwa

Vanua Vatu   Oneata

Southern Lau Group

Moala   Olorua   Moce
Komo   Karoni
Tavu-Na-Sici   Namuka-i-Lau
Moala Group   Vuaqava   Navutu-i-Ra
Totoya   Kabara   Navutu-i-Loma   Yagasa Cluster
Marabo   Ogea Levu
Matuku   Fulaga
Ogea Driki

FIJI AT A GLANCE

DIVISION/PROVINCE	HEADQUARTERS	AREA (square km)	POPULATION (1999 est.)	PERCENT FIJIAN
Central Division	**Suva**	**4,293**	**312,819**	**59.5**
Naitasiri	Vunidawa	1,666	135,220	56.1
Namosi	Navua	570	6,027	91.4
Rewa	Nausori	272	105,458	58.6
Serua	Navua	830	16,125	55.1
Tailevu	Korovou	955	49,989	67.7
Western Division	**Lautoka**	**6,360**	**307,393**	**39.4**
Ba	Lautoka	2,634	220,917	33.2
Nadroga	Sigatoka	2,385	54,859	52.5
Ra	Nanukuloa	1,341	31,617	59.4
Northern Division	**Labasa**	**6,198**	**145,128**	**46.9**
Macuata	Labasa	2,004	83,852	28.2
Bua	Nabouwalu	1,378	15,319	73.6
Cakaudrove	Savusavu	2,816	45,957	72.0
Eastern Division	**Levuka**	**1,422**	**40,928**	**89.4**
Kadavu	Vunisea	478	9,454	99.2
Lau	Lakeba	487	11,700	98.6
Lomaiviti	Levuka	411	16,932	91.2
Rotuma	Ahau	46	2,842	5.8
FIJI	**Suva**	**18,272**	**806,268**	**51.1**

Navua. Some 29 well-defined peaks rise above Viti Levu's interior; most of the inhabitants live in the river valleys or along the coast.

The Nadi River slices across the Nausori Highlands, with the Mount Evans Range (1,195 meters) towering above Lautoka. Other highland areas of Viti Levu are cut by great rivers like the Sigatoka, the Navua, the Rewa, and the Ba, navigable far inland by outboard canoe or kayak. Whitewater rafters shoot down the Navua and occasionally the Ba, while the lower Sigatoka flows gently through Fiji's market garden "salad bowl." Fiji's largest river, the Rewa, pours into the Pacific through a wide delta just below Nausori. After a hurricane the Rewa becomes a dark torrent worth a special visit to Nausori just to see. Sharks have been known to enter both the Rewa and the Sigatoka and swim far upstream.

Vanua Levu

Vanua Levu has a peculiar shape, with two long peninsulas pointing northeastward. Natewa Bay, the South Pacific's largest bay, almost cuts the island in two. A mountain range between Labasa and Savusavu reaches 1,032 meters at Nasorolevu. Navotuvotu (842 meters), east of Bua Bay, is Fiji's best example of a broad shield volcano, with lava flows built up in layers. The mountains are closer to the southeast coast, and a broad lowland belt runs along the northwest. Of the rivers, the Dreketi is the largest, flowing west across northern Vanua Levu; navigation on the Labasa River is restricted to small boats. The interior of Vanua Levu is lower and drier than Viti Levu, yet scenically superb: The road from Labasa to Savusavu is a visual feast.

Other Islands and Reefs

Vanua Levu's bullet-shaped neighbor Taveuni soars to 1,241 meters, its rugged southeast coast battered by the trade winds. Taveuni and Kadavu are known as the finest islands in Fiji for their scenic beauty and agricultural potential. Geologically, the uplifted limestone islands of the Lau Group have more in common with Tonga than with the rest of Fiji. Northwest of Viti Levu is the rugged volcanic Yasawa Group.

Fringing reefs are common along most of the coastlines, and Fiji is outstanding for its 33 barrier reefs. The Great Sea Reef off the north coast of Vanua Levu is the fourth-longest in the world, and the Great Astrolabe Reef north of Kadavu is one of the most diverse. Countless other unexplored barrier reefs are found off northern Viti Levu and elsewhere. The many cracks, crevices, walls, and caves along Fiji's reefs are guaranteed to delight the scuba diver.

Climate

Along the coast the weather is warm and pleasant, without great variations in temperature. The southeast trades prevail from June to October, the best months to visit. In February and March the wind often comes directly out of the east. These winds dump 3,000 mm of annual rainfall on the humid southeast coasts of the big islands, increasing to 5,000 mm inland. The drier northwest coasts, in the lee, get only 1,500–2,000 mm.

The official dry season (June–October) is not always dry at Suva, although much of the rain falls at night. In addition, Fiji's winter (May–November) is cooler and less humid, the preferred months for mountain trekking. During the drier season the reef waters are clearest for the scuba diver. Yet even during the rainy summer months (December–April), bright sun often follows the rains, and the rain is only a slight inconvenience. The refreshing trade winds relieve the high humidity. Summer is hurricane season, with Fiji, Samoa, and Tonga receiving up to five tropical storms annually.

In Fiji you can obtain prerecorded weather information by dialing 330-1642. The same information is available online at www.met.gov.fj.

Flora

Over 2,000 species of plants grow in Fiji, of which 476 are indigenous to Fiji and 10 percent of those are found only here. Patterns of rainfall are in large part responsible for the variety of vegetation here. The wetter sides of the high islands are heavily forested, with occasional thickets of bamboo and scrub. Coconut groves fill the coastal plains. On the drier sides open savanna, or *talasiga*, of coarse saw grasses predominates where the original vegetation has been destroyed by

NADI'S CLIMATE

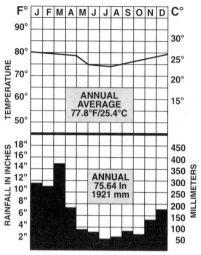

ANNUAL AVERAGE 77.8°F/25.4°C

ANNUAL 75.64 In 1921 mm

SUVA'S CLIMATE

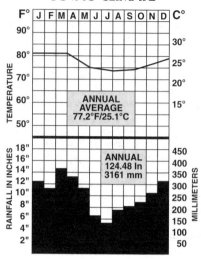

ANNUAL AVERAGE 77.2°F/25.1°C

ANNUAL 124.48 In 3161 mm

slash-and-burn agriculture. Sugarcane is now cultivated in the lowlands here, and Caribbean pine has been planted in many dry hilly areas, giving them a Scandinavian appearance.

Fauna

The only native mammals are the monkey-faced fruit bat, or flying fox, called *beka* by the Fijians, and the smaller, insect-eating bat. Two species of snakes inhabit Fiji: the very rare, poisonous *bolo loa,* and the harmless Pacific boa, which can grow up to two meters long. Venomous sea snakes are common on some coasts, but they're docile and easily handled. Fijians call the common banded black-and-white sea snake the *dadakulaci.*

One of the more unusual creatures found in Fiji and Tonga is the banded iguana, a lizard that lives in trees and can grow up to 70 centimeters long (two-thirds of which is tail). The iguanas are emerald green, and the male is easily distinguished from the female by his bluish-gray cross stripes. Banded iguanas change color to control their internal temperature, becoming darker when in the direct sun. Their nearest relatives

are found in Central America, and how they could have reached Fiji remains a mystery. In 1979 a new species, the crested iguana, was discovered on Yaduataba, a small island off the west coast of Vanua Levu. It's estimated that 6,000 crested iguanas are presently on Yaduataba.

The Indian mongoose was introduced by planters in the 1880s to combat rats, which were damaging the plantations. Unfortunately, no one realized at the time that the mongoose hunts by day, whereas the rats are nocturnal, so the two seldom meet. Today, the mongoose is the scourge of chickens, native ground birds, iguanas, and other animals, though Kadavu, Koro, Gau, Ovalau, and Taveuni are mongoose-free (and thus the finest islands for bird-watching). Feral cats do the same sort of damage.

Some Fijian clans have totemic relationships with eels, prawns, turtles, and sharks, and are able to summon these creatures with special chants. Red prawns are revered on Vanua Vatu in Southern Lau, on a tiny island off Naweni in southern Vanua Levu, and on Vatulele Island. The Nasaqalau people of Lakeba in southern Lau call sharks, and villagers of Korolevu in central Viti Levu call eels. The women of Namuana on Kadavu summon giant sea turtles with their chants. Turtle calling is also practiced at Nacamaki village, in the northeast corner of Koro. Unfortunately, sea turtles are becoming so rare that the turtle callers are having less and less success each year.

HISTORY AND GOVERNMENT
The Pre-European Period
The first people to arrive in Fiji were members of an Austronesian-speaking race, probably the Polynesians. They originated in Taiwan or insular Southeast Asia and gradually migrated east past the already occupied islands of Melanesia. Distinctive *Lapita* pottery, decorated in horizontal geometric bands and dated from 1290 B.C., has been found in the sand dunes near Sigatoka, indicating they had reached here by 1500 B.C. or earlier. Much later, about 500 B.C., Melanesian people arrived, bringing with them their own distinct pottery traditions. From the fusion of these primordial peoples the Fijian race was born.

The hierarchical social structure of the early Fijians originated with the Polynesians. Status and descent passed through the male line, and power was embodied in the *turaga* (chief). The hereditary chiefs possessed the mana of an ancestral spirit, or *vu*. Yet under the *vasu* system, a chiefly woman's son could lay claim to the property of his mother's brothers, and such relationships, combined with polygamy, kept society in a state of constant strife. This feudal aristocracy combined in confederations, or *vanua*, which extended their influence through war. Treachery and cannibalism were an intrinsic part of these struggles; women were taken as prizes or traded to form alliances. For defense, villages were fortified with ring ditches, or built along ridges or terraced hillsides.

The native aristocracy practiced customs that today seem barbarous and particularly cruel. The skull cap of a defeated enemy might be polished and used as a *yaqona* (kava) cup to humiliate a foe. Some chiefs even took delight in cooking and consuming body parts as their agonized victims looked on. Men were buried alive to hold up the posts of new houses, war canoes were launched over the living bodies of young girls, and the widows of chiefs were strangled to keep their husbands company in the spirit world. The farewells of some of these women are remembered today in dances and songs known as *meke*.

These feudal islanders were, on the other hand, guardians of one of the highest material cultures of the Pacific. They built great oceangoing double canoes *(drua)* up to 30 meters long, constructed and adorned large solid thatched houses *(bure)*, performed marvelous song-dances called *meke*, made *tapa*, pottery, and sennit (coconut cordage), and skillfully plaited mats. For centuries the Tongans came to Fiji to obtain great logs for making canoes and sandalwood for carving.

European Exploration
In 1643, Abel Tasman became the European discoverer of Fiji when he sighted Taveuni, although he didn't land. Tasman was searching for *terra australis incognita*, a great southern continent believed to balance the continents of the north. He also hoped to find new markets and trade routes. Unlike earlier Spanish explorers, Tasman entered the Pacific from the west rather than the east. He was the first European to see Tasmania, New Zealand, and Tonga, as well as Fiji. By sailing right around Australia from the Dutch East Indies, he proved New Holland (Australia) was not attached to the elusive southern continent.

In 1774, Captain Cook anchored off Vatoa in southern Lau. Like Tasman he failed to proceed farther or land. It was left to Capt. William Bligh to give Europeans an accurate picture of Fiji for the first time. After the *Bounty* mutiny in May 1789, Bligh and his companions were chased by canoe-loads of Fijian warriors just north of the Yasawa Islands as they rowed through on their escape route to Timor. Some serious paddling, a timely squall, and a lucky gap in the Great Sea Reef saved the Englishmen from ending up as the main course at a cannibal feast. The section of sea where this happened is now known as Bligh Water. Bligh cut directly across the center of Fiji between the two main islands, and his careful observations made him the first real European explorer of Fiji, albeit an unwilling

FIJI ISLANDS

CANNIBALISM

It has been said that the Fijians were extremely hospitable to any strangers they did not wish to eat. Native voyagers who wrecked on their shores, who arrived "with salt water in their eyes," were liable to be killed and eaten, since all shipwrecked persons were believed to have been cursed and abandoned by the gods. Many European sailors from wrecked vessels shared the same fate. Cannibalism was a universal practice, and prisoners taken in war, or even women seized while fishing, were invariably eaten. Most of the early European accounts of Fiji emphasized this trait to the exclusion of almost everything else; at one time, the island group was even referred to as the "Cannibal Isles." By eating the flesh of the conquered enemy, one inflicted the ultimate revenge. One chief on Viti Levu is said to have consumed 872 people and to have made a pile of stones to record his achievement. By eating the flesh of the conquered enemy, one inflicted the ultimate revenge. One chief on Viti Levu is said to have consumed 872 people and to have made a pile of stones to record his achievement. The leaves of a certain vegetable *(Solanum uporo)* were wrapped around the human meat, and it was cooked in an earthen oven. Wooden forks were employed at cannibal feasts. Men who usually relied on their fingers to eat other food, used the implements because it was considered improper to touch human flesh with fingers or lips.

one. Bligh returned to Fiji in 1792, but once again he stayed aboard his ship.

Beachcombers and Chiefs

All of these early explorers stressed the perilous nature of Fiji's reefs. This, combined with tales told by the Tongans of cannibalism and warlike Fijian natives, caused most travelers to shun the area. Then in 1800 a survivor from the shipwrecked American schooner *Argo* brought word that sandalwood grew in abundance along the Bua coast of Vanua Levu. This precipitated a rush of traders and beachcombers to the islands. A cargo of sandalwood bought from the islanders for $50 worth of trinkets could be sold to the Chinese in Canton for $20,000. By 1814 the forests had been stripped to provide joss sticks and incense, and the trade collapsed.

During this period Fiji was divided among warring chieftains. The first Europeans to actually mix with the Fijians were escaped convicts from Australia, who showed the natives how to use European muskets and were thus well received. White beachcombers such as the Swedish adventurer Charles Savage and the German Martin Bushart acted as middlemen between traders and Fijians and took sides in local conflicts. In one skirmish Savage was separated from his fellows, captured, and eaten. With help from the likes of Savage, Naulivou, the cannibal chief of tiny Bau Island just off eastern Viti Levu, and his brother Tanoa extended their influence over much of western Fiji.

From 1820 to 1850 European traders collected bêche-de-mer, a sea cucumber which, when smoked and dried, also brought a good price in China. While the sandalwood traders only stayed long enough to take on a load, the bêche-de-mer collectors set up shore facilities where the slugs were processed. Many traders such as David Whippy followed the example of the beachcombers and took local wives, establishing the part-Fijian community of today. By monopolizing the bêche-de-mer trade and constantly warring, Chief Tanoa's son and successor, Ratu Seru Cakobau (tha-kom-BAU), became extremely powerful in the 1840s, proclaiming himself Tui Viti, or king of Fiji.

The beginnings of organized trade brought a second wave of official explorers to Fiji. In 1827, Dumont d'Urville landed on Bau Island and met Tanoa. The Frenchmen caused consternation and confusion by refusing to drink *yaqona* (kava), preferring their own wine. The American Exploring Expedition of 1840, led by Commodore Charles Wilkes, produced the first recognizable map of Fiji. When two Americans, including a nephew of Wilkes, were speared in a misunderstanding on a beach at Malolo Island, Wilkes ordered the offending fortified village stormed and 87 Fijians were killed. The survivors were made to water and provision Wilkes's ships as tribute. Captain H.M. Denham of the HMS *Herald* prepared accurate navigational charts of the island group in 1855–1856, making regular commerce possible.

European and Tongan Penetration

As early as the 1830s an assortment of European and American beachcombers had formed a small settlement at Levuka on the east coast of Ovalau Island just northeast of Bau, which whalers and traders used as a supply base. In 1846, John Brown Williams was appointed American commercial agent, one step below a consul. On July 4, 1849, Williams's home on Nukulau Island near present-day Suva burned down. Though the conflagration was caused by the explosion of a cannon during Williams's own fervent celebration of his national holiday, he objected to the way Fijian onlookers carried off items they rescued from the flames. A shameless swindler, Williams had purchased Nukulau for only $30, yet he blamed the Tui Viti for his losses and sent Cakobau a $5,001.38 bill. American claims for damages eventually rose to $45,000, and in 1851 and 1855 American gunboats called and ordered Cakobau to pay up. This threat hung over Cakobau's head for many years, the 19th-century equivalent of 20th-century third world debt. Increasing American involvement in Fiji prompted the British to appoint a consul, W.T. Pritchard, who arrived in 1858.

The early 1830s also saw the arrival from Tonga of the first missionaries. Though Tahitian pastors were sent by the London Missionary Society to Oneata in southern Lau as early as 1830, it was the Methodists based at Lakeba after 1835 who made the most lasting impression by rendering the Fijian language into writing. At first, Christianity made little headway among these fierce, idolatrous people, and only after converting the powerful chiefs were the missionaries successful. Methodist missionaries David Cargill and William Cross were appalled by what they saw during a visit to Bau in 1838. A white missionary, Rev. Thomas Baker, was clubbed and eaten in central Viti Levu by the *kai colo* (hill people) as late as 1867.

In 1847, Enele Ma'afu, a member of the Tongan royal family, arrived in Lau and began building a personal empire under the pretense of defending Christianity. In 1853, King George of Tonga made Ma'afu governor of all Tongans resident in Lau. Meanwhile, there was continuing resistance from the warlords of the Rewa River area to Cakobau's dominance. In addition, the Europeans at Levuka suspected Cakobau of twice ordering their town set afire and were directing trade away from Bau. With his power in decline, in 1854 Cakobau accepted Christianity in exchange for an alliance with King George, and in 1855, with the help of 2,000 Tongans led by King George himself, Cakobau was able to put down the Rewa revolt at the Battle of Kaba. In the process, however, Ma'afu became the dominant force in Lau, Taveuni, and Vanua Levu.

During the early 1860s, as Americans fought their Civil War, the world price of cotton soared, and large numbers of Europeans arrived in Fiji hoping to establish cotton plantations. In 1867, the USS *Tuscarora* called at Levuka and threatened to bombard the town unless the still-outstanding American debt was paid. The next year an enterprising Australian firm, the Polynesia Company, paid off the Americans in exchange for a grant from Cakobau of 80,000 hectares of choice land, including the site of modern Suva. The British government later refused to recognize this grant, though they refunded the money paid to the Americans and accepted the claims of settlers who had purchased land from the company. Settlers soon numbered around 2,000 and Levuka boomed.

It was a lawless era, and a need was felt for a central government. An attempt at national rule by a confederacy of chiefs lasted two years until failing in 1867, then three regional governments were set up in Bau (western), Lau (eastern), and Bua (northern), but these were only partly successful. With prices for Fiji's "Sea Island" cotton collapsing as the American South resumed production, a national administration under Cakobau and planter John Thurston was established at Levuka in 1871.

However, Cakobau was never strong enough to impose his authority over the whole country, so with growing disorder in western Fiji, infighting between Europeans and Fijian chiefs, and a lack of cooperation from Ma'afu's rival confederation of chiefs in eastern Fiji, Cakobau decided he should cede his kingdom to Great Britain. The British had refused an invitation to annex Fiji in 1862, but this time they accepted rather than risk seeing the group fall into the hands of another power, and on October 10, 1874, Fiji became a British colony. A punitive expedition into central Viti Levu in 1876 brought the hill tribes *(kai colo)* under British rule. In 1877, the Western Pacific High Commission was set up to protect British interests in the surrounding unclaimed island groups as well. In 1881, Rotuma was annexed to Fiji. At first Levuka was the colony's capital, but in 1882 the government moved to a more spacious site at Suva.

The Making of a Nation

The first British governor, Sir Arthur Gordon, and his colonial secretary and successor, Sir John Thurston, created modern Fiji almost single-handedly. They realized that the easiest way to rule was indirectly, through the existing Fijian chiefs. To protect the communal lands on which the chieftain system was based, they ordered that native land could not be sold, only leased. Not wishing to disturb native society, Gordon and Thurston ruled that Fijians could not be required to work on European plantations. Meanwhile, the blackbirding of Melanesian laborers from the Solomons and New Hebrides had been restricted by the Polynesian Islanders Protection Act of 1872.

By this time sugar had taken the place of cotton and there was a tremendous labor shortage on the plantations. Gordon, who had previously served in Trinidad and Mauritius, saw indentured Indian workers as a solution. The first arrived in 1879, and by 1916, when Indian immigration ended, there were 63,000. To come to Fiji the Indians had to sign a labor contract *(girmit)* in which they agreed to cut sugarcane for their masters for five years. During the next five years they were allowed to lease small plots of their own from the Fijians and plant cane or raise livestock. Over half the Indians decided to remain in Fiji as free settlers after their 10-year

contracts expired, and today their descendants form nearly half the population, many of them still working small leased plots.

Though this combination of European capital, Fijian land, and Indian labor did help preserve traditional Fijian culture, it also kept the Fijians backward—envious onlookers passed over by European and (later) Indian prosperity. The separate administration and special rights for indigenous Fijians installed by the British over a century ago continue today.

In early 1875, Cakobau and two of his sons returned from a visit to Australia infected with measles. Though they themselves survived, the resulting epidemic wiped out a third of the Fijian population. As a response to this and other public health problems the Fiji School of Medicine was founded in 1885. At the beginning of European colonization there were about 200,000 Fijians, approximately 114,748 in 1881, and just 84,000 by 1921.

The Colonial Period

In 1912, a Gujerati lawyer, D.M. Manilal, arrived in Fiji from Mauritius to fight for Indian rights, just as his contemporary Mahatma Gandhi was doing in South Africa. Several prominent Anglican and Methodist missionaries also lobbied actively against the system. Indentured Indians continued to arrive in Fiji until 1916, but the protests led to the termination of the indenture system throughout the empire in 1920 (Manilal was deported from Fiji after a strike that year).

Although Fiji was a political colony of Britain, it was always an economic colony of Australia: The big Australian trading companies Burns Philp and W.R. Carpenters dominated business. (The ubiquitous Morris Hedstrom is a subsidiary of Carpenters.) Most of the Indians were brought to Fiji to work for the Australian-owned Colonial Sugar Refining Company, which controlled the sugar industry from 1881 right up until 1973, when it was purchased by the Fiji government for $14 million. After 1935, Fiji's gold fields were also exploited by Australians. Banking, insurance, and tourism are largely controlled by Australian companies today.

Under the British colonial system the Governor of Fiji had far greater decision-making authority than his counterparts in the French Pacific colonies. Whereas the French administrators were required to closely follow policies dictated from Paris, the governors of the British colonies had only to refer to the Colonial Office in London on special matters such as finance and foreign affairs. Otherwise they had great freedom to make policy decisions.

No representative government existed in Fiji until 1904, when a legislative council was formed with six elected Europeans and two Fijians nominated by the Great Council of Chiefs (Bose Levu Vakaturaga), itself an instrument of colonial rule. In 1916, the governor appointed an Indian member to the council. A 1929 reform granted five seats to each of the three communities: three elected and two appointed Europeans and Indians, and five nominated Fijians. The council was only an advisory body and the governor remained in complete control. The Europeans generally sided with the Fijians against any demands for equality from the Indians—typical colonial divide and rule.

During WW II, Fijians were outstanding combat troops on the Allied side in the Solomon Islands campaign. In 1952–1956, Fijians helped suppress Malaya's national liberation struggle. So skilled were the Fijians at jungle warfare against the Japanese that it was never appropriate to list a Fijian as "missing in action"—the phrase used was "not yet arrived." The war years saw the development of Nadi Airport. Until 1952, Suva, the present Fijian capital, was headquarters for the entire British Imperial Administration in the South Pacific.

In 1963, the Legislative Council was expanded (though still divided along racial lines), and women and indigenous Fijians got the vote for the first time. Wishing to be rid of the British, whom they blamed for their second-class position, the Indians pushed for independence, but the Fijians had come to view the British as protectors and were somewhat reluctant. A Constitutional Convention was held in London in 1965 to move Fiji toward self-government, and after much discussion a constitution was adopted in

1970. Some legislature members were to be elected from a common roll (voting by all races), as the Indians desired, while other seats remained ethnic (voting in racial constituencies) to protect the Fijians. On October 10, 1970, Fiji became a fully independent nation and the first Fijian governor-general was appointed in 1973—none other than Ratu Sir George Cakobau, great-grandson of the chief who had ceded Fiji to Queen Victoria 99 years previously.

Political Development

During the 1940s, Ratu Sir Lala Sukuna, paramount chief of Lau, played a key role in the creation of a separate administration for indigenous Fijians, with native land (83 percent of Fiji) under its jurisdiction. In 1954, he formed the Fijian Association to support the British governor against Indian demands for equal representation. In 1960, the National Federation Party (NFP) was formed to represent Indian cane farmers.

In 1966, the Alliance Party, a coalition of the Fijian Association, the General Electors' Association (representing Europeans, part-Fijians, and Chinese), and the Fiji Indian Alliance (a minority Indian group) won the legislative assembly elections. In 1970, Alliance Party leader Ratu Sir Kamisese Mara led Fiji into independence and in 1972 his party won Fiji's first post-independence elections. Ratu Mara served as prime minister almost continuously until the 1987 elections.

The formation of the Fiji Labor Party (FLP), headed by Dr. Timoci Bavadra, in July 1985 dramatically altered the political landscape. Fiji's previously nonpolitical trade unions had finally come behind a party that campaigned on bread-and-butter issues rather than race. Late in 1986, Labor and the NFP formed the Coalition with the aim of defeating the Alliance in the next election. In the April 1987 elections the Coalition won 28 of 52 House of Representatives seats; 19 of the 28 elected Coalition members were Indo-Fijians. What swung the election away from Alliance was not a change in Indo-Fijian voting patterns but support for Labor from urban Fijians and part-Fijians, which cost Alliance four previously "safe" seats around Suva.

FIJI ISLANDS

The Coalition cabinet had a majority of Indo-Fijian members, but all positions of vital Fijian interest (Lands, Fijian Affairs, Labor and Immigration, Education, Agriculture and Rural Development) went to indigenous Fijian legislators, though none of them was a traditional chief. Coalition's progressive policies marked quite a switch from the conservatism of the Alliance—a new generation of political leadership dedicated to tackling the day-to-day problems of people of all races rather than perpetuating the privileges of the old chiefly oligarchy. Given time, the Coalition might have required the high chiefs to share the rental monies they received for leasing lands to Indo-Fijians more fairly with ordinary Fijians. Most significant of all, the Coalition would have transformed Fiji from a plural society where only indigenous Melanesian Fijians were called Fijians into a truly multiracial society where all citizens would be Fijians.

The First Coup

After the election, the extremist Fiji-for-Fijians Taukei (landowners) movement launched a destabilization campaign by throwing barricades across highways, organizing protest rallies and marches, and carrying out firebombings. On April 24, 1987, Senator Inoke Tabua and former Alliance cabinet minister Apisai Tora organized a march of 5,000 Fijians through Suva to protest "Indian domination" of the new government. Mr. Tora told a preparatory meeting for the demonstration that Fijians must "act now" to avoid ending up as "deprived as Australia's aborigines." (In fact, under the 1970 constitution the Coalition government would have had no way of changing Fiji's land laws without indigenous Fijian consent.)

At 1000 on Thursday, May 14, 1987, Lt. Col. Sitiveni Rabuka (ram-BU-ka), an ambitious officer whose career was stalled at number three in the Fiji army, and 10 heavily armed soldiers dressed in fatigues, their faces covered by gas masks, entered the House of Parliament in Suva. Rabuka ordered Dr. Bavadra and the Coalition members to follow a soldier out of the building, and when Dr. Bavadra hesitated the soldiers raised their guns. The legislators were loaded into army trucks and taken to Royal Fiji Military Forces headquarters. There was no bloodshed, though Rabuka later confirmed that his troops would have opened fire had there been any resistance. At a press conference five hours after the coup, Rabuka claimed he had acted to prevent violence and had no political ambitions of his own.

Australia and New Zealand promptly denounced the region's first military coup. Governor-General Ratu Sir Penaia Ganilau attempted to reverse the situation by declaring a state of emergency and ordering the mutineers to return to their barracks. They refused to obey. The next day Rabuka named a 15-member Council of Ministers, which he chaired, to govern Fiji, with former Alliance prime minister Ratu Mara as foreign minister. Significantly, Rabuka was the only military officer on the council; most of the others were members of Ratu Mara's defeated administration. Rabuka claimed he had acted to "safeguard the Fijian land issue and the Fijian way of life."

On May 19, Dr. Bavadra and the other kidnapped members of his government were released after the governor-general announced a deal negotiated with Rabuka to avoid the possibility of foreign intervention. Rabuka's Council of Ministers was replaced by a 19-member caretaker Advisory Council appointed by the Great Council of Chiefs. The council would govern until new elections could take place. Ratu Ganilau would head the council, with Rabuka in charge of Home Affairs and the security forces. Only two seats were offered to Dr. Bavadra's government, and they were refused.

Until the coup, the most important mission of the Royal Fiji Military Forces was service in South Lebanon and the Sinai with peacekeeping operations. Half of the 2,600-member Fiji army was on rotating duty there, the Sinai force financed by the United States, the troops in Lebanon by the United Nations. During WW II, Indo-Fijians refused to join the army unless they received the same pay as European recruits; indigenous Fijians had no such reservations and the force has been 95 percent Fijian ever since. Service in the strife-torn Middle East gave the Fiji military a unique preparation for its often-political role in Fiji today. (Not many people outside Fiji realize that, after Australia and New Zealand, Lebanon is the foreign country most familiar to indigenous Fijians.)

The Second Coup

In July and August 1987, a committee set up by Governor-General Ganilau studied proposals for constitutional reform, and on September 4 talks began at Government House in Suva between Alliance and Coalition leaders under the chairmanship of Ratu Ganilau. With no hope of a consensus on a revised constitution, the talks were aimed at preparing for new elections.

Then, on September 26, 1987, Rabuka struck again, just hours before the governor-general was to announce a government of national unity to rule Fiji until new elections could be held. The plan, arduously developed over four months and finally approved by veteran political leaders on all sides, would probably have resulted in Rabuka being sacked. Rabuka quickly threw out the 1970 constitution and pronounced himself "head of state." Some 300 prominent community leaders were arrested and Ratu Ganilau was confined to Government House. Newspapers were shut down, trade unions repressed, the judiciary suspended, the public service purged, the activities of political opponents restricted, a curfew imposed, and the first cases of torture reported.

At midnight on October 7, 1987, Rabuka declared Fiji a republic. Rabuka's new Council of Ministers included Taukei extremists Apisai Tora and Filipe Bole, Fijian Nationalist Party leader Sakeasi Butadroka, and other marginal figures. Rabuka appeared to have backing in the Great Council of Chiefs, which wanted a return to the style of customary rule threatened by the Indian presence and Western democracy. Regime ideologists trumpeted traditional culture and religious fundamentalism to justify their actions. Ratu Mara himself was annoyed that Rabuka's second coup had destroyed an opportunity to salvage the reputations of himself and Ratu Ganilau. On October 16, Ratu Ganilau resigned as governor-general and two days later Fiji was expelled from the British Commonwealth.

The Republic of Rabuka

Realizing that Taukei/military rule was a recipe for disaster, on December 5, 1987, Rabuka appointed Ratu Ganilau president and Ratu Mara prime minister of the new republic. The 21-member cabinet included 10 members of Rabuka's military regime, four of them army officers. Rabuka himself (now a self-styled brigadier) was once again Minister of Home Affairs. This interim government set itself a deadline of two years to frame a new constitution and return Fiji to freely elected representative government. By mid-1988 the army had been expanded into a highly disciplined 6,000-member force loyal to Brigadier Rabuka, who left no doubt he would intervene a third time if his agenda was not followed. The Great Council of Chiefs was to decide on Fiji's republican constitution.

The coups transformed the Fijian economy. In 1987, Fiji experienced 11 percent negative growth in the gross domestic product. To slow the flight of capital, the Fiji dollar was devalued 33 percent in 1987, and inflation was up to nearly 12 percent by the end of 1988. At the same time, civil servants (half the workforce) had to accept a 25 percent wage cut as government spending was slashed. Food prices skyrocketed, causing serious problems for many families. At the end of 1987, the per capita average income was 11 percent *below* what it had been in 1980. Between 1986 and 1996 some 58,300 Indo-Fijians left Fiji for Australia, Canada, New Zealand, and the United States. Nearly three-quarters of Fiji's administrators and managers, and a quarter of all professional, technical, and clerical workers departed taking tens of millions of dollars with them, a crippling loss for a country with a total population of under 750,000.

On the other hand, the devaluations and wage-cutting measures, combined with the creation of a tax-free exporting sector and the encouragement of foreign investment, brought about an economic recovery by 1990. At the expense of democracy, social justice, and racial harmony, Fiji embarked on a standard IMF/World Bank-style structural adjustment program. In 1992, the imposition of a 10 percent value-added tax (VAT) shifted the burden of taxation from rich to

FIJI ISLANDS

poor, standard IMF dogma. In effect, Rabuka and the old oligarchs had pushed Fiji squarely back into the third world.

In November 1989, Dr. Bavadra died of spinal cancer at age 55 and 60,000 people attended his funeral at Viseisei, the largest in Fijian history. Foreign journalists were prevented from covering the funeral. The nominal head of the unelected interim government, Ratu Mara, considered Rabuka an unpredictable upstart and insisted that he choose between politics or military service. Thus in late 1989, the general and two army colonels were dropped from the cabinet, though Rabuka kept his post as army commander.

On July 25, 1990, President Ganilau promulgated a new constitution approved by the Great Council of Chiefs, which gave the chiefs the right to appoint the president and 24 of the 34 members of the Senate. The president had executive authority and appointed the prime minister from among the ethnic Fijian members of the House of Representatives. Under this constitution the 70-member House of Representatives was elected directly, with voting racially segregated. Ethnic Fijians were granted 37 seats from constituencies gerrymandered to ensure the dominance of the eastern chiefs. The constitution explicitly reserved the posts of president, prime minister, and army chief for ethnic Fijians. Christianity was made the official religion, and Rabuka's troops were granted amnesty for any crimes committed during the 1987 coups. The Coalition promptly rejected this supremacist constitution as undemocratic and racist.

Not satisfied with control of the Senate, in early 1991 the Great Council of Chiefs decided to project their power into the lower house through the formation of the Soqosoqo ni Vakavulewa ni Taukei (SVT), commonly called the Fijian Political Party. Meanwhile, Fiji's multiethnic unions continued to rebuild their strength by organizing garment workers and leading strikes in the mining and sugar industries.

In June 1991, Major-General Rabuka rejected an offer from Ratu Mara to join the cabinet as Minister of Home Affairs and co-deputy prime minister, since it would have meant giving up his military power base. Instead, Rabuka attempted to widen his political appeal by making public statements in support of striking gold miners and cane farmers, and even threatening a third coup.

By now Rabuka's ambition to become prime minister was obvious, and his new role as a populist rabble-rouser seemed designed to outflank both the Labor Party and the chiefs (Rabuka himself is a commoner). President Ganilau (Rabuka's paramount chief) quickly applied pressure, and in July the volatile general reversed himself and accepted the cabinet posts he had so recently refused. As a condition for reentering the government, Rabuka was forced to resign as army commander and the president's son, Major-Gen. Epeli Ganilau, was appointed his successor. With Rabuka out of the army everyone breathed a little easier, and the chiefs decided to co-opt a potential troublemaker by electing Rabuka president of the SVT.

Return to Democracy

The long-awaited parliamentary elections took place in late May 1992, and the SVT captured 30 of the 37 indigenous Fijian seats. Another five went to Fijian nationalists, while the 27 Indian seats were split between the NFP with 14 and the FLP with 13. The five other races' seats went to the General Voters Party (GVP).

Just prior to the election, Ratu Mara retired from party politics and was named vice-president of Fiji by the Great Council of Chiefs. An intense power struggle then developed in the SVT between Ratu Mara's chosen successor as prime minister, former finance minister Josevata Kamikamica, and ex-general Rabuka. Since the SVT lacked a clear majority in the 70-seat house, coalition partners had to be sought, and in a remarkable turn of events, populist Rabuka gained the support of the FLP by offering concessions to the trade unions and a promise to review the constitution and land leases. Therefore Rabuka became prime minister thanks to the very party he had ousted from power at gunpoint exactly five years earlier!

The SVT formed a coalition with the GVP, but in November 1993 the Rabuka government was defeated in a parliamentary vote of no confidence over the budget, leading to fresh elections in February 1994. In these, Rabuka's SVT increased its representation to 31 seats. Many Indo-Fijians had felt betrayed by FLP backing of Rabuka's prime ministership in 1992, and FLP representation dropped to seven seats, compared to 20 for the NFP.

Ratu Ganilau died of leukemia in December 1993, and Ratu Mara was sworn in as president in January 1994. Meanwhile, Rabuka cultivated a pragmatic image to facilitate his international acceptance in the South Pacific, and within Fiji itself he demonstrated his political prowess by holding out a hand of reconciliation to the Indo-Fijian community. The 1990 constitution had called for a constitutional review before 1997, and in 1995 a three-member commission was appointed, led by Sir Paul Reeves, a former governor-general of New Zealand, together with Mr. Tomasi Vakatora representing the Rabuka government and Mr. Brij Lal for the opposition.

The report of the commission titled *Towards a United Future* was submitted in September 1996. It recommended a return to the voting system outlined in the 1970 constitution with some members of parliament elected from racially divided communal constituencies and others from open ridings on a common roll of racially mixed electorates. The commissioners suggested that the post of prime minister no longer be explicitly reserved for an indigenous Fijian but simply for the leader of the largest grouping in parliament of whatever race.

The report was passed to a parliamentary committee for study, and in May 1997 all sides agreed to a power-sharing formula to resolve Fiji's constitutional impasse. The number of guaranteed seats for indigenous Fijians in the lower house was reduced from 37 to 23, and voting across racial lines was instituted in another third of the seats. The prime minister was to be required to form a cabinet comprised of ministers from all parties in proportion to their representation in parliament—a form of power sharing unique in modern democracy. Nearly half the members of the senate and the country's president would continue to be appointed by the Great Council of Chiefs. Human rights guarantees were included.

The Constitution Amendment Bill passed both houses of parliament unanimously, and was promulgated into law by President Mara on July 25, 1997. In recognition of the rare national consensus that had been achieved, Fiji was welcomed back into the British Commonwealth in October 1997. The new constitution formally took effect in July 1998.

For many years it was unfashionable to look upon Fiji as a part of Melanesia, and the nation's Polynesian links were emphasized. The 1987 coups had a lot to do with rivalry between the eastward-looking chiefs of Bau and Lau and the Melanesian-leaning western Fijians. Ironically, some of the political friction between the commoner Rabuka and the aristocrat Ratu Mara can also be seen in this light. The latter was always networking among Fiji's smaller Polynesian neighbors, and it was only in 1996 that Rabuka brought Fiji into the Melanesian Spearhead Group that had existed since 1988. Of course, the pragmatist Rabuka was merely acknowledging the vastly greater economic potential of Melanesia, but he was clearly much more comfortable socializing with the other Melanesian leaders at regional summits than Ratu Mara ever would have been.

People's Coalition Government

In May 1999, Fiji's 419,000 eligible voters participated in the first election under the 1997 constitution. The IMF-style structural adjustment program of the previous government and a strong desire for change were key issues, and although Rabuka himself was elected, his SVT Party took only eight of the 71 parliamentary seats. The NFP allied with Rabuka was wiped out entirely by the Labor Party, which won all 19 Indo-Fijian seats, plus 18 of the 25 common roll seats elected by all voters. Two indigenous Fijian parties, the Fijian Alliance and the Party of National Unity, won a total of 14 seats. They formed an alliance with Labor's 37 members to give "People's Coalition" an overwhelming 51 seats.

Among the seven women elected to parliament were Adi Kuini Vuikaba Speed, widow of former prime minister Timoci Bavadra, and Adi Koila Mara Nailatikau, daughter of President

Mara. Labor leader Mahendra Chaudhry was appointed prime minister—the first Indo-Fijian ever to occupy the post. Two-thirds of Chaudhry's cabinet were indigenous Fijians, but it was quite different from the two previous governments, which had included no Indo-Fijians. Rabuka resigned from parliament soon after the election and was made chairman of the Great Council of Chiefs. His departure contributed to a feeling among grassroots Fijians that the Indians had taken over. If Dr. Tupeni Baba, Labor's second-in-command and an indigenous Fijian, had become prime minister, the situation might have been different, but Chaudhry's struggle had been long and his victory was so complete that he insisted on getting the top job. Baba became deputy prime minister. NFP leader Jai Ram Reddy issued a portentous warning at the time: "Fiji is not yet ready for an Indian prime minister."

Fiji's first democratic government in a dozen years survived 365 days. Chaudhry vigorously pushed forward his reforms and applied the brakes to privatization, which won him few friends, and his relations with business and the media were antagonistic. In February 2000, the government introduced a "leadership honesty code" bill, which would have required politicians to disclose their personal assets in private to the Ombudsman's office. Corruption had been rife during the Rabuka years, culminating in the collapse of the National Bank of Fiji in 1995 after F$295 million had been siphoned off by politicians and the Fijian chiefs through bad loans and other devices. Mismanagement and cronyism had led to huge losses by the Fiji Development Bank and provincial councils, and kickbacks were routine at Customs & Excise and other government departments. The Chaudhry government's anti-corruption drive was a blast of fresh air.

Reducing poverty was a high priority for the Chaudhry team. People's Coalition attempted to help Fijian villagers through affirmative action programs. The value added tax and customs duty on basic food items were lowered, utility rates were slashed, and loans were made available for small business.

People's Coalition also bucked the trend to-

ward "globalization" and lobbied hard for fairer terms of trade. In recognition, Fiji was selected as the venue for the signing of what would have been the Suva Convention, a 20-year successor to Lomé Agreement governing trade between 77 African, Caribbean, and Pacific (ACP) nations and the 15 European Union states. Dozens of ministers and high officials from these countries were scheduled to be in Suva on June 8, 2000, for the launch of this historic partnership agreement, but it was not to be.

After the May 1999 election, leaders of the defeated SVT party began working on strategies to bring down the People's Coalition government and return to power. In April 2000, the ultra-nationalist Taukei Movement was revived by Apisai Tora, a fringe politician deeply involved in the 1987 coups. Taukei's declared aim was to revise the 1997 constitution to ensure Fijian political supremacy. The SVT supported Taukei, as did some provincial administrations, but the Fiji army declared that it would not be drawn into any attempt to overthrow the government. Taukei agitators tried to make the future of Indo-Fijian land leases an issue, and demonstrations began in Lautoka and Suva.

The Third Coup

On May 19, 2000, a Taukei protest march wound down Victoria Parade in central Suva. When the thousands of marchers reached the gates of the Presidential Palace, they were told that gunmen had stormed Fiji's parliament, which had been in session, and had taken its members hostage. Many of the marchers rushed to the building, joining terrorists who were only too happy to have willing human shields. In central Suva gangs of thugs and protesters responded to news of the takeover by looting and burning Indian shops. Around 160 shops were emptied or destroyed in the three hours before the police began making arrests.

The initial assault on parliament was led by a failed businessman named George Speight, along with seven renegade members of the army's elite Counter Revolutionary Warfare Unit (also known as the First Meridian Squadron) and 35 ex-soldiers, half of them ex-convicts. The highest ranking soldier present was retired major Ilisoni Ligairi, a former British Special Air Services warrant officer who had set up the CRW anti-terrorist unit in 1987. Speight had appeared in the Suva High Court on extortion charges five days before the coup, yet he declared he was acting to defend indigenous Fijian rights. In 1997, Speight had been forced to flee Australia after a pyramid scheme he had a hand in collapsed with A$130 million in losses for gullible investors.

Yet to understand what was really happening, we have to back up a bit. In early 1999, a bitter struggle was being waged in government circles over who would gain the right to market Fiji's valuable mahogany forests worldwide. The Rabuka government was known to favor a U.S. company called Timber Resources Management, while the incoming Chaudhry government announced they intended to give the contract to the British-based Commonwealth Development Corporation on the basis of a recommendation from the Australian office of the accountancy firm Pricewaterhouse Coopers. Speight had previously worked as a consultant for the Americans, and in June 1999 Chaudhry's Forestry Minister removed him from his position as managing director of the state-owned Fiji Hardwood Corporation and Fiji Pine Limited because Speight had been a political appointee of the former regime. Chaudhry's surprise election in May 1999 had cost Speight and associates the chance to control the exploitation mahogany and pine tracts worth hundreds of millions of dollars. Just prior to his assault on parliament, Speight had been trying to foment unrest among landowners by spreading disinformation about the rival bids and the Chaudhry government's intentions. Important figures in the previous Rabuka government were involved in the ongoing mahogany affair, including Rabuka's Minister of Finance and former Speight patron Jim Ah Koy. Speight's coup attempt may have had much more to do with timber rights than indigenous rights.

Among the 45 persons taken hostage by Speight's gang were Prime Minister Chaudhry, and the minister of tourism and transport, President Mara's daughter. Ratu Mara immediately declared a state of emergency, and the Fiji Military Forces commander, Commodore Voreqe Bainimarama, ordered his men to surround the parliamentary compound. Unlike the situation during the 1987 coups, the army's high command and the bulk of its troops did not support the coup attempt. Bainimarama declined to use force to free the captives for fear of triggering a bloodbath, and many of the hostages were to spend the next 56 days sitting on mattresses with their lives in the hands of heavily armed thugs.

On May 27, 80-year-old President Mara officially dismissed the elected Chaudhry government after Speight threatened to kill his daughter. The next day a mob of Speight supporters ransacked the offices of Fiji TV to protest coverage critical of the coup. Soon after a Fijian policeman was shot dead by gunmen near parliament. On May 29, with the situation deteriorating, the army asked President Mara to "step aside" while it restored order. Mara thereupon withdrew to his power base on remote Lakeba in the Lau Group, the ignominious end of a long and distinguished career. That day Commodore Bainimarama declared martial law, announced the abrogation of the 1997 constitution, and assumed executive authority. Bainimarama ruled out any return to power by Chaudhry.

Meanwhile, as the negotiations continued, Speight was constantly making fresh demands. A struggle for power was underway among the Fijian elite. The Great Council of Chiefs wanted to appoint the vice president, Ratu Josefa Iloilo, to replace Mara, but Speight insisted that Ratu Jope Seniloli, a retired schoolteacher with close ties to the chiefly Cakobau family of Bau but no previous political standing, must become vice president. Since the death of Ratu Sir George Cakobau in 1989, the once powerful Cakobaus of eastern Viti Levu had been eclipsed by their historic "Tongan" enemies from Lau, led by Ratu Sir Kamisese Mara. Seven weeks into the crisis, Speight moved to have persons with Cakobau connections granted high positions in an interim administration. His choice for prime minister was Adi Samanunu Cakobau, Fiji's high commissioner in Malaysia and Sir George's eldest daughter.

That was the signal for Bainimarama, a long-time Mara ally, to order his army to tighten the noose around Speight by declaring parliament and nearby streets a "military exclusion zone." The next day (July 3), the Great Council of Chiefs named a civilian cabinet led by the former head of the Fiji Development Bank, Laisenia Qarase, another Mara man. This interim government had the army's blessing, and to win acceptance from the international community, high-profile Speight elements were shut out. These developments triggered widespread disturbances by grassroots Speight supporters throughout the country, including the occupation of a few tourist resorts, the blocking of highways, and the burning of the historic Masonic Lodge in Levuka. There was intimidation of Indo-Fijians living in rural areas of northeastern Viti Levu and central Vanua Levu, traditional Cakobau strongholds, with arson, looting, and ethnic cleansing. The military was unable to cope.

Visibly shaken, on July 9 Bainimarama agreed to an amnesty for Speight and the others on the condition that they free the 27 remaining hostages and surrender all arms. The Qarase interim government would be replaced, and Iloilo and Seniloli would become president and vice president. On July 13, the hostage crisis came to a peaceful end at a kava ceremony when Chaudhry magnanimously said that he harbored no personal animosity toward Speight, though the army noted that not all of the missing weapons were turned in. Upon his release, Chaudhry confirmed that he had been beaten by Speight's thugs early on in the hostage crisis.

It's said that only the threat of a military coup from Bainimarama prevented President Iloilo, who was seen as overly sympathetic to Speight's cause, from accepting Adi Samanunu as prime minister. Former prime minister Rabuka (who remained on the sidelines during most of the crisis) remarked that Speight was only a puppet, brought in at the last minute by persons unknown.

Speight is only part-Fijian, and the Taukei extremists represent a small minority of opinion in Fiji. The concerns of indigenous Fijians to protect their lands and culture were and are legitimate, but those interests have been enshrined in all three of Fiji's constitutions and no government would have be able to negate them. As previously in recent Fijian history, the race issue was manipulated by defeated politicians and power hungry individuals, and rural villagers and marginalized urban Fijians proved effective tools in the hands of rabble-rouser George Speight.

Interim Government

After the hostages were freed, Qarase simply stayed on as prime minister. In late July he appointed a cabinet consisting mostly of indigenous Fijian civil servants and opposition politicians, without any overt Speight insiders. Qarase announced that his military-backed regime would last 18 months, to give time for a new constitution to be drawn up and fresh elections arranged. However, during the week of July 17, Australia, Britain, and New Zealand announced sanctions against Fiji because the elected government had not been restored.

Speight's agitating continued with Qarase now the target of choice. On July 27, Speight was arrested at an army checkpoint between Suva and Nausori, and the next day the army rounded up 369 of his commoner followers in a forceful manner. Speight and cohorts were charged with carrying arms in contravention of the amnesty deal, and a week later the charge of treason was added. Speight and a dozen key figures in the coup attempt were sent to await trial on tiny Nukulau Island, a former picnic spot off Suva. In protest, pro-Speight soldiers kidnapped 50 Indo-Fijians at Labasa, but released them quickly when the army threatened to intervene.

In September, the interim government set up a 12-member commission to review the 1997 constitution. Asesela Ravuvu, an academic with a long history of advocating hardline indigenous Fijian positions, was appointed chairman, and among the other members were three Speight supporters. Most Indo-Fijians boycotted the process.

On the afternoon of November 2, 2000, the final act in this tragedy unfolded at Suva's Queen Elizabeth Barracks, as 39 soldiers from the Counter Revolutionary Warfare Unit staged a surprise raid on army headquarters in an attempt to murder Commodore Bainimarama and seize control of Fiji for Speight. Loyal officers helped Bainimarama escape down a gully, and just before dusk the Third Fiji Infantry Regiment launched a fierce counter attack. Five rebels and three government soldiers died in the attempted mutiny, including several rebels who were kicked to death by army troops after being captured. Two dozen soldiers and civilians were wounded, and the army quickly rounded up the remaining mutineers. The nation was shocked by this unprecedented brutality. The plot thickened when it was revealed that ex-general Rabuka had been present at the barracks during the mutiny. Rabuka claimed he had only gone there to mediate, but Bainimarama ordered him not to re-enter the facility.

After the hostage's release, a number of lawsuits were filed before the Fiji High Court claiming that the change in government was unconstitutional. On November 15, 2000, Chief Justice Anthony Gates issued a ruling in response to a plea brought by an ordinary Indo-Fijian farmer, Chandrika Prasad, who claimed that his constitutional rights had been violated by the coup. Gates agreed and declared the Speight coup null and void, the interim government illegal, and the 1997 constitution still the law of the land. Gates ruled that Ratu Mara was still the legal president of Fiji and that he had a duty to appoint a new prime minister from among the parliamentarians elected in 1999. Gates suggested that the interim government resign and allow the formation of a government of national unity comprised of elected members of parliament. That would get Fiji back on track.

Interim Prime Minister Qarase referred the case to the Fiji Court of Appeal, which upheld Chief Justice Gates' ruling in an historic decision on March 1, 2001. Qarase and Iloilo both announced that the court's decision would be respected. Fiji's top judges had suggested that the president recall parliament, and 40 of the 71 parliamentarians deposed by George Speight signed a petition asking that this be done. Yet instead of recalling parliament, President Iloilo dissolved the old parliament and appointed Qarase to run a caretaker government until fresh elections could be held. Qarase quickly brought back his old 30-minister cabinet, and the un-

elected government the judges had declared illegal just two weeks before was back in business.

As could be expected, the Fiji Crisis had a disastrous impact on the economy. After positive growth of 7.8 percent in 1999, there was 2.8 percent negative growth in 2000. By the end of 2000, over 7,400 people had lost their jobs. Tourist arrivals for the three months following the coup were only 37,126 compared to 120,156 for the same period in 1999, and the industry was losing US$1 million a day. A US$100 million Hilton Hotel project for Nadi was put on hold, and other major resorts at Natadola Beach and elsewhere were canceled. Only in 2001 did the economy again begin to grow. The crisis has seriously widened the gap between the haves and have-nots in Fiji.

Elections and Aftermath

The judges had ruled that the 1997 constitution remained in force, thus attempts by the caretaker government to draft a new constitution weighted toward Fijians were halted. The international sanctions against Fiji continued, and in August 2001 Qarase called early elections to legitimize his rule. Qarase's SDL party won 32 of the 71 parliament seats, Labor 27 seats, and the pro-coup Conservative Alliance six. Despite being imprisoned, George Speight was elected as the Conservative Alliance member from Korovou in northeastern Viti Levu. Qarase formed a government in coalition with the Conservative Alliance after they dropped a demand for an amnesty for Speight, who was formally expelled from parliament in December for failing to attend the sessions.

The 1997 constitution stipulates that any party winning at least 10 percent of the 71 parliamentary seats has a right to be represented in cabinet. This meant Labor was entitled to eight of the 20 cabinet posts, but Qarase claimed that having Labor ministers in his cabinet was "unworkable" and in September 2001 he formed a government without the participation of Labor. Labor filed suit, and in February 2002, the Fiji Court of Appeal ruled that Qarase had to include Labor in his cabinet. Qarase appealed to Fiji's Supreme

Court, which in July 2003 ordered the government to include Labor ministers in the cabinet. In response, Qarase offered to enlarge his cabinet from 22 to 36 ministers with Labor granted 14 minor portfolios in fields such as libraries and health promotion. All ministers would be required to support government policies or resign. Chaudhry refused to accept this "bloated cabinet" and the matter was referred back to court.

In February 2002, George Speight was sentenced to death for treason, but within hours President Iloilo commuted his sentence to life imprisonment. Speight had entered a guilty plea to avoid a trial that might have revealed the names of those behind the coup. During an April 2001 TV interview, Ratu Mara accused Rabuka and Police Commissioner Isikia Savua of involvement in the coup. Chaudhry also pointed a finger at Savua, who prior to May 2000 had assured him that rumors of a coup were unfounded. During the coup itself, Savua stood by while Suva was sacked, but he was later "cleared" of involvement during a secret inquiry by Chief Justice Sir Timoci Tuivaga, author of the military decrees which attempted to scrap the 1997 constitution. Savua is currently Fiji's ambassador to the United Nations in New York.

In a provocative article in the February 2003 issue of *Pacific Magazine,* Michael Field revealed the existence of a mystery coup conspirator Speight expected to emerge on the day of the coup but who has yet to be identified. In May 2003, Vice President Seniloli, two cabinet ministers, and the deputy speaker of parliament were charged with taking unlawful oaths to commit capital offences during the coup. There has been much speculation about other key figures behind the coup, believed to include several prominent businesspeople, and reports of a cover-up in the investigations and trials continue to emerge.

Both President Iloilo and Prime Minister Qarase owe their positions to the Speight coup, and Qarase's SDL party presently governs in coalition with the pro-Speight Conservative Alliance. Although Qarase's government was elected, the political situation remains shaky, with fresh upheavals to be expected if the agenda of the ultra nationalists is not followed. It's also quite likely that the last has not been heard from George Speight himself. He's currently being held on Nukulau Island within sight of the parliament building in Suva, a little Napoleon in exile on Elba. It's said that only international opinion and strong objections from Commodore Bainimarama have thus far prevented a pardon for Speight. The shadow of May 19, 2000, continues to hang over Fiji.

Government

The 1997 constitution provides for a parliamentary system of government with a 71-seat House of Representatives or "lower house" consisting of 46 members from communal ridings and 25 from multiracial ridings with elections every five years. Twenty-three communal seats are reserved for indigenous Fijians, 19 for Indo-Fijians, three for general electors (part-Fijians, Europeans, Chinese, etc.), and one for Rotumans. The leader of the largest party or coalition of parties in parliament is the head of government or prime minister. Voting is compulsory (F$20 fine for failing to vote).

The 32-member "upper house" or Senate has 14 members appointed by the Great Council of Chiefs, nine by the prime minister, eight by the leader of the opposition, and one by the Council of Rotuma. Any legislation affecting the rights of indigenous Fijians must be approved by nine of the 14 senators appointed by the chiefs. The Great Council of Chiefs also chooses Fiji's head of state, the president, for a five-year term. The three traditional Fijian confederacies are Burebasaga, Kubuna, and Tovata.

Aside from the national government, there's a well-developed system of local government. On the Fijian side, the basic unit is the village *(koro)* represented by a village herald *(turaga-ni-koro),* who is chosen by consensus. The 1,169 villages and 483 settlements are grouped into 189 districts *(tikina),* the districts into 14 provinces *(yasana).* The executive head of each provincial council is the *roko tui,* appointed by the Fijian Affairs Board.

The national administration is broken down into four divisions (central, eastern, northern, and western), each headed by a commissioner. These civil servants and the 19 district officers work for the Ministry of Regional Development. The Micronesians of Rabi and Polynesians of Rotuma govern themselves through island councils of their own. Ten city and town councils also function at the local level.

Fiji has a High Court, a Fiji Court of Appeal, and a Supreme Court. The chief justice and eight other judges are appointed by the president after consulting the prime minister. After the collapse of parliament and a change of president in the wake of the Speight coup, the courts emerged as the last bastion of legality in Fiji's national system of government. Criminal and civil cases of lesser importance are handled in magistrates courts.

ECONOMY

Fiji has a diversified economy based on tourism, garment manufacturing, sugar production, fishing, gold mining, timber, mineral water, vegetables, and coconut products. Although eastern Viti Levu and the Lau Group have long dominated the country politically, western Viti Levu remains Fiji's economic powerhouse, with tourism, sugar, timber, and gold mining all concentrated there.

Aside from the cash economy, subsistence agriculture is important to indigenous Fijians in rural areas, where manioc, taro, yams, sweet potato, and corn are the principal subsistence crops. Coastal subsistence fishing is twice as important as commercial fishing in terms of actual catch.

Sugar

It's estimated that a third of Fiji's population relies on sugar for its livelihood. Although the F$235 million a year Fiji earns from sugar is half of what it makes on tourism, more people rely on sugar than on tourism. Almost all of Fiji's sugar cane is grown by small independent Indo-Fijian farmers on contract to the government-owned Fiji Sugar Corporation. Some 20,000 farmers cultivate cane on holdings averaging 4.5 hectares leased from indigenous Fijians, and current problems in renewing these leases could mean that Fiji's

sugar industry is ultimately doomed. For many years the corporation has used 595 km of 0.610-meter narrow-gauge railway to carry the cane to mills at Lautoka, Ba, Rakiraki, and Labasa, and the current shift to truck transport is hurting farmers by increasing costs. Fiji's four aging, inefficient sugar mills are in urgent need of modernization. A distillery at Lautoka produces rum and other liquors from the by-products of sugar.

Over a quarter of a million metric tonnes of sugar are exported annually to Britain, Japan, and other countries, providing direct or indirect employment for 40,000 people. The 14,000 seasonal workers cutting cane earn F$10 a day and two meals. Some 125,000 metric tons of Fiji sugar is sold to the European Union each year at fixed rates four times above world market levels, thanks to import quotas set forth in the Cotonou Agreement. The EU uses this agreement as a way of providing aid to 77 former colonies in Africa, the Caribbean, and the Pacific. Without these subsidies (worth F$100 million a year), Fiji's sugar industry would collapse, since the cost of production is higher than the world market price. Now the World Trade Organization and big producers like Australia and Brazil are putting pressure on the EU to phase out the subsidies after the current protocol expires in 2008.

Other Crops and Water

In the past, Fiji has grown almost half its requirements of rice but the industry has been damaged by competition from imported rice. Much of Fiji's rice is grown around Nausori and Navua, and on Vanua Levu.

Most of Fiji's copra is produced in Lau, Lomaiviti, Taveuni, and Vanua Levu, half by European or part-Fijian planters and the rest by indigenous Fijian villagers. Copra production has slipped from 40,000 tons a year in the 1950s to about 6,000 tons today due to the low prices paid to producers.

In 1998, F$35 million worth of kava root was exported to Germany, the United States, and other countries, where it was used by pharmaceutical firms to make antidepressants and muscle-relaxers. In late 2001, kava exports plummeted after the European Union imposed import restrictions on the roots over allegations that kava-based medicines might cause liver damage, and in 2002 only F$2 million was exported.

Another unique export is natural artesian water drawn from a well at Yaqara on northwestern Viti Levu and bottled in a modern plant (www .fijiwater.com) set up by Canadian David Gilmour, owner of the Wakaya Club island resort. Gilmour gave the indigenous landowners of the watershed a 25 percent interest in his company, making them the richest clan in Fiji, as sales of Fiji Water in the United States are booming. In 2002, Fiji sold almost F$32 million in water, the sixth largest export.

Timber

Timber is increasingly important as 40,730 hectares of softwood planted in western Viti Levu and Vanua Levu by Fiji Pine and private landowners in the late 1970s reach maturity. Milling and marketing is done by Tropik Timber, a Fiji Pine subsidiary. Processing facilities for the 16,000 hectares of pine on Vanua Levu are inadequate and round logs must be transported to Viti Levu by truck and ferry at great expense.

In addition to softwood, around 18,000 hectares of hardwood (74 percent of it mahogany) planted by the British after 1952 are matured and ready for harvesting (another 22,000 hectares in southeastern Viti Levu and in central Vanua Levu will be mature in a decade). With buyers in Europe and elsewhere increasingly averse to natural rainforest timber, Fiji is in the enviable position of possessing the world's largest "green" mahogany forest. The government-controlled Fiji Hardwood Corporation was set up in 1997 to manage this asset, which has been valued as high as F$400 million. Thus far, squabbling between the various stakeholders has delayed exploitation of this resource. Fiji already exports about F$42 million a year in sawed softwood lumber, wood chips, and other wood products (the export of raw logs was banned in 1987).

Yet outside the managed plantations, Fiji's native forests are poorly protected from the greed of foreign logging companies and short-sighted local landowners, and each year large tracts of pristine rainforest are lost. Now that all of the lowland forests have been cleared, attention is turning to the highlands. The planted pine and mahogany have had the corollary benefit of reducing pressure on the natural forests to supply Fiji's timber needs. A factory between Nadi and Sigatoka uses senile coconut trees to make quality furniture, flooring, and panels.

Fishing

Commercial fishing is increasingly important, with a government-owned tuna processing plant at Levuka supplied in part by Fiji's own fleet of longline vessels. Only about 6 percent of the skipjack and albacore tuna is now canned, and most the rest is chilled and sent to canneries in the United States (see the Ovalau section for more information). Chilled yellowfin tuna is flown to Hawaii and Japan to serve the sashimi (raw fish) market. Fish is now Fiji's third-largest export and overfishing has resulted from too many fishing licenses being issued to foreign companies by the government.

Related to fishing is the marine aquarium industry which exports tropical fish and live coral. Walt Smith International (www.walt smith.com) in Lautoka is a world leader in coral farming, with thousands of living rocks currently growing on iron racks in undersea farms off western Viti Levu.

Mining

Mining activity centers on gold from the Emperor Gold Mine at Vatukoula on northern Viti Levu. Elsewhere on Viti Levu, Emperor controls a rich gold deposit at Tuvatu, unfortunately within the Nadi water catchment area and thus an environmental hazard. In 1998, the Mount Kasi gold mine on Vanua Levu closed due to low world prices, and the development of other gold fields has been frozen. In 2002, gold exports were worth F$78 million.

Since 1984, Placer Pacific has spent US$10 million exploring the extensive low-grade copper deposits at Namosi, 30 km northwest of Suva, but in 1997, despite offers of near tax-free status from the government, the company put the US$1 billion project on hold saying it was not economical.

Garment Industry

Garments produced by 150 companies that export their clothes mainly to Australia, New Zealand, and the United States are now Fiji's largest export. Some foreign manufacturers have moved their factories to Fiji to take advantage of the low labor costs, and the South Pacific Regional Trade and Economic Cooperation Agreement (SPARTECA) allows Fiji products with at least 50 percent local content partial duty- and quota-free entry into Australia and New Zealand. The value of SPARTECA is gradually eroding and garment exports seem to have peaked.

The garment industry employs 20,000 people, with the mostly female workers earning an average of F$60 a week. At peak periods the factories operate three shifts, seven days a week. Women working in the industry have complained of body searches and sexual harassment; those who protest or organize industrial action are often fired and blacklisted. About 1,000 recently arrived Asian workers are also employed in the factories. In 2002, Fiji exported textiles worth F$245 million.

Other Manufacturing

Companies that process food or make furniture, toys, or shoes are also prominent in the tax-free exporting sector. Until recently it was believed that manufacturing would eventually overtake both sugar and tourism as the main source of income for the country, but the globalization of trade and the progressive reduction of tariffs worldwide is cutting into Fiji's competitiveness. SPARTECA's local-content rule discourages local companies from reducing costs by introducing labor-saving technology, condemning them to obsolescence in the long term.

Economic Problems

In spite of all this potential, unemployment is a major social problem. The economy generates only 2,000 new jobs a year, but 17,000 young people leave school every year, and in 2002 unemployment stood at 14.1 percent. To stimu-

late industry, firms based in Fiji that export 95 percent of their production are granted 13-year tax holidays, the duty-free import of materials, and the freedom to repatriate capital and profits. An increasing list of incentives is being added to the books.

In 1995, Fiji's financial standing was severely shaken when it was announced that the government-owned National Bank of Fiji was holding hundreds of millions of dollars in bad debts resulting from politically motivated loans to indigenous Fijians and Rotumans. The subsequent run on deposits cost the bank another F$20 million, and the government was forced to step in to save the bank. Vast sums were diverted from development projects to cover the losses, an indication of systemic corruption not usually noticed by visitors. In 1999, Colonial Life Insurance paid F$9.5 million for a 51 percent interest in what was left of the National Bank.

Fiji's government debt is currently F$1,910 million, 42.8 percent of the gross domestic product. Cronyism and corruption, which the Chaudhry government attempted to control, have returned full force since the May 2000 coup. Bribery by American business interests trying to obtain contracts to harvest Fiji's mahogany reserves may have played a major role in the Speight coup itself, and more recently government officials have been accused of accepting bribes to grant fishing licenses to Asian companies. It's become a standard practice to provide "gifts" to officials when bidding for government contracts. Foreign reserves are falling as the Qarase government borrows tens of millions from the World Bank and Asian Development Bank to cover budget deficits. Debt, deficit spending, and corruption have been identified as major obstacles to aid and investment in Fiji.

Trade and Aid

Although Fiji imports 39 percent more than it exports, much of the imbalance is resold to tourists and foreign airlines who pay in foreign exchange. Garments are the nation's largest visible export earner, followed by raw sugar, fish, unrefined gold, wood products, mineral water, fruits and vegetables, shoes, fabrics, molasses, coconut oil, and kava, in that order. Large trade imbalances exist with Australia, New Zealand, and most Asian countries.

Mineral fuels used to eat up much of Fiji's import budget, but this has declined since the Monasavu Hydroelectric Project and other self-sufficiency measures came online in the 1980s. Manufactured goods, petroleum products, textiles, food, chemicals, and motor vehicles account for most of the import bill.

Fiji is the least dependent South Pacific nation. Overseas aid totals only F$40 million a year or less than F$50 per capita (as compared to several thousand dollars per capita in French Polynesia). Development aid comes from Australia, the European Union, Japan, New Zealand, and China. North American aid to Fiji is negligible. The New Zealand Government deserves credit for devoting much of its limited aid budget to the creation of national parks and reserves.

Aside from conventional aid, Fiji's army earns money through its participation in multinational forces. The United Nations is currently millions of dollars in arrears in its payments to Fiji for peacekeeping, and in 2002 the last 600 Fiji soldiers returned from service in Lebanon. In late 2003, some 400 Fijian ex-soldiers and police were sent to Iraq by a private British security firm to serve as security guards. The Fiji Army was not involved in this operation, as it was not sanctioned by the United Nations. Over 5,000 people serve in Fiji's armed forces, costing the country F$80 million a year, more than is spent on any other public institution. Many Fijians also enlist in the British Army.

Remittances from Fijians resident abroad are also very important, bringing in around F$200 million a year.

Tourism

Tourism has been the leading moneymaker since 1989, earning over F$500 million a year—more than garments and sugar combined. In 2002, some 397,859 tourists visited Fiji—50 percent more than visited Tahiti and over 10 times as many as visited Tonga. Things appear in better perspective, however, when Fiji is compared to Hawaii, which is about the same size in surface area. Overpacked Hawaii gets nearly seven million tourists, 20 times as many as Fiji. About 29 percent of Fiji's tourists come from Australia, 18 percent from New Zealand, 15 percent from the United States, 10 percent from Britain, 9 percent from Japan, 7 percent from continental Europe, and 3 percent from Canada.

Gross receipts figures from tourism are often misleading, as $.56 on every dollar is repatriated overseas by foreign investors or used to pay for tourism-related imports. Because of this, sugar is more profitable for Fiji than tourism. In 2003, the hotel industry employed around 7,000 people with an estimated 40,000 jobs in all sectors related to tourism. Management of the top hotels is usually expatriate, with Indo-Fijians filling technical positions such as maintenance, cooking, accounting, etc., and indigenous Fijians working in more visible positions such as receptionists, waiters, guides, and housekeepers. With an eye to profitability, the resorts try to use as many part-time workers as possible.

Fiji has 220 licensed hotels with a total of around 6,000 rooms, over a third of the South Pacific's tourism plant. Most of the large resort hotels in Fiji are foreign owned (the Cathay, Hexagon, and Tanoa hotel chains are Fiji-based exceptions). The Fiji Government is doing all it can to promote luxury hotel development by offering 20-year tax holidays on new projects. The May 2000 coup halted resort development and had a heavy impact on upscale ventures dependent on high occupancy levels. Backpacker resorts were far less affected.

Many of the upmarket tourist resorts are centered along the Coral Coast of Viti Levu and in the Mamanuca Islands off Nadi. Backpacker tourism now focuses on the Yasawa Islands. Investment by U.S. hotel chains has increased in recent years as Japanese firms have pulled out. In 1996, ITT-Sheraton bought two luxury hotels on Nadi's Denarau Island from a group of Japanese banks. In 2000, Outrigger Hotels of Hawaii built a major resort on the Coral Coast. Developments by Hilton, Marriott, and Novotel are currently in the works around Nadi.

THE PEOPLE

The Fijians

Fiji is a transitional zone between Polynesia and Melanesia. Indigenous Fijians bear a physical resemblance to the Melanesians, but like the Polynesians, they have hereditary chiefs, patrilineal descent, a love of elaborate ceremonies, and a fairly homogeneous language and culture.

The Fijians live in villages along the rivers or coast, with anywhere from 50 to 400 people led by a hereditary chief. To see a Fijian family living in an isolated house in a rural area is uncommon. The traditional thatched *bure* is fast disappearing from Fiji as villagers rebuild in tin and panel (often following destructive cyclones). Grass is not as accessible as cement, takes more time to repair, and is less permanent.

Away from the three largest islands the population is almost totally Fijian. *Mataqali* (clans) are grouped into *yavusa* (tribes) of varying rank and function. Several *yavusa* form a *vanua,* a number of which make up a *matanitu.* Chiefs of the most important *vanua* are known as high chiefs. In western Viti Levu the groups are smaller, and outstanding commoners can always rise to positions of power and prestige reserved for high chiefs in the east.

Fijians work communal land individually, not as a group. Each Fijian is assigned a piece of native land. They grow most of their own food in village gardens, and only a few staples, such as tea, sugar, flour, etc., are imported from Suva and sold in local coop stores. A visit to one of these stores will demonstrate just how little they import and how self-sufficient they are. Fishing, village maintenance work, and ceremonial presentations are done together. While village life provides a form of collective security, individuals are discouraged from rising above the group. Fijians who attempt to set up a business are often stifled by the demands of relatives and friends. The Fijian custom of claiming favors from members of one's own group is known as *kerekere.* This pattern makes it difficult for Fijians to compete with Indo-Fijians, for whom life has always been a struggle. It's estimated that fewer than 100 of the 5,000 companies operating in Fiji are owned and operated by indigenous Fijians.

The Indo-Fijians

Most of the Indo-Fijians now in Fiji are descended from indentured laborers recruited in Bengal and Bihar a century ago. In the first year of the system (1879), some 450 Indians arrived in Fiji to work in the cane fields. By 1883, the total had risen to 2,300 and in 1916, when the last indentured laborers arrived, 63,000 Indians were present in the colony. In 1920, the indenture system was finally terminated, the cane fields were divided into four-hectare plots, and the Indian workers became tenant farmers on land owned by Fijians. Indians continued to arrive until 1931, though many of these later arrivals were Gujerati or Sikh businesspeople.

In 1940, the Indian population stood at 98,000, still below the Fijian total of 105,000, but by the 1946 census Indians had outstripped Fijians 120,000 to 117,000—making Fijians a minority in their own homeland. In the wake of the 1987 coups, the relative proportions changed as thousands of Indians emigrated to North America and Australia, and by early 1989 indigenous Fijians once again outnumbered Indo-Fijians. The 1996 census reported that Fiji's total population was 772,655, of which 50.8 percent were Fijian while 43.7 percent were Indian (at the 1986 census 46 percent were Fijian and 48.7 percent Indian). Between 1986 and 1996 the number of Indians in Fiji actually decreased by 12,125, with the heaviest falls in rural areas. Since 1987, more than 70,000 people have emigrated from Fiji, 90 percent of them Indians, and more than 5,000 a year continue to leave. Aside from emigration, the more widespread use of contraceptives by Indian women has led to a lower fertility rate. The crude birth rate per 1,000 population is 28.4 for Fijians and 21.0 for Indo-Fijians. It's estimated that by the year 2016 Indo-Fijians will comprise only 30–35 percent of the population while Fijians reach 60–65 percent, largely due to the lower Indo-Fijian birthrate and emigration.

Unlike the village-based Fijians, a majority of Indo-Fijians are concentrated in the cane-growing areas and live in isolated farmhouses, small settlements, or towns. Many Indo-Fijians also live in Suva, as do an increasing number of Fijians. Within the Indo-Fijian community there are divisions of Hindu (80 percent) versus Muslim (20 percent), north Indian versus south Indian, and Gujerati versus the rest. The Sikhs and Gujeratis have always been somewhat of an elite as they immigrated freely to Fiji outside the indenture system.

The different groups have kept alive their ancient religious beliefs and rituals. Hindus tend to marry within their caste, although the restrictions on behavior, which characterize the caste system in India, have disappeared. Indo-Fijian marriages are often arranged by the parents, while Fijians generally choose their own partners. Rural Indo-Fijians still associate most closely with other members of their extended patrilineal family group, and Hindu and Muslim religious beliefs continue to restrict Indo-Fijian women to a position subservient to men.

Fiji's laws prevent Indo-Fijians, or anyone else, from purchasing native communal land, driving other ethnic groups to find different means of economic survival. Today, Indo-Fijian business interests dominate the country's service and retail sectors, including the lucrative duty-free outlets around Nadi, small general stores, and road transportation throughout the country. As a group, they earn 70 percent of the income and pay 80 percent of the taxes in Fiji. The perceived economic disparity between indigenous Fijians and Indo-Fijians is a source—though by no means the only—of tension between the two groups. In reality, however, the per capita incomes of ordinary indigenous Fijians and Indo-Fijians are not that different. Indo-Fijian farmers have been especially hard hit by changes in the sugar industry and the expiration of land leases, and most would happily emigrate to North America, Australia, or New Zealand if they could only find a way.

Other Groups

The 3,000 Fiji-born Europeans, or *kai Vavalagi,* are descendants of Australians and New Zealanders who came to build cotton, sugar, or copra plantations in the 19th century. Many married Fijian women, and the 12,000 part-Fijians or *Kai*

loma of today are the result. There is almost no intermarriage between Fijians *(kai Viti)* and Indo-Fijians *(kai Idia)* (though Fijians intermarry freely with Chinese and Solomon Islanders). Many other Europeans are present in Fiji on temporary contracts or as tourists.

Most of the 5,000 Chinese in Fiji are descended from free settlers who came to set up small businesses a century ago, although since 1987 there has been an influx of Chinese from mainland China who were originally admitted to operate market gardens but who have since moved into the towns. Chinese garment workers continue to arrive. Fiji Chinese tend to intermarry freely with the other racial groups.

The 10,000 Rotumans, a majority of whom now live in Suva, are Polynesians. On neighboring islands off Vanua Levu are the Micronesians of Rabi (from Kiribati) and the Polynesians of Kioa (from Tuvalu). The descendants of Solomon Islanders blackbirded during the 19th century still live in communities near Suva, Levuka, and Labasa. The Tongans in Lau and other Pacific islanders who have immigrated to Fiji make this an ethnic crossroads of the Pacific.

Social Conditions

Some 98 percent of the country's population was born in Fiji. The partial breakdown in race relations since 1987 has been a tragedy for Fiji, though racial antagonism has been exaggerated. At the grassroots level, the different ethnic groups have always gotten along remarkably well, with little animosity. Unfortunately, race relations in Fiji have been manipulated by agitators with hidden agendas unrelated to race. Of equal importance to race are the variations between rich and poor, or urban (46 percent) and rural (54 percent). Avenues for future economic growth are limited, and unemployment is reflected in an increasing crime rate. Two-thirds of the rural population is without electricity.

Although Fiji's economy grew by 124 percent between 1970 and 2000, the number of people living in poverty increased by two-thirds over the same period. The imposition in 1992 of a 10 percent value-added tax combined with reductions in income tax and import duties shifted the burden of taxation from the haves to the have-nots. A third of the population now lives in poverty, and contrary to the myth of Indian economic domination, Indo-Fijians are more likely to be facing abject poverty than members of other groups. Eighty percent of cane farmers now live below the poverty line, and the number of Indo-Fijian beggars on Suva streets has increased in recent years. Single-parent urban families cut off from the extended-family social safety net are the specific group most affected, especially women trying to raise families on their own. As a Fijian woman on Taveuni told us, "Life is easy in Fiji, only money is a problem."

Literacy is high at 87 percent. Although education is not compulsory at any level, 98 percent of children age 6–14 attend school. Many schools are still racially segregated. Over 100 church-operated schools receive government subsidies. The Fiji Institute of Technology was founded at Suva in 1963, followed by the University of the South Pacific in 1968. The university serves the 12 Pacific countries that contribute to its costs. Medical services in Fiji are heavily subsidized. The divisional hospitals are at Labasa, Lautoka, and Suva, and there are also 19 sub-divisional or area hospitals, 74 health centers, 100 nursing stations, and 409 village clinics scattered around the country. The most common infectious diseases are influenza, gonorrhea, and syphilis.

Land Rights

When Fiji became a British colony in 1874, the land was divided between white settlers who had bought plantations and the *taukei ni gele*, the Fijian "owners of the soil." The government assumed title to the balance. Today the alienated (privately owned) plantation lands are known as "freehold" land—about 10 percent of the total. Another 7 percent is Crown land, 80 percent of it currently leased for periods of up to 99 years. The remaining 83 percent is inalienable Fijian communal land, which can be leased (about 30 percent is) but may never be sold. Compare this 83 percent (much of it not arable) with only 3 percent Maori land in New Zealand and almost zero native Hawaiian land. Land ownership has

provided the Fijians with a security that allows them to preserve their traditional culture, unlike indigenous peoples in most other countries.

Communal land is administered on behalf of some 6,600 clan groups *(mataqali)* by the Native Land Trust Board, an inept government agency established in 1940. The NLTB retains 25 percent of the lease money to cover administration, and a further 10 percent is paid directly to regional hereditary chiefs. In 1966, the British colonial administration established a system which allowed native land to be leased for 10 years, and in 1976 the Agricultural Landlord and Tenants Act (ALTA) increased the period to 30 years. In 1997, the 30-year leases began coming up for renewal, and of the 4,221 which had expired by 2001, only 1,164 were renewed. Thousands of Indo-Fijian farmers have been evicted and the uncertainty has led to properties being allowed to deteriorate.

Many Fijian clans say they want their land back so they can farm it themselves, and Fiji's remaining 20,000 Indo-Fijian sugarcane farmers are becoming highly apprehensive. If rents are greatly increased or the leases terminated, Fiji's sugar industry will be badly damaged and an explosive social situation created. In the event of a lease not being renewed, the Chaudhry government had been giving farmers the choice of being resettled or of receiving F$28,000 in compensation money for improvements they had made. After the Speight coup, this program was withdrawn. To date, most of the agricultural land taken back by Fijian clans has simply gone out of production.

At the First Constitutional Conference in 1965, Indian rights were promulgated, and the 1970 independence constitution asserted that everyone born in Fiji would be a citizen with equal rights. These rights are reaffirmed in the 1997 constitution. But land laws up to the present have very much favored "Fiji for the Fijians." Indo-Fijians have always accepted Fijian ownership of the land, provided they were granted satisfactory leases. Now that the leases are gradually coming to an end, many Indo-Fijians are driven from the only land they've ever known. The stifling of land development may keep Fiji quaint for tourists, but it also condemns a large portion of the population of both races to backwardness and poverty.

Religion

The main religious groups in Fiji are Hindus (290,000), Methodists (265,000), Catholics (70,000), Muslims (62,000), Assemblies of God (33,000), and Seventh-Day Adventists (20,000). Around 40 percent of the total population is Hindu or Muslim due to the large Indo-Fijian population, and only 2 percent of Indo-Fijians have converted to Christianity, despite Methodist missionary efforts dating back to 1884. About 78 percent of indigenous Fijians are Methodist, and 8.5 percent are Catholic.

Since the 1987 military coups, an avalanche of well-financed American fundamentalist missionary groups has descended on Fiji, and membership in the Assemblies of God and some other new Christian sects has grown at the expense of the Methodists.

LANGUAGE

Fijian, a member of the Austronesian family of languages spoken from Easter Island to Madagascar, has more speakers than any other indigenous Pacific language. Fijian vowels are pronounced as in Latin or Spanish, while the consonants are similar to those of English. Syllables end in a vowel, and the next-to-last syllable is usually the one emphasized. Where two vowels appear together they are sounded separately. In 1835, two Methodist missionaries, David Cargill and William Cross, devised the form of written Fijian used in Fiji today. Since all consonants in Fijian are separated by vowels, they spelled *mb* as *b*, *nd* as *d*, *ng* as *g*, *ngg* as *q*, and *th* as *c*.

Though Cargill and Cross worked at Lakeba in the Lau Group, the political importance of tiny Bau Island just off Viti Levu caused the Bauan dialect of Fijian to be selected as the "official" version of the language, and in 1850 a dictionary and grammar were published. When the Bible was translated into Bauan, that dialect's dominance was assured, and it is today's spoken and written Fijian. From 1920 to 1970, the use of Fijian was discouraged in favor of English, but since independence there has been a revival.

Hindustani or Hindi is the household tongue of most Indo-Fijians. Fiji Hindi has diverged from that spoken in India with the adoption of many words from English and other Indian languages such as Urdu. Though a quarter of Indo-Fijians are descended from immigrants from southern India where Tamil and Telegu are spoken, few use those languages today, even at home. Fiji Muslims speak Hindi out of practical considerations, though they might consider Urdu their mother tongue. In their spoken forms, Hindi and Urdu are very similar.

English is the second official language in Fiji and is understood by almost everyone. All schools teach exclusively in English after the fourth grade. Indo-Fijians and indigenous Fijians usually communicate with one another in English. Gilbertese is spoken by the Banabans of Rabi.

CUSTOMS

Fijians and Indo-Fijians are very tradition-oriented peoples who have retained a surprising number of their ancestral customs despite the flood of conflicting influences that have swept the Pacific over the past century. Rather than a melting pot where one group assimilated another, Fiji is a patchwork of varied traditions.

The obligations and responsibilities of Fijian village life include not only the construction and upkeep of certain buildings, but personal participation in the many ceremonies that give their lives meaning. Hindu Indians, on the other hand, practice firewalking and observe festivals such as Holi and Diwali, just as their forebears in India did for thousands of years.

Fijian Firewalking

In Fiji, both Fijians and Indo-Fijians practice firewalking, with the difference being that the Fijians walk on heated stones instead of hot embers. Legends tell how the ability to walk on fire was first given to a warrior named Tui-na-viqalita from Beqa Island, just off the south coast of Viti Levu, who had spared the life of a spirit god he caught while fishing for eels. The freed spirit gave to Tui-na-viqalita the gift of immunity to fire. Today his descendants act as *bete* (high priests) of the rite of *vilavilairevo* (jumping into the oven). Only members of his tribe, the Sawau, perform the ceremony. The Tui Sawau lives at Dakuibeqa village on Beqa, but firewalking is now only performed at the resort hotels on Viti Levu.

Fijian firewalkers (men only) are not permitted to have sex or to eat any coconut for two weeks prior to a performance. A man whose wife is pregnant is also barred. In a circular pit about four meters across, hundreds of large stones are first heated by a wood fire until they are white-hot. If you throw a handkerchief on the stones, it will burst into flames. Much ceremony and chanting accompanies certain phases of the ritual, such as the moment when the wood is removed to leave just the white-hot stones. The men psyche themselves up in a nearby hut, then emerge, enter the pit, and walk briskly around it once. Bundles of leaves and grass are then thrown on the stones and the men stand inside the steaming pit again to chant a final song. They seem to have complete immunity to pain, and there is no trace of injury. The men appear to fortify themselves with the heat, gaining some psychic power from the ritual.

Indian Firewalking

By an extraordinary coincidence, Indo-Fijians brought with them the ancient practice of religious firewalking. In southern India, firewalking occurs in the pre-monsoon season as a call to the goddess Kali (Durga) for rain. Indo-Fijian firewalking is an act of purification, or fulfillment of a vow to thank the god for help in a difficult situation.

In Fiji there is firewalking in most Hindu temples once a year, at full moon sometime between May and September according to the Hindu calendar. The actual event takes place on a Sunday at 1600 on the Suva side of Viti Levu, and at 0400 on the Nadi/Lautoka side. In August, firewalking takes place at the Mahadevi Sangam Temple on Howell Road, Suva. During the 10 festival days preceding the walk, participants remain in isolation, eat only unspiced vegetarian food, and spiritually prepare themselves. There are

prayers at the temple in the early morning and a group singing of religious stories evenings from Monday through Thursday. The yellow-clad devotees, their faces painted bright yellow and red, often pierce their cheeks or other body parts with spikes or three-pronged forks as part of the purification rites. Their faith is so strong they feel no pain.

The event is extremely colorful; drumming and chanting accompany the visual spectacle. Visitors are welcome to observe the firewalking, but since the exact date varies from temple to temple according to the phases of the moon (among other factors), you just have to keep asking to find out where and when it will take place. To enter the temple you must remove your shoes and any leather clothing.

The Yaqona Ceremony

Yaqona (yang-GO-na) is a tranquilizing, nonalcoholic drink that numbs the tongue and lips. Better known as kava, it's made from the *waka* (dried root) of the pepper plant *(Macropiper methysticum)*. This ceremonial preparation is the most honored feature of the formal life of Fijians, Tongans, and Samoans. It is performed with the utmost gravity according to a sacramental ritual to mark births, marriages, deaths, official visits, the installation of a new chief, etc.

New mats are first spread on the floor, on which a hand-carved *tanoa* (a wooden bowl nearly a meter wide) is placed. A long fiber cord decorated with cowry shells leads from the bowl to the guests of honor. At the end of the cord is a white cowry, which symbolizes a link to ancestral spirits. As many as 70 men take their places before the bowl. The officiates are adorned with tapa, fiber, and croton leaves, their torsos smeared with glistening coconut oil, their faces usually blackened.

The guests present a bundle of *waka* to the hosts, along with a short speech explaining their visit, a custom known as a *sevusevu*. The *sevusevu* is received by the hosts and acknowledged with a short speech of acceptance. The *waka* are then scraped clean and pounded in a *tabili* (mortar). Formerly they were chewed. Nowadays the pulp is put in a cloth sack and mixed with water in the *tanoa.* In the ceremony, the *yaqona* is kneaded and strained through *vau* (hibiscus) fibers.

Kava drinking is an important form of Fijian entertainment and a way of structuring friendships and community relations. Even in government offices a bowl of grog is kept for the staff to take as a refreshment at *yaqona* breaks. Some say the Fijians have *yaqona* rather than blood in their veins. Excessive kava drinking over a long period can make the skin scaly and rough, a condition known as *kanikani.*

Individual visitors to villages are invariably invited to participate in informal kava ceremonies. Clap once when the cupbearer offers you the *bilo,* then take it in both hands and say *"bula"* just before the cup meets your lips. Clap three times after you drink. Remember, you're a participant, not an onlooking tourist, so don't take photos if the ceremony is formal. Even though you may not like the appearance or taste of the drink, do try to finish at least the first cup. Tip the cup to show you are done.

In formal situations, it's considered extremely bad manners to turn your back on a chief during a kava ceremony, to walk in front of the circle of people when entering or leaving, or to step over the long cord attached to the *tanoa.* During a semi-formal ceremony, you should remain silent until the opening ritual is complete, signaled by a round of clapping.

Presentation of the Tabua

The *tabua* is a tooth of the sperm whale. It was once presented when chiefs exchanged delegates at confederacy meetings and before conferences on peace or war. In recent times, the *tabua* is presented during chiefly *yaqona* ceremonies as a symbolic welcome for a respected visitor or guest, or as a prelude to public business or modern-day official functions. On the village level, *tabuas* are still commonly presented to arrange marriages, to show sympathy at funerals, to request favors, to settle disputes, or simply to show respect.

Old *tabuas* are highly polished from continuous handling. The larger the tooth, the greater its ceremonial value. *Tabuas* are prized cultural property and may not be exported from Fiji. Endangered species laws prohibit their entry into the United States, Australia, and many other countries.

The Rising of the Balolo

This event takes place only in Samoa and Fiji. The *balolo (Eunice viridis)* is a thin, segmented worm of the Coelomate order, considered a culinary delicacy throughout these islands—the caviar of the Pacific. It's about 45 centimeters long and lives deep in the fissures of coral reefs. Twice a year it releases an unusual "tail" that contains its eggs or sperm. The worm itself returns to the coral to regenerate a new reproductive tail. The rising of the *balolo* is a natural almanac that keeps both lunar and solar times, and has a fixed day of appearance—even if a hurricane is raging—one night in the last quarter of the moon in October, and the corresponding night in November. It has never failed to appear on time for over 100 years now, and you can even check your calendar by it.

Because this rising occurs with such mathematical certainty, Fijians are waiting in their boats to scoop the millions of writhing, reddish brown (male) and moss green (female) spawn from the water when they rise to the surface before dawn. Within an hour after the rising, the eggs and sperm are released to spawn the next generation of *balolo.* The free-swimming larvae seek a suitable coral patch to begin the cycle again. This is one of the most bizarre curiosities in the natural history of the South Pacific, and the southeast coast of Ovalau is a good place to observe it.

CONDUCT

It's important to know that the dress code in Fiji is strict. Wearing short shorts, halter tops, and bathing costumes in public shows a lack of respect. In Fijian villages it's considered offensive to reveal too much skin. Wrap a *sulu* around you to cover up. Men should always wear a shirt in town, and women should wear dresses that adequately cover their legs while seated. Nothing will mark you so quickly as a tourist nor make you more popular with street vendors than scanty dress. Of course, it is permissible to wear skimpy clothing on the beach in front of a resort hotel.

Yet in a society where even bathing suits are considered extremely risqué for local women, public nudity is unthinkable, and topless sunbathing by women is also banned in Fiji (except at isolated island resorts).

Dangers and Annoyances

In Suva, beware of the seemingly friendly Fijian men (usually with a small package or canvas bag in their hands) who will greet you on the street with a hearty *Bula!* These are "sword sellers" who will ask your name, quickly carve it on a mask, and then demand F$20 for a set that you could buy at a Nadi curio shop for F$5. Other times they'll try to engage you in conversation and may offer a "gift." Just say "thank you very much" and walk away from them quickly without accepting anything, as they can suddenly become unpleasant and aggressive. Their grotesque swords and masks have nothing to do with Fiji.

Similarly, overly sociable people at bars may expect you to buy them drinks and snacks. This may not be a problem in the beginning, but know when to disengage. In the main tourist centers such as Nadi and Suva, take care if a local invites you to visit his home, because you may be seen mainly as a source of beer and other goods. Also, don't be fooled by anyone on the street who claims to work at your resort and offers to show you around. They only want to sell you something.

Although *The Fiji Times* is often full of stories of violent crimes including assaults, robberies, and burglaries, it's partly the novelty of these events that makes them worth reporting. Fiji is still a much safer country than the United States, and tourists are not specifically targeted for attack, but normal precautions should still be taken. Keep to well-lit streets at night, take a taxi if you've had more than one drink, and steer clear of poorly dressed Fijian men who may accost you on the street for no reason. Don't react if offered drugs. It's wise to lock your valuables in your bag in your hotel room before going out on the town.

Women should have few real problems traveling around Fiji on their own, so long as they're prepared to cope with frequent offers of marriage. Although a female tourist has less chance of facing violence than a local woman does, it's smart to be defensive and to lie about where you're staying. If you want to be left alone, conservative dress and purposeful behavior will work to your advantage. In village situations, seek the company of local women.

Littering is punished by a minimum F$40 fine and breaking bottles in public can earn six months in jail (unfortunately seldom enforced).

Exploring the Islands

HIGHLIGHTS

Fiji is brimming with colorful attractions, splendid scenery, friendly people, and exciting things to do. From the gateway city **Nadi,** with its numerous shopping and dining possibilities, it's only a quick commuter hop to the enticing **Mamanuca Group,** with about half of Fiji's island resorts. The clear waters, golden sands, dazzling reefs, and good facilities have made this a popular vacation destination for Australians and New Zealanders, but islands like Malololailai, Malolo, and Mana also attract scuba divers and yachting enthusiasts. The long, narrow **Yasawa Group,** off the sugar city Lautoka, is wilder, mightier, and less developed than the Mamanucas: The beaches are longer, the jungle-clad mountains higher, and the accommodations rougher. It's Fiji's most magnificent island chain.

Fiji's mainland, **Viti Levu,** is the "real" Fiji, where much of the country's history has unfolded and the bulk of the Fijian people live out their lives. The 486-km highway around the island passes a series of appealing towns and cities with bustling markets, bus stations, shops, cafés, clubs, monuments, and facilities of every kind. The **Coral Coast** in the south is the country's second resort area, with a series of large hotels nicely spaced between Nadi and Pacific Harbor. Visitors looking for more than only beach life often pick these resorts for the numerous tours and sporting activities available. **Pacific Harbor** itself offers access to some of the best diving, fishing, kayaking, white-water rafting, and golfing in the South Pacific, and **Nananu-i-Ra Island** off Viti Levu's north coast is a favorite of divers, windsurfers, and backpackers.

Fiji's contemporary capital, **Suva,** has the country's finest cinemas, monuments, museums, nightclubs, restaurants, stores, and all of the excitement of the South Pacific's biggest town. Ships, buses, and planes depart Suva for every corner of the republic. The campus of the region's main university, the headquarters of international organizations, government ministries, embassies, libraries, and the large trading companies are all here. It's a fascinating place to explore.

Several adjacent islands allow one to escape from Suva. **Kadavu** to the south is a characteristic Fijian island of small villages strewn between beaches and hills, but its also a mecca for scuba divers who come for the Great Astrolabe Reef, and for surfers who have discovered Kadavu's waves. Several well established backpacker camps and upscale resorts make visiting Kadavu easy. Back toward Viti Levu are **Beqa,** with several upscale scuba resorts, and **Yanuca,** with inexpensive beach camps full of enthusiastic surfers.

Anyone with even the slightest interest in Fiji's vivid history won't want to miss **Ovalau Island** and the timeworn old capital **Levuka.** The town's long row of wooden storefronts looks like the set of a Wild West film, and there are abundant monuments, museums, and historic buildings to discover, all of it set below towering volcanic peaks. Despite these attractions, Levuka remains remarkably unvisited by most tourists, largely thanks to the absence of a good beach. It's the best-preserved relic of the old South Seas anywhere between San Francisco and Sydney.

Across the Koro Sea from Ovalau is Fiji's second island, **Vanua Levu,** heart of the "friendly north." Because a slight effort is required to get there, far fewer tourists ply these exotic shores. Yet **Savusavu** is Fiji's most picturesque town after Levuka, set along a splendid wide bay with an attractive waterfront promenade. Long a center of the Fiji copra trade, planters from the surrounding farms still congregate at the town's colonial-style club on Sundays. Two spectacular highways sweep away from Savusavu: One travels through the mountains to the mill town of Labasa, and another snakes east along the verdant coast to Buca Bay.

Repeat visitors and local Fijians often assert that **Taveuni** is Fiji's finest island, a claim which is difficult to deny. The island's high spine is draped in impenetrable rainforest, with huge coconut plantations tumbling to the coast. Magnificent waterfalls pour down the steep slopes, and the scuba diving is world famous. Yet Fiji doesn't end here: There are many little-known isles in the Lau and Lomaiviti groups, including some like **Vanua Balavu,** with satisfactory facilities for visitors.

Budget travelers often appreciate Tavewa, Nacula, and adjacent islands of the Yasawas, which rank high for their spellbinding environment, stimulating activities, and agreeable company. Waya and Wayasewa are similar. City slickers won't bore easily in Suva, and it's *the* place to be if you like studying. The city's excellent libraries and museums are meant to be savored slowly. Kadavu and Ono both have backpacker camps offering unlimited swimming, snorkeling, scuba, and exploring. Leleuvia just south of Ovalau is also great for a relaxing holiday with abundant diving. Two weeks is the absolute minimum required to get a feel for Fiji, and after a month you'll be in a position to begin planning your next visit.

Suggested Itineraries

Most visitors arrive in Nadi, with a large percentage immediately transferring to resorts in the Mamanucas and Yasawas or along the Coral Coast. Overland travelers intent on seeing Fiji on their own should start moving the morning after they arrive. Save your sightseeing around Nadi until the end of your trip.

Those with **one week** in Fiji can easily circumnavigate Viti Levu by public bus, and since there are far fewer places to stop along Kings Road, it's best to cover the north side of the island first. Starting from Nadi or Lautoka, you can easily make it through to Suva in a day. After a night or two there, fly to Levuka for two nights.

Return to Suva on the early morning Patterson Brothers bus (daily except Sunday), then catch a connecting bus to somewhere on the Coral Coast. The next day you can head back to Nadi with time for a stop at the Sigatoka Sand Dunes. However, if beaches and natural beauty mean more to you than history and culture, consider spending your entire week in the Yasawa Islands.

Visitors with **two weeks** at their disposal can also visit "the friendly north." The most practical way to get started is to fly directly from Nadi to Taveuni, then work your way back overland. Depending on your schedule, there are ferries from Taveuni straight to Savusavu and Suva, or you can fly to Savusavu and catch a ferry from there. Then follow the Levuka-Coral Coast route described above. Otherwise spend your first week in the Yasawas and the second circling Viti Levu.

Visitors with **three weeks** can see a lot of Fiji. Begin with a one-week trip to the glorious Yasawa Islands, then either fly directly to Taveuni or begin working your way around Viti Levu. You could stop at Nananu-i-Ra Island off northern Viti Levu for two nights, from where there are ferries to Vanua Levu. Or continue to Suva and catch a ferry to Savusavu or Taveuni from there. Otherwise, make a side trip to Levuka from Suva and return to Nadi via the Coral Coast. If you still have ample time after Levuka, fly from Suva to Kadavu, where you'll want to spend three or four nights. From Kadavu you can fly directly to Nadi or return to Suva and be bused along the Coral Coast. Toward the end of your trip, a few nights on one of the Mamanuca Islands is an appropriate choice. For ecotourists, Koroyanitu National Heritage Park is nearby.

Parks and Reserves

The **National Trust of Fiji** (tel. 330-1807, fax 330-5092) administers several nature reserves and historic sites. Of these, the Sigatoka Sand Dunes National Park between Nadi and Sigatoka has a visitor center easily accessible by public bus. The Momi Bay Gun Site south of Nadi and the Waisali Nature Reserve near Savusavu are also accessible, but advance clearance is required to visit the iguana sanctuary on Yaduatabu Island off Vanua Levu.

Koroyanitu National Heritage Park, inland from Lautoka, is easily reached and has accommodations for hikers. Although not an official reserve, the forested area around Nadarivatu in central Viti Levu is similar. Bouma National Heritage Park around Bouma and Lavena on the northeastern side of Taveuni features unspoiled rainforests and waterfalls reachable along hiking trails. Colo-i-Suva Forest Park behind Suva also beckons the nature lover with quiet walks through a mahogany forest.

Fiji's only official marine conservation areas are a stretch of fringing reef off Ono Island near Kadavu, and the Waitabu Marine Park, part of the Bouma National Heritage Park project off northeastern Taveuni. Some resorts such as Beachcomber, Navini, and Namenalala islands have banned fishing on their fringing reefs. These places are ideal for beach-based snorkeling, but many other easily accessible areas have been fished out by locals with spearguns, and most scuba diving is done from boats.

SPORTS AND RECREATION
Scuba Diving

Fiji has been called "the soft coral capital of the world" and seasoned divers know well that Fiji has some of the finest diving in the South Pacific, with top facilities at the best prices. You won't go wrong choosing Fiji. The worst underwater visibility conditions here are the equivalent of the finest off Florida. In the Gulf of Mexico you've about reached the limit if you can see for 15 meters; in Fiji the visibility begins at 15 meters and increases to 45 meters in some places. Many fantastic dives are just 10 or 15 minutes away from the resorts by boat (whereas at Australia's Great Barrier Reef, the speedboats often have to travel over 60 km to get to the dive sites). Here are some of Fiji's most popular diving locations:

- Great Astrolabe Reef, Kadavu (caves, marinelife)
- Namena Barrier Reef, south of Savusavu (giant clams)
- Rainbow Reef, west of Taveuni (crevices, soft coral)

- Sidestreets, Beqa Lagoon (soft corals, sea fans)
- Supermarket, west of Mana Island (shark feeding)
- Wakaya Passage, east of Levuka (rays, hammerheads)

Diving is possible year-round, with the marinelife most bountiful July–November. The best diving conditions are March–December, the calmest seas in April and May. Visibility is tops June–October, then slightly worse November–February due to rainfall and plankton growth. Water temperatures vary from 24°C in June, July, and August to 30°C in December, January, and February. Wetsuits are recommended during the winter months.

Facilities for scuba diving exist at most of the resorts in the Mamanuca Group, along Viti Levu's Coral Coast and at Pacific Harbor, on Kadavu, Leleuvia, Beqa, Nananu-i-Ra, Naviti, Tavewa, and Wayasewa, at Levuka, Nadi, and Savusavu, and on Taveuni and adjacent islands. Low-budget divers should turn to the Kadavu, Leleuvia, Nadi, Tavewa, and Wayasewa sections in this book and read. Specialized nonhotel dive shops are found at Levuka, Nadi, Pacific Harbor, Savusavu, and on Taveuni. When choosing a place to stay, pick somewhere as close as possible to the sites you wish to dive, because scuba operators generally resist spending a lot of money on fuel to commute to distant reefs.

Serious divers will bring along their own mask, buoyancy compensator, and regulator. If you've never dived before, Fiji is an excellent place to learn, and the Kadavu, Leleuvia, Levuka, Musket Cove, Nadi, Nananu-i-Ra, Pacific Harbor, Taveuni, Tavewa, and Wayasewa scuba operators offer open-water certification courses lasting four or five days. The best course prices are usually offered by the Nadi-area dive shops, which can afford to charge less due to their high volume of customers. Leleuvia is also good. Learning to dive on Taveuni is more than a hundred dollars more expensive. If you have children, Subsurface Fiji at Musket Cove Resort and on Beachcomber Island specializes in teaching diving to kids as young as 12! Many of the scuba operators listed in this book also offer introductory "resort courses" for those who want only a taste of

scuba diving. For information about live-aboard dive boats see Scuba Cruises, which follows.

Snorkeling

Even if you aren't willing to put the necessary money and effort into scuba diving, you will want to investigate the many snorkeling possibilities. Some dive shops take snorkelers out in their boats for a nominal fee, but there are countless places around Fiji where you can snorkel straight out to the reef for free, mostly on smaller outer islands. The beach snorkeling off Viti Levu and Vanua Levu is usually poor, and it's a complete waste of time around Nadi, Lautoka, Pacific Harbor, Suva, and Labasa. The snorkeling along the Coral Coast is fair, but only at high tide and even then you must take care with currents in the channels. Around Savusavu sharp rocks make it hard to get into the water at all (and the top beaches are private). On the other hand, you'll have no trouble finding glorious reefs in the Mamanuca Group, the Yasawas, off Nananu-i-Ra, Kadavu, Ono, and Taveuni, and at the small resort islands near Ovalau.

Surfing

A growing number of surfing camps are off southern and western Viti Levu. The most famous is Tavarua Island in the Mamanuca Group, accessible only to American surfers on prepackaged tours from the States. Other mortals can also use speedboats from Seashell Cove and Rendezvous resorts to surf nearby reef breaks at far less expense, or try to get a booking at the top-end surf resort on Namotu Island right next to Tavarua. Beach break surfing (as opposed to more challenging reef break surfing) is possible at Club Masa near Sigatoka, and budget surfing camps have been built on Yanuca and Kadavu islands. In 2000, a surfing resort opened at Nagigia Island just off west Kadavu, and the Batiluva Beach Resort on Yanuca is very accessible. Surfing is the main activity at the Waidroka Bay Resort on the Coral Coast. Few of Fiji's waves are for the beginner, especially the reef breaks, and of course, you must bring your own board(s). One of the few companies actively renting surfboards is Viti Surf Legend in Nadi. There's surf throughout the year, with the best swells out of the south March–October.

Fijian clans control the traditional fishing rights *(qoli qoli)* on their reefs, and on many islands they also claim to own the surfing rights. This can also apply at breaks off uninhabited islands and even ocean reefs. In the past, upscale surfing camps like Tavarua, Marlin Bay, and Namotu have paid big bucks to try to corner the right to surf famous waves like Cloudbreak and Frigate, and they often attempt to keep surfers from rival resorts away. Although none of this is enshrined in law, it's wise to keep abreast of the situation. When surfing in a remote area without facilities it's essential to present a *sevusevu* to the local chief and to be on your best behavior.

Windsurfing

Windsurfing is possible at a much wider range of locales than surfing, and many upmarket beach hotels off southern and western Viti Levu include equipment in their rates. Windsurfing is possible at most of the Mamanuca resorts, including Castaway, Musket Cove, Malolo Island, Plantation Island, Tokoriki, and Treasure Island. Other offshore resorts around Fiji offering windsurfing are Matana Resort, Naigani Island, Qamea Beach, Toberua Island, Turtle Island, and Vatulele. Windsurfing tours to Nananu-i-Ra are well promoted. Almost all of the surfing camps also offer windsurfing.

Boating

Exciting **white-water rafting** on the cliff-hugging rapids of the Upper Navua River is offered by Rivers Fiji at Pacific Harbor. More white-water rafting is available on the Ba River below Navala. In central Viti Levu, villagers will pole you through the Waiqa Gorge on a bamboo raft from Naitauvoli to Naivucini villages or down the Navua or Wainibuka rivers.

In the past, organized **ocean kayaking** expeditions have been offered among the Yasawa Islands, around Beqa and Kadavu, in Vanua Levu's Natewa Bay, and off Taveuni and Vanua Balavu (see Getting There, below, for details of sea kayaking tours). Those who only want to dabble can hire kayaks at Kadavu, Taveuni, Savusavu, and a number of other places. Several upmarket Mamanuca Resorts loan kayaks to their guests.

Get in some **sailing** by taking one of the day cruises by yacht offered from Nadi. Yacht charters are available at Musket Cove Resort in the Mamanuca Group.

Hiking

All of the high islands offer hiking possibilities, and many remote villages are linked by well-used trails. The most important hike described in this book is the two-day Sigatoka River Trek down the Sigatoka River from Nadarivatu. Fiji's highest mountain Tomaniivi can be climbed in the same area. Levuka makes an excellent base, with the trail to The Peak beginning right behind the town, and a challenging cross-island trail to Lovoni nearby. Easy day hikes are found in Colo-i-Suva Forest Park near Suva, and the waterfall and coastal hikes in Bouma National Heritage Park on Taveuni. More arduous is the all-day climb to Lake Tagimaucia on Taveuni. Koroyanitu National Heritage Park near Lautoka offers many hiking possibilities, including the famous Mount Batilamu Trek. The cane railway lines of western Viti Levu provide excellent hiking routes, such as from Sigatoka to the Tavuni Hill Fort and from Shangri-La's Fijian Resort to Natadola Beach. For some outer island hiking, you can walk right around Nananu-i-Ra in under a day, or across Waya or Wayasewa. Kadavu provides more of the same.

Bicycling

If you brought along a bicycle, you'll have several possibilities. Queens Road around the southern side of Viti Levu is favored by kamikaze drivers, so you're better off following the northerly Kings Road from Nadi Airport. At Ellington Wharf near Rakiraki you can board the Vanua Levu ferry. The Hibiscus Highway east from Savusavu to Buca Bay is undulating and picturesque. At Natuvu you can connect with the boat to Taveuni, one of Fiji's finest islands for cycling. From Taveuni, catch a ship to Suva and return to Nadi via Kings Road. A side trip to Ovalau on the Natovi ferry is highly recommended, if you have the time.

Golf

Golfers are well catered to in Fiji. The two most famous courses are the fantastic Denarau Golf Club, next to the Sheraton hotels at Nadi, and the renowned Pacific Harbor Country Club, one of the finest courses in the Pacific. Many tourist hotels have golf courses, including the Mocambo at Nadi; Shangri-La's Fijian Resort and Naviti Beach Resort on the south side of Viti Levu; Naigani Island Resort and The Wakaya Club in Lomaiviti; and Taveuni Estates on Taveuni. More locally oriented are the city golf courses at Nadi Airport, Lautoka, and in Suva, and the company-run courses near Rakiraki and Labasa sugar mills and at the Vatukoula gold mine, all built to serve former expatriate staffs. All are open to the public, and only the Sheraton course could be considered expensive.

Team Sports

The soccer season in Fiji is February–November (www.fijifootball.com), while rugby is played almost year-round. The main rugby season is June–November, when there are 15 players on each side. November–March rugby is played as "sevens," with seven team members to a side. (The Fijians are champion sevens players, "wild, intuitive, and artistic," and in 1997 they defeated South Africa to take the Rugby World Cup Sevens in Hong Kong.) Rugby is played only by Fijians, while soccer teams are both Fijian and Indo-Fijian. Cricket is played November–March, mostly in rural areas. Lawn bowling is also popular. Saturday is the big day for team sports (only soccer and lawn bowling are practiced on Sunday).

ENTERTAINMENT

It's cheap to go to the movies in towns such as Ba, Labasa, Lautoka, Nadi, Nausori, and Suva, if a repertoire of romance, horror, and adventure is to your liking (only in Suva can you see the latest Hollywood films). Most Indian films are in Hindi, sometimes with English subtitles. These same towns have local nightclubs where you can enjoy as much drinking and dancing as you like without spending an arm and a leg. When there's live music, a cover charge is collected.

A South Pacific institution widespread in Fiji is the old colonial clubs that offer inexpensive beer in safe, friendly surroundings. Such clubs are found in Labasa, Lautoka, Levuka, Nadi, Savusavu, Sigatoka, Suva, and Tavua, and although they're all private clubs with Members Only signs on the door, foreign visitors are allowed entry (except at the pretentious Union Club in Suva). Many of these are male domains, although women are not refused entry. The yacht clubs in Savusavu and Suva also have good bars. Many bars and clubs in Fiji refuse entry to persons dressed in flip-flops, boots, rugby jerseys, shorts, tank tops, or T-shirts, and one must remove one's hat at the door.

Fiji's unique spectacle is the **Fijian firewalking** performed several times a week at the large hotels along the southwest side of Viti Levu: Sheraton-Fiji (Wednesday), Shangri-La's Fijian Resort (Friday), Outrigger Reef Resort (Friday), Hideaway Resort (Thursday), The Naviti (Wednesday), the Warwick (Monday and Friday), and the Pacific Harbor Cultural Center (Thursday). A fixed admission price is charged, but it's well worth going at least once. For more information on firewalking, see Customs earlier in this chapter's Introduction. The same hotels that present firewalking usually stage a Fijian *meke* (described below) on an alternate night.

Fijian Dancing (Meke)

The term *meke* describes the combination of dance, song, and theater performed at feasts and on special occasions. Brandishing spears, their faces painted with charcoal, the men wear frangipani leis and skirts of shredded leaves. The war club dance reenacts heroic events of the past. Both men and women perform the *vakamalolo*, a sitting dance, while the *seasea* is danced by women flourishing fans. The *tralala,* in which visitors may be asked to join, is a simple two-step shuffle danced side-by-side (early missionaries forbade the Fijians from dancing face-to-face). As elsewhere in the Pacific, the dances tell a story, though the music now is strongly influenced by Christian hymns and contemporary pop. Less sensual than Polynesian dancing, the rousing Fijian dancing evokes the country's violent past. Fijian *meke* are often part of a *magiti,* or feast, performed at hotels.

PUBLIC HOLIDAYS AND FESTIVALS

Public holidays in Fiji include New Year's Day (January 1), National Youth Day (variable), Good Friday and Easter Monday (March/April), Ratu Sukuna Day (a Monday around May 29), Queen Elizabeth's Birthday (a Monday around June 14), Prophet Mohammed's Birthday (variable), Fiji Day (a Monday or Friday around October 10), Diwali (October or November), and Christmas Days (December 25 and 26).

Check with the Fiji Visitors Bureau to see if any festivals are scheduled during your visit. The best known are the Bula Festival in Nadi (July), the Hibiscus Festival in Suva (August), the Sugar Festival in Lautoka (September), and the Back to Levuka Festival (early October). Around the end of June there's the President's Cup Yacht Series at Nadi. Before Diwali, the Hindu festival of lights, Hindus clean their homes, then light lamps or candles to mark the arrival of spring. Fruit and sweets are offered to Lakshmi, goddess of wealth. Holi is an Indian spring festival in February or March. The Third Melanesian Arts Festival will be held in Fiji in 2006.

The International Triathlon at Nadi is in May. One of the main sporting events of the year is the **International Bula Marathon** held in June. The main event involves a 42-km run from Lautoka to the Sheraton at Nadi.

When to Go

Compared to parts of North America and Europe, the seasonal climatic variations in Fiji are not extreme. There's a hotter, more humid season from November–April, and a cooler, drier time from May–October. Hurricanes can occur during the "rainy" season, but they only last a few days a year. The sun sets around 1800 year-round, and there aren't periods when the days are shorter or longer.

Seasonal differences in airfares are often more influential in deciding when to go. On Air New Zealand flights from North America, the low

season is mid-April to August, the prime time in Fiji. Christmas is busy, but in February and March many hotels stand half empty and special discount rates are on offer. In short, there isn't really any one season that is the "best" time to go, and every season has its advantages.

ARTS AND CRAFTS

The traditional art of Fiji is closely related to that of Tonga. Fijian canoes, too, were patterned after the more advanced Polynesian type, although the Fijians were timid sailors. War clubs, food bowls, *tanoas* (kava bowls), eating utensils, clay pots, and *tapa* cloth *(masi)* are considered Fiji's finest artifacts.

There are two kinds of woodcarvings: the ones made from *vesi (Intsia bijuga)*—ironwood in English—or *nawanawa (Cordia subcordata)* wood are superior to those of the lighter, highly breakable *vau (Hibiscus tiliaceus).* In times past it often took years to make a Fijian war club, because the carving was done in the living tree and left to grow into the desired shape. The finest *tanoas* are carved in the Lau Group.

Although many crafts are alive and well, some Fijians have taken to carving "tikis" or mock New Guinea masks smeared with black shoe polish to look like ebony for sale to tourists. Also avoid crafts made from endangered species such as sea turtles (tortoise shell) and marine mammals (whales' teeth, etc.). Prohibited entry into most countries, these will be confiscated by customs if found.

Tapa Cloth

This is Fiji's most characteristic traditional product. Tapa is light, portable, and inexpensive, and makes an excellent souvenir to brighten up a room back home. It's made by the women on Vatulele Island off Viti Levu and on certain islands of the Lau Group.

To produce tapa, the inner, water-soaked bark of the paper mulberry *(Broussonetia papyrifera)* is stripped from the tree and steeped in water. Then it's scraped with shells and pounded into a thin sheet with wooden mallets. Four of these sheets are applied one over another and pounded together, then left to dry in the sun.

While Tongan tapa is decorated by holding a relief pattern under the tapa and overpainting the lines, Fijian tapa *(masi kesa)* is distinctive for its rhythmic geometric designs applied with stencils made from green pandanus and banana leaves. The only colors used are red, from red clay, and a black pigment obtained by burning candlenuts. Both powders are mixed with boiled gums made from scraped roots. Sunlight deepens and sets the colors. Each island group had its characteristic colors and patterns, ranging from plantlike paintings to geometric designs. Sheets of tapa feel like felt when finished. On some islands tapa is still used for clothing, bedding, and room dividers, and as ceremonial red carpets. Tablecloths, bedcovers, place mats, and wall hangings of tapa make handsome souvenirs.

SHOPPING

Most large shops in Fiji close at 1300 on Saturday, but smaller grocery stores are often open on Sunday. After the 1987 military coups, most commercial business was suspended on Sunday, but these restrictions were dropped in 1996 and you'll find many restaurants and bars now open on Sunday. Indo-Fijians dominate the retail trade. If you're buying from an Indo-Fijian merchant, always bargain hard and consider all sales final. Indigenous Fijians usually begin by asking a much lower starting price, in which case bargaining isn't so important.

Fiji's "duty-free" shops such as Prouds or Tappoo are not really duty-free, as all goods are subject to various fiscal duties plus the 12.5 percent value-added tax. Bargaining is the order of the day, but to be frank, Americans can usually buy most of the Japanese electronics sold "duty-free" in Fiji cheaper in the States, where more recent models are available. If you do buy something, get an itemized receipt and international guarantee, and watch that they don't switch packages and unload a demo on you. Once purchased, items cannot be returned, so don't let yourself be talked into anything. Camera film is inexpensive, however, and the selection is good—stock up.

If you'd like to do some shopping in Fiji, locally made handicrafts such as tapa cloth, mats, kava bowls, war clubs, woodcarvings, etc., are a much better investment (see Arts and Crafts, above). The four-pronged cannibal forks available in most souvenirs stores make unique souvenirs, but avoid the masks, which are made only for sale to tourists and have nothing to do with Fiji. If you're spending serious money for top-quality work, visit the Fiji Museum or the Government Handicraft Center in Suva beforehand to see what is authentic.

To learn what's available on the tourist market and to become familiar with prices, browse one of the half-dozen outlets of **Jack's Handicrafts** around Viti Levu. You'll find them in downtown Nadi, Sigatoka, and Suva. If the sales person is overenthusiastic and begins following you around too closely, just stop and say you're only looking today and they'll probably leave you alone.

You can often purchase your souvenirs directly from the Fijian producers at markets, etc. Just beware of aggressive indigenous Fijian "sword sellers" on the streets of Suva, Nadi, and Lautoka who peddle fake handicrafts at high prices, or high-pressure duty-free touts who may try to pull you into their shops, or self-appointed guides who offer to help you find the "best price." If you get the feeling you're being hustled, walk away.

ACCOMMODATIONS

A 12.5 percent government tax is added to all accommodations prices. Most hotels include the tax in their quoted rates, but some don't. If this might have a bearing on your choice, ask beforehand.

Fiji offers a wide variety of places to stay, from low-budget to world-class. Standard international hotels are found in Nadi and Suva, while many of the upmarket beach resorts are on small islands in the Mamanuca Group off Nadi or along the Coral Coast on Viti Levu's sunny south side. The Mamanuca resorts are secluded, with fan-cooled *bure* accommodations, while at the Coral Coast hotels you often get an air-conditioned room in a main building. The Coral Coast has more to offer in the way of land tours, shopping, and entertainment/eating options, while

low budget *bure* at Coral View Resort, Tavewa Island, Yasawas Group

the offshore resorts are preferable if you want a rest or are into water sports. The Coral Coast beaches are only good at high tide and the reefs are degraded, while on the outer islands the reefs are usually pristine. Some resorts cater almost exclusively to scuba divers or surfers and these may not be the best places to stay if you aren't interested in those activities.

In recent years smaller luxury resorts have multiplied in remote locations, from former plantations near Savusavu and on Taveuni to isolated beach resorts on outlying islands such as Beqa, Kadavu, Matangi, Naigani, Namenalala, Nukubati, Qamea, Toberua, Turtle, Vatulele, Wakaya, and Yasawa. Prices at the "boutique" resorts begin at several hundred dollars a day and rise to four figures, so some care should be taken in selecting the right one. A few such as Beqa, Kadavu, and Taveuni are marketed almost exclusively to scuba divers, and Namenalala is a good ecotourism choice. If you delight in glamorous socializing with other upscale couples, Turtle and Vatulele are for you. Families are most welcome at Beachcomber, Castaway, Cousteau, Koro Sun, Malolo, Maravu, Matangi, Naigani, Naviti, Outrigger Reef, Plantation, Shangri-La's Fijian, Sonaisali,

Toberua, Treasure, and Warwick, but children are generally not accepted at all at Katafaga, Lomalagi, Matamanoa, Matana, Namale, Namotu, Natadola, Nukubati, Qamea, Taveuni, Tokoriki, Turtle, Vatulele, Wadigi, Wakaya, and Yasawa. The very wealthy will feel at home on Katafaga, Turtle, and Wakaya, whereas Mamanuca resorts like Castaway, Mana, and Plantation are designed for larger numbers of guests interested in intensive sporting and social activities.

The low-budget accommodations are spread out, with concentrations in Korotogo, Nadi, Lautoka, Levuka, Suva, and Savusavu, and on Taveuni. Low-cost outer island beach resorts exist on Caqalai, Kadavu, Kuata, Leleuvia, Mana, Nacula, Nananu-i-Ra, Nanuya Lailai, Naviti, Ono, Tavewa, Waya, Wayasewa, and Yanuca. The largest budget chain in Fiji is Cathay Hotels, with properties in Suva, Lautoka, and on the Coral Coast (visit their Fiji For Less website at www.fiji4less.com). Since September 2000, several dozen new backpacker resorts have appeared in the Yasawa Islands under the auspices of the Nacula Tikina Tourism Association (www.fiji budget.com), with the support of millionaire environmentalist Richard Evanson. Most of these

FIJI ISLANDS

cater to a younger crowd who decide where they'll stay as they go, and the easiest way to book rooms is to call them up after you get to Fiji or to work through an agent in Nadi.

A few of the cheap hotels in Suva, Nadi, and Lautoka double as whorehouses, making them cheap in both senses of the word. At all of the low-budget hostels, women should exercise care in the way they deal with the male staff; we've received complaints about harassment. Many hotels, both in cities and at the beach, offer dormitory beds as well as individual rooms. Most of the dorms are mixed. Women can sometimes request a women-only dorm when things are slow, but it's usually not guaranteed. Some budget-priced city hotels lock their front doors at 2300 (or at 2200 in Labasa), so ask first if you're planning a night on the town. Several islands with air service from Suva, including Moala, Gau, and Cicia, have no regular accommodations for visitors at all, so it's best to know someone who lives there before heading to those islands.

Camping

Camping facilities (bring your own tent) are found at backpacker resorts on Caqalai, Kadavu, Kuata, Leleuvia, Mana, Nacula, Nanua Lailai, Naviti, Ono, Ovalau, Taveuni, Tavewa, Waya, Wayasewa, and Yanuca Lailai Islands. A few shoestring hostels in Nadi and Suva also allow it, as do Viti Levu beach resorts like Seashell Cove, The Beachouse, and the Coral Coast Christian Camp. On Vanua Levu, you can camp at Mumu Resort.

Elsewhere, get permission before pitching your tent, since all land is owned by someone and land rights are sensitive issues in Fiji. Some freelance campers on beaches such as Natadola near Nadi and around Pacific Harbor have had their possessions stolen, so take care.

In Fijian villages don't ask a Fijian friend for permission to camp beside his house. Although he may feel obligated to grant the request of a guest, you'll be proclaiming to everyone that his home isn't completely to your liking. If all you really want is to camp, make that clear from the start and get approval to do so on a beach or by a river, but *not* in the village. A *sevusevu* should al-

ways be presented in this case. There's really nowhere to camp totally for free.

Staying in Villages

The most direct way to meet the Fijian people and learn a little about their culture is to stay in a village for a couple of nights. A number of hiking tours offer overnight stays in remote villages, and it's also possible to arrange it for yourself. **Fiji bure.com** (www.fijibure.com) organizes stays at Namatukula, Namuamua, and Navutulevu villages in southern Viti Levu at F$50 pp a night. In places well off the beaten track where there are no regular tourist accommodations, you could just show up in a village and ask permission of the *turaga-ni-koro* (village herald) to spend the night. Both Indo-Fijians and native Fijians will probably spontaneously invite you in to their homes. The Fijians' innate dignity and kindness should not be taken for granted, however.

All across the Pacific it's customary to reciprocate when someone gives you a gift—if not now, then sometime in the future. In Fiji this type of back and forth is called *kerekere*. Visitors who accept gifts (such as meals and accommodations) from islanders and do not reciprocate are undermining traditional culture and causing resentment, often without realizing it.

It's sometimes hard to know how to repay hospitality, but Fijian culture has a solution: the *sevusevu*. This can be money, but it's usually a 500-gram "pyramid" of kava roots *(waka)*, which can be easily purchased at any Fijian market for about F$15. *Sevusevu* are more often performed between families or couples about to be married, or at births or christenings, but the custom is a perfectly acceptable way for visitors to show their appreciation.

We suggest travelers donate at least F$20 pp per night to village hosts (carry sufficient cash in small denominations). The *waka* bundle is additional, and anyone traveling in remote areas of Fiji should pack some (take whole roots, not powdered kava). If you give the money up front together with the *waka* as a *sevusevu*, they'll know you're not a freeloader and you'll get VIP treatment, though in all cases it's absolutely essential to contribute something.

VILLAGE ETIQUETTE IN FIJI

- It's a Fijian custom to smile when you meet a stranger and say something like "Good morning," "Bula," or at least "Hello." Of course, you needn't do this in large towns, but you should almost everywhere else. If you meet someone you know, stop for a moment to exchange a few words. As you shake hands, tell the person your name.

- Fijian villages are private property and you should only enter after you've been welcomed. Of course it's okay to continue along a road that passes through a village, but make contact before leaving the road. Wait until someone greets you, then say you wish to be taken to the *turaga-ni-koro* (village herald). This village spokesperson will accept your *sevusevu* of kava roots and grant you permission to look around unless something important is happening, such as a funeral, celebration, feast, or church service (avoid arriving on a Sunday). A villager will be assigned to act as your guide and host. Yet even after this, you should still ask before taking pictures of individuals or inside buildings.

- If you wish to surf off a village, picnic on a village beach, or fish in the lagoon near to a village, you should also ask permission. You'll almost always be made most welcome and granted any favors you request if you present a *sevusevu* to the village herald or chief. If you approach the Fijians with respect, you're sure to be treated the same way in return.

- Take off your footwear before entering a *bure* and stoop as you walk around inside. Fijian villagers consider it offensive to walk in front of a person seated on the floor (pass behind) or to fail to say *tulou* (excuse me) as you go by. Clap three times when you join people already seated on mats on the floor. Shake hands with your hosts.

- In a *bure,* men should sit cross-legged, women with their legs to the side. Sitting with your legs stretched out in front or with your knees up during presentations is disrespectful. After a meal or during informal kava drinking, you can stretch your legs out, but never point them at the chief or the kava bowl. Don't sit in doorways or put your hand on another's head.

- If offered kava *(yaqona),* clap once with cupped hands, take the bowl, say *bula,* and drink it all in one gulp. Then hand the bowl back to the same person and clap three times saying *vinaka* (thanks). Don't stand up during a *sevusevu* to village elders—remain seated. When you give a gift hold it out with both hands, not one hand. Otherwise just place the bundle on the floor before them.

- It's good manners to take off your hat while walking through a village, where only the chief is permitted to wear a hat. Some villagers also object to sunglasses. Objects such as backpacks, handbags, and cameras should be carried in your hands rather than slung over your shoulders.

- Dress modestly in the village, which basically means a shirt for men and covered shoulders and thighs for women. Short shorts are not the best attire for men or women (long shorts okay), and bikinis are analogous to nudity (this also applies when swimming in a village river, pool, or beach). Wrapping a *sulu* around you will suffice.

- Don't point at people in villages. Do you notice how the Fijians rarely shout? In Fiji, raising your voice is a sign of anger. Don't openly admire a possession of someone, as they may feel obligated to give it to you. If sharing a meal, wait until grace has been said before eating. Alcohol is usually forbidden in villages.

- Fijian children are very well behaved. There's no running or shouting as you arrive in a village, and they'll leave you alone if you wish. The Fijians love children, so don't hesitate to bring your own. You'll never have to worry about finding a baby-sitter. Just make sure your children understand the importance of being on their best behavior in the village.

The *sevusevu* should be placed before (not handed to) the *turaga-ni-koro*, or village herald, so he can accept or refuse. If he accepts (by touching the package), your welcome is confirmed and you may spend the night in the village. It's also nice to give some money to the lady of the house upon departure, with your thanks. Just say it's your goodbye *sevusevu* and watch the smile. A Fijian may refuse the money, but he/she will not be offended by the offer if it is done properly. Of course, developing interpersonal relationships with your hosts is more important than money, and mere cash or gifts are no substitute for making friends.

Once you're staying with one family, avoid moving to the home of another family in the same village, as this would probably be seen as a slight to the first. Be wary of readily accepting invitations to meals with villagers other than your hosts, because the offer may only be meant as a courtesy. Don't overly admire any of the possessions of your hosts or they may feel obligated to give them to you. If you're forced to accept a family heirloom or other item you know you cannot take, ask them to keep it there for you in trust. Never arrive in a village on a Sunday, and don't overstay your welcome.

Village Life

As you approach a Fijian village, people will usually want to be helpful and will direct or accompany you to the person or place you seek. It's customary to present a *sevusevu* to the *turaga-ni-koro* if you'd like to be shown around. If you show genuine interest in something and ask to see how it is done, you'll usually be treated with respect and asked if there's anything else you'd like to know.

Initially, Fijians may hesitate to welcome you into their homes because they may fear you will not wish to sit on a mat and eat native foods with your fingers. Once you show them this isn't true, you'll receive the full hospitality treatment. Staying in a village is definitely not for everyone. Many houses contain no electricity, running water, toilet, furniture, etc., and only native food will be available. Water and your left hand serve as toilet paper.

You should also expect to sacrifice most of your privacy, to stay up late drinking grog, and to sit in the house and socialize when you could be out exploring. On Sunday you'll have to stay put the whole day. The constant attention and lack of sanitary conditions may become tiresome, but it would be considered rude to attempt to be alone or refuse the food or grog.

With the proliferation of backpacker resorts, staying in villages has become far less a part of visits to the remoter parts of Fiji than it was a decade ago, and relatively few travelers do it today. The Australian mass-market guidebooks also discourage travelers from going off the beaten track. However, so long as you're prepared to accept all of the above and know beforehand that this is not a cheap (or easy) way to travel, a couple of nights in an outlying village could well be the highlight of your trip.

FOOD AND DRINK

Unlike some other South Pacific destinations, Fiji has many good, inexpensive eateries. The ubiquitous Chinese restaurants are probably your best bet for dinner, and you can almost always get alcohol with the meal. At lunchtime look for an Indian place. The Indian restaurants are lifesavers for vegetarians, as all too often a vegetarian meal elsewhere is just the same thing with the meat removed. Many restaurants are closed on Sunday, and a 12.5 percent tax is added to the bill at some upmarket restaurants, although it's usually included in the menu price. The service at restaurants is occasionally slow.

The ancient Pacific islanders stopped making pottery over a millennium ago and instead developed an ingenious way of cooking in an underground earth oven known as a *lovo*. The *lovo* feasts staged weekly at many large hotels around Nadi or on the Coral Coast offer a good opportunity to taste authentic Fijian food and see traditional dancing. These feasts are usually accompanied by a Fijian *meke*, or song and dance performance, in which legends, love stories, and historical events are told in song and gesture. Alternatively, firewalking may be presented.

The famous Fiji Bitter beer is brewed in Suva

FIJIAN AND INDIAN SPECIALTIES

Traditional Fijian food is usually steamed or boiled instead of fried, and dishes such as baked fish *(ika)* in coconut cream *(lolo)* with cassava *(tapioca)*, taro *(dalo)*, breadfruit *(uto)*, and sweet potato *(kumala)* take a long time to prepare and must be served fresh, which makes it difficult to offer them in restaurants. Many resorts bake fish, pork, and root vegetables wrapped in banana leaves in a *lovo* (earth oven) at least once a week. Don't pass up an opportunity to try *duruka* (young sugar cane) or *vakalolo* (fish and prawns), both baked in *lolo*. *Kokoda* is an appetizing dish made of diced raw fish marinated in coconut cream and lime juice, while smoked octopus is *kuita*. Taro leaves are used to make a spinach called *palusami* (often stuffed with corned beef), which is known as *rourou* when soaked in coconut cream. Taro stems are cut into a marinated salad called *baba*. Seasoned chicken *(toa)* is wrapped and steamed in banana leaves to produce *kovu*. *Miti* is a sauce made of coconut cream, oranges, and chilies.

Indian dishes are spicy, often curries with rice and *dhal* (lentil soup), but practicing Hindus don't consume beef and Muslims forgo pork. Instead of bread Indians eat *roti*, a flat, tortilla-like pancake also called a *chapati*. *Puri* are small, deep-fried *rotis*. Baked in a stone oven *roti* becomes *naan*, a Punjabi specialty similar to pita bread. *Papadam* is a crispy version of the same. *Palau* is a main plate of rice and vegetables always including peas. *Samosas* are lumps of potato and other vegetables wrapped in dough and deep-fried. *Pakoras* are deep-fried chunks of dough spiced with chili and often served with a pickle chutney. A set meal consisting of *dhal, roti,* rice, one or two curries, and chutney, served on a metal plate, is called a *thali*. If meat is included, it's called simply a non-vegetarian *thali*. Yogurt mixed with water makes a refreshing drink called *lassi*. If you have the chance, try South Indian vegetarian dishes like *iddili* (little white rice cakes served with *dhal*) and *masala dosai* (a rice potato-filled pancake served with a watery curry sauce called *sambar*).

by Australian-owned Carlton Brewery Ltd., part of the famous Fosters Brewing Group. The 750-ml beer bottle is called a "long neck," while the smaller "stubbie" is a "short neck." Another Carlton-owned company, South Pacific Distilleries Ltd., produces Bounty Rum, Regal Whisky, Czarina Vodka, and eight other alcoholic beverages at their plant in Lautoka. Beer and other alcohol is only available at supermarkets in Fiji weekdays 0800–1800, Saturday 0800–1300. By law, licensed restaurants can only serve alcohol to those who order meals. Drinking alcoholic beverages on the street is prohibited. Unlike Australia and New Zealand, it's not customary to bring your own (BYO) booze into restaurants.

INFORMATION AND SERVICES
Information
The government-funded **Fiji Visitors Bureau** (tel. 330-2433, fax 330-0970, www.bulafiji.com) mails out general brochures free upon request. In Fiji they have walk-in offices at Nadi Airport

and in Suva. Their overseas offices are listed on www.southpacific.org/info.html.

The Fiji Visitors Bureau sends out a useful tourism newsletter called *Bula News Update* via email twice a month. To subscribe, simply send a blank email to bulanews@fijifvb.gov.fj with "Subscribe" in the subject heading and your email address will be automatically added to the distribution list. To be removed from the list, repeat the process with "Unsubscribe" in the subject heading.

Book buyers should browse the two book centers at the University of the South Pacific in Suva, as only these have a wide selection of titles.

Travel Agencies
If you like the security of advance reservations but aren't interested in joining a regular packaged tour, several local companies specialize in booking cruises, hotel rooms, airport transfers, sightseeing tours, rental cars, etc. Only the Blue Lagoon and Captain Cook mini-cruises mentioned in Getting There really need to be booked well in advance from abroad; upon arrival you'll have dozens

of hotels and resorts competing for your business at prices much lower than what your travel agent back home will charge. So rather than risk being exiled to one of Fiji's most expensive resorts by some agent only thinking of their commission, wait to make most of your ground arrangements upon arrival at Nadi Airport.

Fiji's largest in-bound tour operator is **Rosie The Travel Service** (tel. 672-2935, fax 672-2607), with a 24-hour office in the arrivals arcade at Nadi Airport and 16 branches around Viti Levu. This handbook will give you an idea what's out there, and upon arrival in Fiji, Rosie can make your accommodations bookings for you on the spot at rates lower than you'll pay working through travel agents overseas.

Rosie's main competitor is the **United Touring Company** (tel. 672-2811) with an office at Nadi Airport and tour desks at many Nadi and Coral Coast hotels. **Coral Sun Fiji** (tel. 672-2268) is also very reliable. Numerous other private travel agencies have offices at Nadi Airport and in town, many of them oriented toward backpackers or budget travelers. These are discussed in this book's Nadi section.

Internet Resources

Fiji's official tourism site, **www.bulafiji.com,** provides comprehensive travel information, and a drop-down menu gives access to six regional sites in five languages. Rob Kay's Fiji Islands Travel Guide, **www.fijiguide.com,** is an online travel guide covering subjects like accommodations, recreation, natural history, and facts about Fiji. The site's bulletin board allows you to ask questions and share experiences. Fiji Accommodation and Travel, **www.fiji.travelmaxia.com,** documents dozens of upscale resorts and hotels, with details of packages and specials, plus maps, photos, and online forms. Fiji Island Travel, **www.fiji-island.com,** has interactive travel maps which show the locations of resorts all around Fiji, with pictures of beaches and scenery. Additional interactive maps leading to photos and travel information are available on Fiji Beaches, **www.fijibeaches.com,**. The Fiji Islands Backpackers Guide, **http://fiji-backpacking.com,** is a well-organized website full of budget saving tips, back-

ground on Fiji and the Fijians, accommodations listings, information on transportation and activities, and even a Fijian language section.

Fiji Government Online, **www.fiji.gov.fj,** is well worth visiting to taste the image local politicians and bureaucrats wish to present to the world. You can listen to Fiji's national anthem, peruse recent news briefs, and consult topographical maps. The press releases are often edifying. David Robie's Café Pacific, **www.asiapac.org.fj/cafepacific,** is brimming with links to provocative articles and analysis not found elsewhere. Two Fiji-based news sites, Fiji Live, **www.fijilive.com,** and Fiji Village, **www.fijivillage.com,,** now require payment for access beyond their front page. The Rotuma Website, **www2.hawaii.edu/oceanic/rotuma/os/hanua.html,** covers every niche relating to Rotuma, including history, culture, language, maps, population, politics, news, photos, humor, proverbs, recipes, art, and music. Come Meet the Banabans, **www.banaban.com,** is dedicated to the Banabans of Rabi and Ocean Island. Dick Watling's Pacific Birds, **www.pacificbirds.com,** lists 173 species of birds confirmed to exist in Fiji, plus a further 22 unconfirmed species. Wildlife of Fiji, **http://ice.ucdavis.edu/~beckon,** offers a series of close-up photos of Fiji's unique fauna.

Visas and Officialdom

Everyone needs a passport valid at least three months beyond the date of entry. No visa is required of visitors from 101 countries (including Western Europe, North America, Japan, Israel, and most Commonwealth countries) for stays of up to four months. A complete list of exempt nationalities is on www.bulafiji.com. Tickets to leave Fiji are officially required but usually not checked. No vaccinations are necessary if you're arriving from North America, New Zealand, or Australia.

Extensions of stay are given out by the immigration offices at Lautoka, Nadi Airport, Savusavu, and Suva. You must apply before your current permit expires. After the first four months, you can obtain another two months to increase your total stay to six months by paying a F$82.50 fee. Bring your passport, onward or return ticket, and proof of sufficient funds. After six months you must leave and stay away at least four days, after which you can return and start on another four months. An exception is yachties who can obtain extensions up to one year.

Residence permits are difficult to obtain and the fastest means of obtaining one is to invest F$200,000 or more in the country. For information on business opportunities in your field of expertise, contact the **Fiji Trade and Investment Bureau** (tel. 331-5988, fax 330-1783, www .ftib.org.fj), Civic Tower, Level 6, directly behind the Suva City Library on Victoria Parade. Foreigners holding professional or technical qualifications in fields required by Fiji also receive preference. Fiji's trade commissioners in Los Angeles, Taiwan, and Australia should be able to assist with the process.

Fiji has four ports of entry for yachts: Lautoka, Levuka, Savusavu, and Suva. The Ports Authority can be contacted over VHF channel 16. Calling at an outer island before clearing customs is prohibited. Levuka is the easiest place to check in or out, as all of the officials have offices right on the main wharf, and Savusavu is also convenient. Lautoka is the most inconvenient, because the popular yacht anchorages off western Viti Levu are far from Lautoka. To visit the outer islands, yachts require a letter of authorization from the Ministry of Foreign Affairs in Suva, or the commissioner (at Labasa, Lautoka, or Nausori) of the division they wish to visit. Yacht clubs in Fiji can advise on how to obtain permission. Yacht Help (www.yachthelp.com) also has useful information for yachties.

Money

The currency is the Fiji dollar, which is about two to one to the U.S. dollar in value. To obtain the current rate, visit www.xe.com/ucc. The Fiji dollar is a stable currency, pegged to a basket of the U.S., New Zealand, and Australian dollars, the yen, and the pound.

The first Fijian coins were minted in London in 1934, but Fiji continued to deal in British currency until 1969, when dollars and cents were introduced (at the rate of two Fiji dollars to one pound). There are coins of one, two, five, 10, 20, and 50 cents and one dollar, and bills of F$2,

F$5, F$10, F$20, and F$50 (be careful as the F$5 and F$50 notes and F$2 and F$20 notes have confusingly similar colors and designs).

Banking hours are Monday–Thursday 0930–1500, Friday 0930–1600. A 24-hour bank is at Nadi Airport. Commercial banks operating in Fiji include the ANZ Bank, Indian-owned Bank of Baroda, Pakistani-owned Habib Bank, Colonial National Bank, Merchant Bank, and Westpac Banking Corporation. There are bank branches in all the main towns, but it's usually not possible to change traveler's checks or foreign banknotes in rural areas or on the outer islands. Avoid the ANZ Bank which charges a F$5 commission on traveler's checks (but not on cash exchanges). At last report, the Westpac Bank and Colonial National Bank charged no commission. Also take care when changing at the luxury hotels, since they often give a rate much lower than the banks. Recent cases of stolen traveler's checks being changed in Fiji has caused many hotels and restaurants to refuse them. It's a good idea to plan ahead and change enough money at a bank to get you through the weekends. Always have an ample supply of small notes to pay small bills and carry cash to the outer islands.

Credit cards are strictly for the cities and resorts (the most useful cards to bring are American Express, Diners Club, JCB International, Master-Card, and Visa). The ANZ Bank gives cash advances on MasterCard and Visa, but remember that cash advances are considered personal loans and accrue interest from the moment they are paid. If you're forced to get a cash advance through a large supermarket or resort, they'll probably take 10 percent commission for the favor. Many tourist facilities levy a 5 percent surcharge on credit card payments.

Both the ANZ Bank and Westpac Bank now have automated teller machines (ATMs) outside their branches and these provide local currency at good rates against most debit cards. Some ATMs at Westpac Bank and Colonial National Bank branches still accept only local debit cards.

The import of foreign currency is unrestricted, but only F$500 in Fiji banknotes may be imported or exported. Avoid taking any Fiji banknotes out of the country at all, as Fiji dollars are difficult to change and heavily discounted outside Fiji. The Thomas Cook offices in Suva and Nadi will change whatever you have left into the currency of the next country on your itinerary (don't forget to keep enough local currency to pay your airport departure tax at the check-in counter). Officially, you're only allowed to export a maximum of F$5,000 in foreign cash, although this will only become an issue if they catch you for something else, such as narcotics, pornography, firearms, or immigration offenses.

For security, the bulk of your travel funds should be in traveler's checks. American Express is probably the best kind to have, as they're represented by Tapa International in Suva (Level 4, Downtown Boulevard Plaza, Ellery Street; tel. 330-2333, fax 330-2048). If your American Express checks or card are lost or stolen, contact them. Thomas Cook has offices of their own at 30 Thomson St., Suva (tel. 330-1603, fax 330-0304), and in Nadi (tel. 670-3110).

If you need money sent in an emergency, Western Union can receive fast transfers from anywhere in the world at their offices in Suva (tel. 331-4812) and Lautoka (tel. 665-2509) or most post offices in Fiji. The sender pays the fee. Many banks will hold a sealed envelope for you in their vault for a nominal fee—a good way to avoid carrying unneeded valuables with you all around Fiji on an extended visit.

In 1992, Fiji introduced a value-added tax (VAT), currently 12.5 percent, which is usually (but not always) included in quoted prices. Among the few items exempt from the tax are unprocessed local foods, books printed in Fiji, and bus fares. Despite VAT, Fiji is still one of the least expensive countries in the South Pacific, although costs have been creeping up in recent years (inflation was 4.7 percent in 2003). Tipping isn't customary in Fiji, although some

visitors are working hard to change this. A few resorts have a staff Christmas fund to which contributions are always welcome. Maybe have a quality baseball cap or a small bottle of nice perfume in your bag to give to anyone who has really gone out of their way for you.

Post

Post offices are generally open weekdays 0800–1600 and they hold general delivery mail two months. Postcard postage is inexpensive, so mail lots of them from here! Consider using airmail for parcels, since surface mail takes up to six months. The weight limit for overseas parcels is 10 kilograms. Post Fiji's *fast* POST service guarantees that your letter or parcel will get on the first international airline connection to your destination for a small surcharge. Express mail service (EMS) is more expensive but faster and up to 20 kilograms may be sent. Main post offices around Fiji accept EMS mail.

When writing to Fiji, use the words "Fiji Islands" in the address (otherwise the letter might go to Fuji, Japan) and underline Fiji (so it doesn't end up in Iceland). Also include the post office box number, because there's no residential mail delivery in Fiji. If it's a remote island or small village you're writing to, the person's name will be sufficient. Sending a picture postcard to an islander is a very nice way of saying thank you.

Aside from EMS, the other major courier services active in Fiji are **CDP** (tel. 331-3077) at Ba, Labasa, Lautoka, Levuka, Nadi, Savusavu, Sigatoka, and Suva, **DHL** (tel. 331-3166) with offices at Levuka, Nadi, Savusavu, and Suva, **TNT** (tel. 330-8677) at Nadi and Suva, and **UPS** (tel. 331-2697) at Lautoka, Nadi, and Suva. To Europe or North America, DHL charges F$175 for a small box up to 10 kilograms or F$290 for a big box up to 25 kilograms.

Telecommunications

Card telephones (www.payphones.com.fj) are very handy, and if you're staying in Fiji more than a few days and intend to make your own arrangements, it's wise to purchase a local telephone card upon arrival, since coin telephones don't exist. In this handbook we provide all the numbers you'll need to make hotel reservations, check restaurant hours, find out about cultural shows, and compare car rental rates, saving you a lot of time and inconvenience.

Tele Cards (www.telecard.com.fj) are sold at all post offices and many shops in denominations of F$3, F$5, F$10, F$20, and F$50 (foreign phone cards cannot be used in Fiji). It's wiser to get a F$3 or F$5 card rather than one of the higher values in case you happen to lose it. With a Tele Card you scratch off a strip on the back of the card to reveal a code number. On hearing a dial tone, dial 101 and follow the voice prompts. The Tele Card can be used from all types of phones, but you must enter the code numbers slowly, one by one, otherwise you'll get a message telling you the code is invalid.

As far as telephone charges go, Fiji is divided into three regions. Western includes all of Viti Levu west of Rakiraki and Sigatoka, plus the Yasawas. Eastern is all of Viti Levu east of Korolevu, plus Ovalau and Kadavu. Northern is Vanua Levu and Taveuni. Calls within a region are F$.20 per 45 seconds, while inter-regional calls are F$.20 per 15 seconds. Thus you can call anywhere in the country for a mere F$.20, though you get more time if the call is within the same region. On local calls you get 10 minutes for your F$.20.

Trunk Radio System (TRS) calls can be direct dialed from inside Fiji, but must go through an operator through from overseas. All such seven-digit numbers have 11 in the first three numbers and many are only answered at certain times of day (usually 0800–1000 and 1400–1600). Many resorts in the Yasawa Islands or interior of Viti Levu have very high frequency (VHF) radio telephone connections. In these cases, dial the number provided in this book, wait for two beeps, then key in the extension number. Be aware that only one person at a time can speak over radio telephone hookups.

Because rural telephone services in Fiji are poor, many people carry mobile phones supplied by Vodafone. These numbers begin with a nine and you should avoid using them, as such calls cost a minimum of F$.80 a minute and your phone card will soon be devoured.

You can search for any telephone number in Fiji at www.whitepages.com.fj and www.yellowpages.com.fj. Within Fiji, domestic directory assistance is 011, international directory assistance 022, the domestic operator 011, the international operator 022. In emergencies, dial 911.

Fiji's international access code from public telephones is 00, so insert your card, dial 00, the country code, the area code, and the number (to Canada and the United States the country code is always 1). To call overseas collect (billed to your party at the higher person-to-person rate), dial 031, the country code, the area code, and the number. If calling Fiji from abroad, dial your own international access code, Fiji's telephone code **679**. There are no area codes in Fiji. If the line is inaudible, hang up immediately and try again later.

The basic long-distance charge for three minutes is F$4.26 to Australia or New Zealand, F$7.20 to North America, Europe, or Japan. All operator-assisted international calls have a three-minute minimum charge and additional time is charged per minute, whereas international calls made using telephone cards have no minimum and the charges are broken down into flat six-second units (telephone cards with less than F$3 credit on them cannot be used for international calls).

Faxes can be sent from the post offices in Labasa, Lautoka, Ba, Nadi, Sigatoka, and Suva. Outgoing faxes cost F$9.65/12.15 for the first page to regional/other countries, additional pages F$6/9. You can also receive faxes at these post offices for F$1.65 a page. The numbers you'll probably use are fax 670-2467 at Nadi Airport Post Office, fax 670-2166 at Nadi Town Post Office, fax 666-4666 at Lautoka Post Office, and fax 330-2666 at Suva General Post Office.

If a fax you are trying to send to Fiji from abroad doesn't go through smoothly on the first or second try, wait and try again at another time of day. If it doesn't work then, stop trying, because the fax machine at the other end may not be able to read your signal, and your telephone company will levy a minimum charge for each attempt. Call the international operator to ask what is wrong.

The Internet

Fiji is the most advanced country in the South Pacific as far as the Internet goes. Most tourism-related businesses in Fiji now have email addresses and websites, making communication from abroad a lot cheaper and easier.

In 2002, Connect Internet Services (www.connect.com.fj) changed all Fiji email addresses ending @is.com.fj to @connect.com.fj. This change is reflected in this handbook, but older brochures (and many websites!) may still list the original form. If you come across an address ending with ending @is.com.fj, just substitute @connect.com.fj and it should work. (Also in 2002, Telecom Fiji increased all Fiji telephone numbers from six to seven digits. We've updated all the phone numbers in this book, but you'll still see six-digit numbers in older brochures.)

When sending email to Fiji, never include attachments such as Excel or Word files or photos with your message unless it has been specifically requested, as the recipient may be forced to pay stiff long distance telephone charges to download it. Many people delete such files unopened for security reasons.

In Fiji, public Internet access is available in Nadi, Lautoka, Sigatoka, Pacific Harbor, Suva, Savusavu, and a few other places. Some resorts also provide computers at slightly higher rates than the public Internet cafés. If your Internet service provider doesn't have an electronic mailbox you can use on the road, you should open a free online email account at www.yahoo.com or www.hotmail.com before leaving home.

Print Media

The *Fiji Times* (tel. 330-4111, fax 330-2011), "the first newspaper published in the world today," was founded at Levuka in 1869, but is currently owned by the Rupert Murdoch News Ltd. group. The Fiji government has a controlling 44 percent interest in the *Daily Post* (tel. 331-3342, fax 331-3320), which is also partly owned by Colonial Mutual Insurance. The *Daily Post* appeared just after the Rabuka coups in 1987. The more critical *Fiji Sun* (tel. 330-7555, fax 331-1455, www.sun.com.fj) was established in 1999.

The region's leading newsmagazines are *Islands*

Business (tel. 330-3108, fax 330-1423), published monthly in Suva, and Hawaii-based *Pacific Magazine* (www.pacificislands.cc). There's also a fortnightly Fijian news and business magazine called *The Review* (tel. 330-0591, fax 330-2852, www.fijilive.com). Turn to Resources at the end of this book for more Pacific-oriented publications.

TV

Television broadcasting began in Fiji in 1991. Fiji 1 (www.fijitv.com.fj) is on the air daily 1600–midnight, with Australian programming rebroadcast at other hours. Fiji 1 gives the Fiji news at 1800 and 2155 daily, the BBC world news at 1830 weekdays. Government-owned Yasana Holdings has a majority interest in the station. In addition to this free station, there's a paid service for which a decoder must be rented. The three paid channels are Sky Plus (English language programming), Sky Entertainment (Hindi programming from India), and Star Sports. The daily papers provide program guides or call tel. 186-0100.

Radio

Fiji doesn't have a shortwave broadcaster, but privately owned **Communications Fiji Ltd.** (tel. 331-4766, www.fijivillage.com) rebroadcasts the BBC World Service over 88.2 MHz FM and Radio Australia at 92.6 MHz FM 24 hours a day (available around Suva only). Communications Fiji Ltd. also operates four lively commercial FM stations, which broadcast around the clock throughout the country: **FM 96** (www.fm96.com.fj) and **Legend** in English, Viti FM in Fijian, and Radio Navtarang in Hindi. FM 96 caters to the under 30 age group, while Legend is aimed at a more mature audience.

In addition, the public **Fiji Broadcasting Corporation** (tel. 331-4333, fax 330-1643, website: www.radiofiji.org) operates five AM/FM radio stations: **Bula 100 FM** in English, Radio Fiji One (RF1) in Fijian for older listeners, Bula 102 FM in Fijian for younger listeners, Radio Fiji Two (RF2) in Hindi for older listeners, and Bula 98 FM in Hindi for younger listeners. The Bula stations (or "Bula Network") are funded by commercial advertising, while the public service Radio Fiji stations are supported by a government grant.

At Suva you can pick up the local stations at the following frequencies: **FM 96** at 96.0 MHz, Bula 98 FM at 98.0 MHz, Navtarang at 98.8 MHz, **Bula 100 FM** at 100.4 MHz, Bula 102 FM at 102.0 MHz, Viti FM at 102.8 MHz, RF2 at 105.2 MHz FM, **Legend** at 106.8 MHz, and RF1 at 558 kHz AM.

At Nadi and Lautoka check the following frequencies: **FM 96** at 95.4 MHz, Navtarang at 97.4 MHz, Bula 98 FM at 98.2 MHz, Viti FM at 99.6 MHz, Bula 102 FM at 102.4 MHz, RF2 at 105.4 MHz, and **Legend** at 106.4 MHz. At Lautoka you'll also get **Bula 100 FM** at 94.6 and 100.0 MHz. Privately-run ZFM Classic at 101.0 MHz is based in Lautoka.

On the Coral Coast it's Bula 98 FM at 98.2 MHz, **FM 96** at 99.0 MHz, **Bula 100 FM** at 100.6 MHz, Navtarang at 102.2 MHz, Bula 102 FM at 103.0 MHz, **Legend** at 107.2 MHz, Viti FM at 107.8 MHz, RF1 at 927 kHz, and RF2 at 1206 kHz.

Around Rakiraki look for Bula 98 at 93.0 MHz, Navtarang at 97.0 MHz, **Bula 100 FM** at 100.0 MHz, Viti FM at 104.8 MHz, RF1 at 1152 kHz, and RF2 at 1467 kHz. At Ba you can get ZFM Classic at 88.8 MHz, **Bula 100 FM** at 94.6 MHz, **FM 96** at 99.2 MHz, Navtarang at 101.6 MHz, and Viti FM at 103.8 MHz.

On Vanua Levu, check the following frequencies at Labasa: **FM 96** at 95.4 MHz, Navtarang at 97.4 MHz, Bula 98 FM at 98.2 MHz, Viti FM at 99.6 MHz, **Bula 100 FM** at 100.0 MHz, Bula 102 FM at 102.4 MHz, RF1 at 684 kHz, and RF2 at 810 kHz. At Savusavu it's Bula 98 FM at 98.4 MHz, **Bula 100 FM** at 100.0 MHz, Bula 102 FM at 102.4 MHz, and RF2 at 1152 kHz. On Taveuni, you may hear **Bula 100 FM** at 100.6 MHz and Bula 102 FM at 103.0 MHz.

The local stations broadcast mostly pop music and repetitive advertising with very little news or commentary (the presenters sometimes get things hilariously mixed up). Bula 100 FM broadcasts local news and a weather report on the hour weekdays 0600–2200 (weekends every other hour) with a special news of the day report at 1745, followed by the BBC world news just after 1800. The BBC news is also broadcast on Bula 100 FM at 1900 and 2100. Radio FM 96 broadcasts news and weather on the hour weekdays 0600–1800, Saturday and Sunday at 0800, 0900, 1000, 1200, 1300, 1700, and 1800.

Health

Fiji's climate is a healthy one, and the main causes of death are non-communicable diseases such as heart disease, diabetes, and cancer. Health care is good, with an abundance of hospitals, health centers, and nursing stations scattered around the country. The largest hospitals are in Labasa, Lautoka, Levuka, Ba, Savusavu, Sigatoka, Suva, and Taveuni.

To call an ambulance dial 911. In case of scuba diving accidents, a dive recompression chamber (tel. 330-5154 in Suva or 885-0630 in Savusavu) is available at the excellent Suva Private Hospital. The 24-hour recompression emergency numbers are tel. 999-3506 and 999-5500.

TRANSPORTATION
Getting There

Fiji's geographic position makes it the hub of transport for the entire South Pacific, and Nadi is the region's most important international airport, with long-haul services to points all around the Pacific Rim. Twelve international airlines fly into Nadi: Aircalin, Air Fiji, Air Nauru, Air New Zealand, Air Pacific, Air Vanuatu, Freedom Air, Korean Air, Pacific Blue, Polynesian Airlines, Qantas Airways, and Solomon Airlines. Air Pacific and Air Fiji also use Suva's Nausori Airport.

Fiji's national airline, **Air Pacific,** was founded in 1951 as Fiji Airways by Harold Gatty, a famous Australian aviator who had set a record with American Willy Post in 1931 by flying around the world in eight days. In 1972, the airline was reorganized as a regional carrier and the name changed to Air Pacific. The carrier flies from Nadi to Apia, Auckland, Brisbane, Honiara, Honolulu, Los Angeles, Melbourne, Port

Vila, Sydney, Tokyo, Tongatapu, and Vancouver, and from Suva to Auckland and Sydney.

Qantas owns 46.5 percent of Air Pacific (the Fiji government owns the rest) and all Qantas flights to Fiji are actually code shares with the Fijian carrier. Qantas is Air Pacific's general sales agent in Europe, and you'll fly Air Pacific to Fiji if you booked with Qantas. Air Pacific code shares with Solomon Airlines when going to Honiara and Port Vila.

Air New Zealand and Air Pacific are the major carriers serving Fiji out of Los Angeles. Air Pacific flies nonstop from Los Angeles to Nadi four times a week (10.5 hours) and from Honolulu three times a week (six hours). Air Pacific also flies to Fiji from Vancouver, Canada, via Honolulu twice a week—convenient, since no transfers from one aircraft to another are required. Air New Zealand operates three nonstop flights from Los Angeles to Nadi every week, plus one Coral Route island hopper via Tahiti and Rarotonga. Air New Zealand passengers originating in Canada must change planes in either Honolulu or Los Angeles.

From Australia, Air Pacific offers nonstop flights to Nadi from Brisbane, Melbourne, and Sydney. From Sydney, Air Pacific also has direct flights to Suva. Air New Zealand is competing fiercely in the Australian market, and they offer competitive fares to many South Pacific points via Auckland. Both Air New Zealand and Air Pacific fly from Auckland to Nadi daily, and Air Pacific also flies from Auckland to Suva twice a week.

A number of regional carriers fly to and from Fiji. Samoa's Polynesian Airlines arrives from Apia twice a week. Aircalin flies to Fiji from Nouméa and Wallis. From Suva, Air Fiji flies north to Funafuti in Tuvalu and east to Tongatapu. Air Nauru flies to Nadi from Nauru and Tarawa twice a week. Air Vanuatu arrives from Port Vila. Solomon Airlines links Fiji to Honiara and Port Vila.

Getting Around by Air

While most international flights are focused on Nadi, Fiji's domestic air service radiates from Suva and two local airlines compete fiercely. **Air Fiji** (tel. 331-3666, fax 330-0771, www.air

fiji.net) flies Brazilian-made Embraer Brasilias (30 seats), fast Embraer Bandierantes (18 seats), sturdy Canadian-made Twin Otters (18 seats), efficient TriIslanders (16 seats), and pocket-sized Britten Norman Islanders (nine seats). From Suva's Nausori Airport, flights operate six times a day to Nadi (F$104), five times a day to Labasa (F$139), twice a day to Levuka (F$52), Savusavu (F$111), and Taveuni (F$138), daily except Sunday to Kadavu (F$81), three times a week to Gau (F$64), and weekly to Cicia (F$121), Koro (F$92), Lakeba (F$131), Moala (F$118), Vanua Balavu (F$130), and Rotuma (F$339). Savusavu to Taveuni (F$74) is twice daily (all quoted fares are one-way). From Nadi they fly to Labasa (F$163), Savusavu (F$148), and Taveuni (F$183) twice a day. Air Fiji's 30-day "Discover Fiji Air Pass" (US$270) is valid on any four flights between Kadavu, Nadi, Savusavu, Suva, and Taveuni, but it must be purchased prior to arrival in Fiji. Buying tickets as you go is a better value than this pass.

Sun Air (tel. 672-3016, fax 672-0085, www.fiji.to) bases much of its domestic network at Nadi, with three flights a day to Labasa (F$175), twice daily to Suva (F$104), Savusavu (F$159), and Taveuni (F$183), and daily to Kadavu (F$104). Also from Nadi, the resort island of Malololailai (F$48) gets four to eight flights a day, while Mana Island (F$58) is visited five times a day. From Suva, Sun Air has flights to Labasa (twice daily, F$147) and Nadi (two daily, F$104). From Taveuni, they go to Savusavu (twice daily, F$75) and Labasa (three times a week, F$75). Flying in their nine-passenger Britten Norman Islanders, speedy eight-passenger Beechcraft, and versatile 19-passenger Twin Otters is sort of fun.

Turtle Airways Ltd. (tel. 672-1888, fax 672-0095, www.turtleairways.com), owned by Richard Evanson of Turtle Island Resort, flies their five four-seat Cessna 206 floatplanes and one seven-seat DeHaviland Beaver three times a day from Nadi to Castaway and Mana Islands (F$134/268 one-way/round-trip). Turtle Airways also services the Yasawas. The Beaver is a classic aircraft, performing remarkable whitewater takeoffs and landings.

Because only Nadi and Nausori airports have electric lighting on their runways, all flights are during daylight hours. Always reconfirm your return flight immediately upon arrival at an outer island, as the reservation lists are sometimes not sent out from Suva. Failure to do this could mean you'll be bumped without compensation.

Be aware that flights on the domestic carriers booked from abroad or over the Internet are 25 percent more expensive than the same tickets purchased in Fiji. In this book we quote the reduced local fare, though you won't always be able to get it (the staff at the check-in counters at Nadi Airport usually charge foreigners full fare). The big advantage to booking ahead from overseas is that you'll be guaranteed a seat on these heavily booked flights and will be first in line if the carrier decides to downsize the plane and bump a few passengers.

Add a F$3.50 insurance surcharge to the cost of each flight. Student discounts are for local students only and there are no standby fares. Children aged 12 and under pay 50 percent, infants two and under carried in arms pay 10 percent. Both Sun Air and Air Fiji allow passengers with full fare international tickets to carry 20 kg of baggage, while tickets issued in Fiji at the reduced local residents rate cover only 15 kg. The allowance on Turtle Airways is always 15 kg.

Getting Around by Boat

Since most shipping operates out of Suva, passenger services by sea both within Fiji and to neighboring countries are listed in the Suva section. Ferries to the Mamanuca and Yasawa groups are covered under Nadi and Yasawa Islands, while those between Vanua Levu and Taveuni are under Buca Bay and Taveuni.

The largest local company is **Patterson Brothers Shipping,** set up by Levuka copra planter Reg Patterson and his brother just after WW I. Patterson's Japanese-built car ferry, the *Princess Ashika,* is usually used on the Buresala-Natovi-Nabouwalu-Ellington Wharf run. (In August 2003, a sister ship, the MV *Ovalau,* sank two km off Nananu-i-Ra Island after springing a leak the pumps could not control. Passengers and crew were rescued by the *Princess Ashika* before

the ship went down. A replacement, the *Ovalau III,* may enter service soon.) Patterson's other ferry, the *Island Navigator,* does trips to Lau and Rotuma. Delays or reduced schedules due to mechanical failures are routine.

Consort Shipping Line runs the large car ferry *Spirit of Fiji Islands* from Suva to Koro, Savusavu, and Taveuni twice a week. The car ferry *Adi Savusavu* of **Beachcomber Cruises** (www.beachcomberfiji.com) also visits Savusavu and Taveuni from Suva three times a week.

Other regular boat trips originating in Suva include the Patterson Brothers "Sea Road" shuttle to Levuka, and the weekly ferries to Kadavu. From Nadi, **South Sea Cruises** operates fast catamaran shuttles to the Mamanuca Group on the *Tiger IV* and to the Yasawas on the *Yasawa Flyer.* A sea voyage is essential part of any authentic Fiji experience.

Tourist Cruises

Blue Lagoon Cruises Ltd. (P.O. Box 130, Lautoka, Fiji; tel. 666-3938, fax 666-4098, www.bluelagooncruises.com) has been offering upscale minicruises from Lautoka to the Yasawa Islands since its founding by Captain Trevor Withers in 1950. The two-night trips (from F$1,609) and three-night trips (from F$2,419) leave twice a week, while the six-night cruise (from F$4,354) is weekly. Prices are per cabin (two persons) and include meals (but not alcohol), entertainment, shore excursions, and tax (no additional "port charges" and no tipping). We quote the high season fares charged from April to December (low season from January to March is 30 percent cheaper). Single occupancy is F$248–619 less. "A" deck is about 15 percent more expensive than the main deck, but you have the railing right outside your cabin door instead of a locked porthole window. On the shorter cruises Blue Lagoon uses older three-deck, 40-passenger vessels, while larger four-deck, 60-passenger mini-cruise ships are used on the longer voyages. Since 1996, the 72-passenger luxury cruiser *Mystique Princess* has operated three-night "gold club" cruises from F$3,150 double. The meals are often beach barbecue affairs, with Fijian dancing. You'll have plenty of opportunities to snorkel in the calm, crystal-clear waters (bring your own gear). A special scuba diving cruise leaves on the first Saturday of each month. Though a bit expensive, Blue Lagoon Cruises has an excellent reputation. There are almost daily departures yearround, but reservations are essential.

Captain Cook Cruises (P.O. Box 23, Nadi, Fiji; tel. 670-1823, fax 670-2045, www.captain cook.com.fj) operates out of Nadi's Denarau Marina rather than Lautoka and it's also recommended. Like Blue Lagoon Cruises they offer three/four-night cruises to the Yasawa Islands aboard the 63-meter MV *Reef Escape,* departing Nadi Tuesday and Saturday. The 60 double-occupancy cabins begin at F$1,270/1,694 pp twin with bunk beds. The two itineraries vary considerably, and there's a discount if you do both in succession. The *Reef Escape* was formerly used for cruises along Australia's Great Barrier Reef and it's considerably larger than the Blue Lagoon vessels. The food is good, cabins bright, activities and entertainment fun, and there's even a miniature swimming pool and spa! Most of your fellow passengers will be Australians, which can be stimulating, and the Fijian staff will spoil you silly.

In addition, Captain Cook Cruises operates two/three-night cruises to the southern Yasawas on the 33-meter topsail schooner *Spirit of the Pacific*—a more romantic choice than the mini-cruise ships. These trips depart Nadi every Monday and Thursday morning and cost F$540/684 pp for two/three nights (children under 12 not accepted). You sleep ashore in a double *bure,* the food is good with lots of fresh vegetables and salads, and the staff is friendly and well organized. Captain Cook Cruises also sometimes uses the 34-meter square-rigged brigantine *Ra Marama* on these trips. It's a fine vessel built of teak planks in Singapore in 1957 for a former governor-general of Fiji. These trips can be booked through most travel agents in Fiji or via the website; readers who've gone report having a great time.

Awesome Adventures (P.O. Box 718, Nadi, Fiji; tel. 675-0499, www.awesomefiji.com) at the Denarau Marina offers two-night "Wanna Taki" cruises around the tiny islands off the south end of Naviti in the Yasawa Group aboard the 27-meter catamaran *Taralala.* Everyone sleeps in an air-conditioned dormitory or under the stars on the upper deck at F$350 pp (extra nights F$99 each). Meals, kayaks, swimming with manta rays (maybe), and transfers from Nadi on the *Yasawa Flyer* are included.

The 39-meter three-masted schooner *Tui Tai* of **Tui Tai Adventure Cruises** (P.O. Box 474, Savusavu, Fiji; tel. 885-3032 or 999-6375, www .tuitai.com) based at Savusavu also caters to younger travelers. The four-night cruise departing Savusavu on Tuesday is F$1,700/2,250 single double in the six double cabins with shared bath, or F$915 per bunk in an air-conditioned 28-bed dorm or on deck. If you board at Taveuni for a three-night cruise it's F$1,350/1,800 or F$733. Both trips tour Koro or the Lau Group and end at Savusavu on Saturday. Meals and activities (bicycling, snorkeling, kayaking) are included, but scuba diving is extra.

Scuba Cruises

Several **live-aboard dive boats** ply Fiji waters. A seven-night stay aboard one of these vessels could run as high as F$6,500 pp (airfare, alcohol, and tax extra), but the boat anchors right above the dive sites, so no time is wasted commuting back and forth. All meals are included and the diving is unlimited. Singles are usually allowed to share a cabin with another diver to avoid a single supplement. Bookings can be made through any of the scuba wholesalers previously mentioned under Scuba Tours.

The five-stateroom *Sere Ni Wai* (or "song of the sea") is a 30-meter boat based at the Raffles Tradewinds Hotel in Suva and operating around Beqa, Kadavu, Lomaiviti, and northern Lau. Captain Greg Lawlor's family has been in Fiji for four generations, but his boat is relatively new, launched in 1995. If you're already in Fiji, try calling **Mollie Dean Cruises** (P.O. Box 3256, Lami, Fiji; tel. 336-1174, www.sere.com.fj), which books divers on the *Sere Ni Wai* locally. In the United States, the *Sere Ni Wai* is marketed as the *Fiji Aggressor II* (www.pac-aggressor.com). Another famous boat is the 34-meter, eight-cabin *Nai'a*, which does seven-day scuba cruises to Lomaiviti and northern Lau at US$2,700, or 10 days for US$3,850 excluding airfare. Captain Rob Barrel and Dive Director Cat Holloway have a longstanding interest in dolphins and whales, and whale-watching expeditions to Tonga are organized annually. Long exploratory voyages are occasionally made to places as far afield as Vanuatu and the Phoenix Islands of Kiribati (in June). Local bookings are accepted when space is available and you might even be able to swing a discount. **Nai'a Cruises** (P.O. Box 332, Deuba, Fiji; tel. 345-0382, fax 345-0566, www.naia.com.fj) has an office in the Cultural Center complex at Pacific Harbor, though the *Nai'a* itself is based at Lautoka. In North America call tel. 866/776-5572.

Also based at Pacific Harbor is the 18-meter live-aboard *Beqa Princess,* operated by **Tropical Expeditions** (Charles Wakeham, P.O. Box 129, Deuba, Fiji; tel. 345-0666, fax 330-9551). The three spacious air-conditioned cabins accommodate six divers on three-night cruises to the Beqa Lagoon for around F$500 pp a day. Get a half dozen friends together and charter this boat for an unforgettable trip at F$3,600 daily.

Yacht Tours and Charters

Due to the risks involved in navigating Fiji's poorly marked reefs, yacht charters aren't at all as common in Fiji as they are in Tonga or Tahiti. "Bareboat" charters (where you're given a yacht to sail around on your own) aren't available and all charter boats are required by law to carry a local skipper or guide.

Musket Cove Yacht Charters (Private Mail Bag NAP 0352, Nadi Airport, Fiji; tel. 672-2488, fax 672-3773, www.musketcovefiji.com) offers crewed yacht charters among the Mamanuca and Yasawa islands from their base at the Musket Cove Marina on Malololailai Island in the Mamanuca Group. Surfing and diving charters are available. For example, the ketch *Hobo* can be chartered for Yasawa cruises at F$950/1,100 a day for two/four people, provisions and crew included. The 14-meter catamaran *Take a Break* is also available at F$1,200/1,600 for two/four passengers.

Valentino Sailing Safaris (P.O.Box 10562, Nadi Airport, Fiji; tel. 672-4428 or 992-9182, www.sailsafari.com.fj) offers Mamanuca and Yasawa charters on the crewed 11-meter catamaran *Moana Uli Uli* based at Nadi. It's F$750 for up to four guests, meals and drinks included (minimum of two nights).

Sailing Adventures Ltd. (Peter Kinsey, P.O. Box 7531, Lautoka, Fiji; tel. 666-5244, fax 666-5335, www.fijisail.com), based at the Vuda Point Marina between Nadi and Lautoka, offers charters on the three-cabin, 15.5-meter yacht *Tavake.* A one-week cruise around the Mamanuca and Yasawa groups will cost F$12,600 for two people or F$18,522 for six persons including meals, taxes, crew, guides, and most activities. Scuba diving can be arranged at additional cost. You're promised a cultural experience!

Larger groups could consider the 27-meter ketch *Tau* at the Raffles Tradewinds Hotel, Suva, which costs US$1,800/12,000 a day/week for up to four persons, including all meals, drinks, and an experienced crew (scuba diving is extra). It's available year-round. For full information contact **Tau Charter Yacht** (Tony Philp, tel. 336-2128).

By Bus

Scheduled bus service is available all over Fiji, and the fares are low. If you're from North America, you'll be amazed how accessible, inexpensive, and convenient the bus service really is. Most long-distance bus services operate several times a day and bus stations are usually adjacent to local markets. Buses with a signboard in the window reading Via Highway are local "stage" buses that will stop anywhere along their routes and can be excruciatingly slow on a long trip. Express buses are faster, but they'll only stop in a few towns and some won't let you off at resorts along the way. Strangely, the times of local buses are not posted at the bus stations, and it's often hard to find anyone to ask about buses to remote locations. The people most likely to know are the bus drivers themselves, but you'll often receive misleading or incorrect information about local buses. Express bus times *are* posted at some stations and it's sometimes possible to pick up printed express bus timetables at tourist offices.

FIJI ISLANDS

On Viti Levu, the most important routes are between Lautoka and Suva, the biggest cities. If you follow the southern route via Sigatoka you'll be on Queens Road, the smoother and faster of the two. Kings Road via Tavua is longer and it can be rough and dusty, but you get to see a bit of the interior. Fares from Suva are F$2.95 to Pacific Harbor, F$6.95 to Sigatoka, F$10.10 to Nadi, F$10.55 to Nadi Airport, F$11.60 to Lautoka, and F$13.35 to Ba. Fares average just over F$2 for each hour of travel.

Pacific Transport Ltd. (tel. 330-4366) has 11 buses a day along Queens Road, with expresses leaving from across the street from the Flea Market in Suva for Lautoka at 0645, 0830, 0930, 1210, 1500, and 1730 (221 km, five hours). Eastbound, the expresses leave Lautoka for Suva at 0630, 0700, 1210, 1550, and 1730. An additional Suva-bound express leaves Nadi at 0900. These buses stop at Navua, Pacific Harbor, Sigatoka (coffee break), Nadi, and Nadi Airport, plus a few major resorts upon request (ask). The 1500 bus from Suva continues to Ba. If you want off at a smaller place, you might have to take one of the five local "stage" buses, which take six hours to reach Lautoka via Queens Road. Sunbeam Transport operates five daily express buses between Sigatoka and Suva stopping at many resorts along the way.

The daily **Sunset Express** (Island Buses Ltd., tel. 331-2504) leaves Suva for Sigatoka, Nadi, and Lautoka at 0845 and 1600 (four hours, F$10). From the Lautoka end, it leaves at 0930 and 1515, passing Nadi Airport at 1000 and 1545. The Sunset Express is faster than the Pacific Transport expresses, since it makes fewer and shorter stops.

Sunbeam Transport Ltd. (tel. 338-2704) services the northern Kings Road from Suva to Lautoka five times a day, with expresses leaving Suva at 0600, 0645, 0815, 1200, 1330, and 1715 (265 km, six hours, F$13.90). From Lautoka, they depart at 0615, 0630, 0815, 1215, and 1630. A Sunbeam express bus along Kings Road is a comfortable way to see Viti Levu's picturesque back side, though some of their buses play insipid videos. The expresses stop only at Nausori, Korovou, Ellington, Vaileka (Rakiraki), Tavua, Ba, and a few other places. If time doesn't matter, there's also a "stage" bus which leaves Suva at 0750 and Lautoka at 0835, spending nine fun-filled hours on Kings Road.

Coral Sun Fiji (tel. 672-2268) operates daily air-conditioned tourist expresses called the "Fiji Express" and "Queens Express" between Nadi and Suva via the Coral Coast resorts. These cost twice as much as the regular expresses.

There are many local buses, especially closer to Suva or Lautoka, some with big open windows with roll-down canvas covers which give you a panoramic view of Viti Levu. The local buses often show up late, but the long-distance buses are usually right on time. Bus service on Vanua Levu and Taveuni is also good but there are no buses on Kadavu and most outer islands. In rural areas, passenger trucks called "carriers" charge set rates to and from interior villages.

Running Taxis

Shared "running" taxis and minibuses also shuttle back and forth between Suva, Nadi, and Lautoka, leaving when full and charging only a few dollars more than the bus. Look for them in the markets around the bus stations. They'll often drop you exactly where you want to go; drawbacks include the less than safe driving style and lack of insurance coverage. In a speeding minibus you miss out on much of the scenery, and tourists have been killed in collisions. It's possible to hire a complete taxi from Nadi Airport to Suva for about F$90 for the car, with brief stops along the way for photos, resort visits, etc.

Often the drivers of private or company cars and vans try to earn a little extra money by stopping to offer lifts to persons waiting for buses beside the highway. They ask the same as you'd pay on the bus but are much faster, and you'll probably be dropped off exactly where you want to go. Many locals don't understand hitchhiking, and it's probably only worth doing on remote roads where bus service is inadequate. In such places almost everyone will stop. Be aware that truck drivers who give you a lift may also expect the equivalent of bus fare; locals pay this without question. It's always appropriate to offer the bus fare.

Taxis

Fiji's taxis are plentiful and among the cheapest in the South Pacific, affordable even for low-budget backpackers. Only in Suva do the taxis have meters, and even there it's sometimes easier to ask the driver for a flat rate before you get in. If the first price you're quoted is too high you can often bargain (although bargaining is much more accepted by Indo-Fijian than by indigenous Fijian drivers). A short ride across town might cost F$2, a longer trip into a nearby suburb about F$3. Taxis parked in front of luxury hotels will expect much more than this, and it may be worth walking a short distance and flagging one down on the street. Taxis returning to their stand after dropping off other passengers will often pick up people waiting at bus stops and charge the regular bus fare (ask if it's the "returning fare"). All taxis have their home base painted on their bumpers, so it's easy to tell if it's a returning car.

Don't tip your driver; tips are neither expected nor necessary. And don't invite your driver for a drink or become overly familiar with him, as he may abuse your trust. If you're a woman taking a cab alone in the Nadi area, don't let your driver think there is any "hope" for him, or you could have problems (videos often portray Western women as promiscuous, which leads to mistaken expectations).

Car Rentals

Rental cars are expensive in Fiji, due in part to high import duties on cars and the 12.5 percent value added tax, so with public transportation as good as it is here, you should think twice before renting a car. By law, third-party public liability insurance is compulsory for rental vehicles and is included in the basic rate, but collision damage waiver (CDW) insurance is F$12–22 per day extra. Even with CDW, you're still responsible for a "nonwaivable excess," which can be as high as the first F$500–5,000 in damage to the car! Many cars on the road have no insurance, so you could end up paying for damage even if you're not responsible for the accident.

Your home driver's license is recognized for your first three months in Fiji, provided it's readable in English. Driving is on the left (as in Britain and Australia) and you should request an automatic if you might be uncomfortable shifting gears with your left hand. Seat belts must be worn in the front seat and the police are empowered to give roadside breath-analyzer tests. Around Viti Levu they occasionally employ hand-held radar. Speed limits are 50 kph in towns, 80 kph on the highway. Pedestrians have the right-of-way at crosswalks.

Unpaved roads can be very slippery, especially on inclines. Fast-moving vehicles on the gravel roads throw up small stones, which can smash your front window (and you'll have to pay the damages). As you pass oncoming cars, hold your hand against the windshield just in case. When approaching a Fijian village, slow right down, as poorly marked speed humps usually cross the road. Also beware of narrow bridges, and take care with local motorists, who sometimes stop in the middle of the road, pass on blind curves, and drive at high speeds. Cane-hauling trains have the right of way at level crossings. Driving can be an especially risky business at night. Many of the roads are atrocious (check the spare tire), although the 486-km road around Viti Levu is now fully paved except for a 62-km stretch on the northeast side, which is easily passable if you go slowly. Luckily, there isn't a lot of traffic.

If you plan on using a rental car to explore the rough country roads of Viti Levu's mountainous interior, think twice before announcing your plans to the agency, as they may suddenly decline your business. The rental contracts all contain clauses stating that the insurance coverage is not valid under such conditions. Budget and a few others have 4WD vehicles that may be driven into the interior. You're usually not allowed to take the car to another island by ferry. Tank up on Saturday, as many gas stations are closed on Sunday, and always keep the tank over half full. If you run out of gas in a rural area, small village stores sometimes sell fuel from drums. At regular gas stations expect to pay around F$1.21 a liter (or F$4.58 a US gallon).

Several international car rental chains are represented in Fiji, including Avis (www.avis.com.fj), Budget (www.budget.com.fj), Hertz, and Thrifty (www.rosiefiji.com). Local companies like Central

Rent-a-Car (www.central-rent-car.com.fj), Dove Rent-a-Car, Kenns Rent-a-Car, Khan's Rental Cars (www.khansrental.com.fj), Quality Rent-a-Car, Satellite Rentals, Sharmas Rental Cars (www.sharmasrental.com), and Tanoa Rent-a-Car are often cheaper, but check around, as prices vary. The international companies rent only new cars, while the less expensive local companies may offer secondhand vehicles. If in doubt, check the vehicle carefully before driving off. The international franchises generally provide better support should anything go wrong. Budget, Central, Kenns, and Khan's won't rent to persons under age 25, while most of the others will as long as you're over 21.

The main companies have offices in the arrivals concourse at Nadi Airport and three are also at Nausori Airport. Agencies with town offices in Suva include Avis, Budget, Central, Dove, and Thrifty. In Lautoka you'll find Central. Avis and Thrifty also have desks at or near many resort hotels on Viti Levu. In northern Fiji, Budget has offices at Labasa and Savusavu and on Taveuni, but rental cars are not available on the other islands.

Both unlimited-kilometer and per-kilometer rates are offered. **Thrifty** (tel. 672-2935), run by Rosie The Travel Service, has unlimited-kilometer prices from F$128/691 daily/weekly, which include CDW (F$700 nonwaivable) and tax. **Budget** (tel. 672-2735) charges F$141/696 for their cheapest mini including insurance (F$500 nonwaivable). **Avis** (tel. 672-2233) begins at F$125/735 including insurance (F$2,000 nonwaivable). Prices with Avis and Budget may be lower if you book ahead from abroad. Though more expensive, the international chains are more likely to deliver what they promise.

The insurance plans used by all of the local companies have high nonwaivable excess fees, which makes renting from them more risky. Also beware of companies like Satellite and Tanoa, which add the 12.5 percent tax later (most of the others include it in the quoted price). Of the local companies, **Sharmas Rental Cars** (tel. 672-1908), next to the ANZ Bank in Nadi town, offers unlimited-kilometer rates starting at F$55 (three-day minimum), plus F$12.50 a day insurance. **Khan's Rental Cars** (tel. 672-3506), in office No. 10 upstairs from arrivals at Nadi Airport, charges F$420 a week plus F$10 a day insurance (F$2,000 nonwaivable) for their cheapest car. **Central** (tel. 331-1866, fax 330-5072) in Nadi, Suva, and Lautoka charges F$105/450 a day/week including insurance (F$1,500 nonwaivable) for their cheapest car.

Many of the local car rental agencies offer substantial discounts on their brochure prices for weekly rentals, and you shouldn't hesitate to bargain, because there's lots of competition. Some companies advertise low prices with the qualification in fine print that these apply only to rentals of three days or more. Ask how many kilometers are on the speedometer and beware of vehicles above 50,000, as they may be unreliable. On a per-kilometer basis, you'll only want to use the car in the local area. Most companies charge a F$15–40 delivery fee if you don't return the vehicle to the office where you rented it, although Thrifty allows you to drop the car off at any of their numerous offices around Viti Levu at no additional charge. If you want the cheapest economy subcompact, reserve ahead. Also be prepared to put up a cash deposit on the car.

AIRPORTS
Nadi International Airport
Nadi Airport (NAN) is between Lautoka and Nadi, 22 km south of the former and eight km north of the latter. There are frequent buses to these towns until around 2200. To catch a bus to Nadi (sixty-five cents), cross the highway; buses to Lautoka (F$1.30) stop on the airport side of the road. A few express buses drop passengers right outside the international departures hall. A taxi from the airport should be F$7 to downtown Nadi or F$25 to Lautoka.

An ANZ Bank "Currency Express" window in the baggage collection area opens for all international flights. Two ATMs are there, and another is next to the 24-hour ANZ Bank branch just beyond the customs controls (Visa and MasterCard accepted). These banks deduct F$5 commission on exchanges but give rates similar to those of other banks in Fiji. A third banking counter (for changing leftover Fiji dollars back into other currencies) is in the departure lounge.

As you come out of customs, uniformed tour guides will ask you where you intend to stay, in order to direct you to a driver from that hotel. Most Nadi hotels offer free transfers (ask) but you ought to change money before going. Agents of other hotels will try to sign you up for the commission they'll earn, so be polite but defensive in dealing with them. The people selling stays at the outer island backpacker resorts can be persistent. Many of the Yasawas and Mamanuca resorts have offices in the airport concourse in front of you—the upmarket places downstairs, the backpacker resorts upstairs. The office of the Fiji Visitors Bureau (tel. 672-2433) is hidden away in office No. 20, upstairs in a back corner of the arrivals terminal.

Many travel agencies and car rental companies are also located in the arrivals arcade. The rent-a-car companies you'll find here are Avis, Budget, Europcar, Hertz, Khan's, Sharmas, Tanoa, and Thrifty. Most of the international airlines flying into Nadi have offices upstairs from this same arcade (Air Fiji represents Air Vanuatu and Polynesian Airlines).

The airport post office is across the parking lot from the arrivals terminal (ask). If you'd like to use a public telephone at the airport to check reservations, you can buy a phone card at the gift shop near the international departures gate in the departures terminal.

The left luggage service in the domestic departures area opposite the Sun Air check-in counter is open 24 hours (bicycles or surfboards F$6.15 a day, suitcases and backpacks F$4.10 a day, other smaller luggage F$3.10 a day). Most hotels around Nadi will also store luggage, often for free. A three-dog sniffer unit checks all baggage passing through NAN for drugs.

Several places to eat are in the departures terminal, including an overpriced snack bar (daily 0500–2230) near the domestic check-in counters and the air-conditioned Café International just before the international departures gate. The best coffee is served at the Republic of Cappuccino on the right near the departures gate and they also offer Internet access at F$.25 a minute. To save

money, visit the open-air food market between the guard post at the entrance to the airport compound and the bus stop on the main highway. The women there sell excellent potato rotis for only a dollar.

Duty-free shops (www.dutyfreefiji.com.fj) are found in both the departure lounge and in the arrivals area next to the baggage claim area. If you're arriving for a prebooked stay at a deluxe resort, grab two bottles of cheap Fiji rum, because drinks at the resort bars are expensive (you can usually get mix at the hotel shops). You can spend leftover Fijian currency on duty free items just before you leave Fiji (the famous Bounty Rum brewed in Lautoka costs around F$18). For security reasons, souvenir cannibal forks are not sold at the departure lounge shops, so purchase these beforehand and pack them in your suitcase.

A departure tax of F$30 in cash (in Fijian currency) is payable on all international flights, but transit passengers connecting within 12 hours and children under the age of 12 are exempt (no airport tax on domestic flights). The international departure tax is sometimes included in the ticket price, so ask your airline if you've already paid. The international departures gates are upstairs, but the nicest seating area is hidden downstairs in front of the VIP lounges below the escalator. You can stretch out and sleep on the comfortable long padded benches there if you happen to get stuck in the departure lounge overnight (but you can't see the departure gates from here, so beware of missing your flight). Nadi airport never closes. NAN's 24-hour flight arrival and departure information number is tel. 672-2777 (www.ats.com.fj).

Nausori Airport

Nausori Airport (SUV) is on the plain of the Rewa River delta, 23 km northeast of downtown Suva. Air Fiji runs an aviation academy at the airport. After Hurricane Kina in January 1993 the whole terminal was flooded by Rewa water for several days.

There's no special airport bus, and a taxi direct to/from Suva will run about F$18. You can save money by taking a taxi from the airport only as far as Nausori (four km, F$3), then a local bus to

Suva from there (19 km, with services every 10 minutes until 2100 for F$1.40). When going to the airport, catch a local bus from Suva to Nausori, then a taxi to the airport. It's also possible to catch a local bus to Nausori on the highway opposite the airport about every 15 minutes for F$.50.

The ANZ Bank branch opens for most international flights (except those to/from Tuvalu). They charge F$5 commission. Avis and Budget have car rental offices in the terminal, and a lunch counter provides light snacks. You're not allowed to sleep overnight at this airport. The departure tax is F$30 on all international flights, but no tax is levied on domestic flights. The Air Fiji information number at Nausori Airport is tel. 347-8077.

Nadi

At 10,531 square km, Viti Levu is the second largest island in the South Pacific, about the same size as the Big Island of Hawaii. This 1,323-meter-high island accounts for over half of Fiji's land area, and Nadi itself is a main gateway to the entire South Pacific region.

Nadi International Airport faces Nadi Bay in the center of an ancient volcano the west side of which has fallen away. A small airstrip existed at Nadi even before WW II, and after Pearl Harbor the Royal New Zealand Air Force began converting it into a fighter strip. The U.S. military soon arrived to construct a major air base with paved runways for transport aircraft supplying Australia and New Zealand. In the early 1960s, Nadi Airport was expanded to accommodate jet aircraft, and today the largest jumbo jets can land here. This activity has made Nadi what it is.

The area's predominantly Indo-Fijian population works the cane fields surrounding Nadi. There aren't many sandy, palm-fringed beaches on this western side of Viti Levu—for that you have to go to the nearby Mamanuca and Yasawa groups where a string of sun-drenched resorts soak up vacationers in search of a place to relax. The long gray mainland beaches near Nadi face shallow murky waters devoid of snorkeling possibilities, but okay for windsurfing and water-skiing. Fiji's tropical rainforests are on the other side of Viti Levu, not on this dry side of the island.

In recent years Nadi (NAN-di) has grown into Fiji's third largest town, with a population of 32,000. The town center's main feature is a long stretch of restaurants and shops with high-pressure sales staffs peddling luxury goods and mass-produced souvenirs. It's easily the most tourist-oriented place in Fiji, yet there's also a surprisingly colorful vegetable market and the road out to the airport is flanked by an excellent choice of places to stay. Nadi is Fiji's "border town," and to experience "real Fijian life" you have to get beyond it. Nearby Lautoka (see the separate Lautoka section later in this chapter) is far less foreigner oriented, though it doesn't have as wide a choice of activities and places to stay.

SIGHTS

To get a glimpse of the "real Fiji," visit **Nadi Market** off Hospital Road between the bus station and downtown Nadi. It's open daily except Sunday, but busiest on Saturday when city folk and villagers mix to buy and sell the week's produce. One corner of the market is assigned to *yaqona* (kava) vendors and it's possible to order a whole bowl of the rooty drink for about a dollar (the locals will gladly help you finish the bowl, so don't worry about having to drink more than you want). Some market stalls also sell a few homemade souvenirs, and there are lots of cheap places to eat in the surrounding streets (observe what others are having and order the same). It's all quite a contrast to the tourist scene along Main Street!

Nadi's only other substantial sight is the **Sri Siva Subrahmaniya Swami Temple,** off Queens Road at the south entrance to town, erected by local Hindus in 1994 after the lease on their former temple property expired. This colorful South Indian-style temple, built by craftspeople flown in from India itself, is the largest and finest of its kind in the South Pacific. Visitors may enter this consecrated place of worship, but shoes must

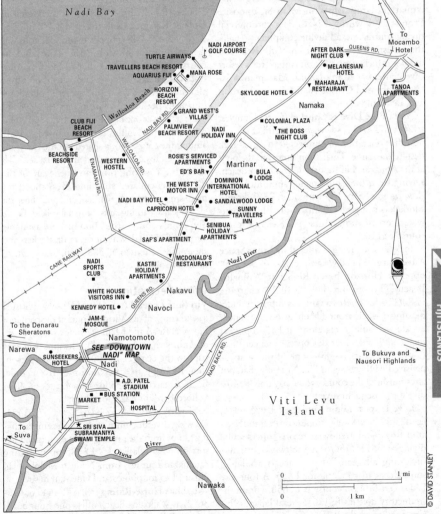

NADI

Nadi Bay

To Lautoka

TOKATOKA RESORT HOTEL

RAFFLES GATEWAY HOTEL

NADI INTERNATIONAL AIRPORT

TERMINAL BUILDING

To Mocambo Hotel

NADI AIRPORT GOLF COURSE

AFTER DARK NIGHT CLUB

QUEENS RD.

MELANESIAN HOTEL

TURTLE AIRWAYS

TRAVELLERS BEACH RESORT

AQUARIUS FIJI

MANA ROSE

SKYLODGE HOTEL

MAHARAJA RESTAURANT

TANOA APARTMENTS

HORIZON BEACH RESORT

Wailoaloa Beach

Namaka

GRAND WEST'S VILLAS

NADI BAY RD.

PALMVIEW BEACH RESORT

NADI HOLIDAY INN

COLONIAL PLAZA

THE BOSS NIGHT CLUB

CLUB FIJI BEACH RESORT

WAILOALOA RD.

ROSIE'S SERVICED APARTMENTS

Martinar

BEACHSIDE RESORT

ENAMANU RD.

WESTERN HOSTEL

ED'S BAR

BULA LODGE

THE WEST'S MOTOR INN

DOMINION INTERNATIONAL HOTEL

NADI BAY HOTEL

SANDALWOOD LODGE

CAPRICORN HOTEL

SUNNY TRAVELERS INN

SENIBUA HOLIDAY APARTMENTS

SAF'S APARTMENT

Nadi River

CANE RAILWAY

MCDONALD'S RESTAURANT

NADI SPORTS CLUB

KASTRI HOLIDAY APARTMENTS

QUEENS RD.

Nakavu

WHITE HOUSE VISITORS INN

Navoci

KENNEDY HOTEL

JAM-E MOSQUE

To the Denarau Sheratons

Namotomoto

SEE "DOWNTOWN NADI" MAP

Narewa

SUNSEEKERS HOTEL

Nadi

NADI BACK RD.

To Bukuya and Nausori Highlands

A.D. PATEL STADIUM

BUS STATION

MARKET

HOSPITAL

Viti Levu Island

To Suva

SRI SIVA SUBRAMANIYA SWAMI TEMPLE

Otuna River

Nawaka

MOON

FIJI ISLANDS

0   1 mi

0   1 km

© DAVID STANLEY

be removed at the entrance and you must cover bare shoulders or legs with a *sulu*. Smoking and photography are prohibited inside the compound (open daily 0500–2000, admission free).

SPORTS AND RECREATION
Scuba Diving and Snorkeling

Aqua-Trek (tel. 670-2413, fax 670-2412, www.aquatrekdiving.com), on Main St. opposite Prouds in downtown Nadi, is a commercial diving contractor and diving equipment retailer that doesn't offer diving from Nadi itself. You can get information here on Aqua-Trek's resort dive centers at Mana Island, Matamanoa Island, Robinson Crusoe Island, Pacific Harbor, and Taveuni.

Aqua Blue Dive & Snorkel (Carol Douglas, tel./fax 672-6111, www.aquabluefiji.com) is a new dive operation unconnected to Aqua-Trek despite the name. Their shop is next to the pool at the Aquarius Fiji Resort on Wailoaloa Beach. Diving from their nine-meter aluminum boat *Aquarium* is F$95/135 with one/two tanks and snorkelers can go for F$30. Aqua Blue's open-water certification course is F$425, a resort course F$110.

Inexpensive diving is offered by **Inner Space Adventures** (Frank Wright, tel./fax 672-3883), opposite Horizon Beach Resort at Wailoaloa Beach. They go out daily at 0900, charging F$80/110 for one/two tanks, equipment and a pickup anywhere around Nadi included. Snorkelers are welcome to tag along at F$30 pp, gear included. Frank's four-day open-water certification course costs F$380—one of the least expensive PADI courses in Fiji. Not only that, but after finishing the course, you'll pay only F$40 a dive for subsequent dives!

Dive Tropex (Eddie Jennings, tel. 675-0944, fax 675-0955, www.divetropex.com), at the Sheraton Royal and Trendwest resorts, offers scuba diving at F$115/180/610 one/two/eight tanks including all gear. When space is available, snorkelers can go along for F$55. A four-day PADI certification course is F$650. For an introductory dive it's F$170. Several Japanese instructors are on the staff.

Golf

The 18-hole, par-70 **Nadi Airport Golf Club** (tel. 672-2148) is pleasantly situated between the airport runways and the sea at Wailoaloa Beach. Green fees are F$15, plus F$20 for clubs and F$10 for a caddy. There's a bar and billiard table in the clubhouse (tourists are welcome). The course is busy with local players on Saturday, but quiet during the week.

The 18-hole, par-72 course at the **Denarau Golf & Racquet Club** (tel. 675-9710 or 675-9711, fax 675-0484) opposite the Sheratons was designed by Eiichi Motohashi. This fabulous course features bunkers shaped like a marlin, crab, starfish, and octopus, and water shots across all four par-three holes (the average golfer loses four balls per round). Green fees are F$95 for those staying at one of the Sheratons or F$100 for other mortals. Golfers are not allowed to walk around the course, but a shared electric cart is included. Clubs can be rented at F$30 a set. Call ahead for a starting time, and be aware of the dress code: collared shirt and dress shorts for men, smart casual for women, and golf shoes for all (no jeans, bathing suits, or metal spiked shoes). Ten tennis courts (four floodlit) are available here at F$15/20 day/night per hour. Rackets and shoes can be rented at F$8 each, and a can of balls is F$5.

Other Recreation

Viti Surf Legend (tel. 670-5960, www.vitisurflegend.com), above Victory Tours at the corner of Hospital Road and Main St. in downtown Nadi, organizes three-hour surfing lessons and surf trips to the coast at F$100 for the first person, then F$50 pp to a maximum of five people. Board rentals cost F$35 for a longboard, F$30 for a shortboard, or F$25 for a bodyboard.

Skydive Fiji (tel. 672-1415, fax 672-1451, www.skydivefiji.com.fj) offers tandem skydiving jumps from their base at Plantation Island Resort on Malololailai. It's F$385 pp including catamaran transfers from Nadi to Malololailai, plus F$175 for photos and videos, if desired.

Babba's Horse-Riding (tel. 672-4449 or 670-3652) at Wailoaloa Beach offers one-hour beach rides at F$20, 1.5 hours cross-country at F$25, or a two-hour combination at F$30. Longer rides can be arranged. Ask for Baba at Travelers Beach Resort.

See rugby or soccer on Saturdays at the A. D. Patel Stadium, near Nadi Bus Station. You might also see soccer on Sundays.

ACCOMMODATIONS

Most of the hotels offer free transport from the airport, which is lucky because only a couple are within walking distance of the terminal itself. In front of you as you leave customs, you'll see a group of people representing the hotels. If you know which hotel you want, tell them the name, and if a driver from that hotel is present, you should get a free ride (ask). (Be aware that the road from the north side of Nadi town across the bridge to the Sunseekers, White House, and Kennedy hotels, and the isolated roads around Wailoaloa Beach, may be unsafe, and a bus or taxi is recommended in those areas after dark, especially if you'll be carrying a backpack.)

Most repeat visitors know that many Nadi hotels, including the Raffles Gateway, Rosie's Serviced Apartments, Sandalwood Lodge, and the West's Motor Inn, regularly discount their official "rack rates" for walk-in bookings, and you could pay considerably less than the full undiscounted prices quoted herein (in this book, we provide the published rates). Rosie The Travel Service at the airport sometimes arranges specials at the Dominion International and other hotels.

Under US$25

There are three budget choices in the downtown area, two with confusingly similar names but under separate management. The seedy **Nadi Downtown Motel** (tel. 670-

0600, fax 670-1541, www.pacificvalley.com.fj), also known as the "Backpackers Inn," occupies the top floor of an office building opposite the BP service station in the center of Nadi. It's main attraction is the price: F$25/30 single/double with fan, F$35/40 with air-conditioning, both with private bath. The five-bed dormitory is F$8 pp, and basic rooms with shared bath are F$20. This place looks sleazy from the outside, but some of the rooms upstairs are okay. The adjacent Nite Life Night Club projects a steady disco beat toward the north side of the motel well into the morning. PVV Tours below the motel arranges transport to Nananu-i-Ra Island at F$25/35/45 pp for four/three/two people.

Around the corner on Koroivolu Street is the two-story, 31-room **Nadi Hotel** (tel. 670-0000,

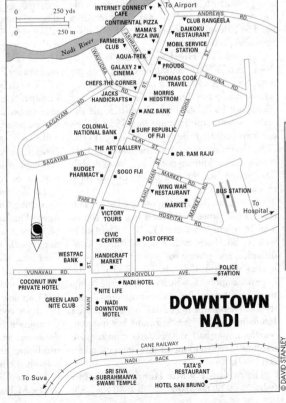

DOWNTOWN NADI

fax 670-0280, www.nadi-hotel.com). Spacious rooms with private bath begin at F$48 twin standard with fan, F$58 superior with air-conditioning, or F$15 pp in a basic 12-bed dorm. Deluxe rooms with fridge are F$68 single/double. Baggage storage is F$1. The neat courtyard with a swimming pool out back can make this a pleasant, convenient place to stay, provided there aren't a lot of rowdy local guests in the house. The standard and deluxe rooms are subjected to the same nightclub noise, so ask for a superior room in the block at the back beyond the pool. The hotel restaurant is okay for breakfast, but skip the dinner.

The two-story **Coconut Inn Private Hotel** (tel. 670-1169, fax 670-0616, coconutinn2000@ yahoo.com), 37 Vunavau St., is around the corner from the Westpac Bank. The 22 upstairs rooms with private bath begin at F$30/40 single/double (plus F$10 for air-conditioning), and downstairs is a F$11 dorm (three beds). Beware of dirty rooms without windows.

The two-story **Hotel San Bruno** (tel. 670-0444, fax 670-3067, sanbruno@connect.com.fj) is on Nadi Back Road east of the Sri Siva Subrahmaniya Swami Temple. The 13 fan-cooled rooms are F$40/50 single/double, while the seven with air-conditioning are F$50/60. The one/two-bedroom family "villas" are F$70/100 each. Dormitory accommodations are F$12 pp. A miniature swimming pool is in front of the billiard room, but the San Bruno doesn't have much atmosphere.

On Narewa Road at the north edge of Nadi town is the **Sunseekers Hotel** (tel. 670-1655). The 24 rooms here are F$33/38 single/double with fan but shared bath, F$39/44 with air-conditioning and private bath, or F$9 for a bunk in the six or 10-bed dorms. There's a bar on the large deck out back, which overlooks the swimming pool (often dry) and surrounding countryside. Despite the sign, this is not an approved Hosteling International associate, but it's quite popular among backpackers. Airport pickups are free, but to return to the airport you must take a taxi (F$7).

The two-story **White House Visitors Inn** (tel. 670-0022, fax 670-2822), is at 40 Kennedy Ave., behind Dainty Restaurant just off Queens Road, a 10-minute walk north of central Nadi. The 12 fan-equipped rooms are F$30 double with shared bath, F$33/44 single/double with private bath, or F$11 pp in the dorm. Rooms with air-conditioning cost F$5.50 extra. The beds are comfortable, and a weight-watchers' toast-and-coffee breakfast is included in the price. You can cook your own meals in the communal kitchen, and there's a tiny grocery store across the street. You'll probably find the small swimming pool too dirty to use. Baggage storage is F$1 per day (but only if you make your outer island bookings through them). Houseguests get a 15 percent discount at the adjacent Dainty Chinese Restaurant.

Half a block up Kennedy Avenue from the White House is the three-story **Kennedy Hotel** (tel. 670-2360, fax 670-2218). The 16 air-conditioned rooms with private bath, TV, and coffee-making facilities are F$60 single or double without fridge, F$70 with fridge, tax included. Deluxe two-bedroom apartments with cooking facilities are F$109. Rooms with shared bath are F$25. Beds in the four fan-cooled, 10-bed dormitory blocks cost F$10 pp, or F$15 for a bed in the four-bed air-conditioned dorm. The Kennedy is quite popular, but the cheaper rooms are small and shabby, so have a look before committing yourself. Advantages are the spacious grounds and large swimming pool, and there's a restaurant/bar on the premises.

The following listings are arranged by location along Queens Road from the airport into town. The **Kon Tiki Private Hotel** (tel. 672-2836) is in a quiet if isolated location, a 15-minute walk inland from Queens Road past the Fiji Mocambo Hotel (Votualevu bus). The 18 rooms go for F$25/35 single/double with private bath and fan, F$45 with air-conditioning, F$11 pp dormitory (four beds), plus tax. Avoid the noisy rooms near the television and bar. Camping is F$8 pp. Breakfast is included with the rooms, and you can use their kitchen. Several small stores are nearby. There's a nice swimming pool in the back yard. Call for a free airport pickup (taxi F$4).

The **Melanesian Hotel** (Hexagon Group of

Hotels, tel. 672-2438, fax 672-0425, melnesian hotl@connect.com.fj), at Namaka, has two wings separated by a swimming pool, bar, and restaurant. The 16 rooms with bath in the old wing begin at F$45/50 single/double, or F$55/60 with air conditioning. Six five-bed dorms (F$18 pp) are also available. The new **Grand Melanesian Apartment Hotel** wing right on the highway has 22 deluxe air-conditioned rooms with fridge and TV at F$78 for up to three people.

The single-story **Nadi Holiday Inn** (tel. 672-5076, www.pacificvalley.com.fj), on Queens Road just north of Martinar, has a dubious reputation (no connection with the famous Holiday Inn chain). Rooms with private facilities are F$35 single or double (plus F$10 for air-conditioning). A bar is on the premises, and there's a lot of in/out action late at night.

Across the street from the Shell service station in Martintar and above the Bounty Restaurant is **Mountainview Apartments** (tel. 672-1880, fax 672-1800) with six fan-cooled rooms with bath at F$35/40 single/double. The two air-conditioned rooms are F$45/50. It's also questionable, and is overpriced to boot.

The **Hotel Martintar** (tel. 651-1777, fax 672-0807, hotelmartintar@connect.com.fj), 22 Kennedy St. around the corner from Ed's Bar in Martintar, has three rooms with bath and fan at F$44 single or double, four air-conditioned rooms at F$55, and an air-conditioned two-bedroom flat at F$88. Fully renovated in 2002, it's a good value at these prices.

The **Sunview Motel & Hostel** (tel. 672-4994) is 300 meters down Gray Road behind the Bounty Restaurant. The seven rooms in their new two-story building are F$30/35 single/double, or F$15 pp in a six-bed dorm, with toast, coffee, and juice in the morning included. Cooking facilities are available, and it's clean, quiet, and friendly.

A new place to stay in Martintar is **Senibua Holiday Apts** (tel. 672-2574), near Wearsmart Textiles on Northern Press Road. The three units with double bed are F$40, while the four with one double and one single are F$60. All units are in a long single-story block and have air-conditioning and cooking facilities.

The 14-room **Sunny Travelers Inn** (tel. 672-5883), 67 Northern Press Road, is F$28 single or double with shared bath, F$35 with private bath, or F$10 in the five-bed dorm. Self-contained apartments with cooking facilities are F$45. It's a little noisy from the nocturnal comings and goings of certain guests and cannot be recommended.

Three-story **Saf's Apartment** (tel. 672-3988), on Queens Road just south of Martintar, has 17 rooms with bath at F$35/45 with fan/air-conditioned single or double. It's also pretty sleazy and not suitable for respectable travelers.

Kastri Holiday Apartment (tel. 672-5056), on Queens Road not far from McDonalds, only opened in 2003. The 14 air-conditioned rooms with fridge, basic cooking facilities, and bathroom are F$35 single or double. Noise levels in this prefabricated building would depend on who else is staying there.

Wailoaloa Beach (also known as New Town Beach) is for backpackers what Denarau Island is for tourists on upscale package tours. A half dozen inexpensive places to stay are near the seaplane base and golf club on the opposite side of the airport runway from the main highway, a three-km hike from the Nadi Bay Hotel. Ask for their free shuttle buses at the airport or take a taxi (F$6 from the airport or F$3 from the junction at Martintar). The Shahabud Transport bus (F$.55) to Wailoaloa New Town leaves Nadi Bus Station Monday to Saturday at 0615, 0815, 1115, 1510, and 1700 (no service on Sunday). It leaves the beach to return to town about 20 minutes after these times.

Wailoaloa is probably your best bet on the weekend, and sporting types can play a round of golf on the public course or go jogging along the beach (the swimming in the knee-deep, murky water is poor). Inner Space Adventures and Aqua Blue Dive & Snorkel are here, and horseback riding is also offered. Remain aware of your surroundings if you stroll far down the lonely beach, because assaults on tourists have occurred.

On your way to the beach you'll pass the **Western Hostel** (tel. 672-4440) on Wailoaloa Road. Rooms with shared bath here are F$45 single or double, or F$12 pp in the nine-bed dorm, continental breakfast included. The rooms are overpriced although the dorm is okay. This hostel provides communal cooking, laundry, and TV facilities. It's a little far from everything and few people stay here.

The **Horizon Beach Resort** (tel. 672-2832, fax 672-0662, www.horizonbeachfiji.com), 10 Wasawasa Road, is a large wooden two-story building just across a field from the beach. The 14 rooms with bath begin at F$35/40 single/double with fan, F$55/70 with air-conditioning. Horizon's 10-bed dormitory is F$10 pp (F$18 pp with air-conditioning) including a cup of tea and a piece of toast for breakfast. No cooking facilities are provided, but there's a medium-priced restaurant/bar and a tiny swimming pool. To use the washer/drier is F$10 a full load.

The **Tropic of Capricorn Backpackers Retreat** (tel. 672-3089, fax 672-3050, chopkins@bigpond.net.au), right next to Horizon Beach Resort at 11 Wasawasa Road, faces the sea. There's a 12-bed dorm at F$15 pp including breakfast, one four-bed room next to the swimming pool at F$60, and five self-catering rooms upstairs at F$30/50 single/double. This smart new place run by Mama Selena opened in 2001.

A hundred meters inland from Horizon is the friendly, two-story **New Town Beach Motel** (tel. 672-3339 or 672-3420, fax 672-0087), 5 Wasawasa Road. The seven clean rooms with fan are F$39 single or double, $50 triple (or F$14 pp in the five-bed dorm), plus tax. There's no cooking, but a huge dinner can be ordered at F$8. A nice protected swimming pool is in the back yard.

Edgewater Backpackers Accommodation (tel. 672-5868, edgewater@connect.com.fj), 33 Wasawasa Road, on the opposite side of Inner Space Adventures from Horizon, is an older wooden building with an eight-bed dorm at F$12 pp, one single at F$25, and a family room for F$40. Camping space in their fenced yard is F$6 pp—one of the only places around Nadi where you can camp!

A few minutes walk north along the beach from the Aquarius Fiji Resort is **Travelers Beach Resort** (tel. 672-3322, fax 672-0026, beachvilla@connect.com.fj). The 12 fan-cooled standard rooms with private bath are F$33/40 single/double, the eight air-conditioned rooms F$40/55,

the two air-conditioned beachfront rooms F$70 single or double, and the 13 villas with kitchenette F$66/77 fan/air-conditioned double (or F$99 for up to four). Four four-bed dorms are available at F$11 pp. The villas are tightly packed in a compound a block back from the beach. There's an overpriced restaurant/bar and a swimming pool, but many of the other facilities listed in their brochure seem to have vanished. Somehow this place has an unpleasant air and you're better off staying elsewhere.

Opposite the Travelers Beach Resort villas is a large modern house called **Mana Rose Apartments** (tel. 672-3333, fax 672-0552). Ratu Kini Bokoniqiwa uses this place to accommodate backpackers on their way to his hostel on Mana Island. The three six-bed air-conditioned dorms are F$15 pp including breakfast, private rooms F$40/45 single/double, and there's a plush lounge downstairs. If you're not on your way to Mana, you'll probably find the transient atmosphere unappealing.

US$25–50

The medium-priced selections that follow are highly competitive and most offer walk-in specials that reduce the quoted rack rates by a third. **Rosie's Deluxe Serviced Apartments** (tel. 672-2755, fax 672-2607, www.rosiefiji.com), in Martintar near Ed's Bar, offers studio apartments accommodating four at F$45/69 walk-in/rack rate, one-bedrooms for up to five at F$68/92, and two-bedrooms for up to eight at F$80/123. All eight air-conditioned units have cooking facilities, fridge, and private balcony. You may use the communal washer and drier for free. Martintar Bakery next door sells bread, muffins, and newspapers. Rosie's is used mostly by people in transit, and there's no swimming pool. The Rosie The Travel Service office at the airport books this place and arranges free airport transfers in both directions at any time of night or day.

Bula Lodge (Karl Hofman, tel. 672-5909, info@bulalodge.com), 49 McElrath Cres. off Gray Road behind the Bounty Restaurant in Martintar (ask directions), has four double rooms with shared bath at F$50 pp. This upscale homestay has a lounge where you can listen to music in the evening or chat with other visiting couples. It's not your usual backpacker hangout.

Sandalwood Lodge (Ana and John Birch, tel. 672-2044, fax 672-0103, sandalwood@connect.com.fj), 250 meters inland on Ragg Street behind the Dominion International Hotel, has 33 air-conditioned rooms with bath, Sky TV, fridge, and cooking facilities at F$66/74/82 single/double/triple, plus tax. Two of the two-story blocks were built in 1992 and a third was added in 2001 (all rooms face the swimming pool). Sandalwood caters to those in search of a quiet, safe, thoroughly respectable place to stay.

The West's Motor Inn (tel. 672-0044, fax 672-0071), also near the Dominion International, is another good choice. The 62 air-conditioned rooms with private bath and fridge begin at F$60 single or double standard (or F$75 for a larger deluxe room). The name really doesn't do justice to this pleasant two-story resort hotel with its courtyard swimming pool, piano bar, restaurant, conference room, secretarial services, and UTC tour desk. The West's Motor Inn is considered Nadi's most gay-friendly hotel, although you probably wouldn't have noticed if you weren't told. It's owned by Hexagon Hotels.

The **Capricorn International Hotel** (tel. 672-0088, fax 672-0522, www.capricorn-hotels-fiji.com), beside The West's Motor Inn, consists of two-story blocks surrounding a swimming pool. The 62 small air-conditioned rooms with fridge begin at F$85 single or double. The 17-bed dorm here is F$20 pp. Cooking facilities are not provided, but there's a restaurant/bar on the premises. UTC Tours has a desk here.

Next door to the Capricorn is **Traveler's Holiday Apartments** (tel. 672-4675), a new three-story hotel containing 14 rooms with bath starting at F$50 double (F$10 extra for air-conditioning). Beware of a misleading sign outside advertising super cheap rooms that have yet to be built!

A few hundred meters down Wailoaloa Road off the main highway is the **Nadi Bay Hotel** (tel. 672-3599, fax 672-0092, www.fijinadibayhotel.com), a two-story concrete edifice enclosing a swimming pool. The 25 rooms are F$48/56 single/double with fan, F$72/88 with private bath and air conditioning. An air-conditioned apartment with cooking facilities is F$85/110 single/double. Beds in the 10/four-bed dorms are F$18/22 pp. Other features include a congenial bar and an inexpensive restaurant. Breakfast is included with the rooms but not in the dorm. The Nadi Bay is run by an old Fiji hand named Errol Fifer, who built upscale resorts on Mana and Malolo islands—an interesting person to meet. The Nadi Bay Hotel is something of a staging point for young tourists on "Feejee Experience" packages or headed for the low-budget beach resorts in the Yasawas. It's the sort of place where you're likely to see bored backpackers lounging by the pool reading Lonely Planet, or posing in the restaurant and bar. The airport flight path passes right above the Nadi Bay.

Right on Wailoaloa Beach between the Tropic of Capricorn Backpackers Retreat and Travelers Beach Resort is the new **Aquarius Fiji Resort** (Louise and Terry Buckley, tel. 672-6000, tblp fiji@connect.com.fj). This large mansion contains four garden view rooms at F$75 double, and four ocean view rooms at F$85. Third persons pay F$23. Otherwise there are two two-bed dorms at F$26 pp, plus six- and 10-bed dorms at F$23 pp. Aquarius has a swimming pool right on the beach with the Aqua Blue dive shop to one side. It's a trendy place to stay at the moment.

On Wailoaloa Beach, a kilometer southwest of the places near the golf course, is **Club Fiji Beach Resort** (tel. 670-2189, fax 672-2324, www.clubfiji-resort.com). It's three km off Queens Road from McDonald's (F$3 one way by taxi). The 24 thatched duplex bungalows, all with veranda, private bath, solar hot water, and fridge, are priced according to location: F$68 single or double for a garden unit, F$90 ocean view, or F$124 on the beach. The eight air-conditioned so-called "beachfront villas" in a two-story building are strangely overpriced at F$152/167 double/triple. One duplex has been converted into a pair of 12-bunk dormitories at F$14 pp. The atmosphere is friendly and relaxed, and you'll meet other travelers at the bar. Tea- and coffee-making facilities are provided, but there's no cooking, and main plates at the

Club's restaurant are overpriced at F$15–24. Special evening events include the *lovo* on Thursday (F$25) and the beach barbecue on Sunday night (F$15–22). Horseback riding is F$20 an hour, the Hobie Cat is F$40 an hour, and windsurfing and paddle boats are complimentary. The day tour to Natadola Beach costs F$45 with lunch. At low tide the beach resembles a tidal flat, but there's a small clean swimming pool, and the location is lovely.

Also very good is the **Beachside Resort** (tel. 670-3488, fax 670-3688, www.beachsideresort fiji.com), next to Club Fiji at Wailoaloa. The 15 clean air-conditioned rooms in the main building are F$70/90 double or triple downstairs/upstairs. The rooms have a fridge and tea/coffee, but no cooking facilities. Adjacent to the main building are two smaller studios at F$45 double and four mountainview rooms with fan at F$55 single or double. These units are duplexes with connecting doors—convenient for families and small groups. There's an attractive dining room serving breakfast at F$12.50, while the blackboard menu lists dinner dishes priced F$15–18. Despite the name, the Beachside isn't right on the beach, although it does have a pleasant swimming pool.

US$50–100

Once again, the listings that follow are arranged starting from the airport and heading south toward town. The **Tokatoka Resort Hotel** (Hexagon Group of Hotels, tel. 672-0222, fax 672-0400, www.tokatoka.com.fj), a short walk north on Queens Road from the airport terminal, caters to families with young children by offering 116 air-conditioned villas and rooms with cooking facilities, mini-fridge, and video beginning at F$144/159 single/double. Eight rooms for guests with disabilities are available. The restaurant serves a buffet dinner Sunday (F$20) and a buffet lunch Saturday and Sunday (F$15). Happy hour by the swimming pool is from 1700–1900 daily. The large designer swimming pool with a water slide is usually full of noisy kids. A Jack's Handicrafts outlet is on the premises.

The two-story, colonial-style **Raffles Gateway Hotel** (tel. 672-2444, fax 672-0620, www .rafflesgateway.com), just across the highway

from the airport, is within easy walking distance of the terminal. Its 92 air-conditioned rooms are officially F$117 single or double (though 22 standard rooms without TVs are offered at a discount). The Gateway's poolside bar is worth checking out if you're stuck at the airport waiting for a flight. A Rosie Travel desk is here.

People on brief prepaid stopovers in Fiji are often accommodated at one of three hotels off Votualevu Road, a couple of kilometers inland from the airport (take a taxi). The closest to the terminal is **Tanoa Apartments** (tel. 672-3685, fax 672-1193, www.tanoahotels.com), on a hilltop overlooking the surrounding countryside. The 20 self-catering apartments begin at F$169 (weekly and monthly rates available). Local rate reductions are possible for walk-in bookings. Facilities include a swimming pool, tennis courts, hot tub, and sauna. First opened in 1965, this property was the forerunner of today's locally owned Tanoa hotel chain.

A few hundred meters inland from Tanoa Apartments is the Malaysian-owned **Fiji Mocambo Hotel** (tel. 672-2000, fax 672-0324, www.shangri-la.com), a sprawling two-story hotel with mountain views from the spacious grounds on Namaka Hill. The 127 air-conditioned rooms with patio or balcony and fridge begin at F$180/203 single/double including breakfast. It's overpriced unless you get a discount. A swimming pool is available, and there's a par-27, nine-hole executive golf course on the adjacent slope (free/F$11 for guests/non-guests). Lots of in-house entertainment is offered, including a *meke* on Mondays. A live band plays in the Marau Lounge Friday and Saturday from 2030. A Rosie Tours desk is here.

Across the street from the Fiji Mocambo is the two-story **Tanoa International Hotel** (tel. 672-0277, fax 672-0191, www.tanoahotels.com), formerly the Nadi Travelodge Hotel. It's now the flagship of the Tanoa hotel chain, owned by local businessman Yanktesh Permal Reddy. The 133 superior air-conditioned rooms with fridge start at F$190 single or double and children under 16 may stay free. Walk-in local rate discounts are possible. They also have a half-price day-use rate, which gives you a room from noon until midnight if you're leaving in the middle of the night (airport transfers are free). A swimming pool, fitness center, floodlit tennis courts, and a UTC tour desk are on the premises. The Tanoa International is a cut above the Fiji Mocambo, but no nonhotel shops or restaurants are within walking distance of either hotel.

Several kilometers southwest of the airport on Queens Road is **Nomad's Skylodge Fiji** (tel. 672-2200, fax 672-4330, www.nomadsskylodge .com.fj), which was constructed in the early 1960s while Nadi Airport was being expanded to take jet aircraft. Airline crews on layovers originally stayed here, and in 2004 the Skylodge was purchased from Tanoa Hotels by the Nomads chain and backpackers replaced business travelers as the target clientel. The 53 air-conditioned units vary considerably, from eight-bed dormitories at F$20 pp to F$110 double for a deluxe room. Try to get into one of the four-unit clusters well-spaced among the greenery, rather than a smaller room in the main building or near the busy highway. A swimming pool, internet cafe, and tour desk are on the grounds, and party-style entertainment is laid on. Feejee Experience groups and backpackers bound for the Yasawa Islands often stay here. Airport transfers are free.

The **Dominion International Hotel** (tel. 672-2255, fax 672-0187, www.dominion-inter national.com), at Martintar halfway between the airport and town, is one of Nadi's nicest large hotels. This appealing three-story building was built in 1973, and they've done their best to keep the place up. The 85 air-conditioned rooms with balcony or terrace are F$125/130/140 single/double/triple, plus F$22 extra if you want a "deluxe" with a TV and a bathtub instead of a "shower. The 40 percent discount late checkout rate allows you to keep your room until 2200. If you stay six nights, the seventh is free. Lots of well-shaded tables and chairs surround the swimming pool, and the nearby hotel bar has a happy hour 1700–1900 daily. On Saturday night you'll be treated to a *meke* (F$22). There's a Rosie Travel Service desk at the Dominion, a barber shop/beauty salon, and a taxi stand. The hotel bottle shop facing the highway is open Monday–Friday 1100–2100,

Saturday 1100–1400 and 1600–2100, should you wish to stock your fridge. The tennis court is free for guests (day use only).

Grand West's Villas (tel. 672-4833, fax 672-5015, grandwestvillas@connect.com.fj), near Wailoaloa Beach between Nadi Bay Road and the airport runway, was built by the Hexagon Group of Hotels in 2001. The 20 luxurious, two-story townhouses in several long blocks are F$125/145 double/triple. These spacious, self-catering apartments are a good value for the money and a small grocery store is on the premises, but unfortunately the location is poor, as the beach is some distance away. The new **Palmview Beach Resort** next door shares the same disadvantage.

Ocean's Edge (Penny and Steve Ellis, tel. 651-1560, fax 670-7222, www.oceansedge.org) is beside the river at Fantasy Estates, just beyond the Beachside Resort at Wailoaloa. The four duplex rooms are F$99 single or double, continental breakfast included. Lunch and dinner can be ordered at around F$10 for lunch or F$12–20 for dinner mains. What is special here is the fitness and health spa with a studio providing skin and body treatments beginning at F$9.50 (F$97 for the three-hour pamper package). Steam and sauna rooms, a 20-meter exercise pool, and a gym are on the premises.

US$250 and up

Nadi's big transnational resorts, the Sheraton Royal and the Sheraton Fiji, are on Denarau Island (www.denarau.com) opposite Yakuilau Island, seven kilometers west of the bridge on the north side of Nadi town. It's a 15-minute drive from the airport. The murky waters lapping the gray sands of Sheraton shores aren't the best for swimming, but two pontoons have been anchored in deeper water. There's no point in snorkeling here; windsurfing, water-skiing, and sailing are better choices as activities. If you came to Fiji mainly for the beach, you should skip Denarau entirely and head for a resort in the Mamanuca Islands.

Sidestepping the Waikiki syndrome, neither Sheraton is taller than the surrounding palms, though the manicured affluence has a dull

Hawaiian neighbor-island feel. In 1993, a F$15-million championship golf course opened on the site of a former mangrove swamp adjacent to the resort, and in 1996 ITT-Sheraton bought both resorts from Japanese interests that had controlled them since 1988. Two-thirds of the hotel staff and all of the taxi drivers based here belong to the land-owning clan. Plans for additional resort development in this area by Hilton and Accor/Novotel were put on hold after the May 2000 coup, but are now being revived.

Almost all of the tourists staying at the Denarau resorts arrive on package tours, and they pay less than the rack rates quoted below. These hotels are rather isolated, and the hotel restaurants are pricey, so you should take the meal package if you intend to spend most of your time here. Bring insect repellent unless you want to be on the menu yourself, and have something warm to wear in your room, as the air-conditioning is strong enough to give you pneumonia in this climate.

The **Sheraton Royal Denarau Resort** (tel. 675-0000, fax 675-0259, www.sheraton.com/denarauresort) opened in 1975 as The Regent of Fiji. This sprawling series of two-story clusters with traditional Fijian touches contains 273 spacious rooms (from F$415 plus tax single or double including breakfast) between the golf course and beach. Facilities include an impressive lobby with shops to one side, a thatched pool bar you can swim right up to, and 10 floodlit tennis courts.

The Sheraton Royal's neighbor to the south, the modern-style **Sheraton Fiji Resort** (tel. 675-0777, fax 675-0818, www.sheraton.com/fiji), has 292 rooms that begin at F$575 single or double plus tax but including a buffet breakfast and nonmotorized sports. For the presidential suite it's F$1,145. This US$60-million, two-story hotel opened in 1987, complete with a 16-shop arcade and an 800-seat ballroom. Outstanding among the hotel boutiques is Michoutouchkine Creations, with hand-decorated clothing by two of the Pacific's most famous artists, and the Pacific Art Shop (www.pacificart.com.fj), with local paintings. Avis Rent-a-Car, UTC Tours, and the Westpac Bank all have counters at the Sheraton Fiji.

Between the two Sheratons and opposite the golf club is a cluster of two-story buildings called the **Sheraton Denarau Villas** (tel. 675-0777, fax 675-0818, www.sheraton.com/denarau villas), which opened in 1999. The 82 condos with one, two, or three bedrooms have kitchenettes, washer/drier, TV, and lounge, starting at F$781 plus tax for a family of two adults and two children, breakfast included. The swimming pool and bar face the beach.

Another new development, a bit south of the Sheraton Fiji Resort, is the **Trendwest Resort** (tel. 675-0442, fax 675-0441, www.trendwest.com). It features a series of two- and three-story blocks between the reception and a large beachside pool (which compensates for the lousy beach). Most of the 138 spacious self-catering apartments in this "vacation ownership resort" have been sold to individual buyers under a timeshare arrangement with WorldMark. All stays are prebooked and walk-in guests are not accepted. The Seafront Restaurant near the pool is part of the Chefs chain. There's a Rosie Tours desk at the reception. Dive Tropex runs the scuba concession here.

A local bus marked "Westbus" operates between Nadi and the Sheratons about every hour (F$.55). It leaves Nadi Bus Station Monday–Saturday at 0700, 0800, 0830, 0930, 1015, 1100, 1215, 1300, 1430, 1545, 1700, and 1800, Sunday at 0700, 0830, 0930, 1300, 1430, and 1700. For the departure times from the Sheratons, add about 25 minutes to these times (which could change). Resort receptionists sometimes pretend not to know about this bus.

The taxis parked in front of the hotels ask a firm F$10 to/from Nadi town or F$22 to the airport. Walk down the road a short distance and stop any returning taxi headed for Nadi—most will take you for F$3. If your travel agent booked you into any of these resorts, you'll be wrapped in North American security and sheltered from the real Fiji.

FOOD

Downtown Restaurants

Several places along Sahu Khan St. near the market serve a good cheap breakfast of coffee and egg sandwiches. The **Wing Wah Restaurant** is typical of these.

A real find if you like Indian food is **Tata's Restaurant** (tel. 670-0502; weekdays 0900–2100, Sat. 0900–1700), on Nadi Back Road between the Siva Temple and the Hotel San Bruno. The vegetable curries are a great value at F$3, and other inexpensive dishes are listed on a blackboard. Though this place is surrounded by automotive workshops, the seating is pleasantly outside on a terrace.

Chopsticks Restaurant (tel. 670-0178; daily 0900–1500/1800–2200), upstairs from the Bank of Baroda on Main Street, offers a large selection of Chinese dishes, curries, and seafood at excellent prices (entrées F$6–11). A second Chopsticks location (tel. 672-1788) is near Morris Hedstrom at Namaka toward the airport. Plenty of local Asians eat here—a recommendation.

Package tour buses often park in front of **Chefs The Corner** (Mon.–Sat. 0900–2130), Sagayam Road and Main Street opposite Morris Hedstrom. This rather expensive self-service restaurant (entrées F$6–7) does have some of the best-selling ice cream in town (F$2–4). Just down Sangayam Road are **Chefs The Edge** (Mon.–Sat. 0900–2200) and **Chefs The Restaurant** (tel. 670-3131; Mon.–Sat. 1100–1400, 1800–2200, www.chefs.com.fj), both run by former Sheraton chef Eugene Gomes (and owned by Jack's Handicrafts). At dinner the seafood and meat entrées average F$38, or you can order something from the grill. It's international dining at its finest.

Two pizza places are opposite the Mobil service station on Main Street at the north end of Nadi town. **Mama's Pizza Inn** (tel. 670-0221; daily 1000–2300) serves pizzas at F$6–23. Mama's has a second location in Colonial Plaza halfway out toward the airport. A better bet is **Continental Cakes & Pizza** (tel. 670-3595; daily 0900 until late), just down from Mama's, which has three sizes of pizza from F$7–22, plus deli rolls for F$3.50, and delicious cakes for F$2.50 and up. Their coffee is about the best in town, and the clean washrooms are a relief. The German owner Dietmar Luecke makes sure everything is just right.

The **Daikoku Japanese Restaurant** (tel. 670-3622; Mon.–Sat. 1130–1400, 1800–2200, Sun. 1800–2100), facing the bridge at the north end of Nadi, is the place to splurge on *teppan-yaki* dishes (F$20–48) cooked right at your table. Ask for the special seafood sauce.

Denarau Marina Restaurant

Cardo's Steakhouse & Bar (tel. 675-0900; daily 1000–2300), at the Denarau Marina, offers charbroiled steaks of 250, 300, or 400 grams for F$19–35. Other meals from prawns to pizza cost F$9–29. You'll have a good view of Nadi's bustling tourist port from their terrace. It's an okay place to eat out if you're staying at the Sheraton, a 15-minute walk away.

Restaurants Toward the Airport

Poon's Restaurant (tel. 672-5396), also called the Jun Sang Seafood Restaurant, beside a textile factory on Northern Press Road just east off Queens Road in Martintar, offers filling meals at reasonable prices. Ordinary Chinese dishes are F$3–10, special Chinese dishes F$7–14, and European dishes F$5–11. Complete Cantonese meals are F$35/62 for two/four people.

RJ's for Ribs (Hans Kehrli, tel. 672-2900; Tues.–Sun. 1800–2300), in the Millennium Center opposite the Dominion International Hotel, has a sister establishment in Beverly Hills, California. Pork barbecue ribs run F$19, cordon bleu F$27, and a skewer of garlic prawns F$29 (all meals include the salad bar). The Skytop Bar on the roof prepares a Mongolian barbecue for F$6.

The **Bounty Restaurant** (Veronika and Brian Smith, tel. 672-0840), a bit north and across the highway from RJ's, has Chinese or Fijian dishes and hamburgers for lunch, steaks and seafood for dinner. Lunch specials here average F$8, while dinner plates are F$16–28. There's also a popular tourist bar (happy hour 1700–1900).

Rik's Café (tel. 672-2110; daily 0700–2200), across the street from the Bounty Restaurant, offers things like breakfast (F$6.50), sandwiches (F$4), fish burgers (F$4.50), and fish and chips (F$6). Beer is not sold.

The **Masala Restaurant** (tel. 672-2275; Mon.–Sat. 0730–2030), opposite Rik's Café, serves Indian dishes from the warmer at F$6–7.

FIJI ISLANDS

The **Ed's Bar** complex in Martintar is probably the top place to eat out in Nadi. It's fun to dine on appetizers at the bar, such as a plate of six big, spicy barbecued chicken wings for F$6. Otherwise, go through the connecting door into the adjacent **West Coast Café** (Mon.–Sat. 1730–2300) for fried fish or steak and eggs at F$12. The upscale dining room called the **Seafood Grill** (tel. 672-4650; daily 1730–2300) beyond the bar serves dishes like *kokoda* (F$7), grilled fish (F$19), pork chops (F$20), seafood hot combo (F$28), steaks, and lobster tails in a gentile setting.

The cheapest place to eat in Martintar is **Millennium Fast Food** (tel. 672-5548; daily 0700–1800), at the Shell service station across the street from the Bounty Restaurant. Taxi drivers often drop in here and order meals from what's in the warmer on the counter.

The **Maharaja Restaurant** (tel. 672-2962; Mon.–Sat. 0900–2200, Sun. 1700–2200), out near the Skylodge Hotel, is popular with flight crews who come for the spicy Indian curries, tandoori dishes, and local seafood (main dishes F$10–18). It's one of Fiji's finest Indian restaurants (dinner is generally better than lunch here).

ENTERTAINMENT AND SHOPPING

Nadi has two movie houses: **Galaxy 2 Cinema** (tel. 670-0176), on Ashram Road between Tappoo and the Farmers Club; and **Novelty Cinema** (tel. 670-0155), upstairs from the mall at the Nadi Civic Center, not far from the post office. They usually show Indian films in Hindi.

Bars and Clubs

The **Nadi Farmers Club** (tel. 670-0415; Mon.–Thurs. 1000–2200, Fri. and Sat. 1000–2300, Sun. 0900–2100), just up Ashram Road from the Mobil station in Nadi town, is a male drinking place where tourists are welcome. The club's restaurant at back of the building serves Indian curries in the F$4–7 price range.

Nite Life (tel. 670-0000), next to the Nadi Hotel, has a live rock band 2100–0100 on Friday and Saturday nights (Tues.–Thurs. recorded music). It's not a tourist scene, so be prepared. Locals call it "the zoo."

Another rough place is **Green Land Nite Club** (Aiyaz Khan, tel. 670-7449; Mon.–Sat. 1800–0100, admission free), 38 Main St. opposite the Nadi Downtown Motel.

Club Rangeela (Moh'd Kaiyum, tel. 670-7171; Thurs.–Sat. 2030–0100, admission F$5), on Andrews Road at the north end of town, caters mostly to Indo-Fijians.

Better than any of the above is **Ed's Bar** (tel. 672-4650), a little north of the Dominion International Hotel in Martintar. You'll enjoy chatting with the friendly staff and meeting the trendy locals and surfers who hang out here. Happy hour is 1730–2000 daily. It's a colorful spot you'll want to visit again.

The Boss Night Club (Wed.–Sat. 1830–0100, admission F$5), in an industrial area behind Colonial Plaza off the road to the airport, is popular among Nadi's Indo-Fijian population. When guest acts like Black Rose appear here, the house is really packed. Drinks are expensive.

After Dark Night Club (daily 2000–0100), above Chopsticks Restaurant at Namaka, just northeast of Morris Hedstrom and not far from the Melanesian Hotel, hosts a mostly indigenous Fijian crowd. They play recorded new release music. You may be viewed as a source of beer by some of the other clients here.

Cultural Shows for Visitors

The **Sheraton Fiji** (tel. 675-0777) has a *meke* and *magiti* (feast) Saturday at 1800 (F$49). Wednesday at 2000 Fijian firewalking comes with the *meke* and a F$12 fee is charged.

You can also enjoy a barbecue and *meke* at the **Dominion International Hotel** (tel. 672-2255) on Saturday (F$22). Mondays the **Fiji Mocambo Hotel** (tel. 672-2000) has a *lovo* feast (F$35).

Shopping

Most shops in Nadi are closed on Sunday. The **Nadi Handicraft Market,** opposite the Nadi Hotel just off Main Street, provides you with the opportunity to buy directly from the handicraft's producers. Several large curio emporia are along Main Street, including **Jack's Handicrafts** (tel.

670-0744, www.jacksfiji.com), opposite Morris Hedstrom. Visit a few of these before going to the market, to get an idea what's available and how much your preferred items should cost.

The Art Gallery (Yogesh Gokal, tel. 670-0722; weekdays 0900–1730, Sat. 0900–1500), 220 Main St. at Sagayam Road, has ties with the Oceania Center for Art and Culture at the University of the South Pacific in Suva. Its shows change monthly. Check out the compact discs (F$40) of panpipe music here.

The Surf Republic of Fiji (tel. 670-5666), Main and Clay Streets, sells trendy resort and swim wear. Don't miss the small art gallery with carefully selected artworks from Fiji, Indonesia, and Papua New Guinea to one side of the shop. The upscale coffee and ice cream bar here is also nice.

Prouds and Tappoo on Main Street sell the type of shiny luxury goods usually seen in airport duty-free shops. **Sogo Fiji** (tel. 670-1614) nearby is the place to pick up tropical clothing and beachwear. Just beware of the friendly handshake in Nadi, for you may find yourself buying something you neither care for nor desire. Lots of visitors get conned in Nadi.

If you have an interest in world literature, you can purchase books on yoga and Indian classics at the **Sri Ramakrishna Ashram** (tel. 670-2786; Mon.–Fri. 0800–1300 and 1400–1700, Sat. 0800–1230), across the street from the Farmers Club. There's a prayer session in the Ashram on Sunday morning, followed by a vegetarian feast.

INFORMATION

The Fiji Visitors Bureau office (tel. 672-2433, fax 672-0141) is well hidden in office No. 20 upstairs in the arrivals concourse at the airport. There's no official tourist information office in downtown Nadi, and the travel agencies masquerading as such give biased information.

The Nadi Town Council Library (tel. 670-0133, ext. 126; Mon.–Fri. 0900–1700, Sat. 0900–1300) is upstairs in the mall at the Nadi Civic Center on Main Street.

Travel Agents

Rosie The Travel Service (tel. 672-2935, www .rosiefiji.com), at Nadi Airport and opposite the Nadi Handicraft Market in town, is an in-bound tour operator that books somewhat upmarket tours, activities, and accommodations. They'll often give you a discount on their day tours and trekking if you book directly with them. Adventure Fiji (tel. 672-5598), two offices down from Rosie at the airport, is a branch of the same company specifically oriented toward backpackers.

The United Touring Company (tel. 672-2811), at the airport and at several hotels, and Coral Sun Fiji (tel. 672-2268, reservations@ csf.com.fj) at the airport are similar to Rosie and quite reliable.

Tourist Transport Fiji (tel. 672-0455, fax 672-0184), next to the washrooms in the arrivals area at Nadi Airport, handles the "Feejee Experience" backpacker bus tours around Viti Levu. They should have information on the Mount Batilamu Trek in Koroyanitu National Heritage Park and on the Abaca day tours.

Many smaller travel agencies upstairs from the arrivals concourse at Nadi Airport book budget resorts in the Yasawa Islands and elsewhere around Fiji. For example, there's Rabua's Travel Agency (tel. 672-1377 or 672-3234) in office No. 23. The friendly manager Ulaiasi "Rambo" Rabua represents Wayalailai Resort on Wayasewa (his home island) and most other offshore backpacker resorts. Louise Blake and Loma at Island Travel Tours (tel. 672-4033 or 672-5930, fax 672-5753, www.travellingfiji.com), in office No. 14 upstairs, Sunset Tours (Poni Natadra, tel. 672-0266), and Western Travel Services (tel. 672-4440), in office No. 4, do the same. Among the backpacker resorts with offices of their own upstairs at the airport are Ratu Kini of Mana Island in office No. 26, David's Place of Tavewa Island in office No. 31, and Dive Trek Wayasewa in office No. 23. The Turtle Island office (tel. 672-2921), downstairs in the arrivals terminal, handles Oarsman's and Safe Landing resorts.

The largest backpacker-oriented travel agency is Victory Tours (tel. 670-0243, fax 670-2746; daily 0730–2000, www.victory.com.fj) with an office at the corner of Main Street and Hospital road in downtown Nadi. Their signpost reads Tourist Information Center, but this is a purely commercial operation. Victory sells a variety of 4WD and trekking "inland safari" excursions into the Nausori Highlands, and books low-budget beach resorts on Mana, Malolo, Tavewa, and Waya islands. Their prices are not fixed and you may feel hustled here.

Pacific Valley View Tours (tel. 670-0600), at the Nadi Downtown Motel, is similar. Better known as PVV Tours, their specialty is Nananu-i-Ra and Mana Island bookings and transfers. Prices vary here as well and bargaining might work.

You can often get a better deal by booking direct with a resort over the phone. The Nadi agents collect commissions as high as 30 percent and the resort owners are often willing to pass along some of their savings to those who call. Always keep in mind that the Nadi travel agents only promote properties that pay them commissions. If they warn you not to go somewhere, it may only be because they don't get an adequate commission from the place.

Airline Offices

Reconfirm your flight, request a seat assignment, or check the departure time by calling your airline: Aircalin (tel. 672-2145), Air Nauru (tel. 672-2795), Air New Zealand (tel. 672-2955), Air Pacific (tel. 672-0888), Air Vanuatu (tel. 672-2521), Korean Airlines (tel. 672-1043), Polynesian Airlines (tel. 672-2521), Qantas Airways (tel. 672-2880), and Solomon Airlines (tel. 672-2831). Most of these offices are at the airport (Air Fiji represents Air Vanuatu and Polynesian Airlines).

SERVICES
Money
The Westpac Bank opposite the Nadi Handicraft Market, the ANZ Bank near Morris Hedstrom, and the Colonial National Bank between these, open Monday–Thursday 0930–1500, Friday 0930–1600. The ANZ Bank charges F$5 commission whereas the others do not. If you need a Visa/MasterCard ATM, go to the ANZ Bank branches in downtown Nadi, at Namaka toward the airport, and at the airport itself. McDonald's Restaurant also has an ATM!

Money Exchange (tel. 670-3366; Mon.–Fri. 0830–1700, Sat. 0830–1300), between the ANZ Bank and Morris Hedstrom, changes cash and traveler's checks without commission at a rate comparable to the banks (and without the line).

Thomas Cook Travel (tel. 670-3110; Mon.–Fri. 0830–1700, Sat. 0830–1200), beside Prouds on Main Street, is a good source of the banknotes of other Pacific countries—convenient if you'll be flying to Australia, New Caledonia, New Zealand, Samoa, Solomon Islands, Tonga, or Vanuatu and don't want the hassle of having to change money at a strange airport upon arrival. They'll also change leftover banknotes of these countries into Fiji dollars.

Post
There are two large post offices, one next to the market in central Nadi, and another between the cargo warehouses directly across the park in front of the arrivals hall at Nadi Airport. Check both if you're expecting general delivery mail. Nadi Town Post Office near the market receives faxes sent to 670-2166. At the Nadi Airport Post Office the public fax number is 672-0467. Both post offices are open Monday–Friday 0800–1600, Saturday 0800–1200.

Internet Access
If you're headed for the Yasawa resorts, Nadi offers your last chance to check email and prices are competitive. Cybercafé (tel. 670-2226; Mon.–Fri. 0800–1730, Sat. 0800–1500), 501 Main Street between Mama's Pizza Inn and Continental Pizza in downtown Nadi, charges F$.10 a minute or F$4 an hour for Internet access in private cubicles.

The Internet Connect Café (tel. 670-3562; weekdays 0800–2000, Sat. 0800–2200, Sun. 1000–1800, www.connect.com.fj), on Main St. beside the bridge at the north end of town, charges F$5 an hour.

Noveix Microsystems (tel. 670-5100; Mon.–Sat. 0800–1830), across the street from the Nadi Civic Center, offers fast Internet access at F$.10 a minute or F$5 for two hours.

Internet service is available in room 201 at the Capricorn International Hotel (tel. 672-0088) in Martintar at F$3 for 30 minutes.

The Internet Café (tel. 672-3758; Mon.–Sat. 0800–2000, Sun. 0800–1300), opposite Rik's Café at Martintar, charges F$.10 a minute.

The Bottle Shop (tel. 672-4650; weekdays 0800–1700, Sat. 0800–1300), next to Ed's Bar in Martintar, provides Internet access at F$2 for 10 minutes.

Immigration Office

Visa extensions can be arranged at the Immigration office (tel. 672-2263; Mon.–Fri. 0900–1300 and 1400–1430), upstairs from near the Sun Air check-in counter at Nadi Airport.

Consulates

The Canadian Consulate (tel./fax 672-1936) is at Nadi. For the Italian Honorary Consul, call Mediterranean Villas (tel. 666-4011).

Launderettes

Self-Service Launderette (tel. 670-5155; Mon.–Sat. 0900–1700), in a two-story building on Queens Road just north of the Bounty Restaurant at Martintar, charges F$6.50 to wash and dry (soap F$.50).

Prabhat Steam Laundry (tel. 672-3061; Mon.–Sat. 0800–1300 and 1400–1600), at the end of Northern Press Road beside Sunny Travelers Inn, charges F$3.50 a kilo to wash, dry, and fold your laundry. Ironing is F$2–3 a piece.

Toilets

Free public toilets are at the corner of Nadi Market closest to the post office, at the bus station, and in the Nadi Civic Center.

Health

The outpatient department at Nadi District Hospital (tel. 670-1128), inland from Nadi Bus Station, is open Monday to Thursday 0800–1630, Friday 0800–1600, and Saturday 0800–1200.

You'll save time by visiting Dr. Ram Raju (tel. 670-1375; Mon.–Fri. 0830–1630, Sat. and Sun. 0900–1230), Lodhia and Clay Streets, a family doctor specializing in travel health.

Dr. Adbul Gani (tel. 670-3776; Mon.–Fri. 0800–1700, Sat. 0800–1300) has his dental surgery downstairs in the mall at the Nadi Civic Center near the post office. (Dr. Gani is also the mayor of Nadi.)

Dr. Shyamendra Sharma (tel. 672-2288) runs the Namaka Medical Center on Queens Road near the Melanesian Hotel. After hours press the bell for service.

Budget Pharmacy (tel. 670-0064) is opposite Sogo Fiji on Main St. in town.

TRANSPORTATION

See Getting Around by Air in the Exploring the Islands chapter for information on regular Air Fiji and Sun Air flights to Malololailai and Mana islands and other parts of Fiji.

Turtle Airways (tel. 672-1888, fax 672-0095, www.turtleairways.com), next to the golf course at Wailoaloa Beach, runs a seaplane shuttle to the main Mamanuca resorts at F$134 one-way, F$268 round-trip (minimum of two passengers, baggage limited to one 15-kg suitcase plus one carry-on). Special backpacker fares to the Yasawa Islands are available at F$119 one-way (minimum of four passengers).

South Sea Cruises (tel. 675-0500, fax 675-0501, www.ssc.com.fj), owned by Fullers of New Zealand, operates a high-speed catamaran shuttle to the offshore island resorts on the 27-meter, 213-passenger *Tiger IV*. The boat leaves from Nadi's Port Denarau daily at 0900, 1215, and 1515 for Treasure (F$46 each way), Malolo (F$56), Castaway (F$56), and Mana (F$56). Connections to Matamanoa or Tokoriki via Mana are available (F$97). Interisland hops between the resorts themselves are F$41 each. Children under 16 are half price on all trips (under five free). Be prepared to wade on and off the boat in ankle deep water at all islands except Mana. If all you want is a glimpse of the lovely Mamanuca Group, a four-island, three-hour, nonstop round-trip cruise is F$56. South Sea Cruises also sends the 25-meter catamaran *Yasawa Flyer* from Nadi to the Yasawa islands daily at 0915 (turn to the Yasawa Islands section for details). Catamaran bookings can be made at any travel agency around Nadi, and bus transfers to the wharf from the main Nadi hotels are included.

Highway Transport

Nadi's bus station adjoining the market is an active place. **Pacific Transport** (tel. 670-0044) has express buses to Suva via Queens Road daily at 0720, 0750, 0900, 1300, 1640, and 1820 (188 km, four hours, F$10). The 0900 bus is the most convenient, as it begins its run at Nadi (all the others arrive from Lautoka). Five other Pacific Transport "stage" buses also operate daily to Suva (five hours). The **Sunbeam Transport** express buses to Suva at 1100 and 1200 make resort stops along the way. Collective taxis and minibuses parked in a corner of Nadi Bus Station take passengers nonstop from Nadi to Suva in three hours for F$15 pp.

Coral Sun Fiji (tel. 672-3105, reservations@ csf.com.fj) at Nadi Airport operates the air-conditioned "Fiji Express" luxury coach to Suva via the Coral Coast resorts, departing Nadi Airport at 1300 daily (F$31 to Suva). The "Queens Deluxe Coach" leaves the airport for Suva at 0730 daily (F$19), calling at all of the Coral Coast resorts.

Local buses to Lautoka (33 km), the airport, and anywhere in between pick up passengers at a bus stop on Main St. opposite Morris Hedstrom.

Unmarked white "Viti Mini" minibuses shuttle frequently between the bus stop on the highway outside Nadi Airport and Nadi town at F$.50 a ride. Collective taxis cruising the highway between the airport and Nadi do the same, taking about what you'd pay on a bus, but ask first.

For information on car rentals, turn to the Getting Around section in this chapter's Exploring the Islands section.

Local Tours

Numerous day cruises and bus tours operating in the Nadi area are advertised in free tourist brochures. Reservations can be made through Rosie The Travel Service or UTC, with several offices around Nadi. Bus transfers to/from your hotel are included in the price, though some trips are arbitrarily canceled when not enough people sign up.

The "road tours" offered by **Rosie The Travel Service** (tel. 672-2935, www.rosiefiji.com), at Nadi Airport and opposite the Nadi Handicraft

Market in town, are cheaper than those of other companies because lunch isn't included (lunch is included on all the cruises and river trips). Rosie's day trips to Suva (F$49) involve too much time on the bus, so instead go for the Sigatoka Valley/Tavuni Hill Fort (F$63 including entry fees) or Emperor Gold Mine (F$55) full-day tours. If you're looking for a half-day tour around Nadi, sign up for the four-hour Vuda Lookout/Viseisei Village/Garden of the Sleeping Giant tour, which costs F$50, including admission to the garden (the lookout and garden are not accessible on public transport). These trips only operate Monday–Saturday, but on Sunday morning Rosie offers a half-day drive to the Vuda Lookout and the Garden of the Sleeping Giant at F$44 pp. On Thursdays there's a tour to Pacific Harbor (F$92) which includes firewalking and a *meke*. Also ask about the full-day hiking tours to the Nausori Highlands (daily except Sunday, F$69), the easiest way to see this beautiful area.

The **United Touring Company** (tel. 672-2811, fax 672-0389, www.utcfiji.com), or UTC, is in the office marked "accommodation information" near the public toilets in the airport's arrivals terminal, to the left as you come out of customs. They offer the same kind of day tours as Rosie, such as a half-day Orchid Tour to Viseisei and the Garden of the Sleeping Giant at F$50. UTC can also book budget-priced beach resorts on Viti Levu, such as Saweni and Tubakula, with air-conditioned bus transfers.

Victory Tours (tel. 670-0243), also known as the "Tourist Information Center," offers "Adventure Jungle Treks" with stays in different Fijian villages at F$199/230 for one/two nights. The hiking trips offered by **Adventure Fiji,** a division of Rosie The Travel Service, are more expensive than these, but the quality is more consistent (see Hiking Tours in the Exploring the Islands chapter of the book).

Wacking Stick Adventure Tours (tel. 672-4673, www.wackingstickadventures.com) operates quality mountain bike tours to Natadola Beach (F$95) and the Sleeping Giant Mountain Range (F$125). Bikes, lunch, admissions, and Nadi hotel transfers are included.

Day tours are easily arranged with taxi drivers

© DAVID STANLEY

the catamaran *Tiger IV* at Mana Island, Mamanuca Group

around Nadi, costing around F$70 as far as Lautoka or Korotogo (three hours) or F$120 to Pacific Harbor (five hours)—worth considering if there are a few of you. The collective taxis at Nadi Bus Station can be hired for leisurely one-way tours to Suva (offer around F$100 for a five-hour ride with lots of stops). Write out a list of everything you want to see and agree on the price and time length beforehand.

Should you not wish to join an organized bus tour from Nadi, you can easily organize your own **self-guided day tour** by taking a local bus (not an express) to the Sigatoka Sand Dunes National Park visitor center on Queens Road. After a hike over the dunes, catch another bus on to Sigatoka town for lunch, some shopping and sightseeing, and perhaps a taxi visit to the Tavuni Hill Fort. Plenty of buses cover the 61 km from Sigatoka back to Nadi until late. All of this will cost you far less than the cheapest half-day tour, and you'll be able to mix freely with the locals.

Day Cruises

Food and accommodations at the Mamanuca island resorts are expensive, and a cheaper way to enjoy the islands—for a day at least—is by book-

ing a day cruise to Castaway (F$99), Malolo (F$99), or Mana (F$99) on the fast catamaran *Tiger IV,* operated by **South Sea Cruises** (tel. 675-0500, www.ssc.com.fj). These all leave from Port Denarau and the price includes transfers from most Nadi hotels, the boat trip, a buffet lunch on the island of your choice, nonmotorized sporting activities, and a day at the beach (children under 16 are half price). South Sea Cruises also has day trips to the outer Mamanuca islands (including Monuriki from *Castaway,* the Tom Hanks movie) on the two-masted schooner *Seaspray* (F$165 with lunch and drinks).

Several companies offer day cruises to imaginatively named specks of sand such as Daydream Island (tel. 670-2774), Malamala Island (tel. 670-2443), Bounty Island (tel. 672-2852 or 672-2869), and South Sea Island (tel. 675-0500) costing F$69–89, always including lunch and Nadi hotel pickups, and usually drinks and nonmotorized sporting activities as well. Children under 16 are usually half price. These trips are fine if all you want is a day at the beach, otherwise you'll find them a colossal bore. Any hotel tour desk can book them. Ask about reduced "early bird" prices, if you're willing to arrive and leave early.

M

FIJI ISLANDS

Youthful travelers will enjoy a day cruise to **Beachcomber Island** (tel. 672-3828, www.beach comberfiji.com), Fiji's unofficial Club Med for the under 35 set. Operating daily, the F$69 pp fare includes bus transfers from Nadi hotels, the return boat ride via Lautoka, and a buffet lunch. Families should consider Beachcomber, because children under 16 are half price and infants under two are free. Beachcomber has an office downstairs in the arrivals terminal at Nadi Airport, or book through any Rosie Tours or UTC desk.

Captain Cook Cruises (tel. 670-1823) runs day cruises to tiny Tivua Island on the sailing vessel *Ra Marama* for F$89 including a picnic lunch, four drinks, and non-motorized watersports. Two bungalows on Tivua host those who'd like to stay overnight at F$353/520 single/double all-inclusive. Three-hour starlight dinner cruises on the ship *City of Nadi* are F$85.

The **Oceanic Schooner Co.** (tel. 672-2455 or 672-3590, funcruises@connect.com.fj) does upscale "fun cruises" on the 30-meter schooner *Whale's Tale,* built at Suva's Whippy Shipyard in 1985. You get a champagne breakfast and gourmet lunch served aboard ship, an open bar, and sunset cocktails in the company of a limited number of fellow passengers at F$165 pp. *Whale's Tale* is a nicer vessel than the *Seaspray* mentioned above, but both cruises are good.

Several other companies run Mamanuca charters and cruises, often with the promise of dolphin encounters. Hotel receptions often display brochures from **Coral Cats** (tel. 672-5961), **Crystal Blue** (tel. 675-0950), and **Sea Fiji** (tel. 672-5961). Some of the same companies offer deep-sea fishing at around F$700/1,050 a half/full day (six anglers maximum).

The most ambitious day cruise from Nadi is aboard the 20-meter catamaran *Tamusua Explorer* to the Sawa-i-Lau Cave in the Yasawa Islands, departing Lautoka every Tuesday, Thursday, and Saturday at 0800. It's F$189 roundtrip including a buffet lunch and Nadi hotel pickups. Contact **Yasawa Island Eco Tours** (tel. 672-1658, fax 672-5208, yiet@con nect.com.fj) next to Rik's Café in Martintar, or any hotel tour desk.

Thirty-minute jet boat rides around the mouth of the Nadi River are offered by **Shotover Jet** (tel. 675-0400, fax 675-0666) about every half hour daily 0800–1600 from Port Denarau (adults F$75, children under 15 years F$35, hotel transfers included). It's fairly certain the birds and fish of this mangrove area are less thrilled by these gas-guzzling, high-impact craft than the tourists seated therein.

Flightseeing

Turtle Airways (tel. 672-1888) offers scenic flights in their Cessna floatplanes at F$190 pp for 30 minutes (minimum of two persons). **Coral Air** (tel. 672-4490, www.coralair.com) has an amphibious seaplane used mostly for flightseeing around Nadi (F$239 pp for 30 minutes, minimum of two), but also available for trips to the Sawa-i-Lau Caves and the Blue Lagoon (F$645 pp, minimum of two). **Island Hoppers** (tel. 672-0410, www.helicopters.com.fj), in a separate terminal behind the airport post office, proposes helicopter tours around Nadi and the Mamanucas starting at F$144 pp (minimum of two).

NORTH OF NADI

A popular legend invented in 1893 holds that **Viseisei village,** on the old road between Lautoka and Nadi, was the first settlement in Fiji. It's told how the early Fijians, led by Chiefs Lutunasobasoba and Degei, came from the west, landing their great canoe, the *Kaunitoni,* at Vuda Point, where the oil tanks are now. A Centennial Memorial (1835–1935) in front of the church commemorates the arrival of the first Methodist missionaries in Fiji, and opposite the memorial is a traditional Fijian *bure*—the official residence of Tui Vuda. Fiji's current president, Ratu Josefa Iloilo, holder of the Tui Vuda title, lives in the green-roofed house behind this central *bure.*

Near the back of the church is another monument topped by a giant war club, the burial place of the village's chiefly family. The late Dr. Timoci Bavadra, the prime minister of Fiji deposed during the Rabuka coup in 1987, hailed from Viseisei and is interred here. Dr. Bavadra's traditional-style home faces the main road near the church. His son presently lives there, and with his permission you'll be allowed to enter to see the photos hanging on the walls.

All of the above is only a few minutes' walk from the bus stop, but you're expected to have someone accompany you through the village. Most visitors arrive on sightseeing tours, and if you come on your own, you should ask permission to visit of anyone you meet at the bus stop. They'll probably send a child along with you, and as you part, give the child a pack of chewing gum or similar (give something else if your escort is an adult). There's a fine view of Nadi Bay from Viseisei and the bus tours often stop here, as the souvenir vendors in the village indicate. In any case, don't come on a Sunday. A bypass on Queens Road avoids Viseisei, and only local buses between Lautoka and Nadi take the back road past the village.

A couple of kilometers from the village on the airport side of Viseisei, just above Lomolomo Public School, are two **British six-inch guns** set up here during WW II to defend the north side of Nadi Bay. Between 1939 and 1941 coastal defense batteries were established at five points around Viti Levu. It's a fairly easy climb from the main highway, and you'll get an excellent view from the top.

Many tours visit **Perry Mason's Orchid Garden** (Mon.-Sat. 0900–1700, Sun. 0900–1200, admission F$10), also known as the Garden of the Sleeping Giant, 2.5 km down Wailoka Road off Queens Road north of the airport. The brochure claims 2,000 kinds of orchids are kept in these gardens at the foot of the hills, though they're slightly overrated.

Accommodations

The **Stoney Creek Resort** (Gary and Michelle Jones, tel. 672-2206, www.stoneycreekfiji.com) is on Sabeto Road six km east of Queens Road, about 11 km northeast of Nadi Airport. There are two *bure* at F$55/75 double/triple, plus a beautifully designed hilltop dormitory with a splendid mountain view at F$20 pp. A deluxe room behind the restaurant is F$120 double. The 16 dorm beds are divided among four separate cubicles, and there are hammocks from which to take in the scene. The restaurant and bar serves

lunch at F$7.50–8.50, dinner F$17.50–18.50, and a Sunday buffet dinner (F$16). There's a swimming pool. Half-day hiking and kayaking tours are F$25 pp, horseback riding F$20 a half day, bicycle rentals F$10 a day (guests only). Situated above the Sabeto River and below scenic mountains, this is an excellent eco-tourism alternative to the Nadi hotels. The Sabeto bus runs to Stoney Creek five times a day, or hire a carrier from Queens Road for F$5.

Mediterranean Villas (tel. 666-4011, fax 666-1773, medvillas@connect.com.fj), on Vuda Hill overlooking Viseisei village just off Viseisei Back Road, has six individually decorated self-catering villas with fridge priced F$110–260 single or double. There's a pool, but the beach is far from here. This hotel acts as the honorary Italian consulate in Fiji. Local buses between Lautoka and Nadi stop nearby.

Two km down Vuda Road from Mediterranean Villas is the **Anchorage Beach Resort** (tel. 666-2099, fax 666-5571, www.tanoa hotels.com), which was taken over by the Tanoa hotel chain in 1996. It's on a hilltop just before the descent to First Landing Resort, a 15-minute walk along the cane railway line or beach from Viseisei. The eight garden-view rooms are F$132 single or double, the four ocean view rooms F$143, and the two panoramic rooms F$154. The only two rooms with cooking facilities are also F$143 (other guests must use the restaurant). All units are air-conditioned and each has a fridge and balcony. A swimming pool is on the premises. The shoreline below Anchorage isn't as good for swimming as the beach at nearby First Landing Resort, but the views across Nadi Bay are nice.

First Landing Resort (tel. 666-6171, fax 666-8882, www.firstlandingfiji.com) is next to the Vuda Point Yacht Marina, three km down Vuda Road from Mediterranean Villas. The beach here is much better than those in and around Nadi but you'd only call it good at high tide. The 14 deluxe/superior duplex units facing the swimming pool are F$195/255 single or double, while the 18 duplex beachfront units go for F$325 (extra persons F$35). All units have fully screened porches and are equipped with a fridge and coffee-making facilities (but no cooking facilities). Connecting doors make the units ideal for large families or small groups. Three units are wheelchair accessible. One beach villa opposite the reception has its own kitchen and pool at F$650. A continental breakfast is included in all rates. The large garden restaurant on the premises bakes pizza (F$10–26), seafood (including lobster), and bread in a wood-fired stone oven. Menu items average F$17–31. The cafe in the adjacent Vuda Point Marina (daily 0700–1500, also Tues., Thurs., and Sat. until 2100) is far less expensive and recommended. Stephen and Julie Lynn of Aquacadabra Diving (tel./fax 664-5911, www.aquacadabra diving.com) organize scuba diving from First Landing Resort using the dive boat *Merlynn's Magic*. The places just mentioned are okay for a night or two, but you'd be making a mistake to plan your whole vacation around them.

SOUTH OF NADI

Sonaisali Island Resort

Opened in 1992, this upscale resort (tel. 670-6011, fax 670-6092, www.sonaisali.com) is on Naisali, a long, low island surrounded by mangrove flats in Momi Bay, just 300 meters off the coast of Viti Levu. The turnoff is 10 km south of Nadi, then it's three km down Nacobi Road (paved) to the landing. The 32 air-conditioned rooms with fridge in the two main two-story buildings are F$335 single or double, and there are 49 thatched *bure* at F$405–550 including tax (no cooking facilities). It's necessary to make dinner reservations and you may have difficulty arranging a convenient time (the food and drink itself is overpriced and the dining room service poor). The water pressure at Sonaisali is low and it takes ages to fill the spa baths built into some of the units. The resort features a marina, large swimming pool (which could use a cleaning), tennis courts, a children's program, and free nonmotorized water sports, but the snorkeling off their artificial beach is nothing. Scuba diving is available and Rosie The Travel Service has a desk at Sonaisali. A taxi from the airport might cost F$25. Nonguests wishing to take the "free"

shuttle boat across to the island must first pay F$25/12.50 per adult/child for a nonrefundable food and beverage credit. Frankly, this place is not recommended.

Surf & Dive Rendezvous

In 2001, Ben and Naoko Seduadua established a backpacker camp called **Surf & Dive Rendezvous** (tel. 651-0571, www.infofiji.com/rendezvous) on Uciwai Beach north of Nabila village, right next to the landing for Tavarua and Namotu islands. Accommodations include one room with private bath (F$75 pp), a Fijian *bure* with private bath (F$70 pp), four rooms with shared bath (F$65/130 single/double), a 20-bed dorm (F$55 pp), and camping space (F$45 pp), all with three meals included in the rates. Scuba diving is F$140 for two tanks, plus F$30 for gear. Ben's three- to four-day open-water certification course is F$500. Surfing trips to the reefs off Namotu and Malolo islands are F$55 pp (to Cloudbreak Saturday mornings only). Surfboard rental, sale, and repair is available. Other activities include surfing lessons, fishing, and horseback riding. The beach is okay for Viti Levu. Internet access is F$.20 a minute. The turnoff to Rendezvous is at Uciwai Junction, 15 km south of Nadi town on Queens Road, then it's another six km west on a gravel road. Get there on the Uciwai bus from Nadi at 0800, 1300, and 1700 daily except Sunday (or pay F$25 for a taxi).

Momi Battery Historic Park

On a hilltop overlooking Momi Bay, 28 km from Nadi, are two **British six-inch guns** named Queen Victoria (1900) and Edward VII (1901). Both were recycled from the Boer War and set up here by the New Zealand Army's 30th Battalion in 1941 to defend the southern approach to Nadi Bay. The only shots fired during the war were across the bow of a Royal New Zealand Navy ship that forgot to make the correct signals as it entered the passage. It quickly turned around, made the proper signals, and reentered quietly. You get a great view of the Mamanuca Group, reefs, and surrounding countryside from the guns. This historic site is managed by the National Trust for Fiji (tel. 997-1508, daily

0900–1700, admission F$3). To reach the battery, catch the Nabila Bus Station at 0900, 1600, and 1715 (only the 0900 bus returns to town the same day). The turnoff from Queens Road is at Nawai Junction, 17 km south of Nadi town, then it's another nine km along a gravel road to the guns. Seashell Cove Resort is nine km south.

Seashell Cove

Seashell Cove Resort (Virginia Smith, tel. 670-6100, fax 670-6094, www.seashellresort.com), on Momi Bay, 29 km southwest of Nadi, has been around since the 1980s. They have six duplex *bure* with fans, fridge, and cooking facilities at F$150 for up to three, and 17 lodge rooms with lumpy beds and shared bath at F$60 single or double, F$70 triple. Six larger units near the restaurant are available for families at F$195 for up to six, and baby-sitters are provided. The two honeymoon suites attached to a lodge are also F$195. Not all of the rooms face the water. The dormitory above the bar includes three six-bed rooms at F$55 per bed including three meals. Otherwise, pitch your own tent beside the volleyball court for F$10. Everything other than the dormitory is a bit overpriced.

Cooking facilities are not provided for campers or lodge guests, although the good-value meal plan is F$35 pp and there's a small grocery store just outside the resort. A *meke* and Fijian feast (F$20) occurs on Friday. Some surfers stay up all night drinking kava with the friendly staff, a great opportunity to get to know them. Baggage storage is available free of charge. Internet access at the office is F$6 for 15 minutes.

A small saltwater swimming pool is near the shore, but there's no beach here, only a concrete seawall. At low tide it's a 10-minute trudge across the mudflats to the water. Amenities and activities include a swimming pool, day trips to Natadola Beach (F$35 including lunch), tennis, and volleyball. There's a horse used to walk kids under 10 around the resort, but the free kayaks leak and become unstable after 20 minutes. A two-island, three-resort day cruise from here costs F$65.

Daily at 0700 the Seashell boat shuttles surfers out to the reliable left at Namotu Island breakers or long hollow right at Wilkes Passage (F$30 pp). The boat also goes to Swimming Pools, Desperations, and Mini Cloudbreak, staying with the surfers while they surf. The famous Cloudbreak lefthander at Navula Reef between Wilkes and Seashell is visited only on Saturday (F$40 pp), provided the Tavarua people aren't using it. Even then, expect crowds of 25 guys in the water—all other spots are less crowded. There's also an offshore break near the Momi Bay Lighthouse. This type of reef break surfing can be dangerous for the inexperienced.

Seashell Cove's scuba diving operation, **Scuba Bula** (www.scubabula.com), can handle to up to 24 divers at a time from beginners to advanced. The cost is F$75/110 for two tanks plus F$20 for gear and F$440 for a PADI certification course (minimum of two). Seashell divers experience lots of fish/shark action at Navula Lighthouse, and there's great drift diving at Canyons (the guides really know their spots). When there's space, snorkelers are welcome to go along at F$20 pp.

The turnoff to Seashell Cove is at Nawai Junction, 17 km south of Nadi town on Queens Road, then it's another 12 km to the resort on a rough gravel road. Airport transfers arranged through the resort are F$15 pp each way. A taxi from Nadi Airport will cost F$40, from Nadi town F$30, from Sigatoka F$50. Dominion Transport (tel. 670-1505) or Ram Dayal Transport (tel. 670-0236) has buses direct to Seashell from Nadi Bus Station Monday–Saturday at 0830, 1430, and 1600 (F$1.70). From Sigatoka Bus Station, buses to Seashell leave Monday–Saturday at 1030 (F$2.65).

The Mamanuca Group

The Mamanuca Group is a paradise of eye-popping reefs and sand-fringed isles shared by traditional Fijian villages and jet-age resorts. The white coral beaches and super snorkeling grounds attract visitors aplenty; boats and planes arrive constantly, bringing folks in from nearby Nadi. These islands are in the lee of big Viti Levu, which means you'll get about as much sun here as anywhere in Fiji. Some of the South Pacific's finest scuba diving, surfing, game fishing, and yachting await you, and many nautical activities are included in the basic resort rates.

The Mamanucas are fine for a little time in the sun, though much of it is a tourist scene irrelevant to Fiji life. The only resort islands also inhabited by Fijian villagers are Mana and Malolo,

and the Mana people have established low-budget backpacker accommodations in their village to make a little money on the side. If the beach is your main focus, you won't mind staying on a tiny coral speck like Beachcomber, Bounty, Matamanoa, Namotu, Navini, Tavarua, and Treasure, but if hiking and land-based exploring are also on your agenda you'll do better on the larger Yasawa Islands.

MALOLOLAILAI ISLAND

Malololailai, or "Little Malolo," 22 km west of Nadi, is a 216-hectare island eight km around (an interesting walk). In 1880, an American sailor named Louis Armstrong purchased Malololailai

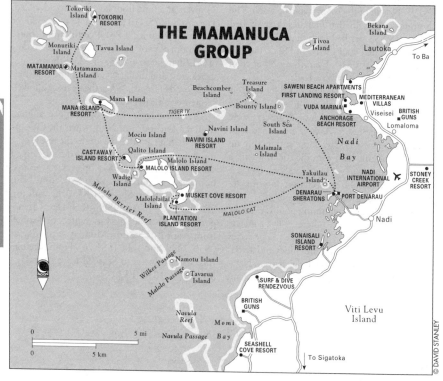

from the Fijians for one musket; in 1964, Dick Smith bought it for many muskets. You can still be alone at the beaches on the far side of the island, but with two growing resorts, a marina, a nine-hole golf course, and projects for lots more time-share condominiums in the pipeline it's becoming overdeveloped. An airstrip across the island's waist separates its two resorts; inland are rounded, grassy hills.

Plantation Island

Plantation Island Resort (tel. 666-9333, fax 672-0620, www.plantation-island.com), on the southwest side of Malololailai, is one of the largest resorts off Nadi. It belongs to the Raffles Group, which has other large hotels in Nadi and Suva. The 142 rooms are divided between 41 air-conditioned hotel rooms in a two-story building and 101 individual or duplex *bure*. Rates start at F$209 single or double plus tax for one of the 26 garden rooms and increase to F$462 for a beachfront *bure*. The rooms have a fridge but no cooking facilities, so add F$55 pp for all meals. A supermarket is at the airport end of the resort. Plantation Island Resort tries hard to cater to families, with two children under 16 accommodated free when sharing with their parents and a children's meal plan at F$33. Creche and babysitting services (F$3 an hour) are available, and there's a 20-meter waterslide and two pools.

Free activities here include snorkeling gear, windsurfing, paddle boats, and Hobie Cat sailing, and daily snorkeling and fishing trips are offered at no charge. Scuba diving with Snuba Reef Tours is F$77/132 for one/two tanks, while a scuba certification course is F$570/470 pp for one/two students. Snuba will give you a sample lesson in the resort's pool for only F$5. Plantation Island's golf course toward the airport offers a F$40/50 single/double package which includes greens fees, clubs, and cart. When things are slow they'll probably allow you to go around the nine holes twice during the same session at no additional cost; just don't drive their golf cart anywhere other than on the course unless you're looking for trouble. Plantation Island has a better beach than neighboring Musket Cove and is much more of

an integrated resort. Musket Cove is a funky do-it-yourself kind of place.

A budget section of Plantation Island Resort called **Lailai Lodge** or "Dive Lodge" (www.lailai lodge.com) is along the road behind the tennis courts. The two 12-bed dormitories are F$54 pp, and kitchens and bathrooms are shared. Guests have access to most resort facilities. Reservations must be made in advance through the Raffles Gateway Hotel (tel. 672-2444) in Nadi.

Musket Cove

Also on Malololailai Island is **Musket Cove Resort** (Dick and Carol Smith, tel. 666-2215, fax 666-2633, VHF 68, www.musketcovefiji.com), which opened in 1977. This is one of the few Mamanuca resorts that provides cooking facilities for its guests, but these vary according to the class of accommodations. Full facilities are provided in the six two-bedroom villas, costing F$530 for four persons, plus F$25 per extra adult to a maximum of six. The eight seaview and four garden *bure* also have kitchenettes at F$375 single or double. However, only breakfast bars are provided in the 18 beachfront and lagoon *bure* (from F$410 single or double). The six air-conditioned rooms (F$240 single or double) upstairs in the resort's administration building have no cooking facilities at all. You can tell that Musket Cove has been patched together over time, as the accommodations are so dissimilar.

Musket Cove's well-stocked grocery store sells fresh fruit and vegetables, and a coin laundry is near the store. A F$50/62 pp two/three meal plan is available at Dick's Place Restaurant by the pool. Otherwise lunch/dinner entrées average F$13/24. Entertainment is provided every night except Sunday. The bar on Ratu Nemani Island, a tiny coral islet connected to the marina by a floating bridge, is popular among yachties off the many boats anchored here.

Activities such as snorkeling, windsurfing, canoeing, kayaking, line fishing, and taking village boat trips are free for Musket Cove guests. Paid activities include the Hobie Cats (F$12.50 an hour) and waterskiing (F$12.50). Four-seat golf carts are for rent at F$60 a day. The launch

Anthony Star is available for deep-sea game-fishing charters at F$75 pp for four hours with a four-person minimum. The 10-meter cruiser *Dolphin Star* can be chartered for longer fishing trips at F$130 an hour (maximum four people). The 17-meter ketch *Dulcinea* does cruises to Castaway Island (F$50 pp without lunch), dolphin-watching trips (F$45 pp), and sunset viewing (F$30 pp). Unfortunately, some of the Musket Cove staff seem rather jaded and not entirely happy with their jobs.

Subsurface Fiji (www.fijidiving.com) runs the scuba diving concession at the Musket Cove marina, and many famous dive sites are less than 15 minutes away. It's F$84/164 for one/two tanks including equipment, or pay F$570 for the four-day PADI certification course (minimum of two persons). Children 12 years and up are accepted at their scuba school. **Musket Cove Yacht Charters** has a small fleet of charter yachts stationed here. The ketch *Hobo* can do a five-day crewed cruise to the Yasawas.

Malololailai is a favorite stopover for cruising yachts, with water and clean showers provided at the marina (mooring is F$8/46/172 a day/week/month). Fuel and groceries are also available. The marked anchorage is protected and 15 meters deep, with good holding. Most of the boats in the Auckland to Fiji yacht race in June end up here just in time for the President's Cup, Fiji's prestige yachting event. In mid-September there's a yachting regatta week at Musket Cove, culminating in a 965-km yacht race from Fiji to Port Vila timed for the boats' annual departure, prior to the onset of the hurricane season. If you're on a boat in Fiji at this time, Musket Cove is *the* place to be, and if you're trying to hitch a ride as crew you won't go wrong. There are even stories of people being *paid* to serve as crew for the race!

Getting There

Malololailai's grass-and-gravel airstrip is the busiest in the Mamanuca Group and serves as a distribution point for the other resorts. Sun Air has flights from Nadi four to eight times a day between 0730–1730. The one-way fare is F$48. Otherwise, take the catamaran *Malolo Cat* from Nadi's Port Denarau at 1030, 1400, or 1700 (50 minutes,

F$40 one way). A F$49 same-day return fare is also offered. From Malololailai, the *Cat* departs at 0900, 1230, and 1530. Call 672-2444 or 666-2215 for a free pickup at any Nadi area hotel.

MALOLO ISLAND

At low tide you can wade from Malololailai to nearby Malolo Island, largest of the Mamanuca Group. Yaro, one of two Fijian villages on Malolo, is known to tourists as "shell village" for what the locals offer for sale. In 2003, a New Zealand television company called Touchdown took over the former Lako Mai Resort near Yaro with the intention of producing a series of reality TV programs there.

Malolo Island Resort (tel. 666-9192, fax 666-9197, www.maloloisland.com), formerly Naitasi Resort, is at Malolo's western tip. The resort is owned by the Whitton family of Nadi, which also runs Rosie The Travel Service. Malolo Island Resort offers 30 oceanview bungalows at F$487 double, 18 deluxe oceanview bungalows at F$568, and one family bungalow at F$1,013 for up to eight persons. All but the family bungalow are duplexes. Up to two children under 12 can stay with their parents free. The meal plan costs F$72 pp (half price for children under 12). The Rosie office at Nadi Airport sometimes offers walk-in specials here. Malolo Island Resort has a two-tier freshwater swimming pool, and most nonmotorized water sports are free. Scuba diving with Subsurface Fiji costs extra.

The *Tiger IV* catamaran arrives from Nadi's Port Denarau three times a day at F$56 each way. South Sea Cruises offers a day trip to Malolo Island Resort at F$99 including lunch and snorkeling gear (children half price). Otherwise, fly Sun Air to Malololailai (F$48), then catch a connecting speedboat straight to the resort at F$90 one way for the boat. The Turtle Airways seaplane from Nadi is F$134 pp one-way.

THE SURFING CAMPS
Tavarua Island

Tavarua Island Resort (Jon Roseman, tel. 670-6513, fax 670-6395, www.tavarua.com), just south of Malololailai, is the South Pacific's most famous surfing resort. It caters to more affluent and mature surfers than the places on Viti Levu, Yanuca, and Kadavu. Although you can sometimes surf the same waves as the Tavarua crowd from budget resorts like Seashell Cove and Rendezvous on the mainland, you won't have the constant immediate access you have here.

Guests are accommodated in 12 newly renovated beach *bure* with hot showers and private bath, plus two larger family *bure*. A one-week package from Los Angeles will cost US$2,631 including airfare. The facilities have been upgraded, with a lagoon-style swimming pool and a large hot tub.

Amenities aside, it's the exclusivity you pay for here, as Tavarua has negotiated sole access to some of Fiji's finest waves. There are both lefts and rights in Malolo Passage at Tavarua, although the emphasis is usually on the lefts. When the swell is high enough you'll have some of the best surfing anywhere in the world. On the off days you can get in some deep-sea fishing, windsurfing, snorkeling, or scuba diving (extra charge). Surfing guests are expected to have had at least three years experience in a variety of conditions.

Bookings must be made six months in advance through Tavarua Island Tours in Santa Barbara, California. See Getting There in the Exploring the Islands chapter for details. Local bookings from within Fiji are not accepted, and they're usually sold out anyway, since Tavarua has become *the* place to go for top U.S. surfers.

Namotu Island

Just across Malolo Passage from Tavarua Island on tiny Namotu Island is **Namotu Island Resort** (Scott and Amanda O'Connor, tel. 670-6439, fax 670-6039, namotu@connect.com.fj), a "Blue Water Sports Camp" for surfers. It's similar to Tavarua but slightly more accessible. They have one double *bure,* three triple *bure,* one villa with two double rooms, and two "VIP" dorm-style *bure* with six single beds in each. Children under 12 are generally not accepted.

All guests arrive on seven-night package tours from Los Angeles, costing US$$2,700 pp including airfare, accommodations, meals, and un-

limited access to the local surf breaks. The price is same regardless of how many people are in the room. All reservations must go through Waterways Travel in Malibu, California (www.waterwaystravel.com). Local bookings from within Fiji are only possible in January and February, if space happens to be available. However, Namotu is usually sold out.

You must bring your own surfboards, sailboards, and kite sails, because none are available on island. Snorkeling gear, kayaks, outrigger canoes, and wake boards are loaned free of charge. Fishing is also included, although lost lures must be paid for. Scuba diving is arranged with Subsurface Fiji at F$95 per dive including gear. Massage also costs extra.

As at Tavarua, Namotu's market is mostly American watersports enthusiasts who fly down from the United States to ride Fiji's spectacular waves. Namotu Left is a worldclass reef break that's more forgiving than its fearsome, famous neighbor, Cloudbreak. At five meters, Cloudbreak is the thrill of a lifetime; at two meters, it's a longboarder's paradise. The powerful right barrels of Wilkes Passage are good anywhere from one to three meters. Rounding out the scene is Swimming Pools, a playful, full wraparound right break on the leeward side of Namotu that, with it crystal blue water and sheltered position, has to be one of the world's most remarkable breaks.

THE TINY ISLANDS
Beachcomber Island

Beachcomber Island (Dan Costello, tel. 666-1500, fax 666-4496, www.beachcomberfiji.com), 18 km west of Lautoka, is Club Med at a bargain price. Since the 1960s, this famous resort has received many thousands of young travelers, and it's still a super place to meet the opposite sex. You'll like the informal atmosphere and late-night parties; there's a sand floor bar, dancing, and floor shows four nights a week. The island is so small you can stroll around it in 10 minutes, but there's a white sandy beach and buildings nestled among coconut trees and tropical vegetation. This is one of the few places in Fiji where both sexes might be able to sunbathe topless. A beautiful coral reef with numerous well-fed fish extends far out on all sides and scuba diving is available with Subsurface Fiji (F$84/164 for one/two tanks, PADI open water certification F$570). A full range of other sporting activities is available at an additional charge (parasailing F$60, windsurfing F$22 an hour, water-skiing F$32, jet skis F$60 for 15 minutes).

Accommodations include all meals served buffet style. Most backpackers opt for the big, open, mixed dormitory where the 42 double-decker bunks (84 beds) cost F$75 each a night. Secure lockers are provided. The 14 simple lodge rooms at F$179/238 single/double (fridge and fan provided) are a good compromise for budget-conscious couples. You can also get one of 22 thatched beachfront *bure* with ceiling fan, fridge, and private facilities for F$270/320/395 single/double/triple. The *bure* are ideal for young families, as children under 16 enjoy reduced rates. The resort's former water problems have been solved by laying pipes from the mainland and installing solar water heating. Drinks at the bar are pricey and a duty free bottle purchased upon arrival at the airport will come in handy here.

Of course, there's also the F$69 round-trip boat ride from Nadi or Lautoka to consider, but that includes lunch on arrival day. You can make a day trip to Beachcomber for the same price if you only want a few hours in the sun. There's a free shuttle bus from all Nadi hotels to the wharf; the connecting catamaran *Drodrolagi* leaves from Port Denarau daily at 0900. From Lautoka, the pickup is at 1030 daily except Tuesday and Thursday. The *Yasawa Flyer* picks up passengers for the Yasawas every morning at 1000, and it can also drop you off here on the way back to Nadi (but it can't carry you between Beachcomber and Nadi).

Beachcomber has been doing it right for decades, and the biggest drawback is its very popularity, which makes it crowded and busy. Reserve well ahead at their Nadi Airport or Lautoka offices, or at any travel agency.

Bounty Island

Bounty Island Sanctuary Resort (tel. 651-1271, fax 651-1390, www.fiji-bounty.com), run by the same company as nearby Treasure Island Resort, imitates the Beachcomber Island formula with 28 bunks in two dorms at F$71 pp. Otherwise the eight set tents are F$140 for up to four persons, plus F$25 pp a day for meals. The eight fan-cooled rooms with shared bath are F$140 for up to five persons, plus F$25 pp (children under 12 half price). The included food is great. At 20 hectares, Bounty is much larger than Beachcomber, with more nature to explore; otherwise, most of the information above also applies here. Choose Bounty over Beachcomber if you like to party now and then, but don't wish to be part of a 24-hour circus. Transfers are via the Vuda Point Marina and cost F$40 pp each way including hotel pickups. The South Sea Cruises catamaran from the Denarau Marina will drop you here for F$46, and you can also transfer to the *Yasawa Flyer* at South Sea Island. Bounty Island reservations are handled by Hunts of the Pacific (tel. 672-2852, fax 672-0397) at Nadi Airport.

Castaway Island

Castaway Island Resort (tel. 666-1233, fax 666-5753, www.castawayfiji.com), on 174-hectare Qalito Island just west of Malolo, was built by Dick Smith in 1966 as Fiji's first outer-island resort. Today it's owned by Geoff Shaw, who also owns the Outrigger Reef Resort on the Coral Coast. It has always been one of Fiji's most popular resorts. The 66 closely-packed thatched *bure* sleep four—F$583 and up. No cooking facilities are provided, but the all-meal plan is F$70 pp. The *lovo* and *meke* are on Wednesday night, the beach barbecue on Saturday.

Among the free water sports are sailing, windsurfing, paddle boats, tennis, and snorkeling, but sportfishing and scuba diving (with Geof and Trudy Loe) are extra. Diving is F$90/180 for one/two tank dives with shark feeding. Otherwise pay F$565 for three tanks a day for the duration of your stay! The PADI certification course is F$710 for one or F$560 pp for two or more, and several other courses are also available. There's a swimming pool. Many Australian holidaymakers return to Castaway year after year; families with small children are welcome. A free "kids club" operates from 0900–1600 and 1900–2100 daily with lots of fun activities for those aged three and over, while mom and dad have some time to themselves.

There's the catamaran *Tiger IV* three times a day from Nadi's Port Denarau (F$56 each way), and Turtle Airways has three seaplane flights a day from Nadi for F$134. Castaway Island Resort's own boat, the 10-meter *Teivovo*, takes only 30 minutes to travel between Nadi and the island at speeds exceeding 100 kph. South Sea Cruises offers day trips to Castaway at F$99 including lunch and snorkeling gear (children half price). Only 10 persons a day are allowed to book the day cruises, so inquire early.

Navini Island

Navini Island Resort (Arthur, Helen, and Simone Reed, tel. 666-2188, fax 666-5566, www.navinifiji.com.fj) is a secluded eco-resort on a 2.5-hectare coral isle with just 10 beachfront *bure* nicely ensconced in the low island's shrubbery. Rates vary from F$470 double for a fan-cooled unit with a motel-like bathroom and small beds to F$650 for the deluxe honeymoon *bure* with a bathtub and enclosed courtyard. Discounts are available for stays of more than a week and for children. The compulsory two/three meal package is F$80/87 pp a day—excellent food and you have a choice. Everyone gets to know one another during pre-dinner cocktails and by eating together at long tables at fixed times. Navini is ideal for couples and families looking for a quiet holiday—those interested in an intense social life or lots of organized activities might get bored. Complimentary morning boat trips are offered, as are snorkeling gear, paddle boats, sailboats, and kayaks. Scuba diving with Subsurface Fiji can be arranged and the snorkeling right off their beach is good (abundant marinelife, since fishing has been banned here for many years). Massage is F$50 an hour. Car/boat transfers from Nadi via the Vuda Point Marina are arranged anytime upon request (F$180 pp return, or free if you stay a week). Only overnight guests are accepted (no day-trippers).

South Sea Island

This is one of the smallest Mamanuca islands, a sandbank reminiscent of the shipwreck cartoons.

Thirty people are packed into a thatched dormitory upstairs in a two-story building at F$70 pp, or sleep in a hut at F$170 double, good buffet meals and lots of watersports included. Even though the beach is fine, the developers have constructed a tacky little swimming pool in the center of the island. Boat transfers from Nadi are F$40 each way, but most guests use the free stopover here allowed on *Yasawa Flyer* tickets to the Yasawa Islands. Awesome Adventures and South Sea Cruises deliver as many day-trippers to this tiny island as they possibly can. It's overcrowded and not as clean as it could be, but fine if swimming and socializing are the things you like most to do. In short, South Sea (tel. 651-0506) is a party island for young backpackers.

Treasure Island

Beachcomber's little neighbor, **Treasure Island Resort** (tel. 666-1599, fax 666-3577, www.fiji-treasure.com), caters to couples and families. It's extremely popular among packaged New Zealand and Australian vacationers and occupancy levels seldom drop below 80 percent. The resort is half owned by the Tokatoka Nakelo land-owning clan, which also supplies most of the workers, although the management is European. The 67 air-conditioned units, each with three single beds (F$495 single or double), are contained in 34 functional duplex bungalows packed into the greenery behind the island's white sands. Cooking facilities are not provided, so add F$68 pp daily for the meal plan. Special dinners and evening entertainment are scheduled every other night. Some nautical activities such as windsurfing, sailing, canoes, and spy board, which cost extra on Beachcomber, are free on Treasure Island. Scuba diving with Subsurface Fiji (www.fijidiving.com) is F$99/150 including gear for one/two-tank boat dives. Unlike Beachcomber, Treasure doesn't accept any day-trippers. Guests arrive on the shuttle boat *Tiger IV*, which departs Nadi's Port Denarau three times a day (F$40 each way, half price under age 16).

Wadigi Island

In 1998, a tiny resort called **Wadigi Island** (Ross and Jeni Allen, tel. 672-0901, www.wadigi.com)

FIJI ISLANDS

opened on the isle of the same name off the west end of Malolo. Each group of visitors gets exclusive use of the entire three-suite resort, costing F$2,310 for a couple, plus F$880 pp for the first two additional persons and F$770 pp for the next two up to six maximum (children under 12 not accepted). Included in the tariff are all meals, drinks, and sporting equipment such as kayaks, windsurfers, spy boards, fishing rods, and snorkeling gear. Only deep-sea fishing, surfing trips, and scuba diving (with Subsurface Fiji) cost extra. Transfers to the island from Nadi are also not included.

MANA ISLAND

Mana Island, 32 km northwest of Nadi, is well known for its scuba diving and luxury resort, but in recent years a whole slew of backpacker hostels have sprouted in the Fijian village on the eastern side of the island. There's much bad blood between the Japanese investors who run the resort and the Fijian villagers who accommodate the backpackers, and a high fence has been erected down the middle of the island to separate the two ends of the market. Uniformed security guards patrol the perimeter and shoestring travelers are most unwelcome anywhere in the resort, including the restaurants, shop, bars, and dive shop. In contrast, tourists from the resort are quite welcome to order drinks or meals at the backpacker camps.

Although this situation does poison the atmosphere on Mana Island slightly, there are lots of lovely beaches all around the island, most of them empty because the packaged tourists seldom stray far from their resort. The long white beach on the northeast side of the island is deserted. At the resort, the snorkeling is better off South Beach at low tide, off North Beach at high tide, but the nicest beach is Sunset Beach at the western end of the island. There's a great view of the Mamanucas and southern Yasawas from the highest point on Mana, a 10-minute hike from the backpacker camps, and splendid snorkeling on the reef. The Mana Main Reef is famous for its drop-offs, with visibility never less than 25 meters, and you'll see turtles, fish of all descriptions, and the occasional crayfish.

The presence of the resort supports the frequent air and sea connections from Nadi, and the budget places allow you to enjoy Mana's stunning beauty at a fraction of the price tourists at the Japanese resort are paying. But to be frank,

© DAVID STANLEY

South Beach, Mana Island

both of the main backpacker camps on Mana are rather squalid, and the places in the Yasawa Islands offer better accommodations for only a bit more money.

Sports and Recreation

Resort guests may patronize **Aqua-Trek** (tel. 666-9309, www.aquatrekdiving.com), which offers boat dives at F$83 for one tank plus F$11 for equipment or F$462 for a six-dive package. Night dives are F$99. They run a variety of dive courses, beginning with a four-day PADI open-water certification course (F$660). Underwater shark feeding is Aqua-Trek Mana's specialty, usually every Wednesday and Saturday at 0830.

Aqua Trek doesn't accept divers from the backpacker camps, who must dive with Ratu Kini's dive operation **Mana Pacific Divers** (tel. 666-9143), on the beach adjacent to Mereani's Inn. It charges F$80 for a one-tank lagoon dive, F$150 for a two-tank outer reef dive, or F$100 for a night dive. Snorkeling gear is rented out at F$10, while guided snorkeling trips are F$20 pp.

Awesome Adventures operates the watersports concession on South Beach at the resort, offering waterskiing, jet-skiing, water scooters, knee boarding, wake boarding, sky riding, banana riding, and parasailing. Unlike Aqua-Trek, it doesn't discriminate against backpackers and everyone is welcome (this could change).

The Backpacker Camps

Right up against the security fence near an enclosed sentry box is **Mereani's Backpackers Inn** (Mereani Ratunavu, tel. 666-3099, fax 670-3466), a large house with two five-bunk dormitories at F$45 pp and four double rooms at F$80 double. When the dorms in the main hostel fill up, they open a 19-bed dorm in the village. A separate "beach house" unit has one double at F$95 and a five-bed family room at F$130. If you have your own tent, you can camp at F$25 pp. All rates include three generous meals served to your table (breakfast is a buffet). You can get drinks at their bar all day. Activities include deep-sea fishing trips and four-island boat excursions (F$35 pp). Those staying a week get an extra night free and several complimentary trips.

Ratu Kini's Resort or "Mana Backpackers" (tel. 672-9143, fax 672-1959, rtkinihostel@con nect.com.fj) has their reception and dining areas alongside the resort's security fence right next to Mereani's Inn, but the large accommodations building is 100 meters back in the village. The concrete main house has a 22-bunk dorm downstairs and a 26-bunk dorm upstairs, plus another four-bunk dorm in the corridor. Nearby are two thatched dormitory *bure* with seven and 14 bunks, all costing F$45 pp. The main house also contains three double rooms with shared bath at F$65/85 single/double, and six better rooms with private bath at F$75/95. A thatched four-bed *bure* in the backyard is F$130 double, plus F$25 per additional person. Have a look around before committing yourself, as all of the rooms are different. Camping is F$35 pp. Buffet-style meals are included in all rates (on Thursdays they prepare a *lovo* and nonguests are welcome at F$10 pp). Reader reviews of the food vary from "awful" to "outstanding." A full-day boat trip to Malololailai Island is F$35 pp with lunch. A two-hour snorkeling trip is F$20 pp for the boat (minimum of four). Ratu Kini works out of office No. 26, upstairs from arrivals at Nadi Airport. People on their way to Ratu Kini's often stay at Mana Rose Apartments near Travelers Beach Resort at Wailoaloa Beach in Nadi. Both Ratu Kini's and Mereani's have electricity generators. Expect water shortages, occasional overcrowding, nocturnal animal sounds, a party atmosphere, and a lack of privacy in the mixed dorms of both hostels. Unattended gear may disappear from the beach.

Rara Cava's **Mana Lodge** (no phone) is a new place on the beach near Mereani's. There are four rooms with bath in one house at F$120 double, plus a separate beach *bure* at F$200, meals included. Mana Lodge has a large beach bar.

Another backpacker resort called **Dream Beach** (no phone) is run by Jerry and Kelera on a splendid beach on the north side of Mana Island, across the hill from Ratu Kini's. Since a fire destroyed one of the houses in 2001, there's only an eight-bunk dorm here. The owners say they intend to build five bungalows, but they'll need to solve their water problems first. For now, it's just a basic place to crash. Dream Beach is nicely secluded from the village and resort, so it's always worth asking about.

US$150–250

Juxtaposed against the backpacker camps is **Mana Island Resort** (tel. 666-1455, fax 666-1562, www.manafiji.com), by far the biggest of the tourist resorts off Nadi, with numerous tin-roofed bungalows clustered between the island's grassy rounded hilltops, white sandy beaches, and crystal-clear waters. The 40 "garden bungalows" are F$338 single or double, while the 20 "deluxe oceanview bungalows" and 32 hotel rooms are F$400. The 12 "executive oceanview bungalows" are F$500. Then there are the six "beachfront bungalows" with whirlpool tub at F$800 and seven "honeymoon bungalows" west of the airstrip at F$900. In 2003, 30 "ocean-front suites" were added in a hotel section near the wharf at F$731. Yuppie backpackers who find Mereani's and Ratu Kini's too basic can get a third off these rates by requesting the "walk-in special." Mana Island Resort caters to guests of all ages and has a daily "Kids Club" program. Children under 12 sleep free if sharing with one or two adults. All prices include a buffet breakfast and some nonmotorized watersports, but add 12.5 percent tax. Cooking facilities are not provided, so you'll need to patronize their restaurants (entrées F$20 and up). Live entertainment is presented nightly, and there's a Fijian *meke* on Tuesday and Saturday and a Polynesian show on Friday.

Getting There

The airstrip on Mana receives five Sun Air flights a day from Nadi (F$58 each way). The terminal is a seven-minute walk west of the resort (to get to the backpacker camps, head for the wharf from which the security fence will be visible).

If you're already staying in Nadi it's just as easy to arrive on the *Tiger IV* catamaran, which runs three times a day from Port Denarau (F$56 each way including Nadi hotel pickups). Otherwise, South Sea Cruises runs a day trip from Nadi including lunch at Mana Island Resort for F$99 (children under 16 half price). The ferry ties up to a wharf at South Beach; in fact, Mana is the only Mamanuca island with a wharf, so you don't need to take off your shoes.

Ratu Kini's own shuttle boat leaves Wailoaloa Beach at 1100 daily, costing F$40/70 one way/return including bus transfers from Nadi hotels. Mereani's guests must use the safer *Tiger IV.* Any Nadi travel agency or hotel can book these transfers.

THE OUTER ISLANDS

Matamanoa Island

Matamanoa Island Resort (tel. 666-0511 or 672-3620, fax 666-1069 or 672-0282, www .matamanoa.com), to the northwest of Mana Island, is the closest resort to Monuriki Island, the uninhabited island seen in the Tom Hanks film *Castaway.* It has 13 air-conditioned motel-style rooms at F$291 single or double, and 20 fan-cooled *bure* at F$470, tax included. Children under 12 are not accepted. The full American breakfast included in the basic price is good, but the same cannot be said of the lunch and dinner (limited choice, same all the time, too much deep frying). Even so, the meal plan costs F$68 pp extra. Complimentary afternoon tea is served at the bar, followed by snacks during happy hour 1730–1830. Bring along a few packets of instant soup and some freeze-dried food so you can spare yourself the meals! Loud cruise ship style entertainment is laid on at meal times and during the evening. The tiny island's beach is complemented by a small swimming pool. Scuba diving is with Aqua-Trek.

Boat transfers from Nadi on the *Tiger IV* cost F$97 pp each way with a change of boats at Mana Island. If you fly to Mana, it's F$45 each way for the boat between Mana and Matamanoa. The schooner *Seaspray* operates all-inclusive day cruises from Matamanoa for F$125.

Tokoriki Island

Tokoriki Island Resort (tel. 666-1999 or 672-5926, fax 666-5295 or 672-5928, www.toko riki.com) is the farthest Mamanuca resort from Nadi and the most private and secluded. There are 29 spacious fan-cooled *bure* from F$690 double (no cooking facilities). The three-meal plan is

CASTAWAY, THE MOVIE

In early 2001 moviegoers worldwide got a taste of the savage beauty of Fiji's westernmost islands from Robert Zemeckis' film *Castaway*. The story revolves around a Federal Express employee (Tom Hanks) who becomes stranded on an uninhabited tropical isle after his plane goes down in the Pacific. The plane-wrecked air courier eventually spends four years on the island, and to achieve the desperate look needed to play his role, Hanks had to lose 40 pounds and grow a ragged beard. Thus *Castaway* was filmed in two stages eight months apart, with the second portion shot on location in the western Mamanucas in early 2000. For this event, around a hundred members of the film crew descended on tiny Monuriki Island, between Matamanoa and Tokoriki.

At the time, concerns were raised that there might be a repeat of the damaging controversy surrounding the filming of *The Beach* in Thailand, when producers were accused of inflicting environmental damage on Maya Beach in Krabi's Phi Phi Islands National Park. The avoid this, Zemeckis was careful to have veteran naturalist and author Dick Watling do an environmental impact assessment before the filming, and the film crew followed Watling's recommendations carefully. Later, when naturalists from the World Wide Fund for Nature in Suva investigated the affair, they gave Zemeckis and his team high marks.

Ironically, 50-odd feral goats have long ravaged the vegetation on Monuriki, threatening the island's rare crested iguanas with extinction. The filmmakers offered to pay the Fijian landowners a bounty of F$100 per goat to remove the beasts, but their offer was refused. To Monuriki's customary owners on nearby Yanuya Island, a steady supply of goat meat is worth more than money or iguanas. Although no Fijians appear in *Castaway*, it conveys well the spellbinding scenery of this exotic region. (Day cruises to Monuriki can be booked through hotel tour desks in Nadi.)

F$94 pp. To enhance the attraction for honeymooners and romantic couples, children under 12 are not accepted. The resort faces west on a kilometer-long beach and water sports such as reef fishing, windsurfing, and Hobie Cats are free (sportfishing available at additional charge). Scuba diving with Dive Tropex (www.tokorikidiving.com) also costs extra. At the center of the island is a 94-meter-high hill offering good views of the Yasawa and Mamanuca groups.

As on Matamanoa, you must take the fast catamaran *Tiger IV* to Mana, then a launch to Tokoriki (F$97 pp each way). If you fly to Mana, you can catch this launch straight to Tokoriki for F$45 one-way. Turtle Airways charges F$154 pp to fly from Nadi to either Matamanoa or Tokoriki (Pacific Island Seaplanes charges F$193 pp). Island Hoppers (tel. 672-0410) at Nadi Airport offers direct helicopter transfers to either Tokoriki or Matamanoa at F$98 pp (minimum of two persons).

Vomo Island

Standing alone midway between Lautoka and Wayasewa Island (see the Yasawa Islands map), 91-hectare Vomo is a high volcanic island with a white beach around its west side. Since 1993, the coral terrace and slopes behind this beach have been the site of the luxurious **Vomo Island Resort** (tel. 666-7955 or 666-8122, fax 666-7997 or 666-8500, www.vomofiji.com). The 28 large air-conditioned villas with individual hot tubs run F$770 pp double occupancy, including all meals and non-motorized activities, plus 12.5 percent tax (minimum stay three nights). Once part of the Sheraton chain, Vomo Island Resort offers swimming and snorkeling infinitely better than anything at Denarau. Scuba diving is with Aquacadabra Diving. The nine-hole pitch and putt golf course is free to guests. Pacific Island Seaplanes (tel. 672-5644) charges F$135 pp each way for transfers, while Turtle Airways is F$148 pp.

Southern Viti Levu

The southwest side of Viti Levu along the Queens Road is known as the Coral Coast for its fringing reef. Sigatoka and Navua are the main towns in this area with most accommodations at Korotogo, Korolevu, and Pacific Harbor. This shoreline is heavily promoted as one of the top resort areas in Fiji, probably because of its convenient location along the busy highway between Nadi and Suva, but to be honest, the beaches here are second rate, with good swimming and snorkeling conditions only at high tide. Much of the coral has been destroyed by hurricanes and beaches have been washed away. To compensate, most of the hotels have swimming pools and in some places you can go reef walking at low tide. Top sights include the Sigatoka sand dunes and the impressive gorge of the Navua River. The possibility of rainfall and the lushness of the vegetation increase as you move east.

Getting Around

An easy way to get between the Coral Coast resorts and Nadi/Suva is on the air-conditioned **Fiji Express** shuttle bus run by Coral Sun Fiji (tel. 672-3105). The bus leaves the Holiday Inn, Tanoa Plaza, and other top hotels in Suva (F$31) at 0730 and calls at the Pacific Harbor International Hotel (F$27), The Warwick Hotel (F$22), Naviti Resort, Hideaway, Tambua Sands, Outrigger Reef Resort (F$20), Fijian Hotel (F$18), most Nadi hotels, and the Sheratons (F$7), arriving at Nadi Airport at noon (quoted fares are to the airport). It leaves Nadi Airport at 1300 and returns along the same route, reaching Suva at 1730. Bookings can be made at hotel tour desks. At Nadi Airport, contact Coral Sun Fiji (tel. 672-2268) in the arrivals area.

Coral Sun Fiji also books the air-conditioned **Queens Coach,** which runs in the opposite direction, leaving Nadi Airport for Suva at 0730, The Fijian Hotel at 0910, the Warwick and Naviti at 1010, and Pacific Harbor at 1110. The return trip departs the Holiday Inn around 1615, arriving at the airport at 2040. It's cheaper at F$19 between Nadi and Suva.

Many less expensive non-air-conditioned express buses pass on the highway, but make sure you're waiting somewhere they'll stop (any local will know). Pacific Transport's "stage" or "highway" buses between Lautoka/Nadi and Suva will stop anywhere along their routes, but the express buses call only at Sigatoka, Pacific Harbor, Navua, and some Coral Coast resorts.

NATADOLA AND ROBINSON CRUSOE

Natadola Beach

The long, white sandy beach here is easily the best on Viti Levu and a popular picnic spot with day-trippers arriving on the sugar train from The Fijian Hotel on the Coral Coast. Care should be taken while swimming in the ocean, because the waves can be unexpectedly strong. The small left point break at Natadola is good for beginning surfers, but one must always be aware of the currents and undertow. The left-hand breaks outside the reef are only for the experienced.

Plans to erect three or four luxury hotels on Natadola have been stalled by limited water supplies at the site. In 1999, it was announced that a 500-room resort to be managed by the Four Seasons chain would be erected here after the Fiji Government agreed to spend millions on infrastructure. Unfortunately, the project was scrapped after the May 2000 coup, but the Natadola Marine Resort Company (www.natadolafiji.com) is getting ready to try again. Shangri-La Hotels also has property here. A modern highway has been built from Queens Road directly to the beach at government expense.

At the moment, very few facilities are available, although the local villagers offer horseback riding to a cave at F$10. It's possible to rent a *bure* in Sanasana village at the south end of the beach at F$25 pp including meals. In the past, travelers have camped on Natadola Beach, but theft is a real problem here. Don't leave valuables unattended on this beach.

The dusty, Santa Fe style **Natadola Beach**

Resort (Thomas Hovelle, tel. 672-1001, fax 672-1000, www.natadola.com), across the road from the public beach, offers one block of six suites, plus another block of four suites, at F$308 single or double including continental breakfast. The luxurious "sandcastle" villa is F$369. Honeymooners are the target clientele and children under 16 are not accepted. Each of the 10 fan-cooled units has a fridge, but no cooking facilities are provided. The resort's restaurant serves sandwiches (F$11), salads (F$11), and hamburgers (F$12.50) at lunch, while dinner mains cost F$27–42. A long swimming pool meanders between huge native trees in a garden setting. Unfortunately, shell peddlers and horse riders waiting outside the resort gate can be a nuisance.

Paradise Transport (tel. 650-0028) has buses on weekdays from Sigatoka to Vusama village about four km from the beach at 0900, 1130, 1300, and 1500 (ask the driver if the bus is going on to Sanasana). Otherwise get off any Nadi bus at the Tuva Indian School stop on Queens Road and hitch the eight km straight to the beach. It's also possible to hike to Natadola in three hours along the coastal railway line from opposite Shangri-La's Fijian Resort.

Robinson Crusoe Island

The most popular offshore resort in this area is Robinson Crusoe Island (tel. 670-0026, fax 651-0100, www.robinsoncrusoeislandfiji.com), on Likuri Island, a small coral isle just north of Natadola. Not to be confused with Crusoe's Retreat on the Coral Coast toward Pacific Harbor, Robinson Crusoe caters to more active crowd. The 11 simple *bure* with shared bath are F$79 pp, while the dorm *bure* with 20 beds upstairs and 38 downstairs is F$65 pp. Prices include three good meals, fishing, and snorkeling. Aqua-Trek has a dive shop on the island, charging F$80/120 for one/two tanks or F$450 for an open-water certification course (minimum of two persons). **Tropical Fishing and Watersports** (Bret Roberts, tel. 992-3233, www.sportfishingfiji.com) offers game fishing from the island at F$485/800 a half/full day (five anglers). Boat transfers at 1000 and 1630 from the Tuva River Jetty near Nata-

dola are F$49 pp roundtrip, bus transfers from Nadi included. Day tours to Robinson Crusoe Island are offered on Tuesday, Thursday, and Sunday, costing F$79 pp including Nadi hotel transfers and a *lovo* lunch. The beach here is great, and this is a good alternative to the better-known Mamanuca resorts for the young at heart.

THE FIJIAN AND VICINITY

Shangri-La's Fijian Resort (tel. 652-0155, fax 650-0402, www.shangri-la.com) occupies all 40 hectares of Yanuca Island (not to be confused with another island of the same name west of Beqa). "The Fijian" (as it's often called) is connected to Viti Levu by a causeway 10 km west of Sigatoka and 61 km southeast of Nadi Airport. Opened in 1967, this Malaysian-owned complex of three-story Hawaiian-style buildings was Fiji's first large resort and it's still Fiji's biggest hotel, catering to a predominantly Japanese clientele. The 436 air-conditioned rooms are F$370 single or double in the "lagoon wings," F$405 in the "ocean wings," F$505 for a family room, F$680 for a suite, or F$950 for one of the four beach *bure*, plus 12.5 percent tax. Included is a buffet breakfast for two people per room. A third adult is F$55, but two children 18 or under sharing their parents' room stay free (kids 12 and under also eat for free). This makes Shangri-La's Fijian an ideal choice for families. The resort offers a nine-hole golf course (par 31), five tennis courts, numerous restaurants and bars, three swimming pools, and a white sandy beach. Every Friday night there's firewalking, a *meke*, and a *lovo* (F$57). Avis Rent A Car has a desk in The Fijian, and an ANZ Bank ATM is available.

John Anthony's **Coral Coast Scuba Ventures** (tel. 652-8793, fax 652-0356, www.coralcoastscuba.com) has the diving concession at Shangri-La's Fijian Resort. There are morning and afternoon dives, costing F$117/195 for one/two tanks including gear. Night diving (on Tuesday and Thursday) is F$145. Daily at 1300, there's a free scuba lesson in the resort's pool. Dive sites such as Nabaibai Passage, Barracuda Drift, The Wall, Golden Reef, and The Pinnacles are within a few minutes of the resort jetty.

VITI LEVU

Waya Island

Wayasewa Island

Bligh Water

White Rock

Vatia Point

Tavua

Vatukoula

Vomolailai Island

Vomo Island

Nacilau Point

Ba

Nadarivatu

LOLOLO PINE SCHEME

Saweni Beach

Lautoka

Navala

Beachcomber Island

Treasure Island

Koroyanitu (1,195 m)

Koro River

Anchorage Beach

Abaca

Nadrau

Malolo Island

Navini Island

Nadi Bay

Mamanuca Group

SHERATON HOTEL

VATURU DAM

Bukuya

Nanoko

Nubutautau

Malololailai Island

Nadi

Nausori Highland

Nadi River

Nadrau Plateau

Tavarua Island

Koroba (1,076 m)

Tubarua

Korolevu

Monavatu (1,131 m)

Momi Bay

SEASHELL COVE RESORT

Tau

Sigatoka River

Viti

Levu

Island

Lomawai

Robinson Crusoe Island

Tuvutau (Mt. Gordon) (933 m)

Natadola Beach

Navua River

Navua Gorge

Cuvu

Sigatoka

Nabukelevu

THE FIJIAN HOTEL

Korotogo

QUEENS

Korolevu

RD.

TAMBUA SANDS

HIDEAWAY RESORT

THE NAVITI

THE WARWICK

BEACHOUSE

CRUSOE'S RETREAT

WAIDROKA BAY RESORT

Serua Island

Coral Coast

0   10 mi

0   10 km

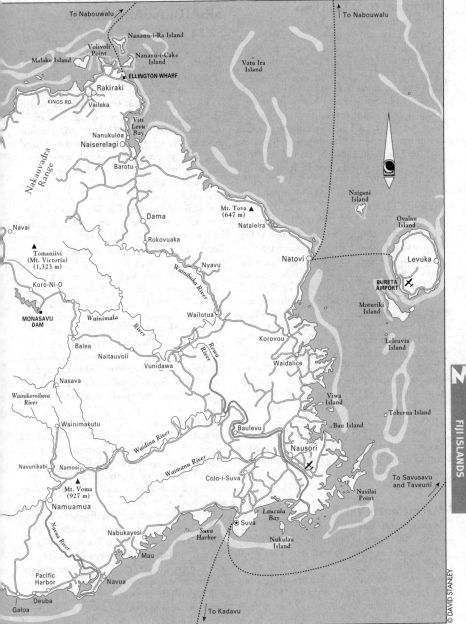

To Nabouwalu

To Nabouwalu

Nananu-i-Ra Island

Volivoli Point

Nananu-i-Cake Island

Malake Island

ELLINGTON WHARF

Rakiraki

Vatu Ira Island

KINGS RD.

Vaileka

Viti Levu Bay

Nanukuloa

Naiserelagi

Barotu

Nakauvadra Range

Dama

Mt. Tova (647 m)

Nataleira

Naigani Island

Navai

Rokovuaka

Ovalau Island

Tomaniivi (Mt. Victoria) (1,323 m)

Nyavu

Natovi

Levuka

Koro-Ni-O

Wainibuka River

BURETA AIRPORT

MONASAVU DAM

Wainimala

River

Wailotua

Korovou

Moturiki Island

Balea

Naitauvoli

Rewa River

Vunidawa

Waidalice

Leleuvia Island

Nasava

Wainikoroiluva River

Viwa Island

Toberua Island

Wainimakutu

Waidina River

Baulevu

Bau Island

Nausori

Navunikabi

Namosi

Waimanu River

Colo-i-Suva

Mt. Voma (927 m)

To Savusavu and Taveuni

Namuamua

Nasilai Point

Navua River

Nabukayesi

Suva Harbor

Laucala Bay

Suva

Nukulau Island

Mau

Pacific Harbor

Navua

Deuba

Galoa

To Kadavu

FIJI ISLANDS

© DAVID STANLEY

Attractions Near The Fijian

Train buffs won't want to miss the *Fijian Princess*, a restored narrow-gauge railway originally built to haul sugarcane. It now runs 16-km day trips along the coast to Natadola Beach daily at 1000. The station is on the highway opposite the access road to Shangri-La's Fijian Resort, and the ride costs F$79 pp including a picnic lunch. Another train tour goes to Sigatoka and the Tavuni Hill Fort. Otherwise, there's a trip that combines Natadola with Robinson Crusoe Island. For information about hotel pickups, call the **Coral Coast Railway Co.** (tel. 652-0434 or 652-8731).

Across the road from the train station is the **Kalevu Cultural Center** (tel. 652-0200, fax 652-0322; Tues.–Sun. 0900–1700, www.fiji culturalcentre.com), a recreated Fijian village dispensing instant Fijian culture to tourists. The basic one-hour tour is F$20, while a full day at the center costs F$79 including tours of the Fiji, Samoa, Tonga, Rotuma, New Zealand, and Kiribati villages, a dance show, hotel transfers, and a *lovo* lunch. This tour is offered Tuesday, Thursday, and Saturday from 1000–1600, and if you can make your own way to the Center and don't require a hotel pickup, the price drops to F$49. The Ka Levu Cultural Center also provides accommodations with three large dormitories at F$55 pp and double rooms at F$65 pp. Both options include all meals and a guided tour.

Pacific Green Fiji (tel. 650-0055, www.paci ficgreenfiji.com), on Queens Road 3.5 km east of the Ka Levu Cultural Center, manufactures stylish tropical furniture from coconut tree logs. Visitors are welcome.

Malaqereqere Villas

Malaqereqere Villas (tel. 652-0704, fax 652-0708), 500 meters off Queens Road, 2.5 km east of Shangri-La's Fijian Resort, stands on a hill overlooking Cuvu Bay. The four deluxe villas, each with three bedrooms, kitchen, fridge, and lounge are F$394 single or double, F$475 for three to six persons (minimum stay three nights). The local walk-in rate is about 40 percent lower than this. There's a swimming pool.

SIGATOKA SAND DUNES

From the mouth of the Sigatoka River westward, five kilometers of incredible 20-meter-high sand dunes separate the cane fields from the beach. These dunes were formed over millennia as sediments brought down by the river were blown back up onto the shore by the southeast trades. The winds sometimes uncover human bones from old burials, and potsherds lie scattered along the seashore—these fragments have been carbon dated at up to 3,000 years old. Now and then giant sea turtles come ashore here to lay their eggs.

It's a fascinating, evocative place, protected as a national park since 1989 through the efforts of the National Trust for Fiji. The **Visitors Center** (tel. 652-0243; daily 0800–1800, admission F$5, persons 18 and under F$2) is on Queens Road, about seven km east of Shangri-La's Fijian Resort and four km west of Sigatoka. Exhibits outline the ecology of the park, and you can hike along trails over dunes that reach as high as 50 meters in one area. For an extra F$3, a park ranger will give you a personal guided tour. It's well worth a visit to experience this unique environment. (Sandboarding down the side of the dunes is not allowed.) Most buses between Nadi and Sigatoka will drop you right in front of the Sand Dunes Visitors Center on the main highway (though some express buses won't stop here).

Kulukulu

Fiji's superlative surfing beach is near Kulukulu village, five km south of Sigatoka, where the Sigatoka River breaks through Viti Levu's fringing reef to form the Sigatoka Sand Dunes. The surf is primarily a river-mouth point break with numerous breaks down the beach. It's one of the only places for beach-break surfing on Viti Levu, and unlike most other surfing locales around Fiji, no boat is required here. The windsurfing in this area is fantastic, as you can either sail "flat water" across the river mouth or do "wave jumping" in the sea (all-sand bottom and big rollers with high wind). The surfing is good all the time, but if you want to combine it with windsurfing, it's good planning to surf in the morning and windsurf in the afternoon when the wind comes up. You can also bodysurf here. Be prepared, however, as these waters are treacherous for novices. There's a nice place nearby where you can swim in the river and avoid the ocean's currents. The beach itself looks like an elephant graveyard, covered with huge pieces of driftwood.

American surfer Marcus Oliver runs a small budget resort behind the dunes called **Club Masa** (tel. 650-1282), also known as Oasis Budget Lodge, three km off Queens Road. The rates including two good meals are F$28 pp in the 10-bed dormitory or F$50 pp in the two double rooms and a four-bedded room. Camping is F$22 pp. There's no electricity, but the layout is attractive and the location excellent. Have a beer on their pleasant open porch. Food and drinks are not available during the day, but you can use their kitchen to prepare lunch (bring snack foods). Leave your valuables behind before going out for an evening stroll, however, as this is an isolated area. Snorkeling trips are F$10 including gear, horseback riding F$20, and fishing F$10–30 pp. Surfboard rentals are F$30 a day. When Marcus is away, his father Gordon Oliver manages the property. It's a good base from which to surf this coast.

Sunbeam Transport (tel. 650-0168) has buses (F$.60) from Sigatoka to Kulukulu village nine or 10 times a day from Monday to Saturday, but none on Sunday and holidays. Taxi fare to Club Masa should be around F$5, and later you may have to pay only a dollar for a seat in an empty taxi returning to Sigatoka. Due to a land dispute with the local village, taxis cannot drive right up to Club Masa and you must walk the last ten minutes from a reception building.

SIGATOKA

Sigatoka (sing-a-TO-ka) is the main business center for the Coral Coast and headquarters of Nadroga/Navosa Province. The racially mixed population numbers around 8,000. A new bridge over the Sigatoka River opened here in 1997, replacing an older bridge damaged during a 1994 hurricane but still used by pedestrians and the cane railway. The town has a picturesque riverside setting and is pleasant to stroll around. The pink and white fantasy mansion up on the hill above Sigatoka and visible from afar is owned by local businessman Bal Krishna Naidu.

Upriver from Sigatoka is a wide valley known as Fiji's "salad bowl" for its rich market gardens beside Fiji's second-largest river. Vegetables are grown in farms on the west side of the valley, while the lands on the east bank are planted with sugarcane. Small trucks use the good dirt road up the west side of the river to take the produce to market, while a network of narrow-gauge railways collects the cane from the east side. You can drive right up the valley in a normal car. The locals believe that Dakuwaqa, shark god of the Fijians, dwells in the river.

The valley also supplies South Pacific Foods Ltd., an organic food producer owned by the French transnational entrepreneur Pernod Ricard. The company's Sigatoka cannery produces juices from bananas, mangos, guava, papayas, and tomatoes purchased from villagers who harvest fruit growing wild on their land. Large plantations have never flourished here due to the threat of hurricanes.

Near Sigatoka, five km up the left (east) bank of the river from the bridge, is the **Tavuni Hill Fort** on a bluff at Naroro village. The fort was established by the 18th-century Tongan chief Maile Latemai and destroyed by native troops under British control in 1876. The nearby village is still inhabited by persons of Tongan descent. An interpretive center and walkways have been established here, and admission is F$6 for adults or F$3 for children (closed Sun.). There's a good view of the river and surrounding countryside from this site. Those without transport can take a taxi from Sigatoka to the reception area (about F$15 return including a one-hour wait). Otherwise the Mavua bus will bring you here from Sigatoka at 0830 or 1030. To hike there from Sigatoka takes about an hour or so each way and it's more pleasant to walk along the cane railway line than on the dusty road.

Accommodations

The **Riverview Hotel** (tel. 652-0544), above Melrose Restaurant facing the new bridge in town, has six rooms with bath and balcony at

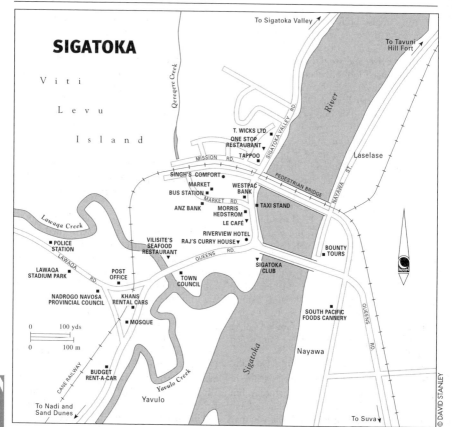

SIGATOKA

V i t i

L e v u

I s l a n d

Qereqere Creek

Lawaqa Creek

T. WICKS LTD.
ONE STOP RESTAURANT
TAPPOO

SIGATOKA VALLEY RD.

River

To Sigatoka Valley

To Tavuni Hill Fort

Laselase

PEDESTRIAN BRIDGE

NAVAWA ST.

SINGH'S COMFORT
MARKET
BUS STATION
WESTPAC BANK
ANZ BANK
MORRIS HEDSTROM
TAXI STAND
LE CAFÉ
RIVERVIEW HOTEL
VILISITE'S SEAFOOD RESTAURANT
RAJ'S CURRY HOUSE

MISSION RD.
MARKET RD.
QUEENS RD.

POLICE STATION
LAWAQA RD.
POST OFFICE
LAWAQA STADIUM PARK
TOWN COUNCIL
NADROGO NAVOSA PROVINCIAL COUNCIL
KHANS RENTAL CARS
MOSQUE

SIGATOKA CLUB
BOUNTY TOURS

SOUTH PACIFIC FOODS CANNERY

QUEENS RD.

Sigatoka

Nayawa

0   100 yds
0   100 m

CANE RAILWAY
BUDGET RENT-A-CAR
Yavulo Creek
Yavulo

To Nadi and Sand Dunes

To Suva

© DAVID STANLEY

F\$35/45 single/double. A large public bar is downstairs, so be prepared for noise.

The **Sigatoka Club** (tel. 650-0026), across the traffic circle from the Riverview, has four fan-cooled rooms with private bath at F\$35/45 single/double. Check that there's water before checking in and bring mosquito coils. The rooms are often full, but the Club's bar is always good for a beer or a game of pool (three tables). The bar is open Monday–Saturday 1000–2200, Sunday 1000–2100.

Singh's Travelers Comfort (tel. 650-0514), also known as "Singh's Millennium Backpackers Motel," upstairs in a gloomy two-story building behind The Chemists facing Sigatoka market, has a few rooms at F\$20/30 single/double. Ask at

Singh's Chinese Restaurant in the arcade of the same building.

Food

A number of basic restaurants around the bus station and market dispense greasy fast food to bus passengers during their 15-minute stop here. Some of the worst food in Fiji is served here.

If you don't have to catch a bus, it's worth the short stroll to **One Stop Restaurant** (tel. 652-0602; Mon.–Sat. 0700–1700), near Tappoo on Sigatoka Valley Road. Don't take the fast food in the warmer on the counter—ask for the hot Indian curries made to order at around F\$4 a plate. The same family operates another restaurant of the same name a bit farther along the same way and you should check both (the duplication in names is to avoid buying another business license).

Le Café (tel. 652-0877; Mon.–Sat. 0900–1700), next to Jack's Handicrafts, offers a choice of nine set lunches for F$6.50 (pizzas F$7–16). Connect to the Internet at Le Surf Café here for F$.20 a minute. Le Café is sort of touristy and always full of day-trippers from the resorts.

Sigatoka's top Indian restaurant is **Raj's Curry House** (tel. 650-1470; daily 0800–2300), on Queens Road next to the Riverview Hotel. The curries listed on their printed menu are priced F$5.50–9.50, including five vegetarian dishes at around F$5. It's always full of savvy locals.

The chef at Raj's used to cook for the **Sigatoka Club** (tel. 650-0026) across the street where meals cost F$7.50–15.50 (printed menu). You're better off eating at Raj's, then crossing the street for a beer.

Vilisite's Seafood Restaurant (tel. 650-1030; daily 0800–2130), on Queens Road, has sandwiches (F$3), curries, fried rice, chop suey (F$5–8), and fish and chips (F$6–12) for lunch. At dinner from 1900–2130 you have a choice of six complete meals priced F$20–45. Taxi drivers get a commission to bring tourists here, but it's still a good value compared to the resorts.

Shopping

Sigatoka has ubiquitous souvenir shops and a colorful local market with a large handicraft section (especially on Wednesday and Saturday). **Jack's Handicrafts** (tel. 650-0810, www.jacks fiji.com) facing the river sells the traditional handmade **Fijian pottery** made in Nakabuta and Lawai villages near Sigatoka.

For quality snorkeling gear, try **Nats** (tel. 650-0064), upstairs between the Colonial National Bank and Big Bear on the street facing the river.

Services

There are four banks in Sigatoka. The ANZ Bank opposite the bus station and the Westpac Bank have Visa/MasterCard ATMs outside their offices.

Sigatoka Money Exchange (tel. 652-0422; weekdays 0830–1700, Sat. 0830–1300), between

Jack's Handicrafts and the Riverview Hotel, changes money at rates similar to the banks without commission.

T-Wicks Ltd. (tel. 652-0505), on Sigatoka Valley Road, offers Internet access at F$.20 per minute.

Health

The District Hospital (tel. 650-0455) is 1.5 km southwest of Sigatoka, out on the road to Nadi.

Dr. Gurusmarna D. Dasi (tel. 650-0369) and Dr. Rudy Gerona and Dr. (Mrs.) Aida Gerona (tel. 652-0128) all work out of offices on Sigatoka Valley Road, facing the river a bit north of the old bridge. They're open weekdays 0730–1600, Saturday 0730–1300.

Patel Chemist (tel. 650-0213) is behind the market.

Transportation

Pacific Transport (tel. 650-0088) express buses leave Sigatoka for Suva at 0845, 0910, 1010, 1425, 1800, and 1945 (127 km, 3.5 hours, F$7.45), and for Nadi Airport at 0935, 1115, 1220, 1500, 1800, and 2020 (70 km, 1.5 hours, F$4.05). **Sunbeam Transport** has express buses to Suva at 0640, 0800, 1220, 1320, and 1500. Many additional local services also operate to/from Nadi (61 km). Beware of taxi drivers hustling for fares at the bus station who may claim untruthfully that there's no bus going where you want to go.

Weekdays you can arrange your own 4.5-hour, F$6 tour by taking the 0900 **Paradise Transport** (tel. 650-0028) bus up the west side of the Sigatoka Valley to Tubarua and back. Other buses to Tubarua leave at 1130, 1430, 1730, and 1900. Carriers to places farther up the valley like Korolevu (F$7) and Namoli (F$7) leave weekdays just after noon, returning the next day. They park beside a mango tree at the market, just around the corner from Sigatoka Bus Station.

Budget Rent-a-Car (tel. 650-0986) is at Niranjan's, opposite the Mobil Service Station at the west entrance to town. **Khans Rental Cars** (tel. 650-1229) has an office at Midas Automotive next to the mosque in Sigatoka.

KOROTOGO

A cluster of budget places to stay and one large American-run resort are at Korotogo, eight km east of Sigatoka, with only the Outrigger Reef Resort, Sandy Point Beach Cottages, and Tubakula Beach Resort right on the beach itself. Most of the places to stay farther east at Korolevu are more upmarket. East of Korotogo the sugar fields of western Viti Levu are replaced by coconut plantations, with rainforests creeping up the green slopes behind.

A road almost opposite the Outrigger Reef Resort leads to a bird park called **Kula Eco Park** (tel. 650-0505, fax 652-0202; daily 1000–1630, admission F$15, children under 12 half price, www.fijiwild.com). It's your only chance to get a close look at the *kula* lorikeet, the Kadavu musk parrot, the goshawk, flying fox fruit bats, and others in near natural settings. The park has a captive breeding program for the endangered crested iguana and peregrine falcon. Displays explain it all.

Sports and Recreation

Aqua Safari (Kaylee Birch, tel. 652-0901, fax 652-0907, aquasafari@connect.com.fj), on the traffic circle at Korotogo, does two-tank dives each morning at F$140. In the afternoon there's a snorkeling trip costing F$30 pp including gear. Their PADI certification course is F$575.

Mountain View Horse Riding (tel. 923-4783), on the beach opposite The Crow's Nest, charges F$10/20 for a short/long ride.

Accommodations

Under US$25: Just west of the Outrigger Reef Resort at Korotogo is **Waratah Lodge** (tel. 650-0278), with three large A-frame bungalows at F$45 double, plus F$10 per additional person up to six maximum. The two rooms below the reception in the main building are F$39 single or double. Cooking facilities are provided. The swimming pool and charming management add to the allure. It's a good value and recommended.

A bit east of the Outrigger and right on the beach, **Tubakula Beach Resort** (tel. 650-0097, fax 650-0201, www.fiji4less.com) offers a holiday atmosphere at bargain rates. The 22 pleasant A-frame bungalows with fan, cooking facilities, and private bath, each capable of sleeping three or four, vary in price from F$66 triple near the highway or F$73 in the garden (F$13.50 extra for a fourth person). Renovated bungalows are F$85 double poolside, F$90 garden, or F$96 beachfront (third persons F$17.50). One self-catering house has three rooms with shared bath at F$39/43 single/double. Their "Beach Club" dormitory consists of eight rooms, each with four or five beds at F$17.50 a bed. Tubakula caters to independent travelers rather than people on "Feejee Experience" style packages. Prices have remained relatively low because the owners don't pay commissions to Nadi travel agents, which works to your advantage. Instead, small discounts are available to youth hostel, VIP, and Nomads cardholders, and if you stay a week it's 10 percent off. A communal kitchen is available to all, plus a swimming pool, restaurant, games room, nightly videos, and mini-market. Late readers will like the good lighting. Tubakula's conference building can host conferences, meetings, and seminars for up to 250 people (it's often used by NGOs). Several sightseeing attractions and local cafes are within walking distance. Ask about the Thursday night *lovo* (underground oven feast) at Malevu village, 500 meter east of Tubakula. The snorkeling here is good, there's surfing and scuba diving nearby, and bus or taxi excursions are available. What more do you want? Basically, Tubakula is a quiet, do-your-own-thing kind of place for people who don't need lots of organized activities. Seated on your terrace watching the sky turn orange and purple behind the black silhouettes of the palms along the beach, a bucket of cold Fiji Bitter stubbies close at hand, you'd swear this was paradise! It's one of the most popular backpacker's resorts in Fiji and well worth a couple of nights.

US$25–50: Grayelen Lodge (Graham and Helen Mulligan, tel./fax 652-0677), off Queens Road, four km east of Sigatoka and two km west of the Korotogo traffic circle, has three self-catering units with fridge at F$50 for up to four persons. There's a swimming pool and a large porch with a deck, though it's on a hill rather than the beach. It's still a good value.

The **Marau Motel** (tel. 652-0807, fax 652-0829, maraumotel@connect.com.fj), 19 Queens Road north of the traffic circle in Korotogo, has four self-catering apartments at F$35/55/70 single/double/triple including a light breakfast. A backpackers dorm upstairs with five beds and its own kitchen is F$18 pp. It's some distance from the beach.

Uncle T's Lodge (tel./fax 652-0235), on Queens Road a bit closer to the traffic circle, has a self-catering, two-bedroom flat on the back side of the owners home at F$100. Taken separately, the two doubles and one single room are F$40/50 single/double with breakfast, or F$20 pp in a four-bed dorm.

The **Crow's Nest Resort** (tel. 650-0230, fax 652-0354, www.crowsnestfiji.com), on Sunset Strip a few hundred meters southeast of the traffic circle, offers 18 split-level duplex bungalows with cooking facilities and verandah at F$88 single or double, plus F$20 pp to four maximum. The Crow's Nest Dormitory behind the reception is F$20 pp for the eight beds. The restaurant facing the swimming pool often has inexpensive curry specials. The nicely landscaped grounds are just across the road from the beach, and good views over the lagoon are obtained from the Crow's Nest's elevated perch. "Feejee Experience" groups often stay here.

The **Vakaviti Motel and Dorm** (tel. 650-0526, fax 652-0424, www.vakaviti.com), next to the Crow's Nest, has four self-catering units facing the pool at F$65 single or double, and a five-bed family *bure* with one double and three single beds at F$75 double. Children under 12 are free. The six-bed dormitory is F$15 pp. Stay a week and the eighth night is free. Facilities include a swimming pool and a large lending library/book exchange at the reception. Day trips to Natadola Beach are F$15 pp.

The **Casablanca Hotel** (tel. 652-0600), next door to Vakaviti, is a two-story hillside building on the inland side of Sunset Strip. Its eight rooms with cooking facilities and arched balconies begin at F$45/60 single/double.

Sandy Point Beach Cottages (Bob Kennedy, tel. 650-0125, fax 652-0147, cbcom@connect.com.fj) shares the same beach with the adjacent Outrigger Reef Resort. Three fan-cooled beachfront units with full cooking facilities are offered at F$75 single, F$85 double or triple, one garden bungalow is F$75 double, and a five-bed cottage is F$135. Set in spacious grounds right by the sea, Sandy Point has its own freshwater swimming pool. The eight huge satellite dishes you see on their lawn allow you to pick up 10 channels on the TV in your room. It's a good choice for families or small groups, but it's often full so you must reserve well ahead.

US$50–100: The **Bedarra Inn** (tel. 650-0476, fax 652-0116, www.bedarrafiji.com), 77 Sunset Strip, a bit west of the Outrigger, has 21 air-conditioned rooms with fridge in a two-story block at F$125/145/165 double/triple/quad. It's all tastefully decorated, but only four rooms have microwaves. A swimming pool, video room, and lounge round out the facilities.

US$150–250: The 254-room **Outrigger Reef Resort** (tel. 650-0044, fax 652-0074, www.outrigger.com/fiji) plunges down the hillside from Queens Road to a sandy beach. A great view of this Fijian village-style complex can be had from the reception. In 2000, this property underwent a US$23.3 million redevelopment, and to provide more building space the main highway was rerouted away from the coast. The new hotel is owned by Australians Geoff Shaw and Bob Cliff, who also run Castaway Island Resort in the Mamanucas, and it's managed by Outrigger Hotels of Hawaii. The Outrigger Reef caters to the middle market, providing comfortable, unpretentious facilities at affordable package prices. The four-story main building on the hill has 167 air-conditioned rooms with ocean views and balconies, beginning at F$410 for up to four people. Down near the huge million-liter swimming pool by the beach is a three-story block remaining from the old Reef Resort with 40 air-conditioned rooms starting at F$440. Scattered around the grounds are 47 regular thatched *bure* with fan from F$475, and five big duplex *bure* at F$1,150 for a family of up to six. Rates include tax and a buffet breakfast, and a reduced local walk-in rate is often offered. Wheelchair accessible rooms are available. A free "kids club" operates from 0900–2100. Even if you're not staying here, it's worth coming for the Fijian firewalking Friday at 1830 (F$15), followed by *meke* and buffet (F$45) in the restaurant. There's a small shopping mall, and Thrifty Car Rental and Rosie The Travel Service have desks just off the lobby. A tunnel under the highway near the tennis courts leads to the Kula Eco Park. Internet access is F$5 for 15 minutes.

Food

Facing the beach just west of the Outrigger Reef Resort is the **Beach Side Restaurant** (tel. 652-0584; daily 0800–2130) with chicken, meat, and seafood dishes for F$5–14, vegetarian food at F$5.50–7. Pizza is F$7–15 (dinner only). A minimarket and handicraft shop adjoin the restaurant. To get there from the Outrigger, go down onto the beach and walk west.

Le Café Garden Restaurant (tel. 652-0877; daily 1000–2300) is between the Beach Side Restaurant and Waratah Lodge. Pizzas are F$7–16, specials F$6.50 (choice of six). Happy hour is 1700–1900, and there's disco dancing after 2200 Friday and Saturday. Under Swiss management, this place has class although the food receives varied reviews.

Another evening you could walk 800 meters west to the **Crow's Nest Restaurant** (tel. 650-0230; daily 0700–1500 and 1800–2130) with dinner mains at F$10. The nicest place for a meal out along this way is the **Bedarra Inn** (tel. 650-0476; daily 0700–1500 and 1800–2200), with main dishes ranging from pasta Bedarra at F$15 to lobster for F$38. Their specialty is seafood curry (F$23). The **Sinbad Pizza Restaurant** (tel. 652-0600) at the Casablanca Hotel isn't as nice as these (pizza F$8–22).

Getting There

Local buses on Queens Road stop at the doors of the Outrigger Reef Resort and Tubakula Beach Resort. For the Crow's Nest, Vakaviti, Casablanca, Bedarra, and Waratah, get off the bus at the traffic circle on the coast, just where the highway turns inland and heads east toward the Outrigger. From there, follow the old highway (Sunset Strip) south along the beach to your hotel.

Car Rentals and Tours

Thrifty Car Rental (tel. 652-0242) has a desk in the lobby of the Outrigger Reef Resort. The **Avis** office (tel. 652-0144) is on the beach opposite Waratah Lodge just west of the resort.

Coastal Rental Cars (tel. 652-0228, fax 652-0888, coastalrentalcar@connect.com.fj), on Korotogo Back Road near the traffic circle at Korotogo, rents cars at F$115/500 for one/six days including tax and insurance.

The **Beach Side Restaurant** (tel. 652-0584), across the street from Avis, rents cars at F$100 a day all inclusive. They also offer taxi tours to Natadola (F$80) and Pacific Harbor (F$80) or a full day of sightseeing at F$100—all prices are for the car. Jiten Kumar of **Sunstrip Tours** (tel. 924-7161) offers the same and is very accommodating.

Adventures in Paradise (tel. 652-0833, fax 652-0848, wfall@connect.com.fj) operates tours to Biausevu Falls (F$89 including lunch, drinks, and guides) and the Naihehe Cave (F$99). For pick-ups around Nadi, add F$20 to these prices. Book through your hotel tour desk (and wear disposable shoes on the falls hike). These trips are highly rated.

Vatukarasa

This small village between Korotogo and Korolevu is notable for its quaint appearance and **Baravi Handicrafts** (tel. 652-0364), 7.5 km east of the Outrigger Reef Resort. Baravi carries a wide selection of Fijian handicrafts at fixed prices and it's worth an outing if you're staying at one of the Coral Coast resorts. If you swim here, beware of dangerous currents.

KOROLEVU

At Korolevu, east of Korotogo, the accommodations tend to cater to a more upscale crowd, and cooking facilities are usually not provided for guests. These places are intended primarily for people on packaged beach holidays who intend to spend most of their time unwinding. Distances between the resorts are great, so for sightseeing you'll be dependent on your hotel's tour desk. An exception is The Beachouse, which opened in 1996. The Coral Village Resort and Waidroka

Bay Resort farther east also accommodate budget travelers, but they're both far off the highway.

Mike's Divers (Mike and Phylis Jaureguy, tel./fax 653-0222, www.dive-fiji.com), at Votua village near Korolevu, offers diving at F$75/125/350/500 for one/two/six/10 tanks, plus F$20 for gear. Night diving is F$95. Non-divers can snorkel from the boat for F$20 (or free from their beach). All the usual courses are offered, including open-water certification at F$450. Drift diving along Morgan's Wall is Mike's specialty (giant sea fans, soft corals, lion fish). Or ask to go to Turtle Town where all good turtles sleep.

South Pacific Adventure Divers (tel. 653-0055, fax 672-0719, www.divetravelfiji.com), based next to the pool at The Warwick Resort, also handles diving at The Naviti, Hideaway Resort, and Tambua Sands (free pick-ups). They frequent the top dive sites in the Beqa Lagoon, 40 minutes away by boat, as well as colorful sites closer to home. For Coral Coast dives, it's F$75/140 for one/two tanks including gear and lunch. Dive excursions to the Beqa Lagoon or Vatulele are F$255 for two tanks including gear (six-person minimum). SPAD's PADI four-day, open-water course is F$580.

Several companies offer tours to **Biausevu Falls,** a 25-minute hike from Biausevu village, itself just under three km inland from Queens Road between The Warwick and Vilisite's Restaurant. The trail to the falls zigzags across the river a half dozen times (expect to get your feet wet), but you'll enjoy a refreshing swim in the pool at the foot of the cascading waterfall. The village charges F$10 pp admission (children F$3) to the area. Call Adventures in Paradise (tel. 652-0833) in Korotogo for information on tours.

Accommodations

US$25–50: Vilisite's Restaurant (tel./fax 653-0054; daily 0800–2200), by the lagoon between The Warwick and The Naviti resorts at Korolevu, has four spacious air-conditioned rooms with bath and fridge at F$55/66 single/double, plus one four-person family room at F$75. Though the accommodations are a good value, "Felicity's Place" is better known for its restaurant, as this is *the* place to stop for food between Nadi and

Suva. You might bump into your country's ambassador on their beachside terrace. The favorite lunch dish is fish and chips at F$6/12 for a small/large portion. Otherwise there's chop suey or curries from F$5–8. Dinner consists of a choice of six set seafood menus costing F$20–45. The champagne sunsets here from 1800–1900 are unforgettable. Vilisite's gift shop has good prices on handicrafts. It's worth the taxi ride if you're staying at The Warwick or The Naviti.

One of the South Pacific's best budget resorts, **The Beachhouse** (tel. 653-0500 or 653-0530, www.fijibeachouse.com), is on a palm-fringed white beach just off Queens Road, between Navola and Namatakula villages, five km east of The Warwick. It's 35 km east of Sigatoka and 43 km west of Pacific Harbor. Their slogan is "low cost luxury on the beach" and the whole project was painstakingly designed to serve the needs of backpackers (and not as a dormitory tacked onto an upmarket resort as an afterthought). The two wooden accommodation blocks each have four five-bunk dorms downstairs (F$19 pp) and four fan-cooled loft rooms upstairs (F$22/25 pp in a three/two-bed dorm). In addition, 12 neat little units in a quadrangle at the heart of the property are F$60 single or double. Campers are allowed to pitch their tents on the wide lawn between the rooms and the beach at F$12 pp. Tax is included. Stay six nights and the seventh night is free. Separate toilet/shower facilities for men and women are just behind the main buildings, and nearby is a communal kitchen and dining area. It's all very clean and pleasant. Daily afternoon tea and scones is free for guests (a beach volleyball game usually follows). Meals in their beachfront Coconut Cafe consist of fish and chips, steak burgers, and vegetarian fare, costing F$9 or less (open until midnight). The closest grocery store is in Korolevu (there's only a tiny cooperative store in Namatakula). Not only is the ocean swimming good at high tide (unlike the situation at many other Coral Coast hotels where you may end up using the pool), but they'll take you out to the nearby reef in their launch for snorkeling (F$8 for a mask and fins, if required). However, do ask about the currents before going far off on your own—

tourists have drowned after being swept out through the reef passage here. A shopping/shuttle to Suva can be arranged (F$14 pp return, minimum of five). A vigorous four-hour round-trip hike to Navola Falls is possible. Sea kayaks (F$3 an hour) and bicycles (F$3 for two hours) are available, and there's a bush track up into the hills behind the resort. The lending library serves those who only came to relax. Check your email for F$.20 per minute. The Beachouse does get crowded whenever the "Feejee Experience" groups arrive, so call ahead for reservations.

Coral Village Resort (tel. 650-0807, corvill@connect.com.fj) is just beyond Namaqumaqua village, 4.5 km off Queens Road down the same difficult access road as Crusoe's Retreat (see below). Coral Village is set in a narrow valley that opens onto a lovely white beach (one of the Coral Coast's best) facing a protected lagoon. The eight large rooms with fan and fridge are F$60 pp including two meals. There's also a five-bed dorm at F$30 pp including two meals. Cooking your own food is not possible and lunch is extra (sandwiches F$5). Massage is F$30 an hour. Diving and other sporting activities must be arranged through Crusoe's Retreat. Unfortunately, Coral Village has gone downhill in recent years and now has a rundown, abandoned air.

The **Waidroka Bay Resort** (Michael Kaz, tel. 330-4605, fax 330-4383, www.waidroka.com) is up the steep, rough gravel road leading to the Dogowale Radio Tower between Korovisilou and Talenaua, four km off Queens Road. Operating since 1995, Waidroka has earned a reputation as one of Fiji's top surfing resorts. Accommodations include a 12-bed dormitory at F$18 pp, and three lodge rooms with shared bath at F$54 triple. The five neat little oceanfront bungalows with private bath, fan, bamboo walls, and covered deck are F$99/134 double/triple. The two superior bungalows are F$139/174/209 double/triple/quad, while five terrace rooms in a long building on the hillside are F$89 single or double, F$124 triple. The optional meal plan is F$38 pp a day (cooking facilities are not provided), otherwise dinner entrées in the restaurant are F$12–23. Videos are shown in the jungle bar at night. The surfing crowd loves this place, and

it's the only "mainland" resort surfing Frigate Passage and six other local breaks. Three breaks are just a five-minute boat ride from the resort, and they'll ferry you out there at F$20 pp for two hours. Snorkeling trips, which cost the same, are necessary, because Waidroka's beach is mediocre. Waidroka's 10-meter dive boat *Fiji Explorer* has two 200-hp engines, which enables it to reach Frigate Passage in just 20 minutes (surfers pay F$45 pp including lunch, with a F$180 minimum charge for the boat). Scuba diving is F$70/130 for one/two tanks, plus F$25 for equipment—perhaps the best diving on the Coral Coast. Open-water certification is F$499 (advanced courses available). Sportfishing aboard *Fishing Machine* is F$600/1,000 a half/full day for four persons. All this is fine, but you should be aware that the Waidroka Bay Resort is only of interest to those intending to participate in the various sporting activities. Those more interested in a relaxing seaside vacation probably won't like the fishing camp atmosphere. Call ahead and they'll pick you up at Korovisilou village on Queens Road at F$10 for the car. Reservations are necessary, because the Waidroka Bay Resort is often full.

US$50–100: Two self-catering flats are for rent at **Don's House** (no phone, http://members.optusnet.com.au/~jflight), a duplex building above Queens Road just west of Namada village, between the Baravi Handicraft Boutique and the Tambua Sands Beach Resort. Each air-conditioned unit has a full kitchen, lounge, floor-to-ceiling windows, and laundry facilities, and there's a small saltwater pool on the large covered deck out front. A sandy beach is across the highway. The price for up to five persons is F$140 for one unit and F$160 for the other or F$270 for both. Discounts are offered for stays over four nights. Reservations must be made through James and Lyndae Flight (tel. 61-2-9546-6256, fax 61-2-9594-1217, jflight@optusnet.com.au) in Sydney, Australia, as the on-site caretaker is unable to rent the units. Visiting celebrities in need of privacy often book this place.

The good value **Tambua Sands Beach Resort** (tel. 650-0399, fax 652-0265, www.tambuasandsfiji.com), in an attractive location facing the sea about 10 km east of the Outrigger Reef Resort, conveys a feeling of calm and peace. The 31 beach bungalows are F$125 double garden or F$135 beachfront (third persons F$30), continental breakfast included. No cooking facilities are provided. Though the restaurant is nothing special, there's a swimming pool, excellent live music most evenings, and a *meke* on Saturday night if enough guests are present. UTC has a tour desk at this hotel.

US$100–150: The 100-room **Hideaway Resort** (tel. 650-0177, fax 652-0025, www.hide awayfiji.com) at Korolevu, is three km east of Tambua Sands and 20 km east of Sigatoka. Set on a palm-fringed beach before a verdant valley, the 30 fan-cooled *bure* are F$280 triple, while the 58 *bure* with air conditioning go for F$305. The 10 air-conditioned villas are F$364. Four larger family units suitable for up to six people go for F$482. Some rooms get a lot of disco noise from the bar or traffic noise from the adjacent highway. A full buffet breakfast is included in all rates (no cooking facilities). The lunch and dinner plan is F$40 pp a day (minimum of three days). This big resort provides entertainment nightly, including a *meke* on Tuesday and Friday (free), firewalking on Thursday (F$15), and an all-you-can-eat Fijian feast Sunday night (F$26.50). The resort's oceanside pool is one of the largest on the Coral Coast. Surfing is possible on a very hollow right in the pass here (not for beginners), and scuba diving can be arranged. Beware of unperceived currents and expect dead coral if you snorkel here (possible at high tide only). The Rosie The Travel Service desk arranges other trips and Thrifty Car Rental bookings.

Crusoe's Retreat (Liam and Cathie Costello, tel. 650-0185, fax 652-0666, www.crusoes retreat.com), by the beach four km off Queens Road from Naboutini, was formerly called the Man Friday Resort. It's the most isolated place to stay on the Coral Coast. The 28 large *bure* each have two double beds, a fridge, and a porch. The 11 "seaside" *bure* are F$236 double, while the 17 "seaview" bungalows on the hillside are F$195. Only units 1–6 have thatched roofs (No. 1 is the closest to the beach). Readers have complained about salty, damp rooms and low water

pressure here. Children under 12 sleep free. Prices include a buffet breakfast, afternoon tea, and non-motorized sports such as kayaks, sail boards, and paddle boards. The mangrove jungle tour is free and a daily activity program is prepared. The lunch and dinner plan is F$45 pp. Don Wood runs the on-site dive shop (www.dive crusoes.com), charging F$92/169 for one/two tanks including gear. The resort's name alludes to Daniel Defoe's novel *Robinson Crusoe,* and the footprint-shaped freshwater swimming pool symbolizes Man Friday. This resort is much more upscale than nearby Coral Village Resort, although the beach isn't as nice. If you call ahead, they'll pick you up from the bus stop on the main highway at F$5 per carload.

US$150–250: The Naviti Resort (tel. 653-0444, fax 653-0099, www.navitiresort.com.fj), five km east of Hideaway Resort and 100 km from Nadi Airport, has 140 spacious air-conditioned rooms and suites in a series of two-story blocks beginning at F$364/472 single/double. The price includes all meals with unlimited wine or beer plus many activities. Breakfast is the best meal of the day. The all-inclusive price allows you to enjoy your holiday without mounting bills (a room alone is F$282 single or double). Kids under 16 stay and eat free when sharing with parents on the Naviti's comprehensive all-inclusive plan. The Naviti is also one of the more wheelchair accessible resorts on this coast. There's firewalking on Wednesday (F$15) and a *lovo* on Friday (F$30). The five tennis courts are floodlit at night. Nonguests may use the nine-hole golf course for F$20, and scuba diving is offered. Other facilities include a swimming pool, mini fitness center, beauty center, Internet access (F$.30 a minute), ATM in the lobby, and a boutique. Rosie The Travel Service has a desk at The Naviti. Scuba diving is with South Pacific Adventure Divers. This spacious resort shares its beach with a Fijian village.

The Warwick Fiji (tel. 653-0555, fax 653-0010, www.warwickfiji.com), on the Queens Road six km east of The Naviti, is the third-largest hotel on the Coral Coast (after The Fijian and the Outrigger Reef). Erected in 1979 and part of the Hyatt Regency chain until 1991, it's now owned by the same Singapore-controlled company as The Naviti and there's a shuttle bus between the two. The 250 air-conditioned rooms are in three-story wings running east and west from the soaring Hyatt-style lobby. It's F$332 double for the 51 rooms with mountain views, F$371 for the 166 with ocean views, F$523 for the 23 club rooms, and F$697 for the 10 suites, buffet breakfast included. Two children 12 and under sleep and eat free when sharing with their parents. The Wicked Walu seafood restaurant on a small offshore islet connected to the main beach by a causeway serves large portions but is expensive (dinner only). The other hotel restaurants can be crowded with Australian families and you might even end up waiting in line (F$53 meal plan). There's live music in the Hibiscus Lounge Wednesday–Saturday until 0100 and nightly disco dancing. The firewalking is on Monday and Friday at 1830 (F$15). This plush resort is very much oriented toward organized activities with a complete sports and fitness center. South Pacific Adventure Divers' dive shop is next to the pool. Thrifty Rent A Car and UTC Tours have desks at The Warwick. The Avis Rent a Car office (tel. 653-0833) is 1.5 km west at the BP service station in Korolevu. If you enjoy the excitement of large resorts full of guests, The Warwick may be for you.

PACIFIC HARBOR

Southeastern Viti Levu from Deuba to Suva is wetter and greener than the coast to the west, and the emphasis changes from beach life to cultural and natural attractions. Pacific Harbor satisfies sporting types, while Fiji's finest river trips begin at Navua. In this area, scattered Indo-Fijian dwellings join the Fijian villages that predominate farther west. All of the places listed below are easily accessible on the fairly frequent Galoa bus from Suva market.

Pacific Harbor is a sprawling South Florida-style condo development and instant culture village, 148 km east of Nadi Airport and 49 km west of Suva. It was begun in the early 1970s by Canadian developer David Gilmour (the current owner of Wakaya Island) and his father Peter

Munk, and good paved roads meander between the landscaped lots with curving canals to drain what was once a swamp. Many residents have boats tied up in their back yard, and if it weren't for the backdrop of deep green hills you'd almost think you were in some Fort Lauderdale suburb. Many of the 180 individual villas are owned by Australian or Hong Kong investors.

In recent years Pacific Harbor has been eclipsed by the sunnier Denarau area near Nadi, and after the May 2000 coup, tourism to Pacific Harbor dropped to nearly nothing. Some relief came in mid-2003 when Columbia Pictures filmed *Anaconda 2: The Black Orchid* around Pacific Harbor, injecting millions of dollars into the local economy. Where Pacific Harbor sparkles is in the excellent scuba diving in the Beqa Lagoon to the south and the river trips into the interior to the north. The beach here is the last reasonable beach before Suva.

Sights

At last report, Pacific Harbor's imposing **Cultural Center** (tel. 345-0095, www.pacific-harbour.com) presented shows only on Thursdays. For their F$18 admission, visitors are shown around a recreated Fijian village featuring a small "sacred island" dominated by a 20-meter-tall Bure Kalau (Spirit House). A tour guide "warrior" carrying a spear gives a spiel to visitors seated in a double-hulled *drua,* and Fijians attired in jungle garb demonstrate traditional canoe making, weaving, *tapa,* and pottery at stops along the route. Performances by the Dance Theater of Fiji or Fijian firewalking end the program. The Center's Waikiki-style **Marketplace of Fiji,** made up of mock-colonial boutiques and assorted historical displays, is open daily and accessible free of charge. It's always worth a stop, since you'll be able to see quite a bit of the Cultural Center from the catwalk and there are a few tourist shops and restaurants (but no bank). The main Pacific Harbor post office (with two card phones) is next to the Cultural Center.

Sports and Recreation

The 65 km of barrier reef around the 390-square-km Beqa Lagoon south of Pacific Harbor fea-

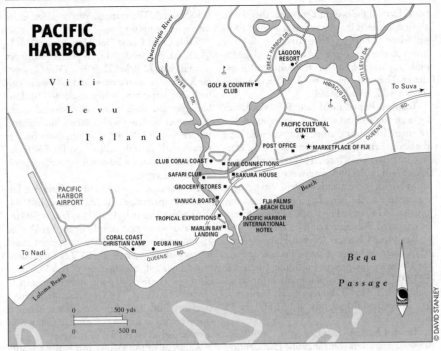

PACIFIC HARBOR

V i t i

L e v u

I s l a n d

Quaraniqio River

GREAT HARBOR DR.

LAGOON RESORT

RIVER DR.

GOLF & COUNTRY CLUB ■

HIBISCUS DR.

VITI LEVU DR.

To Suva

QUEENS RD.

PACIFIC CULTURAL CENTER ★

POST OFFICE ★ MARKETPLACE OF FIJI

CLUB CORAL COAST ■ ● DIVE CONNECTIONS

SAFARI CLUB ■ ■ SAKURA HOUSE

GROCERY STORES ■

YANUCA BOATS ■

TROPICAL EXPEDITIONS ■

MARLIN BAY LANDING ■

FIJI PALMS BEACH CLUB ■

PACIFIC HARBOR INTERNATIONAL HOTEL ■

Beach

PACIFIC HARBOR AIRPORT

CORAL COAST CHRISTIAN CAMP ■

DEUBA INN ■

To Nadi

QUEENS RD.

Loloma Beach

B e q a

P a s s a g e

0   500 yds

0   500 m

© DAVID STANLEY

tures multicolored soft corals and fabulous sea fans at **Sidestreets,** and an exciting wall and big fish at Cutter Passage. Aside from its surfing potential, **Frigate Passage** on the west side of the Beqa barrier reef is one of the top scuba diving sites near Suva. A vigorous tidal flow washes in and out of the passage, which attracts big schools of fish, and there are large coral heads. **Sulfur Passage** on the east side of Beqa is equally good. The top dive sites just north of Yanuca Island, such as Sidestreets, Soft Coral Grotto, Caesar's Rocks, and Coral Gardens, are easily accessible from Pacific Harbor.

Dive Connections (tel. 345-0541, fax 345-0539, diveconn@connect.com.fj) at 16 River Dr., just across the bridge from the Sakura Japanese Restaurant, visits all the best dive sites off Yanuca Island on their spacious 12-meter dive boat *Scuba Queen.* They charge F$90/110 for one/two tank dives. Night dives are F$80. You can rent gear at F$30 a day, but it's better to bring your own. Four-day PADI open water cer-

tification is F$450 (medical examination not required), otherwise there's an introductory two-dive package for F$150. Snorkelers are welcome to go along on their daily dive trips at F$50 pp including a nice lunch and snorkeling gear (they'll drop you off on Yanuca for snorkeling). The dive boat is also available for fishing charters. Dive Connections is run by a Kai Vavalagi couple, Leyh and Edward Harness, descendents of European settlers who arrived in Fiji a century and a half ago. Ask about the self-catering flat next to their office that they rent at F$50 double. They'll pick up anywhere within eight kilometers of the Pacific Harbor bridge.

Aqua-Trek Beqa (Brandon Paige, tel./fax 345-0324, www.aquatrekdiving.com) at the Pacific Harbor International Hotel's marina is an efficient operation with good rental equipment. They send their 11-meter boat, the *Aqua-Sport,* to the Beqa Lagoon twice daily. A two-dive excursion costs F$165, plus F$15 for gear. You may be offered a discount if you just walk in and

FIJI ISLANDS

book direct. If the boat isn't crowded, they'll take along non-divers for snorkeling at around F$40 pp. Some of Fiji's top shark diving is on offer here: you may see several three-meter bull sharks, plus gray reef, black tip, white tip, and nurse sharks. They only do the shark dive a couple of times a week, so call ahead.

Tropical Expeditions (tel. 345-0666), run by personable Charles Wakeham, operates the 18-meter live-aboard *Beqa Princess,* based near the bridge across the river from the Pacific Harbor International Hotel. This relatively small live-aboard carries only six divers on three-night scuba cruises to the islands south of Viti Levu, or on day trips to the Beqa Lagoon. Two-tank day trips are F$140 including lunch, or the boat may be chartered. A compressor is on board.

Baywater Charters (Steven Hay, tel. 345-0573), near the bridge at Pacific Harbor, operates the 18-meter *Turaga Levu* for fishing charters at F$1,500 a full day including lunch for six to eight anglers. They'll also rent the six-berth boat as a live-aboard fishing boat at F$1,800 for 24 hours all-inclusive.

Xtasea Charters (Rob Krause, tel. 345-0280, www.xtaseacharters.com) at Pacific Harbor offers game fishing from 10-meter aluminum boat *Xtasea* at F$700/1,200 a half/full day (six anglers).

Pacific Harbor's focal point is the soggy 18-hole, par-72 championship course at the **Pacific Harbor Golf and Country Club** (tel. 345-0048, fax 345-0262), designed by Robert Trent Jones Jr. The big event here is the Pacific Harbor Open in September. Green fees are F$15/30 for nine/18 holes; electric cart rental is F$20/35 for nine/18 holes and club hire is a further F$20. The clubhouse is a couple of kilometers inland off Queens Road. Unfortunately, the greens and fairways aren't being maintained as well as previously.

Accommodations

Under US$25: The 10-room **Pacific Safari Club** (tel. 345-0498, fax 345-0499, www.pacific safari.com) is just down Atoll Place from Sakura House Restaurant. A bed in a clean, modern four-bed dorm here is F$20, otherwise it's F$40/45 single/double with bath, fan, TV, and full cooking facilities (use of the air-conditioning

is F$5 extra). The manager can organize scuba diving discounts for you.

Club Coral Coast (Tak Hasegawa, tel. 345-0421, fax 345-0900, clubcoralcoast@connect .com.fj) is at 12 Belo Circle near Dive Connections. There are four air-conditioned rooms with bath in a self-catering villa at F$90/110 double/triple, plus three non-air-conditioned rooms in another building with a larger kitchen and terrace at F$80/90. In addition, three budget rooms with shared facilities go for F$20 pp. Amenities include a 20-meter swimming pool, tennis, and a gym.

For a cheaper room you must travel one km west from the bridge at Pacific Harbor. In 1994, the **Deuba Inn** (tel. 345-0544, fax 345-0818, theislander@connect.com.fj) opened at Deuba, 13 km west of Navua. They have eight small rooms with shared bath at F$17/27 single/double and five self-catering units at F$50/60 double/triple. The five-bed dorm and camping space are both F$10 pp. The Inn's restaurant serves excellent meals and their Sand Bar is handy if you're staying at the "dry" Christian Camp next door. Email access is F$.25 a minute.

Adjacent to the Deuba Inn is the friendly **Coral Coast Christian Camp** (tel. 345-0178, coralcoastcc@connect.com.fj). They offer four five-bed Kozy Korner rooms with a good communal kitchen and cold showers at F$12/21/30 single/double/triple (the warm shower in the ladies bathroom takes a F$.50 token). The five adjoining motel units go for F$21/34/43, complete with private bath, kitchen, fridge, and fan. Camping costs F$6 pp. A small selection of snack foods is sold at the office. No alcoholic beverages are permitted on the premises. The Camp is just across the highway from long golden Loloma Beach, the closest public beach to Suva. Watch your valuables if you swim there (place everything in the trunk if you have a rental car). The snorkeling is good in calm, dry weather. This beach may soon be redeveloped as the five-star Taunovo Bay Resort (www.taunovo bay.com). The CCCC is a good place to spend the night while arranging to get out to the surfers' camps on Yanuca Island. Just avoid arriving on a weekend, as it's often fully booked by church groups from Friday afternoon until Sunday afternoon.

US$25–50: Harbor Property Services Ltd. (tel./fax 345-0959, www.fijirealty.com), with an office at the Marketplace of Fiji, rents out five of the Pacific Harbor villas at F$95–110 for up to eight persons. All villas have kitchens, lounge, and washing machine, and some also have a pool. The minimum stay is three nights and there's a reduction after a week. A onetime cleaning fee of F$25 is charged, and F$5 a day for electricity is extra. It's a good value and well worth considering for a longer stay.

US$50–100: The 84 air-conditioned rooms at the three-story **Pacific Harbor International Hotel** (tel. 345-0022, fax 345-0262) are F$158 single or double plus tax. Specials are often available for a few musty, non-air-conditioned rooms. Formerly known as the Centra Resort, the Pacific Harbor International Hotel dates back to 1972 and has undergone several changes of ownership in recent years. It's at the mouth of the Qaraniqio River, between Queens Road and a long sandy beach, on attractive grounds and with a nice deep swimming pool. Unfortunately, an unpleasant sharp smell from the nearby mangroves can engulf the rooms after heavy rains.

The **Fiji Palms Beach Club and Resort** (Wendy Montgomery, tel. 345-0050, fax 345-0025, fijipalms@connect.com.fj), right next to the Pacific Harbor International Hotel, has 14 two-bedroom apartments with cooking facilities. Although most of the units have been sold as part of a timeshare scheme, they're sometimes available on a casual basis at F$165/990 a day/week (Sat.–Sat.) for up to six people.

The **Lagoon Resort** (Heather and Jim Sherlock, tel. 345-0100, fax 345-0270, www.lagoonresort.com), inland a couple of kilometers behind the Cultural Center, is beautifully set on Fairway Place between the river and the golf course, a 10-minute walk from the clubhouse. The 22 plush rooms with marble bathrooms and TV start at F$130 double. This hotel started out in 1988 as the Atholl Hotel, an upscale brothel for Middle Eastern potentates. It's a little secluded and VIP parties often stay here. In 2003, the Hollywood crew filming *Anaconda 2* spent 24 weeks here and a few props from the film are on the resort grounds.

Food

Kumarans Restaurant (tel. 345-0294; daily 0800–2000), across the highway from the Pacific Harbor International Hotel, has curry specials at lunchtime (F$4–5), but the dinner menu is pricey (F$8–12).

Curry House Fast Food (daily 0800–1700), at the back of the Shell service station opposite the Pacific Harbor International Hotel, serves tasty curries in the F$4–5 range.

Et's Eatery (Mon.–Sat. 0700–1800, Sun. 0900–1800), at the Pic'n Pac Supermarket in the Marketplace of Fiji, serves sandwiches at F$2.50, hamburgers or fish and chips F$4.

The **Oasis Restaurant** (tel. 345-0617; daily 0930–1430 and 1800–2200), in the Marketplace of Fiji, has a sandwich (F$5), salad, and burger (F$7.50) menu at lunchtime, and more substantial mains for dinner (F$15–30). A pot of tea is F$2.50. Internet access here is F$.30 a minute, and a large selection of paperbacks is for sale at F$2.50 a book.

There are five small grocery stores beside Kumarans near the bridge at Pacific Harbor and a supermarket in the Marketplace of Fiji. For fruit and vegetables you must go to Navua.

Transportation

Only group charter flights from Nadi Airport land at Pacific Harbor's airstrip, but all of the Queens Road express buses stop here. The express bus to Pacific Harbor from Suva stops next to the highway near the Pacific Harbor International Hotel, a kilometer from the Cultural Center. The slower Galoa buses will stop right in front of the Cultural Center itself (advise the driver beforehand).

The air-conditioned Queens Coach leaves from the front door of the Pacific Harbor International Hotel for Suva (F$12) at 1110, for Nadi at 1715 (F$15). The air-conditioned Fiji Express leaves the hotel for Nadi at 0830 (F$27) and for Suva at 1630 (F$16). Much cheaper and just as fast are the regular Pacific Transport express buses, which stop on the highway: to Nadi Airport at

0750, 0930, 1035, 1315, 1605, and 1835 (148 km, three hours, F$8); to Suva at 1015, 1100, 1155, 1555, 1930, 2115 (49 km, one hour, F$2.95). Sunbeam Transport buses to Lautoka stop here at 1100, 1210, and 1415.

Rosie The Travel Service (tel. 345-0655) in the Marketplace of Fiji can make any required hotel or tour bookings, and they also represent Thrifty Rent-a-Car. Call ahead if you want to pick up a car here.

NAVUA

The bustling riverside town of Navua (pop. 4,500), 39 km west of Suva, is the market center of the mostly Indian-inhabited rice-growing delta area near the mouth of the Navua River. It's also the headquarters of Serua and Namosi Provinces. If low-grade copper deposits totaling 900 million metric tons located just inland at Namosi are ever developed, Navua will become a major mining port, passed by four-lane highways, ore conveyors, and a huge drainpipe for copper tailings. For at least 30 years, millions of tons of waste material will be dumped into the ocean every year by an operation consuming more fossil fuel energy than the rest of the country combined. The present quiet road between Navua and Suva will bustle with new housing estates and heavy traffic, Fiji's social and environmental balance will be turned on its head, and the change from today will be total!

For visitors, Navua town is important as the gateway to the fabulous Navua River. The lower Navua below Namuamua is navigable in large outboard motorboats, while rubber rafts are used on the much faster upper Navua through the narrow Navua Gorge. Either way, a river trip will give you a memorable glimpse of central Viti Levu.

Transportation

All buses between Suva and Nadi stop at Navua. Large village boats leave from the wharf beside Navua market for Beqa Island south of Viti Levu daily except Sunday, but more depart on Saturday (F$15 pp one way). Be aware that safety equipment is usually absent on such boats. Regular flat-bottomed punts carry local villagers 25 km up the Navua River to Namuamua village on Thursday, Friday, and Saturday afternoons and they'll probably agree to take you along for around F$7. You can charter an outboard from Navua wharf to Namuamua almost anytime at F$70 for the boat round-trip. The hour-long ride takes you between high canyon walls and over boiling rapids with waterfalls on each side. Above Namuamua is the fabulous **Upper Navua,** accessible only to intrepid river-runners in rubber rafts. It's also possible to reach the river by road at Nabukelevu.

River Tours

An easy way to experience the picturesque lower Navua is with **Discover Fiji Tours** (Lionel Danford, tel. 345-0180 or 346-0480, fax 345-0549, discoverfiji@connect.com.fj), which has an office on the riverside in Navua. They offer a "Jewel of Fiji Day Tour" up the Navua River by motorized canoe, leaving Navua at 1030 daily and returning at 1630. You then have a choice of any two of three activities: a swim at a waterfall, a visit to a Fijian village with a welcoming kava ceremony, or a float down the river on a bamboo raft (no village visits on Sunday). The cost is F$90 pp from Suva (minimum of two), lunch included. Call to arrange a pick-up or meet them at their river base office in Navua (open 0930–1130 and 1530–1700).

Wilderness Ethnic Adventure Fiji (Donald Mani, tel. 331-5730, fax 330-5450, www.wildernessfiji.com.fj) also runs full-day motorized boat trips 20 km up the river from Navua to Nukusere village, where lunch is served and visitors get an introduction to Fijian culture. Any travel agent in Suva can make the bookings (adults F$79, children F$44, minimum of 10). Wilderness also has canoe and rubber raft trips down the Navua River (F$89, minimum of four). You must call ahead, because they don't hang around in Navua waiting for customers to appear.

In addition, **Mr. Sakiusa Naivalu** (tel. 346-0641) of Navua organizes upriver boat trips to Namuamua village at F$80 pp (minimum of three) with the possibility of spending the night there. These trips depart Navua at 1000, returning at 1600. Readers found Sakiusa's tour "enjoyable."

The brochures of some of the Navua River tour companies promise a kava ceremony and other events, but these are only organized for groups. If only a couple of you are going that day, nothing much of the kind is going to happen. Ask when booking, otherwise just relax and enjoy the boat ride and scenery, and wait to see dancing elsewhere. And even if there is a ceremony, you may find sitting on the hard floor uncomfortable. The bamboo raft trip may also be shorter than you expected, and the climb to the highest waterfall could be strenuous. At some point, you may be asked to make a "contribution" to the village, and the ladies will display their handicrafts in a manner that makes it difficult to refuse to buy. Although this visit isn't for everyone, it could also be the highlight of your trip. (If saving money is a priority and you can get a small group together, it's much cheaper to go to Navua by public bus and hire a market boat from there.)

White-Water Rafting

Exciting white-water rafting trips on the Upper Navua River west of Namuamua are offered by **Rivers Fiji** (tel. 345-0147, fax 345-0148, www .riversfiji.com), with an office on the grounds of the Pacific Harbor International Hotel. You're driven over the mountains to a remote spot near Nabukelevu where you get in a rubber raft and shoot through the fantastic Upper Navua Gorge (inaccessible by motorized boat). Experienced paddlers can do the same on their own in an inflatable kayak, upon request. Due to the class III rapids involved, children under 12 are not accepted, but for others it's F$180 including lunch.

Rivers Fiji also does a less strenuous run down the Wainikoroiluva River north of Namuamua, on which it's possible to paddle your own inflatable kayak. This costs F$160 for adults, or F$80 for children under the age of 12 who are floating with a paying adult. Two days of kayaking on the Wainikoroiluva is F$430. If you're really keen, ask about overnight camping expeditions on the Upper Wainikoroiluva. These trips conclude with a motorized punt ride down the Lower Navua Gorge from Namuamua to Nakavu village, where you reboard the van to your hotel.

Rivers Fiji also offers one-day sea kayaking trips to Beqa Island (F$150 pp, minimum of eight). You cross to Beqa by catamaran, then explore a tiny uninhabited island and paddle into Malumu Bay. Deep inside this cliff-lined bay, hundreds of fruit bats are seen clinging to the trees. A secret mangrove tunnel provides an escape south to the great blue beyond. A different trip takes you along the coast of Viti Levu from Pacific Harbor in a two-person sea kayak at F$65 pp. It's a great way to explore the mangroves or glide across the reefs. All prices above include pick-ups around Pacific Harbor. Transfers from other Coral Coast and Suva hotels are F$30 pp extra, from Nadi F$45 extra.

Discover Fiji Tours (tel. 346-0480, discover fiji@connect.com.fj) also does a Wainikoroiluva River trip between Naqarawai and Navunikabi villages, with white-water rafting, swimming at a waterfall, and a long boat ride down the river. It's F$145/165 pp from Navua/Nadi (two-person minimum).

OFFSHORE ISLANDS
Vatulele Island

This small island, 32 km south of Viti Levu, reaches a height of only 34 meters at its north end; there are steep bluffs on the west coast and gentle slopes facing a wide lagoon on the east. Both passes into the lagoon are from its north end. Five different levels of erosion are visible on the cliffs from which the uplifted limestone was undercut. There are also rock paintings, but no one knows when they were executed. Vatulele today is famous for its *tapa* cloth *(masi)*.

Other unique features of 31-square-km Vatulele are the sacred **red prawns,** which are found in tidal pools at Korolamalama Cave at the foot of a cliff near the island's rocky north coast. These scarlet prawns with remarkably long antennae are called *ura buta,* or cooked prawns, for their color. The red color probably comes from iron oxide in the limestone of their abode. It's strictly *tabu* to eat them or remove them from the pools. If you do, it will bring ill luck or even shipwreck. The story goes that a princess of yesteryear rejected a gift of cooked prawns from a suitor and

FIJI ISLANDS

threw them in the pools, where the boiled-red creatures were restored to life.

In 1990, Vatulele got its own luxury resort, the **Vatulele Island Resort** (tel. 672-0300, fax 672-0062, www.vatulele.com) on the island's west side. The 18 futuristic villas in a hybrid Fijian/New Mexico style sit about 50 meters apart on a magnificent white sand beach facing a protected lagoon. The emphasis is on luxurious exclusivity: villas cost F$2,700 per couple a night, including meals, alcohol, and tax. "The Point," a two-story unit on a low cliff over the ocean, is F$5,850 with private pool. The minimum stay is four nights, and to make the resort more attractive to couples, children under 12 are not accepted. To preserve the natural environment, motorized water sports and a swimming pool are not offered, but there's lots to do, including sailing, snorkeling, windsurfing, paddling, fishing, tennis, and hiking, with guides and gear provided at no additional cost. Other than airfare to the island (see below), about the only things you'll be charged extra for are scuba diving (F$130/220 for one/two tanks) and massage (F$100 an hour). Vatulele's desalination plant ensures abundant fresh water. This world-class resort is a creation of Australian film producer Henry Crawford and thus appeals to the show business set, as well as upscale honeymooners (weddings arranged, bring your own partner). At Nadi Airport, you'll find them in office No. 15 upstairs from arrivals.

The 990 inhabitants live in four villages on the east side of Vatulele. Village boats from Viti Levu leave Paradise Point near Korolevu Post Office on Tuesday, Thursday, and Saturday if the weather is good. Resort guests arrive on a daily charter flight from Nadi, which costs F$792 pp roundtrip (or F$1,620 one way for a special four-person flight). The charters are operated by **Pacific Island Seaplanes** (tel. 672-5644, fax 672-5641), which uses a four-seat Beaver seaplane able to land on the lagoon near the resort. If weather conditions prevent use of the seaplane, a Twin Otter aircraft is sent. It lands on the island's small private airstrip near the villages, six km from Vatulele Island Resort.

Yanuca Island

This island west of Beqa should not be confused with the Yanuca Island on which Shangri-La's Fijian Resort is found. In a coconut grove tucked below the jungly green peaks on the northwest side of the island is the **Batiluva Beach Resort** (tel. 992-0019, tel./fax 345-1019, www.batiluva.com). Batiluva is one of Fiji's top surf resorts, and since its opening in 1998, Americans Sharon Todd and Dan Thorn have had to pay a high premium to the landowners to be able to operate here. The single 12-bed dorm is F$100 pp and a double "honeymoon" *bure* is available at F$120 pp—excellent value compared to places like Namotu and Tavarua. There's only kerosene lighting here, but the grounds are nicely landscaped with lots of places to sit and hammocks under the trees. Included are gourmet meals, appetizers, kayaks, paddle boats, surfing, snorkeling, village tours, and transfers. Fishing and scuba diving are available at additional cost. This is the closest resort to Frigate Passage and Batiluva's surfing boats go there every day (30–40 minutes away). This resort is on the leeward side of the island, so it's usually calm, and you can snorkel among the colorful fish right off their excellent white beach. Several top dive sites, including Three Nuns, Sidestreets, Soft Coral Grotto, and Gilligan's Tower, visited daily by the dive boats from Pacific Harbor, are only a km straight out from this beach. During the sailing season, yachts rock offshore.

A 10-minute walk east of Batiluva over a rocky headland is a second surfing camp called the **Yanuca Island Resort** (Ratu Penaia Drekeni, tel. 345-0801 or 996-5937, www.frigatesreef.com), also known as Frigate Surfriders or Pena's Resort. It offers bunks in a 12-bunk dormitory *bure* at F$120 pp, plus tax. Private *bure* are F$180/290/420 single/double/triple. Included are accommodations and meals, surf transfers, and sportfishing. Boat transfers from the mainland are F$40 pp return. In 2004 this resort was completely rebuilt, so check their website for the latest details.

The lefthander in Frigate Passage southwest of Yanuca has been called the most underrated wave in Fiji: "fast, hollow, consistent, and deserted." Pena's leaflet describes it thus:

Frigate Passage, out on the western edge of the Beqa Barrier Reef, is a sucking, often barreling photocopy of Cloudbreak near Nadi. The wave comprises three sections that often join up. The outside section presents a very steep take-off as the swell begins to draw over the reef. The wave then starts to bend and you enter a long walled speed section with stand-up tubes. This leads to a pitching inside section that breaks onto the reef, and if your timing is right you can backdoor this part and kick out safely in deep water.

All surfing is banned on Sunday. Yet even without the surfing, Yanuca is still well worth a visit (great beach-based snorkeling). The resorts are across the island from Yanuca's single Fijian village, a 30-minute walk. Shells, mats, and necklaces can be purchased from the locals. And as on neighboring Beqa, Fijian firewalking is a tradition here. Village boats to the one Fijian village on Yanuca depart on Monday and Saturday afternoons from the bridge near the Pacific Harbor International Hotel. Call Batiluva or Pena's for direct transfers.

Beqa Island

Beqa (MBENG-ga) is the home of the famous Fijian firewalkers; Rukua, Naceva, and Dakuibeqa are firewalking villages. Nowadays they perform mostly at the hotels on Viti Levu, although the local resorts occasionally stage a show. At low tide you can hike part of the 27 km around the island: Rukua to Waisomo and Dakuni to Naceva are not hard, but the section through Lalati can be difficult. Malumu Bay, between the two branches of the island, is thought to be a drowned crater. Climb Korolevu (439 meters), the highest peak, from Waisomo or Lalati. Kadavu Island is visible to the south of Beqa.

The **Lawaki Beach House** (Sam and Christine Tawake-Bachofner, tel. 992-1621 or 338-1273, fax 330-7386, www.lawakibeachhouse.com) faces the golden sands of Lawaki Beach west of Naceva village. This resort has two double *bure* at F$80/140 single/double and one six-bed family *bure* or dormitory at F$60 pp, all meals included

(reduced rates for children under 12). To camp (own tent) is F$40 pp including meals (no self-catering facilities provided). There's a spacious lounge in the main house and good snorkeling right offshore. Boat transfers from Navua are F$140 roundtrip for the first person, then F$20 per additional person. You can also get there on village boats departing the wharf beside Navua market around noon daily except Sundays (F$12–15 pp one way). Ask for the Naceva boat (Sam or Christine can arrange this for you).

Beqa's newest top end place is the **Kulu Bay Resort** (tel. 331-6444, www.kulubay.com) which opened on the south side of Beqa a bit closer to Naceva in 2003. The seven spacious *bure* are F$2,000 pp all-inclusive. Scuba diving is available at an additional charge.

The **Marlin Bay Resort** (tel. 330-4042, fax 330-4028, www.marlinbay.com), on the west side of Beqa between Raviravi and Rukua villages, dates back to 1991. The 25 *bure* start at F$370 single or double. The meal plan is F$110 pp a day (no cooking facilities). In practice, almost everyone arrives on a prearranged package tour, so these prices are only indicative. Most guests are scuba divers who come to dive the Beqa Lagoon, and it's worth noting that the famous dive sites like Golden Arch and Sidestreets are almost as far from Marlin Bay as they are from Pacific Harbor (where diving costs a lot less). It's F$160 for a two-tank boat dive (plus F$50 for equipment, if required). Surfing runs to Frigate Pass are arranged at F$160/320 pp a half/full day. The Marlin Bay boat picks up guests at Pacific Harbor for F$100 pp roundtrip. Add 12.5 percent tax to all rates.

The more upscale **Lalati Resort** (tel. 347-2033, fax 347-2034, www.lalati-fiji.com), at the north opening of Malamu Bay, has six two-bedroom *bure* at F$660/860/1,110 single/double/triple including meals, kayaking, and windsurfing. A two-tank dive is F$180, plus F$60 for gear. Lalati has cast itself as an upscale sports resort with gourmet meals and spacious accommodations. There's a swimming pool and spa. Compulsory bus/boat transfers from Suva or Nadi are F$190 pp roundtrip.

Suva and Vicinity

The pulsing heart of the South Pacific, Suva is the largest and most cosmopolitan city in Oceania. The port is always jammed with ships bringing goods and passengers from afar, and busloads of commuters and enthusiastic visitors stream constantly through the busy market bus station. In the business center there are Indo-Fijian women in saris, friendly Fijians, expatriate Australians and New Zealanders in shorts, industrious Asians, and wavy-haired Polynesians from Rotuma and Tonga.

Suva squats on a hilly peninsula between Laucala Bay and Suva Harbor in the southeast corner of Viti Levu. The verdant mountains north and west catch the southeast trades, producing damp conditions year-round. Visitors sporting sunburns from Fiji's western sunbelt resorts may appreciate Suva's warm tropical rains (which fall mostly at night). In 1870, the Polynesia Company sent Australian settlers to camp along mosquito-infested Nubukalou Creek on land obtained from High Chief Cakobau. When efforts to grow sugarcane in the area failed, the company convinced the British to move their headquarters here, and since 1882 Suva has been the capital of Fiji.

Today this exciting, diverse city of 170,000—a fifth of Fiji's total population and half the urban population—is also about the only place in Fiji where you'll see a building taller than a palm tree. Growing numbers of high-rise office buildings and hotels overlook the compact downtown area. The British left behind imposing colonial buildings, wide avenues, and manicured parks as evidence of their rule. The Fiji School of Medicine, the University of the South Pacific, the Fiji Institute of Technology, the Pacific Theological College, the Pacific Regional Seminary, and the headquarters of many regional organizations and diplomatic missions have been established here. In addition, the city offers some of the hottest nightlife between Kings Cross (Sydney) and North Beach (San Francisco), plus shopping, sightseeing, and many good-value places to stay and eat. About the only thing Suva lacks is a beach.

Keep in mind that on Sunday the shops may be closed, restaurants keep reduced hours, and fewer taxis or buses are on the road. In short, the city is very quiet—a good time to wander around in relative peace. If you decide to catch a boat or flight to Levuka and spend the weekend there, you should book your ticket a couple of days in advance. Otherwise, it's worth dressing up and attending church to hear the marvelous choral singing. Most churches have services in English, but none compare with the 1000 Fijian service at Centenary Methodist Church on Stewart Street.

The lovely *Isa Lei,* a Fijian song of farewell, tells of a youth whose love sails off and leaves him alone in Suva, smitten with longing.

SIGHTS
Central Suva

Suva's colorful **municipal market,** off Rodwell Raod next to the bus station, the largest retail produce market in the Pacific, is a good place to dabble. If you're a yachtie or backpacker, you'll be happy to hear that the market overflows with fresh produce of every kind. Bundles of kava roots are sold, and liquid kava is consumed at *yaqona* dens upstairs in the market. On the street outside, Fijian women sell fresh pineapple and guava juice from glass "fish tank" containers.

From the market, walk south on Scott Street to the **Fiji Visitors Bureau** in a former customs house (1912) opposite Suva's General Post Office. At the corner of Thomson and Pier Streets opposite the visitors bureau is the onetime **Garrick Hotel** (1914), with a Sichuan Chinese restaurant behind the wrought-iron balconies upstairs. Go east on Thomson to the picturesque colonial-style arcade (1919) along **Nubukalou Creek,** a campsite of Suva's first European settlers. The block behind the arcade is the site of a former Morris Hedstrom store, which burned in late 1998. Carpenters Fiji Ltd. is now redeveloping the property.

Cumming Street, Suva's main shopping area,

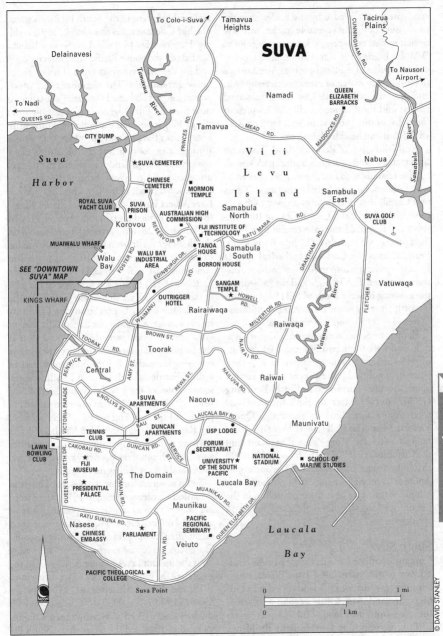

To Colo-i-Suva

Tamavua
Heights

Tacirua
Plains

SUVA

Delainavesi

To Nausori
Airport

Namadi

QUEEN
ELIZABETH
BARRACKS

To Nadi

QUEENS RD.

Suva

Harbor

CITY DUMP

Tamavua

MEAD   RD.

V i t i

Nabua

L e v u

★ SUVA CEMETERY

CHINESE
CEMETERY

MORMON
TEMPLE

I s l a n d

Samabula
East

SUVA GOLF
CLUB

ROYAL SUVA
YACHT CLUB

SUVA
PRISON

AUSTRALIAN HIGH
COMMISSION

Samabula
North

Korovou

FIJI INSTITUTE OF
TECHNOLOGY

RATU MARA   RD.

MUAIWALU WHARF

TANOA
HOUSE

Samabula
South

Walu
Bay

WALU BAY
INDUSTRIAL AREA

BORRON HOUSE

SEE "DOWNTOWN
SUVA" MAP

SANGAM
TEMPLE

★ HOWELL
RD.

Vatuwaqa

KINGS WHARF

OUTRIGGER
HOTEL

Rairaiwaqa

MILVERTON RD.

Raiwaqa

TOORAK
RD.

BROWN ST.

Toorak

NAIRAI RD.

Raiwai

Central

SUVA
APARTMENTS

Nacovu

LAUCALA BAY RD.

Maunivatu

TENNIS
CLUB

DUNCAN
APARTMENTS

DUNCAN RD.

USP LODGE

FORUM
SECRETARIAT

LAWN
BOWLING
CLUB

CAKOBAU RD.

FIJI
MUSEUM

UNIVERSITY
OF THE SOUTH
PACIFIC

★

NATIONAL
STADIUM

SCHOOL OF
MARINE STUDIES

The Domain

PRESIDENTIAL
PALACE

Laucala Bay

RATU SUKUNA RD.

MUANIKAU RD.

Nasese

CHINESE
EMBASSY

PACIFIC
REGIONAL
SEMINARY

L a u c a l a

★ PARLIAMENT

Maunikau

Veiuto

B a y

PACIFIC THEOLOGICAL
COLLEGE

Suva Point

0   1 mi

0   1 km

Moon

FIJI ISLANDS

© DAVID STANLEY

runs east from the park by the bridge over the creek. Suva's original vegetable market was here until it moved to its present location just prior to WW II. During the war, Cumming Street became a market of a different sort as Allied troops flocked here in search of evening entertainment, and since the early 1960s Cumming has served tourist and local shoppers alike in its present form. To continue your walk, turn right on Renwick Road and head back into town.

At the junction of Renwick Road, Thomson Street, and Victoria Parade is a small park known as **The Triangle** with five concrete benches and a white obelisk bearing four inscriptions: "Cross and Cargill first missionaries arrived 14th October 1835; Fiji British Crown Colony 10th October 1874; Public Land Sales on this spot 1880; Suva proclaimed capital 1882." Inland a block on Pratt Street is the **Catholic cathedral** (1902) built of sandstone imported from Sydney, Australia. Between The Triangle and the cathedral is the towering **Reserve Bank of Fiji** (1984), which is worth entering to see the currency exhibition (Mon.–Fri. 0900–1600, www.rbf.gov.fj).

Return to Suva's main avenue, Victoria Parade, and walk south past **Sukuna Park,** the site of pro-democracy demonstrations in 1990 and occasional political protests even today. Farther along are the colonial-style **Fintel Building** (1926), nerve center of Fiji's international telecommunications links, the picturesque **Queen Victoria Memorial Hall** (1904), later Suva Town Hall and now the Ming Palace Restaurant, and the **City Library** (1909), which opened in 1909 thanks to a grant from American philanthropist Andrew Carnegie (one of 2,509 public library buildings Carnegie gave to communities in the English-speaking world). All of these sights are on your right.

South Suva

Continue south on Victoria Parade past the headquarters of the **Native Land Trust Board,** which administers much of Fiji's land on behalf of indigenous landowners. Just beyond and across the street from the Holiday Inn is Suva's largest edifice, the imposing **Government Buildings** (1939), once the headquarters of the British colonial establishment in the South Pacific. A statue of Chief Cakobau stares thoughtfully at the building. Here on May 14, 1987, Col. Sitiveni Rabuka carried out the South Pacific's first military coup and for the next five years Fiji had no representative government. The chamber from which armed soldiers abducted the parliamentarians is now used by Fiji's high court, accessible from the parking lot behind the building. Prime Minister Timoci Bavadra and the others were led out through the doors below the building's clock tower (now closed) and forced into the back of army trucks waiting on Gladstone Road.

The main facade of the Government Buildings faces **Albert Park,** where aviator Charles Kingsford Smith landed his tri-motor Fokker VII-3M on June 6, 1928, after arriving from Hawaii on the first-ever flight from California to Australia. (The first commercial flight to Fiji was a Pan Am flying boat, which landed in Suva Harbor in October 1941.) Facing the west side of the park is the elegant, Edwardian-style **Grand Pacific Hotel,** built by the Union Steamship Company in 1914 to accommodate its transpacific passengers. The 75 rooms were designed to appear as shipboard staterooms, with upstairs passageways surveying the harbor, like the promenade deck of a ship. For decades the Grand Pacific was the social center of the city, but it has been closed since 1992. In 2002, the Government of Fiji purchased the building for F$4.7 million from the Republic of Nauru, which had been doing nothing with it. Hopefully a suitable partner willing to renovate the property will appear and the Grand Pacific will again be grand.

South of Albert Park are the pleasant **Thurston Botanical Gardens,** opened in 1913, where tropical flowers such as cannas and plumbagos blossom. The original Fijian village of Suva once stood on this site. (It's fun to observe the young Indo-Fijian couples enjoying brief moments here away from the watchful eyes of their families.) On the grounds of the gardens is a clock tower dating from 1918, and the **Fiji Museum** (tel. 331-5944, fax 330-5143; Mon.–Sat. 0930–1600, admission F$7, children under 13 F$5, www.fijimuseum.org.fj), founded in 1904 and the oldest in the South Pacific. The first hall deals in archaeology, with much information about Fiji's unique pottery. The centerpiece is a double-hulled canoe made in 1913, plus five huge *drua* steering oars each originally held by four men, several large sail booms, and a bamboo house raft *(bilibili)*. The cannibal forks near the entrance are fascinating, as are the whale tooth necklaces and the large collection of Fijian war clubs and spears. The history gallery beyond the museum shop has a rich collection of 19th-century exhibits featuring items connected with the many peoples who have come to Fiji, including Tongans, Europeans, and Solomon Islanders. Notice the rudder from HMS *Bounty.* An air-conditioned room upstairs contains an exhibition of *tapa* cloth and displays on Indo-Fijians. The museum shop sells copies of the museum journal, *Domodomo,* plus other interesting books.

South of the gardens is the **Presidential Palace,** formerly called Government House, the residence of the British governors of Fiji. The original building, erected in 1882, burned after being hit by lightning in 1921. The present edifice, which dates from 1928, is a replica of the former British governor's residence in Colombo, Sri Lanka. The grounds cannot be visited.

From the seawall south of the palace you get a good view across Suva Harbor to Beqa Island (to the left) and the dark, green mountains of eastern Viti Levu punctuated by Joske's Thumb, a high volcanic plug (to the right). Follow the seawall south past a few old colonial buildings, and turn left onto Ratu Sukuna Road, the first street after the Police Academy.

About a kilometer up this road is the **Parliament of Fiji** (1992, www.parliament.gov.fj), an impressive, traditional-style building with an orange pyramid-shaped roof. From May 19 to July 13, 2000, Fiji's prime minister and several dozen members of parliament were held hostage in the parliamentary complex by a gang of rebel soldiers and assorted thugs led by bankrupt businessman George Speight, who claimed his coup attempt was in defense of indigenous Fijian rights. Thankfully, things are almost back to normal now, and the gatekeeper at the main entrance around the corner off Vuna Road will give you a Visitors Pass to go inside. Huge *tapa* banners hang from parliament's walls, and skillfully plaited coconut fiber ropes from the Lau Group highlight the decor. The parliamentary mace is Chief Cakobau's historic war club originally presented to Queen Victoria and later returned to Fiji by Britain. It's only brought out when Parliament is in session. The location is spectacular with scenic sea and mountain views.

Both Protestants and Catholics have their most important regional training facilities for ministers and priests in South Suva, and the **Pacific Theological College** is just down Vuna Road from Parliament. From **Suva Point** nearby you get a good view of **Nukulau,** a tiny reef island southeast of Suva. This was the site of residence of the first U.S. consul to Fiji, John Brown Williams, and the burning of Williams's house on July 4, 1849, set in motion a chain of events that led to Fiji becoming a British colony. Later Nukulau was used as the government quarantine station, and most indentured Indian laborers spent their first two weeks in Fiji here. Until recently it was a public park, but coup master George Speight is now serving a life sentence in jail on Nukulau.

From Suva Point it's a good idea to catch a taxi to the University of the South Pacific (F$2.50). The Nasese bus does a scenic loop through the beautiful garden suburbs of South Suva: Just flag it down if you need a ride back to the market. In the other direction, catch it from the southwest corner of the bus station.

University of the South Pacific

A frequent bus from in front of the Vanua Arcade opposite Sukuna Park on Victoria Parade brings you directly to the University of the South Pacific (get off when you see a McDonalds on the left). Founded in 1968, this beautiful 72.8-hectare campus on a hilltop overlooking Laucala Bay is jointly owned by 12 Pacific countries. Although over 70 percent of the 3,750 full-time and 4,750 part-time students here are from Fiji, the rest are on scholarships from every corner of the Pacific. The site of the USP's Laucala Campus was a Royal New Zealand Air Force seaplane base before the land was turned over to the USP.

From Laucala Bay Road follow the main walkway to the **University Library,** erected in 1988 with Australian aid. Across a wooden bridge behind the library, past the ANZ Bank and university bookstore, is a traditional Fijian *bure* called the Vale ni Bose, which is used for workshops and seminars. To the left of the *bure* is the **Oceania Center for Arts and Culture,** the university's art gallery (free) with a curvilinear mosaic floor. The center's director is the famous Tongan novelist Epeli Hau'ofa. To the right of (and behind) the *bure* is the **Institute of Pacific Studies,** housed in the former RNZAF officers' mess. This Institute is a leading publisher of insightful books written by Pacific islanders; these books may be perused and purchased at their bookroom inside the building.

Students from outside the Pacific islands pay F$1,390 tuition for each undergraduate course they take at the USP. Room and board are available at F$4,580 a year, and books will run another F$780. There are academic minimum-entry requirements and applications must be received by December 31 for the following term. The two semesters are late February to the end of June, and late July until the end of November. Many courses in the social sciences have a high level of content pertaining to Pacific culture, and postgraduate studies in a growing number of areas are available. Check the university's website www.usp.ac.fj for more information.

The USP is always in need of qualified staff, so if you're from a university milieu and looking for a chance to live in the South Seas, this could be it. If your credentials are impeccable you should write to the registrar from home. On the spot it's better to talk to a department head about his/her needs before going to see the registrar.

Northwest of Suva

The part of Suva north of Walu Bay accommodates much of Suva's shipping and industry. Carlton Brewery on Foster Road cannot be visited. About 600 meters beyond the brewery is the vintage **Suva Prison** (1913), a sinister colonial structure with high walls and barbed wire. Plans to replace this anachronism with a more modern facility have been on the back burner for years. Despite the colorful murals along Foster Road, one look at this place and you'll be a law-abiding

citizen for the rest of your stay in Fiji! Opposite the prison is the **Royal Suva Yacht Club,** where you can sign in and buy a drink, meet some yachties, and maybe find a boat to crew on. In the picturesque **Suva Cemetery,** just north, the Fijian graves are wrapped in colorful *sulus* and *tapa* cloth, and make good subjects for photographers. Gangs of inmates from the nearby jail are often assigned to dig the graves, a common practice in Fiji.

Catch one of the frequent Shore, Lami, or Galoa buses west on Queens Road, past the city dump and **Suvavou** village, home of the Suva area's original Fijian inhabitants, to the **Raffles Tradewinds Hotel** beyond Lami town, seven km from the market. Many cruising yachts tie up at the marina here, and the view of the Bay of Islands from the hotel is good.

Colo-i-Suva Forest Park

This lovely park, at an altitude of 122–183 meters, offers 6.5 km of trails through the lush forest flanking the upper drainage area of Waisila Creek. The mahogany trees you see here are natives of Central America and were planted after the area was logged in the 1950s. The park first opened in 1973. Enter from the Forestry Station along the Falls Trail. A half-kilometer nature trail begins near the Upper Pools, and aside from waterfalls and natural swimming pools there are thatched pavilions with tables at which to picnic. With the lovely green forests behind Suva in full view, this is one of the most breathtaking places in all of Fiji, and you may spot a few native butterflies, birds, reptiles, and frogs. The park is so unspoiled it's hard to imagine you're only 11 km from Suva.

The park (tel. 332-0211) is open daily 0900–1600, and there's a F$5 pp entry fee (under age 14 F$1, under two free) to cover maintenance and management. Security has improved since a police post was set up opposite Raintree Lodge, but you must still keep an eye on your gear if you go swimming in the pools (valuables can be left at the park office). Colo-i-Suva is easily accessible on the Sawani or Serea buses (F$.90), which leave from Lane No. 3 at Suva Bus Station every hour (Sunday every two hours). A 22-seater minibus

(F$1.60) also operates and is much faster than the regular buses. It picks up passengers from a different part of Suva Bus Station—ask the drivers of the Nausori minibuses parked on the corner closest to the market. The last bus back to Suva is around 1800. A taxi will be F$8. Make a circle trip of it by catching a bus from the park on to Nausori, rather than returning directly to Suva. And try to come on a dry day, as it's even rainier than Suva and the creeks are prone to flooding.

Also consider spending the night at Raintree Lodge, 50 meters from the entrance to the park (see Accommodations for details). Lunch and drinks can be ordered at the lodge's attractive restaurant/bar (tel. 332-0562), which overlooks a small lake.

Sports and Recreation

Beqa Divers (tel. 336-1088, www.beqadivers .com), 75 Marine Dr., near the Lami Shopping Center, is the country's oldest dive shop (established as Scubahire by Dave and Lorraine Evans in 1970). Their four-day PADI certification course (F$800) employs Fiji's only purpose-built diver training pool on their Lami premises. You'll need to show a medical certificate proving you're fit for diving. Beqa Divers arranges full-day diving trips to the Beqa Lagoon from their Pacific Harbor base for F$143, including two tanks, weight belt, backpack, and lunch. Other equipment can be rented. Beqa Divers will also take snorkelers out on their full-day dive trips for F$66 pp, snorkeling gear and lunch included. When things are slow they may offer a "special" reduced rate for the all-day scuba trip, if you ask. All diving is out of Pacific Harbor—the Suva office only takes bookings, does certification courses, and sells equipment.

Dive Center Ltd. (tel. 330-0599, fax 330-2639), 4 Matua St., Walu Bay (opposite Budget Rent-a-Car), fills scuba tanks but doesn't rent equipment or offer diving.

Surfers should call Matthew Light (tel. 999-8830), who runs a shuttle out to Sandspit Lighthouse, where there's good surfing on a southwest swell at high tide (F$25 pp round-trip).

At the 18-hole, par-72 **Fiji Golf Club** (tel. 338-2872), 15 Rifle Range Rd., Vatuwaqa, the course record is 65. Green fees are F$15/20 for nine/18 holes, club hire F$20 for a full set, plus pull trolley rental at F$5. Call ahead to ask if any competitions are scheduled as the course may be closed to the public at those times. Don't carry large amounts of cash or valuables with you around the course.

The **Olympic Swimming Pool,** 224 Victoria Parade, charges F$1.65 admission. It's open Monday–Friday 1000–1800, Saturday 0800–1800 (April–Sept.), or Monday–Friday 0900–1900, Saturday 0700–1900 (October–March). Lockers are available.

The **Suva Lawn Tennis Club** (tel. 331-1726; closed Sun.), Cakobau Road opposite the Fiji Museum, charges F$5 an hour to use their courts during the day or F$6.50 from 1800–2100. You can order lunch and drinks here.

The Fijians are a very muscular, keenly athletic people who send champion teams far and wide in the Pacific. You can see rugby (April–September) and soccer (March–October) on Saturday afternoons at 1400 at the **National Stadium** near the University of the South Pacific. Rugby and soccer are also played at Albert Park on Saturday, and you could also see a cricket game here (mid-Oct.–Easter). Soccer is also played on Sunday (but rugby is only on Saturday).

ACCOMMODATIONS

Suva offers a wide variety of places to stay, and the low-budget accommodations can be neatly divided into two groups. The places on the south side of the downtown area near Albert Park are mostly decent and provide communal cooking facilities to bona fide travelers. However, some of those northeast of downtown are dicey and cater mostly to "short-time" guests; few of these bother providing cooking facilities. Many of the medium-priced hotels and self-catering apartments are along Gordon Street and its continuation, MacGregor Road. If you want to spend some time in Suva to take advantage of the city's good facilities and varied activities, look for something with cooking facilities and weekly rates.

Some of the medium-priced hotels along Gordon Street offer specials when things are slow.

DOWNTOWN SUVA

To Nadi

Walu Bay

ELIZA ST.
FOSTER RD.

MAY ST.

EDINBURGH DR.

To Nausori Airport

Suva

KINGS WHARF

Harbor

PRINCES WHARF

WILLIAMS & GOSLING

BALI HAI NIGHTCLUB

CARPENTERS SHIPPING

RICHARDS AVE.

RENOWN RD.

JELLICOE

HARRIS

ESCOTT

RODWELL RD.

ROBERTSON RD.

MOTEL CAPITOL

SAF'S HOTEL

MOTEL 6

TROPIC TOWERS MOTEL

HARBOR LIGHT INN

NEW HAVEN MOTEL

COLONIAL WAR MEMORIAL HOSPITAL

WAIMANU RD.

LAUTOKA BUSES

SUVA FLEA MARKET

CARRIERS

COLONIAL LODGE

ANNANDALE APARTMENTS

BROWN ST.

BUS STATION

NADI TAXIS

STRUAN ST.

NINA ST.

TOP VIEW HOTEL

CAPRICORN HOTEL

OCEANVIEW HOTEL

DAVEY

MARKET

ROBERTSON

PATTERSON BROTHERS

ST. FORT ST.

WAIMANU RD.

BREWSTER

MINIBUS STATION

CENTENARY CHURCH

STEWART ST.

KOREA HOUSE

SUVA PRIVATE HOSPITAL

BREWSTER ST.

VILLAGE 6 CINEMAS

HARBOR TERMINAL

MARKS ST.

KINGS HOTEL

UPTOWN MOTEL

PACIFIC CONCERNS RESOURCE CENTER

TOURIST MOTOR INN

HANDICRAFT MARKET

EDWARD ST.

VISITORS BUREAU

THOMSON

POST OFFICE

CUMMING ST.

RENWICK

RADIBHA RD.

FIJI INDIAN CULTURAL CENTER

TOORAK

DUDLEY MEMORIAL CHURCH

CENTRAL ST.

THE TRIANGLE

GREIG ST.

ELLERY ST.

GANGARAM'S LAUNDRY

HIGH ST.

SHIRDI SAI MANDIR

STINSON

YWCA

RESERVE BANK

PRATT ST.

SPRING ST.

Sukuna Park

POLICE STATION

DOWNTOWN BOULEVARD CENTER

Nubukalou

PATEL

SUVA RD.

JOHNSON ST.

AMY ST.

AIR NEW ZEALAND

JOSKE

CATHOLIC CATHEDRAL

JAME MOSQUE

HUON ST.

CITY HALL

FINTEL BUILDING

GORDON ST.

MURRAY ST.

TOWN HOUSE HOTEL

FORSTER ST.

GREENPEACE

BUTT ST.

SUNSET MOTEL

HERCULES ST.

SELBORNE ST.

TOWER ST.

LAXMI NARAYAN TEMPLE

EDEN ST.

OLYMPIC POOL

SARITA FLATS

MACARTHUR ST.

Creek

CIVIC TOWER

CITY LIBRARY

SUKUNA HOUSE

ANGLICAN CATHEDRAL

HOLLAND ST.

HOLLAND

KNOLLYS

NATIONAL ARCHIVES

KIMBERLY ST.

SOUTHERN CROSS HOTEL

DESVOEUX ST.

DISRAELI RD.

FNPF PLACE

ELIXIR MOTEL

GOODENOUGH ST.

WOMEN'S CRISIS CENTER

MALCOLM ST.

TANOA PLAZA

BERRY ST.

U.S. EMBASSY

LOFTUS ST.

GORDON ST.

NATIVE LAND TRUST BOARD

CARNARVON ST.

THURSTON ST.

TUVALU HIGH COMMISSION

MARION RD.

GLADSTONE RD.

TRAVEL INN

GORRIE ST.

PENDER RD.

SUVA APARTMENTS

HOLIDAY INN SUVA

VICTORIA

GOVERNMENT BUILDINGS

GLADSTONE

BRITISH HIGH COMMISSION

MITCHELL ST.

SUVA MOTOR INN

PENDER ST.

PENDER COURT

MACGREGOR RD.

SOUTHERN CROSS RD.

ALLIANCE FRANÇAISE

PENINSULA HOTEL

NORMANBY

GRAND PACIFIC HOTEL

Albert Park

WILLIAMSON RD.

SOUTH SEAS PRIVATE HOTEL

0   200 yds

0   200 m

© DAVID STANLEY

FIJI ISLANDS

You might save money by calling a few of the places listed below to inquire about the day's "local rate," then take a taxi to the place of your choice. When things are slow, the receptionist may also agree to upgrade you to deluxe at no additional charge, provided you agree to stay for a few nights. Of course, these deals don't apply to overseas bookings.

South Suva

Under US$25: The 42-room **South Seas Private Hotel** (tel. 331-2296, fax 330-8646, www.fiji4less.com), 6 Williamson Rd., one block east of Albert Park, really conveys the flavor in its name. The building originally housed workers involved in laying the first telecommunications cable across the Pacific, and until 1983 it served as a girl's hostel. Things changed when backpackers took over the dormitories (and break-ins through the floorboards by amorous young men came to an end). Today you can get a bed in a five-bed dorm for F$13.50, a fan-cooled room with shared bath at F$22/32 single/double, or a better room with private bath at F$45 double. The owners have decided to keep their costs down by not paying commissions to the Nadi travel agencies—the only reason they aren't promoted by these outfits. You won't find the "Feejee Experience" crowd here either. Instead, you'll receive a F$1 discount if you have a youth hostel, VIP, or Nomads card. This quiet hotel has a pleasant veranda and a large communal kitchen. For a refundable F$10 deposit, you may borrow a plate, mug, knife, fork, and spoon, but there's a longstanding shortage of pots and pans. It's possible to leave excess luggage at the South Seas for free while you're off visiting other islands, but lock your bag securely. The staff changes money at bank rates. Catch a taxi here from the market (F$2) the first time you go.

Travel Inn (tel. 330-4254, www.fiji4less.com), a two-story building opposite the Fiji Red Cross at 19 Gorrie St., is owned by the same company as the South Seas Private Hotel. There are 16 fan-cooled rooms with shared bath at F$23/33 single/double, all with access to communal cooking facilities (shortage of utensils), and four self-contained apartments for F$45 triple daily (F$13 extra for a fourth person). A small discount is offered to youth hostel, VIP, and Nomads cardholders. There are plenty of blankets and good locks on the doors. Visitors from other Pacific islands often stay here, as this is one of Suva's better buys.

Pender Court (tel. 331-4992), 31 Pender Street, has 13 rooms beginning at F$35 single or double. There are also six one-bedroom studios for F$45. It's sometimes a little noisy, and maybe sleazy.

The high-rise **YWCA** (tel. 330-4829, fax 330-3004) on Sukuna Park has two singles and one double available for female foreign visitors only at F$10 pp.

US$25–50: Several apartment hotels on the hill behind the Central Police Station are worth a try. The congenial **Town House Apartment Hotel** (tel. 330-0055, fax 330-3446), 3 Forster St., is a five-story building with panoramic views from the rooftop bar (happy hour 1700–1900). The 28 air-conditioned units with cooking facilities and fridge are good value at F$48/60/72 single/double/triple and up.

Nearby and under the same ownership is the four-story **Sunset Apartment Motel** (tel. 330-1799, fax 330-3446), corner of Gordon and Murray Streets. Avoid the four rooms without cooking facilities that go for F$42/48 single/double, and instead ask for one of the 10 two-bedroom apartments with kitchens and fridge at F$50/65, or the deluxe apartment at F$70/90. The two-bedroom apartments cost F$11 per additional person. Some of the cheaper rooms are noisy and have uncomfortably soft beds. Sunset has a 12-bed dorm, which at F$9 pp is a bit cheaper than the one at the South Seas Private Hotel. The central location is great, but Sunset's dorm is three times as big as the one at the South Seas and cooking facilities are not provided. Security could be a problem here, since the dorm door is left open all day.

The Town House reception also handles bookings at **Sarita Flats** (tel. 330-0084), nearby at 39 Gordon St., where a bed-sitting room apartment with cooking facilities will be F$80 single or double (extra adult F$12). This two-story building lacks the balconies and good views of the Town House but is well maintained.

The **Southern Cross Hotel** (tel. 331-4233, fax 331-1819) is a high-rise concrete building at 63 Gordon Street. The 32 air-conditioned rooms accommodating up to three people start at F$95 for a standard room on the fourth floor, or F$135 for the deluxe rooms on the second, third, and fifth floors. The hotel restaurant on the 6th floor serves Korean dishes.

Four-story **Elixir Motel Apartments** (tel. 330-3288, fax 330-3383, plantworld@connect.com.fj), on the corner of Gordon and Malcolm Streets, has 15 two-bedroom apartments with cooking facilities and private bath at F$63 without air conditioning for up to three people, or F$74 with air conditioning. Weekly rates are 10 percent lower.

Twenty self-catering units owned by the National Olympic Committee are available at **Suva Apartments** (tel. 330-4280, fax 330-1647, fasanoc@fasanoc.org.fj), 17 Bau St., a few blocks east of Pender Court. The 10 fan-cooled units in this new four-story building are F$40/55/70 single/double/triple, while the 10 air-conditioned apartments are F$50/65/80. Ten percent is taken off on weekly rentals. By staying here you help support organized sports in Fiji!

Duncan Apartments (tel. 330-0377, fax 330-8716), 9 Duncan Road, has 15 self-catering air-conditioned flats with TV at F$60/350/800 a day/week/month for up to three people (add about F$100 to the monthly rate for gas, water, and electricity). This well-kept two-story complex is in a nice residential area east of Albert Park.

Anyone with any sort of business at the University of the South Pacific should consider staying at **USP Lodges** (tel. 321-2005, fax 331-4827, usplodges@usp.ac.fj). The accommodations here are in two clusters. The Upper Campus Lodge, overlooking the Botanical Garden on the main campus, has six small flats with TV and cooking facilities at F$54/64 single/double (or F$360/430 a week). Four rooms with shared bath in an older wooden building here are F$39/45. Down beside Laucala Bay near the School of Marine Studies is Marine Lodge with 20 self-contained rooms at F$44 single, and five self-catering units with TV at F$59/69 single/double. The reception for Marine Lodge is at Upper Campus Lodge. For a longer stay, ask about Waqavuka Flats near Upper Campus Lodge, which

offers monthly rates of F$475/750. Rooms in both sections of USP Lodges are often occupied by students on a semi-permanent basis, so it's best to call ahead to check availability.

US$50–100: The 10-story **Tanoa Plaza Hotel** (tel. 331-2300, fax 330-1300, www.tanoahotels.com), formerly known as the Berjaya Hotel, at the corner of Malcolm and Gordon Streets, is the tallest hotel in Fiji. The 60 air-conditioned rooms with fridge and TV all face the harbor. It's F$179 single or double (or F$410 for one of four penthouse suites). The local "corporate rate" is F$143. Completely renovated in 2003, the Tanoa Plaza has a business center and conference facilities for groups of up to 200 people, plus a swimming pool behind the building.

The **Suva Motor Inn** (tel. 331-3973, fax 330-0381, suvamotorinn@connect.com.fj), a three-story complex near Albert Park, corner of Mitchell and Gorrie Streets, has 36 air-conditioned studio apartments with kitchenette at F$103 single or double, F$118 triple (10 percent discount by the week). The nine two-bedroom apartments capable of accommodating five persons are F$173 for the first two, plus F$10 for each extra person. A courtyard swimming pool with waterslide and cascade faces the restaurant/bar. This building (erected in 1996 by the Hexagon Group of Hotels) is well worth considering by families who want a bit of comfort.

The **Peninsula International Hotel** (tel. 331-3711, fax 331-4473, peninsula@connect.com.fj), at the corner of MacGregor Road and Pender Street, is a stylish four-floor building with a swimming pool. The 32 standard air-conditioned rooms are F$90/110 single/double, while the eight suites with kitchenettes run F$100/115. In 2000, another eight deluxe rooms were added, costing F$110/125.

US$100–150: Suva's largest hotel is the **Holiday Inn Suva** (tel. 330-1600, fax 330-0251, sales@holidayinnsuva.com.fj), on the waterfront opposite the Government Buildings. Formerly a Travelodge, the Holiday Inn is a big American-style place with 130 air-conditioned rooms with fridge and TV beginning at F$205 single or double. The newly renovated "superior" rooms are F$320 (the standard rooms are rather musty).

The swimming pool behind the two-story buildings compensates for the lack of a beach, and the view of Viti Levu from here is splendid. A UTC tour desk is at the hotel, and there's a brasserie-style restaurant, bar, lounge, and three conference rooms.

North Suva

Under US$25: The four-story **Top View Motel** (tel. 331-2612, fax 330-2101), 58 Robertson Road, a six-minute walk up the hill from the market bus station, has 12 rooms with shared bath and ceiling fans at F$20 single or double, and 13 with private bath at F$30/35 single/double. It's basic but okay for one night.

Certainly the nicest budget place in this area is **Colonial Lodge** (tel. 330-0655, coloniallodge@connect.com.fj), 19 Anand Street. This old wooden house on a side street near town has three fan-cooled rooms with shared bath at F$38/48 single/double. The large open dormitory downstairs is F$20 pp, or you can camp in the garden for F$15 pp. All rates include a cooked breakfast; dinner is a good value at F$6. The large sitting room and terrace upstairs are pleasant, but Colonial Lodge is sometimes noisy due to a loud television, excited children, and barking dogs.

An alley at the end of Anand Street leads straight up to **Annandale Apartments** (tel. 331-1054), 265 Waimanu Road opposite the Oceanview Hotel. The 12 spacious two-bedroom apartments are F$45/315/900 a day/week/month for up to three or four people. A fridge, kitchen, sitting room, and balcony are provided in each, but it's all a bit scruffy (you only get what you pay for). Washing machines and dryers are available downstairs.

The colorful, 44-room **Oceanview Hotel** (tel. 331-2129), 270 Waimanu Rd., has two singles at F$15, 33 doubles at F$25, and nine four-person family rooms at F$35. All rooms have shared bath. They usually try to put foreigners in the rear block rooms (No. 10 is the best of those) but some of the "local" rooms in the old wooden building closer to the main street are actually nicer. The Oceanview has a pleasant hillside location and it's one of the only "lowlife" hotels in this area with any atmosphere.

Three raunchy establishments just down Robertson Road from the Oceanview cater mostly to short time clients. The 15-room **Harbor Light Inn** (tel. 330-5495), 124 Robertson Rd., is cheap at F$20 single or double, but it's used mostly for one purpose. Also of ill repute is the 23-room **Motel Capitol** (tel. 331-3246), 91 Robertson Rd., with seven rooms with shared bath at F$20 single or double, and 16 with private bath at F$25–30.

The same crowd uses **Saf's Apartment Hotel** (Safique Mohd, tel. 330-1849), 100 Robertson Road between the Crossroad and Capitol. The 40 bare rooms with bath in this three-story concrete building are F$25 single or double downstairs, F$35 upstairs, or F$45 with TV and cooking facilities (F$10 extra for air-conditioning). A bed in the six-bed dorm is F$7 pp.

Just up Waimanu Road from the Oceanview is the seedy, 14-room **New Haven Motel** (tel. 331-5220), another one to avoid. It's F$30 single or double a night upstairs or F$10 an hour downstairs.

Up the hill is the two-story **Outrigger Hotel** (tel. 331-4944), at 349 Waimanu Road near the hospital. The 20 air-conditioned rooms with bath and fridge are F$48 single or double. Most of the rooms have a good view of Suva Harbor. There's a pizza restaurant on the roof (daily 1600–2200; pizzas F$6–14). Unfortunately, feedback about the Outrigger is mixed (and it has no connection with the Hawaiian Outrigger chain).

Back down near the center of town, the **Kings Suva Hotel** (tel. 330-4411, beater@connect.com.fj) on Waimanu Road is rough, with four rowdy bars and more tramps than travelers. The 20 noisy rooms with shared bath are F$20 single or double, while the five with private bath cost F$25.

The **Uptown Motel** (tel./fax 330-6094), 55 Toorak Rd., has 12 spacious self-contained rooms with balcony, phone, fridge, sofa, table and chairs, and coffee-making facilities at F$35 single or double with fan, F$45 with air conditioning. One room has been converted into a six-bunk dorm at F$20 a bed. It's convenient to the shopping district.

The 23 units at the **Tourist Motor Inn** (tel.

331-5745), at 98 Amy St. several blocks east of Waimanu Road, are F$25/30 single/double with fan. This three-story building painted pink and cream is seldom full. It can be rather noisy with shouts and laughter echoing through the halls.

Lami Lodge (tel. 336-2240, fax 331-2875, volau@connect.com.fj), on Queens Road next to Beqa Divers at Lami, has two doubles (F$45), three singles (F$25), and one 12-bed dorm (F$15 pp) in two wooden houses between the highway and the lagoon. Camping in their front yard is F$5 pp. You can cook your own food and there's a lounge.

Raintree Lodge (Tom Davis, tel. 332-0562, fax 332-0113, www.raintreelodge.com), near the entrance to Colo-i-Suva Forest Park, 11 km north of Suva, caters well to both ends of the market. Their 20-bed split-level dormitory (F$18 pp) shares toilet, cooking, and bathing facilities with the thirteen double rooms at F$50. Camping is F$10 pp. More upscale are the four lodges or bungalows in another section just up the hill. These cost F$110 single or double, and are quite luxurious with a sitting room, TV, fridge, private bath, and deck overlooking a small lake (but no cooking facilities). If you'll be using the cooking facilities in the dorm, bring groceries from Suva, because there's no store here. Raintree's large thatched restaurant/bar overlooks a former rock quarry, which has been converted into a lovely lake teaming with tiny tilapia fish. It's possible to borrow a bamboo raft and paddle out to the center of the lake for swimming. Aside from its easy access to the forest park, the lodge can be used as a base for visiting Suva (the last bus back is at 1900 daily). Bus connections are covered in the Colo-i-Suva listing above. A taxi from Suva will cost F$8 (if arriving by air at Nausori, a taxi will be F$12). Call ahead, as Raintree Lodge does fill up some nights. The whole complex is a model for ecotourism in Fiji.

US$25–50: Up in the Waimanu Road area, the **Capricorn Apartment Hotel** (tel. 330-3732, fax 330-3069, www.capricorn-hotels-fiji.com), 7 St. Fort St., has 34 spacious air-conditioned units with cooking facilities, fridge, and TV beginning at F$94 single or double, plus tax. A room upstairs is F$11 more, a one-bedroom flat another

F$22. The three- and four-story apartment blocks edge the swimming pool, and there are good views of the harbor from the individual balconies.

Tropic Towers Apartment Motel (tel. 330-4470, fax 330-4169, tropictowers@connect .com.fj), 86 Robertson Rd., has 34 air-conditioned apartments with cooking facilities, fridge, and TV in a four-story building starting at F$51/62 single/double. Ask about the 13 "budget" units in the annex, which are F$34 single or double with shared bath. Washing machines (F$9) and a swimming pool are available for guests. Both Tropic Towers and the Capricorn are good choices for families.

Motel 6 (tel. 330-7477, fax 330-7133), 1 Walu St. off Waimanu Road, is one of Suva's best deals. Of the 16 clean, comfortable air-conditioned rooms in the main building, the eight with fridge only are F$55 single or double, while those with a balcony, cooking facilities, and a separate bedroom are F$88. Nine self-catering units facing the car park are F$99. All have a regular TV, but only the deluxe rooms have Sky TV. There's a swimming pool, and some of the balconies have an excellent view of Walu Bay.

Nanette's Homestay (Nanette MacAdam, tel. 331-6316, fax 331-6902, www.nanetteshome stay.com), 56 Extension St., off Waimanu Rd. just past the entrance to the Outpatients Department at Colonial War Memorial Hospital, is a modern bed and breakfast run by an Australian-Fijian couple. The four upstairs rooms (F$75 single or double) share a kitchen and lounge area. Downstairs are three self-catering apartments (F$110). All rooms have private bath, air conditioning, and breakfast included in the price. It's an excellent value.

US$50–100: The **Raffles Tradewinds Hotel** (tel. 336-2450, fax 336-1464, www.raffles tradewinds.com), at Lami on the Bay of Islands seven km west of Suva, includes a 500-seat convention center, waterside swimming pool, and oceanfront seafood restaurant. The 109 rooms in this tasteful two-story building are F$113/144 double/triple standard or F$174/206 deluxe with private bath, fridge, and air conditioning (reduced walk-in "local rates" are often available). Internet access is F$.30 a minute. Many cruising yachts anchor here, and the location is the most picturesque of any Suva hotel. Although far from the center, bus service into Suva is good.

FOOD

Fast Food

Familiar, easy eating is available in the American-style food courts in the **Downtown Boulevard Center** (weekdays 0730–1800, Sat. 0730–1700), on Ellery Street, the **Harbor Center** (Mon.–Sat. 0700–1900), along Nubukulou Creek between Scott and Thomson Streets, and **Dolphins Food Court** (tel. 330-7440; daily 0900–2100) at FNPF Place, Victoria Parade and Loftus Street.

One of the few places serving a regular cooked breakfast (F$6.50) is the **Palm Court Bistro** (tel. 330-4662; Mon.–Fri. 0700–1630, Sat. 0700–1430), in the Queensland Insurance Arcade behind Air New Zealand on Victoria Parade. Their burgers and sandwiches are good at lunchtime.

pick of the produce at Suva's colorful market

The **Headworks Café** (tel. 330-9449; weekdays 0800–1900, Sat. 0900–1700), upstairs from The Triangle, Renwick Road opposite the Westpac Bank, serves coffee and cakes on a nice outdoor terrace with a view of downtown.

Jackson Takeaway (tel. 330-3986; Mon.–Sat. 0700–1800, Sun. 0900–1700), in the old town hall next to the Ming Palace Restaurant on Victoria Parade, serves Chinese lunches at F$3 or fish and chips at F$2. It's also good for a quick cup of coffee.

Shooters Tavern (tel. 995-1954; Mon.–Sat. 0730–1500), 54 Carnarvon St., has a pleasant outdoor terrace serving breakfast or lunch for F$5. There's a regular menu priced F$5–15 in addition to the blackboard specials.

An inexpensive snack bar (tel. 330-1443; Mon.–Sat. 0800–1600) with concrete outdoor picnic tables is at the back side of the **Handicraft Market** facing the harbor. Dishes like chop suey, chow mein, fried rice, long soup, and rump steak cost F$3–5 and the portions are gargantuan. This place is really packed with locals around lunchtime—the best deal in town.

Low-budget snacks are also served at **Donald's Kitchen** (tel. 331-5587), 103 Cumming Street. One block over on Marks Street are cheaper Chinese snack bars, such as **Kim's Cafe** (tel. 331-3252), 128 Marks St., where you can get a toasted egg sandwich and coffee for about F$1.50. Kim's has been there for ages. There are scores more cheap milk bars around Suva, and you'll find them for yourself as you stroll around town.

Fijian

A popular place to sample Fijian food is the **Old Mill Cottage Cafe** (tel. 331-2134; Mon.–Sat. 0700–1700), 49 Carnarvon St.—the street behind the Dolphins Food Court. Government employees from nearby offices and staff from the adjacent U.S. Embassy descend on this place at lunchtime for the inexpensive curried freshwater mussels, curried chicken livers, fresh seaweed in coconut milk, taro leaves creamed in coconut milk, and fish cooked in coconut milk. It's also very good for breakfast.

Also try the food stalls between the market and bus station, on the back side of the bus station closer to the harbor. The best deal here is the fish in *lolo* (coconut milk) served at two open kiosks with red tiles on the walls for F$3 a plate. Ask for Emi Whippy, who is famous for her food. You have to eat standing at a counter using a spoon and your hands, but there are taps between the kiosks where you can wash up. Arrive before 1300, because they sell out fast!

Indian

The **Hare Krishna Vegetarian Restaurant** (tel. 331-4154; closed Sun.), at the corner of Pratt and Joske Streets, serves ice cream (12 flavors), sweets, and snacks downstairs, main meals upstairs (available Mon.–Fri. 1100–1400). If you want the all-you-can-eat vegetarian *thali* (F$7.50), just sit down upstairs and they'll bring it to you. No smoking or alcohol is allowed.

A cheaper Indian place is the very popular **Curry House** (tel. 331-3756; Mon.–Fri. 0900–1745, Sat. 0900–1430) at 87 Cumming Street. Their special vegetarian *thali* (F$3.30) is a good lunch and they also have meat curries from F$5. Try the takeaway *rotis*.

Govinda Vegetarian Restaurant (Mon.–Fri. 0800–1700, Sat. 0900–1400), 93 Cumming St., has a combination *thali* for F$6.50, plus sweets, ice cream, milkshakes, and masala tea.

Singh's Curry House (tel. 359-1019; Mon.–Sat. 0930–2130, Sun. 1030–2000), Gordon St. off Victoria Parade, serves spicy South Indian dishes in the F$3–8 range. Choose from the warmer on the counter.

Suva's only upscale Indian restaurant is **Ashiyana** (tel. 331-3000; Tues.–Sat. 1130–1430, 1800–2200, Sun. 1800–2130), in the old town hall next to the Ming Palace Restaurant on Victoria Parade. Their hot and spicy dishes are prepared in a tandoor (clay oven) by a chef from India.

Asian

Not many Indian restaurants in Suva are open evenings or on Sunday, so this is when you should turn to Suva's many excellent, inexpensive Asian restaurants. Most serve beer, while the Indian restaurants are usually "dry."

Two good-value Chinese places are adjacent to one another on Pratt Street near Hare Krishna.

Dishes in the glass-covered steam table at the **Lantern Palace Cafeteria** are F$4, while those at the **Guang Wha Restaurant** next door start at F$3. The Guang Wha is more likely to be open on holidays and nothing on their regular menu is over F$8. The **Lantern Palace Restaurant** (tel. 331-4633; Mon.–Sat. 1130–1400/1700–2100) between these two offers individually prepared dishes priced F$6–16.

The **Sichuan Pavilion Restaurant** (tel. 331-5194; Mon.–Sat. 1100–1400/1700–2200, Sun. 1730–2300), upstairs in the old Garrick Hotel building at 6 Thomson St., is perhaps Suva's finest Asian restaurant. Employees of the Chinese Embassy frequent it for the spicy-hot Chinese dishes (though they're not as hot as Sichuan food elsewhere). Almost everything is good, but avoid the lamb. Entrees average F$8–13. Weather permitting, sit outside on the balcony and watch all of Suva go by.

The **Phoenix Restaurant** (tel. 331-1889), 155 Victoria Parade, has inexpensive Chinese dishes like red pork with fried rice (F$5) in their steam table. Big bottles of beer are sold. They're also open on Sundays 1100–2100.

Suva's most imposing Chinese restaurant by far is the 300-seat **Ming Palace** (tel. 331-5546; Mon.–Sat. 1130–1430/1800–2200, Sun. 1800–2200) in the old town hall next to the public library on Victoria Parade. Weekdays 1130–1430 there's a lunch buffet for F$9 (dinner entrées are F$9–18).

Fong Lee Seafood Restaurant (tel. 330-4233; Mon.–Sat. 1130–1400 and 1800–2200, Sun. 1800–2200), 293 Victoria Parade, is more expensive than the places just mentioned but the food is said to be the tastiest in Suva (notice the many affluent local Chinese having dinner there).

For upscale Japanese food, it's **Daikoku** (tel. 330-8968; Mon.–Sat. 1200–1400, 1800–2200), FNPF Place, 359 Victoria Parade. The Teppan-Yaki dishes (F$10–25) are artistically prepared right at your table.

The **Zen Restaurant** (tel. 330-6314; weekdays 1130–1430 and 1630–2130, Sat. 1130–1430), in Pacific House, Butt and Gordon Streets, has lunch specials at F$7. Dinner will cost around F$16 and photos of their dishes are in the menu.

The **Da Kyung Korean Restaurant** (tel. 359-1224; Mon.–Sat. 1000–2200, Sun. 1600–2200), 43 Gordon St., also has a nifty photographic menu depicting dishes like bulgogy (F$11), steak barbecue (F$15), and vegetarian tofu soup (F$11). A variety of side dishes are included with each order. The pleasant open dining room is in an old colonial house.

International Cuisine

Elegant **Tiko's Floating Restaurant** (tel. 331-3626; weekdays 1200–1400 and 1800–2200, Sat. 1800–2200) is housed in the MV *Lycianda,* an ex-Blue Lagoon cruise ship launched at Suva in 1970 and now anchored off Stinson Parade behind Sukuna Park. Their steaks and seafood are good. A real mountain of crabs will run F$31. A bar called "Tingles" downstairs is open Friday and Saturday 1700–0100. It's a romantic spot, and you can feel the boat rock gently in the waves.

The **Metal Ox Bar & Grill** (tel. 331-4330; weekdays 1100–1400/1800–2230, weekends 1800–2230), in Regal Lane around behind the Qantas and Air Pacific offices, allows you to sit at a table with a view of Suva Harbour and consume steaks of 250, 300, or 400 grams priced from F$19–27. Fancier dishes on the main menu cater to other tastes.

The Nadi tourist-caterer Chef's has opened branches in Suva. **Chef's The Corner** (Mon.–Sat. 0800–2130), Thomson and Pier streets beside Jack's Handicrafts, serves coffee and snacks to trendy youths who wish to be seen here. Upstairs tourists and the affluent consume meat and seafood at **Chef's The Restaurant** (tel. 330-8325). The casual lunches (F$10–22) are from 1100–1400, while candlelit dinners (F$28–38) run from 1800–2200.

JJ's On The Park (tel. 330-5005; daily 1130–2200), in the YWCA Building on Sukuna Park, is a casual restaurant of quality with daily specials listed on blackboards. If you don't want any of the main courses (F$11–32), order a couple of appetizers (F$7–14), such as the sashimi (F$7/10 small/large) or the calamari rings (F$12). Otherwise, there are hamburgers (F$11), catch of the day (F$18.50), and lobster (F$32). One reader recommended the chicken. You'll like the gentle atmosphere and harbor views. Coup master George Speight once owned in a small stake in JJ's, and you never know who you'll meet at JJ's classic long wooden bar (which stays open until 0200).

ENTERTAINMENT AND EVENTS

In 1996, **Village Six Cinemas** (tel. 330-6006) opened on Scott Street next to Nubukalou Creek, giving you a choice of six top Hollywood films several times a day. Regular admission is F$5, reduced to F$4 on Tuesday. The air conditioning is a relief on a hot day.

The best time to be in Suva is in August during the **Hibiscus Festival,** which fills Albert Park with stalls, games, and carnival revelers.

Nightclubs

There are numerous nightclubs in Suva, all of which have F$3–5 cover charges on weekends and require neat dress. Nothing much happens until after 2200, and women shouldn't enter these places alone. Late at night, it's wise to take a taxi back to your hotel. Suva is still a very safe city, but nasty, violent robberies do occur.

The Barn (tel. 330-7845; Tues.–Thurs. 1900–0100, Fri. 1800–0100, Sat. 1930–0100), 54 Carnarvon St., is a popular country and western club with live entertainment and a cover charge from 2100. The crowd here is a bit older than in some of the other clubs.

The **Golden Dragon** (tel. 331-1018; Sat. 1830–0100, Sun.–Fri. 1700–0100), 379 Victoria Parade, is frequented by university students and islanders from other parts of the Pacific (such as Samoa and Tonga).

Signals Night Club (tel. 331-3590; daily 1800–0100), at 255 Victoria Parade opposite the Suva City Library, is popular among Asian seamen (F$3 cover charge after 2000). Gays will feel comfortable here.

Bourbon Bluez (tel. 331-3927), beside Air Nauru across the street from O'Reilly's Pub, caters to an older, Fijian crowd.

Birdland R&B Club (tel. 330-3833; daily from 1800), 6 Carnarvon St., up and around the corner from O'Reilly's Pub, has outstanding live jazz from 2000 on Sunday. Other nights there's recorded music. It's a late night place where people come after they've been to the other clubs.

Bojangles Night Club (tel. 330-3776; Mon.–Sat. from 1800), adjacent to Birdland, is a disco where Fijian students come to dance (cover charge after 2200).

Purple Haze Night Club (tel. 330-3092; Wed.–Sun. from 1930), Butt and MacArthur streets (above The Merchants Club), just up the hill from O'Reilly's Pub, is a predominately Indo-Fijian disco. It's one of the few places in town where you'll see mostly straight men dancing with each other!

Liquids Night Club (tel. 330-0679; closed Sun.), upstairs in the Harbor Center (access from beside Wishbone outside on the Nubukalou Creek side of the building), is crowded with local sports teams on weekends.

Be aware that the places north of Nubukalou Creek are considerably rougher than those just mentioned. **Friends Bar and Niteclub** (Mon.–Sat 1700–0100), 34 Cumming Street, has live music Tuesday and Wednesday (happy hour 1700–2000). Security is tight.

Club 2000 (tel. 330-9754), in the former Metropole Hotel building upstairs at Usher and Scott streets near the market, supplies cheap mugs of beer and it's safe enough during the day. At night, you better know what you're doing. It's loud, hot, and dirty—great. The outside terrace to the right as you come in is quieter than the bar on the left.

Wildest of all is the **Bali Hai Night Club** (tel. 331-7164), 194 Rodwell Road north of the bus station, with dances Thursday to Saturday nights. The middle floor is okay but the top floor is very rough.

Bars

O'Reilly's Pub (tel. 331-2884), 5 MacArthur St. just off Victoria Parade, has a happy hour daily 1600–2000. It's a nice relaxed way to kick off a night on the town, and the big sports screen and canned music are tops.

The whimsically named **Bad Dog Cafe** (tel. 331-2968; Mon.–Wed. 1100–2300, Thurs.–Sat.

1100–0100, Sun. 1700–2300), next door to O'Reilly's, is a trendy wine bar serving margaritas, sangria, and 25 different brands of imported beers. At happy hour 1700–1900 you can order a jug of sangria for F$11 or get F$2 off the mixed drinks. The regular menu features Thai food, steaks, and fish for F$9–14, pizza F$12, appetizers F$5–8, and the food has a reputation for being among Suva's best. For F$6 corkage you may BYO bottle of wine from the nearby Victoria Wines shop. A back door from Bad Dog leads into O'Reilly's.

A block up from O'Reilly's is **The Merchants Club** (tel. 330-4256; Mon. and Tues. 1600–2130, Wed. and Thurs. 1600–2230, Fri. 1600–2330, Sat. 1100–2230, Sun. 1100–1830), 15 Butt St. at MacArthur. Properly dressed overseas visitors are welcome in this classic South Seas bar with a largely male clientele.

Traps Bar (tel. 331-2922; weekdays 1700–0100, weekends 1800–0100), at 305 Victoria Parade next to the Shell service station, is a groupie Suva social scene with a happy hour until 2000 (drunks and youths under 18 are unwelcome here). There's live music from 2200 on Tuesday, *the* night to be there. If you can only visit one Suva bar, pick this one.

Shooters Tavern (tel. 995-1954), at 54 Carnarvon St. next to The Barn, has a happy hour Monday–Saturday 1730–2000. They play harder rock music than the others and the atmosphere is somewhere between O'Reilly's and Traps. Shooters is a youth hangout where you might even bump into high school kids.

The bar at the **Suva Lawn Bowling Club** (tel. 330-2394; daily 0900–2300), facing the lagoon opposite Thurston Botanical Gardens and just off Albert Park, is a very convenient place to down a large bottle of Fiji Bitter—the perfect place for a cold one after visiting the museum. You can sit and watch the bowling, or see the sun set over Viti Levu.

Those in search of more subdued drinking should try the **Piano Bar** in the lobby at the Holiday Inn (tel. 330-1600), which often presents rather good jazz singers, or the **Rooftop Garden Bar** at the Town House Apartment Hotel (tel. 330-0055) which has a happy hour 1700–1900.

SHOPPING

The **Government Handicraft Center** (tel. 331-5869; Mon.–Fri. 0800–1630, Sat. 0800–1230) behind Ratu Sukuna House, MacArthur and Carnarvon Streets, is a low-pressure place to familiarize yourself with what is authentic. **Jack's Handicrafts** (tel. 330-8893, www.jacksfiji.com), Renwick Road and Pier St., has Fijian crafts, postcards, and other tourist goods with prices clearly marked.

The large **Curio and Handicraft Market** (Mon.–Sat. 0800–1700) on the waterfront behind the post office is a good place to haggle over crafts, so long as you know what is really Fijian (avoid masks and "tikis"). Unfortunately, many of the vendors are rather aggressive and it's not possible to shop around in peace. Never come here on the day when a cruise ship is in port—prices shoot up. And watch out for the annoying "sword sellers" mentioned in the main introduction, as they could accost you anywhere in Suva. (Strangers who greet you on the street in Suva almost always want something from you.)

Cumming Street is Suva's busiest shopping street. Expect to obtain a 10–40 percent discount at the "duty-free" shops by bargaining, but *shop around* before you buy. Be especially wary when purchasing gold jewelry, as it might be fake. Commission agents may try to show you around and get you a "good price." If the deal seems too good to be true, it probably is.

The **Suva Flea Market** on Rodwell Road opposite the bus station features a large selection of island clothing and many good little places to eat. You won't be hassled here.

For more upmarket apparel, examine the fashionable hand-printed clothing and beachwear at **Sogo Fiji** (tel. 331-5007), on Cumming Street and on Victoria Parade next to Air New Zealand. You could come out looking like a real South Seas character at a reasonable price.

Bob's Hook Line & Sinker (tel./fax 330-1013), Thomson St. in an outside corner of the Harbor Center, sells snorkeling and fishing gear.

Wai Tui Surf (tel. 330-0287), Parade Arcade, Victoria Parade opposite McDonald's, sells surfing paraphernalia, including stylish bathing suits and trendy beach wear.

The **Philatelic Bureau** (tel. 321-8377, www.stampsfiji.com), next to the General Post Office, sells the stamps of Niue, Pitcairn, Papua New Guinea, Samoa, Solomon Islands, Tonga, Tuvalu, and Vanuatu, as well as those of Fiji.

Fuji Film in the Vanua Arcade, opposite Sukuna Park on Victoria Parade, does one-hour photo finishing.

INFORMATION

The Fiji Visitors Bureau (tel. 330-2433; Mon.–Fri. 0800–1630, Sat. 0800–1200) is on Thomson Street across from the General Post Office. They have a good supply of brochures and can answer most questions. Ask for a copy of the free Jasons map of Fiji and *Fiji What's On.*

The South Pacific Tourism Organization (tel. 330-4177, fax 330-1995, www.spto.org), FNPF Plaza, 3rd floor, 343-359 Victoria Parade at Loftus St., provides information on the entire South Pacific.

The Bureau of Statistics (tel. 331-5822, fax 330-3656, www.statsfiji.gov.fj), 8th floor, Ratu Sukuna House, Victoria Parade and MacArthur Street, has many interesting technical publications on the country and a library where you may browse.

The Maps and Plans Shop (tel. 321-1395; Mon.–Fri. 0800–1300 and 1400–1530) of the Lands and Survey Department, Ground Floor, Government Buildings, sells excellent topographical maps of Fiji.

Carpenters Shipping (tel. 331-2244, www.carpship.com.fj), on Edinburgh Road across from the BP service station, sells British navigational charts of Fiji at a whopping F$81 each (buy these overseas). The Fiji Hydrographic Office (tel. 331-5457; Mon.–Fri. 0800–1300 and 1400–1600), top floor, Freeston Rd., Walu Bay, with navigational charts of the Yasawas, Kadavu, eastern Vanua Levu, and the Lau Group at F$23 a sheet (all other areas are covered by the British charts).

Bookstores

The Dominion Book Center (tel. 330-4334),

Dominion House Arcade behind the Fiji Visitors Bureau, has some books on Fiji.

The Fiji Museum shop also sells a few excellent books at reasonable prices.

Suva's number one bookstore is the USP Book Center (tel. 321-2500, fax 330-3265; Mon.–Thurs. 0800–1700, Fri. 0800–1630, Sat. 0830–1300, www.uspbookcentre.com), next to the ANZ Bank branch at the main Laucala Bay university campus. Not only do they have one of the finest Pacific sections in the region, but they stock the publications of several dozen occasional publishers affiliated with the university and you can turn up some truly intriguing items. Also visit the Book Display Room in the **Institute of Pacific Studies** building (tel. 321-2332), not far from the Book Center. They sell assorted books by local authors published by the IPS itself.

The Government Bookstore (Mon.–Thurs. 0900–1630, Fri. 0900–1530, Sat. 0900–1300), Harbor Terminal, corner of Usher and Scott Streets (enter through one of the shops), sells Fijian dictionaries and grammar books.

The New Coconut Frond (tel. 331-1963), at the back of the Suva Flea Market on Rodwell Road, has a large stock of used paperbacks.

Libraries

The Suva City Library (tel. 331-3433, ext. 241; Mon., Tues., Thurs., Fri. 0930–1800, Wed. 1200–1800, Sat. 0900–1300), at 196 Victoria Parade, allows visitors to take out four books upon payment of a refundable F$20 deposit.

The National Archives of Fiji (tel. 330-4144; Mon.–Fri. 0800–1300, 1400–1600), 25 Carnarvon St., has an air-conditioned library upstairs with a large collection of local newspapers.

The excellent Fiji Museum Library (tel. 331-5944; Mon.–Fri. 0830–1300 and 1400–1600) is directly behind the main museum in a separate building. They charge F$1 to use the facilities.

The library at the Laucala Campus of the University of the South Pacific (tel. 321-2322) is open Monday–Friday 0800–1600 year-round. During semesters they also open Saturday, Sunday afternoon, and in the evening. You'll find a reading room with international newspapers downstairs. Tourists can request a free one-day

visitors card to visit the Pacific Collection upstairs once only. Otherwise, it's possible to buy a two-week visitors card for F$11, which allows access to the Pacific Collection during that time. Prior to entry, bags must be left in a cloakroom behind and below the library.

The Alliance Française (tel. 331-3802, fax 331-3803), 14 MacGregor Road, has an excellent selection of French books, magazines, and newspapers. You're welcome to peruse materials in the reading room Mon.–Fri. 0900–1800. Ask about their video and film evenings.

Ecology Groups

The Greenpeace Pacific Campaign (tel. 331-2861, fax 331-2784; Mon.–Fri. 0830–1700) is above the Ming Palace Restaurant in the old town hall on Victoria Parade.

The Pacific Concerns Resource Center (tel. 330-4649, fax 330-4755, www.pcrc.org.fj), 83 Amy St., has a library open to the public Monday, Tuesday, Thursday, and Friday 0900–1300 and 1400–1630, Wednesday 0900–1300. A large collection of periodicals on Pacific environmental and social issues can be accessed here, and some books are for sale. The Center is the directing body of the Nuclear-Free and Independent Pacific (NFIP) movement, a regional grass-roots coalition.

The National Trust for Fiji (tel. 330-1807, fax 330-5092), 3 Ma'afu St., manages several nature reserves and historic sites around Fiji. Their neighbor, the World Wide Fund for Nature (tel. 331-5533, fax 331-5410, www.wwfpacific.org.fj), 4 Ma'afu St., assists various projects for the support of wildlife and wild habitats.

Travel Agents

Hunts Travel (tel. 331-5288, fax 330-2212), upstairs from the Dominion House arcade behind the Fiji Visitors Bureau, is the place to pick up air tickets. They often know more about Air Pacific flights than the Air Pacific employees themselves!

Rosie The Travel Service (tel. 331-4436), 46 Gordon St. near Sarita Flats, books tours and accommodations all around Fiji. The UTC Tour Desk (tel. 331-2287) in the lobby of the Holiday Inn Hotel does the same.

Nina and Oro at Rainbow-way Travel Services (tel. 330-6613, fax 330-6593, rainboway1@ connect.com.fj), second floor, back section, Honson Building, Thomson St. (opposite the Fiji Visitors Bureau), can arrange stays on Rotuma at F$40 pp a night including meals. They can also organize stays at villages in the interior and Tailevu.

Airline Offices

Reconfirm your onward flight reservations at your airlines' Suva office: Air Fiji (tel. 331-3666), 185 Victoria Parade (also represents Air Vanuatu and Polynesian Airlines); Air Nauru (tel. 331-2377), Ratu Sukuna House, 249 Victoria Parade; Air New Zealand (tel. 331-3100), Queensland Insurance Center, 9 Victoria Parade; Air Pacific (tel. 330-4388), Colonial Building, Victoria Parade; Qantas Airways (tel. 331-3888), Colonial Building, Victoria Parade; Solomon Airlines (tel. 331-5889), Global Air Service, 3 Ellery St., and Sun Air (tel. 330-8979), Parade Arcade on Victoria Parade opposite McDonalds. While you're there, check your seat assignment.

SERVICES

Money

Rates at the banks vary slightly and you might get a dollar or two more on a large exchange by checking the Westpac Bank, ANZ Bank, and Bank of Hawaii before signing your checks (and remember the F$5 commission deducted at the ANZ Bank). All of them have branches on Victoria Parade near The Triangle. The ANZ Bank has a special exchange office open weekdays 0900–1700, Saturday 0900–1300, at 51 Renwick Road.

The ANZ Bank has Visa/MasterCard ATMs at their Victoria Parade and Renwick Road branches, outside Village Six Cinemas, at the food court in Downtown Boulevard Center on Ellery St., at the ANZ Bank branch in Lami, and at 14 other locations around Suva.

Lotus Foreign Exchange (tel. 331-7755), 103 Cumming St. off Renwick Road, gives a better rate than the banks for traveler's checks without commission.

Money Exchange (tel. 330-3566; Mon.–Fri. 0830–1700, Sat. 0830–1300), Thomson and Pier streets opposite the Fiji Visitors Bureau, is similar.

Thomas Cook Travel (tel. 330-1603; Mon.–Fri. 0900–1600, Sat. 0930–1200), on Victoria Parade in the center of town, changes foreign currency at competitive rates, and sells the banknotes of neighboring countries like New Caledonia, Samoa, Solomon Islands, Tonga, and Vanuatu—convenient if you're headed for any of them.

If you need a quick infusion of funds, Global Transfers Ltd. (tel. 331-4812, weekdays 0800–1645, Sat. 0800–1345), Victoria Parade at Gordon St., is the Western Union agent. Money can be send to you here from almost anywhere in world through the Western Union network.

On Sunday and holidays changing money is a problem (try your hotel if you get stuck).

Telecommunications

Fintel, the Fiji International Telecommunications office (tel. 331-2933, fax 330-1025, www.fintel.com.fj), 158 Victoria Parade, is open Monday–Saturday 0800–2000 for long-distance calls and telegrams.

Telecom Fiji (tel. 330-3300, www.tfl.com.fj) operates a telephone center at Downtown Boulevard Center in the mall off Ellery Street.

The public fax at Suva General Post Office on Edward Street is fax 330-2666, should you need to receive a fax from anyone. Otherwise, have your fax sent via Fintel at fax 330-1025.

Internet Access

Several places around Suva offer Internet access at F$.8 a minute, including the Alpha Computer Center (tel. 330-0211; Mon.–Fri. 0800–2000, Sat. 0800–1700, Sun. 1000–1600), 181 Victoria Parade between Gordon and MacArthur, and Cyber Zone (tel. 331-6967), upstairs at 107 Victoria Parade opposite Sukuna Park. The noisy cyber games being played by kids are a drawback at Cyber Zone.

At last report, the cheapest Internet access in Suva was F$.5 a minute, available at Lamtec Services (tel. 992-6719; weekdays 0730–1930, Sat. 0730–1800), third floor, Honson Building, Thomson St. (across the street from the Fiji

Visitors Bureau). You may have to wait a while for a computer.

Connect Internet (tel. 330-0777; weekdays 0800–1900, Sat. 0900–1700, www.connect .com.fj), 10 Thomson St. across the street from Thomas Cook, provides Internet access in air-conditioned comfort at F$5 an hour.

The Republic of Cappuccino (tel. 330-0333; Mon.–Fri. 0700–2300, Sat. 0800–2300, Sun. 0900–1900), in Dolphins Food Court at FNPF Place, Victoria Parade and Loftus, is Suva's original Internet café. Aside from Internet access at F$.15 a minute, they serve a variety of teas and coffees (F$2–3).

Immigration

The Immigration Office (tel. 331-2622; Mon.– Fri. 0830–1230, 1400–1500) for extensions of stay, etc., is in the Civic Tower behind the library on Victoria Parade.

Yachts must report to the Customs and Excise Boarding Office (tel. 330-2322; weekdays 0800–1300 and 1400-1600) in the Ports Authority Tower on Kings Wharf.

Consulates

The following countries have diplomatic missions in Suva:

- Australia (tel. 338-2219, www.austhighcomm .org.fj), 10 Reservoir Rd., off Princes Road, Samabula
- China (tel. 330-0215), 147 Queen Elizabeth Dr., Suva Point
- Chile (tel. 330-0433), Asgar & Co. Optometrists, Queensland Insurance Building behind Air New Zealand, Victoria Parade
- European Union (tel. 331-3633), 4th floor, Development Bank Center, 360 Victoria Parade
- Federated States of Micronesia (tel. 330-4566), 37 Loftus St.
- Finland (tel. 331-3188), 42 Gorrie St.
- France (tel. 331-2233), 7th floor, Dominion House, Scott St.
- Germany (tel. 332-2405), 30 Deovji St., Tamavua Heights
- Japan (tel. 330-4633), 2nd floor, Dominion House, Scott St.

- Kiribati (tel. 338-0599), 36 Gordon St.
- Korea (tel. 330-0977), Vanua House, Victoria Parade
- Malaysia (tel. 331-2166), 5th floor, Pacific House, Butt and MacArthur Streets
- Marshall Islands (tel. 338-7899), 41 Borron Rd., Samabula
- Nauru (tel. 331-3566), 7th floor, Ratu Sukuna House, Victoria Parade and MacArthur
- Netherlands (tel. 330-1499), Cromptons, Queensland Insurance Building behind Air New Zealand, Victoria Parade
- New Zealand (tel. 331-1422), 10th floor, Reserve Bank Building, Pratt St.
- Papua New Guinea (tel. 330-4244), 3rd floor, Credit House, Gordon and Malcolm Streets
- Pakistan (tel. 338-4981), 12 Leka St.
- Sweden (tel. 331-3188), 42 Gorrie St.
- Taiwan (tel. 331-5922), 6th floor, Pacific House, Butt and MacArthur Streets
- Tuvalu (tel. 330-1355, fax 330-8479), 16 Gorrie St.
- United Kingdom (tel. 331-1033, fax 330-1406), 47 Gladstone Rd.
- U.S.A. (tel. 331-4466, fax 330-0081, www .amembassy-fiji.gov), 31 Loftus St.

The Suva City Council has asked the U.S. embassy to relocate away from downtown Suva. The street in front of the heavily guarded embassy was closed in 1999 after threats were received, creating traffic and security problems for the city.

Everyone other than New Zealanders requires a visa to visit Australia, and these are available at the Australian High Commission weekdays 0830–1200. To get there it's probably easier to go by taxi, then return to town by bus. Canada and Italy have consuls at Nadi.

Launderettes

Gangaram's Laundry (tel. 330-2269; Mon.–Fri. 0730–1800, Sat. 0730–1400), 126 Toorak Road, offers same day cleaning services.

Public Toilets

Free public toilets are just outside the Handicraft Market on the side of the building facing the harbor; in the Thurston Botanical Gardens; in

Downtown Boulevard Center on Ellery St.; on the food court level at the Harbor Center; beside Nubukalou Creek off Renwick Road; and between the vegetable market and the bus station.

The public toilets in Sukuna Park (Mon.–Sat. 0800–1535) cost F$.65 or you can also have a shower here for F$1.10.

Yachting Facilities

The Royal Suva Yacht Club (tel. 330-4201, fax 330-4433, VHF channel 16, rsyc@connect .com.fj), on Foster Road between Suva and Lami, offers visiting yachts such amenities as mooring privileges, warm showers, laundry facilities, restaurant, bar, email, and the full use of club services by the whole crew at F$39 a week (F$20 for solo mariners). There have been reports of thefts from boats anchored here, so watch out. Many yachts anchor off the Raffles Tradewinds Hotel on the Bay of Islands, a recognized hurricane anchorage.

HEALTH

Suva's Colonial War Memorial Hospital (tel. 331-3444), about a kilometer northeast of the center, is available 24 hours a day for emergencies. You can see a doctor in the Outpatients Department on Extension St. off Waimanu Rd. weekdays 0800–1600 for a F$20 nonresident fee, but you'll have to line up, since there will be many locals waiting for free service. Built in 1914, this hospital may be an interesting sightseeing attraction, but if you actually need medical attention you're better off seeing a private doctor.

Suva Private Hospital (tel. 330-3404, fax 330-3456, healthcare@connect.com.fj), 120 Amy St. at Brewster, which opened in 2001, offers state-of-the-art facilities. The medical center here is open 24 hours a day (F$20/50 to see a general practitioner/specialist) providing service vastly superior to Colonial War Memorial for the same price (if you're a foreigner). There's an excellent pharmacy here. The Fiji Recompression Chamber Facility (tel. 330-5154 or 885-0630, recom pression@connect.com.fj), donated by the Cousteau Society in 1992, is also here, but it's only open for emergencies—you must call ahead.

The Downtown Boulevard Medical Center (tel. 331-3355; Mon.–Fri. 0830–1700, Sat. 0830–1130), in the mall off Ellery Street, has several foreign doctors (one female) on their roster, and a good pharmacy (tel. 330-3770) is nearby.

Two dentists are Dr. David M. Charya (tel. 330-2160), The Dental Center, 59 Cumming St.; and Dr. Abdul S. Haroon (tel. 331-3870), Suite 12, Epworth House off Nina Street (just down the hall from Patterson Brothers).

The Fiji Women's Crisis Center (tel. 331-3300 answered 24 hours, www.fijiwomen.com), 88 Gordon St. opposite the Tanoa Plaza Hotel, offers free and confidential counseling for women and children. Their office is open Monday–Friday 0830–1630, Saturday 0900–1200.

TRANSPORTATION

Although nearly all international flights arrive at Nadi, Suva is Fiji's main domestic transportation hub. Interisland shipping crowds the harbor, and if you can't find a ship going exactly your way, Air Fiji and Sun Air fly to all the major Fiji islands, while Air Pacific serves Australia and New Zealand and Air Fiji goes to Tonga and Tuvalu—all from Nausori Airport. Make the rounds of the shipping offices listed below, then head over to Walu Bay to check the information. Compare the price of a cabin and deck passage, and ask if meals are included.

Keep in mind that all of the ferry departure times mentioned in this book are only indications of what was true in the past. It's essential to check with the company office for current departure times during the week you wish to travel. Quite a few ships leave Suva on Saturday, but none depart on Sunday. Readers have questioned safety standards on these ships, some of which seem to be nearing the end of their working lives—use them at your own risk.

A solid block of buses awaits your patronage at the market bus station near the harbor, with continuous local service, and frequent long-distance departures to Nadi and Lautoka. Many of the points of interest around Suva are accessible on foot, but if you wander too far, jump on any bus headed in the right direction and you'll wind up back in the market. Taxis are also easy to find and relatively cheap.

Suva's bus station can be a little confusing, as there are numerous companies and time tables are not posted. Most drivers know where a certain bus will park, so just ask. For information on bus services around Viti Levu and domestic flights from Nausori Airport, see Getting Around in the Exploring the Islands chapter. Shipping services from Suva are covered below.

Ferries to Ovalau Island

The Suva to Levuka service is operated by **Patterson Brothers Shipping** (tel. 331-5644, fax 330-1652, patterson@connect.com.fj), Suite 1, 1st floor, Epworth Arcade off Nina Street. Patterson's "Sea-Road" bus leaves from the bus station opposite the Suva Flea Market Monday–Saturday at 1400 (F$24). At Natovi (67 km) it drives onto the *Princess Ashika,* an old Japanese ferry, for Buresala on Ovalau, then continues to Levuka, where it should arrive around 1745. For the return journey you leave the Patterson Brothers office in Levuka Monday–Saturday at 0500, arriving in Suva at 0800. Bus tickets must be purchased in advance at the office, and on Saturdays and public holidays reservations should be made at least a day ahead. These trips should take four or five hours right through, but can be late if the ferry connection is delayed. This is most likely to happen on the afternoon trip to Levuka, making it wise to fly to Ovalau (F$52) and return to Suva on the boat.

On Tuesday, Thursday, Friday, and Saturday, the 50-passenger boat *Viro* operates to Levuka (F$16). The connecting carrier leaves from opposite the Suva Flea Market at 0800. Call **Turtle Island Transport** (tel. 339-4996 or 992-1297) for information.

Ships to Northern Fiji

Patterson Brothers Shipping (tel. 331-5644, patterson@connect.com.fj), Suite 1, 1st floor, Epworth Arcade off Nina Street, takes reservations for the Suva-Natovi-Nabouwalu-Labasa "Sea-Road" ferry/bus combination, which departs the bus station opposite the Suva Flea Market Monday, Wednesday, and Friday at 0530.

Fares from Suva are F$48 to Nabouwalu or F$54 right through to Labasa, an interesting 10-hour trip. Forthcoming departures are listed on a blackboard in Patterson's Suva office and the schedule varies slightly each week. Patterson Brothers also has offices in Labasa, Lautoka, and Levuka.

Taina's Travel Services (tel. 330-5889, fax 330-6189), upstairs in Epworth House opposite Patterson Brothers, handles bookings on the 65-meter MV *Adi Savusavu,* a former Swedish Scarlett Line ferry once used on the Landskrona-Copenhagen run. Now operated by **Beachcomber Cruises,** this ferry generally leaves Walu Bay, Suva, northbound for Savusavu and Taveuni Tuesday at 1000, Thursday at noon, and Saturday at 1800. Fares from Suva are F$42/62 economy/first class to Savusavu or F$47/67 to Taveuni. A bus connection from Savusavu to Labasa is an extra F$6. The air-conditioned first-class lounge contains 30 airline-style seats, plus six long tables with chairs. If you're fast, it's possible to rent a mattress in first class at F$5 pp for the trip. Downstairs in economy are another 246 padded seats and space in which to spread a mat. Ask when lunch and dinner will be served in first class, because they're a good value. The *Adi Savusavu* also carries 12 cars and 15 trucks. Beachcomber Cruises' main office is on Freeston Road, Walu Bay.

Consort Shipping Line (tel. 331-3344 or 330-2877, fax 330-3389, consortship@connect .com.fj), in the Dominion House arcade on Thomson Street, operates the MV *Spirit of Fiji Islands* or "Sofi," an old Greek ferry with 182 airline-style seats in two video rooms, plus numerous long wooden benches outside on deck. First class consists of 20 four-berth cabins. The ship leaves Suva on Wednesday at 1000 and Saturday at 1800 for Koro (nine hours, F$35), Savusavu (14 hours, F$42/77), and Taveuni (23 hours, F$47/87 deck/cabin). The snack bar on board sells basic meals, but you're better off taking along your own food. Consort Shipping's main office is on Matua St., Walu Bay.

Ships to Kadavu and Rotuma

Kadavu Shipping Co. (tel. 331-1766, fax 331-2987), in the Ports Authority office building hidden between hangers Nos. 11 and 12, Rona Street, Walu Bay, runs the MV *Bulou-ni-ceva* to Kadavu twice a week. The boat leaves Suva Monday and Thursday at midnight, with the Monday trip going to Matana and Vunisea and not calling at Jona's, Albert's, or Matava. The Thursday boat reaches Kavala Bay near Albert's Place around 1400. Saturday around 1000 they pick up passengers to return to Suva, arriving at 1700. Fares are F$47/66/90 deck/cabin/lounge, but only the cabin and lounge fares include meals. The cabins have four bunks, the lounge two beds, and deck passengers can stretch out on long benches on the middle deck when it isn't crowded. Once a month this ship sails to Rotuma, a two-day journey costing F$100/170/190 deck/cabin/lounge. The *Bulou-ni-ceva* is a former Chinese riverboat now owned by Kadavu Province (the entire crew is from Kadavu).

Western Shipping (tel. 331-4467), in a yellow container on Muaiwalu Wharf, operates the *Cagi Mai Ba* to Kadavu twice a week, usually leaving for Vunisea Monday at midnight and Kavala Bay Thursday at midnight (F$47 on deck, F$48 in an air-conditioned lounge, and F$57 in a 10-bed salon). The monthly trip to Rotuma is F$98/ 118/148 deck/lounge/salon.

Khans Shipping (tel. 330-8786), hanger No. 16 at the end of Rona St., operates the *Cagidonu* to Kadavu and Rotuma on an irregular schedule. The *Degei II* goes to Lomaiviti and Lau occasionally.

Ships to Other Islands

Salia Basaga Shipping (tel. 330-3403) runs the MV *Tunatuki II* to the Lau Group twice a month. This large metal trading ship styles itself the "inter island trail blazer." There are two four-bunk cabins, and the fare to Lakeba or Vanua Balavu is F$82/113 deck/cabin one-way, meals included. A 4–5-day round-trip to Cicia, Vanua Balavu, Tuvuca, Nayau, Lakeba, and Oneata will cost F$180/250 deck/cabin including meals. Their office is in a green container on Muaiwalu Wharf.

The **Kabua Development Corporation** (tel. 330-2258), near Consort Shipping on Matua St. near Muaiwalu Wharf, runs the *Taikabara*

to Lakeba and the other islands of southern Lau every fortnight (F$68 deck or F$79 in one of two two-berth cabins).

Patterson Brothers Shipping, mentioned above, operates the car ferry *Island Navigator* to Gau (F$60), Moala (F$75), Lakeba (F$85), and Vanua Balavu (F$85) every week or two. They also handle the small wooden copra boat *Adi Lomai* to Lomaiviti, Lau, and Rotuma. Other small boats, such as the *Cagidonu* and *Taikabara,* run from Suva to Lau every week or two. Ask the crews of vessels tied up at Muaiwalu Jetty, Walu Bay, for passage to Nairai, Gau, Koro, Lau, etc. Don't believe the first person who tells you there's no boat going where you want—*keep trying.*

Food is usually included in the price and on the outward journey it will probably be okay, but on the return don't expect much more than rice and tea. If you're planning a long voyage by interisland ship, a big bundle of kava roots to captain and crew as a token of appreciation for their hospitality works wonders.

Ships to Other Countries

The Wednesday issue of the *Fiji Times* carries a special section on international shipping, though most are container ships that don't accept passengers. Most shipping is headed for Tonga and Samoa—there's not much going westward, and actually getting on any of the ships mentioned below requires considerable persistence. Ships from neighboring countries sometimes come to Suva for repairs and they carry passengers back on their return. It's often easier to sign on as crew on a yacht, and they'll probably be heading west. Try both yacht anchorages in Suva: Put up a notice, ask around, etc.

Williams & Gosling Ltd. Ships Agency (tel. 331-2633, fax 330-7358, www.wgfiji.com.fj), 189 Rodwell Road near the market bus station, handles the monthly departure of the *Nivaga II* or *Manu Folau* to Funafuti, but the dates are variable. Fares in Australian dollars are A$234 one-way in a four-person cabin, A$166 in an eight-person cabin, and A$58 deck. Meals will be another A$57.50 cabin class or A$15 deck. Unless you have an onward plane ticket from Funafuti, you'll be required to pay for a round-trip.

Williams & Gosling will only know about a week beforehand approximately when the ship may sail. After reaching Funafuti, the ship cruises the Tuvalu Group.

Williams & Gosling also books passengers on the Kiribati Shipping Services vessel *Nei Matangare*, which leaves Suva for Funafuti and Tarawa occasionally. The three-day trip to Funafuti costs A$95/190 deck/cabin one way, otherwise the seven-day journey Suva-Tarawa with a day at Funafuti is A$184/368, meals included. Unless you have a ticket to leave Tuvalu or Kiribati, you're required to purchase a round-trip and no refund will be given until you can show an air ticket. Deck passengers sleep at the back of the ship and often get wet at night.

Pacific Agencies (tel. 331-5444, fax 330-2754), on Robertson Road between Rodwell Road and Nina Street, knows about Pacific Forum Line container ships from Suva to Apia, Pago Pago, and Nuku'alofa, such as the Samoan government-owned *Forum Samoa* (every two weeks) and the *Forum Fiji*. This office doesn't sell passenger tickets, so just ask when these ships will be in port, then go and talk to the captain, who is the only one who can decide if you'll be able to go.

Carpenters Shipping (tel. 331-2244, fax 330-1572, www.carpship.com.fj) on Edinburgh Road is an agent for the monthly **Bank Line** service to Lautoka, Port Vila, Luganville, Honiara, Papua New Guinea, and on to the United Kingdom. Again, they cannot sell you a passenger ticket and will only tell you when the ship is due in port and where it's headed. It's up to you to make arrangements personally with the captain, and the fare will be higher than airfare. Most passengers book months in advance.

Long-Distance Taxis and Minibuses

Minibuses to Nadi and Lautoka (F$12 to either) park at the **Stinson Parade Mini Bus Station** on the waterfront behind Village 6 Cinemas. Service is throughout the day until 1930. The regular buses at the bus station are slower and safer, and you see more.

Long-distance taxis to Nadi and Lautoka park

outside Foodland, corner of Robertson Road and Struan Street near the market. To Nadi it's F$15 pp or F$60 for the whole car. For an extra F$40 or so, you should be able to negotiate a slower trip with stops along the way. Write out a list of the places you might like to stop and show it to the driver beforehand, so he can't demand more money later on.

Taxis

Taxi meters are set at level one daily 0600–2200 with F$1 charged at flag-fall and about F$.50 a km. From 2200 to 0600 the flag-fall is F$1.50 plus F$.50 a km. Always ask the driver to use the meter. Fares average F$2 in the city center or F$3 to the suburbs. To hire a taxi for a city tour might cost around F$15 an hour.

Nausori Taxi (tel. 330-4178 or 331-2185), based at the taxi kiosk in the parking lot at the Holiday Inn, offers a shuttle service from Suva to Nausori Airport at F$3 pp. Trips are scheduled at 0545, 0845, 0945, 1100, 1330, and 1445 weekdays, and perhaps also on weekends, but only if bookings have been made. Thus it's important to reserve the day before if you want to be sure of getting this fare.

Car Rentals

Car rentals are available in Suva from **Avis** (tel. 331-3833, www.avis.com.fj), on Foster Road, Walu Bay, **Budget** (tel. 331-5899, www.budget.com.fj), 123 Foster Rd., Walu Bay, **Central** (tel. 331-1866, www.central-rent-car.com.fj), 295 Victoria Parade, **Dove** (tel. 331-1755), Brewster Street near Korea House, and **Thrifty** (tel. 331-4436, www.rosiefiji.com), 46 Gordon Street.

Tours

For information on day trips from Suva offered by **Wilderness Ethnic Adventure Fiji** (tel. 331-5730, fax 331-5450, www.wildernessfiji.com.fj), turn to the Navua section in this book. Wilderness also runs two-hour city sightseeing tours (adults F$49, children under 13 years F$33). These trips can be booked through the UTC tour desk at the Holiday Inn or through Rosie Tours on Gordon Street.

NAUSORI

In 1881, the Rewa River town of Nausori, 19 km northeast of Suva, was chosen as the site of Fiji's first large sugar mill, which operated until 1959. In those early days it was incorrectly believed that sugarcane grew better on the wetter eastern side of the island. Today cane is grown only on the drier, sunnier western sides of Viti Levu and Vanua Levu. The old sugar mill is now a rice mill and storage depot, as the Rewa Valley has become a major rice-producing area. Chicken feed is also milled here.

Nausori is Fiji's fifth-largest town and the headquarters of Central Division and Rewa Province. There are several banks in Nausori. The Rewa is Fiji's largest river and the nine-span bridge here was erected in 1937. Long lines of vehicles crawl across this narrow bridge throughout the day, with a policeman directing traffic at the Nausori end right next to the bustling market. Construction of a new Rewa River bridge was delayed for several years by sanctions imposed on Fiji after the May 2000 coup, but in 2003 tenders were finally taken (12.2 million euros in overseas assistance for the bridge has been budgeted by the European Union).

The town is better known for its large international airport three km southeast, built as a fighter strip to defend Fiji's capital during WW II. The population of 22,000 is predominantly Indo-Fijian. In mid-2000, the interior regions upriver from Nausori were scenes of terror as indigenous Fijian nationalists carried out ethnic cleansing operations against Indo-Fijians living in isolated farmhouses. Some 300 people from Baulevu village alone were evacuated to refugee camps.

The **Syria Monument** (1983), at the end of the Rewa bridge, commemorates the wreck of the iron sailing ship *Syria* on Nasilai Point in May 1884. Of the 439 indentured Indian laborers aboard ship at the time, 57 were drowned. The monument tells the story of the rescue of the others.

Accommodations and Food

The only place to stay is **Riverside Accommodations** (tel. 995-0484), near the Nausori Club

down the alley behind Big Bear furniture store in the vicinity of the Shell service station on Kings Road. The three rooms with shared bath are F$35 single or double. A pleasant sitting room is provided in this colonial-style wooden house with a veranda and lovely garden on the river. Don't be put off by the House Full sign you may see outside, as this probably only applies to a separate section used by the locals for "short times." The rooms for foreigners are in the next building.

Krishna Milk Bar (tel. 347-7825; closed Sun.), 3 Ross Street, down from the Westpac Bank and on the right, is Nausori's only vegetarian restaurant. You can get a vegetarian thali meal (F$3), samosas, and flavored masala tea.

The **Whistling Duck Pub,** around the corner from Krishna Milk Bar, and **KB's Bar and Night Club** (Fri. and Sat. 1900–0300, F$5 admission), opposite the bus station, are worth a look. Also try the **Nausori Club** (tel. 347-8287), on the river behind Big Bear.

Transportation

Local buses to the airport (F$.50) and Suva (F$1.40) are fairly frequent, with the last bus to Suva at 2200. A taxi to the airport will be F$3. You can catch Sunbeam Transport express buses from Nausori to Lautoka at 0635, 0715, 0855, 1240, 1405, and 1745 (246 km, 5.5 hours, F$12).

EAST OF NAUSORI
Rewa Delta

Take a bus from Nausori to Nakelo Landing to explore the heavily populated Rewa River Delta. Many outboards leave from Nakelo to take villagers to their riverside homes and passenger fares are around a dollar for short trips. Larger boats leave Nakelo sporadically for Levuka, Gau, and Koro, but finding one would be pure chance. Some also depart from nearby Wainibokasi Landing. At **Nailili** in the delta, French Catholic missionaries built St. Joseph's Church (1905) of solid limestone with stained glass windows.

Bau Island

Bau, a tiny, eight-hectare island just east of Viti Levu, has a special place in Fiji's history, as this was the seat of High Chief Cakobau, who used European cannons and muskets to subdue most of western Fiji in the 1850s. At its pinnacle Bau had a population of 3,000, hundreds of war canoes guarded its waters, and over 20 temples stood on the island's central plain. After the Battle of Verata on Viti Levu in 1839, Cakobau and his father Tanoa presented 260 bodies of men, women, and children to their closest friends and allied chiefs for gastronomical purposes. Fifteen years after this slaughter, Cakobau converted to Christianity and prohibited cannibalism on Bau. In 1867, he became a sovereign, crowned by European traders and planters desiring a stable government in Fiji to protect their interests.

Sights of Bau

The great stone slabs that form docks and seawalls around much of the island once accommodated Bau's fleet of war canoes. The graves of the Cakobau family and many of the old chiefs lie on the hilltop behind the school. The large, sturdy stone church located near the provincial offices was the first Christian church in Fiji. Inside its nearly one-meter-thick walls, just in front of the altar, is the old sacrificial stone once used for human sacrifices, today the baptismal font. Now painted white, this font was once known as King Cakobau's "skull crusher" and it's said a thousand brains were splattered against it. Across from the church are huge ancient trees and the thatched Council House on the site of the onetime temple of the war god Cagawalu. The family of the late Sir George Cakobau, governor-general of Fiji from 1973–1983, has a large traditional-style home on the island. You can see everything on the island in an hour or so.

Getting There

Take the Bau bus (five daily, F$.80) from Nausori to Bau Landing where there are outboards to cross over to the island. Be aware that Bau is not considered a tourist attraction, and from time to time visitors are prevented from going to the island. It's important to get someone to invite you across, which they'll do willingly if you show a genuine interest in Fijian history. Bring a big bundle of *waka* for the *turaga-ni-koro,* and ask permission very politely to be shown around. There could be some

confusion about who's to receive the *sevusevu,* however, as everyone on Bau is a chief! The more respectful your dress and demeanor, the better your chances of success. If you're told to contact the Ministry of Fijian Affairs in Suva, just depart gracefully, as that's only their way of saying no. After all, it's up to them.

Viwa Island

Before Cakobau adopted Christianity in 1854, Methodist missionaries working for this effect resided on Viwa Island, just across the water from Bau. Here the first Fijian New Testament was printed in 1847; Rev. John Hunt, who did the translation, lies buried in the graveyard beside the church that bears his name.

Viwa is a good alternative if you aren't invited to visit Bau itself. To reach the island, hire an outboard at Bau Landing. If you're lucky, you'll be able to join some locals who are going. A single Fijian village stands on the island.

Toberua Island

Created in 1968, **Toberua Island Resort** (tel. 347-2777 or 330-2356, fax 347-2888, www .toberua.com), on a tiny reef island off the east tip of Viti Levu, was one of Fiji's first luxury outer-island resorts. The 15 thatched *bure* are designed in the purest Fijian style, yet it's all very luxurious and the small size means peace and quiet. The tariff is F$490/540 single/double, plus F$110 for the three-meal plan (five-night minimum stay). Discounts are available for children under 16 sharing with adults. Toberua is outside eastern Viti Levu's wet belt, so it doesn't get a lot of rain as does nearby Suva, and weather permitting, meals are served outdoors. There are no mosquitoes.

Don't expect tennis courts or a golf course at Toberua, though believe it or not, there's tropical golfing on the reef at low tide! (Nine holes from 90–180 meters, course par 32, clubs and balls provided free.) Sportfishing is F$90 an hour and scuba diving F$88/450 for one/six tanks. Massage is F$55 an hour. All other activities are free, including snorkeling, sailing, windsurfing, and boat trips to a bird sanctuary or mangrove forest. A swimming pool is provided. Launch transfers from Nakelo Landing to Toberua are F$38 per person each way.

Northern Viti Levu

Northern Viti Levu has far more spectacular landscapes than the southern side of the island, and if you can only travel one way by road between Suva and Nadi, you're better off taking the northern route. Kings Road is now paved from Suva north to Korovou, then again from Dama to Lautoka, but between Korovou and Dama is a 62-km gravel stretch. (Roadwork from the Dama end may have extended the pavement 13 km or so by the time you get there, but at the present rate it will be decades before the asphalt reaches Korovou.) If driving, check your fuel before heading this way. Since Kings Road follows the Wainibuka River from Wailotua village almost all the way to Viti Levu Bay, you get a good glimpse of the island's lush interior, and the north coast west of Rakiraki is breathtaking. In years gone by, the Fijians would use bamboo rafts to transport bundles of bananas down the Wainibuka to markets in Vunidawa and Nausori, and the road is still called the "Banana Highway." These days, many visitors stop for a sojourn on Nananu-i-Ra Island near Rakiraki, and intrepid hikers occasionally trek south down the Sigatoka River from the hill station of Nadarivatu. The rugged north coast is known as the Sunshine Coast for its relatively dry climate.

NORTHEASTERN VITI LEVU

Korovou and the Tailevu Coast

A good paved highway runs 31 km north from Nausori to Korovou, a small town of around 350 souls on the east side of Viti Levu. Korovou is at the junction of Kings Road and the road to Natovi, terminus of the Ovalau and Vanua Levu ferries, and this crossroads position makes it an important stop for buses plying the northern route around the island. Sunbeam Transport express buses leave Korovou for Lautoka at 0720, 0800, 0940, 1325, 1500, and 1830 (215 km, five hours), with local westbound buses departing at 0920 and 0950 (7.5 hours). (Be aware that because "korovou" means "new village," there are many places called that in Fiji—don't mix them up.)

Korovou is the headquarters of Tailevu Province and the district officer's office is in Waimaro House on the south side of town. The Seventh Day Adventist Church operates Fulton College, a large Bible college just south of Korovou. Coupmaster George Speight hails from near Korovou and a rather unpleasant atmosphere hangs over the town.

The dilapidated **Tailevu Hotel** (Warrick Williams, tel. 343-0028, fax 343-0244), on a hill overlooking the Waibula River just across the bridge from Korovou, has three double rooms in an old building at F$45 double, or F$55 for a four-person family room. Better are the six new air-conditioned units in a long block facing an unfinished swimming pool at F$60 double. Two basic single rooms in a nearby cottage are F$25 (or F$15 if you request the "backpackers rate"). This rustic colonial-style hotel features a large bar and restaurant, and a disco opens on Friday and Saturday nights.

North of Korovou is Natovi, terminus of ferry services from Vanua Levu and Ovalau. The **Natalei Eco-Lodge** (tel. 881-1168) at Nataleira village, up the coast beyond Natovi, offers dormitory accommodations at F$35 pp and *bure* at F$100 double, meals included. Buses to Nataleira leave Suva bus station weekdays at 1330, 1430, and 1630 (F$4). Horse riding, hiking, waterfall visits, snorkeling, and cultural activities can be arranged. Natalei Eco-Lodge makes an ideal base from which to climb **Mt. Tova** (647 meters) for its sweeping view of the entire Tailevu area. The trail begins at Silana village, a couple of km northwest of Nataleira.

Kings Road to Viti Levu Bay

The large dairy farms along the highway west of Korovou were set up after WW I. **Dorothy's Waterfall** on the Waimaro River, a kilometer east of Dakuivuna village, is 10 km west of Korovou. It's a nice picnic spot if you have your own transportation.

At Wailotua No. 1, 20 km west of Korovou, is a large **snake cave** (admission F$5) right beside the village and easily accessible from the road. One stalactite in the cave is shaped like a six-headed snake. "Feejee Experience" groups are taken *bilibili* rafting on the Wainibuka River here. At Dama the paved road starts again and continues 45 km northwest to Rakiraki. (As you drive along this road you may be flagged down by Fijians emphatically inviting you to visit their village. At the end of the tour you'll be asked to sign the visitors book and make a financial contribution. If you decide to stop, don't bother trying to present anyone with kava roots, because hard cash is all they're after.)

The old Catholic Church of St. Francis Xavier at **Naiserelagi,** on a hilltop above Navunibitu Catholic School, on Kings Road about 25 km southeast of Rakiraki, was beautifully decorated with frescoes by Jean Charlot in 1962–1963. Typical Fijian motifs such as the *tabua, tanoa,* and *yaqona* blend in the powerful composition behind the altar. Father Pierre Chanel, who was martyred in 1841 on Futuna Island between Fiji and Samoa, appears on the left holding the weapon that killed him, a war club. Christ and the Madonna are portrayed in black. Charlot had previously collaborated with the famous Mexican muralist Diego Rivera, and his work (restored in 1998) is definitely worth stopping to see. Flying Prince Transport (tel. 669-4346) runs buses from Vaileka to Naiserelagi at 0845, 1130, 1200, 1330, 1430, 1545, 1630, and 1730 (F$2), otherwise all the local Suva buses stop there. A taxi from Vaileka might cost F$22 one-way or F$30 roundtrip with waiting time. At **Nanuku-loa** village just north of here is the headquarters of Ra Province.

Near Ellington Wharf

Adventure Water Sports (Warren Francis, tel. 669-3333, fax 669-3366, www.safarilodge.com.fj) on Ellington Wharf offers catamaran cruises (from F$55 pp), two-hour snorkeling tours (F$25/30 pp to the inner/outer reef), kayak tours (F$149 a full day), game fishing (F$115/195 pp for two/four hours), and windsurfing lessons (F$60/110 beginner/advanced an hour, plus F$40/85 board hire). A minimum of two persons is required for most trips. You can also rent windsurfers, snor-

keling gear, and Hobie Cats. Their shop serves basic meals at F$4–5 or coffee for F$1. You can use the phone here to call the island at F$1 a call or check your email at F$.18 a minute. Boat transfers to Nananu-i-Ra can be arranged.

The **Make It Happen Store** (tel. 927-9678 or 991-7684), opposite Adventure Water Sports, can arrange half-day treks to the top of Uluisupani (540 meters), the highest peak behind Ellington Wharf, via Navolau II village, at F$30 pp.

The upscale **Wananavu Beach Resort** (John Gray, tel. 669-4433, fax 669-4499, www.wananavu.com), on a point facing Nananu-i-Ra Island, three km off Kings Road, is near Viti Levu's northernmost tip. There are 15 air-conditioned bungalows costing F$300–365 single or double—reasonable value for the quality. No cooking facilities are provided, but each room does have a fridge. Adjacent to the resort are three two-bedroom villas with kitchens renting for F$372 for up to four persons. Local rate discounts are possible. The three-meal plan is F$85 pp. The resort has a swimming pool, tennis court, and small brown beach. The Nananu-i-Ra dive shops offer scuba diving from the Wananavu, and a variety of other water sports are available. Daily snorkeling trips are organized to different sites, and a picnic lunch on the beach is included in the F$28 pp charge.

NANANU-I-RA ISLAND

This small 355-hectare island, three km off the northernmost tip of Viti Levu, is a good place to spend some quality time amid tranquility and beauty. The climate is dry and sunny, and there are great beaches, reefs, snorkeling, walks, sunsets, and moonrises over the water—only roads are missing. Seven or eight separate white sandy beaches lie scattered around the island, and it's big enough that you won't feel confined. In the early 19th century Nananu-i-Ra's original Fijian inhabitants were wiped out by disease and tribal warfare, and an heir sold the island to the Europeans whose descendants now operate small family-style resorts and a 219-hectare plantation on the island.

The northern two-thirds of Nananu-i-Ra Island, including all of the land around Nananu

windsurfers on Nananu-i-Ra's Long Beach

© DAVID STANLEY

669-4511, fax 669-4611, www.radivers.com) has been operating on Nananu-i-Ra for over a decade. They offer scuba diving at F$85/150/650 for one/two/10 tanks, plus F$15 for gear. Night diving is F$100. Snorkelers can go along for F$25 (mask and snorkel supplied). Ra Diver's resort course costs F$160; full four-day PADI or NAUI certification is F$600 if you're alone or F$525 pp for two or more. They pick up clients regularly from all of the resorts. Ra Divers tends to stay close to Nananu-i-Ra, and the diving here is only spectacular if you observe the small details—there's not the profuse marinelife or huge reefs you'll find elsewhere. The underwater photographer will like it.

An American named Dan Grenier runs a more upscale dive operation called **Crystal Divers** (tel. 669-4747, fax 669-4877, www.crystaldivers.com) at the south end of Nananu-i-Ra. Many of Dan's clients book from overseas via his Internet site, paying F$150/190 for two tank dives to the fringing/outer reef, plus F$40 a day for gear (if required). Third tanks are F$80. Dan prefers to work with experienced divers and usually doesn't have time for certification courses unless a group is interested. His 12-meter jet boat *Crystal Explorer* allows him to offer live-aboard quality diving from a land-based location. He frequents extraordinary Bligh Water sites and he's constantly searching for new locations. Crystal Divers closes for annual leave in January and February.

Accommodations

Under US$25: Accommodation prices on Nananu-i-Ra have crept up in recent years and the number of beds is limited. With the island's growing popularity it's best to call ahead to one of the resorts and arrange to be picked up at Ellington Wharf. None of the innkeepers will accept additional guests when they're fully booked and camping is often not allowed. There's no public telephone at Ellington Wharf, but the staff of Adventure Water Sports on the wharf will make local calls for you at F$1 each.

If you want an individual room or *bure* make 100 percent sure one is available, otherwise you could end up spending a few nights in the dormitory waiting for one to become free. All the

Island Lodge, is owned by Mrs. Louise Harper of southern California, who bought it for a mere US$200,000 in 1966 (she also owns a sizable chunk of Proctor & Gamble back in the States). Today Harper cattle graze beneath coconuts on the Harper Plantation.

To hike right around Nananu-i-Ra on the beach takes about four hours of steady going, or all day if you stop for picnicking and snorkeling. The thickest section of mangroves is between Nananu Island Lodge and the Bamboo Beach Resort, on the west side of the island, and this stretch should be covered at low tide. However you do it, at some point you'll probably have to take off your shoes and wade through water just over your ankles or scramble over slippery rocks. The entire coastline is public, but only as far as two meters above the high tide line. Avoid becoming stranded by high tide.

Scuba Diving

Ra Divers (Elizabeth and Graham Burnett, tel.

budget places have cooking facilities and a few also serve snacks and meals. MacDonald's, Betham's, and Nananu Island Lodge have mini-markets with a reasonable selection of groceries (including beer). Bring enough cash, as only the Bamboo Beach Resort accepts credit cards.

Nananu Island Lodge (tel./fax 669-4290, www.nananu-island-lodge.com), formerly known as Kontiki Island Lodge, has been upgraded since a change of ownership in 2001. It's at the unspoiled north end of the island, with the long deserted beach facing One Bay just a 20-minute walk away. Hike up onto the hill behind the lodge for the view. They offer three modern self-catering bungalows, each capable of sleeping four at F$110/125/140 double/triple/quad, plus tax. If you want more privacy, ask for one of the four rooms in the two thatched duplex *bure* and two rooms in another building, which are F$54 double. The two dorms each have six beds at F$20 pp. Camping is F$10 pp. There's no hot water. All guests have access to a fridge and cooking facilities, and a small shop is on the premises. Otherwise, you can order meals. The "Feejee Experience" people stay here, so reservations are essential. On Saturday night they're always full.

At the other end of Nananu-i-Ra, a one-hour walk along the beach at low tide, are several other inexpensive places to stay, all offering cooking facilities. They're less crowded than Nananu Island Lodge and perhaps preferable for a restful holiday. They almost always have a few free beds in the dorms, but advance bookings are recommended.

MacDonald's Nananu Beach Cottages (tel. 669-4633, fax 669-4302) offers two attractive beach houses and one garden house, all with bath and fridge, at F$80 single or double, plus F$9 pp per additional person to four maximum. A duplex is F$70 for each of the two units, while a larger two-story house accommodating up to six is F$175. The four-bunk dorm is F$20 pp. All units have access to cooking facilities and a three-meal package is available at F$33 pp. Mabel MacDonald's Beachside Café serves excellent grilled cheese sandwiches (F$5) and pizzas (F$15–20) as well as selling groceries. Dinner (F$10–16) must be ordered by 1500. A Fijian *lovo* feast (F$15/25 for vegetarians/carnivores)

is arranged once a week. It's peaceful and attractive with excellent snorkeling (lots of parrot fish) from the long private wharf off their beach. Ryan MacDonald takes guests on a snorkeling trip to the outer reef at F$25 pp (minimum of four). A two-person kayak is F$12.50/25 a half/full day. The atmosphere at MacDonald's is excellent.

Right next to MacDonald's and facing the same white beach is friendly **Betham's Beach Cottages** (Peggy and Oscar Betham, tel./fax 669-4132, www.bethams.com.fj). They have four units in two cement-block duplex houses, each sleeping up to six, at F$90 single or double, F$100 triple. The one wooden beachfront bungalow costs the same. Two mixed dormitories, one with eight beds and another with six, are F$20 pp. There's no hot water, but cooking facilities and a fridge are provided. The electric generator is switched off at 2200. A paperback lending library is at your service. Betham's impressive grocery store also sells alcohol and their well-stocked beachfront bar serves dinner at F$12–20, though the food is better at MacDonald's. A snorkeling trip is F$15, plus F$10 for gear.

Sharing the same high sandy beach with the above is **Charley's Place** (Charley and Louise Anthony, tel. 669-4676). Each of the two houses on the hillside has a three-bed dorm (F$20 pp) in the same area as the kitchen and one double room with shared bath (F$45). You can watch the sunrise on one side of the hill and the sunset on the other. Charley's also rents another house at F$70 double.

Just a few minutes walk across the peninsula via a 200-meter right of way next to Charley's is **Morrison's Beach Cottage** (Phyl and John Morrison, tel./fax 669-4516, tipple@connect.com.fj), on Long Beach on the east side of the island. The two-bedroom bungalow is F$85/95/105 double/triple/quad, the five-bed dorm F$20 pp. Two people can reserve the entire dorm for themselves at F$75. Both units are fully screened and have cooking facilities, fridge, and private bath (no meals served). It's cleaner and quieter than some of the other places. John is a retired engineer from the Emperor Gold Mine who loves to go fishing, and he'll gladly take you out in his boat at F$40/65 a half/full day plus fuel. He also rents paddle boats at F$10/15 a half/full day, snorkeling gear at F$10/15. Morrison's closes for holidays in January and February.

US$150–250: The **Bamboo Beach Resort** (tel. 669-4444, fax 669-4404), formerly known as Mokusigas Island Resort, is owned by the same people who run the Marlin Bay Resort on Beqa Island. Completely rebuilt in 2003, the 20 bungalows with fridge and outdoor shower go for F$370 single or double, with another F$110 pp payable for the meal plan (no cooking facilities). Scuba divers are the target market, and Dan Grenier of Crystal Divers manages the diving operation. To create a diving attraction, the 33-meter *Papuan Explorer* was scuttled in 22 meters of water, 150 meters off the 189-meter Bamboo Beach jetty, which curves out into the sheltered lagoon. Only a skimpy little beach facing a mudflat is on the west side of the property, but there's a mile-long picture-postcard beach over the hill on the other side of the island. All the resort facilities, including the restaurant, bar, and dive shop, are strictly for houseguests only.

Getting There

Boat transfers from Ellington Wharf to Nananu-i-Ra are about F$20 pp return (20 minutes), though the resorts may levy a surcharge for one person alone. Check prices when you call to make your accommodation booking. The Nadi Downtown Motel arranges minibus rides from Nadi direct to Ellington Wharf costing anywhere from F$25–45 pp depending on how many people are going, though it's cheaper to take an express bus from Lautoka to Vaileka, then a taxi to the landing at F$10 for the car. Otherwise, all of the express buses will drop you on the highway, a two km walk from Ellington Wharf. Coming from Nadi, you will have to change buses in Lautoka.

Patterson Brothers operates a vehicular ferry between Ellington Wharf and Nabouwalu a few times a week, a great shortcut to/from Vanua Levu (F$39 one-way). The ferry leaves Ellington Wharf at 0700, departing Nabouwalu for the return at 1130. There's a connecting bus to/from Labasa at Nabouwalu (112 km). Often you'll be allowed to spend the night on the boat at Ellington Wharf. Patterson's best customers

are large trucks carrying pine logs from Vanua Levu to the mills of Lautoka. The schedule changes all the time and the only way to find out which days they'll going that week is to call Patterson's Lautoka office at tel. 666-1173.

RAKIRAKI

This part of northern Viti Levu is known as Rakiraki, but the main town is called **Vaileka** (population 5,000). The Penang Sugar Mill was erected here in 1881. The mill is about a kilometer from the main business section of Vaileka, beyond the golf course. The sugar is loaded aboard ships at Ellington Wharf, connected to the mill by an 11-km cane railway. There are three banks and a large produce market in Vaileka, but most visitors simply pass through on their way to/from Nananu-i-Ra Island.

Right beside Kings Road, just a hundred meters west of the turnoff to Vaileka, is the grave of **Ratu Udreudre,** the cannibal king of this region who is alleged to have consumed 872 corpses. A rocky hill named **Uluinavatu** (stone head), a few kilometers west of Vaileka, is reputed to be the jumping-off point for the disembodied spirits of the ancient Fijians. A fortified village and temple once stood on its summit. Uluinavatu's triangular shape is said to represent a man, while a similar-looking small island offshore resembles a woman with flowing hair.

The **Nakauvadra Range,** towering south of Rakiraki, is the traditional home of the Fijian serpent-god Degei, who is said to dwell in a cave on the summit of Mt. Uluda (866 meters). This "cave" is little more than a cleft in the rock. To climb the Nakauvadra Range, which the local Fijians look upon as their primeval homeland, permission must be obtained from the chief of Vatukacevaceva village who will provide guides. A *sevusevu* must be presented.

Accommodations and Food

The **Rakiraki Hotel** (tel. 669-4101, fax 669-4545, www.tanoahotels.com), on Kings Road a couple of kilometers north of Vaileka, has 36 air-conditioned rooms with fridge and private bath at F$99 single or double, F$123 triple in

FIJI ISLANDS

the new blocks, and 10 rather musty fan-cooled rooms at F$35/48 single/double in the old wing. Reduced rates are sometimes offered on the air-conditioned rooms. The reception area, restaurant, and old wooden wing occupy the core of the original hotel dating back to 1945; the two-story accommodations blocks were added much later. Extensive gardens surround the hotel, and the Rakiraki's outdoor bowling green draws middle-aged lawn bowling enthusiasts from Australia and New Zealand. Those folks like old-fashioned "colonial" touches like the typed daily menu featuring British-Indian curry dishes, and gin and tonic in the afternoon. The manager can arrange for you to play at the nearby nine-hole golf course owned by the Fiji Sugar Corporation (green fees are F$20 and you must bring your own clubs). The Tui Ra (or king of Ra) lives in the village across the highway from the hotel. Only the local or "stage" buses will drop you off on Kings Road right in front of the hotel (the express buses will take you to Vaileka). A taxi from Vaileka will be F$2.50.

A number of restaurants near the bus station at Vaileka serve basic Chinese meals. At F$6.50 and up a plate, **Gafoor & Sons** (tel. 669-4225) is the most expensive, since the Sunbeam express buses stop there. **Rakiraki Lodge** (tel. 669-4336) on the west side of the square serves some excellent curry meals for F$4.50 from a glass-covered warmer at the rear counter. The **Cosmopolitan Club** (tel. 669-4330), two blocks from Vaileka bus station, is the local drinking place.

Transportation

A taxi from Vaileka to Ellington Wharf, where outboard motorboats from Nananu-i-Ra resort pick up guests, will run F$10. Otherwise, take a local bus east on Kings Road to the turnoff and walk two km down to the wharf. All buses from Lautoka and Suva stop at this turnoff.

Sunbeam Transport has express buses from Vaileka to Lautoka (108 km) at 1010, 1035, 1230, 1605, 1730, and 2105, and to Suva at 0830, 0900, 1100, 1440, and 1850. Flying Prince buses to Suva (157 km, F$9) leave Vaileka at 0745, 0845, and 1230. More frequent local buses also operate.

NORTHWESTERN VITI LEVU

West of Rakiraki, Kings Road passes the government-run Yaqara Cattle Ranch where Fijian cowboys keep 5,500 head of cattle and 200 horses on a 7,000-hectare spread enclosed by an 80-km fence. In 1996, an ultramodern artesian water bottling plant owned by Canadian businessman David Gilmour opened here, and plastic bottles of Fiji Water are now the country's fastest growing export. In 2003, an Australian company leased 5,000 hectares of land around Yaqara with the intention of creating a Studio City for foreign film producers.

Tavua

Tavua (population 2,500), an important junction on the north coast, is useful mostly as a base for visiting the gold mine at Vatukoula. Of the three banks in Tavua, the ANZ Bank has a Visa/MasterCard ATM.

The two-story **Tavua Hotel** (tel. 668-0522), a wooden colonial-style building on a hill, is only a five-minute walk from the bus stop. Fully renovated in 2002, the 11 air-conditioned rooms with bath are now reasonable value at F$45/68 single/double. The five-bed dormitory is F$18 pp. Meals are F$10 here. This hotel looks like it's going to be noisy due to the large bar downstairs, but all is silent after the bar and restaurant close at 2100. It's a good base from which to explore Vatukoula or break a trip across northern Viti Levu.

Roy's Wine & Dine (Michael Roy, tel. 668-1474; Mon.–Sat. 0700–1800), on Leka St. near the post office, serves a fish and chips lunch for under F$2. Socialize at the **Tavua Farmers Club** (tel. 668-0236) on Kings Road toward Ba, or the more elitist **Tavua Club** (tel. 668-0265) on Nasivi Street.

Sunbeam Transport has express buses from Tavua to Suva (198 km) at 0725, 0750, 1000, 1340, and 1750, and to Lautoka (67 km) at 1105, 1130, 1320, 1655, 1825, and 2200. Local buses from Tavua to Vaileka (41 km), Vatukoula (8 km), or Lautoka are frequent, but the bus service from Tavua to Nadrau via Nadarivatu has been suspended.

Vatukoula

In 1932, an old Australian prospector named Bill Borthwick discovered gold at Vatukoula, eight km south of Tavua. Two years later Borthwick and his partner, Peter Costello, sold their stake to an Australian company, and in 1935 the **Emperor Gold Mine** opened. In 1977, there was a major industrial action at the mine and the government had to step in to prevent it from closing. In 1983, the Western Mining Corporation of Australia bought a 20 percent share and took over management. Western modernized the facilities and greatly increased production, but after another bitter strike in 1991 they sold out, and the mine is now operated by the Emperor Gold Mining Company once again. The 700 miners who walked out in 1991 have been replaced by other workers who belong to a more amenable union.

The ore comes up from the underground area through the Smith Shaft near "Top Gate." It's washed, crushed, and roasted, then fed into a flotation process and the foundry where gold and silver are separated from the ore. Counting both underground operations and an open pit, the mine presently extracts 130,000 ounces of gold annually from 600,000 metric tons of ore. A ton of silver is also produced each year and waste rock is crushed into gravel and sold. Since 1935, the Emperor has produced five million ounces of gold worth over a billion U.S. dollars at today's prices. Proven recoverable ore reserves at Vatukoula are sufficient for another 20 years of mining, with another 3.5 million ounces awaiting extraction underground. In 1999, the Smith Shaft was deepened to allow easier access to high-grade ores, followed by work on the Cayzer Shaft in 2000 and the Philips Shaft in 2002.

The Emperor is Fiji's largest private employer and Vatukoula is a typical company town of 10,000 inhabitants, with education and social services under the jurisdiction of the mine. The 2,500 miners employed here, most of them indigenous Fijians, live in WW II-style Quonset huts in racially segregated ghettos. In contrast, tradespeople and supervisors, usually Rotumans and part-Fijians, enjoy much better living conditions, and senior staff and management live in colonial-style comfort. Women are forbidden by law from working underground.

To arrange a guided tour of the mine you must contact the Public Relations Officer, Emperor Gold Mining Co. Ltd. (tel. 668-0477, ext. 201, fax 668-0779, www.emperor.com.au), at least 24 hours in advance. Surface tours cost F$30 per group of between one and 30 persons, plus F$1 per additional person for groups of over 30 (underground tours not offered). The tour office is behind the Credit Union, 100 meters from "Bottom Gate." Rosie The Travel Service in Nadi runs gold mine tours (F$55 pp without lunch).

From Tavua, minibuses (F$.70) marked "Loloma" go to Bottom Gate every half hour, while those marked "Korowere" go to Top Gate. Even if you don't get off, it's worth making the round-trip to see the varying classes of company housing, to catch a glimpse of the nine-hole golf course and open pit, and to enjoy the lovely scenery. Cold beer is available at the **Bowling Club** (tel. 668-0719; Mon.–Fri. 1600–2300, Sat. 0830–2300) near Bottom Gate, where meals are served upon request.

Ba

The large Indo-Fijian town of Ba (population 15,000) on the Ba River is seldom visited by tourists. As the attractive mosque in the center of town suggests, nearly half of Fiji's Muslims live in Ba Province. Small fishing boats depart from behind the Shell service station opposite the mosque, and it's fairly easy to arrange to go along on all-night trips. A wide belt of mangroves covers much of the river's delta. Ba's original town site was on the low hill where the post office is today, and the newer lower town is often subjected to flooding. Ba is well known in Fiji for the large Rarawai Sugar Mill, built by the Colonial Sugar Refining Co. in 1886. In 2002, the transnational Nestlé established a large food processing plant at Ba.

The **Ba Hotel** (tel. 667-4000, fax 667-0559), 110 Bank St., has 13 air-conditioned rooms with bath at F$57/67 single/double—very pleasant with a swimming pool, bar, and restaurant.

Of the many places along Main Street serving Indian and Chinese meals, your best choice is probably **Chand's Restaurant** (tel. 667-0822;

daily 0800–2100), just across the bridge from the mosque. Their upstairs dining room serves an Indian vegetarian thali for F$6.50, other meals F$4–11. Chand's fast food center downstairs serves quick lunches from the warmer on the counter at F$3. It's great for a hot cup of tea, coffee, or milo. **Jolly Good** (tel. 667-1885; daily 0900–2100), across Main St. from the bus station and toward town, is clean and pleasant with main dishes from F$4.

The **Town Square Cinema** (tel. 667-4048), on Tabua Park just up the hill from the hotel, shows mostly Indian films. For drinks it's the **Farmers Club** (tel. 667-5511), on Bank St. near the Ba Hotel, or the **Central Club** (tel. 667-4348) on Tabua Park.

The ANZ and Westpac banks on Bank St. both have Visa/MasterCard ATMs outside facing the street. Otherwise try Money Exchange (tel. 667-0766; Mon.–Fri. 0800–1700, Sat. 0830–1300), around the corner on Main Street.

Important express buses leaving Ba daily are the regular Sunbeam Transport buses to Suva via Tavua at 0655, 0715, 0915, 1300, and 1715 (227 km, five hours), and the one Pacific Transport bus to Suva via Sigatoka at 0615 (259 km, six hours, F$13.35). Local buses to Tavua (29 km, F$1.60) and Lautoka (38 km, F$2) are frequent. Buses to Navala are at 1200 and 1715 daily except Sunday (F$2.25).

Vatia Point

Noted photographer Jim Siers operates a sport fishing lodge at Vatia Point between Ba and Tavua. **Angler's Paradise** (tel. 668-1612 or 651-2105, www.fijifishing.com) has a three-room guesthouse (F$154 plus tax pp a day for room and board), a couple of fast fishing boats (F$1,163 plus tax a day for up to four anglers), and good giant trevally fishing! Fishing rods, reels, and lures are available for hire or bring your own. Fishing trips to the Yasawa Islands are easily arranged.

INTO THE INTERIOR

Although Navala receives white-water rafters and sightseers, and regular tours from Nadi visit the Nausori Highlands, the rest of central Viti Levu is seldom visited. The dirt roads are too rough for ordinary rental vehicles, and facilities for tourists don't exist. Yet Fiji's highest mountains and deepest valleys are there, and some spectacular hiking possibilities await self-sufficient backpackers. Nadarivatu is the still the undiscovered jewel of central Viti Levu.

Nausori Highlands

A rough unpaved road runs 25 km southeast from Ba to Navala, a large traditional village on the sloping right bank of the Ba River. It then climbs another 20 km south to Bukuya village in the Nausori Highlands, from where other gravel roads continue south into the Sigatoka Valley and 40 km due west to Nadi. The Nadi road passes Vaturu Dam, which supplies Nadi with fresh water. Gold strikes near Vaturu may herald a mining future for this area, if the water catchment can be protected. The forests here were logged out in the 1970s, but the open scenery of the highlands still makes a visit well worthwhile.

Navala is the last fully thatched village on Viti Levu, its *bure* standing picturesquely above the Ba River against the surrounding hills, and the villagers have made a conscious decision to keep it that way. When water levels are right, white-water rafters shoot the rapids through the scenic Ba River Gorge near here, and guided hiking or horseback riding can also be arranged. Sightseers are welcome, but one must pay a F$15 pp admission/photography fee toward village development. Access is fairly easy on the two buses a day that arrive from Ba, but they only depart Navala to return to Ba at 0600 and 0800, so you must stay for the night. **Bulou's Lodge** (tel. 666-6644, ext. 2116), one km past Navala, provides accommodations at F$45 pp including meals. To hire a taxi from Ba to Navala will cost F$30 one-way or F$45 round-trip with an hour's waiting time. By rental vehicle you'll probably need a 4WD. During the rainy season, the Navala road can be flooded and impassable.

Bukuya in the center of western Viti Levu's highland plateau is far less traditional than Navala, and some of the only thatched *bure* in the village are those used by visitors on hiking/village stay tours organized by backpacker travel agencies in Nadi. The Tui Magodro, or high chief of the region, resides in Bukuya. During the Colo War of 1876, Bukuya was a center of resistance to colonial rule.

The easiest way to experience this area is on a day trip from Nadi. For example, Rosie The Travel Service (tel. 670-2726), opposite the Nadi Handicraft Market and at numerous other locations, operates full-day hiking tours to the Nausori Highlands daily except Sunday at F$69 including lunch, tax, and a souvenir *sulu*. **Victory Tours** (tel. 670-0243) in downtown Nadi offers day tours to a waterfall in the Nausori Highlands at F$95 pp including lunch. Tours to Navala are also offered.

Nadarivatu

An important forestry station is at Nadarivatu, a small settlement above Tavua. Its 900-meter altitude means a cool climate and fantastic panorama of the north coast from the ridge. Beside the road right in front of the Forestry Training Center is **The Stone Bowl,** official source of the Sigatoka River, and a five-minute walk from the Center is the **Governor General's Swimming Pool** where a small creek has been dammed. Go up the creek a short distance to the main pool, though it's dry much of the year and the area has not been maintained. The trail to the fire tower atop **Mt. Lomalagi** (Mt. Heaven) begins nearby, a one-hour hike each way. The tower itself has collapsed and is no longer climbable, but the forest is lovely and you may see and hear many native birds. Pine forests cover the land.

In its heyday Nadarivatu was a summer retreat for expatriates from the nearby Emperor Gold Mine at Vatukoula, and the mine still has two 14-bed guesthouses at Nadarivatu which can be rented at F$33 for a whole house. To reserve, call the mine office in Vatukoula (tel. 668-0477, ext. 201 or 406, fax 668-0779), which will inform the caretaker of your arrival. You can cook, but bring groceries with you. Visitors with tents are allowed to camp at the Forestry Training Center. Ask permission at the Ministry of Forests office as soon as you arrive. Some canned foods are available at the canteen opposite the mine

guesthouse, but bring food from Tavua. Cabin crackers are handy.

Only carriers operate between Tavua and Nadarivatu, leaving Tavua in the early afternoon and Nadarivatu in the morning—a spectacular one-and-a-half-hour ride (F$3). Ask the market women in Tavua where and when to catch the trucks. They often originate/terminate in Nadrau village, where you might also be able to stay (take along a *sevusevu* if you're thinking of this). It's also possible to hitch.

Mount Victoria

The two great rivers of Fiji, the Rewa and the Sigatoka, originate on the slopes of Mt. Victoria (Tomaniivi), highest mountain in the country (1,323 meters). The trail up the mountain begins near the bridge at Navai, 10 km southeast of Nadarivatu. Turn right up the hillside a few hundred meters down the jeep track, then climb up through native bush on the main path all the way to the top. Beware of misleading signboards. There are three small streams to cross; no water after the third. On your way back down, stop for a swim in the largest stream. There's a flat area on top where you could camp—if you're willing to take your chances with Buli, the devil king of the mountain. Local guides (F$20) are available and advisable, but permission to climb the mountain is not required, since this a nature reserve under the Forestry Department. Allow about six hours for the round-trip. Bright red epiphytic orchids (*Dendrobium moh-li-anum*) are sometimes in full bloom, and if you're very lucky, you might spot the rare red-throated lorikeet or pink-billed parrotfinch. Mount Victoria is on the divide between the wet and dry sides of Viti Levu, and from the summit you should be able to distinguish the contrasting vegetation of these zones.

Monasavu Hydroelectric Project

The largest development project ever undertaken in Fiji, this massive F$230 million scheme at Monasavu, on the Nadrau Plateau near the center of Viti Levu, took 1,500 men six years to complete. An earthen dam, 82 meters high, was built across the Nanuku River to supply water to the four 20-megawatt generating turbines at the Wailoa Power Station on the Wailoa River, 625 meters below. The dam forms a lake 17 km long, and the water drops through a 5.4-km tunnel at a 45-degree angle, one of the steepest engineered dips in the world. Overhead transmission lines carry power from Wailoa to Suva and Lautoka. At present Monasavu is filling 95 percent of Viti Levu's needs, representing an annual savings of F$22 million on imported diesel oil.

The Cross-Island Highway that passes the site was built to serve the dam project. Bus service ended when the project was completed and the construction camps closed in 1985. At the present time buses go only from Tavua to Nadrau and from Suva to Naivucini, although occasional carriers go farther. In 1998, there were tense scenes near the dam as landowners set up roadblocks to press claims for land flooded in the early 1980s. In July 2000, during the hostage crisis at Fiji's parliament, landowners occupied the dam and cut off power to much of Viti Levu for almost a month. At last report, lawyers for the landowners were demanding F$52.8 million in compensation from the Fiji Electricity Authority.

The Sigatoka River Trek

One of the most rewarding trips available on Viti Levu is the three-day hike south across the center of the island from Nadarivatu to Korolevu on the Sigatoka River. Northbound the way is much harder to find. Many superb campsites can be found along the trail, and luckily this trek isn't included in the Australian guidebooks, so the area isn't overrun by tourists. Have a generous bundle of *waka* ready in case you're invited to stay overnight in a village. (Kava for presentations on subsequent days can be purchased at villages along the way.) Set out from Nadarivatu early in the week, so you won't suffer the embarrassment of arriving in a village on a Sunday. Excellent topographical maps of the entire route can be purchased at the Lands and Survey Department in Suva.

Follow the dirt road south from Nadarivatu to **Nagatagata,** where you should fill your canteen, because the trail ahead is rigorous and there's no water to be found. From Nagatagata walk south

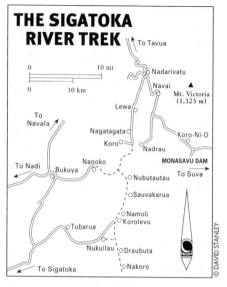

about one hour. When you reach the electric high-power line, where the road turns right and begins to descend toward Koro, look for the well-worn footpath ahead. The trail winds along the ridge, and you can see as far as Ba. The primeval forests that once covered this part of Fiji were destroyed long ago by the slash-and-burn agricultural techniques of the Fijians.

When you reach the pine trees the path divides, with Nanoko to the right and Nubutautau down to the left. During the rainy season it's better to turn right and head to Nanoko, where you may be able to find a carrier to Bukuya or all the way to Nadi. If you do decide to make for Nanoko, beware of a very roundabout loop road on the left. Another option is to skip all of the above by taking a carrier from Tavua to Nadrau, where your hike would then begin.

Reverend Thomas Baker, the last missionary to be clubbed and devoured in Fiji (in 1867), met his fate at **Nubutautau.** Jack London wrote a story, "The Whale Tooth," about the death of the missionary, and the ax that brought about Reverend Baker's demise is still kept in the village (other Baker artifacts are in the Fiji Museum). You should be able to stay in the community center in Nubutautau. In 2003, Baker's descendents traveled to Nubutautau from Australia for a *matani-gasau* ceremony during which the villagers apologized this old crime, and a curse which had hung over the village for 136 years was lifted. The Nubutautau-Korolevu section of the trek involves 22 crossings of the Sigatoka River, which is easy enough in the dry season (cut a bamboo staff for balance), but almost impossible in the wet (Dec.–April). Hiking boots will be useless in the river, so wear a pair of old running shoes.

It's a fantastic trip down the river to **Korolevu** if you can make it. The Korolevu villagers can call large eels up from a nearby pool with a certain chant. A few hours' walk away are the pottery villages, Draubuta and Nakoro, where traditional, long Fijian pots are still made. From Korolevu you can take a carrier to Tubarua, where there are five buses a day to Sigatoka. A carrier leaves Korolevu direct to Sigatoka very early every morning except Sunday (F$7), departing Sigatoka for the return around 1400 (if you want to do this trip in reverse).

Lautoka and Vicinity

Fiji's second city, Lautoka (population 45,000), is the focus of the country's sugar and timber industries, a major port, and the Western Division and Ba Province headquarters. It's a likable place with a row of towering royal palms along the main street. Although Lautoka grew up around the Fijian village of Namoli, the temples and mosques standing prominently in the center of town reflect the large Indo-Fijian population. In recent years things have changed somewhat, with many Indo-Fijians abandoning Fiji as indigenous Fijians move in to take their place, and Lautoka's population is now almost evenly balanced between the groups. Yet in the countryside Indo-Fijians still comprise a large majority.

The Lautoka Sugar Mill, one of the largest in the Southern Hemisphere, was founded in 1903. It's busiest from June to December with trains and trucks constantly depositing loads of cane to be fed into the crushers. Mill tours are not offered, but you can get a good view of the operation from the main gate on the south side of the complex. South Pacific Distilleries on Navutu Road south of the mill is a government-owned plant bottling rum, whisky, vodka, and gin under a variety of labels and, of course, molasses from the sugar mill is the distillery's main raw material. The fertilizer factory across the highway from the distillery uses mill mud from the sugar-making process. To the north, just beyond the conveyor belts used to load raw sugar onto the ships, is a veritable mountain of pine chips ready for export to Japan where they are used to make paper.

This is the main base for Blue Lagoon cruises to the Yasawa Islands, yet because Lautoka doesn't depend on tourism, you get a truer picture of ordinary life than you would in Nadi, and the city has a rambunctious nightlife. There's some shopping, but mainly this is just a pleasant place to wander around on foot.

SIGHTS

Begin at Lautoka's big, colorful **market** (next to the bus station), which is busiest on Saturday (open Mon.–Fri. 0700–1730, Sat. 0530–1600). From here, walk south on Yasawa Street to the photogenic **Jame Mosque.** Five times a day, local male Muslims direct prayers toward a small niche known as a *mihrab,* where the prayers fuse and fly to the *Kabba* in Mecca and thence to Allah. You can visit the mosque outside prayer times if you're conservatively dressed and willing to remove your shoes. During the crushing season (June–Nov.) narrow-gauge trains rattle past the mosque along a line parallel to Vitogo Parade, bringing cane to Lautoka's large sugar mill.

Follow the line east a bit to the **Sikh Temple,** rebuilt after a smaller temple was burned by arson in 1989. To enter you must wash your hands and cover your head (kerchiefs are provided at the door), and cigarettes and liquor are forbidden inside the compound. The teachings of the 10 Sikh gurus are contained in the Granth, a holy book prominently displayed in the temple. Sikhism began in the 16th century in the Punjab

LAUTOKA

FIJI ISLANDS

Bligh Water

YACHT ANCHORAGE

FORMER NEISAU MARINA

NAMOLI VILLAGE

SEA BREEZE HOTEL

SOUTH SEAS CLUB

PATTERSON BROTHERS

BAYLY CLINIC

TUINEAU ACCOMMODATION

MORRIS HEDSTROM

LAUTOKA HOTEL

COCO'S NIGHT CLUB

Shirley Park

WATERFRONT HOTEL

CITY COUNCIL

WESTPAC BANK

BEACHCOMBER CRUISES

BLUE LAGOON CRUISES

POST OFFICE

LIBRARY

MARINE DR.

WALU ST.

NABARA PARADE

VITOGO PARADE

BLUE LAGOON BOATS

BEACHCOMBER BOAT

MAIN WHARF

PINECHIP STORAGE

WESTSIDE WATERSPORTS

FIJI MEATS

SUGAR STORAGE SHEDS

SUGAR WHARF

FISHERIES WHARF

LAUTOKA SUGAR MILL

SOUTH PACIFIC DISTILLERIES

FERTILIZER FACTORY

NAMOLI

BUS STATION

MARKET

GLOBE CINEMA

JOLLY GOOD

GANGA

YASAWA ST.

RAVOUVOU ST.

NASAKI ST.

NAVAI ST.

BOUWALU ST.

SAUTAMATA ST.

LUKANI

VIDILO ST.

VAKABALE ST.

NALOVO ST.

TAVEWA AVE.

NARARA PARADE

CATHAY HOTEL

SUPREME COURT

IMMIGRATION OFFICE

R.S.L. HOTEL

SRI KRISHNA KALIYA TEMPLE

CHURCHILL PARK

JAME MOSQUE

MANA ST.

YAWINI ST.

VITOGO

VERONA ST.

NANUYA ST.

MALOLO ST.

THOMSON AVE.

NAMOSAU ST.

TAGIMAUCIA ST.

DRASA AVE.

TAVAKUBU RD.

BOTANICAL GARDEN

PUNJAS CHILDRENS PARK

LAUTOKA HOSPITAL

CRESENT

NAVA ST.

SHRI VISHNU MANDIR

SIKH TEMPLE

CENTRAL CAR RENTAL

VILLAGE 4 CINEMAS

VAKABALE MEDICAL CLINIC

POLICE STATION

DIAMOND HOTEL

KINGS RD.

To Ba

Namoli Creek

KADAVU ST.

DRAVUNI ST.

NACEVA ST.

CAKAU ST.

VOMO ST.

WAINUMU ST.

VIO ST.

VOMO ST.

LOMO ST.

NAMAKU RD.

VEITARI ST.

WATERFRONT RD.

To Golf Course

To Nadi

0   250 yds
0   250 m

© DAVID STANLEY

The Jame Mosque in Lautoka is symbolic of Fiji's Indo-Fijian heritage.

region of northwest India as a reformed branch of Hinduism much influenced by Islam: For example, Sikhs reject the caste system and idolatry. The Sikhs are easily recognized by their beards and turbans.

Follow your map west along Drasa Avenue to the **Sri Krishna Kaliya Temple** on Tavewa Avenue, the most prominent Krishna temple in the South Pacific (open daily until 1900). The images on the right inside are Radha and Krishna, while the central figure is Krishna dancing on the snake Kaliya to show his mastery over the reptile. The story goes that Krishna chastised Kaliya and exiled him to the island of Ramanik Deep, which Indo-Fijians believe to be Fiji. (Curiously, the indigenous Fijian people have also long believed in a serpent-god, named Degei, who lived in a cave in the Nakauvadra Range.) The two figures on the left are incarnations of Krishna and Balarama. At the front of the temple is a representation of His Divine Grace A.C. Bhaktivedanta Swami Prabhupada, founder of the International Society for Krishna Consciousness (ISKCON). Interestingly, Fiji has the highest percentage of Hare Krishnas in the population of any country in the world. The temple gift shop

(tel. 666-4112; daily 0900–1630) sells stimulating books, compact discs, cassettes, and posters, and it's possible to rent videos. On Sunday there's a lecture at 1100, *arti* or prayer *(puja)* at 1200, and a vegetarian feast at 1300, and visitors are welcome to attend.

Opposite the hospital half a km south on Thomson Crescent is the entrance to Lautoka's **botanical garden** (weekdays 0800–1800, weekends 1000–1800; admission free). It's a pleasant shady spot with a varied array of plants. Birds are surprisingly numerous in the gardens and picnic tables are provided. **Punjas Children's Park** (admission free), across the street from the gardens, is perfect if you're with the kids, and it has a snack bar.

Sports and Recreation

There aren't any dive shops in Lautoka, although **Westside Watersports** (tel. 661-1462, www.fiji-dive.com) has an office on Wharf Road that handles bookings for their Tavewa Island operation.

The **Lautoka Golf Club** (tel. 666-1384), a nine-hole, par-69 course, charges F$10 green fees plus F$20 club rentals. A taxi from the market should cost around F$3–4.

All day Saturday you can catch exciting rugby (April–Sept.) or soccer (Sept.–May) games at the stadium in Churchill Park. Ask about league games.

ACCOMMODATIONS

Under US$25

A good choice is the clean, quiet, three-story **Sea Breeze Hotel** (tel. 666-0717, fax 666-6080), at 5 Bekana Lane on the waterfront near the bus station. They have 26 rooms with private bath from F$33/37 single/double (air-conditioned rooms F$40/45, seaview F$45/49). A good breakfast is F$8 extra. The pleasant lounge has a color TV, and a swimming pool overlooks the lagoon.

Tuineau Accommodation (tel. 666-0351), above Harry's Printery on Nede St., occupies the top two floors of a three-story building (entrance from the side alley—no sign). The 11 basic rooms with shared bath are F$25 single or double, or F$9 pp in a 10-bed dorm. It's rather grim but cheap.

To be closer to the action, stay at the 38-room **Lautoka Hotel** (tel. 666-0388, fax 666-0201, ltkhotel@connect.com.fj), 2 Naviti St., which has a nice swimming pool. Room prices vary from F$30 single or double for a spacious fan-cooled room with shared bath to F$49 single or double with air-conditioning and private bath, or F$62 with TV and fridge. It's F$15 pp in the six-bed dorm. The new rooms are good, but those above the reception in the old building are subjected to a nocturnal rock beat from nearby discos most nights.

Better are the 40 rooms at the friendly **Cathay Hotel** (tel. 666-0566, fax 666-0136, www.fiji4less.com) on Tavewa Ave., which features a swimming pool, TV room, and bar. The charge is F$35/44 single/double with fan and private bath, F$46/55 with air conditioning. Some of the rooms in less desirable locations have been divided into dormitories with three to six beds or bunks. Each dorm has its own toilet and shower at F$12/18 pp fan/air-conditioned (F$1 discount for youth hostel, VIP, or Nomads cardholders). The dorms here are the best deal in the city, otherwise take one of the superior air-con-

ditioned rooms upstairs. The Cathay offers free luggage storage for guests, and the notice board at the reception often has useful information on travel to Fijian villages and the outer islands. The hotel bar upstairs is pleasant. The only reason you won't hear a lot of hype about this place at Nadi Airport is because the owners refuse to pay commissions to the Nadi travel agents.

The **R.S.L. Hotel** (tel. 665-1679), on Tavewa Ave. opposite the Sri Krishna Kaliya Temple, has six clean rooms with bath at F$50 single or double. Owned by the Fiji Ex-Servicemen League, there's a large public bar on the premises.

The 14-room **Diamond Hotel** (tel. 666-6721) on Nacula Street charges F$25/29 single/double for a room with fan. The new manager is trying to upgrade the place, but they still have water problems.

US$25–50

Lautoka's top hotel is the **Waterfront Hotel** (tel. 666-4777, fax 666-5870, www.tanoahotels.com), a two-story building erected in 1987 on Marine Drive. The 47 waterbed-equipped air-conditioned rooms are F$88 single or double, F$107 triple (children under 12 are free if no extra bed is required). There's a swimming pool. The Waterfront's Fins Restaurant serves a dinner mains from F$18–28.

The **Bekana Garden Island Resort** (Kim Waters, tel. 651-1600, fax 651-0628, bekanaisland fiji@connect.com.fj), on the long low island opposite the Lautoka waterfront, has four deluxe beachfront *bure* at F$350 single or double, plus two one-bedroom units at F$265. Low budget travelers are catered to with six thatched *bure* at F$95/108 single/double and a 12-bed dormitory at F$53 pp. Continental breakfast and lunch are included in the Fijian *bure* and dorm rates, but not with the deluxe *bure*. Camping is F$18 pp. The beach here is poor, but it's fun to borrow a kayak and paddle through the nearby mangroves. Windsurfers, fishing lines, and snorkeling gear are also loaned free, and transfers from Lautoka's Neisau Marina are provided at no cost. A dozen free moorings are available for cruising yachties.

Saweni Beach Apartment Hotel (tel. 666-1777, fax 666-6001, www.fiji4less.com), a kilometer off the main highway south of Lautoka, offers two rows of flats each with six self-catering apartments with fan and hot water at F$70/85 poolside/ocean view for up to three persons. A renovated four-bedroom "beach house" (www .fiji-beach-house.com) with full kitchen, air-conditioned bedrooms, living room, and TV is F$300 for up to four, then F$50 per additional person to a maximum of eight. Four dormitories in the annex with two beds each are F$13 pp, or you can pitch your own tent here at F$10 pp and still use the dorm's communal kitchen. Guests unwind by the pool. Birdwatchers can observe waders on the flats behind the hotel. The so-so beach comes alive on weekends when local picnickers arrive from Lautoka. During the season over a dozen yachts are generally anchored offshore and the crews often come ashore here for curry dinners. A bus runs right to the hotel from bay No. 14 at Lautoka Bus Station six times a day. Otherwise, any of the local Nadi buses will drop you off a 10-minute walk away (a taxi from Lautoka is F$7 for the 18 km).

FOOD

Chandu's Restaurant (tel. 666-5877; Mon.–Sat. 0700–2100, Sun. 0800–1830), Tukani St. on the ocean side of the bus station, serves cheap meals like fish and chips (F$2.50) or meat and rice (F$3) to the drivers of the taxis parked outside.

Jolly Good Fast Food (tel. 666-9980; daily 0800–2200), at Vakabale and Naviti Streets opposite the market, is a great place to sit and read a newspaper over a Coke. Their best dishes are listed on the "made on order" menu on the wall beside the cashier. Beef and pork are not offered, so have fish, chicken, mutton, or prawns instead—the portions are large. Eating outside in their covered garden is fun, and the only drawback is the lack of beer.

Yangs Restaurant (tel. 666-1446; Mon.–Sat. 0700–1900), 27 Naviti St., is an excellent breakfast or lunch place with inexpensive Chinese specialties.

Morris Hedstrom (tel. 666-2999; Mon.–Sat. 0730–1930, Sun. 0800–1300), Vidilio and Tukani Streets, is Lautoka's largest supermarket.

At the back of the store is a foodcourt that offers fish or chicken and chips, hot pies, ice cream, and breakfast specials. It's clean and only a bit more expensive than the market places.

More trendy is the **Chilli Tree Café** (tel. 665-1824; weekdays 0900–1800, Sat. 0800–1700, Sun. 1000–1400, www.chillitreecafe.com), corner of Nede and Tukani Streets. They serve a good, filling breakfast for F$8.50, plus cakes and specially brewed coffee. You can "build your own" salad and sandwich from the menu.

The **Pizza Inn** (tel. 666-4592) in the Lautoka Hotel, 2 Naviti Street, serves pizzas for F$6–22.

Indian

The unpretentious **Hot Snax Shop** (tel. 666-1306; Mon.–Fri. 0830–1800, Sat. 0830–1600), 56 Naviti St. opposite Yangs, may be the number one place in Fiji to sample South Indian dishes, such as *masala dosai*, a rice pancake with coconut chutney that makes a nice light lunch, or *samosas, iddili, puri,* and *palau.* The deep-fried *puri* are great for breakfast, and you can also get ice cream. This spot is recommended.

The **Ganga Vegetarian Restaurant** (tel. 666-2990; Mon.–Fri. 0700–1800, Sat. 0700–1700), on the corner of Naviti and Yasawa Streets near the market, has a vegetarian *thali* plate lunch for F$4.75.

For spicy curries (F$5–10) and authentic tandoori dishes (F$6–8) try **Dharshan's Indian Restaurant** (tel. 664-5566; Mon.–Sat. 1000–2200, Sun. 1100–1500/1800–2200), 42 Vitogo Parade beside the Jame Mosque. If you're not sure what to order, ask for a *thali* (plate meal) consisting of several vegetarian (F$5.50) or non-vegetarian (F$7.50) specialties, accompanied by rice or roti. Dharshan's is air-conditioned, the staff is in uniform, the decor is nice, and you can get meat dishes and beer.

ENTERTAINMENT

Lautoka has a flashy new mega-theater called **Village 4 Cinemas** (tel. 666-3555) at 25 Namoli Avenue. It costs about F$4 to view a film on one of their four screens. Your only other choice is

Globe Cinema (tel. 666-1444), opposite the market, which usually shows Indian films.

The **Hunter's Inn** (tel. 666-0388; Mon.–Wed. 1700–0100, Thurs.–Sat. 1600–0100), next to the Lautoka Hotel, is often the venue of special functions advertised on placards outside, though it's rather rough and dark. During the day the same place is called **City Pub** (Thurs.–Sat. 1200–1600). Also at the Lautoka Hotel is the **Ashiqi Nite Club** (Thurs.–Sat. 2000–0100), which caters to the city's Indo-Fijian residents, whereas Hunter's Inn is patronized mostly by indigenous Fijians.

Rougher than these are **The Zone Nite Club** (tel. 666-1199; Wed.–Sat. 1900–0100), upstairs in a building almost opposite the Chilli Tree Café on Naviti St., and **Bollywood Nite Club,** above Ganga Vegetarian Restaurant.

A safer place to go is **Coco's** (tel. 666-8989; Mon.–Sat. 1700–0100), 151 Vitogo Parade. Happy hour is 1700–2000 and a live rock band plays on Friday and Saturday from 2200. Admission is free until 2100 daily (F$5 cover charge Friday and Saturday after 2100).

The **South Seas Club** (tel. 666-0784), on Nede St., is a predominately male drinking place where you'll be welcome.

Sunday Puja

The big event of the week is the Sunday *puja* (prayer) at the **Sri Krishna Kaliya Temple** (tel. 666-4112), 5 Tavewa Avenue. The noon service is followed by a vegetarian feast at 1300, and visitors may join in the singing and dancing, if they wish. Take off your shoes and sit on the white marble floor, men on one side, women on the other. Bells ring, drums are beaten, conch shells blown, and stories from the Vedas, Srimad Bhagavatam, and Ramayana are acted out as everyone chants, *"Hare Krsna, Hare Krsna, Krsna Krsna, Hare Hare, Hare Rama, Hare Rama, Rama, Rama, Hare, Hare."* It's a real celebration of joy and a most moving experience. At one point children will circulate with small trays covered with burning candles, on which it is customary to place a donation; you may also drop a small bill in the yellow box in the center of the temple. You'll be readily invited to join the vegetarian feast later, and no more money will be asked of you.

INFORMATION AND SERVICES

Information

Caroline Tawake at Tawake Travel Center (tel. 651-2148, tawakestravels@yahoo.com), 159 Vitogo Parade (in back of Tawake's Craft Designs near the Colonial National Bank), takes bookings for most of the Yasawa backpacker resorts.

The people staffing the tour desks at the Lautoka and Cathay hotels can also organize any sort of Yasawa Islands trip.

Rosie World Travel (tel. 666-0311), 157 Vitogo Parade next to the Colonial Bank, is a more traditional travel agent.

The Lautoka City Bookshop (tel. 666-1715), 19 Yasawa St., sells used books.

The Western Regional Library (tel. 666-0091) on Tavewa Avenue is open Monday–Friday 1000–1700, Saturday 0900–1200.

Services

There's a Westpac Bank branch on Vitogo Parade, a little west of the post office beyond the Shell station. The ANZ Bank on Vitogo Parade diagonally opposite the post office, and on Naviti Street near the market, has Visa/MasterCard ATMs. Other ANZ Bank ATMs are found next to Rajendra Prasad Foodtown on Yasawa Street opposite the bus station and at Village 4 Cinemas.

Money Exchange (tel. 665-1941; Mon.–Fri. 0830–1700, Sat. 0830–1300), 161 Vitogo Parade just up from the ANZ Bank, changes traveler's checks without commission and buys/sells banknotes of other Pacific countries.

The public fax number at Lautoka Post Office is fax 666-4466.

Cyberzone Netcafe (tel. 665-1675; Mon.–Sat. 0800–1800, Sun. 1000–1700), next to Tavake Travel Center just down the alley beside Money Exchange near the ANZ Bank on Vitogo Parade, provides Internet access at F$.10 a minute or F$5 an hour (F$4 an hour on weekends).

Compuland Cyberlink (tel. 666-6457; weekdays 0800–1900, Sat. 0800–1700, Sun. 1000–1600), upstairs at 145 Vitogo Parade, charges identical rates and is air-conditioned!

The Immigration Department (tel. 666-

1706) is on the ground floor of Rogorogoivuda House on Tavewa Avenue almost opposite the Sri Krishna Kaliya Temple. Customs is in an adjacent building.

Free public toilets are next to Bay No. 1A, on the back side of the bus station facing the market, in Shirley Park between the Waterfront Hotel and Lautoka City Council, and at the botanical gardens.

Yachting Facilities

The Neisau Marina Complex, at the end of Bouwalu Street, fell on hard times after a hurricane twisted their wharf. At last report it was half abandoned, although some yachts still anchor there.

The Vuda Point Marina (tel. 666-8214, fax 666-8215, vudamarina@connect.com.fj) is between Lautoka and Nadi, three km down Vuda Road off Viseisei Back Road. Here yachts moor Mediterranean style in a well protected oval anchorage blasted through the reef. The excellent facilities include a yacht club, chandlery, workshop, general store (daily 0730–1900), inexpensive cafe (daily 0700–1500, until 2100 Tues., Thurs., and Sat.), fuel depot, laundry, showers, and sail repair shop.

Health

The emergency room at the Lautoka Hospital (tel. 666-0399), off Thomson Crescent south of the center, is open 24 hours a day.

Otherwise there's the Bayly Clinic (tel. 666-4598; Mon.–Fri. 0800–1300/1400–1630, Sat. 0800–1300) at 4 Nede Street. You can see a dentist (Dr. Mrs. Suruj Naidu) and an eye doctor, as well as general practitioners here.

Dr. Suresh Chandra's dental office (tel. 666-0999; Mon.–Fri. 0800–1700, Sat. 0800–1200) is opposite Village 4 Cinemas on Namoli Avenue.

The Vakabale Medical Center (Dr. Mukesh C. Bhagat, tel. 665-2955 or 995-2369; weekdays 0830–1700, Sat. 0830–1300), 47 Drasa Ave., charges F$15 for consultations. You'll receive good service at this convenient suburban office.

TRANSPORTATION

Sun Air (tel. 666-4753) is at 27 Vidilio Street.
Patterson Brothers (tel. 666-1173), upstairs at 15 Tukani Street opposite the bus station, runs a bus/ferry/bus service between Lautoka, Ellington Wharf, Nabouwalu, and Labasa (F$60), departing Lautoka a couple of times a week at around 0500. Call or visit their office for the current schedule.

Beachcomber Cruises (tel. 666-1500), Walu St. at Vitogo Parade toward the main wharf, books cruises to **Beachcomber Island** (F$69 pp including lunch, reductions for children), departing Lautoka daily except Tuesday and Thursday at 1030—a great way to spend a day.

The **Awesome Adventures** (tel. 675-0499) ferry *Yasawa Flyer* leaves Lautoka for the Yasawa Islands daily at 0800, although most passengers board at Nadi.

Buses, carriers, taxis—everything leaves from the bus stand beside the market. **Pacific Transport** (tel. 666-0499) has express buses to Suva daily at 0630, 0700, 1210, 1550, and 1730 (221 km, five hours, F$11.60) via Sigatoka (Queens Road). Five other "stage" buses also operate daily along this route (six hours). The daily **Sunset Express** leaves for Suva via Sigatoka at 0900, 1330, and 1515 (four hours, F$10). **Sunbeam Transport** (tel. 666-2822) has expresses to Suva via Tavua (Kings Road) at 0615, 0630, 0815, 1215, and 1630 (265 km, six hours, F$13.90), plus two local buses on the same route (nine hours). Sunbeam also has buses to Suva via Sigatoka at 1010, 1110, and 1240. The northern route is more scenic than the southern, although some Sunbeam buses play insipid videos that detract from the ride. Local buses to Nadi (33 km, F$1.90) and Ba (38 km, F$2) depart every half hour or so.

Collective taxis to Suva (F$15 per seat) park on Tukani St. behind the bus station. Pick one that's almost full if you're in a hurry.

Car rentals are available in Lautoka from **Central** (tel. 666-4511) at 75 Vitogo Parade.

KOROYANITU NATIONAL HERITAGE PARK

With help from New Zealand, an ecotourism reserve has been created between Abaca (am-BA-tha) and Navilawa villages in the Mount Evans Range, 15 km east of Lautoka. Koroyanitu

National Heritage Park takes its name from the range's highest peak, 1,195-meter Koroyanitu, and is intended to preserve Fiji's only unlogged tropical montane forest and cloud forest by creating a small tourism business for the local villagers. The village carrier used to transport visitors also carries the local kids to and from school, the women earn money by staffing the office or arranging room and board, and the men get jobs as drivers, guides, and wardens. By visiting Koroyanitu, you not only get to see some of Fiji's top sights but support this worthy undertaking.

Four waterfalls are close to the village, and Batilamu, with sweeping views of the western side of Viti Levu and the Yasawas, is nearby. More ambitious hikes to higher peaks beckon. The landscape of wide green valleys set against steep slopes is superb. Doves and pigeons abound in the forests, and you'll also find honeyeaters, Polynesian starlings, Fijian warblers, yellow breasted musk parrots, golden whistlers, fantailed cuckoos, and woodswallows. It's an outstanding opportunity to see this spectacular area. The park entry fee is F$5 pp.

Sights

You can swim in the pools at **Vereni Falls,** a five minute walk from the park lodge. Picnic shelters are provided. From the viewpoint above the falls, it's 15 minutes up the Navuratu Track to **Kokobula Scenic Outlook** with its 360 degree view of the park and coast. The trail continues across the open grassland to **Savuione Falls,** passing an old village site en route (guide required). From Savuione there's a trail through the secondary forest directly back to the park lodge (watch for pigeons and doves). You can do all this in just over two hours if you keep going and don't lose your way.

The finest hike here is to **Mount Batilamu** along a trail which begins at the visitor center in Abaca village. You'll pass large kauri trees *(makadre)* and get a terrific view from on top. This part of the range is also known as the "Sleeping Giant" because that's how it appears from Nadi. Allow half a day return from Abaca to Batilamu.

The Batilamu Track continues across the range to **Navilawa** village, from which a six-km road runs south to Korobebe village where there's regular bus service to/from Nadi. Trekkers often spend the night in Fiji's highest *bure* on Batilamu, although less than a hundred people a year actually do this walk. An even more ambitious trek is northeast to **Nalotawa** via the site of Navuga, where the Abaca people lived until their village was destroyed by a landslide in the 1930s. To explore the various archaeological sites of this area and to learn more about the environment and culture, you should hire a guide (F$5–20 depending on how far you want to go).

Accommodations

The **Nase Forest Lodge,** 400 meters from Abaca village, has two six-bunk rooms at F$25 pp (or F$80 for the whole room). Camping is F$10 pp. Children under 15 are half price and all prices include the park entry fee. Good cooking facilities are provided, but bring food, as there's no shop. Meals can be ordered at F$5/7/10 for breakfast/lunch/dinner. Otherwise you can stay with a family in Abaca or Navilawa villages at F$30 pp including meals.

For information call Abaca village at tel. 666-6644 (wait for two beeps, then dial 1234). The receptionist at the Cathay Hotel in Lautoka should also be able to help you. (On Sunday, avoid entering the village during the church service 1000–1200. Village etiquette should be observed at all times.)

Getting There

The closest public bus stop to the park is Abaca Junction on the Tavakuba bus route, but it's 10 km from Abaca village. An official village carrier to the park leaves the Cathay Hotel in Lautoka around 0900, charging F$10 pp (F$20 if only one person). It returns to Lautoka in the afternoon.

At Nadi Airport contact **Tourist Transport Fiji** (tel. 672-0455, fax 672-0184, www.batila mutrek.com), next to the washrooms in the international arrivals area, which books a three-day Mount Batilamu Trek package at F$300 pp. Their day trek to Abaca is F$75 pp from Nadi. During the rainy season, floods can close the road to Abaca and the trekking possibilities may also be limited.

The Yasawa Islands

The Yasawas are a chain of 16 large volcanic islands and dozens of smaller ones, stretching 80 km in a north-northeast direction, roughly 35 km off the west coast of Viti Levu. In the lee of Viti Levu, the Yasawas are dry and sunny, with beautiful, isolated beaches, cliffs, bays, and reefs. The waters are crystal clear and almost totally shark-free. The group was romanticized in two movies about a pair of child castaways who eventually fall in love on a deserted isle. The original 1949 version of *The Blue Lagoon* starred Jean Simmons, while the 1980 remake featured Brooke Shields. (A 1991 sequel *Return to the Blue Lagoon* with Milla Jovovich was filmed on Taveuni.)

It was from the north end of the Yasawas that two canoe-loads of cannibals sallied forth and gave chase to Capt. William Bligh and his 18 companions in 1789, less than a week after the famous mutiny. Two centuries later, increasing numbers of ferries and mini-cruise ships ply the islands, but there are still no motorized land vehicles or roads. The thousand-dollar-a-day crowd is whisked straight to Turtle Island by seaplane, while most backpackers arrive from Nadi on a highspeed catamaran.

Super exclusive Turtle Island Resort and the backpacker camps on Tavewa Island have coexisted for decades, but only since 2000 have the Yasawans themselves recognized the money-making potential of tourism. Now a bumper crop of budget "resorts" is bursting forth, up and down the chain, as the villagers rush to cash in. The **Nacula Tikina Tourism Association** (tel. 672-2921, www.fijibudget.com) coordinates the development of locally-owned backpacker resorts on the central islands around the Blue Lagoon. Thankfully the resorts associated with the scheme have committed to a code of conduct to preserve and protect the natural environment. Some of the backpacker resorts are better than others, but shared bathrooms, a lack of electricity, water shortages, and variable food are to be expected. What you pay for is the superb natural beauty of this region.

Resort Booking Tips

At Nadi Airport, the **Turtle Island Resort office** (tel. 672-2921, nacula@hotmail.com), on the left in the arrivals concourse, should be able to provide information about the Yasawa Islands resorts. Other booking agents at Nadi Airport include **Island Travel Tours** (Louise Blake, tel. 672-4033 or 672-5930, www.travellingfiji.com), in office No. 14 upstairs from arrivals, **Western Travel Services** (tel. 672-4440), in office No. 4, **Sunset Tours** (Poni Natadra, tel. 672-0266), and **Rabua's Travel Agency** (Ulaiasi "Rambo" Rabua, tel. 672-1377 or 672-3234) in office No. 23. Caroline Tawake at **Tawake Travel & Tourist Information Center** (tel. 651-2148, tawakestravels@yahoo.com), 159 Vitogo Parade, Lautoka, can book any of the Yasawa places. Resort-specific booking offices are mentioned in the listings that follow.

Only book your first two nights if you wish to allow yourself the flexibility of moving elsewhere after arrival or bargaining for a lower rate. The Nadi travel agents take 30 percent commission, so you can often get a better deal by booking direct over the phone. Most of the Yasawa backpacker resorts have radio telephones accessed via tel. 666-6644. Dial this number, then key in the extension after hearing two beeps. Only one party can speak at a time over these connections.

The rates quoted in this section usually include all meals and taxes (only Oarsman's and Safe Landing resorts on Nacula Island sometimes quote rates with meals and tax additional). Virtually all of the resorts have mixed dormitories where you pay per person and *bure* intended for two persons. Singles who don't wish to sleep in the dormitory are at a disadvantage, since many resorts charge the same single or double for their *bure*, even though they only have to feed one person instead of two. The Yasawas backpacker resorts are ideal for campers, because virtually all have unlimited tent space and reservations are unnecessary. Campers with their own tents pay slightly less than people in the dorm.

One shouldn't expect gourmet cuisine at any of the backpacker resorts, and at times the meals

THE YASAWA ISLANDS

Yawini Island

Yasawairara

YASAWA ISLAND LODGE

Yasawa Island

Bukama

SOUTH

Vawa
Island

Teci

PACIFIC

Tamasua

Nabukeru

Nanuya Island

Navotua

OCEAN

Nacula Island

Sawa-i-Lau
Island

Nacula

Malakati

Tavewa
Island

Naisilisili

Matacawalevu Island

Nanuya Lailai Island

Matacawalevu

Vuake

TURTLE ISLAND LODGE

Matayalevu

Nanuya Levu
Island

Yaqeta
Island

Naivalavala Passage

Yasawa Islands

Gunu

QEREQERE CROSS RESORT

Sosomo

KOROVOU/COCONUT BAY

Naviti Island

Soso

Kese

BOTAIRA RESORT

Muaira

*Soso
Bay*

Drawaqa Island

Nanuya Balavu
Island

Bligh

Narara Island

Water

Nalauwaki

Wayalevu

Yalobi

Waya Island

Natawa

*Yulobi
Bay*

Wayasewa Island

Namara

Kuata Island

White Rock

Eori Island

Navadra Island

Vomolailai
Island

Vanua Levu Island

Kadomo Island

Vomo Island

Mamanuca Group

Ba

Monu
Island

Tokoriki Island

Yanuya Island

Monuriki
Island

Tavua Island

Viti Levu
Island

Matamanoa
Island

Beachcomber
Island

Saweni
Beach

Lautoka

Treasure
Island

Bekena Island

0   5 mi

0   5 km

can be pretty basic. A vegetarian meal is often the same thing with the meat removed. At times it seems like the numerous vegetarian requests have resulted in plates of cabbage and rice being served to one and all! You should ask other travelers for their opinion of the food at the places where they stayed, just keep in mind that the person's standards and expectations may be different from yours—impressions vary considerably. All too often, what you pay for isn't what you get.

Money

Don't expect to be able to use your credit card in the Yasawas (although Oarsman's and Safe Landing resorts on Nacula accept *only* credit cards). Changing foreign currency is also usually not possible. Thus it's important to bring along sufficient Fijian currency in cash. Even if you've prepaid all your food, accommodations, and interisland transportation, you'll still need a minimum of F$20 pp extra per day to cover alcohol drinks, bottled water, excursions, equipment rentals, etc. The more optional activities you plan to book, the more cash you'll need. Failure to budget for your expenses accurately may force you to return to Nadi early or miss out on some activities.

Prices continue to creep up in the Yasawas, and on a visit of a week or less you'll spend at least F$100 pp a day on transportation, food, and dormitory accommodations alone. On stays of over a week, the transportation component falls exponentially and long-stay discounts kick in.

Getting There

Turtle Airways (tel. 672-1888, www.turtleair ways.com) offers reduced F$119 one-way fares to backpackers headed for the low-budget resorts in the Yasawas. These discounted flights are based on availability, but if they have four backpacker bookings, they'll schedule a special service. Ask at the Turtle Island Resort office at Nadi Airport. It only takes 30 minutes by air from Turtle's Nadi base at Wailoaloa Beach all the way to the seaplane landing area off Nacula Island. The emerald lagoons and colorful reefs are truly dazzling when seen from above.

The vast majority of visitors arrive on the fast 25-meter catamaran *Yasawa Flyer* operated by **Awesome Adventures** (tel. 675-0499, fax 675-0501, www.awesomefiji.com), a subsidiary of South Sea Cruises. The *Flyer* zips up and down the Yasawa Chain daily, leaving Nadi's Port Denarau at 0915 and arriving at Beachcomber Island at 1000, Kuata at 1045, Waya at 1115, Naviti at 1215, and Nacula at 1315. The return trip leaves Nacula at 1330 with stops at Naviti at 1420, Waya at 1550, Kuata at 1600, Beachcomber Island at 1645, and reaching Port Denarau at 1730. Fares from Nadi are F$70 one-way to Kuata or Waya, F$80 to Naviti, and F$90 to Nacula or Tavewa, bus transfers in Nadi included. Interisland fares within the Yasawas vary between F$25 from Kuata to Octopus Resort, F$40 from Waya to Naviti, or F$50 from Kuata to Nacula. The *Flyer* is actually based in Lautoka and you can begin or end your journey there for the same price, if you want.

Awesome Adventures offers a "Bula Pass," which includes one roundtrip transfer between Nadi and Nacula on the *Yasawa Flyer* with unlimited stops at Kuata, Wayalailai, Waya, Naviti, or anywhere else along their route (the only limitations are that only one trip back to Nadi is included and the pass cannot be used between Beachcomber Island and Nadi at all). The Bula Pass costs F$235/350/399 for seven/14/21 days, and it's worth considering if you plan to make a stop or two on the way to Nacula. The 21-day pass includes a one-night Wanna Taki Cruise. Though there are 150 seats on the ferry, reservations are sometimes necessary. Each individual sector can be booked at the time you buy your pass, thus it's a good idea to work out an itinerary in advance. Reservations can also be made by phone 24 hours in advance. Awesome Adventures sells optional accommodations packages along with the pass, but these carry heavy cancellation penalties if not used exactly as specified and you'll have no control over where you stay. Skip the "Full Monty" package, which includes all sorts of add-ons you can purchase for the same price once you're there.

The "yellow boat" is the safest and most comfortable way to go. Awesome Adventures doesn't have an office of their own at Nadi Airport, but

FIJI ISLANDS

any travel agency in Fiji can book their services. There are no refunds on unused tickets. Outboards from the backpacker resorts pick up passengers from the *Yasawa Flyer's* rear deck and transfer them to the beach. Some resorts do this for free, while others will charge you F$5–10 pp each way to go ashore (none of the islands has a wharf). Know where your backpack is at *Yasawa Flyer* stops, because cases of people grabbing the wrong pack in the rush to disembark do occur.

Yasawa Island Eco Tours (tel. 672-1658, fax 672-5208, yiet@connect.com.fj), next to Rik's Café in Martintar (Nadi), operates the 20-meter catamaran *Tamusua Explorer* to the Yasawas every Tuesday, Thursday, and Saturday, departing Lautoka at 0800. It's basically intended as a day cruise to the Sawa-i-Lau Cave, costing F$189 roundtrip including lunch. However, they also drop passengers on Nacula or Tavewa at F$89 pp one-way including Nadi hotel pickups (or F$70 if you book direct and find your own way to the wharf).

Some of the Yasawa backpacker camps have boats of their own (costing around F$70/120 one way/round-trip from Lautoka), and when booking with them, it's best to avoid prepaying your return boat fare. Safety can be an issue on some of the smaller resort and village boats, which often carry more passengers than life jackets (if any). One traveler reported that the local boat he was on ran out of gas a kilometer short of Lautoka and ended up drifting in high seas until it bumped into a container ship that was able to radio for help. Cases of local boats being lost at sea are not unknown. There are few government controls over the village boats, and they aren't that much cheaper than the perfectly safe *Yasawa Flyer*.

However you go, it's risky to schedule a return to Nadi on the same day you must catch an international flight, as adverse weather conditions can lead to the cancellation of all boat trips. This does happen at times, and even allowing two days leeway won't be sufficient if a hurricane warning has been issued.

KUATA ISLAND

Kuata is the *Yasawa Flyer's* first stop in the Yasawa Islands. Like neighboring Wayasewa and Waya,

it's a scenically spectacular island though without any Fijian villages. You can climb to the island's summit (171 meters) for the view. With a buddy you could also snorkel across the open channel to Wayasewa in half an hour, although this activity involves obvious risks and we cannot recommend it.

The **Kuata Island Resort** (tel. 666-6644, ext. 3233), on a nice beach on the side of the island facing Wayasewa, accommodates up to 52 guests at F$40 pp in a 15-bed dorm or F$110 double in a thatched *bure* with private bath. Three average meals are included. There's no electricity, and the food and accommodations aren't overwhelming, but the location is great. An optimum snorkeling area is just across the point on the southwest side of Kuata. Look for the cave near the seagull rocks at the point itself.

WAYASEWA ISLAND

Wayalailai Resort (tel. 666-9715 or 666-1572, www.bbr.ca/wayalailai), formerly known as Dive Trek Wayasewa, is spectacularly situated on the south side of Wayasewa opposite Kuata Island. It's directly below Wayasewa's highest peak Vatuvula (349 meters), with Viti Levu clearly visible behind Vomo Island to the east. Photos don't do this place justice.

The resort is built on two terraces, one 10 meters above the beach and the other 10 meters above that. The lower terrace has the double, duplex, and dormitory *bure,* while the upper accommodates the restaurant/bar and the former village schoolhouse of Namara village, now partitioned into 14 tiny double rooms. Simple rooms with shared bath and open ceiling in the school building are F$50 pp (a good option for singles), while the five individual *bure* with private bath and a small porch are F$120 double. One duplex *bure* with four beds on each side serves as an eight-bed dormitory or *burebau* at F$45 pp. The camping space nearby is F$35 pp. The minimum stay is three nights. Upon arrival, ask the staff to change the sheets if they haven't already done so.

Three meals are included in all rates. Wednesday and Sunday evenings a *lovo* is prepared. An electric generator is used in the evening and there's no shortage of water. Informal musical entertainment occurs nightly, and because this resort is collectively owned by the village, the staff is like one big happy family.

There's lots to see and do at Wayalailai, with hiking and scuba diving the main activities. Aside from scuba and snorkeling trips, the resort's dive shop offers a PADI open-water certification course. For groups of six or more, there are snorkeling trips to a reef halfway to Vomo.

The most popular hike is to the top of Vatuvula, the fantastic volcanic plug hanging directly over the resort. The well trodden path circles the mountain and comes up the back, taking about 1.5 hours total excluding stops (a guide really isn't necessary). From the top of Vatuvula you get a sweeping view of the west side of Viti Levu, the Mamanucas, and the southern half of the Yasawa chain—one of the scenic highlights of the South Pacific. From Vatuvula you can trek northwest across the grassy uplands to another rock with a good view of Yalobi Bay (also known as Alacrity Bay).

Transfers from Lautoka on Wayalailai's own boat depart Monday–Saturday at 1300 (1.5 hours, F$55 pp each way). The boat leaves Wayalailai to return to Lautoka Monday–Saturday at 0900. In both directions the boat fare includes bus transfers to/from Nadi/Lautoka hotels. You can also get there on the Awesome Adventures shuttle from Nadi at F$70 one-way. Passengers on the *Yasawa Flyer* are picked up by a boat from Wayalailai at Kuata. Rabua's Travel Agency (tel. 672-1377 or 672-3234, wayalailai@connect .com.fj), in office No. 23 upstairs at Nadi Airport, takes Wayalailai bookings.

WAYA ISLAND

The high island clearly visible to the northwest of Lautoka is Waya, closest of the larger Yasawas to Viti Levu and just 60 km away. At 579 meters, it's also the highest island in the chain. Waya is an excellent choice for the hyperactive traveler, as the hiking possibilities are unlimited. The beaches are very nice and it's a great place to experience unspoiled Fijian culture. So if you can live with a few rough edges, Waya is *the* place to go.

Four Fijian villages are sprinkled around Waya: Nalauwaki, Natawa, Wayalevu, and Yalobi. The rocky mass of Batinareba (510 meters) towers over the west side of Yalobi Bay and in a morning or afternoon you can scramble up the mountain's rocky slope from the west end of the beach at Yalobi. Go through the forested saddle on the south side of the highest peak, and follow the grassy ridge on the far side all the way down to Loto Point. Many wild goats are seen along the way. An easier hike from Yalobi leads southeast from the school to the sandbar over to Wayasewa.

One of the most memorable walks in the South Pacific involves spending two hours on a well-used trail from Yalobi to Nalauwaki village. Octopus Resort is just a 10-minute walk west over a low ridge, and from there it's possible to hike back to Yalobi down Waya's west coast and across Loto Point in another two or three hours. Due to rocky headlands lapped by the sea you can only go down the west coast at low tide, thus one must set out from Yalobi at high tide and from Octopus at low tide. It's a great way to fill a day.

Accommodations

The **Sunset Resort** (tel. 666-6644, ext. 6383) is right next to the sandbar linking Waya to Wayasewa. The three *bure* are F$90/140 single/double, the 20-bed dorm F$45 pp, and camping space F$30 pp, meals included. Scuba diving is available at F$70/130 for one/two tanks, plus F$25 for gear, and there's good snorkeling right offshore anytime. At low tide it's possible to cross to Wayasewa without removing your shoes, and two villages, Naboro and Yamata, are nearby. It's even possible to hike over the mountains to the Wayalailai Resort in about three hours. However, the vast majority of guests headed for the three backpacker places in this area, Sunset, Bayside, and Adi's, arrive on the *Yasawa Flyer,* which stops nearby.

A 30-minute walk northwest toward Yalobi village is the **Bayside Resort** (tel. 666-6644, ext. 6383), run by a guy named Manasa, the brother of Adi Sayaba of Adi's Place. Count on paying around F$100 double to stay in a simple *bure* here, or F$40 pp in a 14-bed dorm (all prices include meals).

Adi's Place (tel. 665-0573), at Yalobi village on the south side of Waya, is a small family-operated resort in existence since 1981. Although primitive, it still makes a good hiking base, with prices designed to attract and hold those on the barest of budgets. The accommodations consist of one eight-bunk dorm at F$35 pp, a solid European-style house with three double rooms with shared bath at F$40 pp, and camping space at F$25 pp. Lighting is by kerosene lamp. The rates include three meals of variable quality. The beach looks good from shore, but it's hard to swim here due to the corals (don't leave valuables unattended on this beach). It's all a little messy and shouldn't be your first choice.

On a high white-sand beach in Likuliku Bay on northwestern Waya is **Octopus Resort** (Nick Woods, tel. 666-6442 or 666-6337, fax 666-6210, www.octopusresort.com), one of the nicest budget resorts in the South Pacific. The 17 comfortable *bure* with private bath are F$135/155/185 garden/oceanview/beachfront single or double. Otherwise it's F$60 pp in a clean 13-bed dorm, or F$100 double to sleep in one of Octopus's four safari tents. If you bring your own tent it's also F$50 pp. A good lunch and dinner are included in all rates (the menu rotates every 21 days, so there's some variety). The minimum stay is two nights. Drinks are served at their large restaurant/bar and a generator provides electricity. Octopus has it's own dive shop, which also gives PADI certification courses. The snorkeling here is best at high tide (beware of receiving coral cuts at low tide). The Awesome Adventures ferry *Yasawa Flyer* from Nadi calls here, and Octopus has its own launch from Lautoka's Fisheries Wharf daily at 1000. Both charge F$70 each way and the *Yasawa Flyer* is a smoother ride. Some readers have reported confusion over their reservations and bills at Octopus.

NAVITI ISLAND

Naviti, at 33 square km, is the largest of the Yasawas. All of Naviti's villages are on the east coast, including Soso, residence of one of the group's highest chiefs. Soso's church houses fine woodcarvings, and on the hillside above the village are two caves containing the bones of ancestors. Yawesa, the secondary boarding school on Naviti, is a village in itself. The Awesome Adventures shuttle from Nadi (F$80 one way) cruises right up the west side of Naviti, where most of the resorts are found

Natuvalo Bay

Three backpacker resorts, Coconut Bay, Korovou, and White Sandy Beach, share a beach on Natuvalo Bay directly across Naviti from Kese village. From the beach, a huge mango tree is visible atop the ridge to the southeast. A shady, well trodden path leaves the beach 20 meters before the first rocky headland south of Coconut Bay Resort and climbs to the tree, a 40-minute walk. Go south along the ridge a few hundred meters to a grassy hill with great views as far as Wayasewa. The trail continues to Kese village. Do this hike right after breakfast while it's still relatively cool.

A much easier walk is to Honeymoon Point, the peninsula overlooking the north end of Natuvalo Bay. The trail begins next to White Sandy Beach Resort Dive Center and takes only 15 minutes. You'll have a view of the entire west side of Naviti, plus the long low island of Viwa at 1100 o'clock on the horizon far to the west.

The **White Sandy Beach Dive Center** on Natuvalo Bay does one-tank dives at F$70–80 depending on the site, two-tank dives F$130–160. An introductory dive is F$75. Snorkeling trips to a plane wreck in three meters of water are F$20, while snorkeling with manta rays is F$16. A boat trip around the island including both of these sites is F$30 (minimum of eight persons). Snorkeling gear is for rent at F$6/10 a half/full day. Only Fijian currency in cash is accepted.

Accommodations

The **Botaira Resort** (tel. 666-2266), on the southwest side of Naviti, has seven upscale *bure* with bath tubs at F$350/425 double/triple. The two 10-bed dorms are F$90 pp. All prices include meals, tax, and some sporting activities. The travel agents at Nadi Airport should be able to discount these rack rates by a third.

On Natuvalo Bay a few km north of the Botaira Beach Resort is the **Coconut Bay Resort** (Milika and Veretariki Buli, tel. 666-6644, ext. 1300, coconutbay@yahoo.com). The 10 duplex units with private bath are F$150 for up to three persons or F$200 for four (you can reduce this to F$110 double if you book direct by phone). The two large 20-bed dorms are F$46 pp, camping F$35 pp. The meals are served in an enclosed building with no view, but the food is good with a buffet dinner nightly. Water shortages happen here. A snorkeling trip is F$10 pp.

The **Korovou Eco-Tour Resort** (Eta and Siairo Seutinaviti, tel. 666-6644, ext. 2244, korovoultk@connect.com.fj), a few minutes on foot from the Coconut Bay Resort, has four older duplex *bure* and two thatched *bure* at F$120 double, plus four newer *bure* with private bath at F$150/183 double/triple. The 24-bed dorm is F$46 pp, camping F$35 pp. All prices include meals. Korovou's *bure* are more private than those at Coconut Bay and a generator provides electricity in the evening. In 2003, a spacious new restaurant with a large deck right over the beach was constructed at Korovou. Activities include snorkeling with manta rays and an evening fire dancing show.

The **White Sandy Beach Dive Resort,** run by Peter and Sulu Seutinaviti on the beach next to Korovou, has two neat little bungalows with tin roofs at F$110 double including meals. The dorm is F$45 pp. All three resorts just mentioned include afternoon tea in their prices and provide free transfers from the ferry to shore. Drinking water is scarce and you'll be expected to buy bottled water. The swimming on Natuvalo Bay is only good at high tide.

TAVEWA ISLAND

Tavewa is much smaller and lower than Waya and twice as far from Nadi, yet it's also strikingly beautiful with excellent bathing in the warm waters off a picture-postcard beach on the southeast side, and a good fringing reef with super snorkeling. Tall grass covers the hilly interior of this two-km-long island. Tavewa is in the middle of the Yasawas and from the summit you can behold the long chain of islands stretching out on each side with Viti Levu in the background. The sunsets can be splendid from the hill.

There's no chief here, as this is freehold land. In the late 19th century an Irishman named William Doughty married a woman from Nacula who was given Tavewa as her dowry. A decade or two later a Scot named William Bruce married into the Doughty family, and some time thereafter beachcombers called Murray and Campbell arrived on the scene and did the same, with the result that today some 50 Doughtys, Bruces, Murrays, and Campbells comprise the population of Tavewa. William Doughty himself died in 1926 at the ripe age of 77.

The islanders are friendly and welcoming; in fact, accommodating visitors is their main source of income. Coral View, David's, and Otto's have been operating since the 1980s, long before the current crop of backpacker resorts appeared on Naviti, Nacula, and Nanuya Lailai, and their experience shows (better food, accommodations, and tours). Most of their guests are backpackers who usually stay six nights, and most are sorry to leave. It's idyllic, but bring along mosquito coils, toilet paper, a flashlight (torch), bottled water, and a *sulu* to cover up. Be prepared for water shortages.

Sports and Recreation

Westside Watersports (tel./fax 661-1462, www.fiji-dive.com) has a dive center on the beach between David's and Otto's where the price gets cheaper the more diving you do (F$95/155 for one/two dives, subsequent dives F$55 each). Open-water scuba certification is F$565. Credit cards are accepted for diving. Their two dive boats *Absolute II* and *Aftershock* go out at 0900 and 1330, and which side of the island you'll dive on depends upon the wind. Aside from the spectacular underwater topography, encounters with sea turtles, reef sharks, and eagle rays are fairly common. Westside's equipment is good and you can also rent snorkeling gear (F$5).

Accommodations

Coral View Resort (Don Bruce, tel. 666-2648 or 651-0730, coral@connect.com.fj), nestling in a cozy valley on a secluded beach with high hills on each side, is one of the nicest low-budget places to stay in Fiji. It has 14 thatched *bure* with shared bath at F$85/95 single/double, two hotel-style rooms with private bath at F$150 double, and one four-bunk and two eight-bunk dorms at F$40 pp. Camping with your own tent is F$30 pp. Mosquito nets are supplied. Included are three decent meals and one free organized activity a day. Coral View's beach isn't that great, but boat trips to Honeymoon Island and Blue Lagoon Beach are only F$5 (minimum of five). The boat trip to the Sawa-i-Lau caves requires a minimum of five people willing to pay F$35 pp to operate. Snorkeling gear is F$5 extra. Trolling is F$30 pp (minimum of two). Although there are lots of organized activities, Coral View is also a place where people come to relax and socialize, and most guests tend to be under 35. You'll be touched when the genuinely friendly staff gathers to sing *Isa Lei,* the Fijian song of farewell, when the time comes for you to go. Transfers to/from the *Yasawa Flyer* are free.

Kingfisher Lodge (Joe Doughty, tel. 665-2830 or 666-6644, ext. 2288), next to David's Place, offers one self-contained beach bungalow at F$130/160 single/double including meals. Plastic canoes are for rent at F$5 an hour. Westside Watersports (tel. 666-1462) handles bookings here.

David's Place (David Doughty and Fi Liu-taki, tel. 665-2820, davidsplaceresort@yahoo.com) stands in a breezy coconut grove near a small church on the island's longest beach. There are 14 thatched *bure* with shared bath at F$80/110 single/double, one larger bungalow with private bath at F$100/150, a five-bed dorm at F$50 pp, and an eight-bed dorm at F$45 pp. Camping is F$35 pp with your own tent. The minimum stay is two nights. David's *bure* are larger and more comfortable than those at Coral View, though the communal toilets and showers are inadequate when the place is full. Three meals are included in the price with the Thursday *lovo* and Saturday barbecue part of the regular meal plan (opinions about the food vary). David's takes credit cards. At David's you don't get the free trips provided at Coral View (beach visits are F$10 each), and the optional tours cost F$35 for the

cave trip or to visit Naisisili village (minimum of seven). David's caters to all ages. Bookings can be made through David's Travel Service (tel. 672-1820), office No. 31 upstairs in the arrivals concourse at Nadi Airport.

Otto's Place (Otto and Fanny Doughty, tel. 666-6481), on spacious grounds near the south end of the island, caters to a more mature clientele less interested in activities and partying. They have two large bungalows with toilet, shower, and sink at F$90 single or double, F$105 triple. Two thatched *bure* with private bath cost the same. The single 10-bed dormitory is F$40 pp. Because the units aren't right on the beach, they tend to be a bit hotter than David's or Coral View. Camping is not allowed. Add F$40 pp to all rates for three good meals. The generator is on until 2300, but the light is dim. The *bure* are nicely scattered through the plantation, but they don't overlook the beach. Credit cards are accepted. Yachties anchored at the nearby Blue Lagoon are welcome to order dinner here (F$20 pp), so long as 24 hours notice is given. From 1500–1630 afternoon tea is served to both guests and nonguests at Aunty Fanny's Tea House, costing F$3 for tea with some of the richest banana or chocolate cake in Fiji. It's an island institution. Ice cream is also available. You can book Otto's Place through Westside Watersports (tel. 661-1462) in Lautoka, which can also arrange transfers on their own boat at F$80 pp each way.

Getting There

Most visitors arrive from Nadi on the Awesome Adventures catamaran *Yasawa Flyer* at F$90 one way. An island hop from Tavewa to Naviti or Waya on the catamaran is F$50. Outboard transfers from Tavewa to Nacula or Nanuya Lailai are F$10 pp each way. Turtle Airways (tel. 672-1888) offers special "backpacker rates" on seaplane transfers from Nadi to Tavewa.

NACULA ISLAND

Ten-km-long Nacula, between Tavewa and Yasawa islands, is the third largest in the chain. From its contorted coastline rise hills like Naisau (238 meters) and Korobeka (258 meters). Of the four villages, Naisisili and Nacula are the most important, and the Tui Drola, or chief of the middle Yasawas, resides on the island. Some of Fiji's best snorkeling is available just off the high white sands of Long Beach in the southwest corner of Nacula opposite Tavewa. Since 2000, several small resorts have been built on Nacula. Meals are included in most of the rates quoted below, but be aware that water taxi transfers to/from the *Yasawa Flyer* cost F$5–10 pp.

On a good beach on the southeast side of Nacula is **Nabua Lodge** (Sailasa Ratu, tel. 666-9173 or 666-6644, ext. 6369) with six thatched *bure,* four with shared bath at F$89 double and two with private bath at F$120. The five-bed dorm is F$45 pp, camping F$35 pp. Great sunsets can be seen from the hill just above the lodge, and you can hike along the ridge right to the center of the island (take water).

Melbravo Lodge (Laite Nasau, tel. 665-0616 or 666-6644, ext. 7472), right next to Nabua Lodge, has six thatched GI>bure, two with private bath at F$120 double and four with shared bath at F$88 including meals. The eight-bed dorm is F$44 pp. If you call direct rather than booking through a Nadi travel agent these prices are reduced to F$100/70/30. There's electricity in the dining area but none in the rooms. The food can be monotonous and the portions small, but drinking water is supplied free. Activities here include a Sawa-i-Lau cave tour (F$30, minimum of six persons), Blue Lagoon snorkeling (F$10), village entertainment (F$10), and snorkeling gear rental (F$3). Both Melbravo and Nabua Lodge charge F$5 pp for the transfer from the *Yasawa Flyer.*

Safe Landing Resort (Tevita and Kara Volavola, tel. 672-2921) is on a white sand beach tucked between two dark headlands, on the next bay over from Melbravo. The five well constructed Fijian *bure* with shared bath are F$117 double, while the six duplex units with bath are F$179. The six-bunk dorm is F$64 pp, camping F$59 pp. The meals are good and include a lot of fish. It's a nice spot with good swimming at high tide, though the beach at Oarsman's Bay Lodge is much better. Profits from Safe Landing go to community projects in nearby Naisisili village.

Oarsman's Bay Lodge (Ratu Epeli Vuetibau, tel. 672-2921) is on fabulous Long Beach at the southwest end of Nacula. There's a 13-bed dormitory above the restaurant/bar at F$73 pp, six high-quality, self-contained bungalows with solar panels at F$190 double, and two large family bungalows sleeping six at F$428. The units have fans but they can still be a little stuffy due to the lack of breeze (which also means more bugs). Camping with your own tent costs F$61 pp. Paddle boats, kayaks, and snorkeling gear are loaned free. These rates include tax and three good meals, but Oarsman's often quotes prices for accommodations only, so assume that's what's happening if you're told a lower price. Most of the staff hail from Nacula village on the north side of the island and resort profits go to village projects. If you're staying at Safe Landing or one of its neighbors and wish to visit Oarsman's for the day, it takes a bit over an hour to walk utilizing a shortcut trail across the island to/from Suntan Beach. It's only easy to walk there along the beach at low tide—at high tide you'll need to wade part of the way.

Oarsman's and Safe Landing have many things in common. Both were built in 2000 with interest free loans provided by the owner of Turtle Island Resort. To ensure that the loans are repaid, both resorts are now managed by Turtle Island, and bookings are controlled by the Turtle Island office (tel. 672-2921 or 672-2780, nacula @hotmail.com) at Nadi Airport. To further control finances, all accounts must be paid by credit card (cash not accepted anywhere, not even at the bar). The transfer fees from the *Yasawa Flyer* are F$10 pp each way at both, and both resorts operate on "Bula Time" (one hour ahead of Fiji time) to give guests an extra hour of daylight. Oarsman's and Safe Landing are run as businesses rather than family operations, and a high percentage of the guests tend to be middle aged tourists (rather than young backpackers) who "discovered" these places on the Internet. Compared to the rest of the Yasawa backpacker resorts, Oarsman's and Safe Landing are rather expensive, yet compared to Mamanuca resorts like Malolo, Castaway, and Matamanoa, they're dirt cheap. So this is your chance to stay at a trendy—even pretentious—tourist resort at something approaching backpacker rates! Needless to say, bookings are tight, and you should reserve as far ahead as possible.

Adjacent to Oarsman's is **Nalova Bay Lodge,** with four *bure* of similar quality to those at Oarsman's. It started out much like its neighbor, but the Waqa family fell out with the Turtle Island people and financing for Nalova Bay Lodge was abruptly terminated. The family is now attempting to finish the resort from their own resources. If they succeed, it will probably be a better buy than Oarsman's Bay.

AROUND THE BLUE LAGOON
Nanuya Lailai Island
Nanuya Lailai, between Tavewa and Nanuya Levu islands, is best known for Blue Lagoon Beach on the island's west side. The snorkeling here is about the finest in the area, and this beach is often visited by cruise ship passengers. Many yachts anchor just offshore. You can tell that the fish have been fed at the Blue Lagoon by the way they swim straight at you. Unfortunately, much of the coral is now dead.

Since 2000, the island's seven families, related to the Naisisili people on Nacula, have established five small backpacker resorts along Enandala Beach on Nanuya Lailai's east side. Expect water shortages (bring bottled water), a lack of electricity (this could change), and no credit cards accepted (all prices include meals). Transfers from the *Yasawa Flyer* to Nanuya Lailai are F$10 pp each way. It's only a 10-minute walk across the island from the backpacker camps to Blue Lagoon Beach. To avoid conflicts with powerful tour operators, your hosts may ask you to stay away from groups of cruise ship passengers swimming in the Blue Lagoon—the beach is long enough for everyone.

Sunrise Lagoon Resort (Poasa Naivalu, tel. 666-6644, ext. 9484), at the north end of Enandala Beach, charges F$102 double in six thatched *bure* with shared bath and F$150 in one garden *bure* with private bath. Both the seven-bed family beach *bure* and a 14-bed dorm are F$46 pp. At last report Sunrise Lagoon was the only resort

on Nanuya Lailai with electricity, but opinions about the quality of the food and accommodations here vary considerably. This place is well promoted by the Nadi travel agents, so there are usually lots of guests.

On a long stretch of beach next door to Sunset Lagoon is the more spacious **Seaspray Lodge** (Daniel Bokini, tel. 666-8962) with eight simple *bure* with shared bath at F$95 double, plus an eight-bed dorm at F$45 pp. Lighting is by kerosene lamp but the outdoor eating area is nice and the food okay. Sadly, we've heard reports of petty theft from the dorm at Seaspray.

Al's Place (Amelia and Alosio Bogileka, tel. 666-6644, ext. 9484) has six *bure* with shared bath on a low hill behind Seaspray. The poor location means it shouldn't be your first choice.

The **Gold Coast Inn** (Philomena Saucoko, tel. 666-6644, ext. 9484), on the beach right next to Seaspray, has five *bure* with shared bath at F$88 double, and two *bure* with private bath at F$120. It's worth considering.

At the south end of the strip is **Kimi's Place** (tel. 666-6644, ext. 9484) with two basic thatched *bure* with shared bath at F$45 pp. It's more of a place to buy souvenirs or to have afternoon tea and cakes (F$3) than a resort. At low tide you can easily walk across the sandbar behind Kim's Place to Nanuya Levu Island, though you'll be most unwelcome there.

Nanuya Levu Island
In 1972, an eccentric American millionaire named Richard Evanson bought 200-hectare Nanuya Levu Island in the middle of the Yasawa Group for US$300,000. He still lives there, and his **Turtle Island Resort** (tel. 672-2921 or 666-3889, fax 672-0007, www.turtlefiji.com) has gained a reputation as one of the South Pacific's ultimate hideaways. Only 14 fan-cooled, two-room *bure* grace Turtle, and Evanson swears there'll never be more.

Turtle is Tavewa at 25 times the price. The 28 guests pay F$2,850 per couple per night (or F$3,450 in a grand *bure*), but that includes all meals, drinks, and activities (12.5 percent tax is extra). You'll find the fridge in your cottage well stocked with beer, wine, soft drinks, and champagne, refilled daily, with no extra bill to pay when you leave. Sports such as sailing, snorkeling, scuba diving, canoeing, windsurfing, deep-sea fishing, horseback riding, guided hiking, and moonlight cruising are all included in the tariff. Resort staff will even do your laundry at no additional charge (only Lomi Lomi massage costs extra).

If you want to spend the day on any of the dozen secluded beaches, just ask and you'll be dropped off. Later someone will be back with lunch and a cooler of wine or champagne (or anything else you'd care to order over the walkie-talkie). Otherwise, use the beach a few steps from your door. Meals are served at remote and romantic dine-out locations, or taken at the community table; every evening Richard hosts a small dinner party. He's turned down many offers to develop the island with hundreds more units or to sell out for a multimillion-dollar price. That's not Richard's style, and he's quite specific about who he *doesn't* want to come: "Trendies, jetsetters, obnoxious imbibers, and plastic people won't get much out of my place. Also, opinionated, loud, critical grouches and anti-socials should give us a miss."

Of course, all this luxury and romance has a price. Aside from the per diem, it's another F$1,380 per couple for round-trip seaplane transportation to the island from Nadi. There's also a six-night minimum stay, but as nearly half the guests are repeaters that doesn't seem to be an impediment. Actress Julia Roberts was a recent visitor. (Turtle Island is off-limits to anyone other than hotel guests.) Turtle's success may be measured by its many imitators, including Vatulele Island Resort, Lalati Resort, the Wakaya Club, Nukubati Island Resort, Qamea Beach Resort, Katafanga Island Resort, and the Yasawa Island Resort.

Turtle Island has also set the standard for environmentally conscious resort development. Aside from planting tens of thousands of trees and providing a safe haven for birds, Evanson has preserved the island's mangroves, cleverly erecting a boardwalk to turn what others might have considered an eyesore into a major attraction. A model of sustainability, the resort grows 90 percent of its own herbs and vegetables in an organic garden, gets honey from its own apiary, uses solar water heaters and wind-powered generators, and makes its own furniture from local timber. And some of Evanson's guests do more than sun themselves. Every year since 1991, a group of California eye specialists has briefly converted Turtle Island into an unlikely clinic for dozens of Fijian villagers requiring eye surgery or just a recycled pair of prescription glasses, all for free. Nearly 160 local Fijians have jobs here, all to serve 28 guests!

Recently Evanson began an innovative program to save the endangered green and hawksbill turtles of the Yasawas. The resort now purchases all live turtles brought in by hunters, and auctions them to resort guests, with all profits going to the staff fund. The names of the new "owners" are painted on the shells, and the reptiles are released. Although the paint does no harm to the turtles, it renders their shells worthless in the turtle shell market, thereby prolonging the animals' lives.

Evanson has a reputation in Fiji, and some former Fijian employees have complained about being paid low wages, fed vegetarian food, and subjected to authoritarian discipline. Contemporary Captain Bligh or not, Richard certainly is a character. During the 2000 coup turmoil, Turtle Island was briefly occupied by villagers from Naisisili on nearby Nacula. They claimed that the island had been wrongfully given away by a Fijian chief in 1868 and still belonged to them. Over many bowls of kava, Evanson and the villagers came to an understanding, and Turtle Island is again as safe as safe can be. In true Hollywood fashion, some of the interlopers have now established backpacker resorts of their own on neighboring islands—all with Richard's blessing and full support! And so life continues on these legendary isles.

Matacawa Levu Island

Matacawa Levu, west of Nanuya Levu, is less developed touristically, although this is changing fast. **Long Beach Resort** (tel. 666-6644, ext. 3032) stands on the long white beach on Matacawa Levu's south side. A mattress on the mat-covered floor of the eight-bed dorm costs F$55

CAPTAIN WILLIAM BLIGH

In 1789, after being cast adrift by the mutineers on his HMS *Bounty*, Captain Bligh and 18 others in a seven-meter longboat were chased by two Fijian war canoes through what is now called Bligh Water. His men pulled the oars desperately, heading for open sea, and managed to escape the cannibals. They later arrived in Timor, finishing the most celebrated open-boat journey of all time. Captain Bligh did some incredible charting of Fijian waters along the way.

pp with meals, but unfortunately we've received complaints about the primitive conditions and poor food here. At low tide you can walk across to nearby Deviulau Island and good snorkeling is available. Passengers are transferred from the *Yasawa Flyer* at the south end of Matacawa Levu at F$5 pp each way. Ask about the newer **Vanuamali Resort** opposite Tavewa on the north side of Matacawa Levu.

SAWA-I-LAU ISLAND

On Sawa-i-Lau is a large limestone cave illuminated by a crevice at the top. There's a clear, deep pool in the cave where you can swim, and an underwater opening leads back into a smaller, darker cave (bring a light). A Fijian legend tells how a young chief once hid his love in this cave when her family wished to marry her off to another. Each day he brought her food until they could both escape to safety on another island. In the 1980 film *Blue Lagoon*, Brooke Shields runs away to this

very cave. Many cruise ships stop at the cave, and the backpacker resorts on Tavewa and Nacula also run tours. Yachties should present a *sevusevu* to the chief of Nabukeru village, just west of the cave, to visit.

YASAWA ISLAND

The Tui Yasawa, highest chief of the group, resides at Yasawairara village at the north end of Yasawa, northernmost island of the Yasawa group.

For many years the Fiji government had a policy that the Yasawas were "closed" to land-based tourism development, and it was only after the 1987 coups that approval was granted for the construction of **Yasawa Island Resort** (Garth and Denise Downey, tel. 666-3364 or 672-2266, fax 666-5044 or 672-4456, www.yasawa.com). This exclusive Australian-owned resort opened in 1991 on a creamy white beach on Yasawa's upper west side. Most of the resort's employees come from Bukama village, which owns the land.

The accommodations consist of four air-conditioned duplexes at F$1,500 double, 10 one-bedroom deluxes at F$1,700, and a honeymoon unit at F$2,400. All meals are included, but, unlike at most other resorts in this category, alcoholic drinks are *not*. Scuba diving (www.diveyasawa.com), game fishing, and massage also cost extra. The resort often grants a 10 percent discount for off-season, last-minute bookings made in person at their Nadi airport office. The only swimming pool in the Yasawa Islands is here. Guests arrive on a chartered flight (F$620 pp return), which lands on the resort's private airstrip. Children under 12 are only admitted in January.

Kadavu

This big, 50-by-13-km island 100 km south of Suva is the third largest in Fiji (450 square km). A mountainous, varied island with waterfalls plummeting from the rounded rainforested hilltops, Kadavu is outstanding for its vistas, beaches, and reefs. The three hilly sections of Kadavu are joined by two low isthmuses, with the sea biting so deeply into the island that on a map its shape resembles that of a wasp. Just northeast of the main island is smaller Ono Island and the fabulous Astrolabe Reef, stretching halfway to Suva. A process is now underway to have Ono's fringing reefs declared a marine conservation area.

The birdlife is rich, with some species of honeyeaters, fantails, and velvet fruit doves found only here. The famous red-and-green Kadavu musk parrots are readily seen and heard. But Kadavu really stands out for what it lacks. There are not only no mongoose, but also no mynas, or bulbuls, or cane toads. Few islands of this size anywhere in the Pacific have as much endemic biodiversity left as Kadavu.

In the 1870s, steamers bound for New Zealand and Australia would call at the onetime whaling station at Galoa Harbor to pick up passengers and goods, and Kadavu was considered as a possible site for a new capital of Fiji. Instead Suva was chosen and Kadavu was left to lead its sleepy village life; only in the past two decades has the outside world made a comeback with the arrival

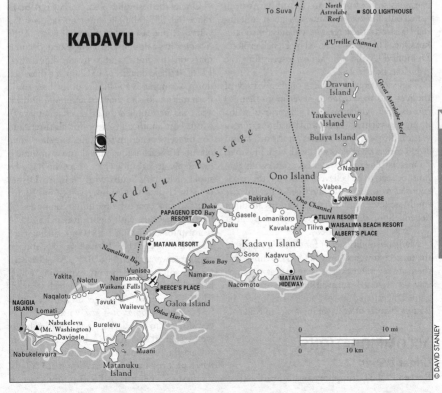

© DAVID STANLEY

FIJI ISLANDS

of roads, planes, and just under a dozen small resorts, many of them on the channel between Kadavu and Ono.

Some 10,000 indigenous Fijians live in 60 remote villages scattered around the island. Kadavu's airstrip and main wharf are each a 10-minute walk, in different directions, from the post office and hospital in the small government station of Vunisea, the largest village and headquarters of Kadavu Province. Vunisea is strategically located on a narrow, hilly isthmus where Galoa Harbor and Namalata Bay almost cut Kadavu in two.

The Great Astrolabe Reef

The Great Astrolabe Reef stretches unbroken for 30 km along the east side of the small islands north of Kadavu. One km wide, the reef is unbelievably rich in coral and marinelife, and because it's so far from shore, it still hasn't been fished out. The reef surrounds a lagoon containing 10 islands, the largest of which is 30-square-km Ono. The reef was named by French explorer Dumont d'Urville, who almost lost his ship, the *Astrolabe,* here in 1827.

There are frequent openings on the west side of the reef and the lagoon is never more than 20 meters deep, which makes it a favorite of scuba divers and yachties. The Astrolabe also features a vertical drop-off of 10 meters on the inside and 1,800 meters on the outside, with visibility up to 75 meters. The underwater caves and walls here must be seen to be believed. However, the reef is exposed to unbroken waves generated by the southeast trades and diving conditions are often dependent on the weather. Surfing is possible at Vesi Passage (boat required).

Many possibilities exist for ocean kayaking in the protected waters around Ono Channel, and there are several inexpensive resorts at which to stay. Kayak rentals are available and several companies mentioned in this book's Exploring the Islands chapter offer kayaking tours to Kadavu.

ACCOMMODATIONS

Under US$25

Reece's Place (Humphrey and Edward Reece,

tel. 333-6097), on Galoa Island just off the northwest corner of Kadavu, was the first to accommodate visitors to Kadavu. It's a 15-minute walk from the airstrip to the dock, then a short launch ride to Galoa itself (F$12 pp return). To stay in a *bure* or European-style house here is F$25/40 single/double, or pay F$12 pp in the dormitory. Pitch your tent for F$6 pp. Three meals are another F$24 pp, and add 12.5 percent tax to all charges. There are longstanding water problems here and the electric generator is seldom used at night. The view of Galoa Harbor from Reece's Place is nice, but snorkeling in the murky water off their so-so beach is a waste of time. For a fee they'll take you out to the Galoa Barrier Reef, where the snorkeling is vastly superior. Scuba diving may be offered—call to ask. There's good anchorage for yachts just off Reece's Place.

One of the best value places to stay is **Albert's Place** (tel. 333-6086), a family operation at Lagalevu at the east end of Kadavu. Each of the five *bure* has a double and a single bed, coconut mats on the floor, and kerosene lighting at F$16/30 single/double, or F$12 pp in a three-bed dorm. Camping is F$10. The units share rustic flush toilets and cold showers, and mosquito nets and coils are supplied (bring repellant anyway). Meals cost another F$25 pp for all three, and you'll receive generous portions. The snorkeling off Albert's beach is fine, though the swimming is only good at high tide (Jona's on Ono has a far superior beach). Scuba with **Naiqoro Divers** (run by Bruce O'Connor) is F$65/110 for one/two tank boat dives including equipment. A four-day package with eight dives is F$400. A reef trip for snorkeling is F$10 pp, surfing trips F$15, fishing trips F$10, kayaking F$5, and the two/three waterfall trip F$20/35. Ask Elizabeth to give you her garden tour, explaining which herbs she uses in her cooking and which are medicinal. The cheapest way to get there from Suva is by boat on the *Bulou-ni-Ceva,* which will bring you directly to Kavala Bay (a good three hours west of Albert's on foot). A boat pickup from Kavala Bay will cost F$30 per trip, otherwise they'll pick you up at Vunisea Airport at F$60 for the first two persons or F$30 pp for three or

a backpacker *bure* at Albert's Place, Kadavu

more for the two-hour boat ride (these prices are fixed, so don't bother bargaining).

US$25–50

Manueli and Tamalesi Vuruya run **Biana Accommodation** (tel. 333-6010), on a hill overlooking Namalata Bay near the wharf at Vunisea. The three rooms with cold showers are F$40/60 single/double including breakfast, plus F$5 each for lunch or dinner. They ask that you call ahead before coming.

The **Waisalima Beach Resort** (tel./fax 331-6281, www.waisalimafiji.com) faces a golden two-km beach with a lovely panorama on the north side of Kadavu, between Albert's and Kavala Bay. The three *bure* with shared bath are F$50/65 single/double, while the three with private bath are F$130/150. *Bure* guests pay F$47 pp extra for three meals, while those staying in the six-bed dorm are charged F$60 pp including meals. It's a bit overpriced compared to Jona's and Albert's, and rather basic for the price, though they do have a permanent electricity supply. Campers can pitch their tents at the end of the property, a few hundred meters down the beach and across a small bridge, at F$8/12 single/double. Two-tank dives are

F$120, plus F$25 for gear. A four-day open-water certification course will cost F$500. Kayaks are for rent at F$15 a day. Waisalima is a one-hour walk from Albert's. Their launch will pick you up at Kavala wharf for F$15 pp (over two hours walk). From Vunisea airport they charge F$50 pp each way with a two-person minimum.

Jona's Paradise Resort (tel. 330-7058, fax 330-9696, www.jonasparadise.com) is at Vabea on the southern tip of Ono Island opposite Kadavu. The accommodations are good, with two deluxe *bure* (private bath) at F$105 pp, three standard *bure* (shared bath) at F$95 pp, two four-bed dorm *bure* at F$70 pp, and camping space at F$53 pp. Children under 12 sharing with their parents are 50 percent off. All prices include three tasty meals, but bring a few snack foods with you since the portions are sometimes skimpy. Jona's generator is unreliable and the lights can go off as early at 2140. Surprisingly, there are no trails leading away from the resort to local villages. This small, family-style resort has a steep, non-tidal white-sand beach, which is always right for swimming and very safe for the kids (no currents or big waves). The snorkeling is great (hundreds of clownfish in crystal-clear water), and the gorgeous Great Astrolabe Reef is only a five-minute boat ride away. Jonas is the closest Kadavu area resort to the top dive sites. Turtles, sharks, and big fish are seen on most channel dives, and the fish and coral on the reefs are first rate, too. Australian Russell Thornley (married to Albert O'Connor's daughter) runs the dive operation, charging F$130 for a two-tank dive including gear. A "discover scuba" course for novices costs F$120 pp including three dives and gear. The high-speed one-hour boat trip from Vunisea Airport costs F$55 pp each way. The 200 HP engine on their custom-built eight-meter aluminum dive boat allows the scuba staff to make regular trips to Suva and they'll happily bring you back with them from the Tradewinds Marina at F$100 pp (call ahead to find out when this might be possible).

US$50–100

Not to be confused with the more expensive Matana Resort is **Matava, The Astrolabe Hideaway** (tel. 333-6098 or 330-5222, fax 333-6099, www.matava.com), a 30-minute walk east of Kadavu village and almost opposite tiny Waya Island on the southeast side of the island. Opened in 1996, this is one of the most eco-conscious resorts in Fiji. The managers Jeanie from New York and Richard and Adrian from the United Kingdom have installed solar electricity and water heating, an organic vegetable garden, and a spring water system. There's no beach in front of Matava, but the snorkeling in the marine reserve off Waya is fine. There are three thatched oceanview *bure* with private bath and solar lighting at F$120 single or double, three waterfront *bure* with private bath at F$100, two waterfront *bure* with shared bath at F$55, and one four-bed dormitory at F$18 pp. The meal plan is F$50 pp and you eat at communal tables, which is fun. A local village store is a 20-minute walk away. Most guests come to scuba dive on the nearby Great Astrolabe Reef, which costs F$60/115/540 for one/two/10 tanks, plus F$25 for equipment. The manta dive is exceptional. PADI open-water certification is F$550. Surfing trips are F$35 (own board). Kayaks and canoes are for rent. Snorkeling trips are F$15 pp, plus F$10 for gear

(if required). Game fishing is F$100 an hour plus fuel. Boat transfers from the airport are F$30 pp each way. It's rustic and remote, but just fine for the diehard diver.

US$150–250

In April 2000, a surfing camp called **Nagigia Island** (tel. 331-5774, www.fijisurf.com) opened on tiny Denham Island off Cape Washington at the west end of Kadavu. The seven neat little bungalows perched on a limestone cliff are F$154 pp if you're willing to share a double or F$200 single. A dorm bed is F$114. Reductions are offered after one week. The meal plan is F$54 pp extra, unlimited surf transfers F$28 a day, and boat transfers to Vunisea Airport F$58 pp each way. Scuba diving and fishing also cost extra. There's good swimming directly below the units and at nearby sandy beaches. The traditional surfing season is April to November, but this resort has excellent surf during the other months as well, due to its outer reefs curving 270 degrees. For surfing details and advice on transporting your boards, consult their website.

The **Matana Beach Resort** (tel. 331-1780, fax 330-3860, www.matanabeachresort.com) at Drue, six km north of Vunisea, caters mostly to scuba divers who've booked from abroad with Dive Kadavu (www.divekadavu.com). The two oceanview *bure* on the hillside and six larger beachfront units are F$275/475/660/800 single/double/triple/quad (local rate discounts often available). All rates include three meals of variable quality (three-night minimum stay). Windsurfers, kayaks, and paddle-boards are free. The morning two-tank boat dive is F$165 without gear. The snorkeling off Matana's golden beach is good, and the Namalata Reef is straight out from the resort (the east end of the Great Astrolabe Reef is an hour away). Boat transfers from Vunisea airport are free. The feedback has been mixed.

The **Papageno Eco Resort** (tel. 330-3355, fax 330-3533, www.papagenoecoresort.com) is on the north side of Kadavu, 15 km east of Vunisea and accessible only by boat. The four colonial-style cottages are F$300/600/750 single/double/triple including meals, airport transfers, and tax. The main house on this 140-hectare property is used as the resort's dining room. Scuba diving and combined village-wildlife trips can be arranged. Papageno offers two-week marine biology course costing F$2,000 pp including room and board, instruction, and materials. They also have a Kadavu Shining Parrot conservation project for which they accept long-term (minimum three months) volunteers who pay to work on the project.

Kadavu's newest place is the **Tiliva Resort** (tel./fax 331-5127, www.tilivaresortfiji.com), near Tiliva village between Kavala Bay and Waisalima on east Kadavu, facing a golden beach with a nice view of Ono. Opened in late 2002, it's run by an ex-British soldier named Kemu Yabaki and his wife Barbara. They have one honeymoon beachfront bungalow at F$500 double, and five spacious fan-cooled twin bungalows at F$250/400 single/double. All meals in the modern restaurant/bar overlooking the resort are included. There's 24-hour electricity. Scuba diving is F$55/30/70 for boat/shore/night dives and sport fishing can be arranged. Airport transfers are included in the rates (minimum stay three nights).

OTHER PRACTICALITIES

Vunisea has no restaurants, but a coffee shop at the airstrip opens for flights, and six small general stores sell canned goods. Vunisea Market opens Monday–Saturday 0800–1600 with cooked meals, hot coffee, and stacks of fruit available. A woman at the market sells roti, pies, and juice.

The small National Bank agency at the post office in Vunisea doesn't deal in foreign currency, so change enough money before coming (and don't leave it unattended in your room or tent).

Occasional carriers ply the rugged, muddy roads of west Kadavu, but there are no buses.

GETTING THERE

Air Fiji arrives from Suva once a day (F$81) and **Sun Air** has daily flights from Nadi (F$104). Be sure to reconfirm your return flight immediately upon arrival. Boat pickups by the resorts on east Kadavu and Ono should be prearranged. The speedboats to east Kadavu are often without safety equipment or roofs, and in rough weather everything could get wet. Have sunblock and a hat ready if it's sunny, rain gear if it's not, as it's a one- to two-hour ride to east Kadavu or Ono. There's no road from Vunisea to east Kadavu.

Ships like the *Bulou-ni-Ceva* and *Cagi Mai Ba* ply between Suva and Kadavu twice a week, calling at villages along the north coast. These vessels are only of interest to low-budget travelers headed for Waisalima or Albert's, who can disembark at Kavala Bay. Take seasickness precautions before boarding. For details turn to Transportation in the Suva section.

The Lomaiviti Group

The Lomaiviti (or central Fiji) Group lies in the Koro Sea near the heart of the archipelago, east of Viti Levu and south of Vanua Levu. Of its nine main volcanic islands, Gau, Koro, and Ovalau are among the largest in Fiji. Lomaiviti's climate is moderate, neither as wet and humid as Suva, nor as dry and hot as Nadi. The population is mostly Fijian, engaged in subsistence agriculture and copra making.

The old capital island, Ovalau, is by far the best known and most visited island of the group, and several small islands south of Ovalau on the way to Suva bear backpackers' resorts. Naigani also has a tourist resort of its own, but Koro and Gau are seldom visited, due to a lack of facilities for visitors. Ferries ply the Koro Sea to Ovalau, while onward ferries run to Vanua Levu a couple of times a week.

OVALAU ISLAND

Ovalau, a large volcanic island just east of Viti Levu, is the main island of the Lomaiviti Group. Almost encircled by high peaks, the Lovoni Valley in the center of Ovalau is actually the island's volcanic crater and about the only flat land. The

FIJI ISLANDS

crater's rim is pierced by the Bureta River, which escapes through a gap to the southeast. The highest peak is 626-meter Nadelaiovalau (meaning, the top of Ovalau), behind Levuka. Luckily Ovalau lacks the magnificent beaches found elsewhere in Fiji, which has kept the package-tour crowd away, and upscale scuba divers have better places to go, so it's still one of the most peaceful, pleasant, picturesque, and historic areas to visit in the South Pacific.

Levuka

The town of Levuka on Ovalau's east side was Fiji's capital until the shift to Suva in 1882. Founded as a whaling settlement in 1830, Levuka became the main center for European traders in Fiji, and a British consul was appointed in 1857. The cotton boom of the 1860s brought new settlers, and Levuka quickly grew into a boisterous town with over 50 hotels and taverns along Beach Street. Escaped convicts and debtors fleeing creditors in Australia swelled the throng, until it was said that a ship could find the reef passage into Levuka by following the empty gin bottles floating out on the tide. The honest traders felt the need for a stable government, so in 1871 Levuka became capital of Cakobau's Kingdom of Fiji. The disorders continued, with extremist elements forming a "Ku Klux Klan," defiant of any form of Fijian authority.

On October 10, 1874, a semblance of decorum came as Fiji was annexed by Great Britain and a municipal council was formed in 1877. British rule soon put a damper on the wild side of the blackbirding. Ovalau's central location seemed ideal for trade, and sailing boats from Lau or Vanua Levu could easily enter the port on the southeast trades. Yet the lush green hills that rise behind the town were to be its downfall, as colonial planners saw that there was no room for the expansion of their capital, and in August 1882 Gov. Sir Arthur Gordon moved his staff to Suva. Hurricanes in 1888 and 1895 destroyed much of early Levuka, with the north end of town around the present Anglican church almost flattened, and many of Levuka's devastated buildings were not replaced.

Levuka remained the collection center for the

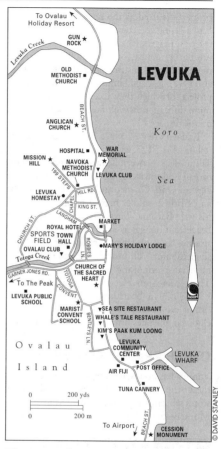

Fiji copra trade right up until 1957, and the town seemed doomed when that industry, too, moved to a new mill in Suva. But with the establishment of a fishing industry in 1964, Levuka revived, and today it's is a minor educational center, the headquarters of Lomaiviti Province, and a low-key tourist center. Thanks to the tuna cannery, there's a public electricity supply.

It's rather shocking that Levuka still hasn't been approved by UNESCO as a World Heritage Site, because Levuka is to Fiji what Lahaina is to Hawaii, a slice of living history. Each year another century-old building is lost due to the lack of an internationally-sanctioned conservation program. In 2003, the historic Mavida Guesthouse burned to the ground, followed in February 2004 by the supermarket, bank, and Air Fiji office on Beach Street. It doesn't take much imagination to see how the rest of Levuka's old wooden buildings are similarly threatened.

Yet the false-fronted buildings and covered sidewalks which survive along **Beach Street** still give this somnolent town of 4,000 mostly Fijian or part-Fijian inhabitants a 19th-century, Wild West feel. From the waterfront, let your eyes follow the horizon from left to right to view the islands of Makogai, Koro, Wakaya, Nairai, Batiki, and Gau respectively. Levuka's a perfect base for excursions into the mountains, along the winding coast, or out to the barrier reef a kilometer offshore.

It's customary to say "Good morning," *"Bula,"* or simply "Hello" to people you meet while strolling around Levuka, especially on the backstreets, and the locals have been rather put off by tourists who failed to do so. This is one of the little adverse effects of tourism, and a very unnecessary one at that.

Sights

Near Levuka Wharf is the old Morris Hedstrom general store, erected by Percy Morris and Maynard Hedstrom in 1880s, great-granddaddy of today's Pacific-wide Morris Hedstrom chain. The store closed when the lease expired in 1979 and the building was turned over to the National Trust for Fiji. In 1981, the facility reopened as the **Levuka Community Center** (tel. 344-0356; weekdays 0800–1630, Sat. 0800–1300) with a museum and library, where cannibal forks vie with war clubs and clay pots for your attention. The many old photos of the town in the museum are fascinating, and a few relics of the mystery ship *Joyita* are on display. The Community Center receives no outside funding and your F$2 admission fee helps keep this place going.

Stroll north on Beach Street along Levuka's sleepy waterfront past a long row of wooden store fronts that haven't changed much in a century. The sea wall opposite was constructed by the Royal Engineers in 1874. Just beyond the wall is the **Church of the Sacred Heart,** erected by French Marist priests who arrived in 1858. The church's square clock tower was added in 1898 to

Levuka photographed from Gun Rock

© DAVID STANLEY

commemorate the first priest, Father Breheret. The green neon light on the stone tower lines up with another green light farther up the hill to guide mariners into port. The tower's French clock strikes the hour twice with a minute interval in between. Go through the gate behind the church to the formidable **Marist Convent School** (1892), originally a girls' school operated by the sisters and still a primary school.

Totogo Lane leads north from the convent to a small bridge over Totogo Creek and the **Ovalau Club** (1904), adjoining the old **Town Hall** (1898), also known as Queen Victoria Memorial Hall. Next to the town hall is the gutted shell of the **Masonic Lodge building,** erected in 1913. The "Little Polynesia" chapter of the Masonic Order was formed here in 1875. In July 2000, the lodge was burned down by a frenzied mob from Lovoni, which had been told by superstitious preachers that it was a center of devil worship.

Follow Garner Jones Road west up the creek to the **Levuka Public School** (1881), the birthplace of Fiji's present public educational system.

M

FIJI ISLANDS

Before WW I, the only Fijians allowed to attend this school were the sons of chiefs. Other Levuka firsts include Fiji's first newspaper (1869), first Masonic Lodge (1875), first bank (1876), and first municipal council (1877).

Continue straight up Garner Jones Road for about 15 minutes, past the lovely colonial-era houses, and you'll eventually reach a locked gate at the entrance to the town's water catchment. A trail on the right just before the gate leads down to a **pool** in the river below the catchment where you can swim. Overhead you may see swallows that live in a cave just upstream. The path to **The Peak** branches off to the left between a large steel water tank and the gate at the end of the main trail. It takes about an hour to scale The Peak through the dense bush, and an experienced guide will be required (arranged through the Royal Hotel at F$6/8 single/double).

As you come back down the hill, turn left onto Church Street and follow it around past the sports field (once a Fijian village site) to **Navoka Methodist Church** (1862). From beside this church, 199 concrete steps ascend **Mission Hill** to Delana Methodist High School, which affords fine views. The original mission school formed here by Rev. John Binner in 1852 was the first of its kind in Fiji. A stairway leads down through the high school to the hospital.

North of Levuka

On a low hill farther north along the waterfront is the **European War Memorial,** which recalls British residents of Levuka who died in WW I. Before Fiji was ceded to Britain, the Cakobau government headquarters was situated on this hill. The 1870s cottage on the hilltop across the street from the monument is called **Sailors Home** for the steamship *Sailors Home,* which worked the England to China route in the 1850s. The **Holy Redeemer Anglican Church** (1902) farther north has period stained-glass windows.

Follow the coastal road north from Levuka to a second bridge, where you'll see the **old Methodist church** (1869) on the left. Ratu Seru Cakobau worshiped here, and in the small cemetery behind the church is the grave of the first U.S. consul to Fiji, John Brown Williams

(1810–1860). For the story of Williams's activities, see "History and Government" in the main introduction. Levuka Creek here marks the town's northern boundary. In the compound across the bridge and beneath a large *dilo* tree is the tomb of an old king of Levuka. The large house in front of the tree is the residence of the present Tui Levuka, customary chief of this area (ask permission before entering the compound).

Directly above this house is **Gun Rock,** which was used as a target by the captain of the HMS *Havanah* in 1849. The intention, of course, was to demonstrate to Cakobau the efficacy of a ship's cannon so he might be more considerate to resident Europeans. In 1874, Commodore Goodenough pumped a few more rounds into the hill to entertain a group of Fijian chiefs, and the scars can still be seen. Long before that, the early Fijians had a fort atop the Rock to defend themselves against the Lovoni hill tribes. Ask permission of the Tui Levuka (the "Roko") or a member of his household to climb Gun Rock for a splendid view of Levuka. If a small boy leads you up and down, it wouldn't be out of place to give him something for his trouble.

Continue north on the road, around a bend and past the ruin of a large concrete building, and you'll reach a cluster of government housing on the site of a cricket field where the Duke of York (later King George V) played in 1878.

There's a beautiful deep pool and waterfall behind **Waitovu** village, about two km north of Levuka. You may swim here, but please don't skinny-dip; this is offensive to the local people and has led to confrontations in the past. Also, avoid arriving on a Sunday.

At Cawaci, a 30-minute walk beyond the Ovalau Holiday Resort, is a small white **mausoleum** (1922) high up on a point with the tombs of Fiji's first and second Catholic bishops, Bishop Julien Vidal and Bishop Charles Joseph Nicholas. The large coral stone church (1893) of **St. John's College** is nearby. This is the original seat of the Catholic Church in Fiji, and the sons of the Fijian chiefs were educated here from 1894 onwards. The French-style church's walls are three meters thick around the buttresses.

South of Levuka

The **Pacific Fishing Company** tuna cannery (tel. 344-0055, fax 344-0400) is just south of Queen's Wharf. A Japanese cold-storage facility opened here in 1964, the cannery in 1975. After sustaining losses for four years, the Japanese company involved in the joint venture pulled out in 1986, turning the facility over to the government, which now owns the cannery. Major improvements to the wharf, freezer, storage, and other facilities were completed in 1992. The plant is supplied by Taiwanese fishing boats. In 2002, a seven-year agreement was signed with the U.S. seafood company Bumble Bee to supply tuna loins to a cannery in San Diego, California, now Pafco's largest market. Nearly a thousand residents of Ovalau (85 percent of them women) have jobs directly related to tuna canning, and the government has heavily subsidized the operation.

A little farther along is the **Cession Monument,** where the Deed of Cession, which made Fiji a British colony, was signed by Chief Cakobau in 1874. The traditional *bure* on the other side of the road was used by Prince Charles during his 1970 visit to officiate at Fiji's independence. It's now the venue of provincial council meetings. A nearby European-style bungalow is **Nasova House** (1869), the former Government House or residence of the governor and now the Levuka Town Council.

One of Fiji's most rewarding hikes begins at Draiba village, a kilometer south of the Cession Monument. A road to the right around the first bend and just after a small bridge, marks the start of the 4.5-hour hike through enchanting forests and across clear streams to **Lovoni** village. Go straight back on this side road till you see an overgrown metal scrap yard on your right, near the end of the road. Walk through the middle of the scrap yard and around to the right past two huge mango trees. The unmarked Lovoni trail begins at the foot of the hill, just beyond the trees.

The Lovoni trail is no longer used by the locals and requires attentiveness to follow, so consider Epi's Midland Tour if you're not an experienced hiker. Be sure to reach Lovoni before 1500 to be able to catch the last carrier back to Levuka. In

1855, the fierce Lovoni tribe, the Ovalau, burned Levuka, and they continued to threaten the town right up until 1871, when they were finally captured during a truce and sold to European planters as laborers. In 1875, the British government allowed the survivors to return to their valley, where their descendants live today. In July 2000, a Lovoni mob again ran amuck through Levuka during the George Speight coup attempt.

If you forgo this hike and continue on the main road, you'll soon come to the old **Town Cemetery** a little south of Draiba. Many of the graves here date back to the early colonial period. A few kilometers farther along is the **Devil's Thumb,** a dramatic volcanic plug towering above **Tokou** village, one of the scenic highlights of Fiji. Catholic missionaries set up a printing press at Tokou in 1889 to produce gospel lessons in Fijian, and in the center of the village is a sculpture of a lion made by one of the early priests. It's five km back to Levuka.

Wainaloka village on the southwest side of Ovalau is inhabited by descendants of Solomon Islanders from the Lau Lagoon region who were blackbirded to Fiji over a century ago.

Sports and Recreation

Ovalau Watersports (tel. 344-0166, www.owl fiji.com) not far from the wharf is run by Nobi and Andrea Dehm with help from Ned Fisher, all of whom worked as divemasters at Leleuvia Island Resort for many years. They offer diving around Levuka at 0900 daily at F$140/600 for two/10 tanks including gear (minimum of two divers). An open-water certification course is F$480 (taught in English or German). They also take out snorkelers at F$35 pp—just show up at their dive shop around 0845. You'll visit the two sites used by the divers that day. Nobi and Ned also rent bicycles at F$5/10/15 an hour/half day/full day. Andrea can help you arrange any land tours you may require.

Inn's Boutique Fashion Wear (tel. 344-0374 or 344-0059), below Kim's Paak Kum Loong Restaurant, rents bicycles at F$3/10/15 an hour/half day/full day.

At high tide, the river mouth near the Royal Hotel is a popular swimming hole for the local kids (and some tourists). The rest of the day some locals cool off by just sitting in the water fully dressed.

PRACTICALITIES

Accommodations

There are a couple of budget places to stay around Levuka (but thankfully no luxury resorts). **Mary's Holiday Lodge** (tel. 344-0013), formerly known as the Old Capitol Inn, on Beach Street, occupies a large wooden house on the waterfront. The 12 basic fan-cooled rooms with shared bath are F$20/30 single/double, or F$12 pp in a three-bed dorm. A cooked breakfast is included, while dinner (order by 1400) is F$6. A cool breeze blowing in from the east helps keep the mosquitoes away.

For the full Somerset Maugham flavor, stay at the 15-room **Royal Hotel** on Robbies Lane (tel. 344-0024, fax 344-0174, www.royallevuka.com). Originally built in 1852 and rebuilt in 1913 by Captain David Robbie after a fire in the 1890s, this is Fiji's oldest hotel, run by the Ashley family since 1927. The platform on the roof is a "widow's watch" where wives would watch for the overdue return of their husband's ships. In the lounge, ceiling fans revolve above the rattan sofas and potted plants, and upstairs the 15 fan-cooled rooms with private bath are pleasant, with much-needed mosquito nets provided. Each room in the main building is in a different style, including six singles (F$21), six doubles (F$29), and three triples (F$39). The section between the hotel and Beach Street contains five cottages, of which only the three closer to the ocean have kitchens (all cost F$80 double). The garden section beside the main building includes the "Captain Robbie" duplex with two air-conditioned apartments (F$90), the "Captain Kaad" cottage with two air-conditioned rooms (F$58 double), and the "Captain Volk" house with four budget rooms with shared bath at F$11 pp in shared three-bed rooms. Communal cooking facilities are available in this dorm. Checkout time is 1000, but you can arrange to stay until 1500 by paying another 50 percent of the daily rate (no credit cards accepted). The restaurant serves breakfast at F$4.50–6.50 and dinner (order before 1500) at F$7.50. The

service is slow and the food rather bland. The bar, beer garden, snooker tables, dart boards, swimming pool, gym, and videos (at 2000) are strictly for guests only. The anachronistic prices and colonial atmosphere make the Royal about the best value in Fiji.

The more upscale **Levuka Homestay** (John and Marilyn Milesi, tel. 344-0777, www.levuka homestay.com), on Church St. behind the Royal Hotel, has four rooms with bath at F$118/133 single/double, including breakfast and tax. The three lower air-conditioned rooms in this custom-built house, which climbs the hillside on five levels, are preferable to the fourth room tucked away directly below the owners' apartment.

The folks at Ovalau Watersports (tel. 344-0166, www.owlfiji.com) rent the **Levuka Holiday Cottage** in front of Gun Rock, a 15-minute walk north of Levuka. This self-catering bungalow (F$70/420 double a day/week) is ideal for couples who want to melt into the local scene for a while.

Around the Island

The **Ovalau Holiday Resort** (tel. 344-0329) is opposite a rocky beach at Vuma, four km north of Levuka (taxi F$5). The five two-room bungalows with kitchen and fridge are F$35/66/86 single/double/triple. There's also a four-bed dorm which costs F$12.50 pp. If you plan to use the cooking facilities, make sure your groceries are protected from mice. Given sufficient advance notice, the resort's restaurant does some fine cooking. Their Bula Beach Bar in a converted whaler's cottage adjoins the swimming pool, and the snorkeling off their beach is okay. It's a nice place for an afternoon at the beach, even if you prefer to stay in Levuka.

Bobo's Farm (Karin and Bobo Ahtack, tel. 344-0166 or 993-3632), near Rukuruku, provides accommodations for four people in two rooms at F$25 pp, plus F$6/6/10 for breakfast/lunch/dinner (real Fijian food). It's a great place to relax. You can book this homestay through Ovalau Watersports.

Food

Coffee in the Garden (tel. 344-0471; Mon.–Sat.

0800–1800), on the waterfront in Patterson Gardens between the Levuka Community Center and the power plant, is the perfect place for a breakfast of tea and muffins, or a coffee anytime.

Kim's Paak Kum Loong Restaurant (tel. 344-0059; Mon.–Sat. 0700–2100, Sun. 1200–1400 and 1800–2100), upstairs in a building near Court's Furniture Store, is Levuka's most popular restaurant. A full breakfast is F$8. Lunch from the glass warmers near the door is F$3.50, while the dinner menu includes Chinese dishes for F$5–10 (meals ordered from the menu are individually prepared). On the dinner menu are several Fijian dishes (F$7–9) and six vegetarian choices for under F$5. Sundays from 1800 there's a buffet (F$13.50), which includes salad and ice cream. Beer is available. If you can get a table, dine on their breezy front terrace with a view of the waterfront.

The **Whale's Tale Restaurant** (Liza Ditrich, tel. 344-0235; Mon.–Sat. 1130–1500 and 1700–2100) on Beach Street is a favorite for its real home cooking at medium prices. Buttered pasta for lunch costs F$8.80 and the three-course dinner special with a choice from among three main plates is F$16.90. They're licensed, so you can get a beer with your meal, and their specially percolated coffee (F$2.75) is the best in town. They also sell bags of pounded kava (F$1).

The **Sea Site Restaurant** (tel. 344-0553), a bit north of Whale's Tale, is basic, but decent for ice cream.

Emily Cafe (tel. 344-0382), between the Sea Site and the Church of the Sacred Heart, is a good place for coffee and cakes during the day. Daily from 1800–2100 the locale becomes **Ovalau Pizza** with pizzas from F$6–16.

Entertainment

Despite the Members Only sign, you're welcome to enter the **Ovalau Club** (tel. 344-0507; Mon.–Thurs. 1600–2230, Fri. 1400–midnight, Sat. 1000–midnight, Sun. 1000–2100), just across Totoga Creek from the police station, said to be the oldest membership club in the South Pacific. You'll meet genuine South Seas characters here, and the place is brimming with atmosphere. The original billiard table is still

in use. Ask the bartender to show you the framed letter from Count Felix von Luckner, the WW I German sea wolf. Von Luckner left the letter and some money at the unoccupied residence of a trader on Katafaga Island in the Lau Group, from which he took some provisions. In the letter, Count von Luckner identifies himself as Max Pemberton, an English writer on a sporting cruise through the Pacific.

The **Levuka Club** (tel. 344-0272) on Beach Street is a good place for sunsets, especially from the picnic tables in their nice backyard beside the water.

Information

Metuisela Tabaki at the Levuka Community Center (tel. 344-0356) may have information on the offshore island resorts and various land tours around Ovalau. You can borrow up to three books from the Community Center library for a F$2.50 fee (plus a refundable F$10 deposit).

Liza at the Whale's Tale Restaurant (tel. 344-0235) will be happy to give you her frank opinion of the offshore resorts—invaluable when planning a trip. Andrea at Ovalau Watersports is also very helpful.

Services

The Westpac Bank (with an ATM) and Colonial National Bank on Beach Street change traveler's checks.

Ovalau Watersports provides Internet access at F$.20 a minute (F$1 minimum). The Royal Hotel also charges F$.20 a minute for Internet access.

Public toilets are available across the street from the Colonial National Bank and behind the post office. Ovalau Watersports does laundry at F$10 a load, while the Royal Hotel charges F$7 a bag.

Levuka's new sub-divisional hospital (tel. 344-0088) is on the north side of town. In 2000, F$3.6 million were spent rebuilding this facility.

Transportation

Air Fiji (tel. 344-0139) has two flights a day between Bureta Airport and Suva (F$52). The minibus from Levuka to the airstrip is F$4 pp. A taxi to the airport will run F$20.

Inquire at **Patterson Brothers Shipping** (tel. 344-0125), beside the market on Beach Street, about the direct ferry from Ovalau to Nabouwalu, Vanua Levu, via Natovi. The connecting bus departs Levuka Monday–Saturday at about 0500. At Nabouwalu, there's an onward bus to Labasa, but bookings must be made in advance (F$55 straight through).

The bus/ferry/bus service between Suva and Levuka was discussed previously under Transportation in the Suva section. It should take just under five hours right through, and cost F$24. The Patterson Brothers combination involves an express bus from Levuka to Buresala departing daily except Sunday at 0500, a 45-minute ferry ride from Buresala to Natovi, then the same bus on to Suva (change at Korovou for Lautoka). Bicycles are carried free on the ferry. Advance bookings are required on the Patterson Brothers bus/ferry/bus service. In the opposite direction, the bus to Natovi leaves Suva at 1400 and the ferry is often late. Thus it's a good idea to fly from Suva to Levuka, returning to Suva by bus.

Metuisela Tabaki at the Levuka Community Center (tel. 344-0356) sells tickets for the 50-passenger boat *Viro* from Levuka to Suva (F$16). The connecting carrier to the landing leaves Levuka at 0800 on Tuesday, Thursday, Friday, and Saturday. Also ask about the "Bureta boat," whose carrier picks up passengers in front the Community Center at 0730 Monday, Wednesday, Friday, and Saturday.

Both taxis and carriers park across the street from the Church of the Sacred Heart in Levuka. Due to steep hills on the northwest side of Ovalau, there isn't a bus right around the island. Carriers leave Levuka for Taviya (F$1.50) or Rukuruku (F$2) villages Monday–Saturday at 0730, 1130, and 1700 along a beautiful, hilly road. During the school holidays only the 1200 trip may operate. Occasional carriers to Bureta (F$1.50), Lovoni (F$2), and Viru (F$2) park across the street from Kim's Paak Kum Loong Restaurant. To Lovoni, they leave Levuka at 0630, 1100, and 1700, Saturday at 1100 only. There's no service on Sunday.

A truck direct to Rukuruku leaves Levuka at 1200 on Tuesday, Thursday, and Saturday, and it's possible to do a round-trip for F$4 since the carrier returns immediately to Levuka. Monday to Saturday you can have a day at the beach at Rukuruku by taking the 0730 carrier to Taviya, then walking the remaining kilometer to Rukuruku (from the top of the hill, turn right down the sideroad to the beach). A vanilla plantation and beautiful verdant mountains cradle Rukuruku on the island side. Return to Levuka on the 1500 carrier from Taviya (check all this with the driver).

Tours

Epi's Midland Tour (tel. 923-6011) is a guided hike to Lovoni that departs Levuka Monday–Saturday around 1000 (F$30 pp including lunch). You hike over and return by truck (or you can just go both ways by truck if you don't wish to walk). The route is steep, and rugged footwear is essential. At Lovoni you may go for a swim in the river or ask to meet the village chief. Epi is an enthusiastic guy very knowledgeable about forest plants, and there have been very good reports about his tour. His reservations book is at Ovalau Watersports. This tour is recommended.

Ovalau Watersports (tel. 344-0146; weekdays 0800–1600, Sat. 0800–1300, www.owl fiji.com), beside the Levuka Community Center, arranges a variety of tours. The 1.5-hour historical town walking tour with Henry Sahai (tel. 344-0096), who has lived here since 1919, is good value at F$8 pp (at 0900 and 1400 daily). He's still very fit and quite a character (if there's only one of you, no problem). The "tea and talanoa" program with Duncan Crichton (tel. 344-0481) or Bubu Kara allows you to meet local residents in their own homes for tea and conversation (F$15 pp). Ovalau Watersports also organizes village visits at F$30 pp including a *lovo* lunch (minimum of five). You can even stay in a village at F$25 pp including breakfast and participate in activities like fishing, trolling, canoeing, rafting, and snorkeling at additional cost.

If you wish to organize your own tour, it costs F$85 for the vehicle to hire a taxi or 15-person carrier right around the island. (A taxi tour to

Cawaci with stops along the way should cost F$20 for a four-passenger car.)

ISLANDS OFF OVALAU

Caqalai Island

Caqalai (THANG-ga-lai) is owned by the Methodist Church of Fiji, which operates a small backpacker resort (tel. 343-0366) on this palm-fringed isle. The 12 simple *bure* are F$40 pp, the three-bed dorm F$30 pp, and camping space F$25 pp, three meals included. A communal fridge is provided. You must take your own alcohol, as none is sold on the island. It's primitive but adequate, and the island and people are great. Dress up for Sunday service in the village church and enjoy the *lovo* that afternoon. There's good snorkeling all around the island and you can wade to Snake Island, where banded sea snakes congregate. With nearby Leleuvia Island Resort showing signs of age, Caqalai has increased in popularity. Information is available at the Royal Hotel (boat from Ovalau/Viti Levu F$20/25 pp each way). The Royal Hotel also arranges day trips to Caqalai Monday–Saturday at 1000 (F$50 pp, minimum of two). Those already staying on Caqalai can make shopping trips to Levuka at a reduced rate.

Leleuvia Island

Leleuvia is a lovely isolated 17-hectare reef island with nothing but coconut trees, fine sandy beaches, and a ramshackle assortment of tourist huts scattered around. The small backpacker resort (tel. 330-1584, www.owlfiji.com/leleuvia.htm), originally built in the 1980s, is now run by Epenisa Cakobau, a member of the indigenous Fijian nobility from Bau Island,. Unfortunately, Leleuvia has gone downhill in recent years.

Accommodations including three basic meals run F$30 pp in the dorm, F$35 pp in a thatched hut, F$42 pp in a wooden bungalow, or F$24 pp if you camp. Water is in short supply on Leleuvia, and bathing is with a bucket of brackish water. You should watch your gear here.

A few activities are laid on, such as reef trips by boat and scuba diving, and on Sunday they'll even take you to church! For a nominal amount

they'll drop you off on one-tree "Honeymoon Island." Leleuvia's diving concession **Nautilus Dive** offers scuba diving at F$75/130 for one/two tanks. The resident instructor—a German named Thomas—has taught diving to quite a few guests. This isn't surprising because at F$390, Nautilus' PADI open-water certification course is one of the least expensive in Fiji (this price only applies if several people are taking lessons at the same time). Many backpackers learn to dive at Leleuvia before going to Taveuni, where such courses are F$250 more expensive. The snorkeling here is also excellent, though the sea is sometimes cold.

Getting there from Levuka costs F$25 pp each way (two-person minimum) from Levuka. Book through Ovalau Watersports. To arrange a transfer from Suva (F$40 pp), call the island direct for instructions. The resort may arrange your taxi from Suva to Waidalice Landing between Nausori and Korovou, where you'll transfer to the Leleuvia boat.

Moturiki Island

In 2002, a 2,600-year-old female skeleton was discovered on the southeast coast of Moturiki Island. The burial style and fragments of Lapita pottery found nearby suggest a connection with Santa Cruz in the Solomon Islands dating back as far as 3,170 years.

Small outboards to Moturiki Island depart Naqeledamu Landing on Ovalau most afternoons. The finest beaches are on the east side of Moturiki. Camping is officially discouraged, but possible.

Naigani Island

Naigani, 11 km off Viti Levu, is a lush tropical island near Ovalau at the west end of the Lomaiviti Group. It's just the right size for exploring on foot, with pristine beaches and only one Fijian village in the southwest corner.

Naigani Island Resort (tel. 330-0925 or 331-2069, www.naigani.com) offers 12 comfortable two-bedroom fan-cooled villas at F$320 for up to five people. Three of the villas have double rooms attached that go for F$185 double by themselves. The meal plans are F$45/65 pp for two/three meals (no cooking facilities). Children under 13 are charged half price for meals and transfers. There's a swimming pool with water slide. Some nonmotorized water sports are free, but fishing trips are charged extra. Scuba diving to sites like Nursery and Swim Through costs F$95/110 for one/two tanks, plus F$20 for gear. At high tide when the sea is calm, some of Fiji's best snorkeling is here. The friendly staff organize many activities for families with children. The daily minibus/launch connection from Suva at 1030 is F$70 pp round-trip. From Levuka, call them up and arrange to be collected by the speedboat at Taviya village on the northwest side of Ovalau (accessible by carrier) at F$35 pp roundtrip.

Yanuca Lailai Island

It was on tiny Yanuca Lailai Island, just off the south end of Ovalau, that the first 463 indentured Indian laborers to arrive in Fiji landed from the ship *Leonidas* on May 14, 1879. To avoid the introduction of cholera or smallpox into Fiji, the immigrants spent two months in quarantine on Yanuca Lailai. Later Nukulau Island off Suva became Fiji's main quarantine station.

It's possible to stay on Yanuca Lailai at **Lost Island Resort**. *Bure* accommodations are F$30 pp, camping F$15 pp. Meals are extra. Current information should be available from Mr. Tavaki (tel. 344-0356) at the Levuka Community Center. Expect to pay F$15 pp each way for the boat over. A day trip from Levuka will be F$30 pp (1000–1600).

OTHER ISLANDS OF THE LOMAIVITI GROUP

Batiki Island

Batiki has a large interior lagoon of brackish water flanked by mudflats. A broad barrier reef surrounds Batiki. Four Fijian villages are on Batiki and you can walk around the island in four hours. Waisea Veremaibau of Yavu village on the north side of the island has accommodated guests in past. Fine baskets are made on Batiki. Due to hazardous reefs, there's no safe anchorage for ships.

Gau Island

Gau is the fifth-largest island in Fiji, with 16 villages and 13 settlements. There's a barrier reef on the west coast, but only a fringing reef on the east. The coop and government station (hospital, post office, etc.) are at Qarani at the north end of Gau. Two ships a week arrive here from Suva on an irregular schedule, but there is no wharf so they anchor offshore. The wharf at Waikama is used only for government boats. The airstrip is on Katudrau Beach at the south end of Gau. The three weekly flights to/from Suva on Air Fiji are F$64 each way.

No guesthouses are currently on Gau. A designer resort called the **Nukuyaweni Outpost** (Kevin Wunrow, tel. 344-0880, www.bayof angels.com) is slowly going up on a point a couple of kilometers southwest of Somosomo. Conceived as a sort of artists' hideaway, it will have four upscale cottages, each with an outdoor bathing grotto. Aside from the swimming pool, guests will be able to enjoy the great snorkeling off the 500-meter beach. There's extraordinary diving in Nigali Passage, just 15 minutes away by boat (large schools of big fish and manta rays).

Koro Island

Koro is an eight-by-16-km island shaped like a shark's tooth. A ridge traverses the island from northeast to southwest, reaching 561 meters near the center. High jungle-clad hillsides drop sharply to the coast. Among Koro's 14 large Fijian villages is Nasau, the government center with post office, hospital, and schools. The road to west coast climbs from Nasau to the high plateau at the center of the island. The coconut trees and mangoes of the coast are replaced by great tree ferns and thick rainforest.

The **Dere Bay Resort** (tel. 330-2631, fax 331-2306, www.derebayresort.com), on a long white beach at the northwestern tip of Koro, opened in October 2000. The three spacious bungalows are F$200 pp including meals (children under 16 half price). There's also a three-bedroom house that rents at the same rate. The *Captain Dan* takes divers out from Dere Bay's dive shop. Sea kayaks are also available. Transfers from the airport/harbor are F$30/20 pp each way.

Koro has an unusual inclined **airstrip** on the east side of the island near Namacu village. You land uphill, take off downhill. Air Fiji can bring you here from Suva once a week (F$92), and several carriers meet the flight.

The weekly **Consort Shipping Line** ferry *Spirit of Fiji Islands* plying between Suva and Savusavu/Taveuni ties up to the wharf near Muanivanua Point. The ship calls northbound in the middle of the night on Wednesdays and Sundays; the southbound trips stop at Koro late Monday and Thursday nights. The fare to/from Suva is F$35 deck one-way.

Makogai Island

Makogai shares a figure-eight-shaped barrier reef with neighboring Wakaya. The anchorage is in Dalice Bay on the northwest side of the island. From 1911 to 1969 this was a leper colony staffed by Catholic nuns and many of the old hospital buildings still stand. Over the years some 4,500 patients sheltered here including many from various other Pacific island groups.

Among the 1,241 souls interred in the patients' cemetery on the hill is Mother Marie Agnes, the "kindly tyrant" who ran the facility for 34 years. Both the British and French governments honored her with their highest decorations, and upon retiring at the age of 80 she commented that "the next medal will be given in heaven." Also buried here is Maria Filomena, a Fijian sister who worked at the colony from its inception. After contracting leprosy in 1925, she joined her patients and continued serving them for another 30 years. Only in 1948 was an effective treatment for leprosy introduced, allowing the colony to be phased out over the next two decades.

Today Makogai is owned by the Department of Agriculture, which runs an experimental sheep farm here, with some 2,000 animals. A new breed intended as a source of mutton and bearing little wool was obtained by crossing British and Caribbean sheep.

Nairai Island

Seven Fijian villages are found on this 336-meter-high island between Koro and Gau. The inhabitants are known for their woven handicrafts. Hazardous reefs stretch out in three directions, and in 1808 the brigantine *Eliza* was wrecked here. Among the survivors was Charles Savage, who served as a mercenary for the chiefs of Bau for five years until falling into the clutches of Vanua Levu cannibals.

Wakaya Island

A high cliff on the west coast of Wakaya is known as Chieftain's Leap, for a young chief who threw himself over the edge to avoid capture by his foes. In those days a hill fort sat at Wakaya's highest point so local warriors could scan the horizon for unfriendly cannibals. Chief Cakobau sold Wakaya to Europeans in 1840, and it has since had many owners. In 1862, David Whippy set up Fiji's first sugar mill on Wakaya.

The German raider Count Felix von Luckner was captured on Wakaya during WW I. His ship, the *Seeadler,* had foundered on a reef at Maupihaa in the Society Islands on August 2, 1917. The 105 survivors (prisoners included) camped on Maupihaa, while on August 23 von Luckner and five men set out in an open boat to capture a schooner and continue the war. On September 21, 1917, they found a suitable ship at Wakaya. Their plan was to go aboard pretending to be passengers and capture it, but a British officer and four Indian soldiers happened upon the scene. Not wishing to go against the rules of chivalry and fight in civilian clothes, the count gave himself up and was interned at Auckland as a prisoner of war. He later wrote a book, *The Sea Devil,* about his experiences.

In 1973, Canadian industrialist David Harrison Gilmour bought the island for US$3 million, and in 1990 he and wife Jill opened **The Wakaya Club** (tel. 344-8128, fax 344-8406, www.wakaya.com), with nine spacious cottages starting at F$3,200 double plus tax, all-inclusive (five-night minimum stay). Children under 16 are not accommodated. The service is excellent, the snorkeling superb, and there's scuba diving, a nine-hole golf course, a swimming pool, and an airstrip for charter flights (F$1,660 roundtrip per couple from Nadi). Only game fishing and massage cost extra. As you might expect at these prices (Fiji's highest!), it's all very tasteful and elegant—just ask Pierce Brosnan, Carol Burnett, Russell Crowe, Tom Cruise, Celine Dion,

Bill Gates, Nicole Kidman, Michelle Pfeiffer, or Burt Reynolds. It's a sort of country club for the rich and famous rather than a trendy social scene. This is one of the only places in Fiji were it's possible to discreetly swim nude. Profits from the resort are used to fund public health and education throughout Fiji. A third of Wakaya has been subdivided into 100 parcels, which are available as homesites; red deer imported from New Caledonia run wild across the rest.

Vanua Levu

Though only half as big as Viti Levu, 5,587-square-km Vanua Levu (Great Land) has much to offer. The transport is good, scenery varied, and people warm and hospitable. Far fewer visitors reach this part of Fiji than heavily promoted Nadi, the Coral Coast, and the Yasawas. Fijian villages are numerous all the way around the island—here you'll be able to experience real Fijian life, so it's well worth making the effort to visit Fiji's second-largest island.

The drier northwest side of Vanua Levu features sugarcane fields and pine forests, while on the damper southeast side copra plantations predominate, with a little cocoa around Natewa Bay. Toward the southeast the scenery is more a bucolic beauty of coconut groves dipping down toward the sea. Majestic bays cut into the island's south side, and one of the world's longest barrier reefs flanks the north coast. There are some superb locations here just waiting to be discovered, both above and below the waterline.

Indo-Fijians live in the large market town of Labasa and the surrounding cane-growing area; most of the rest of Vanua Levu is Fijian. Together Vanua Levu, Taveuni, and adjacent islands form Fiji's Northern Division (often called simply "the north"), which is subdivided into three provinces: The west end of Vanua Levu is Bua Province; most of the north side of Vanua Levu is Macuata Province; and the southeast side of Vanua Levu and Taveuni make up Cakaudrove Province. You won't regret touring this area.

WESTERN VANUA LEVU
Nabouwalu
The ferry from Viti Levu ties up to a wharf in this friendly little government station (the headquarters of Bua Province), near the southern tip of Vanua Levu. The view from the wharf is picturesque, with Seseleka (421 meters) and, in good weather, Yadua Island visible to the northwest. Nabouwalu has a high-technology 24-hour electricity supply system based on windmills and solar panels installed in early 1998. Most of the 600 residents of this area are indigenous Fijians. Three small stores nearby sell groceries. Fijian women in the small market on the corner of the coastal and wharf roads serve a good lunch of fish in *lolo* (coconut milk) for F$3.

The large Patterson Brothers car ferry sails from Natovi on Viti Levu to Nabouwalu around 0800 several times a week (four hours, F$38), returning from Nabouwalu to Natovi at 1230. At Natovi there are immediate bus connections to/from Suva and the boat continues to Ovalau Island where it spends the night. Other days there's a direct Patterson Brothers ferry from Nabouwalu to Ellington Wharf near Rakiraki at 1030 (F$39), where there are connections to Nananu-i-Ra Island and Lautoka. Getting a car onto the ferry without reservations can be difficult, as over a dozen logging trucks are often lined up waiting to go. The schedule often varies due to mechanical problems with Patterson's decrepit fleet. Patterson Brothers runs an express bus between Nabouwalu and Labasa for ferry passengers only (must be booked in conjunction with a ferry ticket). This bus takes only four hours to cover the 137 km to Labasa compared to the six hours required by the four regular buses, which make numerous detours and stops.

East of Nabouwalu
There's a 141-km road along the south coast of Vanua Levu from Nabouwalu to Savusavu, but eastbound only carriers reach as far as Daria, westbound buses as far as Kiobo beyond the for-

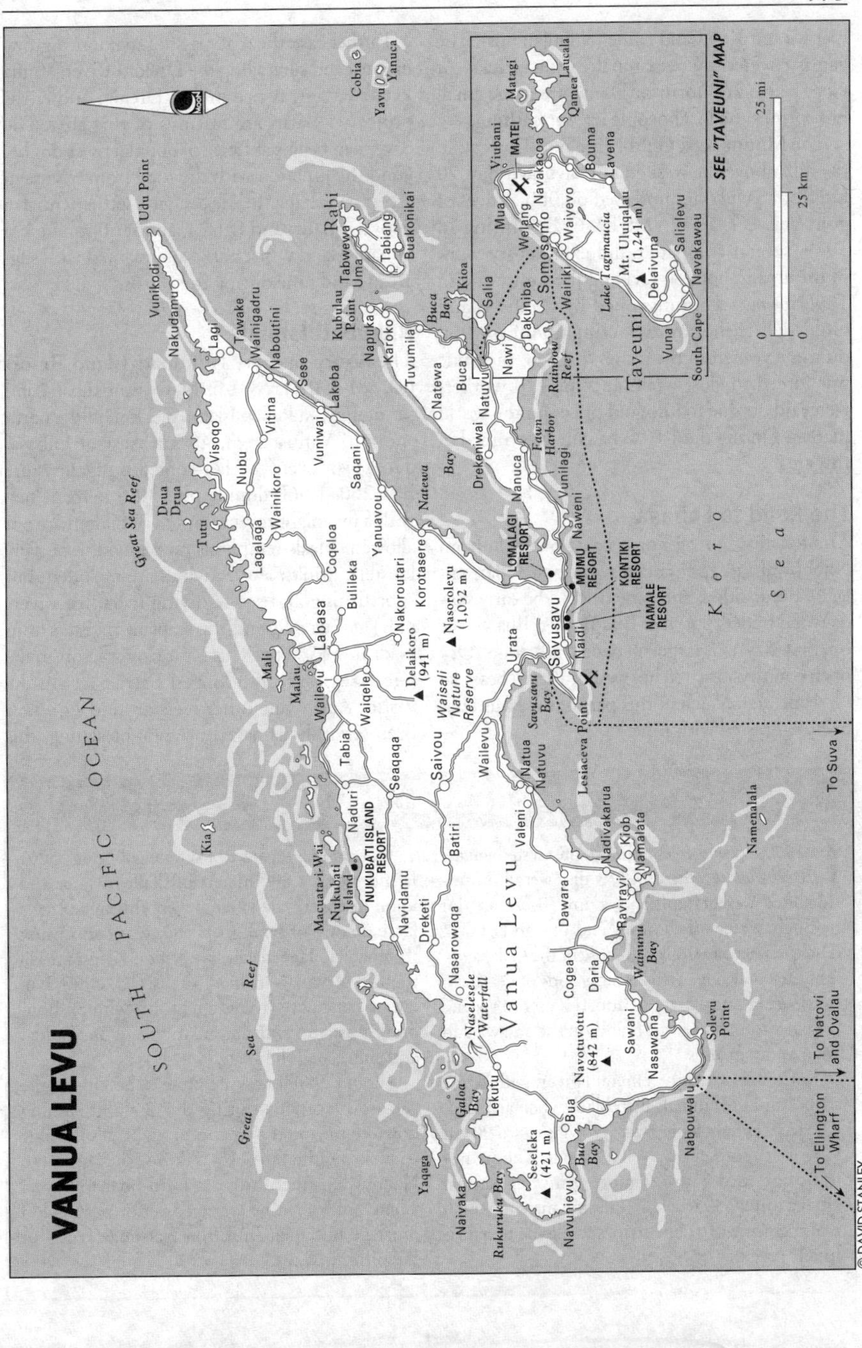
VANUA LEVU
SOUTH PACIFIC OCEAN
Great Sea Reef
Koro Sea
Vanua Levu
Taveuni
Rabi
Udu Point
Vunikodi
Nakudamu
Lagi
Tawake
Wainigadru
Naboutini
Sese
Lakeba
Vitina
Vuniwai
Visoqo
Nubu
Wainikoro
Saqani
Drua Drua
Tutu
Lagalaga
Wainikoro
Coqeloa
Yanuavou
Natewa Bay
Kia
Mali
Malau
Labasa
Bulileka
Nakoroutari
Korotasere
Wailevu
Waiqele
Delaikoro (941 m)
Nasorolevu (1,032 m)
Waisali Nature Reserve
Tabia
Naduri
Seaqaqa
Saivou
Macuata-i-Wai
Nukubati Island
NUKUBATI ISLAND RESORT
Navidamu
Batiri
Dreketi
Nasarowaqa
Naselesele Waterfall
Wailevu
Natua
Natuvu
Valeni
Lesiaceva Point
Savusavu Bay
Savusavu
Naidi
Urata
NAMALE RESORT
KONTIKI RESORT
MUMU RESORT
LOMALAGI RESORT
Naweni
Vunilagi
Nanuca
Fawn Harbor
Drekeniwai
Natuvu
Buca
Natewa
Tuvumila
Karoko
Napuka
Kubulau Point
Buca Bay
Kioa
Salia
Nawi
Dakuniba
Rainbow Reef
Somosomo
Wairiki
Welang
Mua
Navakacoa
Matei
Viubani
Waiyevo
Lake Tagimaucia
Mt. Uluigalau (1,241 m)
Delaivuna
Vuna
South Cape
Navakawau
Salialevu
Lavena
Bouma
Qamea
Laucala
Matagi
Tabwewa
Uma
Tabiang
Buakonikai
Cobia
Yavu
Yanuca
SEE "TAVEUNI" MAP
0 25 mi
0 25 km
Nadivakarua
Kiob
Namalata
Dawara
Raviravi
Wainunu Bay
Cogea
Daria
Sawani
Nasawana
Navotuvotu (842 m)
Solevu Point
Nabouwalu
To Natovi and Ovalau
To Suva
To Ellington Wharf
Bua
Bua Bay
Lekutu
Galoa Bay
Seseleka (421 m)
Yaqaga
Naivaka
Rukuruku Bay
Navunievu
Namenalala

mer Mount Kasi Gold Mine (Kubulau bus). The gap is covered by occasional carrier trucks. At Cogea, five km north of Daria, are some small hot springs the local people use for bathing.

The **Mount Kasi Gold Mine** near Dawara, in the hills above the west end of Savusavu Bay, 70 km from Savusavu, produced 60,000 ounces of gold between 1932 and 1946. Beginning in 1979, several companies did exploratory work in the area in hope of reviving the mine, and in 1996 it was recommissioned by Pacific Island Gold, which began extracting about 40,000 ounces a year from the mine. In 1998, the mine was forced to close again and the 170 workers were laid off due to low gold prices on the world market. During the 1970s, bauxite was mined in this area.

The Road to Labasa

The twisting, tiring north coast bus ride from Nabouwalu to Labasa takes you past Fijian villages, rice paddies, and cane fields. The early sandalwood traders put in at **Bua Bay.** At Bua village on Bua Bay is a large suspension bridge. Dry open countryside stretches west of Bua to Seseleka (421 meters). Much of this part of the island has been reforested with pine.

Farther east, the road passes a major rice-growing area and runs along the **Dreketi River,** Vanua Levu's largest. A rice mill at Dreketi and citrus project at Batiri are features of this area. The pavement begins at Dreketi, but older sections beyond the junction with the road from Savusavu are in bad shape. In the Seaqaqa settlement area between Batiri and Labasa, about 60 square km of native land were cleared and planted with sugarcane and pine during the 1970s.

Nukubati Island

The luxury-category **Nukubati Island Resort** (tel. 881-3901, fax 881-3914, www.nukubati.com) sits on tiny Nukubati Island, one km off the north shore of Vanua Levu, 40 km west of Labasa. The seven oversized fan-cooled bungalows are F$1,260–1,560 double plus 12.5 percent tax, with a five-night minimum stay. Children are not allowed. Meals (emphasis on seafood, especially lobster), drinks, and activities are included, but sportfishing and scuba diving (certified divers only) are extra. Round-trip seaplane transfers from Nadi are F$700 pp. This is the closest resort to the Great Sea Reef, fifth longest barrier reef in the world. And while other reefs around Fiji have been seriously damaged by coral bleaching, this

THE CRESTED IGUANA

In 1979 a new species of lizard, the crested iguana *(Brachylophus vitiensis),* was discovered on uninhabited Yaduatabu Island, a tiny 70-hectare dot in Bligh Water off the west end of Vanua Levu. These iguanas are similar to those of the Galapagos, and they may have arrived thousands of years ago on floating rafts of vegetation. The same species was later found on some islands in the Yasawa and Mamanuca groups.

Both sexes are shiny emerald green with white stripes and the animals turn black when alarmed. The females have longer tails, growing up to 90 cm long. Both sexes have a yellow snout. They're not to be confused with the more common banded iguana found elsewhere in Fiji, the male of which is also green with white stripes while the female is totally green.

Yaduatabu is separated from neighboring Yadua Island by only 200 meters of shallow water and upon discovery the iguanas were threatened by a large colony of feral goats that was consuming their habitat. Fortunately, the National Trust for Fiji took over management of the island, created an iguana sanctuary (www.icffci.com) with an honorary warden from the Fijian village on Yadua, and eliminated the goats.

About 6,000 lizards are present, basking in the sun in the canopy during the day and coming down to the lower branches at night. It's possible to visit Yaduatabu by taking the ferry to Nabouwalu, then hiring a local boat to Yadua where guides can be arranged. Prior permission must be obtained from the National Trust for Fiji office in Suva.

area is less affected. No swimming pool is provided, but the beach consists of white coral sand.

LABASA AND VICINITY

Labasa is a busy Indian market town that services Vanua Levu's major cane-growing area. It's Fiji's fourth-largest town, with 25,000 inhabitants, four banks, and the Northern Division and Macuata Province headquarters. Vanua Levu's only sugar mill is here. Labasa was built on a delta where the shallow Labasa and Oawa rivers enter the sea; maritime transport is limited to small boats. Large ships must anchor off Malau, 11 km north, where Labasa's sugar harvest is loaded. Labasa's lack of an adequate port has hindered development.

Other than providing a good base from which to explore the surrounding countryside and a good choice of places to spend the night, Labasa has little to interest the average tourist. That's its main attraction: Since few visitors come, there's adventure in the air, good food in the restaurants, and fun places to drink for males (a bit rowdy for females). It's not beautiful, but it is real, and the bus ride that brings you here is great. This truly is the "friendly north."

Sights

Labasa has an attractive riverside setting with one long main street lined with shops and restaurants. The park along the riverside near the Labasa Club is quite pleasant.

Sports and Recreation

The **Municipal Swimming Pool** (tel. 881-6387; daily 0900–1800), just before the hospital, is the place to cool off. Admission is F$1.10. A snack bar adjoins the pool, and the Friendly North Inn's nice open bar is only a short walk away.

The **Labasa Sugar Mill**, beside the Oawa River two km east of town, opened in 1894. At the height of the crushing season from May to December there's usually a long line of trucks, tractors, and trains waiting to unload cane at the mill—a picturesque sight. From the road here you get a view of **Three Sisters Hill** to the right.

Around Labasa

The **Snake Temple** (Naag Mandir) at Nagigi, 12 km northeast of Labasa, contains a large rock shaped like a cobra that Hindu devotees swear is growing. Frequent buses pass Naag Mandir.

On your way back to Labasa from Nagigi, ask to be dropped at Bulileka Road, just before the sugar mill. Here you can easily pick up a yellow and blue bus to the **hanging bridge,** a suspension footbridge at Bulileka, six km east of Labasa. Get off the Bulileka bus at Boca Urata where it turns around. The hanging bridge is 150 meters down the road from that point (ask). Cross the bridge and continue through the fields a few hundred meters to the paved road where you can catch another bus back to Labasa. The main reason for coming is to see this picturesque valley, so you may wish to walk part of the way back.

The **Waiqele hot springs** are near a Hindu temple called Shiu Mandir, 14 km southwest of town, about four km beyond Labasa airport, (green and yellow Waiqele bus). Again, the only reason to come is to see a bit of the countryside.

You can get a view of much of Vanua Levu from the telecommunications tower atop **Delaikoro** (941 meters), 25 km south of Labasa, farther down the same road past the airport. Only a 4WD vehicle can make it to the top.

Farther afield is the **Floating Island** in a circular lake at Kurukuru, between Wainikoro and Nubu, 44 km northeast of Labasa (accessible on the Dogotuki, Kurukuru, and Lagalaga buses). It's a 45-minute walk from the turnoff at Lagalaga to Kurukuru. North of Labasa, the pavement ends at Coqeloa.

If you're a surfer, ask about hiring a boat out to the **Great Sea Reef** north of Kia Island, 40 km northwest of Labasa.

Accommodations

Under US$25: The 10-room **Riverview Private Hotel** (tel. 881-1367) is in a quiet two-story concrete building on Namara Street beyond the police station. The four fan-cooled rooms with shared bath are F$25/30 single/double, while another four with private bath are F$30/40. There are also two deluxe air-conditioned rooms with TV, fridge, and hot plate at F$48. The best

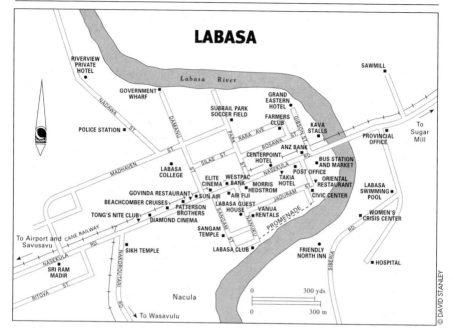

LABASA

deal is the breezy five-bed dormitory with a terrace overlooking the river at F$15 pp (one of the nicest dorms in Fiji). Communal cooking facilities are available. There's a very pleasant riverside bar here. The friendly manager Pardip Singh will do his best to make you feel at home. The gate closes at 2200.

The **Labasa Guest House** (tel. 881-2155), on Nanuku Street, has eight fan-cooled rooms at F$24/30 single/double. Some rooms have a toilet and shower, while others don't, but the price of all is the same (the two back rooms are the best). You can put your own padlock on your door. Communal cooking facilities are provided. There's a laundry room in which to do hand washing. The doors are locked at 2200 and you'll hear a lot of dog and rooster noise through the night.

The four-story **Takia Hotel** (tel. 881-1655, fax 881-3527), at 10 Nasekula Rd. next to the post office, has seven fan-cooled rooms at F$35/45 single/double, 26 air-conditioned rooms at F$66/70, and one family suite at F$90/100, all with private bath. The fan rooms are along the

corridor between the disco and the bar, and will only appeal to party animals (free admission to the disco for hotel guests).

A better medium-priced place is the **Friendly North Inn** (tel. 881-1555, fax 881-6429, countdown@connect.com.fj) on Siberia Road opposite the hospital, about a kilometer from the bus station (F$2 by taxi). They have four rooms with fan at F$35/45 single/double, eight air-conditioned rooms with TV and fridge at F$45/55, two with fan and cooking facilities at F$55 single or double, and two more with air-conditioning and cooking facilities at F$65. Opened in 1996, it's just a short walk from the municipal swimming pool, and the Inn's large open-air bar is a very pleasant place for a beer.

US$25–50: The **Centerpoint Hotel** (tel. 881-1057, fax 881-5057, centerp@connect .com.fj), 24 Nasekula Road, has one fan-cooled room at F$45/55 single/double and 10 air-conditioned rooms at F$55/63. One free breakfast is included with each room (F$6.50 for a second person's breakfast). The upstairs hotel restaurant is not recommended.

The splendid **Grand Eastern Hotel** (tel. 881-1022, fax 881-4011, grest@connect.com.fj) on Gibson Street overlooking the river, just a few minutes' walk from the bus station, reopened in late 1997 after a complete renovation by Hexagon Hotels and is now one of Fiji's top hotels. The 10 standard rooms with terraces in the wing facing the river are F$72 single or double, while the larger deluxe rooms facing the swimming pool are F$98. There are also four suites upstairs in the main two-story building, each capable of accommodating a family of up to five at F$123 double plus F$25 per additional person (children under 12 free). All rooms have air-conditioning, fridge, and private bath. The Grand Eastern's atmospheric dining room and bar retain much of the colonial flavor of the original hotel despite modernization.

Food

The **Oriental Restaurant & Bar** (Mon.–Sat. 1000–1500, 1830–2200, Sun. 1830–2200), next to the bus station, is surprisingly reasonable, with Chinese dishes at F$4–7, grilled dishes at F$5–15, vegetarian dishes at F$2–7, curries at F$3–10, and lobster at F$10–27. Cold bottles of "long neck" Fiji Bitter are served. Thankfully, there's no smoking inside, only out on the balcony.

Simple Fijian, Chinese, and Indian meals are available for under F$4 at many places along Nasekula Road, including the **Wun Wah Cafe** (tel. 881-1653), across from the post office, **Joe's Restaurant** (tel. 881-1766; Mon.–Sat. 0730–2130, Sun. 1100–1500 and 1800–2130), and the **Golden Terrace Restaurant** (tel. 881-8378) below the Centerpoint Hotel, a few doors down.

The **Kwong Tung Restaurant** (tel. 881-1980; Mon.–Sat. 0730–1930, Sun. 1100–1500), 18 Nasekula Road opposite the Takia Hotel, is hugely popular for breakfast and lunch, with large crowds of locals (no beer served).

The **Govinda Restaurant** (tel. 881-1364; Mon.–Sat. 0730–1800), on Nasekula Road next to Sun Air, offers a choice of four tasty vegetarian *thali* (plate meals) priced F$2–7 (the F$4 *thali* includes three curries, dhal, chutney, two roti, and palau rice).

Breakfast is hard to order in Labasa, although several places along the main street will serve buttered cakes and coffee.

Entertainment

Elite Cinema (tel. 881-1260) has films in English and Hindi, and there are shows at 1300 and 2000. **Diamond Cinema** (tel. 881-1471) is often used for special events, including local variety shows.

This is a predominantly Indo-Fijian town, so most of the nightlife is male oriented. The **Labasa Club** (tel. 881-1304) and the **Farmers Club** (tel. 881-1633) both serve cheap beer in a congenial atmosphere. Couples will feel more comfortable at the Labasa Club than at the Farmers, and there are two large snooker tables inside and a nice terrace out back facing the river (both open daily 1000–2200).

The **Bounty Nightclub** (tel. 881-1655; Wed.–Sat. 2100–0100) at the Takia is accessible via an orange stairway on the side of the building. A much rougher place frequented mostly by indigenous Fijians is **Tong's Nite Club** (tel. 925-4918; Wed.–Sat. 2000–0100), 66 Nasekula Road near Diamond Cinema.

Indian **firewalking** takes place once a year sometime between June and October at Agnimela Mandir, the Firewalkers Temple at Vunivau, five km northeast of Labasa.

Information and Services

There's a public library (tel. 881-2617; Mon.–Fri. 0900–1300, 1400–1700, Sat. 0900–1200) in the Civic Center near Labasa Bus Station.

The ANZ Bank is opposite the bus station, and the Westpac Bank is farther west on Nasekula Road. Both provide ATMs outside their offices.

The public fax number at Labasa Post Office is fax 881-3666.

You can check your email at the Govinda Internet Café (tel. 881-1364) in the back of the restaurant of the same name on Nasekula Road.

Public toilets are behind the market.

Health

The Northern District Hospital (tel. 881-1444), northeast of the river, is open 24 hours a day for emergencies.

Less serious medical problems should be taken to a private doctor, such as Dr. Pardeep Singh (tel. 881-3824; weekdays 0800–1300 and 1400–1600, Sat. 0800–1200), on Reddy Place next to the Civic Center. A private dentist, Dr. Ashwin Kumar Lal (tel. 881-4077), is on Jaduram Street near the Labasa Guest House.

The Labasa Women's Crisis Center (tel. 881-4609; weekdays 0830–1430, www.fijiwomen .com), in Bayly House on Siberia Road near the Municipal Swimming Pool, offers free and confidential counseling for women.

Nasekula Drug Store (tel. 881-1178) is on Nasekula Road opposite the post office.

Transportation

Air Fiji (tel. 881-1188), on Nasekula Road opposite the Westpac Bank, has service five times a day between Labasa and Suva (F$139). **Sun Air** (tel. 881-1454; Mon.–Fri. 0800–1700, Sat. 0800–1200), at Northern Travel on the corner of Nasekula Road and Damanu Street, flies to Nadi (F$175) and Suva (F$147) twice daily, to Taveuni (F$75) twice a week. Most flights to Nadi are via Suva. Check signs outside their office for special reduced fares.

To get to the airport, 10 km southwest of Labasa, take a taxi (F$8) or the green and yellow Waiqele bus. Sun Air has a bus based at the airport that brings arriving passengers into town free of charge, but departing passengers must sometimes find their own way from Labasa to the airport. Air Fiji's bus takes passengers to/from the airport at F$.85 pp (free for Air Fiji passengers).

Patterson Brothers Shipping (tel. 881-2444; Mon.–Fri. 0830–1330, 1430–1630, Sat. 0830–1200) has an office near Sun Air on Nasekula Road where you can book your bus/ferry/bus ticket through to Suva via Nabouwalu and Natovi (10 hours, F$54). This bus leaves Labasa at 0600 several times a week, and passengers arrive in Suva at 1830. There's also a direct bus/boat/bus connection from Labasa to Lautoka (F$60) via Ellington Wharf (near Nananu-i-Ra Island) several times a week, and another service straight through to Levuka.

The Wun Wah Cafe (tel. 881-1653), across from the post office, books the **Raja Ferry Ser**vices (tel. 881-8587) bus/boat to Taveuni, departing weekdays at 0530 (seven hours, F$20).

There are three regular buses a day (at 0630, 1030, and 1400) to Nabouwalu (210 km, F$8), a dusty, tiring six-hour trip. Another five buses a day (at 0700, 0800, 0930, 1230, and 1615) run from Labasa to Savusavu (94 km, three hours, F$6), a very beautiful ride on an excellent paved highway over the Waisali Saddle between the Korotini and Valili mountains and along the palm-studded coast. Take the early bus before clouds obscure the views.

Rental cars are available from **Vanua Rentals** (tel. 881-3512, fax 881-3754), in the Mobil service station on the corner of Nanuku and Jadaram Streets. Their cars start at F$125 a day, insurance included (F$1,500 deductible). **Budget Rent A Car** (tel. 881-1999) is at Niranjans Mazda dealership on Zoing Place up Ivi Street from opposite the Jame Mosque west of town. Obtaining gasoline outside the two main towns is difficult, so tank up.

NATEWA BAY AND UDU POINT

Natewa Bay is the largest bay in the South Pacific, almost dissecting the island of Vanua Levu. It's an area seldom visited by tourists, although a daily bus service between Labasa and Savusavu makes it easily accessible. The sea kayaking is often good along this coast.

A unique feature of Natewa Bay is the "dolphin calling" trips when a Fijian boatman "calls" dolphins using traditional magic. It's said to work every time when the bay is flat and calm, and that two pods totaling as many as 100 dolphins can be seen!

At Udu Point, Vanua Levu's northeastern-most tip, a Meridian Wall was built in 1999 just west of Vunikodi village to mark the spot where the 180-degree meridian and international date line cut across the island. Both sunset and sunrise can be observed from the wall.

Accommodations

Don and Seta Chute operate the **Udurara Resort** (no phone) at Udu Point. Until Hurricane Ami devastated the area in January 2003 they had six *bure,* but four were destroyed. Backpack-

FIJI'S FINEST BUS RIDE

The scenic seven-hour bus ride between Labasa and Savusavu via Natewa Bay is like a trip through two distinct countries. For the first few hours you're among sugar fields or dry barren hills, and the bus passengers around you will be mostly Indo-Fijian. Then you climb through a thickly forested area with few farms, and as the road drops again, extensive coconut plantations begin to appear. You look over your shoulder and notice that most of the bus passengers are now indigenous Fijians. Then comes the spectacular ride down Natewa Bay, climbing over lush headlands or roaring along the beach. Your first glimpse of Savusavu Bay as the bus lumbers slowly over the hill beyond the airport is a thrilling culmination to this fascinating trip.

here across to the mountains of southwestern Vanua Levu and down the coast toward Nabouwalu is superlatively lovely. In the 1860s, Europeans arrived to establish coconut plantations. They mixed with the Fijians, and even though the copra business went bust in the 1930s, their descendants and the Fijian villagers still supply copra to a coconut oil mill, eight km west of Savusavu, giving this side of Vanua Levu a pleasant agricultural air. In 2000, the first pearl farms were established on the far side of Nawi Island, and this is an industry that is bound to grow. Savusavu's urban population of 5,000 is almost evenly split between Indo-Fijians and indigenous Fijians, with many part-Fijians here too. One of Fiji's largest white expatriate communities is also present.

Savusavu is Vanua Levu's main port, and cruising yachts often rock at anchor offshore, sheltered from the open waters of Savusavu Bay by Nawi Island. The surrounding mountains and reefs also make Savusavu a well-protected hurricane refuge. The diving possibilities of this area were recognized by Jean-Michel Cousteau in 1990 when he selected Savusavu as the base for his Project Ocean Search. Access to good snorkeling is difficult, however, as the finest beaches are under the control of the top-end resorts and much other shore access is over extremely sharp karst. Although much smaller than Labasa, Savusavu is the administrative center of Cakaudrove Province and has three banks. In recent years, tourism has taken off around Savusavu, with new resorts springing up, though the town is far from spoiled.

ers now stay in the remaining two at F$50 pp including meals. The Chutes have an electric generator, but one should not expect to find luxuries in this remote location. To get there you must "charge" (charter) hire a boat from Wainigadru, where the Natewa Bay buses call. This will cost F$50 if it's a 15-hp outboard (one hour trip) or F$80 for a 40-hp boat (35 minute trip). If you're lucky you'll find a "returning boat" (one that is planning to make the trip anyway) from Wainigadru to Udu Point and will only need to pay F$13 pp. For information on staying at the Udurara Resort, speak to Mr. Pat Chute (tel. 881-6749) who owns Valu City, the shop closest to the river behind the Oriental Restaurant at Labasa.

Transportation

A Vishnu Holdings (tel. 885-0276) bus between Labasa and Savusavu takes the roundabout route via Natewa Bay, departing both ends at 0900 every morning (seven hours, F$11.50). Other Natewa Bay buses from Savusavu may finish their runs at Yanauavou or Wainigadru.

SAVUSAVU AND VICINITY

Savusavu is a picturesque little town opposite Nawi Island on Savusavu Bay. The view from

Sights

The one main street through Savusavu consists of a motley collection of Indian and Chinese shops, parked taxis, loitering locals, and a clutch of tourists. The **market** in the center of town always bustles, but is biggest early Saturday morning. Notice the kava dens behind the market. Nearby, the **Handicraft Center** (tel. 888-3095; weekdays 0730–1700, Sat. 0730–1400), behind the Savusavu Town Council opposite the ANZ Bank, displays numerous grotesque masks with a few good objects mixed in.

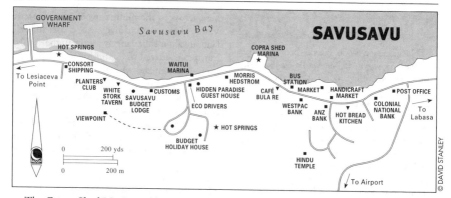

The **Copra Shed Marina** is like a small museum with map displays and historical photos, information boards, fancy boutiques, and many of Savusavu's tourist services. In front of the marina is a stone dated to 1880, which is said to be from Fiji's first copra mill. To the west is Savusavu's second yachting center, the **Waitui Marina,** run by Curly Carswell of Eco Divers. A wonderful scenic viewpoint (and romantic spot to watch a sunset) is on the hill just above and west of the Hot Springs Hotel, above the Waitui Marina.

Visit the small **hot springs** boiling out among fractured coral below and behind the Hot Springs Hotel. Residents use the springs to cook native vegetables; bathing is not possible. These and smaller hot springs along the shore of Savusavu Bay across the street from Consort Shipping near the main wharf remind one that the whole area was once a caldera.

For a good circle trip, take a taxi from Savusavu past the airport to **Nukubalavu** village (six km, F$7), at the end of road along the south side of the peninsula. From here you can walk west along the beach to the Cousteau Fiji Islands Resort on **Lesiaceva Point** in about an hour at low tide. Try to avoid cutting through the resort at the end of the hike, as the Cousteau management disapproves (all beaches in Fiji are public up to two meters above the high tide mark). From Lesiaceva it's six km by road back to Savusavu.

For some mountain hiking ask one of the Labasa buses to drop you at the entrance to the **Waisali Nature Reserve** established by the National Trust for Fiji in 1991, about 40 km northwest of Savusavu. This 116-hectare reserve protects one of Vanua Levu's last unexploited tropical rainforests with native species such as the *dakua, yaka,* and *kuasi* well represented. Some of Fiji's few remaining giant kauri trees are here. A nature trail leads to viewpoints offering sweeping views.

Sports and Recreation

Eco Divers (Curly Carswell, tel. 885-0122 or 885-0345, fax 885-0344, channel 16 or 80, www.ecodivers-tours.com), behind the BP service station opposite the Waitui Marina, offers scuba diving, snorkeling, sailing, village visits, rainforest tours, and guided hiking. They charge F$146 for a two-tank boat dive (plus F$22 for gear), or F$557 including the manual for a PADI open-water certification course. Snorkeling from the boat is F$25 pp for two people (two hours). Eco Divers and the Cousteau Fiji Islands Resort use 21 of the same buoyed dive sites off southern Vanua Levu. Ocean kayak rental is F$30/40 a day for a single/double kayak, a catamaran F$15 an hour, mountain bikes F$15/25 for four/eight hours.

Savusavu Game Fishing (tel. 885-0195), based at the Hot Springs Hotel, has a fast game fishing boat for hire at F$400/600 a half/full day for the boat. Two or three people can go for that price. You'll be trawling for trevally, tuna, sailfish, marlin, or wahu (they recommend "tag and release" for billfish).

Accommodations

Under US$25: The **Copra Shed Marina Apartments** (tel. 885-0457, coprashed@connect.com.fj), above the Captain's Café in the Copra Shed Marina, has two apartments for rent. One is F$45 for up to three persons with the shower downstairs, the other F$75 accommodating four with private bath. Both have cooking facilities.

Hidden Paradise Guest House (Graham and Elenoa Weatherall, tel. 885-0106), just beyond Morris Hedstrom, has six rather hot wooden rooms at F$15 pp with fan and shared bath (F$20 pp with air conditioning), including a good self-service breakfast. Cooking and washing facilities are provided, and it's clean and friendly—don't be put off by the plain exterior. The restaurant here is inexpensive and good.

David Manohar Lal's six-room **Budget Holiday House** (tel. 885-0149), also known as "David's Place," is just behind the Hot Springs Hotel. Five rooms with shared bath cost F$25/30 double/triple and one four-person family room is F$30. The seven-bed dorm is F$15 pp, while camping is F$9/15 single/double. Stay more than a week and you'll get 10 percent off and free laundry service. The shortage of blankets and sheets is a drawback. All rates include a cooked breakfast and there's a well-equipped kitchen. David's a delightful character to meet and also a strict Seventh-Day Adventist, so no alcoholic beverages are allowed on the premises. A cacophony of dogs, roosters, and the neighbor's kids will bid you good morning. It's often used by people from Eco Divers.

Savusavu Budget Lodge (tel. 885-3127, fax 885-3157), a two-story concrete building on the main street, has eight standard rooms with bath at F$17/30 single/double and five air-conditioned rooms at F$45 single or double, breakfast included. Their restaurant (daily 0800–2300) serves meals in the F$3.50–5 range. Though this place was recently renovated, it shouldn't be your first choice.

US$25–50: The **Hot Springs Hotel** (Lorna Eden, tel. 885-0195, fax 885-0430, hotsprings hotel@connect.com.fj), on the hillside overlooking Savusavu Bay, is named for the nearby thermal springs and steam vents. There are 48 rooms, all with balconies offering splendid views. Fan rooms on the second floor are F$80 single or double, while the air-conditioned rooms on the third and fourth floors are F$125. The four ground floor rooms each have three dorm beds at F$25 pp including breakfast. No beach is nearby, but the swimming pool terrace is pleasant. Many sporting activities can be arranged. This former Travelodge is a convenient, medium-priced choice, and the hotel bar is open daily including Sunday. Catch the sunset here.

The **Vatukaluvi Holiday House** (tel. 885-0397, coprashed@connect.com.fj), on the south side of the peninsula, one km west of Savusavu airport, accommodates four people at F$100 for the whole breezy house (or a reduced rate for two weeks). Cooking facilities and fridge are provided, and there's good snorkeling off the beach. Ask for Geoff Taylor, vice-commodore of the Savusavu Yacht Club, at the Copra Shed Marina. A taxi to Vatukaluvi will cost F$4 from the airport, F$6 from Savusavu.

US$50–100: Until recently the **Daku Resort** (Robin Irwin, tel. 885-0046, fax 885-0334, www.dakuresort.com), one km west of the ferry landing, was called Beachcomber's Driftwood Village and was run by the Beachcomber Island crowd from Lautoka. Beachcomber couldn't make a go of it, and in 2004 this "upscale budget" property was relaunched. The four tin-roofed garden *bure* with fan and fridge (but no cooking) on the nicely landscaped grounds just below the pool go for F$95 single or double, while two larger family bungalows above the restaurant rent for F$110. If you want a kitchen, there's a cottage (F$110) and villa (F$135) on the hill. A self-catering, two-bedroom "beach house" next to the entrance is F$150. Included in all rates is tax and a "Planter's Breakfast" served in the large restaurant next to the swimming pool (dinner here is F$15 but lunch is not available). A mediocre beach just across the dusty road has some snorkeling possibilities though the visibility isn't the best (and don't leave valuables unattended). Airport transfers are F$5 pp each way.

US$250 and up: In 1994, oceanographer Jean-Michel Cousteau, son of the famous Jacques Cousteau, purchased a hotel on Lesiaceva Point, six km southwest of Savusavu. The **Jean-Michel Cousteau Fiji Islands Resort** (tel. 885-0188, fax 885-0340, www.fijiresort.com) stylishly recreates a Fijian village with 25 authentic-looking thatched *bure*. Garden accommodations, airport transfers, and all meals begin at F$875 double, plus 12.5 percent tax. In line with the eco-tourism theme, all rooms have fans but no air-conditioning, telephones, or cooking facilities. Bring insect repellent. The restaurant is built like a towering pagan temple, and nonguests wishing to dine there *must* reserve (it's pricey and the food could be better). Children under 13 eat and sleep free when sharing with their parents, and the resort's Bula Camp (operating from 0900–2100) is designed to help those aged three to nine learn while having fun. This resort also caters to the romantic couples market with spa and massage treatments (beginning at F$120), private island picnics (F$88 per couple), and pier dining by candlelight (F$62 for the set-up). Free activities include sailing, kayaking, glass bottom boat trips, tennis, yoga, water aerobics in the freshwater pool, videos, slide shows, tours and evenings with the on-site marine biologist or cultural host, rain forest trips, and visits to a local Fijian village. In addition, the outstanding on-site dive operation "L'Aventure Cousteau" offers scuba diving (F$135/230 for one/two tanks plus tax and gear), PADI/TDI scuba instruction (F$905 plus tax for full certification), and underwater photography courses (F$300 plus tax). Cousteau himself is in residence occasionally and he joins guests on the morning dive when he's in the mood. There's good snorkeling off their beach (ask about Split Rock), though the resort's large Private Property signs warn nonguests to keep out. A taxi from Savusavu will run F$6.

Food

Italian Pizza (tel. 925-9604; daily 1130–2100), below Savusavu Budget Lodge, is run by a Napoletano named Alberto and his local wife Ana. They serve 14 varieties of real Italian pizza priced F$7–20.

The breakfast buffet (F$3.50, or F$5 including eggs) at the **Seaview Restaurant** (tel. 885-0106; daily 0700–1000), at Hidden Paradise Guest House near the Waitui Marina, is an outstanding value. Monday to Saturday from 0900–1600 you can get an excellent curry lunch here for F$3.50.

The **Captain's Café** (tel. 885-0511; open Mon.–Fri. 0830–2030, Sat. 0900–2100, Sun. 1100–2030) at the Copra Shed Marina is a yachtie hangout. Breakfast is F$6–9, pizzas F$7–24, dinner F$10–15. In the evening the outdoor seating on the wharf is nice but the food is nothing special.

The trendy **Bula Re Restaurant** (tel. 885-0307; Mon.–Sat. 0900–2100, Sun. 1700–2200), opposite the bus station, is the place to be seen by other tourists. They offer breakfast (F$5–8), crepes (F$6–8.50), lunch specials (F$6–9), ice cream with coffee (under F$5), Chinese dishes (F$6–10), and a wide range of dinner dishes for under F$20. The food is "absolutely okay."

The **Country Kitchen** (tel. 885-0829; daily 0600–1800), near the Westpac Bank opposite the bus station, offers large servings of curries, chop suey, and fried rice at F$3.50. **Charans Food Center** (tel. 885-0448; Mon.–Sat. 0700–1800, Sun. 0700–1600) nearby is more crowded and not as good.

The spacious **Chong Pong Restaurant** (tel. 885-0588), above a supermarket opposite Savusavu Market, serves local chicken, pork, beef, mutton, seafood, and vegetarian meals at F$4–8. You can even order a beer!

Savusavu's best Chinese restaurant, however, is the **Wing Yuen Restaurant** (tel. 885-0108), near the Colonial National Bank. Most of their chicken, beef, pork, seafood, fried rice, and chow mein plates are F$6–10. Don't be deceived by the shabby exterior or surly staff: The food is good and alcohol is available.

Entertainment

Drinkers can repair to the **Planters Club** (tel. 885-0233; Mon.–Thurs. 1000–2200, Friday and Sat. 1000–2300, Sun. 1000–2000) toward the wharf—this place never runs out of Fiji Bitter. The weekend dances at the club are local events. Despite the Members Only sign, visitors are welcome. It's a vintage colonial club.

The **White Stork Tavern,** next to the Planters Club, is a rough public bar open Mon.–Sat. 1130–2100.

The bar at the **Copra Shed Marina** (daily 1100–2200) is rather hidden in the northeast corner of the building—ask. Happy hour is Wednesday and Friday 1730–1830.

The bar at the **Waitui Marina** (tel. 885-0122; daily 1130–2200, until midnight Tues., Thurs., and Sat.) organizes a *lovo* or curry night on Thursdays and a barbecue on Saturdays (both F$8). Book before 1000 at Eco Divers across the street.

The beer on tap at the **Hot Springs Hotel** (tel. 885-0195) is produced in their own microbrewery at the bottom of the hill below the hotel. Savusavu Draft comes in bitter, lager, and ale varieties.

Information and Services

A shop in the Copra Shed Marina sells nautical charts.

The ANZ Bank (with an ATM), Colonial National Bank, and Westpac Bank all have branches in Savusavu.

Internet access is available for F$.35 a minute at Savusavu Real Estate (tel. 885-0929; Mon.–Fri. 0800–1700, Sat. 0830–1200, savusavurealest@ connect.com.fj) in the Copra Shed Marina.

DHL Express Internet (tel. 885-0801; weekdays 0900–1600), at Plantation Real Estate next to Morris Hedstrom, also charges F$.35 a minute and is less crowded.

At the Bula Re Restaurant (tel. 885-0307), opposite the bus station, you can use a computer to check email for a mere F$.30 a minute.

Free public toilets are behind the Town Council office opposite the ANZ Bank.

Yachting Facilities

The Copra Shed Marina (tel. 885-0457, fax 885-0989, coprashed@connect.com.fj) near the bus station allows visiting yachts to moor alongside at F$10 a day. Anchorage and use of the facilities by the whole crew is F$6 a day. You can have your laundry done for F$7 (wash and dry).

The Waitui Marina (tel. 885-0122) offers similar services. In fact, Waitui's owner, Curly Carswell of Eco Divers, will probably come out to meet you in his boat and will guide you to the anchorage, provided he gets wind of your arrival over channels 16 or 80. Curly's a great source of local information and quite a character.

Yachts can clear Fiji customs in Savusavu. Ar-

riving yachts should contact the Copra Shed Marina over VHF 16. The customs office (tel. 885-0727; weekdays 0800–1300 and 1400–1600), where yachties must report after the quarantine check, is next to Savusavu Budget Lodge west of the Waitui Marina. After clearing quarantine and customs controls, yachties can proceed to the Immigration Department, across the street from the Waitui Marina. If you check in after 1630 or on weekends or holidays there's an additional charge on top of the usual quarantine fee.

Health

The District Hospital (tel. 885-0444; open 0830–1600) is two kilometers east of Savusavu on the road to Labasa (taxi F$2).

Dr. Joeli Taoi's Savusavu Private Health Center (tel. 885-0721; Mon.–Thurs. 0830–1600, Friday 0830–1400) is between the Colonial National Bank and the post office.

Transportation

Air Fiji (tel. 885-0538), at the Copra Shed Marina, flies into Savusavu twice daily from Suva (F$111) and Taveuni (F$74). **Sun Air** (tel. 885-0141), in the Copra Shed Marina, has flights to Savusavu twice daily from Nadi (F$159) and Taveuni (F$75). The airstrip is beside the main highway, three km east of town. Local buses to Savusavu pass the airport about once an hour, or take a taxi for F$4.

Consort Shipping Line Ltd. (tel. 885-0443, fax 885-0442), beside the Planters Club, runs the large car ferry MV *Spirit of Fiji Islands* from Suva to Savusavu (14 hours, F$42/77 deck/cabin). The ferry leaves Savusavu southbound Monday and Thursday at 1900, calling at Koro on the way to Suva. Wednesday at midnight and Sunday at 0900, the "Sofi" leaves Savusavu for Taveuni (F$22 deck). These schedules often change.

Beachcomber Cruises (tel. 885-0266, fax 885-0499), at the Copra Shed Marina, runs the 65-meter car ferry MV *Adi Savusavu* from Savusavu direct to Suva Wednesday, Friday, and Sunday at 1900 (F$43/64 economy/first class). It leaves Savusavu for Taveuni Wednesday and Friday at 0100 and Sunday at 0600 (F$22/42).

Charans Food Center (tel. 885-8587), next to the Westpac Bank opposite the bus station, sells tickets on the **Raja Ferry Services** bus/boat to Taveuni, departing weekdays at 0830 (F$15).

If you're interested in getting aboard a cruising yacht as unpaid crew, put up a notice advertising yourself at both yacht clubs and ask around.

Regular buses leave Savusavu for Labasa at 0730, 0930, 1300, 1430, and 1530, Sunday at 0930, 1300, and 1530 only (92 km, three hours, F$6). This ride over the Waisali Saddle is one of the most scenic in Fiji.

Otherwise, there's the seven-hour bus ride from Savusavu to Labasa via Natewa Bay (F$11.50), over twice as long but even more intriguing. It departs each end at 0900 daily.

The Kubulau bus to Kiobo, west of Savusavu toward Nabouwalu, departs weekdays at 0900 and 1500, Saturday at 1400.

Buses along the Hibiscus Highway from Savusavu to Buca Bay and Napuka leave at 1030 and 1430 daily except Sunday (three hours, F$6.30). Shorter runs to villages like Naweni are more frequent.

Buses leave Savusavu for Lesiaceva Point at 0730, 1200, 1400, and 1600 (F$.70). For more information on buses headed south or east of Savusavu, call Vishnu Holdings at tel. 885-0276.

Numerous taxis congregate at Savusavu market; they're quite affordable for short trips in the vicinity.

Tours

Eco Divers (tel. 885-0122, www.ecodivers-tours.com), opposite the Waitui Marina, offers a variety of day tours, including a village tour (F$25), plantation tour (F$25), and a Waisali Reserve tour (F$40). They only need two participants to run a tour.

Trip 'N Tour Travel (tel. 885-3154, fax 885-0344), in the Copra Shed Marina, also arranges local sightseeing tours at F$25–90 (minimum of two persons) depending on what's offered. Trip 'N Tour also represents Budget Rent a Car with 4WD vehicles starting at F$122 a day, plus F$22 insurance.

Cruises to Koro or the Lau Group on the three-masted schooner *Tui Tai* discussed under Get-

ting There in this book's Exploring the Islands chapter can be booked at **Tui Tai Adventure Cruises** (tel. 885-3032, fax 885-3026, www.tuitai.com) in the Copra Shed Marina. They also offer a day cruise around Savusavu Bay Tuesdays from 1000–1600 at F$99 pp including lunch and kayaking on the Nasekawa River.

SeaHawk Charters (tel. 885-0787, seahawk@connect.com.fj) offers a five-hour yacht cruise on Savusavu Bay at F$85 pp including lunch (minimum of two). The two-hour sunset cruise is F$50 pp (two-person minimum). The 16-meter yacht *SeaHawk* can be chartered at reasonable rates. Eco Divers takes SeaHawk bookings.

NAMENALALA ISLAND

Moody's Namena (tel. 881-3764, fax 881-2366, www.moodysnamenafiji.com), on a narrow high island southwest of Savusavu in the Koro Sea, is one of Fiji's top hideaways. In 1984, Tom and Joan Moody leased Namenalala from the Fiji government, which needed a caretaker to protect the uninhabited island from poachers. Their present resort occupies less than 10 percent of Namenalala's 45 hectares, leaving the rest as a nesting ground to great flocks of red-footed boobies, banded rails, and Polynesian starlings. Giant clams proliferate in the surrounding waters within the 24-km **Namena Barrier Reef,** and from November to March hawksbill turtles haul themselves up onto the island's golden sands to lay their eggs (Namenalala is the last important nesting site for hawksbills left in Fiji). The corals along the nearby drop-offs are fabulous, and large pelagic fish glide in from the Koro Sea. Sea snakes abound. The Moodys have fought long and hard to protect Namenalala's fragile reefs from live-aboards that sometimes use them for high impact night diving.

Each of the Moody's six bamboo and wood hexagonal-shaped *bure* are perched on clifftops, allowing panoramic views, while still well tucked away in the lush vegetation to ensure maximum privacy. Illuminated by romantic gas lighting, each features a private hardwood terrace with 270-degree views. Alternative energy is used as much as possible to maintain the atmosphere (though a diesel generator used to do the laundry and recharge batteries).

The cost to stay here is F$498/708 single/double plus tax, including all meals (five-night minimum stay). The food is excellent, thanks to Joan's firm hand in the kitchen and Tom's island-grown produce. (One reader found the food too "American" and would have preferred more fresh fish.) The ice water on the tables and in the *bure* is a nice touch, but they don't sell liquor, so bring your own. In the evening it's very quiet. Namenalala is in a rain shadow so insects are not a problem.

This resort is perfect for bird-watching, fishing, and snorkeling, and scuba diving is available at F$169 plus tax for two tanks (certification card required). The soft corals at Namenalala are among the finest in the world and the diversity of species is greater than on the Barrier Reef. If you want a holiday that combines unsullied nature with interesting characters and a certain elegance, you won't go wrong here. The remoteness is reflected in the price of getting there. Pacific Island Seaplanes charges F$2,400 round-trip per couple for transfers from Nadi. Transfers from Savusavu in an 11-meter Searov boat are F$250 pp each way. Moody's closes in March and April every year.

BUCA BAY
Along the Hibiscus Highway

This lovely coastal highway runs 75 km east from Savusavu to Natuvu on Buca Bay, then up the east coast of Vanua Levu to the Catholic mission station of **Napuka** at the end of the peninsula. In 2001, the first 20 km or so east of Savusavu was paved.

Old frame mansions from the heyday of the 19th-century planters and 21st-century homes of newly-arrived foreigners can be spotted among the palms, and offshore you'll see tiny flowerpot islands where the sea has undercut the coral rock. Buca Bay is a recognized "hurricane hole," where ships can find shelter during storms. Former Prime Minister Rabuka hails from **Drekeniwai** village on Natewa Bay.

Buses to Savusavu leave Buca Bay at 0800 and 1600 (75 km, three hours, F$5). The ferry *Raja* leaves Natuvu for Taveuni weekdays at 1100 (F$7). It's a beautiful boat trip, but can be rough if the wind is up.

Accommodations

The most pretentious place around Savusavu is the **Namale Fiji Resort** (Anthony Robbins, tel. 885-0435, fax 885-0400, www.namalefiji.com) on a white-sand beach nine km east of Savusavu. The superb food, great entertainment, and refined atmosphere amid exotic landscapes and refreshing beaches make this one of Fiji's most exclusive resorts. The 13 thatched *bure* begin at F$1,580 single or double, and rise to F$2,180 for the honeymoon *bure* with a private wading pool on its deck (add 12.5 percent tax to these nightly rates). Included are gourmet meals and drinks, airport transfers, and all activities other than scuba diving. Private seminars in a 60-seat conference center are now Namale's stock in trade. It caters only to in-house guests—there's no provision for sightseers who'd like to stop in for lunch. Children under 12 are also banned.

The **Koro Sun Resort** (tel. 885-0262, fax 885-0352, www.korosunresort.com) is 14 km east of Savusavu on the Hibiscus Highway. The 13 tasteful hillside and garden bungalows start at F$454/555 single/double, plus 12.5 percent tax. Three of the two-bedroom bungalows are F$566/667, while another with two bathrooms is F$647/748. Included are meals but not drinks. Set in a well-kept coconut grove, the Koro Sun has nearby many interesting caves, pools, trails, falls, ponds, and lakes to explore. The resort's own "Rainforest Spa" offers massage and body treatments. Scuba diving is available at Koro Sun's private marina (F$190 plus tax for two tanks), including underwater weddings! A dive site known as Dream House (a deep water pinnacle) is right at Koro Sun's front door. The snorkeling is fine as well, but the nearest swimmable beach is a kilometer away. There are two swimming pools, a waterslide, two tennis courts, sportfishing, sea kayaking, mountain biking and many other activities (non-motorized sports are included). The nine-hole golf course is pitted with crab holes and gets swampy after rains, but it's picturesque. It's too hilly for golf carts to be used.

Vanua Levu's only real backpacker camp, **Mumu Resort** (Rosie Edris, tel. 885-0416), 17 km east of Savusavu, occupies on the site of the spiritual home of Radini Mumu, a legendary queen of Fiji. The nine *bure* are F$45 single or double, the four bunkhouse rooms F$40 single or double, and the four-person "dream house" F$130. There's also a six-bed dorm at F$17 pp, and you can camp for F$8 pp. Communal cooking and bathing facilities are available, and Mumu's kitchen serves tasty Fijian and European dishes. Mumu is surrounded by the Koro Sea on three sides, and two small uninhabited islands nearby are easily accessible. Although the scenery is good, the snorkeling is poor; it's a very long swim over a shallow flat before reaching a snorkelable area. There's no hot water, and one must be aware of their dogs. A taxi here from Savusavu should be F$15, a bus around F$1.

Ms. Collin McKenny from Seattle owns and operates the upscale **Lomalagi Resort** (tel. 881-6098, fax 881-6099, www.lomalagi.com) on Natewa Bay, three km west of Nasinu village. It's three km off the Hibiscus Highway up unpaved Salt Lake Road, about 25 km from Savusavu airport. The six deluxe self-catering villas start at F$800 double including tax, airport transfers, laundry, and meals (children under 12 not admitted, three-night minimum stay). For an additional F$170 per couple per day, all drinks can be added to the package. The villas are well spaced along the hillside above 500 meters of beach and each has an excellent view. Two artificial waterfalls drop into the S-shaped saltwater swimming pool. Kayaks, mountain bikes, and snorkeling gear are loaned free. Beatle George Harrison is well remembered at Lomalagi for an evening of song he shared with local villagers during his stay. Nonguests are welcome to stop by for drinks, but call ahead to say you're coming if you'd like to order a meal.

Hannibal's Eco-Adventure Resort (tel./fax: 885-3131, www.hannibalsresort.com), at Fawn Harbor 62 km east of Savusavu, has five *bure* at F$600 double plus 12.5 percent tax. Included are all meals (but not drinks), airport transfers, and non-motorized activities such as kayaking. Sportfishing, scuba diving, and sailing charters are extra. The electricity comes from solar panels, water is recycled into their organic garden, and wastes are composted.

Vanaira Bay

Dolphin Bay Divers Retreat (tel. 888-0531 or 992-0531, www.dolphinbaydivers.com) is on Vanaira Bay at the far east end of Vanua Levu, directly across Somosomo Strait from Taveuni. It's run by a German woman named Viola Koch who formerly managed Susie's Plantation on Taveuni. The accommodations are in two Fijian *bure* at F$50 single or double and three large safari tents at F$35, plus F$30 pp for all meals. It's an electricity-free hideaway with snorkeling and hiking possibilities. Dive kayaks are for rent at F$10/50 an hour/day. The resident PADI diving instructor, Roland, offers boat dives at F$130/350/550 for two/six/10 tanks including gear. Shore dives are F$50, and Dolphin Bay offers night dives at F$75. Dolphin Bay is the only dive resort right on the famous Rainbow Reef. Their four-day scuba certification course (taught in English or German) costs F$500 if you're alone or F$480 pp if there are two of you. Boat transfers from the Korean Wharf on Taveuni are F$20 per group each way. The regular supply boat often goes to Taveuni on Friday afternoon and they may take you for free if they're going anyway, so call ahead. It's also possible to be picked up at Buca Bay (F$25 pp each way) if you're coming from Savusavu.

KIOA ISLAND

The Taveuni ferry passes between Vanua Levu and Kioa, home to some 300 Polynesians from Vaitupu Island, Tuvalu (the former Ellice Islands). Captain Owen of the ship *Packet* obtained Kioa from the Tui Cakau in 1853, and since then it was operated as a coconut plantation. In 1946 it was purchased by the Ellice islanders, who were facing overpopulation on their home island.

The people live at **Salia** on the southeast side of Kioa. The women make baskets for sale to tourists in Savusavu, while the men go fishing alone in small outrigger canoes. If you visit, try the coconut toddy *(kaleve)* or more potent fermented toddy *(kamanging)*. There are no facilities for tourists on Kioa.

RABI ISLAND

In 1855, at the request of the Tui Cakau on Taveuni, a Tongan army conquered some Fijian rebels on Rabi. Upon the Tongans' departure a few years later, a local chief sold Rabi to Europeans to cover outstanding debts, and until WW II the Australian firm Lever Brothers ran a coconut plantation here. In 1940, the British government began searching for an island to purchase as a resettlement area for the Micronesian inhabitants of Ocean Island (Banaba) in the Gilbert Islands (presently part of Kiribati), whose home island was being ravaged by phosphate mining. At first Wakaya Island in the Lomaiviti Group was considered, but the outbreak of war and the occupation of Ocean Island by the Japanese intervened. Back in Fiji, British officials decided Rabi Island would be a better homeland for the Banabans than Wakaya, and in March 1942 they purchased Rabi from Lever Brothers using £25,000 of phosphate royalties deposited in the Banaban Provident Fund.

Meanwhile, the Japanese had deported the Banabans to Kosrae in the Caroline Islands to serve as laborers, and it was not until December 1945 that the survivors could be brought to Rabi, where their 4,500 descendants live today. Contemporary Banabans are citizens of Fiji and live among Lever's former coconut plantations in the northwest corner of the island. The nine-member Rabi Island Council administers the island.

Rabi lives according to a different set of rules than the rest of Fiji; in fact, about all they have in common are their monetary, postal, and educational systems, kava drinking (a Fijian implant), and Methodism. The local language is Gilbertese and the social order is that of the Gilbert Islands. Most people live in hurricane-proof concrete-block houses devoid of furniture, with personal possessions kept in suitcases and trunks. The cooking is done outside in thatched huts. The islanders fish with handlines from outrigger canoes.

Alcoholic beverages are not allowed on Rabi, so take something else as gifts. On Friday nights the local *maneaba* (community hall) in Tabwewa village rocks to a disco beat and dancing alternates with sitting around the omnipresent kava bowl, but on Sunday virtually everything grinds to a halt. Another charming feature: adultery is a legally punishable offense on Rabi.

The island reaches a height of 472 meters and is well wooded. The former Lever headquarters is at Tabwewa, while the disused airstrip is near Tabiang at Rabi's southwest tip. Rabi's other two villages are Uma and Buakonikai. At Nuku between Uma and Tabwewa is a post office, Telecom office, clinic, handicraft shop, and general store. The hill behind the Catholic mission at Nuku affords a fine view. Enjoy another fine view from the Methodist church center at Buakonikai.

Accommodations

Up on the hillside above the post office at Nuku is the four-room **Rabi Island Council Guest House.** This colonial-style structure is the former Lever Brothers manager's residence, and is little changed since the 1940s except for the extension now housing the dining area and lounge. View superb sunsets from the porch. One of the rooms is reserved for island officials; the rest are used mostly by contract workers. Other guests pay F$50 pp a night, which includes three meals. The facilities are shared (no hot water) and the electric generator operates 1800–2200 only—just enough time to watch a video (the library next to the court house rents *Go Tell It to the Judge*, a documentary about the Banaban struggle for compensation).

Considering the limited accommodations and the remoteness of Rabi, it's important to call the **Rabi Island Council** (tel. 881-2913, ext. 30) for guesthouse bookings and other information before setting out. Foreign currency cannot be changed on Rabi and even Fijian bills larger than F$10 may be hard to break. Insect repellent is not sold locally.

Transportation

To get to Rabi, catch the daily Napuka bus at 1030 from Savusavu to Karoko. A chartered speedboat from Karoko to the wharf at

FIJI ISLANDS

Nuku on the northwest side of Rabi costs F$60 each way, less if people off the Napuka bus are going over anyway. The ferries *Raja* from Taveuni and *Adi Savusavu* from Suva visit Rabi occasionally.

Motorized transport on Rabi consists of two or three island council trucks plying the single 23-km road from Tabwewa to Buakonikai weekdays and Saturday mornings (less than a dollar each way).

Taveuni

Long, green, coconut-covered Taveuni is Fiji's fourth-largest island. It's 42 km long, 15 km wide, and 442 km square in area. Only eight km across the Somosomo Strait from Vanua Levu's southeast tip, Taveuni is known as the Garden Island of Fiji because of the abundance of its flora. Around 60 percent of the land is tropical rainforest and virtually all of Fiji's coffee is grown here. Its surrounding reefs and those off nearby Vanua Levu are some of the world's top dive sites. The strong tidal currents in the strait nurture the corals, but can make diving a tricky business for the unprepared.

Because Taveuni is free of the mongoose, there are many wild chickens, *kula* lorikeets, red-breasted musk parrots, honeyeaters, silktails, ferntails, goshawks, and orange-breasted doves, making this a special place for birders. Here you'll still find the jungle fowl, banded rail, and purple swamp hen, all extinct on Viti Levu and Vanua Levu. The Fiji flying fox and mastiff bat are also seen only here. The Taveuni longhorn beetle is the largest beetle in Australasia.

The island's 16-km-long, 1,000-meter-high volcanic spine causes the prevailing trade winds to dump colossal amounts of rainfall on the island's southeast side, and considerable quantities on the northwest side. Southwestern Taveuni is much drier. At 1,241 meters, Uluiqalau in southern Taveuni is the second-highest peak in Fiji, and Des Voeux Peak (1,195 meters) in central Taveuni is the highest point in the country accessible by road. The European discoverer of Fiji, Abel Tasman, sighted this ridge on the night of February 5, 1643. Vuna in southwestern Taveuni is presently dormant, but it's considered Fiji's most active volcano, having erupted within the past 350 years. The almost inaccessible southeast coast features plummeting waterfalls, soaring cliffs, and crashing surf. The 12,000 inhabitants live on the island's gently sloping northwest side. Indigenous Fijians make up the bulk of the population, but Indo-Fijians run many of the shops, hotels, buses, and taxis.

The deep, rich volcanic soil nurtures indigenous floral species such as *Medinilla spectabilis*, which hang in clusters like red sleigh bells, and the rare *tagimaucia (Medinilla waterhousei)*, a climbing plant with red-and-white flower clusters 30 cm long. *Tagimaucia* grows only around Taveuni's 900-meter-high crater lake and on Vanua Levu. It cannot be transplanted and blossoms only from October–January. The story goes that a young woman was fleeing from her father, who wanted to force her to marry a crotchety old man. As she lay crying beside the lake, her tears turned to flowers. Her father took pity on her when he heard this and allowed her to marry her young lover.

Taveuni is a popular destination among for scuba divers, and the nature reserves of northeastern Taveuni make it an ideal eco-tourism destination. In 1991, the producers of the film *Return to the Blue Lagoon* chose Taveuni for their remake of the story of two adolescents on a desert isle. This is a beautiful, scenic, and friendly island on which to hang out, so be sure to allow yourself enough time there.

TRANSPORTATION
Getting There
Matei Airstrip at the north tip of Taveuni is served twice daily by **Air Fiji** (tel. 888-0062) from Nadi (F$183), Suva (F$138) and Savusavu (F$74), and by **Sun Air** (tel. 888-0461) from Nadi (F$183) and Savusavu (F$75). Sun Air also arrives from Labasa (F$75) three times a week. Flights

TAVEUNI

Laucala Island

Matagi Island
MATAGI ISLAND RESORT

Qamea Island
QAMEA BEACH RESORT
Niubavu
Vatosogosogo
Kocoma
Dreketi

Nanuku Passage

Viubani Island

Tasman Strait

Naselesele Point
Naselesele
Mua
MATEI
Welagi
Pagai
Qeleni
Navakacoa
Waitabu
Bouma
Vidawa
Korotuaga (864 m)
Lavena Point
TAVORO FOREST PARK
Lavena
Ravilevo Coast

PRINCE CHARLES BEACH
Lamini
Somosomo
Naqara
Lovonivonu
Waiyevo
Wairiki

Bouma National Heritage Park

Lake Tagimaucia

Des Voeux Peak (1,195 m)

Ravilevu Nature Reserve

Taveuni Island

Garden Island Resort
Korolevu Island

Somosomo Strait

Mt. Uluiqalau (1,241 m)

Salialevu

DOLPHIN BAY DIVERS RETREAT
Vanaira Bay

Naucunilawe (814 m)
Naqarawalu
Delaivuna
Navakawau

SOQULU PLANTATION

Kioa Island
Saliao

NOK'S DIVE CENTER

Vuna
Kanacea
Vuna Lagoon

MATAMAIQI BLOWHOLE

Vagai
Dakuniba

Rainbow Reef

SUSIE'S PLANTATION
VATUWIRI FARM RESORT
VUNA LAGOON LODGE

South Cape

Vanua Levu Island
Buca Bay
Buca
Natuvu
Nawi

To Savusavu and Suva

5 mi
5 km

© DAVID STANLEY

to/from Taveuni are often heavily booked, so re-confirm to avoid being bumped. You get superb views of Taveuni from the plane: sit on the right side going up, the left side coming back. Krishna Brothers (tel. 888-0504) in Naqara is the agent for Air Fiji. Sun Air has an office at the airport and the Garden Island Hotel also takes bookings.

Consort Shipping operates the twice weekly *Spirit of Fiji Islands* service from Taveuni to Suva via Koro and Savusavu (23 hours, F$47/87 deck/cabin). Taveuni to Savusavu is F$22. This ferry departs Taveuni southbound Monday and Thursday at noon, having left Suva northbound Wednesday at 1100 and Saturday at 1800. The Consort agent is the First Light Inn (tel. 888-0339; weekdays 0800–1300 and 1400–1700, Sat. 0800–1300) in Waiyevo, and it's F$10 cheaper to purchase your ticket there rather than on the ferry itself.

The **Beachcomber Cruises** car ferry *Adi Savusavu* departs Taveuni for Savusavu and Suva Wednesday, Friday, and Sunday around noon. It takes five hours to reach Savusavu, and after a three-hour stop continues to Suva, where it arrives at Thursday, Saturday, and Monday mornings (F$48/68 economy/first class). The agent is Ian Simpson (tel. 888-0187 or 888-0261) at the fish market opposite the Garden Island Resort (F$2 discount on advance ticket sales here).

The small passenger boat MV *Raja* departs Taveuni for Natuvu weekdays at 0900 (two hours, F$7). Through boat/bus tickets with a bus connection at Natuvu are available to Savusavu (four hours, F$15) and Labasa (six hours, F$20). The *Raja* also does trips to Rabi whenever there's cargo. Information on the *Raja* is available at an upstairs office (tel. 888-0134) opposite Kaba's Supermarket in Naqara.

If you arrive by boat at Taveuni, you could disembark at one of three places. The large ferries from Suva tie up at an old wharf a kilometer north of Waiyevo or a new wharf just south of the Garden Island Hotel. There's a third wharf called the "Korean Wharf" at Lovonivonu village, a kilometer north of the old Waiyevo wharf, midway between Waiyevo and Naqara. This wharf is usually used by the Vanua Levu ferries and other smaller cargo boats.

Getting Around

Monday–Saturday at 0900, 1100, and 1645 **Pacific Transport** (tel. 888-0278) buses leave Waiyevo and Naqara northbound to Bouma (F$2.95) and southbound to Vuna (F$2.75). Buses to Lavena (F$3.35) are more complicated. On Tuesdays and Thursdays the 0900, 1100, and 1645 Bouma buses continue to Lavena, but on Saturdays only the 1100 and 1645 buses do so. Other days, only the 1645 bus goes to Lavena. Both the northbound and southbound 1645 buses stop and spend the night at their turn-around points, Lavena and Navakawau, heading back to Naqara the next morning at 0600 (at 0730 on Sun.). Sunday service is infrequent, although there are buses to Lavena and Vuna at around 1600. Check the current schedule carefully as soon as you arrive and beware of buses leaving a bit early. The buses begin their journeys at the Pacific Transport garage at Naqara, but they all go to Waiyevo hospital to pick up passengers before heading north or south.

The sporadic bus service and rather expensive taxi fares make getting around rather inconvenient. Taveuni's minibus taxis don't run along set routes, picking up passengers at fixed rates as they do on other islands, but only operate on an individual charter basis. The taxi fare from the wharf to Naqara is reasonable at F$3, but from the airport to Naqara it's expensive at F$15. In general, the taxi fare will be about 10 times the corresponding bus fare. Save money by using the buses for long rides and taxis for shorter hops. Hitchhiking also works fine (drivers often expect you do give them the equivalent of bus fare).

You could hire a minibus taxi and driver for the day. Write out a list of everything you want to see, then negotiate a price with a driver. The Garden Island Resort minibus is F$110 to Bouma or F$140 to Lavena for up to five people (six persons and up is F$25/30 pp to Bouma/Lavena). To the Matamaiqi Blowhole in southern Taveuni it's F$100.

Mr. Nand Lal (tel. 888-0705) operates a regular shuttle service to Bouma National Heritage Park at F$40/60 round-trip from Matei to Bouma/Lavena for up to five people including waiting time. Call him up, or ask at Lal's Restaurant in Matei.

Garden State General Merchants, beside the BP service station opposite Kaba's Motel in Naqara, represents **Budget Rent-a-Car** (tel. 888-0291) with Suzuki jeeps at F$210 a day all inclusive, reduced to F$150 after bargaining.

NORTHERN TAVEUNI

The bulk of Taveuni's tourist facilities, including accommodations, restaurants, and dive shops, are within walking distance of the airport at Matei. It's an ideal area in which to stay if you're arriving by air, although boat passengers and those planning to use public transportation for sightseeing may find central Taveuni more convenient. When selecting a place to stay, be aware that the beach east of Matei Point is little more than a broad mud flat at low tide and the best places for swimming are west of the airport in the vicinity of Beverly's Campground.

Sports and Recreation

Taveuni and surrounding waters have earned a reputation as one of Fiji's top diving areas. The fabulous 32-km **Rainbow Reef** off the south coast of eastern Vanua Levu abounds in turtles, fish, overhangs, crevices, and soft corals, all in 5–10 meters of water. Favorite dive sites here include Annie's Bommie, Blue Ribbon Eel Reef, Cabbage Patch, Coral Garden, Jack's Place, Jerry's Jelly, Orgasm, Pot Luck, The Ledge, The Zoo, and White Sandy Gully. At the Great White Wall, a tunnel in the reef leads past sea fans to a magnificent drop-off and a wall covered in awesome white soft coral. Unfortunately, the hard corals on the Rainbow Reef have been heavily impacted by coral bleaching. The soft corals are still okay, and the White Wall is as spectacular as ever. Beware of strong currents in the Somosomo Strait.

Snorkelers should be aware that shark attacks are not unknown on northern Taveuni. Never snorkel out to the edge of the reef alone anywhere around Matei. This is less of a problem elsewhere around the island, although one should always seek local advice. Northern Taveuni is one of the few places in Fiji where sharks are a problem.

Aquaventure (tel./fax 888-0381, www.aquaventure.org), run by Tania de Hoon, has its base on the beach a 20-minute walk south of Matei Airport. Trips start at 0800 and 1300, costing F$140 for two tanks, plus F$30 for gear (F$620 for 10 dives). Aquaventure offers an introductory scuba dive for F$140. Tania also books guided snorkeling tours to the Waitabu Marine Park (F$50 pp all inclusive, minimum of four), an excellent option if you're a bit nervous about snorkeling here on your own.

A few minutes walk north of Aquaventure is **Swiss Fiji Divers** (tel. 888-0586, fax 888-2587, www.swissfijidivers.com), between the beaches of the Taveuni Island Resort and Maravu Plantation. Divemasters Dominique Egerter and Evi Antonietti charge F$180 for a two-tank dive, plus F$20 for rental gear. For those staying longer, they have five-day packages for F$830 or ten days for F$1,400. Their five to six day PADI open-water course is F$760, and many other specialized dive courses are offered. A "discover diving" experience is F$160. This is Taveuni's newest dive shop and their equipment is first rate. They guarantee a ratio of not less than one guide for every three divers. From 0900–1700 you can check your email here at F$.25 a minute.

Matei Game Fishing (Geoffry Amos, tel. 888-0371 or 888-2667), opposite Rauf Mohammed Enterprises at Matei, does game fishing trips on his boat the *Lucky Strike*. It's F$570/900 for a half/full day for up to four people.

Island Pizza (Ken Madden, tel. 888-2888), adjacent to Aquaventure, rents single/double fiberglass kayaks at F$10/14 an hour. Half-day snorkeling trips are F$30 pp (minimum of four), while full-day boat trips to Qamea/Yanuca islands are F$150/200 for the boat (four persons). Fishing trips are also possible.

Accommodations

Places to stay are scattered all around Taveuni, with the main cluster within walking distance of Matei Airport. There are several good places to eat out in this vicinity, so avoiding booking with hotels that try to force you to prepay all your meals. Also beware of misleading resort websites or the glowing reports of travel agents and glossy magazine writers who came on freebie trips. For some reason, a good many of the complaints we receive regarding tourist accommodations in Fiji relate to places on northern Taveuni and its adjacent islands.

Taveuni still doesn't have a public electricity supply, but most of the places to stay have their own generators, which typically run 1800–2100 only.

Under US$25: Beverly's Campground (tel. 888-0684) is on a good beach a bit over one km south of the airport. Run by Bill Madden, it's a peaceful, shady place, adjacent to Maravu Plantation's beach. It's F$8 pp in your own tent, or F$10 pp to sleep in a set tent. The toilet and shower block is nearby. Cooking facilities are available, but bring groceries (Bill provides free fresh fruit from his garden daily). The kitchen shelter by the beach is a nice place to sit and swap traveler's tales with the other guests, and the clean white beach is just seconds from your tent.

A few hundred meters south is **Lisi's Accommodation** (tel. 888-0194), in a small village across the highway from a white-sand beach. It's F$8 pp to camp or F$15/25 single/double in a clean four-room bungalow with shared cooking and bathing facilities. Your friendly hosts Mary and Lote Tuisago serve excellent Fijian meals at F$6/8 for breakfast/dinner. Horseback riding (F$10 an hour) can be arranged here.

US$25–50: Tuvununu Paradise Garden Inn (tel. 888-0465, taveuni@paradisefiji.com), 700 meters east of Naselesele village in northern Taveuni, offers eight rooms in a large wooden building overlooking Viubani Island at F$55/75 single/double, or F$24 pp in the backpacker dorm. Camping is F$9 pp. The tidal flat in front of the inn is beautiful but not ideal for swimming. The Tuvununu has been closed for several years and is in need of major renovations before it can reopen.

The Petersen family runs the **Tovu Tovu Resort** (tel. 888-0560, fax 888-0722, tovutovu@connect.com.fj) at Matei just east of Bhula Bhai & Sons Supermarket. It's across the road from a shallow beach with murky water, and guests often

walk the two km to Beverly's Campground to swim. The two front *bure* capable of sleeping three are self-catering at F$75 single or double. Just behind are another two *bure* with private bath but no cooking at F$65. A larger self-catering bungalow sleeping four is F$85. The three-meal plan is F$35 pp, and the restaurant terrace is a nice place to sit and socialize.

Little Dolphin (tel. 888-0130), opposite Bhula Bhai & Sons Supermarket, less than a kilometer east of the airport, has an airy, two-story cottage with cooking facilities called the "treehouse." At F$80/90 single/double a night it's a good value, and the view from the porch is great. Little Dolphin is run by an Australian named Scott, who is a mine of information. He has a three-person outrigger canoe and a double kayak, which he rents to guests at F$30 a day for either (F$40 a day to non-guests).

Niranjan's Budget Hotel (tel. 888-0406) is just a five-minute walk east of the airport. The four rooms in the main building, each with two beds and fan, go for F$44/55 single/double. The electric generator is on 1800–2200. Niranjan himself is very hospitable guy.

Bibi's Hideaway (tel. 888-0443), about 600 meters south of the airport, has some of the gracious atmosphere of neighboring properties without the sky-high prices. A variety of accommodations is available. The film crew making *Return to the Blue Lagoon* stayed here for three months, and with the extra income the owners built a honeymoon *bure* with a picture window, which is F$80 double. Nearby is a two-room house at F$50 per room or F$80 for the whole house. A small cottage is F$60 double, while a mini-*bure* with two single beds is F$25 pp. There's also a larger family unit accommodating eight at F$100. All five units have access to cooking facilities and fridge. Bibi's is located on lush, spacious grounds, and James, Victor, and Pauline Bibi will make you feel right at home. It's an excellent medium-priced choice if you don't mind being a bit away from the beach.

US$50–100: Audrey of **Audrey's Café** (tel. 888-0039), half a km east of the airport, has a cute cottage with tile floors which she rents at F$125 (children not admitted).

Directly opposite the airport terminal is the **Garden of Eden Villa** (Peter Madden, tel. 888-2344), a large two-bedroom house with cooking facilities at F$100 double or F$120 for four if you book direct. Set on a bluff above the sea, this place was once a favorite retreat of Fiji's former president Ratu Mara.

Matei Point Bungalows (tel. 888-0422), right on the point at the end of the driveway opposite the airport access road, has three self-catering villas at F$140 double, plus F$20 per additional person.

Karin's Garden (tel./fax 888-0511), almost opposite Bibi's Hideaway 650 meters south of the airport, overlooks the same coast as the overpriced Taveuni Island Resort next door. The two screened rooms with fan in a large self-catering bungalow are each F$115 single or double. It's nice but the beds are a bit soft. Don't stay here unless you like dogs.

US$100–150: A retired American tour operator named Bob Goddess (tel. 888-0522, www.fiji-rental-accommodations.com) rents three beachfront houses near Matei Airport. **Sere-ni-Ika,** a six-minute walk east of the terminal, has three bedrooms at F$415 per group. **Lomalagi,** two houses west of Sere-ni-Ika, has two bedrooms at F$265 for both. A hundred meters west toward the terminal is **Marau Vale,** a two-bedroom house in a large garden costing F$455. Bob offers low season and long stay discounts. It's all very nice, although the beach in front of these houses is a mud flat at low tide.

US$250 and up: About 600 meters south of the airport are two of Taveuni's most exclusive properties. **Maravu Plantation Resort** (Angela and Jochen Kiess, tel. 888-0555, fax 888-0600, www.maravu.net) is a village-style resort on a 20-hectare copra-making plantation. Maravu consists of five "planters" *bure* at F$420/640 single/double and five "honeymoon" *bure* at F$480/760. The four "honeymoon suites," each with a private spa and sundeck, are F$880 double. Included are meals, transfers, taxes, horseback riding, bicycles, and some other activities. Two children under 14 can stay free, paying only for their meals (F$60 per day per child). When space is available, you might get the local walk-in rate

of F$198/396 single/double all-inclusive. On the landscaped grounds are an elegant bar, spa, and swimming pool. The resort often arranges a *meke* to go with dinner (F$60 for non-guests) on Wednesday or Thursday. If you're not staying there, you must reserve meals in advance. Maravu's wine menu is way overpriced.

Almost across the street from Maravu Plantation is the **Taveuni Island Resort** (tel. 888-0441, fax 888-0466, www.taveuniislandresort.com), run by the Cammick family. This resort started out in the 1970s as a low-budget scuba camp known as Ric's Place, but today it's patronized by an eclectic mix of divers, anglers, honeymooners, and "romantic couples" who arrive on prepaid package tours. The eight *bure* range in price from F$1,156–1,520 single or double, including meals, transfers, and tax. In addition, the cliff-top honeymoon *bure* with private staff is F$2,400 double all-inclusive. Unlike Maravu, which encourages visits by families, children under 15 are not accepted here. The open terrace dining area and swimming pool added in 1997 merge scenically with the sea on the horizon. Be aware that only registered houseguests are welcome on the property (a sign on the gate says Beware of the Dogs).

Food

The nicest place to eat out around Matei is the **Vunibokoi Restaurant** (tel. 888-0560) at the Tovu Tovu Resort, east of Bhula Bhai & Sons Supermarket. From 1800–2000, upscale dinners (F$13–17) prepared by Mareta are served on a terrace overlooking the sea. The Friday night *lovo* buffet here is F$17.50. Reservations are recommended.

Audrey's Island Café & Pastries (tel. 888-0039; daily 1000–1800), run by a charming American woman at Matei, serves afternoon tea (F$7 pp) to guests who also enjoy the great view from her terrace, and Audrey has various homemade goodies to take away.

Lal's Restaurant (tel. 888-0705; daily 1100–2030), just east of the airport, serves spicy boneless chicken, lamb, fish, and vegetarian Indian curry dishes at F$10 a serve.

The **Matei Restaurant** (tel. 888-0406), at

Niranjan's Budget Hotel just east of the airport terminal, can prepare an excellent curry buffet dinner (F$15 pp), provided your order before 1700.

The snack bar at Matei Airport (open only at flight times) sells tasty curry *rotis*. They're kept under the counter, so ask. The two supermarkets in this area also sell *roti* packets at F$.70.

Island Pizza (Ken Madden, tel. 888-2888; daily 1000–2130), on the beach next to Aquaventure, has pizzas priced F$17/20 regular/large.

The **Tramonto Restaurant** (Peter Madden, tel. 888-2224; Mon.–Thurs. 1100–1400 and 1800–2100, Fri. 1100–2100), on a hilltop at the southwest end of the Matei tourist strip, serves lunch/dinner at around F$7.50/15.50. When available, lobster is F$20. The portions tend to be small here. If you can get a group of at least six persons together, the Tramonto lays out an excellent smorgasbord dinner at F$20 pp. There's a superb view of the beach and Somosomo Strait from their open terrace.

Groceries

Those staying at Matei will appreciate the well-stocked **Bhula Bhai & Sons Supermarket** (tel. 888-0369; Mon.–Sat. 0730–1800, Sun. 0800–1000) at the Matei Postal Agency between the airport and Naselesele village. A second grocery store, **Rauf Mohammed Enterprises** (tel. 888-0431; Mon.–Sat. 0630–1900), Sun. 0700–1100 and 1500–2000), is between Bhula Bhai and the airport. Public telephones are outside both stores.

EASTERN TAVEUNI
Bouma National Heritage Park

This important nature reserve between Bouma and Lavena in northeastern Taveuni has been developed with New Zealand aid money. In 1990, an agreement was signed with the communities of Waitabu, Vidawa, Korovou, and Lavena putting this area in trust for 99 years, and the Tavoro Forest Park at Bouma was established a year later. The Lavena Coastal Walk, Vidawa Rainforest Hike, and Waitabu Marine Park are other features of the park, and the various admission fees and tour charges are used for local

community projects, to provide local residents with an immediate practical reason for preserving their natural environment.

There are three lovely **waterfalls** just south of Bouma (admission F$8). From the information kiosk on the main road it's an easy 10-minute walk up a broad path along the river's right bank to the lower falls, which plunge 20 meters into a deep pool. You can swim here, and changing rooms, toilets, picnic tables, and a barbecue are provided. A well-constructed trail leads up to a second falls in about 30 minutes, passing a spectacular viewpoint overlooking Qamea Island and Taveuni's northeast coast. You must cross the river once, but a rope is provided for balance. Anyone in good physical shape can reach this second falls with ease, and there's also a pool for swimming. The muddy, slippery trail up to the third and highest falls involves two river crossings with nothing to hold onto, and it would be unpleasant in the rain. This trail does cut through the most beautiful portion of the rainforest with

Taveuni's Bouma Falls are among the most impressive in Fiji.

the richest birdlife, and these upper falls are perhaps the most impressive of the three, as the river plunges over a black basalt cliff, which you can climb and use as a diving platform into the deep pool. The water here is very sweet.

A new activity in this area is the six-hour **Vidawa Rainforest Hike** during which local guides introduce the birdlife, flora, and archaeological sites of the area to visitors. You scramble over volcanic ridges offering spectacular views and explore old village sites with their temple platforms and ring ditches still clearly visible. Your guide brings it all to life with tales of the old ways of his people. A picnic lunch is served next to a spring-fed stream deep in the interior. The trek ends at Bouma Falls where hikers are rewarded with a refreshing swim. The F$60 pp cost (F$40 for children) includes park entry fees and transportation from anywhere on northern Taveuni (call 888-0390 to book).

Similar is the **Waitabu Marine Park** where a lagoon area two km before Bouma has been declared a "no fishing" sanctuary for fish and snorkelers. The F$50 pp tour price also includes snorkeling gear, transportation, and food. Book five-hour snorkeling tours here through the dive shop Aquaventure (tel. 888-0381) south of Matei Airport. Reductions for children are available. The departure time varies according to tide and weather conditions. These tours are a good value, and you'll be supporting a worthy cause.

Bouma is accessible by public bus. If you depart Waiyevo or Naqara on the 0900 bus, you'll have about two hours to see the falls and have a quick swim before catching another bus back to Waiyevo. On Tuesdays and Thursdays this second bus does a round-trip to Lavena, six km south, and it's worth jumping on for the ride even if you don't intend to get off at Lavena. Other days the second bus only goes as far at Bouma. Verify the time of the return bus with the driver of the 0900 bus.

Lavena

The **Lavena Coastal Walk** officially opened in 1993. You pay your F$8 admission fee (separate from the F$8 fee charged at Bouma) at the Lavena Lodge Visitor Center, right at the end of the road at Lavena. Guides are available at F$18. From the Visitor Center you can hike the five km down the Ravilevo Coast to **Wainibau Falls** in about an hour and a half. You'll pass Naba village, where the descendants of black-birded Solomon Islanders live to this day, and a suspension bridge over the Wainisairi River, which drains Lake Tagimaucia in Taveuni's interior. The last 15 minutes is a scramble up a creek bed, which can be very slippery as you wade along. Two falls here plunge into the same deep basalt pool and during the rainy season you must actually swim a short distance to see the second pool. Diving into either pool is excellent fun. Be on guard, however, as flash flooding often occurs. Keep to the left near the base of the falls. Several lovely beaches and places to stop are along the trail (allow four hours there and back from Lavena with plenty of stops).

If you also want to see **Savulevu Yavonu Falls,** which plummet off a cliff directly into the sea, you must hire a boat at F$75 for up to three people or F$25 pp for up to six. Intrepid ocean kayakers sometimes paddle down this back side of Taveuni, past countless cliffs and waterfalls. The steep forested area south of Wainibau Stream forms part of the Ravilevu Nature Reserve.

It's not possible to visit Lavena as a day trip by public bus (taxis charge F$60 return to bring you here). Buses depart Lavena for Naqara Monday–Saturday at 0600, Tuesday and Thursday also at 1400, and Sunday at 0730—beware of them leaving a bit early.

Accommodations

At Bouma, visitors can camp by the river behind the park information kiosk (tel. 888-0390) at F$10 per head. Toilets and showers are provided. Meals can be ordered or you can cook your own in a communal kitchen.

Lavena Lodge, next to Lavena village at the end of the bus route, is a pleasant European style building with running water and lantern lighting. The four rooms (two doubles and two three-bed dorms) are F$15 pp. Sinks are provided in the rooms, but the bath is shared. Good cooking facilities are provided and you can eat at a picnic table on a hill overlooking the beach or on the lodge's terrace. Dinner can be ordered for F$10. A village store is opposite the lodge, and two other small trade stores are nearby (however it's best to bring groceries with you). Mosquito coils are essential (the flies are a nuisance too). An excellent golden beach is right in front of the lodge, and at Ucuna Point, a five-minute walk away, is a picnic area where you can spend an afternoon (be careful with the currents if you snorkel). It's a great place to hang out for a few days—the film *Return to the Blue Lagoon* was filmed here. To book, call Lavena via radio telephone at 811-6801 (answered 0800–0900 and 1400–1500 only).

CENTRAL TAVEUNI

Taveuni's police station, hospital, and government offices are on a hilltop at **Waiyevo,** above the Garden Island Resort. On the coast below are the island's post office and largest hotel.

The 180th degree of longitude passes through a point marked by a display called **Taveuni's Time Line** at Waiyevo, 500 meters up the road from the shops near the Garden Island Resort. It's said that one early Taveuni trader overcame the objections of missionaries to his doing business on Sunday by claiming the international date line ran through his property. According to him, when it was Sunday at the front door, it was already Monday around back. Similarly, European planters got their native laborers to work seven days a week by having Sunday at one end of the plantation, and Monday at the other. An 1879 ordinance ended this by placing all of Fiji west of the date line, so you're no longer able to stand here with one foot in the past and the other in the present. Despite this, it's still the most accessible place in the world crossed by the 180th meridian.

To get to the **Waitavala Sliding Rocks,** walk north from the Garden Island Resort about five minutes on the main road, then turn right onto the side road leading to Waitavala Estates. Take the first road to the right up the hill, and when you see a large metal building on top of a hill, turn left and go a short distance down a road through a coconut plantation to a clearing on the right. The trail up the river to the sliding

rocks begins here. The water slide in the river is especially fast after heavy rains, yet the local kids go down standing up! Admission is free.

At **Wairiki,** a kilometer south of Waiyevo, are a few stores and the picturesque Catholic mission, with a large stone church containing interesting sculptures and stained glass. There are no pews: The congregation sits on the floor Fijian style. From Wairiki Secondary School you can hike up a tractor track to the large **concrete cross** on a hill behind the mission in 30 minutes each way. You'll be rewarded with a sweeping view of much of western Taveuni and across Somosomo Strait. A famous 19th-century naval battle occurred here when Taveuni warriors turned back a large Tongan invasion force, with much of the fighting done from canoes. The defeated Tongans ended up in Fijian ovens and the French priest who gave valuable counsel to the Fijian chief was repaid with laborers to build his mission.

A jeep road from Wairiki climbs to the telecommunications station on **Des Voeux Peak.** This is an all-day trip on foot with a view of Lake Tagimaucia as a reward (clouds permitting). The lake itself is not accessible from here. This peak is one of Taveuni's best bird-watching venues, and the rare monkey-faced fruit bat (*Pteralopex acrodonta*) survives only in the mist forest around the summit. Unless you hire a jeep to the viewpoint, it will take four arduous hours to hike the eight km up and another two to walk back down.

Around Somosomo

Somosomo, four km north of Waiyevo, is the chiefly village of Cakaudrove and the seat of the Tui Cakau, Taveuni's "king"; the late Ratu Sir Penaia Ganilau, last governor general and first president of Fiji, hailed from here. The two distinct parts of the village are divided by a small stream where women wash their clothes. The southern portion called **Naqara** is the island's commercial center with several large Indo-Fijian stores, the island's bank, and a couple of places to stay. Pacific Transport has its bus terminus here.

Somosomo, to the north of Naqara, is the chiefly quarter with the personal residence of the Tui Cakau on the hill directly above the bridge (no entry). Beside the main road below is the large hall built for the 1986 meeting of the Great Council of Chiefs. Missionary William Cross, one of the creators of today's system of written Fijian, who died at Somosomo in 1843, is buried in the attractive new church next to the meeting hall. There's even electric street lighting in this part of town!

The challenging trail up to lovely **Lake Tagimaucia,** 823 meters high in the mountainous interior, begins at the south end of Naqara. The first half is the hardest. You'll need between six hours and a full day to do a round-trip, and a guide (F$20) will be necessary because there are many trails to choose from. You must wade for a half-hour through knee-deep mud in the crater to reach the lake's edge. Much of the lake's surface is covered with floating vegetation, and the water is only five meters deep. From October–January you have a chance of seeing the red-and-white *tagimaucia* flower mentioned previously blossoming near the lake.

Sports and Recreation

Aqua-Trek Taveuni (tel. 888-0544, fax 888-0288, www.aquatrekdiving.com), at the Garden Island Resort, does daily two-tank dives at F$165 plus gear (no one-tank dives). PADI scuba certification costs F$660, or take a one-tank "discover scuba course" at F$148). You'll find cheaper dive shops, but Aqua-Trek's facilities are first rate. This is the closest dive shop to the famous Rainbow Reef.

The dive shop at the Garden Island Resort rents kayaks at F$15/50 an hour/half day. In good weather, Korolevu Island opposite the resort would make a great destination.

Accommodations

Under US$25: The original budget hotel on Taveuni was **Kaba's Motel & Guest House** (tel. 888-0233, fax 888-0202, kaba@connect.com.fj) at Naqara, which charges F$25/35/40 single/double/twin in one of four double rooms with shared facilities in the guesthouse. The cooking facilities are very good. The newer motel section is F$45/55/60 for one of the six larger units with kitchenette, fridge, fan, and private bath. The water is solar-heated, so cold showers are de rigueur in overcast weather (ask for a discount in that case). Kaba's Supermarket is just up the street. No check-ins are accepted after 1800. Naqara is a convenient place to stay for catching buses, but at night there's nothing much to do other than watch the BBC on TV.

A friendly Indo-Fijian family runs **Kool's Accommodation** (tel. 888-0395), opposite Kaba's Supermarket at Naqara. The six rooms in two long blocks facing the eating area are F$15 pp, and cooking facilities are provided (but no fridge).

Sunset Accommodation (Baiya Kondaiya, tel. 888-0229), on a busy corner near the Korean Wharf at Lovonivonu, has two rooms with shared bath in the main house at F$15/25 single/double. A separate bungalow with kitchen and bath is F$40 for up to three. They prepare tasty Indian meals (F$5) upon request.

For information on the **Dolphin Bay Divers Retreat** (tel. 888-0531 or 992-0531, www.dolphinbaydivers.com), on Vanua Levu but most easily accessible from Taveuni, turn to Buca Bay and Rabi in the Vanua Levu section.

US$25–50: The **First Light Inn** (tel. 888-0339, fax 888-0387, firstlight@connect.com.fj), near the Garden Island Resort at Waiyevo, was built in late 1999 just in time for the millennium celebrations. This large, two-story concrete building has 20 rooms with bath and TV at F$52/60 fan/air conditioned for up to three people. Communal cooking facilities are provided. Local contract workers sometimes book rooms here on the weekends to watch the football games on TV and have fun, so be prepared.

US$50–100: The **Garden Island Resort** (tel. 888-0286, fax 888-0288, garden@connect.com.fj) is by the sea at Waiyevo, three km south of Naqara. Formerly known as the Castaway, this was Taveuni's premier (and only) hotel when it was built by the Travelodge chain in the 1960s. In 1996, the scuba operator Aqua Trek USA purchased the property. The 28 air-conditioned rooms in an attractive two-story building are F$154/194 single/double, or F$35 pp in the two four-bed dorms. The buffet meal plan is F$80 pp and eating by the pool is fun (dinner reservations before 1700 required). The food won't win any awards but the house band is pretty good! There's no beach, but the Garden Island offers evening entertainment, a swimming pool, excursions, and water sports. Snorkeling trips (F$10 pp, plus F$11 for snorkeling gear, if required) are arranged to Korolevu Island at 1000 and 1400, and a large dive shop is on the premises. Airport transfers are F$30 pp round-trip (unless you're alone, a taxi will be cheaper). The Garden Island is an okay place to hang out-a better value than the high end places around Matei.

Food

Frank Fong's **Waci-Pokee Restaurant** (tel. 888-0036; Mon.–Fri. 0700–2000, Sat. 0700–1400), below the First Light Inn in Waiyevo, serves tasty Chinese and local meals for around F$5. You can eat outside in the thatched **Cannibal Cafe** directly behind the Waci-Pokee, a nice terrace overlooking Vanua Levu. A piece of chocolate cake is less than a dollar, but their slogan is "we'd love to have you for dinner." Order dinner beforehand, if possible.

Several unpretentious places in the fish market opposite the Garden Island Resort serve cheap picnic table meals. Of these, the **Makuluva Restaurant** (tel. 994-5394; Sun.–Thurs. 0800–1630 and 1800–2000, Fri. 0800–1630) serves a good fish lunch/dinner for F$5/10. You must order dinner before 1600.

Dinner mains at the restaurant of the **Garden Island Resort** (tel. 888-0286) will set you back F$23. The hotel organizes a *meke* and *lovo* (F$35 pp) if enough paying guests are present to make it worth their while.

Jack's Restaurant (tel. 888-0173; daily 0700–2000), diagonally opposite the bus station in Naqara, serves mediocre curries in the F$4 range. For breakfast order an egg sandwich with coffee for F$2. Verify prices while ordering.

Groceries

The variety of goods available at **Kaba's Supermarket** (tel. 888-0088) in Naqara is surprising, and a cluster of other small shops is adjacent. The **Morris Hedstrom** supermarket (tel. 888-0053) is a bit north in Somosomo. Small grocery stores also exist at Wairiki and Waiyevo.

Shopping

Ross Handicrafts (tel. 888-0972), below the First Light Inn in Waiyevo, has a typical selection of Fijian handicrafts.

Services

Traveler's checks can be changed at the Colonial National Bank (weekdays 0900–1600) in Naqara. The bank doesn't give cash advances on credit cards. In a pinch, supermarkets on Taveuni may agree to do it but you'll pay a 10 percent surcharge.

Taveuni's main post office is below the First Light Inn at Waiyevo.

Card phones are at Matei Airport, at Bhula Bhai & Sons Supermarket and Rauf Mohammed Enterprises in Matei, at Krishna Brothers Store in Naqara, at the fish market in Waiyevo, and several other locations.

Garden State General Merchants (tel. 888-0291), beside the BP service station opposite Kaba's Motel in Naqara, provides Internet access at F$.40 a minute.

The island's hospital (tel. 888-0444) at Waiyevo received a F$2.4 million upgrade in 2003.

SOUTHERN TAVEUNI

The southern end of Taveuni is one of the island's most beautiful areas, but transportation is spotty, with bus service from Naqara Monday–Saturday at 0900, 1100, and 1645 only. Since the 1645 bus spends the night at Vuna and doesn't return to Naqara until the next morning, the only way to really see southern Taveuni is to also spend the night there. If this isn't possible, the round-trip bus rides leaving Naqara at 0900 and 1100 are still worth doing.

The bus from Naqara runs south along the coast to Susie's Plantation Resort, where it turns inland to Delaivuna. There it turns around and returns to the coast, which it follows southeast to Navakawau via South Cape. On the way back it cuts directly across some hills to Kanacea and continues up the coast without going to Delaivuna again. Southeast of Kanacea there is very little traffic.

A hike around southern Taveuni provides an

interesting day out for anyone staying at Susie's Plantation Resort. From Susie's a road climbs east over the island to **Delaivuna**, where the bus turns around at a gate. The large Private Property sign here is mainly intended to ward off miscreants who create problems for the plantation owners by leaving cattle gates open. Visitors with enough sense to close the gates behind themselves may proceed.

You hike one hour down through the coconut plantation to a junction with two gates, just before a small bridge over a (usually) dry stream. If you continue walking 30 minutes down the road straight ahead across the bridge you'll reach **Salialevu,** site of the Bilyard Sugar Mill (1874–1896), one of Fiji's first. In the 1860s, European planters tried growing cotton on Taveuni, turning to sugar when the cotton market collapsed. Later, copra was found to be more profitable. A tall chimney, boilers, and other equipment remain below the school at Salialevu.

After a look around, return to the two gates at the bridge and follow the other dirt road southwest for an hour through the coconut plantation to **Navakawau** village at the southeast end of the island. Some of Fiji's only Australian magpies (large black-and-white birds) inhabit this plantation.

Just east of South Cape as you come from Navakawau is the **Matamaiqi Blowhole,** where trade wind-driven waves crash into the unprotected black volcanic rocks, sending geysers of sea spray soaring skyward, especially on a southern swell. The viewpoint is just off the main road.

At **Vuna,** lava flows have formed pools beside the ocean, which fill up with fresh water at low tide and are used for washing and bathing.

Sports and Recreation

Nok's Dive Center (tel. 888-0246, fax 888-0072), at Kris Backplace north of Susie's Plantation Resort, offers diving at F$75/130 for one/two dives, plus F$20 a day for gear. Night dives are F$80. Snorkelers can go along in the boat for F$15, although some dive sites are not really suitable for snorkeling (ask). They dive on both the Vuna and Rainbow reefs.

One of the only stretches of paved road on southern Taveuni is at **Soqulu Plantation** or

"Taveuni Estates" (tel. 888-0044), about eight km south of Waiyevo. This upscale residential development features an attractive nine-hole golf course (green fees F$20) by the sea, tennis courts, dive shop (tel. 888-0063, www.taveunidive.com), and a bowling green. Visitors are sometimes accommodated in a 120-year-old plantation house a four-minute walk from the golf course.

Accommodations

Susie's Plantation Resort (Susie Leonard, tel. 888-0125, www.susiesplantation.com), just north of Vuna Point at the south end of Taveuni, offers peace and quiet amid picturesque bucolic surroundings. The two rooms with shared bath in the main house are F$25–30 single or double depending on size, while the one suite with private bath is F$35. The three seaside *bure* with bath rent for F$40–50 double, plus F$10 per additional person to four maximum. Dorm beds are F$15 each or pay F$10 pp to camp. Meals in the restaurant (housed in the oldest missionary building on the island) are F$6/10 for continental/full breakfast, F$5–8 for lunch, or F$16 for dinner. Otherwise you can cook your own food in a common kitchen for a F$2 charge (but not in the *bure* or rooms), and Kutty's Grocery Store is a 10-minute walk up the road to Delaivuna. At sundown the Sunset Boys serenade you from behind the kava bowl. Nok's Dive Center offers daily trips to the Great White Wall and Rainbow Reef. Even if you're not a diver, you'll enjoy snorkeling off their rocky beach. Horseback riding (F$35 for a half day) and bird-watching tours can be arranged at this atmospheric resort on spacious landscaped grounds.

Vuna Lagoon Lodge (tel. 888-0627), on the Vuna Lagoon near Vuna village, a kilometer south of Vatuwiri Farm, consists of two European-style houses just back from a black lava coastline highlighted by small golden beaches. The two rooms with shared bath are F$30 single or double, the two with private bath F$50, and the two dorms with three or four beds are F$15 pp. Cooking facilities are provided (two tiny stores are in the village) or you can order meals. Namoli Beach a 10-minute walk away is good for swimming and snorkeling (better at low tide, as the current picks up appreciably when the tide comes in). The friendly proprietor, Adi Salote Samanunu, is a daughter of the chief of Vuna.

ISLANDS OFF TAVEUNI

Qamea Island

Qamea (ngga-ME-a) Island, just three km east of Taveuni, is the 12th-largest island in Fiji. It's 10 km long with lots of lovely bays, lush green hills, and secluded white-sand beaches. Land crabs *(lairo)* are gathered in abundance here during their migration to the sea at the beginning of their breeding season in late November or early December. The bird life is also rich, due to the absence of the mongoose.

In 2001, Dr. Patrick D. Nunn of the University of the South Pacific conducted excavations of settlement sites on Qamea and surrounding islands and discovered *lapita* era remains dating back 2600–3000 years. Vatusogosogo, one of six villages on Qamea, is inhabited by descendants of blackbirded Solomon islanders. Outboards from villages on Qamea land near Navakacoa village on the northeast side of Taveuni. The best time to try for a ride over is Thursday or Friday afternoons.

The upscale **Qamea Beach Resort** (tel. 888-0220, fax 888-0092, www.qamea.com), on the west side of Qamea, has 11 air-conditioned *bure* at F$1,180 double, and one split-level honeymoon villa at F$1,450 (children under 13 not accepted). Substantial meals, airport transfers, and tax are included. All units have a ceiling fan, mini-fridge, giant outdoor showers, lawn furniture, and hammock-equipped front deck. Meals are served in a tall central dining room and lounge designed like a *burekalou* (temple), and a trio sings around dinnertime. Drink prices are astronomical, so bring along a duty free bottle. The new owners, Ron and Bryce, go out of their way to assist physically challenged guests, although Qamea is not fully wheelchair accessible. The swimming off Qamea's 400 meters of fine white sands is good, with lava pools emerging at low tide, and there's also a small freshwater swimming pool. Activities such as snorkeling, sailing, windsurfing, village tours, and hiking are included in the basic price, but tours to Taveuni and Lau-

cala, fishing, and scuba diving are extra. Unfortunately, we've received mixed feedback about the dive shop. A waterfront spa (one-hour massage F$70, facial F$95) was added in 2002.

Matangi Island

Matangi is a tiny horseshoe-shaped volcanic island just north of Qamea, its sunken crater forming a lovely palm-fringed bay. The island is privately owned by the Douglas family, which has been producing copra on Matangi for five generations and still does. In 1988, they diversified into the hotel business.

Matangi Island Resort (Noel Douglas, tel. 888-0260, fax 888-0274, www.matangiisland .com), 10 km northeast of Taveuni, markets itself as a honeymoon destination by advertising in the U.S. bridal magazines. It tries to do the same as far as scuba diving goes, but the prime dive sites in the Somosomo Strait are a long way from this resort. Matangi's three treehouse *bure* are intended for the recently wed (F$1,100 double). Other guests are accommodated in the neat thatched *bure* scattered among the coconut palms below Matangi's high jungly interior. The seven "deluxe" *bure* are F$490/620 single/double, while the two standards and one duplex are F$370/620. Family *bure* are F$1,120/1,350 standard/deluxe. Prices include meals, snacks, laundry, some excursions, and tax, but return boat transfers from Taveuni are F$124 pp extra. Scuba diving with Tropical Dive (tel./fax 888-0776, www.matangidive.com) is F$195 plus gear for two tanks. Reader feedback on Matangi Island has been mixed.

Laucala Island

Laucala Island, which shares a barrier reef with Qamea, was depopulated and sold to Europeans in the mid-19th century by the chief of Taveuni, after the inhabitants sided with Tongan chief Enele Ma'afu in a local war. In 1972, the late billionaire businessman and New York publisher Malcolm Forbes bought 12-square-km Laucala from the Australian company Morris Hedstrom for US$1 million. He then spent additional millions on an airstrip, wharf, and roads, and on replacing the thatched *bure* of the 300 Fijian inhabitants with 40 red-roofed houses with electricity and indoor plumbing. Forbes died in 1990 and is buried on the island. His former private residence stands atop a hill overlooking the native village, the inhabitants of which make copra. In 1984, Forbes opened a small resort called "Fiji Forbes" on Laucala. During the turbulence following the Speight coup attempt in mid 2000, Laucala Island was invaded by thugs with scores to settle, and the resort managers were beaten and held 24 hours. Although peace has now returned to the island, the resort has closed. In 2003, the island was sold to Dietrich Mateschitz, the Austrian founder of the energy drink producer Red Bull, for US$10 million. Tourists from Qamea visit occasionally to snorkel in Laucala's tidal pools.

The Lau Group

Lau is by far the most remote region of Fiji, its 57 islands scattered over a vast area of ocean between Viti Levu and Tonga. Roughly half of them are inhabited. Though all are relatively small, they vary from volcanic islands to uplifted atolls to some combination of the two. Tongan influence has always been strong in Lau, and the westward migrations continue today: More than 40,000 Lauans live on Viti Levu and under 13,000 on their home islands. Historically the chiefs of Lau have always had a political influence on Fiji far out of proportion to their economic or geographical importance.

Vanua Balavu (52 square km) and Lakeba (54 square km) are the largest and most important islands of the group. These are also the only islands with organized budget accommodations, and Vanua Balavu is the more rewarding of the two. Once accessible only after a long sea voyage on infrequent copra-collecting ships, four islands in Lau—Lakeba, Vanua Balavu, Moala, and Cicia—now have regular air service from Suva. Occasional private ships also circulate through Lau, usually calling at five or six islands on a single trip. No banks are to be found in Lau and it's important to bring sufficient Fijian currency.

Few of these islands are prepared for tourism, so it really helps to know someone. But contrary to what is written in some guidebooks, individual tourists *do not* require a special permit or invitation to visit Lau or Rotuma—you just get on a plane and go. (Cruising yachties do need a permit.) Since the best selection of places to stay is on Vanua Balavu in Northern Lau, that's the logical place to head first. Words like pristine, untouched, and idyllic all seem to have been invented for Lau and Rotuma, and the unconditional friendliness of the local people is renowned. This is one area where you don't need to worry about bumping into a McDonald's!

NORTHERN LAU
Vanua Balavu
The name means the "long land." The southern portion of this unusual, seahorse-shaped island is mostly volcanic, while the north is uplifted coral. This unspoiled environment of palm-fringed beaches backed by long grassy hillsides and sheer limestone cliffs is a wonderful area to explore. Varied vistas and scenic views are on all sides. To the east is a 130-km barrier reef enclosing a 37 by 16 km lagoon. The Bay of Islands at the northwest end of Vanua Balavu is a recognized hurricane shelter. The villages of Vanua Balavu are impeccably clean, the grass cut and manicured. Large mats are made on the island and strips of pandanus can be seen drying before many of the houses.

In 1840, Commodore Wilkes of the U.S. Exploring Expedition named Vanua Balavu and its adjacent islands enclosed by the same barrier reef the Exploring Isles. In the days of sail, Lomaloma, the largest settlement, was an important Pacific port. The early trading company Hennings Brothers had its headquarters here. The great Tongan warlord Enele Ma'afu conquered northern Lau from the chiefs of Vanua Levu in 1855 and made Lomaloma the base for his bid to dominate Fiji. A small monument flanked by two cannons on the waterfront near the wharf recalls the event. Fiji's first public botanical garden was laid out here over a century ago, but nothing remains of it. History has passed Lomaloma by. Today it's only a big sleepy village with a hospital and a couple of general stores. Some 400 Tongans live in Sawana, the south portion of Lomaloma village, and many of the houses have the round ends characteristic of Lau. Fiji's first prime minister and later president, Ratu Sir Kamisese Mara, was born in Sawana.

Accommodations

Moana's Guesthouse (tel. 889-5006, www .moanasguesthouses.com) in Sawana village is run by Tevita and Carolyn Fotofili, with the help of daughter Moana. They offer a three-bedded dorm and double room in an oval-ended Tongan-style house in the village, plus another room in an adjacent house. In 2000, the eager-to-please Fotofilis built three traditional-style Tongan *bure* on the beach about a kilometer away. Either way it's F$50 pp including all meals and snacks (children under 12 half price). The food is outstanding and plentiful with lots of fresh fruit. Some very good snorkeling is available, although it takes a bit of effort to get to it. A motorboat is for hire for use on trips around Vanua Balavu or even to nearby islands like Kanacea and Mago. There's also a Fijian outrigger sailing canoe and horseback riding. If you enjoy peace and solitude and aren't too worried about amenities, this is the place.

You can also stay at Joe and Hélène Tuwai's **Nawanawa Estate** (tel. 811-6833), a kilometer from Daliconi village near the airport on the northwest side of the island. They meet all flights (transfers F$30 pp return) and can accommodate 10 persons in their own home on the estate. In the unlikely event that they are full, something else could be arranged. The Tuwais charge F$55/100 single/double including three meals (children under 10 F$25). You'll share their attractive colonial-style home with solar electricity (no generator noise). Aside from hiking, snorkeling, and fishing, you can ask to be dropped on a deserted island for a small charge. If you have a tent, you can camp there all by yourself for a small fee. Boat trips to the pristine Bay of Islands for caving and snorkeling are also possible (F$10 an hour plus fuel). All three

VANUA BALAVU

Bay of Islands
Nabavatu
Masomo Bay
Vutuna
Avea
Adavaci Island
Dakuirasia
Tota
Matavura
Mavana
Yanucaloa
Daliconi
Malaka
Adavaci Passage
Naruarua
Muamua
Mualevu
Vanua Balavu Island
Boitace
Levukana
Uruone
Lomaloma
Dakuilomaloma
Yanuyanu
Lagoon
Narocivo
Nakama
Namalata
Raviravi Lagoon
Malata
Susui
Munia
SOUTH PACIFIC OCEAN
Susui
Urone
0   4 mi
0   4 km

© DAVID STANLEY

places just mentioned accept cash only (take insect repellent and sunscreen too).

Getting There

Air Fiji flies to Vanua Balavu twice a week from Suva (F$130). The flights are heavily booked, so reserve your return journey before leaving Suva. Even then, if it has been raining too hard, the soggy airstrip may be closed. You can hitch a ride from the airstrip to Lomaloma with the Air Fiji agent for F$1.50. After checking in at the airstrip for departure you'll probably have time to scramble up the nearby hill for a good view of the island. Boat service from Suva on the *Tunatuki II* is only once every two weeks (F$82/113 deck/cabin).

Several carriers a day run from Lomaloma north to Mualevu, and some continue on to Mavana.

Other Islands of Northern Lau

After setting himself up at Lomaloma on Vanua Balavu in 1855, Chief Ma'afu encouraged the establishment of European copra and cotton plantations, and several islands are freehold land to this day. **Kanacea,** to the west of Vanua Balavu, was sold to a European by the Tui Cakau in 1863, and the Kanacea people now reside on Taveuni. **Mago** (20 square km), a copra estate formerly owned by English planter Jim Barron, was purchased by the Tokyu Corporation of Japan in 1985 for F$6 million.

Naitauba is a circular island about 186 meters high with high cliffs on the north coast. Originally owned by Hennings Brothers, in 1983 it was purchased from TV star Raymond Burr by the California spiritual group Johannine Daist Communion for US$2.1 million. Johannine Daist holds four-to-eight-week meditation retreats on Naitauba for longtime members of the communion. The communion's founder and teacher, Baba Da Free John, the former Franklin Albert Jones, who attained enlightenment in Hollywood in 1970, resides on the island.

There's a single Fijian village and a gorgeous white-sand beach on **Yacata Island.** Right next to Yacata and sharing the same lagoon is 260-hectare Kaimbu Island, where a small adults-only luxury resort opened in 1987. In 2004, **Kaimbu Island Resort** (Nigel Douglas, tel. 888-0333, fax 888-0334, kaimbu@connect.com.fj) was closed for renovations. In the past, the three spacious octagonal guest cottages have cost F$2,250 per couple per night, including meals, drinks, snorkeling, sailing, windsurfing, sportfishing, and scuba diving (minimum stay seven nights). The only thing lacking was a swimming pool. Kaimbu catered to folks in search of personalized service and total privacy at any price. The chartered flight from Suva or Taveuni to Kaimbu's central airstrip cost another F$2,225 per couple roundtrip, and 12.5 percent government tax had to be added to all rates. If this sounds interesting, check to see if they've reopened.

Vatu Vara to the south, with its soaring interior plateau, golden beaches, and azure lagoon, is privately owned and unoccupied much of the time. The circular, 314-meter-high central limestone terrace, which makes the island look like a hat when viewed from the sea, gives it its other name, Hat Island. There is reputed to be buried treasure on Vatu Vara.

Katafaga to the southeast of Vanua Balavu was at one time owned by Harold Gatty, the famous Australian aviator who founded Fiji Airways (later Air Pacific) in 1951. In 2004, the super deluxe **Katafanga Island Resort** (tel. 330-7333, www.katafanga.com) opened on this 1.5-km-long private island. The main complex with the dining pavilion and spa is on a coral cliff, while the 20 air-conditioned villas with individual whirlpool tubs and dipping pools are along a white lagoon beach. Rates start at F$2,900 double including meals, drinks, activities, and spa treatments, plus F$800 pp return airfare from Suva and 12.5 percent tax (five-night minimum stay). Children under 17 are only accepted on certain dates. Scuba diving is available at additional cost. A nine-hole golf course separates Katafaga's airstrip from the rest of the resort.

Cicia, between Northern and Southern Lau, receives Air Fiji flights from Suva (F$121) once a week. Five Fijian villages are found on Cicia, and much of the 34-square-km island is covered by coconut plantations. Fiji's only black-and-white Australian magpies have been introduced to Cicia and Taveuni.

Wailagi Lala, northernmost of the Lau Group, is a coral atoll bearing a lighthouse, which beckons to ships entering Nanuku Passage, the northwest gateway to Fiji.

SOUTHERN LAU
Lakeba Island

Lakeba is a rounded volcanic island reaching 215 meters. The fertile red soils of the rolling interior hills have been planted with pine, but the low coastal plain, with eight villages and all the people, is covered with coconuts. To the east is a wide lagoon enclosed by a barrier reef. From the Catholic church you get a good view of Tubou, an attractive village on the south side of the island, with a hospital, wharf, several stores, and the Lau provincial headquarters.

The Tongan chief Enele Ma'afu (died 1881) is buried on a stepped platform behind the Provincial Office near Tubou's wharf. In 1847, Ma'afu arrived in Fiji with a small Tongan army ostensibly to advance the spread of Christianity, and by 1855 he dominated eastern Fiji from his base at Vanua Balavu. In 1869, Ma'afu united the group into the Lau Confederation and took the title Tui Lau. Two years later he accepted the supremacy of Cakobau's Kingdom of Fiji, and in 1874 he signed the cession to Britain. When the Nayau clan conquered the island, their paramount chief, the Tui Nayau, became ruler of all of Southern Lau from his seat at Tubou. From the 1970s to the 1990s, Ratu Sir Kamisese Mara, the current Tui Nayau, served as prime minister and later president of Fiji. Alongside Ma'afu is the grave of Ratu Sir Lala Sukuna (1888–1958), an important figure in the development of indigenous Fijian self-government. David Cargill and William Cross, the first Methodist missionaries to arrive in Fiji, landed on the beach just opposite the burial place on October 12, 1835. Here they invented the present system of written Fijian.

There are numerous limestone caves to explore on Lakeba. A 29-km road runs all the way around the island, and many forestry roads have been built throughout the interior. You can walk across the island from Tubou to Yadrana in a couple of hours, enjoying excellent views along the way. Aiwa Island, which can be seen to the southeast, is owned by the Tui Nayau and is inhabited only by flocks of wild goats.

Jekesoni Qica's Guesthouse (tel. 882-3035) in Tubou offers rooms with shared bath at F$40 pp for room and board. The locals at Tubou concoct a potent homebrew (uburu) from cassava—ask Jack where you can get some.

Air Fiji flies to Lakeba three times a week from Suva (F$131). A bus connects the airstrip to Tubou, and buses run around the island four times daily on weekdays, three times daily weekends.

Other Islands of Southern Lau

Unlike the islands of northern Lau, many of which are freehold and owned by outsiders, the isles of southern Lau are communally owned by the Fijian inhabitants. This is by far the most remote corner of Fiji. In a pool on **Vanua Vatu** are red prawns similar to those of Vatulele and Vanua Levu. Here the locals can summon the prawns with a certain chant.

Oneata is famous for its mosquitoes and tapa cloth. In 1830, two Tahitian teachers from the London Missionary Society arrived on Oneata and were adopted by a local chief who had previously visited Tonga and Tahiti. The men spent the rest of their lives on the island, and there's a monument to them at Dakuloa village.

Moce is known for its tapa cloth, which is also made on Namuka, Vatoa, and Ono-i-Lau. **Komo** is famous for its handsome women and dances (meke), which are performed whenever a ship arrives. Moce, Komo, and Olorua are unique in that they are volcanic islands without uplifted limestone terraces.

The **Yagasa Cluster** is owned by the people of Moce, who visit it occasionally to make copra. Fiji's finest tanoa are carved from vesi (ironwood) at **Kabara,** the largest island in southern Lau. The surfing is also said to be good at Kabara, if you can get there.

Fulaga is known for its woodcarving; large outrigger canoes are still built on Fulaga, as well as on **Ogea.** Over 100 tiny islands in the Fulaga lagoon have been undercut into incredible mushroom shapes. The water around them is tinged with striking colors by the dissolved limestone, and there are numerous magnificent beaches. Yachts can enter this lagoon through a narrow pass.

Ono-i-Lau, far to the south, is closer to Tonga than to the main islands of Fiji. It consists of three small volcanic islands, remnants of a single crater, in an oval lagoon. A few tiny coral islets sit on the barrier reef. The people of Ono-i-Lau make the best magi magi (sennit rope) and tabu kaisi mats in the country. Only high chiefs may sit on these mats. Ono-i-Lau formerly had air service from Suva, but this has been suspended and the only access now is by ship.

The Moala Group

Structurally, geographically, and historically, the high volcanic islands of Moala, Totoya, and Matuku have more to do with Viti Levu than with the rest of Lau. In the mid-19th century, the Tongan warlord Enele Ma'afu conquered the islands, and today they're still administered as part of the Lau Group. All three islands have varied scenery, with dark green rainforests above grassy slopes, good anchorage, many villages, and abundant food. No tourist facilities of any kind exist in the Moala Group.

Triangular **Moala** is an intriguing 68-square-km island, the ninth largest in Fiji. Two small crater lakes on the summit of Delai Moala (467 meters) are covered with matted sedges, which will support a person's weight. Though the main island is volcanic, an extensive system of reefs flanks the shores. Ships call at the small government station of Naroi, also the site of an airstrip that receives **Air Fiji** flights twice a week from Suva (F$118).

Totoya is a horseshoe-shaped high island enclosing a deep bay on the south. The bay, actually the island's sunken crater, can only be entered through a narrow channel known as the Gullet, and the southeast trades send high waves across the reefs at the mouth of the bay, making this a dangerous place. Better anchorage is found off the southwest arm of the island. Five Fijian villages are found on Totoya, while neighboring **Matuku** has seven. The anchorage in a submerged crater on the west side of Matuku is one of the finest in Fiji.

Rotuma

Rotuma is on the opposite side of the country from Lau, 600 km north of Viti Levu. This isolated five-by-14-km volcanic island is surrounded on all sides by more than 322 km of open sea. There's a saying in Fiji that if you can find Rotuma on a map it's a fairly good map. Rotuma's climate is damper and hotter than other parts of Fiji. The Rotumans are a Polynesian people linked to Melanesian Fiji by historical and geographical chance.

According to legend, Rotuma was formed by Raho, a Samoan folk hero who dumped two basketfuls of earth here to create the twin islands, joined by the Motusa Isthmus. Tongans from Niuafo'ou conquered Rotuma in the 17th century and ruled from Noa'tau until they were overthrown.

The first recorded European visit was by Captain Edwards of HMS *Pandora* in 1791, while he was searching for the *Bounty* mutineers. Tongan Wesleyan missionaries introduced Christianity in 1842, followed in 1847 by Marist Roman Catholics. Their followers fought pitched battles in the religious wars of 1871 and 1878, with the Wesleyans emerging victorious. Tiring of strife, the chiefs asked Britain to annex the island in 1879. Cession officially took place in 1881 and Rotuma has been part of Fiji ever since. European traders ran the copra trade from their settlement at Motusa until local cooperatives took over.

On Rotuma today the administration in the hands of a district officer responsible to the district commissioner at Levuka. Most decisions of the 15-member Rotuma island council pertain to local concerns. The island remains remote from the rest of Fiji, and a desire for independence is felt among some Rotumans. Some 2,800 Rotumans presently inhabit the island, and another 4,700 live in Suva and Naitasiri. The women weave fine white mats. Fiji's juiciest oranges are grown here and Rotuma kava is noted for its strength. Most visitors to Rotuma are relatives or friends of local residents and the number of foreign tourists arriving here is negligible.

Sights

Ships arrive at a wharf on the edge of the reef, connected to Oinafa Point by a 200-meter coral causeway, which acts as a breakwater. There's a lovely white beach at **Oinafa**. The airstrip is to the west, between Oinafa and Ahau, the government station. At **Sisilo** near Noa'tau visit a hill with large stone slabs and old cannons scattered about, marking the burial place of the kings of yore. Look for the fine stained-glass windows in the Catholic church at **Sumi** on the south coast. Inland near the center of the island is Mt. Suelhof (256 meters), the highest peak; climb it for the view.

Maftoa, across the Motusa Isthmus, has a graveyard with huge stones brought here long ago. It's said four men could go into a trance and carry the stones with their fingers. **Sororoa Bluff** (218 meters) above Maftoa can be climbed, though the view is obstructed by vegetation. Deserted **Vaioa Beach** on the west side of Sororoa Bluff is one of the finest in the Pacific. A kilo-

BASIC FIJIAN

Although most people in Fiji speak English fluently, mother tongues include Fijian, Hindi, and other Pacific languages. Knowledge of a few words of Fijian, especially slang words, will make your stay more exciting and enriching. Fijian has no pure *b*, *c*, or *d* sounds as they are known in English. When the first missionaries arrived, they invented a system of spelling, with one letter for each Fijian sound. The reader should be aware that the sound "mb" is written *b*, "nd" is *d*, "ng" is *g*, "ngg" is *q*, and "th" is *c*.

Au lako mai Kenada: I come from Canada

Au ni lako mai vei?: Where do you come from?

Au sa lako ki vei?: Where are you going?

bula: a Fijian greeting

Daru lako!: Let's go!

dua: one

dua oo: said by males when they meet a chief or enter a Fijian

dua tale: once more

io: yes

kana: eat

kauta mai: bring

kauta tani: take away

kaivalagi: foreigner

koro: village

Kocei na yacamu?: What's your name?

lailai: small

lako mai: come

lako tani: go

levu: big, much

lima: five

loloma yani: please pass along my regards

maleka: delicious

magimagi: coconut rope fiber

magiti: feast

marama: madam

mataqali: a clan lineage

moce: goodbye

Na cava oqo?: What is this?

ni sa bula: Hello, how are you? (can also say *sa bula* or *bula vinaka:* the answer is *an sa bula vinaka*)

ni sa moce: good night

ni sa yadra: good morning

qara: cave

rua: two

sa vinaka: it's okay

sega: no, none

sega na leqa: you're welcome

sota tale: see you again

talatala: reverend

tolu: three

tulou: excuse me

turaga: sir, Mr.

uro: a provocative greeting for the opposite sex

va: four

vaka lailai: a little, small

vaka levu: a lot, great

vaka malua: slowly

vaka totolo: fast

vale: house

vale lailai: toilet

vanua: land, custom, people

vinaka: thank you

vinaka vakalevu: thank you very much

vu: an ancestral spirit

wai: water

yalo vinaka: please

yadra: good morning

yaqona: kava, grog

BASIC HINDI

aao: come
accha: good
bhaahut julum: very beautiful (slang)
chota: small (male)
choti: small (female)
dhanyabaad: thank you
ek aur: one more
haan: yes
hum jauo: I go (slang)
jalebi: an Indian sweet
jao: go
kab: when
kahaan: where
kahaan jata hai: Where are you going?
kaise hai?: How are you?
khana: food
kitna?: How much?
kya: what
laao: bring
maaf kijye ga: excuse me
nahi: no
namaste: hello, goodbye
pani: water
rait: okay
ram ram: same as *namaste*
roti: a flat Indian bread
seedhe jauo: go straight
theek bhai: I'm fine
yeh kia hai: what's this?
yihaan: here

---

meter southwest of Vaioa Beach is **Solmea Hill** (165 meters), with an inactive crater on its north slope. On the coast at the northwest corner of Rotuma is a natural **stone bridge** over the water. A cave with a swimmable freshwater pool is at **Fapufa** on the south coast.

Visitors are expected to request permission before visiting sites like Sisilo or the cave at Fapufa. Inquire at Ahau about whom to ask (permission will always be given unless something peculiar has come up), but it is a courtesy expected by the Rotumans and will avoid unpleasant misunderstandings.

Accommodations

Though the airport opened as far back as 1982, places to stay on Rotuma are few. Many Rotumans live in Suva, however, and if you have a Rotuman friend he/she may be willing to send word to his/her family to expect you. Ask your friend what you should take along as a gift. It's appropriate to make a financial contribution to your host family soon after you arrive to compensate them for your stay (F$40 a day per couple is the minimum you should offer). When deciding on the amount, bear in mind that groceries purchased in the small stores around Rotuma cost about double what they would on Viti Levu. Rainbow-way Travel Services (tel. 330-6613, fax 330-6593, rainboway1@connect.com.fj) in Suva arranges stays on Rotuma.

The only official place to stay is **Mojito's Barfly** (tel. 889-1144) across the street from Motusa Primary School. The four rooms with shared bath in two Polynesian-style houses are used to accommodate government workers who pay F$65 pp including meals and laundry, or F$30 pp without meals (no cooking facilities provided). Despite the name, the bar no longer functions here.

There's no bank on Rotuma so be sure to change enough money to cover all local expenditures before leaving Suva. In emergencies, you might be able to have someone wire money to you via Western Union care of the Post Shop at Ahau.

Getting There

Air Fiji flies from Suva to Rotuma weekly (F$339 one way). Ships like the *Bulou-ni-ceva* and *Cagi Mai Ba* operate from Suva to Rotuma once a month (two days, F$100/170/190 deck/cabin/lounge each way). Turn to Transportation in the Suva section for more information.

Be aware that transportation to and from Rotuma, either by boat or plane, can be erratic, and you should be as flexible as possible. It's not uncommon for the boat from Suva to be delayed two weeks with engine trouble, and the plane has also been known not to go on schedule, or flights can be cancelled.

FIJI ISLANDS

New Caledonia

Introduction

New Caledonia—or Kanaky, as the indigenous Melanesian inhabitants call it—is unique. In Nouméa, the capital, the fine French restaurants, designer boutiques, and cosmopolitan crowds all proclaim that this is the Paris of the Pacific. Yet over on the east coast of the main island and on all of the outliers, the Kanaks (from *kanaka,* the Hawaiian word for "human") and *la coutume* (native custom) have survived a century and a half of pervasive colonial domination.

During the 1980s, the clash of the irresistible force of Kanak nationalism against the immovable mass of entrenched French settlers catapulted the territory into world headlines more than once. Then in 1988, a 10-year truce was signed, consolidated in a 1998 referendum. A phased increase in local autonomy has been approved, and the possibility of full independence after a 15 to 20-year transitional period is being held out. In the meantime, peace has returned to the "Great Land" and its adjacent islands.

New Caledonia can be a troubling place to visit. The French authorities try to keep the ter-

© SOUTH PACIFIC TOURISM ORGANIZATION

ritory's contradictions tucked away from the eyes of tourists, but unless you spend all your time in Nouméa, you're bound to notice the striking differences between the affluent French and the displaced, disadvantaged Kanaks. New Caledonia is an anachronism in the South Pacific, a bastion of old-fashioned European colonialism held aloft by massive subsidies from France. In recent years, the French government has thrown huge sums at the Kanak elite, with the clear intent of making the entire concept of independence irrelevant. And as long as the subsidies keep flowing and the Melanesian masses can be sufficiently intimidated, not a lot is likely to change.

Though many tourists visit Nouméa, surprisingly few cross the Chaîne Centrale to Grande Terre's exotic east coast, or travel by sea or air to the charming outer islands. Yet this is something you simply must do to see the real New Caledonia. The possibilities are limitless, and it's a lot easier to travel around New Caledonia than it is to tour rural Vanuatu or Solomon Islands. Wherever you go, you'll be received with warmth and interest, especially when people hear you speaking English. This enigmatic French colony just north of the tropic of Capricorn, midway between Fiji and Australia, is quite unlike any of its neighbors and will surprise you in every respect.

The Land

New Caledonia consists of a cigar-shaped mainland (Grande Terre), the Isle of Pines, the Loyalty Group, and the small uninhabited dependencies of Walpole Island (125 hectares), the d'Entrecasteaux Reefs (64 hectares), and the more distant Chesterfield Islands (101 hectares). The d'Entrecasteaux Reefs consist of two separate lagoons centered on tiny Huon and Surprise Islands, with a deep strait 10 km wide between. The territory's 18,735 square km are divided into three provinces: North Province (9,663 square km), South Province (7,092 square km), and Loyalty Islands Province (1,981 square km).

Grande Terre is part of the great fold in the earth's surface that runs from the central highlands of Papua New Guinea to the northern peninsula of New Zealand. The geology is complex, with metamorphic, sedimentary, and vol-

---

NEW CALEDONIA HIGHLIGHTS

Hienghène, Grande Terre: spectacular coastline, scene of Kanak martyrdom (p. 858)

Kanuméra/Kuto, Isle of Pines: lovely beaches, hiking, penal colony remains (p. 865)

Lifou Island: largest uplifted atoll in the world (p. 871)

Ouvéa Atoll: 25 km of unbroken white sand beach, monument to the Ouvéa Massacre (p. 874)

Tjibaou Cultural Center, Nouméa: museum, art gallery, library, botanical garden (p. 833)

---

canic rock present. Grande Terre is 400 km long and 50 km wide, the sixth-largest island in the Southwest Pacific (after New Guinea, the two islands of New Zealand, Tasmania, and New Britain). This island is a fragment on the ancient continent of Gondwana of 60 million years ago. It's slowly sinking as the Indo-Australian Plate pushes under the Pacific Plate to the east; the winding, indented coastline is a result of this submergence. Ten km off both coasts is the second-longest barrier reef in the world, which marks how big the island once was. New Caledonia has a larger area of coral reefs than all the other entities covered in this handbook combined.

Locals refer to Grande Terre as "Le Caillou" or "La Roche" (The Rock). The interior is made up of row upon row of craggy mountains throughout its length, such as Mt. Panie (1,639 meters) in the north and Mt. Humboldt (1,618 meters) in the south, and it contains 20 percent of the world's known reserves of nickel ore (enough to last another century at the present rate of extraction), as well as profitable deposits of other minerals such as tungsten, cobalt, copper, gold, manganese, iron, and chromium. The landscape, you'll notice, is wounded in many locales by huge open-pit mines—the Great Red Menace. Bulldozer tracks and drill holes leave ugly scars, and sediments unleashed by the mining turn the rivers thick red and wash out to kill the reefs. The verdant northeast coast of this island is broken and narrow, cut by tortuous rivers and jagged

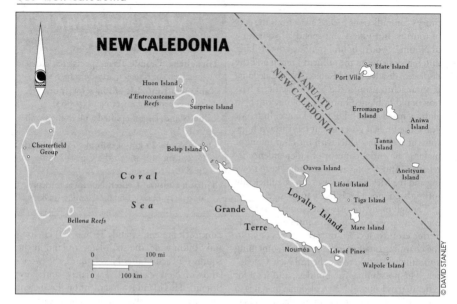

NEW CALEDONIA

peaks falling directly into the lagoon. The drier southwest coast is low, swampy, and mosquito-ridden, with wide coastal plains and alluvial lowlands. In the far south is a lowland plain of lakes.

The Loyalty Islands, on the other hand, are uplifted atolls with no rivers but many limestone caves. Maré, Tiga, Lifou, and Ouvéa form a chain 100 km east of Grande Terre. The Belep Islands and Isle of Pines are geological extensions of the main island. Walpole Island, 130 km east of the Isle of Pines, is also an uplifted limestone island three km long and 400 meters wide, with no protective reef around its 70-meter-high cliffs. Guano (fertilizer) was exploited here in 1910-36. The Huon Islands consist of four tiny coral islands 275 km northwest of Grande Terre, while the Chesterfields are 11 coral islets on a reef in the Coral Sea 550 km west-northwest of the main island. All of these dependencies are home to many species of seabirds.

Climate

New Caledonia is farther south than most other South Pacific islands; this, combined with the refreshing southeast trade winds, accounts for its sunny, moderate climate, similar to that of the south of France. The average annual temperature is 23.6°C. It can even be cool and windy from June to September, and campers will need sleeping bags. The ocean is warm enough for bathing year-round.

December to March is warmer and rainier; it's also the hurricane season. The cyclonic depressions can bring heavy downpours and cause serious flooding. The windward northeast coast of Grande Terre catches the prevailing winds and experiences as much as 3,000 mm of precipitation a year, while the leeward southwest coast is a rain shadow with only 800 to 1,200 mm. Strong currents and heavy seas off the northeast coast make the southwest coast, where navigation is possible behind protective reefs, a better choice for cruising sailors.

Flora

New Caledonia's vegetation has more in common with Australia's than it does with that of its closer tropical neighbor, Vanuatu. Seventy-five percent of the 3,250 botanic species are endemic. There are extensive areas of mangrove swamp and savanna grassland along the west coast. The only sizable forests are in the mountains.

The territory's most distinctive tree is a pine known as the *Araucaria columnaris,* which towers 30–45 meters high, with branches only two meters long. It's common along the more forested east coast and in the south, standing on low hills along the rockier shorelines and on the offshore islands. Often confused with the better-known Norfolk pine or *Araucaria excelsa,* the *Araucaria columnaris* or "candelabra" pine has a cylindrical profile whereas the Norfolk pine is conical. They're the most prominent floral features of these neighboring islands when viewed from the sea, and European mariners from Captain Cook onwards have been suitably impressed.

The most characteristic tree of the savannas of northern and western of Grande Terre is the *niaouli,* a relative of the eucalyptus. This tree has a white, almost completely fireproof bark, which peels off in papery layers and is used as an excellent medicinal oil, somewhat like eucalyptus oil. Through its ability to survive bush fires, the *niaouli* plays an important environmental role in this mountainous country by maintaining the continuity of the vegetation.

Fauna

The only native mammals are the flying fox, the bat, and the rat. The pig was unknown to the indigenous people prior to European contact. The deer that inhabit the savannas of Grande Terre are descended from two pairs introduced in 1862. Some of the butterflies possess a rare beauty. Eighty-eight species of birds are found in New Caledonia, 18 of them endemic. Only a few hundred specimens of the Ouvéa parakeet still exist. The purple swamp hen with its red beak and blue body is often seen running around west coast campgrounds.

The national bird is the flightless *cagou (Rhynochetos jubatus),* or kagu, about the size of a small rooster. This bird has lovely soft gray plumage, contrasted by striped brown-and-white wings. The *cagou's* crest rises when the bird is angered, and its cry is like the bark of a dog. It eats insects, worms, and snails. Since it hatches only one egg a year and is slow on the ground, the *cagou* is threatened with extinction: Dogs often outrun and kill it. Fewer than 2,000 survive in Rivière

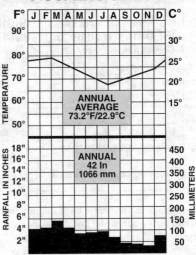

NOUMÉA'S CLIMATE

ANNUAL AVERAGE 73.2°F/22.9°C

ANNUAL 42 In 1066 mm

Bleue Provincial Park at the west end of Yaté Lake and elsewhere.

The extreme richness of life on the reefs compensates for the lack of variety on land. New Caledonia's 1,600 km of barrier reefs are home to 350 species of coral, 1,500 species of fish, and 20,000 species of invertebrates. The territory's protected lagoons total 23,000 square km, with an average depth of 20 meters—the largest lagoon complex in the world.

HISTORY
Prehistory

It's not certain when the Papuan peoples reached New Caledonia. Some 300 earth mounds dating from 6000 B.C. discovered on the Isle of Pines were once thought to prove habitation for at least 8,000 years, but the mounds are now accepted as having been constructed by extinct giant birds. What is known for sure is that Austronesian-speakers have been here for more than 3,000 years. *Lapita* sites have been found near Koné and on the Isle of Pines, the pottery carbon-dated at earlier than 1000 B.C. Prehistoric rock carvings are found

NEW CALEDONIA

NEW CALEDONIA AT A GLANCE

ISLAND	AREA (square km)	HIGHEST POINT (m)	POPULATION (2002 est.)	PERCENTAGE KANAK
Grande Terre	16,648	1,639	189,714	36.9
Isle of Pines	152	262	1,861	93.7
Mare	657	138	7,758	97.2
Lifou	1,146	90	11,131	96.7
Ouvea	132	39	4,408	97.8
Isles Belep	70	283	1,032	99.3
New Caledonia	18,735*		215,904	44.1

* includes other dependencies

throughout the territory. Back migrations of Polynesians reached the Loyalty Islands just a few hundred years before the Europeans.

The Kanak clans lived in small villages of 50 people and farmed their own land, using sophisticated irrigation systems and terraced taro gardens. Kanak culture has been called the "yam civilization," because of the importance of this tuber as a staple and in ceremonial exchanges. Land was owned collectively but controlled by the oldest son of the first clan to settle in a place.

The center of the village was the *grande case,* a large conical-roofed house where the chief lived and ceremonies were performed. Religion was animistic. Of the many spirits loose in the land, the most powerful were the clan ancestors. Society was based around a relationship between the living and their ancestors, both of whom the chief represented, in a sense.

A number of clans formed an autonomous tribe. Local tribes had little contact with each other, and thus many languages evolved; most people lived in the interior, and language groups extended across the main island, rather than down the coasts. When Captain Cook, the first European, arrived in September 1774, there were more than 70,000 Kanaks living in these islands.

Contact and Conquest

Cook landed at Balade, on the northeast coast of Grande Terre, and gave New Caledonia its name—the mountainous island reminded him of the Scottish Highlands (Caledonia was the Romans' name for Scotland). After more navigators (d'Entrecasteaux and Huon de Kermadec), traders arrived looking for sandalwood and bêche-de-mer. The first missionaries were Protestants from the London Missionary Society, who established themselves on Maré (1841) and Lifou (1842) islands. French Catholic missionaries arrived at Balade in 1843, but Kanak hostility and British protests caused them to withdraw four years later.

At this time France was enviously observing the establishment of successful British colonies in Australia and New Zealand. So in 1853, with the idea of creating a penal colony similar to that in New South Wales, Emperor Napoléon III ordered the annexation of New Caledonia. The Loyalties were claimed in 1866. Île Nou, an island in Nouméa Bay, never attained the notoriety of its contemporary, Devil's Island off South America, but between 1864 and 1897 some 20,000 French convicts sentenced to more than eight years hard labor were transported there, although no more than 8,000 were present at any one time. They were used for public works and construction projects in the early days.

Some 3,900 political prisoners from the Paris Commune were held at Ducos near Nouméa and on the Isle of Pines during 1871–1879. Unlike the common criminals who had preceded them, many of the *communards* were cultured individuals. For example, Louise Michel, the "red virgin," taught Kanak children in Nouméa and took an active interest in the indigenous way of life. In her memoirs, Michel compared the freedom struggle of the Kanaks to that of Paris in 1871.

Colonialism and War

In 1864, Jules Garnier, a French mining engineer, discovered nickel on the banks of the Diahot River. Copper was found at Balade in 1872, cobalt in 1875. The Société le Nickel (SLN) was established in 1876, and mining began in earnest. This lead to an increase in the land seizures already underway, causing food shortages and the destruction of the Kanak way of life. In 1878, High Chief Atai of La Foa managed to unite many of the central tribes and launched a guerrilla war that cost 200 Frenchmen and 1,200 Kanaks their lives. Eventually Atai was betrayed by a rival tribe and assassinated.

The French government used the revolt as an excuse to establish a series of "indigenous reservations" for the confinement of the natives in areas the French miners and settlers didn't want, opening the rest of Grande Terre to mining and stock raising. Many clans were forced off their own lands onto that of other clans, leading to further rivalry and disruption. Most of the French political prisoners on the island, who had fought for their own freedom just a few years previously, assisted the colonial regime in repressing the "savages" (Louise Michel was an exception).

The French government assumed title to two-thirds of Grande Terre, another quarter was eventually given or sold to white settlers, and only 10 percent of the main island (in scattered, hilly areas) was left to the original inhabitants. Title to even these crowded holdings was uncertain. The *colons* (settlers) brought in cattle and sheep, and occupied the river valleys and coastal plains. Tribes were relocated in 150 villages under puppet chiefs and were easily controlled by French gendarmes. To obtain cheap labor, the French imposed a heavy poll tax on the Kanaks, effectively forcing them to work for the *colons* in order to obtain the money to pay. With their traditional way of life disrupted, the Kanak population declined from around 60,000 in 1878 to 42,500 in 1887, and 27,000 in 1926. Only during the 1930s did their numbers again increase.

In 1917, the forced recruitment of Kanaks into the French army led High Chief Noel to appeal to his people to fight the French as well at home as Kanak soldiers had fought the Germans abroad (1,000 Kanaks were killed in WW I). Although not as widespread as the 1878 revolt, the fighting lasted two months in north and northwest Grande Terre, and 11 Europeans and 200 Kanaks died. Further land alienations followed. The depression of the 1930s wiped out many small French farmers, and land was concentrated in the hands of a few, as it is today.

In June 1940, after the fall of France, the Conseil Général of New Caledonia voted unanimously to support the Free French government, and in September the pro-Vichy governor was forced to leave for Indochina. The territory became an important Allied base in March 1942, and the fleet that turned back the Japanese navy in the Battle of the Coral Sea (May 1942) was based at Nouméa. Hundreds of thousands of American troops and a lesser number of New Zealand troops passed this way; in the Pacific, only San Francisco handled more wartime cargo. Several Nouméa neighborhoods still bear names like "Receiving" and "Motor Pool" bestowed at this time. Kanaks employed by the Americans received far better treatment than they had come to expect from the French.

Political Development

After WW II, France had a fairly progressive colonial policy. Partly due to a shortage of labor in the nickel industry, the Kanaks were finally given French citizenship in 1946, and the repressive "indigenous regulations" that forbade them from leaving their reservations without police permission were repealed. In 1951, the French parliament gave the right to vote to a large number of indigenous people throughout the French Union, and Maurice Lenormand of the multiracial Union Calédonienne was elected to the French National Assembly. Lenormand's lobbying won an elected territorial assembly with the power to make laws, and in 1957, New

Caledonia became an Overseas Territory and seemed on the road to independence.

Then came an armed uprising by French settlers on June 18, 1958, and the rise to power in France of Général de Gaulle, who dissolved the territorial assembly and appointed a repressive new governor. In 1963, Lenormand was jailed for a year, and deprived of his civil liberties by the French government for five years in a frame-up involving the bombing of the Territorial Assembly. The same year, the French National Assembly scrapped New Caledonia's limited autonomy and returned full control to the governor.

Lenormand's successor, Roch Pidjot, Kanak chief of the La Conception tribe near Nouméa, represented the Union Calédonienne in the French National Assembly for two decades until his retirement in 1986. His many proposals for self-government were never considered. A 1977 gerrymander created a second National Assembly seat for Nouméa and the west coast of Grande Terre, and this was taken a year later by businessman Jacques Lafleur, the wealthiest person in New Caledonia. In 1979, the Union Calédonienne united with four other pro-independence parties to form the Front Indépendantiste, which took 14 of the 36 seats in the Territorial Assembly.

On September 19, 1981, Pierre Declercq, secretary-general of the Union Calédonienne, was shot through a window of his Mont-Dore home. No one has ever been brought to trial for this crime. Declercq's murder further united the independence movement, and in the 1982 elections, the Front Indépendantiste gained a majority in the territorial assembly. Jean-Marie Tjibaou (pronounced Chi-BOW), a former Catholic priest, became vice-president of the government council.

Crisis

Prior to the May 1981 election of François Mitterrand, the French left had assured the Kanaks that their right to self-determination would be respected. Once in power, the Socialists' promises proved empty. Thus disillusioned Kanak activists reorganized their movement into the Front de Libération Nationale Kanake et Socialiste (FLNKS), and de-

cided to actively boycott the territorial assembly elections of November 18, 1984. Their demand was immediate independence.

Roadblocks were set up and ballot boxes destroyed. Though thousands of transient French cast ballots, voter turnout dropped from 75 percent in the 1979 elections to less than 50 percent in 1984. By default, the anti-independence Rassemblement pour la Calédonie dans la République (RPCR) won 34 of the 42 seats. On December 1, 1984 the FLNKS proclaimed a Provisional Government of Kanaky and tightened its roadblocks throughout the territory. President Mitterrand's personal envoy Edgard Pisani arrived on December 3, 1984 and declared that he would work out a plan for self-government within two months.

Two nights later, on December 5, 1984, a gang of French *colons* armed with automatic weapons, dynamite, dogs, and searchlights ambushed a group of 17 unarmed FLNKS militants as they drove home up a valley near Hienghène. Stopped by a felled tree and caught in a crossfire, the Kanaks tried to escape across a river. For half an hour the killers hunted them down like animals, finishing off the wounded until the river ran red with blood. In the end, 10 Kanaks died, including two brothers of Jean-Marie Tjibaou, head of the provisional government. French gendarmes stationed five km away didn't bother to visit the scene for 16 hours, although they were called shortly after the incident. A week later, seven of the killers, including members of third- and fourth-generation settler families, gave themselves up and were jailed.

Appalled by this atrocity, Pisani sought a solution that would bring the two sides together in a semi-independent state freely associated with France. On January 7, 1985, Pisani announced a plan calling for a referendum on independence on July 1, 1985, and self-government in association with France from January 1, 1986. France would control defense and foreign affairs, and French citizens would have special status. Then on January 12, 1985, police sharpshooters shot and killed schoolteacher Éloi Machoro, minister of the interior in the provisional government, and Marcel Noraro, an aide, as they stood outside their rural headquarters near La Foa. (It's believed the same French secret service elements that later planned the *Rainbow Warrior* bombing at Auckland of July 1985 were responsible for this and other provocations in New Caledonia.) In retaliation, the giant French-owned Thio and Kouaoua nickel mines were blown up by the Kanaks as whites rioted against independence in Nouméa. The FLNKS rejected Pisani's "neocolonial" plan (which the RPCR also strongly opposed for daring to take seriously any notion of independence).

In March 1985, an undaunted Pisani submitted his plan to Mitterrand, and in April French Prime Minister Laurent Fabius announced a new decentralization program featuring greater autonomy, land reform, and a say for the Kanaks in the territory's affairs. The territorial assembly elected in November 1984 was to be abolished, and a 43-seat territorial congress created to represent four regions, northern and central Grande Terre, the Loyalty Islands, and Nouméa. Nouméa would have 18 seats elected by universal suffrage, the other three regions (with Kanak majorities), 25 seats. The congress was to decide on independence before the end of 1987.

After protests that the French population was not properly represented, the number of Nouméa seats was increased to 21 in a 46-seat body. In August 1985, President Mitterrand recalled the French National Assembly from holidays to enact the legislation. Territorial elections took place on September 29, 1985. The pro-independence FLNKS won the three rural regions, while the anti-independence RPCR took Nouméa (more than 80 percent of Kanaks voted for the FLNKS). After this election, the political situation quieted down. Thirty-two people, Kanaks and French, died during the 1984–1985 confrontations.

Reaction

In March 1986, conservatives under Prime Minister Jacques Chirac took over the French national assembly from the Socialists. Chirac immediately adopted a hard, anti-independence stance: The concessions granted under the Socialists were to be undone. Chirac's Minister of Overseas Territories, Bernard Pons, recentralized power in the high commissioner by transferring the funds intended for regional development away from the regional councils. The economic agency created to promote development in Kanak areas through soft loans and outright grants was abolished, and land purchased under the Socialists for redistribution to Kanak tribes was turned over to extremist French settlers. French elite troops were stationed at mobile camps next to Kanak villages, the same "nomadization" tactics the French army had used in Algeria and Chad to study and intimidate potential opponents.

These backward steps convinced the South Pacific Forum, meeting at Suva in August 1986, to vote unanimously to ask the United Nations to reinscribe New Caledonia on its list of non-self-governing territories (the territory had previously been on the list until 1947). On December 2, 1986 the U.N. General Assembly voted 89–24 to reinscribe New Caledonia on the decolonization list—a major diplomatic defeat for France. The situation in the territory was to be reviewed annually by the U.N. Committee of 24, focusing international attention on the situation.

Responding to international criticism, the French government held a referendum on independence in the territory on September 13, 1987. The Socialists had proposed a referendum giving voters the option of independence in association with France. Under Chirac the choice was simply complete independence or remaining part of France. The FLNKS insisted that only those with one parent born in the territory (be they Kanak or French settler) be allowed to vote. (Though Kanaks themselves couldn't vote at all until 1953, the 25,000 immigrants who had entered the country between 1969 and 1974 were now to decide its fate.) Chirac insisted that everyone who had been there longer than three years must be allowed to vote. So, with the outnumbered Kanaks boycotting the vote, the result was 98 percent in favor of France.

In October 1987, Pons announced a plan that would redefine the council boundaries to ensure that Kanaks and settlers each controlled two regions, a net loss to the Kanaks of one. Henceforth the regional councils would only be responsible for municipal affairs, road maintenance, agriculture, and folklore. Authority was to be centralized in a 10-member executive council that would replace the territorial congress, overturning Fabius reforms granting the Kanaks limited autonomy in the regions outside Nouméa. Pons's plan denationalized the Kanaks by claiming that only French citizens existed in New Caledonia; the existing native reserves were to be considered freehold land available for sale to anyone. Kanak claims to land rights and independence were to be considered totally irrelevant. In January 1988, the right-wing French National Assembly voted 289–283 to adopt the Pons Statute. After this the Chirac regime simply refused to negotiate with the Kanaks. By now 14,000 French troops were present in the colony, one soldier for every five Kanaks.

The Ouvéa Massacre

In September 1986, a French examining magistrate named Semur ordered the release of the seven self-confessed killers of the 10 Kanaks murdered at Hienghène in December 1984 because they had acted in "self defense." This provoked an international furor, and on November 20 an appeal court ruled that the seven men had to stand trial. This took place in Nouméa in October 1987, and a jury of eight whites and one Indonesian deliberated over dinner for two hours before acquitting the defendants in a major travesty of justice.

From its founding in 1984, the FLNKS had preached nonviolence (although some of their supporters were not aloof from it). This policy seemed to have failed, so just prior to the April 24, 1988, elections for the four redistributed regions the FLNKS declared a "muscular mobilization" to accompany their election boycott. Throughout the territory, Kanaks erected roadblocks and fired on police who attempted to remove them. A general uprising was planned, but at dawn on April 22 a commando of 40 Kanaks acted prematurely and captured the gendarmerie at Fayaoué on Ouvéa in the Loyalty Islands, killing four police and capturing another 27. Sixteen of the prisoners were taken to a cave near the north end of the island and held hostage. Forewarned, every other gendarmerie in the territory went on alert.

On May 4, 1988, just three days prior to the French presidential elections, Chirac ordered an assault on the cave to garner right-wing support for his election campaign against Mitterrand. During "Operation Victor" at 0600 the next morning, 300 elite counterinsurgency troops attacked the cave, massacring 19 Kanaks and freeing the hostages unharmed, for a loss of two of the assaulting force. Kidnap leader, Kanyiapa Dianou (1959–1988), a former student priest, was beaten to death by the troops as he lay wounded on a stretcher, and six other Kanaks were executed by the French troops after they surrendered. There were no Kanak survivors—their bullet-ridden bodies were unrecognizable. Other Ouvéa residents were tortured by the French secret service agents, and 33 prisoners were deported to France. The soldiers who carried out these atrocities have never been brought to justice.

The Matignon Accords

The policies of Chirac and Pons had propelled New Caledonia to the brink of civil war, costing another 25 people their lives. Yet the Kanak blood spilled at Ouvéa didn't rally sufficient support for Chirac to win the French presidency, and Mitterrand was reelected. A month later, parliamentary elections were held in France, and the Socialists returned to power. The renewed violence had chastened everyone, so on June 26, 1988, the FLNKS leader Jean-Marie Tjibaou and the RPCR chief Jacques Lafleur met in Paris under the auspices of Socialist Prime Minister Michel Rocard to work out a compromise. The settlers were worried the Socialists would be sympathetic to independence, while the Kanaks wanted back the economic powers they had enjoyed briefly under the Fabius plan.

Under the peace accords signed at the Matignon Palace in Paris by the French government, the RPCR, and the FLNKS on August 20, 1988, all sides agreed to direct rule from Paris for one year, followed by a federal system for nine. The Pons Statute was to be scrapped and the territory divided into three self-governing provinces, North Province, South Province, and Loyalty Islands Province, with provincial elections in June 1989. There was to be balanced economic development based on decentralization and new training programs for Kanaks. Tens of millions of dollars in development funds were to be channeled into the Kanak regions. A new referendum on independence was to take place in 1998, with voting restricted to those eligible to vote in 1988 and their children of voting age. Amnesty was to be granted to 200 Kanak militants and to settlers charged with crimes against Kanaks. What the Matignon Accords didn't do was significantly increase territorial autonomy, nor did they guarantee a more equal division of the territory's wealth, most of which remained concentrated in the settler-controlled South Province. The Kanak leaders who signed the accords failed to consult their followers to seek approval or to demand an inquiry into the Ouvéa Massacre.

On November 6, 1988, a referendum was held in France, and 80 percent of voters approved the plan. This meant that the agreement couldn't be altered by a simple act of parliament should the government in Paris change—a major Kanak demand. Yet FLNKS hardliners strongly opposed the accords as a sellout that didn't guarantee independence. They argued that the FLNKS should refuse to cooperate with continued colonial rule and mount a last-ditch, all-or-nothing independence struggle. The split deepened as several FLNKS factions refused to participate in the June 1989 elections. The Ouvéa people felt especially betrayed.

Then, on May 4, 1989, at a commemorative service on Ouvéa for the massacre victims, the final act: The moderate FLNKS leaders Jean-Marie Tjibaou, 53, and Yeiwéné Yeiwéné, 44, were shot and killed at point-blank range by Djoubelly Wea, whose father had died from electric shocks inflicted by French troops on Ouvéa a year before. Wea himself, who acted alone, was immediately slain by Tjibaou's bodyguard.

These events served to freeze the Matignon Accords—which Tjibaou had considered a transitional arrangement—into a permanent solution, the foundation for New Caledonia's current colonial regime. Since 1989, the French government has carefully fostered the cult of Jean-Marie Tjibaou to legitimize this system. Most subsequent Kanak leaders had been weak figures, easily bought off and manipulated by the French. The lost struggle for independence of the 1980s is now euphemistically referred to as *les événements* (the events).

Recent Events

In June 1989, elections were held for the three provincial assemblies created under the Matignon Accords. The FLNKS gained majorities in North and Loyalty Islands provinces, while the settler-based RPCR won in South Province. The RPCR's large majority in Nouméa also gave it enough seats to control the Territorial Congress. The 1995 and 1999 elections largely duplicated these results, with the neo-fascist National Front growing steadily in South Province.

During the 1990s, the French government threw over a billion U.S. dollars at New Caledonia in the form of schools, infrastructure, and administration buildings, all with the intent of tying the colony firmly to France by making it more economically dependent than ever. Yet despite the job training programs, Kanak unemployment has remained high, and many of the new jobs created by the projects have gone to newly arrived immigrants from France. The 20 percent of the population that is unemployed is almost entirely Kanak.

In 1998, when the date of the promised referendum on independence rolled around, the French government called together representatives of the various parties to sign the Nouméa Accord, which calls for a gradual devolvement of authority to the territory over a period of 15 to 20 years. This was approved by 72 percent of New Caledonia voters in a November 1998 referendum. A decade or two from now, longtime residents of the territory may have the opportunity to vote in yet another independence referendum. In the meantime, France retains full control over justice, law and order, defense, and the currency, and a wave of French immigration continues to pour into the territory, creating irreversible facts on the ground.

Discontent continues to simmer, and many Kanak urban youth and rural villagers who don't share in the spoils of French colonialism are dissatisfied with an arrangement that has given their leaders luxurious lifestyles but themselves much less. To enforce the status quo, some 3,500 French soldiers and police backed up by helicopters and armored cars are currently stationed in New Caledonia, about one heavily armed French serviceman for every eight young Kanaks. And no one doubts France's willingness to employ deadly force to hang onto New Caledonia's mineral riches, both on land and undersea, and to preserve the role this important colony plays in projecting French power around the world.

GOVERNMENT

New Caledonia is a French associated territory with a high commissioner (www.etat.nc) appointed by the president of France. In addition to the powers vested in France, the high commissioner has some control over international relations, foreign investment, immigration, television broadcasting, navigation and air traffic, finance, research, and higher education.

Each of three provinces has a regional assembly in charge of planning, economic development, social welfare, housing, culture, and environmental protection within its area. The 32 members of the South Province Assembly, 15 members of the North Province Assembly, and seven members of the Loyalty Islands Province Assembly are elected by proportional representation every five years.

Together the members of the provincial assemblies make up the 54-member Territorial Congress, which controls public health, social services, primary education, employment, sports and culture, public transport, highways, electricity, communications, natural resources, mining, foreign trade, taxation, and the territorial budget. Under the Nouméa Accord, congressional president has replaced the high commissioner as head of government. The territory's executive council consists of 10 ministers chosen by the president.

Local government is organized into 33 communes, each with an elected mayor and municipal council. The communes are grouped into four administrative subdivisions, with headquarters at La Foa, Koné, Poindimié, and Wé (Lifou). Nouméa has a separate municipal government. In the French system, civil servants comprise an elite class not seen in English-speaking countries, and most government departments are headed by professionals seconded from France. The appointed bureaucrats running the subdivisions can override the decisions of local councils and mayors.

Everyone born in New Caledonia is legally a French citizen and can vote in French presidential elections. Two deputies are elected to the French National Assembly, one from the east coast of Grande Terre and outer islands, one from the west coast and Nouméa. A senator, elected by the municipal and provincial councils, is also sent to Paris.

ECONOMY

New Caledonia supplies France with raw materials while providing a market for finished French goods. France supplies 40 percent of the territory's imports and takes 32 percent of its exports. Japan is another major customer for New Caledonia's mineral wealth. Yet despite exports averaging Australian $750 million a year, imports exceed Australian $1,250 million, and the territory has the second-largest trade deficit in the South Pacific (after French Polynesia).

Economic power is centered in Greater Nouméa, with all of the industry except mining, 70 percent of the retail trading space, and most tourism and government services. Each year the French state transfers almost a billion U.S. dollars to New Caledonia, but much of it is used to pay the salaries of French civil servants and military personnel. Infrastructure expenditures profit mostly French contractors. Economic development plans have granted tax write-offs to French businesses, and encouraged metropolitan French immigrants to purchase existing small companies. The subsidies have made the territory a consumer colony with a transfer economy, which explains why most non-Melanesians are so devoted to France.

The territory's taxation system is based on high indirect taxes on imports and exports (thereby inflating the cost of living), plus a 4 percent Taxe Générale sur les Services (TGS). Direct company and income taxes (which would fall most heavily on Europeans) remain extremely low. The per capita gross domestic product is over 10 times that of neighboring Vanuatu, but the income of the average Kanak family is only a third that of a Caledonian French family. A few powerful French families—Ballande, Barrau, Lafleur, Frogier, Daly, de Rouvray, and Pentecost—control the local economy and politics. They profit most from colonial rule and are firmly committed to continuing it.

Mining

New Caledonia ranks third in world nickel production (after Canada and Russia), and nickel accounts for 89 percent of territorial exports. The nickel ore is high grade, being free of arsenic, although the presence of asbestos has been linked to a high lung cancer rate among miners. Chrome and iron ore were formerly exported, but these operations have closed due to market conditions.

There are large nickel mines at Thio, Poro, Tiébaghi, and Népoui, and many of the deposits are on mountaintops. In 1990, Kanak-controlled North Province purchased Jacques Lafleur's Société Minière de Sud Pacifique for US$19 million. The other large mining company, Société le Nickel (SLN), which owns the pyrometallurgic smelter at Nouméa, belonged to the Rothschild conglomerate until its nationalization in 1982. Today it's part of the Eramet consortium and 30 percent of SLN shares are owned by the provincial governments. Five smaller mining companies also operate.

To break the French monopoly over nickel processing and to rebalance economic power in the territory, the SMSP has negotiated an agreement with the Canadian mining corporation Falconbridge to build a second nickel refinery in North Province, an arrangement long opposed by Eramet. In 1997, the FLNKS suspended all political negotiations with the French government until the issue was resolved, and in early 1998 Eramet finally agreed to transfer unused nickel reserves at Koniambo near Koné to the SMSP, thereby making the project feasible. World nickel prices permitting, Falconbridge may eventually invest US$1.5 billion in a pyrometallurgic smelter at Koné with construction to begin in 2005. By 2008, the plant could be producing 60,000 tonnes of nickel a year.

In 2001, another Canadian mining giant, Inco, began preparations for a US$1.8 billion hydrometallugic smelter on the Goro Plateau between Goro and Prony Bay in the south. This massive project is receiving 75 percent financing by Inco and 25 percent by Japan's Sumitomo Bank, and by 2006 the smelter should be producing 54,000 tonnes of nickel and 5,400 tonnes of cobalt each year. Environmentalists have pointed to the heavy price that will be paid as the unique flora of the Plaine des Lacs is disrupted and vast quantities of liquid wastes are pumped into the sea, killing the reefs. In 2002, Southern Province politicians torpedoed efforts to have New Caledonia's barrier reefs declared a UNESCO World Heritage Site out of concern that such recognition might impact mining developments.

In 1999, it was announced that one of the world's largest deposits of natural gas had been discovered in 600 meters of water 230 km southwest of Grande Terre, close to the boundary with Australia. Huge oil deposits may also be present in the area.

Agriculture and Fishing

Agriculture represents just 2.5 percent of the gross domestic product. Beef cattle raising has always been the most important monetary agricultural activity, consisting mostly of large herds kept by Europeans on the west coast. Venison is exported to Europe. Pig and shrimp farming are well developed, and there's scallop fishing in the north. Tuna is the most important fish catch, while farmed shrimp are the territory's second largest export.

Among the Kanaks, yams are the main subsistence crop, followed by taro, manioc, and sweet potatoes. Coffee, introduced in the first days of French colonization, is still grown here today, mostly the *robusta* type.

Only 4 percent of Europeans work in agriculture, compared to 60 percent of Kanaks, yet two-thirds of the arable land is controlled by 1,000 French settlers with large estates. Land remains a basic issue in New Caledonia as a Melanesian land-*using* culture continues to find itself confronted by a European land-*owning* culture.

Tourism

After nickel, tourism is the most important industry, with Japan, France, Australia, and New Zealand providing the most visitors. New Caledonia is the only South Pacific country where Japan is a leading supplier of tourists—well over a quarter of the 103,933 arrivals in 2002 were Japanese honeymooners and "office ladies," a result of nonstop flights from Tokyo. A large proportion of the French arrivals come to visit friends or relatives.

Most tourism development in North Province has been built around the concept of eco-tourism, with smaller groups staying in accommodations more in tune with their surroundings. South Province promotes conventional consumer tourism with large hotels and package tours, while Loyalty Islands Province styles itself as a beach holiday paradise.

In the tribal areas, the Kanaks have long resisted outside efforts to set up large resorts. Instead, a system of Melanesian-owned *gîtes* provides accommodations in these areas. As guests of Kanak people, visitors to remote areas are not viewed as intruders. The upscale Drehu and Nengone resorts on Lifou and Maré respectively are owned by Loyalty Islands Province.

THE PEOPLE

Of the 215,000 inhabitants of New Caledonia, 44 percent are Melanesian, 34 percent European, 9 percent Wallisian, 3 percent Tahitian, 3 percent Indonesian, and 2 percent Vietnamese. Other Asians, ni-Vanuatu, West Indians, and Arabs make up the remaining 4 percent. The Vietnamese and Indonesians were brought in to work in the mines early this century; by 1921 some 4,000 of them were present.

Only about half the Europeans were actually born in New Caledonia. The rest are a mix of French civil servants and their families temporarily present in the territory, French refugees from former colonies in Algeria, Vietnam, and Vanuatu, and recent French immigrants referred to as *métros* or *zoreilles* (the ears).

Of the 21,630 convicts transported to New Caledonia from 1864–1897, just over a 1,000 stayed on as settlers *(colons)* on land granted them when they were freed. These and other early French arrivals are called *Caldoches*. French shopkeepers and small ranchers in the interior are known as *broussards*, while the 2,500 French who migrated to the territory from Algeria are the *pieds noir* (black feet). The *Caldoches* are very friendly, and it's mostly the *métros* who react arrogantly toward anyone unable to speak their language fluently.

During the nickel boom of 1969–1973, the European population increased in size by a third, and the number of Polynesians doubled. An average of 2,800 French immigrants have arrived every year since 1985, and the proportions of Kanaks and French may soon be reversed. These migrations are encouraged by the French government to ensure continued French rule, a violation of United Nations resolutions on the norms of conduct for colonial powers in non-self-governing areas. In 2003, a territorial census was postponed after President Chirac objected to a question about ethnic origin which would have revealed a sharp increase in the European population. The 1998 Nouméa Accord created a special New Caledonian French citizenship status intended to discourage immigration from France by making it possible to restrict voting and employment rights, but in 1999 the French Constitutional Court ruled that the provision was unconstitutional.

The Kanaks are also known as Ti-Va-Ouere, the Brothers of the Earth. They own all of the smaller islands surrounding Grande Terre and their reservations on the main island. There's a striking contrast between the affluent French community around Nouméa and the poverty of Kanak villages on the northeast coast of Grande Terre and on the outer islands.

Prior to European colonization there were no cities anywhere in Melanesia, but today nearly 60 percent of New Caledonia's population lives in Nouméa and vicinity, including 80 percent of the Europeans, 85 percent of the Asians, and 90 percent of the Polynesians. The capital is growing fast as regional centers such as La Foa, Bourail, Koumac, and Poindimié stagnate, with populations stuck below the 5,000 mark. With 71 percent of the total population living in cities and towns, New Caledonia is the most heavily urbanized entity in the South Pacific. The life expectancy rate at birth (72 years for men, 78 years for women) is the highest in the region, and the infant mortality rate (5 per 1,000) is the lowest.

About 67 percent of the inhabitants are Catholic, 21 percent Evangelical, and 4 percent Muslim, but religion is polarized, with 90 percent of French settlers Catholic, and Kanaks constituting 90 percent of the membership of the two branches of the Église Évangélique.

La Coutume

In essence, most of the conflicts in New Caledonia have been a clash of cultures. For more than a century, the Kanaks have been obliged to adopt a foreign way of life that styled itself as superior to their own. Yet despite the Kanaks' acceptance of a foreign language, religion, dress, and a monetary economy, indigenous custom *(la coutume)* continues to exert a surprising hold beneath the surface. The term *la coutume* has many meanings, and in the case of visitors it sometimes refers to a small gift (usually money), which can be given to show appreciation for some favor. If you're granted permission to camp, allowed to visit a custom area, or invited to stay in a local home, it's not amiss to offer *la coutume*.

Language

Twenty-eight indigenous languages are still spoken, all of them Austronesian. They can be broadly organized into eight related areas: five on Grande Terre and one on each of the Loyalties. The Kanak languages all developed from a single mother tongue, but are today mutually incomprehensible (thus it's incorrect and denigrating to call them "dialects"). Lifou is the language with the most speakers: about 11,000 on Lifou itself, plus a few thousand in Nouméa. French is the common language understood by most. Very few people in New Caledonia understand English

and you'll get a lot more out of your stay if you know a little French.

Language Courses

The **Université de la Nouvelle Calédonie** (B.P. 4477, 98847 Nouméa; tel. 26-58-58, fax 26-38-26, www.univ-nc.nc), with campuses a km beyond Magenta Airport and at Nouville, offers courses in the arts, social sciences, languages, law, and science. The academic year for CUNC's 2,200 students runs from February to September, with examinations continuing into October. Foreign students are welcome, but application must be made through the cultural adviser at the French consulate or embassy in the country of residence, and pre-enrollment formalities must be complete by December. Annual tuition fees are reasonable at CFP 28,507, and students arriving under an exchange program are eligible for accommodations at subsidized rates at university hostels, although space is limited. The lectures are in French, so foreigners may have to take a refresher course, and there are other academic requirements.

French language and culture courses especially designed for English speakers are offered by the **Centre de Rencontres et d'Echanges Internationaux du Pacifique** (B.P. 3755, 98846 Nouméa; tel. 25-41-24, fax 25-40-58, www.creipac.nc). CREIPAC is based in the old chapel at Nouville, 100 avenue James Cook, just outside Nouméa. Most of the students are part of university groups from Australia and New Zealand which come to round out their French studies. Groups of six persons or more are charged CFP 1,200 an hour pp with a minimum of 12 hours. Individual courses are CFP 4,700 a hour with a nine-hour minimum. CREIPAC can arrange room and board in local homes at CFP 3,500 pp including breakfast, dinner, and transfers.

Dangers and Annoyances

Most of the people you'll meet in New Caledonia will be friendly and helpful, but there's a small minority who are out to rip you off. If you pay for anything with a CFP 10,000 note, watch carefully what is happening, as the person may try to distract you by asking for small change or something else, then switch your CFP 10,000 note for a similar looking CFP 1,000 bill and claim that's all you gave them. Credit card fraud is also not unknown in New Caledonia, and if you sign a charge slip to guarantee a rental car, for example, it's best to let the charge go through and not offer to pay cash in the end or you could be billed twice. Don't let your credit card out of sight for a moment, no matter how nice the person seems. Verify all charges beforehand. It's usually the *métros* who play these tricks, and you shouldn't go by appearances.

Exploring the Islands

Highlights

New Caledonia's greatest attractions are undoubtedly its glamorous capital, the scenic northeast coast of the main island, and the colorful neighbor islands. Nouméa combines the ambience of a French provincial town with the excitement of a Côte d'Azure resort. Hienghène on Grande Terre's east coast is a place of remarkable natural beauty, with high mountains dropping dramatically into the sea. The Isle of Pines's Kuto/Kanuméra area is postcard perfect with exquisite white beaches backed by towering pines. New Caledonia's finest beach runs right up the west side of Ouvéa—a scene of martyrdom in the Kanak people's struggle against French colonialism.

Sports and Recreation

Organized sporting activities are most easily arranged at Nouméa and on the Isle of Pines. The Yacht Charters section under Transportation in this chapter lists several bareboat and crewed yacht charter opportunities, and the sheltered waters from Nouméa to Prony Bay and the Isle of Pines are a prime cruising area. Windsurfers ply the waters off Nouméa's Anse Vata and the Isle of Pines's Kuto Bay. The Isle of Pines is also ideal for sea kayaking, and both canoeing and kayaking are offered on the Néra River at Bourail.

Several companies offer scuba diving from Nouméa, but it's also possible to rent tanks and head off on your own. Other dive shops are on the Isle of Pines, Lifou, and Ouvéa, at Bourail and Poindimié, at the Hienghène Club Med, and at the Hôtel Malabou Beach north of Koumac. There's no recompression chamber in New Caledonia, and in emergencies, patients must be evacuated to Sydney, Australia. There are few places to snorkel on Grande Terre and you really do need a boat to get out to the barrier reef. To see coral from shore, you must go to the Loyalty Islands or the Isle of Pines.

Horseback riding is the favorite terrestrial recreational activity among the local French, and several well established ranches are near Koné. There are numerous hiking opportunities around these large islands. The best-known long-distance hike is across the mountains from the Hienghène valley to Voh. Nouméa has two 18-hole golf courses, and another 18-hole course is near Boulouparis.

Music

Traditional Kanak musical culture is divided into household music (lullabies, vocal games, healing and religious songs, flute tunes) and that of public ceremonies (rhythmical speeches, mimic dances, male songs, Protestant hymns). The ceremonial music is performed during funerals or mourning, at the feast of the first yam, during Christian religious services, and at modern cultural events. Despite the linguistic diversity, Kanak music and dance are remarkably uniform across Grande Terre, though there are differences with the Loyalty Islands.

The closing ceremony of the yearlong period of mourning for an important chief involves a great ceremonial exchange between members of the paternal and maternal lines. A male orator standing on a wooden platform delivers a rhythmical speech as men around him utter hushing sounds and the gifts are exchanged. In the Loyalties such speakers stand on the ground, and rhythm is not employed.

The climax of many ceremonies is a round dance, which lasts an entire night. A dozen musicians pounding bamboo tubes on the ground, shaking and scraping beaters, urge on two male singers as the dancers circulate counterclockwise around the group stamping their feet. The relays of singers relate historical events and claim magical inspiration. Hundreds of people may participate in a round dance at a major ceremony, and there must be no pause in the music or dancing until dawn.

Mimic dance tells a story through gestures and often imitates nature, such as the hopping or strutting of birds. The dancers stand in two lines, with lead dancers weaving between them as bamboo tubes are pounded or struck. On Grande Terre male mimic dancers, dressed in coconut leaves or grass, their bodies painted black, act out legends, history, or important cycles such as yam growing. Only in the Loyalties are such dances accompanied by a mixed choir. Mimic dancers in the Loyalties wear coconut rattle garters and strike bundles of hand-held leaves as they perform mimic dances of events such as the hauling of a canoe onto a beach.

Polyphony (music with several independent but harmonious melodic parts) comes naturally to most Pacific peoples, and the four-part mixed choirs of New Caledonia demonstrate how strongly Kanak vocal music has been influenced by 19th-century Protestant hymns. For contemporary urban Kanaks, reggae is all the rage.

Public Holidays and Festivals

Public holidays include New Year's Day (January 1), Easter Monday (March/April), Labor Day (1 May), 1945 Victory Day (May 8), Ascension Day (a Thursday in May), Pentecost (a Monday in May or June), Bastille Day (July 14), Assumption Day (August 15), New Caledonia Day (September 24), All Saints' Day (November 1), Armistice Day (November 11), and Christmas Day (December 25). The school holidays run from December 15 until the end of February.

The Festival of the Yam is observed in Kanak villages in mid-March. Bastille Day (July 14) features a military parade and aerial show at Anse Vata in Nouméa. Lots of free performances are staged during the August jazz festival in Nouméa. The Agricultural Fair at Bourail in late August features rodeos and other colorful activities. The parade on New Caledonia Day (September 24) recalls the day in 1853 when Admiral Despointes took possession of New Caledonia for France.

There's a triathlon the third Sunday in May, the Dumbéa open golf tournament in July, an international marathon the third Sunday in July, and a bicycle race around Grande Terre in August or September.

Accommodations

Prices at the hotels are manageable for two, but high for one. Expect 4 percent tax to be tacked onto all accommodation rates. In South Province, an additional room tax of CFP 350, 600, or 900 depending on the category of the hotel is added to the price. A small French country hotel is called a *relais*, while an *auberge de jeunesse* is a youth hostel.

New Caledonia's well-developed system of *gîtes* is unique in the Pacific. Basically a *gîte* offers simple Melanesian-style accommodations in thatched cottages, usually near a beach. Toilet facilities may be private or shared, and electricity may or may not be installed. Since the *gîtes* are operated by the Kanaks themselves, you'll be accepted in the community if you're staying there. Though some are poorly run, the best *gîtes* are a good value. The main flaw in the system is that Air Calédonie and the tour operators require the *gîte* owners to charge exorbitant prices to allow for the high commissions paid to travel agents for their bookings. Airport transfers are way overpriced. Bargaining isn't possible because the package tourism people have created strict rules to prevent any undercutting of their prices. About the only way for independent travelers to get around the absurdly high package tour tariffs is to ask to camp on the premises, which in most cases the Kanak owners will happily allow for a reasonable fee. Some *gîtes* offer accommodations in Kanak *case* (pronounced kahz), a conical thatched hut, and this is always much cheaper than European-style accommodations. For food, the *gîtes* are also required to charge prices similar to those at top Nouméa restaurants and the price may not correspond to what you get. The *gîtes* are concentrated on the Loyalty Islands and Isle of

Pines, but many are also found around Grande Terre. To reserve a bungalow at any of the *gîtes,* go to **Air Calédonie** (tel. 28-78-88, fax 28-13-40, www.aircaledonieholidays.com), 39 rue de Verdun, Nouméa. If you only want to camp at a *gîte,* you can just show up.

Women should keep in mind that while mono-kini sunbathing is okay in Nouméa, it could lead to serious problems anywhere else in the territory. *Never* swim topless or naked in front of a Kanak village. There are lots of isolated beaches where you can do it, and if you want to be seen, there's always Nouméa.

Camping

New Caledonia is one of the few places in the South Pacific where camping is widely understood and accepted. French soldiers on leave from Nouméa do it all the time, and French locals consider it a legitimate way to spend a weekend. There are many organized campgrounds on Grande Terre (but none in Nouméa). On the west coast, the municipal campgrounds are usually far off the main highway and not accessible by public transport, while those at *gîtes* on the east coast are often right on bus lines. On the outer islands, you also camp at the *gîtes.*

Almost anyone you ask will readily give you permission to pitch your tent, but do ask. Otherwise you might be violating custom and could create a needless problem. If camping for free on a public beach, take care of your gear.

Food and Drink

New Caledonian's restaurants are good but very expensive. The easiest way to keep your bill down is to stick to one main plate *(plat de résistance)* and eschew appetizers, salads, alcohol, coffee, and dessert. The bread and water on the table are free and tipping is not expected. Also watch for the *plat du jour,* a reasonably priced businessperson's lunch of one or two courses, bread, and dessert. Outside Nouméa most hotel restaurants offer a *prix fixe* dinner, though it's cheaper to order one plate à la carte if you can. Expect 4 percent tax (TGS) to be added to the price of restaurant meals unless the menu states clearly that it's included.

A *bougna* is a Kanak food parcel consisting of sliced root vegetables such as taro, manioc, and yams soaked in coconut milk, wrapped in banana leaves with pork, chicken, or seafood, and cooked over hot stones in an earthen oven for a couple of hours. If you attend a Kanak feast you'll see dozens of *bougna* packages consumed by countless relatives. At some *gîtes* you can order a *bougna* capable of feeding four persons for about CFP 3,500.

Virtually all towns on the west coast of Grande Terre are well equipped with stores, while shopping facilities on the east coast are sometimes poor. Since New Caledonia is associated with the European Union, the foods available in the supermarkets are different from those offered in most other South Pacific countries. Buy long crusty baguettes and flaky croissants to complement the pâté, wine, and cheese. Together these are the makings of a memorable picnic. The Oro fruit juice sold in one-liter plastic bottles is a great buy at CFP 180. Beer and wine are very cheap at supermarkets, but these stores are not allowed to sell alcohol from Saturday at 1200 to Monday at 0600.

Internet Resources

South Province's tourism promotion site Discover New Caledonia, **www.newcaledonia tourism-south.com,** has abundant information on travel and accommodations. Isle of Pines Tourism, **www.isle-of-pines.com,** introduces a small paradise with perfect white beaches backed by tall trees. Loyalty Islands: Lifou, Mare, Ouvea, **www.iles-loyaute.com,** is an official guide to New Caledonia's glorious offshore islands. Traveller's Island, **www.travellers-island.com,** is a commercial travel site that provides a good overview of the facilities available for visitors to New Caledonia. The New Caledonia Accommodation and Resorts Directory, **www.new-caledonia.islands-resorts.com,** provides resort and hotel listings accessible via a searchable online form. Endemia, **www.endemia.nc,** has photos of the territory's flora and fauna.

The site of the Chamber of Commerce and Industry of New Caledonia, **www.cci.nc,** is a good source of business-related information. The

Chamber of Commerce operates New Caledonia's international airport, so there are complete flight listings. The New Caledonia Economic Development Agency is intended to promote trade and investment, and their site, **www.adecal.nc**, is an excellent source of information on the economy. The official website of the South Province Government, **www.province-sud.nc**, provides more economic information on this business-oriented French territory. North Province, **www.province-nord.nc**, also has a site. Kanaky Online, **http://membres.lycos.fr/kanaky**, is devoted to the independence struggle of the Kanak people. Though entirely in French, New Caledonia's own Internet search engine Yahoue, **www.yahoue.com**, is easy to navigate and opens a thousand doors.

Visas and Officialdom

Citizens of the European Union, Canada, the United States, Japan, Australia, and New Zealand do not require a visa. Others should check with their airline a few weeks ahead. Visitors from the United States, Japan, Switzerland, and most Commonwealth countries are allowed to stay one month. Citizens of European Union countries and Australia get three months, and French are admitted for an unlimited stay. Everyone (French included) must have an onward ticket. This requirement is strictly enforced and there's no chance of slipping through without one.

For an extension of stay, go to the Haut-Commissariat de la République (tel. 26-63-00; weekdays 0745–1100 and 1200–1400), corner of avenue Paul Doumer and rue Georges Clémenceau, Nouméa, and enter the office marked *Étrangers*. Extensions are free, but bring along your plane ticket and be prepared to be sent to the police station for an interview before the extension is granted. You must apply at least a week before your current permit expires, as they're quite slow completing the paperwork.

Nouméa is the only port of entry for cruising yachts. Arriving yachts should contact the Capitainerie de Port Moselle (tel. 27-71-97, fax 27-71-29, VHF channel 67), who will send customs and immigration to meet them at a dock opposite the charter boats on Moselle Bay. Otherwise call Nouméa Radio at channel 16. The formalities here are simpler than those in French Polynesia and no bond is required.

Money

The currency is the French Pacific franc or CFP (pronounced "say eff pay"). There are banknotes of 500, 1,000, 5,000, and 10,000 and coins of one, two, five, 10, 20, 50, and 100. The CFP is linked to the Euro (worth CFP 119.25). As an approximate rule of thumb, US$1 = CFP 100. Beware of the 1,000 and 10,000 notes, which look confusingly similar. When changing money, ask for CFP 5,000 notes instead.

New Caledonia's banks are among the biggest rip-offs in the South Pacific, charging 1 percent commission with a CFP 500–1,900 minimum for each foreign currency transaction, whether buying or selling. Thus it's important to plan ahead and not have to change too often. They usually give a better rate for traveler's checks than for cash. The banks are generally open weekdays 0730–1530, and it's difficult or impossible to change foreign currency in rural areas—do it before you leave Nouméa. The American Express representative in Nouméa, Center Voyages, changes traveler's checks without commission (see the Nouméa section for details).

Euros in cash (but not traveler's checks) are converted back and forth at a fixed rate without commission, so that's the best type of money to bring by far. When leaving, you can change surplus CFP into Euros without paying commission or losing anything on the exchange, but many banks refuse to do it for persons without an account at their branch, even if they originally changed with them. New Caledonia and French Polynesia use exactly the same currency, so just hang onto any leftover Pacific francs if you'll be continuing to Papeete. Credit cards are only useful in Nouméa or at upscale resorts. Most banks in Nouméa and provincial towns have ATMs, but they're often out of service and have low weekly limits. It's unwise to be entirely dependent on ATMs.

New Caledonia's form of taxation—high import and export duties—and the elevated salaries paid to local French officials make this the South Pacific's most expensive country by far. You'll be hard pressed to find a cup of coffee for less than CFP 200, or the simplest *plat du jour* meal for even CFP 1,000. Paradoxically, that can also make visiting New Caledonia cheap, since you'll be forced to limit purchases to the basics if you're on a budget. Backpackers can survive because the hitchhiking is easy, camping is accepted, and the supermarkets sell excellent picnic fare, but the cost of living will wallop you if you try to travel in style. Camera film is much less expensive in Fiji, Vanuatu, and Australia, so bring a good supply.

On the positive side, tipping isn't usually done in New Caledonia and is sometimes even considered offensive. Notice how the locals never tip in restaurants. New Caledonia is one of the few South Pacific destinations where worthwhile discounts are available to seniors or those with ISIC student cards. Inflation is less than 2 percent a year, so the prices in this book should be fairly accurate.

Communications

Faxes *(télécopies)* can be sent from any post office, but it's expensive. Postage is also exorbitant here, so save your postcard writing for the next country on your trip.

The way to make telephone calls is with a telephone card *(télécarte)*, available at any post office in denominations of CFP 1,000 (25 units), CFP 3,000 (80 units), and CFP 5,000 (140 units). Calls within New Caledonia are CFP 12 a minute weekdays from 0700–1900, and CFP 6 a minute weekdays from 1900–0700 and all day weekends. There's a CFP 144 charge to call information (tel. 12), so first look in the telephone book *(annuaire)*. An online version is at http://annu.opt.nc.

To place an international call with a card, dial the international access code 00, the country code, the area code, and the number. Using a card, it's CFP 72 a minute to Australia or New Zealand, CFP 96 a minute to Canada, and CFP 130 a minute to the United States or Europe. A one-third reduction is available 2100–0700 weekdays and all day weekends. International calls placed from hotel rooms are charged double, and a three-minute minimum may apply. Collect calls cannot be placed from public telephones. New Caledonia's telephone code is 687.

The two Internet service providers here are Lagoon (www.offratel.nc) and Can'L (www.canl.nc). Internet access is available at several locations around Nouméa and elsewhere for about CFP 250 per 15 minutes. The French keyboards on the computers at these places take some getting used to!

Media

The daily newspaper, *Les Nouvelles Calédoniennes* (tel. 27-25-84, fax 27-94-43, www.info.lnc.nc), is owned by French press baron Robert Hersant, proprietor of the Paris daily *Le Figaro*.

The largest TV broadcaster is the government-owned Réseau France Outremer (tel. 23-99-99, fax 23-99-75, www.rfo.fr). A private television station, Canal Calédonie (tel. 26-53-30), operates on a subscription basis with an encrypted signal.

RFO-Radio broadcasts local programming over 89.0 MHz from Nouméa. Their main news of the day (in French) is daily at 0630, 1200, and 1800. In addition, RFO rebroadcasts France Inter received by satellite from France on 666 kHz AM and 93.0 MHz FM in Nouméa. Elsewhere, look for RFO at 91 MHz in Bourail, 90 MHz in Hienghéne, 91 MHz at Koumac, 90.5 or 91.5 MHz on Lifou, 88.5 MHz on Maré, 89.5 MHz on Ouvéa, and 90 MHz at Yaté.

A private commercial FM station called **Radio Rythme Bleu** or RRB (tel. 25-46-46, fax 28-49-28) is at 100.4 MHz in Nouméa. There's also a 24-hour, youth-oriented music station called **Nouméa Radio Joker** or NRJ (tel. 26-34-34, fax 27-94-47, www.nrj.nc) at FM 93.5 MHz, which doesn't present news.

The pro-independence station, **Radio Dji-ido** (tel. 25-35-15, fax 27-21-87), also broadcasts over various FM frequencies: Boulouparis 96 MHz, Houaïlou 103 MHz, Koumac 103 MHz,

Lifou 98.5 MHz, Maré 97.5 MHz, Nouméa 97.4 MHz, Ouvéa 96.5 MHz, Pouébo 97 MHz, Poya 97 MHz, Touho 96 MHz, and Voh 102 MHz. Radio Djiido tends to play more international music (English, Spanish, Italian, reggae) and not just songs in French. There's no English broadcasting in New Caledonia.

Health

A yellow fever vaccination is required, but only if you've been in an infected area (South America or Africa) within the previous six days. New Caledonia has one of the highest per capita incidences of HIV infections in the South Pacific, though still very low by U.S. standards. New Caledonia's tap water contains high levels of heavy metals resulting from mining, but it's unlikely to cause problems on a short visit. In 2003, a dengue fever outbreak affected 4,000 people and claimed 13 lives. On the bright side, there's no malaria. Public hospitals exist in Nouméa, Poindimié, and Koumac, but it's cheaper and easier to see a private doctor.

Business Hours and Time

Business hours are weekdays 0730–1130 and 1330–1800, and Saturday 0730–1100, though large supermarkets in Nouméa remain open Monday to Saturday 0730–1900, and Sunday 0730–1130 and 1500–1900. Banking hours are weekdays 0730–1530. Main post offices are open weekdays 0745–1115 and 1215–1500.

New Caledonia follows the same hour as Vanuatu, an hour before Sydney and an hour behind Auckland and Fiji. In summer (Dec.–Feb.) the sun comes up at 0430 and sets at 1830, while in winter (June–Aug.) daylight hours are something like 0630–1730. Thus it pays to be an early riser.

TRANSPORTATION

Getting There

Aircalin (tel. 26-55-00, fax 26-55-61, www.air calin.nc), previously known as Air Calédonie International, a local carrier 55 percent owned by the territorial government, links New Caledonia to Auckland, Brisbane, Nadi, Osaka, Papeete, Port Vila, Sydney, Tokyo, and Wallis Island. In Tokyo, Aircalin connects with Air France flights to Paris. The most direct access to New Caledonia from North America is on Aircalin's twice weekly flight to/from Nadi, Fiji, although connections through Tahiti or Australia are more frequent. It's often difficult to get a booking on flights between Fiji and Nouméa because the planes arrive full from Wallis Island.

The national airlines of several neighboring countries also fly straight to Nouméa: **Air New Zealand** (tel. 28-66-77) from Auckland four times a week; **Air Vanuatu** (tel. 28-66-77) from Port Vila four times a week; and **Qantas** (tel. 28-65-46) from Brisbane three times a week and from Sydney daily. All of the above flights operate out of La Tontouta Airport (NOU).

Nouméa fits into the **Visit South Pacific Pass** described in the Exploring the Islands chapter of this book.

By Ship

The **Compagnie Maritime des Îles** (tel. 27-36-73), corner of rue Jules Ferry and avenue de la Victoire, operates the passenger-carrying freighter *Havannah* to Port Vila (CFP 12,500), Lakatoro (CFP 15,300), and Espiritu Santo (CFP 18,000) once a month. Passengers must book passage one week in advance and a ticket to leave Vanuatu is required. The ship stops at the Loyalty Islands en route but you're not allowed to board there.

Joining a yacht as crew is possible. From September to November plenty of boats will be leaving for Australia or New Zealand, and you can also hitch rides to Vanuatu and the Solomon Islands. Skippers sometimes post notices at the youth hostel.

Getting Around by Air

Air Calédonie (tel. 28-78-88, fax 25-03-26, www.air-caledonie.nc), the domestic commuter airline, uses Magenta Airport (GEA) near Nouméa. Several times a day their 46-passenger ATR 42s and 19-passenger Dornier 228s fly to the Loyalty Islands (Maré, Lifou, and Ouvéa), CFP 9,460 one-way. The interisland link between the three larger Loyalties and Tiga costs CFP 3,280 to CFP 6,380 per sector. There are three or more flights a day to the Isle of Pines, CFP 6,380 one-way. Twice a week you can fly from Koumac to remote Belep off the northwest coast of Grande Terre, CFP 8,730 one-way. Add CFP 700 per flight tax to all prices.

Ask Air Calédonie about special package tickets that allow a visit to the Loyalty Islands from Nouméa for one price with accommodations and airport transfers included. Their **Air Pass,** only available to nonresidents, allows any four flights for CFP 26,220 (additional flights CFP 5,460 each). The pass is valid two months, and a special 20-kilogram baggage allowance is included. Reservation changes cost CFP 1,000.

Otherwise, the baggage allowance is 10 kilograms, with overweight costing CFP 105–170 a kilo (CFP 500 minimum charge). There's a CFP 1,000 penalty if you change or cancel a reservation less than 48 hours in advance. Reconfirm your return reservation immediately upon arrival at an outer island. It's usually easy to get a seat to the Loyalty Islands, but the flights to the Isle of Pines are often fully booked by Japanese day-trippers, so inquire well ahead. If you're told the plane is full, the ferry *Betico* is a good alternative.

Getting Around by Other Means

For information on the high-speed vessel *Betico,* turn to Transportation in the Nouméa section. It can zip you to the Isle of Pines or the Loyalties in less than five hours and costs significantly less than the plane, but check the current schedule well ahead.

Buses link most Grande Terre towns at least once a day, and the fares are reasonable (turn to the Nouméa section for information). All around the island *beware of buses leaving 15 minutes early!* The buses will accept bicycles as checked luggage. Hitchhiking is a snap (when there's traffic) and you'll have some very interesting conversations, if you speak French. Payment is never expected. It's always easier to hitch toward Nouméa than in any other direction. Renting a car is the easiest way to go, and it allows you to save money by car camping and eating picnic fare.

Yacht Charters

Nouméa Yacht Charter (tel. 28-66-66; fax 28-74-82, n.y.c@canl.nc), in a kiosk on Baie de la Moselle, offers bareboat or skippered charters out of Nouméa. The usual trip is to sail to the Isle of Pines and back in five to seven days. **Pacific Charter** (tel. 26-10-55, pachart@canl.nc) nearby specializes in crewed charters on catamarans like the *Highlander* and *Bayou.* The yacht charter companies listed in the Getting There section of this book's Exploring the Islands chapter can handle reservations.

Many crewed charter boats work out of Nouméa, including the catamaran sailboat *Nirvana* (tel. 25-94-61, www.nirvana-yacht-charter.com). The actual fleet changes all the time as boats come and go, so check with the tourist office for current information. The optimum sailing months are April to November.

AIRPORTS

International Airport

La Tontouta Airport (NOU, tel. 36-67-18) is 53 km northwest of Nouméa and 112 km southeast of Bourail. As your plane is taxiing up to the terminal, glance at the French air force hangars across the runway to see if their Puma counterinsurgency helicopters are in.

The Arc en Ciel (tel. 27-19-80, www.arc enciel-voyages.nc) and S.C.E.A. airport buses, to the right as you leave the terminal, charge a stiff CFP 2,500 for the ride to Nouméa. You can also wait for the CarSud bus (tel. 25-16-15; CFP 370), to the left as you leave the terminal. They leave the airport once an hour Monday to Saturday 0500–1740. On Sunday (a bad day to arrive) there are only a couple of public buses in the early morning and one more in the early afternoon (at 1335). Airport-bound, don't plan a tight connection if you travel this way. A taxi to Nouméa will be CFP 8,000. If hitching is your thing, just walk one km out to the main highway—you'll have a ride to Nouméa in no time. Wait at the bus stop opposite Super U Supermarket where all the buses from northern Grande Terre also stop.

The car rental companies with counters at La Tontouta Airport are A5 Location (tel. 35-12-43), Avis (tel. 35-11-74), Budget (tel. 27-60-60), Europcar/Mencar (tel. 27-61-25), Hertz (tel. 35-12-77), Thrifty/Discount Location (tel. 24-10-42), and Visa Location (tel. 35-14-20). They're usually staffed only when they have reservations.

The airport BCI Bank branch inside the customs area is open for most arrivals, but not all departures. They charge CFP 520 commission, and give a rate similar to the banks in town. An ATM is next to the airport post office beyond customs. Another bank is on the main highway near the airport but it only opens weekdays 0815–1145. The airport post office opens irregularly, and the duty free shop in the departure lounge is just expensive. A reasonable self-service restaurant is upstairs in the airport (a *plat du jour* is served daily 1100–1400 at CFP 1,050). Due to security considerations, it's not possible to store excess luggage at the airport. The terminal building closes at night. The airport tax is included in the ticket price.

Domestic Airport

Magenta Airport (GEA) is five km northeast of downtown Nouméa. A blue city bus will drop you right at the door (every 15 minutes 0530–1900, CFP 140). A taxi from the Place des Cocotiers costs about CFP 1,000. There are no coin lockers, so leave excess baggage elsewhere.

Nouméa

Nouméa was founded in 1854 by Tardy de Montravel, who called it Port-de-France, and in 1860 the French moved their capital here from Balade. A French governor arrived two years later and convicts condemned to the penal colony on Île Nou followed in 1864. In 1866, the town was renamed Nouméa. Robert Louis Stevenson, who visited in 1890, remarked that Nouméa was "built from vermouth cases." Like Rome, Nouméa stands on seven hills. The town remained a backwater until 1942, when American military forces arrived to transform this landlocked port into a bastion for the war against Japan. Admiral "Bull" Halsey directed the Solomon Islands campaign from his headquarters on Anse Vata.

Today this thriving maritime center near the south end of the New Caledonian mainland is a busy, cosmopolitan city made rich by nickel and tourism. Well over half the population of the territory resides here: 130,000 people if residents of nearby Mont-Dore, Dumbéa, and Païta are included. It's the only South Pacific town with a white majority (less than a quarter of the city's population is Kanak). Bathing beauties bask at Nouméa's swank Anse Vata beach, where most of the luxury hotels are found. Windsurfers, funboarders, and sailboaters hover offshore, and it's clear that this is a moneyed tourist's paradise.

Nouméa is very French city, and you sense that the Kanaks feel out of place. The swank French suburbs of southern Nouméa contradict the Kanak tenements and squatter settlements to the north. Leave touristy Nouméa, and you're back in Melanesia, among the island's original inhabitants, who still value land and custom more highly than money. From European consumers to traditional tribes, it's quite a contrast, and you can't claim to have seen the territory until you get across to the northeast coast or out to one of the neighbor islands.

When planning your day, remember that on weekdays nearly everything in Nouméa closes for the 1130–1330 siesta—a two-hour break! Afternoon hours can be variable, so it's best to attend to important business first thing in the morning.

SIGHTS

Historic Nouméa

The **Place des Cocotiers,** with its statues, fountains, *pétanque* players, and tourist information office is the ideal place to begin your tour. From November to January the poincianas (flame trees) set this wonderful central park alight in hues of red and orange. Points of interest include the vintage bandstand, at the east end of the square, the Celeste Fountain (1892), point zero for all highway mileages on the mainland, in the middle, and the statue of Admiral Olry, governor

Anse de Tir

To La Tontouta
Airport

To Parc
Forestier

PORT OF
NOUMÉA

AVENUE JAMES COOK

ROND
POINT

NOUMÉA

ROUTE DES DEUX VALLÉES

ROUTE STRATEGIQUE

AVIS
RENT-A-
CAR

GENERAL
HOSPITAL

CARSUD BUS TO
LA TONTOUTA
AIRPORT

VALLEE
DU GENIE

FERRY *BETICO*

RUE DU GENERAL GALLIENI

AVENUE PAUL DOUMER

RUE GEORGES CLEMENCEAU

AVENUE DU MARECHAL FOCH

★ GOVERNMENT
HOUSE

BINGO
HALL

RUE DE LA RÉPUBLIQUE

TERRITORIAL
CONGRESS ★

CHAMPION
SUPERMARKET ■

RUE D'AUSTERLITZ

★ PROTESTANT
CHURCH

RUE OLRY

RUE DE L'ALMA

RUE DU GENERAL MANGIN

BOULEVARD VAUBAN

RUE DE SEBASTOPOL

RUE OLRY

RUE JULES FERRY

RUE JEAN JAURES

TOURIST
OFFICE ■

MUSÉE DE ★
LA VILLE

CRUISESHIP
TERMINAL

MENCAR
RENT-A-CAR ■

★
CITY
HALL

PLACE DES COCOTIERS

MOON

CASINO
SUPERMARKET ■

RUE ANATOLE FRANCE

HOTEL
● LAPÉROUSE

YOUTH
HOSTEL

RUE DE VERDUN

AMERICAN
EXPRESS ■

To
Magenta
Airport

*Baie de la
Moselle*

MARINE
CORAIL ■

RUE DRIANT

GOUVERNEUR SAUTOT

AIR CALÉDONIE

RUE DE LA SOMME

NORTH PROVINCE
TOURIST OFFICE ■

★ ST. JOSEPH'S
CATHEDRAL

INTERCITY BUS
TERMINAL ■

BERHEIM
LIBRARY ★

HOTEL LE
PARIS ●

RUE FREDERIC SURLEAU

PLACE BIR
HAKEIM

HAVANNAH
OFFICE ■

AVENUE DE LA VICTOIRE

AVENUE DE LA VICTOIRE

HOTEL
SAN FRANCISCO ●

RUE DU DOCTEUR GUEGAN

RUE DU DOCTEUR LESCOUR

RUE CHARLES DE VERNEIL

ROUTE DE L'ANSE VATA

★ ARMY
BARRACKS

LA VALBONNE

POST
OFFICE ■

CHEZ ■
CAMILLE

RUE LEON COURSIN

MARKET ■

RUE EUGENE PORCHERON

YACHT
CHARTER ★
OFFICES

NEW
CALEDONIA ★
MUSEUM

LATIN
QUARTER

RUE AUGUSTE BRUN

RUE BICHAT

★ PALAIS DE
JUSTICE

RUE DE METZ

PORT
MOSELLE

RUE GEORGES

RUE TOURVILLE

RUE DUQUESNE

SOUTH PROVINCE
HEADQUARTERS ■

AXXESS ■
TRAVEL

RUE SUFFREN

AVENUE DU MARECHAL FOCH

RUE GENERAL SARRAIL

RUE DU GENERAL LECLERC

MONT COFFYN
VIEWPOINT ★

ROUTE DES ARTIFICES

AVENUE DU CLEMENCEAU

POINT ROUGE ■
RENT-A-CAR

0   250 yds

0   250 m

To Anse Vata

© DAVID STANLEY

1878–1880, at the west end. The old town hall (1880), facing the north side of the square, is now the **Musée de la Ville** (tel. 26-28-05; Mon.–Sat. 0900–1700) with an excellent collection of old photos and a 1/400 scale model of Nouméa in 1897. Admission is free.

Walk north on rue du Général Mangin past trendy rue de l'Alma to the **old military hospital,** built by convict laborers in the 1880s and still Nouméa's main medical facility. Only in 1982 did the territory take over the hospital from the army. Turn right on avenue Paul Doumer and you'll come to **Government House,** the residence of the French High Commissioner. Go right, then left up rue de la République two blocks, to the **Territorial Congress** on your right. A small collection of local rocks and shells is showcased upstairs from the reception, in front of the room where the 54-seat congress meets.

Go up the ramp off boulevard Vauban to the **Protestant Church** (1893) at the head of rue de l'Alma, then continue south on Vauban to **St. Joseph's Catholic Cathedral** (1893), which was also built by convict labor. Enter this fine old building overlooking the city through the side doors to see the stained-glass windows, timber roof, and wooden pulpit. Continue east from the cathedral along rue Frédéric Surleau to the **French army barracks** (caserne) on Place Bir Hakeim. A war memorial flanked by guns which once guarded the entrance to Nouméa harbor stands in front of these barracks dating from 1869.

Return west along avenue de la Victoire to 41 avenue du Maréchal Foch and the **Bernheim Library** (tel. 24-20-90, fax 27-65-88, www.bernheim.nc; capriciously open Tues., Thurs., and Fri. 1300–1730, Wed. 0900–1730, Sat. 0900–1600). In 1901, Lucien Bernheim, a miner who made his fortune in the territory, donated the money for its first library (the only time a local mining mogul has ever given away anything). What had been the New Caledonian pavilion at the Paris Universal Exposition of 1900 was used to house the collection, and the original building still stands alongside the present reading room. To this day it's the only real public library in the territory. By paying CFP 1,000 for a three-month membership (CFP 100 for students), you get the right to freely use the Internet half an hour each day (reserve a time slot the day before).

New Caledonia Museum

This outstanding museum (tel. 27-23-42), 45 avenue du Maréchal Foch, two blocks south of the Bernheim Library, was founded in 1971. Kanak cultural objects are displayed downstairs, including elements from *cases* (traditional houses), masks, wooden statues, fishing, hunting, and farming implements, traditional currency, canoes, war clubs, ceremonial axes, bamboo carvings, baskets, and pottery. Upstairs are artifacts from Vanuatu, Solomon Islands, Papua New Guinea, and Irian Jaya. A *case* from Lifou is mounted inside the building, a botanical collection graces the courtyard, and in the rear garden behind the museum is a traditional full-sized *grande case* in the Canala style. The historic photos are good, and you can watch videos narrated in French. It's open daily except Tuesday and holidays 0900–1130 and 1215–1630; admission is CFP 200 (or CFP 50 for students and persons older than 60)—don't miss it.

If you'd like to clear your head after the museum, climb **Mont Coffyn** for the sweeping view; there's an old ceramic map at the top for orientation. To get there, go south on avenue du Maréchal Foch to the American War Memorial, then left on rue Duquesne at the Maison du Sport and two blocks up to rue Guynemer, where you turn right, then left, and up the hill. Use the map in this book. As you stand beside the immense two-armed Cross of Lorraine, you'll be able to pick out Amédée Lighthouse.

Nearby Beaches

Nouméa's finest beaches are near the southern end of the city's scalloped peninsula. When the wind is blowing at Anse Vata, it will be calm at nearby Baie des Citrons. Very attractive and easily accessible by bus, these bays are also cluttered with hotels and tend to be crowded; elsewhere in New Caledonia you can usually have a beach to yourself.

The **Nouméa Aquarium** (tel. 26-27-31; Tues.–Sun. 1030–1645, admission CFP 650, seniors over 60 CFP 300, students CFP 210,

THE BEACH AREA

Motor Pool

MOTEL LE BAMBOU

Val Plaisance

Ouen Toro Hill

MUNICIPAL SWIMMING POOL

LA GRANDE MURAILLE

GRAND CASINO

PAILLARD PIANO BAR

POST OFFICE

HERTZ

Receiving

LIBRE SERVICE OCEANIE

RACETRACK

MOTEL ANSE VATA

NOUMÉA PARKROYAL

LANTANA BEACH HOTEL

CLUB MEDITERRANEE (CLOSED)

LE MERIDIEN HOTEL

HOTEL LE LAGON

OFFICE DU TOURISME

DESTINATION LOYALTY ISLANDS

GALERIE PALM BEACH

SECRETARIAT OF THE PACIFIC COMMUNITY

Anse Vata

SQUASH COURTS

PORT PLAISANCE MALL

CERCLE NAUTIQUE

YACHT HARBOR

MARINA BEACH HOTEL

MOCAMBO HOTEL

LA FIESTA CHEZ ALBAN

HOTEL IBIS NOUMÉA

CENTRE COMMERCIAL BAIE DES CITRONS

NOUMÉA AQUARIUM

CASINO ROYAL/ SURF NOVOTEL

FRENCH NAVY

Baie de l'Orphelinat

Baie des Citrons

Baie des Pecheurs

Rocher à la Voile

Duck Island

Ilot Brun

500 yds

500 m

0

0

© DAVID STANLEY

children CFP 115), located between Baie des Citrons and Anse Vata, has a good collection of reef fish, sponges, cuttlefish, nautilus, sea snakes, sea slugs, and fluorescent corals. It tends to be a little overrated, however, and the small size and jewelrylike displays are drawbacks. Go early on a fine afternoon, as the lighting is poor. (A new aquarium four times the size is to be built using US$10 million in European Union financing.)

On Anse Vata east of the Aquarium is the headquarters of the **Secretariat of the Pacific Community** (tel. 26-20-00, www.spc.int), formerly known as the South Pacific Commission, which opened in 1995. A description of this regional organization is provided in this book's main introduction under the heading Government. The roof of the main conference building and library (to the left as you enter) is shaped like an inverted canoe. The library (weekdays 0730–1600, except Thurs. until 1200 only) is worth visiting to see the showcased artifacts and publications, or just to relax and browse the newspapers and magazines. There's even a computer for connecting to the Internet free of charge if no one else is using it. Temporary exhibitions are often mounted in the conference center beyond, and the coral pathways across the gardens symbolize Micronesian navigational charts.

A road to the left just beyond the municipal swimming pool at the other end of the bay leads up to **Ouen Toro Hill** and a fine panorama (a 15-minute walk). In 1940, two six-inch cannons were set up here by the Australian army to cover the reef passage in the vicinity of Amédée Lighthouse, visible to the south. Promenade Pierre Vernier along Baie Sainte Marie east of Ouen Toro is an attractive place to stroll between the rows of palms, and there's a training track complete with pull-up bars, balance logs, etc.

Jean-Marie Tjibaou Cultural Center

This extraordinary cultural cocktail sits on the Tina Peninsula near the exclusive Golf de Tina, 12 km northeast of town. Designed by Italian architect Renzo Piano, it was built between 1994 and 1998 by French contractors at a cost of over US$50 million. The center opened on May 4, 1998, 10th anniversary of the assassination of

© DAVID STANLEY

a *grande case* at the Tjibaou Cultural Center outside Nouméa

Jean-Marie Tjibaou, the Kanak leader lionized by the French authorities as a signatory of the Matignon Accords. Sixty-four persons are presently on the staff of this major institution.

A "Kanak Pathway" leads through a spectacular botanical garden interwoven with references to Kanak legends. The garden encircles 10 huge *case* clustered in three villages joined by a central corridor. Inside are a contemporary art gallery, temporary and permanent exhibitions of Kanak and other Pacific art, a library, and an audiovisual room where you can watch videos or listen to music. Other features include a ceremonial area with three *grande case*, and indoor and outdoor theaters.

A room in Village Three provides photos and texts on the life of Jean-Marie Tjibaou, up to his death on May 4, 1989. No explanation is provided as to why he was assassinated, the background of the assassin, or the Ouvéa Massacre (see History, this chapter). Other topics the center ignores include the murder of Éloi Machoro, the 19th century land seizures, and the muscle flexing and maneuvering that has prevented independence. In general, the center presents Kanak culture as a regional folklore rather than a national tradition.

For the French, the Matignon Accords which Tjibaou signed in 1988 were a comfortable outcome of the *événments* of the 1980s. Tjibaou himself intended the Matignon Accords to be only a temporary stop on the road to independence, not the permanent arrangement they have become. Tjibaou was the last real Kanak leader and the French have managed to transform his legacy into a mantra for continuing colonial rule. Don't miss the amazing three-meter-high bronze statue of Tjibaou clad in a Roman toga on the hill overlooking the center.

The Jean-Marie Tjibaou Cultural Center is operated by the French-financed Agency for the Development of Kanak Culture (tel. 41-45-45, fax 41-45-56, www.adck.nc) and is open Tuesday to Sunday 1000–1800. Admission is CFP 500 (free for youths under 18 and for students). Guided tours are offered Tuesday to Saturday at 1030 and 1430 (CFP 1,000/500 adult/student). Admission to special performances at the center is CFP 1,700–2,500. Unfortunately, most of the explanations are in French only—ask for a map of the complex when you arrive.

The center's boutique sells posters, handicrafts (a good place to buy these), T-shirts, videos, music cassettes, and books on Kanak culture and New Caledonia. Included in the admission fee is a ticket for a free drink at the center's Pérui Snack Bar (Tues.–Sat. 1100–1600), which serves a good *plat du jour* lunch for CFP 1,000 Tuesday to Friday. Other snacks are inexpensive, and the salads are great value at CFP 600–800. The blue-line bus will drop you right in front of the Tjibaou Center. Go in the morning and plan to spend most of the day there, because this is one of New Caledonia's top sights.

Île Nou

This former island, jutting west of Nouméa, has been connected to the city by a land-reclama- tion project that used waste from the nickel smelter. English seaman James Paddon had a trading post here as early as 1845. After 1864, Île Nou became notorious when the French converted it into a penal colony called Nouville housing more than 3,000 prisoners at a time. **Camp Est Prison** on Île Nou is still a major jail.

The green-line bus will take you directly to the chapel, workshops, and buildings of the original 19th-century Nouville prison, until recently occupied by a mental health facility, and now part of the Université de la Nouvelle Calédonie. A school teaching French as a foreign language occupies the former prison chapel (1882). There are quiet beaches to the west of the university, and you can walk the dirt road right around the end of Île Nou in about an hour.

An evocative sight is **Fort Tereka** (1878), perched on a hilltop at the far west end of Île Nou. This spot offers one of the finest scenic viewpoints in the South Pacific, with the central chain of Grande Terre in full view. Four big 138-mm cannon mounted on wheels were set up here in 1894–1896 to defend the harbor. Two more, placed opposite to create a crossfire, are now in front of the war memorial on Place Bir Hakeim. From the university, it's a 20-minute walk west to the Kuendu Beach Resort, with the fort access road on the right, just before the descent to the resort. There are shortcuts to come back, and a swim at **Kuendu Beach** would certainly be in order. This is where Nouméa's European residents come on weekends to get away from the tourists at Anse Vata.

Société Le Nickel

The northern section of Nouméa is not as attractive as the southern; here, on Pointe Doniambo, is the giant metallurgical factory, Société le Nickel. Established in 1910 and expanded to its present size in 1958 and 1992, the smelter has about 2,000 employees (only 17 percent of them Kanaks). It processes much of New Caledonia's nickel ore, and the rest is exported to Australia and Japan in its natural state.

Ore for the smelter is collected from a number of giant, open-cut mines around Grande Terre by huge ore carriers, leaving terrible scars in their wake. Two distinct products are smelted: ferro-nickel and matte. The former, sold to a variety of industrialized countries, is 75 percent iron and 25 percent nickel, used in the manufacture of stainless steel. Matte, sent to the company's Le Havre (France) plant, is 80 percent nickel and cobalt, used in the making of high-quality steel products.

Toxic discharges of sulfur dioxide and nickel compounds from this smelter have caused serious health problems among the thousands of Kanaks living in the Cité Pierre Lenquette low-cost housing area directly east of the smelter (company regulations prohibit emissions when the wind is blowing south toward central Nouméa and Anse Vata). New Caledonia has the world's highest incidence of asthma-related deaths due to nickel dust thrown up by the mining and smelting.

If you're interested, the Service des Mines (tel. 27-39-44), on rue Édouard Unger between the smelter and downtown, has a collection of rocks on display weekdays 0730–1115 and 1215–1530 (admission free).

Parc Forestier

Visit this botanical garden and zoo five km northeast of downtown to see the flightless and rapidly disappearing cagou (Rhynochetos jubatus), New Caledonia's official territorial bird. The excellent ornithological collection also includes the rare Ouvéa parakeet. There are a few mammals, of which the flying foxes stand out. Allow two hours to see the birds and animals, and another two to study the plants, many of which are labeled. The garden (tel. 27-89-51) is open Tuesday to Sunday 1015–1700, admission CFP 300 (children 12 and under CFP 100).

You can get to the Parc Forestier by taking the white-line or violet-line buses to the Cité Pierre Lenquette low-cost housing complex at Montravel, then walking 1.5 km uphill. Otherwise it's a 35-minute walk from the Nouméa Youth Hostel. Follow the ridge road north, turn up the signposted road beside the Notre Dame du Pacifique statue, and go past the three towers of the Centre Récepteur Radioelectrique. Keep heading toward the huge light blue tower with two circular terraces on top.

There are many excellent scenic views along the way, especially from the light blue telecommunications tower on **Montravel** (167 meters), accessible up a steep road just before you reach the Parc. Amédée Lighthouse is visible on the horizon south of the summit, just to the left of Ouen Toro. To the northeast the twin peaks of Mt. Koghi (1,061 meters) dominate the horizon, while due east the oval profile of Mont-Dore (772 meters) stands alone. Closer in, just on the far side of Magenta Airport, is the Tjibaou Cultural Center. Two orientation tables indicate points of interest. You also get a good view of the apartment blocks of Cité Pierre Lenquette.

The Barrier Reef

Amédée Lighthouse, on a tiny island 18 km south of Nouméa, was prefabricated in Paris and set up here in 1865 to guide ships through Grande Terre's barrier reef. At 56 meters high, it's still the tallest metal lighthouse in the world, and you can mount the 247 steps. Several companies offer day trips to Amédée at around CFP 10,600 pp including a glass-bottom boat trip, barrier reef cruise, shark feeding, Polynesian music, and a buffet lunch. Among the boats doing this trip is the 30-meter cruiser Mary D Princess (tel. 26-31-31, fax 26-39-79, www.amedee.ws), with an office on the waterfront near the Parkroyal Nouméa. It leaves from pontoon K1 at Baie de la Moselle daily at 0830, and from the Club Med wharf daily around 0900, returning by 1700.

A cheaper way to get to Amédée Lighthouse is on the Amédée Diving Club's catamaran Spanish Dancer (see below). This departs the Club Med wharf daily except Tuesday at 0745, and costs only CFP 5,200 pp without lunch. The capacity is limited, so book a day or two ahead (scuba divers have priority and it's easiest to get aboard during the week).

Sports and Recreation

The **Amédée Diving Club** (Bernard Andreani, tel. 26-40-29, fax 28-57-55, www.amedee.spon line.com; weekdays 1300–1800) is based at Marine Corail, 26 rue du Général Mangin in central Nouméa. They offer morning and afternoon dives on a choice of a dozen sites around Amédée Lighthouse. Two-tank dives are CFP 9,880, plus CFP 1,560 for equipment (if required). Otherwise a one-tank dive is CFP 8,632 including gear. An introductory initiation dive is CFP 8,300. When space is available, snorkelers can go along at CFP 5,200, mask and snorkel rental included.

Scubaventure (tel. 28-58-18, scubaventure@ lagoon.nc; closed Mon.), on the beach at Hôtel Le Méridien, offers scuba diving at CFP 9,000/ 42,000 for two/10 dives, plus CFP 2,000 for equipment. They'll also do scuba certification courses at CFP 38,000.

Manta Diving (tel. 28-88-67; daily 1630– 1900) at the Hôtel Ibis does diving at CFP 8,320/10,000 for one/two dives. **Alize Scuba Diving** (tel. 26-25-85) in the Galerie Palm Beach, Anse Vata, has an almost exclusively Japanese clientele.

Some of Nouméa's top scuba locales are near the Passe de Dumbéa where there's good shark action. Turtles are sometimes seen near Îlot Maître, and the reef near Amédée Lighthouse is also visited.

In 1995, the 5,603-meter **Golf de Tina** (tel. 43-82-83, fax 43-82-84, golftina@canl.nc) opened on Tina Bay, four km beyond Magenta Airport and 11 km northeast of downtown Nouméa. It's very posh, with lovely ocean and mountain views. Greens fees for nine/18 holes are CFP 3,120/4,680 weekdays or CFP 4,160/6,240 weekends. Proper dress is mandatory: T-shirts, jeans, bathing suits, and tennis outfits are not permitted. Another rule states that you must finish nine holes in 2.25 hours, 18 holes in 4.5 hours. The blue-line bus will drop you near the course (or call to request a CFP 1,560 return hotel transfer).

The attractive **municipal swimming pool** (tel. 26-18-43), just beyond Club Med at the far end of Anse Vata, is open Monday to Saturday until 1700, Sunday until 1600, admission CFP 180. The adjacent **municipal tennis courts** are lighted at night.

Have a workout at the **Squash Club** (tel. 26-22-18; Mon.–Sat. 1000–2300, Sunday 1600–2100), 21 rue Jules Garnier opposite the Port Plaisance Mall on Baie de l'Orphelinat. A half

hour costs CFP 400 before 1600 and after 1600, or CFP 600 from 1600–2000. Rackets are available and there's an inexpensive bar on the premises (a hangout for English-speaking yachties).

On Sunday afternoons about once a month there's horse racing at the **Hippodrome Municipal** at Anse Vata. Most afternoons you'll see men playing *pétanque* next to the beach at Anse Vata and in Place des Cocotiers. Metal balls the size of baseballs are thrown, not rolled, at the other balls in this French bowling game.

ACCOMMODATIONS
US$25–50
You can camp free on Îlot Ste. Marie, accessible by taxi boat from the Baie de la Moselle tour boat wharf at CFP 2,500 pp roundtrip (minimum of four). Free camping is also possible on Îlot Larégnére, CFP 4,500 pp return by taxi boat (minimum of four persons).

The budget traveler's best headquarters is the Nouméa Youth Hostel (tel. 27-58-79, fax 25-48-17), or *auberge de jeunesse,* on Colline de Semaphore just east of downtown (fantastic sunsets from here). The four-story accommodations wing built in 1990 contains 10 double rooms, 14 four-bed dorms, and three six-bed dorms. It's CFP 1,300 pp in a dorm, or CFP 3,100 double in a twin room. If you don't have a valid youth hostel card there will be a CFP 200 pp per day surcharge, otherwise you can buy a one-year card valid around the world at CFP 1,400 pp. Pillows and sheets are supplied. The office hours for checking in, reserving, or paying are 0700–1000 and 1700–1930 only. The double rooms are almost always taken by young *métros* who spend their first few weeks or months in New Caledonia living here, but dorm beds are usually available. Always call ahead if you know you'll be arriving after the office closes at 1930. If you happen to get there during the day, put your pack in the attic above the Ping-Pong tables and return at 1700 to check in.

In each of the spacious dorms you have a secure personal locker in which to store your gear (lock provided), and all guests receive keys to individual kitchen and refrigerator lockers. One of the hostel's biggest advantages is the excellent cooking facilities, which allow you to save a lot of money on food. Cups, plates, cutlery, and cooking pots are provided, and alcohol is allowed in moderation. Token-operated washing machines are available at CFP 400 to wash (soap included), plus another CFP 100 to dry (or use the adjacent drying lines). Unlike some hostels, there's no age limit, you can stay as many nights as you like, and the premises remain open throughout the day (though the kitchen is closed for cleaning 1400–1600). The staff do their utmost to keep the place clean, and you'll be reminded of the need to cooperate if they see you leaving dirty dishes in the sink, etc.

Not only is this 94-person capacity hostel an inexpensive place to stay, but it's a center for exchanging information with other travelers. The *métros* staying here stick together in their own superficially intimate cliques and don't mix much, but the other guests are friendly. Ads or offers of employment, apartments, and vehicles are often posted on the walls. The hostel will store excess luggage for you. There's ample free parking on the street in front of the hostel, or in the parking area at the top of the adjacent hill. The hostel is accessible on foot up the stairway at the east end of rue Jean Jaures. Even if you don't usually stay at youth hostels, this one is so pleasant and convenient, it's well worth considering by virtually anyone on a budget. Wardens Jacky Sorin and Andrea Schaefer run a tight little ship—the finest and only *real* youth hostel in the South Pacific.

US$50–100

The nicest inexpensive hotel in the city center is the five-story **Hôtel Lapérouse** (tel. 27-22-51, fax 25-90-37), 33 rue de Sébastopol opposite Brasserie Saint Hubert just off Place des Cocotiers. The 29 rooms are CFP 5,550 single or double with shared bath, CFP 6,800 with private bath. There are no cooking facilities.

The flashy **Best Western Hôtel Le París** (tel. 28-17-00, fax 28-09-60, www.leparishotel.com), just below the Catholic cathedral at 45 rue de Sébastopol, has 50 a/c rooms at CFP 8,350/ 9,150/10,150 single/double/triple with TV, bath, and coffee making facilities. Noise from the Safari Club downstairs is a drawback on the lower floors.

The four-story **Hôtel San Francisco** (tel. 28-26-25), 59 rue de Sébastopol, is CFP 5,000 single or double, CFP 6,200 triple a night, or CFP 30,000 single or double, CFP 35,000 triple a week for a reasonable room with bath and cooking facilities. Little notices on all entrances read *Attention au Voleur* (Beware of Thieves). The hotel bar looks like something out of a Clint Eastwood flick.

The 62-room **Paradise Park Motel** (tel. 27-25-41, fax 27-61-31) is at 34 rue du P.R. Roman in Vallée des Colons, a 15-minute walk east of Place Bir Hakeim. An a/c studio with bath, kitchen, and TV is CFP 5,650 single or double a night. Reductions are available for stays of one, two, three, or four weeks. The Paradise Park is inhabited mostly by French contract workers, as the four *pétanque* courts next to the swimming pool indicate. It's the only budget place with a resort atmosphere within walking distance of town. The blue-line and violet-line buses pass nearby.

The **Mocambo Hôtel** (tel. 26-27-01, fax 26-38-77, mocambo@canl.nc), 49 rue Jules Garnier, a four-story building just off Baie des Citrons, has 40 rooms with TV, fan, and fridge beginning at CFP 8,850 single or double, CFP 9,850 triple.

Just around the corner from the Mocambo Hôtel is the **Marina Beach Hôtel** (tel. 28-76-33, fax 26-28-81, marinab@canl.nc), 4 rue Auguste Page. The 20 self-catering studio apartments begin at CFP 8,320 single or double. A sauna and spa pool are provided.

The **Hôtel Ibis Nouméa** (tel. 26-20-55, fax 26-20-44, www.ibis.grands-hotels.cc), 8 promenade Roger Laroque, is opposite Baie des Citrons. The 60 a/c rooms with fridge and TV in this neat four-story building begin at CFP 9,150 single or double, CFP 10,150 triple (CFP 1,000 extra if you want a view of the sea).

Le Lagon Nouméa (tel. 26-12-55, fax 26-12-44, www.lelagon.com), 143 route de l'Anse Vata, is a six-story high-rise just inland from the beach. Le Lagon has four standard rooms at CFP 9,000 single pr double, 41 studios at CFP 10,000, 13 one-bedrooms at CFP 13,000, and one two-bedroom at CFP 16,000, plus CFP 350 tax. Most of the 59 tastefully decorated units have a kitchenette, fridge, and TV. Specify whether you want a double or twin beds.

The four-story **Hôtel Lantana Beach** (tel. 26-22-12, fax 26-16-12, lantana@canl.nc), 113 promenade Roger Laroque, faces Anse Vata (ask for a top floor room with a balcony overlooking the sea). The 37 a/c rooms start at CFP 7,750/8,750/9,750 single/double/triple. A small shopping arcade is downstairs, and on weekends you have to be prepared for disco noise on the lower floors. Stay here if you want to sleep in the belly of the tourist strip.

Two reasonably priced motels are in Val Plaisance near Anse Vata Beach, but both are often full. The three-story, 22-unit **Motel Anse Vata** (tel. 26-26-12, fax 25-90-60, cirypierre@offratel .nc), 19 rue Gabriel Laroque, is only a five-minute walk from Anse Vata beach: CFP 6,450 single or double. On a monthly basis, it's CFP 115,000 double. The rooms are attractive and the French managers friendly.

The two-story, 16-unit **Motel Le Bambou** (tel. 26-12-90, fax 26-30-58) is at 44 rue Spahr, a 10-minute walk farther inland: CFP 6,150 single/double with fan. The rooms at both motels have balcony, private bath, fridge, and cooking facilities, and monthly rates are available.

US$100–150

The **Novotel Surf** (tel. 28-66-88, fax 28-52-23, www.novotel.grands-hotels.cc), on the point separating Anse Vata from Baie des Citrons, has 235 air-conditioned rooms with TV, bath, and fridge in several connected high-rise buildings beginning at CFP 14,000 single or double garden view, CFP 16,800 sea view. Rows of slot machines and the Casino Royal gambling hall are right on the premises, and a swimming pool and fitness center are available. It's only of interest as part of a cheap package tour.

The **Kuendu Beach Resort** (tel. 24-30-00, fax 27-60-33, kuendubeach@lagoon.nc) is on Kuendu Beach, near the west end of the Île Nou peninsula, six km from town. The 20 thatched bungalows with cooking and laundry facilities are CFP 12,150/14,000 garden/beach single or double, while the six overwater bungalows are CFP 35,000 double. On Sunday there's a buffet lunch with folksy entertainment. Kayaks, pedal boats, snorkeling gear, and a swimming pool are provided free of charge. There's scuba diving with Sub-Austral (free initiation dive if you stay a week) and horseback riding is arranged. It's good if you're looking for more natural surroundings than are found in the city. The greenline bus comes this far every half hour, and the resort also offers a shuttle.

Residôtel Le Stanley (tel. 23-23-23, fax 23-23-33, www.stanotel.com), 33 rue la Riviéra, is on a breezy hillside overlooking Baie Sainte Marie at Ouémo, beyond Magenta Airport. The 58 a/c studios and suites with kitchenette, balcony, TV, and fridge begin at CFP 12,600 single or double. On a weekly basis, it's excellent value at CFP 34,650 double plus tax. The accommodations are clean and new, with a view of Mont-Dore. Le Stanley's swimming pool is wedged between the main four-story building and a rocky shore. No shops are nearby, but the violet-line bus goes right there.

US$150–250

The **Parkroyal Nouméa** (tel. 26-22-00, fax 26-16-77, resa.parkroyal@mls.nc), 123 promenade Roger Laroque, is just across the road from the beach at Anse Vata. The three separate sections of this hotel are arranged around the central swimming pool. The original four-story Nouvata wing facing the beach has 72 rooms starting at CFP 22,900 single or double. In 1999, the eight-story Sunshine building was added behind the pool with 113 rooms starting at CFP 27,900. The 11-story Le Pacifique building next door was built in 2000 and has 120 smaller rooms from CFP 15,350. Japanese groups are the main clientele here.

Nouméa's seven-story, 280-room **Club Méditerranée**, directly below Ouen Toro at the southeast end of Anse Vata, was closed in 2003. High labor costs and shifting tastes have cut into profitability and this resort may never reopen. Whatever the future holds, Club Med's beach and wharf are still freely accessible down the stairs on the Anse Vata side.

US$250 and up

Next door to Club Med is Nouméa's top hotel, the five-star **Le Méridien** (tel. 26-50-00, fax 26-51-00, www.lemeridien-noumea.com), owned by local politician Jacques Lafleur. This is the only operating Anse Vata resort without a road between it and the beach. The 253 rooms begin at CFP 30,000 single or double. For a suite you'll pay CFP 50,000, but most guests are here on package tours and pay far less. Two of the hotel's three curving high-rise wings built in 1995 enclose lovely garden and a large swimming pool. A range of sporting facilities are available, including scuba diving with Scubaventure. Nouméa's second gambling casino, a 400-seat ballroom, and five classy restaurants are here.

FOOD

Budget

Nouméa's ubiquitous snack bars will prepare a filling sandwich (*le sandwich*) for CFP 200 and up. This consists of a generous length of baguette-style bread with your favorite filling, plus lettuce and tomatoes. It's a meal in itself. One place serving this is the Vietnamese-run **Snack le Vilbar** (tel. 28-48-48), 55 rue de Sébastopol at Hôtel San Francisco.

The **Alimentation Générale Stop 14** at 14 rue de Sébastopol (next to Brasserie Saint Hubert) has excellent sandwiches and takeaway meals, and the picnic-perfect benches in the Place des Cocotiers are just around the corner. **Libre Service Austerlitz** (tel. 25-99-30) at 28 rue de Austerlitz opposite the taxi stand is similar.

Chez Camille (tel. 28-59-86), 1 rue Charles de Vernheil in the Latin Quarter, is a Vietnamese takeaway with baguette sandwiches from CFP 250, Asian takeaways from CFP 450, and whole barbecued chickens from CFP 850.

Brasserie des Arts (tel. 28-14-27), corner of rues Eugène Porcheron and Sébastopol behind the post office, is a good place for a coffee and croissants breakfast.

Snack Esquimo (tel. 28-21-25; daily 1000–1400/1700–2100), 59 rue de Sébastopol at avenue de la Victoire, serves large portions of Asian-

style chicken, beef, pork, shrimps, omelettes, fish, and chow mein in the CFP 700–900 range.

The Vietnamese-operated **Restaurant Le Hameau II** (tel. 28-48-32; Mon.–Fri. 0600–1700, Sat. 0600–1330), 32 rue de Verdun, offers filling Asian dishes at reasonable prices. Inexpensive beer is available with the meals.

Café L'Annexe (tel. 26-22-30; Mon.–Sat. 0600–1700), near the tourist office right on Place des Cocotiers, is a nice place for sandwiches and drinks.

Better Restaurants

Nouméa has more than 130 restaurants serving dishes like *coq au vin* (chicken in wine sauce) and *champignons provençales* (mushrooms seasoned with garlic and parsley). The cuisine is *très bon;* indeed, given the prices, it has to be! The restaurants start serving lunch around 1100, and by 1200 the *plats du jour* could be gone, so arrive early. Most establishments catering mainly to the locals stop serving lunch at 1300 and dinner at 1900 (the top restaurants stay open until 2200). Many upscale places have a special tourist menu for a set three-course meal, varying anywhere from CFP 1,500 to CFP 2,500. It's often better value to order just one main plate à la carte.

Places offering a *plat du jour* lunch for around CFP 1,000 weekdays include **Café Le Flore** (tel. 28-12-47), 39 rue de Sébastopol, and **Chez Lolo et Pascale** (tel. 28-42-21; closed weekends), 37 rue de Verdun. They're closed in the evening.

Brasserie Saint Hubert (tel. 27-21-42), 44 rue Anatole France on Place des Cocotiers, is *the* place for reasonable pizza, draft beer, and local atmosphere. During the *événements* of the 1980s, this was a stronghold of the local *pied noir,* but Kanaks are allowed in these days. The attached **Restaurant Le Troquet** serves an excellent *plat du jour* lunch on their terrace overlooking the square. It's recommended.

The **Nikko Sushi Bar** (tel. 25-11-88; Mon.–Fri. 1100–1800), 4 rue de Barleux near Place des Cocotiers, is fun for a change. The dishes rotating on the counter cost CFP 200–500 each (or CFP 1,000 for any three). Sample plates stuck to the wall explain the color coding.

Restaurant La Chaumière (tel. 27-24-62;

weekdays 1100-1330/1900-2100, Saturday 1900-2100), 13 rue du Docteur Guégan in the Latin Quarter, is one of Nouméa's finest French restaurants. They offer a three-course meal with a choice of anything on their menu at CFP 1,700/2,600 for lunch/dinner. It's a worthy choice for a splurge.

Restaurant Huong-Xua (tel. 27-47-68), 1 rue Bichat in the Latin Quarter, has Vietnamese dishes priced CFP 1,100–1,300.

Baie des Citrons

A row of terrace restaurants faces the southern portion of Baie des Citrons, and it's great to have sundowners on the terrace of **Desperados Bar La Plage** or similar. Nouméa's trendy groupies all hang out here.

La Fiesta Chez Alban (tel. 26-21-33), 5 promenade Roger Laroque next to the Hôtel Ibis at Baie des Citrons, is run by Basques—good food at normal prices.

Anse Vata

Bambino (tel. 26-11-77) and **Jullius** (tel. 26-13-38), next to the Parkroyal Nouméa and Lantana Beach hotels, have things like hamburgers, *croques monsieurs* (grilled ham-and-cheese sandwiches), and French waffles at fair prices. **Snack Ulysse** (tel. 28-69-28), next to Libre Service Oceania, around the corner at 145 route de l'Anse Vata, is a bit cheaper but it doesn't have a terrace overlooking the sea.

Pizzeria San Rémo (tel. 26-18-02), 119 promenade Roger Laroque, next to the Lantana Beach Hôtel, has some of the tastiest pizza in the Southern Hemisphere (CFP 900 and up for one person). At lunchtime on weekdays the San Remo offers a *plat du jour* for under CFP 1,000. Wednesday nights there's live music.

The Cantonese food at **La Grande Muraille** (tel. 26-13-28; closed Sun. night and all day Mon.), near Hôtel Le Méridien, is a good value.

Surprisingly, the cheapest place to eat at Anse Vata is the bar in the slots area of the **Grand Casino de Nouméa** (tel. 24-20-20) at Hôtel Le Méridien. To hold their gambling clientele they serve draft beer and huge baguette sandwiches at low prices. Casino Royal's **Tanda Café** at Le Novotel Surf also offers meal deals.

Groceries

The **public market** (daily 0400–1200), beside Baie de la Moselle, is the place to buy fish, fresh fruit, vegetables, and pastries. (Some of Nouméa's only free public toilets are here too.) Daily 1700–2300 a row of food vans parked along rue Georges Clémenceau, between the market and the New Caledonia Museum, dish out inexpensive takeaway curries in a colorful night market.

Nouméa has more than a half dozen large supermarkets and department stores. **Casino** (tel. 24-30-60; Mon.–Sat. 0730–1930, Sun. 0730–1230), opposite the Maritime Passenger Terminal two blocks west of Place des Cocotiers, is about the cheapest. There's another Casino open identical hours in the Port Plaisance Mall at Baie de l'Orphelinat. **Champion** (tel. 26-96-72; Mon.–Sat. 0730–1830), off rue du Général Mangin between rue de l'Alma and rue de la République, is another of the few places open through lunchtime. **Oceania** (tel. 26-14-88; Mon.–Fri. 0600–1930, weekends 0600–1230 and 1500–1930), 145 route de l'Anse Vata near Hôtel Le Lagon, is a bit more expensive. With a baguette, Camembert cheese, and French table wine from any of these, you'll be ready for a memorable picnic.

ENTERTAINMENT

Nouméa cinemas include the **Hickson City** (tel. 24-21-39), 6 rue Frédéric Surleau (behind Hôtel de Paris), the **Rex** (tel. 24-21-38), on avenue de la Victoire, and the **Plaza Twin** (tel. 28-87-87), 65 rue de Sébastopol. In 2003, **Cine City,** rue de la Somme at General Mangin, opened with 12 projection rooms. All foreign movies are dubbed into French, with no subtitles (admission CFP 850). Admission fees are reduced to CFP 700 on Monday at the Hickson City and on Tuesday at the Plaza Twin.

Night Club Le Tunnel (tel. 27-21-42), 44 rue Anatole France below Brasserie Saint Hubert, features live rock concerts on Saturday nights. If Le Tunnel fails to please, try **La Corrida** (tel. 26-34-26), 46 rue Anatole France, which opens daily at 1800. (A recent report indicates that the city authorities have closed down many bars and clubs frequented by Kanaks in the city center, while bars in the predominately French neighborhoods of Anse Vata and Baie des Citrons are unaffected.)

If you enjoy French chanson singing, seek out **Paillard Piano Bar** (tel. 26-28-80), 5 rue Jules Garnier, Baie de l'Orphelinat (hidden between L'Ancre de Marine and Restaurant Flamboyant). It's brimming with atmosphere, and Friday and Saturday nights from 2100, you'll enjoy listening to Jean-Pierre's piano playing as Marie-Jo sings. Tuesday at 2100 there are tarot readings. Arrive early if you want a table, or try to reserve.

English speakers will feel right at home at *Bar Le Galapagos* (tel. 26-22-18, www.legalapagos .com; Mon.–Sat. 1000–2300, Sun. 1600–2100), upstairs in the Squash Club, 21 rue Jules Garnier, Port Plaisance. Happy hour is Wednesday 1930–2030, while a special cheese dinner (CFP 1,750) is served Thursday at 1930. Friday there's live music starting at 2030, often jazz, folk, or Latin (no cover charge). This friendly place is a favorite of yachties anchored in nearby Baie de l'Orphelinat.

Anse Vata

Miti Nui Night Club (tel. 24-03-93), below the Lantana Beach Hôtel, operates as a disco Friday and Saturday from 2200 (CFP 1,000 cover charge). Sundays they open at 1600 with no cover charge. Also check **Disco L'Acropole** (tel. 24-19-38), next to Bambino Snack Bar nearby.

Fun and Games

High rollers frequent the **Casino Royal** (tel. 26-00-10) at Le Novotel Surf on Anse Vata. The female casino staff wear evening gowns, the male croupiers black tie, and punters are also required to dress smartly to enter the gaming salon (no shorts, jeans, thongs, or running shoes). You must show your passport at the door—locals and persons under 21 aren't admitted. Dress requirements and admission restrictions don't apply at the casino's slot machine section. The slots are operating from 1100 daily, the gambling salon from 2000 (Sun. from 1500).

The newer **Grand Casino de Nouméa** (tel. 24-20-20), at Hôtel Le Méridien, also has slot machines and a games room, open identical hours.

Less risky than the casinos are the **bingo games** held daily except Monday from 1400 onwards at 7 rue Jules Ferry (tel. 28-11-10; CFP 100 a card). Of course, you'll need to know French (or find a helper).

Trials and Tribulations

One of the top free shows in town is the proceedings at the **Palais de Justice** (tel. 27-93-50) on rue de Metz, just off route de l'Anse Vata downtown. Cases begin being heard in the Salle du Tribunal downstairs weekdays around 0800, and continue until the docket of that day has been cleared. Upstairs the Cour d'Appel evaluates more complicated appeals, also from 0800 onwards. The seats are comfortable, the air conditioning a relief, the situations intriguing, and the opportunity to learn some French unexcelled.

Cultural Shows for Visitors

Polynesian dancing (and the attempts of Japanese tourists to join in) may be witnessed at the **Parkroyal Nouméa** (tel. 26-22-00) during the Wednesday night *Soirée des Îles* and Friday *Soirée Merveilleuse*. If you're not up to having the buffet (island foods for CFP 5,000 Wed., seafood at CFP 7,000 Fri.), just enter the bar and order a drink. On Sunday afternoons Polynesian dancing comes with the seafood buffet at the **Kuendu Beach Resort** (tel. 24-30-00).

No regular programs feature Kanak dances or culture.

SHOPPING

Rue de l'Alma, with its numerous boutiques and specialty shops, is Nouméa's most exclusive shopping street. Watch for the *soldes* sign, which indicates a sale.

Artifacts from the other Melanesian countries are shown at **Galerie Galéria** (tel. 28-49-09), 7 rue de la République.

The **Atelier des Femmes** (tel. 88-87-81), rue Anatole France at Gouverneur Sautot, sells handicrafts made by local women, while the **Association des Sculpteurs de Nouvelle Calédonie** (tel. 83-77-60), half a block up rue Anatole France, displays the works of Kanak woodcarvers.

Compact Megastore (tel. 24-35-35; Mon.–Sat. 0800–1900, Sun. 0900–1200), rues d'Austerlitz and Anatole France, has a large selection of recordings of Pacific music.

Buy camping and snorkeling gear at **R. Deschamps** (tel. 27-39-61), 34 rue de la Somme. Better quality snorkeling and diving gear is available from **Marine Corail** (tel. 27-58-48), 26 rue du Général Mangin. **Nauticus Center** (tel. 27-51-41), 79 rue de Sébastopol, also sells first-rate diving gear.

While rue de l'Alma may be Nouméa's trendiest shopping street, the Latin Quarter is more fun to wander around and make little discoveries for yourself. Check out **Arte Bello Galerie d'Art** (tel. 25-31-00), 30 rue Auguste Brun in the Latin Quarter.

Nouméa has several smart shopping malls with many visitor-oriented shops, restaurants and activities offices. The largest of these are the **Galerie Palm Beach,** 127 promenade Roger Laroque next to the Parkroyal Nouméa on Anse Vata, the **Center Commercial Baie des Citrons,** promenade Roger Laroque, and the **Port Plaisance Mall,** 10 rue James Garnier, Baie des Pêcheurs (green-line bus).

INFORMATION AND SERVICES

Information

The Office du Tourisme (tel. 28-75-80, fax 28-75-85, www.ville-noumea.nc; weekdays 0800–1730, Sat. 0900–1200), in the center of the Place des Cocotiers and with a branch office at Anse Vata (daily 0900–1730), doles out free brochures on Nouméa and South Province, and can answer questions. Ask for the free Jasons map of Nouméa and New Caledonia.

North Province has an information office (tel. 27-78-05, fax 27-48-87, www.tourismeprovincenord.nc; Mon. 1230–1630, Tues.–Fri. 0900–1130 and 1200–1630, Sat. 0900–1200) at 35 avenue du Maréchal Foch.

Destination Îles Loyauté (tel. 27-66-27, fax 27-48-27, www.iles-loyaute.com), 2nd floor, Immeuble Central, 27 rue de Sébastopol, and at 113 avenue Roger Laroque (in front of the Lantana Beach Hôtel) on Anse Vata has outstanding brochures on the Loyalty Islands.

The Institut de la Statistique (tel. 28-31-56, fax 28-81-48), 2nd floor, 5 rue Galliéni, has specialized statistical publications.

Marine Corail (tel. 27-58-48), 26 rue du Général Mangin, handles nautical charts.

The Direction des Ressources Naturelles de la Province Sud (tel. 24-32-55; weekdays 0730–1130 and 1215–1600), second floor, 19 rue Maréchal Foch, has free hiking brochures (in French) on Rivière Bleue and other territorial parks and reserves.

Caledo Livres (tel. 27-38-11), 23 rue Jean Jaures, has the best selection of books on the South Pacific, including many in English.

Librairie Montaigne (tel. 27-34-88, fax 28-45-30, montaigne@canl.nc), 23 rue de Sébastopol, has an excellent selection of books in French on New Caledonia and Tahiti. Librairie Pentecost (tel. 28-88-82, fax 28-54-24), 34 rue de l'Alma, is better for maps. Both bookstores have the colored IGN topographical maps of New Caledonia, including the excellent 1:500,000 "Carte Touristique" of New Caledonia (CFP 1,665). Pentecost also carries the 41 detailed 1:50,000 "Serie Orange" topographical maps (CFP 1,300) and sells nautical charts at CFP 3,700 each.

Photo Vata (tel. 26-24-07), next to the Parkroyal Nouméa at Anse Vata, also sells IGN topographical maps.

Airline Offices

Reconfirm your international flight reservations at Aircalin (tel. 26-55-00), 8 rue Frédéric Surleau opposite St. Joseph's Cathedral, Air France (tel. 25-88-00), 41 rue de Sébastopol, Air New Zealand (tel. 28-66-77), 22 rue Duquesne (Axxess Travel), Air Vanuatu (tel. 28-66-77), 22 rue Duquesne (Axxess Travel), or Qantas (tel. 28-65-46), 36 rue de Verdun.

Money

Numerous banks are along avenue de la Victoire toward Place Bir Hakeim. The rates vary slightly, and they're worth comparing if you're changing a lot of money. A more important consideration are the rip-off commissions deducted by the banks, such as CFP 780/1,780 on cash/traveler's checks taken by the Société Général or CFP 1,248/1,872 subtracted by the Banque de Nouvelle Calédonie. The Banque Calédonienne d'Investissement or BCI (www.bcinet.nc) takes 1 percent of the payout, while the BNP Paribas (www .bnp.nc) charges a flat CFP 728 on any transaction (these fees could change). There's usually no commission if you're changing Euros in cash, though Euro traveler's checks may be subject to commission (ask). Saturdays 0730é1130 you can change money at the Banque Calédonienne, rue Anatole France and rue du Général Mangin (CFP 520 commission). Many banks have ATMs that give cash advances.

You can change American Express traveler's checks without paying a commission at Center Voyages (tel. 28-40-40, fax 27-26-36, center tours@cvoyages.nc; weekdays 0730–1730), 27 bis, avenue du Maréchal Foch. Their rate is similar to the banks. Center Voyages holds mail for American Express clients.

Post

The main post office (tel. 26-84-00), 7 rue Eugène Porcheron in the Latin Quarter, is open weekdays 0745–1530, Saturday 0730–1100. The poste restante counter here holds mail only 15 days before returning to sender and there's a fee of CFP 70 per letter to pick up mail (not rigorously applied). To have mail forwarded for three months, fill out an *ordre de réexpedition*.

It's possible to receive faxes addressed to fax 28-78-78 at this office, but it costs CFP 500 for the first page, plus CFP 100 for additional pages. To send a one-page fax here costs CFP 600 to Oceania, CFP 800 to France, CFP 900 to North America, or CFP 1,000 to other areas.

To mail a parcel, go to the Centre des Colis Postaux (tel. 26-86-00; weekdays 0745–1530), 17 rue de l'Alma.

Internet Access

Le Cyber Café (tel. 24-15-41, www.lecyberpoint.nc; Mon.–Sat. 0800–2000, Sun. 0800–

1200), 75 rue de Sébastopol directly behind the museum, charges CFP 250 for 15 minutes Internet access.

Cyber Citron (Mon.–Sat. 0930–1930, Sun. 1200–1930), on the side of the Centre Commercial Baie des Citrons closest to the Aquarium, offers Internet access at the same rate.

Consulates

The Australian Consulate General (tel. 27-24-14; Mon.–Fri. 0800–1200), 7th floor, 19 avenue du Maréchal Foch, opposite the Musée de la Ville, issues tourist visas. They also represent Canadians.

Other countries with diplomatic offices in Nouméa are Belgium (tel. 28-46-46), 4 rue Montchovet; Indonesia (tel. 28-25-74), 2 rue Lamartine, Baie de l'Orphelinat; Germany (tel. 26-16-81), 19 rue Gazelle, Magenta (behind the university); Italy (tel. 25-13-15), 17 rue de Docteur Tiburzio; Japan (tel. 25-37-29), 45 rue de 5 Mai, Magenta; Netherlands (tel. 28-48-58), Hôtel Lapérouse, 33 rue de Sébastopol; New Zealand (tel. 27-25-43), 4 boulevard Vauban; Switzerland (tel. 26-11-59), 18 rue Jim Daly, Val Plaisance (near Motel Le Bambou); United Kingdom (tel. 28-21-53), 14 rue du Général Sarrail, Mont Coffyn; and Vanuatu (tel. 27-76-21), 53 rue de Sébastopol. There's no U.S. diplomatic representation in New Caledonia (the U.S. Embassy in Fiji has responsibility).

Launderettes

Pat Pressing (tel. 27-11-81; weekdays 0700–1800, Sat. 0730–1230), 14 rue du Docteur Guégan, charges CFP 1,100 to wash and dry five kilos of laundry.

Lav Service (tel. 28-68-86; weekdays 0730–1800, Sat. 0730–1200, 47 rue Jeane Jaures, is also CFP 1,100 to wash and dry five kilos.

Pressing New Wash (tel. 26-24-74; Mon.–Sat. 0700–1800), in the Port Plaisance Mall, charges CFP 1,100 to wash and dry five kilos.

Laverie Flipper (tel. 24-14-04; Mon.–Sat. 0800–1830), on the side of the Centre Commercial Baie des Citrons nearest the Aquarium, will wash and dry five kilos of laundry for CFP 1,090.

Health

The Hôpital "Gaston Bourret" (tel. 25-66-35 or 25-66-66), avenue Paul Doumer, accepts emergency cases 24 hours a day. A business-hours consultation here will cost CFP 4,000 (otherwise CFP 5,700 Sat. from 1200–1800 and Sun. 0600–1800 or CFP 7,600 daily from 1800–0600). To call a doctor in emergencies, dial 15.

Dr. Jacques Gourand (tel. 27-53-00), 20 rue Austerlitz (upstairs from beside the Pharmacie in the Nouméa Center Mall) charges CFP 3,200 for a general consultation. He speaks English, and is on duty mornings from 0730 Monday to Saturday (no appointment required).

Dr. Louis Lagarde (tel. 27-20-63; Mon.–Fri. 0830–1115 and 1430–1730, Sat. 0830–1100), 30 rue de Verdun (upstairs), also charges CFP 3,200 for consultations.

TRANSPORTATION

For information on domestic flights from Nouméa to other parts of New Caledonia, see the Transportation section earlier in this chapter.

Interisland Ferries

The **Armement Loyaltien Sarl** (tel. 26-01-00, fax 28-98-97, betico@lagoon.nc; weekdays 0730–1730, Sat. 0600–1000), based at the Gare Maritime des Îles on the Quai des Voluntaires, 1 avenue James Cook, operates the high-speed 360-passenger catamaran NGV *Betico* (pronounced be-ti-CHU) to the islands. This sleek catamaran cruises at 35 knots, reaching the Isle of Pines in 2.5 hours, Maré in 3.5 hours, and Lifou in 4.5 hours. During holiday periods the ferry is fully booked, and advance reservations are recommended at all times. All departures from Nouméa are at 0700. The ferry leaves from downtown Nouméa and also avoids costly airport transfers on the islands. The wharves on Maré and Lifou especially are much more convenient places to arrive than the airports on those islands. Fares from Nouméa are CFP 5,450 to the Loyalty Islands, or CFP 3,650 to the Isle of Pines. Interisland fares between Lifou and Maré are CFP 2,750 (children half price). Bicycles are carried at CFP 500 a trip. *Betico* costs about half what Air Calé-donie charges on the same routes, while allowing 20 kilos of luggage rather than the usual 10 kilos. Passengers on ferries to the Loyalties are almost all Kanak—the French usually fly. It's a relaxing trip with comfortable airline-style seating.

The **Compagnie Maritime des Îles** (tel. 27-36-73), corner of rue Jules Ferry and avenue de la Victoire, operates the 158-passenger-carrying freighter *Havannah* between Nouméa and the Loyalty Islands about once a week. Fare are CFP 4,000 one-way from Nouméa to any of the Loyalty Islands or CFP 3,000 a hop between the islands. The same company operates the freighter *Lady Geraldine,* which does a similar run. They're much slower and less regular than *Betico* and not worth the small savings unless you just happen to connect.

Inter-City Buses

Three distinct bus networks are based in Nouméa: *les bus interurbains* (inter-city buses), *les bus suburbains* (regional buses), and *les bus urbains* (city buses). Each operates from a different terminal. Most inter-city buses leave from the Gare Routière at 36 rue d'Austerlitz opposite the market. The times quoted below could change, so check the schedule at the ticket office (tel. 88-83-12; Mon.–Fri. 0730–1200 and 1330–1600, Sat. 0730–1200) the day before. The buses do fill up, so arrive at the station early. If the ticket office is closed, simply pay the driver.

The bus to Yaté (two hours, CFP 700) leaves daily except Sunday at 1130. To Thio (two hours, CFP 1,000) the bus leaves Monday to Saturday at 1130, Sunday at 1700. Buses to Canala via La Foa (3.5 hours, CFP 1,100) are Monday to Thursday at 1400, Friday at 1700, Saturday at 1200, and Sunday at 1600.

The west coast is well served, with buses to Bourail (three hours, CFP 1,100) at Monday to Saturday at 0600, 0800, 0930, 1030, 1130, 1200, and 1230, Sunday at 1000, 1130, 1200, and 1500. If you miss these, the bus to La Foa (two hours, CFP 900) is Monday, Tuesday, and Thursday at 1530, Wednesday and Friday at 1730, and Saturday at 1130. To Koné (four hours, CFP 1,300) there are buses Monday to Saturday at 0600, 0930, and 1130, Sunday at 1000 and 1500.

© DAVID STANLEY

The catamaran *Betico* provides fast, inexpensive service from Nouméa to the outer islands.

Buses to Koumac (5.5 hours, CFP 1,650) are Monday to Saturday at 0600 and 1130, Sunday at 1000. Buses to Pouébo (seven hours, CFP 1,850) via Koumac are Wednesday at 0800 and Friday at 1130 and 1730.

To the east coast, buses run to Houaïlou (four hours, CFP 1,250) Monday to Saturday at 0800, 1030, and 1200, Sunday at 1130 and 1200. To Poindimié (five hours, CFP 1,450) Monday to Friday at 1030, and Saturday and Sunday at 1130. The Poindimié continues to Touho. Buses to Hienghène (six hours, CFP 1,650) via Houaïlou leave Monday to Thursday and Saturday at 0800, Friday at 1730.

Regional Buses

The CarSud bus to La Tontouta Airport (tel. 25-16-15; one hour, CFP 370) departs from a stop called "Passeport" on rue Georges Clemenceau near the corner of rue Paul Doumer. It runs almost hourly weekdays from 0400–1900, Saturday 0450–1735, but only in the morning on Sundays. You pay the driver.

Other CarSud buses operate to Dumbéa, Païta, St. Louis, and Mont-Dore. Ask the tourist office for schedule information.

Arc en Ciel (tel. 27-19-80, www.arcenciel-voyages.nc) and S.C.E.A. (tel. 43-31-41) operate special airport buses which will pick you up right at your hotel and cost CFP 2,500.

City Buses

Nouméa's city bus system is excellent. There are eight color-coded bus routes, serving such places as Anse Vata (green-line and orange-line), Baie des Citrons (green-line), Île Nou (green-line), Magenta Airport (blue-line), and the Tjibaou Center (blue-line). Study the route maps posted at all stops. Monday to Friday the buses run every 15 minutes 0530–1900 (every 30 minutes weekends). Catch them at the Place des Cocotiers, or at marked bus stops along the routes. A flat fare of CFP 140 is charged (children under 10 CFP 100) and you pay the driver.

Tourist Train

Le Petit Train (tel. 43-37-43, www.petittrain .com), a miniature tourist train, shuttles between Anse Vata and most of the tourist sites around Nouméa, including the youth hostel and the Parc Forestier. A board in front of the Galerie Palm Beach at Anse Vata outlines the route.

There are four trips a day from Palm Beach Station (at 0915, 1055, 1330, and 1515), and the day ticket (CFP 500/1,000 child/adult) allows you to stop off anywhere and catch a later service on. This is convenient on Sundays when other transportation is limited. On Wednesday, Thursday, and Saturday at 1315 there's a special trip to the Tjibaou Cultural Center (CFP 1,300 roundtrip). The funny little blue *cagou* signs you see around town are Petit Train stops.

Taxis and Hitching

The main Nouméa taxi stand is on rue d'Austerlitz just off the Place des Cocotiers. All taxis have meters (CFP 280 flag fall, plus CFP 105 per km 0600–1800, or CFP 140 per km 1800–0600 weekdays and anytime weekends). Trips outside Nouméa are CFP 162 a kilometer. Expect to pay CFP 800 to Anse Vata, CFP 1,000 to the Parc Forestier, CFP 1,600 to the Golf de Tina or Tjibaou Cultural Center, or CFP 8,000 to La Tontouta Airport for four persons maximum. If you speak French you can call a radio taxi 24 hours a day by dialing 28-35-12. An extra CFP 130 is charged in that case.

To hitch, take a black-line or blue-line city bus to Normandie (Saint-Quentin) at the junction of RT 1 to Bourail and RT 2 to Yaté. But unless saving a few hundred francs is crucial, it's much better to take the La Tontouta bus to the airport to get well out on the road to Bourail, or the Robinson, St. Louis, or Plum buses for the road to Yaté. Hitching up the southwest coast is easy, but it's slow elsewhere due to a lack of traffic. Also, very few drivers speak English.

Taxi Boats

The Air Mer Loisirs information kiosk (tel. 28-29-01, www.aml.nc; daily 0800–1200/1400–1700) on Baie de la Moselle near the fish market sells taxi boat tickets to Îlot Maître, a reef islet surrounded by a white sandy beach just southwest of Nouméa. The fare is CFP 2,100 pp round-trip (minimum of two).

Plages Loisirs (tel. 26-90-00) at the Office du Tourisme on Anse Vata operates a taxi boat to Île aux Canards at CFP 750 pp round-trip and to Îlot Maître at CFP 2,200 round-trip. They also rent bicycles, peddle boats, kayaks, sailboards, canoes, and catamarans.

Vehicle Rentals

Car rental rates begin around CFP 4,000 a day including 150 kilometers. The mileage can add up, so you're better off getting an unlimited kilometer rate (often with a two-day minimum rental). Many of the smaller car rental agencies not associated with the international chains will give you a large discount on their published rates if you take the car for a week or more. Bargaining may be possible, but hang onto all the paperwork until you get home, because cases of credit card fraud have occurred here. Most companies will allow you to drop the car off at La Tontouta Airport at no additional charge.

Full collision insurance is CFP 1,500 a day and up, although the unlimited km rates usually include it. When checking the car rental insurance, ask how much the "franchise" is, as that's the deductible amount you'll have to pay if you're found to be at fault, insurance or no insurance. It varies from CFP 50,000 with AB to CFP 100,000 at Budget, Europcar, and Hertz. Any driver's license will do, but Avis, Hertz, Europcar/Mencar, Euro Car, and some of the others will only rent to those 25 and older (age 21 or older at AB). Expect to pay CFP 115 a liter for gasoline (about US$3.75 per American gallon), and in remote areas tank up every chance you get. Gasoline is exactly the same price everywhere on Grande Terre.

Some companies don't want their cars taken out of South Province, and a clause in the rental contract may stipulate that the insurance will be void and the renter responsible for full damages and towing charges if the car is taken beyond Bourail. Riviére Bleue Provincial Park, roads south of Yaté, and all unpaved roads may also be banned. Chances are, the agency won't mention this to you, but it will be printed in the contract. Thus it's wise to read the contracts carefully when deciding whom to rent from, and make sure North Province is included in the insurance coverage if you intend to go there.

Compared to the other Pacific islands, the roads of New Caledonia are excellent and a joy to drive. Surprisingly, however, the signposting is often poor, and there's a general absence of picnic or rest areas along the highways and benches in the town parks (except occasionally in Nouméa). Driving is on the right, and the use of seat belts is compulsory. The speed limit is 50 kph in town, and up to 110 kph on the open road (beware of speed traps). If two cars meet at an unmarked town intersection, the car on the right has priority. In case of an accident, report to the nearest gendarmerie.

Euro Car (tel. 25-20-20, eurocar@lagoon.nc), 40 avenue Maréchal Foch at avenue de la Victoire, has small cars at CFP 28,080 a week including taxes, insurance, and 1,100 km (extra kms CFP 25). The weekend rate (Fri. at 1600 to Mon. at 1000) is CFP 10,710 with 400 km free. English is spoken here.

AB Location de Voitures (tel. 28-12-12, fax 27-71-55, www.ablocation.com), 36 avenue du Maréchal Foch, offers competitive unlimited-kilometer rates for two weeks (from CFP 54,500, plus 4 percent tax). Insurance is included but you're still responsible for the first CFP 50,000 in damages.

Europcar/Mencar (tel. 27-61-25, fax 28-17-59, www.mencar.nc), 8 rue Jean Jaurès, rents Peugeot cars at CFP 33,000 a week plus tax, unlimited kilometers and insurance included.

Avis (tel. 27-54-84, fax 28-62-90) is at 2 rue Georges Clémenceau behind the Total service station at the north end of downtown.

At Anse Vata, try **Discount Rent a Car** (tel. 27-26-99), 137 route de l'Anse Vata, two blocks inland from Libre Service Oceania. **Hertz** (tel. 26-18-22, fax 26-12-19, www.hertz-nc.com), 113 route de l'Anse Vata, has 4WD jeeps at CFP 10,900 a day plus tax but including insurance and unlimited mileage (minimum two days). Hertz has the advantage of branch offices in Koné (tel. 47-22-61) and Touho (tel. 42-88-38).

Budget Rent a Car (tel. 27-60-60, www.agence-budget.com) is at the Centre Commercial Baie des Citrons, and **Visa Rent a Car** (tel. 26-24-44, www.visa-location.nc) is also on Baie des Citrons.

Take care when parking in the center of Nouméa, because you are required purchase a ticket from an automatic machine on the corner, and this must be placed face up on the dash inside the car for inspection. The fee is CFP 50 every 30 minutes, payable weekdays 0800–1100 and 1300–1600, Saturday 0800–1000. The minimum ticket amount for infractions is CFP 1,000. At last report, parking at Anse Vata was still free. There's plenty of free downtown parking in the lot on the west side of Baie de la Moselle, between the market and the American War Memorial. Elsewhere in the territory, you'll have no trouble finding free parking (except at Mont-Dore on the weekend).

Scooter and Bicycle Rentals

Point Rouge Rent a Car (tel. 28-59-20, www.pointrouge.com), 75 avenue Maréchal Foch, rents one-person scooters at CFP 1,800/11,900 a day/week plus 4 percent tax. A regular drivers license is all you need, and the provided helmet must be worn.

Plages Loisirs (tel. 26-90-00) at the Office du Tourisme on Anse Vata rents bicycles at CFP 1,040/1,560 a half/full day.

Tours

South Pacific Tours (tel. 25-95-05), at the Parkroyal Nouméa Hotel, has organized sightseeing tours from Nouméa. The half-day trips to Mt. Koghi (CFP 5,200) and the full-day trips to Rivière Bleue Provincial Park (CFP 9,360 pp) and Yaté (CFP 9,360) operate on alternate days. Also ask about the less frequent La Foa/Farino tour (CFP 9,360).

The best excursion available from Nouméa is the day trip to Isle of Pines on the high-speed ferry *Betico* every Wednesday, Saturday, and Sunday at 0700 (CFP 6,300 round-trip). The price only includes the boat ride, but you get seven hours free time on the island. It's easy to pass the day exploring the Kuta/Kanumera area on foot, or sign up for one of the organized bus tours offered at the wharf (the lunch can be expensive on these, so bring picnic fare). Between Nouméa and the Isle of Pines, the ferry goes through the narrow Canal de Woodin separating Ouen Island from Grande Terre, and then passes Prony Bay, scenic highlights. This trip is highly recommended—verify the departure times as soon as you arrive in Nouméa. Except on major holidays, you can buy your ticket at the office just prior to boarding the ferry.

A local environmental group, the **Association pour la Sauvegarde de la Nature Neo-Calédonienne** (tel. 28-32-75, asnnc@canl.nc; weekdays 0730–1130 and 1430–1800), room 12, 12 boulevard Vauban, organizes hikes once or twice a month from March to November. These leave

Sundays at 0745, and visitors are welcome to join upon payment of a CFP 1,000 pp insurance fee. The friendly staff will probably help organize transportation to the trailhead with one of their members. Drop into their office near the stairway up to the youth hostel to check the list of *sorties-nature*. They also sell books, and hand out free trail guides and brochures (in French). It's a great way to meet an interesting group of local residents while getting in some hiking.

Grande Terre

Grande Terre is by far the largest island covered in this handbook, and also the most varied. It's so big, the southern part of the island is noticeably cooler than the north. A mountain chain averaging 1,000 meters high runs right up the middle of the island for most of its 400-km length, crossed at intervals by six main highways linking the brown southwest coast to the green northeast. The island is divided into two provinces by a line cutting across Grande Terre to the north of Thio, La Foa, and Bourail. Although North Province is a third larger in land area, South Province has over three times as many inhabitants.

It's very easy to hitch up the west coast and you can thumb your way almost anywhere if you have the time, but the only comfortable way to travel around Grande Terre and discover its hidden beauty is by rental car. You'll save money on accommodations by being able to drive to out-of-the-way campsites, and by picnicking along the way. Buses do exist, but their timetables are designed to serve the needs of local commuters and they don't always coincide with those of travelers. As a supplement to hitching, they're fine, but you'll find them of limited use in touring the island extensively.

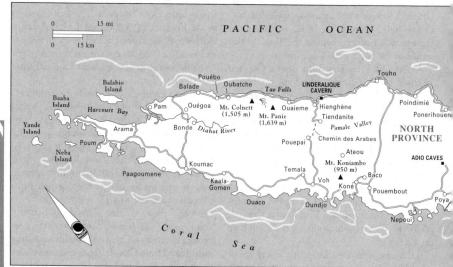

Strangely, once you leave Nouméa, you probably won't meet English-speaking tourists anywhere on Grande Terre. Virtually all of the travel facilities around the island cater almost exclusively to the French visitors, especially local French who often go on weekend trips. This is a tremendous advantage to those of us in the know, as you'll find everything fresh and unspoiled by package tourism. A knowledge of French is an important asset, but everyone is so friendly and helpful even monoglots will get by. A great adventure awaits you.

YATÉ AND THE SOUTH
East of Nouméa
La Conception Church (1874), south of the highway just a few kilometers outside Nouméa, contains many plaques left to thank the Virgin Mary for favors and miracles. In the graveyard beside the road to the church is the tomb of the former secretary-general of the Union Calédonienne, Pierre Declercq, murdered on September 19, 1981, by persons unknown. His tombstone reads: *assassiné dans le combat pour la libération de peuple Kanak.* Roch Pidjot (1907–1990), co-founder of the Union Calédonienne, is also buried here.

Set in lovely grounds seven km east of La Conception Church is picturesque **St. Louis Mission,** founded in 1859, with New Caledonia's oldest church. A footbridge below the east side of the church leads to the Tribu de St. Louis and the impressive **Grande Chefferie de St. Louis** (no entry). In recent years, serious clashes have occurred between local Kanaks and the large Wallisian settler community in the area. CarSud buses link La Conception and St. Louis to Nouméa several times a day.

Yaté
Excellent views of Grande Terre's grandiose, empty interior are obtained from **Col de Mouirange** (260 meters), eight km down the Yaté road from the Plum turnoff. The access road to **Parc Provincial de la Riviére Bleue** (tel. 27-26-74; Tues.–Sat. 0700–1700, Sun. 0700–1400) is just before Yaté Lake, another 13 km northeast of the pass. This 9,045-hectare reserve harbors many endemic plant and animal species, including the endangered *cagou.* The park entry kiosk is 2.5 km off the main road, and admission is CFP 500 per car, plus CFP 100 pp. Camping is free. On rainy days, the park may close if there's a chance of flooding. From near the

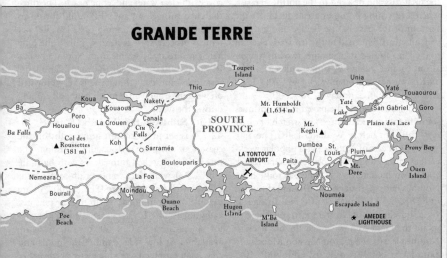

© DAVID STANLEY

turnoff to the park, a *piste rouge* (red dirt track) leads two km southeast to **Le Bois du Sud** where you can camp free.

The road to Yaté winds 30 km along the south shore of Yaté Lake, with the deep blue waters of this 48-square-km reservoir juxtaposed against Grande Terre's bright red soil. A *piste rouge* to the **Chutes de la Madeleine** is 17 km east of the provincial park access road. The falls (admission CFP 300) are 11 km south of the lake, and two km beyond them is the **Site de Netcha** where you can camp at CFP 1,000 per tent. The **Plaine des Lacs** here is noted for its fascinating variety of drought-resistant, flowering shrubs. The dirt road ends at Prony Bay.

On the left, six km east of the Chutes de la Madeleine road, is a two-km side road to the giant **hydroelectric dam** that holds back Yaté Lake. Erected in 1959, the **Barrage de Yaté** is 61 meters high and 641 meters long, and produces about 270 million kilowatt-hours a year (a quarter of the territorial requirements). An old road accessible only on foot continues past the dam and seven km down to the **Yaté Generating Station** in Yaté village, passing a beautiful, high waterfall on the way.

Back on the main highway, you climb over the final pass and descend to the northeast coast, where everything becomes green again. At the bottom of the pass is Yaté Bridge and a three-way junction. The road to the left leads two km to the Unia Bridge, then another two km straight ahead to Yaté village. A supermarket near the Yaté powerhouse is open weekdays 0700–1200 and 1430–1800, Saturday 0730–1200.

Across Yaté Bridge, the paved road continues south to Goro, with a three-km stretch of dusty *piste* four km before Wadiana Falls. The Yaté area, 81 km east of Nouméa, is a popular weekend resort for Nouméa people, and several Kanak *gîtes* accommodate visitors. The bus route from Nouméa ends at **Touaourou Mission,** founded in 1888, 6.5 km southeast of Yaté Bridge. If you're traveling by public transport, you'll have to spend the night somewhere, as the bus back to Nouméa leaves Touaourou Mission Monday to Saturday at 0600 (two hours, CFP 700). Getting there is easier, with departures from Nouméa

Monday to Saturday at 1130. It's possible to camp on the beach at Touaourou Mission (ask permission at the *chefferie* and offer a CFP 500 gift as you do so). Otherwise hitching is easiest on the weekend.

The coastal plain is narrow here, and the alternate views of inlets, mountains, and sea are fine. At the southern tip of Grande Terre, about 22 km from Yaté Bridge, is Goro village. **Wadiana Falls** is visible from the road a kilometer beyond Goro. You can swim in a clear pool at the base of the falls, 20 meters from road (use a mask to see the fish), and climb to the top of the falls for the view across to the Isle of Pines and all the intermediate reefs (beware of loose rocks). The pavement ends nearby. In the 1930s, Indonesian laborers built an iron and chrome mine on the plateau above Goro. A pair of giant rusting **cantilever loaders,** which once fed ore from conveyors directly into waiting ships, are beside the main road less than two km beyond the falls. The scenery is superb.

Accommodations at Yaté

A kilometer and a half north of Touaourou Mission is **Gîte Iya** (Paul Vouti, tel. 46-90-80), on landscaped grounds overlooking a lovely little cove with clear water and a fine beach. The three thatched bungalows are CFP 5,000 for up to three people, while camping is CFP 1,500 per tent. A grocery store is nearby. This is the only Yaté *gîte* directly accessible from Nouméa by bus (it's only 600 meters off the road). The large restaurant and everything else is very crowded on weekends, and you're much better off coming during the week.

Gîte Saint Gabriel (Mr. Abel Atti, tel. 46-42-77) is set in a coconut grove right on the coast, four km south of Touaourou Mission. The three older thatched bungalows with bath are CFP 4,500, while the two newer tin-roofed bungalows with hot water are CFP 5,800. All are capable of accommodating up to four persons. Camping is CFP 1,500 per tent. If you just stop for a picnic here, it's CFP 500 per car. Meals are available. At low tide, explore the pools and crevices in the raised reef a kilometer northwest of Saint Gabriel along the beach. One deep pool full of eels appears to extend back into a submerged cave. The snorkeling is only so-so. On weekends, the conspicuous consumption and heavy drinking here are best avoided.

Gîte Kanua (Robert Attiti, tel. 46-90-00, fax 46-91-22) opened in 1998 at Port Boisé, 16 km southeast of Wadiana Falls on a good road. If you have a 4WD vehicle, you can return to Nouméa via Chutes de la Madeleine and La Capture, rejoining the main Yaté highway after 41 km of *piste rouge*. The four deluxe bungalows in traditional style are CFP 8,000 double with bath, and there's a small camping area with covered picnic tables at CFP 1,500 double. In the attractive thatched restaurant you can get an excellent seafood meal for CFP 4,500, a *bougna* at CFP 2,500 pp, or a regular meal at CFP 2,000. Scuba diving (kanuadiving@offratel.nc) can be arranged. Gîte Kanua is on a white beach with clear water, and is surrounded by high forest—a very special retreat.

THE CENTER
North of Nouméa

The 17-km toll road *(péage)* between Nouméa and La Tontouta Airport costs CFP 150 and saves time, but the old road through Dumbéa and Païta is more picturesque. The **Auberge du Mont Koghi** (tel. 41-29-29, fax 41-96-22, koghiland@offratel.nc), 20 km northeast of Nouméa, is at 500 meters elevation, five km off the old road to Dumbéa. A dozen well marked hiking trails wind through the majestic rainforest, and there's a splendid walk to the viewpoint on Malaoui Peak (636 meters). One tree in the park is estimated to be more than 2,000 years old. Admission is free. The local French come to the Auberge for the *fondue savoyarde* (CFP 3,200 pp, minimum of two) in the restaurant (daily 0930–2130). Nearby are two wooden chalets with kitchen and private bath at CFP 7,500 for up to four people. In the forest, a 10-minute walk from the restaurant is a three-person treehouse at CFP 7500. There are also two refuges in the forest accommodating three or four persons at CFP 6000. Sleeping bags and sheets are CFP 1000 pp extra (optional). You may only occupy

rooms after 1600 on arrival day, but may stay until 1400 on departure day. Camping near the restaurant is free if you eat there.

The 18-hole **Golf Municipal de Dumbéa** (tel. 41-80-00, www.golf.dumbea.net) is 26 km north of Nouméa, in a river valley surrounded by green hills. It's a kilometer inland from the old highway, but easily accessible on the Dumbéa, Païta, and La Tontouta buses. Greens fees are CFP 4,200/5,500 for 18 holes weekdays/weekends. Club rentals and chariots are extra. The New Caledonia International Golf Open takes place here in July.

In you have transportation, camping is also possible on **Plage d'Enghoué,** 19 kilometers off the main highway from Païta on an unpaved road via Tiare. It's quiet and nicely isolated with lots of camping space along the beach, but no toilets or showers are provided, and water is only available from a hose at the caretakers office (CFP 200 per tent).

The small settlement on the main highway at the turnoff to **La Tontouta Airport** includes a large supermarket called Super U (Mon.–Sat. 0630–1200 and 1430–1915, Sunday 0630–1200), next to the bank, less than a kilometer from the terminal. A smaller Alimentation Générale nearby keeps slightly longer hours and opens Sunday afternoon.

If you're bumped from a flight due to overbooking, the airline may put you up at the dreary **Tontoutel** (tel. 35-11-11, fax 35-13-48, ecotel@canl.nc), also called the "Ecotel," two km from the airport terminal and 52 km from Nouméa. It's run by a hotel school and costs about double what it should at CFP 8,470 double. The 20 a/c motel rooms are in long single-story blocks. Hopefully the swimming pool, bar, and TV will keep you entertained.

A well-known hiking trail right across Grande Terre begins 400 meters after the bridge over the Tontouta River, six km northwest of the airport. An unpaved mining road runs 17 km up the river valley to the ruins of the Gallieni Mine. Several hours beyond is the Refuge de Vulcain (970 meters), where most hikers spend the first night. The second night is spent at the Refuge du Humboldt (1,380 meters), an hour short of the summit of **Mont Humboldt** (1,618 meters), second-highest peak in New Caledonia. After visiting the peak in the early morning, one can either return to La Tontouta in a day, or continue east to the Kanak village of Petit Borindi on the east coast. Experienced hikers can complete this memorable trek on their own in three days, using detailed maps and trail guides obtained in Nouméa.

Boulouparis

About 24 km northwest of La Tontouta Airport is **Les Paillottes de la Ouenghi** (tel. 35-17-35, fax 35-17-44, www.hotel-golf-paillottes.nc), an attractive resort near the Ouenghi River, up against the mountains three km off the main highway. The 15 thatched bungalows are CFP 9,150 single or double. There's an acclaimed restaurant/bar, swimming pool, tennis court, 18-hole golf course (greens fees CFP 3,500/4,500 weekdays/weekends plus CFP 2,000 for clubs and chariot), kayaking, and horseback riding.

Nine km beyond the Ouenghi River is Boulouparis, a French village at the foot of Mt. Ouitchambo, 78 km northwest of Nouméa. Here a paved road forks 47 km northeast to Thio over the Col de Nassirah (349 meters). Free camping is available in the small park at **Plage de Bouraké,** on Baie de St. Vincent opposite Leprédour Island, 15 km southwest of Boulouparis. It's easily accessible on a good paved road (signposted) through a French farming area. One of the best-equipped campsites in New Caledonia, there are concrete picnic tables, toilets, showers, and water taps, all of it seldom used. **Bouts d'Brousse Leisure Center** (tel. 43-29-62, fax 43-34-62, bdb@mls.nc) based at Bouraké organizes trips to Ténia Island Marine Park for snorkeling, surfing, and dolphin-watching at CFP 3,640/5,200 pp a half/full day (lunch CFP 2,800 extra, if required). You can scuba dive on these trips for another CFP 2,600.

Thio

Since 1880, Thio has been the most important mining center in New Caledonia, with one of the world's largest nickel deposits in the surrounding hills. Thio leapt into international prominence in late 1984, when 200 FLNKS militants under Éloi Machoro overwhelmed the gendarmerie and captured the town, holding it for almost two months in a standoff against the French army. Seven roadblocks were set up, but when the FLNKS began house-to-house searches for arms and ammunition, the French sent in snipers to eliminate Machoro. Unfortunately, the police helicopter landed in the wrong place, and the marksmen were captured by the Kanaks. In January 1985, the French decided to take no chances and sent 300 gendarmes to surround an isolated farmhouse near La Foa where Machoro and some others were meeting. Soon after, another French death squad arrived and murdered Machoro and a second man in cold blood as they stood outside the building. In retaliation, Kanaks blew up the French mines at Thio, causing US$3 million in damages.

On arriving from Boulouparis, turn right to **Thio Mission,** Bota Méré Hill, and the beach. The Marist mission church dates from 1868. From the beach you can see the nickel workings on the plateau to the northwest and the port to the southeast. The ore is brought down by truck and loaded into ships bound for Nouméa and Japan for processing. Southeast of Thio Mission, a paved road leads to Borindi with a ferry crossing a few km before the village. Moara Beach, 10 km southeast of Thio Mission, offers white sands and lots of shady picnic or camping space. It's worth driving another four km beyond Moara for the view of Baie de Port-Bouquet.

Thio village is beside the Thio River at the foot of the plateau, two and a half km northwest of Thio Mission. It's a colonial-style town, with a post office, bank, gendarmerie, and clinic. The **Musée de la Mine SLN** mining museum (tel. 44-51-77; Wed. 0830–1200, Sat. and Sun. 0900–1200), a block from the bridge, is CFP 200 to visit. The bus to Nouméa departs Thio Monday to Saturday at 0500, and Sunday at 1515 (CFP 1,000).

The **Gîte d'Ouroué** (tel. 44-50-85), on Ouroué Beach, six km north of Thio, is in a beautiful location two km off the road to Canala. The four neat thatched bungalows with electricity are CFP 3,000 double, and there's lots of camping space (CFP 500 per tent) in a coconut grove along the beach. All guests share a common kitchen, with toilets and bathing facilities behind the dining hall. Meals can be ordered at CFP 450/1,600 for breakfast/dinner. The long brown beach here drops off sharply and should be used with caution.

A one-way dirt road to Canala begins nine km north of Thio, with a timetable *(horaire)* for traveling in each direction. You can travel northbound at 0500, 0700, 0900, 1100, 1300, 1500, and 1700, and anytime during the night. Southbound you can begin on the even hours. It takes about 40 minutes to cover the 14-km one-way portion over the Col de Petchécara.

Independence martyr Éloi Machoro is buried next to the church in **Nakéty** village, at the northwest end of this road. Machoro's tomb is in the form of a small Kanak *case* next to the old church. The paved road begins again at Nakéty, and continues 10 km to Canala. There's no bus from Thio to Nakéty, and buses from Nakéty to Nouméa via Canala and La Foa leave before dawn. If you don't have a car you'll almost certainly have to hitch.

Around Canala

Canala Bay is the finest hurricane refuge for shipping on the northeast coast, and during the days of sail in the late 19th century this feature and mining activity made Canala an important center. Today it's Kanak country. The turnoff for **Ciu Falls** is two km southeast of Canala, then it's another four km in to the falls themselves. There's great swimming at the top of the falls (free), and a sweeping view of Canala Bay. Buses leave Canala for Nouméa before dawn (CFP 1,100).

At La Crouen, 11 km west of Canala, are **thermal hot springs,** where you can bathe in a 42° C sulfur pool. It's especially good for anyone suffering from arthritis, asthma, or rheumatism. Turn inland at a large bridge and follow the paved road one km to the Établissement Thermal. At last report, the main bathhouse was closed, but a small pool of thermal water beside the building was accessible anytime. A nice picnic spot overlooks the river and you could camp around here. Farther west is the turnoff to the mining center of Kouaoua, 45 km northwest of

Canala. From this junction, the main highway cuts south across the mountains to La Foa, passing tons of cascading water from several fantastic waterfalls along the way.

Around Sarraméa

Sarraméa, about 15 km before La Foa, is in a lovely valley. There's a large Kanak *case* in **Petit Couli** village, a few hundred meters north of the turnoff to Sarraméa. For CFP 1,000 per tent you can camp in the municipal campsite (tel. 44-39-55) beside the river below the sports field at Sarraméa. If no one is around, ask at the nearby *mairie* (town hall) weekdays during business hours.

Caldoche-operated **Évasion 130** (tel./fax 42-32-35) is four km off the Canala road. The 14 bungalows with private bath are CFP 4,000/5,500 single/double, and a picturesque swimming pool and restaurant are on the premises. Évasion 130 is surrounded by verdant hills abounding in swimmable streams, and it makes an excellent base for hikers. An old mule track that once connected La Foa to Canala winds five km through the forest to the top of the **Dogny Plateau** from the hotel parking lot. It's a wonderful day hike, also possible on horseback. If you're not staying or eating at the hotel, you should park your car at the *mairie*, 700 meters away. If you're well prepared, you could camp at 950 meters elevation up on the plateau.

La Foa

La Foa, 65 km northwest of La Tontouta Airport, is an alternative place to spend the night before catching a flight. It's an orderly *Caldoche* town surrounded by lush fields, acacia trees, and stately *Araucaria columnaris* pines. People from nearby farms and villages come to shop at La Foa's supermarkets, and there are two banks and a tourist office (www.lafoa.com). Fairly frequent buses up the west coast stop in front of the post office. The regular Nouméa bus begins its run here at 0600 daily except Sunday (CFP 900). At the south entrance to La Foa is a small metal bridge erected in 1909 by two students of Gustave Eiffel.

To visit the abandoned farmhouse where independence activists **Éloi Machoro** and Marcel

Noraro were murdered by French police snipers in 1985, take the road inland from opposite the BCI Bank in La Foa. The pavement ends after 2.5 km at a complex marked "Distribution d'eau de La Foa." Keep left here and straight ahead another 11.5 km on a dirt road along the La Foa River, until you see a building with a red tin roof to the right of the road. Lengths of cloth hang from trees in front of the house in memory of Machoro and Noraro.

Hôtel Banu (tel. 44-31-19, fax 44-35-50), opposite the post office in the center of town, occupies an historic colonial-style building with a quaint bar where you should avoid making any pro-Kanak comments. The nine rooms in a two-story building behind the restaurant are CFP 4,350 single or double without bath. In the back yard are five a/c bungalows with bath at CFP 6,350. The Banu's miniature swimming pool is usually empty. The restaurant (closed Sun. night) at the hotel has a reasonable *plat du jour* lunch, but the seafood dinner is expensive.

The **Naïna Park Hôtel** (tel. 44-35-40, fax 44-39-35), 1.5 km south of La Foa, has 11 bungalows at CFP 5,650 double. There's a large swimming pool.

If you have a car you can camp (CFP 900 pp) at the **Complexe Convivia** (tel. 46-90-90) in the park on Plage de Ouano, 24 km south of La Foa (the last 10 km of it on a washboard gravel road off the west coast highway). It's a large open area near a local boat-launching ramp. Picnic tables, barbecues, toilets, and showers are provided, plus plenty of mosquitoes after dark.

The turnoff to **Fort Teremba** is 14 km west of La Foa, then it's another three km south on a paved road to the fort. Built by convict labor in 1874, Fort Teremba's round tower affords a good view of Teremba Bay and the surrounding area. Beyond Fort Teremba, a dirt road leads 5.5 km to **Plage de Tanguy** where you can camp free on the beach, though it's rather swampy and mosquito infested. No services are provided. On the way there you pass the territory's largest prawn farm.

Farino

Farino is on a cool hilltop overlooking the west coast, 3.5 km off the Canala road and 10 km from La Foa. The *mairie* is on the ridge as you enter the village, with the Carrefour Farino supermarket at a crossroads a km beyond. Another km along, if you take the left road at the junction, is a waterfall with a deep pool for diving (free admission). Just under three km up the right-hand road at the crossroads is the **Refuge de Farino** (tel. 44-37-61, fax 44-10-08, refuge .farino@lagoon.nc), a small resort with four wooden four-person bungalows of different sizes at CFP 4,000/6,000 weekdays/weekends. Camping is CFP 1,000 per tent. Communal cooking facilities are provided. You can rent all-terrain vehicles and horseback riding can be arranged. A clear stream runs past the foot of the property, and the Refuge is a natural choice for anyone traveling alone. You're expected to bring your own sheet and sleeping bag. The second Sunday of each month, there's a big market at Farino.

Bourail

Although this town of 5,000 inhabitants, 167 km northwest of Nouméa, is the second largest in the territory, it's a disappointing little place after Nouméa. Along the one main street are the church (1877), post office, banks, supermarkets, gas stations, gendarmerie, town hall, and school, eight essential facilities you'll find in most New Caledonian towns. Two companies of French infantry are stationed at Camp Nandai, seven km north of Bourail beyond the turnoff to Houaïlou. Use Bourail as a stopover on a trip around the island, or as a base for visiting the surrounding area. In mid-August a major agricultural fair is held here—the best time to meet *les broussards* (country people).

There's not a lot to see in Bourail, although a small market is held at the northwest end of town on Tuesday and Saturday mornings. Worth a visit is the **Bourail Museum** (tel. 44-12-18), on the highway just south of the center, in a storehouse remaining from the penitentiary set up here in 1867. The museum displays the history of the region, in particular the life of early French settlers, Kanak artifacts, seashells, and photos from WW II. A Kanak *case* and petroglyphs are in the museum yard. It's open Wednesday, Saturday, and Sunday 0830–1130 and 1300–1700; admission CFP 200.

Plenty of buses pass through Bourail, but the drivers will only let you on if there's an empty seat. This can be a problem on Sunday and with buses headed for the east coast, which arrive full from Nouméa. Thus it's smart to visit Bourail on your way back to Nouméa rather than getting out here on your way north. The bus which begins its run to Nouméa in Bourail (CFP 1,100) leaves Monday to Thursday and Saturday at 0630, Friday at 1230. Strangely, hitchhiking out of Bourail can be unpredictable, with waits of more than three hours not uncommon.

Vicinity of Bourail

About 11 km southeast of Bourail is an **Arab cemetery,** where convicts sent to New Caledonia after the Berber insurrection in Algeria in 1871 and their descendants (who still live in nearby Nessadiou village) are buried. A Centre Islamique is beside the road just north of the cemetery, and another km north is a **New Zealand military cemetery,** to the right of the main highway from Nouméa. Bourail was an important New Zealand training base during WW II, and the peaceful cemetery has a striking location overlooking a valley. An account of the campaigns in which the servicemen died is posted.

One recommended trip from Bourail takes in **Pierced Rock** (Roche Percée), on a side road six km west of the Néra Bridge. A natural tunnel cuts through an eroded quartz cliff here, and at low tide you can get through to the other side. An anthropomorphic rock formation here has been called "le Bonhomme." Nearby is a good beach for swimming and snorkeling.

One km farther along the main road is a track up to **Belvédère Viewpoint,** with a fine view of Néra River, the coast, and Turtle Bay. **Turtle Bay** (Baie des Tortues), backed by towering *Araucaria columnaris* trees, is just up the coast from Pierced Rock, accessible by car from the road to the viewpoint. Be there early in the morning between November and March to see nesting turtles (extremely rare). Freelance camping is possible here.

Ten km past Pierced Rock along the same road is **Poé Beach,** the longest beach on Grande Terre. A camping ground and small resort share 18 km of unbroken sands. This is one of the few coastlines around Grande Terre not protected by an offshore barrier reef.

Accommodations at Bourail

Le Relais Gourmand (tel. 44-23-23, fax 44-23-24, relais.gourmand@lagoon.nc), in a two-story building on rue Simone Drémon at the north end of downtown Bourail, has four air-conditioned rooms with TV at CFP 4,950/5,450 single/double. Continental breakfast in the restaurant is CFP 500, and a *plat du jour* (CFP 1,980) is available weekdays. Otherwise have pizza at the Ch'ti Bar (tel. 44-13-94) across the street.

Hôtel La Néra (tel. 44-16-44, fax 44-18-31, lanera@lagoon.nc) overlooks the Néra River Bridge, two km southeast of central Bourail. The nine a/c rooms with bath in a long block facing the swimming pool are CFP 6,650 double (CFP 9,150 for the suite). It's an attractive location for a highway hotel.

Hôtel El Kantara (tel. 44-13-22, fax 44-20-33) is beside the Néra River, a couple of km southeast of the Pierced Rock and 10 km southwest of downtown Bourail. The *pied noir* owner has endowed his hotel with an Algerian air. The 20 rooms with bath in parallel zigzag blocks are CFP 4,992 single or double. There's a swimming pool and tennis court, it's a good base for sports such as kayaking on the river (kayak and canoe rentals are nearby). Scuba diving is available with **Bourail Sub-Loisirs** (tel. 44-20-65, butterfly.diving@lagoon.nc) at the mouth of the Néra River, two km south of the hotel.

At the beginning of Poé Beach, 18 km southwest of Bourail, is an attractive **campsite** (tel. 41-28-78) offering plenty of sand, banyan trees, songbirds, fresh water, showers, toilets, and excellent surfing (CFP 500 pp). If you don't wish to pay, you can camp free farther down the beach.

The **Hôtel Poé Beach** (tel. 44-18-50, fax 44-10-70, poebeach@lagoon.nc), about a kilometer farther up the same beach, has 24 fan-cooled duplex rooms with fridge and TV from CFP 13,606/19,846 double weekday/weekend including breakfast and dinner, plus six a/c bungalows for a couple of thousand more (no cooking facilities). The resort, which opened in 1991, has a restaurant, bar, pool, tennis courts, scuba diving, and other activities. You have to wade out quite a distance from their beach to reach deep water.

THE NORTHEAST COAST

Vicinity of Houaïlou

The winding road from Bourail follows sparkling rivers and crosses the **Col de Roussettes** (381 meters), a pass named for the big red fruit bats of the region. The border between north and south provinces runs along this ridge. There are good views along the way, especially of the abandoned Kanak taro terraces.

At the Coula River, 35 km north on the road to Houaïlou from the junction of the west coast highway, there's a road upstream to a viewpoint over a large waterfall (keep right). Thirty km farther east is a bridge over the Houaïlou River, with the road to Poindimié across the bridge to the left and Houaïlou town one km to the right.

The riverside town of Houaïlou, four hours from Nouméa by bus, was the base of the famous Huguenot missionary Maurice Leenhardt from 1902 to 1920. Leenhardt taught the Kanaks to read and write, and Ajië, the language spoken around Houaïlou, is still one of the most widely used Kanak languages on Grande Terre.

No regular accommodations exist in Houaïlou, but in a pinch you could camp free on the wild, deserted beach adjacent to abandoned Houaïlou airstrip *(aerodrome)*. The paved access road is two km north of the bridge, then it's another two km to the beach (go around the south end of the airstrip). There's plenty of driftwood for campfires here, but this site is very exposed to the wind and sea.

The **Camping de Kaora** (tel. 42-53-75), on Baie Lebris 11 km north of Houaïlou, charges CFP 1,000 per tent.

Up the Coast

As you continue up the coast, your first stop will be **Bâ Falls,** 14 km northwest of Houaïlou bridge and on the mountain side, only 1.5 km upstream from the highway. There's a large swimming area at the base of the falls. After a swim, climb to the top for the view. (There have been reports of break-ins to the parked cars of visitors to the falls.)

Ponérihouen, 44 km northwest of Houaïlou, is a picturesque little town by the river of the same name. Coffee is the main cash crop in this area, and there's an experimental station in the town. The long one-way steel bridge two km west of Ponérihouen dates from WW II. Mr. Michel Blanchet (tel. 42-85-14) operates **Camping Amenagé de Tiakan** on a brown beach opposite his store, 11 km north of Ponérihouen. Many small thatched picnic shelters among the coconut trees provide shelter in case of rain. Toilets, barbecue pits, and showers are also provided. To camp is CFP 500 pp, plus CFP 1,000 per car. Picnicking is CFP 200 pp.

Poindimié

This small town of under 5,000 inhabitants, 308 km from Nouméa, was founded during WW II, as several Quonset huts attest, and today it's the administrative center of the northeast coast. Stock up at the supermarkets or change money at one of the banks. Buses to Hienghène leave Monday to Saturday at 1130, Tuesday to Friday and Sunday at 1300, and again on Sunday at 1510. Buses to Nouméa (CFP 1,450) leave Poindimié weekdays at 0545, Saturday at 0500, Sunday at 1215. If you're driving, be sure to tank up at Poindimié, because there's no gasoline at Hienghène, and unleaded fuel may not be available again until Koumac.

Koyaboa Hill offers a fine overlook from its 390-meter summit. Take the first paved road up the hill after the Quonset huts west of Hôtel Le Tapoundari. This soon becomes a grassy track, and you must walk to reach the radio towers on top. The **public swimming pool** at the east entrance to town features a 1951 mosaic by Victor Vasarely, the famous Hungarian creator of op-art. A traditional Kanak *case* is between the traffic circle at the west end of town and the beach.

Tieti Diving (tel. 42-64-00, www.tieti-diving .com), based at the Monitel, offers scuba diving at CFP 5,000/6,500 without/with equipment. The scuba diving in this area is good because there isn't any mine-produced erosion killing the reefs with sediment. It's wise to book your diving here a few days in advance.

At the Tiwaka River, 13 km north of Poindimié, a new road cuts across the island to Koné.

Accommodations at Poindimié

The lack of reliable budget accommodations makes it a risky business to plan a stop here if you're traveling by bus or hitching. **Hôtel Le Tapoundari** (tel. 42-71-11, fax 42-76-11), opposite Poindimié's bridge, has 12 a/c rooms with private bath. The six rooms in a block next to the restaurant go for CFP 6,000/6,500 single/double, while the six older units in a row at the back are CFP 5,000/5,500. They're overpriced and often booked out by French contract workers.

Poindimié's most upmarket place to stay is the **Monitel de Tiéti** (tel. 42-64-00, fax 42-64-01, moniteltiem@canl.nc), right on Tiéti Beach, with four rectangular beach bungalows, six a/c rooms in a long block, and two houses with four rooms each, all costing CFP 7,500/8,500 single/double. There's a swimming pool. Despite the hotel's category, the surrounding area is rather shabby.

There's also a free municipal camping area at **Tiéti Beach.** It's a nice, grassy spot, with lots of camping space below the coconut palms behind the light brown beach, and toilets and showers are provided. It's a bit of a local hangout, and there's a longstanding problem of theft, so once your tent is up, you won't be able to go off and leave it.

Gîte Napoémien (tel. 42-73-83), in the verdant Napoémien Valley five km inland from Poindimié, has two bungalows with cooking facilities at CFP 2,000 pp. Camping is CFP 1,500 per tent (toilets and showers provided). There's no sign at the *gîte,* and the whole operation is poorly managed. The owner lives a kilometer back toward Poindimié (next to the bridge with a welcoming sign), and it's best to stop there for information. Better yet, call ahead for reservations, as this place is often closed.

Touho

This small settlement on a bay, 27 km northwest of Poindimié, is a good destination if you're traveling by bus, since there are several inexpensive places to stay. A few local fishing boats are based here, and Touho is a pleasant place to hang

out for a few days. Mandarin orchards, coffee plantations, and tall pines are hallmarks of this area. **Touho Mission** with its evocative old church (1889) is two km west of Camping Lévéque and one km off the main road (ocean side). For a splendid view of the entire area, hike up to the cross on the hill above the mission. The track leads off the main road from the top of the hill, 500 meters north of the mission turnoff. Go between the house and the water tank, and it's less than 10 minutes to the top. Touho's airport is three km southeast of Camping Lévéque, out on the road to Poindimié.

Camping Aménagé Lévéque (tel. 42-88-19), behind the grocery store in Touho, charges campers CFP 350 per tent. There are also five small bungalows, each with two beds, a table, two chairs, and shelves, at CFP 1,500 single or double. No bedding is provided, so roll out your sleeping bag. There's electricity, but the toilets and shower are outside. This is one of the few places in New Caledonia where you can still get a cheap room, but mosquito coils are essential and a net would be much better. It's right on a sheltered beach with clear water ideal for swimming, and next to the road to/from the small boat harbor if you've arrived by yacht.

Relais Alison (Madam Pisniak, tel. 42-88-12), opposite Camping Lévéque, offers five a/c rooms with private bath in a long block behind the Total service station at CFP 4,500/5,000 single/double. Meals are pricey here.

Camping Gastaldi (tel. 42-88-14, fax 42-43-42) is five km from Camping Lévéque. Take the Hienghène road over the hill to a turnoff to the right, then it's a kilometer farther in toward the beach. This free camping ground rates among the nicest and most peaceful on the island. Since it's at the mouth of a small river, the beach isn't as good as the one at Camping Lévéque, but there's a lot more privacy, and toilets and showers are provided. A grocery store is nearby.

Gîte de Mangalia (tel. 42-87-60), across the road from a pebble beach, 16 km northwest of Touho, has eight thatched duplex bungalows starting at CFP 4,000 single or double. Cooking facilities are not provided and breakfast/dinner are CFP 600/1,800 pp.

HIENGHÈNE AND THE NORTH

The scenery around the small town of Hienghène (pronounced "yang-GAIN"), 376 km from Nouméa, is unquestionably the finest in New Caledonia. Hienghène is also a symbol of the Kanak struggle against foreign domination. A hundred years ago Kanaks under Bouarate fought French colonialism here; in December 1984, 10 unarmed Kanaks on their way home from a political meeting were ambushed and murdered just up the river by French settlers.

At Tiouandé, 30 km northwest of Touho on the way to Hienghène, is a rocky crag known as **Napoleon's hat** next to the road. The entrance to Club Med is 5.5 km farther along, and beyond that you see high **limestone cliffs** on the right with a salt lake at their base. Five km beyond Club Med is a narrow one-km coral road leading to the huge **Lindéralique Cave** *(grotte)*, on the far side of the cliffs (CFP 200 admission to the cave).

A kilometer closer to Hienghène at the top of the pass is a turnoff to the viewpoint *(point de vue)*—one of the most beautiful spots on the island. From here, you'll see huge isolated rocks named **Sphinx** (150 meters high) and **Brooding Hen** (60 meters high) guarding the mouth of Hienghène Bay. The town itself is on a rocky spur at the mouth of the river. Across the bay are nestled the tiny white buildings of **Waré Mission,** with the high coastal mountains behind. Four fine coral islets are seen offshore. From town the Brooding Hen looks more like the **Towers of Notre Dame,** its other name.

As you come into Hienghène, between the viewpoint and the bridge is the **Centre Culturel Goa Ma Bwarhat** (tel. 42-80-64), which should be visited for its mixture of modern and traditional architecture. The exhibition room (open Mon. 1300–1700, Tues.–Fri. 0800–1200 and 1300–1700, Sat. and Sun. 0900–1600; admission CFP 100) displays traditional doorjambs, war clubs, spears, tools, pottery, baskets, and indigenous currency. Authentic handicrafts are sold here, and the center also contains an impressive library. Outside are two large *cases* with an open-air theater between.

For a sweeping view, hike up to the TV tower on **Pwihâ Duét** (499 meters). Take the Wérap road upriver from the bridge. After 1.5 km, the jeep track to the summit cuts straight up the hill to the left from a bend of the river.

The **Base nautique de Pai-Kaléon** (tel. 88-27-37), on the beach below the football field in the middle of Hienghène, rents kayaks and canoes.

Buses to Nouméa leave Hienghène at 0630 weekdays and at 1000 on Sunday (CFP 1,650). Hitchhikers will find that very little traffic circulates between Hienghène and Pouébo and 10-hour waits in the hot sun are not unusual.

Tiendanite

Tiendanite, the home village of former FLNKS leader Jean-Marie Tjibaou, has a special place in the history of New Caledonia. Fourteen Kanaks from this village were killed in a 1914 uprising against the French. During the 1917 uprising, the village was burnt to the ground, the men sent to prison in Nouméa, the women to work as servants for the *colons.* Later, Tjibaou's grandfather assembled some people to rebuild the village. In 1984, 10 men from this village of 120 people were brutally murdered by French *colons* who were eventually set free by a French jury.

Eight km up the river from Hienghène on a rough gravel road are the rusting wrecks of two small trucks flanked by a flagpole and strips of cloth marking the spot where 10 men from Tiendanite were killed by French settlers on December 5, 1984, in the Wan'yaat ambush. A black marble stone bears their epitaph and names. The road continues along the Hienghène River another five km, to a turning to the left and a bridge across the river. A side road runs up a small stream four km to Tiendanite village, deep in the mountains. The 10 victims of the Wan'yaat ambush are buried in a row next to the Catholic church in the village. The grave of Jean-Marie Tjibaou (1936–1989) is on the opposite hill facing the church.

Accommodations around Hienghène

Hienghène's tourist office (tel. 42-43-57) opposite the public market is very helpful. They can arrange village-based accommodations, such as camping or sleeping in a *case* for CFP 800 pp, plus CFP 400/1,200 for breakfast/dinner.

The **Gîte Ka Waboana** (tel./fax 42-47-03), near the tourist office in the center of Hienghène, has three bungalows at CFP 6,000 single or double and three self-catering apartments at CFP 7,000. Breakfast/dinner are CFP 600/1,800, and activities like boat trips, horseback riding, and hiking can be arranged.

There's a campsite with running water on the beach 600 meters down the side road to Lindéralique Cave, four km from Hienghène (CFP 800 per tent).

In 1992, the **Koulnoué Village Club Méditerranée** (tel. 42-81-66, fax 42-81-75, www.koulnoue.grands-hotels.cc) opened on attractively landscaped grounds behind a long brown beach, 10 km south of Hienghène and 1.5 km off the main road. The local Kanak villagers received a 10 percent interest in the resort, plus 40 hotel jobs in exchange for providing the land. The 50 neat tin-roofed duplex bungalows with a/c are CFP 9,880 double. Unlike most Club Meds, this one isn't a closely guarded camp, and they'll gladly rent you a room if they have one. Meals are extra at CFP 1,300/1,800/2,800 for buffet breakfast/lunch/dinner. Activities include the swimming pool, tennis, horseback riding, and other standard Club Med features. Babou Plongée (tel. 42-83-59, koulnoue.dive@lagoon.nc) offers scuba diving from the resort. Bicycles are CFP 500 an hour. The Lindéralique rock formations are just a 15-minute walk away (have your bathing suit on under your shorts if you wish to wade across to the caves—they're only 700 meters down the road on the other side of a small lagoon). When you consider what you get, it's actually a good value compared to many other hotels around the island.

Northwest from Hienghène

The coastline northwest from Hienghène features towering mountains with slopes falling right to the sea, empty beaches with fine coral just offshore, numerous high waterfalls clearly visible from the road, and deep green-blue rivers full of small fish such as you've never seen before. This is also the most traditional area on Grande Terre, with the greatest number of *cases*.

On the main road just north of Hienghène,

stop for the excellent view from the **Col de Tanghene**. The church of the **Mission de Waré**, 3.5 km north of Hienghène, has colorful stained glass windows. The pavement ends at Tiluny, six km north of Hienghène.

The Wan Pwéc tribe, between Waré and Ouaïème, about eight km northwest of Hienghène, runs the **Gîte Wéouth** (tel. 42-45-16) in a small village near a beach. The eight rooms in four bungalows are CFP 1,900 pp. Camping is CFP 800 per tent.

You can also camp at **Chez Maria** at Wâjik, a couple of km northwest of Wan Pwéc (CFP 800 per tent).

There's a free ferry operating 24 hours a day at Ouaïème, 17 km northwest of Hienghène. A local legend explains that a bridge can never be built here because of a giant who lives up the river. The giant is part shark, and such a structure would block its route to the sea. What's known for sure is that the river is shark-infested, and it's unlikely you'll see any locals swimming here.

The **Camping de Panié**, 3.5 km north of the Ouaïème ferry, has a grassy camping area in a coconut grove right on an attractive gray beach relatively free of mosquitoes. A long thatched shelter provides refuge in case of rain. It's CFP 800 per tent—a nice place to stop for the night. A grocery truck passes daily (ask the times). The turnoff to **Panié Falls** is 2.5 km northwest of the campground (CFP 600 per car to bathe in the pool).

Tao Falls is 10 km northwest of the Ouaïème ferry. The falls are clearly visible from the bridge, but to go to the base of the falls on foot is CFP 200 pp.

It's possible to climb to the top of **Mt. Panié** (1,639 meters), New Caledonia's highest peak, from near Tao Falls, and there are several shelters on the mountain for hikers. To climb Mt. Panié in one day would involve leaving at 0400 and only returning at dusk, so it might be better to spend a night on the mountain. A guide will cost CFP 7,000 per group.

Gîte de Galarino (Léon Foord, tel. 47-53-30), 20 km northwest of the Ouaïème ferry, has three thatched bungalows with private bath and cooking facilities at CFP 3,000/3,500 single/double, and a beachside camping area at CFP 1,000 per tent. It's an idyllic, end-of-the-world type of place. Colnett Falls is only two km northwest.

The pavement recommences 28 km northwest of the Ouaïème ferry, and the first grocery store on this road is at **Yambé,** 50 km northwest of Hienghène. Also at Yambé is the home of Pierre "Ehna" Teimbouec (tel. 88-14-45), who offers horseback riding. Ask for Ehna 400 meters southeast of the store. From Yambé it's only 11 km to Pouébo.

Pouébo

The first Catholic missionaries arrived at Pouébo in 1847, but were soon driven off by the Kanak inhabitants. The unrelenting fathers returned in 1852 for a more successful second try at establishing a mission. A gold rush here in the 1860s led to much French land grabbing and a Kanak revolt. **Pouébo Mission Church** dates from 1874, and it's worth visiting for its stained glass. At the entrance is a relic of Hippolyte Bonou, the first local chief to convert to Catholicism, who died on the Isle of Pines in 1867. The tomb of the colony's first Catholic priest, Guillaume Douarre, who died at Ballade in 1853, is inside the church.

A free municipal campground is on **St. Mathieu Beach,** 1.5 km north of Pouébo Church on the main road, then another 1.5 km northeast to the beach. Toilets, showers, and picnic tables are provided, and you get nice views of the mountains, but it's not the greatest beach for swimming (and the mosquitoes are a pain in the proverbial).

Buses leave Pouébo for Koumac Monday and Thursday at 1600, and Wednesday and Friday at 0825; for Nouméa (CFP 1,850) via Koumac Monday and Thursday at 0600 and Sunday at 1015. This haphazard schedule calls for careful planning unless you have a car or are prepared to hitch.

Balade to Ouégoa

Balade, 16 km northwest of Pouébo, also has a notable place in New Caledonian history, as this is where Captain Cook landed in 1774. Later, Rear Admiral Fébvrier-Despointes annexed New Caledonia for France at a ceremony near Balade on September 24, 1853, as an iron obelisk (erected in 1913) on a hill above the highway proclaims.

Just before the monument is the short access road to lovely **Mahamate Beach,** where Cook's men observed an eclipse of the sun on September 6, 1774. The first Catholic mass was celebrated here on Christmas Day, 1843. A traditional double-hulled canoe that sailed here from the Isle of Pines in 1993 for the 150th anniversary can be seen behind a plaque here. Lots of nice little secluded spots to camp freelance can be found along this beach, and there's even a water tap just before the canoe. Keep an eye on your gear here.

For CFP 500 per tent you can camp at **Camping Col d'Amos** (Léon Dubois) at Amos, on the way to Ouégoa, down a road to the right just before the beginning of the climb up the Col d'Amos Pass, eight km northwest of the obelisk.

The Diahot River, draining the far north of Grande Terre into Harcourt Bay, is navigable for 32 km. **Ouégoa** is a *Caldoche* farming community that attends church in a Quonset hut behind the *mairie.* **Le Normandon** (tel. 47-54-19), near the Diahot River Bridge, two km from the center of Ouégoa, has five basic rooms in a block called Le Caillou next to the restaurant. The two rooms with a/c and private bath are CFP 4,000/4,500 single/double, the one with private bath but no a/c is CFP 3,000/4,000, and two more with shared bath are also CFP 3,000/4,000. Camping is free if you take the CFP 2,200 dinner at the restaurant. It's not a very good value, and is often full with contract workers. After the bridge, traffic along the road to Koumac increases.

THE NORTHWEST COAST

Koumac

This town of 3,000 inhabitants, 370 km northwest of Nouméa, has a **Catholic church** (1950) on the roundabout that was originally an aircraft hangar! Inside is a striking modern stained glass window, and a number of outstanding Melanesian-style woodcarvings. The *cagou* lectern is by Léonce Weiss, while the altar formed from an outrigger canoe, tabernacle shaped like a Kanak *case,* and holy water bearer in the form of a man are by Léonce's father, Charles Weiss. The Christ figure is by his grandfather, Victor Weiss. **Léonce Weiss** (tel. 47-65-32, www .noumeanc.com/neacom/weiss.htm) himself currently has a studio three km out on the road to Nouméa (turn in at a white block marked "Sous-Station Koumac"). His miniature *flèches faîtières* make excellent souvenirs. More woodcarvings and other souvenirs are available at **Curios de Koumac** (tel. 47-54-71), in the commercial center behind Restaurant Escale de Koumac.

The road inland beside the Catholic church leads eight km to some rather intriguing **limestone caves** (admission free, bring a flashlight). The first cave is back to the right and up some rocks, and the longest stretches three km underground. You could camp free at the entrance to the caves and there are picnic tables, but no water in the vicinity. The **Club Hippique La Crinière** (tel. 35-66-51; closed Monday), 4.5 km east of Koumac off the road to the caves, offers horseback riding.

Koumac's small boat harbor is three km southwest of the traffic circle (turn left on the first road after the *gendarmerie* and keep straight). Several charter yachts operate out of here, and it's a nice picnic spot with tables overlooking the beach. A large army base is at the southeastern entrance to the city.

Accommodations and Food

Camping de Pandop (Monsieur Robert Frouin, tel. 47-62-46) is windy but nicely situated by the sea, only two km from Koumac (take the road opposite the church at the traffic circle and keep left after the *gendarmerie*). Camping is CFP 500 pp. Toilets and showers and provided, and shelters with picnic tables. A security fence surrounds the property.

Hôtel Le Grand Cerf (tel./fax 47-61-31), on the traffic circle in the center of Koumac, has nine wooden a/c bungalows with private facilities from CFP 5,400/6,000/6,600 single/double/triple. The restaurant is good and there's a swimming pool.

Cheaper, but not as nice, is **Hôtel Le Passiflore** (tel. 47-62-10), 800 meters up the road to the caves. The six rooms with shared bath are CFP 3,500 single or double; the five with private bath cost CFP 4,500. **Restaurant Escale de Koumac** (tel. 42-35-85), on rue Georges Baudoux near Le Passiflore, is a good place for lunch or a beer. **Libre-Service Chez Nino** (tel. 47-67-82) next door has whole barbecued chickens on the weekend (you have to arrive around 1000 or 1600 to get one), and takeaway pizza is available upstairs at **Pizza Pedro** (tel. 47-55-55; closed Wed.).

Koumac's most upmarket place is **Monitel de Koumac** (tel. 47-66-66, fax 47-62-85, monitel koumac@lagoon.nc), a kilometer down the road to Nouméa, with 16 a/c rooms in a long block, and six duplex bungalows (another 12 rooms), all costing CFP 6,800/7,300/7,800 single/double/triple. The Monitel has a pleasant swimming pool, and an attractive restaurant/bar with a good value weekday *plat du jour* lunch. They have rental cars.

Transportation

Koumac's airport is four km northwest of the traffic circle. Air Calédonie has flights from Koumac to the Belep Islands (CFP 9,430 one-way) and Nouméa (CFP 12,370) twice a week. The Air Calédonie agent (tel. 47-53-90) is at Hôtel Le Grand Cerf in the center of town.

Buses to Nouméa leave Koumac weekdays at 0430 and 1145, Saturday at 0430, and Sunday at 1145 (5.5 hours, CFP 1,650). Buses to Poum leave Koumac Monday 0345, Wednesday at 1315, and Friday at 1615. To Pouébo you can leave Monday and Thursday at 1315, and Wednesday and Friday at 0530. Koumac's bus station (*gare routière*) is just 500 meters southeast of the traffic circle in town.

Drivers must be aware that the gas stations in Ouégoa and Pouébo don't sell unleaded gas, and no gas at all is available at Hienghène. Thus it's important to tank up at Koumac if you're headed east.

North of Koumac

The paved coastal highway runs 56 km northwest of Koumac to the small town of Poum on Banaré Bay, with good views along the way. About 18.5 km north of Koumac is the entrance road to the **Dôme de Tiébaghi** mining area. From the main road the mining town is visible high up on the side of the 587-meter-high plateau. In 2002, Société le Nickel announced that it was increasing the output of this mine from 250,000 tonnes to a million tonnes a year.

Facing the white sands of Néhoué Bay, 45 km northwest of Koumac and 15 km southeast of Poum, is the **Malabou Beach Resort** (tel. 47-60-60, fax 47-60-70, www.malabou.grands-hotels.cc), part of the Accor/Novotel hotel chain. Opened in 1991, the hotel has 37 spacious a/c bungalows at CFP 9,500 double, plus three suites at CFP 18,500 for four persons. Meals are CFP 1,300/1,850/2,800 for breakfast/lunch/dinner (no cooking facilities). Tennis courts, freshwater swimming pool, and full sporting facilities are offered, but car rentals are not available. The Malabou Beach is in a picturesque but isolated and desolate location, and the water off their beach is rather murky (though teaming with fish). To see coral you must engage the services of **Manta Diving** on the resort wharf. An 850-meter airstrip has been built adjacent to the property. This resort doesn't quite match the standards of the Club Med Koulnoué Village at Hienghène, and there's much less to see and do in the vicinity.

Just past the Malabou Beach Resort is the turnoff to **Camping Amenagé Golonne** (tel. 47-90-78), on Tanle Bay, a recognized hurricane shelter for shipping. It's accessible on a rough, steep five-km dirt track that winds around the resort airstrip. The campground is on a better beach than the Malabou, and is very peaceful once you're there. It's CFP 500 pp with toilets and showers provided (tents can be rented at CFP 700 a night). A bungalow with private bath is CFP 4,000 single or double. There's a lovely view from the hill just before the final descent to the campground.

There's isn't much to see in **Poum village,** but you can climb barren Mt. Poum (413 meters) in about an hour. You can camp freelance on the beach off the road to Poum wharf, opposite a small white church, but it's not a very attractive spot. Don't go off and leave your gear unattended here. There's no water tap, but the swimming is good. The bus back to Koumac leaves Poum Monday at 0535, Wednesday at 1500, and Friday at 1800.

Some 31 km north of Poum (26 km of it on a gravel road), near Boat-Pass, the northernmost tip of Grande Terre, is the **Relais de Poingam** (Henry Fairbank, tel. 47-92-12), with seven thatched bungalows accommodating up to four persons at CFP 6,800 single or double. Camping is CFP 500 per tent. The seafood served in the restaurant is excellent (dinner CFP 2,500). You'll need your own transport to get here.

Belep Islands

The Belep Islands, some 50 km beyond Grande Terre's northern tip, receive twice weekly Air Calédonie services from Koumac (CFP 9,430) and Nouméa (CFP 17,000). There are both morning and afternoon flights from Koumac, making a six-hour day trip possible. The flight lands near Waala on Art Island. This trip is worth taking if you want to get well off the beaten track, but book ahead in Nouméa and be prepared to camp. A small ferry plies the waters between Waala and Poum about once a week (CFP 2,000 each way). Call Tramanord (tel. 47-57-18) in Poum for the times.

From 1892 to 1898, these islands were used as a leper colony, and the French forcibly exiled all the inhabitants to Balade. There's still a bit of resentment over this, but once the locals know you're not French, they're more friendly. The entire group is an indigenous reserve. Scallop fishing is done offshore by an Australian company in partnership with the Kanak communities of Belep and Poum.

Voh

You can hike across the mountains from Voh to the Hienghène valley along the "Chemin des Arabes" in a couple of days. The trail begins at Pouépaï, with access from Voh on a rough road.

Camping at **Plage de Gatope,** five km west of the war memorial in Voh (keep left where the roads divide), is CFP 500 pp. Toilets, showers, and picnic shelters are provided, and the palm-fringed beach is pretty. On weekends it can get crowded with local picnickers.

Koné

The 100-km road southeast from Koumac to

Koné offers only occasional gum trees to break the monotony—this is cattle country. Koné (population 4,500) is the capital of the North Province and a growing administrative center; several banks are here. Koné market is Saturday mornings (just down the road to Baco). Although Koné has some appeal, the main reasons for stopping are the horseback expeditions organized by two local companies. Both offer weeklong excursions across the mountains from Koné to Hienghène and back, or shorter three-day rides into the Pamalé Valley.

Koné Rodeo (Patrick Ardimanni, tel. 47-21-51), near Hôtel Koniambo, 400 meters down the road beginning at the east end of the airstrip, does a seven-day Hienghène ride and three-day mountain rides (CFP 23,000 pp). The price is all-inclusive (typical French Caledonian food, lodging, evening campfires, horses, etc.). A minimum of eight persons is required to do a trip, but they do as many as 30 a year, and individuals can join them, so call ahead. Patrick has 40 horses and speaks good English.

The other horseback company is **Randonnées Equestres** (Eric Tikarso, tel. 47-23-68), based in the Kanak village of Atéou. Eric lives in Koné, 500 meters from the market out on the road to Baco (ask). Randonnées requires five participants, and you'll need to know a little French. The three-day ride to Atéou and Paoué or the five-day trip to Tipindjé in the Hienghène Valley must be booked in advance either by phoning, or through a travel agent in Nouméa. If you're looking to join a group, weekends are best.

Southbound buses to Nouméa leave Koné Monday to Saturday at 0805, and Sunday at 1215 (CFP 1,300). Northbound, you can catch a bus to Koumac Monday to Saturday at 1540, and Friday and Sunday at 1410.

Accommodations at Koné

Budget travelers usually stay at **L'Escale de Koné** (tel. 47-21-09), near the post office and right at the bus stop in Koné. The eight rooms with bath and TV in a two-story block behind the restaurant are CFP 4,000 single or double. To get a room, you must arrive when the restaurant is open (weekdays 0600–1400 and 1700–2200, Sat. 0900–1400 and 1700–2200), and on Sunday

you'll have difficulty getting in. Good, inexpensive Vietnamese dishes are served in the restaurant.

A block south of L'Escale de Koné is **Hôtel Restaurant Le Joker** (tel. 47-37-07, fax 47-35-09), just up from the war memorial in the center of town. The four a/c rooms with bath in a neat block behind the restaurant are CFP 4,750/5,750 single/double, and once again, you can only check in when the restaurant is open (0900–1400 and 1900–2200). They serve a good *plat du jour* lunch at CFP 900.

The 20-room **Monitel l'Hibiscus** (tel. 47-22-61, fax 47-25-35, hibiscus@canl.nc), 100 meters down the road to Nouméa from the war memorial in the center of town, starts at CFP 5,750 for an a/c room in a two-story building. A restaurant and bar face the swimming pool just beyond the reception. It's the flashiest place in town. The Hertz agent is here.

The **Hôtel Le Koniambo** (Yannick Girard, tel. 47-39-40, fax 47-39-41), directly opposite the airstrip three km west of Koné, has 13 self-catering rooms with bath and 12 a/c bungalows without cooking facilities, all CFP 6,000/6,500 single/double (plus CFP 800 if you use the air-conditioning). Ask about their special weekend rate. The Koniambo allows camping in the garden free of charge for those taking dinner (CFP 1,750 set menu) at their restaurant. They have a swimming pool, and car rentals are arranged.

High up in the mountains in the next valley over from the Pamalé Valley is the **Gîte de Atéou** (tel. 47-26-13) with one Kanak *case* without electricity at CFP 900 pp. Camping is CFP 600 pp if you order meals here (you must have a warm sleeping bag). The *gîte* is used mostly as a base for persons on horseback riding tours, but it might also be of interest to hikers. It's 20 km north of Koné on a steep mountain road best covered on horseback or by 4WD (but also possible by normal car if you're a bit crazy). To get there, turn up the road beside Koné post office and go between the gendarmerie and the hospital to the cemetery. Turn left on the dirt road just after the cemetery and keep straight all the way.

There's free camping in the park at **Foué Beach,** seven km southwest of the bridge at the south end of Kone. The toilets and showers are good, and tables and chairs are along the beach, but there can be some radio noise at night from the adjacent fishing village. Turn left to the beach just before you reach the ocean.

South of Koné

The new headquarters of North Province, the **Hôtel de Province Nord,** is four km south of Koné on the road to Nouméa. A traditional *case* stands in front of the provincial assembly building. As part of the development of this area, a new road has been built across the island from this complex to Poindimié.

Four km farther south is Pouembout and the **Hôtel Le Bougainville** (tel. 47-20-60, fax 47-29-84, bougainville@mls.nc) with seven thatched bungalows at CFP 6,500 single or double, and seven a/c rooms in a long wooden block facing the valley at CFP 5,500. The hotel's restaurant and reception area share a mock Kanak *grande case.* You can order a *bougna* (a traditional dish made from seafood, meat, vegetables, and fruit) or the set dinner menu for CFP 1,750.

The territory's agricultural college or Lycée Agricole is three km east of Pouembout, and several French-operated places to stay are in the Tamaon Valley farther east. **Gîte Le Tamaon** (tel. 47-27-26), 13 km east of Pouembout, is far up the arid valley, just above the Pouembout River. The two rooms three self-catering bungalows with bath are CFP 4,000/5,000/6,000. Camping is CFP 700 pp. Horseback riding can be arranged. From near Hôtel Le Bougainville, take the road to Paouta and go past the Lycée Agricole. Six km from Pouembout, take the turn to the right direct to Le Tamaon, which is another seven km along.

Five km beyond Le Tamaon (over the bridge and left) is **Paddock de la Boutana** (Bernard and Marie-Claude Gaûzere, tel. 47-90-00), which offers stays on a more remote working cattle ranch with horseback riding available (CFP 1,500 an hour). A two-night package is CFP 15,500 pp, meals included.

Both Le Tamaon and La Boutana will be booked out by people from Nouméa on weekends and holidays, but they'd probably have a place

for you from Sunday to Thursday. Of course, you'll need a car to get there. Ouendé Falls can be visited from both of these, but the area around Le Tamaon and La Boutana is only interesting if you're into horseback riding and ranching.

You can camp free at Plage de Franco, a few km off the highway southwest of Pouembout. Toilets and picnic tables are provided, and non-potable water for washing only. The beach isn't great but at least it's safe for swimming.

Just before the Rouge River, 18 km south of Pouembout, is the short access road to a **war memorial** with a splendid view of the Plaine des Gaïacs, where there was a large airfield during WW II.

Free camping with a water tap and picnic shelter provided is at **Plage de Pindaï,** 11 km off the main road 35 km south of Pouembout. It's a lovely isolated spot backed by mangroves with a white beach and clear water for swimming. The turnoff is four km west of the Népoui access road.

Between Pouembout and Poya is the old nickel port of Népoui, now being redeveloped as an alternative port to Nouméa for North Province. Large open-cut nickel mines are here. **Hôtel-Restaurant Le Passage** (Mr. and Mrs. Sinem, tel. 47-12-28) at Népoui, six km off the main highway, rents 12 rooms and three bungalows at CFP 3,500 single or double, CFP 4,000 triple. Meals are CFP 750/1,800 for breakfast/dinner. Scuba diving is available here with Plongée Népoui (Marceau Martel, tel. 47-13-02, fax 47-13-06, solange.hervieux@canl.nc).

The turnoff to the **Adio Caves** is 2.5 km north of Poya, 16 km east of the Népoui access road. A wide gravel road leads 14 km northeast to the Col de Böewe, a mountain pass, where a jeep track on the left descends to the caves (admission free). The **Vallée des Roches d'Adio** begins at the bottom of the pass, three km farther along the main road (keep left). Here towering limestone pinnacles, not unlike those at Hienghène, line both sides of the road for about a km. This road ends at the mountain village of Goipin in the very center of the island. There's little traffic up here, so forget it unless you have your own transportation.

Isle of Pines

Across a strait of shoals and coral banks, 70 km southeast of Grande Terre, is the stunningly beautiful Île des Pines, famous for the white beaches of Kanuméra/Kuto. In 1774, Captain Cook named the 18-by-14-km island for its extraordinary 60-meter-high *columnaris,* but the Kanak name is Kwenyii (Kunié). Centuries before, the chiefs of this enticing isle had arrived from Aneityum in present Vanuatu, and the Kwenyii people were always great traders, sailing far and wide in their big outrigger canoes.

British Protestant missionaries landed in 1841, but were killed a year later when they became involved in a dispute between sandalwood traders and the Kwenyii islanders. Subsequently, the island served as a French penal colony. Today this southernmost island of Melanesia remains largely untouched—a tropical paradise of the first order. During the **Festival of the Yams,** which coincides with the yam harvest in March or April, you'll see *pilou* dancing and formal presentations of yams. A good variety of birds can be seen on the Isle of Pines.

SIGHTS

Kanuméra/Kuto

Kanuméra/Kuto is one of the gems of the Pacific: Kuto with its long rolling surf, Kanuméra with its gentle turquoise waters. The talcum-soft beaches curve around a narrow neck of sand, which joins the Kuto Peninsula to the rest of the island. Towering pines contrast with curving palms, casuarinas, gum trees, ferns, wild orchids, and other flowers to create an environment of exotic richness, separated from the sea by a wide strip of snowy white sand. Kanuméra is a photographer's dream, and al-though the snorkeling is second-rate, the windsurfing is excellent.

During the penal colony period the **Kuto Peninsula** was isolated from the rest of the island by a high stone wall intended to protect the prison administrators in the event of a convict revolt. The present gendarmerie is the former home of the prison's doctor, while the governor lived in the red-roofed building a bit along toward the wharf. Opposite the side entrance to the governor's compound is a trail leading south and around the peninsula past a series of scenic views. Another good walk is to the northwest around Kuto Bay, then across the rocky headland on the trail to wild and lovely **Kutema Beach.**

ISLE OF PINES

© DAVID STANLEY

NEW CALEDONIA

For a sweeping panorama of the entire island and a profile of Grande Terre on the horizon, climb to the cross atop **Pic Nga** (262 meters) in an hour (easy). The signposted trailhead is midway on the Kanuméra/Kuto cutoff, southeast of the house with several pine trees in the front yard.

Farther Afield

During 1871–1879, around 3,900 political prisoners from the Paris Commune were held on the Isle of Pines. After an amnesty in 1880, the *communards* were allowed to return to France but the island continued as a regular prison colony until 1912. Pigs now forage in the old prison yard and the narrow, cheerless brick cells—snuffling scavengers in the gloomy and forbidding atmosphere. Some of the most impressive ruins are opposite the bakery at Ouro. The water supply building can be reached via the track inland on the other side of the highway.

To get to the **Deportees' Cemetery,** continue one km north on the airport road and take the first turn on the right. The cemetery where some 260 deportees are buried is to the left, about 500 meters inland. To the right is a track right across the island.

The administrative center and largest village on the island is **Vao,** five km east of Kanuméra. French Catholic missionaries arrived at Vao in 1848, and the present church dates from 1860. Climb up to the chapel above the church for the view. The chief's house *(chefferie)* at Vao is surrounded by a driftwood palisade.

Two km due east of the church is **St. Joseph Beach,** with as fine a collection of large dugout sailing canoes *(pirogues)* as you'll find anywhere in the Pacific. Oupi Bay is dotted with their sails and tiny mushroom-shaped islands.

Speleology

The Isle of Pines boasts three important caves, each one different from the others. Using the map, **Paradise Cave** is very easy to find: Take the obvious path to the right at the end of the access road. Much of the cave is flooded, and there are refreshing pools where you can take a dip.

The **Oumagne Caves** are near Touété village,

a 30-minute walk from the airport. The cave floor is relatively level, and a large opening at the far end provides lighting. A fast-flowing stream disappears into the cave as swarms of swallows circle overhead. Admission to the cave is CFP 200.

The trail to **Ouatchia Cave** begins about a 40-minute walk southeast of the Oumagne Caves. It's a bit hard to find and getting a guide to lead you along the narrow underground passage past some sparkling white formations would be a good idea. Ouatchia Cave is by far the most difficult of these three caves, but it's also the best.

Scuba Diving

Scuba diving is offered by the **Kunié Scuba Center** (tel./fax 46-11-22, www.kunie-scuba.com), based at the Relais de Kodjeue. Two-night packages with diving, transfers, accommodations, and meals included cost CFP 45,200/37,600/33,500 pp for one/two/four divers. There's always a surcharge if fewer than four divers are present.

The top reef diving is at **Gadji Pass** off the north end of the island, especially the **Gie Island Drop-off** and fantastic **Oupere Grotto.** The strong tidal flow means abundant marinelife and spectacular coral and sponge coloration, which can be appreciated through rents in the reef. The Scuba Center also offers freshwater diving into **Paradise Cave,** with its huge stalactites and stalagmites—truly a unique experience.

ACCOMMODATIONS

Under US$25

Chez Yvette (Yvette Kouathe, tel. 46-10-20), between Snack Tadey and the Ouro bakery, offers six simple dorm rooms, each with three to five beds, at CFP 1,000 pp. Communal toilets and showers are outside. Cooking facilities are not provided but Yvette will cook dinner for you at CFP 750.

Camping des Rouleaux (Gaby and Christine, tel. 46-11-16) faces a lovely unspoiled white beach on Kutema Bay, a km down the dirt road running west from Snack Tadey just north of Kuto. Once you're there, you can use a shortcut trail along the coast back to Kuto. Camping is CFP 940 pp, and if you don't have a tent you can rent one at CFP 500/1,000 for two/three persons. The optional breakfast is CFP 600. It's the best camping on the island.

US$50–100

Gîte Nataïwatch (Guillaume et Eulalie Kouathe, tel. 46-11-13, fax 46-12-29), a bit inland from Kanuméra Bay, offers a variety of accommodation options. The four bungalows with a fridge, cooking facilities, and shared bath, and the eight duplex units with private bath but no kitchens, are all CFP 6,650/7,150 single/double. The eight-bed dormitory is CFP 3,000 single or double, CFP 4,500 for four persons. Camping is in a separate area with a shelter and amenities block (CFP 1,500 single or double). Tent rental is CFP 1,500, if required. The restaurant at the Nataïwatch is pleasant (CFP 850/2,000 for breakfast/dinner). Saturdays at 1900 the Nataïwatch offers a special evening with traditional songs and dances by the group Olobath accompanied by a lobster buffet (CFP 3,750). Rental cars are CFP 4,400/7,280 a half/full day, bicycles CFP 1,040/1,560. Island tours cost CFP 1,500.

Just inland from Kuto Bay and behind the restaurant of the same name is **Relais de Kuberka** (Caroline Vendegou, tel. 46-11-18, fax 46-11-58), with three bungalows at CFP 7,150/7,650 double/triple with private bath, TV, and fridge. The eight rooms are CFP 6,150/6,650/7,150 single/double/triple. Camping is CFP 1,040/1,760 single/double. There's a swimming pool, but no cooking facilities for guests. Various set menus in the restaurant are CFP 1,560–2,080. Rental cars are available here at CFP 7,280, plus CFP 40 a kilometer.

Gîte Manamaky (Nazaire Vakoume, tel. 46-11-11) is on lovely St. Joseph Beach, two km east of Vao. The four bungalows with TV and fridge are CFP 6,750 double (no cooking facilities). If you'd like to tour the island by *pirogue*, ask here.

Scuba divers often stay at the **Relais de Kodjeue** (Jojo et Agnès Lepers, tel. 46-11-42, fax 46-10-61, kodjeue@canl.nc) on an excellent beach at Ouaméo Bay, nine km from Kuto

Beach. The 15 bungalows with private bath (six of them also with cooking facilities) are CFP 7,800 single or double. Eight newer beach bungalows without kitchens are CFP 14,100, while the four beach suite bungalows are CFP 19,100. The Relais de Kodjeue has a swimming pool. You can rent a car or motor scooter, but check them carefully before you ride off. The food in the restaurant is excellent, and you can even buy groceries here if you want to cook.

Gîte d'Oro Chez Régis (tel./fax 43-45-55) at Oro Bay charges CFP 7,500 double for one of the four thatched duplex bungalows with bath or CFP 500 pp to camp. Breakfast/dinner is CFP 750/1,000.

US$150–250

The **Hôtel Kou-Bugny** (Yvar Petersen, tel. 46-18-00, fax 24-92-81, www.kou-bugny.com) is across the road from Kuto Bay. The 12 air-conditioned bungalows are CFP 17,950 for a triple unit, CFP 21,050 for a five-person family unit. The hotel restaurant caters mostly to Japanese day-trippers who have lunch here (CFP 2,600). Car rentals begin at CFP 8,000 a day with reduced rates for guests.

US$250 and up

Ouré Lodge (tel. 43-13-15, www.ourelodge.com), at the east end of beautiful Kanuméra Bay, was redeveloped in 2003 with 30 three-star bungalows starting at CFP 28,600 single or double. There's a swimming pool, restaurant, and bar. Cars, scooters, and bicycles are for rent.

In late 1998, **Le Méridien Resort** (tel. 46-15-15, fax 46-15-16, www.lemeridien-iledespins .com) opened at Oro Bay on the northeast side of the island. There are 10 a/c rooms at CFP 45,160 single or double, five freestanding bungalows at CFP 52,160, and 12 duplex bungalows at CFP 56,160. Third persons pay CFP 7,080. Add CFP 1,000 tax to these extravagant rates, and don't forget the CFP 3,640/4,680 pp for breakfast/dinner. Airport transfers are CFP 2,000 pp. Le Méridien is reached by a small bridge and a beachside swimming pool is provided. Nearby are a natural rock pool and stunning white beaches.

OTHER PRACTICALITIES

Food

All of the *gîtes* serve meals which should be ordered half a day in advance, though eating at them two or three times a day quickly becomes expensive. Luckily there are four small grocery stores at Vao, open Monday to Saturday 0700–1200 and 1500–1900, Sunday 1000–1200. Early Saturday morning a small market materializes at Vao.

Snack Tadey (tel. 46-10-68), just north of Kuto, serves a daily *plat de jour* 1130–1300 for CFP 1,000). A small market beside Snack Tadey open Saturdays 0630–0800 only. The bakery at Ouro, a bit farther north of Kuto, opens Monday to Saturday 0630–1000 and 1630–1800.

Restaurant Kuberka (tel. 46-11-18), just inland from Kuto, specializes in upscale seafood, like small sweet lobster, marinated squid, and fried fish. You must order ahead. The French military *village vacances* (tel. 46-19-19) on Kuto Beach has a well-stocked bar, but you're not welcome. If you're a drinker, bring your own supply from Nouméa.

Shopping

Boutique Créations Île des Pins (tel. 46-12-68; daily 0900–1130 and 1400–1730), near the gendarmerie on the Kuto Peninsula, sells beachwear hand-painted by Albert, plus an excellent guide to the island (CFP 850) by Hilary Roots.

Services

The post office, bank, and clinic are in Vao, while the gendarmerie is at Kuto.

Transportation

Air Calédonie flies to the Isle of Pines from Nouméa between three and seven times a day (CFP 7,590). Japanese day-trippers often pack the planes, so book well ahead. The isle's wartime airport sits on an 81-meter-high plateau at the center of the island, nine km from Kanuméra. All of the *gîtes* provide airport transfers for those who have reserved a room, with the price varying from CFP 1,200 to CFP 1,700 pp round-trip. A taxi (tel. 78-49-84) between Kuto/Kanuméra and the airport will cost CFP 1,200 for up to four passengers. Air Calédonie has an office (tel. 44-88-50) at Kuto.

The interisland ferry *Betico* ties up to the wharf on Kuto Bay, charging CFP 3,650 each way for the 2.5-hour trip from Nouméa. The ferry usually leaves Nouméa on Wednesday, Saturday, and Sunday at 0700, departing Kuto for the return trip at 1700, which allows seven hours on the island if you want to make a day trip of it. A bus that meets the ferry offers a day trip to Oro Bay at CFP 1,000 round-trip, not including lunch.

The *gîtes* can arrange car rentals. The Shell service station (tel. 46-11-47; Mon.–Sat. 0630–1130 and 1400–1800, Sun. 0700–0830) between Kuto and Kanuméra rents scooters at CFP 2,710/4,100 a half/full day (CFP 20,000 deposit). They're often all taken, so reserve the day before.

Traffic is thin around the island, but most people will give you a lift, and if you don't mind doing some walking, you should be able to complete the 40-km loop around the island in one day.

The Loyalty Islands

Loyalty Islands Province accounts for just over 10 percent of New Caledonia's land area and population. This coralline group, 100 km east of Grande Terre, consists of the low-lying islands of Ouvéa, Lifou, Tiga, and Maré, each about 50 km apart, plus several islets. Though Captain Cook never saw them, the Loyalties are visible from the tops of New Caledonia's mountains. The people are mostly Kanak, although Ouvéa was colonized by Polynesians from Wallis Island hundreds of years ago. In 1899, the French government declared the Loyalties an indigenous reserve, thus they were spared the worst features of colonialism, and almost 99 percent of the 24,000 residents are Kanak.

The Protestant missionaries who arrived on Maré in 1841 and Lifou in 1842 had already converted most of the inhabitants by the time the French colony was declared in 1853. French Catholics arrived at Maré in 1866, and a period of religious strife ensued. After a battle on Maré in 1871, some 900 Catholicized islanders were exiled with their French missionaries to the Isle of Pines. Be aware that almost nobody in the Loyalties speaks English.

The lifestyle in the Loyalties is unhurried, and many people grow their own yams, taro, and sweet potatoes in bush gardens. Traditional round houses resembling beehives with conical roofs are still common on these islands. Though a thatched Kanak *case* may look primitive (or quaint) from the outside, it's likely to have a clean tiled floor, electric lighting, and a TV inside. During the cool season, the locals often light a fire in the stone hearth of their *case*. Many families also have an adjacent European style house, but you can tell how they feel more comfortable in their *case*.

If you're here for the sand and sun, the Loyalty Islands have some of the finest beaches in the world. The locals are pleasant and friendly, and the camping is fine, but meals, transportation, and a good part of the accommodations are overpriced. Ouvéa tends to be easier than Lifou or Maré, since you can walk to many places, and some *gîtes* will prepare a *repas simple* if you don't wish to pay outlandish prices to consume lobsters, coconut crabs, flying foxes, and other endangered species. Unfortunately, the *gîtes* cater mostly to highly paid French civil servants on weekend trips, and their tariffs are set accordingly.

MARÉ

Maré (Nengone) is an uplifted atoll, its elevated plateau flanked by dramatic cliffs and punctuated with caves. The island's 8,000 inhabitants speak a language known as Nengone, and there are divisions between Protestants and Catholics. Oranges were once common on Maré (harvested

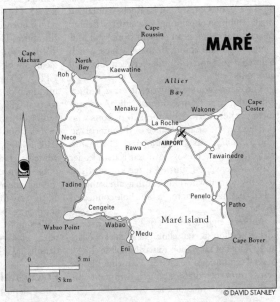

© DAVID STANLEY

in May and June), but the orchards have not been replanted. Shotgun shells strewn along the roadsides in the center of the island account for the rarity of the flying foxes once common on Maré. Despite this, it's a friendly, welcoming island. The big event of the year is the avocado festival in late May.

Around Maré

Maré Airport is only two km from the large Catholic mission at La Roche. Massive stone walls enclose the mission compounds, and a tall, white neo-Gothic church towers above the settlement, itself dominated by a high limestone cliff topped by a cross. You'll need sturdy shoes to climb up to the cross on a path departing from the north side of the church (sharp left at the top of the cliff); there's a sweeping view of the pine-studded island. In times of war, the Maré people have always sought refuge on this cliff, and it's called "La Roche qui Pleure" (the rock that weeps). Religious fighting took place here in 1869, 1880, and 1890. A road leads north from La Roche Mission a km to the picturesque cliffs on the coast (no beach).

The **Yeiwéné Yeiwéné Cultural Center** (tel. 45-44-79), two km west of La Roche, contains a small exhibition of paintings and artifacts. Behind the cultural center is an ancient stone wall four meters high and about 10 meters thick which belonged to a fortress built between A.D. 250 and 580.

The island's administrative center is at **Tadine,** where the ferry from Nouméa calls. A monument at the wharf recalls the 126 persons who perished in the disappearance of the interisland trader *Monique* in 1953. No trace of the ship was ever found. The assassinated Kanak leader Yeiwéné Yeiwéné is buried three km south of this, his hometown. A km south again is the so-called "natural aquarium," a blue hole connected to the sea.

At Nécé, eight km north of Tadine, is the residence of Nidoish Naisseline, grand chief of Maré and a leader of Liberation Kanak Socialiste (LKS). Several monuments near Chief Naisseline's house across from the adjacent church commemorate early Protestant missionaries.

Yedjélé Beach at Ceigeïté, eight km south of Tadine, is Maré's finest, its palm-fringed white sands and clear waters inviting the swimmer and snorkeler. Just before **Medu** village, southeast of Wabao, is a deep karst cave. The 138-meter-high coastal cliffs south of Medu are the highest point on the Loyalty Islands.

Accommodations

Most of Maré's places to stay are at Ceigeïté just west of Wabao, 20 km southwest of the airport. **Camping Fare de la Plage** (Celine Wadrobert, tel. 45-42-24), opposite fabulous Yedjélé Beach, has a traditional *case* at CFP 1,500 pp and ample camping space at CFP 1,100 pp. Meals at Celine's Snack Amaini are around CFP 1,200 and two small stores are nearby.

A few hundred meters west of Fare de la Plage is **Motel Yedjélé Beach** (Martine Wadrobert, tel. 45-40-47) with four self-catering bungalows with fridge and TV at CFP 6,500/7,000 single/double. The cooking facilities are an advantage. Car rentals are CFP 7,000 a day. Airport transfers run CFP 2,400 pp return.

Maré's top accommodations, the **Nengone Village Hôtel** (Henry Fairbank, tel. 45-45-00, fax 45-44-64, www.nengone.grands-hotels.cc), which opened in 1996, is about two km west of the above. The 15 a/c bungalows with bath and TV (but without kitchens) are CFP 8,500 single or double, CFP 10,500 triple, plus tax. Add CFP 1,200 pp for breakfast, plus CFP 2,500 each for lunch or dinner. The resort organizes island tours at CFP 2,500 and rentals of bicycles (CFP 600/1,000 half/full day) and scooters (CFP 2,500/3,500) are offered. Airport transfers are CFP 2,000 pp. The Nengone Village faces a small white beach and there's a beachfront swimming pool. From the resort, a shady trail leads west through the forest past three fine deserted beaches all the way to Plage de Pede, one of Maré's best snorkeling spots, three km from the hotel.

Beyond Medu southeast of Wabao, **Léon Duhnara** (tel. 45-43-70) at Eni offers *case* accommodations at CFP 1,500 pp. A nice beach is nearby.

Practicalities

There's a post office, bank, stores, gendarmerie,

and clinic at Tadine. A market functions in the hall opposite La Roche Airport on Wednesday and Friday mornings.

Transportation

Air Calédonie (tel. 45-55-10), with an office at the airport, has two or more flights a day from Nouméa (CFP 10,160) and three or four flights a week from Lifou (CFP 7,080). Public transport doesn't exist on Maré, but the *gîte* owners pick up guests at the airport for a fee of CFP 2,000–4,000 pp round-trip if they've been forewarned.

No car rentals are available at the airport, but the *gîtes* rent cars at CFP 7,500 a day. If you take one, make sure the fuel tank is full; Maré has been known to run out of gasoline. Renting a bicycle at a *gîte* is another option and hitching is also possible.

The interisland ferry *Betico* calls at Tadine on its way to Lifou or Nouméa. Check the times before leaving Nouméa.

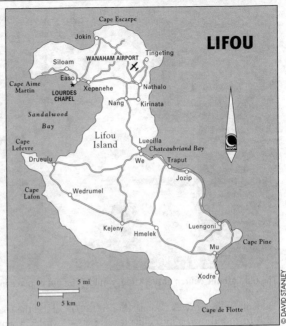

TIGA

The Air Calédonie flight between Lifou and Maré stops on this two-by-six-km island twice a week (CFP 4,800 from Lifou or CFP 3,980 from Maré). Legend tells how a rat once tried to hitch a ride from Lifou to Maré on the back of a passing turtle. The turtle eventually tired of this and threw the rat off its back, forming the tiny island of Tiga.

The one 350-inhabitant village, near the airstrip in the northwest corner of the island, has a small store and a good beach. A north-south track approaches the cliffs at the south end of Tiga. You'll have to camp or sleep in the airport if you stop over.

LIFOU

The most populous of the Loyalties, Lifou (Drehu) is the largest elevated atoll in the South Pacific,

an island bigger than Tahiti or Samoa's Upolu. The cliffs and terraces of the various periods of geologic emergence are clearly visible from the air. Lifou is the most touristically developed of the three Loyalty Islands and many excellent snorkeling venues are accessible from shore. Some of the world's finest vanilla is grown here.

Some 11,000 people live on Lifou, and Drehu, the local language, is the most widely spoken of the Kanak languages. Wé, the main town, is the administrative center of the Loyalty Islands, but the three grand chiefs of Lifou reside at Nathalo, Dueulu, and Mu. Fao, a Polynesian Protestant missionary, arrived at Mu in 1842 and converted the local chief. When the Catholics landed after the French takeover in 1853, a rival chief in northern Lifou welcomed them, and a period of religious strife began that was finally settled when a French military expedition conquered Lifou in 1864.

Around Lifou

Wé is situated on Châteaubriand Bay at the south end of a magnificent white beach, 22 km

The old Catholic church at Wé, Lifou, wouldn't be out of place in Mexico.

© DAVID STANLEY

south of the airport. Wé's Catholic church (1897) with its round towers looks like it was transported here from Mexico. In recent years, Wé has been developed with the large new Loyalty Islands Provincial Headquarters, a town hall, upscale resort, and wide boulevard. In 2003, a yacht harbor with 40 berths was constructed next to the main wharf at Wé.

The highway from Wé to Mu and Xodré follows the coast beside a cliff thick with stalagmites and passes a superb protected beach with talcum sand at **Luengöni**. A large cave with an underground pool is found here. The road ends at Xodré, 42 km south of Wé, where huge waves crash into the coastal cliffs.

The *case* (1976) of the grand chief of **Nathalo**, three km from the airport, is the largest of its kind in New Caledonia. A low palisade surrounds this imposing structure held aloft by great tree trunks set in a circle. You're allowed to go inside. Even more massive is nearby Nathalo Church (1883), a monument to the zeal of early French Catholicism. The interior retains its original decoration.

About 17 km northwest of Nathalo is **Jokin** village, where tourist bungalows are perched

above the coastal cliffs. There's a chance to see whales in September and October, and the snorkeling here is good.

A cave and underground pool are near the highway on the east side of Xépénéhe—in fact, you'll find these everywhere on Lifou if you ask. One of the most picturesque spots on the island is the **Chapel of Our Lady of Lourdes** (1886), perched atop a peninsula above Sandalwood Bay beyond the end of the road at Easo, five km west of Xépénéhe. The view from the chapel is breathtaking, and there's a fair beach nearby (on any other island it would be considered excellent).

Sports and Recreation

Lifou Fun Dive (tel. 45-02-75, www.lifoufun dive.com) at Easo charges CFP 6,500/10,000 for one/two-tank dives.

Deep-sea fishing is organized by **Lifou Marine** (Rénato Antoniazza, tel. 45-19-98, www.lifou marine.nc) in Wé at CFP 55,000/70,000 a half/full day for up to four anglers.

Accommodations

US$25–50: Faré Falaise (Georges Kahlemu, tel. 45-02-01), on a 40-meter cliff at Jokin, 16 km northwest of the airport, offers three bungalows with shared bath and terraces perfect for sunset viewing at CFP 4,000/5,000 single/double. *Case* accommodations are CFP 1,500 pp, and camping is CFP 1,500. Meals cost CFP 500/1,000 for breakfast/dinner, airport transfers CFP 800 pp each way. There's a stone stairway down to the water.

You can pitch your tent at **Chez Benoit Bonua** (tel. 45-90-08), on a nice beach near the end of the road at Easo, 14 km west of the airport, for CFP 800 plus CFP 100 pp. The three basic bungalows with shared bath are CFP 1,500 pp. A light breakfast will be another CFP 400. Fishing trips are arranged and a scuba diving center is nearby.

The closest budget accommodations to Wé are offered by **Marcel and Suzanne Wajoka** (tel. 45-15-69) at Traput, seven km southeast from the harbor. The three traditional *case* are CFP 3,500 pp including all meals. Camping is CFP 500 pp. Airport transfers are CFP 2,000 pp return.

Noel Pia (tel. 45-03-09) on Luengöni Beach in southeastern Lifou, 14 km south of the Oasis de Kiamu or 26 km from Wé, provides mats in a six-person *case* at CFP 1,500 pp. Camping space costs CFP 1,000 per tent plus CFP 100 pp. Meals here are CFP 400/800 breakfast/dinner and a store is within walking distance. Noel offers a three-hour guided forest walk with a visit to a cave where you can swim at CFP 1,500 pp.

Jeanne Forrest (tel. 45-16-56), a few hundred meters beyond Chez Noel at Luengöni, charges CFP 6,000/6,500 single/double for the three bungalows, and camping and *case* accommodations are offered.

Gîte Neibash (tel. 45-15-68), near Jeanne Forrest at Luengöni, has three bungalows at CFP 6,000/6,500 single/double, and one traditional *case* at CFP 2,500/3,000. Camping is CFP 1,500 per tent.

Perhaps the nicest place to stay on the south side of the island is **Gîte Bout du Monde** (tel. 45-02-46) at Xodré near the end of the road, 41 km south of Wé. *Case* accommodations are CFP 1,500 pp, or you can camp at CFP 1,000 per tent, plus CFP 200 pp. The beach is excellent and the fantastic cliffs of Xodré are just a km

away. The only drawbacks here are the endangered species such as coconut crabs and flying foxes served in the restaurant. Luckily a grocery store is nearby.

US$50–100: Gîte Le Servigny (Jacqueline Albert; tel. 45-12-44, www.hotel-servigny.nc) at Kumo, 15 km north of Wé, is only three km from the airport. *Case* accommodations are CFP 3,000 pp, air-conditioned rooms CFP 6,000/7,000 single/double. A large swimming pool and fancy French restaurant are on the premises.

The village you see across Châteaubriand Bay from the wharf at Wé is Luécila. On the fine white beach near the village is **Motel Chez Rachel** (Emile Peteissi, tel. 45-00-78), also known as the Motel Luécila. The eight bungalows with private bath and TV are CFP 6,500/7,000/7,500 single/double/triple, while the four rooms are CFP 6,000/6,500/7,000. Cooking facilities are provided in all of these. Otherwise you can camp at CFP 800 pp. Bicycles are CFP 1,000 a day.

Lifou's most upscale place is the **Hôtel Drehu Village** (tel. 45-02-70, fax 45-02-71, www.drehu.grands-hotels.cc), at Wé and right on Châteaubriand Bay. It opened in 1996 with 20 air-conditioned duplex bungalows with bath and TV at CFP 8,500 single or double, CFP 10,500 triple. Breakfast costs CFP 1,200 pp, lunch or dinner CFP 2,500 each. The Drehu Village has a swimming pool, and snorkeling gear is loaned free. Airport transfers are CFP 1,700 pp return.

At Jozip, 12 km southeast of Wé, is the **Oasis de Kiamu** (tel. 45-15-00, www.oasis-de-kiamu.com) with three blocks of four rooms each at CFP 7,000 single or double. Also available here are two eight-bunk dorms at CFP 1,500 pp. The Oasis de Kiamu is pleasant with a swimming pool, and small beach is just across the road, but the meals in the restaurant are expensive and no stores are anywhere nearby.

Food

Virtually all of the places to stay serve meals and several large grocery stores are at Wé. **Snack Wenehoua** (tel. 45-17-98), opposite the large Loyalty Islands Provincial Headquarters, serves a two-plate lunch weekdays at CFP 1,000. Every Wednesday and Friday, Wé market sets up in this area.

Other Practicalities

Strewn along the main street at Wé you'll find the post office, two banks, snack bars, the provincial headquarters, town hall, clinic, Air Calédonie office (tel. 45-55-50), and gendarmerie (tel. 45-12-17).

The helpful Cemaid information office (tel. 45-18-85 or 45-00-32, cemaid@lagoon.nc; weekdays 0730–1130 and 1300–1630), in front of the mairie and opposite the war memorial on the main street in Wé, can provide information and will help you make reservations. The local women display their handicrafts in a traditional *case* behind Cemaid.

Getting There

Air Calédonie flies to Wanaham Airport, 19 km north of Wé, from Nouméa (CFP 10,160) between three and nine times a day, and from Maré (CFP 7,080) and Ouvéa (CFP 4,860) three or four times a week.

The interisland ferry *Betico* will deposit you on the wharf at the far east end of Wé, a 10-minute walk from the center of town. The service to Maré (CFP 2,750) and Nouméa (CFP 5,450) is several times a week, to Ouvéa (CFP 2,750) once a week, although this does vary. Cruise ships usually anchor in Sandalwood Bay off Xépénéhe.

To/From the Airport

The *gîtes* pick up guests with reservations at the airport for CFP 2,000 round-trip. There's also a public bus *(navette)* from the airport to Wé (CFP 300) at 0700, but it's not often used by tourists and obtaining information can be difficult. Many people come to the airport to drop off friends for flights, so hitching is pretty easy. Otherwise, it's only a 10-minute walk out to the traffic circle where lots of cars pass.

Getting Around

Lifou is so big that to really see the island you'll have to rent a car or take a bus tour. The hitching on Lifou is good since there are more cars than on Maré and Ouvéa and almost everyone stops.

An irregular city bus service (CFP 150 pp) operates between the main wharf and Luécila

weekdays 0730–1500. Shuttle buses *(navettes)* leave outlying villages for Wé weekdays at 0600, returning around 0930 (CFP 450 one way). The **Sometrans** bus (tel. 45-14-78) operates between Mu and Wé while **Transport Wenissö** travels from Jokin to Wé. Ask about both *navettes* at Snack Wenehoua (tel. 45-17-98) next to the market in Wé around 0900.

Auto Pro Location (tel. 45-15-10; weekdays 0730–1130 and 1330–1730, Sat. 0730–1130), near the wharf at Wé, has cars from CFP 6,900 all inclusive. **Loca V** (tel. 45-07-77), two km north of Wé on the road to the airport, rents cars at around CFP 6,000 a day. **Aero Location** (tel. 81-31-21) has a counter at Wanaham Airport that opens at flight times only (cars from CFP 7,000). Most of the accommodations can arrange cars.

Sightseeing tours arranged through the hotels are an inexpensive way of seeing Lifou without renting a car. Excursions to the north and south ends of the island are CFP 2,300 each or CFP 4,100 for both. The commentary will be in French.

OUVÉA

Ouvéa (Iaai) is everything you'd expect in a South Pacific island. Twenty-five km of unbroken white sand borders the western lagoon and extends far out from shore, giving the water a turquoise hue. The necklace of coral islands and barrier reef protecting this lagoon is unique in the Loyalties. Croissant-shaped Ouvéa is tilted, with rocky cliffs pounded by surf on the eastern ocean side of the island, but fine beaches are found here too. At one point on this narrow atoll, only 45 meters separates the two coasts. To watch the sun dip below the lagoon from anywhere along Ouvéa's western beach is a sublime experience.

Traditional circular houses with pointed thatched roofs still predominate in the villages, and the compound of each village chief on Ouvéa is surrounded by a high palisade of driftwood logs. Two of the finest of these are at St. Joseph. Due to a Polynesian invasion in the 18th century, the inhabitants of the far ends of the island (St. Joseph, Lékine, Mouli) speak the Wallisian language (Ua), while those in the center speak Iaai, the original Kanak tongue. All 4,500 Ouvéa islanders speak French as well. Ouvéa produces most of the territory's copra, and a few small industries are based on this product, including a coconut oil soap factory near the main wharf, a coconut fiber rope factory at Mouli, and a coconut oil burning electricity generator. A coconut oil-fueled desalination plant between Wadrilla and the wharf ensures a steady water supply.

On May 5, 1988, this enchanted island was the scene of the Ouvéa Massacre when 300 French police stormed a cave near Gossanah to rescue 16 gendarmes held hostage after being captured on April 22 by Kanak freedom fighters. Nineteen Kanaks died in the assault, including several who suffered extrajudicial execution at the hands of the French police after being wounded and taken prisoner. None of the hostages had been harmed. Thus Ouvéa is a symbol of martyrdom and the heroic resistance of the Kanak people to French colonialism.

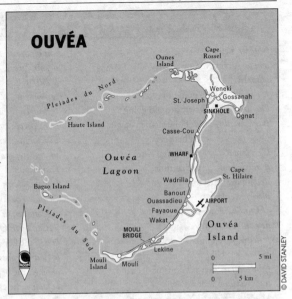

Northern Ouvéa

A paved highway extends south from St. Joseph to Wadrilla (19 km), the administrative center, then on to Mouli (another 21 km). **St. Joseph** is strung along the lagoon, with several general stores and a large Catholic mission (1912). Near the mission is the low stockade of the local chief's *case*.

To reach a large natural **sinkhole** (*trou d'eau*) near the coast, several km southeast of St. Joseph, take the Ognat road east and turn right at Weneki just after a curve. Keep straight ahead past an abandoned quarry. At the fork a kilometer beyond this, go left. The sinkhole is at the end of the road on the left. The Grand Chief of Weneki keeps turtles in the brackish water of the hole until they are required for his table, but never mind, you can swim. No one has ever found the bottom of this deep, dark hole.

There's another sinkhole, the **Trou d'Anawa**

(admission CFP 200 pp or CFP 1,000 per car), at Casse-Cou between St. Joseph and Wadrilla.

The **Grotte de Gossanah** where the Ouvéa Massacre occurred is a few km east of St. Joseph. The trail begins beside an old quarry midway between Gossanah and Ognat (ask permission in Gosannah before visiting the cave, but don't count on it being granted). Every May 5 a pilgrimage is made here in memory of the dead. Djoubelly Wea, the assassin who fired the last shots of the *événiments* of the 1980s killing Jean-Marie Tjibaou and Yeiwéné Yeiwéné (see History under this chapter's Introduction section), is buried in front of his traditional *case* opposite the small store in the center of Gossanah.

It's now known that the people of Gossanah had nothing to do with the hostage taking, which was carried out by youths from other parts of the island. Yet they were rounded up by French troops and assembled on the village football field in front of the church, where they were beaten and tortured by French police trying to extract information. Wea's father was among those who died during the torture and many of the survivors (Wea included) were flown to French prisons. The broken concrete building in the middle

BASIC FRENCH

bonjour: hello

bonsoir: good evening

salut: hi

Je vais à . . .: I am going to . . .

Où allez-vous?: Where are you going?

Jusqu'où allez-vous?: How far are you going?

Où se trouve . . .?: Where is . . .?

C'est loin d'ici?: Is it far from here?

À quelle heure?: At what time?

un horaire: timetable

hier: yesterday

aujourd'hui: today

demain: tomorrow

Je désire, je voudrais . . .: I want . . .

J'aime . . .: I like . . .

Je ne comprends pas: I don't understand

une chambre: a room

Vous êtes très gentil: You are very kind

Où habitez-vous?: Where do you live?

Il fait mauvais temps: It's bad weather

le gendarmerie: police station

Quel travail faites-vous?: What work do you do?

la chômage, les chômeurs: unemployment, the un-employed

Je t'aime: I love you

une boutique, un magasin: a store

le pain: bread

le lait: milk

le vin: wine

le casse-croûte: snack

les conserves: canned foods

les fruits de mer: seafood

un café très chaud: hot coffee

l'eau: water

le plat du jour: set meal

Combien ça fait?: How much does it cost?

   Combien ça coûte?

   Combien? Quel prix?

la clef: the key

la route, la piste: the road

la plage: the beach

la falaise: the cliff

la cascade: waterfall

les grottes: caves

Est-ce que je peux camper ici?: May I camp here?

Je voudrais camper: I would like to camp

le terrain de camping: campsite

Devrais-je demander la permission?: Should I ask permission?

s'il vous plaît: please

---

of the village is the former French school, which the villagers themselves destroyed after the French police had left, to show their disgust for France and the French.

Southern Ouvéa

At **Wadrilla,** visit the graves of the 19 Kanaks murdered by French troops during and after the storming of the Gosannah cave in 1988. In 1990, a large monument designed with two curving white walls to resemble a cave was constructed beside the road in the center of the village. The monument bears the photo, name, and date of birth of each victim, and their traditional war clubs have been placed on the back side of the monument. Their remains are interred below.

During a commemorative ceremony for these

men exactly one year after the massacre, the Kanak leaders Jean-Marie Tjibaou and Yeiwéné Yeiwéné were assassinated by Djoubelli Wea in the *chefferie* (chief's hut) across the road from the monument. Wea felt Tjibaou and Yeiwéné had sold out the independence cause by making a deal with the French government. Ironically, however, the death of the two leaders froze the Matignon Accords into a sort of holy writ, which no one has dared to tamper with since. No monument to Jean-Marie Tjibaou exists on Ouvéa, but the French have constructed a massive cultural center to his memory in their stronghold Nouméa.

Ouvéa's administrative offices, bank, and library are 500 meters inland from the massacre monument at Wadrilla, a tiny contemporary

oui: yes	*onze:* 11
merci: thank you	*douze:* 12
cher: expensive	*treize:* 13
bon marché: cheap	*quatorze:* 14
	quinze: 15
DAYS	*seize:* 16
lundi: Monday	*dix-sept:* 17
mardi: Tuesday	*dix-huit:* 18
mercredi: Wednesday	*dix-neuf:* 19
jeudi: Thursday	*vingt:* 20
vendredi: Friday	*vingt-et-un:* 21
samedi: Saturday	*vingt-deux:* 22
dimanche: Sunday	*vingt-trois:* 23
	trente: 30
NUMBERS	*quarante:* 40
un: 1	*cinquante:* 50
deux: 2	*soixante:* 60
trois: 3	*soixante-dix:* 70
quatre: 4	*quatre-vingts:* 80
cinq: 5	*quatre-vingt-dix:* 90
six: 6	*cent:* 100
sept: 7	*mille:* 1,000
huit: 8	*dix mille:* 10,000
neuf: 9	*million:* 1,000,000
dix: 10	

complex oddly out of place in this traditional thatched village.

The post office and several small stores are strung along the lagoon near the middle of the atoll at **Fayaoué,** a few km south of Wadrilla. The large gendarmerie at Fayaoué is still very well defended with barbed wire, a watchtower, and numerous paramilitary vehicles. The numerous white French police you see here underline the continuing colonial realities of New Caledonia. Unless you're French, your presence probably won't go unnoticed.

Twelve km farther south, many tropical fish are visible from the narrow **bridge** connecting Mouli to the rest of Ouvéa, and the swimming in the clear blue water here is good (but beware of the strong tidal currents). The famous cliffs of Lékine are also clearly visible from this bridge. Approach them by following the beach around. Long ago, before the island was uplifted, wave action undercut these towering walls of limestone, and massive stalactites tell of the great caverns for which this area is noted. On this island of superb beaches, the nicest is at Mouli.

Sports and Recreation

Ouvéa Plongée (tel. 45-09-90, ouveaplongee @raid-ngatahi.nc) based at Mouli offers scuba diving at CFP 12,000 (two tanks).

Saturdays at 1300 there's usually a soccer game at the stadium just beyond the east end of the airport runway, 500 meters from the terminal. It's a great chance to mix with the locals (make it obvious you're not French).

NEW CALEDONIA

Accommodations

Gîte Beaupré (Suzanne Oine, tel. 45-71-32, fax 45-70-94) is opposite the beach at Banout, just north of the junction of the airport and lagoonside roads. The three rooms with shared bath in an older block are CFP 3,850/4,400 single/double, while the three bungalows with private bath are CFP 6,050 single or double. Good food is served here (dinner CFP 1,980), and they rent bicycles (CFP 1,500 a day).

South of the junction of the airport road is **Gîte Marguerite** (Marguerite Aben, tel. 45-73-22) with four bungalows at CFP 6,000/6,600 single/double. Camping in the fenced yard is CFP 1,500 per tent. A large restaurant is on the premises and kayaks are for rent.

Several inhabitants of Ouassadieu between Banout and Fayaoué rent rooms with shared bath at CFP 3,000/3,500 single/double, and allow camping. Meals are CFP 500/1,500 for breakfast/dinner. Of these, the accommodations offered by Jöel Henere at **Gîte Ireital** (tel. 45-70-56) are slightly better than those of Benoît Kalepe at **Gîte Bougainvillier** (tel. 45-72-20), although the price is the same. The wharf used by the ferry *Betico* is about 12 km north of the *gîtes,* while the airport is only a few km east of these.

Gîte Cocotier (Samuel Gogny, tel. 45-70-40) is opposite a splendid white beach (with little shade), five km south of the Mouli Bridge. The traditional *case* is CFP 2,000 for the first person, then CFP 500 for each after that to a maximum of eight. The two thatched bungalows are CFP 3,500/4,000 single/double, or you can pitch your tent directly on the beach across the road at CFP 1,000 per tent, plus CFP 100 pp. The Co-cotier's restaurant is much favored by French tourists (CFP 1,500 a meal). This place is worth considering if the beach is your main interest, though the accommodations in Fayaoué are better situated for sightseeing. A grocery store is near Gîte Cocotier.

The Japanese-owned **Paradis d'Ouvéa** (tel. 45-54-00, fax 45-54-01, www.hotelparadis .com), on a wide white beach just southwest of the Mouli Bridge, has 10 duplex bungalows at CFP 33,000 single or double, and five freestanding villas at CFP 50,000. An artificial waterfall drops from a cliff directly into the hotel pool. Even if you're not willing to spend those amounts, it's still worth stopping here for a coffee at the bar or lunch on the terrace (from CFP 2,000). Most of the guests are rather bored Japanese on package tours.

Transportation

Air Calédonie (tel. 45-55-30) lands at Ouloup Airstrip, six km east of Fayaoué. There are several flights a day from Nouméa (CFP 10,160) and three or four a week from Lifou (CFP 4,860).

The interisland catamaran *Betico* ties up to a wharf on the lagoon side between Wadrilla and St. Joseph. The schedule varies, although the ferry often arrives from Nouméa (CFP 5,450) or Lifou (CFP 2,750) on Monday night, departing again for Lifou on Tuesday morning. You can check the date by calling 26-01-00.

Magasin Ocean Beach (tel. 45-72-65), near the junction of the airport and coastal roads, rents cars at CFP 7,000 a day. Bicycles can be hired from a signposted house at Banout, just north of the airport road.

Vanuatu

Introduction

This string of lush green islands, 2,445 km northeast of Sydney and 800 km west of Fiji, was transformed from the ponderous Anglo-French New Hebrides Condominium into the Ripablik Blong Vanuatu in 1980. Since then, the country has expressed its independence by developing a new national identity based on Melanesian *kastom*. It's a colorful land of many cultures, full of fascinating surprises. Make discoveries for yourself by asking any Ni-Vanuatu (indigenous inhabitant) for the nearest cave, waterfall, swimming hole, hot spring, blowhole, or cliff. The general beauty and relaxed way of life are its biggest attractions.

No other South Pacific country harbors as many local variations. The glamorous duty-free shops, casinos, and gourmet restaurants of the cosmopolitan capital, Port Vila, contrast sharply with unchanging, traditional villages just over the horizon. You'll be moved and touched by the friendliness, warmth, and sincerity of the Ni-Vanuatu, certainly Vanuatu's biggest attraction. Away from the packaged day tours and commercial resorts, this unpolished jewel of the South Pacific is still a land of adventure.

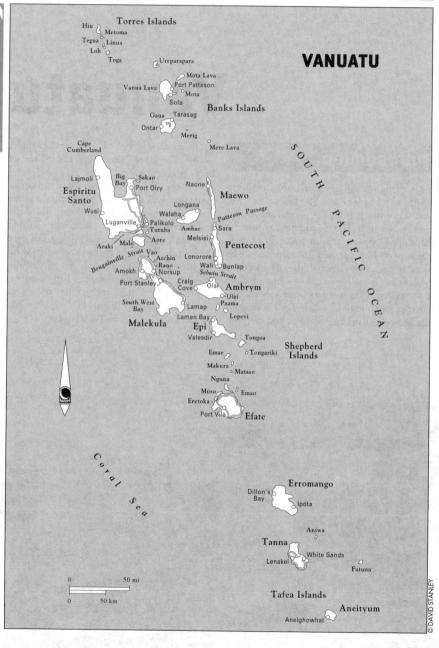

VANUATU

Torres Islands

Hiu
Metoma
Tegua — Linua
Loh
Toga

Ureparapara

Mota Lava
Port Patteson
Vanua Lava — Mota
Sola

Banks Islands

Gaua — Tarasag
Ontar
Merig

Mere Lava

Cape
Cumberland

Lajmoli — Big Sakao
Bay — Port Olry

Naone

Espiritu
Santo

Maewo

Longana

Wusi

Walaha

Palikulo
Luganville
Tutuba
Aore

Ambae

Melsisi

Sara

Patteson Passage

Pentecost

Araki — Malo

Bougainville Strait Vao

Atchin
Rano
Norsup

Lonorore

Wali — Bunlap

Amokh

Selwin Strait

Port Stanley

Craig
Cove

Olal

Ambrym

Ulei

South West
Bay

Paama

Lamap

Lopevi

Lamen Bay

Malekula

Epi

Valesdir

Tongoa

Tongariki

Emae

Shepherd
Islands

Makura

Mataso

Nguna

Moso — Emao

Eretoka

Port Vila

Efate

SOUTH PACIFIC OCEAN

Coral Sea

Erromango

Dillon's
Bay

Ipota

Aniwa

Tanna

White Sands

Lenakel

Futuna

0   50 mi
0   50 km

Tafea Islands

Aneityum

Anelghowhat

© DAVID STANLEY

The Land

The 83 islands of Vanuatu (the name means "Land Eternal") stretch north-south 1,300 km, from the Torres Islands near Santa Cruz in the Solomons to minuscule Matthew and Hunter Islands (also claimed by France) east of New Caledonia. This neat geographical unit is divided into three groups: the Torres and Banks Islands in the north, the Y-shaped central group from Espiritu Santo and Maewo to Efate, and the Tafea islands (Tanna, Aniwa, Futuna, Erromango, and Aneityum) in the south. Together they total 12,189 square km, of which the 12 largest islands account for 93 percent. Espiritu Santo and Malekula alone comprise nearly half of Vanuatu's land area.

Vanuatu is composed of ash and coral: Volcanic extrusion first built the islands, then limestone plateaus were added through tectonic uplift. Vanuatu has more active volcanoes than any other South Pacific country, and these islands form part of a long chain of volcanic activity stretching from New Zealand up through Vanuatu and the Solomons to the islands off New Guinea. Besides Yasur Volcano on Tanna, there are active volcanoes on Lopevi, Ambrym, and Gaua, plus a submarine volcano near Tongoa.

Vanuatu sits on the west edge of the Pacific Plate next to the 8,000-meter-deep New Hebrides Trench. This marks the point where the Indo-Australian Plate slips under the Pacific Plate in a classic demonstration of plate tectonics. Its islands are pushed laterally 10 centimeters a year in a northwest direction, accompanied by earthquakes and volcanic eruptions. In the past three million years, Vanuatu has also been uplifted 700 meters, or approximately two millimeters a year. Although Vanuatu is relatively young geologically, this uplifting has created the series of stepped limestone plateaus you'll see on many islands.

Climate

Vanuatu has a hot, rainy climate—tropical in the north and subtropical in the south. The rainy season is from November to April, but sudden tropical showers can occur anytime. May to July are the optimum months for hiking—cooler and drier, and from June to September, evenings on

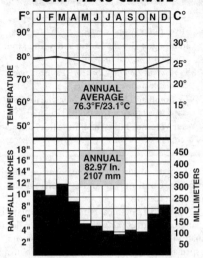

PORT VILA'S CLIMATE

ANNUAL AVERAGE 76.3°F/23.1°C

ANNUAL 82.97 In. 2107 mm

the southern islands can even be brisk. The southeast trade winds blow steadily year-round, though they're stronger and more reliable from April to October. During the wet season, winds from the north or west occur under the influence of hurricanes and tropical lows.

Vanuatu is the most hurricane-prone country in the South Pacific. On average, two or three hurricanes occur each year and any given locality can expect to be hit by a hurricane every other year (usually between December and April). As in other parts of the South Pacific, hurricanes have become more frequent and stronger in recent years (this may be related to climate change). The southernmost islands are less vulnerable to hurricanes, and get less rain than the hotter islands north of Efate.

For weather information dial 22932.

Flora and Fauna

The eastern, or windward, sides of the islands are equatorial, with thick rainforests. The leeward sides, which get less rain, are often open tropical woodlands or savanna, especially in the south. Higher up on the mountains is a humid zone of shrub forest. About 75 percent

VANUATU

Ambrym Island: remote active volcanoes, native culture, woodcarvings (p. 952)

Champagne Beach, Santo: soft white sand, turquoise lagoon (p. 948)

SS *President Coolidge,* Santo: 210-meter wreck available to divers (p. 938)

Wan Smolbag Theater, Port Vila: didactic, village-based theater troupe (p. 915)

Yasur Volcano, Tanna: South Pacific's most accessible active volcano (p. 924)

of the natural forest cover remains, although pressure from logging and agricultural clearing is increasing.

A principal botanical curiosity of Vanuatu is giant banyan trees *(nabangas),* which often dominate village meeting or dancing places *(nasaras),* especially on Tanna. The multirooted banyan begins by growing around another tree, which it eventually strangles out of existence. These massive twisting mazes of trunks and vines are among the earth's largest living organisms. Also unique is a prehistoric giant tree fern called *namwele,* which has great cultural significance and is used in many of the large carvings sold in Port Vila.

The indigenous fauna includes flying foxes, lizards, spiders, and butterflies. Four of the 12 species of bats are fruit bats (flying foxes), Vanuatu's only indigenous land mammals. Unfortunately, their survival is threatened in part by Port Vila restaurateurs, who are not above including this endangered species on their menus. Since the bats live in large colonies in caves or banyan trees, they are easily killed.

Of Vanuatu's two snakes, the Pacific boa and flowerpot snake, only the latter is poisonous, though innocuous and rare. Three species of banded sea snakes are found in Vanuatu (of 52 species worldwide). The snakes crawl up on shore and hide among the rocks at night. Although poisonous, they're timid and no threat to snorkelers or scuba divers (though it would be foolish to try to handle them). Occasionally people wading through murky water will step on one, and they sometimes get caught in fishing nets, but even

then, the bites are seldom fatal, as the snakes inject only a small amount of poison.

Vanuatu's colorful reefs hold its greatest store of life, including potentially dangerous tiger sharks in some areas (especially the corridor between Ambrym and eastern Malekula). Sharks are much less of a problem in southern Vanuatu (including around Efate) than they are in the north. In Vanuatu sharks are associated with a particular type of magic that involves certain individuals who can either become sharks or control sharks. Bottlenose dolphins and pilot whales migrate through Vanuatu waters in large numbers, heading north in April, south in October.

Though introduced by man, the pig is now considered indigenous. Ni-Vanuatu in the central and northern islands knock out the male animal's upper canine teeth so its lower tusks have nothing to grind against, and in six or seven years the tusks grow into a full circle. The pigs are highly valued by their owners, and the meat and tusks are prized at initiation rites and feasts. Culturally, even more valuable than tusker pigs are the rare hermaphrodite pigs *(naravé),* usually found on northern islands such as Espiritu Santo, Malo, Ambae, Maewo, northern Pentecost, and

a tangle of vines on one of Vanuatu's mighty banyans

Gaua, where the world's highest ratio of inter-sexual pigs per generation is found. Nowhere else in the world are pigs of this type found in such numbers.

Birdlife is rich; 54 native species include honeyeaters, fantails, finches, goshawks, kingfishers, parrots, peregrine falcons, pigeons, robins, swiftlets, thrushes, trillers, and warblers. Espiritu Santo has the greatest variety of birds, from great flocks of tiny red cardinals by the roadside to the chestnut-bellied kingfisher and the rare Santo mountain starling unique to the island's highest peaks. Large numbers of brown boobies nest on Monument Rock near Mataso Island in the Shepherd Islands.

HISTORY AND GOVERNMENT
Taem Blong Bifoa

Vanuatu may have been populated since before 3000 B.C., though little is known for certain, since the early habitation sites are probably now below sea level. *Lapita* pottery found on Malo near Espiritu Santo dates 1300–1100 B.C., on Efate from 350 B.C. Around 700 B.C., new arrivals from the Solomons brought a second type of pottery called *Mangaasi*, with incised and applied relief designs, which they carried on to Fiji and New Caledonia. Fresh immigrants under the legendary Chief Roy Mata occupied the central islands circa A.D. 1200. Excavations conducted by French archaeologist Jose Garanger on Eretoka Island off western Efate in 1967 uncovered a burial involving the sacrifice of 40 members of this chief's entourage, dating to 1265—a remarkable confirmation of oral tradition by modern science.

As today, the first inhabitants probably lived in small villages, and had a greater variety of languages and customs than the whole of Europe. Each clan was autonomous; relations between groups were often based on ceremonial gift giving, while families bonded through arranged marriages. Wives, considered property, were exchanged between villages to create links. Spirits were controlled by magic. To work one's way up through the graded societies and become a "big man," an individual had to amass sufficient wealth in the form of pigs to purchase his rank. This *nimanke* system was more widespread in the north than in the center and south, where descent was usually hereditary. The borrowing and loaning of pigs between men created a complex system of bonds and obligations, which strengthened the group and relationships between groups (still a common practice). Only the most able men could rise in this system. Clans raided one another and the victim's bodies were eaten to capture the power of their spirits; these cannibal raids being reciprocal, and one never wandered far from his home village. One was relatively free from the danger of attack along traditional trade routes and within the area of traditional ritual links.

European Contact

The first European to arrive was the Hispanic explorer Pedro Fernandez de Quirós, who pulled into Espiritu Santo's Big Bay on April 29, 1606, believing he had found the "lost" southern continent. When he and his men landed, pious, God-fearing Quirós knelt and kissed the sand, naming the island Terra Austrialis del Espiritu Santo, after the Holy Ghost. He claimed possession of it and everything to the south as far as the South Pole in the name of the king of Spain and the Catholic Church. Quirós planned to build a model Christian settlement on the site, but his treatment of the inhabitants soon led to open hostility which, together with sickness and dissent among his own men, drove this visionary mystic away after only three weeks.

White men did not return for 162 years, when Bougainville sailed between Espiritu Santo and Malekula in 1768, disproving Quirós's hypothesis that they were part of a southern continent. Bougainville named the northern islands the Great Cyclades. In 1774, Captain Cook became the first European to really explore and chart the entire group, naming it New Hebrides, after the Scottish islands. The notorious Captain Bligh first sighted and named the Banks Islands in 1789.

Christianity and Depopulation

The sandalwood traders operated in the islands from 1825 to 1865. Their methods created deep

VANUATU AT A GLANCE

ISLAND	AREA (square km)	HIGHEST POINT (m)	POPULATION (1999)	POPULATION DENSITY (persons per square km)
Espiritu Santo	3,955	1,879	30,900	8.0
Malekula	2,041	863	18,984	9.4
Efate	899	647	42,128	47.5
Erromango	888	886	1,560	1.8
Ambrym	667	1,270	7,369	11.1
Tanna	555	1,084	25,840	46.1
Pentecost	490	946	14,057	28.2
Epi	445	833	4,554	10.3
Ambae	402	1,496	9,418	23.6
Vanua Lava	335	946	1,933	5.6
Gaua	328	797	2,031	6.4
Maewo	303	811	3,171	10.6
Vanuatu	**12,189**	**1,879**	**186,678**	**15.3**

resentment among the islanders, so when the first white members of the London Missionary Society landed on Erromango (Martyr Island) in 1839, they were clubbed and eaten. Samoan missionaries were sent next, but many were also killed or died from malaria. Worse still, they introduced diseases such as measles, influenza, and dysentery, which devastated whole populations. Well-wishers in Australia and elsewhere sent secondhand garments to clothe the naked savages. Regrettably, these were also impregnated with disease, and some sandalwood traders deliberately distributed clothes they knew to be infected with smallpox to wipe out the inhabitants of the areas they wished to exploit.

Since converts—who had the closest contact with missionaries—were the most affected by these epidemics, the newcomers were thought to be evil sorcerers, and the Ni-Vanuatu resisted any way they could. From a precontact population of about half a million, the number of Ni-Vanuatu dropped to 40,000 in 1920. Islands like Erromango remain relatively unpopulated today,

and only after 1920 did Vanuatu's population begin to rise. Some Ni-Vanuatu still refuse to accept Christianity and regard all white men with suspicion. Although a majority had been "converted" by 1900, their understanding of doctrine was shallow, and mass defections from the church have occurred since WW II, especially on Tanna. About 16 percent of the population continues to follow *kastom*.

The Melanesian Mission (Anglican) and the Presbyterians divided the group into spheres of influence, with the Anglicans in the northeast and the Presbyterians in the center and south. Rather than risk establishing a mission in the islands, Anglican Bishop George Selwyn took young Ni-Vanuatu to New Zealand and Norfolk Island for training. Catholicism became established in the central islands after 1887, but little headway was made on Malekula and Espiritu Santo until recently. The missionaries managed to stop village warfare and cannibalism, facilitating the entry of the next two groups—the labor recruiters and European settlers.

The Blackbirders

From 1863 to 1904, some 40,000 Ni-Vanuatu were recruited to work in the canefields of Queensland, Australia, and another 10,000 went to Fiji and New Caledonia. As much as half the adult male population of some islands went abroad. Though many young men welcomed the chance for adventure and escape from the restrictions of village life, conditions were hard. The blackbirders sometimes resorted to kidnapping the islanders, or herding them together by brute force. Outriggers were sunk and the survivors "rescued"; others were bought outright from chiefs for beads, tobacco, mirrors, and muskets. Returnees often brought with them diseases and alcohol, which decimated the home population.

In the end, most of the laborers were deported from Australia in 1906 when the White Australia Policy took effect, but a large percentage died abroad. Some of the returnees to Tanna were so irate about being evicted from Australia that they drove all whites off the island. An enduring legacy of the labor trade was the evolution of a pidgin tongue called Bislama, the national language.

Planters and Land

The first impetus for establishing European plantations in Vanuatu was the high price of cotton during the American Civil War. When cotton collapsed, the planters switched to bananas, cacao, coffee, and copra. The first plantations were on Tanna and Efate, followed later by Espiritu Santo. Though British subjects from Australia arrived first, in 1882 the Compagnie Calédonienne des Nouvelles Hébrides began acquiring large tracts of native land. The Australian-based trading company Burns Philp followed in 1895, but by 1900 French colonists outnumbered British two to one.

Though the first traders and missionaries had been mostly English, the French recognized the agricultural potential of the islands and wanted another colony to strengthen their position in New Caledonia. This alarmed the Australians, who thought one French colony on their doorstep was enough. In 1878, the British and French governments agreed not to annex Vanuatu without consulting one another. To protect the planters' interests and regulate the labor trade, the two nations established a Joint Naval Commission in 1887 with jurisdiction over the islands. It could only intervene in the event of war; during the hurricane season, when the Naval Commission vessels had to be withdrawn, there was no law other than the musket.

During this period, 12 percent of Vanuatu's land, including the choicest tracts, was permanently alienated, 10 percent by French companies and 2 percent by Australian. Traditionally, land could not be sold in Vanuatu, only the *use* of the land temporarily assigned. Many sales were instigated by a few individuals and not agreed upon by consensus as custom required. The Ni-Vanuatu had little understanding of the alienation taking place; when they tried to resist, British and French warships were sent to bombard coastal villages.

The Colonial Period

In 1902, the Germans began to show an interest in these "unclaimed" islands, so the British and French quickly appointed resident commissioners. In 1906, three years after an auspicious visit to Paris by the francophile English King Edward VII, the Anglo-French New Hebrides Condominium was established. The arrangement was formalized in the Protocol of 1914, then proclaimed in 1923.

The Condominium system of government resulted in an expensive duplication of services and administration, as each colonial power implemented its own judiciary, police force, hospitals, schools, etc. Each power had jurisdiction over its own citizens and the natives, but the Ni-Vanuatu were not permitted to claim either British or French nationality, and in effect became stateless. A Joint Court was set up, and land titles registered before 1896 could not be challenged. This institutionalized the large European plantations. In addition, the Ni-Vanuatu didn't have the right of appeal from native courts to the Joint Court. Actually, this combination of administrations had little impact on the Ni-Vanuatu, other than freezing an unjust social structure, and they could simply ignore the Condominium pandemonium if they wished.

Education remained in the hands of the missionaries right into the 1960s. Although a teachers' college opened in 1960, there wasn't a British secondary school (Malapoa College) until 1966, a French secondary school (the lycée) until 1968.

Despite the fact that the budget of the French Residency was twice that of the British, the latter were more effective, due to a long-standing policy of localization and advanced training for Melanesians. France wasted much of its money on a large staff of expatriates, failing to train a French-speaking native elite capable of assuming power. In the early 1970s, the French began a crash program to build a French-speaking majority, but it was too late.

On July 20, 1940, New Hebrides became the first French colony to recognize the Free French forces of General de Gaulle, two months before New Caledonia did so. During WW II, major American bases on Espiritu Santo and Efate were used as staging areas for the Solomon Islands campaign. These islands didn't suffer as the Solomons and New Guinea did. The Japanese bombed Espiritu Santo once, but only managed to kill a cow. On Tanna the apparent wealth of the U.S. soldiers gave fresh impetus to the Jon Frum cargo cult, which had already existed before the war. In turn, the romance of these islands inspired novelist James A. Michener to write *Tales of the South Pacific,* his first book, with Ambae starring as "Bali Hai."

The Road to Independence

The independence of Vanuatu was not generously granted, as it had been elsewhere in the South Pacific, but was won through a long, bitter struggle against bungling colonial administrators, entrenched settlers, and opportunists. In 1971, the New Hebrides Cultural Association emerged to resist large land purchases and subdivisions by an American businessman, one Eugene Peacock. Three months later, the Association became the New Hebrides National Party, headed by Father Walter Lini of Pentecost (an Anglican priest). The party soon won grassroots support throughout the islands, mostly among English-speaking Protestants, by calling for a return of all alienated land to its customary owners. Several French-oriented parties (the "moderates") were also created; they favored prolonged collaboration with the British and French governments.

These factions forced the ruling powers to establish a Representative Assembly in 1975, but it was dissolved in 1977 following a boycott by the Vanua'aku Party (formerly the National Party), which demanded the elimination of appointed members, as well as immediate independence. The crisis was resolved in 1978, with the creation of a Government of National Unity temporarily uniting the two factions. A constitution was signed in October 1979, and in elections a month later the Vanua'aku Party won a two-thirds majority. Understandably, little of this was popular with the French! Most of the plantations were owned by French nationals, who outnumbered British subjects three to one, and their influence was especially strong on Espiritu Santo. The French administration adopted a disruptive policy of encouraging local divisions and disturbances as a means of wringing concessions from the pro-independence side. The British, who just wanted to get out as soon as possible, were unable to interfere with their partner because all Condominium decisions had to be bilateral and the French just stonewalled.

The Republic of Vemarana

The key figure in the independence disruptions was Jimmy Stevens, a charismatic Tongan/Scottish half-caste with a large following on Espiritu Santo and some of the central islands. Basically he was a nonconformist, suspicious of the Vanua'aku Party leadership, which was composed mainly of Ni-Vanuatu British civil servants and Protestant clergy. They in turn regarded Jimmy as a dangerous cargo cultist. His Nagriamel Party began as an agricultural reform movement centered at Fanafo village in the bush 22 km north of Luganville. Nagriamel represented a turning away from European influence and a return to native ways. In 1971, Nagriamel petitioned the United Nations to halt further sales of land on Espiritu Santo to American interests for development as hotel and investment properties.

Ironically, by May 1980 Stevens had come full circle, after accepting US$250,000 in aid, arms, and radio transmitting equipment from the Phoenix Foundation, an American far right organization run by millionaire businessman Michael Oliver. In 1972, Oliver and associates had attempted to declare a tax-free Republic of Minerva on Tonga's Minerva Reef, until the king gave them the boot. Later Phoenix attempted to engineer the secession of Abaco Island in the Bahamas. When this failed, Oliver turned his attention to Espiritu Santo, which was to become a capitalist's paradise, free of government controls. Already four areas on the island had been subdivided into 5,000 lots, of which 2,000 had been sold to individual Americans. Aore Island, off Espiritu Santo, was to have a health resort and casino. Stevens, who now styled himself "President Moli Stevens," declared Espiritu Santo the independent "Republic of Vemarana," and Vanua'aku Party supporters were driven off the island. The Coconut War had begun.

Escalation

During it all, French police stood by and took no action. Stevens had visited Paris and received encouragement from French President Giscard d'Estaing prior to the rebellion. The French apparently intended to have Espiritu Santo continue as a separate French colony, as had occurred with Mayotte when Comoros in the Indian Ocean achieved independence from France in 1975. Chief Minister Walter Lini responded by imposing an economic boycott on Espiritu Santo, but he was unable to prod the British and French authorities into putting down the revolt, as no unilateral action was permitted under Condominium laws. A simultaneous disorder on Tanna dwindled when Alexis Yolou, its "moderate" leader, was shot dead.

There was talk of delaying the independence scheduled for July 30, 1980, but Lini announced that he would declare Vanuatu's independence unilaterally if Britain and France reneged on their promises. Additionally, neighboring countries such as Australia, New Zealand, and Papua New Guinea indicated that they would recognize such independence (Samoa was the first to actually do so). Thus, the colonial powers were forced to adhere to their original timetable, and

Vanuatu became an independent republic on the scheduled day. To prevent bloodshed, the British and French sent military forces to Espiritu Santo to disarm Stevens's followers just a week before independence. Forced to leave afterward, the French ripped out telephones, air-conditioners, and anything else they could move from their offices to make things as difficult as possible for the new government. Had the British not been involved, the French might never have agreed to independence.

The Outcome

In August 1980, Papua New Guinea troops replaced the British/French forces on Espiritu Santo and arrested Jimmy Stevens, who was sent to Port Vila for trial. Stevens's son Eddie was killed by a grenade when he tried to run a roadblock. This was the first military intervention by the forces of one Pacific country in the territory of another since the 19th century, and it fostered a wave of Melanesian solidarity that led to the creation of the Melanesian Spearhead regional grouping in 1988.

Jimmy Stevens was sentenced to 14.5 years imprisonment for his part in the rebellion, during which Luganville was looted and burned. Most of the 70 Ni-Vanuatu arrested along with Stevens were released within a year, but over the next two months, 260 French residents who had sided with the rebellion were rounded up and deported to New Caledonia. Documents captured at the rebel headquarters at Fanafo implicated aides to French Resident Commissioner Jean-Jacques Robert (who himself had come to New Hebrides from Comoros) as direct accomplices in the secession.

After Independence

The first years of independence were uneventful, with the Vanua'aku Party government employing anticolonial, antinuclear rhetoric to forge a regional identity while quietly pursuing the capitalistic domestic policies established during the Condominium. The tax haven created in 1971 was left in place, and confiscated land could be leased back for up to 75 years at low rates. In short, little changed, and fears of "Melanesian socialism" proved unfounded. Development and power became centralized in Port Vila with an indigenous political elite working in tandem with expatriate business interests.

In 1982, Vanuatu closed its ports to American warships that refused to confirm or deny whether they were carrying nuclear weapons—the first Pacific country to do so. In 1983, legislation was passed that made Vanuatu the first totally nuclear-free nation in the Pacific: nuclear weapons, ships, power plants, and waste dumping were all prohibited. Vanuatu was the first South Pacific country to acquire full membership in the Non-Aligned Movement. These positions proved useful in playing different groups of foreigners off against one another, and Vanuatu has been able to garner support from both right-wing libertarians and left-wing internationalists as a result.

Recent Events

In May 1988, there was serious rioting in Port Vila after the government seized the Vila Urban Land Corporation (VULCAN), holder of property leases in the city on behalf of customary landowners in Erakor, Ifira, and Pango. VULCAN was supposed to return income from the leases to the villages; instead, money was being reinvested in other commercial enterprises, and there were allegations that millions of dollars had "disappeared." The government failed to explain to the landowners what was happening, and when VULCAN's chairman Barak Sope (from Ifira) made an inflammatory radio broadcast about land rights, concerned villagers took to the streets to denounce Lini (from rural Pentecost). What began as a peaceful demonstration soon turned into a drunken antigovernment riot that inflicted over a million dollars of damage on the capital.

After order was restored, Sope and four supporters were expelled from parliament. They turned to the pro-French opposition for support, the crisis deepened when all 18 opposition members were expelled for boycotting parliament. A rump parliament then called for by-elections to replace the expelled members. Sope and the main pro-French party boycotted those by-elections in December 1988.

At this point the largely ceremonial head of state, President Ati George Sokomanu (Sope's uncle), greatly exceeded his authority by attempting to dissolve parliament and form an interim government with Sope as prime minister. Sokomanu accused Lini of trying to create a one-party state, while Lini charged Sope with coercion, opportunism, and corruption. Within hours Sope, Sokomanu, and the interim government were arrested by the Vanuatu Mobile Force and charged with sedition. In February 1989, Presbyterian pastor Fred Timakata replaced Sokomanu as president, and in March, Sokomanu was sentenced to six years in prison for attempting to overthrow the elected government, while Sope and Carlot Korman each got five years. A month later, a court of appeal overturned these convictions and set the men free.

A split developed in the Vanua'aku Party in 1991, and ex-foreign minister Donald Kalpokas replaced Lini as prime minister. To mark the 20th anniversary of the founding of the Vanua'aku Party in August 1991, Jimmy Stevens was finally freed, after serving 11 years of his sentence at Port Vila's jail. His followers throughout the archipelago assembled 20 pigs with fully circled tusks to present to the government as an act of atonement (the pigs were later returned to their owners). Stevens had been under hospital treatment for high blood pressure for some time, and his release, just weeks before Lini himself left office, culminated an era in the country's history. In 1994, Jimmy Stevens died at Fanafo.

The elections of December 1991 ushered in an era of instability as parties split and formed coalitions with former opponents. Maxime Carlot Korman of the pro-French Union of Moderate Parties formed a coalition with Lini supporters to take power, and in mid-1995 Carlot Korman was the only Pacific leader who refused to condemn French nuclear testing, even ordering Radio Vanuatu not to report the testing at all. In August 1996, Barak Sope, now minister of finance, was sacked after the ombudswoman, Marie-Noelle Patterson, disclosed details of a US$100 million bank guarantee scam that could have bankrupted Vanuatu. Sope complained to parliament that the ombudswoman had violated a Melanesian custom that holds that women must not criticize men. A month later, the government changed and Sope was back as deputy prime minister. In October 1996, the paramilitary Mobile Force staged a mini-coup, holding the president hostage until a wage arrears claim was settled.

In late 1997, after the ombudswoman initiated court action against the prime minister and several cabinet ministers for accepting unlawful kickbacks, these same leaders pushed a bill through parliament repealing the Ombudsman Act itself. President Jean-Marie Leye refused to sign the bill, referring it to the Supreme Court. In January 1998, there was serious rioting in Port Vila after the ombudswoman revealed that senior politicians and their cronies had been using overgenerous loans from Vanuatu's National Provident Fund, a compulsory pension plan, to illegally purchase government housing. A four-week state of emergency followed.

To restore stability, fresh elections were called for March 1998, and just a month prior to the vote, yet another ombudswoman report alleged that the prime minister had received tens of thousands of dollars from Asian businessmen in exchange for Vanuatu passports and honorary diplomatic posts. Despite all of this, most of the politicians named in the corruption reports were reelected thanks to entrenched party organizations and patronage. In June 1998, a Leadership Code was enacted by the new parliament to reduce future opportunities for abuses of power, although the investigative powers of the ombudswoman were also diminished. Another landmark event was the February 1999 death of Walter Lini.

In November 1999, the opposition succeeded in enticing a number of government members to defect, and none other than Barak Sope was voted in by parliament as prime minister, replacing reformer Donald Kalpokas. In early 2001, it emerged that a Thai citizen had provided Sope with a 82.5 kilogram ruby allegedly worth US$175 million to be used as collateral on government bond sales worth US$300 million. Of course, the "largest ruby in the world" turned out to be worthless mining waste, and only intervention by Australian regulators prevented Vanuatu from quadrupling its national debt.

This and other shady dealings with Asian businessmen shocked the country, and Sope's majority in parliament crumbled, allowing Edward Natapei of the Vanua'aku Party to take over as prime minister in April 2001. Natapei retained his post in the May 2002 elections, but Sope also managed to get himself reelected by claiming that he was the victim of a neo-colonial plot by Australia. In July 2002, Vanuatu's Supreme Court sentenced Barak Sope to three years in jail for forgery relating to the fraudulent loan guarantees supported by the ruby, but in November President John Bani, an old friend of Sope's, used his discretionary powers to pardon the convict against the wishes of the government. Since then, Prime Minister Natapei has worked hard to bring honesty and consistency back into public life.

Government

Vanuatu has a parliamentary system of government (www.vanuatu.gov.vu) with a prime minister who is the leader of the majority party in parliament. Parliament's 52 members are elected for four-year terms, and the prime minister appoints his cabinet from among those members. A National Council of Chiefs (Malvatumauri) advises on matters relating to custom. Parliament and the heads of the provincial governments elect a president, who serves a five-year term as ceremonial head of state.

In 1994, the 11 local government councils were replaced by six provinces: Torba (Torres and Banks), Sanma (Santo and Malo), Penama (Pentecost, Ambae, and Maewo), Malampa (Malekula, Ambrym, and Paama), Shefa (Shepherds, Epi, and Efate), and Tafea (Tanna, Anatom, Futuna, Erromango, and Aniwa).

Vanuatu's cultural, political, and economic diversity is mirrored in the nation's politics. Close political allies can become foes overnight, and former bitter adversaries have no compunctions about forming alliances. Call it democracy or simply the Melanesian tradition of shifting alliances, much time and effort that should be going into solving the country's social and economic problems is devoted to politicking for personal gain. The six political parties represented in parliament are the Vanua'aku Pati, the Union of Moderate Parties, the National United Party, the Melanesian Progressive Party, the Jon Frum Movement, and the Vanuatu Republikan Party.

ECONOMY

Agriculture and Land

Roughly 77 percent of the population lives by subsistence or small scale agriculture. Root crops such as yams, taro, manioc, and sweet potatoes are grown, with copra produced for cash sale. Cattle bred from light-colored French Charolais and Limousin stock roam under the coconuts to provide beef for canning and export. Until recently, copra accounted for almost half of Vanuatu's exports, but hurricane damage, low world prices, and government inefficiency have reduced production. The Commodity Marketing Board has subsidized copra prices with European Union aid money, to ensure a regular income for the village producers who account for 80 percent of Vanuatu's copra. Mismanagement and bad investments have cost the Board millions of dollars. In 1998, Vanuatu exported US$6.83 million worth of kava, but these sales largely came to an end in late 2001 when the European Union began limiting kava imports allegedly over public health concerns.

The constitution specifies that land can only be owned by indigenous Ni-Vanuatu. At independence, all alienated land was returned to its customary owners; former landlords were given five years to go into partnership, lease the land, or otherwise dispose of it. Leases of up to 75 years are available. Land disputes are routine in Vanuatu, as many Ni-Vanuatu claim the same areas. Although about 40 percent of the land is arable, only 17 percent is presently utilized, mostly in coastal areas. International bankers and consultants usually view land title issues as obstacles to development, and politicians often favor land registration as a way of extending the tax base. Ni-Vanuatu villagers, on the other hand, generally recognize their customary land rights as their best defense against subservience and poverty.

Vanuatu receives one of the highest per capita levels of development aid in the region, with contributions nicely diversified between Australia, France, the European Union, Japan, New Zealand, the Asian Development Bank, and Britain.

Trade

Vanuatu imports four times more than it exports, and has a large imbalance with its largest trading partner, Australia, which sells Vanuatu 13 times as much as it buys. New Zealand buys almost nothing from Vanuatu but is its second-largest supplier. The most important exports by value are sawn timber (sold to Australia and New Caledonia), copra (shipped mostly from Luganville to Holland), chilled beef (sold to Japan), cacao (sold to France, Holland, and Germany), and pumpkins (sold to Japan). The export of unprocessed logs was halted in 1994, after it became clear that logging already underway would have stripped the country bare in five years. A flourishing sawmill industry at Luganville is the result.

The import economy is dominated by large European and Chinese trading companies. In rural areas, cooperatives once collected agricultural exports and handled marketing, but individually owned stores are now becoming more common. In 1990, the Swedish brewer Pripps launched Vanuatu Brewing Ltd. as a 50-50 joint venture with the government to produce Tusker beer and Pripps Lager. An industrial park has been created on Espiritu Santo.

Until recently, some 600 Ni-Vanuatu served as crew on Taiwanese fishing boats, on which they were reportedly overworked and otherwise exploited. In 1999, it was revealed that the fishermen's accumulated wages, held in trust by the government-run company which had arranged the contracts with foreign fishing companies, had been pilfered by corrupt officials. After years of heartbreaking work at sea, many men were left with nothing.

Taxation and Evasion

Although Vanuatu has periodically pursued a confrontational left/center foreign policy, its domestic policies (inherited from the Condominium) are ultra-right. There are no company taxes, personal income taxes, estate duties, capital gains taxes, or exchange controls. Instead, government revenue is obtained from customs duties, export taxes, company registration fees, licensing fees, property taxes (Port Vila and Espiritu Santo only), various tourist taxes, and fishing licenses.

In the past, import duties accounted for more than half of government income, and were the major cause of the high cost of living. The American-controlled Asian Development Bank lobbied again this trade barrier, and in August 1998, the tariffs were replaced by a 12.5 percent value-added tax (VAT) on goods and services. About the same time, interest rates were hiked 5 percent to protect the local currency. These moves damaged local businesses by encouraging imports while increasing the cost of borrowing.

Vanuatu has the South Pacific's oldest, largest, and best established "finance center," which offers excellent facilities to foreigners wishing to evade their own country's public auditing and taxation laws. In 1971, the British Companies Regulation was enacted, giving tax-free status to companies registered in what was then New Hebrides. Today almost 6,000 foreign companies participate in the tax-haven scheme, providing jobs for over 500 people, paying US$2 million a year in government fees, and bringing in an estimated US$15 million in flow-on benefits. Several dozen accounting, banking, legal, and investment services help Asian corporations avoid taxation, and foreign currency operations of around US$6 billion are transacted each year. In 1991, the Australian and New Zealand governments passed legislation greatly restricting the use of tax havens by their citizens after televised revelations that large corporations were paying only one percent tax by channeling their profits through these facilities. Vanuatu claims to run a clean operation, with money laundering from illegal sources strictly taboo. Despite this, Vanuatu has come under strong pressure from the Organization for Economic Cooperation and Development to relax their banking secrecy laws. For more information on the tax haven, log onto www.moores rowland.com or www.financial.com.vu.

In 1981, Vanuatu established a shipping registry or flag-of-convenience law modeled on Liberia's, which allows foreign shipping companies to duck taxation, safety regulations, union labor, and government controls. With the political chaos in Vanuatu's main competitors, Liberia and Panama, the annual number of ships registered has jumped from 76 in 1985 to about 500 today, with the main users being American, Japanese, and Hong Kong ship owners. It's all explained on www.vanuatuships.com.

Tourism

Tourism is Vanuatu's leading industry though the country is a long way behind Fiji. Since Vanuatu isn't on a main air route, well over half of the 55,000 airborne tourists are from Australia, with New Zealand providing another 15 percent and New Caledonia 8 percent. Thanks to its proximity to Australia, Vanuatu receives more cruise ship passengers than any other South Pacific country. Cruise ships such as the *Pacific Sky* and *Pacific Sun* call frequently at Port Vila, "Mystery Island" (Aneityum), and Champagne Beach (Santo), unloading about 50,000 one-day visitors a year, and P&O Cruises hopes to increase this to an incredible 150,000 passengers a year. Land-based tourism focuses on the resorts of Port Vila and Espiritu Santo, with Tanna serving as a day-trip destination.

Vanuatu's two-tier neocolonial economy is strikingly obvious in tourism. In the top tier are the overwhelming majority of tourist hotels and resorts in Port Vila and Luganville, owned and operated by foreign companies or resident expatriates. In recent years, the Ni-Vanuatu owners of basic rural guesthouses have united to form the Vanuatu Island Bungalows Association (VIBA), which markets its services through Island Safaris, a joint venture of the VIBA and Vanair. Island Safaris charges Australian-level prices for their adventure tourism packages, which makes them expensive compared to backpacker-style travel in other Pacific countries.

THE PEOPLE

Sixty-eight of Vanuatu's 83 islands are populated, but most of the country's 187,000 people live on 16 main islands. At 15 persons per square

WOMEN IN VANUATU

Women have a higher status on the northern matrilineal islands; on islands like Ambrym, Malekula, south Pentecost, and Tanna, where descent is patrilineal, males dominate society. In times past, women on the central and northern islands belonged to secret societies, but always societies of lower grade than those of the men. Though men and women work together in the villages, the women are responsible for chores considered less prestigious, such as cooking and caring for gardens and pigs. The burdens of a subsistence economy usually fall more heavily on the women. Too often, the men in Port Vila spend much of their time drinking kava and gossiping with friends, while the women keep the families going.

A woman cannot become a "big man" by accumulating wealth—in fact, she herself is considered part of her husband's wealth. The payment of bride-price is still common throughout Vanuatu, and some young girls have even been called "Toyotas," an indication of their market value as potential wives. To control inflation, the Malvatumauri, Vanuatu's National Council of Chiefs, has placed a Vt.300,000 ceiling on bride-prices (a Toyota costs more than Vt.1.5 million). Being viewed as tradable objects is a heavy burden for Ni-Vanuatu women; girls are often deprived of educational opportunities by their own families, who consider them primarily child-bearers for the clan of their future husband. Some educated women refuse to marry, as it would mean forfeiting all rights to the family's property.

Most women treated for injuries at hospitals are victims of domestic violence, and the police only take action in the most extreme cases. Desertion of families by men is also a big problem. Interestingly enough, maltreatment of women is often more common in missionized communities and towns than in traditional areas where customary law prevails. A husband in a "kastom area" will try to avoid beating his wife ("without cause") as she might run away ("with just cause"), back to her original family, and the husband would thus lose the bride-price he paid. Since independence, things have begun to change. There are now 50:50 quotas for both sexes in forms one to four, to give girls an equal chance to attend secondary school.

---

km, the population density is low. Yet after a century of depopulation due to warfare, blackbirding, and introduced diseases, Vanuatu now has one of the highest birthrates in the Pacific, and 43 percent of the population is under the age of 15. Vanuatu's infant mortality rate is also the highest in the South Pacific and the life expectancy at birth is the lowest in the region. Thirty-six percent of the population lacks access to a safe water supply.

Ni-Vanuatu continue to migrate to Port Vila from rural areas in search of jobs, excitement, and better services. One in six now lives in the capital, with people from the same outer islands congregating in their own suburban communities. Although 4,000 young people enter the job market each year, formal employment opportunities exist only for 400 of them. Almost half of Ni-Vanuatu children aged 5–19 don't attend school, and 66.5 percent of adults are illiterate. In Port Vila, wandering the streets or "spearing

the public road" (SPR) is one way of *kilem taem* (killing time).

Just over a third of the population is Presbyterian, with Anglicans, Roman Catholics, and followers of the Jon Frum Cargo Cult making up a sixth each. Smaller groups include the Seventh-Day Adventists, Church of Christ, and Assemblies of God. About 10,000 people still follow traditional Pacific religions. Jon Frummers account for more than a quarter of the population of Tanna.

Although 98 percent of the population is Melanesian (Ni-Vanuatu), there are also Europeans, Chinese, and Vietnamese. Thousands of indentured Vietnamese laborers were imported earlier this century to work on the French plantations, but most were repatriated by 1963. The proportion of non-Ni-Vanuatu has declined since independence and over half of them now live in Port Vila.

Although the Melanesians arrived in Vanuatu from the northwest thousands of years ago, a back migration of Polynesians from the east occurred less than 1,000 years ago. Polynesian languages are still spoken on Futuna, Emae, and Ambae islands, and in Ifira and Mele villages on Efate. A Polynesian hierarchy of chiefs is still evident in much of central and southern Vanuatu. In physical appearance the Polynesians have been almost totally assimilated by the surrounding Melanesian peoples, largely due to a custom requiring a young man to take his bride from a neighboring clan.

Language

With 113 indigenous languages, most having several dialects, Vanuatu boasts the world's highest density of languages per capita. All of these tongues (none with more than 5,000 speakers) belong to the Austronesian family of languages spoken from Madagascar to Easter Island. Bislama is the national language understood by 90 percent of the population, although English and French are also official languages. About 40 percent of the population knows English and 20 percent speak French. Many Ni-Vanuatu are fluent in five or six languages: a few in local languages, Bislama, English, and French.

Bislama developed as a traders' tongue in the 19th century and took hold among the indentured native laborers in Queensland. The name derives from bêche-de-mer, an edible sea slug sought by early traders. This dialect of Pidgin English is now spoken by around 60 percent of Ni-Vanuatu and is the main communication medium between persons from different language groups, though they speak their mother tongues at home. Most parliamentary debates are conducted in Bislama, but education is still conducted in either English or French.

Bislama verbs have no tenses: Finished and unfinished actions are defined by adverbs. Nouns are often descriptions of use. *Blong* indicates possession, while *long* takes the place of most other prepositions. Vowels are pronounced as in Spanish. English speakers usually can't distinguish between *b* and *p*, *d* and *t*, *f* and *v*, and *g* and *k*. The letter *b* is preceded by an "m" sound, *d* by an "n" sound.

Bislama can sound deceptively simple to the untrained ear, but the meaning is not always what one would expect from a literal translation into English. Over the years it has developed into a complex language by adopting indigenous linguistic structures. Bislama is a lot further from English than Solomon Islands pidgin, and you'll only understand fragments without study (there are several dictionaries). The University of the South Pacific has a university-level Bislama course.

Exploring the Islands

Highlights

The overwhelming majority of tourists visit only Efate, Espiritu Santo, and Tanna, and indeed these three islands contain Vanuatu's best-known sights, including the country's only towns, Port Vila and Luganville. Tanna is acclaimed for Yasur Volcano and the Jon Frum Cargo Cult, Efate has an interesting road around its coast, and Espiritu Santo boasts Champagne Beach, one of the South Pacific's finest. Ambrym is less known but outstanding for its active volcanoes. Virtually all of the islands are worth visiting by those willing to slow down and enjoy the unspoiled local environment and friendly people. It's easy to get lost and found in Vanuatu.

Sports and Recreation

Scuba diving is well developed with several active dive shops in Port Vila and a couple more on Espiritu Santo. Diving is also possible from charter vessels off the north side of Efate. Game fishing is available at Port Vila. Other active sports to pursue are windsurfing in Vila's Erakor Lagoon, horseback riding at one of the two ranches on opposite sides of Port Vila, and yachting on charter vessels based at Port Vila.

Golf is big here, with two major 18-hole golf courses on Efate and smaller resort courses at two Port Vila hotels. There's also a golf course on Santo.

All of the above is the domain of tourists, expatriates, and affluent locals; hiking is the sport most commonly practiced by the vast majority of the population, although they'd hardly think of it as such. Well-used trails exist on all the outer islands, with Tanna especially accessible in this regard. It's quite possible to hike right across islands like Tanna, Malekula, and Erromango. Hiking around Espiritu Santo is a much bigger undertaking, with local guides required.

Mountain climbers should consider the active volcanoes of Ambrym: Benbow and Marum in the south and Vetlam in the north. All are quite accessible to those willing to hire local guides and pay custom fees to the local chiefs. Ambae also has a central peak worth a climb. There are many other possibilities.

If surfing is Polynesia's finest gift to the world of sport, Melanesia's greatest contribution is perhaps bungee jumping, which A.J. Hackett saw on Pentecost Island in 1979 and later introduced to New Zealand. Hackett replaced the islanders' vines with expandable rubber lines, and today thousands of people a year prove something to themselves and others by taking the jump, just as the Pentecost men have been doing for hundreds of years.

Public Holidays and Festivals

Public holidays include New Year's Day (January 1), Father Walter Lini Day (February 21), Custom Chiefs Day (March 5), Good Friday, Easter Monday (March/April), Ascension Day (April/May), Labor Day (May 1), Children's Day (July 24), Independence Day (July 30), Assumption Day (August 15), Constitution Day (October 5), National Unity Day (November 29), Christmas Day (December 25), and Family Day (December 26). The Monday or Friday before Independence Day is Children's Day, also a public holiday.

Important annual events include the Jon Frum Festival at Sulphur Bay, Tanna, on February 15, and the Pentecost Land Dive weekly in April and May. Independence Day sees a parade, food and kava stalls, sporting events, and custom dancing in Port Vila. Expect all of the events to begin an hour late.

ACCOMMODATIONS AND FOOD
Accommodations
The 12.5 percent value-added tax is not included in some of the prices listed in this book. Hotels often quote the basic price and add the tax to your bill later. Meals at licensed restaurants serving alcohol are also taxed 12.5 percent, but unlicensed snack bars and small outer-island resorts are tax-free.

The only commercial tourist accommodations are on Efate, Tanna, and Espiritu Santo. Most of the outer islands served by Vanair have basic guesthouses operated by the churches, provincial administrations, women's groups, village chiefs, or others. Thatched resthouses run by local villagers exist on most islands. Such places rarely have electricity, and the water supply may be poor, but there's often some means of cooking your own food. These places almost never have telephones, but it's usually possible to announce your arrival by calling the local government or provincial office and asking them to convey the message. Bookings are not essential, however, and it's almost always possible to arrange something upon arrival with the help of the Vanair agent or otherwise.

Outer island guesthouses belonging to the Vanuatu Island Bungalows Association are packaged by **Island Safaris** (tel. 23288, fax 26779, www.islandsvanuatu.com). Their tours are fine if you want to climb a volcano and aren't too worried about the cost. However, to protect their commissions, Island Safaris requires all 21 guesthouses working with them to price their accommodations, meals, transfers, and activities at Australian levels, and persons not on their tours are expected to pay the same inflated rates. Thus, before heading to any place marketed by Island Safaris, it's important to check the prices carefully, in order to avoid getting a severe shock. Otherwise avoid the Island Safaris lodgings altogether. Herein we've tried to identify village guesthouses booked by Island Safaris and other tour operators.

Camping is possible and safe elsewhere, but always get permission from the landowner or chief. Some eco-lodges in remote areas allow camping at reduced rates. Often people will invite you into their own homes if they think you're in a jam, and in such cases it doesn't hurt to offer payment (gifts or money). Always give back as

TRADITIONAL CULTURE

The Ni-Vanuatu possess an amazing variety of cultures, from the "land-diving" clansmen of South Pentecost to the festival-rich society of the inhabitants of volcanic Tanna. Customs differ from island to island, and remain strong despite generations of missionary influence. In the interiors of the two largest islands, Malekula and Espiritu Santo, are some of the most traditional peoples in the Pacific. Penis wrappers *(nambas)* are still worn by men in remote regions of south Malekula, North Ambrym, South Pentecost, and Tanna. Traditional magic is still practiced throughout Vanuatu, with that of Maewo, Ambrym, and Epi reputed to be the strongest.

Traditional culture revolves around the pig, of which each clan or leader tries to acquire the greatest number. Almost any social offense can be compensated for with the payment of pigs. On the islands north of the Shepherds, the pigs are killed ritually when the tusks, used for body decoration, reach their greatest length. This ritual killing raises the social status of the individual in the village hierarchy *(nimangki)*. In the south, during the *nekowiar,* a clan alliance ritual, one clan gives gifts to another in the form of dances, songs, kava, yams, and taro, and these will eventually have to be given back in yet another *nekowiar.*

Even today, traditional art objects are often associated with public rituals or male secret societies, and a man has to accumulate considerable wealth to advance through the graded levels. Large carved figures, masks, and slit drums often still have to be provided for the advancement ceremony, in addition to payments of pigs. In some areas, different helmet masks are made for each level; these masks become temporary homes for ancestral or other types of spirits. In southern Malekula, curved pig's tusks ornamented them and are kept after pig sacrifices as evidence of wealth.

---

much as you receive, be considerate and polite, and make sure you don't overstay your welcome.

Food

Lap lap is the national dish. Bananas and root vegetables such as yams, taro, and manioc are grated, then kneaded to a paste, to which coconut cream and aromatic leaves are added. Pork or seafood can be included. The mixture is then wrapped in the leaves of a plant resembling the banana tree and cooked using hot stones in an earth oven. The best *lap lap* is made in remote villages, though it's also sold at the Port Vila market. In the northern islands breadfruit is pounded in a wooden bowl to make a food called *nalot.*

Other local specialties include mangrove oysters (served cold) and freshwater prawns (steamed with young bamboo stalks and mayonnaise). If you see "poulet" on a restaurant menu, don't assume it's chicken, as the local deep-water red snapper also goes by that name. Sadly, coconut crab is featured on the menus of several Port Vila restaurants, with the result that

the slow-growing creatures are rapidly becoming an endangered species.

The French-operated restaurants tend to give small portions of expertly prepared food, while the Australian-run establishments usually provide larger portions of conventional dishes. Many Port Vila restaurants allow you to Bring Your Own (BYO) wine and pay a corkage fee to have it with your meal, which works out much cheaper than ordering from the wine menu (watch for the letters BYO in restaurant advertising).

Kava

Kava is consumed in many Pacific countries, but the kava of Vanuatu is the strongest, bearing little resemblance to weak Fijian kava. It's especially potent because the roots are not dried as they are in Fiji, but are diced while still green, then mashed and mixed with water (not strained as in Fiji). Prior to independence, kava drinking in the towns was discouraged by missionaries and government officials, but today it has become a cultural icon, the indigenous alternative to Western alcohol. Traditionally, kava is a ritual *kastom* drink, but in Port Vila it's now entirely social, with the many kava saloons called kava bars or *nakamals* doing brisk business from 1800 onward. Several also cater to visitors.

Genetic and chemical analysis has demonstrated that kava has been cultivated in northern Vanuatu for at least 3,000 years, and from here its use may have spread to other areas. Some 72 varieties of kava exist here—more than anywhere else in the Pacific—with Tanna and northern Pentecost especially famous for their kava. Its medicinal use as a natural tranquilizer has been recognized by the European pharmacological industry.

Kava is narcotic, rather than alcoholic. One coconut shell of it is enough; after several shells you won't be able to lift your arms or walk, and your mouth will feel as if the dentist had just given you novocaine. Don't eat anything before drinking kava or mix alcohol with it. Although it looks and tastes like dishwater, kava is pure relaxation, leaves no hangover, and never prompts aggression (unlike beer). The mind remains clear, and there are no hallucinations. It's not exactly hygienic though, because in central and southern Vanuatu, children chew the roots (at least on the outer islands). Most urban *nakamals* now use meat grinders to crush the roots.

INFORMATION AND SERVICES

Information

The National Tourism Office of Vanuatu (P.O. Box 209, Port Vila; tel. 22515, fax 23889, www .vanuatutourism.com) provides information either in person at their Port Vila office, by mail, or over the internet.

Internet Resources

Destination Vanuatu, **www.vanuatuparadise .com,** is an online visitors guide with mini-maps and specific information about all the main islands. The Vanuatu A-Z Visitors Guide, **www .vanuatuatoz.com,** arranges quirky, personal observations and little known facts on alphabetical pages that are fun to browse. The Cruising Guide to Vanuatu, **www.cruis**

ing-vanuatu.com, is a rich resource for cruising yachties, with a weather analysis center and sailing information around Vanuatu. Honeymoon Vanuatu, **www.honeymoonvanuatu.com,** offers advice about resorts, attractions, dining, and getting around aimed at those planning a honeymoon or wedding in Vanuatu. Vanuatu Resorts Pacific, **www.vanuatu.resortspacific.com,** provides maps and information about upscale Vanuatu vacations, honeymoon resorts, and hotels.

Vanuatu Online, **www.vanuatu.net.vu,** is a general portal with business and tourism listings, plus descriptions of the individual islands. The Vatu.com Portal, **www.vatu.com,** provides a local weather report, exchange rates, a searchable telephone directory, tide tables, flight schedules, news reports, tourism listings, local cinema offerings, a chat room, and a forum.

Stan Combs's Vanuatu: A Canadian's Perspective, **http://members.shaw.ca/scombs/van uatu.html,** explores the "Hidden Vanuatu" not often experienced by casual visitors. Packed with interesting asides about rural areas, pidgin English, local customs, aid donors, and kava, these pages are the perfect antidote to the hype of the conventional tourism sites. The Nguna Island website, **http://plaza.ufl.edu/lumina,** introduces the unspoiled primary forest, stunning coral gardens, ancient volcanoes, steaming springs, and timeless cultural tradition of the islands off northern Efate. The Jon Frum Home Page, **http://enzo.gen.nz/jonfrum/index.htm,** tells you everything you ever wanted to know about this active cargo cult.

Visas and Officialdom

Most nationalities don't require a visa for a stay of one month or less, although onward tickets are required. The immigration officer may ask at which hotel you intend to stay, but just name any of those listed in this book. Three extensions, one month at a time, are possible. The only immigration offices are in Port Vila and Luganville. Elsewhere, take your passport to a police station; they'll send it to Port Vila for the extension. Visa extensions are free. It's possible to obtain a residence permit by investing more than US$50,000 in a local business (the rules are explained on www.transpacificproperty.com). Ten years residency is required for naturalization.

Port Vila and Luganville are ports of entry for cruising yachts. It's also possible to clear in and out at Lenakel (Tanna) and Sola (Vanua Lava) upon payment of a special Vt.6,000 outer islands clearance fee. There are heavy fines for calling at outer islands before checking in, and special permission is required to call at an outer island after checking out. At Port Vila the protected anchorage behind Iririki Island is good but deep.

Doing any sort of research in Vanuatu involves getting advance clearance from the Vanuatu Cultural Center (tel. 22129, fax 26590). One should take care not to appear to be conducting research in the social sciences, as this requires prior approval. Cinematographers and others doing documentaries also require advance approval from the Cultural Center.

Money

The vatu is the unit of currency in Vanuatu; US$1 = Vt.120 approximately (the word *vatu* means "stone"). There are notes of 500, 1,000, and 5,000, coins of one, two, five, 10, 20, 50, and 100. Though linked to special drawing rights (SDR) in the International Monetary Fund, the vatu is not well known abroad and can be hard to get rid of, so change your excess into the currency of the next country on your itinerary. Inflation is low, but remember the 12.5 percent value-added tax, which is often added at the cash register or checkout counter.

The main banks serving Vanuatu are the ANZ Bank and the Westpac Bank, with main branches at Port Vila and Luganville. The National Bank of Vanuatu also has branches at Lakatoro (Malekula), Craig Cove (Ambrym), and Lenakel (Tanna), and although these do change trav-

eler's checks, it's a good idea to make sure you have enough vatu (in small notes) to see you through before leaving for an outer island. Rates of exchange differ slightly from bank to bank, so check around before changing large amounts. At last report there was no American Express representative in Vanuatu, although the Westpac Bank gives cash advances on American Express, MasterCard, and Visa credit cards. Credit cards are generally accepted only in Port Vila and Luganville. Some merchants add a 4 percent surcharge if you pay by credit card.

Vanuatu is an expensive country by South Pacific standards, with a cost of living noticeably higher than neighboring Fiji or Solomon Islands, but a bit lower than New Caledonia. There aren't many ways to spend money out in the bush, but most of the facilities associated with modern life come dear. So-called "custom fees" are often collected from visitors to cultural or natural sites in rural areas, such as old burial places, caves, dancing grounds, etc. The local chiefs have little understanding of the value of money, and will often ask ridiculous sums, such as Vt.1,000 pp to see a heap of stones or a few rotting *tamtams* (drums). Tanna is notorious for this, but you can encounter it anywhere. It's rather discouraging to go to a lot of trouble (and expense) to reach a remote site, only to have someone demand a stiff fee just to be able to look at something out in the open with no amenities provided. Government officials who view tourists as an economic resource often encourage villagers to levy these fees. On the plus side, there's no tipping in Vanuatu.

Communications

Main post offices (www.postvanuatu.com) sell telephone cards in denominations of 10 units (Vt.225), 20 units (Vt.450), 40 units (Vt.900), 60 units (Vt.1,350), 80 units (Vt.1,800), and 120 units (Vt.2,700). Card phones have been installed on many islands, and by using them for international calls you avoid three-minute minimum charges. To call abroad, dial the international code 00, the country code, the area code (if any), and the number. To get the local operator dial 90, directory assistance 91.

There are public card phones at numerous locations all around Vanuatu. A complete list is provided in the front of the telephone directory. Although Telecom Vanuatu (www.vanuatu.com.vu) has managed to install these phones, they're incompetent when it comes to keeping their sales outlets supplied with cards. It can be almost impossible to buy telephone cards on the outer islands (even in places that have card telephones), and you can't even count on being able to pick up a card at Port Vila Airport. Thus it's important to be sure you always have a card with sufficient units to cover all potential calls for the next few days. Consider buying a couple of extra cards to present as gifts in remote areas.

Calls anywhere in the country cost Vt.20 every two minutes, with a reduced rate for calls over five minutes in effect weekdays 1800–0600 and all day on weekends. For international calls, a reduced off-peak rate is available Monday to Saturday 1800–0600 and all day Sunday. Calls to Australia, New Zealand, New Caledonia, and Fiji cost Vt.133/108 peak/off-peak per minute, and to all other countries Vt.216/168. In general, Vanuatu's international telephone rates are the highest in the South Pacific, and you're better off waiting to call from Fiji or Solomon Islands. Postage is also very expensive here.

Vanuatu's telephone code is 678.

Media

For intriguing insights into the local scene be sure to pick up a copy of the *Vanuatu Daily Post* (tel. 23111, fax 24111, www.vanuatudaily.com), published Tuesday to Saturday. You'll get a good mix of local, regional, and international news for your Vt.100. Publisher Marc Neil-Jones isn't shy about reporting on official corruption, and the paper's vicissitudes are a weathervane of Vanuatu democracy.

There's a second paper called the *Port Vila Presse* (tel. 27999, www.presse.com.vu) published every Saturday in English and French.

Television broadcasting began in 1991 with 50-50 programming in English and French. **Television Blong Vanuatu** (TBV) is on the air daily 1630–2200. The news is at 1900 weekdays.

Government-owned **Radio Vanuatu** (tel. 22999, fax 22026) broadcasts from Port Vila over 1125 kHz AM and 96.0 and 98.0 MHz FM, and from Luganville over 1179 kHz AM. Radio Vanuatu has long been subject to official interference as the party in power seeks to deny a platform to its opponents. The station is on the air Monday to Saturday 0600–2215, Sunday 0600–2100. Radio Vanuatu rebroadcasts the Radio Australia news at 0700 daily, the Radio France International news at 0800 daily, the BBC news at 0900 weekdays, and the local news in English at 1215 and 1800 weekdays. Shipping news and a weather report in Bislama are at 1930 daily. In Port Vila you can listen to the **BBC World Service** 24 hours a day at 99.0 MHz FM.

Health

Vanuatu is in the Melanesian malaria belt, which continues up through the Solomon Islands into Papua New Guinea; there's none in New Caledonia or Fiji. Warmer temperatures in recent years may be contributing to an increase in the number of reported cases of malaria in Vanuatu. Although malaria is mostly a problem on the islands north of Port Vila during summer (Nov.–May), prophylactic pills should always be taken, as the disease has been reported everywhere year-round. Begin taking pills a week before you arrive and continue for four weeks after you leave.

Officially, you're supposed to have a prescription to buy malaria pills in Vanuatu, but the pharmacies in Port Vila usually sell the pills over the counter without bothering about prescriptions. Chloroquine-resistant *Plasmodium falciparum* malaria accounts for 73 percent of infections here, so turn to Health in the Solomon Islands chapter introduction and follow that advice. The malarial mosquito here is the female *Anopheles farauti*, which feeds at night or on overcast days and rests outdoors. The use of a mosquito net (available for Vt.500 at most Chinese stores in Port Vila) greatly reduces the chance of getting bitten.

Dengue fever and hepatitis B are also present in Vanuatu, so read up on them in the main introduction. Recommended (but not compulsory) vaccinations are immune globulin or the Havrix vaccine (for viral hepatitis A), and the one against typhoid fever. All minor cuts should be treated seriously: A little iodine at the right time can save you a lot of trouble later. The tap water in Port Vila and Luganville is safe to drink, but elsewhere one should take precautions. Public hospitals exist at Port Vila (Efate), Lenakel (Tanna), Norsup (Malekula), Luganville (Espiritu Santo), Lolowai (Ambae), and Nduindui (Ambae).

Business Hours and Electricity

Business hours are weekdays 0730–1130 and 1400–1700, Saturday 0730–1130. Post offices are usually open 0730–1630. Banking hours are generally weekdays 0800–1500. Most bureaucratic offices (including post offices) are closed for lunch 1130–1330, although shops, banks, and travel agencies remain open all day. Large supermarkets stay open until 1900 weekdays, the Chinese stores until 2000 or later.

The electric voltage is 220–240 volts, 50 cycles, with two- or three-pronged plugs.

TRANSPORTATION
Getting There

The country's flag carrier, **Air Vanuatu** (tel. 23848, fax 26591, www.airvanuatu.com), flies a Boeing 737 to Port Vila from Nouméa and Sydney five times a week, from Brisbane four times a week, from Auckland twice a week, and from Honiara and Nadi weekly. Air Vanuatu's 5/30-day roundtrip excursion fare from Port Vila to Nouméa is Vt.30,100/37,100, plus tax. In the United States you can obtain information about Air Vanuatu by calling 800/677-4277.

Qantas code shares with Air Vanuatu's Brisbane and Sydney flights, allowing a direct connections to Adelaide and Melbourne. From Europe, you can also connect through Brisbane or Sydney. Other code shares include **Solomon Airlines** from Honiara and **Air Pacific** from Nadi, both weekly. Air Pacific offers direct connections in Nadi to/from Auckland and Los Angeles.

The New Caledonian carrier **Aircalin** (tel. 22739) has a service from Nouméa twice a week.

Vanuatu is included in Air Pacific's 30-day Pacific Air Pass (US$462), providing easy access from Fiji, and in the Visit South Pacific Pass, which allows a variety of routings. These passes are described in the Exploring the Islands chapter of this book, under Getting Around.

Getting Around By Air

Government-owned **Vanair** (tel. 22753, fax 23910, vias@vanuatu.com.vu) offers more than 180 weekly services to 29 airstrips on 18 islands, with three 19-passenger Twin Otters, two six-passenger Islanders, and one 36-seat Dash 8-100 based at Port Vila and Espiritu Santo. You can fly from Port Vila to Espiritu Santo (Vt.13,450) three or four times a day (five times a week via Norsup). Flights from Port Vila to Tanna (Vt.11,770) run once or twice a day (via Dillon's Bay, Ipota, and Aniwa weekly). Vanair also operates reduced Sunday service to Espiritu Santo, Norsup, and Tanna. Details of Vanair's many local services appear throughout this chapter.

In recent years, fares on Vanair (which has a monopoly on internal air service) have continued to rise, making getting around Vanuatu an expensive proposition. Vanair uses its profits from the popular Santo and Tanna runs to subsidize service to remote outer islands, which might not otherwise receive regular flights. Stopovers cost extra—the fare from Port Vila to Espiritu Santo is Vt.15,890 with a stop at Norsup. A routing Vila-Walaha-Santo-Norsup-Craig Cove-Vila will be Vt.36,040 in total. Round-trip fares are double the one-way fares. A non-refundable departure tax of Vt.400 is added to the price of all flights from Port Vila, Santo, and Tanna, or Vt.250 per flight from other airports (included in the ticket price). Because airfares are so high, the planes are seldom fully booked (except when a group of politicians suddenly decides to travel). You can obtain a 20 percent discount on Vanair fares by showing your international plane ticket (this fact isn't advertised and you have to ask to get the discount).

A 30-day **Discover Vanuatu Pass** is available at US$236 for four flights to Ambrym, Efate, Espiritu Santo, Malekula, and Tanna only. Extra coupons to a maximum of six are US$60 each and local taxes are extra. On a routing Port Vila-Espiritu Santo-Port Vila-Tanna-Port Vila, this represents a 50 percent savings over regular airfare! The pass must be purchased in conjunction with an international ticket, including at the Vanair office in Port Vila upon presentation of your ticket to leave Vanuatu. In North America, the pass can be preordered through Air Promotion Systems (tel. 800/677-4277, www.pacificislands.com). It's worth looking into.

Reservation changes must be made one day in advance, and "no shows" forfeit the full value of their ticket. Reconfirm your onward reservations immediately *upon arrival* at an outer island. Sometimes a plane will be diverted to make an unscheduled stop at an airstrip along the way if there are passengers to pick up or drop off. This can also work in reverse: They may forget to pick you up even though you've booked. Flights can be cancelled if an airstrip becomes waterlogged or the grass grows too long. Beware of flights leaving early! On some flights you may be allowed to sit up front with the pilot if you ask nicely, and perhaps even fly a more scenic route (such as over Ambrym's volcano). You'll get some excellent views from these planes.

Although the baggage limit is 10 kilograms, they probably won't say anything if you're only a bit overweight. Just carry heavy items in your hand luggage. Excess luggage is around Vt.100 a kilo. Folding kayaks up to four meters long can be carried on the Twin Otters. At last report the government was attempting to privatize Vanair, and if a sale goes ahead, some of the information above may change.

Getting Around By Boat

Interisland boat travel has improved considerably since 2000, when parliament repealed the Coastal Trading Act, which had required all vessels operating wholly within Vanuatu waters to be owned by Ni-Vanuatu. Several expatriate-owned companies have now begun offering regular Port Vila to Luganville services, and they're worth considering for the experience of the voyage and the chance to see the coastlines of many remote islands at stops along the way. Boat fares are about half of airfare. These services are described under Port Vila, following.

Fishing boats and outboards can be hired to take you between nearby islands north of Efate, but it's only cheaper than flying if there are two or three of you. To be really independent, take along a small folding sea kayak and see delightful islands, bays, lagoons, beaches, and reefs on your own. The west coasts are better sheltered from the southeast trades, but avoid the hurricane season. Between the islands are big rollers and strong currents, so don't risk going interisland this way.

Rental cars, taxis, and minibus services are available on Efate and Espiritu Santo. Northeast Malekula also has minibus services with set fares but no car rentals. Elsewhere you can hitch rides in trucks, but traffic is sparse and you're expected to pay the driver. Getting around Tanna is a real challenge, as the drivers of the pickup truck taxis are used to receiving exorbitant charter rates from tourists and you'll be expected to pay the same.

Tourist Cruises

The live-aboard dive boat *Silent World* (also known as the MV *Silent One*) does five-day cruises from Port Vila or Santo. The ship has 16 berths at around Vt.150,000 pp, plus a Vt.3,000 "reef tax." Included are all meals, snacks, and unlimited diving. You're allowed to spend the last (sixth) night aboard ship. In Port Vila, contact Peter Brickland in The Insurance Shop (tel. 23428, fax 26090, www.silentworld.com.au) next to the Olympic Hotel for information.

The ship *Island Explorer* does backpacker adventure tours from Santo with the passengers sleeping in villages along the way. Book through the Adventure Center (tel. 22743) in Port Vila.

Airport

Port Vila International Airport (VLI, www.air ports.vu) is six km north of Port Vila. This wartime airstrip is popularly known as Bauerfield, for Lt. Col. Harold M. Bauer, USMC, who was shot down over Guadalcanal in 1942. Bauer himself supervised construction of the airstrip in just 30 days in May 1942. There are separate terminals for domestic and international flights. The present international terminal was built with Japanese aid money in 1991; the old international terminal is now the domestic terminal.

Taxis cost anywhere from Vt.1,000–1,500 for

the trip into town, depending on the destination. Otherwise walk 100 meters to the exit where the main road leaves the airport parking lot and wait for a regular public bus, which will take you into town for Vt.100. These buses aren't supposed to compete by picking up passengers right in front of the terminal, but there's no problem using them once you get past the taxis.

Avis, Budget, Discount, and Hertz all have rental car drop-off desks near the international check-in counters, but these are unstaffed unless prior arrangements have been made. The head office of Avis (tel. 22570) is right next to the international terminal and they're open business hours.

The National Bank has a window (tel. 22189) also near the check-in counters, which opens for all international flights. They change traveler's checks without commission at a good rate. An ANZ Bank ATM is also at the airport. There's a duty-free shop in the departure lounge selling alcohol, cigarettes, perfume, and not much more. You'll find that the snack bar in the adjacent domestic terminal is much cheaper than the one opposite the international check-in counters.

A departure tax of Vt.2,800 in local currency is payable on international flights, although it's usually included in the price of your plane ticket. Children aged 11 and under are exempt from the airport tax, as are transit passengers who continue on a connecting flight within 24 hours (round-trips to/from a single city excluded). On domestic flights the tax is Vt.250–400 and you pay it when you buy your ticket.

Efate

The South Pacific's most beautiful capital city, Port Vila, sits on the southwest side of 42-by-23-km Efate (Vate) Island, in the lower middle of the Vanuatu chain. Havannah Harbor, on the northwest side of the island, was the original European settlement, but in the late 1870s, drought and malaria forced the settlers to shift 31 km to the site of Port Vila. Plantations were created, and a few traders set up shop, but only after the establishment of the Condominium in 1906 did a town form. Commercial activities occupied the waterfront; the colonial administration settled into the hills above. The town expanded quickly during WW II, and again during the New Caledonian nickel boom of the early 1970s as the French reinvested their profits. Today it's one of the fastest growing cities in the South Pacific.

You can ride right around Efate on a variable, 132-km highway, passing lonely coastlines, little villages, war relics, and countless coconut trees. Vast plantations with herds of grazing Charolais cattle characterize much of Efate's coastal plain, while the interior of this 899-square-km island is impenetrable rainforest. Vanair flights depart Efate's Bauerfield for all parts of Vanuatu.

PORT VILA

Port Vila (pop. 30,000) is the commercial, administrative, touristic, and strategic heart of Vanuatu, the crossroads of the islands to the north and south. Aside from being the national capital, Port Vila is the headquarters of Shefa Province. A cosmopolitan, attractive town, with many yachts anchored in the harbor, Port Vila snuggles around a picturesque bay, well protected from the southeast trades by a jutting peninsula. A narrow neck of land separates the harbor from the plush resorts on L-shaped Erakor Lagoon.

This compact, modern city features excellent facilities, scenic beauty, and a relaxed atmosphere. Add the French *joie de vivre* that pervades the town to the varied shopping, easy transport, sophisticated inhabitants, and many things to see and do, and you'll have one of the most exciting cities in the Pacific. Settle in for a week until you get your bearings, just don't spend all your time here, as Tanna, Espiritu Santo, Ambrym, and the other islands also have much to offer.

Be aware too that Port Vila is small enough for a cruise-ship-load of tourists to have an overwhelming impact. Thus it's well worth knowing when the next cruise ship will dock so you

VANUATU

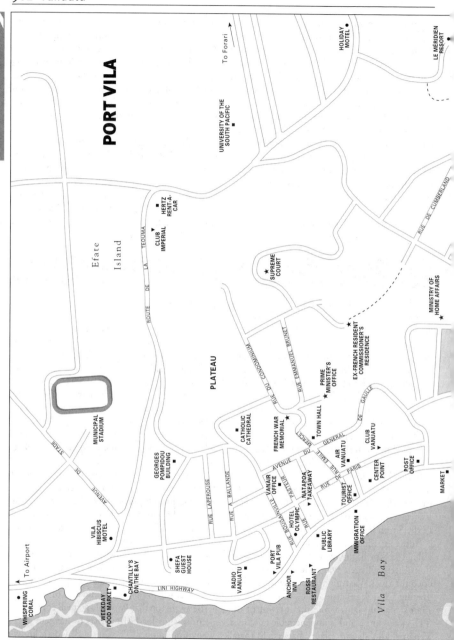

PORT VILA

To Forari →

HOLIDAY MOTEL

LE MERIDIEN RESORT

UNIVERSITY OF THE SOUTH PACIFIC

Efate Island

ROUTE DE LA TEOUMA

HERTZ RENT-A-CAR

CLUB IMPERIAL

RUE DE CUMBERLAND

SUPREME COURT

MINISTRY OF HOME AFFAIRS

MUNICIPAL STADIUM

PLATEAU

RUE DU CORDONNIUM

RUE EMMANUEL BRUNET

PRIME MINISTER'S OFFICE

EX-FRENCH RESIDENT COMMISSIONER'S RESIDENCE

GEORGES POMPIDOU BUILDING

CATHOLIC CATHEDRAL

FRENCH WAR MEMORIAL

TOWN HALL

RUE DE GAULLE

CLUB VANUATU

AVENUE DE STADE

RUE LAPEROUSE

RUE A BALLANDE

AVENUE DU MERCE

VANAIR OFFICE

NATAPOA TAKEAWAY

RUE EMILE

AIR VANUATU

GENERAL

CENTER POINT

POST OFFICE

VILA HIBISCUS MOTEL

RUE PASTEUR

RUE BOUGAINVILLE

HOTEL OLYMPIC

RUE DE PARIS

TOURIST OFFICE

MARKET

To Airport →

CHANTILLY'S ON THE BAY

SHEFA GUEST HOUSE

RADIO VANUATU

PORT VILA PUB

PUBLIC LIBRARY

IMMIGRATION OFFICE

WHISPERING CORAL

WEEKDAY FOOD MARKET

LINI HIGHWAY

ANCHOR INN

ROSSI RESTAURANT

Vila Bay

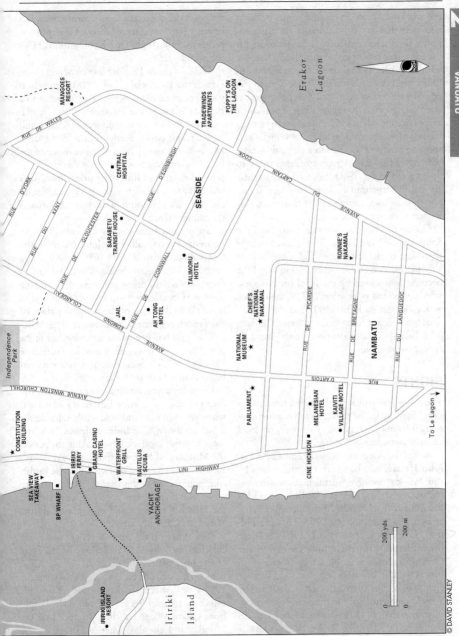

VANUATU

Erakor Lagoon

MANGOES RESORT

RUE DE WALES

RUE D'YORK

RUE DU KENT

RUE DE GLOUCESTER

RUE DU CARDEAU

CENTRAL HOSPITAL

RUE D'EDINBURGH

SARABETU TRANSIT HOUSE

SEASIDE

TRADEWINDS APARTMENTS

POPPY'S ON THE LAGOON

AVENUE DU CAPTAIN COOK

RONNIE'S NAKAMAL

RUE DE CORNWALL

TALIMORU HOTEL

AVENUE EDMOND

JAIL

AH TONG MOTEL

CHIEF'S NATIONAL NAKAMAL

NATIONAL MUSEUM

RUE DE PICARDIE

RUE DE BRETAGNE

RUE DU LANGUEDOC

NAMBATU

Independence Park

AVENUE WINSTON CHURCHILL

PARLIAMENT

RUE D'ARTOIS

CONSTITUTION BUILDING

MELANESIAN HOTEL

KAIVITI VILLAGE MOTEL

SEA VIEW TAKEAWAY

IRIRIKI FERRY

GRAND CASINO HOTEL

WATERFRONT GRILL

NAUTILUS SCUBA

CINE HICKSON

LINI HIGHWAY

To Le Lagoon

BP WHARF

YACHT ANCHORAGE

Iririki Island

IRIRIKI ISLAND RESORT

200 yds
200 m

© DAVID STANLEY

can avoid the Australian carnival hordes by being elsewhere that day. Adventures in Paradise, opposite the French Embassy, arranges tours for the cruise ship passengers, so they should have the schedule. Otherwise ask at the National Tourism Office nearby. Vessels like the *Pacific Sky* and *Pacific Sun* unload as many as 1,900 passengers at Port Vila every two weeks. Even if you don't mind large crowds, it's still important to be forewarned of their arrival, as all rental vehicles and sporting activities will be monopolized by boat passengers that day. A recommended thing to do on a cruise ship day is to go on a day cruise aboard the trimaran *Golden Wing* (see Transportation below), something the cruise ship passengers never have time to do.

On the bright side, visitors arriving from the South Pacific Bible Belt will be relieved to hear that some of the restaurants and shops of Port Vila are open on Sunday. Just keep in mind the peculiar hours kept by the local bureaucracy, who usually start work around 0730, then knock off for a long siesta 1130–1400. Attend to any official business first thing in the morning. To date, it has been quite safe to wander around Port Vila at night—have fun.

SIGHTS

The exhibition hall at the **French Embassy,** on Lini Highway in the center of town, often presents informative temporary displays on local themes, and admission is free.

Across the side street from the embassy is **Pilioko House,** adorned with colorful reliefs by Aloi Pilioko, one of Vanuatu's best-known contemporary artists. Aloi is a Wallisian, and his Russian associate, Nicolai Michoutouchkine, has an exquisite dress shop (tel. 27753) in the building. Have a look upstairs at Nicolai's brilliant line of hand-printed clothing created in the Oceanic tradition of usable art. You'll often find him at work in his shop, and this could be your chance to obtain a garment custom designed by a world-renowned artist in the astrological colors of your star sign. (Michoutouchkine's fashion parade at Le Méridien Resort Wednesdays at 1800 is also worth attending.) High up on the

wall outside, above the shop's corner door, is a bronze plaque announcing that "on this spot was proclaimed the Anglo-French convention of October 20th, 1906."

The road beside Pilioko House leads up to the **French war memorial** (1914–1918), from which you'll get an excellent view of Port Vila and Vila Bay. The island on the left nearest town is Iririki, once the British commissioner's residence and now a major resort. Farther out is Ifira Island, where the customary landowners of much of the Port Vila townsite live (the name Vila is a European corruption of Ifira). The **prime minister's office,** the large building with the Vanuatu flag on the same hill a bit south of the war memorial, is the former French Residency (no entry).

Up the hill from here is the colonial-style **Supreme Court,** called the Joint Court in the Condominium days. During WW II the building served as a U.S. military headquarters. De Querros Street between the prime minister's office and the Supreme Court leads south and winds around to the right to the ruins of the onetime **palace of the French resident commissioner.** After independence the building served as the domicile of the president, until it was destroyed by Hurricane Uma in 1987. The view from the terrace is even better than the one from the war memorial.

Continue southeast on a footpath behind the former palace to avenue Edmond Colardeau, where you turn right and head south watching for a gate on the right to **Independence Park,** the former British Paddock. Overlooking the park is the **Ministry of Home Affairs,** the old British Residency. Under the Condominium, the British community lived in this vicinity, while the more numerous French were on the plateau behind the French Residency, and in a quarter northeast of the Catholic cathedral.

Back down on the main street are two more colorful murals by Aloi Pilioko, one on the front of the **post office,** the other facing the ANZ Bank on the wall of a building across the street. In 1994, a new covered **market** opened at the south end of the pleasant Sea Front Promenade. People from Erakor village sell their produce here on Monday and Tuesday, whereas villagers from north Efate dominate the market Wednesday to

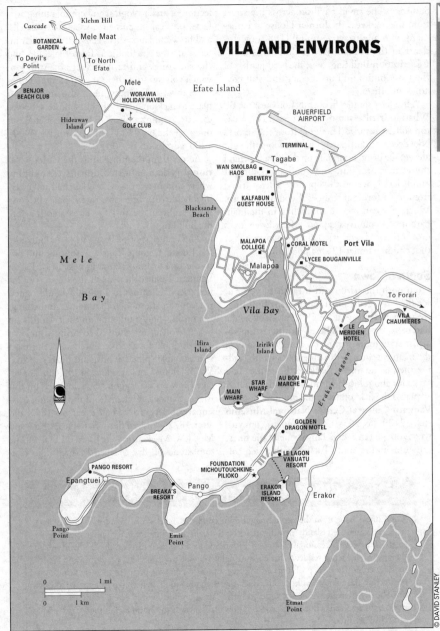

VILA AND ENVIRONS

Cascade

Klehm Hill

BOTANICAL
GARDEN ★

Mele Maat

To Devil's
Point

To North
Efate

BENJOR
BEACH CLUB

Mele

WORAWIA
HOLIDAY HAVEN

Efate Island

Hideaway
Island

GOLF CLUB

BAUERFIELD
AIRPORT

TERMINAL

Tagabe

WAN SMOLBAG
HAOS

BREWERY

KALFABUN
GUEST HOUSE

Blacksands
Beach

MALAPOA
COLLEGE

CORAL MOTEL

Port Vila

Malapoa

LYCEE BOUGAINVILLE

M e l e

B a y

Vila Bay

To Forari

VILA
CHAUMIERES

Ifira
Island

Iririki
Island

LE
MERIDIEN
HOTEL

Erakor Lagoon

STAR
WHARF

AU BON
MARCHE

MAIN
WHARF

GOLDEN
DRAGON MOTEL

PANGO RESORT

Epangtuei

BREAKA'S
RESORT

FOUNDATION
MICHOUTOUCHKINE
PILIOKO ★

Pango

LE LAGON
VANUATU
RESORT

ERAKOR
ISLAND
RESORT

Erakor

Pango
Point

Emis
Point

Etmat
Point

0   1 mi
0   1 km

MOON

© DAVID STANLEY

Saturday. The small pavilion across the street from the market is the former House of Parliament with an attractive mural (1980) by students of the French *lycée*. Behind this is the **Constitution Building,** once the headquarters of the Condominium bureaucracy and still government offices.

A free ferry shuttles frequently from near the BP Wharf to **Iririki Island,** site of one of Port Vila's top tourist resorts. The view from the resort's pool deck is unsurpassed. There's a footpath right around the island beginning up the hillside behind the watersports hut, and good snorkeling at Snorkeler's Cove on the opposite side of Iririki from town (bring reef shoes if you have them). Where else can you go snorkeling in the main harbor of a country's capital? Many lovely trees grow on Iririki, and it's definitely worth a visit (but children under 12 are not admitted).

South of Town

From both the Iririki and Ifira boats, you can see the large, red-roofed **Parliament building,** erected with Chinese aid in 1992, overlooking the harbor to the south. There's an interesting socialist-style monument of a family in front of the main entrance to Parliament (it's worth reading the plaque on the back of the statue, as it says a lot about local attitudes toward women).

Across the field opposite the monument is the **Vanuatu Cultural Center National Museum** (tel. 22129, fax 26590, vks@vanuatu.com.vu), which opened in 1995. This is one of the finest museums in the South Pacific, with a rich collection of archaeological and ethnographic artifacts, musical instruments, weapons, seashells, and flora and fauna specimens. Of particular interest are the ritual objects from Malekula, and the slit gongs and fern carvings of Ambrym, which you can study here at your leisure. It's not to be missed. The museum is also an excellent place to pick up quality T-shirts, posters, books, cassettes, compact discs, and video-cassettes. It's open weekdays 0900–1630, Saturday 0900–1200, admission Vt.500.

Across from the museum is the **Chief's National Nakamal,** a traditional-style building where custom marriages are celebrated and meetings held. An impressive totem-pole slit gong from Ambrym, bearing five faces, stands before the building.

The beauty spot of Port Vila is undoubtedly the Erakor Lagoon. Take any southbound bus to the Erakor Island landing next to Le Lagon Vanuatu Resort, then catch the free ferry (24-hour service) across to **Erakor Island,** a good place for an afternoon of lounging, sunbathing, swimming, and snorkeling on their white-sand beach. You're not allowed to bring your own food or drinks for a picnic, but lunch at the resort is reasonable (pizza, salads, and burgers priced Vt.750–900). Until a cyclone in 1959, Erakor village (now on the lagoon's east side) was on this island. Samoan teachers from the London Missionary Society arrived here as early as 1845, and after 1872, Presbyterian missionaries Rev. and Mrs. J.W. Mackenzie were based on Erakor. The tombstones of Mrs. Mackenzie, three of her chil-

WHY DRIVING IS ON THE RIGHT

While driving is on the left in many Pacific countries such as Australia, Fiji, New Zealand, and Solomon Islands, in Vanuatu it's on the right due to an unusual chain of events. Prior to 1919 there was occasional chaos as British residents drove their carts on the left-hand side of the road while French residents drove on the right. To resolve the problem, the British and French resident commissioners promulgated a decree stipulating that the origin of the next vehicle imported into the colony would decide which side everyone would henceforth be required to drive on. Shortly thereafter a buggy ordered by a Catholic priest arrived from Nouméa and the matter was resolved. The historic coach is now on display at the National Cultural Center Museum in Port Vila.

dren, and some early Polynesian missionaries can still be seen on the island.

When you return to the mainland, wait at the landing for a city minibus to arrive, then ask the driver to take you to the **Foundation Nicolai Michoutouchkine et Aloi Pilioko** (tel. 23053, fax 24224), just under two km southwest of here. This trip should cost no more than Vt.100 pp. These well-known artists, whose work we saw in the city center earlier, have studios on the grounds, and the foundation's art gallery (daily 0900–1700, admission free) contains many tastefully arrayed South Pacific artifacts and works of art. The gardens crowded with fern figures and tamtams all the way down to the seawall have an incredible aura—don't miss this.

University Complex

The Emalus Campus of the **University of the South Pacific** (tel. 22748, fax 22633, www.van uatu.usp.ac.fj), east of downtown at the beginning of the Forari highway, was erected with New Zealand aid in 1989 to house the USP's Pacific Languages Unit and Law Department. The Pacific Languages Unit was established in 1984 to elevate the status of the Pacific vernaculars and protect them from foreign influence. In 1996, the Emalus Campus Library opened at the rear of a central courtyard adorned with slit gongs from Ambrym and other artworks. Outstanding, inexpensive books on the Pacific written by the island people themselves are sold in the Bursary Office. If you're academically inclined, the campus is worth a visit, and any city minibus will bring you directly here for Vt.100.

North of Town

Take another bus (Vt.200) west past the Port Vila Golf and Country Club (where U.S. troops waded ashore on March 2, 1942) to **Mele** village, the largest village in Vanuatu. The big Presbyterian church reflects the British influence here. The tourist resort on nearby **Hideaway Island** is popular among scuba divers. A launch (Vt.500 round-trip) ferries tourists over to the island, but don't come on a cruise ship day, as it will be completely jammed. Other days, you can get in some good snorkeling here, with lots of well-

fed small fish on the reef and a few big ones at the drop-off (fishing isn't allowed). Bringing your own food and drink onto Hideaway Island is also prohibited.

The road around Efate turns inland to Mele Maat, just northwest of Mele, where people from Ambrym were resettled after a big eruption on their home island in 1950. The **Mele Cultural Center and Tropical Garden** (tel. 26222, admission Vt.600/300 adult/child) here features a nakamal, caged animals, a kava garden, and plants.

Just beyond Mele Maat there's a signposted **cascade** (admission Vt.1,000/250 adult/child, www.evergreen.com.vu), accessible from the bridge at the foot of Klehm Hill. Hike up the river to a waterfall that tumbles down from the plateau into this beautiful jungle green setting like a miniature Iguazu. Many lovely pools are near this upper falls.

SPORTS AND RECREATION

Port Vila is a favorite of serious scuba divers. Several efficient operators are based here, and places like Mele Reef, Cathedral Cavern, and Outboard Reef are only half an hour away from the hotels and restaurants of this cosmopolitan resort town. Right in the harbor itself is the wreck of the *Star of Russia,* a fully rigged clipper ship that sank near the main wharf in 1950. Nutrient-rich seawater constantly cleans and feeds the sealife, and the visibility is excellent. You'll see lava tubes, huge table corals, coral columns, clown fish, and feather starfish—the underwater photographer will go octopus here. Only sharks are rare.

Port Vila's most experienced scuba operator is **Nautilus Scuba** (tel. 22398, fax 25255, www .nautilus-scuba.com), next to the Waterfront Bar and Grill. They offer morning and afternoon scuba trips at Vt.5,000 without gear (reductions on four-, six-, and 10-dive packages available). Equipment rental is Vt.1,000. Snorkelers are welcome to go along for Vt.1,000 (plus Vt.500 for snorkeling gear, if required). This professional diving center offers complete PADI open-water certification courses for Vt.25,500 including all equipment. Scuba gear can be purchased here. Nautilus Scuba also arranges parasailing at Vt.6,000/10,000 single/double and does sport fishing charters.

The **Hideaway Island Dive Shop** (tel. 26660, fax 23867, www.hideaway.com.vu) charges Vt.3,800 for one dive, plus Vt.1,500 for equipment. PADI certification courses are Vt.26,000. Most of the dive sites at Hideaway are on the back side of the island, so travel time is minimal.

Tranquility Dive (tel. 25020), at the Coongoola Cruises office opposite Ma Barker's, books scuba diving at the Tranquility Island Dive Base on Moso Island in Havannah Harbor. A two-dive package with transfers, lunch, and gear is Vt.8,800.

Cutting Edge Adventures (tel. 22176, cutting@vanuatu.com.vu), at Chantilly's on the Bay, offers sea kayaking tours to the Eratap islands off southern Efate at Vt.7,400 pp. They also organize kayak tours lasting 2–10 days to the islands off northern Efate.

Game fishing charters are offered on several powerboats based at the Waterfront Bar and Grill or Nautilus Scuba (Vt.25,000/35,000 for three/four hours for two to four anglers). These operators know their waters, and the catches are impressive (retained by the captain).

Touvannah Sport Fishing (Gideon George, tel. 26226), based at Havannah Harbor, offers basic fishing from a five-meter fiberglass boat. Gideon charges Vt.14,000/17,000/22,500/28,000 for one/two/three/four persons, including transfers from Port Vila, refreshments, and lunch. You're allowed to keep your catch!

The **Club Hippique** (tel. 23347), seven km east of Port Vila, offers horseback riding at Vt.2,300/3,500 for one/two hours. The Adventure Center (tel. 22743) runs half-day riding tours at Vt.3,900 pp including transfers.

The 18-hole championship golf course at the **White Sands Country Club** (tel. 22090, fax 27221, whitesan@vanuatu.com.vu), 18 km east of Port Vila, is the venue of the Vanuatu Golf Open in July or August. Greens fees are Vt.1,500/3,000 for nine/18 holes. You can also rent a bungalow here at Vt.11,250. Call them up for information on their shuttle bus or ask the Port Vila tour operators about golfing tours.

The 18-hole **Port Vila Golf and Country Club** (tel. 22564) at Mele is Vt.2,000 greens fees, plus Vt.800 for clubs and a buggy. It's open daily. Both Le Méridien Resort and Le Lagon Vanuatu Resort have smaller golf courses for guests.

See soccer from the bleachers at the municipal stadium every Saturday afternoon. Cricket is played in Independence Park on Saturday.

ACCOMMODATIONS

US$25–50

The longtime favorite of backpackers and budget travelers is **Kalfabun Guest House and Bungalows** (tel./fax 24484, kalfabun@vanuatu.com.vu), on the main road into town, two km from the airport. Bob Kalfabun and family have two dormitory rooms with 10 bunks each at Vt.1,000 pp. The four individual bungalows are Vt.1,500/3,000 single/double. If you pay seven consecutive nights in advance, the eighth is free. Camping is Vt.500 pp, but they only allow it when all of the rooms are occupied. Facilities include a communal kitchen and fridge, TV lounge, and luggage storage room. Au Bon Marché Supermarket is just a five-minute walk away. Bob offers guests a tour around the island at Vt.2,000 pp, and a Melanesian feast, also Vt.2,000. For some strange reason, this place isn't included in the mass-market Australian guidebooks.

Also unknown to the Australian guidebook researchers is the three-story **Talimoru Hotel** (tel. 23740), on Cornwell St., Seaside, owned by controversial political player Barak Sope. The 42 fan-cooled rooms (18 singles and 24 doubles) are Vt.1,500 pp. The toilet and shower are down the hall. Aside from the restaurant and bar, there are poker machines off the lobby. Though the staff are friendly and helpful, the Talimoru is a bit rundown.

The two-room Church of Christ **Sarabetu Transit House** (tel. 22187), closer to the hospital, is Vt.1,500 per person, and communal cooking facilities are provided.

Whispering Coral Guest House (tel./fax 26515), next to the Trading Post office north of town, has two rooms at Vt.3,500/4,000 single/double without terrace, plus Vt.500 with terrace. The one family room is Vt.6,000–7,000. A good breakfast is included and they have a nice seaside garden.

Vila Hibiscus Motel (Marie Ng, tel. 28289, fax 26816, vilahibiscusmotel@vanuatu.com.vu), on the north side of town, opened in 2002. This well-arranged two-story motel has 21 clean rooms with fan, varying from a seven-person dorm at Vt.1,800 pp, twin rooms with cooking facilities at Vt.3,900/4,500 single/double to Vt.4,500/4,900 depending on the size of the room, and complete two-bedroom apartments at Vt.5,900/6,500/7,500 single/double/triple or Vt.2,000 pp to a maximum of six. Ten simpler rooms with shared bath and cooking facilities are Vt.2,500/3,000 single/double.

The recently-renovated **Shefa Guest House** (tel. 22752, www.shefaprovince.vu), on the plateau within walking distance north of town, has seven rooms at Vt.2,000 pp for the room. Shared cooking facilities are provided. During business hours, go to the provincial office within the same compound; otherwise ask at the guesthouse itself. It's mostly locals who stay here.

The **Holiday Motel** (tel. 23088, fax 22699, holidaymotel@vanuatu.com.vu), across the street from Le Méridien Resort, has 12 new self-catering apartments in three blocks. The three studios are Vt.5,500, the six one-bedrooms Vt.6,500, and the three two-bedrooms Vt.7,500. You can get a 10 percent discount if you pay by the week.

The **Ah Tong Motel** (tel. 23218, fax 22910), near the Talimoru Hotel, has 27 self-catering units which are officially Vt.6,000/7,000 single/double, though this is quickly reduced to Vt.4,500/5,000 if you agree to stay a few nights. The motel's Chinese restaurant (daily 0700–2200) serves meals in the Vt.460–580 range.

The **Golden Dragon Motel** (Mok Tsi Wei, tel. 23933, fax 27410, mokinternational@vanuatu.com.vu), in an L-shaped block on the hill just above Le Lagon Vanuatu Resort, has nine self-catering air-conditioned rooms for up to three persons at Vt.5,000 a night or Vt.25,000 a week. Each room has its own individual direct telephone number. It's a reasonable value, but they're often full.

In a garden setting opposite the Foundation Nicolai Michoutouchkine et Aloi Pilioko on the road to Pango is **Tree Tops Lodge** (tel./fax 22944, swedcons@vanuatu.com.vu) with a 10-bed dorm at Vt.1,500 pp. The two rooms with shared bath in the dorm building are Vt.3,000 double. A large terrace and cooking facilities are shared. Breakfast is included in these prices and other meals can be ordered. On the cliff above the owner's house is a two-bedroom bungalow accommodating up to four persons at Vt.6,000 for the unit. Tree Tops is run by the Swedish consul, Karl Waldeback, who is a mine of information on Vanuatu. Karl's guests receive discounts on watersports at nearby resorts—ask Karl to fill you in. Adjacent to Tree Tops is a local nakamal under a huge banyan tree. It's the best option for low-budget backpackers on this side of town.

For long-term rentals of houses and apartments, check the notices in the windows at Au Bon Marché and Center Point, and the classified ads in *The Trading Post*. Also inquire at **Alliance Reality** (tel. 26600, fax 24683, www.property.vu) in Pilioko House. A furnished one-bedroom apartment could run Vt.75,000 a month.

US$50–100

The three-story **Coral Motel** (tel. 24755, fax 23569, coralmotel@vanuatu.com.vu) is at the head of Vila Bay on the main road between the airport and Port Vila. The 10 modern studios with cooking facilities and TV are Vt.5,900/6,800 downstairs/upstairs single or double, plus Vt.500 extra for a third person. Weekly rates are available, and bus service to town is good.

The three-story **Olympic Hotel** (tel. 22464, fax 22953, olympichotel@vanuatu.com.vu) is the only hotel in downtown Port Vila. The 11 air-conditioned rooms with fridge are Vt.6,500 single or double, while the four studios with cooking facilities are Vt.7,200 and the three apartments are Vt.11,250. The Olympic caters to businesspeople by providing direct-dial telephones, telex, and secretarial services.

At the top of the hill directly above Poppy's on the Lagoon behind Central Hospital is **Tradewinds Apartments** (tel. 27018, fax 28100, www.tradewinds.com.vu) with five self-catering units at Vt.9,500. There's a swimming pool.

The three-story **Kaiviti Village Motel** (tel. 24684, fax 24685, kaiviti@vanuatu.com.vu), next to the Melanesian Hotel, has nine two-bedroom apartments and 28 studio apartments at Vt.8,400 single or double, Vt.13,500 for four people, Vt.14,500 for five, Vt.15,500 for six. Only the downstairs units have air conditioning, but those upstairs have ceiling fans and balconies, and all have kitchens. This easygoing motel also features a swimming pool, bar, Internet access (Vt.45 a minute), and laundry facilities, and Au Bon Marché Supermarket is conveniently nearby.

Pacific Lagoon Apartments (tel. 23860, fax 24377, www.pacificlagoon.com) faces the Erakor Lagoon, a few hundred meters southwest of Le Lagon Vanuatu Resort toward Pango. The 10 two-bedroom units with fan and a fully equipped kitchen vary in price from Vt.9,800–13,800 for up to four persons, depending on the location of the apartment.

Worawia Holiday Haven (tel. 25498, fax 25499, www.resort-vanuatu.com), next to the Port Vila Golf Club at Mele, is partly owned by Saipir and Alice Solomon, who organize Solo's Feast here on Thursdays. The three neat bungalows facing the swimming pool are Vt.9,000 double, while one larger family unit is Vt.12,000 (two adults and two children). A dormitory bungalow has four four-bunk rooms at Vt.3,300 pp, breakfast included. All units are decorated in the local style and are equipped with cooking facilities. Free airport transfers are provided.

Hideaway Island Resort (tel. 22963, fax 23867, www.hideaway.com.vu), on Mele Island, nine km northwest of Port Vila, is promoted as a scuba camp for packaged-tour Australian divers. The 15 ocean view bungalows are priced Vt.9,000/12,500 single/double standard or Vt.10,500/16,250 one-bedroom, tax included. The six double rooms with shared bath in a two-story building near the dive shop on the beach are Vt.6,800, while a dormitory with six four-bunk rooms behind the restaurant is Vt.2,280 pp (males and females stay in separate rooms). Hot water is available in the common shower block. The five bungalows are nicely secluded at the

far end of the island, but a bit too close to the generator. Cooking facilities are not provided in any of the accommodations, so you must use their efficient restaurant. This tiny coral island can get crowded on weekends, and on cruise ship days it's literally flooded with day-trippers.

US$100–150

Le Méridien Resort (tel. 22040, fax 23340, www.lemeridien-portvila.com), at the north end of the Erakor Lagoon, is a former Intercontinental Hotel originally built in the 1960s. The waters here aren't as clear as those at Le Lagon Vanuatu Resort, and Iririki Island is more convenient to town, but backed by rainforest, surrounded by gardens, and facing a bright, sandy beach, Le Méridien is still a pleasant place to stay. The 155 air-conditioned rooms (most with balcony) begin at Vt.16,000 single or double, plus 12.5 percent tax; the 10 lagoon bungalows on an island accessible from the main resort by suspension bridge are Vt.50,000. Don't accept one of the noisy rooms facing the taxi rank at the back of the building. Most guests are on cheap package tours from Australia and pay prices much lower than these. A gambling casino is at this hotel, and there's a nine-hole golf course. Nonmotorized sporting activities such as windsurfing, snorkeling, catamaran boating, row boating, outrigger canoeing, golf, and tennis are free to guests, but nautical gear must stay within sight of the hotel.

The **Mangoes Resort** (tel. 24923, fax 24037, www.mangoes.com.vu) opened in 2001 on a ridge behind Central Hospital. It's far from the beach but has two swimming pools. The 20 bungalows start at Vt.15,000 including tax (children and youths under 18 are not accommodated here). Businesspeople are the target market— the "adults-only" angle is designed to appeal to couples interested in a quiet holiday, not swingers.

Poppy's on the Lagoon (tel./fax 23425, www.poppys.com.vu), on the Erakor Lagoon down a steep road behind Central Hospital, caters to families with small children as well as couples. The 14 units range from a garden view bungalow at Vt.14,000 double, beachfront Vt.15,500, and a three-bedroom beachfront house accommodating six at Vt.31,500. All units are fan cooled (no air conditioning) and have full cooking facilities, creating a homey environment. Poppy's has two swimming pools

The three-story **Melanesian Hotel** (tel. 22150, fax 22678, melanesian@vanuatu.com.vu) combines a resort atmosphere (swimming pool) with businesslike convenience to Port Vila. The 20 studios are Vt.13,700 single or double, while the 11 one-bedroom suites are Vt.19,100 single or double. There are also two two-bedroom apartments with washing machines at Vt.20,500. All of the older fan-cooled rooms in the two-story blocks have kitchens, but the 54 air-conditioned "orchid suites" in the new three-story blocks (Vt.16,000 single or double) lack cooking facilities. All units have fridge, fan, and private bath. The rates include a continental breakfast. Gino's Pizza is hidden away below the Club 21 Gaming Lounge here. Nearby entertainment options make it worth considering by those used to a fast lifestyle.

Another new addition to the Port Vila accommodations scene is **Breaka's Resort** (tel. 23670, fax 24710, www.breakas.com), on a white sea beach at Pango village, three km west of Le Lagon Vanuatu Resort. The 10 bungalows are Vt.16,000–20,000 single or double (children under 15 not admitted). A spectacular swimming pool faces right onto the beach. Breaka's is a good bet if you enjoy swimming or surfing in the open ocean.

The **Pango Paradise Cove Resort** (tel. 22701, fax 22693, pangoresort@vanuatu.com.vu) toward Pango Point, seven km west of Le Lagon Vanuatu Resort turnoff, has 10 self-catering bungalows at Vt.14,175 for a one-bedroom (two people) or Vt.16,200 for a two-bedroom (up to five people). Continental breakfast and airport transfers are included. There's a seawater swimming pool (no chlorine or chemicals), mountain bike rentals (Vt.1,000 a day), Italian restaurant (delicious homemade pasta), and bar. Challenge the staff to a game of beach volleyball.

On the opposite side of town, the **Benjor Beach Club** (tel. 26078, www.benjor.vu), 2.5 km along the Devil's Point road from Mele, has four one-bedroom units at Vt.15,000 and two four- or five-bedroom villas with cooking facilities at Vt.36,500, continental breakfast included. Re-

duced weekly rates are available. The large Officer's Club Restaurant is on the premises. Benjor has three beaches on their 600 meters of waterfront, and small do-it-yourself groups may like it here. The city minibuses will drop you here for Vt.300.

US$150–250

Chantilly's on the Bay (tel. 27079, fax 28111, chantillys@vanuatu.com.vu) is a new three-story boutique hotel on Lini Highway just north of town. It's rather overpriced with 12 self-catering studios at Vt.21,500 single or double, six one-bedrooms at Vt.25,700, and two one-bedrooms with large decks at Vt.28,000. There's no beach but the seaside swimming pool and Tilly's Restaurant are nice.

The seven-story **Grand Casino Hotel** (www .theoaksgroup.com.au), next to the Iririki Island wharf opposite the Ballande Center, has 74 rooms with private balconies overlooking the bay. Built in 2004 by local investor Pierre Brunet, this highrise edifice is rather jarring in the center of Port Vila. There's a large casino on the ground floor and a VIP private casino on the top floor. The Grand Casino is run by Oaks Resort and Hotel Management of Sydney, Australia, and specific room rates were unavailable at press time.

Iririki Island Resort (tel. 23388, fax 23880, www.iririki.com), on an island in Vila Bay directly opposite downtown Port Vila, opened in 1986. The 70 air-conditioned bungalows are priced according to whether they face the garden (Vt.22,800 single or double), or are right down on the water (Vt.35,700). Rooms facing the harbor from above are Vt.29,100. Each has one queen-size and one single bed, fridge, video, and furnished balcony. Children under 12 are not accommodated at this adults-only resort aimed at the "romantic couples" market. Included in the complex is an open-plan restaurant with an elevated terrace overlooking the pool, which offers great views of the harbor. There's a one-for-one paperback exchange in the lobby. Nonmotorized water sports (catamarans, windsurfers, kayaks) are free, but the beach isn't as good as those on the Erakor Lagoon. The snorkeling, on the other hand, is much better. A convenient free ferry to town operates round-the-clock.

VANUATU

Le Lagon Vanuatu Resort (tel. 22313, fax 23817, lagonres@vanuatu.com.vu) is near the mouth of the Erakor Lagoon, three km from Port Vila. Formerly known as the Crowne Plaza Vanuatu Resort, it was purchased outright by the Hong Kong-based Warwick International hotel chain in 2003. Aside from 116 air-conditioned hotel rooms (from Vt.18,972 single or double, plus tax) in seven two-story buildings, Le Lagon has 28 bungalows (from Vt.27,498). All rooms are fridge-equipped, and a few have a whirlpool tub (ask). As usual, a lagoon view costs more than a garden view. Le Lagon has a swimming pool, tennis courts, a 12-hole golf course, and nautical activities. Rebuilt in concrete after a hurricane in 1987, Le Lagon lacks some of the character of its competitors.

Erakor Island Resort (tel./fax 26983, erakor@vanuatu.com.vu) has a better beach than Le Lagon Vanuatu Resort just across the water. The resort was completely refurbished in 2002 with a new restaurant and reception area. The 18 well-appointed, fan-cooled bungalows on a long sandy lagoon island start at Vt.24,000 single or double, while the four two-story family bungalows accommodating up to five are Vt.29,120. For the young and sporty types, there's a dorm called "Starfish Lodge" with eight four-bunk rooms at Vt.2,800 pp (often used by dive groups). No cooking facilities are provided, so you must eat at their restaurant. Happy hour at the bar is 1700–1900 and there's live music on Sunday afternoons. The bungalows are well away from the public beach in front of the restaurant, so resort guests aren't bothered by day-trippers. Get Wet Watersports (Dave Cooke, tel. 24970, getwet@vanuatu .com.vu) at the Erakor Island arranges scuba diving, sport fishing, and other nautical activities. Snorkeling tours are daily at 1500. Access to Port Vila is quick and easy via their free ferry and public buses.

FOOD

Tax-Free Places to Eat

The 12.5 percent value-added tax only applies to licensed restaurants serving alcoholic beverages;

the alcohol-free establishments which follow are gastronomical tax havens. Cheapest are the picnic table lunches served by local women in the waterfront park next to Chantilly's on the Bay. They're only there weekdays from 0800–1300, charging Vt.250 a plate.

Best avoided is **Olympic Takeaway** (tel. 27355), between Goodies and the Olympic Hotel, with cheap hamburgers, fish and chips, and other second-rate fast food. On cruise ship days it's packed with passengers in search of the familiar.

In contrast, the **Lapita Café** (tel. 26516; weekdays 0830–1700, Sat. 0830–1500), opposite Goodies, serves real island foods like fish in coconut milk, root vegetables, and casseroles, plus a number of vegetarian choices. You can see what you'll be getting in the warmer on the counter. Most dishes are Vt.450–750.

The locals eat at **Natapoa Takeaway and Snack** (tel. 26377; Mon.–Sat. 0600–2000) on rue de Paris opposite Hua Store in Chinatown, inland a block from Goodies. A heaping plate of curry chicken and rice is Vt.300, with free cold water to wash it down. Most of the dishes are based on chicken or beef, but a surprising variety of vegetables comes with the meals. Coffee and croissants are available for breakfast. It's a good value, and the mural on the wall is great.

The **Chill Out Cafe,** at the back of the Center Point parking lot, has doner kebab for Vt.600.

Jill's Cafe (tel. 25125; weekdays 0700–1800, Sat. 0700–1330), opposite Lolam House, serves American-style country breakfasts (Vt.500–750 without coffee), Tex-Mex dishes (Vt.600–800), burgers, hot dogs, sandwiches, chili, and ice cream.

A more local place is **Cheng Chinese Snack** (tel. 24374; Mon.–Sat. 0730–2030), back behind the Naviti Internet Café opposite the market. They serve a good meat and rice lunch for under Vt.400.

The **Sea View Takeaway** (tel. 27207; daily 0900–2200), beside Au Bon Marché on the south side of the market, has cheap sandwiches, hamburgers, pizza, chicken, fish and chips, and ice cream. The food isn't very good, but you get to eat it at tables right by the water. A more upscale restaurant is upstairs.

Licensed Restaurants

The classy **Rossi Restaurant** (tel. 22528, www
.therossi.com) in the center of town has a garden
terrace overlooking the harbor, great for a leisurely
lunch. If you come for dinner, don't arrive too late
and miss the sunset. It's also a fine place to stop
for a morning or afternoon coffee, and a selection
of newspapers is available for free reading. The
cakes and pies are impressive.

El Gecko Restaurant (tel. 25597; Mon.–
Thurs. 0630–1830, Fri. 0630–2200, Sat. and
Sun. 0630–1430), in the courtyard between the
Olympic Hotel and Goodies, is a quiet, friendly
oasis in the heart of town. The imaginative menu
features main dishes in the Vt.1,440–1,550 range
(the lunchtime express menu provides two/three
courses for Vt.1,100/1,300). Continental breakfast is Vt.650. El Gecko is perhaps the nicest
place in town for an afternoon coffee break.

Ma Barker's (tel. 22399) in the center of town
is perhaps okay if you're dying for an oversized
Aussie-style steak. The adjacent Mamu Bar serves
a counter lunch including a beer for only Vt.800.
Whenever a cruise ship is in port, you'll find the
Mamu Bar packed with semi-drunken passengers
dancing on the bar, shooting water guns at one
another, etc.

The **Harborside Restaurant** (tel. 26155;
Mon.–Sat. 0630–1400/1630–2200), across the
street from the seven-story Grand Casino Hotel,
specializes in French cuisine using fresh ingredients. A bargain is their three-course "early bird
special" offered from 1800–1900 at Vt.1,500.

Le Café du Village (tel. 27789; daily 0800
until late), a bit south of the Grand Casino, has a
smart harborfront location opposite Iririki Island. Their menu features upscale Mediterranean-
style seafood, and keg beer is on tap.

The thatched **Waterfront Bar and Grill** (tel.
23490, www.waterfront.vu; daily 1100 until
late), by the bay south of the center, offers better
steaks than Ma Barker's (local organic beef),
plus Mexican food. They serve some of the freshest fish in town, delivered daily by the fishing
boats you see tied up to their wharf (about
Vt.1,600 a main). Check out the salad bar, and
don't forget the coconut pie. The bar here is a
yachtie hangout.

L'Houstalet (tel. 22303; daily 1100–1300
and 1800–2230), just past Au Bon Marché Supermarket and on the opposite side of the road,
offers 16 varieties of crisp oven-baked pizza
(which are also available takeaway) and five kinds
of spaghetti, priced mostly Vt.790–890. The
mindset of the French owner (and some of his
customers) is indicated by the list of endangered
species on L'Houstalet's regular menu.

For something special, consider French-operated **Vila Chaumières** (tel. 22866; Mon.–Sat.
1130–1400 and 1800–2300), east of town,
which serves a variety of seafood on a terrace
overlooking the lagoon. At lunchtime the city
buses will drop you here, but for dinner you'll
probably have to call a taxi to get home (unless
you have a car). Honeymooners often come here
for a romantic dinner.

Several of the large hotels have Sunday specials. The poolside barbecue buffet at **Iririki Island Resort** (tel. 23388), Sunday from 1200–
1400, is good value at Vt.1,500. Sunday brunch
(1130–1400) at La Verandah Restaurant at **Le
Méridien Resort** (tel. 22040) includes wine for
Vt.2,500, plus tax. The **Rossi Restaurant** (tel.
22528) in town offers a Sunday roast (Vt.1,450)
from 1800 (bookings required).

Groceries

Port Vila's picturesque **market** operates Monday
to Saturday (including all night on Friday in an-
ticipation of the big Saturday market). In addition
to fresh fruit and vegetables, a few handicrafts
are sold. No one will hassle you to buy anything,
so look around as you please, just don't bargain—
the prices are low enough to begin with.

For other groceries try the large supermarkets,
Center Point and Au Bon Marché. **Center Point**
(tel. 22631; daily 0600–1930) is especially well
stocked, and has a good grocery section with
fresh croissants and *pain au chocolat*. Tasty ice
cream is dispensed from a cart in front of Center
Point. **Au Bon Marché** has several locations
around Port Vila, including one beside the market downtown, another at Nambatu near the
road to the main wharf, and a third on the road
to Tagabe. The stores in Chinatown sometimes
have cheaper canned goods.

Ah Pow Bakery (tel. 22215), on Dauphine St. just behind L'Houstalet Restaurant near Au Bon Marché, sells croissants and other pastries (this bakery delivers bread all around Efate every night, leaving at 0100 and returning at 0900). French baguettes are a great buy at Vt.45.

Be aware that the supermarkets are not allowed to sell beer or alcohol after 1130 on Saturday and all day Sunday.

ENTERTAINMENT

Cine Hickson (tel. 22431) shows Hollywood films dubbed into French on a large screen nightly except Thursday at 2000 (admission Vt.400).

Cinema Studio 7 (tel. 22615), at Club Vanuatu, screens videos in English throughout the day (admission Vt.100).

The **Palms Casino** (tel. 24308, fax 22394) at Le Méridien Resort features blackjack, baccarat, roulette, and slots. It's open daily from 1130 until the last customer leaves (admission free). Unfortunately, many Ni-Vanuatu are addicted to the gambling machines, both here and at Club Vanuatu and the Talimoru and Melanesian Hotels, and entire weekly pay packets are often swallowed by the monsters, leading to real hardship for local families. Several important members of parliament are casino shareholders, which explains why this dirty business is allowed to continue.

Bars

The **Port Vila Pub** (tel. 27716; daily 1100 to late), on Lini Highway just north of town, is an unpretentious English-style pub with pool tables. The food menu at the adjacent Flaming Bull Steakhouse is medium-priced.

The **Anchor Inn** (tel. 22582; daily 1100–2200), on Lini Highway a bit closer to the center, home of the Vanuatu Cruising Yacht Club, has a pleasant seaside terrace bar—a great place to have a beer at the best prices in town. Friday is a big night here.

Smuggler's Nite Club & Sports Bar (tel. 25708; Mon.–Sat. 1900–0300), on rue de Paris in Chinatown, plays a variety of new music. It's friendly.

Club Vanuatu (tel. 22615; Mon.–Wed. 1000–midnight, Thurs.–Sat. 1000–0300, Sun. 1000–2300), next to the Unelco electric generating plant on the back street behind the post office, is a private club, but tourists are welcome. The bistro facing the bar downstairs serves reasonably priced hot meals (Vt.350) at lunchtime, while the more upscale Bamboo Royal Restaurant on the top floor has pizza priced Vt.700–1,650. The club's other facilities include a movie room, billiards, bingo, slot machines, and bars with Tusker on tap. Watch television on a huge screen. Reynolds Herena's hot local reggae band Vatdoro often plays at the Club's Friday and Saturday night dances (Vt.400 cover).

Happy hour is from 1700–1900 in the **Sunset Bar** (tel. 22150) at Club 21 Gaming Lounge, next to Cine Hickson.

Club Imperial (no phone), next to the Suzuki dealership up toward the university, is more of a local place, and on Friday and Saturday nights it really gets lively.

Kava Nakamals

Around a hundred *nakamals* or kava bars in Port Vila serve that strong Vanuatu kava at Vt.50–100 a shell. Your best choice for a first experience is **Ronnie's Nakamal** (daily 1700–2200), a few blocks back from the Melanesian Hotel, where the expatriate community congregates for happy hour around sunset. Ronnie Watson works for a telecommunications company during the day, and he and Ruby Watson (a former journalist) do their best to keep the atmosphere amenable and the quality of the kava consistent. The **Shefa Bay-view Nakamal** on the cliff face just below the Shefa Guest House is great for sunset viewing. A more local place to try kava is the **Red Laet** (tel. 27048; closed Sun.), near the Talimoru Hotel, or one of four other *nakamals* on the same street. Also good are the **Rainbow Nakamal** (Jamali Nunue) near Mangoes Resort and the one under the huge banyan next to Tree Tops Lodge.

Most of these have a regular clientele from a particular outer island, and they function as social clubs. You'll be welcome if you enter with respect, keep your voice down, and don't make any abrupt movements (you might disturb someone "listening" to the kava). In the villages, local women aren't allowed to frequent the *nakamals,* but in Port Vila it's usually no problem (and definitely no problem at Ronnie's). Kava drinkers are generally pretty mellow, but the local places are predominantly male enclaves. Chances are there will be a kava bar near your hotel, so ask.

Cultural Shows for Visitors

If you're at all interested in live theater, you won't want to miss a performance by the **Wan Smolbag Theater** (www.wan-smolbag-theatre.org), a local troupe that brings contemporary social issues to the stage with unexpected professionalism and talent. Founded in 1989 by an English couple, Peter Walker and Jo Dorras, Wan Smolbag's success has sparked an interest in didactic theater throughout the Pacific. It's a mix of historical skits, storytelling, custom dancing, kava sampling, etc. You're freely allowed to take photos of the performances, and during the intermission, *lap lap* is sometimes served in the foyer for a nominal fee. The kava after the show is on the house. At last report performances were Tuesday or Thursday at 1900 in Wan Smolbag Haos, around the corner from Vanuatu Brewing at Tagabe, 50 meters up the road to Mele. Watch for posters around town, ask at the tourist office, or call 27119. Tickets (Vt.500 pp) are sold at the door. Even if nothing is scheduled, Wan Smolbag Haos is still worth visiting to buy videos and cassettes of the performances. (If you're very lucky, you may encounter Wan Smolbag in some remote village staging a performance in Bislama with a theme such as "building your own toilet," "family planning," or "violence against women," courtesy of some overseas aid donor.)

Foot-stompin' **custom dancing** accompanies the weekly barbecues and feasts at the major hotels, usually on Tuesday at Iririki Island Resort (tel. 23388), from 1830 on Thursday at Le Méridien Resort (tel. 22040; Vt.3,200 for the buffet), and on Wednesday and Sunday at Le Lagon Vanuatu Resort (tel. 22313). The Melanesian Hotel (tel. 22150) presents custom dancing and kava tasting by the swimming pool Wednesday, Friday, and Sunday at 1800. Erakor Island (tel. 26983) stages Tahitian dancing Thursday evening. If you're not that hungry, a drink at the bar should get you in to any of these. Call ahead to verify the show times.

Village feasts are held at Mele, Pango, and Erakor villages several nights a week with string band music, custom dancing, kava drinking, and island food served buffet style. Admission including transportation is usually Vt.3,000. **Solo's Feast** at Mele village is every Thursday night 1900–2200. The Adventure Center (tel. 22743) takes bookings for a Friday night feast at the Mele Cultural Center and Tropical Gardens (Vt.3,000). Unlike the tourist shows at the resorts, attending one of these is sort of like being invited to a private village party.

SHOPPING

You can buy one of those colorful Mother Hubbard dresses at the Chinese stores on the street running inland from Ma Barker's. The **Hebrida Market Place,** across the parking lot from Center Point Supermarket, also has authentic Mother Hubbards. These dresses are highly recommended for women thinking of visiting remote areas, and they make great party attire at home.

In quite another category are the designer clothes available at many smart boutiques around Port Vila; just beware of fake products bearing counterfeit brand names. Better yet, stick to the autographed apparel available at **Michoutouchkine Creations** (tel. 27753), in Pilioko House, previously mentioned.

Vila Duty Free Gifts (tel. 23443) opposite the post office sells cheap postcards, film, T-shirts, and souvenirs. The **Philatelic Bureau** (tel. 22000), inside the post office, has some very colorful stamps.

Avoid buying anything on a cruise ship day, as some prices are jacked up 15 percent. This practice is intended to compensate for the hard bargaining tactics employed by ship's passengers rather than a desire to rip anyone off.

Handicrafts

A good place to pick up authentic crafts is the **Handikraf Blong Vanuatu** shop (tel. 23228), a nonprofit outlet just south of the market. They sell stone- and woodcarvings, fern figures, slit gongs both large and small, bowls, war clubs, pig killing clubs, spears, bows and arrows, fish traps, model canoes, canoe prows, masks, rattles, panpipes, combs, shell necklaces, grass skirts, shoulder bags, mats, native pottery, and curved boar tusks. The finest articles come from Ambrym. Also watch for the Pentecost money mats with batik designs.

Goodies Treasure Chest (tel. 23445), near the Olympic Hotel, has a representative selection of handicrafts, including items from the other Melanesian countries.

L'Atelier Art Gallery (tel. 23654), across the street from the Westpac Bank, has some very authentic-looking Malekula helmet masks for sale to serious collectors.

Before buying wooden artifacts, check them for cleanliness and freedom from borer pests.

INFORMATION

The friendly National Tourism Office (tel. 22813, fax 23889; weekdays 0730–1130 and 1330–1630, Sat. 0800–1100), in Pilioko House on the main street, supplies useful maps and information sheets. Ask for free copies of *Destination Vanuatu*, the Jasons map of Vanuatu, and *Vanuatu What's On*.

The Statistics Office (tel. 22110, fax 24583), in the Government Building opposite the market, sells informative reports on the economy. Ask for a copy of their free publication *Vanuatu Facts and Figures*.

The Lands Survey Department (tel. 22427, fax 25973; weekdays 0900–1100 and 1400–1600), downstairs in the Georges Pompidou Building, sells excellent topographical maps of all the islands of Vanuatu at Vt.1,000 each. The black-and-white maps were published in 1979 and don't show more recent roads, although new colored sheets exist for many islands. A few marine navigational charts are also sold here (Vt.4,200).

The Port Vila Public Library (tel. 22721; weekdays 0900–1800, Sat. 0800–1130), in the center of town, issues cards at Vt.500, plus a refundable Vt.1,000 deposit. You're allowed to take out three books at a time. The large iron anchor embedded in cement in front of the library was recovered in 1958 from the *Astrolabe,* one of the ships of French explorer La Pérouse, lost at Vanikolo in the Solomons in 1788. The library building itself was Vanuatu's first parliament.

The Alliance Française (tel. 22947, fax 26700, alliafra@vanuatu.com.vu; Mon. 1200–1745, Tues.–Fri. 0900–1745, Sat. 0900–1200), just behind the French Embassy but in the same compound, has a library with the latest French newspapers and magazines. The Alliance offers French language courses with two two-hour classes a week, and organizes interesting activities, such as video nights (Thursdays at 1930), concerts, exhibitions, and dancing classes.

Bookstores

Port Vila has several good bookstores. Stop Press (tel. 22232, fax 26776), opposite the French Embassy, carries some books on the Pacific. Le Kiosque (tel. 22044), on Bougainville St., sells a handy French-Bislama phrasebook called *Apprenons le Bichlamar* (Vt.435). Snoopy's Stationery (tel. 22328, fax 24604), opposite Goodies, is also worth checking.

Airline Offices

Air Vanuatu (tel. 23848), behind Center Point, also represents Qantas and Solomon Airlines. Aircalin (tel. 22019) is opposite Hotel Olympic.

South Pacific Travel (tel. 22836), in Anchor House just before the Waterfront Bar & Grill, south of the center, represents Air Pacific and Air Niugini. Surata Tamaso Travel (tel. 22666), in La Casa d'Andrea e Luciano on the north side of town, represents Air New Zealand, British Airways, and Cathay Pacific.

SERVICES

Money

The Westpac Bank opposite the post office changes traveler's checks without commission. The adjacent ANZ Bank charges a fee of Vt.500 per transaction. The National Bank next to Air Vanuatu also charges no fees. The ANZ and Westpac banks have ATMs outside. All banks close at 1500 weekdays and exchange rates vary slightly—check around.

Goodies (tel. 23445; weekdays 0800–1730, Sat. 0800–1600, Sun. 0830–1200), near the Olympic Hotel, gives rates almost as good as the banks with fewer delays.

Post and Telecommunications

The post office opens weekdays 0730–1630, Saturday 0730–1130. Poste restante mail is held three months. The mail moves slowly out of Vanuatu and parcel postage is very expensive. It's much cheaper to wait and mail your things from Fiji or Solomon Islands, if you're headed that way. Their beautiful aerogram costs Vt.80.

Place long-distance telephone calls and send faxes at Telecom Vanuatu (tel. 22005; weekdays 0800–1200/1330–1600), adjacent to the main post office. At Vt.300 per page, you can receive faxes addressed to the public fax 678/24681 at this office. Long distance calls can be made from any of the card telephones around town.

Internet access at the post office is Vt.25 a minute. The Naviti Internet Café (tel./fax 26525, naviti@vanuatu.com.vu; weekdays 0800–1800, Sat. 0800–1200), in the Prouds building facing the market, provides access for the same price.

Immigration Office

The Immigration office (tel. 22354, fax 25492; weekdays 0730–1130 and 1330–1630), above the French Pharmacy in central Port Vila, gives free visa extensions (return air ticket required).

Consulates

The French Embassy (tel. 22353) is on Lini Highway in the center of town. The New Zealand High Commission (tel. 22933) is in BDO House, across the street from the French Embassy. If you need a P.N.G. visa, call the honorary consul of Papua New Guinea (tel. 22930).

The European Union office (tel. 22501) is in PKF House at the north end of town. The Chinese Embassy (tel. 23598) is south of town, up the street from Au Bon Marché Supermarket. Other countries with diplomatic missions in Port Vila include Australia (tel. 22777), Britain (tel. 23100), Italy (tel. 22243), and Sweden

(tel. 22944). Canada is represented by Australia, but the United States has no representation in Vanuatu.

Laundrettes and Public Toilets

Pacific Wash and Dry (tel. 26416; Mon.–Fri. 0730–1800, Sat. 0730–1230), in the Ballande Center near BP Wharf, is a genuine coin-operated launderette costing Vt.400 to wash or dry.

EZY Wash (tel. 24386; Mon.–Fri. 0730–1800, Sat. 0730–1400, Sun. 0900–1300), below the Olympic Hotel, is another self-service launderette charging identical rates.

Public toilets are at the water end of the market. They're Vt.40 per use. Another Vt.40 public toilet is toward the Port Vila Pub, on the north side of town. Free toilets (for customers) are available at Sea View Takeaway on the waterfront near the market and at Club Vanuatu.

Yachting Facilities

Yachting World (tel. 23273, VHF channel 60, www.yachtingworld-vanuatu.com), next to the Waterfront Bar and Grill, charges visiting yachts Vt.1,600 a day for sea wall tie up with power and water, or Vt.1,000 a day for the 10 harbor moorings. When arriving, beware of the overhead power lines to Iririki Island, which sag to 17 meters at high tide.

The Vanuatu Cruising Yacht Club (tel. 24634), at the Anchor Inn Bar at the north end of town, offers a book swap, mail forwarding, local information, and cruising guides to Vanuatu. Visiting yachts that use the facilities are charged Vt.1,000 per yacht for annual membership. They may also know about yachts out of Port Vila (October is a good month to get on a yacht here as crew, since many boats will be leaving). The office is only staffed during the cruising season from May to October.

A 20-ton mobile crane is at the Star Wharf, the only haul-out facility here. Slipways are available at Luganville.

Health

The Vila Central Hospital (tel. 22100) accepts outpatient consultations weekdays 0700–1630 (Vt.3,000 for tourists). On weekends and holidays only emergency cases are accepted. You can fill prescriptions at the hospital dispensary.

It's faster and more efficient to see a private doctor, such as Dr. Jean-Luc Bador (tel. 22826) upstairs on the back side of The Drug Store (consultations Vt.4,000). Dr. Bador speaks good English and he's very helpful to travelers. His specialty is acupuncture. Two other well-qualified doctors share the office with Dr. Bador.

ProMedical Vanuatu (tel. 25566, fax 27125, VHF channel 16; www.promedical.com.vu) has a diving recompression chamber or hyperbaric unit at their Port Vila location on Freswota Road.

Dr. Hervé Collard (tel. 22306) has a well-equipped private dental surgery practice upstairs in the Oceania Building on rue de Paris.

The Drug Store (tel. 22789; weekdays 0730–1800, Sat. 0730–1200, Sun. 0830–1200), opposite the Westpac Bank, and Heathwise Pharmacy (tel. 25722), opposite Goodies, sell malaria pills without prescription. Mosquito nets can be purchased at most shops in Chinatown for Vt.500.

TRANSPORTATION
By Air
Vanair (tel. 22753) has southbound flights from Port Vila to Tanna (Vt.11,770) once or twice a day (via Dillon's Bay, Ipota, and Aniwa weekly). Twice a week the Tanna flights continue to Aneityum and Futuna. Northbound there are three or four flights a day to Espiritu Santo (Vt.13,450), five times a week via Norsup, and a few also via Lamap or Southwest Bay. Once a week the Port Vila-Espiritu Santo service goes via Lonorore, Sara, Longana, and Walaha. Other routes from Port Vila are to Craig Cove (Vt.9,070), Emae (Vt.5,020), Lamen Bay (Vt.7,720), Paama (Vt.8,390), Tongoa (Vt.6,700), Ulei (Vt.8,620), and Valesdir (Vt.6,700), once or twice a week. For more information on internal flights, see Transportation in the Vanuatu chapter introduction.

Ships to Other Countries
Surata Tamaso Travel (tel. 22666, tamasotours@vanuatu.com.vu), in La Casa d'Andrea e Luciano on the north side of town, represents the New Caledonian freighter MV *Havannah*

which sails to Santo (Vt.6,700) and Nouméa (Vt.14,400) once a month.

Local Shipping
Passenger-carrying cargo boats depart Port Vila for Luganville once or twice a week, with stops at Malekula, Epi, Paama, Ambrym, Pentecost, Maewo, and Ambae. The through trip takes two to four days, depending on ports of call, and the deck fare often includes very basic meals. Take along food, as the journey's length varies according to cargo and the weather. Cabins are usually not available.

The barges *Tina I* and *Brisk* operated by **Sealink Vanuatu** (tel. 36517, fax 36628) in Santo are supposed to depart Port Vila for Luganville every Thursday night. They don't have an office in Port Vila, so call the Santo number to confirm this. In Port Vila, they leave weekly from the Vanuatu Sea Transit coconut oil mill next to the Fisheries Wharf before the turnoff to the main wharf. You buy your ticket (Vt.7,000 deck, no cabins) at the landing when the ship arrives.

Dinh Shipping (tel. 25919), at the BP Wharf, operates the barge *Roena* from Port Vila to Malekula and Santo (Vt.6,500 including meals) about once a week. The newer and larger barge *Dinh I* also does this trip less frequently. The old freighter MV *Killian* operates to Tanna (Vt.5,000 deck including meals) three times a month.

If you don't connect with a boat from Port Vila to Santo and still want a taste of sea travel, consider flying to Espiritu Santo, then look for a ship back to Malekula, a journey of only half a day. Luganville—not Port Vila—is the shipping capital of Vanuatu. From there you might even find an interisland trading ship setting out on a two-week cruise to places few tourists ever see.

By Bus and Taxi
Although no regular public buses travel right around Efate, bus service is frequent within Port Vila itself. The minibuses are all privately owned by the drivers, and there aren't any set routes. You just flag down a bus headed in the right direction and tell the driver where you want to go. If it harmonizes with the previously requested destinations of the other passengers, he'll take you

VANUATU

© DAVID STANLEY

the barge *Dinh I* loading at Port Vila

anywhere in the town area between Pango village, Le Lagon Vanuatu Resort, Korman Stadium, and the airport for a flat fare of Vt.100, not always by the most direct route. To Mele Hideaway or the Mele Maat cascades is Vt.200. The public buses are mostly the smaller 11-seat minibuses; the bigger 22-seat (usually white) buses are for package tours. A bus with its four-way flashers on is out of service. Taxi drivers prevent the buses from picking up right at the airport door; so if you're there, walk down the road a short distance and flag down a bus. Service is frequent, and the last bus to Tagabe leaves at 2300.

Taxis have a red letter T in the license number, while public buses have a red letter B. Most taxis have meters that begin at Vt.100 for the first km, then Vt.10 for every 71 meters. At night (1830–0530), the Vt.100 only covers the first 76 meters, then it's Vt.10 per 71 meters again. Strangely, some meters are cheaper than others. It's always possible to ask the fare before setting out and get a fixed rate, without using the meter. From the airport it's Vt.1,000 to the center of town or Vt.1,500 to Le Lagon Vanuatu Resort. Considering how the local bus service operates, it should almost never be necessary to take a taxi.

You may be able to arrange a ride to North Efate in the back of a truck by asking the women at the market if they know of any vehicles headed that way. These usually leave after 1500 Monday to Saturday, and cost Vt.500 pp. One truck to Emua wharf leaves from in front of Hua Store on rue de Paris in Chinatown, inland a block from Goodies, Monday to Saturday at around 1330, returning the next morning at 0700.

Car Rentals

Foreign driver's licenses are accepted, but most of the companies won't rent to persons under 25 years of age. Most rentals come with unlimited kilometers, and there are discounts for rentals of more than two days. Add 12.5 percent tax to all charges. Gasoline is around Vt.100 a liter (about US$3 a U.S. gallon). On cruise ship days all vehicles will be taken, a good reason to find out when the next love boat is due in so you can beat the fun-loving masses to the booking office and be gone when they arrive.

Gasoline is hard to come by outside Port Vila, so fill up before you set out around the island. The only gas station on the north side of Efate is next to the store at Emua. Driving is on the right.

Speed limits are 40 kph in town, 60 kph elsewhere; in roundabouts, the vehicle entering from the right has the right of way. Cattle grids and speed bumps across the road are a real hazard for those driving around Efate and they must be crossed slowly. Check the spare tire as you take delivery of the car—you never know.

Discount Rentals (tel. 23242, fax 23898, discount-rentals@vanuatu.com.vu), toward the main wharf south of town, rents cars with 200 km free mileage from Vt.5,820 a day, plus Vt.1,400 insurance. If you rent for two days you get a free night at Beachcomber Lodge on the north coast. On three-day rentals the fourth day is free.

Budget Rent a Car (tel. 23170, fax 23132, budget@vanuatu.com.vu), opposite to Au Bon Marché Supermarket south of town, charges Vt.5,660 a day, but with unlimited kilometers (it's unlikely you'd do more than 200 km anyway). Insurance is Vt.1,500, and even with insurance, you're still responsible for the first Vt.120,000 in damage to the car (reduced to the first Vt.20,000 upon payment of Vt.700 a day "excess insurance"). Budget sometimes tries to unload old wrecks on unsuspecting tourists, so protest if they try to give you what appears to be Uncle Eddie's second car. If they tell you that's all there is left, insist on a discount.

Avis (tel. 22570, fax 24968, avis@vanuatu.com.vu) has an office at the airport, but it's well hidden in a building outside the international terminal (look around the corner to the left as you come out). Their rates are Vt.7,400 a day, plus Vt.1,400 insurance.

Hertz (tel. 25700, fax 25511), at the Suzuki dealership next to Club Imperial near the Emalus Campus, is the most expensive at Vt.7,400 and up, plus Vt.1,500 insurance.

Scooter Rentals

Scooters are for hire at **Nautilus Scuba** (tel. 22398) at Vt.2,600/4,100 for a half/full day. Any driving license will be accepted, and the mandatory helmets are provided.

Budget Rent a Car (tel. 23170, fax 23132) has scooters at Vt.2,800 for a 0900–1700 day or Vt.4,100 for 24 hours. The scooters are not supposed to be used to go around the island, as

they aren't very effective on rough roads or steep slopes.

Local Tours

Island Safaris (tel. 23288, fax 26779), in the back of the Govan Building opposite Ma Barker's Restaurant, is your best bet to organize a package tour to any of the islands beyond Efate and Santo. They book two-night packages to Ambrym, Epi, Erromango, Malekula, Tanna, and other islands starting around Vt.35,000 pp double occupancy, including airfare, transfers, accommodations, meals, and some sightseeing. While these tours provide income to rural villagers, they also make outer island travel and accommodations very expensive as independent travelers not on their tours are expected to pay the same overseas rates.

A growing number of tour operators offer sightseeing and activities packages around Vila and the pricing is competitive. The **Adventure Center** (tel. 22743, www.adventurevanuatu.com), near the post office, acts as a booking office for most sporting and sightseeing activities available around Port Vila, and what's available is described on a large board with prices. Their combined cascades/botanical garden tour is Vt.1,200 pp, plus Vt.1,600 in admissions. There's also a circle-island bus tour (Vt.5,000 including lunch) and the Ekasup Traditional village tour (Vt.3,800). The Adventure Center can book most outer island experiences, including volcano treks, custom villages and dances, and nature walks. Even yacht charters are possible.

Rainbow Adventure Tours (tel./fax 26117), opposite the Waterfront Restaurant, offers the same sort of tours. Ask here about discounted circle-island tours with a sandwich lunch (Vt.3,500) and cut-rate Melanesian feasts (Vt.2,700).

Adventures in Paradise (tel. 25200, www.adventuresinparadise.vu), opposite the French Embassy, offers a circle-island tour including lunch at Vt.4,900. They offer numerous other tours and activities.

Tamaso Aliat Wi Tours (tel. 25600, fax 24275), in La Casa d'Andrea e Luciano opposite Chantilly's on the Bay on Lini Highway, offers a quality circle-island tour in an air-conditioned car or land cruiser on Tuesday, Thursday, and

Saturday with stops at places the other tours often miss. It's Vt.5,500–7,500 pp including lunch, depending on the number of people who have booked.

Day Cruises

Snorkeling trips on the glass-bottom boat *Neptune II*, which ties up by the market on the Port Vila waterfront, are Vt.2,400 pp.

Several companies offer boat trips along the northwest side of Efate from Havannah Harbor. For example, the 13-meter trimaran *Golden Wing* of **Sailaway Cruises** (tel. 25155, fax 24452, sail away@vanuatu.com.vu) operates a day cruise (Vt.7,900) with snorkeling at Hat Island and Paul's Rock, plus a stop at a deserted beach for swimming. Scuba diving can be arranged. Skipper Peter Whitelaw tries to sail (rather than motor) as much as possible, and those prone to seasickness will be happy to know that the seven-meter-wide *Golden Wing* doesn't lean over when it's under sail. Peter's priorities are to take his guests to more remote snorkeling and diving areas, where the marine life is healthy and the water visibility is often more than 50 meters. Book through the Adventure Center near the post office.

The classic 23-meter sailing ketch *Coongoola* (tel. 25020, fax 22979, drewco@vanuatu.com.vu), built at Brisbane in 1949, is geared to scuba diving rather than sailing, and non-divers might end up spending most of their time on the beach at the Tranquility Island Dive Base on Moso Island. The Vt.7,400 pp price includes bus transfers from Port Vila, snorkeling gear, and a barbecue lunch. Scuba diving is available at Vt.1,400 extra, gear included. They operate daily except Monday and their office is opposite Ma Barker's. If you can spare the cash, either of the Havannah Harbor trips makes for a great day out, and is a perfect way to see the other side of the island at its best.

AROUND EFATE

The American servicemen who built the 132-km road around Efate during WW II dubbed it U.S. Route No. 1. Today the road is steep and rough from Mele Maat to Emua, then a bit flat-

ter and smoother from Emua back to Port Vila. In January 2001, an earthquake damaged several bridges along this road but it's still passable. There's no bus service beyond Port Vila and vicinity, but you could try hitching around the island (difficult), take a circle-island bus tour (Vt.3,500–5,000 depending on the lunch), or rent a car. If there are a few of you, consider chartering one of the Port Vila city buses for a full-day ride around the island at Vt.10,000. A taxi around the island will run Vt.12,000 for the car. Be aware that the far side of Efate is much less developed than the Port Vila side, so take enough to eat and drink, as shops are few and far between. You may be asked to pay custom fees to use village beaches.

The highway climbs steeply from Mele Maat to the top of **Klehm Hill**, which provides an excellent view. The road then crosses a plateau and descends to the beach at **Creek Ai**, 24 km from Port Vila. If you want to go across to Lelepa Island for a look around, ring the gong and they'll come to pick you up (Vt.1,000 pp round-trip). Near the landing on the main island is the Naguswai Mooring Base where tourist boats such as *Golden Wing* and *Coongoola* pick up day passengers for cruises around Havannah Harbor and beyond.

During WW II, the U.S. Navy had a field hospital and base for the repair of damaged ships at **Havannah Harbor**, and several vestiges from this period remain. Five hundred meters east of Tanaliu village is Ulei School, and next to the road just beyond, a freshwater reservoir that once supplied the 10,000 American troops stationed here with drinking water. At the next bridge east of the pool is an American half track under a huge banyan tree, also next to the road. Close by to the east is one of the oldest colonial buildings in Vanuatu, a remnant of the days before Port Vila became capital. The edifice served as an officers' club during the war, and in the bush behind is an overgrown American airstrip.

Another beach is at **Samoa Point**, four km farther along. From Tanaliu cemetery, a km west of Tanaliu village, a five-kilometer jeep track leads up to the radio repeater station on the 392-meter summit of **Mt. Erskine**. Farther up is **Mt.**

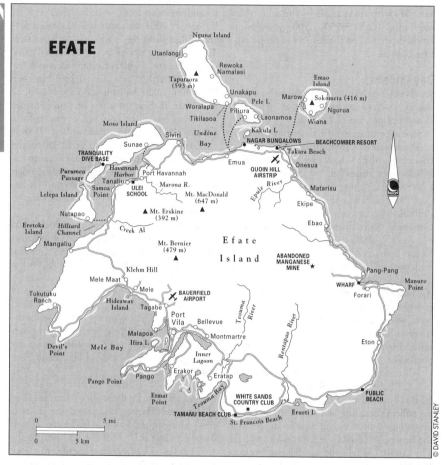

EFATE

Nguna Island

Utanlangi

Rewoka
Namalasi

Taputaora
(593 m)

Unakapu

Emao
Island

Marow

Sokometa (416 m)

Woralapa

Pele I.

Piliura

Ngurua

Moso Island

Tikilasoa

Laonamoa

Wiana

Siviri

Kakula I.

Undine

Sunae

Bay

NAGAR BUNGALOWS

BEACHCOMBER RESORT

TRANQUILITY
DIVE BASE

Emua

Takara Beach

Purumea
Passage

Havannah
Harbor

Port Havannah

QUOIN HILL
AIRSTRIP

Onesua

Tanaliu

Marona R.

Samoa
Point

ULEI
SCHOOL

Matarisu

Lelepa Island

Mt. MacDonald
(647 m)

Epule River

Natapao

Ekipe

Eretoka
Island

*Hilliard
Channel*

▲ Mt. Erskine
(392 m)

Ebao

Mangaliu

Creek Al

Mt. Bernier
(479 m)

E f a t e

I s l a n d

Klehm Hill

ABANDONED
MANGANESE
MINE

Pang-Pang

Mele Maat

Manuro
Point

Tukutuku
Ranch

Mele

BAUERFIELD
AIRPORT

WHARF

Forari

Hideaway
Island

Tagabe

Teouma River

Malapoa

Port
Vila

Bellevue

Ifira I.

Montmartre

Eton

*Devil's
Point*

Mele Bay

Rentapao River

Pango

Erakor

Eratap

Pango Point

Inner
Lagoon

*Etmat
Point*

Teouma Bay

WHITE SANDS
COUNTRY CLUB

PUBLIC
BEACH

TAMANU BEACH CLUB

Erueti I.

St. Francois Beach

Eton

0   5 mi

0   5 km

© DAVID STANLEY

Bernier (479 meters), from which you get a clear all-around view.

Villagers commute to the large islands of Nguna and Pele off northern Efate from the wartime wharf at **Emua** on the north coast of Efate, 44 km from Port Vila. Village outboards to Emao Island leave from **Takara Beach,** 10 km farther east. The U.S.-built Quoin Hill fighter airstrip near here is kept usable. A couple of small resorts in this area offer bungalow accommodations and restaurants (see below). Eric Tom's **Matanawora War Museum** (tel. 25600; admission Vt.500), a km east of Nagar Beach Bunga-

lows, has a collection of war relics including two planes, one in the mangroves and the other offshore in two meters of water.

The broad, gravel road down the east side of Efate passes white sandy beaches and green lagoons bordered by coconut and pandanus palms, yellow acacia bushes, and huge banyan trees. At **Forari,** 25 km south of Takara, are remains from a French **manganese mine** that operated from 1962 until 1978, when reduced deposits and falling prices forced its closure. The ruins of a large cantilever loader and metal warehouses can still be seen next to an old wharf beside the road.

The road opposite the Forari village access road leads four km east to **Manuro Point,** where an abandoned resort overlooks a fine white beach in very attractive surroundings. From Forari it's 50 km back to Port Vila.

Eton Beach, seven km south of Forari, is great for a swim and snorkel (Vt.300 admission pp), but beware of poorly marked speed bumps at Eton village just beyond Eton Beach. West of Eton are a few public beaches and cattle country, then just across the Rentabao River bridge, a turnoff on the left to the **White Sands Country Club,** Vanuatu's top golf course. When you reach the Erakor Lagoon, you're almost full circle back to Port Vila.

Accommodations Around Efate

Gideon George of **Touvanna Sport Fishing** (tel. 26226), two km north of Creek Ai, allows beach camping at Vt.1,000/1,500 with your own/his tent. He'll also shuttle you over to Lelepa Island for camping in a more isolated location at Vt.1,000 per group for the boat, plus Vt.1,500 to camp (own tent).

Tranquility Island Eco-Tourism Dive Base (tel. 27211 or 25020, fax 22979, www.south pacdivecruise.com.vu), on Moso Island in Havannah Harbor, has six thatched bungalows with bath at Vt.4,000 pp, a seven-bed dorm at Vt.2,500 pp, and camping space at Vt.1,200 pp. Meals are served at Vt.3,500 pp for all three. Transfers from Port Vila are Vt.500 pp each way. Scuba diving is Vt.2,700 per dive, or take an open-water certification course for Vt.26,000. Ask about the "mid-week special," which includes one nights accommodation, meals, and transportation from Port Vila at Vt.11,200 pp (or Vt.13,000 including two dives). Tranquility Island shares an office with Coongoola Cruises opposite Ma Barker's in Port Vila. It's an excellent alternative to touristy Hideaway Island if you're into scuba diving.

Nagar Beach Bungalows (tel. 23221, is.vil.adven@vanuatu.com.vu) is at Paonangisu on the north side of Efate, 50 km from Port Vila clockwise on a rough, steep road, or 82 km counterclockwise on a wide, flat road. It's one of the only resorts on the island owned and operated by Ni-Vanuatu. Fanny and Henry Cyrel have two two-bedroom bungalows accommodating up to six persons at Vt.7,000, and four double bungalows with shared bath at Vt.2,000 pp plus tax. Camping on the grounds costs Vt.500 pp. The units are attractive, each with a veranda and chairs. There are no cooking facilities, but a bowl of tropical fruit and a flask of hot water are provided free. The Cyrels' restaurant is open daily—try the steak sandwich (Vt.550). Their beach is poor, but for Vt.2,300 return per group they'll drop you on the white sands of Kakula (Rabbit) Island. Nagar is an ideal place to break a trip around the island, but be prepared for large groups on circle-island bus tours that often take lunch here. Any of the afternoon market trucks headed for Emua wharf could drop you here.

Beachcomber Lodge (tel. 23576, fax 26458, beachc@vanuatu.com.vu), three km east of Nagar, is another convenient stop on your way around the island. It's slightly more upmarket than Nagar, but it has the advantage of a unique circular thermal hot-spring pool for the exclusive use of houseguests and restaurant patrons. The eight self-contained duplex units cost Vt.6,000 for up to four persons, tax additional. Three rooms are Vt.5,000. There's hot water in the showers, but no fridge or coffee-making facilities in the rooms. Meals in the restaurant are pricey. Some car rental agencies in Port Vila offer a free night at Beachcomber for those taking a car for two days, so ask around.

There's also a simple guesthouse (tel. 23120) in Tukilasoa village on **Nguna Island** off North Efate, where you can stay for Vt.1,000 pp. The chief's meeting house in Tukilasoa is unique, and there are many opportunities on Nguna for hiking, snorkeling, and camping. It's a great way to visit an outer island without really leaving Efate! Get there on a market truck to Emua wharf, where you can join the other passengers on the afternoon boat to Nguna at Vt.400 pp (a special charter will be Vt.2,000). Return boats and buses to Port Vila leave Tukilasoa very early in the morning Monday to Saturday.

Tanna

INTRODUCTION

Vanuatu's second-most visited island (after Efate), Tanna is renowned for its active volcano, potent kava, coffee plantations, custom villages, cargo cultists, exciting festivals, strong traditions, magnificent wild horses, long black beaches, gigantic banyan trees, two-meter-long yams, and day-tripping packaged tourists. Due to its southerly location it's cooler than Efate, and there's no problem with malaria. The alternating black and white beaches, often separated only by a narrow headland, are unusual. The island is Vanuatu's most heavily populated, and well-used trails crisscross the landscape. Leave the roads and you'll enter a wonderland of charming, innocent people living as close to nature as their ancestors did before them. Here the real Tanna remains, almost untouched by a century and a half of traders, missionaries, officials, and other visitors.

Kava

Every village has its *nasara,* an open area surrounded by gigantic banyan trees, where the men gather nightly to drink kava at the *nakamal* (men's house). Tanna kava is strong and sudden. One cup will stone you; two cups will knock you out. The green roots of a pepper shrub *(Piper methysticum)* are first chewed into a pulp, spit out on a leaf, then mixed with a little water and squeezed through a coconut frond into a cup to be drunk all at once.

If a man touches any part of the campfire during the ceremony, it's thought that his house will burn down. After finishing the kava, speaking above a whisper is extremely bad manners. Women in the villages are still forbidden to take part in this gathering or even to see it. If they're caught trying, they have to pay a fine of one good kava root. Way back when, they would have been put to death.

Events

Custom dances are held on the occasion of marriages, circumcisions (many in July), and other events. Ask around to find out where the next one will be held. The most important event of the year is the Nekowiar Festival, with its famous Toka Dance. This ritual may be held in August or around the end of the year. The Toka celebrates the circumcision of young boys and is accompanied by pig killing, feasting, and dancers with painted faces and grass skirts—the works.

It can take six or seven years to prepare for these massive ceremonial gift-giving sessions, which cement alliances between villages and clans. The festival lasts three to five days and on the eve of the last day, thousands of men from every village on the island participate in a wild dance, which continues through the night. The next morning, more than 100 pigs may be slaughtered. There's usually a Nekowiar on Tanna every year, and tourists pay Vt.5,000 admission to attend this stirring event (cameras and videos for personal use Vt.10,000, film crews on assignment Vt.15,000).

Jon Frum festivals are held Friday nights at Sulphur Bay with music, singing, and dancing. A similar Friday night Jon Frum ceremony (Vt.300 admission) takes place at **Imanaka,** near White Grass on the other side of the island. The Jon Frum Cult is also active at **Middle Bush,** although custom people are in a majority. On 15 February the Jon Frum Festival is held at Sulphur Bay.

SIGHTS

Yasur Volcano

Yasur Volcano (361 meters high and 1.5 km wide at its base), the chief attraction of Tanna, is 30 km from Lenakel in the eastern part of the island. It's one of the most accessible volcanoes of its kind in the world, and for the convenience of tour groups, a road goes almost to the summit on the mountain's south side. It's also possible to climb the path up the north slope, to the left between the vegetation and the ash field (40 minutes). Either way, you'll pay a Vt.2,000 pp "Volcano Landing Fee" to the "Volcano Committee" for

VANUATU

TANNA

SOUTH PACIFIC OCEAN

Tanna Island

Ehniu

Green Hill

Black Sands Beach

WHITE GRASS OCEAN RESORT

EVERGREEN BUNGALOWS

White Grass

AIRPORT

Imanaka

Middle   Bush

Fetukai

Waisisi

FRIENDLY BUNGALOWS

Dip Point

Lownakariang

Loanialu Pass (552 m)

Nikity

White Sands

Sulphur Bay

Port Resolution

Loanatom

Lowkatai

Yaneumakel

Yanakwa

Ipeukel

HOT SPRINGS

Ireupuow

OCEAN VIEW GUESTHOUSE

Imai

Isaka

Yasur (361 m)

Lenakel

Isangel

Yaohnanen

Lake Isiwi

Manuapen

Captain Cook

Bethel

Yakel

Loanengo

JUNGLE OASIS

Yapilmai

Enfitana

Tukosmera (1,084 m)

Yatukwei

Ikeuti

BLOWHOLES

Yaneumra

Mareun (1,047 m)

Isakwai

Imaki

Isiai

Coral Sea

Green Point

Kwamera

0   4 mi

0   4 km

© DAVID STANLEY

© M.E. DE VOS

Yasur Volcano, Tanna (the lake in the foreground has since drained)

each visit (only one of many inflated custom fees collected on Tanna).

At 940°C, Yasur hisses, rumbles, and spits, constantly erupting in minor explosions, which emit small filaments of volcanic glass called Pele's Hair. Cargo cultists believe that Jon Frum lives beneath the fires of Yasur, where he commands an army of 5,000 souls. The slopes are scattered with boulders considered sacred by the Tannese, and black dust from the crater covers everything for kilometers. Some days are better for viewing than others, depending on smoke, wind, etc. At night it's an unforgettable fireworks display.

The prime time to climb Yasur is around 1700, to see it and the surroundings in daylight, then stay for the sunset and to see the crater at night—the most spectacular time by far as molten lava shoots up into the sky every few minutes. The views down into the crater are quite spectacular—steam and masses of black ash seethe furiously, discharging cinders and rocks, while gas burns your throat. The sulfur fumes can be choking, the noise deafening. Restrictions on how close to the crater's edge visitors are permitted to go were imposed in 1995, after two tourists and a local guide were killed by a projectile that

hurled them eight meters. During a particularly active period in 2002, all visits were suspended.

A barren ash plain surrounds Yasur, with freshwater Lake Isiwi to the west. You could spend hours walking across the ash plain and around Lake Isiwi watching the ash clouds billow from Yasur's summit as the volcano roars. A road along the north side of Lake Isiwi leads up to **Isaka** village; a 2.5-hour hike along a bush trail beyond Isaka is Vecel Falls. After heavy storms in May 2000, Lake Isiwi cut through its banks and much of the water rushed down to the sea.

Sulphur Bay

Just northeast of Yasur is Sulphur Bay village, stronghold of the Jon Frum movement (see the sidebar Cargo Cults), where American flags fly from tall bamboo poles. As you arrive you'll be shown the Headquarters where the flags are kept at night. A signboard on the wall lists the names of three chiefs imprisoned by the British for 17 years. In 1957 they were released, and on February 15 that year the American flags were first raised, a date commemorated by a major feast here each year.

The grave of one of these chiefs, Tommy Nam-

CARGO CULTS

The Tannese were declared converted to Presbyterianism in the early years of this century, yet just prior to WW II a movement to reestablish traditional values emerged in southern Tanna when a spirit began appearing at Green Point around sunset. In 1942, 1,000 men from Tanna were recruited by the Americans to work at military bases on Efate, and the sight of huge quantities of war materiel and black soldiers gave this movement a new meaning.

A sort of cultural hero emerged who would come from across the sea bringing wealth in abundance: Jon "from" America. As the symbol of their newfound religion, the Tannese took the red cross seen on wartime ambulances on Efate, and today the villages north of Yasur Volcano and elsewhere are dotted with little red crosses neatly surrounded by picket fences, bearing witness to this extraordinary chain of events.

The priests and prophets of these cargo cults are called "messengers," and they foretell the return of the ships laden with cargo for Man Tanna, escorted by Jon Frum, the reincarnation of an ancient deity. Towers with tin cans strung from wires, imitating radio stations, were erected so Jon Frum could speak to his people. The movement declares that money must be thrown away, pigs killed, and gardens left uncared for, since all material wealth will be provided in the end by Jon Frum.

Formerly it was felt that missionaries and government administrators had interfered with this Second Coming; thus the movement sometimes manifested itself in noncooperation with them. Beginning in 1940 the British authorities arrested cult leaders and held them without trial in Port Vila, but new devotees sprang up to take their places. There's also a Prince Philip cult among the custom people at Yaohnanen dating back to the prince's visit to what was then New Hebrides in 1974. Followers believe the prince originally came from Tanna in another form and will eventually return to rule over them. An Austrian reader had this comment:

The special thing about the Jon Frum Movement seems to be that (not unlike Jamaica's early Rastafarians) they detached Christian belief systems from church authority and power, and combined it with local traditions and customs, thereby doing a lot for an oppressed and underprivileged community's self-respect. A standard answer of Jon Frummers as to why they follow the movement was "em i wan muvmen blong mifela."

pus, an important Jon Frum leader, stands on the east (or ocean) side of the village common. At the far end of the common is the Jon Frum church with its red cross and other iconography. Ask to speak to prophet Elizabeth, a daughter of Nampus, who lives just behind the church. To the right of Sulphur Bay's beautiful black beach, steam from Yasur Volcano curls among the cliffs flanking the bay. You may be charged Vt.500 admission to the village.

On Friday nights, Jon Frum supporters from most of East Tanna converge on Sulphur Bay for a ceremony, which begins around 2000. Various "teams" take turns singing and playing music while villagers in grass skirts dance outside the shelter. The ceremony goes on most of the night, and if you wish to stay late you'll be able to sleep in the

Headquarters or on the floor of a hut just opposite that serves as a village guesthouse. If you attend the Friday night ceremony on your own, take along a pack of cigarettes or a few sticks of tobacco for Chief Isaak Wan and the others, who will be sitting under a large tree at one end of the square. You'll find them interesting to talk to. There's no set admission fee for attendance at the Jon Frum ceremony on Fridays, although a donation of Vt.300 pp towards the cost of their kerosene lamps is appropriate, if you're asked. You can purchase hibiscus-fiber grass skirts from the Sulphur Bay villagers, a beautiful and genuine buy.

Port Resolution

It's a pleasant 2.5-hour hike straight over the mountains on a well-trodden footpath from

Sulphur Bay to Port Resolution. The trail is easy to find from the Sulphur Bay end. If beginning at Port Resolution, go to the hot springs at the northwest end of the beach near the cliffs and ask someone there to show you the way. The Port Resolution locals use the hot springs for washing and cooking. A 250-kg male dugong (sea cow) named Chief Kaufis used to be a big attraction here, but the animal died in 2000. Captain Cook sailed into this bay in 1774 and named it after his ship. Upon landing, he pointed to the ground with a questioning look, and the locals thought he wanted to know their name for the earth, and Tanna has been called that ever since. The Tannese wouldn't allow Cook to visit Yasur Volcano. Today Port Resolution offers good anchorage for yachts.

Continue to **Ireupuow** village and have a look at the splendid high white beach. Several red Jon Frum crosses stand on Ireupuow's central square. A half hour from here is a point featuring a rock pyramid called **Captain Cook,** where the famous navigator made observations. A beautiful golden beach is next to the point. The main road goes back to Sulphur Bay or White Sands between Lake Isiwi and Yasur. Immense banyan trees line the way.

Across the Island

Tanna's largest village and administrative center is **Lenakel** on the west coast. The market and a cluster of general stores are near a large concrete wharf built by the Japanese. Most government offices are at Isangel, the headquarters of Tafea Province, on a hill about two km southeast. Coffee grown in northern Tanna is roasted in a factory at Lowkatai just north of Lenakel.

Village footpaths cross the island. One trail begins near the hospital, another next to the driveway into the Agriculture Station at Isangel (the "Melbourne" trail). A truck can drive six km up the latter route to Yanakwa, then it's another 10 km on foot through dense forest to Lake Isiwi. The path follows a ridge and from Isangel it's an easy uphill walk for about four hours, the first half through villages and the second through the jungle. The last two hours or so of the hike is downhill and across the ash plain to either White Sands

or Sulphur Bay. These trails are well known, regularly used, and easy to learn about and follow. A good hiker could make it across in a day.

There are many more such hikes in both south and north Tanna, and the 1:50,000 topographical map (obtainable at the Survey Office in Port Vila) is the only guide you need. Hiking on Tanna is safe and easy, as there are no thorns on the trees, no dangerous lizards on the ground, and even the local dogs are mellow. You'll pass through some of the 92 villages where people still live in the traditional way (no Christians or Jon Frummers). Almost no one does this, so you'll be a real explorer.

The Custom Villages

The road to the custom villages begins at the top of the incline a few hundred meters south of the Tanna Beach Resort. **Yapilmai Falls** are about midway between the main road and Yaohnanen, down the hill to the right. **Yaohnanen** is the center of the custom area where the men wear penis sheaths or *nambas,* and the women wear colorful grass skirts. They attended church until the 1940s, when they returned to their traditional religion. Only in the 1970s did they shed Western clothing. Packaged tourists are often brought to Yaohnanen to see custom dances, buy grass skirts, and tour the "primitive" village.

Chief Jack Naiva of Yaohnanen is friendly to visitors who respect his customs, and he may allow you to stay in the village if he likes you (a small gift helps). If you're willing to put on a *namba* or a grass skirt and perhaps do some gardening you'll be very welcome. They'll feed you on rats and cicadas—actually, rat tastes quite good, sort of like chicken. Chief Jack's son Jack Malia can arrange dancing at **Yakel** village, about 500 meters up the road past the Kustom Skul. Here you'll probably see a few men and boys with long hair bound in the traditional style.

Consider making a full day out of Yaohnanen and Yakel, walking there and back. When you enter the village *nasara,* sit down and wait for somebody. A custom fee of Vt.1,500 pp is charged to look around Yakel and to visit the Prince Philip house. After the evening kava, you could walk back to the main road and try to catch a lift.

PRACTICALITIES

Accommodations in West Tanna

White Grass Ocean Resort (John and Silvana Nicholls, tel. 68688, fax 68677, www.white grassvanuatu.com.vu) is on the beach, a 20-minute walk north from the airport. The 12 thatched bungalows with private bath are Vt.13,700/18,900/24,100/25,850 single/double/triple/quad including breakfast, airport transfers, and tax. Main plates in their oceanside restaurant average Vt.1,200, including a fruit platter for dessert. Tennis courts and pitch and put golf are provided, and a rock pool off their beach serves as a sea turtle sanctuary where turtles purchased from local villagers are kept until they can be released. Five-hour Yasur tours are Vt.8,400 pp, volcano landing fee included. A three-hour tour to an authentic custom village is Vt.5,200 pp. The Friday night Jon Frum tour is Vt.2,300 pp. Deep sea fishing is also offered. This quality resort manages the airport bar and shop, so information will be available there.

Less expensive lodging is available at **Tanna Evergreen Bungalows** (Samuel Namake and Iaken Kiero, tel.68774, fax 68624, tevergreen@ vanuatu.com.vu), between the airport and the White Grass Ocean Resort. The two ocean bungalows with private bath are Vt.5,500/7,000 single/double including breakfast, while the four garden bungalows with shared bath are Vt.3,500 double. Camping space is Vt.1,000. Meals in their restaurant are priced Vt.500–2,500. Tours to the volcano and the custom/cargo cult villages are offered.

Tanna Ocean View Guest House (tel. 68695, fax 68846), also known as Paradise View Guesthouse or Tafea Guest House, is a European-style frame house directly behind the Tafea Cooperative Store at Lenakel. The six rooms with shared bath are Vt.2,500/3,000 single/double, or Vt.1,500 pp in a dorm. Three of the rooms are only separated from the rest of the house by thin partitions, so peace and quiet will depend on who your neighbors are. You'll probably be allowed to camp next to the guesthouse when all of the rooms are full. Good communal cooking facilities are provided. This is the former personal residence of island traders Bob and Russell Paul, who decided to return to Australia after independence. A nice common lounge faces the garden, and the guesthouse is in a pleasant location overlooking the coast. (A female reader traveling alone complained of nocturnal prowlers outside the guesthouse.)

The **Uma Guesthouse** (tel. 68768) south of the wharf at Lenakel has three bungalows with shared bath and one four-person room in the guesthouse at Vt.2,500 pp. There's no electricity. It's overpriced because Island Safaris sends people here (charging them a ridiculous Vt.2,700 pp each way for airport transfers). You may be able to camp for Vt.500. The owners run a local restaurant here (meals Vt.700).

Accommodations at White Sands

Rather than putting up on the west coast, you're better off staying in East Tanna, close to the attractions you've come to visit. **Friendly Bungalows** (Barry and Amanda, tel./fax 26856, www .friendlybungalows.com.vu) is on the beach near the French school at Lownasunen, just before White Sands and about six km from the volcano. The large thatched house with three budget rooms with shared bath is Vt.2,250/2,700 single/double. The two smaller bungalows with private bath cost Vt.5,625 single or double, while the two larger two-bedroom bungalows are Vt.5,625/ 6,795/8,325 double/triple/quad. Camping is Vt.500 pp, but it's only allowed when all of the rooms are full. Be prepared to get some ash on your tent if the wind starts blowing this way. Mosquito nets are provided, and an electric generator runs at night, but there are no facilities to cook your own food. Good three-course meals are Vt.1,575 each (breakfast Vt.675). Canoes, horseback riding, hiking trips, tours, and custom dancing are arranged. It's quiet and attractive, well worth a three-night stay. You can hear the roar of the volcano from your bed. Airport transfers are Vt.4,000 pp round-trip (children Vt.2,000) in their own nine-seat Land Rover.

Nengau Entani Tours (David and Eileen Kiel, tel./fax 68676 or 68638, tafea@vanuatu.com.vu) books the **Volcano Adventure Lodge,** also known as Yasur Guesthouse, in Loanengo Village, near the access road up Yasur. The four basic thatched bungalows with shared bath are Vt.3,550/5,560 single/double including breakfast. A full range of minibus tours is offered, and most guests arrive on prebooked package tours.

Jungle Oasis Bungalow (Kelson Hosea, tel. 68676 or 68000, www.jungle-oasis.com), right next door to Volcano Adventure Lodge, is slightly cheaper at Vt.2,000/2,500 single/double including breakfast.

Accommodations at Port Resolution

Adjacent to Ireupuow village near the eastern tip of Tanna is the **Port Resolution Yacht Club** (tel. 68791) with eight thatched bungalows with shared bath at Vt.2,000/3,000 single/double including breakfast if you find your own way here (or Vt.3,720/5,640 if you book through a tour operator like Island Safaris). Other meals are around Vt.1,000 each. Lighting is by kerosene lamp. Kava is served at the club *nakamal*. The location is splendid, atop a cliff overlooking Port Resolution, with several good beaches nearby. You'll see flying foxes in the evening. The friendly staff takes guests out on interesting bush hikes to local hot springs, beaches, the Captain Cook rock, and gardens. The tour companies quote high prices for any sightseeing from Port Resolution and it's much cheaper to hire the yacht club's taxi for island visits, including tours to Yasur Volcano. Yachts may anchor offshore at no charge and yachties are welcome at the bar.

The French-operated **Turtle Bay Inn** (tel. 68850, fax 68885), near the Captain Cook Rock, has four thatched bungalows at Vt.4,000/6,000 single/double with breakfast. There's also a "longroom" dorm at Vt.3,000 pp. There's even hot spring water in the bathrooms! Dinner is around Vt.1,700. This place has had it's ups and downs, so check before heading that way.

Food and Drink

A cluster of general stores is near the old airstrip at Lenakel. The village women spread out their produce on the ground at various locations weekdays. On Mondays and Fridays local markets take place beside the Tafea Cooperative Store in Lenakel and under the large banyan tree opposite the wharf. Bread is baked locally, but it's often sold out by noon. Take all your own food with you if you go walkabout on the east coast.

Next to the National Bank and Tafea Cooperative in Lenakel is the **Kosalos Restaurant** with a menu priced Vt.250–1,000. You can get a filling local meal of meat and rice, and everyone pays the same there! South of the wharf is John Loughman's **Uma Restaurant** (tel. 68768) where similar fare is available at higher prices (be sure to ask first).

Services

The National Bank (tel. 68615), next to the Tafea Cooperative Store at Lenakel, changes traveler's checks weekdays 0800–1100 and 1330–1500. Bring plenty of cash with you to Tanna, as anything associated with package tourism costs heaps of money. There's a card telephone at the co-op. The post office (tel. 68687) and hospital (tel. 68659) are at Isangel.

Transportation

Vanair (tel. 68667) has flights from Port Vila to Tanna (Vt.11,770 one-way) one or twice a day, weekly via Erromango. Southbound, sit on the left side of the plane for the best views. Tanna's new airport is at White Grass, 15 km north of Lenakel (Vt.1,000/200 by taxi/bus). Expect to pay Vt.2,000 pp for a ride in a pickup truck taxi from the airport to the east coast (although the driver will probably start out asking Vt.3,000 pp). A chartered taxi to the east coast will be around Vt.6,000.

You can also come from Port Vila by ship. Lenakel receives a boat from Port Vila two or three times a month, often the barge *Roena* or the freighter MV *Killian* (Vt.5,000 deck including meals).

A couple of open-backed pickup trucks and minibuses offer unscheduled service between Lenakel and White Sands every weekday. The local price to Lonoo village, three km from Friendly Bungalows, is Vt.300 pp, but you'll be expected to pay Vt.2,000 pp right to wherever you want to go. You may be able to bargain this down to Vt.1,000 pp, but it's essential to fix the price with the taxi-truck drivers before setting out, and even then they may ask more when you arrive. So that it obviously won't be a special trip just for you, wait at the junction by the stadium on the road leading to White Sands for a truck headed the right direction. There's quite a bit of traffic between Lenakel and White Sands, so if you suspect a rip-off, just wait for the next one. The drivers are quite accustomed to collecting large sums for transportation from tourists on prearranged packages, so be prepared.

All of the west coast tourist lodgings offer overpriced sightseeing tours, such as the half-

day trip to a custom village and Yasur by 4WD jeep (Vt.11,250 pp). A morning trip to Yakel to see people wearing *nambas* is Vt.5,630 pp (kava included). The above prices are valid assuming at least two people are going; if you're alone it's 50 percent extra. The tour operators try to discourage independent sightseeing that doesn't fit into their packages, and some of the guides have been known to behave aggressively toward low-budget backpackers, though this is mostly a problem on the west coast.

Other Tafea Islands

Erromango

In 1825, Irish trader Peter Dillon discovered vast stands of sandalwood here. Dillon managed to obtain very little of the precious wood, and the ships that followed soon clashed with the inhabitants. Plaques in the church at Unpongkor commemorate the martyrdom of John Williams and James Harris (1839), George and Ellen Gordon (1861), and George's brother, James Gordon (1872). On the other side of the river in the village cemetery are monuments to these well-meaning missionaries, killed by the Erromangans as a consequence of the methods used by the traders and the diseases introduced by the messengers of God themselves.

Later, many Erromangans were carried off to labor in the Australian cane fields, and those few who returned brought back further disease and discord. From 20,000 in the early 1800s, Erromango's population plummeted to 400 by 1930. There are only 1,560 inhabitants today. Old burial caves dot the cliffs along the west and south coasts. As the sun sets across the Coral Sea, you know you've reached one of the farthest ends of the earth.

Although rugged and untouristed, Erromango is a possible stopover between Port Vila and Tanna, because Vanair flights call at Dillon's Bay and Ipota once a week in each direction. This makes it possible to arrive at one, hike across the island, and leave from the other. It's not easy, though, and you'll need a guide. A minimum of three (and preferably four) days is required to

do this. Begin from the Dillon's Bay side, going to Ipota via Happy Land. There are lots of ups and downs, so pack light. A tent is essential—you can't always count on staying with the locals. Water is available at villages, but bring your own food, plus gifts. Take a compass, good boots, and a reliable companion.

Erromango has only two roads, one from Dillon's Bay airstrip to Unpongkor village and a logging road across the island to Port Narvin. Maps show a network of logging roads spreading out from Ipota, but these are overgrown and difficult to follow, even on foot. Besides, there are no motor vehicles at Ipota, and only three at Dillon's Bay. The locals travel around the island by outboard speedboat (expensive) or on trails through the bush.

A truck sometimes meets the flights at Dillon's Bay airstrip and carries passengers the eight km to Unpongkor village for about Vt.600 pp (or Vt.4,500/4,900 single/double each way when booked through Island Safaris). The road drops sharply into the Williams River Valley to the village, beautifully situated at the river mouth.

Meteson's Guest House (William Mete, tel. 68792), in the center of Unpongkor, consists of one room with four beds at Vt.4,220/5,640 single/double including breakfast. It may be possible to pay less if you're not on a package tour, but don't count on it. Meals can be ordered and there's a small co-op store nearby. You may also be able to camp on the grass beside the river.

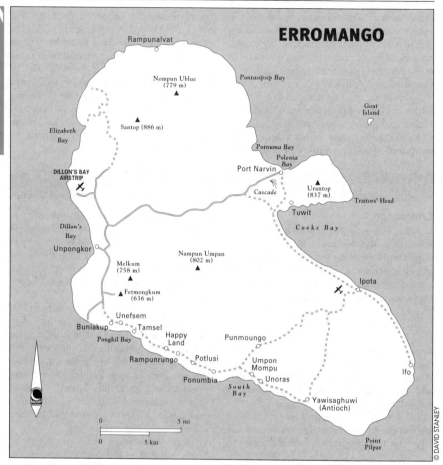

Aniwa and Futuna

These two small islands east of Tanna, each with a population of around 400, are quite different. Aniwa (eight square km) is a low island covered with orange trees, the fruit of which is very sweet and juicy. The villages are near the airstrip and the people very friendly. A magnificent snorkeling spot is north of the airstrip, and there's good anchorage.

The people of 11-square-km Futuna are Polynesian. You could stay at one of the villages near the airstrip but there's not much to do other than climb the 643-meter extinct volcano. Getting

around is difficult, as the tracks go over ladders of bamboo, and in some cases you'll find yourself clinging to rocks 30 meters directly above the sea along the forbidding coast. Vanair flies to Futuna from Tanna (Vt.5,990) twice a week and from Aneityum (Vt.6,220) weekly.

Aneityum

Aneityum (Anatom), southernmost inhabited island in Vanuatu, is somewhat cooler and drier than the rest of the country. Its 160 square km rise to 852 meters, but ample flat areas are available for cultivation. Totemic petroglyphs and

VANUATU

kauri stands are found on Aneityum, and 80 species of orchid flourish here. In the 1840s, whalers from far and wide were based at Inyeug, a sandy islet just off the southwest side of Aneityum where the airstrip is today.

The Rev. John Geddie, first Presbyterian missionary to establish himself in Vanuatu, arrived in 1848 and built a 1,000-seat stone church, the ruins of which can still be seen. His efforts were in vain, however, as introduced diseases such as measles and dysentery ravaged the population, which eventually fell from 3,500 to 800, only 350 of whom were Geddie's converts. Today, about 550 people live in two villages on the south coast.

Vanair flies to Aneityum from Tanna (Vt.5,990) twice a week and from Futuna (Vt.6,220) weekly. The three-room **Mystery Island Guest House** (Francois Wanieg, tel. 68672) on Inyeug, the airstrip island, accommodates visitors in a single thatched building at Vt.2,250 pp, which is high for what you get. The toilet is outside and there's no electricity or running water. You're expected to bring all your own food and to prepare it yourself in the communal kitchen. Be aware that every other week an Australian cruise ship drops as many as 1,900 tourists at a time on this "Mystery Island" to enjoy the long white beaches.

Matthew and Hunter

These small, uninhabited islands are subjects of a territorial dispute between France and Vanuatu, one of the few such disputes in the South Pacific. The islands were discovered in the late 18th century, but largely forgotten until 1962, when two New Hebrides expatriates tried to claim them by means of a legal action before the Joint Court in Port Vila. This attracted the interest of French Condominium officials, who tried to send a warship to Matthew to claim the island for France. The party was unable to land, due to high seas, but later one of the expats managed to swim ashore and plant a coconut tree to validate his own claim.

In 1965, the French announced that the British government had agreed that the islands could be attached to New Caledonia, despite the fact that they had always appeared on the map of New Hebrides and been considered a part of that colony. In 1975, the French did manage to get ashore and erect plaques, but their claims were not recognized by the incoming Vanuatu government, which had the Vanuatu flag raised and sovereignty proclaimed shortly after Independence Day 1980. The two islands are still claimed by both countries, and though of little economic value in themselves, they would form an important addition to the Exclusive Economic Zone of either Vanuatu or New Caledonia. In 1985, the French sent troops to occupy Matthew as a precaution against colonization from Vanuatu. The Forum Fisheries Agency recognizes Vanuatu's claim for fisheries licensing purposes.

Matthew, 350 km southeast of Aneityum and 450 km east of Grande Terre, is an actively volcanic island a little over a kilometer long. The two peaks are separated by a narrow isthmus of sand and ashes: The west peak is older and reaches 177 meters, while the younger east peak (142 meters) features smoking fumaroles in its rocky crater.

Hunter, 69 km east of Matthew, is an abrupt basalt block 297 meters high. No anchorage is possible, due to the great depths, and there are sulfur-colored cliffs on the west side. Seabirds are the only inhabitants of both Matthew and Hunter.

Malekula

Shaped like a sitting dog, Malekula (Mallicollo) is a big 2,041-square-km island of 24,000 inhabitants speaking 30 different languages. The rugged interior of southern Malekula is inhabited by some of the most traditional clans on earth, while the island's east coast features the gentle beauty of continuous coconut plantations. Together with Ambrym and Paama, Malekula forms part of Malampa Province.

It's easy to visit Malekula on your way from Port Vila to Luganville. Vanair offers stopovers at Norsup for Vt.2,440 extra airfare, or come by ship from Luganville. Although there are a few basic resthouses, Malekula is more for the adventuresome traveler who requires few amenities. The traditional areas of southern Malekula are still riddled with taboos, and visitors must tread very carefully. Offshore sharks can be a problem, so get local advice before swimming anywhere off Malekula.

The Big Nambas

The once-feared Big Nambas formerly lived on the plateau at Amokh in the northwest of the island, but since the death of Chief Virhambat in 1988, they've all moved down to the coast, and the fortified village at Amokh is now deserted. Up until the 1930s, internecine tribal fighting was conducted almost constantly among the 2,000 clansmen, and cannibalism was frequently practiced by the powerful hereditary chiefs (the last recorded case was in 1969). The men would barter yams and pigs for women, and if a man valued his wife highly, he would honor her by arranging an expensive, secret ritual, during which the woman's two front teeth were knocked out. The women wore large headdresses of red fibers, and the men wide bark belts and large red penis sheaths (nambas)—from which the tribe derived its name. For better or worse, all of this is now a thing of the past.

The Small Nambas

The jungles of the interior of south Malekula are home to the Small Nambas. Because missionaries penetrated here very late, the 400–500 clanspeople living in many scattered villages retained their traditional customs long after most other Ni-Vanuatu had adopted European ways. A few older men still wear small nambas made of banana leaves, and put on gaudy face masks and body paint worn during funeral rites. No roads penetrate their territory, although the Small Nambas sometimes come to Mbwitin and South West Bay to trade. Some Small Nambas live at Melken, which is connected to the coast by a road through Mbwitin, but most have now adopted Christianity and Western dress. As Small Nambas society disintegrates, the inhabitants spread to new settlements scattered around the southern part of the island.

Tourists on "Small Nambas" packages often stay at **Alo Lodge** (tel. 48659), next to Wintua Airstrip at South West Bay. The four rooms with shared bath cost Vt.4,300/5,800 single/double, including breakfast. Everyone flying into South West Bay must pay a Vt.1,600 "community fee" and all sightseeing tours are extra. Otherwise, **Banam Bay Bungalows** (no phone), on the beach at Fartapo village on the opposite side of Malakula, has five thatched bungalows with shared facilities at Vt.5,000/7,000 including meals. Small Nambas custom dancing can be arranged at Vt.3,000 pp. The speedboat transfer from Lamap Airport to Banam Bay is Vt.11,250 each way for the boat, although the regular weekday truck to Lakatoro or Lamap would be much cheaper. Island Safaris in Port Vila books tours to these places, which explains the pricing.

Lamap

Lamap, at the southeast corner of Malekula, adjoins Port Sandwich, where Captain Cook came ashore to a friendly welcome. Port Sandwich is the finest harbor in Vanuatu, as it affords protection from all winds and has a good holding ground. Dinghies can be taken five km up the river at the head of the bay. The wharf, three km west of the police station, affords a lovely view of the area (but don't swim, as this area is notorious for sharks).

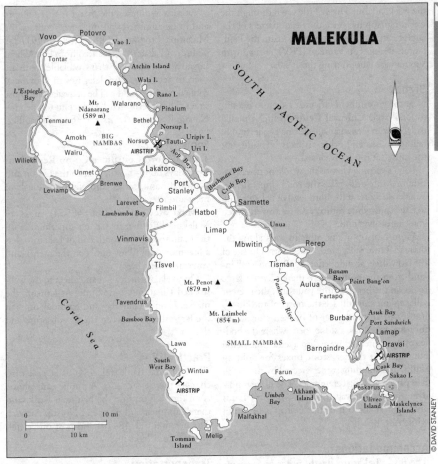

MALEKULA

SOUTH PACIFIC OCEAN

Vovo
Potovro
Vao I.
Tontar
Atchin Island
Wala I.
Orap
Rano I.
L'Espiegle
Bay
Walarano
Pinalum
Mt.
Ndanarang
(589 m)
Bethel
Tenmaru
Norsup I.
Amokh
BIG
NAMBAS
Norsup
Tautu
Uripiv I.
Wairu
AIRSTRIP
Uri I.
Wiliekh
Aop Bay
Lakatoro
Unmet
Brenwe
Port
Stanley
Bushman Bay
Crab Bay
Larevet
Sarmette
Lambumbu Bay
Filmbil
Hatbol
Leviamp
Unua
Limap
Vinmavis
Mbwitin
Rerep
Tisvel
Tisman
Banam
Bay
Point Bang'on
Mt. Penot ▲
(879 m)
Aulua
Fartapo
Tavendrua
Coral Sea
Bamboo Bay
Mt. Laimbele
(854 m)
Burbar
Asuk Bay
Port Sandwich
Lamap
Lawa
SMALL NAMBAS
Barngindre
Dravai
South
West Bay
Wintua
AIRSTRIP
Farun
Cook Bay
Sakao I.
AIRSTRIP
Peskarus
Umbeb
Bay
Akham
Island
Uliveo
Island
Maskelynes
Islands
Malfakhal
Tomman
Island
Melip

0   10 mi
0   10 km

© DAVID STANLEY

You'll probably arrive at the airstrip near Dravai village, five km south of the police station. Vanair calls here once or twice a week between Port Vila, Norsup, and Espiritu Santo. Camp on the grass beside the airstrip or proceed north to Lamap, where a small council resthouse (Vt.1,000 pp) adjoins the police station. For advance information about staying there, call Lamap post office (tel. 48444). Two private guest houses on the road to the airport are around Vt.1,500 pp. Bread and other supplies are available from local stores. A truck to Lakatoro (Vt.1,000) leaves Lamap weekdays at 0500. Ambrym Island is just northeast of Lamap, but speedboats across are rare. Lopevi Island's volcanic cone looms exotically behind Paama Island in the distance.

NORSUP/LAKATORO

Five times a week, Vanair flights between Port Vila and Espiritu Santo land at Norsup airstrip, midway between Lakatoro and Norsup, the former British and French administrative centers in northeastern Malekula. Today Lakatoro is the headquarters of Malampa Province. It's dead on the weekend, but a lively little town through the week. Norsup has once the headquarters of the largest coconut plantation in Vanuatu, the Plantations Reunies du Vanuatu (PRV), created with Vietnamese labor during the 1920s.

Sights

Near the government offices at Lakatoro is a traditional-style **Cultural Center,** which opened in 1991 with Canadian aid. A small collection of helmet masks and other artifacts is inside, but the museum is usually closed.

For a sweeping view of the whole northeastern side of Malekula, take the road opposite SK Wholesale Store, at the north end of Lakatoro, up to a red-and-white **radio repeater tower,** which you can easily climb.

From Norsup, it's possible to walk along the shore to **Tautu** village near the airport. The site of the old village, abandoned in 1918, is on a hill inland from the point where there are two large rocks on the beach before you reach the present village. You can still see the posts of the chief's house, an amphitheater of broken stone slabs for tribal meetings, a stone "bed" where the bodies of dead enemies were displayed before being consumed at dinner, stone boxes for holding skulls, and standing stones erected by men who had passed grading ceremonies. The place is now overgrown and ravaged by pigs. Beyond Tautu and right at the end of the airstrip is beautiful white Aop Beach.

Accommodations

The rustic **Lakatoro Resthouse** is on spacious grounds near the Cultural Center in the hilltop administrative compound, seven km south of Norsup. It has three rooms with six bunks each, and one double room for married couples. There's a communal fridge and cooking facilities, plus a video room. The white prefabricated **Norsup Resthouse** is in a residential area on the plateau, up the hill from the Norsup Co-op. The four rooms have bunk beds, and share the bathrooms, kitchen, fridge, and a tiny video player. The Lakatoro Resthouse is larger and more convenient, but the Norsup Resthouse is in better condition and more private.

At both resthouses, the charge is Vt.1,500 pp, and to be admitted you must first contact the Malampa Provincial Office (tel. 48491, fax 48442) in Lakatoro. Call ahead from Port Vila or Luganville to find out what's available. Both are used to accommodate delegates to provincial council meetings, and will be unavailable at those times. The officials may be reluctant to open the Norsup Resthouse, which is far from their office.

Food

The **Lakatoro Consumer Co-op Restaurant** (weekdays 0630–1730), next to the Co-op and National Bank, serves unpretentious meals of meat and rice and coffee.

Maxi Restaurant (tel. 48554), next to Malekula Distributors Center supermarket on the main road at the south end of Lakatoro, has a few more ambitious meals on the menu, and you can order a beer.

On weekdays there's a market next to the well-stocked Lakatoro Co-op Store. At Norsup, the market is on Wednesday and Saturday only, in the large shelter between the Co-op Store and the sea.

Practicalities

The National Bank (tel. 48400) at Lakatoro changes traveler's checks. A public card phone is on the wall outside the National Bank, and there's another card phone at Norsup Airport. The hospital (tel. 48410) and post office (tel. 48406) are at Norsup.

Transportation

A pickup truck taxi from Norsup Airstrip to either settlement will be Vt.400. A bus would cost Vt.100 (weekdays only). Grab any form of transport you see, or be prepared to walk the four km south to Lakatoro.

The Vanair office (tel. 48552) is between the Shell service station and Malekula Distributors Center at Lakatoro. The interisland ships tie up to a wharf at Litslits, a couple of km south of Lakatoro.

On weekdays minibuses circulate between Lakatoro and Vao every hour or so (from Lakatoro it's Vt.100 to Norsup, Vt.250 to Wala, Atchin, or

Vao). Ask about the weekday trip right around the north end of the island (Vt.500). A truck to Lamap (Vt.1,000) leaves Lakatoro weekdays at 1300.

NORTH OF NORSUP

Many French-speaking villages are strung along the coast north of Norsup and on the small offshore islands. These islands are famous for their megalithic culture, especially the stone-lined dancing grounds *(nasara)* and drums *(tamtam)*. Only the people of Vao and Wala actually continue to use their dancing grounds for traditional ceremonies such as circumcisions. Those on Atchin, Rano, and Uripiv are more or less abandoned. The peoples of Vao, Atchin, Wala, and Rano speak different languages, and can only communicate among themselves in Bislama, English, or French. Ships between Norsup and Luganville call at these islands several times a week, and minibuses run periodically from Norsup to Atchin and Vao (Vt.250).

Take a minibus all the way north to the landing opposite **Vao,** where a motorboat across to the island will cost Vt.1,000 each way. You'll probably be able to find someone to paddle you over in a dugout canoe for the same round-trip, with an hour or so waiting time. Upon arrival, walk past the Catholic church with its two well-carved *tamtam* drums, and when you reach a store, turn left toward the middle of the island. This will eventually bring you to a large *nasara* with slit gongs, stone seats, banyan trees, a *nakamal* (kava drinking venue)—the works. Turn right here, and walk south toward a couple more of the seven *nasara* on Vao. If you're friendly, someone will offer to guide you around, and there's no charge to visit the *nasara,* although you may have to pay custom fees to take photos.

The woodcarvers of Vao produce both raw or "ethnic" masks and canoe prows they're reluctant to sell, and polished airport art. There's a long white beach near the Catholic mission where you'll first arrive, and the tidy island houses are wonderfully picturesque with stone walls or fences made of empty bottles. Vao has an almost magical air, and it's said that magic also controls the sharks and makes it safe to swim anywhere around the island. As yet, Vao is almost untouched by tourism.

Return to the mainland and walk south to **Atchin** in an hour. After sleepy Vao, the contrast of Atchin—mecca of Ni-Vanuatu capitalism and a big SDA village—is startling. A long black-sand beach faces Atchin. Mr. Maxim Metsan has built a few small bungalows for tourists beside the road at Wormet, between Atchin and Wala.

At the mouth of Orap River on the mainland opposite Wala Island is **Rose Bay Bungalows** (Peter Fidelio, tel. 48602) with five bungalows at Vt.3,360/4,050 pp with shared/private bath, breakfast and dinner included. You may be able to get a local booking rate if you call direct, although tour operators like Island Safaris try to discourage any undercutting of their prices. Peter can arrange transportation and tours all around Malekula. In the village on Wala Island is the site of a traditional dancing ground where wooden *tamtams* stand. Some old burials and magical stones on Wala may be taboo, so ask about that and the safety of swimming in these waters.

Mrs. Madeleine Reganvanu runs the two-room **Ngaim Orsel Resthouse** on Uripiv Island, charging Vt.1,500 pp. The snorkeling here is good. A speedboat charter from the wharf just south of the Shell service station at Lakatoro would cost Vt.1,500 one way, or Vt.100 pp if they're going anyway.

Espiritu Santo

With 3,955 square km, Espiritu Santo is Vanuatu's largest island. Mt. Tabwemasana (1,879 meters), highest peak in the country, has never known a recorded climb, and it's believed that still-uncontacted "pygmy" tribes reside in the impassable interior jungles. Espiritu Santo has played a central role in the history of the country, from Quirós's 1606 settlement on Big Bay, to the giant support base set up by the Americans during WW II, and the Coconut Rebellion of 1980. In 1994, Espiritu Santo and Malo were united as Sanma, the largest of Vanuatu's six provinces.

Wusi on the isolated west coast (accessible only by boat or on foot) is the source of some of Vanuatu's only native pottery, made as part of a ceremony in May and June. This beautiful island possesses great economic potential and much to offer the visitor, including untouched beaches, wild jungle hikes, friendly country villages, good communications, and an attractive, untouristed main town.

LUGANVILLE

Apart from Port Vila, Luganville is the only incorporated community in Vanuatu and the headquarters of Sanma Province. It lies at the island's southeast corner on the Segond Channel, a 13-km-long waterway that offers anchorages sheltered enough for a ship to ride out a hurricane. Luganville is called Canal by the locals because of this strait; to people in Port Vila, it's simply Santo.

Luganville is a mixture of French, Chinese, Vietnamese, and American influences, with a certain Wild West air. In May 1942, more than 100,000 American servicemen arrived on Espiritu Santo to construct an instant city, complete with telephones, radio station, movie houses, hospitals, crushed-coral roads, bridges, airfields, and wharves, so by the end of the war a whole infrastructure had been installed. Three bomber airfields and two fighter strips were here, and a major dry dock functioned at Palikulo. Even today, many of the buildings in Luganville are vintage Quonset huts.

With a population of 11,000, the town is an important economic center. Ninety percent of Vanuatu's copra, two-thirds of its frozen meat, most of its cut timber, and all of its cacao pass through Luganville's main wharf. The town doesn't get nearly as many tourists as Port Vila, yet it has all the facilities and there's a large choice of places to stay. It also lacks some of the flair of the capital.

SIGHTS

Unity Park along Segond Channel near the mouth of the Sarakata River is the site of the PT-boat facility where John F. Kennedy and his *PT-109* were based until being transferred to the Solomons in 1943. Adjoining it are the town hall, market, and a traditional-style chiefs' *nakamal.* The **Women's Handicraft Center** (weekdays 0800–1130 and 1400–1630, Sat. 0800–1130) in Unity Park sells woodcarvings, baskets, mats, and other such items.

The Sarakata is one of Vanuatu's largest rivers, and Luganville originally occupied its west bank; the east bank, site of the present downtown, was a marsh until reclaimed by the Americans in 1942. Across the bridge over the river is the French high school at **Saint Louis,** site of the original prewar French settlement. Farther southwest, the road inland just before a high radio tower leads two km steeply up to **Bomber Three,** an abandoned WW II airfield. Picturesque **St. Michel Mission** (1912) is five km from town.

Palikulo Peninsula

The area east of Luganville as far as the Palikulo Peninsula is usually done as a day trip. A large Malaysian-run lumber mill called Santo Veneer is a kilometer past the airport. About two km beyond the airport turnoff, just before the white monument on the left to Captain Elwood J. Euart of the 103rd Field Artillery Battalion (1942), is a road to the shore of Segond Channel. The wreck of the **SS *President Coolidge,*** a 22,000-ton prewar luxury liner converted into a troop ship, lies completely submerged here on

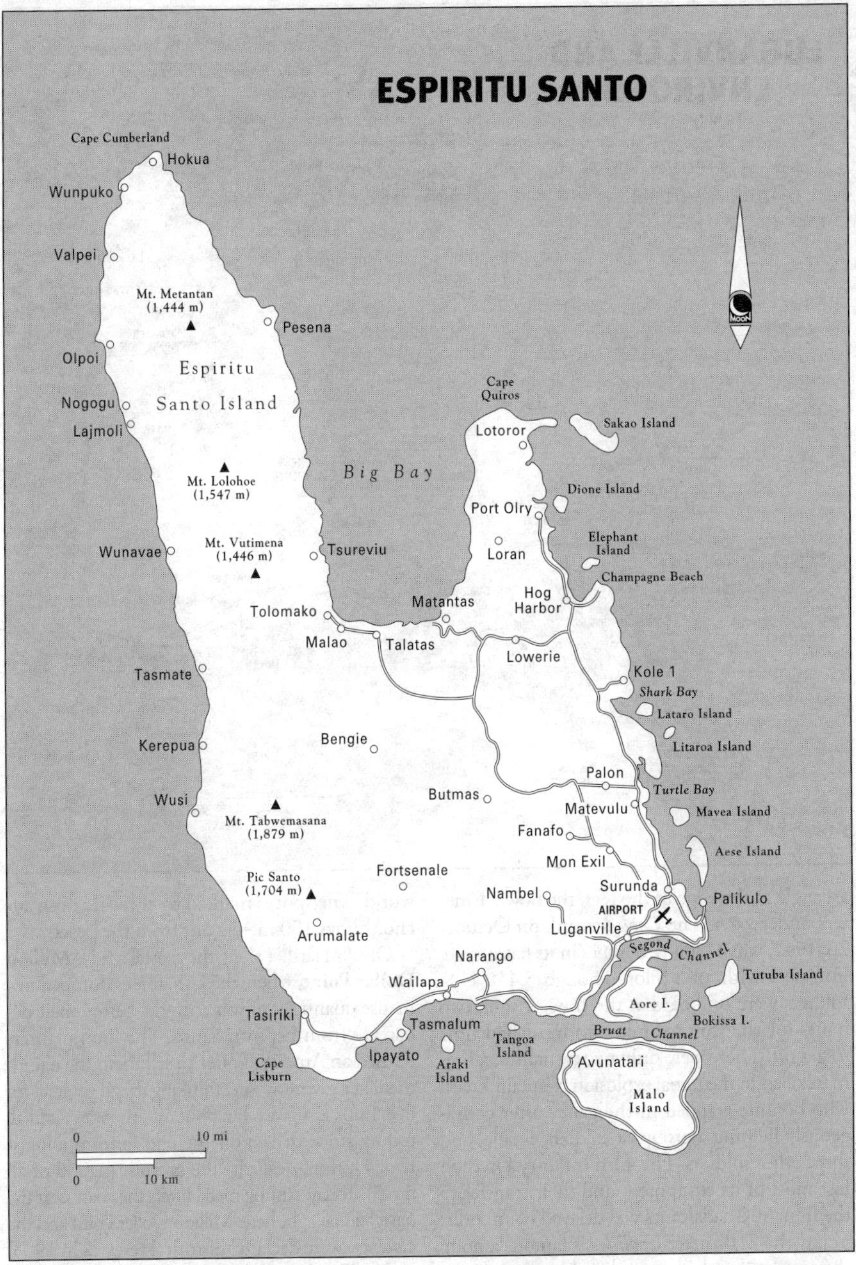

ESPIRITU SANTO

Cape Cumberland
Hokua
Wunpuko
Valpei
Mt. Metantan
(1,444 m)
Pesena

Espiritu
Santo Island

Olpoi
Nogogu
Lajmoli

Big Bay

Cape
Quiros
Lotoror
Sakao Island
Port Olry
Dione Island
Loran
Elephant
Island
Champagne Beach

Mt. Lolohoe
(1,547 m)

Wunavae
Mt. Vutimena
(1,446 m)
Tsureviu
Matantas
Hog
Harbor
Tolomako
Malao
Talatas
Lowerie
Kole 1
Shark Bay
Lataro Island
Tasmate
Litaroa Island
Kerepua
Bengie
Palon
Turtle Bay
Wusi
Butmas
Matevulu
Mavea Island
Mt. Tabwemasana
(1,879 m)
Fanafo
Aese Island
Mon Exil
Pic Santo
(1,704 m)
Fortsenale
Nambel
Surunda
Palikulo
AIRPORT
Luganville
Arumalate
Narango
Segond Channel
Tutuba Island
Wailapa
Aore I.
Tasiriki
Tasmalum
Bokissa I.
Bruat Channel
Ipayato
Araki
Island
Tangoa
Island
Avunatari
Cape
Lisburn
Malo
Island

0   10 mi
0   10 km

© DAVID STANLEY

VANUATU

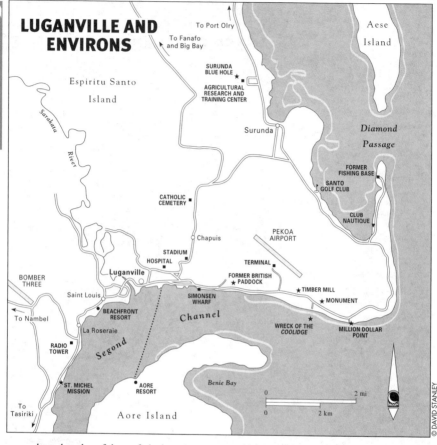

LUGANVILLE AND ENVIRONS

To Port Olry
To Fanafo and Big Bay

Aese Island

Espiritu Santo Island

Sarakata River

SURUNDA BLUE HOLE
AGRICULTURAL RESEARCH AND TRAINING CENTER

Surunda

Diamond Passage

FORMER FISHING BASE
SANTO GOLF CLUB

CATHOLIC CEMETERY

Chapuis

PEKOA AIRPORT

CLUB NAUTIQUE

STADIUM
HOSPITAL
Luganville

TERMINAL
FORMER BRITISH PADDOCK

BOMBER THREE

Saint Louis

To Nambel

BEACHFRONT RESORT
La Roseraie

SIMONSEN WHARF

Channel

TIMBER MILL
MONUMENT

WRECK OF THE COOLIDGE

MILLION DOLLAR POINT

RADIO TOWER

Segond

ST. MICHEL MISSION

AORE RESORT

Benie Bay

To Tasiriki

Aore Island

0   2 mi
0   2 km

© DAVID STANLEY

an angle at the edge of the reef, the bow 21 meters underwater. The *Coolidge* sank on October 26, 1942, when it hit two mines in its haste to get into port without a pilot. Though 5,440 U.S. soldiers were on board at the time, it took two hours for the ship to sink, and most had time to get off. There were only five casualties, a fireman killed in the initial explosion, Captain Euart, who became trapped in the galley after courageously helping a group of soldiers escape, and three other soldiers. The 43rd Infantry Division lost most of its equipment and their transfer to the front at Guadalcanal was delayed by months. Today the 210-meter *Coolidge* is famous among the scuba set as the largest diveable wreck in the

world. The spot is marked by three floating anchor buoys 100 meters out from the beach.

One km farther along the coastal road is **Million Dollar Point,** where the U.S. forces dumped immense quantities of war materiel before their departure from Espiritu Santo. The local planters refused an American offer to sell them the equipment at a giveaway rate, thinking they'd get it all for free. But a ramp was built out into the water and all rolling stock driven off the end (anthropologist Kirk Huffman calls it "the greatest pig kill of all time"). Today, rusting metal litters the coast near the navigational light here. Million Dollar Point and the *Coolidge* were declared historical reserves in 1983, and it's illegal to take any souvenirs from this area.

VANUATU

Abandon ship! Troops are taken off the SS *President Coolidge*, which hit a mine off Santo on October 25, 1942. The wreck is now a favorite of scuba divers.

COURTESY OF THE NATIONAL ARCHIVES, WASHINGTON, D.C.

After another four km on the coastal road, take the turnoff to the right, which leads north a short distance to the **Club Nautique.** There's a beach and picnic area here, and since Palikulo Bay is better protected from the southeast trades than Segond Channel, cruising yachts often anchor off the Club and use the facilities.

Sports and Recreation

Aquamarine Dive Shop (Kevin and Mayumi Green with Barry Holland, tel./fax 36196, VHS channel 69, www.aquamarine-santo.com), next to Santo Chinese Restaurant down the road from the Unity Shell service station, offers shore diving at Vt.3,800/3,400/3,000 per dive for one/six/10 dives without equipment. Boat diving is Vt.5,200/4,700/4,200 per dive for one/six/10 dives (minimum of two divers). You can rent equipment such as buoyancy compensators, regulators, wetsuits, snorkeling gear, and torch at Vt.1,450. Night dives are shore dives only and cost the same (minimum of four). An introductory one-dive resort course is Vt.8,000, while open-water certification is Vt.38,000/31,250 pp for one/two people (medical certificate required).

Their new dive shop on the water is a pleasant place to relax and log your dives over a coffee or cold drink. Aquamarine's two seven-meter, twin-outboard dive boats can be at the *Coolidge* in 15 minutes and several excellent reef sites are reached in less than half an hour.

Allan Power Dive Tours (tel./fax 36822, www.allan-power-santo.com), across the street from Hotel Santo, specializes in diving on the *President Coolidge* and Million Dollar Point. His nine-meter dive boat *The Lady* can reach all dives sites around Luganville. Diving is Vt.3,900/5,600 for shore/boat dives, plus Vt.1,560 for equipment. PADI scuba courses start at Vt.30,000. Free pickups are offered from all accommodations. Allan has done 20,000 *Coolidge* dives since 1969, and he knows every nook and cranny. Ask Allan to introduce you to Boris, a grouper as big as a seal, which also frequents the wreck.

Pro Dive Espiritu Santo (Dave Cross, tel. 36911, fax 36912, VHS channel 68, pdsanto@ vanuatu.com.vu) is based on Aore Island. They charge certified divers Vt.4,500 a dive, plus Vt.1,900 for equipment (if required), with reductions for six or more dives. All of Dave's dives are boat dives and they're particularly suited to families with younger divers or small groups. PADI open-water certification courses (Vt.37,500 plus gear rental) are offered.

The nine-hole **Santo Golf Club** (tel. 37777) is at Palikulo. Greens fees are Vt.1,000 and club rental Vt.500. You're unlikely to encounter other golfers during the week, and the weekly competition starts at 1500 Saturday (the bar is only open on Saturday afternoon). The last Sunday of each month is family day, with volleyball and swimming off the beach next to the club, followed by a barbecue (Vt.500). Cows bathe in the lagoon near the clubhouse where a spring provides fresh water, but the crocodiles that once frequented the seventh tee are long gone.

ACCOMMODATIONS

Under US$25

The single-story **Riviere Motel** (tel. 36782), between the market and the Sarakata River bridge, has nine rooms with shared bath and communal cooking at Vt.1,500/2,400 single/double. It's run by the Catholic mission.

The **Bamboo Garden Motel** (tel. 36837, fax 36061, valiant@vanuatu.com.vu), upstairs overlooking the market, has 10 basic rooms at Vt.1,500/2,500/3,000 single/double/triple with shared bath or Vt.2,800/3,800/4,500 with private bath.

The two-story **Unity Park Motel** (tel. 36052, fax 36025, locm@vanuatu.com.vu) overlooks Unity Park in the center of town. The 13 clean rooms with communal cooking and bathing facilities are Vt.1,350/2,100/2,400/3,200 single/double/triple/quad downstairs, or Vt.2,400/2,900 triple for a back/front room upstairs (Vt.600 extra for air-conditioning). If the motel is full, they may let you camp in the fenced back yard for Vt.700 pp. You can use the washing machine for Vt.450 per load.

Loran Guest House (tel. 36863), near the USP Center, has four basic rooms with shared bath at Vt.1,200 pp (singles must be prepared to share). Breakfast is Vt.300 or you can cook for yourself. Check the place out before agreeing to stay.

Eight-room **Asia Motel** (tel. 36323), opposite the Westpac Bank, is a good value at Vt.2,000/2,500 single/double with private bath and fan. Room no. 9 at the back of the complex gets a nice sea breeze and is quieter than those in front. Communal cooking facilities are available.

The **Church of Christ Transit House** (tel. 36633 or 36781) has two houses near Simonsen Wharf, east of town. There's a two-room guesthouse near Vunamele Church, and a newer eight-room Conference Transit House adjacent. Rooms are Vt.1,000/1,800 single/double, and good shared cooking facilities are available. Once you have a room it's fine, but it may take a bit of searching to find the person with the keys. Alcohol is not allowed.

US$25–50

The **Natapoa Motel** (tel. 36643), two blocks back behind Hotel Santo, has seven units with cooking facilities, fridge, and private bath at Vt.3,000/4,000 single/double—a good value.

The **New Look Hotel** (tel. 36440, fax 36095, newlook@vanuatu.com.vu) on the waterfront has nine clean fan-cooled rooms with private bath at Vt.2,820/3,940 single/double. The two rooms with air conditioning are Vt.600 extra. Cooking facilities are provided and there's a lounge with a view of Segond Channel. Look for the manager in the store below the motel.

Kalmer's Guest House (tel. 36108 or 36153, fax 36720, kalmer@mpeo.org), on the hillside behind Jungle Juice Kava Bar just east of town, has two rooms at Vt.4,000 each or Vt.6,000 for both. The kitchen, lounge, and bathing facilities are shared. There's a great view of Segond Channel from the balcony.

US$50–100

Hotel Santo (tel. 36250, fax 36749, hotelsanto@vanuatu.com.vu) is a stylish two-story establishment in the middle of town. Its 22 air-conditioned rooms with bath upstairs in the main building are Vt.10,380/11,590/12,800 single/double/triple. The regular rooms are overpriced, but Hotel Santo also caters to scuba divers who usually stay in eight "budget" rooms facing the swimming pool at Vt.6,500/7,690 with

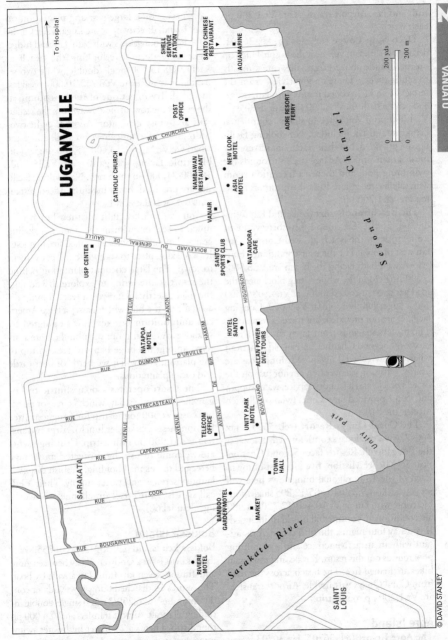

To Hospital

LUGANVILLE

SHELL
SERVICE
STATION

SANTO CHINESE
RESTAURANT

AQUAMARINE

POST
OFFICE

AORE RESORT
FERRY

RUE CHURCHILL

CATHOLIC CHURCH

NAMBAWAN
RESTAURANT

NEW LOOK
MOTEL

ASIA
MOTEL

VANAIR

BOULEVARD DU GENERAL DE GAULLE

USP CENTER

SANTO
SPORTS CLUB

NATANGORA
CAFE

HIGGINSON

Channel

Segond

PASTEUR

NATAPOA
MOTEL

PICANON

HOTEL
SANTO

HAKEIM

ALLAN POWER
DIVE TOURS

RUE DUMONT D'URVILLE

BIR

DE

Unity Park

RUE D'ENTRECASTEAUX

TELECOM
OFFICE

AVENUE

AVENUE

UNITY PARK
MOTEL

BOULEVARD

RUE LAPÉROUSE

SARAKATA

RUE

TOWN
HALL

RUE COOK

BAMBOO
GARDEN MOTEL

MARKET

RUE BOUGAINVILLE

RIVIERE
MOTEL

Sarakata River

SAINT
LOUIS

200 yds

200 m

0

0

© DAVID STANLEY

bath and fan. Airport transfers are Vt.1,200 pp each way.

Deco Stop Lodge (tel. 36175, fax 36101, deco@vanuatu.com.vu), near the hospital high up on the hillside above Luganville, caters mostly to scuba divers. There's a great view from the terrace. The 11 screened rooms with fan, fridge, and private bath are Vt.8,000 single or double (or Vt.4,000 pp if you agree to share), continental breakfast and tax included. No cooking facilities are provided, but their restaurant serves tasty meals at fair prices. A large deck surrounds the swimming pool and there's a recreation room with satellite television. Round-trip airport transfers are Vt.1,200 pp.

The Beachfront Resort (Mike and Kay Windle, tel. 36881, fax 36882, bfresort@vanuatu .com.vu) is on the beach at "Red Corner," two km west of town. The three air-conditioned bungalows with bath facing the beach are Vt.6,500/8,500 single/double, while a long block near the road has two fan-cooled rooms at Vt.4,500/6,500 and a larger family room at Vt.9,000. Cooking facilities are not provided, but there's a restaurant. The motel's spacious front lawn catches a nice breeze off Segond Channel, and an old American wharf and wrecked Taiwanese fishing boat are nearby. Cruising yachts often anchor just off the motel's beach, and a laundry service, water supply, and ice are provided for yachties (who you'll often meet at the bar).

The **Coral Quays Resort** (tel. 36257, fax 36647, www.coralquays.com), formerly known as the Bougainville Resort, faces Segond Channel near St. Michel Mission, five km west of town. Each of the 18 hexagonal bungalows here will set you back Vt.9,250/10,885/12,895 single/double/triple with fan or Vt.10,440/12,720/14,990 air-conditioned, continental breakfast included. If you stay four nights, the fifth is free. A restaurant with an attractive terrace and a swimming pool rounds out this resort. Kayaks and mountain bikes are loaned free. The beach across the road from Coral Quays isn't usable. Airport transfers are Vt.1,200 pp round-trip.

Aore Island

The **Aore Resort** (tel. 36705, fax 36703, www

.aore.net) is on a large working plantation on Aore Island, directly opposite Luganville. Of the 10 thatched bungalows with bath, fan, and fridge, eight have decks overlooking the beach at Vt.11,000/13,400 single/double, while two set back in the garden are Vt.8,750/10,600, breakfast included. Try to get one of the beach units at the end of the row farthest away from the restaurant and noisy generator. Another eight two-bedroom family bungalows on a hill above the wharf are Vt.11,000/13,400/17,100 single/double/triple facing the garden or Vt.13,700/16,600/21,000 on the beach. No cooking facilities are provided, but a medium-priced restaurant/bar faces the wharf.

You can snorkel right off their beach (not much to see) or swim in the pool. Snorkeling gear and mountain bikes are loaned free to guests. It's a relaxing place to stay while still convenient to town. The large coconut plantation behind the resort is interesting to explore. If you take the road directly inland you'll reach a ramp diagonally up the hill, which passes a large American ammunition bunker now populated by swallows. A dozen more such bunkers are scattered among the huge banyan trees on top of the plateau, and you'll see herds of beef cattle and cacao plantations.

The resort operates a boat shuttle to Luganville four times a day, which is free for guests but costs Vt.500 round-trip for nonguests (free for nonguests who order lunch). Airport transfers are Vt.900 pp round-trip. Cruising yachts are welcome to use the protected anchorage here, and there's mail holding, rubbish disposal, laundry service, and water supply. Their VHF call sign is "Aore" (call-up channel 16, working channel 68).

Bokissa Island

Bokissa Eco Island (tel. 36913, fax 36855, www .bokissa.vu) is on a sandy coral cay between Aore and Tutuba, seven km from Luganville by boat. The resort's 14 thatched bungalows with air conditioning are Vt.26,250/31,500 single/double including all meals. Airport transfers are Vt.4,000 pp round-trip. There's a 25-meter freshwater swimming pool with a swim-up bar. It takes a bit more than an hour to walk around Bokissa's 70 hectares on the beach, and the reef diving is incredible. The 47-meter coastal trader MV *Henry Bonneaud* was scuttled 200 meters offshore in 1989 to create an attraction. Bokissa's two dive boats give access to over 20 dive sites. Most guests arrive on all-inclusive package tours from Australia, and local bookings from within Vanuatu are rare.

OTHER PRACTICALITIES
Food
Local meals are served in a double row of thatched huts in Unity Park, and from counters along one side of the market itself. A large plate of beef, chicken, or fish and rice will be around Vt.250.

KC's Cafe and Snack Bar (tel. 36675; weekdays 0630–1630, Sat. 0630–1300), opposite Vanair, is a good place for breakfast, lunch, or just a cup of coffee on their pleasant breezy terrace with picnic tables.

Leslie Bianchessi's **Natangora Café** (tel. 36811; weekdays 0730–1600, Sat. 0800–1300), on the main street, has a cozy atmosphere. The lunch special (such as chicken pie and salad) changes daily, and aside from the tasty cakes, pies, burgers, and omelettes, they have Luganville's top ice-cream cones. The coffee comes with one free refill. The kitchen closes at 1630 weekdays and at noon on Saturday.

The **Nambawan Restaurant** (Carina and Terry Sims, tel. 37303; weekdays 0730–2100, weekends 1000–1400 and 1700–2100), opposite the ANZ Bank, serves a Vt.200 rice and stew lunch which may be the best bargain in town, plus burgers (from Vt.950) and pizza (Vt.750). This is the place to taste the organic Santo beef in the form of a sirloin steak (Vt.1,550) or filet mignon (Vt.1,750). An Internet café is also here.

The **Santo Sports Club** (tel. 36373; Mon.–Thurs. 0900–midnight, Fri. and Sat. 0900–0100, Sun. 0900–2300) serves an inexpensive chicken and rice lunch, or try the poulet fish for a bit more. The cozy little bar upstairs through the casino offers satellite TV and you can eat on a balcony overlooking the main street. Happy hour is

1730–1930 daily. All this is fine, but it's sad to see how the locals are exploited by the noisy slot machines in the adjacent gaming room.

Groceries
Lo Chan Moon (tel. 36530), between the Santo Sports Club and Hotel Santo, is the largest supermarket. Their expensive imported fruits and vegetables arrive by ship once a month and sell out fast. LCM and the many other Chinese stores around town stay open till sundown, even on weekends and holidays.

Luganville Market next to the town hall is open from early Monday morning until Tuesday noon, Wednesday morning until Thursday noon, and Friday morning until Saturday noon. Different villages supply the market during these three periods, and prices can vary according to who is there. Expect to find local produce such as island and Chinese cabbage, sweet potatoes, taro, pumpkins, peppers, tomatoes, lettuce, spring onions, papaya, limes, bananas, watermelon, grapefruit, and pineapple, depending on the season. Buy a piece of the local tapioca pudding called *raprap* or some flowers for your room. Also watch for women weaving baskets or mats, or selling handicrafts.

The **French Bakery** (no sign) is in a white two-story building almost opposite Hardware Santo at the east end of town. They have buns and croissants as well as baguettes, but sell out by early afternoon.

Entertainment
The bar at the Santo Sports Club pretty well sums up Luganville's social scene. Kava is what people drink here, and a good choice is **Green Light Nakamal,** just around the corner from the Unity Shell gas station on the main street. They open at 1800 daily, and kava is Vt.50-100 a cup. Many other *nakamals* are in the Chapuis area beyond the stadium north of town.

Information
The Santo Tourist Information Center (weekdays 0730–2100, weekends 1000–1400 and 1700–2100) is inside the Nambawan Restaurant opposite the ANZ Bank.

The USP Center Library (tel. 36438), inland four blocks on the road from the Santo Sports Club, opens Tuesday to Thursday 0800–1700, Friday 0830–1630, and Saturday 0830–1030. The adjacent business office sells a variety of textbooks on the Pacific.

Services

The Westpac Bank (weekdays 0830–1600) is opposite the Motel New Look behind Nambawan Restaurant, while the ANZ Bank (weekday 0900–1530) with its ATM is opposite the post office a block east. The National Bank (weekdays 0800–1500) is next to the Santo Sport Club. Evenings and weekends, you may be able to change money at the Sports Club at a poor rate.

The post office (tel. 36342; weekdays 0730–1130 and 1330–1630) opposite the ANZ Bank contains a philatelic bureau. Card telephones are available at the Telecom office, a block back from Unity Park.

The CNS Internet Café (weekdays 0730–1130 and 1330–1700), beside the Westpac Bank in the same building as Air Vanuatu, charges Vt.25 a minute for Internet access. Luganville Stationary (tel. 36144; weekdays 0730–1200 and 1330–1700), next to the ANZ Bank, charges the same for access. They also do two-hour photo developing.

The Immigration office (tel. 36724) is at the east end of town.

The public pay toilets are provided in Unity Park.

Health

The Northern District Hospital (tel. 36345) is on the hill above Luganville.

In non-life threatening circumstances, turn to Dr. Timothy Robert Vocor who has a clinic at Luganville Drug Store (tel. 36678 or 36141), behind the Westpac Bank. He works for the Health Department during business hours, so you've a better chance of catching him from 1130–1330 and after 1630.

Santo Pharmacy (tel. 36260; weekdays 0800–1145 and 1400–1700) is opposite the Santo Sports Club.

TRANSPORTATION

By Air

Vanair (tel. 36421), with an office near the Westpac Bank, flies from Espiritu Santo to Port Vila (Vt.13,450) three or four times a day, five times a week via Norsup. Another route from Espiritu Santo to Port Vila goes via Walaha, Longana, Sara, and Lonorore weekly, making stopovers on Ambae and Pentecost possible to/from Port Vila. Aircraft based at Espiritu Santo also fly to Gaua (Vt.8,280), Sola (Vt.9,370), Mota Lava (Vt.9,520), and Torres (Vt.14,020) twice a week, and to Craig Cove (Vt.7,040) weekly. Many offbeat interisland flights operate between remote outer islands, so study the Vanair timetable.

By Ship

To learn about ships doing the Luganville-Port Vila run (around Vt.6,500 one way), go down to the wharf and start asking. There are several departures a week, with the ships stopping at many smaller islands along the way.

Sealink Ltd. (tel. 36517, fax 36628, sealink@ vanuatu.com.vu), near Luganville College across the Sarakata bridge from town, operates the barges *Tina I* and *Brisk* to Ambae (Vt.2,500), Pentecost (Vt.3,500), Ambrym (Vt.4,000), Paama (Vt.4,500), Epi (Vt.5,000), and Port Vila (Vt.7,000) once a week. These one-way deck fares include basic food, but you should definitely carry additional food with you. The official schedule is a departure from Santo on Monday night, arriving at Port Vila Wednesday night, departing Port Vila again Thursday night, and arriving back at Santo on Saturday morning.

Ask about the local barges *Roena* and *Dinh I* at Dinh Shipping (tel. 36750) at Melcoffee Sawmill, west of town.

Smaller copra boats shuttle between Luganville and Malekula stopping at places such as Vao, Atchin, Wala, and Rano which take less than a day. Look for such boats at the Simonsen Wharf, east of Luganville, or at Melcoffee Sawmill, three km west of town. While making your enquiries, you might also find a Chinese trading ship doing two-week trips out of Espiritu Santo collecting copra.

The 158-passenger freighter *Havannah* sails directly from Santo to Nouméa, New Caledonia, about once a month. The agent in Santo is Coulon Agencies (tel. 36172). You must book a week in advance and a ticket to leave New Caledonia is mandatory. The one-way fare will be around US$200.

The ferry to Aore Island leaves the BP Wharf four times daily (Vt.500 pp round-trip).

By Road

Half a dozen minibuses run up and down the east coast between Hog Harbor and Luganville, leaving Hog Harbor in the morning and Luganville around 1600 in the afternoon. This timing makes it impossible to use them for a day trip, but fine to get to Lonnoc Beach Resort. The locals catch them at Luganville market, but another good place to wait is the benches in front of the Unity Shell service station (tel. 36623) in the center of town. Most buses and trucks gas up here before leaving. Tuesday is market day for the South Santo people, so you can be sure of a ride to Tangoa Island (Vt.300) that afternoon. The East Santo people come in on Thursday, so that day you'll have a choice of rides to Big Bay, Hog Harbor (Vt.300), and Port Olry (Vt.400). On Saturday, both groups arrive simultaneously, so you might get a ride almost anywhere.

"Service" minibuses around town charge Vt.100 pp anywhere between the hospital, Chapuis, former British Paddock, Melcoffee Sawmill, and St. Michel Mission. To the airport is Vt.150 pp, to Palikulo or Surunda Vt.200 pp, to Turtle Bay Vt.300 pp, to Hog Harbor Vt.400 pp. A taxi to the airport is Vt.500, to Million Dollar Point Vt.600, to Palikulo Vt.800.

Espiritu Santo is a large island and getting around is difficult unless you hire a minibus or rent a car. Car rentals are available from **Hotel Santo** (tel. 36250, fax 36749) at Vt.3,800 a day, plus Vt.38 a kilometer, plus Vt.1,350 insurance. Unlimited km rentals are Vt.9,000 a day, plus Vt.1,350 insurance, reduced to Vt.8,000 a day for rentals of three days or longer.

Santo 4WD Hire (Joyce Graham, tel. 37259, benbay@vanuatu.com.vu; weekdays 0800–1700), below the Santo Sport Club, charges Vt.12,000/ 13,000 for a small/large pickup truck including insurance and unlimited kilometers. Rentals of three days or more are a bit cheaper. The number of vehicles available at Luganville is limited, so it's a good idea to reserve.

Tours

Glen Russell of **Butterfly Tours** (tel. 36537 or 44314, fax 36116) operates a six-hour "Tales of the South Pacific" sightseeing tour that takes in the plantation where James Michener stayed during WW II, the blue holes, and Champagne Beach. Glen charges Vt.4,500 pp for two people minimum, with reductions for groups of eight or more. He can also organize tours to remote villages and to see fire dancing. His 12-seater minibus with driver can be hired for the day at Vt.12,000. Contact him through Hotel Santo, where he has a reservation book, and also ask about tours at KC's Cafe.

Timmy Rovo of **Santo Heritage Tours** (tel. 36862, VHS channel 12) does tours to Fanafo, plus trips to Timmy's secret snorkeling spots at Vt.2,500–4,000 pp. Kenneth Kelmin of **Santo Bus Tours** (tel. 36601), based at Hotel Santo, has half-day tours from Vt.2,000 pp.

It's also possible to hire one of the Luganville "service" minibuses and organize your own sightseeing tour at Vt.5,000/10,000 a half/full day with an 11-seater vehicle, gas, and driver included. Write out a complete list of everything you might wish to see, then negotiate.

Airport

Pekoa Airport (SON), between Luganville and Palikulo, is five km east of town. Pekoa is a reconditioned WW II airstrip, one of five remaining in the area. Taxis (Vt.500 for the car) and occasional minibuses (Vt.150 pp) connect the airport to town.

EAST SANTO

The pavement on the east coast road ends five km north of Luganville, then it's a potholed coral road all the way to Port Olry. Two km north of Surunda (nine km northeast of Luganville), at the back of the Agricultural Research and Training

Center, is a deep, spring-fed pool known as the **Surunda Blue Hole,** with transparent water. Turn in near the research center where you see a public telephone beside the road.

Seven km north of the Agricultural Research and Training Center is a narrow bridge over a clear river. Turn right on the side road just after the bridge, and about 300 meters along, watch for the wreck of a small American fighter aircraft on the left. At the end of this road is a lovely beach by the river, where you could ask permission to swim.

A short distance north on the main highway is a turnoff to the left to Matevulu College, nine km north of Surunda. Here you'll find an abandoned American airstrip, which explains the presence of the plane. Near the west end of the airstrip, keep left on the track, and go straight into a dip and a bit ahead to the 17-meter-deep **Matevulu Blue Hole,** 1.5 km off the main highway. It's rather green and too muddy for swimming (although the cows like it). The college itself, up on the plateau, was built with Australian aid money in 1983.

On the right, seven km north of Matevulu College, is the signposted **Jerimboo Blue Hole,** where a fee is charged to swim. The limestone rock of this area explains these numerous pools.

Just north of Shark Bay, a five-km side road leads to the village of Kole 1 on Santo's east coast, two km north of which is the **Loru Protected Area** (admission Vt.500, www.positiveearth .org/vpai) with 220 hectares of virgin lowland rainforest. The Loru Environment Centre, built in the style of a traditional meetinghouse, contains colorful display boards outlining conservation issues. Guided hikes (Vt.500 pp) through the forest to a bat cave are offered, during which the legends of the area are recounted. It's possible to stay in the chief's guest house for about Vt.2,000 pp, plus Vt.1,000 pp for meals. Otherwise you can camp or sleep in a hammock on the beach. The Wan Tok Environment Centre (tel. 36153, fax 36720) in the Rural Lands Building near Police Headquarters in Luganville will have information.

A 50-km ride up the coastal highway from Luganville, through coconut plantations crowded with cattle, brings you to friendly **Hog Harbor,** Espiritu Santo's second-largest village. An English-speaking village, Hog Harbor has a large *nakamal* where you can while away the hours getting to know the inhabitants. The Co-op Store nearby sells cold drinks. In front of the Presbyterian church overlooking the village is a monument to Dr. John Bowie who introduced Christianity here in 1898. An American base was at Hog Harbor during WW II, and in the early 1970s, American land developer Eugene Peacock attempted to subdivide and sell choice beachfront property near his Lokalee Beach Resort to American Vietnam war veterans. Peacock's land grab set in motion the movement toward independence.

Champagne Beach, one of the finest in the Pacific, is three km off the main road near Hog Harbor (Vt.300 per person "honesty box" admission fee). The talcum white sands curve around a turquoise lagoon, with a coconut plantation and high, jungle-clad slopes behind, and picturesque Elephant Island offshore. Look for a freshwater spring on the east side of the beach at low tide. Cows often stop there for a sunset drink.

Four km north of Hog Harbor on the road to Port Olry is the signposted **Blue Lagoon,** an arm of clear brackish water cut off from the sea by high cliffs. A fee is charged to visit or swim.

At the end of the road 13 km north of Hog Harbor is the French-speaking community of **Port Olry,** with its large Catholic mission. The site is idyllic, and two lakes are on nearby Dione Island, accessible on foot at low tide. Swim in a transparent, spring-fed pool, inland before the second gate on the track north from the village. Visit **Rennet Wharf** for the view, or climb the bush track west of Port Olry for a panorama of the entire area.

Accommodations in East Santo

The landing for **Oyster Island Resort** (Anna Rodot, tel./fax 36283, oysteril@vanuatu.com.vu) is 300 meters northeast of the Matevulu College access road, then 500 meters off the main highway, 20 km northeast of Luganville. It lies on a small island about 200 meters offshore, and visitors are picked up at a dock near the mouth of the river that originates at the Matevulu Blue Hole. The seven rustic local-style lagoonside bungalows with private bath are

Vt.4,300/4,800/6,800/8,500 single/double/triple/quad, breakfast included. The Melanesian-style restaurant right on the beach serves dishes like poulet fish, fresh oysters, lobster, and pepper steak, all prepared by a French chef. Dugout canoes for paddling around the lagoon are provided, and scuba diving can be arranged with Aquamarine. Airport transfers are Vt.840 pp each way (minimum of two) or pay Vt.200 pp on one of the afternoon minibuses and walk the last 500 meters. Yachties are welcome to drop in for a sundowner or a meal (good holding in 6–10 meters of heavy sand).

One km west of Champagne Beach, 55 km north of Luganville and a bit more than a kilometer off the main road near Hog Harbor, is Kalmer Vocor's **Lonnoc Beach Resort** (tel. 36153, tel./fax 36141, www.positiveearth.org/lonnoc). It has by far the most attractive setting of any of Espiritu Santo's resorts, on an idyllic beach with superb views. The seven thatched bungalows cost Vt.3,000/5,000 single/double including breakfast. Camping is Vt.500 pp. Meals are available, or you can ask permission to use the restaurant kitchen to cook your own food. This may be allowed when they're not too busy, in which case it's wise to inquire when booking and to bring groceries from Luganville. The kerosene lighting adds a romantic touch. It's set slightly back from the beach and is meticulously maintained. You can't beat the swimming, and there are neighboring villages to visit. Several tours are offered to the Loru and Vatthe conservation areas, caves, gardens, and a blue hole. The Hog Harbor minibuses will bring you here most afternoons for Vt.500 pp.

INTO THE INTERIOR
Matantas

Some 46 km north of Luganville, a road runs west through Sara to the **Vatthe Conservation Area** at Matantas on Big Bay. The turnoff is a few km south of Hog Harbor. Ten km west of the coastal highway, you'll pass the junction with the rough jeep track south toward Fanafo (which connects with the road to the western side of Big Bay). Keep straight and another seven km

west toward Matantas you'll reach a spectacular viewpoint over Big Bay and the Vatthe reserve. From here the road drops sharply, reaching Matantas after another seven km (or 70 km total from Luganville).

It was here on Big Bay that the Spanish conquistador Quirós established his "New Jerusalem" in 1606. A wall eight meters long with two gun openings, near the point where the Jordan River empties into the bay, is reputed to date from this time. In 1995, most of this area was set aside as a nature reserve run by the communities of Sara and Matantas. This ecotourism project is intended to protect 4,470 hectares of rainforest from logging, and it's a terrific place to visit, with all income going to a worthy cause. Visitors pay a Vt.600 pp conservation fee upon arrival.

Guests stay in six attractive thatched bungalows with shared bath at Vt.2,150 pp, breakfast included. Otherwise you can camp at Vt.500 pp. Lunch is Vt.600 and at dinner you can order vegetarian/meat dishes for Vt.600/1,000 (or Vt.1,400 for a three-course meal). If you wish to cook your own food, there's a Vt.500 charge to use the facilities. Airport transfers are Vt.5,000 pp each way. Weekdays at 1500 a minibus departs Unity Shell Station in Luganville, charging Vt.2,500 per group of up to five persons. Activities include guided nature walks (Vt.700 pp), a three-hour garden tour (Vt.1,000), a five-hour Jordan River trek (Vt.1,500/2,500 without/with a barbecue lunch), a village tour (Vt.1,500 including dinner), a custom dance ceremony (Vt.1,450), and a custom medicine tour with Chief Moses (Vt.1,000). Book through the Wan Tok Environment Centre (tel. 36153, fax 36720, vatthe@vanuatu.com.vu) in the Rural Lands Building beside the Fire Department on the traffic circle near Police Headquarters in Luganville.

Fanafo

Fanafo (also known as Tanafo or Vanafo), 22 km north of Luganville, was the center of the 1980 Santo Rebellion and Jimmy Stevens' Nagriamel Custom Movement (see History in the Vanuatu Introduction section). A taxi from Luganville should run Vt.4,000 round-trip. Until early 1992, Fanafo officially didn't exist. Officials weren't allowed to visit, and no taxes were paid. Today it's quieter, and tourists are even bused in to see traditional dances and similar activities. The villagers cling to custom as a political statement, although most have adopted Western dress.

Several large WW II ammunition storage bunkers and a number of dwarf coconut trees are beside the road from Luganville. The place where Eddie Stevens was killed, at Mon Exil before Fanafo, is now marked by flowers. A sign at the entrance to Fanafo itself announces a Vt.500 pp village admission fee, collected daily 0800–1130 and 1330–1730. Ask for a guide to show you around. Near the information hut and a huge banyan tree is the spot where the pre-1980 cargo cult met in one of Vanuatu's most striking *nakamals,* narrow and very long. This was demolished in 1989, and your entry fee goes toward a new traditional-style *nakamal,* shorter than the old one, slowly being erected here.

In the center of the village is the concrete Nagriamel Upper Council office where Jimmy Stevens was captured as he sat outside with his family, drinking kava. Jimmy had 15 natural sons, 12 daughters, and 28 adopted children, and you may be introduced to Frankie Stevens, a former member of parliament and current Nagriamel leader. Adjoining the office is a flagpole, and nearby the tin-roofed Ten Head Committee building. In 1980, Nagriamel radio broadcast from the small green hut here. Facing the flagpole is the unfinished Federation Bank, construction of which was halted in 1980.

Not far from this area is the Stevens family compound where Jimmy was laid to rest in a circular thatched hut in 1994, after spending 11 years in jail. To enter the compound, your guide must sound a gong at the gate, and you may have to pay an additional fee to Yanki Stevens if you want to see Jimmy's tomb. Jimmy's house is the long thatched building behind the grave. A footpath beside the Stevens compound leads down to the Sarakata River, where you can swim.

You'll probably also be taken to meet Chief Tari Puluk (Terry Bullock) who lives at the end of a road, past peanut and kava plantations. Near an old *nakamal* halfway there is the tomb of Chief Paul Puluk, founder of Nagriamel, who died in 1982. Paul was imprisoned three times for his political activities, and a Bislama history of the movement is posted. Activities might include a walk to the large waterfall nearby, or a three-hour hike to the interior village of Butmas.

North of Fanafo

From Fanafo a steep, rough coral road leads 37 km north to the Jordan River, and on to Talatas, Maiao, and Tolomako on **Big Bay.** It's necessary to ford the Jordan on a concrete ramp, which is only possible in dry weather. Some 12 km before the Jordan, an overgrown bush track continues north to Matantas and Hog Harbor, but this should only be attempted in a 4WD vehicle. A much easier route to Hog Harbor is to the right, nine km north of Fanafo, just where the main road toward the Jordan turns sharp left. This shortcut goes via Palon village, straight to Turtle Bay.

If one is *very* keen (and a bit crazy), it's possible to walk from Big Bay to Wailapa in South Santo in six hard days. It's damp and slippery, and you'll have to cross fast rivers up to your neck, but you'll see some of the most remote people in the Pacific. Just don't go during the rainy season (Jan.–April) if you're not into drowning. You can buy food from villagers along the way, but you'll need a strong stomach. Take plenty of stick tobacco to give them. A guide, of course, would be required. Ask for Chief Robert at **Talatas.** Longer, but less rigorous, is the walk along the coast to Cape Cumberland. In fact, it's possible to hike right around Espiritu Santo this way, if you're experienced and well equipped.

Another option would be to fly into the new airstrip at Lajmoli on the west coast of Espiritu Santo on the weekly Vanair flight from Luganville (Vt.6,550). From Lajmoli you could hike north along the coast to Cape Cumberland, across the peninsula to Big Bay, or south to the end of the road at Tasiriki in under a week. Steep cliffs south of Wusi will force you to detour inland with the help of a guide.

SOUTH SANTO

To see a bit of the island and experience village life, go to Santo market on Tuesday or Saturday before

VANUATU

1500, and look for a truck west on the road along Segond Channel through endless coconut plantations to **Tangoa Island**. In 1895, a Presbyterian Bible College intended to spread the Gospel to northern Vanuatu was established on Tangoa by Canadian missionary Joseph Annand, who spent 18 years on the island. At Tangoa, ask for local fisherman John Pama Vari and he'll put you up in his house. The people in the fish market by the river behind Luganville Market know John well, and can help put you in touch. You may borrow his outrigger canoe to paddle up and down the strait between Tangoa and the mainland (excellent anchorage for yachts here), but don't swim—too many sharks. Hike up to **Narango** for the view. This is an easy, rewarding trip.

The Eastern Chain

Although the most visited parts of Vanuatu have already been described, there's still a long eastern chain of islands awaiting adventurers who wish to tread where few previous visitors have been. Epi and Paama, just north of Efate, are the closest outer islands to Port Vila, and relatively inexpensive to fly to, yet few tourists arrive. Ambrym occasionally attracts those interested in its volcanoes or traditional culture. Pentecost is best known for its land diving, and very few foreigners arrive at other times, although North Pentecost offers sundry natural beauties. Ambae is a natural stepping-stone for Santo-bound travelers interested in a taste of outer island life. The remote Banks and Torres islands are the least visited of all, lonely outposts of Pacific life beyond the horizons of tourism. Vanair flies to all these islands and each has a special character of its own.

EPI

Epi (445 square km) and smaller Tongoa were once a single island, until a volcanic explosion separated them around the year 1450. An undersea volcano is now trying to link them again. See it all from Epi's radio tower. Lamen Bay airstrip is at Epi's northwest end, with **Paradise Sunset Bungalows** (Tasso Welawo, tel. 28230) only a 10-minute walk away. The three simple bungalows with shared bath are Vt.5,630/7,600 including two meals if booked through Island Safaris or about Vt.1,000 pp less if booked direct. You may be allowed to camp for Vt.500 pp. The two-room **Rovo Bay Resthouse** (Shefa Provincial Council, tel. 28041) five km from Lamen Bay is Vt.2,000 pp. Lamen Bay is a favorite anchorage for cruising yachts, and it's possible to swim with a tame dugong, which resides in the bay. Vanair charges Vt.7,570 to fly to Lamen Bay from Port Vila (twice weekly).

Epi's second airstrip at Valesdir is 30 km south of Lamen Bay by road. The **Epi Island Guesthouse** (Rob Crapper, tel./fax 28225, www.epi-island-guesthouse.com.vu), on a white beach near Valesdir, is in a large wooden building with four rooms at Vt.5,625 pp including all meals. Only one of the rooms has a private bathroom but all cost the same. There's electricity, a bar, library, and porch. Vanair flights from Port Vila to Valesdir are Vt.6,550 one way.

PAAMA AND LOPEVI

Lush little Paama (32 square km) sits between two of Vanuatu's most spectacular volcanoes. Tavie Airport is at Paama's north end, almost opposite Ulei Airport on Ambrym. The administrative center and main wharf are at Liro, a few km southeast of Tavie via a roller-coaster road. Two small resthouses are available at Liro: a two-room guesthouse operated by the Presbyterian Church at Vt.500 pp, and the privately operated **Tavira Guest House** with three rooms at Vt.1,200 pp. Both have cooking facilities. Information should be available through the Malampa Provincial Office (tel. 48411) in Liro. A road runs right across the center of Paama. Ask before swimming anywhere off Paama, as sharks are a problem here. Vanair has flights to Paama from Port Vila (Vt.8,240) twice a week, and Ulei (Vt.2,840) and Lamen Bay (Vt.2,950) weekly. The local Vanair agent is quite strict about overweight baggage.

Paama's eastern neighbor **Lopevi** has a classic symmetrical cone 1,413 meters high, with a five-km base. It's one of the three most active volcanoes in Vanuatu, and after an eruption in the early 1970s, Lopevi's population was permanently relocated to Epi. Another eruption in June 2001 dropped a thick blanket of ash over neighboring Paama.

AMBRYM

Ambrym, like Tanna, is famous for its traditional culture and active volcanoes, yet it's less impacted by tourism. Periodic eruptions have left an ash plain near the center of the island, lava valleys, and a rocky, broken coastline. Black sandy beaches run right along the south coast, and Ambrym's dark volcanic soil contrasts sharply with the deep green vegetation.

The island's 12-km-wide caldera probably formed during a cataclysmic eruption 2,000 years

ago. It's the most active volcano in Vanuatu, and the only real reason to visit. The lava from Marum (1,270 meters) drains out onto the caldera floor, while Benbow (1,159 meters) drains through fissures into the western part of the island. During the last 200 years there have been at least eight large eruptions with lava flowing from the caldera. The most recent was in 1929.

The 8,000 inhabitants live in the three corners of this triangular island, and their only links are by foot or sea. Two of these communities, Craig Cove in the west and Ulei in the east, have airstrips, with Vanair flights from Port Vila (Vt.8,920) three times a week, from Espiritu Santo (Vt.6,890) and Norsup (Vt.4,640) weekly. North Ambrym is accessible only from the sea.

Traditional Culture

The Ambrym islanders produce high-quality woodcarvings and tree fern figures in large quantities. As in most of northern Vanuatu, a power-

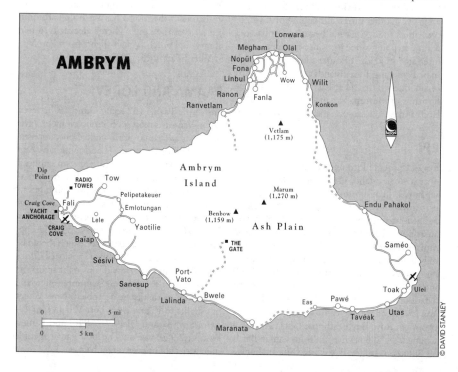

ful system of traditional copyright applies, and only those with the traditional rights to make certain types of objects are allowed to do so.

Vanuatu's most famous handicrafts come from North Ambrym, especially the tall slit drums called *tamtams* in Bislama. Craftsmen slot and hollow two-meter breadfruit logs, then carve faces on them, and these are used as signal drums. Also characteristic are the black tree ferns carved for the *mhehe* graded rituals, and bamboo flutes up to a meter long with burnt-in geometric designs. Painted masks with hair of bleached banana fiber are worn in rites to increase the yield of yams. Masks worn by participants in Rom dances during the Ole ceremony in July and August represent certain spiritual aspects of power associated with yams.

Storytellers on Ambrym use intricate sand drawings to illustrate their tales. Up to 180 stylized patterns that the artist draws without removing his finger from the sand can convey a variety of messages. Ambrym sorcerers are famous throughout Vanuatu for their magic, often associated with the destructive power of the island's volcanoes.

Southwest Ambrym

A dramatic black cliff blocks the north end of **Craig Cove,** where a high black beach curves around to the Catholic mission at Fali. Cruising yachts, interisland boats, and local speedboats anchor off this beach, and buy supplies at the adjacent co-op. Craig Cove airstrip is a 10-minute walk away.

Have a look at the fern carvings in front of the Craig Cove Co-op and the slit gong behind Fali's Catholic church. You can hike up to the radio tower on **Menei Hill** (375 meters) in about an hour. The road begins near Fali village, and follows the ridge of Merak Crater all the way. From atop the tower you'll have a sweeping view of western Ambrym, with Malekula and Pentecost also visible in the distance. At the final turn of the road up to the tower, a trail drops sharply to **Lake Fanteng** (visible from the tower) and the black beach beyond.

Halfway back to Craig Cove from the tower, another road runs east down into a coconut plan-

tation. It's an interesting area to explore, and if you take the turn to the right each time the road divides, you should eventually return to the south coastal road. A number of "custom villages" are up this way (including Lele, Pelipetakeuer, and Emlotungan), but you could be asked to pay as much as Vt.1,000 pp to visit their dancing grounds *(nasara)* and assorted *tamtam*. Several totem-pole-like *tamtam* at Lele village have five heads (you can see the same thing in Port Vila for free). Near the Catholic mission at **Sesivi** is a swimmable hot spring in the sea.

The corrugated-metal **Co-op Resthouse** (tel. 48499), facing the anchorage at Craig Cove and sometimes referred to as the "Commercial Center Resthouse," has three rooms at Vt.1,000 pp. Cooking is possible, but there's no electricity.

The **Presbyterian Resthouse,** next to the church and school in Wuro village, a five-minute walk from Craig Cove airstrip or the co-op, has two basic rooms at Vt.500 pp with mats on the floor in place of furniture. There's a gas stove and outhouse toilet, but the only place to bathe is the beach. It's primitive, but you'll have the opportunity to observe typical village life.

No market exists at Craig Cove, but the Co-op may have tomatoes and onions, and the local baker produces bread when he's in the mood. Small bags of peanuts are sold at the co-op.

The National Bank office next to the co-op can change traveler's checks. The Craig Cove Post Office is a kilometer east of the Craig Cove Co-op on the road to Sanesup.

The Volcano

Anyone interested in climbing the volcano in a reasonable length of time will stay at **Milee Sea Bungalows** (tel. 48657), on a rocky shore at Sanesup, about 12 km from Craig Cove airstrip. The four traditional-style bungalows with shared bath are Vt.5,850/8,760 single/double, including breakfast and dinner (or somewhat less if you book direct rather than through Island Safaris). The pickup truck ride from Craig Cove airstrip to Sanesup is Vt.2,500 per group each way (ask), but you may be able to go for less if you're alone and the resthouse owner, Enos Falau, happens to be there anyway. If three people are going, the Benbow volcano trip costs around Vt.5,000 pp, including guide, transport, and the "volcano fee." A cultural show with dancing and traditional magic is Vt.8,000 per group. Ask Enos about the art of sand drawing. Island Safaris in Port Vila books packages to Milee.

The route up to the vast ash plain in the center of the island begins near Lalinda, and you follow a creek bed. If your climb hasn't been prearranged, you'll have to pay the Vt.1,000 pp volcano fee to the village chief, who will be able to supply a guide. Allow three hours' hard climbing to the Gate (750 meters). From here you can look across the vast ash plain to Benbow and Marum. Clouds can roll in and cover you quite suddenly, and your guide may claim he doesn't know the way to Marum and refuse to take you beyond Benbow. It's strictly business for the locals, and you only get what you pay for. In rainy weather the route becomes slippery and impossible to do as a round-trip in one day.

Southeast Ambrym

No specific tourist sites exist on southeast Ambrym. The airstrip at **Ulei** ends at a cliff, and few facilities such as resthouses or stores are available. You might be able to stay in the guesthouse of Rakonven Rural Training Center (tel. 48786) at Toak, a little more than a kilometer west of Ulei Airstrip. There are two rooms, and you can cook. Ask for the manager, Tias James. A road runs along part of the south coast, and it's possible to hike along the beach between the ends of the roads at Eas and Maranata in about five hours. This will put you near the route up the volcano.

North Ambrym

North Ambrym is one of the most traditional areas in Vanuatu. Paramount Chief Tofor resides at Fanla, less than an hour's walk from the SDA mission at Linbul. He'll show you an adze made from iron allegedly given to his ancestors by Captain Cook. Otherwise all there is to see at Fanla is a few slit drums on the dance platform and some statues. To take photos (and maybe just look around), stick tobacco and Vt.1,000 must be presented. There's a Catholic mission at Olal. The northernmost villages are mostly French-speaking.

From Linbul it's a three-hour hike through gardens and bush to the top of Mt. Vetlam (1,175 meters), with good views in clear weather.

Isiah Bong operates **Vat-Mer Bungalows** (tel. 48527) next to Henyal Orkon Store at Ranvetlam. It's Vt.2,200 pp including all meals to stay in this thatched four-bed guesthouse (or almost double if you book through Island Safaris). Local guides to Marum can be hired here, and don't forget the Vt.1,000 volcano fee (this route is longer than the one from Lalinda).

Solomon Douglas Guest House (tel. 48541 or 48507), a 15-minute walk from the co-op in Ranon, has two small bungalows with shared bath at Vt.4,500/6,760 including breakfast if you book through Island Safaris or about Vt.1,000 less if you book direct. Clarify all prices beforehand. If you find Solomon Douglas too expensive, ask about staying at the Women's Club House (ask for Sarah), a five-minute walk from Ranon co-op, or the **Good Samaritan Resthouse,** right near the Co-op itself (Vt.1,500 pp).

There's no airport on North Ambrym. You can hike southeast along the coast to Ulei in two days, but not southwest to Craig Cove, as the way is blocked by lava flows. A motorboat from Ranon to Craig Cove will cost around Vt.10,000 (three hours), which can be shared among other passengers. Whenever flights arrive at Craig Cove airstrip, an outboard boat will probably set out for North Ambrym the same afternoon.

PENTECOST
Land Diving

South Pentecost is renowned for its land diving *(Nangol),* a thrilling spectacle on this thickly forested island. Men tie liana vines to their ankles, then jump head-first from atop 30-meter man-made towers, jerking to a halt just centimeters from the ground. Slack in the lifeline vine eases the shock as it stretches to its limit, and the platforms are designed to sway, so the jumpers are rarely injured. During the two weeks it takes to build a tower, women are banned from the area, and guards are posted each night to protect it from the "poison man."

The story goes that the custom originated

when a woman trying to escape an angry husband lured him into a trap by climbing a banyan tree. As the fellow climbed after her, she tied previously prepared liana vines to her ankles and jumped, followed by the man—he fell to his death while she was saved by the vines.

Today this daring feat is part of festival of yams, and there's no stigma attached to any diver who "chickens out." Before jumping, a participant can make a speech refuting allegations against him, or he can criticize anyone he likes, including the chief, on the assumption that if he lies, the spirit of the tower will let him die. The jumping is optional and done for fun—many men and boys do so at every opportunity. Even eight-year-olds prove their courage by hurling themselves from these giddy heights. Only speakers of the Sa language may perform the ritual.

When the plunging diver is about to smash to the ground, the vines stretch out fully. This slows—and finally stops—his fall just as his head brushes the spaded soil, symbolically refertilizing the earth for the next crop of yams. The diving takes place every Saturday in April and May, soon after the yam harvest. Today the diving has assumed on a second function: Paying spectators have become the main cash crop for these villagers. It's a rare opportunity to witness an event that has unexpectedly become a part of modern life in the form of bungee jumping.

Port Vila tour operators run day trips from Efate to see the land diving on Pentecost, every Saturday in April and May for Vt.40,000 pp. Included in the package are a flight over Ambrym's crater with the possibility of a peek at the bubbling lava inside, transfers, and a light lunch (unless someone forgot to bring it along). Island Safaris offers a two-night land diving package at Vt.65,000 pp including admissions, flights, accommodations, meals, and a village tour. To use a video camera is Vt.20,000 extra, and television crews filming for commercial purposes are charged Vt.100,000–400,000.

The jumps were originally held at Bunlap village, on the southeast side of Pentecost, but in recent years they've been held at Wali near Lonorore airstrip to spare tourists an exhausting four-hour hike across the island. A new road runs across the south end of Pentecost from Bay Homo to Ranwas near Bunlap, so don't get alarmed if you hear that the diving is at Bunlap again.

Although the tour companies will deny it, it's possible to stay with the locals and pay a custom fee of about Vt.5,000–7,500 pp to see the jump, plus Vt.8,000 per camera. Any visitors who make it across to Bunlap are accommodated in the village at a negotiable rate. Bunlap is picturesque, built in the traditional style on a slope. This is a strong custom area, so inquire about taboo days, especially pertaining to women.

South Pentecost

The people of Pentecost are divided into two matrilineal cross-marrying clans whose gardens and swimming areas are marked off by stones or trees. Ask someone to point these out to you. A white-gray beach runs up the southern part of the west coast. A series of waterfalls is behind **Melsisi,** a Catholic station on the central west coast. You can climb all but the last waterfall, and super swimming/jumping holes accompany them. There's great snorkeling, too, on the reef off Melsisi, with caves, canyons, and abundant fish. Climb the hill behind the village for the view. The Melsisi Catholic mission (tel. 38191) rents rooms. There's also a hospital (tel. 38366) at Melsisi.

Chief Willie Orion Bebe runs **Nangol Bungalows** (tel. 38444) at Bay Homo, 15 km south of Lonorore airstrip. The three thatched bungalows at a rivermouth on the coast are Vt.5,630/9,000 single/double including all meals. There's no electricity. Land diving tourists often stay here, and tour operators like Island Safaris have imposed these high prices.

The **Penama Provincial Guesthouse** (Aspinold Melsul, tel. 38814 or 38327), at Pangi on Bay Homo, has three rooms at Vt.1,000 pp.

Vanair has flights to Lonorore from Port Vila (Vt.11,170), Espiritu Santo (Vt.6,670), Walaha (Vt.5,320), Longana (Vt.4,870), and Sara (Vt.4,190) a couple of times a week.

North Pentecost

Land diving aside, the north is the most scenically lovely part of Pentecost. High cliffs mark the northern tip of this verdant island, falling away to white beaches with colorful reefs offshore. It's an interesting area to explore without the tourism hype of the south.

Several small local resthouses (around Vt.1,000 pp) are available on north Pentecost; for information call the Penama Provincial Offices at Abwatuntora (tel. 38304) or Loltong (tel. 38394). Camping is possible at Philip Varean's **Tiare Resort** is just southwest of Loltong, 12 km south of Sara airstrip. Philip's restaurant is popular among cruising yachties. Alfred Loli runs the three-room **Loli Guest House** at Angoro village, just a few km north of Sara. You can cook or order meals at Vt.250 apiece.

Sara receives direct Vanair flights from Port Vila (Vt.12,520), Longana (Vt.3,290), Lonorore (Vt.4,190), Walaha (Vt.4,300), and Espiritu Santo (Vt.6,550). Sara airstrip is short and rough, with a cliff at each end. It's subject to closure after rains. Unfortunately there's no connection to Craig Cove and Ulei on Ambrym. The flights between Port Vila and Pentecost pass right over Ambrym's volcanoes, and on a flight to Pentecost or Ambae, you should sit on the right-hand side for a view of central Efate, Epi, Lopevi, Paama, and Ambrym.

AMBAE

When early European explorers visited Ambae, they asked a local chief for the name of the island. He didn't quite understand them, but at that very moment a bird called an aoba flew past, and the chief assumed that was what they wanted to know. Thus, throughout the colonial period, Ambae was known as Aoba. During WW II, a U.S. serviceman named James Michener was stationed at Espiritu Santo, and the sight of Ambae on the horizon fascinated him so much that he called it "Bali Hai"—much better than the name "Leper Island," which Bougainville gave it in 1768 (there were no lepers on Ambae). Only after independence in 1980 did Ambae revert to its original name.

Ambae resembles a capsized canoe, with Maewo and Pentecost the broken outriggers. During the colonial period, women from Ambae were considered good potential wives by local

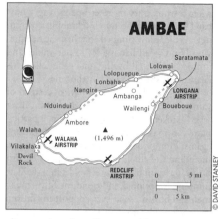

planters, though no European plantations were ever set up on Ambae itself. Today Ambae forms part of Penama Province, along with Pentecost and Maewo.

Ambae is noted for its massive volcanic peak, which rises 1,496 meters above sea level, or 3,900 meters from the sea floor. Lombenden Volcano is one of the world's few active volcanoes with warm-water sulfurous crater lakes. The summit has two large calderas containing three lakes. Manaro Ngoru is a dry lake, while Manaro Lakua is a dammed lake on the edge of the caldera. Lake Vui is two km in diameter. The lakes are thought to be the eyes of the mountain. The god Tagaro took the fire from these craters and threw it across to neighboring Ambrym. There are seven islands in the lakes, and a fumarole beside one. As you swim around, test the echo against the walls of the crater rim.

Serious eruptions may have occurred in 1575, 1670, and 1870, and over the past few hundred years there has been a number of devastating mudflows on both sides of the mountain, caused by heavy rains eroding ash deposits. In 1991, Lake Vui boiled, and the vegetation was burned as much as 120 meters above the waterline. This phenomenon was reported by a Vanair pilot; it had been unnoticed by local residents. The presence of the lakes makes Ambae the most dangerous volcano in Vanuatu, as a strong explosion could send mountains of ash and water crashing down to the coast. In December 1994, a sharp increase in volcanic activity was noted, and the volcano came close to erupting on March 5, 1995. Tremors were felt, and the volcano began emitting thick black clouds of ash and smoke. Scientists now consider a major eruption only a matter of time, and emergency evacuation plans have been prepared. During the 1994–1995 activity, Lake Vui's level dropped six meters.

The mountain can be climbed from **Ambanga** in four hours each way, but it's often socked in by fog. It's better to climb to the lakes from West Ambae, however, and a guide will be required in any case. Unless you plan to camp on top, it will take a full day, so set out before 0700. It's a difficult (but fantastic) hike, with bush knives chopping all the way.

A variety of Vanair flights service Ambae's three airstrips. Walaha receives flights from Espiritu Santo (Vt.4,190) three times a week; Lonorore (Vt.5,320) and Sara (Vt.4,300) twice a week; and Port Vila (Vt.12,970) weekly. Longana is served from Espiritu Santo (Vt.5,650) four times a week; and from Lonorore (Vt.4,870), Maewo (Vt.3,520), Port Vila (Vt.13,300), and Sara (Vt.3,290) once or twice a week. Redcliff gets a weekly flight from Espiritu Santo (Vt.4,870). With careful planning you could fly into one airstrip and out from another.

East Ambae

Saratamata, at the east end of Ambae, is the headquarters of Penama Province. **Longana** airstrip, three km from Saratamata, is on a slope, forcing the plane to land uphill and take off downhill. The Church of Melanesia mission, hospital, and post office (tel. 38347) are six km north at Lolowai, where Lake Wai Memea occupies a volcanic crater. The pretty village of Lolopuepue on the north coast is the former French headquarters, attested to by its Catholic church and stone buildings. The interisland ship ties up to a wharf here.

Due to high cliffs near the center of the island, no road runs right along the north coast, although the footpath between ends of the road is commonly used. A good plan would be to hike the 35 km from Longana to Walaha airstrip, with the strong possibility of a ride at least part of the way. A new road along the south coast connects Longana to Walaha via Redcliffe.

The **Provincial Resthouse** is near the Penama Provincial Office (tel. 38348) at Saratamata, about three km from Longana Airport. The six rooms are Vt.1,000 pp, and several stores and the beach are close at hand, which makes it a very convenient place to stay. Call ahead for reservations.

The hospital (tel. 38302) at Lolowai has one guest room available, as does Vureas High School (tel. 38378), two km northwest. Inquire about these locally.

West Ambae

If you're arriving from Longana, the road will have ended at Loloaru. A well-used footpath leads four km west to Lolombaeko, then there's a steep and winding road another four km to the Catholic mission at Loone Lakua, just above a small black-sand beach. **Nduindui,** the administrative and commercial center of West Ambae, is five km west of there. Nduindui has a small National Bank agency, open Monday, Wednesday, and Friday. **Walaha** airstrip is seven km southwest.

You can climb to Lake Vui from several points along the north coast, including Lovutialao and Lokwainavoaha above Loone Lakua. Allow at least four hours each way, plus the time you wish to spend on top. Expect the mountain to be cloud-covered.

If you have a bit of time to kill before your flight out of Walaha, walk southeast about 15 minutes up the road from Halelulu Guest House to Redcliffe. At the top of a grade, look for a track up through the bush to the tall **radio repeater tower** on Vuti Ngoro Ngoro. It's possible to climb the tower for the view.

Devil Rock is a one-hour walk south from Walaha airstrip. A local custom story tells how the spirits of deceased islanders pass this way, before assuming the form of sharks in the deep sea. All burials on Ambae are arranged so the feet of the deceased point this way. The solitary black rock pounded by the ocean was once part of an adjacent cliff, which frames a red sandy beach. There's good snorkeling in the clear water below the cliff, with pastel-colored corals and huge tropical fish. After your swim, go southeast through the coconut plantation and cut back down to another magnificent and totally different shoreline, with black tongues of lava separating beaches of white coral sand. A small corner of Pentecost is visible on the horizon to the left, and the whole unspoiled scene certainly matches Michener's image of Bali Hai.

A good base for climbing up to Lake Vui is **Toa Guest House** (Tom Hakwa, tel./fax 38405, tel. 41145, tom.hakwa@tvl.net.vu) near the Nduindui Health Center, six km northeast of Walaha airstrip. The three rooms are Vt.1,000–1,500. An electrical generator can be switched on to run the satellite television. Several small stores and fruit markets are nearby.

Halalulu Community Guest House (tel. 38320) is in a large community center building, about a 15-minute walk up the road toward Redcliffe from Walaha airstrip. The two adequate rooms with cooking facilities are Vt.1,000 pp. There's always a lot of activity around the community center and adjacent Apostolic church, so you get to meet people at the expense of some of your privacy.

If Halalulu happened to be occupied, try the church-run guesthouse near another Apostolic church in Walaha village down on the coast. None of these places have electricity, and outhouse toilets/showers are the norm. Friendly people make the difference.

Banks and Torres Islands

The Banks and Torres islands are due south of the Santa Cruz Islands in the Solomons. These out-of-the-way isles are noted for their handicrafts and traditional dancers. Together they form 882-square-km Torba Province with a population of around 7,000. Most travelers arrive on Vanair's scheduled flights from Luganville. Local guides can be hired on most islands at Vt.1,000 a day.

Gaua

Gaua (Santa Maria) is a circular green island with many stone house foundations that recall the large prehistoric population ravaged by blackbirding and disease. Gaua is interesting for its fumaroles and sulfur springs, and especially the deep crater lake drained by a waterfall on smoking Mt. Garet (797 meters). Six-km-long Lake Letas lies at an elevation of 350 meters, a tiring four-hour hike from the coast. To climb the volcano, one must cross the lake by canoe and camp, as it's too much to do in a day. Flying foxes hang from vine-encrusted banyan trees around the lake, while large eels swim through the water.

The **Charles Bice Wongrass Bungalow** (tel. 38519) is a three-minute walk from Saramolo airstrip, not far from Namasari village on the northeast side of Gaua. The two rooms in one duplex bungalow are Vt.3,250/4,300 single/double including all meals. Camping is Vt.1,200

pp, plus Vt.300 per meal (or you can cook). Island Safaris asks an exorbitant Vt.4,000 pp with breakfast alone to stay at Wongrass, so call ahead to verify prices. George Atkin, who lives opposite Wongrass, guides visitors on overnight treks to the volcano, lake, and waterfall (separate Vt.1,500 pp custom fee for each).

Gaua receives Vanair flights from Espiritu Santo (Vt.8,130), Mota Lava (Vt.4,640), Sola (Vt.3,970), and Torres (Vt.8,130), once or twice a week.

Vanua Lava

Vanua Lava, 22 km north of Gaua, is the largest and most populous of the Banks Islands. The main airstrip for the Banks is four km northwest of Sola, headquarters of Torba Province. Vanair services from Espiritu Santo (Vt.9,370), Gaua (Vt.3,970), Mota Lava (Vt.3,180), and Loh (Vt.6,890) arrive at Sola, once or twice a week. Sola is on the south side of Port Patteson, a natural harbor with safe anchorage year-round. Jets of steam rise from the hot springs on the slopes of Mt. Sere'ama (921 meters), an active volcano that erupted in 1965.

Father Luke Dini operates **Leumerus Guest House** (tel. 38823), near the Torba Provincial Office at Sola, with four bungalows at Vt.2,500 pp including meals-a good value. It's easy to call ahead for reservations, and you'll be made most welcome. Beware of saltwater crocodiles if you swim here!

Mota Lava

Ablow Airstrip is at the east end of Mota Lava, with weekly Vanair flights from Loh (Vt.7,340), Sola (Vt.3,180), Gaua (Vt.4,640), and Espiritu Santo (Vt.9,370). Near the airstrip is an interesting cave, one of the few accessible caves in the Banks. If you don't mind crawling, you'll get a spectacular view from the far end of the cave. To visit the cave, ask for Stander Haward of nearby Valuwa village.

Most of the people live at the southwest end of Motu Lava. The truck from the airstrip charges Vt.1,500 pp for the 10 km or you can walk in a couple of hours. The **Award Edgard Guesthouse** (tel. 38563), on the beach at Ngerenigman village, has two small bungalows at Vt.1,500 pp. A separate kitchen is nearby.

Facing a white-sand beach on the tiny island of Ra opposite Ngerenigman is the **Harry Memorial Guest House** (tel. 38585), 500 meters off the main island by canoe (or by wading at low tide). The four small bungalows and two three-room guest houses are Vt.2,500 pp including three meals. Verify these prices before going as Island Safaris charges Vt.5,625/7,880 for the same thing. There's a superb view of Vanua Lava from here. A speedboat hire from Sola to Ra will cost Vt.10,000 for the boat.

Other Islands

Mere Lava is a circular volcanic island, four km in diameter, with a beautiful symmetrical cone 1,028 meters high. The volcano erupted in 1606 and 1906, yet terraced villages stand on its steep slopes.

Ureparapara Island is a sunken volcano with a drowned crater that large ships can sail into. Some 300 people live there.

Torres Islands

Surfers should consider the Torres Islands, an outlying corner of the Pacific not explored until the mid-1800s. The pure white beaches here are stunning. Linua airstrip at the north end of **Loh** has a weekly Vanair service from Espiritu Santo (Vt.13,870), Gaua (Vt.8,130), Mota Lavu (Vt.7,340), and Sola (Vt.6,890).

The **Torres Guest House** in the post office building at Lungharigi on Loh is operated by the community. It's a lovely 15-minute walk from the airstrip, across the reef at low tide. The two rooms are Vt.1,000 pp and you can cook over an open fire if the cooking gas is finished. **Linua Guest House,** run by Father Luke Dini, is beside the lagoon under a km from the airstrip. It's Vt.2,500 pp including meals (bring insect repellant). Nearby is Whitely Toa's **Kamilisa Memorial Resort** with two thatched bungalows at Vt.1,700 pp including all meals (or considerably more through Island Safaris). Bucket showers are provided.

BASIC BISLAMA

bilong baim: for sale

Em ia haumas?: How much is it?

Em i hat smol smol: It's warm

Em i lait nau: It's late

go insait nating: admission fee

gut moning: good morning

gut naet: good night

i gut nomo: just fine

karim olsem yu laik: help yourself

Lukim yu: See you later

Me les lilbit: I feel a little tired

Mi mus paiim long hau mas?: How much should I pay?

Mi no harim?: Beg your pardon?

Mi no save: I don't understand/know

Mi tekem emia: I'll take this one

Nam bilong mi . . . .: My name is . . .

Olgeta samting bilong mi hia: These are my things

ol men: men's

ol woman: women's

plis: please

pusim: push

taim i ren: rainy season

tata: goodbye

tenk yu tumas: thank you very much

tumora: tomorrow

Wanem nem bilong yu?: What's your name?

Wanem taim?: What time is it?

yo no toktok: silence

Yu orait?: How are you?

Yu save?: Do you understand/know?

Yumi mit wea?: Where can we meet?

Solomon Islands

Introduction

One of the last areas of the world to fall under European religious and political control, the Solomon Islands remain today the best-kept secret in the South Pacific. It's all there: shark-callers, war wreckage, gold, and malaria; every Pacific race is present, from Papuans to Melanesians, Micronesians, and Polynesians. The variety of cultures and customs is striking, and the traditional ways are remarkably alive.

Like neighboring Vanuatu, it's a land of contrast and adventure, with jungle-clad peaks, mighty volcanoes, crashing waterfalls, mist-enshrouded rainforests, dark lagoons, scattered islands, uplifted atolls, and brilliant coral reefs. No other Pacific island group has a greater diversity of landforms. Once you figure out where the Solomon Islands actually are and finally get there, you won't wish to leave.

Unless you're on a tour, you'll find travel outside the capital, Honiara, an unstructured, make-your-own-arrangements affair. The number of

© DAVID STANLEY

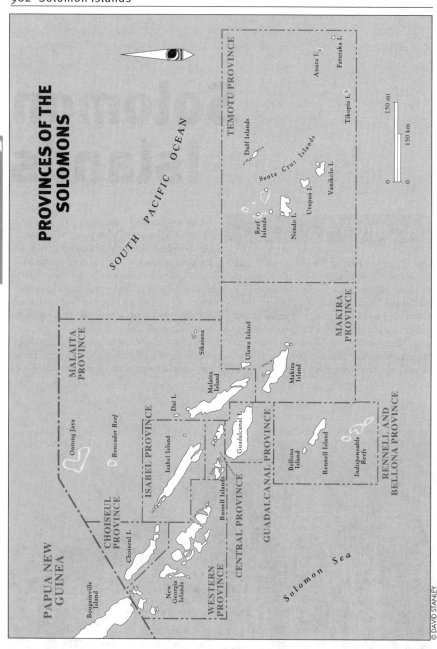

SOLOMON ISLANDS

PROVINCES OF THE SOLOMONS

SOUTH PACIFIC OCEAN

TEMOTU PROVINCE

Anuta I.
Fatutaka I.
Tikopia I.
Duff Islands
Santa Cruz Islands
Vanikolo I.
Utupua I.
Nendo I.
Reef Islands

150 mi
150 km

MALAITA PROVINCE

Sikaiana

Ulawa Island
Makira Island

MAKIRA PROVINCE

Ontong Java
Roncador Reef

ISABEL PROVINCE

Dai I.

Malaita Island

Isabel Island

Guadalcanal I.

GUADALCANAL PROVINCE

Bellona Island
Rennell Island
Indispensable Reefs

RENNELL AND BELLONA PROVINCE

CHOISEUL PROVINCE

Choiseul I.

Russell Islands

CENTRAL PROVINCE

PAPUA NEW GUINEA

Bougainville Island

New Georgia Islands

WESTERN PROVINCE

Solomon Sea

© DAVID STANLEY

SOLOMON ISLANDS HIGHLIGHTS

Gizo, Western Province: quaint town, diving, hiking, canoe trips (p. 1023)

Lake Tenggano, Rennell: South Pacific's largest lake, UNESCO World Heritage Site (p. 1008)

Marovo Lagoon, Western Province: double barrier reef, diving, snorkeling, kayaking (p. 1013)

Poporang, Shortland Islands: intact Japanese relics from WW II (p. 1030)

Savo Island: active volcano, megapode birds (p. 1011)

visitors is negligible, and most of those who do come stay only a few days, mainly in the capital or scuba diving at Gizo or Uepi Island. This gives slightly intrepid travelers an unparalleled opportunity to get well off the beaten track and have a genuine South Sea paradise all to themselves. So you're in for something totally original!

Travel Advisory

In June 2000, the "Hapi Isles" spun into auto-destruct as tribal tensions culminated in the overthrow of a reformist government. Rival militias clashed on the main island Guadalcanal, ethnic cleansing was carried out, and the central authority broke down. At the time of writing, the "troubles" seemed over thanks to an Australian-led regional military intervention in July 2003. Right from the start, the conflict was between rival tribes from Malaita and Guadalcanal, and foreign tourists weren't involved. The Western Solomons—the nicest part of the country—and the provinces of Rennell and Bellona, Central, Choiseul, Isabel, Makira, and Temotu were scarcely affected by a conflict, which left the economy in a shambles.

Yet even today after peace has returned, Solomon Islands still isn't for everyone. Those interested in a programmed beach holiday with few variables should look elsewhere. But for the independent traveler in search of adventure, there's no better place to go in the Pacific islands. The Solomon Islanders have always been friendly and

respectful, and a devaluating local currency translates into low prices in terms of foreign currency. The capital city, Honiara, is quite safe, but visitors should begin trying to get to the other islands as soon as they arrive. Solomon Airlines is often stressed out, and you could well be told their limited schedule of flights is fully booked. In that case, go down to the harbor and catch the first available boat to somewhere like Munda or Gizo. Don't hang around Honiara waiting for a flight that may never materialize. It's much easier to fly back to Honiara from an outer island.

In short, Solomon Islands is now as safe as Fiji, Vanuatu, or many other better known destinations. The no-go zones prior to July 2003 were rural areas of Guadalcanal and Malaita—places tourists seldom visited anyway. Honiara bears no resemblance to many African and Latin American cities, where foreigners are specifically targeted by organized gangs. In the Solomons, it's more a matter of common sense, such as taking care in the towns after dark. You may hear stories about the Malaita and Guadalcanal peoples—listen, but avoid offering opinions. Just remain neutral and be friendly to everyone, and you'll have an unforgettable experience.

The Land

With its 27,556-square-km area and 5,313 km of coastline, the Solomons is the second-largest insular nation of the South Pacific (after Papua New Guinea). This thickly forested, mountainous country, 1,860 km northeast of Australia, is made up of six large islands in a double chain (Choiseul, Isabel, Malaita, and New Georgia, Guadalcanal, Makira), about 20 medium-size ones, and numerous smaller islets and reefs—922 islands in all, 347 of them inhabited. The group stretches more than 1,800 km from the Shortlands in the west to Tikopia and Anuta in the east, and nearly 900 km from Ontong Java (the South Pacific's largest true atoll) in the north to Rennell Island (one of the world's largest uplifted atolls) in the south.

The main islands of the Solomons are the outer limit of the drowned ancient Australian continent and the group is on the edge of the Indo-Australian and Pacific plates, which accounts for volcanic activity, past and present.

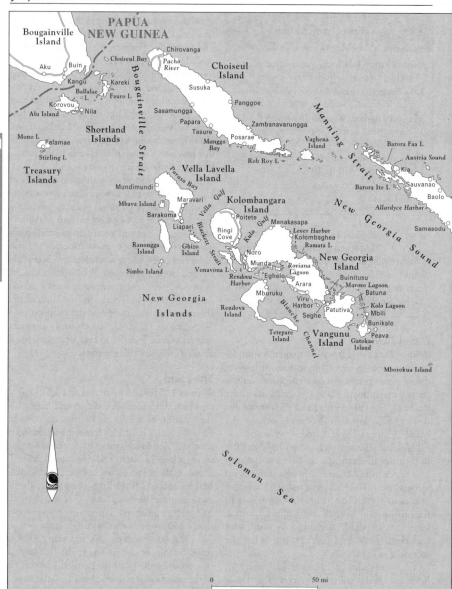

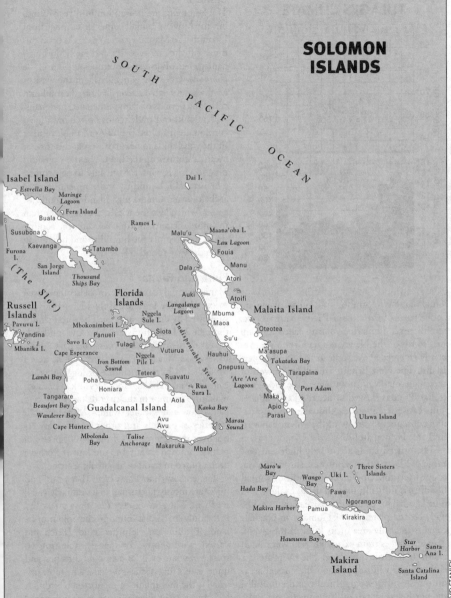

SOLOMON ISLANDS

SOUTH PACIFIC OCEAN

Isabel Island
Estrella Bay
Maringe Lagoon
Buala
Fera Island
Susubona
Kaevanga
Furona I.
San Jorge Island
Tatamba
Thousand Ships Ships Bay

(The Slot)

Russell Islands
Pavuvu I.
Yandina
Mbanika I.
Savo I.
Cape Esperance
Iron Bottom Sound
Lambi Bay
Poha
Tangarare
Honiara
Beaufort Bay
Wanderer Bay
Cape Hunter
Mbolonda Bay
Talise Anchorage
Makaruka
Mbalo

Florida Islands
Mbokonimbeti I.
Panueli
Tulagi
Nggela Sule I.
Siota
Nggela Pile I.
Vuturua
Tetere
Ruavatu
Rua
Sura I.
Aola
Guadalcanal Island
Avu Avu
Kaoka Bay
Marau Sound

Dai I.
Ramos I.
Malu'u
Maana'oba I.
Lau Lagoon
Fouia
Dala
Manu
Atori
Auki
Atoifi
Langalanga Lagoon
Mbuma
Maoa
Su'u
Hauhui
Onepusu
'Are 'Are Lagoon
Maka
Apio
Parasi

Malaita Island
Oteotea
Ma'asupa
Takataka Bay
Tarapaina
Port Adam

Indispensable Strait

Ulawa Island

Maro'u Bay
Wango Bay
Uki I.
Three Sisters Islands
Hada Bay
Pawa
Ngorangora
Makira Harbor
Pamua
Kirakira
Haununu Bay
Star Harbor
Santa Ana I.
Makira Island
Santa Catalina Island

© DAVID STANLEY

SOLOMON ISLANDS

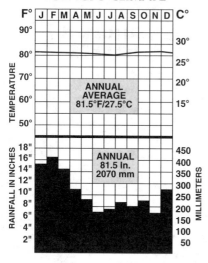

TULAGI'S CLIMATE

ANNUAL AVERAGE 81.5°F/27.5°C

ANNUAL 81.5 In. 2070 mm

Climate

The Solomons are hot and humid year-round, but the heaviest rainfall comes in summer from December to March. Hurricanes build up at this time, but they move south and rarely do much damage here. Between November and April, the *komburu* winds are generally from the west or northwest, though occasionally from the southeast, with long periods of calm punctuated by squalls.

The southeast trade winds *(ara)* blow almost continually from the end of April to November (if the wind shifts to north or west at this time, it means a storm is on the way). The most pleasant time to visit is winter, from July to September, when rainfall, humidity, and temperatures are at their lowest. On the high islands the southeast coasts, which face the winds, are far wetter than the more sheltered north coasts. Yet the cooling sea breezes temper the humidity and heat along all coasts year-round.

Flora and Fauna

Mangroves and coconut groves shelter the coastal strips, while the interiors of the high islands are swallowed by dense rainforest. The forest climbs through 24 belts, from towering lowland hardwoods to the mosses atop Guadalcanal's 2,300-meter peaks. Where the forests have been destroyed by slash-and-burn agriculture or logging, grasslands have taken hold. Crocodiles lurk in brackish mangrove swamps in the river deltas, while sago palms grow in freshwater swamps. More than 230 varieties of orchids and other tropical flowers brighten the landscape. Of the 4,500 species of plants recorded so far, 143 are known to have been utilized in traditional herbal medicine.

The endemic land mammals (bats, rats, and mice) are mostly nocturnal, so it's unlikely you'll see them. The gray cuscus *(Phalanger orientalis)* is the only marsupial found in the Solomon Islands. Birdlife, on the other hand, is rich and varied, with about 223 species including 16 species of white-eyes, fantails, rails, thrushes, and honeyeaters that occur only here. The most unusual is the megapode, or incubator, a bird that lays large eggs in the warm volcanic sands of the thermal areas. After about 40 days, the newly hatched megapodes dig themselves out and are

Tinakula, Savo, Simbo, and Vella Lavella are active parts of the circum-Pacific Ring of Fire, and there's a submarine volcano called Kavachi just south of the New Georgia Group that recently emerged above sea level to become a new island. The New Britain Trench, southwest of the chain, marks the point where the Indo-Australian Plate is shoved under the Pacific Plate. This causes frequent earthquakes and uplifting; consequently, many of the Polynesian outliers are elevated atolls.

The other islands are mostly high and volcanic, with luxuriant rainforest shrouding the rugged terrain. Under these conditions, road building is difficult; only Malaita, Makira, and Guadalcanal have fairly extensive networks. The wide coastal plain east of Honiara on Guadalcanal is the only area of its kind in the group. The soil ranges from extremely rich volcanic to relatively infertile limestone. The rivers are fast and straight, and often flood the coastal areas during storms. Geographically and culturally, the northwest islands of Bougainville and Buka belong to the Solomons, but are politically part of Papua New Guinea.

THE SOLOMONS AT A GLANCE

PROVINCE	MAIN TOWN	POPULATION (1999)	AREA (square km)	HIGHEST POINT (m)
Guadalcanal	Honiara	109,382	5,336	2,447
Malaita	Auki	122,620	4,243	1,303
Rennell and Bellona	Tingoa	2,377	276	220
Central	Tulagi	21,577	1,000	510
Western	Gizo	62,739	5,279	1,661
Choiseul	Taro	20,008	3,294	1,060
Isabel	Buala	20,421	4,014	1,392
Makira	Kirakira	31,006	3,188	1,250
Temotu	Lata	18,912	926	923
Solomon Islands	**Honiara**	**409,042**	**27,556**	**2,447**

SOLOMON ISLANDS

able to fly short distances as soon as their wings dry. There are many species of colorful parrots and 130 species of butterflies, including several species of birdwings.

Sharks are common offshore, so ask local advice before swimming. These creatures earned a certain notoriety among sailors and airmen during WW II, but the problem seems to have receded. White-sand beaches are safer than black. No shark attacks have been reported in the Santa Cruz Islands in recent memory. Many islanders have a curious rapport with the shark and believe that the souls of their ancestors live on in them. Shark worship has made Malaita relatively free of shark attacks.

The 70 species of reptiles include crocodiles, frogs, lizards, skinks, snakes, toads, and marine turtles. The five species of sea turtles nest from November to February. Several of the 20 species of snake are poisonous, but fortunately they're not common and are no threat. Centipedes and scorpions are two other potentially dangerous but seldom-encountered jungle creatures. The isolated Santa Cruz Group has fewer indigenous species than the main island chain. Each year thousands of rare birds, reptiles, amphibians, aquarium fish, and butterflies are exported from the Solomons to be sold in Asia, North America, and Europe. Large numbers of captive bottlenose

dolphins has been air freighted to amusement parks in Mexico for use in lucrative Swim With Dolphins programs.

HISTORY AND GOVERNMENT
Prehistory
The first inhabitants were Papuan-speaking hunters and gatherers, who may have arrived as early as 30,000 years ago. Some 4,000 years ago, Austronesian-speaking agriculturists joined their predecessors. The earliest date of known human habitation, provided by the radiocarbon dating of remains from Vatuluma Posovi Cave near the Poha River, Guadalcanal, is 1300–1000 B.C. Stone tools found here date from 4000 B.C. Due to the nature of the objects discovered and the absence of pottery (the 19th-century inhabitants of the island still had no pottery), it's believed that the occupants of this quite sizable cave were the direct ancestors of the present-day people of Guadalcanal. On the other hand, the many different languages currently spoken by the Melanesians illustrate a long period of mixed settlement.

Lapita pottery has been found in the Santa Cruz Islands, and New Britain obsidian was carried through the Solomons to Santa Cruz and New Caledonia some 3,000 years ago, probably by the first Polynesians. Today's Polynesian enclaves in the Solomons bear no relation to these original eastward migrations, however. Their forebears arrived in a back-migration within the last 1,500 years to Anuta, Tikopia, Bellona, and Rennell from Wallis and Futuna, and to Taumako (Duff Islands), Pileni (Reef Islands), Sikaiana, and Ontong Java from Tuvalu.

The Spanish Episode

There were three Spanish expeditions to Melanesia in the late 16th and early 17th centuries: two by Álvaro de Mendaña (in 1568 and 1595) to the Solomon Islands, and one in 1606 by Mendaña's pilot Pedro Fernandez de Quirós to Vanuatu. Incan legends told of a rich land 600 leagues west of Peru, so the rapacious conquistadores prepared an expedition to find the elusive El Dorado.

Mendaña set out from Peru in November 1567 and arrived on February 7, 1568, at Estrella Bay, Isabel Island, to become the first European to "discover" the Solomons. Mendaña established a base on Isabel, where his men built a small, five-ton, undecked vessel to explore reefs that would have destroyed a bigger, clumsier ship. At the beginning of March, a fleet of war canoes paddled near the Spanish ship, presenting Mendaña with a quarter of baked boy, nicely garnished with taro roots. Mendaña sailed his brigantine among the islands, giving them the Spanish names still used today.

In retaliation for violence and treachery initiated earlier on Guadalcanal by a subordinate commander, the islanders massacred nine members of a watering party sent out by Mendaña. The Spaniards then burned every village within reach, and when they departed, Guadalcanal was left in ashes and death. Mendaña left Makira for Peru on the morning of August 17, 1568.

He returned in 1595, stopping en route to discover and name the Marquesas Islands in eastern Polynesia. This time Mendaña landed on Nendo, in the Santa Cruz Group, where he hoped to found a Spanish colony. For this reason a number of women accompanied the expedition, including Mendaña's ambitious wife, Doña Isabel Barreto, who hoped to be queen of the wealthy Solomon Islands. Yet Mendaña himself and many others soon died of malaria. The three

surviving Spanish ships left for the Philippines, though one became separated and probably sank off San Cristobal (Makira). In 1606, Mendaña's pilot, Pedro Fernandez de Quirós, made another attempt at colonization on Espiritu Santo in Vanuatu before the Spanish gave up on the area.

Mendaña found no gold in the Solomons, but he gave the islands their exotic name, implying to his royal patrons that they were as rich as, or even the source of, King Solomon's treasure—an early example of a real-estate salesman's trickery. The name soon appeared on maps and in formal reports, and was eventually adopted as official. Mendaña placed the Solomons far to the east of their actual location, and for the next 200 years they were lost to European explorers.

Recontact and Exploitation

In 1767, Captain Philip Carteret rediscovered Santa Cruz and Malaita; he was followed a year later by Bougainville, who visited and named Choiseul and other islands to the north. Captain John Shortland sailed past Guadalcanal and San Cristobal in 1788, the same year the La Pérouse expedition was lost at Vanikolo. These explorations opened the door to traders, missionaries, and labor recruiters. Beginning in the 1830s, traders passed through regularly, purchasing bêche-de-mer, mother-of-pearl, turtle shell, and sandalwood. By 1860, stone tools had been replaced almost everywhere with iron. Some traders cheated the islanders and spread disease in their wake.

Copra became important in the 1870s, and labor recruitment for the cane fields of Queensland and Fiji also began about this time. The treacherous methods of the blackbirders, who often kidnapped workers, sparked a wave of intense anti-European feeling, which resulted in the murder of many honest traders and missionaries. Some recruiters even dressed in priests' gowns to ensure a peaceful reception on an island. Between 1870 and 1910, some 30,000 people were removed from the islands; 10,000 never returned. In retaliation, the natives killed Monseigneur Epalle, their first real Catholic bishop, on Isabel in 1845; Anglican Bishop John Coleridge Patteson on Nukapu, Reef Islands, in 1871; and Commodore Goodenough on Nendo, Santa Cruz, in 1875. The recruiting became more voluntary in the later 19th century, but it still amounted to economic slavery. This system died out in Queensland in 1904, when most blacks were expelled from Australia, and in Fiji in 1910.

The Missionaries

The earliest attempts to implant Christianity in the Solomons were by Catholics: first Mendaña in the 16th century, then the Society of Mary in the 1840s. Mendaña failed, and the Marists withdrew in 1848. A decade later, the Anglicans of New Zealand began to take an interest in the Solomons. Rather than sending white missionaries directly into the area, they used the more cautious technique of taking Solomon Islanders to a facility on Norfolk Island (between New Caledonia and New Zealand) for training. The Melanesian Mission of those days, covering both northern Vanuatu and the Solomons, has grown into today's Church of Melanesia.

The Catholics returned at the end of the 19th century and established missions on Guadalcanal and Malaita. Around 1904, Solomon Islands laborers returning to Malaita from the cotton and sugar plantations of Queensland brought back the South Seas Evangelical Mission. Some who had worked in Fiji returned as Methodists; as a result, the United Church (created by a merger of Methodists and Congregationalists in 1968) is active in the Western Solomons. The Seventh-Day Adventist (SDA) Church here dates from 1914, with the largest number of followers around the Marovo Lagoon and on Malaita.

Although the missionaries effaced many old traditions, they also pioneered education, health care, and communications, transforming the country from one of the most dangerous areas on earth to one of the most peaceful. Their influence remains strong today. The churches are one of the few institutions unshaken by the current "troubles" in the Solomon Islands, an indispensable calming influence. Of the 97 percent of the population that now professes Christianity, 35 percent belongs to the Church of Melanesia, 20 percent is Catholic, 18 percent South Seas Evangelical, 11 percent United, and 10 percent SDA. Around 5,500 Solomon Islanders still follow traditional religions, although this number is declining.

The Colonial Period

In 1884, Britain declared a protectorate over Papua in response to Australian alarm at German expansion into New Guinea. By the 1890s, the Germans had established interests in the North Solomons (Bougainville and Buka), so in 1893 the British also declared a protectorate over New Georgia, Guadalcanal, Makira, and Malaita to limit German advances, protect resident Europeans, and to control the labor trade, in response to pleas from missionaries.

In 1896, C.M. Woodford, the first resident commissioner, set up headquarters at Tulagi in the Florida Group, with orders to raise sufficient local revenue to cover his own expenses. The Santa Cruz Group, Rennell, and Bellona became part of the British Solomon Islands Protectorate in 1898 and 1899. In 1900, Germany ceded to Britain the Shortlands, Choiseul, Isabel, and Ontong Java in exchange for a free hand to annex Samoa.

The first decade of the 20th century saw the establishment of large coconut plantations by Levers (1905), Burns Philp (1906), and Fairymead (1909), as well as expansion of the missions, which retained full control of education. British control often didn't extend far beyond the coastal strip, and government officials seemed to appear in villages only to collect taxes and punish people. Life led a sleepy course until the Japanese seized the Solomons in 1942.

The Pacific War

After Singapore fell in February 1942, the South Pacific was fully exposed to Japanese attack. Stung by the Doolittle air raid on Tokyo in April, the Japanese moved south and occupied Tulagi, Florida Group, in May 1942. A Japanese invasion fleet sailed toward Port Moresby in Papua, but was turned back in the Battle of the Coral Sea. On June 4, another invasion fleet was stopped at the Battle of Midway, in which Japan lost four aircraft carriers.

In the Solomons, however, the war was just

beginning, as the Japanese landed on Guadalcanal on July 7. They quickly began constructing an air base on the site of today's international airport, from which they could strike at Australia and counter an American base already underway at Espiritu Santo, Vanuatu. A month later, 10,000 U.S. Marines went ashore at Red Beach and quickly captured the partly completed airstrip and unarmed Korean construction workers, but the next day Japanese planes prevented U.S. transports from unloading supplies. That night, a Japanese task force of eight warships stole silently past a destroyer patrol near Savo Island and sent four Allied cruisers and two destroyers to the bottom of Iron Bottom Sound—one of the worst naval defeats ever suffered by the United States. These savage attacks forced Allied naval forces to withdraw.

The Japanese then began an intense campaign to push the 10,000 Marines into the sea. Supplies and troops were funneled down The Slot (a wide channel that divides the Solomons into two chains of islands) on the "Tokyo Express," and Japanese planes nicknamed "Washing Machine Charlie" and "Louie the Louse" bombed Guadalcanal from dusk to dawn. The Marines held out for six months against malaria, bloodcurdling banzai charges, and bombardment by land and sea. By this time, however, American reinforcements and supplies were pouring in, so in February 1943, the Japanese secretly evacuated their 12,000 surviving troops to a newly built airfield on New Georgia, thereby shortening the communication distance to their headquarters at Rabaul. The Americans followed them to New Georgia in July, with major actions at Rendova and Munda, but a few die-hard Japanese detachments held out on Choiseul and in the Shortlands until 1945.

Guadalcanal is significant because it was the first U.S. victory against land-based Japanese forces during WW II. Some 25,000 Japanese and 5,000 American soldiers were killed or wounded on Guadalcanal itself, plus many more in the surrounding sea and air. Official histories do not mention how many Solomon Islanders were killed.

Highly active was the coast-watching organization, which used radio transmitters to report on Japanese movements from behind enemy lines. Many of these coast-watchers were members of the British administration who knew the area well, but they were aided by militant churchmen, nuns, planters, mission nurses, and hundreds of loyal islanders. Throughout the conflict villagers risked their lives to rescue downed airmen and seamen, and many American lives were saved, including that of future President John F. Kennedy.

The Aftermath

World War II left deep scars on the Solomons. The former capital, Tulagi, was devastated when the Americans recaptured it, so the returning British administration chose to establish a new capital at Honiara to take advantage of the infrastructure installed by the Americans during the conflict. A high percentage of the Solomons' current roads and airstrips date from the war. Military dumps and scattered wreckage can still be found in the bush east of the international airport, although time and souvenir-hunters have taken their toll.

Perhaps the most unexpected outcome of the campaign was the rise of the Ma'asina Ruru movement (the Brotherhood), dubbed "Marching Rule" by local expatriates. Thousands of islanders who'd been forced into the bush to avoid the fighting returned and found great American armies possessed of seemingly limitless wealth and power. This spectacle, coupled with dissatisfaction in a colonial system that treated natives like naughty children, gave birth to a widespread cargo cult on Malaita. Ma'asina Ruru attempted to reorganize society on the basis of "custom," but in 1948 the British administration decided that things were moving in an undesirable direction and used police to crush the movement. By 1949, some 2,000 islanders had been imprisoned for refusing to cooperate with the government.

This adversity united the Malaita people for the first time, and the British were forced to respond. The Malaita Council, formed as a compromise in 1953, was the beginning of the system of local government followed in the Solomons today. Unlike cargo cults in Vanuatu and New Guinea, little remains of the original "Marching Rule," although individual

Americans are still popular. By 1964, the local government councils were handling all regional affairs. A nominated Legislative Council was created in 1960; some elected members were added in 1964. In 1974, this became an almost entirely elected Legislative Assembly. Internal self-government followed in 1976, and full independence on July 7, 1978. A 1977 ordinance converted all alienated land owned by foreigners into 75-year, fixed-term estates on lease from the government, a system that continues today.

The Solomons Crisis

In 1988, Solomon Islands joined Papua New Guinea and Vanuatu to form the Melanesian Spearhead Group to support the independence struggle in New Caledonia. In 1992, however, relations with P.N.G. worsened abruptly after incursions into the Shortland Islands by the P.N.G. Defense Force in pursuit of rebels from Bougainville Island. In 1993, additional police were sent to the Western Solomons after two boatloads of P.N.G. troops landed on Mono Island and exchanged fire with Solomons police. In response to the crisis, Solomon Islands created a paramilitary field force independent of its police.

After the 1997 election, the corrupt administration of Solomon "Solo" Mamaloni was replaced by a reformist government led by Bartholomew Ulufa'alu of the Alliance for Change. In early 1998, it was revealed that prior to his defeat, Mamaloni had ordered US$4 million in arms and ammunition, two light aircraft, and a helicopter gunship from American sources, allegedly for the defense of the country's northern border. Ulufa'alu tried to cancel the order, asserting that in Solo's hands the weapons might have led to a war with Papua New Guinea, and at least part of the weaponry seemed destined for the Bougainville rebels. The change in government in Honiara sidelined politicians like Mamaloni who had been taking bribes from Malaysian loggers. Unable to defeat Ulufa'alu by parliamentary means, his opponents began manipulating ethnic divisions within the country to destabilize the Alliance for Change government.

Since WW II, economic development in the Solomons had been concentrated on northern Guadalcanal while the neighboring island of Malaita remained largely undeveloped, and this situation had attracted large numbers of Malaitans to Guadalcanal in search of work. For largely cultural reasons, the patrilineal Malaitans were well equipped to take advantage of employment opportunities, and they came to monopolize paid employment in the capital. The indigenous Guadalcanalese have a less aggressive, matrilineal culture, and they found it hard to compete. Guadalcanal landowners received only a tiny royalty on the vast oil palm estates east of Honiara, and Malaitan agricultural settlements on northern Guadalcanal grew steadily. A huge Australian-owned gold mine was under construction in the center of the island with Malaitan labor.

In November 1998, Premier Ezekiel Alebua of Guadalcanal Province demanded massive "compensation" from the central government for the use of Honiara as Solomon Islands' capital. On the Weather Coast of southern Guadalcanal, ragtag gangs of youths armed with homemade weapons took this as a signal to begin moving toward Honiara, terrorizing Malaitans in rural areas. Calling themselves variously the "Guadalcanal Liberation Front" or "Guadalcanal Revolutionary Army," the militants forced 1,800 Malaitan laborers to flee the huge oil palm plantations east of Honiara, leading to the total collapse of an industry that was providing a fifth of the country's income. By early 1999, 32,000 people had been forced from their homes on northern Guadalcanal and some 20,000 ethnic Malaitans (most of whom had been born on Guadalcanal) left for Malaita. Honiara itself became a Malaitan enclave, jammed with thousands of displaced persons. Over 100 people were killed.

In June 1999, Ulufa'alu declared a state of emergency throughout the Solomon Islands. The former prime minister of Fiji, Sitiveni Rabuka, was brought in on behalf of the Commonwealth to negotiate a peace agreement between the Guadalcanal rebels, now styled the "Isatabu Freedom Fighters," and the provincial and national governments. The militants agreed to turn in their weapons in exchange for recognition of Guadalcanal's "grievances" and SI$2.5 million in "compensation." After further fighting, Honiara's hardline British police chief was fired and a new Panatina Peace Agreement was signed in August. These deals (and several more which were to follow) collapsed after the rebels failed to turn in their weapons. Honiara became a city under siege with roadblocks east and west of town. In early 2000, Solomon Mamaloni died of malaria, leaving his country in ruins.

In late 1999, an armed group called "Red Cobra" was formed on Malaita to seek revenge. In January 2000, a group of Malaitan militants raided the police station at Auki on Malaita and stole 34 high-powered rifles and a grenade launcher. They announced the formation of the "Malaita Eagle Force" to obtain compensation from the government. By March 2000, the Eagle Force had moved to Honiara where they began "pay back" attacks on the Guadalcanal people. In May, the Ulufa'alu government requested Australian intervention to restore order, but the request was denied. The situation deteriorated and many Malaitans blamed Ulufa'alu (himself from Malaita) for not doing more.

The crisis climaxed in June 2000, when the Malaita Eagle Force and Malaitan members of the paramilitary police took control of Honiara, forcing Prime Minister Ulufa'alu to resign. Parliament was reconvened and a new cabinet was chosen including discredited ministers from the former Mamaloni government. The new government didn't waste any time in paying itself huge doses of "compensation" taken from government coffers and in accepting massive kickbacks on import duty exemptions. During the coup, the police arsenal was seized by the Malaita Eagle Force, and fierce fighting between the rival ethnic militias broke out at the edges of the city. The Malaitans used a hijacked naval patrol boat to shell Isatabu Freedom Fighter positions just east of the airport, causing international air service to be temporarily suspended.

Meanwhile, the Guadalcanal rebels raided the Gold Ridge mine in the center of the island, and gold mining—which was producing half of the Solomons' gross domestic product at the time— came to a halt. The Japanese fishing company Solomon Taiyo stopped fishing and closed their Noro cannery after one of their fishing boats was hijacked. At Gizo in the Western Solomons, members of the Bougainville Revolutionary Army made a brief incursion and murdered several Malaitans. The government (and country) were now effectively bankrupt. Thousands of job losses, combined with recession, negative growth, and insecurity, convinced many well-educated Solomon Islanders to leave the country.

A ceasefire was agreed to in August 2000, leaving the Malaitans in control of the airport and Honiara and the Guadalcanal rebels holding the surrounding countryside. In October 2000, the Malaita Eagle Force, the Isatabu Freedom Movement, and the government signed a peace agreement at Townsville, Australia, granting amnesty in exchange for the surrender of weapons and the return of stolen property. The Townsville Agreement succeeded where half dozen previous agreements had failed largely because millions of dollars of development assistance provided by Taiwan was used to pay compensation to shady politicians and gunmen who complained of such offenses as "being threatened" or "sworn at." In early 2001, Solomon Telekom cut off the government's telephone lines over unpaid bills.

Fresh elections in December 2001 brought in Sir Allan Kemakeza as prime minister. Although only 18 of the 50 members of the previous parliament retained their seats, many new members quickly sold their votes to the corrupt old guard. Kemakeza was a holdover from the previous administration who had paid himself SI$800,000 in "compensation" a year before the election. Kemakeza's main backer is a former finance minister who awarded tens of millions of dollars in tax exemptions to his cronies. The corruption that had fostered the ethnic divisions continued to plague the country.

Under the Townsville Agreement, the former rebels became "special constables" of a "Neutral Force." The Malaitan militia was folded back into the police force, but some of the Guadalcanal rebels continued operating as common bandits, particularly a gang led by Isatabu militant Harold Keke who was able to evade police patrols on southern Guadalcanal's Weather Coast. In August 2002, Keke murdered a cabinet minister who had gone to visit him, and an estimated 50 additional deaths in the area have been attributed to him and his men. In all, some 3,000 weapons were turned in under the Townsville Agreement, but hundreds more remained unaccounted for on Guadalcanal and Malaita. In late 2002 and early 2003, there were a number of high profile murders and assassination attempts in Honiara and on Malaita. A former police commissioner was murdered at Auki in February 2003 while working with a team trying to demobilize the "special constables."

With an insolvent central government and shattered economy, only traditional culture (or "custom") and the church retained any influence over the 85 percent of the population living peacefully in rural villages. Then international events caused a dramatic change in the situation. In mid-2003, the American war in Iraq seemed a success, and there was a taste for foreign interventions in the higher echelons of the Australian government. Prime Minister John Howard had been clever enough to pull Australian troops out of Iraq immediately after President Bush declared major combat operations over, and the situation in the Solomon Islands seemed like a low-risk opportunity for a little military muscle flexing to enhance Australian influence.

In April 2003, the bankrupt Kemakeza government had created alarm in Australia by secretly inviting Indonesia to intervene in the Solomons. Prime Minister Kemakeza was summoned to Canberra and encouraged to endorse an Australian intervention in his country, which he did. Howard quickly obtained the approval of the foreign ministers of 16 Pacific Forum countries, and in July 2003, 2,250 soldiers, police, and public service advisors from Australia, New Zealand, Fiji, and several other Pacific countries arrived for Operation Helpum Fren (Help A Friend). The Australian-led Regional Assistance Mission to Solomon Islands (RAMSI) was warmly welcomed by an overwhelming majority of Solomon Islanders fed up after the period of massive corruption from 1987–1997, followed by low intensity tribal warfare from 1998–2003.

The "Visiting Contingent" (as the Solomons government preferred to call RAMSI) had some re-

markable early successes. Within little more than a month, 3,712 illegal weapons were collected and destroyed. Rebel leader Harold Keke was convinced to surrender on the Weather Coast and sent to Honiara for trial. Several dozen corrupt officers within the police force were rooted out and the ex-militants faded into the population or were arrested. Australia promised Solomon Islands A$850 million in reconstruction aid over 10 years. Most Solomon Islanders viewed Operation Helpum Fren as a second chance for their country, and one can only hope that they are right.

Government

The head of state is an appointed governor-general who represents the British Crown. The 50-member National Parliament elects a prime minister from its ranks, while the cabinet is chosen by the prime minister from among those members of parliament who supported him; opposition members routinely cross the floor after being tempted with ministerial appointments or paid bribes by special interests. Most members of parliament belong to one of several political parties based on personalities rather than issues; others are nominally independent and sell their votes to the highest bidder. There's a 50 percent turnover of members each election as voters try to toss the rascals out, but it isn't long before the new parliamentarians are doing the same things the former members were wont to do.

In 1981, seven provinces were created, each with an elected premier and provincial assembly. In 1991, Choiseul Province was separated from Western Province, and in 1993 Rennell and Bellona Province was created out of Central Province. Honiara is administered separately from Guadalcanal Province by the Honiara Town Council. Although many powers have been transferred from the national to the provincial governments, the latter are largely dependent on the former for financing. The provincial governments are supported by the head tax called "basic rate," a colonial levy originally intended to force the islanders to sell part of their produce or to work for planters. Within each province are various area councils—each with a president—that deal with local or village matters.

ECONOMY

From 1999 to 2003, the Solomon Island's economy was devastated by the ethnic fighting, leading to the destruction of infrastructure and a withdrawal of foreign investment. Exports of most commodities dried up and tourism evaporated. The gross domestic product shrank 14 percent in 2000 and another 25 percent in 2001. The country was almost bankrupt, and in 2002 government salaries stopped being paid and government-run social services virtually came to a standstill in rural areas. By late 2003, however, Operation Helpum Fren had put the country back on track.

The monetary economy has been largely based on the exploitation of the country's rich natural resources by foreign corporations; expatriates still control most business. Timber is the main export, followed by fish. Until 2000, palm oil was the third largest export, but this ended when rebels occupied the plantations on Guadalcanal and destroyed the oil mill. The government operates vast coconut plantations in the Russell Islands on tracts formerly leased to Lever Brothers, and copra and cacao are also grown on the outer islands. In 1998, a large gold mine opened on Guadalcanal, and the metal briefly topped the list of exports, but Guadalcanal rebels trashed the company's equipment and all mining activity ceased. Imports are primarily manufactured goods, fuels, and processed food. Australia profits greatly from trade with the Solomons, selling it far more than it buys.

The government owns a huge chunk of the economy through the Investment Corporation of Solomon Islands (ICSI), a statutory authority under the Ministry of Finance. The ICSI holds equity in the Development Bank of the Solomon Islands (100 percent), Kolombangara Forest Products Ltd. (49 percent), Sasape Marina Ltd. (100 percent), Solomon Airlines (100 percent), Solomon Islands Plantations Ltd. (30 percent), Solomon Telekom (7.1 percent), Soltai Fishing and Processing (100 percent), and Solomon Islands Printers Ltd. (100 percent). In 1995, the government's Commodities Export Marketing Authority was forced to take over Levers Solomons Ltd., which announced that it was technically bankrupt, and CEMA now operates the company as Russell Islands Plantations Limited.

Solomon Islands has the weakest currency in the South Pacific, a result of the government printing money to cover budget deficits. This has led to double-digit inflation and several major devaluations. Solomon Islands is indebted to the tune of SI$2 billion, or SI$4,890 per person, a huge sum for most Solomon Islanders. After 1999, the Government defaulted on all interest and some principle payments, and failed to bring spending under control.

Solomon Islands receives about SI$200 million a year in foreign aid from the European Union, Taiwan, Australia, New Zealand, the United Kingdom, and Japan, in that order. Taiwan pays the expenses of Solomon Islands' mission to the United Nations and isn't concerned if politicians siphon off their aid money so long as it buys them influence. Most Japanese aid money is spent on infrastructure, such as bridges, airports, harbors, and roads to support Japanese business activities. Australia and New Zealand have tried to channel their aid into projects more directly beneficial to the people. Prior to 2003, much aid money was used to pay "compensation" to armed groups or siphoned off through corruption.

Tourism plays only a small role in the economy, although airport improvements now allow the largest jets to land at Honiara. In 1990, the government founded Solomon Airlines, which operated a Boeing 737-400 on east-west routes until Qantas cancelled its lease on the aircraft after heavy fighting between rival militias near Honiara airport in June 2000. The flights are now operated using a chartered Air Vanuatu plane. After 1999, tourism almost stopped, and in 2001 Solomon Islands received only 3,418 arrivals, less than a tenth the number that visited Vanuatu and only one percent as many as Fiji. Internal Solomon Airlines flights are difficult to book, limiting many of those visitors who do come to Honiara. Discussions about a second international airport at Munda or Gizo to allow tourist flights from Australia to bypass the Honiara bottleneck have gone on for years without much getting done. Land disputes have hindered resort development, and the existence of malaria is hardly a selling point.

Logging

Throughout the Solomons, some of the Pacific's last untouched rainforests are falling to the chainsaw in a hit and run operation by Asian timber companies that export raw logs to Japan (only 10 percent of the exported wood is sawn timber, the rest is logs). Logging for export began only in 1961, but already about half the accessible lowland rainforest has been logged. During the mid 1990s, logging was going ahead at a rate of 750,000 cubic meters of logs a year, nearly three times the sustainable rate of 270,000 cubic meters a year. Logging is the only section of the economy that wasn't affected by the recent political crisis; in fact, log exports increased 14 percent between 1998 and 2000. Two-thirds of all logging in 2001 was carried out in Western Province. Currently, the loggers are stripping Isabel of trees as quickly as they can.

During the 1990s, the comparatively small South Pacific forests attracted the attention of Malaysian corporations due to sharply increased prices for tropical hardwood on world markets caused by the phasing out of log exports from Malaysia and Indonesia. Government ministers, provincial premiers, civil servants, local officials, and village chiefs have routinely pocketed substantial bribes from the Asian logging companies to facilitate concessions and avoid taxation. It's estimated that in 1993 alone Solomon Islands was defrauded of SI$40 million through under-reporting, transfer pricing (the sale of assets by one subsidiary to another at below market value), and other tricks. In 1995, the *Solomon Star* reported that seven cabinet ministers had received US$2 million in bribes from a Malaysian company.

Local villagers have had to fight ongoing battles against these companies and their own government for control of their lands. A sustainable alternative to this "robber economy" does exist in the form of portable or walkabout sawmills. Portable chainsaw milling by local people brings villagers 100 times the return of large-scale logging by foreign companies, and does far less harm to the environment. But with big royalties coming in, most government officials and international agencies are uninterested in options that bring in no royalties and few taxes.

Reforestation takes 30-40 years in areas that have been carefully logged, or 45-200 years where environmental controls are disregarded (as is usually the case). Less than a tenth of the areas presently being logged are replanted, and the lack of reforestation has caused rapid erosion—fouling water supplies and leaving the land infertile. The largest reforestation projects are on Choiseul and Kolombangara, with mostly fast-growing exotic species planted. As the giant slow-growing native trees disappear, many rare endemic species of birds and butterflies face extinction due to the destruction of their habitat.

Fishing

Commercial fishing is the Solomons' largest industry, with over SI$100 million worth of fish exported in a good year. In 1972, the Japanese firm Taiyo Fisheries and the government set up a jointly run cannery at Tulagi, and in 1991 this facility was moved to Noro, near Munda in Western Solomons Province. Thanks to transfer pricing, Taiyo only reported a profit twice during its 29 years of operations, allowing it to pay little or nothing in taxes. The Noro cannery closed temporarily during the political crisis of 2000, and in 2001 the Japanese withdrew from the operation, leaving the government to run the operation as Soltai Fishing and Processing. Soltai freezes two-thirds of its tuna catch at Noro, and ships it to Japan, Thailand, and Fiji for processing. Most of the canned fish is sold locally since the European Union halted imports due to quality concerns.

Solomons waters are among the richest tuna fishing grounds in the Western Pacific, and the Forum Fisheries Agency (www.ffa.int) is headquartered on a hill just east of Honiara. This body carries on the wartime tradition of coast-watching by attempting to police the 200-nautical-mile Exclusive Economic Zones of the 16 South Pacific Forum member states, and by negotiating licensing fees with overseas fishing interests.

Mining

Since 1936, Solomon Islanders have collected alluvial gold by hand panning and sluicing along

SOLOMON ISLANDS

the Chovohio River at Guadalcanal's Gold Ridge. About 200 locals hold alluvial gold mining permits, selling around 30,000 grams of unrefined gold a year to 10 licensed traders. Large quantities of gold are smuggled out of the country, creating a drain on the balance of payments and robbing customary landholders.

The gold ore site at Gold Ridge is estimated to harbor reserves of 1.3 million metric tonnes, and in 1998 the Australian company, Ross Mining, commenced open pit operations that it expected would produce 100,000 ounces of gold a year for 13 years. In 2000, the company's equipment at Gold Ridge was looted and the mine closed. Escalating demands from landowners and the poor security situation have prevented its reopening to date. There are undeveloped bauxite deposits on Rennell and Vaghena, phosphates on Bellona, and nickel on San Jorge.

Alternative Development Agendas

The most active nongovernment organization bringing villagers into the mainstream of the development process is the **Solomon Islands Development Trust** (sidt@solomon.com.sb) founded in 1982. Since 1984, the SIDT's outreach program has sent village development workers to hundreds of remote village groups to conduct workshops on natural resources, forestry, minerals, water supplies, health, butterfly ranching, and bait fish. Team members teach the villagers how to understand and prepare for disasters, both natural and man-made, while also covering themes such as balanced cash cropping, sanitation, and family planning.

SIDT teams have stymied rainforest destruction on some islands, while assisting with the reforestation of customary land on others. The SIDT theater group SEI! enhances villagers' awareness by acting out environmental and nutrition skits for village audiences. A women's section stresses issues of particular interest to their village sisters. The programs center on improving village life as a way of beginning and sustaining grassroots development.

Most of the SIDT's funding comes from church or development groups abroad, plus the governments of Australia, Canada, New Zealand,

and the United Kingdom. The SIDT's quarterly magazine, *Link,* carries fascinating articles on subjects like gold mining, tourism, education, and youth, all seen from an authentic indigenous point of view. In Honiara, pick up a copy at their office in New Chinatown (see the Honiara map).

THE PEOPLE

About 94 percent of the country's 410,000 people are Melanesian. Another 4 percent of the population consists of Polynesians living on Rennell, Bellona, Sikaiana, Ontong Java, the Reef Islands, Anuta, and Tikopia—the so-called "Polynesian Fringe." To add to the variety, between 1955 and 1971, thousands of Micronesian Gilbertese were resettled near Honiara and Gizo, where small European and Chinese communities are also found.

Social Issues

Some 77 percent of the population relies on subsistence agriculture. In 1999, only 57,472 people were in paid employment (including part-time work), and of this group, just one in three was a woman. A third of all jobs are in the public sector, and almost 60 percent of all paid employment is found in and around Honiara.

There's strong opposition to family planning, and the birthrate is 3.4 percent. Each Solomon Islands woman has an average of 4.8 children, the highest fertility rate in the South Pacific. Nearly half the inhabitants are under the age of 15 and the population doubles every 20 years. The life expectancy is also the South Pacific's lowest at 60.6 years for men and 61.6 for women.

Education is neither compulsory nor free. Almost half the population has no formal education whatever and 70 percent of adults are illiterate. Some 44 percent of children between the ages of 5 and 19 are not attending school. Only 16 percent of households have access to electricity and just 23 percent have modern toilet facilities. Forty percent have no regular water supply.

Some 7,500 young people leave school each year, but only 15 percent find work, and the gap between the haves and have-nots is increasing. Many young men hang on in Honiara for years as

This early-20th-century photo of three men at Makira exemplifies how Solomon Islanders once dressed.

COURTESY OF THE FIELD MUSEUM OF NATURAL HISTORY, CHICAGO

SOLOMON ISLANDS

liu, a word that means "wanderer" but which we would translate as "unemployed." Thousands of *masta liu* from Malaita live in Honiara, and the influx of village people has strained the traditional custom of providing hospitality to visiting relatives. Squatter settlements have sprung up on the ridges behind Honiara, and some of the suburbs are potentially dangerous after dark. Alcoholism and crime, though still modest compared to Papua New Guinea, are growing problems, and one need only look at the "rascal" situation in Port Moresby to appreciate the threat.

Village Life

Eight out of 10 Solomon Islanders live in small rural villages and practice shifting, subsistence agriculture, operating much as they did before the white man arrived. Most villages are near the shore, so fresh fish plays an important role in the diet, supplemented by wild pigs hunted with dogs and spears, plus the occasional chicken. On Malaita many people live in the interior and keep small herds of cattle for food. Everywhere native vegetables, including taro, yams, sweet potato, and cassava, are grown on small individual plots and provide the bulk of the diet.

The basic social unit is the extended family or clan, which may consist of about 200 "wantoks." Some clan members can recite a genealogy of ancestors going back 10 generations. Villagers work collectively on community projects, and there's much sharing among clans, yet individuals keep their own gardens and can readily tell you what land they own. Land may be passed on by the mother or father, depending on local custom. Customary land accounts for 87 percent of the Solomons, another 9 percent is owned by the government, and the rest by individual Solomon Islanders. About 2 percent is leased to foreigners, though only people born in the Solomons may own land. Disputes over land and boundaries are common.

The achievements of individuals are evaluated by their value to the community as a whole, and a villager who shows too much initiative or ability in his own affairs is more likely to inspire jealousy and resentment rather than admiration. Social status among the Melanesians is based on land ownership, but an individual can also increase his standing in the community by displaying his wealth at a ritual feast. A successful feast-giver becomes a "big man" in this way—

descent is less important. (In Polynesia chiefs are hereditary.) Throughout the Solomons, custom, or *kastom,* is used to justify any number of differing traditional social orders.

Language

Approximately 87 distinct indigenous languages are presently in use in the Solomons, the most widely spoken of which are Kwara'ae (25,000 speakers on Malaita), Lau (10,000 speakers on Malaita), Roviana (9,000 speakers around New Georgia), and Cheke Holo (8,000 speakers on Isabel). Most of these derive from the same parent tongue, Austronesian, and all of the Polynesian languages are also Austronesian. Smaller groups speaking 11 Papuan languages are scattered throughout the Solomons and are perhaps remnants of an earlier population largely replaced or absorbed by the Austronesians. The most-used Papuan language is Bilua (6,000 speakers on Vella Lavella).

Today, most Solomon Islanders understand Pijin, and it has become the everyday tongue of tens of thousands of outer islanders living in the Honiara melting pot. Pijin takes its vocabulary largely from English, though the grammar is Melanesian. Pijin was introduced by sandalwood traders in the early 19th century ("pijin" is the Chinese pronunciation of "business"). It has always been used as a contact language between different groups.

Although the vocabulary may be limited, there's a richness and freshness to the grammatical constructions that always delights newcomers. Pijin has only two prepositions, *bilong,* which shows possession, and *long,* which covers all other prepositions. Solomon Islands Pijin varies considerably from the pidgins of New Guinea or Vanuatu. Trying to communicate in Pijin will add enjoyment to your visit, as only about 20 percent of the population speaks English.

CONDUCT AND CUSTOMS
Conduct

Though it's okay to walk through a village along a road, ask permission of whoever's there before leaving the road. All lagoon waters are considered village property, and permission must be obtained before fishing or sometimes even snorkeling. Some Solomon Islanders resent being "exploited" by tourists who earn big money by selling their snapshots to magazines, so ask before you shoot.

Keep your body well covered if you want to be treated with respect. Women should take care when visiting isolated areas or hiking alone in the Solomons, as cases of physical and sexual abuse by aggressive local males have been reported. Local women are subject to myriad taboos, and foreign women visiting remote villages should always ask if it's allowed to do certain things, such as sitting in a place reserved for men.

Custom Fees and "Compensation"

From time to time you'll encounter a situation whereby people ask you to pay money to visit an archaeological or historic site, to see natural phenomena such as a hot spring or cave, or to enter a traditional village. Some people even claim to be the customary owners of Japanese and American war wreckage! Often local villagers will paddle out to a yacht as soon as the anchor goes down and demand a fee to use their reef, even a reef far offshore. The way the villagers look at it, these things belong to them, so how can wealthy outsiders expect to be able to use them for nothing?

They may start off by asking a ridiculously high amount (SI$50 pp), but will usually (though not always) come down after negotiations. The operators of the live-aboard dive boats pay SI$5 pp to dive on village reefs, and SI$100 per group to visit the villages themselves. Have small bills with you, and try to avoid paying fees over SI$20 pp.

Actually, the custom fees are not only aimed at tourists: Villagers short of cash regularly demand "compensation" from each other for offenses such as speaking to a girl, walking under a clothesline, etc. Anyone unfortunate enough to have such a claim made against them should tread very lightly indeed. Much of the political unrest from 2000–2003 revolved around compensation claims.

Exploring the Islands

Highlights

Solomon Islands has many highlights, beginning with the war remains around the international airport and the panpipe players who perform regularly at Honiara hotels. Another great experience is the boat trip from Honiara to Gizo, passing many romantic outer islands. Gizo itself is a charming little town with adequate facilities, and the *Toa Maru*, which the American scuba newsletter *Undercurrent* calls "one of the top five wreck dives in the world." The small eco-tourism resorts of the Marovo Lagoon are a delight to visit. Once you've "done" these well-known sights, you'll be ready for some real exploring.

Sports and Recreation

Solomon Islands offers some of the finest scuba diving in the South Pacific. In Western Province, the Uepi Island Resort on the Marovo Lagoon caters almost exclusively to scuba divers, and several dive shops are in Gizo. The Solomon's top diving facilities, however, are the live-aboard dive boats described in the Transportation section that follows. When diving, keep in mind that the nearest recompression chamber is in Townsville, Australia, and emergency air evacuation will cost over A$30,000.

Golfers have at their disposal a flat nine-hole course outside Honiara. It's a friendly, inexpensive course worth trying if you happen to be there.

There are unlimited possibilities for hikers in the Solomons. Good day hikes are from Honiara to Mataniko Falls and Gizo to Titiana. The really adventurous hiker will find many fascinating hiking areas on outer islands such as Choiseul, Isabel, and Makira. The Marovo Lagoon area is being developed for sea kayaking.

Anglers are well catered to at the Zipolo Habu Resort on Lola Island near Munda. The resort boat is available for trolling in the lagoon or open sea, with rods, reels, and lures provided. Some of the Pacific's most productive fishing is in and around the Vonavona Lagoon, and manager Joe Entrikin is one of the Solomon's top fishermen. Game fishing is also offered at Gizo.

The most popular spectator sports here are rugby and soccer, with basketball and volleyball also seen.

Public Holidays and Events

National holidays include New Year's Day (January 1), Good Friday, Easter Monday (March/April), Whitmonday (May/June), Queen's Birthday (the Friday closest to June 14), Independence Day (July 7), and Christmas Days (December 25 and 26).

In addition, there's a provincial holiday called "Second Appointed Day": Choiseul (February 25), Isabel (June 2), Temotu (June 9), Central (June 30), Rennell and Bellona (July 21), Guadalcanal (August 1), Makira (August 4), Malaita (August 15), and Western (December 8). These dates can vary a day or two either way. The Church of Melanesia prohibits all custom dancing during the 40 days before Easter (March/April).

Gizo's Festival of the Sea in early December features canoe races, fishing and diving competitions, and traditional events.

Music

The traditional music of the Solomons varies greatly between the different cultural regions. One of the most interesting instruments is the panpipe, a bundle of about a dozen tubes of different sizes open at both ends or closed at the lower end. The open-ended panpipes sound an octave higher than the closed variety, thus the closed pipes are longer. The player moves his head to blow the different tubes—the bundle itself remains stationary. The panpipe players stand or sit in two rows facing one another while whistles or bamboo trumpets produce a continuous background drone. The songs often imitate sounds of nature, such as the calls of birds, and are related to the spirit world. The panpipe ensembles play at funeral cycles, which can last up to eight years, or at important public events. The most famous contemporary panpipe bands are from Malaita.

A distant relative of these is the characteristic bamboo band of the Western Solomons, invented here in the 1920s. Some 15 to 24 horizontal pieces of bamboo of varying length are struck on their open ends with rubber thongs, to the accompaniment of guitar and ukulele. As yet little known to the world of music, bamboo rhythms will win you at once.

Vocal choirs often sing while sitting in two rows, each person shaking a hand-held rattlestick. Men's narrative songs may be accompanied by clapping sticks. Both the instrumental and vocal music of the Solomons is polyphonic (made up of several independent but harmonious melodic parts).

Arts and Crafts

All traditional handicrafts are either ceremonial or functional. The woodcrafts generally range from small domestic items such as combs and bowls, through a variety of figures and heads to objects as large as whole canoes, complete with decorated hulls and figureheads. Nontraditional carvings of fish, birds, or humans, although often good, are made solely to sell to visitors. Some traditional items, such as war clubs, masks, and *nguzunguzu*, are made in miniature to increase their desirability to tourists.

The fantastic cultural diversity of this country is reflected in its artwork. The most distinctive local carving is the *nguzunguzu* (pronounced "noozoo noozoo") of Western Province. The carved sharks and dolphins of the same area are made to European taste but are of exceptional workmanship. The shark is a popular figure because it's believed that the soul of a successful fisherman is reincarnated in a shark. Carving in the west is done in brown-streaked kerosene wood *(Corsia subcordata)* or black ebony, both hardwoods, which may be inlaid with nautilus shell or mother-of-pearl.

Another excellent purchase is the shell money of Malaita, made into beautiful necklaces. Handicrafts from Malaita are often useful items like combs, bamboo lime containers (for use with betelnut), rattles, flutes, panpipes, and fiber carrying bags. Watch too for traditional jewelry, such as headbands, earrings, nose and earplugs, pendants, breastplates, and armbands, mostly made from shell. Bone and shell fishhooks make authentic souvenirs.

Guadalcanal people excel in weaving strong, sturdy bags, baskets, and trays from the *asa* vine *(Lygodium circinnatum)*. These items are known collectively as Bukaware. The Polynesians of the Solomons make fine miniature canoes. The small woven pandanus bags of Bellona are commonly used by the people. Santa Ana and Santa Catalina in Makira Province are other sources of quality handicrafts, especially the striking black ceremonial pudding bowls inlaid with shell.

Solomon Islands handicrafts are of high quality. Bargaining is not practiced, but if you feel the cost is too high, hesitate a few moments, then ask the seller if he has a second price. Remember that any handicrafts incorporating the body parts of sea turtles or marine mammals (e.g., dolphin or whale teeth) cannot be taken into the United States, Australia, and many other countries.

ACCOMMODATIONS

The only large hotels are in Honiara and Gizo. There are tourist lodges at Auki and Munda, cottages at Marau Sound and on Pigeon Island (Reef Islands), and beach resorts at Munda and Uepi Island. Numerous low-budget eco-resorts are found around the Marovo Lagoon. Provincial resthouses are found at Buala, Kirakira, Lata, Taro, Tulagi, and elsewhere, and these always have cooking facilities. A 10 percent hotel tax is charged, and most room prices quoted in this book are without tax. Only the main hotels in Honiara and Gizo accept credit cards—everywhere else you must pay cash. Some hotels and dive shops in the Solomons quote rates in Australian dollars to make them look lower. High inflation means you'll often pay higher prices than those quoted herein, though they should be more or less relative. In general, however, the Solomons offer some of the least expensive places to stay in the South Pacific in all categories.

INFORMATION AND SERVICES

Information

The **Solomon Islands Visitors Bureau** (tel.

22442, fax 23986) publishes a number of useful brochures on the country.

Solomon Airlines offices and agents on the outer islands are good sources of information about accommodations, transport, diving, etc., in their area.

Internet Resources

The Solomon Islands Visitors Bureau website, **www.visitsolomons.com.sb,** offers information about sightseeing, island hopping, diving, fishing, boat charters, accommodations, and travel agents. Also check Solomon Islands Resorts, **www .solomon.islands-resorts.com,**, a searchable resort, hotel, and dive-operator directory. Melanesian Handicraft **www.melanesianhandicraft.com.sb** provides a useful introduction to the arts, crafts, and handicrafts of the Solomon Islanders.

The site of the Solomon Islands Ministry of Commerce, Employment, and Trade, **www.com merce.gov.sb,** is a rich source of travel, business, and government information. The section on the East Rennell World Heritage Site contains numerous photos of the western edge of Polynesia. The Solomon Islands Meteorological Service's site, **www.met.gov.sb,** lets you brush up on the weather patterns of this far-flung South Pacific island group. There's a useful section about climate change. The Vaka Taumako Project of the Pacific Traditions Society, **http://planet-hawaii.com/vaka,** is dedicated to the construction of Polynesian voyaging canoes, to educate a new generation in building authentic canoes and sailing by traditional navigational methods.

Visas and Officialdom

Everyone needs a passport and an onward ticket. Commonwealth citizens, Americans, and most Western European nationals are given a passport stamp allowing a 30-day stay, or until the flight date on their plane ticket. Almost everyone with a confirmed onward reservation within seven days is eligible for a transit visa issued upon arrival.

Extensions of stay to a total of six months maximum in any 12-month period, can be had at the Immigration Office in Honiara. Extensions up to three months are free, then it's SI$33 a month up to the permitted six months. You must bring along your air ticket with a confirmed reservation; the extension will be to the date of your flight out. Don't bother claiming that you're doing some sort of research as a way of getting more time; this requires prior clearance and will only raise questions.

Permanent immigration to the Solomons is very difficult. If you marry a Solomon Islander you can apply for a permit to stay two years, after which it may be possible to obtain permanent residence. Citizenship is possible after 10 years, and you must renounce your former citizenship. To obtain a work permit, you must apply from outside the country, enclosing a letter from your prospective employer.

There are regular immigration offices at Gizo, Honiara, Korovou, Lata (Graciosa Bay), and Munda. It's possible to check out from any of these ports (the fee is SI$50 to check in and another SI$50 to check out). In addition, all visiting yachts must pay a lighthouse fee (despite this fee, many navigational lights are out of order and perilous reefs are unmarked—beware). If your boat will be entering through an obscure port, try to bring some Solomon Islands currency with you, or be prepared for customs officials and locals who insist that American, Australian, and Solomon Islands dollars are all worth the same!

Money

The Solomon Islands dollar (SI$) is linked to a trade-related basket of currencies, and the rate is adjusted daily. Before independence in 1978, the Australian dollar was the currency used in Solomon Islands, and the SI$ was originally introduced at a rate of one to one. Since then it has depreciated to about A$1 = SI$4.50, or US$1 = SI$7. Inflation is high and visitors should be prepared to pay higher

SOLOMON ISLANDS

TRADITIONAL CURRENCY IN THE SOLOMONS

The shell money of the Langa Langa Lagoon, on the northwest side of Malaita, is made by breaking shells into small pieces, boring them with a drill, and stringing them together. Patient rubbing of the shell pieces between two grooved stones gives them their circular shape. Thousands of minute discs go into a *tafuliae,* or string, which contains 10 strands of shells two to three meters long and bears a fixed rate of exchange to the official currency. This auxiliary form of currency is used for quasi-ceremonial transactions, such as buying wives (10 strings), pigs, canoes, or land, and as settlement or compensation for injuries.

Shells vary in value according to the color and size of the shell parts used: pink is the most expensive, then orange, white, and lastly black. Generally, the smaller the size of the shell piece, the more expensive it is. Pink-lipped *spondylus* ("pink money") is made only from the lip of the shell and is the most valuable, worth four or five times as much as white.

Dolphin teeth are also used as custom money on Malaita (1,000 teeth for a wife, at 40 cents a tooth), and dolphin drives to obtain teeth are conducted at Mbita'ama Harbor (northwest Malaita), Port Adam (Maramasike Island), and Sulufou (Lau Lagoon). A sorcerer in a canoe taps magical stones together underwater to attract the dolphins, which are then led ashore by other villagers in canoes, butchered, and the meat divided. Flying-fox teeth and pigs are also exchanged on Malaita.

In the Western Solomons, ceremonial currency is in the form of large heavy rings, four centimeters thick and 24 centimeters in diameter, cut out of the shell of the giant clam. A ring with a small patch of yellow on the edge is worth more than a plain white one. In Santa Cruz, great rolls of red-feather money are used as bride price. The men who have the customary rights to make the coils pluck a few feathers from captured scarlet honeyeaters before releasing the birds.

local currency prices than those quoted in this book. There are banknotes of two, five, 10, 20, and 50 dollars, and coins of one, two, five, 10, 20, and 50 cents, plus a seven-sided SI$1 coin depicting a *nguzunguzu,* which makes an excellent souvenir.

Banking hours in Honiara are weekdays 0900–1500. Otherwise you can change money at the Mendaña Hotel at a 10 percent lower rate. The National Bank, Westpac Bank, or ANZ Bank have branches where traveler's checks may be changed in Auki, Gizo, Kirakira, Lata, Munda, Noro, and Tulagi. Elsewhere, you must have enough local currency to tide you over, since the minor National Bank agencies don't handle foreign currency.

If you don't like carrying a lot of cash around with you, consider opening a SI$ passbook account at the National Bank, which will allow you to withdraw money at any of their outer-island agencies (the branches mentioned above, plus agencies in Afio, Atoifi, Batuna, Buala, and Taro).

Before leaving, be sure to change all your leftover

Solomon Islands dollars into the currency of the next country on your itinerary, as SI$ are almost worthless outside the country. Credit cards are accepted only in Honiara and Gizo, and the use of them can be expensive since the amount will first be converted into Australian dollars, then into your own currency. A 5 percent surcharge is often added to credit card payments. Obtaining cash advances is also expensive for the same reason, plus you'll have to pay interest. American Express is not represented. The sales tax rate is 10 percent on restaurant meals, hotel rooms, car rentals, and professional services. There's no tipping.

Communications

Operator-assisted calls are not available in Honiara, so to make a long-distance call you must purchase a telephone card, sold in denominations of SI$20, SI$50, and SI$100. The cards are good for both domestic and international calls, and can be used at card phones all around the Solomons. Be sure to buy your card before you leave Honiara, as they're hard to find elsewhere.

The cost of calls per minute (using a card) is SI$2.50 to Auki or Gizo, SI$6.50 to Australia, Fiji, New Zealand, Vanuatu, and most other South Pacific countries, and SI$12.50 to North America and Europe. International calls are charged in segments of one minute. Domestic direct-dial calls are much cheaper weekdays 1800–0800 and all day weekends and holidays.

The international access code for overseas calls is 00. The information number is 101. For emergencies, it's 999 (police) or 911 (ambulance). Solomon Islands' telephone code is 677.

You can send or receive faxes via the "public fax" at Solomon Telekom offices (www.telekom.com.sb) throughout the country. These offices will also deliver faxes to post office boxes or individuals within their local areas, so it's a good way to make contact if the numbers provided herein prove inadequate: Auki (fax 40220), Buala (fax 35056), Gizo (fax 60128), Honiara (fax 23110), Kirakira (fax 50145), Lata (fax 53036), Munda (fax 61150), Noro (fax 61075), Tulagi (fax 32180). All of these places except Noro also have post offices.

A regular Internet café operates in Honiara and some Telekom offices in provincial capitals also provide Internet access. The People First Network (www.peoplefirst.net.sb) has established email stations in remote locations using solar-powered short-wave radios to connect village-based computers to a hub in Honiara. For details, visit their website.

Print Media

The main local newspaper, the *Solomon Star* (tel. 22062, fax 21572, solstar@solomon.com.sb), appears on weekdays and presents a readable selection of news. The *National Express* (tel. 20717) is published on Friday.

Solomon Airlines has an interesting in-flight magazine called *Solomons,* which you can pick up free at their Honiara office.

Radio

The Solomon Islands Broadcasting Corporation (tel. 20051, fax 23159, www.sibconline.com.sb), or "Radio Hapi Isles," transmits from Honiara over AM 1035 kHz, 0600–2200 daily. The Gizo

SIBC frequency is 945 kHz AM, or "Radio Hapi Lagoon," broadcasting weekdays 0600–1000 and 1600–1900. If you have a shortwave receiver, you'll be able to listen to the SIBC over 5020 MHz, a strong signal also heard in Vanuatu and parts of Fiji.

The SIBC news in English is at 0700, 1800, and 2100 daily, and also at 1200 on weekdays. In addition, they rebroadcast the Radio New Zealand International news at 0800 weekdays, the Radio Australia news Monday to Saturday at 0900, on Sunday at 1000, and daily at 1300, and the BBC news weekdays at noon and 1700, and again daily at 2200. In Honiara, the SIBC rebroadcasts the BBC World Service when their own programming is off the air. You can hear the *World Business Report* from London in some pretty remote locations!

Paoa FM (tel. 38984, fax 38980), a commercial Honiara station owned by the *Solomon Star* newspaper, broadcasts a lively mix of pop, reggae, and island music to Honiara at 97.7 MHz FM and to Malaita and Isabel at 101.7 MHz FM. A second private station, Z FM 100 at 99.5 MHz, plays mostly golden oldies, plus a few hot contemporary songs. The SIBC also caters to the youth market with Wantok FM at 96.3 MHz.

HEALTH

A yellow fever vaccination is required if you've been exploring the jungles of Africa or South America within the previous six days, otherwise there are no requirements. Suggested (but not obligatory) vaccinations include the hepatitis A vaccine or immune globulin, typhoid fever, tetanus, and cholera.

All tap water should be considered suspect. Take along insect repellent, sunscreen, and something to treat cuts. Even the smallest coral scratch can turn septic in no time at all if left untreated. Sexually transmitted diseases are rampant in Honiara (one reader suggested steering clear of any person wearing makeup).

Malaria

Solomon Islands has the highest rate of malaria in the world, with more than a third of the population infected each year. Half of all cases of malaria are on Guadalcanal, with Malaita and Central Province also heavily affected. It's found almost everywhere in the country below 400 meters altitude, including Honiara, and the rainy season is the worst time. A full-scale eradication program began in 1970, with DDT house spraying, case detection, and treatment, and by 1975 malaria seemed to be on the way out. As a result, funding was cut, and from 1977 to 1990, the number of cases treated in the Solomons increased from 10,496 to 86,820 (a third of the population). Between 1992 and 1999, the incidence of malaria in Honiara was reduced by 83 percent, but from 1999 to 2001 malaria cases in the capital increased by 37 percent due to the breakdown of public health facilities.

Today health officials no longer talk of eradication, only control, primarily by encouraging villagers to sleep under mosquito nets, cleaning up stagnant waters where mosquitoes breed, and introducing fish that eat the eggs. In this way, it's hoped that the present rate of 450 cases per 1,000 inhabitants will eventually be reduced to 30 per 1,000. Unbelievably, spraying is no longer considered effective because studies have shown that the mosquitoes learned not to land on sprayed areas! In any case, the subsidized distribution of mosquito nets is much cheaper than spraying and does no damage to the environment. Mosquito nets treated with icon permethrine kill insects, but the chemical is harmless to birds and mammals.

Malaria is a blood disease involving a parasite called *Plasmodium* that destroys red blood cells. A mosquito sucks in blood from a person or animal with malaria, then injects it into the next individual it bites. This is the only way malaria can be transmitted. The parasites multiply in the liver and only cause symptoms when they are periodically released back into the bloodstream, which is why bouts of malaria come and go. Symptoms begin 10 days to one year after the bite.

Avoid being bitten by wearing long pants and a long-sleeved shirt from dusk to dawn, using a good insect repellent, burning a mosquito coil at night, and sleeping under a mosquito net (check

for gaps—mosquitoes are attracted by the carbon dioxide you exhale and will search for hours for an opening). Dark clothing, perfume, and aftershave lotion attract mosquitoes.

The two nocturnal malarial mosquitoes found in the Solomons, *Anopheles farauti* and *Anopheles punctulatus,* both rest outdoors, so by sleeping in screened quarters you're partly protected. The first feeds in- and outdoors at night or during overcast days, while the second feeds only outdoors. The prime biting time is 1800–1900, and 90 percent of bites are on the ankles. The buzzing of the malaria mosquito can be heard, and their sting feels like a prick by a tiny hypodermic needle.

Since 1980, Chloroquine-resistant *Plasmodium falciparum* malaria has established itself in the Solomons and now accounts for a majority of cases. The Australian Army antimalarial unit recommends that its personnel visiting Melanesia take a 100-mg Doxycycline tablet once a day, beginning a day before they arrive and continuing for four weeks after they leave. This is a fairly strong dose that should not be continued longer than six weeks in any case. For trips of more than two weeks, they prescribe 50 mg of Doxycycline per day, beginning a day before and continuing four weeks after, plus a 250-mg Chloroquine tablet taken once a week for the same period. Doxycycline is not advisable for women in pregnancy and children under eight, and it can also make you susceptible to sunburn.

Lariam is also very effective against *Plasmodium falciparum* malaria. Start taking the drug (after a meal) a week before you arrive, and more importantly, continue four weeks after you leave (one 250-mg tablet each week). Point Cruz Chemists in central Honiara sells Lariam over the counter without prescription at about US$5 per pill (a less expensive generic version of the same thing called Mefloquine is also available). Lariam is not recommended for persons with a history of depression, heart disease, seizures, or epilepsy. Scuba divers may experience malaria-like symptoms underwater if they take Lariam, and are probably better off using Doxycycline. However, 85 percent of those taking Lariam have no problems, and most of the rest suffer only minor headaches and dizziness. If you experience no adverse side effects during the first few weeks, it means you can probably continue taking Lariam as long as you like.

Though budget-priced Chloroquine (sold under various brand names, including Nivaquine and Avloclor) may not prevent a *falciparum* malaria breakthrough, it will lessen the severity of an infection and prevent fatal malaria (two 250-mg tablets once a week). If in doubt, ask the pharmacist at any pharmacy in Honiara which drug they recommend. Whichever you choose, read the instructions on the package carefully and/or consult your doctor (the tips provided above are purely anecdotal and we accept no responsibility for them).

If you develop a fever, get a blood smear as soon as possible (any doctor or clinic in the Solomons can arrange it). Later, if you become sick in another country (even *months* later), don't forget to tell the doctor you've been in the Solomons, because doctors often misdiagnose the symptoms as flu. Always assume it's malaria until the blood test proves otherwise. See Health in the Exploring the Islands chapter of this book for more information. Don't let this situation prevent you from visiting the Solomons, but do take the precautions.

TRANSPORTATION
Getting There
The government-owned carrier, **Solomon Airlines** (tel. 20031, www.solomonairlines.com.au), flies to Honiara twice a week from Brisbane, Nadi, and Port Vila. These services are code shares with Air Pacific, Air Vanuatu, and Qantas, and since Solomon Airlines doesn't have a plane of their own, they're operated by Air Vanuatu. In Brisbane, there are immediate connections to/from Melbourne and Sydney. From North America, the most direct way to get there is via Fiji. From Europe, you have a choice of Fiji or Australia. The various air passes available to the Solomons are discussed in this book's Introduction chapter.

Air Niugini (tel. 22895) has flights from Port Moresby twice a week.

Getting Around by Air
Solomon Airlines (tel. 20031) offers nearly 600 scheduled flights a month linking 31 airstrips in the Solomons. Their 18-passenger Twin Otters and nine-passenger Britten-Norman Islanders are fun to fly in. Island-hopping routes such as Honiara-Gizo-Munda-Seghe-Honiara and Honiara-Bellona-Rennell-Honiara allow you to see several islands without backtracking. They don't allow stopovers on through tickets, however, so you'll have to pay for each sector separately. The baggage allowance is 16 kilos on domestic flights, 20 kilos on international.

From Honiara there are flights to Auki (SI$176), Ballalae (SI$593), Bellona (SI$277), Choiseul Bay (SI$593), Fera/Buala (SI$223), Gizo (SI$445), Kirakira (SI$291), Mono (SI$600), Munda (SI$392), Parasi (SI$223), Rennell (SI$297), Santa Ana (SI$372), Santa Cruz (SI$721), Seghe (SI$324), and Yandina (SI$156). These are the one-way fares, and a regular round-trip is double. Add an insurance surcharge of SI$37.50 per flight and a government tax of SI$10 per ticket to these prices.

All domestic flights are heavily booked—reserve as far in advance as possible. Because airfares are relatively low, the flights from Honiara to Munda and Gizo are often full, and it can be hard to organize a visit if you're staying two weeks or less in the Solomons. Thus you might consider booking from abroad in conjunction with your international ticket. Yet even with a reservation, it's quite possible you'll be bumped at the last minute if the plane is "overweight." The onus is entirely on you, and no shows who miss their flights forfeit their tickets. Always reconfirm your flights, and beware of flights leaving early!

If you can't get a booking locally, buy a ticket anyway and ask to be put on the waiting list. You've got a fair chance of getting on the flight if you simply go to the airport and try to fly standby, especially on the very early morning flights.

The advantage of air travel is that the planes have a set schedule and you can pack a number of far-flung destinations into a relatively short trip. On a brief visit, boat travel is really only practical to a few main centers like Auki, Buala, Tulagi, and Gizo.

SOLOMON ISLANDS

Getting Around by Boat

Interisland travel by ship is more colorful and economical than air travel. Boat service from Honiara to Auki and Gizo is frequent and fairly regular, and virtually every island in the country is accessible by boat. **Wings Shipping** (tel. 22811) and the **Malaita Shipping Company** (tel. 23502, fax 23503) are the largest private lines. Some of the oldest ships in the Pacific spend their last years in the Solomons, often ending up as scrap metal on the Honiara or Gizo waterfronts. Due to the country's financial crisis, ships withdrawn from service often aren't replaced, and those that remain only get that much more overcrowded. A few hours checking around the shipping offices in Honiara will give you an idea what's still operating.

Fares are reasonable, with cabins costing only double the deck fare, so do try to get a cabin if you'll be aboard more than one or two nights. You'll be expected to bring your own bedding. Buy food before boarding, as you may not have another chance to shop until the next day; on a long trip, take enough food to see you through (including a good supply of navy biscuits and canned fish). Hot water is supplied, but you'll need your own cooking and eating utensils. A large water bottle is also recommended. Don't overeat before boarding and avoid greasy food. Purchase a grass mat to use for sleeping on deck or bring newspapers or a piece of cardboard. Below deck, it may be hot and crowded. Keep your bag locked and know where your stuff is at port calls. Waterproof anything that shouldn't get wet with plastic bags. One of the main drawbacks on all the ships is the loud videos, which play well into the night and come back on before dawn. If you arrive somewhere like Honiara or Gizo late at night and the ship isn't leaving, stay aboard until morning, as the guesthouses will probably by closed and it's not safe to walk around with luggage late at night. The ship's schedule is up to the captain, so ask him when he's leaving before you go ashore at some remote port of call. See Transportation under Honiara for individual routes.

You can also get around by wooden or fiberglass outboard canoe, especially from Honiara to Savo or Nggela and to many outer islands from Gizo. If you do a long trip this way you won't be able to sit down again for a couple of days! To find out about a pre-arranged trip, you must ask around. Chartering can be very expensive, as gasoline costs up to SI$10 a liter in remote areas. There are never any life jackets aboard these boats and trips across open sea this way are risky.

Scuba Tours and Charters

Ask any knowledgeable diver about the Solomon Islands and they'll probably mention the two liveaboard dive boats operated by **Bilikiki Cruises Ltd.** (Jane and Rick Belmare, tel. 20412, fax 23897, www.bilikiki.com). Their Honiara office is upstairs in a building near the Point Cruz Yacht Club. The original vessel was the 38-meter, 10-stateroom MV *Bilikiki,* based here since 1989. In 1992, a sister ship, the 13-cabin MV *Spirit of the Solomons,* joined the fleet. Groups on cruises of 7, 10, or 14 nights anchor right at the remote wrecks and reefs of the Florida, Russell, and New Georgia islands, most of them accessible only in this way. The ships have been specially adapted for scuba diving, with low platforms for easy entries and exits, and dive tenders are used. Trips arranged at their Honiara office start at US$300 pp double occupancy per night all-inclusive with a seven-night minimum. However, signing onto one of these ships locally would be pure chance, so buy an all-inclusive package through one of the scuba wholesalers mentioned in the Exploring the Islands chapter of this book.

The 10-meter catamaran *Lalae* of **Lalae Charters** (Steve and Elmah Goodhew, tel. 38888, www.lalae.com.sb) is available for fishing, snorkeling, transfers, and sightseeing charters. It has two double cabins and two single berths. It anchors off the Point Cruz Yacht Club in Honiara.

Airport

Honiara International Airport (HIR), known as Henderson Field until 2003, is 13 km east of Honiara. In 1942, this historic airfield was started by the Japanese and finished by the Americans, and in early 1998 a new international terminal building was added with Japanese aid money. To the west outside the terminal are a couple of American war memorials and a Japanese AA gun. The original WW II control tower, a solitary steel-frame structure, still overlooks the airport's runway.

Public minibuses to/from town charge only SI$3 but they're very infrequent. If you have a backpack, the terminus of the Honiara minibus system is a couple of km west. Airport bound, take any minibus to KG6. Once there, offer the driver an extra SI$10 to continue on to the airport. The taxi fare to/from town is SI$50.

The Visitors Bureau desk at the airport opens for flights from Australia but usually not those from Port Vila or Port Moresby. They may agree to call a hotel on your behalf, otherwise use the public phone next to the snack bar. The exchange counter opens for all international flights but gives a poor rate (they often run out of foreign currency, so don't wait to change back here). A duty-free shop is inside the departure lounge. The departure tax is SI$40 on international flights only.

Guadalcanal

Totaling 5,353 square km, Guadalcanal is the largest island in the Solomons. The northern coastal plain contrasts with the Weather Coast in the south, where precipitous cliffs plunge into the sea. The interior is extremely rugged, rising to Mt. Makarakomburu (2,447 meters), the highest peak in the South Pacific islands (excluding Papua New Guinea).

The nation's capital, Honiara, on Guadalcanal's north side, began as an army camp during WW II. After the war, the British administration decided to utilize the abandoned American facilities here rather than return to their former headquarters, Tulagi, which had been devastated during the fighting. Protected from the rain by high mountains to the south, Honiara is also drier than Tulagi, and it's well placed to serve the North Guadalcanal plain. There are few safe anchorages on Guadalcanal, and Honiara's harbor is also poor—secure for yachts only from April to October. Still, it's the major port of the group, and interisland ships bustle along the waterfront.

Places to stay are abundant around Honiara, and some of the WW II battlefields east of Honiara can be seen on a day trip from the capital. Much of the island was off limits during the "troubles" of 1999–2003, including north Guadalcanal east of the airport and west to Kakambona. Beyond those points, many bridges and facilities were destroyed. Since July 2003, when the Australian-led intervention force began collecting weapons and arresting self-styled rebels and thugs, this area is open again.

HONIARA AND ENVIRONS

The name Honiara derives from the indigenous name for Point Cruz, *naho-ni-ara*, meaning "facing the east and southeast trade winds." Here in 1568, Mendaña, the European discoverer of the Solomons, raised a cross and claimed the island for Spain. Almost 400 years later in September 1942, the town area was the scene of heavy fighting, and the Mataniko River, which runs through the city, was the Japanese/American front line for several months. Quonset huts remain on the back streets from the U.S. base established after the Japanese withdrawal.

Today Honiara is a dusty, untidy minimetropolis of 52,000. Businesses and government offices crowd the narrow coastal strip behind Point Cruz, and residential areas cover the adjacent hillsides. Chinatown stretches along the right bank of the Mataniko River. East of Honiara on the road to the airport are the suburbs of Kukum and Vura, then the new Panatina Plaza shopping center, Ranadi with the golf course and light industry, and finally King George VI High School, where many of the city buses turn around. A steady stream of traffic crawls up and down Mendaña Avenue all day.

Over the past decade, the city's population has doubled, and 12 percent of the country's population now lives here, about 60 percent of them males. Honiara has been swollen with refugees from outlying areas (the 1999 census reported 6,339 displaced persons in Honiara

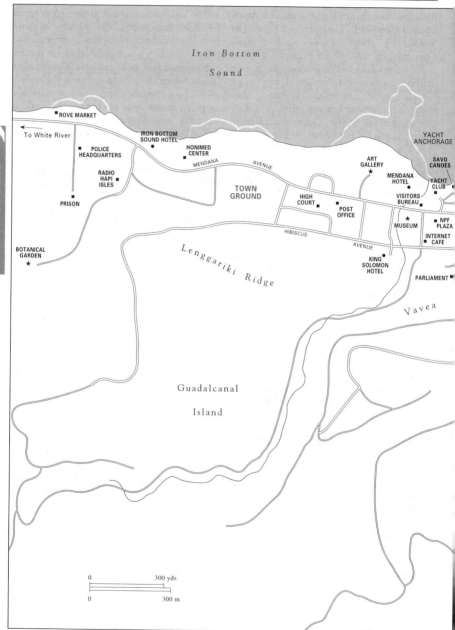

Iron Bottom Sound

To White River

ROVE MARKET

POLICE HEADQUARTERS

IRON BOTTOM SOUND HOTEL

HONIMED CENTER

MENDANA   AVENUE

YACHT ANCHORAGE

ART GALLERY

RADIO HAPI ISLES

PRISON

TOWN GROUND

HIGH COURT

POST OFFICE

MENDANA HOTEL

YACHT CLUB

VISITORS BUREAU

SAVO CANOES

MUSEUM

NPF PLAZA

INTERNET CAFE

HIBISCUS

AVENUE

BOTANICAL GARDEN

Lenggariki   Ridge

KING SOLOMON HOTEL

PARLIAMENT

Vavea

Guadalcanal

Island

0   300 yds

0   300 m

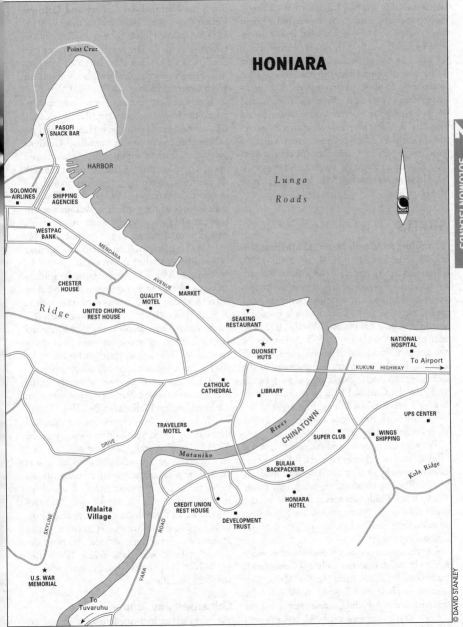

HONIARA

Point Cruz

PASOFI
SNACK BAR

HARBOR

SOLOMON
AIRLINES

SHIPPING
AGENCIES

WESTPAC
BANK

MENDANA

AVENUE

CHESTER
HOUSE

QUALITY
MOTEL

MARKET

UNITED CHURCH
REST HOUSE

Ridge

SEAKING
RESTAURANT

Lunga
Roads

QUONSET
HUTS

NATIONAL
HOSPITAL

To Airport

KUKUM   HIGHWAY

CATHOLIC
CATHEDRAL

LIBRARY

TRAVELERS
MOTEL

DRIVE

Mataniko

River

CHINATOWN

SUPER CLUB

UPS CENTER

WINGS
SHIPPING

Kola Ridge

BULAIA
BACKPACKERS

Malaita
Village

CREDIT UNION
REST HOUSE

HONIARA
HOTEL

VARA   ROAD

SKYLINE

DEVELOPMENT
TRUST

U.S. WAR
MEMORIAL

To
Tuvaruhu

alone and this number has grown since then). Young men continue to be drawn to the bright lights, especially from Malaita and Western Province, and people with jobs are outnumbered by *masta liu,* the unemployed. There always seem to be a lot of people hanging around, watching and waiting for something to happen. Still, the atmosphere in Honiara is relaxed and friendly, and it's safe enough to wander around town during the day. At night, keep to well lit streets and seriously consider investing in a taxi, particularly if you have to pass the market area. Yet compared to Port Moresby, Honiara is a breeze, and this city is a lot less touristy that Port Vila. It's *the* gateway to the Hapi Isles.

SIGHTS

The **Solomon Islands National Museum** (tel. 22309; weekdays 0800–1700, Sat. 0900–1200; admission SI$5), opposite the Visitors Bureau, once provided a good introduction to the life, crafts, and natural environment of the country. Sadly, the museum suffered multiple break-ins during the political chaos of 2001–2002, and many priceless artifacts were lost. At last report, the museum was closed, although some booklets and handicrafts could still be purchased at the museum shop. You can walk around the grounds and tour the **Cultural Village** with its collection of traditional buildings from eight of the Solomon's nine provinces, constructed in the same compound in 1991.

Between the museum and the police station is "Pistol Pete," a 155-mm Japanese howitzer that caused havoc by shelling the American-held airport during the Guadalcanal campaign. Inside the **Central Bank** (www.cbsi.com.sb) on the other side of the police station are Rennellese woodcarvings, and an excellent collection of traditional currency.

On the grounds directly opposite the police station is the **Melanesian Cultural Center** with traditional buildings from the five Melanesian countries. These were erected in 1998 for the first Melanesian Arts and Culture Festival, but the venue is slowly deteriorating. Weekdays an open-air food market functions on the site. Behind

this is the **National Art Gallery and Cultural Center** (weekdays 0900–1600; admission SI$5) in Government House, former residence of the governor-general. The center's waterfront gardens (free) are nice but there isn't a lot to see inside. Farther west, beyond the post office, is the **High Court Building** (1963–1964).

Continue west past the Town Ground. Opposite the Iron Bottom Sound Hotel (closed), take the road inland past Radio Hapi Isles and the prison checkpoint to the **Botanical Gardens** (admission free), where the grounds are always open. There are many attractive paths through the rainforest adjoining the gardens, though the entire area is overgrown. Upstream but still within the confines of the gardens is **Watapamu village** (named for the nearby water pump), fairly typical of rural villages in the Solomons. A lily pond is a bit upstream from Watapamu. It might be unwise to visit the gardens alone.

Return to Mendaña Avenue from the gardens and walk west about 500 meters to **Rove Market,** where you can buy a fresh coconut to drink. Next to Police Headquarters across the street is the **Sergeant Major Jacob Vouza War Memorial** (1992) in memory of the country's most-decorated WW II hero. Captured and tortured by the Japanese, Vouza escaped to tell his story.

Back in the center of town, scramble up the hill behind the Mobil service station to visit the huge, conical **Parliament Building** (1993), which the United States government bankrolled to the tune of US$5 million in memory of the 450 U.S. soldiers and 1,200 marines who died on Guadalcanal. Ironically, the building was erected by a Japanese construction company. Enter the 600-seat public gallery if it's open. In theory, parliament meets for three- to four-week sessions three times a year (March/April, July/August, and November/December), and at these times you can watch debates from the public gallery weekdays 0930–1200 and 1400–1600. In practice, parliamentary sessions are often cancelled.

Chinatown and Around
Take any bus east to the pedestrian overpass near **National Referral Hospital.** Locally known as

© DAVID STANLEY

Honiara's Chinatown is an authentic South Seas wild west.

Nambanaen, this American-built wartime hospital began life as the "Ninth Station." In 1993, the Taiwanese Government erected the modern extension on the west side of the hospital. Across the overpass is **Chinatown,** an Asian Wild West of photogenic high-porched wooden buildings adjacent to the riverside. Chinatown and the area around the old Mataniko bridge are among the prettiest parts of Honiara.

A level, mostly shaded road follows the Mataniko River 2.5 km upstream to friendly **Tuvaruhu village,** where it's possible to swim in the river. Galloping Horse Ridge, a major WW II battlefield, towers over Tuvaruhu to the west, and high grassy ridges almost surround the valley. It's a scenic one-hour round-trip walk providing a glimpse of rural Guadalcanal, and there's just enough traffic along the road to make it safe.

From Chinatown cross the old Mataniko River bridge and proceed up **Skyline Drive** from the Catholic cathedral (notice the row of WW II-era Quonset huts across the road from the cathedral). Keep left and go up the ridge right to the top, a steep 15-minute climb. If it's a hot day, seriously consider catching a taxi from the Catholic cathedral to the U.S. War Memorial.

It will only cost around SI$7 and you can easily walk back down.

You'll end up directly above a large squatter village of Malaita people. Notice the sago palms they use to roof their houses. It's also well worth coming up for the knockout view of Chinatown, the Mataniko Valley, the grassy hills behind Honiara, and the WW II battle sites. The main point of interest up this way, however, is the **U.S. War Memorial,** dedicated on August 7, 1992, to mark the 50th anniversary of the Red Beach landings. A stimulating account of the campaign from the American standpoint is inscribed on red marble tablets inside the monument compound. Skyline Drive, a WW II jeep track, meanders back into the boonies from here.

Mount Austin

Walk, drive, or take a taxi up the paved highway to the summit of Mt. Austin (410 meters) for a sweeping aerial view of the north coastal plains and across to Savo and the Florida Islands. Most of the historic battlefields are visible from here. For five months in the latter part of 1942, Japanese troops held Mt. Austin and used it to direct artillery fire on the American marines around the airport below. Even after the main mountain fell, surrounded Japanese held out another month on ridges such as Gifu, Sea Horse, and Galloping Horse, until starvation, suicide, or banzai assaults finally cut them down.

The easy way to get there is to ride the Naha minibus to the end of its line, then stroll 15 minutes to the large white **Solomon Peace Memorial Park,** erected on the hillside in 1981 by Japanese veterans to commemorate all who perished in the Guadalcanal campaign. Facing the memorial is a bronze sculpture, *Sound of the Tide* by Eikichi Takahashi, a Japanese soldier killed in battle here. This stark memorial contrasts sharply with the grandiose U.S. War Memorial on Skyline Ridge that proclaims American military prowess.

An ordinary car driven with care can easily reach the summit of Mt. Austin, and a taxi from the memorial should cost around SI$15, if you can find one. On foot, allow about an hour. The Forestry Department plots, which you see along the way, have scientific names posted on some of the trees (notice the stand of kauri). The river you see below from the mountaintop is the Lungga. In October 1942, a Japanese army under General Maruyama plodded around behind Mt. Austin from White River in an abortive attempt to take the airport from the rear. It's rumored that at least six big artillery pieces and much war materiel are strewn along the Lungga River north of the mountain.

The potholed paved road continues down to the jungle-clad Lungga Canyon itself, but don't try driving it unless you've got a jeep or pickup truck. On foot, the river is only 30 minutes from the summit. The last stretch of road is badly eroded, but if you walk a bit, you will reach a lovely pool and sandy beach at a bend of the river. In the rainy season the current can be too strong for safe swimming, but it's a good picnic spot anytime. The British built this road as part of a hydroelectric project that was stopped by land disputes and the discovery of limestone in the bedrock, which would have led to heavy leakage. The trail up the river from the end of the road passes two large tunnels constructed as part of the scheme.

There's no permanent habitation along the Mt. Austin road and no custom fees to pay. Go early, pack a lunch, and make a day of it. If it's not too late you can hike back down to Honiara via Mbarana village, over some of the old wartime battlefields. The dirt road westbound just before the Forestry Department plots leads to Mbarana, then it becomes a footpath called the **Tuvaruhu Trail,** which winds along grassy ridges with good views on all sides. Keep straight ahead on the path and generally to the left and you'll come out at Vara, near Chinatown. This may be the best part of the trip.

Mataniko Falls

One of the most amazing waterfalls in the South Pacific is only a two-hour walk south of Honiara up the Mataniko River. Follow the road from Chinatown up the riverside 2.5 km to its end at Tuvaruhu. Cross the river (knee deep) to Lelei village from just beyond the church at Tuvaruhu. It's a good idea to hire a resident of Lelei (not Tuvaruhu) to show you the way to the falls (agree on a price beforehand). You'll follow a trail up over the grassy hillsides and down toward a forest. You pass to the left of a small coconut grove and Harahei village. Here the traditional landowner may collect a custom fee (have small bills). The final descent to the falls is down a steep, slippery, forested incline.

There are many large pools for cooling off after this exhausting hike, but the main sight is a gigantic, swallow-infested, stalagmite-covered cave, with an arm of the river roaring right through. The river itself pours out of a crack in a limestone cliff just above and tumbles down into the cave through a crevice totally surrounded by white water. You'll never forget this excursion.

Sports and Recreation

The only dive shop presently operating in Honiara is **Aqua Action** (tel. 21737, fax 20376) at the Honiara Hotel. You must arrange the diving a few days in advance. The main site visited is Bonegi, northwest of Honiara, with two wrecked Japanese transport ships.

The **Honiara Golf Club** (tel. 30181), across the road from King George VI High School between Honiara and the airport, charges greens fees of SI$25 for the nine holes. One of the staff will rent you a set of clubs for SI$30. Caddy fees are about SI$10 per nine holes (the caddies will tell you it's more, but that's the normal charge). There's a good bar here (open weekdays 1400–2200, weekends 0900–2200), and you should buy the caddy a soft drink if he has been helpful. Food is available after 1700. The course is laid out on the old Kukum "Fighter Two" airstrip so it's dead flat, though the club's pleasant colonial atmosphere is fun. Visitors are welcome.

The **Honiara Hash House Harriers** do a recreational run every Monday at 1730. For the location, look for the notice in the window of Acor Bookstore near Solomon Airlines on Monday afternoon.

On Saturday afternoon catch a game of soccer (April–Sept.) at the **Lawson Tama Stadium** opposite Central Referral Hospital. The action starts about 1600, and the entrance fee is cheap. Rugby (Jan.–April) is played at King George VI High School east of town.

ACCOMMODATIONS

Under US$25

Just under a dozen resthouses and hostels around Honiara offer reasonable shared bath accommodations, usually with communal cooking facilities provided. A few charge *per bed* and singles can often get the per person rate, though some bargaining may be required.

Bulaia Backpackers Lodge (tel. 28819), directly across the street from the Honiara Hotel in Chinatown, opened in early 2003. There are eight two-bed rooms with fan at SI$55 pp, or SI$100/110 single/double if you don't wish to share. A large common kitchen is available, and they keep everything fairly clean.

The **Solomon Islands Credit Union League** (tel. 23564, fax 20131) has a 14-room hostel behind their business office opposite the Red Cross in New Chinatown. The 12 rooms with shared bath are SI$50/90 single/double, the two air-conditioned rooms with bath SI$110 single or double. Each room has a sink and two bunk beds, and rather grubby communal cooking and bathing facilities are provided. It's primarily intended for Credit Union staff attending training seminars, but empty rooms are available to travelers willing to accept basic conditions. Ask what time they lock the gate before going out at night.

The **Travelers Motel** (tel. 25721, fax 25735) has a good location in the "Fijian Quarters" just up the road inland on the west side of the Mataniko Bridge near Chinatown. The 17 rooms in this two-story building include three fan-cooled rooms with shared bath at SI$80 single or double, seven downstairs rooms and another seven upstairs rooms with private bath at SI$90. There are good communal cooking facilities. The screened windows are not very soundproof, so you hear everything around you.

The Melanesian Brotherhood operates **Chester House** (tel. 26355, fax 23079), the gray and blue two-story building with the crosses on the walls standing on the hillside off Hibiscus Avenue, directly back from the Hot Bread Kitchen. This spacious guesthouse has nine rooms upstairs and another seven downstairs at SI$120 single or double. Communal toilets/showers/cooking facilities are provided, and the terrace has a great view of Iron Bottom Sound.

A dirt road east from Chester House leads to the 10-room **United Church Resthouse** (tel. 20028). From town, follow Cluck Street up from Mendaña Avenue and turn right at the top of the hill. The cost is SI$50 pp, and singles will be expected to share. It can be rather noisy due to people chatting on the front porch late at night and locals preparing breakfast in the early morning. Keep your room door firmly locked at all times (even if you're only out on the porch) as there have been thefts. As at Chester House, no alcohol is allowed in the resthouse. This place will be full if any sort of church meeting is taking place.

If none of the above work out, two shoestring places with lots of local color are up the road inland from Club Supreme, behind Kukum Police Station, three km east of downtown (good bus service). The **Kukum Transit House** (tel. 24810), near the Kukum Shopping Center, has six rooms with private bath at SI$90 for the room (up to three people). Communal cooking facilities are provided.

Binaboli Resthouse (tel. 25211), next to Kukum Clinic, two blocks from the Kukum Transit House, has 11 fan-cooled rooms with shared bath and cooking facilities at SI$50/77 single/double.

Tropicana Beach Resort (tel. 23759), on the coast a km west of Rove Market, has nine rooms with fan and shared bath at SI$100–120 single or double. The eight rooms with bath in an adjacent two-story block are SI$165. Communal cooking facilities are available. There's no beach, but you get a nice view of Iron Bottom Sound from the terrace.

US$25–50

The 56-room **Honiara Hotel** (tel. 21737, fax 20376, www.honiarahotel.com.sb), near Chinatown, is a pleasant hotel with reasonable facilities. There are 13 non-air-conditioned "budget" rooms with twin beds and shared bath at SI$120 single or double, plus 26 "standard" air-conditioned rooms with private bath and fridge at SI$240 (the budget rooms are often unavailable). A filling continental breakfast buffet is included. On an upper terrace connected to the rest of the hotel by an offbeat funicular elevator are 12 "deluxe" rooms and five "executive" rooms, but these are currently closed. There's a swimming pool, and the hotel bar and adjacent restaurant are good.

The **Quality Motel** (tel. 25150, fax 25277, qml@solomon.com.sb) is on the hillside directly above the market. The 30 rooms in this two-story building begin at SI$190 single or double with fan, fridge, and bath. The large family rooms are SI$323 without air conditioning, SI$392 with air conditioning, cooking facilities included. The regular rooms don't have access to cooking facilities, but television sets are for rent at SI$35 a night, creating a big disturbance.

US$50–100

Since 1967 Honiara's premier hotel has been the 94-room **Kitano Mendaña** (tel. 20071, fax 23942, kitano@mendana.com.sb), which the Japanese construction company Kitano purchased from the government in 1990. The standard air-conditioned rooms with fridge and private bath are SI$440/480 single/double, deluxe rooms SI$550/580, plus 10 percent tax. There's a freshwater swimming pool, and the hotel's seaside terrace bar has pitchers of draught beer at SI$35. The Sunday noon barbecue (SI$65) and the continental buffet breakfast (SI$28) are good. Change money here only in emergencies, as they give a rate 10 percent lower than the banks.

The **King Solomon Hotel** (Shane and Sue Kennedy, tel. 21205, fax 21771, kingsol@solomon .com.sb), on Hibiscus Ave. across the street from the Australian High Commission, provides a higher standard of accommodations than the Mendaña for a similar price though without the seaside location. The rooms are up on the hillside accessible via a funicular elevator similar to the one at the Honiara Hotel. The 40 deluxe hillside rooms are SI$431 single or double, while the 16 seaview rooms are SI$480. There are also 10 self-catering units at SI$696. Extra persons in the room are SI$139 each, but children under 12 may stay with their parents free. With its upper level swimming pool and "leaf haus" restaurant/bar, the King Solomon is a pleasant place to stay.

FOOD

Snack Bars

Lots of basic eateries around town serve curry beef with rice for SI$15. Many close at night, so if you have access to kitchen facilities, plan on cooking your own dinner and having lunch on the run. Several places at the Central Market serve rice or noodle lunches. Weekdays women at stalls on the Town Ground, just west of the center, sell plates of chicken or fish and rice at SI$10.

The back counter at **Amy's Snack Bar** (weekdays 0600–2030, weekends 0700–1830), next to the Westpac Bank, serves a good selection of dishes, such as sweet and sour pork, fried chicken, noodles, fish and chips, spring rolls, *rotis,* hot dogs, sausages, and meat pies. Most dishes are SI$15, and the cold coconuts are a real treat at SI$2. There are plenty of plastic picnic tables at which to sit.

In the center of town, **Kingsley's Fastfood Center** (tel. 22936; weekdays 0730–1700, Sat.

0930–1500, Sun. 1000–1500), on the street running inland from Solomon Airlines, specializes in barbecued chicken, rice dishes, hamburgers, and noodle soup.

Inexpensive meals can be obtained at the food court of the **NPF Plaza** (closed Sun.) opposite the National Museum. One place sells better than average fish and chips at S$5 a bag. Also watch for the SI$4 *rotis*.

Pasofi Snack Bar (tel. 21295), on Point Cruz, has fish and chips and beef curries. The chili fish is superb at S$16 a plate. There are seats outside, and it's open till 1630 weekdays and until 1400 Saturday.

The food court at **Panatina Plaza** (weekdays 0600–1630, Sat. 0600–1400), between Kukum and Ranadi, has several places serving good cooked meals for SI$17.

Upscale Restaurants

Other than the good-value meals available at the Point Cruz Yacht Club (see below), and the Wednesday and Friday night buffets (SI$120) at the Kitano Mendaña Hotel, the options for fine dining in Honiara are dismal.

There are lots of Chinese restaurants around town, but they're overpriced. Watch the cost of drinks (usually not listed on the menus). Prices are higher at dinner, and you can count on spending double what a comparable meal would cost in Fiji. Expect 10 percent tax to be added to your bill.

The **Seaking Restaurant** (tel. 23678; Mon.–Sat. 1730–2130), on the waterfront opposite the Catholic cathedral, is a large Chinese dining room serving pork, chicken, beef, and fish dishes at SI$55, fried noodles at SI$40, chop suey at SI$45, and lobster at SI$85. White rice is SI$6 extra.

The **JGP Restaurant** (tel. 27547; daily 0700–2200), on Hibiscus Avenue directly behind the Westpac Bank, is an excellent alternative to the hotel restaurants. Appetizers cost SI$15–25, soups SI$10–15, and mains SI$28–55. The catch of the night (SI$35) is always a good choice, and there's lots more seafood, including lobster. Though the service is slow, the atmosphere and food are good.

Groceries

It pays to shop around, as grocery prices vary considerably in Honiara. The best-stocked supermarkets are in Chinatown.

Wings Supermarket (tel. 20108; Mon.–Fri. 0800–1700, Sat. 0830–1300), at the back of NPF Plaza, is the largest in the center of town.

ELO 24 Retail Shop, on Cluck St. below the South Sea Restaurant, sells basic groceries 24 hours a day, seven days a week.

ENTERTAINMENT

Weekdays after work, Honiara's expatriate community congregates at the **Point Cruz Yacht Club** (tel. 22500, fax 22073; daily 1100–2100, until 2200 Wed. and Sat.), and at happy hour Friday afternoon 1730–1830 the place is packed. Have the doorman sign you in. Sit at a beachside table and enjoy the view of ships in the harbor and of Savo Island on the horizon. Cruising yachts anchor in Mbokona Bay opposite the naval vessels, straight out from the yacht club beach, and the club has the usual notice board if you're looking for a yacht/crew. The club's food counter is open daily 1130–1330 and 1800–2030. To find out what's cooking, check the blackboard menu.

Honiara currently has three local discos, all of them open Thursday to Saturday 2100–0200 and charging SI$20 admission. Things don't get moving until after 2300 and intrusive local drunks can be a problem. **The Warehouse,** on Hibiscus Avenue next to the Shell station, a block back from the Westpac Bank, is the largest and perhaps the safest. **Club Paradise VIP Lounge** is next to the Honiara Casino on Mendaña Ave., a bit east of the Westpac Bank. **Club Marimba,** formerly Super Club, in Chinatown just beyond the Shell service station near the Honiara Hotel, is a rough local club (ask to be let into the "VIP Room").

After dark, you've got a good chance of being mugged if you're caught wandering anywhere between Chinatown and the market, so take a taxi. At the bars, beware of smooth talking conmen who are expert at separating visitors from their money, and "dugongs" (ladies of the night) after money and beer. Of course, not all of the women at the clubs are dugongs, but male visitors should find out which island their female dance partners are from and avoid those from Malaita. Otherwise, someone pretending to be a close relative may later demand "compensation," with or without the knowledge of the woman.

Cultural Shows for Visitors

The top events of the week are the **panpipe performances** at the main hotels. The top panpipe band is Narasirato from Are'are in South Malaita (internationally renowned since their tours to England, Canada, and Australia). Narasirato T-shirts and cassettes are sold at the performances. The Mao Dancers from Kwara'ae and the Wasi Ka Nanara Pan Pipers from Waimarau, both on Malaita, and the Oruitolo Pipe Band from Ugi Island, are also very good. Some of the panpipe groups incorporate bamboo band music into their performances.

The panpipe musicians often appear with **Gilbertese dancing,** but unfortunately, most of the Gilbertese groups now perform Tahitian *tamure* dances. These can be rather boring due to the absence of Polynesian drummers able to execute sudden changes in rhythm. Tahitian dancing to recorded music or singing just isn't the same, and it's a pity these people stopped doing their own authentic Gilbertese dances. Be careful if a dancer comes up and places a garland of flowers on your head. Next thing you know she'll have you dancing with her up on the stage!

The programs tend to vary, but a group often performs at the Kitano Mendaña Hotel on Wednesday or Friday night. Panpipers also perform, perhaps with Gilbertese dancing as a warmup. A Gilbertese dance group from White River often does *tamure* dances. The shows start around 1900.

Saturday at 1930, panpipers and *tamure* dancers alternate at the King Solomon Hotel. The *tamure* dancing on the large shell stage at the Honiara Hotel is currently suspended. You can watch any of these for the price of a drink.

SHOPPING

The **Central Market** (open all day but best before 1030) is the place to buy fruit, vegetables,

and shell money. Prices vary considerably from one stall to another, so shop around. Don't bargain, just keep looking. Notice how there are more stores around Honiara selling used clothing than new clothes.

The **Philatelic Bureau** (tel. 21821, fax 21472) beside the post office sells beautiful stamps and first-day covers, which make excellent souvenirs. They also have interesting postcards. The **Central Bank** (tel. 21791) nearby sells commemorative coins, many of which are on display in the lobby.

Afga Film (tel. 20644), Room 39, NPF Plaza, does developing.

Crafts

Without question, Honiara's top buys are traditional handicrafts. Carvers peddle their wares at the entrance to the Kitano Mendaña Hotel, but it's mostly nontraditional tourist art. The handicraft shop at the National Museum is much better.

The **King Solomon Arts and Crafts Center** (no phone), opposite Solomon Airlines, is one of the least expensive places to buy handicrafts. **Melanesian Handcrafts** (tel. 22189), also on Mendaña Ave., also sells a variety of handicrafts.

Nautilus Books and Gift Shop (tel. 26105), room 17, upstairs in the NPF Plaza, sells and trades used paperbacks, plus a variety of local crafts.

INFORMATION

The helpful Visitors Bureau (tel. 22442, fax 23986; weekdays 0800–1630, Sat. 0900–1200), across from the museum, can supply useful brochures. This is one of the few tourist offices in the South Pacific that is only too happy to advise on ways of getting off the beaten track, staying with local people, arranging rides in outboard canoes, etc. They're especially knowledgeable about low-budget ecotourism options in Western Province. If you're looking for real adventure, they'll have plenty of suggestions.

BJS Agencies (tel. 22393, bjs@solomon .com.sb) on Mendaña Avenue sells their annual *Solomon Islands Trade Directory,* which provides considerable information on business conditions and regulations.

The National Land Center Map Sales Office

(weekdays 0800–1130 and 1300–1600), Hibiscus Ave. and Koti Lane, has detailed topographical maps of the whole country at SI$30 a sheet.

The Hydrographic Office (tel. 28647), opposite the National Land Center, sells navigational charts. The four locally produced charts exhibited on the wall are SI$80, while foreign charts sell for SI$165, although very few are available.

Bookstores and Libraries

Riley's Pocket Bookstore in the lobby of the Honiara Hotel, is the only commercial bookstore in Honiara. They carry several intriguing books by local authors, such as *The Confession* by Julian Maka'a and *The Alternative* by John Saunana. It's always closed, but the hotel receptionist has a key.

The University of the South Pacific Center (tel. 21307, fax 21287), behind the National Gymnasium east of Chinatown, also carries books by Solomon Islanders. The library here is open weekdays 0800–1800 and Saturday 0900–1200.

The Public Library (tel. 23227) is on Belama Ave. between the market and Chinatown. Better is the National Library (tel. 27412; weekdays 0830–1200 and 1300–1600), in the building directly behind the Public Library. You may be asked to pay SI$5 to "use" the books, though you won't be allowed to take them out.

Nongovernment Organizations

The Solomon Islands Development Trust (Abraham Baeanisia, tel. 21130, sidt@solomon.com.sb), in New Chinatown, publishes a fascinating quarterly magazine called *Link* on local social and environmental issues.

The Development Services Exchange (tel. 23760, fax 21339), also in New Chinatown, is an umbrella organization founded in 1991 that represents 90 NGOs active in Solomon Islands.

Airline Offices

Solomon Airlines (tel. 20031), on Mendaña Ave. in the center of town, also represents Air Niugini, Air Vanuatu, and Air New Zealand. Guadalcanal Travel Services (tel. 22586, fax 26184, kevin@gts.com.sb), across the street from Solomon Airlines, represents Air Pacific and Qantas. Guadalcanal Travel books domestic flights for exactly the same fares as the crowded Solomon Airlines office across the street and provides better service.

SERVICES

Money

The Westpac Bank, the ANZ Bank, and the National Bank are all near one another in the center of town (weekdays 0900–1500). The ANZ Bank and National Bank both charge SI$15 commission to change traveler's checks but none on cash. The Westpac Bank deducts no commissions but gives a slightly worse rate. An ATM is outside the downtown ANZ Bank branch and there's a second branch with an ATM at Panatina Plaza on the road to the airport.

When the banks are closed, the cashier at the Kitano Mendaña Hotel will change money for about 10 percent less.

Post and Telecommunications

The main post office (tel. 21821) is open weekdays 0800–1630, Saturday 0800–1200. Honiara's post office is uncrowded, the staff are friendly and cooperative, and postal rates in the Solomons are low. Send all your parcels, postcards, and aerograms from here. Always use airmail, even for parcels, as sea mail to Europe or North America can take six months. Poste restante at the post office holds letters three months.

The parcel section at the rear of the main post office opens Monday, Wednesday, and Friday 0800–1600, Tuesday and Thursday 0800–1500, and Saturday 0800–1100. The convenient Post Shop inside the post office sells all sorts of envelopes. The attractive aerograms are SI$2 and first day covers for the value of the stamps.

The DHL Courier Service office is at BJS Agencies/Melanesian Handcraft (tel. 22393, bjs@solomon.com.sb; weekdays 0800–1630, Sat. 0900–1100), on Mendaña Avenue.

Solomon Telekom (tel. 21164, fax 24220; weekdays 0800–1530), next to the post office, has four private booths for making calls with telephone cards. Operator-assisted calls are not available. If you want to receive a fax at this office, have it sent to fax 23110 (SI$4.50 a page to receive). Many other public card phones are found around town.

The People First Network Internet Cafe (tel. 26560; weekdays 0800–1700, Sat. 0800–1500), on the ground floor of the Anthony Saru Building near the museum, charges SI$12 an hour for Internet access.

Immigration

The Immigration office (tel. 26392), in the Ministry of Commerce across Mendaña Ave. from the post office, is open weekdays 0900–1100 and 1300–1500.

Consulates

The Australian High Commission (tel. 21561, www.solomon.emb.gov.au), across the street from the King Solomon Hotel, also represents Canadians, as an official signboard proclaims. (If you need an Australian visa, try to get it through your airline, not here.)

The British High Commission (tel. 21705) is in Telekom House next to the post office. The New Zealand High Commission (tel. 21502) and European Union representation (tel. 22765) are on the second floor of the Y. Sato Building (above Guadalcanal Travel Service). Tradco Shipping Ltd. (tel. 22588), next to Guadalcanal Travel Service, acts as the honorary consulate of Germany and France. The Japanese Embassy (tel. 22953) is on the third floor of the NPF Building behind the Westpac Bank. The Papua New Guinea High Commission (tel. 20561; tourist visas SI$34) is on second floor of the Anthony Saru Building, behind NPF Plaza next to the Solomon Islands National Museum. The consular agent of the U.S. Embassy in Port Moresby, Papua New Guinea, is in the same building as BJS Agencies/Melanesian Handcraft (tel. 23426, fax 27429, bjs@solomon.com.sb), on Mendaña Avenue. The Taiwanese Embassy (tel. 22590) is upstairs in Panatina Plaza east of town.

Public Toilets

Public toilets are available in the Kitano Mendaña Hotel, the Honiara Hotel, and at the Point Cruz Yacht Club. Bring your own toilet paper. At last report, there were no launderettes in Honiara.

HEALTH

The National Referral Hospital (tel. 23600) is overcrowded, so if you need medical attention, consider visiting a private doctor rather than spending a long time waiting there. Any of the clinics mentioned below should be able to do a malaria slide check quickly for about SI$10.

Popular among local expatriates is the Panatina Medical Center (tel. 38185; weekdays 0800–1630, Sat. 0900–1400) opposite the pharmacy in Panatina Plaza. They charge SI$80 for consultations and SI$10 for malaria checks.

The Chinatown Medical Center (tel. 21773; weekdays 0800–1630, weekends 0800–1200) is beside the Shell service station almost opposite the Honiara Hotel.

Dr. Pimbo Ogatuti of the Island Medical Center (tel. 23139; weekdays 0800–1200 and 1300–1600, Saturday 0800–1200), is on Cluck St. on the way up to the United Church Resthouse.

Dr. H. Posala's Honimed Clinic (tel. 22029; Mon., Tues., and Thurs. 0800–1200 and 1330–1600, Wed. 0800–1200, Fri. 0800–1200 and 1330–1500, Sun. 0900–1200), is next to the Iron Bottom Sound Hotel west of the center. It's SI$50 for a consultation or SI$10 for a prescription.

The Honiara Dental Center (tel. 22029; Mon.–Thurs. 0800–1200 and 1330–1630, Fri. 0800–1200) is next to the Honimed Clinic. There's also a Dental Clinic (tel. 23600) at Central Hospital.

For malaria prevention, Point Cruz Chemists (tel. 22911), opposite Solomon Airlines, has Paludrine at SI$32 for 30 tablets (one a day). The Dispensary (tel. 23587) in NPF Plaza sells Paludrine at 65 cents a pill and they have Chloroquine at SI$2.50 for 10 pills. At last report, Lariam was SI$280 for eight tablets at Point Cruz Chemists, or SI$127 for a set of eight at The Dispensary. See Health in this chapter's Exploring the Islands section for a discussion of these drugs.

TRANSPORTATION

For domestic air services from Honiara, see Transportation in this chapter's Exploring the Islands section.

Travel around the Solomons by boat is fairly easy, and it's one of the main attractions of the country. There are many services, and fares are reasonable—plan on doing much of your interisland travel this way. You'll make numerous friends on board and really get to see the Solomons.

Orient yourself by looking over the ships in Honiara harbor; then seek out the shipping company offices. Some ships won't accept passengers for safety reasons, and you should pick the larger vessels if your ability as a sailor is in doubt. Cabin fares (when available) are about double one-way deck fares, and meals usually aren't included. If you want a cabin, try to book a few days in advance. Forget attempting to catch a boat just before Christmas when schedules and routes change at a moment's notice and everything's full.

Ships to Western Province

The 26-hour boat trip from Honiara to Gizo is one of the finest scenic cruises in the South Pacific. It's less rough westbound from Honiara to Gizo than eastbound from Gizo to Honiara because you go with the prevailing winds. Thus if you were planning to fly one way, it's a good plan to go out by boat and return to Honiara by plane. However, you only get to see the Marovo Lagoon by day on the way back to Honiara.

Every Sunday at 1000, **Wings Shipping** (tel. 22811) in Chinatown sends the *Compass Rose II* to Patutiva (SI$109 deck), Munda (SI$129 deck), and Gizo (SI$143 deck). First class costs a third to a half more, a cabin about double. The ship arrives in Gizo on Monday afternoon and starts back toward Honiara a few hours later, calling at the New Georgia and Marovo Lagoon pickup points on Tuesday and arriving in Honiara early Wednesday morning. On the way to Gizo, there will be markets with cooked food at some of the ports of call, but you have to be quick or you'll miss out. It's best to take your own food along. The *Compass Rose II* is small, slow, and dirty but it will get you there.

The MV *Tomoko* of **Transwest Shipping** (tel. 27605) should leave Honiara Sundays at 1900, arriving at Gizo Monday at 1600, calling at Bunikalo, Gasina, Chea, Patutiva, Viru Harbor,

Ughele, Monda, Noro, and Ringi Cove on the way. A second weekly trip, leaving Honiara at 1800 on Wednesday, may be offered. This noisy, ex-Chinese ship is owned by Western Province. There are three decks, all of which will be very crowded, and you must arrive several hours early to get a reasonable place. The benches on the top deck may seem fine, but the tarpaulin roof leaks and water pours onto deck from the outlet pipes when it rains. First class is air-conditioned, but the doors are left open since most people walk through it on the way to the toilets. Get a cabin, if you can. There's a cafeteria on board, but bringing food is still a good idea. Fares are similar to those of Wings Shipping. At last report, you bought your ticket on board before sailing, but check this.

Lauru Shipping Services (tel. 26784) operates the *Lauru I* to Noro, Gizo, Vaghena, and Choiseul (SI$150 deck) about twice a month. If they're transporting fuel, only a few passengers will be allowed on board. This ship is slow, old, and dirty, so make it your last choice.

Ships to Malaita

The **Malaita Shipping Co.** (tel. 23502, fax 23503), just down toward the harbor from the ANZ Bank, runs the MV *Ramos III* from Honiara to Auki Tuesday and Friday at 1800 (arriving 2330). Fares are SI$70 economy, SI$94 first class, and SI$118 cabin. On alternate Sundays, the *Ramos III* sails overnight from Honiara to northeast or south Malaita. On an overnight trip, first class or a cabin might be worth considering, although there's a large protected room downstairs for economy passengers. When it's not crowded, first class on the **Ramos III** is good, with long padded benches on which to stretch out. Unfortunately, noisy nocturnal videos will disturb your sleep in both the downstairs room and the first class lounge. Trips are sometimes cancelled if not enough tickets are sold.

Several smaller wooden boats, such as the *Sa'alai* and the *Memory,* also ply between Honiara and Auki (SI$60 deck) a couple of times a week. Safety would be a concern if they became overcrowded, as often happens.

Seaways Ltd. (tel. 26308), in the aluminum

warehouse facing the wharf, operates the MV *Baruku* to South Malaita weekly (SI$90 deck). Every two months they make a trip to Ontong Java (SI$50 deck). Also ask about the MV *Belama* to Ontong Java and Sikaiana.

Olifasia Shipping Services, in the same aluminum warehouse, runs the MV *Liofai* to Su'u and Masupa every Thursday at 2100.

Ships to Isabel

The **Isabel Development Co.** (tel. 22126, fax 22009), in the aluminum warehouse facing the waterfront, runs the MV *Isabella* to Buala (SI$78 deck) once a week. Twice a month it continues up the west coast of Isabel as far as Kia. Take along a sleeping mat, food, and water.

Ships to Choiseul and Makira

Wings Shipping (tel. 22811), in Chinatown, operates the MV *Compass Rose II* to Choiseul once a month. They call at all ports between Wagina and Taro, following the north or south coasts on alternative trips. Fares from Honiara are SI$148 to Wagina or SI$150 to Taro. The ship travels to Makira monthly, visiting all ports as far east as Santa Ana. Fares from Honiara are SI$98 to Kirakira and SI$115 to Santa Ana.

Ships to Tulagi

Sasape Marina Ltd. (tel. 22111), upstairs in the Marine Division Building, runs the *Kangava* to Tulagi on Monday, Wednesday, and Friday, departing at 1400 at the earliest (later if there is additional cargo to load). It's SI$25 each way. This boat is often out of service due to special charters.

Other Ships

The 304-passenger MV *Temotu* of the **Temotu Shipping Line** (tel. 27558), in the warehouse next to Pasofi Snack Bar on Point Cruz, sails to Temotu Province once or twice a month (SI$171/184/196 economy/second/first class to Lata, SI$189/202/214 to the Reef Islands). They also sail to Gizo (SI$130 economy) when the ships that usually serve that route are out of service. The *Temotu* is newer and cleaner than many of the other ships. You can sometimes help yourself to rice from a large pot in the mess—great

with tinned fish. The same company also uses the *Eastern Trader* for trips to Temotu.

The **Church of Melanesia Shipping Office** (tel. 21892, fax 21098), diagonally opposite the Hot Bread Kitchen, operates three well-maintained mission ships. The *Charles Fox* does the mail run to the Florida Islands (Taroaniara on Gela Island), departing Honiara on Monday, Wednesday, and Friday (SI$35 deck, no cabins). The *Southern Cross* and the *Kopuria* serve Malaita, Isabel, Makira, and Temotu on an irregular basis. This pair is well worth checking as each has three or four double cabins, costing only double per bunk what is costs to travel deck. All three are quite small, so only go if you're sure of your sailing and social abilities.

Less well-known are the old Chinese trading boats, full of South Seas flavor, that run between Honiara and Gizo fortnightly. There are also mission ships to many points; ask the crews along the waterfront.

By Canoe

To reach Savo Island, catch one of the motorized canoes from the landing beside the Point Cruz Yacht Club. Ask for the "passenger rate" of SI$50 pp or you'll be expected to pay SI$250 for a special trip. Try to do the canoe journey in the early morning before the wind wakes up the sea, and be prepared to get soaked even on an apparently calm day. You'll pass through schools of dolphins and flying fish.

Outboard canoes used to make the much shorter crossing from Savo to Visale on west Guadalcanal, then passengers would continue to Honiara by road, but since the "troubles," all canoes go direct to Honiara.

By Bus

Scores of private minibuses cruise up and down the main road from White River to KG6 (King George VI High School), passing every few minutes. Some buses go as far west as White River. Buses marked Naha turn inland at Kukum before reaching KG6. Buses within the town area operate until 2100 daily. All buses have destination boards in the front window, and fares are SI$2 anywhere between White River and KG6. Baggage is free and the conductors are fairly honest, but it's wise to have small bills. Make a hissing sound when you want to get off.

Taxis
Taxi drivers are also honest, but always ask the price beforehand, as they don't have meters, and expect prices to increase at night. Estimate how much you might be willing to pay, then offer that amount to the driver before getting in. It's usually SI$3–4 a kilometer and SI$30–50 to the airport (don't tip the driver). Single passengers sit in front.

You could hire a taxi for the day to tour the battlefields west of the airport for only a bit more than it would cost to rent a car (around SI$50 an hour). Make a list of the places you want to see, then get a flat rate, including waiting time, gas, and mileage. If taking a taxi beyond the Honiara town area (for example, if you want to go past the airport), look for one with a Guadalcanal driver (rather than a Malaitan) to avoid problems.

Car Rentals
The only rent-a-car company currently operating in the country is **Economy Car Rentals** (tel. 27100, fax 23593; weekdays 0800–1700, Sat. 0800–1200), next to the gas station near the Mendaña Hotel. An unlimited-mileage Mazda costs SI$140/840 daily/weekly, plus SI$30/180 mandatory collision insurance (SI$3,500 deductible), plus 10 percent tax. Ask about their reduced half-day rate (valid 0900–1500). Drivers under 21 or over 65 are not accepted.

There's a shortage of vehicles, so book as far in advance as possible, especially on weekends. Hiring a taxi for sightseeing is a good alternative. If you do decide to drive, beware of minibuses stopping suddenly, and at night be on the lookout for people walking along the edge of the road and drunken drivers everywhere. Expect rough roads and narrow bridges, and don't leave valuables unattended in a parked car. Driving is on the left. On the positive side, gasoline is cheap at SI$3.17 a liter.

Tours
With tourism on the rocks, guided sightseeing tours to the WW II sites are scarce. Dennis

Anii (tel. 39757 or 27896) does three-hour Guadalcanal battlefield tours at SI$140 pp for two or more persons (or SI$240 for one person alone). Ask about other tours of this kind at the Visitors Bureau.

EAST OF HONIARA
The Coastal Plain
Catch a KG6 minibus east along the Kukum Highway (known as "Highway 50" to American troops) past King George VI School. The bus route ends a kilometer east of the school at the access road to the **Betikama Carving Shop** (tel. 30223, fax 30174), on the grounds of Betikama Adventist College, 1.5 km off the main road. There's a good display of woodcarvings made at SDA villages in the Marovo Lagoon area, beaten copper and pottery, a collection of WW II relics including several plane parts, a small war museum, and some caged parrots. The storyboards and carved tables sold here are excellent quality, if you can spare the weight. It's open Sunday to Friday 0800–1700 (admission free).

Return to the Kukum Highway and cross the Lungga River bridge, from which two tunnels are visible slightly to the right. The first was General Vandegrift's command post and later a communications center. The tunnel has many rooms on each side and goes under the hillock to the other side. An **underground wartime hospital** is farther to the right at a higher elevation and goes under the nearby hill with a house on top. Both tunnels are accessible with a flashlight, though prominent signs warn that it could be dangerous to enter.

Bloody Ridge, perhaps the most meaningful WW II site in the Solomons, was the turning point of the ground war in the Pacific. If you'd like to visit, follow the dirt road around the west end of the airstrip and turn right at the T-junction. A white triangular memorial crowns Bloody Ridge, also known as "Edson's Ridge" for the American field commander. This is a hot 40-minute walk each way (no shade), but the views from the ridge are rewarding. A **Japanese War Memorial** is a kilometer farther along in the same direction.

Henderson Field, the current international airport, was the center of fierce fighting during the first part of the Solomon Islands campaign. The initial Japanese counterattack came from the east on August 21, 1942, at Alligator Creek, but this thrust was turned back. On the nights of September 13 and 14, Edson's Raiders, which had arrived fresh from the capture of Tulagi, faced other Japanese troops who had landed east of Henderson and attacked the U.S. forces on Bloody Ridge, three km south of the airstrip. They were broken up, but five weeks later a third Japanese army struggled along the Maruyama Trail from White River, passing behind Mt. Austin. On the nights of October 23 and 24, they struck once more at Bloody Ridge but were again defeated, after suffering more than 2,000 casualties.

Eight km east of the airport is **Red Beach,** where the first U.S. Marine Division landed on August 7, 1942 to begin its costly six-month offensive to capture Guadalcanal. One cannon still points out to sea, a silent, rusted sentinel.

Beyond the sawmill near Red Beach, you'll pass some copra and cacao estates, before reaching the rundown palm-oil plantations at **CDC2** (named for the Commonwealth Development Corporation, which financed the project). The huge palm oil mill here was destroyed during the "troubles" of 2000. Rice was also once grown in this area. Continue 2.5 km straight down the road that passes the palm oil mill to **Tetere Beach.** Follow the beach a few hundred meters to the right till you see the monument to five Austrian explorers from the *Albatross* expedition, murdered in 1896 by natives who wanted to prevent them from climbing sacred Mt. Tatuba (Tatuve) near Gold Ridge. Come back and follow the road along the beach to the west and turn inland on a track to see a large number of abandoned WW II **amphibious alligators** (LVT) lined up in hoary rustiness. As many as 27 of these are visible, and more are hidden from view in the bush (admission SI$20 pp).

The main road east from Honiara ends at **Aola** (60 km), the capital of Guadalcanal before WW II. Charles Woodward, the British naturalist who became resident commissioner in

1896, lived on Mbara Island just off Aola in 1885 and 1886.

You can easily visit the Betikama Carving Shop and Bloody Ridge on your own, but you should ask the Visitors Bureau for advice before going to Red Beach or CDC2.

Accommodations

The **Airport Motel** (tel. 36255, fax 36411), beside Don Bosco Technical School about 500 meters east of the airport terminal, has 12 air-conditioned rooms with bath beginning at SI$159/189 single/double. The motel also has a beachfront section called the "Guadalcanal Beach Resort" a kilometer from the motel, which contains another 10 units. Cooking facilities are not provided in either section, although there's a restaurant, store, and bar. It's worth considering if you have to catch a very early flight.

WEST OF HONIARA

At **Bonegi Private Beach,** 14 km west of Poha, are the wrecks of two Japanese freighters sunk offshore in November 1942. One is partly above water, the other only three meters down, and it's easy to swim out from shore and snorkel over both. Bonegi is labeled Koilo Point on topographical maps. It's a nice picnic spot. No fishing is allowed. Admission to the beach is SI$20 per person. To visit an old U.S. tank called *Jezebel* on the other side of the hill from Bonegi costs extra.

West of Bonegi you pass coastal plantations where cattle graze below orange tinted coconut trees. The pavement ends at Ndoma, 23 km west of Honiara. Drive slowly on the gravel road west of here, because it's easy to start sliding.

About 24 km west of Honiara is the **Vilu War Museum** (daily 0800–1800; admission SI$20 pp, video cameras extra) at Vilu village, 650 meters off the main road. The open-air collection includes four large Japanese field guns from Camp Express near Visale, two Douglas dive bombers, a Corsair with W-shaped wings and body, a B-38 Lightning aircraft raised from the sea at Ranadi, four wings of F46 hellcats, a carrier-based Grumman Wildcat with one wing still capable of being folded back, the wing of a B17 bomber, part of a

Japanese Betty bomber, an antiaircraft gun, several smaller field guns, and a piece of a Japanese tank. A number of small war memorials have been set up here and the site is of interest to WW II buffs.

Cape Esperance Lighthouse, 36 km west of Honiara, is close to Visale village, with its large Catholic mission, is about two km west of the cape. Japanese submarine *I-123* is on the reef just offshore from Veuru, 1.5 km west of Visale. It's only a few hundred meters offshore in two meters of water, and a fee is charged to visit.

Selwyn College, at Maravovo, 47 km west of Honiara, opened in 1991. This large modern complex run by the Church of Melanesia accommodates 500 students in forms 7–12. Opposite the college is a long gray public beach, but better white sandy beaches are to the southwest. Beyond these are four or five small rivers all vehicles must ford, and Verahui village, 57 km west of Honiara.

The end of the drivable road for ordinary cars is just beyond Nuku Plantation, eight km short of Lambi Bay, where a larger river with no bridge and a quickly deteriorating road bring most trips to an end. The north coast highway terminates at **Lambi Bay,** 69 km west of Honiara.

SOUTHEAST GUADALCANAL

It used to be possible to hike right across the island from CDC1, east of Honiara, to Kuma on the south coast or "Weather Coast" via **Gold Ridge** in three days of hard slugging. Villages like Old Case and Tinomeat date from the 1936 gold rush, and until recently the locals could earn pocket money from gold won from the streams. In 1998, Gold Ridge Mining Ltd. opened an open-cut mine at a site 45 km from Honiara, which was expected to produce 100,000 ounces of gold a year for 10 years. The mine offered the landowners a tiny royalty, but with the help of corrupt government officials in Honiara, took away their right to practice subsistence mining. This caused much bad feeling among local residents, and the Gold Ridge mine was looted during the "troubles" and remains closed. In

2002 and early 2003, the Weather Coast was terrorized by a murderous gang led by Guadalcanal rebel Harold Keke, who was arrested after the Australian military intervention in July 2003. Peace has now returned to the area.

Marau Sound

Marau Sound at the east tip of Guadalcanal has an extensive system of barrier reefs, offshore islands, and secure anchorages for yachts. Giant clams are found in this area. Marau Sound was relatively unaffected by the recent ethnic fighting. Motorized canoes often leave at Honiara's Point Cruz on Friday afternoons, and you can easily arrange to come back to Honiara Monday morning.

Most visitors come to stay in one of the six tall thatched *vales* at the **Tavanipupu Island Resort** (no phone), set on the emerald lagoon flanked by fine white beaches. Six large traditional-style buildings serve as a lounge, dining room, and reception. Originally purchased by Norwegian trader Oscar Svensen in 1890 for five rifles, the present owner Dennis Bellote bought the place from the Humphrey family in 1986 and has created this exotic hideaway since then. The price for rooms is SI$500 pp including three good meals. Book at the Guadalcanal Travel Service (tel. 22586, kevin@gts.com.sb) in Honiara. Since Solomon Airlines stopped flying to Marau Sound in 2001, it's only accessible by boat.

The Moro Cult

In 1953, a cargo cult led by visionary Chief Moro was founded at **Makaruka,** a village three km up the Alualu River between Avu Avu and Marau Sound. In 1957, Moro called for a return to the *kabilato* and grass skirts after a visit by a spirit who instructed him to lead his people in a return to the old ways. He taught people how to live in harmony with each other and nature. Today the Moro movement, known as the Gaenalu Association, has 5,000 followers scattered around Guadalcanal. Of the four associated villages, today only **Komuvaolu** is totally traditional, and the custom house "bank" brimming with shell money and *tambu* objects is still well guarded there.

Malaita Province

This hot, humid, thickly forested island is the second-largest and most densely populated of the Solomons: Its 125,000 inhabitants comprise almost a third of the country's population. Malaita is one of the country's few islands where people reside in the jungle-clad interior. The bush people live in isolated hamlets of two or three houses, and as many as 10,000 still believe in ancestral spirits (though tenacious missionaries are working to change this).

Many Malaitans have tried to escape their island's limited economic opportunities by emigrating to other islands; there's a large community of them in Honiara. In blackbirding times, nearly 10,000 Malaitans labored in the cane fields of Queensland, Australia. Today, they work on plantations throughout the Solomons. Copra production is one of the few ways most Malaitans have of making cash money, although there have been attempts to introduce cattle and cacao. Only 12 percent of Malaita's population does paid work—the rest live from subsistence activities.

History

The Malaitans have a reputation of cantankerousness, and during the 19th century, shipwrecked sailors were regularly cooked and eaten. The tribes conducted headhunting raids against the Isabel islanders and each other, forcing the people to live in fortified villages. When blackbirders kidnapped villagers, the Malaitans took revenge by attacking visiting European ships. Punitive raids followed the murder of missionaries, leading to new retaliatory attacks, and the traditional conflict between the peoples of the coast and interior intensified with the introduction of firearms by returning workers.

In 1927, the British district officer and a police party were massacred during a campaign to collect head taxes and all outstanding rifles. The British responded by sending an Australian cruiser to shell coastal villages, turning native police from rival tribes loose on those responsible, poisoning Kwaio taro gardens, and arresting 200 Kwaio tribesmen (of whom 30 died in captivity, six of them hanged).

Even before WW II, Malaitan plantation workers were refusing to obey overseers who kept them in line with whips and dogs. When war came, many Malaitan men went to work for the Americans on Guadalcanal. The fair, generous treatment they received and the sight of black Americans dressed like whites and enjoying equal, though separate, rights had an impact. In the hope of trading American rule for British, the Marching Rule cargo cult emerged in 1944. Villages were reorganized under new chiefs and surrounded by stockades with watchtowers, and huts were prepared to store the cargo soon to arrive from the United States.

By 1949, the British decided things were getting out of hand and suppressed the movement by arresting 2,000 of its followers. Things calmed down in 1952 when local councils were established to represent the people, but many Malaitans still distrust outsiders, and large numbers in the interior resist all forms of Western influence. They in turn are often resented by other Solomon Islanders, who see them forming communities on other islands and playing a disproportionately active role in today's cash economy.

Malaita was deeply involved in the "troubles" of 1999–2003, as thousands of refugees returned from Guadalcanal. North Malaita has the most extensive road network in the Solomons, but you should seek local advice before leaving Auki, since the full authority of the central government has yet to be reestablished in some areas.

AUKI

Auki (population 2,000), at the northern end of the Langa Langa Lagoon, has been the administrative center since 1909. It's a laid-back little town with frequent ferry service from Honiara (106 km). The setting is picturesque, and there are several interesting places to visit in the vicinity. Auki is closer to the bush than Honiara, more colorful and relaxed, so it's a fast, easy escape from the dusty capital. Few visitors come here, and although the security situation in Auki is okay during the day, you should exercise caution around town after dark. If your ship arrives during the night, stay aboard until morning.

Lilisiana

For 18 generations, the saltwater people of the Langa Langa Lagoon have lived on tiny artificial-reef islands, which offered protection from raids by the bush people of the interior and were free of mosquitoes. A perimeter was made in the lagoon from blocks of coral, filled with more coral and covered with earth to form an island. The inhabitants remained dependent on their mainland gardens and fresh water, but a unique culture evolved.

One such artificial island is Auki Island, within view of Auki wharf. The two families on this island still maintain a few traditional sites, but most inhabitants moved away after a hurricane devastated their homes. It's now possible to walk (20 minutes) to Lilisiana, the new village on the mainland—to the right as you look out to sea from Auki. Here you can observe shell money being manufactured in authentic surroundings. If you show an interest, people will bring out shell money necklaces for sale. There are isolated stretches of sandy beach along the track to the right just before you reach Lilisiana.

Other Sights of Auki

Take the road inland just before the bridge, less than a km south of Auki wharf, to cool off in the clear waters of the **Kwaibala River** near the pump house. You could rent a dugout canoe at **Ambu** village near here.

Ask about the new **Mt. Ila Nature Trail,** 11 km south of Auki. You'll see bat caves and pagan artifacts, and get a view of the Langa Langa Lagoon.

Accommodations

The spotless **South Seas Evangelical Church Transit House** (tel. 40173), behind Auki Bookshop, has three rooms (eight beds) at SI$50 pp.

There are cooking facilities and a sitting room. It's a clean, quiet place to stay (no smoking allowed).

The **Auki Motel** (tel. 40014, fax 40220), above Solomon Airlines on the road to Malu'u, is SI$60 per bed in five three-bed rooms. Their restaurant (open all day on weekdays, lunch only on Saturday) is reasonable and a good place for a coffee.

The **Golden Dragon Motel** (tel. 40113), above the ANZ Bank, has seven rooms at SI$100 single or double without bath, SI$160 with bath. Go to Auki Store across the street to check in. The Chinese owner Mr. Sing is an interesting character.

Most visitors stay at **Auki Lodge** (Cecil Jack Inifiri, tel. 40131, fax 40044), which has a veranda overlooking the landscaped grounds. The eight rooms start are S$130/160 single/double with fan or S$180/250 deluxe. There's a restaurant (expensive), a bar (reasonable) where you can watch CNN, and a nice veranda.

Food

Auki market functions daily except Sunday, but is best early Wednesday and Saturday mornings. The butcher shop by the market is cheap.

Louisa's Food Palace, near the post office, serves breakfast (0730–1000), lunch (1030–1500), and dinner (1900–2130) daily, but on Sunday it's only dinner. The food is surprisingly good for such an unpretentious place.

Services

The ANZ and National banks have branches in Auki that will change foreign currency and traveler's checks. Kilu'ufi Hospital (tel. 40272) is three km north of Auki.

Transportation

Gwaunaruu airstrip (AKS) is 11 km north of Auki; the airline minibus is SI$20 pp. Solomon Airlines (tel. 40163) has daily flights from Honiara (111 km, SI$176).

Auki is also well serviced by passenger ships to Honiara (six hours, SI$70). The **Malaita Shipping Co.** (tel. 40076) opposite the wharf sells tickets to Honiara on the MV *Ramos,* which leaves Auki Wednesday and Saturday at 0900.

LANGA LANGA LAGOON

The artificial islands in the Langa Langa Lagoon were home to some of the last of the shark callers. Until recently people worshipped their ancestors, whose spirits are embodied in sharks that the high priest could summon. Should a fisherman be capsized in the deep sea, he can call a shark, using a special language the shark understands. After the shark has carried him ashore, the fisherman must offer a sacrificial pig, otherwise he will be eaten on his next fishing trip.

Laulasi

On this small island, 13 km south of Auki, are large spirit houses with high pitched roofs, the names of famous priests inscribed on the gables. When a priest died, his body was taken to neighboring Alite to rot. Later the skull was retrieved and placed in the House of Skulls. A large snake would appear on Alite if offered the head of a goat. At these times believers would ask favors of the animal and enlist its help in punishing enemies.

Offerings are still presented at shark-calling ceremonies in the gap between the two islands. The pigs used for these offerings are held by the shore in pens big enough for a man—the offering in times past, before pigs were substituted.

Women and children are forbidden to enter the custom houses, and no one dressed in red or black will be permitted to land on the island. Tourists are shown how to make shell money using manual stone drills; after they're gone, the metal-headed drill bits come back out. The village on Alite is similar.

A current source of income for the Langa Langa islanders is seaweed farming. Some of the islanders now plant and grow coral as a way of increasing the number of fish in the lagoon.

Getting There

Laulasi Tour Guide (tel. 40006 or 40271, fax 40220), Joachim Baeanisia at Auki Market, and others organize outboard tours to Laulasi or Alite islands (five hours). Included are custom dancing, a demonstration of shell moneymaking, a tour of the custom places, and lunch. Book 24 hours in advance, and find out what kind of custom fees you'll have to pay upon arrival.

Sometimes you can hire a motorized canoe to Laulasi from near Auki Market, then pay the islanders a variable custom fee for the right to look around (no dances or lunch).

NORTH MALAITA

The little government station of **Malu'u** at the island's northern tip, halfway between Auki and Fouia, is the center of heavily populated North Malaita. On the beach at Malu'u is a monument to the first missionary to land on Malaita (in 1894). Out across the lagoon, good surf breaks at the west end of the reef, and surfers used to come between November and March. During the "troubles" of 1999–2003, North Malaita was risky to visit. Although the situation is much better now, it's still wise to exercise caution and make inquiries before heading far off the beaten track. In the past, Malu'u Lodge has provided adequate accommodations at SI$50 pp.

Lau Lagoon

More than 60 artificial islands are found in the 36-km-long Lau Lagoon on the northeast side of Malaita. These are inhabited by the so-called island builders, who bring coral blocks, sand, and earth on log rafts to convert lagoon shallows into solid land. With the constant cool breezes, the air is incredibly fresh out on these man-made islands. On the mainland they grow taro, yams, potatoes, papaya, leafy vegetables, bananas, and sugarcane. The women travel back and forth from their island homes to the gardens, and the men fish most of the time. The large canoes for dolphin-hunting are made by sewing together long planks of wood and caulking the seams with a putty made from the nut of the *tita* tree (*Parinari glaberrima*).

Though Christianity now predominates, some people on islands such as Foueda, Funaafou, and Adagege still practice the same custom religion as the people of Laulasi/Alite. Here you'll find a *beu* (men's house) where chiefs are buried in their canoes, plus places of worship, with a sacrificial altar, cemetery, House of Skulls, etc. Entry to the *beu* is prohibited, but you can often see in from outside. There is no *beu* at Sulufou, which is now thoroughly Christianized. After childbirth, women are sent to a *bisi* (women's house) for 30 days. Shark calling is also practiced here on special occasions, announced by the pagan priests.

Sulufou

The road from Auki ends at **Fouia** wharf (120 km), on the mainland opposite the artificial islands of Sulufou and Adagege. For a few dollars, someone will paddle you the 500 meters over to Sulufou, largest and oldest of the artificial islands. The picturesque village is partly built on stilts over the lagoon. In front of the big Anglican church is a stone where fugitives from northern Malaita sat to obtain sanctuary and protection.

SOUTHEAST MALAITA
East Malaita

The road from Auki to Atori via Dala has a bridge over the Auluta Gorge midway at Nunulafa. **Kwai,** three km across the water from Atori, is a beautiful island. Village houses are densely packed here and on neighboring Ngongosila Island.

A road is underway from Atori to Atoifi, presently as far as Nazareth. **Atoifi** on Uru Harbor is a center for those Kwaio tribespeople who have accepted Christianity, and a large Seventh-Day Adventist hospital and School of Nursing are there. There's an airstrip with flights from Honiara. The pagan population lives in small, scattered hamlets on the upland plateaus. Kwaibaambaala, in the foothills between Atoifi and Sinalanggu, is one traditional village sometimes visited. **Kwaio Country** above Sinalanggu is home to the "Hidden People." Even today, the Kwaios in the hills follow the traditions and taboos of their ancestors, and outsiders aren't always welcome. In 1965, a missionary from New Zealand was killed here, and in 2003 an Australian missionary was beheaded by a local at Atoifi in a random pay-back killing over an unrelated issue. The Solomon Island government collects taxes from these people but provides no services, and even the Seventh-Day Adventist Church links desperately needed medical aid to conversions.

South Malaita

South Malaita was not affected by the Solomons crisis of 2000 and has always been safe to visit. No road connects South Malaita to Auki, so either fly to Parasi (SI$197 one-way from Auki) or take a truck south to Hauhui, then a motorized canoe on south. The Wairaha River, south of Hauhui, is Solomon Island's largest.

Apio is at the southwest entrance to Maramasike Passage. Just 3.7 meters deep near the center, this passage is only open to vessels of light draft. A bush road now runs from Apio, opposite Maka on Malaita, to Olusu'u, near the southeast end of Maramasike, or Small Malaita. The **Ma'asupa Beach Hut** on Takataka Bay, a two-hour canoe ride from Parasi airfield through Maramasike Passage, has two rooms. Few tourists come here.

THE POLYNESIAN OUTLIERS
Sikaiana

This tiny atoll, 177 km northeast of Malaita, is inhabited by the descendants of Tongans, as proved by a variety of filarial mosquito found on Sikaiana and Tonga but nowhere else in the world. Four reef islets mark the triangular Te Moana Lagoon. There's no anchorage, and access is by small boat through the surf. Less than 500 people live here.

Ontong Java

This 70-by-26-km boot-shaped atoll encloses 1,400 square km of lagoon, making it the second-largest atoll in the world (after 2,174-square-km Kwajalein in the Marshall Islands). Ontong Java's 122 islands total only 12 square km of dry land. This is the northernmost point in the Solomon Islands, and only 70 km separate Ontong Java from Nukumanu atoll in Papua New Guinea. The inhabitants are related and often travel in outboards between the two, trading in bêche-de-mer.

Ke Avaiko Passage, just south of Luangiua Island, leads directly to the lagoon anchorage off the village. The supply ship calls at Luangiua,

Labaha, and Pelau, the only permanently inhabited islands, but the people reside part-time on many others, fishing and making copra. All the islets are planted with coconuts, and production is large; swamp taro is cultivated in deep pits in the interior of several islands. Bêche-de-mer (sea cucumbers) and trochus shells are shipped to Honiara.

Ontong Java was named by Tasman on March 22, 1643. Ontong was probably derived from the Malay *untung* (luck, fortune, destiny, fate); in other words, "Java Luck." Tasman's ships had been subjected to squalls for months on end, and he was most likely congratulating himself on the improved conditions. In 1791, Captain Hunter renamed it Lord Howe Island, but the previous name stuck. The local Polynesians believe they originated on Niue; Luangiua means literally "Niue number two" (Luaniue). In 1907, Ontong Java had 5,000 inhabitants, but epidemics reduced it to only 700 by 1927. Now it's back up to about 1,400 (1,000 in Luangiua and 400 in Pelau).

This atoll is one of the few places in the Solomons where houses are built directly on the ground (dirt floor—no stilts). The cemeteries here are striking for their large carved tombstones. Casual visitors are welcome to look around the villages, but the chiefs want to be sure you leave on the same ship. You might be able to spend a night or two in Luangiua, however, while the ship visits the other settlements to pick up copra. Bring your own food, as little is available from the two stores.

Rennell and Bellona Province

Two hundred km south of Guadalcanal are two Polynesian islands, Rennell and Bellona, about 25 km apart. This is the westernmost land colonized by Polynesians. The trademark symbol of the people of the "two canoes" (Rennell and Bellona) is a tuna fish tattoo on the upper arm. Due to the murder of three Melanesian Seventh-Day Adventist missionaries in 1910, Rennell was closed to Europeans until 1934. Conversion to SDA Christianity took place in 1938, when a picture of Christ was seen to speak. A dozen Rennellese volunteered to be put to death and brought back to life, but the group fled in haste after the first two refused to rise from the dead! Even so, the people gave up their traditional ways overnight and adopted Western dress. In 1993, Rennell and Bellona (or "Renbel") separated from Central Province to form a province of their own.

There's no malaria on Rennell or Bellona, but the mosquitoes are of a type that bite all night (not just at dusk), so bring plenty of repellent. These islands would be major destinations if access weren't so difficult. Although regular flights exist from Honiara, they're usually booked solid two weeks in advance, with long waiting lists. Very few tourists ever make it here, so if you get the chance, don't hesitate a minute.

RENNELL

Rennell (Mu Nggava), an 86-by-15-km raised atoll surrounded by sheer 100-meter cliffs, is much larger than Bellona. In fact, at 660 square km it's one of the largest elevated atolls on earth. **Lake Tenggano** (155 square km), on the southeast side of Rennell, is the largest lake in the South Pacific. It's the former lagoon of this uplifted island, and about 200 small islands are dotted around its edge. The saline water in the lake is at sea level but it's surrounded by high cliffs. The islands at the east end of the lake are teaming with seabirds. In 1998, East Rennell was added to UNESCO's World Heritage List, only the third South Pacific site to achieve this status (Henderson Island and Easter Island are also honored).

Eighty percent of Rennell is forested and the island has more endemic bird species than any other in Oceania, excluding much larger places like New Caledonia. Of the 50 species of birds on Rennell, 21 are endemic. The docile Rennell Island krait *(Laticausa crockeri)*—or Tugihono as the Rennellese call it—a unique sea snake, lives only in Lake Tenggano.

Other than a few tiny stores, no business of any

kind exists on Rennell, and all 2,500 villagers live from their gardens. The local stores have little more than canned fish, corned beef, and stick tobacco, so bring food. A potent homebrew is made from green coconut water and sugar. Among the many handicrafts made on Rennell are walking sticks, hardwood crocodile carvings, miniature weapons, woven bags, and mats. Bauxite deposits exist here, and in 1977 the Japanese mining company Mitsui did exploratory work, pulling out when bauxite prices fell. Mining companies continue to pressure the chiefs to allow bauxite strip mining, a potential social and ecological catastrophe.

Accommodations

The Visitors Bureau in Honiara should have information on places to stay and can make bookings by radio telephone. This is important because if they don't know you're coming, they may not have any food available to feed you!

Neitasi Lodge at Tebaitahe, where the road from the airport meets the lake, has three rooms at SI$45 pp.

Kiakoe Lodge, owned by Lenz Tango, is on the northwest side of the lake five minutes by canoe from Tebaitahe. To stay at this fine purpose built lodge on a hillock overlooking the lake costs SI$50 pp, plus SI$70 for three meals. Canoe rentals are around SI$75 an hour.

The nicest place to stay is Jeffrey Kaitu'u's **Tenggano Lodge,** a two-story guesthouse on a promontory on the southwest side of the lake. The six rooms with shared bath are SI$50 pp. It's a 20-minute boat ride from the end of the road. From Tenggano village, one of four on the lake, it's a four-km stroll to a steep stairway known as "ten story" which descends the sharp limestone cliffs to Tuhungganggo on the coast east of Lavanggu. Before the road was built, this was the only access to the lake.

Paul Tauniu operates the **Tahamatangi Guesthouse,** an airy European-style building on the shores of Lake Tenggano beyond Tenggano Lodge. Up to five persons are accommodated in the one main building at SI$50 pp. Paul organizes bushwalking and lake tours to see the unique wildlife of the area. Locally produced meals of crab, fish, chicken, pineapple, papaya, banana, and taro are served (additional charge and not cheap).

By the airstrip at Tingoa is the large **Moreno Guest House,** run by the Solomon Airlines agent Solo, with rooms at SI$50 pp.

Getting There

Solomon Airlines flies into Tingoa airstrip (RNL), at Rennell's west end, twice a week from Honiara (SI$297) and Bellona (SI$143). A crushed coral road leads from Tingoa through

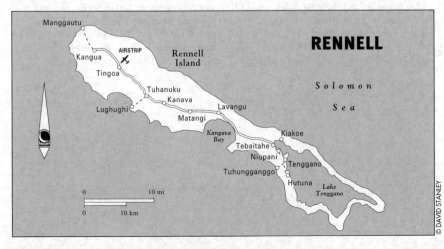

© DAVID STANLEY

lush rainforest to the small port, Lavangu, where the occasional ship from Honiara calls. To walk from Tingoa to Lavangu will take six hours if you go straight, or eight with stops (under a full moon, this walk is magic). The beach at Lavangu is great, and there's a splendid view of it from the village above. For yachts, there's good anchorage on the south shore of cliff-lined Kangava Bay with excellent snorkeling.

From Lavangu, a new European Union-financed road continues to Tebaitahe village right on Lake Tenggano. To walk from the airport right to the lake would take 12 hours. The government tractor/trailer takes six hours to go from the airstrip to the lake at SI$50 pp. You can hire a "Hilux" (a twin-cab 4WD Toyota pickup) for the trip at SI$500 each way, and it will take only two or three hours to cover the distance (only half a dozen vehicles are on the island). If they're going anyway, you should be able to negotiate a much lower price.

BELLONA

Like Rennell, Bellona (Mu Ngiki) is a cliff-girdled uplifted atoll. Rich phosphate deposits exist here, but the islanders rightly fear that strip mining would devastate their homeland. Since it's smaller (12 by three km) than Rennell, Bellona is much easier to visit. The finest beaches are at the west end of the island and along the north coast. The Polynesians first migrated to this island 26 generations ago and upon arrival wiped out the Hiti, a race of Melanesian cave dwellers who previously inhabited the island. The Hiti caves still dot the cliffs and are fascinating to explore, though they're very cramped.

The handsome, intelligent people are a very sociable, fun-loving bunch descended from the same lineage as the Rennellese. Most live in the fertile interior. If you make an effort to communicate, you'll be drawn into island life. But if you keep to yourself, you'll be regarded with suspicion. Solomon Airlines has heavily-booked flights to Bellona from Honiara (SI$277) and Rennell (SI$143) twice a week.

Accommodations

John and Nita Ta'ea run the enchanting **'Aotaha Cave Lodge** beyond Matangi village, about five km east of the airstrip by road. The accommodations are in a natural set of caves below high cliffs at the eastern end of the island. Crushed white coral covers the floor, the air is cool, and mosquito nets are provided. The three double and three single beds are SI$70 pp, otherwise two thatched bungalows above the cave are the same price. It's possible to cook your own food in the cave kitchen, and there's a small trade store on the site. Otherwise, fresh local meals can be ordered (often lobster). You can see across to Rennell from the cave sitting room, and the rock pools below are good for swimming. The Visitors Bureau in Honiara may be able to help you contact 'Aotaha by radio telephone. For the trip from the airstrip, the area council tractor and trailer can be hired.

Suani Resthouse, in Bellona's lush interior several km west of the airstrip, offers shared accommodations in the main seven-bed building at SI$60 pp. Meals are about SI$15 each.

Central Province

Central Province comprises an odd assortment of islands, including the Florida Islands, Savo, and the Russell Islands, which are linked to Honiara but not to each other or to the provincial headquarters on Tulagi. With a bit of planning, one can easily spend a couple of days at Tulagi, and Savo is worth the effort for its volcanic wonders. The Florida Islands are there for adventurers in search of the "real" Solomon Islands, while the Russells are one big coconut plantation.

Tulagi

Tulagi (population 500), a small island about five km in circumference in the Florida Group, was the island capital of the Solomons 1896-1942. The Australian trading company Burns Philp had its head station on Makambo Island, nearby. The Japanese entered unopposed on May 3, 1942, after a hasty British evacuation, and Tulagi was badly damaged during the American invasion three months later. The Americans upgraded an existing British seaplane base just east of Tulagi on Tanambogho Island, which is joined to Ghavutu Island by a small causeway. A good concrete wharf built by Lever Brothers in the 1930s remains on Ghavutu. The American PT-boat squadrons were also based at Tulagi. Another remnant of the old days on Tulagi is the marine base, where shipbuilding and repairs are still carried out.

The deep strait between Tulagi and Nggela Sule forms a good harbor, well sheltered from the southeast trade winds. In 1973, the Japanese Taiyo Corporation took advantage of this by establishing a fish-freezing and canning plant here, but in 1990 this facility was shifted to Noro in Western Province. There's a striking hand-hewn passage cut by prewar prisoners between the wharf and the provincial resthouse. The British resident commissioners lived at Nambawan Haos, on the hill above the cut. Follow a footpath (three hours) clockwise around the island for great views.

Tulagi Dive (Neil Yates, tel. 32052, fax 32131, www.tulagidive.com.sb), based at Vanita Lodge, organizes scuba diving on the destroyer USS *Aaron Ward* only eight km from Tulagi and the oil tanker USS *Kanawha* under two km from the wharf. Numerous reefs are also accessible.

Vanita Lodge (tel. 32186 or 32052), near the wharf, has eight fan-cooled rooms at SI$100/120 single/double. There are no cooking facilities for guests; instead meals are served in their restaurant/bar. **Tulagi Hill View Lodge** is also quite adequate. The rather basic **Central Province Resthouse** (tel. 32074 or 32100) has six double rooms with shared cooking facilities at SI$50 pp. Finally, **Fr. Derick's Guesthouse** may suit low-budget backpackers. Tulagi has a market and two Chinese stores.

The Florida Islands

There are two large islands here, Nggela Sule and Nggela Pile, separated by narrow Utaha Passage. Tulagi is off the south coast of Nggela Sule. In May 2000, the cruise ship *World Discover* struck an uncharted reef in Sandfly Passage off the northwest side of Nggela Sule and had to be beached by her captain to avoid sinking. In July, just as the vessel was being refloated, villagers for nearby islands appeared claiming ownership of the wreck and drove off the salvage team at gunpoint. Then they looted the ship. The wreck currently lies on its side just offshore in Roderick Bay.

The 12-room **Maravagi Island Resort** (tel. 29065) sits on Mangalonga Island beyond Sandfly Passage at the northwest end of the Florida Islands group. Opened in 1996, it's run by Mathias Sake and family of Olevugha village on nearby Mbokonimbeti Island. The simply furnished island-style accommodations are SI$300 pp, seafood meals included. The water here is crystal clear and scuba diving is available. Visits to skull caves and other custom areas are arranged. Two-hour motor canoe transfers from Honiara are SI$250 pp round-trip (minimum of two).

Savo

Savo is a cone-shaped island on Iron Bottom Sound, named for the number of warships sunk in the vicinity during WW II. Savo's volcano last erupted in 1840, but it's still considered potentially dangerous. Near the center of the island are two craters, one inside the other. A trip up to the steaming, 485-meter-high crater is worth trying—if you can find a guide and you're fit. Two boiling hot springs are on the crater's edge, and other springs on the volcano's sides are used for cooking. The chief of Kaonggele collects a custom fee to use the village path to the crater.

Savo is also famous for its megapode bird *(Megapodius freycinet)* or *skrab dak*. This small dark bush turkey lays billiard-ball-sized eggs underground, then leaves them to hatch by heat from either the sun or the island's warm volcanic sands. After two months the fledglings dig themselves out and can run at birth. Unfortunately, the number of megapodes is declining fast due to unrestrained harvesting of the eggs. See them in the early morning near Panueli.

A tractor track runs right around 31-square-km Savo's shark-infested shores, passing 14 villages. The inhabitants all speak a Papuan language, Savosavo, one of the few non-Austronesian languages of the Solomons. Traditionally, Savo people fish by suspending a hook from a kite behind the canoe. There's a fissure just a short distance inland from Siata village where the locals cook their food. All drinking and washing water on Savo comes from wells, and the water in them is also often warm: Boil it before drinking. A rural water supply project is gradually improving this situation, but there's still no electricity.

There are no hotels but it's also possible to stay with local villagers, such as John Tome at Kakalaka village.

The Russell Islands

The Russell Islands consist of two adjacent larger islands, Mbanika and Pavuvu, plus many smaller islets. In 1905, the Australian company Levers Pacific Plantations Ltd. purchased vast tracts here and began creating the huge coconut plantations that cover the islands today. The Solomon's first coconut-oil mill opened here in 1989. In 1995, the government's Commodities Export Marketing Authority took over from Levers and now runs the operation under the name Russell Islands Plantations Limited (in 2001 this company declared itself bankrupt).

The United States captured the Russells unopposed in February 1943 and built a pair of airstrips from which to launch attacks on New Georgia. The American Quonset huts facing Yandina wharf are now used for copra storage. Local children can show you a WW II military dump near Renard Airfield, featuring what's left of a U.S. fighter plane.

In 1995, the corrupt Mamaloni government deployed its paramilitary police to protect loggers sent by the Malaysian company Maving Brothers to clearcut the pristine rainforests of Pavuvu, over the heated objections of local residents. Anti-logging activist Martin Apa was brutally murdered by persons unknown in October 1995, yet the police refused to investigate and the case was never solved.

Many outlying estates are inhabited by Polynesians from Tikopia and Bellona who came to work on the plantations. Several small villages are still inhabited by indigenous Russell Islanders, descendants of a Papuan-speaking people decimated by headhunters from the Roviana Lagoon and Savo long ago. Some 2,000 head of cattle range across the islands, and wild water buffalo dwell in the swamps of Mbanika, descendants of escaped domestic stock. Wild donkeys are also seen in and around Yandina at night.

The upscale **Yandina Plantation Resort** (tel. 21779, fax 21785, www.yandinaresort.com.sb), which opened in October 2000, is conveniently located only 800 meters from the main wharf in Yandina and about two km from the airport. The 12 air-conditioned rooms with bath, fridge, and TV in a long block facing the beach go for SI$630/650 single/double. The meal package is SI$260 pp a day. Let's Go Diving organizes scuba diving on WW II wrecks and colorful reefs from the resort (SI$260/435 for one/two tanks without gear). All rates are based on Australian dollars, so you'll pay that much more if the Solomons dollar continues to decline. The managers have connections with the dive shop at Tulagi, so you can easily combine a stay here with diving in the Florida Islands. Other activities include snorkeling trips, plantation tours, fishing, hiking, and horseback riding.

Groceries are sold at two stores, a block to the right of the post office and main wharf as you arrive by boat. The butcher shop near the post office sells cheap beef, but there's a four-kilogram-per-day limit on purchases. Yachties often share their quota among others and stock up here. Ask the butcher when they'll be dumping the offal at Shark Point, as sharks appear from nowhere whenever this happens and go into a feeding frenzy, which is fun to watch from the cliff. Bring adequate mosquito repellent to the Russells.

Getting there is easy, as most ships between Honiara and Gizo call at Yandina on the east side of Mbanika. The ship ties up at a wharf right in town, a little more than a kilometer from the airport terminal. Solomon Airlines flies to Renard Airfield (XYA) from Honiara (95 km, SI$156 one-way) twice a week. The Solomon Airlines office (tel. 29779) is in the administration building in Yandina.

Western Province

Western Province with the New Georgia Group at its core is easily the most attractive and varied area in the country. High vegetation-shrouded volcanoes buttress the enticing lagoons of Marovo and Roviana, respectively off the eastern and southern coasts of New Georgia. These vast stretches of dazzling water are dotted with hundreds of little green islets, either covered in dense jungle or planted with coconuts. To the north, the remote Shortland and Treasury groups form Western's outback. Sadly, commercial logging is gradually decimating the great rainforests of New Georgia, Rendova, and Kolombangara.

More than a dozen different languages are spoken, but people in this province have long had contact with missionaries, and you'll find very eloquent, well-informed individuals in the most unlikely places. Here the women own the land, which is passed down through the oldest daughter. Headhunting once forced the inhabitants to build their homes on inaccessible interior ridges (where many custom places are now found), but with the demise of interisland raiding the people soon moved down to cooler coastal sites. In the 1950s and 1960s, thousands of Micronesian Gilbertese were resettled at Gizo, Shortland, and Vaghena, adding to the diversity.

Travel among the many islands of the New Georgia Group is almost totally by sea, which makes getting around easy, yet there are also feeder roads from the main centers of Munda, Noro, Ringi Cove, and Gizo, which help the hiker and hitcher. There are many villages, and the people are helpful and hospitable. In recent years, scuba diving on the many wrecks and reefs

has become a big attraction here, and good facilities are available at Munda and Gizo. Sportfishing is being developed. The scheduled weekly passenger ship from Honiara to Gizo via Patutiva, Viru Harbor, Mburuku, Munda, and Ringi Cove offers an excellent introduction to the New Georgia Islands. New Georgia was relatively unaffected by the 1999–2003 political upheaval on Guadalcanal, and is as safe to visit as any other island group in the South Pacific.

The Marovo Lagoon

On the ship from Honiara, you travel first through the 700-square-km Marovo Lagoon, the largest lagoon in the world with a double barrier reef system. James A. Michener called it "one of the seven natural wonders of the world." Two strings of long narrow islands shelter this semicircular lagoon as it swings around Vangunu Island from Gatokae to New Georgia. West of Njae Passage it's known as the Nono Lagoon. The greater part of Marovo is less than 25 meters deep, whereas the Nono Lagoon is as deep as 50 to 60 meters.

Marovo is 35 km long and between eight and 50 km wide, and its 200 tiny islands are a mix of sandy cays, mangrove islets, raised reefs, and small volcanic islands. The nicest beaches are on the oceanside coral islands; mangrove swamps are more common along the volcanic shorelines within. The reef drop-offs are characterized by gorgonian fan forests, black coral gardens, giant clams, sea turtles, manta rays, eels, barracuda, gray whaler sharks, and cruising shoals of pelagic fish. Almost 11,000 people live in the over 50 villages on the lagoon. Despite the fact that the

SOLOMON ISLANDS

Tatama Island

Avavasa
Island

Uepi
Island

Charapoana Island

Inavo
Island   CHARAPOANA ISLAND RESORT

One   UEPI
             ISLAND
             RESORT

Lumalihe
Island

Lokiana Is.   Karikana
                     Island   Sambulo
New Georgia   Island

  Island   Ngaringari   Lagoon
                  I.

Bunitusu   Bukibuki

                  Sasaghana

Chuchulu   Marovo
                  Island   Telina

VANUA RAPITA LODGE   LAGOON   KAJORO
       Michi   LODGE   SUNSET
                                     LODGE
Njae
Passage
Nazareth   Patutiva

Nono   Kele Bay
Monro   Mbareho   Lagoon
Bay   Seghe
         HORENA
         HOLIDAY
         LODGE

Reynolds
  Bay   Vangunu   Kaiere Bay
                                          Sumbolo Ridge
Akara Island   Island

                      Mbale   Hotoanivena
                                     Island
Hele Bar
                      Vura   Ulukoru I.
Riana I.
                      Mbotuano I.

MATIKURI
LODGE
Matikuri I.

Hasana I.
                      ▲
                      (1,123 m)

Hele

Ngirasa I.   Islands

Mariu I.

0   5 mi

0   5 km

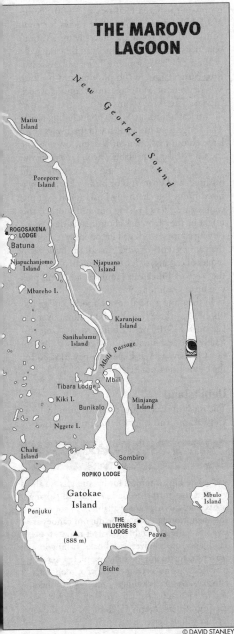

THE MAROVO LAGOON

New Georgia Sound

Matiu Island

Porepore Island

ROGOSAKENA LODGE
Batuna

Njapuchanjomo Island

Njapuana Island

Mbareho I.

Karunjou Island

Sanihulumu Island

Mbili Passage

MOON

Tibara Lodge

Mbili

Kiki I.

Bunikalo

Minjanga Island

Nggete I.

Chalu Island

Sombiro

ROPIKO LODGE

Gatokae Island

Mbulo Island

Penjuku

THE WILDERNESS LODGE

▲ (888 m)

Peava

Biche

© DAVID STANLEY

Marovo Lagoon has been considered for UN-ESCO World Heritage Site status, in 1999 government officials in Honiara announced a plan to create an environmentally destructive 10,000-hectare oil palm plantation on Vangunu, plus increased logging, mining, and commercial fishing in the area.

A cruise through the lagoon makes for great scenic viewing, though some of the ships from Honiara pass at night. The southern gateway is through Mbili Passage at the north end of Gatokae Island. For years Marovo has been a favorite of scuba divers, and recently kayak tours have been developed from Uepi Island. You can also launch your own folding kayak from the ferry landing at Patutiva and hop your way around the lagoon between the growing number of eco-lodges.

You won't see any dancing anywhere around the Marovo Lagoon, as the Seventh-Day Adventist Church has banned it (rumor indicates that dancing leads to pregnancy). The SDA devotees frown on all "heathen" customs, but will carve and market many a *nguzunguzu* for profit. The SDA Sabbath runs from sundown on Friday to sundown on Saturday—a bad time to arrive.

Gatokae Island

One of the best choices in this area is **The Wilderness Lodge** (Corey Howell, no phone, www.thewildernesslodge.org) near Paeva village of the east side of Gatokae. The four double rooms are SI$330 pp including meals, airport transfers, tax, and local guides (the price is based on U.S. dollars and does vary). There's solar electricity. The lodge wharf points at a main building attractively constructed in the traditional island style. Activities include scuba diving, snorkeling, surfing, fishing, mountain biking, and lagoon tours (extra charge). The bush walk from Bunikalo to Penjuku is recommended. Trips can also be made to see the spectacular underwater volcano island Kavachi. Their fast new boat makes getting around much easier.

Letina Lodge, at the custom village of Biche on southern Gatokae, has three rooms. A nearby stream is full of eels and a waterfall is nearby. The **Mariu Resort** is at Sombiro village, a two-minute walk from Gatokae airstrip on the northeast side of the island. The bungalows are equipped with solar electricity, fans, and mosquito nets. Mariu is accessible on the weekly Western Provinces boat MV *Tomoko*.

Ropiko Lodge, a 20-minute walk north of Gatokae airstrip, has three leaf houses at SI$100 pp including meals. The dining area has a deck overlooking the white sandy beach. The snorkeling is good.

Serere Lodge (tel. 39708, serere@solomon .com.sb), on the northeast side of Gatokae Island toward Mbili Passage, has two leaf houses with four rooms at SI$110 pp including all meals. Good snorkeling is available on the fringing reef just offshore. It's run by a guy named Ferol who can arrange bush hikes and fishing trips.

Chief Luten of **Tibara Lodge** on Mbili Passage has two beach houses at SI$100 pp including meals. A wrecked B24 bomber from WW II is in the bush nearby.

Northeast Vangunu

There's a large Seventh-Day Adventist mission at **Batuna** on Vangunu Island, with a post office, hospital, sawmill, agricultural school, shop, and Thursday market. High quality handicrafts can be purchased at Batuna Vocational School. Solomon Airlines flies directly here from Honiara (SI$316) and Munda (SI$153) once a week.

Rogosakena Lodge, a five-minute boat ride from Batuna, has a leaf house containing two rooms with shared facilities at SI$50/85 single/double, plus SI$60 pp for meals (or cook your own). Ask to see the butterfly tree. Various boat trips and other activities can be arranged.

West of Cheke opposite Telina village is **Kajoro Sunset Lodge** (no phone), run by John Wayne, one of Marovo's most famous woodcarvers. The three rooms with shared facilities in two leaf houses are SI$90 pp including meals. The Lodge is set in a garden with pathways and a large communal open-air leaf hut overlooking the sea. Meals are available or you can cook your own food. Good snorkeling is accessible right offshore, and boat trips or bush hikes are organized. John is a charming host, and if you just want somewhere to hang out and snorkel, this might be the place. Ask about his six-day woodcarving course, which will introduce you about to the various types of woods used, the basic techniques of carving, styles, etc. If you book through the Visitors Bureau in Honiara, John will pick you up at Gasini, Batuna, or Seghe.

In the same general area, **Lagoon Lodge** (no phone) has three thatched bungalows over the lagoon at SI$100 pp including meals. Unfortunately, the restaurant is fully enclosed, so you don't get any views. Expect to pay SI$200 for the canoe ride from Seghe.

Uepi Island

The most upscale resort on the lagoon by far is Uepi Island (no phone), 12 km northeast of

CRAFTS OF THE WESTERN SOLOMONS

The Westerners are skilled carvers, shaping *nguzunguzus*, masks, turtles, dolphins, sharks, and model canoes from kerosene wood or black ebony inlaid with mother of pearl. The *kapkap* or *dala* is a forehead ornament made from a circular clamshell disk but embossed with turtle shell, which makes it a prohibited import into many countries. Unfortunately, some carvers have begun working in a grotesque nontraditional style (the so-called "Spirit of the Solomons" series).

Village carvers around the Marovo Lagoon are famous for their workmanship. Cruising yachts are big customers for handicrafts, so the villagers use mirrors to flash a signal to passing boats that carvings are available. No sooner is the anchor dropped than the dugout canoes arrive. It's quite acceptable to barter radios, tools, sandpaper, bush knives, fish hocks, fishing line, batteries, medicine, bed sheets, plates, sewing machines, paint, perfume, tobacco, foodstuffs, raincoats, women's clothing, jeans, T-shirts, shoes, and toys for crafts. Actually, you can buy Marovo carvings just as cheaply in Honiara, and the selection will be better.

Patutiva, on a white coral beach midway down the chain of islands forming Marovo's western barrier. The four beachfront bungalows, two garden bungalows, and two semi-detached lagoon-view units go for SI$725/1,050 single/double. There are also two guest rooms at SI$490/735. Although there's no hot water, the accommodations are adequate for such a remote location and a generator provides electricity. The compulsory meal add-on is SI$435 pp per day. They'll give you a picnic-basket lunch, and the three-course buffet dinner is served at two long communal tables, so you soon get to know everyone. The food is good (ample seafood and fresh fruit). Guests are flown into Seghe, then taken by canoe to Uepi (OO-pee). Transfers from Seghe to the island are SI$330 pp round-trip. Add 10 percent tax to all rates.

At those prices Uepi caters mostly to packaged Australians on scuba or kayaking tours (www .kayaksolomons.com). You're charged extra for everything you do here, except playing volleyball with the staff or paddling a dugout canoe. Paid activities include the custom village tour, the river tour, and lagoon fishing. Scuba diving is SI$350 per dive. Bring your own snorkeling gear with you or be prepared to shell out more money. There's good snorkeling right off their dock on Charapoana Channel at the east end of Uepi—lots of fish. Yachties are not welcome at Uepi Island.

Uepi Island bookings must be confirmed by Tropical Paradise Pty. Ltd. in Melbourne, Australia (tel. 61-3/9787-7904, fax 61-3/9787-5904, www.uepi.com). Fluctuating exchange rates and 20 percent commissions can result in prices considerably higher than those quoted above, especially if you book through a travel agent in the United States. Americans might be able to save a little money by booking locally through Guadalcanal Travel Service (tel. 22586) in Honiara, at the risk of arriving to find no rooms available on Uepi Island. Residents of Australia generally pay lower rates because Australian travel agents accept lower commissions than American agents.

Charapoana Island

Charapoana Island Resort (tel. 30156, www .charapoana.com) on the reef island directly ad-jacent to Uepi Island is newer and less known that its neighbor. It's run by a Czech guy named Jiri Holba and his local partner. To stay in one of the four double and two single rooms with shared bath in the thatched guesthouse is SI$500 pp including meals, non-alcoholic cold drinks, and transfers from Seghe Airport. Jiri's wife Zusye prepares a variety of international dishes with the emphasis on seafood. As at Uepi, most people come here to scuba dive, and this costs SI$275 per dive. A great number of fish are seen on the drift dive through the passage between Charapoana and Uepi, and the diving and snorkeling are superb just offshore. Apart from diving, there's an emphasis on wildlife observation and cultural experiences. Charapoana Island is one of the few upscale resorts in the Solomons offering unique activities such as crocodile spotlighting and traditional "buna" fishing using poisonous plants. Most of their lagoon adventure tours cost SI$150 pp.

Ramata Island

The four-room **Mavo Rest House** (no phone) is on Ramata Island, at the narrow north end of the Marovo Lagoon. It's SI$85 pp including seafood meals in the pleasant thatched restaurant. Most guests come for the excellent fishing around here. Mavo is a few minutes walk from Ramata Airstrip, with a weekly flight from Honiara (SI$372) and Seghe (SI$143), which continues on to Munda (SI$143).

Vanua Rapita

In 1995, an ecotourism resort was established on a tiny island near Michi village just off northern Vanguna. Vanua Rapita (no phone) consists of an attractive tin roofed central building with an open terrace right over the lagoon, plus two leaf houses also built over the lagoon, one with two double rooms and another with three double rooms. The "honeymoon" bungalow has one room. It's SI$110 pp including meals. The accommodations are clean and supplied with mosquito nets, and you can use the fridge (bring your own alcohol, if necessary). Snorkeling is possible and two dugout canoes are supplied. Vanua Rapita is well known for its cultural programs, and most activities are offered. Transfers from Seghe/Patutiva are SI$40 pp each way (25 minutes). Information and bookings are available from Adventure Sports in Gizo.

Seghe Point

Seghe, on New Georgia Island at the southwest end of the lagoon, is the communications hub of Marovo. Solomon Airlines has almost daily flights from Munda (71 km, SI$143), Gizo (122 km, SI$189), and Honiara (256 km, SI$324) to a wartime airstrip (EGM) the Americans built in only 10 days. There's a sunken P38 Lightning fighter in the water off the passage end of the airstrip. During WW II, coast-watcher Donald Kennedy and a small force of Solomon Islanders carried out many daring guerrilla raids against the Japanese near Seghe and supplied vital information on their movements. Author James Michener called Seghe Point, "my favorite spot in the South Pacific."

The **Seghe Resthouse** (no phone) at Seghe has four basic rooms with shared bath.

The passenger ships all stop at **Patutiva** wharf on Vangunu Island, just across scenic Njae Passage from Seghe. A good, cheap market materializes at Patutiva whenever the Honiara ship arrives—jump off and back on quickly to buy oranges and bananas. Dugout canoes propelled by outboard, paddle, or sail carry people around the lagoon from Patutiva, and hitching a ride isn't too hard. However, even low-budget backpackers look rich to some, so agree on a price beforehand. Expect to have to pay for all boat trips anywhere around the lagoon.

Nono Lagoon

Eddie Tivupo and family operate **Horena Hideaway Lodge** (no phone) on a tiny coconut-covered island near Mbareho. Accommodations in two leaf houses are SI$70 pp including meals served in a separate building with a large veranda. Snorkeling, carvings, taboo places, war wreckage, good anchorage, friendly people, and crocodile-watching canoe trips through the mangroves are attractions here. Eddie is a composer well known for his songs about the lagoon. The canoe transfer to Horena from Seghe is SI$80 per group.

Farther south is Benjamin and Jilly Kaniotoku's **Matikuri Lodge** (no phone) on eight-hectare Matikuri Island just off Vangunu's attractive mangrove-fringed coast. The restaurant and entertainment area is on stilts over the lagoon, and three small cottages by the shore accommodate travelers at SI$110 pp, plus tax (children under 16 half price). There's no electricity, but meals are included and a kerosene fridge is provided. Take basic staples with you, because there's only a market at nearby Patutiva twice a week when the boat from Honiara calls. Activities include canoeing, snorkeling, fishing, boat trips up the Nema River or to Hele Bar, rainforest hikes, and village visits. Transport from Seghe/Patutiva to Matikuri is SI$30 pp each way, and motorized canoes are for rent. Benjamin also has a cottage at Seghe. You can also contact Matikura by radio telephone from any Solomon Telekom office (they listen 0800–0830, 1200–1300, and 1600–1700).

Viru Harbor

The ship from Honiara next enters beautiful, landlocked Viru Harbor and calls briefly at Tetemara landing. As you come in between the high coral cliffs, look up above the white triangular navigational aid on the left to see the long barrel of a Japanese gun, still pointing skyward. Five Melanesian stone fortresses, two on the north and three on the south, guarded the harbor entrance in ancient times.

Today Viru Harbor serves as a logging camp and is a stronghold of Seventh-Day Adventist fundamentalism. The offices of Kalena Timber are at Itemi, just a short distance farther up the harbor from Tetemara. A free ferry shuttles between Tetemara, Itemi, and Tombe (a woodcarving village). There's a Forestry Station at Arara, 10 km from Tetemara by road. Aside from the Honiara-Gizo ships, you can get out of Viru Harbor by taking a canoe to Seghe. Ask about the mail run.

Rendova

The Honiara-Gizo ship ties up at Mburuku (Ughele) on the high volcanic island of Rendova, another major WW II battlefield. You'll have about 10 minutes to get off and buy food at the impromptu market on the wharf. Grab a pineapple, some bananas, and a green coconut before they're gone. The native pudding is also good. If you make prior arrangements, you can be picked up here by the Lubaria Island Resort boat (see Munda and Vicinity, below).

Rendova's neighboring island, Tetepare, is one of the largest uninhabited islands in the South Pacific. The original population left more than 200 years ago due to disease, and their descendants are now scattered throughout Western Province. Tetepare's lowland forest is one of the last totally undisturbed rainforests of its kind in the Pacific, yet logging companies are busy lobbying to harvest it.

MUNDA AND VICINITY

Munda, the metropolis of New Georgia, is little more than a string of villages centered on Lambete beside the Roviana Lagoon; the name "Munda" describes the whole area. The government wharf, administration offices, air terminal (MUA), and resthouses are all at **Lambete,** while the United Church maintains its Solomon Islands head-

quarters and runs Helena Goldie Hospital at **Kokenggolo** near an old wharf, two km west of Lambete. The United Church also operates **Goldie College** near the Diamond Narrows. A vast wartime airstrip stretching from Lambete to Kokenggolo still dominates Munda, a huge plain of crushed coral. The Americans built the fine coral roads here by dredging up limestone, crushing it with a steamroller, then pumping saltwater over the road to harden it like cement.

The people of the Roviana Lagoon were once much-feared cannibals who raided far and wide in their long canoes. In 1892, a punitive raid by a British warship broke the power of the headhunters, and a few years later Methodist missionaries converted the survivors. Though the change from those days is striking, much remains the same around this lagoon. You might see old men netting fish, outriggers bringing in live turtles, and fish leaping through the sea.

Sights

Have a swim in the spring-fed freshwater pool near the canoe house at Lambete wharf. Next,

SOLOMON ISLANDS

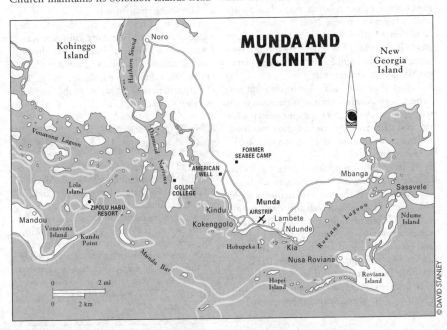

© DAVID STANLEY

follow the coastal road east from Lambete a kilometer to **Kia** village. In the bush just behind the houses of Kia is a large U.S. military dump with huge landing craft deliberately cut in half, amphibious tanks, trucks, aircraft engines, guns, and even a small Japanese tank, all piled up where the Americans left them when they pulled out after the war. Many beautiful pink and blue orchids bloom in the bush beyond. The village chief will be happy to show you around for a SI$20 pp custom fee. Much more war materiel is sunken or dumped in the lagoon off Kia, and small copra driers along the waterfront still utilize wartime 44-gallon petrol drums.

Now head for **Kokenggolo.** The Japanese secretly built the gigantic airstrip that dominates this area. They camouflaged their work by suspending the tops of coconut trees on cables above the runway—surely one of the more remarkable accomplishments of the war. The Americans captured Munda on August 5, 1943, after heavy fighting. Avid snorkelers should visit the sunken aircraft in the lagoon just off the beach near Kokenggolo hospital: A single-engine Corsair fighter is beside a pole near shore, while a larger two-engine Nelly bomber in good condition is farther out in about seven meters of water. If there are a few of you, try hiring a motorized canoe at Lambete wharf, as these planes can be hard to find on your own.

Follow the coastal road northwest from Kokenggolo to **Kindu** village. Women are often seen washing clothes in a large spring-fed pool at the end of the village, right beside the road. Swim here or continue one km to a clear freshwater stream.

Midway between pool and stream is a road leading inland toward Noro. About a kilometer up this road, on the left just before a slight rise, is an old American well and water supply system. Continue along the road till it meets the new highway to Noro. Cross the highway and go straight ahead on a bush trail five minutes to two large **Japanese AA guns** flanking a flagpole foundation, all that's left of the big U.S. Seabee Camp that once covered this area. Hitch back to Munda along the highway for a circle trip.

Vicinity of Munda

Noro, 16 km northwest of Munda by road or by boat through the Diamond Narrows, is the second largest township in the Solomons (3,500 inhabitants). The Soltai cannery established at Noro in 1991 cans 20,000 tons of tuna a year, including the dark-meat Solomons Blue *tin pis* (canned fish). A copra-exporting facility is near the fish freezer plant. There are three wharfs at Noro: the government wharf where the Honiara-Gizo ship ties up, the Fisheries wharf, and the Soltai wharf next to the cannery.

At **Enoghae Point,** east of Noro, four 140-mm Japanese coastal defense guns still lurk in the bush. Only one of the guns is still in good shape; the others have been pulled apart by scrap-metal scavengers. There's a sunken Japanese freighter in shallow water at Mbaeroko Bay nearby.

Roviana Island, just southeast of Munda across the lagoon, was the stronghold of the notorious headhunter Ingava, whose ferocity led to the sacking and burning of his ridgetop fortress by Commander David of the *Royalist* in 1892. The sacred **Dog Stone** is near the southeast end of this broken coral fortress.

There are a few other custom places near Munda, such as the **Island of Skulls** near Kundu Point, or the **Stones of Bau** deep in the interior, but access is difficult, and you'll be charged outlandish customary admission fees to visit. Unfortunately, this also applies to the Dog Stone and the "Cave of the Giant."

THE CRAWL

In 1898 a 12-year-old Roviana islander named Alick Wickham introduced the world to the traditional swimming technique we now know as the crawl. Alick had gone to Sydney two years earlier with his Australian father, and when he easily beat all the Aussie kids at a local swimming carnival, an Australian coach noticed. The technique was perfected and became a sensation at the 1900 Olympics. Alick later worked as a stuntman in a circus, served with the coast-watchers during WW II, and died in Honiara in 1967 at the ripe old age of 81.

During WW II, the Americans had a PT-boat base at **Rendova Harbor,** and a local man, Mr. Kettily Zongahite, has set up a **John F. Kennedy Museum** on Lubaria Island facing the harbor, in memory of JFK's brief stay here. The easiest way to visit is by arranging to spend a few days at the Lubaria Island Resort.

Sports and Recreation

Diving is offered by Trevor Cumberland and Sunga Boso of **Dive Munda** (tel. 61107, www.dive munda.com) at Anges Lodge in Munda. The Roviana Lagoon waters offer limited visibility, but Dive Munda visits many sites beyond the reef.

Accommodations at Lambete

About 150 meters west of Lambete Police Station is **Sunflower House,** a large two-room leaf house with cooking facilities and electric lighting. The separate bungalow near the water has a superb view. It's around SI$50 pp a night, and the friendly owners, Milton and Natsha Aqorau, may offer you fresh fruit each morning. Camping is possible at negotiable rates. The food served here isn't cheap, but you get what you pay for: large servings of well prepared dishes like lasagna, Thai fish, garlic calamari, etc. For dessert, try the pineapple caramel cake. Ask at PX Merle Aqorau store next to the Educational Division office, a five-minute walk from the airport.

The **Sobar Rest House** (tel. 61153), just a five-minute walk from Munda Airport but hard to find, is sometimes called "Sogabule's Lodge" after the owner, John Sogabule. There's no sign on the building. The three double rooms with fan are SI$44 pp and communal cooking facilities are provided—a good value. The folks at Paradise Lodge in Gizo can book you into this place.

Just a stone's throw from the air terminal and government wharf is 22-room **Agnes Lodge** (Derek Kera, tel. 61133, fax 61225, www.agnes lodge.com). It's SI$270/380 single/double for the four rooms with bath in the old wing or SI$435/610 for the 12 deluxe rooms in the new wing. There's also a "backpackers' rate" of SI$82 per bed in three shared rooms in the old wing. Add 10 percent tax to all rates, plus another 20 percent commission if you book through a travel

agent in Australia. The breakfast and dinner package is SI$190 pp extra. During the off-season (Nov.–Apr.) you can stay seven nights for the price of five (backpacker accommodation excluded). No cooking facilities are provided, so you must patronize their restaurant. Sandwiches are available, but a sign at the bar advises patrons that nonguests must order full meals after 1800. This is the only place in Munda to get a beer (check your change). The staff will pressure you to sign up for their half-day lagoon trips, which are artificial and rather expensive.

Noro Lodge (tel. 61238, fax 61225), about a five-minute walk from the government wharf at Noro, is run by David Kera, who is related to the folks at Agnes Lodge. The four rooms without bath are SI$110 single or double, while another four rooms with bath are SI$165.

Island Resorts

Trevor and Zahi Cumberland accept guests on tiny **Hombupeka Island** (tel. 61107, www.hom bupeka.com), just 800 meters offshore from Lambete. There's a leaf house capable of accommodating one family, or you can camp. Trevor runs Dive Munda at Agnes Lodge, so ask for him there.

If you want to have an island to yourself, Agnes Lodge rents out a lovely part-leaf cottage on nearby **Hopei Island,** just offshore from Munda, complete with fridge, oven, and toilet. It's SI$380/530/685 single/double/triple. You can bring your own food, otherwise full provisions can be ordered. It may seem remote, but be aware of theft.

One of the nicest little hideaways in these parts is Joe and Lisa Entrikin's **Zipolo Habu Resort** (tel. 61178, fax 61179, www.zipolohabu.com .sb), on Lola Island at the east entrance to the Vonavona Lagoon. Lola's a medium-size island with a white sandy beach from which one gets a lovely lagoon view. Set in a coconut grove, all buildings on the premises are built from local materials. The four two-bedroom cottages with fridge, gas stove, and mosquito nets are SI$210/300/345 single/double/triple including tax. You can bring food and cook for yourself or order seafood meals in their restaurant (SI$245 meal

SOLOMON ISLANDS

plan). The Fishing Bar staff will happily use your carry-on duty free bottle to mix your drinks— it's that kind of place. As you lie in bed, the jungle sounds lull you to sleep. Twenty minutes from Munda by boat, this resort has been a favorite among anglers since 1989, and the resort's three boats are available for fishing or surfing trips, sightseeing, and shopping excursions at fixed rates. Scuba diving is SI$260/480 with one/two tanks, not including gear (SI$175 surcharge if you're the only diver). Snorkeling trips are SI$150 pp. Transfers cost SI$270 per cottage from Munda or Noro round-trip (free if you stay five nights or longer). All prices are based on Australian dollars, so they fluctuate with the daily rate.

Food and Entertainment

There are four general stores at Lambete. The **Hot Bread Kitchen** near the police station by the airport bakes bread daily (arrive early on Sunday). Sporadic markets happen near Lambete wharf and Kokenggolo hospital, but the selection is poor.

There's custom dancing at Munda on May 23, anniversary of the arrival of the first missionaries (in 1902), July 7 (Independence Day), Christmas, and New Year's Day. The singing and dancing show the influence of Tongan missionaries. Ask if any bamboo bands will be playing while you're there.

Services

The National Bank has a branch next to the airport terminal at Lambete and another at Noro; both change traveler's checks.

Getting There

Solomon Airlines (tel. 61152) has daily flights to Honiara (327 km, SI$392) and several flights a week to Gizo (SI$143), Seghe (71 km, SI$143), and Yandina (SI$297).

The Solomon Airlines office, the customs office, and the immigration office are all inside the airport terminal. The small coffee counter in the terminal opens at flight times.

The Wings Shipping boat calls here Monday morning bound for Gizo, Monday afternoon for Honiara.

Due to the lack of a main wharf at Munda, the ships from Honiara cannot tie up here and you must negotiate with a private canoe owner to take you to/from the small wharf next to Agnes Lodge at Lambete. The Munda-Honiara boat stops some distance offshore, and canoe operators will want SI$20 pp to take you there. One way to avoid this is by disembarking at Noro, where there is a wharf, and try to hitch down to Munda (16 km). If arriving from Honiara during daylight you'll get the added bonus of seeing the Diamond Narrows (which are just after Munda).

Since the airfare from Munda to Gizo is relatively low, consider taking the boat from Honiara direct to Noro, hitching a ride down to Munda in the back of a truck, flying from Munda to Gizo, then either taking the boat or flying from Gizo back to Honiara. Try to book the Munda-Gizo leg before leaving Honiara.

Getting Around

Good roads connect Munda to Mbanga landing (near Sasavele) and Noro. The Port Authority truck (marked "SIPA") carries passengers from Noro to Munda sporadically at SI$5 pp. Otherwise you could simply hitch, although there isn't a lot of traffic, and if you get stuck, it will cost at least SI$150 to hire a truck from Noro to Munda. It's easier to go from Lambete to Noro. Weekdays just before 0800, you can usually get a ride from Lambete to Noro in the truck that brings children to school at Lambete. Ask around the night before. To hire a motorized canoe between Munda and Noro will cost about SI$250.

KOLOMBANGARA

Kolombangara is a classic cone-shaped volcano 30 km across and almost circular in shape that soars to 1,700 meters. The native name of this island-volcano is Nduke. You can climb it from Iriri or Vanga villages, accessible by canoe from Gizo market, where the locals sell their products and shop. To go up and down in one day would be exhausting, so camp partway and reach the top early the next morning; by midday the summit is shrouded in clouds and you'd miss the view. But in the mist, the stunted, moss-covered forest on top will haunt you. The extinct crater is four km across and as much as 1,000 meters deep, with the Vila River, which passes Ringi, draining it on the southeast side.

A coastal road runs around the island's 688 square km, with old logging roads up most of the ridges. Ringi, two km from the wharf (where the Honiara ships stop), is the former headquarters of Levers Pacific Timbers, which logged Kolombangara from 1968 to 1986. At the moment, Kolombangara Forest Products (www.kfpl .com.sb), which is 51 percent owned by the Commonwealth Development Corporation, has a 16,000-hectare hardwood reforestation project on Kolombangara, intended to provide a sustainable alternative to uncontrolled logging of old growth forests. Since 1995 the project has been self-supporting, and eco-friendly timber from the island supplies a niche market in Europe.

The wharf and airport are on opposite sides of Ringi Cove station, both a 15-minute walk away. There's a small market in Ringi. Vilu Plantation, on Blackett Strait just south of the cove airstrip, was an important Japanese base during WW II. Rusted Japanese guns molder in the bush near the airstrip. At last report, there were no regular Solomon Airlines flights to Ringi Cove. Find outboard canoes to Noro or Munda near the canoe shed at the Ringi Cove wharf.

GIZO

The administrative center of the Western Solomons since 1899, Gizo (3,000 inhabitants) is a pleasant little town. It's quite a "modern" place, with electric streetlights, a hospital, banks, and many Chinese stores. Downtown Gizo is like a second version of Honiara's Chinatown. The name recalls a legendary warrior Izo, and although the town is called Gizo, the island name is spelled Ghizo, yet both are pronounced the same.

An important shipping and shopping center for the Western

Solomons, Gizo lies 383 km northwest of Honiara. A large Gilbertese community has been resettled here since 1955. Gizo has a lovely setting with several small islands just offshore. Logha Island directly opposite Gizo is owned by the Catholic Church, which operates a seminary there. Nusaburaku village, on Ghizo Island to the left, is populated by Gilbertese people from Wagina Island, while farther out is a fishing village of Malaita people. The view of Kolombangara looming across Blackett Strait to the right is particularly picturesque.

After their PT boat was cut in half by a Japanese destroyer on August 1, 1943, John F. Kennedy and his 10 shipmates took shelter on Kasolo, or Plum Pudding Island, between Ghizo and Kolombanga, from which he was rescued by a Solomon Islander. The ship from Honiara passes right beside Plum Pudding (anyone aboard could point it out).

Although you'll probably like the leisurely lifestyle and variety of things to see and do, Gizo is becoming rather commercialized as it caters more and more to packaged scuba divers from Australia. Shore diving or snorkeling isn't

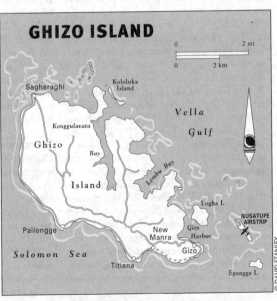

GHIZO ISLAND

possible here, and the expense of always going out by boat to dive adds up. You have to spend money to do almost anything at Gizo.

Sights

Near Gizo's police station is a memorial to Captain Alexander McKenzie Ferguson, master of the *Ripple*—"Killed by natives at Bougainville Island." Another monument in front of the station remembers Captain Thomas Woodhouse, "The Old Commodore," who died at Gizo in 1906. From here a road climbs the hill behind town, and it's worth the effort for the great view of the harbor and surrounding islands. During WW II the Japanese had a major barge-repair base in the bay you see below.

A good half-day trip from town involves taking a truck from Gizo market to the end of the line at the Gilbertese village of **Titiana,** then returning to town along the beach in a couple of hours. You may have to use the road from Titiana to New Manra village to avoid mangroves, and the section from New Manra to Gizo jail is best done at low tide, but all in all, it's an easy scenic walk. If you can't find a truck to Titiana at the market, do the walk in reverse, following the road east out of town past the hospital and jail, and along the beautiful beach, then return to Gizo by road directly from New Manra village. The boys in these villages prepare a smelly homebrew called "Hawaiian tea" from fermented toddy and tea leaves. Unfermented toddy *(te karewe)* is much nicer.

Ghizo Island is 11 km long, five km wide, and 180 meters high. A major all-day hike begins by crossing the island, then following the beach road past the Gilbertese villages of New Manra and Titiana to Pailongge, a Melanesian village. Continue along the beach road for a few more hours to **Sagheraghi,** where an overgrown lumber road along the hilltops leads back to town (branch tracks off the high road lead nowhere). This hike gives you the chance to see central Ghizo, which Levers Pacific Timbers clearcut during the 1960s, leading to the extinction of the unique Ghizo white-eye. You'll still encounter some red-and-green coconut lorries and giant white cockatoos along the way. The snorkeling off Sagheraghi is superb, with a double reef and 25-meter drop-off between.

Scuba Diving

Danny and Kerrie Kennedy's **Adventure Sports** (tel. 60253, fax 60297, www.divegizo.com), or "Dive Gizo," opposite Koburutavia Divers Lodge and with a desk at the Gizo Hotel, offers scuba diving from their boat at SI$260 including tank, belt, and weights, SI$350 with all equipment (two dives SI$600). Snorkeling is SI$65/110 for a half/full day without equipment. If you've never done scuba before, you can take their "resort course" for SI$520 or a full PADI/NAUI scuba certification course for SI$2,600/2,175 pp for one/two persons all-inclusive. Prices are based on Australian dollars and fluctuate daily. You won't find a more relaxed place than Gizo in which to learn how to dive. Danny himself is something of a South Seas beachcomber who has been here since 1985. You'll find his easygoing enthusiasm and good humor contagious. Adventure Sports also sells handicrafts.

Be sure to dive on the 140-meter Japanese transport ship *Toa Maru,* if nothing else. This enormous wreck 18 meters below in Kololuka Bay is still intact in 8–35 meters of water, with sake bottles in the galley and two-man tanks in the hold. Grand Central Station, a sloping drop-off off the north end of Ghizo, is the ultimate fish and coral dive. Other dive spots include the shallow reef at Nusatupe Island, Naru Wall, the Hellcat fighter near Q-Island in the Vonavona Lagoon, and a Zero aircraft in five meters of water just off Gizo's market—ideal to finish off a tank. According to Danny Kennedy, there have never been any problems with sharks in the waters he frequents off Ghizo.

Accommodations

Under US$25: One of the best buys is the nine-room **Naqua Resthouse** (tel. 60012, fax 60278), also known as the "KML Resthouse," run by Meshach Ngodoro and family on the hill just above the wharf. There are great views of Kolombangara from the breezy balcony, and the communal cooking facilities and fridge are excellent, all at SI$50 pp. Alcohol is not allowed. Information is available at KML Hardware next to the National Bank.

On a breezy slope a bit farther up the same way

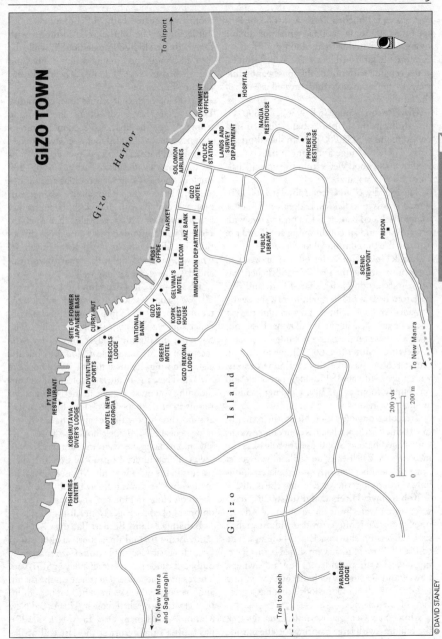

GIZO TOWN

Gizo Harbor

Gizo Harbor

To Airport

SOLOMON ISLANDS

Ghizo Island

Island

© DAVID STANLEY

To New Manra and Sagheraghi

Trail to beach

To New Manra

PARADISE LODGE

FISHERIES CENTER

KOBURUTAVIA DIVER'S LODGE

PT 109 RESTAURANT

ADVENTURE SPORTS

SITE OF FORMER JAPANESE BASE

MOTEL NEW GEORGIA

TRESCOLS LODGE

CURRY HUT

NATIONAL BANK

GIZO NEST

GREEN MOTEL

GIZO REKONA LODGE

KOPIK GUEST HOUSE

GELVINA'S MOTEL

POST OFFICE

MARKET

TELECOM

ANZ BANK

IMMIGRATION DEPARTMENT

GIZO HOTEL

SOLOMON AIRLINES

POLICE STATION

GOVERNMENT OFFICES

LANDS AND SURVEY DEPARTMENT

NAQUA RESTHOUSE

HOSPITAL

PHOEBE'S RESTHOUSE

PUBLIC LIBRARY

SCENIC VIEWPOINT

PRISON

0   200 yds
0   200 m

past Naqua is **Phoebe's Resthouse** (Phoebe Piti-sopa, tel. 60336, fax 60035) with four double rooms with shared bath at SI$45 pp. There's a comfortably furnished lounge, cooking facilities, and a veranda with one of the most panoramic views in the South Seas. You're treated like one of the family.

Gizo Rekona Lodge (tel. 60368, fax 60021), just up from the National Bank, has 10 fan-cooled rooms at SI$50/99 pp with shared/private bath. There's a fridge and communal cooking facilities, and good views from the upstairs balcony. It's very popular.

The friendly, clean **Green Motel** (tel. 60005), directly across from Rekona Lodge, has six rooms, four with shared bath at SI$50 pp and two with private bath and air conditioning at SI$100 pp. You can use the communal kitchen.

Kopik Guest House (tel. 60374), above LCC Enterprises next to the Daily Bread Kitchen, has two double rooms with shared bath and one with four beds at SI$50 pp. In theory, the owner provides cooking facilities, but examine the gas bottle before checking in. It's all rather basic, but okay for those on the barest of budgets.

Gelvina's Motel (tel. 60276), next to Kopik Guest House, has five air-conditioned rooms with private bath at SI$250 single or double and one family room at SI$300. Cooking facilities are not provided.

Trescols Lodge (tel. 60090), in the center of town behind ES Snack Bar, has eight double rooms with shared bath at SI$50 pp. Trescols lacks the nice views and self-catering facilities you get at some of the other similarly-priced places, and is only worth trying when everything else is full.

Koburutavia Divers Lodge (tel. 60257) has a seven-room waterfront lodge opposite Adventure Sports that is often crowded with Australian scuba divers on short packaged holidays. The cost is SI$70 pp plus tax with shared bath. Cooking facilities are provided. The kind owners, Lawry and Regina Wickham, also operate a restaurant/bar behind the lodge that has a great view of Gizo harbor.

Motel New Georgia (Kevin Paia, tel. 60607), the building with large paintings on the outside walls just behind Adventure Sports, has eight

rooms with shared bath and communal cooking facilities. The four fan-cooled rooms with twin beds are SI$40/80 single/double, while the four air-conditioned rooms with a double and a single bed are SI$120 double. There's a breezy elevated terrace here.

Up on top of the hill behind town is **Paradise Lodge** (tel. 60024, fax 60200, plodge@solomon.com.sb). The "backpackers" section downstairs includes three five-bedded rooms and two doubles with shared bath at SI$55 pp, plus tax. Upstairs are four rooms with private bath at SI$165–220 single or double. Communal cooking and a fridge are provided downstairs; upstairs are a bar, restaurant, and veranda with great views. For upmarket accommodations, it's better value than the Gizo Hotel if you don't mind being away from the action. Paradise Lodge is run by May Sogabule, who will pick you up at the wharf if you call ahead. Otherwise it's a long walk.

US$25–50: The **Gizo Hotel** (tel. 60199, fax 60137, gizohtl@solomon.com.sb), in the center of town, has 45 rooms, all with private bath, fridge, and tea- and coffee-making facilities. The seven hot and dumpy "budget" rooms above the reception are SI$200 single or double, while the eight "old wing" rooms at the rear of the hotel are SI$370. These rooms are fan cooled. For air conditioning you must upgrade to the 14 "poolside" rooms in an L-shaped two-story block angled around the shallow figure-eight-shaped swimming pool at SI$500 single/double. The 16 "seaview" rooms along the main street are also SI$500. Two children under 12 can stay free with their parents in the old wing only. Meals are extra. It's owned by the same folks who run the King Solomon Hotel in Honiara, and most guests are on pre-booked packages from Australia.

Babanga Island Resort: Babanga is a long sandy island beyond the airport, six km east of Gizo. It's easily accessible from Gizo market by outboard canoe several times a day at SI$10 pp. There's just one Gilbertese village on the island, and the people there seem to fit a lot better into their environment than those in Titiana and New Manra. A local man, Osia Ta'asi (tel. 60128), has built a small resort at the east end of Babanga, a 20-minute walk from the village. You'll stay in a thatched house on stilts at SI$35 pp, plus another SI$40 for all meals. Mattresses, pillows, sheets, and mosquito nets are provided. There are two beaches here, one with a good view of Plum Pudding Island just opposite. Activities include snorkeling and fishing, and picnic trips to Plum Pudding can be arranged. Ask about this place at Gizo market.

Food

Bridgit Nickols House Snack Bar (weekdays 1030–1630), the last building on the west side of the market, serves local meals.

The **Gizo Nest Restaurant** (George Taylor, no phone), on the main street near Kopik Guest House, serves basic Asian meals.

Iden's Kitchen, on the waterfront between the Chinese stores, also has good plates of rice and meat.

RTC Fast Food Snack Bar (weekdays 0900–1700), almost opposite Trescols Lodge, has cheap snacks you eat while standing up.

The Curry Hut, opposite Trescols Lodge, is about the best place in town for lunch, with a bag of yellowfin tuna and chips for SI$7.

Perhaps the top place in town is the **PT 109 Restaurant** (tel. 60257), overlooking the lagoon behind Koburutavia Divers Lodge. You can order a three-course meal here with tea or coffee for less than SI$50, but dinner must be reserved before 1600. It's a better value than the restaurant at the Gizo Hotel.

Gizo's Favourite (John Leong, no phone, daily 0600–2200), at Motel New Georgia behind Adventure Sports, serves tasty Chinese food and pizza in the SI$20–28 range. The bar here is called the "Vinakiki Bar" after the highest mountain on New Georgia.

The Western Fishermen's Coop (tel. 60040) and Indian Pacific Seafood, both on the waterfront west of town, sell fresh fish in the morning (only frozen fish in the afternoon). Fresh fish are also sold at the weekday market along the waterfront, usually in the afternoon.

Gizo tap water is not fit for drinking.

Entertainment

The **Gizo Hotel** (tel. 60199) presents a bamboo band on Wednesday and Gilbertese *tamure* dancing on Friday. The spectacles are accessible to both diners at the hotel restaurant and to those who only buy a drink at the hotel bar. The action begins around 1930, but it's all canceled when the hotel is short of guests. The occasional Friday night dances at the PT 109 Restaurant tend to be rougher, with fistfights not uncommon.

Services

The ANZ Bank (tel. 60262) and the National Bank (tel. 60134) at Gizo change traveler's checks. ANZ gives cash advances against Visa and MasterCard credit cards (telex fee charged).

The post office is in a temporary building at the market. The Telekom office (tel. 60127, fax 60128), opposite the market, has public phone booths just inside. You can access the Internet here for SI$.60 a minute.

Extensions of stay can be arranged at the Immigration Department, up the street opposite Gizo market.

Adventure Sports (tel. 60253) runs a mini-travel agency and can book you into outer island resorts all around Western Province (including Vanua Rapita). They also arrange early morning birdwatching walks in the hills around Gizo at SI$110 pp.

Transportation

Solomon Airlines (tel. 60173), across the street from the police station, has daily service from Gizo to Honiara (377 km, SI$445), several flights a week to Munda (51 km, SI$143), Seghe (122 km, SI$189), and Choiseul Bay (166 km, SI$230), and weekly to Ballalae (159 km, SI$230), Mono (SI$230), and Kagau (SI$189). Don't forget to reconfirm your onward bookings. The airstrip (GZO) is on Nusatupe Island, a quick boat ride (SI$20 pp) from the wharf in front of the Gizo Hotel. The transfer is free for Gizo Hotel guests.

Between Gizo and Honiara the plane follows an easterly flight path, while northbound it flies more to the west. For optimum views, one should sit on the right side of the aircraft in both directions.

The Wings Shipping ship *Compass Rose* departs Gizo for Honiara Monday at 1500 (SI$143 deck). On the journey from Gizo to Honiara, the

Compass Rose sleeps anchored off Noro, calls at the New Georgia and Marovo Lagoon ports on Tuesday, and arrives in Honiara Wednesday at 0500. Tickets can be purchased at the Gizo Hotel reception.

The MV *Tomoko* of Transwest Shipping should depart Gizo for Honiara Tuesday and Friday at 1900, but the schedule usually varies. This ship also makes trips to Mono and the Shortland Islands.

The Shipping Officer in the Provincial Office opposite the police station may know about boats from Gizo to the Shortland Islands and elsewhere. Several small trading vessels based at Gizo, including the *Lauru I*, serve the Shortland Islands and Choiseul (SI$90 deck).

Outboard canoes leave Gizo market for Vella Lavella, Kolombangara, Ranongga, and Simbo. Ask along the waterfront. You can hire an outboard canoe to go right around Gizo or elsewhere at SI$250 for a full day, petrol included. Ten people can go for that price.

Two minibuses provide passenger service between Gizo market and Titiana about five times a day (SI$3). Ask about the blue truck, which travels between the market and Pailongge.

VELLA LAVELLA

This large island across the Ghizo Strait is easily accessible by outboard canoe from Gizo. Transport can be unreliable, however, so expect to stay a day or two longer than you might want. A wartime road runs right up the southeast side of the island, but all the bridges have long since been washed out. At Niarovai, a couple of hours' walk northeast of Maravari (with several big rivers to cross), is a **New Zealand War Memorial.** As recently as 1978, a Japanese straggler was found on Vella Lavella, and rumors of additional Japanese soldiers still holding out in the bush were circulated for years, in hope of attracting Japanese tourists to the island!

The most unusual attraction of Vella Lavella is the **thermal area,** an hour's walk inland from Paraso Bay on the northeast side of the island. There are megapode birds, hot springs, and bubbling mud in a desertlike area near the Ngokosole River (crocodiles). The only access to Paraso is by

chartered canoe. Ask the driver to take you right around Vella Lavella, rather than coming back the same way. If you decide to snorkel off Vella Lavella, ask local residents if crocodiles pose any danger before you go in the water.

The Americans built an airstrip (VEV) on the beach at Barakoma, between Liapari and Maravari, but Solomon Airlines doesn't have any regular flights here.

SIMBO

Simbo, the westernmost island of the New Georgia Group, was once a base for 19th-century headhunting raids. Later in the 1880s, northbound sea captains called at Simbo on their way from Sydney to Canton, and it became one of the first islands in the Solomons to accept Christian missionaries. The islanders still make tapa, which they dye blue-green in one of the island's sulfurous hot springs.

Today this tiny island (12 square km), 40 km southwest of Ghizo, is better known for its **thermal area,** one of only four in the Solomons (the other three are on Vella Lavella, Savo, and Tinakula). Smoking fumaroles and a sulfur-stained hillside are clearly visible from the sea at Ove, on the southwest side of Simbo. Sulfur-rich seepage points drain into a brackish lake, the habitat of megapodes. The hot springs are too hot to touch. Visitors must pay a stiff fee to the customary landowners to tour the thermal area; if a large group arrives, there's quite a ruckus over who's going to get all the money. The only access to Ove is by boat (not included in the fee) or along a roundabout trail that crosses the mountain from Karivara.

Megapode rookeries at Nusa Simbo village opposite Karivara can be seen with permission of the chief, who also sells the eggs of the fast-disappearing birds. Don't let yourself be hustled here. The **hot springs** easiest to enjoy are near the bridge on the trail linking Nusa Simbo to Lengana, the main village. The hot water mixes with tidal water in the lagoon, and you can have a good swim.

There's good anchorage for yachts at Lengana, a freshwater shower on the wharf, and several general stores nearby. For accommodations, ask around at Lengana. Every Monday and Friday there's an outboard canoe from Lengana to Gizo. A trail leads north from Lengana to Tapurai, where the two chiefs who own the thermal area reside. Negotiate with them for a visit.

THE SHORTLAND ISLANDS

The Shortland Islands are one of most isolated outposts in the Pacific. Together with the adjacent Treasury Islands, the group is traditionally known as Famoa for Fauro, Mono, and Alu, the three largest islands. This intriguing area receives no more than a dozen individual visitors a year, so you'll be in for something totally original!

Though officially part of Solomon Islands' Western Province, the Shortlands are much closer geographically, culturally, and linguistically to North Solomons Province in Papua New Guinea. The modern partition of the area dates from 1899, when the Germans ceded the Shortlands to Britain but held onto Bougainville itself. During WW II, the Japanese fortified the islands to shield their large bases in southern Bougainville. Though the New Zealanders took the Treasury Islands just to the southwest in October 1943, the Japanese entrenched in the Shortlands themselves were bombed and bypassed by the Allies.

In early 1992, fighting between the secessionist Bougainville Revolutionary Army and the Papua New Guinea Defense Force spilled over into the Shortlands when P.N.G. patrol boats and troops made incursions into Solomon Island territory in pursuit of BRA fighters and persons supplying contraband gasoline to the Bougainville rebels. As a result of the 1992 border incidents, Solomon Islands set up a paramilitary field force that presently has several bases in the area.

Although the Shortlands might seem like a natural stepping stone between Solomon Islands and Papua New Guinea, there are no immigration facilities in this area and crossing 20 km of water from Ballalae to Kangu Beach near Buin on Bougainville is officially prohibited. Villagers from Alu and Fauro islands often go to Kangu Beach on Saturdays to sell fish, and some travelers have gone along for the ride in past. This is illegal and we cannot recommend it.

Ballalae

The airstrip (BAS) serving the Shortlands is on uninhabited Ballalae Island, with access to and from Korovou by motorized canoe (30 minutes, SI$30 pp). Be prepared to get wet. There are Solomon Airlines flights from Ballalae to Gizo (159 km, SI$230) and Honiara (536 km, SI$593) twice a week.

During WW II, the Japanese forced several hundred British civilian prisoners brought from Singapore to build the airstrip on Ballalae and none left the island alive. Sadly, no memorial has been erected to those who suffered and died here, and the victims have been forgotten. What can be seen are numerous vestiges of Japanese military might. Japanese propellers flank the small airport terminal, and on the short trail from the terminal to the beach you pass one wrecked plane and a half dozen Japanese trucks in various stages of decay. Three small steamrollers used to build the airport are in the bush west of the terminal and another is behind the beach.

A Japanese AA gun is between the southwest end of the airstrip and the point, but the real attraction here is the large number of wrecked Japanese planes, including fighters and twin-engined "Betty" bombers. They're in the bush on both sides of the airstrip: Turn right at the terminal and walk northeast about halfway down the airstrip. There, cut in on either side and search (the planes are easy to find and no guide is required). The planes are surrounded by large circular craters left by the bombs that destroyed them, and if you look long enough, you might see the crumpled aluminum fuselages of several dozen aircraft, a few still in fair condition despite the years. Bring insect repellent and be prepared for black stinging ants.

Alu

Alu, the largest island of the group, is off the southern tip of Bougainville. The tiny government station of **Korovou** is in Alu's southeast corner, and cruising yachts can clear the Solomons here. The boat to Gizo usually ties up at one of two wharfs near the copra shed at Korovou, directly opposite Faisi Island. In the water near the shore just west of Korovou are a Japanese bomber and a Zero aircraft, clearly visible from the surface.

The Solomon Airlines agent runs BBE Store on tiny Teulu Island near Maleai village. It's well stocked with beer and other essentials. One small trading boat does the 11-hour trip between the wharf at Teulu Island and Gizo every week or two. The Catholic mission station of Nila on Poporang Island is just across the water from Korovou. On the northwest side of Alu Island are the Gilbertese re-settlement villages of Kamaleai and Harapa.

An interesting half-day motorized canoe trip is to **Nankai Point** at the south tip of Alu, where the Japanese set up three large coastal defense guns pointing at Allied-occupied Mono Island. To get there, you travel along the back of Magusaisai Island, reaching the open sea just beyond Nuhu village. West of here is a large coconut plantation at Haleta, where one can land on the beach and follow it around to the guns, which are right by the shore just west of tiny Manualai Island. About 50 meters east of the first gun is a short trail up the hill to a stockpile of ammunition with live Japanese shells still piled high.

Faisi

The only regular place to stay in this area is at the southwest end of Faisi Island, directly opposite Korovou and 10 km south of Ballalae airport. The two-room **Faisi Island Guest House** (no phone), run by a woman named Silvester Gali, is the former personal residence of ex-governor general Sir George Lepping, and it's a great budget place to rest. A covered porch faces a lovely white beach, and some nice coral and lots of fish are right offshore. Silvester asks SI$80 pp for a room with communal cooking and bathing facilities, but this price may be negotiable, especially for long stays. Assume that the guesthouse generator will be out of service during your stay. Silvester lives a few hundred meters away on the southeast side of Faisi, so you'll have the whole house to yourself unless there are other guests. To give advance warning of your arrival, radio the Administration Officer at Korovou.

Bring some food with you for the first day or two (protect your food from mice and ants). Women paddling past in canoes may stop to sell you fruit or vegetables, and you can order fresh coconuts from any of the island men. Also bring adequate toilet paper and mosquito coils.

Silvester can help with the necessary canoe hires, but make sure the price is well understood. Expect to pay SI$100 a day plus gasoline, or SI$60 each way for a special trip to Ballalae Airstrip. For example, Dennis Tanutanu offers canoe trips to Nankai Point and elsewhere at reasonable rates. It's not hard to hitch rides on passing canoes to Nila or elsewhere from the end of the stone wharf near the guesthouse. Almost anyone at Ballalae airport will bring you directly to Faisi for SI$30 pp.

Faisi is a pleasant little island inhabited by three families who earn a living cutting copra and by running the guesthouse. Two cows, one dog, and many pigs are also on the island. Red and green parrots and white cockatoos screech and clatter between the coconut trees that circle the island, and frigate birds glide by. The wreck of a small plane is beside the trail at the north end of Faisi, and a more complete plane, its tail wedged between a rock and a tree, its engine on the ground in front, is on the east side of the island. Blue glass from broken Japanese sake bottles is seen on the ground near the wharf and the copra driers not far from the guesthouse.

Poporang

The highlight of any visit to the Shortlands is a tour of Poporang Hill where the Japanese had their main base during WW II. Upon arrival on Poporang Island it's customary to pay a courtesy call on the Catholic priest at Nila, who may be able to suggest someone willing to act as a guide (ask for Billy). An overgrown Japanese road, complete with a truck stalled halfway down, winds around the hill from the mission cattle ranch. On top of Poporang are two intact Japanese radar trailers, and just beyond that, at least four anti-aircraft batteries, one with two metal shell boxes alongside. Your guide will then show you a huge searchlight, a few of the seven 140-mm coastal defense guns remaining on the hill (several others have been removed), an underground metal ammunition bunker the size of a container, and a Japanese motorcycle with its sidecar still attached. You'll pass numerous trenches cut into the coral rock, and go down another wartime road directly to Sapusapuai village.

Also ask to see the six Japanese seaplanes by the shore next to Kopokopana village, a few minutes walk southwest of Nila. Two more planes are in shallow water a stone's throw from the others. Other sunken seaplanes are at the bottom of the bay between Alu and Poporang Islands, with one nearly intact Japanese bomber in eight meters of snorkeling water just east of Nila. All of the abovewater relics can be seen in a couple of hours with the help of a guide who will have earned his gratuity. Wednesday is a good day to come, as there will be a small market at Nila. (Heavy fines are imposed on anyone attempting to remove war relics from these islands.)

Treasury Islands

The Treasury Islands are the westernmost islands included in this handbook. All of the people live on larger Mono Island, but the airstrip and a lot of war wreckage are on adjacent Stirling. No vehicles or roads are found on these remote islands, and all travel is by foot or canoe. Although few visitors get this far, there are weekly Solomon Airlines flights from Gizo (SI$230) and Honiara (SI$600). Mr. R. Adrian (aka "Queensland" because his grandfather was blackbirded to Australia) has set up **Eco-Tourist Lodge** here. It's about SI$115 including meals, and information may be available from Adventure Sports in Gizo.

Choiseul Province

Choiseul (pronounced Choysle), which separated from Western Province in 1991, is far more closely linked to the Shortlands and Gizo than to distant Honiara. At 2,971 square km, Choiseul is the fifth-largest island in the Solomons. In 1768, French explorer Louis-Antoine de Bougainville named Choiseul after a French minister, but traditionally the island is known as Lauru. Lots of footpaths cross central Choiseul, for instance Sasamungga to Susuka, but a guide would be essential. The new provincial capital, **Taro**, is on the tiny airport island in Choiseul Bay, near the northwest end of the island. Choiseul Bay is an interesting little place worth a two-day visit.

The airstrip cuts across Taro from north to south, and all of the offices, shops, houses, and the wharf are on the east side of the island facing the mainland. In wet weather there are many mosquitoes, in dry weather water shortages. Taro's shoreline consists of mangroves alternating with white sandy beaches. Watch the sun set over the Shortland Islands and Bougainville from the small beach near the south end of the airstrip. Dogs are not allowed on Taro.

The locals often take their motorized canoes a couple of km up the winding Sui River directly east of Taro to a high cascade where they collect fresh water, do their washing, and have a swim. If you offer to supply five liters of petrol, it shouldn't be that hard to convince someone to go. It's a scenic 30-minute trip up the river between the mangroves, and at low tide you might even spot the odd crocodile on a sandbank. These animals are thought to embody the spirits of ancestors, and are thus protected from hunters. In return, no crocodile attack has ever been recorded here.

Accommodations and Food

The **Provincial Resthouse,** the long yellow building overlooking the soccer field, 200 meters from Taro's airport terminal, is SI$40 per bed in the seven double rooms (SI$80 if you want a room to yourself). A shared kitchen is available in this new one-story building.

Billy's Resthouse (Billy Savevai, tel. 63129) is a comfortable private resthouse above the National Bank, almost adjacent to the air terminal. The four airy rooms with shared bath are SI$50 pp, and a common kitchen is provided downstairs. It's clean, and there's a generator in case the public electrical supply goes off. Billy is one of the chiefs of this area, and his outboard motorboat is available for trips.

Near Taro wharf are four or five small grocery stores with rice, noodles, tinned fish, and biscuits. A bakery is next to Billy's Resthouse.

On Tuesday and Friday mornings, a market forms near the wharf at Taro. On Saturday mornings, there's a small market near Choiseul Bay Secondary School at Tarekukure, just across the bay. If your luggage isn't overweight, bring food from Gizo or Honiara.

Getting There

Solomon Airlines flies direct to Choiseul Bay (CHY) from Gizo (166 km, SI$230) and Honiara (SI$593) twice a week.

The real way to "do" Choiseul, however, is to take a weeklong trip around the island on the fortnightly supply ship such as the *Lauru I.* You might visit up to 45 villages this way, some only for a few minutes to drop off passengers, some others for a few hours. As almost all the villages are on the coast, you get a good value for your money. Smaller boats like the *Ozama Twomey* arrive at Choiseul Bay from Gizo.

Vaghena

Since 1963, a large Gilbertese community has been resettled on Vaghena (Wagina) Island off the southeast end of Choiseul. The original Melanesian inhabitants of Vaghena were wiped out by headhunters from Choiseul. Vaghena's 78 square km of uplifted coral contain significant bauxite deposits considered not economically viable to mine. The remote Arnavon Islands in Manning Strait between Vaghena and Isabel are a nesting area for hawksbill turtles in November and December.

Solomon Airlines flies to Kagau Airstrip (KGE) on Vaghena once a week from Honiara (SI$439) and Gizo (SI$189). A Serbian cattle rancher named Eric lives on the small airport island Kagau and serves as the local Solomon Airlines agent. You can contact him by radio telephone, and it might be possible to arrange a place to stay. Kagau has lovely white sandy beaches, but the three villages on Vaghena are a 45-minute canoe ride southeast of Kagau.

Isabel Province

Isabel is perhaps the most peaceful large island in the Solomons. Named for Álvaro de Mendaña's wife, Isabel's 240-km-long northwest-southeast landmass is the longest in the Solomons, and at 3,665 square km, it's the third-largest island in the country. The indigenous name for Isabel is Bughotu. The jungly interior is thick with towering vine-clad trunks and umbrella ferns, forming a habitat for monitor lizards and an array of birds. Isabel has a unique tree-dwelling rat that can weigh up to a kilo and eats only nuts and fruit. On small islands such as Leghahana near Sisiga Point off the northeast coast are flightless megapode birds. Sadly, three-quarters of Isabel's forests have been stripped by Asian loggers despite strong local opposition.

Headhunters from Simbo and the Roviana Lagoon depopulated much of northern Isabel during the early 1800s, and today most of the inhabitants live in the southeast corner of the island, the point farthest away from New Georgia. As in Santa Cruz, most extended families on Isabel are matrilineal; descent and land pass through the mother. Some villages like Kia have quite an assortment of husbands from all around the Solomons! The unique Mere (women's) dance of Isabel is quite hypnotic to watch. One of the Pacific's rarest varieties of tapa originates on Isabel: stained pale blue with a leaf dye.

Most rural villages on Isabel have a simple leaf house to accommodate visitors, but only southwest Isabel is laced with footpaths from village to village. The 22-km road across Isabel from Kolomola near Buala to **Kaevanga** wharf on Ortega Channel is the longest on Isabel. From Kaevanga you can hike northwest along the coast to Susubona and Kilokaka. Otherwise, try to get a lift from Kaevanga to **San Jorge,** a really weird island where all the "spirits" of Isabel are supposed to be. Visit the vanishing lake, caves full of skulls, islands covered with snakes, etc. An elderly chief on San Jorge is able to call not only sharks but crocodiles as well. Sounds like fun, but it's actually very serious. There's a village on San Jorge, but it's uncertain how welcome visitors would be. Catholic Bishop Epalle was murdered here in 1845.

Southeast down the coast from Kaevanga is Vulavu. A pleasant trail crosses the hills to Kamaosi Secondary School in two hours and continues on to Tatamba, from where you should be able to catch a boat to Buala or Honiara. This same path splits at one point with that branch, ending up in Sepi—handy for transport in either direction. Aside from the government boats, quite a few fishing boats call at Sepi, and you might score a quick lift back to Honiara. Tatamba's a government station with a resthouse and post office. It's an easy three-day hike along the coast from Tatamba to Buala past lots of villages.

Southeast Isabel

The administrative center is at **Buala** (population 500) on the Maringe Lagoon in southeast Isabel. The seven-room **Mothers' Union Resthouse** (tel. 35035) in Buala provides accommodations with shared cooking facilities at around SI$43 pp. This Church of Melanesia-operated place is super friendly, provided you don't drink. The five-room **Provincial Government Resthouse** (tel. 35031) is SI$20 pp. The **Diocesan Resthouse** (tel. 35011, fax 35071) has nine rooms at SI$45 pp, and you can cook. A post office, Telekom center, police station, and a good hospital (tel. 35016) complete the amenities of Buala.

An hour's walk southeast of Buala is **Thitiro Falls,** where the Sana River falls straight into the sea. The river dries up during the dry season. Another hour or two inland from the falls is Tirotonga village, with a sweeping view of the entire Maringe Lagoon and even Malaita. You can also climb Mt. Kubonitu (1,392 meters), just southwest of Buala and the highest peak on Isabel.

Northwest Isabel

The reefs and lagoons of northwest Isabel are pristine and teem with fish and dolphins, but beware of crocodiles. **Kia,** a large village (two stores, clinic) on Austria Sound at the northwest end of Isabel, is perhaps the most interesting on Isabel. The Kia people once worshiped the stars and sacrificed the bodies of slaves to protective sharks. Some of Kia's houses are built on the steep hills surrounding the bay, but most are on stilts over the lagoon. The people visit their gardens on other small islands in the lagoon by canoe. There are virtually no roads at the northwest corner of Isabel, and even trails are rare. Government boats sailing around Isabel often spend the night at Kia, and 12 hours is enough at a place where you can't walk far. There's no connection between Kia and Vaghena Island.

Transportation

Solomon Airlines has flights from Honiara (156 km, SI$223) three times a week to the airstrip (FRE) on Fera, a four-km-long offshore island from which motorized canoes cross to Buala (SI$10 pp).

Ships ply between Honiara and Buala about weekly. One especially attractive stop is Furona Island halfway down the west coast. Only Buala, Kia, Thiamba, and Keavanga have wharves.

Makira/Ulawa Province

Makira (San Cristobal) has some level land in the north, but the south coast falls precipitously to the sea. **Makira Harbor,** on the southwest coast, is the most secure anchorage in the Solomons, and **Star Harbor,** at the east end of the island, is also good. The best surfing beach in the Solomons (June–Nov.) is at Olosu'u on **Ulawa Island** between Makira and Malaita. There's no reef off the white beach at this picturesque location.

In 1595, the *Santa Isabel,* one of the four ships of Mendaña's ill-fated second expedition, became separated from the others at Santa Cruz. It sailed on to Makira, where passengers and crew camped on a hilltop at Pamua on the north coast, west of Kirakira (near the site of the present St. Stephen's High School). Their eventual fate is unknown.

Local craft items include carved figures, black inlaid ceremonial food bowls from Santa Ana, and talking drums. Ngali nuts from the canarium nut tree are harvested from a protected forest in the center of the island.

KIRAKIRA AND AROUND

Kirakira (population 1,000), the administrative center of the province, lies on the middle north coast of Makira. This verdant little town with huge trees shading its sleepy streets and inaccessible slopes rising behind is untouched by tourism. There are few specific attractions around Kirakira, just the chance to observe the quiet life of a small provincial settlement and enjoy some pleasant walks in the surroundings. The National Bank opposite the post office will change traveler's checks.

Sights

A Santa Ana-style custom house stands next to the soccer field in the center of Kirakira. Nearby, fiberglass canoes are pulled up on the shore by the concrete breakwater. A bit south is the mouth of Puepue Creek with a market alongside, and from here a long brown beach stretches west almost to the airstrip, a 20-minute walk away. At low tide it's worth going out on the reef beyond the airstrip to watch the waves surging through the deep rock crevices here.

The road behind the resthouse leads north to a large coconut plantation with a small white beach halfway to Honighoro Point, another nice walk.

Roads run along Makira's north coast in both directions from Kirakira, 18 km east to the Warihito River and about 100 km west to Maro'u Bay. The road west is well maintained as far as St. Stephens High School at Pamua, but west of Pamua it deteriorates and there are many rivers to ford (no bridges). Two-thirds of the way along, another road cuts south to Omaanihioro on the south coast. A settlement of Tikopian people is at Nukukaisi, 34 km west of Kirakira.

Taratarau village is a pleasant 20-minute walk east of Kirakira, past some huge betel nut trees. It's typical of rural leaf villages all around the island, and there's a small brown beach a bit beyond. The walking beyond Taratarau is not productive, as you can't see a lot from the unshaded road. The Ravo River, eight km east of Kirakira, must be forded, and from here a high brown beach stretches along Wanione Bay, east from Arohane. The heavy surf stirs up the sand and makes it unsuitable for swimming.

Uki and the Three Sisters are flat islands, yet still visible on the horizon from Kirakira. Crocodiles inhabit a pool on Malaupaina Island, largest of the Three Sisters. There's a lovely white sandy beach and coral lagoon at Pio Island, northwest of Uki. To hire a canoe from Kirakira to Pio, ask at the provincial fisheries office near the landing in Kirakira.

Accommodations and Food

The nine-room **Kirakira Provincial Resthouse** provides Spartan fan-cooled accommodations with shared bathing and cooking facilities at SI$30 pp. The resthouse has water problems. Also ask about the new guesthouse run by Obed Masina and family at Kirakira.

The market down by the river only has a good selection of foods in the morning. However, you can get betelnuts and coconuts all day, plus fish and chips, and often pineapples.

Transportation

Solomon Airlines (tel. 50198) flies from Honiara to Kirakira (237 km, SI$291) four times a week. Unfortunately, direct Kirakira-Santa Cruz flights are no longer offered. For good views, sit on the right side of the aircraft on the way from Honiara to Kirakira. Ngorangora Airstrip (IRA) is three km west of Kirakira by road, and you can easily hitch a ride into town.

The ship from Honiara arrives every two weeks (tickets sold on board). The ship also does trips right around Makira, or to Ugi, Ulawa, and the Three Sisters. Also ask about ships to Star Harbor, Santa Ana, and Santa Catalina, the most beautiful areas in the province. No wharf is available at Kirakira, and passengers and cargo must go ashore by canoe or aluminum longboat.

There are no regular passenger trucks with set fares around Kirakira, and the big trucks you see with loads of passengers in back are either privately owned or have been hired by someone. It's possible to hitch rides in these, and the favorite places to wait are in front of the store next to the Catholic church if you're headed east, or at the store between the hospital and public works garage if westbound.

STAR HARBOR

About 100 skilled carvers live in the Star Harbor area at the southeast end of Makira. The oldest and most expert bear the title *mwane manira*, and their work is avidly sought by museums and serious collectors. Visitors can buy directly from these craftspeople. Although full-sized canoes and houseposts are the most famous carvings, model canoes, decorated bowls, skull containers, human figures, and sharks are all crafted and sold.

Santa Ana

There's an excellent, reefless beach on Santa Ana where sea turtles come ashore. Traditional Natagera village is just behind; ask to see the war canoes and two custom houses rebuilt after a hurricane in 1971. Though only men are actually allowed inside the house, women get an adequate view through the open walls. The local carvers make unique wooden fish floats. There are two freshwater lakes on Santa Ana, and safe, secure anchorage for yachts on the west side of the island. Solomon Airlines flies directly here weekly from Honiara (312 km, SI$372) and Kirakira (76 km, SI$143), if operating. The airstrip on Santa Ana has been closed from time to time due to land disputes.

The Mako Mako Dance

This burlesque or mime is performed on Santa Catalina, a small island off the southeast end of Makira. On the village green the males, their bodies smeared with reddish clay, don hideous makeup and high conical masks. These dancers play the "men of the trees"—primitive jungle folk. The dance is accented by the dull notes of a conch shell. Suddenly the "canoe people" arrive from across the waters, and the "men of the trees" run in panic. Then a very realistic mock battle takes place between these two levels of Pacific Island civilization.

Temotu Province

Temotu Province, 665 km east of Honiara, is by far the most remote of the major island groupings. It's closer to the northernmost islands of Vanuatu than it is to the rest of Solomon Islands. Included are 43-by-24-km Santa Cruz, the Reef Islands, the Duff Islands, and the high islands of Utupua and Vanikolo. Tinakula, just north of Santa Cruz, is a surpassingly graceful, almost symmetrical, active volcano. The Reef Islands are composed of low coral terraces and sandy cays, while the others are mostly volcanic, with steep jungle slopes. Hundreds of kilometers southeast are tiny Tikopia and Anuta.

The Melanesians settled on the larger islands, the Polynesians on the smaller, more isolated outliers. *Lapita* pottery has been found on both Santa Cruz and the Reef Islands. A dozen languages are spoken in Temotu Province, and intriguingly, all of the non-Polynesian languages are Papuan.

The first European to arrive was the Spaniard Mendaña, who attempted to establish a colony at the south end of Graciosa Bay on Santa Cruz in 1595. Days later, when mutiny set in, Mendaña went ashore and executed his camp commander. After Mendaña himself died here on October 18, 1595, the settlement was abandoned. The crew, sick and dying, called Santa Cruz "a corner of hell in the claws on the devil." Of Mendaña's 378 men, death claimed 47 within a month. The next to arrive was Carteret, on August 12, 1767. As he anchored off Santa Cruz, he observed a "wild country and black, naked, woolly-haired natives."

The province is famous for its feather money, and a single roll can bear the red feathers of 3,000 scarlet honeyeaters stuck onto a coiled band as much as 10 meters long. The honeyeater is a very territorial bird, and to capture it the islanders would use a decoy to lure the bird to a branch where its feet would become stuck with a type of glue. After some feathers were taken, the bird would be released. Feathers from the gray Pacific pigeon were used as a backing. Feather money was traded for women and canoes from Santa Cruz to the Reefs and Tau-mako. Ten belts was the traditional price of a bride (widows half price).

SANTA CRUZ

Santa Cruz (Nendo) is by far the largest island of Temotu Province, its densely wooded hills rising to a height of 517 meters. The island has considerable reserves of bauxite. The mangrove-fringed south and east coasts contrast with the rocky northern shores, where fine beaches are often found. The usual rule here is "sun in the morning means rain in the afternoon, while rain in the morning means rain all day," but recently these islands have suffered prolonged droughts.

The administrative center of Temotu Province is at Lata (population 1,500), at the northwest corner of Santa Cruz on the west side of Graciosa Bay. Malo (Temotu) Island partly closes this bay to the north. The airstrip and wharf are both within minutes of Lata.

At Venga, on the sandy west shore of Santa Cruz, people perform custom dances unchanged since time immemorial. Dancers at Banua village wear traditional shell and feather ornaments as they dance and sing around a betel tree all night. August and September are the best months to see custom dancing on Santa Cruz, but no dancing at all takes place in Temotu Province during Lent (the 40 days before Easter).

Sights

The heavily populated area west of Graciosa Bay consists of a series of coral terraces, with the Lata on the first terrace 40 meters above the bay. The provincial government offices are on one side of the soccer field, a double row of small stores on the other. The people's gardens are on the main plateau to the south, 80 to 160 meters above sea level.

The **Lata Coconut Oil Mill** is next to the main wharf. Here copra is squeezed to produce oil to be sent to Honiara for use in the manufacture of soap. The leftover copra cake is used locally as animal feed. If you ask permission nicely, you'll be shown around.

At high tide there's good snorkeling over colorful corals off the white sandy beach at **Luowa,** north of the airstrip. Enter the water where you see the dugouts pulled up on the beach. The residents of Luowa are related to those of Malo village, just across West Passage on Temotu Island, and it's not hard to hitch a paddled ride across. The closest white sandy beach to Lata is at **Nela,** a small collection of houses just south of the west end of the airstrip.

The seven-km road south along the west side of Graciosa Bay passes 14 beautifully situated villages. Each day the villagers scale the forested cliffs behind the coastal strip to plant taro, sweet potatoes, bananas, pineapples, green peppers, pumpkins, manioc, and cabbage to feed their families or to sell at Lata market. Most of the villages have a dancing circle visible from the main road, where dancers adorn themselves with shell and feather ornaments on important holidays such as Second Appointed Day (June 8). Just beyond **Pala,** the southernmost village and site of Mendaña's camp in 1595, is a clear freshwater pool fed by springs draining much of the interior plateau. Swimming is not allowed in the pool itself, which supplies Lata with drinking water, but it's possible to bathe a bit downstream.

A trail across to **Nea** on the south coast begins just beyond the point where the main road crosses the stream from the pool. This eventually joins a forestry road and it's possible to return to Lata by truck over the plateau. This would be too much to accomplish in one day, but it should be possible to spend the night at Nea. Several local men at Nea make tapa cloth as part of an ecotourism project.

Continuing our walk around Graciosa Bay, vehicular traffic comes to an end at the Luembalele River, a few hundred meters beyond the Nea trail. If there hasn't been too much rain, you can wade across the river mouth in knee deep water at low tide, and continue north up the east side of Graciosa Bay to **Luesalo** (Shaw Point), where Levers Pacific Timbers once loaded logs and had a sawmill. The Anglican bishop still resides here. Luesalemba High School is around on the north coast.

For a striking view of Tinakula rising above the treetops of Malo Island, walk inland about three km on the road from the radio towers in Lata to the top of the plateau. The road continues south past many bush gardens and tracks leading down to isolated coastal settlements such as Nea.

Another good hike follows the west coast road three km to **Venga,** a lovely village on a palm-fringed white beach. Two dancing circles are beside the road through the village, and there's an excellent view of Tinakula from here. Several more fine white beaches are south of Venga, and lush rainforests on the steep side of the plateau.

An anchor allegedly from one of Mendaña's ships lies on the south side of **Nemba** village, on the coast eight km southwest of Venga. Of course, it's of much more recent origin, yet the villagers still demand custom fees as high as SI$200 just to set eyes on it. Thus it's prudent to show no interest at all if you happen to pass through Nemba. An excited crowd will gather if you approach the anchor, or even stop to look at it from the main road, and you'll probably end up having to pay something, so take care.

The coastal road ends at **Banyo,** and only a coastal footpath goes on to Nea. A footpath climbs up onto the plateau from Banyo, allowing a return to Lata by the plateau road for a full-day circle trip. It's also possible to climb up onto the plateau from Nemba and this would be much shorter than going via Banyo, if you can avoid getting ensnared in the anchor scam.

At the entrance to Carlisle Bay on the north shore of Santa Cruz is an overgrown memorial to Commodore Goodenough, killed here in 1875. The scenic white beach and good yacht anchorage are Carlisle Bay's other attractions.

Canoe your way to Nangu on the south coast, where there's a damaged wharf, store, radio operator, etc. Temotu Noi Island, just 15 minutes from Nangu by outboard, has a crocodile-infested freshwater lake.

Accommodations

The Temotu Development Authority operates the **Lata Resthouse** (tel. 53145, fax 53174), at the end of the road to the left of the SIBC Santa Cruz studio. The four rooms with shared bath, cooking facilities, and fridge are SI$30 pp. There are chronic water problems here, and some of the rooms have awful sagging beds. No fans are provided. Otherwise it's in a nice hilltop location and is fine. You could have difficulty finding the caretaker to get a room unless you booked ahead.

The best place to stay is the new **Diocese of Temotu Transit House** (tel. 53068, fax 53092), a 24-room conference center operated by the Church of Melanesia at Luowa, a 20-minute walk from the airport terminal toward the beach. In addition to the double rooms, there are four large 20-bed dormitories, and cooking facilities are provided. Information is available at the church bookstore next to the National Bank in Lata.

Lata's only real hotel is **Luelta Resort** (tel. 53144), 100 meters south of the main wharf, run by the Solomon Airlines agent, Simon Barclay. The 12 small rooms in this two-story building are SI$35 pp. Each has a fan, but the toilets and showers are in a separate block. Cooking facilities are not provided, but meals are served. Bring insect repellent. On weekends the Luelta's bar is the favorite local drinking place, and to avoid loud music or video noise, you should ask for an upstairs room on the side facing away from the restaurant. If you find the atmosphere in the bar insalubrious, you can sit and drink on the upstairs balcony, still enjoying a good view of everything.

Brown Teai, nicknamed "Paul," runs a resthouse at Freshwater Point, 50 meters north of the wharf via a footpath along the shore. There's a small beach just below the rocks and a cooling sea breeze, but the facilities are basic (SI$30 pp). Gas cooking and electric lighting may or may not be available. Still, it's very friendly, and the location is the nicest of any of Lata's places to stay.

Food

George Paia's **PLGP Snack Shop** (tel. 53095), among the row of small grocery shops facing the soccer field, theoretically opens Monday to Saturday 0600–2200.

Some fruit and vegetables are also sold under the large mango tree across the street from the National Bank up on the plateau (check again in the afternoon when people return from their gardens). More of the same is also sold every Wednesday and Saturday morning, when a small produce market forms under the trees near the

wharf. The Fisheries Department by the wharf sells fresh fish.

Services

The National Bank has an agency at Lata that changes foreign currency. The immigration office, between the hospital and the Telekom dish up on the plateau, will give visa extensions, and yachts can check in and out here. If they're closed, ask at the police station on the next corner.

At last report, the only public email connection in Temotu Province was Kati Pfnet (weekdays 0800–1600; kati@pipolfastaem.gov.sb), at Kati Primary School up the hill between Moneu and Mbanua villages, a half-hour walk from Lata. They charge SI$3 to send a message or SI$.50 to receive. Ask for the operators Christina or Hellen who live nearby.

Transportation

Solomon Airlines (tel. 53157) arrives at Santa Cruz (SCZ) weekly from Honiara (647 km, SI$721). The flights are often full. Overweight luggage is SI$9 a kilo. Solomon Airlines has an office (usually closed) 150 meters east of the airport terminal.

Ships tie up to the wharf on the west side of Graciosa Bay just below Lata. The MV *Temotu* of the Temotu Shipping Line plies between Honiara and Temotu Province once or twice a month (SI$171/184/196 economy/second/first class).

Ask around the wharf for outboards to Nangu or the Reef Islands and contribute for gas. Fisheries near the wharf rent out their large motorized canoe with driver.

OTHER ISLANDS

The Reef Islands

These low coral islands, 70 km northeast of Graciosa Bay, have long sandy beaches and no malaria. The inhabitants are mostly Melanesians, excepting the Polynesians on tiny Nifiloli and Pileni, as well as Nupani Island to the northwest. Nalogo, a tiny islet near Nupani, is home to tens of thousands of sea birds. Gnimbanga or Temoa Island has a series of caverns containing freshwater pools. Anglican bishop J.C. Patteson was murdered on Nukapu in 1871 after a black-birding ship spread ill will through the area.

One of the remotest outer island resorts in the South Pacific is the **Ngarando Faraway Resort** (tel. 53072, H4E241@sailmail.com) on Pigeon Island, Mohawk Bay. The accommodations on offer are Ngarando House, a European-style bungalow with two bedrooms at SI$270/425/585 single/double/triple; and Nanivo Cottage, a leaf house costing slightly less. Both units have shower, toilet, and cooking facilities. Meals with the host family cost SI$36/45/68 for breakfast/lunch/dinner (add 10 percent tax to all charges). Cash payment only will be accepted. Videos are shown for a small fee, and the resort's satellite dish picks up TV stations from around the world. Snorkeling gear, canoes, and outboards are provided free (you pay only for the gas). There's excellent snorkeling, and scuba-diving gear is for rent (certification card required).

Ngarando is run by the Hepworth clan, including twin brothers Bressin and Ross and their mother Diana, a colorful bunch of genuine South Seas characters who've been here longer than anyone can remember. In 1997, Ross Hepworth was elected president of Temotu Province. The Hepworth's general store sells local vegetables, fresh fruit and fish, canned groceries, and other trade goods as if this were still the 19th century. The wild parrots add to Pigeon Island's veritable Robinson Crusoe air.

Transfers from Graciosa Bay to Pigeon Island are by motorized canoe, a three-hour, 100-km trip, costing SI$675/810/900 for one/two/three persons. Construction of an airstrip on adjacent Lomlom Island has been pending for years. Check in Honiara for a ship direct to Mohawk Bay.

The Duff Islands

The Duff Islands, 88 km northeast of the Reef Islands, consist of nine small volcanic islands in a line 27 km long. Taumako Island, the largest, is 366 meters high. The inhabitants are Polynesian.

Vanikolo

This Melanesian volcanic island (also called Vanikoro) was stripped of its kauri trees by an Australian firm earlier this century. Both ships of the La Pérouse expedition, the *Boussole* and the *Astrolabe,* were wrecked on the reef at Vanikolo during a terrible storm in 1788. Despite a search for La Pérouse by d'Entrecasteaux four years later, his fate was unknown to the world for four decades until Irish sea captain Peter Dillon happened upon the remains in 1826 and solved the mystery (Dillon was knighted by the French government and given a pension for his efforts). Two years later, Dumont d'Urville visited Vanikolo, recovered some cannon and anchors, and set up a memorial to La Pérouse on the south side of the island.

The two wrecked French frigates are about 500 meters apart on the northwest side of the island. From the wreckage, archaeologists have theorized that the *Boussole* dropped its anchors as it was driven toward the reef; the ship swung round and had its stern ripped apart. Evidently, the *Astrolabe* tried to go through a false pass nearby in an attempt to rescue the crew of the first ship from behind, but was also wrecked. The Vanikolo people told Peter Dillon how the French survivors had built a small ship from the wreckage and sailed away. Their eventual fate has never been learned, and even today expeditions continue to visit Vanikolo in search of relics of this dramatic episode in Pacific history.

TIKOPIA AND ANUTA

Tikopia

This three-by-five-km dot in the ocean, 120 km southwest of the nearest other dot (Anuta), is an ancient volcano with a crater lake, Te Roto, rising to 366 meters. Pandanus trees surround the brackish lake waters, which are home to ducks and fish. Tikopia and Anuta are the southern and eastern limits of betel chewing in the Pacific. The inhabitants of both islands are Polynesians who arrived in planned expeditions from Wallis Island some 14 generations ago. Wallis itself was colonized from Tonga, thus this is an outpost of the old Tongan culture. Anthropologist Raymond Firth did fieldwork here in 1928–1929, and his book *We, The Tikopia* is still the classic on the island. Firth returned in 1952 and wrote *Social Change in Tikopia.*

Tikopia is ruled by four chiefs. Until recently

these chiefs did not recognize the central government, but now the number-two chief, Ariki Tafua, has indicated his willingness to submit, much to the fury of the other three. The British inserted a clause in the Solomon Islands constitution asserting that Tikopia and Anuta would be self-governing until the chiefs jointly decided to integrate with the rest of the country, and there will probably be a legal challenge if Honiara attempts to take control on the basis of only one "yes" vote.

Shops, government offices, and police don't exist on Tikopia, though there is a well-equipped clinic at Faea and a two-way radio. Visitors can usually stay at the nurse's house near the clinic for a small fee. The reef is the only toilet. Take care with the amiable chief of Faea District and his family, as they're out to get what they can—be it in the nicest way—and will give a distorted view of the place. Spend more time in Ravenga and Namo districts; the three chiefs of Ravenga are all very welcoming.

There's no electricity, all the houses are traditional, and the ground is cultivated with sticks. As a precaution against famine, food is fermented in the ground for up to two years. The dead used to be buried inside the houses and provided with food, but missionaries have stopped that practice. Some of the teenage girls still use lime to bleach their hair blonde, and many of the men wear their hair, along with their beards, at maximum length. Many are tattooed and wear tapa loincloths. The women cut their hair very short. Most Tikopians go topless.

Now the church and government schools are educating the young in another culture, and Tikopia's traditional life is starting to die. Materialism is catching on, and the children don't feel comfortable with their parents. The chiefs tried to outlaw bras and long trousers, but those responsible for enforcing this decision were ineffectual, and the younger generation now wears western dress.

Yachties sometimes visit Tikopia without clearing Solomon Islands Customs. They're allowed to stay if they present each of the four chiefs a nice gift, such as four-gallon drums of kerosene, lanterns, flashlights, bush knives, files, axes, spades, fishing nets, mosquito nets, spear guns and rubbers, or perfume.

Very few people speak English; Pidgin or a Polynesian language are more useful. It's forbidden to purchase old artifacts from the people; if you do, the chiefs will confiscate the goodies. Bring mosquito repellent.

Anuta

Anuta is the easternmost inhabited island of the Solomons. It's less than a kilometer across and 65 meters high. The people speak a language related to Samoan, and it's ruled by two traditional chiefs whose genealogies go back to the 16th century. Radiocarbon dating reveals that the first habitation was around 900 B.C. Anuta was abandoned around A.D. 500, only to be resettled a few centuries later. Like Tikopia, the influence of the Solomon Islands government is minimal here, and many people still dress in tapa, though some of the young now wear Western garb. Advance permission is required to stay on the island. Fatutaka Island (Mitre), 42 km southeast of Anuta, is uninhabited. In December 2002, Hurricane Zoe's 360 kph winds swept 10-meter-high waves onto Tikopia and Anuta.

BASIC SOLOMON ISLANDS PIJIN

aesboks: refrigerator
arakwao: white man
bagarap: broken down
bele ran: diarrhea
belo: noon
bia blong Solomon: betel nut
basta yu man!: damn you!
bulumakao: cattle
daedae: to be in love with
garem: to have
gudfala: nice
haomas?: how much?
hem i stap wea?: where is he (it)?
iu go baek!: go away!
kabilato: loincloth
kabis: edible greens
kago: luggage, goods
kaikai: food
kalabus: jail
kaliko: clothes
kasem: to reach
kastom kaliko: traditional dress
kastom mani: traditional currency
katkat wani: hey good lookin!
kokorako: chicken
klosap: near, close
kros: angry
liu: jobless
longwe: far

luksave: to recognize
mere: woman
mifala: us
mi no save: I don't understand
moabetta: better
naes bola!: hey good lookin!
nambaten: the worst
nambawan: the best
nating: no
pikinini: child
raosem: to clear out
saedgo: that side
saedkam: this side
samting nating: it doesn't matter
sapos: if
save: to know
save tumas: wise
smol rod: footpath
staka: plenty
susu: milk, breast
taem bifoa: the past
tanggio tumas: thank you very much
wanem: what did you say?
wantok: kinsperson
waswas: shower, swim
waswe: why
wetim: with
yumi: we

SOLOMON ISLANDS

Resources

Glossary

ahimaa: *see* umu

ahu: a Polynesian stone temple platform

anse: cove (French)

aparima: a Tahitian hand dance

archipelago: a group of islands

ariki: a Polynesian high chief; the traditional head of a clan or tribe; in Tahitian, *ari'i:*

Arioi: a pre-European religious society that traveled among the Society Islands presenting ceremonies and entertainments

atoll: a low-lying, ring-shaped coral reef enclosing a lagoon

Australasia: the region comprised of the South Pacific islands, Australia, New Zealand, New Guinea, and eastern Indonesia

Austronesian: all Pacific languages belong to this family, except for the Papuan languages spoken in some parts of Melanesia

balolo: in Fijian, a reef worm *(Eunice viridis),* called *palolo* in Samoa

bareboat charter: chartering a yacht without crew or provisions

bark cloth: *see* tapa

barrier reef: a coral reef separated from the adjacent shore by a lagoon

bêche-de-mer: sea cucumber; an edible sea slug; in Tahitian, *rori;* in French, *trépang;* see also pidgin

betel nut: the seed of the fruit of the betel palm *(Areca catechu),* chewed in Melanesia with a little lime and leaves from the pepper plant

blackbirder: A 19th-century European recruiter of island labor, mostly Ni-Vanuatu and Solomon Islanders taken to work on plantations in Queensland and Fiji.

breadfruit: a large, round fruit with starchy flesh grown on an **uru** tree *(Artocarpus altilis)*

BYO: Bring Your Own (an Australian term used to refer to restaurants that allow you to bring your own alcoholic beverages)

caldera: a wide crater formed through the collapse or explosion of a volcano

Caldoche: Early French settlers in New Caledonia, some of whom had originally been convicts. Now used to distinguish long-time residents of French origin from more recent arrivals called Métros.

cargo cult: Melanesian religious movement or movements promising salvation through the return of ancestors who will bring European-introduced goods (cargo) to their descendants

cassava: manioc; the starchy edible root of the tapioca plant

CFP: *Cour de Franc Pacifique;* the currency in the three French Pacific territories

chain: an archaic unit of length equivalent to 20 meters

ciguatera: a form of fish poisoning caused by microscopic algae

CMAS: Confédération Mondiale des Activités Subaquatiques; the French counterpart of PADI

coastwatchers: Allied intelligence agents who operated behind Japanese lines during WW II

coir: coconut husk sennit used to make rope, etc.

confirmation: A confirmed reservation exists when a supplier acknowledges, either orally or in writing, that a booking has been accepted.

copra: dried coconut meat used in the manufacture of coconut oil, cosmetics, soap, and margarine

coral: a hard, calcareous substance of various shapes, composed of the skeletons of tiny marine animals called polyps

coral bank: a coral formation more than 150 meters long

coral bleaching: the expulsion of symbiotic algae by corals

coral head: a coral formation a few meters across

coral patch: a coral formation up to 150 meters long

CUSO: Canadian University Students Overseas, the Canadian equivalent of the Peace Corps

custom owner: traditional tribal or customary owner based on usage

cyclone: Also known as a hurricane (in the Caribbean) or typhoon (in Japan). A tropical storm that rotates around a center of low atmospheric pressure; it becomes a cyclone when its winds reach force 12 or 64 knots. At sea the air will be filled with foam and driving spray, the water surface completely white with 14-meter-high waves. In the Northern Hemisphere, cyclones spin counterclockwise, while south of the equator they move clockwise. The winds of cyclonic storms are deflected toward a low-pressure area at the center, although the "eye" of the cyclone may be calm.

dalo: see taro

deck: Australian English for a terrace or porch

desiccated coconut: the shredded meat of dehydrated fresh coconut

direct flight: a through flight with one or more stops but no change of aircraft, as opposed to a nonstop flight

dugong: a large plant-eating marine mammal; called a manatee in the Caribbean

EEZ: Exclusive Economic Zone; a 200-nautical-mile offshore belt of an island nation or seacoast state that controls the mineral exploitation and fishing rights

El Niño: a weather pattern occurring every four or five years, featuring wet weather in the east and drought in the west; often followed by *la niña* with drought in the east and wet weather in the west

endemic: native to a particular area and existing only there

ESCAP: Economic and Social Commission for Asia and the Pacific

expatriate: a person residing in a country other than his/her own; in the South Pacific such persons are also called "Europeans" if their skin is white, or simply "expats."

fa'afafine: the Samoan term for men who act and dress like women; called *mahu* in French Polynesia, *fakaleiti* in Tonga

FAD: fish aggregation device

fafa: a "spinach" of cooked taro leaves

fale: Samoan house; in Tahitian *fare*

farani: French; *français*

fautau: the highest formal representative of the Samoan people

filaria: parasitic worms transmitted by biting insects to the blood or tissues of mammals. The obstruction of the lymphatic glands by the worms can cause an enlargement of the legs or other parts, a disease known as elephantiasis.

fissure: a narrow crack or chasm of some length and depth

FIT: foreign independent travel; a custom-designed, prepaid tour composed of many individualized arrangements

fringing reef: a reef along the shore of an island

gendarme: a French policeman on duty only in rural areas in France and French overseas territories

GPS: Global Positioning System, the space age successor of the sextant

greenhouse effect: also referred to as global warming or climate change, the impact on the South Pacific will come in the form of the flooding of low-lying islands, the bleaching of coral reefs, more and stronger hurricanes, and frequent droughts

guano: manure of seabirds, used as a fertilizer

guyot: a submerged atoll, the coral of which couldn't keep up with rising water levels

Havaiki: legendary homeland of the Polynesians

hurricane: see cyclone

IDEA: International Diving Educators Association

jug: a cross between a ceramic kettle and a pitcher used to heat water for tea or coffee in Australian-style hotels

kanaka: a human being in both Polynesia and Melanesia; formerly used in the pejorative sense for "native"

kava: a Polynesian word for the drink known in the Fijian language as *yaqona* and in English slang as "grog." This traditional beverage is made by squeezing a mixture of the grated root of the pepper shrub *(Piper methysticum)* and cold water through a strainer of hibiscus-bark fiber.

knot: about three kilometers per hour

kumara: sweet potato *(Ipomoea batatas)*

lagoon: an expanse of water bounded by a reef

langi: a megalithic tomb for early Tonga kings, in the form of a stepped limestone pyramid

Lapita pottery: pottery made by the ancient Polynesians from 1600 to 500 B.C.

laplap: see pareu

lavalava: see pareu

lava tube: a conduit formed as molten rock continues to flow below a cooled surface during the growth of a lava field. When the eruption ends, a tunnel is left with a flat floor where the last lava hardened.

LDS: Latter-day Saints; the Mormons

leeward: downwind; the shore (or side) sheltered from the wind; as opposed to windward

lei: a garland, often of fresh flowers, but sometimes of paper, shells, etc., hung about the neck of a person being welcomed or feted

le truck: a truck with seats in back, used for public transportation on Tahiti

live-aboard: a tour boat with cabin accommodation for scuba divers

LMS: London Missionary Society; a Protestant group that spread Christianity from Tahiti (1797) across the Pacific

maa Tahiti: Tahitian food

mahimahi: dorado, Pacific dolphinfish (no relation to the mammal)

mahu: a male Tahitian transvestite, sometimes also homosexual; in Tongan the term is *fakaleiti,* in Samoan *fa'afafine*

mairie: town hall (French)

makatea: an uplifted reef around the coast of an elevated atoll

mama ruau: actually "grandmother," but also used for the Mother Hubbard long dress introduced to Tahiti by missionaries

mana: authority, prestige, virtue, "face," psychic power, a positive force

manahune: a commoner or member of the lower class in pre-Christian Tahitian society

mangrove: a tropical shrub with branches that send down roots forming dense thickets along tidal shores

manioc: cassava, tapioca, a starchy root crop

maohi: a native of French Polynesia

Maori: the Polynesians of New Zealand and the Cook Islands

marae: a Tahitian temple or open-air cult place, called *me'ae* in the Marquesas; a Samoan village green *(malae);* a Maori meeting place. The Fijian word is *rara.*

masi: see tapa

matrilineal: a system of tracing descent through the mother's familial line

Melanesia: the high island groups of the western Pacific (Fiji, New Caledonia, Vanuatu, Solomon Islands, Papua New Guinea); from *melas* (black)

Micronesia: chains of high and low islands mostly north of the Equator (Carolines, Gilberts, Marianas, Marshalls); from *micro* (small)

MIRAB economy: an economy based on migration, remittances, aid, and bureaucracy

moai: an Easter Island statue

monoï: perfumed coconut oil

motu: a flat reef islet

nakamal: in the villages of Vanuatu, an open area surrounded by gigantic banyan trees, where men gather nightly to drink kava

namba: a penis wrapper or sheath worn by the Big and Small Namba tribes of interior Malekula, Vanuatu

NAUI: National Association of Underwater Instructors

NGO: Nongovernment organization

Ni-Vanuatu: an indigenous inhabitant of Vanuatu

Oro: the Polynesian god of war

ORSTOM: Office de la Recherche Scientifique et Technique d'Outre-Mer *ote'a:* a Tahitian ceremonial dance performed by men and women in two columns

overbooking: the practice of confirming more seats, cabins, or rooms than are actually available to ensure against no-shows

pa: ancient Polynesian stone fortress

Pacific rim: the continental landmasses and large countries around the fringe of the Pacific

PADI: Professional Association of Dive Instructors

palagi: a Polynesian word used throughout the region to refer to Europeans; also *papalagi, palangi;* in Tahitian *papa'a*

palolo: see balolo

palusami: a Samoan specialty of coconut cream wrapped in taro leaves and baked

pandanus: screw pine with slender stem and prop roots. The sword-shaped leaves are used for plaiting mats and hats. In Tahitian, *fara.*

parasailing: a sport in which participants are carried aloft by a parachute pulled behind a speedboat

pareu: a Tahitian saronglike wraparound skirt or loincloth; *lavalava* in Samoan, *sulu* in Fijian, *laplap* in Melanesia, *sarong* in Indonesian

pass: a channel through a barrier reef, usually with an outward flow of water

passage: an inside passage between an island and a barrier reef

patrilineal: a system of tracing descent through the fathers familial line

pawpaw: papaya

pelagic: relating to the open sea, away from land

peretane: Britain, British in Tahitian

pidgin: a form of speech with a limited vocabulary and simplified grammar used for communication between groups speaking different languages; also known as *bêche-de-mer, Bislama,* and Neo-Melanesian.

pirogue: outrigger canoe (French), in Tahitian *vaa*

PK: *pointe kilométrique,* a system of marking kilometers along highways in the French territories

poe: a sticky pudding made from bananas, papaya, pumpkin, or taro mixed with starch, baked in an oven, and served with coconut milk

poisson cru: raw fish marinated in lime (French), in Tahitian *ia ota;* in Fijian *kokoda;* in Japanese *sashimi*

Polynesia: divided into Western Polynesia (Tonga and Samoa) and Eastern Polynesia (French Polynesia, Cook Islands, Hawaii, Easter Island, and New Zealand); from *poly* (many)

punt: a flat-bottomed boat

pupu: traditional Tahitian dance group

purse seiner: a large fishing boat which circles a school of tuna with a net, which is then closed and lifted like a purse

Quonset hut: a prefabricated, semicircular, metal shelter popular during WW II; also called a Nissan hut

raatira: Tahitian chief, dance leader

rain shadow: the dry side of a mountain, sheltered from the windward side

Ratu: a title for Fijian chiefs, prefixed to their names

reef: a coral ridge near the ocean surface

sailing: the fine art of getting wet and becoming ill while slowly going nowhere at great expense

scuba: self-contained underwater breathing apparatus

SDA: Seventh-Day Adventist

self-contained: a room with private facilities (a toilet and shower not shared with other guests); the brochure term "ensuite" means the same thing; as opposed to a "self-catering" unit with cooking facilities

sennit: braided coconut-fiber rope

shareboat charter: a yacht tour for individuals or couples who join a small group on a fixed itinerary

shifting cultivation: a method of farming involving the rotation of fields instead of crops

shoal: a shallow sandbar or mud bank

shoulder season: a travel period between high/peak and low/off-peak seasons *siapo:* see tapa

SPARTECA: South Pacific Regional Trade and Economic Cooperation Agreement; an agreement that allows certain manufactured goods from Pacific countries duty-free entry to Australia and New Zealand

SPREP: South Pacific Regional Environment Program

subduction: the action of one tectonic plate wedging under another

subsidence: geological sinking or settling

sulu: see pareu

symbiosis: a mutually advantageous relationship between unlike organisms

tabu: also *tapu, kapu;* taboo, sacred, set apart, forbidden, a negative force

tahua: in the old days a skilled Tahitian artisan or priest; today a sorcerer or healer

tamaaraa: a Tahitian feast

Tamaha: daughter of the *Tu'i Tonga Fefine* (queen of Tonga)

tamure: a new name for Ori Tahiti, a very fast erotic dance

tanoa: a special wide wooden bowl in which *yaqona* (kava) is mixed; used in ceremonies in Fiji, Tonga, and Samoa

ta'ovala: a mat worn in Tonga by both sexes over a kilt or skirt

tapa: a cloth made from the pounded bark of the paper mulberry tree *(Broussonetia papyrifera).* It's soaked and beaten with a mallet to flatten and intertwine the fibers, then painted with geometric designs; called *siapo* in Samoan, *ngatu* in Tongan, *masi* in Fijian.

tapu: see tabu

taro: a starchy elephant-eared tuber *(Colocasia esculenta),* a staple food of the Pacific islanders; called *dalo* in Fijian

tatau: the Tahitian original of the adopted English word tattoo

tavana: the elected mayor of a Tahitian commune (from the English "governor")

tifaifai: a Tahitian patchwork quilt based on either European or Polynesian motifs

tiki: a humanlike sculpture used in the old days for religious rites and sorcery

timeshare: part ownership of a residential unit with the right to occupy the premises for a certain period each year in exchange for payment of an annual maintenance fee

tinito: Tahitian for Chinese

TNC: transnational corporation (also referred to as a multinational corporation)

toddy: The spathe of a coconut tree is bent to a horizontal position and tightly bound before it begins to flower. The end of the spathe is then split, and the sap drips down a twig or leaf into a bottle. Fresh or fermented, toddy *(tuba)* makes an excellent drink.

to'ere: a hollow wooden drum hit with a stick

trade wind: a steady wind blowing toward the equator from either northeast or southeast

trench: the section at the bottom of the ocean where one tectonic plate wedges under another

tridacna clam: eaten everywhere in the Pacific, its size varies between 10 centimeters and one meter

tropical storm: a cyclonic storm with winds of 35 to 64 knots

tsunami: a fast-moving wave caused by an undersea earthquake

tu'i: (Polynesian)—king, ruler

umara: see *kumara*

umu: an underground, earthen oven; called *ahimaa* in Tahitian, *lovo* in Fijian. After A.D. 500, the Polynesians had lost the art of making pottery, so they were compelled to bake their food, rather than boil it.

vigia: a mark on a nautical chart indicating a dangerous rock or shoal

volcanic bomb: lumps of lava blown out of a volcano, which take a bomblike shape as they cool in the air

VSA: Volunteer Service Abroad, the New Zealand equivalent of the Peace Corps

VSO: Voluntary Service Overseas, the British equivalent of the Peace Corps

VTT: *vélo à tout terrain;* mountain bike

wantok: a pidgin English term for a member of the same clan or tribe

windward: the point or side from which the wind blows, as opposed to leeward

yam: the starchy, tuberous root of a climbing plant

yaqona: see kava

zories: rubber shower sandals, thongs, flip-flops

Alternative Place Names

Alu: Shortland
Ambae: Aoba
Anatom: Aneityum
Aneityum: Anatom
Aoba: Ambae
Bellingshausen: Motu One
Choiseul: Lauru
Drehu: Lifou
Easter Island: Isla de Pascua
Easter Island: Rapa Nui
Ellice Islands: Tuvalu
Efate: Vate
Espiritu Santo: Santo
Falcon: Fonuafo'ou
Fonuafo'ou: Falcon
Futuna: Hoorn
Gaua: Santa Maria
Gilbert Islands: Kiribati
Hervey: Manuae
Hoorn: Futuna
Hull: Maria
Isabel: Santa Isabel
Isla de Pascua: Easter Island
Kanaky: New Caledonia
Kiribati: Gilbert Islands
Kolombangara: Nduke
Lauru: Choiseul
Lifou: Drehu
Lord Howe: Ontong Java
Luangiua: Ontong Java
Luganville: Santo
Maiao: Tapuaemanu
Makira: San Cristobal
Malekula: Mallicollo
Mallicollo: Malekula
Manuae: Hervey
Manuae: Scilly
Maré: Nengone
Maria: Hull
Maupihaa: Mopelia
Mohotani: Motane
Mopelia: Maupihaa
Moruroa: Mururoa
Motane: Mohotani
Motu Iti: Tupai
Motu One: Bellingshausen
Mururoa: Moruroa
Nduke: Kolombangara
Nendo: Santa Cruz
Nengone: Maré
New Caledonia: Kanaky
New Hebrides: Vanuatu
Niue: Savage
Olohega: Swains
Ontong Java: Lord Howe
Ontong Java: Luangiua
Penrhyn: Tongareva
Port Vila: Vila
Rapa Nui: Easter Island
San Cristobal: Makira
Santa Cruz: Nendo
Santa Isabel: Isabel
Santa Maria: Gaua
Santo: Espiritu Santo
Santo: Luganville
Savage: Niue
Scilly: Manuae
Shortland: Alu
Sikaiana: Stewart Island
Stewart Island: Sikaiana
Swains: Olohega
Taha'a: Uporu
Tapuaemanu: Maiao
Tokelau: Union Group
Tongareva: Penrhyn
Tupai: Motu Iti
Tuvalu: Ellice Islands
Union Group: Tokelau
Uporu: Taha'a
Uvéa: Wallis
Vanuatu: New Hebrides
Vate: Efate
Western Samoa: Samoa

Abbreviations

A$—Australian dollars
ATM—automated teller machine
B.P.—boîte postale
C—Centigrade
C$—Canadian dollars
CDW—collision damage waiver
CFP—French Pacific Franc
EEZ—Exclusive Economic Zone
E.U.—European Union
F$—Fiji dollars
4WD—four-wheel drive
km—kilometer
kph—kilometers per hour
LDS—Latter-day Saints (Mormons)
LMS—London Missionary Society
MV—motor vessel
No.—number

N.Z.—New Zealand
NZ$—New Zealand dollars
PK—pointe kilométrique
P.N.G.—Papua New Guinea
pp—per person
P.W.D.—Public Works Department
S$—Samoan tala
SDA—Seventh-Day Adventist
SI$—Solomon Islands dollars
STD—sexually transmitted disease
tel.—telephone
T$—Tongan pa'anga
U.S.—United States
US$—U.S. dollars
VHF—very high frequency
Vt.—Vanuatu vatu
WW II—World War Two

Suggested Reading

Guidebooks and Maps

Amsler, Kurt. *The French Polynesia Dive Guide.* New York: Abbeville Press, 2001. Describes and maps the territory's 27 top dives.

Bier, James A. *Reference Map of Oceania.* Honolulu: University of Hawaii Press, 1995. A fully indexed double-sided map of the Pacific Islands with 51 detailed inset maps of individual islands. Useful details such as time zones are included. The cartographer, James A. Bier, also produced the worthwhile *Islands of Samoa* map.

Cornell, Jimmy. *World Cruising Routes.* International Marine/Ragged Mountain Press, 2002. Details more than 500 cruising routes worldwide. Cornell's *World Cruising Handbook* covers yachting practicalities on 187 countries.

Hinz, Earl R. *Landfalls of Paradise: Cruising Guide to the Pacific Islands.* Honolulu: University of Hawaii Press, 1999. With 97 maps and 144 illustrations, this is the only cruising guide to Oceania's 75 ports of entry and many lesser harbors and anchorages.

Levy, Neil. *Moon Handbooks Micronesia.* Emeryville, CA: Avalon Travel Publishing. Covers the North Pacific countries of Nauru, Kiribati, the Marshall Islands, the Federated States of Micronesia, the Republic of Palau, Guam, and the Northern Marianas.

Parkinson, Susan, Peggy Stacy, and Adrian Mattinson. *Taste of the Pacific.* Honolulu: University of Hawaii Press, 1995. More than 200 recipes of South Pacific dishes.

Ryan, Paddy. *The Snorkeler's Guide to the Coral Reef.* Honolulu: University of Hawaii Press, 1994. An introduction to the wonders of the Indo-Pacific reefs. The author spent 10 years in Fiji and knows the region well.

Seward, Robert. *Radio Happy Isles: Media and Politics at Play in the Pacific.* Honolulu: University of Hawaii Press, 1998. An insightful and unexpected look at radio stations all across the Pacific.

Description and Travel

Bell, Gavin. *In Search of Tusitala.* London: Picador, 1994. A young Scottish journalists' experiences in the Marquesas, Tahiti, Hawaii, Kiribati, and Samoa in the footsteps of Robert Louis Stevenson.

Birkett, Dea. *Serpent in Paradise.* London: Picador, 1997. The candid tale of a British woman who spent several months on Pitcairn secretly preparing a memoir. In the end she became involved in an affair and was forced to flee on a passing tanker, leaving her book rather tarnished by negativity. Despite this, Birkett's book gives us a fascinating glimpse of contemporary Pitcairn.

Brunes, Evangeline. *Traveling the South Pacific Without Reservations.* Mechanicsville, Virginia: Penrith Publications, 2001. A timid grandmother's account of eight months on the road in Fiji, the Samoas, and Cook Islands.

Frisbie, Robert Dean. *The Book of Pukapuka, A Lone Trader on a South Sea Atoll.* Honolulu: Mutual Publishing. A delightful depiction of daily life on one of the Northern Cook Islands in the interwar period.

Heyerdahl, Thor. *Kon-Tiki: Across the Pacific by Raft.* Rand McNally, 1950. Heyerdahl believed that the mysterious disappearance of the pre-Incan Indians of Peru was related to the equally mysterious origins of the Polynesians. To add weight to his theory, he sailed some 6,500 km across the Pacific in a balsa raft.

Horwitz, Tony. *Blue Latitudes: Boldly Going Where Captain Cook Has Gone Before.* New York: Henry Holt & Company, 2002. A Pulitzer Prize-winning author journeys in the wake of the greatest of all Pacific explorers.

Lewis, David. *We, the Navigators.* Honolulu: University of Hawaii Press, 1994. A second edition of the 1972 classic on the ancient art of land-finding in the Pacific. Lewis' 1964 journey from Tahiti to New Zealand was the first in modern times on which only traditional navigational means were used.

Randall, Will. *Solomon Time: An Unlikely Quest in the South Pacific.* New York: Scribner, 2003. An English schoolteacher, who arrives in the Solomon Islands as a volunteer, ends up establishing a chicken farm on Rendova.

Stevenson, Robert Louis. *In the South Seas.* New York: Scribner's, 1901. The author's account of his travels through the Marquesas, Tuamotus, and Gilberts by yacht in the years 1888–1890.

Sylvain, Adolphe. *Sylvain's Tahiti.* Los Angeles, CA: Taschen America, 2001. Timeless black-and-white images of Tahiti by a romantic photographer who spent 45 years in the islands.

Theroux, Paul. *The Happy Isles of Oceania.* London, Hamish Hamilton, 1992. The author of classic accounts of railway journeys sets out with kayak and tent to tour the Pacific.

Thorpe, Nick. *Eight Men and a Duck: An Improbable Voyage by Reed Boat to Easter Island.* New York: Free Press, 2002. A humorous travel book introduced on www.nickthorpe.co.uk.

Geography

Nunn, Patrick D. *Oceanic Islands.* Cambridge, MA: Blackwell, 1994. A basic text on island formation, coral reefs, and sea level change.

Nunn, Patrick D. *Pacific Island Landscapes.* Suva: Institute of Pacific Studies, 1998. A leading geographer demystifies the geology and geomorphology of Fiji, Samoa, and Tonga, with emphasis on the origin of the islands.

Quanchi, Max. *Atlas of the Pacific Islands.* Honolulu: Bess Press, 2002. This attractive volume provides a collection of general maps, photos, and charts seemingly designed for high school use.

Ridgell, Reilly. *Pacific Nations and Territories.* Honolulu: Bess Press, 1995. A high school geography text that provides an overview of the region and also focuses on the individual islands. *Pacific Neighbors* is an elementary school version of the same book, written in collaboration with Betty Dunford.

Natural Science

Allen, Gerald R, and Roger Steene. *Indo-Pacific Coral Reef Field Guide.* El Cajon, CA: Odyssey Publishing, 1998. Essential for identifying the creatures of the reefs.

Doughty, Chris, Nicolas Day, and Andrew Plant. *Birds of the Solomons, Vanuatu, and New Caledonia.* London: A&C Black, 1999. A unique field guide to a fascinating area.

Goldin, Meryl Rose. *Field Guide to the Samoan Archipelago.* Honolulu: Bess Press, 2002. A beautifully illustrated field guide to the fish, wildlife, and protected areas.

Harrison, Peter. *Seabirds of the World.* Princeton, NJ: Princeton University Press, 1996. An ideal field guide to carry aboard a yacht or ship.

Lebot, Vincent, Lamont Lindstrom, and Mark Marlin. *Kava—the Pacific Drug.* Yale University Press, 1993. A thorough examination of kava and its many uses.

MacLeod, Roy M., and Philip F. Rehbock. *Darwin's Laboratory.* Honolulu: University of Hawaii Press, 1994. Evolutionary theory and natural history in the Pacific.

Myers, Robert F., and Ewald Lieske. *Coral Reef Fishes.* Princeton University Press, 2002. An inexpensive field guide to the marinelife of the tropical Pacific.

Nunn, Patrick D. *Environmental Change in the Pacific Basin.* Hoboken, NJ: John Wiley, 1999. This landmark text traces the physical development of the region and concludes with an examination of how environmental changes have impacted human lifestyles over the past 12,000 years.

Randall, John E., Gerald Robert Allen, and Roger C. Steene. *Fishes of the Great Barrier Reef and Coral Sea.* Honolulu: University of Hawaii Press, 1997. An identification guide for amateur diver and specialist alike.

Safina, Carl. *Song for the Blue Ocean.* New York: Owl Books, 1999. Safina chronicles the decline of the world's marine resources due to human activities—an enthralling and alarming read.

Veron, J.E.N. *Corals of Australia and the Indo-Pacific.* Honolulu: University of Hawaii Press, 1993. An authoritative, illustrated work.

Watling, Dick. *A Guide to the Birds of Fiji & Western Polynesia.* Suva: Environmental Consultants, 2001. The guide has detailed species accounts for the 173 species with confirmed records in the region, and notes a further 22 species with unconfirmed records. Copies can be ordered through www.pacificbirds.com.

Whistler, W. Arthur. *Flowers of the Pacific Island Seashore.* Honolulu: University of Hawaii Press, 1993. A guide to the littoral plants of Hawaii, Tahiti, Samoa, Tonga, Cook Islands, Fiji, and Micronesia.

Whistler, W. Arthur. *Wayside Plants of the Islands.* Honolulu: University of Hawaii Press, 1995. A guide to the lowland flora of the Pacific islands.

History

Denoon, Donald, et al. *The Cambridge History of the Pacific Islanders.* Australia: Cambridge University Press, 1997. A team of scholars examines the history of the inhabitants of Oceania from first colonization to the nuclear era. While acknowledging the great diversity of Pacific peoples, cultures, and experiences, the book looks for common patterns and related themes, presenting them in an insightful and innovative way.

Field, Michael J. *Mau: Samoa's Struggle for Freedom.* Auckland: Pasifika Press, 1991. The story of a nonviolent freedom movement.

Hough, Richard. *Captain James Cook.* W.W. Norton and Company, 1997. A readable new biography of Captain Cook that asserts that Cook's abrupt manner on his third journey may have been due to an intestinal infection that affected his judgment and indirectly led to his death at the hands of Hawaiian islanders.

Howe, K.R. *Nature, Culture, and History.* Honolulu: University of Hawaii Press, 2000. A wide range of contemporary Pacific issues are examined in this timely book.

Howe, K.R., Robert C Kiste, and Brij V Lal, eds. *Tides of History: The Pacific Islands in the Twentieth Century.* Honolulu: University of Hawaii Press, 1994. A comprehensive survey by specialists in a variety of fields.

Irwin, Geoffrey. *The Prehistoric Exploration and Colonization of the Pacific.* Cambridge, UK: Cambridge University Press, 1992. Geoffrey Irwin uses an innovative model to establish a detailed theory of prehistoric navigation.

Kirch, Patrick Vinton. *On the Road of the Winds.* Berkeley, CA: University of California Press, 2000. This archaeological history of the Pacific islands before European contact is easily the most important of its kind in two decades.

Maclellan, Nic, and Jean Chesneaux. *After Moruroa: France in the South Pacific.* Melbourne: Ocean Press, 1998. This timely examination of French colonialism from the French Revolution to the Matignon Accords and the end of nuclear testing also speculates on France's future in the region in light of the political changes in Europe.

McEvedy, Colin. *The Penguin Historical Atlas of the Pacific.* New York: Penguin USA, 1998. Through stories and maps, McEvedy brings Pacific history into sharp focus—a truly unique book.

Moorehead, Alan. *The Fatal Impact.* Honolulu: Mutual Publishing. European impact on the South Pacific from 1767 to 1840, as illustrated in the cases of Tahiti, Australia, and Antarctica. Much information is provided on Captain Cook's three voyages.

Samson, Jane. *Imperial Benevolence: Making British Authority in the Pacific Islands.* Honolulu: University of Hawaii Press, 1998. An insightful analysis of the impulses behind British imperialism.

Social Science

Ewins, Rory. *Linking the Islands: Pacific Implications of the Web.* A 2002 paper exploring the history of the Internet in the South Pacific and its potential as a vehicle for communication and change. The use of the web by academics, the news media, expatriates, governments, and political parties is described, and there's a revealing comparison of the cost of net access in Western and developing countries. The text is available online at http://speedysnail.com/pacific/linking.

Fitzpatrick, Judith M, ed. *Endangered Peoples of Oceania: Struggles to Survive and Thrive.* Westport, CT: Greenwood Publishing Group, 2000. An outstanding survey of the issues and concerns of Pacific peoples today.

Freeman, Derek. *Margaret Mead and Samoa: The Making and Unmaking of an Anthropological Myth.* Cambridge, Mass.: Harvard University Press, 1983. An Australian academic refutes Margaret Mead's theory of Samoan promiscuity and lack of aggression.

Huntsman, Judith, and Antony Hooper. *Tokelau, A Historical Ethnography.* Honolulu, University of Hawaii Press, 1997. This readable ethnographical study provides a wealth of background information on this little-known island group.

Kwa'ioloa, Michael. *Living Tradition: A Changing Life in Solomon Islands.* London: British Museum Press, 1997. The story of a Kwara'ae man who spent his childhood in the forests of Malaita before moving to Honiara, as told to Ben Burt. Distributed in North America by the University of Hawaii Press.

Lindstrom, Lamont. *Cargo Cult.* Honolulu: University of Hawaii Press, 1993. Strange stories of desire from Melanesia and beyond.

Lynch, John. *Pacific Languages: An Introduction.* Honolulu: University of Hawaii Press, 1998. The grammatical features of the Oceanic, Papuan, and Australian languages.

McDonald, Ross. *Money Makes You Crazy.* Dunedin, New Zealand: University of Otago Press, 2003. This 96-page book deals with custom and change in the contemporary Solomon Islands.

McCall, Grant. *Rapanui: Tradition and Survival on Easter Island.* Honolulu: University of Hawaii Press, 1994. A comprehensive summary of what is known about the island and its current inhabitants.

Mead, Margaret. *Letters from the Field.* Edited by Ruth Nanda. New York: Harper & Row, 1977. Describes Mead's experiences in American Samoa, Manus, the Sepik, and Bali. Mead's *Coming of Age in Samoa* perpetuated the old myth of South Seas free love.

Oliver, Douglas L. *Polynesia: In Early Historic Times.* Honolulu: Bess Press, 2002. This new account by veteran anthropologist Douglas Oliver outlines what is known about Polynesian life and culture at the time of first European contact.

Orans, Martin. *Not Even Wrong: Margaret Mead, Derek Freeman, and the Samoans.* Novato, CA: Chandler and Sharp, 1996. By carefully examining Mead's field materials, Orans found that her findings regarding Samoan female sexuality had been influenced by ideology and were thus "not even wrong."

Welsch, Robert L., ed. *An American Anthropologist in Melanesia.* Honolulu: University of Hawaii Press, 1998. The story of Albert Buell Lewis' 1909–1913 expedition, which laid the basis for the outstanding Melanesian collection at Chicago's Field Museum of Natural History.

Literature

Bermann, Richard A. *Home from the Sea.* Honolulu: Mutual Publishing. A reprint of the 1939 narrative of Robert Louis Stevenson's final years in Samoa.

Day, A. Grove, and Carl Stroven, eds. *Best South Sea Stories.* Honolulu: Mutual Publishing. Fifteen extracts from the writings of famous European authors.

Figiel, Sia. *Where We Once Belonged.* Auckland: Pasifika Press, 1996. The acclaimed first novel by a female storyteller, which recounts the experience of growing up in a Samoan village. Sex, violence, and the struggle for a personal identity appear in an island setting. Available in North America through the University of Hawaii Press. Figiel's second novel, *The Girl in the Moon Circle,* about Samoan life as seen through the eyes of a 10-year-old girl, is published by the Institute of Pacific Studies.

Hall, James Norman. *The Forgotten One and Other True Tales of the South Seas.* Honolulu: Mutual Publishing. A book about expatriate writers and intellectuals who sought refuge on the out-of-the-world islands of the Pacific.

Hall, James Norman, and Charles Nordhoff. *The Bounty Trilogy.* Boston, MA: Little Brown and Company, 1985. Retells in fictional form the famous mutiny, Bligh's escape to Timor, and the mutineers' fate on Pitcairn.

Hau'ofa, Epeli. *Tales of the Tikongs.* Auckland: Longman Paul Ltd., 1983. Reprinted by Beake House (Fiji) in 1993 and the University of Hawaii Press in 1994. An amusingly ironic view of Tongan life: "Our people work so hard on Sunday it takes a six-day rest to recover." The development aid business, exotic religious sects, self-perpetuating bureaucracy, and similar themes provide a milieu for the tales of the Tikongs: in Tiko nothing is as it seems. The University of Hawaii Press has also reprinted Hau'ofa's *Kisses in the Nederends,* a satire of life in a small Pacific community.

London, Jack. *South Sea Tales.* Honolulu: Mutual Publishing. Stories based on London's visit to Tahiti, Samoa, Fiji, and the Solomons in the early 20th century.

Maka'a, Julian. *The Confession and Other Stories.* Suva: Institute of Pacific Studies, 1985. A collection of nine short stories about young

Solomon Islanders attaining manhood. Though unpolished, the stories contrast the alienation of city life with social control of the village.

Maugham, W. Somerset. *The Trembling of a Leaf.* Honolulu: Mutual Publishing. The responses of a varied mix of white males—colonial administrator, trader, sea captain, bank manager, and missionary—to the peoples and environment of the South Pacific. Maugham is a masterful storyteller, and his journey to Samoa and Tahiti in 1916–1917 supplied him with poignant material.

Melville, Herman. *Typee, A Peep at Polynesian Life.* In 1842 Melville deserted from an American whaler at Nuku Hiva, Marquesas Islands. This semifictional account of Melville's four months among the Typee people was followed by *Omoo* in which Melville gives his impressions of Tahiti at the time of the French takeover.

Michener, James A. *Return to Paradise.* New York: Random House, 1951. Michener takes a second look at his wartime haunts in this collection of short stories. Michener's *Tales of the South Pacific,* the first of more than 30 books, opened on Broadway in 1949 as the long-running musical *South Pacific.*

Wendt, Albert. *Flying Fox in a Freedom Tree.* Auckland: Longman Paul Ltd., 1974. A collection of short stories in which the men cannot show fear or emotion, while the women appear only as sex objects.

Wendt, Albert. *Leaves of the Banyan Tree.* Honolulu: University of Hawaii Press, 1994. A reprint of the 1980 Wendt classic. Wendt was the first South Pacific novelist of international stature and his semiautobiographical writings are full of interest.

Wendt, Albert. *Pouliuli.* Auckland: Longman Paul Ltd., 1977. This is probably Wendt's finest novel, masterfully depicting the complex values and manipulative nature of Samoan society. No other book explains more about Samoa today.

Wendt, Albert. *Sons for the Return Home.* Auckland: Longman Paul Ltd., 1973. The story of a Samoan youth brought up amid discrimination in New Zealand, yet unable to readjust to the cultural values of his own country. The University of Hawaii Press distributes reprints of Wendt's early works, plus his 1995 novels *Ola* and *Black Rainbow.*

The Arts

Barbieri, Gian Paolo. *Tahiti Tattoos.* Los Angeles, CA: Taschen America, 1998. An outstanding reference on the Polynesian art of tattooing.

Bonnemaison, Joël, Kirk Huffman, Christian Kaufmann, and Darrell Tryon. *Arts of Vanuatu.* Honolulu: University of Hawaii Press, 1997. This book goes far beyond the visual arts reflected in the title to present a complete anthropological picture of the country. Some 383 illustrations accompany the text.

Herle, Anita, et al. *Pacific Art: Persistence, Change, and Meaning.* Honolulu: University of Hawaii Press, 2002. A collection of essays on themes currently shaping the study of Pacific art.

Kaeppler, Adrienne L. *Polynesian Dance.* Honolulu: Bishop Museum Press, 1983. Describes the traditional dances of Hawaii, Tahiti, the Cook Islands, Tonga, and Niue.

Kaeppler, Adrienne, C. Kaufmann, and Douglas Newton. *Oceanic Art.* Abrahams, 1997. The first major survey of the arts of Polynesia, Melanesia, and Micronesia in more than three decades, this admirable volume brings the reader up to date on recent scholarship in the field. Of the 900 illustrations, over a third are new.

Meyer, Anthony J.P. *Oceanic Art.* New York: Konemann, 1996. This two-volume work provides 800 stunning color photos of art objects from all across the Pacific.

St Cartmail, Keith. *The Art of Tonga.* Honolulu: University of Hawaii Press, 1997. The first book solely devoted to this powerfully fresh art style.

Thomas, Nicholas. *Oceanic Art.* London: Thames and Hudson, 1995. Almost 200 illustrations grace the pages of this readable survey.

Reference Books

Crocombe, Ron. *The South Pacific.* Suva: University of the South Pacific, 2001. Parameters, patterns, perceptions, property, power, and prospects in the 28 nations and territories of Oceania.

Craig, Robert D. *Historical Dictionary of Polynesia.* Metuchen, NJ: Scarecrow Press, 1994. This handy volume contains alphabetical listings of individuals (past and present), places, and organizations, plus historical chronologies and bibliographies by island group.

Douglas, Ngaire and Norman Douglas, eds. *Pacific Islands Yearbook.* Suva: Fiji Times Ltd, 1994. First published in 1932, this is the 17th edition of the original sourcebook on the islands. Although the realities of modern publishing have led to the demise of both the *Yearbook* and its cousin *Pacific Islands Monthly,* this final edition remains an indispensable reference work for students of the region.

Fry, Gerald W., and Rufino Mauricio. *Pacific Basin and Oceania.* Oxford: Clio Press, 1987. A selective, indexed Pacific bibliography, which actually describes the contents of the books, instead of merely listing them.

Lal, Brig V., and Kate Fortune, eds. *The Pacific Islands: An Encyclopedia.* Honolulu: University of Hawaii Press, 2000. This important book combines the writings of 200 acknowledged experts on the physical environment, peoples, history, politics, economics, society, and culture of the South Pacific. The accompanying CD-ROM provides a wealth of maps, graphs, photos, biographies, and more.

Motteler, Lee S. *Pacific Island Names.* Honolulu: Bishop Museum Press, 1986. A comprehensive gazetteer listing officially accepted island names, cross-referenced to all known variant names and spellings.

Booksellers and Publishers

Some of the titles listed above are out of print and not available in bookstores. Major research libraries should have a few, otherwise try the specialized antiquarian booksellers or regional publishers which follow. Most of these titles can be ordered online through www.southpacific.org/books.html.

Antipodean Books, P.O. Box 189, Cold Spring, NY 10516, U.S.A. (tel. 845/424-3867, fax 845/424-3617, www.antipodean.com). They have a complete catalog of out-of-print and rare items.

Bibliophile, 24A Glenmore Rd., Paddington, Sydney, NSW 2021, Australia (tel. 61-2/9331-1411, fax 61-2/9361-3371, www.bibliophile.com.au). An antiquarian bookstore specializing in books about Oceania. View their extensive catalog on line.

Bishop Museum Press, 1525 Bernice St., Honolulu, HI 96817-0916, U.S.A. (tel. 808/848-4135, fax 808/848-4132, www.bishopmuseum.org/press). They have an indexed list of books on the Pacific; a separate list of "The Occasional Papers" lists specialized works.

Bluewater Books & Charts, 1481 S.E. 17th St., Fort Lauderdale, FL 33316, U.S.A. (tel. 954/763-6533 or 800/942-2583, fax 954/522-2278, www.bluewaterweb.com). An outstanding source of navigational charts and cruising guides to the Pacific.

Book Bin, 228 S.W. Third St., Corvallis, OR 97333, U.S.A. (tel. 541/752-0045, fax 541/754-4115, www.bookbin.com). Their searchable catalog of books on the Pacific Islands lists hundreds of rare books, including some from the Institute of Pacific Studies.

Books of Yesteryear, P.O. Box 257, Newport, NSW 2106, Australia (tel./fax 61-2/9918-0545, www.abebooks.com/home/booksof yesteryear). Another source of old, fine, and rare books on the Pacific.

Books Pasifika, P.O. Box 68-446, Newtown, Auckland 1, New Zealand (tel. 64-9/303-2349, fax 64-9/377-9528, www.ak.planet.gen.nz/pasi fika/Pasifika.html). Besides being a major publisher, Pasifika Press is one of New Zealand's best sources of mail order books on Oceania, including those of the Institute of Pacific Studies.

Hema Maps Pty. Ltd., P.O. Box 4365, Eight Mile Plains, Queensland 4113, Australia (tel. 07/3340-0000, fax 07/3340-0099, www .hemamaps.com.au). Maps of the Pacific, Fiji, Solomon Islands, Vanuatu, and Samoa.

Institut Géographique National, 136 bis, rue de Grenelle, 75700 Paris, France (www.ign.fr). The publisher of excellent maps of French Polynesia, New Caledonia, and Wallis and Futuna, available at bookstores in Papeete and Nouméa.

Institute of Pacific Studies, University of the South Pacific, P.O. Box 1168, Suva, Fiji Islands (www.usp.ac.fj/ips). Their catalog, *Books from the Pacific Islands,* lists numerous books about the islands written by the Pacific islanders themselves. Some are rather dry academic publications of interest only to specialists, so order carefully. For Internet access to the catalog, see the University Book Centre listing below.

International Marine Publishing Co., www .internationalmarine.com. This branch of McGraw-Hill publishes all the books you'll ever need to teach yourself how to sail. They also have books on sea kayaking.

Jean-Louis Boglio, P.O. Box 72, Currumbin, Queensland 4223, Australia (tel. 61-7/5534-9349, fax 61-7/5534-9949, www.maritime books.com.au). An excellent source of new and used books on the French territories in the Pacific.

Mutual Publishing Company, 1215 Center St., Suite 210, Honolulu, HI 96816, U.S.A. (tel. 808/732-1709, fax 808/734-4094, www.mu tualpublishing.com). The classics of expatriate Pacific literature, available in cheap paperback editions.

Pacific Island Books, 2802 East 132nd Circle, Thornton, CA 80241, U.S.A. (tel. 303/920-8338, www.pacificislandbooks.com). One of the best U.S. sources of books about the South Pacific. They stock many titles published by the Institute of Pacific Studies.

Pan Pacifica, 4662 Sierra Dr., Honolulu, HI 96816, U.S.A. (fax 808/739-2326, www.Pan Pacifica.com). A source of recent official publications and research-level documents from museums and universities. Their primary clients are large research libraries.

Peter Moore, P.O. Box 66, Cambridge, CB1 3PD, United Kingdom (tel. 44-1223/411177, fax 44-1223/240559, www.aus-pacbooks.co.uk). The European distributor of books from the Institute of Pacific Studies of the University of the South Pacific, Fiji. Moore's catalog also lists antiquarian and secondhand books.

Serendipity Books, P.O. Box 340, Nedlands, WA 6009, Australia (tel. 08/9382-2246, fax 08/9388-2728, http://members.iinet.net.au/ ~serendip). The largest stocks of antiquarian, secondhand, and out-of-print books on the Pacific in Western Australia.

South Pacific Regional Environment Program, P.O. Box 240, Apia, Samoa (www.sprep.org.ws). They have a list of specialized technical publications on environmental concerns.

University Book Centre, University of the South Pacific, P.O. Box 1168, Suva, Fiji Islands (tel. 679/321-2500, fax 679/330-3265, www.usp bookcentre.com). An excellent source of books written and produced in the South Pacific itself.

University of Hawaii Press, 2840 Kolowalu St., Honolulu, HI 96822-1888, U.S.A. (tel. 808/956-8255, www.uhpress.hawaii.edu). Their *Hawaii and the Pacific* catalog is well worth requesting if you're trying to build a Pacific library.

Periodicals

Commodores' Bulletin. Seven Seas Cruising Assn., 1525 South Andrews Ave., Suite 217, Fort Lauderdale, FL 33316, U.S.A. (tel. 954/463-2431, fax 954/463-7183, www.ssca.org; US$57 a year worldwide by airmail). This monthly bulletin is chock-full of useful information for anyone wishing to tour the Pacific by sailing boat. All Pacific yachties and friends should be Seven Seas members!

The Contemporary Pacific. University of Hawaii Press, 2840 Kolowalu St., Honolulu, HI 96822, U.S.A. (www.uhpress.hawaii.edu, published twice a year, US$35 a year). Publishes a good mix of articles of interest to both scholars and general readers; the country-by-country "Political Review" in each number is a concise summary of events during the preceding year. The "Dialogue" section offers informed comment on the more controversial issues in the region, while recent publications on the islands are examined through book reviews. Those interested in current topics in Pacific island affairs should check recent volumes for background information.

Islands Business. P.O. Box 12718, Suva, Fiji Islands (tel. 330-3108, fax 330-1423, www.pacificislands.cc; annual airmailed subscription A$35 to Australia, NZ$55 to New Zealand, US$45 to North America, US$55 to Europe). A monthly newsmagazine with in-depth coverage of political and economic trends around the Pacific. It even has a "Whispers" gossip section that is an essential weather vane for anyone doing business in the region. Travel and aviation news gets some prominence.

Journal of Pacific History. Division of Pacific and Asian History, RSPAS, Australian National University, Canberra, ACT 0200, Australia (fax 61-2/6249-5525, http://sunsite.anu .edu.au/spin/RSRC/HISTORY/jphsite.htm). Since 1966 this publication has provided reliable scholarly information on the Pacific.

Journal of the Polynesian Society. Centre for Pacific Studies, University of Auckland, Private Bag 92019, Auckland, New Zealand (www.arts.auckland.ac.nz/ant/JPS/jour nal.html). Established in 1892, this quarterly journal contains a wealth of material on Pacific cultures past and present written by scholars of Pacific anthropology, archaeology, language, and history.

Pacific Magazine. P.O. Box 913, Honolulu, HI 96808, U.S.A. (www.pacificislands.cc; US$15 a year). This monthly newsmagazine, published in Hawaii since 1976, will keep you up to date on what's happening in the South Pacific and Micronesia.

Pacific News Bulletin. Pacific Concerns Resource Center, 83 Amy St., Toorak, Private Mail Bag, Suva, Fiji Islands (fax 330-4755, www .pcrc.org.fj: US$$15 a year in the South Pacific, US$20 in North America and Asia, US$30 elsewhere). A 16-page monthly newsletter with up-to-date information on nuclear, independence, environmental, and political questions.

Rapa Nui Journal. P.O. Box 6774, Los Osos, CA 93412-6774, U.S.A. (www.islandheritage.org; quarterly, US$40 a year in North America, US$50 elsewhere). An interesting mix of scholarly reports and local news of interest to Rapanuiphiles.

Surfer Travel Reports. P.O. Box 1028, Dana Point, CA 92629, U.S.A. (tel. 949/661-5147, fax 949/496-7849, www.surfermag.com/travel/pacific). Each month this newsletter provides a detailed analysis of surfing conditions at a different destination. Back issues on specific countries are available, including a 13-issue "South Pacific Collection" at US$65. This is your best source of surfing information by far.

Tahiti Pacifique. Alex W. du Prel, B.P. 368, 98728 Moorea, French Polynesia (tel. 689/56-28-94, fax 689/56-30-07, www.tahiti-pacifique.com; annual subscription US$85). For those who read French, this monthly magazine offers a style of informed and critical commentary quite unlike that seen in the daily press of the French territories.

Undercurrent. 125 East Sir Francis Drake Blvd., Suite 200, Larkspur, CA 94939-9809, U.S.A. (tel. 800/326-1896 or 415/461-5906, www.undercurrent.org; US$78 a year). A monthly consumer protection-oriented newsletter for serious scuba divers. Unlike virtually every other diving publication, *Undercurrent* accepts no advertising or free trips, which allows its writers to tell it as it is.

Discography

Air Mail Music: South Pacific Songs and Rhythms. Playasound, 2001. A collection of music largely from Tahiti, with a few pieces from Tuvalu, Solomon Islands, and Samoa also included. This recording and those which follow can be ordered through www.southpacific.org/music.html.

Bula Fiji Bula. New York: Arc Music, 2001. Music of the Fiji Islands, including famous *Isa Lei.*

Coco's Temaeva. Manuiti/Playasound, 1994. Founded by Coco Hotahota in 1962, Temaeva has won more prizes at the annual Heiva i Tahiti festivals than any other professional dance troupe. These recordings are from 1966–1972.

Fanshawe, David, ed. *Exotic Voices and Rhythms of the South Seas.* New York: Arc Music, 1994. Cook Island drum dancing, a Fijian tralala meke, a Samoan fiafia, a Vanuatu string band, and Solomon Islands panpipes selected from 1,200 hours of tapes in the Fanshawe Pacific Collection.

Fanshawe, David, ed. *Heiva i Tahiti: Festival of Life.* New York: Arc Music, 1994. Fanshawe has captured the excitement of Tahiti's biggest festival in these pieces recorded live in Papeete in 1982 and 1986. Famous groups led by Coco Hotahota, Yves Roche, Irma Prince, and others are represented.

Fanshawe, David, ed. *Spirit of Melanesia.* United Kingdom: Saydisc Records, 1998. An anthology of the music of Fiji, New Caledonia, Vanuatu, Solomon Islands, and Papua New Guinea. Recorded in 1978, 1983, and 1994.

Fanshawe, David, ed. *Spirit of Polynesia.* United Kingdom: Saydisc Records, 1995. An anthology of the music of 12 Pacific countries recorded between 1978 and 1988. More than half the pieces are from French Polynesia

and the Cook Islands.

Fanshawe, David, ed. *South Pacific: Island Music.* New York: Nonesuch Records, 2003. Originally released in 1981, this recording takes you from Tahiti to the Cook Islands, Tonga, Samoa, Fiji, Kiribati, and the Solomons.

Linkels, Ad, and Lucia Linkels, eds. *Fiafia.* The Netherlands: Pan Records, 1994. The traditional dances of 11 Pacific countries recorded during six field trips between 1979 and 1992. This and many other PAN Records compact discs by the Linkels of Tongan, Samoan, Cook Islands, Tuvalu, and Easter Island music form part of the series "Anthology of Pacific Music" and extensive booklets explaining the music come with the records.

Linkels, Ad, and Lucia Linkels, eds. *Hula, Haka, Hoko!* The Netherlands: Pan Records, 1997. A selection of traditional Polynesian dance music recorded on Easter Island, Cook Islands, Tuvalu, Rotuma, Tonga, and Samoa between 1982 and 1996.

Linkels, Ad, and Lucia Linkels, eds. *Viti Levu.* The Netherlands: Pan Records, 2000. This unique recording provides 20 examples of real Fijian music, from *Isa Lei* to Bula rock, plus four Indo-Fijian pieces. Recorded between 1986 and 1998, it's the best of its kind on the market.

Magic of the South Seas. New York: Arc Music, 2000. An anthology of music from Tahiti, the Marquesas, Tonga, and Fiji.

Te Vaka, The Canoe. New York: Arc Music, 2000. Te Vaka's dynamic interpretations of Tokalauan music and dance created a sensation during the 10-member band's 1997 European tour. A few New Age elements are entwined with the Pacific sounds in this delightful recording.

Internet Resources

Top 20 Pacific Websites

Asia Pacific Network
www.asiapac.org.fj

Journalist David Robie's portal to independent news media, progressive movements, environmental groups, and Pacific research sites.

Charting the Pacific
www.abc.net.au/ra/pacific/places/countries.htm

Via a clickable map, Radio Australia provides statistical data, country profiles, and an overview of the key issues in the island nations of the South Pacific.

Dive Adventures
www.diveadventures.com

This Australian scuba diving site provides detailed information on diving at eight Pacific destinations.

Journalist Michael Field
www.michaelfield.org

The New Zealand and Pacific correspondent for Agence France-Presse provides his illuminating stories on the region.

Map South Pacific
www.mapsouthpacific.com

South Pacific maps and travel guides to Tahiti, Fiji, Samoa, Vanuatu, Easter Island, and more. The De Rienzi Gallery displays 60 antique engravings.

Noonsite
www.noonsite.com

Jimmy Cornell's global site for cruising sailors featuring information of interest to anyone planning an offshore voyage around the South Pacific.

Pacific Islands Report
http://pidp.eastwestcenter.org/pireport

A joint project of several educational institutions in Hawaii, it's your best source of recent political and economic news from the islands. Around 15 stories are posted daily and you can browse through recent issues.

Pacific Magazine
www.pacificislands.cc

The online version of the region's two premier monthly magazines. Aside from the regular features, there's a daily news update and a useful annual almanac.

Pacific Peoples' Partnership
www.pacificpeoplespartnership.org

The site of an NGO working in solidarity with peoples of the South Pacific to promote their aspirations for peace, justice, security and sustainable development.

Pacific Studies WWW Monitor
http://coombs.anu.edu.au/pacific-www-monitor.html

This unique bibliography from the Australian National University offers independent scholarly reviews of online resources of significance to research, teaching, and communications in the field of Pacific Studies. It provides web surfers with a balance to the commercial tourism sites.

Pacific Travel Guides
www.pacific-travel-guides.com

A travel and accommodations guide including maps and pictures of Hawaii, Fiji, Cook Islands, French Polynesia, Samoa, Tonga, Niue, Tokelau, Tuvalu, Micronesia, Kiribati, and New Zealand.

South Pacific Employment
www.southpacificemployment.com

A website designed to help job seekers identify opportunities in the tourism, resort, and dive sectors, and to assist local businesses in finding qualified staff.

South Pacific Organizer
www.southpacific.org

Guidebook writer David Stanley provides mini-guides to South Pacific destinations, island maps, listings of films, music, and books, answers to FAQs, and links to numerous other travel sites relating to the South Pacific.

South Pacific Real Estate
www.southpacificrealestate.com

It can be revealing to peruse the listings of hotels and resorts currently for sale, as listed on this site.

South Pacific Tourism Organization
www.spto.org

The official site of the regional tourism body serving American Samoa, Cook Islands, Fiji Islands, Kiribati, New Caledonia, Niue, Papua New Guinea, Samoa, Solomon Islands, Tahiti, Tonga, Tuvalu, and Vanuatu.

Tahiti Explorer
www.tahiti-explorer.com

Here you can learn about black pearls, cruises, diving, flights, hotels, the weather, people and geography, etc. The photo albums and trip reports are a huge resource, and there's a travel forum.

Travelmaxia
www.travelmaxia.com

This Internet portal provides a vast amount of information on accommodations all across the Pacific. You're able to email the properties directly using the online forms—this is not a tour company.

Vanuatu A to Z
www.vanuatuatoz.com

It's great fun to browse the alphabetical listings on this "small guide to a tropical paradise." The quirky, personal observations, little known facts, and brilliant design make it unique.

Visiting the Pacific Islands
www.geocities.com/TheTropics/
Island/8000/

Young Dutch traveler Wouter Adamse made two extensive trips around the region, and through this personal site he shares his impressions and photos.

WWF South Pacific Program
www.wwfpacific.org.fj

News and information on environmental matters in the Cook Islands, Fiji, Papua New Guinea, and Solomon Islands.

Information Offices

Regional

South Pacific Tourism Organisation, Box 13119, Suva, Fiji Islands (tel. 679/330-4177, fax 679/330-1995, www.spto.org)

South Pacific Tourism Organization, 48 Glentham Road, Barnes, London SW13 9JJ, United Kingdom (tel. 44-20/8741-6082, fax 44-20/8741-6107, www.interfaceinternational.co.uk)

South Pacific Tourism Organization, Petersburg Strasse 94, D-10247 Berlin, Germany (tel. 49-304/225-6026, fax 49-304/225-6287, germany@spto.org)

French Polynesia

Tahiti Tourisme, B.P. 65, Papeete, 98713 Tahiti, Polynésie Française (tel. 689/50-57-00, fax 689/43-66-19, www.tahiti-tourisme.com)

Tahiti Tourisme, 300 North Continental Blvd., Suite 160, El Segundo, CA 90245, U.S.A. (tel. 310/414-8484, fax 310/414-8490, www.gototahiti.com)

Tahiti Tourisme, Level 1, 26 Ponsonby Rd., Ponsonby, Auckland, New Zealand (tel. 64-9/360-8880, fax 64-9/360-8891, www.tahiti-tourisme.co.nz)

Tahiti Tourisme, 12 Ann St., Surry Hills, NSW 2010, Australia (tel. 61-2/9281-6020, fax 61-2/9211-6589, www.tahiti-tourisme.com.au)

Pacific Leisure Group, 8th floor, Maneeya Center Building, 518/5 Ploenchit Rd., Bangkok 10330, Thailand (tel. 66-2/255-9966, fax 66-2/652-2850)

Tahiti Tourisme, Sankyo Building (No. 20) Room 802, 3-11-5 Ildabashi, Chiyoda-Ku, Tokyo 102, Japan (tel. 81-3/3265-0468, fax 81-3/3265-0581)

Oficina de Turismo de Tahiti, Casilla 16057, Santiago 9, Chile (tel. 56-2/251-2826, fax 56-2/233-1787, tahiti@cmet.net)

Tahiti Tourism, c/o CIB Group, 1 Battersea Church Rd., London, SW11 3LY, United Kingdom (tel. 44-20/7771-7023, fax 44-20/7771-7059)

Office du Tourisme de Tahiti, 28 Boulevard Saint-Germain, 75005 Paris, France (tel. 33-1/5542-6121, fax 33-1/5542-6120, www.voyageatahiti.com)

Fremdenverkehrsamt von Tahiti, Bockenheimer Landstrasse 45, D-60325 Frankfurt/Main, Germany (tel. 49-69/971-484, fax 49-69/729-275, www.tahititourisme.de)

Tahiti Tourisme, Piazza Caiazzo 3, 20124 Milano, Italy (tel. 39-2/6698-0317, fax 39-2/669-2648, www.tahiti-turismo.com)

Easter Island

Cámara de Turismo Isla de Pascua, Atamu Tekena s/n, Hanga Roa, Rapa Nui, Chile (tel./fax 56-32/550-055, www.turismo.rapanui.cl)

Cook Islands

Cook Islands Tourism Corporation, P.O. Box 14, Rarotonga, Cook Islands (tel. 682/29-435, fax 682/21-435, www.cook-islands.com)

Cook Islands Tourism Corporation, 2250 E. Imperial Highway, Suite 2000, El Segundo, CA 90245, U.S.A. (tel. 888/994-2665, fax 877/468-6643)

Cook Islands Tourism Corporation, 280 Nelson Street, Suite 202, Vancouver, BC V6B 2E2, Canada (tel. 604/301-1190, fax 604/687-3454)

Cook Islands Tourism Corporation, 1/127 Symonds St., P.O. Box 37391, Auckland, New Zealand (tel. 64-9/366-1106, fax 64-9/309-1876)

Cook Islands Tourism Corporation, P.O. Box H95, Hurlstone Park, NSW 2193, Australia (tel. 61-2/9955-0446, fax 61-2/9955-0447)

Niue

Niue Tourism Office, Box 42, Alofi, Niue (tel. 683/4224, fax 683/4225, www.niueisland.com)

Niue Tourism Office, P.O. Box 489, Newfarm, Queensland 4005, Australia (tel. 61-7/3252-3228 or 300/136-483, fax 61-7/3252-7522, niuetourism@bigpond.com)

Kingdom of Tonga

Tonga Visitors Bureau, Box 37, Nuku'alofa, Kingdom of Tonga (tel. 676/25-334, fax 676/23-507, www.tongaholiday.com)

Tonga Visitors Bureau, Box 18, Neiafu, Vava'u, Kingdom of Tonga (tel. 676/70-115, fax 676/70-666, tvbvv@kalianet.to)

Tonga Visitors Bureau, 41 Eastbourne Rd., Homebush West, Sydney, NSW 2140, Australia (tel. 61-2/9746-0898, fax 61-2/9746-3587)

Tonga Visitors Bureau, P.O. Box 24-054, Royal Oak, Auckland 1003, New Zealand (tel. 64-9/634-1519, fax 64-9/636-8973)

Tongan High Commission, 36 Molyneux St., London W1H 6AB, United Kingdom (tel. 44-171/724-5828, fax 44-171/723-9074)

Tonga Visitors Bureau, Italy (www.tongaturismo.info)

American Samoa

Office of Tourism, P.O. Box 1147, Pago Pago, American Samoa 96799, U.S.A. (tel. 684/633-1092, fax 684/633-2092, www.amerikasamoa.info)

Samoa

Samoa Tourism Authority, P.O. Box 2272, Apia, Samoa (tel. 685/63-500, fax 685/20-886, www1.visitsamoa.ws)

Samoa Tourism Authority, Level 1, Samoa House, 283 Karangahape Road, P.O. Box 68423, Newton, Auckland, New Zealand (tel. 64-9/379-6138, fax 64-9/379-8154, samoa@samoa.co.nz)

Samoa Tourism Authority, P.O. Box 361, Minto Mall, Minto, NSW 2566, Australia (tel. 61-2/9824-5050, fax 61-2/9824-5678, samoa@ozemail.com.au)

Tokelau

Office for Tokelau Affairs, Box 865, Apia, Samoa (tel. 685/20-822, fax 685/21-761)

Tuvalu

Ministry of Tourism, Trade, and Commerce, Private Mail Bag, Vaiaku, Funafuti, Tuvalu (tel. 688/20184, fax 688/20829, mttc@tuvalu.tv)

Tuvalu High Commission, P.O. Box 14449, Suva, Fiji Islands (tel. 679/330-1355, fax 679/330-8479)

Fiji Islands

Fiji Visitors Bureau, GPO Box 92, Suva, Fiji Islands (tel. 679/330-2433, fax 679/330-0970; www.bulafiji.com)

Fiji Visitors Bureau, P.O. Box 9217, Nadi Airport, Fiji Islands (tel. 679/672-2433, fax 679/672-0141, fvbnadi@is.com.fj)

Fiji Visitors Bureau, Suite 220, 5777 West Century Blvd., Los Angeles, CA 90045, U.S.A. (tel. 310/568-1616 or 800/932-3454, fax 310/670-2318, www.bulafijinow.com)

Fiji Visitors Bureau, Level 12, St. Martin's Tower, 31 Market St., Sydney, NSW 2000, Australia (tel. 61-2/9264-3399, fax 61-2/9264-3060, www.bulafiji-au.com)

Fiji Visitors Bureau, P.O. Box 1179, Auckland, New Zealand (tel. 64-9/376-2533, fax 64-9/376-4720, www.bulafiji.co.nz)

Fiji Visitors Bureau, 14th floor, NOA Bldg., 3-5, 2-Chome, Azabuudai, Minato-ku, Tokyo 106, Japan (tel. 81-3/3587-2038, fax 81-3/3587-2563, www.bulafiji-jp.com)

Fiji Visitors Bureau, Petersburger Strasse 94, 10274 Berlin, Germany (tel. 30/4225-6285, www.bulafiji.de)

New Caledonia

Nouvelle-Calédonie Tourisme, B.P. 688, 98845 Nouméa, New Caledonia (tel. 687/24-20-80, fax 687/24-20-70, www.newcaledonia tourism-south.com)

Destination Iles Loyauté, B.P. 343, 98845 Nouméa Cedex, New Caledonia (tel. 687/27-66-27, fax 687/27-48-27, www.iles-loyaute.com)

North Province Tourism, B.P. 115, 98845 Nouméa, New Caledonia (tel. 687/27-78-05, fax 687/27-48-87, www.tourismeprovince nord.nc)

New Caledonia Tourism, Suite 402, Level 4, 117 York St., Sydney, NSW 2000, Australia (tel. 61-2/9261-8688, fax 61-2/9261-8182)

New Caledonia Tourism, P.O. Box 4300, Auckland, New Zealand (tel. 64-9/585-0257, fax 64-9/585-0259)

Maison de la France, Landic No. 2, Akasaka Building 2-10-9 Akasaka, Minato-ku, Tokyo 107, Japan (tel. 81-3/3583-3280, fax 81-3/3505-2873)

Nouvelle-Calédonie Tourisme, 7 rue Général Bertrand, 75007 Paris, France (tel. 33-1/4273-2414, fax 33-1/4773-6989)

Vanuatu

National Tourism Office of Vanuatu, P.O. Box 209, Port Vila, Vanuatu (tel. 678/22685, fax 678/23889, www.vanuatutourism.com)

Solomon Islands

Solomon Islands Visitors Bureau, P.O. Box 321, Honiara, Solomon Islands (tel. 677/22442, fax 677/23986, www.visitsolomons.com.sb)

Solomon Islands High Commission, 19 Napier Close, Deakin, ACT, Australia (tel. 02/6282-7030, fax 02/6282-7040, www.solomon.emb.gov.au)

Index

Index

Acknowledgments

The nationalities of those listed below are identified by the following signs which follow their names: at (Austria), au (Australia), ca (Canada), ch (Switzerland), ck (Cook Islands), cl (Chile), cy (Cyprus), de (Germany), dk (Denmark), fj (Fiji), gb (Great Britain), gr (Greece), nl (Netherlands), no (Norway), nz (New Zealand), pf (French Polynesia), pn (Pitcairn), sb (Solomon Islands), se (Sweden), to (Tonga), us (United States), vu (Vanuatu), and ws (Samoa).

Some of the antique engravings by M.G.L. Domeny de Rienzi are from the classic three-volume work *Oceanie ou Cinquième Partie du Monde* (Paris: Firmin Didot Frères, 1836).

Special thanks to Dr. Patrick D. Nunn (fj) of the University of the South Pacific for correcting part of the main introduction, to Robert Suggs (us) for help with dating Polynesian prehistory, to Barbara Gaston (us), Francis Mortimer (nz), Lucy Powell (us), and Dulcie Wong (ca) for updating airfares, to Chantale Phan Thi Ngoc (pf) for the French Polynesia census results, to Paul Atallah (us) for doing a complete update of the Huahine section, to Betty Christian (pn) and Prof. Herbert Ford (us) for feedback on Pitcairn, to Georgia Lee (us), Conny Martin (cl), Grant McCall (au), and Shawn McLaughlin (us) for detailed feedback on Easter Island, to Elliot Smith (us) and Ron Crocombe (ck) for help with the Cook Islands, to Andrea Eimke (ck) for information on Atiu, to Jan Kristensson (ck) for updating Mangaia, to James Conway (us) for helping to revise the Tuvalu chapter, to Carolyn Fotofili (fj) for updating Vanua Balavu, to Alan Howard (us) and Kim Birkedahl (dk) for information on Rotuma, to Gabriel Teoman (at) for feedback on New Caledonia, to Mayumi Green (vu) for doing a thorough revision of the Espiritu Santo section, to David Leeming (gb) for information on Rennell Island and the Solomons in general, to Danny and Kerrie Kennedy (sb) for information on Gizo, to Gary Hawkins (gb) for extensive notes on five countries, to Wouter Adamse (nl) for detailed feedback on six countries, and to my wife Ria de Vos for her continuing assistance, suggestions, and support during the two and a half years it took to research and write this book.

Thanks to all of the following readers who took the trouble to write us letters about their trips:

J.D. Anderson (us), Paul Arnold (us), Christopher Bartlett (us), Susan Bejeckian (us), Judith Beldner (us), Ron Bently (ws), Linnea Berg (us), Larry Berkowitz (us), Inger Best (us), David Bishop (ca), Stephanie Boisson (pf), Rochard Bondurant (us), Claude and Martine Bordier (pf), Andrew Brown (fj), Steve Brown (ws), Christy Butterfield (to), Ed Candela (us), Lisa Carangelo (us), Lee Carsley (us), Les Charters (nz), Vijendra Chaudhary (fj), Rob and Susan Clemens (us), Larry J. Cohen (au), Jimmy Cornell (gb), Tony Cottrell (fj), Buford A. Crites (us), Marjorie Crocombe (ck), Nari Crocombe (ck), Nancy Daniels (us), John E. Davies (ca), Nick Deahl (gb), Kim and Dan Digardi (us), Feng Ding (us), Steve Evers (us), Warren Francis (fj), Mary T. Crowley (us), Heleen Curtis (us), Martine and Hayden Falloon (cy), Jono Feldman (us), Lee Fewster (au), Mark Frederick (us), Richard Gebert (ca), Fred George (us), Brendan Geeves (ws), Brenda Ger (nl), Cindy and Mark Gibbs (us), Michael Gildersleeve (us), Jean-Francois Giroux (ca), Sylvia Gaudet (ca), Bob Goddess (us), Chris Godfrey (ca), John Goese (us), Scott Graham (fj), Chuck Grobe (us), Sandra and Henk Gros (to), Jerome Guedj (pf), George Hadley (ws), Philip Hand (us), Merrill Hartman (us), Heinz Hermann (ch), Bob Hirsch (us), Anreas Holo (no), Roman Horoszewski (us), Arthur Hoyle (us), Gordon Hull (us), Suein Hwang (us), Carole Jacobs (us), Rob Jenneve (us), Lindsay Johnson (us), Lupe Johnston (us), Oscar Junzell (se), Karen and Paulo Kaiser (us), Ron Killian (us), Stacey King (au), Viola Koch (fj), Rolf Köpke (de), Edwin R. Koeppen (au), Dr. Siegrun Krauss (au), Swan Krejcarek (ca), Jorgen Langballe (no), George Leslie (au), Pat Marsh (us), Steve Maurer (us), Elmah McBirney (ck), Peter McQuarrie (nz), Melissa McCoy (us), Richard McElroy (us), James K. McIntyre (us), Rich McIntyre (us), Terry Meanwell (au), Jibralta Merrill (us), Natalie Minnis (gb), Emily Mulloy (us), Marcus Myers (us), Paul and Cheryl Negro (fj), John and Silvana Nicholls (vu), Erica Noorlander (nl), Pat O'-Connell (us), Cheryl Olson (us), Thanos Papadimitinou (gr), Don Parker (us), Jean Parker (us), John Penisten (us), Talia Pereira (nz), Annie-Claude Petitjean (gb), Jon Peverley (gb), Toro-toro Piiti (ck), Ivan Pisoni (fj), Gerhard Plume (de), Steven A. Rasmussen (us), Julia Ratzmann (de), Andrew Rayner (us), Katrin Reuter (de), Larry Richards (us), Brian Rutherford (au), Timothy and Carol Scheck (us), Harald Schierer (us), Bill Schrader (us), Mike Shallcross (gb), Mikey Sheahan (us), Arnold Siegel (us), Beth Sigren (us), Rolf Sigrist (ch), Joel Simon (us), Laura W. Simpkins (us), Charles R. Simpson, Jr. (us), Jeri Solomon (us), Bill Southworth (nz), Louise Spergel (us), Dennis Sullivan (au), E.J.D. Swabey (gb), Helen Sykes (fj), Sara Tatro (us), Wendy Traver (us), Mathias Ulmer (de), Peter van der Vlies (nl), Rosemary Wakeman (nz), Dieter Walden (de), Rob Weltman (us), Brian Whitcombe (au), Rikke Willums (no), Brandon Wilson (us), Thomas Woltmann (au), Philip James Worthington (ca), and Pauline Youssef (pf).

All their comments have been incorporated into the volume you're now holding. To have your own name included here next edition, write: David Stanley, *Moon Handbooks South Pacific*, Avalon Travel Publishing, 1400 65th St., Suite 250, Emeryville, CA 94608, U.S.A., atpfeed back@avalonpub.com.

Hotel keepers, tour operators, and divemasters are also encouraged to send us current information about their businesses. If you don't agree with what we've written, please tell us why—there's never any charge or obligation for a listing. Thanks to the numerous island tourism workers and government officials who wrote in or answered queries from the author but are far too numerous to list here.

From the Author

While researching this 8th edition, I was able to visit and personally inspect facilities on the following islands: Aitutaki, Atiu, Bora Bora, Easter Island, Efate, Fakaofo, Fatu Hiva, Funafuti, Futuna, Grande Terre, Guadalcanal, Hiva Oa, Isle of Pines, Kadavu, Lifou, Lifuka, Makatea, Mal-ololailai, Mana, Maré, Moorea, Nacula, Nananu-i-Ra, Nanayu Lailai, Naviti, Niue, Nuku Hiva, Ouvéa, Ovalau, Palmerston, Raiatea, Rangiroa, Rarotonga, Tahiti, Tahuata, Takapoto, Taveuni, Tavewa, Tongatapu, Ua Huka, Ua Pou, Upolu, Vanua Levu, Vava'u, Viti Levu, and Yanuca.

In addition, during preparation of the 7th edition, I visited these islands: Alu, Ambae, Ambrym, Ballalae, Choiseul, Espiritu Santo, Faisi, Ghizo, Huahine, Makira, Malekula, Mauke, Mitiaro, New Georgia, Nila, Poporang, Santa Cruz, Savai'i, Tanna, Tutuila, Vao, Waya, and Wayasewa. For the 6th edition, I also got to these islands: Foa, Malaita, Manono, and Norfolk.

Of course, it's impossible to visit every island each edition, and on my trips I give priority to those I haven't been to for a while. The sections on islands not mentioned above have had to be updated through secondary sources, and that information should be used with a bit more care. However, over the past 25 years I've visited almost every island group included herein.

While out researching my books I find it cheaper to pay my own way, and you can rest assured that nothing in this book is designed to repay freebies from hotels, restaurants, tour operators, or airlines. I prefer to arrive unexpected and uninvited, and to experience things as they really are. On the road I seldom identify myself to anyone. The essential difference between this handbook and the myriad travel brochures free for the taking in airports and tourist offices all across the region is that this book represents you, the traveler, while the brochures represent the travel industry. The companies and organizations included herein are there for information purposes only, and a mention in no way implies an endorsement. Similarly, the fact that a business is not listed in this handbook does not necessarily imply any criticism of the establishment.

U.S.~Metric Conversion

1 inch = 2.54 centimeters (cm)
1 foot = .304 meters (m)
1 yard = 0.914 meters
1 mile = 1.6093 kilometers (km)
1 km = .6214 miles
1 fathom = 1.8288 m
1 chain = 20.1168 m
1 furlong = 201.168 m
1 acre = .4047 hectares
1 sq km = 100 hectares
1 sq mile = 2.59 square km
1 ounce = 28.35 grams
1 pound = .4536 kilograms
1 short ton = .90718 metric ton
1 short ton = 2000 pounds
1 long ton = 1.016 metric tons
1 long ton = 2240 pounds
1 metric ton = 1000 kilograms
1 quart = .94635 liters
1 US gallon = 3.7854 liters
1 Imperial gallon = 4.5459 liters
1 nautical mile = 1.852 km

To compute Celsius temperatures, subtract 32 from Fahrenheit and divide by 1.8. To go the other way, multiply Celsius by 1.8 and add 32.

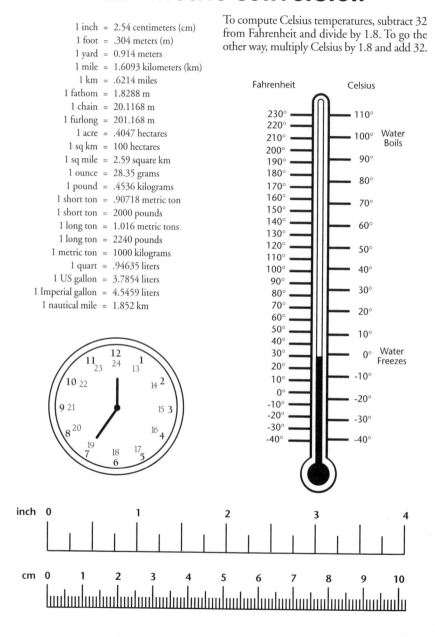

*S*tay in touch ...

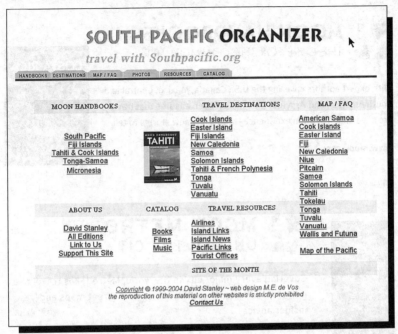

SOUTH PACIFIC ORGANIZER

travel with Southpacific.org

HANDBOOKS   DESTINATIONS   MAP / FAQ   PHOTOS   RESOURCES   CATALOG

MOON HANDBOOKS	TRAVEL DESTINATIONS	MAP / FAQ
	Cook Islands	American Samoa
	Easter Island	Cook Islands
South Pacific	Fiji Islands	Easter Island
Fiji Islands	New Caledonia	Fiji
Tahiti & Cook Islands	Samoa	New Caledonia
Tonga-Samoa	Solomon Islands	Niue
Micronesia	Tahiti & French Polynesia	Pitcairn
	Tonga	Samoa
	Tuvalu	Solomon Islands
	Vanuatu	Tahiti
		Tokelau
ABOUT US	CATALOG	Tonga
		Tuvalu
David Stanley		Vanuatu
All Editions	Books	Wallis and Futuna
Link to Us	Films	
Support This Site	Music	Map of the Pacific

ABOUT US	CATALOG	TRAVEL RESOURCES
		Airlines
David Stanley	Books	Island Links
All Editions	Films	Island News
Link to Us	Music	Pacific Links
Support This Site		Tourist Offices

SITE OF THE MONTH

Southpacific.org takes you beyond Fiji to Tahiti and French Polynesia, the Cook Islands, Tonga, Samoa, Niue, New Caledonia, the Solomons, and everything in between.

Guidebook writer David Stanley's personal website provides mini-guides to South Pacific destinations, island maps, listings of films, music, and books, FAQ's, and links to numerous other travel sites.

www.southpacific.org

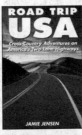

Keeping Current

Although we strive to produce the most up-to-date guidebook humanly possible, change is unavoidable. Between the time this book goes to print and the moment you read it, a handful of the businesses noted in these pages will undoubtedly change prices, move, or even close their doors forever. Other worthy attractions will open for the first time. If you have a favorite gem you'd like to see included in the next edition, or see anything that needs updating, clarification, or correction, please drop us a line. Send your comments via email to atpfeedback@avalonpub.com, or use the address below.

Moon Handbooks South Pacific
Avalon Travel Publishing
1400 65th Street, Suite 250
Emeryville, CA 94608, USA
www.moon.com

Editor: Grace Fujimoto
Series Manager: Kevin McLain
Acquisitions Editor: Rebecca K. Browning
Copy Editor: Kay Elliott
Graphics Coordinator: Justin Marler
Production Coordinator: Darren Alessi
Cover Designer: Kari Gim
Interior Designers: Amber Pirker,
 Alvaro Villanueva, Kelly Pendragon
Map Editor: Naomi Adler Dancis
Cartographers: Mike Morgenfeld, Kat Kalamaras
Indexer: Deana Shields

ISBN: 1-56691-411-6
ISSN: 1085-2700

Printing History
1st Edition—1979
8th Edition—November 2004
5 4 3 2 1

Text and maps © 2004 by David Stanley.
All rights reserved.

Avalon Travel Publishing,
An Imprint of
Avalon Publishing Group, Inc.

AVALON
publishing group incorporated

Front cover photo: © Douglas Peebles
Table of contents photos: © David Stanley, courtesy of Tahiti Tourisme, © Paul J. Lareau, South Pacific Tourism Organization, © Richard Eastwood, © M.E. de Vos, © Mikaele Maiava, Courtesy of the Field Museum of Natural History, Chicago

Printed in China through Colorcraft Ltd., Hong Kong